# AAAI-04 / IAAI-04

# Proceedings

Nineteenth National Conference on
Artificial Intelligence (AAAI-04)

Sixteenth Innovative Applications of
Artificial Intelligence Conference (IAAI-04)

AAAI PRESS/THE MIT PRESS

MENLO PARK, CALIFORNIA • CAMBRIDGE, MASSACHUSETTS • LONDON, ENGLAND

AAAI Press
445 Burgess Drive
Menlo Park, California 94025



Distributed by The MIT Press, Massachusetts Institute of Technology,
Cambridge, Massachusetts and London, England.

ISBN 0-262-51183-5

Printed on acid-free paper in the United States of America

# Contents

## Complexity



## Constraint Satisfaction and Satisfiability

## Game Theory and Economic Models



## Knowledge Representation and Reasoning

## Perception



## Planning and Scheduling

## Qualitative Modeling



## Robotics

## Search



## Uncertainty



## User Modeling

## Innovative Applications of Artificial Intelligence Papers

### Deployed Application Papers



### Emerging Application Papers

## Student Abstracts

## SIGART/AAAI Doctoral Consortium

## Intelligent Systems Demonstrations

# AAAI Organization

# Program Committees

## Conference Committee

**Conference Committee Chair**
James A. Hendler, *University of Maryland*

**AAAI-04 Program Cochairs**
George Ferguson, *University of Rochester*
Deborah L. McGuinness, *Stanford University*

**IAAI-04 Chair**
Randall Hill, *Institute for Creative Technologies, University of Southern California*

**IAAI-04 Cochair**
Neil Jacobstein, *Teknowledge Corporation*

**Intelligent Systems Demonstrations Chair**
Christopher Welty, *IBM Research*

**Student Abstract and Poster Cochairs**
Avi Pfeffer, *Harvard University*
Mark Craven, *University of Wisconsin, Madison*

**Robot Competition and Exhibition Cochairs**
Bill Smart, *Washington University in St. Louis*
Sheila Tejada, *University of New Orleans*

**SIGART/AAAI Doctoral Consortium Chair**
Robert St. Amant, *North Carolina State University*

**Tutorial Forum Chair**
Matthew Stone, *Rutgers University*

**Workshop Chair and Cochair**
Milos Hauskrecht, *University of Pittsburgh*
Dieter Fox, *University of Washington*

## AAAI-04 Senior Program Committee

Yiannis Aloimonos, *University of Maryland*
Chitta Baral, *Arizona State University*
Michael Berthold, *University of Konstanz*
Craig Boutilier, *University of Toronto*
Vinay K. Chaudhri, *SRI International*
William Cohen, *Carnegie Mellon University*
Tim Finin, *University of Maryland, Baltimore County*
Kenneth D. Forbus, *Northwestern University*
Eugene C. Freuder, *University College Cork*
Eric Horvitz, *Microsoft Research*
Henry Kautz, *University of Washington, Seattle*
Michael Kearns, *University of Pennsylvania*
Craig Knoblock, *University of Southern California*
James Lester, *North Carolina State University*
Vladimir Lifschitz, *University of Texas*
Mark T. Maybury, *The MITRE Corporation*
Robin Murphy, *University of Florida*
Karen Myers, *SRI International*
Tuomas Sandholm, *Carnegie Mellon University*
Jonathan Schaeffer, *University of Alberta*
Peter Stone, *University of Texas at Austin*
Mirek Truszczynski, *University of Kentucky*
Ramasamy Uthurusamy, *General Motors Corporation*

## AAAI-04 Program Committee

Julie A. Adams, *Vanderbilt University*
Kamal Ali, *Yahoo!*
Eyal Amir, *University of Illinois, Urbana-Champaign*
Chris Atkeson, *Carnegie Mellon University*
Fahiem Bacchus, *University of Toronto*
Tucker Balch, *Georgia Technical Institute*
Ken Barker, *University of Texas at Austin*
Bettina Berendt, *Humboldt University Berlin*
Christian Bessiere, *LIRMM-CNRS*
Yngvi Bjornsson, *University of Alberta*
David Blei, *University of California, Berkeley*
Jim Blythe, *USC Information Sciences Institute*
James Bowen, *University College Cork*
Michael Bowling, *University of Alberta*
Jeffrey Bradshaw, *Institute for Human and Machine Cognition*
Ronen Brafman, *Ben-Gurion University*
Karl Branting, *North Carolina State University*
Gerhard Brewka, *Leipzig University*
Michael Buro, *University of Alberta*
Mark Burstein, *BBN Technologies*
Mary Elaine Califf, *Illinois State University*
Charles Callaway, *ITC-irst*
Tristan Cazenave, *Labo IA, Universite Paris 8*
Timothy Chklovski, *USC Information Sciences Institute*
Peter Clark, *The Boeing Company*
Michael Collins, *Massachusetts Institute of Technology*
Richard Cost, *University of Maryland, Baltimore County*
Paul Dagum, *Rapt, Inc.*
Laurie E. Damianos, *The MITRE Corporation*
David Danks, *Carnegie Mellon University*
Trevor Darrell, *Massachusetts Institute of Technology*
Adnan Darwiche, *University of California, Los Angeles*
Hasan Davulcu, *Arizona State University*
Johan de Kleer, *Palo Alto Research Center*
James Delgrande, *Simon Fraser University*
Yiannis Demiris, *Imperial College London*
Marc Denecker, *K. U. Leuven*
Marie desJardins, *University of Maryland, Baltimore County*
Giuseppe Di Fatta, *ICAR-CNR*
Scott Dick, *University of Alberta*
Frank Dignum, *Utrecht University*
Juergen Dix, *TU Clausthal*
AnHai Doan, *University of Illinois, Urbana-Champaign*
Christine Doran, *The MITRE Corporation*
Gregory Dudek, *McGill University*
Susan Dumais, *Microsoft Research*
Uwe Egly, *University of Vienna*
Gal Elidan, *Hebrew University*
Esra Erdem, *Vienna University of Technology*
Oren Etzioni, *University of Washington*
Boi Faltings, *Swiss Federal Institute of Technology*
Hany Farid, *Dartmouth College*
Adam Farquhar, *British Library*
Usama M. Fayyad, *DMX Group*
Ariel Felner, *Bar Ilan University*
Robert Fisher, *University of Edinburgh*
Susan Gauch, *University of Kansas*
Michael Gelfond, *Texas Tech University*
Abigail Gertner, *The MITRE Corporation*
Lise Getoor, *University of Maryland, College Park*
Yolanda Gil, *USC Information Sciences Institute*
Robert Givan, *Purdue University*
Kurt Godden, *General Motors R&D*
Randy Goebel, *University of Alberta*
Keith Golden, *NASA Ames Research Center*
Geoff Gordon, *Carnegie Mellon University*
Arnulf Graf, *MPI for Biological Cybernetics*
Jonathan Gratch, *University of Southern California*
Carlos Guestrin, *Intel Research – Berkeley*
Alon Halevy, *University of Washington*
Ulf Hermjakob, *USC Information Sciences Institute*
Frank Hoeppner, *University of Applied Sciences Braunschweig/Wolfenbuettel*
Holger Hoos, *University of British Columbia*
Ian Horswill, *Northwestern University*
Adele Howe, *Colorado State University*

Charles Isbell, *Georgia Insitute of Technology*
Christian Jacob, *University of Calgary*
Tomi Janhunen, *Helsinki University of Technology*
Sverker Janson, *SICS*
Ulrich Junker, *ILOG S.A.*
Sham Kakade, *University of Pennsylvania*
Subbarao Kambhampati, *Arizona State University*
Gal Kaminka, *Bar Ilan University*
Kaz Kawamura, *Vanderbilt University*
Jihie Kim, *USC Information Sciences Institute*
David Kortenkamp, *Metrica Inc./TRACLabs*
Jana Kosecka, *George Mason University*
Vladik Kreinovich, *University of Texas at El Paso*
Benjamin Kuipers, *University of Texas at Austin*
Nicholas Kushmerick, *University College Dublin*
Daniel Lee, *University of Pennsylvania*
Jimmy Lee, *The Chinese University of Hong Kong*
Nicola Leone, *University of Calabria*
Hector Levesque, *University of Toronto*
Kevin Leyton-Brown, *University of British Columbia*
Fangzhen Lin, *HKUST*
Michael Littman, *Rutgers University*
Jorge Lobo, *Open Presence*
Victor Marek, *University of Kentucky*
Shaul Markovitch, *Technion—Israel Institute of Technology*
Maja Mataric, *University of Southern California*
Bruce Maxwell, *Swarthmore College*
Lyle McGeoch, *Amherst College*
David Mitchell, *Simon Fraser University*
Nick Montfort, *University of Pennsylvania*
Alexander P. Morgan, *General Motors Research*
Leora Morgenstern, *IBM T.J. Watson Research Center*
Isabelle Moulinier, *Thomson Legal and Regulatory*
Martin Mueller, *University of Alberta*
Kevin Murphy, *Massachusetts Institute of Technology*
Kenneth Murray, *SRI International*
Ion Muslea, *SRI International*
Gholamreza Nakhaeizadeh, *DaimlerChrysler AG, Research and Technology*
Abhaya Nayak, *University of Australia, Sydney*
Randal Nelson, *University of Rochester*
Hwee Tou Ng, *National University of Singapore*
Ilkka Niemela, *Helsinki University of Technology*
Kamal Nigam, *Intelliseek, Inc.*
Uri Nodelman, *Stanford University*
Natasha Noy, *Stanford University*
Andreas Nuernberger, *Otto-von-Guericke University Magdeburg*
Tim Oates, *University of Maryland Baltimore County*
Luis Ortiz, *University of Pensylvania*
Barry O'Sullivan, *University College Cork*
Lynne Parker, *The University of Tennessee*
David Parkes, *Harvard University*
Aarati Parmar, *Google Inc.*
Ronald Parr, *Duke University*
Simon Parsons, *City University of New York*
Don Perlis, *University of Maryland*
Paulo Pinheiro da Silva, *Stanford University*
John Platt, *Microsoft Research*
Robert Pless
Dimitris Plexousakis, *University of Crete*
David Poole, *University of British Columbia*
James Pustejovsky, *Brandeis University*
Rajesh P. N. Rao, *University of Washington*
Christopher Riesbeck, *Northwestern University*
Jussi Rintanen, *Albert-Ludwigs-University, Freiburg*
Andres Rodriguez, *SRI International*
Amir Ronen, *Technion—Israel Institute of Technology*
Jeffrey S. Rosenschein, *Hebrew University*
Francesca Rossi, *University of Padova*
Wheeler Ruml, *Palo Alto Research Center*
Nestor Rychtyckyj, *Ford Motor Company*
Sudeshna Sarkar, *IIT Kharagpur*
Torsten Schaub, *Universitat Potsdam*
Richard Scherl
Alan Schultz, *Naval Research Laboratory*
Dale Schuurmans, *University of Alberta*
Fabrizio Sebastiani, *Consiglio Nazionale delle Ricerche*
Bart Selman, *Cornell University*
Ishwar Sethi, *Oakland University*
Jianbo Shi, *University of Pennsylvania*
Yoav Shoham, *Stanford University*
Howie Shrobe, *Massachusetts Institute of Technology*
Elizabeth Sklar, *Columbia University*
Barbara Smith, *University of Huddersfield*
David Smith, *NASA Ames Research Center*
Stephen F. Smith, *Carnegie Mellon University*
Tran Cao Son, *New Mexico State University*
Finnegan Southey, *University of Alberta*
John Spletzer, *Lehigh University*
Biplav Srivastava, *IBM India Research Laboratory*
Jaideep Srivastava, *University of Minnesota*
Reinhard Stolle, *Palo Alto Research Center*
Moshe Tennenholtz, *Technion—Israel Institute of Technology*
Belinda Thom, *Harvey Mudd College*
Cynthia Thompson, *University of Utah*
Hans Tompits, *Vienna University of Technology*
Ioannis Tsamardinos, *Vanderbilt University*
Edward Tsang, *University of Essex*
Hudson Turner, *University of Minnesota, Duluth*
Tomas Uribe, *SRI International*
Peter van Beek, *University of Waterloo*
Jaap van den Herik, *Universiteit Maastricht*
Wiebe van der Hoek, *University of Liverpool*
Frank van Harmele, *Vrije Universiteit Amsterdam*
Pascal Van Hentenryck, *Brown University*
Miroslav Velev, *Carnegie Mellon University*
Manuela Veloso, *Carnegie Mellon University*
Toby Walsh, *University College Cork*
Rich Washington, *Google Inc*
Michael Wellman, *University of Michigan*
Michael White, *University of Edinburgh*
Jan Wiebe, *University of Pittsburgh*
Steven Willmott, *Universitat Politècnica de Catalunya*
Michael Witbrock, *Cycorp, Inc.*
Stefan Woltran, *TU Wien*
Michael Wolverton, *SRI International*
Andrew Wong, *University of Waterloo*
Michael Wooldridge, *University of Liverpool*
Peter Wurman, *North Carolina State University*
Holly Yanco, *University of Massachusetts Lowell*
Qiang Yang, *Hong Kong University of Science & Technology*
Makoto Yokoo, *Kyushu University*
R. Michael Young, *North Carolina State University*
Yuanlin Zhang, University College Cork

## Auxiliary Reviewers

Markus Ackermann
Fabio Aiolli
Corin Anderson
Grigoris Antoniou
Avi Bab
Marcello Balduccini
Robert Baumgartner
Darse Billings
Adi Botea
George Boukeas
Thierry Boy de la Tour
Rodrigo Braz
Daniel Bryce
Hung Bui
David Cabanillas
Gangshu Cai
Mats Carlsson
David Carmel
Xiaoyong Chai
Tim Chklovski
Waiyian Chong
Vincent Conitzer
Alvaro Cortes
Joseph Culberson
William Cushing
Leonardo Dagum
David Danks
Romuald Debruyne
Minh B. Do
Carmel Domshlak
Jeroen Donkers
Hani El Sakkout
Austin I. Eliazar
Saher Esmeir
Wolfgang Faber
Adam Feldman
Christian G. Fermueller
Paolo Ferraris
Lev Finkelstein
George Flouris
Jeremy Frank
Alan Frisch
Ulises Cortes Garcia
Cormac Gebruers
Ian Gent
Melinda Gervasio
Eugene Goldberg
Gianluigi Greco
David Grimes
Greg Hamerly
Warwick Harvey
Michael Holmes
Frank Hutter
Chad Jenkins
Terence Kelly

Tom Kelsey
Vladik Kreinovich
Javier Larrosa
Ricky Lau
Scott Lenser
Ho-fung Leung
Olivier Lhomme
Jayant Madhavan
Rudolph Mappus IV
Maarten Marien
Bhaskara Marthi
Pedrito Maynard-Zhang
Colin McMillen
Carlos Mérida
Ian Miguel
Pragnesh Jay Modi
Peter Mork
Bradford Mott
John Mount
Yakov Novikov
Keith O'Hara
Mehmet Orgun
Mark Paskin
Reinhard Pichler
Gerald Pfeifer
Ana-Maria Popescu
Enrico Pontelli
Matt Powers
Pilar Pozos
Steve Prestwich
Patrick Prosser
David Pynadath
Colin Quirke
Sailesh Ramakrishnan
Amit Ramesh
Jan Ramon
Christopher Raphael
Daniel Reeves
Jean-Charles Regin
Ioannis Rekleitis
Jochen Renz
Emma Rollón
Paul Rybski
Thomas Russ
Lawrence Ryan
Romeo Sanchez
Jun Sawada
Francesco Scarcello
Evgeny Selensky
Guy Shani
Aaron Shon
Laurent Simon
Spiros Skiadopoulos
Kevin Smyth
Daniel Sonntag
Mark Stickel
Peter Stuckey
Nathan Sturtevant
Ashish Sureka
Omid D. Tabibi
Giorgio Terracina
Igor Tatarinov
Dave A.D. Tompkins
Vivek Vaidya
Menkes van den Briel
Marc van Dongen
Kristen Brent Venable
Joost Vennekens
Gerard Verfaillie
Deepak Verma
Toby Walsh
Mark Winands
Stefan Woltran
Huayue Wu
Jia-Hong Wu
Roland Yap
Jie Yin
Yingqian Zhang
Jie Zhong
Lin Zhu
Thomas Zielund
Dav Zimak

## IAAI-04 Program Committee

Steve Chien, *Jet Propulsion Laboratory*
Diane Cook, *University of Texas at Arlington*
Marie desJardins, *University of Maryland, Baltimore County*
Yolanda Gil, *USC Information Sciences Institute*
Alexander Hartemink, *Duke University*
Micheal Hewett, *Hewett Research*
Kevin Knight, *USC Information Sciences Institute*
Diane Litman, *University of Pittsburgh*
Bruce Porter, *University of Texas at Austin*
John Riedl, *University of Minnesota*
Ted Senator, *DARPA/IPTO*
Imran Shah, *University of Colorado School of Medicine*
Howie Shrobe, *Massachusetts Institute of Technology*
Reid Smith, *Medstory, Inc.*
James Spohrer, *IBM Almaden Research Center*
Ramasamy Uthurusamy, *General Motors Corporation*
Manuela Veloso, *Carnegie Mellon University*
Peter Wurman, *North Carolina State University*

### Auxiliary Reviewers

Gangshu Cai
Neha Jain
Scott Lenser
Shou-De Lin
Pragnesh Jay Modi
Tom Murray
Michael J. Smith
Marc Spraragen
Ashish Sureka
Liang Zhou

## Student Abstract Reviewers

Eyal Amir, *University of Illinois, Urbana-Champaign*
Berthe Choueiry, *University of Nebraska-Lincoln*
Richard Dearden, *NASA Ames Research Center*
Nando de Freitas, *University of British Columbia*
Patrick Doyle, *Stanford University*
Carlos Guestrin, *Stanford University*
Alex Hartemink. *Duke University*
Luke Hunsberger, *Vassar College*
Rebecca Hwa, *University of Pittsburgh*
Terran Lane, *University of New Mexico*
Uri Lerner, *Stanford University*
Kevin Leyton-Brown, *University of British Columbia*
Pedrito Maynard-Zhang, *Miami University*
Kevin Murphy, *Massachusetts Institute of Technology*
Nicola Muscettola, *NASA Ames Research Center*
Andrew Ng, *Stanford University*
David Parkes, *Harvard University*
Hanna Pasula, *Massachusetts Institute of Technology*
Barney Pell, *NASA Ames Research Center*
Leon Peshkin, *Massachusetts Institute of Technology*
Aviv Regev, *Harvard University*
Wheeler Ruml, *Palo Alto Research Center*
Mehran Sahami, *Stanford University*
Christian Shelton, *Stanford University*
Peter Stone, *The University of Texas at Austin*
David Sullivan, *Harvard University*
Belinda Thom, *Harvey Mudd College*

## SIGART/AAAI Doctoral Consortium Reviewers

Marie desJardins, *University of Maryland, Baltimore County*
Christopher Elsaesser, *The MITRE Corporation*
David Jensen, *University of Massachusetts*
Tessa Lau, *IBM T. J. Watson Research Center*
Ted Pederson, *University of Minnesota at Duluth*
Tim Oates, *University of Maryland, Baltimore County*
Robert St. Amant, *North Carolina State University*
Kiri Wagstaff, *Jet Propulsion Laboratory, California Institute of Technology*

# AAAI-04 Outstanding Paper Award

This year, AAAI's National Conference on Artificial Intelligence honors three papers that exemplify high standards in technical contribution and exposition. During the blind review process, members of the Program Committee recommended the papers to consider for the Outstanding Paper Award. A subset of the Senior Program Committee, carefully chosen to avoid conflicts of interest, reviewed all such papers and selected the winning paper:

## Outstanding Paper Award

Learning and Inferring Transportation Routines

*Lin Liao, Dieter Fox, and Henry Kautz, University of Washington*

## Honorable Mention

Interactive Information Extraction with Constrained Conditional Random Fields

*Trausti Kristjansson, Microsoft Research, Aron Culotta, University of Massachusetts Amherst, Paul Viola, Microsoft Research, and Andrew McCallum, University of Massachusetts Amherst*

## Honorable Mention

Loop Formulas for Circumscription

*Joohyung Lee, University of Texas, Austin and Lin Fangzhen, Hong Kong University of Science and Technology*

# Sponsoring Organizations

- American Association for Artificial Intelligence
- ACM/SIGART
- Defense Advanced Research Projects Agency (DARPA)
- Google, Inc.
- IBM Research
- Microsoft Research
- NASA Ames Research Center
- National Science Foundation
- Naval Research Laboratory

# Preface

## The AAAI–04 Conference

Welcome to the Nineteenth National Conference on Artificial Intelligence, AAAI-04.

This year's conference provides a comprehensive survey of the best research in the various areas within the field of artificial intelligence. Our goal is to provide you with five days of immersion in the wonderful variety of problems that the best researchers in the field are tackling. We hope you will find something to interest you throughout the entire conference, and that you will leave San Jose with your intellectual batteries recharged and ready for another year.

The conference's highlight is the technical program. The papers in the technical program were selected by a highly competitive peer review process. Each paper was reviewed by three members of the program committee, supervised by a member of the senior program committee. The reviewing period was followed by discussion between reviewers, leading to an accept or reject recommendation. These recommendations were reviewed and approved by the senior program committee and program chairs in a face-to-face meeting. In all, out of 453 submitted papers, 120 were accepted and published. We hope you will agree with us that these papers represent significant contributions across a wide range of subject areas.

In addition, three papers were selected for special mention. The AAAI-04 Outstanding Paper award goes to Lin Liao, Dieter Fox, and Henry Kautz for their paper "Learning and Inferring Transportation Routines." Honorable mention goes to Lee Joohyung and Lin Fangzhen for their paper "Loop Formulas for Circumscription," and to Trausti Kristjansson, Aron Culotta, Paul Viola, and Andrew McCallum for their paper "Interactive Information Extraction with Constrained Conditional Random Fields."

The technical program is the heart of the conference, and we would like to gratefully acknowledge the very substantial contributions of the program committee members, and particularly the members of the senior program committee who pulled everything together.

In addition to the technical program, AAAI-04 includes tutorials (organized by Mathew Stone), workshops (organized by Milos Hauskrecht and Dieter Fox), the student abstract program (organized by Avi Pfeffer and Mark Craven), the AAAI/SIGART Doctoral Consortium (organized by Robert St. Amant), intelligent systems demonstrations (organized by Chris Welty), and the robot competition and exhibition (organized by Bill Smart and Sheila Tejada). We would like to thank the organizers of these programs for their efforts, and we hope you will enjoy participating in them. We would also like to thank our invited speakers for sharing their ideas with us, and we hope you will enjoy their talks.

Finally, we would like to remind the AI community that this conference would not be the institution that it is without the never-ending work of the AAAI staff, particularly Carol McKenna Hamilton, Keri Harvey, and Rick Skalsky; and Mike Hamilton of AAAI Press. It has been a pleasure to work with them and serve the AI community. We hope you enjoy the show.

*- George Ferguson, University of Rochester*
*- Deborah McGuinness, Stanford University*

## The IAAI–04 Conference

The Sixteenth Annual Conference on Innovative Applications of Artificial Intelligence (IAAI-04) continues the IAAI tradition of including both case studies of deployed applications and papers on emerging AI applications. The deployed applications papers all include concrete measurements of the benefits provided by AI technology.

IAAI is organized as an independent program within the AAAI national conference, with schedules coordinated to allow attendees to move freely between AAAI and IAAI sessions. We appreciate the cooperation of the AAAI organizers, since we believe the collocated conferences both benefit from each other.

AI applications developers benefit from learning about the latest AI techniques that will enable the next generation of applications. Basic AI research benefits by exposure to the challenges of real-world domains and difficulties and successes in applying AI techniques to real business problems. IAAI-04 addresses the full range of AI techniques including knowledge-based systems, planning and scheduling, perception and monitoring, knowledge formation, knowledge management, learning, intelligent design, natural language processing, and diagnostic reasoning.

Deployed applications are case studies that provide a valuable guide to designing, building, managing, and deploying systems incorporating AI technologies. This year's papers address applications in a wide variety of domains, including natural language processing, secure mobile agents, sales support, securities fraud detection, and scheduling. These applications provide clear evidence of the impact and value that AI technology has in today's world.

Papers on emerging applications and technologies describe efforts whose goal is the engineering of AI applications. They inform AI researchers about the utility of specific AI techniques for applications domains and also inform applications developers about tools and techniques that will enable the next generation of new and more powerful applications.

The invited Robert Engelmore Memorial Lecture for 2004 will be given by Dr. Edward Feigenbaum. Ed will be speaking on one of Bob Engelmore's favorite topics: "The Unexploited Power of Blackboards." Ed is the perfect person to deliver this lecture, because he knew Bob since they roomed together at Carnegie Technical Institute (now CMU), and Ed is a passionate champion for the power of blackboards in applying knowledge to solve challenging problems.

This year we are very pleased to have two in-depth panels. The "AI in Robotics" panel will be moderated by Neil Jacobstein. The panel will feature participants covering robotics at NASA, DARPA, Sony, iRobot and Hasbro. Manuela Veloso will provide her vision of the state of AI in robotics, including robot soccer and other developments. The panel will feature a 360-degree view covering AI, systems engineering, marketing, business, and user adoption aspects of the topic. Robotics has been an emerging AI area for many years. It fuses difficult hardware and software problems to provide new capabilities for digital interactions with the physical world. AI in robotics applications has just recently begun to rack up several commercial and government project successes.

The eScience panel will be moderated by Yolanda Gil. eScience is an emerging way to conduct large and small scale scientific enterprises. It leverages the power of AI in document management and search, collaboration tools, simulation, sequencing, and other forms of problem solving. The panel will address the multidisciplinary requirements of scientific research and how the growing cyber-infrastructure will support progress in the field.

The Innovative Applications of Artificial Intelligence Conference could not take place without the generous help of many people. In particular, we very much appreciate the hard work and dedication of the IAAI-04 program committee, without whom the technical program would be impossible: Steve Chien, Diane Cook, Marie desJardins, Alex Hartemink, Yolanda Gil, Micheal Hewett, Kevin Knight, Diane Littman, Bruce Porter, John Riedl, Ted Senator, Imran Shah, Howie Shrobe, Reid Smith, Jim Spohrer, Ramasamy Uthurusamy, Manuela Veloso, and Peter Wurman. Further, we extend a special thanks to Keri Harvey and Carol Hamilton and the entire AAAI staff for their professionalism, organization, and expertise.

Enjoy the conference!

*– Randy Hill and Neil Jacobstein*

# Invited Talks and Panels

*AAAI-04 Keynote Address:*

## Intelligent Systems and the Nation's Vision for Space Exploration

*Daniel J. Clancy, NASA Ames Research Center*

Over the past few months, NASA has been in the news numerous times both for the exciting discoveries of the pair of Mars Rovers as well as the country's "Vision for Space Exploration." This vision focuses on the joint human and robotic exploration of the solar system starting with a return to the moon and then the human exploration of Mars. In addition, the vision includes a continued array of exciting robotic missions to Mars as well as other destinations. There are numerous challenges that must be addressed to accomplish this vision. One critical area of technology is the broad area of information technology with a particular emphasis on intelligent systems. Future human exploration will require a new level of technology enabling NASA to deploy smarter, more adaptive systems. These systems must be designed to complement their human partners. In this talk, Daniel Clancy will present a brief overview of the new vision and then will talk in depth about a range of technologies that have been developed and demonstrated by NASA over the past few years. In particular, he will focus on how advanced artificial intelligence technologies have been developed and demonstrated within a robust environment and then in some cases deployed on NASA missions. Technologies that will be discussed include: automated planning and scheduling, human-centered computing, remote collaboration tools, machine learning and multi-model interaction using EEG and EMG signals.

*The Joint AAAI-04/IAAI-04 Robert S. Engelmore Memorial Lecture:*

## The Power of "Clear and Demonstrative Knowledge": In Honor of a "True Son of Science"

*Edward Feigenbaum, Stanford University*

This talk, given to honor the memory and work of Robert S. Engelmore, revisits some of the themes that were central to his work by giving them a contemporary context. What is an up-to-date view of the "knowledge is power" hypothesis? What about knowledge webs, new applications of knowledge-based systems, and particularly the blackboard-architectures that Engelmore helped to develop?

*AAAI-04 Invited Talk:*

## AI And Biomedicine: Helping Scientists Reason about Genomes, Drugs, Diseases

*Russ B. Altman, Stanford University Medical Center*

Biology and medicine are now generating data at a pace far exceeding the ability of scientists completely to analyze it. Bioinformatics has responded with a number of powertools for reducing large data sets into manageable chunks. These tools are limited in two ways: they can't read the published literature (or textbooks) and they don't have biological common sense, so they sometimes propose things that are already well-known or don't make sense (and thus can lose credibility). We are trying to ameliorate these problems with technology squarely within, or closely related to AI.

*AAAI-04 Invited Talk:*

## “If not the Turing Test, then What?”

*Paul Cohen, University of Massachusetts, Amherst, and USC Information Sciences Institute*

Turing proposed his indistinguishability test more than half a century ago, and although it is never far from the thoughts of AI researchers, it has done us little good. While other sciences seem motivated by their grand challenges, AI does not strive to pass Turing's test. It is too remote a prospect, and the test itself provides no compass or route markers. It is mired in philosophical problems, it ignores physical and perceptual aspects of intelligence, and it has too many prerequisites. Yet Turing's test has virtues we should preserve in more effective grand challenges: it emphasizes common sense, universal scope, and understanding; success is judged by ordinary people; and the test provides ample rope to hang oneself. These are good criteria for grand challenge problems in general.

But there are other criteria that Turing's test does not satisfy. We need progressions of challenges, spaced at two-to-five year intervals, which will get us to Turing's goal within twenty years, and parallel series of challenges in the perceptual/physical realm. We need “come as you are” challenges that do not require something else to be achieved before we can start work. These problems should drive the development of new technologies but discourage “self-inflicted” research. Ph.D. students should be able to trace very short paths from their dissertation topics to one or more of these problems, and should see clearly the progression from it to longer-term challenges. The grand challenge problems should be updated regularly to deal with unforeseen impediments.

Cohen will give several possible examples of progressions of grand challenge problems. It is time to put aside the Turing Test and replace it with challenges that work for us.

*AAAI-04 Invited Talk:*

## Strength of Character: AI Personalities in Video Games

*Ian Lane Davis, Mad Doc Software*

Davis will examine the upcoming great frontier in AI, which is the construction of believable characters in video games. He will touch on all the aspects of making believable characters from animations to behaviors to internal models of AI.

*AAAI-04 Invited Talk:*

## Agents Meet the Semantic Web in the Aether

*Tim Finin, University of Maryland, Baltimore County*

The software agents paradigm has received considerable research but has not yet found broad application. The vision is still sound and will be re-invigorated by two new developments: semantic web languages, which provide stronger knowledge sharing technology, and the emergence of pervasive computing environments, whose requirements match the strengths of multiagent systems.

*AAAI-04 Invited Talk:*

## Applications of Artificial Intelligence to Web Search

*Peter Norvig, Google*

Web search engines have accumulated billions of pages of text. A corpus of this size provides an interesting opportunity for techniques in machine learning, natural language processing, and other areas of artificial intelligence. This talk will examine how these techniques can be used in a large, practical web search engine.

*AAAI-04 Invited Talk:*

## Human Dynamics

*Alex (Sandy) Pentland, MIT Media Laboratory*

Important and complex discussions are almost always face-to-face, with little or no technology intervention. The result is that current computer and communication tools are largely restricted to mechanizing back-office and support functions. Pentland believes that we can radically improve the functioning of the organizations through active analysis of face-to-face interactions. By using wearable machine perception to characterize, annotate, and influence face-to-face interactions we can augment peoples' memory, initiate productive interactions, improve group decision making, and better understand and manage the functioning of distributed workforce. Examples of each type of augmentation will be shown, and privacy concerns addressed.

*AAAI-04 Invited Talk:*

## Intelligent Technology for Adaptive Aging

*Martha E. Pollack, University of Michigan*

The world's population is rapidly aging, and some are predicting a coming "crisis in caregiving." Intelligent technologies have the potential to help avoid this crisis, by providing people with ways to adapt to the physical and cognitive changes that can accompany aging. This talk will survey the state-of-the-art in such technology, highlight the important role of AI techniques in its design, and describe open research challenges.

*AAAI-04 Invited Talk:*

## Building a Life Science Company Around Statistical Machine Learning

*Astro Teller, BodyMedia, Inc.*

A tour through five years of challenges and discoveries building a wearable body monitoring business using statistical machine leaming techniques. The talk will cover challenges gathering data, building body state models, validating the models with the medical community, and place AI within the larger context of the company and the industry.

*AAAI-04 Invited Talk:*

## Real Robots for the Real World

*Sebastian Thrun, Stanford University*

In 2002, nine coal mines were almost buried alive in Somerset, PA, when accidentally breaching a neighboring mine submersed in water, and thought to be several hundred yards away. According to a 1991 survey "tens of thousands, perhaps even hundreds of thousands, of abandoned mines exist today in the United States. Not even the U.S. Bureau of Mines knows the exact number, because federal recording of mining claims was not required until 1976." An improved understanding of the sizes, locations, and conditions of abandoned mines could substantially reduce the many risks to society that arise from subsidence, contamination, and other factors characteristic of many abandoned mines today.

This talk describes the Groundhog robot system, developed to acquire volumetric maps abandoned mines. Sebastian Thrun will discuss some of the challenges that arise when sending a robot into mines, where it has to operate truly autonomously, outside the communication range of its creators. Specifically, Thrun will present some recent innovations on large-scale robotic mapping, exploration, and navigation in unknown and hazardous environments. These techniques leverage some of the most advanced work in large-scale graphical models, probabilistic inference, and decision making under uncertainty---topics that have been at the heart of AI research for more than a decade.

The Groundhog project was jointly conducted with Red Whittaker and Scott Thayer, who led the robot development, and the CMU Mobile robot design class. Some of the material presented was contributed by researchers from the Fraunhofer Institute in Germany.

# AAAI-04
# Technical Papers

# Agents and Multiagent Systems

# Performance Bounded Reinforcement Learning in Strategic Interactions

**Bikramjit Banerjee** and **Jing Peng**
Dept. of Electrical Engineering & Computer Science
Tulane University
New Orleans, LA 70118
{banerjee, jp}@eecs.tulane.edu

### Abstract

Despite increasing deployment of agent technologies in several business and industry domains, user confidence in fully automated agent driven applications is noticeably lacking. The main reasons for such lack of trust in complete automation are scalability and non-existence of reasonable guarantees in the performance of self-adapting software. In this paper we address the latter issue in the context of learning agents in a Multiagent System (MAS). Performance guarantees for most existing on-line Multiagent Learning (MAL) algorithms are realizable only in the limit, thereby seriously limiting its practical utility. Our goal is to provide certain meaningful guarantees about the performance of a learner in a MAS, *while* it is learning. In particular, we present a novel MAL algorithm that (i) converges to a best response against stationary opponents, (ii) converges to a Nash equilibrium in self-play and (iii) achieves a constant bounded expected regret at any time (no-average-regret asymptotically) in arbitrary sized general-sum games with non-negative payoffs, and against any number of opponents.

## Introduction

Agent technologies are being increasingly deployed in several business and industry domains, including B2B exchanges, supply chain management, car manufacturing etc, and are already providing sustained dramatic benefits. Demands from e-Commerce, particularly on-line auctions, and distributed computing communities are also producing revolutionary ideas in the Agents and MAS research domains. However, user confidence in fully automated agent driven applications is noticeably lacking and a "human in the loop" mind set seems hard to overcome. The main reasons for such lack of trust in complete automation are scalability and non-existence of reasonable guarantees in performance of self-adapting software.

Existing on-line learning algorithms in single agent environments do provide some performance guarantees during learning, but such assurances in multiagent environments are not only lacking but also significantly difficult to provide. In a MAS, a learning agent also forms a part of the environment for every other learning agent. As such, the environments of the learners are usually *non-stationary* which is the key challenge for MAL. It is apparently also a challenge for a learner to learn the moving target of a most beneficial behavior through exploration in such environments, and at the same time ensure "good" performance during the exploration. So much so that the latter property has not been investigated in depth so far. In MAS, either such guarantees are realizable only in the limit, thereby seriously limiting its practical interest, or are realizable in polynomial time (e.g. R-MAX (Brafman & Tennenholtz 2002b)) but only for limited classes of games (e.g., constant-sum games). Our goal is to address this aspect of MAL, i.e., to provide certain meaningful guarantees about the performance of a learner in a MAS, *while it is learning* in general-sum games. We develop a novel algorithm for MAL that maintains the existing policy convergence properties of MAL, viz. *rationality* and *convergence* (Bowling & Veloso 2002), and in addition (i) applies to arbitrary sized general-sum games with non-negative payoffs, (ii) ensures a *bounded regret* at any time such that it is asymptotically *no-regret*. This property guarantees that a learner cannot perform much worse than the best fixed policy at any time while it is learning. The current paper contributes this algorithm with the relevant analyses and is organized as follows: the next section presents definitions from the domain of Multiagent Reinforcement Learning in repeated games, followed by a section on the existing work related to the present endeavor. Thereafter we present the algorithm, the analysis, and conclude with a short summary.

## Multiagent Reinforcement Learning

A Multiagent Reinforcement Learning task is usually modeled (Littman 1994) as a Stochastic Game (SG, also called *Markov Game*), which is a Markov Decision Process with multiple controllers. We focus on stochastic games with a single state, also called repeated games. This refers to a scenario where a matrix game (defined below) is played repeatedly by multiple agents. We shall represent the action space of the $ith$ agent as $A_i$.

**Definition 1** *A matrix game with $n$ players is given by an $n$-tuple of matrices, $\langle \mathbf{R}_1, \mathbf{R}_2, \ldots, \mathbf{R}_n \rangle$ where $\mathbf{R}_i$ is a matrix of dimension $|A_1| \times |A_2| \ldots \times |A_n|$, such that the payoff of* *the ith agent for the joint action $(a_1, a_2, \ldots, a_n)$ is given by the entry $R_i(a_1, a_2, \ldots, a_n)$, $\forall i$.*

A *constant-sum game* (also called competitive games) is a special matrix game where $\sum_i R_i(a_1, a_2, \ldots, a_n) = c$, $\forall (a_1, a_2, \ldots, a_n) \in \prod_k A_k$, $c$ being a constant. If $c = 0$, then it is also called a zero-sum game. An example of such a game with 2 players appears in Table 1. This game is called Rock-Scissor-Paper. Here $A_1 = A_2 = \{R, S, P\}$ and the game payoffs for any joint action sum to 0 as shown in Table 1.

Table 1: Rock-Scissor-Paper Game. $(a, b)$ in the $(i, j)th$ cell is the tuple of payoffs for Row agent and Column agent (in that order) for each combination of their actions $(i, j) \in \{R, S, P\} \times \{R, S, P\}$.

| Actions | Rock (R) | Scissor (S) | Paper (P) |
|---|---|---|---|
| Rock (R) | (0,0) | (1,-1) | (-1,1) |
| Scissor (S) | (-1,1) | (0,0) | (1,-1) |
| Paper (P) | (1,-1) | (-1,1) | (0,0) |

A *mixed policy*, vector $\pi_i \in PD(A_i)$ for agent $i$, is a probability distribution over $A_i$, where $PD$ is the set of probability distributions over the action space. If the entire probability mass is concentrated on a single action (some actions), it is also called a *pure policy* (*partially mixed policy*). The joint policies of the opponents of the $ith$ agent will be given by the vector $\pi_{-i}$. We shall usually refer to the $ith$ agent as the learner and the rest of the agents as the opponents. The expected payoff of the learner at any stage in which the policy tuple $\langle \pi_1, \pi_2, \ldots, \pi_n \rangle$ is followed is given by $V_i(\pi_i, \pi_{-i}) = \sum_{(a_1,\ldots,a_n)\in\prod_k A_k} \pi_1(a_1)\ldots\pi_n(a_n)R_i(a_1, \ldots, a_n)$.

**Definition 2** *For an $n$-player matrix game, the best response ($BR^i_{\pi_{-i}}$) of the ith agent to its opponents' joint policy ($\pi_{-i}$) is given by $BR^i_{\pi_{-i}} = \{\pi_i | V_i(\pi_i, \pi_{-i}) \geq V_i(\pi'_i, \pi_{-i}), \forall \pi'_i \in PD(A_i)\}$.*

**Definition 3** *A mixed-policy Nash Equilibrium (NE) for a matrix game $\langle \mathbf{R}_1, \mathbf{R}_2, \ldots, \mathbf{R}_n \rangle$ is a tuple of probability vectors $\langle \pi^*_1, \pi^*_2, \ldots, \pi^*_n \rangle$ (policy profile) such that each is a best response to the rest, i.e., $\pi^*_i \in BR^i_{\pi^*_{-i}}$ $\forall i$. In terms of payoffs, these conditions can be restated as $V_i(\pi^*_i, \pi^*_{-i}) \geq V_i(\pi_i, \pi^*_{-i})$ $\forall \pi_i \in PD(A_i)$ , $\forall i$.*

No player in this game has any incentive for unilateral deviation from the Nash equilibrium policy, given the others' policy. There always exists at least one such equilibrium profile for an arbitrary finite matrix game (Nash 1951). As an example, the only NE for the 2 player RSP game in Table 1 is $[\frac{1}{3}, \frac{1}{3}, \frac{1}{3}]$ and $[\frac{1}{3}, \frac{1}{3}, \frac{1}{3}]$ for the two agents.

**Definition 4** *For a given time range $t = 0 \ldots T$, the regret of a learner (agent i), $Rg^T_i$ is given by $Rg^T_i = \max_{\pi_i} \sum_{t=1}^{t=T} V_i(\pi_i, \pi^t_{-i}) - \sum_{t=1}^{t=T} V_i(\pi^t_i, \pi^t_{-i})$.*

This means that if the sum of expected payoffs of the learner in the given time range against the actual unknown policies played by the non-stationary opponent were compared to that of an oracle who *knows* the actual policies to be played by the opponent *ahead of time* and can statically compute a fixed policy $\pi_i$ that maximizes $\sum_{t=1}^{t=T} V_i(\pi_i, \pi^t_{-i})$ but is *limited* to play only that policy all through the time window $T$, then the difference would be the former player's regret. In hindsight (after $t = T$) he finds that always playing $\pi_i$ instead of the sequence $\{\pi^t_i\}$ would have yielded a total payoff higher than his actual payoff by $Rg^T_i$.

## Related Work

Multiagent Reinforcement Learning has produced primarily two types of algorithms. One type learns some fixed point of the game e.g., NE (Minimax-Q (Littman 1994; Littman & Szepesvari 1996), Nash-Q (Hu & Wellman 1998; 2002), FFQ (Littman 2001)) or correlated equilibrium (CE-Q (Greenwald & Hall 2002)). These algorithms can guarantee a certain minimal expected payoff asymptotically, but it may be possible to guarantee higher payoff in certain situations if the learner is adaptive to the opponents' play, instead of learning the game solution alone. This brings us to the other type of learners that learn a best response to the opponents' actual play e.g., IGA (Singh, Kearns, & Mansour 2000), WoLF-IGA (Bowling & Veloso 2001; 2002), AWESOME (Conitzer & Sandholm 2003a). Since mutual best response is an equilibrium, two similar best responding players (such situations referred to as *self-play*) should be able to converge to an equilibrium. WoLF-IGA achieves this in $2 \times 2$ games and AWESOME achieves it for arbitrary sized games. Simple Q-learning (Sutton & Burto 1998) is also capable of learning a best response to an arbitrary opponent's policy provided that latter is stationary. Nevertheless, a straightforward application of Q-learning has been shown to perform well in MAL problems (Tan 1993; Sen, Sekaran, & Hale 1994; Sandholm & Crites 1996; Claus & Boutilier 1998). There has also been some work on playing team games (where the game matrices of all agents are identical) (Claus & Boutilier 1998; Wang & Sandholm 2002) with stronger convergence guarantees owing to the correlation of the game matrices.

However, the existing literature in MAL seldom provides any performance guarantees *during* the learning process. One significant line of work with possible impact on MAL in this regard is that on *regret matching* learners. Algorithms have been proposed that achieve $\lim_{T\to\infty} \frac{Rg^T_i}{T} = 0$ (called *no-regret* algorithms) but their convergence properties in policies are unknown (Auer *et al.* 1995; Fudenberg & Levine 1995; Freund & Schapire 1999; Littlestone & Warmuth 1994) or at best limited (Jafari *et al.* 2001). Thus we see that existing MAL algorithms either do not provide any performance assurances during learning or they do without any convergence assurances. Our goal is to achieve both. Recent work by Zinkevich (2003) shows that IGA (Singh, Kearns, & Mansour 2000) has a no-regret property (even with extension to larger games) but this algorithm is not guaranteed to converge to Nash policies in self-play. Even WoLF-IGA cannot guarantee convergence to NE in self-play in larger games (Bowling & Veloso 2002). A more recent work (Conitzer & Sandholm 2003b) establishes a bounded loss learning framework (BL-WoLF) in classes of zero-sum games allowing an agent to learn the minimax solution of such a game with the least amount of cumulative loss against the worst possible opponent (one who knows the game beforehand). Though this does provide performance assurances during learning, the framework does not address general-sum games, or learning adaptive best responses.

There is a fundamentally different notion of equilibrium from a NE of the one-shot game that we address. This is Efficient Learning Equilibrium (ELE) (Brafman & Tennenholtz 2002a), where the players' learning algorithms are required to reach an equilibrium in polynomial time, but which may not exist under imperfect monitoring settings. Though the computational complexity of a NE is an open problem, its advantage is its guaranteed existence. Also, we do not assume perfect monitoring for our work since the learner does not need to observe the opponents' payoffs.

## Performance Bounded Multiagent Learning

No-regret property is of great interest for MAL domains since it provides a meaningful performance bound for a learner in a non-stationary environment. We use this notion of performance bound for our learning algorithm. Our goal is to present a MAL algorithm that satisfies the *rationality* and *convergence* criteria of (Bowling & Veloso 2002), i.e.

- Converges to the stationary best response against stationary opponents. This is a base case that ensures consistency of a learning algorithm against non-learners.
- Converges to the NE policy profile of the one-shot game in repeated self-play of a matrix game.

and in addition has the following properties

- Applies to arbitrary sized games, unlike IGA or WoLF-IGA.
- Achieves no-regret payoff against any opponent.

AWESOME (Conitzer & Sandholm 2003a) also has the first 3 properties but the case where the opponents are *neither stationary nor following the same algorithm as the learner* has not been dealt with explicitly. In (Conitzer & Sandholm 2003a), when such agents are encountered the learner will reset repeatedly each time starting off with playing its NE policy and gradually moving toward a best response until the next reset. This does not provide any guarantee that its average payoff will be "good" in such cases. The behavior of WoLF-IGA in such cases is also unspecified. We posit that a "good" payoff in such cases is the *no regret* payoff. We propose to ensure that in situations where the opponents are neither stationary, nor following the learner's algorithm, at least the learner's average payoff will approach its no-regret payoff. This property does not conflict with either rationality or convergence; in fact they are in agreement since best response payoff (achieved asymptotically in rational and convergent play) cannot be worse than no-regret payoff. We make the following assumptions for the current work,

1. that *either* the learner knows its own bounded game payoffs (like AWESOME) *or* the payoffs are unknown but non-negative and bounded, i.e., in the range $[\underline{r}, \bar{r}]$ such that $\underline{r} \geq 0$. We call such games *non-negative games*. If a learner knows its game payoffs but they can be negative, then he can always imaginably transform that game into a non-negative game, then compute policy using the transformed game and use it in playing the actual game. The expected payoffs will differ only by a constant and the no-regret property will remain unchanged.
2. that the agents can observe each other's instantaneous policies and can use vanishing step sizes for policy improvement (similar to IGA and WoLF-IGA). It can also observe the expected payoffs of all of its actions at any iteration (trivially computable if game payoffs are known).
3. that the agents are given at the start, their portions of an equilibrium policy profile which they converge to if all the agents are following the same prescribed algorithm (similar to WoLF-IGA and AWESOME).

We write the probability of the $jth$ action of the $ith$ agent at time $t$ as $\pi_i^t(j)$ and the expected payoff of this action against the opponent's current policy as $V_i(j, \boldsymbol{\pi}_{-i}^t)$ and note that

$$\sum_j \pi_i^t(j) V_i(j, \boldsymbol{\pi}_{-i}^t) = V_i(\boldsymbol{\pi}_i^t, \boldsymbol{\pi}_{-i}^t). \quad (1)$$

### The ReDVaLeR Algorithm

We propose to use the *Replicator* (Fudenberg & Levine 1998) rule for policy update of our target algorithm with a WoLF-like modification, which we call ReDVaLeR (*Re*plicator *D*ynamics with a *Va*riable *Le*arning *R*ate).

$$\begin{aligned} \pi_i^{t+1}(j) &= \pi_i^t(j) + \eta \pi_i^t(j) \times [l_i^t(j) V_i(j, \boldsymbol{\pi}_{-i}^t) - \\ &\quad \sum_j l_i^t(j) \pi_i^t(j) V_i(j, \boldsymbol{\pi}_{-i}^t)] \end{aligned} \quad (2)$$

for $\eta$ being a vanishing step size and base condition: $\pi_i^0(j) = \frac{1}{|A_i|}$, learning rates $l_i^t(j)$ are defined later. As $\eta \to 0$, the above difference equation yields the following differential equation [1] for the dynamics of the $n$-player system

$$\begin{aligned} \frac{d}{dt}(\pi_i^t(j)) &= \pi_i^t(j) \times [l_i^t(j) V_i(j, \boldsymbol{\pi}_{-i}^t) - \\ &\quad \sum_j l_i^t(j) \pi_i^t(j) V_i(j, \boldsymbol{\pi}_{-i}^t)] \end{aligned} \quad (3)$$

$j = 1 \ldots |A_i|$, $i = 1 \ldots n$. This is similar to the Replicator rule except for the learning rates, $l$. The Replicator Dynamics (RD) (Fudenberg & Levine 1998) have been extensively studied in population genetics and evolutionary game theory. It is known that the NE may not be asymptotically stable for RD in many games, e.g., RSP game in Table 1. A recent result in (Hart & Mas-Colell 2003) explains why. They show that if the dynamics are uncoupled (as in RD), i.e., if the agents do not use the opponents' payoff information in its dynamics, then it is unable to overcome an "information barrier" and consequently unable to guarantee convergence. This also explains why IGA (Singh, Kearns,

[1] The RHS is discontinuous but we do not need to completely solve the system. Our approach is only to show that a chosen fixed point can be made asymptotically stable under the dynamics.

& Mansour 2000) fails to guarantee convergence to NE but WoLF-IGA succeeds. As in WoLF-IGA, the learning rates $l$ may be one way to provide the necessary coupling, and we define $l_i^t(j)$ for ReDVaLeR as

$$l_i^t(j) = \begin{cases} 1 & \text{if } \pi_{-i}^t \text{ is fixed} \\ \left\{ \begin{array}{ll} 1+\sigma & \text{if } \pi_i^t(j) < \pi_i^{*j} \\ 1-\sigma & \text{when } \pi_i^t(j) \geq \pi_i^{*j} \end{array} \right\} & \text{otherwise} \end{cases} \tag{4}$$

where $\pi_i^*$ is an NE policy. We typically require a constant $0 < \sigma \ll 1$. We note that when $\pi_i^t(j) \geq \pi_i^*(j)$, $\pi_i^t(j)V_i(j, \pi_{-i}^t) \geq \pi_i^*(j)V_i(j, \pi_{-i}^t)$ since $V_i(j, \pi_{-i}^t) \geq 0\ \forall j$, which is similar to the situation described as *winning* in (Bowling & Veloso 2002), excepting that now it is defined for *each action*. Thus this scheme of variation in the learning rate is in the spirit of WoLF (Win or Learn Fast). Likewise, we call the situation $\pi_i^t(j) \geq \pi_i^*(j)$ as *winning*, and the situation $\pi_i^t(j) < \pi_i^*(j)$ as *losing*.

## Analysis of ReDVaLeR

For the sake of brevity, we write $V_i(j, \pi_{-i}^t)$ simply as $V_i^j$. Let $D_i(\tilde{\pi}_i, \pi_i^t)$ be the Kullback Leibler divergence between the $ith$ agent's policy at time $t$ and an *arbitrary* distribution $\tilde{\pi}_i$, given by

$$D_i(\tilde{\pi}_i, \pi_i^t) = \sum_j \tilde{\pi}_i(j) \log\left(\frac{\tilde{\pi}_i(j)}{\pi_i^t(j)}\right) \tag{5}$$

**Lemma 1** *The following holds,*

$$\frac{d}{dt}(D_i(\tilde{\pi}_i, \pi_i^t)) = \sum_j l_i^t(j)\pi_i^t(j)V_i^j - \sum_j l_i^t(j)\tilde{\pi}_i(j)V_i^j$$

**Proof** : Differentiating both sides of equation 5 and using equation 3 we get the result. ∎

**Corollary 1** *If $\pi_i^t$ follows RD instead of ReDVaLeR, then the derivative of the corresponding divergence measure can be given by $\frac{d}{dt}(D_i^{RD}(\tilde{\pi}_i, \pi_i^t)) = \sum_j (\pi_i^t(j) - \tilde{\pi}_i(j))V_i^j$*

The following theorem establishes the *rationality* property (Bowling & Veloso 2002) of ReDVaLeR.

**Theorem 1** *If the opponents are playing stationary policies, then the policy sequence of ReDVaLeR converges to the best response to the opponents' policy.*

**Proof** : Let $\bar{\pi}_i$ be the best response of the $ith$ agent to the opponents' fixed joint policy, given by $\pi_{-i}$. Then putting $\bar{\pi}_i$ in place of the arbitrary policy in Lemma 1, we have

$$\begin{aligned} \frac{d}{dt}(D_i(\bar{\pi}_i, \pi_i^t)) &= \sum_j l_i^t(j)\pi_i^t(j)V_i^j - \sum_j l_i^t(j)\bar{\pi}_i(j)V_i^j \\ &= \sum_j \pi_i^t(j)V_i^j - \sum_j \bar{\pi}_i(j)V_i^j \text{ , by (4)} \\ &= V_i(\pi_i^t, \pi_{-i}) - V_i(\bar{\pi}_i, \pi_{-i}) \text{ , by (1)} \\ &\leq 0 \text{ , since } V_i(\pi_i^t, \pi_{-i}) \leq V_i(\bar{\pi}_i, \pi_{-i}) \end{aligned}$$

That $V_i(\pi_i^t, \pi_{-i}) \leq V_i(\bar{\pi}_i, \pi_{-i})$ is evident since otherwise $\pi_i^t$ would have been the best response to $\pi_{-i}$. Now since the divergence measure ($D_i$) is not strictly decreasing, it is possible that $D_i(\bar{\pi}_i, \pi_i^t)$ converges to a non-zero positive value and thus the sequence $\{\pi_i^t\}$ converges to a policy other than $\bar{\pi}_i$, say $\pi_i'$. But even in that case $V_i(\pi_i', \pi_{-i})$ must be equal to $V_i(\bar{\pi}_i, \pi_{-i})$, which implies that $\pi_i'$ must also be a best response. ∎

The following theorem establishes that ReDVaLeR produces performance bounded learning.

**Theorem 2** *The following holds,*

$$\int_0^T V_i(\pi_i^t, \pi_{-i}^t)dt \geq \left(\frac{1-\sigma}{1+\sigma}\right) \max_{\pi_i} \int_0^T V_i(\pi_i, \pi_{-i}^t)dt - \frac{\log|A_i|}{(1+\sigma)}$$

*That is, as $\sigma \rightarrow 0^+$, the maximum regret of the ith agent playing against $n-1$ arbitrary opponents who play fixed sequences of non-stationary policies in the first $T$ steps is $Rg_i^T \leq \log|A_i|$.*

**Proof** : Note that the integrals exist since $V_i$ is continuous and bounded. We write $D_i(\tilde{\pi}_i, \pi_i^0)$ i.e., the initial divergence as $D_0$. Integrating the expression in Lemma 1 in the given time range and noting that $D_i(\tilde{\pi}_i, \pi_i^T) \geq 0$ we have

$$\begin{aligned} -D_0 &\leq \int_0^T \left( \sum_j l_i^t(j)\pi_i^t(j)V_i^j - \sum_j l_i^t(j)\tilde{\pi}_i(j)V_i^j \right) dt \\ &\leq (1+\sigma)\int_0^T V_i(\pi_i^t, \pi_{-i}^t)dt - \\ &\quad (1-\sigma)\int_0^T V_i(\tilde{\pi}_i, \pi_{-i}^t)dt \text{ , by (1), the} \\ &\quad \text{bounds on } l_i^t(j)\text{, and non-negative games} \\ &\leq (1+\sigma)\int_0^T V_i(\pi_i^t, \pi_{-i}^t)dt - \\ &\quad \max_{\pi_i}(1-\sigma)\int_0^T V_i(\pi_i, \pi_{-i}^t)dt \end{aligned}$$

since $\tilde{\pi}_i$ was arbitrarily chosen. Rearranging and noting that $D_0 \leq \log|A_i|$ if the initial policy is uniform, we get the result. ∎

This result is obtained along the same line as the no-regret property of the multiplicative weight algorithm in (Freund & Schapire 1999). It tells us that the player can ensure a constant bound expected regret at any time provided it uses $\sigma \rightarrow 0^+$ and that the average regret of the learner is $\frac{Rg_i^T}{T} \leq \frac{\log|A_i|}{(1+\sigma)T}$, thus ensuring no-regret asymptotically. Using the technique of Freund & Schapire (1999) we can extend this result to arbitrary adaptive (non-oblivious) opponents in a discrete version of ReDVaLeR (future work).

Finally the following theorem establishes the crucial *convergence* property (Bowling & Veloso 2002) of ReDVaLeR.

**Theorem 3** *When all the $n$ agents are following ReDVaLeR algorithm, the sequence of their policies converge to their NE in non-negative games of any size, provided they choose their portions of the same equilibrium, and they all choose $\sigma = 1$ (this requirement may be relaxable).*

**Proof** : The goal is to prove that players using the ReDVaLeR algorithm on a repeated matrix game can converge to a NE of the one-shot game. That they need to choose their portions of the *same* equilibrium (for rule 4) is not really an extra burden, as discussed in (Conitzer & Sandholm 2003a), for agents sharing a single algorithm. We define the sum of the divergence measures of the $n$ agents (from equation 5) from their respective equilibria $\pi_i^*$, for ReDVaLeR and Replicator Dynamics respectively as

$$S = \sum_{i=1}^{n} D_i(\pi_i^*, \pi_i^t) \text{ and } S^{RD} = \sum_{i=1}^{n} D_i^{RD}(\pi_i^*, \pi_i^t)$$

Note that just as $D_i, D_i^{RD} \geq 0$ and differentiable at all times, so are $S, S^{RD} \geq 0$. The general strategy of the proof is to show that $\frac{d}{dt}(S) < 0$ under appropriate assumptions at any time $t$. We accomplish this by comparing $\frac{d}{dt}(S)$ with $\frac{d}{dt}(S^{RD})$ at that time had RD been using the same instantaneous policies. Since $S \geq 0$ and $S = 0$ holds only when all agents have reached their respective equilibria, $\frac{d}{dt}(S) < 0$ implies that $S$ is a Lyapunov function [2] for the dynamic system, i.e., the system converges to the equilibrium. Now at any time $t$ we consider two distinct cases

**Case 1 :** $\frac{d}{dt}(S^{RD}) \leq 0$. Then we have,

$$\begin{aligned}
\frac{dS}{dt} &\leq \frac{d}{dt}(S) - \frac{d}{dt}(S^{RD}) \\
&= \sum_i \frac{d}{dt}(D_i(\pi_i^*, \pi_i^t)) - \sum_i \frac{d}{dt}(D_i^{RD}(\pi_i^*, \pi_i^t)) \\
&= \sum_i \sum_j (\pi_i^t(j) - \pi_i^*(j))(l_i^t(j) - 1)V_i^j \\
&= \sum_i \sum_{j, \pi_i^t(j) \geq \pi_i^*(j)} (\pi_i^t(j) - \pi_i^*(j))(-\sigma)V_i^j \\
&\quad + \sum_i \sum_{j, \pi_i^t(j) < \pi_i^*(j)} (\pi_i^t(j) - \pi_i^*(j))(\sigma)V_i^j \\
&= \sum_i (< 0) < 0.
\end{aligned}$$

It can easily be seen why the $\sum_j$ terms above must be strictly negative. If $\pi_i^t \neq \pi_i^*$ then $\exists j$ s.t. $0 < \pi_i^t(j) < \pi_i^*(j)$. The contribution of this term could be zero only if $V_i^j = 0$, otherwise this term contributes a strictly negative term to the sum. But note that the opponents are all using ReDVaLeR which allows only mixed policies while learning, and partially mixed or pure policies only in the limit. Given this constraint, $V_i^j$ can be zero only if all the payoffs for action $j$ in $\mathbf{R}_i$ are zeroes. This means the $jth$ action of the learner must be dominated by all other actions and strictly dominated by at least one other action (unless of course all the payoffs are zero, which is a degenerate case that we ignore). This means the equilibrium probability for the $jth$ action must be zero, i.e., $\pi_i^*(j) = 0$. But this contradicts the fact that $\pi_i^t(j) < \pi_i^*(j)$ for some $\pi_i^t(j) > 0$. Hence the contribution of term $j$ in the $\sum_j$ must be strictly negative, and consequently the entire sum must be strictly negative. Note that in this case, we do not need to assume $\sigma = 1$, but any $0 < \sigma \ll 1$ will do, thus ensuring asymptotic no-regret payoffs by Theorem 2.

This case actually encompasses all non-negative games where NE is stable under RD but not asymptotically stable, including all non-negative $2 \times 2$ games with a unique mixed equilibrium. For all other types of non-negative $2 \times 2$ games, we also have convergence as simplifying the ReDVaLeR update rule (equation 3) for two action games shows that it is identical to a gradient ascent rule (albeit an extra multiplicative term involving the product of both action probabilities, which changes only the magnitude, not the direction of the gradient in such games), which we know converges in policies in these games (Singh, Kearns, & Mansour 2000). That result also extends to ReDVaLeR.

**Case 2 :** $\frac{d}{dt}(S^{RD}) > 0$. Then we have,

$$\begin{aligned}
\frac{dS^{RD}}{dt} - \frac{dS}{dt} &= \sum_i \frac{d}{dt}(D_i^{RD}(\pi_i^*, \pi_i^t)) - \\
&\quad \sum_i \frac{d}{dt}(D_i(\pi_i^*, \pi_i^t)) \\
&= \sum_{ij} (\pi_i^t(j) - \pi_i^*(j))(1 - l_i^t(j))V_i^j \\
&= \sigma \sum_{ij} \left|\pi_i^t(j) - \pi_i^*(j)\right| V_i^j, \text{ by (4)} \\
&> \frac{d}{dt}(S^{RD}), \text{ if } \sigma = 1, \forall i
\end{aligned}$$

This implies again that $\frac{d}{dt}(S) < 0$. The strict inequality in the last step is explained as in case 1. Thus we see that $S$ is Lyapunov for the system of ReDVaLeR adaptation, though in case 2, it needs $\sigma = 1$ which is counterproductive to Theorem 2. ∎

When $\sigma = 1$, the player essentially *stops* learning (learning rate is 0) when it is winning but continues when losing (learning rate is 2). This principle has been explored before under the title of *Win Stay, Lose Shift* (Posch & Brannath 1997; Nowak & Sigmund 1993). We note that this assignment of learning rates ensures that KL divergence is Lyapunov, i.e., divergence decreases monotonically. However, monotonic convergence is not essential for convergence, and the original schedule of learning rates ($0 < \sigma \ll 1$) may also produce convergence, though KL divergence may sometimes increase in that case. Figure 1 shows that in a non-negative version of the RSP (produced by adding +1 to all payoffs) game, where Case 2 always applies, convergence can be achieved in self-play using $0 < \sigma \ll 1$. However, in the Shapley game where no-regret algorithms usually cycle exponentially (Jafari *et al.* 2001), ReDVaLeR has been found to converge (not shown) in self-play only if $\sigma \geq \frac{1}{3}$.

[2]This is true only for internal starting policies since all pure policies are fixed points of (3). So $S$ cannot be global Lyapunov.

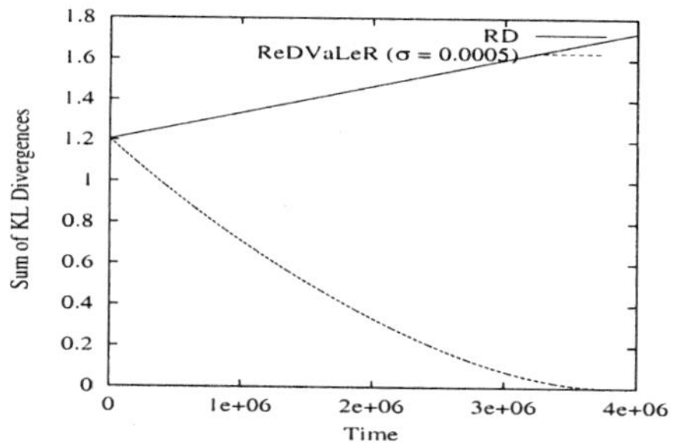


Figure 1: The sum of KL Divergences (S) in the non-negative version of RSP game of Table 1.

## Summary

This paper introduces a novel MAL algorithm, ReDVaLeR, which unlike the previous algorithms has a specific desirable property against opponents that are neither stationary nor using the same algorithm as the learner. It does not attempt to explicitly identify the opponents' algorithms, and as such are unaware of any desirable point of convergence (in policies) against such opponents. Therefore, instead of policy convergence, it achieves constant bounded regret at any time (no-regret payoff asymptotically) against such opponents, while preserving the earlier properties of convergence against stationary opponents and in self-play. We have established the following properties of ReDVaLeR in arbitrary sized general-sum non-negative games: (i) It converges to a stationary best response against an arbitrary number of stationary opponents, (ii) It achieves no-regret payoff against an arbitrary number of opponents playing arbitrary fixed sequences of non-stationary policies, and (iii) If all the players are following ReDVaLeR, then they converge to their portions of a NE, but one case requires a learning rate schedule that conflicts with property (ii). A simple experiment shows that even in this case, the learning rates sometimes can be such that convergence in self-play is maintained and no-regret payoff is achieved.

## References

Auer, P.; Cesa-Bianchi, N.; Freund, Y.; and Schapire, R. E. 1995. Gambling in a rigged casino: The adversarial multi-arm bandit problem. In *Proceedings of the 36th Annual Symposium on Foundations of Computer Science*, 322 – 331. Milwaukee, WI: IEEE Computer Society Press.

Bowling, M., and Veloso, M. 2001. Rational and convergent learning in stochastic games. In *Proceedings of the Seventeenth International Joint Conference on Artificial Intelligence*, 1021 – 1026.

Bowling, M., and Veloso, M. 2002. Multiagent learning using a variable learning rate. *Artificial Intelligence*.

Brafman, R. I., and Tennenholtz, M. 2002a. Efficient learning equilibrium. In *Proceedings of Neural Information Processing Systems*.

Brafman, R. I., and Tennenholtz, M. 2002b. R-max - A general polynomial time algorithm for near-optimal reinforcement learning. *Journal of Machine Learning Research* 3:213 – 231.

Claus, C., and Boutilier, C. 1998. The dynamics of reinforcement learning in cooperative multiagent systems. In *Proceedings of the 15th National Conference on Artificial Intelligence*, 746–752. Menlo Park, CA: AAAI Press/MIT Press.

Conitzer, V., and Sandholm, T. 2003a. AWESOME: A general multiagent learning algorithm that converges in self-play and learns a best response against stationary opponents. In *Proceedings of the 20th International Conference on Machine Learning*.

Conitzer, V., and Sandholm, T. 2003b. BL-WoLF: A framework for loss-bounded learnability in zero-sum games. In *Proceedings of the 20th International Conference on Machine Learning*.

Freund, Y., and Schapire, R. E. 1999. Adaptive game playing using multiplicative weights. *Games and Economic Behavior* 29:79 – 103.

Fudenberg, D., and Levine, D. 1995. Consistency and cautious fictitious play. *Journal of Economic Dynamics and Control* 19:1065 – 1089.

Fudenberg, D., and Levine, K. 1998. *The Theory of Learning in Games*. Cambridge, MA: MIT Press.

Greenwald, A., and Hall, K. 2002. Correlated q-learning. In *Proceedings of the AAAI Symposium on Collaborative Learning Agents*.

Hart, S., and Mas-Colell, A. 2003. Uncoupled dynamics do not lead to nash equilibrium. *American Economic Review*.

Hu, J., and Wellman, M. P. 1998. Multiagent reinforcement learning: Theoretical framework and an algorithm. In *Proc. of the 15th Int. Conf. on Machine Learning (ML'98)*, 242–250. San Francisco, CA: Morgan Kaufmann.

Hu, J., and Wellman, M. 2002. Multiagent Q-learning. *Journal of Machine Learning*.

Jafari, A.; Greenwald, A.; Gondek, D.; and Ercal, G. 2001. On no-regret learning, fictitious play, and nash equilibrium. In *Proceedings of the Eighteenth International Conference on Machine Learning*, 226 – 223.

Littlestone, N., and Warmuth, M. 1994. The weighted majority algorithm. *Information and Computation* 108:212 – 261.

Littman, M. L., and Szepesvari, C. 1996. A generalized reinforcement learning model: Convergence and applications. In *Proceedings of the 13th International Conference on Machine Learning*, 310 – 318.

Littman, M. L. 1994. Markov games as a framework for multi-agent reinforcement learning. In *Proc. of the 11th Int. Conf. on Machine Learning*, 157–163. San Mateo, CA: Morgan Kaufmann.

Littman, M. L. 2001. Friend-or-foe Q-learning in general-sum games. In *Proceedings of the Eighteenth International Conference on Machine Learnig*.

Nash, J. F. 1951. Non-cooperative games. *Annals of Mathematics* 54:286 – 295.

Nowak, M., and Sigmund, K. 1993. A strategy of win-stay, lose-shift that outperforms tit-for-tat in the prisoner's dilemma game. *Nature* 364:56 – 58.

Posch, M., and Brannath, W. 1997. Win-stay, lose-shift. A general learning rule for repeated normal form games. In *Proceedings of the Third International Conference on Computing in Economics and Finance*.

Sandholm, T., and Crites, R. 1996. On multiagent Q-learning in a semi-competitive domain. In Weiß, G., and Sen, S., eds., *Adaptation and Learning in Multi-Agent Systems*. Springer-Verlag. 191–205.

Sen, S.; Sekaran, M.; and Hale, J. 1994. Learning to coordinate without sharing information. In *National Conference on Artificial Intelligence*, 426–431. Menlo Park, CA: AAAI Press/MIT Press.

Singh, S.; Kearns, M.; and Mansour, Y. 2000. Nash convergence of gradient dynamics in general-sum games. In *Proceedings of the Sixteenth Conference on Uncertainty in Artificial Intelligence*, 541–548.

Sutton, R., and Burto, A. G. 1998. *Reinforcement Learning: An Introduction*. MIT Press.

Tan, M. 1993. Multi-agent reinforcement learning: Independent vs. cooperative agents. In *Proceedings of the Tenth International Conference on Machine Learning*, 330–337.

Wang, X., and Sandholm, T. 2002. Reinforcement learning to play an optimal nash equilibrium in team markov games. In *Advances in Neural Information Processing Systems 15, NIPS*.

Zinkevich, M. 2003. Online convex programming and generalized infinitesimal gradient ascent. In *Proceedings of the 20th International Conference on Machine Learning*.

# Searching for Stable Mechanisms : Automated Design for Imperfect Players

**Andrew J. Blumberg**
Department of Mathematics
University of Chicago
blumberg@math.uchicago.edu

**abhi shelat**
CSAIL
Massachusetts Institute of Technology
abhi@mit.edu

**Abstract**

Recently Conitzer and Sandholm (Conitzer & Sandholm 2002) introduced the concept of "automated mechanism design", whereby mechanism design problems are solved using constraint-satisfaction methods.

Traditionally, mechanism design has focused on producing games which yield the desired outcomes when played by ideal rational players. However actual players are never perfectly rational — human irrationality has been exhaustively studied and computational agents have both resource bounds and potentially implementation flaws. In this paper, we discuss extensions of the techniques of automated mechanism design to produce games which are robust in the face of player imperfections.

We model limited rationality by examining agents which converge on their strategy by using a simple variant of "fictitious play" (simulation of repeated play) (Singh, Kearns, & Mansour 2000). This model associates to each game a system of differential equations describing the trajectory of the agent's strategies. We describe additional constraints which guarantee that automated mechanism design search problems yield *stable* mechanisms. In particular, we present negative results for structural stability and positive results for asymptotic stability by considering strict Bayesian-Nash equilibria and by employing Lyapunov techniques.

## Introduction

Mechanism design is the problem of designing the rules of a game such that individually selfish behavior by the players leads to a "globally optimal" outcome. Mechanism design is relevant whenever there are preferences to be aggregated — examples of such situations include auctions, elections, and public goods problems. Classical approaches to mechanism design in the economics literature focused on the construction of general mechanisms which would function for a wide class of possible preference relations for the players. For example, a seminal result due to Maskin (Osborne & Rubinstein 1994) demonstrates by explicit construction that the mechanism design problem is always solvable (in undominated Nash equilibria) when there are more than two players and the player's preferences satisfy certain fairly general conditions (e.g. monotonicity). Other such results include the celebrated Vickrey-Clark-Groves second-price auctions.



However, the classical approach is unsatisfactory on a number of grounds. For one thing, impossibility results such as the Gibbard-Satterthwaite theorem state that such general constructions cannot be obtained in many important areas of mechanism design. Moreover, the mechanisms used in the proofs of these results are extremely intricate and sometimes perverse (for example, many employ tie-breaking "integer games" which require the players to declare unbounded integers (Osborne & Rubinstein 1994)). To circumvent these problems, Conitzer and Sandholm (Conitzer & Sandholm 2002) introduced the notion of automated mechanism design. Their key insight is that in a particular instance, the preferences of the players are known and so the mechanism can be designed with these specific preferences in mind. This observation enables one to translate the problem of designing a mechanism to a numerical programming problem which can be solved using standard techniques.

Viewing mechanism design problems as constraint-satisfaction problems creates an opportunity to add more constraints to search for games with additional structure. Our work herein demonstrates that it is now possible to reasonably perform mechanism design for games with nuanced and complicated solution concepts. It is hard to imagine such problems being tractable from a general perspective.

The formulation of the traditional mechanism design problem presumes that the players are perfectly rational and error-free. This is an idealization which is simply false in practice. For example, human players are known to consistently deviate from ideal rationality in a complicated collection of ways. In the electronic setting, computational agents are likely to have limited computational power and potentially flawed algorithms or implementations. It is therefore desirable to attempt to construct mechanisms which are robust in the face of player failure. Larson and Sandholm considered a model of bounded computational resources for players which they call "strategic computation", in which players rationally seek to deploy their limited computation (Larson & Sandholm 2001). We study a different approach to the problem.

Repeated play is a common model of learning and bounded rationality. In such a setting, players are assumed to learn to play the game by repeatedly playing and improving their strategies between rounds. It may be the case that the game is actually played many times, or the players may be individually simulating the repetition of the game in order to converge on a strategy to play in a one-shot game (this is called "fictitious play"). Such learning processes can be modeled by a system of differential equations describing the updates of the strategy profiles of the players. We study the stability of a potential mechanism by examining the stability of this associated system of differential equations. A robust mechanism is one for which the associated system is stable and robust in the face of noise both in the description of the game and in the specification of the strategies.

In the following sections, we explore several notions of stability. We examine structural stability (the robustness of qualitative behavior of the trajectories in the face of perturbation of the system of equations) and prove that for some classes of games, automated mechanism design will never yield structurally stable solutions. In general, we discuss how to determine if the associated system is structurally stable. Then we consider asymptotic stability of equilibrium points (the robustness of an equilibrium in the face of small perturbations of the state of a system). We describe how to write constraints which guarantee that solutions to the automated mechanism design search problem have asymptotically stable equilibria by searching for Lyapunov functions (Merkin 1997).

## Background

A central solution concept in games of incomplete information is the Bayesian-Nash equilibrium, which we review here (see (Fudenberg & Tirole 1991) for a detailed presentation). In a Bayesian-Nash setting, each of the $n$ players in a game know their own *type* $\theta_i$ (private information), but only have a probability distribution over the types of the other players. Each player also has a set of actions, $A_i$. An *outcome*, or action profile, is the tuple of actions chosen by all the players and is a member of $A = A_1 \times A_2 \times \cdots \times A_n$. Each player also has a utility function which maps their type and an outcome of the game to a particular payoff.

**(Informal) Bayesian-Nash Equilibrium** A set of strategies is a Bayesian-Nash equilibrium if for each player, and for each possible type of that player, the expected utility of the player's strategy (given the distribution of other players' types and that their strategies are fixed) is greater than or equal to the expected utility of any other strategy for that player.

### Automated mechanism design

Now we review the formal setting for automated mechanism design problems.

**Definition** In an automated mechanism design setting, we are given :

1. A finite set of players $N$.
2. A finite set of outcomes $O$.
3. For each player $i$, a set of types $\theta_i$, and a probability distribution over $\theta_i$.
4. For each player $i$, a utility function $u_i : \theta_i \times O \to \mathbb{R}$ which maps types and outcomes to utilities.
5. A social objective function whose expectation the designer is to maximize.
6. A solution concept (e.g. Bayesian-Nash equilibrium).
7. Additional constraints — for example, whether the mechanism can employ randomness or side-payments.

The goal of a mechanism design problem is to produce a game $G$ which is a map $G : S_1 \times S_2 \times \ldots \times S_n \to \chi(O)$, where $\chi(O)$ is the space of probability distribution over $O$ and each $S_i$ is a set of actions for player $i$ to play. When randomized outcomes are not allowed, $\chi$ is restricted to distributions with all of their weight on a single outcome. Note that the set of pure strategies for each player in this game are the same as the set of types– in other words, in the game, each player is to announce a type, and the collective actions of all players determines the outcome.

The mechanism $G$ is a *truth-telling* mechanism if the set of strategies in which all players announce their types honestly forms an equilibrium with respect to the solution concept.

We assume in the remainder of the paper that the solution concept is Bayesian-Nash equilibrium, randomized outcomes are permitted, and the utility function is the sum of expected utilities for all players. Conitzer and Sandholm (Conitzer & Sandholm 2002) present a procedure for expressing mechanism design problems of this type as linear programming problems.

**LP For Mechanism Design** Let $S = S_1 \times S_2 \times \cdots \times S_n$ represent the action profiles, which in this case coincides with the set of types, $\Theta = \theta_1 \times \cdots \times \theta_n$. The variables, $\{x_{s,o}\}$, are indexed on $S \times O$ and represent the probability that a particular outcome $o$ occurs given a specified action profile $s = (s_1, \ldots, s_n)$. The objective function of the program is the social welfare function (the sum of the players' expected utilities). The constraints of the program are:

1. For each action profile $s \in S$, the probabilities associated with that action profile must sum to 1.

$$\forall_{s \in S} \sum_{o \in O} x_{s,o} = 1$$

2. For each player $i$, the expected utility for the truth-telling strategy must be greater than or equal to 0. This specifies that there is nonnegative benefit to the players for participating.

$$\forall_{s \in S} \sum_{o \in O} x_{s,o} u_i(s_i, o) \geq 0$$

Note that in the truth-telling strategy, player $i$'s utility at a particular outcome is simply $u_i(s_i, o)$ since $s_i$ is her true type.

3. For a given player, the expected utility for the truth-telling strategy (when all other players are playing the truth-telling strategy) must be greater than or equal to the expected utility for any other pure strategy. This guarantees that truth-telling is a Bayesian-Nash equilibrium.

$$\forall_{s \in S} \forall_{\sigma \in S_i} \sum_{o \in O} x_{s,o} u_i(s_i, o) \geq \sum_{o \in O} x_{s',o} u_i(\sigma, o)$$

(where $s'_j = s_j$ for $j \neq i$ and $s'_i = \sigma$)

**Remark** If we forbid randomized outcomes, this program becomes a mixed-integer programming problem with linear constraints. Mixed integer programs are still solvable (although not as efficiently), but in some subsequent constructions we will generate polynomial constraints. Mixed-integer programs with polynomial constraints are undecidable, and so we focus on randomized outcomes which lead to general nonlinear programming problems.

## An example

We employ the following divorce settlement example, also discussed in (Conitzer & Sandholm 2003), to illustrate our techniques and methodology.

**Divorce Settlement.** A husband and a wife are getting divorced. An arbitrator must allocate a prized painting.

1. The husband and the wife are each either of type low ($L$) or high ($H$) with respect to their interest in the painting.
2. The possible outcomes are to give the painting to the husband ($h$), to give it to the wife ($w$), joint ownership ($j$), or to burn the painting ($b$).
3. The utilities, which are the same for each player, are as follows: $u_L(b) = -10$, $u_L(\text{other has}) = 0$, $u_L(\text{own}) = 2$, $u_(j) = 1$, $u_H(b) = -10$, $u_H(\text{other has}) = 0$, $u_H(\text{own}) = 100$, $u_H(j) = 50$.
4. Each person is type $L$ with probability 0.8 and type $H$ with probability 0.2.

In our linear program formulation , the variable $x^a_{yz}$ represent the probability that the outcome is $a$ given that husband and wife announce types $y$ and $z$ respectively. Solving the this linear program as described in yields the following mechanism:

| ♀/♂ | $L$ | $H$ |
|---|---|---|
| $L$ | $h = w = j = \frac{1}{3}$ | $h = 1$ |
| $H$ | $w = 1$ | $h = w = j = \frac{2}{11}, b = \frac{5}{11}$ |

Figure 1: Divorce Settlement Mechanism. The Husband's actions are across the columns, and the Wife's actions are on the rows. The expected utility for both players is $17\frac{302}{550}$.

Note that these numbers are different then the solution presented in (Conitzer & Sandholm 2003) — there are many optimal solutions. Interestingly, the solution in (Conitzer & Sandholm 2003) does not have symmetric utilities: the husband's utility is $18\frac{8}{11}$ and the wife's utility is $16\frac{102}{275}$.

## The dynamical system induced by repeated play

We consider the simple repeated-play gradient-ascent dynamics discussed in (Singh, Kearns, & Mansour 2000). In this model, each player updates their strategy between simulations of the games by adjusting the probabilities of action selection along the gradient of their expected utility. A brief description of the framework follows.

The strategy profile for player $i$ is represented as a collection of variables $\{\alpha_{i,j}\}$ indexed on all but one of the possible actions in $S_i$, where $\alpha_{i,j}$ is the probability of playing action $j$. The probability of the deleted action is implicitly $1-\sum_j \alpha_{i,j}$ in order to ensure that the probabilities sum to 1. In our case, the set of pure strategies for player $i$ corresponds to the set of types $S_i = \Theta_i = \{\theta^1_i, \ldots, \theta^k_i\}$, and so $\alpha_{i,j}$ is the probability that player $i$ announces type $\theta^j_i$. Define the gradient vector for player $i$ as $\hat{\alpha}_i = (\dot{\alpha}_{i,1}, \ldots, \dot{\alpha}_{i,k})$ where

$$\dot{\alpha}_{i,j} = \frac{\partial E[u_i]}{\partial \alpha_{i,j}}$$

The gradient-ascent method begins at some initial strategy profile $s \in S$ and repeatedly updates the strategies by taking a small step along $\hat{\alpha}$. To extend the dynamics to the Bayesian-Nash case, we compute the expected utility assuming that both a player's own type and the types of the other players are drawn from given distributions — we assume the player does not use knowledge about their own type as they simulate. This is reasonable in some circumstances (a player simulating their auction behavior might well assume that their valuation of an item will fluctuate) and unreasonable in others. See also (Dekel, Fudenberg, & Levine 2001) for a discussion of related concerns.

In the same manner as (Singh, Kearns, & Mansour 2000), we consider the modified dynamics in which steps which go outside the boundaries of the unit cube are projected back into the cube. This has the effect that equilibrium points of the modified dynamics may not be equilibrium points of the unconstrained dynamics. As such, we have to use modified versions of the analytic tools for stability determination. See (Blumberg & shelat 2004) for an analysis of this situation.

In addition, it should be noted that the system of differential equations we describe is obtained as the limit for very small step size of a discrete update process. However, it can be shown that as the step size decreases the dynamics approach the "continuous dynamics" — we defer further discussion of this to the full paper.

In order to illustrate the gradient-descent repeated-play dynamics for our running example, we first compute the expected utility for the husband, which we denote $V$. Here $\alpha_1$ is the probability that the husband plays low when his type is low, $\alpha_2$ is the probability he plays low when his type is high, and the same applies to $\alpha_3$ and $\alpha_4$ for the wife. Also, $u^x_{yz}$ is the husband's expected payoff when the his type is $x$ and the actions $y$ and $z$ are played (that is, it is $\sum_a x^a_{yz} u_y(a)$). For notational convenience, let $\overline{x}$ represent $(1-x)$.

$$\begin{aligned} V = \\ &(t_1 t_2)(\alpha_1\alpha_3 u^L_{LL} + \alpha_1\overline{\alpha_3} u^L_{LH} + \overline{\alpha_1}\alpha_3 u^L_{HL} + \overline{\alpha_1}\overline{\alpha_3} u^L_{HH}) + \\ &(\overline{t_1} t_2)(\alpha_2\alpha_3 u^H_{LL} + \alpha_2\overline{\alpha_3} u^H_{LH} + \overline{\alpha_2}\alpha_3 u^H_{HL} + \overline{\alpha_2}\overline{\alpha_3} u^H_{HH}) + \\ &(t_1 \overline{t_2})(\alpha_1\alpha_4 u^L_{LL} + \alpha_1\overline{\alpha_4} u^L_{LH} + \overline{\alpha_1}\alpha_4 u^L_{HL} + \overline{\alpha_1}\overline{\alpha_4} u^L_{HH}) + \\ &(\overline{t_1}\overline{t_2})(\alpha_2\alpha_4 u^H_{LL} + \alpha_2\overline{\alpha_4} u^H_{LH} + \overline{\alpha_2}\alpha_4 u^H_{HL} + \overline{\alpha_2}\overline{\alpha_4} u^H_{HH}) \end{aligned}$$

where $t_1 = t_2 = 0.8$. The gradient is obtained by differentiating this expression :

$$\frac{\partial V}{\partial \alpha_1} = t_1 t_2(\alpha_3 u^L_{LL} + \overline{\alpha_3} u^L_{LH} - \alpha_3 u^L_{HL} - \overline{\alpha_3} u^L_{HH}) + t_1 \overline{t_2}(\alpha_4 u^L_{LL} + \overline{\alpha_4} u^L_{LH} - \alpha_4 u^L_{HL} - \overline{\alpha_4} u^L_{HH})$$

(the other derivatives are similar and omitted).

## Searching for stability

There are many ways in which the dynamical system defined above might be unstable. For example, the system might never converge to any Nash equilibrium, no matter what the initial conditions are. Or the system might have many Nash equilibria in addition to the desired one, and each might have large basins of convergence.

**Remark** One difficulty with automated mechanism design is the inability to prevent the existence of extraneous equilibria in addition to the desired solution. This is in contrast to the mechanisms obtained from the classical general theorems, which do not have any additional equilibria (with respect to the solution concept) — although it should be noted that much of the unpleasantness of the results obtained there (e.g. "integer games") arises from the need to rule out unwanted equilibria. Since "generic" games have large numbers of Nash equilibria (McLennan 1999), this is an issue worthy of future work.

We are particularly concerned with two types of stability under perturbation, *structural stability* and *asymptotic stability*.

## Structural stability

A system of differential equations is structurally stable if given a specific trajectory, small changes in the coefficients of the system produce a system with a "nearby" trajectory to the original (see (Hirsch & Smale 1974) for details). Equilibrium points near which the system is structurally stable are called *hyperbolic*. A necessary condition for structural stability is that all equilibrium points are hyperbolic. This can be checked by inspecting the Jacobian matrix of the system of differential equations — if there are no eigenvalues with zero real parts, then the point is structurally stable (Hirsch & Smale 1974).

Unfortunately, our running example never has structurally stable equilibria. In fact, we have the following general result.

**Lemma 1** *The Bayesian-Nash gradient dynamics for games with two players and two types is never structurally stable. In particular, the divorce settlement mechanism is always structurally unstable.*

**Proof Sketch** Consider the Jacobian for the dynamics:

$$\begin{pmatrix} 0 & 0 & \frac{\partial \dot\alpha_1}{\partial \alpha_3} & \frac{\partial \dot\alpha_1}{\partial \alpha_4} \\ 0 & 0 & \frac{\partial \dot\alpha_2}{\partial \alpha_3} & \frac{\partial \dot\alpha_2}{\partial \alpha_3} \\ \frac{\partial \dot\alpha_3}{\partial \alpha_1} & \frac{\partial \dot\alpha_3}{\partial \alpha_2} & 0 & 0 \\ \frac{\partial \dot\alpha_4}{\partial \alpha_1} & \frac{\partial \dot\alpha_4}{\partial \alpha_2} & 0 & 0 \end{pmatrix}$$

Computing, we find that the the $2 \times 2$ submatrix in the top right corner is

$$\begin{aligned} \frac{\partial \dot\alpha_1}{\partial \alpha_3} &= t_1 t_2(u^L_{LL} - u^L_{LH} - u^L_{HL} + u^L_{HH}) \\ \frac{\partial \dot\alpha_1}{\partial \alpha_4} &= t_1 \overline{t_2}(u^L_{LL} - u^L_{LH} - u^L_{HL} + u^L_{HH}) \\ \frac{\partial \dot\alpha_2}{\partial \alpha_3} &= \overline{t_1} t_2(u^H_{LL} - u^H_{LH} - u^H_{HL} + u^H_{HH}) \\ \frac{\partial \dot\alpha_2}{\partial \alpha_4} &= \overline{t_1 t_2}(u^H_{LL} - u^H_{LH} - u^H_{HL} + u^H_{HH}) \end{aligned}$$

Hence, the two top rows are linearly dependent and so this submatrix is singular. Similarly, we obtain that the bottom two rows are linearly dependent, which implies that there are two nonzero eigenvectors with eigenvalue 0 (one of the form $(0\ 0\ x\ y)^T$ and the other of the form $(z\ w\ 0\ 0)^T$, where $(x, y)$ is a nonzero solution to the singular $2 \times 2$ system in the upper righthand corner and $(z, w)$ is a nonzero solution to the singular $2 \times 2$ system in the lower lefthand corner). □

This result is not surprising as a little bit of experimentation makes it clear that the dynamics are sensitive to small changes in the payoff matrix. Larger games are not necessarily structurally unstable, and in a forthcoming paper we determine more precisely the conditions for the Bayesian-Nash gradient dynamics to be structurally stable in general. Unfortunately, searching for structural stability is hard — writing constraints that prevent the Jacobian from having eigenvalues with nonzero real part seems to be infeasible. Moreover, as some of the equilibrium points of the projected dynamics are not necessarily equilibrium points of the unconstrained dynamics, this method is not sufficient to analyze behavior on the boundary of the unit cube.

## Asymptotic stability

*Asymptotic stability* means that for small perturbations away from the equilibrium, over time the system converges back to that equilibrium point. In contrast to our negative result for structural stability, we are able to generate games for which the desired Bayesian-Nash equilibrium is asymptotically stable. We take two approaches to searching for asymptotically stable systems — a "direct" approach and an approach via an adaptation of Lyapunov's criterion (Merkin 1997).

### Strict Bayesian-Nash equilibria

One of the fundamental insights from evolutionary game theory is that a major source of instability within various kinds of response dynamics is the presence of alternative optimal choices — if there are multiple actions available to a player which achieve a Bayesian-Nash equilibrium value (assuming all the other players are fixed and playing their Bayesian-Nash equilibrium strategies), best-response dynamics can slip between these actions (Samuelson 1997). Although the concept of an evolutionary Bayesian-Nash equilibrium does not seem to be easily expressed via constraints (as the definition involves an existential quantification), we can consider instead the (stronger) notion of

Bayesian-Nash equilibrium. As the name suggests, strict Bayesian-Nash equilibrium is defined identically to ordinary Bayesian-Nash equilibria except that the inequalities are made strict. In other words, there is a unique best response to the equilibrium action profile. When the number of actions is finite, strict Bayesian-Nash equilibria are asymptotically stable.

In our running example, truth-telling is a Bayesian-Nash equilibrium. However, any strategy of the form $(x, 0)$ (the husband is type $L$ and lies about his type with probability $(1-x)$) is also a best-response to the truth-telling strategy for the wife. Therefore, the truth-telling strategy is not asymptotically stable — small perturbations lead to another best-response, at which point the gradient will not change the solution. For example, at the point $(0.99, 0, 1, 0)$ the gradient is $(0, -8.9, 0.03, -8.9)$ which implies that neither party can improve their situation since their gradients force them into the boundaries. Thus, even very small deviations from the truth-telling equilibrium $(1, 0, 1, 0)$ do not return. Fortunately, it is straightforward to modify the linear program described before in order to search for strict Bayesian-Nash equilibria.

To produce the strict linear program, we replace the third set of constraints with

$$\forall_{s \in S} \forall_{s'_i \in S_i} \sum_{o \in O} x_{s,o} u_i(s_i, o) \geq \sum_{o \in O} x_{s,o} u_i(s'_i, o) + \epsilon$$

where $\epsilon$ controls the precision needed to see the strictness. Setting $\epsilon = 0.1$, and solving the new linear program, we obtain the following solution:

| ♀/♂ | $L$ | $H$ |
|---|---|---|
| $L$ | $w = h = j = \frac{1}{3}$ | $h = 1$ |
| $H$ | $w = 1$ | $h = w = j = \frac{43}{264}, b = \frac{135}{264}$ |

Figure 2: Strict BNE mechanism. The payoff for each player at the equilibrium is slightly lower than it was before ($17\frac{227}{550}$ vs $17\frac{302}{550}$), but now truth-telling is a strict Bayesian-Nash equilibrium.

A problem with this method is that there exist games with asymptotically stable equilibria which are not strict equilibria, i.e. the condition is too strong. Moreover, picking $\epsilon$ is a tradeoff which requires consideration.

## The method of Lyapunov functions

The definitive method for proving the asymptotic stability of a solution trajectory is to provide a Lyapunov function (Merkin 1997) for the dynamics.

**Lyapunov Function.** A Lyapunov function for a system of differential equations in variables $x_1, \ldots, x_n$ is a function $Y(x_1, x_2, \ldots, x_n)$ which is positive definite and such that $\frac{dY}{dt}$ is negative (semi)-definite.

The existence of such a function implies stability at the origin, and if the derivative is negative definite, the origin is asymptotically stable. To utilize this method, we produce additional constraints for the linear program which induce a simultaneous search for a mechanism and for a Lyapunov function which guarantees that the desired equilibrium point is stable or asymptotically stable (usually the latter). In general, the resulting program will have nonlinear polynomial constraints. In addition, it is a straightforward matter to transform coordinates so that the desired equilibrium point is at the origin.

However, because we are working with a system which is externally constrained to lie in the unit cube, we must employ a slight modification of the Lyapunov method. This technique is further developed in (Blumberg & shelat 2004).

**Recursive Lyapunov Function.** A recursive Lyapunov function for a system of differential equations constrained to lie on the unit cube in variables $x_1, \ldots, x_n$ is a function $Y(x_1, x_2, \ldots, x_n)$ which is positive definite on the unit cube and such that $\frac{dY}{dt}$ is negative definite on the unit cube. In addition, the restriction of $\frac{dY}{dt}$ obtained by setting a subset of the variables $\{x_j\}$ and the derivatives $\{\dot{x_j}\}$ to 0 is also negative definite.

We show elsewhere (Blumberg & shelat 2004) the following result, which we employ herein.

**Theorem 2** *For a given constrained dynamics on the unit cube, if there exists a recursive constrained Lyapunov function, $L$, then the dynamics have an asymptotic equilibrium point at* 0.

In the remaining portion of this section, we will use our theorem in our running example. For the divorce mechanism, we consider a candidate Lyapunov function written as

$$Y = \sum_{i>j} a_{ij} \alpha_i \alpha_j$$

Evaluating the derivative, we find that

$$\frac{dY}{dt} = 2a_{11}\alpha_1\dot{\alpha}_1 + a_{12}(\dot{\alpha}_1\alpha_2 + x_1\dot{\alpha}_2) + a_{13}(\dot{\alpha}_1\alpha_3 + \alpha_1\dot{\alpha}_3) + \ldots + a_{44}\alpha_4\dot{\alpha}_4$$

We now augment our original program with the extra variables, $a_{11}, \ldots, a_{44}$ and now determine additional constraints in order to guarantee that $Y$ is positive definite. To assure definiteness, we could employ the following constraints:

1. For every $i$, $a_{ii} > 0$. This ensures that when all the other variables are set to 0 the form is still positive.
2. For every $i$ and $j$, $a_{ij} \geq 0$.

In order to ensure that $dY/dt$ is negative definite over the unit cube, we must place additional constraints on the variables $x^a_{yz}$ and $a_{ij}$. For the divorce example, calculation shows that $dY/dt$ is a multivariate polynomial of degree 2. Consider a generic multivariate polynomial of degree 2,

$$\sum_k c_k x_k + \sum_{i,j} d_{ij} x_i x_j$$

For this to be negative definite on the unit cube, it suffices for the following conditions to hold:

1. For every $i$, $c_i \leq 0$ and $c_i + d_{ii} < 0$. This ensures that when all the other variables are set to 0 the form is still negative.
2. For every $i$ and $j$, $d_{ij} \leq 0$.

Now, in the running example the $\{c_i\}$ and $\{d_{ij}\}$ are algebraic expressions involving the $a_{ij}$, the constants $t_1, t_2$ and $u^*_{**}$, and the other decision variables in the numerical program — $\{x_{s,o}\}$. Expanding this out, we obtain a program with quadratic constraints. For example, the constraint on $c_1$ requires the following expression be negative:

$$
\begin{aligned}
&-8/5a_{13}x_{HH,h}+8a_{13}x_{HH,b}-4/5a_{13}x_{HH,j}-8a_{13}x_{HL,b} \\
&+8a_{11}x_{HH,b}+20a_{12}x_{LH,h}-20a_{12}x_{HH,h}+2a_{14}x_{HH,b} \\
&-20a_{14}x_{HH,h}+8/5a_{13}x_5+4/5a_{13}x_{HL,j}+8/5a_{11}x_{LH,h} \\
&+10a_{14}x_{HL,j}-2a_{12}x_{12}-4/5a_{11}x_{HH,j}-8a_{11}x_{LH,b} \\
&+10a_{12}x_{LH,j}+2a_{12}x_{HH,b}+4/5a_{11}x_{LH,j}-10a_{14}x_{HH,j} \\
&-2a_{14}x_{HL,b}-8/5a_{11}x_{HH,h}-10a_{12}x_{HH,j}+20a_{14}x_{HL,h}
\end{aligned}
$$

Finally, we require the constraints which guarantee that $Y$ is a recursive Lyapunov function — for every subset of the variables $\{x_i\}$, we must have that $Y$ remains a negative definite form when all of the members of the subset and their derivatives are set to 0. These constraints are generated using the same criterion for negative definiteness specified above.

**Remark** One might be concerned by the quantity of additional constraints required for performing the simultaneous search for a game and a Lyapunov function. Indeed, the number of constraints required in the simultaneous search is exponential in the number of players and actions. Although this is unpleasant, it is no worse than the general mechanism design problem, which also requires constraints exponential in the number of players and actions.

When we solve this program, the game generated has a strict Bayesian-Nash equilibrium — but in addition we are provided with a proof of asymptotic stability in the form of the Lyapunov function encoded in the additional program variables.

**Remark** The conditions to ensure definiteness which we employ are sufficient, but considerably stronger than necessary — we use them for simplicity, but there are benefits in generality to be obtained by utilizing more precise conditions. Also, larger games will involve higher degree polynomials for which somewhat different conditions are required.

## Conclusions

In this paper we have demonstrated extensions of the techniques of automated mechanism design which permit us to search for (and obtain) mechanisms which possess complicated additional properties beyond those implied by the basic problem statement. We believe that this general method of exploiting the flexibility of automated mechanism design to find mechanisms satisfying additional constraints will have broad applicability. For example, one could construct mechanisms which are insensitive to certain kinds of collusion.

We apply this methodology to the problem of finding mechanisms which are robust against player errors by presenting an algorithm which simultaneously searches for a game and a proof that the desired equilibrium point is asymptotically stable. We also discuss the difficulties of finding structurally stable mechanisms. Although we focus on the dynamics associated to a particular simple model of learning, any model of bounded rationality which leads to a dynamical system associated to repeated play is amenable to a similar analysis. In future work, we plan to extend our analysis to the system of stochastic differential equations that is associated to the classical economic notion of fictitious play.

## References


Blumberg, A. J., and shelat, a. 2004. Lyapunov methods for constrained dynamics. Submitted.

Conitzer, V., and Sandholm, T. 2002. Complexity of mechanism design. In *Proceedings of the 18th Annual Conference on Uncertainty in Artificial Intelligence (UAI-02)*, 103–110.

Conitzer, V., and Sandholm, T. 2003. Applications of automated mechanism design. In *Proceedings of the UAI-03 Bayesian Modeling Applications Workshop.*

Dekel, E.; Fudenberg, D.; and Levine, D. K. 2001. Learning to play bayesian games. In *Discussion Papers*, number 1322 in 1. Northwestern University, Center for Mathematical Studies in Economics and Management Science.

Fudenberg, D., and Tirole, J. 1991. *Game Theory.* The MIT Press.

Hirsch, M. W., and Smale, S. 1974. *Differential Equations, Dynamical Systems, and Linear Algebra.* San Diego, CA: Academic Press.

Larson, K., and Sandholm, T. 2001. Bargaining with limited computation: Deliberation equilibrium. *Artificial Intelligence* 132(2):183–217.

McLennan, A. 1999. On the expected number of nash equilibria of a normal form game. University of Minnesota working paper.

Merkin, D. R. 1997. *Introduction to the Theory of Stability.* Springer-Verlag.

Osborne, M. J., and Rubinstein, A. 1994. *A Course in Game Theory.* The MIT Press.

Samuelson, L. 1997. *Evolutionary Games and Equilibrium Selection.* The MIT Press.

Singh, S.; Kearns, M.; and Mansour, Y. 2000. Nash convergence of gradient dynamics in general-sum games. In *Proceedings of the Sixteenth Conference on Uncertainty in Artificial Intelligence*, 541–548. Morgan Kaufmann.

# Affective Recruitment of Distributed Heterogeneous Agents

**Aaron Gage** and **Robin R. Murphy**
{agage, murphy}@csee.usf.edu
Center for Robot-Assisted Search and Rescue
University of South Florida
4202 E. Fowler Ave. ENB 118 Rm. 342
Tampa, FL 33620

**Abstract**

Members of multi-robot teams may need to collaborate to accomplish a task due to differences in capabilities. This paper describes an extension of the ALLIANCE architecture that enables agent recruitment within a decentralized UAV-UGV robot team without task preemption but 1) uses a formal model of emotions and 2) handles heterogeneity. Affective computing allows recruitment to be robust under loss of communication between agents and minimizes the number of messages passed. Data from 66 simulations show that the *affective* strategy succeeds with a random message loss rate up to 25% and requires 19.1% fewer messages to be sent compared to *greedy* and *random*, and that of these, *affective* scales best with team size. Comparisons of broadcast to unicast messaging are also made in simulation.

## Introduction

Collaboration among members of a heterogeneous multi-robot team is motivated by a need to complete tasks that require more capabilities than a single robot can provide. This paper contributes an *affective* recruitment protocol that enables robots to request and receive assistance from other members of the team using an emotional model. Simulation results show that this approach is robust in terms of communication losses, requires less communication than other obvious methods, and that it scales well with the number of robots in the team. Thus, although the task domain for this work is landmine detection, other areas (such as low-power systems, swarms, sensor networks, and stealth applications) may also benefit.

The recruitment protocol described in this paper borrows the *standards-based* emotion SHAME from Ortony's formal model of emotions (Ortony 2002). Emotions are useful in robots, as they provide a mechanism for self-regulation, such that a change in a robot's state or behavior can be induced (Murphy *et al.* 2002) if the robot is making no progress on a task. Emotions have been shown to produce emergent social interactions and improve task performance of a team of heterogeneous robots (Murphy *et al.* 2002). In this work, emotions determine when a robot decides to help another. The protocol is designed for a fully decentralized robot team, without task preemption, and to be tolerant of unreliable communications. It is assumed that the robots have a common coordinate frame for the purposes of estimating distances and for locating each other.

This paper presents a formal description of the protocol and emotional model. This work is motivated by a landmine detection task using a robot team with a single unmanned aerial vehicle (UAV) and multiple unmanned ground vehicles (UGVs). The UAV is tasked with performing a raster scan over a minefield, identifying possible mines. When a possible mine is detected, the UAV recruits a UGV, using the *affective recruitment* strategy, to investigate further. Results from 72 simulations testing scalability, robustness under communication failures, and the impact of unicast versus broadcast messaging are presented and discussed. Four additional simulations of illustrative use-cases demonstrate where *greedy* recruitment does not produce optimal results, but *affective* does.

## Related Work

(Cao *et al.* 1995) provides a survey of the issues inherent in multi-robot cooperation. The work in this paper is an extension of the ALLIANCE architecture (Parker 1998) for coordinating distributed multi-robots. ALLIANCE's *impatience* and *acquiescence* produce a behavior that closely resembles recruitment: when a robot is having difficulty completing a task, another robot will come over and relieve it. However, there are four important differences between this work and ALLIANCE. First, ALLIANCE assumes that the robots in the team are all on the same task, and that any of them can substitute for another. In our approach, teams of heterogeneous robots on different tasks can be used. Second, ALLIANCE implicitly assumes that the communication among all members of the robot team is reliable, whereas in our approach, it is expected that communications (or even entire robots) may fail at any time. Further, the recruitment protocol will compensate for temporary communication failures. Third, ALLIANCE assumes that a robot can be preempted from its task, whereas in this approach, there is no preemption. The final difference is that this approach is based on a formal theory of emotions by Ortony (Ortony 2002), where SHAME is a *standards-based* emotion.

The work in this paper uses a contract-net protocol (CNP)

(Smith 1980) with a first-price auction (Monderer & Tennenholtz 1998). MURDOCH (Gerkey & Mataric 2002) is an instantaneous greedy task scheduler that also uses CNP with a first-price auction; its communications impact increases linearly with team size (Gerkey & Mataric 2003), whereas the approach in this paper scales more slowly. Other auction-based approaches include LEMMING (Ohko, Hiraki, & Anzai 1996) that reduces communications by applying the outcome of one auction to successive auctions but assumes that robots will stay in contact, and CEBOT (Cai, Fukuda, & Arai 1997) that uses a World Model, which is not appropriate for a decentralized approach.

## Approach

In this approach, a fixed recruitment protocol begins with a robot (*requester*) broadcasting a request for assistance (in the form of a *HELP* message), and ends when another robot (*responder*) has arrived and begun performing a task on behalf of the *requester*. Our approach uses one primary *standards-based* emotion (SHAME) to modulate responses to *HELP* messages and determine when a robot will allow itself to be recruited. As a robot refuses to help its teammates (by ignoring *HELP* messages), its SHAME increases. When its level of SHAME passes a threshold, the robot will respond. Once the robot decides to respond, its SHAME will be reset to zero (just as motivations in ALLIANCE are reset when they cross a threshold (Parker 1998)). SHAME will also decay over time.

Three communication issues guide the design of this protocol. First, the recruitment algorithm should use a minimal amount of bandwidth. Applications that require low-power or stealthy behavior benefit from prevention of unnecessary transmissions, and in any case, the communication requirement should scale well with the number of agents. Second, the delivery method for messages is broadcast. In our test domain, the real robots will be using a wireless network to communicate. Wireless Ethernet channels are a shared medium, so any transmissions are automatically broadcasts, and received packets that are not intended for a particular robot are simply ignored. As a beneficial side-effect, the amount of network traffic scales slowly with the size of the robot team as seen in Results. The third design issue is that the protocol must be robust in terms of network failure. In a fully distributed system, it is assumed that anything can fail at any time, and that no member of the team should wait forever for a failed robot to respond. Therefore, the recruitment protocol is based on a 3-way TCP/IP handshake and recovers gracefully from lost messages or failed robots.

## Implementation

The recruitment protocol uses a set of six messages. Each message contains the ID number of the sender, the ID number of the recipient, if any, whether the message is broadcast or unicast, and a message type. There are six message types in the recruitment protocol: *HELP*, *ACCEPT*, *RESPONDER*, *ARRIVAL*, *AGREE*, and *ACKACK*.

The protocol is shown graphically in Figure 1. It begins when the *requester* robot broadcasts a *HELP* message with its location and a percept that a robot must have to be a *responder*. If another robot decides to assist, then it responds with an *ACCEPT* message that contains an estimate of the time needed to reach the *requester* based on the location provided in the *HELP* message and the robot's rate of travel. The process by which a robot decides whether to assist is described after the protocol messages.

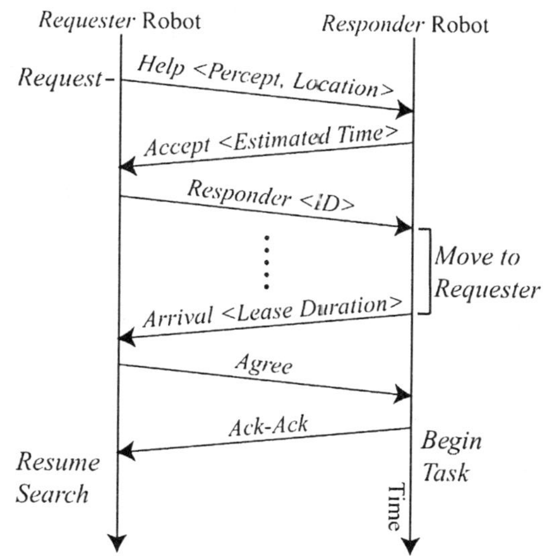


Figure 1: Recruitment protocol in terms of the messages sent between robots.

When the *requester* robot receives an *ACCEPT* message, it broadcasts a *RESPONDER* message to all robots with the ID of the *responder*. For the *responder* robot, this serves as confirmation that its offer to help was accepted, and it will begin moving to assist. For all other robots, this message is an explicit notification that their help is not needed.

The second stage of the protocol begins when the *responder* robot arrives near the *requester* robot and provides an *ARRIVAL* message, which contains the duration of a lease. The purpose of the lease is to compensate for a complete failure of either robot or a loss of communications (as the recruitment ends when the lease expires). If the *requester* robot agrees to the lease, then it will respond with an *AGREE* message. Finally, the *responder* robot will send an *ACKACK* message and take over the investigation of the possible mine. Once the analysis is complete, the agreed lease duration will expire and the recruitment ends.

The *affective recruitment* strategy uses an emotional model to determine under what conditions a robot will respond to a *HELP* message, assuming that it is otherwise available (not on task, able to provide the required percept). At the heart of this model is the affective variable SHAME. The notation for this model will be presented first, followed by details on how to choose the parameters.

Given a team of $n$ robots, $\{r_1, \ldots, r_n\}$, each robot $r_i$ in the team maintains a level of SHAME, $s$, such that $0 \leq s \leq 1$, and $s$ is initialized to zero. Each $r_i$ also has a threshold, $t$, where $t \leq 1$. Three additional parameters affect the behavior of *affective recruitment*: $c$ is a constant that is added to $s$ each time $r_i$ ignores a *HELP* message. $d()$ is a function of the distance $D$ between the *requester* and $r_i$, and is also used to increase $s$. $k()$ is a decay function in terms of elapsed time $\Delta T$ since the previous *HELP* message.

When a *HELP* message arrives, each robot $r_i$ will first account for the decay of its SHAME since the previous request: $s$ is updated as $s = s - k(\Delta T)$. Next, if $s > t$, then robot $r_i$ sends an *ACCEPT* message to the *requester*. Otherwise, if $s \leq t$, then $r_i$ ignores the request and $s$ is updated as $s = s + c + d(D)$.

The parameters were chosen based on experience as follows. $t$ determines how resistant $r_i$ is to being recruited. If $t < 0$, then *affective recruitment* will become *greedy*, in which $r_i$ immediately offers its help when a request is made. The more $t$ approaches 1, the more $r_i$ will ignore requests before responding. In this work, the value $t = 0.75$ was used. The terms $c$ and $d()$ are related to $t$. $c$ controls how quickly a distant robot will respond to a request. If $r_i$ and the *requester* are infinitely far apart, then $t/c$ is approximately the number of requests $r_i$ will ignore before responding (considering that $s$ will decay between requests). In this work, the value $c = 0.2$ was used, so $r_i$ would tend to respond after approximately 4 requests. $d()$ penalizes $r_i$ for ignoring a request from a close neighbor, and should increase as the distance $D$ decreases. In this work, $d(D) = 0.5/D$ so that $r_i$ responds within two requests if it is within 1 unit of the *requester*, and $d()$ has little effect beyond 10 units. The decay function $k()$ determines how quickly $r_i$ will lose its SHAME after ignoring a request. The function $k(\Delta T) = 0.005 \times \Delta T$ was used so that $r_i$ would lose SHAME acquired from a single request in about 40 seconds, and would require 200 seconds to go from $s = 1$ to $s = 0$. This relatively low rate of decay keeps $r_i$ responsive to the needs of the team; if the decay were faster, then periodic requests would tend to be ignored. If the decay were negative, then $r_i$ would tend to "want" to help more over time until it was recruited and $s$ was subsequently reset to zero.

The *requester* robot will continue to send *HELP* messages periodically until it receives an *ACCEPT* message in reply. If the *requester* receives more than one *ACCEPT* message in response to a single *HELP* broadcast, then it will examine the *ACCEPT* messages and choose the sender that specified the least time needed to arrive.

## Experiments

Three recruitment strategies (*greedy, random,* and *affective*) were tested in simulation for a mine detection task. The purpose of these experiments was to measure the performance of the recruitment strategies according to two metrics: the number of messages sent among robots in the team, and the total amount of time that a robot had to wait for assistance. The size of the robot team, rate of random message loss, and messaging type (unicast or broadcast) were varied to test the impact on the recruitment process for each strategy.

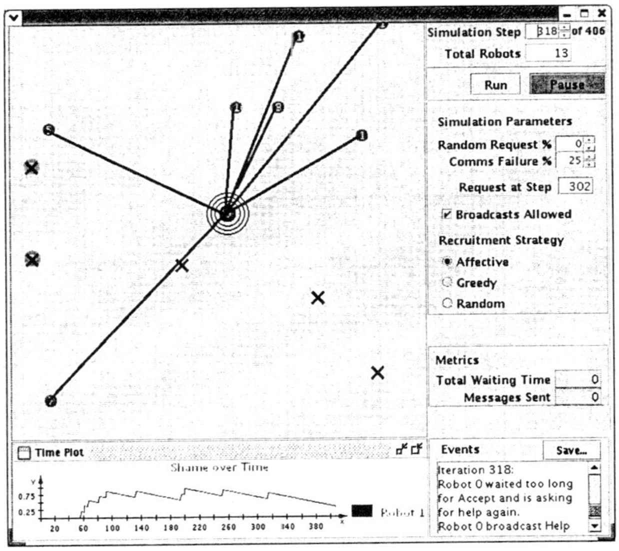


Figure 2: User interface for recruitment simulator. The UAV (center) requests assistance, and all eligible robots with sufficient SHAME respond (solid lines). Those that ignore the request are marked with an $X$.

### Simulated Scenario

In this task, one robot was designated as an unmanned aerial vehicle (UAV) and performed a raster scan over a $100 \times 100$-unit grid at a rate of 3 units per iteration. At five locations in this scan, the UAV stopped, requested assistance, and waited for another robot to arrive. At the end of the raster scan, the UAV stopped for 20 seconds before performing the scan again in the opposite direction.

Between 3 and 22 other simulated robots, representing unmanned ground vehicles (UGVs), were placed in the $100 \times 100$-unit grid. Two of these robots were tasked with raster scans of half of the grid each, at a rate of one unit per iteration, stopping for 20 seconds (and becoming temporarily available for recruitment) at the end of the scan before restarting in the opposite direction. An additional one to twenty idle robots were distributed across the grid. The number of idle robots was varied from one to twenty to test the effect of team size on performance. These idle robots were available for recruitment by the UAV at any time. For each simulation testing the performance of a recruitment strategy, the locations and behavior of all robots were the same unless otherwise noted.

The simulator was coded in Java, using JINI, to test robot recruitment. The simulator controlled three experimental parameters: which recruitment strategy to use, the rate of random communication failures, and which messaging method (unicast or broadcast) to use. The simulator is shown in Figure 2.

### Recruitment Strategies

Three recruitment strategies were tested in simulation. The first was *affective recruitment*, in which the closest idle robot

| | 4 | 8 | 13 | 23 |
|---|---|---|---|---|
| Affective | 48 | 51.67 | 61 | 79.7 |
| Greedy | 29 | 50 | 75 | 125 |
| Random | 29 | 50 | 75 | 125.7 |

Table 1: Average number of messages transmitted for each strategy for varying team size. The total number of robots in the team is shown across the top of the table.

| | 4 | 8 | 13 | 23 |
|---|---|---|---|---|
| Affective | 377.4 | 214.2 | 176.2 | 175.3 |
| Greedy | 260.2 | 120 | 93 | 92 |
| Random | 261 | 203.1 | 261.6 | 326 |

Table 2: Average UAV wait time according to team size, measured in seconds. The total number of robots in the team is shown across the top of the table.

whose SHAME was above a threshold was recruited for each request.

The second recruitment strategy was *greedy recruitment*, in which the idle robot with the minimum estimated time to arrive was recruited for each request. While *greedy recruitment* will tend to have the faster response times than *affective recruitment*, because it does not spend time building up SHAME, it requires an additional message to be sent from every idle robot so the *requester* can choose the least arrival time, and thus does not scale well in terms of communication overhead.

The third recruitment strategy was *random recruitment*, in which an idle robot was chosen at random for recruitment. When the *requester* transmitted a *HELP* message, each idle robot replied to indicate its availability, and one of these was then chosen randomly. As with *greedy recruitment*, this will lead to a faster decision than *affective recruitment*, but does not scale as well for communication. Further, *random* may choose robots that are far away, which will tend to result in longer response times.

## Results

The results of three sets of simulations are provided below. In these experiments, the team size, rate of communication failures, and messaging type were varied to measure the effect on the recruitment strategies.

### Effects of Team Size

The effect of varying the size of the robot team was measured using twelve simulations: for each of the three recruitment strategies, a simulation was performed with 1, 5, 10, and 20 idle robots. The metrics for this test were the total number of messages sent among the robots, and the amount of time that passed, in seconds, from the initial UAV requests until a UGV arrived and was acknowledged. The results of these simulations are shown in Tables 1 and 2.

These results indicate that the *affective recruitment* strategy requires more messages to be sent than *greedy* or *random* when there is only one robot that can be recruited but that once the number of robots increases, *affective recruitment* requires much less communication. The reason behind this difference is that in *affective recruitment*, the UAV only needs to send out *HELP* messages and wait for a single reply to begin negotiating recruitment. As a result, the number of messages that must be sent is almost constant. The variation in the number of messages for *affective recruitment* occurs when more than one robot responds to a particular *HELP* message, or when all UGVs are far from the UAV and additional *HELP* messages must be sent to push their level of SHAME over the threshold. On the other hand, *greedy* and *random* must solicit messages from all other members of the team in order to make a choice, and the number of messages per recruitment increases linearly with the team size.

These results also show that the amount of time that the UAV spent waiting for help to arrive favors the *greedy recruitment* strategy over *affective recruitment*. This is an expected result because *affective recruitment* requires time to build up the level of SHAME in the robots before they will respond. In these simulations, the UAV waited 3 seconds between requests for help before calling again, and needed to request from five to ten times per recruitment before it received a response. If the parameters for updating SHAME were tuned or learned, this difference between *greedy* and *affective* could be reduced. Learning these parameters is a direction for future work. In general, the faster a robot's SHAME exceeds the threshold, the closer *affective recruitment* will resemble *greedy*, to the point that if the SHAME exceeds the threshold after a single request, then the two strategies are equivalent. One advantage of the *affective recruitment* strategy is that it allows for a flexible trade-off between response time and the number of messages transmitted.

Finally, these results show that *affective recruitment* outperformed *random*, because although a recruitment choice was made immediately with *random*, the closest *responder* was typically not chosen, so the time required for it to arrive was higher than for the other strategies.

Note that in this set of simulations, the locations at which the UAV made requests were fixed, and to prevent any bias from the UGV positions, three randomly generated arrangements of robots were used. The results reported above represent 36 simulations, and the averages are shown.

### Effects of Communication Loss

An additional 27 simulations tested the effects of random message loss for the recruitment strategies. Each of the three strategies was tested with 5%, 10%, and 25% of the messages between robots being randomly dropped (not transmitted, but with no notification to the sender). Ten idle robots plus the two tasked UGVs and the UAV were used in each simulation, for a total of 13 robots. In these simulations, the choice of what messages to drop was made randomly by the simulator, and the impact of that choice varied. Thus, each of these tests was conducted three times to capture the typical performance of each strategy. The results from these simulations are shown in Tables 3 and 4.

These results show that the recruitment protocol continues to function despite network losses, and that the relative

|  | 0% | 5% | 10% | 25% |
|---|---|---|---|---|
| Affective | 61 | 81.3 | 67.3 | 147.3 |
| Greedy | 75 | 107.3 | 117.7 | 161.7 |
| Random | 75 | 93 | 99.3 | 189.7 |

Table 3: Average number of messages transmitted according to network failure rate. The rate of random message loss is shown across the top of the table. Note that the 0% column is repeated from Table 1.

|  | 0% | 5% | 10% | 25% |
|---|---|---|---|---|
| Affective | 176.2 | 311.7 | 190.1 | 587.4 |
| Greedy | 67 | 148.4 | 167.8 | 330.6 |
| Random | 261.6 | 385.8 | 340.3 | 897.7 |

Table 4: Average UAV wait time, in seconds, according to network failure rate. The rate of random message loss is shown across the top of the table. Note that the 0% column is repeated from Table 2.

performance of each of the recruitment strategies remains consistent as the rate of message loss increases. As before, *affective recruitment* requires the fewest messages to be sent, on average, followed by *greedy* and *random*. In fact, *random* performs better than *greedy*, when it was expected that they would perform equally well (since they send the same number of messages when there are no losses). By the time that losses reach 25%, the particular recruitment strategy used does not make much difference, because at that point, there is only an 18% likelihood that the six consecutive recruitment messages required by the protocol will all be sent properly. As before, *greedy recruitment* still resulted in the least time spent waiting by the UAV, followed by *affective recruitment*.

A particular weakness of *greedy recruitment* is that the UAV must obtain the locations of all eligible robots before it can choose the nearest one. Assuming a decentralized team, this requires an explicit communication from all other robots to the UAV, which may be impacted by network losses. If the nearest robot to the UAV fails to receive a *HELP* message or to send a reply, then the UAV may commit to recruiting a different, more distant robot, and be forced to await its arrival. On the other hand, using *affective recruitment*, the UAV will tend to make multiple requests, which reduces the reliance on any single *HELP* message. Suppose that an eligible robot, $r_1$, is nearest to the UAV and fails to send a reply due to network problems. Provided that no other robots had sufficient SHAME to respond to that request (for instance, if they were far away and accrued SHAME more slowly), the UAV would quickly request again and have another chance to recruit $r_1$. In other words, requesting over time can find solutions that even outperform *greedy recruitment*, if the time between requests is less than the additional time a more distant robot needs to arrive.

|  | Broadcast | Unicast |
|---|---|---|
| Affective | 67.3 | 379.3 |
| Greedy | 117.7 | 194 |
| Random | 99.3 | 183.3 |

Table 5: Average number of messages transmitted according to messaging type. Note that the Broadcast column is the same as the 10% column in Table 3.

## Broadcast versus Unicast Messaging

Nine simulations were conducted to test the effect of using unicast (single-sender, single-receiver) transmissions instead of broadcast in the recruitment protocol. In these simulations, instead of sending a single *HELP* message to all other robots, the UAV would attempt to send *HELP* messages to all other robots individually. As with the network failure tests, 13 robots were used, of which 10 were untasked. A network failure rate of 10% was used. If there had been no losses in this test, then the number of messages would have trivially been a function of team size. The results of these simulations are shown in Table 5. Note that due to the random nature of the message losses, each strategy was tested three times and the results were averaged.

These results show that *affective recruitment* relies on broadcast messaging to minimize the total number of messages. Since *affective recruitment* sends multiple *HELP* messages before another robot has high enough SHAME to respond, these requests are multiplied by the number of idle team members, which goes well beyond the number of messages required by *greedy* or *random* (for which a single *HELP* message is sufficient). Thus, broadcast messaging is better suited for this application than unicast.

## Illustrative Use Cases

Although the results above indicate that *greedy recruitment* will tend to produce the shortest wait times for the UAV, this is not universally true. There are cases in which the *affective recruitment* strategy results in shorter wait times than *greedy*. Suppose that there are three UGVs, $r_1, r_2, r_3$, such that $r_1$ is untasked, and $r_2$ and $r_3$ perform a raster scan. Let $r_2$ move two units per iteration, while $r_1$ and $r_3$ move one unit. Thus, $r_2$ and $r_3$ will finish their tasks at different times. Next, suppose that at time step $t_0$, the UAV sends a *HELP* message, and two robots, $r_1$ and $r_3$ are idle, and although $r_2$ can reach the UAV faster than $r_1$ or $r_3$, it is on task and cannot respond. In the *greedy* and *random* strategies, $r_1$ or $r_3$ would be chosen for recruitment immediately, whereas with *affective recruitment*, no selection would be made, but all of the UGVs would increase their levels of SHAME. If $r_2$ finishes its task at time step $t_1$, it can then be recruited by the UAV and arrive sooner than $r_1$ or $r_3$. This particular case was tested in simulation, and it was found that using *affective recruitment*, $r_2$ was chosen and arrived after 65.4 seconds. The *greedy* and *random* strategies selected $r_1$ which arrived after 95.2 seconds and 95.4 seconds, respectively.

Another simple use case demonstrates that through *affective recruitment*, the UAV will choose the nearest robot without requiring that all robots reveal their locations (as with the *greedy* strategy). Suppose that, as above, three robots $r_1, r_2, r_3$ are idle at a particular time $t_1$ when the UAV makes a request, but the UAV is nearest $r_2$. After each ignored request, $r_2$'s SHAME will increase faster than that of $r_1$ or $r_3$, because $r_2$ is closest to the UAV. As a result, $r_2$ will be the first to exceed its threshold for SHAME and will respond before $r_1$ or $r_3$. Thus, the UAV recruits the closest robot without requiring all robots to transmit their locations. This behavior has been verified in simulation. In this scenario, the UAV broadcast 5 *HELP* messages, at which point $r_2$ responded, and the recruitment completed normally. Neither $r_1$ or $r_3$ ever broadcast any messages. If this were a low-power or stealth application, $r_1$ and $r_3$ would have been spared an unnecessary transmission by using *affective recruitment* rather than *greedy*.

### Robot Tests

The recruitment protocol was demonstrated on a pair of ATRV-Jr. robots, where the robots responded to requests from a simulated UAV. In these tests, the robots determined their positions via GPS, and when recruited, navigated to a specified waypoint. Further robot tests are ongoing.

## Conclusions

Results from 66 simulations have shown that the *affective* strategy resulted in 19.1% lower communications overhead overall compared to *greedy* and *random*, and that *affective* scaled better (18.6% fewer messages sent with 10 idle robots, 36.3% fewer with 20 idle robots). These simulations have also shown that *greedy* required 39.4% less time to complete recruitments overall when compared to *affective*.

Note that although *affective recruitment* required more wait time to complete than *greedy*, the choice of parameters in the simulation influenced the total time required. With a careful selection or adaptation of parameters, *affective recruitment* can compromise between response time and communication requirements as needed for a particular domain.

These simulations also demonstrated that the recruitment protocol is robust in terms of communication failures such that it still functioned in an environment where 25% of all messages were lost. With communication losses, *affective recruitment* still required fewer transmissions than *greedy* and *random*, though as above, *greedy* required the least time to complete recruitments. The simulations have also provided experimental justification for using broadcasts instead of unicast messaging when performing recruitment, as *affective recruitment* required 464% more messages (and *greedy* required 65% more) using unicast than with broadcast.

These simulations assumed no preemption of robots from their tasks, and it is expected that if this restriction were lifted, *affective recruitment* would behave more intelligently than *greedy*. In particular, *affective* builds up a level of activation (SHAME) in the robots over time, whereas *greedy* makes decisions based only on the current instant in time. In terms of fairness (that is, which robots are chosen to assist), *affective* is less likely to call on the same robot twice in a row than *greedy* (because a robot's SHAME resets to zero when it is recruited). SHAME may also control other aspects of behavior, such as causing a robot to suspend or abandon its own task in order to help another, or at least make it "hurry up."

Future work will examine the impact of preemption in recruitment as well as fit-matching perceptual capabilities of robots to determine how well a given robot can perform the task it is being recruited for (expanding on the *metric evaluation* in (Gerkey & Mataric 2002)). Methods for learning the parameters used in *affective recruitment* will also be developed. Finally, the effect of non-linear parameters for updating SHAME will be examined.


## Acknowledgments

Portions of this work were supported by ONR Grant N00014-03-1-0786 and DOE Grant DE-FG02-01ER45904.


## References


Cai, A.; Fukuda, T.; and Arai, F. 1997. Information sharing among multiple robots for cooperation in cellular robotic system. In *Proceedings of the 1997 IEEE/RSJ International Conference on Intelligent Robot Systems (IROS '97)*, volume 2, 1768–1774.

Cao, Y.; Fukunaga, A.; Kahng, A.; and Meng, F. 1995. Cooperative mobile robotics: Antecedents and directions. In *Intelligent Robots and Systems 95. 'Human Robot Interaction and Cooperative Robots', Proceedings. 1995 IEEE/RSJ International Conference on*, 226–234.

Gerkey, B. P., and Mataric, M. J. 2002. Sold!: Auction methods for multirobot coordination. *IEEE Transactions on Robotics and Automation* 18(5):758–768.

Gerkey, B. P., and Mataric, M. J. 2003. Multi-robot task allocation: analyzing the complexity and optimality of key architectures. In *Proc. IEEE Int. Conf. Robotics and Automation (ICRA '03)*, 3862–3868.

Monderer, D., and Tennenholtz, M. 1998. Optimal auctions revisited. In *Proceedings Fifteenth National Conference on Artificial Intelligence*, 32–37.

Murphy, R.; Lisetti, C.; Tardif, R.; Irish, L.; and Gage, A. 2002. Emotion-based control of cooperating heterogeneous mobile robots. *IEEE Transactions on Robotics and Automation*.

Ohko, T.; Hiraki, K.; and Anzai, Y. 1996. Reducing communication load on contract net by case-based reasoning — extension with directed contract and forgetting. In *Proceedings of the Second International Conference on Multiagent Systems*, 244–251.

Ortony, A. 2002. *On Making Believable Emotional Agents Believable*. The MIT Press. chapter 6, 189–211.

Parker, L. 1998. Alliance: An architecture for fault tolerant multirobot cooperation. *IEEE Transactions on Robotics and Automation* 14(2):220–240.

Smith, R. G. 1980. The contract net protocol: High-level communication and control in a distributed problem solver. *IEEE Transactions on Computers* c-29(12).

# Visibility-based Pursuit-evasion with Limited Field of View

**Brian P. Gerkey** gerkey@stanford.edu
**Sebastian Thrun** thrun@stanford.edu
**Geoff Gordon** ggordon+@cs.cmu.edu
**Artificial Intelligence Lab**
**Stanford University**
**Stanford, CA 94305, USA**

## Abstract

We study a form of the *pursuit-evasion* problem, in which one or more searchers must move through a given environment so as to guarantee detection of any and all evaders, which can move arbitrarily fast. Our goal is to develop techniques for coordinating teams of robots to execute this task in application domains such as clearing a building, for reasons of security or safety. To this end, we introduce a new class of searcher, the $\phi$-searcher, which can be readily instantiated as a physical mobile robot. We present a detailed analysis of the pursuit-evasion problem using $\phi$-searchers. We show that computing the minimum number of $\phi$-searchers required to search a given environment is NP-hard, and present the first complete search algorithm for a single $\phi$-searcher. We show how this algorithm can be extended to handle multiple searchers, and give examples of computed trajectories.

## Introduction

In this paper we address a form of the problem known as *pursuit-evasion*. The goal of this problem is to direct the actions of one or more *searchers* through a given environment in such a way as to guarantee that any *evaders* present in the environment will be found. As an example, consider the problem of closing a museum for the night. In order to be sure that no thieves or other malcontents remain inside after closing, the guards must perform a thorough search of the building. They must keep in mind that any intruders may try to avoid the guards. For example, if a guard is checking each room along a hall, an intruder might sneak behind the guard while he is checking one room and hide in a room that was already checked. In this case, one solution might be to use two guards, with one always keeping watch on the hall.

Our goal is to derive strategies for robots that allow them to play the role of guard. In particular, we are interested in scalable techniques for coordinating the actions of teams of robots to clear entire buildings. In this paper, we establish an analytical foundation for studying this problem by introducing the concept of a $\phi$-searcher, which is a robot equipped with a $\phi$-radian field of view (FOV) sensor for detecting evaders. The $\phi$-searcher reflects the realities of physical robots, most of which have limited FOV sensors, and thus the techniques we develop can be applied to robots.



Furthermore, the $\phi$-searcher is a qualitatively different kind of searcher from those previously studied in pursuit-evasion scenarios, and so warrants the fresh analysis that we present here.

After proving that computing the minimum number of $\phi$-searchers required to search an environment is NP-hard, we present the first complete search algorithm for the case of one $\phi$-searcher in a known environment. We show how this algorithm can be extended to handle multiple robots (albeit at a loss of completeness). We have implemented and tested this algorithm in a variety of environments and present example solution trajectories.

## Background and related work

The first rigorous formulation of the pursuit-evasion problem is due to Parsons (1976), who restricted his study to the case in which the environment is a discrete graph. Nothing is known about the location or motion of the evader, who is assumed to be able to move arbitrarily fast through the graph. The evader can occupy any edge in the graph; to find the evader, a searcher must walk along the edge occupied by the evader and "touch" the evader. The entire graph is initially *contaminated*, which means that the evader could be anywhere. As the search progresses, an edge is *cleared* when it is no longer possible for the evader to occupy that edge. Should it later happen that the evader could have moved back to a previously clear edge, that edge is said to be *recontaminated*. Using this terminology, the goal of the problem can be restated as follows: find a trajectory for each searcher such that the entire graph is cleared.

A visibility-based version of the pursuit-evasion problem was introduced by Suzuki & Yamashita (1992), who changed the domain from discrete graphs to continuous polygonal free spaces and coined the term *k-searcher*. In this formulation, in order to find an evader, a $k$-searcher need not touch the evader, but can instead "see" the evader from a distance. The $k$-searcher is equipped with $k$ infinitely thin "flashlights" with which it can search the environment. These flashlights have unlimited range (but cannot see through walls) and can be freely rotated about the searcher at bounded speed and independently of the searcher's motion. Commonly studied are the cases when $k = 1$, $k = 2$, and $k = \infty$ (LaValle *et al.* 1997; Guibas *et al.* 1999; Lee, Park, & Chwa 2002). The $\infty$-searcher can see in all directions at once.

In addition to such analytical study, there has recently been some work on forms of pursuit-evasion with physical robots. Roy & Gordon (2002) model the single-robot action-selection problem as a POMDP, which is made tractable by compression of the sparse belief space. A similar probabilistic framework is employed by Vidal *et al.* (2002), who use heuristic search to find strategies for coordinating teams of air and ground vehicles to search an unknown outdoor environment. More distantly related is the large body of work on cooperative tracking of moving targets with fixed sensors and/or mobile robots (Werger & Matarić 2001; Stroupe 2003; Spletzer & Taylor 2003).

## The $\phi$-searcher

The existing body of analytical work on visibility-based pursuit-evasion is concerned with some form of the $k$-searcher, and is not readily applicable to physical robots, few of which are equipped with movable flashlights or omnidirectional sensing. Since our target domain is teams of physical robots, we introduce a new class of searcher, which to our knowledge has not yet been studied, and which we call the *$\phi$-searcher.* The *$\phi$-searcher* is a holonomic (i.e., omnidirectional drive) mobile robot with a limited FOV sensor having angular aperture $\phi \in (0, 2\pi]$. The sensor has unlimited range, but cannot penetrate obstacles. This robot can move (i.e., rotate and/or translate) at bounded speed. When $\phi = 2\pi$, we have an $\infty$-searcher. For $\phi < 2\pi$, however, we have a different kind of searcher, with significantly diminished capabilities. Since the sensor's FOV can be freely rotated about the searcher at bounded speed and independently of the searcher's motion (this follows from the holomonicity of the robot), the capabilities of the $\phi$-searcher lie somewhere between those of a 1-searcher and those of a 2-searcher. Shown in Figure 1 is an example of a $\phi$-searcher, for $\phi = \pi$.

Given a connected polygonal free space $F$, the pursuit-evasion problem is to find a trajectory through $F$ (called a *search schedule*) for $\phi$-searchers that guarantees detection of an arbitrarily fast *evader*, whose trajectory and initial location are unknown.[1] Analogously to the graph search problem, any part of $F$ where the evader can be hiding is called *contaminated* and any part of $F$ where the evader cannot be hiding is called *clear.* Whenever there exists a path between contaminated space and clear space, that clear space is said to be *recontaminated.* The space $F$ is initially contaminated and the goal is to clear it.

It is known that for the discrete graph search problem, establishing the minimum number of searchers required to search a given graph, known as the *search number* of the graph, is NP-hard (Megiddo *et al.* 1988). For the visibility-based version, establishing the minimum number of $\infty$-searchers required to search a given polygonal free space is also NP-hard (Guibas *et al.* 1999). We have a similar result for $\phi$-searchers:

**Theorem 1.** *Computing the minimum number of $\phi$-searchers required to search a given polygonal free space $F$ is NP-hard.*

**Proof.** We use the same reduction as Guibas *et al.* (1999): any planar graph $G$ can be mapped onto an equivalent polygonal free space $F$ by making vertices into convex rooms and edges into "kinked" hallways. Each hallway has a kink, or bend, in the middle, such that the searcher cannot see from one end of the hall to the other. As a result, to clear a hall, the searcher must walk its entire length, just as with an edge in $G$. The kink removes all advantages of visibility, and thus has the same effect on the $\phi$-searcher as it does on the $\infty$-searcher. Since any planar graph can be mapped onto an equivalent polygonal free space, and since computing the search number of a planar graph with maximum vertex degree 3 is NP-hard (Monien & Sudborough 1988), computing the minimum number of $\phi$-searchers required to search a polygonal free space is also NP-hard. □

## A complete algorithm for a single $\phi$-searcher

Since, by Theorem 1, we cannot easily determine the minimum number of $\phi$-searchers required to search a given environment, we focus initially on the case of controlling a single $\phi$-searcher. In this section, we present a complete search algorithm for the case of a single $\phi$-searcher. That is, we are interested in finding a trajectory for a single $\phi$-searcher that will search a given polygonal free space $F$, under the assumption that such a trajectory exists. We address the extension to multiple searchers later.

We take inspiration in the design of our algorithm from the work of Guibas *et al.* (1999), who have previously given a complete algorithm for the case of a single $\infty$-searcher. Their algorithm does not suffice for a $\phi$-searcher with $\phi < 2\pi$, because it does not account for the searcher's limited FOV. However, we borrow from their work in several ways.

The basic steps of our algorithm are: (i) by a series of partitions, retract the given free space into a network of curves that represent the visibility constraints induced by the environment and the searcher's FOV; (ii) construct an *information graph* that encodes the possible information states of the problem as the searcher moves, using the network of intersecting curves as a roadmap; then (iii) search this graph for a goal state, and read the desired trajectory out from the resulting path. The key to this algorithm is identifying the critical points in the environment; it is only by moving through these points that the searcher will change the information state of the problem.

### Identifying critical changes in information state

The area visible to a $\phi$-searcher when it is positioned at a point $p$ with orientation $\theta$ in $F$ is called its *visibility polygon*, $V_\phi(F, p, \theta)$, abbreviated to $V_\phi$ when $F$, $p$, and $\theta$ are clear from the context. When a point $q$ lies within $V_\phi$, we say that $q$ is *in view* (Figure 1(c)). The visibility polygon is

[1] It may be the case with physical robots that the available map, having been acquired from sensor data, is grid-based, rather than polygonal. If so, then the first step is to generate an approximate polygonal representation of the grid-based map, either automatically (e.g., via smoothing and line-fitting) or manually (e.g., with the aid of an architectural fborplan).

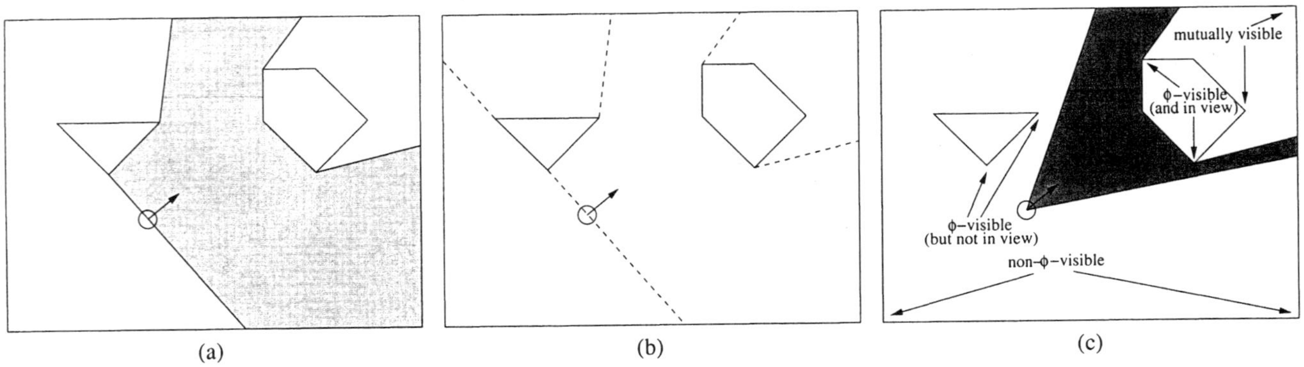


Figure 1: *Introduction to the $\phi$-searcher Shown in (a) is an example of a $\pi$-searcher positioned at a point p with orientation $\theta$ in a polygonal free space F. The shaded region is the searcher's visibility polygon, $V_\pi(F, p, \theta)$. Shown as dashed lines in (b) are the induced gap edges for the $\pi$-searcher, which partition the free space into 4 regions. Shown in (c) are examples of vertices that are* in view, visible, *and/or* $\phi$-visible, *for $\phi = \frac{\pi}{3}$.*

defined by a set of line segments, some of which lie on the boundary of $F$ and some of which do not. The latter segments, which cross through the interior of $F$, are called *gap edges* (Figure 1(b)). These edges, combined with the edges of $F$, form a *planar map* that partitions the free space of $F$ into a set of *faces*, which we call *regions*. We can attach to each region a binary label that indicates whether it is clear ("0") or contaminated ("1").

We model the information state of the problem as $(p, \theta, B(p, \theta))$, where $(p, \theta)$ is the searcher's pose and $B(p, \theta)$ is the list of binary labels on the regions induced by its gap edges. To monitor progress, we need only take notice when this information state changes *combinatorially*; that is, when the set of regions or region labels changes. A combinatorial, or critical, change in information state corresponds to a move of the searcher that changes the topology of contaminated space. During such a move, one or more gap edges will: disappear, split, or merge (it can also happen that a new gap edge appears during a move, but new gap edges always border clear space, and so such a move does not change the topology of the contaminated space).

Other moves can deform the contaminated space of $F$, but do not change its topology. We can characterize critical changes in information state with the following necessary (though not sufficient) condition:

**Lemma 1.** *Given a single $\phi$-searcher in a polygonal free space $F$, there can be a change in the topology of the contaminated space in $F$ only if there is a change in the set of vertices of $F$ that lie in $V_\phi$.*

**Proof.** We treat the three cases separately:

1. **Edge disappearance.** For a gap edge $e$ to disappear, one of two events must occur. Either the concave vertex of $F$ that induced $e$ moves out of $V_\phi$, or $e$ becomes coincident with the boundary of $F$ and terminates at a previously non-visible convex vertex of $F$. In the first case, $e$ disappears because it falls out of view (and thus is no longer part of $V_\phi$); in the second case, $e$ disappears because it becomes part of the boundary of $F$ (and thus is no longer a gap edge).
2. **Edge splitting.** A gap edge $e$ can be split only if a previously non-visible concave vertex of $F$, say $v$, moves into $V_\phi$ such that $v$ lies on $e$. The gap edge $e$ will then split into two new edges, with the first terminating at $v$ and the second originating at $v$.
3. **Edge merging.** Merging is simply the reverse of splitting. Two gap edges $e1$ and $e2$ can merge only if $e1$ terminates at the same concave vertex of $F$, say $v$, from which $e2$ originates, and $v$ moves out of $V_\phi$. The result is a single new edge, having the same origin as $e1$.

In each case, at least one vertex of $F$ moves into or out of $V_\phi$. □

This lemma tells us that any critical change in information state will be accompanied by (actually, caused by) a change in the set of vertices of $F$ that lie within $V_\phi$. So we need to identify the points at which there can be a change in the set of vertices that are in view.

Before continuing, we define two notions of visibility from a point $p \in F$ (Figure 1(c)). We say that two points $p$ and $q$ are *mutually visible* if the line segment between $p$ and $q$ does not cross the boundary of $F$ (this is the traditional geometric notion of visibility). Equivalently, we may say that $p$ is *visible* from $q$ or that $q$ is *visible* from $p$. We say that a pair of points $(p, q)$ is *$\phi$-visible* from a point $s$ if there exists an orientation, say $\theta$, for a $\phi$-searcher located at $s$ such that both $p$ and $q$ lie within $V_\phi$, with $p$ and $q$ ordered counterclockwise about $s$. That is, if we rotate a sweep line counterclockwise about $s$ through the FOV of a searcher positioned at $s$ with orientation $\theta$, we encounter both $p$ and $q$, with $p$ coming before $q$ (angular ties are broken by distance from $s$). Clearly, if $(p, q)$ is $\phi_1$-visible from $s$, then $(p, q)$ is also $\phi_2$-visible from $s$ for any $\phi_2 \geq \phi_1$. Thus, if the pair $(p, q)$ is $\phi$-visible from $s$, then $p$ and $q$ are also both visible from $s$ (traditional visibility is just $2\pi$-visibility).

## Partitioning the environment

We now partition $F$ into a set of regions $R$. Our goal is that the following condition hold for each region $r \in R$: given

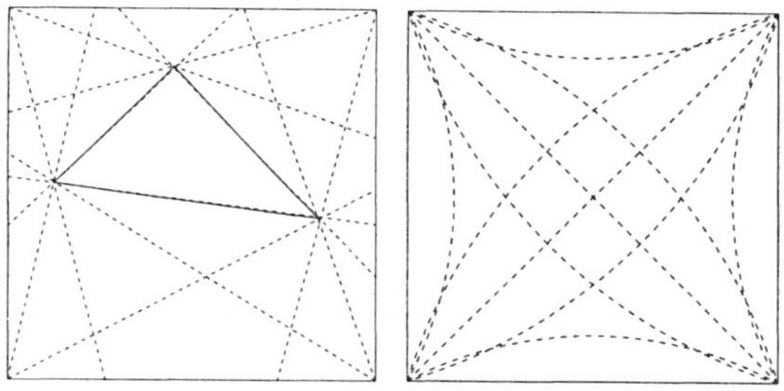

(a) (b)

Figure 2: *Shown in (a) is the partition $P_\pi(F)$ for a space $F$ consisting of a square containing a triangular hole. Shown in (b) is the partition $P_\phi(F)$ for a square free space $F$, with $\phi = \frac{2\pi}{3}$. In both cases, the dashed lines are the segments used in the construction of the partition (the boundaries of the square and/or triangle are also included). Either visibility (a) or $\phi$-visibility (b) of boundary vertices is constant across the resulting regions.*

a $\phi$-searcher located anywhere in $r$, the set of $\phi$-visible vertex pairs does not change. First, we ensure that there is no change in the set of visible vertices. For each pair of mutually visible vertices $v_1$ and $v_2$ of $F$ (including when $v_1$ and $v_2$ are endpoints of the same segment of $F$), we construct the segment $v_1v_2$, then extend this segment in either direction as far as possible without crossing the boundary of $F$. The intersections of the resulting segments form a partition of $F$ into a set of convex regions. The intuition behind this technique is that we identify all places where the set of visible vertices can change due to occlusion (Figure 2(a)). The resulting partition, $P_\pi(F)$, has the following property:

**Lemma 2.** *Given any region $r$ from the partition $P_\pi(F)$ of a polygonal free space $F$, the set of visible vertices of $F$ is the same for all points in the interior of $r$.*

**Proof.** Assume by contradiction that some vertex $v_1$ of $F$ is visible from a point $p$ and not visible from another point $q$, with both $p$ and $q$ in the interior of $r$. Consider any continuous path $\gamma$ from $p$ to $q$ such that $\gamma$ is contained in the interior of $r$. Then there is some point along $\gamma$, say $s$ (possibly equal to $q$), where $v_1$ disappears from view. For this to occur, there must be another vertex of $F$, say $v_2$, that occludes $v_1$. The three points $v_1$, $v_2$ and $s$ will be collinear; $v_1$ and $v_2$ will be mutually visible; and $v_2$ and $s$ will be mutually visible. Then in the construction of $P_\pi$, the extension of the segment $v_1v_2$ would pass through $s$, which means that $s$ does not lie in the interior of $r$. Thus there is no path between $p$ and $q$ that remains in the interior of $r$, which contradicts the assumption that both $p$ and $q$ lie in the interior of $r$. □

So we know that the set of visible vertices cannot change within a region $r \in P_\pi(F)$. However, for $\phi < 2\pi$, it is still possible for the set of $\phi$-visible vertex pairs to change within a region. We want to refine the partition $P_\pi(F)$ so that there is no change in $\phi$-visibility of vertices as a $\phi$-searcher moves within a single region. For this purpose, we introduce *visibility curves*:

**Definition (Visibility curve).** *Given $0 < \phi \leq \pi$ and two distinct points $v_1$ and $v_2$, the* visibility curve, *denoted $C_\phi(v_1, v_2)$, is the locus of $\phi$-searcher positions closest to the midpoint of the segment $v_1v_2$ such that an appropriate orientation of the searcher will place both $v_1$ and $v_2$ in $V_\phi$. For $\pi < \phi < 2\pi$, $C_\phi = C_{(2\pi-\phi)}$. The curve $C_\phi$ is undefined for $\phi = 2\pi$.*

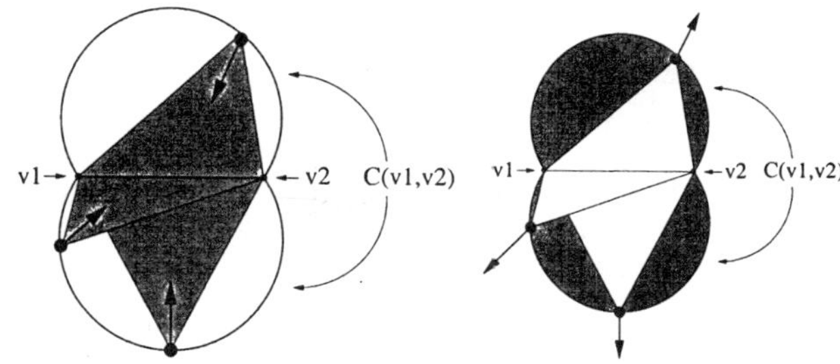


(a) (b)

Figure 3: *The visibility curve $C_\phi(v_1, v_2)$ for two points $v_1$ and $v_2$. Shown in (a) is the case when $\phi = \frac{\pi}{3}$; these arcs are the closest that a $\frac{\pi}{3}$-searcher can come to the midpoint of $v_1v_2$, while maintaining visibility of both points. Shown in (b) is the case when $\phi = \frac{5\pi}{3}$; these arcs are the farthest that a $\frac{5\pi}{3}$-searcher can move after crossing $v_1v_2$ while maintaining visibility of both points. Three example poses along each curve are shown, with the relevant portions of the visibility polygons shaded.*

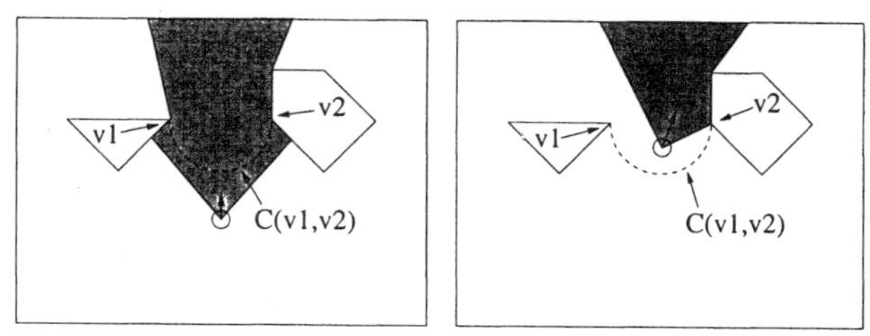


Figure 4: *An example of how $\phi$-visibility changes when crossing a visibility curve, for $\phi = \frac{\pi}{2}$. As the searcher crosses $C_{\frac{\pi}{2}}(v_1, v_2)$, it must lose sight of at least one of $v_1$ and $v_2$.*

As can be seen in Figure 3(a), the visibility curve for $0 < \phi < \pi$ is composed of two arcs. Each arc is part of a circle defined by the locus of points from which the segment $v_1v_2$ subtends the angle $\phi$ (the segment $v_1v_2$ is always a chord in each circle; when $\phi = \frac{\pi}{2}$ the two circles are the same and the segment $v_1v_2$ is a diameter). To maintain visibility of both vertices from a point along this curve, the searcher must be oriented toward the midpoint of $v_1v_2$. As $\phi$ approaches $\pi$, these arcs flatten, until they meet to form a single line when $\phi = \pi$. In this case, a $\pi$-searcher positioned on the line must be oriented orthogonal to the line in order to maintain visibility of $v_1$ and $v_2$. As shown in Figure 3(b), for $\pi < \phi < 2\pi$, the visibility curve is composed of the same two arcs as for $2\pi - \phi$, but the orientation of the searcher is rotated by $\pi$.

The importance of the visibility curve is that it makes concrete the constraints induced by the requirement to maintain visibility of a given pair of vertices with a $\phi$-searcher. For $0 < \phi \leq \pi$, the visibility curve is the closest that a $\phi$-searcher can approach two vertices while keeping them both in view (Figure 4). If the searcher moves forward from a point on this curve, it will necessarily lose visibility of at least one vertex. For $\pi \leq \phi < 2\pi$, the interpretation is slightly different: if two vertices are currently in view and a $\phi$-searcher passes between them, the visibility curve is the farthest that the searcher can travel while keeping both vertices in view. When the searcher reaches a point on the visibility curve, its blind spot becomes wedged between the two vertices; any further forward motion will cause at least one vertex to fall out of view.

We now refine our partition of $F$ with a set of visibility curves. For every pair of vertices $v_1$ and $v_2$ of $F$ (including when $v_1$ and $v_2$ are endpoints of the same segment of $F$) for which there exists some point on the curve $C_\phi(v_1, v_2)$ that lies in the free space of $F$ and from which $(v_1, v_2)$ and/or $(v_2, v_1)$ is $\phi$-visible , we add $C_\phi(v_1, v_2)$ to $F$. The intuition behind this step is that we need only include those curves that represent visibility changes that can actually occur for a searcher moving through $F$. For example, if the searcher can never simultaneously see two vertices, then the visibility curve between them is not a meaningful constraint on the searcher's motion. For the same reason, we discard from each curve any portion that lies outside $F$. It is possible to further prune the visibility curves by removing from $C_\phi(v_1, v_2)$ *any* portion from which one or both of $v_1$ and $v_2$ is not visible. This further pruning would speed up trajectory planning, but has no effect on the completeness of our algorithm.

Note that when $\phi = \pi$, the addition of visibility curves is redundant: the existence of a third point on $C_\pi(v_1, v_2)$ from which $v_1$ and $v_2$ are $\phi$-visible is equivalent to $v_1$ and $v_2$ being mutual visible, and $C_\pi(v_1, v_2)$ is just the line through $v_1$ and $v_2$, which was included in the coarser partition (hence the name $P_\pi(F)$).

The intersections of the resulting arrangement of curves and lines form a partition of $F$ into a set of (not necessarily convex) regions (Figure 2(b)). This partition, $P_\phi(F)$, has the following two properties:

**Lemma 3.** *Given any region $r$ from the partition $P_\phi(F)$ of a polygonal free space $F$, the set of $\phi$-visible vertices is the same for all points in the interior of $r$.*

**Proof.** Since $P_\phi(F)$ is a refinement of $P_\pi(F)$, $r$ must be contained within a single region, say $r_\pi$, of $P_\pi(F)$. As the set of visible vertices cannot change within $r_\pi$ (Lemma 2), the set of visible vertices likewise cannot change within $r$.

So we are left to show that, among the (constant) set of visible vertices, the set of $\phi$-visible vertices does not change. Assume by contradiction that this condition does not hold. In particular, assume that the vertex pair $(v_1, v_2)$ is $\phi$-visible from some point $p$ and not $\phi$-visible from some other point $q$, with both $p$ and $q$ in the interior of $r$. Since $(v_1, v_2)$ is $\phi$-visible from $p$, both $v_1$ and $v_2$ must also be visible from $p$. And since the set of visible vertices is the same for both $p$ and $q$ (because they are both in $r$), $v_1$ and $v_2$ must also be visible from $q$. Then, by the definition of a visibility curve, $p$ and $q$ must lie on opposite sides of $C_\phi(v_1, v_2)$, which contradicts the assumption that $p$ and $q$ lie in the same region $r$. □

**Lemma 4.** *Given any region $r$ from the partition $P_\phi(F)$ of a polygonal free space $F$, any vertex pair that is $\phi$-visible from the interior of $r$ is also $\phi$-visible from the boundary of $r$.*

**Proof.** Assume by contradiction that the vertex pair $(v_1, v_2)$ is $\phi$-visible from some point $p$ in the interior of $r$ (by Lemma 3, the particular choice of $p$ makes no difference), and not $\phi$-visible from some point $q$ on the boundary of $r$. It is clear that, since $v_1$ and $v_2$ are visible from $p$, they must also be visible from $q$. Then, by the definition of a visibility curve, $p$ and $q$ must lie on opposite sides of $C_\phi(v_1, v_2)$, which contradicts the assumption that $q$ is on the boundary of the region containing $p$. □

These lemmas tell us that a $\phi$-searcher that is positioned within a region $r$ can move onto the boundary of $r$ without losing visibility of any vertices (it may gain visibility of some vertices). At this point, to avoid possible ambiguity, it will be necessary to order to the set of vertices that are in view.[2] For a $\phi$-searcher positioned at $p$ with orientation $\theta$, we denote by $S_\phi(F, p, \theta)$ the ordered set of vertices of $F$ that are in view (i.e., in $V_\phi(F, p, \theta)$), sorted counterclockwise about the searcher (angular ties are broken by distance from the searcher). For brevity we may abbreviate this set as $S_\phi$. We now show that a searcher positioned in the interior of a region can move to the region's boundary without removing or reordering any vertices that are initially in view:

**Lemma 5.** *Given any region $r$ from the partition $P_\phi(F)$ of a polygonal free space $F$, and a $\phi$-searcher with pose $(p, \theta)$ such that $p$ lies in the interior of $r$, the searcher can move to any point $q$ on the boundary of $r$ without removing or reordering any vertices in $S_\phi$.*

**Proof.** Consider any continuous path $\gamma$ from $p$ to $q$ such that $\gamma \setminus q$ is contained in the interior of $r$ and $q$ is visited exactly once (i.e., the path $\gamma$ intersects the boundary of $r$ only at $q$, where it terminates). Each vertex pair that is in $S_\phi(F, p, \theta)$ must be $\phi$-visible from $p$ and so, by Lemmas 3 & 4, also be $\phi$-visible from all other points on $\gamma$ (since $\gamma$ is confined to $r$). So it is possible for the searcher to move continuously along $\gamma$ without losing sight of any vertices. Furthermore, because $\phi$-visibility guarantees an ordering on each vertex pair, it is possible for the searcher to move continuously along $\gamma$ such that no vertex pair in $S_\phi$ is reordered. As a result, the searcher can move from $p$ to $q$ without removing or reordering any vertices in $S_\phi$. □

This lemma tells us that we can move a searcher from the interior of a region to its boundary, with the only change in $S_\phi$ being the *addition* of vertices of $F$. To put it another way, a searcher that is positioned in the interior of a region may as well move to the region's boundary, for at the worst its vertex coverage will remain the same. As a result, without loss

[2]When $\phi > \pi$, it may be possible to change the information state without changing the set of vertices that are view, by wedging the searcher's blind spot between different vertex pairs. In this case, only the *order* of the in-view vertices will change, and so we must keep track of this order to be able to distinguish among these information states.

of generality we can restrict our attention to the boundaries of the regions of $P_\phi(F)$, and ignore their interiors. Furthermore, no vertices $S_\phi$ will be removed or reordered as the searcher moves along a single component (i.e., segment or arc) of the boundary of a region; such a change can only occur at the intersection of two components. By moving to an intersection, the searcher is in fact moving from the interior to the boundary of a larger region that would exist if the boundary component along which it is traveling were excluded from the partition. So we can further focus our attention on the intersections of region boundaries.

Of course, the searcher may have to rotate as it moves; $\phi$-visibility only guarantees that it is *possible* for the searcher to simultaneously see a given pair of vertices. In general, for a point $p$ that is an intersection of one or more region boundaries, there will be an interval of orientation for which the set of vertices in $V_\phi$ will remain unchanged. Equivalently, there is an interval of orientation for which each $\phi$-visible vertex pair is in $V_\phi$. By intersecting all such intervals, we can partition the space of possible searcher orientations, $[0, 2\pi)$. The intervals produced by this partition, $\Theta_\phi(F, p)$, have the following property: the set of vertices in $V_\phi$ is the same for any two orientations in the same interval.

So all orientations in a given interval, say $i$, of $\Theta_\phi(F, p)$ are equivalent, in the sense that there can be no critical change in information as a $\phi$-searcher, positioned at $p$, rotates within $i$. We can identify each orientation interval by a pair of vertices $(v_{first}, v_{last})$, which are, respectively, the first and last vertices in view, according to the order in which each vertex is encountered by rotating a sweep line counterclockwise through the searcher's FOV. Without loss of generality, we can assume that a $\phi$-searcher that is oriented within an interval $(v_{first}, v_{last})$ is always oriented such that either its minimum FOV boundary intersects $v_{first}$ or its maximum FOV boundary intersects $v_{last}$.

## Building the information graph

We now have the roadmap along which the searcher will travel as it moves through $F$, and we can build a directed *information graph*, $G_I$, that encodes all possible critical changes in the information state. For each point $p$ that is the intersection of two or more components of region boundaries in $P_\phi(F)$, compute the orientation intervals $\Theta_\phi(F, p)$. We add to $G_I$ a node for each possible region labeling that can result from placing the searcher at $p$ and rotating it through each orientation interval in $\Theta_\phi(F, p)$.

We complete the construction of $G_I$ by adding edges that correspond to the feasible changes in information state. First we must define the actions that are allowed for the searcher. Assume the searcher is positioned at a point $p$ that is the intersection of two or more region boundary components, and oriented within an interval defined by $(v_{first}, v_{last})$. This searcher can:

1. Rotate into any adjacent orientation interval.
2. Translate along the length of any boundary component $c$ incident to $p$ such that the orientation interval $(v_{first}, v_{last})$ is valid at the opposite end of $c$. During the move the searcher servos its rotation so as to maintain visibility of both $v_{first}$ and $v_{last}$ (and thus all vertices in between).

For each node $n$ in $G_I$, we determine the information states that would result from taking each allowable action at the configuration that $n$ represents, and add edges from $n$ to the nodes that encode these new states.

Given an information state from which to start, we can then search $G_I$ for a goal state, which represents all of $F$ being clear. In a start state, all in-view regions are clear and all others are contaminated. In a goal state, all regions are clear. Given a feasible path through $G_I$ from start to goal, we can read from it the required searcher trajectory, as a series of in-place rotations and constrained translations. We now establish the completeness of this approach:

**Theorem 2.** *An algorithm that will find any path to a goal vertex from a start vertex in $G_I$ is complete for the visibility-based pursuit-evasion problem with a single $\phi$-searcher.*

**Proof.** Given a polygonal free space $F$ and a single $\phi$-searcher, take any solution trajectory, say $\tau$. Our goal is to map $\tau$ onto an equivalent path in $G_I$. That is, we wish to show that $\tau$ can be transformed into an equivalent trajectory along the curves that make up the roadmap used in constructing $G_I$.

Denote by $(p, \theta)$ the searcher's pose at the start of $\tau$. If $p$ lies in the interior of a region $r$ in $P_\phi(F)$ then, by Lemma 5, we can move the searcher to any point on the boundary of $r$, without losing or reordering any in-view vertices of $F$. In particular, we can move the searcher to any intersection along the boundary of $r$. If $p$ already lies on a region boundary, then we can slide the searcher along that boundary to the nearest intersection, again without losing or reordering any in-view vertices.

As $\tau$ progresses, we can replicate its moves within our roadmap in the following way. While $\tau$ remains in the interior of a region $r$, we keep the searcher at an intersection, say $q$, on the boundary of $r$, and achieve any necessary changes in vertex visibility by simply rotating the searcher through its orientation intervals. If $\tau$ crosses into an adjacent region $r'$ such that $q$ is also on the boundary of $r'$, we can continue to rotate the searcher in place. If, on the other hand, $q$ is not on the boundary of $r'$, we move the searcher along any boundary component that is incident to both $q$ and some other intersection, say $s$, that does lie on the boundary of $r'$. During this translation, the searcher's rotation is controlled so as to remain within its current orientation interval and not lose or reorder any in-view vertices (Lemma 5 guarantees that this is possible).

In this way, we create a new trajectory $\tau'$ that moves along the roadmap and is at as least as good as $\tau$. That is, $S_\phi$ at each point on $\tau'$ is a superset of $S_\phi$ at the corresponding point on $\tau$. Compared to $\tau$, a searcher moving along $\tau'$ may see additional vertices, but it will never miss any, nor will it see them in a different order. As we can construct a solution $\tau'$ given any solution $\tau$, the algorithm is complete. □

## Multiple searchers

One way to extend this algorithm to handle multiple searchers is to include in the construction of $G_I$ the joint information and action spaces of all searchers. Unfortunately, this approach is not complete. The reason is that the visibility polygons of multiple searchers can interact and overlap in such a way that the information state can change without any searcher crossing a region boundary in $P_\phi$.

A more serious drawback to extending our algorithm to multiple searchers in this way is that the joint information and actions space grow exponentially in the number of searchers. Even in simple environments and with only two searchers, the information graph $G_I$ requires a prohibitively large amount of memory to store and a correspondingly long time to search. Nevertheless, we have implemented this extension, and show in the next section that it computes valid clearing trajectories.

## Implementation and computed examples

We have implemented and tested the algorithm described above, using the CGAL computational geometry library (Burnikel *et al.* 1999). For reasons of efficiency and convenience, our implementation thus far computes trajectories only for the special case of $\phi = \pi$. In this case, the roadmap in $P_\phi(F)$ consists only of linear objects, and so the underlying geometric computation can be done with rational numbers. For $\phi \neq \pi$, circular arcs are introduced, and the exact computation of their intersections requires the use of arbitrary precision real numbers, which are far slower to work with than rationals. Efficiency concerns aside, the case of $\phi = \pi$ is of particular interest and value to roboticists, because a sensor that is commonly found on robots today is a scanning laser range-finder with a 180° FOV (e.g., the SICK LMS). So trajectories computed by our implementation can be executed directly on holonomic robots that are equipped with such sensors.

We now present a few computed examples. In all the figures, light gray (or yellow) areas are currently in view (and thus clear), white areas are clear (but not in view), and dark gray areas are contaminated. For reasons of space, not all steps in each trajectory are shown. For clarity of presentation, the searcher's approximate trajectory is shown in the last frame. Shown in Figure 5 is an office-like environment composed of a hallway connecting two rooms. Shown in Figure 7 is a more complex environment, for which the computed trajectory had 42 steps. Figure 6 shows a simple environment that requires two searchers to clear (a single $\phi$-searcher is incapable of clearing any loops, even when $\phi = 2\pi$). We used the multi-searcher extension mentioned above to compute this solution, in which two searchers work together to clear the environment.

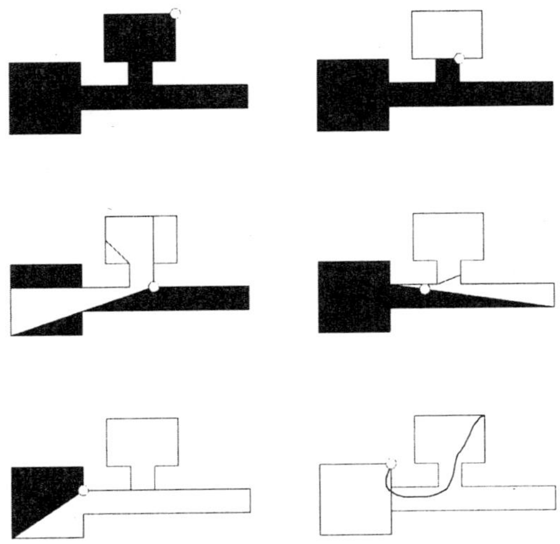

Figure 5: *A computed clearing trajectory for a $\pi$-searcher. In this case the searcher clears the environment by moving backward out of the upper room, down the hall, and into the left room.*

## Summary

We have presented a novel form of the visibility-based pursuit-evasion problem by introducing a new class of searcher, the *$\phi$-searcher*, which we chose because it can readily be instantiated as a physical mobile robot. Because the $\phi$-searcher is qualitatively different from the previously studied $k$-searcher, existing motion-planning techniques do not suffice. As part of a detailed analysis of this new kind of searcher, we showed that computing the minimum number of $\phi$-searchers required to search a given environment is NP-hard and derived the first complete search algorithm for a single $\phi$-searcher. We showed how this algorithm can be extended to find strategies for multiple searchers by planning in their joint action space, and gave examples of computed trajectories for single searchers and for teams of two searchers.

Planning in the joint action space of all searchers is clearly not the best approach, as it is centralized and scales badly as the number of searchers increases. We are currently designing more parsimonious techniques for coordinating multiple searchers, such as distributed negotiation. For example, if a searcher encounters a hallway with many contaminated rooms, it may ask of another searcher, "Watch my back from the end of the hall while I clear these rooms." It is interesting to note that this kind of cooperative mini-strategy arises naturally in the joint action space plans. We are investigating the possibility of learning from these plans such higher-level primitives as "watch my back" and "guard this intersection."

## References

Burnikel, C.; Fleischer, R.; Mehlhorn, K.; and Schirra, S. 1999. Efficient exact geometric computation made easy. In *Proc. of the ACM Symp. on Computational Geometry*, 341–350.

Guibas, L. J.; Latombe, J.-C.; LaValle, S. M.; Lin, D.; and Motwani, R. 1999. A Visibility-Based Pursuit-Evasion Problem. *Intl. J. of Computational Geometry & Applications* 9(4 & 5):471–493.

LaValle, S. M.; Lin, D.; Guibas, L. J.; Latombe, J.-C.; and Motwani, R. 1997. Finding an Unpredictable Target in a Workspace with Obstacles. In *Proc. of the IEEE Intl. Conf. on Robotics and Automation (ICRA)*, 737–742.

Figure 6: *This example, with one loop, is the simplest environment that requires two π-searchers to clear. In this case, the searcher in the upper left corner remains stationary, watching the upper and left corridors, while the other searcher moves to clear the right and lower corridors.*


Lee, J.-H.; Park, S.-M.; and Chwa, K.-Y. 2002. Simple algorithms for searching a polygon with flashlights. *Information Processing Letters* 81:265–270.

Megiddo, N.; Hakimi, S.; Garey, M.; Johnson, D.; and Papadimitriou, C. 1988. The Complexity of Searching a Graph. *J. of the ACM* 35(1):18–44.

Monien, B., and Sudborough, I. 1988. Min cut is NP-complete for edge weighted trees. *Theoretical Computer Science* 58:209–229.

Parsons, T. 1976. Pursuit-evasion in a graph. In Alavi, Y., and Lick, D., eds., *Theory and Applications of Graphs*, Lecture Notes in Mathematics 642. Berlin: Springer-Verlag. 426–441.

Roy, N., and Gordon, G. 2002. Exponential Family PCA for Belief Compression in POMDPs. In *Proc. of Advances in Neural Information Processing Systems (NIPS)*.

Spletzer, J. R., and Taylor, C. J. 2003. Dynamic sensor planning and control for optimally tracking targets. *The Intl. J. of Robotics Research* 22(1):7–20.

Stroupe, A. 2003. *Collaborative Execution of Exploration and Tracking Using Move Value Estimation for Robot Teams (MVERT)*. Ph.D. Dissertation, Robotics Institute, Carnegie Mellon University, Pittsburgh, Pennsylvania.

Suzuki, I., and Yamashita, M. 1992. Searching for a mobile intruder in a polygonal region. *SIAM J. on Computing* 21(5):863–888.

Vidal, R.; Shakernia, O.; Kim, H. J.; Shim, D. H.; and Sastry, S. 2002. Probabalistic Pursuit-Evasion Games: Theory, Implementation, and Experimental Evaluation. *IEEE Transactions on Robotics and Automation* 18(5):662–669.

Werger, B. B., and Matarić, M. J. 2001. Broadcast of Local Eligibility for Multi-Target Observation. In Parker, L. E.; Bekey, G.; and Barhen, J., eds., *Distributed Autonomous Robotic Systems 4*. New York: Springer-Verlag. 347–356.


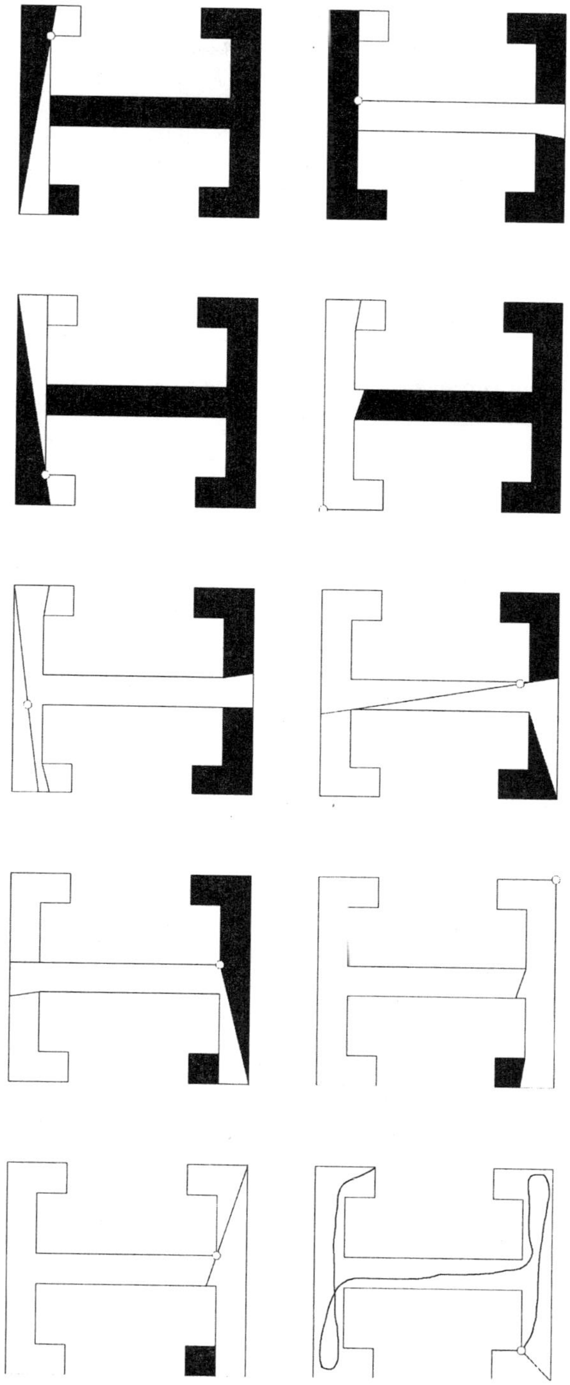

Figure 7: *In this more complicated example, the π-searcher first clears the left hand side from top to bottom, then moves through the horizontal hallway to clear the right hand side, from top to bottom.*

# Task Allocation via Self-Organizing Swarm Coalitions in Distributed Mobile Sensor Network

**Kian Hsiang Low** and **Wee Kheng Leow**
Department of Computer Science
National University of Singapore
3 Science Drive 2, Singapore 117543, Singapore
{lowkh, leowwk}@comp.nus.edu.sg

**Marcelo H. Ang, Jr.**
Department of Mechanical Engineering
National University of Singapore
10 Kent Ridge Crescent, Singapore 119260, Singapore
mpeangh@nus.edu.sg

### Abstract

This paper presents a task allocation scheme via self-organizing swarm coalitions for distributed mobile sensor network coverage. Our approach uses the concepts of ant behavior to self-regulate the regional distributions of sensors in proportion to that of the moving targets to be tracked in a non-stationary environment. As a result, the adverse effects of task interference between robots are minimized and sensor network coverage is improved. Quantitative comparisons with other tracking strategies such as static sensor placement, potential fields, and auction-based negotiation show that our approach can provide better coverage and greater flexibility to respond to environmental changes.

## Introduction

Sensor network has recently received significant attention in the areas of networking, embedded and multi-agent systems (Lesser, Ortiz Jr., & Tambe 2003) due to its wide array of real-world applications (e.g., disaster relief, environment monitoring). In these applications, the distributed sensing task is achieved by the collaboration of a large number of static sensors, each of which has limited sensing, computational, and communication capabilities.

One of the fundamental issues that arises in a sensor network is coverage. Traditionally, network coverage is maximized by determining the optimal placement of static sensors in a centralized manner, which can be related to the class of art gallery problems (O'Rourke 1987). However, recent investigations in sensor network mobility reveal that mobile sensors can self-organize to provide better coverage than static placement (Yadgar, Kraus, & Ortiz Jr. 2003). Existing applications have only utilized uninformed mobility (i.e., random motion or patrol) (Lesser, Ortiz Jr., & Tambe 2003). In contrast, our work here focuses on informed, intelligent mobility to further improve coverage.

Our network coverage problem is motivated by the following constraints that discourage static sensor placement or uninformed mobility: a) no prior information about the exact target locations, population densities or motion pattern, b) limited sensory range, and c) very large area to be observed. All these conditions may cause the sensors to be unable to cover the entire region of interest. Hence, fixed sensor locations or uninformed mobility will not be adequate in general. Rather, the sensors have to move dynamically in response to the motion and distribution of targets and other sensors to maximize coverage. Inspired by robotics, the above problem may be regarded as that of low-level motion control to coordinate the sensors' target tracking movements in the continuous workspace. Alternatively, it can be cast as a high-level task allocation problem by segmenting the workspace into discrete regions (Fig. 1a) such that each region is assigned a group or *coalition* of sensors to track the targets within. We will now refer to mobile sensors as robots since they are the same in this paper's context.



This paper presents a two-level integrated approach (Fig. 1b) to distributed mobile sensor network coverage in complex, dynamic environments. At the lower level, each robot uses a reactive motion control strategy proposed by Low, Leow, & Ang, Jr. (2003) known as *Cooperative Extended Kohonen Maps* (EKMs) to coordinate their target tracking *within* a region without the need of communication. This strategy is also responsible for obstacle avoidance, robot separation to minimize task interference, and navigation between regions via beacons or checkpoints plotted by a motion planner. Low, Leow, & Ang, Jr. (2003) showed that cooperative EKMs perform more efficient target tracking than the well-known potential fields method (Parker 2002) in complex, unpredictable environments.

At the higher level, the robots use a dynamic *ant-based task allocation* scheme to cooperatively self-organize their coalitions in a decentralized manner according to the target distributions *across* the regions. This is the focus of the paper. It contrasts with the other works of biologically-inspired robot swarms (Balch & Arkin 1998; Matarić 1997) that emphasize control- rather than task-level cooperation. Our ant-based scheme addresses the following issues, which distinguish it from the other task allocation mechanisms:

**Task Allocation for Multi-Robot Tasks** Existing Multi-Robot Task Allocation (MRTA) algorithms (i.e., auction- and utility-based) (Gerkey & Matarić 2002; Parker 1998) generally assume that a multi-robot task can be partitioned into several single-robot tasks. But this may not be always possible or the multi-robot task can be more efficiently performed by coalitions of robots. Furthermore, the partitioned single-robot tasks are sometimes assumed to be indepen-

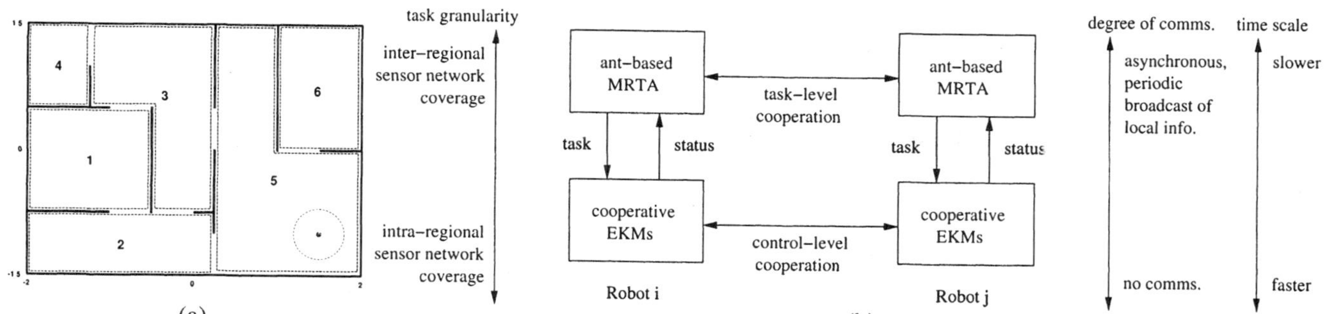


(a) (b)

Figure 1: (a) A 4 m × 3 m environment that is divided into 6 regions. The circle at the bottom right represents the robot's sensing radius of 0.3 m (drawn to scale). The environment is 42.44 times as large as the robot's sensing area. (b) Two-level integrated framework for multi-robot cooperation (MRTA = Multi-Robot Task Allocation, EKM = Extended Kohonen Map).

dent, i.e., no interference would result. However, the robots are bound to interfere with each other's ongoing activity either physically (e.g., space competition) or non-physically (e.g, shared radio bandwidth, conflicting goals). In the extreme case, when too many robots are involved, little or no work gets done as they totally restrict each other's movement. Hence, task interference has an adverse effect on the overall system performance (Goldberg & Matarić 1997). Knowing that physical interference can be implied from robot density (Goldberg & Matarić 1997), our decentralized task allocation scheme dynamically distributes robots in real-time by estimating robot densities in different regions to minimize interference. Bucket brigade algorithm (Schneider-Fontań & Matarić 1998) can also eliminate interference by assigning the robots to separate regions. However, it cannot respond in real-time to changes in regional distributions of targets due to target motion.

**Coalition Formation for Minimalist Robots** Existing multi-agent coalition formation schemes (Sandholm *et al.* 1999; Shehory & Kraus 1998) require complex planning, explicit negotiation, and precise estimation of coalitional cost. Hence, they may not be able to operate in real-time in a large-scale sensor network. Our task allocation method via self-organizing swarm coalitions is reactive, dynamic, and can operate with uncertain coalitional cost and resource-limited robots.

**Cooperation of Resource-Limited Robots** Robots with limited communication and sensing capabilities can only extract local, uncertain information of the environment. As such, distributed methodologies are required to process and integrate the noisy, heterogeneous information to improve its quality so that it can be effectively utilized to boost the task performance. Furthermore, if the robots have limited computational power, their cooperative strategies cannot involve complex planning or negotiations. Existing task allocation mechanisms have either assumed perfect communications, high computational power, centralized coordination or global knowledge of the task and agents (Gerkey & Matarić 2002; Krieger, Billeter, & Keller 2000; Parker 1998; Simmons *et al.* 2000). For example, recent coverage applications (Yadgar, Kraus, & Ortiz Jr. 2003) employ coalition leaders, one in each region, to negotiate with each other. This negotiation is conducted iteratively using an auction-based mechanism and attempts to balance the proportion of robots to that of the targets across all regions. To do so, each coalition leader must be able to obtain the exact number of robots and targets in its region as well as the task performance of these robots. Furthermore, it has to synchronize its negotiation with the coalition leaders in other regions via long-range communication. Note that this negotiation can be conducted entirely by a central coordinator but it requires even more resources. In contrast, our proposed method does not require such expensive resources, thus catering to resource-limited robots. The robots endowed with our ant-based scheme require only local sensing information and short-range communication. The robot coalitions can also be self-organized asynchronously without negotiation.

## Ant-Based Multi-Robot Task Allocation

Many multi-robot tasks, e.g., foraging, transportation, manipulation, sensing and exploration, have been inspired by social insects (Bonabeau, Dorigo, & Théraulaz 1999), in particular, ants. Our MRTA scheme encapsulates three concepts of ant behavior to self-organize the robot coalitions according to the target distributions across regions: (a) encounter pattern based on waiting time, (b) self-organization of social dominance, and (c) dynamic task allocation.

### Encounter Pattern Based on Waiting Time

Encounter patterns provide a simple, local cue for ants with sensory and cognitive limitations to assess regional densities of ants and objects of interest, which are crucial to regulating the division of labor (Gordon 1999). Instead of relying on global communication to relay target positions and density estimation (Jung & Sukhatme 2002), our scheme uses encounter patterns to predict target density via local sensing. Regional robot density is captured in a similar way using local communication.

An encounter pattern can be derived from a series of waiting time or interval between successive encounters. This simple form of information processing has accounted for the complex adaptive process of task allocation in ant colonies (Hirsh & Gordon 2001). In our coverage task, the waiting time of a robot is defined in terms of its encounters with the other robots and targets. A robot encounter is defined as a reception of a message from another robot in the same region. A target encounter is defined as an increase in the number of targets tracked between the previous and the current time steps. For a robot $i$ in region $r$, the waiting time for other robots $w_{ir}(k)$ and targets $w'_{ir}(k)$ is the time interval between the $(k-1)$th and $k$th encounters. Note that each waiting time is subject to stochastic variation. Hence, multiple samplings of waiting time have to be integrated to produce an accurate estimation of the regional density. The average waiting time $W_{ir}(k)$ between the $(k-1)$th and $k$th robot encounters for a robot $i$ in region $r$ is computed as:

$$\begin{aligned} W_{ir}(k) &= \frac{1}{n}w_{ir}(k) + \frac{n-1}{n}W_{ir}(k-1) \\ n &= \min(k, n_{max}) \end{aligned} \quad (1)$$

where $n_{max}$ is the maximum number of encounters that is monitored. This limit allows the robot to forget the early samplings of waiting time, which have become obsolete. The average target waiting time $W'_{ir}(k)$ is updated in the same manner. Both waiting times are updated according to the changing environment, and are inversely proportional to the robot and target densities in region $r$. The target density directly reflects the task demand of the region. The robot density reflects the amount of physical interference in the region, which is inversely proportional to the task demand. Therefore, the task demand $S_{ir}(k)$ of a region $r$ can be determined by robot $i$ as the ratio of the waiting times:

$$S_{ir}(k) = \frac{W_{ir}(k)}{W'_{ir}(k)} \,. \quad (2)$$

The task demand $S_{ir}(k)$ will be used in the self-organization of social dominance as well as in dynamic task allocation.

## Self-Organization of Social Dominance

The division of labor in an ant colony is strongly influenced by its social dominance order (Camazine *et al.* 2001), which self-organizes to match the task demands of the colony and the changing environment. Our scheme is inspired by this concept to move robots out of a region that has a lower target-to-robot density ratio than the other regions. Instead of fixing the dominance order (Goldberg & Matarić 1997), the social dominance of the robots in each coalition is self-organized according to their individual task performance. Robots in the same coalition engage in dominance contests at a regular interval $\tau$ if they are within communication range. The winner increases its tendency to stay in the current region while the loser increases its tendency to leave the current region and join another coalition in other regions. When robot $i$ encounters robot $j$ in region $r$, the probability of robot $i$ winning a contest against robot $j$ is defined as:

$$P(\text{robot } i \text{ winning}) = \frac{n_i^2 S_{ir}^2}{n_i^2 S_{ir}^2 + n_j^2 S_{jr}^2} \quad (3)$$

where $S_{ir}$ and $S_{jr}$ are respectively the task demand of region $r$ determined by robot $i$ and robot $j$, and $n_i$ and $n_j$ are the number of targets currently under observation by robot $i$ and robot $j$ respectively. Equation 3 implies that robot $i$ would most likely win the contest if it observes more targets than robot $j$. However, if both are tracking the same number of targets, then their individual evaluation of the task demand can be used to differentiate them. This will distinguish a robot that has been observing the targets for a long time from another that just encounters the same number of targets.

To inject the influence of social dominance on the self-organization of robot coalitions, each time a robot $i$ wins a contest (Eq. 3), it increases its tendency of staying in the current region, which is represented by the response threshold $\theta_i(t)$ to be used for dynamic task allocation:

$$\theta_i(t) = \theta_i(t-1) + \delta \quad (4)$$

where $\delta$ is small constant. Conversely, each time the robot loses, it decreases its tendency of staying in the region:

$$\theta_i(t) = \theta_i(t-1) - \delta \,. \quad (5)$$

$\theta_i$ varies in the range [0,1] to prevent robots from being overly submissive or dominating.

## Dynamic Task Allocation

The distributed task allocation algorithm in ants can efficiently arrange the ants in proportion to the amount of work in the changing environment (Tofts 1993). In a similar manner, our scheme aims to self-organize the robot coalitions according to the target distributions across the regions.

Our dynamic task allocation scheme is based on the notion of response thresholds (Bonabeau, Dorigo, & Théraulaz 1999). In a threshold model, robots with low response thresholds respond more readily to lower levels of task demand than do robots with high response thresholds. Performing the task reduces the demand of the task. If robots with low thresholds perform the required tasks, the task demand will never reach the thresholds of the high-threshold robots. However, if the task demand increases, high-threshold robots will engage in performing the task.

MRTA strategies that utilize fixed response thresholds (Jung & Sukhatme 2002; Krieger, Billeter, & Keller 2000) are incapable of responding effectively to dynamic environments (Bonabeau, Dorigo, & Théraulaz 1999). In contrast, the thresholds in our scheme are continuously updated by the self-organizing process of social dominance.

To be effective in task allocation, a robot must at least have some knowledge of the task demands in its neighboring regions in order to make rational task decisions. To do so, robot $i$ maintains a memory of the task demand $S_{ir}$ of each region $r$ (initialized to 0) and the amount of time $T_{ir}$ that it previously spent in region $r$. $T_{ir}$ can be used as a certainty measure of $S_{ir}$. In addition to computing $S_{ir}$ using Equation 2, $S_{ir}$ can also be updated when robot $i$ receives a message from a neighboring robot $j$ with $S_{jr}$ less than $S_{ir}$. Then $S_{ir}$ and $T_{ir}$ are updated to take the values $S_{jr}$ and $T_{jr}$ respectively. In this manner, the task demands of the regions are kept in memory. Robot $i$ can then predict which region has the greatest task demand and join that region. At every time interval of $\tau$, if $S_{ir}$ receives no update, the certainty value $T_{ir}$ is decreased by $\tau$ while the task demand $S_{ir}$ is increased by a small amount, such that its magnitude reflects the robot's motivation to explore.

Our distributed MRTA scheme uses a stochastic problem solving methodology. It is performed at intervals of $\tau$ to allow for multiple samplings of waiting time during each interval. The probability of a robot $i$ to stay in its current region $c$ is defined as:

$$P(\text{stay}) = \frac{S_{ic}^2}{S_{ic}^2 + (1-\theta_i)^2 + T_{ic}^{-2}} . \quad (6)$$

On the other hand, the probability of a robot $i$ to leave region $c$ to go to region $r$ is defined as:

$$P(\text{leave}) = \frac{S_{ir}^2}{S_{ir}^2 + \theta_i^2 + T_{ir}^{-2} + d_{cr}^2} \quad (7)$$

where $d_{cr}$ is the pre-computed collision-free distance between region $c$ and region $r$, which can be viewed as the cost of task switching. Note that a robot that loses in the dominance contest in a coalition does not always leave the region. If it experiences a higher task demand in its region than in other regions, it will have a high tendency of remaining in its coalition.

From Equations 6 and 7, if the robot does not respond to any regions, it will not switch task and will remain in the current coalition. The robot may also respond to more than one region. This conflict is resolved with a method that is similar to Equation 3. The probability of a robot $i$ choosing a region $r$ that it has responded to is:

$$P(\text{choose}) = \frac{(S_{ir}\ln T_{ir})^2}{\sum_r (S_{ir}\ln T_{ir})^2} . \quad (8)$$

If the robot $i$ chooses region $r$ that is not the current region $c$, then it will employ the reactive motion control strategy to move through the checkpoints plotted by the planner to region $r$. The generation of checkpoints is performed by the approximate cell decomposition method for motion planning (Low, Leow, & Ang, Jr. 2002).

## Experiments and Discussion

This section presents quantitative evaluations of the ant-based MRTA scheme for distributed mobile sensor network coverage in a complex, unpredictable environment. The experiments were performed using Webots, a Khepera mobile robot simulator, which incorporated 10% white noise in its sensors and actuators. 12 directed distance sensors were modelled around its body of radius 3 cm. Each sensor had a range of 17 cm, enabling the detection of obstacles at 20 cm or nearer from the robot's center, and a resolution of 0.5 cm to simulate noise. Each robot could also sense targets and kin robots at 0.3 m or nearer from its center and send messages to other robots that were less than 1 m away via short-range communication. A 4 m × 3 m environment (Fig. 1a) was used to house the Khepera robots and targets, which were randomly scattered initially. The number of robots varied from 5, 10 to 15, which corresponded to total robot sensing area of 11.8%, 23.6%, and 35.3% of the environment size. The mobile targets were forward-moving Braitenberg obstacle avoidance vehicles (Braitenberg 1984) that changed their direction and speed with 5% probability.

### Sensor Network Coverage

The first performance index determines the overall sensor network coverage of the robots (Parker 2002):

$$\text{sensor network coverage} = \sum_{t=1}^{T} 100\frac{n(t)}{NT} \quad (9)$$

where $N$ is the total number of targets, $n$ is the number of targets being tracked by the robots at time $t$, and the experiment lasts $T$ amount of time. $N$ and $T$ are fixed respectively as 30 targets and 10000 time steps at intervals of 128 ms.

Using this index, a quantitative test was conducted to compare the network coverage of the robots adopting five distributed tracking strategies: (1) potential fields, (2) cooperative EKMs, (3) static placement, (4) auction-based negotiation, and (5) ant-based MRTA. Unlike the latter three strategies, potential fields and cooperative EKMs are reactive motion control techniques that do not involve explicit task allocation. With static placement, static sensors are placed at least 0.6 m apart to ensure no overlap in coverage. With auction-based negotiation and ant-based MRTA, the robots are fitted with cooperative EKMs to coordinate their target tracking within a region, avoid obstacles, and navigate between regions.

Test results (Fig. 2a) show that ant-based MRTA provides better coverage than the other strategies. The differences in coverage between any two strategies have been verified using $t$-tests ($\alpha = 0.1$) to be statistically significant. Notice that 5 mobile robots endowed with our method can track better than 10 static sensors. Although auction-based negotiation uses complex negotiation, longer communication range, and more information about the robots and targets, it does not perform better than our ant-based scheme. This will be explained in the section of degree of specialization.

### Total Coalitional Cost

The second performance index determines the total coalitional cost (Shehory & Kraus 1998) of the robots. Given a set of connected regions where coverage tasks are to be performed, and a set $A$ of $M$ robots, the task allocation algorithm assigns a robot coalition $C_r \subseteq A$ to the coverage task in region $r$ such that (a) $\bigcup_r C_r = A$, (b) $\forall r \neq s, C_r \bigcap C_s = \emptyset$, and (c) each $C_r$ has a positive cost $|(n_r/N) - (m_r/M)|$ where $m_r$ and $n_r$ are the number of robots and targets in region $r$ respectively and $N$ is the total number of targets. The objective is to minimize the total coalitional cost (Shehory & Kraus 1998):

$$\text{total coalitional cost} = \sum_r \left| \frac{n_r}{N} - \frac{m_r}{M} \right| . \quad (10)$$

This index varies within the range [0,2]. A coalitional cost of 0 implies that the robot distribution over all regions is exactly proportional to the target distribution. In this manner, interference between robots is at its minimum, which will improve overall coverage. High costs imply the opposite.

Test results (Fig. 2b) show that auction-based negotiation and ant-based MRTA have the lowest coalitional costs. Hence, we can conclude from Figures 2a and 2b that, with

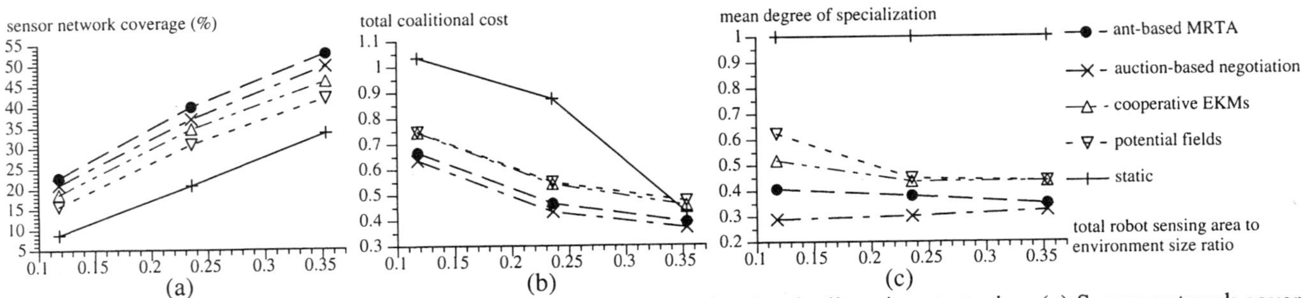


Figure 2: Comparison of performance using different motion control and task allocation strategies: (a) Sensor network coverage, (b) total coalitional cost, and (c) mean degree of specialization.

a lower cost, a higher coverage can be achieved. Although auction-based negotiation achieves slightly lower coalitional cost than ant-based MRTA, its coverage is lower. This will be explicated in the next section. Coalitional cost has been validated using $t$-tests ($\alpha = 0.1$) to be significantly different for various strategies except those without explicit task allocation (i.e., potential fields and cooperative EKMs). This is expected since they do not perform coalition formation, which account for their higher costs.

Coalitional cost is higher with fewer robots because with less robots, it is more difficult to achieve the same proportion of robots to that of the targets over all regions.

## Degree of Specialization

To achieve low coalitional cost, the robot coalitions must be highly responsive, i.e., they can self-organize rapidly according to the changing distributions of targets across regions. In a temporally varying environment, an ant colony has to increase its responsiveness to cope with frequent changes in task demands by employing more generalist ants, which perform a range of tasks (Wilson & Yoshimura 1994). Similarly, we will like to examine the effect of our non-stationary task environment, induced by moving robots and targets, on the degree of specialization in the robots. Based on Shannon-Wiener information variable $H$ (Lehner 1979), the third performance index quantifies the degree to which a robot specializes in a region:

$$\begin{aligned} \text{degree of specialization} &= 1 - H \\ H &= -\sum_{r} p_r \log_R p_r \end{aligned} \qquad (11)$$

where $p_r$ is the proportion of time a robot stays in region $r$ for the task duration of $T$, and $R$ is the total number of regions. This index varies within the range [0,1]. A degree of 1 implies the robot specializes in tracking only one region whereas a degree of 0 means the robot spends equal proportion of time tracking in all $R$ regions.

Figure 2c shows the mean degree of specialization of all the robots, which is lower for auction-based negotiation and ant-based MRTA. Hence, we can conclude from Figures 2b and 2c that a larger number of generalist robots leads to a lower coalitional cost. Although auction-based negotiation achieves lower degree of specialization and coalitional cost than ant-based MRTA, its coverage is lower. This is because reducing the degree of specialization will incur more time in task switching and consequently decrease the time for performing the task (Spencer, Couzin, & Franks 1998). In our test, this means that a robot will switch between several regions, thus incurring longer time in travelling between regions and target searching, and spending less time in target tracking. This accounts for poorer coverage of auction-based negotiation.

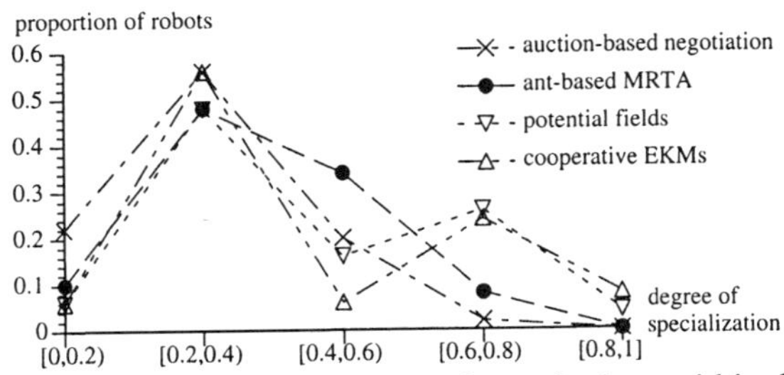


Figure 3: Comparison of proportions of robots within different ranges of degrees of specialization.

For ant-based MRTA, the mean degree of specialization is slightly higher with a smaller number of robots because each robot receives fewer messages from the other robots. As a result, the robots are less certain about the task demands in other regions. This causes the robots to be more specialized and less inclined to explore other regions. With cooperative EKMs or potential fields, fewer robots result in higher mean degree of specialization because the robots interfere less with each other and stay longer in a particular region.

Figure 3 shows the proportions of robots within different ranges of degrees of specialization for the case of 10 robots. Using ant-based MRTA and auction-based negotiation for explicit task allocation, most of the robots have degrees of specialization $< 0.6$. The other two methods without explicit task allocation have comparatively larger number of robots with degrees of specialization $\geq 0.6$. Hence, the methods with explicit task allocation are less rigid to changes in regional task demands and incur lower coalitional cost.

## Summary of Test Results

Compared to the other schemes, ant-based MRTA and auction-based negotiation have lower degree of specialization, coalitional cost, and higher coverage. But the degree of specialization cannot be too low as the cost of generalization would then exceed its benefits. This explains the higher coverage of ant-based MRTA over auction-based negotiation. Also, strategies without explicit task allocation can perform better than static placement by utilizing robot mobility to track the targets.

Our approach has also been tested on the coverage of evasive targets that avoid the tracking robots. In this test of 15 robots, the coverage of the static sensors has dropped to 10% but our ant-based scheme can still maintain a 53% coverage. The coverage of the other schemes have dropped slightly.

Our scheme is robust to robot failures, which is crucial for operating in dynamic, uncertain environments. For example, in the event that 5 robots fail, our scheme can still outperform a fully operational static sensor network (Fig. 2a).

We have also implemented a deterministic version of ant-based MRTA but it performs slightly worse than the stochastic version. This is because robots endowed with the deterministic scheme will move to a region only if information about the region flows out from it. If this region does not contain any robot, no information about this region can be transmitted to robots in other regions. Thus, no robot will move into this region even if it contains many targets to be tracked. Our stochastic scheme resolves this problem.

## Conclusion

This paper describes a task allocation scheme via self-organizing swarm coalitions for distributed mobile sensor network coverage. It uses concepts of ant behavior to self-regulate the division of labor in proportion to the regional task demands in the changing environment. Hence, the sensor network functions like an adaptive multiagent system. Quantitative comparisons with auction-based negotiation, potential fields and static deployment have shown that our approach can provide better coverage. Our work also demonstrates that in a temporally varying task environment, the self-organization of coalitions enables the robots to respond rapidly to frequent changes in regional task demands.

## References


Balch, T., and Arkin, R. C. 1998. Behavior-based formation control for multirobot teams. *IEEE Trans. Robot. Automat.* 14(6):926–939.

Bonabeau, E.; Dorigo, M.; and Théraulaz, G., eds. 1999. *Swarm Intelligence: From Natural to Artificial Systems.* Oxford Univ. Press.

Braitenberg, V. 1984. *Vehicles: Experiments in Synthetic Psychology.* MIT Press.

Camazine, S.; Deneubourg, J.-L.; Franks, N. R.; Sneyd, J.; Theraulaz, G.; and Bonabeau, E. 2001. *Self-Organization in Biological Systems.* Princeton Univ. Press.

Gerkey, B. P., and Matarić, M. J. 2002. Sold!: Auction methods for multi-robot coordination. *IEEE Trans. Robot. Automat.* 18(5):758–768.

Goldberg, D., and Matarić, M. J. 1997. Interference as a tool for designing and evaluating multi-robot controllers. In *Proc. AAAI*, 637–642.

Gordon, D. M. 1999. Interaction patterns and task allocation in ant colonies. In Detrain, C.; Deneubourg, J. L.; and Pasteels, J. M., eds., *Information Processing in Social Insects.* Basel, Switzerland: Birkhäuser Verlag. 51–67.

Hirsh, A. E., and Gordon, D. M. 2001. Distributed problem solving in social insects. *Annals Math. Artif. Intell.* 31(1-4):199–221.

Jung, B., and Sukhatme, G. S. 2002. Tracking targets using multiple robots: The effects of environment occlusion. *Autonomous Robots* 13(3):191–205.

Krieger, M. J. B.; Billeter, J.-B.; and Keller, L. 2000. Ant-like task allocation and recruitment in cooperative robots. *Nature* 406:992–995.

Lehner, P. N. 1979. *Handbook of Ecological Methods.* New York: Garland STPM.

Lesser, V.; Ortiz Jr., C. L.; and Tambe, M. 2003. *Distributed Sensor Networks: A Multiagent Perspective.* Kluwer Academic Publishers.

Low, K. H.; Leow, W. K.; and Ang, Jr., M. H. 2002. A hybrid mobile robot architecture with integrated planning and control. In *Proc. AAMAS*, 219–226.

Low, K. H.; Leow, W. K.; and Ang, Jr., M. H. 2003. Action selection for single- and multi-robot tasks using cooperative extended Kohonen maps. In *Proc. IJCAI*, 1505–1506.

Matarić, M. J. 1997. Behaviour-based control: Examples from navigation, learning, and group behaviour. *J. Expt. Theor. Artif. Intell.* 9(2-3):323–336.

O'Rourke, J. 1987. *Art Gallery Theorems and Algorithms.* Oxford Univ. Press.

Parker, L. E. 1998. ALLIANCE: An architecture for fault tolerant multi-robot cooperation. *IEEE Trans. Robot. Automat.* 14(2):220–240.

Parker, L. E. 2002. Distributed algorithms for multi-robot observation of multiple moving targets. *Autonomous Robots* 12(3):231–255.

Sandholm, T.; Larson, K.; Andersson, M.; Shehory, O.; and Tohmé, F. 1999. Coalition structure generation with worst case guarantees. *Artif. Intell.* 111(1-2):209–238.

Schneider-Fontań, M., and Matarić, M. J. 1998. Territorial multi-robot task division. *IEEE Trans. Robot. Automat.* 14(5):815–822.

Shehory, O., and Kraus, S. 1998. Methods for task allocation via agent coalition formation. *Artif. Intell.* 101(1-2):165–200.

Simmons, R.; Apfelbaum, D.; Burgard, W.; Fox, D.; Moors, M.; Thrun, S.; and Younes, H. 2000. Coordination for multi-robot exploration and mapping. In *Proc. AAAI*, 852–858.

Spencer, A. J.; Couzin, I. D.; and Franks, N. R. 1998. The dynamics of specialization and generalization within biological populations. *J. Complex Systems* 1(1):115–127.

Tofts, C. 1993. Algorithms for task allocation in ants (a study of temporal polyethism: Theory). *Bull. Math. Biol.* 55(5):891–918.

Wilson, D. S., and Yoshimura, J. 1994. On the coexistence of specialists and generalists. *Am. Nat.* 144(4):692–707.

Yadgar, O.; Kraus, S.; and Ortiz Jr., C. L. 2003. Hierarchical information combination in large-scale multiagent resource management. In Huget, M.-P., ed., *Communications in Multiagent Systems.* LNAI 2650, 129–145.

# GrowRange: Anytime VCG-Based Mechanisms

**David C. Parkes**
Division of Engineering and Applied Sciences,
Harvard University,
33 Oxford Street, Cambridge MA 02138
parkes@eecs.harvard.edu

**Grant Schoenebeck**
Harvard College,
Cambridge, MA 02138
schoeneb@fas.harvard.edu

### Abstract

We introduce anytime mechanisms for distributed optimization with self-interested agents. Anytime mechanisms retain good incentive properties even when interrupted before the optimal solution is computed, and provide better quality solutions when given additional time. Anytime mechanisms can solve easy instances of a hard problem quickly and optimally, while providing approximate solutions on very hard instances. In a particular instantiation, GrowRange, we successively expand the range of outcomes considered, computing the optimal solution for each range. Truth-revelation remains a dominant strategy equilibrium with a stage-based interruption, and is a best-response with high probability when the interruption is time-based.

## Introduction

Designing mechanisms to solve distributed optimization problems with self-interested agents is becoming increasingly important in a wide variety of settings, from e-commerce, to the allocation of computational resources in open systems, to planning in multi-agent systems. This field, called *computational mechanism design* (CMD), aims to design solutions that are both incentive-compatible (with truth revelation in a game-theoretic equilibrium) and tractable.

Combinatorial auctions (CAs), with agents that demand bundles of items, are a canonical problem in CMD. All previous work on tractable and strategyproof mechanisms (with truth-revelation in a *dominant-strategy equilibrium*) for CAs has considered restricted domains of agent preferences. For instance, Lehmann et al. (2002) describe a fast and strategyproof CA for single-minded agents that demand only one bundle. But, there are many other examples (Mu'alem & Nisan 2002; Archer *et al.* 2003; Bartal, Gonen, & Nisan 2003). These methods do not apply to the general CA problem.

In this paper, we introduce *anytime mechanisms*, as a new paradigm for the design of incentive-compatible and tractable mechanisms. Anytime mechanism will solve easy instances of a hard family of problems quickly and optimally, while returning approximate solutions and retaining strategyproofness on very hard instances. Provable worst-case approximation results are dropped in favor of good performance on most problems coupled with the ability to terminate the algorithm with an approximate solution on the very hardest of problems.[1] We address the challenge of retaining useful incentive properties, such that truthful bidding is an equilibrium whenever a mechanism is terminated.

It is worth emphasizing that a naive approach, in which a Vickrey-Clarke-Groves (VCG) mechanism (see Nisan & Ronen (2000)) is coupled with an anytime winner-determination algorithm, would not be strategyproof unless the algorithm has enough time to solve the problem optimally. The strategyproofness of the VCG mechanism ordinarily relies on the optimality of its decision.

Our solution builds on *maximal-in-range* VCG mechanisms (Nisan & Ronen 2000).We implement anytime mechanisms as *staged* mechanisms, with a new range of outcomes considered in each stage and the optimal solution computed for each new range. Importantly, the range adopted in each stage must not depend on any information reported by agents. In each stage we also compute the optimal solution to the problem without each agent. When interrupted, the anytime mechanism implements the best solution found so far, and determines VCG-based payments on the basis of the best solutions found so far without each agent. The mechanism will continue to compute a better solution when provided with more time.

To understand the incentive properties we consider two different models of interruption. First, we consider stage-based interruptions, in which the mechanism is interrupted after some number of stages. Truth-revelation remains a dominant strategy equilibrium, because the final solution is optimal over the union of the ranges explored, with individual ranges chosen without regard to agent bids. Throughout the paper it is important that the interruption comes from the center, or some third-party, and not from one of the agents.

A more realistic model is one in which the interruption process is *time-based*, for instance an answer might be required after 10 minutes. A new concern here is that an agent can indirectly affect the sequence of ranges explored by changing the difficulty of the problem through its bids, and thus influence the progress made by the algorithm before interruption. Our solution is to use *consensus functions* (Goldberg & Hartline 2003) to compute a conservative and agent-independent estimate of the number of stages completed by the time of an interruption, with results from any additional stages discarded. Together with additional assump-

[1] Indeed, Nisan & Ronen (2000) and Lavi et al. (2003) suggest that *no* worst-case polynomial time combinatorial auction can be strategyproof and provide good worst-case approximation properties, without assuming a restricted preference domain.

tions about the maximal influence that an agent can have on the run time, this makes truthful bidding a best-response with high probability, whatever the bids of other agents.

We illustrate our methods in the context of CAs. We define GrowRange, which is a particular partition-based instantiation. The empirical results illustrate encouraging performance on hard problems with high run time variance.

## Preliminaries

Mechanism design (MD) considers a system of rational self-interested agents and the problem of choosing an outcome $k$ from a finite set $K$ of possibilities. Let $N$ denote the number of agents. Each agent $i \in \mathcal{I}$ has a *type*, $\theta_i \in \Theta_i$, that defines its value $v_i(k, \theta_i)$ for each possible choice $k$. This information is privately known to each agent. Let $\theta = (\theta_1, \ldots, \theta_N)$ denote a type vector and $\theta_{-i}$ to denote all types except that of agent $i$. Agents have *quasilinear* utility, $u_i(k,p) = v_i(k, \theta_i) - p_i$, in value and payments.

Agents report types (perhaps untruthfully) and the mechanism computes the outcome and payments. The challenge is to implement an outcome with good properties despite the ability to misreport types. For instance, *efficient* MD seeks to implement a choice $k_{\text{eff}}(\theta) \in K$ that maximizes the total value across all agents.

Given reports $\hat{\theta}$, mechanism $M = (k,p)$ defines a choice rule $k(\hat{\theta}) \in K$ and a payment rule $p_i(\hat{\theta}) \geq 0$, that determines the payment made by each agent to the center. Let $V(N) = \max_k \sum_i v_i(k, \hat{\theta}_i)$ and $V(N_{-i}) = \max_k \sum_{j \neq i} v_j(k, \hat{\theta}_j)$.

**Definition 1** *The Vickrey-Clarke-Groves (VCG) mechanism defines choice rule $k_i(\hat{\theta}) = \arg\max_{k \in K} \sum_i v_i(k, \hat{\theta}_i)$, and payment rule $p_i(\hat{\theta}) = v_i(k(\hat{\theta}), \hat{\theta}_i) - [V(N) - V(N_{-i})]$.*

The VCG mechanism has the following properties:

**Strategyproof:** Truth-revelation is a dominant-strategy equilibrium. Formally, $v_i(k_{\text{eff}}(\theta_i, \theta_{-i}), \theta_i) - p_i(\theta_i, \theta_{-i}) \geq v_i(k_{\text{eff}}(\hat{\theta}_i, \theta_{-i}), \theta_i) - p_i(\hat{\theta}_i, \theta_{-i})$ for all $i$, all $\theta_{-i}$, all $\theta_i$, and all $\hat{\theta}_i \neq \theta_i$.

**Efficient:** The choice implemented in the VCG mechanism maximizes the total value across agents, in equilibrium.

Strategyproofness is a useful property for mechanisms because it simplifies the strategic problem facing bidding agents. An agent does not need to model the values or strategies of other agents to compute its equilibrium strategy.

Often times the optimization problem $k(\hat{\theta})$ is intractable, for instance in CAs (Rothkopf, Pekeč, & Harstad 1998). It is interesting to consider a *VCG-based* mechanism, in which the optimal choice rule, $k^*$, is replaced with an approximate choice rule. Everything else is left unchanged, with payments computed by applying the approximate choice rule to solve the optimization problem without each agent.

In particular, Nisan & Ronen (2000) define *maximal-in-range* VCG mechanisms. Consider some range $\tilde{K} \subseteq K$, and let $V(N; \tilde{K}) = \max_{k \in \tilde{K}} \sum_i v_i(k, \hat{\theta}_i)$ and $V(N_{-i}; \tilde{K}) = \max_{k \in \tilde{K}} \sum_{j \neq i} v_j(k, \hat{\theta}_j)$.

**Definition 2** *A maximal-in-range VCG mechanism implements choice rule $\tilde{k}(\hat{\theta}) = \arg\max_{k \in \tilde{K}} \sum_i v_i(k, \hat{\theta}_i)$, and payment rule $p_i(\hat{\theta}) = v_i(\tilde{k}(\hat{\theta}), \hat{\theta}_i) - [V(N; \tilde{K}) - V(N_{-i}; \tilde{K})]$, for some range $\tilde{K} \subseteq K$.*

**Proposition 1** *(Nisan & Ronen 2000) A VCG-based mechanism is strategyproof if and only if it is maximal-in-range.*

That maximal-in-range is sufficient for strategyproof follows immediately from the strategyproofness of VCG mechanisms. Maximal-in-range is also necessary for strategyproofness because otherwise there is always a set of types for which one agent can select the maximal choice in the range by misreporting its type, and thus improve its utility.

Crucially, the strategyproofness of maximal-in-range approximations hinges on the agents retaining an *expressive language* for outcomes in the range, and on the range being selected *independently* of agent bids.

### Combinatorial Auctions

Combinatorial auctions (CAs) have received particular attention in CMD. In a CA, there is a set of $\mathcal{G}$ items to allocate. Agent $i$ with type $\theta_i$ has value $v_i(S, \theta_i) \geq 0$ for a bundle $S \subseteq \mathcal{G}$ of items. For simplicity, it is convenient to drop the explicit dependence on type and write $v_i(S)$. We assume *free-disposal*, with $v_i(T) \geq v_i(S)$ for all $T \supseteq S$ and normalize with $v_i(\emptyset) = 0$. The efficient allocation maximizes $\sum_i v_i(S_i)$ subject to $S_i \cap S_j = \emptyset$ and $S_i \subseteq \mathcal{G}$.

Noting that the strategyproofness of the maximal-in-range approximation requires no restrictions on agent valuations, one might wonder whether a maximal-in-range approximation can provide a CA that is tractable and produce reasonable solutions. Unfortunately, the answer is negative.

**Theorem 1** *(Nisan & Ronen 2000) No strategyproof VCG-based CA can be both tractable and reasonable.*

In particular, an allocation is said to be *reasonable* if whenever a single agent values an item that agent receives the item in the allocation. Without reasonableness there can be no useful worst-case guarantee on efficiency. Thus, this negative result makes the case for an anytime approach. Without this, we must either: (a) impose an *a priori* restriction on the range that will sometimes preclude reasonable behavior even when an instance was actually easy; or (b) seek optimality and accept that sometimes a solution will not be returned quickly; or (c) accept a loss in strategyproofness and an unraveling of incentives.

We note, parenthetically, that although there are many known tractable special-cases of the CAP that arise due to restrictions on the structure of bundles (e.g. *circular-ones, consecutive-ones, two-ones*) (Rothkopf, Pekeč, & Harstad 1998; de Vries & Vohra 2003), and that thus suggest maximal-in-range approximations, all of them assume an *additive-or* language for bids. This language is *not* expressive for general valuations, even on restricted ranges (unless the range only allows each agent to receive a single bundle). Moreover, introducing an expressive language, with *exclusive-or* bids (Nisan 2000), requires introducing additional side constraints that break the very structure that is required for tractability.

## Anytime VCG-Based Mechanisms

We use maximal-in-range VCG approximations to define anytime VCG mechanisms. The mechanisms are defined for a sequence of ranges $K^1, K^2, \ldots,$, that satisfy the following properties:

1. The sequence of ranges is independent of reported types.
2. Optimization $V(N; K^z)$ and $V(N_{-i}; K^z)$ on the range $K^z$ in early stages $z$ tends to be easier than solving the complete problem $V(N; K)$.
3. The union of ranges, $\bigcup_{z'} K^{z'} = K$, *i.e.* the search eventually computes the optimal solution across all choices.

It is critical that the sequence of ranges not depend on the bids from agents to maintain strategyproofness. As an example, this rules out allowing agents to submit 10 bids of their choice, then 20 bids, then 30 bids, ... with the range defined in terms of the bundles in agent bids.[2]

In our staged, maximal-in-range, approach we consider a sequence of ranges, $K^1, K^2, \ldots,$. Let $K^{<z} = \bigcup_{z'<z} K^{z'}$, and $K^{\leq z} = \bigcup_{z' \leq z} K^{z'}$. Let $\tilde{k}^z$ denote the solution to $\max_{k \in K^{\leq z}} \sum_i v_i(k, \hat{\theta}_i)$, and $\tilde{k}^z_{-i}$ denote the solution to $\max_{k \in K^{\leq z}} \sum_{j \neq i} v_j(k, \hat{\theta}_j)$.

**Definition 3 (Anytime VCG Mechanism)** *Given a sequence of ranges $K^1, K^2, \ldots$ and reports $\hat{\theta}$:*

1. *In stage $z$, solve $\max_{k \in K^z} \sum_i v_i(k, \hat{\theta}_i)$ and $\max_{k \in K^z} \sum_{j \neq i} v_j(k, \hat{\theta}_j)$ for all $i \in N$. Update $\tilde{k}^z$ and $\tilde{k}^z_{-i}$, to maintain the best solutions seen so far.*
2. *If an interruption is received during the stage $z'$ then implement outcome $\tilde{k}^{z'-1}$, and payments*

$$p_i = v_i(\tilde{k}^{z'-1}, \hat{\theta}_i) - \left[V(N; K^{<z'}) - V(N_{-i}; K^{<z'})\right].$$

Note that the payments can be quickly computed by evaluating the best solutions determined at the end of stage $z' - 1$; it is not necessary to solve any additional optimization problems. Also, note that this is not simply a sequence of VCG-based mechanisms, because the VCG payments are computed in terms of the best solutions across all stages, regardless of the stage in which they occurred. Not all best solutions (for the main problem and the problem without each agent) need occur in the same stage.

Turning to incentives, consider a stage-based interruption, for instance an answer might be required after 10 stages. More generally, the interruption can follow some p.d.f. $c(z)$, that can be known to the agents.

**Theorem 2** *The anytime VCG mechanism is strategyproof for a stage-based interruption $c(z)$, and will implement the efficient allocation if allowed to run for enough stages.*

**Proof:** The anytime VCG mechanism is strategyproof for any fixed number of stages because the sequence of ranges are independent of agent bids. Thus, the union over some number of ranges defined by an agent-independent distribution is itself agent independent. Efficiency holds once the final stage is implemented because this range contains all feasible solutions. ■

[2]This scheme was proposed in Banks et al. (1989).

### Avoiding Redundant Computation

A number of simple optimizations are possible to avoid the unnecessary duplication of computation across stages.

We describe these in the context of an implementation in which the optimization problems in each stage are formulated as *mixed-integer programs*, and solved via branch-and-cut LP-based search. But the ideas are general, and also hold for other systematic search algorithms.

**Lower-bound Pruning.** When solving $V(N; K^z)$ and $V(N_{-i}; K^z)$ in stage $z$, use the value of the best current solutions, *i.e.* $V(N; K^{<z})$ and $V(N_{-i}; K^{<z})$ to prune the search. For instance, when all solutions under a search node are dominated in value by the current best solution then prune the subtree at that node.

**Second-best Solutions.** When solving $V(N_{-i}; K^z)$ for stage $z$, we know $V(N_{-i}; K^z) \leq V(N; K^z)$. Solve for $V(N; K^z)$ first, and then if a feasible solution to $V(N_{-i}; K^z)$ also has value $V(N; K^z)$ then immediately stop without *proving* optimality. Combining with lower-bound pruning, if $V(N_{-i}; K^{<z}) \geq V(N; K^z)$ then there is no need to solve $V(N_{-i}; K^z)$.

**Disjunctive Search.** Constraints can be added to the formulation of search in a new stage to avoid duplication of effort with earlier searches. For instance, the problem $V(N; K^z)$ can be formulated as $\max_{k \in K^z} \sum_i v_i(k, \hat{\theta}_i)$ s.t. $k \notin K^{<z}$. This is related to the idea of "local branching" in Fischetti & Lodi (2002). In the case of CAs, this means adding a constraint to ensure that at least one agent receives a new bundle.

## An Anytime VCG-Based Mechanism for CAs

GrowRange is a concrete instantiation of an anytime VCG mechanism for CAs. In particular, it adopts a *partition-based* sequence of ranges, and considers only monotonically-increasing sequences of ranges.

### Partition-Based CAs

Let $\Pi = \{A_1, \ldots, A_k\}$ denote a partition of items $\mathcal{G}$ into non-empty parts. Following Holzman et al. (2001), let $\Sigma_\Pi \subseteq 2^{\mathcal{G}}$ denote the set of bundles generated by $\Pi$, *i.e.* containing all bundles of the form $\bigcup_{l \in L} A_l$, where $L \subseteq \{1, \ldots, k\}$. Clearly, the "grand" bundle $\mathcal{G}$ is always in $\Sigma_\Pi$, and we also require that $\Sigma_\Pi$ includes the empty bundle, $\emptyset$. Given all bundles in $\Sigma_\Pi$ we define the *range* to include all allocations $S = (S_1, \ldots, S_N)$ in which $S_i \in \Sigma_\Pi$ for every agent $i$. Loosely, we also find it convenient to simply refer to the bundles, $\Sigma_\Pi$, as the range.

This leads to a concrete instantiation of a maximal-in-range CA. Consider an exclusive-or (XOR) bidding language (Nisan 2000), with bid $(b_i, B_i)$ from agent $i$ defining value $\hat{v}_i(S)$ on all $S \in B_i$ and value $\hat{v}_i(S) = \max_{S' \in B_i, S' \subseteq S} b_i(S')$ on all bundles $S \subseteq \mathcal{G}$, $S \notin B_i$, by free-disposal. Projecting these bids onto the restricted range, $\Sigma_\Pi$, we construct bids $b'_i(S) = \hat{v}_i(S)$ on all bundles $S \in B'_i = \bigcup_{S \in B_i} C(S)$ with $C(S) \in \Sigma_\Pi$ defined as the bundle in $\Sigma_\Pi$ that minimally includes $S$ (Holzman *et al.* 2001). There is a unique such bundle because the field,

$\Sigma_\Pi$, is closed under intersection. The premise behind this approach is that fewer bids tend to make winner determination easier. Note that the input size of the projected bids from agent $i$ is at most $\min\{|B_i|, |\Sigma_\Pi|\}$.

Given these projected bids, a standard "branch-on-bid" winner-determination algorithm such as ILOG's CPLEX mixed-integer programming package, or special-purpose solvers such as CABOB (Sandholm *et al.* 2001) can be used to compute the optimal solution and provide a maximal-in-range VCG mechanism.

As an example, consider an agent with valuation $\{(a, \$50), (b, \$100)\}$, goods $\mathcal{G} = \{a, b, c, d\}$, and partitions $\Pi^1 = \{abc, d\}$, $\Pi^2 = \{a, bc, d\}$, $\Pi^3 = \{a, b, c, d\}$, that define fields $\Sigma_{\Pi^1} = \{\emptyset, abc, d, abcd\}$, $\Sigma_{\Pi^2} = \{\emptyset, a, ad, abc, bc, bcd, d\}$ and $\Sigma_{\Pi^3} = 2^{\mathcal{G}}$. The projected bids are $\{(abc, \$100)\}$, $\{(a, \$50), (bc, \$100)\}$, and $\{(a, \$50), (b, \$100)\}$, for partitions $\Pi^1, \Pi^2$, and $\Pi^3$ respectively.

The additional structure in a partition-based range can also be made available to a solver by defining a new set of "dummy" items, each associated with one bundle in the partition. In fact, the special structure of a partition-based range provides an additional equilibrium property, defined with respect to the bids submitted on the range $\Sigma_\Pi$:

**Theorem 3** *(Holzman* et al. *2001) No agent can benefit by unilaterally submitting a bid outside of a partition-based range $\Sigma_\Pi$, given that bids from other agents are projected onto $\Sigma_\Pi$.*

### Algorithm: GROWRANGE($k_0, \alpha$)

A sequence of partitions, $\Pi^1, \Pi^2, \ldots$, defines the sequence of ranges. Parameter $k_0$ defines the size of the initial partition, and parameter $\alpha$ defines the number of refinements made in between stages:

- To construct $\Pi^0$, choose $k_0$ items uniformly at random, to seed a separate component of $\Pi^0$. Place each remaining item uniformly at random into one of the components.
- To construct $\Pi^z$ from $\Pi^{z-1}$, choose a component $S \in \Pi^{z-1}$ with $|S| > 1$ and split the component (choosing the split uniformly at random) into two new components. Repeat $\alpha$ times (or until all components of the partition are singletons).

Note that because we define refinements of the partition by this subdivision process each successive range will be defined on more and more bundles, *i.e.* $\Sigma_{\Pi^z} \supseteq \Sigma_{\Pi^{z-1}}$. This simplifies the anytime VCG mechanism, because the best solutions to $V(N; K^{\leq z})$ and $V(N_{-i}; K^{\leq z})$, for any $z$, will always be those computed in the most recent stage. Also, we see that the solutions used to determine payments are determined in the *same* stage as the best overall solution.

## Empirical Analysis

In preliminary studies, we have investigated the anytime performance of GROWRANGE for CAs. For winner determination, we use the IBM OSL mixed-integer programming (MIP) solver both to solve optimization problems within

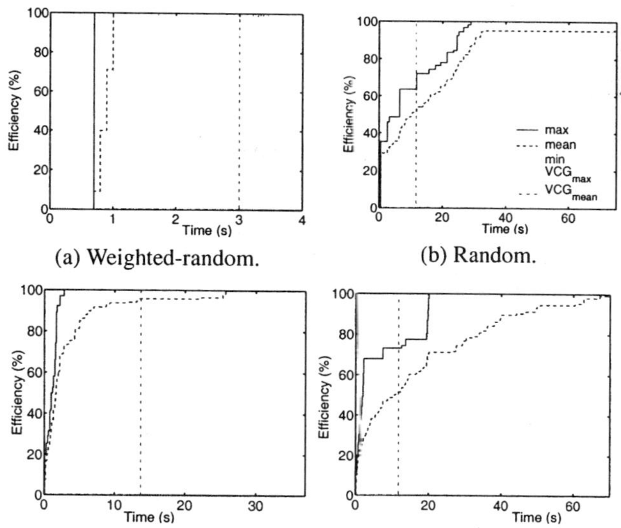

(a) Weighted-random. (b) Random. (c) Uniform. (d) Decay.

Figure 1: Anytime performance of GROWRANGE.

each stage of GROWRANGE, as well as to compute the outcome for the one-shot (optimal) VCG mechanism.

In testing GROWRANGE, we adapt the bid distributions defined in Sandholm (1999), but using Sandholm's models to define *valuations* for agents. It is important to note that we generate values with these distributions, and not bid prices. In particular, we adopt an *exclusive-or* (XOR) logic to define a valuation function in terms of the values on a sparse number of bundles.[3] We adapt the *Weighted-random*, *Random*, *Uniform* and *Decay* distributions. Problem sizes are (agents/bundles-per-agent/goods): 100/4/200, 80/4/160, 40/4/80, and 80/4/160 for each distribution respectively, with Sandholm's Decay parameter set to 0.55 and with bundles of size 5 in Uniform. We adopt parameters $(k_0, \alpha) = (5, 10)$ for all distributions except Uniform, for which we adopt parameters $(k_0, \alpha) = (2, 5)$.

Figure 1 illustrates the performance of GROWRANGE. We plot the average and maximum runtime of the one-shot VCG mechanism, along with the *max*, *min*, and *average* anytime profiles of GROWRANGE. All results are averaged over 10 instances, and experiments were perfomed on a 4 GHz P4, with 512 MB RAM. Note that we measure the total run time for GROWRANGE, including the overhead for projecting bids and constructing partitions.

Given that we use *random* partitions in GROWRANGE and make no effort to tune the sequence of partitions to the prob-

[3]It is a common misconception that these distributions provide easy winner-determination problems. As initially defined in Sandholm (1999) the distributions were used to define bids connected with an *additive-or* bidding language. It is in this form that Andersson et al. (2000), and others, have shown that the Weighted Random, Random, and to some extent the Decay distributions are easy. We are not aware of any studies of the complexity of winner determination when these distributions are used to generate values, and structured as an XOR'ed set.

lem domain we find these initial results quite encouraging. If a system was to use the one-shot VCG mechanism it would need to be prepared to wait for the *maximal* possible run time, because if there was ever a chance that it would be terminated before completion then strategyproofness would be lost and the performance would unravel. Thus, the most interesting test for GrowRange is to look at its anytime performance after some fraction of the maximal VCG run time.

The anytime approach is most promising on problems for which there is a large variance in solution difficulty across instances. This is illustrated on Uniform, for which the run time of the VCG mechanism has a large variance (the mean run time is 13.7s but the maximal run time was 34.3s). GrowRange averages better than 90% allocative-efficiency in 50% of the worst-case VCG run time. We also see good performance on Weighted-random, although this proved to be an easy problem for both methods.

The *Decay* and *Random* distributions proved not to be well suited to the anytime approach because we found little variance in the run time of the VCG mechanism, at least over 10 trials. GrowRange averages only around 50% efficiency in 50% of the worst-case VCG run time. Future analysis should take additional samples to make sure that there is indeed little variance of VCG run time on these problems.

Leyton-Brown et al. (2002) have studied the variance in run time for CAs, given distributions from CATS (**?**). Their analysis suggests a high variance in many problems. We view this as further evidence that anytime mechanisms are necessary in practice.[4]

## Time-Based Interruptions

We now turn to a time-based model of interruption, in which the center interrupts the mechanism according to some random process $T \sim c(t)$ that defines the time $T$ at which a solution is required. Time-based interruptions are appealing because they allow the center to respond when challenged to provide a solution, and also because they can facilitate the integration of cost-of-delay based models of meta-deliberation (Horvitz 1987; Dean & Boddy 1988).

Even when the sequence of ranges $K^1, K^2, \ldots$ remains independent of bids from agents, an agent can try to change the *progress* made across this sequence by a particular time by submitting bids that change the difficulty of the optimization problems in each stage. Consider, for instance, an agent that knows that it is a winner in early stages but not in later stages. If an interrupt will come quite late, this agent could try to state a type that *slows* down computation in early stages. Of course, this is not without drawbacks because the agent must also be careful not to adversely change the outcome in any stages that are searched (it's dominant strategy, contingent on a fixed or random range, remains truth-revelation).

A simple fix would use an optimization algorithm with a run time that is the same for all bids, for any given range. But, this approach is not appealing because we want to solve easy instances quickly rather than design for the worst-case. This is the whole motivation for an anytime approach!

Instead, we define a randomized mechanism and retain strategyproofness with some error probability (Archer *et al.* 2003). We say a mechanism $M$ is *strategyproof with error probability* $p$ if for every $\theta_{-i}$ and every $\theta_i$, the probability that a truthful bid $\theta_i$ is not the best-response for agent $i$ is no greater than $p$.

Let $z(\theta, t)$ denote the number of stages completed by time $t$. We use *consensus functions* (Goldberg & Hartline 2003) to compute a conservative estimate $f(\theta,t) \leq z(\theta,t)$ of the number of stages, that is agent independent and cannot be manipulated by any single agent with probability $p$. The mechanism then "rolls-back" its state to the end of stage $f(\theta, t)$, discarding any results from additional computation.

For now, we provide a high-level description of the mechanism. Let $time(\theta, z)$ denote the total compute time to solve $V(N; K^{\leq z})$ and $time(\theta_{-i}, z)$ denote the total compute time to solve $V(N_{-i}; K^{\leq z})$, given reports $\theta$. We define and construct our agent-independent estimator below.

**Definition 4 (Consensus-Based Anytime VCG Mech.)** *Given a sequence of ranges $K^1, K^2, \ldots$, reports $\hat{\theta}$, and a conservative and agent-independent estimator $f(\theta, t)$:*

1. *In stage $z$, solve $\max_{k \in K^z} \sum_i v_i(k, \hat{\theta}_i)$ and $\max_{k \in K^z} \sum_{j \neq i} v_j(k, \hat{\theta}_j)$ for all $i \in N$. Update $\tilde{k}^z$ and $\tilde{k}^z_{-i}$, to maintain the best solutions seen so far. Update $time(\hat{\theta}, z)$ and $time(\hat{\theta}_{-i}, z)$.*
2. *If an interruption is received at time $t'$, then compute $z' = f(\hat{\theta}, t')$, and implement implement outcome $\tilde{k}^{z_{ce}}$, and payments*

$$p_i = v_i(\tilde{k}^{z'}, \hat{\theta}_i) - \left[V(N; K^{\leq z'}) - V(N_{-i}; K^{\leq z'})\right].$$

*Discard the results from additional computation completed after stage $z'$.*

**Theorem 4** *Consensus-Based Anytime VCG Mechanism, with conservative estimator $f(\theta, t)$ that is agent independent with probability p, and time-based interruption $c(t)$, is strategyproof with probability p.*

**Proof:** Whatever the reports $\theta_{-i}$ of other agents $\neq i$, and whatever the interruption time $t'$, with probability $p$ the mechanism is rolled-back to the same stage $z' = f(\hat{\theta}_i, \theta_{-i}, t')$ for all reports $\hat{\theta}_i$. Agent $i$'s best-strategy is to bid truthfully when this occurs, because the mechanism will implement a maximal-in-range VCG outcome on range $\bigcup_{z \leq z'} K^z$. ∎

Here, it is important that the second-best solutions $V(N_{-i}; K^z)$ are *explicitly* solved in each stage, in order to construct a suitable agent-independent estimator $f(\theta, t)$.[5] Also, it is important that the estimate is close to the true

[4] Subject to the concern, discussed in the next section, that this variance *not* be accompanied by significant opportunities for any *single* agent to change the run time through its bid.

[5] In comparison, these calculations can be skipped in the stage-based interruption model when the solution to $V(N_{-i}; K^z)$ can be readily inferred from $V(N; K^z)$. For instance, in a CA this occurs when agent $i$ receives no items in the efficient solution.

number of stages completed because we must discard any computation performed after the estimated stage $f(\theta, t')$ given interruption at time $t'$.

## An Agent-Independent Stage Estimator

We need an estimator $f(\theta, t)$ for the number of completed stages that is agent independent with high probability.

**Definition 5** *Function $f(\theta, t) \in \mathbb{N}$ is a* ***conservative and agent-independent estimator with probability*** *p, if:*

**P1.** *$f(\theta, t) \leq z(\theta, t)$, for all $\theta$ and all t.*

**P2.** *$f(\hat{\theta}_i, \theta_{-i}, t) = f(\theta_i, \theta_{-i}, t)$, for any $\theta_{-i}, \theta_i$, and t, and all $\hat{\theta}_i \neq \theta_i$, with probability p over coin flips independent of $\theta$ and t.*

A trivial estimator $f(\theta, t)$ would return 0 for small times $t$ and then 1 for larger times, for all $\theta$. This would be conservative and agent independent, but not informative. We will seek an estimator that returns a number of stages $f(\theta, t)$ "close" to the actual number of completed stages, $z(\theta, t)$. Parenthetically, we note that no estimator can be perfectly agent independent and informative:

**Lemma 1** *If f is agent independent, then f depends only on t.*

**Proof:** Suppose not, then there exist $\theta, t$ such that $f(\theta, t) \neq f(\theta', t)$, so we can change $\theta$ to $\theta'$ an agent at a time to get the chain $\theta = \theta^0, \ldots, \theta^n = \theta'$, where $\theta^k$ has the first $k$ types from $\theta'$ and the rest from $\theta$. Then by the agent independence of $f$: $f(\theta^k, t) = f(\theta^{k+1}, t)$ and so $f(\theta, t) = f(\theta', t)$, a contradiction. ■

We require two assumptions about the effect that a single agent's bid can have on the run time.

**Assumption 1 ($\nu$-Closeness)** *No one problem is more than $\nu > 1$ times slower than any other problem across the same sequence of ranges:*

$$\frac{\max[\{time(\theta_{-i}, z) : i \in \mathcal{I}\}, time(\theta, z)]}{\min[\{time(\theta_{-i}, z) : i \in \mathcal{I}\}, time(\theta, z)]} \leq \nu, \quad \forall z$$

*for any sequence of ranges, $K^1, K^2, \ldots$, and for all types $\theta$.*

**Assumption 2 ($\gamma$-bounded single-agent slow-down)** *No single agent can slow down the computation to any problem across any sequence of stages by more that a factor $\gamma > 1$ by stating a false report. For any agent i,*

$$\frac{time(\hat{\theta}_i, \theta_{-ij}, z)}{time(\theta_{-j}, z)} \leq \gamma, \quad \forall \hat{\theta}_i \neq \theta_i, \forall \theta_{-j}, \forall \theta_i, \forall z$$

$$\frac{time(\hat{\theta}_i, \theta_{-i}, z)}{time(\theta, z)} \leq \gamma, \quad \forall \hat{\theta}_i \neq \theta_i, \forall \theta_{-i}, \forall \theta_i, \forall z$$

*for any sequence of ranges, $K^1, K^2, \ldots$.*

Ultimately, both assumptions can be empirically validated for a domain in question. The tighter that $\nu$- and $\gamma$- are in practice, the better the stage estimate will approximate the actual number of stages completed when the mechanism is interrupted.[6]

Following Goldberg & Hartline (2003), who use $g_{u,c}$ in a very different context, we now define a random function $g_{u,c}(t)$ that is a "$\rho$-consensus estimator" at time $t$ with probability $p$, for some $\rho > 1$.

**Definition 6 (consensus-estimator $g_{u,c}$)** *Fix some $c > 1$, then define:*

$$g_{u,c}(t) = \min_{j \in \mathbb{Z}} c^{u+j} \textit{ such that } t \leq c^{u+j} \qquad (1)$$

*with u chosen uniformly at random from* $[0, 1]$.

Parameter $c$ in $g_{u,c}$ can be used to make a trade-off in our mechanism between the probability, $p$, that truthful bidding is an equilibrium and the amount of roll-back that is required on interruption. We discuss this further at the end of this section.

**Definition 7** *We say $g : \mathbb{R}_{\geq 0} \to \mathbb{R}$ is a $\rho$-consensus estimator function at time t if:*

- *$g(t) \geq t$*
- *$g(t) = g(t') \; \forall t'$ such that $t/\rho \leq t' \leq t$.*

*for some $\rho > 1$.*

A function $g$ with these properties is named a "consensus estimator" because given a set of estimates $t_1, t_2, \ldots$, then a consensus estimator $g$ at $\max\{t_1, t_2, \ldots\}$ would return $g(t_1) = g(t_2) = g^*$ for all estimates whenever the individual estimates $t_1, t_2, \ldots$ are clustered within multiplicative factor $\rho > 1$ of each other.

The family, $g_{u,c}$, is defined as a family of *step functions* that are flat on large regions. This ensures that the second condition for a consensus-estimator is often satisfied. The relative size of these flat regions (defined by $c$) makes a tradeoff between the probability of consensus and the accuracy of the estimate.[7] The selection of a random $u$ ensures that the function $g_{u,c}$ is equally likely to be a consensus estimator function at *any* $t$:

**Lemma 2** *Randomly chosen $g_{u,c}$ is a $\rho$-consensus estimator at t with probability $p = 1 - \log_c(\rho)$, for any $\rho > 1$.*

**Proof:** To see this we fix an $t$ and integrate over the possible values for $u$ that give us a $\rho$-consensus estimation function. Let $\pi(u)$ denote the p.d.f. for $u$, Uniform on $[0, 1]$. Without loss of generality, assume that $\frac{t}{\rho} = c^j$ for some $j \in \mathbb{Z}$. Then $c^{j+u} \in [\frac{t}{\rho}, \frac{ct}{\rho})$. Note that $c^{j+u} \in [\frac{t}{\rho}, t)$ iff this is not a $\rho$-consensus estimation function.

$$\int_{c^{u+j}=\frac{t}{\rho}}^{c^{u+j}=t} \pi(u)du = \int_{u=(\log_c \frac{t}{\rho})-j}^{u=(\log_c t)-j} \pi(u)du$$

$$= (\log_c t - j) - (\log_c \frac{t}{\rho} - j) = \log_c \rho = 1 - p.$$

■

[6]Although Leyton-Brown et al. (2002) suggest that the empirical hardness of winner-determination in CAs may vary by orders of magnitude for different instances from a distribution, we are not aware of any research that has considered the possible effect that changing the bid from a *single* agent can have on run time.

[7]Goldberg & Hartline (2003) show there can be no function $g$ that works as a consensus estimator for all values $t$ with certainty.

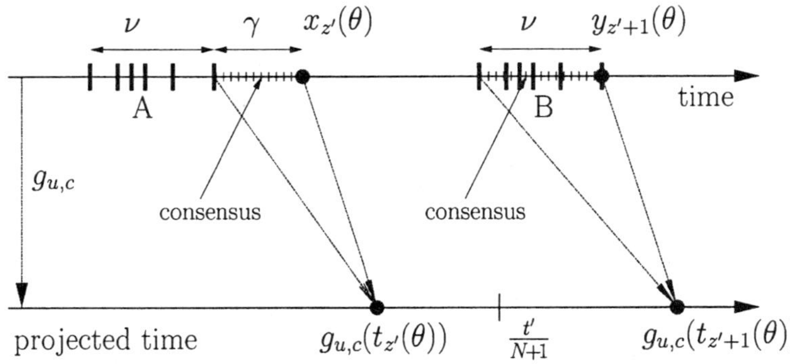


Figure 2: Analysis of Agent-Independent Stage Estimator.

The conservative and agent-independent stage estimator $f(\theta,t)$ is defined in terms of $time(\hat{\theta},z)$, $time(\hat{\theta}_{-i},z)$, and consensus-estimator $g_{u,c}$:

**Definition 8 (agent-independent stage estimator)** *Fix $c > 1$. Given interrupt $t'$, and reports $\hat{\theta}$:*

1. *Select u uniformly at random from* $[0,1]$.
2. *Compute $f(\hat{\theta},t')$ as:*

$$f(\hat{\theta},t') = \max_{z\geq 0} z$$
$$\text{s.t.} \quad (N+1)\cdot g_{u,c}(time(\hat{\theta}_{-i},z)) \leq t', \quad \forall i$$
$$(N+1)\cdot g_{u,c}(time(\hat{\theta},z)) \leq t'$$

*where $N$ is the number of agents.*

Consider Figure 2. Let $z' = f(\theta,t')$, given reports $\theta$ and interrupt $t'$, and define $t_z(\theta) = \max\left[\{time(\theta_{-i},z) : i \in \mathcal{I}\}, time(\theta,z)\right]$, and special points $x_{z'}(\theta)$ and $y_{z'+1}(\theta)$, as follows:

$$x_{z'}(\theta) = \gamma \cdot t_{z'}(\theta)$$
$$y_{z'+1}(\theta) = t_{z'+1}(\theta)$$

**Lemma 3** *Estimator $f(\theta,t')$ is agent independent when $g_{u,c}$ provides a $\gamma$-consensus at $x_{z'}$ and a $\nu$-consensus at $y_{z'+1}$.*

**Proof:** Consider Figure 2. Consider agent $i$, and suppose the reports from other agents are $\theta_{-i}$. Let $z' = f(\theta,t')$. From the definition of $f(\theta,t)$, we know that:

$$g_{u,c}(t_{z'}(\theta)) \leq \frac{t'}{N+1}$$
$$\text{and} \quad g_{u,c}(t_{z'+1}(\theta)) > \frac{t'}{N+1}$$

The report, $\hat{\theta}_i \neq \theta_i$, from agent $i$ can only change the stage returned by $f$ if: a) one of $\{time(\hat{\theta}_i,\theta_{-ij},z') : j \neq i\}$, or $time(\hat{\theta}_i,\theta_{-i},z')$ increases so that $g_{u,c}(t_{z'}(\hat{\theta}_i,\theta_{-i})) > t'/(N+1)$; or b) all of $\{time(\hat{\theta}_i,\theta_{-ij},z'+1) : j \neq i\}$, $time(\theta_{-i},z'+1)$, and $time(\hat{\theta}_i,\theta_{-i},z'+1)$ decrease so that $g(t_{z'+1}(\hat{\theta}_i,\theta_{-i})) \leq t'/(N+1)$. But, a) is not possible because we have a $\gamma$-consensus at $x_{z'}(\theta)$ and therefore $g_{u,c}(x_{z'}(\theta)) = g_{u,c}(t_{z'}(\theta)) = g_{u,c}(t)$ for all $x_{z'}(\theta)/\gamma \leq t \leq x_{z'}(\theta)$ and the most agent $i$ can slow down any time in group **A** (see Figure 2) is by a factor of $\gamma$ because of the $\gamma$-bounded single-agent slow-down assumption. Also, b) is not possible because there is one point, $time(\theta_{-i},z'+1)$, that agent $i$ cannot move, and because a $\nu$-consensus at $y_{z'+1}(\theta)$ implies that all points in group **B** (see Figure 2) map to the same point $g_{u,c}(time(\theta,z'+1))$ to the right of $t'/(N+1)$, and to (at least) $g_{u,c}(time(\theta_{-i},z'+1))$ must remain to the right of $t'/(N+1)$ for any report $\hat{\theta}_i$. ■

**Proposition 2** *Estimator $f(\theta,t')$ is a conservative estimator, and agent independent with probability $p = 1 - \log_c \rho$ for $\rho = \nu\cdot\gamma$, for any time $t'$.*

**Proof:** Let $z(\theta,t')$ denote the number of stages completed by time $t'$. We know that $z' = f(\theta,t') \leq z(\theta,t')$, given interrupt $t'$, because

$$t' \geq (N+1)g_{u,c}(\max\left[\{time(\theta_{-i},z'):i\in\mathcal{I}\},time(\theta,z')\right])$$
$$\geq (N+1)\max\left[\{time(\theta_{-i},z') : i\in\mathcal{I}\}, time(\theta,z')\right]$$
$$\geq \sum_i time(\theta_{-i},z') + time(\theta,z'),$$

which is the actual run time required to complete $z'$ stages.

For agent independence, the probability that we do *not* have a $\gamma$-consensus at $x_{z'}(\theta)$ is $\log_c \gamma$ by Lemma 2, similarly the probability that we do *not* have a $\nu$-consensus at $y_{z'+1}(\theta)$ is $\log_c \nu$. The probability of not having a $\gamma$-consensus or not having a $\nu$-consensus is at most $\log_c \gamma + \log_c \nu = \log_c \rho$, where $\rho$ is defined as $\gamma\cdot\nu$. Thus, the probability of agent independence is at least $1 - \log_c \rho$. ■

This leads to our main result.

**Theorem 5** *The Consensus-Based Anytime VCG Mechanism is strategyproof with probability $1 - \log_c \rho$ for a time-based interruption $c(t)$, and will implement the efficient allocation if allowed to run for enough stages.*

## Cost of Consensus

What is the role of parameter $c$? Well, for larger values of $c$, probability $p$ gets closer to 1 but with an estimate that tends to be further away from the true number of stages completed. Considering the error introduced by consensus-estimator function $g_{u,c}$, we have:

**Lemma 4** *The expectation of $g_{u,c}(t)/t$ given that $g_{u,c}$ is a $\rho$-consensus estimation function at $t$ is $\frac{c-\rho}{(\ln c - \ln \rho)\rho}$.*

**Proof:** Fix $t$, and assume that $\frac{t}{\rho} = c^j$ for some $j \in \mathbb{Z}$. This is a $\rho$-consensus estimation function iff $c^{j+u} \in [t, \frac{ct}{\rho})$. So

$$\int_{c^{u+j}=t}^{c^{u+j}=\frac{ct}{\rho}} \frac{c^{u+j}}{t} \pi(u) du = \frac{c^j}{t(1-\log_c \rho)} \int_{u=(\log_c t)-j}^{u=(\log_c \frac{ct}{\rho})-j} c^u du =$$

$$\frac{c^j}{t(1-\log_c \rho)} \left( \frac{c^{\log_c(\frac{ct}{\rho})-j} - c^{\log_c(t)-j}}{\ln c} \right) = \frac{c-\rho}{(\ln c - \ln \rho)\rho}$$

■

Putting this together, the overhead introduced through the consensus-estimate methods gives a run time for $z' = f(\theta, t')$ usable stages that scales as a multiple:

$$\nu \cdot \frac{c-\gamma}{(\ln c - \ln \gamma)\gamma} \cdot T(z', \theta)$$

of the run time, $T(z', \theta)$, for $z'$ completed stages in the anytime VCG mechanism defined for stage-based interruptions, for the same sequence of ranges. The $\nu$ factor accrues because we must take the maximal time across the $time(\theta, z')$ points rather than the average. The second term follows from the error analysis in Lemma 4 and because we have a $\gamma$-consensus estimator function at $x_{z'}(\theta)$. Rather than include an additional (weak) upper-bound, $(N+1)/2$, on the cost accrued because we must solve all $N$ of the $V(N_{-i})$ problems explicitly (rather than as few as one additional problem), we leave this factor for a tighter empirical analysis. For example, if $\nu = \gamma = 1.2$, then with $c = \rho^{1/1-p}$, we have a slow down of 3.1, 3.7, and 11, for $p = 0.7, 0.8$ and $0.9$.

## Conclusions

Anytime VCG mechanisms are proposed to provide anytime optimization with self-interested agents and retain strategyproofness whenever the mechanism is interrupted and asked for an answer. An anytime mechanism can solve easy instances optimally, while terminating early with approximate solutions on very hard instances. In doing so, we exposed an intriguing tension between flexibility and strategyproofness, through the analysis of agent-independent stage estimators.

In future work we intend to complete an experimental validation of the time-robustness approach, together with a calibration of the $\gamma$- and $\nu$-assumptions in more realistic domains. We are interested to understand the cost of providing robustness against attempts to manipulate via run time, and the sensitivity to the probability $p$. In addition, there should be plenty of opportunity to explore smart methods to expand the range across time and to avoid duplication of effort.

## Acknowledgments

This work is supported in part by NSF grant IIS-0238147, and by the Harvard College Research Program.

## References

Andersson, A.; Tenhunen, M.; and Ygge, F. 2000. Integer programming for auctions with bids for combinations. In *Proc. 4th International Conference on Multi-Agent Systems (ICMAS-00)*.

Archer, A.; Papadimitriou, C.; Talwar, K.; and Tardos, E. 2003. An approximate truthful mechanism for combinatorial auctions with single parameter agents. In *Proc. 14th ACM-SIAM Symposium on Discrete Algorithms*, 205–214.

Banks, J. S.; Ledyard, J. O.; and Porter, D. 1989. Allocating uncertain and unresponsive resources: An experimental approach. *The Rand Journal of Economics* 20:1–25.

Bartal, Y.; Gonen, R.; and Nisan, N. 2003. Incentive compatible multi unit combinatorial auctions. Technical report, The Hebrew University of Jerusalem.

de Vries, S., and Vohra, R. V. 2003. Combinatorial auctions: A survey. *Informs Journal on Computing* 15(3):284–309.

Dean, T. L., and Boddy, M. 1988. An analysis of time-dependent planning. In *Proc. 7th National Conference on Artificial Intelligence (AAAI-88)*, 49–54.

Fischetti, M., and Lodi, A. 2002. Local branching. Technical Report OR-02-6, University of Bologna.

Goldberg, A., and Hartline, J. 2003. Competitiveness via consensus. In *Proc. 14th ACM Symposium on Discrete Algorithms*.

Holzman, R.; Kfir-Dahav, N.; Moncerer, D.; and Tennenholtz, M. 2001. Bundling equilibrium in combinatorial auctions. *Games and Economic Behavior*.

Horvitz, E. J. 1987. Reasoning about beliefs and actions under computational resource constraints. In *Proc. 3rd AAAI Workshop on Uncertainty in Artificial Intelligence*, 429–444.

Lavi, R.; Mu'alem, A.; and Nisan, N. 2003. Towards a characterization of truthful combinatorial auctions. In *Proc. 44th Annual Symposium on Foundations of Computer Science*.

Lehmann, D.; O'Callaghan, L. I.; and Shoham, Y. 2002. Truth revelation in approximately efficient combinatorial auctions. *Journal of the ACM* 49(5):577–602.

Leyton-Brown, K.; Nudelman, E.; and Shoham, Y. 2002. Learning the emprical hardness of optimization problems: The case of combinatorial auctions. In *Proc. 8th Int. Conf. on Principles and Practice of Constraint Programming*.

Mu'alem, A., and Nisan, N. 2002. Truthful approximation mechanisms for restricted combinatorial auctions. In *Proc. 18th National Conference on Artificial Intelligence (AAAI-02)*. .

Nisan, N., and Ronen, A. 2000. Computationally feasible VCG mechanisms. In *Proc. 2nd ACM Conf. on Electronic Commerce (EC-00)*, 242–252.

Nisan, N. 2000. Bidding and allocation in combinatorial auctions. In *Proc. 2nd ACM Conf. on Electronic Commerce (EC-00)*, 1–12.

Rothkopf, M. H.; Pekeč, A.; and Harstad, R. M. 1998. Computationally manageable combinatorial auctions. *Management Science* 44(8):1131–1147.

Sandholm, T. W.; Suri, S.; Gilpin, A.; and Levine, D. 2001. CABOB: A fast optimal algorithm for combinatorial auctions. In *Proc. 17th Int. Joint Conf. on Artificial Intelligence*.

Sandholm, T. W. 1999. An algorithm for optimal winner determination in combinatorial auctions. In *Proc. 16th International Joint Conference on Artificial Intelligence (IJCAI-99)*, 542–547.

# Useful Roles of Emotions in Artificial Agents: A Case Study from Artificial Life

**Matthias Scheutz**
Artificial Intelligence and Robotics Laboratory
Department of Computer Science and Engineering
University of Notre Dame, Notre Dame, IN 46556, USA
mscheutz@cse.nd.edu

### Abstract

In this paper, we discuss the role of emotions in AI and possible ways to determine their utility for the design of artificial agents. We propose a research methodology for determining the utility of emotional control and apply it to the study of autonomous agents that compete for resources in an artificial life environment. The results show that the emotional control can improve performance in some circumstances.

## Introduction

Over the last several years, emotions have received increasing attention in several AI-related fields, most prominently in human-robot/computer interaction, where emotional receptiveness (i.e., being able to perceive and interpret emotional expressions of others) and expressivity (i.e., being able to express emotions in a way that can be perceived and interpreted by others) are crucial. Within AI, believable virtual and robotic agents and human-like synthetic characters are of particular interest, with applications ranging from the entertainment industry, to training and tutoring systems (although there are also other areas of interest, e.g., affective natural language processing). The main focus in most of the employed agents is on the display of emotions (e.g., via animated facial expressions) and/or on their recognition (e.g., in speech signals).

While achieving believable emotion display and reliable emotion recognition are important goals in the context of designing virtual and robotic agents for human-computer/robot interaction, the more general question about what possible roles emotions could have in an agent architecture and in what circumstances they might be useful for the control of agents and possibly even better than other, non-emotional control mechanisms, has received very little attention.

In this paper, we outline a methodological approach, which in practice can provide at least a partial answer to the above questions. After a brief overview of past and present work on emotions in AI, we briefly describe a our approach towards studying the utility of emotions and subsequently apply it to agents in an artificial life environment. Specifically, we introduce an agent model for virtual and robotic agents that is capable of implementing emotional states, and compare the utility of its emotional control mechanism in an evolutionary survival task to other agents that do not use emotional control. The results of these simulations demonstrate the utility as well as the limits of the employed emotional control mechanisms.



## Emotions–Why Bother?

Emotions have been of interest to various researchers throughout the history of AI. From very early on, architectures with emotional components have been proposed for simple and complex agents (e.g., (Toda 1962; Simon 1967; Dyer 1987), and several others; see (Pfeifer 1988) for a discussion of the early models).

Over the recent past, researchers have been particularly interested in endowing artificial agents with emotional expressivity to improve their "believability" and to make them more "life-like" (e.g., (Bates 1994; Hayes-Roth 1995; Rizzo *et al.* 1997)). Such believable virtual agents do not only find applications in the entertainment industry, but increasingly so in the realm of instruction and tutoring (e.g., (Gratch 2000; Shaw, Johnson, & Ganeshan 1999; Conati 2002)), as well as in the design of user-interfaces (e.g., (Olveres *et al.* 1998; Hudlicka & Billingsley 1999; Takeuchi, Katagiri, & Takahashi 2001)).

There is also an increasing number of examples of robotic agents that are based on emotional control (e.g., (Michaud & Audet 2001; Breazeal 2002; Arkin *et al.* 2003)), most of which are intended for human-robot interaction.

And finally, there are researchers interested in "computational models of human emotion" (e.g., (Eliott 1992; Cãnamero 1997; Marsella & Gratch 2002)), which typically are studied in simulations in artificial environments.

This list is by no means intended to give a complete overview of the present activities concerned with emotions in AI (for a more complete overview see (Picard 1997; Trappl, Petta, & Payr 2001; Pfeifer 1988)), but rather to show that an increasing number of researchers are willing to investigate whether emotions *should* have a role in AI in the first place, and if so what that role might be. Before we proceed, we would like to point out that the term "emotion" has different connotations in the AI community: for some emotions are merely facial expressions, while for others emotions are intrinsically concerned with internal processes. Moreover, the same emotional terms used for human concepts (e.g., "embarrassment" or "shame") are often applied to states in artifacts without specifying how the implemented states differ from the human case. For the emotional control processes discussed in this paper we only assume a general characteristic of emotion processes (e.g., (Cãnamero 1997; Marsella & Gratch 2002)) without making any claims about the biological plausibility of the employed states or mechanisms.

## Roles of Emotions in Nature

Emotional control is wide-spread in nature and seems to serve several crucial roles in animals and humans alike.

In simple organisms with limited representational capacities, for example, emotions provide a basic evaluation in terms of *hedonic values*, often causing the organism to be attracted to *what it likes* and to avoid *what it does not like.*[1] If a threat is perceivably caused by another organism, a "fear-anger" system (Berkowitz 2003) may generate "fight-or-flight" behavior (e.g., depending on an estimate of the likelihood that a fight can be won). While emotional states such as fear and anger control immediate actions (LeDoux 1996), other affective states operate on long-term behavioral dispositions (e.g., anxiety leads to increased alertness without the presence of any immediate threat).

In humans, emotions, and more generally, affect, seem to be deeply intertwined with cognition in that they can influence, bias, and direct cognitive processes and, more generally, processing strategies (e.g., negative affect, for example, can bias problem solving strategies in humans towards local, bottom-up processing, whereas positive affect can lead to global, top-down approaches (Bless, Schwarz, & Wieland 1996)). Emotions also seem to play an important role in social contexts (Cosmides & Tooby 2000), ranging from signaling emotional states (e.g., pain) through facial expressions and gestures (Ekman 1993) to perceptions of affective states that cause approval or disapproval of one's own or another agents' actions (relative to given norms), which can trigger corrective responses (e.g., guilt).

## Roles of Emotions in Artificial Agents

Based on the functional roles of emotions proposed by emotion researchers for natural systems, it is worth asking whether emotions could server similar functional roles in artificial systems. Specifically, we can isolate 12 potential roles for emotions in artificial agents (beyond displaying and recognizing emotions in interactions with humans):

- *action selection* (e.g., what to do next based on the current emotional state)
- *adaptation* (e.g., short or long-term changes in behavior due to the emotional states)
- *social regulation* (e.g., communicating or exchanging information with others via emotional expressions)
- *sensory integration* (e.g., emotional filtering of data or blocking of integration)
- *alarm mechanisms* (e.g., fast reflex-like reactions in critical situations that interrupt other processes)
- *motivation* (e.g., creating motives as part of an emotional coping mechanism)
- *goal management* (e.g., creation of new goals or reprioritization of existing ones)
- *learning* (e.g., emotional evaluations as Q-values in reinforcement learning)
- *attentional focus* (e.g., selection of data to be processed based on emotional evaluation)
- *memory control* (e.g., emotional bias on memory access and retrieval as well as decay rate of memory items)
- *strategic processing* (e.g., selection of different search strategies based on overall emotional state)
- *self model* (e.g., emotions as representations of "what a situation is like for the agent")

This list is certainly not exhaustive, but provides a good starting point for systematic investigations of the utility a particular emotional control mechanisms.

## A Case Study of How to Evaluate the Utility of Emotion from Artificial Life

To study the role of emotions in agent architectures and to test their utility for the control of artificial agents, we will focus on a small subset of the above list for the rest of the paper, i.e., on action selection, adaptation, and social regulation, the first three items.

We will use a general methodology for the comparison of different agents with respect to their performance in a given task and environment, which consists of four parts: (1) (emotion) concepts are analyzed and defined in terms of architectural capacities of agent architectures (Sloman 2002a), (2) agent architectures with particular (emotional) states as defined in (1) are defined for a given task together with a performance measure, (3) experiments with agents implementing these architectures (e.g., in the style of (Pollack *et al.* 1994; Hanks, Pollack, & Cohen 1993)) are carried out (either in simulations or on actual robots), and (4) the performance of the agents is measured for a predetermined set of architectural and environmental parameters. The results can then be used to relate agent performance

[1] Hedonic values seem to be at the root of various forms of reinforcement learning.

to architectural mechanisms. Moreover, by analyzing the causes for possible performance differences, it may be possible to generalize the results beyond the given task and set of environments. In the best case, general statements of the form "Mechanism X is better than mechanism Y" can be derived for whole classes of tasks and environments, where "better" is spelled out in terms of the performance ordering obtained from the experiments.

## Agents and Architectures

For the experiments reported here, we used a "one-resource foraging task" for all agents in an unlimited two-dimensional environment, in which the resources appear at random within a predetermined rectangular 1800 x 1800 area at a frequency of one resource per simulation cycle (starting with 50 randomly distributed resources in the beginning). Resources contain energy (800 units), which agents need for movement and processing (agents can consume resources when they are on top of them).

All agents use a basic schema-based architecture for locomotion, which can be used for simulated and robotic agents alike (Arkin 1989). They have a perceptual system that computes directional force vectors $v$ from their visual sensory input to resources ("resource schema") and other agents ("agent schema"). The vectors are subsequently scaled by the square of the distance to the object within their sensory range (of 300 distance units) as well as a multiplicative constant called *schema gain* depending on the type of object ($g_r$ for resources, and $g_a$ for agents) and summed up. The resultant vector $D$ is sent to the motors, thus determining the direction and speed of the agent (the maximum speed is 4). For any given agent $A$ the mapping is given by:

$$D = \sum_n g_r \cdot resource(n) + \sum_m g_a \cdot agent(m)$$

where $resource(n)$ is the vector from the position of $A$ to the $n$-th resource and $agent(m)$ is the vector from the position of $A$ to the $m$-th agent (not including $A$).

The energy expenditure for movement is the square of an agent's speed. In addition, each agent consumes one unit of energy per cycle for processing. Agents have an "energy alarm" for self-preservation that limits the energy expenditure by setting their overall speed to 1 if their energy level drops below $Energy_{crit} = 400$ (the speed will remain at 1 until the energy level is raised above the critical level again).

After $\alpha = 250$ simulation cycles agents can procreate asexually, if their energy levels are above the minimum necessary for procreation (set to 2200). The energy necessary for creating the offspring (2000) is subtracted from the parent, and an identical copy of the parent will be placed in the vicinity of the parent in the subsequent simulation cycle.

All agents compete for resources in order to survive. If two or more agents want to obtain the same resource, they have the option to "fight" for it or to "flee" from the scene. Fighting incurs a cost of 50 units per simulation cycle, whereas fleeing incurs the cost of running at a speed of 7 for about 5 to 10 cycles.

Each agent has a representation of its basic *action tendency*, which it uses to decide what to do in conflict situations. An agent's action tendency is modelled as the probability that it will fight (as opposed to flee). Agents display their action tendency and can use the action tendency displayed by their opponents to modify their own decision. We distinguish two agent kinds, *social* and *non-social* agents, depending on whether they take the opponents' action tendencies into account in a conflict. Social agents decide in the first round of a competition based on the other agents' displayed action tendency whether they will fight or flee: they will only fight if their action tendency is highest, otherwise they will flee. Asocial agents, on the other hand, simply decide their actions probabilistically based on their own action tendencies. Consequently, it is possible for two asocial agents to continue conflicts for several rounds until one finally flees (or dies), which is not possible for two social agents, as they will always determine the winner after one round.

Depending on whether an agent's action tendency can change over time or is fixed, we distinguish *adaptive* and *non-adaptive* agents. Adaptive agents change their action tendencies depending on whether they win or lose in conflicts: if they win, they lower their action tendency, thus increasing the probability that they will lose the next time; if they lose, they will raise their action tendency, thus increasing the probability that they will win the next time. This way adaptive agents implement an approximate sharing mechanism, which gives rise to *altruistic behavior* that we have shown to be beneficial elsewhere (Scheutz & Schermerhorn 2004): an agent that has not received a resource in several competitions in the past is very likely to receive one in the future, while agents that have received several resources in a row will very likely flee in the next conflict, thus giving up the resource.

There are many ways to implement such a mechanism. We use the following way to change an agent's action tendency based on its *basic action tendency* (i.e., its action tendency in the absence of any adaptation):

**Definition** [Adaptation Rule (AR)] Let $r$ be the basic action tendency of agent $A$ and let $m$ be the current action tendency ($r = m$ if AR has never been applied). Then the $AR(m)^+$ is defined (for losses) as follows: if $m \geq r$, then $AR^+(m) = m+(1-m)/2$; if $m \leq r/2$, then $AR^+(m) = 2m$; else $AR^+(m) = r+(2m-r)(1-r)/2r$.[2] Similarly, $AR(m)^-$ is defined (for wins) as follows: if $m \geq r + (1-r)/2$, then $AR^-(m) = m - (1-m)$; if $m \leq r$, then $AR^-(m) = m/2$; else $AR^-(m) = r/2 + r(m-r)/(1-r)$.[3]

[2]This maps values in the interval $(r/2, r)$ into $(r, (1-r)/2))$.

[3]This maps $(r, (1-r)/2)$ into $(r/2, r))$.

This rule effectively keeps track of how often an individual was able to win a conflict by increasing or decreasing the action tendency relative to the basic action tendency and the current action tendency.

Finally, we introduce a third distinction between agents that have fixed schema gains, i.e., a *fixed conflict tendency* for their agent schema, and those that can adjust their agent schema gain $g_a$, i.e., that have a variable *variable conflict tendency.* By adjusting their conflict tendency, an agent can modify its behavioral disposition towards other agents, i.e., whether it seeks conflicts or whether it avoids them.

## Emotional Agents

We can now define *emotional* agents as adaptive agents with variable conflict tendencies that adjust their agent schema gain based on their action tendency according to the following equations: $g_a = action\_tendency \cdot 100 - 50$. Hence, the emotional state of emotional agents (as defined by the current value of $g_a$) is directly coupled to their action tendency. If an agent's conflict tendency is positive and consequently the action tendency is above 0.5, the agent is said to be "angry", if its conflict tendency is less than zero and consequently the action tendency is below 0.5, it is said to be "fearful". Effectively, emotional agents seek conflicts with other agents when they have lost several conflicts in a row in the past (they get "angrier"), while they avoid conflicts with others if they have won conflicts (they get more "fearful"). It is this reaction to events in the environment that causes rapid, yet temporary adjustments of internal states that alter action tendencies, which warrant the attribute emotional. Specifically, the varying influence of the value of $g_a$ on an agent's behavior can be seen as an *amplifying* or *diminishing* modification of the behavior as determined by $g_f$ (i.e., the fixed "drive" to find and consume resources) the drives, which is typical of (some construals of) emotional states (e.g., see (Cãnamero 1997) for a similar view). The implemented states correspond to what some call "primary emotions" (e.g., (Sloman 2002b)) in that they (1) play a regulatory role, (2) are engaged automatically (by virtue of the global alarm system), and (3) alter the internal state of the agent and consequently its behavior.

It is worth mentioning that the mechanisms implemented here resemble what is presumed to be the functional organization of the emotional "fear/anger system" in many animals, given that animals are typically taken to exhibit either a "fight" or a "flee" behavior (e.g., (Berkowitz 2003)). The above model departs from biology, however, by linking the successful outcome of a conflict to an increase in fear based on the adpative sharing mechanisms–in biological systems the opposite is often true, i.e., winners will become more daring, while losers will become more cautious. However, the intent here is not to reproduce a particular biological model, but rather to investigate the utility of directly coupling the altruistic strategy implemented by adaptive agents to their conflict tendency (which, in turn, determines when and how an agent changes its emotional state). It is certainly possible to decouple the two functional components and update emotional states based on a different rule as we have done elsewhere (Scheutz 2001).

Finally, for the sake of comparison, we will also consider agents that are non-adaptive, but have a conflict tendency that is based on their fixed action tendency–they will be called *dispositional.* By default, all non-emotional, non-dispositional agents have $g_a = 0$, while $g_f = 20$ for all agents (including emotional and dispositional agents).

## Experiments and Results

We examined the utility of the above strategies by comparing social and asocial emotional and dispositional agents to four types of agents with fixed conflict tendencies (i.e., non-adaptive and adaptive social and non-social agents). Specifically, we ran 16 sets of experiments, each consisting of 40 different runs for 10000 cycles each with different random initial conditions (the same 40 different initial conditions were used in all 16 sets to guarantee a fair comparison). In all runs, 25 emotional or dispositional agents of one kind and 25 non-emotional, non-dispositional agents of one kind were placed at random locations within the 1800 x 1800 resource area in the environment together with 50 randomly placed resources. The initial energy of all agents was set to 2000 and their initial action tendencies were distributed following a Gaussian distribution with spread 0.125 around 0.5. As performance measure the average numbers of survivors after 10000 cycles was used. Figures 1 and 2 show the results for emotional agents, Figures 3 and 4 for dispositional agents (the error bars indicate the 95% confidence intervals).

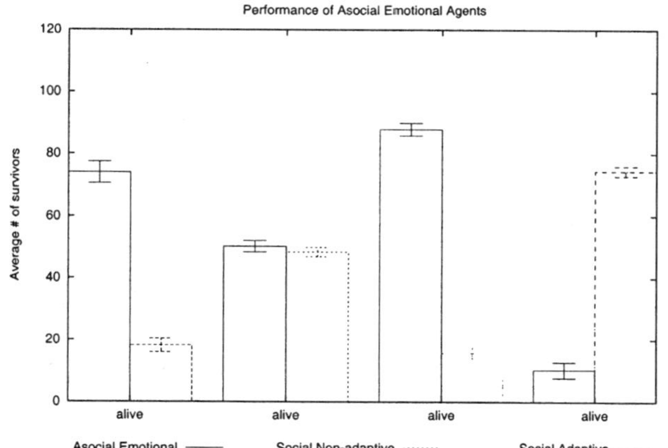


Figure 1: The average number of survivors in the experiment sets comparing asocial-emotional agents to non-emotional agents.

The results demonstrate that emotional and dispositional agents perform better than both adaptive and

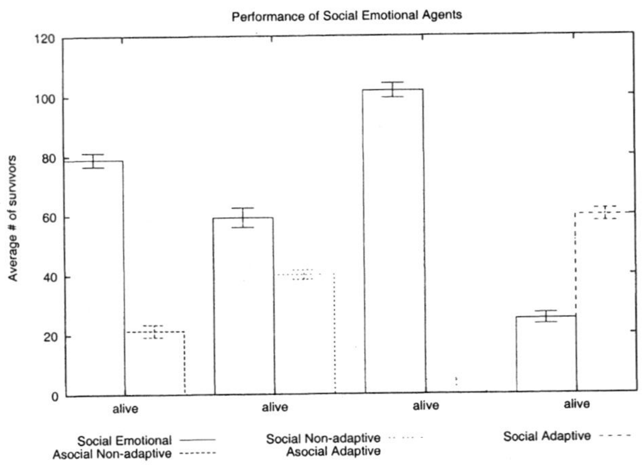


Figure 2: The average number of survivors in the experiment sets comparing social-emotional agents to non-emotional agents.

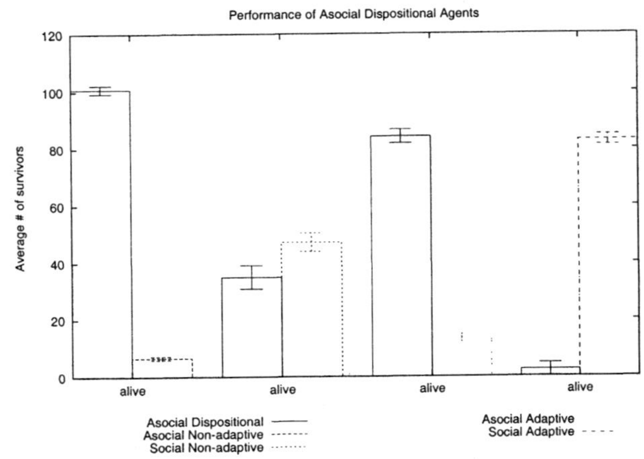


Figure 3: The average number of survivors in the experiment sets comparing asocial-dispositional agents to non-emotional agents.

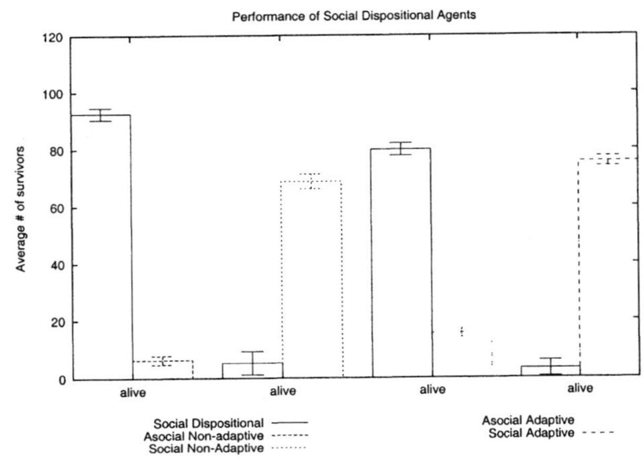


Figure 4: The average number of survivors in the experiment sets comparing social-dispositional agents to non-emotional agents.

non-adaptive asocial agents with $g_a = 0$. Social emotional agents show a better overall performance than non-social emotional agents, whereas social dispositional agents perform overall worse than non-social dispositional agents. Furthermore, dispositional agents perform worse than both social agent kinds with $g_a = 0$, while emotional agents only perform worse than adaptive social agents. This last result indicates that adding conflict tendencies that depend on action tendencies to social adaptive mechanisms reduces performance: loosely speaking, "fear" and "anger" do not improve performance beyond what changing one's action tendency based on the past outcomes in conflicts can achieve, but rather reduce it. It is worth noting, however, that this is only true for social agents. In the asocial case, emotional agents do fare much better, which demonstrates that changing one's conflict tendency based on one's past encounters with others is more beneficial than ignoring signals from others.

## Conclusion

In this paper, we proposed a methodology for studying possible roles of emotions in agent architectures that applies to biological organisms and artificial agents alike. We defined an emotional agent model, in which emotional processes influence the selection of actions in conflicts, the change in conflict tendencies, and consequently the distribution of resources among group members (in social emotional agents based on displaying action tendencies). All emotional agents showed high levels of performance and performed only worse than adaptive social agents. The results show that emotional control is beneficial in most circumstances in the considered environments, but that social adaptive control without influencing conflict tendencies (and thus attractive and aversive behavior)–which basically ignores other agents except in conflict–can do even better. We believe that systematic comparisons of emotional and non-emotional agents in the way suggested in this paper, will allow us, at least in part, to make objectively verifiable claims about the utility of emotional control for both biological and artificial agents in a great variety of tasks.

## References

Arkin, R.; Fujita, M.; Takagi, T.; and Hasegawa, R. 2003. An ethological and emotional basis for human-robot interaction. *Robotics and Autonomous Systems* 42:3–4.

Arkin, R. C. 1989. Motor schema-based mobile robot navigation. *International Journal of Robotic Research* 8(4):92–112.

Bates, J. 1994. The role of emotion in believable agents. *Communications of the ACM* 37(7):122–125.

Berkowitz, L. 2003. Affect, aggression, and antisocial behavior. In (Davidson, Scherer, & Goldsmith 2003). 804–823.

Bless, H.; Schwarz, N.; and Wieland, R. 1996. Mood and the impact of category membership and individuating information. *European Journal of Social Psychology* 26:935–959.

Breazeal, C. L. 2002. *Designing Sociable Robots.* MIT Press.

Cãnamero, D. 1997. Modeling motivations and emotions as a basis for intelligent behavior. In Johnson, L., ed., *Proceedings of the First International Symposium on Autonomous Agents (Agents'97)*, 148–155. New York, NY: ACM.

Conati, C. 2002. Probabilistic assessment of user's emotions in educational games. *Journal of Applied Artificial Intelligence, special issue on "Merging Cognition and Affect in HCI".*

Cosmides, L., and Tooby, J. 2000. Evolutionary psychology and the emotions. In Lewis, M., and Haviland-Jones, J. M., eds., *Handbook of Emotions.* NY: Guilford, 2nd edition. 91–115.

Davidson, R. J.; Scherer, K. R.; and Goldsmith, H. H., eds. 2003. *Handbook of Affective Sciences.* New York: Oxford University Press.

Dyer, M. G. 1987. Emotions and their computations: Three computer models. *Cognition and Emotion* 1(3):323–347.

Ekman, P. 1993. Facial expression and emotion. *American Psychologist* 48(4):384–392.

Eliott, C. 1992. *The Affective Reasoner: A process model of emotions in a multi-agent system.* Ph.D. Dissertation, Institute for the Learning Sciences,Northwestern University.

Gratch, J. 2000. Emile: Marshalling passions in training and education. In *4th International Conference on Autonomous Agents*, 325–332.

Hanks, S.; Pollack, M. E.; and Cohen, P. 1993. Benchmarks, testbeds, controlled experimentation, and the design of agent architectures. *AI Magazine* 14(4):17–42. http://www.cs.pitt.edu/ pollack/distrib/testbeds.ps.

Hayes-Roth, B. 1995. Agents on stage: Advancing the state of the art of AI. In *Proc 14th Int. Joint Conference on AI*, 967–971.

Hudlicka, E., and Billingsley, J. 1999. Affect-adaptive user interface. *Human Computer Interaction* 1:681–685.

LeDoux, J. 1996. *The Emotional Brain.* New York: Simon & Schuster.

Marsella, S., and Gratch, J. 2002. Modeling the influence of emotion on belief for virtual training simulations. In *Proceedings of the 11th Conference on Computer-Generated Forces and Behavior Representation.*

Michaud, F., and Audet, J. 2001. Using motives and artificial emotion for long-term activity of an autonomous robot. In *5th Autonomous Agents Conference*, 188–189. Montreal, Quebec: ACM Press.

Olveres, J.; Billingurst, M.; Savage, J.; and Holden, A. 1998. Intelligent expressive avatars. In *First Workshop on Embodied Conversational Characters.*

Pfeifer, R. 1988. Artificial intelligence models of emotion. In Hamilton, V.; Bower, G. H.; and Frijda, N. H., eds., *Cognitive Perspectives on Emotion and Motivation, volume 44 of Series D: Behavioural and Social Sciences.* Netherlands: Kluwer Academic Publishers. 287–320.

Picard, R. 1997. *Affective Computing.* Cambridge, Mass, London, England: MIT Press.

Pollack, M. E.; Joslin, D.; Nunes, A.; Ur, S.; and Ephrati, E. 1994. Experimental investigation of an agent commitment strategy. Technical Report 94-31, University of Pittsburgh. http://www.cs.pitt.edu/ pollack/distrib/tw.ps.

Rizzo, P.; Veloso, M.; Miceli, M.; and Cesta, A. 1997. Personality-driven social behaviors in believable agents. In *Proceedings of the AAAI Fall Symposium on Socially Intelligent Agents*, 109–114.

Scheutz, M., and Schermerhorn, P. 2004. The role of signaling action tendencies in conflict resolution. *Journal of Artificial Societies and Social Simulation* 7(1).

Scheutz, M. 2001. The evolution of simple affective states in multi-agent environments. In Cañamero, D., ed., *Proceedings of AAAI Fall Symposium*, 123–128. Falmouth, MA: AAAI Press.

Shaw, E.; Johnson, W. L.; and Ganeshan, R. 1999. Pedagogical agents on the web. In *Third International Conference on Autonomous Agents*, 283–290.

Simon, H. A. 1967. Motivational and emotional controls of cognition. Reprinted in *Models of Thought,* Yale University Press, 29–38, 1979.

Sloman, A. 2002a. Architecture-based conceptions of mind. In *Proceedings 11th International Congress of Logic, Methodology and Philosophy of Science*, 397–421. Dordrecht: Kluwer. (Synthese Library Series).

Sloman, A. 2002b. How many separately evolved emotional beasties live within us? In Trappl, R.; Petta, P.; and Payr, S., eds., *Emotions in Humans and Artifacts.* Cambridge, MA: MIT Press. 29–96.

Takeuchi, Y.; Katagiri, Y.; and Takahashi, T. 2001. Learning enhancement in web contents through inter-agent interaction. In Hirose, M., ed., *Eight Conference on Human-Computer Interaction (INTERACT 2001)*, 480–487.

Toda, M. 1962. The design of the fungus eater: A model of human behavior in an unsophisticated environment. *Behavioral Science* 7:164–183.

Trappl, R.; Petta, P.; and Payr, S., eds. 2001. *Emotions in Humans and Artifacts.* MIT Press.

# Automated Reasoning

# Low-Knowledge Algorithm Control*

**Tom Carchrae** and **J. Christopher Beck**
Cork Constraint Computation Center
University College Cork, Ireland
{t.carchrae, c.beck}@4c.ucc.ie

### Abstract

This paper addresses the question of allocating computational resources among a set of algorithms in order to achieve the best performance on a scheduling problem instance. Our primary motivation in addressing this problem is to reduce the expertise needed to apply constraint technology. Therefore, we investigate algorithm control techniques that make decision based only on observations of the improvement in solution quality achieved by each algorithm. We call our approach "low-knowledge" since it does not rely on complex prediction models. We show that such an approach results in a system that achieves significantly better performance than all of the pure algorithms without requiring additional human expertise. Furthermore the low knowledge approach achieves performance equivalent to a perfect high-knowledge classification approach.

## Introduction

Despite both the commercial and academic success of optimization technology and specifically constraint programming, using the technology still requires significant expertise. For non-trivial applications the quality of a system still has much to do with the quality of the person that implemented it (Le Pape *et al.* 2002). In this paper, we investigate algorithm control techniques aimed at achieving strong scheduling performance using off-the-shelf algorithms without requiring significant human expertise. This is done through the application of machine learning techniques to "low-knowledge" algorithm control. Rather than building knowledge-intensive models relating algorithm performance to problem features, we base the control decisions on the evolution of solution quality over time. Such an approach is crucial to our goal of the reduction of expertise.

Given a time limit $T$ to find the best solution possible to a problem instance, we investigate two control paradigms. The first, *predictive*, paradigm runs a set of algorithms during a prediction phase and chooses one to run for the remainder of $T$. A Bayesian classifier is trained on a set of learning instances and used to identify the length of the prediction phase as well as the selected algorithm. In the second, *switching*, paradigm the control decisions allocate computational resources to each algorithm over a series of iterations such that the total run-time is $T$. Reinforcement learning is used during the solving to allocate the run-time.

The contributions of this paper are the introduction of a low-knowledge approach to algorithm control and the demonstration that such an approach can achieve performance significantly better than the best pure algorithm and as good as a perfect high-knowledge approach.

## Low-Knowledge Algorithm Control

Our goal is to build a system that finds the best solution to an instance of a scheduling problem in the following scenario. A problem instance is presented to a scheduling system and that system has a fixed CPU time of $T$ seconds to return a solution. We assume that the system designer has been given a learning set of problem instances at implementation time and that these instances are representative of the problems that will be encountered later. We assume that there exists a set of algorithms, $A$, that can be applied to the problems in question. Algorithm control is the way that the pure algorithms, $a \in A$, are used to solve the problem instance.

Algorithm control and its more specific form, the algorithm selection problem (Rice 1976), have been addressed by building detailed, high-knowledge models of the performance of algorithms on specific problems types. Such models are generally limited to the problem classes and algorithms for which they were developed. For example, Leyton-Brown et al. (Leyton-Brown, Nudelman, & Shoham 2002) developed strong selection techniques for combinatorial auction algorithms that take into account 35 problem features and their interactions based on three problem representations. Lagoudakis & Littman (Lagoudakis & Littman 2000) use a detailed mathematical model of algorithm behavior, Markov decision processes, and reinforcement learning for algorithm control for sorting and order statistic selection tasks. Other work applying machine learning techniques to algorithm generation (Minton 1996) and algorithm parameterization (Horvitz *et al.* 2001; Kautz *et al.* 2002; Ruan, Horvitz, & Kautz 2002) is also knowledge intensive, developing models specialized for particular problems and/or search algorithms and algorithm components.

Our motivation for addressing algorithm control is to

*This work has received support from Science Foundation Ireland (Grant 00/PI.1/C075), Irish Research Council for Science, Engineering, and Technology (Grant SC/2003/82), and ILOG, SA.

lessen the expertise necessary to use optimization technology. While existing algorithm control techniques have shown impressive results, their knowledge-intensive nature means that domain and algorithm expertise is necessary to develop the models. The requirement for expertise has not, therefore, been reduced; it has been shifted from algorithm building to predictive model building. It could still be argued that the expertise will have been reduced if the predictive model can be applied to different types of problems. Unfortunately, the performance of a predictive model tends to be inversely proportional to its generality: while models accounting for over 99% of the variance in search cost exist, they are not only algorithm and problem specific, but problem instance specific (Watson 2003). The model building *approach* is general, but the requirement for expertise remains: an in-depth study of the domain and of different problem representations is necessary in order to identify a set of relevant features that are predictive of algorithm performance. To avoid shifting the expertise to model building, we examine approaches that require little expertise.

The distinction between low- and high-knowledge (or knowledge-intensive) approaches focuses on the number, specificity, and computational complexity of the measurements that need to be made of a problem instance. A low-knowledge approach has very few, inexpensive metrics, applicable to a wide range of algorithms and problem types. A high-knowledge approach has more metrics, that are more expensive to compute, and more specific to particular problems and algorithms. This distinction is independent of the approach taken to build a predictive model. In particular, sophisticated model building techniques (e.g., based on machine learning) are consistent with low-knowledge approaches provided the observations on which they are built do not require significant expertise to identify.

We make some basic assumptions about the pure algorithms for which our techniques are appropriate. First, after a brief start-up time (at most, a few seconds) an algorithm is always able to the return the best, complete solution it has found so far. Second, we require that an algorithm is able to take an external solution and search for solutions that are better. In the latter case, if an algorithm has not found a better solution, when asked for its best solution, the algorithm returns the external solution.

## A Bayesian Classifier for Prediction

Let $t_p$ represent the prediction time and $t_r$ the subsequent time allocated to run the chosen pure technique. It is required that $T = t_p + t_r$. During the prediction phase, each pure algorithm, $a \in A$, is run for a fixed number of CPU seconds, $t$, on the problem instance. The quality of solutions found for each run is used to select the algorithm that will achieve the best performance given the time remaining. We require that $t_p = |A| \times t$. We assume that when a pure algorithm has been selected, it does not have to re-start: it can continue the search from where it left off in the prediction phase. The total run-time for the selected technique is $T_s = t_r + t_p/|A|$.

A simple categorical Bayesian model is constructed to select the algorithm given a predefined $t_p$. For every 10 seconds of prediction time and for each pure algorithm, a binary variable is created with possible values of "best" or "behind". The value is assigned depending on whether the algorithm has found the best solution of all the algorithms, $a \in A$, at that time. Two or more algorithms may have both found the best solution at a particular time. For each algorithm, we also have a binary variable representing the final performance of the algorithm (i.e, at time $T_s$). It also has the value "best" or "behind" depending on the algorithm's comparison with all the other algorithms. For the learning phase, these variables are input. For the test phase, the value of the final performance variables for each algorithm are predicted by the constructed Bayesian classifier.

For example, let $T = 1200$, $t_p = 30$, and $|A| = 3$. We have six input variables: one for each algorithm at time 10 seconds and one for each algorithm at $T_s = 1180$ seconds. We learn a Bayesian classifier that predicts the best algorithm at time 1180. The classifier is used on the learning set to define a hybrid algorithm that runs each pure algorithm for 10 seconds, uses the Bayesian classifier to predict which of the three will be best at 1180 seconds, and then runs the selected algorithm for the remaining 1170 seconds, continuing the search from where it left off. We repeat this procedure, learning a new Bayesian classifier for different values of $t_p \in \{60, 90, \ldots 1200\}$. This results in an assessment of hybrid algorithm performance for each prediction time. The prediction time with the best performance is $t^*$. The Bayesian classifier for $t_p = t^*$, is then used on the test set.

In all cases, ties among the pure algorithms are broken by selecting the algorithm with the best mean solution quality on the learning set at time $T$. The Bayesian classifiers are learned using WinMine 2.0 (Chickering 2002) with default parameters. We refer to this techniques as *Bayes*.

## Reinforcement Learning for Switching

The switching paradigm allocates run-time to the pure algorithms during the search. In contrast to predictive selection, the allocation decision is made multiple times. $N$ iterations are performed such that each iteration, $i$, has a time limit of $t_i$ CPU seconds and $\sum_{1 \le i \le N} t_i = T$. During each iteration, the run-time of each pure algorithm, $a \in A$, is determined using a weight, $w_i(a)$, which is learned as the search progresses. The weights for an iteration are normalized to sum to 1 and therefore, $w_i(a)$ corresponds to the fraction of time $t_i$ allocated to algorithm $a$. For example, if algorithm $a$ has weight $w_i(a) = 0.2$ and $t_i = 60$ seconds, then $a$ is run for 12 seconds during iteration $i$. Weights are initialized to $1/|A|$.

Weights are updated after each iteration by considering the current weight and the performance of each algorithm during the last iteration. Performance is measured in cost improvement per second, which allows us to compare algorithms despite the differing run times. We normalize the cost improvement per second to sum to 1 producing a performance value, $p_i(a)$. The weights are then adjusted using a standard reinforcement learning formula: $w_{i+1}(a) = \alpha \times w_i(a) + (1 - \alpha) \times p_i(a)$. The $\alpha$ value controls the influence of the previous weight and the performance value.

Unlike the predictive paradigm, switching shares information among algorithms. Each invocation of an algorithm begins with the best solution found so far. However, different pure algorithms are able to exploit this information differently. Below, we define the exploitation for each pure algorithm.

Two switching variations are used here. In *rl-static*, the length of each iteration does not vary: $t_i = 60$, for all $i$. For *rl-double* the time for the first two iterations is fixed, $t_1, t_2 = 60$, and subsequently $t_{i+1} = 2 \times t_i$. We switch between algorithms $|A| - 1$ times during an iteration, running each algorithm exactly once. For each iteration, the order in which the algorithms are run is randomly generated with uniform probability. This was done because it is likely to be easier to improve a solution earlier in an iteration since later the easy improvements will already have been made by the earlier algorithms. Similarly, no weight updating is done until after the second iteration, as it is very easy to find large improvements in solution quality in the first iteration. In both rl-static and rl-double, $\alpha = 0.5$. Experimenting with different values of $\alpha$ and $t_i$ is an interesting direction we intend to pursue in our future work.

## Empirical Studies

Three sets of $20 \times 20$ job shop scheduling problems are used. A total of 100 problem instances in each set were generated and 60 problems per set were arbitrarily identified as the learning set for the Bayesian classifier. The rest were placed in the test set. The difference among the three problem sets is the way in which the activity durations are generated. In the **Rand** set durations are drawn randomly with uniform probability from the interval [1, 99]. The **MC** set has activity durations drawn randomly from a normal distribution. The mean and standard deviation are the same for the activities on the same machine but different on different machines. The durations are, therefore, machine-correlated (MC). In the **JC** set the durations are also drawn randomly from a normal distribution. The means and standard deviations are the same for activities in the same job but independent across jobs. Analogously to the MC set, these problems are job-correlated (JC). These different problem structures have been studied for flow-shop scheduling (Watson *et al.* 2002). They were chosen based on the intuition that the different structures may differentially favor one pure algorithm and therefore the algorithms would exhibit different relative performance on the different sets.

Three pure algorithms are taken from the scheduling literature. These were chosen from a set of eight algorithms because they have generally comparable behavior on the learning set. The other techniques performed much worse (sometimes by an order of magnitude) on every problem. The three algorithms are:

- **tabu-tsab**: a sophisticated tabu search due to Nowicki & Smutnicki (Nowicki & Smutnicki 1996).
- **texture**: a constructive search technique using texture-based heuristics (Beck & Fox 2000), strong constraint propagation (Nuijten 1994; Laborie 2003), and bounded chronological backtracking. The bound on the backtracking follows the optimal, zero-knowledge pattern of 1, 1, 2, 1, 1, 2, 4, ... (Luby, Sinclair, & Zuckerman 1993). The texture-based heuristic identifies a resource and time point with maximum competition among the activities and chooses a pair of unordered activities, branching on the two possible orders. The heuristic is randomized by specifying that the resource and time point is chosen with uniform probability from the top 10% most critical resources and time points.
- **settimes**: a constructive search technique using the SetTimes heuristic (Scheduler 2001), the same propagation as texture, and slice-based search (Beck & Perron 2000), a type of discrepancy-based search. The heuristic chronologically builds a schedule by examining all activities with minimal start time, breaking ties with minimal end time, and then breaking further ties arbitrarily. The discrepancy bound follows the pattern: 2, 4, 6, 8, ....

The best solution found so far is shared among the algorithms in the switching paradigm. The constructive algorithms only make use of the bound on the solution quality, searching for a solution that is strictly better than the best solution found so far. Each iteration of tabu-tsab, however, must begin with an initial solution. The best solution found so far is used.

Our control techniques assume that the pure algorithms are able to find a sequence of increasingly good solutions. As we are minimizing a cost function an initial solution (with a very high cost) is always easily available. Each algorithm successively finds better solutions as it progresses either through local search or branch-and-bound, terminating when it has either proved optimality or exceeded a time limit. At any given time, each algorithm can return the best complete solution that it has found so far. If, in a given time interval, no better solution has been found, the solution found in the previous time interval is returned. In the Bayes approach, for example, the binary variables are always constructed based on the best complete solution that the algorithm has found up to a time point.

### Results

Table 1 displays the results on the three problem sets averaged over ten independent runs, R, with an overall time limit $T = 1200$. The evaluation criterion is the mean relative error (MRE), a measure of the mean extent to which an algorithm finds solutions worse than the best known solutions. MRE is defined as follows:

$$MRE(a, K, R) = \frac{\sum_{r \in R} \frac{\sum_{k \in K} \frac{c(a,k) - c^*(k)}{c^*(k)}}{|K|}}{|R|} \quad (1)$$

where $K$ is a set of problem instances, $R$ is a set of independent runs with different random seeds, $c(a, k)$ is the lowest cost found by algorithm $a$ on $k$, and $c^*(k)$ is the lowest cost known for $k$. Also displayed is the mean fraction of problems in each run for which each algorithm finds the best known solution.

| | Rand | | MC | | JC | | All | |
|---|---|---|---|---|---|---|---|---|
| | Frac. Best | MRE | Frac. Best | MRE | Frac. Best | MRE | Frac. Best | MRE |
| tabu-tsab | 0.265 | 0.0211 | 0.385 | 0.0199 | 0.225 | 0.0157 | 0.292 | 0.0189 |
| texture | 0.228 | 0.0206 | 0.09 | 0.0292 | 0.703 | 0.0089 | 0.340 | 0.0196 |
| settimes | 0.0 | 0.0519 | 0.0 | 0.0460 | 0.325 | 0.0168 | 0.108 | 0.0382 |
| Bayes | 0.228 | 0.0186 | 0.230 | 0.0192 | 0.627 | 0.0074 | 0.361 | 0.151 |
| rl-double | 0.453 | **0.0141‡** | 0.453 | 0.0142 | 0.825 | **0.0042*** | 0.577 | **0.0108‡** |
| rl-static | 0.093 | 0.0243† | 0.088 | 0.0265 | 0.754 | 0.0049 | 0.311 | 0.0185 |

Table 1: The performance of each technique on the test set. '*' indicates significantly lower mean relative error (MRE) than all pure techniques, '‡' indicates significantly lower MRE than all other algorithms, and '†' indicates significantly *worse* performance than the best pure technique. "Frac. Best" is the mean fraction of problems in each set for which the algorithm found the best known solution.

Bayes is the only approach that uses the learning set. Recall that the learning set is used to build a Bayesian classifier for each possible prediction time and identify the one with the smallest MRE. The best $t_p$ was found to be 270 seconds, meaning that each pure algorithm is run for 90 seconds and then the Bayesian classifier is used to select the pure algorithm to be run for the subsequent 930 seconds. The Bayes technique achieves an MRE that is not significantly[1] different from the best pure algorithm while finding the best solution in about the same number of problems as the best pure algorithm.

The two reinforcement learning algorithms also achieve strong performance. The better one, rl-double, performs significantly better than all other algorithms based on MRE and able to find the best known solution for over half the instances. One advantage of the switching paradigm is that it can use different pure algorithms in different parts of the search, and therefore, can achieve better performance on a problem instance than the best pure technique. In contrast, predictive selection techniques cannot perform better than the best pure technique. In fact, rl-double finds a better solution than any pure technique in 45 of the problems.

The rl-static technique performs significantly worse than rl-double. The doubling of the time in the iterations appears to be an important part of the performance of rl-double. Nonetheless, rl-static is able to achieve performance that is not significantly worse than the best pure technique. Furthermore, it finds a better solution than any pure technique in 16 of the problems.

The fact that we have created a technique that achieves significantly better performance than the best pure technique is not the main conclusion to be drawn from this experiment. Rather, the importance of these results stems from the fact that the technique does not depend on expertise either in terms of development of new, pure scheduling algorithms or in terms of development of a detailed domain and algorithm model. A low-knowledge approach is able to achieve better performance while *reducing* the required expertise.

## Further Investigations

Our initial experiment demonstrates that, at least for the problem sets, algorithms, and time limit used, it is possible to use low-knowledge approaches to algorithm control to achieve MRE performance that is significantly better than the best pure algorithm. A number of questions can now be asked with respect to these results. How sensitive are the results to different choices of parameters such as the overall time limit? Can we evaluate the extent to which the machine learning techniques are responsible for the performance of the control techniques?

**Other Time Limits** To address the issue of different time limits, we perform a series of experiments using the same design as above with $T \in \{120, 240, \ldots, 1200\}$. Table 2 presents the results. The "Best Pure" column is the MRE of the best pure technique on the test set for each time limit. For $T \in \{120, \ldots, 960\}$, texture achieves the lowest MRE of all pure techniques. For $T \geq 1080$, tabu-tsab is best. The MRE of Bayes is not significantly worse than the best pure algorithm except for $T = 120$. The rl-static approach achieves significantly lower MRE than all pure techniques for three time limits: $T \in \{240, 360, 480\}$. Finally, rl-double achieves MRE significantly lower than all pure techniques for $T \geq 360$ and comparable performance for $T \leq 240$. For $T \geq 600$, rl-double achieves significantly better performance than all other algorithms in Table 2.

We conclude that the results for $T = 1200$ are applicable to other choices for an overall time limit. The rl-double algorithm dominates regardless of time limit and the Bayes approach no worse than the best pure technique except for very low time limits.

**Other Low Knowledge Techniques** To evaluate the impact of the learning techniques in isolation, we create control variations that do not perform learning. We replace the Bayesian classifier with a simple rule: at prediction time, choose the algorithm that has found the lowest cost solution. The learning set is used to evaluate the performance of this *mincost* rule at each prediction time for each $T$ value. The prediction time, $t^*$ that results in the lowest MRE on the learning set for a given $T$ is then used on the test set for that $T$. Similarly, to assess the reinforcement learning, we run rl-static and rl-double with $\alpha = 1$. Each pure algorithm receives an equal portion of the iteration time, regardless of previous performance. We call these "no-learning" variations, *nl-static* and *nl-double*. Finally, to investigate the impact of communication among the algorithms, the *no-com* technique is nl-double without sharing of the best known

[1] All statistical results are measured using a randomized paired-$t$ test (Cohen 1995) and a significance level of $p \leq 0.005$.

| Time Limit | Algorithm | | | | | | | |
|---|---|---|---|---|---|---|---|---|
| | Best Pure | Bayes | mincost | rl-double | rl-static | nl-double | nl-static | no-com |
| 120 | 0.0387 | 0.0406† | 0.0409† | 0.0356 | 0.0340 | 0.0364 | 0.0347 | 0.0560† |
| 240 | 0.0311 | 0.0298 | 0.0315 | 0.0270 | **0.0246*** | 0.0278 | 0.0270 | 0.0440† |
| 360 | 0.0277 | 0.0258 | 0.0266 | **0.0216*** | **0.0211*** | 0.0232 | 0.0238 | 0.0387† |
| 480 | 0.0256 | 0.0232 | 0.0238 | **0.0191*** | **0.0197*** | **0.0203*** | 0.0225 | 0.0353† |
| 600 | 0.0241 | 0.0208 | 0.0216 | **0.0168‡** | 0.0190 | **0.0188*** | 0.0220 | 0.0330† |
| 720 | 0.0225 | 0.0196 | 0.0203 | **0.0147‡** | 0.0187 | **0.0174*** | 0.0218 | 0.0311† |
| 840 | 0.0215 | 0.0181 | 0.0193 | **0.0134‡** | 0.0186 | **0.0158*** | 0.0217 | 0.0298† |
| 960 | 0.0207 | 0.0169 | 0.0181 | **0.0125‡** | 0.0186 | **0.0146*** | 0.0217† | 0.0288† |
| 1080 | 0.0198 | 0.0158 | 0.0171 | **0.0116‡** | 0.0186 | **0.0139*** | 0.0217† | 0.0277† |
| 1200 | 0.0189 | 0.0151 | 0.0163 | **0.0108‡** | 0.0185 | **0.0132*** | 0.0217† | 0.0268† |

Table 2: The mean relative error (MRE) of each algorithm for different time limits. '*' indicates an MRE significantly lower than all pure techniques at the same time limit, '‡' signifies an MRE significantly lower than all other tested algorithms at the same time limit while '†' indicates significantly worse than the best pure technique.

solution among the algorithms: each algorithm is allowed to continue from where it left off in the previous iteration.

The results of these approaches are also presented in Table 2. The mincost technique does not perform significantly worse than the best pure technique, demonstrating that even a simple rule can be applied in a low-knowledge context to achieve competitive performance. Bayes is significantly better than mincost only for $T = 960$ and $T = 1200$. So while the machine learning techniques do provide a benefit, it does not appear to be robust to different time limits.

Reinforcement learning has a stronger impact. Though not displayed in the table, rl-static is significantly better than nl-static for all $T$ and rl-double is significantly better than nl-double at all time limits except $T = 120$. Interestingly, nl-double not only achieves significantly better performance than the pure techniques on seven of the ten time limits but also achieves a significantly lower MRE than all algorithms except rl-double for $T = 840$ and $T = 960$. Finally, no-com performs worse that the best pure algorithm at all time limits: communication between algorithms is clearly an important factor for performance.

**Perfect High-Knowledge Classifiers** We can perform an *a posteriori* analysis of our data to compare our low-knowledge approach with the best performance that can be expected from high-knowledge classifier which seek to select a pure algorithm for a given problem instance. The *best-subset* classifier chooses the pure algorithm that is best, on average, for the subset to which the test instance belongs. This is the best result we can achieve with a high-knowledge classifier that infallibly and with zero CPU time can categorize instances into the three problem sets. The *best-instance* makes a stronger assumption: that, with zero CPU time, the high-knowledge classifier can always choose the best pure algorithm for a given instance. This is the optimal performance that is achievable by *any* technique based on choosing the best pure algorithm for a given instance.

The rl-double technique achieves a lower MRE than best-subset for $T \geq 360$. Furthermore, rl-double performs as well as best-instance for all time limits $T \geq 360$. In other words, without complex model building our best low knowledge approach achieves performance that is as good as the best possible high-knowledge classification approach.

| Time Limit | Algorithm | | |
|---|---|---|---|
| | rl-double | best-subset | best-instance |
| 120 | 0.0356 | 0.0366 | **0.0313‡** |
| 240 | 0.0270 | 0.0291 | **0.0242‡** |
| 360 | **0.0216*** | 0.0259 | 0.0205 |
| 480 | **0.0191*** | 0.0234 | 0.0184 |
| 600 | **0.0168*** | 0.0219 | 0.0170 |
| 720 | **0.0147*** | 0.0203 | 0.0156 |
| 840 | **0.0134*** | 0.0190 | 0.0144 |
| 960 | **0.0125*** | 0.0180 | 0.0133 |
| 1080 | **0.0116*** | 0.0171 | 0.0122 |
| 1200 | **0.0108*** | 0.0164 | 0.0115 |

Table 3: The mean relative error (MRE) for different overall time limits. '*' indicates a significantly lower MRE in the comparison of rl-double and best-subset while '‡' signifies the same thing for the comparison of rl-double and best-instance.

## Future Work

We have examined a number of algorithm control approaches on a single problem type. While there is no reason to expect JSPs to be so unlike other optimization problems that similar results would not be observed, it is necessary to evaluate low-knowledge approaches on other optimization problems. In addition, it may be more relevant to apply algorithm control to problems with particular characteristics. A real system is typically faced with a series of related problems: a scheduling problem gradually changes as new orders arrive and existing orders are completed. As the problem changes, algorithm control techniques may have the flexibility to appropriately change the manner in which underlying pure algorithms are applied.

We have examined a very simple version of reinforcement learning and the best control technique, rl-double, made no use of the off-line learning set. Two obvious uses for the off-line problems is as a basis for setting the $\alpha$ value and as a basis for iteration-specific weights. If it is true that different pure algorithms are more appropriate for different phases of the search, we could use the learning set to weight each algorithm in each iteration. The issue of the ordering of the pure algorithms within an iteration is also an interesting area for future work. It is clear from the result of nl-double that the simple act of switching among a set of algorithms brings problem solving power. Understanding the reasons behind this may help to further leverage such simple techniques.

Finally, we intend to investigate the scaling of these techniques as the number of pure algorithms increases. It seems likely that the prediction-based techniques would suffer: prediction time will need to be longer and/or the time given to each pure technique will be reduced. These implications will both lead to poorer performance as less time is left for the chosen algorithm and the algorithm selection will be less accurate. In contrast, the reinforcement learning, especially if off-line learning is used to set iteration-specific weights, may be able isolate the subset of pure algorithms that are most useful.

## Conclusion

We have shown that low-knowledge metrics of pure algorithm behavior can be used to form a system that consistently and significantly out-performs the best pure algorithm. Machine learning techniques play an important role in this performance, however, even a simpleminded approach that evenly distributes increasing run-time among the pure algorithms performs very well.

Our motivation for investigating low-knowledge algorithm control was to reduce the expertise necessary to exploit optimization technology. Therefore, the strong performance of our techniques should be evaluated not simply from the perspective of an increment in solution quality, but from the perspective that this increment has been achieved without additional expertise. We neither invented a new pure algorithm nor developed a detailed model of algorithm performance and problem instance features. Therefore, we believe low-knowledge approaches are an important area of study in their own right.

## References


Beck, J. C., and Fox, M. S. 2000. Dynamic problem structure analysis as a basis for constraint-directed scheduling heuristics. *Artificial Intelligence* 117(1):31–81.

Beck, J. C., and Perron, L. 2000. Discrepancy-bounded depth first search. In *Proceedings of the Second International Workshop on Integration of AI and OR Technologies for Combinatorial Optimization Problems (CPAIOR'00)*.

Chickering, D. M. 2002. The WinMine toolkit. Technical Report MSR-TR-2002-103, Microsoft, Redmond, WA.

Cohen, P. R. 1995. *Empirical Methods for Artificial Intelligence*. The MIT Press, Cambridge, Mass.

Horvitz, E.; Ruan, Y.; Gomes, C.; Kautz, H.; Selman, B.; and Chickering, M. 2001. A bayesian approach to tacking hard computational problems. In *Proceedings of the Seventeenth Conference on uncertainty and Artificial Intelligence (UAI-2001)*, 235–244.

Kautz, H.; Horvitz, E.; Ruan, Y.; Gomes, C.; and Selman, B. 2002. Dynamic restart policies. In *Proceedings of the Eighteenth National Conference on Artifiical Intelligence (AAAI-02)*, 674–681.

Laborie, P. 2003. Algorithms for propagating resource constraints in AI planning and scheduling: Existing approaches and new results. *Artificial Intelligence* 143:151–188.

Lagoudakis, M. G., and Littman, M. L. 2000. Algorithm selection using reinforcement learning. In *Proceedings of the 17th International Conference on Machine Learning*, 511–518. Morgan Kaufmann, San Francisco, CA.

Le Pape, C.; Perron, L.; Régin, J.; and Shaw, P. 2002. Robust and parallel solving of a network design problem. In *Proceedings of the Eighth International Conference on Principles and Practice of Constraint Programming (CP02)*, 633–648.

Leyton-Brown, K.; Nudelman, E.; and Shoham, Y. 2002. Learning the empirical hardness of optimization problems: The case of combinatorial auctions. In *Proceedings of the Eighth International Conference on Principles and Practice of Constraint Programming (CP02)*, 556–572.

Luby, M.; Sinclair, A.; and Zuckerman, D. 1993. Optimal speedup of Las Vegas algorithms. *Information Processing Letters* 47:173–180.

Minton, S. 1996. Automatically configuring constraint satisfaction programs: A case study. *CONSTRAINTS* 1(1,2):7–43.

Nowicki, E., and Smutnicki, C. 1996. A fast taboo search algorithm for the job shop problem. *Management Science* 42(6):797–813.

Nuijten, W. P. M. 1994. *Time and resource constrained scheduling: a constraint satisfaction approach*. Ph.D. Dissertation, Department of Mathematics and Computing Science, Eindhoven University of Technology.

Rice, J. 1976. The algorithm selection problem. *Advances in Computers* 15:65–118.

Ruan, Y.; Horvitz, E.; and Kautz, H. 2002. Restart policies with dependence among runs: A dynamic programming approach. In *Proceedings of the Eighth International Conference on Principles and Practice of Constraint Programming (CP-2002)*, 573–586. Springer-Verlag.

Scheduler. 2001. *ILOG Scheduler 5.2 User's Manual and Reference Manual*. ILOG, S.A.

Watson, J.-P.; Barbulescu, L.; Whitley, L.; and Howe, A. 2002. Contrasting structured and random permutation flow-shop scheduling problems: search-space topology and algorithm performance. *INFORMS Journal on Computing* 14(1).

Watson, J.-P. 2003. *Empirical Modeling and Analysis of Local Search Algorithms for the Job-Shop Scheduling Problem*. Ph.D. Dissertation, Dept. of Computer Science, Colorado State University.

# Implementing a Generalized Version of Resolution

**Heidi E. Dixon**
CIRL/CIS
1269 University of Oregon
Eugene, OR 97403 USA
dixon@cirl.uoregon.edu

**Matthew L. Ginsberg**
On Time Systems, Inc.
1850 Millrace, Suite 1
Eugene, OR 97403 USA
ginsberg@otsys.com

**David K. Hofer**
CIS
University of Oregon
Eugene, OR 97403 USA
dhofer@cs.uoregon.edu

**Eugene M. Luks**
CIS
University of Oregon
Eugene, OR 97403 USA
luks@cs.uoregon.edu

**Andrew J. Parkes**
CIRL
1269 University of Oregon
Eugene, OR 97403 USA
parkes@cirl.uoregon.edu

### Abstract

We have recently proposed augmenting clauses in a Boolean database with groups of permutations, the augmented clauses then standing for the set of all clauses constructed by acting on the original clause with a permutation in the group. This approach has many attractive theoretical properties, including representational generality and reductions from exponential to polynomial proof length in a variety of settings. In this paper, we discuss the issues that arise in implementing a group-based generalization of resolution, and give preliminary results describing this procedure's effectiveness.

## Introduction

We often say that real-world constraint satisfaction problems contain *structure*. The term 'structure' is somewhat vague, but generally means that a problem contains recognizable patterns. Structured problems might best be described as problems in which subproblems or symmetric variants of subproblems recur throughout the search.

Usually, a problem is originally described using some high level language in which problem structure is explicit. A planning problem, for example, might be represented using first order logic. The Boolean satisfiability methods generally used for solving CSPs are variants of the DPLL "Davis-Putnam" algorithm and are based on conjunctive normal form (CNF) encodings. In practice, the high level encoding is used to generate a much larger CNF or *ground* encoding that unfortunately obscures the original problem structure, making it impossible for solvers to exploit this extra information in solving the problem.

A high price is paid for this approach, since many classes of problems cannot be solved efficiently without appealing to the problem structure in some way. As an example, the pigeonhole problem occurs naturally in many planning and scheduling domains, but DPLL is too weak to produce short proofs of unsatisfiability for these instances. Traditional methods using CNF encodings thus suffer from exponential scaling on these problems.

This roadblock for traditional methods has led some researchers to adapt DPLL to use stronger representations (Barth 1995; Chatalic & Simon 2000; Li 2000). When strong representations are combined with strong inference, the structure of the problem can be leveraged to produce shorter proofs. These lifted methods appear able to overcome the drawbacks of weak encodings without sacrificing the performance achieved by CNF-based methods. The disadvantage is that no single representation has proven sufficient to capture the range of structures present in naturally occurring problem instances.

We have shown (Dixon *et al.* 2004b) that permutation groups provide a general and efficient way of representing problem structure. Group-based axiomatizations generalize cardinality constraints, parity constraints and constraints quantified over finite domains. Inference among different constraint types becomes possible within this unified framework, using a general inference rule called *augmented resolution*. Augmented resolution allows multiple resolutions to be performed in parallel, leading to a powerful yet simple proof system that is still practical for automation. As we will see, the computational issues that arise in this setting can be solved by drawing on the large body of theoretical and algorithmic work that already exists for groups.

## Groups

The collection of permutations on a set $L$ will be denoted $\mathrm{Sym}(L)$. If the elements of $L$ can be labeled $1, 2, \ldots, n$ in some obvious way, $\mathrm{Sym}(L)$ is often denoted simply $S_n$. If we take $L$ to be the integers from 1 to $n$, a particular permutation can be denoted by a series of disjoint cycles, so that the permutation $\omega = (135)(26)$, for example, would map 1 to 3, then 3 to 5, then 5 back to 1. It would also exchange 2 and 6. The order in which the disjoint cycles are written is irrelevant, as is the choice of first element within a particular cycle. If $\omega_1$ and $\omega_2$ are two permutations, it is obviously possible to compose them; we will write the composition as $\omega_1\omega_2$ where the order means that we operate first with $\omega_1$ and then with $\omega_2$.

While composition is associative, it is not necessarily commutative. As an example, $(123)(23) = (12)$ but $(23)(123) = (13)$. The composition operator also has an inverse, since any permutation can obviously be inverted by mapping $x$ to that $y$ with $\omega(y) = x$. In our example, it is easy to see that $\omega^{-1} = (153)(26)$. If we have a set $S \subseteq L$ and a permutation $\omega \in \mathrm{Sym}(L)$, we will denote by $\omega(S)$ the set generated by applying $\omega$ to each element of $S$. We call this set the *image* of $S$ under $\omega$.

We see, then, that the set $S_n$ is equipped with a binary operation that is associative, and relative to which there is an identity element and each element has an inverse. Thus $S_n$ is a *group*. There are many excellent references for group theory generally (Rotman 1994, and others) and computational group theory specifically (Seress 2003).

**Definition 1** *A subset $S$ of a group $G$ is called a* subgroup *of $G$, denoted $S \leq G$, if $S$ is closed under the group operations of inversion and multiplication.*

Groups can be described without enumerating all of their elements; consider the group $S_n$, which is of size $n!$. We can represent a group $G$ by giving only a set $S$ of permutations that *generate* $G$ in that any element of $G$ can be expressed as a product of elements of $S$. If $S$ is such a generating set for $G$, we will write $G = \langle S \rangle$.

The number of generators required to describe any group $G \leq S_n$ is easily shown to be at most $\log_2 |G|$. The reason is that the size of a subgroup always divides the size of the group and so, if $x \notin \langle S \rangle$, then adding $x$ to $S$ at least doubles the size of $\langle S \rangle$. Thus the number of generators needed can never exceed $\log_2 |G|$; a more sophisticated analysis shows that $\lfloor \frac{n}{2} \rfloor$ also serves as a bound for any subgroup of $S_n$ if $n > 3$ (McIver & Neumann 1987). Permutation representations of groups provide highly compact specifications of large objects.

## Axiom Structure as a Group

**Cardinality Constraints** Cardinality constraints have the form

$$x_1 + \cdots + x_m \geq k \tag{1}$$

asserting that at least $k$ of the $x_i$'s must be true. The single axiom (1) is equivalent to $\binom{m}{k-1}$ conventional disjunctions. The representational strength of cardinality constraints allows polynomial length proofs of the pigeonhole problem (Cook, Coullard, & Turan 1987) which is known to be exponentially difficult for any resolution-based method (Haken 1985). Consider the cardinality constraint

$$x_1 + x_2 + x_3 + x_4 + x_5 \geq 3 \tag{2}$$

which can be encoded in conjunctive normal form as

$$\begin{array}{ll} x_1 \vee x_2 \vee x_3 & x_1 \vee x_4 \vee x_5 \\ x_1 \vee x_2 \vee x_4 & x_2 \vee x_3 \vee x_4 \\ x_1 \vee x_2 \vee x_5 & x_2 \vee x_3 \vee x_5 \\ x_1 \vee x_3 \vee x_4 & x_2 \vee x_4 \vee x_5 \\ x_1 \vee x_3 \vee x_5 & x_3 \vee x_4 \vee x_5 \end{array} \tag{3}$$

The constraint (2) could also be encoded by the first ground axiom $x_1 \vee x_2 \vee x_3$, together with the set of permutations

$$\text{Sym}(\{x_1, x_2, x_3, x_4, x_5\}). \tag{4}$$

The remaining ground axioms (3) can be generated by applying the set of permutations (4) to the first axiom. More generally, a cardinality constraint of form (1) can be written as a single clause $x_1 \vee x_2 \vee \cdots \vee x_{m-k+1}$ together with the group $G = \text{Sym}(\{x_i\})$. Operating on $x_1 \vee x_2 \vee \cdots \vee x_{m-k+1}$ with elements of $G$ allows us to generate the full set of CNF clauses that is logically equivalent to (1).

**Parity Constraints** We now consider constraints that are most naturally expressed using modular arithmetic or exclusive or's, such as

$$x_1 \oplus \cdots \oplus x_k = 1 \tag{5}$$

Axiom sets consisting of parity constraints in isolation can be solved in polynomial time using Gaussian elimination, but there are examples that are exponentially difficult for resolution-based methods (Tseitin 1970).

As in the cardinality example, single axioms such as (5) reveal structure that a Boolean axiomatization obscures. In this case, (5) with $k = 3$ is equivalent to:

$$\begin{array}{ll} x_1 \vee x_2 \vee x_3 & x_1 \vee \neg x_2 \vee \neg x_3 \\ \neg x_1 \vee x_2 \vee \neg x_3 & \neg x_1 \vee \neg x_2 \vee x_3 \end{array} \tag{6}$$

These four axioms can be generated from the first using the three permutations in the set

$$\{(x_1, \neg x_1)(x_2, \neg x_2), (x_1, \neg x_1)(x_3, \neg x_3), (x_2, \neg x_2)(x_3, \neg x_3)\}$$

Although literals are now being exchanged with their negations, this set, too, is closed under the group inverse and composition operations. Since each element is a composition of disjoint transpositions, each element is its own inverse. The composition of the first two elements is the third. In general, a constraint of the form (5) can be written as the clause $x_1 \vee x_2 \vee \cdots \vee x_k$ together with the group

$$G = \langle (x_1, \neg x_1)(x_2, \neg x_2), \ldots, (x_{k-1}, \neg x_{k-1})(x_k, \neg x_k) \rangle.$$

**First Order Structure** Consider next a first-order constraint such as

$$P(x, y) \vee Q(y, z) \vee R(x, z) \tag{7}$$

where each variable is universally quantified over a finite domain of size $d$, so that (7) corresponds to $d^3$ ground axioms. If $x$, $y$ and $z$ are all chosen from the two element domain $\{a, b\}$, the single lifted axiom (7) corresponds to the set of ground instances:

$$\begin{array}{c} P(a,a) \vee Q(a,a) \vee R(a,a) \\ P(a,a) \vee Q(a,b) \vee R(a,b) \\ P(a,b) \vee Q(b,a) \vee R(a,a) \\ P(a,b) \vee Q(b,b) \vee R(a,b) \\ P(b,a) \vee Q(a,a) \vee R(b,a) \\ P(b,a) \vee Q(a,b) \vee R(b,b) \\ P(b,b) \vee Q(b,a) \vee R(b,a) \\ P(b,b) \vee Q(b,b) \vee R(b,b) \end{array}$$

If we introduce ground literals $l_1, l_2, l_3, l_4$ for the instances of $P(x, y)$ and so on, we get:

$$\begin{array}{c} l_1 \vee l_5 \vee l_9 \\ l_1 \vee l_6 \vee l_{10} \\ l_2 \vee l_7 \vee l_9 \\ l_2 \vee l_8 \vee l_{10} \\ l_3 \vee l_5 \vee l_{11} \\ l_3 \vee l_6 \vee l_{12} \\ l_4 \vee l_7 \vee l_{11} \\ l_4 \vee l_8 \vee l_{12} \end{array} \tag{8}$$

at which point the structure implicit in (7) has apparently been obscured.

But note that the set of axioms (8) is "generated" by a set of transformations on the underlying variables. For example, we are allowed to swap the values of $a$ and $b$ for variable $x$, and still have a sanctioned ground clause. Since the variable $x$ appears as the first argument of both $P$ and $R$, the permutation

$(P_{(a,a)}, P_{(b,a)})(P_{(a,b)}, P_{(b,b)})(R_{(a,a)}, R_{(b,a)})(R_{(a,b)}, R_{(b,b)})$

corresponds to a swap of $a$ and $b$ as the first argument of both $P$ and $R$, producing the correct action on the relevant ground literals.

In terms of the literals in (8), this becomes

$$\omega_x = (l_1 l_3)(l_2 l_4)(l_9 l_{11})(l_{10} l_{12})$$

In a similar way, swapping the two values for $y$ corresponds to $\omega_y = (l_1 l_2)(l_3 l_4)(l_5 l_7)(l_6 l_8)$ and $z$ produces $\omega_z = (l_5 l_6)(l_7 l_8)(l_9 l_{10})(l_{11} l_{12})$. Now consider the subgroup $G = \langle \omega_x, \omega_y, \omega_z \rangle$ of $\text{Sym}(\{l_i\})$ generated by $\omega_x$, $\omega_y$ and $\omega_z$. As in our earlier examples, this group allows all of the clauses in (8) to be generated from any such clause. Thus operating on the first axiom in (8) with $\omega_x$ produces $l_3 \vee l_5 \vee l_{11}$. This is the fifth axiom, exactly as it should be, since we have swapped $P(a,a)$ with $P(b,a)$ and $R(a,a)$ with $R(b,a)$. Alternatively, a straightforward calculation shows that

$$\omega_x \omega_y = (l_1 l_4)(l_2 l_3)(l_5 l_7)(l_6 l_8)(l_9 l_{11})(l_{10} l_{12})$$

mapping the first axiom in (8) to the next to last, and so on.

**Augmented Clauses** Before proceeding, note that any "reasonable" permutation that maps a literal $l_1$ to another literal $l_2$ should respect the semantics of the axiomatization and map $\neg l_1$ to $\neg l_2$ as well.

**Definition 2** *Given a set of $n$ variables, we will denote by $W_n$ that subgroup of $S_{2n}$ that maps the literal $\neg l_1$ to $\neg l_2$ whenever it maps $l_1$ to $l_2$.*

**Definition 3** *An* augmented clause *in an $n$-variable Boolean satisfiability problem is a pair $(c, G)$ where $c$ is a Boolean clause and $G \leq W_n$. A ground clause $c'$ is an* instance *of an augmented clause $(c, G)$ if there is some $g \in G$ such that $c' = g(c)$. Two augmented clauses $(c_1, G_1)$ and $(c_2, G_2)$ will be called* equivalent *if they have identical sets of instances. This will be denoted $(c_1, G_1) \equiv (c_2, G_2)$.*

**Proposition 4** *Let $(c, G)$ be an augmented clause. Then if $c'$ is any instance of $(c, G)$, $(c, G) \equiv (c', G)$.* ■

**Definition 5** *If $C$ is a set of augmented clauses, we will say that $C$* entails *an augmented clause $(c, G)$, writing $C \models (c, G)$, if every instance of $(c, G)$ is entailed by the set of instances of the augmented clauses in $C$.*

Augmented clauses provide highly compact descriptions of structured clause sets. An augmented clause can be exponentially more concise than its equivalent set of ground clauses.

**Proposition 6** *Let $S$ be a set of ground clauses over $n$ variables, and $(c, G)$ an equivalent augmented clause. Then a set of generators for $G$ can be expressed in $O(n^2)$ space.* ■

## Generalizing Resolution

Of course, presenting a more compact representation is not progress in and of itself; it must also be possible to *reason* with the representation. Augmented clauses possess a natural generalization of the classical Boolean idea of resolution; the essential idea is that the "resolvent" of two augmented clauses $(c_1, G_1)$ and $(c_2, G_2)$ should be, as nearly as possible, the set of all resolvents that can be obtained by resolving an instance of $(c_1, G_1)$ with an instance of $(c_2, G_2)$.

**Definition 7** *Let $(c, G)$ be an augmented clause. By $G(c)$ we will mean the union of all instances $g(c)$ of the augmented clause $(c, G)$. For a permutation $p$ and set $S$ with $p(S) = S$, by $p|_S$ we will mean the restriction of $p$ to the given set, and we will say that $p$ is a* pullback *of $p|_S$ back to the original set on which $p$ acts.*

Note that it is not possible to restrict a group to an arbitrary set; one cannot restrict the permutation $(xy)$ to the set $\{x\}$ because you need to add $y$ as well.

**Definition 8** *Let $(c_1, G_1)$ and $(c_2, G_2)$ be two augmented clauses. A permutation $p$ is called an* extension *of $(c_1, G_1)$ and $(c_2, G_2)$ if there are $g_i \in G_i$ such that for $i = 1, 2$, $p|_{c_i} = g_i|_{c_i}$. We will denote the set of extensions of $(c_1, G_1)$ and $(c_2, G_2)$ by $\texttt{extn}(c_i, G_i)$.*

*An extension will be called* stable *if there are $g_i \in G_i$ such that for $i = 1, 2$, $p|_{G_i(c_i)} = g_i|_{G_i(c_i)}$. We will denote the set of stable extensions of $(c_1, G_1)$ and $(c_2, G_2)$ by $\texttt{stab}(c_i, G_i)$.*

Note that the only difference between an extension and a stable extension is the domain for which the permutation $p$ is required to match elements of the groups $G_i$. For an extension, the match must be only on the given clause $c$; stability requires that the match be on the entire image of $c$ under the $G_i$.

If $(c_1, G_1)$ and $(c_2, G_2)$ are augmented clauses such that the Boolean clauses $c_1$ and $c_2$ resolve to give resolve$(c_1, c_2)$, the set of all clauses of the form $p(\text{resolve}(c_1, c_2))$ where $p \in \texttt{extn}(c_i, G_i)$ is analogous to the set of all resolvents that can be obtained by resolving an instance of $(c_1, G_1)$ and one of $(c_2, G_2)$. Unfortunately, the set of extensions $p$ is not closed under composition and is not a group; it is only for groups that the representational and other efficiencies of the augmented approach can be realized. But the set of stable extensions *is* a group, leading to:

**Definition 9** *Let $(c_1, G_1)$ and $(c_2, G_2)$ be augmented clauses. Then the* resolvent *of $(c_1, G_1)$ and $(c_2, G_2)$, to be denoted by* resolve$((c_1, G_1), (c_2, G_2))$, *is the augmented clause* (resolve$(c_1, c_2)$, $\texttt{stab}(c_i, G_i)$).

The above definition resolves many of the instances of $(c_1, G_1)$ and of $(c_2, G_2)$ in "parallel", allowing us to conclude at a stroke many of the clauses that would have been obtained had we resolved the individual instances of $(c_1, G_1)$ with the instances of $(c_2, G_2)$.

**Proposition 10** *Augmented resolution is sound, in that if $(c, G) =$ resolve$((c_1, G_1), (c_2, G_2))$ and $c'$ is an instance of $(c, G)$, then $(c_1, G_1) \wedge (c_2, G_2) \models c'$.* ■

**Proposition 11** *Augmented resolution is complete, in that if* $(c_1, G_1)$ *and* $(c_2, G_2)$ *are augmented clauses with instances* $c'_1$ *and* $c'_2$ *respectively and* $c' = \text{resolve}(c'_1, c'_2)$, *then* $c'$ *is an instance of* $\text{resolve}((c'_1, G_1), (c'_2, G_2))$. ■

Recall that $(c'_1, G_1) \equiv (c_1, G_1)$ by virtue of Proposition 4, and similarly for $c'_2$.

In some cases, computing the group of stable extensions is easy:

**Lemma 12** *If* $(c_1, G)$ *and* $(c_2, G)$ *are augmented clauses and* $G(c_1) = G(c_2)$, *then* $\text{resolve}((c_1, G), (c_2, G)) \equiv (\text{resolve}(c_1, c_2), G)$. ■

But what can be said about the more general case? We now address this difficulty.

## Augmented resolution

The essence of the augmented resolution computation involves computing the group of stable extensions of the groups in the resolvents. Specifically, we have augmented clauses $(c_1, G_1)$ and $(c_2, G_2)$ and need to compute the group $G$ of stable extensions of $G_1$ and $G_2$. Recalling Definition 8, this is the group of all permutations $\omega$ with the property that there is some $g_1 \in G_1$ such that $\omega|_{c_1^{G_1}} = g_1|_{c_1^{G_1}}$ and similarly for $g_2 \in G_2$ and $c_2$. We have adjusted notation here, replacing the $G_i(c_i)$ in the original Definition 8 with $c_i^{G_i}$. The reason for the notational shift is that the composition of two group elements $fg$ acts with $f$ first and then with $g$. By replacing $g(f(x))$ with $x^{fg}$, the original definition of function composition $g(f(x)) = (fg)(x)$ (note the awkward variable order) becomes the more natural $x^{fg} = (x^f)^g$. As remarked in Definition 7, $c_i^{G_i}$ is the union of the images of $c_i$ under permutations in $G_i$.

As an example, consider the two clauses

$$\begin{aligned}(c_1, G_1) &= (a \vee b, \langle (ad), (be), (bf), (xy) \rangle) \\ (c_2, G_2) &= (c \vee b, \langle (be), (bg) \rangle)\end{aligned}$$

The image of $c_1$ under $G_1$ is $\{a, b, d, e, f\}$ (the $x$ and $y$ appearing in the group are irrelevant), and $c_2^{G_2} = \{b, c, e, g\}$. We therefore need to find those permutations $\omega$ such that $\omega$ restricted to $\{a, b, d, e, f\}$ is an element of $\langle (ad), (be), (bf), (xy) \rangle$, and $\omega$ restricted to $\{b, c, e, g\}$ is an element of $\langle (be), (bg) \rangle$.

From the second condition, we know that $c$ cannot be moved by $\omega$, and any permutation of $b$, $e$ and $g$ is acceptable because $(be)$ and $(bg)$ generate the symmetric group $\text{Sym}\{b, e, g\}$. This second restriction does not impact the image of $a$, $d$ or $f$ under $\omega$.

From the first condition, we know that $a$ and $d$ can be swapped or left unchanged, and any permutation of $b$, $e$ and $f$ is acceptable. But recall from the second condition that we must also permute $b$, $e$ and $g$. These conditions combine to imply that we cannot move $f$ or $g$, since to move either would break the condition on the other. We can swap $b$ and $e$ or not, so the group of stable extensions is $\langle (ad), (be) \rangle$, and that is what our construction should return.

As a preliminary, we need the following:

**Definition 13** *Given a group* $G$ *acting on a set* $L$, *the* point-wise stabilizer *of* $L$, *denoted* $G_L$, *is the subgroup of all* $g \in G$ *such that* $l^g = l$ *for every* $l \in L$. *The* set stabilizer *of* $L$, *denoted* $G_{\{L\}}$, *is that subgroup of all* $g \in G$ *such that* $L^g = L$.

Point stabilizers can be computed in polynomial time. There is no known polynomial algorithm for set stabilizers in general (see (Luks 1993) for a discussion of the complexity of this and related problems), although set stabilizer is not NP-hard unless the polynomial hierarchy collapses to $\Sigma_2^p$ (Babai & Moran 1988).

**Procedure 14** *Given augmented clauses* $(c_1, G_1)$ *and* $(c_2, G_2)$, *to compute* $\texttt{stab}(c_i, G_i)$:

1 $\texttt{c\_image}_i \leftarrow c_i^{G_i}$ for $i = 1, 2$
2 $\texttt{g\_restrict}_i \leftarrow G_i|_{\texttt{c\_image}_i}$ for $i = 1, 2$
3 $C_\cap \leftarrow \texttt{c\_image}_1 \cap \texttt{c\_image}_2$
4 $\texttt{g\_stab}_i \leftarrow \texttt{g\_restrict}_{i\{C_\cap\}}$ for $i = 1, 2$
5 $\texttt{g\_int} \leftarrow \texttt{g\_stab}_1|_{C_\cap} \cap \texttt{g\_stab}_2|_{C_\cap}$
6 $\{g_j\} \leftarrow \{\text{generators of } \texttt{g\_int}\}$
7 $\{l_{ij}\} \leftarrow \{g_j, \text{pulled back to } \texttt{g\_stab}_i\}$ for $i = 1, 2$
8 $\{l'_{2j}\} \leftarrow \{l_{2j}|_{\texttt{c\_image}_2 - C_\cap}\}$
9 **return** $\langle \texttt{g\_restrict}_{1C_\cap}, \texttt{g\_restrict}_{2C_\cap}, \{l_{1j} \cdot l'_{2j}\} \rangle$

**Proposition 15** *Procedure 14 returns* $\texttt{stab}(c_i, G_i)$.

Space prohibits our both proving this result and providing an example of the procedure in action; we work through our example and remark that the proof follows it closely.

**1.** $\texttt{c\_image}_i \leftarrow c_i^{G_i}$. As described earlier, we have $\texttt{c\_image}_1 = \{a, b, d, e, f\}$ and $\texttt{c\_image}_2 = \{b, c, e, g\}$.
**2.** $\texttt{g\_restrict}_i \leftarrow G_i|_{\texttt{c\_image}_i}$. We restrict each group to the corresponding $\texttt{c\_image}_i$. We get $\texttt{g\_restrict}_2 = G_2$ but $\texttt{g\_restrict}_1 = \langle (ad), (be), (bf) \rangle$ as the irrelevant points $x$ and $y$ are removed.
**3.** $C_\cap \leftarrow \texttt{c\_image}_1 \cap \texttt{c\_image}_2$. The construction considers three separate sets – the intersection of the images of the original clauses (where the computation is interesting because the various $g_i$ must agree), and the points in only the image of $c_1$ or only the image of $c_2$. The analysis on these latter sets is straightforward; we just need $\omega$ to agree with any element of $G_1$ or $G_2$ on the set in question. Here we compute the intersection region $C_\cap = \{b, e\}$.
**4.** $\texttt{g\_stab}_i \leftarrow \texttt{g\_restrict}_{i\{C_\cap\}}$. We find the subgroup of $\texttt{g\_restrict}_i$ that set stabilizes $C_\cap = \{b, e\}$. For $\texttt{g\_restrict}_1 = \langle (ad), (be), (bf) \rangle$, this is $\langle (ad), (be) \rangle$ because we can no longer swap $b$ and $f$, while for $\texttt{g\_restrict}_2 = \langle (be), (bg) \rangle$, we get $\texttt{g\_stab}_2 = \langle (be) \rangle$.
**5.** $\texttt{g\_int} \leftarrow \texttt{g\_stab}_1|_{C_\cap} \cap \texttt{g\_stab}_2|_{C_\cap}$. Since $\omega$ must simultaneously agree with both $G_1$ and $G_2$ when restricted to $C_\cap$ (and thus with $\texttt{g\_restrict}_1$ and $\texttt{g\_restrict}_2$ as well), the restriction of $\omega$ to $C_\cap$ must lie within this intersection. In our example, $\texttt{g\_int} = \langle (be) \rangle$.
**6.** $\{g_i\} \leftarrow \{\text{generators of } \texttt{g\_int}\}$. Any element of $\texttt{g\_int}$ will lead to an element of the group of stable extensions provided that we extend it appropriately from $C_\cap$ back to the full set $c_1^{G_1} \cup c_2^{G_2}$; this step begins the process of building up these extensions. It suffices to work with just the generators of $\texttt{g\_int}$, and we construct those generators here. We have $\{g_i\} = \{(be)\}$.

**7.** $\{l_{ki}\} \leftarrow \{g_i, \text{pulled back to } \texttt{g\_stab}_k\}$. Our goal is now to build up a permutation on $\texttt{c\_image}_1 \cup \texttt{c\_image}_2$ that, when restricted to $C_\cap$, matches the generator $g_i$. We do this by pulling $g_i$ separately back to $\texttt{c\_image}_1$ and to $\texttt{c\_image}_2$. Any such pullback suffices, so we can take (for example) $l_{11} = (be)(ad)$ and $l_{21} = (be)$. In the first case, the inclusion of the swap of $a$ and $d$ is neither precluded nor required; we could just as well have used $l_{11} = (be)$.

**8.** $\{l'_{2i}\} \leftarrow \{l_{2i}|_{\texttt{c\_image}_2 - C_\cap}\}$. We cannot simply compose $l_{11}$ and $l_{21}$ to get the desired permutation on $\texttt{c\_image}_1 \cup \texttt{c\_image}_2$ because the part of the permutations acting on the intersection $\texttt{c\_image}_1 \cap \texttt{c\_image}_2$ will have acted twice. In this case, we would get $l_{11} \cdot l_{21} = (ad)$ which no longer captures our freedom to exchange $b$ and $e$.

We deal with this by restricting $l_{21}$ *away* from $C_\cap$ and only then combining with $l_{11}$. Here, restricting $(be)$ away from $C_\cap = \{b, e\}$ produces the trivial permutation $l'_{21} = ()$.

**9. Return** $\langle \texttt{g\_restrict}_{1C_\cap}, \texttt{g\_restrict}_{2C_\cap}, \{l_{1i} \cdot l'_{2i}\}\rangle$. We compute the final answer from three sources: The combined $l_{1i} \cdot l'_{2i}$ that we have been working to construct, along with elements of $\texttt{g\_restrict}_1$ and $\texttt{g\_restrict}_2$ that fix every point in $c_\cap$. These latter two sets consist of stable extensions, since an element of $\texttt{g\_restrict}_1$ pointwise stabilizes the image of $c_2$ if and only if it pointwise stabilizes the points that are in both the image of $c_1$ (to which $\texttt{g\_restrict}_1$ has been restricted) and the image of $c_2$; in other words, if and only if it pointwise stabilizes $C_\cap$.

In our example, we have

$$\begin{aligned} \texttt{g\_restrict}_{1C_\cap} &= \langle (ad) \rangle \\ \texttt{g\_restrict}_{2C_\cap} &= 1 \\ \{l_{1i} \cdot l'_{2i}\} &= \{(be)(ad)\} \end{aligned}$$

The group of stable extensions is $\langle (ad), (be)(ad)\rangle$, identical to the "obvious" $\langle (ad), (be)\rangle$. We can swap either the $(a, d)$ pair or the $(b, e)$ pair, as we see fit. The first swap $(ad)$ is sanctioned for the first "resolvent" $(c_1, G_1) = (a \vee b, \langle (ad), (be), (bf)\rangle)$ and does not mention any relevant variable in the second $(c_2, G_2) = (c \vee b, \langle (be), (bg)\rangle)$. The second swap $(be)$ is sanctioned in both cases.

**Computational issues** We conclude this section by discussing some of the computational issues that arise when we implement Procedure 14, including the complexity of the various operations required.

**1.** $\texttt{c\_image}_i \leftarrow c_i^{G_i}$. Efficient algorithms exist for computing the image of a set under a group. The basic method is to use a flood-fill like approach, adding and marking the result of acting on the set with a single group element, and recurring until no new points are added.

**2.** $\texttt{g\_restrict}_i \leftarrow G_i|_{\texttt{c\_image}_i}$. A group can be restricted to a set that it stabilizes by restricting the generating permutations individually.

**3.** $C_\cap \leftarrow \texttt{c\_image}_1 \cap \texttt{c\_image}_2$. Set intersection is straightforward.

**4.** $\texttt{g\_stab}_i \leftarrow \texttt{g\_restrict}_{i\{C_\cap\}}$. Although set stabilizer is not known to be in P, implementations exist that are efficient in practice.

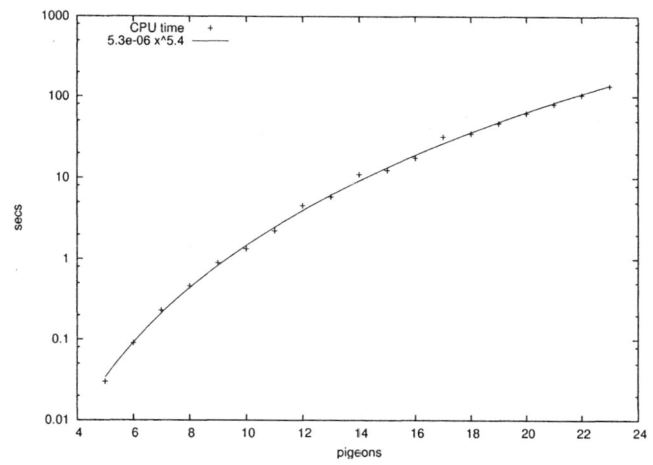


Figure 1: CPU time for a pigeonhole resolution

**5.** $\texttt{g\_int} \leftarrow \texttt{g\_stab}_1|_{C_\cap} \cap \texttt{g\_stab}_2|_{C_\cap}$. Group intersection is also not known to be in polynomial time (and is in fact polynomial time equivalent to set stabilizer (Luks 1993)); once again, practical and efficient implementations exist.

**6.** $\{g_i\} \leftarrow \{\text{generators of } \texttt{g\_int}\}$. Groups are typically represented in terms of their generators, so reconstructing a list of those generators is trivial.

**7.** $\{l_{ki}\} \leftarrow \{g_i, \text{pulled back to } \texttt{g\_stab}_k\}$. Suppose that we have a group $G$ acting on a set $S$, a subset $T \subseteq S$ and a permutation $h$ acting on $T$ such that we know that $h$ is the restriction to $T$ of some $g \in G$. Finding such a pullback is polynomial in the number of variables acted on by $G$.

**8.** $\{l'_{2i}\} \leftarrow \{l_{2i}|_{\texttt{c\_image}_2 - C_\cap}\}$. Restriction is still easy.

**9. Return** $\langle \texttt{g\_restrict}_{1C_\cap}, \texttt{g\_restrict}_{2C_\cap}, \{l_{1i} \cdot l'_{2i}\}\rangle$. Since groups are represented by their generators, we need simply take the union of the generators for the three arguments. The pointwise stabilizers needed for the first two arguments can be computed in polynomial time.

## Experimental results

We have implemented the procedure described in the last section as one of the necessary first steps to building a theorem prover for an augmented resolution system.

The results for the pigeonhole problem are shown in Figure 1. This particular example involves resolving the two basic axioms in a pigeonhole problem containing $n$ pigeons and $n - 1$ holes. (The axioms state that every pigeon is in some hole and no hole contains two pigeons.) We produced the results in the figure by encoding the axioms in a way that obscured the fact that the groups were identical and by also disabling the check to see if the groups were the same.

The solid line gives the observed time (in seconds) for the resolution as a function of the number of pigeons involved, plotted on a log scale. The experiments were performed on a 1.7GHz Pentium-M with 1GB of main memory, although the implementation used only 5MB. Interestingly, the CPU usage was *not* dominated by the non-polynomial steps in Lines 4 and 5 of Procedure 14, but instead by the need to compute "stabilizer chains" in support of the algorithm generally. Stabilizer chains (Sims 1970) are data structures that support a variety of computational manipulations on groups, and can be constructed in time $O(n^5)$ if $n$ is the number of variables being manipulated by the group in question (Knuth 1991). The solid curve in the figure is the best fit between the data and a CPU utilization of $ax^b$, which occurs for $b = 5.4$.

The pigeonhole problem was chosen for our experiments because, although the groups involved are very simple (the direct product of a symmetry over $n$ pigeons and one over $n-1$ holes), the standard stabilizer chain construction generally works poorly on full symmetry groups or products thereof. For this reason, we expect that the computational needs of Procedure 14 in a pigeonhole setting are in fact greater than those that will be encountered in other augmented problems. The running time can be reduced to $O(n^3)$ by using stabilizer chain algorithms designed to work well on full symmetry groups (and only slightly worse than the standard algorithms in the general case). The running time can be reduced to $O(1)$ by recognizing that all of the groups involved are identical and applying Lemma 12 to produce the resolvent group directly.

We have shown elsewhere (Dixon *et al.* 2004b) that actually *solving* the pigeonhole problem in this framework involves a total of $O(n^2)$ resolutions and a similar number of unit propagations. The unit propagations require a single stabilizer chain computation costing $O(n^3)$ (Dixon *et al.* 2004a) but potentially shared among all of the propagations required, since the group is unchanged throughout the problem.[1] The overall scaling on this problem instance can therefore be expected to be $O(n^3)$, which compares favorably with the $O(n^5)$ scaling obtained by exploiting the symmetry directly using symmetry-breaking axioms (Crawford *et al.* 1996), or with the exponential scaling needed by conventional methods. The augmented approach is also far more flexible, since it can deal with theories where no global symmetry is present, or with structure in other forms.

## Conclusion

Augmented resolution is a completely new mechanism for solving satisfiability problems, and has extremely attractive theoretical properties including exponential reductions in both the space needed to store a clausal database and the number of inference steps needed to derive conclusions from it. In this paper, we have begun to investigate the computational properties of this new approach, presenting an algorithm for computing augmented resolution and describing the results of experiments that appear likely to measure that algorithm's worst case performance. The result of those experiments indicate that the time needed for a single resolution remains polynomial in the number $n$ of domain elements being considered, although the time does grow as $O(n^5)$ if full symmetry groups are involved. In practice, it should be possible to reduce the resolution time substantially by exploiting the specific structure of the groups in question.

[1] As with resolution, there are non-polynomial elements to the unit propagation procedure (Dixon *et al.* 2004a) but the evidence is that the stabilizer chain construction dominates.

## References


Babai, L., and Moran, S. 1988. Arthur-Merlin games: A randomized proof system, and a hierarchy of complexity classes. *J. Comput. System Sci.* 36:254–276.

Barth, P. 1995. A Davis-Putnam based enumeration algorithm for linear pseudo-boolean optimization. Technical Report MPI-I-95-2-003, Max Planck Institut für Informatik, Saarbrücken, Germany.

Chatalic, P., and Simon, L. 2000. Zres: the old Davis-Putnam meets ZBDDs. In McAllester, D., ed., *17th International Confernece on Automated Deduction (CADE'17)*, number 1831 in Lecture Notes in Artificial Intelligence (LNAI), 449–454.

Cook, W.; Coullard, C.; and Turan, G. 1987. On the complexity of cutting-plane proofs. *Discrete Applied Mathematics* 18:25–38.

Crawford, J. M.; Ginsberg, M. L.; Luks, E.; and Roy, A. 1996. Symmetry breaking predicates for search problems. In *Proceedings of the Fifth International Conference on Principles of Knowledge Representation and Reasoning*.

Dixon, H. E.; Ginsberg, M. L.; Hofer, D.; Luks, E. M.; and Parkes, A. J. 2004a. Generalizing Boolean satisfiability III: Implementation. Technical report, CIRL, Eugene, Oregon.

Dixon, H. E.; Ginsberg, M. L.; Luks, E. M.; and Parkes, A. J. 2004b. Generalizing Boolean satisfiability II: Theory. Technical report, CIRL, Eugene, Oregon.

Haken, A. 1985. The intractability of resolution. *Theoretical Computer Science* 39:297–308.

Knuth, D. E. 1991. Notes on efficient representation of permutation groups. *Combinatorica* 11:57–68.

Li, C. M. 2000. Integrating equivalency reasoning into Davis-Putnam procedure. In *Proceedings of the Seventeenth National Conference on Artificial Intelligence*, 291–296.

Luks, E. M. 1993. *Permutation Groups and Polynomial-Time Computation*, volume 11 of *DIMACS Series in Discrete Mathematics and Theoretical Computer Science*. Amer. Math. Soc. 139–175.

McIver, A., and Neumann, P. 1987. Enumerating finite groups. *Quart. J. Math.* 38(2):473–488.

Rotman, J. J. 1994. *An Introduction to the Theory of Groups*. Springer.

Seress, A. 2003. *Permutation Group Algorithms*, volume 152 of *Cambridge Tracts in Mathematics*. Cambridge, UK: Cambridge University Press.

Sims, C. C. 1970. Computational methods in the study of permutation groups. In Leech, J., ed., *Computational Problems in Abstract Algebra, Proc. Conf. Oxford, 1967*. Pergamon Press.

Tseitin, G. 1970. On the complexity of derivation in propositional calculus. In Slisenko, A., ed., *Studies in Constructive Mathematics and Mathematical Logic, Part 2*. Consultants Bureau. 466–483.

# SAT-Based Answer Set Programming *

**Enrico Giunchiglia**[1], **Yuliya Lierler**[2], **and Marco Maratea**[1]

[1]DIST - Università di Genova, Genova, Italy
[2]Institut für Informatik, Erlangen-Nürnberg-Universität, Germany
[1]{enrico,marco}@mrg.dist.unige.it, [2]yuliya.lierler@informatik.uni-erlangen.de

### Abstract

The relation between answer set programming (ASP) and propositional satisfiability (SAT) is at the center of many research papers, partly because of the tremendous performance boost of SAT solvers during last years. Various translations from ASP to SAT are known but the resulting SAT formula either includes many new variables or may have an unpractical size. There are also well known results showing a one-to-one correspondence between the answer sets of a logic program and the models of its completion. Unfortunately, these results only work for specific classes of problems.

In this paper we present a SAT-based decision procedure for answer set programming that $(i)$ deals with any (non disjunctive) logic program, $(ii)$ works on a SAT formula without additional variables, and $(iii)$ is guaranteed to work in polynomial space. Further, our procedure can be extended to compute all the answer sets still working in polynomial space. The experimental results of a prototypical implementation show that the approach can pay off sometimes by orders of magnitude.

## Introduction

Propositional satisfiability (SAT) is one of the most studied fields in Artificial Intelligence and Computer Science. Also motivated by the availability of efficient SAT solvers various reductions from logic programs to SAT were introduced in the past.

Fages (1994) showed that if a program $\Pi$ is "tight" then its answer sets (or stable models) are in one-to-one correspondence with the models of its completion (Clark 1978). If the completion is converted to a set of clauses $\Gamma$, state-of-the-art SAT solvers can be used as answer set generators. Since the size of $\Gamma$ is at most twice the size of $\Pi$, and has at most $m$ new variables (where $m$ is the number of rules in the logic program) this is considered a viable and efficient approach. Fages' result was then generalised to include programs with infinitely many rules (Lifschitz 1996), programs tight "on their completion model" (Babovich, Erdem, & Lifschitz 2000), and programs with nested expressions in the bodies of the rules (Erdem & Lifschitz 2003). Still these results do not apply to the whole class of logic programs. It is well known that each answer set corresponds to a model of its completion, but the viceversa in general is not true.

Ben-Eliyahu and Dechter (1996) gave a translation from a class of disjunctive logic programs to SAT. However the translation may need $O(n^2)$ new variables and $O(n^3)$ new clauses (where $n$ is the number of atoms in the logic program). Janhunen (2003) presented an optimized encoding of this translation, which behaves subquadratic in both size and number of atoms.

A reduction to SAT which does not need extra variables was proposed by Lin and Zhao (2002). The drawback of this reduction is that the resulting formula may blow-up in space. Still system ASSAT based on such reduction outperforms state-of-the-art ASP systems like SMODELS (Niemelä 1999; Simons 2000) and DLV (Eiter *et al.* 1998) on many interesting problems.

In this paper the question that we positively answer is: Is it possible to build an efficient SAT-based answer set generator that $(i)$ deals with any (non disjunctive) logic program, $(ii)$ works on a SAT formula without additional variables except for those eventually introduced by the clause form transformation, and $(iii)$ is guaranteed to work in polynomial space? We present a procedure, called ASP-SAT, having the above three but also other features. We integrated ASP-SAT in CMODELS[1] and ran a wide comparative analysis with other state-of-the-art systems. The results show that our procedure has a clear edge over them.

The paper is structured as follows. First we introduce some necessary definitions and terminology. Second we present the main ideas behind our procedure and some details for an effective implementation. We end the paper describing the integration in CMODELS, the experimental results, and the conclusions.

## Formal Background

Let $P$ be a set of atoms. A *rule* is an expression of the form

$$A_0 \leftarrow A_1, \ldots, A_m, not\ A_{m+1}, \ldots, not\ A_n \qquad (1)$$

*We are grateful to Paolo Ferraris and Vladimir Lifschitz for their comments related to the subject of the paper; to Esra Erdem and Keijo Heljanko for providing us with the benchmarks; and to Francesco Calimeri for his support on DLV. This work is partially supported by ASI, MIUR and Texas Higher Education Coordinating Board under Grant 003658-0322-2001.


[1]http://www.cs.utexas.edu/users/tag/cmodels

where $A_0 \in P \cup \{\bot\}$ ($\bot$ is the logical symbol standing for *False*), and $\{A_1, \ldots, A_n\} \subseteq P$ ($0 \leq m \leq n$). $A_0$ is the *head* of the rule, $A_1, \ldots, A_m, not\ A_{m+1}, \ldots, not\ A_n$ is the *body*. A *(non disjunctive) logic program* is a finite set of rules.

In order to give the definition of an answer set we consider first the special case in which the program $\Pi$ does not contain the negation as failure operator $not$ (i.e. for each rule (1) in $\Pi$, $n = m$). Let $\Pi$ be such a program and let $X$ be a set of atoms. We say that $X$ is *closed* under $\Pi$ if for every rule (1) in $\Pi$, $A_0 \in X$ whenever $\{A_1, \ldots, A_m\} \subseteq X$. We say that $X$ is an *answer set* for $\Pi$ if $X$ is the smallest set closed under $\Pi$.

Now consider an arbitrary program $\Pi$. Let $X$ be a set of atoms. The *reduct* $\Pi^X$ of $\Pi$ relative to $X$ is the set of rules

$$A_0 \leftarrow A_1, \ldots, A_m$$

for all rules (1) in $\Pi$ such that $X \cap \{A_{m+1}, \ldots, A_n\} = \emptyset$. Thus $\Pi^X$ is a program without negation as failure. We say that $X$ is an *answer set* for $\Pi$ if $X$ is an answer set for $\Pi^X$.

Our next step is to introduce the relation between the answer sets of $\Pi$ and the models of its completion. In the following we represent an interpretation in the sense of propositional logic as the set of atoms *True* in it. With this convention a set of atoms $X$ can denote both an answer set and an interpretation.

If $A_0$ is an atom or the symbol $\bot$, the *completion of* $\Pi$ *relative to* $A_0$ is the formula

$$A_0 \equiv \bigvee (A_1 \wedge \cdots \wedge A_m \wedge \neg A_{m+1} \wedge \cdots \wedge \neg A_n)$$

where the disjunction extends over all rules (1) in $\Pi$ with head $A_0$. The *completion Comp*($\Pi$) of $\Pi$ consists of the formulas *Comp*($\Pi$, $A_0$), one for each symbol $A_0$ in $P \cup \{\bot\}$.

It is well known that if $X$ is an answer set of $\Pi$ then $X$ satisfies *Comp*($\Pi$) while the converse is not necessarily true. Lin and Zhao (2002) proved that to have a one-to-one correspondence between the answer sets of $\Pi$ and the models of its completion we have to consider the loop formulas of $\Pi$. To state this formally we need the following definitions.

The *dependency graph* of a program $\Pi$ is the directed graph $G$ such that the vertexes of $G$ are the atoms in $\Pi$, and $G$ has an edge from $A_0$ to $A_1, \ldots, A_m$ for each rule (1) in $\Pi$ with $A_0 \neq \bot$. A *loop* of $\Pi$ is a set $L$ of atoms such that for each pair $A, A'$ of atoms in $L$ there is a path from $A$ to $A'$ in the dependency graph of $\Pi$ whose intermediate nodes belong to $L$.

Given a loop $L$, we define $R(L)$ to be the set of formulas

$$A_1 \wedge \ldots \wedge A_m \wedge \neg A_{m+1} \wedge \ldots \wedge \neg A_n$$

for all rules (1) in $\Pi$, with $A_0 \in L$ and $\{A_1, \ldots, A_m\} \cap L = \emptyset$. The *loop formula associated with* $L$ is

$$\bigvee L \supset \bigvee R(L)$$

where $\bigvee L$ denotes the disjunction of the elements in $L$, and similarly for $\bigvee R(L)$. For instance, the only loop formula of the program $\{p \leftarrow p, p \leftarrow not\ q\}$ is $p \supset \neg q$.

**Proposition 1** *(Lin & Zhao 2002) Let* $\Pi$ *be a program, Comp*($\Pi$) *its completion, and* $LF(\Pi)$ *be the set of loop formulas associated with the loops in* $\Pi$*. For each set of atoms* $X$*,* $X$ *is an answer set of* $\Pi$ *iff* $X$ *is a model of Comp*($\Pi$) $\cup$ $LF(\Pi)$.

## SAT-Based Answer Set Solvers

Consider a program $\Pi$. Given Proposition 1 it is clear that if the dependency graph of $\Pi$ has no cycles (in this case we say that $\Pi$ is *tight*) then the models of *Comp*($\Pi$) are also answer sets of $\Pi$. Thus for tight programs answer set systems can use SAT solvers as "black-box" search engines. CMODELS used this approach to compute answer sets for tight programs.

If $\Pi$ is non tight, Lin and Zhao (2002) presented the following procedure $LZ(\Pi)$ which still uses SAT solver as black-boxes:

1. Compute *Comp*($\Pi$) and convert it to a set of clauses $\Gamma$.
2. Find a model $X$ of $\Gamma$ by using a SAT solver. Exit with failure if no such model exists.
3. Compute the set of atoms $X^- = X - Cons(\Pi^X)$, where $Cons(\Pi^X)$ is the set of atoms derivable from the reduct of $\Pi$ relative to $X$.
4. If $X^- = \emptyset$, then return $X$.
5. Otherwise, add the clauses corresponding to the loop formulas of all the maximal (under subset inclusion) loops in $X^-$ to $\Gamma$, and go to step 2.

$LZ(\Pi)$ either returns an answer set for $\Pi$, or failure if $\Pi$ does not have answer sets. In their article Lin and Zhao showed that ASSAT, a system implementing the above procedure, can outperform rival systems often by orders of magnitude. Still, $LZ(\Pi)$ has the following two drawbacks:

1. It is not guaranteed to work in polynomial space. In fact, $\Pi$ can have exponentially many loops: If we assume that each loop formula is not redundant (i.e., that it is not entailed by the rest of the formula under consideration), then
   - If $\Pi$ has an answer set then $LZ(\Pi)$ blows up in space in the worst case, while
   - If $\Pi$ has no answer set then $LZ(\Pi)$ is bound to blow up in space: In $LZ(\Pi)$ adding and keeping loop formulas is essential to guarantee that the SAT solver does not return previously computed models, and ultimately to guarantee ASSAT termination.
2. Considering two successive calls of the SAT solver, the computation done for finding the first model is completely discarded. Thus some branches of the search tree may get computed many times.

These drawbacks can be eliminated if we do not use a SAT solver as a black-box. Instead we can take advantage that state-of-the-art complete SAT solvers are based on the Davis-Logemann-Loveland procedure (DLL) (1962). The basic observation is that DLL can easily work as a SAT enumerator. We can thus compute *Comp*($\Pi$) and then

- *generate* models of *Comp*($\Pi$), and

```
DLL(Γ, S)
  if Γ = ∅ then return True;
  if ∅ ∈ Γ then return False;
  if {l} ∈ Γ then return DLL(assign(l, Γ), S ∪ {l});
  A := an atom occurring in Γ;
  return DLL(assign(A, Γ), S ∪ {A}) or
         DLL(assign(¬A, Γ), S ∪ {¬A}).
```

Figure 1: The DPLL procedure

- *test* whether the generated models are answer sets of $\Pi$.

Consider DLL as in Figure 1, where $l$ denotes a literal; $\Gamma$ a set of clauses; $S$ an *assignment*, i.e. a consistent set of literals. Given an atom $A$, $assign(A, \Gamma)$ is the set of clauses obtained from $\Gamma$ by removing the clauses to which $A$ belongs, and by removing $\neg A$ from the other clauses in $\Gamma$. $assign(\neg A, \Gamma)$ is defined similarly. In the initial call to DLL $\Gamma$ is the set of clauses of which we compute a model and $S$ is the empty set. DLL$(\Gamma, \emptyset)$ returns *True* whenever $\Gamma$ is satisfiable, and *False* otherwise.

Given DLL, we can obtain a SAT-based answer set generator for $\Pi$ by

1. Modifying the first line of DLL in the figure by substituting "**return** *True*" with "**return** *test*$(S, \Pi)$", a new function which
   - prints the set *atoms*$(S) = S \cap P$ and returns *True*, if *atoms*$(S)$ is an answer set of $\Pi$, and
   - returns *False*, otherwise.
2. Defining a function ASP-SAT$(\Pi)$, that calls DLL$(\Gamma, \emptyset)$ where $\Gamma$ is a set of clauses corresponding to *Comp*$(\Pi)$. $\Gamma$ can be computed in many ways. Here, our only assumptions are that $(i)$ $\Gamma$ signature extends $P$, and $(ii)$ for each set $X$ of atoms in $\Gamma$ signature, $X$ satisfies $\Gamma$ iff $X \cap P$ satisfies *Comp*$(\Pi)$. Standard conversion methods satisfy such conditions.

Notice that the set $S$ in *test*$(S, \Pi)$ may be non maximal wrt $P$, i.e., for some atom $A$ in $P$, both $A$ and $\neg A$ may not belong to $S$. Thus, $S \cup \{A\}$ entails *Comp*$(\Pi)$ and in principle we also need to check if *atoms*$(S \cup \{A\})$ is an answer set of $\Pi$. However, this additional check is not needed, as established by the following proposition.

**Proposition 2** *Let $\Pi$ be a program, $X$, $X'$ be two sets of atoms satisfying Comp$(\Pi)$. If $X \subset X'$ then $X'$ is not an answer set.*

From the above proposition, and the fact that each answer set is also a model of *Comp*$(\Pi)$ it follows the correctness and completeness of ASP-SAT$(\Pi)$.

**Proposition 3** *Given a program $\Pi$,* ASP-SAT$(\Pi)$ *returns True if and only if $\Pi$ has an answer set.*

Moreover ASP-SAT$(\Pi)$ $(i)$ performs the search on *Comp*$(\Pi)$ and thus does not introduce any extra variables except for those eventually needed by the clause form transformation; $(ii)$ is guaranteed to work in polynomial space; $(iii)$ can deal with both tight and non tight programs. Further,

- In the case of tight problems each generated model of *Comp*$(\Pi)$ corresponds to an answer set and thus ASP-SAT$(\Pi)$ behaves as a standard SAT solver run on *Comp*$(\Pi)$.
- ASP-SAT$(\Pi)$ can be easily modified for printing all the answer sets of $\Pi$: It is enough to modify *test*$(S, \Pi)$ in order to return *False* also when *atoms*$(S)$ is an answer set.

Compared to ASSAT, ASP-SAT is guaranteed to work in polynomial space and no computation is ever repeated, also when computing all answer sets. Compared to other answer set solvers like SMODELS and DLV, ASP-SAT has the advantage of being SAT-based and thus it can leverage on the great amount of knowledge available in SAT.

Still, most of the state-of-the-art SAT solvers based on DLL, e.g. MCHAFF (Moskewicz *et al.* 2001), use learning when backtracking. With learning, whenever *False* is returned, a "reason" for the failure has to be computed. Intuitively, a reason is a subset $S'$ of the assignment $S$ such that any assignment extending $S'$ will fail. In order to use SAT solvers with learning, it is thus not enough for *test*$(S, \Pi)$ to return *False* when $S$ is not an answer set. Indeed, it has also to compute a reason for such failure, i.e., a subset $S'$ of $S$ such that for any maximal assignment $S''$ $(i)$ extending $S'$ and $(ii)$ entailing *Comp*$(\Pi)$, *atoms*$(S'')$ is not an answer set of $\Pi$. One such set is $S$ itself. However in order to try to maximize the advantages of learning, it is important that $S'$ be as small as possible. Thus, for computing such $S'$, the *test*$(S, \Pi)$ procedure

1. computes the loop formulas associated with the loops in *atoms*$(S) - Cons(\Pi^{atoms(S)})$,
2. determines a subset of $S$ which falsifies one of the loop formulas computed in the previous step.

In our experiments, with such a simple procedure, we are able to compute reasons which are often less than 1% of the size of $S$. Of course, the above method for computing reasons, cannot be applied when returning *False* because the goal is to determine all the answer sets and *atoms*$(S)$ is an answer set. In this case, by Proposition 2, the set *atoms*$(S)$ can work as reason.

In the SAT literature, it is well known that learning can produce exponential speed-ups. We now show that ASP-SAT with learning and the method for computing reasons based on loop formulas, may invoke *test*$(S, \Pi)$ exponentially fewer times than ASP-SAT without learning.

Assume the program $\Pi$ consists of the two rules[2]

$$A_i \leftarrow A_{i+1} \qquad\qquad A_{i+1} \leftarrow A_i$$

for each $i \in \{0, 2, \ldots, 2k\}$. Then $Comp(\Pi)$ includes $A_i \equiv A_{i+1}$ $(i \in \{0, 2, \ldots, 2k\})$ and we can assume that its clausification $\Gamma$ consists of the two clauses $(\neg A_i \vee A_{i+1})$,$(A_i \vee \neg A_{i+1})$, for each $i \in \{0, 2, \ldots, 2k\}$. $\Gamma$ has $2^k$ models while the only answer set of $\Pi$ is the empty set:

[2]In this paragraph for simplicity we assume that the clauses corresponding to the reasons returned by *test*$(S, \Pi)$ are stored and never deleted.

- ASP-SAT without learning or with learning but in which *test*$(S, \Pi)$ computes *atoms*$(S)$ as reason when $S$ is not an answer set, may generate $2^k$ assignments entailing $Comp(\Pi)$.
- ASP-SAT with learning and in which *test*$(S, \Pi)$ computes as reason the subset of $S$ falsifying one of the loop formulas in *atoms*$(S) - Cons(\Pi^{atoms(S)})$, may generate at most $k$ assignments entailing $Comp(\Pi)$.

Still, for such a simple program, the generation and testing of $k$ assignments seems an overkill. Indeed, for programs $\Pi$ without negation as failure, we know that there exists exactly one answer set, $Cons(\Pi)$. For such programs, ASP-SAT can be easily tuned to directly compute such answer set by first assigning the atoms in $P$ to *False* while branching. It can be proved that with this modification and for programs $\Pi$ without negation as failure, the first invocation to *test*$(S, \Pi)$ has $S = Cons(\Pi)$.

## Integration in CMODELS

ASP-SAT was implemented on top of the SIMO system (Giunchiglia, Maratea, & Tacchella 2003) and integrated in CMODELS (Lierler & Maratea 2004) by the last two authors. SIMO is a MCHAFF-like SAT solver (Moskewicz *et al.* 2001), and features two-literal watching data structure, 1-UIP learning, and VSIDS heuristics. However, it does not feature the low level optimizations of MCHAFF and thus it is within a factor of 3 slower than MCHAFF. Our implementation of ASP-SAT incorporates all the techniques presented in previous section, including the idea to assign atoms first to *False* while branching.

Still, the integration of ASP-SAT in CMODELS posed some challenges related to CMODELS expressivity. CMODELS uses LPARSE as frontend and thus its input may contain cardinality expressions (also called "constraint literals" in LPARSE manual[3]) and choice rules, two constructs widely used in answer set programming.[4] Operationally CMODELS performs the following steps:

1. Simplifies the given LPARSE program performing preprocessing similar to those involved in SMODELS.
2. Eliminates cardinality expressions by introducing auxilary atoms and rules. Eliminates choice rules in favor of *nested expressions* in the sense of (Lifschitz, Tang, & Turner 1999). This is done using a procedure defined in (Ferraris & Lifschitz 2003).
3. Verifies that the resulting program with nested expressions is tight: the definition of tightness is generalized to such programs in (Erdem & Lifschitz 2003).
4. Forms the program's completion (see (Lloyd & Topor 1984) for the definition of completion of a program with nested expressions) and calls a SAT solver.

For CMODELS the integration implied calling ASP-SAT instead of the SAT solver. As for ASP-SAT we had to take into account that programs with nested expressions do not satisfy Proposition 2. For instance, the program

$$A \leftarrow not\ not\ A \quad (2)$$

(corresponding to the translation of the choice rule "$\{A\} \leftarrow$") has two answer sets: $\emptyset$, $\{A\}$. The violation of Proposition 2 implied two modifications in our procedure. Consider a program with nested expressions $\Pi$. When we are interested in computing all solutions, we have to guarantee that each set $S$ of literals in *test*$(S, \Pi)$ is maximal. Assuming that the input set of clauses is satisfiable, SIMO always returns maximal assignments but in the signature of the set of clauses resulting after SIMO preprocessing. However SIMO removes tautological clauses in the preprocessing. Tautological clauses can naturally arise during the completion process and removing them may cause the generation of non maximal (wrt the signature of the input program) assignments. By Proposition 2, this is not a problem if $\Pi$ does not have nested expressions; it may be a problem otherwise. For instance, the completion of the program (2) is $A \equiv \neg\neg A$. $(A \vee \neg A)$ is the tautological clause corresponding to this completion. After the preprocessing, the set of clauses corresponding to the program is empty, and ASP-SAT would not find the answer set $\{A\}$. Therefore, we modified ASP-SAT preprocessing in order to keep tautological clauses. The second modification involved the function *test*$(S, \Pi)$. It considers loop formulas as defined in (Lee & Lifschitz 2003) for nested programs. In the case *atoms*$(S)$ is an answer set and we are interested in finding all answer sets of $\Pi$, *test*$(S, \Pi)$ returns the entire set $S$ as a reason since any superset or subset of the atoms in $S$ may be an answer set of $\Pi$.

## Experimental Results

CMODELS2 was comparatively tested against other state-of-the-art systems on a variety of benchmarks. Some of the benchmarks we considered include cardinality constraints and choice rules, and will be called "extended". The systems we considered are SMODELS version 2.27, ASSAT version 1.52 running MCHAFF as SAT solver, DLV release of 2003-05-16. It worths remarking that while SMODELS, ASSAT and CMODELS2 use LPARSE as preprocessor, and thus can be run on the same problems, DLV does not. This explains why DLV appears only in few tables. Further, ASSAT cannot deal with extended programs. Finally, for DLV we have to mention that it is a system specifically designed for disjunctive logic programs, and that very different results can be obtained depending on the specific encoding being used.

All the tests were run on a Pentium IV PC, with 1.8GHz processor, 512MB RAM DDR 266MHz, running Linux. For SMODELS, ASSAT and CMODELS2, the time taken by LPARSE is not counted.[5] Further, each system was stopped after 3600 seconds of CPU time on an instance, or when it exceeded all the available memory: In the tables, these cases

[3]http://www.tcs.hut.fi/Software/smodels/lparse.ps.gz

[4]The input can also contain general weight expressions ("weight literals") However, optimize statements (see LPARSE manual) are not allowed.

[5]Adding the times of LPARSE will not change the picture for DLV when compared to CMODELS2.

| #b | #s | Standard programs | | | Extended programs | |
|---|---|---|---|---|---|---|
| | | SMODELS | ASSAT | CMODELS2 | SMODELS | CMODELS2 |
| 8 | i-1 | 12.32 | 0.80 | 1.19 | 0.81 | 0.47 |
| 11 | i-1 | 71.78 | 2.97 | 4.19 | 2.97 | 1.01 |
| 8 | i | 40.87 | 0.89 | 2.18 | 1.56 | 1.40 |
| 11 | i | 71.42 | 3.17 | 4.52 | 3.41 | 1.16 |
| 8 | i+1 | 23.35 | 0.96 | 0.97 | 4.99 | 0.31 |
| 11 | i+1 | 107.48 | 3.54 | 3.33 | 5.21 | 0.75 |

Table 1: Blocks world: "#b" is the number of blocks.

are denoted with "TIME" and "MEM" respectively. Otherwise, the tables report the CPU times in seconds needed by each solver to solve the problem, or a "–" to denote an abnormal exit of the program.

We start our analysis considering blocks world planning problems, encoded as both standard and extended logic programs, the latter formulation due to Erdem (2002). The results are represented in Table 1. In the table, $(i)$ the column "#b" represents the number of blocks; $(ii)$ an "$i$" in the "#s" (standing for "number of steps") column means that the instance corresponds to the problem of finding a plan in "$i$" steps, where "$i$" is the minimum integer for which a plan exists. Thus, the instances with "$i$" and "$i+1$" in the "#s" column admit at least one answer set, while those with "$i-1$" do not have answer sets. These blocks world problems are tight on their completion models (Babovich, Erdem, & Lifschitz 2000), and thus every model of the completion corresponds to an answer set. As it could be expected, SAT-based systems like ASSAT and CMODELS2 perform (sometimes significantly) better than SMODELS, both on standard and extended programs. On standard programs ASSAT performs slightly better than CMODELS2, and this corresponds to the fact that, on average, MCHAFF is better than SIMO.

We also considered Hamiltonian circuit problems on complete graphs, using both the standard encoding of Niemela (1999), and the extended encoding in the "benchmark problems for answer set programming systems"[6]. These problems are particularly interesting because they are non tight and have exponentially many loops. Thus, one would expect these problems to be difficult for ASSAT, but also for CMODELS2 in the case it will generate and then reject (exponentially) many candidate answer sets. The results are in Table 2. As can be observed, on this test set CMODELS2 performs best, being faster (sometimes by orders of magnitude) than all the other solvers both on standard and extended programs.

The problems in Table 3 are real-world non tight problem related to checking requirements in a deterministic automaton, and are described in (Ştefănescu, Esparza, & Muscholl 2003).[7] Two types of problems are considered and encoded in logic programs. The first type is called IDFD and the results on such problems are reported in the first two rows of the table. The second type of problem is called "Morin", and the results are shown on the last three rows. As can be seen,

[6]http://www.cs.engr.uky.edu/ai/benchmark-suite/ham-cyc.sm

[7]These benchmarks are available at http://www.fmi.uni-stuttgart.de/szs/research/projects/synthesis/benchmarks030923.html

| | Standard programs | | | | Extended programs | |
|---|---|---|---|---|---|---|
| | SMODELS | ASSAT | DLV | CMOD2 | SMODELS | CMOD2 |
| np30c | 11.70 | 1.14 | 22.08 | 0.69 | 0.36 | 0.36 |
| np40c | 62.89 | 41.81 | 97.96 | 1.63 | 2.48 | 0.87 |
| np50c | 219.56 | 14.51 | 314.46 | 3.37 | 8.39 | 1.79 |
| np60c | 594.46 | 48.80 | 770.07 | 5.81 | 20.47 | 3.41 |
| np70c | 1323.61 | 291.60 | 1679.12 | 8.22 | 39.41 | 5.87 |
| np80c | 2354.28 | 32.51 | 3407.35 | 14.20 | 75.36 | 9.18 |
| np90c | TIME | 779.06 | TIME | 22.23 | 122.53 | 14.19 |
| np100c | TIME | – | TIME | 28.63 | 185.52 | 20.76 |
| np120c | TIME | – | TIME | 53.33 | 418.15 | 41.84 |

Table 2: Complete graphs. npXc corresponds to a graph with "X" nodes. CMOD2 is CMODELS2

| | SMODELS | ASSAT | DLV | CMODELS2 |
|---|---|---|---|---|
| mutex4 | 33.92 | (0)0.62 | 840.60 | (0)0.68 |
| phi4 | 0.24 | (168)2.98 | 1.44 | TIME |
| mutex2 | 0.09 | (88)1.78 | | (0)0.12 |
| mutex3 | 229.57 | MEM | | (0)24.16 |
| phi3 | 2.87 | (704)236.91 | | (57)3.91 |

Table 3: Checking requirements in a deterministic automaton. DLV was not run on the last 3 instances.

CMODELS2 times out on one instance that is easily solved by all the other solvers. This is due to the dimension of the related propositional formula. On the other hand, for any other solver, there are one/two instances on which CMODELS is at least 1 order of magnitude faster. Interestingly, ASSAT blows up in memory on one instance (and also on other instances, on which the other systems time out).

Non tight, extended real-world problems corresponding to the bounded model checking (BMC) of asynchronous concurrent systems (see (Heljanko & Niemelä 2003))[8] are shown in Table 4. As for the blocks world, these problems are about proving a certain property in a given number of steps, represented as the last number in the instance name. The problems in the first five rows do not have answer sets, while the remaining (obtained by incrementing the number of steps) do. Here the results are mixed, and sometimes CMODELS2 performs much worse than SMODELS. On these problems, our standard heuristic is not well suited. Given a program $\Pi$, by changing the heuristic in order to

- first assign the atoms occurring within the negation as failure operator, the order and sign of such atoms determined as in SIMO, and
- then assign the remaining atoms first to *False*, the order determined as in SIMO,

we get the better figures represented in the last column, under the label CMODELS'. The idea behind this heuristic is that we should first get to a set of clauses corresponding to a program $\Pi$ without negation as failure, and then we should try to satisfy the remaining set of clauses by assigning the fewest possible atoms to true.

Summing up, the 4 tables show the performances on 45 problems. If for the Table 4 we consider the results in the

[8]http://www.tcs.hut.fi/~kepa/experiments/boundsmodels/

| BMC | SMODELS | CMODELS2 | CMODELS2' |
|---|---|---|---|
| dp-10.i-02-b11 | 382.72 | 1476.72 | 442.14 |
| dp-10.s-02-b8 | 15.24 | 8.20 | 14.22 |
| dp-12.s-O2-b9 | 336.03 | 65.41 | 137.34 |
| dp-8.i-O2-b9 | 8.08 | 12.62 | 10.69 |
| dp-8.s-O2-b7 | 1.19 | 1.02 | 2.28 |
| dp-10.i-O2-b12 | 445.47 | 3295.72 | 163.15 |
| dp-10.s-O2-b9 | 28.87 | 16.07 | 15.08 |
| dp-12.s-O2-b10 | 971.50 | 209.29 | 46.51 |
| dp-8.i-O2-b10 | 5.05 | 40.01 | 6.44 |
| dp-8.s-O2-b8 | 1.76 | 1.99 | 2.03 |

Table 4: Bounded Model Checking Problems.

last column, CMODELS2

- times out on 1 problem, while the other systems do not conclude on at least 3 problems;
- performs better than all the three solvers on 30 problems, and on 26 it has at least a factor of 2; and,
- except for the problem on which it times out, CMODELS2 is either the top performer or within a factor of 2 from it.

We also considered the problem of generating all the answer sets. Here the results are less in favor to CMODELS2 when compared to SMODELS, especially on extended programs. We believe this is because of the very naive way in which reasons are computed by $test(S, \Pi)$, especially when $atoms(S)$ is an answer set.

## Conclusions

We have presented a SAT-based procedure that $(i)$ can deal with any logic program $(ii)$ works on a SAT formula without additional variables, $(iii)$ is guaranteed to work in polynomial space. Further, we have evidenced that ASP-SAT can be easily modified in order to generate all the answer sets. We have shown how to implement ASP-SAT on top of a MCHAFF-like solver, and discussed the modifications needed in the case of extended programs. The experimental evaluation shows that CMODELS2, can have a significant edge over other state-of-the-art systems. Still, we believe that there is a lot of space for improvements, especially in the heuristics, and in the way reasons are computed.

Finally, we believe that ASP-SAT helps in closing the algorithmic gap between answer set and SAT solvers, with beneficial results especially for the former, given the very advanced state of development of the latter.

## References


Babovich, Y.; Erdem, E.; and Lifschitz, V. 2000. Fages' theorem and answer set programming. In *Proc. NMR*.

Ben-Eliyahu, R., and Dechter, R. 1996. Propositional semantics for disjunctive logic programs. *Annals of Mathematics and Artificial Intelligence* 12:53–87.

Clark, K. 1978. Negation as failure. In Gallaire, H., and Minker, J., eds., *Logic and Data Bases*. NY: Plenum Press. 293–322.

Ştefănescu, A.; Esparza, J.; and Muscholl, A. 2003. Synthesis of distributed algorithms using asynchronous automata. In *Proc. of CONCUR*, LNCS 2761.

Davis, M.; Logemann, G.; and Loveland, D. 1962. A machine program for theorem proving. *JACM* 5(7).

Eiter, T.; Leone, N.; Mateis, C.; Pfeifer, G.; and Scarcello, F. 1998. The KR system dlv: Progress report, comparisons and benchmarks. In *Proc. KR*.

Erdem, E., and Lifschitz, V. 2003. Tight logic programs. *Theory and Practice of Logic Programming*, 3:499–518.

Erdem, E. 2002. *Theory and applications of answer set programming*. Ph.D. Dissertation, UT at Austin.

Fages, F. 1994. Consistency of Clark's completion and existence of stable models. *Journal of Methods of Logic in Computer Science* 1:51–60.

Ferraris, P., and Lifschitz, V. 2003. Weight constraints as nested expressions. *Theory and Practice of Logic Programming*. To appear.

Giunchiglia, E.; Maratea, M.; and Tacchella, A. 2003. (In)Effectiveness of look-ahead techniques in a modern SAT solver. In *Proc. CP*, LNCS 2833.

Heljanko, K., and Niemelä, I. 2003. Bounded LTL model checking with stable models. *Theory and Practice of Logic Programming* 3(4&5):519–550.

Lee, J., and Lifschitz, V.. 2003. Loop formulas for disjunctive logic programs. In *Proc. ICLP*.

Lierler, Y., and Maratea, M. 2004. Cmodels-2: SAT-Based Answer Set Solver Enhanced to Non-tight Programs. In *Proc. LPNMR*, 346–350.

Lifschitz, V.; Tang, L. R.; and Turner, H. 1999. Nested expressions in logic programs. *Annals of Mathematics and Artificial Intelligence* 25:369–389.

Lifschitz, V. 1996. Foundations of logic programming. In Brewka, G., ed., *Principles of Knowledge Representation*. CSLI Publications. 69–128.

Lin, F., and Zhao, Y. 2002. ASSAT: Computing answer sets of a logic program by SAT solvers. In *Proc. AAAI*.

Lloyd, J., and Topor, R. 1984. Making Prolog more expressive. *Journal of Logic Programming* 3:225–240.

Moskewicz, M. W.; Madigan, C. F.; Zhao, Y.; Zhang, L.; and Malik, S. 2001. Chaff: Engineering an Efficient SAT Solver. In *Proc. DAC*.

Niemelä, I. 1999. Logic programs with stable model semantics as a constraint programming paradigm. *Annals of Mathematics and Artificial Intelligence* 25:241–273.

Janhunen, T. 2003 A counter-based approach to translating normal logic programs into sets of clauses. *Proc. ASP'03 Workshop*, pp. 166–180.

Simons, P. 2000. Extending and implementing the stable model semantics. In *Doctoral dissertation*, 305–316.

# A Polynomial-time Algorithm for Simple Temporal Problems with Piecewise Constant Domain Preference Functions

**T. K. Satish Kumar**
Knowledge Systems Laboratory
Stanford University
tksk@ksl.stanford.edu

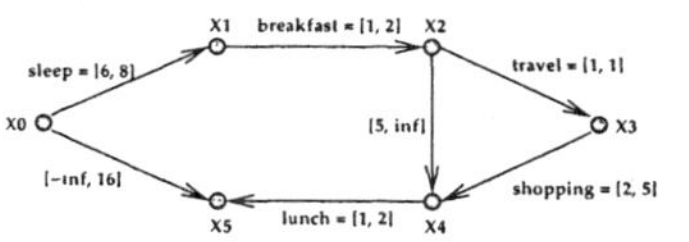


Figure 1: Shows an example of the kind of reasoning possible in STPs. The figure is about an agent who should find a schedule for her day's events that satisfies various constraints (indicated by temporal bounds on the edges). Assuming that $X_0$ corresponds to 12:00 a.m., the agent is allowed to sleep between 6 and 8 hours, have breakfast between 1 and 2 hours, travel to the market for an hour, shop there between 2 and 5 hours, and have lunch between 1 and 2 hours. Further, she should finish having lunch before 4:00 p.m. and should wait for at least 5 hours between having breakfast and having lunch.

## Abstract

In this paper, we provide a polynomial-time algorithm for solving an important class of metric temporal problems that involve simple temporal constraints between various events (variables) and piecewise constant preference functions over variable domains. We are given a graph $\mathcal{G} = \langle \mathcal{X}, \mathcal{E} \rangle$ where $\mathcal{X} = \{X_0, X_1 \ldots X_n\}$ is a set of events ($X_0$ is the "beginning of the world" node and is set to 0 by convention) and $e = \langle X_i, X_j \rangle \in \mathcal{E}$, annotated with the bounds $[LB(e), UB(e)]$, is a simple temporal constraint between $X_i$ and $X_j$ indicating that $X_j$ must be scheduled between $LB(e)$ and $UB(e)$ seconds after $X_i$ is scheduled ($LB(e) \leq UB(e)$). A family of stepwise constant preference functions $\mathcal{F} = \{f_{X_i}(t) : \mathcal{R} \rightarrow \mathcal{R}\}$ specifies the preference attached with scheduling $X_i$ at time $t$. The goal is to find a schedule for all the events such that all the temporal constraints are satisfied and the sum of the preferences is maximized. Our polynomial-time algorithm for solving such problems (which we refer to as extended simple temporal problems (ESTPs)) has important consequences in dealing with limited forms of disjunctions and preferences in metric temporal reasoning that would otherwise require an exponential search space.

## Introduction

Expressive and efficient temporal reasoning is central to many areas of Artificial Intelligence (AI). Several tasks in planning and scheduling for example, involve reasoning about temporal constraints between actions and propositions in partial plans (see (Nguyen and Kambhampati 2001) and (Smith *et al.* 2000)). These tasks may include threat resolution between actions in partial order planning, analyzing resource consumption envelopes to guide the search for a good plan (see (Kumar 2003)) etc. Among the important formalisms used for reasoning with metric time are simple temporal problems (STPs) and disjunctive temporal problems (DTPs) (see (Stergiou and Koubarakis 1998) and (Oddi and Cesta 2000)). Unlike DTPs, STPs can be solved in polynomial time, but are not as expressive as DTPs.



An STP is characterized by a graph $\mathcal{G} = \langle \mathcal{X}, \mathcal{E} \rangle$ where $\mathcal{X} = \{X_0, X_1 \ldots X_n\}$ is a set of events ($X_0$ is the "beginning of the world" node and is set to 0 by convention) and $e = \langle X_i, X_j \rangle \in \mathcal{E}$, annotated with the bounds $[LB(e), UB(e)]$, is a simple temporal constraint between $X_i$ and $X_j$ indicating that $X_j$ must be scheduled between $LB(e)$ and $UB(e)$ seconds after $X_i$ is scheduled ($LB(e) \leq UB(e)$). Figure 1 shows an example of an STP which (like all other instances of the class) can be solved in polynomial time using shortest paths (see (Dechter *et al.* 1991)).

DTPs are significantly more expressive than STPs and allow for disjunctive constraints. The general form of a DTP is as follows. We are given a set of events $\mathcal{X} = \{X_0, X_1 \ldots X_n\}$ ($X_0$ is the "beginning of the world" node and is set to 0 by convention) and a set of constraints $\mathcal{C}$. A constraint $c \in \mathcal{C}$ is a disjunction of simple temporal constraints of the form $s_1 \vee s_2 \ldots s_k$. Here, $s_i$ ($1 \leq i \leq k$) is a simple temporal constraint of the form $l \leq X_b - X_a \leq u$ for $0 \leq a, b \leq n$. Figure 2 shows an example of a DTP which expresses disjunctive constraints.

Although DTPs are expressive enough to capture many tasks in planning and scheduling (like threat resolution and plan merging), they require an exponential search space. The principal approach taken to solve DTPs has been to convert the original problem to one of selecting one disjunct from each constraint and then checking that the set of selected disjuncts forms a consistent STP. Checking the

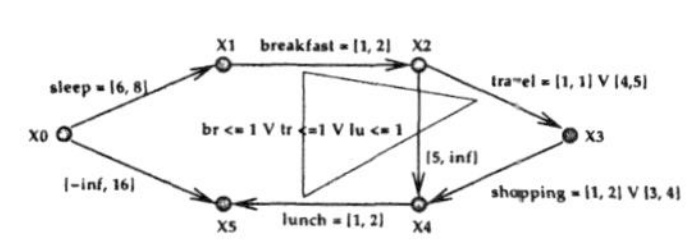


Figure 2: Shows an example of the kind of reasoning possible in DTPs. The scenario is very similar to the that in Figure 1 except that it includes disjunctive constraints like having a travel time between 4 and 5 hours (by walk) or exactly for one hour (by bus), shopping between 1 and 2 hours or 3 and 4 hours, and restricting time spent on at least one of breakfast, lunch or travel time to within an hour.

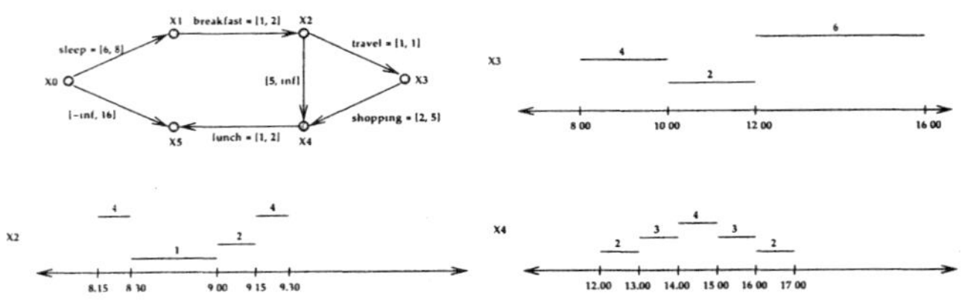

Figure 3: Shows an example of the kind of reasoning allowed by ESTPs. The situation is very similar to that in Figure 1, except that there are preferences attached with various events. If the agent reaches the bus stop between 8:15 a.m. and 8:30 a.m. or between 9:15 a.m. and 9:30 a.m., the buses are readily available and the preference for these intervals is high. Reaching the bus station between 8:30 a.m. and 9:00 a.m. means that she has to wait for at least 15 minutes and therefore has a low preference. Reaching between 9:00 a.m. and 9:15 a.m. means a lower waiting time, and has a slightly higher preference. Similarly if the agent starts shopping early in the morning, the preference is high, it is low during the peak period between 10:00 a.m. and 12:00 a.m. and high again during the non-peak period 12:00 p.m. to 4:00 p.m. Again, for health reasons, starting to have lunch between 2:00 p.m. and 3:00 p.m. is the optimal for the agent and the later the worse beyond 3:00 p.m., and the earlier the worse before 2:00 p.m.

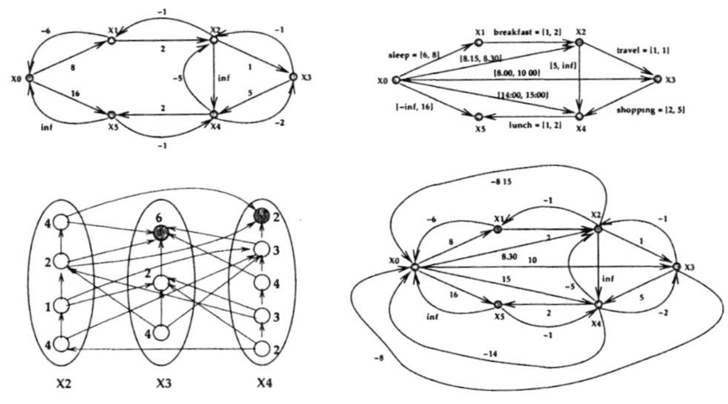

Figure 4: Illustrates how an ESTP (as shown in Figure 3) can be converted to the computation of the largest weighted anti-chain in a POSET. The figure shows the distance graph associated with the temporal constraints to the top-left, and the POSET associated with the size-2 conflicts between various intervals to the bottom-left. The weights on the nodes of the POSET correspond to the preference attached with the respective intervals, the size-2 conflicts are represented by arrows and the size-1 conflicts are represented by dark circles. The top-right figure shows the STP resulting out of replacing the domain preferences with the simple temporal constraints corresponding to the largest weighted anti-chain, and the bottom-right figure shows the corresponding distance graph which is assured of not containing any negative cycle.

consistency of and finding a solution to an STP can be performed in polynomial time using shortest path algorithms (see (Dechter *et al.* 1991)). The computational complexity of solving a DTP comes from the fact that there are an exponentially large number of disjunct combinations possible. The disjunct selection problem can also be cast as a constraint satisfaction problem (CSP) (see (Stergiou and Koubarakis 1998) and (Oddi and Cesta 2000)) or a satisfiability problem (SAT) (see (Armando *et al.* 2000)) and solved using standard search techniques applicable for them. Epilitis is a systems that efficiently solves DTPs using CSP search techniques like conflict-directed backjumping and nogood recording (see (Tsamardinos and Pollack 2003)).

In this paper, we describe a middle ground between STPs and DTPs (which we refer to as extended STPs (ESTPs)) that can deal with limited forms of disjunctions and preferences, and can also be solved in polynomial time. The expressive power of ESTPs along with their tractability makes them a suitable model for many real-life applications. An ESTP is characterized by a graph $\mathcal{G} = \langle \mathcal{X}, \mathcal{E} \rangle$ where $\mathcal{X} = \{X_0, X_1 \dots X_n\}$ is a set of events ($X_0$ is the "beginning of the world" node and is set to 0 by convention) and $e = \langle X_i, X_j \rangle \in \mathcal{E}$, annotated with the bounds $[LB(e), UB(e)]$, is a simple temporal constraint between $X_i$ and $X_j$ indicating that $X_j$ must be scheduled between $LB(e)$ and $UB(e)$ seconds after $X_i$ is scheduled ($LB(e) \leq UB(e)$). A family of stepwise constant preference functions $\mathcal{F} = \{f_{X_i}(t) : \mathcal{R} \rightarrow \mathcal{R}\}$ specifies the preference attached with scheduling $X_i$ at time $t$. The goal is to find a schedule for all the events such that all the temporal constraints are satisfied and the sum of the preferences is maximized. Figure 3 shows an example of an ESTP.

We present a polynomial-time algorithm for solving ESTPs by reducing a given ESTP to the problem of computing the largest weighted anti-chain in a POSET (partially ordered set) which in turn can be solved using *maxflow* techniques. Our algorithm has important consequences in the context of metric temporal reasoning and dealing with limited forms of disjunctions and preferences that would otherwise require an exponential search space. We note again that the disjunctions and preferences are associated only with scheduling individual events at time $t$, and not with the relative time difference between two events. The latter problem has been shown to be tractable when one wants to maximize the minimum preference value, and all the preference functions are known to be concave (see (Khatib *et al.* 2001)).[1] In general, the fact that the disjunctions and/or preference functions allow only one argument does not allow encoding of a general DTP as an ESTP.

## Solving ESTPs: Reduction to Largest Weighted Anti-Chain Computation

We will present a polynomial-time algorithm for solving ESTPs by reducing a given ESTP to the problem of computing the largest weighted anti-chain in a POSET. We will use the following notation.

**Notation.** Let the landmarks in the domain of $X_i$, for which the piecewise constant function $f_{X_i}(t)$ is defined, be $d_{i,1}, d_{i,2} \dots d_{i,T(i)}$. Let $I_{i,1}, I_{i,2} \dots I_{i,T(i)+1}$ be intervals defined as follows: $I_{i,1} = (-\infty, d_{i,1}]$, $I_{i,k} = (d_{i,k-1}, d_{i,k}]$ for $2 \leq k \leq T(i)$ and $I_{i,T(i)+1} = (d_{i,T(i)}, +\infty]$. Let $L((a,b]) = a$ and $R((a,b]) = b$. Let the preference associated with scheduling variable $X_i$ at any time $t \in I_{i,k}$ be denoted by $f_{X_i}(I_{i,k})$.

### Solving Zero-One ESTPs

We will first deal with the case where $f_{X_i}(I_{i,k})$ is restricted to be either 0 or 1 (referred to as zero-one ESTPs). Figure 5 shows the procedure for solving zero-one ESTPs. We note that disjunctions limited only to the domains of variables can be encoded using zero-one ESTPs, and can therefore be solved in polynomial time.

**Lemma 1:** A consistent schedule exists for $X_0, X_1 \dots X_n$ (disregarding the preference functions) in $\mathcal{G} = \langle \mathcal{X}, \mathcal{E} \rangle$ if and only if the distance graph $D(\mathcal{G})$ does not contain any negative cycles (see Figure 5).

**Proof:** see (Dechter *et al.* 1991).

[1] Optimizing the sum of preference values (with the preference functions still remaining concave) is an open problem.

**ALGORITHM:** SOLVE-ZERO-ONE-ESTP
**INPUT:** An instance $\mathcal{G} = \langle \mathcal{X}, \mathcal{E} \rangle$ of the ESTP with $f_{X_i}(I_{i,k}) = 0$ or 1.
**OUTPUT:** A flexible consistent schedule $s$ with only simple temporal constraints that solves $\mathcal{G}$.
(1) Construct the distance graph $D(\mathcal{G})$ on $X_0, X_1 \ldots X_n$ with every edge $e = \langle X_i, X_j \rangle$ in $\mathcal{E}$ compiled to two edges: $\langle X_i, X_j \rangle$ annotated with $UB(e)$, and $\langle X_j, X_i \rangle$ annotated with $-LB(e)$.
(2) Let $dist(X_a, X_b)$ denote the shortest distance from $X_a$ to $X_b$ in $D(\mathcal{G})$.
(3) For every pair of intervals $I_{i,k_1}$ and $I_{j,k_2}$:
(a) Construct a (directed) size-2 conflict from $I_{i,k_1}$ to $I_{j,k_2}$ (denoted $I_{i,k_1} \rightarrow I_{j,k_2}$) if and only if $R(I_{i,k_1}) + dist(X_i, X_j) - L(I_{j,k_2}) < 0$.
(4) Construct a node-weighted directed graph $P(\mathcal{G})$ as follows:
(a) The nodes of $P(\mathcal{G})$ correspond to the intervals.
(b) Remove all nodes that correspond to size-1 conflicts i.e. remove $I_{i,k}$ from $P(\mathcal{G})$ if $dist(X_i, X_0) + R(I_{i,k}) < 0$ or $dist(X_0, X_i) - L(I_{i,k}) < 0$.
(c) The weight on a node corresponding to interval $I_{i,k}$ is equal to $f_{X_i}(I_{i,k})$.
(d) A directed edge $\langle I_{i,k_1}, I_{j,k_2} \rangle$ in $P(\mathcal{G})$ encodes a size-2 conflict $I_{i,k_1} \rightarrow I_{j,k_2}$.
(5) Compute $Q = \{I_{q_1}, I_{q_2} \ldots I_{q_k}\}$ as the largest weighted anti-chain in $P(\mathcal{G})$.
(6) RETURN:
(a) 'inconsistency' if $|Q| < n$.
(b) $s = D(\mathcal{G}) \cup \{\langle X_0, X_i \rangle$ annotated with $R(I_{i,k_1})$ and $\langle X_i, X_0 \rangle$ annotated with $-L(I_{i,k_1}) | I_{i,k_1} \in Q\}$.
**END** ALGORITHM

Figure 5: A polynomial-time algorithm for solving zero-one ESTPs.

**Lemma 2:** Ensuring that variable $X_i$ takes a value in the interval $I_{i,k}$ requires the addition of the edges $\langle X_0, X_i \rangle$ annotated with $R(I_{i,k})$ and $\langle X_i, X_0 \rangle$ annotated with $-L(I_{i,k})$ to the distance graph without creating a negative cycle.
**Proof:** If we have to ensure that the variable $X_i$ is in the interval $I_{i,k}$—i.e. between $L(I_{i,k})$ and $R(I_{i,k})$, we have to make sure that $X_i - X_0 \leq R(I_{i,k})$ and $X_i - X_0 \geq L(I_{i,k})$. Retaining the semantics of the distance graph (where the constraint $X_j - X_i \leq w$ is specified by the edge $\langle X_i, X_j \rangle$ annotated with $w$), this corresponds to the addition of the edges $\langle X_0, X_i \rangle$ annotated with $R(I_{i,k})$ and $\langle X_i, X_0 \rangle$ annotated with $-L(I_{i,k})$ to the distance graph without creating an inconsistency (which by the previous Lemma is characterized by the presence of a negative cycle).
**Definition 1:** We say that an interval $I_{i,k}$ is active if we ensure that the variable $X_i$ takes a value in the interval $I_{i,k}$ by successfully adding the edges $\langle X_0, X_i \rangle$ annotated with $R(I_{i,k})$ and $\langle X_i, X_0 \rangle$ annotated with $-L(I_{i,k})$ to the distance graph.
**Lemma 3:** At most one interval can be activated for every variable.
**Proof:** Consider any variable $X_i$ and two of its intervals $I_{i,k_1}$ and $I_{i,k_2}$, assuming without loss of generality that $R(I_{i,k_1}) \leq L(I_{i,k_2})$. Activating both these intervals would require the addition of the following edges to the distance graph: $\langle X_0, X_i \rangle$ annotated with $R(I_{i,k_1})$, $\langle X_i, X_0 \rangle$ annotated with $-L(I_{i,k_1})$, $\langle X_0, X_i \rangle$ annotated with $R(I_{i,k_2})$ and $\langle X_i, X_0 \rangle$ annotated with $-L(I_{i,k_2})$. This creates the negative cycle $\langle X_0, X_i \rangle$ annotated with $R(I_{i,k_1})$ and $\langle X_i, X_0 \rangle$ annotated with $-L(I_{i,k_2})$, hence establishing the truth of the Lemma.
**Lemma 4:** An ESTP $\mathcal{G}$ is consistent if and only if exactly one interval for all variables can be made active simultaneously.
**Proof:** Suppose exactly one interval for each variable can be made active simultaneously. This means that there is no negative cycle in the resulting distance graph and by Lemma 1, a consistent schedule for $\mathcal{G}$ can be found. Conversely, let $s = \{X_1 = x_1, X_2 = x_2 \ldots X_n = x_n\}$ be a consistent schedule for $\mathcal{G}$. By definition, this means that the distance graph resulting out of adding the edges $\langle X_0, X_i \rangle$ annotated with $x_i$ and $\langle X_i, X_0 \rangle$ annotated with $-x_i$ (for all $1 \leq i \leq n$) does not contain any negative cycles. Let $I_{i,k_i}$ be the interval containing $x_i$ for variable $X_i$. Clearly, $L(I_{i,k_i}) \leq x_i$ and $x_i \leq R(I_{i,k_i})$. This means that the addition of the edges $\langle X_0, X_i \rangle$ annotated with $R(I_{i,k_i})$ and $\langle X_i, X_0 \rangle$ annotated with $-L(I_{i,k_i})$ (for all $1 \leq i \leq n$) instead of $x_i$ and $-x_i$ respectively also does not contain any negative cost cycles (since the weights of edges are only increased). The truth of the Lemma then follows from the fact that the addition of these edges corresponds to the activation of these intervals (Lemma 2) and that at most one interval can be activated for any variable (Lemma 3).
**Definition 2:** A conflict is a set of intervals all of which cannot be made simultaneously active. A minimal conflict is a conflict no proper subset of which is also a conflict.
**Lemma 5:** A set of intervals can be made simultaneously active if and only if there is no subset of them that constitutes a minimal conflict.
**Proof:** By the definition of a conflict, a set of intervals can be made simultaneously active if and only if there is no subset of them that constitutes a conflict. Further, the truth of the Lemma follows from the fact that there exists a subset of actions that constitutes a conflict if and only if there exists a subset of intervals that constitutes a minimal conflict.
**Lemma 6:** The size of a minimal conflict is $\leq 2$.
**Proof:** Suppose we try to activate the set of intervals $I_{i_1,k_1}, I_{i_2,k_2} \ldots I_{i_h,k_h}$. This would involve the addition of the following edges to the distance graph without creating a negative cycle: $\langle X_0, X_{i_p} \rangle$ annotated with $R(I_{i_p,k_p})$ and $\langle X_{i_p}, X_0 \rangle$ annotated with $-L(I_{i_p,k_p})$ for all $1 \leq p \leq h$. We refer to these edges as "special" edges. If a negative cycle is created in our attempt to activate these intervals, it must involve one of the "special" edges. Further, since all "special" edges have $X_0$ as an end point, the negative cycle must contain $X_0$. This also means that the cycle can involve at most 2 "special" edges. Since these "special" edges correspond to the activation of intervals, the size of a minimal conflict is $\leq 2$.
**Lemma 7:** An interval $I_{i,k}$ constitutes a size-1 conflict if $-L(I_{i,k}) + dist(X_0, X_i) < 0$ or $R(I_{i,k}) + dist(X_i, X_0) < 0$.
**Proof:** Continuing the arguments of the previous Lemma, a size-1 conflict contains exactly one "special" edge. In the case that this edge is "incoming" to $X_0$ (say $\langle X_i, X_0 \rangle$ annotated with $-L(I_{i,k})$ for the interval $I_{i,k}$), the negative cycle must be $-L(I_{i,k}) + dist(X_0, X_i)$. In the case that

this edge is "outgoing" from $X_0$ (say $\langle X_0, X_i \rangle$ annotated with $R(I_{i,k})$ for the interval $I_{i,k}$), the negative cycle must be $R(I_{i,k}) + dist(X_i, X_0)$.

**Lemma 8:** The two intervals $I_{i,k_1}$ and $I_{j,k_2}$ constitute a directed size-2 conflict (denoted $I_{i,k_1} \rightarrow I_{j,k_2}$) when $R(I_{i,k_1}) + dist(X_i, X_j) - L(I_{j,k_2}) < 0$.

**Proof:** Continuing the arguments in the proof of the previous two Lemmas, a size-2 conflict involves exactly one incoming "special" edge (say $\langle X_j, X_0 \rangle$ annotated with $-L(I_{j,k_2})$ and exactly one outgoing "special" edge (say $\langle X_0, X_i \rangle$ annotated with $R(I_{i,k_1})$. The weight of the negative cycle created is then $R(I_{i,k_1}) + dist(X_i, X_j) - L(I_{j,k_2})$ as required.

**Lemma 9:** The size-2 conflicts are transitive.

**Proof:** Suppose we have the two directed conflicts $I_{i,k_1} \rightarrow I_{j,k_2}$ and $I_{j,k_2} \rightarrow I_{l,k_3}$. We have to show that $I_{i,k_1} \rightarrow I_{l,k_3}$ is also true. From the previous Lemma we know that $R(I_{i,k_1}) + dist(X_i, X_j) - L(I_{j,k_2}) < 0$ and $R(I_{j,k_2}) + dist(X_j, X_l) - L(I_{l,k_3}) < 0$. Adding the two inequalities and noting that $dist(X_i, X_l) \leq dist(X_i, X_j) + dist(X_j, X_l)$, we have that $R(I_{i,k_1}) + dist(X_i, X_l) - L(I_{j,k_2}) + R(I_{j,k_2}) - L(I_{l,k_3}) < 0$. Further, since $R(I_{j,k_2}) \geq L(I_{j,k_2})$, we have that $R(I_{i,k_1}) + dist(X_i, X_l) - L(I_{l,k_3}) < 0$. This establishes that $I_{i,k_1} \rightarrow I_{l,k_3}$ as required.

**Lemma 10:** The size-2 conflicts are acyclic.

**Proof:** Suppose there was a cycle in the directed size-2 conflicts. By the previous Lemma, this would mean that there is some interval $I_{i,k}$ which conflicts with itself—i.e. $I_{i,k} \rightarrow I_{i,k}$. This would then mean that $R(I_{i,k}) + dist(X_i, X_i) - L(I_{i,k}) < 0$. This is clearly false since $dist(X_i, X_i) = 0$ and $R(I_{i_k}) \geq L(I_{i_k})$. By contradiction, therefore, the truth of the Lemma is established.

**Lemma 11:** The relation $\succeq$ defined as follows forms a POSET—$I_{i,k_1} \succeq I_{j,k_2}$ if and only if $I_{i,k_1} = I_{j,k_2}$ or there is a size-2 conflict $I_{i,k_1} \rightarrow I_{j,k_2}$.

**Proof:** We have to show that the relation $\succeq$ is *reflexive*, *anti-symmetric* and *transitive*. By definition, $\succeq$ is reflexive since $I_{i,k_1} \succeq I_{i,k_1}$. The transitive and anti-symmetric properties follow from the previous two Lemmas.

**Lemma 12:** An ESTP $\mathcal{G}$ is consistent if and only if the size of the largest anti-chain in $P(\mathcal{G})$ is $= n$ (see Figure 5).

**Proof:** From the previous Lemmas, we know that the only minimal conflicts are of size 1 or size 2. $P(\mathcal{G})$ incorporates the deletion of all the size-1 conflicts and any anti-chain in it incorporates the deletion of all size-2 conflicts. The largest anti-chain targets the maximum number of variables that can be assigned a consistent value together, and since exactly one interval must be active for each variable (Lemma 4), the size of the largest anti-chain must be $= n$ for the ESTP to be consistent.

## Solving General ESTPs

In this subsection, we will deal with the most general version of ESTPs where $f_{X_i}(I_{i,k})$ is allowed to be an arbitrary positive real number.

**Lemma 13:** A general ESTP $\mathcal{G}$ is consistent if and only if the largest weighted anti-chain in $P(\mathcal{G})$ (see Figure 5) using the modified weights $f'_{X_i}(I_{i,k}) = f_{X_i}(I_{i,k}) + M$ is $\geq Mn$.

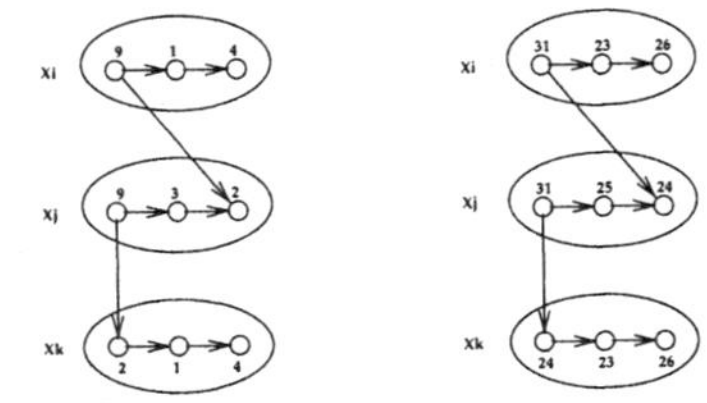


Figure 6: Illustrates the working of Lemmas 13 and 14. The POSET on the left is such that the largest weighted anti-chain in it (9 for $X_i$ and 9 for $X_j$) is not feasible—i.e. it does not choose exactly one node (interval) for each of the variables $X_i$, $X_j$ and $X_k$. The POSET on the right is obtained by adding a factor of 22 to the weights of all the nodes. The largest weighted anti-chain in this POSET (31 for $X_i$, 25 for $X_j$, and 26 for $X_k$) indeed chooses exactly one element from each variable's domain and upon subtracting back the factor 22 from each element in this anti-chain, we get the largest weighted feasible anti-chain for the original POSET (9 for $X_i$, 3 for $X_j$, and 4 for $X_k$). The factor 22 is obtained by summing up the maximum weights in each variable's domain.

Here, $M = \sum_{i=1}^{n} \max\{f_{X_i}(I_{i,k}) : 1 \leq k \leq T(i) + 1\}$.

**Proof:** It suffices to show that any anti-chain that chooses an interval for each variable (feasible) has a greater weight than any anti-chain that does not (infeasible). By the previous Lemma, we know that at most one interval for every variable can be in any anti-chain. This means that the largest value of any infeasible anti-chain is $M(n-1) + \sum_{i=1}^{n} \max\{f_{X_i}(I_{i,k}) : 1 \leq k \leq T(i) + 1\}$ and the smallest value for any feasible anti-chain is $Mn$. Setting $M = \sum_{i=1}^{n} \max\{f_{X_i}(I_{i,k}) : 1 \leq k \leq T(i) + 1\}$ therefore ensures the truth of the Lemma.

**Lemma 14:** The largest weighted anti-chain with the modified weights $f'_{X_i}(I_{i,k}) = f_{X_i}(I_{i,k}) + M$ is the required feasible anti-chain when it is $\geq Mn$.

**Proof:** Continuing the arguments in the proof of the previous Lemma, the largest anti-chain is guaranteed to pick exactly one interval for each variable with the modified weights. Since any other feasible anti-chain also chooses exactly one interval for each variable, the number of nodes in any feasible anti-chain is equal to $n$. Further, since the weights of all intervals are increased by the same additive factor, the largest feasible anti-chain using the weights $f'_{X_i}(I_{i,k})$ is also the largest feasible anti-chain using the weights $f_{X_i}(I_{i,k})$, hence establishing the truth of the Lemma.

Figure 6 shows an example of a possible POSET arising in the context of solving an ESTP (unrelated to the example in Figure 3 and Figure 4) and the weight conversions that must be used to find the largest weighted feasible anti-chain in it. In the example in Figure 4, the largest weighted feasible anti-chain is constituted by the "bottom-most" nodes (intervals) for the variables $X_2$ and $X_3$, and the "middle" node (interval) for the variable $X_4$. This means that the agent should replace the domain preference functions with the set of simple temporal constraints of having to reach the bus stop between 8:15 a.m. and 8:30 a.m., start shopping between 8:00 a.m. and 10:00 a.m. and having lunch between 2:00 p.m. and 3:00 p.m. With such a replacement, the resulting STP can be solved in polynomial time using shortest paths (see (Dechter *et al.* 1991)).

## Largest Weighted Anti-Chain Computation

Figure 7 presents the algorithm for computing the largest weighted anti-chain in a POSET using *maxflow* techniques.

**ALGORITHM:** ANTI-CHAIN-WITH-WTS
**INPUT:** A POSET $P = \langle Y_1, Y_2 \dots Y_N \rangle$ under the relation $\succeq$ and with weights on nodes respectively $\langle w_1, w_2 \dots w_N \rangle$.
**OUTPUT:** The set of nodes $Q$ constituting the largest weighted anti-chain in $P$.
(1) Construct a bi-partite graph $B = \langle U, V, E \rangle$ where $U = \{Y_1, Y_2 \dots Y_N\}$, $V = \{Y'_1, Y'_2 \dots Y'_N\}$ and $(Y_i, Y'_j)$ is an undirected edge in $E$ iff $Y_j \succeq Y_i$ in $P$ and $Y_j \neq Y_i$.
(2) Construct a directed graph $D$ from $B$ as follows:
(a) Add two special nodes $S$ and $T$.
(b) Add directed edges $\langle S, Y_i \rangle$ with capacity $w_i$.
(c) Add directed edges $\langle Y'_j, T \rangle$ with capacity $w_j$.
(d) Impose a direction on all edges $(Y_i, Y'_j)$ in $B$ to get $\langle Y_i, Y'_j \rangle$ and let them be of infinite capacity.
(3) Compute an integral maximum flow $F$ from $S$ to $T$ in $D$. Let the residual graph be $R_F$.
(4) Compute $C = \{\langle S, u \rangle | u$ is unreachable from $S$ in $R_F\} \cup \{\langle v, T \rangle | v$ is reachable from $S$ in $R_F\}$.
(5) Compute $V = \{u | \langle S, u \rangle \in C\} \cup \{v | \langle v, T \rangle \in C\}$.
(6) Compute $S = \{Y_i | Y_i \in V \vee Y'_i \in V\}$.
(7) Compute $Q = \{Y_1, Y_2 \dots Y_N\} \backslash S$.
(8) RETURN $Q$.
**END** ALGORITHM

Figure 7: Illustrates the computation of the largest weighted anti-chain in a POSET using *maxflow* techniques.

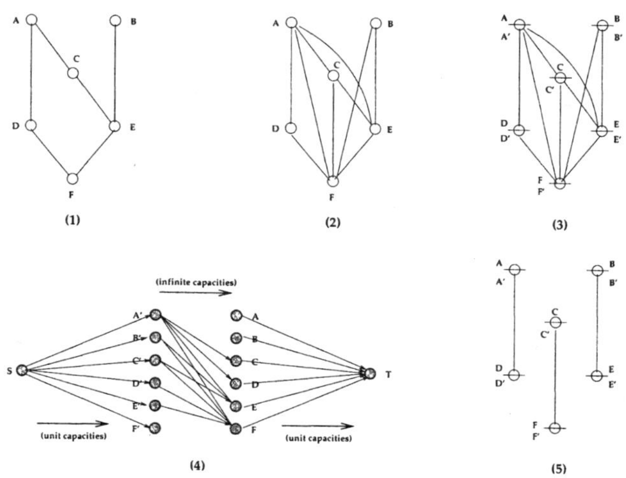


Figure 8: Illustrates the working of the algorithm in Figure 7. Given a POSET under the relation $\succeq$ as in (1), the idea is to first draw all the implicit edges (transitive relationships) to get (2), and split each node into two halves to get (3). Every edge now connects the upper half of some node with the lower half of another and is therefore bi-partite. A *maxflow* (between two auxiliary variables $S$ and $T$) is staged as in (4) to compute a maximum matching on this bi-partite graph. After the maximum matching is computed, the two halves of every node are merged back to get a chain decomposition of the POSET as in (5). Further, the minimum chain decomposition is related to the maximum anti-chain as in Lemmas 19 to 25.

To keep the proof of its correctness simple, we reiterate a series of Lemmas (see (Cormen *et al.* 1990)) that first establish its correctness for unit weights (imagine setting all $w_i = 1$ in Figure 7). We then prove a single concluding Lemma that generalizes the proof for arbitrary positive weights. We make use of the standard result that when edges have integral capacities in an instance of the *maxflow* problem, a maximum flow with integral amount of flow on all edges can be efficiently computed (hence justifying step 3 in Figure 7) (Cormen *et al.* 1990).

**Definition 3:** A matching $M$ in a graph $G$ is a set of edges that do not share a common end-point. The size of a matching (denoted $|M|$) is the number of edges in it, and a maximum matching (denoted $M^*$) is a matching with maximum size. The vertex cover $V$ for a graph $G$ is defined as a set of nodes in $G$ such that all the edges are covered—i.e. for every edge, at least one end point is in $V$. The size of a vertex cover (denoted $|V|$) is the number of nodes in it and a minimum vertex cover (denoted $V^*$) is a vertex cover with minimum size.

**Lemma 15:** If $M^*$ is the maximum matching in $B$, then $|M^*| = F$.

**Proof:** For an integral flow, there cannot exist two edges of the form $\langle Y_i, Y'_{j_1} \rangle$ and $\langle Y_i, Y'_{j_2} \rangle$ both with non-zero flows. This is because the edge $\langle S, Y_i \rangle$ has unit capacity and the flow has to be conserved at $Y_i$. Similarly, there cannot exist two edges of the form $\langle Y_{i_1}, Y'_j \rangle$ and $\langle Y_{i_2}, Y'_j \rangle$ both with non-zero flows (because $\langle Y'_j, T \rangle$ is of unit capacity). Therefore, an integral flow in $D$ defines a matching in $B$ of the same size and hence a maximum flow $F$ in $D$ defines a maximum matching $M^*$ in $B$ of the same size, making $|M^*| = F$.

**Lemma 16:** For any graph $G$, if $M^*$ is the maximum matching in $G$ and $V^*$ is the minimum vertex cover in $G$, then $|V^*| \geq |M^*|$.

**Proof:** For any edge in $M^*$, at least one of its end points must be in $V^*$. Also, since no two edges in $M^*$ share a common end point, they cannot be covered by the same element in $V^*$. This means that $|V^*| \geq |M^*|$.

**Lemma 17:** $V$ constructed in step 5 of Figure 7 is a vertex cover for $B$ and $|V| = F$.

**Proof:** From the construction of $V$, $u$ (belonging to the set $\{Y_1, Y_2 \dots Y_N\}$) is in $V$ if and only if $\langle S, u \rangle$ is in $C$ and $v$ (belonging to the set $\{Y'_1, Y'_2 \dots Y'_N\}$) is in $V$ if and only if $\langle v, T \rangle$ is in $C$. This means that $|V| = |C|$. Since $C$ is formed out of all edges that have one end reachable from $S$ and the other unreachable in $R_F$, it forms a minimum cut between $S$ and $T$ in $D$. From the *maxflow-mincut* theorem, $|C| = F$, and hence $|V| = F$ as required.

**Lemma 18:** For the bi-partite graph $B$, if $V^*$ is the minimum vertex cover, then $|V| = |V^*|$ (where $V$ is the vertex cover constructed for $B$ in step 5 of Figure 7).

**Proof:** From the above Lemmas, we have that $|V| = F$, $|V^*| \geq |M^*|$ and $|M^*| = F$. This implies $|V| = |V^*|$.

**Definition 4:** A chain $c$ in a POSET $P$ is a set of nodes $Y_{i_1}, Y_{i_2} \dots Y_{i_k}$ such that there exists a total order among these nodes under the relation $\succeq$. $Y_{i_2}$ is said to cover $Y_{i_1}$ in $c$ (denoted $\langle Y_{i_2}, Y_{i_1} \rangle$) when $Y_{i_2} \succeq Y_{i_1}$, $Y_{i_2} \neq Y_{i_1}$ and for any distinct third element $Y_{i_j}$ in $c$, $Y_{i_j} \succeq Y_{i_1} \Rightarrow Y_{i_j} \succeq Y_{i_2}$. A chain-decomposition $\rho$ of $P$ is a set of disjoint chains such that all nodes in $P$ are included in exactly one chain. The size of a chain-decomposition $\rho$ (denoted $|\rho|$) is the number of chains constituting it. The minimum chain-decomposition $\rho^*$ of $P$ is a chain-decomposition of $P$ with minimum size.

**Lemma 19:** If $M$ is a matching in $B$, merging $Y_i$ and $Y'_i$ in $M$ produces a chain-decomposition $\rho$ for $P$.

**Proof:** It suffices to prove that merging $Y_i$ and $Y'_i$ in $M$ does not produce cover relationships that share a common end point. Suppose such relationships were produced. They must be of the form $(\langle Y_i, Y_j\rangle, \langle Y_k, Y_j\rangle)$ or $(\langle Y_j, Y_i\rangle, \langle Y_j, Y_k\rangle)$. In the first case, this would mean the existence of the edges $\langle Y_i, Y_j'\rangle$ and $\langle Y_k, Y_j'\rangle$ in $M$, contradicting the fact that no two edges in $M$ share a common point. Similarly, the second case also leads to a contradiction, hence establishing the truth of the Lemma.

**Lemma 20:** If $\rho$ is a chain-decomposition in $P$ corresponding to a matching $M$ in $B$, then $|\rho| + |M| = N$.

**Proof:** Let the chains in $\rho$ be $c_1, c_2 \dots c_{|\rho|}$. The number of edges (cover relationships) in any chain $c_i$ is one less than the number of nodes in it. Let $M_{c_i}$ denote the edges in $M$ that are present in $c_i$. We then have $|M_{c_i}| = |c_i| - 1$. Summing over all chains $c_i$ in $\rho$, we get $|M| = N - |\rho|$ i.e. $|M| + |\rho| = N$.

**Lemma 21:** If $Q^*$ is the largest anti-chain, $|\rho^*| \geq |Q^*|$.

**Proof:** By definition, no two nodes in $Q^*$ are comparable and hence must be in different chains of $\rho^*$. Hence by the pigeonhole principle, we have $|\rho^*| \geq |Q^*|$.

**Lemma 22:** If the minimum vertex cover for $B$ is $V^*$, then $S = \{Y_i | Y_i \in V^* \vee Y_i' \in V^*\}$ is a vertex cover for $P$ with $|S| \leq F$.

**Proof:** For every $Y_i$ in $S$, at least one of $Y_i$ or $Y_i'$ must be present in $V^*$. Therefore, $|S| \leq |V^*| = F$. Also, $S$ forms a vertex cover for $P$, because if there existed an edge $\langle u, v\rangle$ in $P$ not covered by $S$, then there must exist some $Y_j = u$ and $Y_k' = v$ such that $\langle Y_j, Y_k'\rangle$ is in $B$ and is not covered by $V^*$. This contradicts that $V^*$ is a vertex cover for $B$ and hence $S$ must be a vertex cover for $P$.

**Lemma 23:** $Q = P \backslash S$ is an anti-chain and $|Q| \geq N - F$.

**Proof:** $Q$ is an anti-chain because if there existed two nodes $u$ and $v$ in $Q$ that were comparable, then the edge $\langle u, v\rangle$ must have been uncovered by $S$ contradicting that $S$ is a vertex cover for $P$. Also, since $|Q| + |S| = N$ and $|S| \leq F$, $|Q| \geq N - F$.

**Lemma 24:** $Q$ (calculated in step 7 of Figure 7) is the required largest weighted anti-chain.

**Proof:** Suppose $Q^*$ was the optimal. By Lemma 23 we have that $|Q^*| \geq |Q| \geq N - F$. By Lemma 21 we also have that $|\rho^*| \geq |Q^*| \geq |Q| \geq N - F$. Again by Lemma 20 we know that $|\rho^*| \leq N - |M^*|$. Since $|M^*| = F$, we get $|\rho^*| = |Q^*| = |Q| = N - F$, hence making $Q$ optimal as required.

**Lemma 25:** The algorithm presented in Figure 7 works for arbitrary positive weights $w_i > 0$.

**Proof:** From the foregoing Lemmas, we know that the algorithm works for unit weights—i.e. $w_i = 1$. Now suppose that the weights were positive integers (still not the general case). Conceptually, a new POSET can be constructed where node $Y_i$ with weight $w_i$ is replicated $w_i$ times—each of unit weight and incomparable to each other. If $Y_i \succ Y_j$ (short for saying $Y_i \succeq Y_j$ and $Y_i \neq Y_j$), then all $w_i$ copies of $Y_i$ are made to have a $\succ$ relation to all $w_j$ copies of $Y_j$. The staged *maxflow* in $D$ will have all $w_i$ copies of $Y_i$ (denoted $y_{i_1}, y_{i_2} \dots y_{i_{w_i}}$) behaving identically. Also since all edges of the form $\langle y_{i_j}, y'_{k_l}\rangle$ have infinite capacity, we can replace the group of edges $\langle S, y_{i_1}\rangle, \langle S, y_{i_2}\rangle \dots \langle S, y_{i_{w_i}}\rangle$ (each of unit capacity) with a single edge $\langle S, Y_i\rangle$ of capacity $w_i$. Similarly we can replace the group of edges $\langle y'_{i_1}, T\rangle, \langle y'_{i_2}, T\rangle \dots \langle y'_{i_{w_i}}, T\rangle$ (each of unit capacity) with a single edge $\langle Y_i', T\rangle$ of capacity $w_i$. All intermediate edges are of infinite capacity and are defined (as previously) using the $\succ$ relation. Now consider the most general case where $w_i$ is positive but need not be an integer. In such a case, the idea is to conceptually scale all the weights by a uniform factor $L$, such that all of them become integers. The more the precision of the numbers, the larger we can choose $L$—but since this is only conceptual, $L$ does not have a concrete role in the algorithm. The algorithm can then find the largest anti-chain using the scaled weights and since scaling the weights uniformly in a POSET does not affect the largest anti-chain, the same can be used after scaling down the weights by $L$. Computationally however, the idea of scaling is not reflected anywhere except in the fact that the weights $w_i$ can be used as they are to define capacities on the edges in $D$.

## Conclusions

We described a class of metric temporal problems (which we referred to as extended STPs (ESTPs)) that formed a middle ground between STPs and DTPs. We showed that ESTPs could be solved in polynomial time and were expressive enough to deal with limited forms of disjunctions and preferences that would otherwise require an exponential search space. Our polynomial-time algorithm for solving ESTPs was based on the idea of reducing a given ESTP to the problem of computing the largest weighted anti-chain in a POSET which in turn could be solved using *maxflow* techniques. The expressive power of ESTPs along with their tractability makes them a suitable model for many real-life applications that involve metric temporal reasoning.

## References


Armando A., Castellini C. and Giunchiglia E. SAT-based Procedures for Temporal Reasoning. *ECP 2000.*

Cormen T. H., Leiserson C. E. and Rivest R. Introduction to Algorithms. *Cambridge, MA, 1990.*

Dechter R., Meiri I. and Pearl J. Temporal Constraint Networks. *Artificial Intelligence Journal 49. 1991.*

Khatib L., Morris P. H., Morris R. A. and Rossi F. Temporal Constraint Reasoning With Preferences. *IJCAI 2001.*

Kumar T. K. S. Incremental Computation of Resource-Envelopes in Producer-Consumer Models. *CP 2003.*

Nguyen X. and Kambhampati S. Reviving Partial Order Planning. *IJCAI-2001.*

Oddi A. and Cesta A. Incremental Forward Checking for the Disjunctive Temporal Problem. *ECAI 2000.*

Smith D., Frank J. and Jonsson A. Bridging the Gap Between Planning and Scheduling. *Knowledge Engineering Review 15:1, 2000.*

Stergiou K. and Koubarakis M. Backtracking Algorithms for Disjunctions of Temporal Constraints. *In the 15th National Conference on Artificial Intelligence. 1998.*

Tsamardinos I. and Pollack M. E. Efficient Solution Techniques for Disjunctive Temporal Reasoning Problems. *Artificial Intelligence, 2003.*

# Using Performance Profile Trees to Improve Deliberation Control

**Kate Larson** and **Tuomas Sandholm**
Computer Science Department
Carnegie Mellon University
Pittsburgh, PA 15213
{klarson,sandholm}@cs.cmu.edu

## Abstract

Performance profile trees have recently been proposed as a theoretical basis for fully normative deliberation control. In this paper we conduct the first experimental study of their feasibility and accuracy in making stopping decisions for anytime algorithms on optimization problems. Using data and algorithms from two different real-world domains, we compare performance profile trees to other well-established deliberation-control techniques. We show that performance profile trees are feasible in practice and lead to significantly better deliberation control decisions. We then conduct experiments using performance profile trees where deliberation-control decisions are made using conditioning on multiple features of the solution to illustrate that such an approach is feasible in practice.

## Introduction

In many AI applications, bounded rationality is simply a necessary evil that has to be dealt with. The realities of limited computational resources and time pressures caused by real-time environments mean that agents are not always able to optimally determine their best decisions and actions. The field of artificial intelligence has long searched for useful techniques for coping with this problem. Herbert Simon advocated that agents should forgo perfect rationality in favor of limited, economical reasoning. His thesis was that "the global optimization problem is to find the least–cost, or best–return decision, net of computational costs" (Simon 1982).

Considerable work has focused on developing *normative* models that prescribe how a computationally limited agent *should* behave (see, for example (Horvitz 2001; Russell 1997)). In particular, decision theory has proved to be a powerful tool in developing approaches to meta-level control of computation (Horvitz 1990). In general this is a highly nontrivial undertaking, encompassing numerous fundamental and technical difficulties. As a result, most of these methods resort to simplifying assumptions such as myopic search control (Russell and Wefald 1991; Baum and Smith 1997), assuming that an algorithm's future performance can be deterministically predicted using a performance profile (Horvitz 1988; Boddy and Dean 1994), assuming that an algorithm's future performance does not depend on the run on that instance so far (Zilberstein and Russell 1996; Zilberstein *et al.* 1999; Horvitz 2001), resorting to asymptotic notions of bounded optimality (Russell and Subramanian 1995), or using myopic approaches for decision making (Breese and Horvitz 1990). While such simplifications can be acceptable in single-agent settings as long as the agent performs reasonably well, any deviation from full normativity can be catastrophic in multiagent systems. If a multiagent system designer can not guarantee that a strategy (including deliberation actions) is the best strategy that an agent can use, there is a risk that the agent is motivated to use some other strategy. Even if that strategy happens to be "close" to the desired one, the social outcome may be far from desirable. Therefore, a fully normative deliberation control method, which considers all possible information and ways an agent can make a deliberation decision, is required as a basis for analyzing the strategies of agents.

Recently, a fully normative deliberation control method, the *performance profile tree*, was introduced for making stopping decisions for any anytime optimizer (treated as a black box) (Larson and Sandholm 2001). This deliberation control method has been used to analyze (deliberation) strategies of agents in different bargaining and auction settings in order to understand the repercussions that limited deliberation resources have on agents' game-theoretic behavior. However, a weakness of this work is that it has been highly theoretical. While the full normativity provided by the performance profile tree is required theoretically, it has been unclear whether the performance profile tree is of practical use.

In this paper we experimentally study the use of performance profile trees to determine their practicality and usefulness for helping a single agent decide when to stop its anytime optimization algorithm. On data generated from black-box anytime problem solvers, we illustrate that it is feasible to use performance profile tree based deliberation control in hard real-world problems. We also show that this leads to more accurate deliberation control decisions than the use of the performance profile representations presented in prior literature. Furthermore, we demonstrate that the performance profile tree can easily handle conditioning its decisions on (the path of) other solution features in addition to solution quality.

The paper is organized as follows. In the next section we provide an overview of deliberation control along with details of the different methods used in the experiments. After this we provide a description of the setup of the experiments. We describe the problem domains which we use and explain how the performance profiles are created. This is followed by the presentation and discussion of the results, after which we conclude.

## Decision-theoretic deliberation control

We begin by providing a short overview of deliberation control methods, and then describe in detail the different methods that are tested in this paper. We assume that agents have algorithms that allow them to trade off computational resources for solution quality. In particular, we assume that agents have *anytime algorithms*, that is, algorithms that improve the solution over time and return the best solution available even if not allowed to run to completion (Horvitz 1988; Boddy and Dean 1994). Most iterative improvement algorithms and many tree search algorithms (such as branch and bound) are anytime algorithms, additionally there has been many successful applications of anytime algorithms in areas like belief and influence diagram evaluation (Horsch and Poole 1999), planning and scheduling (Boddy and Dean 1994), and information gathering (Grass and Zilberstein 2000).

If agents have infinite computing resources (i.e. no deadlines and free computation), they would be able to compute the optimal solutions to their problems. Instead, in many settings agents have *time-dependent* utility functions. That is, the utility of an agent depends on both the solution quality obtained, and the amount of time spent getting it,

$$U(q,t) = u(q) - \text{cost}(t)$$

where $u(q)$ is the utility to the agent of getting a solution with quality $q$ and $\text{cost}(t)$ is the cost incurred of computing for $t$ time steps.

While anytime algorithms are models that allow for the trading off of computational resources, they do not provide a complete solution. Instead, anytime algorithms need to be paired with a meta-level deliberation controller that determines how long to run the anytime algorithm, that is, when to stop deliberating and act with the solution obtained. The deliberation controller's stopping policy is based on a *performance profile*: statistical information about the anytime algorithm's performance on prior problem instances. This helps the deliberation controller project how much (and how quickly) the solution quality would improve if further computation were allowed.[1] Performance profiles are usually generated by prior runs of the anytime algorithm on different problem instances.

There are different ways of representing performance profiles. At a high level, performance profiles can be classified as being either *static* or *dynamic*.

[1] In the rest of this paper, when it is obvious from the context, we will refer to the combination of the deliberation controller and the performance profile as just the performance profile.

Static performance profiles predict, before the anytime algorithm starts running on the instance at hand, the optimal stopping time for the algorithm. The *performance profile curve (PPCurve)* (Horvitz 1988; Boddy and Dean 1994), Figure 1(a), is an example of a static performance profile. It is created by averaging, at each time point, the solution quality obtained on prior runs (on different instances). Given the curve, specified as solution quality as a function of time, $q(t)$, as well as the cost function $\text{cost}(t)$, the deliberation policy of an agent is to allocate time $t^*$ to the algorithm, where

$$t^* = \arg\max_t \left[u(q(t)) - \text{cost}(t)\right].$$

A potential weakness with static performance profiles is that the time allocation decision is made before the algorithm starts. Instead, by monitoring the current run of the algorithm, it may be possible to gather additional information which leads to better predictions about future changes in solution quality, and thus enables better stopping decisions.

Dynamic performance profiles monitor the run of the algorithm and make online decisions about whether to allow the algorithm more time. Dynamic performance profiles are often represented as a table of discrete values which specify a discrete probability distribution over solution quality for each time step (Zilberstein and Russell 1996), Figure 1(b). The basic table-based representation (Zilberstein and Russell 1996) loses some information that can be useful for making stopping decisions. In particular, it cannot condition the projection on the current solution. Consider Figure 1(b). Once the shaded cell is reached, it is clear that there should be no probability mass at cells of lower solution quality at future steps, but the representation cannot capture that.

To address this, Hansen and Zilberstein (Hansen and Zilberstein 2001) proposed a dynamic programming approach where the projection of solution quality is conditioned on the current solution quality. In particular, by defining the utility of having a solution of quality $q_i$ at time $t_k$ to be $U(q_i, t_k) = u(q_i) - \text{cost}(t_k)$, a stopping rule can be found by optimizing the following value function

$$V(q_i, t_k) = \max_d \begin{cases} U(q_i, t) & \text{if } d = \text{stop} \\ \sum_j P(q_j|q_i, \Delta t)V(q_j, t+\Delta t) & \text{if } d = \text{continue} \end{cases}$$

to determine the policy

$$\pi(q_i, t) = \text{argmax}_d \begin{cases} U(q_i, t) & \text{if } d = \text{stop} \\ \sum_j P(q_j|q_i, \Delta t)V(q_j, t+\Delta t) & \text{if } d = \text{continue} \end{cases}$$

Throughout the rest of this paper, when we compare our methods against the table-based approach, we always use the dynamic program in conjunction with the table in order to give the table-based approach the best possible chance. For short, we will call that combination a *performance profile table (PPTable)*.

Even the PPTable approach yields suboptimal stopping decisions because the representation loses information. In particular, all information about the path of the run is lost. In Figure 1(b), the shaded cell could have been reached by path A or path B. The solution quality projection should be

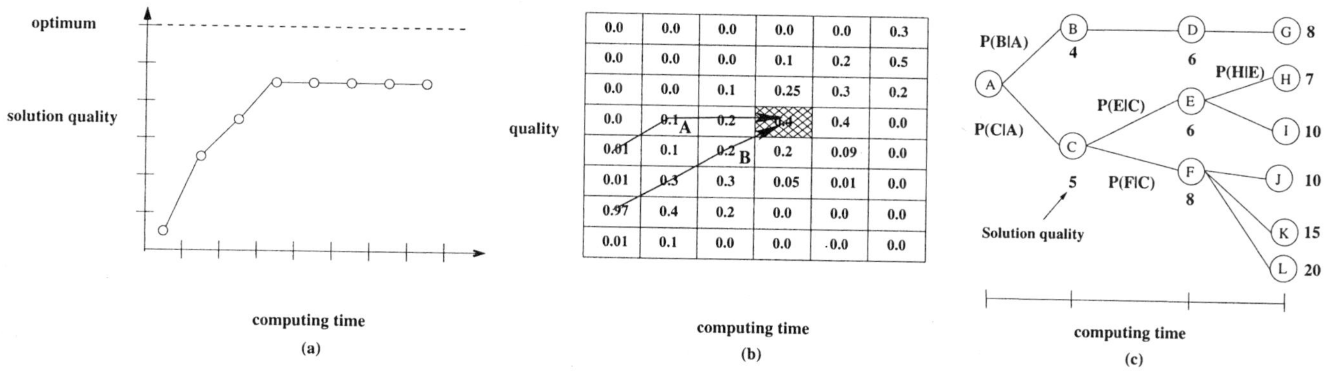

Figure 1: *Three performance profile representations: a) performance profile curve (PPCurve), b) performance profile table (PPTable), and c) a performance profile tree (PPTree).*

more optimistic if the cell was reached via path B, but using the PPTable, the same stopping decision must be made in both cases. (However, the PPTable yields optimal stopping decisions in settings where the current solution quality captures all of the information from the path that is pertinent for projecting solution quality. This Markov assumption is generally not satisfied, as the example above shows.)

In order to capture all of the information available for making stopping decisions, we introduced the *performance profile tree* (PPTree) representation (Larson and Sandholm 2001). In a PPTree, the nodes represent solutions at given time points, while each edge carries the probability that the child node is reached given that the parent was reached. Figure 1(c) exemplifies one such tree. A PPTree can support conditioning on any and all features that are deemed to be of importance for making stopping decisions since the nodes can hold information about solution quality and any other solution feature that may be important. For example, in scheduling applications, often the *slack* in a schedule is a good predictor of future improvement. The solution information stored at a node could therefore include a variable for solution quality and a variable for slack.

A key aspect of the PPTree is that it automatically supports conditioning on the *path* so far. The performance profile tree that applies given a path of computation is the subtree rooted at the current node $n$. This subtree is denoted by $\mathcal{T}(n)$. If an agent is at a node $n$ with solution quality $q(n)$, then when estimating how much additional computing would increase the solution quality, the agent need only consider paths that emanate from node $n$. The probability, $P_n(n')$, of reaching a particular future node $n'$ in $\mathcal{T}(n)$ is simply the product of the probabilities on the path from $n$ to $n'$. The expected solution quality after allocating $t$ more time steps to the problem, if the current node is $n$, is $\sum P_n(n') \cdot q(n')$ where the sum is over the set $\{n' | n'$ is a node in $\mathcal{T}_i(n)$ which is reachable in $t$ time steps$\}$.

Deliberation policies for the PPTree are constructed by optimizing the following rule

$$V(q(n),t) = \max_d \begin{cases} U(q(n),t) & \text{if d=stop} \\ \sum_{n'} P_n(n')V(q(n'),t+\Delta t) & \text{if d=continue} \end{cases}$$

where $n' \in \{$nodes in $\mathcal{T}(n)$ at depth $\Delta t$ time steps$\}$, to determine the policy

$$\pi(q(n),t) = \text{argmax}_d \begin{cases} U(q(n),t) & \text{if d=stop} \\ \sum_{n'} P_n(n')V(q(n'),t+\Delta t) & \text{if d=continue} \end{cases}$$

## Experimental setup

While a fully normative deliberation control method is required for game-theoretic analysis of computationally limited agents, to date no experimental work has been done to show that (1) the performance profile tree based deliberation control method is feasible in practice, and (2) that in practice such sophisticated deliberation control is any better than earlier decision-theoretic deliberation control methods that relied on simpler performance profile representations . In this paper we bridge this gap and show that performance profile trees are desirable in practice also for single-agent deliberation control. In the first set of experiments, we demonstrate (1) and (2). In that experiment we use solution quality as the only feature stored in a tree node (as we mentioned above, the PPTree automatically conditions on the *path* followed to reach the node). In the second set of experiments, we show that it is feasible to use additional problem features to make deliberation decisions.

Our deliberation control method is domain independent and domain problem solver independent—yielding a clean separation between the domain problem solver (a black box) and the deliberation controller. This separation allows one to develop deliberation control methodology that can be leveraged across applications. To demonstrate this we conduct experiments in two different application domains using software which was developed independently from the deliberation controllers.

### Example domain problem solving environments

We conducted our experiments in two different domain environments – vehicle routing and single-machine manufacturing scheduling.

**Vehicle routing** In the real-world vehicle routing problem (VRP) in question, a dispatch center is responsible for a certain set of tasks (deliveries) and has a certain set of resources (trucks) to take care of them (Sandholm 1993; Sandholm and Lesser 1997). Each truck has a depot, and each delivery has a pickup location and a drop-off location. The dispatch center's problem is to minimize transportation cost (driven distance) while still making all of its deliveries and honoring the following constraints: 1) each vehicle has to begin and end its tour at its depot, and 2) each vehicle has a maximum load weight and maximum load volume constraint. This problem is $\mathcal{NP}$-complete.

To generate data for our experiments, an iterative improvement algorithm was used for solving the VRP. The center initially assigned deliveries to trucks in round-robin order. The algorithm then iteratively improved the solution by selecting a delivery at random, removing it from the solution, and then reinserting it into the least expensive place in the solution (potentially to a different truck, and with pickup potentially added into a different leg of the truck's route than the drop-off) without violating any of the constraints. Each addition-removal is considered one iteration. We let the algorithm run until there was no improvement in the solution for some predefined number, $k$, of steps. Figure 2 shows the results of several runs of this iterative improvement algorithm on different instances used in the experiments, with $k = 250$. The algorithm clearly displays diminishing returns to scale, as is expected from anytime algorithms.

The problem instances were generated using real-world data collected from a dispatch center that was responsible for 15 trucks and 300 deliveries. We generated training and testing sets by randomly dividing the deliveries into a set of 210 training deliveries and 90 testing deliveries. To generate a training (testing) instance, we randomly selected (with replacement) 60 deliveries from the training (testing) set.

**Manufacturing scheduling** The second domain is a single-machine manufacturing scheduling problem with sequence-dependent setup times on the machines, where the agent's objective is to minimize weighted tardiness $= \sum_{j\in J} w_j T_j = \sum_{j \in J} w_j \max(f_j - d_j, 0)$, where $T_j$ is the tardiness of job $j$, and $w_j$, $f_j$, $d_j$ are the weight, finish time, and due-date of job $j$.

In our experiments, we used a state-of-the-art scheduler developed by others (Cicirello and Smith 2002) as the domain problem solver. It is an iterative improvement algorithm that uses a scheduling algorithm called Heuristic Biased Stochastic Sampling (Bresina 1996). We treated the domain problem solver as a black box without any modifications.

The problem instances were generated according to a standard benchmark (Lee *et al.* 1997). The due-date tightness factor was set to 0.3 and the due-date range factor was set to 0.25. The setup time severity was set to 0.25. These parameter values are the ones used in standard benchmarks (Lee *et al.* 1997). Each instance consisted of 100 jobs to be scheduled. We generated the training instances and test instances using different random number seeds.

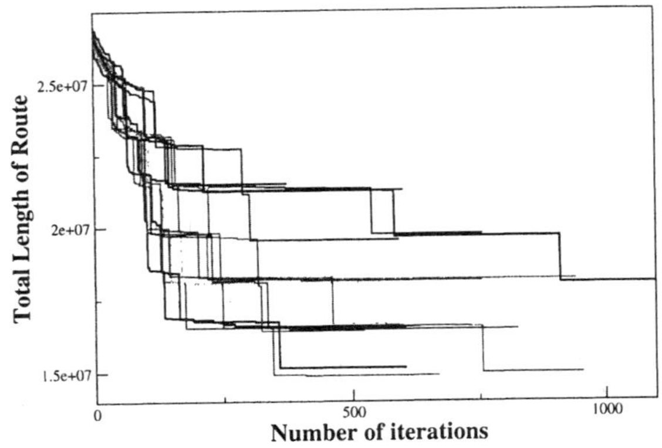


Figure 2: *Runs of the vehicle routing algorithm on different problem instances. The $x$-axis is number of iterations and the $y$-axis is the total distance traveled by all trucks.*

## Constructing performance profiles

Performance profiles encapsulate statistical information about how the domain problem solver has performed on past problem instances. To build performance profiles, we generated

- 1000 instances for the vehicle routing domain. We ran the algorithm on each instance until there was no improvement in solution quality for 250 iterations.
- 10000 instances for the scheduling domain. We ran the algorithm until there was no improvement in solution quality for 400 iterations.

From this data, we generated the performance profiles using each of the three representations: PPCurve, PPTable, and PPTree. Like PPTable-based deliberation control, PPTree requires discretization of computation time and of solution quality (otherwise no two runs would generally populate the same part of the table/tree, in which case no useful statistical inferences could be drawn).[2]

Computation time was discretized the same way for each of the three performance profile representations. We did this the obvious way in that one iteration of each algorithm (routing and scheduling) was equal to one computation step. For the solution quality we experimented with different discretizations. Due to space limitations we present only results where the scheduling data was discretized into buckets of width 100, and the vehicle routing data was discretized into buckets of width 50000.[3] For the vehicle routing domain there turned out to be 1943 time steps, and 551 buckets of solution quality. For the scheduling domain there turned out to be 465 time steps, and 750 buckets of solution quality.

At first glance it may seem that this implies performance profile trees of size $551^{1943}$ for the trucking domain and $750^{465}$ for the scheduling domain. However, most of the paths of the tree were not populated by any run (because

[2]The PPCurve does not require any discretization on solution quality, so we gave it the advantage of no discretization.

[3]The results obtained from these discretizations were representative of the results obtained across all the tested discretizations.

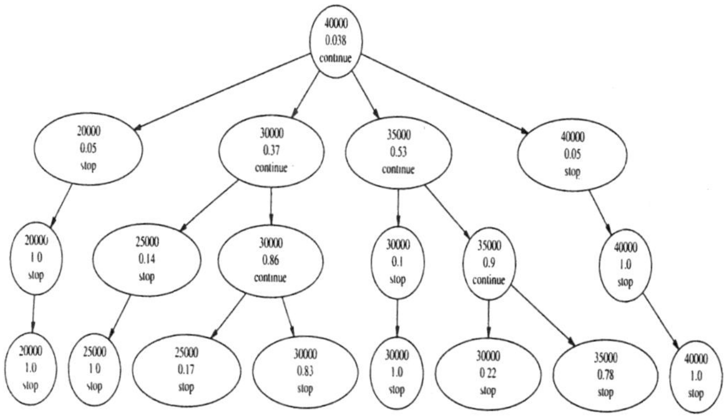


Figure 3: *Subtree of a performance profile tree generated from instances from the scheduling domain. In each node there are three entries. The first entry is the (discretized) solution quality. The second entry is the probability of reaching the node, given that its parent was reached. The final entry represents the stopping policy. An entry labelled "continue" means that the agent should compute another step, while an entry labelled "stop" means that the agent should stop all computation and act with the solution at hand.*

there are "only" 1000 (or 10000) runs, one per instance). We generated the tree dynamically in memory, such that only the populated parts were stored. This way, we could be assured that the number of edges in the tree for trucking was at most 1943 × #instances (because each instance can generate at most one new edge for each compute step). Similarly, for scheduling it was 465 × #instances.

In practice, the trees were easy to generate, but they are much too large to lay out in a paper. Therefore, in Figure 3 we present a subtree of a performance profile tree generated from the same 10000 scheduling instances, but with a much coarser discretization: buckets of width 5000 on solution quality and computing steps that include 150 iterations each (yielding 4 buckets on the computation time axis, i.e., 4 depths to the tree—with root at depth 0).

## Cost functions

In all the experiments we used cost functions of the form $C \cdot t$ where $C$ was an exogenously given cost of one step of computing and $t$ was the number of time steps computed. We studied the behavior of deliberation control methods under a wide range of values of $C$. For the vehicle routing domain we used $C \in \{0, 10, 100, 500, 1000, 5000, 10000, 25000, 35000, 50000, 100000, 1000000\}$ In the scheduling domain we used $C \in \{0, 1, 10, 50, 100, 500, 1000, 5000, 10000, 100000\}$. These value choices span the interesting range: at the bottom end, no controller ever stops the deliberation, and at the top end, each controller stops it immediately.

## Comparison of performance profiles

In the first set of experiments we tested the feasibility of PPTree-based deliberation control and compared its decision-making effectiveness against other performance-profile representations (PPCurve and PPTable).

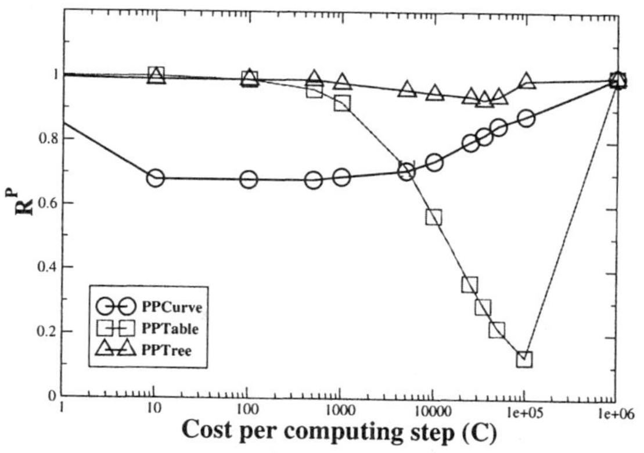


Figure 4: *Performance of the different performance profiles in the vehicle routing domain. Values closer to 1.0 (optimal) are better. PPTree outperforms both PPCurve and PPTable.*

To evaluate the performance, we generated $N = 500$ new test instances of the trucking problem and $N = 5000$ new test instances from the scheduling domain. Each of the three performance profile representations was evaluated on the same test set.

For each test instance we determined the optimal stopping point, $t_i^{\text{opt}}$, given that the entire path of the run was known in hindsight. (This stopping point is optimistic in the sense that it does not use discretization of solution quality. Furthermore, real deliberation controllers do not have hindsight at their disposal.) This allowed us to determine the optimal value that the agent could have possibly gotten on instance $i$ in hindsight: $U_{\text{opt}}(i) = q_i(t_i^{\text{opt}}) + C \cdot t_i^{\text{opt}}$ where $q_i(t)$ is the solution quality after computing for $t$ time steps, and $C$ is the exogenously given cost of one step of computing.[4]

We evaluated the three performance profile representations $P \in \{\text{PPTree}, \text{PPTable}, \text{PPCurve}\}$ separately on the test instances, recording for each instance the stopping point $t_i^{\text{P}}$ that deliberation controller, $P$, imposed and the resulting value. That is, we stored $U_{\text{P}}(i) = q_i(t_i^{\text{P}}) + C \cdot t_i^{\text{P}}$. We determined how far from optimal the resulting value was as a ratio $R_i^{\text{P}} = \frac{U_{\text{opt}}(i)}{U_{\text{P}}(i)}$. Then, $R^{\text{P}} = \frac{1}{N}\sum_i^N R_i^{\text{P}}$ gave an overall measure of performance (the closer $R$ is to 1.0, the better). Figures 4 and 5 display the results.

When computation was free or exorbitantly expensive compared to the gains available from computing, then all the deliberation control methods performed (almost) optimally. With free computing, the deliberation control problem is trivial: it is simply best to compute forever. Similarly, when computation is extremely expensive, it is best to not compute at all. For the midrange costs (i.e., the interesting range), the deliberation controllers performed quite differently from each other. The PPTree outperformed both the PPCurve and the PPTable. In the vehicle routing experiments, the PPTree was, at worst, 93.0% of optimal (when $C = 35000$)

[4]In both application domain, lower solution quality is better. Therefore, we add the cost function, instead of subtracting it in the utility equation.

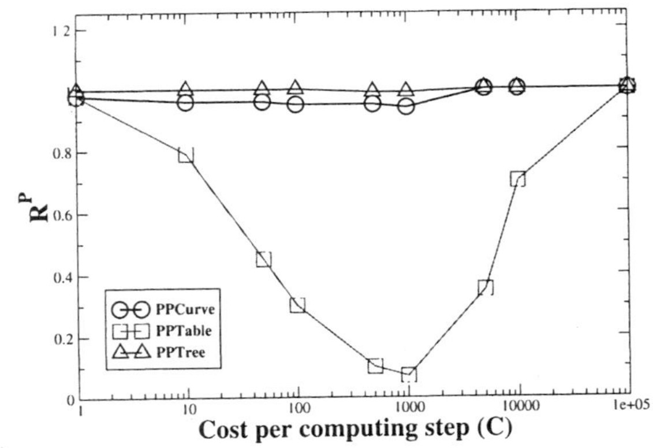


Figure 5: *Performance of the different performance profiles in the scheduling domain. Values closer to 1.0 are better. PPTree out performs both PPTable and PPCurve.*

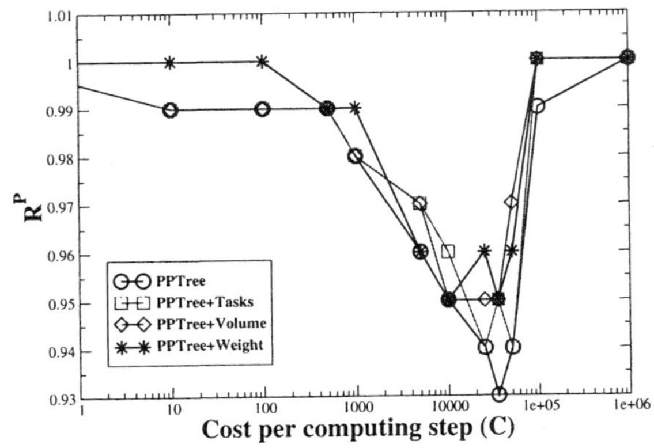


Figure 6: *Performance of the PPTree when deliberation-control decisions are conditioned on both solution quality and an additional solution feature (variance across trucks in number of tasks, variance across trucks of the average volume to max-volume ratio, and variance across trucks in the average weight to max-weight ratio.*

and often performed better (Figure 4). In the scheduling experiments, the PPTree was always within 99.0% of optimal (Figure 5).

In the scheduling domain, the PPCurve performed reasonably well with $R^P$ ranging from 0.95 to 1.00. In the vehicle routing domain, its performance was not as good, with $R^P$ ranging from 0.68 to 1.00. A possible explanation for the difference is that in scheduling there was less variance (in the stopping time) among instances. Therefore, in the scheduling domain the optimal stopping point for the average algorithm run was a better estimate for any given run, compared to the routing domain.

The PPTable had the widest variability in behavior. For both low and high costs it performed well in both application domains. However, for midrange costs it performed poorly, as low as 0.07 in scheduling and 0.13 in vehicle routing. In particular, the PPTable appeared to be overly optimistic when determining a deliberation control policy, as it often allowed too much computing. It was not able to differentiate between algorithm runs which had flattened out and ones in which additional improvement in solution quality was possible. While the dynamic programming approach used in the PPTable produces an optimal policy if solution quality improvement satisfies the Markov property as we discussed earlier, it appears to not be robust when in practice that property does not hold.

While the PPTree performs better than PPCurve and PPTable with respect to absolute difference in performance, it is also important to determine whether there is statistical significance to the results. Using a Fisher sign test, we compared the PPTree against both the PPCurve and the PPTable. We found in both the trucking and scheduling domains that the dominance of the PPTree was truly significant, resulting in $p-$values less than $10^{-13}$ for all costs where there was any difference in the performance between the performance profiles.[5]

[5]When costs were very low ($C = 0$) or very high ($C = 10^6$ in the trucking domain and $C = 10^5$ in the scheduling domain), all performance profiles performed optimally, and thus, identically.

We also experimented using different solution quality and time step discretizations. The general patterns seen in Figures 4 and 5 were again observed. Furthermore, we ran experiments where smaller training sets (of as low as 50 instances) were used. While the performance of all of the deliberation controllers was adversely affected, the relative ranking of their performance did not change.

In summary, this first set of experiments showed that PPTree-based deliberation control is feasible in practice and outperforms the earlier performance profile representations. It also showed that the method is close to optimal even when solution quality and computation time are discretized and conditioning is done only on the path of the solution quality (instead of additional/all possible predictive features).

### Conditioning on (the path of) additional solution features

Using the PPTree as our performance profile representation, we experimented using additional solution features to help in making deliberation control decisions. In the vehicle routing domain, in addition to solution quality (total distance driven) we also allowed conditioning on the following features: 1) variance across trucks in the number of tasks, 2) variance across trucks in the truck's average weight to max-weight ratio, and 3) variance across trucks in the truck's average volume to max-volume ratio. The results are reported in Figure 6. Using the additional solution features did lead to slight improvement in the quality of stopping decisions (a 3.0% absolute improvement for $C = 25000$; less improvement for other values of $C$). Similarly, in experiments conducted in the scheduling domain where slackness in the schedule was used as an additional feature, there was also slight improvement in the deliberation control results.

While the gains from using additional problem instance features in our experiments seem small, it must be recalled that the accuracy from conditioning on only solution quality was close to optimal already. For example when $C = 25000$ the overall performance improved from 94.0% to 97.0% of optimal. So we are starting to hit a ceiling effect. Using a Fisher sign test to analyze the significance of improvement in solution quality when using additional features, we found that for all features there was little significant improvement. Again, we hypothesize that a ceiling effect is in action. In summary, the second set of experiments demonstrated that performance profile trees can support conditioning on (the path of) multiple solution features in practice.

## Conclusions and future research

Performance profile tree based stopping control of anytime optimization algorithms has recently been proposed as a theoretical basis for fully normative deliberation control. In this paper, we compared different performance profile representations in practice, and showed that the performance profile tree is not only feasible to construct and use, but also leads to better deliberation control decisions than prior methods. We then conducted experiments were deliberation control decisions were conditioned on (the path of) multiple solution features (not just solution quality), demonstrating feasibility of that idea.

There are several research directions that can be taken at this point. First, the performance profile tree was developed as a model of deliberation control for multiagent systems. It would be interesting to conduct a series of experiments to see the efficacy of the approach in multiagent settings. Second, we believe that more work on identifying solution features which help in deliberation control would be a beneficial research endeavor.


## Acknowledgements

We would like to thank Vincent Cicirello and Stephen Smith for providing us with both the scheduler and the scheduling instance generator. The material in this paper is based upon work supported by the National Science Foundation under CAREER Award IRI-9703122, Grant IIS-9800994, ITR IIS-0081246, and ITR IIS-0121678.


## References


[Baum and Smith 1997] Eric B Baum and Warren D Smith. A Bayesian approach to relevance in game playing. *Artificial Intelligence*, 97(1–2):195–242, 1997.

[Boddy and Dean 1994] Mark Boddy and Thomas Dean. Deliberation scheduling for problem solving in time-constrained environments. *Artificial Intelligence*, 67:245–285, 1994.

[Breese and Horvitz 1990] John Breese and Eric Horvitz. Ideal reformulation of belief networks. In *Proceedings of UAI'90*, pages 129–144, 1990.

[Bresina 1996] J. L. Bresina. Heuristic-biased stochastic search. In *Proceedings of AAAI'96*, pages 271–278, 1996.

[Cicirello and Smith 2002] Vincent Cicirello and Steven Smith. Amplification of search performance through randomization of heuristics. In *Principles and Practice of Constraint Programming – CP 2002*, pages 124–138, 2002.

[Grass and Zilberstein 2000] Joshua Grass and Shlomo Zilberstein. A value-driven system for autonomous information gathering. *Journal of Intelligent Information Systems*, 14(1):5–27, 2000.

[Hansen and Zilberstein 2001] Eric Hansen and Shlomo Zilberstein. Monitoring and control of anytime algorithms: A dynamic programming approach. *Artificial Intelligence*, 126:139–157, 2001.

[Horsch and Poole 1999] Michael Horsch and David Poole. Estimating the value of computation in flexible information refinement. In *Proceedings of UAI'99*, pages 297–304, 1999.

[Horvitz 1988] Eric J. Horvitz. Reasoning under varying and uncertain resource constraints. In *Proceedings of AAAI'88*, pages 111–116, St. Paul, MN, August 1988.

[Horvitz 1990] Eric Horvitz. *Computation and actions under bounded resources*. PhD thesis, Stanford University, 1990.

[Horvitz 2001] Eric Horvitz. Principles and applications of continual computation. *Artificial Intelligence*, 126:159–196, 2001.

[Larson and Sandholm 2001] Kate Larson and Tuomas Sandholm. Bargaining with limited computation: Deliberation equilibrium. *Artificial Intelligence*, 132(2):183–217, 2001.

[Lee *et al.* 1997] Y. H. Lee, K. Bhaskaran, and M. Pinedo. A heuristic to minimize the total weighted tardiness with sequence-dependent setups. *IIE Transactions*, 29:45–52, 1997.

[Russell and Subramanian 1995] Stuart Russell and Devika Subramanian. Provably bounded-optimal agents. *Journal of Artificial Intelligence Research*, 1:1–36, 1995.

[Russell and Wefald 1991] Stuart Russell and Eric Wefald. *Do the right thing: Studies in Limited Rationality*. The MIT Press, 1991.

[Russell 1997] Stuart Russell. Rationality and intelligence. *Artificial Intelligence*, 94(1):57–77, 1997.

[Sandholm and Lesser 1997] Tuomas Sandholm and Victor Lesser. Coalitions among computationally bounded agents. *Artificial Intelligence*, 94(1):99–137, 1997.

[Sandholm 1993] Tuomas Sandholm. An implementation of the contract net protocol based on marginal cost calculations. In *Proceedings of AAAI'93*, pages 256–262, Washington, D.C., July 1993.

[Simon 1982] Herbert A Simon. *Models of bounded rationality*, volume 2. MIT Press, 1982.

[Zilberstein and Russell 1996] Shlomo Zilberstein and Stuart Russell. Optimal composition of real-time systems. *Artificial Intelligence*, 82(1–2):181–213, 1996.

[Zilberstein *et al.* 1999] Shlomo Zilberstein, François Charpillet, and Philippe Chassaing. Real-time problem solving with contract algorithms. In *Proceedings of IJCAI'99*, pages 1008–1013, Stockholm, Sweden, 1999.

# On Odd and Even Cycles in Normal Logic Programs*

**Fangzhen Lin**
Department of Computer Science
Hong Kong University of Science and Technology
Clear Water Bay, Kowloon, Hong Kong
flin@cs.hst.hk

**Xishun Zhao**
Institute of Logic and Cognition
Sun Yat-Sen University
510275, Guangzhou, P. R. China
hsdp08@zsu.edu.cn

### Abstract

An odd cycle of a logic program is a simple cycle that has an odd number of negative edges in the dependency graph of the program. Similarly, an even cycle is one that has an even number of negative edges. For a normal logic program that has no odd cycles, while it is known that such a program always has a stable model, and such a stable model can be computed in polynomial time, we show in this paper that checking whether an atom is in a stable model is NP-complete, and checking whether an atom is in all stable models is co-NP complete, both are the same as in the general case for normal logic programs. Furthermore, we show that if a normal logic program has exactly one odd cycle, then checking whether it has a stable model is NP-complete, again the same as in the general case. For normal logic programs with a fixed number of even cycles, we show that there is a polynomial time algorithm for computing all stable models. Furthermore, this polynomial time algorithm can be improved significantly if the number of odd cycles is also fixed.

## Introduction

One of the significant events in non-monotonic reasoning in recent years has been the emergence of answer set programming (see, for example (Niemelä 1999)), a constraint programming paradigm based on Gelfond and Lifschitz's stable model and answer set semantics of logic programs (Gelfond&Lifschitz 1988; 1991).

In general, most reasoning problems in ASP are NP-hard. For instance, checking if there exists an answer set of a normal logic program is an NP-complete problem.

Recently, Gottlob *et al* (2002) considered the following decision and search problems in logic programs:

1. Consistency: Determining whether a program $P$ has a stable model.
2. Brave Reasoning: Check whether an atom appears in a stable model of a program $P$.
3. Cautious Reasoning: Check whether an atom appears in all stable models of a program $P$.
4. SM Computation: Find an arbitrary stable model of a program $P$.
5. SM Enumeration: Compute all stable models of a program $P$.

They defined the feedback width of a logic program to be the size of a smallest set of atoms such that when these atoms are deleted from the program's dependency graph, the resulting *un-directed* version of the graph has no cycles with a negative edge, and showed that the above tasks can all be solved in $O(2^k n)$, where $n$ is the size the program and $k$ the feedback width. So for the class of logic programs that have a bounded feedback width, all of the reasoning problems can be solved in linear time on the size of the given input logic program.

One problem with this result is that there are a lot more cycles in the un-directed version than in the directed version of the dependency graph of a logic program. So in this paper, we consider cycles in the directed version of the dependency graph of a logic program. We distinguish two types of cycles. An *even* (*odd*, respectively) cycle is a simple cycle with a non-zero even (odd, respectively) number of negative edges.

Programs that have no odd cycles are also called call-consistent (Kunen ; Sato 1987). An early result by Papadimitriou and Yannakakis (1992), done in the context of deductive databases more than 10 years ago, showed that if a normal logic program is call-consistent, then there is a polynomial algorithm that can return a stable model of the logic program. This would suggest that perhaps other reasoning tasks, such as checking if there is a stable model containing a given atom, would be tractable as well. In this paper we show that this is not the case. In particular, checking if there is a stable model containing a given atom is an NP-complete problem, just as hard as in the general case.

It has also been shown that if a program has no even cycle, then it has at most one stable model (You&Yuan 1994): if the well-founded model of the program is also its stable model, then this is the only one; otherwise, it has no stable model (Zhao 2002). In this paper we extend this result and

*We thank the reviewers for comments to this paper. Much of this work was done during the visit of the second author to HKUST. This work has been supported in part by HK RGC under CERG HKUST6205/02E, and by the NSFC under its major research program "Basic Theory and Core Techniques of Non-Canonical Knowledge".

show that a logic program with at most $k$ even cycles has at most $2^k$ stable models.

In summary, the main results of this paper are as follows:

1. For call-consistent programs we show that the brave reasoning problem is NP-complete, and the cautious reasoning problem is co-NP-complete,
2. If a program has exactly one odd cycle (it could have any number of even cycles), then the consistency problem is NP-complete.
3. If a program has $k$ even cycles (it could have any number of odd cycles), then it has at most $2^k$ stable models. Furthermore, the set of all stable models can be computed in $2^{2k}O(n^{k+2})$ time, where $n$ is the size of the given program.
4. If the number of the total odd and even cycles of a logic program is at most $k$, then we show that the set of all stable models of the program can be computed in $2^{2k}O(n^2)$ time, where $n$ is the size of the program.

As we shall see, besides of theoretical interests, these results suggest that for computing answer sets of a logic program, a good heuristic is to branch on the variable that would break the most number of even cycles.

This paper is organized as follows. In section 2, we review some basic concepts of logic programming. In section 3, we prove our results for call-consistent programs. We discuss programs with exactly one odd cycle in section 4, programs with a fixed number of even cycles in section 5, and programs with a fixed number of odd and even cycles in Section 6. We conclude this paper in section 7.

## Preliminaries

We consider only normal propositional logic programs, which are finite sets of rules of the following form

$$r: \quad a \leftarrow b_1, \cdots, b_m, \texttt{not}\ c_1, \cdots, \texttt{not}\ c_n,$$

where $r$ is the name of the rule, $a$, $b_i$, $1 \leq i \leq m$, and $c_j$, $1 \leq j \leq n$ are atoms, and $m + n \geq 1$. In the following, we let Head($r$)=$a$ (the head of $r$), Pos($r$)=$\{b_1, \cdots, b_m\}$ (the positive body of $r$), and Neg($r$)=$\{c_1, \cdots, c_n\}$ (the negative body of $r$). The body of $r$ is Pos($r$) $\cup$ Neg($r$).

In the following, given a (normal) logic program $P$, we denote by At($P$) the set of atoms occurring in $P$. We shall also call atoms positive literals. A negative literal is an expression of the form $\texttt{not}\ a$, where $a$ is an atom. A literal is either a positive or a negative literal.

Given a logic program $P$, $S \subseteq$ At($P$) is said to be a stable model (Gelfond&Lifschitz 1988) of $P$ if $S$ = Cons($P_S$), where $P_S$ is obtained from $P$ and $S$ by the following Gelfond-Lifschitz transformation:

(1) for each atom $p$ and any rule $r \in P$, if $p \in$ Neg($r$) and $p \notin S$, then remove $\texttt{not}\ p$ from $r$, and

(2) in the set of remaining rules, delete those rules that still contain a negative literal in their bodies,

and Cons($P_S$) is the set of atoms derivable from the definite logic program $P_S$.

A logic program may have zero, one, or more than one stable models. In comparison, the well-founded model semantics (Van Gelder *et al* 1991) produces a unique 3-valued model for a normal logic program. Formally, a 3-valued interpretation $I$ is a pair of two disjoint sets of atoms, $(I^+, I^-)$. Atoms in $I^+$ are assigned *true* and those in $I^-$ *false*. Atoms occurring in neither $I^+$ nor $I^-$ are *undefined*.

Given a logic program $P$, the operation $\Gamma_P$ defined by $\Gamma_P(S)$ := Cons($P_S$), is anti-monotone, i.e., if $S_1 \subseteq S_2$ then $\Gamma_P(S_2) \subseteq \Gamma_P(S_1)$. Thus the operation $\Gamma_P^2$, defined as $\Gamma_P^2(S) := \Gamma_P(\Gamma_P(S))$, is monotone. Therefore, $\Gamma_P^2$ has the least fixed-point, say $S$, and the greatest fixed-point, say $T$. The well-founded model of $P$ is $(S, \mathrm{At}(P) - T)$.

The well-founded model can be computed in quadratic time (Van Gelder *et al* 1991), and has been used to simplify a logic program in almost all of the current answer set programming systems.

In the following, we denote by $\mathrm{WFM}(P) = (\mathrm{WFM}(P)^+, \mathrm{WFM}(P)^-)$ the well-founded model of $P$. We use WFM($P$) to simplify $P$ as follows:

(1) Delete all rules $r \in P$ such that either Head($r$) $\in$ WFM$^+(P)$, Pos($r$) $\cap$ WFM$^-(P) \neq \emptyset$, or Neg($r$) $\cap$ WFM$^+(P) \neq \emptyset$.

(2) From the bodies of the remaining rules, remove all positive literals in WFM$^+(P)$ and all negative literals $\texttt{not}\ q$ with $q \in$ WFM$^-(P)$.

The resulting program is written as $P \setminus$ WFM($P$).

The *dependency graph* (Apt *et al* 1988) of a normal logic program $P$, denoted by $G_P$, is a directed graph with signed edges. The vertices of $G_P$ are atoms in At($P$). There is a positive (negative, respectively) edge from a vertex $p$ to a vertex $q$ if there is a rule $r \in P$ such that Head($r$) = $q$ and $p \in$ Pos($r$) ($p \in$ Neg($r$), respectively). Informally, a positive (negative, respectively) edge from $p$ to $q$ means that $q$ depends positively (negatively, respectively) on $p$.

If a simple cycle of $G_P$ has an odd (a non-zero even, respectively) number of negative edges then we call it an *odd (even, respectively) cycle*. In the following, we denote by NOC($P$) (NEC($P$), respectively) the number of odd (even, respectively) cycles in the dependency graph of $P$.

## Call-Consistent Programs

As mentioned earlier, a call-consistent program is a normal logic program that has no odd cycles. It has been shown that a call-consistent program always has a stable model, and such a stable model can be computed in polynomial time. Despite this, checking if an atom is in a stable model of a call-consistent program is still NP-complete, and checking if an atom is in all the stable models of a call-consistent program is still co-NP complete.

**Theorem 1**

*(a) Brave reasoning for call-consistent programs is NP-complete.*

*(b) Cautious reasoning for call-consistent programs is co-NP-complete.*

*Proof.* (Sketched) Memberships in NP for (a), and co-NP for (b) is obvious. For hardness, consider a set $\varphi$ of clauses with variables $x_1, ..., x_n$. Let $y_1, ..., y_n$, $a$ and $b$ be new variables. Let $P(\varphi)$ be the program consisting of rules in the following groups.

**(I)** For each $x_i$ ($1 \leq i \leq m$), the rules:

$$y_i \leftarrow \texttt{not}\ x_i, \quad x_i \leftarrow \texttt{not}\ y_i.$$

**(II)** For each $C$ in $\varphi$, the rule: $a \leftarrow \overline{C}$, where for a clause $C$, if $\neg x \in C$, then $x \in \overline{C}$, and if an atom $x \in C$, then $\texttt{not}\ x \in \overline{C}$.

**(III)** The single rule: $b \leftarrow \texttt{not}\ a$.

The only cycles of $P(\varphi)$ are generated by rules in group (I), and they are all even cycles. Thus the program is a call-consistent.

We show that $\varphi$ is satisfiable iff $b$ is in at least one stable model of $P(\varphi)$, and $\varphi$ is unsatisfiable iff $a$ is in every stable model of $P(\varphi)$. From these, the NP-hardness of the brave reasoning, and the co-NP-hardness of the cautious reasoning follow.

Suppose $\varphi$ is satisfiable. We can then generate a truth assignment satisfying it using the rules in (I). Under this truth assignment, rules in group (II) are not applicable. Hence we can not use them to get $a$. In this case, we get $b$ by using the rule in (III). Therefore, we get a stable model of $P(\varphi)$ containing $b$. Suppose $\varphi$ is not satisfiable. Then any truth assignment makes some clause $C$ in $\varphi$ false, and hence the rule in (II) is applicable. Thus, $a$ is in every stable model of $P(\varphi)$. ∎

Notice that a well-known technique for finding a stable model containing an atom $a$ is to add the constraint "$\leftarrow$ not $a$" to the original logic program. According to our theorem, and the fact that there is a polynomial time algorithm that can return a stable model of a call-consistent logic program, one cannot replace this constraint by a polynomial number of rules without introducing some odd cycles unless the polynomial hierarchy collapses.

It is worth mentioning here that in disjunctive logic programs, the so-called head-cycle free programs (Ben-Eliyahu-Zohary&Paloponi 1997; Ben-Eliyahu-Zohary *et all* 2000) appear to exhibit similar properties like call-consistent programs. In particular, finding one answer set is tractable for these disjunctive logic programs, but brave reasoning and cautious reasoning are hard.

## Programs with Exactly One Odd Cycle

Programs with odd cycles may or may not have stable models. For instance, consider the following programs

$$P_0 = \{b \leftarrow \texttt{not}\ a,\ \ c \leftarrow \texttt{not}\ b,\ \ a \leftarrow \texttt{not}\ c\},$$
$$P_1 = P_0 \cup \{a \leftarrow\}.$$

Both have exactly one odd loop, but $P_0$ has no stable model while $P_1$ has one $\{a, c\}$.

In general, even cycles generate models while odd cycles eliminate models. For instance, the following set of rules

$$\{x_1 \leftarrow \texttt{not}\ y_1, y_1 \leftarrow \texttt{not}\ x_1, \cdots, x_n \leftarrow \texttt{not}\ y_n, \\ y_n \leftarrow \texttt{not}\ x_n\} \qquad (1)$$

has $n$ even cycles and $2^n$ stable models. Now if we add an odd cycle such as $x_1 \leftarrow \texttt{not}\ x_1$ to it, then in principle, we may have to go through all these $2^n$ models before we are sure that there is no stable model of the new program.

This is basically the reason why the consistency problem for programs with exactly one odd cycle is intractable.

**Theorem 2** *The consistency problem for programs whose dependency graphs have exactly one odd cycle is NP-complete.*

*Proof.* Membership in NP is obvious. The proof of hardness is similar to that of Theorem 1. Consider again a set $\varphi$ of clauses with variables $x_1, ..., x_n$. Let $y_1, ..., y_n$, $a$ and $b$ be new variables. Let $P(\varphi)$ be as in the proof of Theorem 1 but with the rule (III) replaced by the following rule:

**(III')** $b \leftarrow a, \texttt{not}\ b$.

Clearly, $P(\varphi)$ has exactly one odd cycle formed by rule (III'), and it has a stable model if and only if $\varphi$ is satisfiable. ∎

## Programs with a Fixed Number of Even Cycles

From the result in the last section, we see that restricting the number of odd cycles to a fixed positive number cannot reduce the complexity. As we mentioned above, the reason is that even cycles can generate an exponential number of models. We now consider what happens if we restrict the number of even cycles.

As mentioned in Introduction, if a program has no even cycle, then it has at most one stable model (You&Yuan 1994). Furthermore, if the well-founded model of the program is also its stable model, then this is the only one; otherwise, it has no stable model (Zhao 2002). To study the general case, we first introduce the following definition, which was first introduced in (Cholewinski&Truszczynski 1999).

**Definition 1** *Let $P$ be a program, and $a$ an atom in $At(P)$. Define $P_a^+$ to be the program obtained from $P$ by*

1. *deleting all rules whose bodies contain* not *a, and*
2. *removing a from the bodies of remaining rules.*

*Similarly define $P_a^-$ to be the program obtained from $P$ by*

1. *deleting all rules whose bodies contain a, and*
2. *removing* not *a from the remaining rules.*

Notice that $G_{P_a^+}$, $G_{P_a^-}$ are subgraphs of $G_P$, and that in $G_{P_a^+}$, $G_{P_a^-}$ there are no edges going out from $a$.

**Lemma 1** *(Cholewinski&Truszczynski 1999) Let $P$ be a program, $a \in At(P)$. Suppose $S$ is a stable model of $P$. Then*

1. *If $a \in S$ then $S$ is a stable model of $P_a^+$.*
2. *If $a \notin S$ then $S$ is a stable model of $P_a^-$.*

Cholewinski and Truszczynski (1999) also proved that a program with $n$ rules has at most $O(3^{n/3})$ stable models. Our following result gives the upper bound of the number of stable models according to the number of even cycles.

Recall that for a program $P$, NEC($P$) denotes the number of even cycles in $P$, and NOC($P$) the number of odd cycles in $P$.

**Lemma 2** *Let $P$ be a program such that NEC$(P) \leq k$. Then $P$ has at most $2^k$ stable models.*

*Proof.* We show the theorem by induction on $k$, here $k$ is NEC$(P)$.
If $k = 0$ then the lemma follows from the aforementioned result by You and Yuan (1994). Suppose NEC$(P) \geq 1$. Then pick an atom $a \in$ At$(P)$ such that $a$ occurs in an even cycle. Please note that $G_{P_a^+}, G_{P_a^-}$ are subgraphs of $G_P$, and that in $G_{P_a^+}, G_{P_a^-}$ there are no edges going out from $a$.Thus NEC$(P_a^+) \leq k-1$ and NEC$(P_a^-) \leq k-1$. By the induction hypothesis, $P_a^+$ ($P_a^-$, respectively) has at most $2^{k-1}$ stable models. By the above lemma, we know that $P$ has at most $2^{k-1} + 2^{k-1} = 2^k$ stable models. ■

From these two lemmas, and the fact that when NEC$(P)$ is zero, either $P$ has no stable model or its well-founded model is its stable model, a naive way to compute the stable models of a program with NEC$(P) \leq k$ is to choose an atom $a$ that lies in an even cycle, split the current program $P$ into $P_a^+$ and $P_a^-$, and then inductively compute the stable models of $P_a^+$ and $P_a^-$, which have fewer numbers of even cycles than $P$. Unfortunately, finding an atom that lies in an even loop of a program is an intractable problem:

**Lemma 3** *Given a program $P$ and an atom $a$. The problem of determining whether $a$ lies in an even cycle of $G_P$ is NP-complete.*

*Proof.* (Sketched) The proof of this this lemma is similar to the proof of Theorem 16 of (Gottlob *et al* 2002). The membership in NP is obvious. To prove the hardness we reduce the node-disjoint path problem for directed graphs, which is a NP-complete problem (Garey&Johnson 1979), to our problem.
Let $G = (N, E)$ be a directed graph, and $x_1, y_1$ and $x_2, y_2$ two pairs of nodes of $G$.
The problem is deciding whether there are two node-disjoint paths linking $x_1$ to $x_2$ and $y_1$ to $y_2$. From $G$, we construct a logic program $P(G)$ containing a rule $t \leftarrow s$ for each edge $(s, t) \in E$, plus two additional rules $x_1 \leftarrow \texttt{not}\ y_2$, and $y_1 \leftarrow \texttt{not}\ x_2$.
We can show that $x_1$ lies in an even cycle in $P_G$ if and only if there are two node-disjoint paths linking $x_1$ to $x_2$ and $y_1$ to $y_2$ in $G$. ■

So instead of looking for an atom that lies in an even cycle of a program, and split the program on the atom, we simply split the program on every atom of the program. This is the basic idea behind our algorithm for computing Ans$(P, k)$ in Figure 1.

**Lemma 4** *Let $k$ be a fixed natural number, $P$ a program with NEC$(P) \leq k$. Then every stable model of $P$ appears in Ans$(P, k)$.*

*Proof.* We prove the assertion by induction on $k$. When $k = 0$, the assertion follows from the known result. Suppose $k > 0$. If the dependency graph $G_P$ has an even cycle, then the cycle will be broken in $G_{P_a^+}$ and $G_{P_a^-}$ for some $a$. That is, NEC$(P_a^+) \leq k - 1$ and NEC$(P_a^-) \leq k - 1$. By the induction hypothesis, all stable models of $P_a^+$ ($P_a^-$), respectively) appear in Ans$(P_a^+, k - 1)$ (Ans$(P_a^-, k - 1)$, respectively). Now the lemma follows from Lemma 2. ■

**Function** Ans$(P, k)$
**Input** A normal program $P$, and a natural number $k$.
**Output** A set of stable models of $P$
**begin**
**if** $k = 0$ **then**
  **if** WFM$^+(P)$ is a stable model of $P$ **then return** $\{$WFM$^+(P)\}$ **else return** $\emptyset$.
$\Pi := \emptyset$.
**for** each atom $a \in$ At$(P)$
  **for** each $S \in$Ans$(P_a^+, k-1)\cup$Ans$(P_a^-, k-1)$
    **if** $S$ is a stable model of $P$ **then** $\Pi := \Pi \cup \{S\}$.
**return** $\Pi$
**end**

Figure 1: An algorithm for computing the stable models of a logic program with at most $k$ even cycles

**Lemma 5** *Let $P$ be a program, and $k$ a fixed natural number. Then*

1. *Ans$(P, k)$ contains at most $2^k n^k$ sets, where $n$ is the size of $P$.*
2. *Ans$(P, k)$ can be computed in $2^{2k}O(n^{k+2})$ time.*

*Proof.* (1) We shall proceed by induction on $k$. The assertion clearly holds when $k = 0$. Suppose $k > 0$. By the induction hypothesis, Ans$(P_a^+, k-1)$ (Ans$((P_a^-, k-1)$, respectively) contains at most $2^{k-1}n^{k-1}$ sets for each atom $a$. Thus, Ans$(P, k)$ has at most $2n(2^{k-1}n^{k-1}) = 2^k n^k$ sets.
(2) We shall prove the claim by induction on $k$. When $k = 0$ the claim is obviously valid because the well-founded model can be computed in quadratic time and to check whether it is a stable model costs not more than quadratic time. Suppose $k > 0$. By the induction hypothesis, to compute Ans$(P_a^+, k-1)$ and Ans$(P_a^-, k-1)$ for all $a$ will cost time not more than

$$2n(2^{2(k-1)}n^{k+1}) = 2^{2k-1}n^{k+2}.$$

From (1), to check whether the sets in all Ans$(P_a^+, k-1) \cup$ Ans$(P_a^-, k-1)$ are stable models needs time not more than

$$2n(2^{k-1}n^{k-1})O(n^2) = 2^k O(n^{k+2}).$$

Altogether, the total running time is

$$2^{2k-1}n^{k+2} + 2^k n^{k+2} \leq 2^{2k}n^{k+2}.$$

■

From these two lemmas we obtain the following theorem.

**Theorem 3** *For an arbitrary fixed natural number $k$, the set of stable models of a program with at most $k$ even cycles can be computed in $2^{2k}O(n^{k+2})$ time, where $n$ is the size of $P$.*

Notice that in the theorem, the time complexity is bounded by $n^{k+2}$ which is a polynomial *whose degree depends on the parameter $k$*. It remains an open question whether there is an algorithm computing all stable models in time bounded by a polynomial whose degree does not depend on $k$. In the next section, we show that this is true for logic programs with at most $k$ total number of odd and even cycles.

**Function** All-Ans($P$)
**Input:** A normal program $P$
**Output:** The set of stable models of $P$
**begin**
**if** $\text{WFM}^+(P)$ is a stable model of $P$ **then return** $\{\text{WFM}^+(P)\}$.
$Q := P \setminus \text{WFM}(P)$ (now $Q$ is non-empty).
compute a bottom $H$ of $Q$.
pick an atom $a \in H$ such that there is another atom $b$ in $H$, and a negative edge $a$ to $b$ in $G_Q$.
$\Pi := \emptyset$.
**for** each $S \in$ All-Ans($P_a^+$)$\cup$ All-Ans($P_a^-$)
  **if** $S$ is a stable model of $P$ **then** $\Pi := \Pi \cup \{S\}$
**return** $\Pi$
**end**

Figure 2: An algorithm for computing the stable models of a logic program

## Programs with a Fixed Number of Cycles

In this section we show that for any given $k$, there is an algorithm that computes in quadratic time all stable models of any given program $P$ with $\text{NEC}(P) + \text{NOC}(P) \leq k$.

Recall that a strongly connected component of a graph is a set of nodes such that for any two nodes in the set, there is a path from one node to the other, and it is not a proper subset of any such sets. There is a linear time algorithm that can compute all strongly connected components of a graph (Tarjan 1972).

Given a normal program $P$, we call a set $B$ of atoms a *bottom* if it is a strongly connected component of $G_P$, and there is no other strongly connected component $B'$ such that there is a path from an atom in $B'$ to another atom in $B$.

**Proposition 1** *Let $P$ be a normal logic program. If $Q = P \setminus WFM(P)$ is not empty, then every bottom of $Q$ must have a pair of nodes $a$ and $b$ such that there is a negative edge from $a$ to $b$.*

*Proof.* We prove by contradiction. Suppose $Q$ is not empty, $H$ is a bottom of $Q$, and all paths in $H$ are positive.
Let $R(H) = \{r \in Q \mid \text{Head}(r) \in H\}$. Since $H$ is a bottom of $Q$, and $Q$ is the result of simpifying $P$ by its well-founded model, there cannot be any atom $p$ in $Q$ such that $p \notin H$, and there is a path from $p$ to an atom in $H$. For otherwise, since there is no more cycles below $p$, its truth value would have been dertermined in the well-founded model of $P$, thus eliminated when $P$ is simplified using its well-founded model. Thus the bodies of all rules in $R(H)$ must all be in $H$. As a consequence, no rule in $R(H)$ can have a negative literal in its body. Moreover, since $Q = P \setminus \text{WFM}(P)$, every rule in $Q$ has to have a non-empty body. Then according to the procedure for calculating well-founded models, all atoms in $H$ are false in the well-founded model of $P$, and hence they cannot occur in $Q$. This contradicts the assumption that $H$ is a strongly connected component of $Q$. ∎

**Lemma 6** *Let $P$ be a normal logic program. Then All-Ans($P$) defined in Figure 2 contains all stable models of $P$.*

*Proof.* We show the theorem by induction on $k$, the number of cycles of $G_P$.
When $k = 0$, i.e., NEC($P$)=NOC($P$)=0, the theorem follows from the fact that $P$ has exact one stable model which is the well-founded model of $P$.
Suppose $k > 0$ , and NEC($P$)+NOC($P$) $= k$. If WFM($P$) is a stable model of $P$, then it is the unique stable model of $P$, and the theorem follows. So, we assume that WFM($P$) is not a stable model of $P$. Thus $Q := P \setminus \text{WFM}(P)$ is not empty. Suppose $H$ is a bottom of $Q$, let $a$ and $b$ be two atoms in $H$ such that there is a negative edge from $a$ to $b$. Since $H$ is a connected component, there must a path from $b$ to $a$. Thus, there is at least one cycle in $H$ that goes through the negative edge from $a$ to $b$. Then NEC($P_a^+$)+NOC($P_a^+$) $\leq k-1$, and $\text{NEC}(P_a^-) + \text{NOC}(P_a^-) \leq k-1$. We know that every stable model of $P$ is a stable model of either $P_a^+$ or $P_a^-$. By the inductive assumption, every stable model of $P_a^+$ ($P_a^-$, respectively) appears in All-Ans($P_a^+$) (All-Ans($P_a^-$), respectively). Therefore, every stable model of $P$ appears in All-Ans($P$). ∎

**Lemma 7** *For each fixed natural number $k$, the function in Figure 2 runs in time $2^{2k}O(n^2)$ for any given program $P$ such that NEC($P$)+NOC($P$) $\leq k$, where $n$ is the size of $P$.*

*Proof.* We proceed by induction on $k$. When $k = 0$, the lemma follows from the fact that $P$ has exact one stable model, i.e., the well-founded model, which can be computed in quadratic time and that to check whether the well-founded model is a stable model costs no more than quadratic time.
Suppose $k > 0$. To compute the well-founded model of a program costs quadratic time, to computer a bottom takes linear time, and the atom $a$ and $P_a^+, P_a^-$ can be computed in linear time. By the inductive assumption, to compute All-Ans($P_a^+$) and All-Ans($P_a^-$) costs not more than

$$2^{2(k-1)}O((n-1)^2) + 2^{2(k-1)}O((n-1)^2) \leq 2^{2k-1}O(n^2)$$

time. From Lemma 2, we know that All-Ans($P_a^+$) $\cup$ All-Ans($P_a^-$) has at most $2^k$ elements. Thus to check whether they are stable models of $P$ needs no more than time $2^kO(n^2)$.
Altogether the algorithm costs no more than

$$O(n^2) + O(n) + 2^{2k-1}O(n^2) + 2^kO(n^2) \leq 2^{2k}O(n^2)$$

∎

By Lemmas 6 and 7 we obtain the following theorem.

**Theorem 4** *The set of all stable models of a program with a fixed number of even and odd cycles can be computed in quadratic time $2^{2k}O(n^2)$, where $k$ is the number of even and odd loops, and $n$ the size of the given program.*

We want to emphasize that this result assumes a fixed $k$, and the co-efficient $2^{2k}$ means that this number should not be too big for the algorithm in Figure 2 to be practical. Of course, this is the worst case complexity. Problems normally encountered in practice could be much easier even for large $k$.

## Conclusions

We have performed a detailed complexity analysis of normal logic programs with a limited number of odd and/or even cycles. To recast, for a normal logic program without any odd cycles, others have shown that it always has stable models (Dung 1992; You&Yuan 1994), and one of them can be computed in polynomial time (Papadimitriou&Yannakakis 1992). What we have shown here is that despite these positive results, given an atom, checking whether it is in one of its stable models is an NP-complete problem, and checking whether it is in all of its stable models is a coNP-complete problem. We have also shown that if we relax the condition a little bit, allowing just one odd cycle, then whether there is a stable model becomes an NP-complete program, the same as in the general case.

For a normal logic program without even cycles, others have shown that it has at most one stable model (You&Yuan 1994), and if it has a stable model, then the stable model must also be its well-founded model (Zhao 2002). We have extended these results, and shown that if a normal logic program has at most $k$ even cycles, then it has at most $2^k$ stable models, and all of them can be computed in polynomial time for the fixed parameter $k$.

It is clear that there is a disparity between the results for programs with a limited number of odd cycles and those for programs with a limited even cycles. The reason is that these two types of cycles play very different roles. The even cycles are stable model generators, and the odd cycles are stable model eliminators.

We believe that our results are not just of theoretical interest. The algorithms in Figures 1 and 2, suggest that for computing answer sets of general logic programs, a good heuristic is to choose the next variable that would break the most number of even cycles. The key of course is how to efficiently compute the variables that would break a large number of even cycles. One future work for us is to address this problem and to experiment with this heuristic.

## References


Apt, K.R., Blair, H.A., and Walker, A. 1988. Towards a Theory of Declarative Knowledge. In *Foundation of Deductive Database and Logic Programming* (ed. J. Minker), 293–322, Morgan Kaufmann, Los Altos, 1988.

Apt, K.R., and Bol, R.N., 1994. Logic Programming and Negation: A Survey. *Journal of Logic Programming* 19/20:9–71.

Ben-Eliyahu-Zohary, R. and Paloponi, L. 1997. Reasoning with minimal models: efficient algorithms and applications. *Artificial Intelligence* 96(2):421–449.

Ben-Eliyahu-Zohary, R., Paloponi, L., and Zemlyanker, V. 2000. More on tractable disjunctive datalog. *Journal of Logic Programming* 46(1-2):61–101.

Bidoit, N., and Froidevaux, C. 1991. Negation by Default and Unstratifible Logic Programs. *Theoretical Computer Science* 78:85–112.

Cholewinski, P., and Truszczynski, M. 1999. Extremal Problems in Logic Programming and Stable Model Computation. *Journal of Logic Programming* 38:219–242.

Dung, P.M. 1992. On the Relation between Stable and Well-Founded Semantics of Logic Programs. *Theoretical Computer Science: Logic, Semantics and Theory of Programming* 105:7–26.

Eiter, T., Leone, N., Mateis, C., Pfeifer, G., and Scarnello, F. 1998. The KR-System DLV: Progress Report, Comparison and Benchmarks. In *Proceedings of the 6th International Conference on Principles of Knowledge Representation and Reasoning*, 406–417. Morgan Kaufmann Publishers.

Garey, M.R., and Johnson, D.S. 1979. *Computers and Intractability, A Guide to the Theory of NP-Completeness.* Freeman, Newyork.

Gelfond, M., and Lifschitz, V. 1988. The Stable Model Semantics for Logic Programming. In *Proceedings of the 5th International Conference on Logic Programming*, 1070–1080. The MIT Press.

Gelfond, M., Lifschitz, V., 1991. Classical Negation in Logic Programs and Disjunctive Database. *New Generation Computing* 9: 365–385.

Gottlob, G., and Scarcello, F., and Sideri, M. 2002. Fixed-Parameter Complexity in AI and Nonmonotonic Reasoning. *Artificial Intelligence* 138:55–86.

Kleine Büning, H., and Lettmann, T. 1999. *Propositional Logic: Deduction and Algorithms.* Cambridge University Press.

Kunen, K. 1989. Signed Dada Dependencies in Logic Programs. *Journal of Logic Programming*, 7:231–245.

Lifschitz, V., and Turner, H. 1994. Splitting a Logic Program. In *Proceedings of International Conference on Logic Programming*, 23–37.

Lin, F., and You, J.H. 2002. Abduction in Logic Programming: A New Definition and an Abductive Procedure Based on Rewritting. *Artificial Intelligence*, 140(1/2):175–205.

Lin, F., and Zhao, Y. 2002. ASSAT: Computing Answer Sets of a Logic Program by SAT Solvers. In *Proceedings of AAAI-2002*, 112–117.

Niemelä, I. 1999. Logic Programs with Stable Model Semantics as a Constraint Programming Paradigm. *Annals of mathematics and Artificial Intelligence* 25:241–273.

Papadimitriou, C.H., and Yannakakis, M. 1992. Tie-Breaking Semantics and Structural Totality. In *Proceedings of 11th ACM conference on Principles of Database Systems (PODS 1992)*, 16–22.

Sato, T. 1987. On the Consistency of First-Order Logic Programs, ETL Technique Report, TR-87-12.

Tarjan, R.E. 1972. Depth-First Search and Linear Graph Algorithms, *SIAM Journal of on Computing* 1:146–160.

Van Gelder, A., Ross, K.R., and Schlipf, J.S. 1991. The Well-Founded Semantics for General Logic Programs. *Journal of the ACM* 38:620–650.

You, J.H., and Yuan, L. 1994. A Three-Valued Semantics for Deductive Database and Logic Programs. *Journal of Computer and System Science* 49:334–361.

Zhao, J. 2002. A Study of Answer set Programming, MPhil Thesis, Dept. of Computer Science, The Hong Kong University of Science and Technology.

# Logic Programs with Abstract Constraint Atoms

**Victor W. Marek** and **Mirosław Truszczyński**
Department of Computer Science
University of Kentucky
Lexington, KY 40506-0046
{marek,mirek}@cs.uky.edu

## Abstract

We propose and study extensions of logic programming with constraints represented as generalized atoms of the form $C(X)$, where $X$ is a finite set of atoms and $C$ is an abstract constraint (formally, a collection of sets of atoms). Atoms $C(X)$ are satisfied by an interpretation (set of atoms) $M$, if $M \cap X \in C$. We focus here on monotone constraints, that is, those collections $C$ that are closed under the superset. They include, in particular, weight (or pseudo-boolean) constraints studied both by the logic programming and SAT communities. We show that key concepts of the theory of normal logic programs such as the one-step provability operator, the semantics of supported and stable models, as well as several of their properties including complexity results, can be lifted to such case.

## Introduction

In this paper, we study logic programs whose clauses are built of generalized atoms expressing constraints on sets. We show that under the assumption of *monotonicity* of constraints, and with an appropriate handling of nondeterminism inherent in deriving ways to satisfy constraints, basic concepts, methods, semantics and results studied in normal logic programming generalize to the extended setting. Our work provides a theoretical framework for recent extensions of logic programming with weight constraints (Simons, Niemelä, & Soininen 2002) but applies to a much broader class of programs.

In the 1990s researchers demonstrated that normal logic programming with the stable-model semantics is an effective knowledge representation formalism. It provides solutions to problems arising in such contexts as planning, reasoning about action, diagnosis and abduction, product configuration, and modeling and reasoning about preferences. Moreover, due to the emergence of fast methods to compute stable models (Niemelä & Simons 1997; Leone *et al.* 2003; Babovich & Lifschitz 2002; Lin & Zhao 2002), the importance of the formalism increased significantly as it became possible to use it not only as a modeling language but also as a practical computational tool. (Baral 2003) and (Gelfond & Leone 2002) provide a detailed discussion of the formalism and its applications.

In the last few years, researchers proposed extensions of the language of normal logic programming with means to model constraints involving *aggregate* operations on sets. (Simons, Niemelä, & Soininen 2002) proposed a formalism integrating logic programming with *weight constraints*[1], generalized the concept of stable models to this extended setting, and developed fast algorithms to compute them. (Denecker, Pelov, & Bruynooghe 2001; Pelov, Denecker, & Bruynooghe 2004), introduced a formalism allowing for more general aggregates. They extended to this new setting several semantics of normal logic programs, including the stable-model semantics and the well-founded semantics. A related recent work (Dell'Armi *et al.* 2003), incorporated aggregates into the formalism of *disjunctive* logic programs with the *answer-set semantics*. Such extensions are important as they simplify the task of modeling problem specifications, typically result in more direct and concise encodings, and often significantly improve the computational effectiveness of the formalism as a problem-solving tool[2].

However, arguably, all these approaches are subject to limitations. The formalism of (Simons, Niemelä, & Soininen 2002) admits only weight constraints and focuses almost entirely on the semantics of stable models. Furthermore, the connections to normal logic programming are indirect and somewhat obscure. There is a correspondence to logic programs with *nested* expressions (Ferraris & Lifschitz 2004), which helped establish some interesting results on programs with weight constraints (for instance, characterizations of their strong equivalence (Turner 2003)). However, the direct encodings of programs with weight constraints as programs with nested expressions have large size and, more importantly, it is not clear whether that connection applies in the broader context of other types of constraints. The other two approaches consider broader classes of constraints and are more firmly grounded in the core formalism of normal (dis-



[1]These are constraints on the total weight of elements in sets. In the SAT community, they are also referred to as *pseudo-boolean* constraints.

[2]For similar reasons, extending propositional logic with aggregates (most notably, weight constraints) has recently been gaining attention (Aloul *et al.* 2002; Dixon & Ginsberg 2002; Prestwich 2002).

junctive) programs, but are limited in that they do not allow aggregate constructs to appear in the heads of the clauses. In addition, all approaches discussed above focus on specific constraints, and so, they are restricted in their applicability.

Our goal is to address these limitations. We develop a formalism of logic programs with clauses built of generalized atoms that express constraints on sets. To this end, we propose the notion of an *abstract constraint* and its linguistic counterpart — an *abstract constraint atom*. We then use abstract constraint atoms as building blocks of program clauses. We restrict our attention to *monotone* constraints, as monotonicity is essential for preserving a procedural reading of a logic program as a computational device. We show that basic concepts, techniques and results of normal logic programming have direct generalizations to the class of programs built of monotone constraints. In particular, we extend to that setting the *supported-model* and the *stable-model* semantics. We also establish some relevant complexity results. Our work is related to (Marek, Niemelä, & Truszczyński 2004). That work, however, focused only on one specific class of constraints — cardinality constraints.

The key tool in our work is the *nondeterministic one-step provability* operator. It generalizes the one-step provability operator of (van Emden & Kowalski 1976). Thanks to close parallels between these two concepts, we are able to reconstruct operator-based characterizations of models, supported models and stable models, presented in (Apt 1990; Fitting 2002). We also distinguish and discuss the class of *deterministic* programs (programs with clauses whose heads can be satisfied only in one way). For these programs the one-step provability operator becomes deterministic and the theory of normal logic programming extends to deterministic programs without *any* significant change.

## Basic concepts, motivation, examples

We limit our considerations to the propositional case. As we interpret programs with variables by means of Herbrand models, the first-order case reduces to the propositional one.

We consider a language determined by a fixed countable set $At$ of *propositional atoms*. An *abstract constraint* is a collection $C \subseteq \mathcal{P}(At)$. An *abstract constraint atom* is a syntactic expression of the form $C(X)$, where $X \subseteq At$ is *finite* and $C$ is an abstract constraint.

We interpret abstract constraint atoms by means of propositional interpretations (truth assignments), represented as subsets of $At$[3]. An interpretation $M \subseteq At$ *satisfies* an abstract constraint atom $C(X)$ ($M \models C(X)$), if $M \cap X \in C$ (that is, if the set of atoms in $X$ that are true in $M$ belongs to, or satisfies, the constraint $C$). Otherwise, $M$ does not satisfy $C(X)$, ($M \not\models C(X)$). In that case, we also say that $M$ satisfies the *literal* $\mathbf{not}(C(X))$. An abstract constraint atom $C(X)$ is *consistent* if there is an interpretation $M$ such that $M \models C(X)$. We will now illustrate these concepts with several examples of common constraints.

**Weight constraints**. Given a real number $v$ and a weight function $w$, assigning to each atom in $At$ a real number (its *weight*), a weight constraint $W^{\leq}_{w,v}$ imposes a restriction that "a total weight of atoms in an *allowed* subset of $At$ be at least $v$". We represent $W^{\leq}_{w,v}$ as an abstract constraint $W^{\leq}_{w,v} = \{A \subseteq At\colon v \leq \sum_{a\in A} w(a)\}$ (comparison relations $<, >, \geq$ give rise to other types of weight constraints).

**Maximum constraints.** Given a weight function $w$ on the set of atoms and a real bound $v$, the maximum constraint restricts allowed sets of atoms to those with the maximum weight at least $v$. Formally, we express them as abstract constraints of the form $Max^{\leq}_{w,v} = \{A \subseteq At\colon v \leq \max\{w(a)\colon a \in A\}\}$ (or its variants, depending on the comparison relation).

**Even- and odd-cardinality constraints.** They impose a parity requirement on the cardinality of allowed sets. Formally, we express them as abstract constraints $E = \{A \subseteq At\colon |A| \text{ is even}\}$ and $O = \{A \subseteq At\colon |A| \text{ is odd}\}$.

**Containment constraints.** Such constraints require that allowed sets contain some prespecified configurations (subsets). We capture them by abstract constraints $C_{\mathcal{A}}$ that consist of all subsets of $At$ that contain at least one element from a prespecified collection $\mathcal{A}$ of finite subsets of $At$.

Each of these constraints determines associated abstract constraint atoms. Let $At = \{p_1, p_2, \ldots\}$ and let us consider a weight function $w$ such that for every integer $i \geq 1$, $w(p_i) = i$. The expression $W^{\leq}_{w,6}(p_1, p_2, p_5, p_6)$ is an example of an abstract constraint atom. A set $M$ of atoms satisfies $W^{\leq}_{w,6}(p_1, p_2, p_5, p_6)$ if and only if the total weight of atoms in $M \cap \{p_1, p_2, p_5, p_6\}$ is at least 6 (that is, whenever $M$ contains $p_6$, or $p_5$ together with at least one other atom). Similarly, the abstract constraint atom $Max^{\leq}_{w,5}(p_2, p_4, p_6, p_8)$ enforces the restriction that allowed sets contain $p_6$ or $p_8$. An abstract constraint atom $E(p_1, p_7)$ ($E$ stands for the even-cardinality constraint) forces allowed sets of atoms to contain none or both of $p_1$ and $p_7$. All these constraint atoms are consistent. An atom $W^{\leq}_{w,7}(p_1, p_2, p_3)$ is an example of an inconsistent atom. No selection of atoms from $\{p_1, p_2, p_3\}$ satisfies it and, consequently, it has no models.

These examples demonstrate that abstract constraints and constraint atoms can express a broad range of constraints. In the paper, we show that abstract constraint atoms can be combined into logic program clauses to represent even more complex constraints, and that much of the theory of normal logic programs generalizes to the extended setting.

Let $\mathcal{F}$ be a class of abstract constraints over $At$. By an $\mathcal{F}$*-atom* we mean an abstract atom $A(X)$ such that $A \in \mathcal{F}$ and $X \subseteq At$. By an $\mathcal{F}$*-clause* we mean an expression

$$A(X) \leftarrow B_1(X_1), \ldots, B_m(X_m), \mathbf{not}(C_1(Y_1)), \ldots, \mathbf{not}(C_n(Y_n)) \qquad (1)$$

where $A(X)$, $B_i(X_i)$ and $C_j(Y_j)$ are *consistent* $\mathcal{F}$-atoms[4]. By an $\mathcal{F}$*-program* we mean a collection of $\mathcal{F}$-clauses.

If $r$ is a clause of the form (1), $A(X)$ is the *head* of $r$, denoted by $hd(r)$, and $X$ is the *head set* of $r$, denoted by $hset(r)$. We also call the conjunction of literals

[3]We recall that for an interpretation $M \subseteq At$, an atom $p \in At$ is *true* in $M$ if $p \in M$; otherwise, $p$ is *false* in $M$.

[4]The case when inconsistent atoms are allowed is not essentially different and can be reduced to the one we focus on here. We do not discuss that issue in detail due to space restrictions.

$B_1(X_1), \ldots, B_m(X_m), \mathbf{not}(C_1(Y_1)), \ldots, \mathbf{not}(C_n(Y_n))$, the *body* of $r$. Finally, for an $\mathcal{F}$-program $P$, we define $hset(P)$ to be the union of sets $hset(r)$, for $r \in P$. An interpretation $M \subseteq At$ *satisfies* (is a *model* of) an $\mathcal{F}$-clause $r$ if $M$ satisfies the head of the clause whenever if satisfies the body of $r$. An interpretation $M \subseteq At$ *satisfies* (is a *model* of) an $\mathcal{F}$-program $P$ if it satisfies all clauses in $P$.

Our goals are to extend concepts, techniques and results of normal logic programming to the class of $\mathcal{F}$-programs, to provide a uniform theoretical framework for current extensions of logic programs with aggregates, and to identify basic assumptions under which such extensions are possible. To this end, we note that normal logic programs can be viewed as programs with abstract constraint atoms. Let $U_{At} = \{X \subseteq At\colon X \neq \emptyset\}$. Clearly, $U_{At}$ is an abstract constraint and, for every atom $a \in At$ and every interpretation $M$, $M \models a$ if and only if $M \models U_{At}(a)$. That is, propositional atoms are *equivalent* to abstract constraint atoms $U_{At}(a)$. Under this equivalence, a normal logic program $P$ can be viewed as a $\{U_{At}\}$-program, by regarding each atom $a$ as a shorthand for the constraint atom $U_{At}(a)$. Formally, for a normal logic program $P$, we define its corresponding $\{U_{At}\}$-program $P^{ac}$ (the superscript stands for *abstract constraints*) to consist of all $\{U_{At}\}$-clauses obtained from clauses in $P$ by replacing atoms $a$ with abstract constraint atoms $U_{At}(a)$. As a verification of the soundness of our approach, we will show in the paper that several properties of programs with abstract constraints, when applied to programs of the form $P^{ac}$, reduce to well known properties of normal logic programs.

Clauses of normal logic programs are typically regarded as computational devices: *assuming that preconditions of a clause have been established, the clause provides a justification to establish (compute) its head.* Crucial concepts behind formal accounts of that intuition are those of a Horn program, the corresponding *bottom-up* computation, and a least Herbrand model, which defines the *result* of the computation. Computations and their results are well defined due to the *monotone* behavior of Horn programs. To extend normal logic programming to the class of programs with abstract constraint atoms, one needs a generalization of the class of Horn programs supporting an appropriate notion of a computation, with the results of computations playing the same role as that played by the least Herbrand model.

In order to accomplish that, it is not enough simply to disallow the negation operator in the bodies of $\mathcal{F}$-clauses. It is also necessary to restrict the class of constraints to those that are *monotone* (that is, intuitively, once true in an interpretation, they remain true in its every superset). Without that assumption, the "monotonicity" of normal Horn programs does not generalize and there is no straightforward way to define the concept of a computation.

Formally, we say that an abstract constraint $C$ is *monotone* if for every $A, A' \subseteq At$, if $A \in C$ and $A \subseteq A'$ then $A' \in C$ (in other words, monotone constraints are precisely upward-closed families of subsets of $At$). An abstract constraint atom $C(X)$ is monotone if its constraint $C$ is monotone.

**Proposition 1** *Let $C$ be an abstract monotone constraint over $At$, $X \subseteq At$, and let $M, M' \subseteq At$ be two interpretations. If $M \models C(X)$ and $M \subseteq M'$, then $M' \models C(X)$.*

We note that if all the individual weights used by the weight function $w$ are non-negative, the weight constraint $W^{\leq}_{w,v}$, which we discussed earlier, is monotone. The maximum constraint $Max^{\leq}_{w,v}$ is monotone for every weight function $w$. We also note that the constraint $U_{At}$, which we used to interpret normal logic programs as programs with abstract constraints, is monotone as well, which further justifies a central role of monotone constraints. On the other hand, we note that some common constraints, for instance, even- and odd-cardinality constraints $E$ and $O$, are not monotone.

From now on, unless explicitly stated otherwise, we restrict our attention to constraints that are *monotone*. Under this assumption, the concept of a Horn program has an obvious direct generalization. Namely, for any class $\mathcal{F}$ of monotone constraints, an $\mathcal{F}$-program is a *Horn $\mathcal{F}$-program* if it contains no occurrences of the operator $\mathbf{not}$.

## Nondeterministic one-step provability operator

A basic tool in the studies of normal logic programs is that of the *one-step provability operator* (van Emden & Kowalski 1976). It describes the results of updating an interpretation by computing the heads of applicable program clauses. The difficulty with extending that operator to the case of $\mathcal{F}$-programs is that once a clause "fires", there may be many sets of atoms that can be derived on that basis, as there may be many ways to "satisfy" the abstract atom in the head of the clause. In this section, we address that issue.

A *nondeterministic operator* on a set $D$ is any function $f\colon D \to \mathcal{P}(D) \setminus \emptyset$ (that is, for every $d \in D$, $f(d) \neq \emptyset$). One can view the set $f(d)$ as the collection of all possible outcomes of applying $f$ to $d$, one of which (by the definition, at least one is available) can be selected nondeterministically as the *actual* outcome of $f$.

**Definition 1** *Let $\mathcal{F}$ be a class of monotone constraints. Let $P$ be an $\mathcal{F}$-program and let $M \subseteq At$.*
*(1) A clause $r \in P$ is* $M$-applicable, *if $M$ satisfies all literals in the body of $r$. We denote by $P(M)$ the set of all $M$-applicable clauses in $P$.*
*(2) A set $M'$ is* nondeterministically one-step provable *from $M$ by means of $P$, if $M' \subseteq hset(P(M))$ and $M' \models hd(r)$, for every clause $r$ in $P(M)$.*
*(3) The* nondeterministic one-step provability operator $T^{nd}_P$, *is a function from $\mathcal{P}(At)$ to $\mathcal{P}(\mathcal{P}(At))$ such that for every $M \subseteq At$, $T^{nd}_P(M)$ consists of all sets $M'$ that are nondeterministically one-step provable from $M$ by means of $P$.*

Our use of the term *nondeterministic operator* in reference to $T^{nd}_P$ is justified. We have the following property.

**Proposition 2** *Let $\mathcal{F}$ be a class of monotone constraints over a set $At$ and let $P$ be an $\mathcal{F}$-program. For every $M \subseteq At$, $hset(P(M)) \in T^{nd}_P(M)$. In particular, $T^{nd}_P(M) \neq \emptyset$.*

We use the operator $T^{nd}_P$ to introduce and characterize several semantics for $\mathcal{F}$-programs, and to relate the formalism of $\mathcal{F}$-programming to normal logic programming. We will often rely on the intuition that elements of $T_P^{nd}(M)$ can be viewed as possible *updates* of $M$ on the basis of clauses in $P$, none of them distinguished and each available for a nondeterministic selection as an *actual* update.

We conclude this section with a characterization of models of $\mathcal{F}$-programs. It is a generalization of the familiar description of models of normal logic programs as prefixpoints of the van Emden-Kowalski operator (the conditions in the theorem are commonly used as a definition of *prefixpoints* of a nondeterministic operator).

**Theorem 1** *Let $\mathcal{F}$ be a class of monotone constraints over a set $At$. Let $P$ be an $\mathcal{F}$-program and let $M \subseteq At$. The set $M$ is a model of $P$ if and only if there is $M' \in T_P^{nd}(M)$ such that $M' \subseteq M$.*

## Supported models of $\mathcal{F}$-programs

For a set $M$ of atoms, we say that $M$-applicable clauses in an $\mathcal{F}$-program $P$ provide *support* to atoms in the heads of these clauses. For $M$ to be a model of $P$, $M$ must satisfy the heads of all applicable clauses. To this end, $M$ needs to contain some of the atoms appearing in the heads of these clauses (atoms with support in $M$ and $P$) and, possibly, also some atoms that do not have such support. Models that contain only atoms with support form an important class of models generalizing the class of supported models for normal logic programs (Clark 1978; Apt 1990).

**Definition 2** *Let $\mathcal{F}$ be a class of monotone constraints and let $P$ be an $\mathcal{F}$-program. A set of atoms $M$ is a* supported model *of $P$ if $M$ is a model of $P$ and $M \subseteq hset(P(M))$.*

Supported models have the following characterization generalizing a characterization of supported models of normal logic programs as fixpoints of the the van Emden-Kowalski operator (the characterizing condition is commonly used as a definition of a *fixpoint* of a nondeterministic operator).

**Theorem 2** *Let $\mathcal{F}$ be a class of monotone constraints. Let $P$ be an $\mathcal{F}$-program. A set $M \subseteq At$ is a supported model of $P$ if and only if $M \in T_P^{nd}(M)$.*

Our concept of a supported model generalizes that considered in normal logic programming. Specifically, supported models of a normal logic program coincide with supported models of this same program viewed as a $\{U_{At}\}$-program.

**Theorem 3** *For every normal logic program $P$, a set of atoms $M$ is a supported model of $P$ if and only if $M$ is a supported model of the $\{U_{At}\}$-program $P^{ac}$.*

## Horn $\mathcal{F}$-programs

The concepts of a model and supported model extend to $\mathcal{F}$-programs directly. To find a proper generalization of stable models is less straightforward. We will address it in the next two sections. In this section, we will study *Horn $\mathcal{F}$-programs*. The key issues is that of generalization of the concept of a bottom-up computation which, in the case of Horn $\mathcal{F}$-programs is inherently non-deterministic.

Let $\mathcal{F}$ be a class of monotone constraints and let $P$ be a Horn $\mathcal{F}$-program. A *$P$-computation* is a sequence $(X_n)_{n=0,1,\ldots}$ such that $X_0 = \emptyset$ and, for every non-negative integer $n$:

1. $X_n \subseteq X_{n+1}$, and
2. $X_{n+1} \in T_P^{nd}(X_n)$.

Given a computation $t = (X_n)_{n=0,1,\ldots}$, we call $\bigcup_{n=0}^{\infty} X_n$ the *result* of the computation $t$ and denote it by $R_t$.

The following proposition shows that the results of computations contain only atoms with support and that they are supported models (and, thus, also models) of Horn $\mathcal{F}$-programs.

**Proposition 3** *Let $\mathcal{F}$ be a class of monotone constraints and let $P$ be a Horn $\mathcal{F}$-program. For every $P$-computation $t$:*
*1. $R_t \subseteq hset(P(R_t))$, and*
*2. $R_t$, is a supported model of $P$.*

Let $M$ be a model of $P$. We define $X_0^{P,M} = \emptyset$ and, for every $n \geq 0$, we set $X_{n+1}^{P,M} = hset(P(X_n^{P,M})) \cap M$.

**Theorem 4** *Let $\mathcal{F}$ be a class of monotone constraints and let $P$ be a Horn $\mathcal{F}$-program. For every model $M$ of $P$, the sequence $t^{P,M}$ is a $P$-computation.*

We call the $P$-computation $t^{P,M}$, where $M$ is a model of $P$, the *canonical* $P$-computation for $M$. Since every $\mathcal{F}$-program $P$ has models, every Horn $\mathcal{F}$-program has at least one computation. In general, a Horn $\mathcal{F}$-program may have multiple computations with, possibly, different results. Indeed, when deriving $X_{n+1}$ from what was computed so far, we can pick for $X_{n+1}$ *any* element form the collection $T_P^{nd}(X_n)$ which, typically, contains more than one element.

We use computations to distinguish an important class of models of Horn $\mathcal{F}$-programs, which generalizes the concept of a least Herbrand model of a normal Horn program.

**Definition 3** *Let $\mathcal{F}$ be a class of monotone constraints and let $P$ be a Horn $\mathcal{F}$-program. We say that a set of atoms $M$ is a* derivable model *of $P$ if there exists a $P$-computation $t$ such that $M = R_t$.*

It follows from Proposition 3(2) that derivable models of a Horn $\mathcal{F}$-program $P$ are supported models (and therefore models) of $P$. The following theorem shows they are the results of their own canonical computations.

**Theorem 5** *Let $\mathcal{F}$ be a class of monotone constraints. For every derivable model $M$ of a Horn $\mathcal{F}$-program $P$, we have $M = R_{t^{P,M}}$.*

Proposition 3(2) and Theorems 4 and 5 entail additional properties of derivable models of Horn $\mathcal{F}$-programs.

**Corollary 1** *Let $\mathcal{F}$ be a class of monotone constraints and let $P$ be a Horn $\mathcal{F}$-program. Then:*
*1. $P$ has at least one derivable model*
*2. Every model of $P$ contains a derivable model of $P$*
*3. Every minimal model of $P$ is derivable.*

These properties generalize their counterparts holding for normal Horn programs. Indeed, the $\{\mathcal{U}_{At}\}$-program $P^{ac}$, where $P$ is a normal Horn program, has exactly one $P^{ac}$-computation coinciding with the bottom-up computation for $P$, and exactly one derivable model that coincides with the least Herbrand model of $P$.

## Stable models of $\mathcal{F}$-programs

We will now define stable models of $\mathcal{F}$-programs. To this end, we will generalize the concept of the *reduct* (Gelfond & Lifschitz 1988) to the case of $\mathcal{F}$-programs and exploit results on Horn $\mathcal{F}$-programs from the previous section.

**Definition 4** *Let $\mathcal{F}$ be a class of monotone constraints and let $P$ be an $\mathcal{F}$-program. For a set of atoms $M \subseteq At$ we define the* reduct *of $P$ with respect to $M$, $P^M$ in symbols, as a Horn $\mathcal{F}$-program obtained from $P$ by (1) removing from $P$ every clause containing in the body a literal* $\mathbf{not}(A)$ *such that $M \models A$, and (2) removing all literals of the form* $\mathbf{not}(A)$ *from all remaining clauses in $P$.*

It is clear that the reduct $P^M$ is a Horn $\mathcal{F}$-program. Thus, the following definition is sound, as the concept of a derivable model is well defined for the reduct.

**Definition 5** *Let $\mathcal{F}$ be a class of monotone constraints and let $P$ be an $\mathcal{F}$-program. A set of atoms $M$ is a* stable *model of $P$ if $M$ is a derivable model of the reduct $P^M$.*

This definition does not make it explicit that a stable model of an $\mathcal{F}$-program is a model. It is however so and the use of the term *model* is indeed justified. In fact, a stronger property holds: stable models of $\mathcal{F}$-programs are supported.

**Proposition 4** *Let $\mathcal{F}$ be a class of monotone constraints and $P$ be an $\mathcal{F}$-program. If $M \subseteq At$ is a stable model of $P$ then $M$ is a supported model of $P$.*

The notion of a stable model allows us to strengthen Proposition 3(2).

**Proposition 5** *Let $\mathcal{F}$ be a class of monotone constraints and $P$ be a Horn $\mathcal{F}$-program. A set of atoms $M \subseteq At$ is a derivable model of $P$ if and only if $M$ is a stable model of $P$.*

We conclude this section by noting that this concept of a stable model of an $\mathcal{F}$-program extends the concept of a stable model of a normal logic program.

**Theorem 6** *Let $P$ be a normal logic program and let $M$ be a set of atoms. Then, $M$ is a stable model of $P$ if and only if $M$ is a stable model of the $\{U_{At}\}$-program $P^{ac}$.*

## Deterministic $\mathcal{F}$-programs

A monotone constraint atom $C(X)$ is *deterministic* if $X$ is a minimal element in $C$. Deterministic monotone constraint atoms have the following properties.

**Proposition 6** *Let $C(X)$ be a deterministic constraint atom. Then $C(X)$ is consistent and, for every $M \subseteq At$, $M \models C(X)$ if and only if $X \subseteq M$.*

An $\mathcal{F}$-program $P$ is *deterministic*, if the head of every clause in $P$ is a deterministic constraint atom. For deterministic logic programs there is only one way to derive a set of atoms to satisfy the head of an applicable clause. Thus, computing with deterministic $\mathcal{F}$-programs does not involve nondeterminism. Indeed, we have the following result.

**Proposition 7** *Let $\mathcal{F}$ be a class of monotone constraints and let $P$ be a deterministic $\mathcal{F}$-program. Then, for every set of atoms $M$, $|T_P^{nd}(M)| = 1$.*

Consequently, for a deterministic $\mathcal{F}$-program $P$, the operator $T_P^{nd}$ is deterministic and, so, can be regarded as an operator with both the domain and codomain $\mathcal{P}(At)$. We write $T_P^d$, to denote the unique operator such that for every $M \subseteq At$, $T_P^{nd}(M) = \{T_P^d(M)\}$. Models, supported models and stable models of a deterministic $\mathcal{F}$-program can be introduced in terms of the operator $T_P^d$ in exactly the same way as the corresponding concepts are defined in normal logic programming in terms of the operator $T_P$. In particular, the algebraic treatment of logic programming developed in (Fitting 2002; Przymusinski 1990; Denecker, Marek, & Truszczyński 2000) applies literally to deterministic $\mathcal{F}$-programs. We note that this comment extends to 3- and 4-valued semantics of partial models, supported models and stable models (including the Kripke-Kleene semantics and the well-founded semantics)[5]. That is important as we do not have yet a convincing generalization of some of these semantics (most notably, multivalued stable-model semantics and the well-founded semantics) to the case of arbitrary $\mathcal{F}$-programs.

## Complexity

In this section we will briefly discuss the complexity of deciding whether an $\mathcal{F}$-program has a supported (stable) model. We note that an abstract constraint $C$ gives rise to a decision problem $\mathcal{D}_C$: given a finite set $X \subseteq At$, decide whether $X \in C$. For many common constraints that decision problem belongs to the class P. It is so for all constraints considered earlier (in the case of a containment constraint, under the assumption that sets in $\mathcal{A}$ that define the constraint are given by lists of their elements).

**Theorem 7** *Let $\mathcal{F}$ be a nonempty class of abstract monotone constraints such that for every constraint $C \in \mathcal{F}$, the decision problem $\mathcal{D}_C$ is in* P. *If there is a constraint in $\mathcal{F}$ containing at least one finite set then the problem to decide whether an $\mathcal{F}$ program has a supported (stable) model is NP-complete.*

The proof of the upper bound is simple. Once we guess a candidate $M$ for a stable model for $P$, we first verify that $M$ is a model of $P$. Next, we compute the reduct $P^M$ and, finally, we verify that $M$ is a derivable model of $P^M$ by constructing the canonical derivation for $M$. The last task is well defined as it is applied after we first verify that $M$ is a model (we recall that canonical derivations are defined for models only). Moreover, all tasks can be accomplished in polynomial time (by our assumption on the class $\mathcal{F}$). The proof of the NP-completeness is slightly harder. We omit the details due to the lack of space[6].

The arguments in the case of supported models are similar. We also note that Theorem 7 can be generalized so

[5] Results in (Denecker, Pelov, & Bruynooghe 2001) are related to this observation. They deal with programs (with aggregates), whose clauses have heads consisting of *single* atoms.

[6] We note though that the proof is straightforward under a stronger assumption that $\mathcal{F}$ contains the constraint $\mathcal{U}_{At}$. Indeed, normal logic programs, for which the problem of the existence of stable models is NP-complete, can be viewed as $\mathcal{U}_{At}$-programs and, hence, $\mathcal{F}$-programs, as well.

that to give the complexity of the problem of the existence of supported (stable) models of $\mathcal{F}$-programs in terms of the complexity of the decision problems $\mathcal{D}_C$, for $C \in \mathcal{F}$.

## Discussion

In this paper, we discussed a generalization of normal logic programming, in which clauses consist of *abstract constraint atoms*, that is, expressions modeling constraints on sets. We showed that for a broad class of abstract constraints, called in the paper *monotone*, basic concepts, methods and results from normal logic programming generalize.

The results of the paper provide a formal tool to study properties of current extensions of logic programming systems with weight constraints such as those proposed in (Simons, Niemelä, & Soininen 2002). However, they apply equally well to extensions with much broader classes of constraints; the only requirement is their monotonicity. Such extended formalisms have clear modeling and computational advantages. Our work offers for them a solid theoretical basis.

The paper opens several interesting research directions. First, our complexity results indicate that the complexity of automated reasoning tasks for programs with constraints remains NP-complete as long as programs are built on the basis of constraints, for which the membership problem is in P. That indicates that an extension of algorithmic methods to compute stable models of programs with weight constraints in (Simons, Niemelä, & Soininen 2002) to programs with more general constraints might be possible. Second, due to close analogies between our approach and normal logic programming, we believe several other properties and results (splitting theorems, the concept of strong equivalence and its characterizations, Fages lemma, etc.) can be extended to the setting of programs with constraints. Finally, an important problem is to establish under what conditions the assumption of monotonicity can be dropped. Our formalism can easily be extended to the case allowing clauses with inconsistent heads and in such clauses, atoms built of *arbitrary* constraints can occur. Whether that result can be generalized in any significant fashion is an open question.

## Acknowledgments

The authors were supported by the NSF grants IIS-0097278 and IIS-0325063.

## References

Aloul, F.; Ramani, A.; Markov, I.; and Sakallah, K. 2002. PBS: a backtrack-search pseudo-boolean solver and optimizer. SAT02, 346 – 353.

Apt, K. 1990. Logic programming. *Handbook of theoretical computer science*. 493–574.

Babovich, Y., and Lifschitz, V. 2002. *Cmodels package*. `http://www.cs.utexas.edu/users/tag/cmodels.html`.

Baral, C. 2003. *Knowledge representation, reasoning and declarative problem solving*.

Clark, K. 1978. Negation as failure. *Logic and data bases*, 293–322.

Dell'Armi, T.; Faber, W.; Ielpa, G.; Leone, N.; and Pfeifer, G. 2003. Aggregate functions in disjunctive logic programming: semantics, complexity, and implementation in DLV. IJCAI 2003.

Denecker, M.; Marek, V.; and Truszczyński, M. 2000. Approximations, stable operators, well-founded fixpoints and applications in nonmonotonic reasoning. *Logic-Based Artificial Intelligence*, 127–144.

Denecker, M.; Pelov, N.; and Bruynooghe, M. 2001. Ultimate well-founded and stable semantics for logic programs with aggregates. *ICLP 2001*, 212–226.

Dixon, H., and Ginsberg, M. 2002. Inference methods for a pseudo-boolean satisfiability solver. *AAAI-2002*, 635–641.

Ferraris, P., and Lifschitz, V. 2004. Weight constraints and nested expressions. *Theory and Practice of Logic Programming, (forthcoming)*.

Fitting, M. C. 2002. Fixpoint semantics for logic programming – a survey. *Theoretical Computer Science* 278:25–51.

Gelfond, M., and Leone, N. 2002. Logic programming and knowledge representation – the A-prolog perspective. *Artificial Intelligence* 138:3–38.

Gelfond, M., and Lifschitz, V. 1988. The stable semantics for logic programs. *ICLP 1988*, 1070–1080.

Leone, N.; Pfeifer, G.; Faber, W.; Eiter, T.; Gottlob, G.; Perri, S.; and Scarcello, F. 2003. The dlv system for knowledge representation and reasoning. `http://xxx.lanl.gov/abs/cs.AI/0211004`.

Lin, F., and Zhao, Y. 2002. ASSAT: Computing answer sets of a logic program by SAT solvers. *AAAI-2002*, 112–117.

Marek, V.; Niemelä, I.; and Truszczyński, M. 2004. Characterizing stable models of logic programs with cardinality constraints. *LPNMR7*, 154–166.

Niemelä, I., and Simons, P. 1997. Smodels — an implementation of the stable model and well-founded semantics for normal logic programs. In *LPNMR4*, 420–429.

Pelov, N.; Denecker, M.; and Bruynooghe, M. 2004. Partial stable models for logic programs with aggregates. *LPNMR7*, 207–219.

Prestwich, S. 2002. Randomised backtracking for linear pseudo-boolean constraint problems. *CPAIOR-02*, 7–20.

Przymusinski, T. 1990. The well-founded semantics coincides with the three-valued stable semantics. *Fundamenta Informaticae* 13(4):445–464.

Simons, P.; Niemelä, I.; and Soininen, T. 2002. Extending and implementing the stable model semantics. *Artificial Intelligence* 138:181–234.

Turner, H. 2003. Strong equivalence made easy: Nested expressions and weight constraints. *Theory and Practice of Logic Programming* 3, (4&5):609–622.

van Emden, M., and Kowalski, R. 1976. The semantics of predicate logic as a programming language. *Journal of the ACM* 23(4):733–742.

# Adding Time and Intervals to Procedural and Hierarchical Control Specifications*

**Tran Cao Son**
Computer Science Department
New Mexico State University
Las Cruces, NM 88003, USA
tson@cs.nmsu.edu

**Chitta Baral and Le-Chi Tuan**
Computer Science and Engineering
Arizona State University
Tempe, AZ 85287, USA
chitta|lctuan@asu.edu

### Abstract

In this paper we introduce the language Golog+HTN$^{TI}$ for specifying control using procedural and HTN-based constructs together with deadlines and time restrictions. Our language starts with features from GOLOG and HTN and extends them so that we can deal with actions with duration by being able to specify time intervals between the start (or end) of an action (or a program) and the start (or end) of another action (or program). We then discuss an off-line interpreter based on the answer set planning paradigm such that the answer sets of the logic program have a one to one correspondence with the traces of the Golog+HTN$^{TI}$ specification.

## Introduction and Motivation

GOLOG (Levesque *et al.* 1997) is an Algol-like logic programming language for agent programming, control, and execution. It is based on the situation calculus theory of actions (Reiter 2000). GOLOG has been primarily used as a programming language for high-level agent control in dynamical environments (see e.g. (Burgard *et al.* 1998)). Some of the ways GOLOG can be extended are: (*a*) adding new program constructs (and providing the semantics for these constructs thereafter); or (*b*) adapting the language to an extension of situation calculus; or (*c*) combining (*a*) and (*b*). The first approach to extending GOLOG has been taken by (De Giacomo, Lespérance, & Levesque 2000; Baral & Son 1999) where various new constructs such as concurrency, interrupts, prioritized interrupts, or partial ordering are added to GOLOG. The other approaches can be seen in (Reiter 2001; Grosskreutz & Lakemeyer 2000; Boutilier *et al.* 2000) where continuous changes, durative actions, or stochastic actions are considered. In these extensions, time instances are introduced for specifying when an action (or a program) should be executed; in (Grosskreutz & Lakemeyer 2000), it is argued that the explicit specification of time in GOLOG programs – similar to what is used in (Reiter 2001) (also in (Boutilier *et al.* 2000)) – is not adequate for specifying event-driven behaviors and cc-Golog is proposed to address this problem. However, none of the constructs in cc-Golog allows us to express a simple behavior like "action $a$ should start its execution within 3 units of time after action $b$ starts its execution" because the language forces actions to happen as soon as possible, which – given that both $a$ and $b$ are executable at the time 0 – will not allow us to consider "$a$ starts at 0 and $b$ starts at 1" as an acceptable trajectory even though it satisfies the stated constraint.

In this paper, we investigate the introduction of actions with duration into the framework proposed in (Son, Baral, & McIlraith 2001) in which not only GOLOG-constructs such as sequence, while-loop, if-then-else, etc. but also HTN-based constructs such as the partial ordering and temporal constraints are allowed. This leads to a language[1], called Golog+HTN$^{TI}$, that generalizes GOLOG-based and HTN-based specifications with time intervals. Our language differs from the extensions of GOLOG in (Reiter 2001; Grosskreutz & Lakemeyer 2000; Boutilier *et al.* 2000) in that it includes different HTN-based constructs such as partial ordering and temporal constraints. Like cc-Golog, it does not require the explicit specification of time.

To characterize Golog+HTN$^{TI}$ we need an action theory that allows actions to have durations. For that we chose a simple extension of the language $\mathcal{A}$ (Gelfond & Lifschitz 1998), which we will refer to as $\mathcal{AD}$. We give the semantics of $\mathcal{AD}$ using logic programming with answer sets semantics. This (the semantics of $\mathcal{AD}$) allows us to define the notion of a trajectory which we use to define the notion of a trace of a Golog+HTN$^{TI}$ specification. We will begin with a short review of the answer set semantics of logic programs. We then present the language $\mathcal{AD}$ and discuss answer set planning with $\mathcal{AD}$ domains. We define the language Golog+HTN$^{TI}$ and develop a logic programming based interpreter for it. Finally, we conclude with a brief discussion about future work.

## Logic Programs and Answer Set Semantics

A logic program is a collection of rules of the form:

$$a_0 \leftarrow a_1, \ldots, a_m, not\ a_{m+1}, \ldots, not\ a_n \quad \text{or} \quad (1)$$

$$\leftarrow a_1, \ldots, a_m, not\ a_{m+1}, \ldots, not\ a_n \quad (2)$$

where each of the $a_i$'s is a literal in the sense of classical logic. $not$ is the *negation-as-failure* connective. $not\ a$ is called a naf-literal. Intuitively, the first rule means that if $a_1, \ldots, a_m$ are true and $a_{m+1}, \ldots, a_n$ can be safely assumed to be false then $a_0$ must be true. The second rule is

*Supported by NSF grants EIA-0130887, EIA-0220590. NSF grant 0070463, and NASA grant NCC2-1232.


[1]The superscript $TI$ refers to time and intervals.

a constraint that requires that at least one of $a_1, \ldots, a_m$ is false or one of $a_{m+1}, \ldots, a_n$ is true.

The body of a rule (1) or (2) is satisfied by a set of literals $X$ if $\{a_1, \ldots, a_m\} \subseteq X$ and $\{a_{m+1}, \ldots, a_n\} \cap X = \emptyset$. A rule of the form (1) is satisfied by $X$ if either its body is not satisfied by $X$ or $a_0 \in X$. A rule of the form (2) is satisfied by $X$ if its body is not satisfied by $X$.

For a set of literals $X$ and a program $P$, the reduct of $P$ with respect to $X$, denoted by $P^X$, is the program obtained from the set of all ground instances of $P$ by deleting (*1.*) each rule that has a naf-literal $not\ l$ in its body with $l \in X$, and (*2.*) all naf-literals in the bodies of the remaining rules. Answer sets of logic programs are first defined by Gelfond and Lifschitz in (Gelfond & Lifschitz 1990). $S$ is an *answer set* of $P$ if it satisfies the following conditions.

1. If $P$ does not contain any naf-literal (i.e. $m = n$ in every rule of $P$) then $S$ is a minimal set of literals that satisfies all the rules in $P$.
2. If the program $P$ does contain some naf-literal ($m < n$ in some rule of $P$), then $S$ is an answer set of $P$ if $S$ is an answer set of $P^S$. (Note that $P^S$ does not contain naf-literals, its answer set is defined in the first item.)

In what follows, we will refer to logic programming with answer set semantics as *AnsProlog*. Answer sets of propositional programs can be computed using answer set solvers such as **smodels** (Simons, Niemelä, & Soininen 2002), **dlv** (Eiter *et al.* 1998), **cmodels** (Lierler & Maratea 2003), or **ASSAT** (Lin & Zhao 2002). Answer set planning (ASP) (Subrahmanian & Zaniolo 1995; Lifschitz 2002) is an approach to planning using AnsProlog, an application of answer set programming (Marek & Truszczyński 1999; Niemelä 1999) to planning. In this approach, a planning problem is translated into a logic program whose answer sets correspond one-to-one to the solutions of the original problem. To make answer set programming easier, several new types of rules have been introduced. In this paper, we will often make use of *cardinality constraints* of the form: $l\{b_1, \ldots, b_k\}u \leftarrow a_1, \ldots, a_m, not\ a_{m+1}, \ldots, not\ a_n$ where $a_i$ and $b_j$ are literals and $l$ and $u$ are two integers, and $l \leq u$. Intuitively, such a rule enforces the constraint that if the body is true then at least $l$ and at most $u$ literals from the head are also true. Answer sets of programs with cardinality constraints are defined in (Simons, Niemelä, & Soininen 2002).

## Reasoning About Durative Actions Using LP

As we mentioned earlier, to characterize domain constraints, we need to first describe an action description language. The action description language that we plan to use is a simple extension of the language $\mathcal{A}$ (Gelfond & Lifschitz 1998). In our extension, which we will refer to as $\mathcal{AD}$, we will allow actions to have duration and this will be sufficient to help us to justify and illustrate our language for domain constraints with new connectives.

### Syntax of $\mathcal{AD}$

An action theory consists of two finite, disjoint sets of names **A** and **F**, called *actions* and *fluents*, respectively, and a set of propositions of the following form:

| | | | |
|---|---|---|---|
| (3) | **causes**$(a, f)$ | **initially**$(f)$ | (5) |
| (4) | **executable**$(a, \{p_1, \ldots, p_n\})$ | **duration**$(a, v)$ | (6) |

where $f$ and $p_i$'s are fluent literals (a *fluent literal* is either a fluent $g$ or its negation $\neg g$) and $a$ is an action. (3) is called a *dynamic causal law* and represents the effect of $a$ while (4) states an executability condition of $a$. Intuitively, a proposition of the form (3) states that $f$ is guaranteed to be true after the execution of $a$. An executability condition of $a$ says that $a$ is executable in a state in which $p_1, \ldots, p_n$ hold. Propositions of the form (5) are used to describe the initial state. It states that $f$ holds in the initial state. Finally, a proposition of the form (6) is used to say that duration of action $a$ is $v$.

An action theory is a set of propositions of the form (3)-(6). We will assume that each action $a$ appears in one and only one proposition of the form (6) and $v$ is a non-negative integer expression. We will often conveniently write $d(a)$ to denote the value $v$ if **duration**$(a, v) \in D$ and for a set of actions $A$, $d(A) = \max\{d(a) \mid a \in A\}$.

**Example 1** Consider an action theory with the set of fluents $\{f, g, h\}$, the set of actions $\{a, b, c, d\}$, and the following propositions:

| | | |
|---|---|---|
| **causes**$(a, f)$ | **duration**$(a, 3)$ | **executable**$(a, \{g, h\})$ |
| **causes**$(b, h)$ | **duration**$(b, 2)$ | **executable**$(b, \{\})$ |
| **causes**$(c, g)$ | **duration**$(c, 2)$ | **executable**$(c, \{\})$ |
| **causes**$(d, \neg g)$ | **duration**$(d, 1)$ | **executable**$(d, \{\})$ |
| **initially**$(\neg f)$ | **initially**$(\neg g)$ | **initially**$(\neg h)$ |

The propositions about $a$ (the first three propositions on the first line) say that $a$ will cause the fluent $f$ to be true after 3 units of time and is executable only if $g$ and $h$ are true. The propositions for other actions have similar meaning.

Since the characterization of $\mathcal{AD}$ is not the aim of this paper, we do not present an independent characterization of it. (Recall that our goal is to use $\mathcal{AD}$ to show how to plan using a proposed domain constraint language Golog+HTN$^{TI}$.) Instead we give a AnsProlog encoding of prediction and planning using $\mathcal{AD}$. Moreover, a transition function based semantics for $\mathcal{AD}$ can be defined similarly to what has been done for the language $\mathcal{ADC}$ in (Baral, Son, & Tuan 2002). It is worth noticing that the definitions defined herein can be easily adapted to more complex action description language such as $\mathcal{ADC}$.

### Semantics: Prediction in $\mathcal{AD}$

Given a set of propositions $D$ we construct a logic program $\pi_D$ for reasoning about the effects of actions in $D$. The main predicates in $\pi_D$ are:

- $h(f, t)$ – fluent literal $f$ holds at the time $t$;
- $exec(a, t)$ (resp. $in\_exec(a, t)$) – action $a$ is executable (resp. in its execution) at $t$;
- $init(a, t)$ (resp. $ends(a, t)$) – action $a$ starts (resp. ends) its execution at $t$;

The rules of $\pi_D$ are given next.

- For each proposition (5) in $D$, $\pi_D$ contains the following rule: $h(f, 1)$. (7)
  This describes the initial state (which fluents hold at time point 1) as specified by propositions of the from (5) in $D$.
- For each proposition (4) in $D$, $\pi_D$ contains the rules:

$$\begin{array}{lcl} exec(a, T) & \leftarrow & not\ not\_exec(a, T). \\ not\_exec(a, T) & \leftarrow & not\ h(p_1, T). \\ & \ldots & \\ not\_exec(a, T) & \leftarrow & not\ h(p_n, T). \end{array} \quad (8)$$

These rules define when $a$ is executable at a time point $T$, based only on the truth of fluents. These rules establish that $a$ is executable if its executability condition holds.

- For each proposition (6) in $D$, we add the following rules to $\pi_D$,

$$\begin{array}{lll} ends(a, T+v) & \leftarrow & init(a,T). \\ in\_exec(a,T) & \leftarrow & init(a,T'), T' \leq T < T+v. \end{array} \quad (9)$$

These rules define when an action ends and when it is under execution.

- For each action $a$ and an ef-proposition (3), the following rules are added to $\pi_D$,

$$\begin{array}{lll} h(f,T) & \leftarrow & ends(a,T). \\ ab(f,T) & \leftarrow & in\_exec(a,T). \end{array} \quad (10)$$

These rules are used to reason about truth value of fluents at different time points.

**Encoding the frame axiom.** $\pi_D$ contains the following rules that encode the frame axiom. They are slightly different from the normal logic program encoding of the frame axiom in (Gelfond & Lifschitz 1993). For each fluent $f$, the following rules belong to $\pi_D$:

$$\begin{array}{l} h(f,T+1) \leftarrow h(f,T),\ not\ ab(\neg f, T+1). \\ h(\neg f,T+1) \leftarrow h(\neg f,T),\ not\ ab(f, T+1). \end{array} \quad (11)$$

If we now want to find out if $f$ would be true at time point $t$ after starting the execution of actions $a_1$ at time point $t_1$, $a_2$ at time point $t_2, \ldots$ and $a_n$ at time $t_n$ all we need to do is to add the set $\{init(a_i,t_i) \mid i \in \{t_1,\ldots,t_n\}\}$ and the constraints $\leftarrow init(a_i,t_i), not\ exec(a_i,t_i)$ (for $i = 1,\ldots,n$) to $\pi_D$, set the limits for the various variables, and ask if the resulting program entails $h(f,t)$.

One assumption we made in our characterization is that the effect of an action takes into account only after its execution ends, and the fluents, whose value changes due to an action execution, are in a unknown state during the execution. This of course can be changed by appropriately modifying $\pi_D$, in particular the rules in (10).

## Answer Set Planning with $\mathcal{AD}$ Action Theories

We now show how the idea of answer set planning can be extended to $\mathcal{AD}$ action theories. Our AnsProlog planner for an action theory $D$, denoted by $\Pi(D)$, will consist of the program representing and reasoning about actions of $D$, $\pi_D$, the rules representing the goal, and the rules that generate action occurrences. Besides, we will need to set the limit on the maximal number of steps (the length) of the plan. We will call it $plan\_size$. From now on, whenever we refer to a time point $t$, we mean that $1 \leq t \leq plan\_size$.

**Representing goal.** Assume that we have a goal that is a conjunction of fluent literals $g_1 \wedge \ldots \wedge g_m$. We represent this by a set of atoms $\{finally(g_i) \mid i = 1,\ldots,m\}$. The following rules encode when the goal – as described by the $finally$ facts – is satisfied at a time point $T$.

$$\begin{array}{lll} not\_goal(T) & \leftarrow & finally(X),\ not\ h(X,T). \\ goal(T) & \leftarrow & not\ not\_goal(T). \end{array} \quad (12)$$

The following constraint eliminates otherwise possible answer sets where the goal is not satisfied at the time point $plan\_size$.

$$\leftarrow not\ goal(plan\_size). \quad (13)$$

We now define the notion of a *plan*.

**Definition 1** Given an action theory $D$, a goal $G$, and a plan size *plan_size*, we say that a sequence of sets of grounded actions $A_1,\ldots,A_n$ is a *plan* achieving $G$ if $goal(plan\_size)$ is true in every answer set of the program $\pi^{PVer}(D,G)$[2], which consists of

- the rules of $\pi_D$ and the rules representing $G$ (rules (7)-(13)) in which the time variable is less than or equal *plan_size*;
- the set of action occurrences $\bigcup_{i=1}^{n}\{init(a,i) \mid a \in A_i\}$;
- the rules preventing actions with contradictory conclusions to overlap (rules (15), below).

We say that a plan $p = A_1,\ldots,A_n$ is a *concurrent plan* if there exists a pair $i$ and $j$ and an action $a \in A_i \cap A_j$ such that $i + d(a) > j$, i.e., $p$ contains an overlapping of two instantiations of a same actions. $p$ is said to be *non-concurrent* if it is not a concurrent plan.

**Generating Action Occurrences.** The following rules enumerate action initiations. To decrease the number of answer sets we have made the assumption that two action instantiations corresponding to the same action can not overlap each other, i.e., we consider only non-concurrent plans. This need not be the case in general. Our point here is that AnsProlog allows us to express such restrictions very easily. For each action $a$ with the duration $v$, the rules:

$$\begin{array}{l} act(a,T) \leftarrow init(a,T_1), T_1 < T < T_1+v. \\ ninit(a,T) \leftarrow not\ init(a,T). \\ init(a,T) \leftarrow exec(a,T), not\ act(a,T), not\ ninit(a,T). \end{array} \quad (14)$$

can be used to prevent two instantiations of $a$ to overlap. The $1^{st}$ rule defines when $a$ is active and the $3^{rd}$ rule allows $a$ to occur only if it has not been initiated and is not active.

For every pair of $a$ and $b$ such that **causes**$(a,f)$ and **causes**$(b,\neg f)$ belong to $D$, the two rules:

$$\begin{array}{l} overlap(a,b,T) \leftarrow in\_exec(a,T), in\_exec(b,T). \\ \leftarrow overlap(a,b,T). \end{array} \quad (15)$$

can be used to disallow actions with contradictory effects to overlap. Let $\pi^{PGen}(D,G)$ be the set of rules of $\Pi(D)$ with the goal $G$ and $plan\_size{=}n$ and the rules (14)-(15). For an answer set $M$ of $\pi^{PGen}(D,G)$, let $s_i(M) = \{f \mid h(f,i) \in M\}$ and $A_i(M) = \{a \mid init(a,i) \in M\}$. We can prove that there is an one-to-one correspondence between answer sets of $\pi^{PGen}(D,G)$ and non-concurrent plans achieving $G$.

**Theorem 1** For a theory $D$ and a goal $G$, $B_1,\ldots,B_n$ is a non-concurrent plan that achieves $G$ iff there exists an answer set $M$ of $\pi^{PGen}(D,G)$ s.t. $A_i(M){=}B_i$.

## Golog+HTN$^{TI}$: Using Durations in Procedural and Hierarchical Domain Constraints

We begin with an informal discussion on the new construct in Golog+HTN$^{TI}$. Consider the domain from Example 1. It is easy to see that the program $b; c; a$ is a program achieving $f$ from any state and the time needed to execute this plan is the sum of the actions's durations (Figure 1, Case (a)). Observe that $b$ and $c$ are two actions that achieve the condition for $a$ to be executable and can be executed in parallel. Hence it should be obvious that any program that allows $b$ and $c$ to execute in parallel will have a shorter execution time. For the

[2] The $^{PVer}$ stands for *plan verification*.

moment, let us represent this by the program $p_1 = \{b, c\}; a$. The execution of this program is depicted in Figure 1, Case (b). Now consider a modification of the domain in Exam-

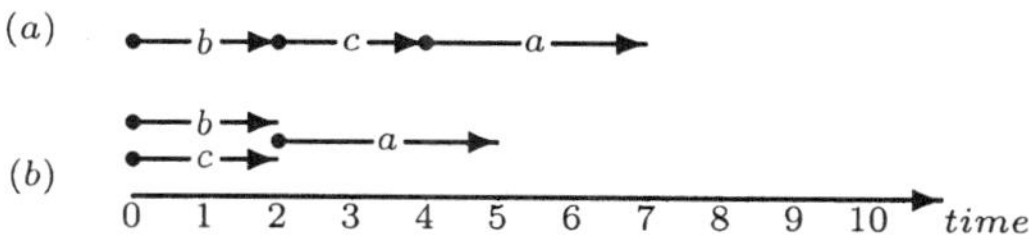


Figure 1: A pictorial view of program execution (the dot indicates when an action starts and the arrow indicates when an action stops)

ple 1, in which the executable propositions of $c$ changes to **executable**$(c, \{\neg g\})$. A program achieving $f$ would be to execute $b$ and $d$ in parallel, then $c$, and lastly $a$. We cannot execute $b$, $c$, and $d$ in parallel all the time because $c$ is not executable until $\neg g$ holds, and hence, it might need to wait for $d$ to finish. It is easy to see, however, that it is better if $c$ starts whenever $d$ finishes. To account for this, we introduce a new construct that allows programs to start even if the preceding program has not finished. We write $(\{b, d\};^s_{[1,1]} c); a$ to indicate that $c$ should start its execution 1 time unit after $\{b, d\}$ and then $a$ and denote this program by $p_2$. The execution of this program can be illustrated as follows.

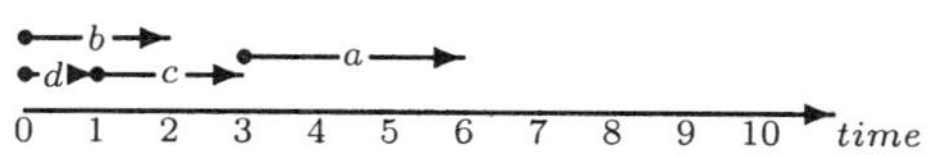


Figure 2: Execution of $(\{b, d\};^s_{[1,1]} c); a$

The above discussion provides a compelling argument for the need of *specifying time constraints in GOLOG programs and its extensions*. In the following, we extend the language proposed in (Son, Baral, & McIlraith 2001) with time constraints and define the language Golog+HTN$^{TI}$.

**Definition 2 (Program)** For an action theory $D$,

1. an action $a$ is a program;
2. a temporal constraint $\phi[t_1, t_2]$, where $\phi$ is a fluent formula (a formula constructed using fluent literals and the propositional connectives), is a program;
3. if $p_1$ and $p_2$ are programs and $0 \leq t_1 \leq t_2$ are two time non-negative integers then so are $(p_1|p_2)$, $(p_1;^s_{[t_1,t_2]} p_2)$, and $(p_1;^e_{[t_1,t_2]} p_2)$;
4. if $p_1$ and $p_2$ are programs and $\phi$ is a fluent formula then so are "**if** $\phi$ **then** $p_1$ **else** $p_2$" and "**while** $\phi$ **do** $p$";
5. if $X$ is a variable and $p(X)$ is a program then **pick**$(X, p(X))$ is a program[3];
6. if $p_1, \ldots, p_n$ are programs then a pair $(S, C)$ is a program where $S = \{p_1, \ldots, p_n\}$ and $C$ is a set of constraints over $S$ of the following form: (i) $p_1 \prec^s_{[t_1,t_2]} p_2$ (or $p_1 \prec^e_{[t_1,t_2]} p_2$), (ii) $(p, \phi[t_1, t_2])$, (iii) $(\phi[t_1, t_2], p)$, and (iv) $(p_1, \phi[t_1, t_2], p_2)$ where $p, p_1, p_2$ are programs, $\phi$ is a fluent formula and $0 \leq t_1 \leq t_2$.

The constructs 1-5 in the above definitions are generalizations of constructs in GOLOG (Levesque *et al.* 1997) and the construct 6 is a generalization of hierarchical task networks (HTN) (Sacerdoti 1974). The main difference is that some of them are attached to a time interval and/or a directive '$s$'/'$e$' which are introduced for the specification of time constraints between program components. Intuitively, $\phi[t_1, t_2]$ says that if it is executed at the time moment $t$ then the fluent formula $\phi$ must hold during the interval $[t+t_1, t+t_2]$. The program $(p_1;^s_{[t_1,t_2]} p_2)$ states that $p_2$ should start its execution at least $t_1$ and at most $t_2$ units of time after $p_1$ *starts* whereas $(p_1;^e_{[t_1,t_2]} p_2)$ forces $p_2$ to wait for $t$ ($t_1 \leq t \leq t_2$) units of time after $p_1$ *finishes*. It is easy to see that $(p_1;^s_{[0,0]} p_2)$ requires that $p_1$ and $p_2$ be executed in parallel whereas $(p_1;^e_{[0,0]} p_2)$ requires that $p_2$ starts its execution at the time $p_1$ finishes. Note that $(p_1;^e_{[0,0]} p_2)$ corresponds to the original notation $p_1; p_2$.

The constraints in item 6 above are similar to truth constraints and ordering constraints over tasks in HTN. Intuitively, $p_1 \prec^s_{[t_1,t_2]} p_2$ (resp. $p_1 \prec^e_{[t_1,t_2]} p_2$) specifies the order and the time constraint for $p_2$ to start its execution. It states that if $p_1$ begins (resp. ends) its execution at a time moment $t$ then $p_2$ must start its execution during the interval $[t + t_1, t + t_2]$. Similarly, $(p, \phi[t_1, t_2])$ (resp. $(\phi[t_1, t_2], p)$) means that $\phi$ must hold from $t_1$ to $t_2$ immediately after (resp. before) $p$'s execution. $(p_1, \phi[t_1, t_2], p_2)$ states that $p_1$ must start before $p_2$ and $\phi$ must hold $t_1$ units of time after $p_1$ starts until $t_2$ units of time before $p_2$ starts.

We note that there is a subtle difference between the constructs $;^e_{[t_1,t_2]}$ (resp. $;^s_{[t_1,t_2]}$) and $\prec^e_{[t_1,t_2]}$ (resp. $\prec^s_{[t_1,t_2]}$) in that the former (inspired by GOLOG) represents a sequential order and the latter (inspired by HTN) represents a partial order between programs. For example, during the execution of the program $(p_1;^s_{[t_1,t_2]} p_2)$, no other program should start its execution. On the other hand, $(p_1 \prec^s_{[t_1,t_2]} p_2)$ only requires that $p_2$ should start its execution between the interval $[t_1, t_2]$ after $p_1$ starts its execution and does not prevent another program to start during the execution of $p_1$ and $p_2$.

**Example 2** In our notation, $p_1$ and $p_2$ (from the discussion before Figure 1) are represented by $((b;^s_{[0,0]} c);^e_{[0,0]} a)$ and $(((b;^s_{[0,0]} d);^s_{[1,1]} c);^e_{[0,0]} a)$, respectively.

We will now define the notion of *a trace of a program*, which describes what actions are done when. But first we need to define the notion of a trajectory. For an action theory $D$ and an integer $n$, let $\pi^{Gen}(D)$ be the set of rules (7)-(11) and (14)-(15) whose time variable belongs to $\{1, \ldots, n\}$.

**Definition 3 (Trajectory)** For an action theory $D$ and an answer set $M$ of $\pi^{PGen}(D)$, let $s_i = \{f \mid h(f, i) \in M\}$ and $A_i = \{a \mid init(a, i) \in M\}$. We say that the sequence $\alpha = s_1 A_1 \ldots s_n A_n$ is a *trajectory* of $D$.

Intuitively, a trajectory is an alternating sequence of states and action occurrences $s_1 A_1, \ldots, s_n A_n$, where $s_i$ is a state at time point $i$ and $A_i$ is the set of actions that are supposed to have started at time point $i$. Observe that because of the assumption that during the execution of an action, value of fluents affected by the action is unknown, i.e., the states $s_i$ might be incomplete. However, $s_i$ will be complete if there

[3]Roughly speaking, programs are allowed to contain variables whose domains are pre-defined. A program with variables is considered as a shorthand for the set of its ground instantiations.

exists no action that is active at $i$. The notion of a trace of a program will be defined in the next four definitions.

**Definition 4 (Trace–Primitive Cases)** A trajectory $\alpha = s_1 A_1 \ldots s_n A_n$ is a trace of a program $p$ if

- $p{=}a$, $n{=}d(a)$ and $A_1{=}\{a\}$ and $A_i{=}\emptyset$ for $i > 1$; or
- $p{=}\phi[t_1, t_2]$, $n{=}t_2$, $A_i{=}\emptyset$ for every $i$, and $\phi$ holds in $s_t$ for $t_1 \leq t \leq t_2$.

The next definition deals with programs that are constructed using GOLOG-constructs ((Levesque *et al.* 1997)).

**Definition 5 (Trace–Programs with GOLOG-Constructs)** A trajectory $\alpha = s_1 A_1 \ldots s_n A_n$ is a trace of a program $p$ if one of the following is satisfied.

- $p = p_1 \mid p_2$, $\alpha$ is a trace of $p_1$ or $\alpha$ is a trace of $p_2$,
- $p =$ **if** $\phi$ **then** $p_1$ **else** $p_2$, $\alpha$ is a trace of $p_1$ and $\phi$ holds in $s_1$ or $\alpha$ is a trace of $p_2$ and $\neg\phi$ holds in $s_1$,
- $p =$ **while** $\phi$ **do** $p_1$, $n = 1$ and $\neg\phi$ holds in $s_1$ or $\phi$ holds in $s_1$ and there exists some $i$ such that $s_1 A_1 \ldots A_i$ is a trace of $p_1$ and $s_{i+1} A_{i+1} \ldots A_n$ is a trace of $p$, or
- $p =$ **pick**$(X, q(X))$, then there exists a constant $x$ such that $\alpha$ is a trace of $q(x)$.

The trace of each program is defined based on its structure. We next deal with the new connectives $;^s_{[t_1,t_2]}$ and $;^e_{[t_1,t_2]}$.

**Definition 6 (Trace–Parallel and Overlapping Programs)** A trajectory $\alpha = s_1 A_1 \ldots s_n A_n$ is a trace of a program $p$ if

- $p{=}p_1;^s_{[t_1,t_2]} p_2$, there exists two numbers $t_3$ and $t_4$ such that $t_1 + 1 \leq t_3 \leq t_2 + 1$ and $t_4 \leq n$ (because the index of the trace starts from 1) and either (i) there exists a trace $s_1 B_1 \ldots s_{t_4} B_{t_4}$ of $p_1$ and a trace $s_{t_3} C_{t_3} \ldots s_n C_n$ of $p_2$ such that $A_i = B_i \cup C_i$ for every $i$; or (ii) $t_3 \leq t_4$ and there exists a trace $s_1 B_1 \ldots s_n B_n$ of $p_1$ and a trace $s_{t_3} C_{t_3} \ldots s_{t_4} C_{t_4}$ of $p_2$ such that $A_i = B_i \cup C_i$ (we write $B_j = \emptyset$ or $C_j = \emptyset$ for indexes that do not belong to the trace of $p_1$ or $p_2$); or
- $p{=}p_1;^e_{[t_1,t_2]} p_2$, there exists two numbers $t_3$ and $t_4$ such that $t_1{+}t_3 \leq t_4 \leq t_2{+}t_3$ and $t_4 \leq n$ and $s_1 A_1 \ldots s_{t_3} A_{t_3}$ is a trace of $p_1$ and a trace $s_{t_4} A_{t_4} \ldots s_n A_n$ is a trace of $p_2$ and $A_i = \emptyset$ for every $t_3 \leq i < t_4$.

This definition is best illustrated using a picture.

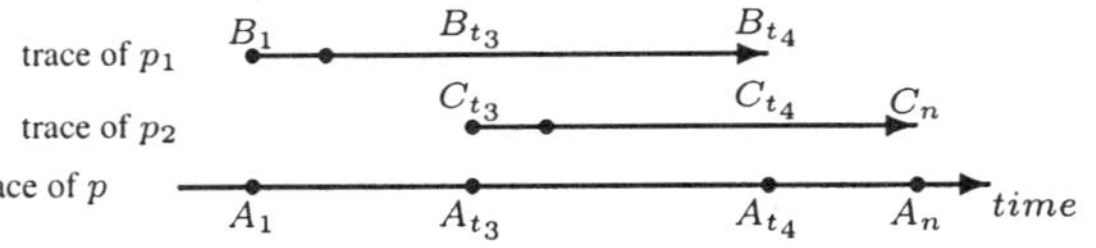


Figure 3: $A_i = B_i \cup C_i$ – First Item, Case 1 (Definition 6)

**Example 3**

- For $p_1{=}((b;^s_{[0,0]} c);^e_{[0,0]} a)$ (wrt. the action theory in Example 1), we can easily check that $\mathbf{s}^1_1 \, \{\mathbf{b}, \mathbf{c}\} \, \mathbf{s}^1_2 \, \emptyset \, \mathbf{s}^1_3 \{\mathbf{a}\} \, \mathbf{s}^1_4 \, \emptyset \, \mathbf{s}^1_5 \, \emptyset \, \mathbf{s}^1_6 \, \emptyset$ where
  $s^1_1 = \{\neg f, \neg g, \neg h\}$ $\quad s^1_2 = \{\neg f\}$ $\quad s^1_3 = \{\neg f, g, h\}$
  $s^1_4 = \{g, h\}$ $\quad s^1_5 = \{g, h\}$ $\quad s^1_6 = \{f, g, h\}$
  is a trace of $p_1$. On the other hand, we can see that $\mathbf{s}^1_1 \, \{\mathbf{b}, \mathbf{c}, \mathbf{d}\} \, \mathbf{s}^1_2 \, \emptyset \, \mathbf{s}^1_3 \{\mathbf{a}\} \, \mathbf{s}^1_4 \, \emptyset \, \mathbf{s}^1_5 \, \emptyset \, \mathbf{s}^1_6 \, \emptyset$ is not a trace of $p_1$ although it contains a trace of $p_1$.
- For $p_2{=}(((b;^s_{[0,0]} d);^s_{[1,1]} c);^e_{[0,0]} a)$ (wrt. the modified action theory), let
  $s^2_1 = \{\neg f, \neg g, \neg h\}$ $\quad s^2_2 = \{\neg f, \neg g\}$ $\quad s^2_3 = \{\neg f, h\}$
  $s^2_4 = \{\neg f, g, h\}$ $\quad s^2_5 = \{g, h\}$ $\quad s^2_6 = \{g, h\}$
  $s^2_7 = \{f, g, h\}$
  we can check that $\mathbf{s}^2_1 \, \{\mathbf{b}, \mathbf{d}\} \, \mathbf{s}^2_2 \, \{\mathbf{c}\} \, \mathbf{s}^2_3 \, \emptyset \, \mathbf{s}^2_4 \{\mathbf{a}\} \, \mathbf{s}^2_5 \, \emptyset \, \mathbf{s}^2_6 \, \emptyset \, \mathbf{s}^2_7 \, \emptyset$ is a trace of $p_2$ but it is easy to see that $\mathbf{s}^2_1 \, \{\mathbf{b}, \mathbf{d}\} \, \mathbf{s}^2_2 \, \emptyset \, \mathbf{s}^2_2 \, \{\mathbf{c}\} \, \mathbf{s}^2_3 \, \emptyset \, \mathbf{s}^2_4 \{\mathbf{a}\} \, \mathbf{s}^2_5 \, \emptyset \, \mathbf{s}^2_6 \, \emptyset \, \mathbf{s}^2_7 \, \emptyset$ is not a trace of $p_2$ because $c$ should start at the time moment 2.

We next deal with programs containing HTN-constructs.

**Definition 7 (Trace–HTN Programs)** A trajectory $\alpha{=}s_1 A_1 \ldots s_n A_n$ is a trace of a program $p{=}(S, C)$ with $S{=}\{p_1, \ldots, p_k\}$ if there exists two sequences of numbers $b_1, \ldots, b_k$ and $e_1, \ldots, e_k$ with $b_j \leq e_j$, a permutation $(i_1, \ldots, i_k)$ of $(1, \ldots, k)$, and a sequence of traces $\alpha_j{=}s_{b_j} A^j_{b_j} \ldots s_{e_j} A^j_{e_j}$ that satisfy the following conditions:

- for each $l$, $1 \leq l \leq k$, $\alpha_l$ is a trace of $p_{i_l}$,
- if $p_t \prec p_l \in C$ then $i_t{<}i_l$,
- if $p_t{\prec}^s_{[q_1,q_2]} p_l{\in}C$ then $i_t{<}i_l$ and $b_{i_t}{+}q_1{\leq}b_{i_l}{\leq}b_{i_t}{+}q_2$,
- if $p_t{\prec}^e_{[q_1,q_2]} p_l{\in}C$ then $i_t{<}i_l$ and $e_{i_t}{+}q_1{\leq}b_{i_l}{\leq}e_{i_t}{+}q_2$,
- if $(\phi[t_1, t_2], p_l) \in C$ (or $(p_l, \phi[t_1, t_2]) \in C$) then $\phi$ holds in the states $s_{b_{i_l}-t_2}, \ldots, s_{b_{i_l}-t_1}$ (or $s_{e_{i_l}+t_1}, \ldots, s_{e_{i_l}+t_2}$), and
- if $(p_t, \phi[t_1, t_2], p_l) \in C$ then $\phi$ holds in $s_{b_{i_t}+t_1}$, …, $s_{b_{i_l}-t_2}$.
- $A_i = \cup^k_{j=1} A^j_i$ for every $i = 1, \ldots, n$ where we assume that $A^j_i = \emptyset$ for $i{<}b_j$ or $i > e_j$.

The intuition of the above definition is as follows. First, each program starts ($b_i$'s) and ends ($e_i$'s) at some time point and it cannot finish before it even starts, hence, the requirement $b_i \leq e_i$. The order of the execution is specified by the ordering constraints and not by the program's number. The permutation $(i_1, \ldots, i_k)$ and $j$'s record the starting time of the programs. The conditions on the trajectories make sure that the constraints are satisfied (first four items) and they indeed create $A_1, \ldots, A_n$ (last item).

## An AnsProlog Interpreter

We have developed an AnsProlog interpreter for programs defined in Definitions 2. For a program $p$ of an action theory $D$, we define $\Pi(D, p)$ as a program consisting of $\Pi(D)$, the rules describing the program $p$, the set of rules for generating action occurrences (14)-(15), the constraint eliminating answer sets in which $trans(p, 1, plan\_size)$ does not hold, and a set of rules that realizes the operational semantics of programs (Definitions 4-7). We follow the approach in (Son, Baral, & McIlraith 2001) and define a predicate $trans(p, t_1, t_2)$ which holds in an answer set $M$ of $\Pi$ iff $s_{t_1}(M) A_{t_1}(M) \ldots s_{t_2}(M) A_{t_2}(M)$ is a trace of $p$[4]. Space limitation does not allow a detailed presentation of $\Pi$. We therefore will concentrate on describing the ideas behind the rules and their meaning rather than presenting the rules in great detail. They can be found on our Web site[5].

We will begin with an informal discussion on the ideas behind the rules defining $trans(p, t_1, t_2)$. Intuitively, because of the rules (14)-(15), each answer set $M$ of the program $\Pi$ will contain a sequence of sets of actions $\alpha = A_1, \ldots, A_n$ where $A_i = \{a \mid init(a, i) \in M\}$. The encoding of the action theory, $\pi_D$, makes sure that whenever an action $a$ is

[4]For an answer set $M$, $s_i(M) = \{f \mid h(f, i) \in M,\ f$ is a fluent literal$\}$ and $A_i(M) = \{a \mid init(a, i) \in M\}$.

[5]URL: `http://www.cs.nmsu.edu/~tson/ASPlan/Duration`

initiated it is executable. Thus, the sequence $\alpha$ is a trajectory of $D$. So, it remains to be verified that $\alpha$ is indeed a trace of the program $p$. We will do this in two steps. First, we check if $\alpha$ contains a trace of $p$, i.e., we make sure that there is a trace $s_1B_1 \ldots s_nB_n$ of $p$ such that $B_i \subseteq A_i$. Second, we make sure that no action is initiated when it is not needed and define two predicates:

- $tr(p, t_1, t_2)$ - $s_{t_1}A_{t_1} \ldots A_{t_2}$ contains a trace of $p$;
- $used\_in(p, q, t, t_1, t_2)$ - a trace of $p$ starting from $t$ is used in constructing a trace of $q$ from $t_1$ to $t_2$. Intuitively, this predicate records the actions belonging to the traces of $q$. The definition of this predicate will make sure that for a simple action $a$, only action $a$ is used to construct its trace, i.e., $used\_in(a, a, t_1, t_1, t_1 + d(a))$ is equivalent to $init(a, t_1)$ and $used\_in(b, a, t_1, t_1, t_1 + d(a))$ is false for every $b \neq a$.

We define that $trans(p, t_1, t_2)$ holds iff $tr(p, t_1, t_2)$ holds and for every action $a \in A_j$ for $t_1 \leq j \leq t_2$, $used\_in(a, p, j, t_1, t_2)$ holds. The rules for $tr(p, t_1, t_2)$ are similar to the rules of the predicate $trans(p, t_1, t_2)$ from (Son, Baral, & McIlraith 2001) with changes that account for action duration and the new constructs such as $;^s_{[t_1,t_2]}$ and $;^e_{[t_1,t_2]}$ and checking for the condition of new constraint on a HTN-program. The construction of $\Pi(D, p)$ allows us to prove the following theorem.

**Theorem 2** For a theory $D$ and a program $p$, (i) for every answer set $M$ of $\Pi(D, p)$, $s_1(M)A_1(M) \ldots s_n(M)A_n(M)$ is a trace of $p$, where $s_i(M) = \{f \mid h(f, i) \in M,\ f$ is a fluent literal$\}$ and $A_i(M) = \{a \mid init(a, i) \in M\}$; and (ii) if $s_1B_1s_2 \ldots s_nB_n$ is a trace of $p$ then there exists an answer set $M$ of $\Pi(D, p)$ such that $s_i = \{f \mid h(f, i) \in M\}$ and $B_i = \{a \mid init(a, i) \in M\}$.

## Conclusion and Discussion

In this paper we propose a control specification language Golog+HTN$^{TI}$ that generalizes procedural (based on GOLOG) and HTN-based specifications to allow time intervals. In the process we generalize the connective ';' to two connectives '$;^s_{[t_1,t_2]}$' and '$;^e_{[t_1,t_2]}$' and make similar generalizations of the HTN constructs. We then discuss the implementation of an AnsProlog-based interpreter for the language Golog+HTN$^{TI}$. Among the features that distinguish Golog+HTN$^{TI}$ from previous extensions of GOLOG are:

1. The underlying action language of Golog+HTN$^{TI}$ allows actions with duration and parallel execution;
2. The program constructs of Golog+HTN$^{TI}$ generalize the constructs of GOLOG and HTN with time and intervals;
3. It does not require an explicit specification of time.

Finally, we notice that the approach presented in this paper can be extended to allow more complex action languages that allow continuous fluents and processes such as $\mathcal{ADC}$ in (Baral, Son, & Tuan 2002). Besides its use as a specification language similar to cc-Golog, Golog+HTN$^{TI}$ can also be viewed as a language for specifying domain-dependent knowledge in a planner, a view explored by (Son, Baral, & McIlraith 2001) with respect to GOLOG. There, they demonstrated that a simplified version of programs discussed in this paper can help improving the performance of planner. To investigate this use of Golog+HTN$^{TI}$, we have developed a prototype of a planner for domains with continuous fluents and durative actions that uses Golog+HTN$^{TI}$ with encouraging results. We will report our experiments with Golog+HTN$^{TI}$ in planning in a future work.

## References


Baral, C., and Son, T. C. 1999. Extending ConGolog to allow partial ordering. Theories, LNCS 1757, ATAL-99, 188–204.

Baral, C.; Son, T. C.; and Tuan, L.-C. 2002. A transition function based characterization of actions with delayed and continuous effects. KR-02, 291–302.

Boutilier, C.; Reiter, R.; Soutchanski, M.; and Thrun, S. 2000. Decision-theoretic, high-level agent programming in the situation calculus. AAAI-00, 355–362.

Burgard, W.; Cremers, A. B.; Fox, D.; Hähnel, D.; Lakemeyer, G.; D., S.; Steiner, W.; and Thrun, S. 1998. The interactive museum tour-guide robot. Artificial AAAI-98, 11–18.

Eiter, T.; Leone, N.; Mateis, C.; Pfeifer, G.; and Scarcello, F. 1998. The KR System `dlv`: Progress Report, Comparisons, and Benchmarks. KR-98, 406–417.

De Giacomo, G.; Lespérance, Y.; and Levesque, H. 2000. *Con-Golog*, a concurrent programming language based on the situation calculus. AIJ 121(1-2):109–169.

Gelfond, M., and Lifschitz, V. 1990. Logic programs with classical negation, ICLP-90, 579–597.

Gelfond, M., and Lifschitz, V. 1993. Representing actions and change by logic programs. *JLP* 17(2,3,4):301–323.

Gelfond, M., and Lifschitz, V. 1998. Action languages. *ETAI* 3(6).

Grosskreutz, H., and Lakemeyer, G. 2000. cc-golog: Towards more realistic logic-based robot controllers. AAAI-00, 476–482.

Levesque, H.; Reiter, R.; Lesperance, Y.; Lin, F.; and Scherl, R. 1997. GOLOG: A logic programming language for dynamic domains. *JLP* 31(1-3):59–84.

Lierler, Y., and Maratea, M. Cmodels-2: SAT-based Answer Set Solver Enhanced to Non-tight Programs. LPNMR-03, 346–350.

Lifschitz, V. 2002. Answer set programming and plan generation. *AIJ* 138(1–2):39–54.

Lin, F., and Zhao, Y. 2002. ASSAT: Computing Answer Sets of A Logic Program By SAT Solvers. AAAI-02.

Marek, V., and Truszczyński, M. 1999. Stable models and an alternative logic programming paradigm. *The Logic Programming Paradigm: a 25-year Perspective*, 375–398.

Niemelä, I. 1999. Logic programming with stable model semantics as a constraint programming paradigm. *AMAI* 25, 241–273.

Reiter, R. 2000. On knowledge-based programming with sensing in the situation calculus. $2^{nd}$ *Int. Cog. Rob. Workshop, Berlin.*

Reiter, R. *KNOWLEDGE IN ACTION: Logical Foundations for Describing and Implementing Dynamical Systems.* MIT Press.

Sacerdoti, E. D. 1974. Planning in a hierarchy of abstraction spaces. *AIJ* 5:115–135.

Simons, P.; Niemelä, N.; and Soininen, T. 2002. Extending and Implementing the Stable Model Semantics. AIJ 138, 181–234.

Son, T. C.; Baral, C.; and McIlraith, S. 2001. Domain dependent knowledge in planning - an answer set planning approach. LPNMR-01, 226–239.

Subrahmanian, V., and Zaniolo, C. 1995. Relating stable models and ai planning domains. ICLP, 233–247.

# Model Checking Temporal Logics of Knowledge in Distributed Systems

**Kaile Su**
Department of Computer Science, Zhongshan University
Guangzhou 510275, P.R. China
isskls@zsu.edu.cn

## Abstract

Model checking is a promising approach to automatic verification, which has concentrated on specification expressed in temporal logic. Comparatively little attention has been given to temporal logics of knowledge, although such logics have been proven to be very useful in the specifications of protocols for distributed systems. In this paper, we address ourselves to the model checking problem for a temporal logic of knowledge (Halpern and Vardi's logic of $CKL_n$). Based on the semantics of *interpreted systems* with *local propositions*, we develop an approach to symbolic $CKL_n$ model checking via OBDDs. In our approach to model checking specifications involving agents' knowledge, the knowledge modalities are eliminated via quantifiers over agents' non-observable variables.

## Introduction

Model checking is most widely understood as a technique for automatically verifying that finite state systems satisfy formal specifications. The success of model checking in mainstream computer science has led to a recent growth of interest in the use of the technology in fields of AI such as planning and multiagent systems. However, the formal specifications for finite state systems are most commonly expressed as formulae of temporal logics such as $LTL$ (linear temporal logic) in the case of SPIN (Holzmann 1997) and FORSPEC (Vardi 2001) and $CTL$ in the case of SMV (McMillan 1993), while the specifications for multiagent systems involve agents' knowledge, belief and other notions of agents' mental states. In this paper, we address ourselves to the model checking problem for a temporal logic of knowledge (Halpern and Vardi's logic of $CKL_n$).

The application of model checking within the context of the logic of knowledge was first mooted by (Halpern & Vardi 1991). A number of algorithms for model checking epistemic specifications and the computational complexity of the related problems were studied in (van der Meyden 1998). However, they did not investigate "practical" model checking for knowledge and time.

(Rao & Georgeff 1993) investigated the model checking problem for situated reasoning systems, but they did not consider S5 logics of knowledge and they did not implement any of the techniques they developed. (Benerecetti, Giunchiglia, & Serafini 1999; Benerecetti & Giunchiglia 2000) developed techniques for some temporal modal logics, but these logics have an unusual (non-Kripke) semantics.

(van der Meyden & Su 2004) took a promising first step towards model checking of anonymity properties in formulas involving knowledge. Nevertheless, they took the assumptions that agents are of perfect recall and considered only a small class of epistemic formulas without any nest of epistemic modalities.

(Hoek & Wooldridge 2002) developed an approach to reduce $CKL_n$ model checking to linear temporal logic ($LTL$) (Pnueli 1977) model checking. However, the verification process of their approach still requires an input from a human verifier (to obtain the so-called local propositions when reducing the $CKL_n$ specification to $LTL$). A "direct" implementation of $CKL_n$ model checking would thus be desirable.

Our approach presents a methodology for symbolic $CKL_n$ model checking, based on the semantics of *interpreted systems* with *local propositions* (Engelhardt, van der Meyden, & Moses 1998), which leads to a "direct" implementation of $CKL_n$ model checking. Moreover, by the results presented, we can provide via OBDD (Bryant 1986) an approach to symbolic verifying $CTL^*$, the combination of $LTL$ and $CTL$ (branching temporal logic). This is interesting because $LTL$ and $CTL$ have been well studied and implemented efficiently into a number of tools (Clark, Grumberg, & Peled 2000; Holzmann 1997) and the community of model checking expects such a tool that can verify specifications in full $CTL^*$ efficiently.

The present paper follows similar lines to (Hoek & Wooldridge 2002), which is based on the idea of local propositions as described in (Engelhardt, van der Meyden, & Moses 1998; Engelhardt, van der Meyden, & Su 2002). The main advantages of the present paper over (Hoek & Wooldridge 2002) are:

1. We explicitly introduce the notion of finite-state program with $n$-agents (which is a symbolic representation of the well-known interpreted systems) and present some interesting results on the theoretical foundations of (Hoek & Wooldridge 2002).
2. In order to determine whether $K_i\varphi$ holds at some point

of an interpreted system, Hoek and Wooldridge (Hoek & Wooldridge 2002) attempt to find an $i$-local proposition $\psi$ which is equivalent to $K_i\varphi$ at that point; whereas, we try to get an $i$-local proposition $\psi$ which is equivalent to $K_i\varphi$ at any point (see Remark 11).

The structure of the paper is as follows. In the next section, we shortly introduce the well-known interpreted system (Fagin *et al.* 1995) and a temporal logic of knowledge, Halpern and Vardi's $CKL_n$ (Halpern & Vardi 1989). Then, we define a class of interpreted systems that are generated by finite-state programs with $n$-agents. The most exciting result is to show how to use OBDDs to implement symbolic $CKL_n$ model checking, based on those interpreted systems generated by finite-state programs with $n$-agents.

## Knowledge in an Interpreted System with Local Variables

In this section, we define the semantic framework within which we study the model checking of specifications in the logic of knowledge. First, we introduce interpreted systems (Fagin *et al.* 1995) and a temporal logic of knowledge $CKL_n$ (Halpern and Vardi's $CKL_n$ (Halpern & Vardi 1989)). Then, we present the notion of a finite-state program with $n$-agents, a finite-state transition representation for those interpreted systems with local variables

### Interpreted systems

The systems we are modelling are composed of multiple agents, each of which is in some state at any point of time. We refer to this as the agent's *local* state, in order to distinguish it from the system's state, the *global* state. Without loss of too much generality, we make the system's state a tuple $(s_1, \cdots, s_n)$, where $s_i$ is agent $i$'s state.

Let $L_i$ be a set of possible local states for agent $i$, for $i = i, \cdots, n$. We take $G \subseteq L_1 \times \cdots \times L_n$ to be the set of *reachable global* states of the system. A *run* over $G$ is a function from the time domain–the natural numbers in our case–to $G$. Thus, a run over $G$ can be identified with a sequence of global states in $G$. We refer to a pair $(r, m)$ consisting of a run $r$ and time $m$ as a *point*. We denote the $i$'th component of the tuple $r(m)$ by $r_i(m)$. Thus, $r_i(m)$ is the local state of agent $i$ in run $r$ at "time" $m$.

The idea of the interpreted system semantics is that a run represents one possible computation of a system and a system may have a number of possible runs, so we say a *system* is a set of runs.

Assume that we have a set $\Phi$ of primitive propositions, which we can think of as describing basic facts about the system. An *interpreted system* $\mathcal{I}$ consists of a pair $(\mathcal{R}, \pi)$, where $\mathcal{R}$ is a set of runs over a set of global states and $\pi$ is a valuation function, which gives the set of primitive propositions true at each point in $\mathcal{R}$ (Fagin *et al.* 1995).

To define knowledge in interpreted systems, we associate with every agent $i$, an equivalence relation $\sim_i$ over the set of points (Fagin *et al.* 1995): $(r, u) \sim_i (r', v)$ iff $r_i(u) = r'_i(v)$.

If $(r, u) \sim_i (r', v)$, then we say that $(r, u)$ and $(r', v)$ are indistinguishable to agent $i$, or, alternatively, that agent $i$ carries exactly the same information in $(r, u)$ and $(r', v)$.

To give a semantics to the "common knowledge" among a group $\Gamma$ of agents, two further relations, $\sim_\Gamma^E$ and $\sim_\Gamma^C$, are introduced (Fagin *et al.* 1995). We define the relation $\sim_\Gamma^E$ as $\bigcup_{i\in\Gamma} \sim_i$ and the relation $\sim_\Gamma^C$ as the transitive closure of $\sim_\Gamma^E$.

Notice that a system as a set of infinite runs seems not well suited to model checking directly as it is generally applied to the finite state systems. In fact, we can represent an interpreted system as a *finite-state program* $(G, G_0, R, V)$, where $G_0$ is a set of initial states, $R$ is a total "next time" relation, and $V$ associates each state with a truth assignment function. A set of infinite runs is then obtained by "unwinding" the relation $R$ starting from initial states in $G_0$.

### Semantics

Given a set $\Phi$ of primitive propositions, we use $Prop$ to denote the set of all propositional formulas over $\Phi$.

The *linear temporal logic LTL* (Manna & Pnueli 1995) is propositional logic augmented by the future-time connectives $\bigcirc$ (next) and $\mathbf{U}$ (until). The other future-time connectives $\diamond$ (sometime or eventually) and $\square$ (always) can be introduced as abbreviations.

The language of $CKL_n$ is the language of propositional temporal logic augmented by a modal operator $K_i$ for each agent $i$, and common knowledge operators $C_\Gamma$, where $\Gamma$ is a group of agents. The semantics of $CKL_n$ is given via the satisfaction relation "$\models_{CKL_n}$". Given an interpreted system $\mathcal{I} = (\mathcal{R}, \pi)$ and a point $(r, u)$ in $\mathcal{I}$, we define $(\mathcal{I}, r, u) \models \psi$ by the induction on the structure $\psi$. The only nontrivial cases are when $\psi$ is of the forms $K_i\varphi$, $C_\Gamma\varphi$, $\bigcirc\varphi$ and $\varphi\mathbf{U}\varphi'$.

- $(\mathcal{I}, r, u) \models_{CKL_n} K_i\varphi$ iff $(\mathcal{I}, r', v) \models_{CKL_n} \varphi$ for all $(r', v)$ such that $(r, u) \sim_i (r', v)$.
- $(\mathcal{I}, r, u) \models_{CKL_n} C_\Gamma\varphi$ iff $(\mathcal{I}, r', v) \models_{CKL_n} \varphi$ for all $(r', v)$ such that $(r, u) \sim_\Gamma^C (r', v)$.
- $(\mathcal{I}, r, u) \models_{CKL_n} \bigcirc\varphi$ iff $(\mathcal{I}, r, (u + 1)) \models_{CKL_n} \varphi$
- $(\mathcal{I}, r, u) \models_{CKL_n} \varphi\mathbf{U}\varphi'$ iff $(\mathcal{I}, r, u') \models_{CKL_n} \varphi'$ for some $u' \geq u$ and $(\mathcal{I}, r, u'') \models_{CKL_n} \varphi$ for all $u''$ with $u \leq u'' < u'$.

We say that $\varphi$ is valid in $\mathcal{I}$, denoted by $\mathcal{I} \models_{CKL_n} \varphi$, if $(\mathcal{I}, r, u) \models_{CKL_n} \varphi$ for every point $(r, u)$ in $\mathcal{I}$. We also write $(\mathcal{I}, r, u) \models_{LTL} \varphi$ for $(\mathcal{I}, r, u) \models_{CKL_n} \varphi$ when $\varphi$ is an $LTL$ formula. For a propositional formula $\varphi$, we use $\models \varphi$ to express that $\varphi$ is a valid formula or tautology.

### Finite-state program with $n$ agents

A *finite-state program with n agents* is a finite-state program associated with a set $O_i$ of observable variables for each agent $i$. To get a symbolic representation of a finite-state program with $n$ agents, we present a symbolic representation of a finite-state program $(G, G_0, R, V)$ in what follows.

1. We use a tuple of boolean variables $\mathbf{x} = \{x_1, \cdots, x_k\}$ and encode a state as an assignment for $\mathbf{x}$, or a subset of $\mathbf{x}$. (For convenience, we sometimes do not distinguish a set and its characteristic function.) Thus, $G_0$ and any set of states can be represented as a propositional formula over $\mathbf{x}$.

2. Further, we use another tuple of boolean variables $\mathbf{x}' = \{x'_1, \cdots, x'_k\}$ and represent the "next time" relation $R$ between two states as a propositional formula $\tau$ over $\mathbf{x} \cup \mathbf{x}'$. In other words, for two assignments $s$ and $s'$ for $\mathbf{x}$, $sRs'$ holds iff $\tau(\mathbf{x}, \mathbf{x}')$ is satisfied by the assignment $s \cup N(s')$, where $N(s')$ denotes $\{x'_j \mid x_j \in s' \text{ and } 0 < j \leq k\}$.
3. We assume that for each $s$, $V(s)$ equals $s$, that is, for each variable $x_j$ $(1 \leq j \leq k)$, $V(s)(x_j) = 1$ iff $s(x_j) = 1$.

Omitting the component $V$, we represent the finite-state program $(G, G_0, R, V)$ just as $(\mathbf{x}, \theta(\mathbf{x}), \tau(\mathbf{x}, \mathbf{x}'))$.

Hence, we formally define a (symbolic) *finite-state program with $n$ agents* as a tuple $\mathcal{P} = (\mathbf{x}, \theta(\mathbf{x}), \tau(\mathbf{x}, \mathbf{x}'), O_1, \cdots, O_n)$, where

1. $\mathbf{x}$ is a set of system variables;
2. $\theta$ is a boolean formula over $\mathbf{x}$, called the *initial condition*;
3. $\tau$ is a boolean formula over $\mathbf{x} \cup \mathbf{x}'$, called the *transition relation*; and
4. for each $i$, $O_i \subseteq \mathbf{x}$, containing agent $i$'s *local variables*, or *observable variables*.

Given a state $s$, we define agent $i$'s local state at state $s$ to be $s \cap O_i$. For convenience, we denote $(s \cap O_1, \cdots, s \cap O_n)$ by $g(s)$. We associate with $\mathcal{P}$ the interpreted system $\mathcal{I}_\mathcal{P} = (\mathcal{R}, \pi)$, where $\mathcal{R}$ is a set of those runs $r$ satisfying that

1. for each $m$, $r(m)$ is of the form $g(s) = (s \cap O_1, \cdots, s \cap O_n)$ where $s$ is a state in $\mathcal{P}$ and the assignment $\pi(s)$ is the same as $s$;
2. $r(0)$ is $g(s)$ for some assignment $s$ that satisfies $\theta$;
3. for each natural number $m$, if $r(m) = g(s)$ and $r(m+1) = g(s')$ for some assignments $s$ and $s'$ for $\mathbf{x}$ , then $s \cup N(s')$ is an assignment satisfying $\tau(\mathbf{x}, \mathbf{x}')$.

The interpreted system $\mathcal{I}_\mathcal{P}$ is called *the generated interpreted system of $\mathcal{P}$*.

For convenience, we fix throughout this paper $\mathcal{P} = (\mathbf{x}, \theta(\mathbf{x}), \tau(\mathbf{x}, \mathbf{x}'), O_1, \cdots, O_n)$ to be a finite-state program with $n$ agents.

### Local propositions

We now introduce the notion of a *local* proposition (Engelhardt, van der Meyden, & Moses 1998). An $i$-local proposition is a formula whose interpretation is the same in each of the points in each equivalence class induced by the $\sim_i$ relation. Formally, given an interpreted system $\mathcal{I}$ and an agent $i$, a formula $\varphi$ is *$i$-local* iff for each point $(r, u)$ in $\mathcal{I}$, if $(\mathcal{I}, r, u) \models_{CKL_n} \varphi$, then $(\mathcal{I}, r', u') \models_{CKL_n} \varphi$ for all points $(r', u')$ such that $(r, u) \sim_i (r', u')$. Further, for a set $\Gamma \subseteq \{1, \cdots, n\}$, we say a formula $\varphi$ is *$\Gamma$-local* if $\varphi$ is *$i$-local* for each $i \in \Gamma$.

The *model checking* problem for $CKL_n$ we are concerned is the problem of determining whether, given an interpreted system $\mathcal{I} = (\mathcal{R}, \pi)$ and a formula $\varphi$, the formula $\varphi$ is true in the initial state of every run in $\mathcal{R}$. More concisely, given an interpreted system $\mathcal{I}$ and a formula $\varphi$, we say that $\mathcal{I}$ realizes $\varphi$, denoted by $mc_{CKL_n}(\mathcal{I}, \varphi)$, if for all runs $r$ in $\mathcal{I}$, we have $(\mathcal{I}, r, 0) \models_{CKL_n} \varphi$.

If $\varphi$ is an $LTL$ formula in the above definition, we also write $mc_{LTL}(\mathcal{I}, \varphi)$ to stand for $mc_{CKL_n}(\mathcal{I}, \varphi)$. We use $l_i(\mathcal{I}_\mathcal{P}, r, u)$ to denote the above formula $(\bigwedge_{x \in r_i(u)} x \wedge \bigwedge_{x \in (O_i - r_i(u))} \neg x)$.

**Proposition 1** *A formula $\varphi$ is $i$-local in the generated interpreted system $\mathcal{I}_\mathcal{P}$ iff there is a propositional formula $\psi$ containing only variables over $O_i$ such that $mc_{CKL_n}(\mathcal{I}_\mathcal{P}, \Box(\varphi \Leftrightarrow \psi))$.*

**Proposition 2** *Let $\Gamma$ be a set of agents. Then, a formula $\varphi$ is $\Gamma$-local in the generated interpreted system $\mathcal{I}_\mathcal{P}$ iff for each agent $i$ in $\Gamma$, there is a propositional formula $\psi_i$ containing only variables over $O_i$ such that $mc_{CKL_n}(\mathcal{I}_\mathcal{P}, \Box(\varphi \Leftrightarrow \psi_i))$.*

We omit the proofs of the two propositions above, which present both necessary and sufficient conditions for $i$-locality and $\Gamma$-locality, respectively, whereas Proposition 1 and 2 in (Hoek & Wooldridge 2002) give only sufficient conditions.

### Reachable global states

Let $\xi$ be an operator from the set of boolean formulas over $\mathbf{x}$ to the set of boolean formulas over $\mathbf{x}$. We say $\psi$ is a *fixed point* of $\xi$, if $\models \xi(\psi) \Leftrightarrow \psi$. We say a $\psi_0$ is a *greatest fixed point* of $\xi$, if $\psi_0$ is a fixed point of $\xi$ and for every fixed point $\psi$ of $\xi$, we have that $\models \psi \Rightarrow \psi_0$. Clearly, any two greatest fixed points are logically equivalent to each other. Thus, we denote a greatest fixed point of $\xi$ by $\mathbf{gfp}Z\xi(Z)$. Similarly, We say a $\psi_0$ is a *least fixed point* of $\xi$, if $\psi_0$ is a fixed point of $\xi$ and for every fixed point $\psi$ of $\xi$, we have that $\models \psi_0 \Rightarrow \psi$. A least fixed point of $\xi$ is denoted by $\mathbf{lfp}Z\xi(Z)$. We say $\xi$ is *monotonic*, if for every two formulas $\psi_1$ and $\psi_2$ such that $\models \psi_1 \Rightarrow \psi_2$, we have $\models \xi(\psi_1) \Rightarrow \xi(\psi_2)$. For a finite set $\mathbf{x}$ of boolean formulas if $\xi$ is monotonic, then there exist a least fixed point and a greatest fixed point (Tarski 1955).

As usual, for a set of boolean variables $\mathbf{v} = \{v_1, \cdots, v_m\}$, $\exists \mathbf{v}\varphi$ $(\forall \mathbf{v}\varphi)$ stands for $\exists v_1 \cdots \exists v_m \varphi$ $(\forall v_1 \cdots \forall v_m \varphi)$, and $\psi(\frac{\mathbf{x}'}{\mathbf{x}})$ is the result of renaming variables in $\mathbf{x}'$ by those in $\mathbf{x}$ respectively.

Let

$$G(\mathcal{P}) = \mathbf{lfp}Z\left[\theta(\mathbf{x}) \vee (\exists \mathbf{x}(Z \vee \tau(\mathbf{x}, \mathbf{x}')))\left(\frac{\mathbf{x}'}{\mathbf{x}}\right)\right].$$

The following lemma says that the (quantified) boolean formula $G(\mathcal{P})$ expresses the set of *reachable global states* .

**Lemma 3** *The following holds:*

1. $\mathcal{I}_\mathcal{P} \models_{CKL_n} G(\mathcal{P})$.
2. *For a boolean formula $\varphi$, $\mathcal{I}_\mathcal{P} \models_{CKL_n} \varphi$ iff $\models G(\mathcal{P}) \Rightarrow \varphi$.*

## Symbolic Model Checking $CKL_n$

The intuition of our approach to symbolic model checking $CKL_n$ is to replace a formula of the form $K_i\varphi$ by some $i$-local formula $\psi$. There are two cases depending on whether $\varphi$ is a pure propositional formula or an $LTL$ formula containing modalities $\mathbf{U}$ or $\bigcirc$.

## Model checking knowledge of state properties

First, we consider the case that $\varphi$ does not contain temporal modalities, this is, $\varphi$ represents a state property.

**Proposition 4** *Let $\varphi$ be a formula that does not containing any temporal modalities. Then*

$$\mathcal{I}_\mathcal{P} \models_{CKL_n} K_i\varphi \Leftrightarrow \forall(\mathbf{x} - O_i)(G(\mathcal{P}) \Rightarrow \varphi).$$

**Proof:** The conclusion of the proposition follows by Proposition 1 and Lemma 3. ▮

**Proposition 5** *Let $\varphi$ be a formula that does not containing any temporal modalities, $\Gamma$ a set of agents, and $\Lambda$ an operator such that*

$$\Lambda(Z) = \bigwedge_{i\in\Gamma} \forall(\mathbf{x} - O_i)(G(\mathcal{P}) \Rightarrow Z).$$

*Then*

$$\mathcal{I}_\mathcal{P} \models_{CKL_n} C_\Gamma\varphi \Leftrightarrow \mathbf{gfp}\ Z(G(\mathcal{P}) \wedge \varphi \wedge \Lambda(Z)).$$

**Proof:** Omitted for limited space. ▮

By Proposition 4 and 5, when we do the task of model checking $CKL_n$ formula, we can replace formulas of the form $K_i\varphi$ ($C_\Gamma\varphi$) by some $i$-local ($\Gamma$-local) proposition, where $\varphi$ does not containing any temporal modalities.

## Model checking knowledge of temporal properties

Now, we deal with the case that $\varphi$ may contain some temporal modalities. We use the idea of the so-called tableau construction as descried in (Lichtenstein & Pnueli 1985) and (E.M. Clarke & Hamaguchi 1994). For a formula, $\psi$, we write $\psi \in \varphi$ to denote that $\psi$ is a sub-formula of (possibly equals to) $\varphi$. Formula $\psi$ is called *principally temporal* if its main operator is temporal operator, i.e., $\psi$ is of the form $\bigcirc\alpha$ or $\alpha\mathbf{U}\beta$.

Given a formula $\varphi$, we define a finite-state program $\mathcal{P}_\varphi = (\mathbf{x}_\varphi, \theta_\varphi, \tau_\varphi, O_1, \cdots, O_n)$ as follows.

**System variables:** The set $\mathbf{x}_\varphi$ of system variables of $\mathcal{P}_\varphi$ consists of $\mathbf{x}$ plus a set of auxiliary boolean variables

$$X_\varphi : \{x_\psi \mid \psi \text{ is a principally temporal sub-formula of } \varphi\}.$$

The auxiliary variable $x_\psi$ is intended to be true in a state of a computation iff the temporal formula $\psi$ holds at the state.

For convenience, we define a function $\chi$ which maps every sub-formula of $\varphi$ into a boolean formula over $\mathbf{x} \cup X_\varphi$.

$$\chi(\psi) = \begin{cases} \psi & \text{for } \psi \text{ a variable in } \mathbf{x} \\ \neg\chi(\alpha) & \text{for } \psi = \neg\alpha \\ \chi(\alpha) \wedge \chi(\beta) & \text{for } \psi = \alpha \wedge \beta \\ x_\psi & \text{for principally temporal } \psi \end{cases}$$

Let $X'_\varphi$ be the primed version of $X_\varphi$. For a formula $\psi$ over $\mathbf{x} \cup X_\varphi$, we use $\chi'(\psi)$ to denote the formula $\psi(\frac{\mathbf{x}\cup X_\varphi}{\mathbf{x}'\cup X'_\varphi})$, i.e., the primed version of $\psi$.

**Initial condition:** The initial condition of $\mathcal{P}_\varphi$ is the same as for $\mathcal{I}_\mathcal{P}$.

**Transition relation:** The transition relation $\tau_\varphi$ of $\mathcal{P}_\varphi$ is the transition relation $\tau$ plus

$$\bigwedge_{\bigcirc\psi\in\varphi} (x_{\bigcirc\psi} \Leftrightarrow \chi'(\psi)) \wedge \bigwedge_{\alpha\mathbf{U}\beta\in\varphi} (x_{\alpha\mathbf{U}\beta} \Leftrightarrow (\chi(\beta) \vee (\chi(\alpha) \wedge x'_{\alpha\mathbf{U}\beta})))$$

For convenience, we introduce now some more notations from the CTL logic (Clark, Grumberg, & Peled 2000). Let $\mathbf{EX}$ be the operator such that for a boolean formula $\psi$ over $\mathbf{x} \cup X_\varphi$,

$$\mathbf{EX}\psi(\mathbf{x}, X_\varphi) = \exists(\mathbf{x}' \cup X'_\varphi)(\psi(\mathbf{x}', X'_\varphi) \wedge \tau_\varphi).$$

In other words, the set of those states satisfying $\mathbf{EX}\psi(\mathbf{x}, X_\varphi)$ is the image of the set of those states satisfying $\psi$ under the transition relation $\tau_\varphi$.

The operators $\mathbf{EF}$ and $\mathbf{EU}$ are defined by the least fixed point of some monotonic operators: $\mathbf{EF}f = \mathbf{lfp}\ Z(f \vee \mathbf{EX}Z)$, and $\mathbf{EU}(f, g) = \mathbf{lfp}\ Z(g \vee (f \wedge \mathbf{EX}Z))$.

Let $\mathcal{J}_\varphi$ be the set of all formulas $\neg x_{\alpha\mathbf{U}\beta} \vee \chi(\beta)$, where $\alpha\mathbf{U}\beta$ is a sub-formula of $\varphi$. To give the knowledge of agent $i$ at some state, we consider the following fairness constraints:

$C^1_\varphi$: There is a computational path for which each formula in $\mathcal{J}_\varphi$ holds infinitely often.

$C^2_\varphi$: There is a finite computational path such that each formula in $\mathcal{J}_\varphi$ holds at the last state of the computational path, and the last state does not have any next state in the system $\mathcal{I}_\mathcal{P}$.

Clearly, if $C^1_\varphi$ holds with $\mathcal{J}_\varphi \neq \emptyset$, then there is a computational path which is infinitely long. If $C^2_\varphi$ holds, then there is a finite computational path at which the last state does not have a next state in the system $\mathcal{I}_\mathcal{P}$.

We suppose that $\mathcal{J}_\varphi$ is not an empty set. This assumption does not lose any generality because we can put $\mathbf{true}$ in $\mathcal{J}_\varphi$.

The constrain $C^2_\varphi$ can be expressed as $\mathbf{EF}(End(\mathcal{P}) \wedge \bigwedge_{\psi\in\mathcal{J}_\varphi} \psi)$ in the standard $CTL$ logic, where $End(\mathcal{P})$ is the formula related to the set of dead states in the system $\mathcal{I}_\mathcal{P}$, it can be represented as $\neg\exists\mathbf{x}'\tau(\mathbf{x}, \mathbf{x}')$.

The constrain $C^1_\varphi$ can be defined as:

$$C^1_\varphi = \mathbf{gfp}\ Z[\bigwedge_{J\in\mathcal{J}_\varphi} \mathbf{EX}(\mathbf{EU}(\mathbf{true}, Z \wedge J))].$$

It is not difficult to see that a state satisfies the condition $C^1_\varphi$ iff the state is at some run where each $J \in \mathcal{J}_\varphi$ holds for infinite times along the run (Clark, Grumberg, & Peled 2000).

We say a run $r_\varphi$ in $\mathcal{I}_{\mathcal{P}_\varphi}$ is *fair*, if either $r_\varphi$ is infinitely long and each $J$ in $\mathcal{J}_\varphi$ is satisfied by infinitely many states at $r_\varphi$, or there is a state, say $s_{end}$, such that $s_{end} \cap \mathbf{x}$ has no successor in $\mathcal{I}_\mathcal{P}$ and each $J \in \mathcal{J}_\varphi$ is satisfied by $s_{end}$. It follows the following assertion.

**Lemma 6** *Let $\varphi$ be an $LTL$ formula, $s_\varphi$ a state of $\mathcal{I}_{\mathcal{P}_\varphi}$. Then, $s_\varphi$ satisfies $C^1_\varphi \vee C^2_\varphi$ iff $s_\varphi$ is at some fair run of $\mathcal{I}_{\mathcal{P}_\varphi}$.*

**Lemma 7** *Let $\varphi$ be an $LTL$ formula. Then for each run $r$ in $\mathcal{I}_\mathcal{P}$, there is a fair run $r_\varphi$ in $\mathcal{I}_{\mathcal{P}_\varphi}$ such that for every natural number $u$ and for every subformula $\psi$ of $\varphi$,*

1. $r(u) = r_\varphi(u) \cap \mathbf{x}$,
2. $(\mathcal{I}_\mathcal{P}, r, u) \models_{LTL} \psi$ *iff* $\chi(\psi)$ *is satisfied by* $r_\varphi(u)$.

**Proof:** Let $r$ be a run in $\mathcal{I}_\mathcal{P}$. We define a fair run $r_\varphi$ in $\mathcal{I}_{\mathcal{P}_\varphi}$ as follows. For each point $r(u)$, let $r_\varphi(u)$ be the variable set

$$r(u) \cup \left\{ x_\alpha \,\middle|\, \begin{array}{l} \alpha \text{ is principally temporal subformula of } \varphi \\ \text{and } (\mathcal{I}_\mathcal{P}, r, u) \models_{LTL} \alpha \end{array} \right\}$$

It follows immediately that $r(u) = r_\varphi(u) \cap \mathbf{x}$ and, for a principally temporal subformula $\psi$ of $\varphi$, we have that $(\mathcal{I}_\mathcal{P}, r, u) \models_{LTL} \psi$ iff $\chi(\psi)$ is satisfied by $r_\varphi(u)$. For other subformula $\psi$ of $\varphi$, we can prove the above assertion holds by induction on $\psi$. It is also easy to see that $r_\varphi$ is a run in $\mathcal{I}_{\mathcal{P}_\varphi}$ and $r_\varphi$ is fair. ∎

**Lemma 8** *Let $\varphi$ be as in Lemma 7. Then, for each fair run $r_\varphi$ in $\mathcal{I}_{\mathcal{P}_\varphi}$, there is a run $r$ in $\mathcal{I}_\mathcal{P}$ such that for every natural number $u$ and for every subformula $\psi$ of $\varphi$,*

1. $r(u) = r_\varphi(u) \cap \mathbf{x}$,
2. $(\mathcal{I}_\mathcal{P}, r, u) \models_{LTL} \psi$ *iff* $\chi(\psi)$ *is satisfied by* $r_\varphi(u)$.

**Proof:** Let $r_\varphi$ be a fair run in $\mathcal{I}_{\mathcal{P}_\varphi}$. We define a run $r$ in $\mathcal{I}_\mathcal{P}$ simply by $r(u) = r_\varphi(u) \cap \mathbf{x}$ for each state $r_\varphi(u)$.

We assume that $r_\varphi$ is infinitely long because the other case, where $r_\varphi$ is finite, can be dealt with in the same way.

Given a subformula $\psi$ of $\varphi$, we show, by induction on the structure of $\psi$, the claim that $(\mathcal{I}_\mathcal{P}, r, u) \models_{LTL} \psi$ iff $\chi(\psi)$ is satisfied by $r_\varphi(u)$. The conclusion of the lemma follows by the above claim. ∎

We now extend the logic $CKL_n$ by introducing two path quantifiers $\mathbf{A}$ and $\mathbf{E}$. The resulting language is denoted by $ECKL_n$. For a finite-state program $\mathcal{P}$ with $n$ agents, a run $r$ in $\mathcal{I}_\mathcal{P}$, a formula $\psi$, and a natural number $u$, we have $(\mathcal{I}_\mathcal{P}, r, u) \models_{CKL_n} \mathbf{E}\psi$ iff there is a run $r'$ such that, for some natural number $v$, $r(u) = r'(v)$ and $(\mathcal{I}_\mathcal{P}, r', v) \models_{CKL_n} \psi$. We define $\mathbf{A}\psi$ as $\neg\mathbf{E}\neg\psi$.

Clearly, if we remove knowledge modalities from $ECKL_n$, we get the well-known logic $CTL^*$. The following proposition presents a methodology of implementing symbolic verifying $CTL^*$ via OBDDs.

**Proposition 9** *Let $\varphi$ be an $LTL$ formula. Then*

$$\mathcal{I}_\mathcal{P} \models_{CKL_n} \mathbf{E}\varphi \Leftrightarrow \exists X_\varphi((C_\varphi^1 \vee C_\varphi^2) \wedge \chi(\varphi)).$$

**Proof:** ($\Rightarrow$) Assume that $(\mathcal{I}_\mathcal{P}, r, u) \models_{CKL_n} \mathbf{E}\varphi$. There is a run $r'$ and a natural number $v$ such that $r'(v) = r(u)$ and $(\mathcal{I}_\mathcal{P}, r', v) \models_{CKL_n} \varphi$. By Lemma 7, there is a fair run $r_\varphi$ in $\mathcal{I}_{\mathcal{P}_\varphi}$, such that $r_\varphi(v)$ satisfies $\chi(\varphi)$ iff $(\mathcal{I}_\mathcal{P}, r, v) \models_{CKL_n} \varphi$. Thus, $r_\varphi(v)$ satisfies $\chi(\varphi)$. Moreover, because $r_\varphi$ is a fair run, every state at run $r_\varphi$ must satisfy $C_\varphi^1 \vee C_\varphi^2$. So, $r_\varphi(v)$ satisfies $(C_\varphi^1 \vee C_\varphi^2) \wedge \chi(\varphi)$. Because $r(u) = r'(v) = r_\varphi(v) \cap \mathbf{x}$, we have that $r(u) \cup (r_\varphi(v) \cap X_\varphi) = r_\varphi(v)$ satisfies $(C_\varphi^1 \vee C_\varphi^2) \wedge \chi(\varphi)$. This is, $(\mathcal{I}_\mathcal{P}, r, u) \models_{CKL_n} \exists X_\varphi((C_\varphi^1 \vee C_\varphi^2) \wedge \chi(\varphi))$.

($\Leftarrow$) Suppose that $(\mathcal{I}_\mathcal{P}, r, u) \models_{CKL_n} \exists X_\varphi((C_\varphi^1 \vee C_\varphi^2) \wedge \chi(\varphi))$. Then, $r(u)$ satisfies $\exists X_\varphi((C_\varphi^1 \vee C_\varphi^2) \wedge \chi(\varphi))$, and there is a state $s_\varphi$ in $\mathcal{I}_{\mathcal{P}_\varphi}$ such that $r(u) = s_\varphi \cap \mathbf{x}$, and $s_\varphi$ satisfies $((C_\varphi^1 \vee C_\varphi^2) \wedge \chi(\varphi))$. By the fact that $s_\varphi$ satisfies $C_\varphi^1 \vee C_\varphi^2$ and Lemma 6, we get that $s_\varphi$ is at some fair run $r_\varphi$ in $\mathcal{I}_{\mathcal{P}_\varphi}$, and there is a natural number $v$ such that $s_\varphi = r_\varphi(v)$. By Lemma 8, there is a run $r'$ in $\mathcal{I}_\mathcal{P}$ such that $r'(v) = r_\varphi(v) \cap \mathbf{x}$ and $(\mathcal{I}_\mathcal{P}, r', v) \models_{CKL_n} \varphi$ iff $r_\varphi(v)$ satisfies $\chi(\varphi)$. Recalling $r_\varphi(v) = s_\varphi$ and $r(u) = s_\varphi \cap \mathbf{x}$, we have $r'(v) = r(u)$. Moreover, by the fact that $r_\varphi(v)$ satisfies $\chi(\varphi)$, we have that $(\mathcal{I}_\mathcal{P}, r', v) \models_{CKL_n} \varphi$. Hence, $(\mathcal{I}_\mathcal{P}, r, u) \models_{CKL_n} \mathbf{E}\varphi$. ∎

Now follow the main results in this section.

**Proposition 10** *Let $\varphi$ be an $LTL$ formula. Then, the following formula*

$$K_i\varphi \Leftrightarrow \forall(X_\varphi \cup \mathbf{x} - O_i)((C_\varphi^1 \vee C_\varphi^2) \wedge G(\mathcal{P}) \Rightarrow \chi(\varphi))$$

*is valid in $\mathcal{I}_\mathcal{P}$.*

**Proof:** We first notice that the formula $K_i\varphi \Leftrightarrow K_i\mathbf{A}\varphi$ is valid in $\mathcal{I}_\mathcal{P}$. Proposition 9 says that the formula $\mathbf{A}\varphi \Leftrightarrow \forall X_\varphi((C_\varphi^1 \vee C_\varphi^2) \Rightarrow \chi(\varphi))$ is valid. Hence,

$$\mathcal{I}_\mathcal{P} \models_{CKL_n} K_i\varphi \Leftrightarrow K_i(\forall X_\varphi((C_\varphi^1 \vee C_\varphi^2) \Rightarrow \chi(\varphi))).$$

By Proposition 4, the following formula

$$K_i\varphi \Leftrightarrow \forall(\mathbf{x} - O_i)(G(\mathcal{P}) \Rightarrow \forall X_\varphi((C_\varphi^1 \vee C_\varphi^2) \Rightarrow \chi(\varphi)))$$

must be valid in $\mathcal{I}_\mathcal{P}$. Because variables in $X_\varphi$ do not appear in $G(\mathcal{P})$, the formula

$$K_i\varphi \Leftrightarrow \forall(X_\varphi \cup \mathbf{x} - O_i)((C_\varphi^1 \vee C_\varphi^2) \wedge G(\mathcal{P}) \Rightarrow \chi(\varphi))$$

is thus valid in $\mathcal{I}_\mathcal{P}$. ∎

**Remark 11** In order to determine whether $K_i\varphi$ holds at some point of an interpreted system, Hoek and Wooldridge (Hoek & Wooldridge 2002) attempt to find an $i$-local proposition $\psi$ such that $K_i\varphi$ holds iff $\psi$ holds at that point. However, how to get such an $i$-local proposition $\psi$ was not presented in (Hoek & Wooldridge 2002). In addition, the local-proposition formula $\psi$ may depend on the point at which we check $K_i\varphi$ (see Proposition 5 in (Hoek & Wooldridge 2002)). Thus, when faced with the problem of determining whether some point satisfies a formula $\alpha$ with a subformula of the form $K_i\varphi$, we could not reduce the problem to determining whether the point satisfies the formula $\alpha(\frac{K_i\varphi}{\psi})$ (which results from $\alpha$ by replacing $K_i\varphi$ with $\psi$.) The main advantage of Proposition 10 over Hoek and Wooldridge's results is that the $i$-local proposition $\psi$ is given out (i.e. $\forall(X_\varphi \cup \mathbf{x} - O_i)((C_\varphi^1 \vee C_\varphi^2) \wedge G(\mathcal{P}) \Rightarrow \chi(\varphi))$) and the proposition $\psi$ does not depend on the point $(r, u)$.

We also remark that Proposition 10 provides a reduction of $CKL_n$ to $LTL$, while Proposition 9 gives a method of model checking $LTL$ formulas. The complexity of our reduction of $CKL_n$ to $LTL$ is $PSPACE$-complete. Nevertheless, because $C_\varphi^1$, $C_\varphi^2$ and quantifications of boolean functions can be dealt with in any $OBDD$ package, the reduction of $CKL_n$ to $LTL$ and the $LTL$ model checking method can be based on OBDDs. Thus, the $CKL_n$ model checking algorithm via Proposition 10 and 9 might be practically implementable.

As for model checking common knowledge of temporal properties, we can see the following proposition holds.

**Proposition 12** *Let $\varphi$ be a formula that may contain some temporal modalities, $\Lambda$ an operator such that*

$$\Lambda(Z) = \bigwedge_{i \in \Gamma} \forall(\mathbf{x} - O_i)(G(\mathcal{P}) \Rightarrow Z).$$

*Then, the following formula is valid in $\mathcal{I}_{\mathcal{P}}$:*

$$C_\Gamma \varphi \Leftrightarrow \textbf{gfp}\ Z[G(\mathcal{P}) \wedge \forall X_\varphi((C_\varphi^1 \vee C_\varphi^2) \Rightarrow \chi(\varphi)) \wedge \Lambda(Z)]$$

**Proof:** By Proposition 9 and Proposition 5. ▮

## Conclusions

In this paper, we have considered the model checking problem for Halpern and Vardi's well-known temporal epistemic logic $CKL_n$. We have introduced the notion of a finite state program with $n$ agents, which can be thought of as a symbolic representation of interpreted systems. We have developed an approach to symbolic $CKL_n$ model checking, using OBDDs. In our approach to model checking specifications involving agents' knowledge, the knowledge modalities are eliminated via quantifiers over agents' non-observable variables. As a by-product, we have presented a methodology of implementing symbolic verifying $CTL^*$ via OBDDs.

We are currently working on an implementation of a $CKL_n$ model checker based on the results in this paper, via CUDD library developed by Fabio Somenzi at Colorado University. We have founded the prototype of the model checking system and finished the kernel part of it. Because of limited space, we do not include experimental results here. As for future work, we are interested in providing automated support for the analysis of knowledge in distributed system protocols and game theoretic examples, and the verification and compilation of knowledge-based programs (Fagin *et al.* 1995).

## Acknowledgement

Thanks to Yanyan Xu, Qingliang Chen and the AAAI reviewers for their valuable comments. This work was supported by the National Science Foundation of China under grants 60073056 and 60273062.

## References

Benerecetti, M., and Giunchiglia, F. 2000. Model checking security protocols using a logic of belief. In Graf, S., and Schwartzbach, M., eds., *Proc. 6th International Conference on Tools and Algorithms for the Construction and Analysis of Systems (TACAS 2000)*, 519–534.

Benerecetti, M.; Giunchiglia, F.; and Serafini, L. 1999. A model checking algorithm for multi-agent systems. In Muller, J.; Singh, M.; and Rao, A., eds., *Intelligent Agents V*, volume LNAI Vol. 1555. Berlin: Springer-Verlag.

Bryant, R. 1986. Graph-based algorithms for boolean function manipulation. *IEEE Transaction on Computers* (C-35(8)).

Clark, E.; Grumberg, O.; and Peled, D. 2000. *Model Checking*. Cambridge, MA: The MIT Press.

E.M. Clarke, O. G., and Hamaguchi, K. 1994. Another look at LTL model checking. In *Proc. 6th Conference on Computer Aided Verification*, 415–427. Springer LNCS Vol. 818.

Engelhardt, K.; van der Meyden, R.; and Moses, Y. 1998. Knowledge and the logic of local propositions. In *Theoretical Aspects of Rationality and Knowledge, Proc. of TARK 1998*.

Engelhardt, K.; van der Meyden, R.; and Su, K. 2002. Modal logics with a hierarchy of local propositional quantifiers (preliminary version). In *Advance in Modal Logic 2002 (AiML)*, 63–76.

Fagin, R.; Halpern, J.; Moses, Y.; and Vardi, M. 1995. *Reasoning about knowledge*. Cambridge, MA: MIT Press.

Halpern, J., and Vardi, M. 1989. The complexity of reasoning about knowledge and time, I: Lower bounds. *Journal of Computer and System Sciences* 38(1):195–237.

Halpern, J., and Vardi, M. 1991. Model checking vs. theorem proving: A manifesto. In *Proc. 2nd Int. Conf. on Principles of Knowledge Representation and Reasoning*, 325–334.

Hoek, W. v. d., and Wooldridge, M. 2002. Model checking knowledge and time. In *9th Workshop on SPIN (Model Checking Software)*.

Holzmann, G. 1997. The spin model checker. *IEEE Transaction on Software Engineering* 23:279–295.

Lichtenstein, O., and Pnueli, A. 1985. Checking that finite-state concurrent programs satisfy their linear apecification. In *Proc. 12th ACM Symp. of Prog. Lang.*, 97–107.

Manna, Z., and Pnueli, A. 1995. *Temporal Verification of Reactive Systems*. Berlin, Germany: Springer-verlag.

McMillan, K. 1993. *Symbolic Model Checking*. Boston: Kluwer Academic Publisher.

Pnueli, A. 1977. The temporal logic of programs. In *Proc. 18th IEEE Symposium on Foundations of Computer Science*, 46–57.

Rao, A., and Georgeff, M. 1993. A model theoretic approach to the verification of situated reasoning systems. In *Proc. 13th International Joint Conference on Artificial Intelligence*, 318–324.

Tarski, A. 1955. A lattice-theoretical fixpoint theorem and its applications. *Pacific J. Math.* 5:285–309.

van der Meyden, R., and Su, K. 2004. Symbolic model checking the knowledge of the dining cryptographers. In *Proc. of 17th IEEE Computer Security Foundation Workshop*.

van der Meyden, R. 1998. Common knowledge and update in finite environments. *Information and Computation* 140(2):115–157.

Vardi, M. 2001. Branching vs. linear time:. In Margaria, T., and Yi, W., eds., *Proc. 7th International Conference on Tools and Algorithms for the Construction and Analysis of Systems (TACAS 2001)*, 1–22.

# Identifying Linear Causal Effects

**Jin Tian**
Department of Computer Science
Iowa State University
Ames, IA 50011
*jtian@cs.iastate.edu*

**Abstract**

This paper concerns the assessment of linear cause-effect relationships from a combination of observational data and qualitative causal structures. The paper shows how techniques developed for identifying causal effects in causal Bayesian networks can be used to identify linear causal effects, and thus provides a new approach for assessing linear causal effects in structural equation models. Using this approach the paper develops a systematic procedure for recognizing identifiable direct causal effects.

## Introduction

Structural equation models (SEMs) have dominated causal reasoning in the social sciences and economics, in which interactions among variables are usually assumed to be linear (Duncan 1975; Bollen 1989). This paper deals with one fundamental problem in SEMs, accessing the strength of linear cause-effect relationships from a combination of observational data and model structures. This problem has been under study for half a century, primarily by econometricians and social scientists, under the name "The Identification Problem". Traditional approaches are based on algebraic manipulation of the linear equations, for example, the rank and order conditions (Fisher 1966), the well-known instrumental variable method (Bowden & Turkington 1984). The applications of these methods are limited in scope and the identification problem is still far from being solved.

In recent years, causal reasoning with graphical models has been an active research area in the artificial intelligence community (Heckerman & Shachter 1995; Lauritzen 2000; Pearl 2000; Spirtes, Glymour, & Scheines 2001; Dawid 2002). The most common representation of graphical causal models involves a directed acyclic graph (DAG) with causal interpretation, called a *causal Bayesian network (BN)*. The relation between linear SEMs and causal BNs, in which no assumptions were made about the functional forms of how the variables interact with each other, is analyzed in (Pearl 1998; 2000; Spirtes, Glymour, & Scheines 2001). Graphical approaches for identifying linear causal effects in SEMs have been developed in which the structure of a SEM is represented by a DAG with bidirected edges, and some sufficient graphical conditions were established (McDonald 1997; Pearl 1998; Spirtes *et al.* 1998). Recently, (Brito & Pearl 2002b) developed a sufficient graphical criterion for the identification of the entire model. (Brito & Pearl 2002a) gave a generalization of the instrumental variable method that allows its application to models with few conditional independences.

The problem of identifying (nonlinear) causal effects in causal BNs concerns the assessment of the effects of actions or interventions from a combination of observational data and causal structures. This problem has been under extensive study over the last ten years (Pearl 1993; 1995; Galles & Pearl 1995; Glymour & Cooper 1999; Pearl 2000; Spirtes, Glymour, & Scheines 2001; Tian & Pearl 2002). In this paper we show that all the results in identifying nonlinear causal effects in causal BNs can be directly used to identify linear causal effects in SEMs, and thus provide a new tool for the identification problem in SEMs.

We consider three types of linear causal effects in SEMs – direct effects, partial effects, and total effects, and show how they can be computed through identifying nonlinear causal effects. Identifiable causal effects are expressed in terms of observed convariances. One feature of this approach is that it may directly identify total effects and partial effects even though some individual parameters involved are not identifiable. We also give a procedure that systematically looks for identifiable direct causal effects. The approach adds another tool to our repertoire of identification methods. However, its application is limited and it may well fail to identify some causal effects that are identifiable by other approaches.

## Linear SEMs and Identification

A linear SEM over a set of variables $V = \{V_1, \ldots, V_n\}$ is given by a set of equations of the form

$$V_j = \sum_{i<j} c_{V_j V_i} V_i + \epsilon_j, \quad j = 1, \ldots, n, \tag{1}$$

where $c_{V_j V_i}$'s are called *path coefficients*, and $\epsilon_j$'s represent "error" terms and are assumed to have normal distribution with zero mean and covariance matrix $\Psi$ with $\Psi_{ij} = Cov(\epsilon_i, \epsilon_j)$. In this paper we consider recursive models and assume that the summation is for $i < j$.

The equations and the non-zero entries in the covariance matrix $\Psi$ define the structure of the model. The model struc-

$X = \epsilon_x$
$Z = aX + \epsilon_z$
$W = bZ + \epsilon_w$
$Y = cX + dZ + eW + \epsilon_y$
$Cov(\epsilon_x, \epsilon_w) \neq 0$
$Cov(\epsilon_z, \epsilon_y) \neq 0$

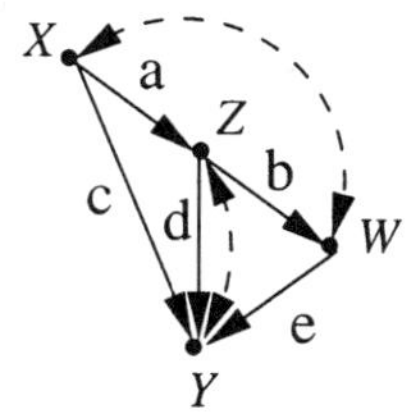


Figure 1: A linear SEM.

ture can be represented by a DAG $G$ with (dashed) bidirected edges, called a *causal diagram* (or *path diagram*), as follows: the nodes of $G$ are the variables $V_1, \ldots, V_n$; there is a directed edge from $V_i$ to $V_j$ in $G$ if the coefficient of $V_i$ in the equation for $V_j$ is not zero ($c_{V_j V_i} \neq 0$); there is a bidirected edge between $V_i$ and $V_j$ if the error terms $\epsilon_i$ and $\epsilon_j$ have non-zero correlation. Figure 1 shows a simple SEM and the corresponding causal diagram in which each directed edge is annotated by the corresponding path coefficient.

In linear SEMs, the observed distribution $P(v)$ is fully specified by a covariance matrix $\Sigma$ over $V$. Let $C$ be the matrix of path coefficients $c_{V_j V_i}$. Given the model structure and parameters $C$ and $\Psi$, the covariance matrix $\Sigma$ is given by (see, for example, (Bollen 1989))

$$\Sigma = (I - C)^{-1}\Psi(I - C)'^{-1}. \tag{2}$$

Conversely, in the identification problem, given the structure of a model, one attempts to solve for $C$ in terms of the (observed) covariance $\Sigma$. If the equation (2) gives a unique solution to some path coefficient $c_{V_j V_i}$, independent of the (unobserved) error correlations $\Psi$, that coefficient is said to be *identifiable*. In other words, the *identification problem* is that whether a path coefficient is determined uniquely from the covariance matrix $\Sigma$ given the causal diagram. Note that the identifiability conditions we seek involve the structure of the model alone, not particular numerical values of parameters, allowing for pathological exceptions.

## Causal BNs and Identification

A causal Bayesian network consists of a DAG $G$ over a set $V = \{V_1, \ldots, V_n\}$ of vertices, called a *causal diagram.* The interpretation of such a diagram has two components, probabilistic and causal. The probabilistic interpretation views $G$ as representing conditional independence assertions: Each variable is independent of all its non-descendants given its direct parents in the graph.[1] These assertions imply that the joint probability function $P(v) = P(v_1, \ldots, v_n)$ factorizes according to the product (Pearl 1988)

$$P(v) = \prod_i P(v_i|pa_i) \tag{3}$$

[1]We use family relationships such as "parents," "children," and "ancestors" to describe the obvious graphical relationships.

where $pa_i$ are (values of) the parents of variable $V_i$ in the graph.[2]

The causal interpretation views the directed edges in $G$ as representing causal influences between the corresponding variables. This additional assumption enables us to predict the effects of interventions, whenever interventions are described as specific modifications of some factors in the product of (3). The simplest such intervention involves fixing a set $T$ of variables to some constants $T = t$, denoted by the action $do(T = t)$ or simply $do(t)$, which yields the post-intervention distribution[3]

$$P_t(v) = \begin{cases} \prod_{\{i|V_i \notin T\}} P(v_i|pa_i) & v \text{ consistent with } t. \\ 0 & v \text{ inconsistent with } t. \end{cases} \tag{4}$$

Eq. (4) represents a truncated factorization of (3), with factors corresponding to the manipulated variables removed. If $T$ stands for a set of treatment variables and $Y$ for an outcome variable in $V \setminus T$, then Eq. (4) permits us to calculate the probability $P_t(y)$ that event $Y = y$ would occur if treatment condition $T = t$ were enforced uniformly over the population. This quantity, often called the *causal effect* of $T$ on $Y$, is what we normally assess in a controlled experiment with $T$ randomized, in which the distribution of $Y$ is estimated for each level $t$ of $T$.

We see that, whenever all variables in $V$ are observed, given the causal diagram $G$, all causal effects can be computed from the observed distribution $P(v)$. Our ability to estimate $P_t(v)$ from observed data is severely curtailed when some variables are unobserved, or, equivalently, if two or more variables in $V$ are affected by unobserved confounders; the presence of such confounders would not permit the decomposition of the observed distribution $P(v)$ in (3). The question of *identifiability* arises, i.e., whether it is possible to express a given causal effect $P_t(s)$ as a function of the observed distribution $P(v)$ in a given causal diagram.

It is convenient to represent a causal BN with unobserved confounders in the form of a DAG $G$ that does not show the elements of unobserved variables explicitly but, instead, represents the confounding effects of unobserved variables using (dashed) bidirected edges. A bidirected edge between nodes $V_i$ and $V_j$ represents the presence of unobserved factors (or confounders) that may influence both $V_i$ and $V_j$. For example, the diagram in Figure 1 can be used to represent a causal BN with unobserved confounders.

In general, identifiability can be decided using *do*-calculus derivations (Pearl 1995). Sufficient graphical conditions for ensuring identifiability were established by several authors and are summarized in (Pearl 2000, Chapters 3 and 4), and see (Tian & Pearl 2002) for latest development. These graphical conditions often use a graphical relation called d-separation defined as follows (Pearl 1988).

[2]We use uppercase letters to represent variables or sets of variables, and use corresponding lowercase letters to represent their values (instantiations).

[3](Pearl 2000) used the notation $P(v|set(t))$, $P(v|do(t))$, or $P(v|\hat{t})$ for the post-intervention distribution, while (Lauritzen 2000) used $P(v||t)$.

**Definition 1 (d-separation)** *A path[4] $p$ is said to be* d-separated *by a set of nodes $Z$ if and only if*

1. *$p$ contains a chain $V_i \to V_j \to V_k$ or a fork $V_i \leftarrow V_j \to V_k$ such that the node $V_j$ is in $Z$, or*
2. *$p$ contains an inverted fork $V_i \to V_j \leftarrow V_k$ such that $V_j$ is not in $Z$ and no descendant of $V_j$ is in $Z$.*

For example, a criterion called "back-door" (Pearl 1993) says that the causal effect $P_x(y)$ of variable $X$ on $Y$ is identifiable if there exists a set of variables $Z$ such that $Z$ satisfies the following *back-door condition* relative to $(X, Y)$: (i) no member of $Z$ is a descendant of $X$; and (ii) $Z$ d-separates all the back-door paths from $X$ to $Y$, where a path from $X$ to $Y$ is said to be a *back-door path* if it contains an arrow into $X$. Moreover, $P_x(y)$ is given by

$$P_x(y) = \sum_z P(y|x, z)P(z). \tag{5}$$

Linear SEMs can be thought of as a special case of causal BNs in which all interactions among variables are assumed to be linear. If a causal effect $P_t(y)$ is identifiable given a causal diagram, it will provide information about the identifiability of certain path coefficients in the SEM with the same causal diagram. In the next section, we show how causal effects $P_t(y)$ are related to path coefficients in SEMs.

## Identifying Linear Causal Effects: from Causal BNs to SEMs

In SEMs, we define three types of linear causal effects as follows. The path coefficient $c_{V_j V_i}$ quantifies the direct causal influence of $V_i$ on $V_j$, and is called a *direct effect*. Assume that there is a directed path $p$ from $V_k$ to $V_i$ in the causal diagram $G$, then the product of path coefficients along the path $p$ is called the *partial effect* of $V_k$ on $V_i$ along the path $p$, and will be denoted by $PE(p)$. For example, in the model shown in Figure 1, the partial effect of $X$ on $Y$ along the path $(X, Z, Y)$ is given by $ad$. Let $\Gamma(V_k, V_i)$ denote the set of all directed paths from $V_k$ to $V_i$, and let $\gamma \subseteq \Gamma(V_k, V_i)$. Then $\sum_{p \in \gamma} PE(p)$ is called the partial effect of $V_k$ on $V_i$ along the set of paths $\gamma$ and will be denoted by $PE(\gamma)$. In particular, $PE(\Gamma(V_k, V_i))$, which represents the summation of products of path coefficients along the directed paths from $V_k$ to $V_i$, is called the *total effect* of $V_k$ on $V_i$ and will be denoted by $TE(V_k, V_i)$. For example, in the model shown in Figure 1, the total effect of $X$ on $Y$ is given by $TE(X, Y) = c + ad + abe$.

The three types of linear causal effects – direct effects, partial effects, and total effects, can be computed from the nonlinear causal effects $P_t(y)$. An identifiable causal effect $P_t(y)$ would mean certain linear causal effects are identifiable in the SEM with the same causal diagram $G$. Let $E[.|do(t)]$ denote the expectations in the post-intervention distribution $P_t(.)$:

$$E[X|do(t)] = \int x P_t(x) dx \tag{6}$$

The following proposition is intuitive and not hard to prove.

[4]A path is a sequence of consecutive edges (of any directionality).

**Proposition 1 (Total Effects)** *The total effect of $V_k$ on $V_i$ is identifiable if $P_{v_k}(v_i)$ is identifiable, and $TE(V_k, V_i)$ can be computed as*

$$TE(V_k, V_i) = E[V_i|do(v_k)]/v_k. \tag{7}$$

For example, in the model shown in Figure 1, if $P_x(y)$ is identifiable, then $TE(X, Y) = c + ad + abe = E[Y|do(x)]/x$.

Let $Pa_j = \{V_{j_1}, \ldots, V_{j_l}\}$ be the set of parents of $V_j$ in the causal diagram ($Pa_j$ is the set of variables that appear in the right hand side of the equation for $V_j$ in Eq. (1)), then it is easy to show that

$$E[V_j|do(pa_j)] = \sum_i c_{V_j V_{j_i}} v_{j_i}, \tag{8}$$

from which we have the following proposition.

**Proposition 2 (Direct Effects)** *The direct effect of $V_k$ on $V_j$ is identifiable if $P_{pa_j}(v_j)$ is identifiable, and the path coefficient $c_{V_j V_k}$ can be computed as*

$$c_{V_j V_k} = \frac{\partial}{\partial v_k} E[V_j|do(pa_j)], \quad V_k \in Pa_j. \tag{9}$$

For example, in the model shown in Figure 1, if $P_{xzw}(y)$ were identifiable, then $E[y|do(xzw)] = cx + dz + ew$ and path coefficients $c, d, e$ would be identifiable.

Let $S = \{V_{i_1}, \ldots, V_{i_m}\}$ be a set of variables that does not contain $V_i$. Let $\gamma_j$ be the set of directed paths from $V_{i_j}$ to $V_i$ that does not pass any other variables in $S$. Then it is easy to show that

$$E[V_i|do(s)] = \sum_j PE(\gamma_j) v_{i_j}, \tag{10}$$

where we define $PE(\emptyset) = 0$. Eq. (10) leads to the following proposition.

**Proposition 3** *Let $S = \{V_{i_1}, \ldots, V_{i_m}\}$, and let $\gamma_j$ be the set of directed paths from $V_{i_j}$ to $V_i$ that does not pass any variables in $S \setminus \{V_{i_j}\}$. If $P_s(v_i)$ is identifiable, then each partial effect $PE(\gamma_j)$, $j = 1, \ldots, m$, is identifiable and is given by*

$$PE(\gamma_j) = \frac{\partial}{\partial v_{i_j}} E[V_i|do(s)]. \tag{11}$$

If we seek to identify some particular partial effects, then Proposition 3 can be modified to obtain the following proposition.

**Proposition 4 (Partial Effects)** *Given a set $\gamma \subseteq \Gamma(V_k, V_i)$ of directed paths from $V_k$ to $V_i$, if there exists a set of variables $S$ such that none of the variables in $S$ lies in the paths in $\gamma$ and each path in $\Gamma(V_k, V_i) \setminus \gamma$ passes a variable in $S$,[5] and if $P_{s,v_k}(v_i)$ is identifiable, then the partial effect $PE(\gamma)$ is identifiable and can be computed as*

$$PE(\gamma) = \frac{\partial}{\partial v_k} E[V_i|do(s), do(v_k)]. \tag{12}$$

[5]Note that such a set $S$ may not exist for some $\gamma$.

For example, in the model shown in Figure 1, the partial effect $c+ad$ of $X$ on $Y$ along the paths $(X,Y)$ and $(X,Z,Y)$ is equal to $\frac{\partial}{\partial x}E[Y|do(xw)]$ if $P_{xw}(y)$ is identifiable.

Propositions 1-4 provide a method for identifying linear causal effects in SEMs by identifying certain causal effects $P_t(y)$ and then computing expectations. Identified causal effects $P_t(y)$ are expressed in terms of the observed joint $P(v)$ which is a normal distribution in SEMs. To compute expectations with respect to the distribution $P_t(y)$, we will often need to compute conditional expectations. Let $S = \{V_{i_1},\ldots,V_{i_m}\}$ and $S_j = S\setminus\{V_{i_j}\}$. We have the following formula for conditional expectations in normal distributions (Cramer 1946)

$$E[V_i|s] = \sum_j \beta_{V_i V_{i_j}.S_j}\, v_{i_j}, \tag{13}$$

where $\beta_{V_i V_{i_j}.S_j}$ denotes the *partial regression coefficient* and represents the coefficient of $V_{i_j}$ in the linear regression of $V_i$ on $S$. (Note that the order of the subscripts in $\beta_{V_i V_j.S}$ is essential.) Partial regression coefficients can be expressed in terms of covariance matrices as follows (Cramer 1946):

$$\beta_{V_i V_j.S} = \frac{\Sigma_{V_i V_j} - \Sigma^T_{V_i S}\Sigma^{-1}_{SS}\Sigma_{V_j S}}{\Sigma_{V_j V_j} - \Sigma^T_{V_j S}\Sigma^{-1}_{SS}\Sigma_{V_j S}}, \tag{14}$$

where $\Sigma_{SS}$ etc. represent covariance matrices over corresponding variables.

Whenever a causal effect $P_t(y)$ is determined as identifiable, we can use Eqs. (7)–(13) to identify certain linear causal effects. We illustrate the computation process by an example. The "back-door" criterion (Pearl 1993) says that if a set of variables $Z$ satisfies the back-door condition relative to an ordered pair of variables $(X,Y)$, then $P_x(y)$ is identifiable and is given by Eq. (5). Then by Proposition 1, the total effect of $X$ on $Y$ is identifiable. Let $Z = \{Z_1,\ldots,Z_k\}$ and $Z^i = Z\setminus\{Z_i\}$. $TE(X,Y)$ can be computed as

$$\begin{aligned}
TE(X,Y) &= E[Y|do(x)]/x \\
&= \sum_z E[Y|x,z]P(z)/x \quad \text{(by Eq. (5))} \\
&= \sum_z (\beta_{YX.Z}\, x + \sum_i \beta_{YZ_i.XZ^i}\, z_i)P(z)/x \quad \text{(by Eq. (13))} \\
&= \beta_{YX.Z} \quad (E[Z_i]=0)
\end{aligned} \tag{15}$$

Therefore, we conclude that if a set of variables $Z$ satisfies the back-door condition relative to $(X,Y)$, then the total effect of $X$ on $Y$ is identifiable and is given by $\beta_{YX.Z}$. This result is given as Theorem 5.3.2 in (Pearl 2000, p. 152).

Using this approach, all the results for identifying causal effects in causal BNs can be used for identifying linear causal effects. Some of these results provide new graphical criteria for the identification of linear causal effects in SEMs. Consider the "front-door" criterion (Pearl 1995), which says that the causal effect $P_x(y)$ of variable $X$ on $Y$ is identifiable if there exists a set of variables $Z$ satisfying the following *front-door condition* relative to $(X,Y)$: (i) $Z$ intercepts all directed paths from $X$ to $Y$; (ii) all back-door paths from $X$ to $Z$ are d-separated by the empty set; and (iii) all back-door paths from $Z$ to $Y$ are d-separated by $X$. Moreover, $P_x(y)$ is given by

$$P_x(y) = \sum_z P(z|x)\sum_{x'} P(y|x',z)P(x') \tag{16}$$

Proposition 1 then leads to the following criterion for identifying total effects in SEMs.

**Theorem 1** *If a set of variables $Z = \{Z_1,\ldots,Z_k\}$ satisfies the front-door condition relative to $(X,Y)$, then the total effect of $X$ on $Y$ is identifiable and is given by $\sum_i \beta_{YZ_i.XS_i}\beta_{Z_iX}$ where $S_i = Z\setminus\{Z_i\}$.*

For $X$ being a singleton a general criterion for identifying $P_x(y)$ is given by Theorem 4 in (Tian & Pearl 2002). Let a path composed entirely of bidirected edges be called a *bidirected path*. Let $An(Y)$ denote the union of $\{Y\}$ and the set of ancestors of $Y$, and let $G_{An(Y)}$ denote the subgraph of $G$ composed only of variables in $An(Y)$. The theorem says that $P_x(y)$ is identifiable if there is no bidirected path connecting $X$ to any of its children in $G_{An(Y)}$. Proposition 1 then leads to the following theorem.

**Theorem 2** *(Tian & Pearl 2002) The total effect of $X$ on $Y$ is identifiable if there is no bidirected path connecting $X$ to any of its children in $G_{An(Y)}$.*

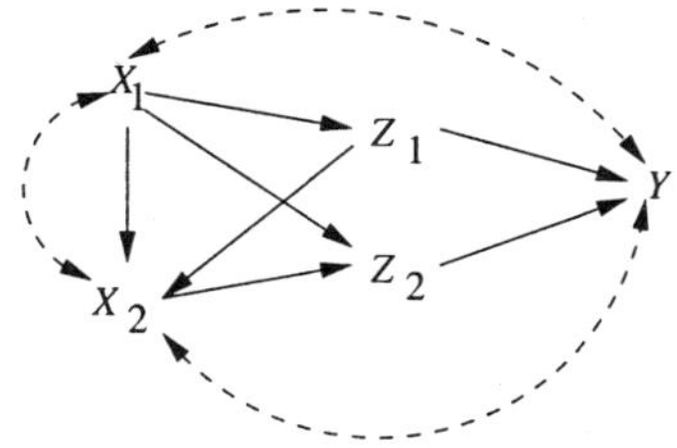


Figure 2: $P_{x_1x_2}(y)$ is identifiable.

Partial effects can be obtained by Proposition 4 from identifying the causal effects $P_t(y)$ of a set of variables $T$ on $Y$. Some graphical criteria for identifying $P_t(y)$ are given in (Pearl & Robins 1995; Kuroki & Miyakawa 1999). Those criteria are complicated and here we show the use of those criteria by an example. It was shown in (Kuroki & Miyakawa 1999) that $P_{x_1x_2}(y)$ in Figure 2 is identifiable. Then by Proposition 3, the partial effect $c_{Z_1X_1}c_{YZ_1} + c_{Z_2X_1}c_{YZ_2}$ of $X_1$ on $Y$ is identifiable, and the total effect $c_{Z_2X_2}c_{YZ_2}$ of $X_2$ on $Y$ is identifiable. The computation of actual expressions for these partial effects are lengthy and will not be shown here.

Direct effects can be thought of as a special case of partial effects, and by Proposition 2, direct effects on a variable $V_j$ can be obtained by identifying $P_{pa_j}(v_j)$, the causal effects of $V_j$'s parents on $V_j$. The criteria in (Pearl & Robins 1995; Kuroki & Miyakawa 1999) can also be used for identifying direct effects. For example, it is shown in (Pearl & Robins 1995) that the causal effect $P_{x_1x_2}(y)$ in Figure 3 is identifiable and is given by (Pearl 2000, page 122)

$$P_{x_1x_2}(y) = \sum_z P(y|x_1,x_2,z)P(z|x_1), \tag{17}$$

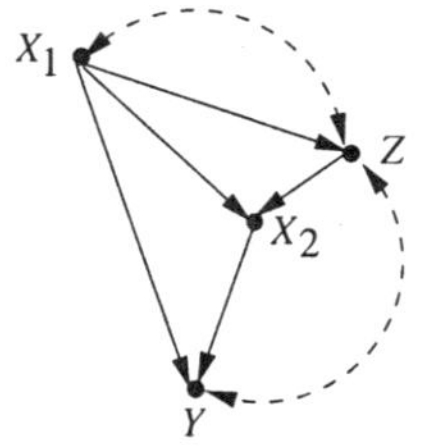


Figure 3: $P_{x_1 x_2}(y)$ is identifiable.

from which we compute

$$E[Y|do(x_1, x_2)]$$
$$= (\beta_{YX_1.X_2Z} + \beta_{YZ.X_1X_2}\beta_{ZX_1})x_1 + \beta_{YX_2.X_1Z}\, x_2. \quad (18)$$

By Proposition 2, we conclude that the direct effects of $X_1$ and $X_2$ on $Y$ are both identifiable and are given by

$$c_{YX_1} = \beta_{YX_1.X_2Z} + \beta_{YZ.X_1X_2}\beta_{ZX_1}, \quad (19)$$
$$c_{YX_2} = \beta_{YX_2.X_1Z}. \quad (20)$$

This method of translating identifiability results in causal BNs to linear models provides another tool for the identification problem in SEMs. Traditional SEM methods (Bollen 1989; Bowden & Turkington 1984) and recent graphical methods (Brito & Pearl 2002a) have focused on the identification of individual path coefficients, i.e. direct effects (with the exception of (Pearl 1998)). The method presented in this paper not only can be used to identify individual path coefficients, but may also directly identify some total effects and partial effects even though some individual path coefficients involved are not identifiable.

Some individual path coefficients that can not be directly identified as direct effects may be identified indirectly by the identification of some other causal effects of which they are a part. For example, in Figure 4(a), the path coefficient $c_{WY}$ can not be identified directly (nonlinear causal effect $P_y(w)$ is not identifiable), yet it can be shown that the total effect of $Z_2$ on $Y$, $c_{YZ_2}$, and the total effect of $Z_2$ on $W$, $c_{YZ_2}c_{WY}$, are both identifiable, and therefore $c_{WY}$ can be computed as $TE(Z_2, W)/TE(Z_2, Y)$. In general, a set of identifiable causal effects means that a set of algebraic expressions (sum of products) of path coefficients are identifiable, which can be treated as a set of equations over path coefficients. Individual path coefficients may be identified by solving those equations. For the purpose of identifying individual path coefficients, in the next section, we develop a procedure that systematically determines identifiable causal effects and solves for path coefficients.

## Identifying Path Coefficients Systematically

Let a topological order over $V$ be $V_1 < \ldots < V_n$ such that if $V_i < V_j$ then there is no directed path from $V_j$ to $V_i$. For $j$ from 2 to $n$, at each step, we will try to identify the path coefficients associated with edges pointing at $V_j$ (i.e., the direct effects on $V_j$, $c_{V_jV_i}$'s). For this purpose we consider the subgraph composed of those variables ordered before $V_j$. Let $V^{(j)} = \{V_1, \ldots, V_j\}$, $j = 1, \ldots, n$, and let $G_{V^{(j)}}$ denote the subgraph composed of the nodes in $V^{(j)}$. At step $j$, we seek identifiable causal effects imposed by other variables on $V_j$. Ideally, if $P_{pa_j}(v_j)$ is identifiable, then all those path coefficients $c_{V_jV_i}$'s are identifiable. In general, this is usually not the case. One general type of causal effects on $V_j$ that is guaranteed to be identifiable is given in (Tian & Pearl 2002), as shown in the following lemma.

**Lemma 1** *(Tian & Pearl 2002) Let a topological order over $V$ be $V_1 < \ldots < V_n$, and let $V^{(j)} = \{V_1, \ldots, V_j\}$, $j = 1, \ldots, n$, and $V^{(0)} = \emptyset$. Let $S_j$ be the set of variables (including $V_j$) that are connected with $V_j$ by a bidirected path (i.e., a path composed entirely of bidirected edges) in $G_{V^{(j)}}$ and let $\bar{S}_j = V^{(j)} \setminus S_j$. Then $P_{\bar{s}_j}(s_j)$ is identifiable and is given by*

$$P_{\bar{s}_j}(s_j) = \prod_{\{i|V_i \in S_j\}} P(v_i|v^{(i-1)}). \quad (21)$$

Using Lemma 1 and Proposition 3, at step $j$, we can compute $E[V_j|do(\bar{s}_j))]$ and identify some partial effects on $V_j$. Next, we study in detail what information we could obtain from these partial effects. Let $Z = \{Z_1, \ldots, Z_k\}$ be the set of variables in $\bar{S}_j$ such that for each $Z_i$ there exists a directed path from $Z_i$ to $V_j$ that does not pass any other variables in $\bar{S}_j$. Let $\gamma_i$ be the set of directed paths from $Z_i$ to $V_j$ that do not pass any other variables in $\bar{S}_j$. By Proposition 3, each partial effect $PE(\gamma_i)$ is identifiable and is given by

$$PE(\gamma_i) = \frac{\partial}{\partial z_i} E[V_j|do(\bar{s}_j)]. \quad (22)$$

Let the set of parents of $V_j$ that are connected with $V_j$ by a bidirected path be $Pa_j \cap S_j = \{Y_1, \ldots, Y_l\}$. Then the partial effect $PE(\gamma_i)$ as a summation of products of path coefficients along directed paths from $Z_i$ to $V_j$ can be decomposed into

$$PE(\gamma_i) = \sum_{m=1}^{l} PE(\delta_{im})c_{V_jY_m}, \quad \text{for } Z_i \notin Pa_j, \quad (23)$$

or when $Z_i$ is a parent of $V_j$,

$$PE(\gamma_i) = c_{V_jZ_i} + \sum_{m=1}^{l} PE(\delta_{im})c_{V_jY_m}, \quad \text{for } Z_i \in Pa_j, \quad (24)$$

where $\delta_{im}$ is the set of directed paths from $Z_i$ to $Y_m$ that do not pass any other variables in $\bar{S}_j$, and the summation is over the parents of $V_j$ that are in $S_j$ because $\gamma_i$ only contains paths that do not pass variables in $\bar{S}_j$.

Since $P_{\bar{s}_j}(s_j)$ is identifiable and $Y_m \in S_j$, by Proposition 3, each partial effect $PE(\delta_{im})$ is identifiable and is given by

$$PE(\delta_{im}) = \frac{\partial}{\partial z_i} E[Y_m|do(\bar{s}_j)], \quad (25)$$

which would have been identified before the step $j$. From Eqs. (22)–(25), we conclude that, at step $j$, we will obtain a set of equations which are linear in path coefficients $c_{V_jV_i}$'s

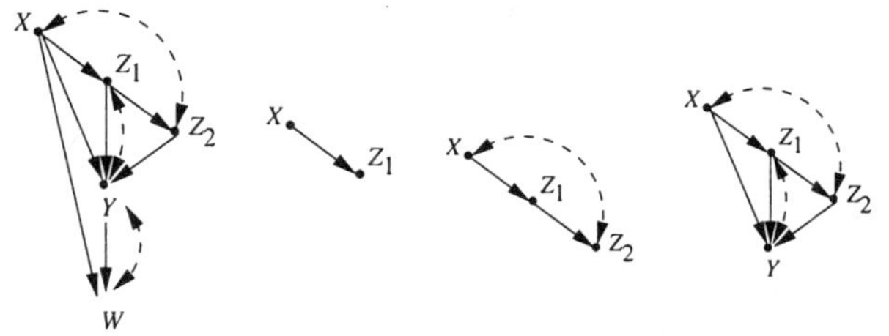


(a) $G$ (b) (c) (d)

Figure 4: Subgraphs for identifying path coefficients in $G$.

associated with edges pointing at $V_j$ and in which $c_{V_jV_i}$'s are the only unknowns. Eq. (24) will be linearly independent with other equations because the path coefficient $c_{V_jZ_i}$ will not appear in any other equations. However, in general, we can not guarantee that Eq. (23) is independent with each other.

In summary, we propose the following procedure for systematically identifying path coefficients.

- Let a topological order over $V$ be $V_1 < \ldots < V_n$ and let $V^{(j)} = \{V_1, \ldots, V_j\}, j = 1, \ldots, n,$
- At step $j$, for $j$ from 2 to $n$, do the following
  1. Let $S_j$ be the set of variables (including $V_j$) that are connected with $V_j$ by a bidirected path in $G_{V^{(j)}}$ and let $\bar{S}_j = V^{(j)} \setminus S_j$.
  2. Find the expression for $P_{\bar{s}_j}(s_j)$ by Lemma 1.
  3. Compute $E[V_j|do(\bar{s}_j)]$ and use Proposition 3 to get a set of equations linear in path coefficients $c_{V_jV_i}$'s associated with edges pointing at $V_j$.
  4. Try to solve the set of linear equations for $c_{V_jV_i}$'s.

We demonstrate this procedure by systematically identifying path coefficients in a SEM with causal diagram shown in Figure 4(a). The only admissible order of variables is $X < Z_1 < Z_2 < Y < W$. At step 1, we consider the subgraph in Figure 4(b). It is obvious that $P_x(z_1) = P(z_1|x)$, and we obtain

$$c_{Z_1X} = E[Z_1|do(x)]/x = \beta_{Z_1X}. \tag{26}$$

At step 2, we consider the subgraph in Figure 4(c). $Z_2$ is connected with $X$ by a bidirected path and Lemma 1 gives

$$P_{z_1}(x, z_2) = P(z_2|z_1, x)P(x), \tag{27}$$

which leads to

$$P_{z_1}(z_2) = \sum_x P(z_2|z_1, x)P(x). \tag{28}$$

Therefore, we obtain

$$c_{Z_2Z_1} = E[Z_2|do(z_1)]/z_1 = \beta_{Z_2Z_1.X}. \tag{29}$$

At step 3, we consider the subgraph in Figure 4(d). $Y$ is connected with $Z_1$ by a bidirected path and Lemma 1 gives

$$P_{xz_2}(y, z_1) = P(y|z_2, z_1, x)P(z_1|x). \tag{30}$$

We then compute the expectation

$$E[Y|do(x, z_2)] = \beta_{YZ_2.Z_1X}\, z_2 + (\beta_{YZ_1.Z_2X}\beta_{Z_1X} + \beta_{YX.Z_2Z_1})x \tag{31}$$

By Proposition 3 we obtain the path coefficient

$$c_{YZ_2} = \beta_{YZ_2.Z_1X}, \tag{32}$$

and the following partial effect

$$c_{YX} + c_{Z_1X}c_{YZ_1} = \beta_{YX.Z_2Z_1} + \beta_{Z_1X}\beta_{YZ_1.Z_2X}, \tag{33}$$

where $c_{Z_1X}$ is identified in Eq. (26) and $c_{YX}$ and $c_{YZ_1}$ are unknown.

Finally, at the last step, we consider the graph in Figure 4(a). $W$ is is connected with $Y$ and $Z_1$ by a bidirected path and Lemma 1 gives

$$P_{xz_2}(w, y, z_1) = P(w|y, z_2, z_1, x)P(y|z_2, z_1, x)P(z_1|x). \tag{34}$$

We then compute the expectation

$$\begin{aligned} E[W|do(x, z_2)] &= (\beta_{WY.Z_2Z_1X}\beta_{YZ_2.Z_1X} + \beta_{WZ_2.YZ_1X})z_2 \\ &+ [\beta_{WY.Z_2Z_1X}(\beta_{YZ_1.Z_2X}\beta_{Z_1X} + \beta_{YX.Z_2Z_1}) \\ &+ \beta_{WZ_1.YZ_2X}\beta_{Z_1X} + \beta_{WX.YZ_2Z_1}]\, x, \end{aligned} \tag{35}$$

and by Proposition 3, the total effect of $Z_2$ on $W$ is identifiable:

$$c_{YZ_2}c_{WY} = \beta_{WY.Z_2Z_1X}\beta_{YZ_2.Z_1X} + \beta_{WZ_2.YZ_1X}, \tag{36}$$

and the following partial effect of $X$ on $W$ is identifiable:

$$\begin{aligned} &c_{WX} + (c_{YX} + c_{Z_1X}c_{YZ_1})c_{WY} \\ &= \beta_{WY.Z_2Z_1X}(\beta_{YZ_1.Z_2X}\beta_{Z_1X} + \beta_{YX.Z_2Z_1}) \\ &+ \beta_{WZ_1.YZ_2X}\beta_{Z_1X} + \beta_{WX.YZ_2Z_1}. \end{aligned} \tag{37}$$

The path coefficient $c_{YZ_2}$ is identified in (32), and from Eq. (36), the path coefficient $c_{WY}$ is identifiable and is given by

$$c_{WY} = \beta_{WY.Z_2Z_1X} + \frac{\beta_{WZ_2.YZ_1X}}{\beta_{YZ_2.Z_1X}}. \tag{38}$$

Then from Eqs. (37), (33), and (38), the path coefficient $c_{WX}$ is identifiable and is given by

$$\begin{aligned} c_{WX} &= \beta_{WX.YZ_2Z_1} + \beta_{WZ_1.YZ_2X}\beta_{Z_1X} \\ &- \frac{\beta_{WZ_2.YZ_1X}}{\beta_{YZ_2.Z_1X}}(\beta_{YZ_1.Z_2X}\beta_{Z_1X} + \beta_{YX.Z_2Z_1}) \end{aligned} \tag{39}$$

## Conclusion

We show how the three types of linear causal effects in SEMs – direct effects, partial effects, and total effects, can be identified through identifying nonlinear causal effects of the form $P_t(y)$ using techniques developed in causal BNs. The approach provides a new tool for the identification problem in SEMs. Every progress in causal effects identification in causal BNs can be directly translated into progress in SEMs. One feature of this approach is that it may directly identify total effects and partial effects even though some individual path coefficients involved are not identifiable. The approach does not mean to be a complete identification rule, and it may fail to identify some path coefficients that are identifiable (possibly by other approaches).

## Acknowledgments

This research was partly supported by NSF grant IIS-0347846.

## References

Bollen, K. 1989. *Structural Equations with Latent Variables*. New York: John Wiley.

Bowden, R., and Turkington, D. 1984. *Instrumental Variables*. Cambridge, England: Cambridge University Press.

Brito, C., and Pearl, J. 2002a. Generalized instrumental variables. In *Proceedings of the Eighteenth Conference on Uncertainty in Artificial Intelligence (UAI)*, 85–93. San Francisco, CA: Morgan Kaufmann.

Brito, C., and Pearl, J. 2002b. A graphical criterion for the identification of causal effects in linear models. In *Proceedings of the Eighteenth National Conference on Artificial Intelligence (AAAI)*, 533–538. Menlo Park, CA: AAAI Press/The MIT Press.

Cramer, H. 1946. *Mathematical Methods of Statistics*. Princeton, N.J: Princeton University Press.

Dawid, A. 2002. Influence diagrams for causal modelling and inference. *International Statistical Review* 70(2).

Duncan, O. 1975. *Introduction to Structural Equation Models*. New York: Academic Press.

Fisher, F. 1966. *The Identification Problem in Econometrics*. McGraw-Hill.

Galles, D., and Pearl, J. 1995. Testing identifiability of causal effects. In Besnard, P., and Hanks, S., eds., *Uncertainty in Artificial Intelligence 11*. San Francisco: Morgan Kaufmann. 185–195.

Glymour, C., and Cooper, G., eds. 1999. *Computation, Causation, and Discovery*. Cambridge, MA: MIT Press.

Heckerman, D., and Shachter, R. 1995. Decision-theoretic foundations for causal reasoning. *Journal of Artificial Intelligence Research* 3:405–430.

Kuroki, M., and Miyakawa, M. 1999. Identifiability criteria for causal effects of joint interventions. *Journal of the Japan Statistical Society* 29(2):105–117.

Lauritzen, S. 2000. Graphical models for causal inference. In Barndorff-Nielsen, O.; Cox, D.; and Kluppelberg, C., eds., *Complex Stochastic Systems*. London/Boca Raton: Chapman and Hall/CRC Press. chapter 2, 67–112.

McDonald, R. 1997. Haldane's lungs: A case study in path analysis. *Multivariate Behavioral Research* 32(1):1–38.

Pearl, J., and Robins, J. 1995. Probabilistic evaluation of sequential plans from causal models with hidden variables. In Besnard, P., and Hanks, S., eds., *Uncertainty in Artificial Intelligence 11*. San Francisco: Morgan Kaufmann. 444–453.

Pearl, J. 1988. *Probabilistic Reasoning in Intelligence Systems*. San Mateo, CA: Morgan Kaufmann.

Pearl, J. 1993. Comment: Graphical models, causality, and intervention. *Statistical Science* 8:266–269.

Pearl, J. 1995. Causal diagrams for empirical research. *Biometrika* 82:669–710.

Pearl, J. 1998. Graphs, causality, and structural equation models. *Socioligical Methods and Research* 27:226–284.

Pearl, J. 2000. *Causality: Models, Reasoning, and Inference*. NY: Cambridge University Press.

Spirtes, P.; Richardson, T.; Meek, C.; Scheines, R.; and Glymour, C. 1998. Using path diagrams as a structural equation modeling tool. *Socioligical Methods and Research* 27:182–225.

Spirtes, P.; Glymour, C.; and Scheines, R. 2001. *Causation, Prediction, and Search*. Cambridge, MA: MIT Press.

Tian, J., and Pearl, J. 2002. A general identification condition for causal effects. In *Proceedings of the Eighteenth National Conference on Artificial Intelligence (AAAI)*, 567–573. Menlo Park, CA: AAAI Press/The MIT Press.

# Complexity

# The Complexity of Global Constraints

**Christian Bessiere**
LIRMM-CNRS
Montpellier, France
email: bessiere@lirmm.fr

**Emmanuel Hebrard** and **Brahim Hnich** and **Toby Walsh***
Cork Constraint Computation Centre
University College Cork, Ireland.
email: {e.hebrard,b.hnich,tw}@4c.ucc.ie

**Abstract**

We study the computational complexity of reasoning with global constraints. We show that reasoning with such constraints is intractable in general. We then demonstrate how the same tools of computational complexity can be used in the design and analysis of specific global constraints. In particular, we illustrate how computational complexity can be used to determine when a lesser level of local consistency should be enforced, when decomposing constraints will lose pruning, and when combining constraints is tractable. We also show how the same tools can be used to study symmetry breaking, meta-constraints like the cardinality constraint, and learning nogoods.

## Introduction

Global constraints are one of the factors central to the success of constraint programming. See, for example, (Régin 1994; 1996; Bessiere & Régin 1997; Régin & Rueher 2000; Beldiceanu & Contegean 1994; Frisch *et al.* 2002). Global constraints specify patterns that occur in many problems, and exploit efficient and effective constraint propagation algorithms for pruning the search space. For instance, we often have sets of variables which must take different values (e.g. activities in a scheduling problem requiring the same resource must all be assigned different times). Most constraint solvers therefore provide a global all-different constraint which is propagated efficiently and effectively (Knuth & Raghunathan 1992; Régin 1994).

What are the limits of reasoning with global constraints? In this paper, we show how the basic tools of computational complexity can be used to uncover many of the basic limits. We will show that reasoning with global constraints is intractable in general. We therefore need to focus on specific constraints like the all-different constraint which are tractable. We then show how these same tools of computational complexity can be used to analyse specific global constraints proposed in the past like the number of values constraint (Pachet & Roy 1999), as well as to help design new global constraints.

*All supported by Science Foundation Ireland and an ILOG grant.


## Formal background

A *constraint satisfaction problem* (CSP) is a set of variables, each with a domain of values, and a set of constraints that specify allowed combinations of values for subsets of variables. We assume a constraint $C$ is given intensionally by a function of the form $f_C : D_1 \times \ldots \times D_n \mapsto \{True, False\}$ where $D_i$ are the domains of the variables in the scope of the constraint $C$. We cannot permit any sort of function. For example, suppose domains are integers of size $m$ and $f_C(X_1, X_2, X_3, \ldots)$ is the function that halts iff $X_1 + X_2 * m + X_3 * m^2 + \ldots$ is the Gödel number of a halting Turing machine. Testing if an assignment satisfies the constraint $C$ is then undecidable. We therefore insist that $f_C$ is computable in polynomial time.

A solution to a CSP is an assignment of values to the variables satisfying the constraints. To find such solutions, we often use tree search algorithms that construct partial assignments and enforce a local consistency like generalized arc consistency to prune the search space. A constraint $C$ is *generalized arc consistent* (GAC) iff, when a variable in the scope of $C$ is assigned any value, there exists an assignment of the other variables in $C$ such that $C$ is satisfied (Mohr & Masini 1988). This satisfying assignment is called *support* for the value. An algorithm like GAC-Schema (Bessiere & Régin 1997) removes values from the initial domains of variables till we have the *maximal* generalized arc consistent subdomains. That is, the set of subdomains that are GAC and any larger set of subdomains are not GAC.

We have derived very similar results to those presented in this paper for other local consistencies. For example, many of these results map over to bounds consistency on finite domain, set or multiset variables. For reasons of space, however, we are only able to present the results here for generalized arc consistency.

## Complexity of global constraints

Reasoning with global constraints is intractable in general. We consider two decision problems at the heart of reasoning with global constraints. The first is GACSupport, the problem of deciding if a value for a variable has support on a constraint. In general, this is NP-complete to decide.

**Theorem 1** GACSupport *is NP-complete.*

**Proof:** Clearly it is in NP as a support is a polynomial witness which can be checked (by definition) in polynomial time. To show completeness, we transform the satisfiability of the Boolean formula $\varphi$ into the problem of determining if a particular value has support. We simply construct the global constraint $C$ involving the variables of $\varphi$ plus an additional variable $X$, and defined by $f_C = (X \rightarrow \varphi)$. If $X = True$ has support then $\varphi$ is satisfiable. ♡

The second decision problem we consider is MAXGAC. Given a constraint and initial domains for its variables, this is the problem of deciding if a given set of subdomains is the maximal GAC set of subdomains. This is in the complexity class $D^P$. This contains problems which are the conjunction of a problem in NP and one in coNP (Papadimitriou & Yannakakis 1984). The class $D^P$ is also known as the second level of the Boolean hierarchy, $BH_2$. A typical example of a $D^P$-complete decision problem is the EXACT TRAVELING SALESPERSON PROBLEM. Given a distance matrix and an integer $B$, EXACT TSP decides if the shortest tour is *equal* to $B$. By comparison, TSP decides if there is a tour of length $B$ *or less*, which is NP-complete. We show that MAXGAC is $D^P$-complete.

**Theorem 2** MAXGAC *is* $D^P$*-complete.*

**Proof:** A problem $Q$ is in $D^P$ if there exist a NP problem $Q_1$ and a coNP one $Q_2$ such that $Q$ answers "yes" iff $Q_1$ and $Q_2$ answer "yes". If $Q_1$ is NP-complete and $Q_2$ is coNP-complete, then $Q$ is $D^P$-complete. We use 3COL and UN3COL as $Q_1$ and $Q_2$. We suppose without loss of generality that $Q_1$ and $Q_2$ both involve the same set $X$ of vertices. $E_i$ is the set of edges in $Q_i$.

We introduce a variable for each vertex with domain $\{R_1, G_1, B_1, R_2, G_2, B_2\}$. We then define a global constraint as follows. For each pair $(x_i, x_j)$ of vertices with an edge between in both $Q_1$ and $Q_2$, we permit pairs of values that are different but have the same subscript (i.e., the set $\{(R_1, G_1), (R_1, B_1), (G_1, R_1), (G_1, B_1), (B_1, R_1), (B_1, G_1), (R_2, G_2), (R_2, B_2), (G_2, R_2), (G_2, B_2), (B_2, R_2), (B_2, G_2)\}$). For each pair $(x_i, x_j)$ of vertices with an edge between in $Q_1$ and not in $Q_2$, we permit pairs of values that are different for the subscript 1, and any combination for subscript 2 (i.e., the set $\{(R_1, G_1), (R_1, B_1), (G_1, R_1), (G_1, B_1), (B_1, R_1), (B_1, G_1)\} \cup \{R_2, G_2, B_2\}^2$). Similarly, for each pair $(x_i, x_j)$ of vertices with an edge between in $Q_2$ and not in $Q_1$, we permit pairs of values that are different for the subscript 2, and any combination for subscript 1. Finally, for each pair $(x_i, x_j)$ of vertices with no edge between in $Q_1$ or in $Q_2$, we permit any pairs of values with the same subscript (i.e., the set $\{R_1, G_1, B_1\}^2 \cup \{R_2, G_2, B_2\}^2$). By construction, $R_i$, $G_i$ and $B_i$ are GAC iff $(X, E_i)$ is 3-colorable. Hence, $\{R_1, G_1, B_1\}$ is the maximal GAC subdomain for each variable iff $(X, E_1)$ is 3-colorable, and $(X, E_2)$ is not 3-colorable. ♡

**Corollary 1** *Enforcing GAC is NP-hard.*

**Proof:** Enforcing GAC directly answers both the GACSUPPORT and MAXGAC problems. ♡

Reasoning with global constraints is thus not tractable in general. Global constraints which are used in practice are therefore usually part of that special subset for which constraint propagation is polynomial. For example, GAC on an $n$-ary `AllDifferent` constraint can be enforced in $O(n^{\frac{3}{2}}d)$ time (Régin 1994). In the rest of this paper, we show how we can further use the tools of computational complexity in the design and analysis of *specific* global constraints.

## Local consistency

Computational complexity results can indicate what level of local consistency to enforce on a constraint. If achieving a given local consistency on a constraint is NP-hard, then enforcing a lower level of consistency is usually advisable. For example, the number of values constraint, `NValue`$(X_1, \ldots, X_n, N)$ (Pachet & Roy 1999; Beldiceanu 2001) ensures that $N$ values are used by the $n$ finite domain variables $X_i$. Note that $N$ can itself be an integer variable. The `AllDifferent` constraint is a special case of the `NValue` constraint in which $N = n$. The `NValue` constraint is useful for reasoning about resources. For example, if the values are workers assigned to a particular shift, we may have a `NValue` constraint on the number of shifts that someone can work. Enforcing GAC on the `NValue` constraint is intractable in general. We therefore look to enforce a lower level of consistency.

**Theorem 3** *Enforcing GAC on a* `NValue`$(X_1, \ldots, X_n, N)$ *constraint is NP-hard, and remains so even if $N$ is ground and different to $n$.*

**Proof:** (Sketch) Reduction from 3SAT. Given a Boolean formula in $k$ variables (labelled from 1 to $k$) and $m$ clauses, we construct the `NValue`$(X_1, \ldots, X_{k+m}, N)$ constraint in which $X_i = \{i, -i\}$ for all $i \in [1, k]$, and each $X_i$ for $i > k$ represents one of the $m$ clauses. If the $j$th clause is $x \vee \neg y \vee z$ then $X_{k+j} = \{x, -y, z\}$. If $N = k$, the constructed `NValue` constraint has a solution iff the original 3SAT problem has a satisfying assignment. Hence testing a value for support is NP-complete, and enforcing GAC is NP-hard. ♡

## Decomposing constraints

Computational complexity results can tell us more than just what level of local consistency to enforce. It can also indicate properties that any possible decomposition of a constraint must possess. We say that a decomposition of a global constraint is *GAC-poly-time* if we can enforce GAC on the decomposition in polynomial time. A decomposition is GAC-poly-time when, for example, the number of decomposed parts is polynomial, and each decomposed part either is a specific constraint that has a polynomial GAC algorithm (like `AllDifferent`) or has a bounded arity. The following result tells us when such decomposition hinders constraint propagation.

**Theorem 4** *If enforcing GAC on a constraint $C$ is NP-hard, then there does not exist any GAC-poly-time decomposition of $C$ that achieves GAC on $C$ (assuming P $\neq$ NP).*

**Proof:** By definition, enforcing GAC on a GAC-poly-time decomposition is polynomial. Hence, if GAC on the decomposition was equivalent to GAC on the original constraint, then P would equal NP. ♡

For example, (Sadler & Gervet 2001) introduce the `Atmost1` constraint. This ensures that $n$ set variables of a fixed cardinality intersect in at most one value. To fit this within the theoretical framework presented in this paper, we consider the characteristic function representation for each set variable (i.e. a vector of 0/1 decision variables). Enforcing GAC on such a representation is equivalent to enforcing bounds consistency on the upper and lower bounds of the set variables (Walsh 2003a). The `Atmost1` constraint can be decomposed into pairwise intersection and cardinality constraints. That is, it can be decomposed into $|X_i \cap X_j| \leq 1$ for $i < j$ and $|X_i| = c$ for all $i$. On the characteristic function representation, this is $\sum_k X_{ik} \cdot X_{jk} \leq 1$ and $\sum_k X_{ik} = c$, which are both GAC-poly-time. Such decomposition hinders constraint propagation.

**Theorem 5** *GAC on any GAC-poly-time decomposition of the* `Atmost1` *constraint is strictly weaker than GAC on the undecomposed constraint (assuming P ≠ NP).*

**Proof:** We show that enforcing GAC on an `Atmost1` constraint is NP-hard, and apply theorem 4.

To show that enforcing GAC on the `Atmost1` constraint is NP-hard, we consider the case when the cardinality $c = 2$. For $c > 2$, we can use a similar construction as in the $c = 2$ reduction but add $c - 2$ distinct values to each set. The proof uses a reduction from 3SAT. For each clause $\sigma$, we introduce a set variable, $X_\sigma$. Suppose $\sigma = x_i \vee \neg x_j \vee x_k$, then $X_\sigma$ has the domain $\{m_\sigma\} \subseteq X_\sigma \subseteq \{m_\sigma, i_\sigma, \neg j_\sigma, k_\sigma\}$. If the intersection and cardinality constraint is satisfied, $X_\sigma$ takes the value $\{m_\sigma, i_\sigma\}$, $\{m_\sigma, \neg j_\sigma\}$, or $\{m_\sigma, k_\sigma\}$. The first case corresponds to $x_i$ being $True$ (which satisfies $\sigma$), the second to $\neg x_j$ being $True$, and the third to $x_k$ being $True$.

We use additional (at most quadratic) set variables to ensure that contradictory assignments are not made to satisfy other clauses. Suppose we satisfy $\sigma$ by assigning $x_i$ to $True$. That is, $X_\sigma = \{m_\sigma, i_\sigma\}$. Consider any other clause, $\tau$ which contains $\neg x_i$. We construct two set variables, $Y_{\sigma\tau i}$ and $Z_{\sigma\tau i}$ with domains $\{m_\sigma\} \subseteq Y_{\sigma\tau i} \subseteq \{m_\sigma, i_\sigma, \neg i_\tau\}$ and $\{\neg i_\tau\} \subseteq Z_{\sigma\tau i} \subseteq \{m_\sigma, m_\tau, \neg i_\tau\}$. Since $X_\sigma = \{m_\sigma, i_\sigma\}$, then $Y_{\sigma\tau i} = \{m_\sigma, \neg i_\tau\}$ and $Z_{\sigma\tau i} = \{m_\tau, \neg i_\tau\}$. Hence, $X_\tau \neq \{m_\tau, \neg i_\tau\}$. That is, $\tau$ cannot be satisfied by $\neg x_i$ being assigned $true$. Some other literal in $\tau$ has to satisfy the clause.

The constructed set variables thus have a solution which satisfies the intersection and cardinality constraints iff the original 3SAT problem is satisfiable. Hence testing a value for support is NP-complete, and enforcing GAC is NP-hard. ♡

A similar result can be given for the `Distinct` constraint introduced in (Sadler & Gervet 2001). This constraint ensures that $n$ set variables of a fixed cardinality intersect in at least one value. Again, GAC-poly-time decomposition of such a constraint hinders constraint propagation (assuming P ≠ NP).

## Combining constraints

Global constraints specify patterns that reoccur in many problems. There are, however, only a limited number of common constraints which repeatedly occur in problems. One strategy for developing new global constraints is to identify conjunctions of constraints that often occur together, and developing constraint propagation algorithm for their combination. For example, (Régin & Rueher 2000) propose a propagation algorithm for a constraint which combines together sum and difference constraints. As a second example, (Carlsson & Beldiceanu 2002) combine together a chain of lexicographic ordering constraints. As a third example, (Hnich, Kiziltan, & Walsh 2004) combine together a lexicographic ordering and two sum constraints.

We can use results from computational complexity to determine when we should combine together constraints. For example, scalar product constraints occur in many matrix models like the balanced incomplete block design, template design and social golfers problems (Walsh 2003b). Often such problems have scalar product constraints between all pairs of rows in a 0/1 matrix. We can enforce GAC on a scalar product constraint between two rows in linear time. Should we consider combining together all the row scalar product constraints into one large global constraint? Such a matrix `ScalarProduct` constraint would ensure that $\forall i < j \sum_k X_{ik} \cdot X_{jk} = m$. The following result shows that enforcing GAC on such a composition of constraints is intractable.

**Theorem 6** *Enforcing GAC on a matrix* `ScalarProduct` *constraint is NP-hard, even when restricted to 0/1 variables.*

**Proof:** (Sketch) We consider the case when the scalar product $m = 1$. For $m > 1$, we use a reduction that adds $m - 1$ additional columns to the matrix, each column containing variables that must take the value 1.

We reduce 1IN3-3SAT on positive formulae (which is NP-complete (Garey & Johnson 1979)) to testing GAC on a matrix `ScalarProduct` constraint over 0/1 variables. The first row of the matrix represents the model which satisfies the 1IN3-3SAT problem. There is a column for each occurrence of a literal in a clause. This is assigned 1 iff the corresponding literal is *True*. There is also a column for the negation of each literal. This is assigned 1 iff the corresponding literal is *False*. There are also "dummy" columns to ensure each pair of rows has the required scalar product.

The remaining rows are divided into two types. First, there is a row for each clause. The columns corresponding to literals in the clause have 0/1 values. Columns corresponding to literals not in the clause only have the value 0. The scalar product constraint between a row representing a clause and the row representing the model ensures that only one of the literals in the clause is *True*. Second, there are rows for each occurrence of a positive literal to ensure that the row representing the model does not assign both a literal and its negation to *True*.

The 1IN3-3SAT problem has a model iff the constructed matrix has a solution. Hence testing a value for support is NP-complete, and enforcing GAC is NP-hard. ♡

Special cases of the matrix `ScalarProduct` constraint are tractable. For instance, if the scalar product is zero and variables are 0/1 then the constraint is equivalent to the pairwise `Disjoint` constraint on set variables, which is tractable (Walsh 2003a).

## Symmetry breaking

Like global constraints, symmetry is an important aspect of constraint programming. Computational complexity results can indicate how difficult it is to deal with particular symmetries. For example, symmetric rows and columns occur in many matrix models (Flener *et al.* 2002). Lexicographical ordering constraints can be posted between the rows to break all such row symmetry, and between all rows and columns to break some (but not all) such row and column symmetry (Frisch *et al.* 2002). Why don't we identify additional constraints to post that will break the remaining symmetry?

Some simple complexity analysis suggests that it will be intractable to do so. We define a symmetry breaking constraint, `MatrixSymmetry` which ensures that all permutations of the rows or columns give "smaller" matrices when the matrices of decision variables are ordered by conjoining their rows and comparing the resulting one-dimensional vectors lexicographically. This constraint eliminates all row and column symmetry from the matrix. Note that the `MatrixSymmetry` constraint implies that the rows and columns are lexicographically ordered (but not vice versa).

To demonstrate the intractability of computing symmetry breaking constraints in general, (Crawford *et al.* 1996) prove that the MAXIMUM INCIDENCE MATRIX problem is NP-complete. This result can be used immediately to show that the `MatrixSymmetry` constraint is intractable. For a graph $(V, E)$, an incidence matrix can be constructed by taking any ordering on $V$ and $E$ and constructing the matrix $A$ in which $A_{ij} = 1$ iff the $i$th vertex in $V$ is connected by the $j$th edge in $E$. Given a graph $(V, E)$ and an incidence matrix $A$ for $(V, E)$, the MAXIMUM INCIDENCE MATRIX problem is to determine if there is another incidence matrix $B$ for $(V, E)$ such that $B >_{\text{lex}} A$. It follows immediately that determining if an assignment satisfies the `MatrixSymmetry` constraint is coNP-complete. This is beyond our assumption that checking if an assignment satisfies a constraint is polynomial. Therefore, on such a "super" constraint, GACSUPPORT and MAXGAC would definitely be NP-hard. In addition, assuming P≠NP, there cannot exist any GAC-poly-time decomposition of the `MatrixSymmetry` constraint since on such a decomposition, satisfiability testing of an assignment would obviously be polynomial. As a result, whilst we may post symmetry breaking constraints in addition to the lexicographical ordering constraints, we cannot break all row and column symmetry in polynomial time.

## Meta-constraints

Computational complexity can also be used to study "meta-constraints" that combine together other constraints. For example, the `Cardinality` constraint (Van Hentenryck & Deville 1991) is provided by many constraint toolkits. It ensures that $N$ constraints from a given set are satisfied, where $N$ is an integer decision variable. The cardinality constraint can be used to implement conjunction, disjunction, negation, as well as a host of other useful constraints. Only a limited form of consistency is enforced on a `Cardinality` constraint. It is easy to show why this is necessary in general.

**Theorem 7** *Enforcing GAC on the* `Cardinality` *constraint is NP-hard, and remains so even if all the constraints are identical and binary and no variable is repeated more than three times.*

**Proof:** (Sketch) We use a reduction from the special case of 3SAT in which at most three clauses contain a variable or its negation. Each Boolean variable $x$ is represented by a CSP variable $X$ with domain $\{0, 1\}$. Each clause $\sigma$ is represented by three CSP variables, $U_\sigma$, $V_\sigma$ and $W_\sigma$, and five binary constraints posted on these variables. The domain of $U_\sigma$ is a strict subset of $\{8, \ldots, 15\}$, of $V_\sigma$ is a strict subset of $\{16, \ldots, 23\}$ and of $W_\sigma$ is a strict subset of $\{24, \ldots, 31\}$. The domain values serve two purposes. First, the bottom three bits indicate the truth values taken by the variables that satisfy the clause. We therefore have to delete one value from each domain. This is the assignment of truth values which does not satisfy the clause. For example, if $\sigma$ is $x \vee \neg y \vee z$ then the only assignment to $X$, $Y$ and $Z$, which does not satisfy the clause is 0, 1, 0. We therefore delete the value 26 from $W_\sigma$ as $26 \bmod 8$ is 2 (or 010 in binary). Similarly, we delete the value 18 from $V_\sigma$ as $18 \bmod 8$ is 2, and 10 from $U_\sigma$. Second, the top two bits of the values of $U_\sigma$, $V_\sigma$ and $W_\sigma$ point to one of the three positions in the clause. We add three binary constraints to the cardinality constraint: $C(U_\sigma, X)$, $C(V_\sigma, Y)$ and $C(W_\sigma, Z)$.

We also need to ensure that $U_\sigma$, $V_\sigma$ and $W_\sigma$ take consistent values. We therefore add two binary constraints: $C(U_\sigma, V_\sigma)$, and $C(V_\sigma, W_\sigma)$. Finally, we define $C(X, Y)$ as follows. If $Y \in \{0, 1\}$, there are three cases. If $8 \leq X \leq 15$ then $C$ is satisfied iff $(X \bmod 8) \operatorname{div} 4 = Y$ (i.e., the third bit of $X$ agrees with $Y$). If $16 \leq X \leq 23$ then $C$ is satisfied iff $(X \bmod 4) \operatorname{div} 2 = Y$ (i.e., the second bit of $X$ agrees with $Y$). If $24 \leq X \leq 31$ then $C$ is satisfied iff $X \bmod 2 = Y$ (i.e., the first bit of $X$ agrees with $Y$). Otherwise $Y \geq 8$ and $C$ is satisfied iff $X \bmod 8 = Y \bmod 8$.

The constructed cardinality constraint has a solution iff there is an assignment to the Boolean variables that satisfies all of the clauses. Hence enforcing GAC is NP-hard. ♡

A more restricted, but nevertheless very useful form of the cardinality constraint is the cardinality path constraint (Beldiceanu & Carlsson 2001). This "slides" a constraint of fixed arity down a sequence of variables and ensures that it holds $N$ times, where $N$ is itself an integer decision variable. This constraint can be used to implement the change, smooth, number of rests, and sliding sum constraints. In (Beldiceanu & Carlsson 2001), a greedy algorithm is given for partially propagating the cardinality path constraint. However, even for binary constraints, the algorithm fails to prune all possible values. Again, it is not hard to show that this constraint is intractable in general to propagate. It is an open question to prove that it remains intractable when no variable is repeated in the sequence.

## Learning nogoods

When we enforce GAC, we are essentially learning unary nogoods. A *nogood* is a partial assignment that cannot be extended to a complete solution. We can also apply the tools of computational complexity to study the learning of larger arity nogoods. We consider here two decision problems at the heart of learning. The first is NOGOOD testing, the problem of deciding if a partial assignment is nogood. In general, this is intractable to decide.

**Theorem 8** NOGOOD *testing is coNP-complete, even for nogoods of bounded size.*

**Proof:** We consider the complement problem of GOOD testing. This is determining if an assignment can be extended to a solution. A polynomial witness to this is a solution that extends this assignment. To show completeness, we reduce SAT to GOOD testing. We construct a CSP with two disjoint parts. The first part accepts the partial assignment whatever. The second part uses disjoint variable names and encodes the SAT problem using a reduction of SAT to CSPs. Note that, even if the nogoods are of bounded size, the second part of the construction is large enough to perform the reduction of SAT to CSPs. ♡

The second problem we consider is MINIMALNOGOOD testing, the problem of determining if a (partial) assignment is nogood, whilst all strict subsets of the assignment are not. This is again $D^P$-complete.

**Theorem 9** MINIMALNOGOOD *testing is $D^P$-complete, even for nogoods of bounded size.*

**Proof:** Recall that a problem $Q$ is in $D^P$ if there exist a NP problem $Q_1$ and a coNP one $Q_2$ such that $Q$ answers "yes" iff $Q_1$ and $Q_2$ answer "yes". If $Q_1$ is NP-complete and $Q_2$ coNP-complete, then $Q$ is $D^P$-complete. We use SAT and UNSAT as $Q_1$ and $Q_2$. Let $\varphi_i$ be the formulae in $Q_i$ being tested for (un)satisfiability. We suppose without loss of generality that $\varphi_1$ and $\varphi_2$ have disjoint sets of Boolean variables. Let $x$ and $y$ be two new Boolean variables. We construct the formula $(x \to \varphi_1) \wedge ((x \wedge y) \to \varphi_2)$. Then $x \wedge y$ is a minimal nogood iff $\varphi_1$ is SAT and $\varphi_2$ is UNSAT. ♡

Connections exist between the complexity of NOGOOD and MINIMALNOGOOD testing. For example, if NOGOOD testing is polynomial then MINIMALNOGOOD testing must also be polynomial. Connections also exist between the complexity of constraint propagation and that of testing nogoods. For example, if NOGOOD testing is polynomial then enforcing GAC is also. The reverse does not hold.

**Theorem 10** *There exist a class of global constraints on which GAC is polynomial but* NOGOOD *testing is coNP-complete and* MINIMALNOGOOD *testing is $D^P$-complete.*

**Proof:** We construct a class of global constraints which encode the 3COL problem but on which GAC is polynomial. Each of the $n$ nodes in the graph is represented by a variable. The domain of each variable contains the three colors and one don't care value. The global constraint is satisfied iff variables representing adjacent nodes in the graph take different colors, or $n-1$ of the variables have the don't care value. This encoding is always GAC (even if the graph is not 3-colorable) since no single value can be removed. However, testing whether an assignment of two different colors to two variables representing adjacent nodes is good is equivalent to determining if the graph can be 3-colored, which is NP-complete. Thus, NOGOOD testing is coNP-complete, and MINIMALNOGOOD testing is $D^P$-complete. ♡

Space prevents us from listing in detail some of the other applications we are exploring related to nogood learning. For example, we have identified a number of special cases where nogood learning is tractable. As a second example, we have studied the computational complexity of size and relevance bounded nogood learning. A related, yet different problem, the number of minimal nogoods, is addressed in (Dechter 1986).

## Related work

For constraints of bounded arity, asymptotic analysis has been extensively used to study the complexity of constraint propagation both in general and for specific constraints. For example, the GAC-Schema algorithm of (Bessiere & Régin 1997) has an $O(d^n)$ time complexity on constraints of arity $n$ and domains of size $d$, whilst the GAC algorithm of (Régin 1994) for the $n$-ary `AllDifferent` constraint has $O(n^{\frac{3}{2}}d)$ time complexity. By comparison, we have considered here what happens when we let the arity of global constraints grow. This happens in many real world problems. For instance, in the balanced incomplete block design problem (prob028 in CSPLib), the arity of the constraints grows with the problem size.

For global constraints like the `Cummulative` and `Cycle` constraints, there are very immediate reductions from the bin packing and Hamiltonian circuit which demonstrate that reasoning with these constraints is intractable in general. It is therefore perhaps not surprising that there has been little comment in the past about their intractability. However, as we show here, there are many other global constraints proposed in the past like `NValue` and `Atmost1` where a reduction is less immediate, but the constraint is intractable nevertheless.

In many constraint problems, the goal is not only to satisfy all the constraints, but also to minimize (or maximize) an objective function. Constraint propagation can be enhanced in these problems by cost-based filtering where we also remove values that are proven sub-optimal. *Optimisation constraints*, that combine a regular constraint of the problem with a constraint on the maximal value the objective function can take have been advocated in (Caseau & Laburthe 1997). GAC on such a combined constraint will not only prune the values having no support on the regular constraint, but also the values that do not extend to any satisfying assignment of the constraint improving the given bound. However, as in the case of combining constraints (see Section on combining constraints), such compositions have to be handled with care. The optimisation version of a constraint for which enforcing GAC is intractable obviously remains intractable (e.g., (Sellmann 2003a)). However, the optimisation version of a constraint for which GAC is polynomial either remains tractable (e.g., (Focacci, Lodi, & Milano 2002; Régin 2002)) or may become intractable. An example of the latter situation is the shorter path constraint, which is the optimization version of the path constraint (Sellmann 2003b).

Beldiceanu has proposed a general framework for describing many global constraints in terms of graph properties on structured networks of simple elementary constraints (Beldiceanu 2000). It is an interesting open question if we can identify properties or elementary constraints within this framework which guarantee that a global constraint is computationally (in)tractable. Finally, computational complexity can help us classify constraints wrt the notions of globality proposed in (Bessiere & Van Hentenryck 2003). Indeed, NP-hardness of enforcing GAC is a sufficient condition for a constraint to be *operationally GAC-global* wrt GAC-polytime decompositions.

## Conclusions

We have studied the computational complexity of reasoning with global constraints. We have shown that it is NP-complete in general to determine if a value has support, and $D^P$-complete to decide if a subdomain is the maximal generalized arc consistent subdomain. We have then demonstrated how the same tools of computational complexity can be used in the design and analysis of specific global constraints like the `NValue` and `Atmost1` constraints. In particular, we have illustrated how computational complexity can be used to determine when a lesser level of local consistency should be enforced, when decomposing constraints will reduce propagation and when constraints can be combined tractably. We have also shown how the same tools can be used to study symmetry breaking, meta-constraints like the `Cardinality` constraint, and learning nogoods. In the future, we plan an extensive study of the computational complexity of global constraints on set and multiset variables. Computational intractability is very common here as there are, in the worst case, an exponential number of sets or multisets between the upper and lower bounds on a variable.

## References


Beldiceanu, N., and Carlsson, M. 2001. Revisiting the cardinality operator and introducing cardinality-path constraint family. In *Proceedings ICLP'01*, 59–73.

Beldiceanu, N., and Contegean, E. 1994. Introducing global constraints in CHIP. *Mathematical Computer Modelling* 20(12):97–123.

Beldiceanu, N. 2000. Global constraints as graph properties on a structured network of elementary constraints of the same type. In *Proceedings CP'00*, 52–66.

Beldiceanu, N. 2001. Pruning for the minimum constraint family and for the number of distinct values constraint family. In *Proceedings CP'01*, 211–224.

Bessiere, C., and Régin, J. 1997. Arc consistency for general constraint networks: preliminary results. In *Proceedings IJCAI'97*, 398–404.

Bessiere, C., and Van Hentenryck, P. 2003. To be or not to be ... a global constraint. In *Proceedings CP'03*, 789–794. Short paper.

Carlsson, M., and Beldiceanu, N. 2002. Arc-consistency for a chain of lexicographic ordering constraints. Technical report T2002-18, Swedish Institute of Computer Science. ftp://ftp.sics.se/pub/SICS-reports/Reports/SICS-T–2002-18–SE.ps.Z.

Caseau, Y., and Laburthe, F. 1997. Solving various weighted matching problems with constraints. In *Proceedings CP'97*, 17–31.

Crawford, J.; Luks, G.; Ginsberg, M.; and Roy, A. 1996. Symmetry breaking predicates for search problems. In *Proceedings KR '96*, 148–159.

Dechter, R. 1986. Learning while searching in constraint-satisfaction-problems. In *Proceedings AAAI'86*, 178–183.

Flener, P.; Frisch, A.; Hnich, B.; Kiziltan, Z.; Miguel, I.; Pearson, J.; and Walsh, T. 2002. Breaking row and column symmetries in matrix models. In *Proceedings CP'02*, 462–476.

Focacci, F.; Lodi, A.; and Milano, M. 2002. Optimization-oriented global constraints. *Constraints* 7:351–365.

Frisch, A.; Hnich, B.; Kiziltan, Z.; Miguel, I.; and Walsh, T. 2002. Global constraints for lexicographic orderings. In *Proceedings CP'02*.

Garey, M., and Johnson, D. 1979. *Computers and Intractability: A Guide to NP-Completeness*. San Francisco CA: Freeman.

Hnich, B.; Kiziltan, Z.; and Walsh, T. 2004. Combining symmetry breaking with other constraints: lexicographic ordering with sums. In *Proceedings of the 8th International Symposium on the Artificial Intelligence and Mathematics*.

Knuth, D., and Raghunathan, A. 1992. The problem of compatible representatives. *SIAM Journal of Discrete Mathematics* 5(3):422–427.

Mohr, R., and Masini, G. 1988. Good old discrete relaxation. In *Proceedings ECAI'88*, 651–656.

Pachet, F., and Roy, P. 1999. Automatic generation of music programs. In *Proceedings CP'99*, 331–345.

Papadimitriou, C., and Yannakakis, M. 1984. The complexity of facets (and some facets of complexity). *J. Comput. System Sci.* 28:244–259.

Régin, J., and Rueher, M. 2000. A global constraint combining a sum constraint and difference constraint. In *Proceedings CP'00*, 384–395.

Régin, J. 1994. A filtering algorithm for constraints of difference in CSPs. In *Proceedings AAAI'94*, 362–367.

Régin, J. 1996. Generalized arc consistency for global cardinality constraint. In *Proceedings AAAI'96*, 209–215.

Régin, J. 2002. Cost-based arc consistency for global cardinality constraints. *Constraints* 7:387–405.

Sadler, A., and Gervet, C. 2001. Global reasoning on sets. In *Proceedings of Workshop on Modelling and Problem Formulation (FORMUL'01)*. held alongside CP-01.

Sellmann, M. 2003a. Approximated consistency for knapsack constraints. In *Proceedings CP'03*, 679–693.

Sellmann, M. 2003b. Cost-based filtering for shorter path constraints. In *Proceedings CP'03*, 694–708.

Van Hentenryck, P., and Deville, Y. 1991. The cardinality operator: a new logical connective for constraint logic programming. In *Proceedings ICLP'91*, 745–759.

Walsh, T. 2003a. Consistency and propagation with multiset constraints: a formal viewpoint. In *Proceedings CP'03*, 724–738.

Walsh, T. 2003b. Constraint patterns. In *Proceedings CP'03*.

# The Backdoor Key: A Path to Understanding Problem Hardness

**Yongshao Ruan, Henry Kautz**
Department of Computer Science
University of Washington
Seattle, WA 98195
ruan@cs.washington.edu
kautz@cs.washington.edu

**Eric Horvitz**
Microsoft Research
Redmond, WA 98052
horvitz@microsoft.com

**Abstract**

We introduce our work on the *backdoor key*, a concept that shows promise for characterizing problem hardness in backtracking search algorithms. The general notion of *backdoors* was recently introduced to explain the source of heavy-tailed behaviors in backtracking algorithms (Williams, Gomes, & Selman 2003a; 2003b). We describe empirical studies that show that the *key faction,i.e.*, the ratio of the key size to the corresponding backdoor size, is a good predictor of problem hardness of ensembles and individual instances within an ensemble for structure domains with large key fraction.

## Introduction

Propositional reasoning (SAT) is the best-known NP-complete problem in computer science. Even though a class of SAT problems may be intractable in the worst case, most of its instances may still be polynomial-time solvable in practice and their hardness may vary significantly. It has proven extremely difficult in practice to define realistic problem ensembles where instances do not vary widely in hardness (Kautz *et al.* 2001). Different instances have widely varying hardness even in the well-known random 3-SAT problem ensembles with fixed clause-to-variable ratios (Kirkpatrick & Selman 1994). In such cases, it is crucial to understand the hidden structures that can be used to identify problem hardness and as points of attack for search heuristics.

There has been considerable research interest in identifying such structures for many years. One example of such hidden structure is the *backdoor* set (Williams, Gomes, & Selman 2003a). Given a SAT formula, a set of variables forms a *backdoor* for a problem instance if there is a truth assignment to these variables such that the simplified formula can be solved in polynomial time via use of the propagation and simplification mechanism of the SAT solver under consideration.

The original motivation of the backdoor concept was to explain the heavy-tailed behavior of backtracking search algorithms (Williams, Gomes, & Selman 2003b). Williams *et al.* went on to describe a variety of simple randomized "guessing" algorithms for solving problems with small backdoor sets, and empirically showed than many interesting benchmark SAT problems have surprisingly small backdoors (on the order of a few dozen variables). These algorithms are best-case exponential in the size of the backdoor, and thus are practical for problems with backdoors up to about size 20. For problems with larger backdoors — which do indeed appear to be the vast majority of satisfiability problems of interest — the best complete algorithms remain ones based on Davis-Putnam-Loveland-Logemann style backtracking search. Therefore it is important to investigate the precise connection between the backdoor properties of an problem instance or ensemble and problem hardness as measured by solution time using backtracking search.



Intuitively, the difficulty of identifying a backdoor set and setting a correct assignment to the backdoor variables by a backtracking solver is positively correlated to problem hardness because once the backdoor set is assigned correctly, the remaining problem becomes trivial. However, as we shall describe below, problem hardness is not a simple function of backdoor size. In particular, the backdoor size does not capture the *dependencies* among backdoor variables. We introduce the concepts of *backdoor key* variables to capture such dependencies. A *backdoor key variable* is a backdoor variable whose value is logically determined by settings of other backdoor variables. We define the *key fraction* of a problem as the ratio of the key size to the corresponding backdoor size, and investigate its relation with instance hardness and ensemble hardness. *Instance hardness* is the hardness of an individual instance, which we take as the median search cost of a set of runs of a search algorithm applied to the given instance. *Ensemble hardness* is the median hardness of an ensemble of instances. Empirical results demonstrate that key fractions are good predictors for both ensemble hardness and instance hardness for structure domains with large key fractions.

## Previous Work on Hidden Structure

We first summarize prior work on identifying hidden structures that are linked to problem hardness. Next, we describe two structure benchmark domains used in our empirical studies.

### Hidden Structures for Problem Hardness

An important step in understanding problem hardness is to relate hardness with observations of phase transitions in problem distributions as the underlying parameters are varied. Many NP-complete problems like satisfiability and constraint satisfaction display phase transition behavior in solubility and the easy-hard-easy pattern of search cost associating with increasing constrainedness. Problems that are under-constrained tend to have many solutions and thus generally easy to solve due to the high probability of guessing a solution. On the other hand, problems that are over-constrained tend to have no solution. These problems are also generally easy to solve because there are many constraints and thus many possible solutions can be pruned efficiently. Hard problems are usually located at a critical-constrained point, where roughly half the instances are satisfiable and half the instances are unsatisfiable. One well-know example is the random 3-SAT problem with varying clause-to-variable ratio: instances with the ratio equals 4.25 are the most difficult ones on average (Mitchell, Selman, & Levesque 1992). Other examples include the average graph connectivity for graph coloring problem (Cheeseman, Kanefsky, & Taylor 1991); constraint tightness (Smith 1994; Prosser 1996) for constraint satisfaction problems. A generalized the notion of constrainedness for an ensemble of instances was introduced by Gent *et al.* (Gent *et al.* 1996).

However, information about the number of solutions does not tell the whole story. Mammem *et al.* (Mammen & Hogg 1997) showed that the easy-hard-easy pattern still appears for some search methods even the number of solution is held constant. In these cases, the pattern appears to be due to changes in the size of the minimal unsolvable subproblems, rather than changing number of solutions.

Another important line of research has been focused on the relationship between hardness and *backbone* variables. For satisfiable SAT instances, the backbone is the set of literals which are logically entailed by the clauses of the instance, that is, backbone variables take on the same values in all solutions.

Achlioptas *et al.* (Achlioptas *et al.* 2000) demonstrated that there is a phase transition phenomenon in the *backbone fraction*–the ratio of the size of backbone to the total number of variables–with changes in the number of unset variables or "holes" created in solutions to Quasigroup with Holes (QWH) instances. They also show that the phase transition coincides with the hardness peak in local search. However, the hardness peak of backtrack algorithms does not coincide with the phase transition of backbone fraction seen in local search. The relationships between the hardness peak and backbone fraction is even less clear for optimization and approximation problems where backbone size has been found to be negatively or positively correlated with hardness depending on the domain at hand (Slaney & Walsh 2001).

In other work, Singer *et al.* (Singer, Gent, & Smaill 2000) found that the number of solutions is only relevant for small-backbone random 3-SAT instances. They introduced a measure of the *backbone fragility* of an instance, which indicates how persistent the backbone is as clauses are removed. The backbone fragility of an instance is positively correlated with the problem hardness for local search.

## Benchmark Domains and Solvers

We shall first investigate hardness and backdoor keys within the benchmark domain of a version of the Quasigroup Completion Problem (QCP) (Gomes & Selman 1997). The basic QCP problem is to complete a partially-filled Latin square, where the "order" of the instance is the length of a side of the square. We used a version called *Quasigroup with Holes* (QWH), where problem instances are generated by erasing values from a solved Latin square (Achlioptas *et al.* 2000; Kautz *et al.* 2001). Note that QWH problems are satisfiable by definition as they are built from previously solved problems.

We also will study problem hardness for a second problem domain, the morphed Graph Coloring Problem introduced by Gent *et al.* (Gent *et al.* 1999). The Graph Coloring Problem (GCP) is a well-known combinatorial problem from graph theory. Given a graph $G = (V, E)$, where $V = \{v_1, v_2, ..., v_n\}$ is the set of vertices and $E$ the set of edges connecting the vertices, we seek to find a coloring $C : V \rightarrow N$, such that connected vertices always have different colors. The challenge is to decide whether a coloring of the given graph exists for a particular number of colors. A $p$-morph of two graphs $A = (V, E_1)$ and $B = (V, E_2)$ is a graph $C = (V, E)$ where $E$ contains all the edges common to $A$ and $B$, a fraction $p$ of the edges from $E_1 - E_2$ (the remaining edges of $A$), and a fraction $1-p$ of the edges from $E_2 - E_1$. The test sets considered here are obtained by morphing regular ring lattices, where the vertices are ordered cyclically and each vertex is connected to its k closest in this ordering, and random graphs from the well-known class $G_{nm}$. The morphing ratio $p$ controls the amount of structure in the problem instances. The test sets used in our studies are from (sat ).

Finally, we consider domains of logistics planning (Kautz & Selman 1996) and circuit synthesis problems (Kamath *et al.* 1993). All instances of these domains are satisfiable and encoded in propositional encodings. The solver we used was Satz-Rand (Gomes, Selman, & Kautz 1998), a randomized version of the Satz system (Li & Anbulagan 1997) with powerful variable selection heuristics, and zChaff (version Z2001.2.17) (Zhang *et al.* 2001).

## Backdoors

The *backdoor* (Williams, Gomes, & Selman 2003a; 2003b) of a problem aims to capture structural properties in a problem that underlie heavy-tailed behaviors in backtracking algorithms. A set of variables forms a backdoor for a problem instance if there is a truth assignment for these variables such that the simplified formula can be solved in polynomial time by the propagation and simplification mechanism of the SAT solver under consideration. That is, after setting the backdoor variables correctly, the simplified formula falls in a polynomially solvable class.

Given a Boolean formula $\mathcal{F}$, let $V$ be the set of variables in $\mathcal{F}$. Let $\mathcal{A}_B : B \subseteq V \rightarrow \{True, False\}$ be a partial truth assignment and $\mathcal{F}[\mathcal{A}_B]$ denote the simplified formula obtained from the formula $\mathcal{F}$ by setting the partial truth assignment $\mathcal{A}_B$.

A set of backdoor variables is defined with respect to a particular search algorithm; once the backdoor variables are assigned certain values, the problem becomes polynomial time solvable by the algorithm. Such algorithms are called *sub-solvers* (Williams, Gomes, & Selman 2003a). A sub-solver $\mathcal{S}$ always runs in polynomial time. Given a formula $\mathcal{F}$ as the input, $\mathcal{S}$ either rejects $\mathcal{F}$, or determines $\mathcal{F}$ correctly as

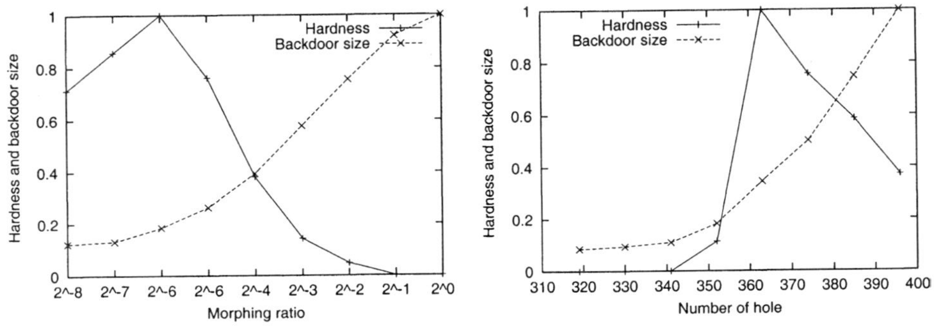


Figure 1: Normalized backdoor sizes and ensemble hardness. Left: Morphed GCP and its x-axis is the morphed ratio. Right: QWH of order 33 and its x-axis is the number of holes. For hardness, each data point represents the median value of the run-time of Satz-rand on 100 instances. For backdoor size, data points represent the mean value of 100 instances

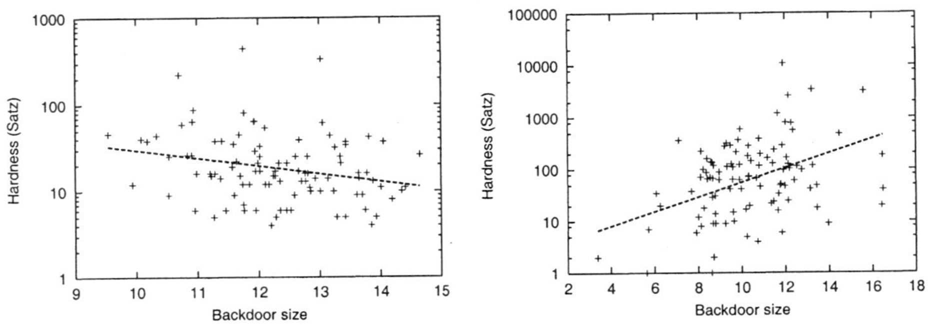


Figure 2: Backdoor sizes and instance hardness. The x-axis represents the backdoor size and the y-axis is the instance hardness. Left: Morphed GCP with morphed ratio = $2^{-6}$. Right: QWH of order 33 and 363 holes. For each data point $(x, y)$, $y$ represents the median search cost of 100 runs of Satz-rand and $x$ represents the mean size of 100 backdoor sets.

unsatisfiable or satisfiable, returning a solution if satisfiable.

Given a sub-solver $\mathcal{S}$, a formula $\mathcal{F}$ and its variables set $V$, we can definite formally the notion of backdoor.

**Definition 1 (Backdoor)** *A nonempty subset $B$ of the variable set $V$ is a backdoor for $\mathcal{F}$ w.r.t $\mathcal{S}$ if for some partial truth assignment $\mathcal{A}_B$, namely, a backdoor truth assignment, $\mathcal{S}$ returns a satisfying assignment of $\mathcal{F}[\mathcal{A}_B]$.*

Note that, by definition, backdoor sets exist only for satisfiable instances. A corresponding notion of *strong backdoors* can be defined for unsatisfiable instances (Williams, Gomes, & Selman 2003a). We will not discuss strong backdoors.

Note that any superset of a backdoor set is also a backdoor set. We are interested in backdoor sets with no unnecessarily variables, which we refer to as *minimal backdoor* sets.

**Definition 2 (Minimal Backdoor)** *A nonempty backdoor set $B$ for $\mathcal{F}$ w.r.t $\mathcal{S}$ is minimal if for any $v \in B$ such that $B - v$ is not a backdoor set for $\mathcal{F}$ w.r.t $\mathcal{S}$.*

For the rest of this paper, unless otherwise specified, we assume that a backdoor set is minimal.

## Backdoor Size and Hardness

We performed empirical studies to test the relation between backdoor sizes and hardness on the morphed GCP, QWH, circuit synthesis, and logistics planning domains. We modified the SAT solver Satz-rand to keep track of the set of variables selected for branching and their truth assignments in a solution. We also used Satz as a sub-solver by turning off its variable branching function, *i.e.*, allowing only unit propagation and simplification. By the definition of backdoor, the set of branching variables in a solution contains a backdoor set. Unnecessary variables were randomly removed one by one from the set of branching variables until the remaining set of variables is a minimal backdoor set. For each ensemble, we collected data of 100 instances; for each instance, we generated 100 backdoor sets.

Recall that a backdoor is a set of variables that, if set correctly, renders the remaining problem trivial to solve. Thus, the difficulty of identifying and assigning backdoor variables correctly is proportional to the difficulty of solving a problem. It is reasonable to assume that the backdoor of a problem reflects a core structural property that is closely linked to the problem hardness of the problem. However, we have found that the straightforward way of using backdoor size as a predictor does not correlate well with ensemble or instance hardness.

Figure 1 shows that there is no significant correlation between backdoor size and ensemble hardness for either morphed GCP or QWH domains. For morphed GCP, the backdoor size increases with increasing morphing ratio $p$, or the declining amount of structure in the problem instances. This is consistent with prior observations that structured domains tend to have smaller backdoor sizes, while random domains tend to have larger backdoor sizes (Williams, Gomes, & Selman 2003a).

We have also noted that ensemble hardness for morphed GCP does not increase monotonically with increasing backdoor size. Instead, the ensemble with the largest backdoor size is the easiest to solve and the peak of hardness is located at some intermediate point between the totally random and totally structured ensembles. The same observation applies to QWH problems: Backdoor size increases monotonically with the increasing number of holes while the peak of hardness is located at some intermediate point.

We additionally discovered that there is poor correlation between backdoor sizes and instance hardness within an ensemble. In Figure 2, the graph on the left captures results obtained with morphed GCP, showing a weak negative correlation while the right figure for QWH shows a weak positive correlation. Empirical studies using zChaff demonstrated similar results, *i.e.*, no significant correlation between backdoor sizes and ensemble or instance hardness, which are not shown here due to limitation of space.

We believe that the reason that the size of a backdoor set alone is not enough to predict hardness is that the backdoor size does not capture the *dependencies* among backdoor variables, *i.e.*, the "dependent" variables whose truth values are completely determined by other variables in the backdoor set. For an example, in the case of morphed GCP, although the backdoor sizes of the totally random ensemble are larger, there are few dependent variables. Therefore, the probability of setting some backdoor variable to the "wrong" value is smaller, even though more backdoor variables must be set. On the other hand, for instances at the hardness peak, the dependencies among backdoor variables are higher and there are more dependent variables. In these cases, it is likely that a backdoor variable will be set to a value that makes the remaining problem unsatisfiable.

This observation suggests that problem hardness is the result of the interaction between backdoor size and dependencies among backdoor variables, which we will address in the next section.

## Backdoor Keys

In the last section, we showed that problem hardness is not a simple function of backdoor size, and proposed the need for considering the dependencies among backdoor variables. To capture such dependencies, we introduce the notion of the backdoor key and examine its relationship with problem hardness.

### Defi nitions

Given a sub-solver $\mathcal{S}$, let $B$ be a backdoor of a formula $\mathcal{F}$ with respect to $\mathcal{S}$, and $\mathcal{A}_B$ be a backdoor truth assignment, *i.e.*, a value setting of $B$ such that $\mathcal{S}$ returns a satisfiable assignment of $\mathcal{F}$. We use $B - v$ as a simple denotation of $B - \{v\}$, for any $v \in V$. Before our exposition of backdoor keys, we need to define the notion of a dependent variable.

**Definition 3 (Dependent Variable)** *A variable $v \in V$ is a dependent variable of formula $\mathcal{F}$ with respect to a partial truth assignment $\mathcal{A}_B$ if $\mathcal{F}[\mathcal{A}_B]$ determines $v$,* i.e., *there is a unique value assignment $x$ of $v$ such that $\mathcal{F}[\mathcal{A}_B \cup \{v/x\}]$ is satisfiable.*

To capture the dependencies among backdoor variables, we introduce the definition of a *backdoor key*, which we define formally as follows:

**Definition 4 (Backdoor Key)** *A backdoor variable $v$ is in the backdoor key set of $B$ with respect to a backdoor truth assignment $\mathcal{A}_B$ if and only if $v$ is a dependent variable in $\mathcal{F}$ with respect to the partial truth assignment $\mathcal{A}_{B-v}$*

In distinction to variables with superficial dependencies, which can be easily detected by unit-propagation and simplification, a backdoor key set represent a deep dependency whose detection requires extra effort beyond unit-propagation and simplification. We believe that such deep dependencies provide a view onto the core structural properties that lay at the foundations of problem hardness.

We know that once the backdoor variables are set correctly, the remaining problem becomes trivial. Thus, the difficulty of solving a problem is proportional to the difficulty of identifying and assigning backdoor variables. We do not yet know how to estimate the difficulty of identifying backdoor variables; this is an open challenge. It is generally believed that modern variable selection heuristics have done reasonably well at identifying backdoor variables from the success of the state-of-the-art backtrack search algorithms.

We believe that the difficulty of *assigning* backdoor variables correctly is captured by the notion of a backdoor key, because the dependent variables are the ones which are likely to be assigned incorrectly. Thus, the size of a backdoor key is a prime candidate for predicting problem hardness. Another candidate is the relative size of a backdoor key set, which we refer to as the *backdoor key fraction*:

**Definition 5 (Backdoor Key Fraction)** *A backdoor key fraction is the ratio of the size of the backdoor key set to the size of the corresponding backdoor set.*

We will see that in many domains the key fraction is a precise predictor of problem hardness.

### Experiments

We performed a set of empirical studies to test our hypothesis. We used the method described in previous section to collect minimal backdoor sets and then calculated the key size for each backdoor set by testing whether a backdoor variable is in the key set with respect to the truth assignment of the backdoor set.

Fig. 3 shows the relation between ensemble hardness and key fractions as well as key sizes. The graph at the left displays results for the morphed GCP domain and the graph on the right shows results for the QWH domain. For both problem domains, the peaks of key fraction coincide with those of ensemble hardness, which illustrates a strong correlation between key fraction and ensemble hardness. On the other hand, there is little or no correlation between key size and problem hardness. For morphed GCP, the peak of backdoor key size shifts to the left of the hardness peak. For QWH, the size of backdoor key increases monotonically, which does not coincide with the easy-hard-easy pattern of problem hardness. Empirical studies using zChaff demonstrated similar results.

In predicting instance hardness within an ensemble, the key fraction also shows the strongest correlation. Fig. 4 shows the correlation between key fraction and instance hardness. For both domains, the overall shapes suggest linear correlations between the key fraction and the log of instance hardness. We performed linear regression on the data and summarized the results in table 1. As a comparison, we

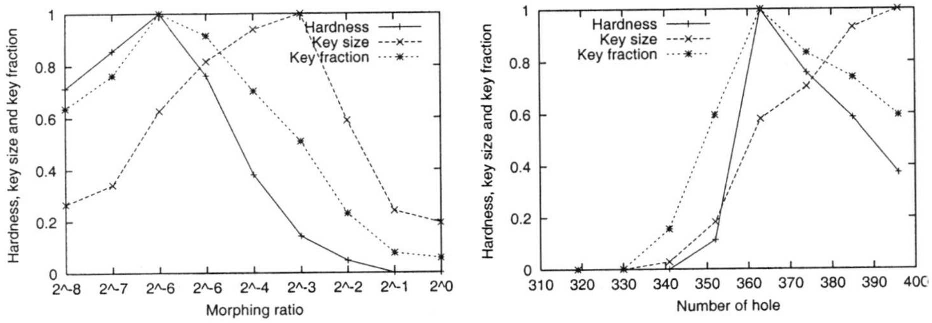


Figure 3: Normalized key sizes, key fractions and ensemble hardness. Left: Morphed GCP where the x-axis represents the morphed ratio. Right: QWH where the x-axis represents the number of unset variables or holes, removed from prior solutions. For hardness, each data point represents the median hardness of 100 instances solved by Satz-rand. For backdoor size, the data points represent the mean value of 100 instances.

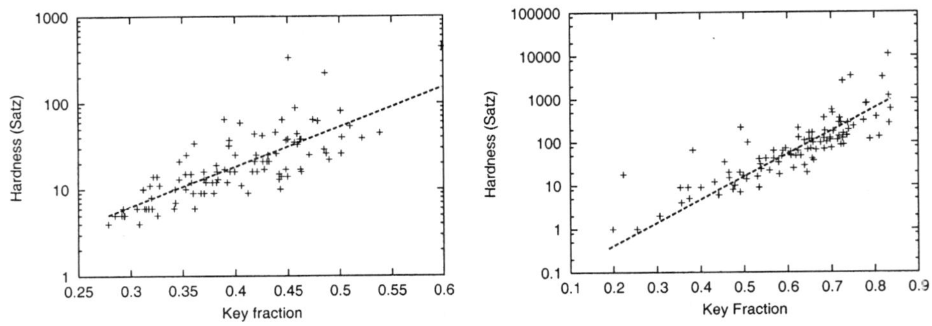


Figure 4: Key fractions and instance hardness. The x-axis is the key fraction (the ratio of key size and backdoor size) and the y-axis is the instance hardness. Left: Morphed GCP with morphed ratio = $2^{-6}$. Right: QWH of order 33 and 363 holes. For each data point $(x, y)$, $y$ represents the median search cost of 100 runs of Satz-rand and $x$ represents the mean key fraction of 100 backdoor sets.

also include results for backdoor size and key size. We report correlation coefficients as well as two error measures for linear regression, the root mean squared error (RMSE) and mean absolute error (MAE). The table shows that the *key fraction is the best predictor for problem hardness in all aspects*.

An intuitive explanation for the success of the key fraction in predicting hardness is that it represents the probability that a backdoor variable is dependent. We have argued that variable selection heuristics essentially attempt to identify backdoor variables, that only dependent backdoor variables can be set to incorrect values (values that rule out all solutions), and that large backtracking trees and long runs result when backdoor variables are initially set to incorrect values. Putting these arguments together makes the prediction that *as the key fraction increases the probability that the solver has a long run should increase as well.* Our experimental results show that this is exactly the case.

The concept of backdoor keys works well for domains with relatively large key fractions, such as QWH and morphed GCP. We did the same investigation for the logistics and circuit synthesis domains but found no significant correlations. It turns out that for the two latter domains, most instances from the two domains have key sets of size zero! In other words, given any backdoor and its corresponding solution, you can flip the truth assignment of any single variable in the backdoor and still extend the backdoor to a solution.

A similar issue was highlighted in work that looked at the phenomena of backbones in graph coloring problems (Culberson & Gent 2001). By the original definition of backbone—a variable that is fixed in all solutions—the problems had no backbones. Culberson and Gent therefore adopted a new definition of backbone in terms of *pairs* of variables that must take on different values in all solutions. We are currently pursuing a similar generalized notion of backdoor key to take into consideration special problems where the key fails to be predictive of hardness. For example, one can define dependent pairs of variables with respect to a partial truth assignment, and then analogously define the set of backdoor key pairs.

## Conclusion and Research Directions

We extended the notion of backdoor variables by introducing and investigating the concept of *backdoor keys*. Backdoor keys capture the link between dependencies among backdoor variables and problem complexity. To examine the relationship between the backdoor key of a problem and its hardness, we performed experiments on several structured domains. Our analysis suggests that the key fraction is a good predictor for both ensemble and instance hardness for domains with relatively large key fractions.

We are pursuing a deeper understanding of backdoors and backdoor keys, as well as their relationships to problem hardness. In parallel, we are seeking to apply the backdoor and backdoor key concepts to inform problem-solving methods. Moving beyond backdoor keys, we are seeking to

| Measures | Satz-rand | | | | | | zChaff | | | | | |
|---|---|---|---|---|---|---|---|---|---|---|---|---|
| | QWH | | | GCP | | | QWH | | | GCP | | |
| | F | K | B | F | K | B | F | K | B | F | K | B |
| Correlation Coefficient | 0.86 | 0.79 | 0.42 | 0.78 | 0.56 | -0.26 | 0.70 | 0.70 | 0.42 | 0.54 | 0.53 | 0.01 |
| RMSE | 0.41 | 0.47 | 0.71 | 0.24 | 0.37 | 0.38 | 0.39 | 0.68 | 0.87 | 0.37 | 0.37 | 0.38 |
| MAE | 0.29 | 0.37 | 0.57 | 0.29 | 0.28 | 0.28 | 0.29 | 0.53 | 0.69 | 0.31 | 0.31 | 0.32 |

Table 1: Results of linear regression analysis for instance hardness, where F represents key fraction, K represents key size and B represents backdoor size

understand more about the hidden structure of problems. We are particularly interested in understanding structure among variables in the backdoor set for domains with small key fractions. The presence and nature of such hidden structures may be related to the difficulty of identifying backdoor variables. Finally, we interested in investigating the effect of clause learning on backdoor and key sizes. Clause learning (Marques-Silva & Sakallah 1996; Bayardo & Schrag 1997; Zhang 1997; Moskewicz *et al.* 2001; Zhang *et al.* 2001) can be seen as a mechanism that helps to identify variable dependencies. Our hypothesis is that the effectiveness of clause learning may be related to the variation in backdoor or key sizes during the learning process.

## References


Achlioptas, D.; Gomes, C. P.; Kautz, H. A.; and Selman, B. 2000. Generating satisfi able problem instances. In *AAAI/IAAI*, 256–261.

Bayardo, R., and Schrag, R. 1997. Using csp look-back techniques to solve real-world sat instances. In *Proceedings of the Fourteenth National Conference on Artificial Intelligence (AAAI-97)*, 203–208. New Providence, RI: AAAI Press.

Cheeseman, P.; Kanefsky, B.; and Taylor, W. M. 1991. Where the Really Hard Problems Are. In *Proceedings of the Twelfth International Joint Conference on Artificial Intelligence, IJCAI-91, Sidney, Australia*, 331–337.

Culberson, J., and Gent, I. 2001. Frozen development in graph coloring. *Theoretical Computer Science* 265(1–2):227–264.

Gent, I. P.; MacIntyre, E.; Prosser, P.; and Walsh, T. 1996. The constrainedness of search. In *AAAI/IAAI, Vol. 1*, 246–252.

Gent, I. P.; Hoos, H. H.; Prosser, P.; and Walsh, T. 1999. Morphing: Combining structure and randomness. In *Proceedings of the Sixteenth National Conference on Artificial Intelligence (AAAI'99)*, 654–660.

Gomes, C. P., and Selman, B. 1997. Problem Structure in the Presence of Perturbations. In *Proceedings of the Fourteenth National Conference on Artificial Intelligence (AAAI-97)*, 221–227. New Providence, RI: AAAI Press.

Gomes, C. P.; Selman, B.; and Kautz, H. 1998. Boosting Combinatorial Search Through Randomization. In *Proceedings of the Fifteenth National Conference on Artificial Intelligence (AAAI-98)*, 431–438. New Providence, RI: AAAI Press.

Kamath, A. P.; Karmarkar, N. K.; Ramakrishnan, K. G.; and Resende, M. G. C. 1993. An interior point approach to Boolean vector function synthesis. *Proceedings of the 36th MSCAS* 185–189.

Kautz, H., and Selman, B. 1996. Pushing the envelope: planning, propositional logic, and stochastic search. In *Proceedings of the Thirteenth National Conference on Artificial Intelligence (AAAI-96)*, 1188–1194. Portland, OR: AAAI Press.

Kautz, H.; Ruan, Y.; Achlioptas, D.; Gomes, C. P.; Selman, B.; and Stickel, M. 2001. Balance and fi ltering in structured satisfi - able problems. In *Proceedings of the Sixteenth International Joint Conference on Artificial Intelligence (IJCAI-01)*, 351–358.

Kirkpatrick, S., and Selman, B. 1994. Critical behavior in the satisfi ability of random Boolean expressions. *Science* 264:1297–1301.

Li, C. M., and Anbulagan. 1997. Heuristics based on unit propagation for satisfi ability problems. In *Proceedings of the International Joint Conference on Artificial Intelligence*, 366–371. AAAI Pess.

Mammen, D. L., and Hogg, T. 1997. A new look at the easy-hard-easy pattern of combinatorial search diffi culty. *Journal of Artificial Intelligence Research* 7:47–66.

Marques-Silva, J., and Sakallah, K. 1996. Grasp – a new search algorithm for satisfi ability. In *Proceedings of the International Conference on Computer Aided Design*, 220–227.

Mitchell, D. G.; Selman, B.; and Levesque, H. J. 1992. Hard and easy distributions for SAT problems. In Rosenbloom, P., and Szolovits, P., eds., *Proceedings of the Tenth National Conference on Artificial Intelligence*, 459–465. Menlo Park, California: AAAI Press.

Moskewicz, M. W.; Madigan, C. F.; Zhao, Y.; Zhang, L.; and Malik, S. 2001. Chaff: Engineering an Effi cient SAT Solver. In *Proceedings of the 38th Design Automation Conference (DAC'01)*.

Prosser, P. 1996. An empirical study of phase transitions in binary constraint satisfaction problems. *Artificial Intelligence* 81:81–109.

www.satlib.org.

Singer, J.; Gent, I.; and Smaill, A. 2000. Backbone Fragility and the Local Search Cost Peak. *Journal of Artificial Intelligence Research* 12:235–270.

Slaney, J. K., and Walsh, T. 2001. Backbones in optimization and approximation. In *IJCAI*, 254–259.

Smith, B. 1994. Phase transition and the mushy region in constraint satisfaction problems. In *In Proceedings of the eleventh European Conference on Artificial Intelligence*, 100–104.

Williams, R.; Gomes, C.; and Selman, B. 2003a. Backdoors to typical case complexity. In *IJCAI03*.

Williams, R.; Gomes, C.; and Selman, B. 2003b. On the connections between backdoors, restarts, and heavy-tailedness in combinatorial search. In *SAT03*.

Zhang, L.; Madigan, C. F.; Moskewicz, M. W.; and Malik, S. 2001. Effi cient conflict driven learning in boolean satisfi ability solver. In *ICCAD*, 279–285.

Zhang, H. 1997. SATO: an effi cient propositional prover. In *Proceedings of the International Conference on Automated Deduction (CADE'97), volume 1249 of LNAI*, 272–275.

# Complexity of Contextual Reasoning

**Floris Roelofsen**[1,2]
[1]University of Twente, P.O. box 217
7500 AE Enschede, Netherlands
Phone: +31 53 4893680
Fax: +31 53 4893503
roelofsen@itc.it

**Luciano Serafini**[2]
[2]ITC-IRST, Via Sommarive 18
38050 Povo, Trento, Italy
Phone: +39 0461 314 319
Fax: +39 0461 314 591
serafini@itc.it

### Abstract

This paper delineates the computational complexity of propositional multi-context systems. We establish NP-membership by translating multi-context systems into bounded modal $K_n$, and obtain more refined complexity results by achieving the so-called bounded model property: the number of local models needed to satisfy a set of formulas $\Phi$ in a multi-context system MS is bounded by the number of contexts addressed by $\Phi$ plus the number of bridge rules in MS.

Exploiting this property of multi-context systems, we are able to encode contextual satisfiability into purely propositional satisfiability, providing for the implementation of contextual reasoners based on already existing specialized SAT solvers.

Finally, we apply our results to improve complexity bounds for McCarthy's propositional logic of context – we show that satisfiability in this framework can be settled in non-deterministic polynomial time $O(|\varphi|^2)$.

Keywords:
Contextual reasoning, computational complexity.

## Introduction

The establishment of a solid paradigm for contextual knowledge representation and contextual reasoning is of paramount importance for the development of sophisticated theory and applications in Artificial Intelligence.

McCarthy (1987) pleaded for a formalization of context as a possible solution to the problem of *generality*, whereas Giunchiglia (1993) emphasized the principle of *locality*: reasoning based on large (common sense) knowledge bases can only be effectively pursued if confined to a manageable subset (context) of that knowledge base.

Contextual knowledge representation has been formalized in several ways. Most notable are the propositional logic of context (PLC) developed by McCarthy, Buvač and Mason (1993; 1998), and the multi-context systems (MCS) devised by Giunchiglia and Serafini (1994), which later became associated with the local model semantics (LMS) introduced by Giunchiglia and Ghidini (2001). MCS has been proven strictly more general than PLC (Bouquet & Serafini 2004).



Contexts were first implemented as microtheories into the CYC common sense knowledge base (Lenat & Guha 1990). However, while in CYC the notion of local microtheories was a choice, in contemporary settings like the semantic web the notion of local, distributed knowledge is a must. Modern architectures impose highly scattered, heterogeneous knowledge fragments, which a central reasoner cannot deal with. This engenders a high demand for distributed, contextual reasoning procedures.

More recently, the idea of grid computing (Foster 1998) has received ample attention and fostered the development of various distributed reasoning systems (G. Behrmann & Vaandrager 2000; Chrabakh & Wolski 2003) which show, from the practical point of view, that implementing logical reasoners as cooperative systems of autonomous local reasoners can indeed improve performance.

The *complexity* of contextual reasoning, however, has so far received little attention. Massacci (1996) accomplishes a non-deterministic tableaux-based decision procedure, which establishes NP-membership for PLC, but leaves MCS/LMS out of consideration. Serafini and Roelofsen (2004) provide a deterministic SAT-based decision procedure that applies to both MCS/LMS and PLC, but they do not consider the effect that introducing non-determinism may have on the inherent complexity of the problem they are facing.

The goal of this paper is exactly this: to characterize the inherent computational complexity of contextual reasoning. The lion's share of our analysis regards reasoning based on MCS/LMS. Towards the end of the paper, however, our results are shown to be applicable to PLC as well.

We proceed as follows. After defining MCS/LMS and explicating the contextual satisfiability problem we establish an equivalence result with bounded modal $K_n$, which directly entails NP-membership. In pursuit of more specific upper bounds, we subsequently embark upon a more direct analysis of contextual satisfiability, which leads to the so-called bounded model property for multi-context systems. Next, we encode the contextual satisfiability problem into a purely propositional one. This encoding paves the way for the implementation of contextual reasoning systems based on already existing SAT solvers. At last, we show how our results can be applied to obtain improved complexity results for PLC. We conclude with a concise recapitulation of our achievements, and some pointers to future research avenues.

## Multi-Context Systems

A simple illustration of the intuitions underlying MCS/LMS is provided by the so-called "magic box" example (Ghidini & Giunchiglia 2001), depicted below.

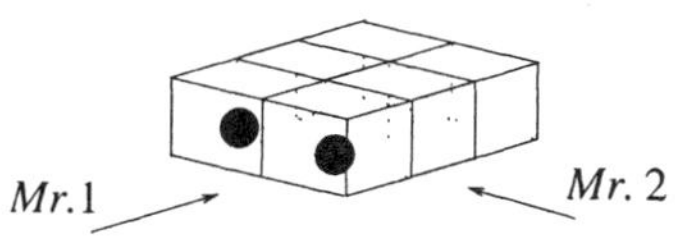


Figure 1: The magic box

**Example 1** *Mr.1 and Mr.2 look at a box, which is called "magic" because the observers cannot make out its depth. Both Mr.1 and Mr.2 maintain a local representation of what they see. These representations must be coherent – if Mr.1's sees a ball, for instance, then Mr.2's must see some ball too.*

We will now show how such interrelated local representations can be captured formally. Our point of departure is a set of indices $I$. Each index $i \in I$ denotes a *context*, which is described by a formal (in this case propositional) language $L_i$. To state that a propositional formula $\varphi$ in the language $L_i$ holds in context $i$ we utilize so-called *labeled formulas* of the form $i : \varphi$ (when no ambiguity arises we will simply refer to *labeled formulas* as *formulas*). Formulas that apply to different contexts may be related by so-called *bridge rules*. These are expressions of the form:

$$i_1 : \phi_1, \ldots, i_n : \phi_n \rightarrow i : \varphi \tag{1}$$

where $i_1, \ldots, i_n, i \in I$ and $\phi_1, \ldots, \phi_n, \varphi$ are formulas. Note that "$\rightarrow$" does not denote implication (we'll use "$\supset$" for this purpose). Also note that our language does not include expressions like $\neg(i : \varphi)$ and $(i : \varphi \wedge j : \psi)$. $i : \varphi$ is called the *consequence* and $i_1 : \phi_1, i_n : \phi_n$ are called *premises* of bridge rule (1). We write $cons(br)$ and $prem(br)$ for the consequence and the set of all premises of a bridge rule $br$, respectively.

**Definition 1 (Propositional Multi-Context System)** *A propositional multi-context system $\langle \{L_i\}_{i \in I}, \mathbb{BR} \rangle$ over a set of indices $I$ consists of a set of propositional languages $\{L_i\}_{i \in I}$ and a set of bridge rules $\mathbb{BR}$.*

In this paper, we assume $I$ to be (at most) countable and $\mathbb{BR}$ to be finite. Note that the latter assumption does not apply to MCSs with *schematic* bridge rules, such as provability - and multi-agent belief systems (Giunchiglia & Serafini 1994). The question whether our results may be generalized to capture these cases as well is subject to further investigation.

**Example 2** *The situation described in example 1 may be formalized by an MCS with two contexts 1 and 2, described by $L_1 = L(\{l, r\})$ and $L_2 = L(\{l, c, r\})$, respectively. The constraint that Mr.2 must see a ball if Mr.1 sees one, can be captured by the following bridge rule:*

$$1 : l \vee r \quad \rightarrow \quad 2 : l \vee c \vee r$$

Let $M_i$ denote the class of classical interpretations of $L_i$. An interpretation $m \in M_i$ is called a *local model* of $L_i$. Interpretations of entire MCSs are called *chains*. They are constructed from sets of local models.

**Definition 2 (Chain)** *A chain $c$ over a set of indices $I$ is a sequence $\{c_i\}_{i \in I}$, where each $c_i \subseteq M_i$ is a set of local models of $L_i$. A chain $c$ is $i$-consistent if $c_i$ is nonempty. It is point-wise if $|c_i| \leq 1$ for all $i \in I$, and set-wise otherwise.*

A chain can be thought of as a set of "epistemic states", each corresponding to a certain context (or agent). The fact that $c_i$ contains more than one local model means that $L_i$ can be interpreted in more than one unique way. So, set-wise chains correspond to partial knowledge, whereas point-wise chains indicate complete knowledge.

**Example 3** *Consider the situation depicted in Figure 1. Both agents have complete knowledge, corresponding to a point-wise chain $\{\{\{l, r\}\}, \{\{l, \neg c, \neg r\}\}\}$. We can imagine a scenario however, in which Mr.1 and Mr.2's views are restricted to the right half and the left-most section of the box, as depicted in Figure 2.*

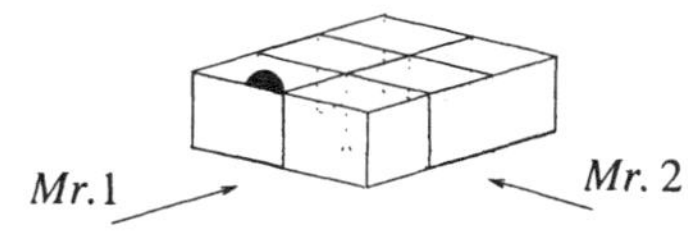


Figure 2: The partially hidden magic box

*Now, both Mr.1 and Mr.2 have only partial knowledge; their observations may be interpreted in several different ways. This is reflected by the set-wise chain:*

$$\left\{ \begin{array}{c} \{\{l, \neg r\}, \{\neg l, \neg r\}\}, \\ \{\{l, \neg c, \neg r\}, \{l, \neg c, r\}, \{l, c, \neg r\}, \{l, c, r\}\} \end{array} \right\}$$

The epistemic states that a chain consists of concern *one and the same* situation. Therefore, arbitrary sets of local models may not always constitute a "sensible" chain. The somewhat vague conception of "sensibility" is captured by the more formal notion of "bridge rule compliance" specified below.

**Definition 3 (Compliance and Satisfiability)** *Let $c$ be a chain, $\varphi$ a formula over $L_i$, and $br$ an element of the set of bridge rules $\mathbb{BR}$ of a multi-context system $MS$.*

1. *$c \models i : \varphi$ if $m \models \varphi$ in a classical sense for all local models $m \in c_i$. We say that $c$ satisfies $i : \varphi$.*
2. *$c$ complies with $br$ if either $c \models cons(br)$ or $c \not\models i : \xi$ for some $i : \xi \in prem(br)$. $c$ complies with $\mathbb{BR}$ if it complies with every $br \in \mathbb{BR}$.*
3. *If there exists an $i$-consistent chain $c$ that satisfies $i : \varphi$ and complies with $\mathbb{BR}$, we say that $i : \varphi$ is consistently satisfiable in $MS$.*

The contextual satisfiability problem, then, is to determine whether or not a set of labeled formulas $\Phi$ is consistently satisfiable in a multi-context system $MS$.

**Example 4** *Consider an MCS with two contexts 1 and 2, described by $L(\{p\})$ and $L(\{q\})$, respectively, and subject to the following bridge rules:*

$$\begin{array}{rcl} 1 : p & \rightarrow & 2 : q \\ 1 : \neg p & \rightarrow & 2 : q \end{array}$$

*The formula $2 : \neg q$ is satisfied in this system by the chain:*

$$\left\{ \begin{array}{c} \{\{p\}, \{\neg p\}\}, \\ \{\{\neg q\}\} \end{array} \right\}$$

This example reflects that an MCS cannot be encoded into propositional logic by simply indexing propositions – such an encoding of the above system would be inconsistent.

Hereafter we refer to the set of bridge rules of MS as $\mathbb{BR}$, and to the set of contexts involved by formulas in $\Phi$ as $J$.

## Encoding Into Bounded Modal $K_n$

A first insight regarding the complexity of contextual SAT may be obtained by investigating its encoding into modal $K_n$ satisfiability. In this section we show that any contextual satisfiability problem may be reduced to that of satisfying some formula in $K_n$, whose depth is at most equal to one. This problem is known to be NP-complete (Ladner 1977; Halpern & Moses 1992).

Let us define a translation $(.)^*$ of labeled formulas into modal formulas:

$$(i : \phi)^* = \Box_i \phi$$

For bridge rules we have:

$$(i_1 : \phi_1, \ldots, i_n : \phi_n \to i : \phi)^* = (i_1 : \phi_1)^* \wedge \ldots \wedge (i_n : \phi_n)^* \supset (i : \phi)^*$$

And a $j$-consistency constraint is captured by:

$$(j\text{-cons})^* = \neg \Box_j \bot$$

**Theorem 1** *There is a kripke model $K = \langle W, \pi, \mathbf{R} \rangle$ such that $K, w_0 \models \psi$ for some $w_0 \in W$ and:*

$$\psi = \bigwedge_{i:\phi \in \Phi} (i : \phi)^* \wedge \bigwedge_{j \in J} (j\text{-}cons)^* \wedge \bigwedge_{br \in \mathbb{BR}} (br)^*$$

*if and only if there is a $J$-consistent chain $c^K$ that satisfies $\Phi$ and complies with $\mathbb{BR}$.*

***Proof.*** ($\Rightarrow$) We demonstrate how to construct $c^K$ from $K$. Let $m_w$ be the interpretation of $\bigcup_{i \in I} L_i$ associated to a world $w \in W$; for any $i \in I$, let $m_w|_i$ be the restriction of $m_w$ to $L_i$ and let $c_i^K = \{m_w|_i \, | w_0 R_i w\}$.

As $K, w_0 \models \Box_i \phi$, we have that $w \models \phi$ for any $w$ with $w_0 R w$. Moreover, as $\phi \in L_i$, we have that $m_w|_i \models \phi$. This implies that $c^K \models i : \phi$. Bridge rule compliance and $J$-consistency are established likewise.

($\Leftarrow$) From $c^K$ we may obtain a suitable kripke model $K$. Let $W$ consist of a world $w_0$ plus one world $w_{m_i}$ for each local model $m_i$ of every component $c_i^K$ of $c^K$. Let every $w_{m_i} \in W/\{w_0\}$ evaluate $L_i$ according to $m_i$, and assign $True$ to the rest of $\bigcup_{i \in I} L_i$. Let $w_0$ evaluate every atomic proposition to $True$. For all $i \in I$, let:

$$R_i = \{\langle w_0, w_{m_i} \rangle \mid w_{m_i} \text{ corresponds to } m_i \in c_i^K\}$$

The resulting model is schematically depicted in Figure 3. One can easily verify that $K, w_0 \models \psi$. □

Contextual satisfiability clearly subsumes classical SAT, and is therefore NP-hard (Cook 1971). The above result, and the fact that satisfiability for bounded modal $K_n$ is in NP (Ladner 1977), imply that contextual satisfiability is also in NP, and therefore NP-complete.

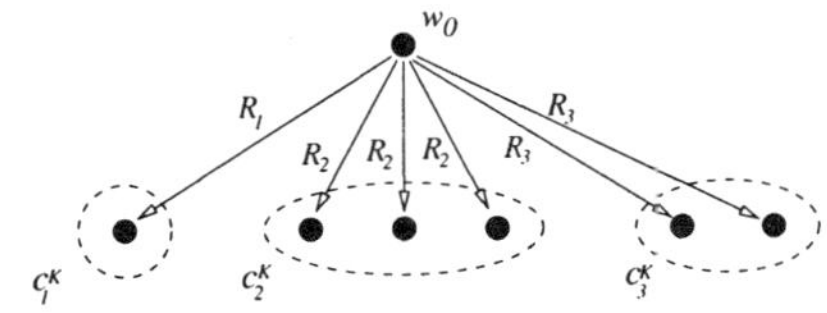


Figure 3: A schematic kripke model for $\psi$.

Moreover, the syntax of the formula that results from our translation is highly constrained: we obtain a conjunction of disjunctions of (negated) boxed formulas. Each disjunction comprises at most one boxed formula that is not negated, and furthermore, each boxed formula is purely propositional. This form strongly alludes to the existence of relatively efficient ways to solve the contextual satisfiability problem. Therefore, to obtain a more nuanced understanding of its complexity, we proceed with a more direct analysis.

## Firsthand Analysis

We first introduce some notation and terminology. The size of a labeled formula $i : \varphi$ is denoted by $|i : \varphi|$. Let $P(i : \varphi)$ and $P(\Phi)$ be the set of propositional atoms appearing in a formula $i : \varphi$ or a set of formulas $\Phi$. Let $G_i$ be the number of local models contained by the $i^{th}$ component of a chain, and let $G$ be the total number of local models comprising that chain. Let $\Xi(br)$ and $\Xi(\mathbb{BR})$ consist of the premises and the consequence(s) of a bridge rule $br$ or a set of bridge rules $\mathbb{BR}$. Finally, let $N$ be the total size of the formulas in $\Phi$ and $\Xi(\mathbb{BR})$:

$$N = \sum_{i:\varphi \in \Phi} |i : \varphi| + \sum_{i:\xi \in \Xi(\mathbb{BR})} |i : \xi|$$

We first consider the *model checking problem*, that is, the problem of determining whether a given chain $c$ consistently satisfies a set of formulas $\Phi$ in a multi-context system MS. This task can be split into three sub-tasks:

1. Check whether $c$ satisfies $\Phi$;
2. Check whether $c$ complies with $\mathbb{BR}$;
3. Check whether $c$ is $J$-consistent.

**Theorem 2** *Model checking can be performed deterministically in time:*

$$O(\sum_{i:\varphi \in \Phi \cup \Xi(\mathbb{BR})} G_i \times |\varphi|)$$

***Proof.*** First consider sub-task 1. Checking whether a particular formula $i : \varphi \in \Phi$ is satisfied by $c$ can be done as follows. Let $\varphi_1, \ldots, \varphi_k$ be an ordering of the subformulas of $\varphi$, such that $\varphi_k = \varphi$ and if $\varphi_i$ is a subformula of $\varphi_j$, then $i < j$. Since $\varphi$ has at most $|\varphi|$ subformulas, we have $k < |\varphi|$. By induction on $k'$ we can label each local model $m$ in $c_i$ with either $\varphi_j$ or $\neg\varphi_j$, for $j = 1, \ldots, k'$, depending on whether or not $m \models \varphi_j$, in time $O(G_i \times k')$. As a result, checking whether $c$ satisfies $\Phi$ can be carried out in time $O(\sum_{i:\varphi \in \Phi} G_i \times |\varphi|)$.

Sub-task 2 takes time $O(\sum_{i:\xi\in\Xi(\mathbb{BR})} G_i \times |\xi|)$, as in the worst case it involves checking whether all the consequences and premises of every bridge rule in $\mathbb{BR}$ are satisfied or not. Sub-task 3 merely consists in checking whether $c_j$ is nonempty, for $j \in J$. This can be done in $O(|J|)$ timesteps. The result follows directly. □

Next, we consider satisfiability. We first show that MCSs enjoy the so-called *bounded model property*. More specifically, we establish that if a chain consistently satisfies $\Phi$ in MS, then it can be reduced to a chain that contains at most $|J| + |\mathbb{BR}|$ local models and still consistently satisfies $\Phi$. Using this result, we reprove contextual satisfiability to be NP-complete, and establish an upper bound for the amount of time it requires.

**Theorem 3 (Bounded Model Property)** *A set of formulas $\Phi$ is consistently satisfiable in a multi-context system MS iff there is a $J$-consistent chain that contains at most $|J|+|\mathbb{BR}|$ local models and satisfies $\Phi$ in compliance with $\mathbb{BR}$.*

***Proof.*** Take any $J$-consistent chain $c$ that satisfies $\Phi$ in compliance with $\mathbb{BR}$. Let $\mathbb{BR}^* \subseteq \mathbb{BR}$ be the set of bridge rules whose consequences are not satisfied by $c$. Every $br \in \mathbb{BR}^*$ must have a premise which is not satisfied in some local model $m_{br}$ contained by $c$. On the other hand, for every $j \in J$, there must be at least one local model $m_j \in c_j$ that satisfies all those formulas in $\Phi$ that apply to context $j$. The chain $c^*$ obtained from $c$ by eliminating all local models except for:

$$\bigcup_{j\in J} m_j \cup \bigcup_{br\in\mathbb{BR}^*} m_{br}$$

is $J$-consistent, satisfies $\Phi$ in compliance with $\mathbb{BR}$ and contains at most $|J| + |\mathbb{BR}^*| \leq |J| + |\mathbb{BR}|$ local models. □

**Theorem 4** *Contextual satisfiability is NP-complete and can be settled in non-deterministic time:*

$$O((|J| + |\mathbb{BR}|) \times N)$$

***Proof.*** We already observed that contextual satisfiability is NP-hard. Now, to determine satisfiability we may proceed as follows. First, we non-deterministically appoint a set $Cons$ of bridge rule consequences, and a set $Prem$ of bridge rule premises, such that for every $br \in \mathbb{BR}$, either $br$'s consequence is in $Cons$, or one of $br$'s premises is in $Prem$. Let $J$, $I_{Cons}$, and $I_{Prem}$ be the set of contexts involved by $\Phi$, $Cons$, and $Prem$, respectively. Furthermore, let $\Phi_i$, $Cons_i$, and $Prem_i$ be the set of $i$-formulas contained by $\Phi$, $Cons$, and $Prem$, respectively. We construct a chain $c$, such that:

- For all $i \in I_{Prem}$, $c_i$ contains $|Prem_i|$ local models;
- For all $i \in J/I_{Prem}$, $c_i$ contains exactly one local model;
- For all $i \notin J \cup I_{Prem}$, $c_i$ is empty;
- For all $i \in I$, each $m \in c_i$ evaluates the propositional atoms *not* appearing in $\Phi_i \cup Cons_i \cup Prem_i$ to $True$.

The only "guessing" involved in constructing $c$, apart from the choice of $Cons$ and $Prem$, are the truth values to which each local model in $c_i$ should evaluate the propositional atoms in $P(\Phi_i \cup Cons_i \cup Prem_i)$. Notice that $c$ contains at most $|J|+|Prem| \leq |J|+|\mathbb{BR}|$ local models, which are distributed over those components $c_i$ of $c$ with $i \in J \cup I_{Prem}$; all the other components of $c$ are empty. Consider a local model $m$ contained in $c_i$ for some $i \in J \cup I_{Prem}$. The number of atomic propositions $|P(\Phi_i \cup Cons_i \cup Prem_i)|$ that $m$ should "explicitly" evaluate is clearly bounded by $N$. We must appoint at most $|J| + |\mathbb{BR}|$ such explicit valuations (one for each local model in $c$), so $c$ can be constructed in non-deterministic time $O((|J| + |\mathbb{BR}|) \times N)$.

It remains to check whether $c$ is $J$-consistent, satisfies $\Phi$, and complies with $\mathbb{BR}$. By theorem 2 this can be done in deterministic time $O((|J| + |\mathbb{BR}|) \times N)$.

Theorem 3 assures that, if $\Phi$ is consistently satisfiable in $MS$, then guessing a chain as described above is bound to result in a suitable one. Thus, consistent satisfiability of $\Phi$ in $MS$ can be determined in non-deterministic polynomial time $O((|J| + |\mathbb{BR}|) \times N)$. □

## Encoding Into Propositional SAT

As contextual satisfiability is in NP, it is tractably reducible to purely propositional SAT. In providing such a reduction, we may loose the particular structure of our problem, but do lay the groundwork for the implementation of purely SAT-based contextual reasoners, which could benefit from the well-advanced techniques developed by the SAT community.

To obtain a purely propositional representation of multi-contextual satisfiability problems, we exploit the understanding we obtained while establishing the bounded model property in the previous section. The key insight there was that a set of formulas $\Phi$ is satisfied by a chain $c$ if and only if it is satisfied by chain $c^b$ such that:

- For each $j \in J$, $c^b_j$ contains at least one local model $m_j$ that satisfies all the formulas in $\Phi$ that apply to context $j$.
- For every bridge rule $br \in \mathbb{BR}$ whose consequence is not satisfied by $c$, there is at least one premise $i : \xi$ of $br$, such that $c^b_i$ contains a local model $m_{br}$ that satisfies $\neg\xi$.

Notice that to meet these requirements, the number of local models in each component of $c^b$ can be kept down to $|\mathbb{BR}|$ (we assume that $|\mathbb{BR}| \geq 1$). Also, if a non-empty component of $c^b$ contains less than $|\mathbb{BR}|$ local models it can be extended to comprise exactly $|\mathbb{BR}|$ models, simply by adding duplicates of already existing models. So we may say that $\Phi$ is consistently satisfiable in MS if and only if it is satisfied by a $J$-consistent chain $c^*$ all of whose components are either empty or contain exactly $|\mathbb{BR}|$ local models.

Now, we construct a propositional formula $\psi$, which is satisfiable if and only if such a chain $c^*$ exists. We express this formula in a language which contains a propositional atom $p^k_i$ for every $p \in L_i$, and for every $k = 1, \ldots, |\mathbb{BR}|$. Intuitively, the truth value assigned to $p^k_i$ by a propositional model of $\psi$ corresponds to the truth value assigned to $p$ by the $k^{th}$ local model in $c^*_i$. The language also contains an atomic proposition $e_i$ for each index $i \in I$. Intuitively, $e_i$ being assigned $True$ corresponds to $c^*_i$ being empty.

We write $K = \{1, \ldots, |\mathbb{BR}|\}$. For any formula $\varphi$, and each $i \in I$ and $k \in K$, let $\varphi_i^k$ denote the formula that results from substituting every atomic proposition $p$ in $\varphi$ with $p_i^k$. Furthermore, let $\varphi_i^K = \bigwedge_{k \in K} \varphi_i^k$. Then, the translation of a labeled formula reads:

$$(i : \varphi)^* = e_i \vee \varphi_i^K$$

For bridge rules we have:

$$(i_1 : \varphi_1, \ldots, i_n : \varphi_n \rightarrow i : \phi)^* = \\ (i_1 : \phi_1)^* \wedge \ldots \wedge (i_n : \phi_n)^* \supset (i : \phi)^*$$

A $j$-consistency constraint is captured by:

$$(j\text{-cons})^* = \neg e_j$$

**Theorem 5** *There is an assignment $V$ to the propositions $\{p_i^k \mid i \in I \text{ and } k = 1, \ldots, |\mathbb{BR}|\} \cup \{e_i \mid i \in I\}$ that satisfies:*

$$\psi = \bigwedge_{i:\phi \in \Phi} (i : \phi)^* \wedge \bigwedge_{j \in J} (j\text{-}cons)^* \wedge \bigwedge_{br \in \mathbb{BR}} (br)^*$$

*if and only if there is a $J$-consistent chain $c^V$ that satisfies $\Phi$ in compliance with $\mathbb{BR}$.*

**Proof** ($\Rightarrow$) From $V$ we construct a chain $c^V$, such that each component $c_i^V$ is empty if $V(e_i) = True$ and consists of exactly $|\mathbb{BR}|$ local models otherwise. In the latter case, the $k^{th}$ local model of $c_i^V$ is made to evaluate each propositional atom $p \in L_i$ to $True$ iff $V(p_i^k) = True$. It's easy to see that $c^V$ is $J$-consistent and satisfies $\Phi$ in compliance with $\mathbb{BR}$.

($\Leftarrow$) By the above observations, if there is a $J$-consistent chain $c$ that satisfies $\Phi$ in compliance with $\mathbb{BR}$, there must also be a $J$-consistent chain $c^*$ each of whose components is either empty or contains exactly $|\mathbb{BR}|$ local models, and which still satisfies $\Phi$ in compliance with $\mathbb{BR}$.

From $c^*$ we may obtain a truth assignment $V$ as follows. To an atomic proposition $e_i$, let $V$ assign $True$ iff $c_i^* = \emptyset$. To an atomic proposition $p_i^k$, let $V$ assign $True$ if the $k^{th}$ local model of $c_i^*$ satisfies $p$, $False$ if the $k^{th}$ local model of $c_i^*$ satisfies $\neg p$, and any truth value if $c_i^*$ is empty. It should be straightforward to see that $V$ satisfies $\psi$. □

## Application to PLC

We apply the results presented above to improve current complexity bounds for the propositional logic of context as described in (McCarthy 1993; McCarthy & Buvač 1998). The best result so far has been established by Massacci (1996). He proposes a tableaux-based decision procedure, which determines satisfiability of a PLC formula $\varphi$ in non-deterministic polynomial time $O(|\varphi|^4)$.

We translate a PLC formula $\varphi$ into a labeled formula $\epsilon : \varphi$ and a multi-context system MCS($\varphi$), so that $\varphi$ is satisfiable in PLC iff $\epsilon : \varphi$ is consistently satisfiable in MCS($\varphi$). The translation is only sketched here – details can be found in (Bouquet & Serafini 2004). Subsequently, we demonstrate that determining whether or not $\epsilon : \varphi$ is consistently satisfiable in MCS($\varphi$) takes non-deterministic time $O(|\varphi|^2)$.

The translation works as follows. For each nesting pattern $ist(k_1, \ldots ist(k_n, \psi) \ldots)$ in $\varphi$, let MCS($\varphi$) contain a context labeled with the sequence $k_1 \ldots k_n$. Let the language of context $k_1 \ldots k_n$ contain all the atomic propositions in $\psi$, plus a new atomic proposition for each formula of the form $ist(k, \chi)$ occurring in $\psi$. Finally, equip MCS($\varphi$) with the following bridge rules[1]:

$$\bar{k}k : \psi \rightarrow \bar{k} : ist(k, \psi) \\ \bar{k} : ist(k, \psi) \rightarrow \bar{k}k : \psi \\ \bar{k} : \neg ist(k, ist(h, \psi)) \rightarrow \bar{k}k : \neg ist(h, \psi) \\ \bar{k} : \neg ist(k, \neg ist(h, \psi)) \rightarrow \bar{k}k : ist(h, \psi)$$

where $\bar{k} = k_1 \ldots k_n$ refers to any context of MCS($\varphi$), whose language contains $ist(k, \psi)$ or $ist(k, ist(h, \chi))$, respectively.

**Example 5** *Consider the following PLC formula:*

$$\varphi = p \vee ist(k, q \supset (ist(h, r \wedge s) \supset ist(j, q)))$$

*MCS($\varphi$) consists of four contexts which are labeled $\epsilon$ (the empty sequence), $k$, $kh$, and $kj$. The language of $\epsilon$, $L_\epsilon$, contains two propositions, $p$ and $ist(k, q \supset (ist(h, r \vee s) \supset ist(j, q)))$; $L_k$ contains two propositions, $q$ and $ist(h, r \wedge s)$; $L_{kh} = L(\{r, s\})$ and $L_{kj} = L(\{q\})$. The bridge rules of MCS($\varphi$) are as stated above.*

**Theorem 6 (Bouquet & Serafini, 2004)** *$\varphi$ is satisfiable in PLC if and only if $\epsilon : \varphi$ is consistently satisfiable in MCS($\varphi$).*

**Theorem 7** *Satisfiability of $\varphi$ in PLC can be computed in non-deterministic polynomial time $O(|\varphi|^2)$.*

***Proof.*** By theorem 6 any satisfiability problem in PLC can be transformed into an equivalent satisfiability problem in MCS. This transformation can be established in linear time.

Every bridge rule in MCS($\varphi$) involves at least one proposition of the form $ist(k, \psi)$. Every such proposition occurs in at most four bridge rules. Every subformula of $\varphi$ of the form $ist(k, \psi)$ (and nothing else) results in a proposition of the form $ist(k, \psi)$ in the language of exactly one context in MCS($\varphi$). The number of subformulas of $\varphi$ of the form $ist(k, \psi)$ is bounded by $|\varphi|$. From these observations, we may conclude that the number of bridge rules $|\mathbb{BR}|$ in MCS($\varphi$) is bounded by $4 \times |\varphi|$. Moreover, by construction, the sum of the lengths of the formulas involved in any bridge rule of MCS($\varphi$) is at most four.

By theorem 4, contextual satisfiability of $\epsilon : \varphi$ in MCS($\varphi$) can be settled in non-deterministic time:

$$O((|\Phi| + |\mathbb{BR}|) \times (\sum_{i:\varphi \in \Phi} |i : \varphi| + \sum_{br \in \mathbb{BR}} \sum_{i:\xi \in \Xi(br)} |i : \xi|))$$

In the light of the above observations, and keeping in mind that $\Phi$ merely consists of $\epsilon : \varphi$, we may rewrite this in terms of $\varphi$ as:

$$O(|\varphi|^2)$$

□

[1]The first two bridge rules correspond to the notions of *entering* and *exiting* contexts (McCarthy & Buvač 1998), while the last two bridge rules correspond to the $\Delta$ axiom introduced by Buvač and Mason (1993).

## Conclusion

We have analysed the complexity of contextual reasoning based on propositional multi-context systems with finite sets of bridge rules.

A first insight was obtained by establishing an encoding of contextual satisfiability into satisfiability in bounded multi-modal $K_n$, which is well-known to be NP-complete. Next, we accomplished a more fine-grained upper bound for the complexity of contextual satisfiability by a direct investigation of its semantical properties. Herein we observed that multi-context systems enjoy the bounded model property.

We also provided a tractable encoding of contextual satisfiability problems into purely propositional ones. In doing so, we laid the groundwork for SAT-based implementations of contextual reasoning systems.

Finally, we obtained improved complexity results for the satisfiability problem in McCarthy's propositional logic of context, by translating it into the satisfiability problem that we have considered in this paper.

Future work will encompass experimentation with both native and SAT-based contextual reasoning systems. Also, we are interested whether, or to what extent, our results may be generalized so as to apply to multi-context systems with schematic bridge rules as well.

## Acknowledgments

We wish to thank Johan van Benthem, Roberto Sebastiani, and the anonymous referees for their very useful comments.

## References

Bouquet, P., and Serafini, L. 2004. Comparing formal theories of context in AI. *Artificial Intelligence*. Accepted for publication.

Buvač, S., and Mason, I. A. 1993. Propositional logic of context. In *National Conference on Artificial Intelligence (AAAI 93)*.

Chrabakh, W., and Wolski, R. 2003. Gridsat: a chaff-based distributed SAT solver for the grid. In *Supercomputing Conference (SC03)*.

Cook, S. 1971. The complexity of theorem proving procedures. In *ACM Symposium on the Theory of Computing*, 151–158.

Foster, I. 1998. *The Grid : Blueprint for a New Computing Infrastructure*. Morgan-Kaufmann.

G. Behrmann, T. H., and Vaandrager, F. 2000. Distributed timed model checking - how the search order matters. In *Computer Aided Design (CAV 00)*, 216–231.

Ghidini, C., and Giunchiglia, F. 2001. Local models semantics, or contextual reasoning = locality + compatibility. *Artificial Intelligence* 127(2):221–259.

Giunchiglia, F., and Serafini, L. 1994. Multilanguage hierarchical logics, or: how we can do without modal logics. *Artificial Intelligence* 65(1):29–70.

Giunchiglia, F. 1993. Contextual reasoning. *Epistemologia* XVI:345–364.

Halpern, J., and Moses, Y. 1992. A guide to completeness and complexity for modal logics of knowledge and belief. *Artificial Intelligence* 54(3):311–379.

Ladner, R. 1977. The computational complexity of provability in systems of modal propositional logic. *SIAM Journal of Computing* 6:467–480.

Lenat, D. B., and Guha, R. V. 1990. *Building Large Knowledge Based Systems*. Addison Wesley.

Massacci, F. 1996. Contextual reasoning is NP complete. In *National Conference on Artificial Intelligence (AAAI 96)*, 621–626.

McCarthy, J., and Buvač, S. 1998. Formalizing context (expanded notes). In *Computing Natural Language*, volume 81 of *CSLI Lecture Notes*. 13–50.

McCarthy, J. 1987. Generality in artificial intelligence. *Communications of ACM* 30(12):1030–1035.

McCarthy, J. 1993. Notes on formalizing context. In *International Joint Conference on Artificial Intelligence (IJCAI 93)*, 555–560.

Serafini, L., and Roelofsen, F. 2004. Satisfiability for propositional contexts. In *Principles of Knowledge Representation and Reasoning (KR 04)*. Accepted for publication.

# Constraint Satisfaction and Satisfiability

# Hiding Satisfying Assignments: Two are Better than One

**Dimitris Achlioptas**
Microsoft Research
Redmond, Washington
optas@microsoft.com

**Haixia Jia** and **Cristopher Moore***
Computer Science Department
University of New Mexico
{hjia,moore}@cs.unm.edu

### Abstract

The evaluation of incomplete satisfiability solvers depends critically on the availability of hard satisfiable instances. A plausible source of such instances are $k$-CNF formulas whose clauses are chosen uniformly at random among all clauses satisfying some randomly chosen truth assignment $A$. Unfortunately, instances generated in this manner are relatively easy and can be solved efficiently by practical heuristics. Roughly speaking, as the number of clauses is increased, $A$ acts as a stronger and stronger attractor. Motivated by recent results on the geometry of the space of solutions for random $k$-SAT and NAE-$k$-SAT instances, we propose a very simple twist on this model that greatly increases the hardness of the resulting formulas. Namely, in addition to forbidding the clauses violated by the hidden assignment $A$, we also forbid the clauses violated by its complement, so that both $A$ and $\overline{A}$ are satisfying. It appears that under this "symmetrization" the effects of the two attractors largely cancel out, making it much harder for an algorithm to "feel" (and find) either one. We give theoretical and experimental evidence supporting this assertion.

## Introduction

Recent years have witnessed the rapid development and application of search methods for constraint satisfaction and Boolean satisfiability. An important factor in the success of these algorithms is the availability of good sets of benchmark problems to evaluate and fine-tune them. There are two main sources of such problems: the real world, and random instance generators. Real-world problems are arguably the best benchmark, but unfortunately are in short supply. Moreover, using real-world problems carries the risk of tuning algorithms toward the specific application domains for which good benchmarks are available. In that sense, random instance generators are a good additional source, with the advantage of controllable characteristics, such as size and expected hardness. Hard random instances have led to the development of new stochastic search methods such as `WalkSAT` (Selman, Kautz, & Cohen 1996) and the breakout procedure (Morris 1993), and have been used in detailed comparisons of local search methods for graph coloring and related graph problems (Johnson *et al.* 1989).

*Supported by NSF grant PHY-0200909.


A key limitation of current problem generators concerns their use in evaluating incomplete local search methods. When a local search algorithm does not find a solution, it can be difficult to determine whether this is because the instance is unsatisfiable, or simply because the algorithm failed in finding a satisfying assignment. The standard way of dealing with this problem is to use a complete search method to filter out the unsatisfiable cases. However, this limits the size and difficulty of problem instances that can be considered. Ideally, one would use problem generators that generate satisfiable instances only. One recent source of such problems is the quasigroup completion problem (Shaw, Stergiou, & Walsh 1998; Kautz *et al.* 2001; Achlioptas *et al.* 2000). However, a generator for random hard satisfiability instances has remained elusive.

A very natural candidate for generating random hard satisfiable 3-SAT formulas is the following. Generate a random truth assignment $A$, and then generate a formula with $n$ variables and $rn$ random clauses, rejecting any clause that is violated by $A$. In particular, if we work close to the transition region $r \approx 4.25$ where the hardest 3-SAT problems seem to be (Cheeseman, Kanefsky, & Taylor 1991; Hogg, Huberman, & Williams 1996; Mitchell, Selman, & Levesque 1992), we might hope that this would generate hard satisfiable instances. Unfortunately, though, this generator is highly biased towards formulas with many assignments clustered around $A$. When given to local search methods such as `WalkSAT`, these formulas turn out to be much easier than formulas of comparable size obtained by filtering satisfiable instances from a 3-SAT generator. More sophisticated versions of this "hidden assignment" scheme (Asahiro, Iwama, & Miyano 1996; Van Gelder 1993) improve matters somewhat but still lead to biased samples.

In this paper we introduce a new generator of random satisfiable problems. The idea is simple: we pick a random 3-SAT formula that has a "hidden" **complementary pair** of satisfying assignments, $A$ and $\overline{A}$, by rejecting clauses that are violated by either $A$ or $\overline{A}$. Our motivation comes from recent work (Achlioptas & Moore 2002b) which showed that moving from random $k$-SAT to random NAE-$k$-SAT (in which every clause in the $k$-CNF must have a true *and* a false literal) tremendously reduces the correlation between solutions. That is, whereas in random $k$-SAT, satisfying assignments tend to form clumps, in random NAE-$k$-SAT the solutions appear to be scattered throughout the hypercube in a rather uniform "mist", even for densities extremely close to the threshold. An intuitive explanation of this phenomenon is that since the complement of every NAE-assignment is also an NAE-assignment, the pull of pairs of solutions largely cancel out. In this paper we impose a similar symmetry on the hidden assignments $A$ and $\overline{A}$, so that *their* attractions cancel out, making it hard for a wide variety of algorithms to "feel" either one.

A key feature of our generator is that it corresponds to an extremely simple probabilistic process, in sharp contrast with, say, 3-SAT generators based on cryptographic ideas (Massacci 1999). As a result, it is *readily amenable to mathematical analysis.* Here we take some significant steps in this direction, indeed using tools similar to those employed in the study of random $k$-SAT formulas.

To ascertain the hardness of our formulas we performed extensive computational experiments comparing them to "1-hidden" and "0-hidden" formulas. That is, we compared our formulas to random 3-SAT formulas with one hidden assignment and to standard random 3-SAT formulas (with no hidden assignment). We examined four leading algorithms: two complete solvers, `zChaff` and `Satz`, and two incomplete ones, `WalkSAT` and the recently introduced `SP`.

For all these algorithms, we find that our formulas are much harder than 1-hidden formulas and, more importantly, *about as hard 0-hidden ones.*

## The space of solutions

In this section we compare 1-hidden and 2-hidden formulas with respect to the expected number of solutions at a given distance from the hidden assignment(s).

Let $X$ be the number of satisfying truth assignments in a random formula with $n$ variables and $m = rn$ clauses chosen uniformly and independently among all $k$-clauses with *at least one positive literal*, i.e., 1-hidden formulas where we hide the all–1s truth assignment. Then, using linearity of expectation, clause independence, the selection of the literals in each clause with replacement, and Stirling's approximation for the factorial, we get (1) below (where $\sim$ suppresses terms polynomial in $n$):

$$\begin{aligned}\mathbf{E}[X] &= \sum_{\sigma\in\{0,1\}^n} \Pr[\sigma \text{ is satisfying}] \\ &= \sum_{z=0}^{n}\binom{n}{z}\Pr\left[\begin{array}{c}\text{a truth assignment with } z \text{ ones}\\ \text{satisfies a random clause}\end{array}\right]^m \\ &= \sum_{z=0}^{n}\binom{n}{z}\left(1-\sum_{j=1}^{k}\binom{k}{j}\frac{(1-z/n)^j(z/n)^{k-j}}{2^k-1}\right)^m \\ &= \sum_{z=0}^{n}\binom{n}{z}\left(1-\frac{1-(z/n)^k}{2^k-1}\right)^m \\ &\sim \max_{\alpha\in[0,1]}\left[\frac{1}{\alpha^\alpha(1-\alpha)^{1-\alpha}}\left(1-\frac{1-\alpha^k}{2^k-1}\right)^r\right]^n \\ &\equiv \max_{\alpha\in[0,1]}\left[f_{k,r}(\alpha)\right]^n \quad . \qquad (1)\end{aligned}$$

From (1) we see that $\mathbf{E}[X]$ is dominated by the contribution of truth assignments with $\gamma n$ ones, where $\gamma$ is the maximizer of $f_{k,r}$ in $[0,1]$. Observe now that $f_{k,r}$ is a strictly increasing function of $\alpha$, maximized at some $\gamma > 1/2$ for *every* $r > 0$. Thus, always, most solutions have a majority of 1s, i.e., the hidden assignment is "felt". Moreover, as $r$ is increased $\gamma \to 1$ (see Figure 1 below).

To study 2-hidden formulas now, let $X$ be the number of satisfying truth assignments in a random formula with $n$ variables and $m = rn$ clauses chosen uniformly among all $k$-clauses with at least one positive *and at least one negative literal*; that is, 2-hidden formulas where we hide the all–1s truth assignment *and* its complement. Proceeding as above, but with the second line replaced by

$$\sum_{z=0}^{n}\binom{n}{z}\left(1-\sum_{j=1}^{k-1}\binom{k}{j}\frac{(1-z/n)^j(z/n)^{k-j}}{2^k-2}\right)^m$$

and carrying through the ensuing changes we find that now $\mathbf{E}[X] \sim \max_{\alpha\in[0,1]}[g_{k,r}(\alpha)]^n$ where

$$g_{k,r}(\alpha) = \frac{1}{\alpha^\alpha(1-\alpha)^{1-\alpha}}\left(1-\frac{1-\alpha^k-(1-\alpha)^k}{2^k-2}\right)^r .$$

Observe that the function $g_{k,r}$ is *symmetric* in $[0,1]$, unlike $f_{k,r}$. Indeed, its global maximum occurs at $\alpha = 1/2$ for all $r$ up to extremely close to the random $k$-SAT threshold. In other words, for such $r$ the hidden assignments do not cause satisfying assignments to cluster around them. More precisely, there exists a sequence $\epsilon_k \to 0$ such that $g_{k,r}(1/2) > g_{k,r}(\alpha)$ for all $\alpha \neq 1/2$, as long as

$$r \le 2^k \ln 2 - \frac{\ln 2}{2} - 1 - \epsilon_k \ . \qquad (2)$$

Contrast this with the fact (implicit in (Kirousis *et al.* 1998)) that there exists a sequence $\delta_k \to 0$ such that for

$$r \ge 2^k \ln 2 - \frac{\ln 2}{2} - \frac{1}{2} - \delta_k \ , \qquad (3)$$

a random $k$-SAT formula with $n$ variables and $m = rn$ clauses is unsatisfiable with probability $1 - o(1)$. Equations (2) and (3) differ by just $1/2$ as $k \to \infty$; for instance, for $k = 10$ they give 708.40 and 708.94 respectively.

Below we plot[1] $f_{k,r}$ and $g_{k,r}$ for $k = 5$ and $r = 16, 18, 20, 22, 24$ (from top to bottom). We see that in the case of 1-hidden formulas, i.e., $f_{k,r}$, the maximum always occurs to the right of $\alpha = 1/2$. Moreover, observe that for $r = 22, 24$, i.e., after we cross the 5-SAT threshold (which occurs at $r \approx 21$) we have a dramatic shift in the location of the maximum and, thus, in the extent of the bias: as one would expect, the only remaining satisfying assignments above the threshold are those extremely close to the hidden assignment.

[1] The reason we plot $k = 5$ is that this is the smallest value of $k$ for which the evolution of $g_{k,r}$ exhibits its full complexity (the evolution is qualitatively the same for all $k \ge 5$). For $k = 3, 4$ there are never more than *two* local extrema, as the emergence of maxima away from $\alpha = 1/2$ coincides with $\alpha = 1/2$ becoming a local minimum.

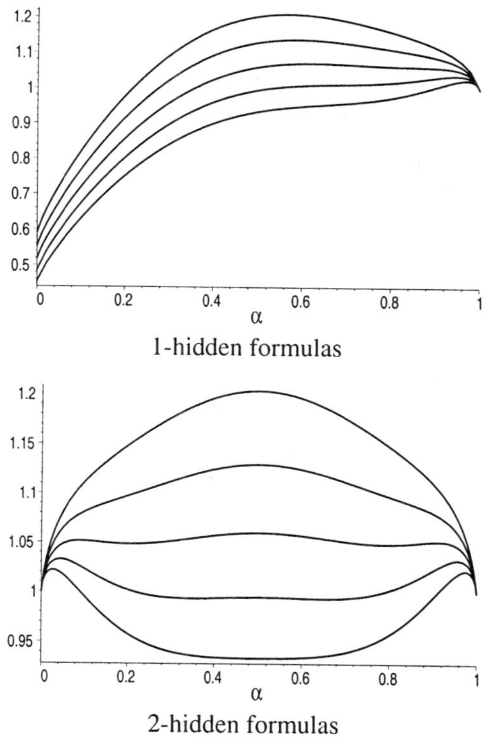


Figure 1: The $n$th root of the expected number of solutions $f$ and $g$ as functions of the fraction $\alpha = z/n$ of 1s. Here $k = 5$ and $r = 16, 18, 20, 22, 24$ from top to bottom.

In the case of 2-hidden formulas, on the other hand, we see that for $r = 16, 18, 20$ the global maximum occurs at $\alpha = 1/2$. For $r = 20$, we also have two local maxima, near $\alpha = 0, 1$, but since $g_{k,r}$ is raised to the $n$th power, these are exponentially suppressed. Naturally, for $r$ above the threshold, i.e., $r = 22, 24$, these local maxima become global, signifying that indeed the only remaining truth assignments are those extremely close to one of the two hidden ones.

## Unit Clause Resolution and DPLL algorithms

Consider the following linear-time heuristic, called Unit Clause (UC): if there are any unit clauses, satisfy them; else (a "free step") pick a random literal and satisfy it. One can think of UC as the first branch of the simplest possible DPLL algorithm $S$: set variables in a random order, each time choosing randomly which branch to take first. Clearly, UC succeeding on a formula $F$ is equivalent to $S$ succeeding on $F$ on its very first try, i.e., without any backtracking. In (Chao & Franco 1986), it was shown that UC succeeds with constant probability on random 3-SAT formulas for $r < 8/3$, and fails w.h.p. for $r > 8/3$.

To analyze UC on random 1-hidden and 2-hidden formulas we actually analyze UC on arbitrary initial distributions of 3-clauses, i.e., where for each $0 \leq j \leq 3$ we specify the initial number of 3-clauses with $j$ positive literals and $3-j$ negative ones. We use the method of differential equations; see (Achlioptas 2001) for a review. To simplify notation, we assume that our 1-hidden formulas forbid clauses where all literals are negative, while our 2-hidden formulas forbid all-negative and all-positive clauses. A *round* of UC is a free step and the ensuing chain of unit-clause propagations. For $0 \leq i \leq 3$ and $0 \leq j \leq i$, let $s_{i,j}$ be the density of clauses of length $i$ with $j$ positive literals and $i-j$ negative ones, and let $x$ be the fraction of variables set so far. Since $s_{1,0} = s_{1,1} = 0$ at the beginning of each round, our "state space" will consist of the variables $s_{i,j}$ for $i \geq 2$.

Let $m_T$ and $m_F$ be the expected number of variables set True and False in a round; we will calculate these below. Then rescaling the expected effect of a round gives the following system of differential equations,

$$\begin{aligned} \frac{ds_{3,j}}{dx} &= -\frac{3s_{3,j}}{1-x} \\ \frac{ds_{2,j}}{dx} &= -\frac{2s_{2,j}}{1-x} + \frac{m_F(j+1)s_{3,j+1} + m_T(3-j)s_{3,j}}{(m_T+m_F)(1-x)} \end{aligned} \tag{4}$$

To see this, note that a variable appears positively in a clause of type $i, j$ with probability $j/(n-X)$, and negatively with probability $(i-j)/(n-X)$. The terms above correspond to clauses being "hit" by the variables set, and the "flow" of 3-clauses to 2-clauses. Then Wormald's theorem (Wormald 1995) ensures that w.h.p. for all $x$, the $s_{i,j}$ are within $o(1)$ of the solutions to this system.

To calculate $m_T$ and $m_F$, we model the chain of unit clauses created in a round as a two-type branching process, which we analyze as in (Achlioptas & Moore 2002a). Since the free step gives the chosen variable a random value, the initial expected population of unit clauses can be represented by a vector $p_0 = (1/2, 1/2)^T$. Moreover, at time $x$, a unit clause procreates according to the matrix

$$M = \frac{1}{1-x}\begin{pmatrix} s_{2,1} & 2s_{2,0} \\ 2s_{2,2} & s_{2,1} \end{pmatrix} .$$

For instance, satisfying a negative unit clause creates, in expectation, $M_{1,1} = s_{2,1}/(1-x)$ negative unit clauses and $M_{2,1} = 2s_{2,2}/(1-x)$ positive unit clauses.

Let $\lambda_1$ be the largest eigenvalue of $M$. If $\lambda_1 < 1$ for all $x$, then the branching process is subcritical, UC succeeds with constant probability, and $(m_F, m_T)^T = (I-M)^{-1} \cdot p_0$ where $I$ is the identity matrix. On the other hand, if $\lambda_1$ ever exceeds 1, then the branching process becomes supercritical, with high probability the unit clauses proliferate and the algorithm fails. Note that

$$\lambda_1 = \frac{s_{2,1} + 2\sqrt{s_{2,0}\, s_{2,2}}}{1-x} . \tag{5}$$

Now, suppose our initial distribution of 3-clauses is symmetric, i.e., $s_{3,0}(0) = s_{3,3}(0)$ and $s_{3,1}(0) = s_{3,2}(0)$. It is easy to see from (4) that in that case, both the 3-clauses and the 2-clauses are symmetric at all times, i.e., $s_{i,j} = s_{i,i-j}$ and $m_F = m_T$. In that case $s_{2,1} + 2\sqrt{s_{2,0}s_{2,2}} = s_2$, so the criterion for subcriticality is $\lambda_1 = \frac{s_2}{1-x} < 1$. Moreover, since the system (4) is now symmetric with respect to $j$, summing over $j$ gives precisely the differential equations $\frac{ds_3}{dx} = -\frac{3s_3}{1-x}$ and $\frac{ds_2}{dx} = -\frac{2s_2}{1-x} + \frac{3s_3}{2(1-x)}$ for UC on random (0-hidden) instances of 3-SAT.

Since 2-hidden formulas correspond to symmetric initial conditions, we have thus shown that UC succeeds on them with constant probability if and only if $r < 8/3$, i.e., that UC *fails on 2-hidden formulas at exactly the same density for which it fails on 0-hidden formulas.* (In contrast, integrating (4) with the initial conditions corresponding to 1-hidden formulas shows that UC succeeds for them at a slightly higher density, up to $r < 2.679$.)

Of course, UC can easily be improved by making the free step choice more intelligent. We believe that a lot of the progress that has been made in analyzing the performance of algorithms on instances of random 3-SAT, i.e., 0-hidden formulas, can be "pushed through" to 2-hidden formulas. Specifically, nearly all DPLL-type algorithms analyzed so far have the property that given as input a symmetric initial distribution of 3-clauses, e.g. random 3-SAT, their residual formulas consist of symmetric mixes of 2- and 3-clauses. As a result, methods as above can be used to show that such algorithms act on 2-hidden formulas exactly as they do on 0-hidden ones, failing w.h.p. at the same density.

This last point acquires additional significance in the light of recent results on the onset of backtracking in DPLL algorithms for random 3-SAT formulas. Specifically, for the algorithm $S$ defined above (the backtracking extension of UC), it was proved (Achlioptas, Beame, & Molloy 2001) that exponential behavior already occurs for $r > 3.81$, well below the conjectured satisfiability threshold $r \approx 4.2$. In fact, non-rigorous but mathematically sophisticated calculations of (Cocco & Monasson 2001a; 2001b) suggest that exponential behavior begins right at the density where UC begins to fail with high probability, i.e., $r = 8/3$. (Indeed, that follows rigorously from the conjecture that the "tricritical" point in random (2+$p$)-SAT is $p_c = 2/5$.) As a single branch of $S$ acts on 2-hidden formulas in exactly the same way as on 0-hidden formulas, a very exciting possibility is to *prove* that $S$ takes exponential time on 2-hidden formulas above a certain density by extending the existing proof for random 3-SAT. Indeed, one can hope to do this for all DPLL algorithms with the symmetry discussed above.

## Experimental results

In this section we report experimental results on our 2-hidden formulas, and compare them to 1-hidden and 0-hidden ones. We use two leading complete solvers, `zChaff` and `Satz`, and two leading incomplete solvers, `WalkSAT` and the new Survey Propagation algorithm `SP`. In an attempt to avoid spurious features often present in "too-small" random instances, we restricted our attention to experiments where $n \geq 1000$. This meant that `zChaff` and `Satz` could only be examined at densities significantly above the satisfiability threshold, i.e., 4.2.., as neither algorithm could practically solve either 0-hidden *or* 2-hidden formulas with $n \sim 1000$ variables and such density. For `WalkSAT` and `SP` on the other hand, we can easily run experiments in the hardest range (around the satisfiability threshold) for $n \sim 10^4$.

### `zChaff` and `Satz`

In order to do experiments with $n \geq 1000$ with `zChaff` and `Satz`, we focused on the regime where $r$ is relatively large, $20 < r < 60$. This is because for $r$ near the satisfiability threshold, 0-hidden and 2-hidden random formulas with $n \sim 1000$ variables seem completely out of the reach of either algorithm. At the same time, in the overconstrained regime we considered, the formulas are still challenging, but the presence of many forced steps allows both solvers to completely explore the space fairly quickly.

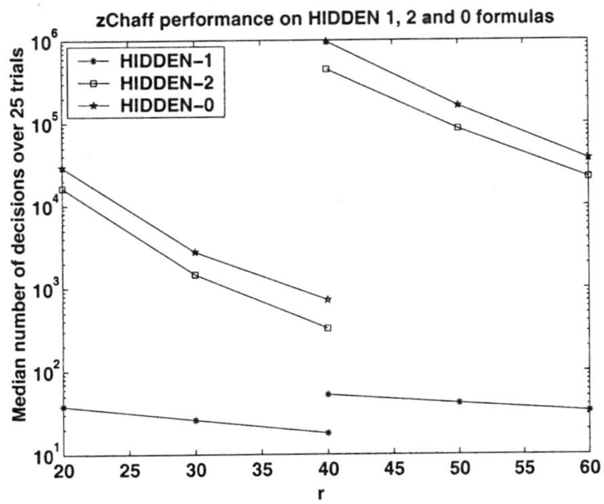


Figure 2: The number of branches of `zChaff`on 0-, 1-, and 2-hidden 3-SAT formulas, with $n = 1000$ for $20 \leq r \leq 40$ and $n = 3000$ for $40 \leq r \leq 60$. Each point is the median of 25 trials. The 2-hidden formulas are almost as hard as 0-hidden ones; the 1-hidden formulas are much easier.

We obtained `zChaff` from Princeton (Zhang ). Figure 2 shows its performance on random 0-hidden, 1-hidden and 2-hidden formulas. We see that for all three types of problems, the number of branches decreases rapidly as $r$ increases, consistent with earlier findings for complete solvers on random 3-SAT formulas.

Figure 2 shows that `zChaff` finds 2-hidden formulas almost as difficult as 0-hidden ones, which for this range of $r$ are unsatisfiable with overwhelming probability. On the other hand, the 1-hidden formulas are much easier, with a number of branchings between 2 and 5 orders of magnitude smaller. It appears that while `zChaff`'s smarts allow it to quickly "zero in" on a single hidden assignment, when there are two hidden assignments it only "stumbles" upon one of them after a search that is nearly as exhaustive as for unsatisfiable random 3-SAT formulas of the same density.

We performed similar experiments on `Satz`, and found that all three types of formulas had roughly the same running time. The reason for this is that while `Satz` makes intelligent decisions about which variable to branch on, it tries these branches in a fixed order, attempting first to set each variable false (Li 1997). Therefore, a given hidden assignment will appear at a uniformly random leaf in `Satz`'s search tree. We believe that if `Satz` were modified to use, say, the majority heuristic to choose a variable's first value, it would find 1-hidden formulas much easier than 2-hidden or 0-hidden ones. We plan to confirm this experimentally.

## SP

SP is a recently introduced incomplete solver (Mézard & Zecchina 2002) based on a generalization of belief propagation the authors call *survey propagation*. We compared SP's performance on the three types of problems near the satisfiability threshold. For $n = 10^4$ SP solves 2-hidden formulas at densities somewhat above the threshold, up to $r \approx 4.8$, while it solves 1-hidden formulas up to $r \approx 5.6$. These results stayed essentially the same when we increased $n$ to $2 \times 10^4$, and when we used 5000 iterations, instead of the default 1000, for SP's convergence procedure.

Presumably the 1-hidden formulas are easier for SP since the "messages" from clauses to variables tend to push the algorithm towards a hidden assignment. Having two hidden assignments appears to cancel these messages out to some extent, causing SP to fail at a lower density. However, this argument doesn't explain why the threshold for 2-hidden formulas should be higher than the satisfiability threshold; nor does it explain why SP doesn't solve 1-hidden formulas for arbitrarily large $r$. Indeed, we find this latter result surprising, since as $r$ increases the messages should point more and more consistently towards the hidden assignment in the 1-hidden case. These observations seem to us like an interesting direction for further investigation of SP.

## WalkSAT

We conclude with a local search algorithm, WalkSAT. Unlike complete solvers, WalkSAT can solve problems with $n = 10^4$ fairly close to the threshold, although not quite up to the densities reachable with SP. We performed experiments on WalkSAT both with a random initial state, and with a biased initial state where the algorithm is lucky enough to start with 75% agreement with one of the hidden assignments (note that this is exponentially unlikely). In both cases, we performed trials of $10^8$ flips for each formula, without random restarts or novelty heuristics, performing random or greedy flips with equal probability. Since random initial states have w.h.p. roughly 50% overlap with both hidden assignments, we expect their attractions to cancel out so that WalkSAT will have difficulty finding either of them. On the other hand, if we begin with a biased initial state, then the attraction from the nearby assignment will be much stronger than the other one; this situation is similar to a 1-hidden formula, and we expect WalkSAT to find it easily.

In Figure 3 we measure WalkSAT's performance on the three types of problems with $n = 10^4$ and $r$ ranging from 3.7 to 5.5, and compare them with 0-hidden formulas for $r$ ranging from 3.7 up to 4.1, just below the satisfiability threshold. We see that, below the threshold, the 2-hidden formulas are just as hard as the 0-hidden ones when WalkSAT sets its initial state randomly, and become the hardest when $r \approx 4.2$ (where $10^8$ flips no longer suffice to solve them). For all $r$ the 2-hidden formulas are much harder than the 1-hidden ones, unless we are lucky enough to start with a biased initial state. In Figure 4, we compare 0-hidden, 1-hidden and 2-hidden problems with both types of initial state as a function of $n$ at $r = 4.25$ (we filter the 0-hidden problems and only count the satisfiable ones). Consistent with experiments of (Barthel *et al.* 2002), the median running time is

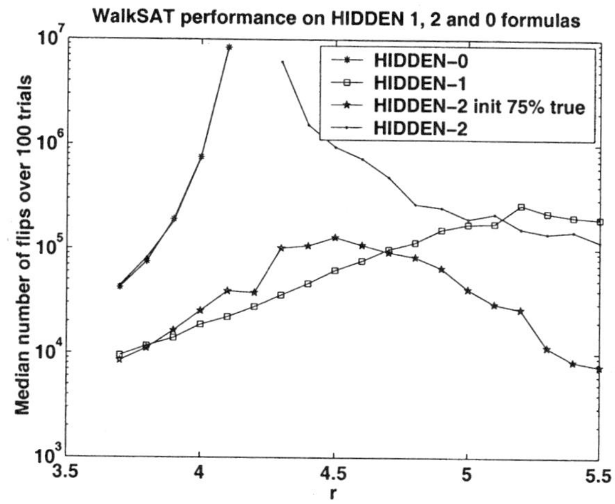


Figure 3: The median number of flips needed by WalkSAT for 3-SAT formulas of all three types as a function of $r$ with $n = 10^4$. Below the threshold, 2-hidden formulas are just as hard as 0-hidden ones, and their running time increases steeply as we approach the threshold. For all $r$, 2-hidden formulas are much harder than 1-hidden ones, unless the algorithm starts with a (very lucky) biased initial state.

polynomial in $n$. However, the power of $n$ (the slope in the the log-log plot) is the same for the 2-hidden and 0-hidden formulas, while for 1-hidden formulas (and 2-hidden with biased initial state) it is much lower.

## Conclusions

We introduce an extremely simple new generator of random satisfiable 3-SAT instances which is amenable to all the mathematical tools developed for the study of random 3-SAT. Our generator appears to produce instances that are as hard as random 3-SAT instances, in sharp contrast to those with a single hidden assignment. Our experiments show that this hardness is quite robust, both above and below the satisfiability threshold, and for very different algorithms, i.e., DPLL solvers (zChaff and Satz), local search algorithms (WalkSAT), and survey propagation (SP).

We believe that random 2-hidden instances could make excellent satisfiable benchmarks, especially just around the satisfiability threshold, say at $r = 4.25$ where they appear to be the hardest for WalkSAT (although beating SP requires somewhat higher densities). We propose several exciting directions for further work:

1. Proving that the expected running time of natural DPLL algorithms on 2-hidden formulas is exponential in $n$.
2. Explaining the different threshold behaviors of SP on 1-hidden and 2-hidden formulas.
3. Understanding how long WalkSAT takes at the midpoint between the two hidden assignments, before it becomes sufficiently unbalanced to converge to one of them.
4. Studying random 2-hidden formulas in the dense case where there are $\omega(n)$ clauses.

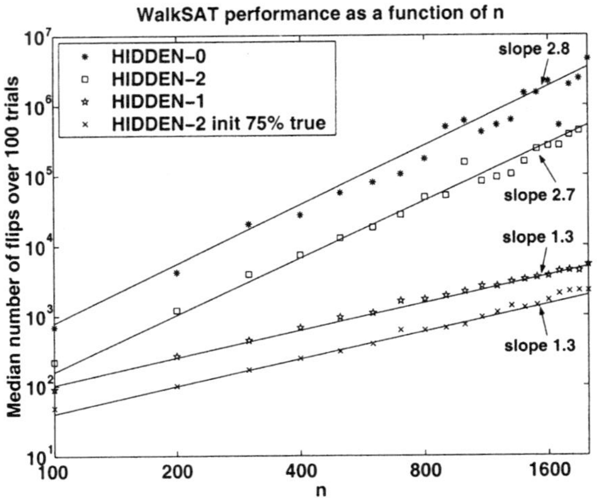


Figure 4: The median number of flips needed by `WalkSAT` to solve 0-, 1-, and 2-hidden 3-SAT formulas at $r = 4.25$, with $n$ ranging from 100 to 2000. While the median running time is polynomial, for 2-hidden problems it grows just as fast as for 0-hidden ones, while 1-hidden problems are similar to 2-hidden problems with a biased initial state.

## References


Achlioptas, D., and Moore, C. 2002a. Almost all graphs with average degree 4 are 3-colorable. *STOC* 199–208.

Achlioptas, D., and Moore, C. 2002b. The asymptotic order of the random k-sat threshold. *FOCS* 779–788.

Achlioptas, D.; Beame, P.; and Molloy, M. 2001. A sharp threshold in proof complexity. *STOC* 337–346.

Achlioptas, D.; Gomes, C.; Kautz, H.; and Selman, B. 2000. Generating satisfiable problem instances. *AAAI* 256–261.

Achlioptas, D. 2001. Lower bounds for random 3-sat via differential equations. *Theor. Comp. Sci.* 265:159–185.

Asahiro, Y.; Iwama, K.; and Miyano, E. 1996. Random generation of test instances with controlled attributes. *DIMACS Series in Disc. Math. and Theor. Comp. Sci.* 26.

Barthel, W.; Hartmann, A.; Leone, M.; Ricci-Tersenghi, F.; Weigt, M.; and Zecchina, R. 2002. Hiding solutions in random satisfiability problems: A statistical mechanics approach. *Phys. Rev. Lett* 88(188701).

Chao, M., and Franco, J. 1986. Probabilistic analysis of two heuristics for the 3-satisfiability problem. *SIAM J. Comput.* 15(4):1106–1118.

Cheeseman, P.; Kanefsky, R.; and Taylor, W. 1991. Where the really hard problems are. *IJCAI* 163–169.

Cocco, S., and Monasson, R. 2001a. Analysis of the computational complexity of solving random satisfiability problems using branch and bound search algorithms. *Eur. Phys. J. B* 22:505–.

Cocco, S., and Monasson, R. 2001b. Trajectories in phase diagrams, growth processes and computational complexity: how search algorithms solve the 3-satisfiability problem. *Physical Review Letters* 86:1654–.

Hogg, T.; Huberman, B.; and Williams, C. 1996. Phase transitions and complexity. *Artificial Intelligence* 81. special issue.

Johnson, D.; Aragon, C.; McGeoch, L.; and C., S. 1989. Optimization by simulated annealing: An experimental evaluation. *Operations Research* 37(6):865–892.

Kautz, H.; Ruan, Y.; Achlioptas, D.; Gomes, C.; Selman, B.; and Stickel, M. 2001. Balance and filtering in structured satisfiable problems. *IJCAI* 351–358.

Kirousis, L.; Kranakis, E.; Krizanc, D.; and Stamatiou, Y. 1998. Approximating the unsatisfiability threshold of random formulas. *Random Structures Algorithms* 12(3):253–269.

Li, C. 1997. Anbulagan, heuristics based on unit propagation for satisfiability problems. *IJCAI* 366–371.

Massacci, F. 1999. Using walk-sat and rel-sat for cyptographic key search. *IJCAI '99* 290–295.

Mézard, M., and Zecchina, R. 2002. Random k-satisfiability: from an analytic solution to a new efficient algorithm. *Phys. Rev. E* 66. Available at: http://www.ictp.trieste.it/~zecchina/SP/.

Mitchell, D.; Selman, B.; and Levesque, H. 1992. Hard and easy distributions of sat problems. *AAAI* 459–465.

Morris, P. 1993. The breakout method for escaping from local minima. *AAAI* 40–45.

Selman, B.; Kautz, H.; and Cohen, B. 1996. Local search strategies for satisfiability testing. *2nd DIMACS Challange on Cliques, Coloring, and Satisfiability.*

Shaw, P.; Stergiou, K.; and Walsh, T. 1998. Arc consistency and quasigroup completion. *ECAI, workshop on binary constraints.*

Van Gelder, A. 1993. Problem generator `mkcnf.c`. *DIMACS.* Challenge archive.

Wormald, N. 1995. Differential equations for random processes and random graphs. *Ann. Appl. Probab.* 5(4):1217–1235.

Zhang, L. zchaff source site. Available at: http://ee.princeton.edu/~chaff/zchaff.php.

# Modeling Choices in Quasigroup Completion: SAT vs. CSP * †

**Carlos Ansótegui**
Computer Science Department
Universitat de Lleida
Jaume II, 69, E-25001 Lleida, Spain
carlos@eup.udl.es

**Alvaro del Val** and **Iván Dotú**
Escuela Politécnica Superior
Universidad Autónoma de Madrid
28049 Madrid, Spain
{delval, ivan.dotu}@ii.uam.es

**Cèsar Fernández** and **Felip Manyà**
Computer Science Department
Universitat de Lleida
Jaume II, 69, E-25001 Lleida, Spain
{cesar, felip}@eup.udl.es

### Abstract

We perform a systematic comparison of SAT and CSP models for a challenging combinatorial problem, quasigroup completion (QCP). Our empirical results clearly indicate the superiority of the 3D SAT encoding (Kautz *et al.* 2001), with various solvers, over other SAT and CSP models. We propose a partial explanation of the observed performance. Analytically, we focus on the relative conciseness of the 3D model and the pruning power of unit propagation. Empirically, the focus is on the role of the unit-propagation heuristic of the best performing solver, Satz (Li & Anbulagan 1997), which proves crucial to its success, and results in a significant improvement in scalability when imported into the CSP solvers. Our results strongly suggest that SAT encodings of permutation problems (Hnich, Smith, & Walsh 2004) may well prove quite competitive in other domains, in particular when compared with the currently preferred channeling CSP models.

## Introduction

The Quasigroup Completion Problem (QCP) is a very challenging benchmark among combinatorial problems, which has been the focus of much recent interest in the area of constraint programming (Gomes & Shmoys 2002b; Dotú, del Val, & Cebrián 2003). It has a broad range of practical applications such as conflict-free wavelength routing in wide band optical networks, statistical design, and error correcting codes (Gomes & Shmoys 2002b); it has been put forward as a benchmark which can bridge the gap between purely random instances and highly structured problems (Gomes & Shmoys 2002a); and its structure as a multiple permutation problem (Walsh 2001; Hnich, Smith, & Walsh 2004) is common to many other important problems in constraint satisfaction. Thus, solutions that prove effective on QCPs have a good chance of being useful in other problems with similar structure.

Motivated by earlier results by (Gomes & Shmoys 2002b; 2002a) and (Dotú, del Val, & Cebrián 2003) with integer programming and CSP models, we perform a systematic study of modeling choices for quasigroup completion, testing a variety of solvers and heuristics on various SAT and CSP encodings. The clear winner is the SAT 3D-encoding proposed in (Kautz *et al.* 2001), specially with the solver Satz (Li & Anbulagan 1997), closely followed by the solver Satzoo (Eén & Sörensson 2003) on the same encoding. As these two solvers are quite different (one uses a strong form of lookahead in its heuristic, but no backjumping or learning, while the other relies heavily on the last two), the 3D encoding appears to be quite robust as a representation. On the other hand, CSP models perform significantly worse with the two solvers we tried, and standard SAT encodings generated from the CSP models are simply too large in practice. These results strongly suggest that the 3D encoding can turn out to be quite competitive in other permutation problems (many of which arise in quite practical problems (Hnich, Smith, & Walsh 2004)) when compared with the currently preferred channeling models.

The reasons for this appear to be twofold. First, we can show that the 3D encoding (which is basically the "SAT channeling model" of (Hnich, Smith, & Walsh 2004) extended to multiple permutations and dual models) exactly captures the channeling models of QCPs as defined e.g. in (Dotú, del Val, & Cebrián 2003), but in a much more concise way, by collapsing primal and dual variables. Further, we can show that the 3D encoding captures the "support SAT encoding" of the channeling model, hence by results of (Gent 2002), that unit propagation on the 3D encoding achieves the same pruning as arc consistency (MAC) in the CSP channeling model. These results appear easy to extrapolate to other permutation problems (or similar ones with "channeling constraints"), which have received a lot of recent attention (Cheng *et al.* 1999; Walsh 2001; Hnich, Smith, & Walsh 2004). Second, empirically, we identify Satz's UP heuristic as crucial to its success in this domain; as shown by the fact that, when importing the heuristic into our CSP solvers, we obtain significant improvements in their scalability. Further, the improvements are much smaller if we only use lookahead to detect potential wipeouts (i.e. for "failed literal detection"), but choose variables instead by some other standard heuristic such as min-domain.

The structure of this paper is as follows. In sections 2 and

*We thank Carla Gomes for the quasigroup generator lsencode and for computational resources to run the experiments, C. Bessiére for the MAC code, and the authors of all solvers.

†This research has been partially supported by projects TIC2001-1577-C03-03 and TIC2000-0539 of the Ministerio de Ciencia y Tecnologia, Spain.

3 we describe the QCP and various SAT and CSP encodings. We then present in Section 4 the main empirical results for someone who just wants to know the fastest way to solve this kind of problem. Section 5 analyzes the theoretical relationships between representations along the lines discussed above on conciseness and propagation power. Sections 6 and 7 inquire into solver-specific features that may explain the success of Satz. As described above, the focus is on Satz's UP heuristic and its incorporation into CSP solvers. Finally, we list some open questions and directions for future work.

## The Quasigroup Completion Problem

A quasigroup is an ordered pair $(Q, \cdot)$, where $Q$ is a set and $\cdot$ is a binary operation on $Q$ such that the equations $a \cdot x = b$ and $y \cdot a = b$ are uniquely solvable for every pair of elements $a, b$ in $Q$ (Gomes & Shmoys 2002b). The order n of the quasigroup is the cardinality of the set $Q$. A quasigroup can be seen as an $n \times n$ multiplication table which defines a Latin Square, i.e. a matrix which must be filled with "colors" (the elements of the set $Q$) so that the colors of each row are all distinct, and similarly for columns. We focus on the quasigroup completion problem (QCP), which is the NP-complete problem (Colbourn ) of coloring a partially filled Latin square. QCP share with many real world problems a significant degree of structure, while at the same time allowing the systematic generation of difficult problems by randomly filling the quasigroup with preassigned colors. It is thus ideally suited as a testbed for constraint satisfaction algorithms (Gomes & Shmoys 2002a). Experimental studies of the problem have confirmed its interest for research, by for example helping to discover important patterns in problem difficulty such as heavy-tailed behavior (Gomes *et al.* 2000).

Among the kind of structure that has been identified in many constraint satisfaction problems, and which is shared by QCPs, is that of permutation problems. These are constraint satisfaction (sub)problems with the same number of variables as values, where a solution is a permutation of the values (Walsh 2001). Each row and column of a Latin Square defines a permutation problem, thus the QCP is a multiple permutation problem with $2n$ intersecting permutation constraints ($n$ row permutation constraints and $n$ column permutation constraints).

## SAT and CSP Encodings

The two SAT encodings of the QCP of order $n$ considered in this paper, introduced in (Kautz *et al.* 2001), use $n$ Boolean variables per cell; each variable represents a color assigned to a cell, and the total number of variables is $n^3$. The most basic SAT encoding, which is known as 2-dimensional (2-D) encoding, includes clauses that represent the following constraints:

1. at least one color must be assigned to each cell (ALO-1);
2. no color is repeated in the same row (AMO-2); and
3.. no color is repeated in the same column (AMO-3).

The other encoding, which is known as 3-dimensional (3-D) encoding, adds to the 2-D encoding redundant clauses that represent the following constraints:

1. each color must appear at least once in each row (ALO-2);
2. each color must appear at least once in each column (ALO-3); and
3. no two colors are assigned to the same cell (AMO-1).

Both encodings have $\mathcal{O}(n^4)$ clauses. The labels associated to each clause set are explained later.

For the sake of brevity and clarity, the only CSP encoding we describe is the "bichanneling model" of (Dotú, del Val, & Cebrián 2003). It consists of:

- A set of *primal variables* $X = \{x_{ij} \mid 1 \leq i \leq n,\ 1 \leq j \leq n\}$; the value of $x_{ij}$ is the color assigned to the cell in the $i$th row and $j$th column, and $n$ is the order of the quasigroup, i.e. the number of rows and columns.
- Two sets of *dual variables*: $R = \{r_{ik} \mid 1 \leq i \leq n,\ 1 \leq k \leq n\}$, where the value of $r_{ik}$ is the column $j$ where color $k$ occurs in row $i$; and $C = \{c_{jk} \mid 1 \leq j \leq n,\ 0 \leq k \leq n\}$ where the value of $c_{jk}$ represents the row $i$ where color $k$ occurs in column $j$.

The domain of all variables is $\{1, \ldots, n\}$, where these values represent respectively colors, columns, and rows. Variables of different types are linked by channeling constraints:

- *Row channeling constraints* link the primal variables with the row dual variables: $x_{ij} = k \Leftrightarrow r_{ik} = j$.
- *Column channeling constraints* link the primal variables with the column dual variables: $x_{ij} = k \Leftrightarrow c_{jk} = i$.

As pointed out in (Dotú, del Val, & Cebrián 2003), this model is a complete model of the problem; in particular, the so called primal constraints, which explicitly state that no two colors can be repeated in any one row or column, are redundant, and hinder propagation. CSP "channeling" encodings for permutation problems similar to the one presented here are discussed at length in (Hnich, Smith, & Walsh 2004).

## Experimental results: Part 1

We considered four state-of-the art SAT solvers: Satz (Li & Anbulagan 1997), Chaff (Moskewicz *et al.* 2001), Berkmin (Goldberg & Novikov 2002). and Satzoo (Eén & Sörensson 2003). We chose Satz because some authors have claimed that it is the best option to solve QCPs; our experimental results provide evidence of this claim too. We chose Chaff and Satzoo because they were the winners of the two last SAT competitions, and Berkmin because it is often competitive with Chaff. In addition, we tested two CSP solvers, the GAC library described in (van Beek & Chen 1999), and the MAC solver by Regin and Bessiere (Bessière & Régin 1996). Note that for binary CSPs they are simply different implementations of the MAC algorithm.

The instances tested in our experiments are of the QWH type (quasigroup with holes (Kautz *et al.* 2001), generated with `lsencode`), are all satisfiable, and are located near the phase transition.[1] Our samples, with 200 instances each,

[1] Specifically, QWH instances of order $n$ are generated with $\lceil 1.6 \times n^{1.55} \rceil$ holes.

| order | % solved Chaff | Berkmin | Satzoo | Satz | mean Chaff | Berkmin | Satzoo | Satz | median Chaff | Berkmin | Satzoo | Satz |
|---|---|---|---|---|---|---|---|---|---|---|---|---|
| 35 | 99 | 100 | 100 | 100 | 59 | 24 | 37 | 6 | 3.2 | 0.5 | 16 | 1.2 |
| 37 | 96 | 99 | 100 | 100 | 232 | 173 | 129 | 42 | 24 | 4.7 | 5 | 5.8 |
| 40 | 82 | 86 | 96 | 99.5 | 518 | 590 | 861 | 539 | 288 | 112 | 142 | 41 |
| 43 | 50.5 | 62 | 78.5 | 84 | 279 | 1487 | 1799 | 1243 | 1085 | 2178 | 815 | 358 |
| 45 | 46 | 46 | 59.5 | 68 | 380 | 1312 | 1021 | 1181 | > 12000 | > 12000 | 1857 | 1184 |

Table 1: Comparison of Chaff, Berkmin, Satzoo and Satz on the 3-D encoding. Time in seconds, mean of solved instances. Cutoff 12000 seconds. 1 GHz.

| order | % solved Satz | GACvo | mean (solved) Satz | GACvo | median Satz | GACvo |
|---|---|---|---|---|---|---|
| 35 | 100 | 37 | 6 | 2970 | 1.2 | > 12000 |
| 37 | 100 | 11 | 42 | 2572 | 5.8 | > 12000 |
| 40 | 99.5 | 7 | 539 | 4546 | 41 | > 12000 |

Table 2: Comparison of Satz on the 3-D encoding and GAC-vo. Time in seconds. Cutoff 12000 seconds. 1 Ghz.

did not contain "balanced" problems, which are reported to be the hardest; still, we did verify that they are much harder for all solvers than the balanced problems tested in (Dotú, del Val, & Cebrián 2003), which were not close enough to the phase transition for their class.

Of all the solutions tried, we can discard the 2D SAT encoding and the primal CSP models, as they give significantly worse results. Of the remaining encodings, the 3D encoding was clearly superior with the four SAT solvers, with Satz scaling somewhat better than Satzoo and both much better than chaff. On the other hand, the CSP approach proposed in (Dotú, del Val, & Cebrián 2003), which uses MAC on the bichanneling model, scaled much worse on the (harder) problems tested in this paper. There is therefore a clear dividing line between SAT and CSP encodings in terms of performance. Table 1 provides the data for SAT solvers, and Table 2 compares our best SAT solver with the CSP approach (labeled GACvo) of (Dotú, del Val, & Cebrián 2003), which seems to be the best one in the literature, using GAC on the bichanneling model with a special value ordering heuristic (named vdom+ in that paper). Note that the ratio of solved problems for GACvo is much lower than reported in (Dotú, del Val, & Cebrián 2003) for problems of the same order, and that's because our instances are harder.[2]

We will now explore potential explanations for these observations, and ways to improve these results for the CSP approaches drawn from these explanations. Our first focus will be on comparing representations; later we consider solver-specific issues (most importantly, the extra level of propagation and the heuristics of Satz).

[2]The improvements reported for the trichanneling model in (Dotú, del Val, & Cebrián 2003) do not affect scaling behavior, and are pretty much subsumed by the stronger forms of lookahead discussed later. Hence we did not test this model for this paper.

## Comparing models

In order to compare our models formally, we need a small detour through *SAT encodings of CSP models*, a third modeling option that we have not considered so far. In this context, the many-valued CSP variables are represented by means of a set of boolean variables, one for each possible assignment. So, for example, a primal variable $x_{ij}$ becomes a set of boolean variables $x_{ij} = 1, \ldots, x_{ij} = n$. The semantics of CSP domains is then captured by including one ALO ("at least one") clause for each variable, specifying that the variable must take at least one of its possible values, and $O(n^2)$ AMO ("at most one") clauses which specify, for every pair of possible values of a variable, that they can not be satisfied simultaneously. In our bichanneling model, we would have variables $x_{ij} = k$, $r_{ik} = j$ and $c_{jk} = i$, for each triple $j, k, i$, for a total of $3n^3$ variables.

Define the *minimal support encoding* of the bichanneling model as that consisting of AMO-ALO clauses for the three variable types, together with the *channeling clauses* $\neg x_{ij} = k \vee r_{ik} = j$ and $\neg r_{ik} = j \vee x_{ij} = k$, which directly encode the equivalence $x_{i1} = j \Leftrightarrow r_{ij} = k$ which defines the constraint between $x_{ij}$ and $r_{ik}$ (and similarly for column channeling constraints). Clearly, the channeling clauses completely characterize the channeling constraints, hence the minimal support encoding is a complete model.

The *support encoding*, as defined in (Gent 2002), encodes a constraint between two variables $X$ and $Y$ by adding, for each possible value $v$ of $X$, the clause $\neg X = v \vee Y = v_1 \vee \ldots \vee Y = v_k$, where $v_1, \ldots, v_k$ is a list of all values $w$ in the domain of $Y$ such that $(v, w)$ satisfies the constraint, i.e. a list of *supports* for the assignment $X = v$. For the bichanneling model, we can observe that the channeling clauses of the minimal support encoding already encode the supports for $x_{ij} = k$ and $r_{ik} = j$. For values $v \neq k$, the supports for $x_{ij} = v$ are given by the clause $\neg x_{ij} = v \vee \bigvee_{h \in \{1,\ldots,n\}, h \neq j} r_{ik} = h$, and for values $v \neq j$, the supports for $r_{ik} = v$ are given by $\neg r_{ik} = v \vee \bigvee_{h \in \{1,\ldots,n\}, h \neq k} x_{ij} = h$.

**Proposition 1** *Unit resolution obtains the same results on the minimal support encoding as in the support encoding of the bichanneling model.*

**Proof:** Consider e.g. the constraint between $x_{i1}$ and $r_{i2}$ (a similar analysis holds for column channeling constraints). Since the channeling clauses are preserved in the minimal encoding, it suffices to show that the effect of unit propagation on the additional support clauses is also obtained without them. For $v \neq 2$ we have the support clause $\neg x_{i1} = v \vee \bigvee_{h\in\{1,\dots,n\},h\neq 1} r_{i2} = h$. We consider two cases. First, suppose $r_{i2} = 2, \dots, r_{i2} = n$ are all false; we must show that unit resolution on the remaining clauses imply $\neg x_{i1} = v$. Unit resolution on the ALO for $r_{i2}$ obtains $r_{i2} = 1$, which together with the channeling clauses yield $x_{i1} = 2$, and with the AMO for $x_{i1}$, $\neg x_{i1} = v$. Second, suppose $x_{i1} = v$ is true and, say, $r_{i2} = 1$ through $r_{i2} = n - 1$ are all false; we need to show that $r_{i2} = n$ follows by unit resolution. Now, $x_{i1} = v$ implies through AMO $\neg x_{i1} = 2$, and thus $\neg r_{i2} = 1$ using the channeling clauses. This together with the hypothesis of the case and the ALO for $r_{i2}$ allows us to obtain $r_{i2} = n$, as desired. ■

Our second observation is that the binary theory consisting of the channeling clauses for all constraints can be simplified using a strongly connected components (SCC) algorithm such as in (del Val 2001). The SCCs will consist precisely of the triplets of boolean variables of the form $x_{ij} = k$, $r_{ik} = j$ and $c_{jk} = i$. The SCC-based algorithm would then replace each such triplet by a single variable, which we may appropriately call $x_{ijk}$, as in the 3D SAT encodings, and perform the appropriate replacements in the remaining clauses. The result is the following:

- The ALO and AMO clauses for the CSP variables become clauses of the 3D-encoding. Specifically, the clauses labeled ALO-k and AMO-k ($1 \leq k \leq 3$) in the 3D-encoding are the result of rewriting the ALO and AMO clauses for the primal variables (k=1), row dual variables (k=2) and column dual variables (k=3) in the minimal channeling encoding.
- The channeling clauses become tautologies after variable replacement, so they can be eliminated.

The SCC-simplification formally captures the intuitive idea that the triplet of variables $x_{ij} = k$, $r_{ik} = j$ and $c_{jk} = i$ all "mean the same" –color $k$ is in cell $(i, j)$–, and hence that each triplet can be "collapsed" into a single boolean variable $x_{ijk}$, as done in the 3D encoding (and in the "SAT channeling model" of (Hnich, Smith, & Walsh 2004)).

**Proposition 2** *Unit resolution on the 3D model has the same pruning power as MAC on the bichanneling model.*

**Proof:** (Gent 2002) shows that unit resolution on the support encoding of a CSP problem is equivalent to MAC on the original problem. We have just shown that unit resolution on the minimal support encoding is equivalent to unit resolution on the support encoding of the bichanneling model, and that the 3D encoding is simply the minimal support encoding after SCC simplification, which does not affect the power of unit resolution. ■

Thus, the 3D model exactly captures the bichanneling model, without loosing any propagation power, but with 3 times fewer variables ($n^3$ instead of $3n^3$) and without the $4n^3$ channeling clauses of the minimal channeling model. We did in fact try to solve QCPs using a direct encoding of the bichanneling model, with very bad results due to the size of the resulting theories. The above propositions seem to go a long way toward explaining the success of the 3D model.

## Satz's heuristic in QCPs

We now turn to solver and domain-specific features that may explain the observed performance. Thus our next step was to analyze in depth the behavior on QCP instances of the best solver, Satz, so as to incorporate new propagation techniques and heuristics into the CSP solvers from the insights gained. Before going into details, let us recall the variable selection heuristic that implements Satz, which combines MOMS (Maximum Occurrences in clauses of Minimum Size) and UP (Unit Propagation) heuristics. In both heuristics, the goal is to maximize the power of unit propagation. MOMS picks one variable among those that occur the most often in minimal size clauses, since these are more likely to result in propagation. UP goes a step further by actually measuring the number of propagations from each choice. It examines each variable $p$ occurring in a given CNF formula $\phi$ by respectively adding the unit clauses $p$ and $\neg p$ to $\phi$, and independently making two unit propagations, which are used to derive a score for each variable. As a secondary effect, UP detects so-called *failed literals* in $\phi$, which when satisfied falsify $\phi$ in a single unit propagation.

**For each** free variable $x$ **such that** $PROP_z(x)$ is true **do**
(let $F'$ and $F''$ two copies of the formula $F$ under consideration)

> $F'$ := unit-propagation($F' \cup \{x\}$);
> $F''$ := unit-propagation($F'' \cup \{\neg x\}$);
> **If** $\square \in F'$ **and** $\square \in F''$ **then return** "$F$ is unsatisfiable"
> **If** $\square \in F'$ **then** $x$:=0, $F$ := $F''$
> **else if** $\square \in F''$ **then** $x$:=1, $F$ := $F'$
> **If** $\square \notin F'$ **and** $\square \notin F''$ **then**
> let $w(x)$ denote the weight of $x$
> $w(x)$ := number of times that non-binary clauses of $F$ have been reduced when deriving $F'$
> $w(\neg x)$ := number of times that non-binary clauses of $F$ have been reduced when deriving $F''$

**For each** free variable $x$ **do**
$H(x) := w(x) * w(\neg x) * 1024 + w(x) + w(\neg x)$;
Branch on the free variable $x$ with greatest $H(x)$

Figure 1: The variable selection heuristic of *Satz* for $PROP(x, 4)$

In order to reduce the time required to propagate all literals, Satz applies UP to a restricted number of variables that occur in binary clauses by applying a unary predicate, called $PROP_z$, which is defined as follows:

**Definition 1** *Let $\phi$ be a CNF formula; let $PROP(x, i)$ be a binary predicate which is true iff variable $x$ occurs both positively and negatively in binary clauses of $\phi$, and there are at least $i$ occurrences of $x$ in binary clauses of $\phi$; and let $T$ be an integer. $PROP_z(x)$ is defined to be the first of the three predicates $PROP(x, 4), PROP(x, 3), true$ (in this order) whose denotational semantics contains more than a fixed number $T$ of variables. $T$ is set to 10 in Satz.*

After applying unit propagation to a restricted number of variables and detecting failed literals, the heuristic of Satz weights literals with different criteria depending on the predicate applied. For example, when $PROP(x, 4)$ is applied, the heuristic scores each literal $(x, \neg x)$ with the number of times that non-binary clauses have been reduced when propagating the literal. The pseudocode of the variable selec-

| order | % solved GAC-HLA | MAC-HLA | Satz | mean GAC-HLA | MAC-HLA | Satz | median GAC-HLA | MAC-HLA | Satz |
|---|---|---|---|---|---|---|---|---|---|
| 35 | 98 | 98.5 | 100 | 428 | 586 | 6 | 131 | 129 | 1.2 |
| 37 | 86 | 89.5 | 100 | 1360 | 1913 | 42 | 882 | 822 | 5.8 |
| 40 | 52 | 58 | 99.5 | 1770 | 3033 | 539 | 5304 | 8411 | 41 |
| 43 | 30 | 39 | 84 | 1342 | 2668 | 1243 | > 12000 | > 12000 | 358 |
| 45 | 24 | 26 | 68 | 2810 | 3585 | 1181 | > 12000 | > 12000 | 1184 |

Table 3: Comparison of GAC-HLA, MAC-HLA and Satz. Time in seconds, mean of solved instances. Cutoff 12000 seconds. 1 Ghz.

| order | % solved MAC-LA | MAC-HLA | mean MAC-LA | MAC-HLA | median MAC-LA | MAC-HLA |
|---|---|---|---|---|---|---|
| 30 | 96 | 100 | 544 | 18 | 482 | 9 |
| 33 | 91 | 100 | 1753 | 187 | 1256 | 52 |
| 35 | 58 | 98.5 | 2714 | 586 | 4487 | 129 |

Table 4: Comparison of MAC-LA and MAC-HLA. Time in seconds, mean of solved instances. Cutoff 12000 seconds. 1 Ghz.

tion heuristic of Satz for $PROP(x, 4)$ is shown in Figure 1. Function $H(x)$ is used to reach a good balance between weights of positive literals and weights of negative literals.

When solving QCP instances using the 3-D encoding with Satz, we observed that Satz almost always uses the predicate $PROP(x, 4)$, which requires $x$ to occur in both positive and negative binary clauses, with at least 4 occurrences in total. A closer look at the 3-D encoding reveals that Boolean variables that fulfill $PROP(x, 4)$ model CSP variables with domain size 2. The reason is that positive literals only occur in the ALO-1, ALO-2 and ALO-3 constraints, hence the only way to have $x$ occur positively in a binary clause is when one of these clauses becomes binary, in which case the corresponding (primal or dual) CSP variable has domain size 2. Further, it is easy to show that the variables in such positive binary clauses have at least three other negative occurrences from AMO clauses, so that $PROP(x, 4)$ holds. This analysis led us to incorporate the technique of failed literals and the heuristic of Satz into CSP solvers as follows:

1. For each free CSP variable of domain size 2, we propagate each value of the domain in order to see if the domain can be reduced. As a result, the domain can remain as before, can be a singleton or can be empty. In the first case, we weight the variable using the balance function $H$ of Satz's heuristics, where $w(x = i)$ is the number of times that domains have been reduced after propagating the value $i$. In the second case, we fix the variable to the only value of its domain. In the third case, we have detected an inconsistency and we backtrack.
2. We select the first free CSP variable of domain size 2 with greatest value of function $H$.
3. If there is no candidate variable in step 2, we apply the default heuristic of the CSP solver (for example, `min-domain`).

The above description corresponds to what we will call simply look-ahead heuristic (LAH). We refer to the version of GAC (MAC) that incorporates LAH as GAC-LAH (MAC-LAH).

## Experimental results: Part 2

To assess the performance of LAH we performed an empirical investigation. In the first experiment we compared Satz with GAC-LAH and MAC-LAH on sets of 200 instances of order 35, 37, 40 and 45 of the hard region of the phase transition. The results obtained are shown in Table 3. We observed that Satz outperforms GAC-LAH and MAC-LAH, but the differences are not so dramatic as with GAC-vo, which was the most competitive CSP option to solve QCPs. MAC-LAH seems to be slightly superior to GAC-LAH.

In the second experiment, we analyzed if the improvements achieved on CSP solvers are due to the use of lookahead to detect potential wipeouts or to the heuristic function. To this end, we compared MAC-LAH with a variant MAC-LA which uses the same lookahead but chooses variables of minimum domain size instead of applying the heuristic function H to a reduced number of variables; we refer to that version as MAC-LA. The results obtained, shown in Table 4, clearly indicate that the heuristic function plays a central role.

Nevertheless, failed literals do achieve an extra-level of consistency in each search node over that of plain unit propagation, and a natural question to ask is whether stronger forms of consistency could yield better results. We experimented with stronger forms of lookahead without success, but did not try `alldifferent` constraints. Hall's Theorem, as presented in (van Hoere 2001), states that: the constraint $\texttt{alldifferent}(x_1, \ldots, x_n)$ with respective variable domains $D_1, \ldots, D_n$ has a solution if and only if no subset $K \subseteq \{x_1, \ldots, x_n\}$ exists such that $|K| > |\bigcup_{x_i \in K} D_i|$. However, we observed experimentally that, for the QCP and the solvers considered, the condition of the theorem is only violated by subsets of three CSP variables with domain size two. It is easy to show that the lookahead phase of our heuristic, when applied to a variable of domain size two, finds a contradiction for the two values of the do-

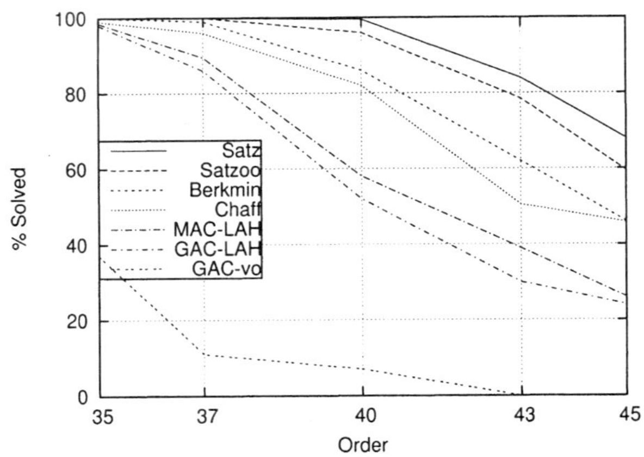


Figure 2: Percent solved for the main solvers.

main and backtracks. So in practice we may be getting the same pruning power as with Hall's theorem.

As a summary of our main results, Figure 2 compares the main approaches discussed in this paper in terms of scalability, plotting percent of solved instances against the order of quasigroups. It can be seen that SAT encodings still scale better, but that the incorporation of the lookahead heuristic inspired by Satz goes a long way toward bridging the gap between the best CSP model available to date, GAC-vo, and the SAT approaches.

## Conclusions and future work

In this paper, we have shown that SAT encodings allow much more scalable solutions to QCP problems, in particular when compared to previous results in the literature. We have explained this performance by properties of the representation and by solver-specific features; and we have shown that those features can also be fruitfully exploited in CSP models to get much better CSP solutions than before.

A number of open questions remain for future work. First, while we can explain Satz's performance and exploit its features in CSP approaches, a similar study could be carried out for Satzoo. This might help in understanding the role of CBJ and learning in QCPs, as in our experience they do not help with QCPs formulated as CSPs. Second, it appears that the single-lookahead heuristic with a MAC-GAC solver may do quite a bit of redundant work, which may already be done when ensuring arc-consistency in the previous search level; exploiting this may lead to a substantially faster implementation of the heuristic. Finally, we plan to study the effect of many-valued models (Ansótegui *et al.* 2002) as an intermediate and potentially more concise representation between SAT and CSP.

## References


Ansótegui, C.; Manyà, F.; Béjar, R.; and Gomes, C. 2002. Solving many-valued SAT encodings with local search. In *Proc. of the Workshop on Probabilistics Approaches in Search, AAAI-2002*.

Bessière, C., and Régin, J. 1996. MAC and combined heuristics: Two reasons to forsake FC (and CBJ?) on hard problems. In *CP-96, 2nd Int. Conf. on Principles and Practice of Constraint Programming*, 61–75.

Cheng, B.; Choi, K.; Lee, J.; and Wu, J. 1999. Constraint propagation by redundant modeling: an experience report. *Constraints* 167–192.

Colbourn, C. 1984. The complexity of completing partial latin squares. *Discrete Applied Mathematics* 25–30.

del Val, A. 2001. Simplifying binary propositional theories into connected components twice as fast. In *LPAR'01, Proc. 8th Int. Conf. on Logic for Programming, Artificial Intelligence and Reasoning*. LNCS, Springer-Verlag.

Dotú, I.; del Val, A.; and Cebrián, M. 2003. Redundant modeling for the quasigroup completion problem. In *Proc. CP-2003*, 288–302. Springer LNCS 2833.

Eén, N., and Sörensson, N. 2003. Satzoo. http://www.math.chalmers.se/~een/Satzoo/.

Gent, I. P. 2002. Arc consistency in SAT. In *Proc. ECAI'2002*.

Goldberg, E., and Novikov, Y. 2002. Berkmin: A fast and robust sat-solver. In *Proc. of DATE'02*.

Gomes, C., and Shmoys, D. B. 2002a. Completing quasigroups or latin squares: A structured graph coloring problem. In *Proc. Computational Symposium on Graph Coloring and Extensions*.

Gomes, C., and Shmoys, D. B. 2002b. The promise of LP to boost CSP techniques for combinatorial problems. In *CP-AI-OR'02*, 291–305.

Gomes, C.; Selman, B.; Crato, N.; and Kautz, H. 2000. Heavy-tailed phenomena in satisfiability and constraint satisfaction problems. *Journal of Automated Reasoning* 24(1/2):67–100.

Hnich, B.; Smith, B. M.; and Walsh, T. 2004. Dual modelling of permutation and injection problems. *Journal of Artificial Intelligence Research*. to appear.

Kautz, H. A.; Ruan, Y.; Achlioptas, D.; Gomes, C. P.; Selman, B.; and Stickel, M. 2001. Balance and filtering in structured satisfiable problems. In *IJCAI'01*, 351–358.

Li, C. M., and Anbulagan. 1997. Look-ahead versus look-back for satisfiability problems. In *CP'97, Proc. Int. Conf. on Principles of Constraint Programming*, 341–355. Springer LNCS 1330.

Moskewicz, M.; Madigan, C.; Zhao, Y.; Zhang, L.; and Malik, S. 2001. Chaff: Engineering an efficient sat solver. In *39th Design Automation Conference*.

van Beek, P., and Chen, X. 1999. Cplan: A constraint programming approach to planning. In *AAAI'99*, 585–590.

van Hoere, W. 2001. The alldifferent constraint: A survey. In *Proc. 6th Annual Workshop of the ERCIM Working Group on Constraints, Prague*.

Walsh, T. 2001. Permutation problems and channeling constraints. In *LPAR-2001*.

# Leap Before You Look: An Effective Strategy in an Oversubscribed Scheduling Problem*

**Laura Barbulescu** and **L. Darrell Whitley** and **Adele E. Howe**
Computer Science Dept.
Colorado State University
Fort Collins, CO 80523
email:{laura,whitley,howe}@cs.colostate.edu

### Abstract

Oversubscribed scheduling problems require removing or partially satisfying tasks when enough resources are not available. For a particular oversubscribed problem, Air Force Satellite Control Network scheduling, we find that the best approaches make long leaps in the search space. We find this is in part due to large plateaus in the search space. Algorithms moving only one task at a time are impractical. Both a genetic algorithm and Squeaky Wheel Optimization (SWO) make long leaps in the search space and produce good solutions almost 100 times faster than local search. Greedy initialization is shown to be critical to good performance, but is not as important as directed leaps. When using fewer than 2000 evaluations, SWO shows superior performance; with 8000 evaluations, a genetic algorithm using a population seeded with greedy solutions further improves on the SWO results.

## Introduction

Variants of local search have been shown to be extremely effective and robust for scheduling problems (Vaessens, Aarts, & Lenstra 1996; Lemaître, Verfaillie, & Jouhaud 2000). When heuristics are available for focusing attention on parts of the schedule, then iterative repair performs well (e.g., (Kramer & Smith 2003)). Both these classes of algorithms adopt an incremental view: propose a change, evaluate the result, accept or retract the change, and identify the next potential changes. The incremental strategy works well because minor changes may cause a cascade effect in the schedule and these cascade effects are difficult to predict.

In contrast, a genetic algorithm, *Genitor* (Whitley 1989), has shown better performance on an oversubscribed scheduling application: Air Force Satellite Control Network (AFSCN) access scheduling (Barbulescu *et al.* 2004b). *Genitor* proposes large changes to a schedule at each iteration. It represents a proposed schedule as a permutation (a prioritization) of the tasks, which can be translated into an actual schedule with assignment of tasks to time slots on resources. The crossover operator (Syswerda 1991) randomly selects about half of the positions in a permutation for re-ordering, typically producing a large change in the schedule.

One hypothesis about the superior performance is that the genetic algorithm is *learning* patterns of task interactions. An analysis of the search space and solutions showed that a simple domain specific pattern emerged and provided evidence for more complex patterns (Barbulescu *et al.* 2004a).

Aside from such patterns, another explanatory hypothesis is that the large leaps taken by *Genitor* at each iteration are needed to effectively traverse the search space. We find evidence to support this hypothesis in the performance of another method that makes directed leaps: Squeaky Wheel Optimization (SWO)(Joslin & Clements 1999). SWO focuses attention on the most contentious tasks in the schedule and simultaneously moves those requests forward in the prioritized permutation, thereby causing other less troublesome tasks to move backward. We show that solutions appear to be residing on plateaus, which tend to be difficult for incremental methods to traverse. We also examine whether the power is obtained from simply starting closer to the best solutions (i.e., the role of initialization) and whether *Genitor* and SWO seem to be following similar paths to their solutions. We find that narrowing the distance to the optimal solutions certainly helps, but is not the only factor at work, and that *Genitor* and SWO follow rather different paths through the search space. Thus, these algorithms represent two different, but almost equally effective methods for making large leaps across the search space.

## AFSCN Scheduling

The U.S.A. AFSCN is responsible for coordinating communications between users on the ground and satellites in space. Communications to more than 100 satellites are performed through 16 antennas at nine ground stations located around the globe. To reserve a particular antenna for a period of time, users submit a task request which includes a required duration, a time window within which the duration must occur and a desired resource. Alternate time windows and antennas may also be specified. Approximately 500 requests are typically received for a single day. Separate schedules are produced for each day.

Some antennas are typically oversubscribed. After human schedulers attempt to fit all tasks into the schedule, often about 120 conflicts, or requests that could not be accommo-

*With apologies to Keith Golden, we have co-opted the clever title to show how it applies to scheduling as well as planning dated, remain. Because satellites are extremely expensive resources and the tasks may be mission critical, absolute rejection of requests is not an option. Rather, human schedulers must engage in a complex, time-consuming arbitration process to create a conflict-free schedule.

For our studies, we use 12 days of actual data from the AFSCN: seven consecutive days from 1992 and five days from 2002-2003[1]. These data demonstrate the changing nature of the task (e.g., differences in size and differences in utilization of resources between 1992 and 2002/2003) and exhibit the complex structure of real problems, which we have not been able to replicate in synthesized problems.

Analyses of these problems have shown a high degree of contention for resources, which leads to a high branching factor for most search algorithms (Barbulescu *et al.* 2004a). *Genitor* has shown the best performance on this problem so far (Barbulescu *et al.* 2004b; 2004a), finding schedules that minimize the number of conflicts. It appears that *Genitor* may be learning patterns, some that are easily translated into heuristics (e.g., schedule the low altitude satellite requests first) and some that are more complex.

The primary criterion that has been used in attempts to automate AFSCN scheduling is minimizing the number of conflicts (e.g., (Gooley 1993; Parish 1994)). This results in a very coarse evaluation function for an NP-hard problem where the search space is exponentially large (Barbulescu *et al.* 2004b). Minimizing conflicts also means that large tasks are generally bumped more often than smaller tasks. Conversations with human schedulers indicate that they often negotiate changes in *duration* of tasks to fit in additional tasks–and that everything must eventually be scheduled, even if tasks must be modified. Thus, a better evaluation criterion and the one used in this paper is to minimize the sum of overlaps between conflicting tasks in a proposed schedule. This provides the human schedulers with a better starting point for negotiations. It also provides a richer evaluation function.

## Related Work

Other examples of multiple resource, oversubscribed problems include applications such as USAF Air Mobility Command (AMC) scheduling (Kramer & Smith 2003), NASA's shuttle ground processing (Deale *et al.* 1994), and satellite scheduling (Frank *et al.* 2001; Globus *et al.* 2003).

AMC scheduling assigns delivery missions to air wings. Kramer and Smith (Kramer & Smith 2003) adopt an iterative repair approach by greedily creating an initial schedule by priority order and then attempting to insert unscheduled tasks by retracting and re-arranging conflicting tasks.

Globus et al.(2003) compared a genetic algorithm, simulated annealing, SWO and hill climbing on a simplified, synthetic form of the satellite scheduling problem (two satellites with a single instrument). The genetic algorithm and SWO techniques were reported to perform poorly. However, similarly to what we found for AFSCN scheduling, multiple moves performed better than single moves.

For both AFSCN scheduling and MAXSAT, it is possible to quickly identify key variables or tasks that are unsatisfied. In both cases, there is an opportunity to resolve these unsatisfied variables or requests and to use a greedy selection strategy for changing a variable or schedule assignment.

Another similarity is that the search spaces in both cases have large flat regions or plateaus (Gent & Walsh 1993). In MAXSAT, these plateaus result from the fact that the evaluation function is a linear combination of subfunctions: each clause is a subfunction. In oversubscribed scheduling problems, moves affecting only requests that do not compete for the same resources or time windows have no impact on the evaluation function. Strategies for "walking" across these flat regions are therefore key components for successful search in both domains. One strategy that is similar in flavor to the SWO strategy used here is JumpSAT (Gent & Walsh 1995). Instead of flipping *one* variable in an unsatisfied clause, one variable is flipped in *each* unsatisfied clause. While not state of the art for MAXSAT, JumpSat was shown to outperform greedy local search (the GSAT algorithm).

MAXSAT and AFSCN differ in two important ways. First, the neighborhood size is $O(N)$ for MAXSAT while it is $O(N^2)$ for scheduling (where $N$ is the number of variables or requests). Second, MAXSAT has a fast partial evaluation that allows one to quickly evaluate a move. Our scheduling domain requires that a new schedule be built from scratch and evaluated after every move.

## Minimizing Overlap in AFSCN

A wide range of approaches have been tested for minimizing conflicts in AFSCN scheduling. One of the earliest, Gooley (1993), exploited complex heuristics and mixed integer programming. Attempts using constraint based methods (e.g., texture-based (Beck *et al.* 1997) and minslack (Smith & Cheng 1993)) worked well on small, synthetic problems, but did not scale well to the actual data (Barbulescu *et al.* 2002); similarly, attempts to use constructive tree search algorithms, such as HBSS (Bresina 1996), have so far not produced good results, probably because the ordering heuristics are inadequate.

Some of the approaches do not translate well for minimizing overlaps because they were carefully tuned for the original evaluation metric. Local search and *Genitor* are easily adapted. Additionally, because the evaluation metric is less coarse, new algorithms such as SWO are viable. This section describes the set of algorithms and their performance.

### Algorithms

The three algorithms considered encode solutions using a permutation $\pi$ of the $n$ task request IDs (i.e., $[1..n]$); a *schedule builder* is used to generate solutions from the permutation. In the order defined by $\pi$, each task request is assigned to the first available resource from its list of alternatives and at the earliest possible starting time. If a request cannot be scheduled without conflict on any of the alternative resources, it overlaps; we assign such a request to the alterna-

[1]We thank Dr. James T. Moore, Associate Professor, Dept. of Operational Sciences, Air Force Institute of Technology and Brian Bayless and William Szary from Schriever Air Force Base for providing the data.

tive resource on which the overlap with requests scheduled so far is minimized.

Genetic algorithms were found to perform well in some early studies (Parish 1994) and for an abstraction of NASA's Earth Observing Satellite (EOS) scheduling problem (Wolfe & Sorensen 2000). For our studies, we use the version of *Genitor* originally developed for a warehouse scheduling application (Starkweather *et al.* 1991). Like all genetic algorithms, *Genitor* maintains a population of solutions. In each step of the algorithm, a pair of parent solutions is selected, and a crossover operator is used to generate a single child solution, which then replaces the worst solution in the population. Selection of parent solutions is based on the rank of their fitness, relative to other solutions in the population. Following Parish (1994), we use Syswerda's (1991) position-based crossover operator.

As the local search algorithm, we implemented a hill-climber. Because it has been successfully applied to a number of well-known scheduling problems, we selected a domain-independent move operator, the *shift* operator. From a current solution $\pi$, a neighborhood is defined by considering all $(N-1)^2$ pairs $(x, y)$ of positions in $\pi$, subject to the restriction that $y \neq x - 1$. The neighbor $\pi'$ corresponding to the position pair $(x, y)$ is produced by *shifting* the job at position $x$ into the position $y$, while leaving all other relative job orders unchanged. Given the large neighborhood size, we use the shift operator in conjunction with next-descent hill-climbing: the neighbors of the current solution are examined in a random order, and the first neighbor with either a lower or equal sum of overlaps is accepted.

SWO (Joslin & Clements 1999) repeatedly iterates through a cycle composed of three phases. First, a greedy solution is built, based on priorities associated with the elements in the problem. Then, the solution is analyzed and the elements causing "trouble" are identified, based on their contribution to the objective function. Third, the priorities of such "trouble makers" are modified, such that they will be considered earlier during the next iteration. The cycle is then repeated, until a termination condition is met.

In our implementation of SWO, we identify the overlapping requests as the "trouble spots" in the schedule. We sort the overlapping requests in increasing order of their contribution to the sum of overlaps. We associate with each such request a distance to move forward, based on its rank in the sorted order. We fix the minimum distance of moving forward to one and the maximum distance to five (this seems to work better than other possible values we tried). The distance values are equally distributed among the ranks. We move the requests forward in the permutation in increasing order of their contribution to the sum of overlaps (smaller overlaps first). We tried versions of SWO where the distance to move forward is proportional with the contribution to the sum of overlaps or is fixed. However, these versions performed worse than the rank based distance implementation described above.

We construct the initial greedy permutation for SWO by sorting the requests in increasing order of their flexibility. Our flexibility measure is identical to that defined for AMC (Kramer & Smith 2003): the duration of the request divided by the average time window on the possible alternative resources. We break ties based on the number of alternative resources available. For requests with equal flexibilities and numbers of alternative resources, the earlier request is scheduled first. For multiple runs of SWO, we restart it from a modified permutation created by performing 20 random swaps in the initial greedy permutation.

### Performance

The results of running each of the algorithms are summarized in Table 1. For each of the three algorithms, we report the best and mean value and the standard deviation observed over 30 runs, with 8000 evaluations per run. CPU times corresponding to 30 runs of each algorithm (on a Dell Precision 650, 3.06 GHz Xeon, running Linux) are also included. "Size" is the number of requests for that date. In the third column, we include the best values we have seen for the sum of overlaps; these values were obtained by running *Genitor* with the population size increased to 400 and up to 50,000 evaluations. Both *Genitor* and local search were initialized from random permutations.

While *Genitor* and SWO perform equally well for the data from 1992 and R5, SWO produces the best results for the remaining data. The performance of local search is relatively poor: worse mins/means and higher variance. If SWO is allowed up to 50,000 evaluations, SWO does not find better solutions, unlike *Genitor* which continues to improve the solution quality.

## Leap or Creep?

Both SWO and *Genitor* make large changes to the permutation at each step before evaluating the resulting schedule. Thus, another hypothesis for *Genitor*'s success is that effectively searching the space requires a large step size or "leaping before looking". Local search adopts a conservative approach by assessing the results of each change. Local search can find close to optimal solutions for these problems provided that it searches for a very long time (500,000 evaluations). In this case, the search space may be too big, and the information gained at each evaluation may be too little to justify the expense of evaluation after each move.

To test the hypothesis that large step size is critical to good performance, we look at four factors. First, we examine the neighborhood of permutations to assess whether the search space does contain plateaus and more specifically, whether solutions appear to reside on them. Second, we assess the role of initialization in traversing the space: are Genitor and SWO succeeding because they just start out closer to the solution? Third, we control for the effects of multiple moves by comparing SWO to a version that makes one move at a time. Finally, we look at the rate of solution improvement over time for both SWO and *Genitor*.

### Plateaus

One reason local search has trouble with AFSCN scheduling are plateaus. We count the number of pairwise shifts in 30 random and 30 best known solutions that produce no

| Day | Date | Size | Best Known | Genitor Min | Genitor Mean | Genitor Stdev | Genitor CPU | Local Search Min | Local Search Mean | Local Search Stdev | Local Search CPU | SWO Min | SWO Mean | SWO Stdev | SWO CPU |
|---|---|---|---|---|---|---|---|---|---|---|---|---|---|---|---|
| A1 | 10/12/92 | 322 | 104 | 104 | 106.9 | 0.6 | 107 | 255 | 375.0 | 54.4 | 96 | 104 | 104 | 0.0 | 97 |
| A2 | 10/13/92 | 302 | 13 | 13 | 13 | 0.0 | 101 | 65 | 174.6 | 50.6 | 92 | 13 | 13.4 | 2.0 | 91 |
| A3 | 10/14/92 | 311 | 28 | 28 | 28.4 | 1.2 | 102 | 144 | 252.0 | 52.9 | 91 | 28 | 28.1 | 0.6 | 89 |
| A4 | 10/15/92 | 318 | 9 | 9 | 9.2 | 0.7 | 107 | 153 | 239.6 | 55.4 | 97 | 9 | 13.3 | 7.8 | 95 |
| A5 | 10/16/92 | 305 | 30 | 30 | 30.4 | 0.5 | 104 | 142 | 220.1 | 59.3 | 93 | 30 | 30 | 0.0 | 91 |
| A6 | 10/17/92 | 299 | 45 | 45 | 45.1 | 0.4 | 105 | 190 | 277.4 | 46.7 | 93 | 45 | 45.1 | 0.3 | 92 |
| A7 | 10/18/92 | 297 | 46 | 46 | 46.1 | 0.6 | 90 | 137 | 219.6 | 40.4 | 81 | 46 | 46 | 0.0 | 79 |
| R1 | 03/07/02 | 483 | 774 | 913 | 987.8 | 40.8 | 189 | 1559 | 1830.9 | 143.4 | 175 | 798 | 841.4 | 14.0 | 178 |
| R2 | 03/20/02 | 457 | 486 | 519 | 540.7 | 13.3 | 162 | 1078 | 1235.5 | 92.8 | 146 | 491 | 503.8 | 6.5 | 148 |
| R3 | 03/26/03 | 426 | 250 | 275 | 292.3 | 10.9 | 144 | 788 | 967.7 | 96.7 | 133 | 265 | 270.1 | 2.8 | 130 |
| R4 | 04/02/03 | 431 | 725 | 738 | 755.4 | 10.3 | 140 | 1139 | 1287.1 | 84.2 | 126 | 731 | 736.2 | 3.0 | 125 |
| R5 | 05/02/03 | 419 | 146 | 146 | 146.5 | 1.9 | 127 | 351 | 457.9 | 69.1 | 112 | 146 | 146.0 | 0.0 | 109 |

Table 1: Performance of *Genitor*, local search and SWO in terms of the best and mean sum of overlaps. All statistics are taken over 30 independent runs, with 8000 evaluations per run. Best values we have obtained for these problems are included in the third column. Dates are given shorthand names to indicate whether they belong to the AFIT set (A) or are recent (R). CPU times (in seconds) corresponding to the 30 runs of each algorithm are also shown.

change in the resulting schedule (non-interacting pairs). Table 2 shows the mean number of non-interacting pairs of tasks. *Average Percentage* corrects for problem size differences. More than 33% of the shifts make no change to the schedule. Best known solutions (except for R3) have slightly more non-interacting pairs than do random solutions.

| Day | Total Pairs | Non-interacting Pairs: Random Perms Mean | Random Perms Avg % | Optimal Perms Mean | Optimal Perms Avg % |
|---|---|---|---|---|---|
| A1 | 51681 | 20767.2 | 40.2 | 22925.8 | 44.3 |
| A2 | 45451 | 19684.3 | 43.3 | 21169.7 | 46.6 |
| A3 | 48205 | 19859.6 | 41.2 | 20373.5 | 42.3 |
| A4 | 50403 | 19491.7 | 38.7 | 20729.1 | 41.1 |
| A5 | 46360 | 18371.3 | 39.6 | 19238.9 | 41.5 |
| A6 | 44551 | 16771.7 | 37.6 | 17811.7 | 39.9 |
| A7 | 43956 | 18406.9 | 41.9 | 20220.7 | 46.0 |
| R1 | 116403 | 39380.1 | 33.8 | 37805.9 | 36.2 |
| R2 | 104196 | 34362.7 | 32.9 | 33894.3 | 37.4 |
| R3 | 90525 | 33470.8 | 36.9 | 41285.6 | 35.5 |
| R4 | 92665 | 34147.1 | 36.8 | 36816.9 | 39.7 |
| R5 | 87571 | 34180.8 | 39.0 | 35891.4 | 40.9 |

Table 2: Mean and average % for the number of pairs of non-interacting requests over 30 random and optimal permutations. Second column is the total number of request pairs in the permutation.

Intuition might suggest that *Genitor* is likely to locate and jump onto the middle of a large plateau, while gradient methods might be more likely to find the edge of a plateau. To test this idea, we apply a random walk to solutions from Genitor and local search with the constraint that after each shift the new permutation has the same value as the initial one. We then compute the pairwise distance after increments of shifts (10, 50, 100 and 500). *Genitor*'s solutions drift somewhat further than do those of local search (average distance of 19869 versus 19350). However, the difference is small, and neither ever revisits the same point in the space even after 500 shifts.

| Day | Seeded Genitor Min | Seeded Genitor Mean | Seeded Genitor Stdev | GreedyStartLS Min | GreedyStartLS Mean | GreedyStartLS Stdev |
|---|---|---|---|---|---|---|
| A1 | 104 | 107.9 | 3.0 | 104 | 122.5 | 10.6 |
| A2 | 13 | 13 | 0.0 | 13 | 23.4 | 14.9 |
| A3 | 28 | 28 | 0.0 | 28 | 33.0 | 6.1 |
| A4 | 9 | 9 | 0.0 | 9 | 14.4 | 10.1 |
| A5 | 30 | 30 | 0.0 | 30 | 43.1 | 13.8 |
| A6 | 45 | 45 | 0.0 | 45 | 47.5 | 5.5 |
| A7 | 46 | 46 | 0.0 | 46 | 81.6 | 22.9 |
| R1 | 794 | 828.3 | 19.3 | 958 | 1062.4 | 41.4 |
| R2 | 486 | 494.5 | 7.7 | 554 | 600.7 | 26.2 |
| R3 | 250 | 257 | 5.9 | 356 | 451.8 | 37.9 |
| R4 | 725 | 730.6 | 6.5 | 754 | 848.5 | 51.6 |
| R5 | 146 | 146 | 0.0 | 146 | 153.4 | 8.1 |

Table 3: Performance of Genitor and local search when initialized from greedy permutations. All statistics are taken over 30 independent runs, with 8000 evaluations per run.

## Role of Initialization

While *Genitor* and local search normally start with random permutations, SWO is initialized with a greedy solution. The greedy solution can be quite good; for two problems (A6 and R5), the greedy solution translated into best known values. In this section, we investigate the effects of initializing the search from similar greedy solutions for all three algorithms considered.

We modify the local search algorithm by starting it from the SWO greedy initial permutation and from variations of it obtained by randomly swapping 20 pairs of tasks (as in the initialization for SWO); we call this *GreedyStartLS*. We also seed the initial population of *Genitor* (size 200) with the greedy initial permutation built for SWO and 199 variations of this permutation, obtained by randomly swapping 20

| Day | Size | SWO1move | | |
|---|---|---|---|---|
| | | Min | Mean | Stdev |
| A1 | 322 | 113 | 115.0 | 4.2 |
| A2 | 302 | 13 | 13.1 | 0.3 |
| A3 | 311 | 28 | 29.2 | 1.9 |
| A4 | 318 | 9 | 11.6 | 3.0 |
| A5 | 305 | 30 | 31.8 | 2.7 |
| A6 | 299 | 45 | 45.9 | 1.7 |
| A7 | 297 | 46 | 49.1 | 3.7 |
| R1 | 483 | 999 | 1125.2 | 54.6 |
| R2 | 457 | 600 | 627.6 | 13.3 |
| R3 | 426 | 288 | 313.7 | 15.8 |
| R4 | 431 | 820 | 842.0 | 10.9 |
| R5 | 419 | 146 | 157.0 | 7.9 |

Table 4: Performance of a modified version of SWO where only one request is moved forward. All statistics are taken over 30 independent runs, with 8000 evaluations per run.

pairs of requests; we call the new algorithm *Seeded Genitor*. We compare the results of random initializations (Table 1) to those of running *GreedyStartLS* and *Seeded Genitor* (shown in Table 3). The initialization from a greedy permutation induces a major improvement in the local search performance. Initializing the *Genitor* population also results in major improvements on the results obtained for the new days of data (in fact, except for R1 all the results are equal to the best known results). Also, while SWO is still better than *GreedyStartLS*, *Seeded Genitor* finds equal or better solutions that does SWO.

### Multiple Moves in the Search Space

We hypothesize that multiple moves are needed to effectively traverse the search space to good solutions. To test this, we implement a version of the SWO where only the request that contributes the most to the sum of the overlaps is moved forward. We use a distance proportional to the contribution of the chosen request to the sum of overlaps. We call this new algorithm SWO1Move. The results obtained by running SWO1Move for 30 runs, with 8000 evaluations per run are presented in Table 4.

The performance of SWO worsens significantly when only one task is moved forward. In fact, *GreedyStartLS* outperforms SWO1move, suggesting just focusing on the major contributors to the evaluation error is not enough. These results support the conjecture that the performance of SWO is due to the simultaneous moves of requests.

### Progress toward the Solution

To further compare the genetic algorithm and SWO, we track the best value obtained so far when running the two algorithms. For each problem, we collect the best value found by SWO and *Seeded Genitor* in increments of 100 evaluations for up to 8000 evaluations. We average these values over 30 runs of SWO and *Seeded Genitor*, respectively. A typical example is presented in Figure 1. In the beginning, SWO progresses very fast to a good solution, but further improvements over time are small. On the other hand, *Seeded Genitor* steadily progresses in smaller steps toward the best solution, and while it takes longer to reach values as good as the ones produced by SWO, it outperforms SWO given enough evaluations.

## Conclusion

For AFSCN oversubscribed scheduling, directed leaping appears to be an effective strategy for traversing its large search space. Both the genetic algorithm and SWO make long leaps in the search space and quickly arrive at good solutions. These leaps may change as much as 50% of the schedule at each iteration. By contrast, local search, by only moving one task at a time, results in a slow creep through the search space. One explanation for the relatively poor performance of algorithms that creep is that large plateaus are present in the search space.

We investigate the role of initializing the search closer to the best solution (as in SWO). We find that initialization helps. However, the multiple moves are more important: the performance of SWO is significantly worse when only one of the conflicting tasks is moved.

Finally, we show that *Genitor* and SWO follow different paths through the search space. SWO finds good solutions fast. Given more evaluations, *Genitor* finds better solutions.

The success in transferring the flexibility measure from Air Mobility Command scheduling suggests the domains may have a great deal in common. Future work will investigate whether our results generalize to other oversubscribed scheduling problems such as AMC.

## Acknowledgments

This research was sponsored by the Air Force Office of Scientific Research, Air Force Materiel Command, USAF, under grant number F49620-03-1-0233. The U.S. Government is authorized to reproduce and distribute reprints for Governmental purposes notwithstanding any copyright notation thereon. Adele Howe was also supported by the National Science Foundation under Grant No. IIS-0138690. Any opinions, findings, and conclusions or recommendations expressed in this material are those of the author(s) and do not necessarily reflect the views of the National Science Foundation. We wish to thank the AAAI reviewers for their insightful comments and an anonymous reviewer of a previous paper for, among other excellent advice, suggesting we take a second look at SWO.

## References

Barbulescu, L.; Howe, A.; Watson, J.; and Whitley, L. 2002. Satellite range scheduling: A comparison of genetic, heuristic and local search. In *Proceedings of The Seventh International Conference on Parallel Problem Solving from Nature(PPSNVII)*.

Barbulescu, L.; Howe, A.; Whitley, L.; and Roberts, M. 2004a. Trading places: How to schedule more in a multi-resource oversubscribed scheduling problem. In *Proceedings of the International Conference on Planning and Scheduling*. to appear.

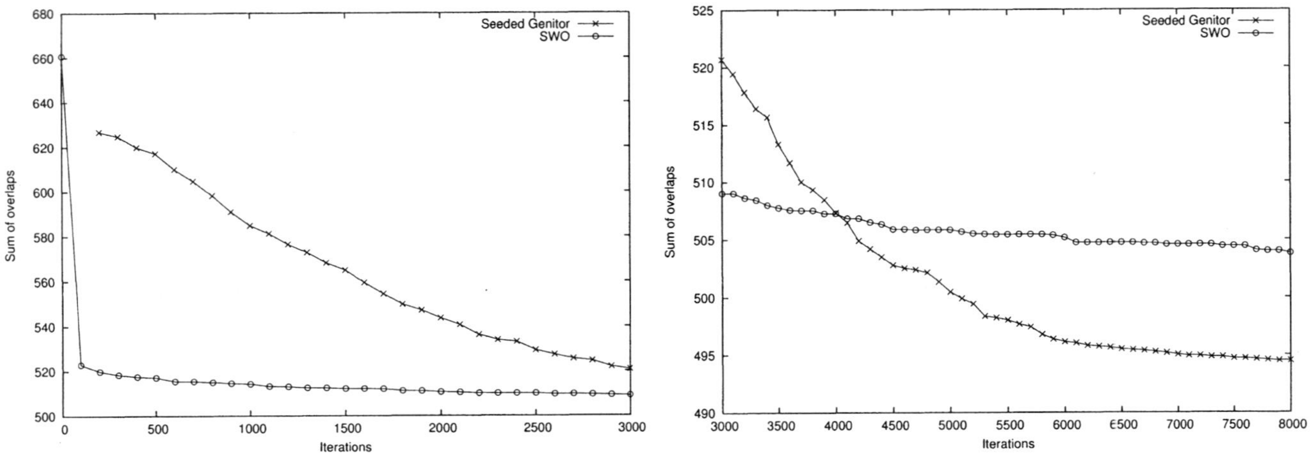


Figure 1: Evolutions of the average best value obtained by SWO and *Genitor* during 8000 evaluations, over 30 runs. The left figure depicts the improvement in the average best value over the first 3000 evaluations. The last 5000 evaluations are depicted in the right figure; note that the scale is different on the y-axis.

Barbulescu, L.; Watson, J.; Whitley, D.; and Howe, A. 2004b. Scheduling space-ground communications for the Air Force satellite control network. *Journal of Scheduling* 7(1):7–34.

Beck, J. C.; Davenport, A. J.; Sitarski, E. M.; and Fox, M. S. 1997. Texture-based Heuristic for Scheduling Revisited. In *Proceedings of the Fourteenth National Conference on Artificial Intelligence (AAAI-97)*, 241–248. Providence, RI: AAAI Press / MIT Press.

Bresina, J. 1996. Heuristic-Biased Stochastic Sampling. In *Proceedings of the Thirteenth National Conference on Artificial I ntelligence*, 271–278.

Deale, M.; Yvanovich, M.; Schnitzuius, D.; Kautz, D.; Carpenter, M.; Zweben, M.; Davis, G.; and Daun, B. 1994. The Space Shuttle ground processing scheduling system. In Zweben, M., and Fox, M., eds., *Intelligent Scheduling*. Morgan Kaufmann. 423–449.

Frank, J.; Jonsson, A.; Morris, R.; and Smith, D. 2001. Planning and scheduling for fleets of earth observing satellites. In *Proceedings of the Sixth International Symposium on Artificial Intelligence, Robotics, Automation and Space*.

Gent, I., and Walsh, T. 1993. Toward and Understanding of Hill-climbing Procedures for SAT. In *Proceedings of the Eleventh National Conference on Artificial Intelligence (AAAI-93)*. AAAI Press.

Gent, I., and Walsh, T. 1995. Unsatisfied variables in local search. In *Hybrid Problems, Hybrid Solutions*, 73–85. IOS Press Amsterdam.

Globus, A.; Crawford, J.; Lohn, J.; and Pryor, A. 2003. Scheduling earth observing satellites with evolutionary agorithms. In *International Conference on Space Mission Challenges for Information Technology*.

Gooley, T. 1993. Automating the Satellite Range Scheduling Process. In *Masters Thesis*. Air Force Institute of Technology.

Joslin, D. E., and Clements, D. P. 1999. "Squeaky Wheel" Optimization. In *Journal of Artificial Intelligence Research*, volume 10, 353–373.

Kramer, L., and Smith, S. 2003. Maximizing flexibility: A retraction heuristic for oversubscribed scheduling problems. In *Proceedings of 18th International Joint Conference on Artificial Intelligence*.

Lemaître, M.; Verfaillie, G.; and Jouhaud, F. 2000. How to manage the new generation of Agile Earth Observation Satellites. In *6th International SpaceOps Symposium (Space Operations)*.

Parish, D. 1994. A Genetic Algorithm Approach to Automating Satellite Range Scheduling. In *Masters Thesis*. Air Force Institute of Technology.

Smith, S., and Cheng, C. 1993. Slack-based Heuristics for Constraint Satisfaction Problems. In *Proceedings of the Eleventh National Conference on Artificial Intelligence (AAAI-93)*, 139–144. Washington, DC: AAAI Press.

Starkweather, T.; McDaniel, S.; Mathias, K.; Whitley, D.; and Whitley, C. 1991. A Comparison of Genetic Sequencing Operators. In Booker, L., and Belew, R., eds., *Proc. of the 4th Int'l. Conf. on GAs*, 69–76. Morgan Kaufmann.

Syswerda, G. 1991. Schedule Optimization Using Genetic Algorithms. In Davis, L., ed., *Handbook of Genetic Algorithms*. NY: Van Nostrand Reinhold. chapter 21.

Vaessens, R. J. M.; Aarts, E. H. L.; and Lenstra, J. K. 1996). Job shop scheduling by local search. *INFORMS J. Comput.* 8(3):302–317.

Whitley, L. D. 1989. The GENITOR Algorithm and Selective Pressure: Why Rank Based Allocation of Reproductive Trials is Best. In Schaffer, J. D., ed., *Proc. of the 3rd Int'l. Conf. on GAs*, 116–121. Morgan Kaufmann.

Wolfe, W. J., and Sorensen, S. E. 2000. Three Scheduling Algorithms Applied to the Earth Observing Systems Domain. In *Management Science*, volume 46(1), 148–168.

# Domain Transmutation in Constraint Satisfaction Problems[*]

**James Bowen** and **Chavalit Likitvivatanavong**
Cork Constraint Computation Centre
University College Cork, Ireland
{j.bowen, chavalit}@4c.ucc.ie

### Abstract

We study local interchangeability of values in constraint networks based on a new approach where a single value in the domain of a variable can be treated as a combination of "sub-values". We present an algorithm for breaking up values and combining identical fragments. Experimental results show that the transformed problems take less time to solve for all solutions and yield more compactly-representable, but equivalent, solution sets. We obtain new theoretical results on context dependent interchangeability and full interchangeability, and suggest some other applications.

## Introduction

Interchangeability of domain values was first reported by (Freuder 1991), where neighborhood interchangeability (NI) and neighborhood substitutability (NS) are identified as local properties that can be exploited to remove redundant values, either as a preprocessing step or during search (Benson & Freuder 1992; Haselböck 1993). NI was later extended to cover interchangeable values in different variables (Choueiry & Noubir 1998).

We present a new approach to local interchangeability in this paper. Normally, each domain value is treated as atomic. Our idea is to "split the atom" — a domain value can be split into several "sub-values" (Figure (2.1),(2.2)) so that interchangeable fragments from other values can then be merged to avoid duplicate search effort during the solving process.

Figure (1.1),(1.2),(1.3) illustrate. The problems depicted are in microstructure form: each edge connects compatible values in the domains of two variables. Figure (1.1) shows the original problem, while (1.2) shows the result of splitting and merging sub-atomic value fragments in the domain of $X$ (a process which, by analogy with Nuclear Chemistry,[1] we call *domain transmutation*). Figure (1.3) shows the result of subsequently transmutating the domain of $Y$.

Consider, for example, the values $a$, $b$ and $c$ shown in (1.1). Value $a$ supports the following tuples in $Y \times Z \times W$:

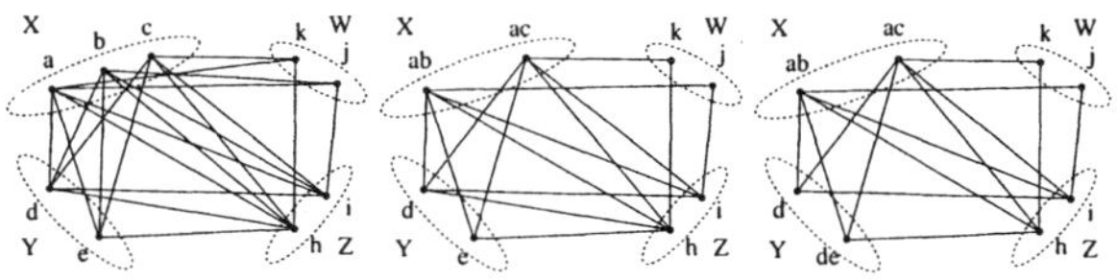

(1.1) (1.2) (1.3)

$(d,h,j)$, $(d,h,k)$, $(d,i,j)$, $(d,i,k)$, $(e,h,j)$, $(e,h,k)$, $(e,i,j)$ and $(e,i,k)$. We denote this support relationship concisely by $(\{\boldsymbol{a}\}, \{d,e\} \times \{h,i\} \times \{j,k\})$. The supports of $b$ and $c$ are $(\{\boldsymbol{b}\}, \{d,e\} \times \{h,i\} \times \{j\})$ and $(\{\boldsymbol{c}\}, \{d,e\} \times \{h,i\} \times \{k\})$. No two of the values $a$, $b$ and $c$ are NI. However, $a$ is neighborhood-substitutable for $b$ and also for $c$.

The value $a$ can be split into two fragments: $(\{\boldsymbol{a}\}, \{d,e\} \times \{h,i\} \times \{j\})$ and $(\{\boldsymbol{a}\}, \{d,e\} \times \{h,i\} \times \{k\})$. The first fragment of $a$ is interchangeable with $b$, while the second fragment of $a$ is interchangeable with $c$. Instead of eliminating one of the interchangeable fragments, we merge them together and use their combined labels as the new value's label, to indicate its origin. Thus, after merging we have two values: $(\{\boldsymbol{a,b}\}, \{d,e\} \times \{h,i\} \times \{j\})$ and $(\{\boldsymbol{a,c}\}, \{d,e\} \times \{h,i\} \times \{k\})$, depicted as $ab$ and $ac$ in (1.2).

Similarly, consider the values $d$ and $e$ in (1.2). The supports of $d$ and $e$ are $(\{\boldsymbol{d}\}, \{ab,ac\} \times \{h,i\})$ and $(\{\boldsymbol{e}\}, \{ab,ac\} \times \{h\})$. However, $d$ can be split into two fragments: $(\{\boldsymbol{d}\}, \{ab,ac\} \times \{h\})$ and $(\{\boldsymbol{d}\}, \{ab,ac\} \times \{i\})$. The first fragment is interchangeable with $e$. The result is (1.3). No two values from the same domain intersect in this problem.

As demonstrated, our approach subsumes both NI and NS, but it does so by applying the NI principle to value-*fragments*. Indeed, while standard NS cannot preserve the solution set of a CSP, our approach can, precisely because it treats value-substitutability as fragment-interchangeability. For example, the solution $(ac, de, h, k)$ in (1.3) corresponds to four solutions in the original problem: $(a,d,h,k)$, $(a,e,h,k)$ $(c,d,h,k)$, and $(c,e,h,k)$.

We will show empirically that domain transmutation can reduce the amount of time needed to find all solutions, as well as enable more compact representations of solution sets. This is essential in certain interactive constraint-based applications, such as interactive design-advice systems (O'Sullivan 2002): sometimes, to make his next interactive decision, a design engineer needs to be able to examine *all* consistent assignments to the variables involved

[*]This work has received support from Science Foundation Ireland under Grant 00/PI.1/C075.


[1]Transmutation — a change in the number of protons in the nucleus of an atom, producing an atom with a different atomic number.

in a sub-region of the overall CSP, and to see how similar they are to each other. Another application involves compiling CSPs (Weigel & Faltings 1999): all solutions to a subproblem are required in order to create a meta-variable, after which NI is employed to reduce domain size.

## Background

We focus on binary CSPs since non-binary constraints can be converted into binary constraints.

**Definition 1 (Binary CSP)** A *binary CSP* $\mathcal{P}$ is a triplet $(\mathcal{V}, \mathcal{D}, \mathcal{C})$ where $\mathcal{V}$ is the finite set of variables, $\mathcal{D} = \bigcup_{V \in \mathcal{V}} D_V$ where $D_V$ is the finite set of possible values for $V$ (sometimes we denote $D_V$ by $\mathcal{D}(V)$), and $\mathcal{C}$ is a finite set of constraints such that each $C_{XY} \in \mathcal{C}$ is a subset of $D_X \times D_Y$ indicating the compatible pairs of values for $X$ and $Y$, where $X \neq Y$. If $C_{XY} \in \mathcal{C}$, then $C_{YX} = \{(y,x) \mid (x,y) \in C_{XY}\}$ is also in $\mathcal{C}$. The *neighborhood* of variable $V$, denoted by $N_V$, is the set $\{W \mid C_{VW} \in \mathcal{C}\}$.

A *partial assignment* is a function $\pi : \mathcal{W} \subseteq \mathcal{V} \rightarrow \mathcal{D}$ such that $\pi(W) \in D_W$ for all $W \in \mathcal{W}$; we denote the function domain by *dom*($\pi$). $\pi$ is *consistent* iff for all $C_{XY} \in \mathcal{C}$ such that $X, Y \in$ *dom*($\pi$), $(\pi(X), \pi(Y)) \in C_{XY}$; we denote consistency of $\pi$ by *cons*($\pi$). $\pi$ is a *solution* iff *dom*($\pi$) = $\mathcal{V}$ and *cons*($\pi$).The set of all solutions for $\mathcal{P}$ is denoted by *Sols*($\mathcal{P}$). We use $\mathcal{P}|_{\mathcal{W}}$ to denote the CSP induced by $\mathcal{W} \subseteq \mathcal{V}$.

Given a partial assignment $\pi$, we define $\pi[a/b]$ to be the partial assignment where $\pi[a/b](V) = b$ if $\pi(V) = a$; otherwise $\pi[a/b](V) = \pi(V)$.

At this point we extend the usual definition of a value to a 2-tuple in order to clearly distinguish between its syntax (label) and semantics (support). This lower-level detail is only of theoretical concern and can be safely ignored in other contexts.

**Definition 2 (Values)** A *value* $a$ is a 2-tuple $(L, \sigma)$ where $L$ is a set of *labels*, while $\sigma$, called *support*, is a function $\sigma : N_V \rightarrow 2^{\mathcal{D}}$ such that $\sigma(W) \subseteq D_W$ for any $W \in N_V$. We use $L_a$ to denote the set of labels of $a$ and use $\sigma_a$ to denote the support of $a$. A value $a$ in $\mathcal{D}$ of the CSP $\mathcal{P} = (\mathcal{V}, \mathcal{D}, \mathcal{C})$ must be *valid*, that is, $\sigma_a(W) = \{b \in D_W \mid (a,b) \in C_{VW}\}$ for any $W \in N_V$.

Let $\mathcal{L} = \bigcup_{a \in \mathcal{D}} L_a$ be the set of all labels. A *partial label assignment* is a function $\lambda : \mathcal{W} \subseteq \mathcal{V} \rightarrow \mathcal{L}$ such that $\lambda(W) \in \bigcup_{a \in D_W} L_a$ for all $W \in \mathcal{W}$. Given a partial assignment $\pi$, we denote $\pi_{label}$ to be the set of partial label assignments $\{\lambda \mid \lambda(V) \in L_{\pi(V)}\}$. For any set of partial assignments $\mathcal{X}$, we use $\mathcal{X}_{label}$ to denote $\bigcup_{\pi \in \mathcal{X}} \pi_{label}$.

The new definition allows a variable domain to contain values having the same label but differrent supports (e.g. Figure (2.2)). Note that NI is still allowed: it is possible to have values with the same supports but different labels. However, values having both the same labels and supports are not permitted. In practice, when structure can no longer be used to differentiate values, each label can still be made unique and yet indicate its origin simply by appending to it some suffix. (e.g. $r_1$ and $r_2$ in Figure (3.2)). A solution can be converted back to the original format in time $O(|\mathcal{V}|)$.

Each value can have multiple labels so that we can combine NI values without losing any solution (unlike the standard practice where only one value is kept). For example ({**a**}, $\{x\} \times \{y\}$) and ({**b**}, $\{x\} \times \{y\}$) can be replaced by a single value ({**a,b**}, $\{x\} \times \{y\}$). Any solution $\pi$ involving ({**a,b**}, $\{x\} \times \{y\}$) can be converted using $\pi_{label}$. Throughout this paper, we always assume CSPs with no NI values since NI values are trivially handled by this approach.

Given a CSP we define the following operations on values, analogous to the usual operations on sets.

**Definition 3 (Operations on Values)** Let $a$ and $b$ be two values in $D_V$.

The *intersection* of $a$ and $b$ (denoted by $a \odot b$) is a value $c$ where $L_c = L_a \cup L_b$ and $\sigma_c(W) = \sigma_a(W) \cap \sigma_b(W)$ for all $W \in N_V$. The intersection is undefined (denoted by $a \odot b = \emptyset$) if there exists a variable $X \in N_V$ such that $\sigma_a(X) \cap \sigma_b(X) = \emptyset$. Two values $a$ and $b$, are said to be *disjoint* if $a \odot b = \emptyset$. A set of values is disjoint if its members are pairwise disjoint.

The *union* of $a$ and $b$ (denoted by $a \oplus b$) is a value $c$ where $L_c = L_a$ and $\sigma_c(W) = \sigma_a(W) \cup \sigma_b(W)$ for all $W \in N_V$. The union is undefined (denoted by $a \oplus b = \emptyset$) if $L_a \neq L_b$ or there exist two or more variables $X \in N_V$ such that $\sigma_a(X) \neq \sigma_b(X)$. The *subtraction* of $b$ from $a$ (denoted by $a \ominus b$) is the smallest set[2] of disjoint values $\mathscr{C}$ such that $\bigoplus(\mathscr{C} \cup \{a \odot b\}) = a$.

Value $a$ is *subsumed*[3] by $b$ (denoted by $a \sqsubseteq b$) if $\sigma_a(W) \subseteq \sigma_b(W)$ for all $W \in N_V$.

We will continue to use cross-product representation to denote supports for a value. For instance, consider values ({**a**}, $\{d,e\} \times \{h,i\} \times \{j,k\}$) and ({**b**}, $\{d,e\} \times \{h,i\} \times \{j\}$), which are depicted by their labels $a$ and $b$ in Figure (1.1). Their intersection is ({**a,b**}, $\{d,e\} \times \{h,i\} \times \{j\}$). Another example: ({**x,y**}, $\{a,b\} \times \{c\}$) $\odot$ ({**y,z**}, $\{a\} \times \{c,d\}$) = ({**x,y,z**}, $\{a\} \times \{c\}$).

It should be emphasized that the result of subtraction may be a *set* of values. Consider ({**a**}, $\{d,e\} \times \{f,g\}$) $\ominus$ ({**b**}, $\{d\} \times \{f\}$). The result is a set {({**a**}, $\{e\} \times \{f,g\}$), ({**a**}, $\{d\} \times \{g\}$)}. (This kind of fragmentation is not uncommon. On a larger scale, extracting subproblems can also fracture the remainder of a CSP (Freuder & Hubbe 1995).)

**Lemma 1** Let $a$ and $b$ be values in $D_V$ and let $W \in N_V$.
(1) Let $S \subseteq D_W$, then $S \subseteq \sigma_a(W)$ iff $a \in \bigcap_{d \in S} \sigma_d(V)$.
(2) $\mathscr{C} = \{a \odot b\} \cup (a \ominus b) \cup (b \ominus a)$ is disjoint[4]. Moreover, $\{\pi \mid \text{cons}(\pi) \wedge (\text{dom}(\pi) = \{V\} \cup N_V) \wedge (\pi(V) \in \{a,b\})\}_{label} = \{\pi \mid \text{cons}(\pi) \wedge (\text{dom}(\pi) = \{V\} \cup N_V) \wedge (\pi(V) \in \mathscr{C})\}_{label}$.
(3) $\odot$ and $\oplus$ are idempotent, commutative, and associative.

We now formally define domain transmutation.

[2] Subtraction is unique, although we do not have enough space to provide the proof.

[3] $a$ is neighborhood substitutable for $b$ if and only if $b \sqsubseteq a$.

[4] Recall that the subtraction of two values may result in a collection of values.

**Definition 4 (Transmutation)** Given a CSP $\mathcal{P} = (\mathcal{V}, \mathcal{D}, \mathcal{C})$. For any $V \in \mathcal{V}$, a *transmutation* of $D_V$ (denoted by *trans*$(D_V)$) is a variable domain $D'_V$ such that,
(1) $D'_V$ is disjoint.
(2) $Sols(\mathcal{P}|_{\{V\}\cup N_V})_{label} = Sols(\mathcal{P}'|_{\{V\}\cup N_V})_{label}$, where $\mathcal{P}'$ is the CSP in which $D_V$ is replaced by $D'_V$ and all constraints involving $V$ have been updated[5] by values in $D_V$. We denote $\mathcal{P}'$ by *trans*$(\mathcal{P}, V)$.

In a domain transmutation, no two values overlap and all the solutions involving the original domain are preserved. An algorithm for transmutating a domain will be given in the next section. Effects of domain transmutation are shown in the following theorem, whose proof is omitted.

**Theorem 1 (Transmutation Effects)** Given a CSP $\mathcal{P} = (\mathcal{V}, \mathcal{D}, \mathcal{C})$, let *trans*$(\mathcal{P}, V) = (\mathcal{V}, \mathcal{D}', \mathcal{C}')$,
(1) If $b \in \mathcal{D}'(V)$, then there exists some $a \in \mathcal{D}(V)$ such that $b \sqsubseteq a$ and such that, for any solution $\pi$ for *trans*$(\mathcal{P}, V)$ where $\pi(V) = b$, there also exists the solution $\pi[b/a]$ for $\mathcal{P}$.
(2) If $\pi$ is a solution for $\mathcal{P}$ such that $\pi(V) = a$, then there is *exactly one* $c \in \mathcal{D}'(V)$, $c \sqsubseteq a$, such that $\pi[a/c]$ is a solution for *trans*$(\mathcal{P}, V)$.

**Proposition 1 (Upper Bound on Search Space)** Given a CSP $\mathcal{P} = (\mathcal{V}, \mathcal{D}, \mathcal{C})$, we denote *maxassign*$(\mathcal{P})$ to be the number of possible partial assignments $\pi$ such that *dom*$(\pi) = \mathcal{V}$. For any binary CSP $\mathcal{P}$, *maxassign*$(trans(\mathcal{P}, V)) \leqslant$ *maxassign*$(\mathcal{P})$ for all $V \in \mathcal{V}$.

In the rest of this section, we will obtain new results on other types of interchangeability based on transmutation.

Context dependent interchangeability (CDI) was proposed in (Weigel, Faltings, & Choueiry 1996) in an attempt to capture interchangeability in a limited situation. CDI is rephrased as follows.

**Definition 5 (Context Dependent Interchangeability)** Values $a$ and $b$ in $D_V$ are *context dependent interchangeable* iff there exist two solutions $\pi_1$ and $\pi_2$ such that $\pi_1(V) = a$ and $\pi_2 = \pi_1[a/b]$.

**Theorem 2 (Intersection of CDI Values)** Values $a$ and $b$ in $D_V$ are CDI for a CSP $\mathcal{P} = (\mathcal{V}, \mathcal{D}, \mathcal{C})$ iff in *trans*$(\mathcal{P}, V) = (\mathcal{V}, \mathcal{D}', \mathcal{C}')$ there is *exactly one* $c \in \mathcal{D}'(V)$ such that $c \sqsubseteq a$ and $c \sqsubseteq b$ and there exists a solution $\pi$ such that $\pi(V) = c$.

*Proof* ($\Rightarrow$) From Theorem 1(2) we have $c_1$ and $c_2$ and two solutions $\pi[a/c_1]$ and $\pi[a/c_2]$ ($= \pi[a/b][b/c_2]$) for *trans*$(\mathcal{P}, V)$. But $c_1$ and $c_2$ must be the same value because otherwise $c_1 \odot c_2 \neq \emptyset$ ($\pi(W) \in c_1(W) \cap c_2(W)$ for all $W \in N_V$), contradicting Definition 4(1).

($\Leftarrow$) Given a solution $\pi$ in *trans*$(\mathcal{P}, V)$ such that $\pi(V) = c$ where $c \sqsubseteq a$ and $c \sqsubseteq b$, then $\pi[c/a]$ and $\pi[c/b]$ are solutions of $\mathcal{P}$ according to Theorem 1(1). □

**Collorary 1 (Necessary Condition for CDI)** If values $a$ and $b$ in $D_V$ are CDI then $a \odot b \neq \emptyset$.

[5] To make values in $D'_V$ valid.

Theorem 2 tells us that two values are CDI iff both share the same sub-value and that sub-value is part of a solution. As a result, CDI can be seen as a local condition followed by a global condition. In (Weigel, Faltings, & Choueiry 1996), however, CDI is viewed as a single global condition and has to be detected indirectly by a non-CSP method.

We can exploit this property to find CDI values by transmutating a domain and then solving the resulting problem *independently using any CSP algorithm*. E.g., to check whether $a$ and $b$ in Figure (1.1) are CDI, one only needs to check whether $ab$ in (1.3) is involved in any solution. If two values do not intersect, such as $h$ and $i$ in (1.1), we can tell immediately that they are not CDI according to Corollary 1.

We next consider the relation between full interchangeability (FI) (Freuder 1991) and transmutation. (Freuder 1991) showed that NI implies FI. But what happens when values are FI but not NI? Theorem 3 gives the answer.

**Definition 6 (Full Interchangeability)** Two values $a$ and $b$ in $D_V$ are FI iff for any solution $\pi$,
(1) if $\pi(V) = a$ then $\pi[a/b]$ is a solution.
(2) if $\pi(V) = b$ then $\pi[b/a]$ is a solution.

In contrast to FI, CDI has a weaker requirement in that values do not need to be interchangeable in all solutions — just some of them. On the other hand, FI values do not need to be involved in any solution, whereas it is necessary for CDI.

**Theorem 3 (FI Pruning)** Two values $a$ and $b$ in $D_V$ are FI iff for any solution $\pi$, $(\pi(V) \in \{a, b\}) \Rightarrow (\pi(W) \in \sigma_{a \odot b}(W)$ for all $W \in N_V)$.

*Sketch of a Proof:* Contrapositive of the fact: there exists a solution $\pi$ such that $\pi(V) = a$ but $\pi[a/b]$ is not a solution iff there exists $W \in N_V$ such that $\pi(W) \notin \sigma_{a \odot b}(W)$. □

**Collorary 2 (Necessary Condition for FI)** If $a \odot b = \emptyset$ then $a$ and $b$ are FI iff neither takes part in a solution.

The common way of finding FI values is to look for two values that can be interchangeable in the solution sets. We will show how to use Theorem 3 to reduce the search effort.

Consider the CSP in (3.1); suppose that there is an extra constraint between $V_1$ and $V_3$, whose only nogoods are $\{(c,f),(d,h)\}$. Suppose we are interested in finding FI values in $V_2$, whose domain is $\{r,g,b,x,y,z\}$, and after transmutation becomes what is shown in (3.2). The potential FI pairs of values are $r$-$g$, $g$-$b$, $r$-$b$, and $x$-$y$. Although any pair of values that do not intersect can still trivially be FI, this is uninteresting since according to Corollary 2 both of them must not take part in any solution; thus interchangeability of $z$ can be ruled out because it does not intersect with other values.

We can remove $rg$, $gb$, and $rb$ from the domain since their involvement in solutions does not affect FI. The domain is now $\{r_1,r_2,g_1,g_2,b_1,b_2,x_1,y_1\}$.

To find all the solutions, suppose we try to instantiate $V_2$ in the order $(r_1,r_2,g_1,g_2,b_1,b_2,x_1,y_1)$. The first solution involves $r_1$. According to Theorem 3, $r$ cannot be FI with any other values and so we can rule out $r$-$g$ and $r$-$b$. Moreover,

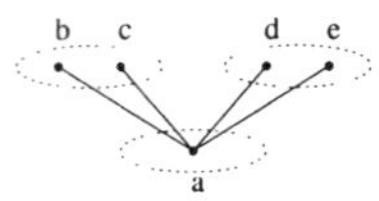

(2.1)

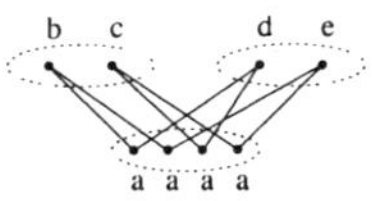

(2.2)

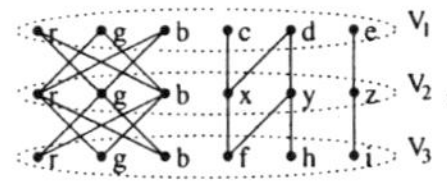

(3.1)

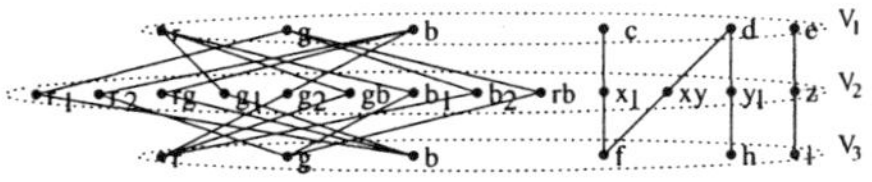

(3.2)

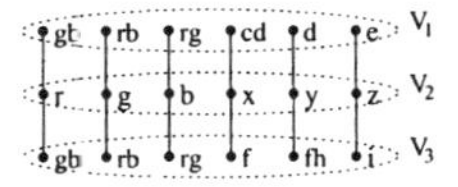

(3.3)

$r_2$ can be removed from the domain since its involvement in a solution does not give us any new information.

Next we try $g_1$, and it too takes part in a solution. By the same reasoning, we infer that $g$ cannot be FI with any other values, and so we can prune $g_2$. We are now done with FI regarding $\{r,g,b\}$ — no FI value involving one of them exists — and so values $b_1$ and $b_2$ can be removed.

We carry on with values $x_1$ and $y_1$ that are left in the domain; neither is involved in a solution. There is no value left and by Theorem 3, we conclude that $x$ and $y$ are FI.

## Domain Transmutation Procedure

The procedure for transmutating the domain of a single variable is stated as pseudo-code below.

**Procedure** `transmutate(V)`

```
0 input ← D_V;
0 output ← ∅;
0 while input ≠ ∅ do
0     Select and delete any a from input ;
0     match ← false ;
0     while (not match) and (next b in output exists ) do
0         if a ⊙ b ≠ ∅ then
0             match ← true ;
0             𝒜 ← a ⊖ b;
0             ℬ ← b ⊖ a;
0             Replace b in output with a ⊙ b and all values in ℬ;
0             Put all values in 𝒜 back to input ;
0     if (not match) then
0         Insert a to output
0 Where possible, union values in output ;
0 D_V ← output ;
0 Update all constraints connecting V;
```

**Theorem 4 (Correctness)** Algorithm `transmutate` produces a domain transmutation.

*Proof* At the end of the algorithm `output` is a disjoint set of values by induction on the size of `output` and Lemma 1(2). Since the algorithm depends only on $\odot$ and $\ominus$ to split values, all solutions are preserved by Lemma 1(2). Therefore `output` satisfies Definition 4 □

The following theorem shows that each variable needs to be transmutated by the algorithm at most once.

**Theorem 5 (Transmutation Quiescence)** If a variable domain $D_V$ is a transmutation, any subsequent transmutation attempt using the algorithm will result in no change.

*Proof* This is obviously true if no variable domain in $N_V$ is altered. Otherwise, we will show that after $D_V$ has been transmutated, it remains disjoint regardless of any domain transmutation in $N_V$.

Let $\mathcal{P}$ be the CSP $(\mathcal{V},\mathcal{D},\mathcal{C})$ just after $D_V$ has been transmutated. Let $a$ and $b$ be values in $\mathcal{D}(V)$. Both are disjoint according to Definition 4(1) and so there must be a variable $W \in N_V$ such that $\sigma_a(W) \cap \sigma_b(W) = \emptyset$. Consider *trans*$(\mathcal{P}, W) = (\mathcal{V}, \mathcal{D}', \mathcal{C}')$ and let us suppose that $c \in \sigma_a(W) \cap \sigma_b(W) \neq \emptyset$ as a result of transmutating $W$, for some value $c \in \mathcal{D}'(W)$.

By Lemma 1(1), $\{a, b\} \subseteq \sigma_c(V)$. Since $c \in \mathcal{D}'(W)$, by Theorem 1(1) $c \sqsubseteq d$ for some $d \in \mathcal{D}(W)$. That means $\{a, b\} \subseteq \sigma_c(V) \subseteq \sigma_d(V)$. By Lemma 1(1), $d \in \sigma_a(W) \cap \sigma_b(W)$ — contradicting $\sigma_a(W) \cap \sigma_b(W) = \emptyset$ for $\mathcal{P}$.

Hence the assumption is false and $\sigma_a(W) \cap \sigma_b(W)$ remains empty after $W$ is transmutated. □

Note that union in line 15 is used in re-combining remaining fragmented values from the same source, although the smallest possible domain transmutation is not required by Definition 4.

During transmutation the size of `output` could be very large if there many fragments of values left after intersection. If so, it is very unlikely that the values inside can be combined so that the resulting domain is smaller than the original. Therefore we use the *transmutation cutoff heuristic* which imposes an upper bound on the size of `output`; if it exceeds the upper bound, transmutation is aborted.

The overall transmutation process involves transmutating each variable domain, one by one, in some order. The order in which variables are processed affects the result. Figure (3.1),(3.2),(3.3) show sample transmutations: (3.1) is the original, (3.2) shows the result of processing in the order $(V_2, V_1, V_3)$, while the CSP in (3.3) is obtained with either $(V_1, V_3, V_2)$ or $(V_3, V_1, V_2)$. (In fact, the CSP in (3.2) results from the transmutation of $V_2$ alone and subsequent attempts to transmutate $V_1$ and $V_3$ result in no change.)

The CSP in (3.2) has larger domains than the original CSP in (3.1), so it can be expected that it would take more time to solve. As a heuristic, we have chosen never to accept a domain transmutation if domain size is increased; we call this the *transmutation acceptance heuristic*. While variable domains can, in principle, be transmutated in any order, we always pick the variable whose transmutation leads to the maximum domain size reduction. To achieve this, we tentatively consider the transmutation of each variable in the network; if there is no variable whose domain size is reduced by the transmutation procedure, we terminate the process. The same approach is applied for subsequent variable transmutations. We need only recompute tentative transmutations for the domains of the variables that are immediate neighbors of the variable whose domain has been transmutated.

## Experimental Results

We tested the `transmutate` algorithm and solved the transmutated problems for all solutions over randomly generated CSPs with ten variables[6] and six values in each domain, varying density from 0.2 to 0.8 with 0.05 increment step,

[6]These problems may appear small but, as will be discussed later, many real-world uses of the approach involve only small regions of larger network.

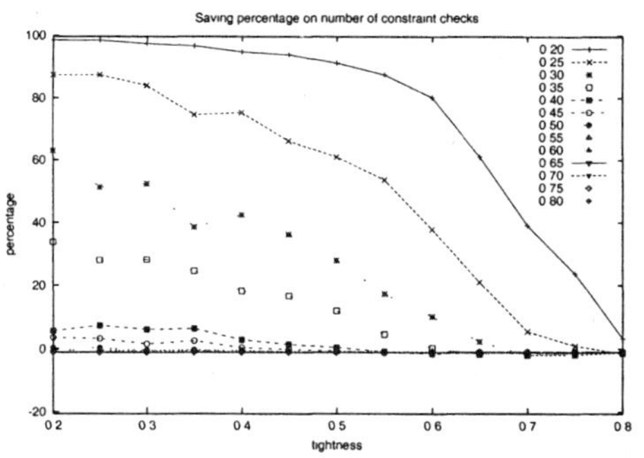


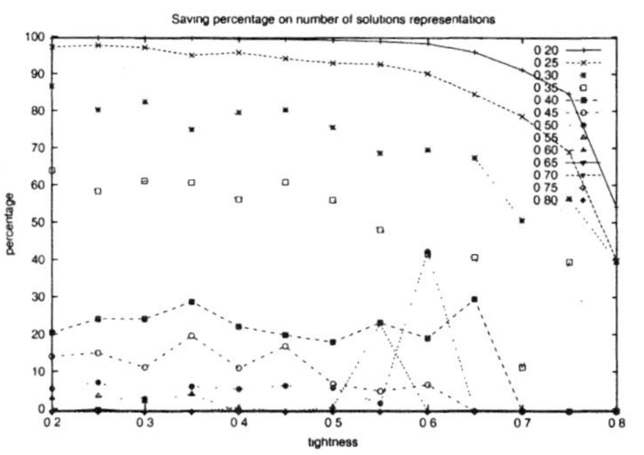


while tightness ranges from 0.2 to 0.8 with the same increment. We used model B random problem generator, with "flawless" constraint generation (Gent *et al.* 2001).

For each data-point, the number of constraint checks required to compute all solutions and the number of representations needed to express these solutions are computed and averaged over 100 problem instances. We gathered the data for both transmutated and original problems. The solver is MAC-3 with dom/deg variable ordering. For the transmutation cutoff heuristic, we fixed the upper bound of the `output` queue to be ten times the size of the domain (60).

It may appear that our experimental problems are too small, but remember that *all* solutions are to be computed. Since the solving time increases exponentially with the problem size, finding all solutions in larger networks therefore has few practical uses, and is not studied here. Indeed, as explained in the introduction, all solutions are needed only for relatively small subnetworks in larger CSPs — for creating meta-variables or for user perspicuity of subnetworks. Furthermore, since we tested the algorithm over a wide range of density and tightness, we had to settle on a relatively small problem size to keep the experimental time in check. However we believe the trend seen in the experiments in this paper can be extrapolated to larger problems without significant loss of accuracy.

Because transmutation time is always an insignificant fraction of the time needed to compute all the solutions of a CSP, it is always worthwhile trying the transmutation. In our setting, it takes just a few seconds to transmutate a (50, 10, 0.5, 0.5)[7] instance.

The results are shown in the graphs, in which the legends refer to density. While the transmutation cannot *guarantee* to reduce the number of constraint checks needed to compute all solutions to a CSP, it can produce huge savings. From the graphs, we see that more domain transmutation occurred for problems with lower density or lower tightness, as either case will lead to a lot of value combination; a similar reduction holds for the solution representation. On the other hand, in the worst case we have seen in the experimental data, which occurred only at a few data-points, the number of extra constraint checks for a transmutated CSP is no more than one or two percent of the untransmutated CSP.

[7]A tuple ($n$, $m$, *density*, *tightness*) denotes a CSP where $n$ is the number of variables and $m$ is the domain size for each variable.

## Other Applications

Domain transmutation can be used for other purposes as well. Three applications are described in this section.

### Robustness

We can exploit the combination of values after transmutation to achieve robustness for a single solution simply by ordering values during search based on the size of their labels. For example, suppose (*a*, *abc*, *b*, *bc*, *c*) is the transmutated domain of some variable. During search, it would be ordered as (*abc*, *bc*, *a*, *b*, *c*). The first solution obtained will be the most robust in this variable. That is, if a solution found involves *abc*, we know that it corresponds to three solutions in the original problem and should one of the three values be unavailable, it can be immediately replaced with either of the other two without any change to the rest of the solution. The advantage of this approach is that the transmutation process is independent of the solving process and thus no specialized solver is required. We can also order the variables for search based on which variables should be more robust to changes.

But, since variables are instantiated in order, there may be a case where the solver would prefer a solution which is very robust at one variable and brittle at another, rather than a uniformly robust solution: e.g., a solution tuple (*abcd*, *efg*, *hi*, *j*) may be found before (*ac*, *ef*, *hi*, *jk*). (Ginsberg, Parkes, & Roy 1998) provides formalization and more details on solution robustness. In contrast, (Lesaint 1994) propose an algorithm that gives a single maximal bundling of solutions.

### Decision Problems

In Definition 3, union is restricted to fragments that come from the same value so as to preserve the solutions. However, satisfiability remains unchanged when the restriction is lifted, although a solution cannot easily be converted back.

**Definition 7 (Extended Union)** Let $a$ and $b$ be two values in $D_V$. The *extended union* of $a$ and $b$ (denoted by $a \otimes b$) is a value $c$ where $L_c = L_a \cup L_b$ and $\sigma_c(W) = \sigma_a(W) \cup \sigma_b(W)$ for all $W \in N_V$. The extended union is undefined (denoted by $a \otimes b = \emptyset$) if there exist two or more variables $X \in N_V$ such that $\sigma_a(X) \neq \sigma_b(X)$.

**Theorem 6 (Satisfaction of Extended Union)** Consider two values $a$ and $b$ in CSP $\mathcal{P}$ such that $a \otimes b \neq \emptyset$, and the resulting CSP $\mathcal{P}'$ where $a$ and $b$ are replaced by $a \otimes b$. $\mathcal{P}$ is satisfiable iff $\mathcal{P}'$ is satisfiable.

For example, consider ($\{a\}$, $\{x\}\times\{y\}$) and ($\{b\}$, $\{x\}\times\{z\}$) in $D_V$, where $y$ and $z$ are in $D_W$, $W \in N_V$. Both can be combined into ($\{a,b\}$, $\{x\}\times\{y,z\}$). Given a solution $\pi$ involving ($\{a,b\}$, $\{x\}\times\{y,z\}$), there must be another solution involving either ($\{a\}$, $\{x\}\times\{y\}$) or ($\{b\}$, $\{x\}\times\{z\}$), although we cannot tell which one without inspecting $\pi(W)$.

In a situation where satisfiability of problems is the only concern, extended union can be used on its own to prune values during preprocessing or during search, similar to NI. And, unlike basic domain transmutation, the resulting domain is *guaranteed* to be smaller than the original.

Using extended union in domain transmutation can sometimes dramatically reduce the domain size. For example, the domain of $V_2$ in Figure (3.2) can be reduced from 13 values to 4 should we use extended union in the algorithm.

### Finding a Single Solution

Even though Proposition 1 tells us that the upper bound on the search space for a transmutated CSP is smaller than its original, this is not in any way an indication of the actual search effort. In fact, in our preliminary, unreported experiments, the results are mixed. This is simply a consequence of conventional CSP solvers, where each value's support is established as the search progresses, and discarded afterward during backtracking. As the problem gets harder (more backtracking) and the domain size gets larger[8], finding a support for each value becomes the main bottleneck as it has to be re-discovered anew.

In this situation, the benefit of AC-4-like data structures (Mohr & Henderson 1986) in which supports for each values are remembered could offset its overhead. Although AC-4 was empirically shown to be inferior than AC-3 — a forgetful algorithm with non-optimal worst-case time-complexity — as far as we know there is no report on its effectiveness compared to other AC algorithms when used during search to solve *hard* problems. ((Sabin & Freuder 1994) compared MAC-4 with only forward checking.)

## Related Work

Cross product representation (CPR) of partial solutions generated during search has been studied in (Hubbe & Freuder 1992). In extending a CPR to complete solutions, a new value is combined into existing CPR if possible; otherwise a new CPR is created. Domain transmutation could be seen as a "dynamic programming" version of the same concept.

Preliminary work on value transformation was reported in a poster paper by the authors of this submission [reference omitted for blind reviewing]. Subsequently and independently (Chmeiss & Saïs 2003) defined Generalized Neighborhood Substitutability, which corresponds exactly to the intersection of values. Rather than extracting identical parts from various values to form new ones, extra constraints are inserted to prevent the same search space from being explored again. However, this approach is undemonstrated, and no other benefits such as compact representation of solutions can be obtained.

[8]Larger domains in transmutated CSP are not uncommon, despite using the best variable ordering.

## Conclusions

We present a new perspective on domain values in CSP where each value is viewed as a combination of smaller values. This allows us to freely manipulate variable domains so as to remove redundant partial assignments. We present an inexpensive method for merging duplicate local solutions in a constraint network, which subsumes NI and NS. The benefits are two-fold: reducing time spent on finding consistent assignments and reducing the complexity of enumerating the members of the complete solution set. Experimental results show that the savings are considerable, especially on loose problems with a low density of constraints. We use the new extended CSP definition, in which values are composed of labels and structures, to obtain new result on CDI and FI and to prove some properties of the algorithm presented. We also suggest how it could be used to find robust solutions, to solve decision problems, and to speed up the search for a single solution.

## References


Benson, B. W., and Freuder, E. C. 1992. Interchangeability preprocessing can improve forward checking search. In *Proceedings of ECAI-92*, 28–30.

Chmeiss, A., and Saïs, L. 2003. About neighborhood substitutability in CSPs. In *CP-03 Workshop on Symmetry in Constraint Satisfaction Problems*.

Choueiry, B. Y., and Noubir, G. 1998. On the computation of local interchangeability in discrete constraint satisfaction problems. In *Proceedings of AAAI-98*, 326–333.

Freuder, E. C., and Hubbe, P. D. 1995. Extracting constraint satisfaction subproblems. In *Proceedings of IJCAI-95*, 548–555.

Freuder, E. C. 1991. Eliminating interchangeable values in constraint satisfaction problems. In *Proceedings of AAAI-91*, 227–233.

Gent, I. P.; MacIntyre, E.; Prosser, P.; Smith, B. M.; and Walsh, T. 2001. Random constraint satisfaction: Flaws and structure. *Constraints* 6(4):345–372.

Ginsberg, M. L.; Parkes, A. J.; and Roy, A. 1998. Supermodels and robustness. In *Proceedings of AAAI-98*, 334–339.

Haselböck, A. 1993. Exploiting interchangeabilities in constraint satisfaction problems. In *Proceedings of IJCAI-93*, 282–287.

Hubbe, P. D., and Freuder, E. C. 1992. An efficient cross-product representation of the constraint satisfaction problem search space. In *Proceedings of AAAI-92*, 421–427.

Lesaint, D. 1994. Maximal sets of solutions for constraint satisfaction problems. In *Proceedings of ECAI-94*, 110–114.

Mohr, R., and Henderson, T. C. 1986. Arc and path consistency revisited. *Artificial Intelligence* 28(2):225–233.

O'Sullivan, B. 2002. Interactive constraint-aided conceptual design. *Journal of Artificial Intelligence for Engineering Design Analysis and Manufacturing (AIEDAM)* 16(4).

Sabin, D., and Freuder, E. C. 1994. Contradicting conventional wisdom in constraint satisfaction. In *Proceedings of ECAI-94*, 125–129.

Weigel, R., and Faltings, B. V. 1999. Compiling constraint satisfaction problems. *Artificial Intelligence* 115(2):257–287.

Weigel, R.; Faltings, B. V.; and Choueiry, B. Y. 1996. Context in discrete constraint satisfaction problems. In *Proceedings of ECAI-96*, 205–213.

# Collapsibility and Consistency in Quantified Constraint Satisfaction

**Hubie Chen**
Department of Computer Science
Cornell University
Ithaca, NY 14853, USA
hubes@cs.cornell.edu

### Abstract

The concept of *consistency* has pervaded studies of the constraint satisfaction problem. We introduce two concepts, which are inspired by consistency, for the more general framework of the quantified constraint satisfaction problem (QCSP). We use these concepts to derive, in a uniform fashion, proofs of polynomial-time tractability and corresponding algorithms for certain cases of the QCSP where the types of allowed relations are restricted. We not only unify existing tractability results and algorithms, but also identify new classes of tractable QCSPs.

## Introduction

The constraint satisfaction problem (CSP) is widely acknowledged as a convenient framework for modelling search problems. An instance of the CSP consists of a set of variables, a domain, and a set of constraints; each constraint consists of a tuple of variables paired with a relation (over the domain) which contains permitted values for the variable tuple. The question is to decide whether or not there is an assignment mapping each variable to a domain element that satisfies all of the constraints. Because the CSP is in general NP-complete, a tremendous amount of research effort has been devoted to identifying solution techniques that are effective in practice, as well as restricted cases of the problem that are polynomial-time tractable.

All of the variables in a CSP can be thought of as being implicitly existentially quantified. A useful generalization of the CSP is the quantified constraint satisfaction problem (QCSP), where variables may be both existentially and universally quantified. Whereas the CSP concerns deciding the existence of a *static* object, a satisfying assignment, the QCSP concerns deciding the existence of a *dynamic* object: a strategy telling how to set the existentially quantified variables in reaction to an arbitrary setting of the universally quantified variables, so that the constraints are satisfied. The generality of the QCSP framework permits the modelling of a variety of artificial intelligence problems that cannot be expressed using the CSP, for instance, problems from the areas of planning, game playing, and non-monotonic reasoning. Of course, the relatively higher expressiveness of the QCSP comes at the price of higher complexity: the QCSP is in general complete for the complexity class PSPACE, which is believed to be much larger than NP.



In contrast to the rich and ever-expanding body of research on the CSP, the study of the QCSP appears to be in its infancy. In light of this age gap, a natural approach to understanding the QCSP is to develop analogs of notions that have been successful in understanding the CSP. *Consistency* is a concept that has pervaded both practical and theoretical investigations of the CSP, and is thus extremely obvious as a candidate notion for import into the QCSP world. From a high-level viewpoint, consistency procedures involve performing computation that is localized, in that a small number of data items are considered at a time. More specifically, consistency procedures allow for the "tightening" of a CSP by the continual consideration of bounded-size sets of variables and elimination of tuples from relations that cannot be used by any satisfying assignment. Although they are simple, such procedures have been used heavily to identify polynomial-time tractable cases of the CSP; as a sampling of work along these lines, we name the papers (Freuder 1978; 1982; 1985; Dechter 1992; van Beek & Dechter 1995; Dechter & van Beek 1996; van Beek & Dechter 1997; Feder & Vardi 1998; Jeavons, Cohen, & Cooper 1998; Dalmau & Pearson 1999; Dalmau, Kolaitis, & Vardi 2002; Bulatov 2002; Bulatov & Jeavons 2003). Indeed, the HORN SATISFIABILITY and 2-SATISFIABILITY problems, two classic tractable cases of the CSP, are solvable by consistency-based algorithms.

In this paper, we introduce two new concepts for use with QCSPs which are inspired by consistency: *collapsibility* and *extended minimality*. A class of QCSP problems has *bounded collapsibility* when, roughly speaking, deciding the truth of an instance can be reduced to deciding the truth of an ensemble of instances, all of which have a bounded number of universally quantified variables and are derived from the original instance by "collapsing" together universally quantified variables. *Extended minimality* extends a notion of consistency called minimality that has been used to study the CSP; it is a "smooth" extension of minimality in that the notions of minimality and extended minimality perfectly coincide for CSPs (equivalently, QCSPs with no universal quantification).

These two new concepts yield a number of ramifications,

which we present and discuss in this paper. First, when used together, the concepts provide a uniform proof technique for deriving the tractability of certain cases of the QCSP where the types of allowed relations are restricted. This technique reconciles and reveals common structure among known tractable cases of the QCSP that were originally proved to be tractable using disparate proof techniques (Aspvall, Plass, & Tarjan 1979; Karpinski, Büning, & Schmitt 1987; Börner *et al.* 2003; Chen 2003b). (These cases generalize tractable cases of the CSP solvable by consistency procedures.) Second, any cases of the QCSP to which this proof technique applies, are solvable by (possibly different parameterizations of) a single algorithm which, as with consistency-based algorithms for the CSP, is not only efficient, but conceptually simple. In fact, we obtain the first unified polynomial-time algorithms for QUANTIFIED HORN SATISFIABILITY and QUANTIFIED 2-SATISFIABILITY as a corollary of our results; these two cases of the QCSP have been known to be polynomial-time tractable for many years (Aspvall, Plass, & Tarjan 1979; Karpinski, Büning, & Schmitt 1987). In addition to unifying known QCSP tractability results, we expand the tractability frontier by identifying new, broad classes of tractable QCSPs. For example, we show that a certain large class of *multi-sorted* QCSPs are tractable; tractability results for multi-sorted CSPs (Bulatov & Jeavons 2003) play a major role in the recent, spectacular dichotomy theorem on CSP complexity for a three-element domain (Bulatov 2002), and we expect that multi-sorted QCSPs will similarly be significant in understanding the complexity of the QCSP.

## Preliminaries

We use $[n]$ to denote the set containing the first $n$ positive integers, that is, $\{1,\ldots,n\}$. For a function $f: A \to B$ and a subset $A' \subseteq A$, we denote by $f_{|A'}$ the restriction of $f$ to $A'$. For a set $F$ of functions $f: A \to B$ and a subset $A' \subseteq A$, we denote by $F_{|A'}$ the set of functions $\{f_{|A'} : f \in F\}$.

**Quantified constraint satisfaction.** A *domain* is a nonempty set of finite size. A *tuple* (over domain $D$) is an element of $D^k$ for some $k \geq 1$, and is said to have arity $k$. The $i$th coordinate of a tuple $\overline{t}$ is denoted by $t_i$. A *relation* (over domain $D$) is a subset of $D^k$ for some $k \geq 1$, and is said to have arity $k$.

A *constraint* is an expression of the form $R(\overline{v})$, where $R$ is a relation and $\overline{v}$ is a tuple of variables such that $R$ and $\overline{v}$ have the same arity. A *constraint network* is a finite set of constraints, all of which have relation over the same domain, and is said to be over the variable set $V$ if all of its constraints have variables from $V$. Throughout, we let $D$ denote the domain of our constraints and constraint networks.

**Definition 1** *A quantified formula is an expression of the form $Q_1v_1 \ldots Q_nv_nC$, where each $Q_i$ is a quantifier from the set $\{\forall, \exists\}$, and $C$ is a constraint network over the variable set $\{v_1,\ldots,v_n\}$.*

We call $Q_1v_1 \ldots Q_nv_n$ the *quantifier prefix* of the quantified formula $Q_1v_1 \ldots Q_nv_nC$. We say that the variable $v_i$ comes (strictly) before the variable $v_j$ if $i \leq j$ ($i < j$). We let $V_\phi$, $Y_\phi$, and $X_\phi$ denote the variables, universally quantified variables, and existentially quantified variables of a quantified formula $\phi$, respectively; we drop the $\phi$ subscript when it is understood from the context. (Notice that $V_\phi$ is the disjoint union of $Y_\phi$ and $X_\phi$). We generally assume that the universally quantified variables (of a quantified formula) are denoted $y_1,\ldots,y_{|Y|}$, where $y_i$ comes strictly before $y_j$ for $i < j$; similarly, we generally assume that the existentially quantified variables (of a quantified formula) are denoted $x_1,\ldots,x_{|X|}$, where $x_i$ comes strictly before $x_j$ for $i < j$. When $W$ is a non-empty subset of the variable set $V_\phi$ (of a quantified formula $\phi$), we use $\mathsf{first}_\phi(W)$ to denote the unique variable in $W$ coming before all of the other variables in $W$, and we use $\mathsf{last}_\phi(W)$ to denote the unique variable $w$ in $W$ such that all of the other variables in $W$ come before $w$. For a subset $W$ of the variable set $V$ (of a quantified formula) and a variable $v$ of $V$, we let $W[\leq v]$ ($W[< v]$) denote the set of variables in $W$ coming (strictly) before $v$. As an example, consider a quantified formula with quantifier prefix $\forall y_1 \exists x_1 \exists x_2 \forall y_2 \exists x_3$. Relative to this formula, $X[\leq x_3]$ denotes the set $\{x_1, x_2, x_3\}$; $X[< x_3]$ denotes the set $\{x_1, x_2\}$; and $Y[\leq x_3]$ and $Y[< x_3]$ both denote the set $\{y_1, y_2\}$.

**Strategies and truth.** A constraint $R(v_1,\ldots,v_k)$ is *satisfied* by an assignment $f$ defined on $\{v_1,\ldots,v_k\}$ if $(f(v_1),\ldots,f(v_k)) \in R$. A constraint network $\mathcal{C}$ (over the variable set $V$) is *satisfied* by an assignment $f: V \to D$ if each constraint $C$ in $\mathcal{C}$ is satisfied by $f$.

**Definition 2** *A* strategy $\sigma$ *is a sequence of mappings*

$$\{\sigma_i : D^{\mathsf{rank}(\sigma_i)} \to D\}_{i \in [n]}$$

*where the $i$th mapping $\sigma_i$ is a function over $D$ having rank* $\mathsf{rank}(\sigma_i) \geq 0$.

Note that when $\sigma_i$ is a mapping of a strategy such that $\mathsf{rank}(\sigma_i) = 0$, we consider $\sigma_i$ to be a constant, that is, an element of $D$.

A *strategy for the quantified formula* $\phi$ is a strategy $\sigma_1,\ldots,\sigma_{|X_\phi|}$ where for $i \in [|X_\phi|]$, the mapping $\sigma_i$ has rank $|Y_\phi[< x_i]|$. An *adversary for the quantified formula* $\phi$ is a function $\tau : Y_\phi \to D$. When $\sigma$ is a strategy and $\tau$ is an adversary for the quantified formula $\phi$, the *outcome* of $\sigma$ and $\tau$, denoted by $\mathsf{outcome}(\sigma,\tau) : V_\phi \to D$, is the assignment defined by $\mathsf{outcome}(\sigma,\tau)(x_i) = \sigma_i(\tau(y_1),\ldots,\tau(y_{|Y[<x_i]|}))$ for $x_i \in X_\phi$ and $\mathsf{outcome}(\sigma,\tau)(y_i) = \tau(y_i)$ for $y_i \in Y_\phi$.

A strategy $\sigma$ for the quantified formula $\phi$ is said to be *winning* if for all adversaries $\tau$ for $\phi$, the assignment $\mathsf{outcome}(\sigma,\tau) : V_\phi \to D$ satisfies the constraint network $\mathcal{C}$ of $\phi$. We consider a quantified formula $\phi$ to be *true* if there exists a winning strategy for $\phi$. (This is one of many equivalent ways to define truth of a quantified formula.)

**Problem formulation.** This paper focuses on the following restricted version of the QCSP, where all relations must come from a *constraint language*. A *constraint language* is defined to be a set of relations (not necessarily of the same arity), all of which are over the same domain.

**Definition 3** *Let $\Gamma$ be a constraint language. The* $\mathsf{QCSP}(\Gamma)$ *problem is to decide, given as input a quantified formula $\phi$ with constraints having relations from $\Gamma$, whether or not $\phi$ is true.*

We define the $\mathsf{CSP}(\Gamma)$ problem to be the restriction of the $\mathsf{QCSP}(\Gamma)$ problem to instances where all quantifiers are existential.

We will find it convenient to use an alternative formulation of the notion of a constraint. A *functional constraint* $C$ consists of a set of variables called the *scope* of $C$, denoted by $\mathsf{scope}(C)$; and, a set of functions from $\mathsf{scope}(C)$ to a domain $D$, denoted by $\mathsf{funs}(C)$. A functional constraint $C$ is considered to be satisfied by an assignment $f : V \to D$ defined on $\mathsf{scope}(C)$ when $f_{|\mathsf{scope}(C)} \in \mathsf{funs}(C)$. A constraint $R(v_1, \ldots, v_k)$ naturally induces the functional constraint $C$ where $\mathsf{scope}(C) = \{v_1, \ldots, v_k\}$ and $\mathsf{funs}(C)$ contains all functions $f : \{v_1, \ldots, v_k\} \to D$ such that $\{(v_i, f(v_i)) : i \in [k]\} = \{(v_i, t_i) : i \in [k]\}$ for some tuple $\overline{t} \in R$. Note that an assignment $f : V \to D$ satisfies a constraint $R(v_1, \ldots, v_k)$ if and only if it satisfies the functional constraint naturally induced by $R(v_1, \ldots, v_k)$. We use functional constraints and constraints interchangeably in this paper.

**Invariance and set functions.** A powerful algebraic theory for studying the complexity of $\mathsf{CSP}(\Gamma)$ problems, which can also be applied to study the complexity of $\mathsf{QCSP}(\Gamma)$ problems, was introduced in (P.G.Jeavons, D.A.Cohen, & M.Gyssens 1997; Jeavons 1998). (We refer the reader to those papers for more information.) Two key definitions of this theory to be used throughout this paper are the following. A relation $R \subseteq D^m$ is *invariant* under an operation $\mu : D^k \to D$ if for all tuples $\overline{t_1}, \ldots, \overline{t_k} \in R$, the tuple $(\mu(t_{11}, \ldots, t_{k1}), \ldots, \mu(t_{1m}, \ldots, t_{km}))$ is in $R$. A constraint language $\Gamma$ is *invariant* under an operation $\mu : D^k \to D$ if all relations $R \in \Gamma$ are invariant under $\mu$.

We consider a *set function* (on domain $D$) to be a mapping from $\mathcal{P}(D) \setminus \{\emptyset\}$ to $D$, where $\mathcal{P}(D)$ denotes the power set of $D$. A set function $f : \mathcal{P}(D) \setminus \{\emptyset\} \to D$ naturally induces a sequence of functions $f_k : D^k \to D$ defined by $f_k(d_1, \ldots, d_k) = f(\{d_1, \ldots, d_k\})$, for $k \geq 1$. We consider a relation (or constraint language) to be invariant under a set function $f : \mathcal{P}(D) \setminus \{\emptyset\} \to D$ if it is invariant under all of the functions $f_k$ (for $k \geq 1$). We say that a set function $f : \mathcal{P}(D) \setminus \{\emptyset\} \to D$ is an *idempotent set function* if all of the functions $f_k$ (for $k \geq 1$) are idempotent.

## Collapsibility

In this section, we develop machinery for demonstrating that a constraint language $\Gamma$ has *bounded collapsibility*; essentially, this means that an arbitrary instance of $\mathsf{QCSP}(\Gamma)$ can be reduced to an ensemble of instances of $\mathsf{QCSP}(\Gamma)$, all of which have a constant number of universally quantified variables. Bounded collapsibility is computationally a very strong condition, since quantified formulas with a constant number of universally quantified variables are, intuitively, very close to being CSPs. After developing sufficient conditions for bounded collapsibility, we give examples of classes of constraint languages that have bounded collapsibility.

**Collapsings of formulas.** Define a quantified formula $\phi'$ to be a $j$-*collapsing* of a quantified formula $\phi$ if there exists a subset $Y'$ of $Y_\phi$ such that $|Y'| = \min(j, |Y_\phi|)$ and $\phi'$ can be obtained from $\phi$ by first eliminating, from the quantifier prefix of $\phi$, all variables in $Y_\phi \setminus Y'$ except for $\mathsf{first}_\phi(Y_\phi \setminus Y')$; and then replacing, in the constraint network of $\phi$, all variables in $Y_\phi \setminus Y'$ with $\mathsf{first}_\phi(Y_\phi \setminus Y')$. For example, the quantified formula

$$\forall y_1 \exists x_1 \forall y_2 \forall y_3 \exists x_2 \{R_1(y_1, x_1), R_2(y_3, x_2), R_3(y_2, y_3, x_2)\}$$

has the following three 1-collapsings:

$$\forall y_1 \exists x_1 \forall y_2 \exists x_2 \{R_1(y_1, x_1), R_2(y_2, x_2), R_3(y_2, y_2, x_2)\}$$

$$\forall y_1 \exists x_1 \forall y_2 \exists x_2 \{R_1(y_1, x_1), R_2(y_1, x_2), R_3(y_2, y_1, x_2)\}$$

$$\forall y_1 \exists x_1 \forall y_3 \exists x_2 \{R_1(y_1, x_1), R_2(y_3, x_2), R_3(y_1, y_3, x_2)\}.$$

We have the following fact concerning the $j$-collapsings of a true quantified formula.

**Proposition 4** *If a quantified formula $\phi$ is true, then for any $j \geq 1$ and any $j$-collapsing $\phi'$ of $\phi$, the quantified formula $\phi'$ is true.*

We will be able to demonstrate classes of formulas for which the converse of Proposition 4 holds; for such formulas, deciding whether or not $\phi$ is true is equivalent to deciding whether or not all $j$-collapsings of $\phi$ are true. The following characterization of when the $j$-collapsings of a quantified formula are true, will be wieldy. Define a set of functions $F$ of the form $\tau : Y \to D$ to be a $j$-*adversary set* for $Y$ if there exists a subset $Y' \subseteq Y$ of size $\min(j, |Y|)$ such that $F$ contains exactly those functions $\tau$ having the property that $\tau(y_1) = \tau(y_2)$ for all $y_1, y_2 \in Y \setminus Y'$. When $\phi$ is a quantified formula and $F$ is a set of adversaries $\tau : Y_\phi \to D$, we say that the formula $\phi$ is $F$-winnable if there exists a strategy $\sigma$ for $\phi$ such that for all $\tau \in F$, the assignment $\mathsf{outcome}(\sigma, \tau)$ satisfies the constraint network of $\phi$.

It is straightforward to verify that the $j$-collapsing of a quantified formula corresponding to a subset $Y'$ is true, if and only if the formula is $F$-winnable, where $F$ is the $j$-adversary set corresponding to $Y'$. Hence, we have the following proposition.

**Proposition 5** *Let $\phi$ be a quantified formula. The $j$-collapsings $\phi'$ of $\phi$ are all true if and only if for each $j$-adversary set $F$ for $Y_\phi$, the formula $\phi$ is $F$-winnable.*

**Collapsibility of constraint languages.** We say that a constraint language $\Gamma$ is $j$-*collapsible* if for every quantified formula $\phi$ that is an instance of $\mathsf{QCSP}(\Gamma)$, the following property holds: if all $j$-collapsings of $\phi$ are true, then $\phi$ is true. We say that a constraint language $\Gamma$ has *bounded collapsibility* if there exists a $j \geq 1$ such that $\Gamma$ is $j$-collapsible. Using the notion of invariance, we will be able to identify classes of constraint languages that have bounded collapsibility. In order to do this, we introduce a notion of composability, with respect to a function $\mu$.

When $\mu : D^k \to D$ is a function, and $F, F_1, \ldots, F_k$ are sets of functions of the form $\tau : \{y_1, \ldots, y_n\} \to D$, we say that $F$ *is* $\mu$*-composable in one step from* $F_1, \ldots, F_k$ if there exist strategies $\pi^1 = \{\pi^1_i : D^i \to D\}_{i \in [n]}, \ldots, \pi^k = \{\pi^k_i : D^i \to D\}_{i \in [n]}$ such that for all $\tau \in F$, the following two properties hold: (1) for all $i \in [k]$, the mapping $\tau^i : \{y_1, \ldots, y_n\} \to D$ defined by $\tau^i(y_j) = \pi^i_j(\tau(y_1), \ldots, \tau(y_j))$ (for all $j \in [n]$) is contained in $F_i$, and (2) it holds that $\tau(y_j) = \mu(\tau^1(y_j), \ldots, \tau^k(y_j))$ (for all $j \in [n]$). The key feature of this definition is the following lemma.

**Lemma 6** *Let $\phi$ be a quantified formula with $\{y_1, \ldots, y_n\}$ as its universally quantified variables and with relations invariant under $\mu$, and suppose that $F$ is $\mu$-composable in one step from $F_1, \ldots, F_k$. If $\phi$ is $F_i$-winnable for all $i \in [k]$, then $\phi$ is $F$-winnable.*

When $\mu : D^k \to D$ is a function, and $F, F_1, \ldots, F_k$ are sets of functions of the form $\tau : \{y_1, \ldots, y_n\} \to D$, we say that $F$ *is* $\mu$*-composable from* $F_1, \ldots, F_k$ if there exist sets of functions $F_{k+1}, \ldots, F_m$ (containing functions of the form $\tau : \{y_1, \ldots, y_n\} \to D$) such that $F_m = F$ and for all $i \in [m]$ with $i > k$, the set of functions $F_i$ is $\mu$-composable in one step from $F_{j_1}, \ldots, F_{j_k}$ for some $j_1, \ldots, j_k \in [i-1]$. A function $\mu : D^k \to D$ is $j$-collapsible if for any $n \geq 1$, the set of all functions from $Y = \{y_1, \ldots, y_n\}$ to $D$ can be composed from the $j$-adversary sets (for $Y$). By use of Lemma 6, the following theorem can be established.

**Theorem 7** *If the operation $\mu$ is $j$-collapsible, then any constraint language $\Gamma$ invariant under $\mu$ is $j$-collapsible.*

**Applications.** We can now derive the collapsibility of a variety of constraint languages. In particular, we now give a number of results which demonstrate that constraint languages invariant under an operation of some type are $j$-collapsible, for some $j$. These results are all obtained by demonstrating the $j$-collapsibility of the operations at hand, and then applying Theorem 7.

A *near-unanimity operation* is an operation $\mu : D^k \to D$ of rank $k \geq 3$ where for all tuples $\bar{t} \in D^k$, if there exists $i \in [k]$ and $d \in D$ such that $t_j = d$ for all $j \in [k] \setminus \{i\}$, then $\mu(\bar{t}) = d$. In words, if all but at most one of the arguments to $\mu$ agree, then $\mu$ returns the "nearly-unanimous" argument.

**Theorem 8** *Any constraint language invariant under a near-unanimity operation of rank $k$ is $(k-1)$-collapsible.*[1]

We say that a set function $f : (\mathcal{P}(D) \setminus \{\emptyset\}) \to D$ is a *set function with default* if there exists a non-empty subset $E \subseteq D$ such that the induced mapping $f_E : (\mathcal{P}(D) \setminus \{\emptyset\}) \to D$ defined by $f_E(S) = f(E \cup S)$ is surjective. Set functions with default provide another class of collapsible constraint languages.

[1]By this theorem, it can be deduced that any constraint language invariant under a *dual discriminator operation* (a particular type of rank 3 near-unanimity operation) is 2-collapsible. However, we can strengthen this implication and show that constraint languages invariant under a dual discriminator are 1-collapsible.

**Theorem 9** *Any constraint language invariant under a set function with default is 1-collapsible.*

A *semilattice operation* is a binary operation $\oplus : D^2 \to D$ that is associative, commutative, and idempotent. Every semilattice operation naturally induces a set function. The semilattice operations can be divided into two classes which yield considerably different behaviors with respect to QCSP complexity. Define a semilattice operation $\oplus$ to be a *semilattice operation with unit* if there exists an element $u \in D$ such that $\oplus(u, d) = \oplus(d, u) = d$ for all $d \in D$, and a *semilattice operation without unit* otherwise. From Theorem 9, we can deduce the following corollary.

**Corollary 10** *Any constraint language invariant under a semilattice operation with unit is 1-collapsible.*

It was shown in (Chen 2003b) that for any constraint language $\Gamma$ invariant under a semilattice operation with unit, the problem QCSP($\Gamma$) is tractable. On the other hand, it was demonstrated in (Chen 2003a) that there exist constraint languages $\Gamma$ invariant under semilattice operations without unit, such that QCSP($\Gamma$) is coNP-hard. By this hardness result and the results in this paper, it follows that demonstrating the $j$-collapsibility of a semilattice operation without unit is not possible, unless P = NP. In fact, we can demonstrate the non-$j$-collapsibility of such operations in a manner that is purely combinatorial, and does not make use of any complexity-theoretic assumptions.

**Theorem 11** *For any semilattice operation $\oplus$ without unit, there exists a constraint language invariant under $\oplus$ that is not $j$-collapsible for any $j \geq 1$.*

Theorem 11 implies that Theorem 9 cannot be improved to address the class of all set functions. Precisely, Theorem 11 implies that for no $j \geq 1$ can it be proved that all set functions are $j$-collapsible.

## Extended Minimality

As mentioned in the introduction, various forms of consistency have been developed for solving the CSP. In this section, we generalize a flavor of consistency called $k$-*minimality* to the QCSP setting, obtaining a new form of consistency for QCSPs which we call *extended $k$-minimality*. There are constraint languages $\Gamma$ for which establishing some level of $k$-minimality and then checking for an empty constraint, is a decision procedure for CSP($\Gamma$); such constraint languages are said to have *bounded relational width*. We will correspondingly say that a constraint language $\Gamma$ has *bounded extended width* if establishing some level of extended $k$-minimality and then checking for an empty constraint, is a decision procedure for QCSP($\Gamma$). Our main result in this section is that, under a mild assumption, bounded relational width implies bounded extended width! With this result in hand, one can take existing results showing constraint languages to have bounded relational width, and immediately infer the constraint languages to have bounded extended width.

Bounded relational width constraint languages are tractable in the CSP setting since any CSP can be converted in polynomial time into one that is $k$-minimal (for each fixed

$k$); the corresponding claim that can be made concerning extended $k$-minimality is that any QCSP *with a constant number of universal quantifiers* can be converted in polynomial time into one that is extended $k$-minimal (for each fixed $k$). As we will discuss in the next section, this latter fact gives rise to a two-phase decision procedure for QCSP($\Gamma$) when $\Gamma$ is both of bounded collapsibility and bounded extended width.

**$k$-minimality.** When $\mathcal{C}$ is a constraint network over variable set $V$ and $S$ is a subset of $V$, we define $\mathcal{C}_{|S}$ to be the constraint network $\{C_{|S} : C \in \mathcal{C}\}$, where $C_{|S}$ is the constraint such that $\mathsf{scope}(C_{|S}) = \mathsf{scope}(C) \cap S$ and $\mathsf{funs}(C_{|S}) = \mathsf{funs}(C)_{|\mathsf{scope}(C) \cap S}$. Intuitively, $\mathcal{C}_{|S}$ is the restriction of the entire constraint network $\mathcal{C}$ to $S$.

**Definition 12** *(Bulatov 2002) A constraint network $\mathcal{C}$ over variable set $V$ is* $k$-minimal *if the following conditions hold:*

- *for all subsets $S \subseteq V$ with $|S| = k$, there exists a constraint $C \in \mathcal{C}$ such that $S \subseteq \mathsf{scope}(C)$, and*
- *for all constraints $C \in \mathcal{C}$, functions $f \in \mathsf{funs}(C)$, and subsets $S \subseteq \mathsf{scope}(C)$ with $|S| \leq k$, the constraint network $\mathcal{C}_{|S}$ is satisfied by $f_{|S}$.*

**Theorem 13** *(Bulatov 2002) For each fixed $k \geq 1$, there is a polynomial-time algorithm that converts an arbitrary constraint network $\mathcal{C}$ into a $k$-minimal constraint network that is equivalent to $\mathcal{C}$ (that is, has the same satisfying assignments as $\mathcal{C}$).*

There are CSP($\Gamma$) problems solvable in polynomial-time by using the algorithms of Theorem 13. Following (Bulatov 2002), we say that a constraint language $\Gamma$ has *relational width $k$* if for every instance $\mathcal{C}$ of CSP($\Gamma$), the constraint network $\mathcal{C}$ is satisfiable if and only if a $k$-minimal constraint network equivalent to $\mathcal{C}$ has no empty constraint. For any constraint language $\Gamma$ of relational width $k$, the problem CSP($\Gamma$) is polynomial-time tractable: to decide satisfiability of an input constraint network, convert it into an equivalent $k$-minimal constraint network, and then report "satisfiable" if and only if the second constraint network has no empty constraint.

Previous work has identified the following classes of constraint languages having *bounded relational width*, that is, of relational width $k$ for some $k \geq 1$.

**Theorem 14** *(Jeavons, Cohen, & Cooper 1998) Any constraint language invariant under a near-unanimity operation of rank $k$ has relational width $k$.*

**Theorem 15** *(Dalmau & Pearson 1999) Any constraint language invariant under a set function has relational width* 1.

**Extended $k$-minimality.** We now generalize the condition of $k$-minimality to one called *extended $k$-minimality*. The first two conditions in the following definition can be thought of as analogs of the first two conditions of Definition 12, while the third condition has no analog in the CSP setting.

**Definition 16** *A quantified formula $\phi$ with constraint network $\mathcal{C}$ is* extended $k$-minimal *if the following conditions hold:*

- *for all subsets $S \subseteq X$ with $|S| = k$, there exists a constraint $C \in \mathcal{C}$ such that $S \cup Y \subseteq \mathsf{scope}(C)$,*
- *for all constraints $C \in \mathcal{C}$, functions $f \in \mathsf{funs}(C)$, and subsets $S \subseteq \mathsf{scope}(C)$ with $|S \cap X| \leq k$ and $\mathsf{last}(S) \in X$, the constraint network $\mathcal{C}_{|S}$ is satisfied by $f_{|S}$, and*
- *for all constraints $C \in \mathcal{C}$, functions $f \in \mathsf{funs}(C)$, universally quantified variables $y \in \mathsf{scope}(C) \cap Y$, subsets $S \subseteq \mathsf{scope}(C)[< y]$, and domain elements $d \in D$, the extension of $f_{|S}$ mapping $y$ to $d$ is in $\mathsf{funs}(C)_{|S \cup \{y\}}$.*

Definition 16 is a smooth generalization of Definition 12 in the sense that a CSP is $k$-minimal if and only if it is extended $k$-minimal. (This is straightforward to verify.)

We have the following analog (indeed, generalization) of Theorem 13.

**Theorem 17** *For fixed $j, k \geq 1$, there is a polynomial-time algorithm that converts a quantified formula $\phi$ with at most $j$ universally quantified variables into an extended $k$-minimal quantified formula that is equivalent to $\phi$ (that is, has the same winning strategies as $\phi$).*

We say that a constraint language $\Gamma$ has *extended width $k$* if for every instance $\phi$ of QCSP($\Gamma$), the quantified formula $\phi$ is true if and only if an extended $k$-minimal quantified formula $\phi'$ equivalent to $\phi$ has no empty constraint; when a constraint language $\Gamma$ has extended width $k$ for some $k \geq 1$, we say that it has *bounded extended width*. The following is our main result concerning extended $k$-minimality; it shows that one can automatically infer bounded extended width from bounded relational width.

**Theorem 18** *Let $\mu$ be an idempotent operation. If every constraint language invariant under $\mu$ has relational width $k$, then every constraint language invariant under $\mu$ has extended width $k$.*

As a testament to the power of Theorem 18, we can immediately deduce the following corollaries from it and Theorems 14 and 15.

**Corollary 19** *Any constraint language invariant under a near-unanimity operation of rank $k$ has extended width $k$.*

**Corollary 20** *Any constraint language invariant under an idempotent set function has extended width* 1.

## Tractability

We say that a constraint language has *quantified width* $(j, k)$ if it is $j$-collapsible and has extended width $k$; a constraint language has *bounded quantified width* if it has quantified width $(j, k)$ for some $j, k \geq 1$ (equivalently, if it is of bounded collapsibility and bounded extended width). By considering Theorems 8, 9 along with Corollaries 19, 20, we can identify the following classes of constraint languages having bounded quantified width.

**Theorem 21** *Any constraint language invariant under a near-unanimity operation of rank $k$ has quantified width $(k-1, k)$.*

**Theorem 22** *Any constraint language invariant under an idempotent set function with default has quantified width* $(1, 1)$.

For any constraint language with quantified width $(j, k)$, the problem QCSP($\Gamma$) is solvable in polynomial-time via a two-phase decision procedure. Given an input formula $\phi$, the procedure is to (1) compute all $j$-collapsings of $\phi$, and (2) for each of these $j$-collapsings, use the algorithm of Theorem 17 to compute an equivalent formula that is extended $k$-minimal, and check for an empty constraint. The formula is true if and only if no empty constraint is detected. Note that, for a fixed $j$, there are polynomially many $j$-collapsings of an input formula.

**Theorem 23** *For any constraint language* $\Gamma$ *with bounded quantified width, the problem* QCSP($\Gamma$) *is decidable in polynomial-time. Moreover, all such problems* QCSP($\Gamma$) *are decidable by (different* $(j, k)$ *parameterizations of) the same algorithm.*

Theorem 23 allows us to derive, in a uniform fashion, a number of different tractability results.

**Corollary 24** *For any constraint language* $\Gamma$ *invariant under a near-unanimity operation, the problem* QCSP($\Gamma$) *is decidable in polynomial-time.*

We remark that near-unanimity operations were shown to be tractable in (Chen 2003b), and dual discriminator operations were shown to be tractable in (Börner *et al.* 2003).

**Corollary 25** *For any constraint language* $\Gamma$ *invariant under an idempotent set function with default, the problem* QCSP($\Gamma$) *is decidable in polynomial-time.*

The problems QCSP($\Gamma$) identified by Corollary 25 constitute a new tractable subclass of the QCSP that has not been previously observed, although the tractability of semilattices with unit (which is implied by Corollary 25) was demonstrated in (Chen 2003b).

From Corollaries 24 and 25, we can derive the following.

**Corollary 26** QUANTIFIED HORN SATISFIABILITY *and* QUANTIFIED 2-SATISFIABILITY *are decidable in polynomial-time.*

We can also show that semilattice operations with unit and near-unanimity operations can be combined to derive tractability results in a multi-sorted setting. The following theorem holds for a multi-sorted analog of bounded quantified width; for its statement, we adopt the terminology of (Bulatov & Jeavons 2003).

**Theorem 27** *Suppose that* $\mathcal{A}$ *is a collection of idempotent algebras such that each algebra in* $\mathcal{A}$ *contains either a semilattice operation with unit or a near-unanimity operation. Any constraint language* $\Gamma$ *invariant under* $\mathcal{A}$ *has bounded quantified width, and hence for such constraint languages* $\Gamma$ *the problem* QCSP($\Gamma$) *is decidable in polynomial-time.*

**Acknowledgements.** The author thanks Víctor Dalmau for useful discussions, and Carla Gomes, Riccardo Pucella, Bart Selman, and Vicky Weissman for helpful comments on drafts of this paper.

## References

Aspvall, B.; Plass, M. F.; and Tarjan, R. E. 1979. A linear-time algorithm for testing the truth of certain quantified boolean formulas. *Information Processing Letters* 8(3):121–123.

Börner, F.; Bulatov, A.; Krokhin, A.; and Jeavons, P. 2003. Quantified constraints: Algorithms and complexity. In *Computer Science Logic 2003*.

Bulatov, A., and Jeavons, P. 2003. An algebraic approach to multi-sorted constraints. In *CP 2003*.

Bulatov, A. 2002. A dichotomy theorem for constraints on a three-element set. In *Proceedings of 43rd IEEE Symposium on Foundations of Computer Science*, 649–658.

Chen, H. 2003a. Quantified constraint satisfaction and small commutative conservative operations. Cornell technical report.

Chen, H. 2003b. Quantified constraint satisfaction problems: Closure properties, complexity, and proof systems. Cornell technical report.

Dalmau, V., and Pearson, J. 1999. Closure functions and width 1 problems. In *CP 1999*, 159–173.

Dalmau, V.; Kolaitis, P. G.; and Vardi, M. Y. 2002. Constraint satisfaction, bounded treewidth, and finite-variable logics. In *Constraint Programming '02*, LNCS.

Dechter, R., and van Beek, P. 1996. Local and global relational consistency. *Theoretical Computer Science*.

Dechter, R. 1992. From local to global consistency. *Artificial Intelligence* 55:87–107.

Feder, T., and Vardi, M. Y. 1998. The computational structure of monotone monadic snp and constraint satisfaction: A study through datalog and group theory. *SIAM J. Comput.* 28(1):57–104.

Freuder, E. C. 1978. Synthesizing constraint expressions. *Commun. ACM* 21(11):958–966.

Freuder, E. C. 1982. A sufficient condition for backtrack-free search. *J. ACM* 29(1):24–32.

Freuder, E. C. 1985. A sufficient condition for backtrack-bounded search. *J. ACM* 32(4):755–761.

Jeavons, P.; Cohen, D.; and Cooper, M. 1998. Constraints, consistency, and closure. *Articial Intelligence* 101(1-2):251–265.

Jeavons, P. 1998. On the algebraic structure of combinatorial problems. *Theoretical Computer Science* 200:185–204.

Karpinski, M.; Büning, H. K.; and Schmitt, P. H. 1987. On the computational complexity of quantified horn clauses. In *CSL 1987*, 129–137.

P.G.Jeavons; D.A.Cohen; and M.Gyssens. 1997. Closure properties of constraints. *Journal of the ACM* 44:527–548.

van Beek, P., and Dechter, R. 1995. On the minimality and global consistency of row-convex constraint networks. *Journal of the ACM* 42(3):543–561.

van Beek, P., and Dechter, R. 1997. Constraint restrictiveness versus local and global consistency. *Journal of the ACM* 44(4):549 – 566.

# Complete Local Search for Propositional Satisfiability

**Hai Fang**
Department of Computer Science
Yale University
New Haven, CT 06520-8285
hai.fang@yale.edu

**Wheeler Ruml**
Palo Alto Research Center
3333 Coyote Hill Road
Palo Alto, CA 94304
ruml@parc.com

### Abstract

Algorithms based on following local gradient information are surprisingly effective for certain classes of constraint satisfaction problems. Unfortunately, previous local search algorithms are notoriously incomplete: They are not guaranteed to find a feasible solution if one exists and they cannot be used to determine unsatisfiability. We present an algorithmic framework for complete local search and discuss in detail an instantiation for the propositional satisfiability problem (SAT). The fundamental idea is to use constraint learning in combination with a novel objective function that converges during search to a surface without local minima. Although the algorithm has worst-case exponential space complexity, we present empirical results on challenging SAT competition benchmarks that suggest that our implementation can perform as well as state-of-the-art solvers based on more mature techniques. Our framework suggests a range of possible algorithms lying between tree-based search and local search.

## Introduction

Algorithms for constraint satisfaction problems have traditionally been divided into two classes: those that are based on a systematic tree-structured search and those that use a repair-based local search scheme. Algorithms that explore a tree containing all possible variable assignments can implicitly prove that a problem is unsatisfiable by traversing the entire tree without finding a feasible solution. Methods based on repairing an initially infeasible solution typically follow a local gradient function and do not record which assignments have been visited and which remain untried. Such methods are therefore incomplete: There is no finite time within which they are guaranteed to find a satisfying assignment if one exists. They will fail to terminate on unsatisfiable problems and are not guaranteed to solve a satisfiable problem. Given the surprising effectiveness of local search methods in practice, there is great interest in understanding how tree-based and repair-based methods can be hybridized and in whether it might be possible to design a complete local search algorithm (Selman, Kautz, & McAllester, 1995; Kautz & Selman, 2003).

In this paper, we will show that it is indeed feasible to record information reflecting the past history of a gradient-based search and to use that information to prove the search complete. Although our basic framework applies to any finite-domain constraint satisfaction problem, we will focus in this paper on propositional satisfiability (SAT). In this problem, one must determine whether it is possible to find a satisfying assignment to the variables of a Boolean formula that is presented in conjunctive normal form—a conjunction of clauses, each of which is the disjunction of one or more literals, where a literal is an instance of a variable or its negation. Each clause thus forms a constraint that disallows certain assignments. Many other problems can be translated into SAT, including STRIPS planning, graph coloring, test pattern generation, logic synthesis, equivalence checking, and model checking.

Our approach is based on using a novel objective function to compute the local gradient. When a local minimum is reached, we generate new implied clauses from the current formula. This can be done in many different ways, including resolution. As we discuss in detail below, the new clauses dynamically change the objective function. This process incrementally smooths the search space. We provide a guarantee that when all possible implied clauses have been generated there will be no local minima left. Although this approach suffers from worst-case exponential space complexity, in practice our implementation usually either finds a satisfying assignment or generates the empty clause well before all implied clauses have been generated.

After presenting our framework for complete local search, we will discuss our instantiation of the scheme for SAT. We then demonstrate the performance of our prototype implementation on challenging benchmarks from the 2003 SAT competition. The results indicate that the guarantee of completeness costs little in overall performance: Our solver surpasses all local search solvers from the competition and performs comparably to the best local search solver known.

## The Framework

An outline of our approach is given in Figure 1. As in most local search algorithms for SAT, the search proceeds by iteratively toggling the value of a single variable in the current assignment. Unlike many other local search schemes, ours does not fundamentally depend on randomness. The search moves to a neighboring assignment only if it is strictly better according to the current objective function (steps 3–4). If no

```
CompleteLocalSearch(φ)
1. α ← generate-initial-assignment(φ)
2. while α does not satisfy φ do
3.     if the best neighbor α' is better than α
4.         α ← α'
5.     else
6.         γ ← generate-implied-clause(φ,α)
7.         if γ is the empty clause
8.             return unsatisfiable
9.         else
10.            φ ← φ ∧ γ
11. return α
```

Figure 1: A framework for complete local search.

adjacent assignment is better, we have reached a local minimum (step 5). A new implied clause is then derived from the current formula (step 6). The clause generator must always generate a new implied clause in finite time, but any procedure that meets this criterion can be used. The generator need not use the current assignment when constructing a new clause, although doing so may improve performance. (We will discuss clause generation at length below.) If the empty clause can be derived, the instance is unsatisfiable, otherwise the formula is augmented with the new clause, thereby implicitly changing the objective function.

The objective function compares two assignments on the basis of the clauses that they each violate. It depends crucially on the lengths of the violated clauses. Although this novel formulation may seem a little strange, it will be important in ensuring the completeness of the search. More formally, let $\phi_\alpha$ denote those clauses of formula $\phi$ that are violated by assignment $\alpha$. If $\phi$ is over $n$ variables, let $\mathcal{D}(\phi_\alpha)$ be the tuple $\langle d_n, \ldots, d_0 \rangle$, where $d_i$ is the number of clauses of length $i$ that are violated by $\alpha$. Given the current formula $\phi$, an assignment $\alpha'$ is better than another assignment $\alpha$ if $\mathcal{D}(\phi_{\alpha'})$ is lexicographically earlier than $\mathcal{D}(\phi_\alpha)$. That is to say $\mathcal{D}(\phi_{\alpha'})$ must have a smaller entry at the leftmost position where the two tuples differ. This might occur, for instance, because the longest clause violated by $\alpha'$ is shorter than the longest clause violated by $\alpha$. Note that as new clauses of various lengths are added to the formula during the search process, the relative superiority of different assignments can change.

The algorithm is clearly sound: Because the new clauses that are added to the formula do not change the set of satisfying assignments, any assignment that satisfies the current formula and is returned (steps 2 and 11) would have satisfied the original formula. Assuming the clause generator terminates, the search will terminate because there are only a finite number of possible implied clauses ($\leq 3^n$, in fact) and there are only a finite number of strictly improving steps the search can make with a fixed objective function, as would be obtained once all clauses were generated. Of course, SAT is NP-complete (Garey & Johnson, 1991) and our scheme has worst-case exponential time complexity. What is perhaps less obvious is that the algorithm is complete.

## Completeness

To show that the algorithm is complete, we need only consider the situation in which all possible implied clauses have already been generated. (Of course, in practice we hope to find a model or generate the empty clause well before this.) We will use $\phi^*$ to denote this implication closure of the original formula $\phi$. If the formula were unsatisfiable, the empty clause would have been generated, so we need only consider the case of a satisfiable formula. We need to show that there are no local minima when using the objective function specified above on $\phi^*$. In other words, a neighboring assignment $\alpha'$ that is closer to a solution than the current assignment $\alpha$ will necessarily appear more attractive.

To prove this, we will first need a few helpful supporting ideas. In the traditional view of SAT, each clause excludes a family of states from the solution set. We explore an alternative view of this phenomenon: Each solution excludes the clauses that are incompatible with it from $\phi^*$.

Let $\mathcal{U}$ denote the set of all clauses that can be formed using variables appearing in $\phi$ and let $\phi^-$ denote those clauses in $\mathcal{U}$ that do not appear in $\phi^*$. We can describe the relationship between $\phi^-$ and partial solutions of $\phi$ precisely:

**Lemma 1** *A clause $\gamma = l_1 \vee \cdots \vee l_k$ appears in $\phi^-$ if and only if the corresponding negated partial assignment $\overline{\gamma} = \{\overline{l}_1, \ldots, \overline{l}_k\}$ is part of some solution of $\phi$.*

***Proof:*** A clause $\gamma$ appears in the closure $\phi^*$ if and only if $\overline{\gamma}$ is not part of any solution of $\phi$. Therefore, $\gamma$ is not in $\phi^*$ iff $\overline{\gamma}$ is part of some solution. If $\gamma$ is not in $\phi^*$, it must be in $\phi^-$. □

Next, we need to note a special property of the objective function:

**Lemma 2** *For any assignment $\alpha$, the componentwise addition $\mathcal{D}(\phi^*{}_\alpha) + \mathcal{D}(\phi^-{}_\alpha)$ will yield the same constant tuple.*

***Proof:*** Note that $\mathcal{D}(\phi^*{}_\alpha) + \mathcal{D}(\phi^-{}_\alpha) = \mathcal{D}(\mathcal{U}_\alpha)$. But $\mathcal{D}(\mathcal{U}_\alpha)$ does not depend on $\alpha$. There are $2^i\binom{n}{i}$ possible clauses of length $i$ on $n$ variables. Any complete assignment to $n$ variables will satisfy exactly one of the two possible literals for each variable and thus will violate exactly $1/2^i$ of all possible clauses of length $i$. So the number of possible clauses of length $i$ that will be violated will be exactly $\binom{n}{i}$ and the tuple $\mathcal{D}(\phi^*{}_\alpha) + \mathcal{D}(\phi^-{}_\alpha)$ will always equal the binomial distribution. □

Now we can consider the objective function on neighboring assignments and show that there are no local optima when $\phi$ has expanded to its closure:

**Theorem 1** *For any unsatisfying assignment $\alpha$ and satisfiable formula $\phi$, any neighbor $\alpha'$ that is closer to the nearest solution will be better than $\alpha$ according to the objective function on $\phi^*$.*

***Proof:*** The intuition here is that as we step closer and closer to the nearest solution, larger and larger implied clauses will always become satisfied. For the proof, $\phi^-$ is simpler to deal with than $\phi^*$, so we will proceed by showing that $\alpha'$ is strictly worse than $\alpha$ with respect to $\phi^-$. Lemma 2 will then give us the opposite result for $\phi^*$.

Without loss of generality, assume that $\alpha$ is of the form $\{l_1, \ldots, l_n\}$, the nearest solution $\alpha^*$ is of the form

```
NeighborhoodResolution(φ,α)
foreach violated clause γ1, oldest first
    foreach literal l in γ1, in random order
        foreach clause γ2 critically satisfied by l̄, oldest first
            γ3 ← resolve γ1 and γ2
            if γ3 ∉ φ then return γ3
return ᾱ
```

Figure 2: A resolution-based implicate generator.

$\{l_1, \ldots, l_k, \bar{l}_{k+1}, \ldots, \bar{l}_n\}$, and $\alpha'$ is $\{l_1, \ldots, l_{n-1}, \bar{l}_n\}$. We first examine $\mathcal{D}(\phi^-{}_\alpha)$. Each clause in $\phi^-{}_\alpha$ has the form $\bar{l}_{i_1} \vee \ldots \vee \bar{l}_{i_r}$, since it is violated by $\alpha$. By Lemma 1, we know that the corresponding $\{l_{i_1}, \ldots, l_{i_r}\}$ are partial solutions. Since $\alpha^*$ is the nearest solution, $\{l_1, \ldots, l_k\}$ must be the longest such partial solution, and therefore all clauses in $\phi^-{}_\alpha$ must have length less than or equal to $k$. So $\mathcal{D}(\phi^-{}_\alpha) = \langle 0, \ldots, 0, d_k, \ldots, d_0 \rangle$.

We will now show that $\mathcal{D}(\phi^-{}_{\alpha'})$ is worse. Note that $\bar{l}_1 \vee \ldots \vee \bar{l}_k \vee l_n$ is a clause that will be violated by $\alpha'$. Because its corresponding negated partial assignment $\{l_1, \ldots, l_k, \bar{l}_n\}$ is a subset of $\alpha^*$, by Lemma 1 this clause is also in $\phi^-$. Therefore $\mathcal{D}(\phi^-{}_{\alpha'})$ will be non-zero at the entry for clauses of length $k+1$, making it worse than $\mathcal{D}(\phi^-{}_\alpha)$. Since $\mathcal{D}(\phi^*{}_\alpha) + \mathcal{D}(\phi^-{}_\alpha)$ is a constant (Lemma 2), this means that $\mathcal{D}(\phi^*{}_{\alpha'})$ is better than $\mathcal{D}(\phi^*{}_\alpha)$. □

We have shown that our complete local search framework is indeed complete provided that the full implication closure of the original formula is eventually generated. At that point, the fitness landscape will have no local minima and the search procedure will head directly to the nearest solution. (If two neighbors are equally promising, random tie-breaking can be used to choose between them.) We might hope, however, that by choosing new clauses carefully, we can often avoid generating most of the closure while still benefiting from the smoothing effect.

## An Instantiation

Within this complete local search framework, many different algorithms can be developed. The most important choice is probably the method of generating new clauses. As long as it eventually generates all implied clauses, the search is guaranteed to be complete (Theorem 1), but the choice of method can greatly influence the efficiency of the resulting algorithm. For example, generating long clauses violated by the current assignment can quickly cause changes in the objective function, allowing escape from a local minimum. However, such specific clauses may not be useful during subsequent search. For unsatisfiable instances, a bias toward short clauses may be preferred, in an attempt to generate the empty clause quickly. This also minimizes the size of the expanding formula. The most promising technique we have evaluated so far is based on resolution.

### Neighborhood Resolution

In resolution, clauses such as $x \vee C_1$ and $\bar{x} \vee C_2$ are combined to yield $C_1 \vee C_2$. Neighborhood resolution (Cha & Iwama, 1996) refers to the special case in which there is exactly one variable that appears positively in one clause and negatively in the other. This guarantees that the result will not be rendered useless by the presence of $x \vee \bar{x}$. The particular variable and clauses that are used can be decided in many ways. In our current implementation (Figure 2), we select a random literal from the oldest violated clause (that is, whose status changed longest ago). We then select the oldest satisfied neighboring clause that depends crucially on the negation of that literal for its satisfaction. In the exceedingly rare case in which a new resolvent cannot be generated, the clause corresponding to the negation of the current assignment is returned. In either case, the new clause is guaranteed to be violated by the current assignment and is therefore potentially helpful for escaping from the current minimum.

To prove that this procedure can always generate a new clause, and thus will preserve the completeness of the search, we need only check its behavior at local minima:

**Theorem 2** *Let $\alpha$ be a local minimum on a formula $\phi$ which already contains the negation of $\alpha$ (call it $\bar{\alpha}$). If $\phi$ does not already contain the empty clause, then neighborhood resolution will generate a new resolvent.*

***Proof:*** We will proceed via the contrapositive, showing that if additional resolvents cannot be generated, the empty clause is present. Let $\mathcal{D}_i(\phi_\alpha)$ be the number of clauses of length $i$ in $\phi$ that are violated by $\alpha$. Note that the clause $\bar{\alpha}$ has length $n$, so $\mathcal{D}_n(\phi_\alpha) = 1$, its maximum possible value. Because $\alpha$ is a local minimum, $\mathcal{D}_n(\phi_{\alpha'}) = 1$ for all neighboring assignments $\alpha'$. This means that the clauses $\overline{\alpha'}$ must also be in $\phi$. A chain reaction is thus initiated. If neighborhood resolution cannot generate any new resolvents, then $\phi$ must already contain the $n$ clauses of length $n-1$ that neighborhood resolution can generate from resolving $\bar{\alpha}$ with the various $\overline{\alpha'}$. These shorter clauses are subsets of $\bar{\alpha}$, so $\mathcal{D}_{n-1}(\phi_\alpha) = n$. Again, because we are at a local minimum, $\mathcal{D}_{n-1}(\phi_{\alpha'}) = n$ for all $\alpha'$. For each $\alpha'$, all $n$ clauses resulting from dropping a single literal from $\overline{\alpha'}$ must be in $\phi$. The chain reaction continues, with neighborhood resolution providing all $\binom{n}{i}$ subsets of $\bar{\alpha}$ of length $i$ and the local minimum property implying the presence of the additional clauses necessary for producing still shorter clauses. Continuing in this manner, we see that the empty clause must already be present in $\phi$. □

### Other Features

Although the algorithm described above yields a respectable SAT solver, additional techniques can be incorporated into the algorithm to improve performance. To allow a meaningful comparison to existing, highly-tuned solvers, the implementation evaluated below included these standard enhancements:

**unit propagation** Whenever a unit clause is generated, the corresponding variable can be set and eliminated. Adding this feature improved performance on handmade and industrial instances (these benchmarks are described below).

**equivalent literal detection** If $l_1 \vee \overline{l_2}$ and $\overline{l_1} \vee l_2$ are both present, $l_2$ can be replaced everywhere by $l_1$. This limited form of equivalency reasoning seemed to improve performance on parity checking and many industrial instances.

**resolution between similar clauses** If two clauses differ only in the polarity of a single literal, their resolvent is generated immediately. In our implementation, it is easy to check for similar clauses in a hashtable, and obtaining these shortened clauses seemed to provide a slight improvement.

**appropriate data structures** Violated and critical clauses are held in doubly-linked lists, allowing constant-time removal as well as tracking clause age (for clause selection during resolution). The critical clause lists are indexed by variable. For each variable, two hashtables hold the clauses in which it occurs positively and negatively. To choose the best neighbor during hill-climbing, the improvement resulting from flipping each variable is calculated explicitly. For efficiency, variables whose attractiveness can only have decreased are not checked. After each resolution, only the variables involved are checked.

## Empirical Evaluation

To assess whether complete local search is of practical as well as theoretical interest, we tested our implementation using the instances and protocol of the 2003 SAT Competition (Simon, 2003; Hoos & Stützle, 2000). This allows us to compare against many state-of-the-art solvers using a broad collection of challenging and unbiased instances. The 996 competition instances are divided into three categories: random problems (produced by a parameterized stochastic generator), handmade problems (manually crafted to be both small and difficult), and industrial problems (encodings of problems from planning, model checking, and other applications). Within each category, closely related instances are grouped into a single 'series'. To minimize the effect of implementation details and emphasize breadth of ability, solvers are ranked according to how many different series they can solve, where a series is considered solved if at least one of its instances is solved. Solvers incorporating randomness are given three separate tries on each instance. Prizes are awarded for best performance in each category, with separate awards for performance on all instances and performance on satisfiable instances only. Prize-winning solvers from the 2002 competition were automatically entered in 2003. In the competition, each solver was allocated 900 seconds on an Athlon 1800+ with 1Gb RAM (a 2.4Ghz Pentium 4 was used for instances in the random family). We attempted to match these conditions in our tests, normalizing across machines using the DIMACS dfmax utility (and SPECint2000 results for the Athlon) and imposing a 900Mb memory limit.[1]

Table 1 presents the performance of complete local search (CLS) together with many state-of-the-art solvers, both in terms of the number of series solved and the number of instances. All data except those for CLS and RSAPS were copied from the published competition results. The first four rows represent all of the local search solvers from the competition. Unitwalk (Hirsh & Kojevnikov, 2003) was the best 2003 entrant on satisfiable random instances. Results of CLS are presented both with and without unsatisfiable instances. RSAPS (Hutter, Tompkins, & Hoos, 2002), while not entered in the competition, represents one of the best current local search solvers, if not the best.[2] It uses a clause weighting scheme that is carefully engineered for efficiency. The remaining seven rows represent complete tree search-based solvers, and include the other prize winners from 2003 and 2002.[3] In several cases, the same solver was best both overall and on only satisfiable instances.

The results convincingly demonstrate that complete local search is of practical interest. CLS surpasses all of the local search-based solvers from the 2003 competition on the primary competition measure, number of series solved, both overall and in each category, as well as on the number of instances solved overall. Even considering satisfiable instances alone, CLS solved more random series and a similar number of series overall. Had it entered the competition, CLS would have garnered best solver on satisfiable random instances. Its ability to prove unsatisfiability allows it to substantially surpass other local search solvers on industrial instances. Compared with RSAPS, CLS solved fewer random series but more series overall and a comparable number of instances overall.

Overall, CLS behaves more like a local search solver than a tree-based solver. It does better on satisfiable random instances than any tree-based solver, but it does not exhibit the overall performance of the best tree-based solvers.

The time CLS takes per flip increases as the size of the clause database grows during search. Techniques developed for other solvers, such as subsumption testing and forgetting irrelevant clauses, may be useful for managing this growth and reducing the time per flip.

Randomness is exploited by the algorithm in three places: to construct the initial assignment, to break ties between equally promising neighbors during hill-climbing, and to select variables to resolve on.

## Related Work

Constraint learning is a popular technique in tree-based search (Bayardo Jr. & Schrag, 1996), where it has been shown to increase the formal power of the proof system (Beame, Kautz, & Sabharwal, 2003). Usually, only clauses that are short or relevant to the current portion of the search tree are retained (Moskewicz *et al.*, 2001). In

[1] In cases in which we did not use a 2.4Ghz Pentium 4, we used 724 seconds on a 2.0 GHz Xeon, and 557 seconds on a 2.6Ghz Xeon.

[2] Tests on smaller instances (Hutter, Tompkins, & Hoos, 2002) suggest that RSAPS surpasses the performance of Novelty+ (Hoos, 1999) and ESG (Schuurmans, Southey, & Holte, 2001), and therefore also WalkSAT (Selman, Kautz, & Cohen, 1994) and DLM (Wu & Wah, 2000). We ran `saps-1.0` ourselves with default parameters and the `-reactive` (self-tuning) flag.

[3] Oksolver was not run on handmade or industrial problems in the 2003 competition.

| | Random ser. | Random inst. | Handmade ser. | Handmade inst. | Industrial ser. | Industrial inst. | Total ser. | Total inst. | |
|---|---|---|---|---|---|---|---|---|---|
| amvo | 0 | 0 | 1 | 10 | 1 | 2 | 2 | 12 | |
| qingting | 9 | 73 | 3 | 12 | 4 | 17 | 16 | 102 | |
| saturn | 14 | 127 | 7 | 29 | 3 | 22 | 24 | 178 | |
| unitwalk | 15 | 139 | 5 | 20 | 4 | 15 | 24 | 174 | best sat. random '03 |
| cls | 16 | 121 | 9 | 22 | 14 | 66 | 39 | 209 | |
| cls (sat only) | 16 | 121 | 5 | 17 | 2 | 15 | 23 | 153 | |
| rsaps | 21 | 177 | 8 | 26 | 1 | 9 | 30 | 212 | |
| kcnf | 25 | 163 | 16 | 51 | 6 | 17 | 47 | 231 | best random '03 |
| satzoo1 | 11 | 67 | 21 | 102 | 31 | 124 | 63 | 293 | best handmade '03 |
| forklift | 11 | 53 | 17 | 63 | 34 | 143 | 62 | 259 | best industrial '03 |
| oksolver | 16 | 96 | na | na | na | na | na | na | best random '02 |
| berkmin561 | 10 | 54 | 16 | 65 | 32 | 136 | 58 | 255 | best sat. handmade '02 |
| zchaff | 10 | 53 | 17 | 67 | 29 | 115 | 56 | 235 | best industrial, handmade '02 |
| limmat | 5 | 24 | 14 | 52 | 28 | 114 | 47 | 190 | best sat. industrial '02 |

Table 1: Performance on the 2003 SAT Competition instances: number of series and instances solved.

local search, techniques that associate a weight with each clause and change those weights over time can simulate the effect of adding duplicate clauses (Morris, 1993; Shang & Wah, 1997). The RSAPS solver takes this approach. Such methods can be seen as attempting to approximate the ideal search surface that complete local search builds. Explicitly adding implied clauses was suggested by Cha & Iwama (1996). They showed how implied clauses could provide improvements over duplicate clauses (see also Yokoo, 1997), although their method does not guarantee completeness. Morris (1993) noted that explicitly recording and increasing the cost of visited states can force an algorithm to eventually solve a satisfiable instance, although his scheme cannot easily detect unsatisfiability.

There have been several recent proposals for hybrids of local and tree-based search. To our knowledge, none achieves completeness without embedding the local search in a tree-like framework. For example, both Mazure, Saïs, & Grégoire (1998) and Eisenberg & Faltings (2003) propose schemes in which local search is used to determine a variable ordering for subsequent tree search.

The weak-commitment search strategy of Yokoo (1994) and the Learn-SAT algorithm of Richards & Richards (2000) are perhaps the previous proposals most similar to complete local search. In these closely related procedures, only the first branch of a search tree is explored. Variable choice is guided in part by a current infeasible assignment. At the first dead-end, a new clause is learned and the search starts again from the root. As in our approach, this no-good learning confers completeness. However, both weak-commitment search and Learn-SAT are fundamentally constructive, tree-like, search methods. Many variables can change their values between one construction episode and the next, and unit propagation lets one variable's value directly dictate the values of several others. In contrast, complete local search is based on hill-climbing with gradient information, always changing exactly one variable assignment at a time. In this sense, the steps of the search are restricted to 'local' changes to one part of the assignment. As in our experiments, Richards & Richards did not find the worst-case exponential space complexity of their method a hindrance in practice. Unfortunately, we cannot easily compare Learn-SAT with complete local search because all published results are in terms of constraint checks and node counts, which are meaningless for CLS, and its source code does not seem to be available on-line.

## Possible Extensions

There are many ways in which this work might be extended. Other strategies to generate new clauses may be useful. General resolution is powerful, but by itself doesn't suggest which clauses should be resolved. Two interesting alternatives to neighborhood resolution are conflict analysis and clause splitting. By conflict analysis, we mean a procedure that incrementally constructs a new assignment, exploiting unit propagation as in a tree search. When the partial assignment cannot be extended, the corresponding clause can be learned (Bayardo Jr. & Schrag, 1996). Such a procedure can perform the equivalent of many resolution steps, and can take advantage of variable choice heuristics developed for tree search algorithms. While this is the major search step in weak-commitment search and Learn-SAT, it can also be used simply as a clause generation technique in support of local search. Our preliminary experience with such a procedure is promising, but not yet as successful as with neighborhood resolution.

In clause splitting, a violated clause $C$ gives rise to $C \vee x_i$ and $C \vee \overline{x}_i$, where $x_i$ doesn't already appear in the clause. Whichever new clause is violated can be usefully learned, and provides a succinct way to make the current minimum less attractive. This method can be made complete when used with resolution between similar clauses, which we mentioned above.

If extended effort in one part of the search space does not yield a solution, there is no reason why the search cannot be restarted at another assignment. As long as the learned clauses are retained, completeness will not be sacrificed.

Preliminary evidence suggests that this approach could result in substantial gains. Using a greedy heuristic to generate the initial assignment might also improve performance, especially when used with a restarting strategy.

It should be possible to use a variation of complete local search to find all possible models of a formula. When a solution $\alpha$ is found, the negated clause $\overline{\alpha}$ can be added to the formula to force the search to another nearby solution, until eventually the formula becomes unsatisfiable.

Our framework applies directly to other constraint satisfaction problems. The size of the closure is increased, and constraint generation may become more complex, but the completeness proof still holds.

## Conclusions

We have presented the first local search algorithm that has been proved complete. This answers one of the major outstanding problems in propositional reasoning and search (Selman, Kautz, & McAllester, 1995; Kautz & Selman, 2003). The algorithm is fundamentally based on following gradient information, rather than relying on an external tree search for completeness. Constraint learning ensures completeness, but does not restrict the motion of the search. Although the completeness proof assumes that all implied clauses have been generated, this is far from necessary in practice. By testing an implementation of the method on challenging SAT instances, we have shown that the completeness guarantee does not hinder the empirical performance of the algorithm compared to other local search solvers. On the contrary, due in part to its ability to prove unsatisfiability, complete local search surpassed all the local search solvers from the 2003 SAT competition and performed comparably to RSAPS, one of the best local search solvers known.

Complex resolution and constraint learning techniques can easily be incorporated into our framework, raising the possibility of mimicking much of the reasoning done by current tree-based solvers. Complete local search suggests that the division between tree-based search and local search may be much more porous than commonly believed.

## Acknowledgments

We thank Jimmy H. M. Lee, Valeria de Paiva, and Johan de Kleer for helpful discussions and comments on a preliminary draft of this work, Wen Xu for help improving the C implementation of CLS, and Dave Tompkins for providing the source code for RSAPS. Much of this research was done while the first author was an intern at PARC. This work was supported in part by the DARPA NEST program under contract F33615-01-C-1904.

## References

Bayardo Jr., R. J., and Schrag, R. 1996. Using CSP look-back techniques to solve exceptionally hard SAT instances. In *Proceedings of CP-96*, 46–60.

Beame, P.; Kautz, H.; and Sabharwal, A. 2003. Understanding the power of clause learning. In *Proceedings of IJCAI-03*, 1194–1201.

Cha, B., and Iwama, K. 1996. Adding new clauses for faster local search. In *Proceedings of AAAI-96*, 332–337.

Eisenberg, C., and Faltings, B. 2003. Making the breakout algorithm complete using systematic search. In *Proceedings of IJCAI-03*, 1374–1375.

Garey, M. R., and Johnson, D. S. 1991. *Computers and Intractability*. New York: W.H. Freeman and Co.

Hirsh, E. A., and Kojevnikov, A. 2003. UnitWalk: A new SAT solver that uses local search guided by unit clause elimination. In *Proceedings of SAT-02*, 35–42.

Hoos, H. H., and Stützle, T. 2000. SATLIB: An online resource for resesarch on SAT. In Gent, I.; van Maaren, H.; and Walsh, T., eds., *SAT 2000*. IOS Press. 283–292.

Hoos, H. H. 1999. On the run-time behavior of stochastic local search algorithms for SAT. In *AAAI-99*, 661–666.

Hutter, F.; Tompkins, D. A. D.; and Hoos, H. H. 2002. Scaling and probabilistic smoothing: Efficient dynamic local search for SAT. In *Proceedings of CP '02*, 233–248.

Kautz, H., and Selman, B. 2003. Ten challenges redux: Recent progress in propositional reasoning and search. In *Proceedings of CP '03*, 1–18.

Mazure, B.; Saïs, L.; and Grégoire, E. 1998. Boosting complete techniques thanks to local search methods. *Annals of Mathematics and Artificial Intelligence* 22:319–331.

Morris, P. 1993. The breakout method for escaping from local minima. In *Proceedings of AAAI-93*, 40–45.

Moskewicz, M. W.; Madigan, C. F.; Zhao, Y.; Zhang, L.; and Malik, S. 2001. Chaff: engineering an efficient SAT solver. In *Proceedings of DAC-01*, 530–535.

Richards, T., and Richards, B. 2000. Nonsystematic search and no-good learning. *J. Auto. Reasoning* 24(4):483–533.

Schuurmans, D.; Southey, F.; and Holte, R. C. 2001. The exponentiated subgradient algorithm for heuristic boolean programming. In *Proceedings of IJCAI-01*, 334–341.

Selman, B.; Kautz, H. A.; and Cohen, B. 1994. Noise strategies for improving local search. In *AAAI-94*, 337–343.

Selman, B.; Kautz, H.; and McAllester, D. 1995. Ten challenges in propositional reasoning and search. In *Proceedings of IJCAI-95*, 50–54.

Shang, Y., and Wah, B. W. 1997. A discrete Lagrangian-based global-search method for solving satisfiability problems. *Journal of Global Optimization* 10:1–40.

Simon, L. 2003. The SAT-03 contest results site. http://www.lri.fr/~simon/contest03/results/.

Wu, Z., and Wah, B. 2000. An efficient global-search strategy in discrete lagrangian methods for solving hard satisfiability problems. In *Proceedings of AAAI-00*, 310–315.

Yokoo, M. 1994. Weak-commitment search for solving constraint satisfaction problems. In *Proc. AAAI-94*, 313–318.

Yokoo, M. 1997. Why adding more constraints makes a problem easier for hill-climbing algorithms: Analyzing landscapes of CSPs. In *Proceedings of CP-97*, 356–370.

# QUICKXPLAIN: Preferred Explanations and Relaxations for Over-Constrained Problems

**Ulrich Junker**
ILOG
1681, route des Dolines
06560 Valbonne
France
ujunker@ilog.fr

### Abstract

Over-constrained problems can have an exponential number of conflicts, which explain the failure, and an exponential number of relaxations, which restore the consistency. A user of an interactive application, however, desires explanations and relaxations containing the most important constraints. To address this need, we define preferred explanations and relaxations based on user preferences between constraints and we compute them by a generic method which works for arbitrary CP, SAT, or DL solvers. We significantly accelerate the basic method by a divide-and-conquer strategy and thus provide the technological basis for the explanation facility of a principal industrial constraint programming tool, which is, for example, used in numerous configuration applications.

## Introduction

Even experienced modelling experts may face over-constrained situations when formalizing the constraints of a combinatorial problem. In order to identify and to correct modelling errors, the expert needs to identify a subset of the constraints that explain the failure, while focusing on the most important ones. Alternatively, the expert can be interested in a subset of the constraints that have a solution, again preferring the important constraints.

In interactive applications, the careful selection of explanations and relaxations is an even more important problem. We consider a simple sales configuration problem, where not all user requirements can be satisfied:

**Example 1** *A customer wants to buy a station-wagon with following options, but has a limited budget of* 3000*:*

| | *Option* | *Requirement* $\rho_i$ | *Costs* |
|---|---|---|---|
| *1.* | *roof racks* | $x_1 = 1$ | $k_1 = 500$ |
| *2.* | *CD-player* | $x_2 = 1$ | $k_2 = 500$ |
| *3.* | *one additional seat* | $x_3 = 1$ | $k_3 = 800$ |
| *4.* | *metal color* | $x_4 = 1$ | $k_4 = 500$ |
| *5.* | *special luxury version* | $x_5 = 1$ | $k_5 = 2600$ |

*where the boolean variable* $x_i \in \{0, 1\}$ *indicates whether the* $i$*-th option is chosen and the costs* $y = \sum_{i=1}^{5} k_i \cdot x_i$ *are smaller than the total budget of* 3000*.*

A constraint solver maintaining bound consistency will successively increase the lower bound for $y$ if the requirements are propagated one after the other (see Table 1). When propagating the last requirement, the lower bound of 4900 exceeds 3000 and a failure is obtained. A straightforward explanation for this failure is obtained if we maintain the set of requirements explaining why $y \geq lb_i$. Unfortunately, the resulting explanations contains all requirements meaning that requirements may be removed without need.

| Requirement | Deduction | Argument/Conflict |
|---|---|---|
| $\rho_1 : x_1 = 1$ | $y \geq 500$ | $\{\rho_1\}$ |
| $\rho_2 : x_2 = 1$ | $y \geq 1000$ | $\{\rho_1, \rho_2\}$ |
| $\rho_3 : x_3 = 1$ | $y \geq 1800$ | $\{\rho_1, \rho_2, \rho_3\}$ |
| $\rho_4 : x_4 = 1$ | $y \geq 2300$ | $\{\rho_1, \rho_2, \rho_3, \rho_4\}$ |
| $\rho_5 : x_5 = 1$ | $y \geq 4900$ | $\{\rho_1, \rho_2, \rho_3, \rho_4, \rho_5\}$ |
| | $fail$ | $\{\rho_1, \rho_2, \rho_3, \rho_4, \rho_5\}$ |

Table 1: Computing a conflict during propagation.

| Requirement | Deduction | Argument/Conflict |
|---|---|---|
| $\rho_4 : x_4 = 1$ | $y \geq 500$ | $\{\rho_4\}$ |
| $\rho_5 : x_5 = 1$ | $y \geq 3100$ | $\{\rho_4, \rho_5\}$ |
| | $fail$ | $\{\rho_4, \rho_5\}$ |

Table 2: Propagation for producing a minimal conflict.

We are therefore interested in minimal (i.e. irreducible) conflicts. Table 2 shows another sequence of propagations, which results into the minimal conflict $\{\rho_4, \rho_5\}$. If the customer prefers a special luxury version to metal color, $\rho_4$ will be removed, meaning that we can get another conflict, e.g. $\{\rho_3, \rho_5\}$. However, the customer prefers an additional seat to the special luxury version and now removes $\rho_5$, meaning that only $\{\rho_1, \rho_2, \rho_3\}$ are kept. This relaxation of the requirements is not maximal, since $\rho_4$ can be re-added after the removal of $\rho_5$. Unnecessary removals can be avoided if we directly produced the conflict $\{\rho_3, \rho_5\}$ containing the preferred requirements. If we take into account user preferences between requirements, we can directly determine preferred explanations as the one shown in Table 3 (we write $\rho_i \prec \rho_j$ iff $\rho_i$ is preferred to $\rho_j$).

Hence, the essential issue in explaining a failure of a constraint solver is not the capability of recording a proof, but selecting a proof among a potentially huge number that does not contain unnecessary constraints and that involves

| Requirement | Deduction | Argument/Conflict |
|---|---|---|
| $\rho_3 : x_3 = 1$ | $y \geq 800$ | $\{\rho_3\}$ |
| $\rho_5 : x_5 = 1$ | $y \geq 3400$ | $\{\rho_3, \rho_5\}$ |
| | $fail$ | $\{\rho_3, \rho_5\}$ |

Table 3: A preferred explanation for $\rho_3 \prec \rho_1 \prec \rho_2 \prec \rho_5 \prec \rho_4$.

the most preferred constraints. We address this issue by a preference-controlled algorithm that successively adds most preferred constraints until they fail. It then backtracks and removes least preferred constraints if this preserves the failure. Relaxations can be computed dually, first removing least preferred constraints from an inconsistent set until it is consistent. The number of consistency checks can drastically be reduced by a divide-and-conquer strategy that successively decomposes the overall problem. In the good case, a single consistency check can remove all the constraints of a subproblem.

We first define preferred relaxations and explanations and then develop the preference-based explanation algorithms. After that, we discuss consistency checking involving search as well as related work.

## Preferred Explanations and Relaxations

Although the discussion of this paper focuses on constraint satisfaction problems (CSP), its results and algorithms apply to any satisfiability problem such as propositional satisfiability (SAT) or the satisfiability of concepts in description logic (DL). We completely abstract from the underlying constraint language and simply assume that there is a monotonic satisfiability property: *if $S$ is a solution of a set $\mathcal{C}_1$ of constraints then it is also a solution of all subsets $\mathcal{C}_2$ of $\mathcal{C}_1$.*

If a set of constraints has no solution, some constraints must be relaxed to restore consistency. It is convenient to distinguish a background $\mathcal{B}$ containing the constraints that cannot be relaxed. Typically, unary constraints $x \in D$ between a variable $x$ and a domain $D$ will belong to the background. In interactive problems, only user requirements can be relaxed, leaving all other constraints in the background. We now define a relaxation of a problem $\mathcal{P} := (\mathcal{B}, \mathcal{C})$:

**Definition 1** *A subset $R$ of $\mathcal{C}$ is a* relaxation *of a problem $\mathcal{P} := (\mathcal{B}, \mathcal{C})$ iff $\mathcal{B} \cup R$ has a solution.*

A relaxation exists iff $\mathcal{B}$ is consistent. Over-constrained problems can have an exponential number of relaxations. A user typically prefers to keep the important constraints and to relax less important ones. That means that the user is at least able to compare the importance of some constraints. Thus, we will assume the existence of a strict partial order between the constraints of $\mathcal{C}$, denoted by $\prec$. We write $c_1 \prec c_2$ iff (the selection of) constraint $c_1$ is preferred to (the selection of) $c_2$. (Junker & Mailharro 2003) show how those preferences can be specified in a structured and compact way. There are different ways to define preferred relaxations on such a partial order (cf. e.g. (Junker 2002)). In this paper, we will pursue the lexicographical approach of (Brewka 1989) which assumes the existence of a unique ranking among the constraints. The partial order $\prec$ is considered an incomplete specification of this ranking. We will introduce three extensions of this partial order:

- A *linearization* $<$ of $\prec$, which is a strict total order that is a superset of $\prec$ and which describes the ranking.
- Two lexicographic extensions of $<$, denoted by $<_{lex}$ and $<_{antilex}$, which are defined over sets of constraints.

Those lexicographic orders will be defined below. For now, we keep only in mind that two relaxations can be compared by the lexicographic extension $<_{lex}$.

Similarly, an over-constrained problem may have an exponential number of conflicts that explain the inconsistency.

**Definition 2** *A subset $C$ of $\mathcal{C}$ is a* conflict *of a problem $\mathcal{P} := (\mathcal{B}, \mathcal{C})$ iff $\mathcal{B} \cup C$ has no solution.*

A conflict exists iff $\mathcal{B} \cup \mathcal{C}$ is inconsistent. Some conflicts are more relevant for the user than other conflicts. Suppose that there are two conflicts in a given constraint system:

- Conflict 1 involves only very important constraints.
- Conflict 2 involves less important constraints.

The intuition is that conflict 1 is much more significant for the user than conflict 2. Indeed, in any way, the user will have to resolve the first conflict, and thus, he will have to relax at least one important constraint. As for the second conflict, a less important constraint can be relaxed and the user will consider such a modification as more easy to do.

We now give a formalization of the above intuitions. We define *preferred relaxations* following (Brewka 1989) and then give an analogous definition for *preferred conflicts*. Firstly, we recall the definition of the lexicographic extension of a total order.

**Definition 3** *Given a total order $<$ on $\mathcal{C}$, we enumerate the elements of $\mathcal{C}$ in increasing $<$-order $c_1, \ldots, c_n$ starting with the most important constraints (i.e. $c_i < c_j$ implies $i < j$) and compare two subsets $X, Y$ of $\mathcal{C}$ lexicographically:*

$$\begin{array}{c} X <_{lex} Y \\ \textit{iff} \\ \exists k : c_k \in X - Y \textit{ and} \\ X \cap \{c_1, \ldots, c_{k-1}\} = Y \cap \{c_1, \ldots, c_{k-1}\} \end{array} \tag{1}$$

Next, we define preferred relaxations, first for a total order over the constraints, and then for a partial order:

**Definition 4** *Let $\mathcal{P} := (\mathcal{B}, \mathcal{C}, <)$ be a totally ordered problem. A relaxation $R$ of $\mathcal{P}$ is a* preferred relaxation *of $\mathcal{P}$ iff there is no other relaxation $R^*$ of $\mathcal{P}$ s.t. $R^* <_{lex} R$.*

**Definition 5** *Let $\mathcal{P} := (\mathcal{B}, \mathcal{C}, \prec)$ be a partially ordered problem. A relaxation $R$ of $\mathcal{P}$ is a* preferred relaxation *of $\mathcal{P}$ iff there is a linearization $<$ of $\prec$ s.t. $R$ is a preferred relaxation of $(\mathcal{B}, \mathcal{C}, <)$.*

A preferred relaxation $R$ is maximal (non-extensible) meaning that each proper superset of $R$ has no solution. If no preferences are given, i.e. $\prec$ is the empty relation, then the maximal relaxations and the preferred relaxations coincide. If $\prec$ is a strict total order and $\mathcal{B}$ is consistent, then $\mathcal{P}$ has a unique preferred relaxation.

The definitions of preferred conflicts follow the same scheme as the definitions of the preferred relaxations. In order to get a conflict among the most important constraints, we prefer the retraction of least important constraints:

**Definition 6** *Given a total order $<$ on $\mathcal{C}$, we enumerate the elements of $\mathcal{C}$ in increasing order $c_1, \ldots, c_n$ (i.e. $c_i < c_j$ implies $i < j$) and compare $X$ and $Y$ lexicographically in the reverse order:*

$$\begin{array}{c} X <_{antilex} Y \\ \textit{iff} \\ \exists k : c_k \in Y - X \textit{ and} \\ X \cap \{c_{k+1}, \ldots, c_n\} = Y \cap \{c_{k+1}, \ldots, c_n\} \end{array} \quad (2)$$

A preferred conflict can now be defined:

**Definition 7** *Let $\mathcal{P} := (\mathcal{B}, \mathcal{C}, <)$ be a totally ordered problem. A conflict $C$ of $\mathcal{P}$ is a* preferred conflict *of $\mathcal{P}$ iff there is no other conflict $C^*$ of $\mathcal{P}$ s.t. $C^* <_{antilex} C$.*

**Definition 8** *Let $\mathcal{P} := (\mathcal{B}, \mathcal{C}, \prec)$ be a partially ordered problem. A conflict $C$ of $\mathcal{P}$ is a* preferred conflict *of $\mathcal{P}$ iff there is a linearization $<$ of $\prec$ s.t. $C$ is a preferred conflict of $(\mathcal{B}, \mathcal{C}, <)$*

A preferred conflict $C$ is minimal (irreducible) meaning that each proper subset of $C$ has a solution. If no preferences are given ($\prec$ is empty), then the minimal conflicts and the preferred conflicts coincide. If $\prec$ is a strict total order and $\mathcal{B} \cup \mathcal{C}$ is inconsistent, then $\mathcal{P}$ has a unique preferred conflict. Hence, a total order uniquely specifies or characterizes the conflict that will be detected by our algorithms. It is also interesting to note that the constraint graph consisting of the constraints of a minimal conflict is connected.

**Proposition 1** *Let $C$ be a conflict for a CSP $\mathcal{P} := (\emptyset, \mathcal{C}, \prec)$. If $C$ is a minimal conflict of $\mathcal{P}$, then the constraint graph of $C$ consists of a single strongly connected component.*

There is a strong duality between relaxations and conflicts with a rich mathematical structure. The relationships between $<_{antilex}$ and $<_{lex}$ can be stated as follows:

**Proposition 2** $X <_{antilex} Y$ *iff* $Y (<^{-1})_{lex} X$.

Conflicts correspond to the complements of relaxations of the negated problem with inverted preferences:

**Proposition 3** *Let $\neg c_j \succ' \neg c_i$ iff $c_i \prec c_j$. $R$ is a preferred relaxation (conflict) of $(\mathcal{B}, \mathcal{C}, \prec)$ iff $\{\neg c \mid c \in \mathcal{C} - C\}$ is a preferred conflict (relaxation) of $(\neg\mathcal{B}, \{\neg c \mid c \in \mathcal{C}\}, \succ')$.*

The definition of preferred relaxations and preferred conflicts can be made constructive, thus providing the basis for the explanation and relaxation algorithms. Consider a totally ordered problem $\mathcal{P} := (\mathcal{B}, \mathcal{C}, <)$ s.t. $\mathcal{B}$ is consistent, but not $\mathcal{B} \cup \mathcal{C}$. We enumerate the elements of $\mathcal{C}$ in increasing $<$-order $c_1, \ldots, c_n$. We construct the preferred relaxation of $\mathcal{P}$ by $R_0 := \emptyset$ and

$$R_i := \begin{cases} R_{i-1} \cup \{c_i\} & \text{if } \mathcal{B} \cup R_{i-1} \cup \{c_i\} \text{ has a solution} \\ R_{i-1} & \text{otherwise} \end{cases}$$

The preferred conflict of $\mathcal{P}$ is constructed in the reverse order. Let $C_n := \mathcal{C}$ and

$$C_i := \begin{cases} C_{i+1} - \{c_i\} & \text{if } \mathcal{B} \cup C_{i+1} - \{c_i\} \text{ has no solution} \\ C_{i+1} & \text{otherwise} \end{cases}$$

Adding a constraint to a relaxation thus corresponds to the retraction of a constraint from a conflict. As a consequence of this duality, algorithms for computing relaxations can be reformulated for computing conflicts and vice versa.

Preferred conflicts explain why best elements cannot be added to preferred relaxations. In fact, the $<$-minimal element that is not contained in the preferred relaxation $R$ of a problem $\mathcal{P} := (\mathcal{B}, \mathcal{C}, <)$ is equal to the $<$-maximal element of the preferred conflict $C$ of $\mathcal{P}$:

**Proposition 4** *If $C$ is a preferred conflict of $\mathcal{P} := (\mathcal{B}, \mathcal{C}, <)$ and $R$ is a preferred relaxation of $\mathcal{P}$, then the $<$-minimal element of $\mathcal{C} - R$ is equal to the $<$-maximal element of $C$.*

Preferred conflicts permit an incremental construction of preferred relaxations while avoiding unnecessary commitments. For example, consider $\alpha \prec \beta \prec \gamma$ and the background constraints $\neg\beta \vee \neg\delta$, $\neg\gamma \vee \neg\delta$. Then $\{\beta, \delta\}$ is a preferred conflict for the order $\alpha < \beta < \gamma < \delta$. Since $\gamma$ is neither an element of the conflict $\{\beta, \delta\}$, nor $\prec$-preferred to any of its elements, we can move it behind $\delta$, thus getting a new linearization $\alpha <' \beta <' \delta <' \gamma$. The linearizations $<$ and $<'$ have the same preferred conflict and the same preferred relaxation. This observation shows that we can construct the head (or start) of a preferred relaxation from a preferred conflict $C$ of $\prec$. We identify a worst element for $C$, precede it by the other elements of $C$ and all constraints $Pred(C)$ that are preferred to an element of $C$. We then reduce the problem to

$$(\mathcal{B} \cup Pred(C) \cup C - \{\alpha\}, \mathcal{C} - Pred(C) - C, \prec)$$

Please note that non-preferred conflicts such as $\{\gamma, \delta\}$ include irrelevant constraints such as $\gamma$ and do not allow this reduction of the problem. Given different preferred conflicts, we can construct different preferred relaxations. This is interesting in an interactive setting where the user wants to control the selection of a relaxation.

## Computing Preferred Explanations

We compute preferred conflicts and relaxations by following the constructive definitions. The basic algorithm will (arbitrarily) choose one linearization $<$ of the preferences $\prec$, thus fixing the resulting conflict or relaxation. It then inspects one constraint after the other and determines whether it belongs to the preferred conflict or relaxation of $<$. It thus applies a consistency checker *isConsistent*$(C)$ to a sequence of subproblems. In this section, we assume that the consistency checker is complete and returns true if $C$ has a solution. Otherwise, it returns false. For a CSP, complete consistency checking can be achieved as follows:

- arc consistency AC is sufficient for tree-like CSPs.
- systematic tree search maintaining AC is needed for arbitrary CSPs.

Incomplete checkers can provide non-minimal conflicts, as will be discussed in the next section.

### Iterative Addition and Retraction

The basic algorithm successively maps a problem to a simpler problem. Initially, it checks whether the background is

**Algorithm** QUICKXPLAIN($\mathcal{B}, \mathcal{C}, \prec$)

1. **if** *isConsistent*($\mathcal{B} \cup \mathcal{C}$) return 'no conflict';
2. **else if** $\mathcal{C} = \emptyset$ **then** return $\emptyset$;
3. **else** return QUICKXPLAIN'($\mathcal{B}, \mathcal{B}, \mathcal{C}, \prec$);

**Algorithm** QUICKXPLAIN'($\mathcal{B}, \Delta, \mathcal{C}, \prec$)

4. **if** $\Delta \neq \emptyset$ and not *isConsistent*($\mathcal{B}$) **then** return $\emptyset$;
5. **if** $\mathcal{C} = \{\alpha\}$ **then** return $\{\alpha\}$;
6. let $\alpha_1, \ldots, \alpha_n$ be an enumeration of $\mathcal{C}$ that respects $\prec$;
7. let $k$ be *split*($n$) where $1 \leq k < n$;
8. $\mathcal{C}_1 := \{\alpha_1, \ldots, \alpha_k\}$ and $\mathcal{C}_2 := \{\alpha_{k+1}, \ldots, \alpha_n\}$;
9. $\Delta_2 :=$ QUICKXPLAIN'($\mathcal{B} \cup \mathcal{C}_1, \mathcal{C}_1, \mathcal{C}_2, \prec$);
10. $\Delta_1 :=$ QUICKXPLAIN'($\mathcal{B} \cup \Delta_2, \Delta_2, \mathcal{C}_1, \prec$);
11. return $\Delta_1 \cup \Delta_2$;

Figure 1: Divide-and-Conquer for Explanations.

inconsistent. If $\mathcal{C}$ is empty, then the problem can immediately be solved:

**Proposition 5** *Let $\mathcal{P} := (\mathcal{B}, \mathcal{C}, \prec)$. If $\mathcal{B}$ is inconsistent then the empty set is the only preferred conflict of $\mathcal{P}$ and $\mathcal{P}$ has no relaxation. If $\mathcal{B} \cup \mathcal{C}$ is consistent then $\mathcal{C}$ is the only preferred relaxation of $\mathcal{P}$ and $\mathcal{P}$ has no conflict.*

If $\mathcal{C}$ is not empty, then the algorithm follows the constructive definition of a preferred relaxation. In each step, it chooses a $\prec$-minimal element $\alpha$ and removes it from $\mathcal{C}$. If $\mathcal{B} \cup R \cup \{\alpha\}$ is consistent, $\alpha$ is added to $R$. A preferred relaxation can be computed by iterating these steps.

The constructive definition of a preferred conflict starts by checking the consistency of the complete set $\mathcal{C} \cup \mathcal{B}$ and then removes one constraint after the other. Whereas the addition of a constraint is an incremental operation for a consistency checker, the removal is a non-incremental operations. Therefore, the computation of a conflict starts with the process of constructing a relaxation $R_i$. When the first inconsistency is obtained, then we have detected the best element $\alpha_{k+1}$ that is removed from the preferred relaxation. According to Proposition 4, $\alpha_{k+1}$ is the worst element of the preferred conflict. Hence, the preferred conflict is a subset of $R_k \cup \{\alpha_{k+1}\}$ and $C_{n-k}$ is equal to $\{\alpha_{k+1}\}$. We now switch over to the constructive definition of preferred conflicts and use it to find the elements that are still missing.

**Example 2** *As a simple benchmark problem, we consider $n$ boolean variables, a background constraint $\sum_{i=1}^{n} k_i \cdot x_i < 3n$ (with $k_i = n$ for $i = 9, 10, 12$ and $k_i = 1$ otherwise) and $n$ constraints $x_i = 1$. The algorithm introduces the constraints for $i = 1, \ldots, 12$, then switches over to a removal phase.*

## Divide-and-Conquer for Explanations

We can significantly accelerate the basic algorithms if conflicts are small compared to the number of constraints. In this case, we can reduce the number of consistency checks if we remove whole blocks of constraints. We thus split $\mathcal{C}$ into subsets $\mathcal{C}_1$ and $\mathcal{C}_2$. If the remaining problem $\mathcal{C}_1$ is inconsistent, then we can eliminate all constraints in $\mathcal{C}_2$ while needing a single check. Otherwise, we have to re-add some of the constraints of $\mathcal{C}_2$. The following property explains how the conflicts of the two subproblems can be assembled.

**Proposition 6** *Suppose $\mathcal{C}_1$ and $\mathcal{C}_2$ are disjoint and that no constraint of $\mathcal{C}_2$ is preferred to a constraint of $\mathcal{C}_1$:*

1. *If $\Delta_1$ is a preferred relaxation of $(\mathcal{B}, \mathcal{C}_1, \prec)$ and $\Delta_2$ is a preferred relaxation of $(\mathcal{B} \cup \Delta_1, \mathcal{C}_2, \prec)$, then $\Delta_1 \cup \Delta_2$ is a preferred relaxation of $(\mathcal{B}, \mathcal{C}_1 \cup \mathcal{C}_2, \prec)$.*
2. *If $\Delta_2$ is a preferred conflict of $(\mathcal{B} \cup \mathcal{C}_1, \mathcal{C}_2, \prec)$ and $\Delta_1$ is a preferred conflict of $(\mathcal{B} \cup \Delta_2, \mathcal{C}_1, \prec)$, then $\Delta_1 \cup \Delta_2$ is a preferred conflict of $(\mathcal{B}, \mathcal{C}_1 \cup \mathcal{C}_2, \prec)$.*

We divide an inconsistent problem in this way until we obtain subproblems of the form $\mathcal{P}' := (\mathcal{B}, \{\alpha\}, \prec)$, where all but one constraint are in the background. We then know that $\mathcal{B} \cup \{\alpha\}$ is inconsistent. According to Proposition 5, it is sufficient to check whether $\mathcal{B}$ is consistent in order to determine whether $\{\alpha\}$ is a preferred conflict of $\mathcal{B}$. Algorithm QUICKXPLAIN (cf. Figure 1) exploits propositions 5 and 6. It is parameterized by a split-function that chooses the subproblems for a chosen linearization of $\prec$ (see line 6):

**Theorem 1** *The algorithm* QUICKXPLAIN($\mathcal{B}, \mathcal{C}, \prec$) *always terminates. If $\mathcal{B} \cup \mathcal{C}$ has a solution then it returns 'no conflict'. Otherwise, it returns a preferred conflict of $(\mathcal{B}, \mathcal{C}, \prec)$.*

QUICKXPLAIN spends most of its time in the consistency checks. A subprocedure QUICKXPLAIN' is only called if $\mathcal{C}$ is a non-empty conflict and if a part of the background, namely $\mathcal{B} - \Delta$ has a solution. Figure 2 shows the call graph of QUICKXPLAIN' for example 2. If no pruning (line 4) occurs, then the call graph is a binary tree containing a leaf for each of the $n$ constraints. This tree has $2n - 1$ nodes. The square nodes correspond to calls of QUICKXPLAIN' that test the consistency of the background (line 4). Successful tests are depicted by grey squares, whereas failing tests are represented by black squares. For example, the test fails for node $n_{11}$, meaning that $n_{11}$ is pruned and that its subtree is not explored (indicated by white circles). The left sibling $n_{10}$ of the pruned node $n_{11}$ does not need a consistency check (line 4) and is depicted by a grey circle. If a test succeeds for a leaf, then its constraint belongs to the conflict (line 5) and will be added to the background.

If we choose *split*$(n) := \frac{n}{2}$ then subproblems are divided into smaller subproblems of same size and a path from the root to a leaf contains $\log n$ nodes. If the preferred conflict has $k$ elements, then the non-pruned tree is formed of the $k$ paths from the root node to the $k$ leaves of those elements. In the best case, all $k$ elements belong to a single subproblem that has $2k - 1$ nodes and there is a common path for all elements from the root to the root of this subproblem. This path has the length $log\ n - log\ k = log \frac{n}{k}$. In the worst case, the paths join in the top in a subtree of depth $log\ k$. Then we have $k$ paths of length $log \frac{n}{k}$ from the leaves of this subtree to the leaves of the conflict. All other cases fall in between these extremes. For problems with one million of constraints, QUICKXPLAIN thus needs between 33 and 270 checks if the conflict contains 8 elements. Table 4 gives the complexities of different split-functions. For lines 2 and 3, the shortest path has length 1, but the longest one has length $n$.

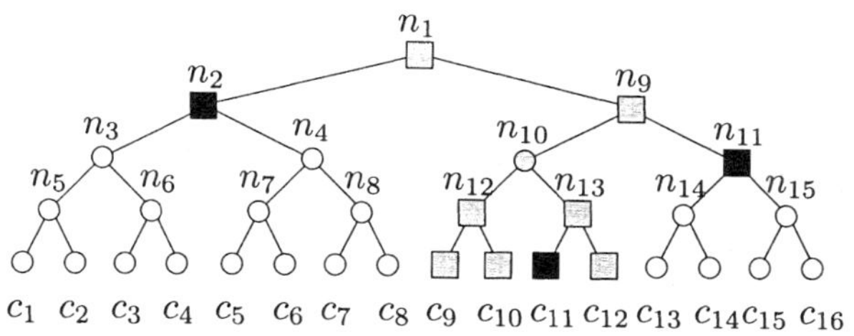


Figure 2: Call graph for QUICKXPLAIN.

| Method | Split | Best Case | Worst Case |
|---|---|---|---|
| 1. | $split(n) = n/2$ | $log\frac{n}{k} + 2k$ | $2k \cdot log\frac{n}{k} + 2k$ |
| 2. | $split(n) = n - 1$ | $2k$ | $2n$ |
| 3. | $split(n) = 1$ | $k$ | $n + k$ |

Table 4: Number of Consistency Checks.

If a problem is decomposable and the preferred conflict is completely localized in one of the subproblems, say $P^*$, then the size of the conflict is bounded by the size of $P^*$. QUICKXPLAIN will prune all subtrees in the call graph that do not contain an element of $P^*$ and thus discovers irrelevant subproblems dynamically. Similar to (Mauss & Tatar 2002), it thus profits from the properties of decomposable problems, but additionally takes preferences into account.

Further improvements of QUICKXPLAIN are possible if knowledge of the constraint graph is exploited. Once an element $c$ of the conflict has been determined, all non-connected elements can be removed. If two elements $c_1, c_2$ have been detected and all paths from $c_1$ and $c_2$ go through a constraint from $X$, then at least one element of $X$ belongs to the conflict. Hence, graph algorithms for strongly connected components and cut detection make QUICKXPLAIN more informed and enable deductions on conflicts.

### Multiple Preferred Explanations

We use preference-based search (Junker 2002) to determine multiple preferred relaxations. It sets up a choice point each time a constraint $c_i$ is consistent w.r.t. a partial relaxation $R_{i-1}$. The left branch adds $c_i$ to $R_{i-1}$ and determines preferred relaxations containing $c_i$. The right branch adds other constraints to $R_{i-1}$ that entail $\neg c_i$. We can adapt PBS to the constructive definition of preferred conflicts. We set up a choice point when $c_i$ is removed from $C_{i+1}$. The left branch removes $c_i$ from $C_{i+1}$ and determines preferred conflicts not containing $c_i$. The right branch removes other constraints from $C_{i+1}$ such the removal of $c_i$ leads to a solution.

## Consistency Checking with Search

If search fails, but not constraint propagation, then the consistency checking of QUICKXPLAIN requires multiple searches through similar search spaces.

We consider a variant of example 1, where the type of each option needs to be chosen from a product catalogue in order to determine its precise price. Furthermore, we suppose that there are several compatibility constraint between those types. A solution consists of a set of options and their types such that the budget and the compatibility constraints are met. Propagation is insufficient to detect the infeasibility of an option if the constraint network contains one or several cycles.

Hence, the consistency checker will search for a solution to prove the consistency of a set $X$ of constraints. If successful, QUICKXPLAIN adds further constraints $\Delta$ and checks $X \cup \Delta$. For example, $X$ may contain a requirement for a CD-player and $\Delta$ may refine it by requiring a CD-player of type A if one is selected. In order to prove the consistency of $X$, the checker must be able to produce a solution $S$ of $X$. If $S$ contains a CD-player of type A, then it satisfies $\Delta$ and it is not necessary to start a new search. Or we may repair $S$ by just changing the type of the CD-player. We therefore keep the solution $S$ as witness for the consistency of $X$. This *witness of success* can guide the search for a solution of $X \cup \Delta$ by preferring the variable values in $S$. It can also avoid a re-exploration of the search tree for $X$ if the new search starts from the search path that produced $S$.

If a consistency check fails for $X$, then QUICKXPLAIN removes some constraints $\Delta$ from $X$ and checks $X - \Delta$. For example, $X$ may contain requirements for all options, including that for a CD-player of type A. Suppose that the inconsistency of $X$ can be proved by trying out all different metal colors. Now we remove the requirement for a CD-player of type $A$ from $X$. If the CD-player type was not critical for the failure, then it is still sufficient to instantiate the metal color in order to fail. Otherwise, we additionally instantiate the type of the CD-player. Since these critical variables suffice to provoke a failure of search, we can keep them as *witness of failure* and instantiate them first when checking $X - \Delta$. Decomposition methods (Dechter & Pearl 1989) such as cycle cutset give good hints for identifying a witness of failure.

This analysis shows that QUICKXPLAIN does not need to start a search from scratch for each consistency check, but can profit from witnesses for failure and success. The witness of success guides a least-commitment strategy that tries to prove consistency, whereas a first-fail strategy is guided by a witness of failure and tries to prove inconsistency.

If problems are more difficult, but search of the complete problem fails in a specified time, then approximation techniques can be used. Firstly, QUICKXPLAIN can be stopped when it has found the $k$ worst elements of a preferred conflict, which is sometimes sufficient. Secondly, a correct, but incomplete method can be used for consistency checking. An arc consistency based solver has these properties. Another example is tree search that is interrupted after a limited amount of time. If such a method reports false, QUICKXPLAIN knows that there is a failure and proceeds as usual. Otherwise, QUICKXPLAIN has no precise information about the consistency of the problem and does not remove constraints. As a consequence, it always returns a conflict, but not necessarily a minimal one. Hence, there is a trade-off between optimality of the results and the response time.

## Related Work

Conflicts and relaxations are studied and used in many areas of automated reasoning such as truth maintenance systems (TMS), nonmononotonic reasoning, model-based diagnosis, intelligent search, and recently explanations for over-constrained CSPs. Whereas the notion of preferred relaxations found a lot of interest, e.g. in the form of extensions of prioritized default theories (Brewka 1989), the concept of a preferred explanation appears to be new. It is motivated by recent work on interactive configuration, where explanations should contain the most important user requirements.

Conflicts can be computed by recording and analyzing proofs or by testing the consistency of subsets. Truth maintenance systems elaborate the first approach and record the proof made by an inference system. Conflicts are computed from the proof on a by-need basis (Doyle 1979) or by propagating conflicts (de Kleer 1986) over the recorded proof. There have been numerous applications of TMS-techniques to CSPs, mainly to achieve more intelligent search behaviour, cf. e.g. (Ginsberg & McAllester 1994; Prosser 1993; Jussien, Debruyne, & Boizumault 2000). More recently, TMS-methods have been embedded in CSPs to compute explanations for CSPs (Sqalli & Freuder 1996).

The computation of minimal and preferred conflicts, however, requires the selection of a suitable proof, which can be achieved by selecting the appropriate subset controlled by preferences. Iterative approaches successively remove elements (Bakker *et al.* 1993) or add elements (de Siqueira N. & Puget 1988) and test conflict membership. QUICKXPLAIN unifies and improves these two methods by successively decomposing the complete explanation problem into subproblems of the same size. (Mauss & Tatar 2002) follow a similar approach, but do not take preferences into account. (de la Banda, Stuckey, & Wazny 2003) determine all conflicts by exploring a conflict-set tree. These checking-based methods for computing explanations work for any solver and do not require that the solver identifies its precise inferences. This task is indeed difficult for global $n$-ary constraints that encapsulate algorithms from graph theory. Moreover, subset checking can also be used to find explanations for linear programming as shown in (Chinneck 1997).

## Conclusion

We have developed algorithms that compute preferred conflicts and relaxations of over-constrained problems and thus help developers and users of Constraint Programming to identify causes of an inconsistency, while focusing on the most important constraints. Since the algorithms just suppose the existence of a consistency checker, they can be applied to all kind of satisfiability problems, including CSPs, SAT, or different combinatorial problems such as graph coloring. A divide-and-conquer strategy significantly accelerates the basic methods, ensures a good scalability w.r.t. problem size, and provides the technological basis for the explanation facility of a principal industrial constraint programming tool (ILOG 2003b) and a CP-based configurator (ILOG 2003a), which is used in various B2B and B2C configuration applications.

QUICKXPLAIN has a polynomial response time for polynomial CSPs. For other problems, multiple searches through similar search spaces are needed. Search overhead can be avoided by maintaining witnesses for the success and failure of previous consistency checks. If response time is limited, the QUICKXPLAIN algorithm can compute an approximation of a minimal conflict by using an incomplete checker.

## Acknowledgements

I thank my colleagues and the anonymous reviewers for helpful comments. Olivier Lhomme made significant contributions to the clarity of the paper.

## References

Bakker, R. R.; Dikker, F.; Tempelman, F.; and Wognum, P. M. 1993. Diagnosing and solving over-determined constraint satisfaction problems. In *IJCAI-93*, 276–281.

Brewka, G. 1989. Preferred subtheories: An extended logical framework for default reasoning. In *IJCAI-89*, 1043–1048.

Chinneck, J. W. 1997. Finding a useful subset of constraints for analysis in an infeasible linear porgram. *INFORMS Journal on Computing* 9:164–174.

de Kleer, J. 1986. An assumption–based truth maintenance system. *Artificial Intelligence* 28:127–162.

de la Banda, M. G.; Stuckey, P. J.; and Wazny, J. 2003. Finding all minimal unsatisfiable subsets. In *PPDP 2003*, 32–43.

de Siqueira N., J. L., and Puget, J.-F. 1988. Explanation-based generalisation of failures. In *ECAI-88*, 339–344.

Dechter, R., and Pearl, J. 1989. Tree clustering for constraint networks. *Artificial Intelligence* 38:353–366.

Doyle, J. 1979. A truth maintenance system. *Artificial Intelligence* 12:231–272.

Ginsberg, M., and McAllester, D. 1994. GSAT and dynamic backtracking. In *KR'94*, 226–237.

ILOG. 2003a. ILOG JConfigurator V2.1. Engine programming guide, ILOG S.A., Gentilly, France.

ILOG. 2003b. ILOG Solver 6.0. User manual, ILOG S.A., Gentilly, France.

Junker, U., and Mailharro, D. 2003. Preference programming: Advanced problem solving for configuration. *AI-EDAM* 17(1):13–29.

Junker, U. 2002. Preference-based search and multi-criteria optimization. In *AAAI-02*, 34–40.

Jussien, N.; Debruyne, R.; and Boizumault, P. 2000. Maintaining arc-consistency within dynamic backtracking. In *CP'2000*, 249–261.

Mauss, J., and Tatar, M. 2002. Computing minimal conflicts for rich constraint languages. In *ECAI-02*, 151–155.

Prosser, P. 1993. Hybrid algorithms for the constraint satisfaction problem. *Computational Intelligence* 9:268–299.

Sqalli, M. H., and Freuder, E. C. 1996. Inference-based constraint satisfaction supports explanation. In *AAAI-96*, 318–325.

# MAX-2-SAT: How Good is Tabu Search in the Worst-Case?

**Monaldo Mastrolilli**
IDSIA
Galleria 2, 6928 Manno, Switzerland
monaldo@idsia.ch

**Luca Maria Gambardella**
IDSIA
Galleria 2, 6928 Manno, Switzerland
luca@idsia.ch

### Abstract

Tabu search algorithms are amongst the most successful local search based methods for the maximum satisfiability problem. The practical superiority of tabu search over the local search alone has been already shown experimentally several times. A natural question addressed here is to understand if this superiority holds also from the worst-case point of view. Moreover, it is well known that the main critical parameter of tabu techniques is the tabu list length. Focussing on MAX-2-SAT problem, the main contribution of this paper is a worst-case analysis of tabu search as a function of the tabu list length. We give a first theoretical evidence of the advantage of a tabu search strategy over the basic local search alone that critically depends on the tabu list length.

## Introduction

In the maximum satisfiability problem (MAX-SAT) we are given a boolean formula in conjunctive normal form, i.e., as a conjunction of clauses, each clause being a disjunction. More formally, $n$ is the number of variables and $m$ the number of clauses, so that a formula has the following form:

$$\bigwedge_{1 \leq i \leq m} \left( \bigvee_{1 \leq h \leq |C_i|} l_{ih} \right)$$

where $|C_i|$ is the number of literals in clause $C_i$ and $l_{ih}$ is a literal, i.e., a propositional variable $v_j$, or its negation $\overline{v}_j$, for $1 \leq j \leq n$. The set of clauses in the formula is denoted by $\mathbb{C} = \{C_1, C_2, ..., C_m\}$. If one associates a positive weight $w_i$ to each clause $C_i$, one obtains the *weighted* MAX-SAT problem. We are asked to find an assignment of values to the variables that maximizes the (weighted) sum of the satisfied clauses.

The interest for MAX-SAT stems from many reasons. On one hand, the decision version SAT was the first example of an NP-complete problem; moreover, MAX-SAT and related variants play an important role in the characterization of different approximation classes like APX and PTAS (Ausiello *et al.* 1999). On the other hand, many issues in mathematical logic and artificial intelligence can be expressed in the form of satisfiability or some of its variants, like constraint satisfaction.



**Local Search Strategies.** Amongst the many different approaches proposed to deal with this problem (see (Battiti & Protasi 1998) for a survey), local search based algorithms play a fundamental role. Local search employs the idea that a given solution may be improved by making "small" changes: starting from some initial solution, move from neighbor to neighbor as long as possible while increasing the objective function value. Most local search based algorithms for MAX-SAT use a *1-flip* neighborhood relation for which two truth value assignments are neighbors if they differ in the truth value of exactly one variable. A basic local search ($LS$) starts with any given assignment, and then repeatedly changes ("flips") the assignment of a variable that leads to the largest decrease in the total number of unsatisfied clauses. A local optimal solution is defined as a state whose local neighborhood does not include a state that is strictly better. Let $OPT_{loc}$ (and $OPT$) be the number of satisfied clauses at a local (global) optimum of any instance of MAX-SAT with at least $k$ literals per clause. Then it is known (Hansen & Jaumard 1990) that

$$OPT_{loc} \geq \frac{k}{k+1} OPT. \quad (1)$$

The idea is simple and natural and it is surprising to see how successful the use of this local search has been on a variety of difficult instances. Moreover, the combination of local optimization and other mechanisms for escaping from local optimal solutions would seem to give them some advantage over either alone. MAX-SAT is among the problems for which many local search based heuristics (like GSAT, tabu search, simulated annealing, etc.) have been proved (experimentally) to be very effective (see the review in (Battiti & Protasi 1998) and (Hoos 1999; Mills & Tsang 2000; Wu & Wah 2000; Smyth, Hoos, & Stuetzle 2003) for more recent results). These algorithms have been widely used and tested. However, the efficiency and effectiveness have never been analyzed analytically. In particular, nothing is known about their performance guarantees.

**Aim of the Paper.** The aim of this paper is not to improve algorithms that achieve the best known approximation ratios[1] for MAX-SAT (for this see (Asano & Williamson

[1]The quality of an approximation algorithm is measured by its so called *performance ratio*. An approximation algorithm for

2000; Goemans & Williamson 1994; 1995; Yannakakis 1994)), but to provide a first worst-case analysis of some tabu search procedures that achieve very good results in 'practice'. The present work was motivated by the current state of the MAX-SAT local search algorithms, where a considerable gap exists between successful applications of heuristics and the theoretical analysis of these various heuristic methods. We remark that our analysis assumes that the initial starting solution is arbitrary (given by an adversary).

**Analysis of Tabu Search for MAX-2-SAT.** A fundamental approach for escaping from local optima is to use aspects of the search history. Tabu Search (TS) is a general local search method which systematically utilizes memory for guiding the search process (Glover 1989; 1990). In the simplest and most widely applied version of TS, a greedy local search algorithm is enhanced with a form of short term memory which enables it to escape from local optima. Overall, TS algorithms are amongst the most successful local search based methods to date. MAX-SAT was one of the first application problems to which TS algorithms were applied. In fact, in one of the papers in which TS algorithms were first proposed (Hansen & Jaumard 1990), the target application was MAX-SAT.

Mazure, Saïs, & Grégoire (1997) considered a simple tabu search algorithm, TSAT, for satisfiability problems. TSAT makes a systematic use of a tabu list of variables in order to avoid recurrent flips and thus escape from local optima. The tabu list is updated each time a flip is made. TSAT keeps a fixed length-chronologically-ordered FIFO list of flipped variables and prevents any of the variables in the list from being flipped again during a given amount of time. TSAT was compared with the Random Walk Strategy GSAT (Selman, Kautz, & Cohen 1993), an important extension of the basic GSAT and amongst the best performing algorithms. TSAT proves extremely competitive in the resolution of many problems, in particular hard random instances at the critical point of the phase transition. In this empirical study, Mazure, Saïs, & Grégoire found that the optimal length of the tabu list is crucial to the algorithm's performance. Interestingly, they observed that the optimal length of the tabu lists for these random problems proves (experimentally) linear with respect to the number of variables.

In this paper we consider the MAX-2-SAT problem, i.e. the restricted version of MAX-SAT in which each clause contains two literals. This problem is known to be NP-Hard (Garey & Johnson 1979). We analyze a tabu search algorithm, $TS(\ell)$ (see Figure 1), which has the same flavor of TSAT (and of many other tabu search implementations), and whose tabu list length is bounded by the parameter $\ell$. The superiority of TS with respect to the local search alone has already been shown experimentally several times. It is well known that the main critical parameter of tabu techniques is the tabu list length. Here the main goal is to understand if there are values of $\ell$ for which $TS(\ell)$ is better

---

MAX-SAT has a performance ratio of $\rho$, if for all input instances it finds a solution of value at least $\rho$ times the optimal solution value.

```
Start with any given truth assignment X⃗;
k ← 0, TT ← ℓ;
LastUsed(x_i) ← −∞, for i = 1...n;
while a termination condition is not met do
    AdmissibleSet ← {x_i ∈ N(X⃗) :
                      LastUsed(x_i) < (k − TT)
                      or x_i satisfies the aspiration criterion};
    if AdmissibleSet ≠ ∅ then
        u ← ChooseBestOf(AdmissibleSet);
    else
        Determine variable u by using a dynamic tabu
        policy;
    end if
    X⃗ ← X⃗ with the truth assignment of u reversed;
    LastUsed(u) ← k;
    k ← k + 1;
end while.
```

Figure 1: Tabu Search algorithm $TS(\ell)$ with tabu tenure at most $\ell$.

than the basic local search even from the worst-case point of view. We show that the approximation ratio for $TS(\ell)$ is $2/3$ for any tabu list length sublinear in the number of variables. This means that, in the worst-case and for any $\ell = o(n)$, $TS(\ell)$ is not better than the basic local search (see (1) when $k = 2$). However we prove a strong separation in the performance of the basic local search and $TS(\ell)$ when the tabu list length is allowed to increase up to $n$. Indeed we show that $TS(n)$ achieves an approximation ratio of $3/4$, whereas the basic local search ensures an approximation ratio of $2/3$ for MAX-2-SAT. To some extent, these results confirm the linearity in $n$ of the optimal length of the tabu lists, as it was observed experimentally in (Mazure, Saïs, & Grégoire 1997). Moreover, we give a first theoretical evidence of the advantage of a tabu search strategy over the basic local search alone even from the worst-case point of view.

The paper is organized as follows. In the next section, we give a detailed description of the $TS(\ell)$ procedure. We then derive an upper bound on the approximation ratio of $TS(\ell)$ as a function of $\ell$. Finally, we show that when the tabu list length is allowed to increase up to $n$ the tabu search procedure achieves an approximation ratio of $3/4$.

## Tabu Search description

The considered Tabu Search algorithm $TS(\ell)$ is as follows (see also Figure 1). The search starts with any given variable assignment and with the tabu list length $TT$ (i.e., the *tabu tenure*) equal to the parameter $\ell$. Each search step corresponds to a single variable flip, which is selected according to the associated change in the number of unsatisfied clauses and its tabu status. More precisely, let $N(\vec{X})$ denote the set of variables that appear in some unsatisfied clauses according to the current variable assignment $\vec{X}$. Let $LastUsed(x_i)$ denote the last time the truth assignment of $x_i$ was reversed ($LastUsed(x_i) = -\infty$ at the beginning).

At each step, a variable $x_i$ is considered *admissible* if $x_i$ appears in some unsatisfied clause (i.e., $x_i \in N(\overrightarrow{X})$) and either

**(a)** $x_i$ has not been flipped during the last $TT$ steps $(LastUsed(x_i) < (k - TT))$

**(b)** or, when flipped, leads to a lower number of unsatisfied clauses than the best assignment found so far (the latter condition defines the so-called *aspiration criterion* (Glover 1989)).

From the set of admissible variables (if not empty), one variable among those that when flipped yield a maximal decrease (or, equivalently, a minimal increase) in the number of unsatisfied clauses, is selected (ties are broken arbitrarily, or even randomly).

If there is no admissible variable, the analysis provided in this paper applies to the following (and possibly to others) alternative *dynamic tabu policies*:

- (*self-adapting tabu list length*) decrease the tabu tenure TT until there is a non-tabu variable that appears in some unsatisfied clause (add this command at line 9 of Figure 1). Each time a variable is flipped set $TT \leftarrow \max\{TT + 1, \ell\}$ (add this command just after line 11 of Figure 1);
- (*least recently used*) flip the least recently used variable that appears in some unsatisfied clause (add this command at line 9 of Figure 1).

Observe that in both strategies the tabu tenure of a variable is at most $\ell$, but it can be less than $\ell$ (dynamic tabu policy). We refer to $\ell$ as the *maximum tabu tenure*.

The algorithm stops when a termination condition is met. For our purposes it is sufficient to assume that the tabu search procedure stops if for $n$ consecutive steps there are no improvements.

Before providing the analysis of algorithm $TS(\ell)$ we make the following considerations about the dynamic tabu policies. One of the main purposes of a tabu list is to prevent from returning to recently visited solutions, and therefore from endless cycling. A list that is too short may not prevent cycling (see the proof of Lemma 5 for an example of this), but a list that is too long may create excessive restrictions. It is often difficult (or even impossible) to find a value that prevents cycling and does not excessively restrict the search for all instances of a given size. In the next section we prove that the useful values of $\ell$ are linear in $n$, and for these large tabu tenures it may easily happen that all the variables that appear in some unsatisfied clauses are tabu. An effective way of circumventing this difficulty is to have a tabu tenure that can be varied during the search, i.e. a dynamic tabu policy. Evidence has shown that dynamic tabu policies are generally more effective. Interesting examples can be found in (Battiti & Protasi 1997; Battiti & Tecchiolli 1994; Dell'Amico & Trubian 1993; Mastrolilli & Gambardella 2000). Advanced ways to create dynamic tabu tenure are described in (Glover 1990).

## An Upper Bound on the Approximation Ratio

Let $c = \frac{n}{\ell}$ be the ratio between the number of variables $n$ and the maximum tabu tenure $\ell$. In this subsection we study the approximation ratio of $TS(\ell)$ as a function of $c$. In particular, we provide the following upper bound on the approximation ratio of $TS(\ell)$.

**Theorem 1** *Starting from any arbitrary initial solution and for $c \geq 3$, the approximation ratio of $TS(\ell)$ for MAX-2-SAT is bounded from above by*

$$R(c) = \frac{2c^2}{3c^2 - 2c + 2}. \tag{2}$$

**Proof.** We prove the theorem by showing that there exists a class of input instances for which $TS(\ell)$ achieves an approximation ratio that asymptotically converges to $R(c)$. With this aim, we borrow and modify an input instance for MAX-2-SAT appeared in (Khanna *et al.* 1994). We assume that $n \geq 2\ell + 5$. The input $S$ consists of a disjoint union of four sets of clauses, say $S_1$, $S_2$, $S_3$ and $S_4$, defined as follows.

$$\begin{aligned}
S_1 &= \bigcup_{1 \leq i < j \leq n} (x_i \vee \overline{x}_j), \\
S_2 &= \bigcup_{1 \leq i < j \leq n} (\overline{x}_i \vee x_j), \\
S_3 &= \left( \bigcup_{0 \leq i \leq \ell+2} T_{2i+1} \right) - \{(\overline{x}_{2\ell+3} \vee \overline{x}_n)\}, \\
S_4 &= \bigcup_{2\ell+6 \leq i \leq n} T_i, \\
T_i &= \bigcup_{i < j \leq n} (\overline{x}_i \vee \overline{x}_j).
\end{aligned}$$

Note that set $S_3$ is obtained by eliminating clause $(\overline{x}_{2\ell+3} \vee \overline{x}_n)$. Clearly, $|S_1| = |S_2| = \binom{n}{2}$, and $|S_3| + |S_4| = \binom{n}{2} - n(\ell+2) + (\ell+2)(\ell+3) - 1$. Assume that $\overrightarrow{X}$ is the starting assignment for which all variables are set to 1 except for $x_{2i-1}$ $(i = 1, ..., \ell+1)$ whose value is 0. The number of clauses from $S_1 \cup S_2$ unsatisfied by the assignment $\overrightarrow{X}$ is $(\ell+1)(n-\ell-1)$, whereas the number of satisfied clauses from $S_3 \cup S_4$ is given by $\sum_{i=0}^{\ell} |T_{2i+1}| = (\ell+1)(n-\ell-1)$.

Let $\overrightarrow{X}(i)$ denote the current solution after $i$ steps of execution. In Lemma 5 (see appendix) we show that $TS(\ell)$ cannot find a solution better than $\overrightarrow{X}$ if the starting solution $\overrightarrow{X}(0)$ of $TS(\ell)$ is $\overrightarrow{X}$. On the other hand, an optimal assignment can satisfy all the clauses by choosing the vector $\overrightarrow{X}_{opt} = (0, 0, ..., 0)$. Thus the approximation ratio of $TS(\ell)$, say $R_\ell$, is

$$R_\ell = \frac{2\binom{n}{2}}{3\binom{n}{2} - n(\ell+2) + (\ell+2)(\ell+3) - 1}.$$

Let $\ell = n/c$ and assume that $c \geq 3$ (which is sufficient to guarantee that $n \geq 2\ell + 5$ for any $n \geq 15$). As soon as the

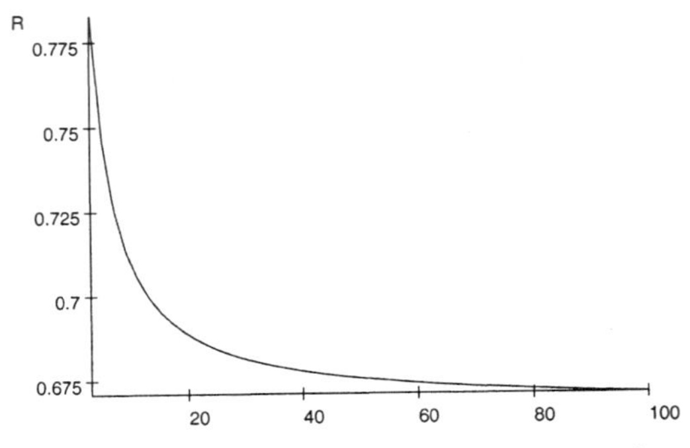


Figure 2: Approximation ratio upper bound of $TS(\ell)$ as a function of $c = n/\ell$.

number $n$ of variables increases, the approximation ratio $R_\ell$ asymptotically converges to

$$\lim_{n\to\infty} R_\ell = \frac{2c^2}{3c^2 - 2c + 2}.$$

■

Figure 2 plots function (2). For any $\ell = o(n)$, this ratio asymptotically converges to $2/3$. Therefore, $TS(\ell)$ cannot improve the basic local search when the maximum tabu tenure $\ell$ is sublinear in $n$ (see (1) when $k = 2$).

**Corollary 2** *Starting from any arbitrary initial solution, the approximation ratio of $TS(\ell)$ for MAX-2-SAT is $2/3$ for any $\ell = o(n)$.*

Moreover, already for $\ell \leq n/5$ the approximation ratio of $TS(\ell)$ is smaller than $3/4$.

## Tabu Search with Linear Tabu Tenure

The main question addressed in this subsection is to understand if there is a value of $\ell = \Theta(n)$ such that $TS(\ell)$ exhibits a worst-case superiority over the basic local search alone. Figure 2 suggests that interesting values can be found when the ratio $c = n/\ell$ is "small". Indeed, we show that $\ell = n$ suffices to our goal. We prove that $TS(n)$ achieves an approximation ratio of $3/4$, whereas the basic local search ensures an approximation ratio of $2/3$.

**Lemma 3** *Assume that for $n$ consecutive steps $TS(n)$ cannot find a better solution. Then the best found solution is a $\frac{3}{4}$-approximate solution.*

**Proof.** The claim follows by analyzing the execution of $TS(n)$. Remember that $\vec{X}(i)$ denotes the current solution after $i$ steps of execution. Moreover, we denote by $\mathbb{C}_h^i$ the subset of clauses that have exactly $h$ literals satisfied by assignment $\vec{X}(i)$. Without loss of generality, assume that $TS(n)$ has performed a number of steps such that the best solution found so far has been found at step $s$ and that $\vec{X}(s)$ is a local optimum for $LS$ (the presence of the aspiration criterion guarantees that, each time an improved solution is found, then that solution is improved until a local optimum is reached).

Now, in at most $n$ steps from step $s$ either a solution better than $\vec{X}(s)$ is found or there is a positive integer $t \leq n$ such that all the variables that appear in some clause from $\mathbb{C}_0^{s+t}$ have been flipped just once during the last $t$ steps. The latter can be easily observed by recalling that the flipped variables have been chosen according to their tabu status, and by using one of the described dynamic tabu policies. Therefore no clause that at step $s$ has at least one unsatisfied literal, can be an unsatisfied clause at step $s+t$. It follows that every clause from $\mathbb{C}_0^s$ belongs to the set $\mathbb{C} - \mathbb{C}_0^{s+t}$ of satisfied clauses at iteration $s + t$. Moreover, within $t$ steps all clauses from $\mathbb{C}_1^s$ are still satisfied, i.e. $\mathbb{C}_1^s \in \mathbb{C} - \mathbb{C}_0^{s+t}$.

Now there are two possibilities:

1. $|\mathbb{C}_0^s| > |\mathbb{C}_0^{s+t}|$
2. $|\mathbb{C}_0^s| \leq |\mathbb{C}_0^{s+t}|$

If case 1 happens then after $t \leq n$ steps the previous best known solution has been improved by solution $\vec{X}(s+t)$ (the latter has a lower number of unsatisfied clauses). The number of times case 1 may happen is clearly bounded by $m$.

If case 2 happens then

$$|\mathbb{C}_0^{s+t}| \leq |\mathbb{C}| - |\mathbb{C}_0^s| - |\mathbb{C}_1^s|,$$

since, by previous arguments, no clause from $\mathbb{C}_0^s \cup \mathbb{C}_1^s$ belongs to the set $\mathbb{C}_0^{s+t}$ of unsatisfied clauses of solution $\vec{X}(s+t)$, i.e. $\mathbb{C}_0^{s+t} \subseteq \mathbb{C}/(\mathbb{C}_0^s \cup \mathbb{C}_1^s)$. It follows that

$$\begin{aligned} |\mathbb{C}| &= |\mathbb{C}| - |\mathbb{C}_0^s| - |\mathbb{C}_1^s| + |\mathbb{C}_0^s| + |\mathbb{C}_1^s| \\ &\geq |\mathbb{C}_0^{s+t}| + |\mathbb{C}_0^s| + |\mathbb{C}_1^s| \geq 2|\mathbb{C}_0^s| + |\mathbb{C}_1^s| \\ &\geq 4|\mathbb{C}_0^s|, \end{aligned} \tag{3}$$

where we have used $|\mathbb{C}_1^s| \geq 2|\mathbb{C}_0^s|$ that holds since $\vec{X}(s)$ is a local optimum (see (Hansen & Jaumard 1990) or pp. 120-121 in (Battiti & Protasi 1998)). We remark that the aspiration criterion suffices to guarantee the latter condition. Inequality (3) immediately implies that the number of unsatisfied clauses at step $s$ is no more than $1/4$ the total number of clauses. Thus this algorithm ensures an approximation ratio of $3/4$. ■

**Theorem 4** *Starting from any arbitrary initial assignment, $TS(n)$ achieves an approximation ratio of $3/4$ for MAX-2-SAT in $O(mn)$ steps.*

**Proof.** The claim easily follows from Lemma 3 and by observing that the number of times a better solution is computed is bounded by the number $m$ of clauses. ■

We note that the same approximation ratio can be obtained for the weighted case of MAX-2-SAT, although the time complexity might be only pseudopolynomially bounded in the input size (simply take multiple copies of the clauses).

## Future Work

In this paper we have approached the problem of understanding the worst-case behavior of tabu search. In particular, we analyzed the worst-case behavior of tabu search as a function of the tabu list length for MAX-2-SAT. Certainly there are many interesting lines for future research. It would be interesting to understand if a similar analysis can be provided for the general MAX-SAT problem. An interesting starting case would be MAX-3-SAT. We believe that results in these directions are necessary steps toward a better understanding of local search strategies for MAX-SAT.

## Acknowledgments

We are grateful to Fred Glover for many helpful comments. This research has been supported by the Swiss National Science Foundation project 200021-100539/1, "Approximation Algorithms for Machine scheduling Through Theory and Experiments", and by the "Metaheuristics Network", grant HPRN-CT-1999-00106.

## Appendix

**Lemma 5** *According to the definitions given in the proof of Theorem 1, if $\overrightarrow{X}(0) = \overrightarrow{X}$ then $TS(\ell)$ cannot find a solution better than $\overrightarrow{X}$ for input $S$ when $n \geq 2\ell + 5$.*

**Proof.** The claim follows by showing that $TS(\ell)$ cycles around a set of solutions that are not better than $\overrightarrow{X}$. More precisely, we start proving that $TS(\ell)$ first flips, in the order, $x_{2(\delta-1)-1}, x_{2(\delta-2)-1}, ..., x_1$, where $\delta = \ell + 2$. Therefore, $TS(\ell)$ reaches solution $(1, 1, ..., 1)$ with a tabu list equal to $(x_1, x_3, ..., x_{2(\delta-2)-1})$. Then we show that $TS(\ell)$ flips, in the order, $x_{2(\delta-1)-1}, x_{2(\delta-2)-1}, ..., x_1$ and again the starting solution $\overrightarrow{X}(0)$ is obtained. Since at this point the tabu list is equal to $(x_1, x_3, ..., x_{2(\delta-2)-1})$, $TS(\ell)$ repeats the same moves generating a cycle.

Let $gain(x_j, s)$ (and $loss(x_j, s)$) denote the number of clauses that become satisfied (unsatisfied) if variable $x_j$ is flipped at step $s$. At step $s$ algorithm $TS(\ell)$ chooses the variable $x_j$ with the highest $\Delta(x_j, s) = gain(x_j, s) - loss(x_j, s)$. In the chosen example and at each step $s$, we will see that there is no more than one variable $x_j$ that when flipped yields a maximal $\Delta(x_j, s)$. Therefore, random moves introduced to break ties are not used.

Starting from $\overrightarrow{X}(0)$, the following analysis reveals that at step $s = \delta - j$ (for $j = \delta - 1, \delta - 2, ..., 1$) $TS(\ell)$ flips variable $x_{2j-1}$. We compute $\Delta(x_j, s = \delta - j)$ for every admissible variable $x_j$. The claim that $TS(\ell)$ flips, in the order, $x_{2(\delta-1)-1}, x_{2(\delta-2)-1}, ..., x_1$, follows by induction.

1. $\Delta(x_{2w-1}, \delta - j) = w - j$, for $w = 1, 2, ..., j$.
   Explanation: by flipping $x_{2w-1}$, for $w = 1, 2, ..., j$, the number of unsatisfied clauses in $S_1 \cup S_2$ reduces from $j(n - j)$ to $(j - 1)(n - (j - 1))$; except for $(j - w)$ that remains satisfied, all the clauses from $T_{2w-1}$ becomes unsatisfied, and the number of unsatisfied clauses in $S_3 \cup S_4$ increases by $n - (2w - 1) - (j - w) = n - (w + j) + 1$. Therefore, $gain(x_{2w-1}, \delta - j) = n - 2j + 1$ and $loss(x_{2w-1}, \delta - j) = n - (w + j) + 1$.
2. $\Delta(x_{2\delta-1}, \delta - j) = j - \delta$.
   Explanation: by flipping $x_{2\delta-1}$ the number of unsatisfied clauses in $S_1 \cup S_2$ increases from $j(n - j)$ to $(j + 1)(n - (j+1))$, i.e. $loss(x_{2\delta-1}, \delta - j) = n - 2j - 1$; all the clauses from $T_{2\delta-1}$ becomes true plus one clause from each set $T_{2i-1}$, for $i = j + 1, j + 2, ..., \delta - 1$, i.e., $gain(x_{2\delta-1}, \delta - j) = n - 2\delta + (\delta - j - 1) = n - \delta - j - 1$.
3. $\Delta(x_{2w}, \delta - j) = -(n - 2j - 1)$, for $w = 1, 2, ..., j$.
   Explanation: this move does not affect clauses from $S_3 \cup S_4$, whereas the number of unsatisfied clauses in $S_1 \cup S_2$ increases from $j(n - j)$ to $(j + 1)(n - (j + 1))$.
4. $\Delta(x_{2w}, \delta - j) = -n + j + w + 1$, for $w = j + 1, j + 2, ..., \delta$.
   Explanation: this move does not affect clauses from $S_4$, whereas it satisfies one clause for each set $T_{2j+1}, T_{2(j+1)+1}, ..., T_{2(w-1)+1}$. The number of unsatisfied clauses in $S_1 \cup S_2$ increases from $j(n - j)$ to $(j + 1)(n - (j + 1))$.
5. $\Delta(x_{2\delta+1+w}, \ell - j) \leq j - \delta$, for $w = 0, 1, ..., n - (2\delta + 1)$.
   Explanation: by flipping $x_{2\delta+1+w}$, the number of unsatisfied clauses in $S_1 \cup S_2$ increases from $j(n - j)$ to $(j + 1)(n - (j + 1))$. At most one clause for each set $T_{2i+1}$ becomes true, for $i = j, ..., \delta - 1$. One clause for each set $T_{2\delta+1+i}$ becomes true, for $i = 0, ..., w - 1$. All the clauses from $T_{2\delta+1+w}$ becomes satisfied. Therefore, $gain(x_{2\ell+1+w}, \ell - j + 1) \leq \delta - j + w + n - (2\delta + 1 + w) = n - \delta - j - 1$ and $loss(x_{2\ell+1}, 1) = n - 2j - 1$.

By the previous analysis, it follows that $TS(\ell)$ flips variable $x_{2j-1}$ (case 1) at step $s = \delta - j$. The latter proves that $TS(\ell)$ flips, in the order, $x_{2(\delta-1)-1}, x_{2(\delta-2)-1}, ..., x_1$; therefore, $TS(\ell)$ reaches solution $(1, 1, ..., 1)$ with a tabu list equal to $(x_1, x_3, ..., x_{2(\delta-2)-1})$.

In the following we show that $TS(\ell)$ starting from solution $(1, 1, ..., 1)$, and with a tabu list equal to $(x_1, x_3, ..., x_{2(\delta-2)-1})$, flips, in the order, $x_{2(\delta-1)-1}, x_{2(\delta-2)-1}, ..., x_1$ and again the initial solution $\overrightarrow{X}(0)$ is obtained. At this point, we can easily observe that $TS(\ell)$ gets stuck into a cycle.

The analysis below reveals that at step $s = 2\delta - j + 1$ (for $j = \delta - 1, \delta - 2, ..., 1$) algorithm $TS(\ell)$ flips variable $x_{2j-1}$. We compute $\Delta(x_j, s = 2\delta - j + 1)$ for every admissible variable $x_j$. The claim that $TS(\ell)$ flips, in the order, $x_{2(\delta-1)-1}, x_{2(\delta-2)-1}, ..., x_1$, follows by induction. Let us start observing that every admissible move causes the increase of unsatisfied clauses in $S_1 \cup S_2$ from $(\delta - 1 - j)(n - (\delta - 1 - j))$ to $(\delta - j)(n - (\delta - j))$, i.e., a loss of $(\delta - j)(n - (\delta - j)) - (\delta - 1 - j)(n - (\delta - 1 - j)) = n + 2j - 2\delta + 1$.

1. $\Delta(x_{2j-1}, 2\delta - j + 1) = \delta - 2j$.
   Explanation: by flipping $x_{2j-1}$, one clause for each set $T_{2i-1}$ becomes true, for $i = 1, ..., j - 1$. All the clauses from $T_{2j-1}$ becomes satisfied, except for $\delta - j - 1$ that are already satisfied. Therefore, $gain(x_{2j-1}, 2\delta - j + 1) = j - 1 + n - (2j - 1) - (\delta - j - 1) = n - \delta + 1$ and $loss(x_{2j-1}, 2\delta - j + 1) = n + 2j - 2\delta + 1$.
2. $\Delta(x_{2\delta-1}, 2\delta - j + 1) = -1 - j$.

Explanation: by flipping $x_{2\delta-1}$ all the clauses from $T_{2\delta-1}$ becomes satisfied plus one clause from each set $T_{2i-1}$, for $i = 1, 2, ..., j$, i.e., $gain(x_{2\delta-1}, 2\delta - j + 1) = n - 2\delta + j$ and $loss(x_{2\delta-1}, 2\delta - j + 1) = n + 2j - 2\delta + 1$.

3. $\Delta(x_{2w}, 2\delta - j + 1) = w - (n + 2j - 2\delta + 1)$, for $w = 1, 2, ..., j$.
   Explanation: one clause for each set $T_{2i-1}$ becomes true, for $i = 1, ..., w$.
4. $\Delta(x_{2w}, 2\delta - j + 1) \leq -j - n + 2\delta$, for $w = j + 1, .., \delta$.
   Explanation: one clause for each set $T_{2i-1}$ becomes true, for $i = 1, ..., j$, plus one clause from $T_{2\delta-1}$ if $w = \delta$.
5. $\Delta(x_{2\delta+1}, 2\delta - j + 1) \leq -j - 1$.
   Explanation: by flipping $x_{2\delta+1}$, one clause for each set $T_{2i-1}$ becomes true, for $i = 1, ..., j$, plus at most one clause from $T_{2\delta-1}$. All the clauses from $T_{2\delta+1}$ becomes satisfied. Therefore, $gain(x_{2\delta+1}, 2\delta - j + 1) \leq j + 1 + n - (2\delta + 1) = j + n - 2\delta$ and $loss(x_{2\delta-1}, 2\delta - j + 1) = n + 2j - 2\delta + 1$.
6. $\Delta(x_{2\delta+2+w}, 2\delta - j + 1) \leq -j - 1$, for $w = 0, 1, ..., n - (2\delta + 2)$.
   Explanation: by flipping $x_{2\delta+2+w}$, one clause for each set $T_{2i+1}$ becomes true, for $i = 0, 1, ..., j$, plus at most one clause from $T_{2\delta-1}$. One clause for each set $T_{2\delta+2+i}$ becomes true, for $i = 0, 1, ..., w - 1$. All the clauses from $T_{2\delta+2+w}$ becomes satisfied. Therefore, $gain(x_{2w-1}, 2\delta - j + 1) \leq j + 2 + w + n - (2\delta + 2 + w) = j + n - 2\delta$ and $loss(x_{2w-1}, 2\delta - j + 1) = n + 2j - 2\delta + 1$.

■

## References


Asano, T., and Williamson, D. P. 2000. Improved approximation algorithms for MAX SAT. In *Proceedings of the Eleventh Annual ACM-SIAM Symposium on Discrete Algorithms*, 96–105. N.Y.: ACM Press.

Ausiello, G.; Crescenzi, P.; Gambosi, G.; Kann, V.; Marchetti-Spaccamela, A.; and Protasi, M. 1999. *Complexity and Approximation*. Springer.

Battiti, R., and Protasi, M. 1997. Reactive Search, a History-Sensitive Heuristic for MAX-SAT. *ACM Journal of Experimental Algorithms* 2:Article 2.

Battiti, R., and Protasi, M. 1998. Approximate Algorithms and Heuristics for MaxSat. In Du, D.-Z., and Pardalos, P. M., eds., *Handbook of Combinatorial Optimization*, volume 1. Kluwer Academic Publishers. 77–148.

Battiti, R., and Tecchiolli, G. 1994. The reactive tabu search. *ORSA Journal on Computing* 6:126–140.

Dell'Amico, M., and Trubian, M. 1993. Applying tabu-search to the job shop scheduling problem. *Annals of Operations Research* 22:15–24.

Garey, M. R., and Johnson, D. S. 1979. *Computers and intractability; a guide to the theory of NP-completeness*. W.H. Freeman.

Glover, F. 1989. Tabu search - Part I. *ORSA Journal on Computing* 1(3):190–206.

Glover, F. 1990. Tabu search - Part II. *ORSA Journal on Computing* 2(1):4–32.

Goemans, M. X., and Williamson, D. P. 1994. New $\frac{3}{4}$-approximation algorithms for MAX SAT. *SIAM Journal on Discrete Mathematics* 7:656–666.

Goemans, M. X., and Williamson, D. P. 1995. Improved Approximation Algorithms for Maximum Cut and Satisfiability Problems Using Semidefinite Programming. *J. Assoc. Comput. Mach.* 42:1115–1145.

Hansen, P., and Jaumard, B. 1990. Algorithms for the maximum satisfiability problem. *Computing* 44:279–303.

Hoos, H. H. 1999. On the run-time behaviour of stochastic local search algorithms for SAT. In *Proceedings of the 16th National Conference on Artificial Intelligence (AAAI-99) and of the 11th Conference on Innovative Applications of Artificial Intelligence (IAAI-99)*, 661–666. AAAI Press.

Khanna, S.; Motwani, R.; Sudan, M.; and Vazirani, U. 1994. On syntactic versus computational views of approximability. In *Proceedings: 35th Annual Symposium on Foundations of Computer Science*, 819–830.

Mastrolilli, M., and Gambardella, L. M. 2000. Effective neighbourhood functions for the flexible job shop problem. *Journal of Scheduling* 3:3–20.

Mazure, B.; Saïs, L.; and Grégoire, É. 1997. Tabu search for SAT. In *Proceedings of the 14th National Conference on Artificial Intelligence (AAAI-97) and 9th Innovative Applications of Artificial Intelligence Conference (IAAI-97)*, 281–285. AAAI Press.

Mills, P., and Tsang, E. 2000. Guided local search for solving SAT and weighted MAX-SAT problems. *JAR: Journal of Automated Reasoning* 24:205–223.

Selman, B.; Kautz, H. A.; and Cohen, B. 1993. Local search strategies for satisfiability testing. In Trick, M., and Johnson, D. S., eds., *Proceedings of the Second DIMACS Challange on Cliques, Coloring, and Satisfiability*.

Smyth, K.; Hoos, H. H.; and Stuetzle, T. 2003. Iterated robust tabu search for MAX-SAT. In *Proceedings of the 16th Canadian Conference on Artificial Intelligence (AI'2003)*, 661–666. LNCS 2671.

Wu, Z., and Wah, B. W. 2000. An efficient global-search strategy in discrete lagrangian methods for solving hard satisfiability problems. In *Proceedings of the 7th Conference on Artificial Intelligence (AAAI-00) and of the 12th Conference on Innovative Applications of Artificial Intelligence (IAAI-00)*, 310–315. AAAI Press.

Yannakakis, M. 1994. On the approximation of maximum satisfiability. *J. Algorithms* 17(3):475–502.

# The Practice of Approximated Consistency for Knapsack Constraints *

**Meinolf Sellmann**
Cornell University, Department of Computer Science
4130 Upson Hall, Ithaca, NY 14853, U.S.A.
sello@cs.cornell.edu

### Abstract

Knapsack constraints are a key modeling structure in discrete optimization and form the core of many real-life problem formulations. Only recently, a cost-based filtering algorithm for Knapsack constraints was published that is based on some previously developed approximation algorithms for the Knapsack problem. In this paper, we provide an empirical evaluation of approximated consistency for Knapsack constraints by applying it to the Market Split Problem and the Automatic Recording Problem.

## Introduction

Knapsack constraints are a key modeling structure in discrete optimization and form the core of many real-life problem formulations. Especially in integer programming, a large number of models can be viewed as a conjunction of Knapsack constraints only. However, despite its huge practical importance, it has been given rather little attention by the Artificial Intelligence community, especially when comparing it to the vast amount of research that was conducted in the Operations Research and the Algorithms communities.

One of the few attempts that were made was published in (Sellmann 2003). In this paper, we introduced the theoretical concept of *approximated consistency*. The core idea of this contribution consists in using bounds of guaranteed accuracy for cost-based filtering of optimization constraints. As the first example, the paper introduced a cost-based filtering algorithm for Knapsack constraints that is based on some previously developed approximation algorithms for the Knapsack problem.

It was shown theoretically that our algorithm achieves approximated consistency in amortized linear time for bounds with arbitrary but constant accuracy. However, no practical evaluation was provided, and until today it is an open question whether approximated consistency is just a beautiful theoretical concept, or whether it can actually yield performant cost-based filtering algorithms.

In this paper, we provide an empirical evaluation of approximated consistency for Knapsack constraints. After briefly reviewing the filtering algorithm presented in (Sellmann 2003), we discuss practical enhancements of the filtering algorithm. We then use our implementation and apply it to two very different problems: First, we devise an algorithm for the Market Split Problem (MSP) and compare it with previous algorithms for the problem based on mathematical programming or constraint programming. Since the MSP represents a computationally very hard problem for which already very small problem instances cause severe problems for standard solution techniques, next we apply approximated Knapsack filtering to the much simpler Automatic Recording Problem (ARP). We compare the performance of Knapsack filtering algorithms based on approximated consistency with filtering algorithms based on linear relaxation bounds.

*This work was supported by the Intelligent Information Systems Institute (AFOSR Grant F49620-01-1-0076).


## A Brief Review of Approximated Consistency for Knapsack Constraints

We start by reviewing approximated consistency for Knapsack constraints as it was introduced in (Sellmann 2003). In the following, denote with $n \in \mathbb{N}$ the number of items in our Knapsack, denote with $w^T = (w_1, \ldots, w_n) \in \mathbb{N}^n$ the weights and with $p^T = (p_1, \ldots, p_n) \in \mathbb{N}^n$ the profits of the items. Furthermore, denote with $C$ the capacity of the Knapsack, and denote with $B$ a lower bound on the objective.

**Definition 1**
*Given $n$ binary variables $X^T = (X_1, \ldots, X_n)$, we define:* A Knapsack Constraint $\mathcal{KC}(X_1, \ldots, X_n, w_1, \ldots, w_n, C, p_1, \ldots, p_n, B)$ *is true, iff* $w^T X \leq C$ and $p^T X \geq B$.

A Knapsack constraint (KC) is the formal expression of our wish to search for a feasible (wrt. to the limited capacity), improving solution. Therefore, we also speak of the KC as an *optimization constraint* (Focacci *et al.* 1999). Now, a prominent task in Constraint Programming is to identify all variable assignments that would yield to an inconsistency. With respect to the KC, these are all decisions to include or remove an item that would either cause the capacity of the knapsack to be exceeded, or that, for all solutions that are feasible with respect to the limited capacity, would force the objective function to drop below $B$. For optimization constraints, this process of eliminating non-profitable variable assignments is called *cost-based filtering*.

Clearly, cost-based filtering for KCs is an NP-hard task, since it requires the solution of some Knapsack problems itself. Therefore, we suggested to relax the requirement that all non-profitable assignments be found and introduced the notion of *approximated consistency*:

**Definition 2**
*Denote with $\mathcal{KC}(X_1, \dots, X_n, w_1, \dots, w_n, C, p_1, \dots, p_n, B)$ a KC where the variables $X_i$ are currently allowed to take values in $D_i \subseteq \{0, 1\}$. Then, given some $\epsilon \geq 0$, we say that $\mathcal{KC}$ is* $\epsilon$-consistent, *iff for all $1 \leq i \leq n$ and $x_i \in D_i$ there exist $x_j \in D_j$ for all $j \neq i$ such that*

$$\sum_{i \leq n} w_i x_i \leq C \quad \text{and} \quad \sum_{i \leq n} p_i x_i \geq B - \epsilon P^*,$$

*whereby $P^* = \max\{\sum p_i y_i \mid y_i \in D_i, \sum w_i y_i \leq C\}$.*

Therefore, to achieve a state of $\epsilon$-consistency for a KC, we must ensure that

1. all items are deleted that cannot be part of any solution that obeys the capacity constraint and that achieves a profit of at least $B - \epsilon P^*$, and
2. all items have to be permanently inserted into the knapsack that are included in all solutions that obey the capacity constraint and that have a profit of at least $B - \epsilon P^*$.

That is, we do not enforce that all variable assignments are filtered that do not yield to any improving solution, but at least we want to remove all assignments for which the performance is forced to drop too far below the critical objective value. It is this property of filtering against a bound of guaranteed accuracy (controlled by the parameter $\epsilon$) that distinguishes the filtering algorithms in (Sellmann 2003) from earlier cost-based filtering algorithms for KCs that were based on linear programming bounds (Fahle and Sellmann 2002).

Of course, it would be nicer if we could use the stronger bound $(1 - \epsilon)B$, but for small lower bound values $B$ we do not know how to perform filtering based on this bound efficiently. Therefore, the optimal Knapsack value $P^*$ is used in the definition of approximated consistency. In the filtering algorithm, we cannot afford to compute $P^*$ of course (since this would require to solve the Knapsack problem), but we can nevertheless prove that this bound is achieved even without computing it exactly.

Now, to achieve a state of $\epsilon$-consistency for a KC, we modified an approximation algorithm for Knapsacks developed in (Lawler 1977). This algorithm works in two steps: First, the items are partitioned into two sets of large ($L$) and small ($S$) items, whereby $L$ contains all items with profit larger than some threshold value $T$. The profits of the items in $L$ are scaled and rounded down by some factor $K$: $\overline{p}_L := \lfloor p_L / K \rfloor$.

In the second step, the algorithm computes a solution $x = (x_L, x_S) \in \{0, 1\}^n$ (whereby $v_L$ and $v_S$ contain all entries of a vector $v$ whose corresponding indices are in $L$ or $S$, respectively) such that:

- If an item in $S$ is included in the solution then so are all items in $S$ that have a higher efficiency (whereby the efficiency of an item is its profit divided by its weight), and
- $K \overline{p}_L^T x_L + p_S^T x_S$ is maximized.

If $T$ and $K$ are chosen carefully, the scaling of the profits of items in $L$ and the additional constraint that a solution can only include items in $S$ with highest efficiency make it possible to solve this problem in polynomial time. Moreover, it can be shown that the solution obtained has an objective value within a factor of $(1 - \epsilon)$ from the optimal solution of the Knapsack that we denoted with $P^*$ (Lawler 1977).

The cost-based filtering algorithm makes use of the performance guarantee given by the algorithm. Clearly, if the solution quality of the approximation under some variable assignment drops below $B - \epsilon P^*$, then this assignment cannot be completed to an improving, feasible solution, and it can be eliminated. We refer the reader to (Sellmann 2003) for further details on how this elimination process can be performed efficiently.

## Practical Enhancements of the Filtering Algorithm

The observation that the filtering algorithm is based on the bound provided by the approximation algorithm is crucial. It means that, in contrast to the approximation algorithm itself, we hope to find rather bad solutions by the approximation, since they provide more accurate bounds on the objective function. The important task when implementing the filtering algorithm is to estimate the accuracy achieved by the approximated solution as precisely as possible. For this purpose, in the following we investigate three different aspects:

- the computation of a 2-approximation that is used to determine $K$ and the filtering bound,
- the choice of the scaling factor $K$, and
- the computation of the filtering bound.

### Computation of a 2-Approximation

A 2-approximation on the given Knapsack is used in the approximation algorithm for several purposes. Most importantly, it is used to set the actual filtering bound $\overline{B}$. From our discussion in the previous section it is clear that $\overline{B}$ can be set to $B - \epsilon P^*$. However, we cannot afford to compute $P^*$ since this would require to solve the Knapsack problem first. Therefore, we showed that it is still correct to filter an assignment if the performance drops below $B - \epsilon P_0$ only, whereby $P_0$ denotes the value of a 2-approximation of the original Knapsack problem.

The standard procedure for computing a 2-approximation $P_0$ is to include items with respect to decreasing efficiency. If an item fits, we insert it, otherwise we leave it out and consider the following items. After all items have been considered, we compare the solution obtained in that way with the Knapsack that is obtained when we follow the same procedure but by now considering the items with respect to decreasing profit (whereby we assume that $||w||_\infty \leq C$[1]). Then, we choose $P_0$ as the solution that has the larger objective function value. It is easy to prove that this procedure yields a 2-approximation.

[1] $||w||_\infty$ denotes the maximum absolute entry of vector w.

Now, with respect to the filtering routine, of course we would like to set $P_0$ as small as possible. Note that it is of no relevance for the correctness of the filtering algorithm that there actually exists a solution that has value $P_0$. All that is required is that $2P_0$ is an upper bound which is indeed essential for the correctness of our algorithm. Therefore, we propose to compute the value $P_0$ in a much simpler way. We can obtain an upper bound by allowing that items can be inserted fractionally and solving the relaxed problem as a linear problem. We obtain an upper bound $U$, and we simply set $P_0 := U/2$. Is is easy to show that this procedure returns a value for $P_0$ that is at most as large as the value returned by the standard 2-approximation algorithm.

### Setting the Scaling Factor

The next issue regards the factor with which the profits in the set of large items $L$ are scaled down. According to the correctness proof in (Sellmann 2003), we need to ensure that $\frac{K}{T} p_L^T x_L^* + p_S^T(x_S^* - \overline{x}_S) \leq \epsilon P_0$, whereby $x^*$ denotes an optimal solution to the Knapsack problem, and $\overline{x}$ denotes the solution found by our approximation algorithm. We proposed to set $K := \frac{\epsilon}{4} T$. Intuitively, we obtain worse approximation results (and consequently more accurate upper bounds) and shorter running times if we scale the profits of the items in $L$ as much as possible. We can choose the scaling factor more aggressively, by setting $K := \frac{\epsilon P_0}{2U_L} T$, where $U_L$ denotes an upper bound on the large item Knapsack problem. Then, it holds that:

$$\frac{K}{T} p_L^T x_L^* + p_S^T(x_S^* - \overline{x}_S) \leq \frac{\epsilon P_0}{2} \frac{p_L^T x_L^*}{U_L} + \frac{\epsilon P_0}{2} \leq \epsilon P_0.$$

Therefore, our setting maintains correctness. In order to compute $U_L$ we use the linear programming upper bound on the large item problem. Nota bene: If $U_L = 0$, the large item problem is trivially solved by the empty Knapsack, and we do not need to scale the profits at all.

### Setting the Filtering Bound

The last important issue regards the bound against which we filter eventually. In the analysis of the approximation algorithm both the large and the small item problem contribute equally to the approximation error made. More precisely, the large item problem contributes an error of $\frac{\epsilon P_0}{2}$, and the small item problem contributes $||p_S||_\infty$. When setting $T := \frac{\epsilon P_0}{2}$, clearly the total deviation from the optimum is bounded by $\epsilon P_0$. Consequently, we proposed to set the filtering bound to $\overline{B} := B - \epsilon P_0$. With respect to the brief discussion above, we can already enhance on this by setting $\overline{B} := B - \frac{\epsilon P_0}{2} - ||p_S||_\infty$. Like that, if the small item problem is actually empty, we are able to half the absolute error made! Similarly, if the large item problem is empty, or if $U_L = 0$, this problem does not contribute to the error made. Then we can even set $\overline{B} := B - ||p_S||_\infty$.

## Approximated Knapsack Filtering for Market Split Problems

We implemented the approximated filtering algorithm including the enhancements discussed in the previous section. To evaluate the practical usefulness of the algorithm, we first apply it in the context of Market Split Problems (MSPs), a benchmark that was suggested for Knapsack constraints in (Trick 2001). The original definition goes back to (Cornuéjols and Dawande 1998; Williams 1978): A large company has two divisions $D_1$ and $D_2$. The company supplies retailers with several products. The goal is to allocate each retailer to either division $D_1$ or $D_2$ so that $D_1$ controls A% of the company's market for each product and $D_2$ the remaining (100-A)%. Formulated as an integer program, the problem reads:

$$\begin{array}{rcll} \sum_j a_{ij} x_j & = & \frac{A}{100} \sum_j a_{ij} & \forall\, 0 \leq i < m \\ x_j & \in & \{0,1\} & \forall\, 0 \leq j < n, \end{array}$$

whereby $m$ denotes the number of products, $n$ is the number of retailers, and $a_{ij}$ is the demand of retailer $j$ of product $i$.

### A Tree-Search-Algorithm for the MSP

We model the problem as a constraint program by introducing one Knapsack constraint for each product, whereby profit and weight of each Knapsack item are equal. Capacity and profit bound are determined by the right hand side of the constraint. Following an idea presented in (Trick 2001), additionally we add one more redundant Knapsack constraint that is the weighted sum of the other constraints:

$$\begin{array}{rcll} \sum_i \lambda^i \sum_j a_{ij} x_j & = & \sum_i \lambda^i \frac{A}{100} \sum_j a_{ij} & \\ x_j & \in & \{0,1\} & \forall\, 0 \leq j < n. \end{array}$$

In (Trick 2001) it was conjectured that, if $\lambda$ was chosen large enough, the summed-up constraint contained the same set of solutions as the conjunction of Knapsack constraints. This is true for Knapsack constraints as they evolve in the context of the MSP where the weight and the profit of each item are the same and capacity and profit bound are matching. However, the example $3 \leq 2x_1 + 7x_2 \leq 8$ in combination with $3 \leq 7x_1 + 2x_2 \leq 8$, $x_1, x_2 \in \{0,1\}$, shows that this is not true in general: The conjunction of both Knapsack constraints is clearly infeasible, yet no matter how we set $\lambda$, no summed-up constraint alone is able to reveal this fact. Note that, when setting $\lambda$ to a very large value in the summed-up constraint, the profit becomes very large, too. Consequently, the absolute error made by the approximation algorithm becomes larger, too, and thereby renders the filtering algorithm less effective. In accordance to Trick's report, we found that $\lambda = 5$ yields very good filtering results for the Cornuéjols-Dawande MSP instances that we consider in our experimentation.

Using the model as discussed above, our algorithm for solving the MSP carries out a tree-search. In every choice point, the Knapsack constraints perform cost-based filtering, exchanging information about removed and included items. On top of that, we perform cost-based filtering by changing the capacity constraints within the Knapsack constraints. As Trick had noted in his paper already, the weights of the items and the capacity of the Knapsack can easily be modified once a Knapsack constraint is initialized. The new weight constraints considered are the capacity and profit constraints of the other Knapsack constraints as well as additional weighted sums of the original capacity constraints,

| $\epsilon$ | | 3 / 20 – 8% CPs | 3 / 20 – 8% Time | 4 / 30 – 29% CPs | 4 / 30 – 29% Time | 5 / 40 – 34% CPs | 5 / 40 – 34% Time |
|---|---|---|---|---|---|---|---|
| 5% | max | 11 | 0.18 | 8699 | 211.8 | - | - |
| | $\phi$ | 3.53 | 0.08 | 1392 | 50.21 | - | - |
| | min | 1 | 0.04 | 7 | 1.04 | - | - |
| 2% | max | 3 | 0.07 | 321 | 31.53 | 505K | 52.6K |
| | $\phi$ | 1.29 | 0.03 | 26.71 | 4.92 | 30.1K | 4867 |
| | min | 1 | 0.01 | 3 | 0.98 | 96 | 36.2 |
| 1% | max | 3 | 0.05 | 19 | 7.68 | 26.8K | 12.6K |
| | $\phi$ | 1.25 | 0.03 | 2.7 | 0.68 | 943.3 | 552.8 |
| | min | 1 | 0.01 | 1 | 0.41 | 25 | 38.85 |
| 5‰ | max | 3 | 0.05 | 7 | 0.99 | 171 | 826.8 |
| | $\phi$ | 1.25 | 0.03 | 2.61 | 0.61 | 60.15 | 174.9 |
| | min | 1 | 0.02 | 1 | 0.42 | 5 | 30.96 |
| 2‰ | max | 3 | 0.04 | 7 | 0.96 | 59 | 47.19 |
| | $\phi$ | 1.25 | 0.03 | 2.61 | 0.61 | 13.9 | 28.99 |
| | min | 1 | 0.01 | 1 | 0.43 | 3 | 16.08 |
| 1‰ | max | 3 | 0.05 | 7 | 0.95 | 59 | 47.75 |
| | $\phi$ | 1.25 | 0.03 | 2.61 | 0.61 | 13.9 | 28.98 |
| | min | 1 | 0.01 | 1 | 0.34 | 3 | 16.19 |
| 0.5‰ | max | - | - | 7 | 0.95 | 59 | 47.8 |
| | $\phi$ | - | - | 2.61 | 0.61 | 13.9 | 28.98 |
| | min | - | - | 1 | 0.44 | 3 | 16.13 |

(Column headers: # Constraints / # Variables – % Feasible)

Table 1: Numerical results for our 3 benchmark sets. Each set contains 100 Cornuéjols-Dawande instances, and the percentage of feasible solutions in each set is given. We apply our MSP algorithm varying the approximation guarantee $\epsilon$ for the Knapsack filtering algorithm between 5% and 0.5‰. For each benchmark set, we report the maximum, average, and minimum number of choice points and computation time in seconds.

whereby we use as weights powers of $\lambda = 5$ again while considering the original constraints in random order. After the cost-based filtering phase, we branch by choosing a random item that is still undecided yet and continue our search in a depth-first manner.

## Numerical Results for the MSP

All experiments in this paper were conducted on an AMD Athlon[tm] 1.2 GHz Processor with 500 MByte RAM running Linux 2.4.10, and we used the gnu C++ compiler version g++ 2.91.

(Cornuéjols and Dawande 1998) generated computationally very hard random MSP instances by setting $n := 10(m-1)$, choosing the $a_{ij}$ randomly from the interval $\{0, \ldots, 99\}$, and setting $A := 50\%$. We use their method to generate 3 benchmark sets containing 3 products (constraints) and 20 retailers (variables), 4 constraints and 30 variables, and 5 constraints and 40 variables. Each set contains 100 random instances. In Table 1 we report our numerical results.

As our results show, the choice of $\epsilon$ has a severe impact on the performance of our algorithm. We see that for the benchmark set (3,20) it is completely sufficient to set $\epsilon := 0.02$. However, even for these very small problem instances, setting $\epsilon$ to 5% almost triples the average number of choice points and computation time. On the other hand, choosing a better approximation guarantee does not improve on the performance of the algorithm anymore. We get a similar picture when looking at the other benchmark sets, but shifted to a different scale: For the set (4,30), the best performance can be achieved when setting $\epsilon :=$ 5‰, for the set (5,40) this value even decreases to 2‰.

In our experiments, we found that choosing higher approximation accuracies can sometimes yield an increase in the number of choice points. This counter intuitive effect is explained by the fact that the approximated filtering algorithm is not monotone in the sense that demanding higher accuracy does not automatically result in better bounds. It may happen occasionally that for a demanded accuracy of 5‰ the approximation algorithm does a rather poor job which results in very tight bound on the objective function. Now, when demanding an accuracy of 1‰, the approximation algorithm may actually compute the optimal solution, thus yielding a bound that can be up to 1‰ away from the correct value. Consequently, by demanding higher accuracy we may actually get a lower one in practice.

When comparing the absolute running times with other results on the Cornuéjols-Dawande instances reported in the literature, we find that approximated consistency is doing a remarkably good job: Comparing the results with those reported in (Trick 2001), we find that approximated Knapsack filtering even outperforms the generate-and-test method on the (4,30) benchmark. Note that this method is probably not suitable for tackling larger problem instances, while approximated consistency allows us to scale this limit up to 5 constraints and 40 variables.

When comparing our MSP algorithm with the best algorithm that exists for this problem (Aardal *et al.* 1999), we find that, for the (4,30) and the (5,40) benchmark sets, we achieve competitive running times. This is a very remarkable result, since really approximated Knapsack filtering is in no way limited or special to Market Split Problems. It could for example also be used to tackle slightly different and more realistic problems in which a splitting range is specified rather than an exact percentage on how the market is to be partitioned. And of course, it can also be used when the profit of the items does not match their weight and in any context where Knapsack constraints occur.

We also tried to apply our algorithm to another benchmark set with 6 constraints and 50 variables. For this set, we were not able to experiment with values for $\epsilon$ that are below 5‰ since then the memory requirements of the filtering algorithm were exceeding the available RAM. We therefore note that the comparably high memory requirements present a clear limitation of the practical use of the approximated filtering routine. Still, the (6,50)-instances can be solved with our approach, but this takes a few hours on average. That this is possible at all is a direct merit of the improvements that we suggested in the previous section. Unfortunately, there is not space enough to present a detailed evaluation here. So we just note our improvements reduce the memory requirements and the accuracy of the algorithm considerably.

It remains to note that our experimentation also confirms a result from (Aardal *et al.* 1999) regarding the probability of generating infeasible solutions by the Cornuéjols-Dawande method. Clearly, the number of feasible instances increases the more constraints and variables are considered by their generator. For a detailed study on where the actual phase-transition for Market Split Problems is probably located, we refer the reader to the Aardal paper.

## Approximated Knapsack Filtering for the Automatic Recording Problem

Encouraged by the surprisingly good numerical results on the MSP, we want to evaluate the use of approximated consistency in the context of a very different application problem that incorporates a Knapsack constraint in combination with other constraints. We consider the Automatic Recording Problem (ARP) that was introduced in (Sellmann and Fahle 2003):

The technology of digital television offers to hide meta-data in the content stream. For example, an electronic program guide with broadcasting times and program annotation can be transmitted. An intelligent video recorder like the TIVO$^{tm}$ system (TIVO ) can exploit this information and automatically record TV content that matches the profile of the system's user. Given a profit value for each program within a predefined planning horizon, the system has to make the choice which programs shall be recorded, whereby two restrictions have to be met:

- The disk capacity of the recorder must not be exceeded.
- Only one program can be recorded at a time.

### CP-based Lagrangian Relaxation for the ARP

Like in (Sellmann and Fahle 2003), we use an approach featuring CP-based Lagrangian relaxation: The algorithm performs a tree search, filtering out assignments, in every choice point, with respect to a Knapsack constraint (capturing the limited disk space requirement) and a weighted stable set constraint on an interval graph (that ensures that only temporally non-overlapping programs are recorded).

For the experiments, we compare two variants of this algorithm: The first uses approximated Knapsack filtering, the second a cost-based filtering method for Knapsack constraints that is based on linear relaxation bounds (Fahle and Sellmann 2002). While CP-based Lagrangian relaxation leaves the weight constraint unmodified but calls to the filtering routine with ever changing profit constraints, we replace, in the Knapsack constraint, each variable $x_i$ by $y_i = 1 - x_i$. Thereby, profit and weight constraint change roles and we can apply the technique in (Trick 2001) again by calling the approximated Knapsack filtering routine with different capacity constraints.

### Numerical Results for the ARP

For our experiments, we use a benchmark set that we made accessible to the research community in (ARP 2004). This benchmark was generated using the same generator that was used for the experimentation in (Sellmann and Fahle 2003):

Each set of instances is generated by specifying the time horizon (half a day or a full day) and the number of channels (20 or 50). The generator sequentially fills the channels by starting each new program one minute after the last. For each new program, a *class* is being chosen randomly. That class then determines the interval from which the length is chosen randomly. The generator considers 5 different classes. The lengths of programs in the classes vary from 5±2 minutes to 150±50 minutes. The disk space necessary to store each program equals its length, and the storage capacity is randomly chosen as 45%–55% of the entire time horizon.

To achieve a complete instance, it remains to choose the associated profits of programs. Four different strategies for the computation of an objective function are available:

- For the *class usefulness (CU)* instances, the associated profit values are determined with respect to the chosen class, where the associated profit values of a class can vary between zero and 600±200.
- In the *time strongly correlated (TSC)* instances, each 15 minute time interval is assigned a random value between 0 and 10. Then the profit of a program is determined as the sum of all intervals that program has a non-empty intersection with.
- For the *time weakly correlated (TWC)* instances, that value is perturbed by a noise of ±20%.
- Finally, in the *strongly correlated (SC)* data, the profit of a program simply equals its length.

Table 2 shows our numerical results. We apply our ARP algorithm using approximated consistency for cost-based filtering and vary $\epsilon$ between 5% and 5‰. We compare the number of choice points and the time needed by this method with a variant of our ARP algorithm that uses Knapsack filtering based on linear relaxation bounds instead of approximated consistency. The numbers reported are the average and (in brackets) the median relative performance for each set containing 10 randomly generated instances.

Consider as an example the set containing instances with 50 channels and a planning horizon of 1440 minutes where the profit values have been generated according to method TWC. According to Table 2, the variant of our algorithm using approximated consistency with accuracy $\epsilon = 5\%$ visits 72.79% of the number of choice points that the variant incorporating linear programming bounds is exploring. However, when comparing the time needed, we see that approximated consistency actually takes 178.80% of the time, clearly because the time per choice point is higher compared to the linear programming variant.

Looking at the table as a whole, this observation holds for the entire benchmark set: even when approximated consistency is able to reduce the number of choice points significantly (as it is the case for the TWC and TSC instances), the effort is never (!) worthwhile. On the contrary, the approximation variant is, on average, 30% up to almost 5 times slower than the algorithm using linear bounds for filtering. In this context it is also remarkable that, in general, a variation of the approximation guarantee had no significant effect on the number of choice points visited. This effect is caused by the fact that an improvement on the Knapsack side need not necessarily improve the global Lagrangian bound.

| obj. | #channels/ horizon | $\phi$ # progs | Time (sec) | $\epsilon = 5\%$ | | $\epsilon = 1\%$ | | $\epsilon = 5‰$ | |
|---|---|---|---|---|---|---|---|---|---|
| | | | | CPs (%) | Time (%) | CPs (%) | Time (%) | CPs (%) | Time (%) |
| CU | 20/720 | 305.3 | 14.3 | 99.7 (104.6) | 163.6 (153.6) | 99.7 (104.6) | 235.0 (224.6) | 99.7 (104.6) | 291.9 (280.0) |
| | 50/720 | 771.3 | 58.7 | 101.5 (100.3) | 168.5 (169.0) | 101.5 (100.3) | 169.6 (170.9) | 101.5 (100.3) | 227.9 (217.4) |
| | 20/1440 | 609.8 | 67.8 | 97.2 (99.0) | 193.3 (195.5) | 97.2 (99.0) | 234.5 (235.3) | 97.2 (99.0) | 359.7 (358.9) |
| | 50/1440 | 1440 | 2426 | 118.1 (110.3) | 165.2 (143.0) | 118.1 (110.3) | 165.2 (140.9) | 112.2 (105.4) | 165.9 (134.7) |
| SC | 20/720 | 317.5 | 4.3 | 138.8 (122.5) | 199.2 (125.8) | 138.8 (122.5) | 157.1 (541.9) | 138.8 (122.5) | 236.4 (1093.7) |
| | 50/720 | 788.5 | 2.1 | 137.3 (128.9) | 250.1 (242.3) | 137.3 (128.9) | 251.2 (245.0) | 137.3 (128.9) | 171.9 (732.9) |
| | 20/1440 | 609.9 | 4.1 | 124.8 (114.2) | 256.6 (317.5) | 124.8 (114.2) | 132.7 (595.2) | 124.8 (114.2) | 324.3 (1683.6) |
| | 50/1440 | 1464 | 1.8 | 108.9 (108.3) | 278.2 (365.7) | 108.9 (108.3) | 280.9 (371.3) | 108.9 (108.3) | 302.7 (405.2) |
| TWC | 20/720 | 305.3 | 15.2 | 92.6 (94.1) | 212.9 (249.5) | 92.5 (94.1) | 314.3 (340.6) | 92.0 (94.1) | 420.7 (388.0) |
| | 50/720 | 771.3 | 60.8 | 72.8 (76.7) | 178.8 (181.1) | 72.8 (76.7) | 181.5 (184.3) | 72.8 (76.7) | 298.1 (288.6) |
| | 20/1440 | 609.8 | 207.0 | 83.4 (83.7) | 189.4 (189.5) | 83.4 (83.7) | 325.4 (297.7) | 83.4 (83.7) | 217.4 (538.8) |
| | 50/1440 | 1440 | 71.2 | 77.5 (80.2) | 177.3 (181.4) | 77.5 (80.2) | 177.9 (181.9) | 77.5 (80.2) | 205.0 (206.8) |
| TSC | 20/720 | 307.2 | 35.5 | 71.2 (71.4) | 199.3 (182.6) | 71.2 (71.4) | 286.4 (268.9) | 69.4 (71.4) | 385.5 (370.3) |
| | 50/720 | 780.8 | 681 | 84.7 (87.3) | 144.5 (133.1) | 84.7 (87.3) | 141.5 (131.7) | 84.7 (87.3) | 192.0 (182.5) |
| | 20/1440 | 609.8 | 239.5 | 82.6 (85.2) | 172.0 (171.5) | 82.6 (85.2) | 267.0 (248.8) | 82.6 (85.2) | 480.3 (467.6) |
| | 50/1440 | 1448 | 7295 | 91.9 (98.4) | 134.6 (128.0) | 91.9 (98.4) | 134.7 (128.0) | 91.9 (98.4) | 140.6 (134.5) |

Table 2: Numerical results for the ARP benchmark. We apply our algorithm varying the approximation guarantee of the Knapsack filtering algorithm between 5% and 5‰. The first two columns specify the settings of the random benchmark generator: the first value denotes the objective variant taken, and it is followed by the number of TV channels and the planning time horizon in minutes. Each set identified by these parameters contains 10 instances, the average number of programs per set is given in the third column. We report the average (median) factor (in %) that the approximation variant needs relative to the variant using Knapsack filtering based on linear relaxation bounds. The average absolute time (in seconds) of the last algorithm is given in the fourth column.

It clearly depends on the application when a more accurate filtering of the Knapsack constraint pays off for the overall problem.

## Conclusions

The most important advantage of approximated consistency is our ability to trade filtering efficiency for computation time. It would be most interesting to have a general understanding of this trade-off that would allow us to develop automated strategies for tuning the filtering effectiveness towards problems and problem instances.

Our numerical evaluation shows that manually tuned approximated consistency for Knapsack constraints can lead to massive improvements for critically constrained problems. Approximated consistency is the first generic constraint programming approach that can efficiently tackle the Market Split Problem (MSP), and is even competitive when compared with specialized state-of-the-art approaches for this problem. Note that, for the Knapsack constraints as they evolve from the MSP where profit and weight of each item are the same, linear relaxation bounds are in most cases meaningless, thus rendering Knapsack filtering based on these bounds without effect.

On the other hand, the application to the Automatic Recording Problem showed that, for combined problems, the effectiveness of a more accurate Knapsack filtering can be limited by the strength of the global bound that is achieved. The practical use of approximated filtering is further limited by high memory requirements for very tight approximation guarantees. And for lower accuracies, Knapsack filtering based on linear relaxation bounds may be almost as effective and overall faster.

## References


K. Aardal, R.E. Bixby, C.A.J. Hurkens, A.K. Lenstra, J.W. Smeltink. Market Split and Basis Reduction: Towards a Solution of the Cornuéjols-Dawande Instances. *IPCO*, Springer LNCS 1610:1–16, 1999.

ARP: *A Benchmark Set for the Automatic Recording Problem*, maintained by M. Sellmann, `http://www.cs.cornell.edu/~sello/-arp_benchmark.tar.gz`

G. Cornuéjols, M. Dawande. A Class of Hard Small 0-1 Programs. *IPCO*, Springer LNCS 1412:284–293, 1998.

T. Fahle, M. Sellmann. Cost-Based Filtering for the Constrained Knapsack Problem. *AOR*, 115:73–93, 2002.

F. Focacci, A. Lodi, M. Milano. Cost-Based Domain Filtering. *CP*, Springer LNCS 1713:189–203, 1999.

E.L. Lawler. Fast Approximation Algorithm for Knapsack Problems. *FOCS*, pp. 206–213, 1977.

M. Sellmann. Approximated Consistency for Knapsack Constraints. *CP*, Springer LNCS 2833: 679–693, 2003.

M. Sellmann and T. Fahle. Constraint Programming Based Lagrangian Relaxation for the Automatic Recording Problem. *AOR*, 118:17–33, 2003.

TIVO. TV your way. TIVO, Inc., `http://-www.tivo.com/home.asp`.

M. Trick. A Dynamic Programming Approach for Consistency and Propagation for Knapsack Constraints. *CP-AI-OR'01*, pp. 113–124, 2001.

H.P. Williams. Model Building in Mathematical Programming. Wiley, 1978.

# Study of Lower Bound Functions for MAX-2-SAT*

**Haiou Shen, Hantao Zhang**
*Computer Science Department*
*The University of Iowa*
*Iowa City, IA 52242*
*{hshen, hzhang}@cs.uiowa.edu*

### Abstract

Recently, several lower bound functions are proposed for solving the MAX-2-SAT problem optimally in a branch-and-bound algorithm. These lower bounds improve significantly the performance of these algorithms. Based on the study of these lower bound functions, we propose a new, linear-time lower bound function. We show that the new lower bound function is admissible and it is consistently and substantially better than other known lower bound functions. The result of this study is a high-performance implementation of an exact algorithm for MAX-2-SAT which outperforms any implementation of the same class.

## Introduction

In recent years, there has been considerable interest in the maximum satisfiability problem (MAX-SAT) of propositional logic, which, given a set of propositional clauses, asks to find a truth assignment that satisfies the maximum number of clauses. The decision version of MAX-SAT is NP-complete, even if the clauses have at most two literals (so called the MAX-2-SAT problem). Because the MAX-SAT problem is fundamental to many practical problems in computer science (Hansen, & Jaumard) and hardware circuit designs (Xu et al), efficient methods that can solve a large set of instances of MAX-SAT are eagerly sought. One important area of applications of MAX-2-SAT is that many NP-complete graph problems such as *maximum cut*, *independent set*, can be reduced to special instances of MAX-2-SAT (Cheriyan et al; Mahajan & Raman). Many of the proposed methods for MAX-SAT are based on approximation algorithms (Dantsin et al); some of them are based on branch-and-bound methods (Hansen, & Jaumard; Borchers & Furman; Bansal & Raman; Hirsch; Hirsch b; Gramm et al; Niedermeier & Rossmanith); and some of them are based on transforming MAX-SAT into SAT (Xu et al).

To the best of our knowledge, there are only six implementations of exact algorithms for MAX-SAT that are variants of the well-known Davis-Putnam-Logemann-Loveland (DPLL) procedure (Davis et al). One is due to (Wallace & Freuder) (implemented in Lisp); one is due to (Borchers & Furman) (implemented in C and publicly available); the next two are made available in 2003 by (Alsinet et al) and (Zhang et al), respectively. The last one is provided by (Zhao & Zhang) in 2004.

Since it is well-known that the tighter the bound the smaller the search tree in a typical branch-and-bound algorithm, it is not a surprise to see that Alsinet et al.'s implementation is better than Borchers and Furman's implementation because a better lower bound function is used in (Alsinet et al), and Shen and Zhang's implementation outperformed Alsinet et al.'s implementation because of another better lower bound function.

After studying these lower bound functions, we present in this paper a new lower bound function to further improve the performance of the branch-and-bound algorithm for MAX-2-SAT. We show that these new lower bound functions are admissible and provide tighter bounds than any known lower bound functions. In order to evaluate the new lower bound function, we present experimental results on many examples. We showed that the improved algorithm is consistently and substantially better than all other known algorithms (Borchers & Furman; Alsinet et al; Zhang et al).

## Preliminary

Let $F$ be a formula in CNF with $n$ variables $V = \{x_1, ..., x_n\}$ and $m$ clauses. An *assignment* is a mapping from $V$ to $\{0, 1\}$ and may be represented by a vector $\vec{X} \in \{0, 1\}^n$, where 0 means false and 1 means true. Let $S(\vec{X}, F)$ be the number of clauses in $F$ satisfied by $\vec{X}$ and $K(F)$ be the minimal number of false clauses under any assignment. That is,

$$K(F) = m - \max\{S(\vec{X}, F) \mid \vec{X} \in \{0, 1\}^n\}.$$

If we use the right-hand side of the above equation for computing $K(F)$, we obtain a naive enumeration algorithm for MAX-SAT. $K(F)$ can also be computed by a simple recursive function as follows:

$$K(F) = \min(K(F_x), K(F_{\overline{x}}))$$

where $F_x$ is the formula obtained from $F$ by replacing $x$ by 1 and $\overline{x}$ by 0. Algorithm based on the above equation

*Partially supported by the National Science Foundation under Grant CCR-0098093

is also called Davis-Putanm-Logemann-Loveland procedure (Davis et al).

To speed up the computation, a lower bound is often introduced and the algorithm is called branch-and-bound algorithm. This paper introduces a new lower bound to improve the performance of the algorithm. To facilitate the discussion, we borrow some convention and the algorithm presented in (Zhang et al).

For every literal $x$, we use variable($x$) to denote the variable appearing in $x$. That is, variable($x$) $= x$ for positive literal $x$ and variable($\overline{x}$) $= x$ for negative literal $\overline{x}$. If $y$ is a literal, we use $\overline{y}$ to denote $x$ if $y = \overline{x}$.

A partial (complete) assignment can be represented by a set of literals (or unit clauses) in which each variable appears at most (exactly) once and each literal is meant to be true in the assignment. If variable($x$) does not appear in a partial assignment $A$, then we say literals $x$ and $\overline{x}$ are *unassigned* in $A$. For an unassigned literal $x$, $\mu(x)$ is the number of the unit clause for literal $x$ in the current clause set, including those generated during the search. Initially, $\mu(x)$ is the number of unit clauses for literal $x$ in the input.

The algorithm taken from (Zhang et al) is presented in Figure 1. In the algorithm, $B(x) = \{y \mid (x \vee y) \in F, \text{variable}(x) < \text{variable}(y)\}$ for each literal $x$. By abuse of notations, we assume $x_i$ is represented by $i$ and $\overline{x_i}$ is represented by $\bar{i}$, where $1 \leq i \leq n$. Hence, we have $\mu(i) = \mu(x_i)$, $B(i) = B(x_i)$, $\mu(\bar{i}) = \mu(\overline{x_i})$ and $B(\bar{i}) = B(\overline{x_i})$..

The following result is provided in (Zhang et al).

**Theorem 1** *Suppose $F_0$ is a set of binary clauses of n variables. Then max_2_sat($F_0, n$) will return the minimum number of false clauses under any assignment. The time complexity of max_2_sat($F_0, n$) is $O(n2^n)$ and the space complexity is $L/2 + O(n)$, where L is the size of the input.*

## Lower Bounds

Since the algorithm is trying to find the minimum number of false clauses under any assignment, lower bounds which estimate the minimum number of false clauses at a given search node are useful for cutting out some search space. In line 3 of bb_max_2_sat in Figure 1, popular lower bound functions can be used to improve its performance. We may also compute upper bound functions to cut off some search space. In practice, we all adopted the two-phase approach used by Borchers and Furman by first calling a local search algorithm for computing an upper bound before the search starts. We found that this approach is much more effective than computing an upper bound in each internal node of the search tree.

However, for lower bounds, we have not found such an effective function which can be computed before the search. Many algorithms from linear programming can be used for computing lower bounds. However, since this lower bound function is called in every internal node of the search tree, it must be very efficient. In fact, the lower bounds proposed in (Alsinet et al), (Shen & Zhang), and our new lower bound function take only linear-time (in terms of the input size).

The following three lower bound functions are used in (Borchers & Furman; Alsinet et al; Shen & Zhang 2004):

Figure 1: An exact algorithm for MAX-2-SAT.

```
function max_2_sat ( F0: clause set, n: integer)
    // initiation
    min_fcl := MAX_INT;
    for i := 1 to n do
        compute B(i) and B(ī) from F0;
        // assuming no unit clauses in F0
        μ(i) := μ(ī) := 0;
    end for
    bb_max_2_sat(1, n, 0);
    return min_fcl;
end function

function bb_max_2_sat( i, n: integer, k: integer )
1   if (i > n) // end of the search tree
2       if (k < min_fcl) min_fcl := k;
3   else if (lower_bound(i) + k < min_fcl)
4       if (μ(ī) + k < min_fcl) ∧ (μ(ī) < μ(i) + |B(i)|)
5           record_unit_clauses(x̄_i);
6           bb_max_2_sat(i + 1, n, k + μ(ī));
7           undo_record_unit_clauses(x̄_i);
8       end if
9       if (μ(i) + k < min_fcl) ∧ (μ(i) ≤ μ(ī) + |B(ī)|)
10          record_unit_clauses(x_i);
11          bb_max_2_sat(i + 1, n, k + μ(i));
12          undo_record_unit_clauses(x_i);
13      end if
14  end if
end function

procedure record_unit_clauses ( x: literal )
    for y ∈ B(x) do
        μ(y) := μ(y) + 1
    end for;
end procedure

procedure undo_record_unit_clauses ( x: literal )
    for y ∈ B(x) do
        μ(y) := μ(y) − 1
    end for;
end procedure
```

Figure 2: The function for computing LB3.

```
function lower_bound3 ( i: integer ) return integer
    LB3 = LB2;
    for (x ∨ y) in S do
        if (t(x) > 0) ∧ (t(y) > 0)
            LB3 = LB3 + 1;
            t(x) = t(x) − 1; t(y) = t(y) − 1;
    end for
    return LB3
end function
```

- Borchers and Furman's lower bound:
  LB1 = the number of conflicting (or empty) clauses by the current partial assignment;
- Alsinet, Manyà and Planes' lower bound:
  LB2 = LB1 + $\sum_{j=i}^{n} \min(\mu(\overline{j}), \mu(j))$;
- Shen and Zhang's lower bound:
  LB3 = lower_bound3$(i)$.

Here $\mu(x)$ is the number of the unit clause for literal $x$ under the current partial assignment and the function lower_bound3 is provided in Figure 2. Using LB2 instead LB1 contributes greatly to the improved performance of Alsinet, Manyà and Planes' implementation over Borchers and Furman's. It is easy to see that LB1 $\leq$ LB2 $\leq K(F)$. In general, a lower bound LB is said to be *admissible* if LB $\leq K(F)$. In other words, both LB1 and LB2 are admissible.

To compute LB3, for any literal $x$, let $t(x) = \mu(\overline{x}) - \mu(x)$ and $S$ be the set of clauses of which both literals are unassigned under the current assignment.

The following theorem is given in (Shen & Zhang 2004):

**Theorem 2** *LB1 $\leq$ LB2 $\leq$ LB3 $\leq K(F)$.*

To prove the above theorem, we may use the following lemma:

**Lemma 3** *If there is a clause $x \vee y$ in $F$ such that $\mu(x) < \mu(\overline{x})$ and $\mu(y) < \mu(\overline{y})$, then LB2 $+ 1 \leq K(F)$.*

**Proof** Given $\mu(\overline{x}) > \mu(x)$ and $\mu(\overline{y}) > \mu(y)$, for a clause $x \vee y$, if we assign 0 to $x$, $\mu(y)$ will be increased by 1. So $\min(\mu(y), \mu(\overline{y}))$ in LB2 will be increased by 1. If we assign 1 to $x$, then $\min(\mu(x), \mu(\overline{x}))$ in LB2 will be increased because $\mu(\overline{x}) > \mu(x)$. In both cases, we can see that it is safe to increase LB2 by 1. []

## A New Lower Bound

We design another lower bound, lower_bound4 in Figure 3, to fully explore the property revealed by Lemma 3.

It is easy to prove the following result.

**Lemma 4** *The worst-case time complexity of lower_bound4$(i)$ is $O((n-i)+\sum_{j=i}^{n} \max(|B(j)|, |B(\overline{j})|))$.*

Before we prove formally that LB4 is indeed an admissible lower bound for MAX-2-SAT, let us look at a simple example.

Figure 3: The function for computing LB4.

```
function lower_bound4 ( i: integer) return integer
    LB4 = LB1;
    while (i ≤ n) do
        LB4 = LB4 + min(μ(ī), μ(i));
        t = |μ(ī) − μ(i)|;
        if μ(ī) > μ(i) Y = B(i) else Y = B(ī)
        for y ∈ Y if (t > 0) do
            t = t − 1;
            μ(y) = μ(y) + 1;
        end for
        i = i + 1
    end while
    return LB4
end function
```

**Example 5** Suppose a 2CNF formula $F$ is represented by $\mu$ and $S$, where $\mu(a) = \mu(b) = \mu(c) = \mu(\overline{c}) = 0$, $\mu(\overline{a}) = \mu(\overline{b}) = 1$ and $S = \{a \vee c, b \vee \overline{c}\}$. It is easy to see $K(F) = 1$. LB3 = 0 because there exists no clause $x \vee y$ in $F$ such that $\mu(\overline{x}) > \mu(x)$ and $\mu(\overline{y}) > \mu(y)$.

Suppose $a < b < c$, then LB4 = 1 because $a \vee c$ will increase $\mu(c)$ by 1 and $b \vee \overline{c}$ will increase $\mu(\overline{c})$ by 1, making $\min(\mu(\overline{c}), \mu(c)) = 1$.

Let $F(i)$ be the remaining nontrivial (neither empty nor tautology) clauses when bb_max_2_sat$(i, n, k)$ in Figure 1 is called. Recall that for any unassigned literal $x$, $\mu(x)$ is the number of the unit clause $x$ and $k$ in the procedure bb_max_2_sat$(i, n, k)$ is the number of empty clauses created by the partial assignment on variables $x_1$ to $x_{i-1}$. Let $\mathbf{u}(x)$ be the multiset of $\mu(x)$ copies of the unit clause $x$ and $xB(x)$ denote the set $\{(x \vee y) \mid y \in B(x)\}$. Then we have

$$F(i) = \mathbf{u}(x_i) \cup \mathbf{u}(\overline{x_i}) \cup x_i B(i) \cup \overline{x_i} B(\overline{i}) \cup F(i+1)$$

where $F(i+1)$ is the subset of $F(i)$ not containing the variable $x_i$ (assuming $F(n+1) = \emptyset$).

Let $F$ be $F(i)$ and $x$ be $x_i$ in

$$K(F) = \min(K(F_x), K(F_{\overline{x}}))$$

we have

$$\begin{aligned} K(F(i)_{x_i}) &= \mu(\overline{i}) + K(B(\overline{i}) \cup F(i+1)) && (1) \\ K(F(i)_{\overline{x_i}}) &= \mu(i) + K(B(i) \cup F(i+1)) && (2) \\ K(F(i)) &= \min(K(F(i)_{x_i}), K(F(i)_{\overline{x_i}})) && (3) \end{aligned}$$

Since $K(F(i+1)) \leq K(Y \cup F(i+1))$ for any clause set $Y$, we have $\min(\mu(\overline{i}), \mu(i)) + K(F(i+1)) \leq K(F(i))$, by discarding $B(i)$ and $B(\overline{i})$ from (1) and (2), respectively. This relation shows why LB2 is an admissible lower bound. To show that LB4 is admissible, we need the following lemma.

**Lemma 6** *For any subset $X \subseteq B(i)$, if $|X| \leq \mu(\overline{i}) - \mu(i)$, then*

$$\min(\mu(\overline{i}), \mu(i)) + K(X \cup F(i+1)) \leq K(F(i)) \quad (4)$$

**Proof** If $|X| = 0$, then (4) is trivially true. If $|X| > 0$, then $\mu(\bar{i}) > \mu(i)$ and (4) becomes

$$\mu(i) + K(X \cup F(i+1)) \leq K(F(i)) \quad (5)$$

According to (3), there are two cases:

Case 1: $K(F(i)_{x_i}) < K(F(i)_{\overline{x_i}})$. So $K(F(i)) = K(F(i)_{x_i}) = \mu(\bar{i}) + K(B(\bar{i}) \cup F(i+1))$ by (1). Because $\mu(\bar{i}) \geq \mu(i) + |X|$ and $K(B(\bar{i}) \cup F(i+1)) \geq K(F(i+1)) \geq K(X \cup F(i+1)) - |X|$, we have $K(F(i)) \geq \mu(i) + |X| + K(X \cup F(i+1)) - |X|$, or (5).

Case 2: $K(F(i)_{x_i}) \geq K(F(i)_{\overline{x_i}})$. So $K(F(i)) = K(F(i)_{\overline{x_i}}) = \mu(i) + K(B(i) \cup F(i+1))$ by (2). Since $X \subseteq B(i)$, $K(B(i) \cup F(i+1)) \geq K(X \cup F(i+1))$. So (5) holds. []

A mirror of the above lemma can be obtained by switching $x_i$ and $\overline{x_i}$.

**Theorem 7** *LB4* $\leq K(F)$.

**Proof** We will use Lemma 6 (or its mirror) at each iteration of $i$ in lower_bound4. If $i = n$, then LB4 = LB3 = LB2 = $\min(\mu(i), \mu(\bar{i}))$. If $i < n$, suppose LB4$'$ is the value computed inside lower_bound4 for $X \cup F(i+1)$, where

$$F(i) = \mathbf{u}(x_i) \cup \mathbf{u}(\overline{x_i}) \cup X_i B(i) \cup \overline{x_i} B(\bar{i}) \cup F(i+1).$$

As an inductive hypothesis, we assume

$$\text{LB4}' \leq K(X \cup F(i+1)).$$

If $\mu(\bar{i}) > \mu(i)$ then $Y = B(i)$ and a subset $X$ of $Y$ is added at lines 6–9, where $|X| \leq t$ as computed at line 4. Since $\text{LB4} = \min(\mu(\bar{i}), \mu(i)) + \text{LB4}'$, by induction hypothesis, $\text{LB4} \leq \min(\mu(\bar{i}), \mu(i)) + K(X \cup F(i+1)) \leq K(F(i))$. The case when $\mu(\bar{i}) \leq \mu(i)$ is similar. In both cases, LB4 $\leq K(F(i))$. []

## Comparison of LB3 and LB4

In (Shen & Zhang 2004), it has been shown by experimental results that LB3 can improve the performance of MAX-2-SAT ten times faster than other lower bounds (LB1 and LB2). Since LB3 and LB4 have the same worst-case time complexity, we wish that LB4 is never smaller than LB3, as Example 5 already showed that LB4 can be greater than LB3.

Let us look at Example 5 again. We saw that LB4 = 1 when $a < b < c$. The same result can be obtained when $b < a < c$, $a < c < b$, or $b < c < a$. However, if $c < a < b$ (or $c < b < a$), then LB4 = 0 because neither $\mu(a)$ nor $\mu(b)$ can be increased by the two binary clauses.

This simple example shows that the value of LB4 depends on how the propositional variables are ordered in the implementation. In contrast, the value of LB3 does not depend on variable ordering. Variable ordering is an important performance issue of the algorithm in Figure 1. Several orderings have been compared in (Shen & Zhang 2004), including an ordering based on the implication graph of $F$.

The next example shows that the ordering for choosing clauses in the computation of LB3 and LB4 affect their values.

Figure 4: The function for computing LB4a.

```
function lower_bound4a ( i: variable) return integer
1   LB4 = LB1;
2   while (i ≤ n) do
3       LB4 = LB4 + min(μ(ī), μ(i));
4       t = |μ(ī) − μ(i)|;
5       if μ(ī) > μ(i) Y = B(i) else Y = B(ī)
6       S = ∅
7       for j ∈ Y if (t > 0) do
8           if (μ(j) ≥ μ(j̄)) S = S ∪ {j} else
9               t = t − 1;
10              μ(j) = μ(j) + 1;
11      end for
12      for j ∈ S if (t > 0) do
13          t = t − 1;
14          μ(j) = μ(j) + 1;
15      end for
16      i = i + 1
17  end while
18  return LB4
end function
```

**Example 8** Let $F$ be represented by $\mu$ and $S$, where $\mu(a) = \mu(b) = \mu(c) = \mu(d) = 0$, $\mu(\bar{a}) = \mu(\bar{b}) = \mu(\bar{c}) = \mu(\bar{d}) = 1$, and $S = \{a \vee b, b \vee c, c \vee d\}$. Obviously, $K(F) = 2$. If $b \vee c$ is chosen first at line 2 of lower_bound3, then LB3 = 1; otherwise, LB3 = 2. Similarly, for computing LB4, if $b \vee c$ is chosen first at line 6 of lower_bound4, (either $b$ or $c$ must be the smallest in the variable ordering.) then LB4 = 1; otherwise LB4 = 2.

This example shows that LB3 may be 2 while LB4 may be 1. Thus LB3 and LB4 are different in general. Now we have the following question: If the same clause ordering is used for computing both LB3 and LB4, is it true that LB3 $\leq$ LB4? The answer is unfortunately no, as illustrated by the following example.

**Example 9** Suppose $F$ is represented by $\mu$ and $S$, where $\mu(a) = \mu(b) = \mu(c) = \mu(\bar{c}) = 0$, $\mu(\bar{a}) = \mu(\bar{b}) = 1$ and $S = \{a \vee c, a \vee b\}$. Then $K(F) = 1$ and LB3 = 1 because of $a \vee b$. However, if the clauses are chosen in the given order, then LB4 = 0 because $t = 1$ for $a$ is used on $c$ when $a \vee c$ is chosen.

To avoid the problem illustrated in the above example, at line 6 of lower_bound4, we may prefer those clauses in $Y$ that will increase the value of LB4. This idea is implemented as function lower_bound4a in Figure 4. Those literals in $Y$ that will not increase the value of LB4 immediately are stored in $S \subseteq Y$ and processed later at lines 13–16.

However, we do not have a proof that LB4 computed by lower_bound4a is always greater than or equal to LB3. To make sure LB4 $\geq$ LB3, let us say a clause ordering $<_c$ is LB3-*compatible* if for any two clauses $(a \vee b)$ and $(c \vee d)$, if $(a \vee b)$ satisfies $(t(a) > 0) \wedge (t(b) > 0)$ but $(c \vee d)$ does not, then $(a \vee b) <_c (c \vee d)$.

**Theorem 10** *If we select clauses from* $Y$ *at line 6 of lower_bound4(*$i$*) using a LB3-compatible clause ordering (from small to big), then LB3* $\leq$ *LB4.*

In Example 9, any LB3-compatible ordering will place $a \vee b$ before $a \vee c$. Using this ordering for computing LB4, we have LB3 = LB4 = 1.

The only extra cost for using a LB3-compatible clause ordering in lower_bound4 is that we have to execute lines 6–9 twice: The first time for those $y \in Y$, $t(y) > 0$, and the second time for those such that $t(y) \leq 0$. In other words, using this ordering will not compromise the worst-case time complexity of lower_bound4. However, our implementation of LB4 using a LB3-compatible clause ordering is slightly slower than lower_bound4a, because of this second visit.

## Experimental Results

We already implemented the algorithm presented in Figure 1 and the lower bound functions LB2 and LB3 (Shen & Zhang 2004). The implementation is written in C++ and the code is available to public. We have also implemented two lower bounds presented in this paper: lower_bound4 and lower_bound4a, and they are denoted by LB4 and LB4a, respectively. Note that the function lower_bound($i$) in bb_max_2_sat (line 3) of Figure 1 returns a lower bound value minus LB1 in our experiments.

Table 1 shows the performance of five implementations on Borchers and Furman's benchmarks. The six implementations are BF (Borchers & Furman), AMP (Alsinet et al), ZZ (Zhao & Zhang), LB3 (Shen & Zhang 2004), LB4 and LB4a. The benchmarks contain randomly generated 2-CNFs of 50, 100, and 150 variables (#var), and are available from their web site. It is clear from that the table that LB4a provides the best result while LB3 and LB4 are ranked second. The harder the problem, the more significant the gain of LB4a over other implementations.

(Shen & Zhang 2004) have shown that LB3 is about ten times faster than other implementations on many random 2-CNFs. Table 2 provides a detailed comparison of LB3 and LB4a. The instances are random 2CNF with 100 or 200 variables and various number of clauses. The data show the average runs on 100 instances (of the same numbers of variables and clauses). It is clear from the table that LB4a explores only $1/4$ of the search space (represented by the number of branches in the search tree) of LB3 and LB4a is about 3 times faster than LB3 on average. Note that the number in the parentheses following the run time is the number of unfinished cases after two hours of running.

## Conclusion

After studying several lower bound functions for the branch-and-bound algorithm of MAX-2-SAT, we have proposed a new lower bound function and proved that it is admissible and it is indeed a better lower bound function than LB2 and LB3. We have implemented this function and our experimental results showed that the lower bound function is consistently and substantially better than other lower bound functions. All the techniques presented in the paper can be applied to the weighted MAX-2-SAT problem where each

Table 1: Experimental results on Borchers and Furman's examples. The times (in seconds) are collected on a Pentium 4 linux machine, 2.4GHz, 1G memory; "–" means the job doesn't finish in one hour; $*$ means the output was erroneous.

| Problem | | #fcl | BF | AMP | ZZ | LB3 | LB4 | LB4a |
|---|---|---|---|---|---|---|---|---|
| #var | #cls | | | | | | | |
| 50 | 100 | 4 | 0.02 | 0.03 | 0.31 | 0.02 | 0.02 | 0.01 |
| | 150 | 8 | 0.06 | 0.03 | 0.46 | 0.02 | 0.02 | 0.02 |
| | 200 | 16 | 4.18 | 0.38 | 0.55 | 0.03 | 0.03 | 0.03 |
| | 250 | 22 | 24 | 0.26 | 0.62 | 0.05 | 0.04 | 0.04 |
| | 300 | 32 | 350 | 4.88 | 1.05 | 0.09 | 0.09 | 0.07 |
| | 350 | 41 | 2556 | 10 | 1.58 | 0.09 | 0.17 | 0.11 |
| | 400 | 45 | 2308 | 4.65 | 1.23 | 0.05 | 0.08 | 0.06 |
| | 450 | 63 | – | 44 | 6.04 | 0.23 | 0.32 | 0.21 |
| | 500 | 66 | – | 17 | 4.15 | 0.12 | 0.17 | 0.15 |
| 100 | 200 | 5 | 0.14 | 0.16 | 0.41 | 0.03 | 0.03 | 0.04 |
| | 300 | 15 | 501 | 29 | 0.69 | 0.42 | 0.66 | 0.4 |
| | 400 | 29 | – | 1204 | 3.92 | 1.26 | 3.15 | 0.98 |
| | 500 | 44 | – | – | 968 | 192 | 180 | 62 |
| | 600 | 65 | – | – | – | 303 | 394 | 130 |
| 150 | 300 | 4 | 0.18 | 0.22 | * | 0.12 | 0.10 | 0.08 |
| | 450 | 22 | – | – | * | 64 | 19 | 7.11 |
| | 600 | 38 | – | – | * | 347 | 385 | 54 |

Table 2: Experimental results on random instances. The times (in seconds) are collected on a Pentium 4 linux machine, 2.4GHz, 1G memory.

| Problem | | LB3 | | LB4a | |
|---|---|---|---|---|---|
| #var | #cls | #branches | sec | #branches | sec |
| 100 | 200 | 3.7e+03 | 0.035 | 1.63e+03 | 0.030 |
| | 250 | 6.22e+04 | 0.15 | 1.39e+04 | 0.082 |
| | 300 | 5.91e+05 | 1.08 | 1.07e+05 | 0.41 |
| | 350 | 2.28e+06 | 4.14 | 3.84e+05 | 1.5 |
| | 400 | 9.5e+06 | 17 | 1.09e+06 | 5.23 |
| | 450 | 1.77e+07 | 44 | 3.14e+06 | 14 |
| | 500 | 3.91e+07 | 81 | 7.32e+06 | 32 |
| | 550 | 7.32e+07 | 158 | 1.27e+07 | 55 |
| | 600 | 1.69e+08 | 373 | 3.38e+07 | 152 |
| | 650 | 3.15e+08 | 632 | 6.85e+07 | 337 |
| | 700 | 4.34e+08 | 1191 | 1.14e+08 | 512 |
| 200 | 400 | 1.61e+06 | 3.41 | 2.09e+05 | 0.88 |
| | 420 | 1.27e+07 | 28 | 1.3e+06 | 5.33 |
| | 440 | 5.79e+07 | 145 | 3.17e+06 | 15 |
| | 460 | 1.24e+08 | 330(3) | 1.81e+07 | 90 |
| | 480 | 1.46e+08 | 405(10) | 2.26e+07 | 117(1) |
| | 500 | 2.69e+08 | 758(21) | 4.31e+07 | 244(2) |

clause has a weight. As future work, we will extend the lower bound function to other optimization problems such as the maximum cut and the maximum clique problems in graph theory.

## References


T. Alsinet, F. Manyà, J. Planes, Improved branch and bound algorithms for Max-SAT. *Proc. of 6th International Conference on the Theory and Applications of Satisfiability Testing*, SAT2003, pages 408-415.

T. Alsinet, F. Manyà, J. Planes, Improved branch and bound algorithms for Max-2-SAT and Weighted Max-2-SAT. *Catalonian Conference on Artificial Intelligence*, 2003.

B. Aspvall, M. F. Plass and R. E. Tarjan, A linear-time algorithm for testing the truth of certain quantified Boolean formulas, *Information Processing Letters*, 1979, 8(3):121-123

N. Bansal, V. Raman, Upper bounds for MaxSat: Further improved. In Aggarwal and Rangan (eds.): *Proceedings of 10th Annual conference on Algorithms and Computation*, ISSAC'99, volume 1741 of Lecture Notes in Computer Science, pages 247-258, Springer-Verlag, 1999.

B. Borchers, J. Furman, A two-phase exact algorithm for MAX-SAT and weighted MAX-SAT problems. *Journal of Combinatorial Optimization*, 2(4):299-306, 1999.

J. Cheriyan, W.H. Cunningnham, L. Tuncel, Y. Wang. A linear programming and rounding approach to Max 2-Sat. *DIMACS Series in Discrete Mathematics and Theoretical Computer Science*, 26:395–414, 1996.

E. Dantsin, A. Goerdt, E.A. Hirsch, R. Kannan, J. Kleinberg, C. Papadimitriou, P. Raghavan, U. Schöning. A deterministic $(2-2/(k+1))^n$ algorithm for $k$–SAT based on local search. *Theoretical Computer Science*, 2002.

M. Davis, G. Logemann, D. Loveland, A machine program for theorem-proving. *Communications of the Association for Computing Machinery*, 7 (July 1962), 394–397.

J. Gramm, E.A. Hirsch, R. Niedermeier, P. Rossmanith: New worst-case upper bounds for MAX-2-SAT with application to MAX-CUT. Preprint, submitted to Elsevier, May, 2001

P. Hansen, B. Jaumard. Algorithms for the maximum satisfiability problem. *Computing*, 44:279-303, 1990.

E.A. Hirsch. A new algorithm for MAX-2-SAT. In *Proceedings of 17th International Symposium on Theoretical Aspects of Computer Science*, STACS 2000, vol. 1770, Lecture Notes in Computer Science, pages 65-73. Springer-Verlag.

E.A. Hirsch. New worst-case upper bounds for SAT. *Journal of Automated Reasoning*, 24(4):397-420, 2000.

M. Mahajan, V. Raman. Parameterizing above guaranteed values: MaxSat and MaxCut. *Journal of Algorithms*, 31:335–354, 1999.

R. Niedermeier, P. Rossmanith. New upper bounds for maximum satisfiability. *Journal of Algorithms*, 36:63-88, 2000.

H. Shen, H. Zhang, An empirical study of max-2-sat phase transitions, *Proc. of LICS'03 Workshop on Typical Case Complexity and Phase Transitions*, Ottawa, CA, June 2003.

H. Shen, H. Zhang, Improving Exact Algorithms for MAX-2-SAT, *Eighth International Symposium on Artificial Intelligence and Mathematics*, Fort Lauderdale, Florida, January 2004.

R. Wallace, E. Freuder. Comparative studies of constraint satisfaction and Davis-Putnam algorithms for maximum satisfiability problems. In D. Johnson and M. Trick (eds.) *Cliques, Coloring and Satisfiability*, volume 26, pages 587-615, 1996.

H. Xu, R.A. Rutenbar, K. Sakallah, sub-SAT: A formulation for related boolean satisfiability with applications in routing. ISPD'02, April, 2002, San Diego, CA.

H. Zhang, H. Shen, F. Manyà: Exact algorithms for MAX-SAT. In *Proc. of International Workshop on First-order Theorem Proving* (FTP 2003).

X. Zhao, W. Zhang. An efficient algorithm for maximum boolean satisfiability based on unit propagation, linear programming, and dynamic weighting. Preprint, Department of Computer Science, Washington University. 2004.

# Additive versus Multiplicative Clause Weighting for SAT

**John Thornton** and **Duc Nghia Pham** and **Stuart Bain** and **Valnir Ferreira Jr.**
Institute for Integrated and Intelligent Systems, Griffith University
PMB 50, Gold Coast Mail Centre, 9726, Australia
email: {j.thornton, d.n.pham, s.bain, v.ferreira}@griffith.edu.au

## Abstract

This paper examines the relative performance of additive and multiplicative clause weighting schemes for propositional satisfiability testing. Starting with one of the most recently developed multiplicative algorithms (SAPS), an experimental study was constructed to isolate the effects of multiplicative in comparison to additive weighting, while controlling other key features of the two approaches, namely the use of random versus flat moves, deterministic versus probabilistic weight smoothing and multiple versus single inclusion of literals in the local search neighborhood.

As a result of this investigation we developed a pure additive weighting scheme (PAWS) which can outperform multiplicative weighting on a range of difficult problems, while requiring considerably less effort in terms of parameter tuning. We conclude that additive weighting shows better scaling properties because it makes less distinction between costs and so considers a larger domain of possible moves.

## Introduction and Background

Clause weighting algorithms for satisfiability testing have formed an important research area since their first introduction in the early 1990s. Since then various improvements have been proposed, resulting in the two best known algorithms of today: the discrete Lagrangian method (DLM) (Wu & Wah 2000) and scaling and probabilistic smoothing (SAPS) (Hutter, Tompkins, & Hoos 2002). While these methods differ in important aspects, both use the same underlying trap avoiding strategy: increasing weights on unsatisfied clauses in local minima and then periodically adjusting weights to maintain reasonable weight differentials during the search.

The earliest clause weighting algorithms, such as Breakout (Morris 1993), repeatedly increased weights on unsatisfied clauses and so allowed unrestricted weight growth during the search. Flips were then chosen on the basis of minimizing the combined weight of the unsatisfied clauses. In 1997, Frank proposed a new weight decay algorithm that updated weights on unsatisfied clauses using a combination of a multiplicative decay rate and an additive weight increase. While Frank's work laid the ground for future advances, his decay scheme produced relatively small improvements over earlier weighting approaches. At this point, clause weighting algorithms proved competitive on many smaller problems but were unable to match the performance of faster and simpler heuristics, such as Novelty, on larger problem instances (McAllester, Selman, & Kautz 1997). As a key reason for developing incomplete local search techniques is to solve problems beyond the reach of complete SAT solvers, the poor scalability of clause weighting was a major disadvantage.



It was not until the development of DLM that a significant performance gain was achieved. In its simplest form, DLM follows Breakout's weight increment scheme, but additionally decrements clause weights after a fixed number of increases. DLM also alters the point at which weight is increased by allowing *flat* moves that leave the weighted cost of the solution unchanged. These flat moves are in turn controlled by a tabu list and by a parameter which limits the total number of consecutive flat moves (Wu & Wah 2000). In empirical tests DLM proved successful at solving a range of random and structured SAT problems, and in particular was able to outperform the best non-weighting algorithms on many larger and more difficult problem instances.

In another line of research, Schuurmans and Southey (2000) developed a fully multiplicative weighting algorithm: smoothed descent and flood (SDF). SDF introduced a new method for breaking ties between equal cost flips by additionally considering the number of true literals in satisfied clauses. In situations where no improving moves are available, SDF multiplicatively increases weights on unsatisfied clauses and then normalizes (or *smooths*) clause weights so that the greatest cost difference between any two flips remains constant. SDF's reported flip performance was promising in comparison to DLM, but these results did not look at the more difficult problems for which DLM was especially suited. In addition, SDF's time performance did not compare well, due to the overhead of adjusting weights on all clauses at each local minimum.

In subsequent work, SDF evolved into the exponentiated subgradient algorithm (ESG) (Schuurmans, Southey, & Holte 2001), which in turn formed the basis of the scaling and probabilistic smoothing (SAPS) algorithm (Hutter, Tompkins, & Hoos 2002). ESG and SAPS dispensed with SDF's augmented cost function, and SAPS further improved on the run-time performance of ESG by only smoothing weights periodically, and only increasing weights on *vio-*

*lated* clauses in a local minimum[1].

The feature of greatest interest to the current study is that, ignoring the issue of additive versus multiplicative clause weighting, the weight update scheme of SAPS is almost identical in structure to the weight update scheme of DLM: both increase weight when a local minimum is identified (although using different identification criteria), and both periodically adjust weights according to a parameter value that varies for different problems[2]. SAPS differs from DLM only in using the parameter to probabilistically determine when weight is reduced, whereas DLM deterministically reduces weight after a fixed number of increases.

The aim of this study is to investigate whether an additive or multiplicative weight update scheme is better for satisfiability testing. Given that SAPS and DLM both have some claim to be considered as the state-of-the-art in local search for SAT and that both have separately hit upon a similar underlying weighting structure, it now becomes possible to compare additive and multiplicative clause weighting without their relative performance being disguised by differing implementation details. To perform this comparison, we started with the authors' original version of SAPS and changed it in small steps until it became an effective additive clause weighting algorithm. By examining and empirically testing the effect of each step, we set out to isolate exactly those features that are crucial for the success of each approach. This resulted in the development of a new pure additive weighting scheme (PAWS). As the published results for SAPS have only looked at relatively small problems, we also decided to evaluate SAPS and PAWS on an extended test set that includes a selection of the more difficult problems for which DLM was developed. In the remainder of the paper we describe in more detail the development of PAWS from SAPS and DLM, and then present the results and conclusions of our empirical study.

## Clause Weighting Algorithms for SAT

DLM has been described as "ad hoc" (Schuurmans, Southey, & Holte 2001) and criticized for requiring a large number of parameters to obtain optimum performance. However, DLM has evolved through several versions, the last of which was developed specifically to solve the larger towers of Hanoi and parity learning problems from the DIMACS benchmarks (Wu & Wah 2000). As already discussed, the basic structure of DLM is similar to SAPS, except for the heuristic used to control the taking of flat moves. In addition, although the latest version of DLM has 27 parameters, in practice only three of these require adjustment in the SAT domain.

[1]ESG's approach is to scale and smooth the weight on all clauses in every local minima.

[2]Additionally, a third clause weighting algorithm, GLSSAT (Mills & Tsang 1999), uses a similar weight update scheme, additively increasing weights on the least weighted unsatisfied clauses and multiplicatively reducing weights whenever the weight on any one clause exceeds a predefined threshold. Although GLSSAT performed well in comparison with Walksat, it could not match DLM on larger problems and so is not considered further in this study.

Of particular interest is that DLM uses a single parameter to control the weighting process (corresponding to $Max_{inc}$ in Figure 2), which determines when weights are to be reduced. In contrast, SAPS requires two further parameters ($\alpha$ and $\rho$) to determine the amount that weights are multiplicatively scaled or smoothed (in DLM clause weight increases and decreases are implemented by adding or subtracting one). The other two DLM parameters ($\theta_1$ and $\theta_2$) are used to control the flat move heuristic: Using the terms from Figure 1, if $best < 0$, DLM will randomly select and flip any $x_i \in L$. Otherwise, if $best = 0$, and the number of immediately preceding consecutive flat moves is $< \theta_1$ and $L_t \neq \emptyset$, then DLM will randomly select and flip any $x_i \in L_t$, where $L_t$ contains all flat move literals that have not been flipped in the last $\theta_2$ moves. Otherwise clause weights are additively updated, as per Figure 2.

Although SAPS implements a fairly "pure" weighting algorithm, there are a few implementation details that distinguish it from DLM (see Figure 1). The first is the $wp$ parameter which probabilistically controls whether a random flip is taken when no improving cost move is available. This acts as an alternative to DLM's flat move heuristic. The second is that the set of local neighborhood of moves for SAPS contains a single copy of each literal that can *make* a false clause (i.e. turn it from false to true). In DLM, the neighborhood consists of all literals in all false clauses. This means that if a literal appears in more than one false clause, it will appear more than once in the local neighborhood, thereby increasing the probability that it will be selected. Finally, as noted earlier, SAPS uses *probabilistic* smoothing when adjusting clause weights, i.e. if $P_{smooth}$ is set to 5% then there is a 1 in 20 chance that weight will be adjusted after an increase. In contrast, DLM's third parameter fixes the exact number of increases before weight is decreased, and so represents a *deterministic* weight reduction scheme.

Overall, there is little difference between DLM and SAPS in terms of parameter tuning. While SAPS has four parameters ($\alpha, \rho, wp$ and $P_{smooth}$) and a basic version of DLM has three, in practice at least one of the SAPS parameters can be treated as a constant and the others adjusted to suit (in this study $wp$ is set at 1%). For both algorithms the process of parameter tuning is time consuming, as optimal performance is highly dependent on the correct settings. This compares poorly with simpler non-weighting algorithms, such as adaptive Walksat (Hoos 2002), which only requires the automatic tuning of a single noise parameter. To address this, a version of SAPS called Reactive SAPS (RSAPS) was developed (Hutter, Tompkins, & Hoos 2002) that automatically adjusts the $P_{smooth}$ parameter during the search. However we found this algorithm did not perform as well as a properly tuned SAPS on our problem set, so we did not consider it further.

Hence, the main design criticism that can be levelled at DLM is that it relies on a somewhat complex flat move heuristic, whereas SAPS can search purely on the basis of weight guidance (while taking the occasional random move). From this it could be argued that multiplicative weighting is superior to additive weighting because it makes finer distinctions between moves and so avoids the need to

```
procedure SAPS
begin
  generate random starting point
  for each clause c_i do: set clause weight w_i ← 1
  while solution not found and not timed out do
    best ← ∞
    for each literal x_i appearing in at least one false clause do
      Δw ← change in false clause Σw caused by flipping x_i
      if Δw < best then L ← x_i and best ← Δw
      else if Δw = best then L ← L ∪ x_i
    end for
    if best < −0.1 then randomly flip x_i ∈ L
    else if probability ≤ wp then randomly flip any literal
    else
      for each false clause f_i do: w_i ← w_i × α
      if probability ≤ P_smooth then
        μ_w ← mean of current clause weights
        for each clause c_j do: w_j ← w_j × ρ + (1 − ρ) × μ_w
      end if
    end if
  end while
end
```

Figure 1: Scaling and probabilistic smoothing (SAPS)

```
procedure PAWS
begin
  generate random starting point
  for each clause c_i do: set clause weight w_i ← 1
  while solution not found and not timed out do
    best ← ∞
    for each literal x_ij in each false clause f_i do
      Δw ← change in false clause Σw caused by flipping x_ij
      if Δw < best then L ← x_ij and best ← Δw
      else if Δw = best then L ← L ∪ x_ij
    end for
    if best < 0 or (best = 0 and probability ≤ P_flat) then
      randomly flip x_ij ∈ L
    else
      for each false clause f_i do: w_i ← w_i + 1
      if # times clause weights increased % Max_inc = 0 then
        for each clause c_j|w_j > 1 do: w_j ← w_j − 1
      end if
    end if
  end while
end
```

Figure 2: The pure additive weighting scheme (PAWS)

search plateau areas. However, this assumes that the overall performance of SAPS is at least as good as DLM's and that the effectiveness of additive weighting depends on plateau searching, both issues we shall address later in the paper.

## The Pure Additive Weighting Scheme (PAWS)

SAPS has demonstrated that effective local search guidance can be given by a reasonably simple manipulation of clause weights. It has also outperformed DLM on a range of SATLIB benchmark problems, both in terms of time and median number of flips (Schuurmans, Southey, & Holte 2001; Hutter, Tompkins, & Hoos 2002). From this work several questions arise: firstly how does SAPS perform on the larger DIMACS benchmark problems for which DLM was developed? Secondly, the SAPS code is based on a very efficient implementation of Walksat[3], so to what extent is the superior time performance of SAPS based on the details of this implementation? And finally, does the success of SAPS depend on multiplicative weighting? i.e. can we obtain the same kind of guidance using additive weighting, avoiding the complication of multiplicative update parameters and without resorting to the further complication of a plateau searching strategy?

To answer all three of these questions we developed a pure additive weighting scheme (PAWS), which we embedded directly into the SAPS source code[4] (so the same efficiencies were obtained), and tested PAWS on both the SATLIB benchmarks used for SAPS and a selection of the DIMACS benchmarks used for DLM. We term PAWS as a pure weighting scheme because it does away with DLM's plateau searching heuristic and only relies on weight guidance to determine the search trajectory. However, PAWS retains DLM's preference for taking flat moves when no improving moves are available, by selecting random moves from the domain of available flat moves. In addition, PAWS retains DLM's deterministic weight reduction scheme and the multiple inclusion of literals that appear in more than one false clause.

Figure 2 shows the complete PAWS procedure which is now controlled by two parameters: $P_{flat}$ which decides whether a randomly selected flat move will be taken (corresponding to $wp$ in SAPS), and $Max_{inc}$ which determines at which point weight will be decreased (corresponding to $P_{smooth}$ in SAPS). As with $wp$ in SAPS, we found that $P_{flat}$ can be treated as a constant, and for all subsequent experiments it was set at 15%. Hence PAWS only requires the tuning of a single parameter, $Max_{inc}$, which we found to have roughly the same settings and sensitivity as the equivalent parameter in DLM. On all our test problems the optimum value of $Max_{inc}$ was relatively easy to find, generally showing a similar concave shaped relationship with local search cost as that observed for Walksat's noise parameter in (Hoos 2002). The requirement to only tune a single parameter with a fairly stable relationship to cost gives PAWS a considerable practical advantage over DLM and SAPS, which typically need considerably more effort to set up for a particular class of problem.

While PAWS comes close to being an additive version of SAPS, as discussed earlier, it differs in three aspects:

- Random Flat (RF): PAWS probabilistically takes a random flat move when no improving move is available (rather than allowing cost increasing moves).
- Deterministic Reduction (DR): PAWS deterministically reduces weights after $Max_{inc}$ number of increases (rather than reducing weights with probability $P_{smooth}$).

[3] http://www.cs.washington.edu/homes/kautz/walksat/walksat-dist.tar.Z.uu

[4] http://www.int.gu.edu.au/~johnt/paws.tar

- Multiple Inclusion (MI): PAWS allows optimal cost flips that appear in $n$ false clauses to also appear $n$ times in its move list $L$ (rather than exactly once).

To test the effects of these differences, three additional versions of PAWS were developed, each with one of these features replaced by the alternative heuristic used in SAPS. Similarly, three further versions of SAPS were developed each using the alternative PAWS heuristic.

## Empirical Study

### Problem Set

We firstly set out to reproduce the problem set reported in the original study on SAPS (Hutter, Tompkins, & Hoos 2002). This involved selecting the median and hardest problems from several SATLIB problem classes. As we were unable to verify the exact problems with the authors, we ran our own tests with SAPS, using the published parameter settings, to identify the median and hardest instances for the flat100, flat200, uf100 and uf250 problem sets. Secondly, to test performance on larger problem instances, we included the SATLIB bw-large.d blocks world problem, the two most difficult DIMACS graph coloring problems (g125.17 and g250.29) and the median and hardest DIMACS 16-bit parity learning problems (par16). We then generated three sets of random 3-SAT problems from the accepted hard region, each containing 20 instances, the first with 400 variables, the second with 800 variables and the last with 1600 variables. To these we added the f400, f800 and f1600 DIMACS problems and repeated the earlier process to identify the median and hardest problem from each set. Finally, we generated a range of random binary CSPs, again from the accepted hard region, and transformed them into SAT problems using the multivalued encoding described in (Prestwich 2003). These problems were divided into 4 sets of five problems each, according to the number of variables (v), the domain size (d), and the constraint density (c) in the original CSP, giving the 30v10d40c, 30v10d80c, 50v15d40c and 50v15d80c problem sets from each of which the hardest problem was selected.

### Complete versus Local Search

One of the key motivations for the development of local search techniques for SAT was to solve problems beyond the reach of existing complete solvers. Complete solvers, even if slower on particular instances, have the advantage of unambiguously reporting if an instance is unsatisfiable. Hence, local search for SAT is most applicable to problems that are too difficult for complete search to solve in a reasonable time frame. This means the scalability of local search is important, and that evaluations on problems that can easily be solved by a complete solver are not conclusive. To clarify this issue we additionally tested our problem set using the well-known complete solver, Satz (Li & Anbulagan 1997).

### The Wilcoxon Rank-Sum Test

Local search run-times can vary significantly on the same problem instance, as determined by the initial starting point and any subsequent randomized decisions. For this reason empirical studies require the same problem to be solved multiple times, and at least for the mean, median and standard deviation to be reported. However, it is still unclear exactly how much confidence we can have in the reported differences between algorithms. Standard deviation is informative for normally distributed data, but local search run-times are generally not normally distributed, often having the median to the left of the mean and a number of unpredictably distributed outliers. Hence standard comparisons that assume normality, such as a two-sample t-test, are not reliable, and the level of statistical confidence in differences between algorithms is rarely investigated.

However, nonparametric measures, such as the Wilcoxon rank-sum test, do not rely on normality, and only assume that the distributions to be compared have a similar shape. To use the Wilcoxon test requires that the run-times (or number of flips) from two sets of observations, $A$ and $B$, are sorted in ascending order. Then each observation is ranked (from $1 \ldots N$) and the sum of the ranks for distribution $A$ is calculated. This value ($w_A$) can now be used to test the hypothesis that distribution $A$ lies to the left of distribution $B$, i.e. $H_1 : A < B$, using the normal approximation to the Wilcoxon distribution (Gibbons & Chakraborti 1992)[5]:

$$z = (w_A - n_A(N+1)/2 - 0.5)/\sqrt{n_A n_B (N+1)/12}$$

where $n_A$ and $n_B$ are the number of observations in distributions $A$ and $B$ respectively and $N = n_A + n_B$. Using the standard $Z \sim \text{Normal}(0, 1)$ tables, $z$ will give the probability $P$ that the null hypothesis, $H_0 : A \geq B$, is true.

### Results

Table 1 shows the results for the original SAPS problem set from (Hutter, Tompkins, & Hoos 2002), except the f400 problems which came from our own problem distribution (as the SAPS uf400 problems were unavailable). Table 2 shows the results for the larger DIMACS benchmarks and our random 3-SAT and binary CSP problems[6]. In both tables, the Wilcoxon values give the probability that the null hypothesis $A \geq B$ is true, where $A$ is the distribution of flips or run-times that has the *smaller* rank-sum value. We record $P$-values against distribution $A$ and take $P < 0.05$ to indicate that $A$ is significantly less than $B$, marking such results with '*'. Also, due to space limitations, we only report the base version performance of SAPS and PAWS, and discuss the overall performance of each variant in the next section.

Table 1 shows SAPS and PAWS to be fairly evenly matched on the original SAPS problem set. SAPS is significantly better on the flat-med and uf250-hard problems, and slightly better on the flat-hard, f400-hard and bw_large.b problems, whereas PAWS is significantly better on the bw_large.c, logistics.c, uf100 and f400-med problems and slightly better on bw_large.a and ais10. However, the results also show that most of these problems are not difficult for

[5] assuming $n_A > 12$, $n_B > 12$ and that no rank values are tied

[6] All results are for 100 runs with a 20 million flip cut-off except 50v15d40c which had a 50 million cut-off.

| | | | Success | Time(secs) | Flips | Satz | Wilcoxon |
|---|---|---|---|---|---|---|---|
| Problem | Method | Params | %100 runs | median<br>mean | median<br>mean | time (secs) | t:time f:flips |
| bw_large.a | SAPS | $P$:6 $\alpha$:1.30 $\rho$:0.80 | 100 | 0.01<br>0.02 | 2,571<br>3,366 | 0.11 | |
| | PAWS | $Max$:34 | 100 | 0.01<br>0.01 | 2,604<br>3,077 | | 0.0749$t$<br>0.2955$f$ |
| bw_large.b | SAPS | $P$:5 $\alpha$:1.30 $\rho$:0.80 | 100 | 0.14<br>0.22 | 24,570<br>38,116 | 0.49 | 0.3124$t$<br>∗0.0267$f$ |
| | PAWS | $Max$:50 | 100 | 0.14<br>0.21 | 29,083<br>45,112 | | |
| bw_large.c | SAPS | $P$:7 $\alpha$:1.10 $\rho$:0.60 | 100 | 17.45<br>26.17 | 1,409,463<br>2,091,311 | 2.38 | |
| | PAWS | $Max$:5 | 100 | 4.54<br>7.15 | 796,261<br>1,251,603 | | ∗0.0000$t$<br>∗0.0005$f$ |
| logistics.c | SAPS | $P$:5 $\alpha$:1.30 $\rho$:0.90 | 100 | 0.04<br>0.05 | 7,454<br>9,187 | 0.53 | |
| | PAWS | $Max$:$\infty$ | 100 | 0.02<br>0.03 | 5,117<br>6,360 | | ∗0.0000$t$<br>∗0.0000$f$ |
| flat100-med | SAPS | $P$:5 $\alpha$:1.30 $\rho$:0.40 | 100 | 0.01<br>0.01 | 3,940<br>6,669 | 0.20 | ∗0.0280$t$<br>∗0.0060$f$ |
| | PAWS | $Max$:16 | 100 | 0.01<br>0.02 | 6,578<br>9,137 | | |
| flat100-hard | SAPS | $P$:6 $\alpha$:1.30 $\rho$:0.80 | 100 | 0.04<br>0.05 | 23,773<br>28,663 | 0.30 | 0.4064$t$<br>0.3147$f$ |
| | PAWS | $Max$:46 | 100 | 0.04<br>0.06 | 24,113<br>36,267 | | |
| flat200-med | SAPS | $P$:8 $\alpha$:1.30 $\rho$:0.40 | 100 | 0.20<br>0.28 | 92,872<br>131,702 | 0.30 | ∗0.0396$t$<br>∗0.0029$f$ |
| | PAWS | $Max$:9 | 100 | 0.26<br>0.35 | 137,267<br>188,652 | | |
| flat200-hard | SAPS | $P$:5 $\alpha$:1.30 $\rho$:0.40 | 100 | 5.51<br>6.15 | 2,748,230<br>3,065,908 | 0.50 | 0.3327$t$<br>0.1556$f$ |
| | PAWS | $Max$:74 | 100 | 5.10<br>7.40 | 2,767,914<br>4,026,639 | | |
| uf100-hard | SAPS | $P$:6 $\alpha$:1.30 $\rho$:0.80 | 100 | 0.01<br>0.01 | 2,442<br>3,666 | 0.03 | |
| | PAWS | $Max$:15 | 100 | 0.01<br>0.00 | 1,697<br>2,644 | | ∗0.0105$t$<br>∗0.0245$f$ |
| uf250-med | SAPS | $P$:5 $\alpha$:1.30 $\rho$:0.40 | 100 | 0.01<br>0.02 | 5,024<br>6,236 | 1.42 | 0.4713$f$ |
| | PAWS | $Max$:15 | 100 | 0.01<br>0.02 | 4,854<br>6,224 | | 0.4518$t$ |
| uf250-hard | SAPS | $P$:6 $\alpha$:1.30 $\rho$:0.70 | 100 | 0.44<br>0.55 | 173,666<br>217,831 | 0.32 | ∗0.0437$t$<br>∗0.0275$f$ |
| | PAWS | $Max$:18 | 100 | 0.54<br>0.78 | 223,331<br>318,772 | | |
| f400-med | SAPS | $P$:5 $\alpha$:1.25 $\rho$:0.20 | 100 | 0.09<br>0.14 | 31,638<br>48,870 | 110.96 | |
| | PAWS | $Max$:9 | 100 | 0.06<br>0.08 | 21,556<br>29,566 | | ∗0.0003$t$<br>∗0.0019$f$ |
| f400-hard | SAPS | $P$:5 $\alpha$:1.30 $\rho$:0.10 | 100 | 2.28<br>3.34 | 819,408<br>1,195,727 | 371.07 | 0.0970$t$<br>0.0632$f$ |
| | PAWS | $Max$:11 | 100 | 3.28<br>3.86 | 1,219,155<br>1,433,813 | | |
| ais10 | SAPS | $P$:4 $\alpha$:1.30 $\rho$:0.90 | 100 | 0.07<br>0.10 | 13,853<br>19,569 | 0.80 | |
| | PAWS | $Max$:52 | 100 | 0.07<br>0.10 | 15,092<br>21,044 | | 0.0893$t$<br>0.2622$f$ |
| Overall | SAPS | | 100 | 0.07<br>2.65 | 22,011<br>490,488 | | |
| | PAWS | | 100 | 0.06<br>1.43 | 22,459<br>527,068 | | ∗0.0499$t$<br>0.3663$f$ |

Table 1: Results for original SAPS problem set

| | | | Success | Time(secs) | Flips | Satz | Wilcoxon |
|---|---|---|---|---|---|---|---|
| Problem | Method | Params | %100 runs | median<br>mean | median<br>mean | time (secs) | t:time f:flips |
| bw_large.d | SAPS | $P$:5 $\alpha$:1.05 $\rho$:0.80 | 100 | 23.48<br>34.33 | 1,400,950<br>2,082,487 | 346.16 | |
| | PAWS | $Max$:4 | 100 | 6.22<br>10.24 | 836,718<br>1,340,809 | | ∗0.0000$t$<br>∗0.0016$f$ |
| f800-med | SAPS | $P$:5 $\alpha$:1.25 $\rho$:0.10 | 100 | 0.83<br>0.92 | 243,511<br>270,383 | >3600 | |
| | PAWS | $Max$:9 | 100 | 0.30<br>0.40 | 96,574<br>131,303 | | ∗0.0000$t$<br>∗0.0000$f$ |
| f800-hard | SAPS | $P$:5 $\alpha$:1.25 $\rho$:0.30 | 100 | 3.93<br>5.27 | 1,148,092<br>1,899,465 | >3600 | |
| | PAWS | $Max$:10 | 100 | 1.91<br>2.93 | 642,537<br>1,012,867 | | ∗0.0000$t$<br>∗0.0017$f$ |
| f1600-med | SAPS | $P$:5 $\alpha$:1.25 $\rho$:0.30 | 100 | 3.59<br>5.70 | 791,484<br>1,222,877 | >3600 | |
| | PAWS | $Max$:10 | 100 | 1.17<br>1.60 | 338,792<br>511,318 | | ∗0.0000$t$<br>∗0.0000$f$ |
| f1600-hard | SAPS | $P$:5 $\alpha$:1.25 $\rho$:0.30 | 92 | 29.01<br>34.67 | 6,444,467<br>7,620,710 | >3600 | |
| | PAWS | $Max$:11 | 99 | 11.55<br>17.05 | 3,003,227<br>4,542,798 | | ∗0.0000$t$<br>∗0.0001$f$ |
| par16-med | SAPS | $P$:7 $\alpha$:2.00 $\rho$:0.25 | 85 | 14.52<br>22.01 | 6,682,149<br>8,020,488 | 1.52 | |
| | PAWS | $Max$:36 | 98 | 6.27<br>8.01 | 3,193,260<br>4,063,500 | | ∗0.0000$t$<br>∗0.0000$f$ |
| par16-hard | SAPS | $P$:4 $\alpha$:1.40 $\rho$:0.90 | 86 | 17.31<br>19.82 | 8,209,360<br>9,402,907 | 0.57 | |
| | PAWS | $Max$:40 | 98 | 5.64<br>9.43 | 2,847,317<br>4,763,523 | | ∗0.0000$t$<br>∗0.0000$f$ |
| g125.17 | SAPS | $P$:5 $\alpha$:1.20 $\rho$:0.05 | 99 | 60.02<br>91.02 | 3,108,428<br>4,663,084 | >3600 | |
| | PAWS | $Max$:4 | 100 | 6.16<br>8.48 | 480,091<br>656,876 | | ∗0.0000$t$<br>∗0.0000$f$ |
| g250.29 | SAPS | $P$:6 $\alpha$:1.15 $\rho$:0.10 | 90 | 100.14<br>219.92 | 563,389<br>2,622,915 | >3600 | |
| | PAWS | $Max$:4 | 100 | 19.73<br>21.89 | 275,782<br>315,937 | | ∗0.0000$t$<br>∗0.0000$f$ |
| 30v10d80c | SAPS | $P$:6 $\alpha$:1.30 $\rho$:0.10 | 100 | 0.06<br>0.08 | 9,577<br>12,689 | 0.29 | |
| | PAWS | $Max$:7 | 100 | 0.05<br>0.06 | 8,839<br>10,523 | | ∗0.0059$t$<br>0.1495$f$ |
| 30v10d40c | SAPS | $P$:6 $\alpha$:1.25 $\rho$:0.50 | 100 | 0.10<br>0.12 | 17,628<br>21,376 | 0.35 | |
| | PAWS | $Max$:7 | 100 | 0.09<br>0.12 | 15,926<br>23,944 | | 0.2245$t$<br>0.2318$f$ |
| 50v15d80c | SAPS | $P$:6 $\alpha$:1.20 $\rho$:0.10 | 100 | 2.24<br>3.53 | 134,936<br>229,951 | >3600 | |
| | PAWS | $Max$:5 | 100 | 1.28<br>1.64 | 124,941<br>158,479 | | ∗0.0000$t$<br>∗0.0280$f$ |
| 50v15d40c | SAPS | $P$:5 $\alpha$:1.25 $\rho$:0.25 | 99 | 96.84<br>149.05 | 7,579,338<br>11,748,482 | >3600 | 0.2535$t$<br>0.0735$f$ |
| | PAWS | $Max$:6 | 98 | 121.12<br>169.55 | 10,866,838<br>15,159,576 | | |
| Overall | SAPS | | 96.23 | 7.63<br>35.97 | 940,756<br>3,145,317 | | |
| | PAWS | | 99.46 | 2.93<br>18.40 | 427,173<br>2,373,633 | | ∗0.0000$t$<br>∗0.0000$f$ |

Table 2: Results for harder problem set

a complete search, with Satz having easily the best performance on bw_large.c and flat200-hard, and only being seriously challenged on the f400 problems.

In contrast, Table 2 shows PAWS to be strongly outperforming SAPS on all problems except the most difficult random binary CSP (50v15d40c). Additionally, Satz is significantly challenged on this problem set, being unable to solve the larger 3-SAT f problems, 50v CSP problems or g125/g250 problems before timing out after an hour[7]. The strong performance of PAWS in Table 2 is therefore doubly important, because it is in a domain where complete search starts to break down.

Figure 3 further illustrates the superior performance of PAWS on the Table 2 problem set by graphing the run-times for all 1300 runs of each algorithm. Here PAWS is consistently better than SAPS, in particular solving 93% versus 78% of instances within 50 seconds.

[7]All experiments were performed on a Sun supercomputer with 8 × Sun Fire V880 servers, each with 8 × UltraSPARC-III 900MHz CPU and 8GB memory per node.

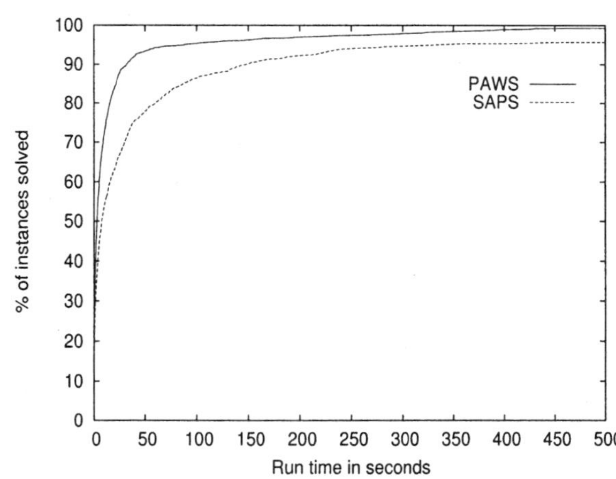


Figure 3: SAPS versus PAWS on the Table 2 problem set

## Analysis and Conclusions

Our analysis of the three variants of each algorithm only showed an overall significant difference in performance ($P < 0.05$) on the Table 2 problems, where the exchange of the deterministic reduction (PAWS-DR, SAPS+DR) and random flat (PAWS-RF, SAPS+RF) heuristics produced a significant worsening of performance for both SAPS and PAWS. Conversely, the multiple inclusion heuristic (MI) did not have a significant effect on the overall performance of either approach. Therefore, we conclude that neither algorithm significantly benefits from the inclusion of the other algorithm's secondary heuristics.

Overall the results indicate that additive weighting tends to perform better than multiplicative weighting on larger and more difficult problems. The most obvious difference between the two schemes is that multipliers create finer distinctions between clause weights: as multiplicative weights are real-valued, the previous history of clause weighting will be retained in small differences, even after smoothing. Hence, in longer term searches, we would expect clause weights to become more and more distinguished, making it increasingly unlikely that any two flips will evaluate to the same cost. Conversely, additive weighting changes clause weights by simply adding or subtracting one, and most weights are returned to a base weight of one at some point in the search. Hence longer term residual weight is eliminated and the likelihood that different flips will evaluate to the same cost remains relatively high, meaning additive weighting will generally have a greater number of possible best cost moves to select from. We confirmed this by measuring the mean number of candidate moves in list $L$ for SAPS and PAWS for a single run of each algorithm on each test problem, eliminating any duplicate flips from the PAWS list. For all instances, except bw_large.b/c and g125/g250, the SAPS list tends to a length of one, whereas the *smallest* average list length for PAWS was 2.05 (ais10), with an average list length ratio of PAWS to SAPS of 3.3

We therefore conjecture that this difference in the available number of moves is important for longer term searches and gives additive weighting the greater freedom of movement needed to navigate difficult cost surfaces (i.e. cost surfaces that produce ambiguous clause weight guidance). However, the fact that SAPS is better on the most difficult problem (50v15d40s), shows this rule cannot be automatically generalized and that for some problems other, as yet unidentified, features are important.

However, the overall case for preferring additive over multiplicative weighting is compelling: firstly, the average flip performance of PAWS does not differ significantly from SAPS for Table 1 and strongly dominates SAPS on the more difficult problems of Table 2 (i.e. those beyond the reach of Satz). Secondly, additive weighting is more time efficient than multiplicative due to using integer rather than real-valued clause weights (the average flips/sec for PAWS on the complete problem set was 148,899 versus 114,665 for SAPS, remembering both algorithms are running within the same software architecture). And finally the search space of possible parameter settings is at least an order of magnitude less for PAWS than for SAPS ($Max_{inc}$ was tested on a domain of less than 100 distinct values ranging from 3 to 75 in steps of one, whereas the search space of $\alpha$, $\rho$ and $P_{smooth}$ was approximately $20 \times 20 \times 5$).

In summary, this paper balances much of the recent work on clause weighting that has concentrated on multiplicative updates, showing that additive weighting can be faster, simpler in terms of parameter tuning, and more applicable to larger problems beyond the reach of complete search methods. However, multiplicative weighting still has the better performance in several problem domains, and in future work it would be worth identifying the problem characteristics and search behaviors that favor a multiplicative approach.

## References

Gibbons, J., and Chakraborti, S. 1992. *Nonparametric Staistical Inference*. Statistics: Textbooks and Monographs. New York: Marcel Dekker, Inc. 241–251.

Hoos, H. 2002. An adaptive noise mechanism for WalkSAT. In *Proceedings of the Nineteenth National Conference on Artificial Intelligence (AAAI-02)*, 655–660.

Hutter, F.; Tompkins, D.; and Hoos, H. 2002. Scaling and probabilistic smoothing: Efficient dynamic local search for SAT. In *Proceedings of the Eighth International Conference on the Principles and Practice of Constraint Programming (CP'02)*, 233–248.

Li, C., and Anbulagan. 1997. Look-ahead versus look-back for satisfiability problems. In *Proceedings of the Third International Conference on the Principles and Practice of Constraint Programming (CP'97)*, 341–355.

McAllester, D.; Selman, B.; and Kautz, H. 1997. Evidence for invariance in local search. In *Proceedings of the Fourteenth National Conference on Artificial Intelligence (AAAI-97)*, 321–326.

Mills, P., and Tsang, E. 1999. Guided local search applied to the satisfiability (SAT) problem. In *Proceedings of the 15th National Conference of the Australian Society for Operations Research (ASOR'99)*, 872–883.

Morris, P. 1993. The Breakout method for escaping local minima. In *Proceedings of the Eleventh National Conference on Artificial Intelligence (AAAI-93)*, 40–45.

Prestwich, S. 2003. Local search on SAT-encoded CSPs. In *Proceedings of the Sixth International Conference on Theory and Applications of Satisfiability Testing (SAT-03)*.

Schuurmans, D., and Southey, F. 2000. Local search characteristics of incomplete SAT procedures. In *Proceedings of the Seventeenth National Conference on Artificial Intelligence (AAAI-00)*, 297–302.

Schuurmans, D.; Southey, F.; and Holte, R. 2001. The exponentiated subgradient algorithm for heuristic Boolean programming. In *Proceedings of the Seventeenth International Joint Conference on Artificial Intelligence (IJCAI-01)*, 334–341.

Wu, Z., and Wah, B. 2000. An efficient global-search strategy in discrete Lagrangian methods for solving hard satisfiability problems. In *Proceedings of the Seventeenth National Conference on Artificial Intelligence (AAAI-00)*, 310–315.

# Tractable Tree Convex Constraint Networks *

**Yuanlin Zhang** and **Eugene C. Freuder**
Cork Constraint Computation Center
University College Cork
Cork, Republic of Ireland
{y.zhang, e.freuder}@4c.ucc.ie

## Abstract

A binary constraint network is tree convex if we can construct a tree for the domain of the variables so that for any constraint, no matter what value one variable takes, all the values allowed for the other variable form a subtree of the constructed tree. It is known that a tree convex network is globally consistent if it is path consistent. However, if a tree convex network is not path consistent, enforcing path consistency on it *may not* make it globally consistent. In this paper, we identify a subclass of tree convex networks which are *locally chain convex and union closed*. This class of problems can be made globally consistent by path consistency and thus is tractable. More interestingly, we also find that some scene labeling problems can be modeled by tree convex constraints in a natural and meaningful way.

## Introduction

A constraint network describes a problem as a set of variables with a finite set (called domain here) of values for each variable, and a set of constraints among the variables. In this paper, we consider only binary constraint networks where each constraint involves at most two variables. A basic task is to solve a constraint network, that is to find an assignment of a value to each variable such that all the constraints in the network are satisfied. Constraint networks, together with the effective techniques developed for them, have many applications in manufacturing, transportation, telecommunication, logistics and bio-informatics.

Since to solve general constraint networks is NP-hard, much effort has been made to identify *tractable* constraint networks which can be solved efficiently. A typical example is that when the graph of a constraint network is a tree, arc consistency is sufficient to make the network globally consistent (Freuder 1982). In this case, the topological structure among variables plays an important role. The structure or semantics of the constraints is also used to identify tractable networks, using the concept of $k$-consistency (Freuder 1978). Dechter (1992) shows that some local consistency in a network whose domains are of limited size ensures global consistency. For *monotone constraints*, path consistency implies global consistency (Montanari 1974). Van Beek and Dechter (1995) generalize monotone constraints to a larger class of *row convex constraints* which are further generalized to *tree convex constraints* by Zhang and Yap (2003).

A binary constraint network is tree convex if we can construct a tree for the domain of the variables so that for any constraint, no matter what value one variable takes, all the values allowed for the other variable form a subtree of the constructed tree. To construct a tree for a domain is to construct a tree such that its vertex set is exactly the domain itself. See Fig. 1(a) for an example of a tree convex constraint. It has been shown that a tree convex network is globally consistent if it is path consistent. However, if a tree convex network is not path consistent, enforcing path consistency on it *may not* make it globally consistent because some constraints may be modified during the enforcing procedure and thus may no longer be tree convex.

In this paper, we examine the tree convex constraints and characterize conditions under which the desirable tree convex property of a network is preserved when path consistency is enforced. We then identify a tractable class of restricted tree convex constraints and show an application. This result generalizes earlier work on monotone and connected row convex constraints (Deville, Barette, & Van Hentenryck 1997). Our work differs from the work by Jeavons et al. (1997) in that we study the tractability of constraint networks whereas they study that of constraint languages. The tractable class reported here may not be closed under the known algebraic operations proposed by these and other researchers.

We first generalize tree convex constraint networks by relaxing the existence of a tree on *all* values to the existence of a tree on *the domain of each variable*. The intuition is that a constraint is defined on the domains of the involved variables, rather than on all possible values in the network. Such a relaxed tree convex network is globally consistent if it is path consistent.

Next, we need to add some restrictions on a relaxed tree convex network to avoid the destruction of its tree convexity during the process enforcing path consistency. Enforcing path consistency involves the intersection and composition of constraints. It can be verified that the intersection of

*This work has received support from Science Foundation Ireland under Grant 00/PI.1/C075.

two constraints is also tree convex, but the composition may not be tree convex any more. We propose a natural restriction on tree convexity which is preserved under composition. Given a tree convex constraint $c_{xy}$ on variables $x$ and $y$ with domains $D_x$ and $D_y$ respectively, the restriction is that for some tree on $D_x$, any two values that are neighbors on the tree should share a common support in $D_y$. The properties are then studied.

Finally, a tractable class of networks is presented.

A careful reader may be concerned about the usefulness of tree convexity even before our discussion of further restrictions on it. There do exist many tractable problems belonging to this class (e.g., monotone and row convex constraints), but the tree structure for a domain seems still too strange to be of any practical use. No new application is given in Zhang & Yap (2003). Interestingly, we find that tree convex constraints help to model some scene labeling problems in a natural and meaningful way, which may not be captured by a general constraint network. In the following example we show that for some problems, there exists a relationship between the constraints and a certain structure on the domain of variables. Consider the inequality on integers: $x < y$ with $x \in \{1, 2, 3\}$ and $y \in \{2, 3, 4\}$. There is a natural total ordering (denoted by $\preceq$ to be distinguished from $<$) on the values. Its graphical representation is a chain of the values {1,2,3,4}. If $x.1 < y.2$ where $x.1$ denotes integer 1 for variable $x$, then $x.1 < y.3$ because $y.2 \preceq y.3$. In fact, the constraint $x < y$ has to conform to the structure $\preceq$ on integers. A more complex example, where the values of each domain form a tree structure, will be presented later.

Related work is discussed and concluding remarks are given in the conclusion.

## Preliminaries

In this section, we introduce the basic concepts and notations used in this paper.

**Constraint Network** A binary *constraint network* consists of a set of variables $V = \{x_1, x_2, \cdots, x_n\}$ with a finite domain $D_i$ for each variable $x_i \in V$, and a set of binary constraints $C$. $c_{xy}$ denotes a constraint on variables $x$ and $y$ which is defined as a relation over $D_x$ and $D_y$. Operations on relations, e.g., *intersection* ($\cap$), *composition* ($\circ$), *and inverse*, are applicable to constraints.

We assume that, between any ordered variables $(x, y)$, there is only one constraint. *$c_{xy}$ and $c_{yx}$ are considered to be two different constraints*, however, we assume the inverse of $c_{xy}$ is equal to $c_{yx}$.

**Image** Given a constraint $c_{xy}$ and a value $u \in D_x$, $v \in D_y$ is a *support* of $u$ if $u$ and $v$ satisfy $c_{xy}$, that is $(u, v) \in c_{xy}$. $u$'s *image* under $c_{xy}$, denoted by $I_y(u)$, is the set of all its supports in $D_y$. The image of a subset of $D_x$ is the union of the images of its values.

**$k$-consistency** A constraint network is *$k$-consistent* if and only if any consistent instantiation of any distinct $k - 1$ variables can be consistently extended to any new variable. A network is *strongly* $k$-consistent if and only if it is $j$-consistent for all $j \leq k$. A strongly $n$-consistent network is called *globally consistent*. 2- and 3-consistency are usually called *arc consistency* and *path consistency* respectively.

Note that under this definition, we need to add a universal constraint between variables which are not explicitly constrained by the network.

**Matrix Representation** A constraint $c_{xy}$ can be represented by a boolean matrix whose rows are named by values in $D_x$ and columns by values in $D_y$. An entry in the matrix is 1 if its row value and column value satisfy $c_{xy}$, and otherwise is 0. For an example, see $c_{xy}$ in Fig. 1(a). The composition of two constraints can be defined as the multiplication of boolean matrices. Path consistency is described by the intersection and multiplication by many authors.

More materials on these concepts can be found in Mackworth (1977), Montanari (1974), Freuder (1978).

**Trees, Chains, and Sets** In the following we review trees which play a fundamental role in the analysis of tree convex constraints and introduce some new notations used in this paper. A tree is a connected graph without any cycles. In the rest of the paper, *we always assume there is a root for a tree*. The path between any two nodes (or vertices) is unique and the *distance* of a node to the root is defined as the number of edges in the path between them. Given a tree, a *subtree* is defined as a connected subgraph of the tree, and its *root* is the node closest to the root of the tree.

A *tree on a set $S$* is a tree whose vertex set is exactly $S$. We also call a set $I$ a *subtree* of a tree $T$ if there exists a subtree of $T$ whose vertex set is exactly $I$. An empty set is a *subtree* of any tree. A tree (subtree respectively) becomes a *chain (subchain)* if each node of the tree (subtree) has at most one child. The *last value* of a subchain is the farthest one away from its root. For example, the graph in Fig. 1(b) is a tree on $\{a, b, c, d\}$. $\{a, b, c\}$ is a subtree of it, and $\{a, b\}$ is a subchain whose last value is $b$.

The *intersection* of two trees is defined as the graph whose vertices and edges are in both trees. It has the following property:

**Proposition 1** (Zhang & Yap 2003) *Let $T_1, T_2$ be two subtrees of some tree. The intersection of $T_1$ and $T_2$ is also a subtree of the tree. Furthermore, if the intersection is not empty, the root of the intersection is either the root of $T_1$ or that of $T_2$.*

Various convex constraints are introduced below.

**Row Convex Constraints** A constraint is *row convex* if and only if in each row of its matrix representation, all 1's are consecutive. It is *connected row convex* if it is row convex and all ones in any two neighboring rows are consecutive.

**Tree Convex Sets** (Zhang & Yap 2003) Sets $E_1, \cdots, E_k$ are *tree convex with respect to a tree $T$ on* $\bigcup_{i \in 1..l} E_i$ if and only if every $E_i$ is a subtree of $T$. For example, given the tree in Fig. 1(b), sets $\{a, b, c\}$, $\{a, b, d\}$, and $\{a, c, d\}$ are tree convex.

**Tree Convex Constraints** A constraint $c_{xy}$ is *tree convex with respect to a tree $T$ on $D_y$* if and only if the images of all values in $D_x$ are tree convex with respect to $T$. That $c_{xy}$ is tree convex might not mean that $c_{yx}$ is tree convex. Consider $c_{xy}$ in Fig. 1(a). The images of $a, b, c$ are $\{a, b, c\}$, $\{a, c, d\}$, and $\{a, b, d\}$ respectively. They are tree convex with respect to Fig. 1(b) and thus $c_{xy}$ is tree convex with respect to that tree. The readers are invited to verify that there is no tree to make $c'_{xy}$ (in Fig. 1(c)) tree convex.

## Relaxed Tree Convex Constraint Networks

In Zhang & Yap (2003), a tree convex constraint network is defined as a network where all constraints are tree convex with respect to a common tree on *the union of all domains* in the network. In the following definition only the tree structures on *individual* domains matter.

**Definition 1** *A constraint network is* tree convex *if and only if there exists a tree on each domain such that every constraint $c_{xy}$ is tree convex with respect to the tree on $D_y$.*

In the rest of the presentation, tree convexity always refers to our new definition. This new definition is equivalent to the old one if the domains are pairwise disjoint. One advantage of the new definition is that even if the domains of two variables of a constraint $c_{xy}$ share some values, it explicitly allows us to use different tree structures for each domain in deciding the tree convexity of $c_{xy}$ and $c_{yx}$. Furthermore, it helps simplify the presentation.

Here is the consistency result on tree convex networks:

**Theorem 1** *A tree convex constraint network is globally consistent if it is path consistent.*

The proof follows directly from the proof in Zhang & Yap (2003) since the new definition does not affect the essential part of that proof.

## Properties of Intersection and Composition of Tree Convex Constraints

A network can be made path consistent by removing from the constraints the tuples which can not be consistently extended to a new variable. It is equivalent to the matrix computation $c_{xy} = c_{xy} \cap (c_{xz} \circ c_{zy})$, where $\circ$ means composition.

As suggested by Theorem 1, we need to study the impact of the intersection and composition operations on the tree convexity of constraints.

**Proposition 2** *Assume constraints $c^1_{xy}$ and $c^2_{xy}$ are tree convex wrt a tree $T$ on the domain $D_y$. Their intersection is also tree convex.*

**Proof.** Let $c_{xy} = c^1_{xy} \cap c^2_{xy}$. For any $v \in D_x$, its images under $c^1$ and $c^2$ are both subtrees of $T$. The intersection of the two images is a subtree of $T$, by Proposition 1. That is, the image of every $v \in D_s$ is a subtree of $T$. Hence $c$ is tree convex. □

The intersection of two subtrees may be an empty set, which means that after the intersection of two tree convex constraints, the image of a value could be empty. Deleting such a value could make a constraint no longer tree convex. An example is shown is Fig. 1.

It is also interesting to note that a constraint $c_{xy}$ may become tree convex after a sufficient number of values are removed from $D_y$.

We identify a special class of tree convex constraints which is closed under the operation of deleting values.

$$c_{xy} = \begin{array}{c} a\,b\,c\,d \\ \begin{bmatrix} 1110 \\ 1011 \\ 1101 \end{bmatrix} \end{array} \begin{array}{c} \\ a \\ b \\ c \end{array}$$

(a)

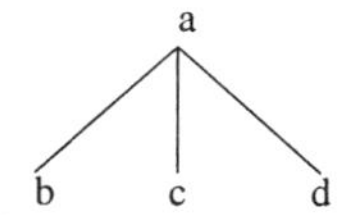


(b)

$$c'_{xy} = \begin{bmatrix} 110 \\ 011 \\ 101 \end{bmatrix}$$

(c)

Figure 1: **(a)** Constraint $c_{xy}$ is represented by a matrix. The column $\{a, b, c\}$ after the matrix is the domain of $x$ and the row $\{a, b, c, d\}$ above the matrix the domain of $y$. **(b)** A tree constructed for the domain of $y$. **(c)** $c'_{xy}$ is obtained from $c_{xy}$ by deleting the value $a$ from the domain of $y$.
$c_{xy}$ is tree convex with respect to the tree on $D_y$ in (b), but $c'_{xy}$ is not tree convex with respect to any tree.

**Definition 2** *A constraint $c_{xy}$ is* locally chain convex *with respect to a tree on $D_y$ if and only if the image of every value in $D_x$ is a subchain of the tree. A constraint network is* locally chain convex *iff there exists a tree on each domain such that every constraint $c_{xy}$ is locally chain convex with respect to the tree on $D_y$.*

For example, under the tree for $D_y$ in Fig. 1(b), the constraint in Fig. 1(a) is not locally chain convex because the image of $a \in D_x$ is $\{a, b, c\}$ which is not a subchain of the tree on $D_y$. In fact, there does not exist any tree to make it chain convex.

**Proposition 3** *A locally chain convex constraint network $(V, D, C)$ is still locally chain convex after the removal of any value from any domain.*

**Proof.** Assume the tree on $D_y$ is $T$ and a value $v$ is removed from $D_y$. The removal of $v$ does not affect the property of constraint $c_{yx} \in C$ for any $x \in V$. We need to show that for all $x \in V$, constraint $c_{xy}$ is locally chain convex. The deletion of $v$ could make some subchain not connected. By constructing a new tree $T''$ on $D_y$, those broken subchains would be connected under $T''$. Let the children of $v$ be $v_1, \cdots, v_l$. Construct a new tree $T'$ from $T$ by removing $v$ and all edges incident on $v$. If $v$ is the root of $T$, construct $T''$ from $T'$ by adding an edge between $v_1$ and $v_i$ for all $i(2 \le i \le l)$. Otherwise, let $p_v$ be the parent of $v$ in $T$, and construct $T''$ from $T'$ by adding an edge between $p_v$ and $v_i$ for all $i(1 \le i \le l)$. In either case, we can verify that the claim holds under $T''$. □

Now let us study a property of the composition of tree convex constraints. Let us use a more intuitive way than matrix multiplication to understand the composition. See Fig. 2. After composing $c_{xy}$ and $c_{yz}$, the image of $a$ under the composition $c_{xz}$ is $\{a, b, c, d\}$ which is exactly the union of the images of $b$ and $d$ in $D_y$ under $c_{yz}$. We know that $\{b, d\}$ is the image of $a$ under $c_{xy}$. In short, the image of $a$ under $c_{xz}$ is the image of $I_y(a)$ under $c_{yz}$.

By this understanding we can construct an example where the composition does not preserve the property of tree convexity; and we are also able to identify conditions under which tree convexity is preserved under the composition. The intuition behind the following special class of constraints is that given a constraint $c_{xy}$, the image of any subtree of $D_x$ should be a connected graph (thus a subtree of

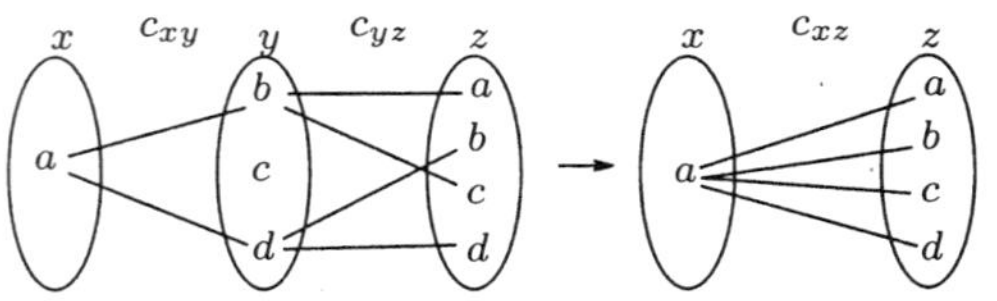

Figure 2: The composition of two constraints. In the diagrams in this paper, a value is drawn as a dot or letter, and a variable is drawn as an ellipse. The values inside an ellipse form the domain of the corresponding variable. The edges between two ellipses form the constraint between the variables.

the tree on $D_y$).

**Definition 3** *A tree convex constraint $c_{xy}$ is* consecutive *wrt a tree $T_x$ on $D_x$ if and only if every two neighboring values on $T_x$ share a common support. A constraint network is* tree convex and consecutive *iff there exists a tree on each domain such that every constraint $c_{xy}$ is tree convex and consecutive wrt the trees on $D_y$ and $D_x$.*

**Proposition 4** *The class of consecutive tree convex constraints is closed under composition.*

**Proof.** Let $c_{xy}$ and $c_{yz}$ be two consecutive tree convex constraints with trees $T_x, T_y$, and $T_z$ on $D_x, D_y$, and $D_z$ respectively, and $c_{xz}$ the composition of $c_{xy}$ and $c_{yz}$. Firstly, we show that $c_{xz}$ is tree convex. Consider any $v \in D_x$. Let its image in $D_y$ be $I_y(v)$. The image of $v$ under $c_{xz}$ would be $\cup_{b \in I_y(v)} I_z(b)$ where $I_z(b)$ is the image of $b$ under $c_{yz}$ (here we need the intuitive understanding of the composition discussed above). Since the intersection of the images of any neighboring values in $I_y(v)$ is non empty, the union of all the images of values in $I_y(v)$ is connected and thus is a subtree of $T_z$.

Secondly, we show that $c_{xz}$ is consecutive. Let $u, v \in D_x$ be neighbors. Let $I_z(u)$ and $I_z(v)$ be their images under $c_{xz}$. Since $c_{xy}$ is consecutive, the images of $u$ and $v$ share a value $w \in D_y$. Hence, the image of $w$ in $D_z$ will appear in both $I_z(u)$ and $I_z(v)$. □

## Tractable Tree Convex Constraint Networks

We are now in a position to explore the conditions under which tree convex constraint networks are tractable. A first attempt is to combine the local chain convexity with consecutiveness. However, the composition may destroy the chain convexity, as shown by the example in Fig. 3(a).

The image of a value under the composition is the union of several subchains. This union can not be guaranteed to be a subchain by the consecutiveness of the constraints. We need a stronger restriction.

**Definition 4** *A locally chain convex constraint $c_{xy}$ (wrt a tree $T_y$ on $D_y$) is* strictly union closed *wrt a tree $T_x$ on $D_x$ iff the image of any subchain of $T_x$ is a subchain of $T_y$.*

**Remark** Strict union closedness implies consecutiveness for a locally chain convex constraint network; but consecutiveness might not imply union closedness as shown by the example in Fig. 3.

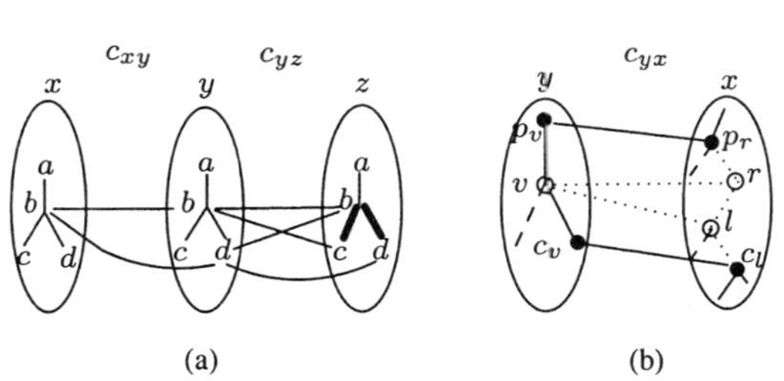

Figure 3: In this diagram, we draw the tree on a domain inside an ellipse. **(a)** Both $c_{xy}$ and $c_{yz}$ are locally chain convex, but their composition is not because the image of $b \in D_x$ under this composition is $\{b, c, d\}$ (the darkened shape), which is not a subchain. **(b)** $t_y$ contains the solid lines in $D_y$. $t_x$ contains $(p_r, r, l, c_l)$. $t_r$ contains $(r, l)$.

Now we have the main result on a class of tractable constraint networks.

**Definition 5** *A constraint network is* locally chain convex and strictly union closed *iff there exists a tree on each domain such that every constraint $c_{xy}$ is locally chain convex (wrt the tree on $D_y$) and strictly union closed (wrt the tree on $D_x$).*

**Theorem 2** *A locally chain convex and strictly union closed constraint network $(V, D, C)$ can be transformed to an equivalent globally consistent network in polynomial time.*

**Proof.** We show that after enforcing arc and path consistency on the given network, it is locally chain convex. In accordance with Theorem 1, the new network is globally consistent. It is known that arc and path consistency enforcing (Zhang & Yap 2001) are of polynomial complexity.

Since arc consistency enforcing only removes values from domains, the consequent network is still locally chain convex.

Next we show that the removal of any value $v \in D_y$ preserves strict union closedness. For all $x \in V$, $c_{xy}$ is still strictly union closed (similar to the proof of Proposition 3). Consider a constraint $c_{yx}$ for any variable $x \in V$. If it is still strictly union closed, the claim is true. Otherwise, there exists a subchain, denoted by $t_y$, of $D_y$ which contains exactly $v$ and its parent and child, such that its image is no longer a connected graph due to the removal of $v$. See Fig. 3(b). Let $t_x$ be the image of $t_y$ before removing $v$. After the removal of $v$, $t_x$ is broken into two chains. Let the gap (removed subchain) in $t_x$ be $t_r$. Note $t_r$ might not be equal to the image of $v$ due to possible overlapping of the image of $v$ and that of its parent and/or child. Let $r$ be the root and $l$ the last node of $t_r$. Let $p_v$ and $p_r$ be the parents of $v$ and $r$ respectively, and $c_v$ and $c_l$ the children of $v$ and $l$ respectively. Consider any node $u \in t_r$. We know that $u$ is supported by $v$, but not by $p_v$ nor by $c_v$ in $t_y$. Further, since $c_{xy}$ is strictly union closed, the image of $t_x$ must be a subchain containing $(p_v, v, c_v)$. It implies that the image of $u$ must be on or contain the subchain $(p_v, v, c_v)$ . Hence, $v$ is the only support of $u$. After it is gone, $u$ should also be removed. After the removal of $t_r$, the image of $t_y$ is now connected and thus a subchain.

Next we show that path consistency enforcing preserves the local chain convexity and strict union closedness. For any constraint $c_{xz}$, path consistency is usually done by first composing $c_{xy}$ and $c_{yz}$, and then setting the new constraint between $x$ and $z$ to be the intersection of the composition and $c_{xz}$.

Firstly, we show that the composition of $c_{xy}$ and $c_{yz}$ is locally chain convex and strictly union closed. 1) For any $v \in D_x$, its image $t_y$ is a subchain. Since $c_{yz}$ is strictly union closed, the image of $t_y$ in $D_z$ is also a subchain. We know that the image of $v$ under the composition is the image of $t_y$ in $D_z$. 2) For any subchain $t_x \in D_x$, its image $t'_y$ under $c_{xy}$ is also a subchain due to the strict union closedness of $c_{xy}$. Thanks to the strict union closedness of $c_{yz}$ again, the image of $t'_y$ is a subchain of $D_z$: that is, the image of $t_x$ under the composition is a subchain.

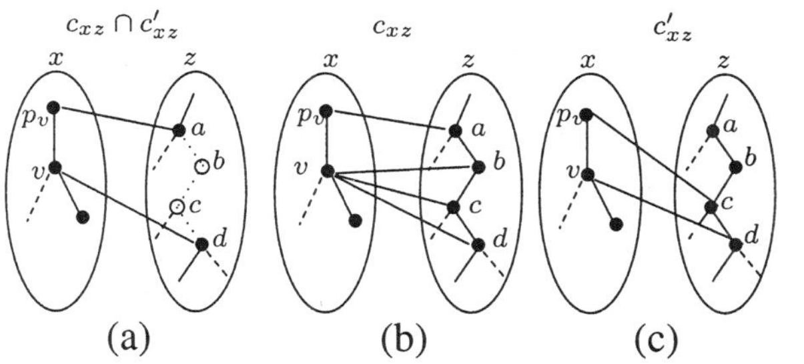


Figure 4: **(a)** $c_{xz} \cap c'_{xz}$. In the intersection, assume $b$ and $c$ are not shared by the images of $v$ under $c_{xz}$ and under $c'_{xz}$. The constraints $c_{xz}$ and $c'_{xz}$ should have a form as shown in **(b)** and **(c)**.

Secondly, we show that the intersection $c''_{xz}$ of $c_{xz}$ and $c'_{xz}$ $(= c_{xy} \circ c_{yz})$ is locally chain convex and strictly union closed. Local chain convexity is preserved under intersection in accordance with Proposition 3.

We now prove the strict union closedness of the constraint $c''_{xz}$. In this paragraph, when we refer to *image*, it is under $c''_{xz}$. Assume there is a subchain $t_x$ in $D_x$ whose image $t''_z$ is not a subchain. Since the intersection does not form a cycle, $t''_z$ must not be connected. Starting from the root of $t_x$, we find the first value $v \in t_x$ whose image is disjoint from the image of its parent $p_v$. Assume the image of $v$ is below the image of $p_v$ (the opposite can be proved similarly). Let $a$ be the last value of $p_v$'s image. Let $d$ be the root of $v$'s image. See Fig. 4(a). Let $u$ be any value between (but not including) $a$ and $d$ in $D_z$. We next prove that there is no support for $u$. Hence it should be removed and thus the image of $t_x$ is a chain after the deletion.

Let $p_v$'s images under $c_{xz}$ and $c'_{xz}$ be $I(p_v)$ and $I'(p_v)$ respectively. The intersection of $I(p_v)$ and $I'(p_v)$ is a subchain of $D_z$. Since both $I(p_v)$ and $I'(p_v)$ are subchains, $a$ must be the last value of either $I(p_v)$ or $I'(p_v)$. Assume it is the last value of $I(p_v)$. See Fig. 4(b). This implies $p_v$ is not in $u$'s image $I(u)$ under $c_{zx}$, since $u$ is between $a$ and $d$. $I(u)$ has to be below $p_v$ (not including it) because $I(u)$ is a chain. Let $I(v)$ and $I'(v)$ be the images of $v$ under $c_{xz}$ and $c'_{xz}$ respectively. $I(v)$ should include at least $d$ and all values between $a$ and $d$ in the tree $D_z$ because the chain $(p_v, v)$ is strictly union closed. For $d$ is the root of $I(v) \cap I'(v)$, $I'(v)$ includes $d$ but does not include values above $d$ (see Fig. 4(c)). Hence, $v$ is not a support of $u$, implying that $I'(u)$ has to be above $v$ (not including it). Therefore, the image of $u$ under $c''_{xz}$ is empty because it is the intersection of $I(u)$ and $I'(u)$. In other words, $u$ has no support in the intersection of $c_{xz}$ and $c'_{xz}$.

Finally, path consistency also involves universal constraints. It can be verified that strict union closedness and local chain convexity of a constraint are preserved when it is composed and intersected with a universal constraint.

There may be universal constraints in the final path consistent network, but the tree convexity of all constraints is sufficient to ensure the global consistency of the network. □

In fact the strict union closedness can be further relaxed in the following way.

**Definition 6** *A locally chain convex constraint $c_{xy}$ is* union closed *if and only if for any subchain of $D_x$, its image is either a subchain of $D_y$ or the whole tree of $D_y$.*

Locally chain convex constraint networks with relaxed union closedness are still tractable.

**Theorem 3** *A locally chain convex and union closed constraint network $(V, D, C)$ can be transformed to an equivalent globally consistent network in polynomial time.*

This can be proved similarly to Theorem 2.

## Application of Tree Convex Networks

Scene labeling problems are NP-hard (Kirousis & Papadimitriou 1988). In the following, we show that some scene labeling instances can be naturally modeled by tree convex constraints.

Consider the labeling of the line drawing in Fig. 5 taken from van Beek & Dechter (1995). Traditionally, it is modeled as a constraint network in the following way. Each vertex $i$ is a variable $x_i$. A value for a variable is the edges incident on this vertex and a label (of +, - or >) on each edge. For example, the edges on vertex 1 form a fork. There are six possible ways to label the fork (Fig. 5), and thus $x_1$ has six values. Similarly, we have two other domains of values: Arrow and Ell as shown in Fig. 5. The constraint is that any two variables should share the same labeling on their shared edge (see Fig. 6).

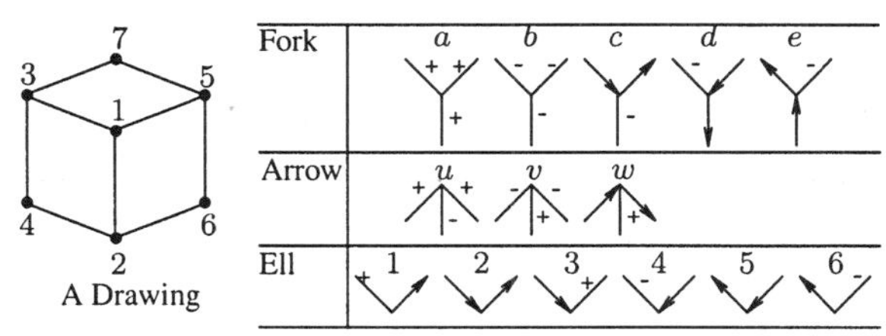


Figure 5: On the left is a line drawing and on the left is a table of the values necessary to model the labeling of this drawing

A distinctive feature of this model is that the values of a variable have complex structures and there is some natural relationship among them. Consider the fork values in Fig. 5. Values $c$, $d$, and $e$ have an edge labeled as $-$, and all three edges of $b$ are labeled as $-$. We can let $b$ be the parent of $c, d$ and $e$, resulting in the subtree $\{b, c, d, e\}$ in Fig. 6(a). Since value $a$ has nothing to do with the rest, we simply connect it with $b$ to make a tree for all fork values. Similarly we have tree structures for Arrow values in Fig. 6(b) and Ell values in Fig. 6(c). The tree on Ell values is not constructed by intuition only, but also by the constraints on the Ell values. Under these trees, the constraints are both locally chain convex and union closed. Note that for constraint $c_{12}$ (and some other constraints), the image of the subchain $(a, b, c)$ of the tree on the domain of $x_1$ ( Fig. 6(a)) is the whole tree of $D_2$ (the Arrow tree in Fig. 6(b)). Note also that an empty set is taken as a (trivial) subchain of any tree.

This network is globally consistent after enforcing arc and path consistency on it.

Constraints $c_{21}, c_{31}$, and $c_{51}$ are not row convex. They are "connected row convex" as defined by Deville, Barette, & Van Hentenryck (1997) in the sense that their reduced forms (by deleting the values without any support) are connected row convex (as defined in the preliminary section of this paper).

To see the difference between connected row convexity, and locally chain convexity and union closedness, we modify $c_{21}, c_{31}$, and $c_{51}$ by allowing $v$ to be compatible with every value in the domains of $x_2$, $x_3$ and $x_5$ respectively. Now the new constraints are no longer connected row convex (as defined by Deville, Barette, & Van Hentenryck (1997)), but are still locally chain convex and union closed.

In this example, we can identify the tree structures for some domains in an intuitive way. However, there also exists some domain to construct a tree for which we need more knowledge about the constraints on it. It is both interesting and challenging to explore the principles of the construction of trees for domain values appearing in the scene labeling problems.

A more general lesson is that by studying the semantics of domain values, we could discover more efficient constraint solving techniques.

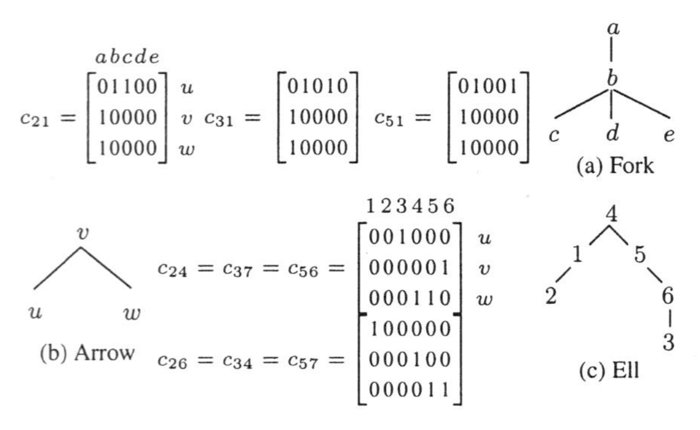


Figure 6: The constraints for labeling the drawing in Fig. 5

## Conclusion

We have identified a new tractable class of networks: locally chain convex and union closed networks. This result not only generalizes the existing work, but also shows an direct interaction between the semantics of constraints and the semantics of domain values in deciding a tractable class of problems. This interaction is reflected in the properties of intersection and composition of tree convex constraints. An application of the new tractable class of networks is also presented, demonstrating that tree convexity is a useful way to characterize the semantics of domain values, in addition to the traditional ones like total ordering.

Compared with the work on connected row convexity by Deville et al. (1997), our work reveals more fundamental properties – local chain convexity and union closedness – that determine the tractability of a class of convex constraints. The new tractable class covers more networks.


## Acknowledgement

We thank Angela Glover for her help with the writing of this paper.


## References


Dechter, R. 1992. From local to global consistency. *Artificial Intelligence* 55:87–107.

Deville, Y.; Barette, O.; and Van Hentenryck, P. 1997. Constraint satisfaction over connected row convex constraints. In *Proceedings of IJCAI-97*, volume 1, 405–411. Nagoya, Japan: IJCAI Inc. (See also Artificial Intelligence 109(1999): 243–271).

Freuder, E. 1978. Synthesizing constraint expressions. *Communications of ACM* 21(11):958–966.

Freuder, E. 1982. A sufficient condition for backtrack-free search. *Journal of The ACM* 29(1):24–32.

Jeavons, P. G.; Cohen, D. A.; and Gyssens, M. 1997. Closure properties of constraints. *Journal of The ACM* 44(4):527–548.

Kirousis, L. M., and Papadimitriou, C. H. 1988. The complexity of recognizing polyhedral scenes. In *Journal of Computer and System Sciences*, volume 37, 14–38.

Mackworth, A. K. 1977. Consistency in networks of relations. *Artificial Intelligence* 8(1):118–126.

Montanari, U. 1974. Networks of constraints: Fundamental properties and applications. *Information Science* 7(2):95–132.

van Beek, P., and Dechter, R. 1995. On the minimality and global consistency of row-convex constraint networks. *Journal of The ACM* 42(3):543–561.

Zhang, Y., and Yap, R. H. C. 2001. Making AC-3 an optimal algorithm. In *Proceedings of IJCAI-01*, 316–321. Seattle: IJCAI Inc.

Zhang, Y., and Yap, R. H. C. 2003. Consistency and set intersection. In *Proceedings of IJCAI-03*, 263–268. Acapulco, Mexico: IJCAI Inc.

# Game Theory and Economic Models

# Eliciting Bid Taker Non-price Preferences in (Combinatorial) Auctions

**Craig Boutilier**
Dept. of Computer Science
University of Toronto
Toronto, ON, M5S 3H5, Canada
cebly@cs.toronto.edu

**Tuomas Sandholm**
Computer Science Dept.
Carnegie Mellon University
Pittsburgh, PA 15213, USA
sandholm@cs.cmu.edu

**Rob Shields**
CombineNet Inc.
Fifteen 27th Street
Pittsburgh, PA 15222, USA
rshields@combinenet.com

## Abstract

Recent algorithms provide powerful solutions to the problem of determining cost-minimizing (or revenue-maximizing) allocations of items in combinatorial auctions. However, in many settings, criteria other than cost (e.g., the number of winners, the delivery date of items, etc.) are also relevant in judging the quality of an allocation. Furthermore, the bid taker is usually uncertain about her preferences regarding tradeoffs between cost and non-price features. We describe new methods that allow the bid taker to determine (approximately) optimal allocations despite this. These methods rely on the notion of *minimax regret* to guide the elicitation of preferences from the bid taker and to measure the quality of an allocation in the presence of utility function uncertainty. Computational experiments demonstrate the practicality of minimax computation and the efficacy of our elicitation techniques.

## 1 Introduction

*Combinatorial auctions (CAs)* generalize traditional market mechanisms to allow the direct specification of bids over *bundles* of items [13; 14] together with various types of side constraints [17]. This form of *expressive bidding* is extremely useful when a bidder's valuation for collections of items—or bidder's costs in reverse auctions—exhibit complex structure. The problem of *winner determination (WD)*, namely, determining a (cost or revenue) optimal allocation of items given a collection of expressive bids, is generally NP-complete [14]. However, algorithms have been designed for WD that work very well in practice [9; 16; 18]. Indeed, recent advances have impelled the application of CAs to large-scale, real-world markets, such as procurement.

Most of the recent literature on CAs has focused on algorithms that find optimal allocations w.r.t. cost or revenue. However, in many settings, features other than cost also play a role in assessing the quality of an allocation. For example, in a procurement auction (or reverse auction), the bid taker may be concerned with the number of suppliers awarded business, the percentage of business awarded to a specific supplier, the average delivery-on-time rating of awarded business, and any of a host of other factors that can be traded off against cost. Most algorithms can be adapted to deal with such features *if*, say, tradeoff weights are made explicit and incorporated into the objective function. However, most bid takers are unable or unwilling to articulate such precise tradeoffs (for reasons we elaborate below).

One way to deal with this issue is to allow users to generate a collection of allocations by imposing various constraints on these feature values (e.g., limiting the number of suppliers to five) and examining the implications on the optimal allocation (e.g., how cost changes) by rerunning WD. When this process ends, the user chooses one of the generated allocations as making the right tradeoffs between cost and the relevant non-price attributes. Unfortunately, this manual process of *scenario navigation* does nothing to ensure sufficient or efficient exploration of allocation or tradeoff space.[1]

In this paper, we explicitly view the process of choosing an optimal allocation as requiring a form of *preference elicitation* with the bid taker (i.e., the party determining the final allocation).[2] We assume that the way in which non-price features influence the choice of allocation can be modeled using a utility function, albeit one that is imprecisely specified. Using this observation, we develop a collection of techniques that can support, or even automate, the preference elicitation required to determine an (approximately) optimal allocation. As such, it can obviate the need for manual creation and exploration of different scenarios. Underlying these methods is the notion of *minimax regret*; this allows us to examine the worst-case error associated with optimizing an allocation in the presence of utility function uncertainty, thus giving *robust* allocations. It also provides valuable information to guide elicitation: it can suggest appropriate refinements of utility information, and when to terminate preference refinement.

We begin in Section 2 with a discussion of CAs and linear utility functions over non-price features. Section 3 addresses the issue of utility functon uncertainty and defines minimax

[1]In procurement settings, the bid taker generally maintains such flexibility in deciding the allocation. This means that there is no predetermined allocation rule (i.e., mapping from bids to allocations), unlike canonical auctions. Therefore, this is sometimes referred to as *procurement optimization* rather than an auction. These observations of typical use of WD software are based on our experiences with large-scale, real-world procurement problems.

[2]We distinguish the preference elicitation we study from forms of elicitation for CAs in which one attempts to minimize the amount of bid information needed from the *bidders* (e.g., [6; 7]).

regret as a suitable criterion for robust decision making. In Section 4 we define several techniques for computing minimax optimal allocations in CAs under different forms of utility function uncertainty. Section 5 describes two methods for preference elicitation based on minimax regret, and empirically evaluates these strategies on random problems with realistic structure and size, demonstrating the feasibility of our methods. We conclude in Section 6 with a discussion of future research.

## 2 CAs and Non-price-based Utility

We begin with a discussion of relevant concepts relating to CAs and utility for non-price features.

### 2.1 Combinatorial Auctions

CAs have found recent popularity as market mechanisms due to their ability to allow expressive bids reflecting the complex utility structure of market participants. As a result, economically efficient allocations of goods and services can be found using combinatorial bids in cases where noncombinatorial bids would not suffice. Recent research has focused on the problem of *winner determination* in various classes of CAs: finding an optimal allocation w.r.t. cost or revenue. While a computationally difficult problem [14], recent advances in optimization methods for CAs have made them a practical market technology [9; 16; 18].

The WD problem for a generic CA can be formulated as an integer program (IP). In this paper, we focus on *reverse CAs* where the goal is to obtain a collection of items at minimal cost, since procurement is a main motivation for our work. However, this is for concreteness only—all of our techniques apply *mutatis mutandis* to most variants of CAs (see [19] for a discussion of a number of such generalizations).

In a reverse CA, a *buyer* (bid taker) wishes to obtain a specific set of items $G$. *Sellers* submit bids of the form $\langle b_i, p_i \rangle$, where $b_i \subseteq G$ is a subset of items, and $p_i$ is the price at which it is offered. Given a set of bids $B = \{\langle b_i, p_i \rangle : i \leq m\}$, we let an *allocation* be any subset of $B$. A *feasible allocation* is an allocation whose bids cover all items in $G$. The WD problem asks for the feasible allocation that supplies $G$ as cheaply as possible, and can be formulated as a (linear) IP. Letting $q_i$ be a boolean variable denoting that bid $\langle b_i, p_i \rangle$ was accepted, we wish to solve:

$$\min p_i q_i \;\; s.t. \;\; \sum_{i:g \in b_i} q_i \geq 1, \; \forall g \in G$$

Note that we assume free disposal (i.e., obtaining multiple copies of any $g$ incurs no penalty). This problem can be generalized to include multiple units of each item, no free disposal, various side constraints on the part of the sellers or the buyer, etc. Notice, however, that existing methods determine the optimal solution by minimizing only the (possibly constrained) *cost* of obtaining $G$.

### 2.2 Linear Utility for Non-price Features

While cost minimization is a primary objective in procurement, other features of the ultimate allocation will often play a role in assessing the quality of that allocation. For example, the buyer may prefer to deal with fewer suppliers, all else being equal, in order to minimize overhead. While a hard constraint might be imposed on the number of suppliers (e.g., less than five), this approach is undesirable, since rarely is a buyer unwilling to consider a larger number of suppliers if that reduces cost significantly. Instead there is a tradeoff—one is willing to pay more for a collection of items if the number of suppliers is less. There are a number of properties that are often used in procurement—to use just one domain of application—to assess the quality of allocations. Among these are: number of winners; (possibly aggregate) quality of certain items; percentage of volume given to a specific supplier; geographical diversity of winners; and many others.

Tradeoffs between price and non-price features can be captured by the buyer's *utility function*. We let $X$ denote the set of feasible allocations given bids $B$. Let $F = \{f_1, \ldots, f_k\}$ be a set of *features* over which the buyer has preferences. We assume that the buyer's preferences for allocations $x \in X$ can be expressed by a *quasi-linear utility function* of the form

$$u(x) = \sum_{i=1}^{k} w_i f_i(x) - c(x), \qquad (1)$$

where $c(x)$ is the cost of the allocation. Thus the utility function is completely characterized by a set of tradeoff weights $w_i$ that express how much of each feature the buyer is willing to sacrifice for a given amount of money. We assume local value functions $v_i$ that convert any non-numeric $f_i(x)$ into a numeric value $v_i(f_i(x))$; but we suppress mention of $v_i$ for notational clarity.

Let $\mathbf{w} = \langle w_1, \ldots, w_k \rangle$ denote a *weight vector*. We assume all weights are non-negative (i.e., $\mathbf{w} \geq 0$), which implies that higher levels of each feature are preferred to lower levels.[3] We will use the notation $u(x; \mathbf{w})$ when we wish to emphasize the fact that utility is parameterized by a weight vector.

The independence and linearity of the local utility functions inherent in our formulation are, admittedly, fairly strong assumptions, but nonetheless often (roughly) hold in practice. Our techniques can be generalized to nonlinear local utility functions and *conditionally independent* features through various encoding tricks. We also assume that each feature $f_i(x)$ can be defined linearly in terms of attributes of allocation $x$. Again, if this is not so, certain approximations are possible. We briefly discuss these generalizations in Section 4.4.

## 3 Utility Function Uncertainty

In this section, we develop techniques for computing *robust* allocations when the parameters of the utility function are not precisely specified.

Given a known weight vector $\mathbf{w}$, our objective would be clear—find the feasible allocation $x^*_{\mathbf{w}}$ with maximum utility: $\max_x u(x)$. A number of WD algorithms can be adapted to this linear optimization problem. Unfortunately, buyers are usually uncertain about their tradeoff weights. This should not be surprising; the decision analysis literature is rife with evidence that decision makers have trouble constructing precise tradeoff weights [11]. And numerous methods for decision making and elicitation have been developed

[3] For instance, if fewer winners are preferred to more, the relevant feature is *negative* number of winners.

that account for this fact, both within decision analysis [23; 15] and AI [10; 5; 2; 4]. Furthermore, in procurement, the buyer is often faced with the difficult task of aggregating the preferences of multiple stakeholders via internal negotiation within the buying organization (the CFO preferring low cost, marketing people preferring high average delivery-on-time rating, plant managers preferring small numbers of suppliers, etc.). Thus, buyers are often unwilling to commit to specific tradeoff weights, often adopting the approach of "preference aggregation through least commitment."

In practice, we have found that buyers are often willing to provide loose bounds on these tradeoff weights, but unwilling to make things more precise without aid. As a result, buyers tend to ignore tradeoff weights altogether. Instead, they frequently use WD software to explore different *scenarios* by imposing various constraints on feature values and generating the corresponding optimal allocations. With a number of such allocations in hand, manual inspection is used to choose the most preferred allocation from this set. Unfortunately, while users find such manual *scenario navigation* appealing, it generally admits neither *sufficient* nor *efficient* exploration of allocation space.

In the next section, we develop techniques that will support, or even automate, this process. However, we first need methods for making allocational decisions in the presence of utility function uncertainty. Assume that through some interaction with the buyer, we have a set of linear constraints on the buyer's weight vector, with $W$ denoting the set of feasible vectors.[4] Without full knowledge of $\mathbf{w}$, we cannot maximize utility (Eq. 1): whatever $x$ we chose, there may be some feasible utility function for which $x$ is far from optimal. Our goal instead is to find a *robust allocation* that, in the worst case, is as close to optimal as possible. In other words, even if an adversary were allowed to choose the utility function, we want $x$ to be as close to optimal as possible.

**Defn** The *regret* of allocation $x$ w.r.t. utility function $\mathbf{w}$ is

$$R(x, \mathbf{w}) = \max_{x' \in X} u(x'; \mathbf{w}) - u(x; \mathbf{w}) \qquad (2)$$

The *maximum regret* of $x$ w.r.t. feasible utility set $W$ is

$$MR(x, W) = \max_{\mathbf{w} \in W} R(x, \mathbf{w}) \qquad (3)$$

The *pairwise max regret* of $x$ w.r.t. $x'$ (with $W$ understood) is

$$MR(x, x') = \max_{\mathbf{w} \in W} u(x'; \mathbf{w}) - u(x; \mathbf{w}) \qquad (4)$$

The *minimax optimal (or robust) allocation* w.r.t. $W$ (i.e., the allocation with *minimax regret*) is

$$x^*_W = \arg\min_{x \in X} \max_{x' \in X} MR(x, x') \qquad (5)$$

Minimax regret is one of the more appealing criteria for decision making under *strict uncertainty* (i.e., where distributional information is lacking) [20; 8]. It has found (in modified form) application to analysis of online algorithms [1]. Only recently has it been used in the explicit modeling of utility function uncertainty and elicitation [3; 15]. The minimax optimal allocation is attractive due to its *robustness* against utility uncertainty. The key difficulty in the application of minimax regret in practical settings is the computation of minimax optimal decisions and its use in elicitation, though recently computationally effective techniques have begun to emerge [22; 4].

[4] The elicitation methods below will make it clear exactly how these constraints arise. Linearity is important computationally, but is not critical to the definition of max regret that follows.

## 4 Computation of Minimax Regret

Most WD methods cannot be applied directly to computation of the minimax optimal allocation. Specifically, Eq. 5 requires solution of a minimax program (with a min over two maxes), preventing the application of very effective linear optimization techniques. In this section we describe an algorithm to compute the minimax optimal allocation in a way that uses standard integer programming or WD methods iteratively. We distinguish two settings. In the first, $W$ is defined by upper and lower bounds for each weight $w_i$, these being quite natural to specify directly. In the second, arbitrary linear constraints on the $w_i$ define $W$; these naturally arise when a buyer compares or ranks two or more alternatives.

### 4.1 Upper and Lower Weight Bounds

**Computing Max Regret** We begin with computation of max regret (Eq. 3). Suppose $W$ is a hyperrectangle in weight space defined by an upper bound $w_i\!\uparrow$ and lower bound $w_i\!\downarrow$ on each parameter $w_i$. The max regret of a specific allocation $x$ w.r.t. $W$ is given by the obvious optimization program:

$$MR(x) = \max_{\mathbf{w} \in W} \max_{x' \in X} \sum_{i=1}^{k} w_i[f_i(x') - f_i(x)] - c(x') + c(x) \quad (6)$$

This poses the difficulty that the objective is quadratic, since both the $w_i$ and the adversarial allocation $x'$ are variables. Fortunately, since $W$ is specified by upper and lower weight bounds, we can rewrite this as follows:

$$\max_{x' \in X} c(x) - c(x') + \sum_{i=1}^{k} \left\{ \begin{array}{lll} w_i\!\uparrow(f_i(x') - f_i(x)) & \text{if} & f_i(x') > f_i(x)) \\ w_i\!\downarrow(f_i(x') - f_i(x)) & \text{if} & f_i(x') \leq f_i(x)) \end{array} \right\}$$

With some clever encoding, we can make this objective linear, and rewrite this optimization as an IP. Specifically, we can linearly define variable $A_i^+$ to indicate that $f_i(x') > f_i(x)$ (and $A_i^-$ the opposite), as well as variable $F_i^+$ (resp., $F_i^-$) that takes value $f_i(x')$ if $A_i^+$ is true and 0 otherwise (resp., if $A_i^-$ is true). We then solve the following objective:

$$\max \sum_{i=1}^{k} \{w_i\!\uparrow[F_i^+ - f_i(x)A_i^+] + w_i\!\downarrow[F_i^- - f_i(x)A_i^-]\} + c(X) - c(x)$$

Thus with a linear IP we can compute the max regret of any given allocation $x$.

**Computing Minimax Regret** Computing the allocation with minimax regret requires a minimax program:

$$\arg\min_{x \in X} \max_{\mathbf{w} \in W} \max_{x' \in X} \sum_{i=1}^{k} w_i[f_i(x') - f_i(x)] + c(x') - c(x)$$

We can convert this to a standard minimization using the following conceptual trick:

$$\min_{x \in X} \delta$$

$$\text{s.t. } \delta \geq \sum_{i=1}^{k} w_i[f_i(x') - f_i(x)] + c(x') - c(x), \ \forall x', \mathbf{w} \quad (7)$$

The difficulty lies in the fact that these constraints over all $x' \in X$ and $\mathbf{w} \in W$ cannot be enumerated explicitly.

Fortunately, for any specific $x'$, we need not enumerate the (continuous) set of possible weight vectors $W$; rather we can identify the unique weight vector $\mathbf{w}$ (hence the only active constraint for $x'$) that maximizes the regret of $x$ w.r.t. $x'$ by setting each $w_i$ to either its upper or lower bound (depending on the relative values of this feature in $x$ and $x'$). This can be accomplished using a strategy much like the one outlined above, using a specific indicator variable for each $x'$. This still leaves the problem of enumerating all allocations $x'$ to form the constraint set above. To circumvent this, we use an iterative constraint generation procedure, whereby we solve relaxed versions of the problem, gradually adding constraints for various $x'$ until we are assured that all active constraints in the full program are present.[5]

Note that in defining this program, we use tricks similar to those used to compute max regret. However, now allocation variables refer to "our" allocation (we are minimizing over these variables), not the adversary's allocation. The adversary's allocations will be fixed within specific constraints. The formulation is similar to the max regret computation except that we require variables $A_i^+[x']$, $A_i^-[x']$, $F_i^+[x']$, and $F_i^-[x']$ for each adversarial $x'$ present in the constraint set (similar in meaning to those above).

The constraint generation procedure works as follows:

1. Let *Gen* $= \{x'\}$ for some arbitrary feasible $x'$.
2. Solve the following IP:

$$\min \delta$$

$$\text{s.t. } \delta \geq \sum_{i=1}^{k} \{ w_i\!\uparrow (f_i(x') A_i^+[x'] - F_i^+[x']) + w_i\!\downarrow (f_i(x') A_i^-[x'] - F_i^-[x']) \} + c(x') - c(X) \quad \forall x' \in Gen$$

and definitional constraints $\forall x' \in Gen$

Let $x^*$ be the IP solution with objective value $\delta^*$.

3. Compute the minimax regret of allocation $x^*$ using the IP above, producing a solution with regret level $r^*$ and adversarial allocation $x''$. If $r^* > \delta^*$, then add $x''$ to *Gen* and repeat from Step 2; otherwise (if $r^* = \delta^*$), terminate with minimax optimal solution $x^*$ (with regret level $\delta^*$).

The correctness of this procedure is easy to verify. The constraints ensure that $\delta$ is greater or equal to the pairwise regret level $MR(x^*, x')$ of the solution $x^*$ and every $x' \in$ *Gen*, and the minimization ensures that $x^*$ has the minimum such regret. Given the solution $x^*$ to this relaxed IP, we can easily determine the adversarial allocation $x''$ that maximizes regret w.r.t. $x^*$. If the max regret of $x^*$ is no greater than the $\delta^*$, we are assured that all unexpressed constraints (for those $x'$ outside *Gen*) are satisfied. If the computed max regret level is greater than $\delta^*$, then the corresponding constraint is added, thus making "maximal" progress towards a true solution.

## 4.2 Arbitrary Weight Constraints

When $W$ is given by a set of arbitrary linear constraints, we can't exploit weight bounds in the manner above. However, we can use an alternating optimization technique to compute max regret when $W$ is so defined using only a sequence of IPs and LPs. Note that if we fix a weight vector $\mathbf{w}$, the quadratic program in Eq. 6 becomes a linear IP; and if we fix the allocation $x'$, it becomes an LP. So to solve Eq. 6 we start by fixing $\mathbf{w}$ to some random feasible weight vector $\mathbf{w}_1$. We then iterate over the following steps:

(a) Given a fixed $\mathbf{w}_i$, solve the IP above, obtaining solution $x'_i$, with max regret $m'_i$.

(b) Given the fixed $x'_i$, solve the LP above, obtaining solution $\mathbf{w}_{i+1}$ with max regret $m_{i+1}$.

This alternation stops whenever the max regret computed at two successive levels is identical. Since the computation of a new $\mathbf{w}$ is an LP, the algorithm will terminate with a solution $\mathbf{w}$ whose value is equal to that of some $\mathbf{w}'$ lies at a vertex of the polytope $W$. This ensures convergence though perhaps only at a local maximum. We can integrate this scheme with a constraint generation procedure to compute an approximately minimax optimal allocation with some minor modifications in a straightforward way.

When the dimensionality of $W$ is small, we can improve the procedure. First, we run a standard vertex enumeration algorithm once to compute the vertices of $W$—this will be a small set if only a few features are relevant to utility. At each iteration of the procedure, rather than repeatedly solving IPs and LPs to generate a new constraint, we can find the adversarial allocation $x'$ that maximizes the regret of $x^*$ as follows: we compute the $x_{\mathbf{w}}$ that maximizes the regret of $x^*$ w.r.t. each weight vector $\mathbf{w}$ in the vertex set; the maximum of these gives the $x'$ and $\mathbf{w}$ at which the regret of $x^*$ is maximized. This $x'$ (with suitable setting of weights) is then added to the constraint set.[6] This removes the LP from each iteration and ensures convergence to a global maximum. Indeed, one can avoid constraint generation altogether and simply impose the constraints for each $\mathbf{w}, x_{\mathbf{w}}$ pair and solve a single IP.

## 4.3 Empirical Evaluation

We tested the effectiveness of our procedures on some large scale, real-world reverse CAs. The goal in this section is to demonstrate the computational feasibility of our constraint generation procedure for practical problems. Here we focus on the computation of minimax regret for problems with weight bounds. (We discuss arbitrary linear constraints in Section 5.2.)

For these experiments, we generated random reverse CAs which have a similar structure to a class of transportation procurement problems encountered frequently in the real world. In these instances, the items to be procured are divided into

[5]This related to Bender's reformulation for mixed IPs [12].

[6]This is much like Bender's decomposition [12].

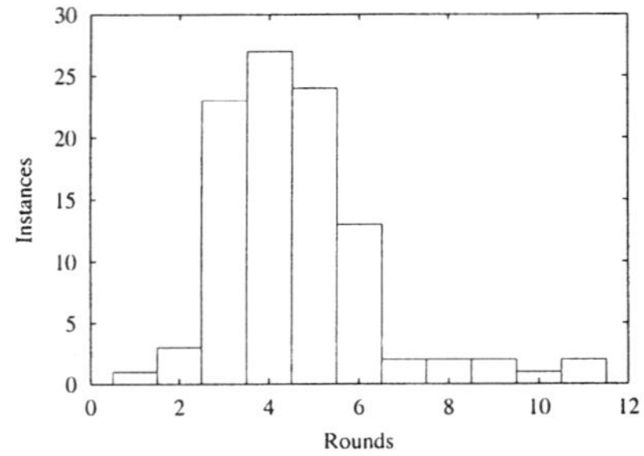

Figure 1: Number of constraints generated.

five regions; the relevant features are the number of winning suppliers in each region, and the number of winning suppliers overall (yielding six features in total). Each instance has ten suppliers, and ten times as many bids as there are items. The bids are on individual items only.[7]

All experiments were conducted for the case where $w$ is defined by upper and lower bounds for each weight $w_i$. The initial bounds were chosen to reflect plausible tradeoff weights for each feature, and are reasonably (but plausibly) loose.

To measure the computational feasibility of the minimax optimization, we tracked how many rounds of constraint generation were required to determine the minimax optimal allocation—since each iteration requires the solution of two WD problems, this gives a sense of how the problem will scale with one's favorite WD algorithm. We first test how the number of generated constraints scales with problem size. Testing problems sizes of 10, 20, 30, 40, and 50 items (at each size, we generated 10 instances), we found the average number of constraints generated to be 3.3., 3.8, 3.6, 3.8, and 3.1, respectively. Figure 1 shows the distribution of constraint generation rounds for a larger set of instances (100 instances with 500 bids and 50 items). The vast majority of instances required only 3 or 4 rounds of constraint generation.[8] Interestingly, the average number generated constraints stays nearly constant as problem size increases. This is very promising for the scalability of this technique to even larger instances (at least from problems in this class), since it seems to depend only on how well the underlying WD method itself scales.

Should the number of required constraints become infeasible, approximate solutions can be obtained in an anytime fashion by early termination of constraint generation (we do not test this behavior here since the number of required constraints is so small). Faster convergence can also be achieved by "seeding" the constraint generation procedure with the constraints used in related versions of the problem; for instance, in the elicitation process, once new utility information is received, the new minimax problem can be seeded with the constraints from the prior, closely related problem. Finally, the solution time per generated constraint can be shortened by using approximate WD.

[7]Here the combinatorial complexity of WD stems solely from consideration of the number of winners.

[8]Average WD solution time for these instances was 19.37s.

### 4.4 Generalizations

In this section, we briefly hint at how the simple linear utility model can be generalized and minimax regret computation adjusted to reflect these changes.

First, we note that independence of features is not critical. If the utilities of some features are conditionally dependent on those of others, but this dependence is sparse (e.g., as captured in a graphical model [3]), the number of utility parameters remains small, and typically the utility of an allocation is a linear function of these parameters.

Uncertainty in a nonlinear local utility function for a specific feature $f_i$ cannot be represented using bounds (or constraints) on a single weight $w_i$. However, even if the utility function has an unknown, or nonparametric form, we can still compute minimax regret if we have upper and lower bounds on the utility of *sampled points* from the domain of $f_i$. We defer details to a longer version of this paper. From the point of view of elicitation, we can address the question of which sampled points offer the greatest (potential) improvement in decision quality. Finally, dealing with certain types of features that cannot be defined by linear constraints is also possible. For certain features, we can impose bounds on their values with linear constraints. This permits the discretization of feature values, allowing one to define utility as a function of the specific discrete level taken by that feature.

## 5 Preference Elicitation

A critical component of WD when non-price features play a role is *preference elicitation* from the bid taker. While the minimax regret methods described above allow robust decisions to be made in the face of utility function uncertainty, these must be coupled with tools that support a buyer in refining her preferences. Uncertainty must be reduced if regret is to reach an acceptable level. Regret methods have a key advantage in this respect—when regret reaches a satisfactory level, further refinement of the utility function can be *proven* to be unnecessary. Thus, in a practical sense, minimax regret can help focus elicitation on the *relevant* parts of the buyer's utility function.[9]

In this section, we describe two classes of techniques in which minimax regret is used to drive the process of elicitation. While a number of methods can be used for elicitation, we focus here on two especially simple techniques, one involving direct manipulation of weight bounds, the second involving comparisons of automatically chosen outcomes.[10] We provide detailed empirical results are presented for the first method, and preliminary results for the second.

### 5.1 Direct Weight-bound Manipulation

In our first method the buyer directly manipulates the upper and lower bounds (via a graphical interface) on the weights $w_i$, using regret-based feedback. We assume the buyer has provided some initial (possibly crude) bounds on each

[9]Also, different stakeholders in the buying organization can decide to end their internal negotiation when the benefit from further negotiation (i.e., max regret) becomes provably small.

[10]We are also exploring various hybrids of these methods, including their combination with manual navigation.

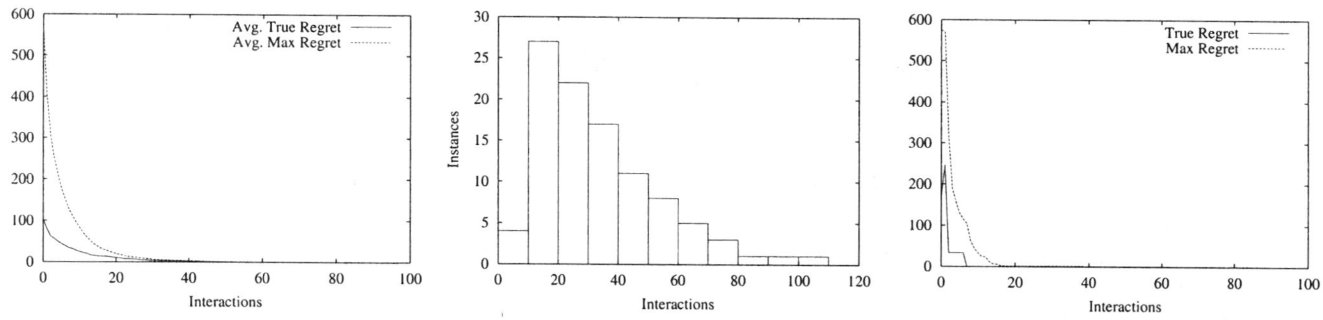


Figure 2: (a) Avg. max regret and avg. true regret as a function of number of slider *interactions* (each interaction is one tightening of one bound of one feature weight); (b) Number of interactions required to reach zero max regret; (c) Reduction of max regret on a specific instance (true regret is zero immediately).

weight. At each round $k$ of interaction, we display the following information: a slider demonstrating the range of values for each $w_i$, with bounds $w_i^k\uparrow$ and $w_i^k\downarrow$ defining the feasible weight set $W^k$ at round $k$; the minimax optimal allocation $x^k$; the adversarial allocation $a^k$; the weights $w_i^a$ chosen by the adversary that maximize regret of $x^k$ (these will lie at either an upper or lower bound, and are highlighted on each slider); and the (adversarial) utility of both $x^k$ and $a^k$, as well as their difference (the minimax regret).

The buyer is asked to manipulate the bounds. If the buyer prefers $x^k$ to $a^k$ (or feels that regret overstates the amount by which $a^k$ is preferred to $x^k$), we ask the buyer to adjust one of the bounds $w_i^a$ at which the adversary's utility function lies. As this bound is adjusted up (in the case of a lower bound) or down (upper bound), the pairwise max regret $MR(x^k, a^k)$ must be reduced, and can be updated in real-time without reoptimization, providing the user with real-time feedback. (The only exception is when $a^k$ and $x^k$ agree on feature $f_i$.) However, if $a^k$ is preferred to $x^k$, the user must adjust one of the $w_i$ bounds opposite from that chosen by the adversary. In this case, pairwise regret is unaffected, and no immediate feedback is provided. After these manipulations, the new (tighter) bounds are used to recompute the minimax optimal allocation and related quantities. The process terminates when minimax regret is reduced to an acceptable level.

For experimental purposes, we simulate a user's behavior with a simple model which favors moving bounds that give immediate feedback. A *true weight* is chosen randomly for each feature using a truncated Gaussian distribution centered at the midpoint of the unknown weight interval $[w_i\uparrow, w_i\downarrow]$, with variance $(0.25(w_i\uparrow - w_i\downarrow))^2$. This reflects the fact that users are more likely to have true utility closer to the middle of their assessed intervals.[11] Each move of a bound by the simulated user removes half of the distance between the current bound and the true weight. At any stage, a user will move an "adversarial bound" (i.e., a bound at which the adversarial utility $w_i^a$ is located) if some such bound is more than $0.1(w_i\uparrow - w_i\downarrow)$ from the true weight $w_i$; such moves provide immediate feedback, and if more than one such feature exists the bound that provides the largest reduction in $MR(x^k, a^k)$ is moved. Otherwise, if the adversarial bound is very close to the true utility weight (within 10% of the total slider range), the user moves an opposite bound.

Despite the rather cautious nature of the "simulated user," we find that the number of interactions required to find robust allocations is typically quite small. The anytime nature of utility refinement is evident in Figure 2(a), which shows max regret of the minimax optimal allocation as a function of the number of interactions (averaged over 100 50-item, 500-bid instances).[12] Max regret reduces very rapidly with the initial interactions. Reducing max regret to zero is more difficult, but only for some instances. On many instances, max regret is driven to zero very quickly, as shown in Figure 2(b). One instance did not reach zero max regret within 100 interactions, but it did reach very low max regret quickly, as exemplified in Figure 2(c). Note that *true regret*—the error in the minimax optimal allocation w.r.t. the true utility function—is considerably less than max regret (see Figure 2(a)). The anytime nature of the approach is critical: it allows one to terminate when max regret reaches an acceptable level, relative to the cost of further interaction.

## 5.2 Comparison Queries

The manipulation of bounds provides the user with direct control of utility function refinement. Alternatively, an elicitation scheme in which we directly *query* the user about specific allocations gives much more control to the system.

We have engaged in preliminary investigation of simple *comparison queries*. This involves asking the user to compare two allocations: "Do you prefer $x'$ to $x$?"[13] A (yes/no) answer to such a query induces a linear constraint on possible weight vectors; for instance, if $x$ is preferred to $x'$, we impose the linear constraint

$$w_i f_i(x) - c(x) > w_i f_i(x') - c(x')$$

[11] We do not exploit this information in the querying process. Experiments with uniformly drawn utilities have qualitatively similar results, but require *slightly* more interaction.

[12] Optimal allocations have average utility of 23,960.

[13] Such comparisons need only involve the utility-bearing features of the allocations in question and the cost of each; the entire allocations need not be presented.

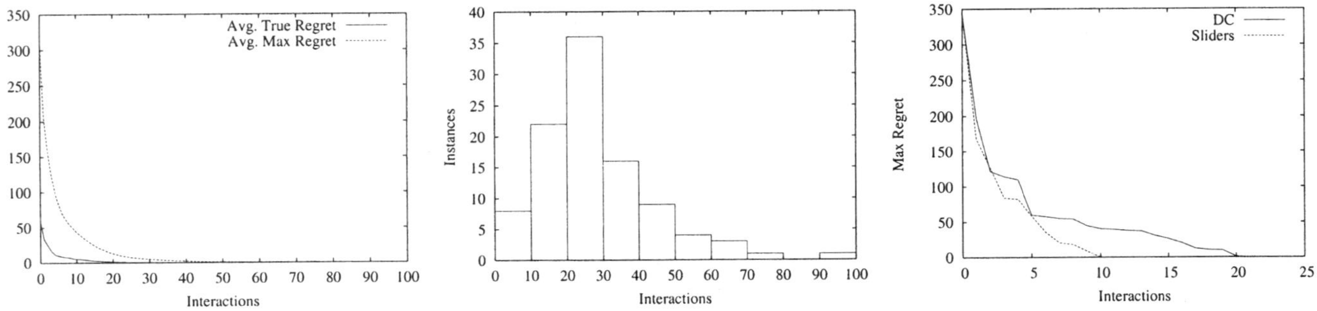


Figure 3: (a) Avg. max regret and avg. true regret as a function of number of *comparison queries*; (b) Number of queries required to reach zero max regret; (c) Reduction of max regret on a specific instance (vs. slider interactions).

on the set of weight vectors. We can also allow the user to express rough indifference by responding "I'm not sure," treating this as meaning $|u(x) - u(x')| \leq \epsilon$ for some small $\epsilon$, and imposing the constraint the these values are $\epsilon$-close.

The goal then is to construct a query plan that reduces the feasible region $W$ in a fashion that reduces the max regret of the minimax optimal allocation quickly. A number of alternative query policies can be considered; to date we have focused on a very simple, yet promising strategy, in which the user is repeatedly asked to compare her minimax optimal allocation with the adversary's allocation. Any response to that query will generally provide valuable information. Should the user prefer the minimax optimal allocation, this immediately rules out the adversary's chosen utility function, and will generally reduce regret. Conversely, should the user prefer the adversary's allocation, this rules out the current minimax optimal allocation, thus imposing a constraint that forces a new (minimax optimal) decision to be made.

The ability to compute minimax regret for arbitrary polytopes $W$, as discussed above, is critical when dealing with comparison queries. We did some preliminary investigation of the comparison query strategy using the vertex enumeration scheme discussed in Section 4.2. After each query response, a new linear constraint is imposed on $W$. The optimal allocation $x_{\mathbf{w}}$ is computed for each vertex $\mathbf{w}$ of $W$ and the minimax optimal allocation is then determined with a single IP. Note that since the vertices of $W$ at each iteration are identical to the previous vertices except for those incident with the new constraint, we need only run a WD algorithm at the (small) set of *new* vertices.

Figure 3(a) shows average max-regret and true-regret reduction offered by the comparison query model (averaged over 100 30-item, 300-bid instances). The same desirable anytime nature as seen with slider interactions is evident, with regret reducing very quickly with just a few initial queries. Figure 3(b) shows the number of queries required to reach zero max regret (though as with sliders, this measure is less important than the anytime profile). Figure 3(c) illustrates performance on a typical instance, showing that regret reduces very quickly with the number of queries. For comparison, we show regret reduction with the slider mode of interaction on the same instance. While sliders generally require slightly fewer interactions, it is important to note that more information is generally being provided with each slider interaction than is contained in the response to a comparison query. A suitable measure of interaction cost is needed to draw definitive conclusions regarding the relative merits of the two approaches.

Computationally, the comparison query approach is quite fast for problems of this size, and is certainly able to support online interaction. Using the simple, non-iterative, vertex-enumeration approach described in Section 4.2 on the 100 30-item, 300-bid instances, we found that the $W$ polytope had on average 253 vertices when querying terminates at the optimal (zero-regret) solution. The WD problem for each vertex is solved in 0.13s on average, but recall that after each interaction, only new vertices need to have their WD problems solved. On average, 54 vertices are added per query (each initial computation is on a hyperrectangle with 64 vertices, reflecting initial bounds). Finally, computation of the minimax optimal solution after each query (using the vertex solutions as constraints) takes an average of 3.5s. Thus average computation time per query is under 11 seconds. There are considerable opportunities for improving this performance as well.

## 6 Concluding Remarks

We have described new methods that allow a bid taker to find an (approximately) optimal allocation despite uncertainty in utility for non-price criteria. These methods rely on the notion of *minimax regret* to guide the elicitation of preferences from the bid taker on an as-needed basis, and to measure the quality of an allocation in the presence of utility function uncertainty. This provides a basis for deciding when to terminate utility refinement and for determining a robust allocation. Our computational experiments demonstrate the practicality of minimax computation and the efficacy of our elicitation techniques.

While we presented our techniques for allocation-level features, they can directly handle item-level (and bid-level) features as well (e.g., color, delivery date, etc.). The bid taker can leave certain item features unspecified, allowing bidders to specify various alternative (e.g., red on Monday for \$10, or blue on Wednesday for \$7).[14] The bid taker's utility function

[14]Preference elicitation *from the bidders* (using techniques analogous to ascending-price auctions), has been studied in single-item

can depend on these features, and our methods can be used if the bid taker is uncertain about that function. Our techniques and notation stay unchanged, but now each allocation (i.e., vector $x$) not only includes a decision variable (accept or reject) for each bid, but also variables describing how the additional features are set (e.g., what delivery date and color the bid taker chooses).

We plan to conduct more systematic experiments with various forms of comparison queries. Apart from the "current solution" strategy for choosing queries, we intend to investigate other methods for choosing the allocations that the user is asked to compare. We will also explore some of the iterative approaches to minimax optimization in the presense of arbitrary weight contraints for problems where vertex enumeration is infeasible.

Other important directions include the study of additional query types. In situations where computational bottlenecks arise, investigation of anytime constraint generation and anytime WD would prove interesting. We also plan to field these techniques in procurement applications.

**Acknowledgements**

This research was conducted at and supported by CombineNet, Inc.

## References

[1] Allan Borodin and Ran El-Yaniv. *Online Computation and Competitive Analysis*. Cambridge University Press, Cambridge, 1998.

[2] Craig Boutilier. A POMDP formulation of preference elicitation problems. In *Proceedings of the Eighteenth National Conference on Artificial Intelligence*, pages 239–246, Edmonton, 2002.

[3] Craig Boutilier, Fahiem Bacchus, and Ronen I. Brafman. UCP-Networks: A directed graphical representation of conditional utilities. In *Proceedings of the Seventeenth Conference on Uncertainty in Artificial Intelligence*, pages 56–64, Seattle, 2001.

[4] Craig Boutilier, Relu Patrascu, Pascal Poupart, and Dale Schuurmans. Constraint-based optimization with the minimax decision criterion. In *Ninth International Conference on Principles and Practice of Constraint Programming*, pages 168–182, Kinsale, Ireland, 2003.

[5] Urszula Chajewska, Daphne Koller, and Ronald Parr. Making rational decisions using adaptive utility elicitation. In *Proceedings of the Seventeenth National Conference on Artificial Intelligence*, pages 363–369, Austin, TX, 2000.

[6] Wolfram Conen and Tuomas Sandholm. Preference elicitation in combinatorial auctions: Extended abstract. In *Third ACM Conference on Electronic Commerce (EC'01)*, pages 256–259, Tampa, FL, 2001. A more detailed version appeared in the IJCAI-2001 Workshop on Economic Agents, Models, and Mechanisms, pp. 71–80.

[7] Wolfram Conen and Tuomas Sandholm. Partial-revelation VCG mechanism for combinatorial auctions. In *Proceedings of the Eighteenth National Conference on Artificial Intelligence*, pages 367–372, Edmonton, 2002.

[8] Simon French. *Decision Theory*. Halsted Press, New York, 1986.

auctions with item-level features (e.g., [21]).

[9] Yuzo Fujisima, Kevin Leyton-Brown, and Yoav Shoham. Taming the computational complexity of combinatorial auctions. In *Proceedings of the Sixteenth International Joint Conference on Artificial Intelligence*, pages 548–553, Stockholm, 1999.

[10] Vu Ha and Peter Haddawy. Problem-focused incremental elicitation of multi-attribute utility models. In *Proceedings of the Thirteenth Conference on Uncertainty in Artificial Intelligence*, pages 215–222, Providence, RI, 1997.

[11] Ralph L. Keeney and Howard Raiffa. *Decisions with Multiple Objectives: Preferences and Value Trade-offs*. Wiley, New York, 1976.

[12] George L. Nemhauser and Laurence A. Wolsey. *Integer Programming and Combinatorial Optimization*. Wiley, New York, 1988.

[13] S. J. Rassenti, V. L. Smith, and R. L. Bulfin. A combinatorial auction mechanism for airport time slot allocation. *Bell Journal of Economics*, 13:402–417, 1982.

[14] Michael H. Rothkopf, Aleksander Pekeč, and Ronald M. Harstad. Computationally manageable combinatorial auctions. *Management Science*, 44(8):1131–1147, 1998.

[15] Ahti Salo and Raimo P. Hämäläinen. Preference ratios in multiattribute evaluation (PRIME)–elicitation and decision procedures under incomplete information. *IEEE Trans. on Systems, Man and Cybernetics*, 31(6):533–545, 2001.

[16] Tuomas Sandholm. An algorithm for optimal winner determination in combinatorial auctions. *Artificial Intelligence*, 153:1–154, 2002.

[17] Tuomas Sandholm and Subash Suri. Side constraints and non-price attributes in markets. In *Proceedings of the IJCAI-01 Workshop on Distributed Constraint Reasoning*, Seattle, 2001.

[18] Tuomas Sandholm, Subash Suri, Andrew Gilpin, and David Levine. CABOB: A fast optimal algorithm for combinatorial auctions. In *Proceedings of the Seventeenth International Joint Conference on Artificial Intelligence*, pages 1102–1108, Seattle, 2001.

[19] Tuomas Sandholm, Subash Suri, Andrew Gilpin, and David Levine. Winner determination in combinatorial auction generalizations. In *Proceedings of the First International Joint Conference on Autonomous Agents and Multiagent Systems*, pages 69–76, Bologna, 2002.

[20] Leonard J. Savage. *The Foundations of Statistics*. Wiley, New York, 1954.

[21] Aditya Sunderam and David C. Parkes. Preference elicitation in proxied multiattribute auctions. In *Fourth ACM Conference on Electronic Commerce (EC'03)*, pages 214–215, San Diego, 2003.

[22] Tianhan Wang and Craig Boutilier. Incremental utility elicitation with the minimax regret decision criterion. In *Proceedings of the Eighteenth International Joint Conference on Artificial Intelligence*, Acapulco, 2003. to appear.

[23] Chelsea C. White, III, Andrew P. Sage, and Shigeru Dozono. A model of multiattribute decisionmaking and trade-off weight determination under uncertainty. *IEEE Transactions on Systems, Man and Cybernetics*, 14(2):223–229, 1984.

# Combinatorial Auctions with Structured Item Graphs

**Vincent Conitzer** and **Jonathan Derryberry** and **Tuomas Sandholm**
Carnegie Mellon University
5000 Forbes Avenue
Pittsburgh, PA 15213
{conitzer, jonderry, sandholm}@cs.cmu.edu

## Abstract

Combinatorial auctions (CAs) are important mechanisms for allocating interrelated items. Unfortunately, winner determination is NP-complete unless there is special structure. We study the setting where there is a graph (with some desired property), with the items as vertices, and every bid bids on a connected set of items. Two computational problems arise: 1) clearing the auction when given the item graph, and 2) constructing an item graph (if one exists) with the desired property. 1 was previously solved for the case of a tree or a cycle, and 2 for the case of a line graph or a cycle.

We generalize the first result by showing that given an item graph *with bounded treewidth*, the clearing problem can be solved in polynomial time (and every CA instance has some treewidth; the complexity is exponential in only that parameter). We then give an algorithm for constructing an item tree (treewidth 1) if such a tree exists, thus closing a recognized open problem. We show why this algorithm does not work for treewidth greater than 1, but leave open whether item graphs of (say) treewidth 2 can be constructed in polynomial time. We show that finding the item graph with the fewest edges is NP-complete (even when a graph of treewidth 2 exists). Finally, we study how the results change if a bid is allowed to have more than one connected component. Even for line graphs, we show that clearing is hard even with 2 components, and constructing the line graph is hard even with 5.

## Introduction

Combinatorial auctions (CAs), where bidders can bid on *bundles* of items, have emerged as key mechanisms for allocating goods, tasks, resources, etc., both in computer science and economics. They are desirable when a bidder's valuation of a bundle might not equal the sum of his valuations of the individual items contained in the bundle.

Unfortunately, determining the winners in a general CA is NP-complete (Rothkopf, Pekeč, & Harstad 1998). Three main approaches have been pursued to address this: 1) designing optimal search algorithms that are often fast (e.g., (Sandholm 2002; Sandholm *et al.* 2001; Fujishima, Leyton-Brown, & Shoham 1999; Boutilier 2002)), but require exponential time in the worst case (unless P = NP), 2) designing approximation algorithms (e.g., (Hoos & Boutilier 2000; Zurel & Nisan 2001; van Hoesel & Müller 2001))—but unfortunately no polytime algorithm can guarantee an approximation (unless ZPP = NP) (Sandholm 2002), and 3) designing optimal polytime algorithms for restricted classes of CAs (e.g., (Rothkopf, Pekeč, & Harstad 1998; Tennenholtz 2000; Penn & Tennenholtz 2000; Sandholm & Suri 2003)).

This paper falls roughly within the third approach: we present hardness and easiness results for natural classes of CAs. However, we also develop a problem instance parameter (treewidth of the item graph, described below), such that *any* CA instance falls within our framework, and winner determination complexity is exponential in the parameter only. Like almost all of the work on polynomial-time solvable combinatorial auctions, we restrict our attention to the case where any two bids on disjoint subsets can be simultaneously accepted (that is, no XOR-constraints between bids are allowed).

Consider graphs with the auction's items as vertices, which have the property that for any bid, the items occurring in it constitute a connected set in the graph. (For instance, the fully connected graph (with an edge between every pair of items) always has this property.) Such graphs can have potentially useful structure (for example, the graph may be a tree). For any type of structure, one can ask the following two questions: 1) how hard is the clearing problem when we are given a valid item graph with the desired structure? 2) if the graph is not given beforehand, how hard is it to construct a valid item graph with this structure (if it exists)? We will investigate both questions. 1 has been solved for the special case where the graph is a tree or a cycle (Sandholm & Suri 2003); 2 has been solved for the special case where the graph is a line (Korte & Mohring 1989) or a cycle (Eschen & Spinrad 1993). In each of these cases, a low-order polynomial algorithm was presented.

One practical use of such polynomially detectable and solvable special cases is to incorporate them into optimal search algorithms (Sandholm & Suri 2003). At every node of the search tree, we can detect whether the remaining problem is polynomially solvable, and if it is, we use the polynomial special-purpose algorithm for solving it. Otherwise the search will continue into the subtree.

Also, there are two pure uses for graph structures which make questions 1 and 2 easy. First, the auctioneer can decide on the graph beforehand, and allow only bids on connected sets of items. (In this case, 1 is most important, but 2 may also be useful if the auctioneer wants to make sure that bids on certain bundles are allowed.) Second, the auctioneer can allow bids on any bundle; then, once the bids have been submitted, attempt to construct an item graph that is valid for these bids; and finally, clear the auction using this graph. Clearly, the second approach is only practical if real instances are likely to have item graphs with some structure. To a lesser extent, this is also important for the first approach: if bidders must bid on bundles too different from their desired bundles, economic value will be lost.

Fortunately, real-world instances are likely to have graphs that are not fully connected. For instance, consider a combinatorial auction for tourist activities in the Bay Area. One item for sale may be a ticket to Alcatraz (in San Francisco). Another may be a ticket to the Children's Discovery Museum (in San Jose). A third item may be a Caltrain ticket to get back and forth between the two cities. Supposing (for now) that there is no alternative transportation between the two cities, the only bundle that is unlikely to receive a bid is {Alcatraz, Children's Discovery Museum}, because the bidder will need transportation (no matter which city she is based out of for the duration of her visit). Thus, a valid graph for this auction is the following line graph (because its only disconnected set is the one we just ruled out).

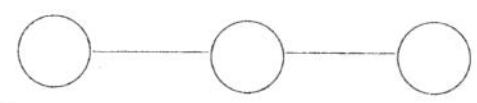


To extend the example, suppose that there are alternative modes of transportation which are also included in the auction: a Rental Car, and a Bus ticket. Now the following bundles are unlikely to receive a bid: {Alcatraz, Children's Discovery Museum} (because the bidder requires a form of transportation) and any bundle containing more than one mode of transportation. Thus, the following is a valid item graph (because we just ruled out all its disconnected sets).

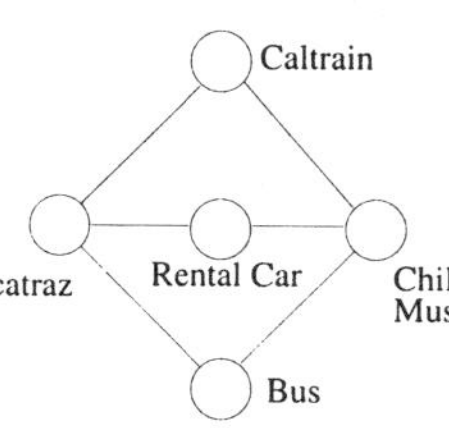


This graph does not fall under any of the previously studied structures (it is not a line, tree, or cycle). Still, it has interesting structure: for instance, it has a treewidth of 2.

The rest of the paper is organized as follows. We first show that given an item graph with bounded treewidth, the clearing problem can be solved in polynomial time. Next, we show how to construct an item tree (treewidth = 1), if it exists, in polynomial time. This answers the proposed open question of whether this can be done (Sandholm & Suri 2003). (We leave open the question of whether an item graph with small treewidth (say, 2) can be constructed if it exists.) We show that constructing the item graph with the fewest edges is NP-complete (even when a graph of treewidth 2 is easy to construct). Finally, we study a variant where a bid is allowed to consist of $k$ connected sets, rather than just one. We show that the clearing problem is NP-complete even for line graphs with $k = 2$, and the graph construction problem is NP-complete for line graphs with $k = 5$.

## Item graphs

We first formally define item graphs.

**Definition 1** *Given a combinatorial auction clearing problem instance, the graph $G = (I, E)$, whose vertices correspond to the items in the instance, is a* (valid) item graph *if for every bid, the set of items in that bid constitutes a connected set in $G$.*

We emphasize that an item graph, in our definition, does *not* need to have an edge connecting every pair of items that occurs in a bid. Rather, each pair only needs to be connected via a path consisting only of items in the bid. In other words, the subgraph consisting of each bid must form only one connected component, but it needs not be a clique.

## Clearing with bounded treewidth item graphs

In this section, we show that combinatorial auctions can be cleared in polynomial time when an item graph with bounded treewidth is given. This generalizes a result by Sandholm and Suri (Sandholm & Suri 2003) which shows polynomial time clearability when the item graph is a tree (treewidth = 1).[1] Linear-time approximation algorithms for clearing when the item graph has bounded treewidth have also been given, where the approximation ratio is the treewidth, plus one (Akcoglu *et al.* 2002). In contrast, we will clear the auction optimally.

First we will give a very brief review of treewidth.

**Definition 2** *A* tree decomposition *$T$ of a graph $G = (I, E)$ is a tree with the following properties.*

1. *Each $v \in T$ has an associated set $I_v$ of vertices in $G$.*
2. *$\bigcup_{v \in T} I_v = I$ (each vertex of $G$ occurs somewhere in $T$).*
3. *For each $(i_1, i_2) \in E$, there is some $v \in T$ with $i_1, i_2 \in I_v$ (each edge of $G$ is contained within some vertex of $T$).*
4. *For each $i \in I$, $\{v \in T : i \in I_v\}$ is connected in $T$.*

*We say that the* width *of the tree is $\max_{v \in T} |I_v| - 1$.*

While the general problem of finding a tree decomposition of a graph with minimum width is NP-complete, when the treewidth is bounded, the tree decomposition can be constructed in polynomial time (Areborg, Corneil, & Proskurowski 1987). Because we are only interested in the case where the treewidth of the item graph is bounded, we may assume that the tree decomposition is given to us as well as the graph itself.

The following (known) lemma will be useful in our proof.

**Lemma 1** *If $X \subseteq I$ is a connected set in $G$, then $\{v \in T : I_v \cap X \neq \{\}\}$ is connected in $T$.*

[1]The special case of a tree can also be solved in polynomial time using algorithms for perfect constraint matrices (de Vries & Vohra 2003), but those algorithms are slower in practice.

We are now ready to present our first result.

**Theorem 1** *Suppose we are given a combinatorial auction problem instance, together with a tree decomposition $T$ with width $tw$ of an item graph $G$. Then the optimal allocation can be determined in $O(|T|^2(|B|+1)^{tw+1})$ using dynamic programming. (Both with and without free disposal.)*

**Proof**: Fix a root in $T$ (the "top" of the tree). At every vertex $v \in T$ with items $I_v$, consider all functions $f : I_v \to B \cup \{0\}$, indicating possible assignments of the items to the bids. ($f(i) = 0$ indicates no commitment as to which bid item $i$ is assigned to.) This set has size $(|B|+1)^{|I_v|}$. Consider the subset $F_{I_v}$ of these functions satisfying: 1. If $f(i) = b$, $b$ must bid on $i$; 2. All bids in the image $f(I_v)$ include items that occur higher up in $T$ than $v$; 3. If $f(i) = b$ and $b$ also bids on item $j \in I_v$, then $f(j) = b$ also.

The interpretation is that each function in $F_{I_v}$ corresponds to a constraint from higher up in the tree as to which bids should be accepted. We now compute, for every node $v$ (starting from the leaves and going up to the root), for every function $f \in F_{I_v}$, the maximum value that can be obtained from items that occur in $v$ and its descendant vertices (but not in any other vertices), and that do not occur in bids in the image of $f$. (We observe that if $v$ is the root node, there can be no constraints from higher up in the tree (that is, there is only one $f$ function), and the corresponding value is the maximum value that can be obtained in the auction.) Denoting this value by $r(v, f)$, we can compute it using dynamic programming from the leaves up in the following manner:

• Consider all assignments $g : \{i \in I_v : f(i) = 0\} \to B \cup \{0\}$,[2] with the properties that: 1. If $g(i) = b$, $b$ must bid on $i$; 2. The image of $g$ does not include any bids that include items that occur higher in $T$ than $v$. 3. If $g(i) = b$ and $b$ also bids on item $j \in I_v$, then $f(j) = 0$ and $g(j) = b$ also. (Thus, $g$ indicates which bids concerning the unallocated items in $I_v$ we are considering accepting, but only bids that we have not considered higher in the tree.)

• The value of such an assignment is $\sum_{b \in g(I_v)} a(b) + \sum_{w \in T: p(w)=v} r(w, q_w(f, g))$, where $g(I_v)$ is the image of $g$, $a(b)$ is the value of bid $b$, $p(w)$ is the parent of $w$, and $q_w(f, g) : I_w \to B$ maps items occurring in a bid in the image of either $f$ or $g$ to that bid, and everything else to 0.

• The maximum such value over all $g$ is $r(v, f)$.

Because we need to do this computation once for each vertex $v$ in $T$, the number of assignments $g$ is at most $(|B|+1)^{|I_v|}$ where $|I_v| \leq tw+1$, and for each assignment we need to do a lookup for each of the children of $v$, this algorithm has running time $O(|T|^2(|B|+1)^{tw+1})$.

The allocation that the algorithm produces can be obtained going back down the tree, as follows: at the root node, there is only one constraint function $f$ mapping everything to 0 (because no bid has items higher up the tree). Thus, consider the $r$-value maximizing assignment $g_{root}$ for the root; all the bids in its image are accepted. Then, for each of its children, consider the $r$-value maximizing assignment under the constraint imposed by $g_{root}$; all the bids in the image of that assignment are also accepted, etc.

To show that the algorithm works correctly, we need to show that no bids that are accepted high up in the tree are "forgotten about" lower in the tree (and its items lower in the tree awarded to other bids). Because the items in a bid constitute a connected set in the item graph $G$, by Lemma 1, the vertices in $T$ containing items from such a bid are also connected. Now, if a bid $b$ is accepted at the highest vertex $v \in T$ containing an item in $b$ (that is, the items in that vertex occurring in $b$ are awarded to $b$), each of $v$'s children must also award all its items occurring in $b$ to $b$; and by the connectedness pointed out above, for each child, either there is at least one such an item in that child, or none of its descendants have any items occurring in $b$. In the former case, $b$ is also in the image of the child's allocation function, and the same reasoning applies to its children, etc.; in the latter case the fact that $b$ has been accepted is irrelevant to this part of the tree. So, either an accepted bid forces a constraint in a child, and the fact that the bid was accepted is propagated down the tree; or the bid is irrelevant to all that child's descendants as well, and can be safely forgotten about. ∎

[2]In the case of no free disposal, $g$ cannot map to 0.

## Constructing a valid item tree

So far we discussed question 1: how to clear the auction *given* a valid item graph. In this section, we move on to the second question of *constructing* the graph. We present a polynomial-time algorithm that constructs an item tree (that is, an item graph without cycles), if one exists for the bids. This closes a recognized open research problem (Sandholm & Suri 2003), and is necessary if one wants to use the polynomial item tree clearing algorithm as a subroutine of a search algorithm, as discussed in the introduction.

First, we introduce some notation. In a combinatorial auction with bid set $B$ and item set $I$, define $items(b) \subseteq I$ to be the set of items in bid $b$. Also, let $T_b$ refer to the subgraph of a tree containing only vertices represented by $items(b)$ and all edges among elements of $items(b)$.

With these definitions in hand, we are now ready to present the main theorem of this section. This theorem shows how to give a tree that "minimally violates" the requirement of an item tree that each bid bids on only one component. Thus, if it is actually possible to give a valid item tree, such a tree will be produced by the algorithm.

**Theorem 2** *Given an arbitrary set of bids $B$ for items $I$, a corresponding tree $T$ that minimizes*

$$\sum_{b \in B} \textit{the number of connected components in } T_b$$

*can be found in $O(|B| \cdot |I|^2)$ time.*

**Proof**: Consider the algorithm MAKETREE$(B, I)$ shown below, which returns the maximum spanning tree of the complete undirected weighted graph over vertices $I$ in which each edge $(i, j)$ has a weight equal to the number of bids $b$ such that $i, j \in items(b)$.

```
MakeTree(B, I)
A ← An |I| × |I| matrix of 0s
for each b in B
   do for each i in items(b)
         do for each j ≠ i in items(b)
               do A(i, j) ← A(i, j) + 1
return the maximum spanning tree of the graph A
```

The running time of MAKETREE$(B, I)$ is $O(|B| \cdot |I|^2)$ from the triply nested **for** loops, plus the time needed to find the maximum spanning tree. The maximum spanning tree can be found in $O(|I|^2)$ time (Cormen, Leiserson, & Rivest 1990), so the running time of the algorithm as a whole is $O(|B| \cdot |I|^2) + O(|I|^2) = O(|B| \cdot |I|^2)$.

To see that MAKETREE$(B, I)$ returns the tree $T$ with the minimum sum of connected components across all $T_b$, note that the total weight of $T$ can be written as

$$\sum_{b \in B} \text{the number of edges in } T \text{ among } items(b).$$

Because $T$ is a tree, each subgraph $T_b$ is a forest, and the number of edges in any forest equals the number of vertices in the forest, minus the number of components in the forest. It follows that we can rewrite the above expression as

$$s = \sum_{b \in B} |items(b)| - \text{ the number of components in } T_b.$$

Because $\sum_{b \in B} |items(b)|$ is a constant, maximizing $s$ is the same as minimizing the sum of the number of connected components across all $T_b$. ■

In particular, if an item tree exists for the given bids, then in that tree, each bid bids on only one connected component, so the summation in Theorem 2 is equal to the number of bids. Because each term in the summation must always be greater than or equal to 1, this tree minimizes the summation. Thus, MAKETREE will return a tree for which the summation in Theorem 2 is equal to the number of bids as well. But this can only happen if each bid bids on only one connected component. So, MAKETREE will return an item tree.

**Corollary 1** MAKETREE *will return a valid item tree if and only if one exists, in $O(|B| \cdot |I|^2)$ time. (And whether a tree is a valid item tree can be checked in $O(|B| \cdot |I|)$ time.)*

## Implications for bid sets without an item tree

The above result presents an algorithm for constructing a tree $T$ from a set of bids that minimizes the sum of the number of connected components across all $T_b$. Even when the tree returned is not a valid item tree, we can still use it to help us clear the auction, as follows. Suppose MAKETREE was "close" to being able to construct an item tree, in the sense that only a few bids were split into multiple components. Then, we could use brute force to determine which of these split bids to accept, and solve the rest of the problem using dynamic programming as in (Sandholm & Suri 2003). If the number of split bids is $k$, this algorithm takes $O(2^k \cdot |B| \cdot |I|)$ time (so it is efficient if $k$ is small). We note, however, that MAKETREE$(B, I)$ does not minimize the number of split bids ($k$), as would be desirable for the proposed search technique. Rather, it minimizes the total number of components (summed over bids). Thus, it may prefer splitting many bids into few components each, over splitting few bids into many components each. So there may exist trees that have fewer split bids than the tree returned by MAKETREE.

Also, MAKETREE does not solve the general problem of constructing an item graph of small treewidth if one exists. The straightforward adaptation of the MAKETREE algorithm to finding an item graph of treewidth 2 (where we find the maximum spanning graph of treewidth 2 in the last step) does not always provide a valid item graph, even when a valid item graph of treewidth 2 exists. To see why, consider an auction instance for which the following graph is the unique item graph of treewidth 2 (for example, because for each edge, there is a bid on only its two endpoints).

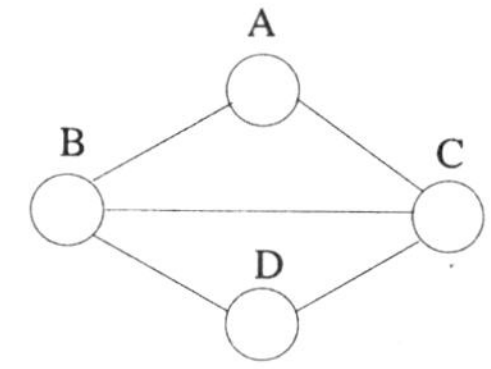


If there are many bids on the bundle $\{A, B, D\}$, and few other bids, the adapted algorithm will draw the edge $(A, D)$. As a result, it will fail to draw one of the other edges (because otherwise the graph would have treewidth 3), and thus the graph will not be a valid item graph.

For now, we leave open the question of how to construct a valid item graph with treewidth 2 (or 3, or 4, ...) if one exists. However, in the next section, we solve a related question.

## Constructing the item graph with the fewest edges is hard

The more edges an item graph has, the less structure there is in the instance. A natural question is therefore to construct the valid item graph with the fewest edges. It should be pointed out that this is not necessarily the best graph to work on. For example, given our algorithm, a graph of treewidth 2 may be more desirable to work on than a graph with fewer edges of high treewidth. On the other hand, assuming that the items cannot be disjoint into two separate components (which is easy to check), a tree is always a graph with the minimum number of edges (and if a tree exists, then only trees have the minimum number of edges). So in this case, generating a graph of minimum treewidth is the same as generating a graph with the minimum number of edges.

We next show that constructing the graph with the fewest edges is hard. Interestingly, the question is hard already for instances with treewidth 2. (For instances of treewidth 1 (forests) it is easy: divide the items into as many separate components (with no bids across more than one component) as possible, and run our MAKETREE algorithm on each.) Thus, if a graph of treewidth 2 can be constructed in polynomial time (and P≠NP), the algorithm for doing so cannot be used to get the fewest edges—unlike the case of treewidth 1.

**Theorem 3** *Determining whether an item tree with fewer than $q$ edges exists is* NP*-complete, even when an item graph of treewidth 2 is guaranteed to exist and each bid is on at most 5 items, and whether or not the item tree we construct is required to be of treewidth 2.*

**Proof**: The problem is in NP because we can nondeterministically generate a graph with the items as vertices and at most $k$ edges, and check whether it is valid item graph. To show that the problem is NP-complete, we reduce an arbitrary 3SAT instance to the following set of items and bids. For every variable $v \in V$, let there be two items $i_{+v}, i_{-v}$. Furthermore, let there be two more items, $i_0$ and $i_1$. Let the set of bids be as follows. For every $v \in V$, let there be bids on the following sets: $\{i_0, i_{+v}\}, \{i_0, i_{-v}\}, \{i_{+v}, i_{-v}\}, \{i_{+v}, i_{-v}, i_1\}$. Finally, for every clause $c \in C$, let there be a bid on $\{i_{+v} : +v \in c\} \cup \{i_{-v} : -v \in c\} \cup \{i_0, i_1\}$ (the set of all items corresponding to literals in the clause, plus the two extra items—we note that because we are reducing from 3SAT, these are at most 5 items). Let the target number of edges be $q = 4|V|$. We proceed to show that the two instances are equivalent.

First, suppose there exists a solution to the 3SAT instance. Then, let there be an edge between any two items which constitute a bid by themselves; additionally, let there be an edge between $i_{+v}$ and $i_1$ whenever $v$ is set to *true* in the SAT solution, and an edge between $i_{-v}$ and $i_1$ whenever $v$ is set to *false* in the SAT solution (for a total of $4|V|$ edges). We observe that all the bids of the form $\{i_{+v}, i_{-v}, i_1\}$ are now connected. Also, for any $c \in C$, because the 3SAT solution satisfied $c$, either $i_1$ is connected to some $i_{+v}$ with $+v \in c$, or $i_1$ is connected to some $i_{-v}$ with $-v \in c$. (And all the items besides $i_1$ in the bid corresponding to $c$ are clearly connected.) So all the bids constitute connected subsets, and there exists a valid item graph with at most $4|V|$ edges. (Also, this is a series parallel graph, and such graphs have treewidth 2.)

Now, suppose there exists a valid item graph with at most $4|V|$ edges. Of course, there must be an edge between any two items which constitute a bid by themselves; and because of the bids on three items, for every $v \in V$, there must be an edge either between $i_{+v}$ and $i_1$, or between $i_{-v}$ and $i_1$. This already requires $4|V|$ edges, so there cannot be any more edges. Because each bid corresponding to a clause $c$ must be connected, there must be either an edge between some $i_{+v}$ with $+v \in c$ and $i_1$, or between some $i_{-v}$ with $-v \in c$ and $i_1$. But then, it follows that if we set $v$ to *true* if there is an edge between $i_{+v}$ and $i_1$, and to *false* if there is an edge between $i_{-v}$ and $i_1$, we have a solution to the SAT instance.

All that remains to show is that in these instances, a valid item graph of treewidth 2 always exists. Consider the graph that has an edge between any two items which constitute a bid by themselves; an edge between $i_{+v}$ and $i_1$ for any $v \in V$; and an edge between $i_0$ and $i_1$ (for a total of $4|V| + 1$ edges). This is a series parallel graph, and such graphs have treewidth 2. ■

## Bids on multiple connected sets

In this section, we investigate what happens if we reduce the requirements on item graphs somewhat. Specifically, let the requirement be that for each bid, the items form *at most* $k$ connected components in the graph. (The case where $k = 1$ is the one we have studied up to this point.) So, to see if a bid is valid given the graph, consider how many connected components the items in the bid constitute in the graph; if (and only if) there are at most $k$ components, the bid is valid. The following figure shows an example item tree. One bid bids on all the items encapsulated by rectangles (2 connected components); the other, on all the items encapsulated by ellipses (3 connected components). Thus, if $k = 2$, then the first bid is valid, but the second one is not. (Equivalently, the graph is not valid for the second bid.)

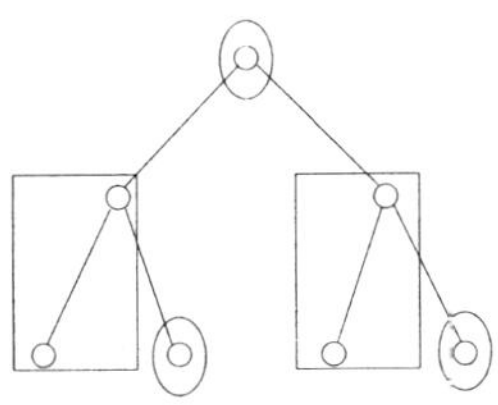

As we will see, both clearing when a simple graph is known, and detecting whether a simple graph exists, become hard for $k > 1$.

### Clearing is hard even with 2 connected sets on a line graph

Even if the item graph is a line, it is hard to clear auctions in which bidders may bundle two intervals together. To show this, we prove the following slightly stronger theorem.

**Theorem 4** *If an item graph is created that consists of two disconnected line graphs, and bidders are permitted to bundle one connected component from each line, then determining if the auction can generate revenue $r$ is* NP*-complete.*

**Proof**: The problem is in NP because the general clearing problem is in NP. To show that it is NP-complete, an arbitrary instance of VERTEXCOVER will be reduced to a corresponding auction problem. In VERTEXCOVER, the goal is to determine whether there exists a set of vertices $C$ of size at most $k$ in a graph $G = (V, E)$ such that for each edge $(x, y) \in E$, either $x \in C$ or $y \in C$.

To perform the reduction, given $G = (V, E)$, create an item $u_i$ for each edge $e_i$. Place all of the $u_i$ items into the upper line. In addition, for each vertex $v_i \in V$, create the items $l_{v_i}^{e_j}$ for each edge $e_j$ that $v_i$ is part of. For each $v_i$, align all of its corresponding $l_{v_i}^{e_j}$ items into a contiguous interval on the lower line. Now, create the following bids: 1. A bid of price 2 for each "edge item pair" $(l_{v_i}^{e_j}, u_j)$. 2. A bid of price 1 for each "vertex interval bundle," $\{l_{v_i}^{e_j}|\text{for all } e_j \text{ for which } v_i \text{ is part of } e_j\}$.

We now show that there exists a vertex cover of size at most $k$ exactly when the optimal revenue of the corresponding auction is at least $2 \cdot |E| + |V| - k$.

Suppose there is a vertex cover of size $k$ for a graph $G = (V, E)$. Then it is possible to sell all $|E|$ of the edge items breaking up only $k$ of the vertex interval bundles. The resulting revenue if only those $k$ intervals are rendered unsellable by matching one or more of their members with edge items is $r = 2 \cdot |E| + |V| - k$ as required; the profit is 2 for each of the edge pairs of the form $(l_{v_i}^{e_j}, u_j)$ that are sold, plus 1 for each of the vertex interval bundles that have not had any of their items matched to edges.

Conversely, suppose there is a way to achieve revenue $r = 2 \cdot |E| + |V| - k$. Suppose all of the edge item pairs were sold in this case. Then, because $|V| - k$ vertex intervals were sold, only $k$ were spoiled by selling some of their items with edge pairs. These $k$ vertices can be used as a vertex cover. On the other hand, suppose not all edge pairs were sold. Then the revenue could be increased by selling the rest of the edge pairs even if it means spoiling additional vertex bundles because edge pairs carry a price of 2 while vertex interval bundles only have price 1. This implies that it is possible, by selling all of the edge item pairs, to acheive revenue $r' = 2 \cdot |E| + |V| - k' > r$ so that $k' < k$, where $k'$ represents the size of a possible vertex cover. ■

**Corollary 2** *The problem of optimally clearing bids that bundle together at most two connected components of a line item graph is* NP*-hard because joining the two lines of item graphs of the form discussed in Theorem 4 constitutes a trivially correct reduction.*

## Constructing a line graph is hard even with 5 connected sets

We now move on to the task of constructing a simple item graph that is valid when bids are allowed to consist of multiple components. The graph construction question is perhaps less interesting here because, as we just showed, clearing remains hard even if we are given an item line graph. Nevertheless, the graph may still be helpful in reducing the clearing time: maybe the clearing time bound can be reduced to a smaller exponential function, or maybe it can reduce the clearing time in practice. In this section, we show that unfortunately, detecting whether a valid line graph exists with multiple (5) components is also NP-complete.

**Lemma 2** *Suppose a bid is allowed to contain up to $k$ connected components of items. Then, if there are $m \geq 2k + 5$ items, there exists a set of $O(m^k)$ bids such that there is exactly one line graph (one ordering of the items, up to symmetry) consistent with these bids.*

**Proof**: Label the items 1 through $m$. For any subset of $k+1$ items of which at least two items are successors ($i$ and $i+1$), let there be a bid on that set of items. We observe that there are at most $(m-1)\binom{m}{k-1}$ such bids (choosing the successive pair of items first, and then the remaining $k - 1$—of course we are double-counting some combinations this way, but we only want an upper bound), which is $O(m^k)$. Ordering the items $1, 2, \ldots, m$ (or equivalently $m, m - 1, \ldots, 1$), we get a valid item graph (because any two successive items are adjacent in this graph, there are at most $k$ components in every bid). What remains to show is that if the items are ordered differently, there is at least one bid with $k + 1$ components. If the items are ordered differently, there is at least one pair of successive (according to the original labeling) items $i, i + 1$ which are not adjacent in the graph. Consider the set of these two items, plus every item that has an odd index in the ordering of this graph (besides the ones that coincide with, or are adjacent to, the first two). This set has at least $2 + (k + 3) - 4 = k + 1$ items, two of which are adjacent in the original labeling, and each of which is a separate component. It follows that there exists a subset of this set which constituted one of the bids, and now has $k + 1$ components. ■

**Lemma 3** *Suppose each bid is allowed to contain at most $k$ connected components, and we have a set of bids that forces a unique ordering of the items (up to symmetry). Then suppose we replace one item $r$ with two new items $n_1$ and $n_2$, and let every bid bidding on the original item bid on both the new items. Then the only valid orderings of the new set of items are the valid orderings for the original set, where $r$ is replaced by $n_1, n_2$ (where these two can be placed in any order). This extends to replacing multiple items by pairs.*

**Proof**: We omit the proof because of space constraint. ■

**Theorem 5** *Given the bids, detecting whether an ordering of the items (a line graph) exists such that each bidder bids on at most 5 connected components is* NP*-complete.*

**Proof**: The problem is in NP because we can nondeterministically generate an ordering of the items, and check whether any bid is bidding on more than 5 components. To show that the problem is NP-hard, we reduce an arbitrary 3SAT instance to the following sets of items and bids. For every variable $v \in V$, let there be four items, $i_v^*, i_v, i_{+v}, i_{-v}$. Let the set of bids be as follows. First, using Lemma 2 and Lemma 3, let there be $O(m^5)$ bids such that the only remaining valid orderings are $i_{v_1}^*, i_{v_1}, \{i_{+v_1}, i_{-v_1}\}, i_{v_2}^*, i_{v_2}, \{i_{+v_2}, i_{-v_2}\}, \ldots, i_{v_n}^*, i_{v_n}, \{i_{+v_n}, i_{-v_n}\}$. (Here, two items are in set notation if their relative order is not yet determined.) Finally, for every clause $c \in C$, let there be a bid bidding on any $i_v$ with $v$ occurring in $c$ (whether it is $+v$ or $-v$), and on any $i_{+v}$ with $+v$ occurring in $c$, and on any $i_{-v}$ with $-v$ occurring in $c$. (So, 6 items in total.) We show the instances are equivalent.

First suppose there exists a solution to the 3SAT instance. Then, whenever a variable $v$ is set to *true*, let $i_{+v}$ be ordered to the left of $i_{-v}$; otherwise, let $i_{+v}$ be ordered to the right of $i_{-v}$. Then, for every clause, for some literal $+v$ (or $-v$) occurring in that clause, $i_{+v}$ (or $i_{-v}$) is adjacent to $i_v$, and it follows that the bid corresponding to the clause has at most 5 connected components. So, there is a valid ordering.

Now suppose there exists a valid ordering. Because of the $i_v^*$ items, the only items in a bid corresponding to a clause that can possibly be adjacent are an $i_{+v}$ and the corresponding $i_v$, or an $i_{-v}$ and the corresponding $i_v$. This must happen at least once for every bid corresponding to a clause (or the bid would have 6 components. But then, if we set a variable $v$ to *true* if $i_{+v}$ and $i_v$ are adjacent, and to *false* otherwise, every clause must have at least one $+v$ in it where $v$ is set to *true*, or at least one $-v$ in it where $v$ is set to *false*. It follows that there is a solution to the 3SAT instance. ■

## Conclusions and future research

Combinatorial auctions (CAs) are important mechanisms for allocating interrelated items. Unfortunately, (even approximate) winner determination is NP-complete unless there is special structure. In this paper, we studied the setting where there is a graph (with some desired property), with the items as vertices, and every bid bids on a connected set of items. Two computational problems arise: 1) clearing the auction when given the item graph, and 2) constructing an item graph (if one exists) with the desired property. 1 was previously solved for the case of a tree or a cycle, and 2 for the case of a line graph or a cycle.

We generalized the first result by showing that given an item graph *with bounded treewidth*, the clearing problem can be solved in polynomial time (and every CA instance has some treewidth; the complexity is exponential in only that parameter). We then gave an algorithm for constructing an item tree (treewidth 1) if such a tree exists, thus closing a recognized open problem. We showed why this algorithm does not work for treewidth greater than 1, but leave open whether item graphs of (say) treewidth 2 can be constructed in polynomial time. We showed that finding the item graph with the fewest edges is NP-complete (even when a graph of treewidth 2 exists). Finally, we studied how the results change if a bid is allowed to have a few connected components (rather than just one). Even for line graphs, we showed that clearing is hard even with 2 components, and constructing the line graph is hard even with 5 components.

For future research, the most important specific question left open is whether item graphs of bounded treewidth $w$ can be constructed in polynomial time (when they exist), for $w \geq 2$. Another question is whether a line graph can be constructed in polynomial time in the variant where a bid is allowed to have $k$ components, when $k < 5$. Also, we can ask whether we can reduce the runtime bound of the tree detection algorithm. More open-ended future research includes doing experimental work with the algorithms presented here (for instance, comparing their running time to solvers such as CPLEX), and integrating these algorithms into search algorithms as subroutines, as discussed in the introduction.

## Acknowledgements

This material is based upon work supported by the National Science Foundation under CAREER Award IRI-9703122, Grant IIS-9800994, ITR IIS-0081246, and ITR IIS-0121678. Discussions with Jason Hartline and Daniel Sleator were helpful in working out ideas about how to construct an item tree from a bid set.

## References

Akcoglu, K.; Aspnes, J.; DasGupta, B.; and Kao, M. Y. 2002. Opportunity cost algorithms for combinatorial auctions. *Applied Optimization: Computational Methods in Decision-Making, Economics and Finance* 455–479.

Areborg, S.; Corneil, D. G.; and Proskurowski, A. 1987. Complexity of finding embeddings in a K-tree. *SIAM Journal on Algebraic and Discrete Methods* 8:277–284.

Boutilier, C. 2002. Solving concisely expressed combinatorial auction problems. In *AAAI-02*, 359–366.

Cormen, T. H.; Leiserson, C. E.; and Rivest, R. L. 1990. *Introduction to Algorithms*. MIT Press.

de Vries, S., and Vohra, R. 2003. Combinatorial auctions: A survey. *INFORMS Journal on Computing*.

Eschen, E. M., and Spinrad, J. 1993. An $O(n^2)$ algorithm for circular-arc graph recognition. In *SODA-93*, 128–137.

Fujishima, Y.; Leyton-Brown, K.; and Shoham, Y. 1999. Taming the computational complexity of combinatorial auctions: Optimal and approximate approaches. In *IJCAI*, 548–553.

Hoos, H., and Boutilier, C. 2000. Solving combinatorial auctions using stochastic local search. In *AAAI*, 22–29.

Korte, N., and Mohring, R. H. 1989. An incremental linear-time algorithm for recognizing interval graphs. *SIAM Journal on Computing* 18(1):68–81.

Penn, M., and Tennenholtz, M. 2000. Constrained multi-object auctions and $b$-matching. *Information Processing Letters* 75(1–2):29–34.

Rothkopf, M. H.; Pekeč, A.; and Harstad, R. M. 1998. Computationally manageable combinatorial auctions. *Management Science* 44(8):1131–1147.

Sandholm, T., and Suri, S. 2003. BOB: Improved winner determination in combinatorial auctions and generalizations. *Artificial Intelligence* 145:33–58. Early version: Improved Algorithms for Optimal Winner Determination in Combinatorial Auctions and Generalizations. *AAAI-00*, pp. 90–97.

Sandholm, T.; Suri, S.; Gilpin, A.; and Levine, D. 2001. CABOB: A fast optimal algorithm for combinatorial auctions. In *IJCAI*, 1102–1108.

Sandholm, T. 2002. Algorithm for optimal winner determination in combinatorial auctions. *Artificial Intelligence* 135:1–54. Conference version appeared at *IJCAI-99*, pp. 542–547.

Tennenholtz, M. 2000. Some tractable combinatorial auctions. In *AAAI-00*.

van Hoesel, S., and Müller, R. 2001. Optimization in electronic marketplaces: Examples from combinatorial auctions. *Netnomics* 3(1):23–33.

Zurel, E., and Nisan, N. 2001. An efficient approximate allocation algorithm for combinatorial auctions. In *Proceedings of the ACM Conference on Electronic Commerce (ACM-EC)*, 125–136.

# Computing Shapley Values, Manipulating Value Division Schemes, and Checking Core Membership in Multi-Issue Domains

**Vincent Conitzer and Tuomas Sandholm**
{conitzer, sandholm}@cs.cmu.edu
Computer Science Department
Carnegie Mellon University
Pittsburgh, PA 15213

**Abstract**

Coalition formation is a key problem in automated negotiation among self-interested agents. In order for coalition formation to be successful, a key question that must be answered is how the gains from cooperation are to be distributed. Various solution concepts have been proposed, but the computational questions around these solution concepts have received little attention.

We study a concise representation of characteristic functions which allows for the agents to be concerned with a number of independent *issues* that each coalition of agents can address. For example, there may be a set of *tasks* that the capacity-unconstrained agents could undertake, where accomplishing a task generates a certain amount of value (possibly depending on how well the task is accomplished). Given this representation, we show how to quickly compute the *Shapley value*—a seminal value division scheme that distributes the gains from cooperation fairly in a certain sense. We then show that in (distributed) marginal-contribution based value division schemes, which are known to be vulnerable to manipulation of the order in which the agents are added to the coalition, this manipulation is NP-complete. Thus, computational complexity serves as a barrier to manipulating the joining order. Finally, we show that given a value division, determining whether some subcoalition has an incentive to break away (in which case we say the division is not in the *core*) is NP-complete. So, computational complexity serves to increase the stability of the coalition.

## 1. Introduction

Coalition formation is a key part of automated negotiation among self-interested agents. A coalition of agents can sometimes accomplish things that the individual agents cannot, or can do things more efficiently. Besides being of interest to the distributed AI / multiagent systems community, coalition formation has electronic commerce applications as well. For example, consider a large number of companies, some subsets of which could form profitable virtual organizations that can respond to larger or more diverse orders than the individual companies can.

In order for coalition formation to be successful, a key question that must be answered is how the gains from cooperation are to be distributed. This question has been studied extensively in cooperative game theory, and some of the resulting solution concepts have already been adopted in the multiagent systems literature (e.g., (Ketchpel 1994; Zlotkin & Rosenschein 1994; Shehory & Kraus 1996; 1998; Conitzer & Sandholm 2003a)). One objective that these solution concepts pursue is that of *fairness*. For instance, the *Shapley value* divides the value fairly in a certain sense. Another objective is that of *stability*. For instance, a value division is in the *core* if no subcoalition of agents has an incentive to break away and form their own coalition.

The computational questions around these solution concepts have received relatively little attention. (As exceptions, constructing solutions in the core has been studied under a concise representation relying on superadditivity (Conitzer & Sandholm 2003a), as well as for a routing game on graphs (Markakis & Saberi 2003), and a facility location game (Goemans & Skutella 2004).) When it comes to coalition formation among software agents (that represent real-world parties), these questions become increasingly explicit. Additionally, there are many potential commercial applications for methods that compute value divisions with certain properties. For instance, one possible application of being able to compute a value division in the core is to determine how much each employee of a company should be paid so that the company does not collapse as a result of a group of employees being bought away by another company.

One important source of computational complexity could be that each potential coalition has some hard optimization problem, making it difficult to ascertain a single coalition's value. For example, when the agents are carrier companies with their own trucks and delivery tasks, they can save costs by forming a coalition (pooling their trucks and tasks), but each potential coalition faces a hard optimization problem: a vehicle routing problem defined by the coalition's trucks and tasks. The effect of such hard optimization problems on coalition formation has been studied by Sandholm and Lesser (Sandholm & Lesser 1997), but the bulk of research on coalition formation (Aumann 1959; Charnes & Kortanek 1966; Shapley 1967; Kahan & Rapoport 1984; van der Linden & Verbeek 1985; Bernheim, Peleg, & Whinston 1987; Chatterjee *et al.* 1993; Ketchpel 1994; Moreno & Wooders 1996; Okada 1996; Ray 1996; Shehory & Kraus 1996; Milgrom & Roberts 1996; Evans 1997; Shehory & Kraus 1998; Conitzer & Sandholm 2003a) does not address this issue.

A second source of computational complexity, more directly related to the coalition formation process itself, is that even if we can compute each coalition's value, we still need a method to choose a value division among the agents that is consistent with the solution concept. Finding such a value division can be a nontrivial problem. How complex is it? There are other, related, important computational questions as well. For instance, how hard is it for an agent to manipulate (to its advantage) which of the consistent value divisions is chosen? Or, can we perhaps use a weaker notion of stability because it is computationally difficult to find a subcoalition that has an incentive to break away? In this paper we address all of these three questions.

We study the questions in a problem representation where the agents are concerned with a number of distinct *issues* that each coalition of agents can address. (That there can be multiple independent issues does not in any way restrict the settings that we can capture; in the worst case the problem is not decomposable, so there will be just one issue.) For example, there may be a set of *tasks* that the agents could undertake, where accomplishing a task generates a certain amount of value (possibly depending on how well the task is accomplished). Here, each coalition of agents would have a different collective skill set, and thereby achieve a different level of success on each task. We assume that each coalition's optimization problem for each individual issue is solved already (or easy to solve), thereby largely assuming away the first source of computational complexity. This paper belongs to the relatively new set of papers that study computational considerations directly related to value division among the agents—the second source of complexity.

The rest of the paper is organized as follows. In Section 2, we formalize our problem representation. In Section 3, we show how to efficiently compute the Shapley value. In Section 4, we show that manipulating marginal-contribution based value division schemes is hard. Finally, in Section 5, we show that it is hard to determine whether a given value division is stable—that is, belongs to the core.

## 2. Multi-issue characteristic function games

### Characteristic function games

Value division in coalition formation is usually studied in *characteristic function games*, where each potential coalition $S$ has a value $v(S)$ that it can obtain. This assumes that utility is transferable (e.g., payments are possible),[1] and that a coalition's value is independent of what nonmembers of the coalition do. In some settings, nonmembers' actions affect the coalition's value, for example, due to usage of shared limited resources. Such general games can be modeled in the characteristic function framework by either optimistically assuming that the nonmembers will do what maximizes the coalition's value, or pessimistically assuming that the nonmembers will do what minimizes the coalition's value. (In either case, the members of the coalition act to maximize the coalition's value.) The optimistic assumption yields stronger stability (in the sense of the core): if a coalition cannot beneficially deviate even if its value is maximized by the nonmembers, then it certainly cannot beneficially deviate.

**Definition 1** *Given a set of agents $A$, a* characteristic function $v : 2^A \to \mathbb{R}$ *assigns a value to each coalition.*

Typically the function is increasing:

**Definition 2** *$v$ is* increasing *if $S_1 \subseteq S_2 \Rightarrow v(S_1) \leq v(S_2)$.*

The function being increasing entails that adding more agents to a coalition never hurts (in the worst case, they can sit on the side and do nothing). All of our results hold both with and without the assumption that $v$ is increasing.

Another common assumption on characteristic functions is that they are *superadditive*:

**Definition 3** *$v$ is* superadditive *if for all disjoint coalitions $S_1, S_2 \subseteq A$, $v(S_1) + v(S_2) \leq v(S_1 \cup S_2)$.*

The motivation behind this is that, at worst, the agents can pretend that they are in two separate coalitions even though they are joined into a single one. However, superadditivity does not always hold, for any of several reasons: 1. There can be coordination overhead. A larger coalition may need to expend more effort in coordinating the agents in the coalition. 2. The problem of deciding how a coalition will handle its tasks can be a hard optimization problem, and the cost of solving it often increases superlinearly with the number of agents in the coalition (Sandholm & Lesser 1997). 3. There may be some penalty to collusion, for example, due to antitrust laws. 4. In games where a coalition's value can depend on what nonmembers do, and the characteristic function is derived using the optimistic assumption described above, the argument of pretending to be in two separate coalitions does not go through. This is because it would implicitly require all agents to act in the best interest of $S_1$, as well as in the best interest of $S_2$, which may not be possible.

### Concise representation of multi-issue games

We are now ready to present our concise representation of characteristic functions, which involves a decomposition over a number of independent *issues*. Each issue has its own characteristic function.

**Definition 4** *The vector of characteristic functions $(v_1, v_2, \ldots, v_T)$, with each $v_i : 2^A \to \mathbb{R}$, is a* decomposition over $T$ issues *of characteristic function $v : 2^A \to \mathbb{R}$ if for any $S \subseteq A$, $v(S) = \sum_{i=1}^{T} v_i(S)$.*

The following lemmas show that if the functions into which the characteristic function decomposes are increasing or superadditive, then so is the characteristic function.

**Lemma 1** *If $v = \sum_{i=1}^{T} v_i$ is a decomposition of $v$, and each $v_i$ is increasing, then $v$ is increasing.*

[1] In the general case where utility transfers are not necessarily possible, each coalition has a set of *utility possibility vectors*, each of which contains a utility for each agent. If utility is transferable, then the set of utility possibility vectors for a coalition is the set of all utility vectors for that coalition with utilities summing to at most the value of the coalition. We will only deal with the transferable utility case in this paper.

**Proof**: If $S_1 \subseteq S_2$, then $v(S_1) = \sum_{i=1}^{T} v_i(S_1) \leq \sum_{i=1}^{T} v_i(S_2) = v(S_2)$. ■

**Lemma 2** *If $v = \sum_{i=1}^{T} v_i$ is a decomposition of $v$, and each $v_i$ is superadditive, then $v$ is superadditive.*

**Proof**: For disjoint $S_1, S_2 \subseteq A$, we have $v(S_1 \cup S_2) = \sum_{i=1}^{T} v_i(S_1 \cup S_2) \geq \sum_{i=1}^{T} v_i(S_1) + v_i(S_2) = \sum_{i=1}^{T} v_i(S_1) + \sum_{i=1}^{T} v_i(S_2) = v(S_1) + v(S_2)$. ■

The decomposition can lead to a more concise representation if the individual $v_i$ are concisely representable. In this paper, we will study the case where each $v_i$ only concerns a subset of the agents that are relevant to issue $i$. For instance, in a setting where the issues correspond to tasks, some of the agents may not have any skills relevant to a given task.

**Definition 5** *We say that $v_i$* concerns only *$C_i \subseteq A$ if $v_i(S_1) = v_i(S_2)$ whenever $C_i \cap S_1 = C_i \cap S_2$. In this case, we only need to define $v_i$ over $2^{C_i}$.*

Our representation requires the specification of only $\sum_{i=1}^{T} 2^{|C_i|}$ values, exponentially fewer than the $2^{|A|}$ we need to specify in general—presuming the $|C_i|$ are small. We will conceive of the $|C_i|$ as being small (for example, a constant) throughout this paper.

## 3. Computing the Shapley value

We will now review a well-known value division scheme known as the *Shapley value* (Shapley 1953). The Shapley value aims to distribute the gains from cooperation in a fair manner. It has many equivalent characterizations; we will review one that gives a formula in closed form for it.

First consider a different value division scheme, which we will call the *marginal-contribution scheme*. It imposes an order $\pi$ on the agents in $A$, and adds in the agents one by one in this order. An agent's payoff is its marginal contribution to the value of the coalition. This simple value division scheme has its advantages, not the least of which is its simplicity, and we will return to it later. A difficulty that it presents is that the value that an agent receives depends on the order, $\pi$, in which the agents join the coalition. The Shapley value resolves this by averaging each agent's payoff over *all* possible orderings.

**Definition 6** *Given an ordering $\pi$ of $A$, for any agent $a$, let $S(\pi, a)$ be the set of agents in $A$ that appear before $a$ in ordering $\pi$. Then the* Shapley value *for agent $a$ is defined as $Sh(A, a) = \frac{1}{|A|!} \sum_{\pi} (v(S(\pi, a) \cup \{a\}) - v(S(\pi, a)))$.*

To operationalize a value division scheme, the scheme should be associated with an algorithm for finding a value division consistent with the scheme. In the rest of this section we derive a fast way of determining the Shapley value.

We first show that to compute the Shapley value in our representation, we can simply compute the Shapley value for each term $v_i$, and sum these. That is, if the characteristic function decomposes, then so does the Shapley value.

**Lemma 3** *If $v = \sum_{i=1}^{T} v_i$ is a decomposition of $v$, then for any agent $a$ we have $Sh(A, a) = \sum_{i=1}^{T} Sh_{v_i}(A, a)$, where $Sh_{v_i}$ is the Shapley value computed with respect to characteristic function $v_i$.*

**Proof**: $Sh(A, a) = \frac{1}{|A|!} \sum_{\pi} (v(S(\pi, a) \cup \{a\}) - v(S(\pi, a))) = \frac{1}{|A|!} \sum_{\pi} (\sum_{i=1}^{T} v_i(S(\pi, a) \cup \{a\}) - \sum_{i=1}^{T} v_i(S(\pi, a))) = \frac{1}{|A|!} \sum_{\pi} \sum_{i=1}^{T} (v_i(S(\pi, a) \cup \{a\}) - v_i(S(\pi, a))) = \sum_{i=1}^{T} \frac{1}{|A|!} \sum_{\pi} (v_i(S(\pi, a) \cup \{a\}) - v_i(S(\pi, a))) = \sum_{i=1}^{T} Sh_{v_i}(A, a)$. ■

Next, we show that to compute the Shapley value of a function that only concerns a subset of the agents, we need to average over the orderings of only those agents.

**Lemma 4** *If $v_i$ only concerns $C_i \subseteq A$, then for any $a \in C_i$, $Sh_{v_i}(A, a) = Sh_{v_i}(C_i, a) = \frac{1}{|C_i|!} \sum_{\pi_{C_i}} (v_i(S(\pi_{C_i}, a) \cup \{a\}) - v_i(S(\pi_{C_i}, a)))$ (where the $\pi_{C_i}$ are orderings of the agents in $C_i$ only, and $S(\pi_{C_i}, a)$ is the set of agents in $C_i$ appearing before $a$ in ordering $\pi_{C_i}$). For any $a \notin C_i$, $Sh_{v_i}(A, a) = 0$.*

**Proof**: Because $v_i(S) = v_i(S \cup \{a\})$ for any $S \subseteq A$ and $a \notin C_i$, the marginal contribution of an agent outside $C_i$ is always 0, and it follows that its Shapley value is 0—proving the second part of the lemma. For any $S \subseteq A$ and $a \in C_i$, we have $v_i(S \cup \{a\}) - v_i(S) = v_i((S \cap C_i) \cup \{a\}) - v_i(S \cap C_i)$. Using the notation $\pi \Rightarrow \pi_{C_i}$ to indicate that $\pi$ and $\pi_{C_i}$ agree on the order of the elements in $C_i$, if $\pi \Rightarrow \pi_{C_i}$, it follows that $S(\pi, a) \cap C_i = S(\pi_{C_i}, a)$. Combining this with our previous observation, we have $v_i(S(\pi, a) \cup \{a\}) - v_i(S(\pi, a)) = v_i(S(\pi_{C_i}, a) \cup \{a\}) - v_i(S(\pi_{C_i}, a))$. Then, $Sh_{v_i} = \frac{1}{|A|!} \sum_{\pi} (v_i(S(\pi, a) \cup \{a\}) - v_i(S(\pi, a))) = \frac{1}{|A|!} \sum_{\pi_{C_i}} \sum_{\pi:\pi \Rightarrow \pi_{C_i}} (v_i(S(\pi, a) \cup \{a\}) - v_i(S(\pi, a))) = \frac{1}{|A|!} \sum_{\pi_{C_i}} \sum_{\pi:\pi \Rightarrow \pi_{C_i}} (v_i(S(\pi_{C_i}, a) \cup \{a\}) - v_i(S(\pi_{C_i}, a))) = \frac{1}{|A|!} \sum_{\pi_{C_i}} \frac{|A|!}{|C_i|!} (v_i(S(\pi_{C_i}, a) \cup \{a\}) - v_i(S(\pi_{C_i}, a))) = \frac{1}{|C_i|!} \sum_{\pi_{C_i}} (v_i(S(\pi_{C_i}, a) \cup \{a\}) - v_i(S(\pi_{C_i}, a))) = Sh_{v_i}(C_i, a)$, proving the first part. ■

Finally, we show that we do not really need to sum over all possible orderings, but rather just over all possible subsets, if we add an appropriate weighting factor to each term.

**Lemma 5** *We can write $Sh(A, a) = \frac{1}{|A|!} \sum_{S \subseteq A - \{a\}} |S|!(|A| - |S| - 1)!(v(S \cup \{a\}) - v(S))$.*

*Similarly, if $v_i$ only concerns $C_i \subseteq A$, then for any $a \in C_i$, we can write $Sh_{v_i}(C_i, a) = \frac{1}{|C_i|!} \sum_{S \subseteq C_i - \{a\}} |S|!(|C_i| - |S| - 1)!(v_i(S \cup \{a\}) - v_i(S))$.*

**Proof**: We have $Sh(A, a) = \frac{1}{|A|!} \sum_{\pi} (v(S(\pi, a) \cup \{a\}) - v(S(\pi, a))) = \frac{1}{|A|!} \sum_{S \subseteq A - \{a\}} \sum_{\pi : S(\pi, a) = S} (v(S \cup \{a\}) - v(S)) = \frac{1}{|A|!} \sum_{S \subseteq A - \{a\}} |S|!(|A| - |S| - 1)!(v(S \cup \{a\}) - v(S))$. The proof for the $v_i$ is exactly the same, because the formula has exactly the same structure. ∎

We can conclude that our representation allows for fast computation of the Shapley value, if the $|C_i|$ are small.

**Theorem 1** *Suppose we are given a characteristic function with a decomposition $v = \sum_{i=1}^{T} v_i$, represented as follows. For each $i$ with $1 \leq i \leq T$ we are given $C_i \subseteq A$, so that each $v_i$ concerns only $C_i$. Each $v_i$ is flatly represented over $2^{C_i}$, that is, for each $i$ with $1 \leq i \leq T$, we are given $v_i(S_i)$ explicitly for each $S_i \subseteq C_i$. Then (assuming that table lookups for the $v_i(S_i)$, as well computations of factorials, multiplications and subtractions take constant time), we can compute the Shapley value of $v$ for any given agent in time $O(\sum_{i=1}^{T} 2^{|C_i|})$, or less precisely $O(T 2^{\max_i |C_i|})$. This holds whether or not the characteristic function is increasing, and whether or not it is superadditive.*

**Proof**: By Lemma 3, we can simply compute the agent's Shapley value for each individual issue, and then sum these together. By Lemmas 4 and 5, to compute the Shapley value of an individual issue, we only need to sum weighted marginal utilities over subsets of the agents that that issue concerns. The computation of each term in the latter summation only takes constant time, by assumptions made in the statement of the theorem. ∎

Thus, the Shapley value can be computed quickly when the $|C_i|$ are small (especially in the case where the $|C_i|$ are bounded by a small constant, as will be the case in the rest of the paper).

## 4. Manipulating marginal-contribution based value division schemes

We now return to marginal contribution schemes for value division where we do not average over all possible orders (unlike in the Shapley value scheme). In such schemes, we should be concerned that an agent may have some influence over which order is chosen, and will attempt to make the chosen order so that its marginal contribution is maximal when it joins. Choosing the order completely at random has been suggested as a solution to this (with the added bonus that the *expected* value to an agent is its Shapley value). This, however, requires either a trusted source of randomness, or a distributed cryptographic protocol—for instance, each agent could pick a permutation of the agents, submit an encryption of it to all the other agents, and then provide the decryption key once everybody has submitted an encrypted permutation. Then, we can choose the composition of all the permutations as the order with respect to which we compute the marginal contributions. For example, consider a 3-agent example where agent 1 submits the permutation $\pi_1$, where $\pi_1(1) = 2$, $\pi_1(2) = 1$, and $\pi_1(3) = 3$, agent 2 submits the permutation $\pi_2$, where $\pi_2(1) = 3$, $\pi_2(2) = 1$, and $\pi_2(3) = 2$, and agent 3 submits the permutation $\pi_3$, where $\pi_3(1) = 2$, $\pi_3(2) = 3$, and $\pi_3(3) = 1$. The final joining order would then be $\pi_3(\pi_2(\pi_1(1)))$, $\pi_3(\pi_2(\pi_1(2)))$, $\pi_3(\pi_2(\pi_1(3)))$, which is 2, 1, 3. Assuming that the decryption cannot be manipulated, if even one agent picks its order uniformly at random, then the final resulting order will be uniformly random. This is the approach suggested by Zlotkin and Rosenschein (Zlotkin & Rosenschein 1994). However, a problem with this approach remains that it may be possible for an agent to change its decryption key (and thus the plaintext of its submission) on the basis of the plaintexts of the other agents' permutations. This way the agent could again manipulate the joining order to its advantage.

We suggest a different approach to resolving this problem. *Even with perfect control over the (final) order chosen, it may be computationally hard for an agent to determine the order most beneficial to it. We want to use this computational complexity as the barrier to manipulation.*[2] The following problem captures the predicament of a manipulating agent with perfect control over the order chosen.

**Definition 7 (MAX-MARGINAL-CONTRIBUTION)** *We are given a characteristic function with a decomposition $v = \sum_{i=1}^{T} v_i$, represented as follows. For each $i$ with $1 \leq i \leq T$ we are given $C_i \subseteq A$, so that each $v_i$ concerns only $C_i$. Each $v_i$ is flatly represented over $2^{C_i}$, that is, for each $i$ with $1 \leq i \leq T$, we are given $v_i(S_i)$ explicitly for each $S_i \subseteq C_i$. Additionally, we are given an agent $a \in A$, and a number $k$. We are asked if there is some $S \subseteq A - \{a\}$ such that $v(S \cup \{a\}) - v(S) \geq k$.*

We show this problem is NP-complete by reducing the MAX2SAT problem to it (Papadimitriou 1995).

**Theorem 2** *MAX-MARGINAL-CONTRIBUTION is NP-complete, even when $|C_i| = 3$ for all $i$, $v_i$ only takes on values in $\{0, 1, 2\}$ for all $i$, and all $v_i$ (and thus, by Lemma 1, $v$) are increasing (but not necessarily superadditive).*

**Proof**: The problem is in NP because for a given $S \subseteq A - \{a\}$, we can easily compute the marginal contribution of $a$ to this set. To show that it is NP-hard, we reduce an arbitrary MAX2SAT instance (given by a set of Boolean variables $V$ and a set of clauses $C$, each of which contains 2 literals (a literal is a variable or its negation), corresponding to different variables; and a target number $r$ of satisfied clauses) to the following MAX-MARGINAL-CONTRIBUTION instance.

[2] Using computational complexity as the barrier to manipulation has previously been studied in the context of the complexity of manipulating voting protocols (Bartholdi, Tovey, & Trick 1989; 1992; Bartholdi & Orlin 1991; Conitzer & Sandholm 2002; 2003b).

For each variable $v \in V$, there is an agent $a_v$; additionally, there is the agent $a$ whose marginal contribution we seek to maximize. For every clause $c \in C$, there is an issue $t_c$ (so that $T = |C|$). The set of agents that $v_{t_c}$ concerns is $C_{t_c} = \{a\} \cup \{a_v : v \in c \vee -v \in c\}$ (exactly 3 agents because we are reducing from MAX2SAT). The characteristic function $v_{t_c} : 2^{C_{t_c}} \to \mathbb{R}$ is defined as follows. Let $P_{t_c} = \{a_v : v \in c\}$ and $N_{t_c} = \{a_v : -v \in c\}$. Then, for a given $S_{t_c} \subseteq C_{t_c}$, $v_{t_c}(S_{t_c}) = 0$ if at least one element of $N_{t_c}$, and $a$, are *not* in $S_{t_c}$; $v_{t_c}(S_{t_c}) = 1$ if at least one element of $N_{t_c}$ is *not* in $S_{t_c}$, but $a$ is in $S_{t_c}$; $v_{t_c}(S_{t_c}) = 1$ if $N_{t_c} \subseteq S_{t_c}$, and: either $a \notin S_{t_c}$, or no element of $P_{t_c}$ is in $S_{t_c}$; $v_{t_c}(S_{t_c}) = 2$ if $N_{t_c} \subseteq S_{t_c}$, $a \in S_{t_c}$, and some element of $P_{t_c}$ is in $S_{t_c}$. (It is easy to see that each $v_{t_c}$ is increasing.) Finally, let $k = r$, that is, the two instances' target values are the same. We now show the instances are equivalent.

Suppose there is a solution to the MAX2SAT instance, that is, an assignment of truth values to the variables so that at least $r$ clauses are satisfied. Let $V+$ be the variables set to *true*. Then, let $S = \{a_v : v \in V+\}$. Now, if $c \in C$ is satisfied in this assignment, either some variable $v$ whose negation occurs in this clause is set to *false*; or, if this is not the case, some variable $v$ that occurs in this clause (not negated) is set to *true*. In the former case, we have $a_v \in N_{t_c}$ and $a_v \notin S$; so that $v(S) = 0$ and $v(S \cup \{a\}) = 1$. In the latter case, we have $N_{t_c} \subseteq S_{t_c}$ (because the former case did not apply), $a_v \in P_{t_c}$, and $a_v \in S$; so that $v(S) = 1$ and $v(S \cup \{a\}) = 2$. In either case, the marginal contribution of $a$ to this issue is at least 1, so that the total marginal contribution of $a$ is at least $r = k$. Thus, $S$ is a solution to the MAX-MARGINAL-CONTRIBUTION instance.

Now suppose there is a solution to the MAX-MARGINAL-CONTRIBUTION instance, that is, a set $S$ so that $v(S \cup \{a\}) - v(S) \geq k = r$. Then, let our assignment be to set $v$ to *true* if $a_v \in S$, and to *false* otherwise. The marginal contribution of $a$ to an issue (relative to $S$) is either 0 or 1. If the marginal contribution of $a$ to $t_c$ is 1 (which by the previous has to be the case for at least $r$ issues), then either some $a_v \in N_{t_c}$ is not in $S$, or we have that $N_{t_c} \subseteq S_{t_c}$ and some element $a_v$ of $P_{t_c}$ is in $S$. In the former case, the negation of $v$ occurs in $c$, and we have set $v$ to *false*, so $c$ is satisfied. In the latter case, $v$ occurs in $c$ (not negated), and we have set $v$ to *true*, so $c$ is satisfied. It follows that the number of clauses satisfied by our assignment is at least $r$. Thus, our assignment solves the MAX2SAT instance. ■

We observe that the MAX-MARGINAL-CONTRIBUTION problem is not necessarily hard if the characteristic function is known to have special structure. For instance, a characteristic function is *convex* if the marginal contribution of an agent is always increasing in the subset of agents to which the agent is added—that is, an agent always adds at least as much value to a coalition as it does to any subcoalition. In this case, it is easy to see that an agent always wants to be the last in the order.

An interesting aspect of convex games is that in such games the Shapley value and any value division stemming from a marginal-contribution based scheme are always in the core, so the resulting value division is stable (Shapley 1971; Mas-Colell, Whinston, & Green 1995; Osborne & Rubinstein 1994). So, these payoff schemes seem particularly desirable in that setting. It is thus frustrating that, as we discussed above, finding a beneficial manipulation of the joining order in convex games is easy!

The complexity of the MAX-MARGINAL-CONTRIBUTION problem remains open if the characteristic function is superadditive, but not convex.

It should also be observed that, even though the problem of maximizing an agent's marginal contribution is hard in the worst case, there may still exist effective heuristics for finding an order that makes the agent's marginal contribution at least relatively large (even if it is not the largest possible). For instance, if most other agents' skills can substitute for this agent's skills, then it is likely beneficial for the agent to be early in the order. On the other hand, with complementary skills, it is likely beneficial for the agent to be late in the order (convex games are an extreme example of this).

## 5. Checking core membership

We finally consider the best-known stability concept, the *core* (Gillies 1953; von Neumann & Morgenstein 1947). A value division is in the core if no subcoalition has an incentive to break away.

**Definition 8** *A value division $d : A \to \mathbb{R}$ is* blocked *by coalition $S$ if $v(S) > \sum_{a \in S} d(a)$. We say that $d$ is in the* core *if it is not blocked by any coalition.*

Our next result shows that under the multi-issue representation, even checking whether a given value division is in the core is coNP-complete. We first define the problem.

**Definition 9 (CHECK-IF-BLOCKED)** *We are given a characteristic function with a decomposition $v = \sum_{i=1}^{T} v_i$, represented as follows. For each $i$ with $1 \leq i \leq T$ we are given $C_i \subseteq A$, so that each $v_i$ concerns only $C_i$. Each $v_i$ is flatly represented over $2^{C_i}$, that is, for each $i$ with $1 \leq i \leq T$, we are given $v_i(S_i)$ explicitly for each $S_i \subseteq C_i$. Additionally, we are given a value division $d : A \to \mathbb{R}$.*[3] *We are asked whether $d$ is outside of the core, that is, if there is some blocking coalition $S$ with $v(S) > \sum_{a \in S} d(a)$.*

We show this problem is NP-complete by reducing the VERTEX-COVER problem to it (Papadimitriou 1995).

[3]We intentionally do not constrain $d$ to be a *feasible* value division relative to the given charcteristic function ($d$ is feasible if $\sum_{a \in A} d(a) \leq v(A)$). This omission is justified because it does not introduce any new instances of the computational problem: when $d$ is not a feasible value division, it is always possible to increase the value of the grand coalition of all agents to the point where the value division is feasible, without changing the value of any other coalition. This new "valid" instance has the exact same strategic structure as the original instance. Apart from streamlining the definition, omitting the constraint that $d$ is feasible also makes it easier to think about scenarios where there is an outside benefactor that gives some of the agents some additional value to prevent them from blocking the value division.

**Theorem 3** *CHECK-IF-BLOCKED is NP-complete, even when $|C_i| = 3$ for all $i$, $v_i$ only takes on values in $\{0, 1\}$ for all $i$, and all the $v_i$ (and thus, by Lemmas 1 and 2, $v$) are increasing and superadditive.*

**Proof**: The problem is in NP because given a subset $S$, we can compute $v(S)$ and $\sum_{a \in S} d(a)$ in polynomial time, and check if the former is larger. To show that it is NP-hard, we reduce an arbitrary VERTEX-COVER instance (given by a graph $G = (V, E)$ ($|V| > 0$, $|E| > 0$) and a maximal number $r > 0$ of vertices to cover all the edges with) to the following CHECK-IF-BLOCKED instance. For every vertex $v \in V$, there is an agent $a_v$; there is one additional agent $a_0$. For every edge $e \in E$, there is an issue $t_e$ (so that $T = |E|$). The set of agents that $v_{t_e}$ concerns is $C_{t_e} = \{a_0\} \cup \{a_v : v \in e\}$ (we say $v \in e$ when one of $e$'s endpoints is $v$). The characteristic function $v_{t_e} : 2^{C_{t_e}} \to \mathbb{R}$ is defined as follows: for a given $S_{t_e} \subseteq C_{t_e}$, $v_{t_e}(S_{t_e}) = 1$ if $a_0 \in S_{t_e}$ and $\{a_v : v \in e\} \cap S_{t_e}$ is nonempty, and $v_{t_e}(S_{t_e}) = 0$ otherwise. (It is easy to see that each $v_{t_e}$ is increasing; each $v_{t_e}$ is also superadditive, because when splitting a coalition into two disjoint subcoalitions, only one of them can have $a_0$ in it, and the other hence will have value 0.) Finally, for the value division, we have $d(a_0) = T - \frac{1}{2}$, and for any $v \in V$, $d(a_v) = \frac{1}{2(r+\frac{1}{2})}$. We now show the instances are equivalent.

Suppose there is a solution to the VERTEX-COVER instance, that is, a subset $W \subseteq V$ such that $|W| \leq r$ and for any $e \in E$, $\{v : v \in e\} \cap W$ is nonempty. Then consider the set $S = \{a_0\} \cup \{a_v : v \in W\}$. It is straightforward to check that $v_{t_e}(S) = 1$ for all issues, and thus $v(S) = T$. On the other hand, $\sum_{a \in S} d(a) = T - \frac{1}{2} + |W|\frac{1}{2(r+\frac{1}{2})} \leq T - \frac{1}{2} + r\frac{1}{2(r+\frac{1}{2})} < T - \frac{1}{2} + r\frac{1}{2r} = T = v(S)$. Thus, $S$ is a blocking coalition, and there is a solution to the CHECK-IF-BLOCKED instance.

Now suppose there is a solution to the CHECK-IF-BLOCKED instance, that is, a subset $S \subseteq A$ such that $v(S) > \sum_{a \in S} d(a)$. We first observe that $a_0 \in S$, because otherwise we would have $v(S) = 0$ and $S$ could not be a blocking coalition. Now consider the set $W = \{v : a_v \in S\}$ of the vertices corresponding to agents in the blocking coalition. Then, $\sum_{a \in S} d(a) = T - \frac{1}{2} + |W|\frac{1}{2(r+\frac{1}{2})}$. Combining this with $T \geq v(S) > \sum_{a \in S} d(a)$, and using the fact that $|W|$ is an integer, we can conclude $|W| \leq r$. Additionally, we have $v(S) > d(a_0) = T - \frac{1}{2}$. It follows that $v_{t_e}(S) = 1$ for every issue $t_e$, and thus, for any edge $e$, there is an agent $a_v \in S$ (and thus a vertex $v \in W$) with $v \in e$. It follows that $W$ covers all the edges, and is thus a solution to the VERTEX-COVER instance. ■

This result not only implies that it is difficult computationally to use the core as the solution concept, but also that the core may be an unnecessarily strong solution concept. If a value division is unstable in the sense that some subcoalition is motivated to break away, but nobody can *find* this coalition because it is too difficult computationally, then the value division is still stable in practice. Of course, NP-completeness is a worst-case measure of hardness, so it is still possible that in many instances, finding a subcoalition that could do better by breaking off is easy. Also, the computational hardness is not a significant barrier if the instances are small enough.

## 6. Conclusions and future research

Coalition formation is a key problem in automated negotiation among self-interested agents. A coalition of agents can sometimes accomplish things that the individual agents cannot, or can do things more efficiently. In order for coalition formation to be successful, a key question that must be answered is how the gains from cooperation are to be distributed. This question has been studied extensively in cooperative game theory, and some of the resulting solution concepts have already been adopted in the multiagent systems literature. However, the computational questions around these solution concepts have received relatively little attention. When it comes to coalition formation among software agents (that represent real-world parties), these questions become increasingly explicit.

We studied a concise representation of characteristic functions which allows for the agents to be concerned with a number of distinct independent *issues* that each coalition of agents can address. For example, there may be a set of *tasks* that the capacity-unconstrained agents could undertake, where accomplishing a task generates a certain amount of value (possibly depending on how well the task is accomplished). Here, each coalition of agents would have a different collective skill set, and thereby achieve a different level of success on each task. We assumed that each coalition's value determination problem (how it would handle the task/issue) for each individual issue is solved already (or easy to solve), and focused on the computational questions related to value division among the agents. To make our representation concise, we also assumed that each individual issue concerns only a small number of agents.

We showed how to quickly compute the *Shapley value*—a seminal value division scheme that distributes the gains from cooperation fairly in a certain sense. We then showed that in (distributed) marginal-contribution based value division schemes, which are known to be vulnerable to manipulation of the order in which the agents are added to the coalition, this manipulation is NP-complete. Thus, computational complexity serves as a barrier to manipulating the joining order. Finally, we showed that given a value division, determining whether some subcoalition has an incentive to break away (in which case we say the division is not in the *core*) is NP-complete. So, computational complexity serves to increase the stability of the coalition. These results yield a positive picture, where even fairly complex value divisions can be computed quickly, even distributed value division schemes are not too vulnerable to manipulation, and economic instability of the coalition is less of a worry.

For future research, an immediate extension would be to study the questions of this paper in settings where utility transfer is not always possible. More interestingly, is it possible to design new value division schemes that are particularly hard to manipulate, for example, PSPACE-hard or average-case complete? Also, could one construct stability concepts that take into account the complexity of finding a beneficial deviation?

## Acknowledgements

This material is based upon work supported by the National Science Foundation under CAREER Award IRI-9703122, Grant IIS-9800994, ITR IIS-0081246, and ITR IIS-0121678.

## References

Aumann, R. 1959. Acceptable points in general cooperative n-person games. volume IV of *Contributions to the Theory of Games*. Princeton University Press.

Bartholdi, III, J. J., and Orlin, J. B. 1991. Single transferable vote resists strategic voting. *Social Choice and Welfare* 8(4):341–354.

Bartholdi, III, J. J.; Tovey, C. A.; and Trick, M. A. 1989. The computational difficulty of manipulating an election. *Social Choice and Welfare* 6(3):227–241.

Bartholdi, III, J. J.; Tovey, C. A.; and Trick, M. A. 1992. How hard is it to control an election? *Math. Comput. Modelling* 16(8-9):27–40. Formal theories of politics, II.

Bernheim, B. D.; Peleg, B.; and Whinston, M. D. 1987. Coalition-proof Nash equilibria: I concepts. *Journal of Economic Theory* 42(1):1–12.

Charnes, A., and Kortanek, K. O. 1966. On balanced sets, cores, and linear programming. Technical Report 12, Cornell Univ., Dept. of Industrial Eng. and Operations Res., Ithaca, NY.

Chatterjee, K.; Dutta, B.; Ray, D.; and Sengupta, K. 1993. A noncooperative theory of coalitional bargaining. *Review of Economic Studies* 60:463–477.

Conitzer, V., and Sandholm, T. 2002. Complexity of manipulating elections with few candidates. In *Proceedings of the National Conference on Artificial Intelligence (AAAI)*, 314–319.

Conitzer, V., and Sandholm, T. 2003a. Complexity of determining nonemptiness of the core. In *Proceedings of the Eighteenth International Joint Conference on Artificial Intelligence (IJCAI)*.

Conitzer, V., and Sandholm, T. 2003b. Universal voting protocol tweaks to make manipulation hard. In *Proceedings of the Eighteenth International Joint Conference on Artificial Intelligence (IJCAI)*.

Evans, R. 1997. Coalitional bargaining with competition to make offers. *Games and Economic Behavior* 19:211–220.

Gillies, D. 1953. *Some theorems on n-person games*. Ph.D. Dissertation, Princeton University, Department of Mathematics.

Goemans, M., and Skutella, M. 2004. Cooperative facility location games. *Journal of Algorithms* 50:194–214. Early version: SODA 2000, 76–85.

Kahan, J. P., and Rapoport, A. 1984. *Theories of Coalition Formation*. Lawrence Erlbaum Associates Publishers.

Ketchpel, S. 1994. Forming coalitions in the face of uncertain rewards. In *Proceedings of the National Conference on Artificial Intelligence (AAAI)*, 414–419.

Markakis, E., and Saberi, A. 2003. On the core of the multicommodity flow game. In *Proceedings of the ACM Conference on Electronic Commerce (ACM-EC)*, 93–97.

Mas-Colell, A.; Whinston, M.; and Green, J. R. 1995. *Microeconomic Theory*. Oxford University Press.

Milgrom, P., and Roberts, J. 1996. Coalition-proofness and correlation with arbitrary communication possibilities. *Games and Economic Behavior* 17:113–128.

Moreno, D., and Wooders, J. 1996. Coalition-proof equilibrium. *Games and Economic Behavior* 17:80–112.

Okada, A. 1996. A noncooperative coalitional bargaining game with random proposers. *Games and Economic Behavior* 16:97–108.

Osborne, M. J., and Rubinstein, A. 1994. *A Course in Game Theory*. MIT Press.

Papadimitriou, C. H. 1995. *Computational Complexity*. Addison-Wesley.

Ray, I. 1996. Coalition-proof correlated equilibrium: A definition. *Games and Economic Behavior* 17:56–79.

Sandholm, T., and Lesser, V. R. 1997. Coalitions among computationally bounded agents. *Artificial Intelligence* 94(1):99–137. Early version appeared at the International Joint Conference on Artificial Intelligence (IJCAI), pages 662–669, 1995.

Shapley, L. S. 1953. A value for n-person games. In Kuhn, H. W., and Tucker, A. W., eds., *Contributions to the Theory of Games*, volume 2 of *Annals of Mathematics Studies, 28*. Princeton University Press. 307–317.

Shapley, L. S. 1967. On balanced sets and cores. *Naval Research Logistics Quarterly* 14:453–460.

Shapley, L. S. 1971. Cores of convex games. *International Journal of Game Theory*.

Shehory, O., and Kraus, S. 1996. A kernel-oriented model for coalition-formation in general environments: Implemetation and results. In *Proceedings of the National Conference on Artificial Intelligence (AAAI)*, 134–140.

Shehory, O., and Kraus, S. 1998. Methods for task allocation via agent coalition formation. *Artificial Intelligence* 101(1–2):165–200.

van der Linden, W. J., and Verbeek, A. 1985. Coalition formation: A game-theoretic approach. In Wilke, H. A. M., ed., *Coalition Formation*, volume 24 of *Advances in Psychology*. North Holland.

von Neumann, J., and Morgenstein, O. 1947. *Theory of games and economic behavior*. Princeton University Press.

Zlotkin, G., and Rosenschein, J. S. 1994. Coalition, cryptography and stability: Mechanisms for coalition formation in task oriented domains. In *Proceedings of the National Conference on Artificial Intelligence (AAAI)*, 432–437.

# Learning Social Preferences in Games

**Ya'akov Gal**
Division of Engineering and Applied Sciences
Harvard University
Cambridge, MA 02138
gal@eecs.harvard.edu

**Avi Pfeffer**
Division of Engineering and Applied Sciences
Harvard University
Cambridge, MA 02138
avi@eecs.harvard.edu

**Francesca Marzo**
Cognitive Science Department
University of Siena
Siena, 53100 Italy
marzo@eecs.harvard.edu

**Barbara J. Grosz**
Division of Engineering and Applied Sciences
Harvard University
Cambridge, MA 02138
grosz@eecs.harvard.edu

### Abstract

This paper presents a machine-learning approach to modeling human behavior in one-shot games. It provides a framework for representing and reasoning about the social factors that affect people's play. The model predicts how a human player is likely to react to different actions of another player, and these predictions are used to determine the best possible strategy for that player. Data collection and evaluation of the model were performed on a negotiation game in which humans played against each other and against computer models playing various strategies. A computer player trained on human data outplayed Nash equilibrium and Nash bargaining computer players as well as humans. It also generalized to play people and game situations it had not seen before.

## Introduction

Technology is opening up vast opportunities for computer agents to interact with people. In many of these settings, agents need to make decisions that affect the other participants. Many human-computer interactions may be modeled as games, in which human and computer players each have their own choices of actions and their own goals. In AI, game theory has often been used as a paradigm for modeling interaction in multi-agent systems; it prescribes rules-of-behavior for all agents in the game.

However, traditional game theory cannot naturally capture the diversity of human behavior. People play quite differently from game theoretic predictions and their play varies considerably (Kagel & Roth 1995). A multitude of social factors, such as altruism, selfishness and reciprocity have been shown to mediate people's play in games (Camerer 2003). It has proven difficult to derive analytically the extent to which these factors affect the play of different people. To design computer agents that interact successfully with humans and adapt to new situations, we must represent these factors explicitly in our model and be able to learn them.

In this paper, we use machine learning techniques to learn models of how people play games. The model learns a utility function that players use, in which social factors are explicitly represented and defined in terms of players' outcomes.

We explicitly model several types of social factors, ranging from pure self-interest to altruism and including a notion of fairness. The model assumes that people reason about the same types of social factors, but that individuals weigh them differently. The model learns the utility functions deployed by different types of people; it also allows individuals to reason about their preferences with some degree of error. Since each utility function provides a guideline for behavior, learning the utility functions is key to developing a model that can predict which action a player will take.

The learned models were incorporated into a computer agent that interacted with humans and used to predict how a human player would likely react to different actions of the computer player. These predictions were then used to determine the best possible strategy for the computer player.

We implemented our model in a two-player negotiation game that uses the Colored Trails framework, developed by Grosz and Kraus (2004), an environment in which each player has a goal and certain resources are needed to reach it. The players can trade resources, leading to interesting negotiation scenarios. We study a scenario in which one player proposes a trade to the other, who then has the opportunity to accept or reject. Our model learns to predict whether the second player accepts or rejects the offer. This model is then used by an agent taking the role of the first player to help it decide which offer to make.

We tested our model in experiments involving human subjects. In the first phase of the experiments, data consisting of human play was collected. This data was used to learn a model of human play. In the second phase, a "social" computer player using the learned model was compared against two other computer players and against the performance of human players themselves. The social computer player was able to perform better than all the other players. It exhibited a variety of interesting behavior, depending on the resources players started out with and their positions in the game. The model generalized well to play people and game situations it had not seen before.

Most of the work on learning in games (Fudenberg & Levine 1998) has been on learning the strategy of a particular opponent from repeated play against that opponent. For example, opponent modeling has been applied successfully to poker (Davidson *et al.* 2000).

Common to the techniques in this approach is that they focus on learning and evolution within a single repeated game, in which the agent keeps playing against the same opponents. In contrast, our approach to learning has been to generalize from the behavior of some human players to the behavior of other players. We aim to develop agents that interact well with human agents, even those they have never seen before.

Work in AI with regard to learning utility functions within MDPs (Ng & Russell 2000) and probabilistic frameworks (Chajewska, Koller, & Ormoneit 2001) differs from ours in fundamental ways. First, they learn a utility function directly in terms of outcomes of the game. No external factors enter into the utility function, and there is no consideration of behavioral aspects in their model. In contrast, we learn utility functions that are influenced by the social preferences that hold between players. Second, they assume that players choose the pure strategy that maximizes their utility function. We allow for the possibility that players' actions will sometimes contradict their supposed utility function, enabling us to handle noise in people's decisions.

## Behavioral Decision-Making

Social factors play a crucial part in players' reasoning, both in repeated and in one-shot interactions. For example, reciprocal behavior has been shown to appear in the ultimatum negotiation game (Guth, Schmittberger, & Schwarze 1982), contradicting the predictions of traditional game theoretic models. In this game, one player proposes a division of some amount of good to another player. If the second player accepts, the good is divided as proposed, otherwise both players get nothing. The unique sub-game perfect Nash equilibrium of the game is to offer the smallest amount possible to the other player, and for the other player to agree to the proposal. However, numerous experiments have shown that individuals behave differently; most offers consist of half of the goods, and most rejections occur for offers consisting of less than a quarter of the goods.

A growing body of research in behavioral economics is concerned with *social preference* models. These models assume that players consider others' outcomes, as well as their own, when they reason about the game. These models allow players to follow a "social" utility function, exogenous to the game description, in which factors such as the following are explicitly represented.

**Self Interest** A key motivation for players is to maximize their individual utility, as specified by the rules of the game. This is the sole motivation considered by classical game theory.

**Social Welfare** Players concerned with social welfare are interested in the welfare of the group as a whole, as well as their own utility. Such players are willing to sacrifice some individual utility to make others better off.

**Inequity Aversion** A player who cares about fairness is concerned that the outcome be as equal as possible for all players. Such a player is willing to sacrifice individual utility, or to decrease others' payoffs, in order to ensure a more balanced outcome.

Social preference models that depend on these factors have been formalized. Bolton (1991) provides a model that assumes people care about inequity-aversion, in addition to self-interest. Charness and Rabin (2002) propose a model in which players also care about reciprocity; one player is able to punish the other. Bolton and Ockenfels (2002) compare models that measure fairness in terms of relative payoff comparisons with models that use reciprocal measures. Lowenstein et.al (1989) compared several social utility forms and found that a utility function including terms for self-interest, as well as a separate term for positive and negative discrepancies between the parties' payoffs, matched data corresponding to one-shot dispute type negotiation.

Common to these approaches is that models were learned and evaluated in simple scenarios; subjects in the laboratory were allowed to choose between two options, each of them corresponding to a different social feature. These approaches did not attempt to model social preferences in a more complex setting, such as a negotiation game which includes many possible deals. Moreover, they did not explicitly model different types of people interacting together.

There has been no work to date on building a computer agent that learns social preferences through repeated observation of human play. If human behavior presents particular regularities such as described above, and if a model can capture different types of players, then it should be possible to identify the factors influencing people's behavior through the use of computational modeling. An agent based on such a model would be able to generalize to playing new situations and examples of interaction it had not seen before.

## Colored Trails

Our study used the game Colored Trails (CT), designed by Grosz and Kraus. CT is played on a board of colored squares with a set of tiles in colors chosen from the same palette as the squares. One square is designated as the "goal square" and each player has a piece on the board, initially located in one of the non-goal squares. The players have a set of colored tiles. To move a piece into an adjacent square a player must turn in a chip of the same color as the square. Tiles may be exchanged by the players, and the conditions of exchange may be varied to model different decision-making situations.

A player's performance in CT is determined by a scoring function. This function may depend on many factors, such as the player's distance from the goal-square, the number of moves made, and the number of tiles the player possesses at the end of the game. In addition, a player's performance in the game can be made to depend on the performance of other players, by including the score of other players in her own scoring function.

For our study, we use a version of CT in which two players played on 4x4 boards with a palette consisting of 4 colors. Each player has full view of the board as well as the other player's tiles. At the beginning of the game, the two players are randomly placed at two locations on the CT board and allocated four tiles at random, which could include any color in the palette. The distribution of tiles is designed such that it is likely that the game is "interesting". A game is considered to be interesting if (1) at least one of the players can reach the goal after trading with the other player; (2) it is not the case that both players can reach the goal without trading.

The scoring function for the players was set as follows.

- 100 points bonus for reaching the goal.
- 5 points for each tile left in a player's possession.
- 10 points deducted for any square in the path between the player's final position and the goal-square. This path is computed by the Manhattan distance.

The parameters were chosen so that while getting to the goal is by far the most important component, if a player cannot get to the goal it is preferable to get as close to the goal as possible. Furthermore, a player's outcome is determined solely by her own performance.

In each game, each player is designated one of two roles, which determines the possible actions that are available during the game. One player is the *allocator*, the other player is the *deliberator*. The allocator is allowed to propose an offer for exchange of tiles to the deliberator. The deliberator can either accept or reject the allocator's offer. If the allocator does not make an offer, then both players are left with their initial allocation of tiles. The deliberator is not allowed to counter the allocator's offer with another proposal. The score that each player receives if no offer is made is identical to the score each player receives if the offer is rejected by the deliberator. We refer to this event as the *no negotiation alternative*. The score that each player receives if the offer is accepted by the deliberator is referred to as the *proposed outcome* score.

Under the conditions specified above, each game consists of a one-shot negotiation deal between the two players, and a deliberator's reply to the exchange proposed by the allocator completely determines the final outcome of the game.

## Model Construction

This work aims to model human deliberators in the CT game. Our task is to predict whether a deliberator will accept a given proposal. The inputs to the model are $NN_A$ and $NN_D$, the no-negotiation alternative scores for the allocator and deliberator, and $PO_A$ and $PO_D$, the proposed outcome scores for the allocator and deliberator.

To develop the model, we introduce the following features, which represent possible social factors that might affect the deliberator for a given deal:

- Individual-benefit ($IB$) $\quad PO_D - NN_D$
- Aggregate-utility ($AU$)

$$(PO_D + PO_A) - (NN_D + NN_A)$$

- Advantage-of-outcome ($AO$) $\quad PO_D - PO_A$
- Advantage-of-trade ($AT$)

$$(PO_D - NN_D) - (PO_A - NN_A)$$

The features Individual-benefit and Aggregate-utility match the social preferences self-interest and social-welfare that have been shown to contribute to players' reasoning in the behavioral economics literature. We add features to distinguish between two types of inequality. Advantage-of-outcome measures inequality in the final outcomes. Advantage-of-trade measures inequality in the gains received from a trade. In both cases this means that the deliberator has a strict preferences to do better than the allocator.

Given any proposed exchange $x$, a particular deliberator's utility $u$ is a weighted sum of features. The utility function is determined by the weights $\mathbf{w} =< w_{IB}, w_{AU}, w_{AO}, w_{AT} >$. The weights measure the relative importance of each of the social preferences to the deliberator. The utility function is normalized around 0, so a utility of 0 corresponds to indifference between accepting the proposal and rejecting it. We interpret the utility to be not only an indication of which decision to make, but also the degree to which one decision is preferred. Thus, accepting a proposal is more strongly preferred when the utility is a large positive number than a small positive number.

We could try to learn a single utility function representing the preferences of all people, but this would be unlikely to fit many deliberators well; it is not likely that all deliberators behave the same way. On the other hand, if we try to learn a separate utility function for each deliberator, we would need to play against the same deliberator for many rounds before we could learn about that person, and we would not be able to generalize from one deliberator to another. Therefore we assume that there are several *types* of deliberators, where each type has its own utility function. We use a mixture model over types, with a probability distribution $P(t)$ over the set of types. Each type $t$ is associated with its own set of social preference weights $\mathbf{w}^t$, defining a utility function $u^t$.

In addition, while a utility function corresponds to a decision rule, we do not assume that deliberators implement the decision rules perfectly, for two reasons. First, the deliberators' play may be noisy; they may make mistakes and act capriciously. Therefore, we expect noise in the data that could not be explained if the deliberators played perfectly. Second, even if a deliberator falls under a certain type, it is unlikely that her utility function will exactly match that of the type. Rather, it may differ in small ways, which cause her to take decisions that are contrary to the type's utility function.

To capture the fact that a decision rule might be implemented noisily, we use a sigmoid function. We define the probability of acceptance for a particular exchange $x$ by deliberator of type $t$ to be

$$P(accept|x,t) = \frac{1}{1 + e^{-u^t(x)}}$$

In particular, the probability of acceptance converges to 1 as the utility becomes large and positive, and to 0 as the utility becomes large and negative. When the decision is less clear-cut, i.e. the utility is close to zero, the probability of acceptance is close to $\frac{1}{2}$, meaning "mistakes", or decisions that are contrary to the utility function, are more likely to happen.

Given that we have a model describing the deliberator's behavior, the next step is to incorporate this model into a computer agent that plays with humans. In our framework, the computer agent plays the allocator and a human is playing the deliberator. The goal of this step is to maximize the score of the allocator, by exploiting the model of how the deliberator acts. The strategy is to propose the deal that maximizes the expected utility to the allocator. The expected utility is the sum of the allocator's utility of the proposal times the probability the proposal is accepted, and the allocator's no-negotiation alternative score times the probability the proposal is rejected.

We take the expectation of this sum with respect to all of the deliberator utility functions. Formally, let $E$ be the set of all possible exchanges that are available to the allocator. Let $T$ be the set of deliberator types. The computer model will choose exchange $e$ s.t.

$$e = \operatorname*{argmax}_{e \in E} \sum_{t \in T} P(t) \cdot [P(accept|x,t) \cdot PO_A(x) + (1 - P(accept|x,t)) \cdot NN_A]$$

## Learning

The goal of the learning task is to complete the model of the deliberators by estimating the parameters from collected data. Since we are learning a mixture model, the task is two-fold; we must learn the distribution $P(T)$ over deliberator types, and for each type $t \in T$, we must learn the feature weights $\mathbf{w} =< w_{IB}, w_{AU}, w_{AO}, w_{AT} >$ , corresponding to the contribution of each social preference. To solve this problem, we interleaved two optimization procedures, a version of the EM algorithm (Dempster, Laird, & Rubin 1977) and the gradient descent technique, as described in the Results section. We began by placing an arbitrary distribution over deliberator types and setting the feature weights with particular parameter values. We varied the number of types and the initial feature weights for each type.

Each observation $d$ consists of inputs $\mathbf{x}^d = (NN_A^d, NN_D^d, PO_A^d, PO_D^d)$, and response $y^d$, which equals 1 or 0 for "accept" or "reject". To speed up learning, the inputs are scaled to lie in the interval [-1,1], by setting -1 to be the smallest value of the feature and 1 to be the largest.

The deliberator type $t^d$ is unobserved, but we can compute the probability of each type for each data case using the current parameter settings:

$$P(t^d|d) = \frac{1}{Z^d} P(y^d|t^d, x^d) \cdot P(t^d)$$

where $Z^d$ is a normalizing factor. Note that $P(y^d|t^d, x^d)$ is the likelihood of the deliberator's response in the game at data point $d$, according to type $t^d$. This can be computed by plugging the social utility function $u^t$ for the observed game into the sigmoid function.

Computing the new values of the $P(t)$ parameters is straightforward. We compute $E(N_t|D) = \sum_{d \in D} P(t^d \mid d)$ and normalize. The maximization for the feature weights for each type is more interesting. The model for each type is a simple sigmoid belief network (Neal 1992). (In fact, it is a particularly simple sigmoid belief network, because it has no hidden layers.) The maximum likelihood problem for such a network can be solved by gradient descent, using a delta rule.

Since these networks participate in a mixture model, each one makes a contribution to the final output of $P(t|d)$. Therefore the gradient for the model associated with type $t$ is proportional to $P(t|d)$. In other words, the degree to which a training example can be used to learn the weights in a network is proportional to the probability that the network actually generated the data. In the delta rules for these networks, therefore, we multiply the learning rate by $P(t|d)$. We obtain the following delta rule for each feature $j$:

$$w_j^t = w_j^t + \alpha P(t|d) \sum_{d \in D} x_j^d (1 - P(y^d|t)).$$

The $1 - P(y^d|t)$ error term comes from assuming that if the network was a perfect predictor, it would have predicted the outcome $y^d$ with probability 1. The difference between 1 and $P(y^d|t)$ is the degree to which the network is not a perfect predictor.

## Experimental Setup

A total of 42 subjects participated in the experiment, 32 in the data-collection phase and 10 in the evaluation phase. Participants were given a 20 minute tutorial of the game, consisting of an explanation of the rules, the scoring function and a practice game.

Each subject was identified by a serial number, and was seated in front of the same terminal for the entire length of the experiment, which was composed of a number of rounds of Colored Trails. A central server was responsible for matching up the participants at each round and for keeping the total score for each subject in all of the rounds of the experiment. No subject was paired up with any other subject more than once in the same role capacity. Subjects could not observe the terminals of other subjects, and they were not told about the identity of their partner. Participants were paid in a manner consistent with the scoring function in the game. For example, a score of 130 points gained in a round earned a \$1.30 payment. We kept a running score for each subject, revealed at the end of the experiment.

The experiment consisted of two separate phases: data-collection and evaluation. In the data-collection study, 16 subjects played consecutive CT games against each other. Each subject played 12 CT rounds, making for a total of 96 games played. The initial settings (board layout, tile distribution, goal and starting point positions) were different in each game. For each round of the game, we recorded the board and tile settings, as well as the proposal made by the allocator, and the response of the deliberator. We ran two instances of the data-collection phase, each one with different subjects, collecting 192 games. The data obtained from the data-collection phase was then used to learn a model of human play.

The evaluation study consisted of two groups, each involving 5 human subjects and 3 computer players. The computer players, only playing allocators, were automatic agents capable of mapping any CT game position to some proposed exchange. Agent $SP$ proposed the exchange with the highest expected utility, according to our learned social preferences model. Agent $NE$ proposed the exchange corresponding to the Nash equilibrium strategy for the allocator. Agent $NB$ proposed the exchange corresponding to the Nash bargaining strategy for the allocator. Nash (1971), who addressed the topic of bargaining, gave several axioms which every reasonable bargaining solution must follow. He then showed that the deal which maximized the product of the agents' utilities is the sole solution to the set of axioms. An interesting point is that the Nash bargaining solution is always Pareto optimal. In the context of CT, this means that if there is no deal in which both parties do better than not negotiating, this player will not propose an exchange.

At each round, eight concurrent games of CT were played in which members of the same group played each other. The set-up was as follows. One of the human subjects, designated as an allocator, played another human subject, designated as deliberator; each computer player, designated as an allocator, played another human subject, designated as deliberator. The game settings, including board layout, start and goal positions, and initial tile distributions, were the same for all of the games played by members of the same group. Therefore, at each round there were 4 matching CT games being played by the eight members of each group.

Participants were given the same instructions and tutorial as in the data-collection experiment. We expected that telling the participants they would be playing computer agents in some of the rounds would alter their behavior. Therefore, participants were led to assume that they were playing a human at each round.

As before, for each round of CT, we recorded the settings of each game, the proposals being offered by the allocators, and the deliberators' response. The first group played 7 games, and the second group played 14 games, for a total of 21 games, where each game was replicated 4 times with different allocators.

## Results and discussion

We learned separate models for one, two and three possible types of deliberators, henceforth referred to as Model1, Model2 and Model3 respectively. We set prior parameter values for the models as follows. For all models, we used random initial values for the distribution over deliberator types. For Model1 we also set random values for the feature weights. For Model2 and Model3, we assigned each deliberator type with initial feature values that corresponded to different points in feature space, by "highlighting" some features and giving them significantly higher initial value than others. In Model2, one of the deliberator types highlighted advantage-of-outcome and advantage-of-trade, while the other highlighted aggregate-utility. In Model3, deliberator types highlighted advantage-of-outcome, aggregate-utility, and Advantage-of-trade separately.

We ran each model on the data from the data-collection phase. We obtained the following posterior parameter values for each model. Model1, which had a single deliberator type, learned feature weights $(7.00, 5.42, 0.40, 4.00)$ for features individual-benefit, aggregate-utility, advantage-of-outcome, advantage-of-trade, respectively. Model1 described a highly competitive deliberator who only cares about her own outcome and would hurt the other to do better. In Model2, the distribution over deliberator types was $(0.36, 0.63)$ and feature weights were $(3.00, 5.13, 4.61, 0.46)$ and $(3.13, 4.95, 0.47, 3.30)$ for each type respectively. Model2 described two partially altruistic deliberators. They both have high weights for social welfare, while still being competitive; one of the types cares more about advantage-of-outcome, and the other type cares more about advantage-of-trade. In Model3, the distribution over deliberator types assigned miniscule probability for the third type, and resembled Model2 in all other parameter values. We decided to use Model2 in the validation study.

The following table presents the results of the evaluation phase for each of the models used in the experiment.

| Model | Total Reward | Proposals Accepted | Proposals Declined | No Offers |
|---|---|---|---|---|
| $SP$ | 2880 | 16 | 5 | 0 |
| $NE$ | 2100 | 13 | 8 | 0 |
| $NB$ | 2400 | 14 | 2 | 5 |
| $HU$ | 2440 | 16 | 1 | 4 |

It lists the total monetary reward, the number of proposals accepted, the number of proposals rejected, and the number of times no offer was proposed. The computer allocator labeled $NE$ always proposed the exchange that corresponded to the allocator's strategy in the (unique) sub-game perfect Nash equilibrium of each CT game. In essence, this resulted to offering the best exchange for the allocator, out of the set of all of the exchanges that are not worse off to the deliberator. As a consequence, many of the exchanges proposed by this agent were declined. We hypothesize this is because they were not judged as fair by the deliberator. This result closely follows the findings of behavioral game theory. The performance of $NE$ was the worst of the four. The computer allocator labeled $NB$ always proposed the exchange that corresponded to the allocator's strategy in the Nash Bargaining profile. This exchange consistently offered more to the deliberator than the $NE$ player did for the same game, when the board and tile distribution enabled it. Because $NB$ tended to offer quite favorable deals to the deliberator, they were accepted more than the other computer players, provided that an offer was made.

The allocator labeled $HU$ combines the monetary rewards for all of the human players. Human offers were almost always accepted, when they were made. The computer allocator that followed our expected utility model, labeled $SP$, achieved a significantly higher reward than $NE$ and $HU$ (T-test comparison for mean reward was $p < .05, p < .1$, respectively). It also had the highest number of accepted proposals, along with the allocations proposed by humans. Interestingly, our model proposed the same offer as the human proposal in 4 of the games, whereas the Nash equilibrium player did not match a human proposal in any game, and the Nash bargaining player matched human proposals in 2 games. This suggests that our computational model would be perceived to be relatively more reasonable, or "human like", by other people.

Next, we describe some interesting behavior displayed by our program. The $NNA$ heading in the following tables represents the no-negotiation alternative situation. First, we show a round in which SP proposed an exchange which was accepted by an altruistic human deliberator. Interestingly, there was only one observation in which an altruistic deliberator agreed to such an exchange, yet it was used 4 times by the allocator in the evaluation phase. This behavior, of asking for a favor when the other player is much better off, was consistently accepted by the human player.

| Model | Allocator Score | Deliberator Score |
|---|---|---|
| $NNA$ | 45 | 170 |
| $SP$ | 70 | 150 |

A second example, in which the proposed outcome of the exchange proposed by $NE$, while beneficial for the deliberator, was lower than the exchange proposed by $SP$. The $NE$ exchange was rejected, while the $SP$ exchange was accepted. This seems to indicate that the responders in this game cared about the equality of outcomes. Note that in this exchange, the $SP$ exchange and the exchange proposed by the human were equal.

| Model | Allocator Score | Deliberator Score |
|---|---|---|
| $NNA$ | 75 | 150 |
| $SP$ | 170 | 170 |
| $NE$ | 180 | 155 |
| $NB$ | 150 | 190 |
| $HU$ | 170 | 170 |

## Conclusion and Future Work

We have presented a computational framework for representing and learning a social preference model of people in one-shot games. The model successfully learns the factors that affect human play and can generalize to people and game situations that were not seen before. We plan to model additional social features, such as the regret that a player might feel from accepting one trade when a more preferable trade was available.

Our current model assumed that observations of play are independent from each-other. We plan to constrain multiple observations from the same subject to originate from the same type.

The CT framework provides a natural test-bed for learning in more complex scenarios, such as repeated games. In repeated games, additional factors are at work, including dynamics of reciprocity and punishment. We also plan to study games involving more than two allocators, where issues of competition between the allocators arise.

While we have focused on one particular game for practical reasons, the learned models we use are cast in terms of general social preferences and do not depend on the specific features of the game. Therefore the learned models should be immediately applicable to other games in which the same social preferences play a role. It will be interesting to see if the model learned for one type of negotiation game will generalize to another type of game.

For our performance measure, we have used the score obtained by our computational agent while playing against humans. One can also imagine setting the goal of trying to play as much like humans as possible. Our learned models would now be used to generate computer play, rather than simply as predictors of human reaction. With the approach described in this paper, it is conceivable that we could build a program to pass a limited Turing test in a negotiation game, in the spirit of the Caltech Turing Test competition[1].

## Acknowledgments

This work was supported by NSF grant IIS-0222892 and NSF Career Award IIS-0091815. We thank Jacomo Corbo and the Harvard AI research group for valuable discussions and programming assistance.

## References

Bolton, G., and Ockenfels, A. 2002. A stress test of fainess measures in models of social utility. Technical report, Max Plank Institute.

Bolton, G. 1991. A comparative model of bargaining. *American Economic Review* (81):1096–1136.

Camerer, C. 2003. *Behavioral Game Theory: Experiments in Strategic Interaction*. Princeton University Press.

Chajewska, U.; Koller, D.; and Ormoneit, D. 2001. Learning an agent's utility function by observing behavior. In *ICML'01*.

Charness, G., and Rabin, M. 2002. Understanding social preferences with simple tests. *Quarterly Journal of Economics* (117):817–869.

Davidson, A.; Billings, D.; Schaeffer, J.; and Szafron, D. 2000. Improved opponent modeling in poker. In *International Conference on Artificial Intelligence(ICAI00)*.

Dempster, A.; Laird, N.; and Rubin, D. 1977. Maximum likelihood from incomplete data via the EM algorithm. *Journal of the Royal Statistical Society* 39(1).

Fudenberg, D., and Levine, D. K. 1998. *The Theory of Learning in Games*. MIT Press.

Grosz, B.; Kraus, S.; Talman, S.; and Stossel, B. 2004. The influence of social dependencies on decision-making. Initial investigations with a new game. In *AAMAS'04*.

Guth, W.; Schmittberger, R.; and Schwarze, B. 1982. An experimental analysis of ultimatum bargaining. *Journal of Economic Behavior and Organization* (3):367–388.

J.Nash. 1971. The bargaining problem. *Econometrica* 18:155–162.

Kagel, J., and Roth, A., eds. 1995. *The hanbook of experimental economics*. Princeton University Press.

Loewenstein, G.; Bazerman, M.; and Thompson, L. 1989. Social utility and decision making in interpersonal contexts. *Journal of Personality and Social psychology* (57)(3):426–441.

Neal, R. 1992. Connectionist learning of belief networks. *Artificial Intelligence* 56:71–113.

Ng, A., and Russell, S. 2000. Algorithms for inverse reinforcement learning. In *ICML'00*.

[1] http://turing.ssel.caltech.edu/

# Methods for Boosting Revenue in Combinatorial Auctions

**Anton Likhodedov and Tuomas Sandholm**
Carnegie Mellon University
Computer Science Department
5000 Forbes Avenue
Pittsburgh, PA 15213
{likh,sandholm}@cs.cmu.edu

**Abstract**

We study the recognized open problem of designing revenue-maximizing combinatorial auctions. It is unsolved even for two bidders and two items for sale. Rather than pursuing the pure economic approach of attempting to characterize the optimal auction, we explore techniques for automatically modifying existing mechanisms in a way that increase expected revenue. We introduce a general family of auctions, based on bidder weighting and allocation boosting, which we call *virtual valuations combinatorial auctions (VVCA)*. All auctions in the family are based on the Vickrey-Clarke-Groves (VCG) mechanism, executed on virtual valuations that are linear transformations of the bidders' real valuations. The restriction to linear transformations is motivated by incentive compatibility. The auction family is parameterized by the coefficients in the linear transformations.

The problem of designing a high revenue mechanism is therefore reduced to search in the parameter space of VVCA. We analyze the complexity of the search for the optimal such mechanism and conclude that the search problem is computationally hard. Despite that, optimal parameters for VVCA can be found at least in settings with few items and bidders (the experiments show that VVCA yield a substantial increase in revenue over the traditionally used VCG). In larger auctions locally optimal parameters, which still yield an improvement over VCG, can be found.

## 1 Introduction

Combinatorial auctions (CAs), where agents can bid on bundles of items, are popular autonomy-preserving ways of allocating items (goods, tasks, resources, services, etc.). They are relatively efficient both in terms of process and outcome, and are extensively used in a variety of allocation problems in economics and computer science.

One of the main open problems in CAs (and the whole field of mechanism design) is designing *optimal auctions*, that is, auctions that maximize the seller's expected revenue (Myerson 1981; Vohra 2001). This problem is unsolved even for auctions with two distinct items on sale (e.g. a TV and a VCR) and two agents. A major advance on the problem was the full characterization of 1-item auctions (Myerson 1981), later extended to the case of selling multiple units of the same item. However, the characterization of multi-item auctions has been obtained only for very specialized models (two items, two agents drawing valuations for the items from the same binary distribution (Avery & Hendershott 2000; Armstrong 2000)).

A related line of research is concerned with bundling decisions of the seller, and the effect they have on revenue. Typically the starting point is the *Vickrey-Clarke-Groves (VCG)* mechanism (Vickrey 1961; Clarke 1971; Groves 1973) (aka. *Generalized Vickrey Auction*), which in the 1-item case is equivalent to the second-price sealed-bid auction. The VCG allocates the items in a way that maximizes the social welfare of the agents (sum of their valuations for the allocated items), and each winning agent pays the minimal valuation that she would have had to bid in order to win the bundle she won. Rather than running a standard VCG, the seller might want to bundle some items together and decide to either sell the whole bundle or not sell it at all (in the extreme case, all items are bundled together). Not surprisingly, a good bundling policy yields higher expected revenue than the VCG. (Palfrey 1983) proves that in certain models, the seller is better off (on an expected revenue basis) bundling the products on sale together when the number of bidders is small and should auction them separately when the number of bidders increases. (Jehiel, ter Vehn, & Moldovanu 2003) show that modifying the objective function of the VCG in favor of allocations that sell all the items together can yield higher expected revenue.

We exploit the benefits of both lines of research. We generalize the idea of artificially making weak bidders more competitive (from Myerson's 1-item auction) and ideas on tweaking the VCG allocation rule (from bundling research). Using these ideas we design a *parametric family* of CAs. Since all attempts to obtain an analytic characterization of the revenue-optimal CA have been unsuccessful, we instead advocate a computer science approach where we algorithmically search for good parameters in this CA family, for the specific setting (seller's prior over the bidders' valuations).[1] Although it may not construct an optimal auction, this practical approach yields significant revenue improvement over the currently used VCG (see Section 6).

[1] In this sense, our approach parallels *automated mechanism design (AMD)* (Conitzer & Sandholm 2002). However, in the AMD work so far, the types of agents had to be discretized, and an optimal mechanism was searched for *without any use of exogenous ideas/results on how to improve the mechanism.* Thus that AMD work only scales to small CAs (Conitzer & Sandholm 2003).

## 2 Framework and notation

We index agents with numbers from 1 to $n$. Index 0 refers to the seller. Items are indexed with numbers from 1 to $k$. The set of all items is denoted by $G = (g_1, \ldots, g_k)$.

In an auction, bidders submit bids for the items and the auction rules determine the allocation $a$ and the payments $t$, where $a_i$ is the bundle that bidder $i$ receives and $t_i$ is the payment by bidder $i$. The pair $(a, t)$ is called the *outcome*.

### 2.1 Utilities and valuations

We make the standard assumption that each bidder $i$ has a quasi-linear utility function $u_i = v_i(a) - t_i$, where $v_i$ is the *valuation function* of bidder $i$. We also make the following standard assumptions: 1) *no externalities*: the valuation of any bidder $i$ for each allocation $a$ depends only on the bundle $a_i$ that bidder receives, not on how the items that $i$ does not receive get allocated, 2) *free disposal*: the value of a subset of a bundle is less than or equal to the value of a bundle ($\forall\, b' \subset b, v_i(b') \leq v_i(b)$), and 3) the valuation for an empty bundle is 0.

Let $V_i$ denote the set of all valuation functions for bidder $i$. $V$ denotes $\times_{i=1\ldots n} V_i$. We make the following standard assumptions from economics:

1. $V_i$ is a convex, compact subset of $\Re^{|2^k|}$.
2. Each valuation function $v_i$ is generated from a continuous density $f_i$ and $f_i$ is positive on all $V_i$.
3. The valuations of different bidders are drawn independently of each other.

A simple example (and an important special case) is the Additive Valuations Model:

**Definition 2.1 Additive Valuations Model (AVM).**

1. *The valuation of bidder $i$ for item $j$, is a realization of the random variable $X_{ij}$ with the density $f_{ij} : [l_i, r_i] \longrightarrow \Re$, and*
2. *The valuation of bidder $i$ for any bundle $b$ is the sum of $i$'s valuations for the individual items contained in $b$.*

The AVM is the most basic model, with no substitutability or complementarity effects (valuation for the bundle of items equals the sum of the valuations for individual items).

In terms of the distributions from which valuations are drawn, two classes of models are considered in literature. In the *symmetric* case, $f_i = f_j$ for all bidders $i$ and $j$. In the *asymmetric* case, valuations of different bidders are drawn from different $f_i$. We will consider both cases.

### 2.2 Mechanism design principles

Each bidder's valuation function is private information (although the auctioneer and other bidders may know the distribution from which it is drawn). Thus a concern is that a bidder might not bid her true valuations for the bundles—she might be able to obtain higher utility by submitting a different valuation function. As is common in much of mechanism design, especially within computer science, we focus on on *deterministic dominant-strategy mechanisms*, that is, mechanisms where each bidder has a strategy that is optimal regardless of what the other bidders do. Such mechanisms are robust in the sense that the bidders do not benefit from counterspeculating each others' valuations and rationality. As is standard in mechanism design, we focus on *incentive-compatible* mechanisms, that is, mechanisms where each bidder's dominant strategy is to bid truthfully. This is without loss of generality in the sense that the well-known *revelation principle* shows that anything that can be accomplished with an arbitrary mechanism can also be accomplished with a truth-promoting mechanism (see e.g. (Krishna 2002)).

It is also important that the mechanism motivates the bidders to participate. A mechanism is *ex post individually rational* if each bidder is no worse off participating than not participating, *for all* possible valuations of other bidders. As does most of auction theory, we focus on such mechanisms.

### 2.3 Vickrey-Clarke-Groves (VCG) mechanism

A classic example that satisfies the above conditions is the following mechanism (Vickrey 1961; Clarke 1971; Groves 1973).

**Definition 2.2 Vickrey-Clarke-Groves (VCG) mechanism.** *Each bidder $i$ submits a valuation function $v_i$. The allocation, $a$, is computed to maximize social welfare*

$$SW(v) = \sum_{i=0}^{n} v_i(a). \tag{2.1}$$

*The payment by bidder $i$ is*

$$t_i = \left[\sum_{j \neq i} v_j(a_{-i}) - \sum_{j \neq i} v_j(a)\right]$$

*where*

$$a_{-i} = argmax_a \sum_{j=0, j\neq i}^{n} v_j(a)$$

*is the allocation that is optimal among the allocations where bidder $i$ does not receive any items. One can also interpret $t_i$ as the minimum valuation for $a_i$ (the bundle won by $i$), which $i$ would have had to bid in order to win $a_i$.*

The VCG is the most popular mechanism in the literature. (In the 1-item case it is also equivalent to the widely used English auction). It maximizes the welfare of the bidders. However, it often yields poor revenue for the seller.

## 3 Revenue maximization in combinatorial auctions (CAs)

In this section we first explain the non-optimal revenue of the VCG, and then describe the general idea of revenue boosting.

### 3.1 Non-optimality of VCG

There are at least two reasons why the VCG mechanism may not yield maximal expected revenue.

1. **Bundling effect.** The following well-known simple example shows that bundling decisions of the seller may affect the revenue.

**Example 3.1** *Consider an auction with $k$ items for sale $(g_1, \ldots g_k)$, and two bidders in the AVM model. The VCG would sell each item separately to the higher bidder, collecting payment equal to the valuation of the lower bidder for each item. So, the revenue is $\sum_{j=1}^{k} \min_{i\in\{1,2\}} v_i(g_j)$. However, should the seller decide to bundle all the items together and sell them as a whole via a second-price mechanism, she would receive revenue $\min_{i\in\{1,2\}} \left[\sum_{j=1}^{k} v_i(g_j)\right]$ which is clearly greater.*

2. **Asymmetry of valuation distributions.** In the asymmetric case, it may happen that the distribution of valuations of bidder $i$ for some bundle $b$ stochastically dominates the distributions of other bidders (we call such bidders "strong" and "weak", respectively). For instance, consider a 1-item auction, where valuation of bidder $i$ for the item is drawn uniformly from the $[2, 3]$ interval, while other bidders' valuations are drawn from $[0, 1]$ interval. Under the VCG allocation scheme bidder $i$ wins the auction, paying just the second-highest bid price, while it would be easy to improve revenue beyond that by charging (at least) 2, which is the lowest possible valuation of bidder $i$.

### 3.2 Priors in mechanism design

Before discussing the methods for boosting revenue, we need to make a point about the use of priors, $f_i$, (on bidders' valuations) in mechanism design. The VCG is prior-free, since it does not use information about $f_i$'s in the allocation rule or payment rule. Although being prior-free is desirable (because the auctioneer can run the mechanism with less information), no prior-free mechanism can guarantee even a fraction of the optimal revenue:

**Proposition 3.1** *For every prior-free, incentive-compatible, individually-rational deterministic CA mechanism $M$, and every $\epsilon > 0$, there exist distributions of valuation functions $V$, such that*

$$\frac{E_v(R_M(v))}{E_v(OPT(v))} < \epsilon$$

*Here $OPT(v)$ denotes the revenue-optimal mechanism and $E_v$ denotes the expectation over $V$.*

Although in some special cases prior-free mechanisms may yield good revenue,[2] Proposition 3.1 shows that in order to construct a good general-purpose mechanism we need to use priors. Therefore, we focus on prior-dependent mechanisms (where the designer of the mechanism knows the distributions $f_i$).

### 3.3 Ideas from the Myerson auction

For boosting revenue in CAs, we will draw some ideas from the optimal 1-item auction (Myerson 1981):

**Definition 3.1 Myerson 1-item auction.** *Each bidder $i$ submits her valuation $v_i$ for the item. The mechanism computes* virtual valuations *for the bidders:*

$$\tilde{v}_i(v_i) = v_i - \frac{1 - F_i(v_i)}{f_i(v_i)} \tag{3.1}$$

*The allocation is computed so as to maximize the following objective:*

$$SW(v) = \sum_{i=0}^{n} \tilde{v}_i. \tag{3.2}$$

*Thus, the item is given to the bidder with highest* virtual *valuation.[3] So, the allocation rule is the same as in the VCG (2.2), except that virtual valuations are used in place of real valuations. The payment by the winning bidder is equal to the minimal bid that she would have had to make in order to win (that is, $\tilde{v}_i^{-1}(v_j)$, where $v_j$ is the second highest bid). The item is sold only if the virtual valuation of the winning bidder is above 0. All losing bidders pay nothing.*

The intuition behind the mechanism is that it is biased in favor of weak bidders, creating an artificial competition between weak and strong bidders, and extracting more revenue from strong bidders. It is easy to check that the transformation (3.1) brings down the valuations of strong bidders more than those of weak bidders. Such a mechanism allows the auctioneer to set a high sell price for a strong bidder while motivating her to stay truthful (even if she is sure that her valuation exceeds valuation of any other bidder).

Drawing from this intuition, we propose increasing revenue in CAs by designing certain virtual valuations, and then running VCG on those valuations. We argue that virtual valuations are capable of improving VCG in both asymmetry handling and bundling aspects. In the next section we discuss the forms of virtual valuations that we use.

## 4 Techniques for boosting revenue in CAs

In this section we introduce two families of CAs that employ virtual valuations, and a hybrid family that combines the two. We then analyze the restrictions that individual rationality and incentive compatibility impose on virtual valuations.

### 4.1 Bidder weighting technique

**Definition 4.1 Weighted auction.** *An allocation, $a$, is chosen that maximizes*

$$SW^{\mu}(v) = \sum_{i=0}^{n} \mu_i v_i(a) \tag{4.1}$$

*The parameters, $\mu$, of the mechanism are positive real numbers, chosen* in advance *by the auctioneer, based on the priors on bidders' valuations. The payments by the bidders are*

$$t_i = \frac{1}{\mu_i}\left[\sum_{j\neq i} \mu_j v_j(a_{-i}) - \sum_{j\neq i} \mu_j v_j(a)\right]$$

The mechanism effectively replaces the valuation function $v_i$ of bidder $i$ with $\mu_i v_i$. This is useful in asymmetric cases when valuations of some bidders are concentrated around higher values than those of other bidders. The proof

[2] For example, in the symmetric case, the VCG revenue is asymptotically optimal as the number of bidders approaches infinity (Monderer & Tennenholtz 1999).

[3] For the mechanism to be incentive compatible, $\tilde{v}_i$ should be increasing in $v_i$. If (3.1) does not satisfy this condition, an "ironing" technique is used to make $\tilde{v}_i$ non-decreasing (Myerson 1981).

of incentive compatibility of this mechanism follows that of the VCG.

In many cases the same bidder can be strong w.r.t. some bundle and weak w.r.t. another bundle. It would thus seem to be helpful to allow the mechanism to assign a bidder different weights for different bundles. However it is easy to show that such a mechanism is not incentive compatible:

**Proposition 4.1** *No mechanism that chooses an allocation, a, that maximizes* $SW^{\mu(a)}(v) = \sum_{i=0}^{n} \mu_i(a_i)v_i(a)$ *is incentive compatible for all possible valuations in the CA domain (unless* $\mu_i(a_i)$ *is constant over* $a_i$*).*

Proofs are omitted due to limited space.

### 4.2 Allocation boosting technique

Proposition 4.1 shows that there does not exist a general bundle- and bidder-specific multiplicative weighting mechanism. However, it turns out that it is possible to give a bidder bundle-specific advantage in an incentive-compatible way by using *additive* terms. Let $\lambda_{\{i,b\}}(a) = c_{\{i,b\}}$ for all allocations $a$ that give bidder $i$ exactly bundle $b$, and $\lambda_{\{i,b\}}(a) = 0$ otherwise (as before, lambda's are chosen *in advance* by the auctioneer, based on the priors on valuations of the bidders). Here, the $c_{\{i,b\}}$ values are real numbers that the auction designer sets. We call this the *allocation boosting technique*.

### 4.3 Bidder weighting *and* allocation boosting

Now, a mechanism that uses both *allocation boosting* and *bidder weighting* can be defined as follows:

**Definition 4.2 Virtual valuations CA (VVCA).** *The mechanism computes an allocation a that maximizes*

$$SW_\lambda^\mu(v) = \sum_{i=0}^{n} [\mu_i v_i(a) + \lambda_{\{i,a(i)\}}(a)] \qquad (4.2)$$

*where* $\mu$ *are positive. The payment rule is*

$$t_i(\mu, \lambda, v) = \frac{1}{\mu_i}\Bigg[\sum_{j\neq i}[\mu_j v_j(a_{-i}) + \lambda_{\{j,a_j\}}(a_{-i})] - \sum_{j\neq i}[\mu_j v_j(a) + \lambda_{\{j,a_j\}}(a)] - \lambda_{\{i,a_i\}}(a)\Bigg]$$

VVCA is a family of mechanisms, parameterized by $\mu$ and $\lambda$. It also includes the VCG. By analogy to Myerson's auction, $\mu_i v_i(a) + \lambda_{\{i,a(i)\}}$ can be viewed as a virtual valuation $[\tilde{v}_i]_\lambda^\mu$ of bidder $i$ for allocation $a$.

The mechanism adds $c_{\{i,b\}}$ to the value of the objective on allocations where bidder $i$ gets bundle $b$.[4] Obviously the probability of bidder $i$ winning $b$ under the rule 4.2 is increasing in $c_{\{i,b\}}$. The proof of the truthfulness of the mechanism above also follows that of the VCG.

[4] The basic idea of adding an allocation-specific constant to the objective was introduced in (Jehiel, ter Vehn, & Moldovanu 2003) for the purpose of tuning the bundling policy. Their $\lambda$-*auction* can be viewed as a special case of the VVCA where 1) no weights are used ($\mu = 1$ for all $i$), and 2) the same fixed additive term is added to the objective whenever all items are sold to the same bidder (*i.e.*, $\lambda_{\{i,b\}}(a) = c$ if all items are sold in one bundle $b$ to bidder $i$, and $\lambda_{\{i,b\}}(a) = 0$ for all other bundles). In the symmetric AVM model, they show that the $\lambda$-auction can increase the revenue over both pure bundling auctions (which always sells all the items together) and separate auctioning of individual items (this is what the VCG does in the AVM model).

### 4.4 Impossibility of nonlinear virtual valuations

Incentive-compatibility imposes limitations on the virtual valuations that can be used in the mechanism. In 1-item auctions, it is sufficient for the virtual valuations $\tilde{v}_i$ to be increasing in $v_i$ (Myerson 1981). However, this is not sufficient in CAs. (Lavi, Mu'Alem, & Nisan 2003) recently showed that under certain natural assumptions, every *(ex post)* incentive-compatible CA is almost[5] an affine maximizer.

**Definition 4.3 Affine Maximizer Auction (AMA).** *The allocation is computed so as to maximize*

$$SW_\lambda^\mu(v) = \sum_{i=0}^{n} \mu_i v_i(a) + \lambda(a) \qquad (4.3)$$

*Here* $\mu_i$ *are positive and* $\lambda(a)$ *is arbitrary. The payments are*

$$t_i = \frac{1}{\mu_i}\Bigg[\sum_{j\neq i} \mu_j v_j(a_{-i}) + \lambda(a_{-i}) - \sum_{j\neq i} \mu_j v_j(a) - \lambda(a)\Bigg]$$

It is easy to see that VVCA mechanisms are a strict subset of AMAs. The results of (Lavi, Mu'Alem, & Nisan 2003) imply that every "reasonable" *(ex post)* incentive-compatible and individually-rational *general* mechanism is an AMA. (Non-AMAs might be truthful for some specific distributions of valuations, only AMAs are truthful for *all* CA settings.) Therefore, among mechanisms that are based on virtual valuations, only those which use linear virtual valuations ($\tilde{v}_i$ linear in $v_i$) are incentive compatible. Our VVCA captures all linear virtual valuations, and is thus the most general class of incentive-compatible CA mechanism that use virtual valuations.

### 4.5 Bidder-specific reserve prices

Despite the simple form of VVCA, manipulating the parameters $(\mu, \lambda)$ is a powerful tool. For instance, it allows the auction designer to enforce or prevent any bidder from receiving a certain bundle. Another important property of the VVCA is that it allows for bidder-specific reserve prices. (Bidder-specific reserve prices are also used in Myerson's revenue-optimal 1-item auction (3.2). Recall that the item is sold only if the virtual valuation of the winning bidder $i$ is above 0, which sets a reserve price for this bidder to $\tilde{v}_i^{-1}(0)$). However, the reserve-price mechanism does not generalize straightforwardly to arbitrary CAs. The standard way to set reserve prices in CAs is to submit fake bids by the seller. That approach does not support *bidder-specific* reserve prices. On the other hand, bidder-specific reserve prices can be achieved in the VVCA: to ensure that bidder $i$ never gets the bundle $b$ for a price below $p_0$, set $\lambda_{\{i,b\}} = -p_0$.

[5] A mechanism is an almost affine maximizer if it is an affine maximizer for sufficiently high valuations. (Lavi, Mu'Alem, & Nisan 2003) conjecture that the "almost" qualifier is merely technical, and can be removed in future research.

## 5 Searching for good parameters

VVCA and AMA define families of mechanisms, parameterized by $(\lambda, \mu)$. Depending on the value of the parameters, the seller's expected revenue may be greater or less than in the VCG. In this section we discuss the problem of choosing parameters that yield high revenue.

The seller's expected revenue in VVCA is

$$R(\mu, \lambda, v) = \sum_{i=1}^{n} t_i(\mu, \lambda, v) = \qquad (5.1)$$

$$-(n-1)SW_\lambda^\mu(v) - \sum_{i=1}^{n} \lambda_{\{i,a(i)\}} + \sum_{i=1}^{n} [SW_{-i}]_\lambda^\mu(v)$$

The following Proposition proves that $E_v\big[R(\mu, \lambda, v)\big]$ is a "well behaved" function of $(\lambda, \mu)$ and therefore suggests the use of numerical methods (as hill-climbing) for estimating (locally) optimal values of those parameters. That requires evaluating $E_v\big[R(\mu, \lambda, v)\big]$ for given $(\lambda, \mu)$, which can be estimated by sampling valuations from the distributions $f_i$.

**Proposition 5.1** *The expected revenue of the AMA (and consequently VVCA) is continuous and almost everywhere differentiable in $\mu$ and $\lambda$.*

Finding $R(\mu, \lambda, v)$ for a given set of valuations $v$ requires determining the affine maximizing allocation (4.2). This winner determination problem is known to be NP-complete, but can be optimally solved for relatively large instances in practice. Any optimal winner determination algorithm for CAs can be used here; the affine maximization problem can be converted into the standard combinatorial auction winner determination problem by preprocessing the bids with the multiplicative and additive terms. In the AVM model, an important special case, the optimal allocation is trivial to find: every item is sold to the bidder with highest $[\tilde{v}_i]_\lambda^\mu$.

The main problem in optimization is that the number of parameters in $(\lambda, \mu)$ is exponential in the number of items for sale: $\mu$ is just a vector of size $n$, but the length of $\lambda$ is $n * 2^k$ (for every bidder we have one parameter for every bundle) for VVCA and $n^k$ for AMA. It would be helpful if we could discard some choices of $\lambda_{\{i,b\}}$ beforehand (e.g. by setting them to 0), thereby simplifying the optimization process. Unfortunately, the theorem below shows that there cannot exist a polynomial-time algorithm capable of always determining the optimal value for *any* $\lambda_{\{i,b\}}$, even if the valuations of the bidders are given. Moreover, no polynomial-time algorithm can always determine whether the mechanism with $\lambda_{\{i,b\}}$ set to some particular value $\lambda_1$ yields higher revenue then the mechanism with $\lambda_{\{i,b\}}$ set to $\lambda_2$.

**Theorem 5.1** *For any bundling parameter in VVCA (and AMA) - $\lambda_{\{i,b\}}$ - and any pair of values of this parameter - ($\lambda_1$ and $\lambda_2$) there does not exist an algorithm that determines whether $R(\mu, (\lambda_{-\{i,b\}}, \lambda_1)) > R(\mu, (\lambda_{-\{i,b\}}, \lambda_2))$ in polynomial time, even if the valuations $v$ of the bidders are given, unless P=NP. (Here $\lambda_{-\{i,b\}}$ denotes the set of all $\lambda$ parameters except for $\lambda_{\{i,b\}}$.)*

Theorem 5.1 shows that there is no easy *general* method to decide whether one set of parameters is better than another. Therefore, there is no easy way to fix some of the parameters up front without compromising optimality. Any search algorithm that guarantees the optimum for *any* distribution of valuations must run optimization in all $n * 2^k$ parameters (and therefore uses an exponential number of optimization runs). A related problem is that the surface of $E_v\big[R(\mu, \lambda, v)\big]$ is non-convex even in simple mechanisms, see Figure 6.1. The latter makes optimization complicated.

However, the problem can be addressed as follows. If the number of items and bidders is small, run optimization in all $n * 2^k$ parameters and find a close to optimal solution (see Section 6). For larger problems we can find the local optimum (for example, by hill climbing with the VCG as the starting point, thus yielding higher revenue than the VCG). Also, for some *special* distributions, mechanisms for finding the optimal values of parameters might exist.

## 6 Experiments

In this section we demonstrate how the suggested methodology can be used. The approach of this paper is a form of automated mechanism design (AMD) (Conitzer & Sandholm 2002; 2003). The main difference is that the mechanisms' space is restricted to mechanisms of the VVCA form. Although this may not yield an optimal mechanism (while traditional AMD does), this approach drastically simplifies the computation. It thus scales to larger problem instances. It also handles settings where the distributions of valuations are continuous (unlike in traditional AMD).

We now consider several example problems. We compare the revenue of VVCA to the revenue of the VCG and AMA. (The parameters of VVCA and AMA were determined using a hill-climbing procedure, starting at all points of a fine multidimensional grid; this does not guarantee optimality of the solution, but it is extremely likely that this method finds the optimum for the examples considered). The expected revenues were computed by sampling the valuations from the specified distributions (100000 samples were drawn, where each sample included one valuation function for each bidder) and running the auction in question on each sample. *Consider an auction setting with 2 items, $g_1$ $g_2$, and 2 bidders with valuation functions $v_1$ and $v_2$, correspondingly. Assume $v_1(g_1)$ and $v_1(g_2)$ are drawn from the distribution $F_1$. $v_2(g_1)$, and $v_2(g_2)$ are drawn from the distribution $F_2$. The valuation of bidder 1 for the bundle of two items is given by $v_1(g_{12}) = v_1(g_1) + v_1(g_2) + c_1$ where $c_1$ is a complementarity parameter drawn from distribution $C$. Similarly $v_2(g_{12}) = v_2(g_1) + v_2(g_2) + c_2$ where $c_2$ is also drawn from $C$.*

The results for various distributions $F_1, F_2, C$ are given in the following table. The columns correspond to the experiments with various valuation models: **Ex. I** - AMA model, **Ex. II** - symmetric model with substitutabilities/complementarities, **Ex. III** - asymmetric model with substitutabilities/complementarities. The first three rows specify distributions $F_1, F_2, C$, the last three - the expected revenue on these distributions in VCG, optimal AMA found and optimal VVCA found. We give the revenue estimate and 95% confidence intervals for the estimated values (in tiny font). $U[a, b]$ denotes a uniform distribution on $[a, b]$.

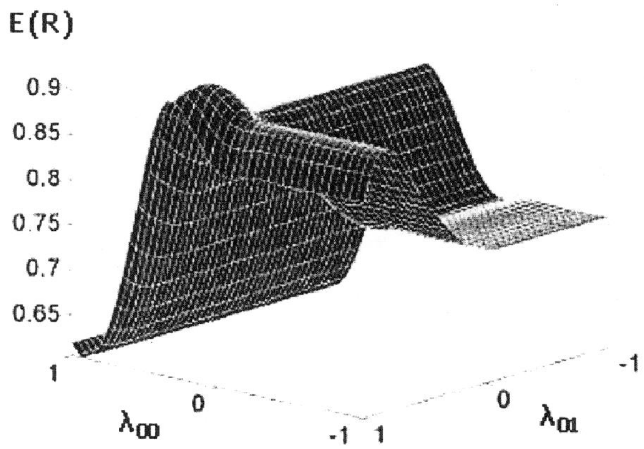


Figure 6.1: *3-dimensional projection in $(\mu, \lambda)$ space of the expected revenue surface of the AMA mechanism in Experiment I. All $\mu$ and $\lambda$ are fixed, except for the following $\lambda$ parameters: $\lambda_{00}$ favors allocations where both items are kept by the seller, and $\lambda_{10}$ favors allocations where item 1 is allocated to bidder 1 and the other item is kept. The analogous parameters $\lambda_{01}$ (referring to bidder 1 and item 2), $\lambda_{20}$ (bidder 2 and item 1) and $\lambda_{02}$ (bidder 2 and item 2) are set equal to $\lambda_{10}$.*

| | Ex. I | Ex. II | Ex. III |
|---|---|---|---|
| $F_1$ | $U[0,1]$ | $U[1,2]$ | $U[1,2]$ |
| $F_2$ | $U[0,1]$ | $U[1,2]$ | $U[1,5]$ |
| $C$ | $0$ | $U[-1,1]$ | $U[-1,1]$ |
| $VCG$ | $2/3$ | $2.45_{(2.72,2.78)}$ | $2.85_{(2.82,2.88)}$ |
| $AMA$ | $0.88_{(0.86,0.9)}$ | $2.78_{(2.75,2.81)}$ | $4.21_{(4.16,4.26)}$ |
| $VVCA$ | $0.87_{(0.85,0.89)}$ | $2.78_{(2.75,2.81)}$ | $4.20_{(4.15,4.25)}$ |

The experiments show that both the general AMA mechanism and our VVCA mechanisms yield substantial improvement over the VCG even in symmetric auctions. Also, the VVCA is as good as AMA (within the confidence)—at least on these small problem instances.

## 7 Conclusions and future research

In this paper we developed a new approach to the problem of maximizing revenue in combinatorial auctions (CAs). Instead of attempting a full characterization (a recognized elusive problem), we developed methods for automatically modifying existing auction mechanisms to increase revenue.

We introduced two techniques: bidder weighting and allocation boosting and a general family of auctions that uses those techniques. We call such auctions *virtual valuations combinatorial auctions (VVCA)*. All auctions in the family are based on the Vickrey-Clarke-Groves mechanism, executed on virtual valuations that are linear transformations of the bidders' valuations. The restriction to linear transformations is motivated by incentive compatibility (truthfulness). The auction family is parameterized by the multipliers and constants in the linear transformations. VVCAs are a subset of an even more general parametric family of *affine maximizer auctions (AMAs)*.

For VVCA and AMA, the problem of mechanism design is therefore reduced to search in the parameter space (AMA has many more parameters). We proved that the revenue of both VVCA and AMA is a well-behaved function, suggesting the use of hill-climbing methods for parameter search. However, finding the optimal parameters turned out to be a computationally hard problem for both families. Despite that, close to optimal parameters for VVCA and AMA can be found at least in settings with few items and bidders (the experiments on small auctions showed that VVCA yields a drastic increase in revenue over the VCG, and the same revenue (within tolerance) as AMA). In larger auctions, locally optimal parameters can be used. This still yields higher revenue than the VCG because the hill-climbing in parameter space can be started from the VCG auction.

We plan to pursue several extensions to this approach. The most important problem is to show that the proposed mechanism yields a good approximation of revenue compared to the (unknown) revenue-optimal mechanism (if the parameters are set optimally). Another line of research is concerned with the organization of the search of the parameter space: although we proved that any search algorithm which guarantees the optimum for *any* given distribution of valuations must run optimization in an exponential number of parameters, better algorithms might exist for specific distributions. Finally, the approach could be extended to combinatorial exchanges with multiple sellers.

## 8 Acknowledgements

This material is based upon work supported by the National Science Foundation under CAREER Award IRI-9703122, Grant IIS-9800994, ITR IIS-0081246, and ITR IIS-0121678.

## References

Armstrong, M. 2000. Optimal multi-object auctions. *Review of Economic Studies* 67:455–481.

Avery, C., and Hendershott, T. 2000. Bundling and optimal auctions of multiple products. *Review of Economic Studies* 67:483–497.

Clarke, E. H. 1971. Multipart pricing of public goods. *Public Choice* 11:17–33.

Conitzer, V., and Sandholm, T. 2002. Complexity of mechanism design. In *Proceedings of the 18th Annual Conference on Uncertainty in Artificial Intelligence (UAI-02)*, 103–110.

Conitzer, V., and Sandholm, T. 2003. Applications of automated mechanism design. In *UAI-03 workshop on Bayesian Modeling Applications*.

Groves, T. 1973. Incentives in teams. *Econometrica* 41:617–631.

Jehiel, P.; ter Vehn, M. M.; and Moldovanu, B. 2003. Mixed bundling auctions. Working Paper.

Krishna, V. 2002. *Auction Theory*. Academic Press.

Lavi, R.; Mu'Alem, A.; and Nisan, N. 2003. Towards a characterization of truthful combinatorial auctions. In *Proceedings of the Annual Symposium on Foundations of Computer Science (FOCS)*.

Monderer, D., and Tennenholtz, M. 1999. Asymptotically optimal multi-object auctions for risk-averse agents. Technical report, Faculty of Industrial Engineering and Management, Technion, Haifa, Israel.

Myerson, R. 1981. Optimal auction design. *Mathematics of Operation Research* 6:58–73.

Palfrey, T. 1983. Bundling decisions by a multiproduct monopolist with incomplete information. *Econometrica* 51:463–484.

Vickrey, W. 1961. Counterspeculation, auctions, and competitive sealed tenders. *Journal of Finance* 16:8–37.

Vohra, R. V. 2001. Research problems in combinatorial auctions. Mimeo, version Oct. 29.

# Using Contracts to Influence the Outcome of a Game*

**Robert McGrew** and **Yoav Shoham**
Computer Science Department
Stanford University
Stanford, CA 94305
{bmcgrew, shoham}@cs.stanford.edu

### Abstract

We consider how much influence a center can exert on a game if its only power is to propose contracts to the agents before the original game, and enforce the contracts after the game if all agents sign it. Modelling the situation as an extensive-form game, we note that the outcomes that are enforceable are precisely those in which the payoff to each agent is higher than its payoff in at least one of the Nash equilibria of the original game. We then show that these outcomes can still be achieved without any effort actually expended by the center: We propose a mechanism in which the center does not monitor the game, and the contracts are written so that in equilibrium all agents sign and obey the contract, with no need for center intervention.

## Introduction

There has been much interest in AI in mechanism design, the area of game theory devoted to designing protocols for self-interested agents. In the literature (Mas-Colell, Whinston, & Green 1995) it is generally assumed that the mechanism designer has complete freedom in designing the rules of the game. Yet the world is full of strategic situations with rules that already exist and cannot be changed arbitrarily. Recent work on *k-implementation* (Monderer & Tennenholtz 2003) restricts the capabilities of the mechanism designer in a particular way – it can add to any given cell in the payoff matrix, but it cannot subtract. (The interesting results in that line of work concern cases in which, despite that addition, the cost to the center in equilibrium is zero.) The opposite of this setting would be one in which the center can impose fines, rather than bonuses. This in and of itself is not interesting, because with sufficiently large fines any outcome can be enforced. However, suppose the mechanism cannot unilaterally impose fines, but it can do so in the context of a signed contract. Specifically, we consider the following class of mechanisms. Given a game $G$, the center can:

1. Propose a contract before $G$ is played. This contract specifies a particular outcome, that is, a unique action for each agent, and a penalty for deviating from it.
2. Collect signatures on the contract and make it common knowledge who signed.
3. Monitor the players' actions during the execution of $G$.
4. If the contract was signed by all agents, fine anyone who deviated from it as specified by the contract.

Our setting is reminiscent of the work on social laws and conventions (Shoham & Tennenholtz 1997). There too the center can offer a *social convention* to the players, where each player agrees to a particular outcome so long as the other players play their part. The difference is that in that work it is assumed that, once all agents agree, the center has the power to enforce that outcome. Here we assume that players still have the freedom to choose whether or not to honor the agreement; the challenge is to design a mechanism such that, in equilibrium, they will.

The technical results of this paper will refer to games of complete information, but for intuition consider the example of online auctions, such as those conducted by eBay. Consider the complete game being played, including the decision after the close of the auction by the seller of whether to deliver the good and by the buyer of whether to send payment. Straightforward analysis shows that that the equilibrium is for neither to keep his promise, and the experience with fraud on eBay (Hafner 2004) demonstrates that the problem is not merely theoretical. It would be in eBay's interest to find a way to enable its customers to bind themselves to their promises.

Our first interest will be to characterize the achievable outcomes: What outcomes may the center suggest, with associated penalties, that the agents will accept? Our first result will be an observation that the center's power is quite broad: Any outcome will be accepted when accompanied by appropriate fines, so long as the payoffs of each agent in that outcome are better than that player's payoffs in *some* equilibrium of the original game.

Although the center can achieve almost any outcome, we note that the helpful center expends a large amount of effort to do so: suggesting an outcome, collecting signatures, observing the game, and enforcing the contracts. If this procedure happens not just for one game, but for hundreds or thousands per day, the center may wish to find a way to avoid this burden while still achieving the same effect.

*This work was supported in part by the National Science Foundation under ITR IIS-0205633.

The bulk of this paper concerns ways in which this reduction in effort can be achieved. We continue to assume that the center still needs to propose a contract. We also simply assume that it does not monitor the game. Nor does it participate in the signing phase; the agents do that among themselves using a broadcast channel. While we might imagine that the players could simply broadcast their signatures, this protocol allows a single player to learn the others' signatures and threaten them with fines. Nonetheless, we can construct a more complicated protocol - using a second stage of contracts - which does not require the center's participation. The only phase in which the center's protocol requires it to get involved under some conditions is the enforcement stage. However, our goal will be to devise contracts so that, *in equilibrium*, at this stage too the center sits idle. Our results here will be as follows. If the game play is *verifiable* (if the center can discover after the fact how the game played out), we can achieve all of the outcomes achievable by a fully engaged center. If the game is not verifiable then we can still achieve all previously achievable outcomes with some contract, but that contract might allow equilibria with additional outcomes.

The rest of the paper is organized as follows: we first formally define our setting. Then we characterize the set of outcomes which are achievable with a busy center using contracts in this game. Finally, we lighten the load on the center first in the enforcement stage, then in the signature exchange stage.

## Formal Setting

The strategic situation the center wishes to influence can be characterized as a *strategic-form game* with consequences in $O$: $G = \langle N, A, O, g, V\rangle$. (We roughly follow the notation of (Osborne & Rubinstein 1994).) Here $N$ is the set of players $\{1...n\}$. $A = A_1 \times A_2 \times ... \times A_n$, where $A_i$ is the set of actions which can be taken by an individual agent. We will use $a_i$ to refer to an action of $i$ in $G$ and $a_{-i}$ to refer to the vector of actions of all other players. $O$ is the space of outcomes; $g : A \to O$ determines the outcome after an action profile. We identify each outcome $o_{(a_i,a_{-i})}$ with a distinct action profile $(a_i, a_{-i})$, and assume $g(a_i, a_{-i}) = o_{(a_i,a_{-i})}$. $V = V_1 \times V_2 \times ... \times V_n$, where $V_i : A \to \mathbb{R}$ is the pay-off function for player $i$.

Before this strategic situation $G$ occurs, the helpful center suggests a contract to the players. This contract specifies the outcome $o$ suggested by the center and what actions $h$ the center will take in response to different action profiles of the players. The center will not enforce this contract unless it is signed by all players. This contract defines the center's protocol in the enforcement stage $H$, as described below. We will denote a contract that describes a particular center protocol $h$ as $c_h$.

Now we will describe the stages of the game, as initially formulated. We will adjust this formulation in later sections so that the center does no work in equilibrium.

**Signature Exchange Stage F** Each player who assents sends his signature on the contract to the center, who collects them. The center notifies all players of the identities of the signers. At the end of this stage, it is common knowledge whether or not the contract will be enforced.

**Execution Stage G** The players play the game $G$. Each player may take his action $a_i$ to achieve $o$ or he may not. The center observes the actions taken by the players.

**Enforcement Stage H** The center takes the actions specified in the contract in response to the actions he observed.

The outcomes are a consequence of the execution stage, but the only way the center can affect the players' actions in the is by fining them in the enforcement stage.

The extended game which arises from playing the stage games one after another we denote by $X = F \cdot G \cdot H$. Together, these define an *extensive-form game with simultaneous moves*. In general, an extensive-form game $X$ can be defined as $X = \langle N, \Omega, A_\omega, P, U\rangle$, where $N$ is again the players, $\Omega$ is the set of histories of actions taken, $A_\omega$ is the set of actions for all players that can be taken after history $\omega$, $P : \Omega \to 2^N$ is the player function that defines which players get to move after a given history, and $U$ is the utility function of players in the entire game.

In our particular setting, the history $\omega$ is just the set of actions taken in each stage game played so far, $A_\omega$ is the set of actions possible in each stage game following history $\omega$, $P$ is the set of all players (all players move simultaneously in each stage), and $U$ is the (undiscounted) sum of the utilities of each stage game. We denote the subgame of $X = \langle N, \Omega_{|\omega}, A_{|\omega}, P_{|\omega}, U_{|\omega}\rangle$ that arises after history $\omega$ by $\Gamma(\omega)$, which simply refers to the play of the remaining stage games following the actions taken in $\omega$. In later sections, we will refer to the strategy space of stage $F$ as $\Gamma^F$, of stage $G$ as $\Gamma^G$, and of stage $H$ as $\Gamma^H$.

A *pure strategy* $\sigma_i$ for player $i$ in a strategic-form game corresponds to the choice of a single action $\sigma_i \in A_i$. A *mixed strategy* corresponds to the choice of a distribution over actions: $\sigma_i \in \Delta A_i$. A pure strategy in an extensive form game is defined as $\sigma_i : \Omega \to A_\omega$; a mixed strategy is defined accordingly. If $\sigma_i$ is a strategy in $X$, then the strategy $\sigma_{i|\omega} : \Omega_{|\omega} \to A_{|\omega}$ induced by $\sigma_i$ in the subgame $\Gamma(\omega)$ is $\sigma_{i|\omega}(\omega') = \sigma_i(\omega, \omega')$. Since it is unobservable whether a player has played a particular mixed strategy (only the realization of that strategy is observed), we will henceforth concentrate on enforcing outcomes that are the consequence of pure strategy profiles.

Our chosen solution concept will be subgame perfect equilibrium. To define this, we must first define a *Nash equilibrium*: a profile of strategies $\sigma$ is a Nash equilibrium in a game if $\forall i \in N, \sigma'_i \in \Delta A_i : U_i(\sigma_i, \sigma_{-i}) \geq U_i(\sigma'_i, \sigma_{-i})$. A profile of strategies $\sigma$ in an extensive form game is a *subgame perfect equilibrium* if for every $\omega \in \Omega$, $\sigma_{|\omega}$ is a Nash equilibrium of the subgame $\Gamma(\omega)$. A subgame perfect equilibrium is resistant to deviations by players even in subgames off the equilibrium path.

## The Power of a Helpful Center

We wish to characterize the power of a helpful center without any resource limitations. In this section, the center is limited only by the voluntary consent required from all agents and by its lack of desire to spend its own money. Specifically, we assume that it collects the signatures in $F$ itself and that it monitors the players' actions in $G$. In later sections we will relax each of these two assumptions.

First, we must precisely define the game which is being played. We model the signature exchange stage as a game form $F$ with players $N$ and action space $\Gamma^F = \{0,1\}^n$. The player $i$ assents to the contract if $\gamma_i^F \in \Gamma_i^F = 1$. Since the center broadcasts the identities of the signers, each player's action is common knowledge. The execution game $G$ thus has an extended action space $\Gamma^G : \{0,1\}^n \rightarrow A$ in which players decide to take action based on the consequences of the signature exchange stage. In the initial formulation, the enforcement stage $H$ requires no action on the part of the players, but only of the center. The center's protocol $h$ sets the payoff function of the enforcement stage. The center observes the signatures it receives and the actions chosen by the players and chooses to fine or reward players. Formally, $h = h_1 \times h_2 \times ... \times h_n$ and $h_i : \{0,1\}^n \times O \rightarrow \mathbb{R}$.

We define the payoff function $U_i : \Gamma \rightarrow \mathbb{R}$ for each player in the extended game $X$ given actions $v \in \{0,1\}^n$ and $(a_i, a_{-i}) \in A$ as $U_i(v, a_i, a_{-i}) = V(g(a_i, a_{-i})) + h_i(v, g(a_i, a_{-i}))$. Thus each player has a quasi-linear utility function over the outcome determined in $G$ and the money taken or given by the center according to $h$.

We say that the center's protocol $h$ is *voluntary* if the center neither fines nor rewards players if the contract is not signed by every player: for all $v \neq 1^n \in \{0,1\}^n$ and for all $o \in O$, it is the case that $h_i(v, o) = 0$. We say that $h$ is *frugal* if the center never spends its own money: for all $v \in \{0,1\}^n$ and all $o \in O$, it is the case that $\sum_{i \in N} h_i(v, o) \leq 0$. As these capture the limitations on the helpful center in our setting, we will henceforth limit $h$ to be frugal and voluntary.

We first wish to characterize what outcomes can occur in a subgame-perfect equilibrium of the extended game $X$. The outcome depends on two things: the contract $c_h$ suggested by the center and the strategies of the players in $X$. We wish to find contracts to which the players will agree that ensure that our chosen outcome is played.

In order to characterize the space of possible outcomes which can be enforced, we must define the notion of a *punishment equilibrium*. $\rho^i$ is a punishment equilibrium for $i$ if $\rho^i$ is the Nash equilibrium of $G$ with minimal payoffs for $i$ among all (mixed) Nash equilibria of $G$.

**Theorem 1** *Let $\rho^i$ be the punishment equilibrium for i. For all $o_{(a_i, a_{-i})}$, if $V_i(a_i, a_{-i}) \geq V_i(\rho^i)$, then there exists a voluntary and frugal center protocol h and a subgame perfect equilibrium $\pi^*$ in which all players agree to $c_h$ and play $(a_i, a_{-i})$, and in no subgame perfect equilibrium do players agree to $c_h$ and then fail to play $(a_i, a_{-i})$. Furthermore, for all i, $U_i(\pi^*) = V_i(a_i, a_{-i})$. If $V_i(a_i, a_{-i}) < V_i(\rho^i)$, then there is no subgame perfect equilibrium in which $(a_i, a_{-i})$ is played.*

**Proof:** First, suppose $V_i(a_i, a_{-i}) < V_i(\rho^i)$. Since player $i$ will get at least $V_i(\rho^i)$ in any subgame perfect equilibrium without fines, $i$ can profit by withholding his assent. As $(a_i, a_{-i})$ cannot be a Nash equilibrium by assumption and no fines are assessed in $H$, there can be no subgame perfect equilibrium in which $(a_i, a_{-i})$ is played.

Second, suppose $V_i(a_i, a_{-i}) \geq V_i(\rho^i)$. We choose $h_i(a_i) = 0$ and $h_i(a'_i \neq a_i) = -M$. If we choose $M$ so that for all $i$, $a'_i$, and $a'_{-i}$, it is the case that $M > V_i(a'_i, a'_{-i}) - V_i(a_i, a_{-i})$, then $(a_i, a_{-i})$ will be the only subgame perfect equilibrium of the subgame $G \cdot H$, supposing all players agree to $c_h$. We also require that all players assent in $F$. If any player does not assent, all players coordinate on his punishment equilibrium $\rho^i$ in $G$. If more than one player fails to assent, we break ties arbitrarily to see which $\rho^i$ is played. No matter which player fails to assent, $\rho^i$ will be a subgame perfect equilibrium of $G \cdot H$, since the center will not assess fines. Thus $i$ will not profit by withholding his assent. □

Thus we show that, with a fully engaged center that takes part in the protocol and monitors the players' actions, we can achieve any payoffs for the players which are at least as good for every player as some Nash equilibrium of $G$. Furthermore, once a contract for $o$ is mutually signed, the unique subgame perfect equilibrium achieves $o$.

We notice that, already, the center takes no action in $H$ in equilibrium. Yet as the center takes action in every other stage, we shall consider how to lighten the load on the center.

## Removing the Center From the Enforcement Stage

In this section, we will drop the assumption that the center does not monitor the players' actions in the execution stage $G$. Instead, we assume that actions and outcomes are common knowledge among the players but are not observed by the center. The center must therefore encourage the players to tell him if there has been a deviation. We will distinguish two cases. In the *verifiable* case, the center can verify that a particular player played a given action if he chooses to do so once the game $G$ has been played. Specifically, we require that the center be able to verify, for each player $i$, whether $i$ played the correct action $a_i$ or some other action $a'_i \neq a_i$. The center saves effort by not paying attention to $G$; we merely require that he can determine the truth after the fact, if necessary. In the *unverifiable* case, the center has no information about players' actions whatsoever.

Because we now require the center to be notified by the players of deviations, the enforcement games we now consider will be of the following form: first, the players observe the outcome and send messages to the center. The center publishes any messages he receives to all players. The players then have the chance to respond to the center's messages. This repeats for some number of rounds. Finally, the center makes monetary transfers between the players based on the messages sent.

For our purposes, this full generality is not needed. Our enforcement stage $H$ is a single-round stage game where each player chooses whether or not to *complain* about other players by sending their names to the center, and the center chooses a fine to impose on each player: $H = \langle N, \Gamma^H, \mathbb{R}^n, h \rangle$. $\gamma_i^H \in \Gamma_n^H : O \rightarrow 2^N$ specifies which complaints player $i$ will send to the center after each outcome. As before, $h$ is the center's protocol which maps outcomes and complaints received to monetary consequences in $\mathbb{R}^n$. The center may make payments based on the outcome (if he can verify it), the identities of the complainers, and the target of their complaints. In the verifiable case, $h : O \times (2^N)^n \rightarrow \mathbb{R}^n$, while in the unverifiable case, $h : (2^N)^n \rightarrow \mathbb{R}^n$.

Now that we have specified an enforcement game, we wish to characterize the set of outcomes obtainable thereby in the extended game corresponding to this enforcement game.

We define a protocol $h_o$ for the center, which will induce an equilibrium under which the center takes no action in the enforcement stage. Let $M$ and $m$ be a large and small amount of money, respectively. In $h_o$, the center punishes each player who deviated by a large-enough amount $M$, but also rewards each player who sent in a correct complaint by $m$ for each correct complaint. The center also punishes any player who sent in an incorrect complaint by $m$. The contract that specifies center protocol $h_o$ we call $c_{h_o}$.

**Theorem 2 (Contracts for Verifiable Games)** *Let $G$ be a game with verifiable consequences in $O$ and let $o_{(a_i,a_{-i})} \in O$ be the desired outcome. Assume that the center has suggested contract $c_{h_o}$ defined above and consider the subgame $G \cdot H$ that follows unanimous agreement to this contract. Then there is a strategy profile $\pi^*$ such that $\pi^*$ is the unique subgame perfect equilibrium of $G \cdot H$, $o_{(a_i,a_{-i})}$ is the equilibrium outcome of $\pi^*$, and $\pi^*$ has payoffs $V(a_i, a_{-i})$. The center takes no action if $\pi^*$ is played.*

[Proof omitted.]

We now consider the unverifiable case. As before, we first define a particular center protocol $h'_o$. In $h'_o$, the center punishes the target of each complaint by a large-enough amount $M$, but does not reward or punish players for complaints. After all, the center cannot distinguish valid complaints from invalid ones. The contract that specifies center protocol $h'_o$ we call $c_{h'_o}$.

**Theorem 3 (Contracts for Unverifiable Games)** *Let $G$ be a game with unverifiable consequences in $O$, and let $o_{(a_i,a_{-i})} \in O$ be the desired outcome. Assume that the center has suggested contract $c_{h'_o}$ and consider the subgame $G \cdot H$ that follows unanimous agreement to this contract. Then there is a strategy profile $\pi^{*\prime}$ such that $\pi^{*\prime}$ is a subgame perfect equilibrium of $G \cdot H$, $o_{(a_i,a_{-i})}$ is the equilibrium outcome of $\pi^{*\prime}$, and $\pi^{*\prime}$ has payoffs $V(a_i, a_{-i})$. The center takes no action if $\pi^{*\prime}$ is played.*

[Proof omitted.]

We have seen that even without verifiability, it is possible to achieve almost any outcome in equilibrium. Unfortunately, these equilibria are no longer unique. As we shall see, in the unverifiable case, a given signed contract may have many possible equilibrium outcomes rather than just the intended one.

Given a game $G$, define the *shortfall* $s_i^\sigma$ of pure-strategy profile $\sigma = (a_i, a_{-i})$ for $i$ as $s_i^\sigma = \max_{a'_i} V_i(a'_i, a_{-i}) - V_i(a_i, a_{-i})$. The shortfall of $i$ in $\sigma$ is the amount $i$'s payoffs would need to rise so that $i$ would have no incentive to deviate from $\sigma$, all else held constant. We can see that there must be some equilibrium of the enforcement game in which an agent $i$ is punished by at least $s_i^{(a_i,a_{-i})}$ whenever he deviates from his action $a_i$. Yet, in an unverifiable game, there is nothing in the center's protocol which makes $(a_i, a_{-i})$ special. The players could just as well coordinate on this equilibrium in the enforcement game when the actions are not some other action $(a'_i, a_{-i})$. This implies that any enforcement scheme for the unverifiable case will not in general have a unique outcome. Here we consider not only our chosen center protocol $h'_o$, but in fact any center protocol $h$ in any form of enforcement game $H$.

**Theorem 4 (Spurious Equilibria)** *Consider an unverifiable enforcement game with a frugal and voluntary $h$ under which $G \cdot H$ has a subgame-perfect equilibrium $\pi$ in which the center does no work, where $(a_i, a_{-i})$ is the strategy profile that $\pi$ plays in $G$. Then if $\sigma'$ is a pure strategy profile of $G$ and $\forall i : s_i^{\sigma'} \leq s_i^{(a_i,a_{-i})}$, then there exists a subgame perfect equilibrium $\pi'$ of $G \cdot H$ such that $\sigma'$ is the strategy profile that $\pi'$ plays in $G$.*

[Proof omitted.]

A consequence of this theorem is that any Nash equilibrium of $G$ can be played in $F \cdot G \cdot H$ regardless of the contract signed.

**Corollary 5 (No Deletion)** *If $\sigma$ is a pure or mixed Nash equilibrium in the unverifiable game $G$, then, for any frugal and voluntary center protocol $h$ that has a subgame perfect equilibrium $\pi$ where the center does no work, there is a subgame perfect equilibrium $\pi'$ of $G \cdot H$ such that $\sigma$ is the strategy profile that $\pi'$ plays in $G$.*

[Proof omitted.]

Thus, if the center cannot verify the players' actions, he cannot in general enforce any outcomes uniquely. After signing the contracts, the players might arrive at an outcome different from the one the center suggested. In a real-world setting, this would substantially weaken the case that the players should sign the contract.

We have shown that a helpful center who neither monitors the player's actions nor fines any player in equilibrium can enforce every outcome that a fully engaged center can enforce with more burdensome contracts. In an unverifiable game, however, the center must generally accept spurious equilibria. Our next task is to remove the center from the signature exchange stage.

## Exchanging Signatures Without The Center

Under the original contract, the center collected signatures on the contract $c_h$ and enforced the contract if every player signed. We now show how the players can exchange signatures on the contract by use of a broadcast channel without requiring any action from the center in equilibrium. In this, our goal is similar to the goal of *optimistic signature exchange* (Garay & MacKenzie 1999), but with rational actors instead of computationally-bounded ones.

If players may communicate without being observed by others, $F$ would be a game of imperfect information. As these games are difficult to analyze and generally admit of many solutions, we require the players to use a broadcast channel, on which all messages sent are common knowledge.

When the center no longer monitors the signature exchange stage, he no longer knows in the enforcement stage $H$ whether the contracts have been signed or not. Therefore, we now require that each complaint sent to the center in the enforcement stage $H$ include a fully signed copy of the contract.

### The Naive Broadcast Protocol

We might hope that the signature collection service performed by the center was superfluous: that we will achieve the same results if we simply require players to broadcast their agreement or disagreement. Unfortunately, this will not be so. Consider the naive broadcast protocol where all players simultaneously broadcast their signatures. Let us formally define $F$ to be the one-round stage game $F = \langle N, \Gamma^F, S, f \rangle$, where $N$ is the set of players and $\Gamma^F = \{0,1\}^n$, where 0 represents the decision not to broadcast one's signature, while 1 represents the decision to do so. $S = (\{0,1\}^n)^n$ is the set of outcomes of the game. Each outcome specifies the set of signatures (represented by $\{0,1\}^n$) possessed by each player in $N$. $f : \Gamma^F \to S$ is the outcome function of $F$: each player knows his own signature and every signature which is broadcast.

The complete set of signatures is thus common knowledge if and only if every player chooses to broadcast his signature. Consider what occurs if exactly one player $i$ fails to reveal his signature: $i$ has received all the signatures of the other players, and he can produce his own. Thus $i$ is the only player to possess all signatures on the contract, and this fact is common knowledge among the players. The center, on the other hand, cannot distinguish this case from the case where all players know all signatures, but only $i$ chooses to complain. Therefore $i$ is able to unilaterally enforce the contract, unlike in the original formulation.

Recall that, in $H$, every message sent by one player to the center is broadcast to all other players. Thus, once one player has sent a complaint about another (which includes a fully signed contract), every player will know all signatures on $c_h$ and be able to complain. A player who deviates in $F$ cannot choose to punish other players while remaining unscathed himself, but he can choose unilaterally whether or not to enforce the contract. Unfortunately, this power implies that our previously specified equilibrium for the extended game $F \cdot G \cdot H$ is no longer an equilibrium.

The equilibrium for $F \cdot G \cdot H$ discussed above requires that, if $i$ fails to reveal his signature on the contract, all players coordinate on $i$'s punishment equilibrium. Consider the case, for instance, where the punishment equilibrium for some $i$ is $(a_i, a'_{-i})$, where $a_i$ is the action $i$ is contractually obliged to play. Suppose $i$ alone fails to reveal his signature and all players play $i$'s punishment equilibrium $(a_i, a'_{-i})$. In stage $H$, then, $i$ will profit by choosing to enforce the contract: the center will punish the other players and reward $i$. Knowing this, the other players will not in general wish to play their part of the punishment equilibrium, so our previous strategy fails.

### The Pre-Contract Protocol

Although the naive broadcast protocol did not allow us to guarantee all the payoffs we wanted, we shall see that we can use a more complicated signature exchange stage $F$ to ensure that either each player receives all signatures on $c_h$, or no players receive all signatures on $c_h$. Our exchange scheme is modelled on the contracts mechanism of the rest of the paper: we will add a *pre-contract* $\hat{c}_h$ that the players will sign before signing $c_h$. This contract authorizes the center to fine players who do not reveal their signature on $c_h$. Surprisingly, this does not lead to infinite regress: this one pre-contract is sufficient to allow for signature exchange.

We will divide $F$ itself into stages: a miniature contract exchange stage $\hat{F}$, a miniature execution stage $\hat{G}$, and a miniature enforcement stage $\hat{H}$. The players will bind themselves in contract $\hat{c}_h$ to reveal their signatures on the contract $c_h$ in such a way that, if they fail to reveal them, they can be fined by the center. We will allow them, however, to recoup that fine by revealing their signatures on $c_h$ to the center and all players after the fact. The after-the-fact alteration of the outcome allows us to use the naive broadcast protocol for $\hat{F}$ where we could not use it for $F$.

Formally, let the signature stage $F = \hat{F} \cdot \hat{G} \cdot \hat{H}$. Let us call the contract signed in $\hat{F}$ the pre-contract $\hat{c}_h$, which binds players to release their signatures on the real contract $c_h$. $\hat{F}$ is the naive broadcast protocol defined above as the stage game $\hat{F} = \langle N, \Gamma^{\hat{F}}, S, \hat{f} \rangle$. $S$ is the set of signatures on $\hat{c}_h$ that each player knows, and $\Gamma^{\hat{F}}$ is each player's choice to broadcast or not broadcast his signature on $\hat{c}_h$. $\hat{G}$ is also the naive broadcast protocol defined above for the signatures on $c_h$: $\hat{G} = \langle N, \Gamma^{\hat{G}}, \Phi, \hat{g} \rangle$, with $\Phi$ the set of known signatures on $c_h$, and $\Gamma^{\hat{G}} : S \to 0, 1^n$ the decision of the players to broadcast their signatures on $c_h$ given what signatures each player knows on $\hat{c}_h$.

$\hat{H} = \langle N, \Gamma^{\hat{H}}, \mathbb{R}^n, \hat{h} \rangle$ is a miniature enforcement stage that is substantially different from the enforcement stage $H$. $\hat{H}$ has two rounds. In the first round, a player $i$ is allowed to complain to the center that he has not received some signature on $c_h$. To do so, $i$ must submit the contract $\hat{c}_h$, all signatures on $\hat{c}_h$, and $i$'s signature on $c_h$. When the center rebroadcasts this message to all players, both the signatures on $\hat{c}_h$ and $i$'s signature on $c_h$ become known to all players. In the second round, each player who did not complain in the first round is given a chance to complain. $\Gamma_i^{\hat{H}}$ simply characterizes whether $i$ will complain to the center after each history.

We now state our chosen center protocol $\hat{h}$ in $\hat{H}$. If the center received a complaint in the first round, then the center fines all players who did not complain in either the first or the second round by a large-enough amount $M$. If the center does not receive any complaints, he does not fine any players. Note that if all players complain, all signatures on $c_h$ become common knowledge and no fines are assessed.

We now specify the strategy $\pi^*$ we expect the agents to play in $F$. In $\hat{F}$, each player first reveals his signature on $\hat{c}_h$. In $\hat{G}$, he will reveal his signature on $c_h$ if and only if he has received the signatures of every other player on $\hat{c}_h$. In the enforcement stage $\hat{H}$, he complains to the center if and only if he has received all signatures on $\hat{c}_h$, but he has not received all signatures on $c_h$, or if some other player has complained.

The remainder of $\pi^*$ for $G$ and $H$ is simple. If all signatures on $c_h$ become known to all players, then the players play $(a_i, a_{-i})$ in $G$ to achieve $o$, just as before, and then complain to the center in $H$ if some player deviates. If, however, some player $i$ deviates from the equilibrium in $F$ (whether by choosing not to reveal in $\hat{F}$, choosing not to reveal in $\hat{G}$, or failing to complain in $\hat{H}$), in such a way that the signatures on $c_h$ do not become commonly known, then the agents coordinate on that player's punishment equilibrium $\rho^i$. If several players deviate during $F$, the agents coordinate on the punishment equilibrium of the last player to deviate.

Our strategy $\pi^*$ is now an equilibrium. Thus, we can achieve any outcome achievable with a busy center with a center that does no work in equilibrium.

**Theorem 6** *Let $X$ be the extended game $\hat{F} \cdot \hat{G} \cdot \hat{H} \cdot G \cdot H$, and let $\rho^i$ be the punishment equilibrium for $i$ in $G$. Then, for any $o_{(a_i,a_{-i})}$ such that for all $i$, $V_i(a_i, a_{-i}) \geq V_i(\rho^i)$, there exists a contract $c_h$ for which there is an strategy profile $\pi^*$ such that $\pi^*$ is a subgame perfect equilibrium of the extended game and $o_{(a_i,a_{-i})}$ is the equilibrium outcome of $\pi^*$. Furthermore, in $\pi^*$, the center takes no action during any stage.*

**Proof:** Let us sketch why this will be a subgame perfect equilibrium. We will proceed by backwards induction.

So long as no single player gains complete knowledge of the signatures on $c_h$, then $\pi^*$ is a subgame perfect equilibrium in $G$ and $H$. This does not occur if $\pi^*$ is played in $F$, so it is sufficient to prove that $\pi^*$ is a subgame perfect equilibrium in $F$. We will show that, even after one deviation, either all players know all the signatures on $c_h$ or no player knows all signatures on $c_h$.

Consider the second round of $\hat{H}$. If no player complained in the first round, second-round complaints have no effect. If a player complained in the first round of $\hat{H}$, then it will be dominant for every other player to complain according to $\pi^*$ to avoid the punishment of $M$ from the center. Thus, all players will know all signatures on $c_h$.

Consider the first round of $\hat{H}$. There are three cases to distinguish. First, if every player knows all signatures on both $\hat{c}_h$ and $c_h$, then complaining will have no effect. Second, if every player knows all signatures on $\hat{c}_h$, but only one player knows all signatures on $c_h$. Every other player will complain in the first round and $i$ must therefore complain in the first or second rounds to avoid losing $M$. Every player will learn all signatures. Third, if only one player $i$ knows all the signatures on $\hat{c}_h$, then $i$ will not know all the signatures on $c_h$. If $i$ does not complain, no player will learn all signatures on $c_h$ and players will coordinate on $i$'s punishment equilibrium. If $i$ does complain, all others will complain in the second round and all players will learn all signatures.

Consider the stage $\hat{G}$. There are now two cases to consider. First, suppose all players know all signatures on $\hat{c}_h$. Then no player $i$ can benefit by failing to reveal his signature on $c_h$, since the other players will complain, $i$ will complain to avoid punishment, and all players will end up learning all signatures on $c_h$. Second, suppose only one player $i$ knows the signatures on $\hat{c}_h$ because he failed to reveal in $\hat{F}$. Then no other players will reveal their signatures, and, whether $i$ reveals or not, all players will coordinate on $i$'s punishment equilibrium.

Finally, consider the stage $\hat{F}$. Suppose one player $i$ deviates in the stage $\hat{F}$ by failing to reveal his signature on the pre-contract $\hat{c}_h$. Then he alone will have all the signatures on $\hat{c}_h$, and no one else will reveal their signatures on $c_h$ in $\hat{G}$. According to the equilibrium, $i$ will complain to the center in stage $\hat{H}$, resulting in complete knowledge of $c_h$ and the decision to play $(a_i, a_{-i})$. □

## Conclusion

We have discussed the power of a helpful center in enabling a group of players to make contracts which require them to play a certain strategy or face penalties. Even if the center brings no money to the system and transfers money from the players only after receiving permission, the center is able to help the players achieve nearly any outcome of the game. Moreover, we find that the center is still able to help the players achieve these outcomes in equilibrium, even if he does not monitor the game and does not participate on the equilibrium path - in other words, even when the center does no work in equilibrium beyond suggesting a contract.

In fact, if the contracts the center would suggest are common knowledge or determined by a negotiation stage between the agents, the center does no work whatsoever in equilibrium. Incidentally, we notice that the center makes a profit to cover his costs whenever his services are used. These two properties are very important for a third party who wishes to influence outcomes in strategic settings that occur frequently, such as in the online auction setting.

## References

Garay, J. A., and MacKenzie, P. D. 1999. Abuse-free multi-party contract signing. In *International Symposium on Distributed Computing*, 151–165.

Hafner, K. 2004. Vigilantes attack eBay fraud. *The New York Times*. Available at http://news.com.com/2100-1038_3-5176525.html.

Mas-Colell, A.; Whinston, M.; and Green, J. 1995. *"Microeconomic Theory"*. Oxford University Press.

Monderer, D., and Tennenholtz, M. 2003. k-implementation. In *Proceedings of the 4th ACM Conference on Electronic Commerce*, 19–28.

Osborne, M., and Rubinstein, A. 1994. *A Course in Game Theory*. MIT Press.

Shoham, Y., and Tennenholtz, M. 1997. On the emergence of social conventions: Modeling, analysis, and simulations. *Artificial Intelligence* 94:139–166.

# Knowledge Representation and Reasoning

# Scaling Up Reasoning about Actions Using Relational Database Technology

**Giuseppe De Giacomo and Toni Mancini**
Dipartimento di Informatica e Sistemistica
Università di Roma "La Sapienza"
Via Salaria 113, I-00198 Roma, Italy
{degiacomo,tmancini}@dis.uniroma1.it

### Abstract

Reiter's variant of the Situation Calculus is tightly related to relational databases, when complete information on the initial situation is available. In particular, the information on the initial situation can be seen as a relational database, and actions, as specified by the preconditions and successor state axioms, can be seen as operations that change the state of the database. In this paper, we show how to exploit such a correspondence to build systems for reasoning about actions based on standard relational database technology. Indeed, by exploiting standard relational DBMS services, a system may be able to perform both Projection, exploiting DBMS querying services, and Progression, exploiting DBMS update services, in very large action theories. A key result towards such a realization, is that under very natural conditions Reiter's basic action theories turn out to be made of "safe formulas" (where basically negation is used as a form of difference between predicates only) and that regression and progression preserve such a safeness. This is a fundamental property to efficiently exploit relational database technology for reasoning. We then show that, even when action theories are not "safe", they can be made so while trying to retain efficiency as much as possible. Finally, we briefly discuss how such results can be extended to certain forms of incomplete information.

## Introduction

Typically, in Cognitive Robotics, we assume that the cognitive agent, the robot, is equipped with a representation of the world and a specification of how its and other agents actions affect the world. There are several choices for the representation and reasoning formalism to adopt for this task. Among them the Situation Calculus as revised by Reiter and others is emerging as a general tool to express action theories (Reiter 1991; 2001).

Often in modelling the world we have to deal with incomplete information of various forms. In the Situation Calculus we typically have incomplete information on the initial situation. However, at least in certain domains, the main issue is not how to cope with incomplete information, but how to deal with hundred thousand facts that describe the current state of the world. In order to do this, we need to be able to scale up action theories, and especially to be able to reason with so many facts.

It is known that Reiter's basic action theories are tightly related to relational databases, when complete information on the initial situation is available. In particular, the information on the initial situation can be seen as a relational database, and actions, as specified by the preconditions and successor state axioms, can be seen as operations that change the state of the database (Reiter 2001; Fangzhen & Reiter 1997).

In this paper we show how to exploit such a correspondence to build systems for reasoning about actions based on standard relational database technology (cf., e.g., (Abiteboul, Hull, & Vianu 1995)). In particular, by exploiting a relational DBMS, systems may be able to perform in very large action theories both Projection, i.e., evaluate a certain (either open or closed) formula in the world resulting from executing a sequence of actions, and Progression, i.e., progress from the initial situation to the situation resulting from executing a sequence of actions. In order to perform the first task, one can exploit standard DBMS querying services, while to perform the second task one can exploit standard DBMS update services.

A key result towards such a realization, is that under very natural conditions Reiter's basic action theories turn out to be made of "safe formulas" (e.g., negation can be used as a form of difference between predicates only) and that regression and progression preserve safeness. This is a fundamental property to exploit relational database technology for reasoning, since these are the only formulas that a DBMS can evaluate. It is possible, under very general assumptions (domain closure), to transform any formula into a safe formula, however this requires the use of very large relations (suitable Cartesian products of a relation containing all domain elements), which put in serious jeopardy the ability of the DBMS to efficiently evaluate queries (formulas). In the paper, we discuss such a problem showing methods to try to retain efficiency as much as possible when transforming a formula into an equivalent safe one.

It is important to stress that the crux of this setting (i.e., using standard relational database technology) is performing reasoning through query evaluation (i.e., formula evaluation), not deduction. This can certainly be done in the case we have complete information of the initial state of the reasoning about the action system, and this is the case we will focus on in this paper. But this can also be done in case missing information can be supplied by sensors (see the notion of *just-in-time-histories* in (De Giacomo & Levesque 1999)). Our results can in principle be extended to such cases of incomplete information.

Finally, we observe that the ability of performing Projection allows for using a reasoning about action system based on relational technology in conjunction with high level robot language interpreters so as to exploit its formula evaluation capabilities for evaluating tests and action preconditions (Levesque *et al.* 1997; De Giacomo, Lespérance, & Levesque 2000).

## Situation Calculus and basic action theories

Our account of action and change is formulated in the language of Situation Calculus (McCarthy & Hayes 1969; Reiter 2001). We will not go over the language here, except to note the following components. The language is multi-sorted, in particular we have a sort *action* for actions, a sort *state* for situations, and a sort *object* for all other terms. In fact, we may allow for specializing the sort *object*, creating sorts corresponding to the various types of objects in the domain, but, for simplicity, here we will stick to a single sort *object*. A special constant $S_0$ is used to denote the *initial situation*, namely the one in which no actions have yet occurred. There is a distinguished binary function symbol do where $\mathrm{do}(a, s)$ denotes the successor situation to $s$ resulting from performing action $a$. Relations whose truth values vary from situation to situation are called (relational) *fluents* [1], and are denoted by predicate symbols taking a situation term as their last argument. A special predicate $\mathrm{Poss}(a, s)$ is used to state that action $a$ is executable in situation $s$.

Within this language, we can formulate action theories that describe how the world changes as the result of the available actions. In this paper, we focus on Reiter's basic action theories (Reiter 1991; 2001). A basic action theory $\mathcal{D}$ is formed by:

- Axioms (denoted by $\mathcal{D}_{S_0}$) describing the *initial situation* $S_0$ which form the initial database $D_0$.
- *Action precondition axioms* ($\mathcal{D}_{ap}$) of the form:

  $$\mathrm{Poss}(a(\vec{x}), s) \equiv \phi_a(\vec{x}, s)$$

  one for each primitive action $a$, characterizing $\mathrm{Poss}(a, s)$.
- *Successor state axioms* ($\mathcal{D}_{ss}$) of the form:

  $$F(\vec{x}, \mathrm{do}(\alpha, s)) \equiv \gamma_F^+(\vec{x}, \alpha, s) \vee \big(F(\vec{x}, s) \wedge \neg\gamma_F^-(\vec{x}, \alpha, s)\big)$$

  one for each fluent $F$, stating under what conditions $F(\vec{x}, \mathrm{do}(\alpha, s))$ holds as function of what holds in situation $s$. For successor state axioms the following consistency requirement must hold:

  $$\neg\exists\vec{x}, \alpha, s.[\gamma_F^+(\vec{x}, \alpha, s) \wedge \gamma_F^-(\vec{x}, \alpha, s)]$$

  which states that it is never the case that both $\gamma_F^+$ and $\gamma_F^-$ hold for the same arguments. Successor state axioms take the place of the so called *effect axioms*, and provide also a solution to the frame problem (Reiter 1991). In fact they are generated automatically starting from standard effect axioms of the form:

  $$\gamma_F^+(\vec{x}, \alpha, s) \supset F(\vec{x}, \mathrm{do}(\alpha, s))$$
  $$\gamma_F^-(\vec{x}, \alpha, s) \supset \neg F(\vec{x}, \mathrm{do}(\alpha, s))$$

  by applying the so called *causal completeness assumption* that intuitively says that the first (second) effect axiom above characterize all the conditions under which action $a$ causes $F$ to become true (false) in the successor situation (cf. (Reiter 2001) for details).
- *Unique names axioms* ($\mathcal{D}_{una}$) for the primitive actions, plus some foundational, domain independent axioms.

In this paper we will only consider Situation Calculus formulas $\phi(s)$ that are *uniform* in $s$. Intuitively, $\phi(s)$ is uniform in $s$ if it talks only about facts that hold in the situation $s$ (cf. (Reiter 2001)).

One of the main reasoning services that a reasoning about actions system must support is solving the so-called *projection problem*: Given a formula $\phi(s)$ uniform in $s$, and a sequence of actions $a_1, \dots, a_n$, determine whether a given formula $\phi(\sigma)$ is entailed by the action theory, where $\sigma = \mathrm{do}(a_n, \mathrm{do}(a_{n-1}, \cdots \mathrm{do}(a_1, S_0) \cdots))$, also written in the following as $\mathrm{do}([\alpha_1, \dots, \alpha_n], S_0)$, in the (ground) situation resulting by performing the sequence of actions $a_1, \dots, a_n$ from the initial situation $S_0$ (cf. (Reiter 2001)). That is, to decide whether:

$$\mathcal{D} \models \phi\,(\mathrm{do}([a_1, \dots, a_n], S_0))\,.$$

One of the main results of Reiter's variant of Situation Calculus is that the projection problem can be reduced to checking whether a certain formula $\mathcal{R}[\phi(\sigma)](S_0)$ holds in the initial situation, formally:

$$\mathcal{D}_{S_0} \cup D_{una} \models \mathcal{R}[\phi(\sigma)](S_0)$$

where $\mathcal{R}[\cdot](S_0)$ is the so called *regression operator* (cf. (Reiter 2001)) which, intuitively, recursively eliminates Poss atoms in favor of their definitions in $\mathcal{D}_{ap}$, and replaces fluent atoms about $\mathrm{do}(a_i, \sigma_{i-1})$ by logically equivalent expressions about $\sigma_{i-1}$ as given in $\mathcal{D}_{ss}$. Applying the regression operator to a uniform formula $\phi(\sigma)$ results into a formula uniform in the initial situation $S_0$, such that: $\mathcal{D} \models \phi(\sigma) \iff \mathcal{D}_{S_0} \cup \mathcal{D}_{una} \models \mathcal{R}[\phi(\sigma)](S_0)$ (Reiter 2001). Notice that the regression operator can be applied to open formulas as well, and in this case the above statement holds for all instantiations of the open formula (Reiter 2001).

## Relational databases

At the highest abstraction level, a relational database is a first-order relational structure $DB$ formed by a finite set of relations of different arities, each associated to a predicate name and formed by a finite set of tuples over a fixed domain. Such a domain can in general be infinite[2]. Unique name assumption and domain closeness is enforced on such a domain, i.e., we have a distinct constant for each object in the domain.

A first-order query $q(\vec{x})$ over a database $DB$ is an open first-order function-free formula with free variables $\vec{x}$, whose predicates are among those associated with the relations of $DB$. The answer to a query $q(\vec{x})$ is the set of tuples constants (domain elements) such that

$$\{\vec{c} \mid DB \models q(\vec{c})\}$$

that is, substituting $\vec{c}$ to the free variables in $q(\vec{x})$, the (closed) formula $q(\vec{c})$ is true in $DB$.

[1] We do not consider functional fluents here.

[2] As long as, we limit our interest to safe query only, see later.

An important issue in databases is the concept of *safe formula* (Abiteboul, Hull, & Vianu 1995). As mentioned, relations in a database may be over an infinite domain (e.g., including the naturals, or strings). Due to this, the problem of avoiding those queries that return infinite answers arises. Suppose, as an example, to deal with a database made of a single monadic relation $R(\cdot)$ on the naturals, with extension $R(0)$, and suppose to write a query $q$ that asks for those tuples that do not belong to $R$, i.e., $q = \{x | \neg R(x)\}$. The answer to the query $q$ will be made of an infinite number of tuples, namely $\{1, 2, \ldots\}$. The same happens if we have the additional relation $S(\cdot, \cdot)$ and want to compute $q' = \{\langle x, y\rangle | R(x) \vee S(x, y)\}$.

It is usual in databases to consider queries that always return answers that are both finite and independent on the database domain. To this end, restrictions on their syntax is needed, mainly on the use of negation and disjunction. We don't go into details here, but just observe that, intuitively, negation is safe when can be written as difference, while disjunction is safe when the two operands relations have the same schema. We will present a formal definition of safe formula specialized for uniform Situation Calculus formulas on a given situation, in the next section.

Before closing the section, we need to mention that usually first-order queries in databases are not expressed in first-order logic but in relational algebra (RA). This is because relational algebra can be seen as a direct abstraction for queries written in SQL, the standard query language adopted by virtually all relational database systems. It is well known (Abiteboul, Hull, & Vianu 1995) that a strong relationship can be identified in general between FO formulas and RA expressions. In particular, Maier (1983) proposes a very simple extension to original Codd's RA, in order to make translation between FO formulas and RA expressions more effective. This extension relies on the concept of *indexed relational table*, i.e., a pair $\langle T, \vec{x}\rangle$ where $T$ is a set of $n$-tuples of constants, for some $n$, and $\vec{x}$ is an $n$-tuple of distinct variables. The intuitive idea behind indexed relational tables is that they represent a first-order query $\phi(\vec{x})$ with free variables $\vec{x}$ by $\langle T, \vec{x}\rangle$, thus allowing to refer both to tuples in $T$ and to the free variables $\vec{x}$ of $\phi(\vec{x})$, $T$ was computed from. This extension of RA is equivalent to the original one proposed by Codd. In particular, all traditional RA operators (i.e., $\cup, \sigma, \pi, \bowtie, -, \ominus$) can be straightforwardly defined by means of operations in the domain of indexed relational tables.

## Situation Calculus and relational databases

In this section we show how to relate the Situation Calculus formalism and relational database technology. To do so, we need to introduce some more constraints on the basic action theories we consider.

- We reinforce $\mathcal{D}_{una}$ by requiring unique name assumption and closure of the sort $object$. In this way we force each element of $object$ to be uniquely denoted by a single distinct constant.
- We additionally require that, for each fluent $F$ and each tuple of objects $\vec{c}$, the theory $\mathcal{D}_{S_0}$ either logically implies $F(\vec{c}, S_0)$ or $\neg F(\vec{c}, S_0)$. That is, we have *complete information on the initial situation*. Under this assumption we have that $F$ is characterized, in the initial situation, simply by the set of facts of the form $F(\vec{c}, S_0)$ that are logically implied by the theory, $\mathcal{D}_{S_0}$ and $\mathcal{D}_{una}$.

The above constraints are quite severe and certainly are not suitable for certain applications (Reiter 2001). However, if our application does allow us to make such assumptions, then we can use, without loss of generality, formula evaluation instead of logical implication (exchanging entailment with truthness) thus getting a quite efficient method to base reasoning on (De Giacomo & Levesque 2000; Liu & Levesque 2003).

These observations indicate that we can exploit standard relational database technology as the base of a system for reasoning about actions. In particular, we can use relational database querying techniques to perform formula evaluation, thus being able to exploit sophisticated optimization techniques developed for databases in order to deal with very large amounts of facts. Relational database technology promises to be a good vehicle to scaling up reasoning about actions (though of a limited form) to realistic domains that require dealing with a lot of information.

In order to develop such a system, we need to decide how to tackle the following issues: (i) how to represent fluents and their values as database states; (ii) how to represent uniform Situation Calculus formulas as queries on the database. We deal with each of these issues in turn.

**Representing system states as database states** We assume that the database does not explicitly store objects of sort *state* inside the tables, but the database itself may be considered as a "snapshot" taken of each fluent in the current situation. In other words, the database keeps track of the truth values of the fluents for all objects in the current situation.

Here we consider, as the current situation, the initial situation $S_0$, and represent it as a database $DB_{S_0}$ defined as follows: each fluent $F(\vec{x}, s)$ of arity $k+1$ defined in the action theory is associated a table $F$ composed by $k$ columns $(f1, ..., fk)$. Table $F$ is populated by the $k$-tuples of objects that make the fluent $F$ true in the situation $S_0$. That is:

$$F = \{\vec{c} \mid \mathcal{D}_{S_0} \cup \mathcal{D}_{una} \models F(\vec{c}, S_0)\}$$

**Uniform Situation Calculus formulas as queries** For the moment, we concentrate on safe formulas.

**Definition 1 (Safe Situation Calculus formulas).** *The set of* safe Situation Calculus formulas *is the smallest set of formulas uniform in s such that:*

- *Atoms of the form $x = c$, $a(\vec{x}) = b(\vec{c})$, $F(\vec{x}, s)$ are safe, where with $x$ and $\vec{x}$ are variables of sort object, $c$ and $\vec{c}$ are constants of sort object, $a$ and $b$ are (possibly distinct) function symbols of sort action, and $F$ is a fluent.*
- *If $\phi$, $\phi'$ and $\phi''$ are safe, then also $\phi \wedge (x_1 = x_2)$, $\phi \wedge (x_1 \neq x_2)$, $\phi' \wedge \phi''$, $\phi' \wedge \neg\phi''$ (provided that every free variable of sort object of $\phi''$ is also free in $\phi'$), $(\exists x)\phi$ are safe, with $x_1$ and $x_2$ variables of sort object occurring free in $\phi$.*
- *If $\phi'$ and $\phi''$ are safe, then also $\phi' \vee \phi''$ is safe, provided that the free variables of sort object in $\phi''$ are the same as in $\phi'$.*

Let now $\phi$ be a safe Situation Calculus formula uniform in $S_0$. Then, we can easily define a function $||\cdot||$, which maps $\phi$ into an indexed relational table (or, equivalently, into a relational algebra expression).

**Definition 2 (The function $||\cdot||$).** *Let $\phi$ be a safe Situation Calculus formula uniform in $S_0$. Then $||\phi||$ is defined as follows:*

1. *If $\phi$ is atomic of the form:*
   - $x = c$, *then* $||\phi|| = \langle\{c\}, x\rangle$;
   - $a(\vec{c}) = a(\vec{x})$, *then* $||\phi|| = \langle\{\vec{c}\}, \vec{x}\rangle$;
   - $a(\vec{c}) = b(\vec{x})$, *then* $||\phi|| = \langle\{\}, \vec{x}\rangle$;
   - $F(\vec{y}, S_0)$, *then* $||\phi|| = \langle\{\vec{c}^{(1)}, \ldots, \vec{c}^{(n)}\}, \vec{y}\rangle$;

   *where $x$, $\vec{x}$ and $\vec{y}$ are variables of sort object, $c$, $\vec{c}$, and $\vec{c}^{(1)}, \ldots, \vec{c}^{(n)}$ are constants of sort object, $a$ and $b$ are distinct function symbols of sort action, and the axiom for fluent $F$ in $\mathcal{D}_{S_0}$ is $F(\vec{x}, S_0) \equiv \vec{x} = \vec{c}^{(1)} \vee \cdots \vee \vec{c}^{(n)}$.*
2. *If $\phi$ is of the form:*
   - $\phi' \wedge (x = y)$ *(resp. $x \neq y$), then* $||\phi|| = \underset{x=y}{\sigma}(||\phi'||)$ *(resp. $x \neq y$);*
   - $\phi' \wedge \phi''$, *then* $||\phi|| = ||\phi'|| \bowtie ||\phi''||$;
   - $\phi' \wedge \neg\phi''$, *provided that every free variable of sort object of $\phi''$ is also free in $\phi'$, then* $||\phi|| = ||\phi'|| \ominus ||\phi''||$;
   - $\phi' \vee \phi''$, *provided that the free variables of sort object in $\phi''$ are the same as is $\phi'$, then* $||\phi|| = ||\phi'|| \cup ||\phi''||$;
   - $(\exists x)\phi'$, *where $\phi'$ is a safe formula, then* $||\phi|| = \underset{x}{\pi}(||\phi'||)$;

   *where $x$ and $y$ are variables of sort object.*

With these definitions in place we formally express how we can make inference on the initial situation by evaluating queries over the corresponding database $DB_{S_0}$.

**Theorem 1.** *Let $\mathcal{D}_{S_0}$ and $\mathcal{D}_{una}$ be as above, and let $\phi(\vec{x}, S_0)$ be a safe Situation Calculus formula uniform in the initial situation $S_0$, and $Q_\phi = ||\phi(\vec{x}, S_0)||$. Then*

$$\{\vec{c} \mid \mathcal{D}_{S_0} \cup \mathcal{D}_{una} \models \phi(\vec{c}, S_0)\} = ans(Q_\phi, DB_{S_0}).$$

In other words, the answer over the database $DB_{S_0}$ to the query modelled by the indexed table corresponding to a safe Situation Calculus formula $\phi$ over the initial situation $S_0$ are exactly all the tuples of constants that substituted to the free variables of $\phi$ make the resulting formula entailed from $\mathcal{D}_{S_0} \cup \mathcal{D}_{una}$, i.e., entailed by the information on the initial situation and the assumptions on constants above.

## Safe basic action theories

If we aim at using formula evaluation as the reasoning engine, it is natural to assume to be able to evaluate at least those formulas for checking if an action is possible, and how a fluent changes by performing such an action. Hence in the relational setting proposed here it is natural to assume that queries for checking action precondition and effect axioms are safe. In other words, it is natural to consider basic action theories where:

- The precondition axioms have the form
$$\text{Poss}(a(\vec{x}), s) \equiv \phi_a(\vec{x}, s)$$
where $\phi_a(\vec{x}, s)$ is safe;
- The effect axioms have the form
$$\gamma_F^+(\vec{x}, \alpha, s) \supset F(\vec{x}, \text{do}(\alpha, s))$$
$$\gamma_F^-(\vec{x}, \alpha, s) \supset \neg F(\vec{x}, \text{do}(\alpha, s))$$
where both $\gamma_F^+(\vec{x}, \alpha, s)$ and $\gamma_F^-(\vec{x}, \alpha, s)$ are safe.

Let us concentrate for a moment on the effect axioms. Does the safeness of the premises of the effect axioms guarantee the safeness of the corresponding successor state axiom obtained by applying the causal completeness assumption? Interestingly, the answer to this question is positive.

**Theorem 2.** *Let $\gamma_F^+(\vec{x}, \alpha, s) \supset F(\vec{x}, \text{do}(\alpha, s))$ and $\gamma_F^-(\vec{x}, \alpha, s) \supset \neg F(\vec{x}, \text{do}(\alpha, s))$ be the effect axioms for the fluent $F$, and let both $\gamma_F^+(\vec{x}, \alpha, s)$ and $\gamma_F^-(\vec{x}, \alpha, s)$ be safe. Then the formula*

$$\gamma_F^+(\vec{x}, \alpha, s) \vee \big(F(\vec{x}, s) \wedge \neg\gamma_F^-(\vec{x}, \alpha, s)\big)$$

*in the corresponding successor state axiom $F(\vec{x}, \text{do}(\alpha, s)) \equiv \gamma_F^+(\vec{x}, \alpha, s) \vee \big(F(\vec{x}, s) \wedge \neg\gamma_F^-(\vec{x}, \alpha, s)\big)$ is also safe.*

Observe that assuming precondition and effect axioms having safe premises seems quite in the spirit of the idea of checking conditions by evaluating them on a database. It is not so for successor state axioms, since they embed a quite sophisticated technique to deal with the frame problem. The theorem above comes about as a nice and welcome surprise.

After this discussion, we feel comfortable in introducing the notion of safe basic action theory.

**Definition 3 (Safe basic action theory).** *A safe basic action theory is a basic action theory in which the right part of each action precondition axiom and the right part of each successor state axiom are safe formulas.*

Safe basic action theories have a very interesting property, namely that regression preserves safeness.

**Theorem 3 (Regression in safe basic action theories).** *Let $\mathcal{D}$ be a safe basic action theory, and $\phi(\vec{x}, \sigma)$ a safe Situation Calculus formula uniform in the (ground) situation $\sigma = \text{do}([a_1, \ldots, a_n], S_0)$. Then, the regression operator $\mathcal{R}$ applied to $\phi(\vec{x}, \sigma)$, returns a formula $\mathcal{R}[\phi(\vec{x}, \sigma)](S_0)$, uniform in $S_0$, that is safe.*

Observe that this theorem, together with Theorem 1, gives us the mean to exploit database technology to deal with the projection problem.

**Theorem 4.** *Let $\mathcal{D}$ be a safe basic action theory, $\phi(\vec{x}, \sigma)$ be a safe Situation Calculus formula uniform in the situation $\sigma = \text{do}([a_1, \ldots, a_n], S_0)$, $\mathcal{R}[\phi(\vec{x}, \sigma)](S_0)$ the formula on the initial situation obtained by regression, and $Q_{\phi_r} = ||\mathcal{R}[\phi(\vec{x}, \sigma)](S_0)||$. Then*

$$\{\vec{c} \mid \mathcal{D} \models \phi(\vec{c}, \sigma)\} = ans(Q_{\phi_r}, DB_{S_0}).$$

This theorem tells us how to exploit relational databases to solve the projection problem, i.e., to get all tuples of constants $\vec{c}$ such that $\phi(\vec{c}, \text{do}([a_1, \ldots, a_n], S_0)$ is entailed by the action theory $\mathcal{D}$. In particular, we can proceed as follows:

1. Apply regression to get a Situation Calculus formula on the initial situation, (we are guaranteed that such a new formula is safe);

2. Transform it into an SQL query (which is immediate once the formula has been transformed into relational algebra);
3. Compute and return the answer of the resulting query over the database $DB_{S_0}$.

## Dealing with unsafe formulas

For now we have a nice solution in case of safe formulas. What about if we cannot enforce safeness? Then Database Theory tells us that we need to enforce the finiteness of the domain, and in fact introduce an additional relation in our database corresponding to the domain itself.

Under the hypothesis of finite domain, every query can be made safe in a trivial way: as an example, the query $q = \{x|\neg R(x)\}$ can be rewritten as $q'' = \{x|U(x) \wedge \neg R(x)\}$, where the relation $U$ is the relation that stores all domain values for $x$.

Observe however that the new relation $U$, and even more Cartesian products such as $U \times U \times \cdots \times U$ that may be involved in a query, are likely to store an huge number of tuples, thus making query answering efficiency critical.

To extend our approach to deal with unsafe formulas, we need to further reinforce the assumption of $\mathcal{D}_{una}$ and state that the sort *object* is finite. This corresponds to introduce a new fluent $obj(\cdot, s)$, which contains initially (i.e., in $S_0$) a *finite* number of elements (the same in every model), each denoted by a distinct constant, and such that its successor state axiom states that it does not change with actions. Predicate $obj(\cdot, s)$ defines the extension of the sort *object*. To reflect such an assumption, we introduce in the database $DB_{S_0}$ a relation `Obj` which denotes exactly the objects in $obj(\cdot, s)$.

With $obj(\cdot, s)$ and `Obj` in place, it is straightforward to make every uniform Situation Calculus formula safe. However caution must be put in order to retain al least some efficiency of query answering once we reduce reasoning to query evaluation on the initial database.

The problem is that, to make a query safe, we are forced to introduce occurrences of the `Obj` table, which is typically formed by a huge number of tuples. Unfortunately, we cannot in general overcome this, but can often carefully choose, among the different alternatives, the best way to translate an unsafe uniform Situation Calculus formula into a query on the current database.

Of course, several functions $||\cdot||'$ can be defined that reduce to $||\cdot||$ given in Definition 2 when dealing with safe formulas, and several heuristics can be defined for choosing the most efficient translation. In this paper, we give a possible heuristic, under the (reasonable) assumption that the size of the `Obj` relation is much larger than the size of any other relation in the database. Under this assumption, our heuristic allows us to choose at each step whether to apply De Morgan laws to our formula or not, by computing a *cost* for each alternative. Let the `Obj` relation consists of $n$ tuples: the cost of evaluating a RA formula is given by the sum of $n^{|\vec{x}|}$ factors, one of each time a table $\langle \underbrace{Obj \times \cdots \times Obj}_{|\vec{x}| times}, \vec{x}\rangle$ (denoted in the following as $\langle Obj^{|\vec{x}|}, \vec{x}\rangle$) has to be built. Moreover, the cost is given in an incremental fashion, i.e., by considering constant the cost of evaluating subformulas. In this way, we are allowed to independently choose at each level of the formula tree whether to apply De Morgan laws or not.

In the following, both $\phi_1(\vec{x}, \vec{y}, S_0)$ and $\phi_2(\vec{y}, \vec{z}, S_0)$ are uniform Situation Calculus formulas in the initial situation $S_0$, which do not have '$\neg$' as the outermost operator, and such to have $\vec{y}$ as common free variables of sort *object*. Moreover, $\phi_1$ has $\vec{x}$ as additional free variables of sort *object* that not occur in $\phi_2$, and $\phi_2$ has $\vec{z}$ as additional free variables of sort *object* not occurring in $\phi_1$. We describe in detail only one case, the others are analogous.

Let the Situation Calculus formula $\phi(\vec{x}, \vec{y}, \vec{z}, S_0)$ to be translated be

$$\neg\,(\phi_1(\vec{x}, \vec{y}, S_0) \vee \phi_2(\vec{y}, \vec{z}, S_0))\,. \tag{1}$$

We identify two possible alternatives for translating it: the first is to translate it directly, the other is to apply De Morgan laws in order to obtain the equivalent formula

$$\neg\phi_1(\vec{x}, \vec{y}, S_0) \wedge \neg\phi_2(\vec{y}, \vec{z}, S_0). \tag{2}$$

Translation of option (1) is the following:

$$\begin{aligned} ||\phi||' \;=\; & ||\neg(\phi_1 \vee \phi_2)||' = \langle Obj^{|\vec{x}|+|\vec{y}|+|\vec{z}|}, \vec{x}; \vec{y}; \vec{z}\rangle - \\ & \Big(||\phi_1(\vec{x}, \vec{y}, S_0)||' \times \langle Obj^{|\vec{z}|}, \vec{z}\rangle \cup \\ & \langle Obj^{|\vec{x}|}, \vec{x}\rangle \times ||\phi_2(\vec{y}, \vec{z}, S_0)||'\Big) \end{aligned} \tag{3}$$

while translation of option (2) is:

$$\begin{aligned} ||\phi||' \;=\; & ||\neg\phi_1 \wedge \neg\phi_2||' = \\ & \Big(\langle Obj^{|\vec{x}|+|\vec{y}|}, \vec{x}; \vec{y}\rangle \dot{-} ||\phi_1(\vec{x}, \vec{y}, S_0)||'\Big) \bowtie \\ & \Big(\langle Obj^{|\vec{y}|+|\vec{z}|}, \vec{y}; \vec{z}\rangle - ||\phi_2(\vec{y}, \vec{z}, S_0)||'\Big)\,. \end{aligned} \tag{4}$$

Assuming that RA expressions $||\phi_1||'$ and $||\phi_2||'$ have already been computed, the cost for formula (3) is $n^{|\vec{x}|+|\vec{y}|+|\vec{z}|} + n^{|\vec{x}|} + n^{|\vec{z}|}$, while that for formula (4) is $n^{|\vec{x}|+|\vec{y}|} + n^{|\vec{y}|+|\vec{z}|}$. If we assume for simplicity that $|\vec{x}| \approx |\vec{y}| \approx |\vec{z}|$, the cost of the second alternative is lower, so the formula is rewritten by pushing negation in.

Using these calculations, in the full paper we rewrite all kind of unsafe formulas in order to achieve the most efficient translation (i.e., the one with less occurrences of Cartesian products of the `Obj` table). Then, we define the function $||\cdot||'$ by firstly applying our heuristic, and then by inserting suitable Cartesian products of the `Obj` table. Details are omitted for lack of space and will be given in the full paper.

## Performing actions and changing the database

Normally, we are interested in querying the current database state, possibly exploiting regression, in order to make some projection on the future. On the other hand, from time to time we want to perform progression, i.e., to transform the action theory by updating the current situation according to the results of performing a given sequence of actions. This results in changing the database content, in order to reflect this new situation.

Under the assumptions we have made (i.e., unique name assumption, closure of the object domain, and complete information on the initial situation), results in (Fangzhen & Reiter 1997) show that progression, which is very difficult in general, becomes simple. Moreover, relational technology can potentially allow to perform progression by exploiting the standard update mechanisms developed for databases, and take advantage of the transactional support to guarantee consistency, even in case of a failure during the progression.

With these observations in mind, we develop an account of progression that is based on the relational setting proposed so far. In order to do this, we need to clarify how the successor state axioms can be exploited as a specification of the updates to perform.

Let the successor state axiom for the fluent $F$ be:

$$F(\vec{x}, do(\alpha, s)) \equiv \gamma_F^+(\vec{x}, \alpha, s) \vee F(\vec{x}, s) \wedge \neg\gamma_F^-(\vec{x}, \alpha, s).$$

We can extract from it *effect axioms* instantiated for each (ground) action $a$:

$$\gamma_F^-(\vec{x}, a, s) \supset \neg F(\vec{x}, do(a, s))$$
$$\gamma_F^+(\vec{x}, a, s) \supset F(\vec{x}, do(a, s)).$$

In order to change the database accordingly, assuming `GammaFminus_a`, and `GammaFplus_a` being the tables corresponding to $\gamma_F^-(\vec{x}, a, s)$ and $\gamma_F^+(\vec{x}, a, s)$ respectively, we need to perform the following SQL commands as a unique transaction:

```
delete from F where exists (
  select x1, ..., xn from GammaFminus_a
  where x1 = f1 and ... and xn = fn );

insert into F (
  select x1 as f1, ... xn as fn
  from GammaFplus_a );
```

That is, a tuple is contained in table $F$ after the update associated with action $a$ if and only if, either the update has inserted it in the table, or the tuple was already in the table and the update has not deleted it. This clearly corresponds to what specified by the successor state axiom instantiated for action $a$. Since the following consistency requirement holds:

$$\neg\exists\vec{x}, s.[\gamma_F^+(\vec{x}, a, s) \wedge \gamma_F^-(\vec{x}, a, s)],$$

tables `GammaFplus_a` and `GammaFminus_a` are disjoint. Hence, exchanging the order of the two statements would not change the result.

Once we have defined the above updates, by exploiting the result on progression mentioned above we get the following theorem:

**Theorem 5.** *Let $\mathcal{D}$ be a safe basic action theory, with $\mathcal{D}_{S_0}$ and $\mathcal{D}_{una}$ defined as usual. Let $\phi(\vec{x}, \sigma)$ be a safe Situation Calculus formula uniform in the (ground) situation $\sigma = \mathrm{do}([a_1, \ldots, a_n], S_0)$, $DB_\sigma$ be the database obtained from $DB_{S_0}$ by performing the updates corresponding to each action $a_i$ in $\sigma$ in order, and $Q_\phi = ||\phi(\vec{x}, S_0)||$. Then*

$$\{\vec{c} \mid \mathcal{D} \models \phi(\vec{c}, \sigma)\} = ans(Q_\phi, DB_\sigma).$$

In other words, in order to evaluate a formula on the situation resulting from executing a sequence of actions, we can update the database, using the above update commands, and evaluate the formula on the resulting database. That is, the above update commands can be used to *progress*, in the sense of (Fangzhen & Reiter 1997), the database and hence the action theory it represents.

It is worth noting that the transactional support of the relational DBMS can be exploited to avoid leaving the database in an undesired state in case the progression fails, by issuing a *commit* statement only when the progression is successfully completed. Actually, it can be exploited further. In those cases where regression generates a query that is too big and complex to be efficiently evaluated, progression can be used as an alternative, with the proviso that after the evaluation, the transaction corresponding to the progression gives an explicit *roll back* command to restore the initial situation. In fact, this technique has shown to be quite effective in practice in dealing with projections involving very long sequences of actions. We also observe that state-of-the-art DBMSs do most of their computations in main memory cashes and not on disks directly, so the updates mentioned so far are usually performed in a fast way in main memory before issuing the *commit* statement.

## Conclusions

In this paper we have described how reasoning about actions, under complete information, can be potentially scaled up exploiting standard relational technology. A prototype of such a system, based on the implementation work reported in (De Giacomo & Palatta 2000), is currently under construction, and first experimental results are very promising.

It is important to stress that more advanced form of reasoning that can still rely on formula evaluation can potentially take advantage from the relational technology proposed here. Along this line, we are currently working on extending such an approach to reasoning with incomplete information when missing information can be supplied by sensors as in the setting of (De Giacomo & Levesque 1999).

## References


Abiteboul, S.; Hull, R.; and Vianu, V. 1995. *Foundations of Databases.* Addison Wesley Publ. Co.

De Giacomo, G., and Levesque, H. 1999. Projection using regression and sensors. In *Proc. of IJCAI'99*, 160–165.

De Giacomo, G., and Levesque, H. 2000. Two approaches to efficient open-world reasoning. In *Logic-based artificial intelligence.* Kluwer. 59–78.

De Giacomo, G., and Palatta, F. 2000. Exploiting a relational dbms for reasoning about actions. In *Proc. of CogRob'00.*

De Giacomo, G.; Lespérance, Y.; and Levesque, H. 2000. ConGolog, a concurrent programming language based on the Situation Calculus. *Artificial Intelligence* 121(1–2):109–169.

Fangzhen, L., and Reiter, R. 1997. How to progress a database. *Artificial Intelligence* 92:131–167.

Levesque, H.; Reiter, R.; Lesperance, Y.; Lin, F.; and Scherl, R. 1997. GOLOG: A logic programming language for dynamic domains. *J. of Logic Programming* 31:59–84.

Liu, Y., and Levesque, H. 2003. A tractability result for reasoning with incomplete first-order knowledge bases. In *Proc. of IJCAI'03*, 83–88.

Maier, D. 1983. *The Theory of Relational Databases.* Computer Science Press, Rockville, Maryland.

McCarthy, J., and Hayes, P. J. 1969. Some philosophical problems from the standpoint of aritificial intelligence. *Machine Intelligence* 4:463–502.

Reiter, R. 1991. The frame problem in the situation calculus. In *Artificial Intelligence and Mathematical Theory of Computation.* Academic Press. 359–380.

Reiter, R. 2001. *Knowledge in action: Logical foundations for describing and implementing dynamical systems.* MIT Press.

# Conservative Belief Change

**James P. Delgrande**
School of Computing Science
Simon Fraser University
Burnaby, B.C.
Canada V5A 1S6
jim@cs.sfu.ca

**Abhaya C. Nayak**
Department of Computing
Macquarie University
NSW, 2109
Australia
abhaya@ics.mq.edu.au

**Maurice Pagnucco**
School of CSE and National ICT Aust.
The University of New South Wales
Sydney, NSW, 2052
Australia
morri@cse.unsw.edu.au

**Abstract**

A standard assumption underlying traditional accounts of belief change is the *principle of minimal change*, that an agent's belief state should be modified minimally to incorporate new information. In this paper we introduce a novel account of belief change in which the agent's belief state is modified minimally to incorporate *exactly* the new information. Thus a revision by $p \vee q$ will result in a new belief state in which $p \vee q$ is believed, but a stronger proposition (such as $p \wedge q$) is not, regardless of the initial form of the belief state. This form of belief change is termed *conservative belief change* and corresponds to a Gricean interpretation of the input formula. We investigate belief revision in this framework, and provide a representation result between a set of postulates characterising this form of belief change and a construction in terms of systems of spheres. This approach is extended to that of belief revision with respect to a specified context. Last, we show how this approach resolves a longstanding problem in belief revision.

## 1 Introduction

An agent interacting with an external environment will need to maintain its stock of beliefs in the face of new information. Such belief change is not arbitrary, but rather is usually taken to be guided by various *rationality criteria*. One of the most widely accepted rationality criteria is the *principle of minimal change*: that a belief state is modified minimally to incorporate new information. This principle has many guises (Makinson 1993; Rott 2000). Perhaps the most evident way in which a change in belief can be said to be minimal is in terms of standard constructions such as systems of spheres (Grove 1988) or epistemic entrenchment (Gärdenfors & Makinson 1988), i.e., orderings of logical interpretations or orderings of sentences.

In this paper we introduce an account of belief change in which "minimal change" is taken with respect to the new information. We examine an account of belief change in which *all* we wish to accept is the new information itself—no more, no less. This is reminiscent of the Gricean principle of *Conversational Implicature*, in particular, *The Maxim of Quantity*, that in interpreting a speaker we should assume that the speaker means no more, and no less, than what she says. Our approach ensures that, in a sense to be specified, *exactly* the sentence accepted as evidence is incorporated. Thus for example if an agent believed that $p \wedge q$ was true and was subsequently informed that $p \vee q$ was the case, then in the resulting belief state the agent would believe only $p \vee q$. This is in contrast with the standard account, in which revision by an implied sentence has no effect; here this has the effect of weakening the belief state. It proves to be the case that a modified knowledge base in this new approach is a *conservative extension* (see Section 3) of the sentence for belief change; consequently we term this *conservative* belief change. We provide a characterisation of this form of belief change in terms of a set of postulates and in terms of a construction involving systems of spheres (i.e., orderings over logical interpretations); a representation result establishes a correspondence between these characterisations. This approach is extended to a context-dependent approach to belief change. A revision of a belief set is now with respect to a context (a set of atoms) and a formula; intuitively the idea is that for a revision, the given formula is *exactly* what is known about the provided context.

The paper is organised as follows. In the next section we give some motivating examples that highlight particular aspects of our proposal; as well we examine related work. Section 3 provides the necessary background material. In Section 4 we outline our proposed method of belief change. Section 5 discusses the significance of these results and Section 6 presents our conclusions. Proofs of theorems are given in an extended version of this paper, as is the treatment of belief update in this approach.

## 2 Motivation and Examples

The following example illustrates the traditional account of integrating new information in accord with the principle of minimal change. We write $K * \alpha$ to denote the belief set resulting from the revision of $K$ by the sentence $\alpha$.

**Example 1 (Exclusive disjunctive revision)** *Leslie and Robin are two students who share a flat above yours. They are independent and have their own circles of friends. One evening, you believe that both are out of town, $K \equiv \neg l \wedge \neg r$. However, you hear unmistakable sounds of domestic activity. You modify your beliefs minimally to account for this new information, and so you conclude just that one of them* *has gone out, i.e.* $K * (l \vee r) \equiv (l \leftrightarrow \neg r)$.[1]

To be sure, this result is not dictated by the standard revision postulates (see Section 3). However, if the assumption that Leslie and Robin are independent and have their own circles of friends is taken seriously, and coded into the system of spheres accompanying the belief set $K$, then this result becomes the most plausible minimal change.[2] This phenomenon recurs in the standard distance-based approaches to update of (Winslett 1990; Forbus 1989), as well as in the belief revision counterparts. The next example illustrates that these results aren't always desirable.

**Example 2 (Inclusive disjunctive revision)** [3] *There are two rooms in a warehouse, one on the left and another on the right. Let* $l$ *and* $r$ *denote the fact that the respective rooms are not empty. You believe that there are a number of boxes (that can fit together in a single room) outside the warehouse and the rooms are empty, and so* $K \equiv \neg l \wedge \neg r$. *You are later informed that it had been raining, and the boxes had been moved inside. You conclude just that the rooms are not empty, i.e.* $K * (l \vee r) \equiv (l \vee r)$.

On the face of it, this example violates the principle of minimal change. As well it conflicts with the aforecited distance-based approaches, which dictate that the result be $l \leftrightarrow \neg r$, that all the boxes are in one room or the other. The next example is expressed in first-order terms, but has an obvious propositional encoding over a finite domain.

**Example 3 (Generalised inclusive disjunctive revision)** *A robbery has taken place; with no other information, we have* $K \equiv \exists x R(x)$, *that someone is a robber. It is subsequently learned that there were exactly three people A, B, and C present at the time of the robbery, that is* $\phi = (R(A) \vee R(B) \vee R(C))$. *We conclude that* $K * \phi \equiv (R(A) \vee R(B) \vee R(C))$ *– i.e. the robber(s) constitutes a (nonempty) subset of* $\{A, B, C\}$. *However standard accounts of minimization (e.g., Dalal's revision operator) stipulate that* $K * \phi$ *entail that* $R$ *is true of exactly one of* $\{A, B, C\}$.

Example 1 comprises the standard interpretation of belief revision: the belief set is modified in a minimal fashion so as to incorporate a formula consistently. Examples 2 and 3 comprise a distinct sense for belief change, in which for a revision by a formula $\phi$, *exactly* $\phi$ is to be incorporated into the belief set. Consider $K * (p \vee q)$. If the idea is that all we know about $p$ and $q$ is that $p \vee q$ is true, then we would want the possible combinations of truth values $\{p, q\}$, $\{\neg p, q\}$, and $\{p, \neg q\}$ to be considered possible, and so be consistent with $K * (p \vee q)$. In this example, the atoms $p$ and $q$ supply an implicit context. We can extend this notion by giving an explicit context, where a context (or, subject matter) is comprised of some set of atoms. Thus a revision of belief set $K$ by $p$ in the context $\{p, q\}$, say $K * (\{p, q\}, p)$, would be intended to convey that, of the context $\{p, q\}$, precisely $p$ will be known to be true; in particular, neither $q$ nor $\neg q$ will be believed in the resulting belief set.

This sense is reminiscent of Gricean conversational implicature (Grice 1989) wherein a speaker is required to be maximally informative. Thus if a listener is told that $p \vee q$ is true, then the communicator does not know which of $p, q$ are true; if they did, they would have conveyed the stronger information to the listener. A similar notion has been studied by Lakemeyer and Levesque (see (Lakemeyer & Levesque 2000)) dealing with "only-knowing" or "only-knowing about". These concepts arise in autoepistemic default reasoning where one may want to assert that all an agent knows is $\phi$ or all that an agent knows about $\alpha$ is $\phi$.

An example similar to Example 2 has been addressed in (Herzig & Rifi 1999) in what is there called "the problem of disjunctive input." Their diagnosis is that the problem arises from how disjunction is interpreted. Here, in contrast, we argue that a deeper issue is manifested in these examples involving disjunction and, further, that there is a second, distinct way in which belief change can be interpreted, in which the input formula for belief change expresses all that is known concerning the propositions expressible in the language of this formula. Technically in our approach this will amount to the result of a belief change being a *conservative extension* (Section 3) of the formula to be incorporated into the belief set. As we discuss later, this division is essentially the dual of the revision/update distinction for types of belief change. As well, we show that this distinction provides a resolution to a longstanding problem concerning the recovery postulate in belief revision.

## 3 Background

The underlying logic will be classical propositional logic. We consider a finitary propositional language $\mathcal{L}$, over a set of atoms, or propositional letters, $\mathbf{P} = \{a, b, c, \ldots\}$, and truth-functional connectives $\neg$, $\wedge$, $\vee$, $\supset$, and $\leftrightarrow$. $\mathcal{L}$ also includes the truth-functional constants $\top$ and $\bot$. To clarify the presentation we shall use the following notational conventions. Upper-case Roman characters ($A$, $B, \ldots$) denote *consistent conjunctions of literals* from $\mathcal{L}$. Lower-case Greek characters ($\phi$, $\psi$, $\xi$, ...) denote arbitrary sentences of $\mathcal{L}$.

An *interpretation* of $\mathcal{L}$ is a function from $\mathbf{P}$ to $\{T, F\}$; $M$ is the set of interpretations of $\mathcal{L}$. A *model* of a sentence $\phi$ is an interpretation that makes $\phi$ true, according to the usual definition of truth. A model can be equated with its defining set of literals. $|\phi|_{\mathcal{L}}$ denotes the set of models of sentence $\phi$ over language $\mathcal{L}$. For interpretation $\omega$ we write $\omega \models \phi$ for $\phi$ is true in $\omega$. For $\phi \in \mathcal{L}$, we will define $\mathcal{L}(\phi)$, the language in which $\phi$ is expressed, as comprising the minimum set of atoms required to express $\phi$, as follows, where $\phi^p_q$ is

[1] We use $\leftrightarrow$ for *material biconditional* and $\equiv$ for *logical equivalence*.

[2] If we assumed to the contrary that Leslie and Robin always do things together, and reflect this information in the system of spheres, then minimal change of beliefs leads you to believe that neither of them has gone out, i.e., $K*(l \vee r) \equiv (l \wedge r)$, as expected. However both in this example as in the next, we take $l \wedge r$ to be less plausible than either of $l \wedge \neg r$ and $\neg l \wedge r$ in order to examine the problem from the same footing.

[3] It is contentious whether this example illustrates update or revision. We take it to be revision since information about the current state of the world is learned.

the result of substituting atom $q$ everywhere for $p$ in $\phi$:

$$\mathcal{L}(\phi) = \{p \in \mathbf{P} \mid \phi^p_\top \not\equiv \phi^p_\bot\} \cup \{\top, \bot\}$$

Thus $\mathcal{L}(p \wedge (q \vee \neg q)) = \mathcal{L}(p) = \{p\}$. This can be extended to sets of sentences in the obvious way. It follows trivially that if $\models \phi \leftrightarrow \psi$ then $\mathcal{L}(\phi) = \mathcal{L}(\psi)$.

We will make use of the notion of a *conservative extension* of one set of sentences by another.

**Definition 1** *For* $\Gamma_1 \subseteq \Gamma_2 \subseteq \mathcal{L}$, $\Gamma_2$ *is a* conservative extension *of* $\Gamma_1$ *iff for every* $\phi \in \mathcal{L}(\Gamma_1)$, *if* $\Gamma_2 \models \phi$ *then* $\Gamma_1 \models \phi$.

Intuitively $\Gamma_2$ is a conservative extension of $\Gamma_1$ iff $\Gamma_2$ extends $\Gamma_1$ but tells us nothing more about sentences that are in the language of $\Gamma_1$. $\Gamma_2$ may entail sentences in its extended language of course but as far as the language which it shares with $\Gamma_1$ is concerned, it says no more than $\Gamma_1$.

### 3.1 Belief Revision

A common approach in addressing belief revision has been to provide a set of *rationality postulates* for belief change functions. The *AGM approach* (see (Gärdenfors 1988)) provides the best-known set of such postulates. Belief states are modelled by sets of sentences, called *belief sets*, closed under the logical consequence operator of a logic that includes classical propositional logic. Thus a belief set $K$ satisfies the constraint: $\phi \in K$ if and only if $K$ logically entails $\phi$. $K$ can be seen as a partial theory of the world. For belief set $K$ and formula $\phi$, $K + \phi$ is the deductive closure of $K \cup \{\phi\}$, the *expansion* of $K$ by $\phi$. $K_\bot$ is the inconsistent belief set (i.e. $K_\bot = \mathcal{L}$).

*Revision* represents the situation in which the new information may be inconsistent with the reasoner's beliefs $K$ and needs to be incorporated in a consistent manner where possible. A revision function $*$ is a function from $2^{\mathcal{L}} \times \mathcal{L}$ to $2^{\mathcal{L}}$ satisfying the following postulates.

$(K*1)$ $K * \phi$ is a belief set.

$(K*2)$ $\phi \in K * \phi$.

$(K*3)$ $K * \phi \subseteq K + \phi$.

$(K*4)$ If $\neg\phi \notin K$, then $K + \phi \subseteq K * \phi$.

$(K*5)$ $K * \phi = K_\bot$ iff $\models \neg\phi$.

$(K*6)$ If $\models \phi \leftrightarrow \psi$, then $K * \phi = K * \psi$.

$(K*7)$ $K * (\phi \wedge \psi) \subseteq (K * \phi) + \psi$.

$(K*8)$ If $\neg\psi \notin K * \phi$, then $(K * \phi) + \psi \subseteq K * (\phi \wedge \psi)$.

Motivation for these postulates can be found in (Gärdenfors 1988). A dual operator, called contraction, is similarly defined, so that for a contraction of $\phi$ from $K$, denoted $K \dot{-} \phi$, the result is a belief set in which $\phi$ is not believed. See (Gärdenfors 1988) for the set of contraction postulates.

Various constructions have been proposed to characterise belief revision. We will make reference to Grove's use of a system of spheres (SOS) model for characterizing AGM revision (Grove 1988). A *system of spheres centred on* $X$ is a total preorder on the set of interpretations (or: *possible worlds*), $\leq_{SOS}$, in $\mathcal{L}$ such that for $\omega \in M$ we have that: $\omega \in X$ iff $\omega \leq \omega'$ for all $\omega' \in M$. (That is, $X$ is the least set of worlds in the preorder.) We will often omit the subscript from $\leq_{SOS}$ for readability. Revision is defined for $|K|_{\mathcal{L}} = X$ by

$$|K * \phi|_{\mathcal{L}} = \min_{\leq_{SOS}} \{\omega \in M \mid \omega \models \phi\} \qquad (1)$$

where $\min\{\}$ denotes the minimal models under $\leq$. Grove shows that for every belief revision operator satisfying the AGM postulates there is a system of spheres characterising that operator, and vice versa.

## 4 Approach

### 4.1 Conservative Belief Revision

We use $\hat{*}$ to denote the type of belief revision described in Section 2, called "conservative belief revision" or "C-revision." The idea we wish to capture is that, for $K \hat{*} \phi$, *$\phi$ is exactly what will be believed in the resulting belief set*, relative to the "subject matter" $\phi$. So for $K \hat{*} ((p \vee q) \wedge r)$ the idea is that $(p \vee q) \wedge r$ constrains the truth values of atoms in $\{p, q, r\}$, and that exactly $(p \vee q) \wedge r$ will be known about these atoms in the resulting belief set. In particular, strengthenings of $p \vee q$, such as $p$ or $p \leftrightarrow \neg q$ will not be true in the resulting belief set. This will be the case even when $K$ implies $p$ or $p \leftrightarrow \neg q$; hence revision may in fact yield a weakening of the belief set. This restriction does not hold for sentences not in $\mathcal{L}(\phi)$. The assumption is that the new information is more reliable than that contained in the current belief set. Further, the new information completely overrides what was previously believed.

The semantic intuition behind our proposal is easily visualised. In Figure 1 we consider a revision where the underlying language is generated from atoms $x, y$ and $z$. The agent believes $x \wedge \neg y \wedge z$ and encounters evidence $\neg x \vee \neg y$. Accordingly the interpretations are partitioned into four cells corresponding to the interpretations over the language $\mathcal{L}(\neg x \vee \neg y)$. The best worlds from each of the three cells satisfying $\neg x \vee \neg y$ are chosen to represent the revised belief set. Clearly, the belief content of the new belief set modulo $\mathcal{L}(\neg x \vee \neg y)$ will be exactly $\neg x \vee \neg y$. Beliefs regarding $z$ will depend on extralogical factors, namely the plausibility of different worlds.

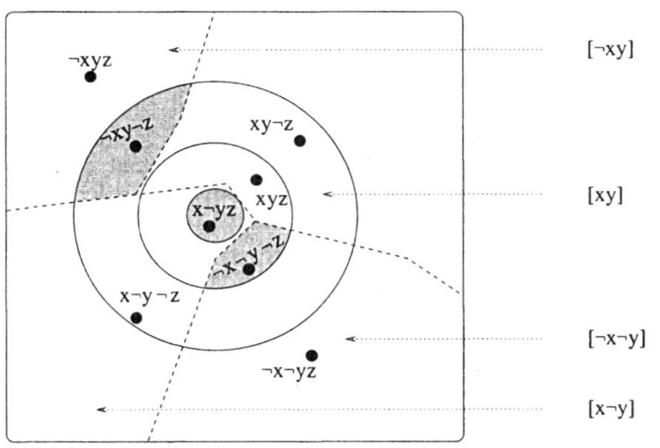


Figure 1: Conservative Revision – Semantics

Now, in determining C-revision, we consider the plausibility of different worlds represented in Figure 1 by the concentric "rings" in the system of spheres model. The worlds that are more centrally located are more plausible. Accordingly, from the $|x\neg y|$ cell, the world $x\neg yz$ is selected, whereas worlds $\neg xy\neg z$ and $\neg x\neg y\neg z$ are selected from the cells $|\neg xy|$ and $|\neg x\neg y|$ respectively. Since some of these selected worlds satisfy $z$ and some $\neg z$, under this plausibility ordering belief $z$ is lost. In fact, new beliefs regarding $z$ are captured by the beliefs $x \leftrightarrow z$ and $y \vee z$. We can formalize this analogously to Grove's system of spheres model for characterizing AGM revision. Revision was defined in (1). We have an analogous definition for C-revision:[4]

$$|K \hat{*} \phi|_{\mathcal{L}} = \bigcup_{\sigma \in |\phi|_{\mathcal{L}(\phi)}} \min_{\leq SOS} \{\omega \in M \mid \omega \models \sigma\}. \quad (2)$$

A key result is captured by the following theorem:

**Theorem 1** *For any belief set $K$ and input sentence $\phi$, $K \hat{*} \phi$ is a* conservative extension *of $\phi$, i.e., for $\psi \in \mathcal{L}(\phi)$, if $K \hat{*} \phi \models \psi$ then $\phi \models \psi$.*

We also obtain the following results relating this approach to AGM revision.

**Theorem 2** *Let $\hat{*}$ be obtained from a systems of spheres $\leq_{SOS}$ and let $*$ be the AGM revision obtained from $\leq_{SOS}$.*

1. $K \hat{*} \phi \subseteq K * \phi$.
2. $K \hat{*} A = K * A$.[5]

This raises the question of whether a specific C-revision function can be captured using the standard definition of revision (1) in a suitably-constructed system of spheres. In general the answer is negative; for a counterexample, consider where $\mathcal{L} = \{p, q\}$ and we are given a C-revision function such that $K \equiv \neg p \wedge \neg q$ and in which $K \hat{*} p = K \hat{*} (p \wedge q)$. This entails the constraints on the ordering: $\{\neg p, \neg q\} < \{p, q\}, < \{p, \neg q\}$. However, as is easily verified, $K \hat{*} (p \vee q) \equiv p \vee q$. This cannot be obtained by standard revision given the above constraints on the ordering, since it requires $\{p, q\}$, $\{\neg p, q\}$ and $\{p, \neg q\}$ at the same level.

While a given system of spheres determines a unique C-revision (as constructed by (2)), the converse in general does not hold. The following example demonstrates this point.

**Example 4** *Consider two SOS's: SOS$_1$: $\ldots < xyz < x\neg y\neg z$ and SOS$_2$: $\ldots < x\neg y\neg z < xyz$, where the $\ldots$ in the orderings represent an identical subsequence. The C-revision based on these SOS's (using (2)) exhibit identical behaviour since no cell of any partition based on a sub-language of $\{x, y, z\}$ will pick up exactly the set $\{xyz, x\neg y\neg z\}$.*

Thus we notice an asymmetry between the classical AGM account of belief revision and C-revision. An AGM revision operation $*$, given a fixed belief set $K$, determines a unique system of spheres. On the other hand, the C-revision operation, given a fixed belief set $K$, corresponds to a class of systems of spheres. It is of interest to characterise the class of systems of spheres that a given C-revision operation $\hat{*}$ determines. We have such a characterisation:

**Definition 2** *Two systems of spheres, $\leq_1$ and $\leq_2$ are $\hat{*}$-equivalent iff for every sentence $\phi \in \mathcal{L}$, $K \hat{*}_{\leq_1} \phi = K \hat{*}_{\leq_2} \phi$, where $|K|$ is the set of $\leq_{\{1,2\}}$-minimal[6] worlds and $\hat{*}_{\leq_1}$ and $\hat{*}_{\leq_2}$ are defined from $\leq_1$ and $\leq_2$ using (2).*

Our goal is to characterise in formal terms the set of SOS's that are $\hat{*}$-equivalent to a given SOS. Toward this end, we offer the following construction:

**Definition 3** *Let $\leq$ be a given SOS. We say an SOS $\leq'$ is a C-transform of $\leq$ iff the former can be constructed from the latter in the following manner: (1) Consider any two worlds $\omega$ and $\omega'$. If there is a consistent set $S$ of literals over $\mathcal{L}$ such that both $\omega \models \bigwedge(S)$ and $\omega' \models \bigwedge(S)$, and $\omega$ is $\leq$-minimal among all worlds satisfying $\bigwedge(S)$, then $\omega \leq \omega'$ iff $\omega \leq' \omega'$ (note that since $\bigwedge(\omega) \equiv \omega$ we obtain a reflexive $\leq'$); and (2) After obtaining all those constraints on $\leq'$, we complete it as we wish to get a total preorder $\leq'$.*

It is easily verified that C-transformation is a symmetric relation, i.e., if $\leq'$ is a C-transform of $\leq$, then $\leq$ is a C-transform of $\leq'$. The following is a simple example illustrating this construction:

**Example 5** *Assume a language based on atoms $\{p, q, r\}$. Let $\leq$ be: $\{\neg p\neg q\neg r, \neg p\neg qr\} < \{\neg pq\neg r, \neg pqr\} < \{p\neg q\neg r\} < \{p\neg qr\} < \{pq\neg r, pqr\}$. If we compare worlds $pq\neg r$ and $p\neg qr$, the only relevant conjuncts are $p$ and $\top$. Since neither of these worlds are $\leq$-minimal either in $|\top|$ (all worlds) or $|p|$ (worlds satisfying $p$), no particular constraint on $\leq'$ is generated by this comparison. On the other hand, if we compare $pq\neg r$ and $\neg pqr$, we notice that the relevant conjuncts are $q$ and $\top$. Since, among worlds satisfying $q$, we have $\neg pqr$ as one of the $\leq$-minimal elements, and also $\neg pqr < pq\neg r$ it follows that $\neg pqr <' pq\neg r$*

The reader is invited to verify that, given this definition, the two SOS's, SOS$_1$ and SOS$_2$ used in Example 4 are actually C-transforms of each other. This suggests that there is a close connection between the two concepts, C-transformation and $\hat{*}$-equivalence. In fact the following theorem shows that C-transformation actually captures the set of total preorders that are $\hat{*}$-equivalent to each other.

**Theorem 3** *Two preorders $\leq$ and $\leq'$ are C-transforms of each other iff they are $\hat{*}$-equivalent.*

We consider next the properties that characterise C-revision functions.

## 4.2 Postulates

Recall that upper-case Roman characters ($A$, $B$, ...) denote *consistent conjunctions of literals* from $\mathcal{L}$, and lower-case Greek characters ($\phi$, $\psi$, $\xi$, ...) denote arbitrary sentences of $\mathcal{L}$. A *C-revision* function is a function $\hat{*} : 2^{\mathcal{L}} \times \mathcal{L} \to 2^{\mathcal{L}}$ satisfying the following postulates.

[4]Since $\phi$ is a formula and by definition finite, a model of $\phi$ over the language of $\phi$ will be finite; hence we are justified in conflating the model $\sigma$ with a formula, viz. a conjunction of literals.

[5]Recall that formulas $A$, $B$, ..., are conjunctions of literals by convention.

[6]The $\leq_1$-minimal worlds and the $\leq_2$-minimal worlds are both equal to $|K|$ otherwise they are not appropriate for revising $K$.

$(K \hat{*} 1)$ $K \hat{*} \phi$ is a belief set

$(K \hat{*} 2)$ $\phi \in K \hat{*} \phi$

$(K \hat{*} 3)$ $K \hat{*} A \subseteq K + A$

$(K \hat{*} 4)$ If $\neg A \notin K$, then $K + A \subseteq K \hat{*} A$

$(K \hat{*} 5)$ $K \hat{*} \phi = K_\perp$ iff $\models \neg\phi$.

$(K \hat{*} 6)$ If $\models \phi \leftrightarrow \psi$, then $K \hat{*} \phi = K \hat{*} \psi$

$(K \hat{*} 7)$ $K \hat{*} (A \wedge B) \subseteq (K \hat{*} A) + B$

$(K \hat{*} 8)$ If $\neg B \notin K \hat{*} A$, then $(K \hat{*} A) + B \subseteq K \hat{*} (A \wedge B)$.

$(K \hat{*} 9)$ If $\phi \not\models \perp$, then there is an $A \not\models \perp$ such that, $A \models \phi$ and for all $B$, $\neg\phi \notin K \hat{*} B$ implies $A \wedge B \models K \hat{*} B$

$(K \hat{*} 10)$ If $A \models \phi$ and $\mathcal{L}(A) \subseteq \mathcal{L}(\phi)$ then $K \hat{*} \phi \subseteq K \hat{*} A$.

$(K \hat{*} 11)$ If $\neg A \notin K \hat{*} \phi$, then there is a $C$ such that $C \models \phi$ and $\neg A \notin K \hat{*} C$, and $\mathcal{L}(C) \subseteq \mathcal{L}(\phi)$.

Postulates $(K \hat{*} 1)$ – $(K \hat{*} 8)$ are the standard AGM postulates with the proviso that postulates $(K \hat{*} 3)$, $(K \hat{*} 4)$, $(K \hat{*} 7)$ and $(K \hat{*} 8)$ are restricted to consistent conjunctions of literals. Postulate $(K \hat{*} 9)$ compensates for the weakening of these postulates. It states that for every consistent formula $\phi$ there is a stronger conjunction of literals $A$ capable of accounting for any other C-revision, consistent with $\phi$, by a conjunction of literals.[7] It is possible to show that the general, AGM, versions of postulates $(K * 3)$ and $(K * 7)$ follow from these postulates. Postulate $(K \hat{*} 10)$ says that if $A \models \phi$, then the only reason for $K \hat{*} \phi$ to not be included in $K \hat{*} A$ is because the language of $A$ is outside the minimum language of $\phi$. Postulate $(K \hat{*} 11)$ essentially states the converse: the only reason that a conjunction of literals $A$ is in $K \hat{*} \phi$ is that there is some conjunction of literals $C$ (in fact, a prime implicant of $\phi$) such that $A$ is in $K \hat{*} C$. It is possible in fact to rephrase $(K \hat{*} 10)$ and $(K \hat{*} 11)$ in terms of prime implicants:

$(K \hat{*} 10')$ If $A \models \phi$ and $K \hat{*} \phi \not\subseteq K \hat{*} A$, then there is a literal $L$ such that $A \models L$, and $L$ is neither entailed nor contradicted by any prime implicant of $\phi$.

$(K \hat{*} 11')$ If $\neg A \notin K \hat{*} \phi$, then $\exists C$ such that $C \models \phi$ and $\neg A \notin K \hat{*} C$, and for all literals $L$, if $C \models L$, then $L$ is either entailed or contradicted by a prime implicant of $\phi$.

The following postulate is also of interest.

$(K \hat{*} 12)$ $K \hat{*} A$ is the largest theory satisfying postulates $(K \hat{*} 1)$ – $(K \hat{*} 10)$.

It is possible to show that this postulate is equivalent to $(K \hat{*} 11)$ in the presence of postulates $(K \hat{*} 1)$ – $(K \hat{*} 10)$.

**Proposition 1** *Postulates $(K \hat{*} 11)$ and $(K \hat{*} 12)$ are equivalent given $(K \hat{*} 1)$ – $(K \hat{*} 10)$.*

For a representation result, the soundness of $(K \hat{*} 1)$ – $(K \hat{*} 11)$ is relatively straightforward:

**Theorem 4** *Let $K$ be a theory and $\leq_{SOS}$ a system of spheres centred on $|K|_\mathcal{L}$. The function $\hat{*}$ induced from $\leq_{SOS}$ via (2) satisfies $(K \hat{*} 1)$ – $(K \hat{*} 11)$.*

[7] This postulate can be better motivated in terms of models where it guarantees that among each non-empty set of models of $\phi$, $|\phi|_\mathcal{L}$, there is a non-empty set of "best" models $|A|_\mathcal{L}$.

For the completeness of the axioms, we proceed in two steps: (i) we consider the special case of consistent conjunctions of literals, for which C-revision reduces to classical AGM revision, and prove the completeness of $(K \hat{*} 1)$ – $(K \hat{*} 9)$, and (ii) extend the results to arbitrary sentences and include $(K \hat{*} 10)$ and $(K \hat{*} 11)$. More precisely, we have:

**Theorem 5**

1. *Let $K$ be a theory and $\hat{*}$ a revision function satisfying $(K \hat{*} 1)$ – $(K \hat{*} 9)$. There exists a system of spheres $\leq_{SOS}$ centred on $|K|_\mathcal{L}$, such that for any consistent conjunction of literals $A$, $|K \hat{*} A|_\mathcal{L} = \min_{\leq_{SOS}}\{\omega \in M \mid \omega \models A\}$*
2. *Let $K$ be a theory and $\hat{*}$ a revision function satisfying $(K \hat{*} 1)$ – $(K \hat{*} 11)$. There exists a system of spheres $\leq_{SOS}$ centred on $|K|_\mathcal{L}$, such that $\hat{*}$ is identical to the C-revision function induced from $\leq_{SOS}$.*

### 4.3 Context-Dependent Revision

We defined $\mathcal{L}(\phi)$ as comprising the least set of atoms *required* to express $\phi$. Thus $\mathcal{L}(\phi)$ provides an implicit context for revision, in that following the C-revision $K \hat{*} \phi$, all conjunctions of literals corresponding to models of $\phi$ over $\mathcal{L}(\phi)$ are satisfied by the resulting belief set. This can be generalised to revision of the form $K \hat{*} (C, \phi)$,[8] such that $\mathcal{L}(\phi) \subseteq C \subseteq \mathbf{P}$, and the intuition is that $K$ is to be revised so that all that is known concerning the context $C$ is $\phi$.

As an example of context sensitive revision, consider the revision of a belief set $\{a \wedge b \wedge c \wedge d\}$ by $a \vee b$. Let $a, b$ and $c$ stand respectively for Albert, Becky and Charles being involved in a bank robbery, and $d$ stand for Doug being a geologist. The input $a \vee b$ suggests that the context is the relevant bank robbery, represented by $\{a, b, c\}$. We would expect that after the revision, we would no longer suspect Charles of robbery, and whether or not we would still believe that Doug is a geologist would depend on extraneous factors. Otherwise, if we let $c$ stand for Charles being a nice dad (and $a, b$ and $d$ as before) we would expect that the context is simply $\{a, b\}$, and as a result of the revision, whether or not $c$ would be maintained will depend on extraneous factors.

We can formalize this analogously to C-revision, as in (2) and again using Grove's system of spheres model. For $K \subseteq \mathcal{L}$, $\phi \in \mathcal{L}$, and $\mathcal{L}(\phi) \subseteq C \subseteq \mathbf{P}$ define:

$$|K \hat{*} (C, \phi)|_\mathcal{L} = \bigcup_{\sigma \in |\phi|_C} \min_{\leq_{SOS}} \{\omega \in M \mid \omega \models \sigma\}. \qquad (3)$$

We obtain for any belief set $K$, context $C$, and input sentence $\phi$, that $K \hat{*} (C, \phi)$ is a *conservative extension* of $C$ in which $\phi$ is true. As well, we obtain the following results:

**Theorem 6** *Let $\hat{*}$ and $*$ (representing AGM revision) be obtained from a system of spheres $\leq_{SOS}$.*

1. *$K \hat{*} (C, \phi) \subseteq K * \phi$.*
2. *If $\mathcal{L}(A) = C$ then $K \hat{*} A = K * A$.*
3. *$K \hat{*} (\mathbf{P}, \phi) \equiv \phi$.*

[8] Writing $K \hat{*} (C, \phi)$ as well as $K \hat{*} \phi$ overloads the symbol $\hat{*}$. However the revision operator intended is clear from the use of $\hat{*}$.

The third result is justified by the fact that we work with a finitary language; it states that, as a special case, when the context is the full set of atoms, context-sensitive revision corresponds to full-meet revision.

Clearly C-revision can be defined in terms of context sensitive revision by defining $K \hat{*} \phi$ as $K \hat{*} (\mathcal{L}(\phi), \phi)$. Conversely, context sensitive revision can be defined in terms of C-revision via: $|K \hat{*} (C, \phi)|_{\mathcal{L}} = \bigcup_{A \in |\phi|_C} |K \hat{*} A|_{\mathcal{L}}$.

## 5 Discussion

Semantically, the distinction between standard AGM revision and C-revision is analogous to the distinction between revision and update, and in fact the two distinctions may be seen as duals of each other. For an (AGM) revision, $K * \phi$, we consider the set of all models of $K$, and revise by selecting the closest models of $\phi$ to that set. For an update, $K \diamond \phi$, for each model of $K$ we look for the closest models of $\phi$; the update is the union of all such models. Analogous, for a C-revision, $K \hat{*} \phi$, we consider each model of $\phi$ (over $\mathcal{L}(\phi)$), and revise $K$ by this model; the C-revision is the union of all such models. This duality between C- and standard belief change on the one hand, and between revision and update on the other, completes a classification of belief change operators, in terms of whether the models of a knowledge base or formula for change are considered *en masse*, or individually.

C-belief change is also of independent interest. We have already noted that it conforms to a Gricean interpretation of the sentence for revision. As well it resolves the problem of disjunction noted by (Herzig & Rifi 1999), but in a general and syntax-independent setting. To conclude, we discuss two further ways in which C-revision contributes to the overall theory of belief change.

First, the approach provides a resolution to a recalcitrant problem concerning the *recovery postulate* of belief contraction: $K \subseteq (K \dot{-} \phi) + \phi$. Thus if one contracts a belief set by a sentence, and then adds that sentence, no information is lost with respect to the original belief set. (Hansson 1999) gives the following counterintuitive example (paraphrased): *Let $K$ entail that "Cleopatra had a son and a daughter" ($s \wedge d$). New information is received that Cleopatra didn't have a child, expressed by $K \dot{-} (s \vee d)$. Then one learns that she had a child, thus $(K \dot{-} (s \vee d)) + (s \vee d)$. Recovery says that $s \wedge d$ is believed – that Cleopatra had a son and daughter. Intuitively, just $s \vee d$ should be believed, that all that is known after these changes is that she had a child.* We note that if $K \models \phi$ then recovery can be written as $K \subseteq (K \dot{-} \phi) * \phi$. Arguably this example is best interpreted as involving conservative revision – that is, concerning $\{s, d\}$, one learns *at most* that Cleopatra has a child $s \vee d$. Under this reading of revision we have possibly $K \not\subseteq (K \dot{-} \phi) \hat{*} \phi$. In our example, if $K \equiv (s \wedge d)$, then we would expect: $K \dot{-} (s \vee d) \equiv \neg s \wedge \neg d$; $(K \dot{-} (s \vee d)) \hat{*} (s \vee d) \equiv (s \vee d)$.

Second, and more speculatively, belief contraction has been criticised for removing too little information from a knowledge base; at the other extreme, *severe* contraction (Rott & Pagnucco 1999) has been criticised as removing too much information. (Hansson 1999) proposes that a realistic contraction operator should lie between AGM-style contraction operators and severe contraction operators. As suggested earlier, a corresponding C-contraction operator $\hat{-}$ is easily defined using the Harper Identity or by direct definition. C-contraction is easily shown to lie between AGM and severe contraction. Given that it comes with (arguably) compelling intuitions and a straightforward semantics, C-contraction can be proposed as a "reasonable" intermediate.

## 6 Conclusion

We have discussed a theory of conservative belief change. The main intuitive motivation for this work stems from an attempt to make the most of the information presented by new evidence that a reasoner acquires. As such, our approach focuses on the content of the new evidence. Our current analysis suggests that the operators we have introduced based on these intuitions possesses some interesting and appealing properties; as well it resolves a problem with the recovery postulate, and may provide a satisfactory contraction operator. Last, the distinction between traditional belief change and C-belief change appears to be a dual to that between revision and update.

## Acknowledgements

The authors would especially like to thank Pavlos Peppas for his invaluable help with this paper.

## References

Forbus, K. 1989. Introducing actions into qualitative simulation. In *International Joint Conference on Artificial Intelligence*, 1273–1278.

Gärdenfors, P., and Makinson, D. 1988. Revisions of knowledge systems using epistemic entrenchment. In *Proceedings of the Second Conference on Theoretical Aspect of Reasoning About Knowledge*, 83–96.

Gärdenfors, P. 1988. *Knowledge in Flux: Modeling the Dynamics of Epistemic States*. Bradford Books, MIT Press, Cambridge Massachusetts.

Grice, H. P. 1989. *Studies in the Way of Words*. Harvard University Press, Cambridge Massachusetts.

Grove, A. 1988. Two modellings for theory change. *Journal of Philosophical Logic* 17:157–170.

Hansson, S. O. 1999. A textbook of belief dynamics: Theory change and database updating. Kluwer Academic Publishers.

Herzig, A., and Rifi, O. 1999. Propositional belief base update and minimal change. *Artificial Intelligence* 115:107–138.

Lakemeyer, G., and Levesque, H. 2000. *The Logic of Knowledge Bases*. Cambridge, Mass.: MIT Press.

Makinson, D. 1993. Five faces of minimality. *Studia Logica* 52:339–379.

Rott, H., and Pagnucco, M. 1999. Severe withdrawal (and recovery). *Journal of Philosophical Logic* 28(5).

Rott, H. 2000. Two dogmas of belief revision. *Journal of Philosophy* 97:503–522.

Winslett, M. 1990. *Updating Logical Databases*. Cambridge University Press.

# Mereological Semantics for Bio-Ontologies

**Udo Hahn**[1] **Stefan Schulz**[2] **Kornél Markó**[1,2]

[1]Text Knowledge Engineering Lab, Freiburg University
Werthmannplatz 1, D-79085 Freiburg, Germany
http://www.coling.uni-freiburg.de

[2]Department of Medical Informatics, Freiburg University Hospital
Stefan-Meier-Str. 26, D-79104 Freiburg, Germany

### Abstract

Biomedical ontologies are typically structured in a biaxial way, reflecting both a taxonomic and a mereological order. Common examples such as the *Gene Ontology* and the *Unified Medical Language System (UMLS)* excel in terms of coverage but lack an adequate semantics of the mereological relations they incorporate. This shortcoming is particularly evident as far as the (non-)mandatory existence of parts for their wholes is concerned, on the one hand, and the propagation of properties across part-whole hierarchies, on the other hand. We provide a formal specification of the semantic foundations of mereology in the biomedical domain that is closely linked to the paradigm of description logics. In essence, we here propose to emulate mereological reasoning by taxonomic reasoning. In an attempt to capture much of the shared intuition underlying merelogical reasoning in the biomedical domain, we distinguish for each mereologically relevant concept four different classes of parts and wholes which allow for the expression of five different propagation patterns.

## Introduction

The notion of 'biological structure' plays a key role in bio-ontologies, since tangible parts of organisms such as organs, tissues, cells, molecules, etc. constitute the location of biological processes and are the targets of experimental, diagnostic and therapeutic interventions. Up until now, most biomedical concept systems encode terminological knowledge in an informal thesaurus-style way (McCray & Nelson 1995) such as the source vocabularies of the *UMLS Metathesaurus* (UMLS 2004) and the *Gene Ontology* (Gene Ontology Consortium 2001). The latter is a nice example of a domain description, which apparently provides "clean", i.e., acyclic *is-a* and *part-of* hierarchies, but refrains from specifying explicitly the semantic nature of its foundational relations (Smith, Williams, & Schulze-Kremer 2003). The *Foundational Model of Anatomy* [FMA] (Rosse *et al.* 1998; Noy *et al.* 2002) has just recently become an exception to this rule as its creators started to develop a proper axiomatic basis (Smith & Rosse 2004). This desideratum has also been formulated after auditing the FMA using formal reasoning devices (Hahn & Schulz 2003; Beck & Schulz 2003).



As an example of semantic underspecification, assertions such as *Cell Has-Part Cell Nucleus* leave open whether *Cell Nucleus* should be interpreted as some kind of sortal restriction (or sanctioning) of the role filler, or as an existential condition for *Cell*. Such existential dependency relationships are, however, crucial for adequate domain models which should *(i)* allow the expression of ontological dependency (e.g., "each *cell nucleus* is part of a *cell*"), *(ii)* permit possible relations ("a *cell* may have *cell nuclei*"), and *(iii)* reject invalid assertions ("there is a *cell nucleus* which is part of a *protein molecule*").

Of equal importance is another reasoning phenomenon, *viz.* the propagation of properties between parts and wholes (Artale *et al.* 1996; Horrocks, Rector, & Goble 1996; Rogers & Rector 2000; Rector 2002; Horrocks & Sattler 2003). The concept *insulin secretion*, e.g., is usually considered to be related to the concept *pancreas* by the role *function-of*, because *pancreatic beta cells* (cells which produce the substance) are considered *part-of* a *pancreas*. In the same way, *contraction* would be classified as a *function-of* a *muscle*, since it is a *function-of* the *actin-myosin complex* which is a *component-of muscle cells*, the latter being *part-of muscle*.

However, there are counterexamples: An *amputation-of toe* cannot be classified as *amputation-of foot* although every *toe* is *part-of* a *foot*. *Mitosis* is a *cell* function, but it is generally not seen as a *pancreas* or *liver* function although these organs have *cells* as parts. Such propagation patterns – attributes propagate from parts to wholes, or from wholes to parts or do not propagate at all – bear subtle intricacies which still have not been sufficiently accounted for in biomedical knowledge engineering although they are relevant in order to enhance the empirical adequacy and expressive power of biomedical ontologies.

In this paper, we will discuss and classify typical reasoning patterns from which we derive our requirements for adequate biomedical domain modeling. Then we propose an ontology engineering approach, based on our previous work on biomedical knowledge representation, in the context of $\mathcal{ALC}$-based description logics (Baader & Nutt 2003). The central idea of this approach (Hahn, Schulz, & Romacker 1999) has already proved useful for the construction of a large terminological biomedical domain knowledge base. (Hahn & Schulz 2003).

## Semantic Distinctions for Parts and Wholes

In this section, we discuss and formalize four dependency patterns by which parts and wholes are conceptually related. We draw on common categories for knowledge representation. Concepts are characterized by their attributes or properties, e.g., *slots* in frame-based representations or *roles* in description logic systems (such as *has-location*, *part-of*, etc.), while role filler restrictions constrain their sortal ranges. For example, the concept *liver* is a reasonable filler of the role *has-location* of *hepatitis*. With $C$ being the concept to be defined (i.e., a unary predicate), $r$ a conceptual relation (i.e., a binary predicate) and $F$ the target concept (role filler), the following distinctions on the role status can be made:

- **Mandatory roles** of a concept $C$ are required to be filled at least once by a filler of the type $F$, as in the case of *has-location liver* when defining the concept *hepatitis*. This allows one to infer that for each concrete *hepatitis* there *must* be a concrete *liver* where it is located.
- **Forbidden roles**. $F$ is *disallowed* to be a filler of the role $r$ of the concept $C$. For the concept *dermatitis* and the relation *has-location*, e.g., a filler such as *liver* must be rejected in order to prevent unintended models.
- **Possible roles** $r$ are used to *allow* an instance of $C$ to be related to an instance of $F$ via $r$, but this is not necessarily an existential condition for $C$.[1] Possible roles constitute the complement to forbidden ones. For example, *has-part* is a possible role with filler *nucleus* when we define the concept *cell*, as cells with and without nuclei exist (e.g., bacteria).

In $\mathcal{ALC}$[2] notation (Baader & Nutt 2003), mandatory roles are specified in terms of existential quantification, whereas possible roles can be implicitly expressed in terms of conceptual constraints.

We now classify mereologically relevant concepts with regard to their role dependence status. Considering part-whole hierarchies, the notion of mandatory roles gives rise to the distinction of (mp) *mandatory* parts, on the one hand, and (sp) *specific* parts, on the other hand. Also taking into consideration *has-part*, the inverse relation of *part-of*, on equal terms, we are able to express in a similar way (mi) *mandatory* wholes (includers), and (si) *specific* wholes (includers).[3] This leads, quite naturally, to the following distinction of four kinds of related concepts for each concept in a partonomy. These dependency patterns describe particular 'views' from parts to a whole or wholes to a part, which we formalize as corresponding existential conditions for parts or wholes.

[1] All mandatory roles are possible roles, too.

[2] $\mathcal{ALC}$ allows for the construction of hierarchies of concepts and relations, where '$\sqsubseteq$' denotes subsumption and '$\equiv$' definitional equivalence. Existential ($\exists$) and universal ($\forall$) quantification, negation ($\neg$), conjunction ($\sqcap$) and disjunction ($\sqcup$) are supported. Role fillers are linked to the relation name by a dot, e.g., $\exists r.C$.

[3] We prefer the term 'includer' as argued for by Schulz & Hahn (2002). This should not be confounded with a solely topological understanding of part-whole relations such as discussed by Schulz & Hahn (2004).

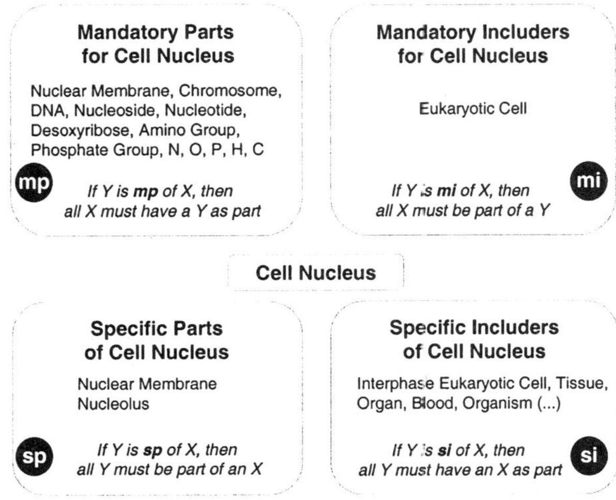


Figure 1: Part-Whole Conceptualizations of *Cell Nucleus*.

- (mp) $W_{mp}$ (**mandatory parts** of a "whole concept" $W$) subsumes all those "part concepts" $P_1$, $P_2$,... $P_n$, which fulfill the following condition: Each instance $w$ of $W$ *must* be related by *has-part* to at least one instance of each "part concept" $p_1, p_2$,... $p_n$ of $P_1$, $P_2$,... $P_n$, respectively. Here, the whole depends on the parts, or in other words, the parts are mandatory for the whole.
- (sp) $W_{sp}$ (**specific parts** of a "whole concept" $W$) subsumes those concepts $P_1$, $P_2$, ... $P_n$, which depend on a given class of wholes $W$. Each instance $p_1$, $p_2$,... $p_n$ of $P_1$, $P_2$,... $P_n$, respectively, *must* be related to $w$ (an instance of $W$) via *part-of*. Here, the parts depend on the whole, or the whole is mandatory for the parts.
- (mi) $P_{mi}$ (**mandatory includers** of a "part concept" $P$) subsumes all those "whole concepts" $W_1$, $W_2$,... $W_n$, which fulfill the following condition: Each instance $p$ of $P$ *must* be related via *part-of* to at least one instance of each "whole concept" $w_1$, $w_2$,... $w_n$ of $W_1$, $W_2$,... $W_n$, respectively. In this case, the part depends on the wholes, or the wholes are mandatory for the part.
- (si) $P_{si}$ (**specific includers** of a "part concept" $P$) subsumes those "whole concepts" $W_1$, $W_2$, ... $W_n$, which depend on a given class of parts $P$. Each instance $w_1$, $w_2$,... $w_n$ of $W_1$, $W_2$,... $W_n$, respectively, *must* be related to $p$ (an instance of $P$) via *has-part*. Here, the wholes depend on the part, or the part is mandatory for the wholes.

Figure 1 illustrates these four concept groups, using *cell* as an example. A cell nucleus has as *mandatory parts* (mp) nuclear membrane, as well as DNA, which is axiomatically constituted by nucleotides etc., the latter by nucleosides, nucleosides by functional groups, and functional groups by atoms. Nuclear membrane and nucleolus are necessarily parts of a cell nucleus, the latter being here a *specific part* (sp). The existence of a cell nucleus implies the existence of a eukaryotic cell as a *mandatory includer* (mi). Finally, interphase (i.e., non-replicating) eukaryotic cells, tissues, organs, blood, organisms necessarily have a cell nucleus as part, they are *specific includers* (si).

$C_{mp}$ can be defined as the common subsumer of all those concepts, for which $C$ is a specific includer; $C_{mi}$ as the common subsumer of those for which $C$ is a specific part. Note that $C_{mp}(x)$ and $C_{mi}(y)$ hold true even for individuals $x$ and $y$ which are *not* part of a $C$ or *do not* have $C$ as their part, e.g., *atom* for physical objects or *organism* for body parts. Rather the extension of $C_{mp}$ ( $C_{mi}$) includes all those individuals which – by their sortal kind – are principally allowed to be a part (respectively includer) of $C$. Subsequently, we will use this 'modal' reading to express the notion of *possible* parts and wholes.

Next, we discuss some algebraic properties of *part-of* and *has-part* (at the instance level). We note that *has-part* is the inverse relation of *part-of*:

$$\forall x, y : part\text{-}of(x, y) :\Leftrightarrow has\text{-}part(y, x) \quad (1)$$

According to Casati & Varzi (1999), the generic parthood relation is reflexive, antisymmetric and transitive. Although the transitivity property is by no means uncontroversial (Winston, Chaffin, & Herrmann 1987), we here claim:

$$\forall x, y, z : (part\text{-}of(x, y) \wedge part\text{-}of(y, z)) \Rightarrow part\text{-}of(x, z) \quad (2)$$

Now, we introduce some new kinds of mereological relations. In contradistinction to *part-of* and *has-part*, they relate concepts (i.e., classes), not individuals.[4] These relations are '*specific part of*' ($SP$), '*specific includer of*' ($SI$), '*mandatory part of*' ($MP$), and '*mandatory includer of*' ($MI$). Given the transitivity of *part-of* and *has-part*, we can show that these relations are transitive, too ($\pi = \{SP, SI, MP, MI\}$):

$$\forall X, Y, Z : (\pi(X, Y) \wedge \pi(Y, Z)) \Rightarrow \pi(X, Z) \quad (3)$$

According to the above definition of the common subsumer concepts $C_{mi}$ and $C_{mp}$, we may also conclude:

$$\forall X, Y : SP(X, Y) \Leftrightarrow MI(Y, X) \quad (4)$$

$$\forall X, Y : SI(X, Y) \Leftrightarrow MP(Y, X) \quad (5)$$

The proposed encoding enables us not only to directly address mandatory and specific parts, mandatory includers, and specific includers of a given concept, but also offers an opportunity to capture *possible parts* ($PP$) as well as *possible includers* ($PI$):

$$\forall X, Y : (MP(X, Y) \vee SP(X, Y)) \Rightarrow PP(X, Y) \quad (6)$$

$$\forall X, Y : (MI(X, Y) \vee SI(X, Y)) \Rightarrow PI(X, Y) \quad (7)$$

provided that there are no parts left that are neither mandatory nor specific. With (4) and (5), we then derive

$$\forall X, Y : PP(X, Y) \Leftrightarrow PI(Y, X) \quad (8)$$

We now illustrate examples of biomedical reasoning which can be stated using the predicates we introduced above. These examples are not meant to be generally valid inference rules. Rather they stand for particular concept instantiations in the context of biomedicine for which the chosen instantiation yields a valid reasoning result that meets the shared intuitions in the biomedical community. Still, these instantiations hint at another challenging problem we will not get into, *viz.* the interaction of part-whole conceptualizations we propose with spatial, functional, etc. relations in terms of *general* inference schemata.

1. *Insulin synthesis* takes place (*has-location*, $HL$) in the pancreatic *Beta Cells*. *Beta Cells* are specific parts of *Pancreas*. We infer that *Insulin Synthesis* is also located in the *Pancreas*:

| *Insulin Synthesis* | $HL$ | *Beta Cells* |
|---|---|---|
| *Beta Cells* | $SP$ | *Pancreas* |
| *Insulin Synthesis* | $HL$ | *Pancreas* |

   Therefore, the role filler of *has-location* needs to be sortally restricted by *Beta Cells* or "whatever mandatorily includes *Beta Cells*", the latter corresponding to $BetaCells_{mi}$. This inference pattern seems to be typical of the *location* of biological processes. It also explains why the following inference appears counter-intuitive:

| *Mitosis* | $HL$ | *Eukaryotic Cells* |
|---|---|---|
| *Eukaryotic Cells* | $MP$ | *Human Body* |
| *Mitosis* | $HL$ | *Human Body* (**FALSE**) |

   In contradistinction to the first example, this part is not specific for the whole: Eukaryotic cells can be found in all plants and animals, they can even constitute organisms of their own. Therefore, the conclusion is not necessarily true.

2. The following example illustrates another case in which an inference across part-whole hierarchies is prohibitive (the relation $HT$ stands for *has-target*):

| *Amputation of Toe* | $HT$ | *Toe* |
|---|---|---|
| *Toe* | $SP$ | *Foot* |
| *Amputation of Toe* | $HT$ | *Foot* (**FALSE**) |

   Obviously, an amputation of a toe is not an amputation of a foot. $HT$ targets an anatomical structure as a whole and does not include any part or includer into its range.

3. In contrast to the above example of invalid "upstream propagation" from the parts to the whole, here is an example of valid "downstream propagation" from the whole to the parts ($IO$ stands for *ingestion-of*):

| *Erythrocyte-Phagocytosis* | $IO$ | *Erythrocyte* |
|---|---|---|
| *Erythrocyte* | $SI$ | *Iron* |
| *Erythrocyte-Phagocytosis* | $IO$ | *Iron* |

   The role filler of *ingestion-of* would therefore be sortally restricted by *Erythrocyte* or "whatever mandatorily constitutes *an Erythrocyte* ", the latter corresponding to $Erythrocyte_{si}$.

4. Another example of "downstream propagation" ($FO$ stands for *function-of*):

| *Immunity* | $FO$ | *Immune System* |
|---|---|---|
| *Immune System* | $MI$ | $\gamma$*Globulin* |
| *Immunity* | $FO$ | $\gamma$*Globulin* |

   The role filler of *function-of* would therefore be sortally restricted by *Immune System* or "any specific part of an *Immune System*", the latter corresponding to $ImmuneSystem_{sp}$. The latter does *not* include components of $\gamma$Globulin such as amino acids, since these are not *specific* (albeit *mandatory*) ones. This inference scheme may

[4]This difference is highlighted by capital letters for concept-to-concept relations, as well as for concept (class) names.

be restricted to functional systems in biology (such as the immune system, the circulatory system, etc.), and cannot be generalized to any composite biological structure.

We observe that once we use the four auxiliary nodes in concept definitions we get a more precise description which yields inference results that match community-wide shared biomedical intuitions.

## Parts and Wholes Recast in Description Logic

Reasoning engines for biomedical applications face large-sized knowledge bases, usually on the order of hundreds of thousands of concepts and relations. Therefore, we intentionally chose $\mathcal{ALC}$ as our formal framework, a rather simple variant of description logics that is supported by most off-the-shelf reasoning engines. Hence, we diverge from most alternative approaches to part-whole reasoning which advocate extensions of the underlying (description) logic (Franconi 1993; Padgham & Lambrix 1994; Bernauer 1996; Rogers & Rector 2000; Horrocks & Sattler 2003). At the methodological level, the gain in expressive flexibility these approaches offer has to be traded against the proliferation of (artificial) concepts and relation hierarchies in our approach. At the system engineering level, however, language extensions always require substantial adaptation or even completely new implementations of the inference engines in order to make these extensions work. Due to the inherent complexity of description classifiers the resulting extended engines usually lack the capability to deal robustly with very large knowledge bases.

Based on the $\mathcal{ALC}$ framework, we will now recast the stipulations from the previous section in terms of what we call the extended **PI** ("parts"/"includer") model which updates our previous work on the *SEP* (Hahn, Schulz, & Romacker 1999) and *Extended SEP* (Schulz & Hahn 2002) models. The extended PI model is centered around the relations *part-of* and *has-part* with the semantics introduced above. We emulate transitive mereological reasoning by taxonomic reasoning. This is achieved through the introduction of additional concepts which serve as 'reificators' of the relations *part-of* and *has-part*. For each concept $S$ we introduce two artificial concepts for both the relations *part-of* and *has-part*. These 'proto' concepts are common subsumers for all those concepts which must have, by definition, the role *part-of* filled by $S$, or the role *has-part* filled by $S$.

$$S_{sp} \equiv \exists part\text{-}of.S \quad (9) \qquad S_{si} \equiv \exists has\text{-}part.S \quad (10)$$

$S_{sp}$ then subsumes all concepts that have $S$ as a *mandatory includer* (whole), and $S_{si}$ subsumes the ones which have $S$ as a *mandatory part*. As an example, the concept $Hand_{sp}$ subsumes both *Finger* and *Thumb*. Cascading subsumption of concepts by 'part' nodes of their mandatory wholes emulates transitivity of the *part-of* relation. The same applies to the emulation of *has-part* transitivity: In this case, concepts – together with their corresponding 'includer' nodes – are subsumed by 'includer' nodes of their mandatory parts.

Figure 2 depicts a scenario in which mandatory parts correspond to mandatory includers (wholes). Each instance of *Cell Membrane* ($M$) has its role *part-of* filled by an instance

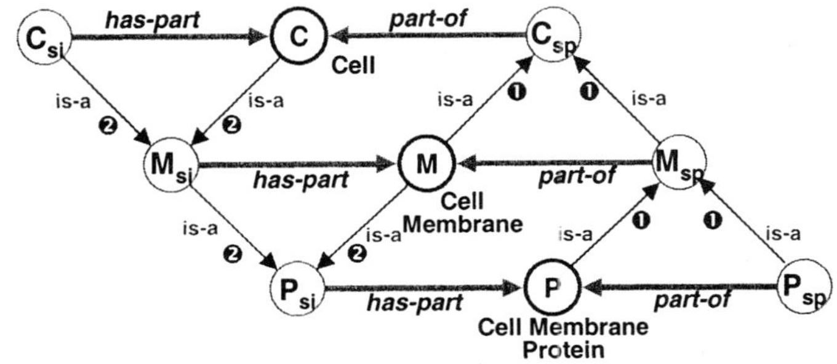


Figure 2: PI Architecture: Emulation of transitivity of both *part-of* and its converse *has-part*. The *is-a* links with label (1) emulate *part-of* hierarchies, those with label (2) emulate *has-part* hierarchies.

of *Cell* ($C$), because $M$ is subsumed by $C_{sp}$. Each *Cell* ($C$) has the role *has-part* filled by an instance of *Cell Membrane*, because $C$ is subsumed by $M_{si}$ (the same applies to *Cell Membrane* ($M$) and *Cell Membrane Protein* ($P$)). As $P$ is subsumed by $M_{sp}$ and $M_{sp}$ by $C_{sp}$, we infer that not only $M$, but also $C$ is a mandatory whole for $P$. Accordingly, $C$ is subsumed not only by $M_{si}$, but also by $P_{si}$, therefore both $M$ and $P$ are mandatory parts of $C$ (in other words, each instance of *Cell* must have an instance of *Cell Membrane* and an instance of *Cell Membrane Protein* related via *has-part*).

For a formal specification of these considerations, let us assume $C$, $M$ and $P$ denote the concepts to be modeled, and $C_{sp}$, $M_{sp}$, and $P_{sp}$ denote "part" nodes, related to $C$, $M$, and $P$ via the role *part-of*, respectively. Accordingly, $C_{si}$, $M_{si}$, and $P_{si}$ denote "includer" nodes related to $C$, $M$, and $P$ via the role *has-part*, respectively. Translating Figure 2 into (redundant) description logic expressions, we get:

$$
\begin{array}{rlrcl}
M \sqsubseteq C_{sp} & (11) & C_{si} & \sqsubseteq & M_{si} \sqsubseteq P_{si} \quad (18) \\
M_{sp} \sqsubseteq C_{sp} & (12) & C_{sp} & \equiv & \exists part\text{-}of.C \quad (19) \\
P \sqsubseteq M_{sp} \sqsubseteq C_{sp} & (13) & M_{sp} & \equiv & \exists part\text{-}of.M \quad (20) \\
P_{sp} \sqsubseteq M_{sp} \sqsubseteq C_{sp} & (14) & P_{sp} & \equiv & \exists part\text{-}of.P \quad (21) \\
M \sqsubseteq P_{si} & (15) & C_{si} & \equiv & \exists has\text{-}part.C \quad (22) \\
M_{si} \sqsubseteq P_{si} & (16) & M_{si} & \equiv & \exists has\text{-}part.M \quad (23) \\
C \sqsubseteq M_{si} \sqsubseteq P_{si} & (17) & P_{si} & \equiv & \exists has\text{-}part.P \quad (24)
\end{array}
$$

It is obvious that, by using this pattern across various physical concepts linked with each other via the *part-of* or the *has-part* relation, we get the same deductions as if *part-of* and *has-part* were really transitive at the level of concepts.

However, using the two auxiliary nodes from expressions (9) and (10), it is still not possible to address mandatory parts and includers, which so far are only available as a filler of the (inherited) roles *has-part* and *part-of*. Therefore, we provide two additional hierarchies, *viz.* the hierarchy of mandatory parts and that of mandatory includers. As all the information is already available in the PI hierarchy the new hierarchies, indeed, contain redundant information. The construction of these hierarchies is straightforward: A $C_{mp}$ node (mandatory part) subsumes all first-level (non-inherited) role fillers of *has-part* at $C$, and $C_{mi}$ (mandatory includer) all first-level role fillers of *part-of* at $C$, as well as their associated *mp* and *mi* nodes.

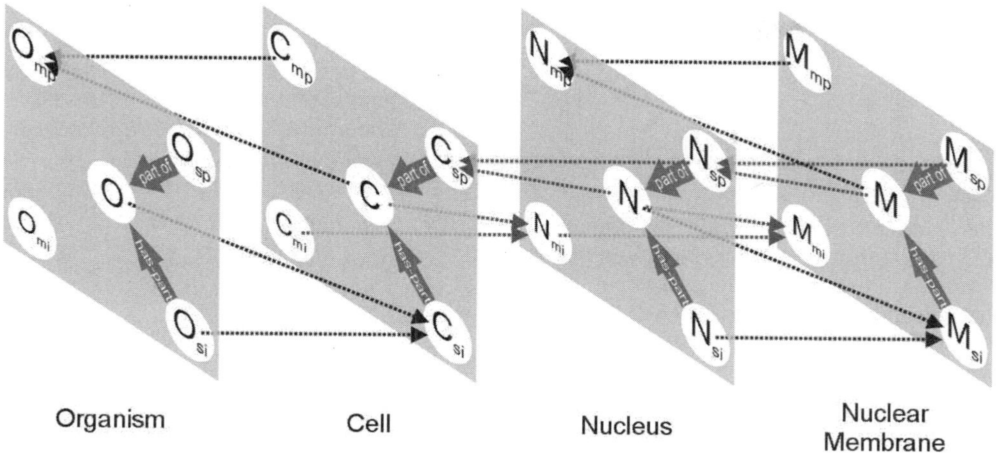


Figure 3: Extended PI Architecture using the quadruple concept encoding pattern. The *si*-nodes are linked to their core concepts by *has-part*, the *sp*-nodes by *part-of* (dotted lines indicate subsumption relations).

In

$$C \sqsubseteq A_{si} \sqcap B_{si} \quad (25)$$

$C$ inherits the roles $has\text{-}part.A$ and $has\text{-}part.B$; the concept $C$ also has $A$ and $B$ as specific includers. Hence, the auxiliary node $C_{mp}$ has to subsume both $A$ and $B$, but also $A_{mp}$ and $B_{mp}$. The following axioms will have to be added:

$$A \sqsubseteq C_{mp} \quad (26) \qquad A_{mp} \sqsubseteq C_{mp} \quad (28)$$
$$B \sqsubseteq C_{mp} \quad (27) \qquad B_{mp} \sqsubseteq C_{mp} \quad (29)$$

The flexibility of this approach is shown in Figure 3:
(i) An *organism* is mandatorily constituted by a *cell*;
(ii) a *cell* is not necessarily part of an organism;
(iii) a *nucleus* is mandatorily part of a *cell*;
(iv) cells without nuclei exist;
(v) a *nucleus* mandatorily has a *nuclear membrane*;
(vi) a *nuclear membrane* is mandatorily part of a *nucleus*.

(i) is reflected by the subsumption of $O$ and $O_{si}$ by $C_{si}$, and, consequently, by the subsumption of $C$ and $C_{mp}$ by $O_{mp}$. Due to (ii), there are no subsumptions by *mi* and *sp* nodes. (iii) is reflected by the subsumptions of $N$ and $N_{sp}$ by $C_{sp}$, and, consequently, by the subsumption of $C$ and $C_{mi}$ by $N_{mi}$. With (iv) there is no subsumption of $C$ by $N_{si}$. (v) and (vi) result from the following subsumptions: $N \sqsubseteq M_{si}$, $N_{si} \sqsubseteq M_{si}$, $N \sqsubseteq M_{mi}$, $N_{mi} \sqsubseteq M_{mi}$, $M \sqsubseteq N_{sp}$, $M_{sp} \sqsubseteq N_{sp}$, and $M \sqsubseteq N_{mp}$, $M_{mp} \sqsubseteq N_{mp}$.

This encoding allows us to introduce a range restriction into concept definitions suitable for allowing "possible" parts and wholes, and obviating "forbidden" role fillers. According to (6) and (7), we constrain the definition of the concept *cell* ($C$) by the following range restrictions:

$$C \sqsubseteq \forall part\text{-}of.(C_{si} \sqcup C_{mi}) \quad (30)$$
$$C \sqsubseteq \forall has\text{-}part.(C_{sp} \sqcup C_{mp}) \quad (31)$$

Thus, an instance of *cell* may have an instance of *nucleus* and *nuclear membrane* as part, as well as an instance of *organism* as includer, but any object not contained in the extension of the two disjunctions[5] would be disallowed to be connected to an instance of $C$.

Finally, we demonstrate how the proposed part-whole model is capable of accounting for the inferences discussed previously (numbers correspond to the examples).

1. $InsulinSynthesis \sqsubseteq \exists has\text{-}location.(BetaCells \sqcup BetaCells_{mi})$
   $InsulinSynthesis \sqsubseteq \forall has\text{-}location.(BetaCells \sqcup BetaCells_{mi} \sqcup BetaCells_{si})$
2. $AmputationOfToe \sqsubseteq \exists has\text{-}target.Toe$
   $AmputationOfToe \sqsubseteq \forall has\text{-}target.Toe$
3. $ErythrocytePhagocytosis \sqsubseteq \exists ingestion\text{-}of.(Erythrocyte \sqcup Erythrocyte_{mp})$
   $ErythrocytePhagocytosis \sqsubseteq \forall ingestion\text{-}of.(Erythrocyte \sqcup Erythrocyte_{mp} \sqcup Erythrocyte_{sp})$
4. $Immunity \sqsubseteq \exists function\text{-}of.(ImmuneSystem \sqcup ImmuneSystem_{sp})$
   $Immunity \sqsubseteq \forall function\text{-}of.(ImmuneSystem \sqcup ImmuneSystem_{sp} \sqcup ImmuneSystem_{mp})$

The *PI* encoding not only provides an elegant way of emulating *part-of* and *has-part* transitivity through taxonomic subsumption, but also grants more flexibility and precision in adapting the ontology to common conceptualizations in the biomedical domain. By adding four "proto-nodes" for every concept we are able to express four propagation patterns (two downstream and two upstream), as well as one pattern without propagation. The "proto-nodes" also support several control mechanisms for the propagation of roles within mereological hierarchies. Hence, our approach cannot be considered just a data structure 'hack' but rather bears ontological plausiblity in the biomedical domain.

[5] In order to simplify the underlying logic, the disjunctions can be avoided by common subsumer concepts.

## Conclusions

Adequate and expressive domain models require not only appropriate ontological categories but also the support of typical reasoning patterns. Our solution is based on a layered modeling strategy for concepts within standard description logics, essentially based upon the introduction of additional concepts such as reifi cators for the relations *part-of* and *has-part*. These artifacts not only enable the propagation of roles across partonomic hierarchies, but also the accommodation of various standard reasoning patterns. Unlike the approaches which advocate language extensions in order to adequately deal with part-whole reasoning, we do not require newly designed (and implemented) terminological inference engines.

In order to deal with the proliferation of concepts we found it imperative to ease the knowledge editing and maintenance phase. We chose to use an intermediate representation format as interface to the knowledge engineer, a frame-based system with a graphical user interface (Noy, Fergerson, & Musen 2000). We combined the ease of knowledge maintenance with the power of a terminological reasoner for our current experiments in which we converted the Foundational Model of Anatomy into a description logic format using the extended PI architecture (Beck & Schulz 2003).

## References


Artale, A.; Franconi, E.; Guarino, N.; and Pazzi, L. 1996. Part-whole relations in object-centered systems: An overview. *Data & Knowledge Engineering* 20(3):347–383.

Baader, F., and Nutt, W. 2003. Basic description logics. In Baader, F.; Calvanese, D.; McGuinness, D.; Nardi, D.; and Patel-Schneider, P., eds., *The Description Logic Handbook. Theory, Implementation and Applications*. Cambridge University Press. 43–95.

Beck, R., and Schulz, S. 2003. Logic-based remodeling of the digital anatomist foundational model. In *AMIA'03 – Proceedings of the 2003 Annual Symposium of the American Medical Informatics Association*, 687–691.

Bernauer, J. 1996. Analysis of part-whole relation and subsumption in the medical domain. *Data & Knowledge Engineering* 20(3):405– 415.

Casati, R., and Varzi, A. C. 1999. *Parts and Places. The Structures of Spatial Representation*. MIT Press.

Franconi, E. 1993. A treatment of plurals and plural quantifi cations based on a theory of collections. *Minds and Machines* 3(4):453–474.

Gene Ontology Consortium. 2001. Creating the Gene Ontology resource: Design and implementation. *Genome Research* 11(8):1425–1433.

Hahn, U., and Schulz, S. 2003. Building a very large ontology from medical thesauri. In Staab, S., and Studer, R., eds., *Handbook on Ontologies in Information Systems*. Springer. 133–150.

Hahn, U.; Schulz, S.; and Romacker, M. 1999. Partonomic reasoning as taxonomic reasoning in medicine. In *AAAI'99 – Proceedings of the 16th National Conference on Artificial Intelligence*, 271–276.

Horrocks, I., and Sattler, U. 2003. The effect of adding complex role inclusion axioms in description logics. In *IJCAI'03 – Proceedings of the 18th International Joint Conference on Artificial Intelligence*, 343–348.

Horrocks, I.; Rector, A.; and Goble, C. 1996. A description logic based schema for the classifi cation of medical data. In *KRDB'96 – Proceedings of the 3rd Workshop Knowledge Representation Meets Databases*, 24–28.

McCray, A. T., and Nelson, S. J. 1995. The representation of meaning in the UMLS. *Methods of Information in Medicine* 34(1/2):193–201.

Noy, F.; Musen, M. A.; Mejino, J. L. V.; and Rosse, C. 2002. Pushing the envelope: Challenges in a frame-based representation of human anatomy. Technical Report SMI-2002-0925, 2002, Stanford University.

Noy, F.; Fergerson, R. W.; and Musen, M. A. 2000. The knowledge model of PROTEGE-2000: Combining interoperability and flexibility. In *Proceedings of the 12th International Conference on Knowledge Engineering and Knowledge Management – EKAW 2000*, 17–32.

Padgham, L., and Lambrix, P. 1994. A framework of part-of hierarchies in terminological logics. In *Principles of Knowledge Representation and Reasoning. Proceedings of the 4th International Conference – KR'94*, 485–496.

Rector, A. L. 2002. Analysis of propagation along transitive roles: Formalisation of the GALEN experience with medical ontologies. In *DL 2002 – Proceedings of the 2002 International Workshop on Description Logics*.

Rogers, J., and Rector, A. 2000. GALEN's model of parts and wholes: Experience and comparisons. In *AMIA 2000 – Proceedings of the Annual Symposium of the American Medical Informatics Association*, 714–718.

Rosse, C.; Mejino, J. L. V.; Modayur, B. R.; Jakobovits, R.; Hinshaw, K. P.; and Brinkley, J. F. 1998. Motivation and organizational principles for anatomical knowledge representation: The DIGITAL ANATOMIST symbolic knowledge base. *Journal of the AMIA* 5(1):17–40.

UMLS. 2004. *Unified Medical Language System*. Bethesda, MD: National Library of Medicine.

Schulz, S., and Hahn, U. 2002. Necessary parts and wholes in bio-ontologies. In *Proceedings of the 8th International Conference – KR 2002*, 387–394.

Schulz, S., and Hahn, U. 2004. Parthood as spatial inclusion: Evidence from biomedical conceptualizations. In *Proceedings of the 9th Intl. Conference – KR 2004*.

Smith, B., and Rosse, C. 2004. The role of foundational relations in the alignment of biomedical ontologies. In *MEDINFO 2004 – Proceedings of the 11th World Congress on Medical Informatics*.

Smith, B.; Williams, J.; and Schulze-Kremer, S. 2003. The ontology of the Gene Ontology. In *AMIA'03 – Proceedings of the 2003 Annual Symposium of the American Medical Informatics Association*, 609–613.

Winston, M.; Chaffi n, R.; and Herrmann, D. J. 1987. A taxonomy of part-whole relationships. *Cognitive Science* 11:417–444.

# CASE$^E$: A Hierarchical Event Representation for the Analysis of Videos

**Asaad Hakeem, Yaser Sheikh, and Mubarak Shah**
University of Central Florida, Orlando, FL 32816
{ahakeem, yaser, shah}@cs.ucf.edu

### Abstract

A representational gap exists between low-level measurements (segmentation, object classification, tracking) and high-level understanding of video sequences. In this paper, we propose a novel representation of events in videos to bridge this gap, based on the CASE representation of natural languages. The proposed representation has three significant contributions over existing frameworks. First, we recognize the importance of causal and temporal relationships between sub-events and extend CASE to allow the representation of temporal structure and causality between sub-events. Second, in order to capture both multi-agent and multi-threaded events, we introduce a hierarchical CASE representation of events in terms of sub-events and case-lists. Last, for purposes of implementation we present the concept of a temporal event-tree, and pose the problem of event detection as subtree pattern matching. By extending CASE, a natural language representation, for the representation of events, the proposed work allows a plausible means of interface between users and the computer. We show two important applications of the proposed event representation for the automated annotation of standard meeting video sequences, and for event detection in extended videos of railroad crossings.

## Introduction

Human community and society are built upon the ability to share experiences of events. Hence, in the enterprize of machine vision, the ability to represent and share observed events must be one of the ultimate, if most abstract, goals. With computer vision techniques maturing sufficiently to provide reliable low-level descriptions of scenes, the necessity of developing semantically meaningful descriptions of these low-level descriptors is becoming increasingly pressing. In this work, one primary objective is to present a coherent representation of events, as a means to encode the relationships between agents and objects participating in an event. We also emphasize, in particular, a representation that allows computers to share observations with other computers and also with humans, in terms of events. An *event* is defined as a collection of actions performed by one or more agents. *Agents* are animates that can perform actions independently or dependently (e.g. people or robots). The practical need for formal representation of events is best illustrated through possible applications. These applications include: (1) *Surveillance*: By definition, surveillance applications require the detection of peculiar events. Event representations can be used for prior definition of what constitutes an interesting event in any given domain, allowing automation of area surveillance, (2) *Video Indexing and Event Browsing*: Given a query for a certain event (defined in terms of an event representation), similar instances can be retrieved from a database of annotated clips, (3) *Annotation*: In the spirit of MPEG-7, video sequences may be annotated autonomously based on their content, (4) *Domain Understanding*: It is noted that causality is an abstract that cannot be directly inferred from a single video sequence. Through the use of event representations, causality can be inferred between events in a single domain (e.g. surveillance of airports) across several extended video sequences for domain understanding.



In literature, a variety of approaches have been proposed for the detection of events in video sequences. Most of these approaches can be arranged into two categories based on the semantic significance of their representations. This distinction is important, since it determines whether humans can exploit the representation for communication. Approaches where representations do not take on semantic meaning include Causal events (Brand 1997), Force dynamics (Siskind 2000), Stochastic Context Free Grammars (Bobick and Ivanov 1998), Spatio-temporal Derivatives (Zelnik-Manor and Irani 2001), and geometric properties and appearance (Malliot, Thonnat, and Boucher 2003). While they differ in approaches, the representations they employ do not lend themselves directly to interpretation or interface to humans. Learning methods such as Bayesian Networks and Hidden Markov Models (Ivanov and Bobick 2000) have been widely used in the area of activity recognition. A known drawback of learning methods is that they usually require large training sets of events and variation in data may require complete re-training. Similarly, there is no straightforward method of expanding the domain, once training has been completed. On the other hand, semantically significant approaches like the state machines (Koller, Heinze, and Nagel 1991), and PNF Networks (Pinhanez and Bobick 1998) provide varying degrees of representation to the actions and agents involved in the events.

What is missing in these representations is coherence in describing low-level measurements as 'events'. Can these representations be used to share knowledge between two systems? Can events be compared on the basis of these representations? How are these representations related to human understanding of events? Can a human communicate his or her observation of an event to a computer or vice versa? By extending automatic generation of a natural language ontology to event representation of a video, a plausible interface between the human and the computer is facilitated. One such natural language representation called CASE was proposed by Fillmore (Fillmore 1968) for language understanding. The basic unit of this representation is a case-frame that has several elementary cases, such as an agentive, an instrumental, and a predicate. Using these case-frames Fillmore analyzed languages, treating *all* languages generically. However, CASE was primarily used for syntactic analysis of natural languages, and while it provides a promising foundation for event representation it has several limitations for that end. Firstly, since events are typically made up of a hierarchy of sub-events it is impossible to describe them as a succession of case-frames. Second, these sub-events often have temporal and causal relationships between them, and CASE provides no mechanisms to represent these relationships. Furthermore, there might be simultaneous dependent or independent sub-events with multiple agentives, and change of location and instrumentals during events. CASE was first investigated for event representation (Neumann 1989), but the author did not investigate the temporal structure of events as the author was not concerned with event *detection*. More recently (Kojima, Tamura, and Fukunaga 2001) addressed some shortcomings in CASE for single person event detection with, SO- (source prefixed to case), GO- (goal prefixed to case) and **SUB** (child frame describing a sub-event). SO- and GO- are prefixed to the **LOC** (locative) case mostly describing the source and destination locations of the agent in the event. A concept hierarchy of action rules (case-frames) was used to determine an action grammar (ontology) for the sequence of events. Also, using case-frames based on events, they reconstructed the event sequence in the form of sentences. Their method worked well for single person action analysis using the CASE representation. However, this work did not address important issues of temporal and causal relationships. Moreover, no mechanisms were proposed for multiple-agents or multi-threaded events.

We propose three critical extensions to CASE for the representation of events: (1) accommodating multiple agents and multi-threaded event, (2) supporting the inclusion of temporal information or *temporal logic* into the representation, and (3) supporting the inclusion of *causal* relationships between events as well. We also propose a novel event-tree representation, based on temporal relationships, for the detection of events in video sequences. Hence, unlike almost all previous work, we use both temporal structure and an environment descriptor simultaneously to represent an event.

## The Extended CASE framework: CASE$^E$

In this section, the three extensions to the CASE framework are presented. Firstly, in order to capture both multi-agent and multi-thread events, we introduce a hierarchical CASE representation of events in terms of sub-events and case-lists. Secondly, since the temporal structure of events is critical to understanding and hence representing events, we introduce temporal logic into the CASE representation based on the interval algebra in (Allen and Ferguson 1994). Lastly, we recognize the importance of causal relationships between sub events and extend CASE to allow the representation of such causality between sub-events.

### Multi-Agent, Multi-Thread Representation

Except in constrained domains, events typically involve multiple agents engaged in several dependent or independent actions. Thus any representation of events must be able to capture the composite nature of *real* events. To represent multiple objects, we introduce the idea of case-lists of elements for a particular case. For example, if there are more than one agents involved in an event we add both in a case-list within **AG**,

[ **PRED**: move, **AG**:{ person1, person2 }, ...]

As in (Kojima, Tamura, and Fukunaga 2001), we use **SUB** to represent a sub-event that occurs during an event. However, this representation offers no means to represent *several* sub-events or multiple threads. To represent multiple threads we add them to a list of sub-events in the **SUB** case. An example is shown below,

"While Jack stole from the cashier, Bonnie robbed from the bank as Clyde was talking to the cashier"

[ **PRED**: steal, **AG**: Jack, **D**: cashier, **SUB**:{
[ **PRED**: rob, **AG**: Bonnie, **OBJ**: bank ],
[ **PRED**: talk, **AG**: { Clyde, cashier } ] }
]

It should be immediately evident to the reader that the above event representation is ambiguous as temporal relations have not been defined. When did Clyde talk to the cashier? Was it before, during or after the steal event. In order to have an unambiguous representation, we need to incorporate temporal relations in our representation. The temporal relations are based on temporal logic, which is described in the next section.

### Temporal Logic

The temporal structure of events is critical to understanding and hence representing events. Events are rarely instantaneous and often largely defined by the temporal order and relationship of their sub-events. In order to represent temporal relationships of sub-events, we introduce temporal logic into the CASE representation based on the interval algebra of (Allen and Ferguson 1994). We use this algebra to represent seven temporal relationships[1]. This interval temporal logic is shown in Fig. 1. Since temporal relationship exist between sub-events, the temporal case is always used in conjunction with **SUB**. The temporal case (e.g. **AFTER**) assumes the value of the predicate of the case-frame with which the temporal relationship exists. Consider, once again, the above example of the bank robbery by Bonnie and

[1]A minor modification was made where **BEFORE** was replaced by **AFTER** with respective modification in the parameters for ease of use in CASE

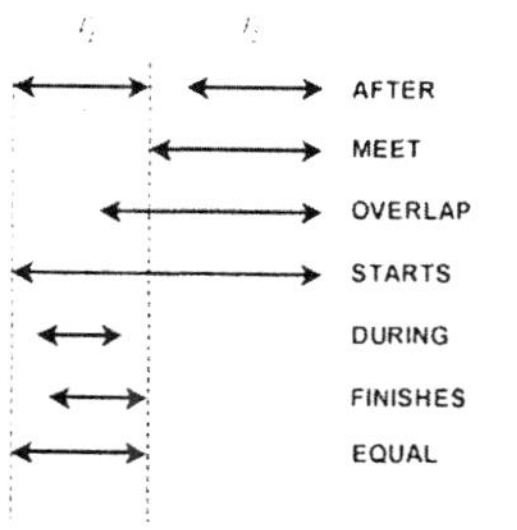


Figure 1: Allen's interval algebra describing temporal logic between durations $T_1$ and $T_2$.

Clyde, the case-frames with the temporal logic incorporated are,

[ **PRED**: steal, **AG**: Jack, **D**: cashier, **SUB**:{
[ **PRED**: rob, **AG**: Bonnie, **OBJ**: bank, **DURING**: steal ],
[ **PRED**: talk, **AG**: { Clyde, cashier }, **OVERLAP**: steal ] }
]

The entire list of temporal cases, for two durations $T_1$ and $T_2$ is as follows,

**AFTER** : $T_2^{start} > T_1^{end}$
**MEETS** : $T_1^{end} = T_2^{start}$
**DURING** : $(T_1^{start} < T_2^{start}) \wedge (T_1^{end} > T_2^{end})$
**FINISHES** : $(T_1^{end} = T_2^{end}) \wedge (T_1^{start} < T_2^{start})$
**OVERLAPS** : $(T_1^{start} < T_2^{start}) \wedge (T_1^{end} > T_2^{start}) \wedge (T_1^{end} < T_2^{end})$
**EQUAL** : $(T_1^{start} = T_2^{start}) \wedge (T_1^{end} = T_2^{end})$
**STARTS** : $(T_1^{start} = T_2^{start}) \wedge (T_1^{end} \neq T_2^{end})$

It is ensured that each temporal case is unique. A little thought should convince the reader that temporal relationships between more than two events are also possible within this scheme.

There is still a requirement for representing the *dependency* of events. Some events require a causal relationship, i.e. they will not occur independently and are conditional upon other events. The representation so far does not have the capability to codify causal relationships, which is addressed in the next section.

### Causality

In understanding the nature of events, the causal relationships between the constituent sub-events are indispensable. Some events might not occur if certain conditions were not satisfied, while some events may be dependent on other events. In order to explain this concept we show a simplistic example below,

"Caravaggio pulled the chair therefore Michelangelo fell down."

[ **PRED**: pull, **AG**: Caravaggio, **OBJ**: chair, **CAUSE**:
[ **PRED**: fall, **D**: Michelangelo, **FAC**: down] ]

In the above example, Michelangelo would not have fallen down if Caravaggio had not pulled the chair. Therefore the 'fall' and 'pull' event have a causal relationship. It should be noted that only definite causal relations are represented by the **CAUSE** case, instead of using **SUB**. While the proposed extension allows the representation of causal relationships, it is noted that causal relationships cannot be inferred from video measurements alone. In other words, it is impossible to make a distinction between two successive events, and two causal events without some reasoning. Thus, from the point of view of on-line processing of measurements, videos are represented in terms of a *temporal representation*. Events and sub-events are arranged in a hierarchy according to the order of their temporal incidence and duration. Inferring causality solely from these temporal representations is a promising future direction.

## Event Detection in Videos

In this section, we address some issues of implementing the proposed representation for event detection in videos. Video data is available as a discrete set of images, sampled on sequential lattices. Let $f(\mathbf{p}, t)$ represent a continuous video signal, indexed by spatial and temporal coordinates respectively. By indexing on the discrete-time variable $k$ we can *temporally* represent the video signal as the set $\{f[\mathbf{x}, k]\}$ for $1 \leq k \leq N$, where $N$ is the temporal support of the video signal, and $\mathbf{x} = (x, y)$ denotes the spatial coordinate (over some support). Here it is assumed that the lower-level tasks of object detection, classification and tracking have been performed for a stationary camera (corresponding to the GSD of Neumann (1989)). Each object is represented in terms of its label and motion, e.g. $\{\text{person}_a, \mathbf{u}_a\}$, where $\mathbf{u}_a = \{ (x_1, y_1), (x_2, y_2), \ldots (x_N, y_N) \}$ is the trajectory of $\text{person}_a$'s centroid. It is important to note that since it is the *relative* concept of motion that we are interested in (e.g. where did $\text{agent}_1$ move to with respect to $\text{object}_2$?), two-dimensional projections of three-dimensional world trajectories are sufficient for event representation (barring some degenerate configurations). Particular to each domain, domain objects and a vocabulary of predicates can be defined. Conceptually, these are the 'input' into a system that represents these inputs in terms of $\text{CASE}^E$. For event *detection*, a set of events are predefined as events of interest. In order to detect these events of interest within an autonomously generated representation of events in a video sequences, we pose the problem as a subtree isomorphism. A similarity measure is defined to guide the search for a match.

### Maximal Subtree Isomorphism

The temporal structure of $\text{CASE}^E$ can be intuitively visualized as a rooted tree, with each vertex corresponding to a sub-event (case-frame), and each edge corresponding to the temporal relationship between two vertices (e.g. **AFTER**, **MEET**). A split occurs at the simultaneous incident of multiple sub-events or when one of several sub-event ends during a parent event. An example sub-tree is shown in Figure 2. The problem of detecting the occurrence of a pre-defined event can be posed as finding a maximal subtree isomorphism. Given a video stream, a rooted tree can be continuously grown based on temporal relations of sub-events. Each pre-defined event itself can be represented as a tree, too. For two rooted trees, $T_1 = (V_1, E_1)$, the event-tree of the pre-defined events of

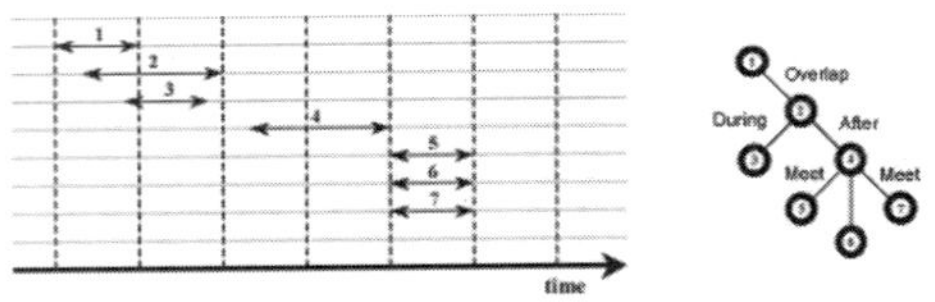


Figure 2: An Event Tree. The plot shows the temporal duration of a succession of sub-events, and to the right of it is a tree representation. Each vertex corresponds to a sub-event, and each edge represents the temporal relationship with the parent vertex.

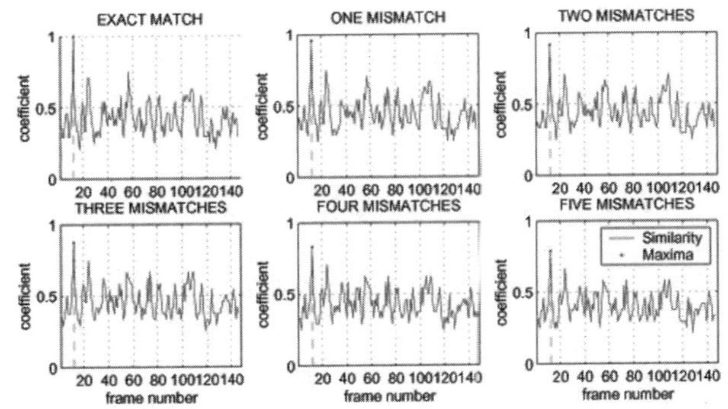


Figure 3: Matching using the Jaccard Coefficient. A predefined event-tree consisting of six vertices (case-frames) is matched with an event-tree of a video sequence consisting of 148 vertices (case-frames). The correct match occurs at the subtree rooted at frame 12 (the similarity maximum by the dotted red line). From top-left to bottom-right the pre-defined predicate is perturbed so that progressively greater number of case-elements within the case-frames mismatch.

interest, and $T_2 = (V_2, E_2)$, the video event-tree, any bijection $\phi : H_1 \rightarrow H_2$, with $H_1 \subseteq V_1$ and $H_2 \subseteq V_2$, is a subtree isomorphism if it preserves the adjacency and the hierarchy between vertices and if $T_1(H_1)$ and $T_2(H_2)$ are trees too. In our implementation, we employ a naive search for the maximal subtree isomorphism. A more sophisticated algorithm has been proposed in (Pelillo, Siddiqi, and Zucker 1999), where it shown that there is a one-to-one correspondence between the maximal subtree isomorphism problem and the maximal clique problem and, moreover, that a continuous formulation of the maximum clique problem can be exploited to find a solution to the original subtree matching problem. The cost function we wish to maximize is the similarity of corresponding vertices, and the number of matching edges. To that end, a measure of similarity between case-frames, which correspond to vertices in the event-tree, is defined next.

**Similarity** Most pattern recognition problems are based on feature vectors of real-valued numbers usually with a natural measure of distance between vectors. On the other hand, in measuring the 'similarity' between nominal data as in our case there is no clear notion of similarity (or metric). However, within a *complete* event domain, where a complete event domain is one where the set of possible objects and vocabulary is *uniquely* defined, it is possible to measure similarity between case-frames. We wish to compare a pair of observations $(\mathbf{C}_1, \mathbf{C}_2)$, where $\mathbf{C}_i = [c_{i1}, c_{i2}, \ldots, c_{ip}]$ corresponds to a case-frame and each element corresponds to a case. If a certain case does not exist (e.g. if the location is unspecified) the value of the element is $\emptyset$. Now for a complete event domain, we can define $\psi(c_{ik}, c_{jk})$,

$$\psi(c_{ik}, c_{jk}) = \begin{cases} \infty & \text{if } c_{ik} = c_{jk} = \emptyset \\ 1 & \text{if } c_{ik} = c_{jk} \neq \emptyset \\ 0 & \text{otherwise} \end{cases}$$

and similarity is measured using the Jaccard coefficient (ratio of sizes of intersection and union),

$$\rho(\mathbf{C}_i, \mathbf{C}_j) = \frac{\sum_{k=1}^{p} \mathbf{I}(\psi(c_{ik}, c_{jk}) = 1)}{\sum_{k=1}^{p} \mathbf{I}(\psi(c_{ik}, c_{jk}) = 1) + \sum_{k=1}^{p} \mathbf{I}(\psi(c_{ik}, c_{jk}) = 0)} \quad (1)$$

where $\mathbf{I}$ is an indicator function. An evaluation of the Jaccard Coefficient is shown in Figure 3.

## Experiments and Discussion

We performed two sets of experiments (corresponding to each domain), both were implemented to run in real time (30 fps) on a 2.1 GHz Pentium Machine. The first experiment set involved the standard PETS test video for hand posture classification, as well as 11 other unconstrained sequences of human interaction. Initial object identification and labelling were performed manually, and further tracking was performed using the MEANSHIFT tracking algorithm. The objective was to perform a real-time generation of CASE$^E$ representations. Figures 4 shows snapshots of individuals interacting in an unconstrained environment and their corresponding event representations.

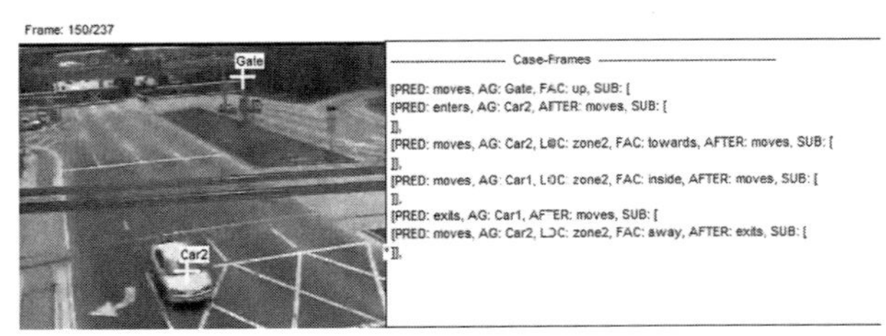


(a)

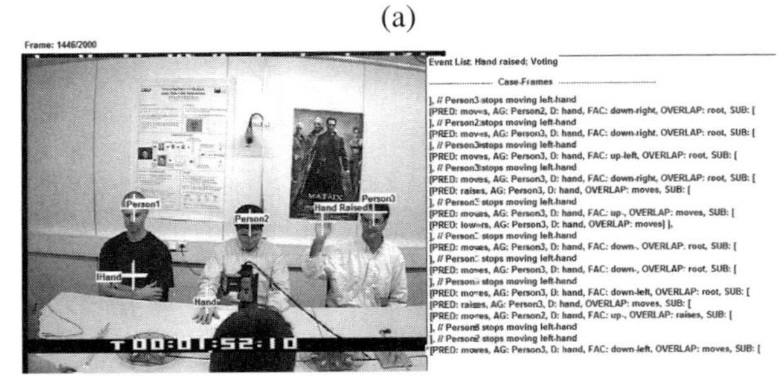


(c)

Figure 4: On-line CASE$^E$ representation of a video sequences. Frames during the online CASE$^E$ generation are shown, with each agent labelled. (a) Representation at Frame 150/237 for the Railroad Monitoring Experiment (b) (PETS Sequence) Representation at Frame 1446/2000.

The second set of experiments was to the application of CASE$^E$ to the domain of monitoring a railroad intersection. In an independent railway study of 25,000 video sequences, ten events of interest were identified in this domain. We encoded each of these events using the CASE$^E$ representation and include CASE$^E$ representations of these ten events. The encoding of human interaction domain using CASE$^E$ is not shown due to space limitation, but CASE$^E$ can represent events of two very different domains. The railroad scenario was selected since it is a closed environment suited to formal representation. For this domain, the CASE$^E$ was coded for events of interest, and as the system produced CASE$^E$ representations for the video stream, it monitored for the incidence of each pre-defined event using the algorithm previously presented. At the instance of each frame, the motion of each agent is analyzed and used to update the current CASE$^E$. Results of the event detection are shown in Figure 5. The experimental results for the precision and recall values are summarized in Table 1.

| No. of Frames | Events Detected | Ground Truth | False Positive | Precision % | Recall % |
|---|---|---|---|---|---|
| 272 | 18 | 17 | 1 | 94.44 | 100 |
| 311 | 24 | 27 | 2 | 91.67 | 81.48 |
| 330 | 40 | 36 | 5 | 87.50 | 97.22 |
| 161 | 18 | 16 | 3 | 83.33 | 93.87 |
| 187 | 39 | 32 | 7 | 82.05 | 100 |
| 184 | 13 | 13 | 1 | 92.03 | 92.03 |
| 165 | 18 | 18 | 0 | 100 | 100 |
| 247 | 40 | 38 | 4 | 90 | 94.73 |
| 342 | 61 | 51 | 11 | 81.96 | 98.03 |
| 2000 | 102 | 108 | 7 | 93.13 | 87.96 |
| 335 | 32 | 29 | 5 | 84.37 | 93.10 |
| 402 | 34 | 28 | 7 | 79.41 | 96.42 |
| 237 | 9 | 10 | 1 | 88.89 | 80 |
| 223 | 4 | 4 | 0 | 100 | 100 |
| 486 | 12 | 9 | 3 | 75 | 100 |
| 192 | 9 | 8 | 1 | 88.89 | 100 |

Table 1: Summary of results for the two experiment sets.

## Application of CASE$^E$ Representation for Monitoring Railroad Intersections

### Domain Entities

| | |
|---|---|
| **Vehicle** | A vehicle in the universe |
| **Person** | A person in the universe |
| **Train** | A train on the tracks |
| **Gate** | Gate at the railroad crossing |
| **Signal** | Signal at the railroad crossing |
| **Zone1** | Zone covering the area of activation for the signal |
| **Zone2** | Zone covering a designated high-risk area |
| **Tracks** | The tracks that the train travels on |

**Domain Predicates** *Moves, Enters, Exits, Switches, Signals, Breaks, Collides, Stops.*

### Domain Events

1. **train approaches ⇒ signal switches on ⇒ gate arm moves down ⇒ vehicle stops outside Zone2**
   [ **PRED**: Moves, **AG**: Train, **D**: Signals, **LOC**: Zone1, **FAC**: Towards, **CAUSE**:
   [ **PRED**: Switches, **AG**: Signals, **FAC**: On, **CAUSE**:
   [ **PRED**: Moves, **AG**: Gate, **FAC**: Down, **AFTER**: Switches, **SUB**:
   [ **PRED**: Stops, **AG**: Vehicle, **LOC**: Zone2, **FAC**: Outside, **AFTER**: Moves ] ] ] ]

2. **train approaches ⇒ signal switches on ⇒ gate arm moves down ⇒ vehicle stops inside Zone2**
   [ **PRED**: Moves, **AG**: Train, **D**: Signals, **LOC**: Zone1, **FAC**: Towards, **CAUSE**:
   [ **PRED**: Switches, **AG**: Signals, **FAC**: On, **CAUSE**:
   [ **PRED**: Moves, **AG**: Gate, **FAC**: Down, **AFTER**: Switches, **SUB**:
   [ **PRED**: Stops, **AG**: Vehicle, **LOC**: Zone2, **FAC**: Inside, **AFTER**: Moves ] ] ] ]

3. **train approaches ⇒ signal switches on ⇒ gate arm moves down ⇒ vehicle breaks the gate arm while entering Zone2**
   [ **PRED**: Moves, **AG**: Train, **D**: Signals, **LOC**: Zone1, **FAC**: Towards, **CAUSE**:
   [ **PRED**: Switches, **AG**: Signals, **FAC**: On, **CAUSE**:
   [ **PRED**: Moves, **AG**: Gate, **FAC**: Down, **AFTER**: Switches, **SUB**:
   [ **PRED**: Enters, **AG**: Vehicle, **LOC**: Zone2, **DURING**: Moves, **SUB**:
   [ **PRED**: Breaks, **AG**: Vehicle, **D**: Gate, **DURING**: Enters ] ] ] ] ]

4. **train approaches ⇒ signal switches on ⇒ gate arm moves down ⇒ vehicle breaks the gate arm while exiting Zone2**
   [ **PRED**: Moves, **AG**: Train, **D**: Signals, **LOC**: Zone1, **FAC**: Towards, **CAUSE**:
   [ **PRED**: Switches, **AG**: Signals, **FAC**: On, **CAUSE**:
   [ **PRED**: Moves, **AG**: Gate, **FAC**: Down, **AFTER**: Switches, **SUB**:
   [ **PRED**: Exits, **AG**: Vehicle, **LOC**: Zone2, **DURING**: Moves, **SUB**:
   [ **PRED**: Breaks, **AG**: Vehicle, **D**: Gate, **DURING**: Exits ] ] ] ] ]

5. **train approaches ⇒ signal switches on ⇒ gate arm moves down ⇒ vehicle enters while gate is in motion**
   [ **PRED**: Moves, **AG**: Train, **D**: Signals, **LOC**: Zone1, **FAC**: Towards, **CAUSE**:
   [ **PRED**: Switches, **AG**: Signals, **FAC**: On, **CAUSE**:
   [ **PRED**: Moves, **AG**: Gate, **FAC**: Down, **AFTER**: Switches, **SUB**:
   [ **PRED**: Enters, **AG**: Vehicle, **LOC**: Zone2, **DURING**: Moves ] ] ] ]

6. **train approaches ⇒ signal switches on ⇒ gate arm moves down ⇒ vehicle exits while gate is in motion**
   [ **PRED**: Moves, **AG**: Train, **D**: Signals, **LOC**: Zone1, **FAC**: Towards, **CAUSE**:
   [ **PRED**: Switches, **AG**: Signals, **FAC**: On, **CAUSE**:
   [ **PRED**: Moves, **AG**: Gate, **FAC**: Down, **AFTER**: Switches, **SUB**:
   [ **PRED**: Exits, **AG**: Vehicle, **D**: Zone2, **DURING**: Moves ] ] ] ]

7. **Vehicle collides with train**
   [ **PRED**: Moves, **AG**: Train, **LOC**: Zone2, **FAC**: Inside, **SUB**:
   [ **PRED**: Moves, **AG**: Vehicle, **FAC**: Inside, **LOC**: Zone2, **DURING**: Move, **CAUSE**:
   [ **PRED**: Collides, **AG**: { Vehicle, Train } ] ] ]

8. **Person being hit by train**
   [ **PRED**: Moves, **AG**: Train, **LOC**: Zone2, **FAC**: Inside, **SUB**:
   [ **PRED**: Moves, **AG**: Person, **FAC**: Inside, **LOC**: Zone2, **DURING**: Move, **CAUSE**:
   [ **PRED**: Collides, **AG**: { Person, Train } ] ] ]

9. **Person enters zone2 while signal was switched on**
   [ **PRED**: Switches, **AG**: Signals, **FAC**: On, **SUB**:
   [ **PRED**: Enters, **AG**: Person, **LOC**: Zone2, **DURING**: Switches ] ]

10. **Train entering zone2 while gates are in motion**
    [ **PRED**: Moves, **AG**: Gates, **FAC**: Down, **SUB**:
    [ **PRED**: Enters, **AG**: Train, **LOC**: Zone2, **DURING**: Moves ] ]

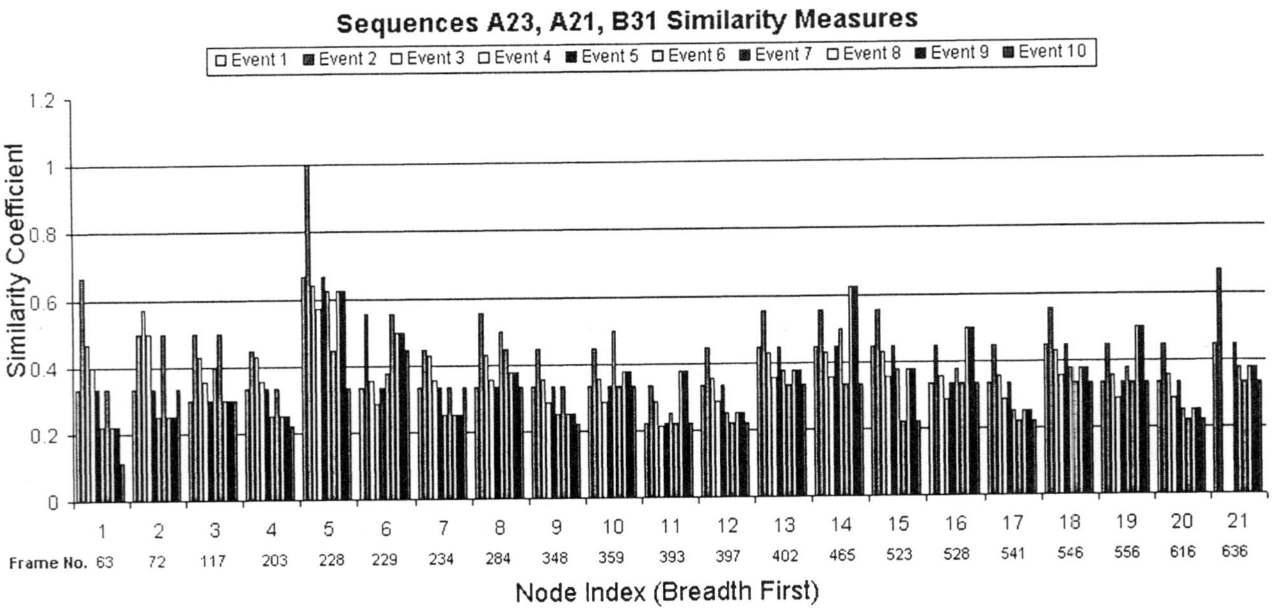


Figure 5: Event Detection using the Jaccard Coefficient. Sequences A23 (223 frames), A21 (237 frames), and B31 (192 frames) monitors railroad crossings (similar to the one shown in Figure 4). All events coded in the Application of CASE, we tested on the autonomously generated case frames and evidently Event 2 occurred at the time instant corresponding to Node Index 5 in sequence A21.

## Conclusion

The problem of formally representing events occurring in a video sequence using measurements in terms of object labels and tracks was identified, and in order to represent events, cases were added to the original framework of (Fillmore 1968) to support multi-agent/thread, temporal logic and causal relationships. Experiments were performed on real sequences, for the on-line generation of CASE$^E$ for human interaction, and a similarity coefficient was defined for the detection of pre-defined events. An instance of a complete event domain (Monitoring of Railroad intersections) was also treated. The essence of the proposition here is that based on the temporal relationships of the agent motions and a description of its state, it is possible to build a formal description of an event. We are interested in several future directions of this work including the inference of causality in video sequences, event-based retrieval of video, and unsupervised learning of event ontologies.

## References


Allen, J. F., Ferguson, G. 1994. Actions and Events in Interval Temporal Logic. In *Journal of Logic and Computation*, Vol.4(5), pp.531-579.

Bobick, A. F., and Ivanov, Y. A. 1998. Action Recognition using Probabilistic Parsing. In *Proc. of Computer Vision and Pattern Recognition*, pp.196-202.

Brand, M. 1997. Understanding Manipulation in Video. In *International Conference on Face and Gesture Recognition*, pp.94-99.

Fillmore, C. J. 1968. The Case for CASE. In Bach, E. and Harms, R. eds., *Universals in Linguistic Theory*, pp.1-88, New York, NY:Holt, Rinehart, and Winston.

Ivanov Y. A., and Bobick A. F. 2000. Recognition of Visual Activities and Interactions by Stochastic Parsing. In *IEEE Trans. on Pattern Analysis and Machine Intelligence*, vol.22, pp.852-872.

Kojima, A., Tamura, T. and Fukunaga, K. 2001. Natural Language Description of Human Activities from Video Images Based on Concept Hierarchy Actions. In *International Journal of Computer Vision*, vol.50, pp.171-184.

Koller, D., Heinze, N., and Nagel, H. H. 1991. Algorithmic Characterization of Vehicle Trajectories from Image Sequences by Motion Verbs. In *Proc. of Computer Vision and Pattern Recognition*, pp.90-95.

Maillot, N., Thonnat, M., and Boucher, A. 2003. Towards Ontology Based Cognitive Vision. In *Proc. of International Conference of Vision Systems*, pp.44-53.

Neumann, B. 1989. Natural Language Description of Time Varying Scenes. In Waltz, D. eds., *Semantic Structures: Advances in Natural Language Processing*, pp.167-206, Hillsdale, NJ: Lawrence Erlbaum Associates.

Pelillo, M., Siddiqi, K., and Zucker, S. 1999. Matching Hierarchical Structures using Association Graphs. In *IEEE Trans. on Pattern Analysis and Machine Intelligence*, vol.21(11), pp.1105-1119.

Pinhanez, C., and Bobick, A. 1998. Human Action Detection Using PNF Propagation of Temporal Constraints. In *Proc. of Computer Vision and Pattern Recognition*, pp.898-904.

Siskind, J. M., 2000. Visual Event Classification via Force Dynamics. In *Proc. of Seventeenth National Conference on Artificial Intelligence*, pp.149-155, Menlo Park, CA:AAAI Press.

Zelnik-Manor, L., and Irani, M. 2001. Event-based Analysis of Video. *Proc. of Computer Vision and Pattern Recognition*, pp.123-130.

# Making Argumentation More Believable

**Anthony Hunter**
Department of Computer Science
University College London
Gower Street
London, WC1E 6BT, UK

### Abstract

There are a number of frameworks for modelling argumentation in logic. They incorporate a formal representation of individual arguments and techniques for comparing conflicting arguments. A problem with these proposals is that they do not consider the believability of the arguments from the perspective of the intended audience. In this paper, we start by reviewing a logic-based framework for argumentation based on argument trees which provide a way of exhaustively collating arguments and counter-arguments. We then extend this framework to a model-theoretic evaluation of the believability of arguments. This extension assumes that the beliefs of a typical member of the audience for argumentation can be represented by a set of classical formulae (a beliefbase). We compare a beliefbase with each argument to evaluate the empathy (or similarly the antipathy) that an agent has for the argument. We show how we can use empathy and antipathy to define a pre-ordering relation over argument trees that captures how one argument tree is "more believable" than another. We also use these to define criteria for deciding whether an argument at the root of an argument tree is defeated or undefeated given the other arguments in the tree.

## Introduction

Argumentation is a vital aspect of intelligent behaviour by humans. There are a number of proposals for logic-based formalisations of argumentation (Prakken & Vreeswijk 2000; Chesnevar, Maguitman, & Loui 2001). These proposals allow for the representation of arguments for and against some conclusion, and for attack or undercut relationships between arguments. In the monological, as opposed to dialectical, approaches we can imagine a knowledgebase $\Delta$ as being a set of possibily conflicting pieces of information (each piece of information is represented by a formula) that has been collated by one or more agents, and the role of argumentation is to construct arguments from $\Delta$. However, a problem with the logic-based formalisations is that no account is taken of the audience of the arguments, and in particular, of how believable the arguments may appear to a typical member of the intended audience.

To motivate this need, consider a politician who is giving a speech on a plan by the government to charge car drivers to be able to drive into the city. This requires monological argumentation, since the audience would not be expected to participate in a dialogue *during* the speech. If the audience is a group of commuters who live in the city, then the politician would want to provide arguments that relate to what the audience is likely to be familiar with, perhaps saying that the money raised would be used to buy much-needed new buses, and there would be less pollution for pedestrians. In contrast, if the audience is a group of business executives, then the politician may argue that the cost of the charge to commercial vehicles (e.g. delivery trucks) would be more than offset by the savings made by their vehicles not being stuck in traffic in the city.

The beliefs of these two audiences are unlikely to be the same. They may even be mutually contradictory. The business executives, for example, may live in a different city, and so they might not know whether or not there are enough buses, or whether there is a lot of pollution in that city. And the commuters may be unaware that businesses have greater expenses to pay when their delivery vehicles are stuck in traffic. So the way the politician has to proceed, is to be selective so that the arguments used are likely to be based on assumptions that are already believed, and if not, on assumptions that do not contradict the intended audience's beliefs.

This need is reflected in many professional domains (e.g. medicine, science, law, journalism, etc), and so to deliver better decision-support technology, we first need to develop appropriate formalisms for argumentation that is more believable by the intended audience.

To address this need, we introduce the beliefs of a typical member of the intended audience into logic-based argumentation. These beliefs are represented by a beliefbase (a set of classical formulae). To present this approach, we extend an existing framework to logic-based argumentation by Besnard and Hunter (Besnard & Hunter 2001). In the next section, we review the existing framework, and then in subsequent sections we present our new extension.

## Review of Argument Trees

We use $\alpha, \beta, \gamma, \ldots$ to denote formulae and $\Delta, \Phi, \Psi, \ldots$ to denote sets of formulae. Deduction in classical propositional logic is denoted by the symbol $\vdash$ and deductive closure by $\mathsf{Th}$ so that $\mathsf{Th}(\Phi) = \{\alpha \mid \Phi \vdash \alpha\}$.

For the following definitions, we first assume a knowledgebase $\Delta$ (a finite set of formulae) and use this $\Delta$ throughout. We further assume that every subset of $\Delta$ is given an enumeration $\langle \alpha_1, \ldots, \alpha_n \rangle$ of its elements, which we call its canonical enumeration. This really is not a demanding constraint: In particular, the constraint is satisfied whenever we impose an arbitrary total ordering over $\Delta$. Importantly, the order has no meaning and is not meant to represent any respective importance of formulae in $\Delta$. It is only a convenient way to indicate the order in which we assume the formulae in any subset of $\Delta$ are conjoined to make a formula logically equivalent to that subset.

The paradigm for the approach is a large repository of information, represented by $\Delta$, from which arguments can be constructed for and against arbitrary claims. Apart from information being understood as declarative statements, there is no a priori restriction on the contents, and the pieces of information in the repository can be as complex as possible. Therefore, $\Delta$ is not expected to be consistent. It need even not be the case that every single formula in $\Delta$ is consistent.

The framework adopts a very common intuitive notion of an argument. Essentially, an argument is a set of relevant formulae that can be used to classically prove some point, together with that point. Each point is represented by a formula.

**Definition 1.** *An* **argument** *is a pair $\langle \Phi, \alpha \rangle$ such that: (1) $\Phi \nvdash \perp$; (2) $\Phi \vdash \alpha$; and (3) there is no $\Phi' \subset \Phi$ such that $\Phi' \vdash \alpha$. We say that $\langle \Phi, \alpha \rangle$ is an argument for $\alpha$. We call $\alpha$ the consequent of the argument and $\Phi$ the support of the argument (we also say that $\Phi$ is a support for $\alpha$). For an argument $\langle \Phi, \alpha \rangle$, the support is given by* $\mathsf{Support}(\langle \Phi, \alpha \rangle) = \Phi$.

**Example 1.** *Let $\Delta = \{\alpha, \alpha \rightarrow \beta, \gamma \rightarrow \neg\beta, \gamma, \delta, \delta \rightarrow \beta, \neg\alpha, \neg\gamma\}$. Some arguments are:*

$$\begin{array}{c} \langle \{\alpha, \alpha \rightarrow \beta\}, \beta \rangle \\ \langle \{\neg\alpha\}, \neg\alpha \rangle \\ \langle \{\alpha \rightarrow \beta\}, \neg\alpha \vee \beta \rangle \\ \langle \{\neg\gamma\}, \delta \rightarrow \neg\gamma \rangle \end{array}$$

Arguments are not independent. In a sense, some encompass others (possibly up to some form of equivalence). To clarify this requires a few definitions as follows.

**Definition 2.** *An argument $\langle \Phi, \alpha \rangle$ is* **more conservative** *than an argument $\langle \Psi, \beta \rangle$ iff $\Phi \subseteq \Psi$ and $\beta \vdash \alpha$.*

**Example 2.** *$\langle \{\alpha\}, \alpha \vee \beta \rangle$ is more conservative than $\langle \{\alpha, \alpha \rightarrow \beta\}, \beta \rangle$.*

Some arguments directly oppose the support of others, which amounts to the notion of an undercut.

**Definition 3.** *An* **undercut** *for an argument $\langle \Phi, \alpha \rangle$ is an argument $\langle \Psi, \neg(\phi_1 \wedge \ldots \wedge \phi_n) \rangle$ where $\{\phi_1, \ldots, \phi_n\} \subseteq \Phi$.*

**Example 3.** *Let $\Delta = \{\alpha, \alpha \rightarrow \beta, \gamma, \gamma \rightarrow \neg\alpha\}$. Then, $\langle \{\gamma, \gamma \rightarrow \neg\alpha\}, \neg(\alpha \wedge (\alpha \rightarrow \beta)) \rangle$ is an undercut for $\langle \{\alpha, \alpha \rightarrow \beta\}, \beta \rangle$. A less conservative undercut for $\langle \{\alpha, \alpha \rightarrow \beta\}, \beta \rangle$ is $\langle \{\gamma, \gamma \rightarrow \neg\alpha\}, \neg\alpha \rangle$.*

**Definition 4.** *$\langle \Psi, \beta \rangle$ is a* **maximally conservative undercut** *of $\langle \Phi, \alpha \rangle$ iff $\langle \Psi, \beta \rangle$ is an undercut of $\langle \Phi, \alpha \rangle$ such that no undercuts of $\langle \Phi, \alpha \rangle$ are strictly more conservative than $\langle \Psi, \beta \rangle$ (that is, for all undercuts $\langle \Psi', \beta' \rangle$ of $\langle \Phi, \alpha \rangle$, if $\Psi' \subseteq \Psi$ and $\beta \vdash \beta'$ then $\Psi \subseteq \Psi'$ and $\beta' \vdash \beta$).*

The value of the following definition of canonical undercut is that we only need to take the canonical undercuts into account. This means we can justifiably ignore the potentially very large number of non-canonical undercuts.

**Definition 5.** *An argument $\langle \Psi, \neg(\phi_1 \wedge \ldots \wedge \phi_n) \rangle$ is a* **canonical undercut** *for $\langle \Phi, \alpha \rangle$ iff it is a maximally conservative undercut for $\langle \Phi, \alpha \rangle$ and $\langle \phi_1, \ldots, \phi_n \rangle$ is the canonical enumeration of $\Phi$.*

An argument tree describes the various ways an argument can be challenged, as well as how the counter-arguments to the initial argument can themselves be challenged, and so on recursively.

**Definition 6.** *An* **argument tree** *for $\alpha$ is a tree where the nodes are arguments such that*

1. *The root is an argument for $\alpha$.*
2. *For no node $\langle \Phi, \beta \rangle$ with ancestor nodes $\langle \Phi_1, \beta_1 \rangle, \ldots, \langle \Phi_n, \beta_n \rangle$ is $\Phi$ a subset of $\Phi_1 \cup \cdots \cup \Phi_n$.*
3. *The children nodes of a node $N$ consist of all canonical undercuts for $N$ that obey 2.*

The second condition in Definition 6 ensures that each argument on a branch has to introduce at least one formula in its support that has not already been used by ancestor arguments. As a notational convenience, in examples of argument trees the $\diamond$ symbol is used to denote the consequent of an argument when that argument is a canonical undercut.

**Example 4.** *Let $\Delta = \{\alpha \vee \beta, \alpha \rightarrow \gamma, \neg\gamma, \neg\beta, \delta \leftrightarrow \beta\}$. For this, two argument trees for the consequent $\alpha \vee \neg\delta$ are given.*

$$\begin{array}{ccc} \langle \{\alpha \vee \beta, \neg\beta\}, \alpha \vee \neg\delta \rangle & & \langle \{\delta \leftrightarrow \beta, \neg\beta\}, \alpha \vee \neg\delta \rangle \\ \uparrow & & \uparrow \\ \langle \{\alpha \rightarrow \gamma, \neg\gamma\}, \diamond \rangle & & \langle \{\alpha \vee \beta, \alpha \rightarrow \gamma, \neg\gamma\}, \diamond \rangle \end{array}$$

For an argument tree $T$, each argument in T is either an **attacking argument** or a **defending argument**. If an argument $a_i$ is a defending argument, then any child $a_j$ of $a_i$ is an attacking argument. If an argument $a_j$ is an attacking argument, then any child $a_k$ of $a_j$ is a defending argument. If an argument $a_r$ is the root, then $a_r$ is the **initiating argument**, and $a_r$ is a defending argument. Finally, for an argument $a_i$ in an argument tree $T$, let the set of children of $a_i$ be given by $\mathsf{Children}(T, a_i)$.

## Pairwise Theory Comparison

When comparing an agent's beliefbase with the support of an argument, we are comparing a pair of theories. To do this we now present a model-theoretic way to compare pairs of theories. Note, we use $\wedge X$ to denote a conjunction of all the formulae in $X$ and we use $\mathsf{Atoms}(X)$ to denote the atom symbols (i.e. propositional letters) used in the formulae in $X$.

**Definition 7.** *Let $\mathcal{A}$ be a set of atoms. Each* **interpretation** *$w$ is represented by a subset of $\mathcal{A}$. For each interpretation $w$, each atom in $w$ is assigned true and each atom in $\mathcal{A} \setminus w$*

*is assigned false. Let $X$ be a set of classical propositional formulae. Let $I(X)$ be the set of interpretations of $X$ delineated by the atoms used in $X$ (i.e. $I(X) = \wp(\mathsf{Atoms}(X))$). Let $M(X,Y)$ be the set of* **models** *of $X$ that are in $I(Y)$. So $M(X,Y) = \{w \models \wedge X \mid w \in I(Y)\}$ where $\models$ is classical.*

**Example 5.** *Let $X = \{\alpha\}$ and $Y = \{\beta \wedge \gamma\}$. So $M(X, X \cup Y) = \{\{\alpha,\beta,\gamma\},\{\alpha,\beta\},\{\alpha,\gamma\},\{\alpha\}\}$, and $M(Y, X \cup Y) = \{\{\alpha,\beta,\gamma\},\{\beta,\gamma\}\}$, where $I(X \cup Y) = \{\{\alpha,\beta,\gamma\},\{\alpha,\beta\},\{\alpha,\gamma\},\{\beta,\gamma\},\{\alpha\},\{\beta\},\{\gamma\},\{\}\}$.*

Obviously $M(X,X) \subseteq I(X)$. When $X$ is non-empty, we get: (1) $M(X,X) = \emptyset$ iff $X$ is inconsistent; and (2) $I(X) = M(X,X)$ iff $X$ is a set of tautologies. Also $M(X, X \cup Y) \subseteq M(Y, X \cup Y)$ iff $X \vdash \wedge Y$.

The degree of entailment of $X$ for $Y$ is the number of models they have in common divided by the total number of models for $X$.

**Definition 8.** *Let $X$ and $Y$ be sets of classical propositional formulae each of which is consistent (i.e. $X \not\vdash \bot$ and $Y \not\vdash \bot$). The* **degree of entailment** *of $X$ for $Y$, denoted $E(X,Y)$, is defined as follows:*

$$E(X,Y) = \frac{|M(X, X \cup Y) \cap M(Y, X \cup Y)|}{|M(X, X \cup Y)|}$$

**Example 6.** $E(\alpha, \alpha \wedge \beta) = 1/2$, $E(\alpha, \alpha \wedge \beta \wedge \gamma) = 1/4$, $E(\alpha, \alpha \wedge \beta \wedge \gamma \wedge \delta) = 1/8$, $E(\alpha \wedge \beta, \alpha \vee \beta) = 1$, $E(\alpha \wedge \beta, \alpha \wedge \epsilon) = 1/2$, $E(\alpha \wedge \beta \wedge \gamma, \alpha \wedge \epsilon) = 1/2$, $E(\alpha \wedge \beta \wedge \gamma \wedge \delta, \alpha \wedge \epsilon) = 1/2$, $E(\alpha \wedge \epsilon, \alpha \wedge \beta \wedge \gamma \wedge \delta) = 1/8$, $E(\alpha \wedge \beta, \alpha \wedge \neg\beta) = 0$.

**Proposition 1.** *Let $X$, $Y$, and $Z$ be sets of classical propositional formulae: (1) $0 \leq E(X,Y) \leq 1$; (2) $X \vdash \wedge Y$ iff $E(X,Y) = 1$; (3) $X \vdash \neg \wedge Y$ iff $E(X,Y) = 0$; (4) If $E(X,Y) = 1$ then $0 < E(Y,X)$; and (5) $E(X,Y) = 0$ iff $E(Y,X) = 0$.*

We now recall the definition for Dalal distance for comparing pairs of models (Dalal 1988). It is the Hamming distance between two models.

**Definition 9.** *Let $X$ be a set of classical propositional formulae, and let $w_i, w_j \in I(X)$. The* **Dalal distance** *between $w_i$ and $w_j$, denoted $\mathsf{Dalal}(w_i, w_j)$, is the difference in the number of atoms assigned true:*

$$\mathsf{Dalal}(w_i, w_j) = |w_i - w_j| + |w_j - w_i|$$

To evaluate the conflict between two theories, we take a pair of models, one for each theory, such that the Dalal distance is minimised. The degree of conflict is this distance divided by the maximum possible Dalal distance between a pair of models in $I(X \cup Y)$ (i.e. $\log_2$ of the total number of models in $I(X \cup Y)$).

**Definition 10.** *Let $X$ and $Y$ be sets of classical propositional formulae, each of which is consistent, and let $\mathsf{Distances}(X,Y) = \{\mathsf{Dalal}(w_x, w_y) \mid w_x \in M(X, X \cup Y)$ and $w_y \in M(Y, X \cup Y)\}$. The* **degree of conflict** *between $X$ and $Y$, denoted $C(X,Y)$, is defined as follows:*

$$C(X,Y) = \frac{\mathsf{Min}(\mathsf{Distances}(X,Y))}{\log_2(|I(X \cup Y)|)}$$

**Example 7.** $C(\alpha \wedge \beta, \alpha \wedge \neg\beta) = 1/2$, $C(\alpha \wedge \beta, \neg\alpha \vee \neg\beta) = 1/2$, $C(\alpha \wedge \beta, \neg\alpha \wedge \neg\beta) = 1$, $C(\alpha \wedge \beta, \neg\alpha \wedge \beta) = 1/2$, $C(\alpha \wedge \beta \wedge \gamma, \neg(\alpha \wedge \beta) \wedge \neg\gamma \wedge \neg\delta) = 1/2$.

**Proposition 2.** *Let $X$ and $Y$ be sets of classical propositional formulae: (1) $0 \leq C(X,Y) \leq 1$; (2) $C(X,Y) = C(Y,X)$; and (3) $C(X,Y) = 0$ iff $X \cup Y \not\vdash \bot$ iff $E(X,Y) \neq 0$.*

In the next section, we use these measures to analyse the believability of arguments.

## Believability of Argument Trees

To evaluate the believability of an argument, we use a consistent set of formulae, called a **beliefbase**, that reflects the beliefs of a typical member of the intended audience of the argument. Argumentation for different intended audiences requires different beliefbases.

**Definition 11.** *Let $\langle\Phi, \alpha\rangle$ be an argument and let $\Gamma$ be a beliefbase. The* **empathy** *for $\langle\Phi, \alpha\rangle$ is $E(\Gamma, \Phi)$. The* **antipathy** *for $\langle\Phi, \alpha\rangle$ is $C(\Gamma, \Phi)$.*

**Example 8.** *Let $\Delta = \{\alpha \vee \beta, \alpha \to \gamma, \neg\gamma, \neg\beta, \delta \leftrightarrow \beta\}$ and consider the following argument tree. If $\Gamma = \{\alpha, \neg\beta\}$, then $E(\Gamma, \{\alpha \vee \beta, \neg\beta\}) = 1$ and $C(\Gamma, \{\alpha \to \gamma, \neg\gamma\}) = 1/3$.*

$$\begin{array}{c}\langle\{\alpha \vee \beta, \neg\beta\}, \alpha \vee \neg\delta\rangle \\ \uparrow \\ \langle\{\alpha \to \gamma, \neg\gamma\}, \diamond\rangle\end{array}$$

In order to improve the believability of an argument tree, we want to maximize the empathy for defending arguments, and maximize the antipathy of attacking arguments.

**Proposition 3.** *Let $\langle\Phi, \alpha\rangle$ be an argument, and let $\langle\Psi, \diamond\rangle$ be a canonical undercut for it, and let $\Gamma$ be a beliefbase: (1) If $E(\Gamma, \Phi) = 1$, then $E(\Gamma, \Psi) = 0$; and (2) If $C(\Gamma, \Phi) = 1$, then $C(\Gamma, \Psi) \neq 1$.*

Now we provide definitions for the measure of recursive empathy and the measure of recursive antipathy for argument trees. Each of these measures gives a value in the $[-1, 1]$ range. The essential idea is that the empathy at a node can be affected by the nodes below it in the tree. Defending arguments may increase the recursive empathy at a node and attacking arguments may decrease the recursive empathy.

**Definition 12.** *The* **recursive empathy** *(r.e.) for an argument tree $T$ with the beliefbase $\Gamma$, denoted $Re(\Gamma, T)$, is given by $F(a_r)$ where $a_r$ is the root of $T$ and the $F$ function is defined for all nodes $a_i$ in $T$ as follows. Let $k_1 = E(\Gamma, \mathsf{Support}(a_i))$. If $\mathsf{Children}(T, a_i) \neq \emptyset$, then let $k_2$ be the maximum $F(a_j)$ value for the nodes $a_j$ in $\mathsf{Children}(T, a_i)$, otherwise let $k_2 = 0$. So $F(a_i)$ is:*

1. *If $k_1 > k_2$, then $F(a_i) = k_1$*
2. *If $k_1 = k_2$, then $F(a_i) = 0$*
3. *If $k_1 < k_2$, then $F(a_i) = -k_2$*

For an argument tree $T$, and a beliefbase $\Gamma$, $Re(\Gamma, T) > 0$ when the root has greater non-zero empathy than the r.e. of any of the undercuts, $Re(\Gamma, T) < 0$ when there is an undercut with r.e. greater then the empathy of the root, and

$Re(\Gamma, T) = 0$ when the best undercut (ie. the undercut with maximum r.e.) has r.e. equal to the empathy of the root or when the best undercut has negative r.e. and the root has zero empathy.

**Definition 13.** *The* **recursive antipathy** *(r.a.) for an argument tree $T$ with the beliefbase $\Gamma$, denoted $Re(\Gamma, T)$, is given by $A(a_r)$ where $a_r$ is the root of $T$ and the $A$ function is defined for all nodes $a_i$ in $T$ as follows. Let $k_1 = C(\Gamma, \mathsf{Support}(a_i))$. If $\mathsf{Children}(T, a_i) \neq \emptyset$, then let $k_2$ be the maximum $A(a_j)$ for the nodes $a_j$ in $\mathsf{Children}(T, a_i)$, otherwise let $k_2 = 0$. So $A(a_i)$ is:*

1. *If $k_1 > k_2$, then $A(a_i) = k_1$*
2. *If $k_1 = k_2$, then $A(a_i) = 0$*
3. *If $k_1 < k_2$, then $A(a_i) = -k_2$*

For an argument tree $T$, and a beliefbase $\Gamma$, $Ra(\Gamma, T) > 0$ when the root has greater non-zero antipathy than the r.a. of any of the undercuts, $Ra(\Gamma, T) < 0$ when there is an undercut with greater r.a. than the antipathy of the root, and $Ra(\Gamma, T) = 0$ when the best undercut (ie. the undercut with maximum r.a.) has r.a. that is equal to antipathy of the root or when the best undercut has negative r.a. and the root has zero antipathy.

**Example 9.** *Consider $\Delta = \{\alpha \leftrightarrow \neg\delta, \beta, \beta \rightarrow \alpha, \gamma \wedge \neg\beta, \neg\gamma, \delta, \neg\delta\}$ giving the argument tree $T_1$ below.*

$$\langle\{\beta \rightarrow \alpha, \beta\}, \alpha\rangle$$
$$\nearrow \qquad\qquad \nwarrow$$
$$\langle\{\gamma \wedge \neg\beta\}, \diamond\rangle \qquad\qquad \langle\{\delta, \alpha \leftrightarrow \neg\delta\}, \diamond\rangle$$
$$\uparrow \qquad\qquad\qquad \uparrow$$
$$\langle\{\neg\gamma\}, \diamond\rangle \qquad\qquad \langle\{\neg\delta\}, \diamond\rangle$$

*For $\Gamma = \{\delta, \neg\gamma\}$, the arguments in $T_1$ are evaluated in the table below, where $E$ is the empathy for the node, $F$ is the r.e. for the node, $C$ is the antipathy for the node, and $A$ is the r.a. for the node, giving $Re(\Gamma, T_1) = -1/2$ and $Ra(\Gamma, T_1) = -1/3$. So r.e. is poor and r.a. is good.*

| *Argument* | *E* | *F* | *C* | *A* |
|---|---|---|---|---|
| $\langle\{\beta \rightarrow \alpha, \beta\}, \alpha\rangle$ | 0 | $-1/2$ | 0 | $-1/3$ |
| $\langle\{\gamma \wedge \neg\beta\}, \diamond\rangle$ | 0 | $-1$ | $1/3$ | $1/3$ |
| $\langle\{\delta, \alpha \leftrightarrow \neg\delta\}, \diamond\rangle$ | $1/2$ | $1/2$ | 0 | $-1$ |
| $\langle\{\neg\gamma\}, \diamond\rangle$ | 1 | 1 | 0 | 0 |
| $\langle\{\neg\delta\}, \diamond\rangle$ | 0 | 0 | 1 | 1 |

**Example 10.** *Consider $\Delta = \{\alpha \leftrightarrow \neg\delta, \beta, \beta \rightarrow \alpha, \gamma \wedge \neg\beta, \neg\gamma, \delta, \neg\delta\}$ giving the argument tree $T_2$ below.*

$$\langle\{\neg\delta, \alpha \leftrightarrow \neg\delta\}, \alpha\rangle$$
$$\uparrow$$
$$\langle\{\delta\}, \diamond\rangle$$

*For $\Gamma = \{\neg\delta\}$, $T_2$ is evaluated in the table below, where $E$, $F$, $C$, and $A$ are as in Example 9, giving $Re(\Gamma, T_2) = 1/2$ and $Ra(\Gamma, T_2) = -1$. So r.e. and r.a. are good.*

| *Argument* | *E* | *F* | *C* | *A* |
|---|---|---|---|---|
| $\langle\{\neg\delta, \alpha \leftrightarrow \neg\delta\}, \alpha\rangle$ | $1/2$ | $1/2$ | 0 | $-1$ |
| $\langle\{\delta\}, \diamond\rangle$ | 0 | 0 | 1 | 1 |

**Example 11.** *Consider $\Delta = \{\alpha \leftrightarrow \neg\delta, \beta, \beta \rightarrow \alpha, \gamma \wedge \neg\beta, \neg\gamma, \delta, \neg\delta\}$ giving the argument tree $T_3$ below.*

$$\langle\{\delta, \alpha \leftrightarrow \neg\delta\}, \neg\alpha\rangle$$
$$\nearrow \qquad\qquad \nwarrow$$
$$\langle\{\beta, \beta \rightarrow \alpha\}, \diamond\rangle \qquad\qquad \langle\{\neg\delta\}, \diamond\rangle$$
$$\uparrow$$
$$\langle\{\gamma \wedge \neg\beta\}, \diamond\rangle$$
$$\uparrow$$
$$\langle\{\neg\gamma\}, \diamond\rangle$$

*For $\Gamma = \{\delta, \neg\gamma\}$, $T_3$ is evaluated in the table below, where $E$, $F$, $C$, and $A$ are as in Example 9, giving $Re(\Gamma, T_3) = 1/2$ and $Ra(\Gamma, T_3) = -1/2$. So r.e. and r.a. are good.*

| *Argument* | *E* | *F* | *C* | *A* |
|---|---|---|---|---|
| $\langle\{\delta, \alpha \leftrightarrow \neg\delta\}, \neg\alpha\rangle$ | $1/2$ | $1/2$ | 0 | $-1/2$ |
| $\langle\{\beta, \beta \rightarrow \alpha\}, \diamond\rangle$ | 0 | 0 | 0 | $-1/3$ |
| $\langle\{\neg\delta\}, \diamond\rangle$ | 0 | 0 | $1/2$ | $1/2$ |
| $\langle\{\gamma \wedge \neg\beta\}, \diamond\rangle$ | 0 | $-1$ | $1/3$ | $1/3$ |
| $\langle\{\neg\gamma\}, \diamond\rangle$ | 1 | 1 | 0 | 0 |

There is an intuitive preference for an argument tree with higher r.e. and there is an intuitive preference for an argument tree with lower r.a. For these two dimensions, the best case argument tree has an r.e. of 1 and an r.a of $-1$, and the worst case argument tree has an r.e. of $-1$ and an r.a. of 1.

**Example 12.** *Let $T$ be the following argument tree. If $\Gamma = \{\alpha \wedge \beta\}$, then $Re(\Gamma, T) = 1$ and $Ra(\Gamma, T) = -1$. If $\Gamma' = \{\neg\alpha \wedge \neg\beta\}$, then $Re(\Gamma', T) = -1$ and $Ra(\Gamma', T) = 1$.*

$$\langle\{\alpha \wedge \beta\}, \alpha\rangle$$
$$\uparrow$$
$$\langle\{\neg\alpha \wedge \neg\beta\}, \diamond\rangle$$

In the extreme case where the empathy for the root is 1, then the r.e. for the tree is automatically 1. Similarly, in the (diametrically opposed) extreme case where the antipathy for the root is 1, then the r.a. for the tree is automatically 1.

**Proposition 4.** *Let $\langle\Phi, \alpha\rangle$ be the root of an argument tree $T$, and let $\Gamma$ be a beliefbase: (1) If $E(\Gamma, \Phi) = 1$, then $Re(\Gamma, T) = 1$; and (2) If $C(\Gamma, \Phi) = 1$, then $Ra(\Gamma, T) = 1$.*

The r.e. and r.a. obtained for a tree are coupled. This is a consequence of a beliefbase being unable to have both a non-zero antipathy and a non-zero empathy for an argument.

**Proposition 5.** *For an argument tree $T$ and a beliefbase $\Gamma$, if $Re(\Gamma, T) > 0$ then $Ra(\Gamma, T) \leq 0$.*

So the most important factor in developing believable aruments is for the initiating arguments to have non-zero empathy (ideally unit empathy) and therefore zero antipathy.

**Definition 14.** *Let $T$ be a argument tree, let $\Gamma$ be a beliefbase, and let $a_i$ be a node in $T$. $a_i$ is* **e-disabled** *iff $\exists a_j \in \mathsf{Children}(T, a_i)$ such that $E(\Gamma, \mathsf{Support}(a_i)) \leq F(\Gamma, \mathsf{Support}(a_j))$. $a_i$ is* **c-disabled** *iff $\exists a_j \in \mathsf{Children}(T, a_i)$ such that $C(\Gamma, \mathsf{Support}(a_i)) \leq A(\Gamma, \mathsf{Support}(a_j))$.*

The definition of e-disabled (and similarly c-disabled) give the grounds for empathy (and similarly for antipathy) for a node to not affect the evaluation of r.e. (and similarly r.a) for ancestor nodes.

**Definition 15.** *Let $T$ be a argument tree, let $\Gamma$ be a beliefbase, let $a_i$ and $a_j$ be nodes in $T$.*

$$a_i \textbf{ e-voids } a_j \textit{ iff } E(\Gamma, \mathsf{Support}(a_i)) > E(\Gamma, \mathsf{Support}(a_j))$$
$$a_i \textbf{ c-voids } a_j \textit{ iff } C(\Gamma, \mathsf{Support}(a_i)) > C(\Gamma, \mathsf{Support}(a_j))$$

The definition of e-voids (and similarly c-voids) gives the grounds for empathy (and similarly for antipathy) for a node to not be affected by the evaluation of r.e. (and similarly r.a) for an offspring node.

**Proposition 6.** *Let $T$ be an argument tree, let $\Gamma$ be a beliefbase, and let $a_i$ be a node in $T$. (1) $a_i$ is not e-disabled iff $\forall a_j \in \mathsf{Children}(T, a_i)$ $a_i$ e-voids $a_j$ or $a_j$ is e-disabled. (2) $a_i$ is not c-disabled iff $\forall a_j \in \mathsf{Children}(T, a_i)$ $a_i$ c-voids $a_j$ or $a_j$ is c-disabled.*

We will use e-disabled, c-disabled, e-voids, and c-voids to characterise undefeated argument trees.

## Improving Believability

Given a knowledgebase $\Delta$, we may be able to generate more than one argument tree for a conclusion such as in Example 4. Using a beliefbase, we can select one of these trees to optimise believability in terms of r.a. and r.e. We can also seek better arguments trees by ignoring some of the formulae in $\Delta$. In other words, we can delete formulae from $\Delta$ to give $\Delta'$ and then generate argument trees from $\Delta'$.

**Example 13.** *Continuing Example 9, we could ignore (i.e. delete) $\delta$ in $\Delta$. From this, we get argument tree $T_4$ below.*

$$\begin{array}{c} \langle\{\beta \rightarrow \alpha, \beta\}, \alpha\rangle \\ \uparrow \\ \langle\{\gamma \wedge \neg\beta\}, \diamond\rangle \\ \uparrow \\ \langle\{\neg\gamma\}, \diamond\rangle \end{array}$$

*For the beliefbase $\Gamma = \{\delta, \neg\gamma\}$, $T_4$ is evaluated in the table below, where E, F, C, and A are as in Example 9. So $Re(\Gamma, T_4) = 0$ and $Ra(\Gamma, T_3) = -1/3$ which is an improvement on the r.e. value for $T_1$.*

| *Argument* | *E* | *F* | *C* | *A* |
|---|---|---|---|---|
| $\langle\{\beta \rightarrow \alpha, \beta\}, \alpha\rangle$ | 0 | 0 | 0 | $-1/3$ |
| $\langle\{\gamma \wedge \neg\beta\}, \diamond\rangle$ | 0 | $-1$ | $1/3$ | $1/3$ |
| $\langle\{\neg\gamma\}, \diamond\rangle$ | 1 | 1 | 0 | 0 |

**Definition 16.** *Let $T$ and $T'$ be argument trees and let $\Gamma$ be a beliefbase. Let $Re(\Gamma, T) = x$, let $Re(\Gamma, T') = x'$, let $Ra(\Gamma, T) = y$, and $Ra(\Gamma, T') = y'$, $T$ is more believable for $\Gamma$ than $T'$, denoted $T \preceq_\Gamma T'$, iff $x \geq x'$ and $y \leq y'$. $T$ is most believable for $\Gamma$ iff for all argument trees $T'$, $T \preceq_\Gamma T'$.*

**Example 14.** *Consider $T_1$ in Example 9 and $T_4$ in Example 13. If $\Gamma = \{\delta, \neg\gamma\}$, then $T_4 \preceq_\Gamma T_1$.*

**Proposition 7.** *Let $T$ be an argument tree and let $\Gamma$ be a beliefbase. $T$ is most believable for $\Gamma$ iff $Re(\Gamma, T) = 1$ and $Ra(\Gamma, T) = -1$.*

Obviously, there is not a unique most believable $T$ for $\Gamma$ since there are many knowledgebases $\Delta$ we can consider.

**Definition 17.** *Let $\mathsf{Trees}(\Delta, \alpha)$ be the set of argument trees constructed from $\Delta$ for $\alpha$ (according to Definition 6). Let* $\mathsf{Treelets}(\Delta, \alpha) = \bigcup_{\Pi \in \wp(\Delta)} \mathsf{Trees}(\Pi, \alpha)$.

So if we want to increase the believability of an argument tree $T \in \mathsf{Trees}(\Delta, \alpha)$, we could try to find an argument tree $T' \in \mathsf{Trees}(\Delta, \alpha)$ where $\Delta' \subset \Delta$ and $T' \preceq_\Gamma T$. In other words, we could examine $\mathsf{Treelets}(\Delta, \alpha)$ for a more believable tree. Note, for a given knowledgebase $\Delta$ and a given beliefbase $\Gamma$, the pre-ordering $(\mathsf{Treelets}(\Delta, \alpha), \preceq_\Gamma)$ does not necessarily have a unique maximal element. Furthermore to maximize believability according to the $\preceq_\Gamma$ pre-ordering may involve a trade-off of increasing r.e. and decreasing r.a.

## Winning Argument Trees

Given an argument tree, we want to determine whether the initiating argument wins (i.e. it is undefeated) or whether it looses (i.e. it is defeated). If an initiating argument wins, then we may regard it as an acceptable inference. A simple approach is to consider the binary judge defined next.

**Definition 18.** *Given an argument tree $T$, the initiating argument wins according to the* **binary judge**, *denoted $\mathsf{win_b}(T) = yes$, iff for each branch of $T$, the leaf is a defending argument. Furthermore $\mathsf{win_b}(T) = yes$ iff $\mathsf{win_b}(T) \neq no$.*

So the initiating argument wins whenever all maximal branches of the argument tree have an even length (though not necessarily the same length). This approach captures the essence of a number of approaches to argumentation (see (Besnard & Hunter 2001) for more details).

Now that we have measures of r.a. and r.e. for argument trees, we can take a finer grained approach to evaluating argument trees. Below we define the empathy judge, the antipathy judge, and the combined judge and give examples in Table 1. All the judges we consider are functions that return either $yes$ (when the initiating argument is undefeated) or $no$ (when the initiating argument is defeated).

Using the empathy judge, the initiating argument wins when the empathy for the initiating argument is greater than the r.e. for the undercuts. In other words, the initiating argument is not disabled (by Definition 14). Hence, the initiating argument can win if empathy is sufficient or if the undercuts have lower empathy than a defending argument.

**Definition 19.** *Given an argument tree $T$, and beliefbase $\Gamma$, the initiating argument wins according to the* **empathy judge**, *denoted $\mathsf{win_e}(\Gamma, T) = yes$, iff $Re(\Gamma, T) > 0$.*

The empathy judge effectively weighs the effect of undercuts, and by recursion undercuts to undercuts, on the initiating argument. This means that the empathy for an undercut can be too low for it to be regarded as sufficient grounds for it to defeat an argument. A consequence of this is that a tree that wins by the binary judge may loose by the empathy judge and vice versa.

**Proposition 8.** *Let $T$ be a argument tree, let $\Gamma$ be a beliefbase, and let $a_r$ be the root of argument tree $T$. $\mathsf{win_e}(\Gamma, T) = yes$ iff for all $a_i \in \mathsf{Children}(T, a_r)$ either $a_r$ e-voids $a_i$ or $a_i$ is e-disabled.*

Using the antipathy judge, the initiating argument wins when the antipathy for the initiating argument is less than the r.a. for the undercuts. Hence, the initiating argument can

| | Tree | r.e. | r.a. | $\mathsf{win_b}$ | $\mathsf{win_e}$ | $\mathsf{win_a}$ |
|---|---|---|---|---|---|---|
| $\Gamma_1$ | $T_1$ | $-1$ | $1/3$ | *yes* | *no* | *no* |
| $\Gamma_1$ | $T_3$ | $1$ | $-1$ | *no* | *yes* | *yes* |
| $\Gamma_2$ | $T_1$ | $-1$ | $1/4$ | *yes* | *no* | *no* |
| $\Gamma_2$ | $T_3$ | $1$ | $-1$ | *no* | *yes* | *yes* |
| $\Gamma_3$ | $T_1$ | $-1/2$ | $1/2$ | *yes* | *no* | *no* |
| $\Gamma_3$ | $T_3$ | $0$ | $-1/2$ | *no* | *no* | *yes* |
| $\Gamma_4$ | $T_1$ | $1/2$ | $-1/2$ | *yes* | *yes* | *yes* |
| $\Gamma_4$ | $T_3$ | $-1/2$ | $0$ | *no* | *no* | *no* |

Table 1: Combinations of beliefbases and argument trees are evaluated with the binary judge, the empathy judge, and the antipathy judge, where $\Gamma_1 = \{\delta, \neg\alpha\}$, $\Gamma_2 = \{\delta, \neg\alpha, \gamma\}$, $\Gamma_3 = \{\neg\beta\}$ and $\Gamma_4 = \{\beta\}$ are beliefbases, and $T_1$ from Example 9 and $T_3$ from Example 11.

win if antipathy for it is sufficiently low or if undercuts have higher antipathy than a defending argument.

**Definition 20.** *Given an argument tree $T$, and beliefbase $\Gamma$, the initiating argument wins according to the* **antipathy judge**, *denoted* $\mathsf{win_a}(\Gamma, T) = yes$, *iff* $Ra(\Gamma, T) < 0$.

The antipathy judge effectively weighs the effect of undercuts, and by recursion undercuts to undercuts, on the initiating argument. This means that the antipathy for an undercut can be too high for it to be regarded as sufficient grounds for it to defeat an argument. Furthermore, this antipathy to the undercut could be sufficient for the intiating argument to win because the undercut has "alienated" the intended audience irrespective of the other undercuts. A consequence of this is that a tree that wins by the binary judge may loose by the antipathy judge and vice versa.

**Proposition 9.** *Let $T$ be a argument tree, let $\Gamma$ be a beliefbase, and let $a_r$ be the root of argument tree $T$.* $\mathsf{win_c}(\Gamma, T) = yes$ *iff there is an $a_i \in$ $\mathsf{Children}(T, a_r)$ such that $a_i$ c-voids $a_r$ and $a_i$ is not c-disabled.*

The combined judge classifies a tree as undefeated iff both the empathy judge and the antipathy judge classify the tree as undefeated.

**Definition 21.** *Given an argument tree $T$, and beliefbase $\Gamma$, the initiating argument wins according to the* **combined judge**, *denoted* $\mathsf{win_c}(\Gamma, T) = yes$, *iff* $\mathsf{win_e}(\Gamma, T) = yes$ *and* $\mathsf{win_a}(\Gamma, T) = yes$.

Argument trees with initiating arguments that win by the combined judge are more believable than those that do not.

**Proposition 10.** *Let $T_1, T_2 \in \mathsf{Trees}(\Delta, \alpha)$ and let $\Gamma$ be a beliefbase. If $\mathsf{win_c}(\Gamma, T_1) = yes$ and $\mathsf{win_c}(\Gamma, T_2) = no$, then $T_2 \not\preceq_\Gamma T_1$.*

A necessary condition for $\mathsf{win_e}(\Gamma, T) = yes$ or $\mathsf{win_c}(\Gamma, T) = yes$ is for $\Gamma \neq \emptyset$. Furthermore, the empathy $\Gamma$ has for the root of $T$ has to be greater than 0. These are natural expectations to have about believable argumentation. If the audience has zero empathy for the initiating argument, then the consequence of the initiating argument should not be regarded as an acceptable inference.

## Discussion

The proposal for evaluating believability of arguments is a way for argumentation systems to interact intelligently with users. Given a beliefbase that reflects the intended audience, the values for empathy/antipathy provide an intuitive ranking over arguments. The definitions for r.a. and r.a. extend this ranking to argument trees. This may then be used to optimize the presentation of argumentation for audiences as part of decision-support technology. It may also be used to define judges that capture important criteria for deciding when an initiating argument should be an inference.

Whilst the presentation is based on a particular approach to logic-based argumentation, the proposal could be adapted for a range of other logic-based approaches to argumentation. It also seems that the proposal in this paper could be generalised for dialectical argumentation where arguments are generated by different agents in a debate or dialogue in a multi-agent system. Furthermore, the beliefbase of an audience could be constructed dynamically as part of a dialogue involving an agent asking questions to determine some of the beliefs of the audience before presenting arguments.

Other approaches to evaluating potentially inconsistent information, such as information-theoretic measures (Lozinskii 1994), possibilistic measures (Dubois, Lang, & Prade 1994), epistemic action measures (Konieczny, Lang, & Marquis 2003), and measures based on four valued models (Hunter 2003), may give interesting alternatives to the empathy and antipathy definitions.

## References


Besnard, P., and Hunter, A. 2001. A logic-based theory of deductive arguments. *Artificial Intelligence* 128:203–235.

Chesnevar, C.; Maguitman, A.; and Loui, R. 2001. Logical models of argument. *ACM Computing Surveys* 32:337–383.

Dalal, M. 1988. Investigations into a theory of knowledge base revision: Preliminary report. In *Proceedings of the 7th National Conference on Artificial Intelligence (AAAI'88)*, 3–7. MIT Press.

Dubois, D.; Lang, J.; and Prade, H. 1994. Possibilistic logic. In *Handbook of Logic in Artificial Intelligence and Logic Programming*, volume 3. Oxford University Press. 439–513.

Hunter, A. 2003. Evaluating the significance of inconsistency. In *Proceedings of the International Joint Conference on AI (IJCAI'03)*, 468–473. Morgan Kaufmann.

Konieczny, S.; Lang, J.; and Marquis, P. 2003. Quantifying information and contradiction in propositional logic through epistemic actions. In *Proceedings of the 18th International Joint Conference on Artificial Intelligence (IJCAI'03)*, 106–111.

Lozinskii, E. 1994. Information and evidence in logic systems. *Journal of Experimental and Theoretical Artificial Intelligence* 6:163–193.

Prakken, H., and Vreeswijk, G. 2000. Logical systems for defeasible argumentation. In Gabbay, D., ed., *Handbook of Philosophical Logic*. Kluwer.

# Towards Higher Impact Argumentation

**Anthony Hunter***
Dept of Computer Science
University College London
Gower Street, London WC1E 6BT,UK

**Abstract**

There are a number of frameworks for modelling argumentation in logic. They incorporate a formal representation of individual arguments and techniques for comparing conflicting arguments. An example is the framework by Besnard and Hunter that is based on classical logic and in which an argument (obtained from a knowledgebase) is a pair where the first item is a minimal consistent set of formulae that proves the second item (which is a formula). In the framework, the only counter-arguments (defeaters) that need to be taken into account are canonical arguments (a form of minimal undercut). Argument trees then provide a way of exhaustively collating arguments and counter-arguments. A problem with this set up is that some argument trees may be "too big" to have sufficient impact. In this paper, we address the need to increase the impact of argumentation by using pruned argument trees. We formalize this in terms of how arguments resonate with the intended audience of the arguments. For example, if a politician wants to make a case for raising taxes, the arguments used would depend on what is important to the audience: Arguments based on increased taxes are needed to pay for improved healthcare would resonate better with an audience of pensioners, whereas arguments based on increased taxes are needed to pay for improved transport infrastructure would resonate better with an audience of business executives. By analysing the resonance of arguments, we can prune argument trees to raise their impact.

## Introduction

Consider reading an article in a current affairs magazine such as the Economist or Newsweek. Such an article only has a relatively small number of arguments. These arguments are quite a small subset of all possible arguments that either the writer or the reader could construct from their own knowledgebases. In producing an article, a writer regards some arguments as having higher impact with the intended audience than others, and only the higher impact ones are used. In a sense, there is some filter on the argument tree that can be constructed.

This perspective raises two questions: (1) What is this notion of impact? (i.e. what does it mean and how do we measure it in practice?) and (2) Given a measure of impact, how do we use it as a filter on arguments? In this paper, we look at some of the issues surrounding these questions.

To characterize these issues we use an existing framework for logic-based argumentation by Besnard and Hunter (Besnard & Hunter 2001). In the next section, we review this framework. Then in subsequent sections, we show how this can be adapted for higher impact argumentation.

## Logic-based argumentation

We consider a propositional language. We use $\alpha, \beta, \gamma, \ldots$ to denote formulae and $\Delta, \Phi, \Psi, \ldots$ to denote sets of formulae. Deduction in classical propositional logic is denoted by the symbol $\vdash$ and deductive closure by $\mathsf{Th}$ so that $\mathsf{Th}(\Phi) = \{\alpha \mid \Phi \vdash \alpha\}$.

For the following definitions, we first assume a knowledgebase $\Delta$ (a finite set of formulae) and use this $\Delta$ throughout. We further assume that every subset of $\Delta$ is given an enumeration $\langle \alpha_1, \ldots, \alpha_n \rangle$ of its elements, which is called its canonical enumeration. This really is not a demanding constraint: In particular, the constraint is satisfied whenever we impose an arbitrary total ordering over $\Delta$. Importantly, the order has no meaning and is not meant to represent any respective importance of formulae in $\Delta$ is imposed. It is only a convenient way to indicate the order in which it is assumed the formulae in any subset of $\Delta$ are conjoined to make a formula logically equivalent to that subset.

The paradigm for the approach is a large repository of information, represented by $\Delta$, from which arguments can be constructed for and against arbitrary claims. Apart from information being understood as declarative statements, there is no a priori restriction on the contents, and the pieces of information in the repository can be as complex as possible. Therefore, $\Delta$ is not expected to be consistent. It need even not be the case that every single formula in $\Delta$ is consistent.

The framework adopts a very common intuitive notion of an argument. Essentially, an argument is a set of relevant formulae that can be used to classically prove some point, together with that point. Each point is represented by a formula.

**Definition 1** *An* **argument** *is a pair $\langle \Phi, \alpha \rangle$ such that: (1) $\Phi \nvdash \bot$; (2) $\Phi \vdash \alpha$; and (3) there is no $\Phi' \subset \Phi$ such that $\Phi' \vdash \alpha$. We say that $\langle \Phi, \alpha \rangle$ is an argument for $\alpha$. We call $\alpha$ the consequent of the argument and $\Phi$ the support of the*

---

*Thanks are due to Philippe Besnard for feedback on this work.

*argument. We also say that $\Phi$ is a support for $\alpha$. For an argument $\langle\Phi,\alpha\rangle$, let* $\mathsf{Support}(\langle\Phi,\alpha\rangle) = \Phi$.

**Example 1** *Let* $\Delta = \{\alpha, \alpha \rightarrow \beta, \gamma \rightarrow \neg\beta, \gamma, \delta, \delta \rightarrow \beta, \neg\alpha, \neg\gamma\}$. *Some arguments are:*

$$\langle\{\alpha, \alpha \rightarrow \beta\}, \beta\rangle$$
$$\langle\{\neg\alpha\}, \neg\alpha\rangle$$
$$\langle\{\alpha \rightarrow \beta\}, \neg\alpha \vee \beta\rangle$$
$$\langle\{\neg\gamma\}, \delta \rightarrow \neg\gamma\rangle$$

Arguments are not independent. In a sense, some encompass others. This is clarified as follows.

**Definition 2** *An argument $\langle\Phi,\alpha\rangle$ is* **more conservative** *than an argument $\langle\Psi,\beta\rangle$ iff $\Phi \subseteq \Psi$ and $\beta \vdash \alpha$.*

**Example 2** *$\langle\{\alpha\}, \alpha \vee \beta\rangle$ is more conservative than $\langle\{\alpha, \alpha \rightarrow \beta\}, \beta\rangle$. Here, the latter argument can be obtained from the former (using $\alpha \rightarrow \beta$ as an extra hypothesis) but this is not the case in general.*

Some arguments directly oppose the support of others, which amounts to the notion of an undercut.

**Definition 3** *An* **undercut** *for an argument $\langle\Phi,\alpha\rangle$ is an argument $\langle\Psi, \neg(\phi_1 \wedge \ldots \wedge \phi_n)\rangle$ where $\{\phi_1, \ldots, \phi_n\} \subseteq \Phi$.*

**Example 3** *Let $\Delta = \{\alpha, \alpha \rightarrow \beta, \gamma, \gamma \rightarrow \neg\alpha\}$. Then, $\langle\{\gamma, \gamma \rightarrow \neg\alpha\}, \neg(\alpha \wedge (\alpha \rightarrow \beta))\rangle$ is an undercut for $\langle\{\alpha, \alpha \rightarrow \beta\}, \beta\rangle$. A less conservative undercut for $\langle\{\alpha, \alpha \rightarrow \beta\}, \beta\rangle$ is $\langle\{\gamma, \gamma \rightarrow \neg\alpha\}, \neg\alpha\rangle$.*

**Definition 4** *$\langle\Psi,\beta\rangle$ is a* **maximally conservative undercut** *of $\langle\Phi,\alpha\rangle$ iff $\langle\Psi,\beta\rangle$ is an undercut of $\langle\Phi,\alpha\rangle$ such that no undercuts of $\langle\Phi,\alpha\rangle$ are strictly more conservative than $\langle\Psi,\beta\rangle$ (that is, for all undercuts $\langle\Psi',\beta'\rangle$ of $\langle\Phi,\alpha\rangle$, if $\Psi' \subseteq \Psi$ and $\beta \vdash \beta'$ then $\Psi \subseteq \Psi'$ and $\beta' \vdash \beta$).*

**Definition 5** *An argument $\langle\Psi, \neg(\phi_1 \wedge \ldots \wedge \phi_n)\rangle$ is a* **canonical undercut** *for $\langle\Phi,\alpha\rangle$ iff it is a maximally conservative undercut for $\langle\Phi,\alpha\rangle$ and $\langle\phi_1, \ldots, \phi_n\rangle$ is the canonical enumeration of $\Phi$.*

An argument tree describes the various ways an argument can be challenged, as well as how the counter-arguments to the initial argument can themselves be challenged, and so on recursively.

**Definition 6** *An* **argument tree** *for $\alpha$ is a tree $T$ where the nodes are arguments such that*

1. *The root is an argument for $\alpha$.*
2. *For no node $\langle\Phi,\beta\rangle$ with ancestor nodes $\langle\Phi_1,\beta_1\rangle, \ldots, \langle\Phi_n,\beta_n\rangle$ is $\Phi$ a subset of $\Phi_1 \cup \cdots \cup \Phi_n$.*
3. *The children nodes of a node $A$ are canonical undercuts for $A$ that obey 2.*

*A* **complete argument tree** *for $\alpha$ is an argument tree for $\alpha$ such that the children nodes of a node $A$ consist of* all *canonical undercuts for $A$ that obey 2.*

As a notational convenience, in examples of argument trees we will use the $\diamond$ symbol to denote the consequent of an argument when that argument is a canonical undercut.

**Definition 7** *Let $T$ be an argument tree and let $T = (N, E)$ where $N$ is a set of nodes and $E$ is a set of edges. The set of nodes in $T$ is given by* $\mathsf{Nodes}(T) = N$.

**Definition 8** *Let $T_1$ and $T_2$ be argument trees. $T_1$ is* **more or equally pruned** *than $T_2$ iff* $\mathsf{Nodes}(T_1) \subseteq \mathsf{Nodes}(T_2)$. *For a complete argument tree $T$, let* $\mathsf{Space}(T) = \{T' \mid T'$ *is more or equally pruned than* $T\}$.

In $\mathsf{Space}(T)$, the least pruned tree is $T$, and the most pruned tree is the tree given by the empty argument tree (i.e. the tree with no nodes or arcs).

Whilst the use of canonical arguments simplifies the complete argument trees enormously, they may still be "too big" in the sense that too many of the arguments used do not resonate with the intended audience. In this paper, we formalize how arguments resonate with the intended audience. By analysing the resonance of arguments, we can prune argument trees to raise their impact.

## Resonance of arguments

The impact of argumentation depends on what an agent regards as important. Different agents think different things are important. We adopt a simple way, called a desideratabase, of capturing what an agent in the intended audience thinks is important, and then use this to measure how arguments resonante with the agent.

**Definition 9** *A* **desideratabase** *for an agent is a tuple $(\Pi,\lambda)$ where (1) $\Pi$ is a set of classical propositional formulae called a set of* **desiderata** *and (2) $\lambda$ is mapping from $\Pi$ to $[0,1]$ called a* **desiderata weighting**. *For $\delta_i, \delta_j \in \Pi$, $\delta_i$ is a* **more important desideratum** *than $\delta_j$ for the agent iff $\lambda(\delta_j) < \lambda(\delta_i)$. A* **unit desiderata weighting** *$\lambda$ is a desiderata weighting such that for all $\delta \in \Pi$, $\lambda(\delta) = 1$. For desiderata weighting $\lambda_1$ and $\lambda_2$, $\lambda_1$ is* **stronger than or equal** *to $\lambda_2$ iff for all $\delta \in \Pi$, $\lambda_2(\delta) \leq \lambda_1(\delta)$.*

Intuitively, a desideratum (a formula in a desiderata) represents what an agent would like to be true in the world. There is no constraint that it has to be something that the agent can actually make true. It may be something unattainable such as "there will be no more wars" or "bread and milk is free for everyone". There is also no constraint that the desiderata for an agent are consistent.

We can view a desiderata weighting $\lambda$ as delineating a ranking over possible worlds (where the set of worlds is the set of classical interpretations given by the propositional language of $\Pi$). We do not provide details in this paper.

**Definition 10** *Let $(\Pi,\lambda)$ be a desideratabase, and let $\langle\Phi,\alpha\rangle$ be an argument. $\langle\Phi,\alpha\rangle$ is a* **resonating argument** *iff for some $\delta \in \Pi$, $\Phi \vdash \delta$ or $\Phi \vdash \neg\delta$.*

So for an argument to have an impact on an agent, the support for the argument must imply a desideratum or the negation of a desideratum.

**Definition 11** *Let $(\Pi,\lambda)$ be a desideratabase, and let $\langle\Phi,\alpha\rangle$ be a argument. The* **echo** *of this argument with respect to the desiderata is defined as follows*

$$\mathsf{Echo}(\Phi,\Pi) = \{\delta \in \Pi \mid (\Phi \vdash \delta \text{ or } \Phi \vdash \neg\delta)\}$$

Note if $(\Pi_1,\lambda_1)$ and $(\Pi_2,\lambda_2)$ are desideratabases, such that $\mathsf{Th}(\Pi_1) \subseteq \mathsf{Th}(\Pi_2)$, and $\Phi$ is the support of an argument, then it is not necessarily the case that $\mathsf{Echo}(\Phi,\Pi_1) \subseteq$

$\mathsf{Echo}(\Phi,\Pi_2)$ or that $\mathsf{Echo}(\Phi,\Pi_2) \subseteq \mathsf{Echo}(\Phi,\Pi_1)$, as illustrated in the next example.

**Example 4** *Let* $\Pi_1 = \{\alpha, \beta \wedge \gamma\}$, $\Pi_2 = \{\alpha \wedge \beta, \gamma\}$, *and let* $\Phi = \{\alpha, \gamma\}$. *So* $\mathsf{Echo}(\Phi,\Pi_1) = \{\alpha\}$ *and* $\mathsf{Echo}(\Phi,\Pi_2) = \{\gamma\}$. *Hence* $\mathsf{Echo}(\Phi,\Pi_1) \not\subseteq \mathsf{Echo}(\Phi,\Pi_2)$ *and* $\mathsf{Echo}(\Phi,\Pi_2) \not\subseteq \mathsf{Echo}(\Phi,\Pi_1)$.

Obviously if an agent has no desiderata, $\Pi = \emptyset$, then for any argument $\langle\Phi,\alpha\rangle$, $\mathsf{Echo}(\Phi,\Pi) = \emptyset$. At the other extreme, if every desideratum that an agent has is inconsistent with itself, i.e. for all $\delta \in \Pi$, $\{\delta\} \vdash \perp$, then $\vdash \top \leftrightarrow \neg\delta$, and so for any argument $\langle\Phi,\alpha\rangle$, $\Phi \vdash \neg\delta$, and hence $\mathsf{Echo}(\Phi,\Pi) = \Pi$.

**Definition 12** *Let* $(\Pi,\lambda)$ *be a desideratabase, and let* $\langle\Phi,\alpha\rangle$ *be a argument. The* **resonance** *of this argument with respect to the desideratabase is defined as follows*

$$\mathsf{Resonance}(\Phi,\Pi,\lambda) = \sum_{\delta \in \mathsf{Echo}(\Phi,\Pi)} \lambda(\delta)$$

The resonance function captures the weighted sum of the echo of the argument. This reflects the importance that the agent attaches to the argument.

**Example 5** *Let* $\Pi = \{\beta,\gamma\}$, $\lambda(\beta) = 1$, *and* $\lambda(\gamma) = 0.5$. *Let* $A_1$ *and* $A_2$ *be arguments as below where* $A_2$ *is a canonical undercut for* $A_1$.

$$A_1 = \langle\{\beta, \beta \rightarrow \alpha\}, \alpha\rangle$$
$$A_2 = \langle\{\neg(\beta \vee \gamma)\}, \neg(\beta \wedge (\beta \rightarrow \alpha))\rangle$$

*Hence we get the following resonance values.*

$$\mathsf{Resonance}(\mathsf{Support}(A_1),\Pi,\lambda) = 1.0$$
$$\mathsf{Resonance}(\mathsf{Support}(A_2),\Pi,\lambda) = 1.5$$

The resonance function is monotonic in the membership of the support of the argument.

**Proposition 1** *Let* $\Phi_1$ *and* $\Phi_2$ *be supports for arguments and let* $(\Pi,\lambda)$ *be a desideratabase. If* $\Phi_1 \subseteq \Phi_2$, *then* $\mathsf{Resonance}(\Phi_1,\Pi,\lambda) \leq \mathsf{Resonance}(\Phi_2,\Pi,\lambda)$.

Similarly, a logically weaker support for an argument has a lower resonance.

**Proposition 2** *Let* $\Phi_1$ *and* $\Phi_2$ *be supports for arguments and let* $(\Pi,\lambda)$ *be a desideratabase. If* $\mathsf{Th}(\Phi_1) \subseteq \mathsf{Th}(\Phi_2)$, *then* $\mathsf{Resonance}(\Phi_1,\Pi,\lambda) \leq \mathsf{Resonance}(\Phi_2,\Pi,\lambda)$.

With unit desiderata weighting, the resonance function is also monotonic in the membership of the desideratabase.

**Proposition 3** *Let* $\Phi$ *be a support for an argument and let* $(\Pi_1,\lambda_1)$ *and* $(\Pi_2,\lambda_2)$ *be desideratabases, where* $\lambda_1$ *and* $\lambda_2$ *are unit desiderata weightings. If* $\Pi_1 \subseteq \Pi_2$, *then* $\mathsf{Resonance}(\Phi,\Pi_1,\lambda_1) \leq \mathsf{Resonance}(\Phi,\Pi_2,\lambda_2)$.

However, if $(\Pi_1,\lambda_1)$ and $(\Pi_2,\lambda_2)$ are desideratabases, such that $\mathsf{Th}(\Pi_1) \subseteq \mathsf{Th}(\Pi_2)$ and $\lambda_1$ and $\lambda_2$ are unit desiderata weightings, and $\langle\Phi,\alpha\rangle$ is an argument, then we see in the next example that it is not necessarily the case that $\mathsf{Resonance}(\Phi,\Pi_1,\lambda_1) \leq \mathsf{Resonance}(\Phi,\Pi_2,\lambda_2)$, and it is not necessarily the case that $\mathsf{Resonance}(\Phi,\Pi_2,\lambda_2) \leq \mathsf{Resonance}(\Phi,\Pi_1,\lambda_1)$.

**Example 6** *Let* $(\Pi_1,\lambda_1)$ *and* $(\Pi_2,\lambda_2)$ *be desideratabases where* $\Pi_1 = \{\alpha,\beta\}$ *and* $\Pi_2 = \{\alpha \wedge \beta, \gamma\}$ *and* $\lambda_1$ *and* $\lambda_2$ *are unit desiderata weightings. So* $\mathsf{Th}(\Pi_1) \subseteq \mathsf{Th}(\Pi_2)$. *Also let* $\Phi = \{\beta\}$ *and* $\Phi' = \{\gamma\}$. *So* $\mathsf{Echo}(\Phi,\Pi_1) = \{\beta\}$, $\mathsf{Echo}(\Phi,\Pi_2) = \emptyset$, $\mathsf{Echo}(\Phi',\Pi_1) = \emptyset$, *and* $\mathsf{Echo}(\Phi',\Pi_2) = \{\gamma\}$. *So* $\mathsf{Resonance}(\Phi,\Pi_2,\lambda_2) < \mathsf{Resonance}(\Phi,\Pi_1,\lambda_1)$ *and* $\mathsf{Resonance}(\Phi',\Pi_1,\lambda_1) < \mathsf{Resonance}(\Phi',\Pi_2,\lambda_2)$

There are various other ways to define one desideratabase being logically weaker than another. One way, given in the following proposition, implies that the logically weaker desideratabase leads to a higher resonance for an argument.

**Proposition 4** *Let* $\Phi$ *be a support for an argument and let* $(\Pi_1,\lambda_1)$ *and* $(\Pi_2,\lambda_2)$ *be desideratabases. If there is a bijection* $G$ *from* $\Pi_1$ *to* $\Pi_2$ *such that for all* $\delta \in \Pi_1$ $\{\delta\} \vdash G(\delta)$ *and* $\lambda_1(\delta) \leq \lambda_2(G(\delta))$, *then* $\mathsf{Resonance}(\Phi,\Pi_1,\lambda_1) \leq \mathsf{Resonance}(\Phi,\Pi_2,\lambda_2)$.

Desiderata weighting can also have a net effect on resonance. At one extreme, if $\lambda(\delta) = 0$ for all $\delta \in \Pi$, then $\mathsf{Resonance}(\Phi,\Pi,\lambda) = 0$. At the other extreme, if $\lambda(\delta) = 1$ for all $\delta \in \Pi$, (i.e. $\lambda$ is a unit weighting) then $\mathsf{Resonance}(\Phi,\Pi,\lambda) = |\mathsf{Echo}(\Phi,\Pi)|$. More generally, increasing the strength of the weighting in a desideratabase also increases resonance as formalised in the next proposition.

**Proposition 5** *Let* $\Phi$ *be a support for an argument and let* $(\Pi,\lambda_1)$ *and* $(\Pi,\lambda_2)$ *be desideratabases. If* $\lambda_1$ *is stronger than or equal to* $\lambda_2$, *then* $\mathsf{Resonance}(\Phi,\Pi,\lambda_2) \leq \mathsf{Resonance}(\Phi,\Pi,\lambda_1)$.

Finally in this section, we need to measure the cost of an argument. We will use an obvious and simple measure: The cost of an argument is the number of different propositional letters used in the support of the argument. So for a support $\Phi$, and using the definition of Propositions given below, the cost is the cardinality of $\mathsf{Propositions}(\Phi)$.

**Definition 13** *The set of propositional letters used in* $\phi \in \mathcal{L}$ *is given by* $\mathsf{Propositions}(\phi)$, *and the set of propositional letters used in* $\Phi \subseteq \mathcal{L}$ *is given by*

$$\mathsf{Propositions}(\Phi) = \bigcup_{\phi \in \Phi} \mathsf{Propositions}(\phi)$$

**Example 7** $\mathsf{Propositions}(\alpha \vee (\beta \rightarrow (\alpha \vee \neg\delta))) = \{\alpha,\beta,\delta\}$.

For this measure of the cost of an argument, we are assuming that an agent in the audience prefers arguments with fewer propositional letters, since they are simpler to read and analyse. We draw Definitions 13 and 12 together in the next section.

## Measuring impact of argument trees

Now we want to consider resonance and cost in the context of an argument tree. For this, we want resonance of a tree to be sensitive to the depth of the arguments in the tree. We formalise this with the following notion of a discount function.

**Definition 14** *For any argument tree $T$, the function* Depth *from* $\mathsf{Nodes}(T)$ *to* $\mathbb{N}$ *is such that for the root* $A_r \in \mathsf{Nodes}(T)$, $\mathsf{Depth}(A_r) = 1$, *and for all nodes* $A_i \in \mathsf{Nodes}(T)$, *if* $\mathsf{Depth}(A_i) = n$, *then for any child* $A_j$ *of* $A_i$ *in* $T$, $\mathsf{Depth}(A_j) = n + 1$.

**Definition 15** *A* **discount function** *is a monotonically decreasing function from* $\mathbb{N}$ *to* $[0, 1]$. *So if* $\mu$ *is a discount function, then* $\mu(n) \geq \mu(n+1)$ *for all* $n \in \mathbb{N}$. *For a discount function* $\mu$, *the* **boundary** *of* $\mu$ *is* $n \in \mathbb{N}$ *such that* $\mu(n) > 0$ *and* $\mu(n+1) = 0$. *A* **unit discount function** *is a discount function* $\mu$ *such that for all* $n \in \mathbb{N}$, $\mu(n) = 1$. *A* **unit-step discount function** *is a discount function* $\mu$ *such that for all* $n \in \mathbb{N}$, $\mu(n) = 1$ *or* $\mu(n) = 0$. *Let* $\mu_1$ *and* $\mu_2$ *be discount functions.* $\mu_1$ *is* **more or equally discounting** *than* $\mu_2$ *iff for all* $n \in \mathbb{N}$, $\mu_1(n) \leq \mu_2(n)$.

**Definition 16** *A* **context** *is a tuple* $(\Pi, \lambda, \mu)$ *where* $(\Pi, \lambda)$ *is a desideratabase, and* $\mu$ *is a discount function. A* **unit context** *is a context* $(\Pi, \lambda', \mu')$ *where* $\lambda'$ *is a unit desiderata weighting, and* $\mu'$ *is a unit discount function.*

A unit context is an extreme context where neither the desiderata weighting nor the discount have any net effect on the outcome. In other words, with a unit context the resonance of an argument tree is only based on the actual desiderata.

We now consider a definition for measuring the resonance of an argument tree. This definition takes a sum of the resonance of the arguments in the tree where the net effect of each argument is scaled by the discount function. The discounting increases going down the tree. So arguments at a greater depth have a reduced net effect on the resonance of the tree.

**Definition 17** *The* **resonance** *of the argument tree* $T$ *with respect to the context* $(\Pi, \lambda, \mu)$, *denoted* $\mathsf{Resonance}(T, \Pi, \lambda, \mu)$, *is defined as follows*

$$\sum_{A \in \mathsf{Nodes}(T)} \mathsf{Resonance}(\mathsf{Support}(A), \Pi, \lambda) \times \mu(\mathsf{Depth}(A))$$

**Definition 18** *The* **propositional cost** *of an argument tree* $T$ *denoted* $\mathsf{Propositionalcost}(T)$ *is the cardinality of the following set.*

$$\bigcup_{A \in \mathsf{Nodes}(T)} \mathsf{Propositions}(\mathsf{Support}(A))$$

The above measure of cost is $\log_2$ of the number of classical interpretations for the supports of the arguments in $T$.

**Definition 19** *For a context* $(\Pi, \lambda, \mu)$, *the* **impact** *of an argument tree* $T$ *with one or more nodes is given by the following ratio,*

$$\mathsf{Impact}(T, \Pi, \lambda, \mu) = \frac{\mathsf{Resonance}(T, \Pi, \lambda, \mu)}{\mathsf{Propositionalcost}(T)}$$

*and for the empty argument tree* $T_\emptyset$ *(i.e. the tree with no nodes),* $\mathsf{Impact}(T_\emptyset, \Pi, \lambda, \mu) = 0$.

Pruning an argument tree may decrease the cost, but this may also decrease the resonance. In a unit context, $\mathsf{Impact}(T, \Pi, \lambda, \mu)$ gives the ratio of desiderata in the echo of the arguments in $T$ to the propositional letters used in the support of the arguments in $T$.

When measuring impact with a non-unit context, we are also taking into account the relative interest in the desiderata and the relative depth of the arguments in the argument trees. These orthogonal factors help to better evaluate the impact for a particular audience. We therefore see selection of an appropriate context as an important design decision in developing an argumentation system. In some applications, we want fewer arguments per argument tree and in other applications we want more arguments per argument tree.

In the following example, we use the impact function to compare three argument trees, $T_1$, $T_2$ and $T_3$, where $T_3$ is a complete argument tree, and $T_1$ and $T_2$ are more pruned than $T_3$.

**Example 8** *Let* $\Delta = \{\beta, \beta \to \alpha, \gamma, \gamma \to \neg\beta, \neg\gamma \wedge \delta\}$ *From this, we obtain the following (non-exhaustive) list of arguments.*

$$A_1 = \langle\{\beta, \beta \to \alpha\}, \alpha\rangle$$
$$A_2 = \langle\{\gamma, \gamma \to \neg\beta\}, \neg(\beta \wedge (\beta \to \alpha))\rangle$$
$$A_3 = \langle\{\neg\gamma \wedge \delta\}, \neg(\gamma \wedge (\gamma \to \neg\beta))\rangle$$

*Let* $\mathsf{Nodes}(T_1) = \{A_1\}$, $\mathsf{Nodes}(T_2) = \{A_1, A_2\}$, *and* $\mathsf{Nodes}(T_3) = \{A_1, A_2, A_3\}$ *giving the following argument trees, where* $T_3$ *is a complete argument tree, and* $T_2$ *is more pruned than* $T_3$, *and* $T_1$ *is more pruned than* $T_2$.

| $T_1$ | $T_2$ | $T_3$ |
|---|---|---|
| $A_1$ | $A_1$ | $A_1$ |
| | $\uparrow$ | $\uparrow$ |
| | $A_2$ | $A_2$ |
| | | $\uparrow$ |
| | | $A_3$ |

*Let* $(\Pi, \lambda, \mu)$ *be a unit context where* $\Pi = \{\beta, \neg\gamma, \delta\}$. $\mathsf{Echo}(A_1, \Pi) = \{\beta\}$, $\mathsf{Echo}(A_2, \Pi) = \{\beta, \neg\gamma\}$, *and* $\mathsf{Echo}(A_3, \Pi) = \{\neg\gamma, \delta\}$. *Hence*

$$\begin{aligned}
&\mathsf{Resonance}(T_1, \Pi, \lambda, \mu)\\
&= (\mathsf{Resonance}(\mathsf{Support}(A_1), \Pi, \lambda) \times \mu(1))\\
&= (1 \times 1) = 1
\end{aligned}$$

$$\begin{aligned}
&\mathsf{Resonance}(T_2, \Pi, \lambda, \mu)\\
&= (\mathsf{Resonance}(\mathsf{Support}(A_1), \Pi, \lambda) \times \mu(1))\\
&\qquad +(\mathsf{Resonance}(\mathsf{Support}(A_2), \Pi, \lambda) \times \mu(2))\\
&= (1 \times 1) + (2 \times 1) = 3
\end{aligned}$$

$$\begin{aligned}
&\mathsf{Resonance}(T_3, \Pi, \lambda, \mu)\\
&= \mathsf{Resonance}(\mathsf{Support}(A_1), \Pi, \lambda) \times \mu(1))\\
&\qquad +\mathsf{Resonance}(\mathsf{Support}(A_2), \Pi, \lambda) \times \mu(2))\\
&\qquad +\mathsf{Resonance}(\mathsf{Support}(A_3), \Pi, \lambda) \times \mu(3))\\
&= (1 \times 1) + (2 \times 1) + (2 \times 1) = 5
\end{aligned}$$

*Since* $\mathsf{Propositionalcost}(T_1) = 2$, $\mathsf{Propositionalcost}(T_2) = 3$, *and* $\mathsf{Propositionalcost}(T_3) = 4$, *we get* $\mathsf{Impact}(T_1, \Pi, \lambda, \mu) = \frac{1}{2}$, $\mathsf{Impact}(T_2, \Pi, \lambda, \mu) = \frac{3}{3}$, *and* $\mathsf{Impact}(T_3, \Pi, \lambda, \mu) = \frac{5}{4}$. *If we use an alternative discount function, where* $\mu_2(1) = 1$, $\mu_2(2) = 0.5$, *and* $\mu_2(3) = 0$, *then* $\mathsf{Impact}(T_1, \Pi, \lambda, \mu_2) = \frac{1}{2}$, $\mathsf{Impact}(T_2, \Pi, \lambda, \mu_2) = \frac{2}{3}$, *and* $\mathsf{Impact}(T_3, \Pi, \lambda, \mu_2) = \frac{2}{4}$. *So with the unit discount* *function $\mu$, the complete argument tree $T_3$ has the highest impact, whereas with the non-unit discount function $\mu_2$, the pruned argument tree $T_2$ has the highest impact.*

When $(\Pi, \lambda, \mu)$ is not a unit context, the following result summarizes the conditions for zero impact.

**Proposition 6** *Let $(\Pi, \lambda, \mu)$ be a context, and let $T$ be an argument tree.* $\mathsf{Impact}(T, \Pi, \lambda, \mu) = 0$ *iff for all* $A \in \mathsf{Nodes}(T)$ ($\delta \in \mathsf{Echo}(\mathsf{Support}(A), \Pi)$ *implies* $(\mu(\mathsf{Depth}(A)) = 0$ *or* $\lambda(\delta) = 0)))$.

The following series of propositions are counterparts to propositions given for the behaviour of resonance.

**Proposition 7** *Let $(\Pi, \lambda)$ be a desideratabase, let $T$ be an argument tree and let $\mu_1$ and $\mu_2$ be discount functions. If $\mu_1$ is more or equally discounting than $\mu_2$ then* $\mathsf{Impact}(T, \Pi, \lambda, \mu_1) \leq \mathsf{Impact}(T, \Pi, \lambda, \mu_2)$.

**Proposition 8** *Let $T$ be an argument tree and let $(\Pi_1, \lambda_1)$ and $(\Pi_2, \lambda_2)$ be desideratabases, where $\lambda_1$ and $\lambda_2$ are unit desiderata weightings, and $\mu$ is a discount function. If $\Pi_1 \subseteq \Pi_2$, then* $\mathsf{Impact}(T, \Pi_1, \lambda_1, \mu) \leq \mathsf{Impact}(T, \Pi_2, \lambda_2, \mu)$.

**Proposition 9** *Let $\Phi$ be a support for an argument and let $(\Pi_1, \lambda_1)$ and $(\Pi_2, \lambda_2)$ be desideratabases. If there is a bijection $G$ from $\Pi_1$ to $\Pi_2$ such that for all $\delta \in \Pi_1$ $\{\delta\} \vdash G(\delta)$ and $\lambda_1(\delta) \leq \lambda_2(G(\delta))$, then* $\mathsf{Impact}(T, \Phi, \Pi_1, \lambda_1) \leq \mathsf{Impact}(T, \Phi, \Pi_2, \lambda_2)$.

Replacing an argument in an argument tree with a logically equivalent argument that does not introduce redundant propositional letters results in the same impact as the original argument tree.

**Proposition 10** *Let $(\Pi, \lambda, \mu)$ be a context. Let $T$ and $T'$ be two isomorphic arguments trees. So $T = (N, E)$ and $T' = (N', E')$ and there is a bijection $F : N \mapsto N'$ such that $(A_i, A_j) \in E$ iff $(F(A_i), F(A_j)) \in E'$. If the bijection $F$ is such that for all arguments $A \in N$,* $\mathsf{Propositions}(\mathsf{Support}(A)) = \mathsf{Propositions}(\mathsf{Support}(F(A)))$ *and* $\mathsf{Th}(\mathsf{Support}(A))) = \mathsf{Th}(\mathsf{Support}(F(A)))$, *then* $\mathsf{Impact}(T, \Pi, \lambda, \mu) = \mathsf{Impact}(T', \Pi, \lambda, \mu)$.

Impact is not a monotonic function (i.e. increasing the size of the tree, can increase or decrease the impact): If $T_1$ is more pruned than $T_2$, then it is not necessarily the case that $\mathsf{Impact}(T_1, \Pi, \lambda, \mu) \geq \mathsf{Impact}(T_2, \Pi, \lambda, \mu)$, and it is not necessarily the case that $\mathsf{Impact}(T_1, \Pi, \lambda, \mu) \leq \mathsf{Impact}(T_2, \Pi, \lambda, \mu)$. This is illustrated in the next example.

**Example 9** *Let $(\Pi, \lambda, \mu)$ be a unit context where $\Pi = \{\beta\}$. Let $A_1 = \langle\{\alpha \wedge \beta\}, \alpha\rangle$ and $A_2 = \langle\{\neg\alpha \wedge \gamma \wedge \beta\}, \neg(\alpha \wedge \beta)\rangle$. Let $T_1$ be a tree consisting of nodes $A_1$ and $A_2$, let $T_2$ be a tree consisting of node $A_1$, and let $T_3$ be the empty tree. Therefore $T_3$ is more pruned than $T_2$ and $T_2$ is more pruned than $T_1$. Yet* $\mathsf{Impact}(T_1, \Pi, \lambda, \mu) \leq \mathsf{Impact}(T_2, \Pi, \lambda, \mu)$, *and* $\mathsf{Impact}(T_3, \Pi, \lambda, \mu) \leq \mathsf{Impact}(T_1, \Pi, \lambda, \mu)$.

By definition, the minimum possible value for impact is 0. At the other extreme, we can set up a knowledgebase and desideratabase to create a complete argument tree with maximum impact. We explore this in the next two propositions.

**Proposition 11** *For a set of $m$ propositional letters, the knowledgebase $\Delta$ and a unit context $(\Pi, \lambda, \mu)$ are defined as follows: For all $\phi, \psi \in \Delta$, $\{\phi, \psi\} \vdash \bot$, and $\Delta = \Pi$ and $|\Delta| = |\Pi| = 2^m$. Now let $T$ be a complete argument tree where the arguments in* $\mathsf{Nodes}(T)$ *are obtained from $\Delta$. If* $A \in \mathsf{Nodes}(T)$, *then*

$$\mathsf{Echo}(\mathsf{Support}(A), \Pi) = \Pi$$
$$\mathsf{Resonance}(\mathsf{Support}(A), \Pi, \lambda, \mu) = |\Pi| = 2^m$$
$$|\mathsf{Propositions}(\mathsf{Support}(A))| = m$$

In the above proposition, the knowledgebase $\Delta$ has the maximum number of pairwise conflicts. This fact, together with $\Delta = \Pi$ holding, leads to a complete argument tree with maximum possible impact as follows.

**Proposition 12** *For a knowledgebase $\Delta$ composed of $m$ propositional letters, the highest possible impact for an argument tree $T$ composed of arguments from $\Delta$, where* $|\mathsf{Nodes}(T)| = k$, *and $(\Pi, \lambda, \mu)$ is a unit context, is*

$$\mathsf{Impact}(T, \Pi, \lambda, \mu) = \frac{\mathsf{Resonance}(T, \Pi, \lambda, \mu)}{\mathsf{Propositionalcost}(T)} = \frac{k \times 2^m}{m}$$

**Example 10** *For the propositional letters $\alpha$ and $\beta$, let $\Delta = \{\alpha \wedge \beta, \neg\alpha \wedge \beta, \alpha \wedge \neg\beta, \neg\alpha \wedge \neg\beta\}$. This knowledgebase can be used to construct a complete argument tree $T$. Each of these trees has 16 nodes. For* $A \in \mathsf{Nodes}(T)$, *if $\Delta = \Pi$, then* $\mathsf{Resonance}(\mathsf{Support}(A), \Pi, \lambda, \mu) = 4$ *and* $\mathsf{Propositionalcost}(T) = 2$. *Hence,* $\mathsf{Impact}(T, \Pi, \lambda, \mu) = 32$.

In general, given some knowledgebase $\Delta$, we can design a context $(\Pi, \lambda, \mu)$ that allows us to tailor the argumentation for the intended audience. In general, a non-unit discount function tends to favour wider and shallower trees rather than deeper and narrower trees. Dense desiderata (i.e. a desideratabase $(\Pi, \lambda)$ where there are many items in $\Pi$) with unit desiderata weighting can favour wider trees, less dense desiderata with non-unit desiderata weighting can favour either wide and shallow or deep and narrow trees. The argument trees with higher impact are therefore obtained by considering the interplay between these dimensions.

## Optimizing impact

To optimize the impact of argumentation, given a complete argument tree, and a context, we need to select a pruned argument tree that maximizes resonance and minimizes propositional cost.

**Definition 20** *Let $T$ be a complete argument tree. An argument tree* $T_i \in \mathsf{Space}(T)$ *is an* **optimal tree** *in a context $(\Pi, \lambda, \mu)$ iff for all* $T_j \in \mathsf{Space}(T)$ $\mathsf{Impact}(T_i, \Pi, \lambda, \mu) \geq \mathsf{Impact}(T_j, \Pi, \lambda, \mu)$.

We can view optimization of impact as a decision problem.

**Theorem 1** *Let $T$ be a complete argument tree and let $k \in \mathbb{R}$. Determining whether there is a* $T_i \in \mathsf{Space}(T)$ *such that* $\mathsf{Impact}(T_i, \Pi, \lambda, \mu) \leq k$ *is an NP-complete decision problem.*

The proof is based on 3-SAT. Whilst in general the search for optimal trees can be expensive, there are some results like the following that can simplify the search space: If an argument in an optimal tree is not a resonating argument, and it adds cost to the tree, then it has an offspring argument in the tree that is a resonating argument. We see this in the following example, and more generally in Proposition 13.

**Example 11** *Let* $(\Pi, \lambda, \mu)$ *be a unit context where* $\Pi = \{\beta, \gamma\}$. *Let* $T$ *be an optimal tree composed of nodes* $\{A_1, A_2, A_3\}$ *where* $\mathsf{Support}(A_1) = \{\alpha\}$, $\mathsf{Support}(A_2) = \{\neg\delta \wedge \beta \wedge \neg\alpha\}$, *and* $\mathsf{Support}(A_3) = \{\beta \wedge \gamma \wedge \neg\alpha\}$. *Hence* $T$ *has the following form.*

$$\begin{array}{ccc} & A_1 & \\ \nearrow & & \nwarrow \\ A_2 & & A_3 \end{array}$$

*So* $\mathsf{Impact}(T, \Pi, \lambda, \mu) = 1/2$. *Now consider* $T'$ *which is* $T$ *extended with* $A_4$ *and* $\mathsf{Support}(A_4) = \{\delta \wedge \epsilon\}$. *So* $A_4$ *is a canonical undercut for* $A_2$. *Since* $\mathsf{Echo}(\mathsf{Support}(A_4), \Pi) = \emptyset$, *and* $\mathsf{Propositionalcost}(T) < \mathsf{Propositionalcost}(T')$, *we see that* $T'$ *is not an optimal tree.*

**Proposition 13** *Let* $T_i \in \mathsf{Space}(T)$ *be an optimal tree in the context* $(\Pi, \lambda, \mu)$. *For all* $A \in \mathsf{Nodes}(T_i)$, *if* $A$ *is a leaf, then* $\mathsf{Echo}(\mathsf{Support}(A), \Pi) \neq \emptyset$, *or* $\mathsf{Propositionalcost}(T_i) = \mathsf{Propositionalcost}(T_i')$, *where* $T_i'$ *is* $T_i$ *without* $A$.

The other substantial overhead in high impact argumentation is in constructing the actual arguments. This is the same for many forms of argumentation (e.g. (Brewka 1989; Benferhat, Dubois, & Prade 1993)) and it is essentially that of finding minimally consistent proofs of a formula (Cadoli 1992). One approach to addressing this complexity is to adopt approximate entailment (Schaerf & Cadoli 1995) for approximate coherence-based reasoning (Koriche 2001).

## Discussion

In the philosophical study of argumentation, the relationship between the person presenting arguments and the audience has been considered, and in particular the need for arguments to be aposite for an audience has been identified (see for example (Walton 1989; Cockcroft & Cockcroft 1992)). The proposal in this paper is, as far as we know, the first attempt to provide a formal logic-based account of maximising the apositeness of augments for an audience. It is clear that aspects of individual arguments in natural langauge can be represented and analysed using classical logic (see for example (Fisher 1988)). Furthermore, a set of such arguments can be related using argument trees (Besnard & Hunter 2001). Now with the framework in the paper, these arguments can be analysed to select an optimal subset that would have the maximum impact for the audience. This analysis could be useful in a variety of professional domains.

An application where wide but shallow argument trees are desirable is in decision-support for drug prescribing. Capsule is a system for identifying pros and cons for each possible drug that can be prescribed for a particular condition for a particular patient (Fox & Das 2000). Arguments are based on information about known benefits and side-effects of each drug, relative cost of each drug, other drugs the patient is using, the patient's known drug allergies, and any preferences the patient may have. The doctors who use the system want the key pros and cons but they do not want a deep structure to the arguments and counter-arguments. As a result, the form of argumentation used in the Capsule system can be formalized in our framework by using a unit-step discount function with a boundary of 2, so that the highest impact trees are of height 2 but with arbitrary width.

An application where deeper argument trees are desirable is in trial by jury. Here, arguments need to be analysed from various angles, leading to deeper branches. However, normally not all argument trees are presented to the jury since this would lead to too much information being presented. Rather a selection of branches is made on the basis of what is likely to resonate with the jury. For some court trials, lawyers are commissioning research based on focus groups for shaping the presentation of cases (see for example www.trialtech.com). This information may be formalisable with a desideratabase.

Finally, discounting as formalised in this paper, may be regarded as a formalization of the notion of serial weakening seen in legal argumentation (Verheij 1996).

## References


Benferhat, S.; Dubois, D.; and Prade, H. 1993. Argumentative inference in uncertain and inconsistent knowledge bases. In *Proceedings of Uncertainty in Artificial Intelligence*, 1449–1445. Morgan Kaufmann.

Besnard, P., and Hunter, A. 2001. A logic-based theory of deductive arguments. *Artificial Intelligence* 128:203–235.

Brewka, G. 1989. Preferred subtheories: An extended logical framework for default reasoning. In *Proceedings of the Eleventh International Conference on Artificial Intelligence*, 1043–1048.

Cadoli, M. 1992. The complexity of model checking for circumscriptive formulae. *Information Processing Letters* 42:113–118.

Cockcroft, R., and Cockcroft, S. 1992. *Persuading people: An Introduction to Rhetoric*. Macmillan Press.

Fisher, A. 1988. *The Logic of Real Arguments*. Cambridge University Press.

Fox, J., and Das, S. 2000. *Safe and Sound: Artificial Intelligence in Hazardous Applications*. MIT Press.

Koriche, F. 2001. On anytime coherence-based reasoning. In *Quantitative and Qualitative Approaches to Reasoning with Uncertainty*, volume 2143 of *LNCS*. Springer. 556–567.

Schaerf, M., and Cadoli, M. 1995. Tractable reasoning via approximation. *Artificial Intelligence* 74:249–310.

Verheij, B. 1996. *Rules, Reasons, Arguments: Formal studies of argumentation and defeat*. Ph.D. Dissertation, Universiteit Maastricht.

Walton, D. 1989. *Informal Logic: A Handbook for Critical Argumentation*. Cambridge University Press.

# Loop Formulas for Circumscription

**Joohyung Lee**
Department of Computer Sciences
University of Texas, Austin, TX, USA
appsmurf@cs.utexas.edu

**Fangzhen Lin**
Department of Computer Science
Hong Kong University of Science and Technology
Clear Water Bay, Kowloon, Hong Kong
flin@cs.ust.hk

### Abstract

Clark's completion is a simple nonmonotonic formalism and a special case of many nonmonotonic logics. Recently there has been work on extending completion with "loop formulas" so that general cases of nonmonotonic logics such as logic programs (under the answer set semantics) and McCain–Turner causal logic can be characterized by propositional logic in the form of "completion + loop formulas". In this paper, we show that the idea is applicable to McCarthy's circumscription in the propositional case. We also show how to embed propositional circumscription in logic programs and in causal logic, inspired by the uniform characterization of "completion + loop formulas".

## Introduction

Clark's predicate completion (Clark 1978) is a simple and intuitive nonmonotonic formalism. Normally it is applicable when the knowledge base is given as a set of rules, and works when the rules do not yield a cycle.

Despite these limitations, surprisingly perhaps, predicate completion has been used to solve some problems that were thought to require more sophisticated nonmonotonic logics. For instance, Reiter (1991) showed that under certain reasonable assumptions, successor state axioms can be computed from action effect axioms by predicate completion, and thus solved the frame problem when there are no state constraints. For state constraints, Lin (1995) argued that they should be encoded using a notion of causality, and once they are encoded this way, successor state axioms can once again be computed using predicate completion for a class of causal rules that includes almost all of the benchmark planning domains (Lin 1995; 2003). The implementation of the fragment of McCain and Turner causal logic (McCain & Turner 1997) in the Causal Calculator (CCALC)[1] is also based on completion; CCALC has been successfully applied to several challenge problems in the theory of commonsense knowledge.

In logic programming where predicate completion is best known and commonly referred to as program completion semantics, its relationships with other semantics, especially the answer set semantics (also known as the stable model semantics) of Gelfond and Lifschitz (1988), have been studied quite extensively. First of all, it is well known that an answer set for a normal (non-disjunctive) logic program is also a model of its completion, while the converse, generally, does not hold. Fages (1994) showed that a certain syntactic condition, which is now called "tightness," is sufficient for establishing the equivalence between them. Erdem and Lifschitz (2003) generalized Fages' theorem and extended it to programs with nested expressions (in the sense of (Lifschitz, Tang, & Turner 1999)) in the bodies of rules.

Instead of looking for conditions that will guarantee the equivalence between the completion semantics and the answer set semantics, Lin and Zhao (2002) considered how to strengthen completion to make it equivalent to the answer set semantics. The idea is that, since cycles are what cause the mismatch between the models of the completion and the answer sets for a program, one should address the problems raised by them directly. Just like the completion semantics captures the intuition that for a predicate to be true, one of the bodies of the rules with the predicate as the head must be true, for each loop, Lin and Zhao associated with it a loop formula that captures the intuition that for the atoms in the loop to be true, there must be a rule whose head is in the loop, and whose body is true but its positive part does not have any atom in the loop. They showed that an interpretation is an answer set for a logic program iff it satisfies the completion and all loop formulas of the program. SAT-based answer set solvers ASSAT (Lin & Zhao 2002) and CMODELS-2 (Giunchiglia, Lierler, & Maratea 2004) are based on this idea.

As it turned out, program completion and loop formulas are not limited to non-disjunctive logic programs. Lee and Lifschitz (2003) extended the Lin/Zhao theorem to disjunctive logic programs and, more generally, to arbitrary programs with nested expressions. Lee (2004) showed that a similar result can be obtained for McCain and Turner causal logic and based on this, discussed the relationship between causal logic and logic programs.

Given these results, one wonders how far this idea of "completion + loop formulas" can go. Is it general enough to capture other nonmonotonic logics? In this paper, we answer this question positively for circumscription (McCarthy 1980; 1986) in the propositional case.



[1] http://www.cs.utexas.edu/users/tag/ccalc/

## Logical Preliminaries

A *literal* is a (propositional) atom or the negation of an atom. A *(propositional) formula* is formed from literals using propositional connectives. A *clause* is a finite set of literals. We identify a clause $C$ with the disjunction of its elements. It is well known that any formula can be transformed into an equivalent set of clauses. Given a set $X$ of literals, $\overline{X}$ is the set of literals complementary to literals in $X$. In the following, given a language $L$, we identify an interpretation of $L$ with a set of atoms in $L$.

We assume some variables ranging over 0-place connectives ($\top$, $\bot$), and quantify over them. For instance, we write $\forall z(z \vee p)$, where $p$ is an atom, to denote $(\top \vee p) \wedge (\bot \vee p)$, and similarly $\exists z(z \vee p)$ to denote $(\top \vee p) \vee (\bot \vee p)$.

In the following, we sometimes write a formula $A$ as $A(P)$ or $A(P, Q)$ for tuples $P$ and $Q$ of atoms. This way, when $z$ is a tuple of variables and atoms of the same length as $P$, we use $A(z)$ or $A(z, Q)$ to denote the result of simultaneously replacing each element of $P$ in $A$ by the corresponding element of $z$. In this notation we sometimes allow a set in place of a tuple when there is no confusion. On the other hand, for convenience, we sometimes treat a tuple as the corresponding set.

For $P = (P_1, ...P_n)$, $Q = (Q_1, ...Q_n)$,

$P \leq Q$ stands for $\bigwedge_{1 \leq i \leq n}(P_i \supset Q_i)$,
$P = Q$ stands for $\bigwedge_{1 \leq i \leq n}(P_i \equiv Q_i)$,
$P < Q$ stands for $(P \leq Q) \wedge \neg(P = Q)$.

Let $P$ and $Z$ be tuples of atoms, and $A(P, Z)$ a formula. The circumscription of $P$ in $A(P, Z)$ with atoms in $Z$ allowed to vary, is the following formula:

$$A(P, Z) \wedge \neg\exists pz(A(p, z) \wedge p < P). \qquad (1)$$

The formula is denoted by $\text{CIRC}[A(P, Z); P; Z]$, which may also be written as $\text{CIRC}[A(P); P]$ when $Z$ is empty.

The following is a model-theoretic account of circumscription. For two interpretations $I$, $J$ of the same signature, we write $I \leq^{P;Z} J$ [2] if

- $I$ and $J$ agree on all atoms that are not in $P$ and $Z$, and
- for each $P_i \in P$, if $P_i \in I$ then $P_i \in J$.

We write $I <^{P;Z} J$ if $I \leq^{P;Z} J$ but not $J \leq^{P;Z} I$.

An interpretation $I$ is a model of (1) iff it is *minimal on $P$ with $Z$ allowed to vary*, that is,

- $I$ is a model of $A(P, Z)$, and
- there is no model $J$ of $A(P, Z)$ such that $J <^{P;Z} I$.

## Positive Dependency Graphs and Loops

A clause like $p \vee q \vee \neg r$ can be rewritten as $(r \wedge \neg q) \supset p$ or $(r \wedge \neg p) \supset q$. So if one wants to count ways an atom can be derived, this clause needs to be counted for both $p$ and $q$. In general, if a clause $C$ contains an atom $p$, then $\neg(C \setminus \{p\})$ [3] implies $p$. This motivates the following definition of a (positive) dependency graph of a set of clauses.

[2] We may even write $I \leq^P J$ when $Z$ is empty.

[3] $\neg(C \setminus \{p\})$ is equal to $\bigwedge_{l \in C \setminus \{p\}} \bar{l}$ according to our convention of identifying a clause with the disjunction of its literals.

Figure 1: The dependency graph of $A_1(P)$ on $P$

**Definition 1** *The (positive) dependency graph of a set $A$ of clauses on a set $P$ of atoms is the directed graph $G$ such that*

- *the vertices of $G$ are the atoms in $P$, and*
- *for each clause $C$ in $A$, $G$ has an edge from each atom in $C \cap P$ to each atom in $\overline{C} \cap P$.*

A nonempty set $L$ of atoms is called a *loop* of $A$ on $P$ if, for every pair $p$, $p'$ of atoms in $L$, there exists a path of nonzero length from $p$ to $p'$ in the dependency graph of $A$ on $P$ such that all the vertices in this path belong to $L$.

For example, let $P = (p, q, r, s)$, and let $A_1(P)$ be the set of clauses: $\{p \vee \neg q,\ \neg p \vee q,\ r \vee \neg s,\ \neg r \vee s,\ p \vee r\}$. The dependency graph of $A_1(P)$ on $P$, shown in Figure 1, has two loops: $\{p, q\}$, $\{r, s\}$.

**Definition 2** *Given a formula $A$, if $B$ is a finite set of clauses that is logically equivalent to $A$, then the dependency graph of $B$ on $P$ is called the dependency graph of $A$ on $P$ under $B$. Similarly, loops of $B$ on $P$ are called loops of $A$ on $P$ under $B$.*

## Computing Propositional Circumscription

We begin with the simple case when there are no constants (atoms) allowed to vary.

### Fixed Constants

For any formula $A$ and any tuple $P$ of atoms, we denote by $A(\hat{P})$ the result of replacing every atom of $P$ in $A$ by $\bot$. The following proposition follows from the definition of circumscription straightforwardly:

**Proposition 1** $\text{CIRC}[A(P); P]$ *is equivalent to the conjunction of $A(P)$ and*

$$\bigwedge K \supset \neg A(\hat{K}) \qquad (2)$$

*for each nonempty subset $K$ of $P$, where $\bigwedge K$ stands for the conjunction of all elements in $K$.*

In fact, including all subsets of $P$ is unnecessary. We will now discuss how Proposition 1 can be improved. As mentioned above, a clause $C$ that contains an atom $p$ is equivalent to $\neg(C \setminus \{p\}) \supset p$. More generally, by Theorem 2 of (Lin 2001), for any formula $A$ and any atom $p$, $A \models \neg A(\hat{p}) \supset p$. Furthermore, $\neg A(\hat{p})$ is the weakest such condition in the sense that for any other formula $B$ that does not mention $p$, if $A \models B \supset p$, then $A \models B \supset \neg A(\hat{p})$. In other words, $\neg A(\hat{p})$ is the weakest sufficient condition for $p$ in $A$. Now to form the completion of $p$, one just makes the weakest sufficient condition also its necessary condition.

**Definition 3** *The completion of a formula $A(P)$ on $P$ is the theory formed by taking the union of $A(P)$ and the set consisting of the formulas*

$$p \supset \neg A(\hat{p}) \qquad (3)$$

*for each $p \in P$.*

It is easy to see that a model of CIRC$[A(P);P]$ is also a model of the completion of $A(P)$ on $P$, but the converse does not hold in general.

**Theorem 1** *Let $A(P)$ be a formula, and $B$ a finite set of clauses equivalent to $A$.* CIRC$[A(P);P]$ *is equivalent to the union of the completion of $A(P)$ on $P$ and the set consisting of the formulas*

$$\bigwedge L \supset \neg A(\hat{L}) \tag{4}$$

*for each loop $L$ of $A(P)$ on $P$ under $B$.*

We call formula (4) the *(conjunctive) loop formula* of $L$ for CIRC$[A(P);P]$ under $B$.

Note that compared with Proposition 1, Theorem 1 tells us that, for a model $X$ of a formula $A(P)$ to be a model of CIRC$[A(P);P]$, it is sufficient to check whether every singleton subset of $X$ and every loop of $A$ in $X$ satisfies formulas (2).

Clearly, a circumscription is equivalent to the completion when there are no loops:

**Corollary 1** *For any formula $A(P)$, if there is an equivalent finite set $B$ of clauses such that there are no loops of $A(P)$ on $P$ under $B$, then* CIRC$[A(P);P]$ *is equivalent to the completion of $A(P)$ on $P$.*

For example, let $A_2(P)$ be the formula $p \lor q$ where $P = (p,q)$. $A_2(P)$ has three models, $\{p\}$, $\{q\}$ and $\{p,q\}$, among which $\{p,q\}$ is not a model of CIRC$[A_2(P);P]$ because $\{p\} <^P \{p,q\}$. Since there are no loops of $A_2(P)$ on $P$, Corollary 1 gives us another way of computing the models of the circumscription, by just computing the models of the completion, $\{p \lor q,\ p \supset \neg q,\ q \supset \neg p\}$.

$A_1(P)$ on $P = (p,q,r,s)$ in the previous section is an example that contains loops. $A_1(P)$ has three models, $\{p,q\}$, $\{r,s\}$ and $\{p,q,r,s\}$, among which the last is not a model of CIRC$[A_1(P);P]$ because $\{p,q\} <^P \{p,q,r,s\}$. Theorem 1 gives us another way of computing the models of the circumscription, by computing the models of the completion and loop formulas. First, the completion of $A_1(P)$ on $P$ is the union of $A_1(P)$ and

$$\{p \supset q \lor \neg r \lor (r \not\equiv s),\ \ q \supset p \lor (r \not\equiv s) \lor \neg(p \lor r),$$
$$r \supset s \lor \neg p \lor (p \not\equiv q),\ \ s \supset r \lor (p \not\equiv q) \lor \neg(p \lor r)\}$$

from (3). We see that the models of the completion are the three models of $A_1(P)$ above. There are two loops of $A_1(P)$ on $P$, $\{p,q\}$ and $\{r,s\}$, and their loop formulas are $p \land q \supset \neg r$ and $r \land s \supset \neg p$ each. Among the models of the completion of $A_1(P)$ on $P$, $\{p,q,r,s\}$ does not satisfy any loop formula, so that it is not a model of CIRC$[A_1(P);P]$. The other two satisfy every loop formula, and are models of the circumscription.

Furthermore, it is easy to see that CIRC$[A_1;p,q]$ is equivalent to CIRC$[A_1;P]$. The completion of $A_1$ on $(p,q)$ is a subset of the completion of $A_1$ on $P$, so that all three models of $A_1$ still satisfy the completion of $A_1$ on $(p,q)$. $\{p,q,r,s\}$ still does not satisfy the only loop formula $p \land q \supset \neg r$ for CIRC$[A_1;p,q]$, which is also a loop formula for CIRC$[A_1;P]$.

According to Theorem 1, to compute the circumscription of $P$ in $A(P)$ with all other atoms fixed, one first converts $A$ to a finite set $B$ of clauses, constructs the dependency graph of $B$ on $P$, computes the loops of the dependency graph, and then computes the completion and loop formulas.

Computationally, there are a few problems here. First of all, without introducing new atoms, the size of $B$ could be exponential in the number of atoms in $A$, although the size of the dependency graph of $B$ is always polynomial. The second problem is that the number of loops can be exponential.

From the complexity point of view, we cannot do much about the second problem as SAT is in NP, and the problem of finding a model of circumscription is $\Sigma_2^P$-hard.

For the first problem, one can introduce new atoms when converting $A$ to its clausal form to avoid combinatorial blow-up when distributing "$\lor$" over "$\land$." One can also try to construct a dependency graph directly without actually generating the set of clauses. However, a formula may be equivalent to many different sets of clauses, which in turn may yield different dependency graphs. Intuitively, for our purpose, everything being equal, the fewer loops that a dependency graph has the better. We believe that in general, given a formula $A$, it is computationally hard to find a set of clauses for $A$ that would yield the smallest number of loops. But we do not have a proof, and it remains an open question.

## Varied Constants

The following fact (Lifschitz 1985, Proposition 2) shows how to eliminate varied constants in general:

**Fact 1** CIRC$[A(P,Z);P;Z]$ *is equivalent to*

$$A(P,Z) \land \text{CIRC}[\exists z A(P,z);P].$$

Thus circumscription with varied constants reduces to the basic case where Theorem 1 applies.

Alternatively, we have the following result by modifying the definitions of a dependency graph and a loop. Intuitively, paths are allowed to have varied atoms and their negations as intermediate vertices.

**Definition 4** *The (positive) dependency graph of a set $A$ of clauses on $P$ with $Z$ allowed to vary is the directed graph $G$ such that*

- *the vertices of $G$ are the literals in $P \cup Z \cup \overline{Z}$, and*
- *for each clause $C$ in $A$, $G$ has an edge from each literal $l$ in $C \cap (P \cup Z \cup \overline{Z})$ to each literal in $\overline{C \setminus \{l\}} \cap (P \cup Z \cup \overline{Z})$.*

A nonempty set $L_0$ of literals is called an *extended loop* of $A$ on $P$ with $Z$ allowed to vary if, for every pair $p$, $p'$ of literals in $L_0$, there exists a path of nonzero length from $p$ to $p'$ in the dependency graph of $A$ on $P$ with $Z$ allowed to vary such that all the vertices in this path belong to $L_0$. A nonempty set $L = L_0 \setminus (Z \cup \overline{Z})$ is called a *loop* of $A$ on $P$ with $Z$ allowed to vary.

For example, let $P = \{p,q\}$, $Z = \{z\}$ and $A_3(P,Z)$ be the set of clauses $\{p \supset \neg z,\ \neg z \supset q,\ q \supset p\}$. The dependency graph of $A_3(P,Z)$ on $P$ with $Z$ allowed to vary is shown in Figure 2. It has only one extended loop, $\{p,q,\neg z\}$, and so has only one loop, $\{p,q\}$.

The above definition of a loop is intuitive, but here is an alternative, more economical definition in terms of the number of loops we get. For a set $A$ of clauses, by $S(A)$ we

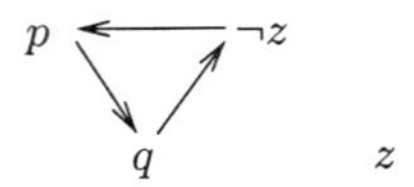


Figure 2: The dependency graph of $A_2$ on $P$ with varied $z$

denote the set of clauses $C$ in $A$ such that $C$ does not contain a pair of complementary literals and there is no proper subset $C'$ of $C$ such that $C' \in A$. Given a set $A$ of clauses and a tuple of atoms $Z = (z_1, \ldots, z_n)$, $B_Z$ is defined as follows.

- $B_{()} = A$,
- $B_{(z_1,\ldots,z_k)} = S(B_{(z_1,\ldots,z_{k-1})}) \cup \{C_1 \cup C_2 : C_1 \cup \{z_k\}, C_2 \cup \{\neg z_k\} \in S(B_{(z_1,\ldots,z_{k-1})})\}$.

We call $S(B_Z)$ the $Z$-collapsed set of $A$.

Let $A_Z$ be the $Z$-collapsed set of $A$ and let $A'_Z$ be the set of clauses in $A_Z$ that do not mention $Z$. Loops of the dependency graph of $A'_Z$ on $P$ are called loops of $A$ on $P$ with $Z$ allowed to vary. A loop according to this alternative definition is also a loop according to the definition above, but not vice versa. The following result holds under either definition.

Here is a counterpart of Proposition 1, where we allow some atoms to vary.

**Proposition 2** CIRC$[A(P,Z);P;Z]$ *is equivalent to the conjunction of* $A(P,Z)$ *and*

$$\bigwedge K \supset \forall z \neg A(\hat{K}, z)$$

*for each nonempty subset* $K$ *of* $P$.

**Definition 5** *The completion of a formula* $A(P,Z)$ *on* $P$ *with* $Z$ *allowed to vary is the theory formed by taking the union of* $A(P,Z)$ *and the set consisting of the formulas*

$$p \supset \forall z \neg A(\hat{p}, z)$$

*for each* $p \in P$.

**Theorem 2** *Let* $A(P,Z)$ *be a formula, and* $B$ *a finite set of clauses equivalent to* $A(P,Z)$. CIRC$[A(P,Z);P;Z]$ *is equivalent to the union of the completion of* $A(P,Z)$ *on* $P$ *with* $Z$ *allowed to vary and the set consisting of the formulas*

$$\bigwedge L \supset \forall z \neg A(\hat{L}, z) \quad (5)$$

*for each loop* $L$ *of* $A(P,Z)$ *on* $P$ *with* $Z$ *allowed to vary.*

We call formula (5) the *(conjunctive) loop formula* of $L$ for CIRC$[A(P,Z);P;Z]$ under $B$.

$A_3(P,z)$ above has two models, $\{p,q\}$ and $\{z\}$, but the first is not a model of CIRC$[A_3(P,z);P;z]$, though it satisfies the completion of $A_3(P,z)$ on $P$, $\{p \supset q,\ q \supset p\}$. There is only one loop of $A_3(P,z)$ on $P$ with $z$ allowed to vary, $\{p,q\}$, and its loop formula is $p \wedge q \supset \bot$. Only the interpretation $\{z\}$ satisfies both the completion and the loop formula.

Similarly to Corollary 1, we get the following corollary to Theorem 2:

**Corollary 2** *For any formula* $A(P,Z)$, *if there is an equivalent finite set* $B$ *of clauses such that there are no loops of* $A(P,Z)$ *on* $P$ *with* $Z$ *allowed to vary under* $B$, *then* CIRC$[A(P,Z);P;Z]$ *is equivalent to the completion of* $A(P,Z)$ *on* $P$ *with* $Z$ *allowed to vary.*

## Relating to Some Known Results

Reiter (1982) was the first to show some relationships between Clark's predicate completion and circumscription. He proved that if a theory is Horn in a predicate $P$, then the circumscription of $P$ logically entails $P$'s completion. In the propositional case, our new contributions are as follows. First, we extended the notion of completion to arbitrary theories, not just those that are Horn. Second, we showed that it is always the case that circumscription of an atom $p$ entails $p$'s completion. Third, we gave a general syntactic condition that guarantees the equivalence between circumscription and completion. Lastly, and most importantly, we defined notions of loops and loop formulas, and showed that circumscription can be reduced to completion plus loop formulas.

Traditionally, computing circumscription means finding classes of first-order theories for which circumscription is equivalent to first-order theories (e.g. (Lifschitz 1985; 1987) and (Doherty, Łukaszewicz, & Szałas 1997) ). In the propositional case, circumscription is always equivalent to a propositional theory. So the problem in the propositional case is not whether circumscription can be reduced to propositional logic, but how well this can be done.

In logic programming, when the positive dependency graph of a program has no loops, the program is called "tight", and the answer sets for such a tight program are exactly the models of the completion. Corollaries 1 and 2 in this paper address a similar syntactic condition for circumscription in the propositional case. In the following, we show that some of the known results about circumscription can be easily explained by our corollaries.

We say an occurrence of an atom in a formula is *positive* if it is in the range of an even number of negations, and *negative* otherwise (assuming that $\supset$ and $\equiv$ have been eliminated in favor of other connectives). A formula $A(P)$ is *positive* (relative to $P$) if all occurrences of $P$ in it are positive, and *negative* if all occurrences of $P$ are negative.[4] We see that if $A(P)$ is positive (or negative) relative to $P$, then there is an equivalent set of clauses whose dependency graph on $P$ has no loops, so that CIRC$[A(P);P]$ is equivalent to the completion of $A(P)$ on $P$. The result can also be extended when some atoms are allowed to vary. The following is the propositional case of Proposition 2a from (Lifschitz 1987).

**Proposition 3** *If* $A(p,Z)$ *is positive relative to an atom* $p$, *then* CIRC$[A(p,Z);p;Z]$ *is equivalent to*

$$A(p,Z) \wedge \neg \exists z (p \wedge A(\bot, z)). \quad (6)$$

**Proof.**

$$\begin{aligned} \text{CIRC}[A(p,Z);p;Z] &\equiv A(p,Z) \wedge (p \supset \forall z \neg A(\hat{p}, z)) \\ &\equiv A(p,Z) \wedge \neg \exists z (p \wedge A(\bot, z)). \end{aligned}$$

[4] A formula is both positive and negative relative to $P$ if it doesn't contain $P$.

The first equivalence holds because there exists a set of clauses equivalent to $A(p, Z)$ such that the dependency graph of $A(p, Z)$ under it has no loops, so that Corollary 2 applies. ∎

The form of circumscription in (6) is the propositional case of what Lifschitz (1987) called *pointwise circumscription*.

Proposition 3 can be extended to parallel circumscription:

**Proposition 4** *(Lifschitz 1987, Proposition 5) If $P$ is a tuple of atoms $p_1, \ldots, p_n$ and $A(P, Z)$ is positive relative to each $p_i$, then* $\text{CIRC}[A(P, Z); P; Z] \equiv \bigwedge_i \text{CIRC}[A(P, Z); p_i; Z]$.

**Proof**. Again, this is easy to see from the facts that there exists a set of clauses equivalent to $A(P, Z)$ such that the dependency graph of $A(P, Z)$ under it has no loops, and that the completion of $A(P, Z)$ on $P$ is equivalent to the conjunction of each completion of $A(p_i, Z)$ on $p_i$. ∎

In fact, Corollary 2 presents us a much more general condition than the one in Proposition 3 (and 4) that shows the equivalence between the circumscription of the form (1) and pointwise circumscription. For example, consider $\text{CIRC}[(p \supset q) \wedge (q \supset r); q, r]$. There are no loops of the formula, and consequently the circumscription is equivalent to its corresponding pointwise circumscription according to Corollary 2. But the conjunction in the formula cannot be divided into two parts so that $q$,$r$ are positive in one part and negative in the other, so Proposition 3 does not apply.

Sometimes it is easy to observe that the dependency graphs of some circumscriptions have the same loops.

**Proposition 5** *(Lifschitz 1987) If $B(P)$ is negative relative to $P$, then $\text{CIRC}[A(P) \wedge B(P); P]$ is equivalent to $\text{CIRC}[A(P); P] \wedge B(P)$.*

**Proof**. There exists a set $B'(P)$ of clauses which is equivalent to $B(P)$ and is negative relative to $P$. Notice that $A(P) \wedge B'(P)$ and $A(P)$ have the same dependency graph on $P$, hence have the same loops. We see that the completion and loop formulas of $A(P) \wedge B'(P)$ on $P$ and those of $A(P)$ on $P$ are equivalent to each other when we notice that $B'(\hat{P})$ is entailed by $B'(P)$. ∎

However, if some atoms are allowed to vary, then $A(P) \wedge B(P)$ may have more loops than $A(P)$ ($A_3(P, z)$ for example), and $B(P)$ may not be easily "factored out".

## Embedding Circumscription in Other Nonmonotonic Logics

As mentioned in the introduction, the idea of "completion + loop formulas" has been applied to logic programs in (Lin & Zhao 2002; Lee & Lifschitz 2003) and to McCain–Turner causal logic in (Lee 2004). The characterizations of these nonmonotonic logics in terms of propositional logic are useful tools for comparing the formalisms. Based on this idea, Lee (2004) showed how to embed logic programs in causal logic.

Inspired by a similar characterization for circumscription, we show how to relate circumscription to logic programs and to causal logic. The propositions below can be proved by turning each formalism into "completion+loop formulas" and then show that the translations are equivalent to each other.

### Logic Programming

For a literal $l$, by $l_{not}$ we denote *not* $l$ if $l$ is positive, and $\bar{l}$ otherwise. Let $A(P)$ be a finite set of clauses. For each clause $C \in A(P)$, the corresponding rule $C_P$ is

$$\mathop{;}_{p \in C \cap P} p \leftarrow \mathop{,}_{q \in C \setminus P} q_{not}$$

By $\sigma_A$ we denote the set of all atoms that occur in $A$.

**Proposition 6** *For any finite set $A(P)$ of clauses, a set of atoms is a model of $\text{CIRC}[A(P); P]$ iff it is an answer set for the logic program*

$$\{C_P \ : \ C \in A(P)\} \ \cup \ \{a \ ; \ not\ a \ : \ a \in \sigma_A \setminus P\}.$$

We may even embed circumscription with varied constants in logic programs. Given a finite set $A(P, Z)$ of clauses, $\Pi_{A;P;Z}$ is the following logic program. Let $A_Z$ be the $Z$-collapsed set of $A$.

- For each clause $C$ in $A_Z$ that does not mention $Z$, $\Pi_{A;P;Z}$ has the rule $C_P$,
- For every other clause $C$ in $A_Z$, $\Pi_{A;P;Z}$ has the rule

$$\leftarrow \mathop{,}_{p \in C} p_{not},$$

- For each atom $a \in \sigma_A \setminus P$, $\Pi_{A;P;Z}$ has the rule $a \ ; \ not\ a$.

**Proposition 7** *For any finite set $A(P, Z)$ of clauses, a set of atoms is a model of $\text{CIRC}[A(P, Z); P; Z]$ iff it is an answer set for the logic program $\Pi_{A;P;Z}$.*

### McCain–Turner Causal Logic

McCain–Turner causal logic is a useful formalism for describing effects of actions, and is a basis of action language $\mathcal{C}$+ (Giunchiglia *et al.* 2004), which is a high level language for describing transition systems.

**Proposition 8** *Let $A(P)$ be a finite set of clauses. An interpretation is a model of $\text{CIRC}[A(P); P]$ iff it is a model of the causal theory*

$$\{C \cap (P \cup \overline{P}) \Leftarrow \neg(C \setminus (P \cup \overline{P})) : C \in A\} \\ \cup \{\neg r \Leftarrow \neg r : r \in \sigma_A\} \cup \{r \Leftarrow r : r \in \sigma_A \setminus P\}$$

*whose signature is $\sigma_A$.*

Proposition 8 is similar to the propositional case of Proposition 1 of (Lifschitz 1997). Extending the result to circumscription with varied constants is similar to the case with logic programs and is omitted here due to the lack of space.

## Conclusion

To recast, the following are our main contributions (all in the propositional case):

- Extend completion to arbitrary theories.

- Introduce a notion of a positive dependency graph for a finite set of clauses, and based on it, notions of loops and loop formulas.
- Show that circumscription is equivalent to completion plus loop formulas, and based on this result, embed circumscription in other nonmonotonic logics.

These results are of both theoretical interest and practical importance. A major obstacle in implementing a reasoning system for propositional circumscription is that checking if an assignment is a model of a circumscription is NP-hard. In comparison, checking if an assignment is a model of a formula in propositional logic or an answer set for a nondisjunctive logic program can be done efficiently. By Theorems 1 and 2, if a given formula has no loop or has only a polynomial number of loops and these loops can be computed in polynomial time, then checking if an assignment is a model of circumscription can be done in polynomial time as well. Hopefully, many applications of circumscription will belong to this class, just as many logic programs for practical problems are "tight" or "tight on the models of completion". Alternatively, one could implement circumscription in logic programming systems like DLV and GnT using Propositions 6 and 7.[5]

Note that we could have defined a loop to allow a path of length 0, which corresponds to each atom. In this sense, the second part of completion is just a set of loop formulas, and circumscribing a theory can be regarded as just adding loop formulas to it.

For future work, there is a need to better understand how loops can be computed. More importantly, there is a need to extend the results of this paper to the first-order case.

## Acknowledgements

We are grateful to Selim Erdoğan, Paolo Ferraris, Vladimir Lifschitz, Hudson Turner and the anonymous referees for useful comments. Joohyung Lee was partially supported by the Texas Higher Education Coordinating Board under Grant 003658-0322-2001. Fangzhen Lin's work has been supported in part by HK RGC under CERG HKUST6205/02E, and by the NSFC under its major research program "Basic Theory and Core Techniques of Non-Canonical Knowledge".

[5]Strictly speaking, the current versions of those systems do not allow negation as failure in the head of a rule, so it cannot handle such a rule as $a; not\ a$. However there is a well-known technique to "simulate" rules of this kind using additional atoms.

## References

Clark, K. 1978. Negation as failure. In Gallaire, H., and Minker, J., eds., *Logic and Data Bases*. New York: Plenum Press. 293–322.

Doherty, P.; Łukaszewicz, W.; and Szałas, A. 1997. Computing circumscription revisited: A reduction algorithm. *Journal of Automated Reasoning* 18(3):297–336.

Erdem, E., and Lifschitz, V. 2003. Tight logic programs. *Theory and Practice of Logic Programming* 3:499–518.

Fages, F. 1994. Consistency of clark's completion and existence of stable of stable models. *Journal of Methods of Logic in Computer Science* 1:51–60.

Gelfond, M., and Lifschitz, V. 1988. The stable model semantics for logic programming. In *Proc. Fifth International Conference and Symposium on Logic Programming*, 1070–1080.

Giunchiglia, E.; Lee, J.; Lifschitz, V.; McCain, N.; and Turner, H. 2004. Nonmonotonic causal theories. *Artificial Intelligence* 153:49–104.

Giunchiglia, E.; Lierler, Y.; and Maratea, M. 2004. SAT-based answer set programming. In *Proc. AAAI-04*. this proceeding.

Lee, J., and Lifschitz, V. 2003. Loop formulas for disjunctive logic programs. In *Proc. Nineteenth Int'l Conf. on Logic Programming*, 451–465.

Lee, J. 2004. Nondefinite vs. definite causal theories. In *Proc. 7th Int'l Conference on Logic Programming and Nonmonotonic Reasoning*, 141–153.

Lifschitz, V.; Tang, L. R.; and Turner, H. 1999. Nested expressions in logic programs. *Annals of Mathematics and Artificial Intelligence* 25:369–389.

Lifschitz, V. 1985. Computing circumscription. In *Proc. IJCAI-85*, 121–127.

Lifschitz, V. 1987. Pointwise circumscription. In Ginsberg, M., ed., *Readings in nonmonotonic reasoning*. San Mateo, CA: Morgan Kaufmann. 179–193.

Lifschitz, V. 1997. On the logic of causal explanation. *Artificial Intelligence* 96:451–465.

Lin, F., and Zhao, Y. 2002. ASSAT: Computing answer sets of a logic program by SAT solvers. In *Proc. AAAI-02*, 112–117.

Lin, F. 1995. Embracing causality in specifying the indirect effects of actions. In *Proc. IJCAI-95*, 1985–1993.

Lin, F. 2001. On strongest necessary and weakest sufficient conditions. *Artificial Intelligence* 128(1-2):143–159.

Lin, F. 2003. Compiling causal theories to successor state axioms and STRIPS-like systems. *Journal of Artificial Intelligence Research* 19:279–314.

McCain, N., and Turner, H. 1997. Causal theories of action and change. In *Proc. AAAI-97*, 460–465.

McCarthy, J. 1980. Circumscription—a form of non-monotonic reasoning. *Artificial Intelligence* 13:27–39,171–172.

McCarthy, J. 1986. Applications of circumscription to formalizing common sense knowledge. *Artificial Intelligence* 26(3):89–116.

Reiter, R. 1982. Circumscription implies predicate completion (sometimes). In *Proceedings of AAAI–82*, 418–420.

Reiter, R. 1991. The frame problem in the situation calculus: a simple solution (sometimes) and a completeness result for goal regression. In Lifschitz, V., ed., *Artificial Intelligence and Mathematical Theory of Computation: Papers in Honor of John McCarthy*. San Diego, CA: Academic Press. 359–380.

# An Instance-based State Representation for Network Repair

**Michael L. Littman** and **Nishkam Ravi**
Department of Computer Science
Rutgers University
Piscataway, NJ
{mlittman,nravi}@cs.rutgers.edu

**Eitan Fenson** and **Rich Howard**
PnP Networks, Inc.
Los Altos, CA
{eitan,reh}@pnphome.com

### Abstract

We describe a formal framework for diagnosis and repair problems that shares elements of the well known partially observable MDP and cost-sensitive classification models. Our cost-sensitive fault remediation model is amenable to implementation as a reinforcement-learning system, and we describe an instance-based state representation that is compatible with learning and planning in this framework. We demonstrate a system that uses these ideas to learn to efficiently restore network connectivity after a failure.

## Introduction

The first, and possibly most important, question to answer when creating a reinforcement-learning system (Sutton & Barto 1998) for an application is how the state space for learning and planning should be defined. A good choice of state representation can make the difference between a problem that is trivial and one that is impossible to solve via learning. There is a great need for learning approaches that can evolve toward a state representation that is natural and efficient for the problem at hand based on relatively raw inputs.

Nowhere is the need for automatic development of state representations more evident than in environments that are not Markov in the decision maker's direct observables. In such partially observable environments (Kaelbling, Littman, & Cassandra 1998), decision makers often must exploit their history of interaction and reason explicitly about their uncertainty about the state of the world during decision making, particularly if they need to take actions to gain information to behave effectively. Attempts to learn complex environments represented with hidden states (Chrisman 1992), histories (McCallum 1995a), and as predictions of future observations (Littman, Sutton, & Singh 2002) have met with some limited success, primarily in simulations.

This paper explores an instance-based representation for a special kind of partially observable environment called a CSFR (cost-sensitive fault remediation) model. The CSFR model captures a diagnosis-and-repair situation in which a system can detect if it has entered a failure mode, take actions to gain information about the failure mode, attempt repair actions, and detect when correct functioning has been restored. Although we believe that the learning approach we describe can be applied in more general environments, we focus here on this specialized subclass.

We demonstrate our approach to learning and planning in the CSFR framework with an implemented network-repair application.

## The CSFR Model

The CSFR model was motivated by an exploration of problems that arise in sequential decision making for diagnosis and repair including problems of web-server maintenance, disk-system replacement, and the network-repair application illustrated later in the paper.

In cost-sensitive fault remediation, a decision maker is responsible for repairing a system when it breaks down. To narrow down the source of the fault the decision maker can perform a *test action* at some cost and to repair the fault it can carry out a *repair action*. A repair action incurs a cost and either restores the system to proper functioning or fails. In either case, the system informs the decision maker of the outcome. The decision maker seeks a minimum cost policy for restoring the system to proper functioning.

CSFR bears many similarities to cost-sensitive classification (CSC, see Turney 1995, Greiner, Grove, & Roth 1996). Like standard classification, CSC is concerned with categorizing unknown instances. However, CSC can be viewed as a kind of sequential decision problem in which the decision maker interacts with a system by requesting attribute values (running test actions). The decision maker's performance is the total of the individual action costs plus a charge for misclassification, if applicable. Diagnosis tasks formulated as CSCs include hidden information—the identity of the fault state—making them a kind of partially observable Markov decision process (POMDP). POMDPs can be notoriously difficult to solve, although there is reason to believe that CSCs result in relatively benign POMDP instances (Zubek & Dietterich 2002, Guo 2002).

The main difference between CSC and CSFR, and the principle novelty of our framework, is that a decision maker in a CSFR model can use feedback on the success or failure of a repair action to attempt an alternate repair. In CSC, classification actions end episodes, whereas in CSFR, episodes continue until the fault is repaired. Although this constitutes a relatively small change, we feel it adds significantly to the degree of autonomy supported by the model. Specifically, CSFRs are amenable to reinforcement learning as they have no dependence on supervisory signals to evaluate the attempted classifications—as long as the system is capable of detecting proper and improper function, learning can take place. We demonstrate this capability in an implemented network-repair scenario later in the paper.

In contrast to general POMDPs, faults in a CSFR remain constant until repaired. This simplifies the construction of policies compared to the general case and may enable efficient approximations. Therefore, the CSFR model lies at an intermediate point on the spectrum from the simple CSC model to the general POMDP model.

## CSFR Definition

A CSFR problem can be defined formally by the quantities:

- $S$, a set of fault states;
- $\Pr(s)$, a prior probability for fault state $s \in S$;
- $A_T$, a set of test actions;
- $A_R$, a set of repair actions;
- $c(s, a)$, a cost function over actions $a \in A_T \cup A_R$ and states $s \in S$;
- $o(s, a)$, an outcome or observation model over actions $a \in A_T \cup A_R$ and states $s \in S$.

In this paper, we assume the range of the outcome model $o(s, a)$ is 0 and 1. For repair actions $a \in A_R$, $o(s, a) = 1$ is interpreted to mean that the repair action $a$ returns the system to proper working order if afflicted with fault $s$. A *repair episode* is the sequence of actions and outcomes from the time the fault is first detected to the time it is repaired. Note that initial fault detection and the determination that the fault is resolved happens in the environment—outside of the CSFR model. In addition, repair episodes are assumed to be independent.

## Finding an Optimal Policy

Note that we are assuming deterministic observations in the CSFR model. As in POMDPs, stochastic observations can be modeled by increasing the size of the state space. Unlike POMDPs, the expansion may require an exponential increase in the number of states, perhaps to one state for each possible combination of stochastic outcomes. In addition, stochastic observations can mean that there is additional information to be gained by repeating a test or repair action more than once. Ignoring this issue is a significant limitation of the current formulation.

Nevertheless, the combination of deterministic observations and the lack of state transitions provides simplifications in the state space for planning that can be exploited. At the beginning of the repair process, the probability of a fault $s$ is simply its prior $\Pr(s)$. An *episode* is a set of actions with associated outcomes. We write $e \subseteq s$ if episode $e$ is *consistent* with fault state $s$, that is, for every action $a$ taken in $e$, the associated outcome is $o(s, a)$. Similarly, we write $e_1 \subseteq e_2$ to mean that all actions that appear in episode $e_1$ also appear in episode $e_2$ with the same outcome. The probability of a given fault state $s$ being the current state is zero if $s$ is inconsistent with the current episode $e$, otherwise it is proportional to its prior probability. This follows from Bayes rule: $\Pr(s|e) = \Pr(e|s)\Pr(s)/\Pr(e)$ where $\Pr(e|s)$ is the indicator function of $e \subseteq s$, $\Pr(s)$ is the prior, and $\Pr(e) = \sum_s \Pr(s)\Pr(e|s)$.

As an episode progresses and assuming that the decision maker only selects test actions that have differing outcomes for the fault states consistent with the episode, each decision results in a shrinking set of fault states with non-zero probability. It follows that the number of decision situations that the decision maker will face is bounded by the size of the power set of $S$. Although this can be a very large number, it is small enough that it has not been a bottleneck in the applications we have examined to date.

We can find an optimal repair policy via dynamic programming. Let $B$ be the power set of $S$, which is the set of belief states of the system. For each $b \in B$ and $a \in A_T \cup A_R$, define the expected value of action $a$ in belief state $b$ as the expected cost of the action plus the value of the resulting belief state:

$$Q(b, a) = \begin{cases} \Pr(b_0)/\Pr(b)(c(b_0, a) + V(b_0)) \\ \quad +\Pr(b_1)/\Pr(b)(c(b_1, a) + V(b_1)), \\ \quad \text{if } \Pr(b_0) > 0 \text{ and } \Pr(b_1) > 0, \\ \quad \text{or } \Pr(b_1) > 0 \text{ and } a \in A_R; \\ \infty, \text{ otherwise.} \end{cases}$$

Here, $b_i = \{s \in b | o(s, a) = i\}$ is the belief state resulting from taking action $a$ in belief state $b$ and obtaining outcome $i \in \{0, 1\}$. If $a \in A_R$ and $i = 1$, we define $V(b_1) = 0$, as there is no additional cost incurred once a repair action is successful. In all other cases, the value of a belief state is the minimum action value taken over all available choices: $V(b) = \min_{a \in A_T \cup A_R} Q(b, a)$. The quantities $\Pr(b)$ and $c(b, a)$ are the probability and cost functions extended to belief states in the natural probability-weighted way. Specifically, let $\Pr(b) = \sum_{s \in b} \Pr(s)$ and $c(b, a) = \sum_{s \in b} \Pr(s)c(s, a)$. The conditions that $\Pr(b_0) > 0$ and $\Pr(b_1) > 0$ (or $\Pr(b_1) > 0$ for a repair action $a \in A_R$) in the recursion ensure that the equations bottom out; no quantity is defined in terms of itself. This restriction rules out only suboptimal policies that include actions that do not alter the belief state and guarantees that the algorithm can be implemented without considering cyclic dependencies.

These equations can be evaluated in time proportional to $2^{|S|}(|A_T| + |A_R|)(|S| + |A_T| + |A_R|)$, at which point the optimal policy can be extracted by choosing the action $a$ in belief state $b$ that minimizes $Q(b, a)$. Such a policy will optimally trade off actions to gain information, actions to repair, and the information gained from a failed attempt at repair, in a way that minimizes the total expected cost of repair.

## Example

Table 1 illustrates a small CSFR example with two fault states, $A$ and $B$.

| | A | | B | |
|---|---|---|---|---|
| DnsLookup | 0 | (2500ms) | 0 | (2500ms) |
| DefaultGateway | 0 | (50ms) | 1 | (50ms) |
| PingIp | 0 | (50ms) | 1 | (250ms) |
| **RenewLease** | 1 | (2500ms) | 0 | (1000ms) |
| **UseCachedIP** | 0 | (10000ms) | 1 | (25000ms) |
| **FixIP** | 1 | (20000ms) | 1 | (20000ms) |

Table 1: A small table of CSFR states. Each row lists the outcome and cost of a test action (DnsLookup, DefaultGateway, and PingIP) or repair action (**FixIP**, **UseCachedIP**, **RenewLease**, in boldface) for each of the states. The priors are $\Pr(A) = .25$ and $\Pr(B) = .75$.

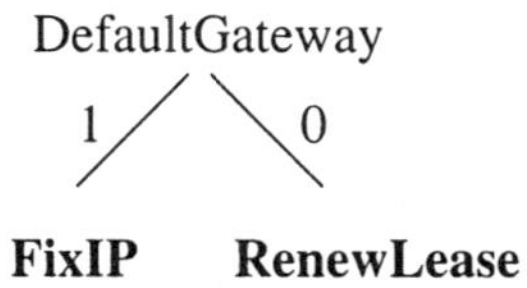


Figure 1: The optimal policy for the small example CSFR.

The planning process for this example begins with the belief state $\{A, B\}$. It considers the test actions DefaultGateway and PingIP and the repair actions **FixIP**, **UseCachedIP**, and **RenewLease**. It does not consider DnsLookup since the action neither provides information (always 0), nor has a non-zero chance of repair. In evaluating the action PingIP, the algorithm finds that outcome 0 has a probability of .25 and outcome 1 has a probability of .75. Its expected cost from belief state $\{A, B\}$ is then

$$.25(50 + \text{cost}(\{A\})) + .75(250 + \text{cost}(\{B\})). \quad (1)$$

The expected cost from belief state $\{A\}$ is computed recursively. Since all test actions have some outcome with an estimated probability of 0, only repair actions are considered. Of these, **RenewLease** is chosen as the optimal action, with a cost of 2500. Similarly, the optimal expected cost from belief state $\{B\}$ is 20000 by taking action **FixIP**. Substituting these costs into Equation 1, we find the optimal expected cost of repair from belief state $\{A, B\}$, starting with PingIP, is 15825. The minimum over all actions from belief state $\{A, B\}$ is achieved by DefaultGateway (expected cost 15675), leading to a repair policy shown in Figure 1.[1]

## Instance-based CSFR Learning

The previous section described how to create optimal repair policies for problems specified as CSFR models. A CSFR model of an application can be created through carefully supervised experimentation and fault injection (Li *et al.* 2002). That is, human experimenters can identify the set of fault states that they would like their repair system to handle, create the symptoms of these faults, and measure the costs and outcomes for each action for each injected fault. In addition to being labor intensive, this fault-injection methodology is limited to collecting data on a small set of artificially created fault states instead of the problems that occur during actual operation.

We are interested in developing learning methodologies that can create and manipulate models based on unstructured interaction with the environment. We now describe an instance-based reinforcement-learning approach we developed for the CSFR setting.

### Instance-based Representations

In instance-based reinforcement-learning, state spaces for learning are constructed from examples of states experienced in interaction with the environment. Instance-based approaches have been primarily explored in continuous-space environments (Moore, Atkeson, & Schaal 1995; Santamaría, Sutton, & Ram 1997; Smart & Kaelbling 2000; Ormoneit & Sen 2002), where learning state-action values for each possible state is infeasible. Instead, a value is learned for each observed state. A similarity function is used to relate non-identical observations, resulting in a pooling of experience information across different episodes.

Whereas continuous-space environments suffer from an overspecificity of information—we may never see the same state twice—observations in partially observable environments are typically inadequate to sufficiently specify the decision maker's situation. One way to make up for this lack of information is to view the "state" as the sequence of actions and observations made during an entire episode. As in the continuous-space case, we now run the risk of never returning to any situation a second time, making generalization between experiences a requirement for successful learning.

Motivated by these concerns, McCallum (1995b) described an application of the instance-based approach to partially observable domains. He defined two histories as being similar if they match in their last $k$ actions and observations. The degree of similarity is the length of the match. He demonstrated successful learning on several simulated partially observable environments.

### CSFR Learning

In the CSFR setting, the number of possible history sequences is on the order of $(2|A_T| + |A_R|)!$ since an episode consists of an ordering of test actions and their outcomes, along with failed repair actions. Because action outcomes are deterministic, there is no need to repeat an action twice. An example episode, which we'll call $e_V$, is: DefaultGateway=1, DnsLookup=0, **UseCachedIP**=0, PingIp=0, **RenewLease**=1.

Note that the order of previous actions is not relevant for decision making in CSFRs. Thus, a significantly smaller space of possible experiences can be derived by summarizing an episode by the set of actions taken along with their outcomes. The revised representation of episode $e_V$, along with four other episodes, is illustrated in Table 2. Using this

[1]Note that optimal CSFR policies are tree structured with each node representing a distinct, reachable belief state. They resemble policy trees (Kaelbling, Littman, & Cassandra 1998) and sparse-sampling trees (Kearns, Mansour, & Ng 1999), which capture distinct histories from a starting state. In contrast, these CSFR policies are derived as optimal policies from a fixed starting state, not sampled approximations or responses to a family of possible starting belief states.

|  | $e_V$ | $e_W$ | $e_X$ | $e_Y$ | $e_Z$ |
|---|---|---|---|---|---|
| DnsLookup | 0 | 0 | ? | ? | ? |
| DefaultGateway | 1 | 0 | 1 | ? | 0 |
| PingIp | 0 | ? | 0 | 1 | 1 |
| **RenewLease** | 1 | 0 | ? | ? | ? |
| **UseCachedIP** | 0 | 1 | 0 | ? | 1 |
| **FixIP** | ? | ? | 1 | 1 | 1 |

Table 2: A small collection of CSFR episodes, $E$.

reordering observation, the number of distinct episodes is no more than $3^{|A_T|} \cdot 2^{|A_R|-1} \cdot 2|A_R|$,since each test action has an outcome that is 0, 1, or ? (not yet executed), at most one repair action can be successful, and the others have outcomes of 0 or ?.

Our instance-based approach begins with a set of episodes $E$. One method for applying the CSFR planning algorithm from the previous section to a set of episodes $E$ would be to take a model-based approach, deriving a small set of fault states that *covers* a set of episodes. That is, we'd want a set of states $S$ such that, for every $e \in E$, there is some $s \in S$ such that $e \subseteq s$ (every episode can be explained as deriving from one of the hypothesized fault states). At this point, it is relatively easy to estimate the parameters of a CSFR model and solve it. However, explicitly finding a minimum set of fault states that covers a set of episodes is NP-hard (by reduction to graph coloring).

Instead of identifying a minimum set of states to cover the set of episodes $E$, we simplify model construction by taking the episodes themselves as the states, $S = E$. We assume a uniform prior $\Pr(e) = 1/|E|$ and define unknown outcomes (?) as differing from 0 or 1. If $E$ is generated by random exploration episodes in a true CSFR, the probability estimates used to generate the policy will converge in the limit to their true probabilities and therefore the model-based algorithm will produce optimal policies. [2]

As an upper bound on planning effort, the number of belief states cannot be larger than $2^{|E|}$, and, in fact, we can construct examples in which the number of constructed belief states is exponentially larger than $2^{|S|}$ for a minimal set of fault states $S$. However, in practice, far fewer belief states are considered during planning (see the results section).

One interesting difference between our instance-based reinforcement-learning algorithm and that of McCallum (1995b) is that the state space for planning is that of belief states formed by subsets of instances instead of individual instances. This provides a more direct approach to the problem of taking actions to gain information. We hypothesize that our representation trades additional computation in the planning stage for more efficient use of available data.

[2] Among those episodes $d \in E$ that contain the current episode $e$, $\Pr(s)/\Pr(e)$ are expected to have been produced by state $s$ and therefore the observed outcomes of actions will reflect the probabilities of the unknown CSFR.

## Experimental Results

In this section, we demonstrate the ideas behind our instance-based learning algorithm for the CSFR model in a network-repair scenario.

### Network Repair

As our dependence on the Internet grows, continuous availability of network services is important. Recoverability from events that impair functionality is therefore becoming a focus of software-systems research. Work has been done to systematically study and classify the kinds of faults that can occur in a system, ranging from hardware and configuration faults (Li *et al.* 2002) to faults generated as a result of executing corrupt processes/applications (Bohra *et al.* 2004). Our initial learning-based approach to diagnosis and repair complements existing systems research by providing a framework for flexibly introducing information gathering and repair actions to a self-healing system without the need for detailed hand tuning; the system discovers the relationship between observed faults and optimal repair actions.

In our first experiments, we focus on recovering from faults that result from a corrupted network-interface configuration. We model the computer system as a CSFR and have implemented a set of triggers to detect faults. A repair episode is initiated if any change is detected in the network configuration. Elapsed time is the cost measure the planner seeks to minimize. A repair episode terminates when the system can reach the wide-area network.

Our test and repair actions were implemented in Java in a Windows XP environment. The test actions were:

- PluggedIn: Runs ipconfig to see whether or not the system is connected to the network.
- IsWireless: Returns 1 if the network interface is wireless, 0 otherwise.
- PingIp: Pings the current IP address of the local machine (as read from system configuration) and indicates whether or not it is reachable.
- PingLhost: Pings 127.0.0.1, returning 1 if it is reachable, 0 otherwise.
- PingGateway: Pings the IP of the network gateway (as read from system configuration), returning 1 if it is reachable, 0 otherwise.
- DnsLookup: Checks to see if DNS (as read from system configuration) is working properly by executing nslookup on an external server. Returns 1 if the attempt is successful, 0 otherwise.
- DefaultIpAddr: Checks to see if the IP address is a valid local address by performing a logical "or" with the netmask.
- DefaultNetmask: Checks to see if the netmask is valid by comparing it with previously stored valid netmask values.
- DefaultNameServer: Returns 1 if the DNS is valid and if an external server can be looked up.
- DefaultGateway: Checks to see if the gateway setting is valid by comparing it with previously stored valid gateway values.

- DHCPEnabled: Returns 1 if the network interface is DHCP enabled, otherwise 0.
- PnPReachDns: Tries to establish an http connection with a remote server. Returns 1 if the attempt is successful, 0 otherwise.

The repair actions were:

- **RenewLease**: Renews DHCP lease.
- **UseCachedIP**: Restores settings for the IP parameters to cached values in an attempt to fix the network configuration.
- **FixIP**: Pops up a dialog box, asking the user to input correct network parameters. For the purpose of our automated experiments, we had the system read correct network parameters from a file.

### Results

The network-repair system runs in the background on a workstation, initiating repair episodes when problems are detected. Although we have anecdotal evidence that the system is able to repair naturally occurring faults, including a loss of authentication on our local wireless network after a timeout, we needed a methodology for collecting fault data more quickly.

We constructed a separately running piece of software we called the "breaker", programmed to introduce any of the following faults:

- Set bad static netmask: Invokes netsh, a windows configuration program, with a bad value for the netmask.
- Set bad static gateway: Invokes netsh with a bad value for gateway.
- Set bad static IP address: Invokes netsh with a bad IP address.
- Set bad static value for DNS server: Invokes netsh with a bad value for DNS.
- Set DNS to DHCP with no lease: Invokes netsh with DNS set to use DHCP and then cancels the DHCP lease.
- Set IP address to DHCP with no lease: Invokes netsh with the IP address set to use DHCP and then cancels the DHCP lease.
- Lose existing DHCP lease: Invokes ipconfig to release the DHCP lease.

For our data collection, we ran the network-repair software concurrently with the breaker to inject faults. Faults were selected uniformly at random from the list above and executed at regular intervals of approximately two minutes, providing ample time for recovery.

During learning, we had the system choose actions greedily according to the best policy found for the previous episodes. If the system reached a current episode $e$ such that $d \not\subseteq e$ for all episodes $d \in E$, the system executed all test actions and all repair actions (until one was successful) approximately in order of increasing cost. Each episode $e$ resulting from executing all actions was clearly a distinct fault state.

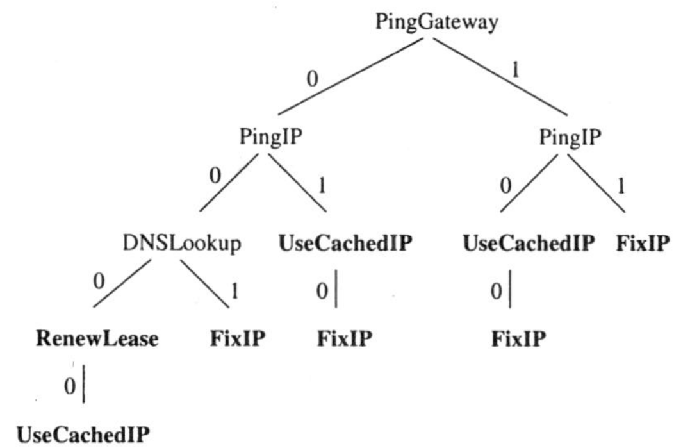


Figure 2: A learned policy for the network-repair domain.

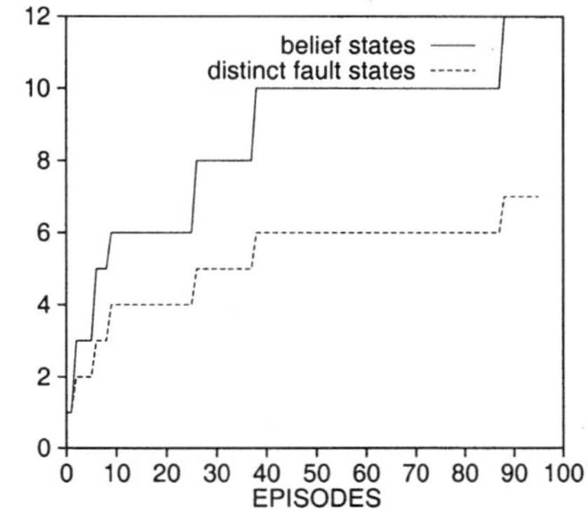


Figure 3: Growth of fault states and belief states with increasing number of episodes.

The learned policy after 95 repair episodes is illustrated in Figure 2. In this policy, **RenewLease** is attempted only when PingGateway, PingIP and DNSLookup all fail, with **UseCachedIP** as the backup repair action. **RenewLease** works differently from **UseCachedIP** and **FixIP** in that it obtains the IP parameters dynamically. In almost all the other cases, **UseCachedIP**, being cheaper than **FixIP**, is tried first with **FixIP** used as a backup action. The exceptions are the two cases where **FixIP** is tried without trying **UseCachedIP**, which stems from the lack of adequate exploration. Aside from these imperfections, the policy appears perfectly suited to our test domain.

We measured the number of belief states encountered during the planning process as a measure of planning complexity, along with the number of distinct fault states encountered. Although our best upper bound on belief states is exponential in the number of episodes, it is evident from Figure 3 that the number of belief states does not grow nearly this fast. It is roughly twice as large as the number of distinct fault states, which itself grows quite slowly with the number of episodes in the database, increasing only when new fault states are encountered.

Five test actions were used as triggers to detect failures and initiate repair episodes. They were DefaultIpAddr, DefaultNetmask, DefaultNameServer and DefaultGateway. A repair episode began if the value of any of the test actions changed. These test actions were run every few seconds. Note that since the outcomes of these tests were known at the beginning of the episode, they can be included in the initial episode used in planning "for free". Our runs that included triggers generally resulted in more efficient policies, although were less interesting from a learning standpoint as they generally needed no additional tests to select an appropriate repair action.

Beyond the network settings discussed above, we also created a preliminary implementation of a test action that monitors processes to identify those consuming more than 90% of CPU time and a corresponding repair action to terminate such processes. We feel a more complete system would include checks to see that other resources such as network bandwidth and memory usage also remain within appropriate limits.

## Conclusions

This work demonstrates an approach to learning for autonomic network repair. Although we have explored several other scenarios to which our cost-sensitive fault remediation model can be applied in simulation, our experience implementing the learning algorithm on a live network helped illustrate the robustness of the basic idea, and also indicated that we should revisit some of the underlying assumptions in our model.

The CSFR model assumes that episodes are independent. While this is true to a first approximation in the network-repair setting, we found many cases in which the effect of a repair action or an injected fault lingered from one episode to the next. For example, several repairs have the side effect of enabling or disabling DHCP. Enabling DHCP in one episode means that the system will not encounter static IP problems in the next, leading to a non-stationary failure distribution.

In our study, we used action-execution time to define costs. In practice, an additional significant action cost is its impact of the user, either due to the need for the user's involvement (like "Check if the network cable is plugged in") or because of the action's effect on other system functions (like "Reboot"). These costs are easily taken into consideration in the model; the difficulty is how to measure them during learning.

Our model also assumes that test and repair actions have no side effects apart from the possibility of fixing a failure. Not only is this assumption violated in the case of repair actions that alter, and possibly worsen, the network configuration, but it limits the types of actions that can be included and how they are used.

Two other issues worth mentioning are the assumption of stationarity in the fault distribution and the lack of explicit exploration to learn more effective repair strategies. These issues are ubiquitous concerns in reinforcement learning and we plan to study them in future work in the context of autonomic diagnosis and repair.

## Acknowledgments

We gratefully acknowledge financial support from DARPA IPTO and the National Science Foundation (IIS-0325363) and coding help from Phil Straw.

## References

Bohra, A.; Neamtiu, I.; Gallard, P.; Sultan, F.; and Iftode, L. 2004. Remote repair of OS state using backdoors. Technical Report DCS-TR-543, Rutgers Univ.

Chrisman, L. 1992. Reinforcement learning with perceptual aliasing: The perceptual distinctions approach. In *Proceedings of the Tenth National Conference on Artificial Intelligence*, 183–188. San Jose, California: AAAI Press.

Greiner, R.; Grove, A. J.; and Roth, D. 1996. Learning active classifiers. In *Proceedings of the Thirteenth International Conference on Machine Learning (ICML-96)*, 207–215.

Guo, A. 2002. Active classification with bounded resources. At http://cs.umass.edu/ anyuan/publications/SSS402AGuo.ps.

Kaelbling, L. P.; Littman, M. L.; and Cassandra, A. R. 1998. Planning and acting in partially observable stochastic domains. *Artificial Intelligence* 101(1–2):99–134.

Kearns, M.; Mansour, Y.; and Ng, A. Y. 1999. A sparse sampling algorithm for near-optimal planning in large Markov decision processes. In *Proceedings of the Sixteenth International Joint Conference on Artificial Intelligence (IJCAI-99)*, 1324–1331.

Li, X.; Martin, R.; Nagaraja, K.; Nguyen, T. D.; and Zhang, B. 2002. Mendosus: A SAN-based fault-injection test-bed for the construction of highly available network services. In *First Workshop on Novel Uses of System Area Networks (SAN-1)*.

Littman, M. L.; Sutton, R. S.; and Singh, S. 2002. Predictive representations of state. In *Advances in Neural Information Processing Systems 14*, 1555–1561.

McCallum, A. K. 1995a. *Reinforcement Learning with Selective Perception and Hidden State*. Ph.D. Dissertation, Department of Computer Science, University of Rochester.

McCallum, R. A. 1995b. Instance-based utile distinctions for reinforcement learning with hidden state. In *Proceedings of the Twelfth International Conference on Machine Learning*, 387–395. San Francisco, CA: Morgan Kaufmann.

Moore, A. W.; Atkeson, C. G.; and Schaal, S. 1995. Memory-based learning for control. Technical Report CMU-RI-TR-95-18, CMU Robotics Institute.

Ormoneit, D., and Sen, S. 2002. Kernel-based reinforcement learning. *Machine Learning* 49:161–178.

Santamaría, J. C.; Sutton, R. S.; and Ram, A. 1997. Experiments with reinforcement learning in problems with continuous state and action spaces. *Adaptive Behavior* 6(2):163–217.

Smart, W. D., and Kaelbling, L. P. 2000. Practical reinforcement learning in continuous spaces. In *Proceedings of the Seventeenth International Conference on Machine Learning (ICML 2000)*, 903–910.

Sutton, R. S., and Barto, A. G. 1998. *Reinforcement Learning: An Introduction*. The MIT Press.

Turney, P. D. 1995. Cost-sensitive classification: Empirical evaluation of a hybrid genetic decision tree induction algorithm. *Journal of Artificial Intelligence Research* 2:369–409.

Zubek, V. B., and Dietterich, T. G. 2002. Pruning improves heuristic search for cost-sensitive learning. In *Proceedings of the International Conference on Machine Learning*, 27–34.

# Logical Foundations of Negotiation: Outcome, Concession and Adaptation

**Thomas Meyer** and **Norman Foo**
National ICT Australia
School of CSE, UNSW
Sydney, Australia
tmeyer@cse.unsw.edu.au

**Rex Kwok**
Knowledge Systems Group
School of CSE, UNSW
Sydney, Australia
rkwok@cse.unsw.edu.au

**Dongmo Zhang**
School of Computing and
Information Technology
University of Western Sydney, Australia
dongmo@cit.uws.edu.au

### Abstract

This paper provides a logical framework for negotiation between agents that are assumed to be rational, cooperative and truthful. We present a characterisation of the permissible outcomes of a process of negotiation in terms of a set of rationality postulates, as well as a method for constructing exactly the rational outcomes. The framework is extended by describing two modes of negotiation from which an outcome can be reached. In the concessionary mode, agents are required to weaken their demands in order to accommodate the demands of others. In the adaptationist mode, agents are required to adapt to the demands of others in some appropriate fashion. Both concession and adaptation are characterised in terms of rationality postulates. We also provide methods for constructing exactly the rational concessions, as well as the rational adaptations. The central result of the paper is the observation that the outcomes obtained from the concessionary and adaptationist modes both correspond to the rational outcomes. We conclude by pointing out the links between negotiation and AGM belief change, and providing a glimpse of how this may be used to define a notion of preference-based negotiation.

## Introduction

Intelligent software agents involved in bargaining and negotiation on behalf of human clients are a reality (Sandholm 2002). As a result, negotiation is currently being investigated from many perspectives, including economics, applied mathematics, psychology, sociology and computer science (Bui & Shakun 1996; Rosenschein & Zlotkin 1994; Kraus, Sycara, & Evenchik 1998; Kraus 2001; Parsons, Sierra, & Jennings 1998). Thus far, most successful approaches have been quantitative in nature. Such approaches are usually game-theoretic in nature, with numeric utility functions forming the basis for decision-making. In many cases, however, numeric utilities are either unreliable or simply unavailable. This paper is a contribution to the body of literature, such as (Sycara 1990; Kraus, Sycara, & Evenchik 1998; Parsons, Sierra, & Jennings 1998; Booth 2001; 2002; Zhang *et al.* 2004) which, instead, views negotiation in a *qualititative* light. Our aim is to provide a logical framework for describing a process of negotiation between agents. The framework shares some similarities with (Wooldridge & Parsons 2000) as well as with work on belief merging (Booth 2001; 2002). It is closely related to and, indeed, inspired by the work in (Zhang *et al.* 2004). For a more detailed treatment of negotiation see (Walton & Krabbe 1995).

In this paper we restrict ourselves to the case involving only two agents. Each agent comes to the negotiation table with an initial set of demands. The parties involved then proceed with a process of negotiation which terminates when they *strike a deal*—that is, when they have converged on a mutually agreed upon set of demands. The purpose of this paper is to define a logical framework for describing exactly those deals that are deemed to be rational.

Crudely speaking, the goal of an agent is two-pronged: it aims to have as many of its initial demands included in the negotiated outcome. At the same time it is also driven to reach an agreement acceptable to all parties. The framework we propose is intended to strike the correct balance between these two, possibly conflicting, goals. Agents are assumed to be truthful, rational and cooperative.

We commence with the provision of a set of rationality postulates, constraining the possible *outcomes* of the negotiation process between two agents. This is followed by a discussion of two different *modes* of negotiation, both also defined in terms of sets of rationality postulates. The first mode is a *concessionary* one. If the demands of two agents conflict, each is required to weaken its demands, by dropping some, in order to come to an agreement. The final negotiated outcome then consists of the *combination* of those demands that each agents chooses to retain. The second mode, termed *adaptation*, is one in which an agent is willing to deviate from its current demands in order to ensure that a settlement is reached. In the case of adaptation the negotiated outcome contains *only* those demands occurring in both adapted sets of demands. We show that the two modes of negotiation are interdefinable and, perhaps surprisingly, interdefinable with the framework for defining negotiated outcomes as well. We provide methods of constructing rational outcomes, concessions, and adaptations and prove, via appropriate representation results, that the sets of rationality postulates characterise these construction methods.

The results in this paper provide a basic logical framework for the definition of qualitative negotiation, but it does not address the question of defining the negotiation process itself, which is left as future work. In the conclusion we elaborate on this, providing a brief discussion on the connection between negotiation and mutual belief revision, and how this connection may be employed to extend the currently defined framework to a preference-based one.

The logic under consideration is finitely generated and propositional, with the language denoted by $\mathcal{L}$, falsum by $\perp$, logical entailment by $\models$, logical equivalence by $\equiv$ and logical closure by $Cn$. A *theory* is a set of sentences closed under logical entailment. $M(K)$ denotes the *models* of a set of sentences $K$ and $M(\alpha)$ that of a single sentence $\alpha$.

A deal $D$ is defined as an abstract object. Any deal is defined with respect to a *demand pair* $K = (K_0, K_1)$, with $K_i$ $(i = 0, 1)$, being a *consistent* theory of $\mathcal{L}$, representing the initial demands, or demand set, of agent $i$. By doing so we are implicitly assuming that our agents are ideal reasoners, aware of all the logical consequences of their explicit demands. We add more structure to the formal definition of a deal as we proceed through the paper.

## Negotiated outcomes

We commence with the assumption that negotiating agents are ultimately interested in the *outcome* of the process of negotiation, irrespective of the mode of negotiation they adopt. Formally, the outcome $O(D)$ of a deal $D$ is a set of sentences representing the demands which both agents have agreed upon. A deal $D$ is *outcome-permissible* iff $O(D)$ satisfies the following rationality postulates:

**(O1)** $O(D) = Cn(O(D))$

**(O2)** $O(D) \not\models \perp$

**(O3)** If $K_0 \cup K_1 \not\models \perp$ then $O(D) = Cn(K_0 \cup K_1)$

**(O4)** $(K_0 \cap K_1) \subseteq O(D)$ or $O(D) \cup (K_0 \cap K_1) \models \perp$

(O1) ensures that outcomes are theories and (O2) that outcomes are consistent. (O3) states that if the initial demand sets do not conflict, an agent is obliged to uncritically add all demands posed by the other to its own, a requirement which might seem unrealistic. After all, why should I be forced to accept *all* demands of the other party involved just because our initial demands do not conflict? The response to this objection hinges on the current (admittedly simplistic) assumption that agents are cooperative. Other agents are seen as participants in a process in which the ultimate aim is to reach common ground. Cooperation implies the intention to meet as many of the demands of the other agent, as long as it does not conflict directly with one's own interests. (O4) prohibits the outcome of any process of negotiation to be consistent with the initial demands that both agents have in common without including *all* these commonly held demands. This can be justified by pointing out that if a potential outcome $O$ is *consistent* with the demands that the agents have in common, it would be to the benefit of both rather to strengthen $O$ to contain *all* commonly held demands.

### A classification of deals

The constraints placed on outcomes by (O1)-(O4) lead naturally to a taxonomy of deals in which we distinguish between four kinds of deals. A *trivial* deal is one for which the

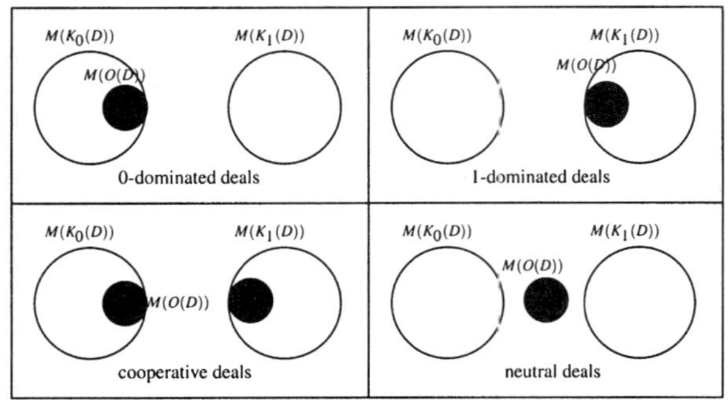


Figure 1: Semantic representations of the outcome-permissible non-trivial deals.

outcome is $Cn(K_0 \cup K_1)$. This can only occur when the combination of the initial demand sets is consistent. In the next type of deal one of the agents, the *master*, gets to keep all its demands. An *i-dominant* deal $(i = 0, 1)$ is one in which agent $i$ plays the role of the master. Observe that the different supersets of the demands of agent $i$ correspond to the different $i$-dominant deals. The third type of deal is the class of *cooperative* deals, where the outcome is consistent with the initial demand set of each agent. Finally, we have the class of *neutral* deals, in which the outcome of negotiation is inconsistent with that which is common to the original demand sets. Figure 1 contains semantic representations of the non-trivial deals.

**Definition 1** *Consider any deal D. If* $K_0 \cup K_1 \not\models \perp$ *then D is the* trivial *deal, where* $O(D) = Cn(K_0 \cup K_1)$. *Otherwise we have the following classification.*

1. *D is an* $i$-dominant *deal iff* $O(D) \models K_i$, *for* $i = 0, 1$.
2. *D is a* neutral *deal iff* $O(D) \cup (K_0 \cap K_1) \models \perp$.
3. *D is a* cooperative *deal iff* $K_i \cup O(D) \not\models \perp$, *for* $i = 0, 1$.

The semantic representation is particularly instructive in the case of the neutral deals. The intention is that a neutral deal will be struck when the starting positions of the two agents are too far apart for them to accommodate each other. In the spirit of cooperation they are then required to move to "neutral territory", which is defined as any theory that is inconsistent with those initial demands that the agents have in common. It is in the justification of the choice of neutral territory that the semantic representation comes in useful: an outcome is neutral with respect to the initial demands of the two agents when it does not share any models with either of the initial demand sets.

It is easily established that the classification above provides a partition of the space of outcome-permissible deals.

**Theorem 1** *Let D be any outcome-permissible deal. Then D is exactly one of a trivial, i-dominant* $(i = 0, 1)$*, neutral, or cooperative deal. Conversely, every deal which is trivial, i-dominant* $(i = 0, 1)$*, neutral, or cooperative is also outcome-permissible.*

This classification is useful when setting protocols for negotation, an issue that will be dealt with in future work.

### Constructing outcomes

We now describe a method for constructing those outcomes sanctioned by (O1)-(O4). Let $\mathcal{OD} = \{D \mid O(D) \in O\}$ where $O = \{Cn(K_0 \cup K_1)\}$ if $K_0 \cup K_1 \nvDash \perp$, and $O = \{\phi \mid \phi \nvDash \perp$ and $(Cn(\phi) \vDash K_0 \cap K_1$ or $\phi \cup (K_0 \cap K_1) \vDash \perp)\}$, otherwise.

As the next result shows, the set $\mathcal{OD}$ contains precisely the outcome-permissible deals.

**Theorem 2** *A deal D satisfies (O1)-(O4) iff* $D \in \mathcal{OD}$.

Whenever the demand sets of two agents do not conflict, the postulates (O1)-(O4) thus allow the agents to converge on any consistent set either containing the commonly held demands, or in conflict with the commonly held demands.

**Example 1** *Let D be a deal such that* $K_0 = Cn(p \wedge q)$ *and* $K_1 = Cn(\neg p \wedge \neg q)$. *Then* $O(D) \in \{Cn(p \wedge q), Cn(\neg p \wedge \neg q), Cn(p \wedge \neg q), Cn(\neg p \wedge q), Cn(p \leftrightarrow \neg q)\}$. *More specifically, D is an 0-dominated deal iff* $O(D) = Cn(p \wedge q)$, *D is 1-dominated iff* $O(D) = Cn(\neg p \wedge \neg q)$, *D is cooperative iff* $O(D) = Cn(p \leftrightarrow q)$ *and D is neutral iff* $O(D) \in \{Cn(p \wedge \neg q), Cn(\neg p \wedge q), Cn(p \leftrightarrow \neg q)\}$.

Having laid down the basic requirements of negotiated outcomes, we now proceed with the description of two modes for obtaining such outcomes.

## Concession

In this section we propose a mode of negotiation which is *concessionary* in nature. Agents are expected to *weaken* their initial demands to reach an outcome acceptable to both parties. For a deal $D$, let $C(D) = (C_0(D), C_1(D))$ be a pair of theories where $C_i(D)$ $(i = 0, 1)$ represents the weakened demands, or *concessions*, of agent $i$, also referred to as an $i$-concession. The outcome of the negotiation is taken to be $Cn(C_0(D) \cup C_1(D))$. Formally, this means that we insist that the following property holds.

**(OC)** $O(D) = Cn(C_0(D) \cup C_1(D))$

The link between outcomes and concessions will be strengthened further once the adaptationist mode of negotiation has also been discussed.

A deal $D$ is *concession-permissible* iff $C(D)$ satisfi es the following rationality postulates:

**(C1)** $C_i(D) = Cn(C_i(D))$ for $i = 0, 1$

**(C2)** $C_i(D) \subseteq K_i$ for $i = 0, 1$

**(C3)** If $K_0 \cup K_1 \nvDash \perp$ then $C_i(D) = K_i$ for $i = 0, 1$

**(C4)** $C_0(D) \cup C_1(D) \nvDash \perp$

**(C5)** If $C_0(D) \cup K_1 \nvDash \perp$ or $C_1(D) \cup K_0 \nvDash \perp$ then $K_0 \cap K_1 \subseteq C_0(D) \cup C_1(D)$

**(C6)** If $C_0(D) \cup K_1 \vDash \perp$ and $C_1(D) \cup K_0 \vDash \perp$ then $C_0(D) \cup C_1(D) \cup (K_0 \cap K_1) \vDash \perp$

(C1) requires a concession to be a theory. (C2) ensures that the concession of an agent is a logical weakening of its initial demand set. (C3) deals with the case in which the initial demand sets are consistent. In this case neither agent has anything to gain by a weakening of its demand set. Note that (C3) expresses the same requirement as (O3) under the assumption that (OC) holds. (C4) is the insistence

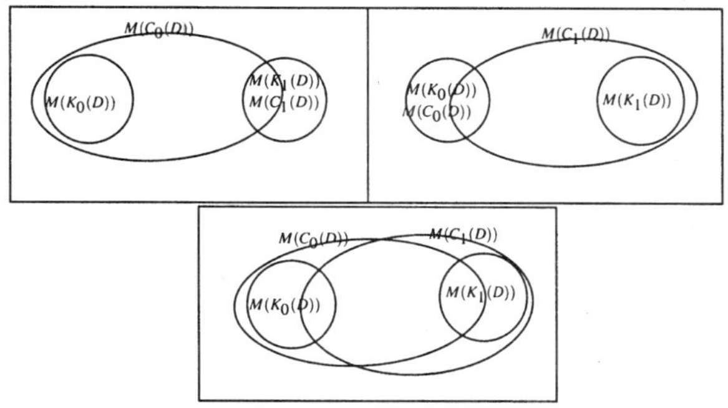


Figure 2: A semantic representation of the concessions in $CC$. Observe that $M(C_1(D)) = M(K_1)$ in the top left diagram, while $M(C_0(D)) = M(K_0)$ in the top right diagram.

that the two agents reach some common ground when negotiating. It is the concessionary analogue of (O2), given that (OC) holds. (C5) is an appeal to the cooperative spirit in which negotiation is assumed to take place. Whenever one agent's concession is consistent with the other's initial demands, this postulate ensures that the demands they initially had in common are all included in the demands they have in common after both have conceded. Observe that in the presence of (C2) the entailment in the consequent of (C5) becomes equivalence. (C6) is a fairness requirement with a dichotomous flavour, and with rationality as the underlying motivation. If the concession of each agent is *inconsistent* with the initial demands of the other, then the fi nal outcome (the two concessions combined) should be inconsistent with the initial demands they had in common. In other words, if neither of us were willing to weaken our position enough to become consistent with the initial demands of the other, we then agree to move to neutral territory.[1]

### Constructing concessions

We now consider a method for constructing the concession-permissible deals. Let $\mathcal{CD} = \{D \mid C(D) \in C\}$ where

$$C = \begin{cases} \{(K_0, K_1)\}, \text{ if } K_0 \cup K_1 \nvDash \perp, \\ CC \cup IC \text{ otherwise} \end{cases}$$

where $CC = \{(Cn(K_0 \cap \phi_1), Cn(K_1 \cap \phi_0)) \mid \phi_0 \nvDash \perp$ or $\phi_1 \nvDash \perp$, and $\phi_i \vDash K_i$ for $i = 0, 1\}$

and $IC = \{(Cn(K_0 \cap \phi), Cn(K_1 \cap \phi)) \mid \phi \nvDash \perp$ and $\phi \cup (K_0 \cap K_1) \vDash \perp\}$.

As shown in Figure 2, $CC$ contains exactly those cases in which both agents retain the initial commonly held beliefs, and at least one agent weakens its initial demand set so as not to conflict with the initial demands of the other. And as shown in Figure 3, $IC$ contains those cases in which each agent picks the same set that conflicts with their commonly held demands, and restricts its initial demands to those occurring in this set as well.

[1] See the section on deal classification for a discussion of "neutral territory".

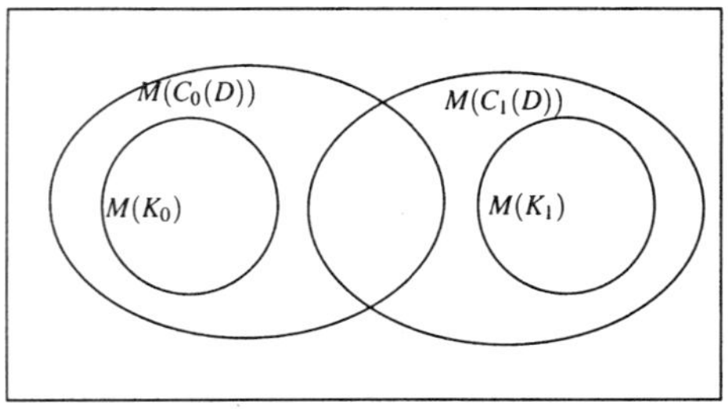


Figure 3: A semantic representation of concessions in $IC$.

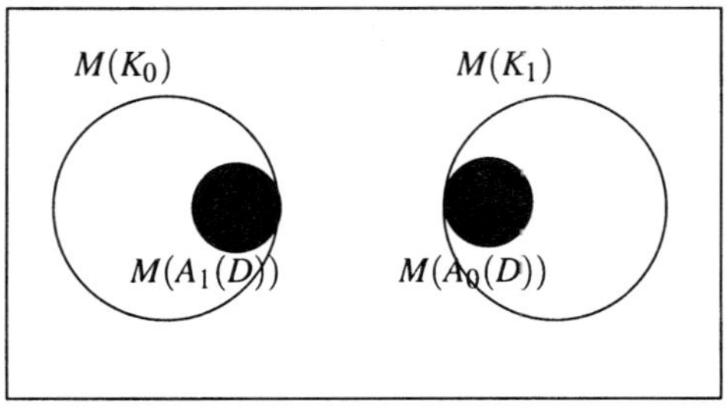


Figure 4: A semantic representation of the adaptations in $C\mathcal{A}$.

**Example 2** *Let $D$ be such that $K_0 = Cn(p \wedge q)$ and $K_1 = Cn(\neg p \wedge \neg q)$. $CC = \{(Cn(p \wedge q), Cn(p \leftrightarrow q)), (Cn(p \leftrightarrow q), Cn(\neg p \wedge \neg q)), (Cn(p \leftrightarrow q), Cn(p \leftrightarrow q))\}$ and $IC = \{(Cn(p), Cn(\neg q)), (Cn(q), Cn(\neg p)), (Cn(p \vee q), Cn(\neg p \vee \neg q))\}$.*

As the next result shows, the set $C\mathcal{D}$ contains precisely the concession-permissible deals.

**Theorem 3** *A deal $D$ satisfies (C1)-(C6) iff $D \in C\mathcal{D}$.*

We now have two classes of deals to consider—the outcome-permissible and concession-permissible deals. Before we look at the relationship between these, it is necessary to consider a second mode of negotiation.

## Adaptation

In this section we turn our attention to the *adaptationist* mode, where both agents are required to adapt their initial demands in such a way as to accommodate the demands of the other. For a deal $D$, let $A(D) = (A_0(D), A_1(D))$ be a pair of theories where the adapted demands of agent $i$ ($i = 0, 1$), also referred to as an $i$-adaptation, are denoted by $A_i(D)$. The outcome of the negotiation process after adaptation has taken place consists of the sentences the two adaptation have in common. This is formalised as follows.

**(OA)** $O(D) = A_0(D) \cap A_1(D)$

As we shall see, $A_i(D)$ may conflict with $K_i$, thereby capturing the intuition that an agent's adaptive demands may differ radically from its initial demands. Such a situation is tenable only because of the assumption that both agents are cooperative and *know* that the other party is cooperative. An agent is therefore willing to risk a drastic departure from its initial demands towards the stated demands of the other only because it knows that the other party will not abuse its trust, and that both will therefore benefi t from such a move.

A deal $D$ is *adaptation-permissible* iff $A(D)$ satisfi es the following rationality postulates:

**(A1)** $A_i(D) = Cn(A_i(D))$ for $i = 0, 1$

**(A2)** $K_0 \cup K_1 \nvDash \bot$ implies $A_0(D) = A_1(D) = Cn(K_0 \cup K_1)$

**(A3)** $K_0 \subseteq A_i(D)$, or $K_1 \subseteq A_i(D)$, or $A_i(D) \cup (K_0 \cap K_1) \vDash \bot$, for $i = 0, 1$

**(A4)** For $i = 0, 1$, if $K_i \nsubseteq A_i(D)$ then $A_0(D) = A_1(D)$

(A1) ensures that adaptations are theories, while (A2) defi nes adaptation to be the combination of all initials demand in the case where the initial demands sets are not conflicting. Given (OA), it expresses the same requirement as (O3) and (C3). (A3) is a dichotomy principle based on rationality as motivation. It ensures that an agent's adaptation either includes at least one of the initial demand sets, or is inconsistent with the initial commonly held demands. The intuition is that an agent has exactly three choices when adapting: including all of its own demands, moving over completely to the viewpoint of the other agent, or otherwise moving to some neutral set of demands.[2] (A4) draws on the assumption of cooperation. If both agents do not include their own initial demands in their respective adaptations, they are required to cooperate completely by settling on identical adaptations.

Observe that the following property is a consequence of these postulates.

**(Rationality)** $A_i(D) \vDash K_i \cap A_{1-i}(D)$ for $i = 0, 1$

(Rationality) was proposed in (Zhang *et al.* 2004). It states that those initial demands of an agent adopted by its opponent should be retained in its own adaptation as well.

### Constructing adaptations

We now provide a method for constructing the adaptation-permissible deals. Let $\mathcal{AD} = \{D \mid A(D) \in \mathcal{A}\}$ where

$$\mathcal{A} = \begin{cases} \{(Cn(K_0 \cup K_1), Cn(K_0 \cup K_1))\} & \text{if } K_0 \cup K_1 \nvDash \bot, \\ C\mathcal{A} \cup I\mathcal{A} & \text{otherwise} \end{cases}$$

where $C\mathcal{A} = \{(Cn(\phi_0), Cn(\phi_1)) \mid \phi_i \nvDash \bot, \phi_i \vDash K_i, i = 0, 1\}$, and $I\mathcal{A} = \{(Cn(\phi), Cn(\phi)) \mid (\phi \cup (K_0 \cap K_1) \vDash \bot,\ \phi \vDash K_0$ or $\phi \vDash K_1)$, and $\phi \nvDash \bot\}$

**Example 3** *Let $D$ be a deal such that $K_0 = Cn(p \wedge q)$ and $K_1 = Cn(\neg p \wedge \neg q)$. Then $C\mathcal{A} = \{(Cn(\neg p \wedge \neg q), Cn(p \wedge q))\}$, and $I\mathcal{A} = \{(Cn(p \wedge q), Cn(p \wedge q)), (Cn(\neg p \wedge \neg q), Cn(\neg p \wedge \neg q)), (Cn(p \wedge \neg q), Cn(p \wedge \neg q)), (Cn(\neg p \wedge q), Cn(\neg p \wedge q)), (Cn(p \leftrightarrow \neg q), Cn(p \leftrightarrow \neg q))\}$.*

Observe that $C\mathcal{A}$ contains those cases in which each agent adopts a consistent superset of the other's initial demands. Figure 4 contains a semantic picture of such cases.

$I\mathcal{A}$, on the other hand, contains those cases in which both agents adopt the *same* consistent set, provided it either contains the initial demands of one of the agents, or it conflicts

[2] See the section on deal classification for a discussion of "neutral territory".

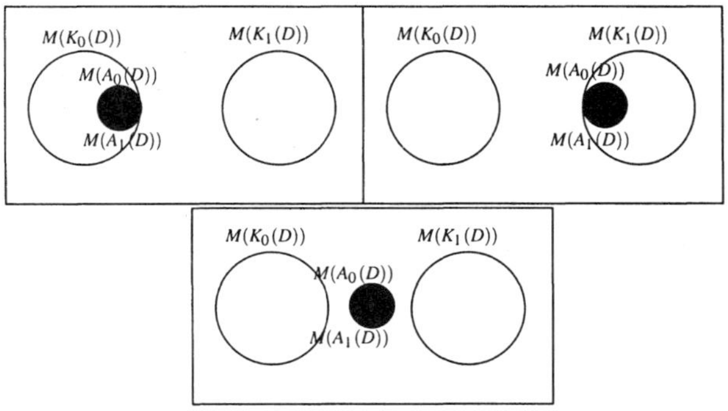


Figure 5: A semantic representation of the adaptations in $\mathcal{IA}$.

with the commonly held initial demands (a move to neutral territory). Figure 5 contains a semantic picture of such cases.

As the next result shows, the set $\mathcal{AD}$ contains precisely the adaptation-permissible deals.

**Theorem 4** *A deal D satisfies (A1)-(A4) iff $D \in \mathcal{AD}$.*

## Outcome, concession and adaptation

We remarked earlier on our assumption that agents are primarily interested in the outcome of the negotiation process and that the mode of negotiation is of secondary concern. Nevertheless, the two different modes of negotiation are important in that they represent different approaches to the problem of characterising negotiation. Of course, measuring whether adaptation and concession yield the same results will have to be done via their common denominator, the *outcome* of the process of negotiation. Based on this, we make the reasonable assumption that both modes of negotiation should produce the same outcome, and it thus follows immediately from (OA) and (OC) that the next property holds:

**(AC)** $Cn(C_0(D) \cup C_1(D)) = A_0(D) \cap A_1(D)$

(AC) insists that the combination of the concessions be equivalent to that which the adaptations have in common.

It is now possible to prove the following important result.

**Theorem 5** $\mathcal{OD} = \mathcal{CD} = \mathcal{AD}$. *That is, the classes of outcome-permissible deals, concession-permissible deals and adaptation-permissible deals are identical.*

In view of theorem 5 we shall refer to an element of any of these classes as *permissible.*

(AC) establishes a relationship between the concession and adaptation associated with a permissible deal, say $D$, but it is possible to go further and defi ne $C(D)$ and $A(D)$ in terms of each other. This can be done with the following constructions.

**(Def $C$ from $A$)** $C_i(D) = K_i \cap A_{1-i}(D)$, for $i = 0, 1$

**(Def $A$ from $C$)** $A_i(D) = \{Cn(C_i(D) \cup C_{1-i}(D))$ if $K_i \cup C_{1-i}(D) \vDash \bot$, and $A_i(D) = Cn(K_i \cup C_{1-i}(D))$ otherwise (for $i = 0, 1$).

**Theorem 6** *For every permissible deal D, $C(D)$ can be defined in terms of $A(D)$ and $K(D)$ using (Def C from A), and $A(D)$ can be defined in terms of $C(D)$ and $K(D)$ using (Def A from C).*

In fact, while we already know that an outcome $O(D)$ obtained for a permissible deal $D$ can be defi ned in terms of $C(D)$ and in terms of $A(D)$, it is also possible to defi ne $C(D)$, as well as $A(D)$ in terms of the outcome $O(D)$. This can be done with the following constructions.

**(Def $C$ from $O$)** $C_i(D) = K_i \cap O(D)$, for $i = 0, 1$

**(Def $A$ from $O$)** $A_i(D) = \{Cn(O(D) \cup K_i$ if $O(K) \cup K_i \nvDash \bot$, and $A_i(D) = O(K)$ otherwise (for $i = 0, 1$).

**Theorem 7** *For every permissible deal D, $C(D)$ can be obtained from $O(D)$ and $K(D)$ using (Def C from O), and $A(D)$ can be obtained from $O(D)$ and $K(D)$ using (Def A from O).*

The next example illustrates the results of theorems 6 and 7.

**Example 4** *Consider any permissible deal D for which $K_0 = Cn(p \wedge q)$ and $K_1 = Cn(\neg p \wedge \neg q)$. By theorem 5 and the results in examples 1, 2 and 3 we know that*

$$O(D) \in \left\{ \begin{array}{ll} Cn(p \wedge q), & Cn(\neg p \wedge \neg q), \\ Cn(p \leftrightarrow q), & Cn(p \wedge \neg q), \\ Cn(\neg p \wedge q), & Cn(p \leftrightarrow \neg q) \end{array} \right\},$$

$$C(D) \in \left\{ \begin{array}{l} (Cn(p \wedge q), Cn(p \leftrightarrow q)), \\ (Cn(p \leftrightarrow q), Cn(\neg p \wedge \neg q)), \\ (Cn(p \leftrightarrow q), Cn(p \leftrightarrow q)), \\ (Cn(p), Cn(\neg q)), \\ (Cn(q), Cn(\neg p)), \\ (Cn(p \vee q), Cn(\neg p \vee \neg q)) \end{array} \right\} \textit{and}$$

$$A(D) \in \left\{ \begin{array}{l} (Cn(p \wedge q), Cn(p \wedge q)), \\ (Cn(\neg p \wedge \neg q), Cn(\neg p \wedge \neg q)), \\ (Cn(\neg p \wedge \neg q), Cn(p \wedge q)), \\ (Cn(p \wedge \neg q), Cn(p \wedge \neg q)), \\ (Cn(\neg p \wedge q), Cn(\neg p \wedge q)), \\ (Cn(p \leftrightarrow \neg q), Cn(p \leftrightarrow \neg q) \end{array} \right\}$$

*By theorems 6 and 7 we know that*

$$\mathcal{OD} = \mathcal{CD} = \mathcal{AD} = \{D_1, D_2, D_3, D_4, D_5, D_6\}$$

*where:*

$$\begin{array}{ll} O(D_1) = Cn(p \wedge q), & O(D_2) = Cn(\neg p \wedge \neg q), \\ O(D_3) = Cn(p \leftrightarrow q), & O(D_4) = Cn(p \wedge \neg q), \\ O(D_5) = Cn(\neg p \wedge q), & O(D_6) = Cn(p \leftrightarrow \neg q) \end{array}$$

*and*

$$\begin{array}{l} C(D_1) = (Cn(p \wedge q), Cn(p \leftrightarrow q)), \\ C(D_2) = (Cn(p \leftrightarrow q), Cn(\neg p \wedge \neg q)), \\ C(D_3) = (Cn(p \leftrightarrow q), Cn(p \leftrightarrow q)), \\ C(D_4) = (Cn(p), Cn(\neg q)), \\ C(D_5) = (Cn(q), Cn(\neg p)), \\ C(D_6) = (Cn(p \vee q), Cn(\neg p \vee \neg q)) \end{array}$$

*and*

$$\begin{array}{l} A(D_1) = (Cn(p \wedge q), Cn(p \wedge q)), \\ A(D_2) = (Cn(\neg p \wedge \neg q), Cn(\neg p \wedge \neg q)), \\ A(D_3) = (Cn(\neg p \wedge \neg q), Cn(p \wedge q)), \\ A(D_4) = (Cn(p \wedge \neg q), Cn(p \wedge \neg q)), \\ A(D_5) = (Cn(\neg p \wedge q), Cn(\neg p \wedge q)), \\ A(D_6) = (Cn(p \leftrightarrow \neg q), Cn(p \leftrightarrow \neg q) \end{array}$$

## Conclusion and future work

This paper has established a basic framework for determining permissible deals. We conclude with a brief discussion of how such a framework is to be used in a process of negotatiation. The details will be the subejct of future research.

The process of reaching an agreement involves a sequence of negotiation steps where, at each step, both agents simultaneously put forward the deal for which they currently have the highest preference. The process terminates when both agents are willing to accept the most recent deal proposed by the other party. Such a process assumes that, at any point, each agent has a preference relation on deals. Roughly speaking, these preferences are analogous to the utility functions used in quantitative settings. While the preferences of an agent can vary considerably, it has to take into account the demands and preferences of the other party involved in the negotatiation process as well. The initial demands are known when the negotiation process commences, but the only other information available to an agent is the sequence of proposed deals it obtains from the other party. An agent thus has to make use of the information contained in these deals, and combine it with its knowledge about the negotiation process to perform a kind of preference extraction to guide it in its choice of deals to propose. This is one of the main topics to be dealt with in future work.

### Negotiation as belief revision

The reader familiar with the area of belief change will be struck by the similarities between adaptation and concession on the one hand, and AGM belief revision and contraction on the other (Alchourrón, Gärdenfors, & Makinson 1985; Gärdenfors 1988).[3] By conceding, an agent weakens its current demands, just as a belief contraction operation weakens the beliefs of an agent to some acceptable level. By adapting, an agent either strengthens its current demands, adopts a set which includes the demands of its adversary, or settles on a set that is inconsistent with the initial commonly held demands. Compare this with belief revision in which an agent either strengthens its own beliefs, or adopts a set which includes the sentence with which to revise and is inconsistent with its original beliefs.

These similarities are no coincidence. It can be shown that negotiation, as defined in this paper, can also be described as mutual belief revision (Meyer *et al.* 2004). Roughly speaking, the idea is the following. If the initial demands of the agents are conflicting, each agent is required to present a weakened version of their demands to the other which, in turn, is obliged to accept this weaker set of demands, by revising its current demands with it. It turns out that a suitably defined set of basic AGM revision operations can be used to obtain the adaptations of all permissible deals.

One of the advantages of looking at adaptation as basic AGM revision is that it provides a crude notion of preference among deals. This notion can be refined by a move to those AGM revision operations satisfying the supplementary AGM postulates as well—a move that proves to be very useful in the definition of appropriate negotiation protocols.

[3] See (van der Meyden 1994) for work on mutual belief revision and (Lau *et al.* 2003) for connections between negotiation and belief revision.

## References


Alchourrón, C. E.; Gärdenfors, P.; and Makinson, D. 1985. On the logic of theory change: Partial meet functions for contraction and revision. *Journal of Symbolic Logic* 50:510–530.

Booth, R. 2001. A negotiation-style framework for non-prioritised revision. In van Benthem, J., ed., *Theoretical Aspects of Rationality and Knowledge: Proceedings of the Eighth Conference (TARK 2001)*, 137–150. San Francisco, California: Morgan Kaufmann.

Booth, R. 2002. Social contraction and belief negotiation. In *Proceedings of KR'02*, 375–384.

Bui, T. X., and Shakun, M. F. 1996. Negotiation processes, evolutionary systems design, and negotiator. In Shakun, M. F., ed., *Negotiation Processes*. Kluwer Academic Publishers. 39–53.

Gärdenfors, P. 1988. *Knowledge in Flux : Modeling the Dynamics of Epistemic States*. Cambridge, Massachusetts: The MIT Press.

Kraus, S.; Sycara, K.; and Evenchik, A. 1998. Reaching agreements through argumentation: a logical model and implementation. *Artificial Intelligence* 104:1–69.

Kraus, S. 2001. *Strategic Negotiation in Multiagent Systems*. MIT Press.

Lau, R.; Essam, B.; Chan, S.; and Huang, Z. 2003. Belief revision for adaptive negotiation agents. 196–202.

Meyer, T.; Foo, N.; Kwok, R.; and Zhang, D. 2004. Logical foundations of negotiation: strategies and preferences. In *Proceedings of KR'04*.

Parsons, S.; Sierra, C.; and Jennings, N. 1998. Agents that reason and negotiate by arguing. *Journal of Logic and Computation* 8(3):261–292.

Rosenschein, J. S., and Zlotkin, G. 1994. *Rules of Encounter*. MIT Press.

Sandholm, T. 2002. e-mediator: A next generation electronic commerce server. *Computational Intelligence* 18(4):656–667.

Sycara, K. 1990. Persuasive argumentation in negotiation. *Theory and Decision* 28:203–242.

van der Meyden, R. 1994. Mutual belief revision (preliminary report). In *Proceedings of KR'94*, 595–606.

Walton, D., and Krabbe, E. C. W. 1995. *Commitment in Dialogue: Basic Concepts of Interpersonal Reasoning*. Albany, State University of New York Press.

Wooldridge, M., and Parsons, S. 2000. Languages for negotiation. In *Proceedings of the Fourteenth European Conference on Artificial Intelligence (ECAI 2000)*, 393–400.

Zhang, D.; Foo, N.; Meyer, T.; and Kwok, R. 2004. Negotiation as mutual belief revision. In *Proceedings of the Nineteenth National Conference on Artificial Intelligence (AAAI-04)*.

# Repeated Observation Models

**Avi Pfeffer**
Division of Engineering and Applied Sciences
Harvard University
avi@eecs.harvard.edu

**Abstract**

Repetition is an important phenomenon in a variety of domains, such as music, computer programs and architectural drawings. A generative model for these domains should account for the possibility of repetition. We present repeated observation models (ROMs), a framework for modeling sequences that explicitly allows for repetition. In a ROM, an element is either generated by copying a previous element, or by using a base model. We show how to build ROMs using $n$-grams and hidden Markov models as the base model. We also describe an extension of ROMs in which entire subsequences are repeated together. Results from a music modeling domain show that ROMs can lead to dramatic improvement in predictive ability.

## Introduction

Repetition is an important phenomenon in many artifacts. It is absolutely essential to music. Much of the art of composition is reusing material in different ways. Quite often, the same rhythm will be repeated with different pitches. In other cases pitch patterns will be repeated and transformed. A good framework for modeling music will take these phenomena into account.

Repetition also appears naturally in other domains. Consider, for example, the task of modeling computer programs. The same identifiers tend to be used again and again within a function. Architectural drawings present another example. The same window design might appear several times within a room, and in many rooms in a building. Text may also contain an element of repetition, with the same names and keywords (such as "repetition") appearing throughout a document.

Existing probabilistic frameworks for modeling sequences of elements, such as hidden Markov models (RJ86), do not take repetition into account. In this paper, we present *repeated observation models (ROMs)*, a probabilistic modeling framework that explicitly allows for repetition. ROMs are not a single model but rather an idea that can be applied to other frameworks in order to yield a new kind of model. We present two instantiations of this idea: the repetition $n$-gram and the repetition HMM. We also present experimental results from a music modeling domain showing the dramatic improvements in predictive power that can be obtained through the use of ROMs.

In the basic ROMs, single elements are repeated one at a time. A more realistic model would allow entire subsequences to be modeled as a whole. We develop an extension of ROMs that allows for repetition of subsequences. Our experimental results show that this extension leads to further improvements in predictive capability.



## Repeated Observation Models

The basic idea of ROMs is simple. Given a generative model $G$ that generates elements of a sequence, we produce a new generative model $G'$ as follows: $G'$ generates elements one by one. As elements are generated, a memory is maintained of how many times each element has appeared. Each time a new element is to be generated, with probability $\rho$ it is generated from memory, and with probability $1-\rho$ it is generated according to the base model $G$. The parameter $\rho$ is called the *memory rate* of the model.

There is one exception to the above generation process. When the very first element of a sequence is to be generated, the memory is empty, so reusing an item from memory is impossible. Therefore the first element of a sequence is generated directly according to $G$.

Let $P^m(o_k \mid o_{1:k-1})$ denote the probability that $o_k$ will be generated from a memory containing $o_{1:k-1}$. This memory model is fixed in advance and not learned. There are a number of ways to implement $P^m$. The simplest approach for generating an element at time $k$ is to choose a time index uniformly from 1 to $k-1$, and to produce the element at that time index. Thus the probability that an element is produced is proportional to the number of times the element appears in the memory. An alternative model would hold that more recent items are more likely to be reproduced than items from the distant past. One way to capture this is with a linear model. When generating element $o_k$, the probability that element $o_j$, where $j<k$, will be chosen is proportional to $a+bj$. Other alternatives such as an exponential model can also be used.

An important issue, whatever memory model is chosen, is its implementation. In a naive implementation, each time we want to compute $P^m(o_k \mid o_{1:k-1})$ we will examine the sequence $o_{1:k-1}$. If we compute $P^m$ for all time points up to time $S$, where $S$ is the length of the sequence, we obtain an

$O(S^2)$ algorithm. A better solution is to precompute $P^m$ for all time points using dynamic programming, obtaining an $O(S)$ algorithm. This can be accomplished for the constant memory model, in which all we need to know is the number of times an element has appeared, not the exact points at which it has appeared. It can also be accomplished easily for the linear model, by storing the total weight associated with each possible element as the sequence is traversed.

It is important to emphasize that the observed variables do indeed need to be observed in a ROM. If the repeating variables are hidden, inference becomes extremely difficult and approximation methods are needed, because one has to sum over all possible values of the repeating elements. Therefore in this paper we assume that the elements of the sequence are always observed, hence the name "repeated observation model". Furthermore, we restrict ourselves to discrete observations. While one could imagine an approximate notion of repetition for continuous elements, exact repetition would be a very rare occurence. We now present two examples of RMs.

## Repetition $n$-grams

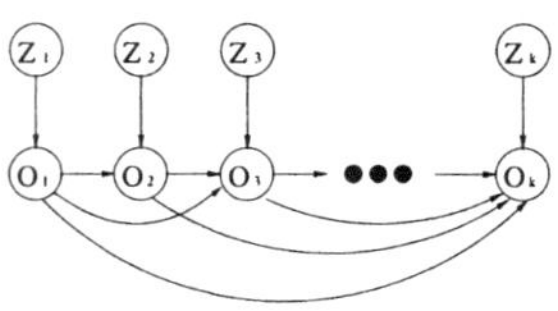

Figure 1: Dependency model for repetition $n$-gram

We begin with repetition $n$-grams. Figure 1 shows the dependency model in the form of a Bayesian network. We see that the $k$-th observation $o_k$ depends on all the previous $k-1$ observations, because of generation from memory. We also introduce a variable $z_k$, which is true if $o_k$ is generated from memory, false if it is generated according to the $n$-gram probabilities. The probability that $z_k$ is true is $\rho$, the memory rate of the model, for all $k > 1$.

In using ROMs, like other probabilistic sequence models, we need a number of algorithms. The most basic algorithm computes the probability of an observation sequence $o_{1:T}$. Let $P^n(o_k \mid o_{k-n+1:k-1})$ denote the $n$-gram probability of $o_k$ given the previous $n-1$ observations. Then for $k > 1$,

$$P(o_k \mid o_{1:k-1}) = \begin{array}{l} \rho P^m(o_k \mid o_{1:k-1}) + \\ (1-\rho) P^n(o_k \mid o_{k-1:k-n+1}) \end{array}$$

$P(o_1)$ is obtained from the unigram model. The probability of an observation sequence is simply the product $\prod_{k=1}^{T} P(o_k \mid o_{1:k-1})$.

The next algorithm computes the most likely assignment to hidden variables given an observation sequence. While $n$-grams do not have hidden variables, repetition $n$-grams do, namely the $z_k$. To find the most likely assignment to the $z_k$, we note from Figure 1 that the $z_k$ are conditionally independent of each other given the observation sequence. Therefore we can choose the most likely value of each $z_k$ independently. To start with, $z_1$ is always false. For $k > 1$, we compute

$$\begin{array}{l} P(z_k = T, o_k \mid o_{1:k-1}) = \rho P^m(o_k \mid o_{1:k-1}), \\ P(z_k = F, o_k \mid o_{1:k-1}) = (1-\rho) P^n(o_k \mid o_{k-1:k-n+1}) \end{array}$$

and choose the $z_k$ that results in higher probability.

Finally, we need an algorithm to learn the values of the parameters from data. In a repetition $n$-gram the parameters are the memory rate $\rho$ and the $n$-gram parameters. A simple version of expectation maximization (EM) (DLR77) will do the trick. In the expectation step, we compute $p_k^i = P(z_k^i = T \mid o_{1:S}^i)$ for each time point $k$ in each training sequence $i$. This is obtained simply by normalizing the results of the above two equations. In the maximization step, we estimate $\rho$ to be the average over all time points $> 1$ in all sequences of $p_k^i$. Meanwhile, the $n$-gram parameters are estimated by counting as usual, except that the $n$-gram ending with $o_k^i$ only contributes a count of $1 - p_k^i$.

## Repetition HMM

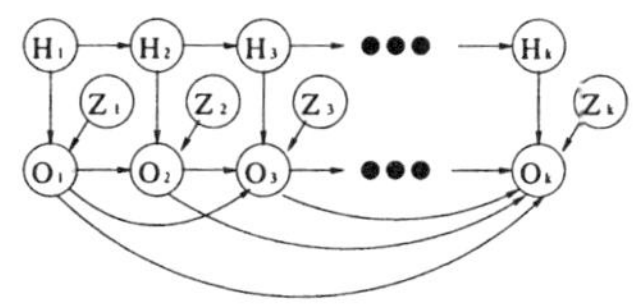

Figure 2: Dependency model for repetition HMM

The repetition HMM is a more powerful model, allowing for a hidden state that varies over time. As in an ordinary HMM, the generative model produces a Markov chain of hidden states, where the initial state is determined by the initial model $P^1(h)$ and the transition probabilities are determined by the transition model $P(h_2 \mid h_1)$. At each point an observation is generated. With probability $\rho$ it is generated from memory, and with probability $1-\rho$ it is generated using the observation model $P(o \mid h)$. The Bayesian network structure for the repetition HMM, shown in Figure 2, appears quite dense. The hidden states $h_k$ form a Markov chain as in ordinary HMMs. Unlike ordinary HMMs, however, each observation depends not only on its hidden state but also on the previous observations. The graph is thus highly multiply connected. However, the graph hides a lot of additional structure in the model in the form of context-specific independence (CSI) (CBK96). CSI is a situation in which two variables are independent of each other given some values of a third variable and not others. In our case, the context variables are the $z_k$. If $z_k$ is true, then $o_k$ depends only on the previous observations and not on its hidden state. If $z_k$ is false, $o_k$ depends only on the hidden state $h_k$. Thus in no circumstances does an observation depend both on the hidden state and its previous observations.

The first algorithm computes the probability of a sequence, and is analogous to the Forward-Backward algorithm for HMMs (RJ86). We present the backward version of the algorithm here. It is similar in principle, but requires some modifications to the HMM algorithm. The algorithm computes $f_k(h_k, z_k) = P(o_{k:S} \mid h_k, z_k, o_{1:k-1})$ at each time step. Note that unlike the HMM algorithm, all previous observations are included as conditioning factors for the future observations. This is because it is no longer the case that future observations are independent of past ones given the hidden state. The computation proceeds separately for the cases $z_k = T$ and $z_k = F$. For $z_k = T$,

$$
\begin{gathered}
f_k(h_k, T) = P(o_{k:S} \mid h_k, z_k = T, o_{1:k-1}) \\
= \\
P(o_k \mid h_k, z_k = T, o_{1:k-1}) P(o_{k+1:S} \mid h_k, z_k = T, o_{1:k}) \\
= \\
\sum_{h_{k+1}, z_{k+1}} \left( \begin{array}{l} P^m(o_k \mid o_{1:k-1}) \times \\ P(h_{k+1} \mid h_k, z_k = T, o_{1:k}) \times \\ P(z_{k+1} \mid h_k, z_k = T, h_{k+1}, o_{1:k}) \times \\ P(o_{k+1:S} \mid h_k, z_k = T, h_{k+1}, z_{k+1}, o_{1:k}) \end{array} \right) \\
= \\
P^m(o_k \mid o_{1:k-1}) \times \\
\sum_{h_{k+1}, z_{k+1}} P(h_{k+1} \mid h_k) P(z_{k+1}) f_{k+1}(h_{k+1}, z_{k+1})
\end{gathered}
$$

For the case where $z_k = F$, we get the similar result of

$$
\begin{array}{l}
f_k(h_k, F) = P(o_k \mid h_k) \times \\
\quad \sum_{h_{k+1}, z_{k+1}} P(h_{k+1} \mid h_k) P(z_{k+1}) f_{k+1}(h_{k+1}, z_{k+1})
\end{array}
$$

These expressions for $f$ form the basis of a dynamic programming algorithm. The interesting point to note is that the second step of the derivation makes use of the CSI properties of the model. This results in two different possible terms at the front of the expression, each of them simple. The dynamic programming algorithm begins by setting $f_S(h_S, T) = P^m(o_S \mid o_{1:S-1})$, and $f_S(h_S, F) = P(o_S \mid h_S)$. In looping backwards, care must be taken at the first time step, in which an element cannot be selected from memory, so $f_1(h_1, T)$ is undefined. Therefore we only compute $f_1(h_1, F)$ at the first time step. We can then return $P(o_{1:S}) = \sum_{h_1} P^1(h_1) f_1(h_1, F)$.

We skip the algorithm for computing the most likely explanation of an observation sequence, which uses similar ideas to the previous algorithm. Instead we move on to the algorithm for learning the parameters of a repetition HMM from data. As for repetition $n$-grams, this algorithm is a variant of EM, and follows along similar lines to the Baum-Welch algorithm. As always, the algorithm iterates between an Expectation step, in which it computes the values of expected sufficient statistics, and a Maximization step in which it reoptimizes the parameters of the model. The expected statistics to be computed are as follows:

$$
\begin{array}{l}
E[N_h] = \sum_{i=1}^{M} \sum_{k=1}^{S^i} P(h_k^i = h \mid o_{1:S^i}^i) \\
E[N_{h_1 h_2}] = \sum_{i=1}^{M} \sum_{k=2}^{S^i} P(h_{k-1}^i = h_1, h_k^i = h_2 \mid o_{1:S^i}^i) \\
E[N_h^F] = \sum_{i=1}^{M} \sum_{k=1}^{S^i} P(h_k^i = h, z_k^i = F \mid o_{1:S^i}^i) \\
E[N_{ho}^F] = \sum_{i=1}^{M} \sum_{k=1}^{S^i} P(h_k^i = h, o_k^i = o, z_k^i = F \mid o_{1:S^i}^i) \\
E[N_z] = \sum_{i=1}^{M} \sum_{k=2}^{S^i} P(z_k^i = z \mid o_{1:S^i}^i) \\
E[N_h^1] = \sum_{i=1}^{M} P(h_1^i = h \mid o_{1:S^i}^i)
\end{array}
$$

Note that instead of computing the number of times observation $o$ appears in hidden state $h$, we compute the number of times that it does so when the generation is not from memory. It is only when the generation is not from memory that we can learn from the coappearance of $h$ and $o$. Once we have estimated these statistics, the maximization step is as one would expect. The only thing to note is that when computing $\rho$, we only consider time points after the first, so the denominator uses $S^i - 1$:

$$
\begin{array}{ll}
P(h_2 \mid h_1) = \frac{E[N_{h_1 h_2}]}{E[N_{h_1}]} & P(o \mid h) = \frac{E[N_{ho}^F]}{E[N_h^F]} \\
P^1(h) = \frac{E[N_h^1]}{M} & \rho = \frac{E[N_T]}{\sum_{i=1}^{M} (S^i - 1)}
\end{array}
$$

It remains to explain how to compute the expected sufficient statistics. Here, like Baum-Welch, we use our version of the backwards algorithm as a subroutine to compute $f_k(h_k, z_k)$ for all time points, ending with the first. We can then iterate forwards to compute the probabilities needed. The iteration forwards computes $P(h_k \mid o_{1:S})$ at each time step. The computation uses the fact that

$$
P(h_{k-1}, h_k, z_k \mid o_{1:S}) = \frac{1}{Z} \begin{array}{l} P(h_{k-1} \mid o_{1:S}) P(h_k \mid h_{k-1}) \\ P(z_k) f_k(h_k, z_k) \end{array}
$$

where $Z$ is a normalizing factor. Once we have computed the joint probability of $h_{k-1}$, $h_k$ and $z_k$, using previously computed terms, we can use marginalization to obtain the probabilities we need for learning.

## Repeating Subsequences

Up to this point, we have considered models of repetition in which single elements are retrieved from memory and reused, one at a time. An alternative model is to have subsequences of elements retrieved from memory and reused in their entirety. This may be a more realistic model for applications. In music, for example, it is quite natural to repeat a four-measure unit, rather than repeat each individual measure separately.

In order to model repetition of subsequences, we introduce two hidden variables. $z_k$ indicates the number of remaining elements of a subsequence to be copied at point $k$. In particular, if $z_k$ is non-zero, $o_k$ is generated from memory, whereas if $z_k$ is zero, $o_k$ is generated according to the underlying model. $w_k$ indicates the position in the sequence from which $o_k$ is derived, if $o_k$ is generated from memory. For example, if $o_k$ is 2 and $w_k$ is 8, $o_k = o_8$ and $o_{k+1} = o_9$. When $z_k = 0$, $w_k$ is immaterial; by convention, it is set to 0.

The dynamic model of $z$ and $w$ is simple. If $z_k > 1$, then deterministically $z_{k+1} = z_k - 1$ and $w_{k+1} = w_k + 1$. If on the other hand $z_k = 1$ or 0, we must make a new decision at time point $k+1$ as to whether $o_k$ is generated from memory, and if so, how long a subsequence is copied. This is achieved by selecting $z_{k+1}$ at random from a multinomial distribution over 0 and possible subsequence lengths. The probability of selecting a particular $z_{k+1}$ will be denoted $\rho(z_{k+1})$, extending the notation from before. If $z_{k+1}$ is non-zero, $w_{k+1}$ is drawn uniformly from the integers 1 to $k$.

An interesting point to note is that the sequence being repeated can overlap with the sequence being generated. For example, if $z_{k+1}$ is chosen to be 2, while $w_{k+1}$ is $k$, then the sequence of length 2 beginning at $k$ is repeated beginning at point $k+1$, with an overlap at point $k+1$. The net result in this situation is that $o_{k+1}$ will be equal to $o_k$, while $o_{k+2}$ will be equal to $o_{k+1}$ and therefore also to $o_k$. This is a useful feature. Situations where the same small group repeats itself several times in succession are quite common. It is advantageous to model them with a single long repetition with high explanatory power, rather than with several shorter repetitions.

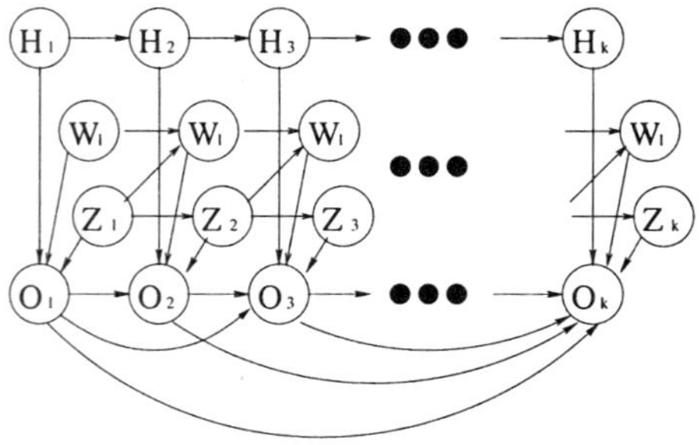


Figure 3: Dependency model for subsequence HMM

We explain the technical details of subsequence repetition models using HMMs as the underlying model. The Bayesian network structure for this model is shown in Figure 3. As before, there is a good deal of structure that is not shown in the figure. $z_k$ and $w_k$ act together as a multiplexer, so that when they are known, $o_k$ either depends on $h_k$ or is equal to a *single* previous observation. Furthermore, $w_{k+1}$ only depends on $w_k$ when $z_k > 1$, in which case $w_k$ deterministically sets $w_{k+1}$, while $z_k$ deterministically sets $Z_{k+1}$. Meanwhile, if $z_k$ is 0 or 1, we do not care which as far as $w_{k+1}$ and $z_{k+1}$ are concerned.

One approach to reasoning with this model is to create a hidden state that consists of $h_k, z_k, w_k$. In a backward pass, we would compute $f(h_k, z_k, w_k) = P(o_{k:S} \mid h_k, z_k, w_k)$. This would be computed by summing over all possible $h_{k+1}, z_{k+1}, w_{k+1}$, using the probability of transitioning from $h_k, z_k, w_k$ to $h_{k+1}, z_{k+1}, w_{k+1}$. A subsequent forward pass would proceed similarly, computing $P(h_k, z_k, w_k \mid o_{1:S})$ at each point.

The problem with this approach is that in both the backward and forward passes, the cost for each time step is quadratic in the number of hidden states. If we let $L$ denote the maximum allowed repetition length, $H$ the number of hidden states of the underlying HMM, and $S$ the length of the sequence, which determines the range of $w_k$, the total cost over all $S$ steps of the sequence is $O(H^2L^2S^3)$. Since $S$ is often quite large, this is unacceptable.

We address this issue using two optimizations. The first is to notice that $f$ and $P$ are quite sparse. In order for $f(h_k, z_k, w_k)$ to be positive, when $z_k > 0$, it must be the case that $o_{w_k} = o_k$. It must further be the case that there is a subsequence of length $z_k$ beginning at $w_k$ that matches a corresponding sequence beginning at $k$. We therefore precompute, for each point in the sequence, all values of $z_k$ and $w_k$ that have these properties. These values are stored in a set $\mathbf{R}_k$. Let $B$ be the maximum number of values in any $\mathbf{R}_k$. It will usually be the case that $B$ is a lot smaller than $LS$, and the inference will cost $O(H^2B^2S)$, which is much better.

The second optimization comes from the observation that we do not need to consider all possible transitions from $h_k, z_k, w_k$ to $h_{k+1}, z_{k+1}, w_{k+1}$, since many of them are impossible. In combination with the CSI noted above, this leads to a more efficient computation in both the backward and forward passes. We begin by breaking up the computation of $f$ into cases, depending on the value of $z_k$.

$$f_k(h_k,0,0) = P(o_k \mid h_k) \textstyle\sum_{h_{k+1}} \sum_{z_{k+1},w_{k+1} \in \mathbf{R}_{k+1}} \\ P(h_{k+1} \mid h_k)\rho(z_{k+1})P(w_{k+1} \mid z_{k+1})f_{k+1}(h_{k+1}, z_{k+1}, w_{k+1})$$

Here $P(w_{k+1} \mid z_{k+1})$ is $1/k$ if $z_{k+1} > 0$, otherwise it assigns probability 1 to $w_{k+1} = 0$. Meanwhile, when $z_k = 1$, and $z_k, w_k \in \mathbf{R}_k$, we get the same expression, except that we no longer need $P(o_k \mid h_k)$:

$$f_k(h_k,1,w_k) = \textstyle\sum_{h_{k+1}} \sum_{z_{k+1},w_{k+1} \in \mathbf{R}_{k+1}} \\ P(h_{k+1} \mid h_k)\rho(z_{k+1})P(w_{k+1} \mid z_{k+1})f_{k+1}(h_{k+1}, z_{k+1}, w_{k+1})$$

Finally, when $z_k > 1$ and $z_k, w_k \in \mathbf{R}_k$, we do not need to sum over $z_{k+1}$ and $w_{k+1}$, and we do not need to include $\rho(z_{k+1})$ or $P(w_{k+1} \mid z_{k+1})$ since $z_{k+1}$ and $w_{k+1}$ are fully determined. We get

$$f_k(h_k, z_k, w_k) = \sum_{h_{k+1}} P(h_{k+1} \mid h_k) f_{k+1}(h_{k+1}, z_k - 1, w_k + 1)$$

Now we can unroll the computation of $f_k$ into two separate loops, each costing $O(H^2B)$.

Forall $h_k$
  total1 = 0
  Forall $h_{k+1}$
    Forall $z_{k+1}, w_{k+1} \in \mathbf{R}_{k+1}$
      total1 $+=$ $P(h_{k+1} \mid h_k)\rho(z_{k+1})P(w_{k+1} \mid z_{k+1})$
        $f_{k+1}(h_{k+1}, z_{k+1}, w_{k+1})$
  $f(h_k, 0, 0) = P(o_k \mid h_k) *$ total1
  Forall $1, w_k \in \mathbf{R}_k$
    $f(h_k, 1, w_k) =$ total1
Forall $h_k$
  Forall $z_k, w_k \in \mathbf{R}_k$ where $z_k > 1$
    total2 = 0
    Forall $h_{k+1}$
      total2 $+=$ $P(h_{k+1} \mid h_k) f_{k+1}(h_{k+1}, z_k - 1, w_k + 1)$
    $f(h_k, z_k, w_k) =$ total2

Similar techniques can be applied to the forward pass, to reduce the cost of computing $P(H_k, W_k, Z_k \mid o_{1:S})$ to $O(H^2B)$ at each time point. Thus the total cost of inference is $O(H^2BS)$. It should be pointed out that despite the optimizations, there is an extra factor of $B$ compared to ordinary HMMs. Even though $B$ is much smaller than $LS$, it may still be reasonably large, making inference with subsequence HMMs considerably slower than for ordinary HMMs or repetition HMMs.

## Results

The models and algorithms in this paper were tested on a musical corpus. The corpus consisted of minuets and trios from Mozart's mature string quartets. Each piece was segmented into measures, and the rhythm of the first violin part was recorded for each measure. Thus the time points were measures, and the observations were the rhythm patterns of each measure. The rhythm of a measure was represented as a sequence of durations. Since the smallest rhythmic value appearing in the corpus was a thirty-second note, durations were represented as multiples of thirty-second note values. For example, in a measure consisting of two quarter notes followed by two eight notes, the observation was the sequence 8 8 4 4. There were twenty sequences in the corpus, ranging in length from 25 to 93 measures.

Each of the experiments described here used twenty-fold cross-validation. In each experiment the model was trained on nineteen of the sequences, and the perplexity of the remaining sequence was measured. The perplexity of a sequence under a model is $2^p$, where $p$ is the mean negative log probability, according to the model, of each observation in the sequence. Intuitively, the perplexity is the number of elements from which each observation is chosen. A lower perplexity corresponds to better predictive power of the model. In each of the following results, the geometric mean of the perplexities for the twenty sequences is reported.

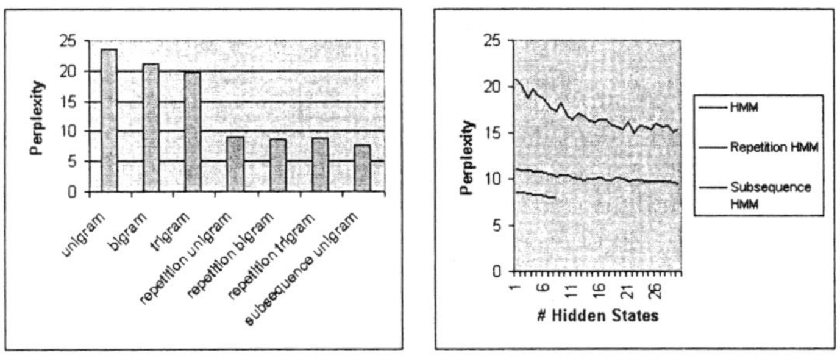


Figure 4: (a) N-gram results (b) HMM results

Figure 4(a) shows the results for the different kinds of $n$-gram. First, for the ordinary $n$-gram, we see slight improvement from unigrams to bigrams to trigrams. This indicates that the preceding two observations are not particularly useful elements for predicting the next observation. When we turn to repetition $n$-grams there is a dramatic improvement, going from 19.84 for the trigram to 9 for the repetition unigram. However there is almost no improvement from the repetition unigram to the repetition bigram and trigram. This suggests that for ordinary $n$-grams, all the structure captured by bigrams and trigrams related to immediate repetition of elements. Since this structure is already captured by the repetition unigram, there is nothing left for the repetition bigram and trigram to capture.

When we move on to subsequence repetition, there is an improvement over the basic ROMs, from 9 to 7.62. However, the worst perplexity among the twenty runs for both models was about the same. It appears that in this corpus, modeling repeating subsequences is a useful idea, but it only produces benefits in some sequences.

The results for HMMs, shown in Figure 4(b), are similar. There is a dramatic improvement for the repetition HMM over the ordinary HMM, and the performance of the subsequence HMM is even better. While adding hidden states helps the ordinary HMM, we find only a slight improvement from increasing the number of hidden states for the repetition HMM. This suggests, again, that the hidden state in the ordinary HMM was being used to capture repetitions. Despite the optimizations described in the previous section, the subsequence repetition HMM took significantly longer to run than the other methods, so a smaller number of experiments were performed. Without the optimizations, however, the method would have been completely infeasible.

Finally, we investigated whether the model by which elements are retrieved from memory makes a difference. All previous results used a model in which elements were selected uniformly. We also tried models in which recent items were more likely to be selected, using the linear model. The results are almost exactly the same as for the uniform model. This shows that, at least in this domain, there is no support for the hypothesis that recent elements are more likely to be repeated.

## Related Work

ROMs bear a superficial resemblance to the Chinese Restaurant Process (CRP), recently applied to learning topic hierarchies (BGJT03). The CRP models a process in which a stream of diners arrives at a restaurant. When a new diner arrives, with some probability she will be seated at an already occupied table, otherwise she will sit at an unoccupied table. The result of this process is a distribution over partitions of integers.

There are a number of fundamental differences between the CRP and ROMs. First, the CRP is not associated with time series. Second, the CRP provides a static probability distribution over partitions. It characterizes how entities are likely to be clumped, but does not attempt to model the entities themselves and how they are generated. Third, the CRP is a self-contained model, while the ROM is an idea that can be attached to existing temporal models.

There have been many extensions to HMMs allowing elements to depend on previous elements.. For example Hierarchical HMMs (FST98) model domains with hierarchical structure and allow dependencies at multiple time scales. Mixed-memory Markov models (SJ99) allow an observation to depend on a number of previous observations. None of the previous extensions of HMMs handle repetition in the manner described in this paper.

Compression algorithms do take advantage of repeated elements in the data. Sequitur (NMW97), for example, is an algorithm that discovers hierarchical structure in sequences by identifying repeated elements. However, compression algorithms are designed to find structure in existing sequences. ROMs, in contrast, are generative models that are able to predict unseen sequences. They make it possible to exploit repetition within the framework of temporal prediction models.

Several authors have applied temporal probabilistic models to problems in music. Cemgil and Kappen (CK03) and Raphael (Rap02) have both applied graphical models to the problems of tempo induction and rhythmic parsing. Vitaniemi et al. (VKE03) have applied a simple probabilistic model of pitch to automated transcription of music. Raphael and Stoddard (RS03) and Sheh and Ellis (SE03) recently applied HMMs to harmonic analysis. Kapanci and Pfeffer (KP03) used HMMs modified to incorporate musical knowledge to model musical rhythm. None of these authors modeled reoccurence of elements, and all of these applications could benefit from ROMs.

## Conclusion and Future Work

Repetition is an important feature of many domains. By making it explicit, repeated observation models are able to achieve greater accuracy when predicting the next element of a sequence, in a domain with repetition. We have shown how to incorporate repetition into $n$-grams and HMMs, and demonstrated that the improvement in prediction can be dramatic. We have also described how to model repeating subsequences, and shown how doing so can lead to further improvements.

Once we consider explicit models of repetition, a variety of extensions come to mind. One possibility is a repetition grammar. Here repetition would be possible at every level of the hierarchy. Whenever we want to expand a non-terminal, we might choose a subtree that has previously appeared for that non-terminal. A repetition grammar would be useful, for example, in modeling computer programs. Another possible extension is a two-dimensional repetition model. Here one would define the memory at a point to be the subset of the plane that is below and to the left of the point.

A deeper and more ambitious extension is to recognize that in many cases elements are not repeated exactly, but are varied and transformed. This extension would require a probabilistic model of the transformation process. Once we have integrated transformations into ROMs, we will be able to perform a deep parsing of sequences such as melodies, to determine not only their hierarchical structure, but how each element is derived from previous elements.

## References


D.M. Blei, T.L. Griffiths, M.I. Jordan, and J.B. Tenenbaum. Hierarchical topic models and the nested Chinese restaurant process. In *Advances in Neural Information Processing Systems 16*, 2003.

M. Goldszmidt C. Boutilier, N. Friedman and D. Koller. Context-specific independence in Bayesian networks. In *Proceedings of the Conference on Uncertainty in Artificial Intelligence (UAI)*, 1996.

A.T. Cemgil and B. Kappen. Monte Carlo methods for tempo tracking and rhythm quantization. *Journal of Artificial Intelligence Research*, 18:45–81, 2003.

A. Dempster, N. Laird, and D. Rubin. Maximum likelihood from incomplete data via the EM algorithm. *Journal of the Royal Statistical Society B*, 39(1), 1977.

Shai Fine, Yoram Singer, and Naftali Tishby. The hierarchical Hidden Markov Model: Analysis and applications. *Machine Learning*, 32, 1998.

E. Kapanci and A. Pfeffer. Learning style-specific rhythmic structures. In *International Computer Music Conference*, 2003.

C.G. Nevill-Manning and I.H. Witten. Identifying hierarchical structure in sequences: A linear-time algorithm. *Journal of Artificial Intelligence Research*, 7:67–82, 1997.

C. Raphael. A hybrid graphical model for rhythmic parsing. *Artificial Intelligence*, 137(1–2):217–238, 2002.

L. Rabiner and B. Juang. An introduction to hidden markov models. *IEEE Acoustics, Speech and Signal Processing Magazine*, 3:4–16, 1986.

C. Raphael and J. Stoddard. Harmonic analysis with probabilistic graphical models. In *Fourth International Conference on Music Information Retrieval*, 2003.

A. Sheh and D.P.W. Ellis. Chord segmentation and recognition using EM-trained hidden Markov models. In *Fourth International Conference on Music Information Retrieval*, 2003.

Larry Saul and Michael Jordan. Mixed memory Markov models: Decomposing complex stochastic processes as mixture of simpler ones. *Machine Learning*, 37(1):75–87, 1999.

T. Viitaniemi, A. Klapuri, and A. Eronen. A probabilistic model for the transcription of single-voice melodies. In *Finnish Signal Processing Symposium*, 2003.

# Encoding Probabilistic Causal Model in Probabilistic Action Language

**Nam Tran** and **Chitta Baral**
Department of Computer Science and Engineering
Arizona State University, Tempe, AZ 85281
{chitta,namtran}@asu.edu

**Abstract**

Pearl's probabilistic causal model has been used in many domains to reason about causality. Pearl's treatment of actions is very different from the way actions are represented explicitly in action languages. In this paper we show how to encode Pearl's probabilistic causal model in the action language PAL thus relating this two distinct approaches to reasoning about actions.

## Introduction and motivation

Normally an action when executed in a world changes the state of the world. Reasoning about actions is important in several 'intelligent' tasks such as planning, hypothetical reasoning, control generation and verification (for dynamical systems), and diagnosis. Often the effect of an action on the world is not deterministic but rather has an uncertainty associated with it. In recent years there have been several approaches to represent and reason with such actions. The first type of approaches include probabilistic generalization of formalisms for reasoning about actions; for example, planning (Kushmerick, Hanks, & Weld 1995; Littman 1997), situation calculus (Bacchus, Halpern, & Levesque 1999; Poole 1998; Reiter 2001; Mateus, Pacheco, & Pinto 2002), and action languages (Baral, Tran, & Le 2002; Eiter & Lukasiewicz 2003). The second type of approaches are based on frameworks of reasoning under uncertainty such as independence choice logic (Poole 1997; 1998) and probabilistic causal model (Pearl 1995; 1999; 2000).

In all these proposals, except in Pearl (1999; 2000), actions are explicitly defined (with names) and their effects on the world are described by various means. In Pearl (1999; 2000) the dynamics of the world is described through relationships between variables (which denote properties of objects in the world) that are expressed through functional relationships between them. Furthermore, probabilities are associated with a subset of variables called background (or exogenous) variables. Together they are referred to as *probabilistic causal models* (PCMs). The effect of actions are then formulated as "local surgery"on these models (Pearl 1995).



In this paper our goal is to study the relationship between reasoning about actions in PCMs and similar reasoning in the action description language PAL (Baral, Tran, & Le 2002) as a representative of the approaches where actions are named and have effects associated with it. The motivation behind studying this relationship is to objectively compare the expressiveness of these two formalisms vis-a-vis each other. We select PCM to study as it is the most successful representative of causal reasoning formalisms (Pearl 2000). We pick PAL as a representative of the high level action description languages (Gelfond & Lifschitz 1993; McCain & Turner 1995; Gelfond & Lifschitz 1998), for this is the most similar to PCM in the way it handles uncertainty among the action languages that have actions named distinctly. Moreover, PAL is inspired by PCM [1], so it is natural to question how they relate to each other. In fact, the formal analysis of this relation has provided us a better understanding of the two frameworks in term of their advantages and limitations.

The rest of this paper is organized as follows. First, we briefly recall the language PAL and PCM. We present an encoding of PCM in PAL together with a correctness result. We also provide the intuition of the encoding as well as of the result and its proof through a detailed example. Finally, we conclude with discussion on related and future works.

## The language PAL: a brief overview

The alphabet of the language PAL (Baral, Tran, & Le 2002) consists of four non-empty disjoint sets $\mathbf{F}$, $\mathbf{U}_I$, $\mathbf{U}_N$, $\mathbf{A}$. The sets respectively contain fluents, *inertial* unknown variables, *non-inertial* unknown variables and actions. Intuitively, both fluents and unknown variables encode properties of the world. An action can have effects on the former but not on the latter. Moreover, inertial variables are unchanged through courses of actions. Unknown variables are assumed to be independent of each other. A *fluent literal* is a fluent or a fluent preceded by $\neg$. An unknown variable literal is an unknown variable or an unknown variable preceded by $\neg$. A *literal* is either a fluent literal or an unknown variable literal. A *formula* is a propositional formula constructed from

[1]Since the proposal of PAL in Baral, Tran, & Le (2002), other action languages have also been extended to allow actions with probabilistic effects; for example see Eiter & Lukasiewicz (2003).

literals.

A state s is an interpretation of fluents and unknown variables that satisfy certain conditions (to be mentioned while discussing semantics). For a state s, the sub-interpretations of s restricted to fluents, inertial unknown variables, and non-inertial unknown variables are denoted by $s_F$, $s_I$, and $s_N$ respectively.

In the following we briefly review the components of PAL.

**The domain description language:** A *domain description* is a collection of propositions of the forms:

$$a \textbf{ causes } \psi \textbf{ if } \varphi \quad (1)$$
$$\theta \textbf{ causes } \psi \quad (2)$$
$$\textbf{impossible } a \textbf{ if } \varphi \quad (3)$$

where $a$ is an action, $\psi$ is a *fluent* formula, $\theta$ is a formula of fluents and *inertial* unknown variables, and $\varphi$ is a formula of fluents and *unknown* variables. Propositions of the form (1), called *dynamic causal laws*, describe the direct effects of actions. Propositions of the form (2), called *static causal laws*, describe causal relations between fluents and unknown variables. Propositions of the form (3), called *executability conditions*, state when actions are not executable.

The semantics of domain descriptions is defined based on transition functions. In the following, let $\mathcal{D}$ be a domain description in the language PAL.

An *interpretation* $I$ of the fluents and unknown variables in $\mathcal{D}$ is a maximal consistent set of literals of $\mathcal{D}$. A literal $l$ is said to be true (resp. false) in $I$ iff $l \in I$ (resp. $\neg l \in I$). The truth value of a formula in $I$ is defined recursively over the propositional connective in the usual way. For example, $f \wedge g$ is true in $I$ iff $f$ is true in $I$ and $g$ is true in $I$. The formula $\psi$ is said to hold in $I$ (or $I$ satisfies $\psi$), denoted by $I \models \psi$, if $\psi$ is true in $I$.

A set of formulas from $\mathcal{D}$ is *logically closed* if it is closed under propositional logic (w.r.t. $\mathcal{D}$). Let $V$ be a set of formulas and $K$ be a set of static causal laws of the form $\theta$ **causes** $\psi$. $V$ is said to be closed under $K$ if for every rule $\theta$ **causes** $\psi$ in $K$, if $\theta$ belongs to $V$ then so does $\psi$. $Cn_K(V)$ denotes the least logically closed set of formulas from $\mathcal{D}$ that contains $V$ and is also closed under $K$. A *state* s of $\mathcal{D}$ is an interpretation that is closed under the set of static causal laws of $\mathcal{D}$.

An action $a$ is *prohibited (not executable)* in a state s if there exists in $\mathcal{D}$ an executability condition of the form **impossible** $a$ **if** $\varphi$ such that $\varphi$ holds in s. The *effect of an action a* in a state s is the set of formulas:

$$E_a(\mathsf{s}) = \{\psi \mid \exists r \in \mathcal{D} : r = a \textbf{ causes } \psi \textbf{ if } \varphi\ ,\ \mathsf{s} \models \varphi\}.$$

Let $\mathcal{S}$ be the set of the states of $\mathcal{D}$. A *transition function* $\Phi$ is a function from $\mathcal{A} \times \mathcal{S}$ to $2^{\mathcal{S}}$. If $a$ is prohibited in s, then $\Phi(a, \mathsf{s}) = \emptyset$; otherwise we have that

$$\Phi(a, \mathsf{s}) = \{\ \mathsf{s}' \mid \mathsf{s}'_{F,I} = Cn_R((\mathsf{s}_{F,I} \cap \mathsf{s}'_{F,I}) \cup E_a(\mathsf{s}))\}$$

where $R$ is the set of the static causal laws of $\mathcal{D}$.

An extended transition function $\hat{\Phi}$ expresses the state transition due to a sequence of actions, which is defined as

$$\hat{\Phi}([a], \mathsf{s}) = \Phi(a, \mathsf{s});$$
$$\hat{\Phi}([a_1, \ldots, a_n], \mathsf{s}) = \bigcup_{\mathsf{s}' \in \hat{\Phi}(a_1, \mathsf{s})} \hat{\Phi}([a_2, \ldots, a_n], \mathsf{s}').$$

Let s be a state in a domain description $\mathcal{D}$. Then s *entails* $\varphi$ **after** $a_1, \ldots, a_n$ , written as $\mathsf{s} \models \varphi$ **after** $a_1, \ldots, a_n$ , if $\varphi$ is true in all states in $\hat{\Phi}([a_1, \ldots, a_n], \mathsf{s})$.

**Probabilities of unknown variables:** A probability description $\mathcal{P}$ of the unknown variables is a collection of propositions of the form

$$\textbf{probability of } u \textbf{ is } p\ ;$$

where $u$ is an unknown variable, and $p \in [0, 1]$. Each proposition above directly gives us the probability distribution of the corresponding unknown variable as: $P(u) = p$.

For any state s, $\mathsf{s}_u$ denotes the interpretation of the unknown variables of s, that is, $\mathsf{s}_u = \mathsf{s}_I \cup \mathsf{s}_N$. The unconditional probability of the various states is defined as:

$$P(\mathsf{s}) = \frac{P(\mathsf{s}_u)}{|\{\mathsf{s}' | \mathsf{s}'_u = \mathsf{s}_u)\}|}$$

**Example 1** Let us consider a domain of coin tossing, in which the coin can be fair or fake with some probability $p$. If it is a fair coin, then it will land head with probability $q_1$. If it is fake, it lands head with probability $q_2$. The PAL domain has an inertial unknown variable $u$ describing the coin's fairness and two non-inertial variables $v_1$, $v_2$ describing the landing head of different coin types:

$$\textbf{probability of } u \textbf{ is } p$$
$$\textbf{probability of } v_1 \textbf{ is } q_1$$
$$\textbf{probability of } v_2 \textbf{ is } q_2$$

Besides, the domain has a fluent *head* describing the outcome of action *toss*. We have that:

$$toss \textbf{ causes } head \textbf{ if } u, v_1$$
$$toss \textbf{ causes } \neg head \textbf{ if } u, \neg v_1$$
$$toss \textbf{ causes } head \textbf{ if } \neg u, v_2$$
$$toss \textbf{ causes } \neg head \textbf{ if } \neg u, \neg v_2$$

**The query language**: Let $\varphi$ be a formula of fluents and unknown variables, $a_i$'s be actions, and $p \in [0, 1]$. A query has the following form:

$$\textbf{probability of } [\varphi \textbf{ after } a_1, \ldots, a_n] \textbf{ is } p\ .$$

The entailment of queries is defined in several steps. First, we define the transitional probability between states:

$$P_{[a]}(\mathsf{s}'|\mathsf{s}) = P_a(\mathsf{s}'|\mathsf{s}) = \begin{cases} \frac{2^{|U_N|}}{|\Phi(a,\mathsf{s})|} P(\mathsf{s}'_N) \text{ if } \mathsf{s}' \in \Phi(a, \mathsf{s}) \\ 0, \text{ otherwise.} \end{cases}$$

The (probabilistic) correctness of a single action plan given an initial state state s is defined as follows.

$$P(\varphi \textbf{ after } a|\mathsf{s}) = \sum_{\mathsf{s}' \in \Phi(a,\mathsf{s}) \wedge \mathsf{s}' \models \varphi} P_a(\mathsf{s}'|\mathsf{s})$$

Next, the transitional probability due to a sequence of actions, is recursively defined starting with the base case.

$$P_{[\,]}(\mathsf{s}'|\mathsf{s}) = \begin{cases} 1 \text{ if } \mathsf{s} = \mathsf{s}' \\ 0, \text{ otherwise.} \end{cases}$$

$$P_{[a_1,\dots a_n]}(\mathsf{s}'|\mathsf{s}) = \sum_{\mathsf{s}''} P_{[a_1,\dots,a_{n-1}]}(\mathsf{s}''|\mathsf{s}) P_{a_n}(\mathsf{s}'|\mathsf{s}'')$$

Finally, we define the (probabilistic) correctness of a (multi-action) plan given an initial state s:

$$P(\varphi \textbf{ after } \alpha|\mathsf{s}) = \sum_{\mathsf{s}' \in \hat{\Phi}([\alpha],\mathsf{s}) \wedge \mathsf{s}' \models \varphi} P_{[\alpha]}(\mathsf{s}'|\mathsf{s}) \quad (4)$$

**The observation language:** An observation description $\mathcal{O}$ is a collection of proposition of the form

$$\psi \textbf{ obs\_after } a_1, \dots a_n \ ;$$

where $\psi$ is a fluent formula, and $a_1, \dots, a_n$ are actions. When $n = 0$, it is simply written as **initially** $\psi$. The probability $P(\varphi$ **obs_after** $\alpha|\mathsf{s})$ is computed by the right hand side of (4).

Using the Bayes' rule, the conditional probability of a state given some observations is given as follows.

$$P(\mathsf{s}_i|\mathcal{O}) = \begin{cases} \frac{P(\mathcal{O}|\mathsf{s}_i)P(\mathsf{s}_i)}{\sum_{\mathsf{s}_j} P(\mathcal{O}|\mathsf{s}_j)P(\mathsf{s}_j)} \text{ if } \sum_{\mathsf{s}_j} P(\mathcal{O}|\mathsf{s}_j)P(\mathsf{s}_j) \neq 0 \\ 0, \text{ otherwise .} \end{cases}$$

The (probabilistic) correctness of a (multi-action) plan given only some observations is defined by

$$P(\varphi \textbf{ after } \alpha|\mathcal{O}) = \sum_{\mathsf{s}} P(\mathsf{s}|\mathcal{O}) \times P(\varphi \textbf{ after } \alpha|\mathsf{s}) \quad (5)$$

An action theory $\mathcal{T}$ in PAL consists of a domain description $\mathcal{D}$, a probability description $\mathcal{P}$ of the unknown variables, and an observation description $\mathcal{O}$: $\mathcal{T} = \mathcal{D} \cup \mathcal{P} \cup \mathcal{O}$.
Let $Q$ be a query:

$$Q = \textbf{probability of } [\varphi \textbf{ after } a_1, \dots, a_n] \textbf{ is } p \ .$$

Then $\mathcal{T}$ entails $Q$, written as $\mathcal{T} \models_A Q$, if and only if $P(\varphi \textbf{ after } a_1, \dots, a_n|\mathcal{O}) = p$. The entailment can be written in the shorter form as

$$\mathcal{T} \models_A P(\varphi \textbf{ after } a_1, \dots, a_n|\mathcal{O}) = p \ .$$

In the next section, we briefly review PCM (Pearl 2000).

## Probabilistic causal models

**Causal model:** A *causal model* is a triple $M = \langle U, V, F \rangle$ where

* $U$ is a set of *background* variables, (also called *exogenous*), that are determined by factors outside the model;
* $V$ is a set $\{V_1, V_2, \dots V_n\}$ of variables, called *endogenous*, that are determined by variables in the model - that is, variables in $U \cup V$; and
* $F$ is a set of functions $\{f_1, f_2, \dots f_n\}$, such that each $f_i$ is a mapping from $U \cup (V \setminus V_i)$ to $V_i$, and such that the entire set $F$ forms a mapping from $U$ to $V$. In other words, each $f_i$ tells us the value of $V_i$ given the values of all other variables in $U \cup V$, and the entire set $F$ has a unique solution for $V$, given a realization of $U$. Symbolically, the set of equations $F$ can be represented by writing

  $$V_i = f_i(PA_i, U_i) \ i = 1, \dots, n$$

  where $PA_i$ is a subset of variables in $V \setminus V_i$ and $U_i$ stands for a subset of variables in $U$.

**Example 2** We have a simple causal model consisting of a background variable $U$, endogenous variables $A$ and $B$, and the set of the following functions:

$$A = U \wedge B;$$
$$B = U \vee A.$$

For each value of $U$, there is a unique solution $A, B$. That is, if $U = 1$, then $A = B = 1$; otherwise $A = B = 0$. □

**Submodel:** Let $M$ be a causal model, $X$ be a set of variables in $V$, and $x$ be a particular realization of $X$. A *submodel* $M_x$ of $M$ is the causal model $M_x = \langle U, V, F_x \rangle$ where $F_x = \{f_i : V_i \notin X\} \cup \{X = x\}$.

Submodels are useful for representing the effect of local actions and hypothetical changes. $M_x$ represents the model that results from a minimal change to make $X = x$ hold true under any realization of $U$.

**Probabilistic causal model:** A *probabilistic causal* model (PCM) is a pair $\langle M, P \rangle$ where $M$ is a causal model and $P$ is a probability distribution over the domain of $U$.

Note that because the set of functional equations forms a mapping from $U$ to $V$, the probability distribution $P$ also induces a probability distribution over the endogenous variables. Hence, given any subsets $X$ and $E$ of $U \cup V$, the conditional probability $P(x|e) = P(X = x|E = e)$ is well-defined in the model $\langle M, P \rangle$.

**Probabilistic queries and their entailment in PCM**

* Given a PCM $\mathcal{M} = \langle M, P \rangle$, the probability of $x$ given an observation $e$ is the conditional probability $P(x|e)$. If $P(x|e) = p$, we write $\mathcal{M} \models_C P(x|e) = p$.
* Given a PCM $\mathcal{M} = \langle M, P \rangle$, the probability of $x$ given an intervention $do(y)$, denoted by $P(x|do(y))$, is the probability of $x$ computed w.r.t the submodel $\mathcal{M}_y = \langle M_y, P \rangle$. If $P(x|do(y)) = p$, we write $\mathcal{M} \models_C P(x|do(y)) = p$.
* Given a PCM $\mathcal{M} = \langle M, P \rangle$, the probability of $x$ given observation $e$ and intervention $do(y)$, denoted by $P(x|e, do(y))$, is the probability $P(x|do(y))$ that is computed w.r.t the modified causal model $\mathcal{M}' = \langle M_y, P_e \rangle$. Here, $P_e$ is the conditional probability $P(\_|e)$ computed w.r.t the model $\mathcal{M} = \langle M, P \rangle$. If $P(x|e, do(y)) = p$ we write $\mathcal{M} \models_C P(x|e, do(y)) = p$.

From the above definition it follows that $\langle M, P \rangle \models_C P(x|do(y)) = p$ if and only if $\langle M_y, P \rangle \models_C P(x) = p$; and $\langle M, P \rangle \models_C P(x|e, do(y)) = p$ if and only if $\langle M_y, P_e \rangle \models_C P_e(x) = p$.

**Example 3** The PCM of the *firing squad example* (Pearl 1999; 2000) has two exogenous variables $U$ and $W$, and endogenous variables $A, B, C$, and $D$; which stand for

$U$ = court orders the execution;
$C$ = captain gives a signal;
$A$ = rifle A shoots;
$B$ = rifle B shoots;
$D$ = the prisoner dies;
$W$ = rifle A pulls the trigger out of nervousness.

The causal relationships between the variables are described by the following functional equations:

$$C = U; \quad A = C \vee W; \quad B = C; \quad D = A \vee B.$$

The goal is to compute the probability $P(\neg D|D, do(\neg A))$, which expresses the *counterfactual* probability that the prisoner would be alive if $A$ had not shot, given that the prisoner is in fact dead. It is shown that the PCM entails:

$$P(u, w|D) = \begin{cases} \frac{P(u,w)}{1-(1-p)(1-q)} & \text{if } u = U \text{ or } w = W \\ 0 & \text{if } u = \neg U \text{ and } w = \neg W \end{cases}$$
$$P(\neg D|D, do(\neg A)) = \frac{q(1-p)}{1-(1-p)(1-q)}$$

where $p = P(U)$ and $q = P(W)$. □

## Encoding PCM in PAL

In this section we give an encoding of PCM in PAL, illustrate the encoding with an example, and show the correspondence between query entailment in PCM and query entailment of the corresponding encoding in PAL.

**General encoding of PCM in PAL:** Given a PCM $\mathcal{M} = \langle M, P\rangle$ and assuming that the functions $f_i(PA_i, U_i)$ in $M$ are logical functions, we construct a PAL action theory $D(\mathcal{M})$ as follows:

- There are no non-inertial unknown variables.
- The inertial unknown variables are the exogenous variables in $M$ with the same probability distributions:

  **probability of** $u$ **is** $P(u)$.

- The endogenous variables in $M$ are fluents in $D(\mathcal{M})$. Moreover, for every fluent $V_i$, there is an additional fluent $ab(V_i)$ in $D(\mathcal{M})$.
- For each functional equation of the form $V_i = f_i(PA_i, U_i)$ in $M$, the following static causal rule is in $D(\mathcal{M})$:

  $\neg ab(V_i)$ **causes** $V_i \Leftrightarrow f_i(PA_i, U_i)$.

- For every fluent $V_i$, $D(\mathcal{M})$ has actions '$make(V_i)$', '$make(\neg V_i)$' with the following effects:

  $make(V_i)$ **causes** $\{ab(V_i), V_i\}$
  $make(\neg V_i)$ **causes** $\{ab(V_i), \neg V_i\}$.

The main intuition is that functional equations of the form $V_i = f_i(PA_i, U_i)$ need to be encoded as $\neg ab(V_i)$ **causes** $V_i = f_i(PA_i, U_i)$ instead of the straightforward encoding $true$ **causes** $V_i = f_i(PA_i, U_i)$. Then the equation $V_i = f_i(PA_i, U_i)$ can be properly inactivated by action $make(V_i)$.

Let us construct the PAL encoding of the PCM in Example 3. The action theory contains inertial unknown variables $U$ and $W$, fluents $A, B, C, D$, $ab(A), ab(B), ab(C)$, and $ab(D)$. Translated into PAL, the functional equations become the following static causal laws:

$$\begin{array}{lll} \neg ab(C) & \textbf{causes} & C \Leftrightarrow U \\ \neg ab(A) & \textbf{causes} & A \Leftrightarrow C \vee W \\ \neg ab(B) & \textbf{causes} & B \Leftrightarrow C \\ \neg ab(D) & \textbf{causes} & D \Leftrightarrow A \vee B \end{array} \quad (6)$$

We now relate the probabilities entailed by the PCM in Example 3 with those entailed by its PAL encoding. (In the following, $\chi$ denotes the indicator function, that is, $\chi(X) = 1$ if $X$ is true and $\chi(X) = 0$ if $X$ is false.)

**Proposition 1** Let $\mathcal{M} = \langle M, P\rangle$ be the PCM of firing squad in Example 3, and let us denote its encoding in PAL by $D(\mathcal{M})$.

Let us denote that

$$init_{\neg ab} = \{\textbf{initially } \neg ab(A), \neg ab(B), \neg ab(C), \neg ab(D)\} .$$

Then for any $u$ and $w$ literals of $U$ and $W$:

$$P(\textbf{initially } \{u, w\}|init_{\neg ab}, \textbf{initially } D) = \begin{cases} \frac{P(u,w)}{1-(1-p)(1-q)} & \text{if } u = U \text{ or } w = W, \\ 0 & \text{if } u = \neg U \text{ and } w = \neg W. \end{cases} \quad (7)$$

$$P(\neg D \textbf{ after } make(\neg A)|init_{\neg ab}, \textbf{initially } D) = \frac{q(1-p)}{1-(1-p)(1-q)} \quad (8)$$

**Proof (*sketch*).**

First we use the Bayes' rule to compute as follows.

$$P(\textbf{initially } \{u, w\}|init_{\neg ab}, \textbf{initially } D) = \frac{P(\textbf{initially } \{u, w\}, \textbf{initially } D|init_{\neg ab})}{P(\textbf{initially } D|init_{\neg ab})} \quad (9)$$

Because of the static causal laws (6), given $init_{\neg ab}$, the variables $U, W$ and the fluents $A, B, C, D$ in the initial state satisfy that

$$\begin{array}{llll} C \Leftrightarrow U, & A \Leftrightarrow C \vee W, \\ B \Leftrightarrow C, & D \Leftrightarrow A \vee B. \end{array} \quad (10)$$

It follows from (10) that $\neg D \Leftrightarrow \neg U \wedge \neg W$ (in the initial state). Hence,

$$\begin{aligned} & P(\textbf{initially } \neg D|init_{\neg ab}) \\ & = P(\textbf{initially } \neg U, \textbf{initially } -W|init_{\neg ab}) \\ & = P(U = 0, W = 0) = (1-p)(1-q). \end{aligned}$$

Therefore, we have:

$$\begin{aligned} &P(\textbf{initially } D | init_{\neg ab}) \\ &= 1 - P(\textbf{initially } \neg D | init_{\neg ab}) \\ &= 1 - (1-p)(1-q). \end{aligned} \tag{11}$$

Because $\neg D \Leftrightarrow \neg U \wedge \neg W$ in the initial state, we also have that: **initially** $D \Leftrightarrow$ **initially** $U \vee$ **initially** $W$. Consequently, if $u = U$ or $w = W$ then:

$$\begin{aligned} &P(\textbf{initially } \{u, w\}, \textbf{initially } D | init_{\neg ab}) \\ &= P(\textbf{initially } \{u, w\} | init_{\neg ab}) = P(u, w). \end{aligned}$$

Otherwise, if $u = \neg U$ and $w = \neg W$ then:

$$P(\textbf{initially } \{u, w\}, \textbf{initially } D | init_{\neg ab}) = 0.$$

Finally, we have that:

$$\begin{aligned} &P(\textbf{initially } \{u, w\}, \textbf{initially } D | init_{\neg ab}) \\ &= \begin{cases} P(u, w) & \text{if } u = U \text{ or } w = W \\ 0 & \text{if } u = \neg U \text{ and } w = \neg W. \end{cases} \end{aligned} \tag{12}$$

It is easy to see that (7) follows from (9), (11) and (12).

For proving (8), we use the formula:

$$\begin{aligned} &P(\neg D \textbf{ after } make(\neg A) | init_{\neg ab}, \textbf{initially } D) = \\ &\sum_{\mathsf{s}} P(\neg D \textbf{ after } make(\neg A) | \mathsf{s}) P(\mathsf{s} | init_{\neg ab}, \textbf{initially } D) \end{aligned} \tag{13}$$

Observe that $P(\mathsf{s} | init_{\neg ab}, \textbf{initially } D) = 0$ if $init_{\neg ab}$ does not hold in s (that is, $\mathsf{s} \not\models init_{\neg ab}$). Hence, the right hand side depends only on the terms containing s such that $\mathsf{s} \models init_{\neg ab}$. In the following we will consider only s such that $\mathsf{s} \models init_{\neg ab}$. Let us assume that $u$ and $w$ are the literals of $U$ and $W$ that hold in the initial state s. The variables and fluents in the initial state s satisfy the functions in (10). Consequently, the variables and fluents in s are uniquely determined by the values of $U$ and $W$, that is, by $u$ and $w$. So s is also uniquely determined by $u$ and $w$. Thus we have:

$$\begin{aligned} &P(\mathsf{s} | init_{\neg ab}, \textbf{initially } D) \\ &= P(\textbf{initially } \{u, w\} | init_{\neg ab}, \textbf{initially } D) \end{aligned} \tag{14}$$

Assume that we reach the state s′ by executing $make(\neg A)$ in the initial state s. The action causes $ab(A)$ and $\neg A$ to be true. Then it follows from the static causal laws (6) that in the state s′: $C \Leftrightarrow U, B \Leftrightarrow C$ and $D \Leftrightarrow B$. Therefore, in the state s′, we have that $D \Leftrightarrow U$. Because $U$ is an inertial unknown variable, its values are the same in s and s′. Consequently,

$$\begin{aligned} &\neg D \textbf{ after } make(\neg A) \Leftrightarrow \neg D \in \mathsf{s}' \\ &\Leftrightarrow \neg U \in \mathsf{s}' \Leftrightarrow \neg U \in \mathsf{s} \Leftrightarrow \textbf{initially } \neg U \end{aligned}$$

Since s uniquely depends on $u, w$:

$$P(\textbf{initially } \neg U | \mathsf{s}) = P(\textbf{initially } \neg U | u, w)$$

Thus we have:

$$\begin{aligned} &P(\neg D \textbf{ after } make(\neg A) | \mathsf{s}) \\ &= P(\textbf{initially } \neg U | \mathsf{s}) = \chi(u = \neg U) \end{aligned} \tag{15}$$

From (13), (14) and (15), we have that:

$$\begin{aligned} &P(\neg D \textbf{ after } make(\neg A) | init_{\neg ab}, \textbf{initially } D) \\ &= \sum_{u,w} \chi(u = \neg U) P(\textbf{initially } \{u, w\} | init_{\neg ab}, \textbf{initially } D) \end{aligned}$$

Note that $\chi(u = \neg U) \neq 0$ only if $u = \neg U$. Furthermore, because of (7), if $u = \neg U$ then $P(\textbf{initially } \{u, w\} | init_{\neg ab}, \textbf{initially } D) \neq 0$ only if $w = W$. So the only possible positive term in the above sum corresponds to the pair $u = \neg U, w = W$. Then:

$$\begin{aligned} &P(\neg D \textbf{ after } make(\neg A) | init_{\neg ab}, \textbf{initially } D) \\ &= P(\textbf{initially } \{\neg U, W\} | init_{\neg ab}, \textbf{initially } D) \\ &= \frac{P(\neg U, W)}{1 - (1-p)(1-q)} = \frac{q(1-p)}{1 - (1-p)(1-q)}. \end{aligned}$$

## Relating PCM and PAL: the main result

We generalize Proposition 1 to the following general result.

**Theorem 1** *Given a PCM $\mathcal{M} = \langle M, P \rangle$, let $D(\mathcal{M})$ be its respectively constructed PAL action theory. Let $init_{\neg ab} = \{\textbf{initially } \neg ab(v) | v \in V\}$. Let $u$ be a subset of background variable, $v$ and $w$ be subsets of endogenous variables. Then we have the following relations between entailments in PCM and PAL:*

- *$\mathcal{M}$ entails $P(u|w) = p$ if and only if $D(\mathcal{M})$ entails*

  $$P(\textbf{initially } u | init_{\neg ab}, \textbf{initially } w) = p$$

- *$\mathcal{M}$ entails $P(w|do(v)) = p$ if and only if $D(\mathcal{M})$ entails*

  $$P(w \textbf{ after } do(v) | init_{\neg ab}) = p$$

- *$\mathcal{M}$ entails $P(\neg w | w, do(\neg v)) = p$ if and only if $D(\mathcal{M})$ entails*

  $$P(\neg w \textbf{ after } make(\neg v)\ | init_{\neg ab}, \textbf{initially } w) = p$$

Due to lack of space, we do not present the proof Theorem 1 in detail. This proof is based on a reasoning similar to that of the proof of Proposition 1.

## Related works and discussion

The works closely related to ours include Poole (1997), Thielscher (1999), Finzi & Lukasiewicz (2003)[2]. These works also provide formal translations between probabilistic formalisms for reasoning about actions.

Poole (1997) introduces *independent choice logic* (ICL) of independent choices and logic programs that specify the consequence of choices and actions. Poole (1997) has shown that many formalisms can be translated into ICL, including influence diagrams, Markov decision problems (MDPs), strategic form of games and (dynamic) Bayesian networks. The relation between ICL and PAL is still unknown.

Thielscher (1999) translates causal models (without probabilities) into Fluent Calculus. Like the fluents $ab(V_i)$, their generic fluent $Denied(x)$ is used to simulate how an action inactivates respective functional equations. Nevertheless, the

[2]We thank anonymous reviewers for pointing this out.

semantics of counterfactuals by Thielscher (1999) is essentially non-probabilistic. We also plan to relate this semantics to PAL in the future extension of our work.

Finzi & Lukasiewicz (2003) provide translations between PCM and ICL then extends the notions of structural causes and explanations to ICL-theories. The translations are restricted to a special class of PCMs whose causal graphs are *acyclic*. This restriction is probably due to the fact that ICL is defined with acyclic logic programs. Moreover, their and our method of analysis are orthogonal. In Finzi & Lukasiewicz (2003), the extended notions are first translated into PCM together with the ICL; then they are semantically interpreted in the translated PCM model. In our case, probabilistic queries can be interpreted separately in PCM and PAL semantics. Our contribution was showing that the translation from PCM to PAL is semantically correct. Finally, counterfactual reasoning was a major point in our work (see (iii) in Theorem 1), which has not been studied in Finzi & Lukasiewicz (2003).

Baral, Tran, & Le (2002) discuss differences between PAL and PCM in detail. With regard to our work in this paper, it is noticeable that we have used only inertial variables in the encoding of PCM. Another important aspect of the PAL encoding is that as the world progresses if we want to reactivate a previously inactivated functional equation $V_i = f_i(PA_i, U_i)$ all we need to do is make $ab(V_i)$ false. (Reactivation need to be done with care though.) In PCMs once a functional equation is inactivated it can no longer be activated.

Finally, the proof of Proposition 1 (as well as that of Theorem 1) has referred to an important assumption of causal model. It is the assumption that the set of functional equations uniquely determines the values of the endogenous variables, given the values of the exogenous variables. Moreover, counterfactual probabilities are not well-defined in PCM without the assumption. While it is not clear how to do extend counterfactual reasoning in PCM without this assumption, it is straightforward to do so in PAL framework.

## Conclusion

In this paper we have presented a translation of probabilistic causal models into the action description language PAL. The translation shows that the language of PCMs is semantically equivalent to a sub-language of PAL, which contains only *inertial* unknown variables and a special set of actions acting on fluents '$ab(V_i)$'. Our result has several important implications: (i) PAL is more expressive than PCM; (ii) PCM does not capture probabilistic effects of actions, which are encoded by *non-inertial* unknown variables in PAL; (iii) PAL is more suitable than PCM for reasoning about actions.

## Acknowledgments

The authors acknowledge the support of NSF through grant number 0070463 and of NASA through grant number NCC2-1232.

## References

Bacchus, F.; Halpern, J. Y.; and Levesque, H. J. 1999. Reasoning about noisy sensors and effectors in the situation calculus. *AI journal* 111(1-2):171–208.

Baral, C.; Tran, N.; and Le, T. 2002. Reasoning about actions in a probabilistic setting. In *Proc. AAAI'02*, 507–512.

Eiter, T., and Lukasiewicz, T. 2003. Probabilistic reasoning about actions in nonmonotonic causal theories. In *Proc. UAI'03*, 192–199.

Finzi, A., and Lukasiewicz, T. 2003. Structure-based causes and explanations in the independent choice logic. In *Proc. UAI'03*, 225–232.

Gelfond, M., and Lifschitz, V. 1993. Representing actions and change by logic programs. *Journal of Logic Programming* 17:301–323.

Gelfond, M., and Lifschitz, V. 1998. Action languages. *ETAI* 3(16).

Kushmerick, N.; Hanks, S.; and Weld, D. 1995. An algorithm for probabilistic planning. *AI journal* 76(1-2):239–286.

Littman, M. 1997. Probabilistic propositional planning: representations and complexity. In *Proc. of AAAI'97*, 748–754.

Mateus, P.; Pacheco, A.; and Pinto, J. 2002. Observations and the probabilistic situation calculus. In *Proc. KR'02*, 327338.

McCain, N., and Turner, H. 1995. A causal theory of ramifications and qualifications. In *Proc. of IJCAI'95*, 1978–1984.

Pearl, J. 1995. Action as a local surgery. In *Working Notes of AAAI Spring Symposium Series*, 157–162.

Pearl, J. 1999. Reasoning with cause and effect. In *Proc. of IJCAI'99*, 1437–1449.

Pearl, J. 2000. *Causality*. Cambridge University Press.

Poole, D. 1997. The independent choice logic for modelling multiple agents under uncertainty. *AI journal* 94:7–56.

Poole, D. 1998. Decision theory, the situation calculus and conditional plans. *ETAI* 2(1-2):105158.

Reiter, R. 2001. *Knowledge in action: logical foundation for describing and implementing dynamical systems*. MIT Press.

Thielscher, M. 1999. In *KI'99*, 137–148.

# Evaluating Ontology Cleaning

**Christopher Welty, Ruchi Mahindru, and Jennifer Chu-Carroll**

IBM T.J. Watson Research Center
19 Skyline Dr.
Hawthorne, NY 10532
{welty,jencc}@us.ibm.com, ruchi_mahindru@yahoo.com

**Abstract**

Ontology as a discipline of Computer Science has made many claims about its usefulness, however to date there has been very little evaluation of those claims. We present the results of an experiment using a hybrid search system with a significant knowledge-based component to measure, using precision and recall, the impact of *improving the quality of* an ontology on overall performance. We demonstrate that improving the ontology using OntoClean (Guarino and Welty, 2002), does positively impact performance, and that having knowledge of the search domain is more effective than domain-knowledge-free search techniques such as link analysis.

*Content Areas:* Ontologies

## Introduction

Ontologies have been proposed as a solution to numerous problems in areas such as search, semantic integration, agents, human-computer interaction, etc. The premise is usually that a clear, high-quality ontology can act as an *interlingua* in which mappings between systems can unambiguously be expressed, or in which understanding of a domain can be gained by a system or shared by users (Smith and Welty, 2001).

For the most part, this claim has not been realized in practice, and one reason for this failure is that there was little agreement on just what makes an ontology "clear" or "high quality." One recent development in ontology research has been the specification of a formal methodology for ontological analysis, OntoClean (Guarino and Welty, 2002), that addresses the problem of defining just what "high quality" is for ontologies. Following this definition and approach, a high quality foundational ontology, Dolce, is being developed (Gangemi, et al, 2002). While OntoClean appears to be widely accepted in the scientific community, and OntologyWorks, a small company providing database integration services, has a proprietary analysis tool based on OntoClean (www.ontologyworks.com), there is very little evidence that it can have impact on knowledge-based systems. In fact, there appears to be a significant obstacle in understanding the methodology, and even without this "learning curve", significant manual effort must be expended to employ the methodology to develop actual "clean" ontologies. Furthermore, there has been no clear argument that such an expenditure will pay for itself in the long run. Indeed, "Why does it matter?" has been the most frequent criticism of the OntoClean approach.

We report here on a series of experiments using a hybrid search system with a significant knowledge-based component to test the impact of improving the quality of ontologies on system performance. The use of search as a test system provides a well understood framework for empirical evaluation, and gives an excellent opportunity to address the "Why does it matter?" question.

Preliminary results of this experiment were presented earlier in a workshop (Welty, et al, 2003). In this paper we present the final data for the full experiment, plus a more detailed analysis of the results.

## Background

The field of ontology has been sorely lacking in formal empirical analysis in general. This deficiency has been recognized, however, and a few examples are starting to appear. Ablation analysis of ontologies at U.T. Austin (Fan, et al., 2003) is one example in which elements of an ontology used by a search system that relied on recognizing noun compounds were systematically removed to determine which level of specificity were most relevant to the results. There have also been several evaluations of the impact of structured knowledge (loosely construed as ontologies) on IR and search systems in general.

Most closely related to this work is the work of Clark, et al, at Boeing (2000), in which a search system was enhanced by employing an ontology-like artifact (a thesaurus of terms with more meaningful structure than a flat list of keywords).

This work showed that precision and recall performance of a retrieval system can be significantly increased by adding this kind of information. It is important to note that while Clarke, et al, did discuss a process for improving the quality of the ontology; they did not formally evaluate the impact of the *improvement*. Furthermore, Kanisa, Inc. (previously AskJeeves Enterprise Solutions – www.kanisa.com) has based their business on providing domain-specific knowledge-enhanced search, and has been turning a profit since 1Q 2002 (Ulicny, 2003).

Similar evaluations of the impact of ontologies on search-based systems have been done in the question-answering community. Moldovan and Mihalcea (2000) use a significantly enhanced version of WordNet to drastically improve question answering performance, and other groups including Woods, et al (2000), Hovy et al (2001), and Prager, et al (2001), have reported similar results. Again, as with the Boeing work, these groups report positively on the impact of adding an ontology to a search system, but make no attempt to determine whether a good quality ontology would improve performance more. In fact, within the IR and QA communities, WordNet is the most common ontology-like artifact to employ, and previous work has shown that WordNet viewed as an ontology is not particularly of high quality (Oltramari, et al, 2002).

## System Overview

The RISQUE system is an evolution of the system reported in (Chu-Carroll, et al, 2002). This system provides a natural-language front end to a conventional search engine, but uses clues in the natural language question, a knowledge-base of industry terms, and knowledge of the web site structure (see below) to construct an *advanced search query* using the full expressiveness of the search engine query language. This search is limited to a corporate web site, in this case our knowledge is of the ibm.com buy and support pages for the ThinkPad™ and NetVista™ product lines.

The main components of RISQUE include a parser, the terminology knowledge base, rules for question types, a hub page finder, a query formulation component, and the search engine.

The parser is a slot-grammar parser (McCord, 1980) that must be seeded with multi-word industry specific terms, so that e.g. "disk drive" will be parsed as a compound noun, rather than a head noun with a pre-modifier. These multi-word terms come from the knowledge-base. From the grammatical structure of the question, we extract the primary verb phrase and the noun phrases. The verb phrase information is the main evidence used to fire rules for recognizing question types, which themselves depend on the web site structure. The ibm.com web site, like many enterprise sites, is divided into a section for support and a section for sales. This gives RISQUE its two most basic question types, "buy" and "support".

The hub-page finder is a system of declarative rules that takes the noun phrases from the question and determines whether they correspond to products listed in the terminology, and if so finds the most appropriate "hub page" or "comparison page" for that product. For example, many questions about IBM Thinkpads can be answered with information on the "ThinkPad home page" on the IBM site. Directing users to these key pages is often the quickest path to an answer. Hub and comparison pages are described in the next section. The rules are broken into two parts, one set is derived directly from the knowledge base and includes *moreImportantThan* relationships and the taxonomy; the second includes rules expressing the relationships between linguistically-derived information and the hub pages. For example, if the question contains a superlative, as in "What is the fastest Thinkpad?", the rules indicate that the Thinkpad comparison page should be returned.

The system iteratively generates complex queries using knowledge of web site structure. The query may include URL restrictions, such as "only consider pages with 'support' in the URL for support questions", or "exclude pages with research.ibm.com in the URL for buy questions". The query will also make use of boolean connectives, disjunction to support synonym expansion, and conjunction of noun phrase terms. If this query does not return enough hits, the query formulation component will relax the query according to a number of heuristics, such as dropping the least important noun phrase. Knowledge of which terms are more important than others, based on manual analysis of the web site, is included in the knowledge-base. RISQUE iteratively formulates search queries and accumulates results until a pre-determined number of result pages are obtained.

The RISQUE system was tested and trained with a set of questions made up by team members. For the initial experiment described in (Welty, et al, 2003), the system was evaluated with questions made up by a domain expert from outside the group. Finally, the system was evaluated with roughly 200 questions collected from students and professors at CCNY.

## Role of Ontology

The central terminology of RISQUE is an ontology-like knowledge-base of industry terms arranged in a taxonomy according to specificity. In addition to the taxonomy, the knowledge base includes important information used by the system:

*Hub page:* Most terms at the top level of the taxonomy have a corresponding "hub page" – a page that gives a general description of the things in that category. For example, there is a hub page for IBM ThinkPad, and also a hub page for IBM T-Series ThinkPad. The ibm.com website, along with most e-commerce websites, are designed to pack a lot of information in these particular pages, with links to as much information as the designers can imagine might be relevant to someone seeking support or seeking to purchase. The taxonomy is used to associate terms with *the most specific* hub page that is relevant. For example, if we know that a "ThinkPad A21" is a "ThinkPad A-Series Model" which itself is a "Thinkpad", then if only the latter two terms have hub pages, the hub page for "Thinkpad A21" would be the "Thinkpad A-Series" hub page – the most specific hypernym that has an associated hub page.

*Comparison Page:* Many e-commerce web sites including IBM's provide the ability to compare two or more similar products. Our knowledge-base stores information on how to find or generate comparison pages for products. These pages will be displayed for questions like, "What is the fastest A-Series ThinkPad?" Similar to hub pages, the taxonomy is used to associate terms with the *most specific common* comparison page.

*Synonyms:* Synonyms account for simple variations on spelling, acronyms, abbreviations, etc., as well as traditional synonyms. This information is used to find the term being referenced in a question, as well as in query expansion. The use of synonyms in query expansion made the notion of an *expansion* (see below) more important.

*moreImportantThan:* e-Commerce websites have an organization that is important to capture in interpreting questions. For example, IBM's web site is organized such that add-on accessory pages list which models they are compatible with, but computer pages do not list which accessories are compatible with them. This knowledge is explicit and intentional for the website maintainers, but is not necessarily obvious to a customer browsing the site for the first time. Thus, when an accessory and a computer are mentioned in the same question, such as, "What CD drive goes with my ThinkPad T23?" we consider the CD drive to be the more important term in the question. The more important term in the question will have its hub page returned in a higher position, and the less important term may, in some circumstances, not have its hub page appear at all. In addition, the less important term will be dropped first during query relaxation. The *moreImportantThan* relation is considered to be transitive, and is also inherited down the taxonomy. Thus we only represent in the knowledge-base that accessories are *moreImportantThan* computers, and from this we infer that "CD drive" is *moreImportantThan* "ThinkPad T23."

*Expansions:* An interesting situation that we had to account for in dealing with questions generated by non-experts was that often people are confused about what industry terms mean. For example, many people think "SCSI" is a kind of disk drive, when in fact is it a type of communications bus. These types of errors do not appear in the web pages, thus making SCSI a simple synonym of "disk drive" would not be productive – synonyms are used in query expansion and therefore searches for disk drives would turn up communication bus technology pages. To solve this, the *expansion* relation between terms is treated as an asymmetric synonym. When "SCSI" appears in a query, it will be considered a synonym of disk-drive, however when disk-drive appears in a query, it will not be considered a synonym of "SCSI".

## Clean-up Process

The original RISQUE system terminology, Quilt, was developed by domain experts with no experience with or knowledge of ontology engineering methods, and contained on the order of 3K synsets and 4.6K terms. We improved this terminology in a number of ways:

1. Developed a "backbone taxonomy" of terms
2. Analyzed terms and their position in the hierarchy
3. Organized terms more logically
4. Ensured every term was grounded in the top level
5. Ensured terminology was logically consistent

We used three tools in performing this cleanup: The OntoClean methodology was used in analysis, and helped with #1-3; an ontology editor was used to view the taxonomy, this was critical in #2-4; a reasoner was used to ensure consistency and coverage of the *moreImportantThan* relation. The analysis and cleanup took on the order of one person-week, and resulted 3K synsets and 10.8K terms.

The main cleanup effort was establishing a *backbone taxonomy* (Guarino and Welty, 2001) of roughly 30 terms. The backbone taxonomy terms represent the terms with the highest organizational utility. They cover the entire domain of discourse: every entity must instantiate a backbone class. The backbone proved a critical resource in organizing the terms, as our requirement was that all other terms "ground up" through hypernym links to one and only one backbone term – the backbone terms were mutually disjoint.

That isn't to say there weren't terms with multiple hypernyms, but no term had more than one ancestor hypernym in the backbone. This was a critical organizational policy that helped keep the taxonomy clean. Analyzing 3,000 terms for their formal meta-properties proved daunting, however it was easy to find terms grounded in more than one backbone term. These terms were analyzed more carefully and in most cases were found to exhibit one of the common modeling pitfalls outlined in (Guarino and Welty, 2002). The most common of these was the confusion between *part-of* and *subclass*. For example, a purpose-built keyboard for a small hand-held computer is not a more specific term than the computer. It is an accessory for that computer.

The initial Quilt taxonomy contained a large number of inconsistent, meaningless, redundant and disconnected terms. These terms were found using an ontology editor and reasoner, and either eliminated or connected properly to the backbone. It is important to note that the cleaned taxonomy did not have any new synsets, other than a few in the relatively small backbone taxonomy. We did, however, find considerable inconsistent usage of synonym patterns. For example, the "Thinkpad T21" might have "T21" as a synonym, however the "Thinkpad T23" might have "TP 23" as a synonym. These abbreviation patterns were normalized with a program, accounting for the large increase in the number of terms. Surprisingly, this increase did not end up impacting the evaluation significantly, as the questions tended to use the full names of computer models when present.

## Experimental Setup

Although the main goal of RISQUE was to show an improvement over traditional web search, the particular experiment described in this paper was to isolate the process of improving the quality of the terminology using ontology-based analysis tools. The RISQUE system architecture treats the terminology as a pluggable module, which allowed us to isolate this particular change while holding all other aspects of the system constant. We then concentrated on how to compare a poorly structured terminology with a cleaned one. After the cleanup was complete, we performed four evaluations as follows:

- *baseline:* basic search over the IBM web pages using a traditional search engine
- *quilt:* The full RISQUE system with the original Quilt terminology
- *clean:* The full RISQUE system with the cleaned terminology
- *google:* Basic search using Google restricted to the ibm.com web pages

The evaluation was performed on 200 natural language questions about IBM products collected mainly from students and faculty at CCNY. Participants were asked to imagine they wanted to purchase something from IBM, or get support for an existing product. The experiments were run against the live ibm.com website, over which we had no control. As a result, we ran the evaluations in parallel, with each question running through all four systems at the same time, in order to prevent changes in the web site from impacting performance of one system in isolation. The google and baseline queries were formulated manually from a conjunction of all the words in the noun phrases from the natural language question. The answer to a question was considered correct if one of the pages in the top ten returned by the search contained an answer to the question – i.e. the answer is on the returned page or a single click (and some reading) away. For comparison questions, e.g. "What is the fastest desktop?", or "What is the lightest ThinkPad?" the answers were considered correct if the comparison page selected by RISQUE contained the relevant data for each type of computer, e.g. the processor speed of each desktop model, or the weight of each ThinkPad model.

## Results and Analysis

Our results are shown in the table below. Each experiment lists the number correct (of 200) and the percent.

| | # correct | % correct | % improvement |
|---|---|---|---|
| Base | 65 | 32% | |
| Quilt | 105 | 52% | 63% |
| Clean | 121 | 61% | over baseline: 91%<br>over Quilt: 17% |

| Google | 43 | 22% | -31% |
|---|---|---|---|

First of all, our results confirm the overwhelming evidence to date that ontologies can significantly improve search results. In the original version of RISQUE, which utilizes the pre-cleaned-up version of the ontology, Quilt, we achieved a 63% relative improvement over our baseline system. This improvement is obtained as a combination of RISQUE's iterative query formulation process, the hubpage finder, and RISQUE's query expansion feature, all of which utilize the set of known industry terms, and their synonyms/expansions provided by the ontology.

Most notably, our results show a clear improvement of the search results when using the higher quality "cleaned" terminology, which shows a 17% relative improvement over the original terminology and, as utilized by RISQUE's processing components, nearly doubles the performance of the baseline system. While the improved terminology contained more actual words, this expansion did not in itself account for the increase in precision – as noted above, questions tended to use the full names of products, rather than abbreviations. This expansion of terms would likely have more of an impact on actual usage of the system, but was not relevant to our evaluation of ontology cleaning.

Many of the correct answers in our system come from hub and comparison pages, so the fact that terms are more consistently connected through the taxonomy with these pages in the cleaned terminology was the major reason the cleanup improved precision. Another important factor was the proper derivation of the *moreImportantThan* relation between terms, which was incorrect or ambiguous in a number of cases in the original search because of missing links in the taxonomy.

The heavy reliance of our system on "hub pages" for correct answers would seem to indicate that link analysis, or a similar technique that ranks highly connected pages over less connected ones, would improve search considerably given the large number of incoming and outgoing links on these pages. If effective, such a technique would clearly be preferable over a knowledge-base, since it requires significantly less manual effort to maintain. This led us to perform an experiment using the Google™ search engine restricted to the ibm.com website. We were very surprised to find that this experiment was the worst performer of all.

The important difference between the knowledge-based search and one based on link analysis is knowledge of the structure of the website, as reflected e.g. in the *moreImportantThan* relation. As discussed above, one of the things captured in the relation is the fact that information about compatibility is located on accessory pages, not the computer pages. Thus the highly-connected ThinkPad hub pages receive high scores from Google™ for questions like, "What modem goes with my ThinkPad t30?", but they do not contain an answer to the question. In fact, the correct page contains so few references to Thinkpad t30 that it does not show up in the top ten, and furthermore for any query that contains the word "thinkpad" google search will return the Thinkpad hub page, as it contains that term numerous times and is very highly connected. This page is typically not the answer for most questions, and our internal hub page finder *knows* this. We believe that explicit knowledge, though expensive to maintain, will always win out over heuristics like link analysis.

These results are consistent with the results previously reported in (Welty, et al, 2003), however the limitations of that experiment, in which questions were taken from a domain expert, were overcome by using students who did not know anything about the experiment being performed or the system being evaluated. The overall precision of our searches decreased in this experiment over the previous, indicating that the difference in subjects did impact the system, however the relative improvements across the three principle evaluations remained roughly the same.

The fourth evaluation, for google, dropped significantly in relative precision; in the previous experiment the google evaluation showed only a 3% relative decrease in precision from the base. In this experiment, google showed a 31% relative decrease in precision over the baseline. The main cause of this decrease was that there were significantly more questions about accessories and comparisons, for which (as described above) link analysis and keyword ranking were poor heuristics.

## Conclusion

We described a system for knowledge-based natural language search called RISQUE, and focused on the knowledge-based components and their role in the system. We performed a controlled experiment to compare the precision of the search system with an unprincipled ontology to the same system with a principled ontology. Our results showed an 17% relative improvement in precision (from 52% to 61%) with no other changes in the system other than applying the OntoClean methodology to analyzing the ontology and cleaning it.

These results provide some evidence that improving the quality of an ontology does improve the performance of an ontology-based search. It stands to reason that any system that has a significant ontology component would benefit from improving the ontology portion. It is our further claim that as systems with an ontology component begin to employ more sophisticated reasoning, improvements in ontology quality will have even more impact. This is the focus of our current investigations.

In light of the results reported in the ablation studies described in (Fan, et al, 2003), in which it was shown that the higher, more abstract, levels of an ontology have significantly more impact on system performance than lower ones, we can address the common complaint about OntoClean, that it takes too long to perform detailed meta-property analysis on large ontologies. Accepting the results of these two empirical evaluations as general indicators, we conclude that focusing this detailed analysis on the top level would have the highest cost-benefit, and could easily justify the expense.

## Acknowledgements

Other contributors to the Risque system were John Prager, Yael Ravin, Christian Lenz Cesar, David Ferrucci, and Jerry Cwiklik. Our thanks to Mike Moran and Alex Holt for supporting the project. This work was supported in part by the Advanced Research and Development Activity (ARDA)'s Novel Intelligence for Massive Data (NIMD) Program under contract number MDA904-01-C-0988.

## References

Chu-Carroll, J., John Prager, Yael Ravin and Christian Cesar. 2002. A Hybrid Approach to Natural Language Web Search. *Proceedings of EMNLP-2002.*

Clark, P., J. Thompson, Heather Holmback, and Lisbeth Duncan. 2000. Exploiting a Thesaurus-Based Semantic Net for Knowledge-Based Search. *Proceedings of IAAI-2000.* Pp. 988-995. Austin:AAAI Press.

Fan, J., K. Barker and B. Porter. 2003. The Knowledge Required to Interpret Noun Compounds. *Proceedings of the Eighteenth International Joint Conference on Artificial Intelligence.* Acapulco:AAAI Press.

Gangemi A., N. Guarino, C. Masolo, A. Oltramari, L. Schneider. 2002. Sweetening Ontologies with DOLCE. *Proceedings of EKAW 2002.* Siguenza:Springer.

Guarino, N. and C. Welty. 2000. A Formal Ontology of Properties. In, Dieng, R., and Corby, O., eds, *Proceedings of EKAW-2000: The 12th International Conference on Knowledge Engineering and Knowledge Management.* Spring-Verlag LNCS Vol. 1937:97-112.

Guarino, Nicola and Chris Welty. 2002. Evaluating Ontological Decisions with OntoClean. *Communications of the ACM.* **45**(2):61-65. New York: ACM Press.

Hovy, E, L. Gerber, U. Hermjakob, C.-Y. Lin, and D. Ravichandran. 2001. Toward Semantics-Based Answer Pinpointing. In *Proceedings of the DARPA Human Language Technology Conference (HLT).* San Diego, CA.

McCord, Michael C. 1980. Slot grammars. *American journal of Computational Linguistics*, **6**(1):255-286, January 1980.

Moldovan, D. and Rada Mihalcea. 2000. Using WordNet and Lexical Operators to Improve Internet Searches. *IEEE Internet Computing.* **4**(1): 34-43.

Oltramari, A., Aldo Gangemi, Nicola Guarino, and Claudio Masolo. Restructuring WordNet's Top-Level: The OntoClean approach. *Proceedings of LREC2002 (OntoLex workshop).* Las Palmas, Spain

Prager, J., Jennifer Chu-Carroll, and Krzysztof Czuba. Use of WordNet Hypernyms for Answering What-Is Questions. *Proceedings of TREC 2001.*

Smith, B. and C. Welty. 2001. Ontology: Towards a new synthesis. In *Formal Ontology in Information Systems.* Ongunquit:ACM Press.

Ulicny, B. Putting your customers' answers to work. 2003. Keynote address, *AAAI Spring Symposium on New Directions in Question Answering.*

Welty, C., R. Mahindru, and J. Chu-Carroll. 2003. Evaluating Ontological Analysis. In *Proceedings of the ISWC-03 Workshop on Semantic Integration.* Sanibel Island.

Woods, W., Stephen Green, Paul Martin, and Ann Houston. Halfway to Question Answering. Proceedings of *TREC 2000.*

# Negotiation as Mutual Belief Revision

**Dongmo Zhang**
School of Computing and Information Technology
University of Western Sydney, Australia
dongmo@cit.uws.edu.au

**Norman Foo** and **Thomas Meyer** and **Rex Kwok**
School of Computer Science and Engineering
The University of New South Wales, Australia
{norman, tmeyer, rkwok}@cse.unsw.edu.au

### Abstract

This paper presents a logical framework for negotiation based on belief revision theory. We consider that a negotiation process is a course or multiple courses of mutual belief revision. A set of AGM-style postulates are proposed to capture the rationality of competitive and cooperative behaviors of negotiation. We first show that the AGM revision and its iterated extension is a special case of negotiation function. Then we show that a negotiation function can be constructed by two related iterated belief revision functions under a certain coordination mechanism. This provides a qualitative method for constructing negotiation space and rational concessions. It also shows a glimpse of how to express game-theoretical concepts in logical framework.

## Introduction

Negotiation has been investigated from many perspectives, including economics, applied mathematics, psychology, sociology and computer science. Significant advances have been made in both quantitative and qualitative analysis of negotiating processes (Pruitt 1981)(Rosenschein and Zlotkin 1994)(Faratin *et al.* 1998) (Kraus *et al.* 1998) (Parsons *et al.* 1998) (Sadri *et al.* 2001). Quantitative approaches, especially those which are inspired by game-theory, dominate much of the existing work. In many cases, however, numeric utility functions are either unreliable or simply unavailable. This paper is a contribution to the body of literature, such as (Sycara 1990) (Kraus *et al.* 1998)(Parsons *et al.* 1998) (Wooldridge and Parsons 2000), which, instead, views negotiation in a qualitative light. Different from most of the existing work, we provide an axiomatic analysis of negotiating processes based on belief revision theory(AGM 1985)(Zhang and Foo 2001).

Negotiation is a process of consensus-seeking among two or more agents. Each agent comes to the negotiation table with an initial set of demands or offers. The parties involved proceed with mutual persuasion or argumentation and terminate when they have converged on a mutually acceptable agreement. If we consider the demands(or offers) of parties as their beliefs on the matter in question, the change of the demands of each party reflects the change of its beliefs during the progress of negotiation. The parties who are convinced to accept part of the other parties' demands would perform a belief revision. New belief states of participants represent their revised demands which are normally closer to each other and apt to reach an agreement. We term such kind of belief revision *mutual belief revision.*

Different from the single agent belief revision, each agent in mutual belief revision tries not only to minimize the loss of its beliefs but also to maximize its gain of information from the other agents. Negotiation behaves in a similar manner. A negotiator attempts to keep as many of her demands as possible and typically tends to selectively accept some demands of his opponents in order to avoid failure of negotiation and maximize gains from negotiation table. The logical framework we propose is intended to strike the correct balance between *competition* and *cooperation* among agents. As a starting point of the investigation, we restrict ourselves to the case of two agents. We propose a set of postulates to model rationality of mutual belief revision and negotiation. These postulates are mostly inspired by the frameworks of AGM theory(AGM 1985), Zhang and Foo's multiple belief revision(Zhang and Foo 2001) and Darwiche and Pearl's iterated belief revision(Darwiche and Pearl 1997).

## Postulates for mutual belief revision and negotiation

We will work in a propositional language $\mathcal{L}$. The language is that of classical propositional logic with an associated consequence operation $Cn$ in the sense that $Cn(X) = \{A : X \vdash A\}$. A set $K$ of sentences is *logically closed* or called a *belief set* when $K = Cn(K)$. If $X$, $Y$ are two sets of sentences, $X + Y$ denotes $Cn(X \cup Y)$.

In this section we propose a set of axioms to specify properties of mutual belief revision and negotiation between two agents. The idea is the following. Suppose that $K_1$ and $K_2$ are the current belief states of two agents. During the mutual belief revision, each agent accepts part of beliefs from the other agent and minimize her change of belief states to preserve consistency. As a result, the revised belief states of the agents, denoted by $N_1(K_1, K_2)$ and $N_2(K_1, K_2)$ respectively, normally get closer each other.

In negotiation setting, the revision of belief states reflects the changes of agent demands or offers. If $X$ and $Y$ represent the initial demands/offers of two agents, $N_1(X,Y)$ and $N_2(X,Y)$ will be their revised demands/offers after negotiation. $N_1(X,Y) \cap N_2(X,Y)$ will be then the agreement reached in the negotiation.

Formally, a mutual revision or negotiation function is a two-input and two-output function

$$N(X,Y) = (N_1(X,Y), N_2(X,Y))$$

where $X$ and $Y$ represent the initial belief sets or demands of each agent and $N_1(X,Y)$ and $N_2(X,Y)$ the revised belief sets or demands, respectively. Note that we do not assume that $X$ or $Y$ to be logically closed.

**Definition 1** A function $N : 2^{\mathcal{L}} \times 2^{\mathcal{L}} \rightarrow 2^{\mathcal{L}} \times 2^{\mathcal{L}}$ is a *mutual belief revision* or *negotiation function* if it satisfies the following postulates:

**(N1)** *Closure:*
$N_1(X,Y) = Cn(N_1(X,Y))$; $N_2(X,Y) = Cn(N_2(X,Y))$

**(N2)** *Inclusion:*
$$N_1(X,Y) \subseteq X + Y;\ N_2(X,Y) \subseteq X + Y$$

**(N3)** *Vacuity:* If $X \cup Y$ is consistent, then
$$X + Y \subseteq N_1(X,Y);\ X + Y \subseteq N_2(X,Y)$$

**(N4)** *Inconsistency:*
$N_1(X,Y)$ is inconsistent iff $X$ or $Y$ is inconsistent;
$N_2(X,Y)$ is inconsistent iff $X$ or $Y$ is inconsistent.

**(N5)** *Extensionality:* If $Cn(X) = Cn(Y)$, then
$$N(X,Z) = N(Y,Z);\ N(Z,X) = N(Z,Y)$$

We call (N1)-(N5) the *basic postulates* for mutual belief revision or negotiation. Intuitively, (N1) says that the resulting belief state of each agent is logically closed. (N2) states that no third party information would be introduced. (N3) says that each agent will accept all the beliefs of the other agent if no conflict arises. (N4) says that mutual belief revision can only happen between rational agents. (N5) assumes that mutual belief revision is syntax-independent, i.e. logically equivalent description of beliefs leads to the same results of mutual belief revision.

Similar interpretation of these postulates can also be given in terms of negotiation. If we localize the belief state of an agent on the matters of a negotiation, its belief set represents its demands in the negotiation, which we call the *demand sets* of the agents. (N1) then states that each negotiator should be aware of that she is responsible to undertake all the items and their consequences of her demands once they are included in an agreement. (N2) assumes that if no conflicts between the demands of two agents, amendments of demands may only be done within the initial demand sets from the negotiators[1]. (N3) reflects the cooperative aspect of negotiation that each agent is willing to accept the other party's demands provided they do not conflict with herself's. (N4) means that no negotiation can proceed from inconsistent demands. (N5) is similar.

[1]Note that if there are conflicts between two agents' demands, the amended demand sets could be anything since $X + Y$ will be inconsistent.

It is easy to see that postulates (N1)-(N5) are counterparts of AGM basic postulates for belief revision(AGM 1985)(see next section for a review of the postulates) except of *the success postulate*. It is unreasonable to assume that one side of negotiation would accept all the demands of the other side.

It is easy to see that for the following two special cases:

- $X \cup Y$ is consistent. In this case, $N(X,Y) = (X+Y, X+Y)$;
- $X$ or $Y$ is inconsistent. In this case, $N(X,Y) = (\mathcal{L}, \mathcal{L})$.

the basic postulates can uniquely determine a negotiation function. However for the most interesting cases when $X$ and $Y$ are consistent but $X \cup Y$ is inconsistent, the postulates do not tell us too much about what the function would be. We need more postulates to capture more characteristics of negotiation behaviors. The following two postulates reflect a common principle in belief revision and negotiation, known as *the principle of information economy*, from two different perspectives: *competitive* and *cooperative*.

**(N6)** *Consistent Expansion:*
If $X \cup N_1(X,Y)$ is consistent, then $X \subseteq N_1(X,Y)$;
If $Y \cup N_2(X,Y)$ is consistent, then $Y \subseteq N_2(X,Y)$.

This postulate capture the conservative or self-interest feature of agents, which says that if an agent is not going to accept any counter-demands that contradict her own, she does not need to give up any of her demands. The postulate comes from Ferme and Hansson's selective revision (Ferme and Hansson 1999), where the postulate was interpreted as *"previous beliefs are given up only if this is required to avoid inconsistency"*.

The following postulate (N7) reflects the cooperative attitude of negotiation agents. It states that every agent should commit herself to keeping her original demands/offers once they have been are accepted by the other side. We call it *the rule of no recantation*. It is a quite common negotiation protocol and is one of conditions to guarantee the convergency of negotiation process. To understand the postulate, note that $Cn(X) \cap N_2(X,Y)$ represents the demands of agent 1 which have been accepted by agent 2 after negotiation and $Cn(Y) \cap N_1(X,Y)$ the demands of agent 2 which have been accepted by agent 1.

**(N7)** *No Recantation:*
$Cn(Y) \cap N_1(X,Y) \subseteq N_2(X,Y)$;
$Cn(X) \cap N_2(X,Y) \subseteq N_1(X,Y)$.

We remark that (N7) does not imply the following condition:

*Intersection:* $K_1 \cap K_2 \subseteq N_1(K_1,K_2) \cap N_2(K_1,K_2)$ which says that common items of initial demands must be included in the last agreement of the negotiation. This condition can be a special negotiation protocol but we can't take it for granted. If both sides decide to give up a common item (in order to keep some more beneficial demands), the item will not be included in the last agreement.

The following postulate describes a property of iterated process of negotiation.

**(N8)** *Iteration:*
If $F \subseteq Cn(Y) \cap N_1(X,Y)$, then $N(N_1(X,F),Y) = N(X,Y)$.
If $F \subseteq Cn(X) \cap N_2(X,Y)$, then $N(X, N_2(F,Y)) = N(X,Y)$.

It is a typical strategy in real-life negotiation that a negotiator poses its demands in several stages. At each stage, the negotiator reveals part of her demands, hiding something tougher or some alternatives behind tying to push her opponent changing mind step by step. (N8) says that if one can expect that some of her demands will be definitely accepted by the other side, it will be useless to pose this part first. As we will see, this postulate posts a constraint on the stability of agent's negotiation policy.

## Multiple belief revision and iterated belief revision

We have seen in the last section that there exists a close relationship between AGM belief revision and mutual belief revision. In this section we show that an AGM revision function is a special case of mutual belief revision. First let's recall some basic facts about multiple belief revision and iterated belief revision in single agent environments.

To best suit the context of mutual belief revision, instead of using the original AGM framework, we shall exploit the multiple version of the AGM theory (Zhang and Foo 2001), which allows us to revise a belief set by another belief set. Formally, for any belief set $K$ and a set $F$ of sentences, $K \otimes F$ stands for the result of belief revision when $K$ is revised by $F$. The operation is required to satisfy the following postulates:

($\otimes$1) $K \otimes F = Cn(K \otimes F)$.
($\otimes$2) $F \subseteq K \otimes F$.
($\otimes$3) $K \otimes F \subseteq K + F$.
($\otimes$4) If $F \cup K$ is consistent, $K + F \subseteq K \otimes F$.
($\otimes$5) $K \otimes F$ is inconsistent if $F$ is inconsistent.
($\otimes$6) If $Cn(F_1) = Cn(F_2)$, $K \otimes F_1 = K \otimes F_2$.
($\otimes$7) $K \otimes (F_1 \cup F_2) \subseteq (K \otimes F_1) + F_2$.
($\otimes$8) If $F_2 \cup (K \otimes F_1)$ is consistent, $(K \otimes F_1) + F_2 \subseteq K \otimes (F_1 \cup F_2)$.

A negotiation process normally consists of several stages of mutual belief revision. To simulate such a process, an iterated mechanism of belief revision is required[2]. The following assumption has been accepted by several different iterated belief revision formalisms:

**($\otimes$IBR)** $(K \otimes F_1) \otimes (F_1 \cup F_2) = K \otimes (F_1 \cup F_2)$

It is easy to see that ($\otimes$IBR) is the multiple version of the postulate ($C1$) in (Darwiche and Pearl 1997). Based on Lehmann's observation (Theorem 1 in (Lehmann 1995)) we can easily prove that ($\otimes$1)-($\otimes$6) and ($\otimes$IBR) implies ($\otimes$7) and ($\otimes$8).

The following theorem is an easy generalization of Lehmann's consistency result presented in (Lehmann 1995).

**Theorem 1** *($\otimes$1)-($\otimes$6) are consistent with ($\otimes$IBR).*

In the following we will call a revision function an *iterated belief revision* if it satisfies the postulates ($\otimes$1)-($\otimes$8) and ($\otimes$IBR). Note that such an iterated revision function is different from Darwiche and Pearl's one since we use the exact AGM postulates. This should be fine because ($\otimes$IBR) goes well with AGM postulates(Zhang 2004).

Now let's consider a special case of mutual belief revision when one agent unconditionally accepts the other agent's beliefs. Formally, a mutual revision function $N$ is a *master-slave* revision if it satisfies

**(M-S)** $X \subseteq N_2(X, Y)$.

The condition says that the second agent (slave) always accepts beliefs of the first agent (master) with no reservation. Interestingly the following observation shows that under protocol ($N7$), the first agent can always keep its beliefs.

**Lemma 1** *Let $N$ be a master-slave revision. If it satisfies ($N7$), then for any $X$ and $Y$, $X \subseteq N_1(X, Y)$.*

The following is the representation theorem for master-slave revision.

**Theorem 2** *Let $N$ be a master-slave revision. If we define a revision function $\otimes$ as $K \otimes F \stackrel{def}{=} N_2(F, K)$, then it satisfies the postulates ($\otimes$1)-($\otimes$6). If $N$ satisfies ($N8$), then it satisfies ($\otimes$IBR).*

*Conversely, if $\otimes$ is an iterated belief revision function which satisfies ($\otimes$1)-($\otimes$6) and ($\otimes$IBR), then the mutual belief revision function defined as follows satisfies (N1)-(N8) and (M-S):*

$$N(X, Y) \stackrel{def}{=} (Cn(Y) \otimes X, Cn(Y) \otimes X).$$

This representation theorem shows that (N1)-(N8) plus (M-S) fully specifies a master-slave revision function. Since an iterated revision function always exists, this theorem also shows the consistency of the postulates (N1)-(N8).

In the next section, we will present a general construction of negotiation function, which will allow more "balanced" negotiation.

## Construction of negotiation functions

In this section we provide a model for negotiation functions. Firstly, we give a simple model of negotiation function that satisfies the basic postulates for mutual belief revision and negotiation.

### Representation theorem for basic postulates

A function $t : 2^{\mathcal{L}} \to 2^{\mathcal{L}}$ is called a *belief transform* if for any set $X$ of sentences,

1. $t(X)$ is a belief set, i.e., $t(X) = Cn(t(X))$.
2. $t(Cn(X)) = t(X)$.
3. if $X$ is consistent, then $t(X)$ is consistent.

**Theorem 3** *A negotiation function $N$ satisfies the basic postulates (N1)-(N5) if and only if there are two belief transforms $t_1$ and $t_2$ such that*

$$N(X, Y) = \begin{cases} (X + Y, X + Y), & \text{if } X \cup Y \text{ is consistent;} \\ (\mathcal{L}, \mathcal{L}), & \text{if either } X \text{ or } Y \text{ is inconsistent;} \\ (t_1(X), t_2(Y)), & \text{otherwise.} \end{cases}$$

This theorem indicates that the basic postulates does not tell us too much except that agents in a negotiation might change their mind.

[2]This is similar to some other settings, say belief fusion (Maynard-Reid II and Shoham 2001).

## Negotiable deals

Now we give a more sophisticated model to capture more properties of negotiation processes. We shall introduce some concepts that are borrowed from game-theory, inspired by the work of (Rosenschein and Zlotkin 1994).

Let $X$ and $Y$ be two sets of sentences, representing the initial demands or offers of two agents, respectively. We call the pair $(X, Y)$ a *negotiation encounter*.

Given two iterated revision functions $\otimes_1$ and $\otimes_2$. A *deal* over an encounter $(X, Y)$ is a pair $(\Psi_1, \Psi_2)$ such that $\Psi_1 \subseteq Cn(X), \Psi_2 \subseteq Cn(Y)$ and satisfies the fix-point condition:

$$Cn(\Psi_1 \cup \Psi_2) = (Cn(X) \otimes_1 \Psi_2) \cap (Cn(Y) \otimes_2 \Psi_1) \quad (1)$$

The set of all possible deals over $(X, Y)$ is called the *negotiation set* of $(X, Y)$, denoted by $\mathcal{NS}(X, Y)$.

Intuitively, $\Psi_1$ represents all the demands of agent 1 that agent 2 is willing to accept. Similarly $\Psi_2$ expresses the demands of agent 2 that agent 1 is willing to accept. Then $Cn(X) \otimes_1 \Psi_2$ is going to be the revised demand set of agent 1 and $Cn(Y) \otimes_2 \Psi_1$ the revised demand set of agent 2 after negotiation. A deal then, is an agreement in which both agents agree on $\Psi_1$ and $\Psi_2$ (as well as their consequences). Therefore $Cn(\Psi_1 \cup \Psi_2)$ will be the common acceptable conditions, $(Cn(X) \otimes_1 \Psi_2) \cap (Cn(Y) \otimes_2 \Psi_1)$, after the negotiation. Negotiation set consists of all possible deals that both agent might consider.

Obviously negotiation set can never be empty since $(Cn(X) \cap Cn(Y), Cn(X) \cap Cn(Y))$ always belongs to $\mathcal{NS}(X, Y)$. We call this deal *the conflict deal* of the encounter.

**Example 1** *Consider an encounter* $(X, Y)$ *where* $X = \{p, q\}$ *and* $Y = \{\neg p, \neg q\}$. *Let* $\otimes_1$ *and* $\otimes_2$ *are any iterated revision functions. Then the conflict deal will be* $(Cn(\{p \leftrightarrow q\}), Cn(\{p \leftrightarrow q\}))$, *which is in the negotiation set. Two other extreme cases,* $(Cn(X), Cn(\{p \leftrightarrow q\}))$ *and* $(Cn(\{p \leftrightarrow q\}), Cn(Y))$, *are also negotiable deals. If each agent is going to take some offers from the other, then more "balanced" negotiation could happen. However the result will heavily depend on the evaluation on their demands and counter-demands. Suppose that for agent 1, p is more entrenched than q and for agent 2* $\neg q$ *is more entrenched than* $\neg p$. *Then* $(Cn(\{p\}), Cn(\{\neg q\}))$ *will be a negotiable alternative whereas* $(Cn(\{q\}), Cn(\{\neg p\}))$ *is not.* □

It seems to be that we are ready to define the negotiation function as follows:

$$N(X, Y) \stackrel{def}{=} (Cn(X) \otimes_1 \Psi_2,\ Cn(Y) \otimes_2 \Psi_1)$$

where $(\Psi_1, \Psi_2)$ is a deal of $(X, Y)$. However, this is not going to be a valid definition since we might have several deals for each encounter. We need to pick up one deal from all the possible deals as the agreement.

## Selection function

We consider that negotiation is a decision-making procedure in which each agent chooses a deal from negotiation set. If both agents choose the same deal, then an agreement is reached; otherwise, the conflict deal will be the result of the negotiation. Formally, a negotiation process is a selection function which chooses a deal from negotiation set. Let $\gamma$ be a selection function which selects an element from a nonempty set. We will abbreviate $\gamma(\mathcal{NS}(X, Y))$ to $\gamma(X, Y)$. As usual, $\gamma_i(X, Y)$ means the $i^{th}$ component of $\gamma(X, Y)$. Now we define a negotiation function as follows:

**Definition 2** *Let* $\otimes_1$ *and* $\otimes_2$ *be two iterated revision functions and* $\gamma$ *a selection function. Define a negotiation function N as follows: for any encounter* $(X, Y)$,

$$N(X, Y) = \begin{cases} (X + Y, X + Y), & \text{if } X \cup Y \text{ is consistent;} \\ (\mathcal{L}, \mathcal{L}), & \text{if either } X \text{ or } Y \text{ is inconsistent;} \\ (Cn(X) \otimes_1 \Psi_2, Cn(Y) \otimes_2 \Psi_2), & \text{otherwise.} \end{cases}$$

*where* $(\Psi_1, \Psi_2) = \gamma(X, Y)$.

It is easy to see that given an encounter $(X, Y)$, if the selection function $\gamma$ selects the conflict deal of the encounter, then $N(X, Y) = (X, Y)$.

The following example shows another extreme case.

**Example 2** *Let* $\otimes$ *be an iterated revision operator and* $\ominus$ *is the associated contraction operator. For any encounter* $(X, Y)$, *let* $\gamma(X, Y) = (Cn(X), Cn(Y) \ominus X)$. *Then* $\gamma$ *is a selection function that defines a master-slave mutual belief revision operator where* $\otimes_1 = \otimes_2 = \otimes$. □

Now let's check whether the defined negotiation function satisfies the proposed postulates. The following observation is easy to verify.

**Proposition 1** *Any function that is defined by Definition 2 satisfies the basic postulates (N1)-(N5) as well as postulate (N6).*

However, To satisfy the other postulates we need to introduce some restrictions on the selection function.

## Rationality and compatibility

A deal $\delta = (\Psi_1, \Psi_2)$ over $(X, Y)$ is called *rational* if it satisfies the following conditions:

$$Cn(X) \cap (Cn(Y) \otimes_2 \Psi_1) \subseteq Cn(X) \otimes_1 \Psi_2$$
$$Cn(Y) \cap (Cn(X) \otimes_1 \Psi_2) \subseteq Cn(Y) \otimes_2 \Psi_1$$

The set of all rational deals is called *rational negotiation set*.

Obviously these conditions correspond to the postulation (N7). Therefore if the function in Definition 2 defined by a selection function over rational negotiation set, then it satisfies (N7).

(N8) requires a kind of uniformity in the selection mechanism over different negotiation situations. Before we present the model for (N8), let's introduce a game-theoretical concept.

A deal $\delta = (\Psi_1, \Psi_2)$ *dominates* a deal $\delta' = (\Psi_1', \Psi_2')$ if $Cn(X) \otimes_1 \Psi_2' = Cn(X) \otimes_1 \Psi_2$ and $Cn(Y) \otimes_2 \Psi_1' = Cn(Y) \otimes_2 \Psi_1$ and either

$\Psi_1' \subseteq \Psi_1$ and $\Psi_2' \subset \Psi_2$, or $\Psi_1' \subset \Psi_1$ and $\Psi_2' \subseteq \Psi_2$.

In the other words, $\delta$ dominates $\delta'$ if at least one agent agrees to accept more demands from the other agent without sacrificing any agent's profits.

A deal $\delta$ is called *pareto optimal* over a set of deals if it is in the set and there do not exist any other deals in the set that dominate $\delta$.

The set of all the deals that are rational and pareto optimal over the rational deals is called *refined negotiation set.*

**Lemma 2** *Let* $(X, Y)$ *be any encounter. For any deal* $(\Psi_1, \Psi_2)$ *in the refined negotiation set,*
$\Psi_1 = Cn(X) \cap (Cn(Y) \otimes_2 \Psi_1)$ *and* $\Psi_2 = Cn(Y) \cap (Cn(X) \otimes_1 \Psi_2)$.

**Definition 3** A selection function $\gamma$ is *downward compatible* if for any $F_1 \subseteq \gamma_1(X, Y)$ and $F_2 \subseteq \gamma_2(X, Y)$,
$\gamma(Cn(X) \otimes_1 F_2, Cn(Y) \otimes_2 F_1) = (\gamma_1(X, Y) + F_2, \gamma_2(X, Y) + F_1)$.

**Example 3** *Let* $\gamma$ *be a selection function such that* $\gamma(X, Y) = (Cn(X) \cap Cn(Y), Cn(X) \cap Cn(Y))$. *Then* $\gamma$ *is downward compatible. In other wards, always-standing-still is a uniform behavior of negotiation.*

Now we come to the main result of the paper.

**Theorem 4** *If* $\gamma$ *is a downward compatible selection function over a refined negotiation set, the negotiation function defined by Definition 2 satisfies (N1)-(N8).*

Since a downward compatible selection function always exists, this theorem shows again the consistency of the negotiation postulates. We remark that downward compatibility is a sufficient condition for postulate (N8) but not necessary. In fact, we can show that any master-slave negotiation function satisfies postulate (N8) but its associated selection function is not necessarily downward compatible. How to find a sufficient and necessary condition for (N8) is open for the future research.

## Related work

There have been several streams of research which related to this work. One stream is the work on arbitration, belief merging and knowledge fusion (Liberatore and Schaerf 1998)(Kfir-Dahav and Tennenholtz 1996)(Konieczny and Pino Perez 1998). All these researches deal with conflicts between agents. With our framework, we can also define an "arbitration" operator that satisfies most of Revesz's postulates and Liberatore and Schaerf's postulates for arbitration operation(Liberatore and Schaerf 1998)(Revesz 1997).

**Proposition 2** *Let* $N$ *be a negotiation function. Define an "arbitration operator"* $\triangle$ *as follows: for any belief set* $K_1$ *and* $K_2$,
$K_1 \triangle K_2 = N_1(K_1, K_2) \cap N_2(K_1, K_2)$
*then* $\triangle$ *satisfies Liberatore and Schaerf's postulates (A1)-(A3)(A5)-(A6) for two-agent case(Liberatore and Schaerf 1998).*[3]

However there is a fundamental difference between arbitration and mutual belief revision or negotiation. An arbitration of two knowledge bases should be fair on both information resources, whereas an outcome of negotiation does not necessarily "fair". We allow an agent totally give up her beliefs and takes all information from the other agent.

Another stream of work is that of non-prioritized belief revision(Booth 2001)(Ferme and Hansson 1999)(Hansson 1999)(Hansson *et al.* 2001). A negotiation function can be viewed as two associated selective revision(Ferme and Hansson 1999). A non-prioritized belief revision function can also be defined by negotiation processes(Booth 2001). However the existing operators proposed under these settings capture only the basic properties of negotiation.

There have been several attempts to consider belief revision in the setting of multi-agent systems(Kfir-Dahav and Tennenholtz 1996)(Malheiro *et al.* 1994)(van der Meyden 1994). In (van der Meyden 1994) a concept of mutual belief revision was defined with a totally different setting from ours, where mutual belief revision is referred to the process of belief change by which an agent in a synchronous multi-agent system revises its beliefs about other agents' beliefs.

In terms of logical approach to negotiation, there are numbers of researches on argumentation-based negotiation(Sycara 1990)(Kraus *et al.* 1998)(Parsons *et al.* 1998)(Sadri *et al.* 2001). This work is more concentrated on agent architectures and procedural analysis of negotiation protocols. Although the goal is similar with ours, the emphases and outcomes of the research are quite different from our work ( we focus on the axiomatic analysis on negotiation processes).

## Conclusion

In this paper we presented a formal framework for describing and modelling rational negotiation behaviors. A set of AGM-style postulates was presented. A representation theorem is given for the basic postulates. The consistency of all the list of postulates was also proved through an explicit construction of negotiation function in which negotiation process was modelled by two related iterated belief revision operations. This model provided a logical method to analyze the competitive and cooperative behaviors of negotiation.

As an initial work towards an axiomatic approach to negotiation, we only presented the basic axiomatic system and its modelling in this paper. In a sequent paper, we will define a notion of preference-based negotiation and concentrate on the construction of negotiation concessions and outcomes(Meyer *et al.* 2004). By then, more computation-friendly examples will be given. There are also many other things to be done. First of all, in this work, we only extended some basic game-theoretical concepts, such as individual rationality and Pareto optimality, into logical form and express a particular equilibrium by using fix-point inference. However, more profound mechanisms of cooperation and competition behind negotiation, especially the large amount of variations of equilibrium concepts in game theory and economics, need to be investigated.

## Proofs of Selected Theorems

Due to the limitation of space, we only list the proof of two main theorems.

**Proof of Theorem 2:** The postulates ($\otimes$1) and ($\otimes$3)-($\otimes$6) are the special case of the postulates (N1)-(N5), respectively. ($\otimes$2) is im-

[3]Note that $\triangle$ does not satisfy (A4) since the inconsistency of $K_1 \triangle K_2$ does not require the inconsistency of both $K_1$ and $K_2$. However, we do not consider this to be a major difference between arbitration and negotiation.

plied by (M-S). To prove ($\otimes$ IBR), we know that $(K \otimes F_1) \otimes (F_1 \cup F_2) = N_2(F_1 \cup F_2, K \otimes F_1)$. Since $F_1 \subseteq F_1 \cup F_2$, it follows from (M-S) that $F_1 \subseteq N_2(F_1 \cup F_2, K)$. Therefore $F_1 \subseteq (F_1 \cup F_2) \cap N_2(F_1 \cup F_2, K)$. By (N8) we yield $N_2(F_1 \cup F_2, N_2(F_1, K)) = N_2(F_1 \cup F_2, K) = K \otimes (F_1 \cup F_2)$.

Conversely, suppose that $\otimes$ satisfies ($\otimes$1)-($\otimes$6) and ($\otimes$IBR). It is obvious that the defined negotiation function satisfies obviously (N1)-(N5). (N6) is implies by ($\otimes$2) and ($\otimes$4). (N7) is trivial.

To prove (N8), assume $F \subseteq Cn(Y) \cap N_1(X,Y)$. Then $Cn(F) \ominus X \subseteq Cn(F) \subseteq N_1(X,Y) = Cn(Y) \otimes X$. Hence $N_1(N_1(X,F),Y) = Cn(Y) \otimes N_1(X,F) = Cn(Y) \otimes (Cn(F) \otimes X) = Cn(Y) \otimes (X \cup (Cn(F) \ominus X)) = (Cn(Y) \otimes X) + (Cn(F) \ominus X) = Cn(Y) \otimes X = N_1(X,Y)$. Similarly we have $N_2(N_1(X,F),Y) = N_2(X,Y)$.

Again assume $F \subseteq Cn(X) \cap N_2(X,Y)$. Then $N_1(X, N_2(F,Y)) = N_1(X, Cn(Y) \otimes F) = (Cn(Y) \otimes F) \otimes X = Cn(Y) \otimes (F \cup X) = Cn(Y) \otimes X = N_1(X,Y)$. $N_2(X, N_2(F,Y))$ is exactly the same. Therefore (N7) is valid. □

**Proof of Theorem 4:** We only need to verify (N8). Assume that $F \subseteq Cn(Y) \cap N_1(X,Y)$. Then $F \subseteq Cn(Y) \cap (Cn(X) \otimes_1 \gamma_2(X,Y))$. It follows from Lemma 2 that $F \subseteq \gamma_2(X,Y)$. According to the construction of negotiation function, $N_1(N_1(X,F),Y) = N_1(X,F) \otimes_1 \gamma_2(N_1(X,F),Y) = (Cn(X) \otimes_1 \gamma_2(X,F)) \otimes_1 \gamma_2(Cn(X) \otimes_1 \gamma_2(X,F),Y)$. Let $F_2 = \gamma_2(X,F)$. Thus $F_2 \subseteq Cn(F) \subseteq \gamma_2(X,Y)$. Since $\gamma$ is downwards compatible, we have $\gamma_2(Cn(X) \otimes_1 F_2, Y) = \gamma_2(X,Y)$. Therefore $N_1(N_1(X,F),Y) = (Cn(X) \otimes_1 F_2) \otimes_1 \gamma_2(Cn(X) \otimes_1 F_2, Y) = (Cn(X) \otimes_1 F_2) \otimes_1 \gamma_2(X,Y)$. By $(\otimes IBR)$ we know $(Cn(X) \otimes_1 F_2) \otimes_1 \gamma_2(X,Y) = Cn(X) \otimes_1 \gamma_2(X,Y) = N_1(X,Y)$. Put them together we yield $N_1(N_1(X,F),Y) = N_1(X,Y)$. For agent 2, similarly we have $N_2(N_1(X,F),Y) = Cn(Y) \otimes_2 \gamma_1(N_1(X,F),Y) = Cn(Y) \otimes_2 \gamma_1(Cn(X) \otimes_1 \gamma_2(X,F),Y) = Cn(Y) \otimes_2 \gamma_1(Cn(X) \otimes_1 F_2, Y)$. By the downward compatibility of $\gamma$, we have $\gamma_1(Cn(X) \otimes_1 F_2, Y) = \gamma_1(X,Y) + F_2$. Since $F_2 \subseteq Cn(Y) \otimes_2 \gamma_1(X,Y)$, Therefore, $Cn(Y) \otimes_2 (\gamma_1(X,Y) + F_2) = Cn(Y) \otimes_2 \gamma_1(X,Y)$. These give us $N_2(N_1(X,F),Y) = Cn(Y) \otimes_2 (\gamma_1(X,Y) + F_2) = Cn(Y) \otimes_2 \gamma_1(X,Y) = N_2(X,Y)$. We have proved $N(N_1(X,F),Y) = N(X,Y)$. The other half of the postulate is symmetric. □

## References


E. Alchourrón,P. Gärdenfors and Makinson, 1985. On the logic of theory change: partial meet contraction and revision functions, *Journal of Symbolic Logic,* 50(2)(1985), 510-530.

R. Booth,2001. A negotiation-style framework for non-priorised revision, *TARK'01*, 137-150.

A. Darwiche and J. Pearl, 1997. On the logic of iterated belief revision. *Artificial Intelligence,* 89(1-2):1-29.

P. Faratin, C. Sierra and N. R. Jennings, 1998. Negotiation decision functions for autonomous agents, *Robotics and Autonomous Systems*, 24(1998):159–182.

E. Ferm and S. O. Hansson,1999. Selective Revision, *Studia Logica*, 63 (3):331-342.

S. O. Hansson, 1999. A survey of non-prioritized belief revision, *Erkenntnis* 50:413-427.

S. O. Hansson, E. Ferm, J. Cantwell, and M. Falappa, 2001. Credibility-limited revision, *Journal of Symbolic Logic*, 66:1581-1596.

D. Lehmann, 1995. Belief revision, revised, *IJCAI-95,* 1534-1540.

W. Li , A logical framework for evolution of specification. in *Programming Language and Systems*, (ESOP'94), Springer-Verlag, 394-408, 1994.

P. Liberatore and M. Schaerf, 1998. Arbitration (or How to merge knowledge bases), *IEEE Transactions on Knowledge and Data Engineering*, 1(10):76-90.

N. E. Kfir-Dahav and M. Tennenholtz, 1996. Multi-agent belief revision, *TARK'96*, 175-194.

S. Konieczny and R. Pino Perez, 1998. On the logic of merging, *KR-98*, 488-498.

S.Kraus, K.Sycara, A.Evenchik, 1998. Reaching agreements through argumentation: a logical model and implementation, *Artificial Intelligence*, 104(1998), 1-69.

B. Malheiro, N. R. Jennings, and E. Oliveira, 1994. Belief revision in multi-agent systems, *ECAI-94*, 294-298.

P. Maynard-Reid II and Y. Shoham, 2001. Belief fusion: aggregating pedigreed belief states, *Journal of Logic, Language and Information* 10 (2):183-209.

R. van der Meyden, 1994. Mutual belief revision (Preliminary Report), *KR'94,* 595-606.

T. Meyer, N. Foo, R. Kwok and D. Zhang, Logical foundations of negotiation, in this proceedings.

S. Parsons, C. Sierra, N. Jennings, 1998. Agents that reason and negotiate by arguing, Journal of Logic and Computation 8(3): 261-292.

D. G. Pruitt, 1981. *Negotiation Behavour*, Academic Press.

P. Z. Revesz, 1997. On the semantics of arbitration, *International Journal of Algebra and Computation,* 7(2):133-160.

J. S. Rosenschein and G. Zlotkin, 1997. *Rules of Encounter*, MIT Press.

C. Sierra, N. R. Jennings, P. Noriega, and S. Parsons, 1997. A framework for argumentation-based negotiation. ATAL-97: 177-192.

F. Sadri, F.Toni, and P. Torroni, 2001. Dialogues for Negotiation: agent varietirs and dialogue sequences, n *Proc. ATAL-2001.*

K. Sycara, Persuasive arguementation in negotiation, *Theory and Decision*, 28:203-242.

M. Wooldridge and S. Parsons, 2000. Languages for negotiation, in: *ECAI2000*, 393-400.

D. Zhang and N. Foo, 2001. Infinitary belief revision,*Journal of Philosophical Logic*, 30(6):525-570.

D. Zhang, 2004. Properties of iterated belief revision, in: *Proc. LPNMR-04.*

# Learning

# Hierarchical Hidden Markov Models with General State Hierarchy

**Hung H. Bui***
Artificial Intelligence Center
SRI International
333 Ravenswood Ave
Menlo Park, CA 94025, USA
bui@ai.sri.com

**Dinh Q. Phung, Svetha Venkatesh**
Department of Computing
Curtin University of Technology
GPO Box U 1987
Perth, Western Australia
{phungquo, svetha}@cs.curtin.edu.au

## Abstract

The hierarchical hidden Markov model (HHMM) is an extension of the hidden Markov model to include a hierarchy of the hidden states. This form of hierarchical modeling has been found useful in applications such as handwritten character recognition, behavior recognition, video indexing, and text retrieval. Nevertheless, the state hierarchy in the original HHMM is restricted to a tree structure. This prohibits two different states from having the same child, and thus does not allow for sharing of common substructures in the model. In this paper, we present a general HHMM in which the state hierarchy can be a lattice allowing arbitrary sharing of substructures. Furthermore, we provide a method for numerical scaling to avoid underflow, an important issue in dealing with long observation sequences. We demonstrate the working of our method in a simulated environment where a hierarchical behavioral model is automatically learned and later used for recognition.

## Introduction

Hierarchical modeling of stochastic and dynamic process has recently emerged as an important research issue in many different applications. The challenging problem is to design algorithms that are robust in noisy and uncertain dynamic environments, and at the same time take advantage of the natural hierarchical organization common in many real-world domains. To this end, the hierarchical hidden Markov model (HHMM) originally proposed by (Fine, Singer, & Tishby 1998) is an extension of the hidden Markov model to include a hierarchy of the hidden states. In this paper, we will refer to this as the FST model. Motivated by the inside-outside algorithm for probabilistic context-free grammar (PCFG) (Lari & Young 1990), Fine et al. presented a method for inference and expectation-maximization (EM) parameter learning in the HHMM with complexity $T^3Sb^2$, where $T$ is the length of the observation sequence, $S$ is the total number of hidden states, and $b$ is the maximum number of substates for each state (branching factor). This model has recently been applied to a number of application domains, including handwritten character recognition (Fine, Singer, & Tishby 1998), robot navigation (Theocharous & Mahadevan 2002), behavior recognition (Luhr *et al.* 2003), video indexing (Xie *et al.* 2003) and information retrieval (Skounakis, Craven, & Ray 2003). In all of these domains, there exists a natural hierarchical decomposition of the modeled process, for example, in the way a sentence is written or a planned behavior is acted out. This property is shared by many other real-world domains, and thus an effective way of capturing this dynamic hierarchical abstraction can be very useful.

The original HHMM, however, has limitations that hinder its applicability. First, the original model considers only state hierarchies that have tree structures, disallowing the sharing of substructures among the high-level states. We argue here that substructure sharing is common in many domains. For example, in models for hand-written scripts, different word-level states should be able to share the same letter-level substates; in models of human behavior, different high-level intentions should be able to share the same set of lower-level actions. From a modeling perspective, sharing the substructures allows us to build more compact models, which facilitates more efficient inference and reduces the sample complexity in learning. Previous work on HHMM (Fine, Singer, & Tishby 1998; Murphy & Paskin 2001) allows sharing of substates only through explicit parameter tieing, although doing this is neither elegant nor efficient: one would need to expand a lattice state structure into a tree, which leads to the unnecessary exponential increase in the size of the representation and in the complexity of inference. To address this problem, we show that inference and EM learning can be done directly on the lattice state-structure, with the same complexity $O(T^3Sb^2)$. Furthermore, we present a method for numerical scaling to avoid underflow when dealing with a long observation sequence, a previously unaddressed issue. We demonstrate the working of our method in a simulated behavior recognition scenario.

This paper is motivated by earlier work. The idea that hierarchical decomposition of a stochastic dynamic process can be modeled in a dynamic Bayesian network (DBN) first appears in (Bui, Venkatesh, & West 2000; Murphy & Paskin 2001). Murphy and Paskin (2001) convert the HHMM to a DBN, and apply general DBN inference to the model to achieve complexity linear in time $T$, but exponential in the depth $D$ of the HHMM. The same analysis applies to the "flattening" method, that is to convert an HHMM to an equivalent HMM for inference purposes (Xie *et al.* 2003). When the state hierarchy is strictly a tree, the number of states $S$ is necessarily exponential in $D$. However, when considering a general lattice state hierarchy, the number of states $S$ can be much smaller than $exp(D)$, or even linear in

*Supported by DARPA under contract NBCHD030010

$D$ , depending on how much sharing is in the model. Thus, methods with complexity linear to the number of states like ours are useful, especially when the level of substate sharing is high. The $T^3$ complexity, however, means that our method is suitable only for batch learning. For online filtering, there exists an efficient approximate method for the abstract hidden Markov memory model (AHMEM) (Bui 2003), which is directly applicable to the HHMM. This can provide a fast approximation (linear in time and in the number of states of the model) for online recognition and classification.

## HHMM: Model Definition and Parameters

In this section, we describe the structural model and parameter for the HHMM. We also briefly summarize the task involved in doing EM parameter reestimation in this model. The actual computational method is deferred until later sections.

### Structural model and parameter

An HHMM is defined by a structural model $\zeta$ and a set of parameters $\theta$. The structural model $\zeta$ specifies the model depth $D$, and for each $d \in 1..D$ a set of states at level $d$: $Q^d$. For convenience, we take the set $Q^d$ to be $\{1..|Q^d|\}$. Level 1 is the top level and consists of a single state: $Q^1 = \{1\}$, while level $D$ is the bottom one. For each state $q^d \in Q^d, d < D$, the structural model also specifies the set of children of $q^d$, denoted by $\text{ch}(q^d) \subset Q^{d+1}$. From this, the set of parents of $q$ can be derived and is denoted by $\text{pa}(q^d)$. Note that the original HHMM assumes that $\text{pa}(q^d)$ always contains a single state; thus, the state hierarchy is strictly a tree. In addition to the states, we also specify an observation model. In the discrete observation case, we let $Y = \{1..|Y|\}$ be the set of observation symbols. It is straightforward to generalize to a Gaussian observation model, although the details are not shown here. Throughout the paper, the structural model $\zeta$ is assumed to be known and fixed; thus, we are not concerned with the problem of model selection.

Given such a structural model $\zeta$, the parameter $\theta$ of the HHMM is specified as follows. For each level $d \in \{1..D-1\}$, $p \in Q^d$, $i, j \in \text{ch}(p)$: $\pi_i^{d,p}$ is the initial probability of the child $i$ given the parent is $p$, $A_{i,j}^{d,p}$ is the transition probability from child $i$ to child $j$, and $A_{i,\text{end}}^{d,p}$ is the probability that state $p$ terminates given its current child is $i$. We require that $\sum_i \pi_i^{d,p} = 1$, $\sum_j A_{i,j}^{d,p} = 1$, and $A_{i,\text{end}}^{d,p} \leq 1$. FST transition parameters $a_{i,j}^{d,p}$ are slightly different from our definition, and can be obtained as $a_{i,j}^{d,p} = A_{i,j}^{d,p}(1 - A_{i,\text{end}}^{d,p})$. Finally, for $i \in Q^D$, $y \in Y$, $B_{y|i}$ is the probability of observing the symbol $y$ given that the state at the bottom level is $i$.

Given the parameter $\theta$, the HHMM defines a joint distribution over a set of variables that represent the evolution of the stochastic process over time. Following (Murphy & Paskin 2001), we specify this distribution by a DBN given in Figure 1. The variable $q_t^d$ denotes the state at time $t$ and level $d$; $e_t^d$ is an indicator variable denoting if the state $q_t^d$ has ended (i.e., its child has gone to an end state[1]).

[1]Note that $q_t^d$ has a different interpretation than the same node in (Murphy & Paskin 2001): it takes a value over $Q^d$, the set of all states at level $d$, as opposed to just over the set of children of some parent state. Thus, in our DBN, $q_t^d$ depends only on $q_t^{d-1}$ and not on the entire set of states above it $q_t^{1:d-1}$.

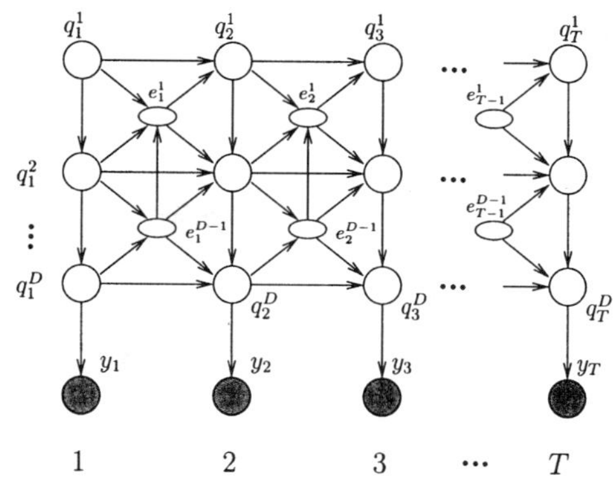


Figure 1: DBN for HHMM

Let $\mathcal{V} = \{q_{1:T}^{1:D}, e_{1:T}^{1:D-1}, y_{1:T}\}$ be the set of all variables. The HHMM defines a JPD over $\mathcal{V}$ following the factorization of the DBN[2]: $\Pr(q_{1:T}^{1:D}, e_{1:T}^{1:D-1}, y_{1:T}) \triangleq \prod_{v \in \mathcal{V}} \Pr(v \mid \text{parent}(v))$. For ease of notation, we also include the set of ending variables at the bottom level $\{e_t^D\}$, and fix their values to 1.

The conditional probability $\Pr(v \mid \text{parent}(v))$ is defined from the parameters of the HHMM and captures the evolution of the variables over time. A state can end only when the state below it has ended, and then does so with probability given by the termination parameter:

$$\Pr(e_t^d = 1 \mid q_t^{d+1} = i, q_t^d = p, e_t^{d+1}) = \begin{cases} A_{i,\text{end}}^{d,p} & \text{if } e_t^{d+1} = 1 \\ 0 & \text{if } e_t^{d+1} = 0 \end{cases}$$

A state stays the same until the next time if it does not end. If it ends and the parent state stays the same, it follows a transition to a new child-state of the same parent. Otherwise, it is initialized by a new parent-state:

$$\Pr(q_t^d = j \mid q_{t-1}^d = i, q_t^{d-1} = p, e_{t-1}^{d-1:d}) = \begin{cases} \delta(i,j) & \text{if } e_{t-1}^{d-1:d} = 00 \\ A_{i,j}^{d-1,p} & \text{if } e_{t-1}^{d-1:d} = 01 \\ \pi_j^{d-1,p} & \text{if } e_{t-1}^{d-1:d} = 11 \end{cases}$$

### Sufficient statistics and EM

The previous two equations show that the HHMM parameter $\theta$ ties together different sets of parameters of the DBN. Thus, it is not surprising that the HHMM can be written in the exponential family form, with the sufficient statistics vector $\tau$ being the count of the different types of configurations in the data $\mathcal{V}$. In this case, maximum likelihood estimation of

[2]Since the top-level state does not end during the HHMM process, the set of well-defined events is restricted to those instantiations of $\mathcal{V}$ such that $e_1^{1:T-1}$ are false. An event that does not satisfy this property is not associated with any probability mass.

$\theta$ from a complete data set $\mathcal{V}$ reduces to setting the parameters to the normalized values of the sufficient statistics $\tau$. Most of the time, however, we can observe only a subset $\mathcal{O}$ of the variables $\mathcal{V}$ so that the remaining variables $\mathcal{H} = \mathcal{V} \backslash \mathcal{O}$ are hidden. In this case, doing EM parameter reestimation reduces to first calculating the expected sufficient statistics (ESS) $\bar{\tau} = \mathrm{E}_{\mathcal{H}|\mathcal{O}}\, \tau$, and then setting the reestimated parameter $\hat{\theta}$ to the normalized value of $\bar{\tau}$.

Space restriction prevents giving the full set of sufficient statistics here. Rather, we describe only a subset of the sufficient statistics that corresponds to the transition parameter $\{\mathrm{A}^{d,p}_{i,j}\}$. Imagine the process of going through $\mathcal{V}$ and counting the number of occurrences of the configuration $\{q^{d+1}_{t+1} = j, q^{d+1}_t = i, q^d_{t+1} = p, e^{d:d+1}_t = 01\}$, resulting in the count $\tau(\mathrm{A})^{d,p}_{i,j}$. The corresponding ESS is then[3]:

$$\bar{\tau}(\mathrm{A})^{d,p}_{i,j} = \underset{\mathcal{H}|\mathcal{O}}{\mathrm{E}}\, \tau(\mathrm{A})^{d,p}_{i,j} = \sum_{t=1}^{T-1} \xi^{d,p}_t(i,j) \Big/ \Pr(\mathcal{O}) \qquad (1)$$

where the auxiliary variable $\xi^{d,p}_t(i,j)$ is defined as the probability $\Pr(q^{d+1}_{t+1} = j, q^{d+1}_t = i, q^d_{t+1} = p, e^{d:d+1}_t = 01, \mathcal{O})$. Most commonly, what we observe is the sequence $y_{1:T}$, together with the implicit fact that the HHMM does not end prior to $T$; thus our observation is $\mathcal{O} = \{y_{1:T}, e^1_{1:T-1} = \mathbf{0}\}$. In the rest of the paper, we will work explicitly with this set of observations.[4] Our method, however, also applies to an arbitrary set of observations in general.

## The Asymmetric Inside-Outside Algorithm

From Equation (1), computing the ESS reduces to evaluating the set of auxiliary variables and the likelihood $\Pr(\mathcal{O})$. We now present a method for doing this.

### Handling multiple parents

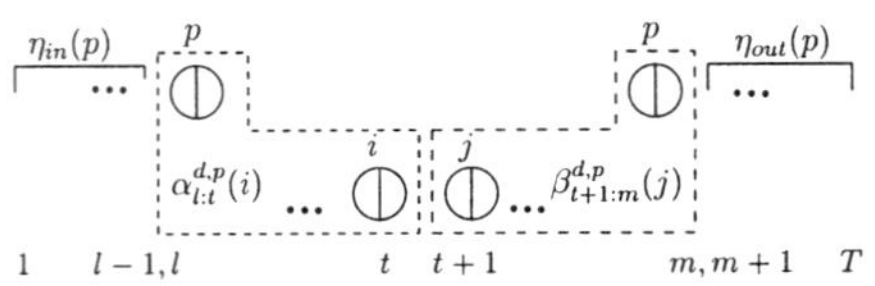

Figure 2: FST's decomposition.

We first describe the main intuition behind the FST method. Suppose we know that the state $q^d_t = p$ starts at time $l \le t$ and stops at time $m \ge t$ (when these times are not known, we can simply sum over all possible values of $l, m$). Fine et al. observe that the auxiliary variable $\xi^{d,p}_t(i,j)$ can then be factorized into the product of four different parts: the "in" part ($\eta_{in}$) consisting of the observations prior to $l$, the "forward" part ($\alpha$) consisting of the observations from $l$ to $t$, the "backward" part ($\beta$) consisting of the observations from $t+1$ to $m$, and the "out" part ($\eta_{out}$) consisting of the observations after $m$ (Figure 2). Although not stated by Fine et al., implicit in this factorization is the assumption that $q^d_t$ has a single parent state. When this does not hold, the unknown parent state of $q^d_t$ destroys the conditional independence between the "in" and the "out" parts, and thus the factorization no longer holds.

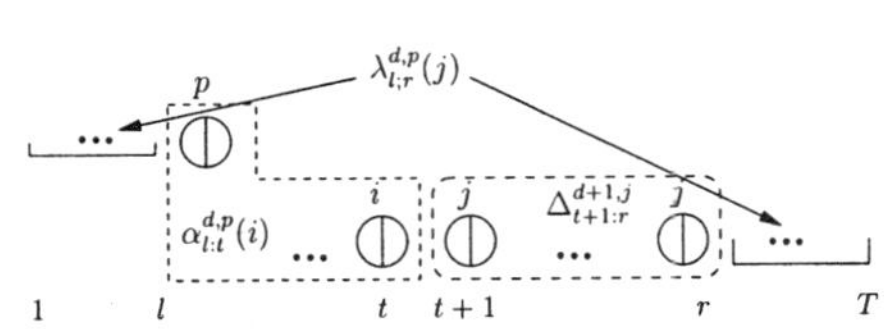

Figure 3: Our asymmetric inside-outside decomposition.

Our fix requires two modifications to the original method. First, rather than summing over the stopping time $m$ of the state $q^d_t$, we sum over the stopping time $r$ of the child state $q^{d+1}_{t+1}$. Second, we appeal to a similar technique used by the inside-outside algorithm in the PCFG, and group all the observations outside the interval $[l, r]$ into one, called the "outside" part ($\lambda$). Thus, the boundary between the inside and outside parts is not symmetrical, hence the term *asymmetric inside-outside*. The inside part is further factorized into an asymmetric inside part (same as FST's forward $\alpha$), and an symmetric inside part ($\triangle$) (Figure 3). The formal definitions of these newly defined inside-outside variables are as follows[5]:

$$\alpha^{d,p}_{l:r}(i) \triangleq \Pr(\mathcal{O}_{in}, q^{d+1}_{r\cdot} = i, e^d_{l:r-1} = \mathbf{0} \mid \cdot q^d_l = p)$$

$$\Delta^{d,i}_{l:r} \triangleq \Pr(\mathcal{O}_{in}, e^d_{l:r-1} = \mathbf{0}, e^d_r = 1 \mid \cdot q^d_l = i)$$

$$\lambda^{d,p}_{l;r}(i) \triangleq \Pr(\mathcal{O}_{out} \mid \cdot q^d_l = p, e^d_{l:r-1} = \mathbf{0}, q^{d+1}_{r\cdot} = i)\Pr(\cdot q^d_l = p)$$

$$\underset{\leadsto}{\alpha}{}^{d,p}_{l:r+1}(i) \triangleq \Pr(\mathcal{O}_{in}, \cdot q^{d+1}_{r+1} = i, e^d_{l:r} = \mathbf{0} \mid \cdot q^d_l = p)$$

where the dot in front of $q^d_t$ represents the event $e^d_{t-1} = 1$, the dot after $q^d_t$ represents the event $e^d_t = 1$, $\mathcal{O}_{in} = y_{l:r}$ is the set of observations "inside", and $\mathcal{O}_{out} = \{y_{1:l-1}, y_{r+1:T}, e^1_{1:T-1} = \mathbf{0}\}$ is the set of observations "outside". Intuitively, the asymmetric inside $\alpha^{d,p}_{l:r}(i)$ contains all the observations between when a parent state $p$ starts and a child state $i$ ends; the asymmetric outside $\lambda^{d,p}_{l;r}(i)$ contains all the remaining observations. The symmetric inside $\Delta^{d,i}_{l:r}$ contains all the observations between when a state $i$ starts and when it ends. For convenience we also define a *started* $\alpha$, denoted by $\underset{\leadsto}{\alpha}{}^{d,p}_{l:r+1}(i)$, which contains the observations from when a parent $d$ starts at $l$ to just before when a child $i$ starts at $r+1$. A summary of these variables in concise diagrammatic forms is given in Figure 4.

[3]When multiple observation sequences are encountered, we need to also sum over the set of observation sequences in the equation.

[4]Note that Fine et al. assume that the observation also includes $e^T_1 = 1$. This limits training data to the set of complete sequences of observations from the start to the end of the HHMM generating process. Removing this terminating condition at the end allows us to train the HHMM with prefix data, e.g., observed data that does not have to last until the end of the process.

[5]The definitions for FST's auxiliary variables include informal use of words such as "started", "finished", and in some cases are incorrect. For example, the correct definition of their backward variable $\beta$ should be $\Pr(\mathcal{O}_{in}, e^d_{l:r-1} = \mathbf{0}, e^d_r = 1 \mid \cdot q^{d+1}_l = i, q^d_l = p)$. Using the formal definitions of our auxiliary variables, all the equations in our paper can be verified formally. Space restrictions, however, prevent us from showing the detailed derivations.

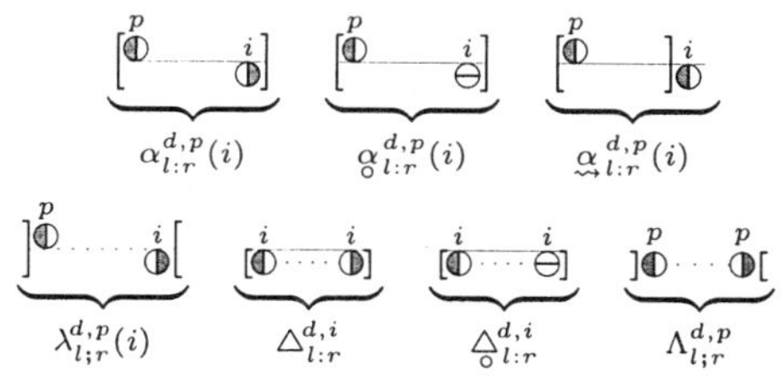

Figure 4: Diagrams for the inside and outside variables. Brackets denote the range of observations. Half-shaded circles denote starting/ending states. Crossed circles denote nonending states.

An important property of the HHMM is that given the event $\{\cdot q_l^d = p, e_{l:r-1}^d = \mathbf{0}, q_r^{d+1} = i\}$, which we call the *asymmetric boundary event*, the observations inside ($\mathcal{O}_{in}$) and outside ($\mathcal{O}_{out}$) of this asymmetric boundary are independent. With this property, we can expand the auxiliary variable $\xi$ in terms of the newly defined variables:

$$\xi_t^{d,p}(i,j) = \sum_{l=1}^{t} \sum_{r=t+1}^{T} \left( \lambda_{l;r}^{d,p}(j) \alpha_{l:t}^{d,p}(i) d_{i,j}^{d,p} \Delta_{t+1:r}^{d+1,j} \right) \quad (2)$$

### Calculating the inside-outside variables

The diagrammatic visualization of the inside and outside variables gives us a good tool for summarizing the recursive relations between these variables. Imagine trying to construct the diagram associated with $\alpha_{l:r}^{d,p}(i)$ using the other diagrams in Figure 4 as the building blocks. Let $t$ be the starting time of the child state $i$ that ends at $r$. We can then break the diagram of $\alpha_{l:r}^{d,p}(i)$ into two subdiagrams: one corresponds to $\underset{\rightsquigarrow}{\alpha}_{l:t}^{d,p}(i)$ and another one corresponds to $\Delta_{t:r}^{d+1,i}$:

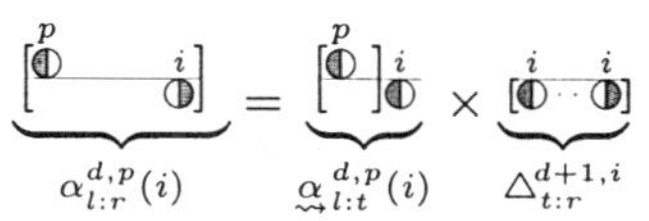

The conditional independence property in the HHMM allows us to simply take the product of the two parts. Summing over the unknown time $t$ then gives us the precise recursion formula for $\alpha_{l:r}^{d,p}(i)$:

$$\alpha_{l:r}^{d,p}(i) = \sum_{t=l}^{r} \underset{\rightsquigarrow}{\alpha}_{l:t}^{d,p}(i) \Delta_{t:r}^{d+1,i}$$

Recursion formulas for other variables can be derived intuitively in a similar way. The appendix provides a summary of all the formulas. Although not shown here, rigorous derivations can be worked out for each of them. Intuitively, each inside variable depends on other inside variables with smaller ranges, or variables at the lower level. The initialization of these variables can be derived straight from their definitions:

$$\underset{\rightsquigarrow}{\alpha}_{r:r}^{d,p}(i) = \pi_i^{d,p}, \Delta_{r:r}^{D,i} = \mathrm{B}_{y_r|i}$$

Based on this, dynamic programming can be used to compute all the inside variables bottom-up. Similarly, the outside variables can be computed top-down.

The remaining problem is to compute the likelihood $\Pr(\mathcal{O})$. Similar to FST, we sum over the asymmetric inside variable at the top level to yield

$$\sum_{i \in Q^2} \alpha_{1:T}^{1,1}(i) = \Pr(\mathcal{O}, e_T^1 = 1 \mid \cdot q_1^1 = 1) = \Pr(\mathcal{O}, e_T^1 = 1)$$

Unfortunately, this is not enough to give us the likelihood $\Pr(\mathcal{O})$. The missing term is $\Pr(\mathcal{O}, e_T^1 = 0)$, and we have not discussed how this can be obtained. To do this, we need to define a new variant of the asymmetric inside variable when the child state does not end at the right time index $r$. We call this the *continuing* $\alpha$, denoted by $\underset{\circ}{\alpha}$:

$$\underset{\circ}{\alpha}_{l:r}^{d,p}(i) \triangleq \Pr(\mathcal{O}_{in}, q_r^{d+1} = i, e_r^{d+1} = 0, e_{l:r-1}^d = \mathbf{0} \mid \cdot q_l^d = p)$$

Similar recursion formulas can be established for $\underset{\circ}{\alpha}$ (see the appendix), which allow us to compute these variables bottom-up. It is then straightforward to verify that

$$\sum_{i \in Q^2} (\alpha_{1:T}^{1,1}(i) + \underset{\circ}{\alpha}_{1:T}^{1,1}(i)) = \Pr(\mathcal{O}) \quad (3)$$

## Numerical Scaling

It is well-known that as the length of the observation sequence increases, naive implementations of the HMM will run into a numerical underflow problem. For this, a method for numerical scaling for the HMM has been derived (Rabiner 1989). It is thus imperative to address this same issue in the HHMM. Equation (1) reveals the source of the problem: both the numerator and the denominator of the RHS are joint probability of $O(T)$ variables that quickly go to zero as $T$ becomes large. We can rewrite Equation (1) as $\bar{\tau}(\mathrm{A})_{i,j}^{d,p} = \sum_{t=2}^{T} \tilde{\xi}_t^{d,p}(i,j)$, where the scaled auxiliary variable $\tilde{\xi}_t^{d,p}(i,j)$ is defined as $\xi_t^{d,p}(i,j)/Pr(\mathcal{O})$, which is $\Pr(q_{t+1}^d = p, q_{t+1}^{d+1} = j, q_t^{d+1} = i, e_t^{d:d+1} = 01 \mid \mathcal{O})$. It is thus desirable to compute $\tilde{\xi}$ directly.

To do this, define the scaled factor at time $t$ as follows: $c_1 = \Pr(y_1)^{-1}$, $c_t = \Pr(y_t, e_{t-1}^1 = 0 \mid y_{1:t-1}, e_{1:t-2}^1 = \mathbf{0})^{-1}$ for $t \geq 2$, so that $\prod_{k=1}^{t} c_k = \Pr(y_{1:t}, e_{1:t-1}^1 = \mathbf{0})^{-1}$. We proceed to scale up each inside and outside variable by the set of scaled factors in the observation range, that is,

$$\tilde{\alpha}_{l:r}^{d,p}(i) = \alpha_{l:r}^{d,p}(i) \prod_{k=l}^{r} c_k, \tilde{\Delta}_{l:r}^{d,i} = \Delta_{l:r}^{d,i} \prod_{k=l}^{r} c_k$$

$$\tilde{\lambda}_{l;r}^{d,p}(i) = \lambda_{l;r}^{d,p}(i) \prod_{k=1}^{l-1} c_k \prod_{k=r+1}^{T} c_k$$

and similarly for the other variables. Since each of the scaled variables effectively carries all the scaled factors within its range of observations, their product would carry the product of all the scaled factors. Thus, Equation (2) still holds if we replace each of the variables by its scaled version. By the same reason, the recursion formulas for the unscaled variables in the appendix also hold for their scaled counterparts.

We will now show that the scaled variables can be computed via dynamic programming in a bottom-up and left-right fashion. Assume that we have computed all the scaled inside variables up to the right index $r - 1$. We can simply apply the recursion formulas to calculate the scaled variables with the right index $r$. However, the remaining difficulty is in the initialization step $\tilde{\Delta}^{D,i}_{r:r} = \mathrm{B}_{y_l|i}c_r$ that requires knowledge of the scale factor $c_r$. Fortunately, we can get around this by a two-stage procedure. In the first stage, we calculate the new scaled variables from their usual recursion formulas, however, using the unscaled initialization $\Delta^{D,i}_{r:r} = \mathrm{B}_{y_l|i}$. The variables computed at this stage are partially scaled, i.e. they carry all the necessary scale factors except $c_r$. When we reach the top level, the partially scaled variables, denoted by $\ddot{\alpha}$, are

$$\ddot{\alpha}^{1,1}_{1:r}(i) = \alpha^{1,1}_{1:r}(i)\prod_{k=1}^{r-1} c_k, \quad \ddot{\underset{\circ}{\alpha}}^{1,1}_{1:r}(i) = \underset{\circ}{\alpha}^{1,1}_{1:r}(i)\prod_{k=1}^{r-1} c_k$$

Substituting these into Equation (3), we obtain

$$\sum_{i \in Q^2} (\ddot{\alpha}^{1,1}_{1:r}(i) + \ddot{\underset{\circ}{\alpha}}^{1,1}_{1:r}(i)) = \Pr(\mathcal{O})\prod_{k=1}^{r-1} c_k = c_r^{-1} \quad (4)$$

In the second stage, once $c_r$ is obtained, it is multiplied into all the partially scaled variables calculated in the first stage. This gives us the final scaled variables at time index $r$.

Finally, the log likelihood $\log\Pr(\mathcal{O})$ can be obtained from the set of scale factors: $\log\Pr(\mathcal{O}) = -\sum_{k=1}^{T}\log c_k$.

## Experimental Results

The first simulation is designed to to verify the EM parameter estimation in the presence of shared structures in the hierarchy (Figure 5). Based on a randomly initialized parameter $\theta$, we generate 40 sequences of observation of length $T = 50$. Using the data, we estimate $\tilde{\theta}$. We found $\tilde{\theta}$ to be very close to $\theta$. In general, the accuracy increases from top to bottom. This is not surprising because recovering the parameters at the higher hidden level is more difficult. An example is shown for the transition matrix $\mathrm{A}^{3,2}$ (estimated values in RHS).

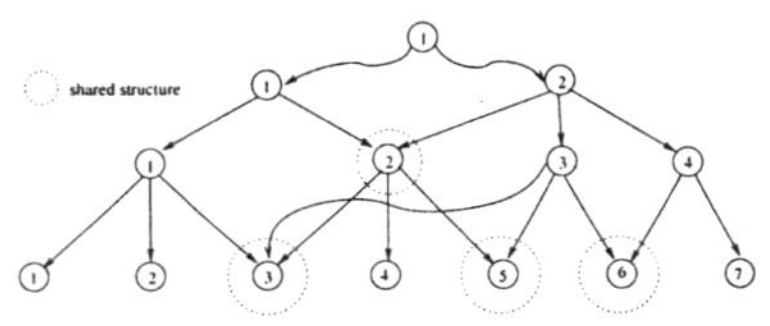


Figure 5: A 4-level hierarchy topology used in the simulation

$$\begin{bmatrix} 0.0459 & 0.2620 & 0.2475 & 0.4446 \\ 0.3716 & 0.2851 & 0.3233 & 0.0201 \\ 0.2296 & 0.2907 & 0.1835 & 0.2962 \end{bmatrix} \begin{bmatrix} 0.0472 & 0.2686 & 0.2549 & 0.4292 \\ 0.3682 & 0.2868 & 0.3272 & 0.0176 \\ 0.2324 & 0.3012 & 0.1896 & 0.2768 \end{bmatrix}$$

The second experiment demonstrates the advantage of our proposed method in comparison with the linear time method (Murphy & Paskin 2001). We construct two different topologies for testing. The first topology has 4 levels containing 3 states each (a total of 12 states excluding the top-level dummy state); the topology is fully connected, that is a state at each level is the parent of all the states at the level below. The second topology is similar except that it has five levels (and thus has 15 states). Figure 6 shows the computational time of the forward pass in one EM iteration using the two methods on two different topologies. While our method exhibits $O(T^3)$ complexity, it scales linearly when we increase the depth of the model. Adding an extra level means that our method only has to deal with an extra 3 states, where as the linear time method has to deal with 3 times the number of states due to its conversion to a tree structure.

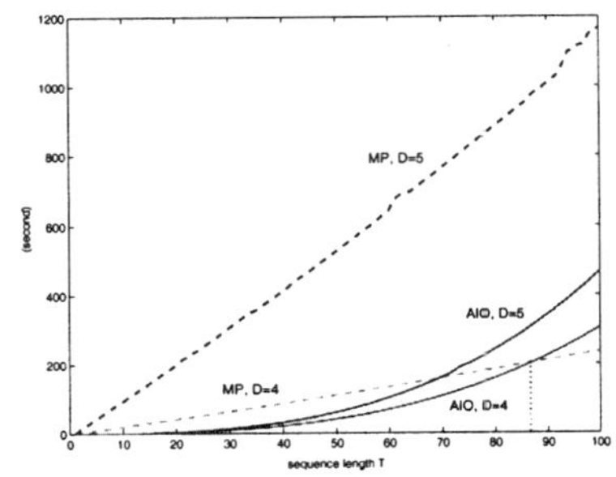


Figure 6: Computation time of MP method (Murphy & Paskin 2001) versus Asymmetric Inside-Outside (AIO) method

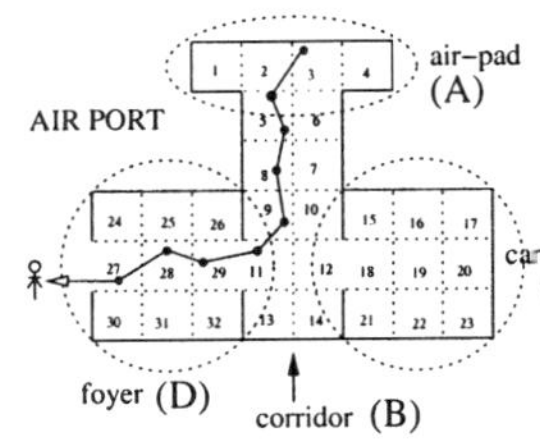


Figure 7: Airport simulation environment.

The third experiment demonstrates the use of our method in learning a hierarchical model for movement trajectories in a simulated "airport" environment, shown in Figure 7. The airport is divided into four subregions: (A) the airpad, (B) the corridor, (C) the carousel, and (D) the foyer for entry and exit. At the top level, we are interested in three behaviors: (1) leaving the plane and exit the airport without collecting luggage (*exit-airport*), (2) collecting the luggage before exiting the airport (*pickup-luggage-exit*), and (3) friends picking up passengers (*meet-pickup*). This behaviors are built from a set of 9 behaviors at the lower level: *exit-airplane* (region A); *turn-left-foyer, turn-right-carousel, pass-left-right, pass-right-left* (region B); *collect-luggage, leave-carousel* (region C); and *enter-foyer, leave-foyer* (region D). The production level includes all the grid cells as its state space $(1 - 32)$. This results in a 4-level HHMM where each state corresponds to a behavior in the hierarchy. The lattice structure allows us to model sharing of subbehaviors among the high-level behaviors. For example, *exit-airport* and *pickup-luggage-exit* would share most of the lower-level subbehaviors, except that *exit-airport* does not involve entering the carousel.

A manually-specified HHMM is used to generate 30 sequences (length $= 30$) of observations as the training data set. The generating model is then thrown away, and the data is used to train a new HHMM. Except for prior knowledge

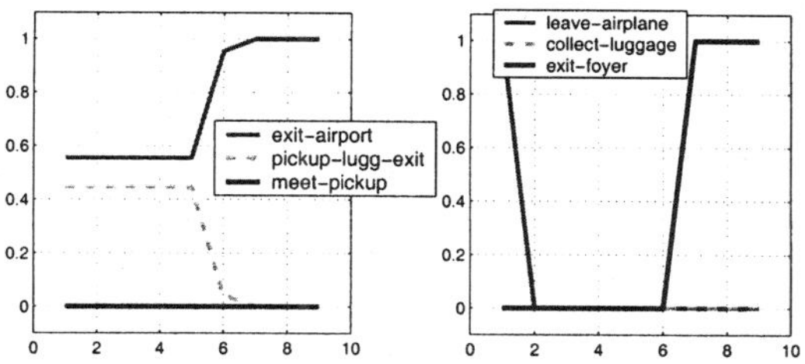


Figure 8: Online tracking result for top-level behaviors (left) and subbehaviors (right)

about the topology of the state hierarchy, learning is done completely unsupervised. Results similar to the first experiment are observed when comparing the original and estimated parameters. This allows us to then relabel the states of the learned model using "semantic" labels from the original model. To see how the learned model can be used for online tracking, we randomly generate trajectories for behaviors at the top level and examine the filtering distributions. For example, a random trajectory generated for *exit-airport* is shown in Figure 7. The filtering probability for this trajectory at two levels of behaviors is plotted in Figure 8. At the top level, the behavior *exit-airport* wins at the end, although the middle part is uncertain when it is not clear if the passenger will pick up the luggage (left diagram). For tracking lower-level behaviors, the graph shows a high probability for *leave-airplane* at the beginning, and a high probability for *exit-foyer* at the end (right diagram).

## Conclusion

We have presented a method for parameter reestimation for the HHMM in the case where the state hierarchy is a general lattice. This allows us to learn models where the high-level states could share the same children at the lower level. Furthermore, we address an important issue when dealing with long observation sequences by providing a method for numerical scaling for the HHMM. Experimental results with simulated data show the potential of our method in building a hierarchical model of behavior from a data set of observed trajectories. We are currently applying our method to a real-world environment for learning hierarchical models of human movement behavior.

## Appendix : Summary of the Formulas

We present the set of all formulas for computating the auxiliary variables defined for the HHMM. In all cases, except where explicitly stated, the level index $d$ will range from 1 to $D-1$, where $D$ is the depth of the model.

$$\alpha_{l:r}^{d,p}(i) \triangleq \Pr(y_{l:r}, q_{r}^{d+1}{\cdot}=i, e_{l:r-1}^{d}=\mathbf{0} \mid \cdot q_{l}^{d}=p) = \sum_{t=l}^{r} \underset{\rightsquigarrow}{\alpha}_{l:t}^{d,p}(i)\Delta_{t:r}^{d+1,i}$$

$$\underset{\circ}{\alpha}_{l:r}^{d,p}(i) \triangleq \Pr(y_{l:r}, q_{r}^{d+1}=i, e_{r}^{d+1}=0, e_{l:r-1}^{d}=\mathbf{0} \mid \cdot q_{l}^{d}=p) = \sum_{t=l}^{r} \underset{\rightsquigarrow}{\alpha}_{l:t}^{d,p}(i)\underset{\circ}{\Delta}_{t:r}^{d+1,i}$$

$$\underset{\rightsquigarrow}{\alpha}_{l:r}^{d,p}(i) \triangleq \Pr(y_{l:r-1}, \cdot q_{r}^{d+1}=i, e_{l:r-1}^{d}=\mathbf{0} \mid \cdot q_{l}^{d}=p) = \begin{cases} \sum_{j\in \mathrm{ch}(p)} \alpha_{l:r-1}^{d,p}(j) a_{j,i}^{d,p} & \text{if } r>l \\ \pi_{i}^{d,p} & \text{if } r=l \end{cases}$$

$$\Delta_{l:r}^{d,i} \triangleq \Pr(y_{l:r}, e_{l:r-1}^{d}=\mathbf{0}, e_{r}^{d}=1 \mid \cdot q_{l}^{d}=i) = \begin{cases} \sum_{s\in \mathrm{ch}(i)} \alpha_{l:r}^{d,i}(s) \mathrm{A}_{s,\mathrm{end}}^{d,i} \\ = \mathrm{B}_{y_r|i} & \text{if } d=D \end{cases}$$

$$\underset{\circ}{\Delta}_{l:r}^{d,i} \triangleq \Pr(y_{l:r}, e_{l:r}^{d}=\mathbf{0} \mid \cdot q_{l}^{d}=i) = \begin{cases} \sum_{s\in \mathrm{ch}(i)} \left[\alpha_{l:r}^{d,i}(s)\left(1-\mathrm{A}_{s,\mathrm{end}}^{d,i}\right) + \underset{\circ}{\alpha}_{l:r}^{d,i}(s)\right] \\ 0 \quad \text{if } d=D \end{cases}$$

Define $\mathcal{O}_{out} \triangleq \{y_{1:l-1:}, y_{r+1:T}, e_{1:T-1}^{1}=\mathbf{0}\}$

$$\Lambda_{l;r}^{d,p} \triangleq \Pr(\mathcal{O}_{out} \mid \cdot q_{l}^{d}=p, e_{l:r-1}^{d}=\mathbf{0}, e_{r}^{d}=1)\Pr(\cdot q_{l}^{d}=p)$$

$$\lambda_{l;r}^{d,p}(i) \triangleq \Pr(\mathcal{O}_{out} \mid \cdot q_{l}^{d}=p, e_{l:r-1}^{d}=\mathbf{0}, q_{r}^{d+1}{\cdot}=i)\Pr(\cdot q_{l}^{d}=p)$$

$$\Lambda_{1;T}^{1,1}=1, \qquad \lambda_{1;T}^{1,1}(i)=\mathrm{A}_{1,\mathrm{end}}^{1,i}$$

$$\lambda_{1;r}^{1,1}(i) = \sum_{r'=r+1}^{\mathrm{RB}(1,1)} \sum_{j} \lambda_{1;r'}^{1,1}(j)\Delta_{r+1:r'}^{2,j} a_{i,j}^{1,1}$$

$$\Lambda_{l;r}^{d,p} = \sum_{q\in \mathrm{pa}(p)} \sum_{l'=1}^{\mathrm{LB}(d,l)} \underset{\rightsquigarrow}{\alpha}_{l':l}^{d-1,q}(p)\lambda_{l';r}^{d-1,q}(p)$$

$$\lambda_{l;r}^{d,p}(i) = \sum_{r'=r+1}^{\mathrm{RB}(d,r)} \sum_{j\in \mathrm{ch}(p)} \lambda_{l;r'}^{d,p}(j) a_{i,j}^{d,p}\Delta_{r+1:r'}^{d+1,j} + \Lambda_{l;r}^{d,p}\mathrm{A}_{i,\mathrm{end}}^{d,p}$$

where $\mathrm{LB}(d,l)$ and $\mathrm{RB}(d,r)$ are two functions used to compute the appropriate index boundary: $\mathrm{LB}(d,l) \triangleq l$ if $l>1, d>2$, and $\triangleq 1$ otherwise; $\mathrm{RB}(d,r) \triangleq T$ if $d<D-1, \triangleq (r+1)$ if $d=(D-1)$, and $\triangleq r$ if $r=T$.

## References

Bui, H. H.; Venkatesh, S.; and West, G. 2000. On the recognition of abstract Markov policies. In *Proceedings of the National Conference on Artificial Intelligence (AAAI-2000)*.

Bui, H. H. 2003. A general model for online probabilistic plan recognition. In *Proceedings of the Eighteenth International Joint Conference on Artificial Intelligence (IJCAI-03)*.

Fine, S.; Singer, Y.; and Tishby, N. 1998. The hierarchical Hidden Markov Model: Analysis and applications. *Machine Learning* 32.

Lari, K., and Young, S. J. 1990. The estimation of stochastic context-free grammars using the Inside-Outside algorithm. *Computer Speech and Language* 4:35–56.

Luhr, S.; Bui, H. H.; Venkatesh, S.; and West, G. 2003. Recognition of human activity through hierarchical stochastic learning. In *IEEE International Conference on Pervasive Computing and Communication (PERCOM-2003)*.

Murphy, K., and Paskin, M. 2001. Linear time inference in hierarchical HMMs. In *NIPS-2001*.

Rabiner, L. R. 1989. A tutorial on Hidden Markov Models and selected applications in speech recognition. *Proceedings of the IEEE* 77(2):257–286.

Skounakis, M.; Craven, M.; and Ray, S. 2003. Hierarchical hidden Markov models for information extraction. In *Proceedings of the Eighteenth International Joint Conference on Artificial Intelligence (IJCAI-03)*.

Theocharous, G., and Mahadevan, S. 2002. Learning the hierarchical structure of spatial environments using multiresolution statistical models. In *IEEE/RSJ International Conference on Intelligent Robots and Systems (IROS)*.

Xie, L.; Chang, S.-F.; Divakaran, A.; and Sun, H. 2003. Unsupervised discovery of multilevel statistical video structures using hierarchical hidden Markov models. In *International Conference on Multimedia and Exhibition (ICME-2003)*.

# An Ensemble Technique for Stable Learners with Performance Bounds

**Ian Davidson**

Department of Computer Science, SUNY - Albany
1400 Washington Avenue, Albany, NY, 12210, davidson@cs.albany.edu

**Abstract**

Ensemble techniques such as bagging and DECORATE exploit the "instability" of learners, such as decision trees, to create a diverse set of models. However, creating a diverse set of models for stable learners such as naïve Bayes is difficult as they are relatively insensitive to training data changes. Furthermore, many popular ensemble techniques do not have a rigorous underlying theory and often provide no insight into how many models to build. We formally define stable learner as having a second order derivative of the posterior density function and propose an ensemble technique specifically for stable learners. Our ensemble technique, *bootstrap model averaging,* creates a number of bootstrap samples from the training data, builds a model from each and then sums the joint instance and class probability over all models built. We show that for stable learners our ensemble technique for infinite bootstrap samples approximates posterior model averaging (aka the optimal Bayes classifier (OBC)). For finite bootstrap samples we estimate the increase over the OBC error using Chebychev bounds. We empirically illustrate our approach's usefulness for several stable learners and verify our bound's correctness.

## 1 Introduction and Motivation

Ensemble approaches are popular because they decrease predictive error. Bagging (Brieman 1996), boosting (Schapire 1992), arcing (Brieman 1998) and DECORATE (Melville, Mooney, 2003) have been empirically shown to have a better generalization error than using a single model.

Although ensemble techniques are popular, they suffer from several problems. They are best suited to unstable learners such as decision trees that readily allow the creation of a diverse set of classifiers (Melville, Mooney, 2003) and do not decrease predictive error as much for stable learners, a claim we empirically verify in this paper. Why an ensemble technique works is not often known meaning when they are applicable is difficult to predict. Therefore, each ensemble technique should be tried for completeness, just in case it works. Finally, how many models to build is not known leaving the number of bags, boosting rounds or data sets to generate another unknown to be investigated empirically. Therefore, though they are useful, ensemble techniques require a large investment of time to verify how many models to build and which technique to apply.

In this paper we propose an ensemble technique for stable learners we refer to as bootstrap model averaging. For now, we define only the behavior of a stable learner as building similar models from slight variations of a data set, precise properties we leave until later sections. Examples of stable learners include naïve Bayes classifiers and belief networks when applied to data sets with no missing values. We show that as the number of models built approaches infinity our ensemble approach is equivalent to the optimal Bayes classifier (OBC) when using the same prior distribution over the model space. The OBC is known to minimize the Bayesian error/risk for a given model space and prior probability distribution over the space: no classifier can perform better, hence its name (Mitchell, 1997). In this respect OBC is highly desirable but it requires integration over the model space making it extremely time consuming. Our approach offers an approximation to OBC with performance bounds dependent on the number of models built. This allows the quantification of the closeness of the approximation and specifying a trade-off between closeness to the OBC error and time (number of models to build).

## 2 Paper Outline

We begin this paper by algorithmically outlining our ensemble approach. Some ensembles approaches such as bagging are known to not perform well for stable learners as it is difficult to create a diverse set of models, we verify this and show similar results for DECORATE. We then formally define stable learners and describe their properties. The subsequent section shows our approach approximates the OBC in the limit as the number of models built approaches infinity. For the non-ideal case, we bound the increase over the OBC error as a function of the number of models built. For artificial data sets, we can measure the error increase and we verify the correctness of our bound. We next empirically demonstrate our approach on real world data sets for naïve Bayes and belief networks showing that the results are better than a single model and bagging. Finally we conclude and describe future work. Throughout this paper we use five standard UCI data sets, similar results were obtained for other data sets but are not presented due to space limitations.

## 3 Bootstrap Model Averaging

From the $n$ instance training data set, $D$, a number of ($T$) bootstrap samples (sampling with replacement) of size $n$ are drawn and a model built for each. Let $\theta_t$ represent the model learnt from bootstrap sample ($X_t$). Each model votes for every class according to the joint probability of the class and the test set instance given the model. Let the sum of the joint probability for class $i$ be $r_i$. Formally bootstrap model averaging chooses the highest probability class:

$$\arg\max_i : r_i = \sum_t^T P(y_i, x \mid \theta_t) \quad (1)$$

Generative learners such as naïve Bayes classifiers and mixture models estimate the joint probability.

## 4 Ensembles and Learner Stability

The purpose of this section is to illustrate empirically that popular ensemble techniques do not work as well for stable learners. Later, we shall show our approach does increase predictive accuracy for these data sets. Creating a diverse set of models appears to be an important property for successful ensemble techniques (Krough and Vedelsby, 1995). However, creating a diverse set for stable learners appears to be difficult. Techniques such as bagging are known to work best with unstable learners (see Table 1 and Table 3) as they reduce variance. We illustrate that techniques such as DECORATE also does not work as well with stable learners (see Table 2 and Table 4 ). Our presented results show the following:

1) The mean error reduction for bagging (DECORATE) C4.5 is 1.5% (1.3%), for naïve Bayes 0.13% (0.5%).
2) Bagging and DECORATE naïve Bayes produced only one statistically significant[1] decrease in error but nine significant decreases for C4.5.
3) Bagging and DECORATE generalization errors are non-monotonic functions of the number of bags/rounds.

Table 1. C4.5 bagging 10 X-fold % error, 100 trials.

| Dataset | Training Data | T=10 | T=50 | T=100 | Improve (Stat. Sig.) |
|---|---|---|---|---|---|
| **Iris** | 5.4 | 4.7 | 5.4 | 4.7 | 0.7 (Yes) |
| **Breast** | 5.2 | 4.2 | 3.4 | 3.2 | 2.0 (Yes) |
| **Soybean** | 7.6 | 6.6 | 6.8 | 6.1 | 1.5 (Yes) |
| **Crx** | 15.2 | 13.5 | 14.2 | 13.8 | 1.8 (Yes) |
| **Adult**[2] | 17.0 | 16.4 | 16.2 | 15.6 | 1.4 (Yes) |

Table 2. Naïve Bayes bagging 10 X-fold % error,100 trials.

| Dataset | Training Data | T=10 | T=50 | T=100 | Improve (Stat. Sig.) |
|---|---|---|---|---|---|
| **Iris** | 5.2 | 5.3 | 5.3 | 5.3 | 0 (No) |
| **Breast** | 2.7 | 2.7 | 2.8 | 2.8 | 0 (No) |
| **Soybean** | 9.25 | 9.35 | 9.2 | 9.3 | 0 (No) |
| **Crx** | 22.5 | 22.1 | 22.4 | 22.0 | 0.48 (No) |
| **Adult** | 19.3 | 19.3 | 19.2 | 19.2 | 0.16 (No) |

[1] Pairwise t-Test for means at the 95% confidence level

[2] Predicting SEX field

Table 3. C4.5 DECORATE 10 X-fold % error, 100 trials.

| Dataset | Training Data | T=10 | T=50 | T=100 | Improve (Stat. Sig.) |
|---|---|---|---|---|---|
| **Iris** | 5.4 | 5.4 | 6.0 | 5.4 | 0.0 (No) |
| **Breast** | 5.2 | 3.6 | 3.6 | 3.4 | 1.8 (Yes) |
| **Soybean** | 7.6 | 5.8 | 6.1 | 6.4 | 1.5 (Yes) |
| **Crx** | 15.2 | 14.9 | 14.5 | 14.5 | 0.7 (Yes) |
| **Adult** | 17.0 | 18.4 | 14.5 | 17.8 | 2.5 (Yes) |

Table 4. Naïve Bayes DECORATE 10 X-fold error, 100 trials

| Dataset | Training Data | T=10 | T=50 | T=100 | Improve (Stat. Sig.) |
|---|---|---|---|---|---|
| **Iris** | 5.2 | 5.2 | 5.2 | 5.1 | 0.1 (No) |
| **Breast** | 2.7 | 3.0 | 3.0 | 3.0 | -0.3 (No) |
| **Soybean** | 9.25 | 9.3 | 9.3 | 9.3 | -0.0 (No) |
| **Crx** | 22.5 | 20.2 | 20.2 | 20.2 | 2.3 (Yes) |
| **Adult** | 19.3 | 19.4 | 19.4 | 19.4 | 0.16 (No) |

## 5 Stable Learners

So far we have only colloquially mentioned that a stable learner converges to a set of similar models from slight variations of the training data set, we now formalize the definition. A stable learner has a posterior density function whose second order derivative with respect to the model parameters **is defined**. This second order derivative is the rate of change, of the rate of change of the posterior probability to changes in the model parameters for a given data set. A learner/estimator that has the above mentioned property and one other is all that is required for the Bayesian central limit theorem (Clarke and Barron) to hold.

The Bayesian central limit theorem tells us precisely what properties a learner must have to produce a Gaussian posterior. Those are:

1) The training data must be independently and identically distributed given the model.
2) The posterior probability density function must be twice differentiable everywhere for all of the training data.

An additional property not required for the theorem to hold but we add into our definition of stable learners is:

3) The learner is a deterministic function of the training data.

Property 1) means that the training set observations can be considered independent of each other and are drawn from the same distribution (pool of data). Property 2) we have discussed earlier in this section may seem prohibitive but holds for many learners in the machine learning literature. Most probability density functions used in learning are from the expotential family and meet the above properties. A few distributions such as the Cauchy distribution do not meet the requirements, but they appear not to be in common use.

Note, the theorem **does not state** that for models of multivariate Gaussians that the posterior will be Gaussian, it states for **any** posterior density function that is twice differentiable and models the data as IID that the posterior will be Gaussian. The smooth Gaussian distribution denotes a well defined functional relationship between the data and the model parameters. Conversely small changes to the data will result in only small changes to the posterior probabilities. We could have defined the second order derivative with respect to changes in the data, but the number of parameters in a model is far less than the number of data points and hence easier to calculate. The Gaussian posterior for stable learners is:

$$\theta \sim N(\mu_\theta = E_{P(\theta|D)}(\theta),\ \sigma_\theta^2 = \mathrm{Var}_{P(\theta|D)}(\theta)) \tag{2}$$

The mean of this Gaussian is the expected model parameters over the posterior distribution (ie. $\Sigma P(\theta|D).\theta$) and the variance is calculated over model parameters multiplied by their posterior probability. As an illustrative example, consider perhaps the simplest stable learner: the majority guesser. The majority guesser simply predicts the most populous class in the training set and for a two class problem effectively has one parameter, $\rho$, the probability of class +. We encode a positive label for the $i^{th}$ instance as $y_i = 1$ and negative label as $y_i = 0$. The posterior density function over the one parameter is:

$$\begin{aligned} P(\rho \mid D) &\propto P(\rho)\prod_{i=1}^{n} P(x_i \mid \rho), \text{assume a uniform prior} \\ &\propto \prod_{i=1}^{n} \rho^{y_i}(1-\rho)^{(1-y_i)} \end{aligned} \tag{3}$$

The mean of the posterior is $\Sigma_i \rho_i P(\rho_i|D) = 0.5$ for all data sets where $i$ indexes all possible parameter values. The posterior standard deviation for a model space of size $k$ is over $\{\rho_1 P(\rho_1|D) \ \ldots \ \rho_k P(\rho_k|D)\}$. We now show that as expected, that naïve Bayes is stable and decision trees unstable according to our definition. Consider a two class naïve Bayes classifier with a single Boolean attribute (true=1, false=0) without loss of generality. This classifier effectively builds a model for each class and we focus on the model to predict one class (+), the other class (-) model will be identical in form. The parameters for the model are {P(+), $p$, $q$=(1- $p$)}. We use the term $n_+$ to indicate the number of instances with a positive label and $n_{+,T}$, $n_{+,F}$ the number of positive labeled instances with a TRUE and FALSE attribute respectively. Writing the posterior distribution for class + yields equation ( 4 ). Taking the second order derivative with respect to $p$ yields equation ( 5 ), a standard result for binomial distributions.

$$\begin{aligned} P(\theta_+ \mid D) &\propto P(+)\prod_{i=1}^{n_+} P(x_i \mid +) \\ &\propto P(+)\prod_{i=1}^{n_+} p^{x_i}(1-p)^{(1-x_i)} \\ &\propto [n_+/n]\, p^{n_{+,x_i=T}}(1-p)^{n_{+,x_i=F}} \end{aligned} \tag{4}$$

For a uniform and hence constant prior

$$\begin{aligned} P'(\theta_+ \mid D) &\propto n_{+,x_i=T}(pe+(1-p))^{n_{+,x_i=T}-1}\, pe \\ P''(\theta_+ \mid D) &\propto n_{+,x_i=T}(n_{+,x_i=T}-1)(pe+(1-p))^{n_{+,x_i=T}-2} + \\ &\quad n_{+,x_i=T}(pe+(1-p))^{n_{+,x_i=T}-1}\, pe \end{aligned} \tag{5}$$

Most learners that involve counting (with no independent attributes having missing values) will have a posterior density function that contain a binomial distribution and hence have posteriors that are twice differentiable. Examples include belief networks and even association rules. These are all considered by the machine learning community to be more stable compared to learners such as decision trees.

Consider the posterior distribution for a decision tree learner with $m$ attributes. If any of the attributes were continuous, the model parameters contain inequalities and hence the posterior density function cannot be differentiated. For Boolean or multistate attributes, the model consists of a disjunction of *nLeafs* conjunctions. Let the parameters for the $i^{th}$ conjunction be $\{X_{i,1} \wedge \ldots X_{i,m}\}$ and the number of training instances following this path be $n_{Path\_i}$. Then the posterior density function is:

$$\begin{aligned} P(\theta \mid D) &\propto P(\theta)\prod_{i=1}^{nLeafs} P(Path_i)^{n_{Path_i}} \\ &\propto P(\theta)\prod_{i=1}^{nLeafs} P(X_{i,1} \wedge \ldots X_{i,m})^{n_{Path_i}} \end{aligned} \tag{6}$$

Colloquially, the first order derivative measures the change in posterior density when the parameters are changed slightly. However, one cannot change the parameters of a conjunction slightly and the derivative of a conjunctive expression is undefined. Therefore, decision trees of either (or both) discrete or continuous attributes are not stable according to our definition.

We now discuss the optimal Bayes classifier and compare it to our ensemble approach bootstrap model averaging.

# 6 Optimal Bayesian Classifier and Bootstrap Model Averaging

We begin this section by describing the OBC and why it is optimal. Then we describe our approach and show it is equivalent to OBC for stable learners in the limit as the number of models approaches infinity. For the finite case we then derive bounds that measure the difference between the two ensemble approaches.

Without loss of generality consider a two class problem, $y_1$ and $y_2$, and a single test instance, $x$, training data $D$ and model space $\Theta$. Generalizing our results for the entire instance space involves just adding another integral over the instance space. The OBC sums the belief that the instance $x$ is in class $y_i$ for each model weighted by the posterior probability of the model. The approach chooses the class that maximizes equation ( 7 ).

$$\arg\max_i : q_i = \int_{\theta\in\Theta} P(y_i, x \mid \theta) P(\theta \mid D)\, d\theta \tag{7}$$

To minimize a zero-one loss function it is well known that the optimal decision rule is to select the class with the highest probability (Duda, Hart, Stork, 2001). The risk associated with selecting class $i$ is then 1-P($Class_i$) . If this approach is applied for all models, the overall risk or expected loss (Duda, Hart, Stork, 2001) associated with choosing class/action $i$ using a model space $\Theta$ and training data $D$ is:

$$R_{i,\Theta,D} = \int_\theta (1 - P(y_i, x \mid \theta))p(\theta \mid D)\, d\theta \qquad (8)$$
$$= \int_\theta p(\theta \mid D)\, d\theta - \int_\theta P(y_i, x \mid \theta)p(\theta \mid D)\, d\theta$$
$$= 1 - \int_\theta P(y_i, x \mid \theta)p(\theta \mid D)\, d\theta$$

Consequently, choosing the class that maximizes ( 7 ) minimizes the risk. For a given data set, model space and prior distribution over the model space, no other approach can yield a smaller risk (Mitchell, 1997). However, OBC is a time consuming process as it involves performing an integration over the entire model space which could be high dimensional.

## 6.1 Bootstrap Model Averaging Approximates Bayesian Model Averaging

In this section we show that bootstrap model averaging approximates the OBC for stable learners. The posterior probability distribution for a stable learner according to the Bayesian central limit theorem is a Gaussian as shown in ( 2 ). We could obtain the exact values of these parameters of this distribution, but this would effectively involve the computation to perform the integration in equation ( 7 ). However, for a Gaussian the sample mean and sample standard deviation are *sufficient statistics* for the population mean and standard deviation and we can use them to perform our inference on the test set instance. Generally, that is $P(\mu_\theta, \sigma_\theta \mid D) = P(\mu_\theta, \sigma_\theta \mid \hat{\mu}_\theta, \hat{\sigma}_\theta)$. We note that the population parameters in our situation are the posterior mean and variance calculated from *all* of the models in the model space (equation ( 2 )) and sample parameters are calculated from a small subset of models sampled. For stable learners this relationship is shown in equation ( 9 ).

$$P(\mu_\theta = \mathrm{E}_{P(\theta|D)}(\theta), \sigma_\theta^{\,2} = \mathrm{Var}_{P(\theta|D)}(\theta) \mid D) \qquad (9)$$
$$= P(\mu_\theta = \mathrm{E}_{P(\theta|D)}(\theta), \sigma_\theta^{\,2} = \mathrm{Var}_{P(\theta|D)}(\theta) \mid \hat{\mu}_\theta, \hat{\sigma}_\theta^{\,2})$$

If the bootstrap model averaging approach yields a *sample* (posterior) mean and standard deviation then it produces sufficient statistics for the posterior distribution. Stable learners are by definition (property 3) deterministic functions written as L(.). The learner when applied to the training data places a fixed probability distribution over the model space with a prescribed mean and variance (equation ( 2 )) and returns the most probable model. When the learner is applied within our ensemble approach of bootstrap model averaging it is effectively a deterministic function of the bootstrap samples. The variability over the models within our approach is due to variability across the bootstrap samples.

In the training data set suppose that Boolean attribute $i$ was TRUE $p$ percent of the time and continuous attribute $j$ was on average $q$. Then across the bootstrap samples the average values of attributes $i$ and $j$ will also be $p$ and $q$ respectively. Therefore, when we average over models learnt from $X_1 \ldots X_T$ we find that Average($L(X_1) \ldots L(X_T)$)$\approx L(D)$ $\approx \mathrm{E}_{P(\theta|D)}(\theta)$ by definition as the learner chooses the most probable model and the posterior distribution is unimodal. Furthermore, Efron (Efron, 1979) created the bootstrapping approach to estimate the population variance. The variance of the attributes across the bootstrap samples approximately equals the variance across randomly drawn samples which is a function of the training data variance. Therefore, Variance($L(X_1) \ldots L(X_T)$) $\approx$ $\mathrm{Variance}_{P(\theta|D)}(\theta)$. An assumption of the above is that it holds in the limit as the number of samples approaches infinity, that is, $\lim_{T\to\infty}$. We now develop a bound on the closeness of the approximation of bootstrap model averaging to the OBC in the non-ideal case when $T << \infty$.

In earlier work Domingos (Domingos 2000) argues that bagging (bootstrapping with uniform votes) is an approximation to Bayesian model averaging by importance sampling. He then provides extensive empirical evidence showing that attempting to improve importance sampling does not yield better results than bagging. We note that the learners used in that work are not stable according to our definition and our work makes no claims on its applicability to unstable learners.

## 6.2 Bounds for a Classifier

We now develop a bound that measures the closeness between both sets of parameters ($(\mu_\theta, \sigma_\theta)$ and $(\hat{\mu}_\theta, \hat{\sigma}_\theta)$) using a Chebychev inequality/bound. The Chebychev inequality (*for repeated experiments*) allows the definition of the number of samples, $T$, (in our case the number of bootstrap samples) required to obtain an estimate ($\hat{p}$) (calculated from those samples) that is within an error ($\varepsilon$, $0<\varepsilon<1$) of the true value ($p$). It is assumed that the samples are drawn from a distribution with mean of $p$ and standard deviation of $\sigma$. The bound in its general form is:

$$P\left[|\hat{p} - p| > \varepsilon\right] < \frac{\sigma^2}{T(\varepsilon)^2} \qquad (10)$$

This expression can be interpreted as an upper bound on the chance that the error is larger than $\varepsilon$. In-turn we can upper bound the right-hand side by $\delta$ $(0 < \delta < 1)$ which can be considered the maximum chance/risk we are willing to take that our estimate and true value differ by more than $\varepsilon$. We can use the posterior standard deviation estimate calculated from the bootstrap samples for $\sigma$. Then rearranging these terms to solve for the error yields:

$$\varepsilon > \sigma \;/ \sqrt{T\delta} \qquad (11)$$
$$|\mu_\theta - \hat{\mu}_\theta| > \varepsilon > \frac{\sigma_\theta}{\sqrt{T\delta}}$$

The question of how close the means are, is now answered with respect to the chance ($\delta$) that their difference threshold ($\varepsilon$) will be exceeded, for $T$ models built. If we treat the numerator as a constant for a given problem we see that as $T$ (number of models built) and $\delta$ (chance of failure) increases the error decreases as expected.

We now derive a bound for the standard deviation. We use a Chebychev bound but need to know the standard deviation of the posterior standard deviation. As the posterior is Gaussian the standard deviation is drawn from a chi-squared distribution, that is: $\mathbf{Stdev}(\hat{\sigma}_\theta) = \sqrt{\sigma_\theta^2 / (2(n-1))}$ .The probability the parameters differ by more than $\varepsilon$ is then:

$$P\left[\left|\sigma_\theta - \hat{\sigma}_\theta\right| > \varepsilon\right] < \sigma_\theta^2 / \left[2(n-1)(T\varepsilon^2)\right] \quad (12)$$

Again we can bound the right hand side by the chance ($\delta$) that this error will be exceeded and solve for $\varepsilon$. Note that these constants can differ from those in equation ( 11 ).

$$\begin{aligned} &\delta > \sigma_\theta^2 / \left[2(n-1)(T\varepsilon^2)\right] \\ &\varepsilon^2 > \sigma_\theta^2 / \left[2(n-1)(T\delta)\right] \\ &\varepsilon > \sigma_\theta / \sqrt{2(n-1)(T\delta)} \\ &\left|\sigma_\theta - \hat{\sigma}_\theta\right| > \varepsilon > \sigma_\theta / \sqrt{2(n-1)(T\delta)} \end{aligned} \quad (13)$$

Therefore, if we use $T$ samples with our ensemble approach, then we know the difference in the calculated mean will be no more (with chance no more than $\delta$) than $\frac{\sigma_\theta}{\sqrt{T\delta}}$ and the error in the standard deviation no more than $\sigma_\theta / \sqrt{2(n-1)(T\delta)}$ .

We can see that the posterior distribution $\mathbf{N}(\mu_\theta, \sigma_\theta)$ and the distribution obtained via bootstrap model averaging from $T$ samples is in the worst case: $\mathbf{N}\left[\mu_\theta \pm \frac{\sigma_\theta}{\sqrt{T\delta}}, \sigma_\theta \pm \sigma_\theta / \sqrt{2(n-1)(T\delta)}\right]$. This is so as our calculations are only for differences and we do not know if the approach will exceed or be less than the true value. We can now substitute these errors into our risk calculations to determine the approximation to the risk which we denote with the estimation symbol (hat).

$$\hat{R}_{i,\Theta,D} = 1 - \int_\theta P(y_i, x \mid \theta) \left[\frac{P(\theta \mid, \mu_\theta \pm \frac{\sigma_\theta}{\sqrt{T\delta}},}{\sigma_\theta \pm \sigma_\theta / \sqrt{2(n-1)(T\delta)}}\right] \quad (14)$$

Performing this integration is equivalent to drawing an infinite number of models according to the bootstrap model averaging distribution over the model space. Note that $\theta_i$ is the $i^{th}$ model drawn from a distribution. Formally:

$$\hat{R}_{i,\Theta,D} = 1 - \sum_{i=1}^{\infty} P(y_i, x \mid \hat{\theta}_i)$$

where $\hat{\theta}_i \sim N(\mu_\theta \pm \frac{\sigma_\theta}{\sqrt{T\delta}}, \sigma_\theta \pm \sigma_\theta / \sqrt{2(n-1)(T\delta)})$

$$\hat{\theta}_i = \{\theta_i \pm \beta_i\},$$

$$\theta_i \sim N(\mu_\theta, \sigma_\theta), \beta_i \sim N(\pm \frac{\sigma_\theta}{\sqrt{T\delta}}, \pm \sigma_\theta / \sqrt{2(n-1)(T\delta)})$$

due to the additive nature of the Normal distribution.

$$\begin{aligned} \hat{R}_{i,\Theta,D} &= 1 - \sum_{i=1}^{\infty} \left[P(y_i, x \mid \theta_i) \pm P(y_i, x \mid \beta_i)\right] \\ &= 1 - \left[\begin{array}{l} \int_\theta [P(y_i, x \mid \theta) P(\theta \mid \mu_\theta, \sigma_\theta) \pm \\ P(y_i, x \mid \theta) P(\theta \mid \frac{\sigma_\theta}{\sqrt{T\delta}}, \sigma_\theta / \sqrt{2(n-1)(T\delta)})] \end{array}\right] \end{aligned}$$

$$\text{therefore, } \left|R_{i,\Theta,D} - \hat{R}_{i,\Theta,D}\right| < \int_\theta P(y_i, x \mid \theta) P(\theta \mid \frac{\sigma_\theta}{\sqrt{T\delta}}, \sigma_\theta / \sqrt{2(n-1)(T\delta)}) \quad (15)$$

As the number of models in the ensemble increases, the distribution in equation ( 15 ) becomes more peaked and its contribution is reduced as expected. This equation is an inequality as we have used upper bounds to perform a worse case analysis.

# 7 Experimental Results

## 7.1 Majority Guesser with Uniform Prior

We provide this illustrate example to indicate how our bounds are used. Again, consider a majority guesser for a two-class problem, where each class is equiprobable in the training set of size 50 (ie. ρ=0.5). Then $\mu_\theta$=0.5, $\sigma_\theta$=.0.057. For $T$=250 and $\delta$=0.05 we find from equations ( 11 ) that the differences in means should be no more than 0.057/sqrt(250x0.05) = 0.00456 five percent of the time. Empirically we find that repeating the bootstrap model averaging approach 1000 times yields 33 (3.3%) occurrences where the means differ by more than the calculated error (0.00456). This is to be expected, as the equations provide an **upper bound** on the chance of failure. Equation ( 13 )specifies that the variances should differ by no more than $0.057 / \sqrt{(98)5} \approx 0.0025$, no more than 5% of the time. Over 1000 experiments, we find that 38 times (3.8%) this error was exceeded.

Given these bounds hold, how can we use them in practice? We know the OBC gives us the optimal results and we have an approximation to this approach which we know the error of. This allows us to quantify the difference between $r_i$ and $q_i$ using equation ( 15 ). We can then produce an error range for $q_i$ to produce a joint probability *region* for each class. So long as these do not overlap, then our results will be the same as for OBC with a chance of failure no greater than $\delta$. We can use as many bootstrap samples as required to prevent the regions from overlapping. In this way we are only drawing as many models as required given our tolerance to risk.

### 7.2 Belief Networks

We now focus on differences in predictive error for the standard Boolean belief network shown in Figure 1.

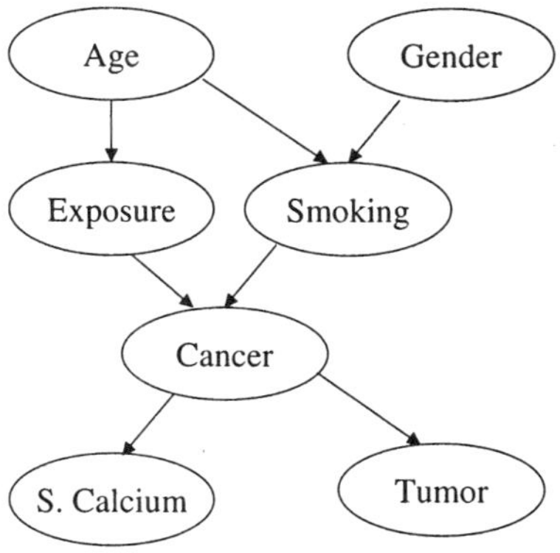


Figure 1. The Cancer Belief Network

As we know the parameters of the generating mechanism we can determine the difference between the true predictive distributions: $r_i$ (equation ( 1 )) and our approaches estimate of it: $q_i$ (equation ( 7 )). We used our ensemble approach to build a collection of enough models ($n$=500) so that the decision regions do not overlap using the chance of failure 5% ($\delta$=0.05). We found that for 1000 random test queries (ie. Of the form P(Tumor = ? | Gender=M, Smoking=T)) that OBC and our approach made differing predictions 2% of the time over one hundred experiment repetitions.

### 7.3 Naïve Bayes for Real World Datasets

For a variety of data sets we empirically compare bootstrap model averaging against building a single model. As we do not know the true population parameters, we can not test the accuracy of our bounds as for artificial data sets. Therefore, in this section we test our approaches' usefulness using empirical experiments. Where as bagging and DECORATE did not increase the predictive accuracy we find that this is not the case for our approach. Furthermore, we find that the improvement increases as a function of the number of bootstrap samples. We find for all but one data set that the decrease in error is significant and that the error decreases as a function of the number of models.

Table 5. Naïve Bayes bootstrap model averaging 10 X-fold error (%) over 100 trials.

| **Dataset** | **Training Data** | **T= 10** | **T= 50** | **T= 100** | **Improvement (Stat. Sig.)[3]** |
|---|---|---|---|---|---|
| **Iris** | 5.2 | 4.9 | 4.6 | 4.5 | 0.7 (Yes) |
| **Breast** | 2.7 | 2.6 | 2.6 | 2.5 | 0.2 (No) |
| **Soybean** | 9.25 | 8.5 | 7.7 | 7.5 | 1.75 (Yes) |
| **Crx** | 22.5 | 22.3 | 22.1 | 22.0 | 0.5 (Yes) |
| **Adult** | 19.3 | 18.9 | 18.7 | 18.2 | 0.9 (Yes) |

We note that all of these data sets contain missing values (with the exception of IRIS) so the naïve Bayes classifier may not be returning the most probable model, a requirement of our approach.

## 8 Conclusion and Future Work

Ensemble approaches are popular but typically require creating a diverse set of models. This is difficult for stable learners. In addition ensemble approaches are not always underpinned by a rigorous theory and increasing the number of models to build does not always decrease predictive error. We formally specified the notion of stable learners as having a defined second order derivative for the posterior density function. Learners with this property that model the data as IID have a Gaussian posterior according to the Bayesian central limit theorem. We created an ensemble technique for stable learners known as bootstrap model averaging that creates bootstrap samples of the data and builds a model from each. Rather than aggregating votes amongst these models (like bagging), the joint probability of the instance and class are summed and the most probable class is predicted. This is equivalent to OBC as the number of models reaches infinity. In the finite situation we developed bounds to determine how far above the OBC error our approach was.

We empirically demonstrate our approach for belief networks with artificial data sets. For the naïve Bayes classifier we were able to obtain statistically significant improvements where bagging and DECORATE could not. Our future work will involve generalization to latent variable models and creating a list of stable and unstable learners.

## References


Brieman, L., Bagging Predictors, *Machine Learning 1996.*

Breiman, L., Arcing classifiers. Ann. Statistics,26(3), 1998.

Clarke B. and Barron A. Entropy, risk and the Bayesian central limit theorem. manuscript.

Domingos, P., Bayesian Averaging of Classifiers and the Overfitting Problem. ICML, 2000.

Duda R., Hart P., & Stork D., Pattern Classification. Wiley, 2001.

Efron, B. 1979. Bootstrap methods. Annals Statistics 7:1-26.

Krogh A. and Vedelsby J., Neural network ensembles, cross validation and active learning. NIPS 1995.

Melville, P. and Mooney, R. Constructing Diverse Classifier Ensembles Using Artificial Training Examples, IJCAI 2003.

Mitchell, T. (1997), Machine Learning, McGraw Hill.

Schapire R.E.. The strength of weak learnability. Machine Learning, 5(2):197-227, 1990.


[3] Pairwise t-Test for means at the 95% confidence level

# On the Optimality of Probability Estimation by Random Decision Trees

**Wei Fan**
IBM T.J. Watson Research
19 Skyline Drive, Hawthorne, NY 10532
weifan@us.ibm.com

## Abstract

Random decision tree is an ensemble of decision trees. The feature at any node of a tree in the ensemble is chosen randomly from remaining features. A chosen discrete feature on a decision path cannot be chosen again. Continuous feature can be chosen multiple times, however, with a different splitting value each time. During classification, each tree outputs raw posterior probability. The probabilities from each tree in the ensemble are averaged as the final posterior probability estimate. Although remarkably simple and somehow counter-intuitive, random decision tree has been shown to be highly accurate under 0-1 loss and cost-sensitive loss functions. Preliminary explanation of its high accuracy is due to the "error-tolerance" property of probabilistic decision making. Our study has shown that the actual reason for random tree's superior performance is due to its optimal approximation to each example's true probability to be a member of a given class.

## Introduction

Given an unknown target function $y = F(\mathbf{x})$ and a set of examples of this target function $\{(\mathbf{x}, y)\}$, a classification algorithm constructs an inductive model that approximates the unknown target function. Each example $\mathbf{x}$ is a feature vector of discrete and continuous values such as age, income, education, and salary. $y$ is drawn from a discrete set of values such as $\{$*fraud, nonfraud*$\}$. A classification tree or decision tree is a directed single-rooted acyclic graph (sr-DGA) ordered feature tests. Each internal node of a decision tree is a feature test. Prediction is made at leaf nodes. Decision trees classify examples by sorting them down the tree from the root to some leaf node. Each non-leaf node in the tree specifies a test of some feature of that example. For symbolic or discrete features, each branch descending from the node specifies to one of the possible values of this feature. For continuous values, one branch corresponds to instances with feature value $\geq$ the threshold and another one $<$ the threshold. Different instances are classified by different paths starting at the root of the tree and ending at a leaf. Some instances, e.g., with missing attribute values etc., may be split among multiple paths. $w$ is the weight of an instance $\mathbf{x}$; it is set to 1.0 initially or other real numbers proportional to the probability that $\mathbf{x}$ is sampled. When $\mathbf{x}$ splits among multiple paths, the weight is split among different paths usually proportional to the probability of that path. If $\mathbf{x}$ has a missing value at an attribute test and the attribute has value 'A' with probability 0.9 and value 'B' with probability 0.1 in the training data, $\mathbf{x}$ will be classified by both path 'A'and path 'B' with weights $0.9w$ and $0.1w$ respectively. Since every path is unique and every possible split is disjoint, the sum of all weights at every leaf node is the sum of the weight of every instance. A leaf is a collection of examples that may not be classified any further. Ideally, they may all have one single class, in which case, there is no utility for further classification. In many cases, they may still have different class labels. They may not be classified any further because either additional feature tests cannot classify better or the number of examples are so small that fails a given statistical significance test. In these cases, the prediction at this leaf node is the majority class or the class label with the most number of occurrences. Since each path from the root to a leaf is unique, a decision tree shatters the instance place into multiple leaves.



The performance of a decision tree is measured by some "loss function" specifically designed for different applications. Given a loss function $L(t, y)$ where $t$ is the true label and $y$ is the predicted label, an optimal decision tree is one that minimizes the average loss $L(t, y)$ for all examples, weighted by their probability. Typical examples of loss functions in data mining are 0-1 loss and cost-sensitive loss. For 0-1 loss, $L(t, y) = 0$ if $t = y$, otherwise $L(t, y) = 1$. For cost-sensitive loss, $L(t, y) = c(\mathbf{x}, t)$ if $t = y$, otherwise $L(t, y) = w(\mathbf{x}, y, t)$. In general, when correctly predicted, $L(t, y)$ is only related to $\mathbf{x}$ and its true label $t$. When misclassified, $L(t, y)$ is related to the example as well as its true label and the prediction. If the problem is not ill-defined, we expect $c(\mathbf{x}, t) \leq w(\mathbf{x}, t, y)$. For many problems, $t$ is nondeterministic, i.e., if $\mathbf{x}$ is sampled repeatedly, different values of $t$ may be given. This is due to various reasons, such as noise in the data, inadequate feature set, insufficient feature precision or stochastic nature of the problem (i.e., for the same $\mathbf{x}$, $F(\mathbf{x})$ returns different value at different time). It is usually difficult to know or measure apriori if a problem is deterministic. Without prior knowledge, it is hard to distinguish noise from stochastic nature of the problem. The optimal decision $y_*$ for $\mathbf{x}$ is the label that minimizes the expected loss $E_t(L(t, y_*))$ for a given example $\mathbf{x}$ when $\mathbf{x}$ is sampled repeatedly and different $t$'s may be given. For 0-1 loss function, the optimal prediction is the most likely label or the label that appears the most often when $\mathbf{x}$ is sampled repeatedly. For cost-sensitive loss, the optimal prediction is the one that minimizes the empirical risk.

To choose the optimal decision, *a posteriori* probability is usually required. In decision tree, assume that $n_c$ is the number or weight of examples with class label $c$ at a leaf node, and $n$ is the total number or weight of examples at the leaf. The raw *a posteriori* probability can be estimated as

$$P(c|\mathbf{x}) = \frac{n_c}{n} \tag{1}$$

It is usually NP-hard to find the most accurate decision tree on a given training data. Most of the practical techniques is to use "greedy" to approximate the simplest model with various heuristics. For decision trees, typical heuristics include information gain (Quinlan 1993), gini index (Mehta, Agrawal, & Rissanen 1996), Kearns-Mansour criterion (Kearns & Mansour 1996) among others. After the model is completely constructed, it is then further simplified via pruning with different techniques such as MDL-based pruning (Mehta, Rissanen, & Agrawal 1995), reduced error pruning (Quinlan 1993), cost-based pruning (Bradford *et al.* 1998), among others. Although no longer NP-hard, most of these techniques still require significant amount of computation as well as storage. Most algorithms require multiple scans of the training data and require data to be held in main memory.

Random decision tree is proposed in (Fan *et al.* Nov 2003). It is an ensemble of decision trees trained randomly. When training each tree, the splitting feature at each node is chosen randomly from any "remaining" features. A chosen discrete feature on a particular decision path (starting from the root of the tree to the current node) cannot be chosen again since it is useless to test the same discrete feature more than once, i.e., each split path will have the same discrete feature value. However, continuous features can be chosen multiple times, each time with a different randomly chosen spliting value. During classification, each tree outputs raw posterior probability. The probabilities from each tree in the ensemble are averaged as the final posterior probability estimate. Although remarkably simple and somehow counter-intuitive, random decision tree has been shown to be highly accurate under both 0-1 loss and cost-sensitive loss functions. Preliminary explanation provided in (Fan *et al.* Nov 2003) is due to the "error-tolerance" property of probabilistic decision making. Borrowing from (Fan *et al.* Nov 2003), assuming 0-1 loss function and a binary problem. The probability threshold to predict $\mathbf{x}$ to be a member of class $y$ is 0.5, i.e., we predict $\mathbf{x}$ to be a member of class $y$ iff $P(y|\mathbf{x}) > 0.5$. Under this situation, an estimated probability of 0.99 and 0.51 will have exactly the same effect, predicting $\mathbf{x}$ to be a member of $y$, since both 0.99 and 0.51 are higher than the decision threshold of 0.5.

Our study has shown that the actual reason for random tree's superior performance is due to its optimal approximation to each example's true probability to be a member of a given class. On the reliablity curve, the probability output by random tree matches the true probability closely throughout the range (between 0 and 1). However, the best single decision tree (one trained with best spliting criteria such as information gain) matches well only at points close to either 0 or 1. In the range around 0.5, single best decision tree either significantly over-estimates or under-estimates.

## Random Decision Tree

The "canonical" form of random decision tree first builds the structure of $N$ random decision trees without the data. It then updates the statistics of each node by scanning the training examples one by one. The feature set is provided to construct the structure of the tree. At each node of the tree, a remaining feature is completely randomly chosen despite of the training data. A discrete feature can be used only once in a decision path starting from the root of the tree till the current node. Continuous features can be discretized and treated as discrete features. Another approach is to pick a random dividing point (i.e., $<$ and $\geq$ the dividing value) each time that this continuous feature is chosen. Since a different dividing point is picked whenever a continuous feature is chosen, it can be used multiple times in a decision path. After the tree structures are finalized, the dataset is scanned only once to update the statistics of each node in every tree. These statistics are simply to track the number of examples belonging to each class that are "classified" by each node. These statistics are used to compute the posteriori probability (Eq. 1). Empty nodes are removed from the random trees. To classify an example, the *a posteriori* probability output from multiple trees are averaged as the final probability estimate. In order to make a decision, a loss function is required in order to minimize the expected loss when the same example is drawn from the universe repeatedly. When the number of features are small, generate empty trees are realistic. However, when the number of features are a large, generated empty trees before scanning the data can lead to astronomical amount of memory usage. In our implementation, we do not generate a node unless some example in the training datasets will actually go there. In other words, we do not generate empty nodes. On average, we find that a random tree is about 2 to 3 times bigger than a single best tree when stored in the Linux file system.

According to (Fan *et al.* Nov 2003), the minimal number of decision trees are 30. That is when the $t$-distribution is nearly identical to normal distribution. When the distribution of the data is extremely skewed, however, it usually requires a sample size of about 50. They have also discussed the depth of the tree. One heuristic suggested in (Fan *et al.* Nov 2003) is to go about half of the number of features, since that is when the combinations to sample half out of $n$ items maximizes in order to create diversity. One restriction of the random decision tree as well as other state-of-the-art decision tree learners (such as c4.5 and dti) is that they all have a "single feature information gain bias". In other words, the data must have features with information gain individually but not "collectively." An example to show "single feature information gain bias" can be found in (Fan *et al.* Nov 2003).

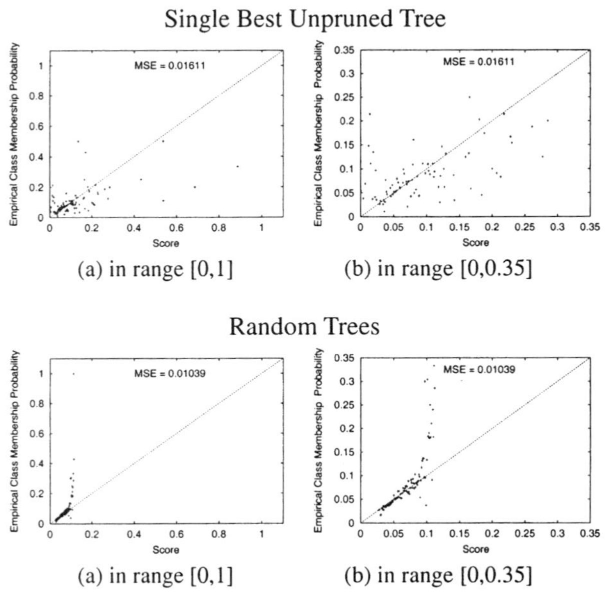


(a) in range [0,1] (b) in range [0,0.35]

(a) in range [0,1] (b) in range [0,0.35]

Figure 1: donation: reliability plot of best and random tree

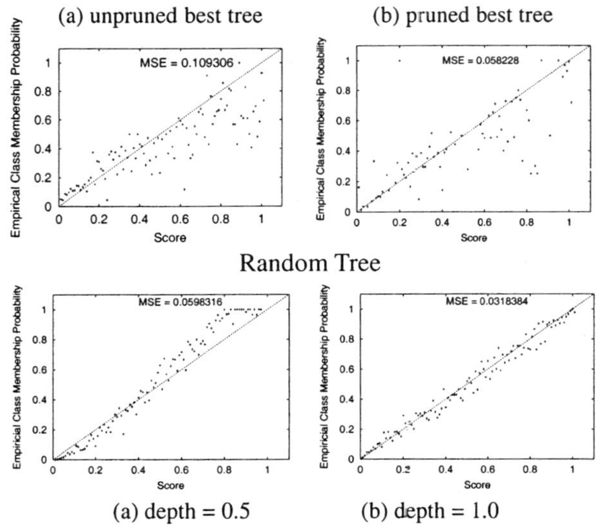


(a) unpruned best tree (b) pruned best tree

(a) depth = 0.5 (b) depth = 1.0

Figure 2: adult: reliability plot of best and random tree

# Experiment

## Data Set

We have chosen three datasets in this study. The first one is the famous donation dataset that first appeared in KDD-CUP'98 competition. Suppose that the cost of requesting a charitable donation from an individual $\mathbf{x}$ is \$0.68, and the best estimate of the amount that $\mathbf{x}$ will donate is $Y(\mathbf{x})$. Its benefit matrix (converse of loss function) is:

| | predict *donate* | predict $\neg$*donator* |
|---|---|---|
| actual *donate* | Y(x) - \$.0.68 | 0 |
| actual $\neg$*donate* | -\$0.68 | 0 |

The accuracy is the total amount of received charity minus the cost of mailing. Assuming that $p(donate|\mathbf{x})$ is the estimated probability that $\mathbf{x}$ is a donor, we will solicit to $\mathbf{x}$ iff $p(donate|\mathbf{x}) \cdot Y(\mathbf{x}) > 0.68$. The data has already been divided into a training set and a test set. The training set consists of 95412 records for which it is known whether or not the person made a donation and how much the donation was. The test set contains 96367 records for which similar donation information was not published until after the KDD'98 competition.

The second data set is a credit card fraud detection problem. Assuming that there is an overhead $v \in \{\$60, \$70, \$80, \$90\}$ to dispute and investigate a fraud and $y(\mathbf{x})$ is the transaction amount, the following is the benefit matrix:

| | predict $fraud$ | predict $\neg fraud$ |
|---|---|---|
| actual $fraud$ | $y(x)$ - $v$ | 0 |
| actual $\neg fraud$ | -$v$ | 0 |

The accuracy is the sum of recovered frauds minus investigation costs. If $p(fraud|\mathbf{x})$ is the probability that $\mathbf{x}$ is a fraud, $fraud$ is the optimal decision iff $p(fraud|\mathbf{x}) \cdot y(x) > v$. The dataset was sampled from a one year period and contains a total of .5M transaction records. The features (20 in total) record the time of the transaction, merchant type, merchant location, and past payment and transaction history summary. We use data of the last month as test data (40038 examples) and data of previous months as training data (406009 examples).

The third dataset is the adult dataset from UCI repository. We use the natural split of training and test sets. The training set contains 32561 entries and the test set contains 16281 records. The feature set contains 14 features that describe the education, gender, country of origin, martial status, capital gain among others. Each data item indicates if an individual earns more than \$50K or less.

## Decision Tree Learner

The experiments were based on C4.5 release 8 (Quinlan 1993). The single best tree is constructed by running C4.5 with all the default settings. It computes both the unpruned and pruned decision trees. The random decision tree algorithm is a modified version of C4.5 that does not compute information gain. It chooses remaining features randomly, i.e., discrete feature is chosen only once in a decision path and continuous feature can be chosen multiple times yet with a different splitting threshold. After a splitting feature is chosen, the data items with the same feature values are grouped. The procedure is run recursively until either the predefined tree depth is met or the splitted node becomes empty.

## Results

**Reliability Plot** "Reliability plot" shows how reliable the "score" of a model is in estimating the empirical probability of an example $\mathbf{x}$ to be a member of a class $y$. To draw a reliability plot, for each unique score value predicted by the model, we count how many examples in the data have this same score (e.g.,$N$), and how many among them have class label $y$ (e.g.,$n$). Then the empirical class membership probability is simply $\frac{n}{N}$. Most practical datasets are limited in

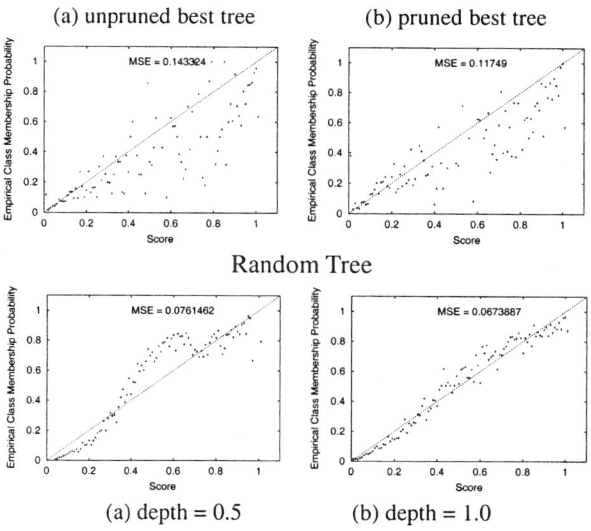


Figure 3: ccf: reliability plot of best and random tree

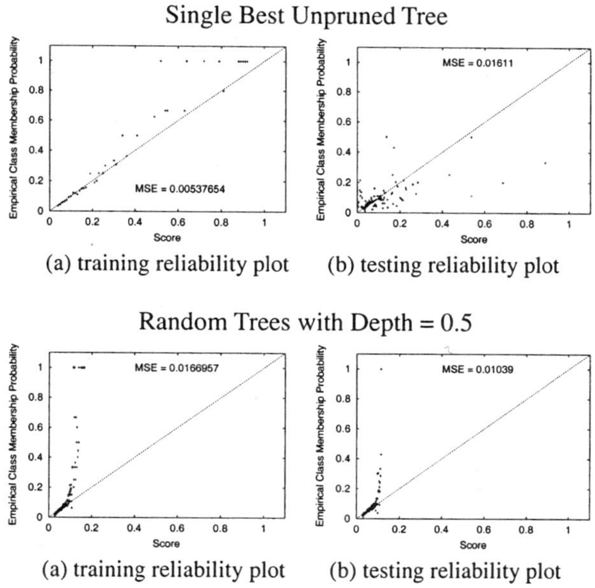


Figure 4: donation: reliability plot of best and random tree show overfitting of single best tree and "non-overfitting" by random tree

size; some scores may just cover a few number of examples and the empirical class membership probability can be extremely over or under estimated. To avoid this problem, we normally divide the range of the score into continuous bins and compute the empirical probability for examples falling into each bin.

The reliability plots for single best tree and random tree are shown in Figures 1 to 3. Figure 1 is for the donation dataset. There are 1000 bins of equal size; in other words, each bin covers a range of 1.0/1000 = 0.001. The $x$-axis is the predicted score by the model and the $y$-axis is the matching empirical class membership probability measured from the data. To visually compare the performance, we also draw the perfect straight line where every score exactly matches the true probability. The top two plots are for single best *unpruned decision tree*. Since the default pruning procedure of C4.5 deems every internal node of the unpruned decision tree as statistically insignificant, the pruned decision tree has just one useless node predicting everybody is a non-donor. Since most points are within the range between 0 and 0.35, we "enlarged" that area on a separate plot on the immediate right. As we can see clearly that the single best unpruned tree's score is like a "cloud" that scatters around the perfect matching line. However, the random decision tree (with depth of 0.5) matches the true probability very well. To summarize these results, we use *mean square error* or MSE to measure how closely the score matches the empirical probability. Assuming that $n_j$ is the number of examples covered in bin $j$, $s_j$ is the score or predicted probability and $p_j$ is the empirical probability, then $MSE = \frac{\sqrt{n_j \cdot (s_j - p_j)^2}}{\sum n_j}$. The MSE for single best unpruned tree and random tree are labelled on the top of each reliability plot. The MSE for single best unpruned tree is 0.01611 while the MSE for random tree is 0.01039.

The reliability plots for the adult and credit card fraud data sets are shown in Figures 2 and 3 respectively (with bin size 100). As we can see clearly that both single best pruned and unpruned tree's posterior probability is far from the empirical class membership probability; the visual effect is that the empirical probability scatters widely around the score value, and this is particularly true in the middle range around 0.5. However, the random tree's probability estimates are very close to the true empirical probability throughout the whole range.

## Overfitting

One interesting observation we have found is that random decision tree doesn't overfit the training data at all. To study the effect of overfitting, we have run an additional test that "trains on the *test data* and then predicts on the same test data" (called "training reliability plot") and compare it with the previous results of "training on *train data* and test on the test data" (called "testing reliability plot"). The results on donation and adult datasets are shown in Figures 4 and 5. One important point is that the exact training reliability plot of a single best tree should be the one where every unique score falls exactly on the "perfect line". Since the whole 0-1 probability range is divided into equal sized bins and we have finite number of examples, there will be some small errors. Visually, some of the points may not be exactly on the "perfect line". However, this is sufficient for comparing single best and random tree because they use exactly the same bin size.

As we can see clearly from Figure 4 and 5, for the single best decision tree, there is a big difference between the training reliability plot and the testing reliability plot. The training reliability plot on the left becomes much less than

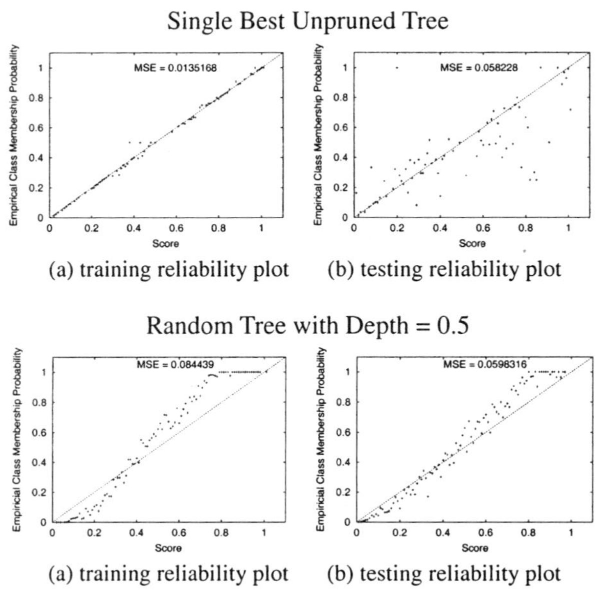


(a) training reliability plot (b) testing reliability plot

(a) training reliability plot (b) testing reliability plot

Figure 5: adult: reliability plot of best and random tree to show overfitting of single best tree and "non-overfitting" of random trees

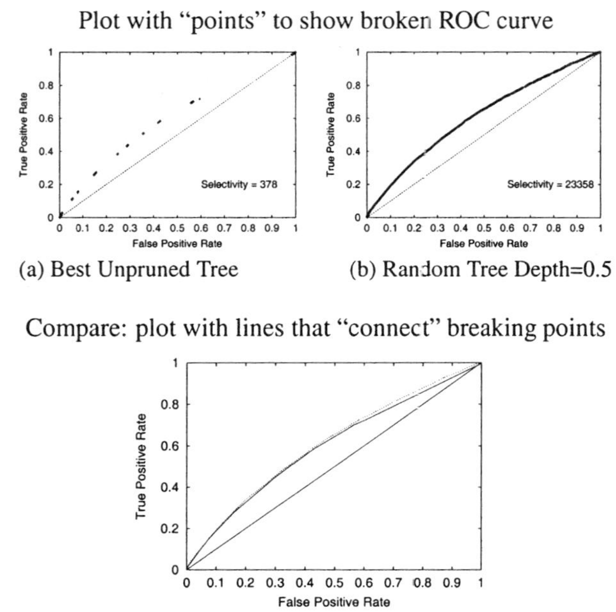


(a) Best Unpruned Tree (b) Random Tree Depth=0.5

Figure 6: donation: exhaustive ROC plot of best and random tree

perfect when the same model is tested on a different dataset, as shown in the testing reliability plot on the right. In the testing reliability plots, we can see that the "points" are scattered widely around the perfect line. The MSE for training and testing on the same dataset is 0.005 [1], and MSE for training and testing on a different dataset is 0.016. On the other hand, the training and testing reliability plots for the random tree are nearly identical for both the donation and adult datasets.

## Selectivity

One important, but often ignored, property of a model is its "selectivity". The problem of selectivity comes from the fact that most models, especially decision trees, can only output a discrete set of "unique probability values" since there are only a limited number of terminal nodes and each node can just output one probability value. This fact has a serious practical consequence. With different threshold values, there will be only a limited number of true positive and false positive values. When we draw the paired true positive and false positive values on the ROC curve, we will actually never see a continuous line ranging from (0,0) to (1,1). What we will see is a discrete set of points that are scattered in this range. Any area *without a point* is undefined. Some suggest to draw a line connecting these defined points. However, the area connecting the points are undefined; we cannot choose any undefined point since there is actually no value there at all. Due to this reason, it is practically not very useful to connect points at all.

[1] The MSE is computed using binning, so it still has a non-zero value

We define "selectivity" to measure how good is an ROC curve. It takes two facts into account. The first fact is how uniform it is between consecutive false positive values. When all available false positives spread evenly between 0-1, the variance between consecutive values will be 0. In other words, the lower this variance is, the more evenly false positive values spreads. The second fact is how many unique false positive values there are. The more unique values there are, the more choices we can choose from. So we define selectivity as the following $d = \frac{u}{s}$, where $s$ is the variance between consecutive false positive values and $u$ is the number of unique false positive values.

We have computed ROC curves for adult and donation datasets exhaustively by choosing all unique probability values in posterior probability output as the decision threshold and record its corresponding false positive and true positive rates. Any duplicate entries are removed and the results are shown in Figures 6 and 7. To show the idea of "selectivity" clearly, we plot with "points" rather than "lines" on the two top plots. This way, any areas in ROC without false positive and true positive rates will be clearly exposed. In each ROC curve, we have also shown the "selectivity" measure as defined previously. The "selectivity" problem for single best decision tree is clearly shown, particularly in the donation dataset. For the donation dataset as shown in Figure 6, the single best tree only has 11 broken clusters spread out the range, while the random tree has visually continuous ROC curve. The selectivity measure is 238 for single unpruned tree and 23358 for random tree (100 times higher than 238). As shown in Figure 7, the ROC curves for adult data have similar phenomenon, but the single best tree's ROC is not as broken as that of the donation data. In the bottom part

Plot with "points" to show broken ROC curve

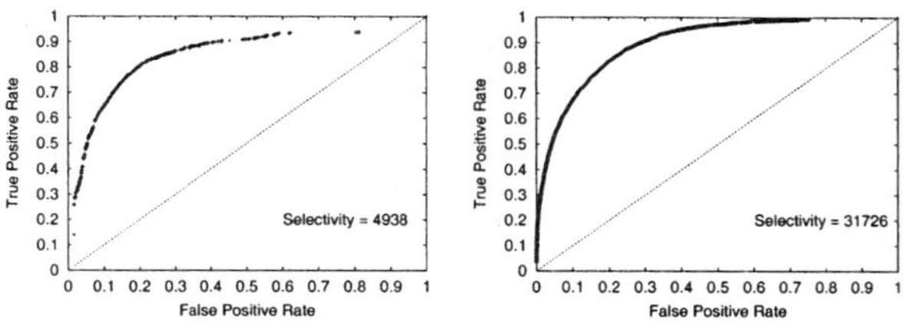


(a) Best Unpruned Tree (b) Random Tree Depth=0.5

Compare: plot with lines that "connect" breaking points

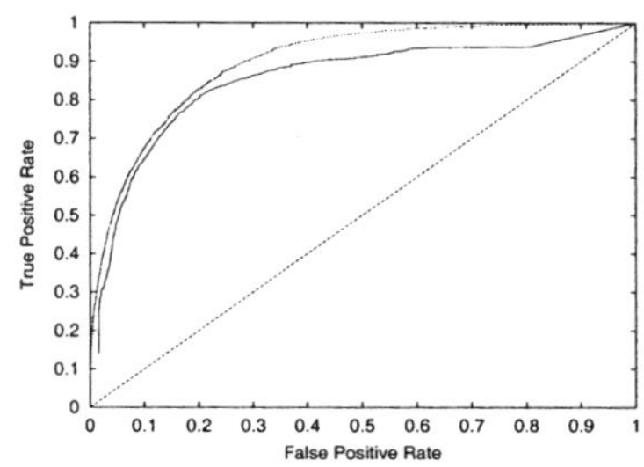


Figure 7: adult: exhaustive ROC plot of best and random tree

of Figure 6 and Figure 7, we plot the ROC curves of single best unpruned tree and random tree in the same figure. For visual clarity, we plot with "lines" to connect broken curves. Strictly speaking, any points not in the top exhaustive ROC curve is not defined. This is just to compare the difference in true positive value for the same false positive value. As we can see in the ROC curve, for the donation dataset, true positive of the random tree is mostly the same or slightly higher than single best unpruned tree for the same false positive value. For the adult data set, the random tree's true positive rate is consistently higher than that of single best unpruned tree.

## Related Work

Breiman has proposed the "random forests" method (Breiman 2001). In random forests, randomness is injected by randomly sampling a subset of remaining features (those not chosen yet by a decision path) and then choosing the best spliting criteria from this feature subset. The chosen size of the subset has to be provided by the user of random forests. However, in random decision tree, the spliting feature is randomly chosen from any remaining features not chosen yet in the current decision path. There is no information gain (or any other criteria) involved in choosing this feature and when it will be chosen. In other words, random decision tree doesn't use any heuristics to choose feature. The data is used to update the class distribution in each node. However, in Breiman's random forests, information gain or other criteria is still used to choose the best feature among randomly chosen feature subsets. This has great impact on the efficiency between training a random forest or a random tree since computing any heuristics is expensive. Another important distinction is that Breiman's random forests performance simple voting on the final prediction. In other words, each tree votes 1 on one of the class labels. The class labels with the highest vote is the final prediction. However, random tree, each tree output raw probability and the probability outputs from multiple tree are averaged as the final probability. .

## Conclusion

We have extensively studied the posterior probability estimation by previously proposed random decision method. We have found that random decision tree can faithfully estimate the empirical class membership probability. In the statistical reliability curve, the estimated probability by random decision tree closely matches the empirical class membership probability measured from the data. We also found that random decision tree's ability to estimate posterior probability does not overfit at all. The probability reliability curve of the training set is very close to the reliability curve on a unseen validation or test dataset. We have also studied the "selectivity" of ROC curve and defined how to measure "selectivity". We have found that the ROC curve of random decision tree is remarkably continuous throughout the range. Comparing with random decision tree, a single best decision doesn't match the empirical class membership probability well, overfits on the training data easily, and has broken or discontinuous ROC curves.

## References

Bradford, J. P.; Kunz, C.; Kohavi, R.; Brunk, C.; and Brodley, C. E. 1998. Pruning decision trees with misclassification costs. In *European Conference on Machine Learning*, 131–136.

Breiman, L. 2001. Random forests. *Machine Learning* 45(1):5–32.

Fan, W.; Wang, H.; Yu, P. S.; and Ma, S. Nov 2003. Is random model better? on its accuracy and efficiency. In *Proceedings of Third IEEE International Conference on Data Mining (ICDM-2003)*.

Kearns, M., and Mansour, Y. 1996. On the boosting ability of top-down decision tree learning algorithms. In *Proceedings of the Annual ACM Symposium on the Theory of Computing*, 459–468.

Mehta, M.; Agrawal, R.; and Rissanen, J. 1996. SLIQ: A fast scalable classifier for data mining. In *Extending Database Technology*, 18–32.

Mehta, M.; Rissanen, J.; and Agrawal, R. 1995. MDL-based decision tree pruning. In *Proceedings of the First International Conference on Knowledge Discovery and Data Mining (KDD'95)*, 216–221.

Quinlan, R. 1993. *C4.5: Programs for Machine Learning*. Morgan Kaufmann.

# Fibring Neural Networks

**Artur S. d'Avila Garcez**[δ] **and Dov M. Gabbay**[γ]
[δ]Dept. of Computing, City University London, EC1V 0HB, UK aag@soi.city.ac.uk
[γ]Dept. of Computer Science, King's College London, WC2R 2LS, UK dg@dcs.kcl.ac.uk

## Abstract

Neural-symbolic systems are hybrid systems that integrate symbolic logic and neural networks. The goal of neural-symbolic integration is to benefit from the combination of features of the symbolic and connectionist paradigms of artificial intelligence. This paper introduces a new neural network architecture based on the idea of fibring logical systems. Fibring allows one to combine different logical systems in a principled way. Fibred neural networks may be composed not only of interconnected neurons but also of other networks, forming a recursive architecture. A fibring function then defines how this recursive architecture must behave by defining how the networks in the ensemble relate to each other, typically by allowing the activation of neurons in one network (A) to influence the change of weights in another network (B). Intuitively, this can be seen as training network B at the same time that one runs network A. We show that, in addition to being universal approximators like standard feedforward networks, fibred neural networks can approximate any polynomial function to any desired degree of accuracy, thus being more expressive than standard feedforward networks. **Keywords**: Neural-Symbolic Integration, Fibring Systems, Recursion.

## Introduction

Neural-Symbolic integration concerns the use of symbolic knowledge in the neurocomputing paradigm of Artificial Intelligence (AI) (d'Avila Garcez, Broda, & Gabbay 2002; 2001). Its goal is to benefit from the integration of the symbolic and connectionist paradigms of AI, by providing either a logical characterisation of a connectionist system, a connectionist, massively parallel implementation of a logic, or a hybrid system bringing together features from neural networks and symbolic AI (Cloete & Zurada 2000; d'Avila Garcez, Broda, & Gabbay 2002; Holldobler, Kalinke, & Storr 1999). Towards this end, efficient, parallel and distributed reasoning and learning capabilities should be at the core of any Neural-Symbolic system and, one may argue, of any AI system. Ultimately, our goal should be to produce an effective AI system with added reasoning and learning capabilities, as recently pointed out by Valiant (Valiant 2003) as a key challenge for computer science.



Neural-Symbolic systems that use simple neural networks, such as single hidden layer feedforward or recurrent networks (Haykin 1999), typically only manage to represent and reason about propositional symbolic knowledge or *if then else* rules (Boutsinas & Vrahatis 2001; d'Avila Garcez, Broda, & Gabbay 2002; Fu 1994; Pinkas 1995; Towell & Shavlik 1994). On the other hand, Neural-Symbolic systems that are capable of representing and reasoning about more expressive symbolic knowledge, such as modal logic and first order logic, normally are less capable of learning new concepts efficiently (Holldobler, Kalinke, & Storr 1999; Sun & Alexandre 1997; Shastri 1999; Kijsirikul, Sinthupinyo, & Chongkasemwongse 2001). There is clearly a need to strike a balance between the reasoning and learning capabilities of Neural-Symbolic systems. Either the simple networks to which, for example, the efficient *backpropagation* learning algorithm is applicable to (Rumelhart, Hinton, & Williams 1986; Werbos 1990) must be shown to represent languages more expressive than propositional logic, or the complex connectionist systems that are capable of representing first order and higher order logics, such as for example CHCL (Holldobler & Kurfess 1992), must have efficient learning algorithms developed for them. This is necessary because real-world applications such as failure diagnosis, engineering and bioinformatics applications, will require the use of languages more expressive than propositional logic. Bioinformatics, in particular, very much requires the ability to represent and reason about relations as used in first order logic (Angelopoulos & Muggleton 2002).

In this paper, we adopt the approach of extending simple networks that use *backpropagation* in order to allow for higher expressive power. We do so by following Gabbay's Fibring methodology (Gabbay 1999), in which several different systems such as logical systems of space and time, neural networks and Bayesian networks (Williamson & Gabbay 2004; d'Avila Garcez 2004; d'Avila Garcez & Lamb 2004), may be put to work together in a co-ordinated manner to solve a particular problem.[1] To this end, we know that a fundamental aspect of symbolic computation lies in the ability to implement recursion. As a result, to make neural networks behave like logic, we need to add recursion to it by allowing networks to be composed not only of interconnected neurons but also of other networks. Figure 1 exemplifies how a network (B) can be embedded recursively into another network (A). Of course, the idea of fibring is not only to organise networks as a number of sub-networks (A, B, etc). In Figure 1, for example, hidden neuron X of Network A is expected to be a neural network (Network B) in its own right. The input, weights and output of Network B may depend on the activation state of neuron X, according to what is known as a fibring function $\varphi$. One such function may be to multiply the weights of Network B by the input potential of neuron X.

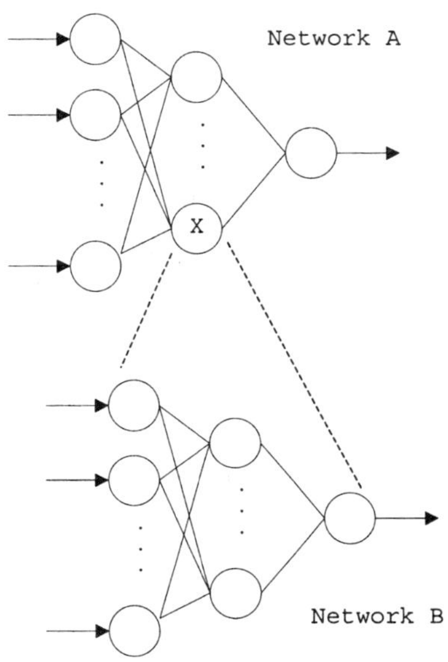


Figure 1: Fibring Neural Networks

Most of the work on how to implement recursion in neural networks has concentrated on the use of recurrent auto-associative networks and symmetric networks to represent formal grammars (Elman 1990; Touretzky & Hinton 1988; Smolensky 1990; 2000; Pollack 1990). In general, the networks learn how to simulate a number of recursive rules by similarity with a set of examples, and the question of how such rules are represented in the network is treated as secondary. In this paper, we give a different treatment to the subject, looking at it from a Neural-Symbolic integration perspective (d'Avila Garcez, Broda, & Gabbay 2002). The idea is to be able to represent and learn expressive symbolic rules, such as rules containing embedded implication of the form $(a \rightarrow b) \rightarrow c$, where $(a \rightarrow b)$ would be encoded into network B, and then $X \rightarrow c$, with $X = (a \rightarrow b)$, would be encoded into network A so that the fibred network represents $(a \rightarrow b) \rightarrow c$.

In what follows, we introduce and define fibred neural networks (fNNs), and show that, in addition to being universal approximators[2], fNNs can approximate any polynomial function in an unbounded domain, thus being more expressive than standard feedforward networks. Briefly, this can be shown by noting that fibred neural networks compute, e.g., the function $f(x) = x^2$ exactly for any given input $x$ in $\mathbb{R}$, as opposed to feedforward networks which are restricted to compact (i.e. closed and bounded) domains (Cybenco 1989; Hornik, Stinchcombe, & White 1989). Intuitively, fibring neural networks can be seen as the running and training of neural networks at the same time. In Figure 1, for example, at the same time that we run network A, we perform a kind of learning in network B because we allow the weights of B to change according to the fibring function. In other words, object-level network running and meta-level network training are occurring simultaneously in the same system, and this is responsible for the added expressiveness of the system.

This paper is organised as follows. Firstly, we introduce and exemplify fibred neural networks. Then, we define the architecture and dynamics of fibred networks precisely, and show that fibred networks approximate polynomials. Finally, we conclude and discuss directions for future work.

## Examples of Fibring

The main idea behind fibring neural networks is to allow single neurons to behave like entire embedded networks according to a fibring function $\varphi$. This function qualifies the function computed by the embedded network so that the embedded network's output depends on $\varphi$. For example, consider Network A and its embedded network (Network B) in Figure 1. Let $\mathbf{W}_A$ and $\mathbf{W}_B$ be the set of weights of Network A and Network B, respectively. Let $f_{\mathbf{W}_A}(\mathbf{i}_A)$ be the function computed by Network A, and $g_{\mathbf{W}_B}(\mathbf{i}_B)$ be the function computed by Network B, where $\mathbf{i}_A$ and $\mathbf{i}_B$ are the input vectors of Networks A and B, respectively. If Network B is embedded into neuron X of Network A with fibring function $\varphi$, the function computed by Network B becomes $g_{\mathbf{W}'_B}(\mathbf{i}_B)$, where $\mathbf{W}'_B = \varphi(\mathbf{W}_B)$, and then the output of neuron X becomes the output of Network B, as the following example illustrates.

Consider the two simple networks (C and D) of Figure 2. Let us assume, without loss of generality, that input and output neurons have the identity as activation function, while hidden neurons have $h(x) = \tanh(x)$ as activation function (Hornik, Stinchcombe, & White 1989). We use bipolar inputs $i_j \in \{-1, 1\}$, $W_{jk} \in \mathbb{R}$, and outputs $o_k \in (-1, 1)$. The output of Network C

[1]For example, a robot's motion control system may require a logic of space, a logic of time, and a visual pattern recognition, neural networks-based system.

[2]Universal approximators, such as feedforward neural networks, can approximate any (Borel) measurable function *in a compact domain* to any desired degree of accuracy.

is $o_C = W_{3C}.h(W_{1C}.i_{1C} + W_{2C}.i_{2C})$, and the output of Network D is $o_D = W_{3D}.h(W_{1D}.i_{1D} + W_{2D}.i_{2D})$. Now, let Network D be embedded into Network C as shown in Figure 2. This indicates that the input potential of neuron Y will influence D according to fibring function $\varphi$. Let us refer to the input potential of Y as $\mathbf{I}(Y)$.[3] In addition, this indicates that the output of D ($o_D$) will influence C (in this example, only the output of C). Suppose $\varphi(\mathbf{W}_D) = \mathbf{I}(Y) \cdot \mathbf{W}_D$, where $\mathbf{W}_D = [W_{1D}, W_{2D}, W_{3D}]$, i.e. $\varphi$ multiplies the weights of D by the input potential of Y. Let us use $\overline{o}_C$ and $\overline{o}_D$ to denote the outputs of networks C and D, respectively, after they are fibred. $\overline{o}_D$ is obtained by applying $\varphi$ to $\mathbf{W}_D$ and calculating the output of such a network, as follows: $\overline{o}_D = (\mathbf{I}(Y).W_{3D}) \cdot h((\mathbf{I}(Y).W_{1D}).i_{1D} + (\mathbf{I}(Y).W_{2D}).i_{2D})$. $\overline{o}_C$ is obtaining by taking $\overline{o}_D$ as the output of neuron Y. In this example, $\overline{o}_C = \overline{o}_D$. Notice how network D is being trained (as $\varphi$ changes its weights) at the same time that network C is running.

Clearly, fibred networks can be trained from examples in the same way that standard feedforward networks are (for example, with the use of *backpropagation* (Rumelhart, Hinton, & Williams 1986)). Networks C and D of Figure 2, for example, could have been trained separately before being fibred. Network C could have been trained, e.g., with a robot's visual system, while network D would have been trained with its planning system. For simplicity, we assume for now that, once defined, the fibring function itself should remain unchanged. Future extensions of fibring neural networks could, however, consider the task of learning fibring functions as well.

Notice that, in addition to using different fibring functions, networks can be fibred in a number of different ways as far as their architectures are concerned. The networks of Figure 2, for example, could have been fibred by embedding Network D into an input neuron of Network C (say, the one with input $i_{1C}$). In this case, outputs $\overline{o}_D$ and $\overline{o}_C$ would have been $\overline{o}_D = \varphi(W_{3D}) \cdot h(\varphi(W_{1D}).i_{1D} + \varphi(W_{2D}).i_{2D})$, where $\varphi$ is a function of $\mathbf{W}_D$ (say, $\varphi(\mathbf{W}_D) = i_{1C} \cdot \mathbf{W}_D$), and then $\overline{o}_C = W_{3C}.h(W_{1C}.\overline{o}_D + W_{2C}.i_{2C})$.

Let us now consider an even simpler example that, nevertheless, illustrates the power of fibring neural networks. Consider two networks A and B, both with a single input neuron ($i_A$ and $i_B$, respectively), a single hidden neuron, and a single output neuron ($o_A$ and $o_B$, respectively). Let all the weights in both networks have value 1, and let the identity ($f(x) = x$) be the activation function of all the neurons (including the hidden neurons). As a result, we simply have $o_A = f(W_{2A} \cdot f(W_{1A} \cdot f(i_A))) = i_A$ and $o_B = f(W_{2B} \cdot f(W_{1B} \cdot f(i_B))) = i_B$, where $W_{1A}$ and $W_{2A}$ are the weights of network A, and $W_{1B}$ and $W_{2B}$ are the weights of network B. Now, assume we embed network B into the input neuron of

[3]Note that, in this particular example, $\mathbf{I}(Y) = o_C$ due to the use of the identity as activation function in the output layer.

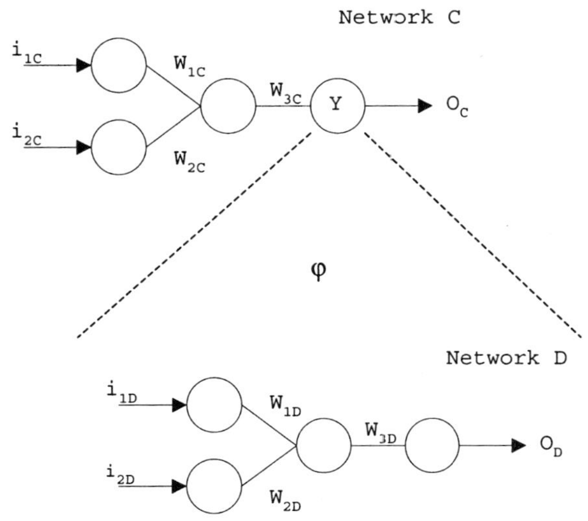


Figure 2: Fibring two simple networks

network A. We obtain $\overline{o}_B = f(\varphi(W_{2B}) \cdot f(\varphi(W_{1B}) \cdot f(i_B)))$, and then $\overline{o}_A = f(W_{2A} \cdot f(W_{1A} \cdot \overline{o}_B))$. Since $f(x) = x$, we have $\overline{o}_B = \varphi(W_{2B}) \cdot \varphi(W_{1B}) \cdot i_B$ and $\overline{o}_A = W_{2A} \cdot W_{1A} \cdot \overline{o}_B$. Now, let our fibring function be $\varphi(\mathbf{W}_A, \mathbf{i}_A, \mathbf{W}_B) = i_A \cdot \mathbf{W}_B$, where $\mathbf{W}_B = [W_{1B}, W_{2B}]$. Since $W_{1A}, W_{2A}, W_{1B}$ and $W_{2B}$ are all equal to 1, we obtain $\overline{o}_B = i_A \cdot i_A \cdot i_B$ and $\overline{o}_A = \overline{o}_B$. This means that if we fix $i_B = 1$, the output of network A (fibred with network B) will be the square of its input. As a result, if the following sequence is given as input to A (fibred with B): $n, 1/n, n+1, 1/(n+1), n+2, 1/(n+2), \ldots$ for $n \in \mathbb{R}$, the corresponding output sequence of A will be: $n^2, 1, (n+1)^2, 1, (n+2)^2, 1, \ldots$ Note that, input $n$ changes the weights of B from 1 to $n$, input $1/n$ changes the weights of B back to 1, input $n+1$ changes the weights of B from 1 to $n+1$, input $1/(n+1)$ changes the weights of B back to 1, and so on.[4] The interest in this sequence lies in the fact that, for alternating inputs, the square of the input is computed exactly by the network for any input in $\mathbb{R}$. This illustrates an important feature of fibred neural networks, namely, their ability to approximate functions in an unbounded domain (Henderson 2002; Hines 1996). This results from the recursive characteristic of fibred networks as indicated by the fibring function, and will be discussed in more detail in the following section. Note that, in practice, the fibring function $\varphi$ is to be defined according to the problem domain.

## Fibred Neural Networks

In this section, we define fibred neural networks (fNNs) precisely, we define the dynamics of fNNs, and we show

[4]Since the fibring function changes the weights of the embedded network, we use $1/n$, $1/n+1$, $1/n+2\ldots$ to *reset* the weights back to 1 during the computation of the sequence.

that fNNs can approximate unbounded functions.

## Fibring Definition

For the sake of simplicity, we restrict the definition of fibred networks to feedforward networks with a single output neuron. We also concentrate on networks with linear input and linear output activation functions, and either linear or sigmoid hidden layer activation function. We believe, however, that the principles of fibring could be applied to any artificial neural network model.[5] In what follows, we allow not only two networks, but any number of embedded networks to be nested into a fibred network. We also allow for an unlimited number of hidden layers per network.

**Definition 1** (Fibring Function) *Let A and B be two neural networks. A function* $\varphi_n : \mathbf{I} \rightarrow \mathbf{W}$ *is called a fibring function from A to B if* $\mathbf{I}$ *is the input potential of a neuron n in A and* $\mathbf{W}$ *is the set of weights of B.*

**Definition 2** (Fibred Neural Networks) *Let A and B be two neural networks. We say that B is embedded into A if* $\varphi_n$ *is a fibring function from A to B, and the output of neuron n in A is given by the output of network B. The resulting network, composed of networks A and B, is said to be a fibred neural network.*

Note that many networks can be embedded into a single network, and that networks can be nested so that network B is embedded into network A, network C is embedded into network B, and so on. The resulting fibred network can be constructed by applying Definition 2 recursively, e.g., first to embed C into B and then to embed the resulting network into A.

**Example 3** *Consider three identical network architectures (A, B and C), each containing a single linear input neuron, a single linear hidden neuron, and a single linear output neuron, as depicted in Figure 3. Let us denote the weight from the input neuron to the hidden neuron of network N,* $N \in \{A, B, C\}$, *by* $W_N^h$, *and the weight from the hidden neuron to the output neuron of N by* $W_N^o$. *Assume we embed network C into the output neuron (Y) of network B, and embed the resulting network into the output neuron (X) of network A (according to Definition 2), as shown in the figure. Let* $\varphi_B$ *denote the fibring function from A to B, and* $\varphi_C$ *denote the fibring function from B to C. As usual, let us define* $\varphi_B = I(X) \cdot \mathbf{W}_B$ *and* $\varphi_C = I(Y) \cdot \mathbf{W}_C$, *where* $I(X)$ *is the input potential of neuron X,* $I(Y)$ *is the input potential of neuron Y,* $\mathbf{W}_B$ *denotes the weight vector* $[W_B^h, W_B^o]$ *of B, and* $\mathbf{W}_C$ *denotes the weight vector* $[W_C^h, W_C^o]$ *of C. Initially, let* $W_A^h = \sqrt{a}$, *where* $a \in \mathbb{R}^+$, *and* $W_A^o = W_B^h = W_B^o = W_C^h = W_C^o = 1$. *As a result, given input x to A, we have* $I(X) = x\sqrt{a}$. *Then,* $\varphi_B$ *will be used to update the weights of network B to* $W_B^h = x\sqrt{a}$ *and* $W_B^o = x\sqrt{a}$. *If we had only networks A and B fibred, input* $y = 1$, *for example, would then produce an output* $o_B = ax^2$ *for network B, and the same* $(o_A = ax^2)$ *for network A. Since network C is also embedded into the system, given input y to network B, fibring function* $\varphi_C$ *will be used to update the weights of network C, using* $I(Y)$ *as a parameter. Thus, if* $y = 1$, *we have* $I(Y) = ax^2$, *and the weights of network C will be changed to* $W_C^h = ax^2$ *and* $W_C^o = ax^2$. *Finally, if* $z = 1$, *the output of network C (and then of networks B and A as well) will be* $a^2x^4$. *This illustrates the computation of polynomials in fNNs. The computation of odd degree polynomials and of negative coefficients can be achieved by adding more hidden layers to the networks, as we will see in the sequel.*

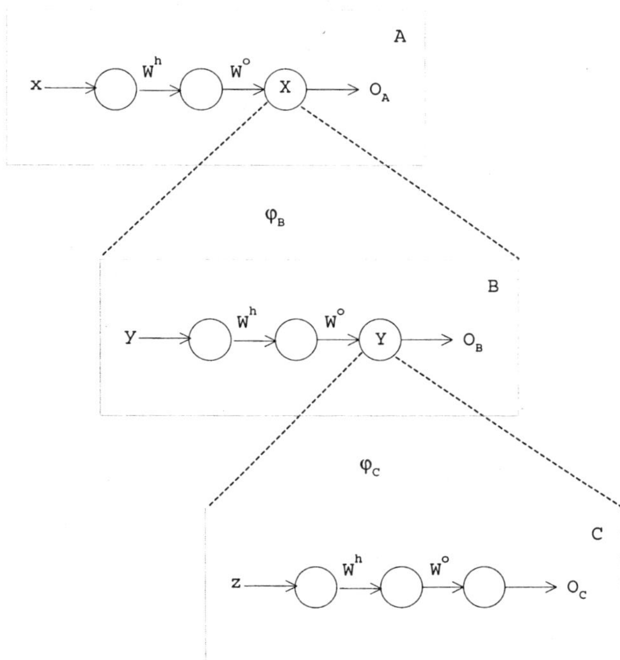


Figure 3: Nesting Fibred Networks

## Fibring Dynamics

Example 3 also illustrates the dynamics of fibred networks. Let us now define such a dynamics precisely.

**Definition 4** (Nested fNNs) *Let* $N_1, N_2, \ldots, N_n$ *be neural networks.* $N_1, N_2, \ldots, N_n$ *form a nested fibred network if* $N_i$ *is embedded into a neuron of* $N_{i-1}$ *with a fibring function* $\varphi_i$ *for any* $2 \leq i \leq n$. *We say that* $j - 1$ $(1 \leq j \leq n)$ *is the level of network* $N_j$.

**Definition 5** (fNNs Dynamics) *Let* $N_1, N_2, \ldots, N_n$ *be a nested fibred network. Let* $\varphi_i$ *be the fibring function from* $N_{i-1}$ *to* $N_i$ *for* $2 \leq i \leq n$. *Let* $\mathbf{i}_j$ *denote an input vector to network* $N_j$, $\mathbf{W}_j$ *the current weight vector of* $N_j$, $\mathbf{I}_n(\mathbf{i}_j)$ *the input potential of* $N_j$*'s neuron* $n_j$ *into which* $N_{j+1}$ *is embedded given input vector* $\mathbf{i}_j$, $\mathbf{O}_{n_j}$ *the output of neuron* $n_j$, *and* $f_{\mathbf{W}_j}(\mathbf{i}_j)$ *the function computed by network* $N_j$ *given* $\mathbf{W}_j$ *and* $\mathbf{i}_j$ *as in the standard way for feedforward networks. The output* $o_j$ *of network* $N_j$

[5] Particularly interesting would be to consider fibring recurrent networks (i.e. networks with feedback connections).

$(1 \le j \le n-1)$ *is defined recursively in terms of the output* $o_{j+1}$ *of network* $N_{j+1}$*, as follows:*

$$\mathbf{W}_{j+1} := \varphi_{j+1}(\mathbf{I}(\mathbf{i}_j), \mathbf{W}_{j+1}), 1 \le j \le n-1$$

$$o_n = f_{\mathbf{W}_n}(\mathbf{i}_n)$$

$$o_j = f_{\mathbf{W}_j}(\mathbf{i}_j, \mathbf{O}_{n_j} := o_{j+1})$$

*where* $f_{\mathbf{W}_j}(\mathbf{i}_j, \mathbf{O}_{n_j} := o_{j+1})$ *denotes the function computed by* $N_j$ *by substituting the output of its neuron* $n_j$ *by the output of network* $N_{j+1}$.

## Fibring Expressiveness

Now that fNNs have been defined, we proceed to show that, in addition to being universal approximators, fNNs can approximate any polynomial function, and thus are more expressive than standard feedforward neural networks.

**Proposition 6** *Fibred neural networks can approximate any (Borel) measurable function in a compact domain to any desired degree of accuracy (i.e. fNNs are universal approximators).*
***proof:*** *This follows directly from the proof that single hidden layer feedforward neural networks are universal approximators (Hornik, Stinchcombe, & White 1989), together with the observation that level zero networks are a generalisation of single hidden layer feedforward networks.* □

**Proposition 7** *Fibred neural networks can approximate any polynomial function to any desired degree of accuracy.*[6]
***proof:*** *Consider the level zero network N of Figure 4. Let* $n+1$ $(n \in \mathbb{N})$ *be the number of input neurons of N,* $0 \le i \le n$, $a_i \in \mathbb{R}$*. Now, embed* $n-1$ *networks into the input neurons of N, all at level 1, as indicated in Figure 4 for networks A, B and C, such that network A is embedded into neuron A of network N, network B is embedded into neuron B of N, and network C is embedded into neuron C of N. Each of the* $n-1$ *embedded networks will be used to represent* $x^2, x^3, ..., x^n$*. In Figure 4, A represents* $x^2$*, B represents* $x^3$*, and C represents* $x^n$*. In the ensemble, all networks, including N, contain linear neurons. A network* $N_j$ *that represents* $x^j$ $(2 \le j \le n)$ *contains two input neurons (to allow the representation of* $a_j \in \mathbb{R}$*),* $j-1$ *hidden layers, each layer containing a single hidden neuron (let us number these* $h_1, h_2, ..., h_{j-1}$*), and a single output neuron. In addition, let* $a_j/2$ *be the weight from each input neuron to* $h_1$*, and let 1 be the weight of any other connection in* $N_j$*. We need to show that* $N_j$ *computes* $a_j x^j$*. From Definition 5, given input x to N and* $\varphi_j = x \cdot \mathbf{W}_j$*, the weights of* $N_j$ *are multiplied by x. Then, given input (1,1) to* $N_j$*, neuron* $h_1$ *will produce output* $a_j x$*, neuron* $h_2$ *will produce output* $a_j x^2$*, and so on. Neuron* $h_{j-1}$ *will produce output* $a_j x^{j-1}$*, and the output neuron will produce* $a_j x^j$*. Finally, by Definition 2, the neuron in N into which* $N_j$ *is embedded will present activation* $a_j x^j$*, and the output of N will be* $\sum_j a_j x^j$*. The addition of* $a_1 x$ *and* $a_0$ *is straightforward (see network N in Figure 4), completing the proof that fNNs compute* $\sum_i a_i x^i$*.* □

[6] Recall that, differently from functions in a compact domain, polynomial functions are not bounded.

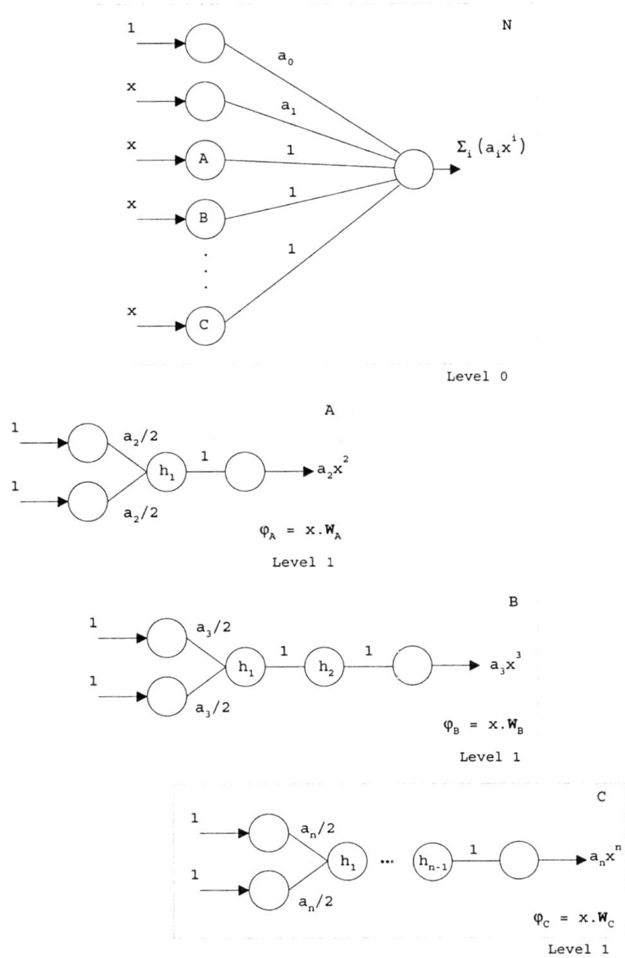


Figure 4: Computing polynomials in fibred networks

## Conclusion and Future Work

This paper has introduced a new neural network architecture named fibred neural networks (fNNs), which combines a number of standard feedforward neural networks (that can be trained using *backpropagation*) with the use of a fibring function. We have shown that, in addition to being universal approximators, fNNs can approximate any polynomial function, therefore being more expressive than standard feedforward neural networks.

The question of which logics could be represented in fNNs is an interesting open question. Our next step is to use the recursive, more expressive architecture of fNNs to perform symbolic computation, giving fNNs a Neural-Symbolic characterisation. We expect to be able to use fNNs to represent variables and to learn and reason about relational knowledge.

Another interesting work to pursue would be to define how recurrent neural networks could be fibred. Recurrent networks already possess a limited ability to compute unbounded functions (Henderson 2002). A comparison of the computational capabilities of these two architectures would be highly desirable.

Finally, the questions of how different networks should be fibred and which fibring functions should be used is a very important one when it comes to practical applications of fNNs. This is clearly domain dependent, and an empirical evaluation of fNNs in comparison with standard neural networks would also be required.

## Acknowledgments

We are grateful to Stefan Rueger for very useful discussions. Artur Garcez is partly supported by the Nuffield Foundation.

## References

Angelopoulos, N., and Muggleton, S. H. 2002. Machine learning metabolic pathway descriptions using a probabilistic relational representation. *Electronic Transactions in Artificial Intelligence* 6. MI-19.

Boutsinas, B., and Vrahatis, M. N. 2001. Artificial nonmonotonic neural networks. *Artificial Intelligence* 132:1–38.

Cloete, I., and Zurada, J. M., eds. 2000. *Knowledge-Based Neurocomputing.* The MIT Press.

Cybenco, G. 1989. Approximation by superposition of sigmoidal functions. In *Mathematics of Control, Signals and Systems 2.* 303–314.

d'Avila Garcez, A. S., and Lamb, L. C. 2004. Reasoning about time and knowledge in neural-symbolic learning systems. In Thrun, S.; Saul, L.; and Schoelkopf, B., eds., *Advances in Neural Information Processing Systems 16*, Proceedings of the NIPS 2003 Conference. Vancouver, Canada: MIT Press.

d'Avila Garcez, A. S.; Broda, K.; and Gabbay, D. M. 2001. Symbolic knowledge extraction from trained neural networks: A sound approach. *Artificial Intelligence* 125:155–207.

d'Avila Garcez, A. S.; Broda, K.; and Gabbay, D. M. 2002. *Neural-Symbolic Learning Systems: Foundations and Applications.* Perspectives in Neural Computing. Springer-Verlag.

d'Avila Garcez, A. S. 2004. On Gabbay's fibring methodology for bayesian and neural networks. In *Laws and Models in Science*, European Science Foundation (ESF). King's College London.

Elman, J. L. 1990. Finding structure in time. *Cognitive Science* 14(2):179–211.

Fu, L. M. 1994. *Neural Networks in Computer Intelligence.* McGraw Hill.

Gabbay, D. M. 1999. *Fibring Logics.* Oxford Univesity Press.

Haykin, S. 1999. *Neural Networks: A Comprehensive Foundation.* Prentice Hall.

Henderson, J. 2002. Estimating probabilities of unbounded categorization problems. In *Proceedings of European Symposium on Artificial Neural Networks*, 383–388.

Hines, J. W. 1996. A logarithmic neural network architecture for unbounded non-linear function approximation. In *Proceedings of IEEE International Conference on Neural Networks.*

Holldobler, S., and Kurfess, F. 1992. CHCL: A connectionist inference system. In Fronhofer, B., and Wrightson, G., eds., *Parallelization in Inference Systems*, 318–342. Springer.

Holldobler, S.; Kalinke, Y.; and Storr, H. P. 1999. Approximating the semantics of logic programs by recurrent neural networks. *Applied Intelligence Journal, Special Issue on Neural Networks and Structured Knowledge* 11(1):45–58.

Hornik, K.; Stinchcombe, M.; and White, H. 1989. Multilayer feedforward networks are universal approximators. *Neural Networks* 2:359–366.

Kijsirikul, B.; Sinthupinyo, S.; and Chongkasemwongse, K. 2001. Approximate match of rules using backpropagation neural networks. *Machine Learning* 43(3):273–299.

Pinkas, G. 1995. Reasoning, nonmonotonicity and learning in connectionist networks that capture propositional knowledge. *Artificial Intelligence* 77:203–247.

Pollack, J. B. 1990. Recursive distributed representations. *Artificial Intelligence* 46(1):77–105.

Rumelhart, D. E.; Hinton, G. E.; and Williams, R. J. 1986. Learning internal representations by error propagation. In Rumelhart, D. E., and McClelland, J. L., eds., *Parallel Distributed Processing: Explorations in the Microstructure of Cognition*, volume 1. MIT Press. 318–362.

Shastri, L. 1999. Advances in SHRUTI: a neurally motivated model of relational knowledge representation and rapid inference using temporal synchrony. *Applied Intelligence Journal, Special Issue on Neural Networks and Structured Knowledge* 11:79–108.

Smolensky, P. 1990. Tensor product variable binding and the representation of symbolic structures in connectionist networks. *Artificial Intelligence* 46:159–216.

Smolensky, P. 2000. Grammar-based connectionist approaches to language. *Cognitive Science* 23:589–613.

Sun, R., and Alexandre, F. 1997. *Connectionist Symbolic Integration.* Lawrence Erlbaum Associates.

Touretzky, D., and Hinton, G. 1988. A distributed connectionist production system. *Cognitive Science* 12(3):423–466.

Towell, G. G., and Shavlik, J. W. 1994. Knowledge-based artificial neural networks. *Artificial Intelligence* 70(1):119–165.

Valiant, L. G. 2003. Three problems in computer science. *Journal of the ACM* 50(1):96–99.

Werbos, P. J. 1990. Backpropagation through time: what does it mean and how to do it. In *Proceedings of the IEEE*, volume 78, 1550–1560.

Williamson, J., and Gabbay, D. 2004. Recursive causality in bayesian networks and self-fibring networks. In *Laws and Models in Science*, European Science Foundation (ESF). King's College London.

# Learning and Inferring Transportation Routines

**Lin Liao  Dieter Fox  Henry Kautz**
Department of Computer Science & Engineering
University of Washington
Seattle, WA 98195

**Abstract**

This paper introduces a hierarchical Markov model that can learn and infer a user's daily movements through the community. The model uses multiple levels of abstraction in order to bridge the gap between raw GPS sensor measurements and high level information such as a user's mode of transportation or her goal. We apply Rao-Blackwellised particle filters for efficient inference both at the low level and at the higher levels of the hierarchy. Significant locations such as goals or locations where the user frequently changes mode of transportation are learned from GPS data logs without requiring any manual labeling. We show how to detect abnormal behaviors (*e.g.* taking a wrong bus) by concurrently tracking his activities with a trained and a prior model. Experiments show that our model is able to accurately predict the goals of a person and to recognize situations in which the user performs unknown activities.

## Introduction

The advent of low-cost GPS (global positioning system) technology has led to great interest in developing commercial applications that take advantage of information about a user's current location — for example, 911 service. But localization based on immediate sensor data is only one small part of inferring a user's spatial context. In this paper we describe a system that creates a *probabilistic model* of a user's daily movements using unsupervised learning from raw GPS data. The model allows one to:

- Infer the locations of usual goals, such as home or workplace;
- Infer a user's mode of transportation, such as foot, car, or bus, and predict when and where she will change modes;
- Predict her future movements, both in the short term (will the user turn left at the next street corner?) and in terms of distant goals (is she going to her workplace?);
- Infer when a user has *broken his ordinary routine* in a way that may indicate that he has made an error, such as failing to get off his bus at his usual stop on the way home;
- Robustly track and predict locations even in the presence of total loss of GPS signals and other sources of noise.

A motivating application for this work is the development of personal guidance systems that help cognitively-impaired individuals move safely and independently throughout their community. Other potential applications include *customized* "just in time" information services (for example, provide the user with current bus schedule information when she is likely to need it or real time traffic conditions on her future trajectories) and self-configuring appointment calendars.

Our approach is based on an abstract hierarchical Markov model (Bui, Venkatesh, & West 2002) of a user from data collected by a small wearable GPS unit. The model is compactly represented by a dynamic Bayesian network, and inference is efficiently performed using Rao-Blackwellised particle filtering both for the low level sensor integration and for the higher levels of the hierarchical model.

The main research contribution in this paper is a method for learning hierarchical predictive models of user location and transportation mode in an unsupervised manner. While previous authors described inference in hierarchical models (Bui, Venkatesh, & West 2002) and learning flat transportation models (Patterson *et al.* 2003), our work is the first to combine the techniques. A second research contribution are initial results on inferring *user errors and deviations from routine* by model selection. We demonstrate the effectiveness of this approach with an example of the system recognizing when the user has missed his bus stop.

This paper is organized as follows. In the next section, we discuss related work. Then, we provide an overview of the activity model, followed by a description of inference and learning mechanisms. Before concluding, we present experimental results that show the capabilities of our approach.

## Related work

Over the last years, estimating a person's activities has gained increased interest in the AI, robotics, and ubiquitous computing communities. (Ashbrook & Starner 2003) learn significant locations from logs of GPS measurements by determining the time a person spends at a certain location. For these locations, they use frequency counting to estimate the transition parameters of a second-order Markov model. Their approach then predicts the next goal based on the current and the previous goals. In contrast to our approach, their model is not able to refine the goal estimates using GPS information observed when moving from one significant location to another. Furthermore, such a coarse representation does not allow the detection of potential user errors. In our previous work (Patterson *et al.* 2003), we estimate a person's location and mode of transportation from GPS measurements using a "flat" model. Since the model has no notion of significant locations, it is not able to predict the high-level goal of a person. By conditioning on goals and segments of a trip, our hierarchical model is able to learn more specific motion patterns of a person, which also enables us to detect user errors.

In the context of probabilistic plan recognition, (Bui, Venkatesh, & West 2002) introduced the abstract hidden Markov model, which uses hierarchical representations to efficiently infer a person's goal in an indoor environment from camera information. (Bui 2003) extended this model to include memory nodes, which enables the transfer of context information over multiple time steps. Bui and colleagues introduced efficient inference algorithms for their models using Rao-Blackwellised particle filters. Since our model has a similar structure to theirs, we apply the inference mechanisms developed in (Bui 2003). Our work goes beyond the work of Bui *et al.* in that we show how to learn the structure and the parameters of the hierarchical activity model from data. Furthermore, our low level estimation problem is more challenging than their indoor tracking problem. In the context of mobile robotics, (Cielniak, Bennewitz, & Burgard 2003) apply a two level model to track and predict the location of people using a mobile robot equipped with a laser range-finder. Their model learns a person's trajectories using a mixtures of Gaussians approach. Due to this representation, they are only able to track a person along paths the robot has observed during training. Thus, the technique is not able to track and detect novel behaviors.

The task of detecting abnormal events in time series data (called *novelty detection*) has been studied extensively in the data-mining community (Guralnik & Srivastava 1999), but remains an open and challenging research problem. We present the first results on abnormality detection in location and transportation prediction using a simple and effective model selection approach based on comparing the likelihood of a learned hierarchical model against that of a prior model.

## Hierarchical Activity Model

We estimate a person's activities using the three level dynamic Bayesian network model shown in Fig. 1. The individual nodes in such a temporal graphical model represent different parts of the state space and the arcs indicate dependencies between the nodes (Murphy 2002). Temporal dependencies are represented by arcs connecting the two time slices $k-1$ and $k$. The highest level of the model, denoted goal level, represents the person's next goal, *e.g.*, her work place. The trip segment level represents the mode of transportation and the locations at which the person transfers from one mode to another. The person's location and motion velocity are estimated from the GPS sensor measurements at the lowest level of the model.

**Locations and transportation modes** We denote by $x_k = \langle l_k, v_k, c_k \rangle$ the location and motion velocity of the person, and the location of the person's car [1] (subscripts $k$ indicate discrete time). As we will describe in the next section, locations are estimated on a graph structure representing a street map. GPS sensor measurements, $z_k$, are generated by the person carrying a GPS sensor. Since measurements are given in continuous $xy$-coordinates, they have to be "snapped" to

[1]We include the car location because it strongly affects whether the person can switch to the car mode.

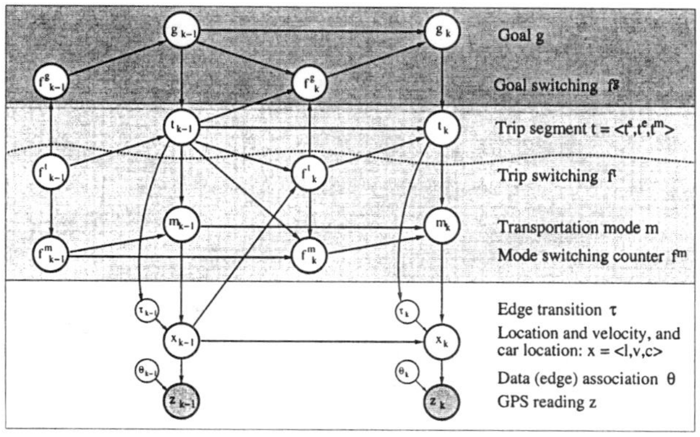


Figure 1: Hierarchical activity model representing a person's outdoor movements during everyday activities. The upper level estimates the current goal, the middle layer represents segments of a trip and mode of transportation, and the lowest layer estimates the person's location. The dashed line indicates the flat model.

an edge in the graph structure. The edge to which a specific measurement is "snapped" is estimated by the association variable $\theta_k$. The location of the person at time $k$ depends on his previous location, $l_{k-1}$, the motion velocity, $v_k$, and the vertex transition, $\tau_k$. Vertex transitions $\tau$ model the decision a person makes when moving over a vertex in the graph, for example, to turn right when crossing a street intersection.

The mode of transportation can take on four different values $m_k \in \{BUS, FOOT, CAR, BUILDING\}$. Similar to (Patterson *et al.* 2003), these modes influence the motion velocity, which is picked from a Gaussian mixture model. For example, the walking mode draws velocities only from the Gaussian representing slow motion. $BUILDING$ is a special mode that occurs only when the GPS signal is lost for significantly long time. Finally, the location of the car only changes when the person is in the $CAR$ mode, in which the car location is set to the person's location.

**Trip segments** A trip segment is defined by its start location, $t^s_k$, end location, $t^e_k$, and the mode of transportation, $t^m_k$, the person uses during the segment. For example, a trip segment models information such as "she gets on the bus at location $t^s_k$ and takes the bus up to location $t^e_k$, where she gets off the bus". In addition to transportation mode, a trip segment predicts the route on which the person gets from $t^s_k$ to $t^e_k$. This route is not specified through a deterministic sequence of edges on the graph but rather through transition probabilities on the graph. These probabilities determine the prediction of the person's motion direction when crossing a vertex in the graph, as indicated by the arc from $t_k$ to $\tau_k$.

The transfer between modes and trip segments is handled by the switching nodes $f^m_k$ and $f^t_k$, respectively. More specifically, the binary trip switching node is set to true whenever the person reaches the end location $t^e_k$ of the current trip segment. In this case, the trip segment is allowed to switch with the constraint that the start location of the next segment is identical to the end location of the current segment. The next trip segment is chosen according to the segment transition of the current goal $g_k$. Once the next trip segment is active, the person still has to change mode of transportation. This does not happen instantaneously, since, for example, a person has to wait for the bus even though he already reached the bus stop (and thus entered the bus trip segment). This semi-Markov property of delayed mode switching is modeled by the node $f_k^m$, which is a counter that measures the time steps until the next transportation mode is entered. The counter is initialized by the next trip segment, then decremented until it reaches a value of zero, which triggers the mode switch.

**Goals** A goal represents the current target location of the person. Goals include locations such as the person's home, work place, the grocery store, and locations of friends. These goals are also contained in the trip segment level. Thus, the goal of the person can only change when the person reaches the end of a trip segment. The goal switching node $f_k^g$ is true only when the trip switching node $f_k^t$ is true and the end of the current trip segment $t_k$ is identical to the goal $g_k$. If the goal switches, the next goal is chosen according to a learned goal transition model.

## Inference, Learning, and Error Detection

### Inference

The independence structure of our hierarchical activity model allows us to use efficient inference developed for abstract hidden Markov memory models (Bui 2003). This technique relies on Rao-Blackwellised particle filters, where the states at the lowest level are estimated using particle filters, and higher levels are solved analytically conditioned on the low level particles. For brevity, we focus on the task of estimating a person's location and mode of transportation using GPS measurements. Inference at higher levels will only be outlined, since it is very similar to (Bui 2003).

**GPS-based tracking on street maps** Our previous work (Patterson *et al.* 2003) uses a "flat" model for location and transportation mode estimation. Such a model is obtained by removing the nodes $g$, $f^g$, and $t$ from the activity model shown in Fig. 1, as indicated by the dotted line. In that model, we estimate a person's location on a street map represented by a graph-structure $S = (V, E)$, where $V$ is the set of vertices, $v_i$, and $E$ is the set of edges, $e_j$. Typically, vertices are intersections and the length of edges corresponds to city blocks. The person can switch mode of transportation whenever she is near her car or a bus stop. While our previous work uses particle filters for inference, we now rely on a more efficient Rao-Blackwellised solution to the problem (Doucet *et al.* 2000), which is based on the following factorization of the posterior:

$$p(x_k, m_k, f_k^t, f_k^m, \theta_k, \tau_k \mid z_{1:k}) = p(x_k|m_k, f_k^t, f_k^m, \theta_k, \tau_k, z_{1:k})\, p(m_k, f_k^t, f_k^m, \theta_k, \tau_k|z_{1:k}) \quad (1)$$

The posterior at time $k$ is conditioned on $z_{1:k}$, the sequence of GPS measurements observed so far. The factorization (1) separates the state space of our estimation problem into its continuous and discrete parts. The continuous part represents the location and motion velocity of the person, $x_k$, and the discrete part represents the remaining quantities including transportation mode $m_k$, edge association $\theta_k$, edge transition $\tau_k$, and switching nodes $f_k^m$ and $f_k^t$.

Rao-Blackwellised particle filters (RBPF) estimate this factorized posterior by sampling the discrete states using a particle filter and then estimating the person's location and motion velocity using Kalman filters conditioned on the samples. More specifically, RBPFs represent posteriors by sets of weighted samples, or particles:

$$S_k = \{s_k^{(i)}, w_k^{(i)} \mid 1 \le i \le N\}$$

Each $s_k^{(i)} = \langle\langle {\mu_k}^{(i)}, {\Sigma_k}^{(i)}\rangle, {m_k}^{(i)}, f_k^{m(i)}, f_k^{t(i)}, {\theta_k}^{(i)}, {\tau_k}^{(i)}\rangle$, where the person's location and velocity are represented by $\langle {\mu_k}^{(i)}, {\Sigma_k}^{(i)}\rangle$, the mean and covariance of the Kalman filter, which represents posteriors by Gaussian approximations (Bar-Shalom, Li, & Kirubarajan 2001). The other components of the particle are instances of the discrete parts of the state space. At each time step, RBPFs first sample the discrete components from the posterior at the previous time $k - 1$. This can be done stepwise by simulating (1) from right to left, using the independence represented in the activity model (see Fig. 1). Then, the continuous part is updated analytically using Kalman filters.

The discrete variables are sampled as follows. The value of the trip switching node $f_k^{t(i)}$ is sampled conditioned on the previous location of the person $x_{k-1}$. For example, whenever the person approaches a bus stop, $f_k^{t(i)}$ is set to true with a small probability. If $f_k^{t(i)} = \mathrm{T}$, then the value of the mode switching counter $f_k^{m(i)}$ is initialized to the waiting time. Otherwise, the value of $f_k^{m(i)}$ is decremented, and when it reaches zero, the new transportation mode ${m_k}^{(i)}$ is sampled according to the mode transition probability; otherwise, ${m_k}^{(i)} = {m_{k-1}}^{(i)}$. The value of the edge transition variable $\tau_k$ determines, for example, whether the person moves straight or turns right at the next intersection. ${\tau_k}^{(i)}$ is sampled based on the previous position of the person and a learned transition model. Finally, the edge association variable $\theta_k$ "snaps" the GPS reading to a street in the map. This step is crucial for the Kalman filter update described below. To sample $\theta_k^{(i)}$, we first determine the distance between the measurement, $z_k$, and the different streets in the vicinity. The probability of "snapping" $z_k$ to one of these streets is then computed from this distance.

At this step of the algorithm, we can assume that all discrete values of a sample are already generated, that is, $s_k^{(i)} = \langle\langle\cdot\rangle, {m_k}^{(i)}, f_k^{m(i)}, f_k^{t(i)}, {\theta_k}^{(i)}, {\tau_k}^{(i)}\rangle$. The RBPF now generates the missing values $\langle {\mu_k}^{(i)}, {\Sigma_k}^{(i)}\rangle$ by updating the Kalman filter conditioned on the already sampled values. To see, let us rewrite the left term on the right hand side of (1):

$$p(x_k \mid m_k^{(i)}, f_k^{m(i)}, f_k^{t(i)}, \theta_k^{(i)}, \tau_k^{(i)}, z_{1:k}) \propto p(z_k|x_k, \theta_k^{(i)}) \int p(x_k|m_k^{(i)}, \tau_k^{(i)}, x_{k-1}^{(i)})\, p(x_{k-1}^{(i)}|z_{1:k-1})\, \mathrm{d}x_{k-1}^{(i)} \quad (2)$$

(2) follows by applying Bayes rule and the independences in our estimation problem. It represents the standard recursive Bayes filter update rule; see (Bar-Shalom, Li, & Kirubarajan 2001) for details. The prior probability is given by the Gaussian of the previous Kalman filter estimate: $p(x_{k-1}^{(i)}|z_{1:k-1}) = \mathcal{N}(x_{k-1}^{(i)}; \mu_{k-1}^{(i)}, \Sigma_{k-1}^{(i)})$. The Kalman filter implements the update rule (2) by two steps: a *prediction step* followed by a *correction step*.

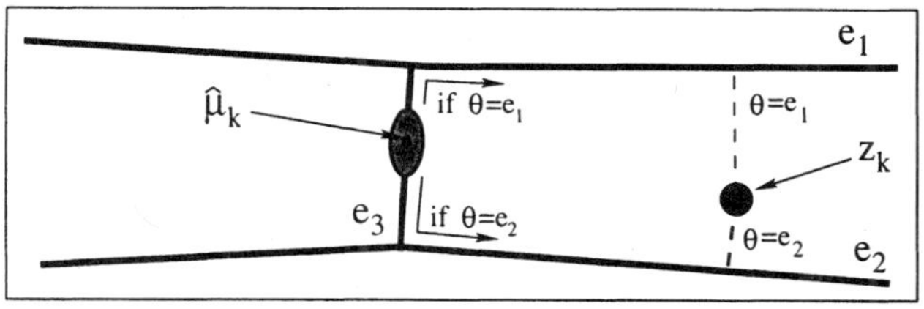


Figure 2: Kalman filter update and data association: The person is located on edge $e_3$. The continuous coordinates of the GPS measurement, $z_k$, are between edges $e_1$ and $e_2$. Depending on the value of the edge association, $\theta$, the correction step moves the estimate up-wards or down-wards.

In the prediction step, the distance traveled since the last filter update is predicted using the previous velocity estimate. The prediction, $\langle \hat{\mu}_k^{(i)}, \hat{\Sigma}_k^{(i)} \rangle$, results then from shifting and convolving the previous estimate by the predicted motion, thereby implementing the integration in (2). This prediction step is straightforward if the person stays on the same edge of the graph. If she transits over a vertex of the graph, then the edge is given by the already sampled edge transition ${\tau_k}^{(i)}$.

In the correction step, the predicted estimate $\langle \hat{\mu}_k^{(i)}, \hat{\Sigma}_k^{(i)} \rangle$ is corrected based on the most recent GPS measurement, $z_k$. Intuitively, this correction compares the predicted mean $\hat{\mu}_k^{(i)}$ with the location of $z_k$ and shifts the mean toward the measurement (under consideration of the uncertainties). The correction step is illustrated in Fig. 2. The predicted location is on edge $e_3$, and the GPS sensor reports a measurement, $z_k$, between edges $e_1$ and $e_2$. Depending on whether $z_k$ originates from $e_1$ or $e_2$, the predicted estimate is corrected either up-wards or down-wards.[2] The already sampled value of the edge association variable ${\theta_k}^{(i)}$ uniquely determines to which edge the reading is "snapped" (see previous paragraph).

After all components of each particle are generated, the importance weights of the particles are updated. This is done by computing the likelihood of the GPS measurement $z_k$, which is provided by the update innovations of the Kalman filters (Doucet *et al.* 2000).

**Goal and trip segment estimation** So far, we concentrated on the estimation in a flat model. To further estimate a person's goal and trip segment, we apply the inference algorithm used for the abstract hidden Markov memory models (Bui 2003). More specifically, we use a Rao-Blackwellised particle filter both at the low level and at the higher levels. Each sample of the resulting particle filter contains the discrete and continuous states described in the previous section, and a joint distribution over the goals and trip segments. These additional distributions are updated using exact inference. To summarize, at each time step, the filter is updated as follows (see (Bui 2003)):

1. For each particle, sample the discrete states, $m_k^{(i)}, f_k^{m(i)}, f_k^{t(i)}, f_k^{g(i)}, \theta_k^{(i)}, \tau_k^{(i)}$, update the continuous state $\langle \mu_k^{(i)}, \Sigma_k^{(i)} \rangle$ by performing one-step Kalman filtering, and compute importance weight $w_k^{(i)}$.
2. Do re-sampling according to the importance weights.
3. For each particle, perform one-step exact inference to update the distribution of goals $g_k^{(i)}$ and trip segments $t_k^{(i)}$.

[2] Alternatively, one could compute the innovation in $xy$-space and project it onto the graph. However, such an approach can result in "stuck situations", for example, in dead ends on the graph.

The first step is extremely similar to the flat model described in the previous section. The main difference lies in the fact that the transportation mode $m_k^{(i)}$, the trip switching $f_k^{t(i)}$, and the edge transitions $\tau_k^{(i)}$ are sampled *conditioned* on the estimates of the high level goal and trip segment. Thereby, the sampling is adjusted to the current high level information.

## Learning

Learning of the hierarchical model includes two procedures: structural learning and parameter learning, both are completely unsupervised. Structural learning searches for the significant locations, *i.e.*, usual goals and mode transfer locations, from GPS logs collected over an extended period of time. To do that, we apply expectation maximization (EM) using the "flat" activity model described above (called flat EM). When it finishes, the structure of the model is determined. EM is then used to estimate the transition probabilities in the hierarchical model (called hierarchical EM).

**Finding goals** We consider goal locations to be those locations where a person typically spends extended periods of time. (Ashbrook & Starner 2003) extract significant locations by detecting places where the GPS signal is lost. The disadvantage of such an approach is that it can only detect indoor goals. To overcome this problem, we store for each edge on the graph how long the person stays on this edge, estimated during the flat EM. Since we model loss of GPS signal by transiting into a "BUILDING" mode, our model can thus detect both indoor and outdoor goals. Once significant edges are detected, they are clustered by combining edges that are connected or very close.

**Finding mode transfer locations** The mode transition probabilities for each street are estimated during the flat EM. Even before learning, knowledge about the bus stops and the fact that the car is either parked or moves with the person, already provides important constraints on mode transitions. In the E-step, both a forward and a backward filtering pass are performed and the transition counts of the two passes are combined. Then in the M-step, the parameters are updated based on the counts. The mode transfer locations for a user, *i.e.*, usual bus stops and parking lots, are then those locations at which the mode switching exceeds a certain threshold.

**Estimating transition matrices** Once goals and trip segments are determined, we can extend the flat model by inserting these significant locations into the higher levels of the activity model. Then, we can re-use the GPS data in the hierarchical EM to estimate the transition matrices between the goals, between the trip segments given the goal, and between the adjacent streets given the trip segment. Hierarchical EM is similar to flat EM. During the E-steps, smoothing is performed by tracking the states both forward and backward in time. The M-steps update the model parameters using the frequency counts generated in the E-step. All transition parameters are smoothed using Dirichlet priors.

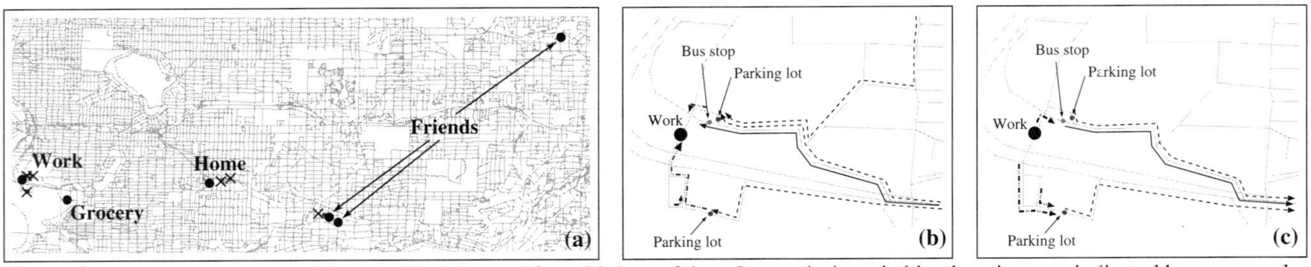


Figure 3: (a) Street map along with goals (dots) learned from 30 days of data. Learned trip switching locations are indicated by cross marks. From home, the person either walks to one of the two bus stops or takes the car, which is not learned as a trip switching location since the car is parked inside the house. (b) Zoom into the area around the work place. Shown are very likely transitions (probability above 0.75), given that the goal is the work place (dashed lines indicate car mode, solid lines bus, and dashed-dotted lines foot). (c) Learned transitions in the same area conditioned on the home being the goal.

### Detection of User Errors

If the person always repeats her past activities, activity tracking can be done with only a small number of particles in the learned model. This is mainly because the model has low uncertainty in where the person switches modes and goals. In reality, however, people often perform novel activities or commit some errors. The most straightforward way to model abnormalities is to add an unknown goal and an unknown mode transfer location to the learned model, and estimate the probability of the unknowns. However, this means the person can change mode and goal *everywhere*, because any place could be an unknown goal or transfer location. This would require a huge number of particles to track correctly.

Instead, we use two different trackers simultaneously and perform model monitoring by computing the Bayes factors between the two models (West & Harrison 1997). The first tracker uses hierarchical inference on the learned model that models the person's ordinary routine. The second uses a flat model with the *apriori* parameter settings; these account for general physical constraints but are not adjusted to the individual's ordinary routines. The trackers are run in parallel, and the probability of each model is calculated from the observation likelihoods of the two models. When the user is following her ordinary routine the hierarchical model has higher likelihoods, but when the user does something unexpected the general flat model becomes more likely.

Both trackers can be run very efficiently. The hierarchical tracker has "expensive" particles, each containing much state information, but requires few particles for accurate tracking. The flat, untrained tracker needs more particles to maintain tracking, but each particle is cheaper to compute. Furthermore, calculating the likelihood of a model introduces no extra expense, because the value already needs to be computed as part of importance weighting.

## Experimental Results

We collected a log of 60 days of GPS data from one person using a wearable GPS unit. We use the first 30 days for learning and the other 30 days for the empirical comparison.

**Activity model learning** The learning was done completely unsupervised without any manual labeling. The structural learning precisely identifies the subject's six most common transportation goals and all frequently used bus stops and parking lots, as shown in Fig. 3 (a). After recognizing the goals and transfer locations, parameter learning estimates the transition matrices at all levels of the model. Fig. 3 (b) and (c) show the learned street transitions given high-level information. The model successfully discovered the most frequent trajectories for traveling from home to the workplace and vice-versa, as well as other common trips, such as to the homes of friends.

**Empirical comparison to other models** The hierarchical model is very expressive and able to answer many useful queries. For example, many applications need to query the probability of a given goal. Here we compare the performance of our hierarchical model to the goal prediction of a flat model (Patterson *et al.* 2003) and a second-order Markov model between goals (2MM for simplicity) (Ashbrook & Starner 2003).

A flat model only keeps a first-order Markov model over the street blocks. Thus, in order to calculate the probability of a goal, one must calculate the sum over all possible paths to the goal, which is intractable if the goal is far away. A reasonable approximation is to compute the probability of the most likely path to the goal. Fig. 4 (a) compares the result of such a query on the probability of the goal being the work place during an episode of traveling from home to work. As one can see, quite early on the hierarchical model assigns a high probability to the true goal, while the estimate from the flat model is meaningless until the user is near the goal.

| Model | Avg. accuracy at given time | | | |
|---|---|---|---|---|
| | beginning | 25% | 50% | 75% |
| 2MM | 0.69 | 0.69 | 0.69 | 0.69 |
| Hierarchical model | 0.66 | 0.75 | 0.82 | 0.98 |

Table 1: Goal predictions using 2MM and hierarchical model

The 2MM models the goal transitions explicitly, but it cannot refine the prediction using the observations collected during transit. To show the difference, we labeled the 30 days of test data with the true goals and computed the prediction accuracy using the 2MM and our hierarchical model, which are learned using the same training data. The average prediction accuracies at the beginning of the trips and after 25%, 50%, 75% of the trips are listed in Table 1. At the beginning, our model predicts the next goal using first-order transition matrices; it performs a little worse than the 2MM. But by integrating real time measurements, our predictions become more accurate while 2MM's estimates remain the same.

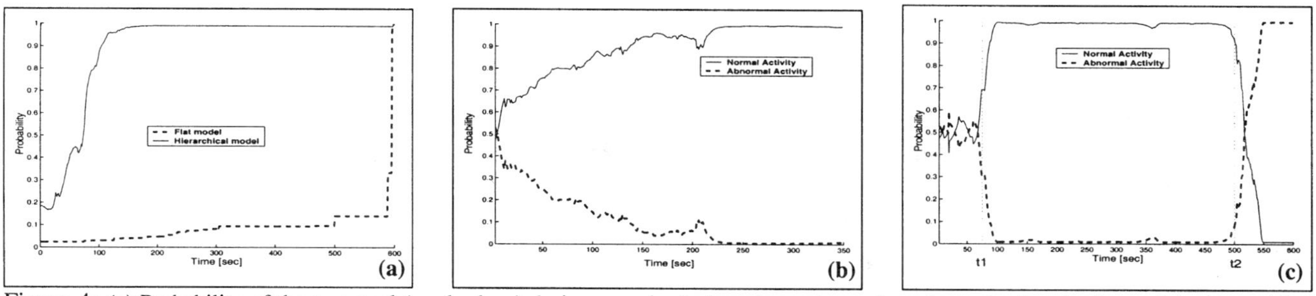


Figure 4: (a) Probability of the true goal (work place) during an episode from home to work, estimated using the flat and the hierarchical model. (b,c) Probability of an activity being normal or abnormal, estimated by the concurrent trackers. (b) Normal activity: driving from home to work. (c) Abnormal activity: missing to get off the bus at time t2.

**Detection of user errors** Another important feature of our model is the capability to capture user errors using the parallel tracking approach. To demonstrate the performance of parallel tracking, we did two experiments, with a subject who sometimes drives and sometimes takes the bus from work to home. In the first experiment, the subject drove from home to work as usual. In the second experiment, the subject took his usual bus toward home but failed to get off the bus at the usual stop. In each experiment, we determine the probability of each tracker over time, as shown in Fig. 4 (b) and (c). In the first experiment, because the trajectory matches the learned model well, the normal tracker quickly becomes dominant. The second experiment starts when the subject is waiting at the bus stop. At time t1, the person gets on the bus. Since the route is already well-learned, the belief that the subject is going home becomes high. At time t2, however, the person misses the usual bus stop. At this point the probability of the learned model quickly drops, while that of the flat "abnormal" model quickly rises. We performed additional experiments in which the goal and transportation mode were instantiated explicitly in the model. In such a setting, the model is able to quickly determine when the user deviates from the desired behavior; an ability that can be very useful to monitor and guide cognitively-impaired individuals.

## Conclusions and Future Work

We have described the foundations and experimental validation of a hierarchical model that can learn and infer a user's daily movements and use of different modes of transportation. The model can be learned using unlabeled data, and online inference can be efficiently performed. Our results show that the approach can provide predictions of movements to distant goals, and support a simple and effective strategy for detecting novel events that may indicate user errors.

Our future work builds upon the foundation laid in this paper in several directions. One obvious extension is to incorporate information about time of day and the day of the week into the model, which we expect to greatly enhance predictive power. We furthermore plan to use probabilistic relational models (Getoor *et al.* 2001) to better represent and learn different types of locations. Using relational model learning, specific features of location types can be learned from data sets collected by several people. The same data can also be used to create loosely-coupled models of several individuals, so that one can predict joint activities, such as when two people will meet. Finally, the approach described here will be incorporated into a safety monitoring and guidance system that we are constructing for cognitively-impaired individuals who often become lost and have difficulty in using public transportation safely.

### Acknowledgments

We thank Donald J. Patterson for providing useful software, data, and discussions in the course of this work. This research is based on work that has been supported by the NSF under grant numbers IIS-0225774 and IIS-0093406, and by DARPA's SDR Programme (grant number NBCHC020073).

## References

Ashbrook, D., and Starner, T. 2003. Using GPS to learn significant locations and predict movement across multiple users. *Personal and Ubiquitous Computing* 7(5).

Bar-Shalom, Y.; Li, X.-R.; and Kirubarajan, T. 2001. *Estimation with Applications to Tracking and Navigation.* John Wiley.

Bui, H.; Venkatesh, S.; and West, G. 2002. Policy recognition in the abstract hidden markov model. *Journal of Artificial Intelligence Research* 17.

Bui, H. 2003. A general model for online probabilistic plan recognition. In *Proc. of the International Joint Conference on Artificial Intelligence.*

Cielniak, G.; Bennewitz, M.; and Burgard, W. 2003. Where is ...? learning and utilizing motion patterns of persons with mobile robots. In *Proc. of the International Joint Conference on Artificial Intelligence.*

Doucet, A.; de Freitas, J.; Murphy, K.; and Russell, S. 2000. Rao-Blackwellised particle filtering for dynamic Bayesian networks. In *Proc. of the Conference on Uncertainty in Artificial Intelligence.*

Getoor, L.; Friedman, N.; Koller, D.; and Pfeffer, A. 2001. Learning probabilistic relational models. In Dzeroski, S., and Lavrac, N., eds., *Relational Data Mining.* Springer-Verlag.

Guralnik, V., and Srivastava, J. 1999. Event detection from time series data. In *5th ACM SIGKDD International Conference on Knowledge Discovery and Data Mining.*

Murphy, K. 2002. *Dynamic Bayesian Networks: Representation, Inference and Learning.* Ph.D. Dissertation, UC Berkeley, Computer Science Division.

Patterson, D.; Liao, L.; Fox, D.; and Kautz, H. 2003. Inferring high-level behavior from low-level sensors. In *International Conference on Ubiquitous Computing.*

West, M., and Harrison, P. 1997. *Bayesian Forecasting and Dynamic Models.* New York: Springer-Verlag, 2nd edition.

# Learning and Applying Competitive Strategies

**Esther Lock and Susan L. Epstein**

Hunter College and The Graduate Center of The City University of New York
Department of Computer Science
New York, New York 10021

### Abstract

Learning reusable sequences can support the development of expertise in many domains, either by improving decision-making quality or decreasing execution speed. This paper introduces and evaluates a method to learn action sequences for generalized states from prior problem experience. From experienced sequences, the method induces the context that underlies a sequence of actions. Empirical results indicate that the sequences and contexts learned for a class of problems are actually those deemed important by experts for that particular class, and can be used to select appropriate action sequences when solving problems there.

Repeated problem solving can provide salient, reusable data to a learner. This paper focuses on programs that acquire expertise in a particular domain. The thesis of our work is that previously experienced sequences are an important knowledge source for such programs, and that appropriate organization of those sequences can support reuse of that knowledge, in novel as well as familiar situations (Lock 2003). The primary contributions of this paper are a learning method for the acquisition of *action sequences* (contiguous subsequences of decisions) and an empirical demonstration of their efficacy and salience as *competitive strategies* in game playing. We claim not that sequences are *all* there is to learn, but that they are a powerful part of expert behavior, and well worth learning. In the work reported here, our method learns many useful action sequences and highlights the ones human experts consider significant.

The *context* of an action sequence is the set of world states where it is relevant. Rather than deduce all possible contexts from the operators available to an agent, or from inspection of the search space, our method exploits the knowledge inherent in experience to learn context. It associates a sequence of actions with the set of *origin states* where the sequence's execution began. The underlying assumption is that some commonality among origin states drives the same sequence of moves. Discovering context is thus reduced to generalization over the origin states to extract it. A learned context is paired with its sequence, and subsequently recommended as a course of action when the context matches the current state of the world.

Macro operators to speed problem solving and planning have been widely studied. MACROPS learned to compose a sequence of operators together, but it was limited to domains with a set of operators with well-defined preconditions and post-conditions, ones where the goal state was a conjunction of well-defined subgoals (Fikes, Hart et al. 1972). Other programs learn to acquire macros that achieve subgoals without undoing previously solved subgoals (Korf 1985; Tadapelli and Natarajan 1996). A game, however, may lack accessible subgoals, and actions in games can have subtle, far-reaching effects that are not clearly delineated. MACLEARN and MICRO-HILLARY use a domain's heuristic function to selectively learn macros from problem solving experience (Iba 1989; Finkelstein and Markovitch 1998). Our method assumes neither the existence of subgoals nor of a heuristic function. Planning for Markov decision processes learns macro actions to achieve subgoals (Moore, Baird et al. 1998; Sutton, Precup et al. 1999; Precup 2000). Most closely related to our method is reinforcement learning work that discovers useful sequences online from successful experience (McGovern 2002). Neither of McGovern's methods generalize context, however.

Our approach uses problem-solving experience to learn the context for a sequence, and uses that knowledge to make decisions. The next section describes how this method learns action sequences and their contexts, and applies them. Subsequent sections describe a program that applies learned competitive strategies, details our experimental design, and discuss results and related work.

## 1. Learning action sequences with contexts

We explore sequence learning first within the domain of two-player, perfect-information, finite board games, using the following definitions. (Broader applicability is addressed in Section 3.) A problem-solving experience is a *contest*, the agents *contestants*, and a legal move an *action*. A *state* is uniquely described by the game board and whose turn it is to move. A place on a game board where a contestant's piece may be placed is a *location*. All locations on a game board are numbered in row order, as in Figure 1. A *blank* is an empty location. A *pattern* is a set of locations and their contents. Our method learns action sequences only from successful experience; in game playing, those are move sequences from contests in which a particular contestant won or drew at a *draw game*, where the value of the root of the game tree is a draw under full minimax.

We consider two games here: lose-tic-tac-toe and five men's morris. *Lose-tic-tac-toe,* where the first to place three pieces in a row in Figure 1(a) loses, is far more difficult for people to learn than ordinary tic-tac-toe. The object is to avoid a certain pattern rather than to achieve it, and a non-optimal move is a fatal error. Flawless lose tic-tac-toe play involves different strategies for each contestant, some of which are non-intuitive and go undiscovered by many people (Cohen 1972). In *five men's morris*, the contestants (black and white) each have five pieces, which they take turns placing on the board in Figure 1(b). Once the pieces are all placed, a move slides a piece from one location on the board to an adjacent, empty location. A contestant who achieves a *mill* (three owned pieces on a line drawn on the board) removes any one opposition piece from the board. A contestant reduced to two pieces or unable to slide, loses. This is a challenging game, with a significantly larger game graph than lose tic-tac-toe.

## 1.1 Overview of the learning method

The program *SeqLearner* observes computer programs of various skill levels in competition at a game. After each contest, SeqLearner examines the contest's actions for sequences of prespecified lengths. It collects action sequences that are *duets* (include both agents' actions) and *solos* (include one agent's actions.) In some two-agent domains, an agent determinedly executes a sequence of actions, so long as they are legal, no matter what the other agent does. If one gathers only sequences that include both agents' actions, the other agent's varied responses to a solo could cast instances of the same solo as different sequences. Therefore, SeqLearner also gathers solos. In the trace of a contest of length $n$, the number of duets of any length is $O(n^2)$, as is the number of solos.

To associate these sequences with states, SeqLearner organizes the collected data into *SeqTable*, a sequence hash table. A key for SeqTable is a sequence; a value stored there is a list of states. For each extracted sequence, SeqLearner records in SeqTable the sequence's origin state, where the sequence's execution began. For repeatedly encountered sequences, SeqLearner extracts a context from the set of origins associated with it. Periodically, SeqLearner sweeps through SeqTable, examining one sequence at a time. For game playing, SeqLearner identifies the maximal common pattern that exists in all the stored states as the context for the sequence. SeqLearner takes

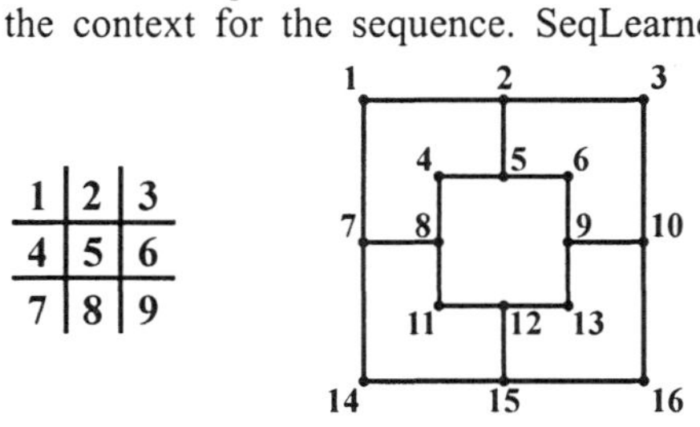

(a) (b)

*Figure 1:* Two game boards and their numbered location for (a) lose tic-tac-toe and (b) five men's morris.

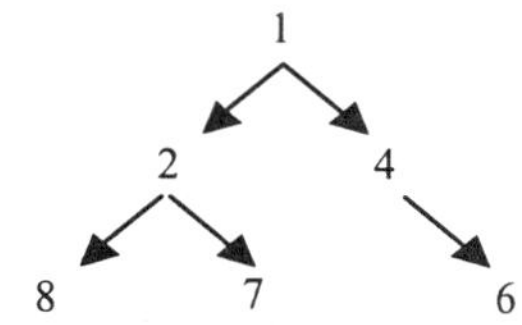

*Figure 2:* A sequence tree merging three sequences that have the same context.

each location of the board as a feature, and examines its value in each of those states, retaining only features with the same value on all the boards. Any location whose value is not retained is labeled # (don't care). The resultant *maximal common pattern* is associated with its sequence in a *context pair.* Both contexts and sequences are normalized for horizontal, vertical, and diagonal reflection, plus rotations of 90°, 180°, and 270°. As a result, a sequence is retrievable whenever its context or a symmetric equivalent arises. With additional experience, the candidate sets for each sequence are likely to grow, engendering new, more general context pairs. If more than one sequence leads to the formation of the same context, those sequences are merged into a *sequence tree* (a tree of alternative, overlapping sequences) to form a single context pair. For example if the three sequences <X to 1, O to 2, X to 8>, <X to 1, O to 2, X to 7>, and <X to 1, O to 4, X to 6> have the identical context, they are merged into the competitive strategy in Figure 2.

Given their inductive origin, these context pairs are not applied immediately in problem solving; the incorrect context pairs must first be carefully filtered out. A variant of *PWL* (Probabilistic Weight Learning) is used to weight them (Epstein 1994). The algorithm determines how well each context pair simulates expert behavior. After every experience, it takes the states where it was the expert's turn to act, checks whether a context pair's advice supports or opposes the expert's decision, and revises the pair's weight in [0,1] accordingly. A context pair's weight rises consistently when it is reliable and frequently applicable.

## 1.2 An example

Figure 3, for example, shows a repeatedly detected lose tic-tac-toe sequence, <X to 1, O to 3, X to 7>, that began at six different states. The sequence is the key to the

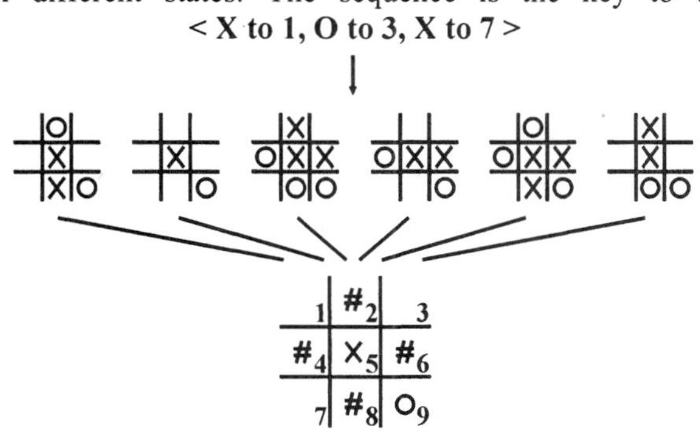


*Figure 3:* The knowledge stored in the SEQTABLE and its associated extracted context.

SeqTable, and the list of states is its stored value. The state descriptions are the data from which context is induced.

Figure 3 also shows the maximal common pattern SeqLearner induces as a context for that sequence. The locations consistently present in the origin states are 1, 3, 5, 7, and 9, containing blank, blank, X, blank, and O, respectively. Rather than associate the sequence with all six states, SeqLearner associates the sequence with the pattern at the bottom of Figure 3. If this pattern matches a state during future play, the duet sequence <X to 1, O to 3, X to 7> can be suggested as a possible course of action, whether or not the state is among the original six. A solo would include only one player's moves, ignoring the opponent's responses.

### 1.3 Using the learned sequences

*SeqPlayer* is a game-playing program created to test SeqLearner. SeqPlayer begins with no knowledge about a game other than the rules. It learns to play a game during training, where it observes programs of various skill levels in competition. During training, SeqPlayer uses SeqLearner to learn and weight context pairs. During testing we evaluate SeqPlayer's performance while it uses the learned context pairs as competitive strategies to make decisions. There are many ways the data acquired by SeqPlayer might be used; we report here on two.

Version 1 of SeqPlayer's decision-making module is a two-tier, hierarchical framework. Tier 1 is a single procedure, Enforcer, which either continues a sequence whose execution has already begun or discards one that becomes inapplicable because of the other contestant's response. Tier 2 is those context pairs whose weights had reached or exceeded a pre-set threshold (.55 in the work reported here) by the end of training. When it is SeqPlayer's turn to choose a move, control begins in tier 1, where Enforcer suggests the next move in an ongoing sequence. If no sequence is being executed or one has just been discarded, control passes to tier 2. Each context pair compares its context with the current state; if they match, it supports the first action in its sequence with the context pair's learned weight. The action with the highest total support is chosen.

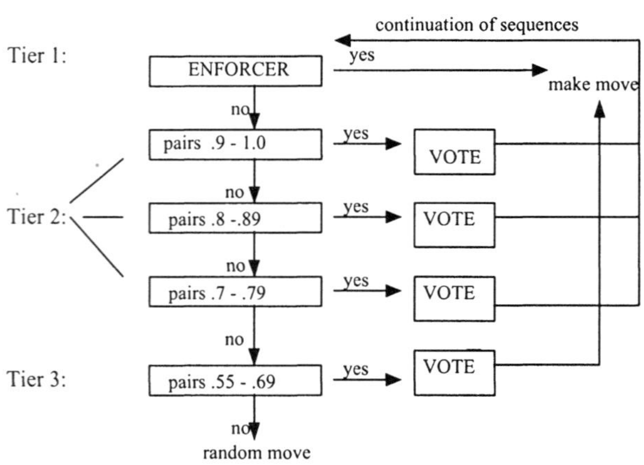


*Figure 4:* Version 2 of SeqPlayer's Decision-making Module

Thus, actions that begin more than one sequence and actions proposed by context pairs with higher weights are more likely to be selected. If a sequence's first action is chosen, the rest of the sequence is sent to Enforcer, which merges the individual sequences it receives into one sequence tree. As the contest continues, Enforcer recommends a next action from the branch in the sequence tree that the opponent followed. If there is no such branch, Enforcer discards the sequence tree. If no move is recommended in tier 2, a random move is chosen.

Version 2 of SeqPlayer's decision-making module has a more sophisticated structure, shown in Figure 4. It uses tier 1 from Version 1, followed by two new tiers. Control passes through the tiers one at a time; if no move is selected, then one is chosen at random. Tier 2 partitions the best of the context pairs into three subclasses by weight: [.9, 1.0], [.8, .9], and [.7, .8]. (Partition criteria were empirically selected.) Each subclass supports actions the way Version 1's tier 2 does. Together, however, they work as a hierarchy: as long as a sequence is not yet selected, the next subclass is consulted. Tier 3 includes all context pairs with weights in [.55, .7]. Like the tier-2 context pairs, those in tier 3 find applicable sequences and select an action based upon them, but tier 3 does not send the continuation of the chosen sequences to Enforcer. Tier 3's one-move advice from low-weight context pairs is expected to be better than choosing a move at random. Rather than enforce the remainder of the sequences associated with these low-weight context pairs, however, the program returns to the higher-weight context pairs on the next move, in anticipation that a better decision can be made, and a more correct sequence will be identified. Because Version 2 considers only one subclass of context pairs at a time, and stops when an action is suggested, the program no longer has to consult the full set of context pairs on every decision. This should decrease execution time.

## 2. Experimental Design and Results

Variously-skilled computer programs were used in our experiments. A *perfect agent* is a hand-crafted external program that plays a randomly-chosen best move in any state. A *reasonable* play makes a winning move one ply away, avoids a losing move two ply away, and otherwise makes a random, non-losing move. An *x-reasonable agent* makes reasonable plays *x*% of the time, and perfect moves 100-*x*% of the time. For purposes of comparison, baseline experiments were conducted for lose tic-tac-toe and five men's morris. In each *baseline experiment* in Table 1, a random agent competed in four 1,000-contest tournaments against four different opponents: a perfect agent, an expert (10%-reasonable), a novice (70%-reasonable), and a random agent.

To evaluate SeqLearner, two experiments were conducted on each game: Experiment 1 with Version 1 of SeqPlayer and Experiment 2 with Version 2. SeqPlayer breaks voting ties at random, so each experiment reported

*Table 1:* Percentage of contests won (power) and won +drawn (reliability) by Baseline and SeqPlayer (Experiments 1 and 2) when tested against four opponents. Statistically improved performance over the previous experiment is highlighted in bold, with standard deviations in parentheses. (Power is not shown against the perfect player, since one cannot win a draw game against perfect play.)

| | Perfect | Expert | | Novice | | Random | |
|---|---|---|---|---|---|---|---|
| | Reliability | Reliability | Power | Reliability | Power | Reliability | Power |
| **Lose tic-tac-toe** | | | | | | | |
| Baseline | 20.50 | 25.80 | 9.00 | 49.20 | 37.70 | 58.40 | 46.10 |
| | (4.14) | (5.33) | (4.12) | (7.57) | (6.67) | (7.28) | (7.84) |
| Experiment 1 | **66.00** | **70.80** | **12.80** | **83.50** | **42.70** | **85.30** | **55.40** |
| | (20.96) | (16.22) | (4.71) | (6.38) | (8.08) | (4.79) | (5.52) |
| Experiment 2 | **82.00** | **83.80** | 12.10 | 85.10 | 46.70 | 87.00 | 57.40 |
| | (13.24) | (9.73) | (4.22) | (5.08) | (7.08) | (4.17) | (7.02) |
| **Five men's morris** | | | | | | | |
| Baseline | 0.20 | 1.60 | 1.20 | 22.40 | 14.20 | 54.00 | 36.00 |
| | (0.60) | (1.20) | (0.98) | (4.27) | (5.90) | (7.27) | (6.81) |
| Experiment 1 | **39.60** | **34.20** | 1.00 | **28.80** | 9.20 | 54.20 | 17.40 |
| | (13.11) | (11.29) | (1.34) | (4.66) | (2.23) | (7.18) | (6.39) |
| Experiment 2 | **57.80** | **45.00** | 0.80 | **45.00** | **29.00** | **73.00** | **51.20** |
| | (13.22) | (10.05) | (1.33) | (4.58) | (5.81) | (8.35) | (7.44) |

here averages data from ten runs. A *run* is a training stage followed by a testing stage. A *tournament* is a set of contests between two agents. During training, SeqPlayer observed a tournament that pitted a perfect agent against a random agent, followed by a tournament against a novice, one against an expert, and one against another perfect agent. This cycle was then repeated (8 tournaments in all) to provide enough exposure to the space to form the context pairs and weight them properly. A training tournament was 20 contests for lose tic-tac-toe, and 40 for five men's morris. The testing stage for both games consisted of four 50-contest tournaments that pitted SeqPlayer against the same four agents used in training. We assumed that shorter sequences would be more frequently applicable in a broader range of unfamiliar situations, and therefore set SeqLearner to learn only shorter sequences, of length 3 for lose tic-tac-toe and lengths 3 and 5 for five men's morris. Although SeqLearner can learn any length sequence, the lengths chosen for the final experiments were hand-tuned. Context pairs were extracted from SeqTable after every training tournament.

Experimental results appear in Table 1, where *reliability* is the number of wins plus the number of draws, and *power* is the number of wins. Recall that SeqPlayer begins without any built-in knowledge, either of game-playing in general or of the particular game itself. SeqPlayer uses only the knowledge it learns from watching sequences in actual play. In light of that, one does not expect SeqPlayer alone (i.e., without other knowledge or learning methods) to lead to superior play. These results demonstrate that much knowledge about a game is contained in experienced sequences; they measure SeqPlayer's ability to capitalize on this knowledge.

For lose tic-tac-toe, Experiment 1 (using context pairs with weights above .55) shows that SeqPlayer was able to win or draw 66-70% of the time against the stronger players and 83-85% of the time against the weaker players. This is a significant improvement in both reliability and power over Baseline for all four opponents. In Experiment 2, recall, context pairs with weights at least .55 were distributed among tier 3 and the subclasses of tier 2. This hierarchical approach enabled SeqPlayer to win or draw the game 82-87% of the time against all opponents, and improved reliability against the perfect and expert players.

Five men's morris, with its significantly larger space, suggests how this method scales. In Experiment 1, SeqPlayer learns enough knowledge to significantly improve reliability over Baseline for the perfect, expert and novice players. Experiment 1 actually demonstrated decreased power against the novice and random players. Basing moves on sequence knowledge alone is

*Table 2:* Number of learned context pairs by tiers and subclasses

| | Lose Tic-Tac-Toe | | Five Men's Morris | |
|---|---|---|---|---|
| **Tier 2** | | | | |
| **Subclass 1 (weight .9 - 1.0)** | 17.80 | (2.79) | 575.50 | (48.79) |
| **Subclass 2 (weight .8 - .89)** | 3.80 | (1.54) | 210.40 | (8.44) |
| **Subclass 3 (weight .7 - .79)** | 6.65 | (1.84) | 277.90 | (20.97) |
| **Tier 3 (weight .55 - .69)** | 3.20 | (1.44) | 496.30 | (20.79) |

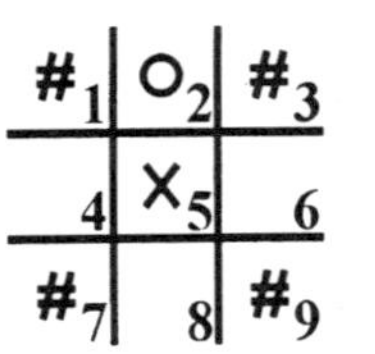


**< X to 8, O to 6, X to 4 >**

*Figure 5:* With this context pair, SeqLearner has learned to reflect through the center in lose tic-tac-toe, a technique people rarely discover for this game.

problematic for two reasons: it does not give a player enough power to win, and it may not provide enough applicable knowledge when competing against weaker players who follow few, if any sequences. Experiment 2 produced better reliability than Experiment 1 against all four opponents, and improved power against the novice and random players. As a result, SeqPlayer was able to win or draw against a perfect player 57.80% of the time, and slightly less against the mid-level opponents.

Table 1 shows that SeqLearner is most useful for learning techniques against better opponents. Realistically, the better the opponent, the more one should expect to rely on learning to produce an expert program. Hence an algorithm like SeqLearner, that leads to better performance against stronger opponents, is an important step in game learning, and a prospective component for multiple-method learning programs.

The average number of sequences collected in SeqTable in Experiment 2 was 78.2 for lose-tic-tac-toe, and 12,234 for five men's morris. These sequences yielded 31.45 context pairs with weights above .55 for lose tic-tac-toe, and 1560.1 for five men's morris. Table 2 examines the quality of the context pairs learned in Experiment 2, by their weights. In both games, context pairs with weights in [.9, 1] form the largest subclass of tier 2, larger than all the other included context pairs together. This means that many retained context pairs give excellent advice. In five men's morris, the second largest group is in tier 3. As a result, Version 2 runs 21% faster than Version 1, since tier 3 is rarely reached in the decision-making process.

## 3. Discussion and Related Work

Inspection indicates that SeqLearner learns salient concepts for each game. Figure 5 shows a context pair learned for lose tic-tac-toe that achieved a perfect weight of 1.00 after 160 training contests. It advises Player X to reflect O's move horizontally or vertically through the center. Although proved to be correct play (Cohen 1972), few people discover it (Ratterman and Epstein 1995).

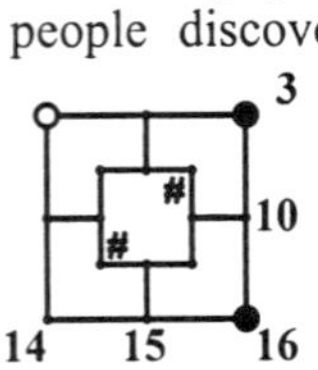


**< W to 10, B to 14, W to 15 >**

*Figure 6:* With this context pair, SeqLearner has learned a duet for five men's morris that anticipates and defends against the formation of two mills by black.

Figure 6 is a context pair learned in the placing stage of five men's morris; it advises White to block Black from creating a mill twice. By moving to position 10, White blocks Black from creating a mill in positions 3-10-16, and by moving to position 15 after Black moves to 14, White blocks Black from creating a mill in 14-15-16. Figure 7 shows a solo sliding context pair learned to create a mill and shuttle in and out of the mill once it is achieved. This is a crucial sequence for winning five men's morris. (An equivalent context pair was also learned for White.) The context pairs in Figures 6 and 7 achieved weights of 1.00 after 320 training contests. All context pairs learned are applicable elsewhere on the board, when a symmetrically equivalent context arises. This shuttle is a sophisticated exploitation of the rules to achieve the goal of reducing the opponent to two pieces.

SeqLearner learns action sequences for generalized states. Results show that SeqLearner, beginning with no knowledge, can learn a great deal about playing the game of lose tic-tac-toe, and scales to the more difficult game of five men's morris. Surprisingly, relying only on learned sequences, SeqPlayer can draw against a perfect five men's morris player more than half the time. Results also show that the most dramatic improvement gained from applying SeqLearner occurs when testing against the better players. This correlates with cognitive science results that better chess players rely on move-sequence structures stored in their long-term memories (Chase and Simon 1973).

Instead of all possible legal sequences, SeqLearner induces contexts from the limited number of sequences seen during experience. This should enable it to scale to larger spaces. However, for induction to be correct in a large space, many training examples will be needed. Therefore, for games with many more moves per contest and much larger boards, the SeqLearner approach may require some adaptation. Instead of collecting all sequences, additional game-specific knowledge could specify when sequences should be collected. For example, one can define locality for a game, and collect only sequences that fall in the same locality. In Go, sequences of moves in the same geographic vicinity are usually related; this could be used to indicate the length of a sequence to be learned. The algorithm that looks for the underlying context would also concentrate on a vicinity instead of the entire board. In a game like chess, however, locality would be defined both by proximity to the locations moved to, and by the squares those moved pieces attack and defend.

Although the algorithm in SeqLearner for the maximal common pattern is efficient, it does not consider the value

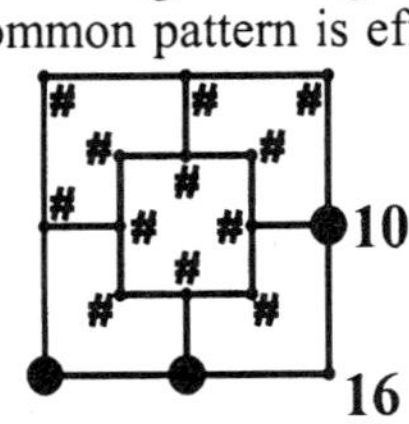


**< B slide from 10 to 16**
**W anywhere**
**B slide from 16 to 10 >**

*Figure 7:* With this context pair, SeqLearner has learned a powerful solo for five men's morris that shuttles in and out of a mill.

of more than one board position at a time as a feature, which may be important to the actual context. Hence the algorithm may over-generalize, that is, drop locations whose values were not identical, but whose combination of values was important. If the feature representation for learning contexts were *complete* (able to express every combination of the locations on the board as a feature) this would not be an issue. Completeness, however, comes at the expense of efficiency. In general, one limitation of SeqLearner is that context learning depends on human-selected features. The wrong features will form incorrect contexts. Learned features are a topic for future work.

Like SeqLearner, case-based planners index a sequence under a context to retrieve for future use. Unlike SeqLearner, however, case-based planners require large quantities of domain knowledge (Hammond, Converse et al. 1993). PARADISE linked chess concepts to formulate plans that guided a small search tree to select the best plan (Wilkins 1980). PARADISE's concepts, however, were taken from a manually constructed chess knowledge base, and not learned. Sequential Instance Based Learning (SIBL) learns to appropriately select actions in new bridge contests based on action patterns (i.e., sequences of consecutive states) played in previous contests (Shih 2001). Rather than learn the context, SIBL treats the sequence that led to an action as the context for the action itself, and trains a database of <sequence, action> pairs based on similarity metrics that measure a new sequence's similarity to known sequences. Kojima's evolutionary algorithm that learns patterns for Go, can also learn sequences of moves (Kojima and Yoshikawa 1999). Kojima's system, however, like SIBL, learns sequences as part of the context for the next single action to take, unlike SeqLearner which learns sequences to follow.

SeqLearner is not restricted to two-agent-domains; it could learn sequences that involve one agent or more than two agents. Although SeqLearner extrapolates a context from limited experience inductively, searching more broadly would be costly. SeqLearner takes a computationally reasonable approach; once it narrows the focus, a deductive method can further refine the acquired knowledge. For example, a narrow search from an induced context could be attempted to prove correctness.

Meanwhile, the work outlined here has demonstrated that previously experienced sequences are an important resource for programs learning expertise in a particular domain. Experience with sequences can support learning their contexts. Future work will experiment with other domains, such as truck-routing, other context extraction methods, and with using domain-specific knowledge to guide the sequence gathering of SeqLearner, rather than gathering all sequences of various lengths.

## Acknowledgements

This work was supported in part by the National Science Foundation under #IIS-0328743 and #9423085.

## References


Chase, W. G. and Simon, H. A. (1973). The Mind's Eye in Chess. *Visual Information Processing*. W. G. Chase. New York, Academic Press: 215-281.

Cohen, D. I. A. (1972). The Solution of a Simple Game. *Mathematics Magazine*. **45:** 213-216.

Epstein, S. L. (1994). Identifying the Right Reasons: Learning to Filter Decision Makers. *Proc. of the AAAI 1994 Fall Symposium on Relevance*, Palo Alto.

Fikes, R. E., Hart, P. E., and Nilsson, N. J. (1972). "Learning and Executing Generalized Robot Plans." *Artificial Intelligence* **3**: 251-288.

Finkelstein, L. and Markovitch, S. (1998). "A Selective Macro-learning Algorithm and its Application to the *N* x *N* Sliding-Tile Puzzle." *JAIR* **8**: 223-263.

Hammond, K. J., Converse, T., and Marks, M. (1993). "Opportunism and Learning." *Machine Learning* **10**: 279-309.

Iba, G. (1989). "A heuristic approach to the discovery of macro-operators." *Machine Learning* **3**: 285-317.

Kojima, T. and Yoshikawa, A. (1999). Knowledge Acquisition From Game Records. *ICML Workshop on Machine Learning in Game Playing*.

Korf, R. (1985). "Macro-Operators: A Weak Method for Learning." *AIJ* **26**: 35-77.

Lock, E. (2003). Learning and Applying Temporal Patterns through Experience. Ph.D. thesis, The Graduate School of The City University of New York.

McGovern, A. (2002). Autonomous Discovery of Temporal Abstractions From Interaction with an Environment. Ph.D. thesis, University of Massachusetts.

Moore, A. W., Baird, L., and Kaelbling, L. P. (1998). Multi-Value-Functions: Efficient automatic action hierarchies for multiple goal MDPs. *NIPS'98 Workshop on Abstraction and Hierarchy in Reinforcement Learning*.

Precup, D. (2000). Temporal abstraction in reinforcement learning. Ph.D. thesis, University of Massachusetts.

Ratterman, M. J. and Epstein, S. L. (1995). Skilled like a Person: A Comparison of Human and Computer Game Playing. *Proc. of the Seventeenth Annual Conference of the Cognitive Science Society*, Hillsdale, NJ, Lawrence Erlbaum Associates.

Shih, J. (2001). Sequential Instance-Based Learning for Planning in the Context of an Imperfect Information Game. *International Conference on Cased Based Reasoning*.

Sutton, R. S., Precup, D., and Singh, S. (1999). "Between MDPs and Semi-MDPs: A framework for temporal abstraction in reinforcement learning." *AIJ* **112**: 181-211.

Tadapelli, P., and Natarajan, B. K. (1996). "A formal framework for speedup learning from problems and solutions." *JAIR* **4**: 419-433.

Wilkins, D. (1980). "Using Patterns and Plans in Chess." *Artificial Intelligence* **14**: 165-203.

# Bayesian Network Classifiers versus $k$-NN Classifier using Sequential Feature Selection

**Franz Pernkopf** *

University of Washington, Department of Electrical Engineering
M254 EE/CSE Building, Box 352500, Seattle, WA, 98195-2500, USA
Graz University of Technology, Institute of Communications and Wave Propagation,
Inffeldgasse 12, A-8010 Graz, Austria, pernkopf@tugraz.at

### Abstract

The aim of this paper is to compare Bayesian network classifiers to the $k$-NN classifier based on a subset of features. This subset is established by means of sequential feature selection methods. Experimental results show that Bayesian network classifiers more often achieve a better classification rate on different data sets than selective $k$-NN classifiers. The $k$-NN classifier performs well in the case where the number of samples for learning the parameters of the Bayesian network is small. Bayesian network classifiers outperform selective $k$-NN methods in terms of memory requirements and computational demands. This paper demonstrates the strength of Bayesian networks for classification.

## Introduction

In most classification tasks the relevant features are often unknown a priori. Thus, many features are derived from a specific classification problem and those which do not contribute or even degrade the classification performance should be removed from the set of extracted features. Feature selection has become important for numerous pattern recognition and data analysis tasks (Jain & Zongker 1997), (Dash & Liu 1997), (Kohavi & John 1997). The main purpose of feature selection is to reduce the number of extracted features to a set of a few significant ones while maintaining the classification rate. The reduction of the feature set may even improve the classification rate by reducing estimation errors associated with finite sample size effects (Jain & Chandrasekaran 1982).

Another approach to achieve an improvement of the classification accuracy is to model statistical dependencies between attributes. Therefore, the framework of Bayesian networks (Pearl 1988) can be used to build classifiers (Friedman, Geiger, & Goldszmidt 1997), (Singh & Provan 1996), (Keogh & Pazzani 1999) to address this effectively.
Bayesian network classifiers have been applied in many different domains. In this paper, we compare the performance of these approaches to the selective $k$-NN classifier. The selective $k$-NN classifier uses a subset of features which maximize the classification performance. This subset is established by means of sequential feature selection methods.

## Bayesian Network Classifier

A Bayesian network (Pearl 1988), (Cowell *et al.* 1999) $B = \langle G, \Theta \rangle$ is a directed acyclic graph $G$ which models probabilistic relationships among a set of random variables $\mathbf{U} = \{X_1, \ldots, X_n, \Omega\} = \{U_1, \ldots, U_{n+1}\}$, where each variable in $\mathbf{U}$ has specific states or values denoted by lower case letters $\{x_1, \ldots, x_n, \omega\}$. The symbol $n$ denotes the number of attributes of the classifier. Each vertex (node) of the graph represents a random variable, while the edges capture the direct dependencies between the variables. The network encodes the conditional independence relationship that each node is independent of its nondescendants given its parents. These conditional independence relationships reduce the number of parameters needed to represent a probability distribution. The symbol $\Theta$ represents the set of parameters which quantify the network. Each node contains a local probability distribution given its parents. The joint probability distribution of the network is uniquely determined by these local probability distributions. Basically, two different techniques for parameter learning are available, the maximum likelihood estimation and the Bayesian approach (Cowell *et al.* 1999). In this paper, the parameters of the network are estimated by the maximum likelihood method. In the following, three different types of Bayesian network classifiers are presented, the naïve Bayes classifier, the tree augmented naïve Bayes classifier, and the selective unrestricted Bayesian network classifier.

### Naïve Bayes Classifier

The naïve Bayes (NB) decision rule (Duda, Hart, & Stork 2000) assumes that all the attributes are conditionally independent given the class label. As reported in the literature (Friedman, Geiger, & Goldszmidt 1997), the performance of the naïve Bayes classifier is surprisingly good even if the independence assumption between attributes is unrealistic in most of the data sets. Independence between the features ignores any correlation among them. The attribute values of $X_i$ and $X_j$ ($X_i \neq X_j$) are conditionally independent given the class label of node $\Omega$. Hence, $x_i$

*The author is grateful to Elisabeth Pernkopf and Prof. Djamel Bouchaffra for the valuable comments on this paper and to Ingo Reindl and Voest Alpine Donawitz Stahl for providing the data for the first experiment.

is conditionally independent of $x_j$ given class $\omega$, whenever $P(x_i|\omega, x_j) = P(x_i|\omega)$ for all $x_i \in X_i, x_j \in X_j, \omega \in \Omega$, and when $P(x_j, \omega) > 0$. The structure of the naïve Bayes classifier represented as Bayesian network is illustrated in Figure 1. Feature selection is introduced to this network by removing irrelevant features by means of a search algorithm (see Section *Search-and-Score Structure Learning*). This extension is known as selective naïve Bayes classifier (SNB). The structure in Figure 1 shows that each attribute is conditionally independent of the remaining attributes given the class label $\omega$ of the class variable. The class variable $\Omega$ is the only parent for each attribute $X_i$ denoted as $\mathbf{pa}_{X_i} = \{\Omega\}$ for all $1 \leq i \leq n$. Hence, the joint probability distribution $P(X_1, \ldots, X_n, \Omega)$ for this network is determined to be $P(X_1, \ldots, X_n, \Omega) = \prod_{i=1}^{n+1} P(U_i|\mathbf{pa}_{U_i}) = P(\Omega) \prod_{i=1}^{n} P(X_i|\Omega)$, and from the definition of conditional probability the probability for the classes in $\Omega$ given the values of the attributes is $P(\Omega|X_1, \ldots, X_n) = \alpha P(\Omega) \prod_{i=1}^{n} P(X_i|\Omega)$, where $\alpha$ is a normalization constant.

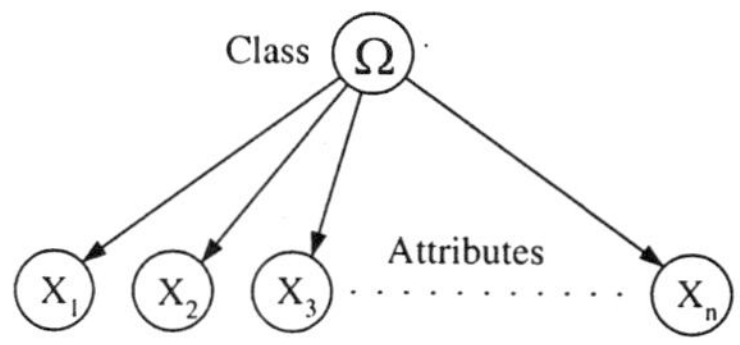


Figure 1: Structure of a naïve Bayes network.

## Tree Augmented Naïve Bayes Classifier

Since the features may be correlated and the independence assumption of the naïve Bayes classifier is unrealistic, Friedman et al. (Friedman, Geiger, & Goldszmidt 1997) introduce the *tree augmented naïve Bayes classifier* (TAN). It is based on the structure of the naïve Bayes network where the class variable is the parent of each attribute. Hence, the posterior probability $P(\Omega|X_1, \ldots, X_n)$ takes all the attributes into account. Additionally, edges (arcs) among the attributes are allowed in order to capture the correlations among them. Each attribute may have at most one other attribute as additional parent which means that there is an arc in the graph from feature $X_i$ to feature $X_j$. This implies that these two attributes $X_i$ and $X_j$ are not independent given the class label. The influence of $X_j$ on the class probabilities depends also on the value of $X_i$. An example of a tree augmented naïve Bayes network is shown in Figure 2. A tree augmented naïve Bayes network is initialized as naïve Bayes network. Additional arcs between attributes are found by means of a search algorithm (see Section *Search-and-Score Structure Learning*). The maximum number of arcs added to relax the independence assumption between the attributes is $n - 1$.

## Selective Unrestricted Bayesian Network Classifier

The selective unrestricted Bayesian network classifier (SUN) (Singh & Provan 1996) (see Figure 3) can be viewed as generalization of the tree augmented naïve Bayes

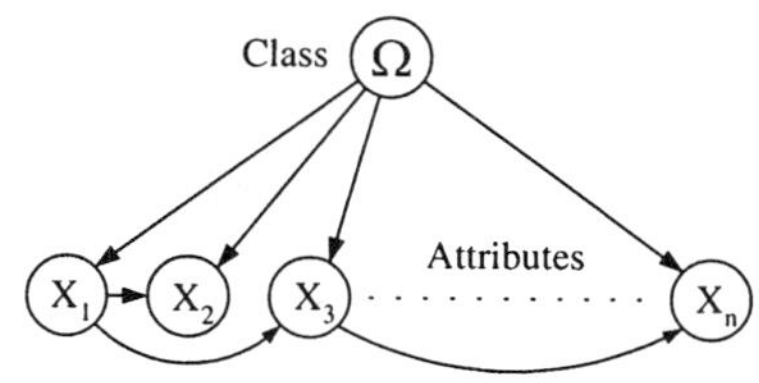


Figure 2: Structure of a tree augmented naïve Bayes network.

network. The class node is equally treated as an attribute node and may have attribute nodes as parents. The attributes need not be connected directly to the class node as for the tree augmented naïve Bayes network. After initialization the network consists of the nodes without any arcs. A search algorithm (see Section *Search-and-Score Structure Learning*) adds arcs to the network according to an evaluation criterion. If there is no arc between an attribute and the classifier network then the attribute is not considered during classification. During the determination of the network structure, irrelevant features are not included and the classifier is based on a subset of selected features. This unrestricted network structure maximizes the classification performance by removing irrelevant features and relaxing independence assumptions between correlated features. Since this network is unrestricted, the computational

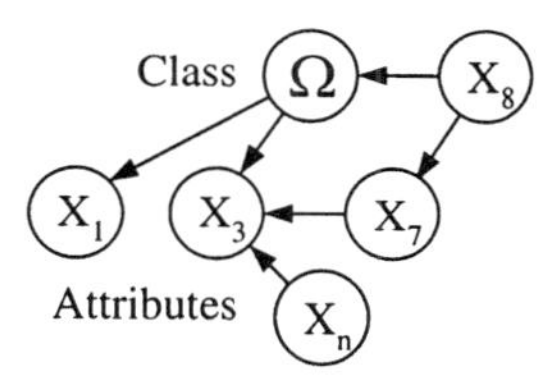


Figure 3: Structure of a selective unrestricted Bayesian network.

demands for determining the network structure is huge especially if there is a large number of attributes available. Additionally, the size of the conditional probability tables of the nodes increases exponentially with the number of parents. This might result in a more unreliable probability estimate of the nodes which have a large number of parents. The posterior probability distribution of $\Omega$ given the value of all attributes is only sensitive to those attributes which form the Markov blanket of node $\Omega$ (Pearl 1988). The Markov blanket of the class node $\Omega$ consists of the direct parents of $\Omega$, the direct successors (children) of $\Omega$, and all the direct parents of the direct successors (children) of the class node $\Omega$. All the features outside the Markov blanket do not have any effect on the classification performance. Introducing this knowledge into the search algorithm reduces the search space and the computational effort for determining the structure of the classifier.

### Search-and-Score Structure Learning

In order to learn the structure of the Bayesian network classifiers, Keogh and Pazzani propose hill climbing search (Keogh & Pazzani 1999). An improvement of the hill climbing search is to apply the classical floating search algorithm (CFS) used for feature selection applications (Pudil, Novovičová, & Kittler 1994). This algorithm is adopted for learning the network structure of tree augmented naïve Bayes classifiers and selective unrestricted Bayesian network classifiers (Pernkopf & O`Leary 2003). We use the cross-validation classification accuracy estimate as scoring function $J$ for evaluating the performance of the networks. For the selective unrestricted Bayesian network this learning approach enables simultaneous feature selection and structure learning. The main disadvantage of hill climbing search is that once an arc has been added to the network structure, the algorithm has no mechanism for removing the arc at a later stage. Hence, this algorithm suffers from the *nesting* effect (Kittler 1978). To overcome this drawback, Pudil et al. (Pudil, Novovičová, & Kittler 1994) present a floating search method for finding significant features which optimize the classification performance in feature selection tasks. This algorithm allows conditional exclusions of previously added attributes and/or arcs from the network. Hence, this algorithm is able to correct disadvantageous decisions which were performed in previous steps. Therefore, it may approximate the optimal solution in a better way than hill climbing search, especially in case of data of great complexity and dimensionality. However, this search strategy uses more evaluations to obtain the network structure and therefore is computationally less efficient than hill climbing search. This floating search algorithm facilitates the correction of disadvantageous decisions made in previous steps.

## Sequential Feature Selection Algorithms

Sequential feature selection algorithms search in a sequential deterministic manner for the best feature subset (suboptimal). Basically, forward and backward algorithms are available. The forward methods start with an empty set and add features until a stopping criterion concludes the search. The backward algorithms begin with all features and remove features iteratively. The well-known suboptimal sequential algorithms are listed in the following.

- Sequential forward selection (SFS): The sequential forward selection algorithm (Kittler 1978) is a bottom up search method. With each iteration one feature among the remaining features is added to the subset, so that the subset maximizes the evaluation criterion $J$.
- Sequential backward selection (SBS): Sequential backward selection (Kittler 1978) is the counterpart of the sequential forward selection. In each step one feature is rejected so that the remaining subset gives the best result of the evaluation criterion $J$.
- Plus $l$-take away $r$ selection (PTA$(l,r)$): The PTA$(l,r)$ algorithm (Kittler 1978) partially avoids nesting of feature sets by allowing a low level backtracking in the selection process. The subset is enlarged by adding $l$ features using the SFS algorithm. Afterwards, $r$ features are rejected by using the SBS method. Both steps are repeated until a particular predetermined subset size is obtained.
- Generalized sequential forward selection (GSFS$(r)$) (Kittler 1978): At each stage $r$ features are added simultaneously instead of adding just one feature to the subset at a time like the SFS method does. This algorithm and the following counterpart does not avoid nesting entirely, since successive added sets may be nested.
- Generalized sequential backward selection (GSBS$(r)$): This algorithm is the counterpart of the GSFS method.
- Generalized plus $l$-take away $r$ selection (GPTA$(l,r)$) (Kittler 1978), (Devijver & Kittler 1982): The difference between the PTA and the GPTA method is that the former approach employs the SFS and the SBS procedures instead of the GSFS and GSBS algorithms.
- Sequential forward floating selection (SFFS): The sequential forward floating algorithm is a bottom up search procedure introduced by Pudil et al. (Pudil, Novovičová, & Kittler 1994). This method was adapted for learning the structure of Bayesian network classifiers (see Section *Search-and-Score Structure Learning*) (Pernkopf & O`Leary 2003). The algorithm includes new features which maximize the criterion $J$ by means of the SFS procedure starting from the current feature set. Afterwards, conditional exclusions of the previously updated subset take place. If no feature can be excluded anymore, the algorithm proceeds again with the SFS algorithm. The floating methods are allowed to correct wrong decisions made in previous steps and they approximate the optimal solution in a better way than the sequential feature selection methods described above.
- Sequential backward floating selection (SBFS). This algorithm is the counterpart to the SFFS method.
- Adaptive sequential forward floating selection (ASFFS$(r_{max}, b, d)$): This search algorithm suggested by Somol et al. (Somol *et al.* 1999) utilizes the best of both, generalized strategies and floating methods. This algorithm is similar to the SFFS procedure, where the SFS and the SBS methods are replaced by their generalized versions GSFS$(r)$ and GSBS$(r)$. The optimal value of $r$ is determined dynamically. The maximum generalization level which is used is restricted by a user defined bound $r_{max}$. The current generalization level $r$ changes during the search depending on the subset size $k$. Therefore, the parameters $d$ and $b$ are necessary. For a detailed description of the algorithm refer to Somol et al. (Somol *et al.* 1999). This algorithm is initialized with an empty subset.
- Adaptive sequential backward floating selection (ASBFS$(r_{max}, b, d)$) (Somol *et al.* 1999). This is the counterpart of the ASFFS method.

## Experiments

A comparative study has been performed on data of a surface inspection task (Pernkopf 2003) and data sets from the UCI repository (Merz, Murphy, & Aha 1997). Throughout the experiments, five-fold cross-validation classification accuracy has been used for learning the structure of the Bayesian networks. Similarly, the five-fold cross-validation classification rate of the $k$-NN approach is used as scoring function $J$ for the feature selection methods. All the structure learning and feature selection experiments are based on exactly the same cross-validation folds of the data sets. The Bayesian network classifiers use discretized features, which were discretized using recursive minimal entropy partitioning (Fayyad & Irani 1993). The partition boundaries for discretization were established only through the training data set. Zero probabilities of the conditional probability tables of the Bayesian network classifiers are replaced with a small epsilon $\varepsilon = 0.00001$. The following abbreviations are used for the different classification approaches:

- **NB**: Naïve Bayes classifier.
- **CFS-SNB**: Selective Naïve Bayes classifier using the classical floating search.
- **HCS-TAN**: Tree augmented naïve Bayes classifier using hill-climbing search.
- **CFS-TAN**: Tree augmented naïve Bayes classifier using classical floating search.
- **CFS-SUN**: Selective unrestricted Bayesian network using classical floating search.
- **SFFS-$k$-NN-C**: $k$-nearest neighbor classifier using continuous-valued data and the SFFS method ($k \in \{1, 3, 5, 9\}$).
- **SFFS-$k$-NN-D**: $k$-nearest neighbor classifier using discrete-valued data and the SFFS method ($k \in \{1, 3, 5, 9\}$).

The $k$-NN classifier requires a scaling of the features, whereby, the scaling parameters were determined only through the training data set of the corresponding cross-validation folds of the data set. Each feature is scaled to zero mean and unit variance (Kaufman & Rousseeuw 1990).

## First Experiment

**Data** Experiments have been performed on a data set $\mathcal{S}$ consisting of 516 surface segments from a surface inspection task, uniformly distributed into three classes. Each sample (surface segment) is represented by 42 features which are described in more detail in (Pernkopf 2003). The data set is divided into six mutually exclusive subsets $\mathcal{S} = \{\mathcal{D}_1, \mathcal{D}_2, \mathcal{D}_3, \mathcal{D}_4, \mathcal{D}_5, \mathcal{H}\}$. The data set parts $\mathcal{D}_1, \mathcal{D}_2, \mathcal{D}_3, \mathcal{D}_4$, and $\mathcal{D}_5$ are used for finding the optimal classifier (five-fold cross-validation). Each part is comprised of 90 samples. The established classifiers are validated on a separate hold-out data set $\mathcal{H}$ which was never employed during the optimization experiments (Kohavi & John 1997).

**Results** First, the sequential forward feature selection algorithms are compared in terms of the achieved cross-validation classification performance using the $3-NN$ classifier (see Figure 4). Generally, the floating algorithms perform better than the methods without floating property. The sequential forward floating algorithm (SFFS) performs in a similar manner as the more complex adaptive floating method (ASFFS(3,4,5)) (With the given parameter setting of the ASFFS algorithm the classification performance of a subset size of 5 within a neighborhood of 4 is optimized

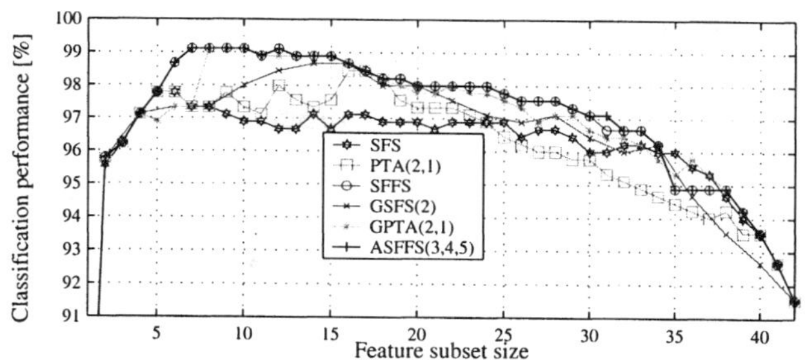


Figure 4: Cross-validation classification performance of different sequential forward feature selection methods for a subset size up to 42.

more thoroughly.). There is only a marginal difference of the result for the feature subset size of 31. However, the number of classifier evaluations used for establishing the optimal subset for classification is for the SFFS only 5086 compared to the ASFFS with 7768. For the floating algorithms, the computational costs depend on the characteristics of the data set due to the floating property. The generalized algorithms (GSFS and GPTA) perform slightly worse than the SFFS method with a computational requirement of 6391 and 13201, respectively. The number of evaluations used for obtaining the optimal subset for all non-floating algorithms is fixed for a given parameter setting. The PTA and SFS search strategies achieve the lowest scores for different sizes of subsets. Therefore, 2623 and 903 evaluations are necessary. Since the SFFS algorithm achieves a good tradeoff between computational demands and achieved classification score and due to the fact that the structure of the Bayesian network classifiers was trained with an equivalent algorithm further feature selection results consider only this method.

Table 1 compares the feature selection results of the SFFS approach to the Bayesian network classification methods. The table shows the five-fold cross validation classification accuracy estimate (%CV5) and the performance on the hold-out data set (%H). It also depicts the number of classifier evaluations (#Evaluations) used for search, the number of independent probabilities (#Parameters), and the number of features (#Features) and/or arcs (#Arcs) used to achieve this classification accuracy estimate. The best achieved classification accuracy is emphasized by boldface letters.

The selective naïve Bayes classifier (CFS-SNB) achieves a better %CV5 classification accuracy estimate than the naïve Bayes (NB) approach based on all available attributes. However, the performance on the hold-out data is similar. The computational demands for establishing the CFS-SNB classifier is relatively small. For the tree augmented naïve Bayes classifier the same result is achieved either with hill climbing or with the classical floating search algorithm. This means that the CFS method does not perform backward steps during the search. This is also observable in the number of used classifier evaluations. The TAN classifier uses all extracted features and 12 arcs are added to the naïve Bayes structure (#Arcs=52). The TAN classifier uses 533 independent probabilities which have to be estimated from the data set and

| | %CV5 | %H | #Arcs | #Features | #Evaluations | #Parameters |
|---|---|---|---|---|---|---|
| NB | 89.11 ± 2.8727 | 95.45 | 40 | 40 | 1 | 275 |
| CFS-SNB | 96.44 ± 2.11 | 96.96 | 20 | 20 | 2098 | 122 |
| HCS-TAN | 97.11 ± 2.02 | 96.96 | 52 | 40 | 17893 | 533 |
| CFS-TAN | 97.11 ± 2.02 | 96.96 | 52 | 40 | 17958 | 533 |
| CFS-SUN | 98.66 ± 0.81 | **98.48** | 14 | 12 | 4097 | 230 |
| SFFS-1-NN-C | **99.33 ± 0.60** | **98.48** | - | 8 | 2873 | 450 samples × 8 features |
| SFFS-3-NN-C | **99.11 ± 0.49** | **98.48** | - | 8 | 5086 | 450 samples × 8 features |
| SFFS-5-NN-C | **98.44 ± 0.60** | **98.48** | - | 7 | 4346 | 450 samples × 7 features |
| SFFS-9-NN-C | **98.44 ± 0.99** | **98.48** | - | 9 | 5086 | 450 samples × 9 features |
| SFFS-1-NN-D | 96.22 ± 2.02 | 86.36 | - | 15 | 6003 | 450 samples × 15 features |
| SFFS-3-NN-D | 96.44 ± 2.53 | 90.90 | - | 23 | 4803 | 450 samples × 23 features |
| SFFS-5-NN-D | 96.22 ± 2.02 | 93.94 | - | 26 | 5302 | 450 samples × 26 features |
| SFFS-9-NN-D | 96.00 ± 1.26 | 93.94 | - | 20 | 4745 | 450 samples × 20 features |

Table 1: Comparison of classification approaches (Experiment 1).

it is only slightly better than the selective naïve Bayes classifier. However, the CFS-SNB classifier has a much simpler structure and a smaller number of parameters is required. The selective unrestricted Bayesian network (CFS-SUN) achieves the best classification accuracy estimate on the five-fold cross-validation and hold-out data set among the Bayesian network classifiers. For achieving this result, 230 probabilties have to be estimated and the structure consists of 12 attributes and 14 arcs, whereas the TAN and NB structure do not enable feature selection. Additionally, the number of classifier evaluations used for determining the structure of the TAN network is high compared to establishing the structure of the CFS-SUN since the Markov blanket is used during the search for the SUN network structure.

The selective $k$-NN classifier on continuous attributes slightly outperforms the CFS-SUN classifier. However, the achieved classification performance on the hold-out data set is the same for both. As mentioned above, the Bayesian network classifiers use a discretized feature space. For discretized features the performance of the SFFS-$k$-NN-D classifier degrades. Basically, the $k$-NN decision rule searches through a labeled reference set for the nearest neighbors which might be time-consuming in case of a large number of samples. Additionally, a large amount of memory is required. Bayesian network classifiers outperform selective $k$-NN methods in terms of memory requirements and computational demands during classification. Especially, the CFS-SUN is simple to evaluate but still maintains high predictive accuracy.

## Second Experiment

The second experiment has been performed on 8 data sets from the UCI repository (Merz, Murphy, & Aha 1997). The main characteristics are summarized in Table 2. The attributes in the data sets are multinomial and continuous-valued. Table 3 compares the CFS-SUN classifier to the SFFS method using the $k$-NN classifier. We select $k \in \{1, 3, 5, 9\}$ which gives the largest classification performance. Both classification approaches are based on the equivalent search algorithm. The table shows the five-fold cross validation classification accuracy estimate (%CV5),

| Data set | #Features | #Classes | #Instances | Attributes |
|---|---|---|---|---|
| australian | 14 | 2 | 690 | mixed |
| flare | 10 | 2 | 1066 | mixed |
| glass | 9 | 7 | 214 | continuous |
| glass2 | 9 | 2 | 163 | continuous |
| heart | 13 | 2 | 270 | continuous |
| pima | 8 | 2 | 768 | continuous |
| vote | 16 | 2 | 435 | discrete |
| vehicle | 18 | 4 | 846 | continuous |

Table 2: Data sets (Experiment 2).

the number of classifier evaluations (#Evaluations) used for search, the number of independent probabilities (#Parameters), the number of nearest neighbors $k$, and the number of features (#Features) and/or arcs (#Arcs) used to achieve this classification accuracy estimate. The best achieved classification accuracy is emphasized by boldface letters. The CFS-SUN classifier outperforms the selective $k$-NN approach five times. In one case the selective $k$-NN classifier using discretized attributes achieves the best classification performance. The selective $k$-NN classifier performs well in domains such as Glass, Glass2, and Heart where the number of samples for learning the parameters (probabilities) of the Bayesian network is small (see Table 2). In general, it is interesting how few parameters are used by the CFS-SUN classifier, especially for the data sets Flare, Glass2, Heart, and Pima. The number of independent probabilities used for classifying the Vehicle data set is large. Basically, the size of the conditional probability tables of the nodes in the network increases exponentially with the number of parents. In this case, this might provide probability estimates that are not robust since the data set is relatively small.

## Conclusion

This paper compares Bayesian network classifiers to the selective $k$-NN classifier. The selective $k$-NN classifier uses a subset of features which is established by means of sequential feature selection methods. In order to learn the structure of the Bayesian networks, hill climbing search and the sequential forward floating algorithm are used.

| | Data set | Australian | Flare | Glass | Glass2 | Heart | Pima | Vote | Vehicle |
|---|---|---|---|---|---|---|---|---|---|
| CFS-SUN | %CV5 | **89.58** | **84.07** | 74.70 | 82.66 | 86.29 | **75.90** | **98.64** | **76.03** |
| | #Arcs | 15 | 3 | 10 | 5 | 7 | 9 | 15 | 13 |
| | #Features | 10 | 3 | 7 | 4 | 5 | 7 | 10 | 13 |
| | #Evaluations | 1647 | 83 | 992 | 184 | 441 | 307 | 6055 | 1922 |
| | #Parameters | 58 | 15 | 273 | 8 | 18 | 29 | 495 | 1808 |
| SFFS-$k$-NN-C | %CV5 | - | - | **78.50** | **88.96** | 86.29 | 75.26 | - | 75.53 |
| | $k$ | - | - | 3 | 1 | 5 | 5 | - | 9 |
| | #Features | - | - | 5 | 5 | 7 | 7 | - | 9 |
| | #Evaluations | - | - | 117 | 87 | 316 | 108 | - | 1130 |
| SFFS-$k$-NN-D | %CV5 | 88.26 | 83.95 | 68.69 | 79.14 | **87.03** | 68.88 | 97.24 | 68.32 |
| | $k$ | 5 | 3 | 9 | 1 | 5 | 9 | 1 | 5 |
| | #Features | 8 | 3 | 4 | 3 | 7 | 5 | 6 | 12 |
| | #Evaluations | 465 | 122 | 87 | 87 | 283 | 165 | 377 | 522 |

Table 3: Comparison of classification approaches (Experiment 2).

Experiments were performed on data of a surface inspection task and data sets from the UCI repository. Bayesian network classifiers more often achieve a better classification rate on different data sets as selective $k$-NN classifiers. The $k$-NN classifier performs well in the case where the number of samples for learning the parameters of the Bayesian network is small. It has been observed that only few parameters are used by the selective unrestricted Bayesian network classifier for certain data sets. Bayesian network classifiers outperform selective $k$-NN methods in terms of memory requirements and computational demands. Especially, the performance of the selective unrestricted Bayesian network classifier demonstrates the strength of Bayesian network classifiers.

## References


Cowell, R.; Dawid, A.; Lauritzen, S.; and Spiegelhalter, D. 1999. *Probabilistic networks and expert systems*. Springer Verlag.

Dash, M., and Liu, H. 1997. Feature selection for classification. *Intelligent Data Analysis* 1(3):131–156.

Devijver, P., and Kittler, J. 1982. *Pattern recognition: A statistical approach*. Prentice Hall International.

Duda, R.; Hart, P.; and Stork, D. 2000. *Pattern Classification*. John Wiley & Sons.

Fayyad, U., and Irani, K. 1993. Multi-interval discretizaton of continuous-valued attributes for classification learning. In *Proceedings of the Thirteenth International Joint Conference on Artificial Intelligence*, 1022–1027.

Friedman, N.; Geiger, D.; and Goldszmidt, M. 1997. Bayesian network classifiers. *Machine Learning* 29:131–163.

Jain, A., and Chandrasekaran, B. 1982. *Dimensionality and sample size considerations in pattern recognition in practice*, volume 2 of *Handbook of Statistics*. Amsterdam: North-Holland.

Jain, A., and Zongker, D. 1997. Feature selection: Evaluation, application, and small sample performance. *IEEE Transactions on Pattern Analysis and Machine Intelligence* 19(2):153–158.

Kaufman, L., and Rousseeuw, P. 1990. *Finding groups in data: An introduction to cluster analysis*. John Wiley & Sons.

Keogh, E., and Pazzani, M. 1999. Learning augmented Bayesian classifiers: A comparison of distribution-based and classification-based approaches. In *Proceedings of 7th International Workshop on Artificial Intelligence and Statistics*, 225–230.

Kittler, J. 1978. Feature set search algorithms. In Chen, C., ed., *Pattern Recognition and Signal Processing*. Sijtho and Noordho. 41–60.

Kohavi, R., and John, G. 1997. Wrappers for feature subset selection. *Artificial Intelligence* 97:273–324.

Merz, C.; Murphy, P.; and Aha, D. 1997. UCI repository of machine learning databases. Department of Information and Computer Science, University of California, Irvine, URL: www.ics.uci.edu/~mlearn/MLRepository.html.

Pearl, J. 1988. *Probabilistic reasoning in intelligent systems: Networks of plausible inference*. Morgan Kaufmann.

Pernkopf, F., and O'Leary, P. 2003. Floating search algorithm for structure learning of Bayesian network classifiers. *Pattern Recognition Letters* 24:2839–2848.

Pernkopf, F. 2003. 3D surface analysis using Bayesian network classifiers. Technical report, Graz University of Technology.

Pudil, P.; Novovičová, J.; and Kittler, J. 1994. Floating search methods in feature selection. *Pattern Recognition Letters* 15:1119–1125.

Singh, M., and Provan, G. 1996. Efficient learning of selective Bayesian network classifiers. In *International Conference of Machine Learning*, 453–461.

Somol, P.; Pudil, P.; Novovičová, J.; and Paclík, P. 1999. Adaptive floating search methods in feature selection. *Pattern Recognition Letters* 20:1157–1163.

# Online Parallel Boosting

**Jesse A. Reichler[1], Harlan D. Harris[2], and Michael A. Savchenko[3]**

[1]Department of Computer Science, University of Illinois at Urbana-Champaign, Urbana, IL 61801, USA, reichler@uiuc.edu
[2]Department of Psychology, Columbia University, New York, NY 10027, USA, harlan@psych.columbia.edu
[3]Department of Aeronautical and Astronautical Engineering, University of Illinois, Urbana, IL 61801, USA, savchenk@uiuc.edu

**Abstract**

This paper presents a new boosting (arcing) algorithm called POCA, Parallel Online Continuous Arcing. Unlike traditional boosting algorithms (such as Arc-x4 and Adaboost), that construct ensembles by adding and training weak learners sequentially on a round-by-round basis, training in POCA is performed over an entire ensemble continuously and in parallel. Since members of the ensemble are not frozen after an initial learning period (as in traditional boosting) POCA is able to adapt rapidly to non-stationary environments, and because POCA does not require the explicit scoring of a fixed exemplar set, it can perform online learning of non-repeating data. We present results from experiments conducted using neural network experts that show POCA is typically faster and more adaptive than existing boosting algorithms. Results presented for the UCI letter dataset are, to our knowledge, the best published scores to date.

## Introduction

Boosting (also known as arcing) is an ensemble learning strategy that works by iteratively constructing and combining experts that are increasingly forced to concentrate on "difficult" training exemplars.

Traditionally, boosting proceeds in a series of sequential rounds. During each round, a new expert is trained and added to the ensemble. Training data for all experts is drawn from a single fixed data set with weights on each exemplar. After each round, exemplars are re-weighted to increase the importance of those exemplars that have been the most difficult for prior experts to learn. Ensemble output is a weighted combination of all expert outputs.

It has been shown that efficient boosting algorithms exist for constructing arbitrarily accurate (on training data) ensembles from individual learners which perform no better than chance (Schapire 1999). One such algorithm, Adaboost, has received a great deal of attention because of its efficiency and unexpectedly good generalization properties (Freund and Schapire 1998). Recently, Breiman introduced Arc-x4 (Breiman 1997), a similar but simpler algorithm, that assigns fixed, equal voting weights for each expert, and re-weights exemplars using a simpler function of the number of mistakes made by prior experts. Breiman (Breiman 1999) has demonstrated that Arc-x4 usually performs as well as Adaboost, and has argued that the success of boosting algorithms is due to the general process of increasing weights on difficult exemplars, rather than to any specific re-weighting or recombination scheme. Pseudo-code for Arc-x4 is shown in Table 1-A.

Current boosting algorithms require that explicit performance scores for each exemplar be calculated after each training round. This can require large memory resources and is unsuitable for use with changing concepts or in environments that lack a fixed, finite training set.

This paper introduces a new multi-class boosting algorithm, POCA (Parallel Online Continuous Arcing), that does not require the use of a fixed, finite training set, and is thus capable of learning in online environments with non-repeating data. Unlike traditional boosting, where prior experts are frozen as new experts are added, POCA continuously trains an entire ensemble in parallel, allowing ensembles to adapt rapidly to non-stationary environments.

Results from multi-class classification tests show that even with a fixed data set POCA performs competitively with existing boosting algorithms and learns faster in terms of improvement per training iteration. Results on the UCI letter dataset are, to our knowledge, the best published scores to date.

Other work on parallel boosting includes parallel boosting of binary concepts using decision trees (Fern and Givan 2003), and boosting with disjoint distributed data sets (Fan et al. 1999; Lazarevic and Obradovic 2001; Chawla et al. 2002).

## POCA: Parallel Online Continuous Arcing

The basic idea behind the POCA algorithm is straightforward: Each exemplar is received from the environment and delivered to an entire ensemble of experts in parallel. Every expert is trained on every exemplar as it is delivered, and experts dynamically modulate each other's learning rates in a manner that approximates traditional boosting schemes for re-weighting training data. In essence, experts form a virtual chain (Figure 1), such that the learning rate of an expert is a function of the performance, on that exemplar only, of the experts preceding it in the chain. After an exemplar is used for training, it is discarded from memory. Pseudo-code for POCA is shown in Table 1-B.

## A Virtual Chain

POCA was designed to approximate the behavior of standard boosting algorithms, but in a parallelizable manner. Here we provide a brief inductive proof outline for the assertion that POCA approximates traditional boosting. Consider the case of learning a fixed set of training data. The first (leftmost) expert in POCA is trained on the un-weighted data, exactly as in traditional boosting. That expert will converge to the same solution as would the initial expert in Adaboost or Arc-x4, except that its training never ends. After the first expert has converged, it sends to the rightward experts an error signal that is weighted in the same way that exemplar mistakes are weighted in standard boosting. Therefore, as experts sequentially converge from left to right, POCA ensembles come to mirror traditional boosting ensembles. While this equivalence holds in the limit, we will show that POCA benefits from not waiting until experts converge before initiating the training of subsequent experts.

## Choice of Experts and Weighting Functions

Because the POCA algorithm must operate in non-stationary environments, it requires experts that are capable of gradual and continuous non-monotonic learning. Here we have used backpropagation and small multi-layer neural network experts, where the learning rate of each expert is simply a baseline rate multiplied by the current output of the expert's paired weighting node. In multi-class classification, weighting nodes compute vector weightings by treating each output class as a separate classification task (Schapire 1999), and we use a slightly modified form of backpropagation described in a subsequent section.

For experts that cannot accept explicit learning rates, a variant of POCA analogous to boosting-by-resampling (Freund and Schapire 1999) can be used: The value computed by each weighting node (scaled from 0 to 1) is used as the probability of training the paired expert on each exemplar, and each expert makes an independent and probabilistic decision about whether to train on each exemplar as it is delivered from the environment.

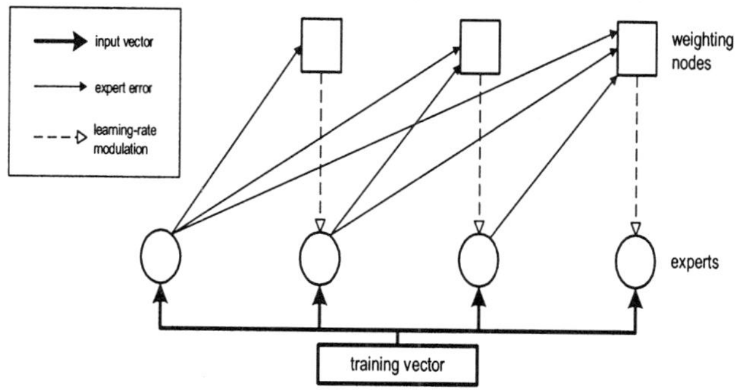


Figure 1: The POCA architecture. Each expert processes the input in parallel and computes its own prediction error. This error is forwarded in parallel to all rightward weighting nodes. Each weighting node computes some function over the incoming errors and projects this value down to its paired expert in order to modulate the learning rate for the current exemplar.

**Table 1-A.** Arc-x4 Algorithm

Given: Training dataset {<$x_1$,$y_1$>,…,<$x_n$,$y_n$>}
  Maximum # of rounds, R, Expert (weak) learning algorithm
Initialize weights and mistakes:
  $w_1(i) = 1/n \quad \forall i \quad m_0(i) = 0 \quad \forall i$
For r=1 to R:
  Build new expert h with weighted dataset.
  Calc. weighted error of current expert:
    $e_r(i) = [\![ 1 \text{ if } h_r(x_i) \neq y_i \text{ else } 0 ]\!] \quad \forall i$
    $\varepsilon_r = \sum w_r(i) e_r(i)$
  If weighted error is greater than chance:
    Reset weights, delete expert, loop
  Update exemplar mistakes, weights:
    $m_r(i) = m_{r-1}(i) + e_r(i) \quad \forall i$
    $w_{r+1}(i) = 1 + m_r(i)^4 \quad \forall i$
  Normalize exemplar weights:
    $w_{r+1}(i) = w_{r+1}(i) / \sum_i w_{r+1}(i) \quad \forall i$
End for loop.
Ensemble output: $h(x) = \arg\max_{y \in Y} \| \{ h_r : h_r(x) = y \} \|$

**Table 1-B.** POCA Algorithm

Given: Expert learning algorithm,
  # of experts, R; Decay, d
Build experts $h_1$,…,$h_R$
Initialize weighted error approximations:
  $\varepsilon(r) = q(r) = 0.5 \quad \forall r \qquad s(r) = 1 \quad \forall r$
While there is an available training exemplar <x,y>:
  Calc. expert errors on <x,y>: $e(r) = [\![ 1 \text{ if } h_r(x) \neq y \text{ else } 0 ]\!] \quad \forall r$
Calc. expert weights for <x,y>:
  $m(r) = \sum_{\{i: i<r \wedge \varepsilon(i)<0.5\}} e(i) \quad \forall r$
  $w_t(r) = 1 + m(r)^4 \quad \forall r$
  $z(r) \approx \max(w_{t-windowsize}(r), \ldots, w_t(r))$
Train experts on <x,y> using $w_t(r)/z(r)$
Update norm. weighted error estimates of experts:
  $q(r) = q(r)(1-d) + w_t(r)e(r)d \quad \forall r$
  $s(r) = s(r)(1-d) + w_t(r)d \quad \forall r$
  $\varepsilon(r) = q(r)/s(r) \quad \forall r$
End while loop.
Ensemble output: $h(x) = \arg\max_{y \in Y} \| \{ h_r : h_r(x) = y \} \|$

Table 1: Pseudo-code for (two-class) Arc-x4 and POCA. Indices in table 1-A index over exemplars in the fixed training set; indices in table 1-B index over experts in the ensemble. See text for discussion of decay, windowsize, and normalization constants in POCA.

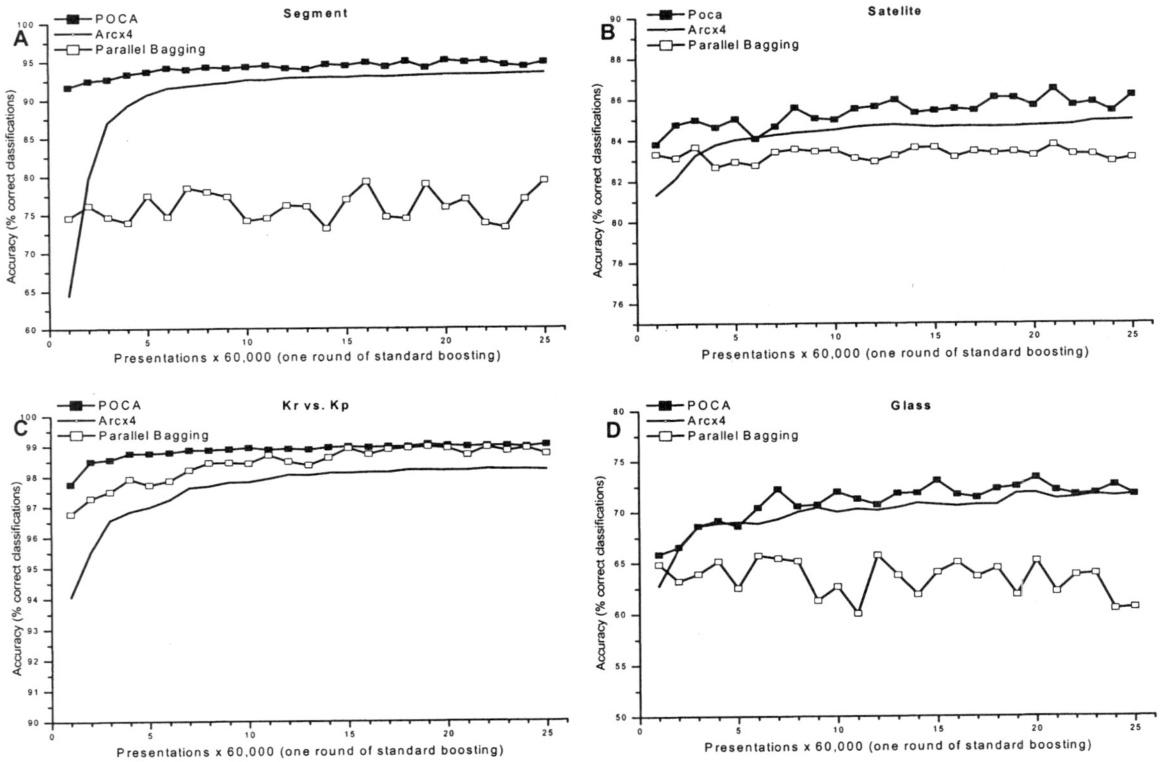


Figure 2: Does POCA boost? Performance on some UCI datasets using simple experts (standard deviations are omitted for clarity, but are generally within one percentage point). Note that significantly better results can easily be obtained on these datasets with more powerful experts; simple experts were chosen to examine the effect of boosting.

In addition to selecting a particular architecture for the experts, it is necessary to choose a particular function to be computed by the weighting nodes. We have implemented parallelizable (Fern and Givan 2003) weighting functions that emulate both the Arc-x4 and Adaboost weighting schemes, and found only minor differences in performance. All experiments in this paper were conducted using the Arc-x4 version of POCA.

## Dynamic Normalization of Weighting Nodes

Traditional boosting algorithms employ an explicit normalization step after each round to ensure that exemplar weights form a valid distribution for sampling. This is important because, depending on the performance of prior experts, the highest weights that a given expert receives may be very small. If left un-normalized, excessively small weights could significantly slow down learning. The difficulty for POCA is that it is impossible to systematically normalize weighting node outputs (i.e. learning rates or training probabilities) between rounds, not only because POCA does not work in discrete rounds, but because we assume an online environment with possibly non-repeating, non-stationary training exemplars.

We employ a heuristic mechanism to approximate the normalization of weighting node outputs: Each expert keeps track of the highest weight it has seen in the recent past, and this value is used to normalize new weights as they are generated. The heuristic ensures that the relative weighting of exemplars is largely preserved, while each expert rescales its weights so that the highest weighted exemplars receive weights (probabilities or learning rates) near 1. The optimal window size for normalization depends on learning rates and concept drift rate, but experimental results show little difference over a wide range of window sizes; experiments presented in this paper normalize over the last 2000 exemplars. Another technique employed in boosting algorithms (Breiman 1999) is to exclude experts that perform worse than chance. We emulate this by tracking each expert's "decaying-weighted-error" over time, which can be used continuously and is suitable for non-stationary concepts. Experiments presented here use a decay of .001.

## Differentially Weighted Backpropagation

When training multi-class neural networks, one commonly presents a vector where the correct class has a value near 1,

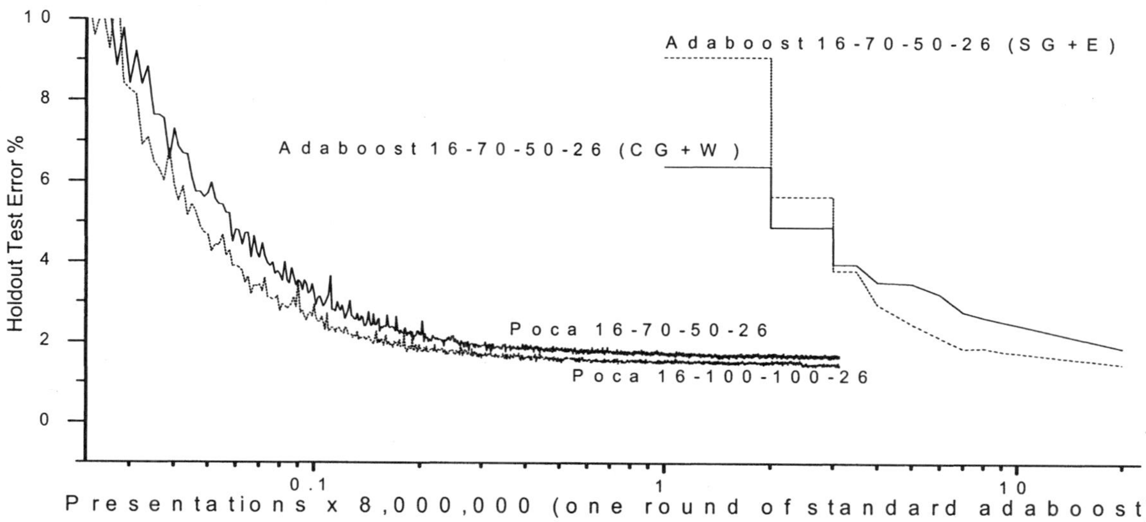


Figure 3: Comparison with previously published (state-of-the-art) results on the UCI Letter dataset by Schwenk et al. Note that test scores in Adaboost are calculated after the completion of each discrete round (which is accompanied by the addition of a new expert to the ensemble), and therefore begin only after completion of the first round. For clarity, standard deviations are not shown, but are consistently below 0.1 during the second half of POCA training. SG+E is stochastic-gradient descent training using weighted resampling; CG+W is conjugate gradient descent training using weighted training exemplars; results taken from (Schwenk and Bengio 2000).

and other classes have a value near 0. Prediction error is the mean-squared-error over the entire output vector. When boosting such multi-class neural network experts, the common practice is to calculate a scalar weight for each training exemplar and use this scalar weight to either modify the learning rate of the neural network or to weight the exemplars for resampling (Drucker et al. 1994; Drucker 1999; Optiz and Maclin 1999; Schwenk and Bengio 2000).

We have obtained slightly better results using a modification of backpropagation that differentially weights individual components of the error vector, rather than modifying the global learning rate of the network. We simply multiply the backpropagation error term on each output node by the associated (normalized) weight of that component, as calculated using the applicable weighting rule (i.e. Arc-x4 variant or Adaboost variant), treating each component of the output as an independent binary learning task, along the lines of Adaboost.M2 (Schapire 1999). This forces the neural networks to concentrate learning on hard-to-distinguish output classes (specific output components). Results using standard backpropagation (not shown) are not qualitatively different, but tend to converge slightly slower.

## Results

This section presents some representative results comparing POCA to other ensemble methods using datasets from the UCI machine learning repository (Blake and Merz 1998).

## Does POCA Boost?

The first set of experiments compares POCA to Arc-x4 and Parallel Bagging, using very simple experts. Experts are standard MLP (multi-layer feed-forward perceptron) neural networks with a single hidden layer of only 3 nodes; training was performed using a slightly modified version of stochastic backpropagation that multiplies output component errors by the component output of the weighting nodes, emulating Schapire's Adaboost.M2 (Schapire 1999) training scheme for multi-class boosting. The baseline learning rate was 0.4, with a momentum of 0.2; each run consists of 25 "rounds" with 60,000 training presentations per round. Note that in POCA and parallel bagging, rounds demarcate chunks of training exemplars seen, and have no greater significance; all algorithms receive the same number of total training exemplars.

Figure 2 shows that POCA performs comparably to standard Arc-x4, and is not simply averaging the votes of independent experts, as in bagging. Plots show accuracy over time, on held-out test data, averaged over 10 runs. Results of Adaboost and POCA-adaboost were similar and are not shown.

It is important to note that significantly better results can be achieved on these UCI datasets with more complex experts; for this set of experiments we specifically chose simple experts as base learners in order to tax the abilities of individual experts and test the ability of POCA to boost. As has been reported elsewhere, with more complex individual experts, the advantages of boosting over bagging become less pronounced (Optiz and Maclin 1999).

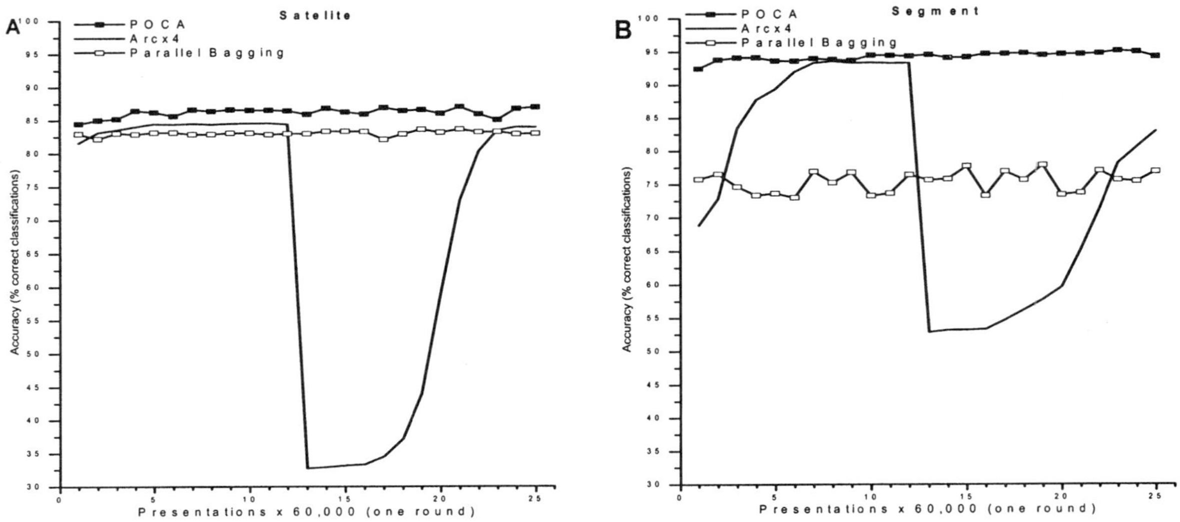


Figure 4: Performance on datasets where the concept changes during training. In traditional boosting, only over time do new experts "drown-out" the old incorrect ones.

## Comparison with State-of-the-art

Recently, Schwenk and Bengio (Schwenk and Bengio 2000) presented state-of-the-art results on the large (20,000 cases) and difficult UCI Letter dataset using boosted neural networks. Schwenk and Bengio's results plateau at 1.47% error after a total of 200 million training-exemplar presentations (25 rounds of 500 epochs each, with 16,000 training exemplars per epoch), which they cite as the best results obtained to date on this data.

Figure 3 shows a comparison of POCA to the Schwenk et al. Adaboost results, using identically sized ensembles and experts (25 neural network experts of size 16-70-50-26) , and also using larger ensembles (50 experts) of larger neural networks (16-100-100-26). Other parameters were identical to the previous experiment. To reduce training time, results for POCA have been averaged over only 3 runs and we stopped training after 25 million exemplars were presented, when learning seemed to plateau.

With neural network experts of identical size to those used in Schwenk et al., POCA plateaus at a slightly higher error of 1.6%, but reaches this much more rapidly. With larger networks, POCA plateaus at an error rate of 1.44%, which is the best published score on this dataset to our knowledge.

We believe that the significance of the results shown in figure 3 lies not so much in the final error rates, but rather in the speed of the learning (in terms of improvement per iteration and potential running time on parallel hardware), and in the flexibility of the underlying algorithm (i.e. suitability for online learning of non-repeating data).

We further note that Schwenk et al. were unable to obtain satisfactory results when using stochastic gradient descent training with a directly-weighted cost function (not shown), and had to use weighted sampling or conjugate-gradient descent, both of which greatly increase computational processing requirements. POCA is able to achieve identical results using a computationally cheaper, online-suitable gradient descent procedure with a directly-weighted cost function (differentially weighted backprop).

## Suitability for Changing Concepts

A major motivation for the development of the POCA algorithm was the possibility of applying boosting principles to online learning in non-stationary environments. Standard boosting algorithms are ill-suited for such tasks both because they require a fixed dataset over which to track explicit performance scores, and because traditional boosting algorithms build ensembles sequentially, so that previously built experts are incapable of adapting to changes in a target concept.

Figure 4 compares the performance of POCA against the standard Arc-x4 algorithm and Parallel Bagging on two UCI Datasets, Satellite and Segment. After the 12th round we change half of the target classes, for both training and testing data, effectively changing the target concept. Arc-x4 exhibits a catastrophic failure and can only recover slowly by building enough new experts to drown out the newly-incorrect votes of previously constructed experts.

# Conclusions

In a recent paper, Breiman (Breiman 1999) states that "in terms of handling large databases, an advantage for bagging, randomized construction, and output randomization is that they can be easily parallelized, while boosting algorithms are essentially sequential." Drucker (Drucker 1999) similarly states that "The big advantage of bagging over boosting is that each machine can be trained independently, hence in parallel." And in (Bauer and Kohavi 1999), Bauer and Kohavi state that "In parallel environments, Bagging has a strong advantage because the sub-classifiers can be built in parallel" and go on to question whether an efficient parallel implementation of boosting/arcing is possible.

We believe that POCA represents a viable, efficient, parallelizable boosting algorithm. It requires no memory for storing exemplars or exemplar scores and can be used for online learning of difficult multi-class concepts in non-stationary environments.

Although the POCA algorithm itself is clearly parallel, one might ask whether the actual adaptation of experts is still in some sense inherently serial. Empirically, the parallel training procedure yields consistently better results over its serial counterpart. We speculate that this is due to the fact that, even though a given expert cannot be expected to completely stabilize until those preceding it in the virtual chain completely stabilize, all experts in POCA are learning gradually, as if tracking a drifting distribution. When training begins, learning in the ensemble resembles a form of parallel bagging, but as experts learn to specialize on certain regions of the input space, they perturb the distribution of weights seen by those experts that follow them in the virtual chain, forcing those experts to adapt to the changing distribution as if the target concept had changed. Because of this, POCA typically learns faster (in improvement per training iteration) than traditional boosting algorithms like Arc-x4 and Adaboost, as can be seen in Figures 2, 3, and 4.

In traditional boosting, at the start of each round a new expert is created, given the full data set, and "trained to completion." Because neural network experts (and similar structures) can get stuck in local minima for prolonged periods, traditional boosting algorithms must adopt criteria for deciding when to stop training a given expert and move on to the next round. Stopping prematurely may result in an unnecessarily large number of rounds, while overtraining experts wastes computational time. The continuous training of experts in POCA ensures that no time is wasted overtraining experts, while still providing each expert with the entire training time in which to reach asymptotic performance. We believe that the higher overall accuracy of POCA seen in our results is due to the ability of POCA to avoid the under and over training of individual experts.

A drawback of the POCA algorithm is that on a single CPU it can run orders of magnitude slower in actual runtime than traditional boosting algorithms. We are currently working on a version of POCA that runs on parallel hardware, using a pipeline system to minimize communication bandwidth. We also hope to explore alternative weight-propagation topologies and learning schemes, which would allow POCA to generalize to parallel forms of other ensemble algorithms such as Multiboosting (Webb 2000) and Mixtures of Experts (Jacobs et al. 1991).

## References


Bauer, E., and Kohavi, R. 1999. An Empirical Comparison of Voting Classification Algorithms: Bagging, Boosting, and Variants. *Machine Learning* 36(1-2): 105-39.

Blake, C. L. and Merz, C. J. 1998. "UCI Repository of machine learning databases." Web page. Available at http://www.ics.uci.edu/~mlearn/MLRepository.html.

Breiman, L. 1997. *Arcing the Edge*, Technical Report #486. University of California, Berkeley.

Breiman, L. 1999. Combining Predictors. *Combining Artificial Neural Nets.* ed. A. J. C. Sharkey, 31-50. London: Springer-Verlag.

Chawla, N. V, Hall, L. O, Bowyer, K. W, Moore, T. E, and Kegelmeyer, W. P. 2002. Distributed Pasting of Small Votes. *In Proceedings of Multiple Classifier Systems 2002.*

Drucker, H. 1999. Boosting Using Neural Networks. *Combining Artificial Neural Nets.* ed. A. J. C. Sharkey, 51-77. London: Springer-Verlag.

Drucker, H., Cortes, C., Jackel, L. D., Lecun, Y., and Vapnik, V. 1994. Boosting and Other Ensemble Methods. *Neural Computation* 6(6): 1289-301.

Fan, W., Stolfo, S. J., and Zhang, J. 1999. The Application of AdaBoost for Distributed, Scalable and On-line Learning. *In Proceedings of the fifth ACM SIGKDD International Conference on Knowledge discovery and Data Mining, KDD-99*, San Diego, California.

Fern, A., and Givan, R. 2003. Online Ensemble Learning: an Empirical Study. *Machine Learning* 53(1-2): 71-109.

Freund, Y., and Schapire, R. E. 1998. Arcing Classifiers - Discussion. *Annals of Statistics* 26(3): 824-32.

Freund, Y., and Schapire, R. E. 1999. A Short Introduction to Boosting. *Journal of the Japanese Society for Artificial Intelligence* 14(5): 771-80.

Jacobs, R. A., Jordan, M. I., Nowlan, S. J., and Hinton, G. E. 1991. Adaptive mixtures of local experts. *Neural Computation* 3(1): 79-87.

Lazarevic, A, and Obradovic, Z. 2001. The Distributed Boosting Algorithm. *In Proceedings of the International Conference on Knowledge Discovery and Data Mining, KDD-2001.*

Optiz, D., and Maclin, R. 1999. Popular Ensemble Methods: An Empirical Study. *Journal of Artificial Intelligence Research* 11: 169-98.

Schapire, R. E. 1999. A Brief Introduction to Boosting. *In Proceedings of the Sixteenth International Joint Conference on Artificial Intelligence.*

Schwenk, H., and Bengio, Y. 2000. Boosting Neural Networks. *Neural Computation* 12(8): 1869-87.

Webb, G. I. 2000. Multiboosting: a Technique for Combining Boosting and Wagging. *Machine Learning* 40(2): 159-96.

# Bayesian Inference on Principal Component Analysis using Reversible Jump Markov Chain Monte Carlo

**Zhihua Zhang**[1] and **Kap Luk Chan**[2] and **James T. Kwok**[1] and **Dit-Yan Yeung**[1]

[1]Department of Computer Science
Hong Kong University of Science and Technology
Clear Water Bay, Hong Kong
{zhzhang,jamesk,dyyeung}@cs.ust.hk

[2]School of Electrical and Electronic Engineering
Nanyang Technological University
Nanyang Avenue, Singapore 639798
eklchan@ntu.edu.sg

### Abstract

Based on the probabilistic reformulation of principal component analysis (PCA), we consider the problem of determining the number of principal components as a model selection problem. We present a hierarchical model for probabilistic PCA and construct a Bayesian inference method for this model using reversible jump Markov chain Monte Carlo (MCMC). By regarding each principal component as a point in a one-dimensional space and employing only birth-death moves in our reversible jump methodology, our proposed method is simple and capable of automatically determining the number of principal components and estimating the parameters simultaneously under the same disciplined framework. Simulation experiments are performed to demonstrate the effectiveness of our MCMC method.

## Introduction

Principal component analysis (PCA) is a powerful tool for data analysis. It has been widely used for such tasks as dimensionality reduction, data compression and visualization. The original derivation of PCA is based on a standardized linear projection that maximizes the variance in the projected space. Recently, Tipping & Bishop (1999) proposed the probabilistic PCA which explores the relationship between PCA and factor analysis of generative latent variable models. This opens the door to various Bayesian treatments of PCA. In particular, Bayesian inference can now be employed to solve the central problem of determining the number of principal components that should be retained. Bishop (1999a; 1999b) addressed this by using automatic relevance determination (ARD) (Neal 1996) and Bayesian variational methods. Minka (2001), on the other hand, adopted a Bayesian method which is based on the Laplace approximation. In this paper, we propose a hierarchical model for Bayesian inference on PCA using the novel reversible jump Markov chain Monte Carlo (MCMC) algorithm of Green (1995).

In brief, reversible jump MCMC is a random-sweep Metropolis-Hastings method for varying-dimension problems. It constructs a dimension matching transform using the reversible jump methodology and estimates the parameters using Gibbs sampling. Richardson & Green (1997), by developing the split-merge and birth-death moves for the reversible jump methodology, performed a fully Bayesian analysis on univariate data generated from a finite Gaussian mixture (GM) with an unknown number of components. This was then further extended to univariate hidden Markov models (HMM) by Robert, Rydén, & Titterington (2000). In general, reversible jump MCMC is attractive in that it can perform parameter estimation and model selection simultaneously within the same framework. In contrast, the other methods mentioned above can only perform model selection separately. In recent years, reversible jump MCMC has also been successfully applied to neural networks (Holmes & Mallick 1998; Andrieu, Djurié, & Doucet 2001) and pattern recognition (Roberts, Holmes, & Denison 2001).

Motivated by these successes, in this paper, we introduce reversible jump MCMC into the probabilistic PCA framework. This provides a disciplined method to perform parameter estimation simultaneously with choosing the number of principal components. In particular, we propose a hierarchical model for probabilistic PCA, together with a Bayesian inference procedure for this model using reversible jump MCMC. Note that PCA is considerably simpler than GMs and HMMs in the following ways. First, PCA has much fewer free parameters than GMs and HMMs. Second, unlike GMs and HMMs, no component in PCA can be empty. Third, using reversible jump MCMC in GMs and HMMs for high-dimensional data is still an open problem, while reversible jump MCMC for PCA is more manageable because, as to be discussed in more detail in later sections, each principal component can be regarded as a point in some one-dimensional space. Because of these, we will only employ birth-death moves for the dimension matching transform in our reversible jump methodology.

The rest of this paper is organized as follows. In the next section, we give a brief overview of probabilistic PCA and the corresponding maximum likelihood estimation problem. A hierarchical Bayesian model and the corresponding reversible jump MCMC procedure are then presented, followed by some experimental results on different data sets. The last section gives some concluding remarks.

## Probabilistic PCA

Probabilistic PCA was proposed by Tipping & Bishop (1999). In this model, a high-dimensional random vector $\mathbf{x}$ is expressed as a linear combination of basis vectors ($\mathbf{h}_j$'s) plus noise ($\epsilon$):

$$\begin{aligned}\mathbf{x} &= \sum_{j=1}^{q} \mathbf{h}_j w_j + \mathbf{m} + \boldsymbol{\epsilon} \\ &= \mathbf{Hw} + \mathbf{m} + \boldsymbol{\epsilon}, \quad (1)\\ \boldsymbol{\epsilon} &\sim \mathcal{N}(\mathbf{0}, \mathbf{V}), \quad (2)\end{aligned}$$

where $\mathbf{x} \in \mathbb{R}^d$, $\mathbf{w} = (w_1, \ldots, w_q)^T \in \mathbb{R}^q$, $q < d$, and $\mathbf{H} = [\mathbf{h}_1, \ldots, \mathbf{h}_q]$ is a $d \times q$ matrix that relates the two sets of variables $\mathbf{x}$ and $\mathbf{w}$. The vector $\mathbf{m}$ allows the model to have non-zero mean. In PCA, the noise variance matrix $\mathbf{V}$ is hyperspherical, i.e.,

$$\mathbf{V} = \sigma^2 \mathbf{I}_d, \quad (3)$$

and the latent variables $w_1, \ldots, w_q$ are independent Gaussians with zero mean and unit variance, i.e.,

$$\mathbf{w} \sim \mathcal{N}(\mathbf{0}, \mathbf{I}_q).$$

Note that the probabilistic PCA is closely related to factor analysis, with the only difference being that the noise variance matrix $\mathbf{V}$ in factor analysis is a general diagonal matrix.

Given an observed data set $\mathcal{D} = \{\mathbf{x}_1, \ldots, \mathbf{x}_N\}$, the goal of PCA is to estimate the matrix $\mathbf{H}$ in (1) and the noise variance $\sigma^2$ in (3). From (1) and (2), we can obtain the conditional probability of the observation vector $\mathbf{x}$ as

$$\mathbf{x}|\mathbf{w}, \mathbf{H}, \mathbf{m}, \sigma^2 \sim \mathcal{N}(\mathbf{Hw} + \mathbf{m}, \sigma^2 \mathbf{I}),$$

and so, by integrating out $\mathbf{w}$, we have

$$p(\mathbf{x}|\mathbf{H}, \mathbf{m}, \sigma^2) = \int p(\mathbf{x}|\mathbf{w}, \mathbf{H}, \mathbf{m}, \sigma^2) p(\mathbf{w}) d\mathbf{w}.$$

Note that (Tipping & Bishop 1999)

$$\mathbf{x}|\mathbf{H}, \mathbf{m}, \sigma^2 \sim \mathcal{N}(\mathbf{m}, \mathbf{C}),$$

with $\mathbf{C} = \mathbf{HH^T} + \sigma^2 \mathbf{I}$. The corresponding likelihood is therefore

$$\begin{aligned}p(\mathcal{D}|\mathbf{H}, \mathbf{m}, \sigma^2) &= \prod_{i=1}^{N} p(\mathbf{x}_i|\mathbf{H}, \mathbf{m}, \sigma^2) \\ &= (2\pi)^{-Nd/2} |\mathbf{HH}^T + \sigma^2 \mathbf{I}|^{-N/2} \\ &\quad \times e^{-\frac{N}{2} \mathrm{tr}((\mathbf{HH}^T + \sigma^2 \mathbf{I})^{-1} \mathbf{S})}, \quad (4)\end{aligned}$$

where

$$\mathbf{S} = \frac{1}{N} \sum_{i=1}^{N} (\mathbf{x}_i - \mathbf{m})(\mathbf{x}_i - \mathbf{m})^T. \quad (5)$$

From (Tipping & Bishop 1999), the maximum likelihood estimates of $\mathbf{m}$ and $\mathbf{H}$ are

$$\begin{aligned}\widehat{\mathbf{m}} &= \frac{1}{N} \sum_{i=1}^{N} \mathbf{x}_i, \quad (6)\\ \widehat{\mathbf{H}} &= \mathbf{U}_q (\boldsymbol{\Lambda}_q - \sigma^2 \mathbf{I}_q)^{1/2} \mathbf{R},\end{aligned}$$

respectively, where $\mathbf{U}_q$ is a $d \times q$ orthogonal matrix in which the $q$ column vectors are the principal eigenvectors of $\mathbf{S}$, $\boldsymbol{\Lambda}_q$ is a $q \times q$ diagonal matrix containing the corresponding eigenvalues $\lambda_1, \ldots, \lambda_q$, and $\mathbf{R}$ is an arbitrary $q \times q$ orthogonal matrix. For $\mathbf{H} = \widehat{\mathbf{H}}$, the maximum likelihood estimate of $\sigma^2$ is given by

$$\widehat{\sigma}^2 = \frac{1}{d-q} \sum_{j=q+1}^{d} \lambda_j,$$

which implies that the maximum likelihood noise variance is equal to the average of the left-out eigenvalues.

## Bayesian Formalism for PCA

### Hierarchical Model and Priors

In a fully Bayesian framework, both the number of principal components ($q$) and the model parameters ($\boldsymbol{\theta} = \{\mathbf{H}, \mathbf{m}, \sigma^2\}$) are considered to be drawn from appropriate prior distributions. We assume that the joint density of all these variables takes the form

$$p(q, \boldsymbol{\theta}, \mathcal{D}) = p(q) p(\boldsymbol{\theta}\,|q)\, p(\mathcal{D}\,|\boldsymbol{\theta}, q)\,. \quad (7)$$

Following (Minka 2001), we decompose the matrix $\mathbf{H}$ as

$$\mathbf{H} = \mathbf{U}_q (\mathbf{L}_q - \sigma^2 \mathbf{I}_q)^{1/2} \mathbf{R},$$

where $\mathbf{U}_q^T \mathbf{U}_q = \mathbf{I}_q, \mathbf{R}^T \mathbf{R} = \mathbf{I}_q$, and $\mathbf{L}_q = \mathrm{diag}(l_1, \ldots, l_q)$. It is easy to extend the $d \times q$ matrix $\mathbf{U}_q$ to a $d \times d$ orthogonal matrix $\mathbf{U}$ such that $\mathbf{U} = (\mathbf{U}_q, \mathbf{U}_{d-q})$ and $\mathbf{U}_{d-q}^T \mathbf{U}_{d-q} = \mathbf{I}_{d-q}$. Letting

$$\mathbf{L} = \begin{matrix} \\ q \\ d-q \end{matrix} \begin{pmatrix} \overset{q}{\mathbf{L}_q - \sigma^2 \mathbf{I}_q} & \overset{d-q}{\mathbf{0}} \\ \mathbf{0} & \mathbf{0} \end{pmatrix},$$

we have

$$\begin{aligned}\mathbf{ULU}^T &= (\mathbf{U}_q, \mathbf{U}_{d-q}) \begin{pmatrix} \mathbf{L}_q - \sigma^2 \mathbf{I}_q & \mathbf{0} \\ \mathbf{0} & \mathbf{0} \end{pmatrix} \begin{pmatrix} \mathbf{U}_q^T \\ \mathbf{U}_{d-q}^T \end{pmatrix} \\ &= \mathbf{U}_q (\mathbf{L}_q - \sigma^2 \mathbf{I}) \mathbf{U}_q^T \\ &= \mathbf{HH}^T.\end{aligned}$$

Hence,

$$\begin{aligned}\mathbf{HH}^T + \sigma^2 \mathbf{I}_d &= \mathbf{ULU}^T + \sigma^2 \mathbf{I}_d \\ &= \mathbf{U} \begin{pmatrix} \mathbf{L}_q & \mathbf{0} \\ \mathbf{0} & \sigma^2 \mathbf{I}_{d-q} \end{pmatrix} \mathbf{U}^T. \quad (8)\end{aligned}$$

Since the matrix $\mathbf{S}$ in (5) is symmetric and positive definite, we can decompose it as $\mathbf{S} = \mathbf{AGA}^T$, where $\mathbf{A}$ is an orthogonal matrix consisting of the eigenvectors of $\mathbf{S}$, and $\mathbf{G}$ is diagonal with diagonal elements $g_i$'s being the eigenvalues of $\mathbf{S}$.

For simplicity, we set $\mathbf{R} = \mathbf{I}_q$ and use the maximum likelihood estimators for $\mathbf{m}$ and $\mathbf{U}$. In other words, we obtain $\mathbf{m}$ from (6) and set $\mathbf{U}$ to be the eigenvector matrix $\mathbf{A}$ of $\mathbf{S}$.

Combining with (4) and (8), we can rewrite the likelihood as:

$$\begin{aligned} p(\mathcal{D}|l_1^{-1},\ldots,l_q^{-1},\sigma^{-2}) &= \prod_{i=1}^{N} p(\mathbf{x}_i|l_1^{-1},\ldots,l_q^{-1},\sigma^{-2}) \\ &= (2\pi)^{-\frac{Nd}{2}} \prod_{j=1}^{q} l_j^{-N/2}\sigma^{-N(d-q)} \times e^{-\frac{N}{2}\sum_{j=1}^{q} l_j^{-1} g_j} \\ &\quad \times e^{-\frac{N\sigma^{-2}}{2}\sum_{j=q+1}^{d} g_j}. \end{aligned}$$

Now, our goal is to estimate the parameters ($l_j$'s and $\sigma^2$) and the number of principal components ($q$) via reversible jump MCMC. First of all, we have to choose a proper prior distribution for each parameter. A common choice for $q$ is the Poisson distribution with hyperparameter $\lambda$. Here, for convenience of presentation and interpretation, we assume that $q$ follows a uniform prior on $\{1, 2, \cdots, d-1\}$.

To ensure identifiability, we impose the following ordering constraint on $l_j$'s and $\sigma^2$:

$$l_1 > l_2 > \cdots > l_q > \sigma^2.$$

The prior joint density for these parameters is then given by:

$$\begin{aligned} p(l_1,\ldots,l_q,\sigma^2|q) &= (q+1)!\,p(l_1,\ldots,l_q,\sigma^2) \\ &\quad \times \mathbf{I}_{l_1>l_2>\cdots>l_q>\sigma^2}(l,\sigma^2), \end{aligned}$$

where $\mathbf{I}$ denotes the indicator function, and the $(q+1)!$ term arises from the ordering constraint.

We assume that $l_1, \ldots, l_q$ and $\sigma^2$ are distributed *a priori* as independent variables conditioned on some hyperparameter. In this case, we consider the prior distributions for the parameters $l_1, \ldots, l_q$ and $\sigma^2$ as conjugate priors:

$$\begin{aligned} l_j^{-1} &\sim \Gamma(r,\tau), \quad j = 1, 2, \ldots, q, \\ \sigma^{-2} &\sim \Gamma(r,\tau), \end{aligned}$$

where $\Gamma(\cdot,\cdot)$ denotes the Gamma distribution.[1] Since the hyperparameter $r > 0$ represents the shape of the Gamma distribution, it is appropriate to pre-specify it. In this paper, $r$ is held fixed while $\tau > 0$ is also given a Gamma prior:

$$\tau \sim \Gamma(\alpha, \eta),$$

where $\alpha > 0$ and $\eta > 0$. We have thus obtained a complete hierarchical model (Figure 1), which can be represented graphically in the form of a directed acyclic graph (DAG).

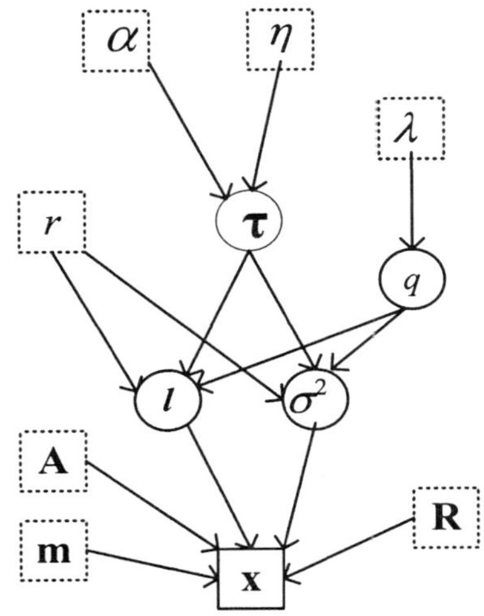


Figure 1: DAG for the proposed probabilistic PCA model.

## Reversible Jump MCMC Methodology

For the hierarchical model proposed above, the goal of Bayesian inference is to generate realizations from the conditional joint density $p(q, \boldsymbol{\theta}|\mathcal{D})$ derived from (7). The reversible jump MCMC algorithm in (Green 1995) allows us to handle this problem even when the number of principal components is unknown. The algorithm proceeds by augmenting the usual proposal step of a random-sweep Metropolis-Hastings method with variable dimensions. It constructs the dimension matching transform with the split-merge or birth-death moves by adding or removing a latent variable. As discussed in the introduction section, we only use the birth-death moves in this paper. Consequently, each sweep of our reversible jump MCMC procedure consists of three types of moves:

(a) update the parameters $l_j$'s and $\sigma$;
(b) update the hyperparameter $\tau$;
(c) the birth or death of a component.

Move types (a) and (b) are used for parameter estimation via Gibbs sampling. Since move type (c) involves changing the number of components $q$ by 1, it constitutes the reversible jump and is used for model selection via the Metropolis-Hastings algorithm. Assume that a move of type $m$, which moves from the current state $\mathbf{s}$ to a new state $\mathbf{s}'$ in a higher-dimensional space, is proposed. This is often implemented by drawing a vector $\mathbf{v}$ of continuous random variables, independent of $\mathbf{s}$, and denoting $\mathbf{s}'$ by using an invertible deterministic function $f(\mathbf{s}, \mathbf{v})$. Then, the acceptance probabilities from $\mathbf{s}$ to $\mathbf{s}'$ and from $\mathbf{s}'$ to $\mathbf{s}$ are $\min(1, R)$ and $\min(1, R^{-1})$, respectively, where

$$R = \frac{p(\mathbf{s}'|\mathbf{x})\, r_m(\mathbf{s}')}{p(\mathbf{s}|\mathbf{x})\, r_m(\mathbf{s}) p(\mathbf{v})} \left| \frac{\partial \mathbf{s}'}{\partial(\mathbf{s},\mathbf{v})} \right|, \tag{9}$$

$r_m(\mathbf{s})$ is the probability of choosing move type $m$ in state $\mathbf{s}$, $p(\mathbf{v})$ is the density function of $\mathbf{v}$, and $\left|\frac{\partial \mathbf{s}'}{\partial(\mathbf{s},\mathbf{v})}\right|$ is the Jacobian arising from the change of variables from $(\mathbf{s}, \mathbf{v})$ to $\mathbf{s}'$. Using (9) for our probabilistic PCA model, the acceptance probability for the birth move from $\{q, l_1^{-1}, \ldots, l_q^{-1}\}$

[1] The Gamma density of a random variable $x \sim \Gamma(\alpha, \lambda)$ is defined as:

$$p(x; \alpha, \lambda) = \frac{\lambda^\alpha}{\Gamma(\alpha)} x^{\alpha-1} e^{-\lambda x},$$

where $\alpha > 0, \lambda > 0$ are the shape and scaling parameters, respectively.

to $\{q+1, l_1^{-1}, \ldots, l_q^{-1}, l_{q+1}^{-1}\}$ is $\min(1, R)$, where

$$R = (\text{likelihood ratio}) \frac{p(q+1)}{p(q)} (q+2) \times \frac{p(l_1^{-1}, \ldots, l_{q+1}^{-1}, \sigma^{-2})}{p(l_1^{-1}, \ldots, l_q^{-1}, \sigma^{-2})} \frac{d_{q+1}}{b_q} \frac{1}{p(l_{q+1}^{-1})}. \quad (10)$$

Here, $d_k$ and $b_k$ are the probabilities of attempting death and birth moves, respectively, when the current state has $k$ latent variables. Usually, $b_j = d_j = 0.5$ when $j = 2, \ldots, d-2$, $d_1 = b_{d-1} = 0$ and $b_1 = d_{d-1} = 1$. Our death proposal proceeds by choosing the latent variable with the smallest eigenvalue.

The correspondence between (9) and (10) is fairly straightforward. The first two terms of (10) form the ratio $\frac{p(\mathbf{s}'|\mathbf{x})}{p(\mathbf{s}|\mathbf{x})}$, the $(q+2)$-factor is the ratio $\frac{(q+2)!}{(q+1)!}$ from the order statistics densities for the parameters $l_j$'s and $\sigma^2$, and the last term is the proposal ratio $\frac{r_m(\mathbf{s}')}{r_m(\mathbf{s})p(\mathbf{v})}$. The Jacobian is equal to unity because we are drawing new principal components independent of the current parameters.

## Reversible Jump MCMC Algorithm for Probabilistic PCA

We use Gibbs sampling (Gilks, Richardson, & Spiegelhalter 1996) to simulate the parameters and hyperparameters in our model. The reversible jump MCMC algorithm for the proposed probabilistic PCA method is described as follows:

**Reversible Jump MCMC Algorithm**

1. Initialization: Sample $(q, \sigma^{-2}, l_1^{-1}, \ldots, l_q^{-1}, \tau)$ from their priors.
2. Iteration $t$:
   - Update the parameters and hyperparameters using Gibbs sampling.
   - Draw a uniform random variable $u \sim \mathcal{U}(0,1)$;
   - If $u \leq b_q$, then perform the Birth move.
   - Else if $u \leq b_q + d_q$, then perform the Death move.
   - End if
3. Set $t = t+1$ and go back to Step 2 until convergence.

**Gibbs Sampler**

1. For $j = 1, \cdots, q$, simulate from the full conditionals

$$l_j^{-1}|\cdots \sim \Gamma\Big(\frac{N}{2}+r, \frac{Ng_j}{2}+\tau\Big)\mathbf{I}_{[l_{j-1}, l_{j+1}]}(l_j),$$

$$\sigma^{-2}|\cdots \sim \Gamma\Big(\frac{N(d-q)}{2}+r, \frac{N\sum_{j=q+1}^{d} g_j}{2}+\tau\Big) \times \mathbf{I}_{(0, l_q]}(\sigma^2).$$

2. Simulate the hyperparameter $\tau$ from its full conditional:

$$\tau|\cdots \sim \Gamma\Big((q+1)r+\alpha, \sum_{j=1}^{q} l_j^{-1} + \sigma^{-2} + \eta\Big).$$

Birth move

1. Draw $l_{q+1}^{-1}$ from its prior $\Gamma(r,\tau)\mathbf{I}_{[l_q, \sigma^2]}(l_{q+1})$.
2. Calculate the acceptance probability $\alpha = \min(1, R)$ of the birth move using (10).
3. Draw a uniform random variable $v \sim \mathcal{U}(0,1)$.
4. If $v < \alpha$, then accept the proposed state; otherwise, set the next state to be the current state.

Death move

1. Remove the $q$th principal component.
2. Calculate the acceptance probability $\alpha = \min(1, R^{-1})$ of the death move using (10).
3. Draw a uniform random variable $v \sim \mathcal{U}(0,1)$.
4. If $v < \alpha$, then accept the proposed state; otherwise, set the next state to be the current state.

## Experiments

In this section, we perform experiments on several data sets to demonstrate the efficacy of the reversible jump MCMC algorithm for probabilistic PCA. We adopt the recommendation of Richardson & Green (1997) on the choice of hyperparameters and set $r > 1 > \alpha$. Also, we set $r = 3.0$, $\alpha = 0.5$, and $\eta = 1.2/V$, where $V$ is the standard deviation of the data. We run our algorithm for 20,000 sweeps in the following two experiments. The first 10,000 sweeps are discarded as burn-in. All our inferences are based on the last 10,000 sweeps.

### Experiment 1

In the first experiment, we generate a data set (Set 1) of 1,000 points from a 6-dimensional Gaussian distribution, with variances in the 6 dimensions equal to 10, 7, 5, 3, 1 and 1, respectively. The eigenvalues of the observed covariance matrix on the data so generated are 8.9580, 7.2862, 5.3011, 2.8964, 1.1012 and 0.9876, respectively. Table 1 shows the posterior probabilities for different numbers of principal components ($q$) and the corresponding estimated values of the parameters ($l_j$'s and $\sigma^2$). As we can see, the posterior probability of $q$ is tightly concentrated at $q = 4$, which agrees with our intuition that there are 4 dominant dimensions in this data set. Moreover, the estimated values of the parameters are very close to the true ones. Figure 2 depicts the jumping in the number of principal components on the last 10,000 sweeps.

Table 1: Posterior probabilities for different numbers of principal components ($q$'s) and the estimated values of $l_j$'s and $\sigma^2$.

| $q$ | $p(q\|\mathcal{D})$ | $\sigma^2$ | $l_j$'s |
|---|---|---|---|
| 4 | **0.8666** | 1.0573 | 9.0342, 7.3198<br>5.2214, 2.9420 |
| 5 | 0.1334 | 1.0263 | 9.0322, 7.3187<br>5.2201, 2.9403, 1.0930 |

Like the variational method in (Bishop 1999b), our proposed MCMC method does not provide one specific value on the number of principal components that should be retained. Instead, it provides posterior probability estimate for each possible dimensionality over the complete range. This leaves room for us to make an appropriate decision. In many applications, however, these probabilities are tightly concentrated at a specific dimensionality or only a few dimensionalities that are close to each other. Notice that the number of principal components $q$ only jumps between 4 and 5 after the burn-in period. Since the noise variance $\sigma^2$ is very close to the variance of either of the last two principal components (Table 1), either one may be treated as a noise term and hence $q$ is sometimes estimated to be equal to 5.

## Experiment 2

In the second experiment, we use three data sets similar to those used by Minka (2001). The first data set (Set 2 in Table 2) consists of 100 points generated from a 10-dimensional Gaussian distribution, with variances in the first 5 dimensions equal to 10, 8, 6, 4 and 2 respectively, and with variance equal to 1 in the last 5 dimensions. The second data set (Set 3 in Table 2) consists of 100 points generated from a 10-dimensional Gaussian distribution, with variances in the first 5 dimensions equal to 10, 8, 6, 4 and 2 respectively, and with variance 0.1 in the last 5 dimensions. The third data sets (Set 4 in Table 2), consisting of 10,000 points, is generated from a 15-dimensional Gaussian distribution, with variances in the first 5 dimensions equal to 10, 8, 6, 4 and 2 respectively, and with variance equal to 0.1 in the last 10 dimensions.

Table 2 shows the posterior probabilities for different numbers of principal components ($q$) and Figure 2 depicts the jumping in the number of principal components during the last 10,000 sweeps. As we can see, the posterior probabilities are all tightly concentrated at $q = 5$, which agrees with our intuition that there are 5 dominant dimensions in these data sets.

## Concluding Remarks

In this paper, we have proposed a Bayesian inference method for PCA using reversible jump MCMC. This allows simultaneous determination of the number of principal components and estimation of the corresponding parameters. Moreover, since each principal component in this PCA framework is considered as a point in a one-dimensional space, the use of reversible jump MCMC becomes feasible. Also, as the proposed probabilistic PCA framework is only one of the possible generative latent variable models, in the future, it is worthy to explore the reversible jump MCMC methodology for other generative models, such as the mixture of probabilistic PCA, factor analysis and its mixture, and independent component analysis.

In our reversible jump method, the dimension matching transform only employs birth-death moves, but not both split-merge and birth-death moves as in the reversible jump method for Gaussian mixtures (Richardson & Green 1997). Note that the birth-death moves of (Richardson & Green 1997) are developed for the empty components, which is only a supplement of the split-merge moves in order to enhance the robustness of the reversible jump method. Apparently, it is possible to use split-merge moves instead of birth-death moves to develop a reversible jump method for PCA. Recently, Stephens (2000) used the birth-death process instead of the reversible jump methodology and described an alternative of the reversible jump MCMC, called the birth-death MCMC. This birth-death MCMC differs from our method in that ours still follows the setting of standard reversible jump MCMC. Moreover, the computational cost of the birth-death MCMC is far higher than that of reversible jump MCMC. The relationship between these two has also been recently studied in (Cappé, Robert, & Rydén 2003).

## Appendix

We assume independence between $\mathcal{D} = \{\mathbf{x}_1, \ldots, \mathbf{x}_N\}$ given all model parameters, and between $l_1^{-1}, \ldots, l_q^{-1}$ and $\sigma^{-2}$ given the hyperparameter $\tau$. For convenience, we denote $\mathbf{l}^{-1} = \{l_1^{-1}, \ldots, l_q^{-1}\}$ and $\boldsymbol{\theta} = \{\mathbf{l}^{-1}, \tau, \sigma^{-2}\}$. The joint distribution of the data and parameters is:

$$
\begin{aligned}
p(\mathcal{D}, \boldsymbol{\theta}) &= \Big\{\prod_{i=1}^{N} p(\mathbf{x}_i|\mathbf{l}^{-1}, \sigma^{-2})\Big\} \\
&\quad \times \Big\{\prod_{j=1}^{q} p(l_j^{-1}|\tau)\Big\} \times p(\sigma^{-2}|\tau)p(\tau) \\
&= (2\pi)^{-\frac{Nd}{2}} \prod_{j=1}^{q} l_j^{-\frac{N}{2}} \sigma^{-N(d-q)} \\
&\quad \times e^{-\frac{N}{2}\left(\sum_{j=1}^{q} l_j^{-1} g_j + \sigma^{-2}\sum_{j=q+1}^{d} g_j\right)} \\
&\quad \times \Big\{\prod_{j=1}^{q} p(l_j^{-1}|\tau)\Big\} \times p(\sigma^{-2}|\tau)p(\tau).
\end{aligned}
$$

Then, the full conditionals for $l_j^{-1}$, $\sigma^{-2}$ and $\tau$ are

$$
\begin{aligned}
l_j^{-1}|\cdots &\sim l_j^{-\frac{N}{2}} e^{-\frac{N}{2} l_j^{-1} g_j} p(l_j^{-1}|\tau) \\
&\sim \Gamma\Big(\frac{N}{2} + r, \frac{N g_j}{2} + \tau\Big), \\
\sigma^{-2}|\cdots &\sim \sigma^{-N(d-q)} e^{-\frac{N\sigma^{-2}}{2}\sum_{j=q+1}^{d} g_j} p(\sigma^{-2}|\tau) \\
&\sim \Gamma\Big(\frac{N(d-q)}{2} + r, \frac{N\sum_{j=q+1}^{d} g_j}{2} + \tau\Big), \\
\tau|\cdots &\sim \Big\{\prod_{j=1}^{q} p(l_j^{-1}|\tau)\Big\} \times p(\sigma^{-2}|\tau)p(\tau) \\
&\sim \Gamma\Big((q+1)r + \alpha, \sum_{j=1}^{q} l_j^{-1} + \sigma^{-2} + \eta\Big),
\end{aligned}
$$

respectively.

## References

Andrieu, C.; Djurić, P. M.; and Doucet, A. 2001. Model selection by MCMC computation. *Signal Processing* 81:19–37.

Table 2: Posterior probabilities for different numbers of principal components ($q$'s).

| Data set | Number of points | Dimen-sionality | $p_i \equiv p(q = i \mid \mathcal{D})$ |
|---|---|---|---|
| Set 2 | 100 | 10 | $p_4 = 0.0231, \mathbf{p_5 = 0.6830}, p_6 = 0.2329, p_7 = 0.0566, p_8 = 0.0043, p_9 = 0.0001$ |
| Set 3 | 100 | 10 | $\mathbf{p_5 = 0.8907}, p_6 = 0.1023, p_7 = 0.0070$ |
| Set 4 | 10000 | 15 | $\mathbf{p_5 = 0.6346}, p_6 = 0.2681, p_7 = 0.0436, p_8 = 0.0532, p_8 = 0.0005$ |

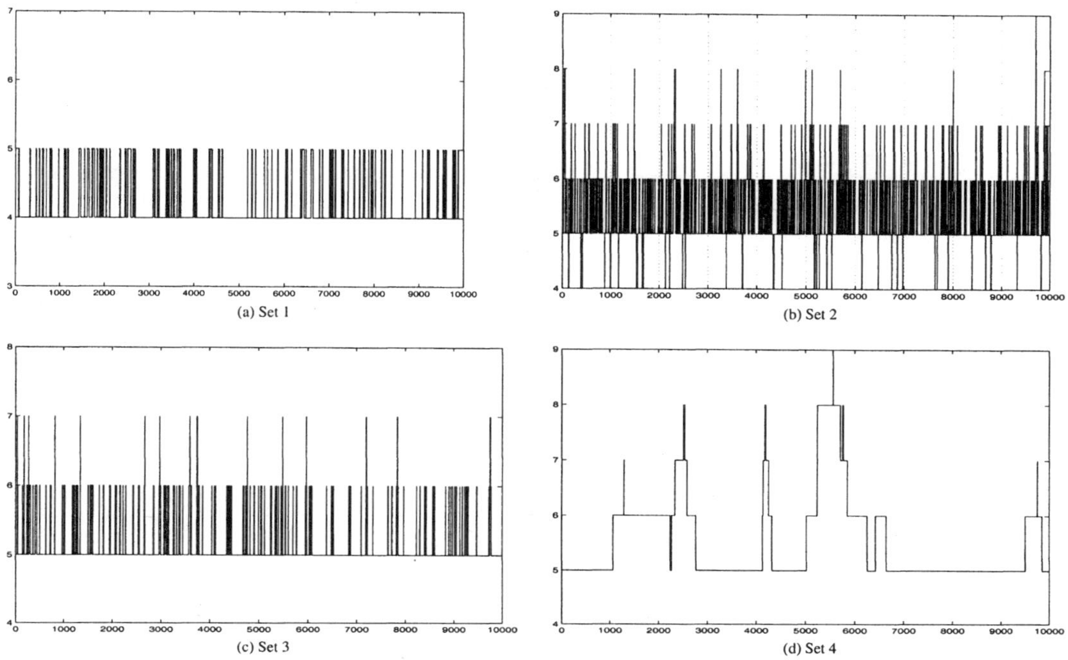

Figure 2: Number of components vs. number of sweeps after the burn-in period of 10,000 sweeps.


Bishop, C. M. 1999a. Bayesian PCA. In *Advances in Neural Information Processing Systems 11*, volume 11, 382–388.

Bishop, C. M. 1999b. Variational principal components. In *Proceedings of the International Conference on Artificial Neural Networks*, volume 1, 509–514.

Cappé, O.; Robert, C. P.; and Rydén, T. 2003. Reversible jump, birth-and-death and more general continuous time Markov chain Monte Carlo samplers. *Journal of the Royal Statistical Society, B* 65:679–700.

Gilks, W. R.; Richardson, S.; and Spiegelhalter, D. J. 1996. *Markov Chain Monte Carlo in Practice*. London: Chapman and Hall.

Green, P. J. 1995. Reversible jump Markov chain Monte Carlo computation and Bayesian model determination. *Biometrika* 82:711–732.

Holmes, C. C., and Mallick, B. K. 1998. Bayesian radial basis functions of variable dimension. *Neural Computation* 10:1217–1233.

Minka, T. P. 2001. Automatic choice of dimensionality for PCA. In *Advances in Neural Information Processing Systems 13*.

Neal, R. M. 1996. *Bayesian Learning for Neural Networks*. New York: Springer-Verlag.

Richardson, S., and Green, P. J. 1997. On Bayesian analysis of mixtures with an unknown number of components (with discussion). *Journal of the Royal Statistical Society Series B* 59:731–792.

Robert, C. P.; Rydén, T.; and Titterington, D. M. 2000. Bayesian inference in hidden Markov models through the reversible jump Markov chain Monte Carlo method. *Journal of the Royal Statistical Society Series B* 62:57–75.

Roberts, S. J.; Holmes, C.; and Denison, D. 2001. Minimum entropy data partitioning using reversible jump Markov chain Monte Carlo. *IEEE Transactions on Pattern Analysis and Machine Intelligence* 23(8):909–915.

Stephens, M. 2000. Bayesian analysis of mixtures with an unknown number of components — an alternative to reversible jump methods. *Annals of Statistics* 28:40–74.

Tipping, M. E., and Bishop, C. M. 1999. Probabilistic principal component analysis. *Journal of the Royal Statistical Society, Series B* 61(3):611–622.

# Error Detection and Impact-Sensitive Instance Ranking in Noisy Datasets

**Xingquan Zhu, Xindong Wu, and Ying Yang**

Department of Computer Science, University of Vermont, Burlington VT 05405, USA
{xqzhu, xwu, yyang}@cs.uvm.edu

## Abstract

Given a noisy dataset, how to locate erroneous instances and attributes and rank suspicious instances based on their impacts on the system performance is an interesting and important research issue. We provide in this paper an Error Detection and Impact-sensitive instance Ranking (*EDIR*) mechanism to address this problem. Given a noisy dataset *D*, we first train a benchmark classifier *T* from *D*. The instances, that cannot be effectively classified by *T* are treated as suspicious and forwarded to a subset *S*. For each attribute $A_i$, we switch $A_i$ and the class label *C* to train a classifier $AP_i$ for $A_i$. Given an instance $I_k$ in *S*, we use $AP_i$ and the benchmark classifier *T* to locate the erroneous value of each attribute $A_i$. To quantitatively rank instances in *S*, we define an impact measure based on the Information-gain Ratio (*IR*). We calculate $IR_i$ between attribute $A_i$ and *C*, and use $IR_i$ as the impact-sensitive weight of $A_i$. The sum of impact-sensitive weights from all located erroneous attributes of $I_k$ indicates its total impact value. The experimental results demonstrate the effectiveness of our strategies.

## 1. Introduction

The goal of inductive learning is to form generalizations from training instances such that the classification accuracy on previously unobserved instances is maximized. This maximum accuracy is usually determined by two most important factors: (1) the quality of the training data; and (2) the inductive bias of the learning algorithm. Given a specific learning algorithm, it is obvious that its classification accuracy depends vitally on the quality of the training data. Basically, the quality of a real-world dataset depends on a number of issues (Wang *et al.* 2001), but the source of the data is a crucial factor. Data entry and acquisition are inherently prone to errors. Unless an organization takes extreme measures in an effort to avoid data errors the field error rates are typically around 5% or more (Orr 1998; Maletic & Marcus 2000).

There have been many approaches for data preprocessing (Maletic & Marcus 2000; Wang *et al.* 2001) and noise handling (Bansal *et al.* 2000; Brodley & Friedl 1999; Gamberger *et al.* 1999; Kubica *et al.* 2003; Little & Rubin 1987; Liu *et al.* 2002; Teng 1999; Wu 1995; Zhu *et al.* 2003) to enhance the data quality, where the enhancement is achieved through noise elimination, missing value prediction, or noisy value correction. Basically, a general noise handling mechanism consists of three important steps: (1) noisy instance identification; (2) erroneous attribute detection; and (3) error treatment.

For errors introduced by missing attribute values, the first two steps are trivial, because the instance itself will explicitly indicate whether it contains noise or not (e.g, a "?" represents a missing attribute value). Therefore, techniques for this type of attribute noise handling mainly focus on predicting correct attribute values (which is called imputation in statistics) by using a decision tree (Shapiro 1987) or other mechanisms (Little & Rubin 1987). If an instance contains an erroneous value, how to distinguish this error becomes a challenging task, because such a noisy instance likely acts as a new training example with valuable information. Teng (1999) proposed a polishing mechanism to correct noisy attribute values by training classifiers for each attribute. However, this correcting procedure tends to introduce new noise when correcting the "suspicious" attributes. A recent research effort from Kubica & Moore (2003) employed probabilistic models to model noise and data generation, in which the trained generative models are used to detect suspicious instances in the dataset. A similar approach was adopted in Schwarm & Wolfman (2000) where a Bayesian model is adopted to identify erroneous attribute values. Unfortunately, since real-word data rarely comply with any generative model, these model-based methods still suffer from a common problem of noise correction: introducing new errors during data correction. Meanwhile, researchers from statistics have also put significant efforts to locate and correct problematic attribute values. Among various solutions from statistics, the Fellegi-Holt editing method (Fellegi & Holt 1976) is the most representative one. To identify and correct errors, this approach takes a set of edits as input, where the edits indicate the rules that attribute values should comply with. For example "age < 16" should not come with "Marital status = Married". The Fellegi-Holt method has the advantage that it determines the minimal number of fields to change (located errors) so that a record satisfies all edits in one pass through the data. This approach has been extended to many editing systems, such as SPEER at the Census Bureau (Greenberg & Petkunas 1990). Unfortunately, the most challenging problem of the Fellegi-Holt method is to find a set of good edits, which turns to be impossible in many situations.

All methods above are efficient in their own scenarios, but some important issues are still open. First of all, due to the fact that noise correction may incur more troubles, such as ignoring outliers or introducing new errors, the reliability of these "automatic" mechanisms is questionable, especially when the users are very serious with their data. On the other hand, for real-world datasets, doing data cleansing "by hand" is completely out of the question given the amount of human labor and time involved. Therefore, the contradiction between them raises a new research issue: how to rank instances' impacts, so that given a certain amount of expenses (e.g, processing time), the data manager can maximize the system performance by putting priority on instances with higher impacts.

In this paper, we provide an error detection and impact-sensitive instance ranking system to address this problem. Our experimental results on real-world datasets will demonstrate the effectiveness of our approach: with datasets from the UCI repository (Blake & Merz 1998), at any noise level (even 50%), our system shows significant effectiveness in locating erroneous attributes and ranking suspicious instances.

## 2. Proposed Algorithms

Our *EDIR* system consists of two major steps: Error Detection and Impact-sensitive Ranking. The system flowchart is depicted in Fig. 1, and the procedures are given in Figs. 2 and 3.

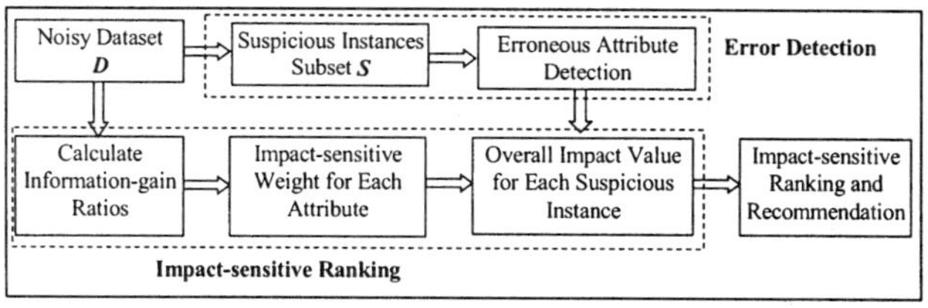


Fig. 1. The flowchart of *EDIR* system

**Procedure:** ***EDIR*** ()
**Input:** Dataset $D$; **Output:** Ranked suspicious instances.
**Parameter:** $K$, # of maximal changes for one instance

(1). $S \leftarrow \phi$; $EA \leftarrow \phi$; $IR \leftarrow \phi$
(2). Train benchmark classifier $T$ from $D$.
(3). For each instance $I_k$ in $D$
(4). If {!*CorrectClassify*($I_k$, $T$) or !*Cover*($I_k$, $T$)}
(5). $S \leftarrow S \cup \{I_k\}$
(6). For each attribute $A_i$
(7). Calculate Information-gain Ratio ($IR_i$) between $A_i$ and $C$
(8). $IR \leftarrow IR \cup \{IR_i\}$
(9). Switch $A_i$ and $C$ to learn $AP_i$ and rule set $AR_i$
(10). Evaluate accuracy of each rule in $AR_i$ on $D$.
(11). For each instance $I_k$ in $S$
(12). $EA_k \leftarrow \phi$; $A\tilde{V}^k \leftarrow \phi$; $CV^k \leftarrow \phi$
(13). For each attribute $A_i$ of $I_k$
(14). Calculate $A\tilde{V}_i^k$ and confidence $CV_i^k$ from $AP_i$
(15). $A\tilde{V}^k \leftarrow A\tilde{V}^k \cup \{A\tilde{V}_i^k\}$; $CV^k \leftarrow CV^k \cup \{CV_i^k\}$
(16). For ($L$=1; $L$<=$K$; $L$++)
(17). If {*ErrorDetection*($I_k$, $L$, $A\tilde{V}^k$, $CV^k$, $T$, &$EA_k$)}
(18). $EA_k \leftarrow$ Located $L$ erroneous attributes
(19). $EA \leftarrow EA \cup \{EA_k\}$
(20). Break
(21). ImpactSensitiveRanking ($S$, $IR$, $EA$) // see Section 2.2

Fig. 2. Error Detection and Impact-sensitive Ranking

**Procedure:** ***ErrorDetection*** ($I_k$, $L$, $A\tilde{V}^k$, $CV^k$, $T$, &$EA_k$)

(1). $EA_k \leftarrow \phi$, $\Omega$ [] $\leftarrow \phi$; *ChgNum* $\leftarrow$ 0; *Iteration* $\leftarrow$ 0; $CV$[] $\leftarrow \phi$
(2). Do { $AV_{i_1}^k \leftarrow A\tilde{V}_{i_1}^k; .., AV_{i_L}^k \leftarrow A\tilde{V}_{i_L}^k$; $A_{i_1},..A_{i_L} \in \Re$;
$A_{i_1},..A_{i_L} \notin \Omega[]$; $A_{i_1} \neq .. \neq A_{i_L}; A_{i_j} \in \forall\Re$
(3). If {*CorrectClassify* ($I_k$, $T$)}
(4). $\Omega[ChgNum] \leftarrow \{A_{i_1},...,A_{i_L}\}$
(5). $CV[ChgNum] = CV_{i_1}^k + ... + CV_{i_L}^k$
(6). *ChgNum*++
(7). Restore old values of $A_{i_1},..A_{i_L}$; *Iteration*++;
(8). } while { *Iteraction* $\leq \binom{N}{L}$}
(9). If {*ChgNum* = 0} Return (0)
(10). Else
(11). $EA_k \leftarrow \Omega$ [l]; $l$=arg{max($CV$[$j$]), $j$=1, 2.., *ChgNum*}
(12). Return (1)

Fig. 3. Erroneous attribute detection

### 2.1 Error Detection

#### 2.1.1 Suspicious Instance Subset Construction

Our first step of error detection is to construct a subset $S$ to separate suspicious instances from the dataset $D$. We first train a benchmark classifier $T$ from $D$, and then use $T$ to evaluate each instance in $D$. The subset $S$ is constructed by using the following criteria, as shown in steps (3) to (5) of Fig. 2.

1. If an instance $I_k$ in $D$ cannot be correctly classified by $T$, we forward it to $S$.
2. If an instance $I_k$ in $D$ does not match any rule in $T$, we forward it to $S$ too.

The proposed mechanism relies on the benchmark classifier (which is also imperfect) trained from the noisy dataset to explore noisy instances. Our experimental analysis has suggested that although the benchmark classifier is not perfect (actually we may never learn a perfect classifier), it can still be relatively reliable to detect some noisy instances.

#### 2.1.2 Erroneous Attribute Detection

Given an instance $I_k$ in $S$, assume $I_k$ contains $N$ attributes $A_1, A_2,.., A_N$ and one class label $C$. Further assume each attribute $A_i$ has $V_i$ possible values. We denote the aggregation of all attributes by $\Re$. To locate erroneous attributes from $I_k$ (where an erroneous attribute means the attribute has an incorrect value), we adopt an Attribute Prediction (*AP*) mechanism, as shown in Figs. 2 and 3.

Basically, Attribute Prediction uses all other attributes $A_1,.. A_j,...A_N$ ($j \neq i$) and the class label $C$ to train a classifier, $AP_i$, for $A_i$ (using instances in $D$). Given an instance $I_k$ in $S$, we use $AP_i$ to predict the value of attribute $A_i$. Assume $I_k$'s current value of $A_i$ is $AV_i^k$, and the predicted value from $AP_i$ is $A\tilde{V}_i^k$. If $AV_i^k$ and $A\tilde{V}_i^k$ are different, it implies that $A_i$ of $I_k$ may possibly contain an incorrect value. Then we use the benchmark classifier $T$ (which is relatively reliable in evaluating noisy instances) to determine whether the predicted value from $AP_i$ makes more sense: If we change $AV_i^k$ to $A\tilde{V}_i^k$, and $I_k$ can be correctly classified by $T$, it will indicate that the change results in a better classification. We therefore conclude that attribute $A_i$ contains an erroneous value. However, if the change still makes $I_k$ incorrectly classified by $T$, we will leave $A_i$ unchanged and try to explore errors from other attributes. If the prediction from each single attribute does not conclude any error, we will start to revise multiple attribute values at the same time. For example, change the values of two attributes $A_i$ (from $AV_i^k$ to $A\tilde{V}_i^k$) and $A_j$ (from $AV_j^k$ to $A\tilde{V}_j^k$) at the same time, and then evaluate whether the multiple changes make sense to $T$. We can iteratively execute the same procedure until a change makes $I_k$ correctly classified by $T$. However, allowing too many changes in one instance may actually have the error detection algorithm make more mistakes. Currently, the *EDIR* system allows to change up to $K$ ($K \leq 3$) attributes simultaneously to locate errors. If all the changes above still make $I_k$ incorrectly resolved by $T$, we will leave $I_k$ unprocessed.

With the proposed error detection algorithm, one important issue should be resolved in advance: which attribute to select if multiple attributes are found to contain errors.

Our solution in solving this problem is to maximize the prediction confidence while locating the erroneous attributes, as shown in Fig. 3. When learning $AP_i$ for each attribute $A_i$, we use a classification rule algorithm, e.g., C4.5rules, to learn an Attribute prediction Rule set ($AR_i$). Assuming the number of rules in $AR_i$ is $M_i$, for each rule $AR_i^r$, $r=1,..M_i$, in $AR_i$, we evaluate its accuracy ($AR_i^r$) on dataset $D$. This accuracy will indicate the confidence that $AR_i^r$ classifies the instance. In our system, we use C4.5rules (Quinlan 1993) to learn the rule set $AR_i$, so the accuracy value has been provided with each learned rule.

When adopting the rule set $AR_i$ to predict the value of $A_i$, we use the first hit mechanism (Quinlan 1993), which means we rank the rules in $AR_i$ in advance, and classify instance $I_k$ by its first coved rule in $AR_i$. Meanwhile, we also use the accuracy of the selected rule as the confidence ($AC_i^k$) of $AP_i$ in predicting $A_i$ of $I_k$.

Given an instance $I_k$, assume the predicted values for each attribute are $A\widetilde{V}_1^k$, .., $A\widetilde{V}_N^k$ respectively, with the confidences for each of them denoted by $AC_1^k,..,AC_N^k$. We first set $L$ to 1 to locate an erroneous attribute by using Eq. (1). If this procedure does not find any erroneous attribute, we increase the value of $L$ by 1 and repeat the same procedure, until we find erroneous attributes or $L$ reaches the maximal allowable changes for one instance ($K$).

$$EA_k = \{A_{i_1},..,A_{i_L}\};\ \arg_{i_1,...,i_L}\{\max\{\sum_{l}^{L} AC_{i_l}^k\};\ CorrectClassify(A\widetilde{V}_{i_1}^k,..,A\widetilde{V}_{i_L}^k,T)=1\}_{\{A_{i_1},..A_{i_l},..A_{i_L}\}\in\Re;\ i_1\neq.i_l,\neq i_L;\ A_{i_l}\in\forall\Re} \quad (1)$$

### 2.1.3 Validity Analysis

Our algorithm above switches each attribute $A_i$ and class $C$ to learn an $AP_i$ classifier, then uses $AP_i$ to locate erroneous attributes. There are two possible concerns with the algorithm: (1) switching $A_i$ and $C$ to learn classifier $AP_i$ does not make much sense to many learning algorithms, because attribute $A_i$ may have very little correlation with other attributes (or not at all); and (2) when the prediction accuracy from $AP_i$ is relative low (e.g., less than 50%), does the algorithm still work? Our experimental results in Section 3 will indicate that even the prediction accuracy from all $AP_i$ classifiers are relatively low, the proposed algorithm can still provide good results.

As we can see from Fig. 3, the prediction from each $AP_i$ classifier just provides a guide for the benchmark classifier $T$ to evaluate whether a change makes the classification better or not. The prediction from $AP_i$ won't be adopted unless $T$ agrees that the value predicted by $AP_i$ will make the instance correctly classified. In other words, the proposed mechanism relies more on $T$ than on any $AP_i$. Even if the prediction accuracy from $AP_i$ is 100%, we won't take its prediction unless it gets the support from $T$. Therefore, a low prediction accuracy from $AP_i$ does not have much influence with the proposed algorithm. However, we obviously prefer a high prediction accuracy from each $AP_i$. Then the question comes to how good $AP_i$ could be with a normal dataset? Actually, the performance of $AP_i$ is inherently determined by correlations among attributes. It is obvious that if all attributes are independent (or conditionally independent given the class $C$), the accuracy of $AP_i$ could be very low, because no attribute could be used to predict $A_i$. However, it has often been pointed out that this assumption is a gross over-simplification in reality, and the truth is that the correlations among attributes extensively exist (Freitas 2001; Shapiro 1987). Instead of taking the assumption of conditional independence, we take the benefits of interactions among attributes, as well as between the attributes and class. Just as we can predict the class $C$ by using the existing attribute values, we can turn the process around and use the class and some attributes to predict the value of another attribute. Therefore, the average accuracy of $AP_i$ classifiers from a normal dataset usually maintains a reasonable level, as shown in Tab. 1.

## 2.2 Impact-sensitive Ranking

To rank suspicious instances by their impacts on the system performance, we define an impact measure based on the Information-gain Ratio ($IR$). We first calculate $IR$ between each attribute $A_i$ and class $C$, and take this value as the impact-sensitive weight ($IW$) for $A_i$. The impact value for each suspicious instance $I_k$, $Impact(I_k)$, is then defined by Eq. (2), which is the sum of the impact-sensitive weights of all located erroneous attributes in $I_k$,

$$Impact(I_k)=\sum_{i=1}^{N} IW(A_i,I_k);\quad IW(A_i,I_k)=\begin{cases} IR_i; & If\ A_i\ contains\ error \\ 0 & otherwise \end{cases} \quad (2)$$

The Information-gain Ratio ($IR$) is one of the most popular correlation measures used in data mining. It was developed from information gain ($IG$) which was initially used to evaluate the mutual information between an attribute and the class (Hunt *et al.* 1966). The recent development from Quinlan (1986) has extended $IG$ to $IR$ to remove the bias caused by the number of attribute values. Since then, $IR$ has become very popular in constructing decision trees or exploring correlations. Due to the space limit of the paper, we omit the technique on calculating $IR$. Interested readers may refer to Quinlan (1986; 1993) for details.

With Eq. (2), instances in $S$ can be ranked by their $Impact(I_k)$ values. Given a dataset with $N$ attributes, the number of different impact values of the whole dataset $D$ is determined by Eq. (3), if we allow the maximal number of changes for one instance to be $K$. For example, a dataset $D$ with $N$=6 and $K$=3 will have $NC(D)$ equal to 41. It seems that $NC(D)$ is not large enough to distinguish each suspicious instance, if the number of suspicious instance in $D$ is larger than 41 (which is likely a normal case). However, in reality, we usually work on a bunch of suspicious instances rather than a single one to enhance the data quality. Therefore it may not be necessary to distinguish the quality of each instance, but to assign suspicious instances into various quality levels. Given the above example, we can separate its suspicious instances into 41 quality levels. From this point of view, it's obvious that this number is large enough to evaluate the quality of instances in $S$.

$$NC(D) = \sum_{l=1}^{K} \binom{N}{l} \quad (3)$$

# 3. Experimental Evaluations

### 3.1 Experiment Settings

The majority of our experiments use C4.5, a program for inducing decision trees (Quinlan 1993). To construct the benchmark classifier $T$ and $AP_i$ classifiers, C4.5rules (Quinlan 1993) is adopted in our system. We have evaluated our algorithms extensively on datasets collected from the UCI data repository (Blake & Merz 1998). Due to the size restrictions, we will mainly report the results on two representative datasets: Monks-3 and Car, because these two datasets have relatively low attribute prediction accuracies, as shown in Tab. 1. If our algorithms achieve good results on these two datasets, they can possibly have good performances on most real-world datasets. In Tab. 1, $AT_i$ represents the average prediction accuracy for attribute $A_i$ (from $AP_i$). For Soybean, Krvskp and Mushroom datasets, we only show the results of the first six attributes. We also report summarized results from these three datasets in Tab. 5.

For most of the datasets that we used, they don't actually contain much noise, so we use manual mechanisms to add attribute noise, where error values are introduced into each attribute with a level $x \cdot 100\%$, and the error corruption for each attribute is independent. To corrupt each attribute $A_i$ with a noise level $x \cdot 100\%$, the value of $A_i$ is assigned a random value approximately $x \cdot 100\%$ of the time, with each alternative value being approximately equally likely to be selected. With this scheme, the actual percentage of noise is always lower than the theoretical noise level, as sometimes the random assignment would pick the original value. Note that, however, even if we exclude the original value from the random assignment, the extent of the effect of noise is still not uniform across all components. Rather, it is dependent on the number of possible values in the attribute. As the noise is evenly distributed among all values, this would have a smaller effect on attributes with a larger number of possible values than those attributes that have only two possible values (Teng 1999). In all figures and tables below, we only show the noise corruption level $x \cdot 100\%$, but not the actual noise level in each dataset.

Tab. 1. The average prediction accuracy for each attribute

| DataSet | $AT_1$(%) | $AT_2$(%) | $AT_3$(%) | $AT_4$(%) | $AT_5$(%) | $AT_6$(%) |
|---|---|---|---|---|---|---|
| Monks-3 | 45.02 | 57.08 | 54.31 | 37.52 | 45.82 | 49.55 |
| Car | 36.48 | 35.47 | 27.68 | 49.57 | 41.24 | 56.5 |
| Soybean | 55.38 | 95.66 | 94.9 | 86.35 | 96.58 | 54.67 |
| Krvskp | 97.74 | 98.63 | 99.17 | 95.59 | 85.92 | 78.98 |
| Mushroom | 46.28 | 55.77 | 44.76 | 100 | 81.25 | 99.79 |

### 3.2 Suspicious Subset Construction

To evaluate the performance of the suspicious subset ($S$) construction, we need to assess the noise level in $S$. Intuitively, the noise level in $S$ should be higher than the noise level in $D$, otherwise the existence of $S$ becomes useless. Also, the size of $S$ should be reasonable (not too large or too small), because a subset with only several instances has a very limited contribution in locating erroneous attributes, even if all instances in $S$ are noise. To this end, we provide the following measures: (1) $S/D$, which is the ratio between the sizes of $S$ and $D$; (2) $I\_S$ and $I\_D$, which are the instance-based noise levels in $S$ and $D$, as defined by Eq. (4); and (3) $A_i\_S$ and $A_i\_D$, which represent the noise levels for attribute $A_i$ in $S$ and $D$, as defined by Eq. (5).

$$I\_X = \#\text{ erroneous instances in } X \,/\, \#\text{ instances in } X \quad (4)$$

$$A_i\_X = \#\text{ instances in } X \text{ with error in } A_i \,/\, \#\text{ instances in } X \quad (5)$$

We have evaluated our suspicious subset construction at different noise levels and provided the results in Tab. 2. Basically, the results indicate that in terms of $S/D$, the proposed algorithm in Section 2.1 has constructed a suspicious subset with a reasonable size. When the noise level increases from 10% to 50%, the size of $S$ also proportionately increases (from 14.17% to 41.07% for the Car dataset), as we have anticipated. If we take a look at the third column with instance-based noise, we can find that the noise level in $S$ is always higher than the noise level in $D$. For the Car dataset, when the noise corruption level is 10%, the noise level in $S$ is about 30% higher than the noise level in $D$. With Monks-3, the noise level in $S$ is significantly higher than $D$. It indicates that with the proposed approach, we can construct a reasonable size of the subset concentrating on noisy instances for further investigation.

The above observations conclude the effectiveness of the proposed approach, but it's still not clear whether $S$ equally captures noise from all attributes or more focuses on some of them. We therefore evaluate the noise level on each attribute, which is shown from columns 5 to 10 in Tab. 2. As we can see, most of the time, the attribute noise level in $S$ ($A_i\_S$) is higher than the noise level in $D$ ($A_i\_D$), which means the algorithm has a good performance on most attributes. However, the algorithm also shows a significant difference in capturing noise from different attributes. For example, the noise level on attributes 2 and 5 in Monks-3 (in $S$) is much higher than the attribute noise level in the original dataset $D$. The reason is that these attributes have significant contributions in constructing the classifier, hence the benchmark classifier $T$ is more sensitive to errors in these attributes. This is actually helpful for us to locate erroneous attributes: if noise in some attributes has less impact with the system performance, we can simply ignore them or put less effort on them.

### 3.3 Erroneous Attribute Detection

To evaluate the performance of our erroneous attribute detection algorithm, we define the following three measures: Error detection Recall ($ER$), Error detection Precision ($EP$), and Error detection Recall for each Attribute ($ERA_i$). Their definitions are given in Eq. (6), where $n_i$, $p_i$ and $d_i$ represent the number of actual errors, the number of correctly located errors and the number of located errors in $A_i$ respectively.

$$ER = \sum_{i=1}^{N} ERA_i,\ ERA_i = \frac{p_i}{n_i};\qquad EP = \sum_{i=1}^{N} EPA_i,\ EPA_i = \frac{p_i}{d_i} \quad (6)$$

We provide the results in Tab. 3, which are evaluated at three noise levels (from 10% to 50%). As we can see from the third column ($EP$) of Tab. 3, the overall error detection precision is pretty attractive, even with the datasets (Monks-3 and Car) that have low attribute prediction accuracies. On average, the precision is maintained at 70%, which means most located erroneous attributes actually contain errors. We have also provided the experimental results from other three datasets in Tab. 5. All these results prove the reliability of the proposed error detection algorithm.

Tab. 2. Suspicious subset construction results

| Dataset | Noise Level | S/D | Instance Noise | | $AT_1$ Noise | | $AT_2$ Noise | | $AT_3$ Noise | | $AT_4$ Noise | | $AT_5$ Noise | | $AT_6$ Noise | |
|---|---|---|---|---|---|---|---|---|---|---|---|---|---|---|---|---|
| | | | $I\_D$ | $I\_S$ | $A_1\_D$ | $A_1\_S$ | $A_2\_D$ | $A_2\_S$ | $A_3\_D$ | $A_3\_S$ | $A_4\_D$ | $A_4\_S$ | $A_5\_D$ | $A_5\_S$ | $A_6\_D$ | $A_6\_S$ |
| Monks-3 | 10% | 6.29 | 32.41 | 97.09 | 6.04 | 6.71 | 6.45 | 44.85 | 4.58 | 5.21 | 6.43 | 9.96 | 7.49 | 54.92 | 5.62 | 5.34 |
| | 30% | 17.14 | 71.06 | 94.78 | 20.22 | 20.95 | 20.33 | 51.46 | 14.94 | 15.83 | 20.75 | 22.29 | 21.63 | 49.2 | 14.73 | 16.02 |
| | 50% | 33.42 | 89.45 | 95.68 | 32.61 | 33.18 | 33.52 | 54.36 | 25.3 | 25.74 | 33.07 | 33.72 | 38.11 | 53.25 | 24.8 | 25.27 |
| Car | 10% | 14.17 | 36.3 | 64.14 | 7.51 | 14.25 | 7.73 | 14.15 | 7.86 | 8.65 | 6.87 | 16.85 | 6.72 | 9.75 | 6.66 | 18.6 |
| | 30% | 33.71 | 76.32 | 85.97 | 22.71 | 26.78 | 22.75 | 26.35 | 22.52 | 22.69 | 19.95 | 28.47 | 20.56 | 21.21 | 20.02 | 29.78 |
| | 50% | 41.07 | 92.06 | 96.61 | 36.82 | 39.45 | 36.42 | 38.67 | 37.65 | 37.27 | 33.29 | 40.71 | 32.56 | 34.64 | 33.52 | 42.79 |

Obviously, having a high precision is only a partial advantage of the algorithm. A system that predicts only one error is likely useless, even if its precision is 100%. We therefore evaluate the error detection recall (*ER*), as shown on columns 4 to 10 in Tab. 3. On average, the algorithm can locate about 10% of errors. Meanwhile, for different attributes, the $ERA_i$ values vary significantly. For example, when the noise level is 30%, the $ERA_1$ for Monks-3 is about 5.4% which is much less than the value (about 24%) of attribute 2. If we go further to analyze the correlations between attributes and the class, we can find that the proposed algorithm actually has a good performance in locating errors for some important attributes. For example, among all attributes in Monks-3, attribute 2 has the highest correlation with class *C*, and its recall value ($ERA_2$) also turns out to be the highest.

Just looking at the *ER* values may make us worry that the algorithm has missed too much noise (90% of errors). We'd like to remind the readers that from the data correction point of view, having a higher precision is usually more important, because an algorithm should avoid introducing more errors when locating or correcting existing errors. Actually, the 10% located errors likely bring more troubles than others (because they obviously cannot be handled by the benchmark classifier *T*). Our experimental results in the next subsection will indicate that correcting this part of the errors will improve the system performance significantly.

Tab. 3. Erroneous attribute detection results

| Data Set | Noise Level | *EP* | *ER* | $ERA_1$ | $ERA_2$ | $ERA_3$ | $ERA_4$ | $ERA_5$ | $ERA_6$ |
|---|---|---|---|---|---|---|---|---|---|
| Monks-3 | 10% | 84.61 | 7.18 | 0.68 | 24.08 | 0.94 | 1.07 | 15.22 | 1.08 |
| | 30% | 77.08 | 11.36 | 5.41 | 24.01 | 4.34 | 6.09 | 20.9 | 7.45 |
| | 50% | 80.58 | 10.54 | 5.61 | 22.21 | 6.35 | 6.17 | 16.58 | 6.57 |
| Car | 10% | 65.84 | 11.35 | 7.31 | 6.91 | 3.43 | 21.91 | 4.85 | 23.69 |
| | 30% | 71.43 | 11.17 | 8.25 | 7.58 | 4.56 | 21.5 | 6.18 | 18.97 |
| | 50% | 73.29 | 8.55 | 6.05 | 6.2 | 5.78 | 14.11 | 5.54 | 13.62 |

### 3.4 Impact-sensitive Instance Ranking

We evaluate the performance of the proposed impact-sensitive instance ranking mechanism in Section 2.2 from three aspects: training accuracy, test accuracy and the size of the constructed decision tree. Obviously, it's hard to evaluate the ranking quality instance by instance, because one instance likely does not impact too much with the system performance. We therefore separate the ranked instances into three tiers, each tier consisting of 30% of instances from the top to the bottom of the ranking. Intuitively, correcting instances in the first tier will produce a bigger improvement than correcting instances in any of the other two tiers, because instances in the first tier have more negative impacts (with relatively larger impact values), so does the second tier to the third tier. Accordingly, we manually correct the instances in each tier (because we know which instance was corrupted, the manual correction has a 100% accuracy), and compare the system performances on the corrected dataset and the original dataset.

We evaluate the system performance at three noise levels and provide results in Tab. 4, where "Org" means the performance (training, test accuracy and tree size) from the original dataset (*D*), and "Fst", "Snd" and "Thd" indicate the performance of only correcting instances in the first, second and third tier respectively.

From Tab. 4, we can find that at any noise level, correcting instances in the first tier always results in a better performance than correcting instances in any of the other two tiers, so does the second tier to the third tier. For example, with the Car dataset at 30% noise level, correcting instances at the first tier will achieve 0.7% and 2.3% more improvements with the test accuracy than correcting instances in the second and third tiers. In terms of the decision tree size, the improvement is even more significant. It proves that our system provides an effective way to automatically locate errors, and rank them by their negative impacts (danger levels). So we can put more emphasis on instances in the top tier than those in the bottom tier.

When comparing the performances from each tier with the performance from the original dataset, we find that correcting recommended instances has a significant improvement, especially when the noise level goes higher. For example, with the Car dataset at 30% noise level, correcting instances at any tier will contribute a 2.1% (or more) improvement with the test accuracy. This also proves the effectiveness of our *EDIR* system in enhancing the data quality, even in high noise-level environments.

When using *EDIR* as a whole system for noise detection and data correction, we'd like to know its performance in comparison with other approaches, such as random sampling. We therefore perform the following experiments. Given a dataset *D*, we use *EDIR* to recommend α% of instances in *D* for correction. For comparison, we also randomly sample α% of instances in *D* for correction. We compare the test accuracies from these two mechanisms (because the comparison of the test accuracies is likely more objective), and report the results in Fig. 4 (b) to Fig. 4 (g), where "*Org*", "*EDIR*" and "*Rand*" represent the performances from the original dataset, the corrected dataset by *EDIR* and the random sampling mechanism respectively. We have evaluated the results by setting $\alpha{\cdot}100\%$ to four levels: 5%, 10%, 15% and 20%. In Tab. 5, we provide summarized results from other three datasets by setting $\alpha{\cdot}100\%$ to 5%. The results from Fig. 4 indicate that when the value of $\alpha$ increases, the performances of *EDIR* and *Rand* both get better. This does not surprise us, because when recommending more and more instances for correction, we actually lower the overall noise level in the dataset, therefore better performances could be achieved. However, the interesting point is that when comparing "*EDIR*" and "Rand", we can find that *EDIR* always has a better performance than *Rand.*

Tab. 4. Impact-sensitive instance ranking results

| DataSet | Noise Level | Training Accuracy (%) | | | | Test Accuracy (%) | | | | Tree Size | | | |
|---|---|---|---|---|---|---|---|---|---|---|---|---|---|
| | | Org | Fst | Snd | Thd | Org | Fst | Snd | Thd | Org | Fnt | Sed | Thd |
| Monks-3 | 10% | 94.31 | 96.27 | 95.9 | 95.48 | 97.45 | 98.94 | 98.52 | 98.13 | 29.2 | 26.1 | 27.8 | 28.6 |
| | 30% | 86.44 | 90.23 | 89.98 | 89.07 | 88.06 | 92.17 | 91.58 | 91.37 | 76.1 | 60.8 | 63.3 | 66.1 |
| | 50% | 81.73 | 86.37 | 85.84 | 84.96 | 76.09 | 82.64 | 82.01 | 81.09 | 112.8 | 93.9 | 101.5 | 107.6 |
| Car | 10% | 90.25 | 92.73 | 92.2 | 91.86 | 87.77 | 90.44 | 89.62 | 89.04 | 250.2 | 215.8 | 225.6 | 232.5 |
| | 30% | 83.77 | 86.9 | 86.32 | 86.14 | 76.77 | 80.98 | 80.21 | 78.69 | 394.1 | 363.3 | 375.2 | 391.3 |
| | 50% | 80.76 | 83.51 | 82.8 | 82.09 | 69.37 | 74.59 | 73.18 | 72.66 | 463.7 | 415.2 | 429.4 | 437 |

Actually, most of the time, the results from *EDIR* by recommending 5% of instances are still better than using *Rand* to recommend 20% of instances. For example, when *EDIR* recommends 5% of instances for correction, the test accuracy for the Car dataset at 10% noise level is 88.51%, which is still better than the results (88.11%) of using *Rand* to recommend 20% of instances. The same conclusion can be drawn from most other datasets. It indicates that *EDIR* has a significantly good performance in locating and recommending suspicious instances to enhance the data quality.

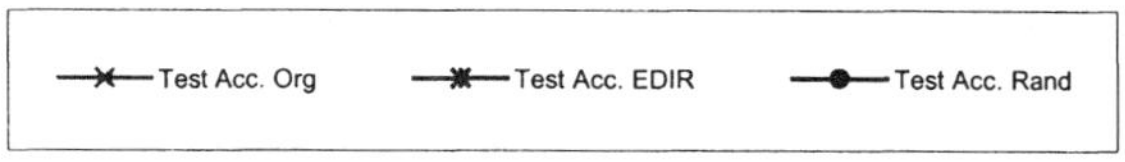


(a) Meaning of each curve in Fig. 4 (b) to Fig. 4 (g)

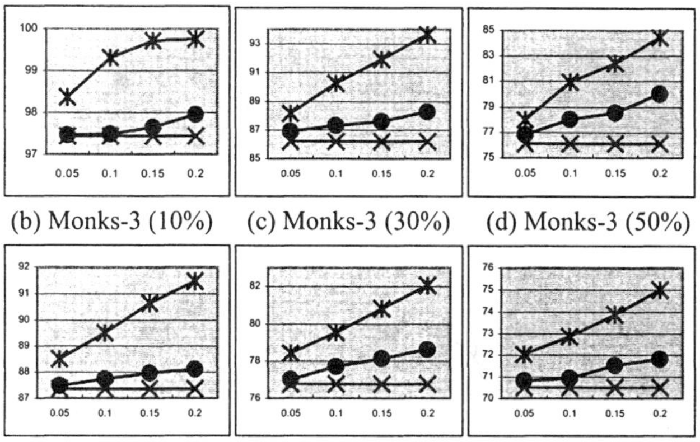

(b) Monks-3 (10%) (c) Monks-3 (30%) (d) Monks-3 (50%)

(e) Car (10%) (f) Car (30%) (g) Car (50%)

Fig. 4. Experimental comparisons of *EDIR* and random sampling approaches from three noise levels: 10%, 30% and 50%

In Figs. 4 (b) to (g), the *x*-axis denotes the percentage of recommended data ($\alpha$) and the *y*-axis represents the test accuracy.

Tab. 5. Experimental summary from other three datasets ($\alpha$=0.05)

| Data Set | Noise Level | *EP* | *ER* | Test Accuracy | | | Tree Size | | |
|---|---|---|---|---|---|---|---|---|---|
| | | | | *Org* | *EDIR* | *Rand* | *Org* | *EDIR* | *Rand* |
| Soybean | 10% | 88.51 | 10.4 | 86.23 | 86.99 | 86.23 | 424.7 | 407.2 | 418.9 |
| | 30% | 87.23 | 12.66 | 76.18 | 77.14 | 76.25 | 496.8 | 485.3 | 497.1 |
| | 50% | 84.17 | 9.42 | 57.44 | 61.64 | 58.09 | 532.1 | 526 | 532.8 |
| Krvskp | 10% | 76.57 | 10.56 | 95.22 | 96.78 | 95.89 | 500.2 | 379.5 | 466.4 |
| | 30% | 72.33 | 8.69 | 80.23 | 85.94 | 82.66 | 986.8 | 887.1 | 964 |
| | 50% | 71.08 | 6.83 | 67.65 | 79.41 | 70.78 | 1096 | 998.3 | 1072 |
| Mushroom | 10% | 90.28 | 9.79 | 99.89 | 100 | 99.97 | 545 | 322 | 529 |
| | 30% | 84.33 | 7.48 | 99.21 | 99.97 | 99.32 | 1644 | 1126 | 1620 |
| | 50% | 81.49 | 7.04 | 98.32 | 99.82 | 99.11 | 3060 | 2383 | 2935 |

## 4. Conclusions

In this paper, we have presented an *EDIR* system, which automatically locates erroneous instances and attributes and ranks suspicious instances according to their impact values. The experimental results have demonstrated the effectiveness of our proposed algorithms for error detection and impact-sensitive ranking. By adopting the proposed *EDIR* system, correcting the instances with higher ranks always results in a better performance than correcting those with lower ranks. The novel features that distinguish our work from existing approaches are threefold: (1) we provided an error detection algorithm for both instances and attributes; (2) we explored a new research topic on impact-sensitive instance ranking, which can be very useful in guiding the data manager to enhance the data quality with minimal expenses; and (3) by combining error detection and impact-sensitive ranking, we have constructed an effective data recommendation system. It's more efficient than the manual approach and more reliable than automatic correction algorithms.

## Acknowledgement


This research has been supported by the U.S. Army Research Laboratory and the U.S. Army Research Office under grant number DAAD19-02-1-0178.


## References


Bansal, N., Chawla, S., & Gupta, A., (2000), Error correction in noisy datasets using graph mincuts, *Technical Report, CMU.*

Blake, C.L. & Merz, C.J. (1998), *UCI Repository of machine learning databases.*

Brodley, C.E. & Friedl, M.A. (1999), Identifying mislabeled training data, *J. of Artificial Intelligence Research*, 11: 131-167.

Greenberg, B. & Petkunas, T. (1990), SPEER: structured programs for economic editing and referrals, *American Statistical Asso., Proc. of the 1990 Section on Survey Research Methods.*

Fellegi, I. P. & D. Holt, (1976), A systematic approach to automatic edit and imputation, *Journal of the American Statistical Association*, vol.71, pp.17-35.

Freitas, A., (2001), Understanding the crucial role of attribute interaction in data mining, *AI Review*, 16(3):177-199.

Gamberger, D., Lavrac, N., & Groselj C. (1999), Experiments with noise filtering in a medical domain, *Proc. of 16th ICML*, CA.

Hunt, E. B., Martin, J. Stone, P. (1966), *Experiments in Induction.* Academic Press, New York.

Kubica, J. & Moore A., (2003), Probabilistic noise identification and data cleaning, *Proc. of ICDM*, FL, USA.

Little, R.J.A. & Rubin, D.B. (1987), *Statistical analysis with missing data*, Wiley, New York.

Liu, X., Cheng, G., & Wu, J. (2002), Analyzing outliers cautiously, *IEEE Trans. on TKDE*, 14:432-437.

Maletic J. & Marcus A. (2000), Data cleansing: Beyond integrity analysis, *Proc. of Information Quality*, pp. 200–209.

Orr, K., (1998), Data quality and systems theory, *CACM,* 41 (2):66-71.

Quinlan, J.R. (1986). Induction of decision trees. *Machine Learning*, 1(1): 81-106.

Quinlan, J.R. (1993). *C4.5: programs for machine learning*, Morgan Kaufmann, San Mateo, CA.

Schwarm S. & Wolfman S., (2000), Cleaning data with Bayesian methods, *Technical Report, University of Washington.*

Shapiro A. (1987), *Structured induction in expert systems*, Addison-wesley.

Teng M. T., (1999), Correcting noisy data, *Proc. of 16th ICML.*

Wang R., Ziad M., & Lee Yang, (2001), *Data quality*, Kluwer.

Wu, X. (1995), *Knowledge acquisition from database*, Ablex Pulishing Corp., USA.

Zhu, X., Wu, X. & Chen Q. (2003). Eliminating class noise in large datasets, *Proc. of 20th ICML*, Washington D.C., USA.

# Natural Language Processing and Information Extraction

# Comparing Cognitive and Computational Models of Narrative Structure

**David B. Christian and R. Michael Young**

Department of Computer Science,
North Carolina State University, Campus Box 7535
Raleigh, NC, 27695
dbchrist@ncsu.edu, young@csc.ncsu.edu

### Abstract

A growing number of applications seek to incorporate automatically generated narrative structure into interactive virtual environments. In this paper, we evaluate a representation for narrative structure generated by an automatic planning system by 1) mapping the plans that control plot into conceptual graphs used by QUEST, an existing framework for question-answering analysis that includes structures for modeling a reader's narrative comprehension and 2) using methods originally employed by QUEST's developers to determine if the plan structures can serve as effective models of the understanding that human users form after viewing corresponding stories played out within a virtual world. Results from our analysis are encouraging, though additional work is required to expand the plan language to cover a broader class of narrative structure.

## Introduction

Detailed, immersive 3D virtual environments are increasingly commonplace in applications ranging from entertainment to social interaction to education and training. While many of these virtual environments include a narrative, the interaction within them is generally prescripted with little dynamic capability. Recent work (André, Rist, & Müller, 1998, Cavazza, Charles & Mead, 2002, Young & Riedl, 2003) seeks to develop algorithms that dynamically generate narratives for such environments. To date, however, there has been little effort to verify that the computational structures created to control interactive narratives correspond to mental models formed by people when comprehending activity within conventional story worlds (e.g., narrative texts).

We are currently developing *Mimesis*, a system that will automatically generate an internal description of the actions
composing a narrative's plot, then use that representation to
drive the action of characters within a 3D gaming environment (Young and Riedl, 2003). The action sequences used in Mimesis are automatically created by an artificial intelligence (AI) planning system called DPOCL (Young, Pollack & Moore, 1994), described briefly in the following section. The research we describe here seeks to measure the correspondence between the data structures that Mimesis generates to represent plot and the mental models that people form when observing the action sequences as they are played out within the 3D story world.

To evaluate the correspondence between DPOCL plans and the mental models that users of our system form regarding an unfolding narrative, we first defined a mapping from DPOCL elements onto a subset of the conceptual graph structures that model narrative defined by Graesser, *et al,* in their work on QUEST, a psychological model of question answering (Graesser & Clark, 1985, Graesser & Franklin, 1990). Next, we generated a DPOCL plan capable of driving a story within our virtual environment and, using the mapping, determined the graph structure corresponding to the plan.

We then had human subjects view a video of the plan as it executed within a 3D virtual world, and asked them to rate the appropriateness of answers to questions regarding the story they had viewed. Their ratings were compared to QUEST's ratings of the same answers, a technique similar to that used in the evaluation of the QUEST algorithms themselves (Graesser, Lang, & Roberts, 1991). The results of the small-scale study are encouraging, indicating a strong correspondence between a number of features of both plans and the intended mental models users form.

## Background

### DPOCL Plan Structure

In this work, we represent the action that unfolds within a narrative-oriented virtual environment using a *plan*, a data structure completely characterizing the actions that occur in the story and the specification of the role that characters, objects and locations play in those actions. Plans and the planning systems that produce them have been widely studied in artificial intelligence research, though they are typically are used to describe specifications of real-world action sequences.

The plan structures we employ are those produced by the DPOCL planner (Young, Pollack and Moore, 1994).

Table 1: QUEST Knowledge Structure (QKS) Arc Types

| Arc Type | Description (A -> B) | Narrative Structure Equivalent |
|---|---|---|
| Consequence | A causes or enables B | Actions have effects, which are state changes. Events cannot yet cause other events. |
| Implies | A implies B, semi-logical reasoning | Syllogistic reasoning is outside of scope, goal equivalency is handled through causal links from actions to goal states |
| Reason | B is a reason or motive for A<br>B is a superordinate goal of A | Causal links – basic plan components – embody reasons for actions |
| Outcome | B specifies whether or not the goal A is achieved | In simple plan sctructures, goals are always achieved |
| Initiate | A initiates or triggers the goal in B | Not covered (plans for future coverage) |
| Manner | B specifies the manner in which A occurs | Not covered (plans for future coverage) |

DPOCL plans are composed of *steps* corresponding to the actions that occur in a story; DPOCL uses the approach used by STRIPS (Fikes & Nilsson, 1971) to represent individual actions.

In DPOCL, each step is defined by a set of *preconditions*, the conditions in the world that must hold immediately prior to the step's execution in order for the step to succeed, and a set of *effects*, the conditions in the world that are altered by the successful execution of the action. In addition to a set of steps, a DPOCL plan contains a set of *temporal constraints* defining a partial temporal ordering on the execution of the plan's steps and a set of *causal links* connecting pairs of steps. Two steps *s1* and *s2* are connected by a causal link with associated condition *c* just when *c* is an effect of *s1* and a precondition of *s2* and the establishment of *c* by *s1* is used in the plan to ensure that *c* holds at *s2*. Further, DPOCL plans contain information about the hierarchical structure of a plan, similar to the representation used by hierarchical task network (HTN) planners (Sacerdotti, 1977). In DPOCL, each abstract step in a plan is connected to a set of more primitive steps that represent a sub-plan for achieving the abstract action's effects. Overall, DPOCL plans contain a fair amount of causal, hierarchical and temporal structure. This structure is added by the planning algorithm in order to guarantee that a plan is *sound*, that is, that, when executed, the plan is guaranteed to achieve it's goals. Recent work (Ratterman, et al, 2002, Young, 1999) suggests that this structure as well as the techniques used by the DPOCL algorithm to create it, make for effective models of human plan reasoning.

## The QUEST Knowledge Structure

Graesser has developed a framework for representing the cognitive structures built by readers while reading texts (Graesser & Clark, 1985). Graesser's model is based on conceptual graph structures, which contain concept nodes and connective arcs. These graphs, referred to here as *QUEST knowledge structures* (QKSs), are used to describe the reader's conception of a narrative text and related general knowledge (Graesser & Clark, 1985). QKSs can be combined and traversed in order to make predictions relating to an idealized reader's conception of a text (Graesser & Clark, 1985; Graesser & Franklin, 1990; Graesser & Hemphill, 1991; Graesser, Lang & Roberts, 1991).

A QKS consists of "statement" nodes connected by directed arcs. Both nodes and arcs are typed based on their meaning and purpose. Below is a short description of the statement nodes and relational arcs; the references above provide a complete discussion.

Statement nodes contain individual pieces of data within a QKS. Statement nodes contain either a simple sentence (e.g. of the form *<subject> <verb> <simple predicate>*) or any number of combinations of such sentences (e.g. "x saw P1" where P1 = *<subject> <verb> <simple predicate>*). These statement nodes are categorized into state, event, goal, style, and concept nodes. A *state* node describes a part of the world-state that can be assumed to remain true unless explicitly changed. An *event* node describes the changing of a state, with or without intention. *Goal* nodes describe the desire of an agent, although such goals do not have to be conscious. Any action taken intentionally has a corresponding goal and node.

Relational arcs connect statement nodes within the QKS, and by doing so describe how the narrative data represented within the QKS are cognitively linked. The six arc types that are crucial to event-oriented storytelling are displayed and described in Table 1 (1991). These arcs focus on events and the reasoning of characters, which constitute most of basic story telling.

## Comparing Computational and Cognitive Structures

To determine whether or not DPOCL plans are cognitively plausible models of a user's understanding of a narrative controlled by those same plans, we developed a mapping from the DPOCL plan representation onto an existing, well-understood cognitive model, namely Graesser's QKS. We then tested whether a correspondence existed between the user's responses to questions about the plan-based QKS and the responses of the QUEST model. The mapping from DPOCL to QKS and the specifics of the experiment to determine the model's effectiveness are described below.

Let $n$ be the number of top-level goals of plan $P$ and $m$ be the number of steps in $P$, then

1. Create a total ordering $o$ for the $m$ steps in $P$ consistent with $P$'s partial ordering over its steps.
2. For each of $P$'s top-level goals $g_i$, $i = 1, .., n$, convert $g_i$ into a goal node $G_i$.
3. For each plan step $s_j$ in $P$, starting with the last step in $o$
   3.1 Convert $s_j$ into a goal node $G_j$ and an event node $E_j$
   3.2 Link $G_j$ to $E_j$ with an outcome arc
   3.3 For each effect $e$ of $s_j$, add a state node $S$ listing $e$ and link $E_j$ to $S$ by a consequence arc
4. For each causal link in $P$ connecting two steps $s_1$ and $s_2$ with condition $c$, connect the state node $S$ created for $s_1$ and $c$ in 3.3 to the event node $E$ createad for step $s_2$ in 3.2
5. Number the nodes based on the total order $o$, using a depth-first algorithm for numbering sub-plan goals
6. For each causal link in $P$ connecting two steps $s_1$ and $s_2$, find the goal nodes $G_1$ and $G_2$ created for $s_1$ and $s_2$ in 3.2. If G1 has a lower node number than $G_2$, connect $G_1$ to $G_2$ with a reason arc.

Figure 1: Mapping a plan structure to QUEST

## Mapping a DPOCL Plan Structure to a QKS

The translation of plans to QKSs is not straightforward due to the expressivity of the QKS and the relative rigidity of plan structures. As noted, plan structures only have one type of arc (the causal link) and one type of node (the plan step) compared to Graesser's many. D espite these difficulties, it is possible to map a standard DPOCL plan structure into a simple yet functional QKS. Figure 1 describes the algorithm to perform this task. The resulting QKS is regularly structured, and is related in form and content to what Graesser calls a goal-oriented substructure (Graesser & Clark, 1985).

This mapping relies on the idea that many of Graesser's arc types have a simple corollary within DPOCL. Table 1 shows a listing of each arc type and its equivalent (or lack thereof) in a standard plan structure. This initial mapping includes only outcome, consequence, and reason arcs. The generated QKS is also limited to the actions of a single character, which makes for a relatively simplistic narrative. Future work will seek to expand the DPOCL plan representation and the mapping algorithm to address these limitations.

## Experimental Evaluation

We wish to test whether the QKS generated by the automatic mapping from a DPOCL plan can be used as an effective means of predicting the "goodness of answers" (GOA) to why, how, and "what enabled" questions regarding the story that the plan describes. If QUEST's predictor variables perform as expected, it would be a strong indication that DPOCL plan structures can serve as an effective model of an idealized user's understanding of the narrative. The hypotheses and methods we use are modeled after Graesser's own tests of the QUEST algorithm's predictive ability (Graesser, Lang, & Roberts 1991): Participants watch a video, rate the goodness of answers (GOA) to questions about that video, and their responses are compared to the QUEST algorithm's predictions.

### QUEST Predictor Variables

Goodness of answer (GOA) ratings are key to Graesser's validation of the QUEST model, and obtaining estimates of these ratings is the purpose of the QUEST predictor variables. There are three major predictor variables which are correlated to the goodness of an answer: an arc search procedure, the structural distance between the question and answer nodes, and constraint satisfaction. Their numeric values are calculated for a question/answer pair, and can then be used to predict human GOA ratings, or the likelihood that an answer will be produced when asked a given question (Graesser & Hemphill, 1991; Graesser, Lang, & Roberts, 1991; Golding, Graesser & Millis, 1990).

The *arc search procedure* differs depending on the question category. In all cases, certain types of arcs are traversed in certain directions starting from the question node. If a node can be reached via those arcs, it is considered to pass the arc search procedure, and receives a value of 1. Otherwise, it receives a value of 0.

The *structural distance* measures the number of arcs that must be traversed to reach the answer node from the question node. If a legal path is found using the appropriate arc search procedure, then the shortest legal path length is used. Otherwise, the shortest path length is used.

The *constraint satisfaction* measurement is an averaging of several variables including argument overlap, temporal compatibility, planning compatibility, plausibility, and causal strength. The value ranges from 0 to 1. For a complete description, see Graesser, Lang, & Roberts (1991).

Table 2: A Sample Training Session Guide

| |
|---|
| You are in a long hall, called the "lava room". Look around with the mouse to see what is in the lava room. In this training session, your job is to raise and then cross the bridge across the lava, which is now lowered. To raise and lower the bridge, you must use your hand on the hand symbol on the left-hand wall. The hand symbol is close to the lava on the same side as the power switch. The hand symbol for operating the bridge does not appear and the bridge does not work unless the power is on. You can turn on the power by using your hand on the yellow power switch. Cross the raised bridge to complete this training session. |

### Method

**Participants.** 15 computer science undergraduates from NC State University were given course extra credit participating in this study. The participants were randomly assigned into one of three subject groups. Each group was asked to rate answers in one of three different categories: answers to "how", "why", or "what enabled" questions.

**Materials.** Participants first completed five training sessions within a virtual environment in order to familiarize themselves with the rules for action within the story world. Each training session required a subject to control a character via the mouse and keyboard. Participants were required to use their character to successfully perform a task composed of individual actions that also made up the story plans they would later observe being executed. Table 2 contains one training session guide, and Fig. 2 contains DPOCL step descriptions defined in the story world.

The 3D story world in which participants interacted modeled a four-room section of a spaceship. Rooms were connected by airlock doors, elevators and drawbridges with simple touch-activated controls. Actions in the story world typically had several preconditions and effects (e.g., the power must be on in order for a machine to process raw materials into medical supplies, pressing the drawbridge control button raises or lowers the bridge).

After the participants completed the five training sessions, they were shown a video that showed the execution of a DPOCL plan by a character acting in the same environment. The story involved the character processing raw materials into medical supplies and delivering them into another room. The video was derived from a plan with 20 actions; using our mapping algorithm this plan expanded into a 71 node QKS with 23 event/goal pairs and 25 state changes.

| **Name:**<br>RaiseBridge(Bridge)<br>**Preconditions:**<br>Lowered(Bridge)<br>PowerOn(Ship)<br>**Effects:**<br>Raised(Bridge) | **Name:**<br>CrossBridgeEast(Bridge)<br>**Preconditions:**<br>Not(Lowered(Bridge))<br>In(EastLavaRoom)<br>**Effects:**<br>In(WestLavaRoom) |
|---|---|

Figure 2: DPOCL Operators for the RaiseBridge and CrossBridge Actions

Seven event nodes and three state nodes from this QKS were chosen from the QKS as the basis for ten questions posed to the participants. The seven chosen event nodes were "cross the bridge," "raise the lift," "close the door from the medicine room to the hallway," "get the keycard," "turn on the power," "go from the lift to the elevated area," and "exit the lift into the medicine room." The three chosen state nodes were "have the medicine's ingredients," "the keycard door was open," and "the door from the hallway to the lava room was open." These nodes were turned into the appropriate questions by putting "Why did the protagonist," or "how did the protagonist," or "what enabled the protagonist to," etc., in front of the node's description.

For each question node, 16 answer nodes were chosen, leading to 160 question/answer pairs. In Graesser's experiment, he used answers previously given to related questions in a previous experiment as a pool from which to draw his answer nodes. However, we did not have such a resource. Because Graesser's earlier experiments showed that the structural distance between the question and answer nodes was a key factor in determining the goodness of an answer and it was a straightforward measure, we picked at random eight nodes with a structural distance of three or less, and eight other nodes from throughout QKS.

Similar to Graesser's study, nodes that were part of a goal/event pair were described as a goal (e.g. "because she *wanted* to open the door"), if the event described in the answer occurs after the event described in the question node and as an event (e.g. "because she *opened* the door) otherwise. Answer nodes that described state changes were described as goals (e.g., "because she wanted the door to be open") if they had not happened yet, and as states ("because the door was open") otherwise. These descriptions were chosen order to give every action in the story its best chance of being rated as a good answer. The answer nodes were described in the same was for every phrasing of question, with the exception that "Because" was placed in front of the answers to why questions. Twelve answer nodes were thrown out because their wording did not follow these rules exactly, meaning that 148 question/answer pairs are used for all further analysis.

**Procedure.** The participants proceeded through the training sessions at their own pace. When they completed all five training sessions, they were told that they would be shown a video that took place in a similar world to the one they had just been working in. They were given the following back story, in order to express the initial goals of the narrative: "The video shows a woman who wants to bring some medicine from the medicine room to the small final room on the other side of the keycard door." They were told they could watch the video as many times as they wanted to, and that they should watch it carefully as they would be asked questions about it afterwards.

After the participants were finished with the video, it was explained that they would be rating answers to questions about the video they had just seen. The difference between good answers and bad answers was explained as described in Graesser, Lang, & Roberts (1991). However, no practice items were given. Participants rated the answers on a fourpoint scale, where answers could be a) bad answer to the question, b) possibly an acceptable answer, c) moderately good answer, or d) very good answer. Participants were timed as in Graesser's studies (Graesser, Lang, & Roberts, 1991) in order to preserve the format of the experiment, but those numbers were not used in our analysis.

**Predictor Variables**. Graesser used seven predictor variables with QUEST in order to examine whether the three main components of the QUEST algorithm were significant predictors of goodness of answer (GOA) ratings. However, the four auxiliary predictor variables are not relevant or calculable for this study. Therefore we examined only the three central components of QUEST: the arc search procedure, structural distance, and constraint satisfaction. These components are described below.

*Arc search procedure.* Answers receive a 1 if there is at least one legal path to an answer using Graesser's arc search procedures for goal hierarchies, and a 0 otherwise. Because state nodes play a larger role in plan structures converted to QKSs, subordinate state changes were included in the arc search procedure wherever Graesser included subordinate actions. The mean arc-search procedure ratings were .22, .12, and .57 for why-, how- and enable- questions respectively (SD=.41, .32, .49).

*Structural Distance* denotes the number of arcs between nodes in the QKS. The shortest path found using the arc-search procedure was used if one existed; otherwise the shortest path was used. Structural distance was predicted to be negatively correlated with GOA scores. The mean structural distance score was 3.75 (SD=1.50).

*Constraint Satisfaction* is a complex variable that measures the argument overlap, temporal compatibility, planning compatibility, plausibility, and causal strength of an answer node. For a complete description, see Graesser, Lang, & Roberts (1991). Graesser had experts calculate these values; we estimated them computationally. These estimations were possible given the extra information about relationships contained within the plan structure. Argument overlap (AO) was derived from plan structures: if the a subset of the objects listed in the plan action for the question node where in the action for the answer node, then the answer received a 1 for this value. Temporal (TC) compatibility received a 1 if the answer was a goal node with a lower number, a 1 if the answer was a state change node that had not been negated by later state changes, a .5 if the answer were the directly previous or next action and a 0 otherwise. Planning compatibility and plausibility were assumed to be 1 and left out of final calculations because we involve only a single actor, and all of our answer nodes are considered plausible.

Causal strength was the combination of four factors: temporality, operativity, necessity, and sufficiency. Temporality (T) was 1 if the answer node had a lower number than the question node. Operativity (O) was considered equivalent to temporal compatibility above. Necessity (N) was 1 if the answer node was a state node and fulfilled a precondition for the question's related action, or if the answer node was an action and some effect of the action was such a state node. Sufficiency (S) was 1 if the answer was a goal node for which a precondition would be filled by taking the action listed in the question.

These numbers were combined to create constraint satisfaction score between 1 and 0 as follows: (AO + TC. + (T x O x ((N + S) / 2)))/3. The mean constraint satisfaction score was .43 (SD=.20). In general, the mean scores for all three predictor variables were not as high in our study as in Graesser's (by QUEST's criteria, our answers were poorer). This is most likely due to the different method used to select answer nodes.

## Results

A multiple regression analysis was run to determine the effects of the three predictor variables, and a second test was run to determine the effects of interactions between the three variables. Graesser's earlier analyses predict that the regression equations will show a significant positive coefficient for arc-search procedures and constraint satisfaction and a significant negative coefficient for structural distance. Graesser's analyses also predict a significant interaction between arc-search and structural distance as well as between constraint satisfaction and structural distance.

Table 3 shows the standardized regression coefficients (β-weights) for each predictor variable. The table shows that arc-search and structural distance are important factors for all three question types. Structural distance is shown to be important only for enable questions.

Table 3: β-Weights of Predictors of Goodness of Answer (GOA), Segregated by Question Category

| Predictor variable | Why | How | Enable |
|---|---|---|---|
| Arc Search | $.40_s$ | $.69_s$ | $.22_i$ |
| Structural Distance | -.11 | -.02 | $-.25_s$ |
| Constraint Satisfaction | $.34_s$ | $.30_s$ | $.28_s$ |
| $R^2$ | .41 | .64 | .29 |

Note: s = significant at $p < .05$ for question/answer pair.

We performed a second multiple regression analysis with the four possible interactions between the predictor variables added. A possible interaction was found between arc search and structural distance for enable questions $F(1,148) = 16, p < .06$. Adding in this interaction increased the variance explained (R2) from .29 to .31. No other interaction was found between the predictor variables.

Mean GOA ratings for why-, how- and enable-questions were calculated to check for ceiling or floor effects. The mean ratings for why-, how- and enables-questions were 1.66, 1.8, and 1.4 respectively, with standard deviations of .76, .88, and .62. These GOA scores are slightly more restrictive than Graesser's, who had means 1.99, 2.07, and 2.32 with standard deviations of .87, .80, and .85. This restricted range is likely due to the different method we used to select answer nodes, which was described in the materials section.

## Discussion

In this study, we examined how well Graesser's QUEST model worked when the knowledge structure on which the algorithm was applied was automatically generated from a plan structure, all predictor variables were computed without human input, and the narrative was shown in a video instead of given in text. Despite the deviation from

Graesser's original design, two out of three of Graesser's QUEST components (arc search and constraint satisfaction) proved to significantly predict goodness of answers (GOA) ($p < .05$).

Structural distance was not shown to be a significant predictor for how and why questions, while in Graesser's study it was shown to be inversely related to GOA for all three question types. This discrepancy could be due to several factors. First, Graesser's β-weights for structural distance were small (-.16, -.13, -.13 for why-, how- and enable- questions); it could be that our sample size (N=15, N=5 for each question type) is too small to measure this effect. Second, it could be that Graesser's distance measures were correlated to the way answer nodes were chosen, and that this effect did not appear in our analysis due to our different method. Finally, our QKS covers only one actor's plan. Structural distance could only be a factor across multiple plans or between different actors.

No significant interactions were found between the three predictor variables ($p < .05$). It should be noted that the interactions found in Graesser's work all involved distance -- not a statistically significant predictor variable in two out of three question types. Thus, it is not surprising that there should be no significant interactions for these question types. In contrast, structural distance was found to be a statistically significant predictor in enable questions, and there is a possible interaction between arc search and structural distance ($p < .06$). However, because of the nature of the interaction and the small sample size, we did not analyze this possibility further.

The variance explained by Graesser's QUEST components was smaller in our study than in Graesser's. Our average R2 was 44.6, whereas Graesser's was 57.6. The variance explained for enable questions was 29%, as opposed to Graesser's 55%. The same factors that made structural distance less important may also have affected the overall effectiveness of QUEST's algorithm.

## Conclusions and Future Work

One long-term goal of our research is to define a cognitively plausible structure for representing a viewer's understanding of a story that a) can be generated automatically and b) is expressive enough to be used to control a virtual environment. The results provided here are encouraging; the data indicate that DPOCL plan structures can be mapped automatically onto a QUEST knowledge structure, and that the resulting QUEST components are satisfactory initial predictors of GOA ratings for why-, how- and enable- questions in their new environment.

## Conclusions and Future Work

This paper was supported by NSF CAREER Award # 0092586.

## References

André, E., Rist, T., & Müller, J. (1998). Integrating reactive and scripted behaviors in a life-like presentation agent. In *Proceedings of the 2nd International Conference on Autonomous Agents* (pp. 261-268).

Cavazza, M., Charles, F. & Mead, S., (2002) Planning characters' behaviour in interactive storytelling. In *Journal of Visualization and Computer Animation 13*(2): 121-131.

Fikes, R., Nilsson, N., (1971) STRIPS: A New Approach to the Application of Theorem Proving to Problem Solving. In *the Proceedings of IJCAI*, pages 608-620.

Graesser, A.C., Clark, L.F., (1985). *Structures and procedures of implicit knowledge*. Norwood NJ: Ablex.

Graesser, A.C, Franklin, S. P. (1990). Quest: A cognitive model of question answering. *Disc. Processes*, 13,279-303.

Graesser, A. C., & Hemphill, D. (1991). Question answering in the context of scientific mechanisms. *Journal of Memory and Language, 30*. 186-209.

Graesser, A.C., Lang, K. L. & Roberts, R.M., (1991). Question answering in the context of stories. *Journal of Experimental Psychology: General, 120*, 254-277..

Graesser, A.C., Singer, M., & Trabasso, T. (1994). Constructing inferences during narrative text comprehension. *Psycological. Review, 101, v.3,* 371-395.

Rattermann, M. J., Spector, L., Grafman, J., Levin, H. and Harward, H. Partial and total-order planning: evidence from normal and prefrontally damaged populations, in *Cognitive Science*, vol. 25, issue 6, pages 941-975.

Sacerdoti, E. (1977) *A Structure for Plans and Behavior*. Elsevier, New York.

Young, R. M, Pollack, M., & Moore, J. (1994) Decomposition and causality in partial-order planning, in *Proceedings of the Second International Conference on AI and Planning Systems*, Chicago, IL, pages 188-193.

Young, R. M. & Riedl, M. (2003) Towards an Architecture for Intelligent Control of Narrative in Interactive Virtual Worlds, in the *Proceedings of IUI,* January, 2003.

Young, R. M. (1999) Using Grice's Maxim Of Quantity To Select The Content Of Plan Descriptions. *Artificial Intelligence*, no 115, 215-256

# Methods for Domain-Independent Information Extraction from the Web: An Experimental Comparison

**Oren Etzioni, Michael Cafarella, Doug Downey, Ana-Maria Popescu Tal Shaked, Stephen Soderland, Daniel S. Weld, and Alexander Yates**
Department of Computer Science and Engineering
University of Washington
Seattle, WA 98195-2350
etzioni@cs.washington.edu

### Abstract

Our KNOWITALL system aims to automate the tedious process of extracting large collections of facts (*e.g.*, names of scientists or politicians) from the Web in an autonomous, domain-independent, and scalable manner. In its first major run, KNOWITALL extracted over 50,000 facts with high precision, but suggested a challenge: How can we improve KNOWITALL's recall and extraction rate without sacrificing precision?
This paper presents three distinct ways to address this challenge and evaluates their performance. *Rule Learning* learns domain-specific extraction rules. *Subclass Extraction* automatically identifies sub-classes in order to boost recall. *List Extraction* locates lists of class instances, learns a "wrapper" for each list, and extracts elements of each list. Since each method bootstraps from KNOWITALL's domain-independent methods, no hand-labeled training examples are required. Experiments show the relative coverage of each method and demonstrate their synergy. In concert, our methods gave KNOWITALL a 4-fold to 19-fold increase in recall, while maintaining high precision, and discovered 10,300 cities missing from the Tipster Gazetteer.

## 1. Introduction and Motivation

Collecting a large body of information by searching the Web can be a tedious, manual process. Consider, for example, compiling a list of the astronauts who have reached earth's orbit, or of the cities in the world, *etc.* Unless you find the "right" document(s), you are reduced to an error-prone, one-fact-at-a-time, piecemeal search. To address the problem of accumulating large collections of facts, we have constructed KNOWITALL, a domain-independent system that extracts information from the Web in an automated, open-ended manner.

KNOWITALL introduces a novel, generate-and-test architecture that extracts information in two stages. First, KNOWITALL utilizes a set of eight domain-independent extraction patterns to *generate* candidate facts (*cf.* (Hearst 1992)). For example, the generic pattern "NP1 such as NPList2" indicates that the head of each simple noun phrase (NP) in NPList2 is an member of the class named in NP1. By instantiating the pattern for class `City`, KNOWITALL extracts three candidate cities from the sentence: "We provide tours to cities such as Paris, London, and Berlin."

Next, extending (Turney 2001), KNOWITALL automatically *tests* the plausibility of the candidate facts it extracts using *pointwise mutual information* (PMI) statistics computed by treating the Web as a massive corpus of text. KNOWITALL leverages existing Web search engines to compute these statistics efficiently. Based on these PMI statistics, KNOWITALL associates a probability with every fact it extracts, enabling it to automatically manage the tradeoff between precision and recall.[1]

In its first major run, KNOWITALL extracted over 50,000 facts regarding cities, states, countries, actors, and films (Etzioni *et al.* 2004). This initial run revealed that, while KNOWITALL is capable of autonomously extracting high-quality information from the Web, it faces several challenges. In this paper we focus on one key challenge:

> *How can we improve* KNOWITALL*'s recall and extraction rate so that it extracts substantially more members of large classes such as cities and films while maintaining high precision?*

We describe and compare three distinct methods added to KNOWITALL in order to improve its recall:

- **Rule Learning (RL):** learns domain-specific rules and validates the accuracy of instances they extract.
- **Subclass Extraction (SE):** automatically identifies subclasses in order to facilitate extraction. For example, in order to identify more scientists, it may be helpful to determine subclasses of scientists (*e.g.*, physicists, geologists, *etc.*) and look for instances of these subclasses.
- **List Extraction (LE):** locates lists of class instances, learns a "wrapper" for each list, and uses the wrapper to extract list elements.

All of the methods dispense with hand-labeled training examples by bootstrapping from the information extracted by KNOWITALL's domain-independent patterns. We evaluate each method experimentally, demonstrate their synergy, and compare with the baseline KNOWITALL system described in (Etzioni *et al.* 2004). Our main contributions are:



[1] Since we cannot compute "true recall" on the Web, the paper uses the term "recall" to refer to the size of the set of facts extracted.

1. We introduce, implement, and evaluate three methods for improving the recall and extraction rate of a Web information extraction system. While our implementation is embedded in KNOWITALL, the lessons learned are quite general.
2. We show that LE is frequently the most powerful generator of candidate extractions, and that its extraction rate is two orders of magnitude faster than that of the other methods. However, LE's precision improves dramatically when combined with KNOWITALL's PMI statistics.
3. We demonstrate, with experiments in three domains, that our methods, when used in concert, can increase KNOWITALL's recall by 4-fold to 19-fold over the baseline KNOWITALL system described in (Etzioni *et al.* 2004).

The remainder of this paper is organized as follows. The paper begins with an overview of KNOWITALL and a comparison with earlier work. Sections 4 to 6 describe our three methods, and Section 7 reports on our experimental results. We conclude with directions for future work in Section 8.

## 2. Overview of KnowItAll

KNOWITALL is an autonomous, domain-independent system that extracts facts, concepts, and relationships from the Web (Etzioni *et al.* 2004). The only domain-specific input to KNOWITALL is a set of classes and relations that constitute its *focus*. KNOWITALL is also given a set of generic extraction patterns (*e.g.*, Figure 1), but these are domain independent. In this paper we concentrate on KNOWITALL's ability to extract instances of classes from the Web.

KNOWITALL begins with a bootstrap learning phase where it automatically instantiates its set of generic extraction patterns into class-specific extraction rules for each of the classes in its *focus*. KNOWITALL uses these rules to find a set of seed instances and uses the seeds to estimate conditional probabilities that are used by its Assessor module. After this bootstrap phase, the Extractor module begins to extract candidate instances from the Web, and the Assessor assigns a probability to each candidate. At each cycle of this main loop, KNOWITALL re-allocates system resources to favor the most productive classes, and to avoid seeking more instances of "exhausted" classes (*e.g.*, continents). We elaborate on KNOWITALL's main modules below.

**Extractor:** The Extractor automatically instantiates extraction patterns (*e.g.*, Figure 1) for each focus class. Some

```
NP1 "such as" NPList2
    & head(NP1)= plural(Class1)
    & properNoun(head(each(NPList2)))
=> instanceOf(Class1, head(each(NPList2)))
keywords: "plural(Class1) such as"
```

Figure 1: **This generic extraction pattern can be instantiated automatically with the (pluralized) class name to create a domain-specific extraction rule. For example, if** `Class1` **is set to "City" then the rule spawns the search engine query "cities such as", downloads the Web pages, and extracts every proper noun immediately following that phrase as a potential city.**

of our domain-independent patterns were adapted from the hyponym patterns of (Hearst 1992), while others were developed independently. Though this paper focuses on unary predicates, our rules extract N-ary predicates as well. The Extractor uses the Brill tagger (Brill 1994) to assign part-of-speech tags and identifies noun phrases with regular expressions based on the part-of-speech tags. Rules that look for proper names also include an orthographic constraint that tests capitalization.

**Search Engine Interface:** KNOWITALL automatically formulates queries based on its extraction rules. Each rule has an associated search query composed of the rule's keywords. For example, if the pattern in Figure 1 was instantiate for the class `City`, it would lead KNOWITALL to 1) issue the search-engine query "cities such as", 2) download in parallel all pages named in the engine's results, and 3) apply the Extractor to the appropriate sentences on each downloaded page. For robustness and scalability KNOWITALL queries multiple different search engines.

Etzioni (Etzioni 1996) introduced the metaphor of an *Information Food Chain* where search engines are herbivores "grazing" on the web and intelligent agents are *information carnivores* that consume output from various herbivores. In terms of this metaphor, KNOWITALL is an information carnivore that consumes the output of existing search engines. Since it would be inappropriate for KNOWITALL to overload these search engines, we limit the number of queries KNOWITALL issues per minute, which has become the major bottleneck for KNOWITALL. In order to overcome this bottleneck, We are in the process of incorporating an instance of the Nutch open-source search engine into KNOWITALL. Since our Web index will be roughly two orders of magnitude smaller than those of commercial engines, KNOWITALL will continue to depend on external search engines for some queries. Thus, we are transforming KNOWITALL from a carnivore to an *information omnivore*.

**Assessor:** KNOWITALL uses statistics computed by querying search engines to assess the likelihood that the Extractor's conjectures are correct. Specifically, the Assessor uses a form of *pointwise mutual information* (PMI) between words and phrases that is estimated from Web search engine hit counts in a manner similar to Turney's PMI-IR algorithm (Turney 2001). The Assessor computes the PMI between each extracted instance and multiple, *automatically generated discriminator phrases* associated with the class (such as "city of" for the class `City`).[2] For example, in order to estimate the likelihood that "Liege" is the name of a city, the Assessor might check to see if there is a high PMI between "Liege" and phrases such as "city of."

More formally, let $I$ be an instance and $D$ be a discriminator phrase. We compute the PMI score as follows:

$$\text{PMI}(I, D) = \frac{|\text{Hits}(D + I)|}{|\text{Hits}(I)|} \quad (1)$$

The PMI score is the number of hits for a query that com-

[2]We use class names and the keywords of extraction rules to automatically generate these discriminator phrases; they can also be derived from rules learned using RL techniques (Section 4).

bines the discriminator and instance, divided by the hits for the instance alone. This can be viewed as the probability that $(D + I)$ will be found on a Web page that contains $I$. Note that the number of search engine queries necessary to compute the PMI for a particular instance $I$ is the number of discriminators plus one additional query to compute $Hits(I)$.

These mutual information statistics are treated as features that are input to a *Naive Bayes Classifier* (NBC). In a standard NBC, if a candidate fact is more likely to be true than false, it is classified as true. However, since we wish to be able to trade precision against recall, we record the numeric probability values computed by the NBC for each extracted fact. By raising the probability threshold required for a fact to be deemed true, we increase precision and decrease recall; lowering the threshold has the opposite effect.

Since the NBC is notorious for producing polarized probability estimates that are close to zero or to one, the estimated probabilities are often inaccurate. However, as (Domingos & Pazzani 1997) points out, the classifier is surprisingly effective because it only needs to make an ordinal judgment (which class is more likely) to classify instances correctly. Similarly, our formula produces a reasonable *ordering* on the likelihood of extracted facts for a given class. This ordering is sufficient for KNOWITALL to implement the desired precision/recall tradeoff.

Each of this paper's new methods (Sections 4–6) reuse the KNOWITALL assessor to considerable benefit.

## 3. Previous Work

KNOWITALL's most distinctive feature is its adaptation of (Turney 2001)'s PMI-IR algorithm to assess the probability that extractions are correct. Another system that uses hit counts for validation is the question answering system of (Magnini, Negri, & Tanev 2002), although their technique of getting hit counts for a specially constructed *validation pattern* is restricted to question-answer pairs.

KNOWITALL is also distinguished from many Information Extraction (IE) systems by its novel approach to bootstrap learning. Unlike IE systems that use supervised learning techniques such as *hidden Markov models* (HMMs) (Freitag & McCallum 1999), rule learning (Soderland 1999), or Conditional Random Fields (McCallum 2003), KNOWITALL does not require manually tagged training sentences. Other *bootstrap* IE systems such as (Riloff & Jones 1999; Agichtein & Gravano 2000; Brin 1998) still require a set of domain-specific seed instances as input, then alternately learn rules from seeds, and further seeds from rules. Instead, KNOWITALL begins with a domain-independent set of *generic extraction patterns* from which it induces a set of seed instances. KNOWITALL's use of PMI validation helps overcomes the problem of maintaining high precision, which has plagued previous bootstrap IE systems.

KNOWITALL is able to use weaker input than previous IE systems because it relies on the scale and redundancy of the Web for an ample supply of simple sentences. This notion of *redundancy-based extraction* was introduced in Mulder (Kwok, Etzioni, & Weld 2001) and further articulated in AskMSR (Banko *et al.* 2002). Of course, many previous IE systems have extracted more complex relational information than KNOWITALL. We believe that KNOWITALL will be effective in extracting $N$-ry relations, but we have yet to demonstrate this experimentally.

Several previous projects have automated the collection of information from the Web with some success. Information extraction systems such as Google's Froogle, Whizbang's Flipdog, and Elion, collected large bodies of facts but only in carefully circumscribed domains (*e.g.*, job postings), and only after extensive domain-specific hand tuning. KNOWITALL is both highly automated and domain independent. In fairness, though, KNOWITALL's redundancy-based extraction task is easier than Froogle and Flipdog's task of extracting "rare" facts each of which only appears on a single Web page.

KNOWITALL was inspired, in part, by the WebKB project (Craven *et al.* 2000). However, the two projects rely on very different architectures and learning techniques. For example, WebKB relies on supervised learning methods that take as input hand-labeled hypertext regions to classify Web pages, whereas KNOWITALL employs unsupervised learning methods that extract facts by using search engines to home in on easy-to-understand sentences scattered throughout the Web.

The next three sections discuss our newly added methods for enhancing KNOWITALL's recall.

## 4. Rule Learning (RL)

While generic extraction patterns perform well in the baseline KNOWITALL system, many of the best extraction rules for a domain do not match a generic pattern. For example, "the film <*film*> starring" and "headquartered in <*city*>" are rules with high precision and coverage for the classes `Film` and `City`. Arming KNOWITALL with a set of such domain-specific rules could significantly increase the number of sentences from which it can extract facts. This section describes our method for learning domain-specific rules.

Our rule learning algorithm starts with a set of seed instances generated automatically by KNOWITALL's bootstrapping phase. We issue search engine queries for each seed instance, $i$, and for each page returned by the search engine we record a *context string*—the substring including the $k$ words before $i$, <*class-name*>, and the $k$ words after $i$ surrounding each instance in the returned documents (in our experiments, we set $k = 4$). The 'best' substrings of the 'best' context strings are converted into extraction rules and added to KNOWITALL.

For our purposes, 'best' means "able to extract new class instances with high precision." The reason is primarily efficiency; we want to minimize the number of rules we execute per unique extraction, and also minimize the number of times we execute the KNOWITALL Assessor on false facts. Precision is also important for another reason – while the KNOWITALL Assessor can eliminate the majority of false positives, the presence of a large number of low precision rules can still degrade the quality of the system's output. Estimating rule quality is difficult for several reasons: 1) we have no labeled negative examples, 2) good extraction rules

| *Rule* | *Correct Extractions* | *Precision* |
|---|---|---|
| the cities of <*city*> | 5215 | 0.80 |
| headquartered in <*city*> | 4837 | 0.79 |
| for the city of <*city*> | 3138 | 0.79 |
| in the movie <*film*> | 1841 | 0.61 |
| <*film*> the movie starring | 957 | 0.64 |
| movie review of <*film*> | 860 | 0.64 |
| and physicist <*scientist*> | 89 | 0.61 |
| physicist <*scientist*>, | 87 | 0.59 |
| <*scientist*>, a British scientist | 77 | 0.65 |

Table 1: **Three of the most productive rules for each class, along with the number of correct extractions produced by each rule, and the rule's overall precision (before assessment).**

are quite rare[3] 3) many of the most precise rules have low recall, and vice versa. We address these challenges with two heuristics:

**H1:** We prefer substrings that appear in multiple context strings across different seeds. By banning all substrings that matched only a single seed, 96% of the potential rules are eliminated. In experiments with the class `City`, H1 was found to improve extraction rate substantially, increasing the average number of unique cities extracted by a factor of five.

**H2:** We wish to penalize substrings whose rules would have many false positives, but have no labeled negative instances. Instead, we exploit the fact that KNOWITALL learns rules for multiple semantic categories at once, and define the positive examples of one class to be negative examples for all other classes.[4] After obtaining context strings for examples from each class, we estimate the precision of each potential rule using a Laplace correction:

$$EstimatedPrecision = \frac{c+k}{c+n+m}$$

where $c$ is the number times the rule matched a seed in the target class, $n$ is the number of times it matched known members of other classes, and $\frac{k}{m}$ is the prior estimate of a rule's precision, obtained by testing a sample of the learned rules' extractions using the KNOWITALL Assessor. On experiments with the class `City`, ranking rules by H2 further increased the average number of unique instances extracted (by 63% over H1) and significantly improved average precision (from 0.32 to 0.58).

As a final step, we take the 200 rules that satisfy H1 and are ranked most highly by H2 and subject them to more detailed analysis, applying each to 100 Web pages and testing their precision with the KNOWITALL Assessor. Examples of the most productive rules for each class are shown in Table 1 along with the number of unique correct extractions and precision (before assessment) of each rule.

[3]In the `City` class, for example, we found that only 2% of the potential rules had a precision of at least 0.5 and non-trivial recall.

[4]This proved useful in practice, even though it was sometimes fooled by an instance that is positive for both classes, such as the movie (and city) "Chicago".

RL is similar to the methods of (Lin, Yangarber, & Grishman 2003) (indeed, they discovered a heuristic similar to H2 and experimentally showed that it increases precision), but there are several differences: 1) They use manually-specified seeds, whereas RL uses seeds generated automatically by KnowItAll's bootstrapping phase 2) In their assessment process, Lin *et al.* apply their rules to their entire corpus — which is impossible at Web scale 3) They have no mechanism similar to KNOWITALL's PMI assessment.

(Riloff & Jones 1999) also extract instances of large semantic classes using *bootstrap learning*, but they use a different heuristic for rule quality and test on a much smaller corpus (again applying their rules to the entire corpus). Like our work, (Ravichandran & Hovy 2002) uses Web search engines to find patterns surrounding seed values. However, their goal is to support *question answering*, for which a training set of question and answer pairs is known. This is easier than our task, because they can measure a rule's precision on seed questions by checking the correspondence between the extracted answers and the answers given by the seed.

Snowball (Agichtein & Gravano 2000) and DIPRE (Brin 1998) use bootstrap learning to alternately learn extraction rules and seeds to generate further rules. In contrast with KNOWITALL, they lack a domain-independent method to validate the accuracy of extracted information. In addition, Snowball relies on a domain-specific named-entity tagger to identified company names and locations. Finally, DIPRE requires manual editing after each bootstrapping cycle.

## 5. Subclass Extraction (SE)

SE identifies subclasses of the class of interest, and feeds the subclasses to the Extractor. For example, if KNOWITALL is extracting instances of the class `Scientist` and learns that physicists, chemists, and geologists are scientists then it can instantiate its generic extraction patterns with each of the learned subclasses (*e.g.*, "physicists such as ...", *etc.*) to increase the set of candidate scientists extracted. Indeed, while a great many scientists are mentioned on the Internet in some form, only a fraction are referred to as "scientists". By sequentially instantiating the generic patterns with subclasses like the ones in Table 3, SE enables KNOWITALL to identify over 2,500 scientists, more than ten times the number found by the baseline (Figure 4).

Extracting subclasses mirrors the extraction of class instances, and can be achieved by a recursive application of the instantiated extraction rules in KNOWITALL's main loop, but the rules need to distinguish between instances and subclasses of a class. Rules for extracting instances contain a proper noun test (using a part-of-speech tagger and a capitalization test). In order to extract subclasses, the rules are modified to check that the extracted noun is a *common* noun (*i.e.* not capitalized).

The SE Assessor ranks the candidate subclasses in order of probability. First, the Assessor checks whether a subclass is a hyponym of the class in WordNet. This test is not sufficient because on average 40% of the correct subclasses discovered by SE were absent from WordNet and, in some cases, the class itself could be absent from WordNet. Second, the Assessor checks the morphology of the candidate

| Pattern | Extraction |
|---|---|
| $C_1\{",\"\}$ 'such as' CN | $isA(CN, C_1)$ |
| 'such' $C_1$ 'as' CN | $isA(CN, C_1)$ |
| CN $\{",\"\}$ 'and other' $C_1$ | $isA(CN, C_1)$ |
| CN $\{",\"\}$ 'or other' $C_1$ | $isA(CN, C_1)$ |
| $C_1\{",\"\}$ 'including' CN | $isA(CN, C_1)$ |
| $C_1\{",\"\}$ 'especially' CN | $isA(CN, C_1)$ |
| $C_1$ 'and' CN | $isA(CN, superclass(C_1))$ |
| $C_1$ $\{","\}$ $C_2\{",\"\}$ 'and' CN | $isA(CN, superclass(C_1))$ |

Table 2: **Sample Rules for Subclass Extraction. CN refers to common noun, *i.e.* one that is not capitalized.**

| | |
|---|---|
| biologist | zoologist |
| astronomer | meteorologist |
| mathematician | economist |
| geologist | sociologist |
| chemist | oceanographer |
| anthropologist | pharmacist |
| psychologist | climatologist |
| paleontologist | neuropsychologist |
| engineer | microbiologist |

Table 3: **Subclasses of Scientist found by SE.**

subclass name, since some subclass names are formed by attaching a prefix to the name of the class (*e.g.*, "microbiologist" is a subclass of "biologist"). If either test holds, then the Assessor assigns the subclass a probability that is close to one. 61% of SE's bona fide subclasses were confirmed using the above tests. Finally, remaining candidates are evaluated using a variant of KNOWITALL's standard Assessor. Because an incorrect subclass choice can result in the extraction of hundreds or thousands of incorrect class instances (*e.g.*, one of SE's candidate subclasses for `Scientist` is 'Doctor'), only candidates whose assessed probability exceeds 0.85 are selected by SE.

Just as the generic extraction rules for instances have limited recall, their counterparts for extracting subclasses generate a limited set of subclasses. Moreover, even those that are generated may have low co-occurrence with the superclass name or the discriminators. Thus, subclass extraction faces the same recall problem as instances extraction. In order to improve subclass recall, we add another extraction-and-verification step. After a set of subclasses for the given class is obtained by SE, high-recall enumeration rules (the last two rules in Table 2) are seeded with subclasses, which are judged very likely to be correct by KNOWITALL's Assessor, and then used to extract additional subclass candidates. For instance, given the sentence "Biologists, physicists and chemists have convened at this inter-disciplinary conference.", such rules identify "chemists" as possible sibling of "biologists" and "physicists".

SE is similar in flavor to work on acquiring domain-specific lexicons and ontologies from corpora by (Phillips & Riloff 2002; Maedche & Staab 2001; Sombatsrisomboon, Matsuo, & Ishizuka 2003) and others. SE's main distinguishing features are its use of domain-independent extraction patterns and of PMI-IR to assess its extractions.

## 6. List Extraction (LE)

All of the techniques we have discussed thus far extract information from natural language sentences, but the Web also contains numerous regularly-formatted lists that enumerate many of the elements of a class. Examples include lists of cities with airport codes, lists of movies with show times, and lists of researchers with their home pages. LE exploits this structure in three stages: 1) finding such lists, 2) extracting list elements, and 3) assessing the accuracy of the resulting extracted instances.

In order to find good lists, LE (like SE and RL) uses the high-probability instances extracted by baseline KNOWITALL as seeds. LE selects a random subset of $k$ of these instances as keywords for a search engine query, and it downloads the documents corresponding to the engine's results. This process is repeated 5000–10,000 times with different random subsets. Space precludes discussion of our experiments varying $k$, but decreasing $k$ led LE to increase recall at the cost of reduced precision; in Section 7 we use $k = 4$.

In each downloaded document, LE searches for a regularly-formatted list that includes these keywords. This is done by a light-weight wrapper induction algorithm similar to the HLRT algorithm of (Kushmerick, Weld, & Doorenbos 1997), but there are several differences: 1) our algorithm exploits the HTML parse tree[5], and would not generalize well to unstructured text, 2) instead of learning from a fully labeled training set or via an oracle with well-defined accuracy, our training is done online from only a few positive instances, 3) Kushmerick's goal is to generate a wrapper for use on a future document stream, but in contrast we generate one or more wrappers per page, discard them after a single use, and return the extracted instances. This extraction process is fast — including network time, it usually takes less than a second to process a document.

After extracting instances from the pages returned in response to a thousand randomly composed queries, the final challenge is to assess the probability of each extracted instance. Intuitively, the more lists that contain a particular instance, the more likely such an instance is to be an actual member of the class. Similarly, the more valid instances are in a list, the higher the list accuracy. This reasoning suggests an iterative assessment algorithm, since intuitively an instance's likelihood is higher if it is in $n$ accurate lists than $n$ with low accuracy. We implemented several approaches to assessment: 1) treat list membership as a feature and use a Naive Bayesian classifier (trained on KNOWITALL baseline's seeds) to determine accuracy of an instance, 2) model each list as a uniform distribution, perform EM to determine the probability that a randomly-drawn element of a list is a class member, and then use naive Bayes to compute the probability of each instance, 3) simply sort the instances according to the number of lists in which they appear. To our

[5]LE 1) parses the document and converts to a DOM tree (`www.w3.org/DOM`), 2) selects subtrees containing positive examples, 3) computes the greatest common prefixes and suffixes of these examples, and 4) finally chooses header and tail strings to limit extraction to good subtrees.

surprise, method 3 outperformed methods 1 and 2, and so we used it in all results marked LE. Our final method ("LE+A") applies KNOWITALL's Assessor to rank the raw LE results. While "LE+A" requires many more search-engine queries than LE methods 1–3, Section 7 shows LE+A performs has much higher recall than LE without assessment.

The bulk of past work on wrapper induction requires manually labeled training examples from each Web site in order to build a wrapper; in contrast, LE learns thousands of wrappers on the fly. LE can be viewed as extending the method of (Doorenbos, Etzioni, & Weld 1997), which queried online stores with known product names and looked for regularities in the resulting pages in order to build e-commerce wrappers, applying it to a different task. LE can also be viewed as a specialization of the list extraction method described in (Cohen, Hurst, & Jensen 2002). *Google Sets*, whose algorithm is unpublished, also generates lists of related items, but LE's recall is much higher. Finally, LE is distinct from work on the problem of table extraction from unstructured text, which focuses on segmenting columns, finding cells, and differentiating between data and labels.

## 7. Experimental Results

We conducted a series of experiments to evaluate the effectiveness of Subclass Extraction (SE), Rule Learning (RL), and List Extraction (LE) in increasing the recall of the baseline KNOWITALL system on three classes `City`, `Scientist`, `Film`. We used the Google API as our search engine. Each of the methods tested associates a probability with each extracted instance. We estimated the number of correct instances extracted by manually tagging samples of the instances grouped by probability, and computed *precision* as the proportion of correct instances at or above a given probability. In the case of `City`, we also automatically marked instances as correct when they appeared in the Tipster Gazetteer.

Figures 2, 3, and 4 compare the number of extractions at precision 0.90 for the baseline system (B), the baseline combined with each method (RL, SE, LE), and the baseline combined with a variant of LE whose extractions were sorted based on probabilities assigned by the Assessor (LE+A)[6]. We chose 0.90 precision as representative of high quality extraction, but our relative results were largely unchanged when we varied the precision from 0.8 to 0.95. The bars labeled "All" show the results of a composite method that returns the union of instances extracted by B, RL, SE, and LE+A.

In each bar, the instances extracted by the baseline (B) exclusively are the white portion, and those extracted by both a new method and the baseline are shown in gray. Since each method begins by running the baseline system, the combined height of the white and gray portions is exactly that of the B bar in each Figure. Finally, instances extracted by one of this paper's methods but *not* by the baseline are in black.

[6]For each method we continued searching for new extractions until the signal-to-noise (STN) ratio fell below 0.30, where STN is defined as the number extractions with probability over .90 divided by extractions with probability under .10.

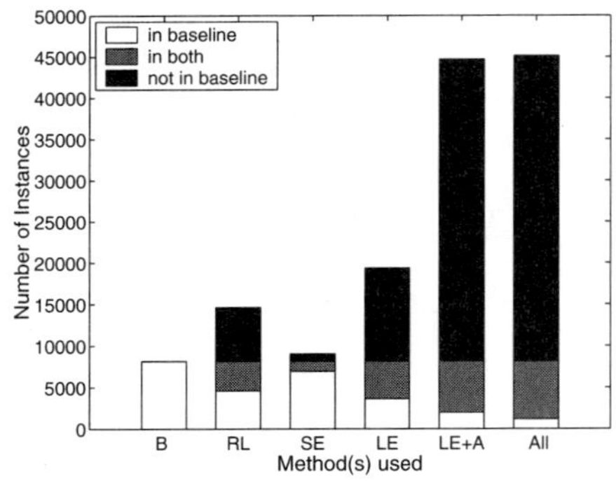


Figure 2: **Instances of City at precision .90.**

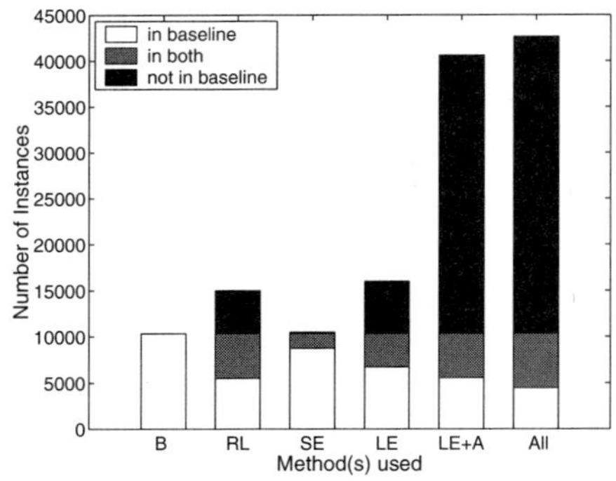


Figure 3: **Instances of Film at precision .90.**

Thus, the black portion shows the "added value" of our new methods over the baseline system described in (Etzioni *et al.* 2004).

In the `City` class we see that each of the methods resulted in some improvement over the baseline, but the methods were dominated by LE+A, which resulted in a 5.5-fold improvement, and found virtually all the extractions found by other methods. We see very similar results for the class `Film` (Figure 3), but different behavior for the class `Scientist` (Figure 4). In the case of `Scientist`, SE's ability to extract subclasses made it the dominant method, though both RL and LE found useful extractions that SE did not. We believe that SE is particularly powerful for general, naturally decomposable classes such as `Plant`, `Animal`, or `Machine` where text usually refers to their named subclasses (*e.g.*, `Flower`, `Mammal`, `Computer`).[7]

While our methods clearly enhance KNOWITALL's recall, what impact do they have on its extraction rate? Search engine queries (with a "courtesy wait" between queries) are the system's main bottleneck. Thus, we measure extraction rate by the number of unique instances extracted per search engine query. We focus on *unique* extractions because each

[7]To use the psychological terminology of (Rosch *et al.* 1976), we conjecture that text on the Web refers to instances as elements of "basic level" categories such as `Flower` much more frequently than as elements of superordinate ones such as `Plant`.

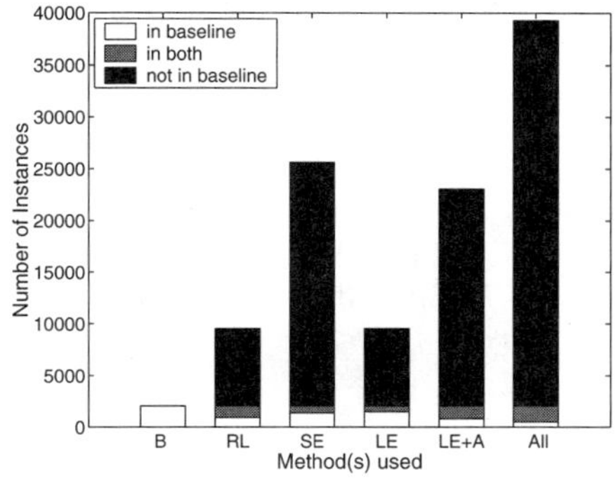


Figure 4: **Instances of Scientist at precision .90.**

| Method | Queries | Extraction Rate |
|---|---|---|
| B | 182,576 | 0.138 |
| RL | 194,564 | 0.125 |
| SE | 98,272 | 0.124 |
| **LE** | **23,400** | **12.3** |
| LE+A | 1,748,118 | 0.164 |
| All | 1,888,325 | 0.148 |

Table 4: **The number of queries issued by the different methods, and the extraction rate as measured by the number of unique extractions per query.**

of our methods extracts "popular" instances multiple times. Table 4 shows that LE+A enhancement to recall comes at a cost. In contrast, LE's extraction rate is two orders of magnitude better than any of the other methods.

While each of the methods tested have numerous parameters that influence their performance, we ran our experiments using the best parameter settings we could find for each method. While the exact results will vary with different settings, or classes, we are confident that our main observations — the massive increase in recall due to our methods in concert, and the phenomenal increase in extraction rate due to LE — will be borne out by additional studies.

## 8. Conclusions & Future Work

In conclusion, our *rule learning* (RL), *subclass extraction* (SE), and *list extraction* (LE) techniques greatly improve on the baseline recall of (Etzioni *et al.* 2004)'s KNOWITALL system, while maintaining precision and improving extraction rate. KNOWITALL's running time increases linearly with the size and number of web pages it examines; KNOWITALL's computational complexity remains linear after the addition of RL, SE, and LE. In practice, the main parameter that impacts KNOWITALL's performance is the rate at which it can issue search-engine queries. To increase this rate, we are incorporating a copy of the Nutch open source search engine into KNOWITALL.

Overall, LE combined with PMI assessment gave the greatest improvement, but SE extracted the most new `Scientists`. Although KNOWITALL is still "young", it suggests futuristic possibilities for systems that scale up Information Extraction (IE), new kinds of search engines based on massive Web-based IE, and the automatic accumulation of large collections of facts to support knowledge-based AI systems. There are numerous directions for future work including, notably, further investigation of EM and related co-training techniques (Blum & Mitchell 1998; Nigam *et al.* 2000) to improve the assessment of extracted instances, and the generalization of our results to the extraction of $N$-ary predicates.

## Acknowledgments

This research was supported in part by NSF grants IIS-0312988 and IIS-0307906, DARPA contract NBCHD030010, ONR grants N00014-02-1-0324 and N00014-02-1-0932, and a gift from Google. Google generously allowed us to issue a large number of queries to their XML API to facilitate our experiments. We thank Jeff Bigham, and Nick Kushmerick for comments on previous drafts, and Bob Doorenbos, Mike Perkowitz, and Ellen Riloff for helpful discussions.

## References

Agichtein, E., and Gravano, S. 2000. Snowball: Extracting relations from large plain-text collections. In *Proceedings of the 5th ACM International Conference on Digital Libraries.*

Banko, M.; Brill, E.; Dumais, S.; and Lin, J. 2002. AskMSR: Question answering using the Worldwide Web. In *Proceedings of 2002 AAAI Spring Symposium on Mining Answers from Texts and Knowledge Bases.*

Blum, A., and Mitchell, T. 1998. Combining labeled and unlabeled data with co-training. In *Proceedings of the Eleventh Annual Conference on Computational Learning Theory.*

Brill, E. 1994. Some advances in rule-based part of speech tagging. In *Proceedings of the Twelfth National Conference on Artificial Intelligence*, 722–727.

Brin, S. 1998. Extracting patterns and relations from the World-Wide Web. In *Proceedings of the 1998 International Workshop on the Web and Databases.*

Cohen, W.; Hurst, M.; and Jensen, L. S. 2002. A flexible learning system for wrapping tables and lists in HTML documents. In *The Eleventh International World Wide Web Conference WWW-2002.*

Craven, M.; DiPasquo, D.; Freitag, D.; McCallum, A.; Mitchell, T.; Nigam, K.; and Slattery, S. 2000. Learning to construct knowledge bases from the World Wide Web. *Artificial Intelligence.*

Domingos, P., and Pazzani, M. 1997. On the optimality of the simple Bayesian classifier under zero-one loss. *Machine Learning* 29:103–130.

Doorenbos, R.; Etzioni, O.; and Weld, D. 1997. A scalable comparison-shopping agent for the World-Wide Web. In *Proc. First Intl. Conf. Autonomous Agents*, 39–48.

Etzioni, O.; Cafarella, M.; Downey, D.; Kok, S.; Popescu, A.; Shaked, T.; Soderland, S.; Weld, D.; and Yates, A.

2004. Web-scale information extraction in KnowItAll. In *Proceedings of the 13th International World Wide Web Conference (WWW-04)*.

Etzioni, O. 1996. Moving up the information food chain: softbots as information carnivores. In *Proceedings of the Thirteenth National Conference on Artificial Intelligence*. Revised version reprinted in AI Magazine special issue, Summer '97.

Freitag, D., and McCallum, A. 1999. Information extraction with HMMs and shrinkage. In *Proceedings of the AAAI-99 Workshop on Machine Learning for Information Extraction*.

Hearst, M. 1992. Automatic acquisition of hyponyms from large text corpora. In *Proceedings of the 14th International Conference on Computational Linguistics*, 539–545.

Kushmerick, N.; Weld, D.; and Doorenbos, R. 1997. Wrapper Induction for Information Extraction. In *Proceedings of the Fifteenth International Joint Conference on Artificial Intelligence*, 729–737. San Francisco, CA: Morgan Kaufmann.

Kwok, C. C. T.; Etzioni, O.; and Weld, D. S. 2001. Scaling question answering to the Web. In *World Wide Web*, 150–161.

Lin, W.; Yangarber, R.; and Grishman, R. 2003. Bootstrapped learning of semantic classes. In *Proceedings of ICML-2003 Workshop on The Continuum from Labeled to Unlabeled Data*.

Maedche, A., and Staab, S. 2001. Learning ontologies for the semantic web. In *Proceedings of the Second International Workshop on the Semantic Web*.

Magnini, B.; Negri, M.; and Tanev, H. 2002. Is it the right answer? exploiting web redundancy for answer validation. In *Proceedings of the 40th Annual Meeting of the Association for Computational Linguistics*, 425–432.

McCallum, A. 2003. Efficiently inducing features or conditional random fields. In *Proceedings of the Nineteenth Conference on Uncertainty in Artificial Intelligence*.

Nigam, K.; McCallum, A.; Thrun, S.; and Mitchell, T. M. 2000. Text classification from labeled and unlabeled documents using EM. *Machine Learning* 39(2/3):103–134.

Phillips, W., and Riloff, E. 2002. Exploiting strong syntactic heuristics and co-training to learn semantic lexicons. In *Proceedings of the 2002 Conference on Empirical Methods in Natural Language Processing*.

Ravichandran, D., and Hovy, D. 2002. Learning surface text patterns for a question answering system. In *Proceedings of the 40th ACL Conference*.

Riloff, E., and Jones, R. 1999. Learning dictionaries for information extraction by multi-level bootstrapping. In *Proceedings of the Sixteenth National Conference on Artificial Intelligence*.

Rosch, E.; Mervis, C. B.; Gray, W.; Johnson, D.; and Boyes-Bream, P. 1976. Basic objects in natural categories. *Cognitive Psychology* 3:382–439.

Soderland, S. 1999. Learning information extraction rules for semi-structured and free text. *Machine Learning* 34(1–3):233–272.

Sombatsrisomboon, R.; Matsuo, Y.; and Ishizuka, M. 2003. Acquisition of hypernyms and hyponyms from the WWW. In *Proceedings of the 2nd International Workshop on Active Mining*.

Turney, P. D. 2001. Mining the Web for synonyms: PMI-IR versus LSA on TOEFL. In *Proceedings of the Twelfth European Conference on Machine Learning*.

# Interpreting Loosely Encoded Questions*

**James Fan** and **Bruce Porter**
Department of Computer Sciences
University of Texas at Austin
Austin, TX 78712 USA
{jfan, porter}@cs.utexas.edu

### Abstract

Knowledge-based question-answering systems have become quite competent and robust at answering a wide range of questions in different domains, however in order to ask questions correctly, one needs to have intimate knowledge of the structure of the knowledge base, and typical users lack this knowledge. We address this problem by developing a system that uses the content of the knowledge base to automatically align a user's encoding of a query to the structure of the knowledge base. Our preliminary evaluation shows the system detects and corrects most misalignments, and users are able to pose most questions quickly.

## Introduction

Knowledge-based question-answering systems have become quite competent and robust. Unlike their expert-system predecessors, modern systems answer a wide range of types of questions. Moreover, they cover broad domains (e.g. infectious disease), not just isolated tasks (e.g. diagnosis of infectious disease). For example, several question-answering systems built for Project Halo (Vulcan Inc. 2003) performed well on a targeted portion of the Advanced Placement (AP) exam in chemistry, answering about 160 widely varying and novel questions (Barker *et al.* 2004; Angele *et al.* 2003).

Despite this success, Project Halo revealed a significant problem that limits the utility of question-answering systems: *posing questions to knowledge-based question-answering systems requires intimate knowledge of the structure of the knowledge base, and ordinary users lack this knowledge.* Consequently, their question encodings are structurally flawed, and no state-of-the-art question-answering system will answer the questions correctly.

One solution to this problem, but a false one, is to restrict the expressiveness of the query language to such a degree that only "legal queries" can be posed. For example, conventional information-retrieval systems use a query language that permits only boolean combinations of keywords. Queries posed in this language are matched with target texts, which are little more than bags of words and their frequencies, so there is no opportunity for structural misalignments. However, the keyword-query language is inappropriate for asking conventional questions, such as this typical one from Project Halo:

> When dilute nitric acid was added to a solution of one of the following chemicals, a gas was evolved. This gas turned a drop of limewater, $Ca(OH)_2$ cloudy, due to the formation of a white precipitate. The chemical was:

(a) household ammonia, $NH_3$
(b) baking soda, $NaHCO_3$
(c) table salt, $NaCl$
(d) epsom salt, $MgSO_4 \cdot 7H_2O$
(e) bleach, 5% $NaOCl$

Another approach to restricting the expressiveness of the query language is to use question templates. The template language permits expressions such as: "what happens to $\langle entity \rangle$ during $\langle process \rangle$?", where $\langle entity \rangle$ and $\langle process \rangle$ are typed variables that can be bound to individuals in the knowledge base. Although question templates have been used successfully (Clark *et al.* 2003; Buchanan & Shortliffe 1984), they have serious limitations. First, the set of templates is small and fixed, which limits their usefulness for novel questions. Second, they lack the expressiveness to describe the context in which the question is posed. For example, the question above arises in the context of a chemical mixture which produces a gas, which in turn mixes with limewater to produce a precipitate.

The goal of our research is to address the problem of posing questions to knowledge-based systems by automating the task of aligning question encodings with the structure of the knowledge base.

## Loose speak

We assume that questions originate in English, or some other natural language, and that some person or program encodes them in the formal language used by the question-answering system. If the question is encoded without regard for the structure of the knowledge base, we call it a *naïve encoding*. If the encoding happens to align with the structure of the

*Full support for this research was provided by Vulcan Inc. as part of Project Halo

| | Pilot ($N$ = 43) | Final ($N$ = 107) |
|---|---|---|
| No loose speak | 2.3% | 0.0% |
| Metonymy | 25.0% | 10.8% |
| Causal factor | 45.5% | 23.5% |
| Role | 9.1% | 7.8% |
| Aggregate | 77.3% | 87.3% |
| Too generic | 34.1% | 40.2% |
| Noun compounds | 22.7% | 29.4% |

Table 1: Types of loose speak, and their frequencies, encountered in two sets of AP-like questions from Project Halo. The pilot set contains 43 questions in total; the final set contains 107 questions in total. The first row shows the percentage of questions that contained no loose speak – i.e. for which a naïve encoding was correct. Note that the sum of the frequencies exceeds 100% because each question may contain multiple occurrences of loose speak.

knowledge base, then it is a *correct encoding* of the question. If, on the other hand, any part of the encoding fails to align with the knowledge base, we call that part *loose speak*, in reference to the imprecise way that people form English expressions.

The term "loose speak" is not meant to be pejorative. To the contrary, question encodings that contain loose speak are often literal translations from the original English expressions– i.e. the form of questions we should expect from typical users. The goal of our project is to improve knowledge-based question-answering systems by developing ways to automate the interpretation of loose speak to produce correct encodings of questions.

## Types of loose speak and their frequencies

Misalignments between queries and the knowledge bases to which they are posed are common and unavoidable because knowledge bases, like many engineered systems, are full of idiosyncratic design decisions. Since a naïve encoding may differ from a correct encoding in many ways, developing and testing a loose-speak interpreter appears to be a daunting task.

However, we have found that occurrences of loose speak cluster into a small set of categories that share interpretation strategies. This section describes a study in which we analyzed two sets of questions from Project Halo. All the questions were given in English. We built naïve encodings for the questions and matched the encodings with the structure of the chemistry knowledge base built for Project Halo (Barker *et al.* 2004). Here are the types of loose speak we encountered:

- Metonymy: referring to an entity or event (the referent) by one of its features or attributes (the metonym). The metonym is related to the referent through a restricted set of relations; a commonly used list of metonymic relations is compiled by (Lakoff & Johnson 1980). It has the following relations: PART-FOR-WHOLE, PRODUCER-FOR-PRODUCT, OBJECT-FOR-USER, CONTROLLER-FOR-CONTROLLED, INSTITUTION-FOR-PEOPLE-RESPONSIBLE, PLACE-FOR-INSTITUTION and PLACE-FOR-EVENT.

  Figure 1 contains an example of metonymy: a property ($conductivity$), which pertains to a part (solutes), is ascribed to the whole (the aqueous solution).

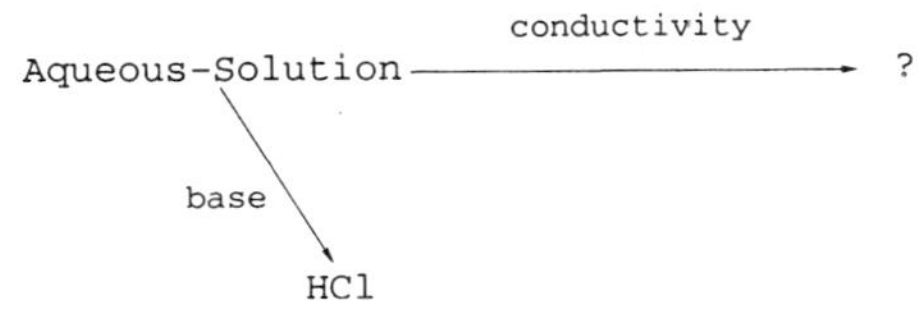


Figure 1: An example of loose speak from the Project Halo question set: "Is a water solution of $HCl$ conductive?". The "?" in the figure indicates an query. With respect to the chemistry knowledge base, this encoding contains two occurrences of loose speak. First, it contains aggregate loose speak: a $HCl$ is a molecule, and a single molecule does not act as the solute of a solution because it does not have properties such as concentration. The $HCl$ in the encoding should be replaced by a $Chemical$ whose basic structural unit is a $HCl$ molecule. Second, it contains metonymy loose speak: the $conductivity$ property belongs to solutes instead of solutions because it is the solutes that determine the conductivity of a solution. The query "the conductivity of Aqueous-Solution" should be placed on the base of the Aqueous-Solution instead. Figure **??** shows the correct encoding of this query.

- Causal factor: referring to a result by one of its causes. For example, a chemistry question might refer implicitly to a chemical reaction by mentioning only the "mix" or "add" event that causes the reaction.
- Aggregate: referring to an aggregate by one of its members, or *vice-versa*. For example, in figure 1, $HCl$ must refer to a set of molecules, i.e. a chemical, not an individual $HCl$ molecule, because a solution of $HCl$ should contain more than one $HCl$ molecule. Although this type of loose speak is similar to PART-FOR-WHOLE metonymy, it differs in terms of the partonomy types to which it applies. The PART-FOR-WHOLE metonymic relation applies to heterogeneous sets (e.g. an entity can have different types of parts, such as the various parts of a car), but the aggregate relation applies to homogeneous sets (e.g. each individual in the set is a basic unit of the set, such as a single soldier in an army).
- Role: referring to an entity by a role played by that entity, or *vice-versa*(Fan *et al.* 2001). For example, a Bronsted acid is a role played by chemicals in the context of reactions, but is often used loosely, omitting the context as in: "these chemicals are Bronsted acids".
- Overly generic concept: referring to a specific concept or instance by the generic class to which it belongs. For example, a "reaction" is used to refer to an "equilibrium reaction".
- Noun compounds: referring to the implicit relation be-

```
Given a triple of the form <C1, r, C2>:

  RESULT = nil
  If domain_violation (C1, r) then
     RESULT = search_head(<C1,r,C2>)
   else if range_violation (C2, r) then
        RESULT = search_tail(<C1,r,C2>)
        else if not(resemblace_test (<C1, r, C2>)) then
             RESULT = search_head(<C1,r,C2>)
             If not (RESULT) then
                RESULT = search_tail(<C1,r,C2>)
             end if
           end if
        end if
  end if
  If RESULT then
     Return RESULT
  else
     Return <C1, r, C2>
  end if
```

Figure 2: The search algorithm used to interpret one triple. The algorithm detects loose speak by checking the domain, range constraints and checking to see if the input expression is similar to any existing knowledge. If loose speak is found, then it calls the two search routine to search for encodings similar to the input, and it returns the search result if any is found, or the original input if nothing else is found.

tween a pair of nouns by using just the noun phrase consisting of the two nouns. For example, "zinc metal" refers to metal *composed of* zinc. Noun compounds are a type of loose speak because they omit the semantic relation between the head noun and its modifier(s), and this omission must be rectified before the reference is clear.

Table 1 reports the results of our study. We can draw several conclusions from this study. First, loose speak is ubiquitous, occurring in virtually every question we analyzed. Second, loose speak concentrates on a small number of types. We found common types of loose speak, some of which occur as frequently as 87% of the time.

## Interpreting loose speak

### Algorithm Overview

The input to our loose-speak interpreter is a question encoding, which may or may not contain loose speak, and the output is the correct encoding of the question. The question encoding is a conceptual graph consisting of a set of labeled edges of the form: $\langle ConceptClass, relation, FillerClass\rangle$. We call $ConceptClass$ the ***head*** and $FillerClass$ the ***tail***. Queries are encoded as a special type of edge in which the tail is unknown (denoted: "?"). Figure 1 is an example of such encoding.

The interpreter makes multiple passes through the set of edges. Each pass is equivalent to traversing the graph. During each pass, the interpreter applies a "test & repair" function to every edge. The interpreter stops when a pass is completed in which all the edges pass the test, so none is repaired. The order of traversal does not matter because (other than "overly generic concept" type of loose speak) the interpreter does not alter the original head or tail. Rather, the interpretation of each edge is a series of connecting edges, and the interpretation of one edge does not affect the interpretation of other edges. For "overly generic concept" type of loose speak, the interpreter replaces the head or the tail of an edge with a more specific class, and a simple backtracking algorithm is used in case the more specific class conflicts with edges connected to the original edge.

### Test & repair

During the traversal of the conceptual graph encoding the question, each edge is tested and repaired. Figure 2 shows the algorithm for the test and repair procedure. The test determines whether the edge contains loose speak. Because the correct encoding is unknown, the test uses this heuristic:

> If the edge violates structural constraints, then it must contain loose speak (because correct encodings are consistent with the structure of the knowledge base).

The only structural constraints used by the interpreter are based on the domain and range of the relation in an edge. Specifically, for an edge $\langle C_1, r, C_2\rangle$, the domain of $r$ must subsume $C_1$, and the range of $r$ must subsume $C_2$.

Although the constraint check returns many true positive cases, it also may return many false negatives. The constraint check is complemented by a resemblance check. The resemblance check is based on the hypothesis that if the input does not resemble any existing knowledge, then it may contain loose speak because studies have shown that "one frequently repeats similar versions of general theories" (Clark, Thompson, & Porter 2000). Even though the knowledge resemblance test may return many false positives, it returns many true negatives as well.

The resemblance test, applied to an edge, is implemented as follows. If the edge represents a query (i.e. the tail of the edge is "?"), the edge passes the test only if the knowledge base can compute one or more fillers for the tail. (This is the basic question-answering function of a knowledge base.) Otherwise, the edge $\langle Head_q, r, Tail_q\rangle$ passes the test only if the knowledge base contains an edge $\langle Head_{kb}, r, Tail_{kb}\rangle$, such that $Head_{kb}$ subsumes or is subsumed by $Head_q$ and $Tail_{kb}$ subsumes or is subsumed by $Tail_q$.

After loose speak has been detected in a edge, it is interpreted by searching the knowledge base for similar edges. The search is conducted by two breadth-first procedures: `search_head` and `search_tail`. Given the edge $\langle C_1, r, C_2\rangle$, the `search_head` function starts at $C_1$, traverses all semantic relations, such as "has-part", "agent" and "subclasses", and stops when a suitable instance is found. An instance, $C_3$, is suitable if the triple $\langle C_3, r, C_2\rangle$ does not contain loose speak. The successful search path is returned as the interpretation for the input.

To avoid unintended interpretations, the semantic relations do not include "superclasses" relation. If both "subclasses" and "superclasses" are included in the search path, then any concept can be found from $C_1$ by climbing up and

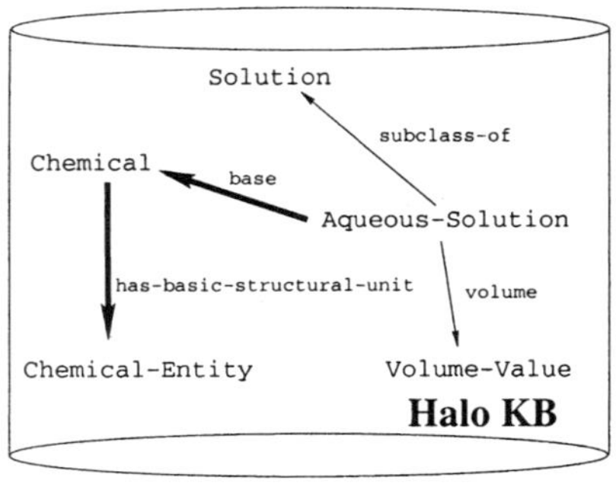


Figure 3: The application of "search-head" function on the edge ⟨ *Aqueous-Solution*, *base*, *HCl* ⟩. The function is called because this edge does not resemble any existing path in the knowledge base. The loose speak is resolved by breadth-first search from *Aqueous-Solution*, along all the semantic relations such as *volume*, *base*, *subclasses*, until a *HCl* or a superclass or subclass of *HCl*, is found. In this example, the search stops at depth 2, and returns the new edge ⟨ *Aqueous-Solution*, *base*, ⟨ *Chemical*, *has-basic-structural-unit*, *HCl* ⟩ ⟩ because *HCl* is a superclass of *Chemical-Entity*. The bold line in the above figure shows how the result is found.

down the taxonomy, and a large number of spurious interpretations may be returned for the given input.

If multiple suitable instances are found, then they are ordered based on their distances from $C_1$. Either users are prompted to choose one correct interpretation from the list of results or the first result is automatically chosen.

If the original input has a domain constraint violation and no result is found, then an additional search is performed. The additional breadth-first search starts from an instance of the domain class, and it searches along all semantic relations until $C_1$ is found.

The `search_tail` function is implemented similarly as a search that starts at $C_2$.

The search is conducted in a breadth-first manner for two reasons. First, because each occurrence of loose speak is a naïve encoding that has a limited number of differences from its correct encoding, a correct interpretation should be closely related to the naïve input. A very deep search will only return encodings that are not closely related to the input. If only a shallow search is needed, then a brute force search such as breadth-first search is sufficient. The maximum search depth in our system is set 4. Second, a breadth-first search returns the shallowest interpretation without examining the whole search space. Such breadth-first searches have been shown to be effective in interpreting noun compound type of loose speak given a top level ontology that contains the fundamental axioms (Fan, Barker, & Porter 2003).

If no interpretation is found when the depth cutoff is reached, the interpreter returns the original encoding. In addition, if loose speak was detected by a constraint violation, the interpreter returns an error report.

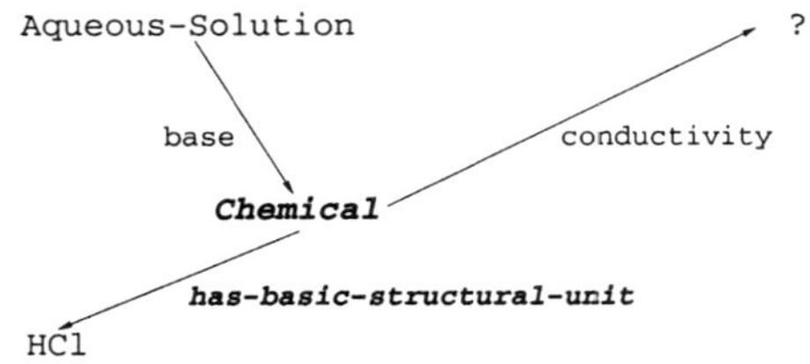


Figure 4: The interpretation of the query in Figure 1 in the context of the chemistry knowledge base built for Project Halo. Notice that *HCl* is replaced by *Chemical*, and the *conductivity* query has been moved from *Aqueous-Solution* to the *base* of *Aqueous-Solution* to conform to the structure of the knowledge base.

This algorithm applies to all types of loose speak, even noun compounds. A noun compound is represented as an unlabeled edge of the form: $\langle ModifierClass, nil, HeadClass \rangle$. Because there is no unlabeled edges in the knowledge base, noun compounds will fail the resemblance test, and consequently trigger `search_head` and `search_tail`.

### Example

For the example in figure 1, the loose-speak interpreter traverses the query graph to test & repair each edge. The edge ⟨ *Aqueous-Solution*, *base*, *HCl* ⟩ is tested first. The domain of *base* is constrained to be a *Solution*, and the range is constrained to be a *Thing*. Both constraints are satisfied because *Aqueous-Solution* is a subclass of *Solution* and *HCl* is a subclass of *Thing*. However, there is no path in the knowledge base that resembles the edge, so the `search-head` function is called to search from the head, *Aqueous-Solution*. The search returns *Chemical*, whose *has-basic-structural-unit* is *Chemical-Entity* (the superclass of *HCl*). See Figure 3. Consequently, the edge is interpreted as ⟨ *Aqueous-Solution*, *base*,*Chemical* ⟩.

The edge ⟨ *Aqueous-Solution*, *conductivity*, ? ⟩ is then tested for loose speak. No constraints are violated, but the query does not yield any result. This prompts a breadth-first search from *Aqueous-Solution*. This search stops at *Chemical*, the *base* of *Aqueous-Solution*, because it has a conductivity value and is a suitable replacement for *Aqueous-Solution* in the original edge.

Figure **??** shows the final interpretation of the query graph. Notice that the solute of the *Aqueous-Solution* is replaced by *Chemical*, and the *conductivity* query has been moved from *Aqueous-Solution* to *Chemical*. After these changes, the two types of loose speak, metonymy and aggregate, are resolved in the query graph and the encoding is correctly aligned with the structure of the knowledge base.

## Experiment

To evaluate our approach, we asked several users to encode a set of questions, and compared their naïve encodings with the corresponding output from the loose-speak interpreter.

| | KE Experience | Chemistry Background | Experiment length | Questions encoded | Correct encodings | Interpreter precision | Interpreter recall |
|---|---|---|---|---|---|---|---|
| User A | 0.5 yr | medium | 10.5 hr | 47 (94%) | 3 (6.4%) | 97.4% | 90.5% |
| User B | 17 yrs | weak | 9.95 hr | 48 (96%) | 4 (8.3%) | 100% | 90.7% |
| User C | 0.25 yr | medium | 10 hr | 44 (88%) | 5 (11.4%) | 96.8% | 87.8% |

Table 2: The evaluation results of the loose-speak interpreter. The first two columns show users' backgrounds in knowledge engineering and chemistry. The next three columns show users' performance: the time required to finish the experiment; the number of questions encoded; and the number of correct encodings. The last two columns measure the interpreter's performance in term of precision recall. As the data have shown, despite different backgrounds, all users were able to encode most of questions, the encodings had many occurrences of loose speak, the interpreter was able to correct most encodings, and to do so with high precision.

## Setup

For this experiment we used a set of fifty multiple choice questions from various mock AP chemistry tests. This set was compiled by a chemist (anonymous to us), who also provided the answers for the questions. This data set is distinct from the two sets of questions used in the frequency study, and it is distinct from the training data that we used to refine the interpreter.

We recruited three users, with varying backgrounds in knowledge engineering and chemistry, to pose questions to the chemistry knowledge base built for Project Halo. All three were familiar with KM (Porter & Clark 1998), the knowledge representation language used in the experiment, but none was familiar with the chemistry knowledge base and its structure. Their knowledge engineering experience varied from a few months to many years. Their chemistry backgrounds varied from weak (high school chemistry decades ago) to medium (college chemistry years ago).

The users were given a short (three page) tutorial on encoding questions. It contains two sections: format and vocabulary. The format section explained that question encodings should have a context part, which gives the contextual information of a question, and an output part, which specifies the value being sought. The format section illustrates this with three examples. The vocabulary section lists commonly used classes and slots in the chemistry knowledge base, and their corresponding chemistry terms. Users were also pointed to a web page containing the complete listing of slots and classes, and they were allowed to take as much time as necessary to complete the questions. These brief instructions were not a complete tutorial on using the knowledge base, as evidenced by the high rate of loose speak in the users' encodings of questions.

We used metrics of precision and recall to evaluate the interpreter's performance. Precision and recall are defined as follows (Jurafsky & Martin 2000):

$$Precision = \frac{\#\ of\ correct\ answers\ given\ by\ system}{\#\ of\ answers\ given\ by\ system}$$

$$Recall = \frac{\#\ of\ correct\ answers\ given\ by\ system}{total\ \#\ of\ possible\ correct\ answers}$$

For our experiment, the correct answers are the number of question encodings that are interpreted correctly. Answers given by the system are the number of question encodings for which the interpreter detects loose speak and finds an interpretation. Finally, all possible correct answers are the number of all the question encodings that contain loose speak. An interpretation is determined to be correct if it completely aligns with the chemistry knowledge base and conveys the intended semantics of the question encoding as judged by us. Precision estimates the likelihood of a correct interpretation when an interpretation is found; recall is a measurement of coverage.

Our experiment does not include noun compound type of loose speak for two reasons. First, the effectiveness of the interpreter on noun compounds has been evaluated separately in (Fan, Barker, & Porter 2003). Second, although noun compounds, such as "carbon monoxide", occur frequently in chemistry questions, their interpretations do not require inferring a variety of semantic relations, therefore chemistry is an unrepresentative domain for evaluating noun compound interpretation.

For this experiment, we ran the interpreter in "batch mode". If the interpreter found multiple interpretations for any question, we treated the first interpretation as its sole response.

## Data analysis and discussion

The experimental results are shown in table 2. The first two columns give the users' background in knowledge engineering and in chemistry; the next three columns record the time it took users to encode the test questions, the number of questions they were able to encode, and the percentages of correct encodings. The last two columns measure how well the interpreter performed.

Based on the data, we can draw three conclusions:

1. Loose speak is very common – just as we found in our preliminary study (described in the "Types of loose speak and their frequencies" section). Only 4% of the encodings on average contain no loose speak. This underscores the importance of the loose-speak interpreter for building useful knowledge-based question-answering systems.
2. The loose-speak interpreter works well. As shown in Table 2, the precision of the interpreter is above 95%, and the recall is around 90%. This shows the search algorithm we used is suitable for interpreting naïve encodings.

In addition we found that 54% of the loose speak occurrences are detected by constraint violations, and the rest by the resemblance check. This suggests both checks are important for detecting loose speak.

3. The loose-speak interpreter significantly assists novice users in posing questions. The results show that there is no clear correlation between users' knowledge engineering experience and the number of questions they are able to encode. Users with little knowledge engineering experience were able to encode large percentages of questions quickly. This is good news; it suggests that with the burden of loose-speak interpretation lifted, knowledge engineering is no longer a significant hurdle to question-answering. Users can concentrate on the content of questions instead of knowledge engineering details.

## Related work

Metonymy is one type of loose speak that has been studied extensively in the computational linguistic community. There are two basic approaches to metonymy interpretation. First, there are systems that interpret metonymic expressions based on a set of rules (Weischedel & Sondheimer 1983; Grosz *et al.* 1987; Lytinen, Burridge, & Kirtner 1992; Fass 1997). These rules contain explicit knowledge about how to interpret some types of metonymy, and they are matched against inputs to produce interpretations. This approach is easy to implement because no large knowledge base is required, but it can handle only a fixed set of metonymy types. Second, there are systems that interpret metonymic expressions based on knowledge-base search (Browse 1978; Markert & Hahn 1997; Harabagiu 1998). Unlike the rule-based systems, they do not contain explicit knowledge of different types of metonymy, instead they rely on searches in a general purpose knowledge base. Our loose speak interpreter is one of them. Although this approach has no limit on the types of metonymy it can handle, the demand for an extensive knowledge base makes it difficult to implement. Because our interpreter is used for knowledge-based question-answering systems, it avoids this cost by operating on an existing knowledge-base.

Another closely related linguistic phenomenon is the use of generics, a technique called "genericity". The study of genericity deals with how to distinguish between classes and instances (Carlson & Pelletier 1995). For example, "potato" refers to the class of potato and an instance of potato in the following two sentences.

a. The potato was first cultivated in South America.

b. The potato was rotten.

This is similar to the aggregate type of loose speak because an individual is used to refer to an aggregate, the class. However aggregate type of loose speak differs from genericity when the aggregate being referred to is not the whole class of concepts. For example, in figure 1, $HCl$ refers to a particular set of molecules that is dissolved in the solution, not the complete class of $HCl$ molecules. Most of the genericity detection methods are either syntax based or require human judgment. They are not suitable for automatic interpretation of loose speak in a knowledge-rich environment such as question-answering.

Techniques similar to knowledge-base search are used for other tasks, such as knowledge acquisition, in addition to loose-speak interpretation (Davis 1979; Kim & Gil 1999; Blythe 2001). Many of these systems build explicit meta-knowledge representation, such as the tree of rule models in (Davis 1979), and use such meta-knowledge to guide knowledge acquisition. Our loose-speak interpreter does not have meta-knowledge representations, instead it uses generic search algorithm directly on the knowledge base itself to find useful knowledge to assist question-answering.

## Conclusion

In this paper, we defined loose speak as the part of a question encoding that misaligns with existing knowledge base structures, and we presented a system that would interpret loose speak automatically. Our preliminary evaluation shows that loose speak is common in question encodings, and that our interpreter can detect and interpret most occurrences of loose speak correctly. Without the burden of manually interpreting every occurrence of loose speak, users were able to pose a good percentage of questions quickly.

In the near future, we will expand the investigation of loose speak into other aspects of knowledge base interaction, such as knowledge acquisition, and evaluate its impact.

## References

Angele, J.; Moench, E.; Oppermann, H.; Staab, S.; and Wenke, D. 2003. Ontology-based query and answering in chemistry: Ontonova@project halo. In *Proceedings of 2nd International Semantic Web Conference.*

Barker, K.; Chaw, S. Y.; Fan, J.; Porter, B.; Tecuci, D.; Yeh, P.; Chaudhri, V. K.; Israel, D.; Mishra, S.; Romero, P.; and Clark, P. E. 2004. A question-answering system for AP chemistry: Assessing KR&R technologies. In *Principles of Knowledge Representation and Reasoning: Proceedings of the Ninth International Conference.*

Blythe, J. 2001. Integrating expectations from different sources to help end users acquire procedural knowledge. In *Proceedings of Seventeenth International Joint Conference on Artificial Intelligence.*

Browse, R. A. 1978. Knowledge identification and metaphor. In *Proceedings of the 2nd Biennial Conferene of the Canadian Society for Computational Studies of Intelligence (CSCSI-2)*, 48–54.

Buchanan, B. G., and Shortliffe, E. 1984. *Rule-Based Expert Systems: The MYCIN Experiments of the Stanford Heuristic Programming Project.* Reading, MA: Addison-Wesley.

Carlson, G. N., and Pelletier, F. J., eds. 1995. *The Generic Book.* Chicago: University of Chicago Press.

Clark, P.; Barker, K.; Porter, B.; Chaudhri, V.; Mishra, S.; and Thomere, J. 2003. Enabling domain experts to convey questions to a machine: a modified, template-based approach. In *Proceedings of Second International Conference on Knowledge Capture.*

Clark, P.; Thompson, J.; and Porter, B. 2000. Knowledge patterns. In *Principles of Knowledge Representation and Reasoning: Proceedings of the Seventh International Conference.*

Davis, R. 1979. Interactive transfer of expertise: Acquisition of new inference rules. *Artificial Intelligence* 12(2):121 – 157.

Fan, J.; Barker, K.; and Porter, B. 2003. The knowledge required to interpret noun compounds. In *Proceedings of Eighteenth International Joint Conference on Artificial Intelligence.*

Fan, J.; Barker, K.; Porter, B.; and Clark, P. 2001. Representing roles and purpose. In *Proceedings of First International Conference on Knowledge Capture.*

Fass, D. 1997. *Processing Metonymy and Metaphor.* Greenwich, Connecticut: Ablex Publishing.

Grosz, B. J.; Appelt, D. E.; Martin, P. A.; and Pereira, F. C. N. 1987. TEAM: An experiment in the design of transportable naturual-language interfaces. *Artificial Intelligence* 32(2):173–243.

Harabagiu, S. 1998. Deriving metonymic coercions from wordnet. In *Proceedings of the Workshop on Usage of WordNet in Natural Language Processing Systems, COLING-ACL*, 142–148.

Jurafsky, D., and Martin, J. 2000. *Speech and Language Processing: An Introduction to Natural Language Processing Computational Linguistics, and Speech Recognition.* New Jersey: Prentice Hall.

Kim, J., and Gil, Y. 1999. Deriving expectations to guide knowledge-base creation. In *Proceedings of Sixteenth National Conference on Artificial Intelligence.* AAAI Press.

Lakoff, G., and Johnson, M. 1980. *Metaphors We Live By.* Chicago: University of Chicago Press.

Lytinen, S. L.; Burridge, R. R.; and Kirtner, J. D. 1992. The role of literal meaning in the comprehension of non-literal constructions. *Computational intelligence* 8(3):416–432.

Markert, K., and Hahn, U. 1997. On the interaction of metonymies and anaphora. In *Proceedings of the Fifteenth International Joint Conference on Artificial Intelligence.*

Porter, B., and Clark, P. 1998. KM - the knowledge machine: Reference manual. Technical report, University of Texas at Austin. http://www.cs.utexas.edu/users/mfkb/km.html.

Vulcan Inc. 2003. Project Halo. http://projecthalo.com.

Weischedel, R. M., and Sondheimer, N. J. 1983. Metarules as a basis for processing ill-formed input. *American Journal of Computational Linguistics* 9(3-4):161–177.

# Learning Indexing Patterns from One Language for the Benefit of Others

**Udo Hahn**[1] **Kornél Markó**[1,2] **Stefan Schulz**[2]

[1]Text Knowledge Engineering Lab, Freiburg University
Werthmannplatz 1, D-79085 Freiburg, Germany
http://www.coling.uni-freiburg.de/

[2]Department of Medical Informatics, Freiburg University Hospital
Stefan-Meier-Str. 26, D-79104 Freiburg, Germany

**Abstract**

Using language technology for text analysis and light-weight ontologies as a content-mediating level, we acquire indexing patterns from vast amounts of indexing data for English-language medical documents. This is achieved by statistically relating interlingual representations of these documents (based on text token bigrams) to their associated index terms. From these 'English' indexing patterns, we then induce the associated index terms for German and Portuguese documents when their interlingual representations match those of English documents. Thus, we learn from past English indexing experience and transfer it in an unsupervised way to non-English texts, without ever having seen concrete indexing data for languages other than English.

## Introduction

Manual indexing or classification requires skilled human experts to perform a routine task, *viz.* to assign index terms or classification codes (usually, taken from a controlled vocabulary) to journal or newspaper articles, technical reports, etc. – once they have at least partially read and understood them. Limiting the choice of allowed descriptors to those conceptually organized in a thesaurus (the *Medical Subject Headings* (MESH 2001; Aronson *et al.* 2000) or the *Unified Medical Language System* (UMLS 2003; Aronson 2001), e.g., in the medical domain) creates additional benefits in that the description space is semantically structured in terms of more general/specific or related subject areas. Consequently, search capabilities become more powerful, e.g., through query expansion that incorporates synonyms, taxonomically more specific terms, etc. Large bibliographic services such as PUBMED (`http://www.ncbi.nlm.nih.gov/PubMed/`), which is maintained by the National Library of Medicine (NLM) and hosts MEDLINE, the largest bibliographic medical online database, still rely on the human indexers' performance, as far as the content description of documents is concerned.

The manual assignment of index terms from a very large set of descriptors is not only a laborious and often tedious task, but it is also quite expensive. In the nineties, the NLM spent over two million dollars and employed 44 full-time equivalent indexers each year just for that task (Hersh *et al.* 1994), facing yearly updates of less than 100,000 bibliographic units. In 2002, more than 350,000 new records were added to MEDLINE. Therefore, costs tend to increase at an even higher rate when indexing is performed by humans only.

MEDLINE includes English as well as non-English documents, though the indexing is only in English. After many years of hard work, more than 12 million bibliographic units have been indexed and classified using the *English* MESH as a controlled vocabulary. A few terminology mappers exist from English to some non-English languages, but their coverage is far from complete (compared with the English MESH). Because the role of the physicians' native languages is much more dominant than in other scientific disciplines, the focus on English as the medical content description language creates a serious bottleneck for tentative users of PUBMED in non-English-speaking countries.

In order to reuse this bulk of scholarly work for languages other than English, we started a project which benefits from that experience in the following way: Assuming that the English indexing of medical documents is a highly valued asset, we determine lexical patterns in the abstracts and relate them to their associated index terms. This mapping is affected by language technology tools, which incorporate light-weight ontologies for interlingual content representation. Once we (can) map lexical items from an arbitrary non-English language (e.g., German or Portuguese) to their English lexical correlates, we may then reuse the English indexing patterns for the non-English languages, once a mediating interlingua is available. Thus, we learn from past English indexing experience and transfer it in an unsupervised way to non-English texts, without ever having seen concrete indexing data for languages other than English.

## Document Analysis

We take a lexicalized, bag-of-words-style approach to document analysis. Our main focus is on morphological analysis, because morphological processes alter the appearance of words but leave their core meaning, by and large, intact. Such morphological variants can generally be described as concatenations of basic sublexical forms (e.g., stems) with additional substrings (affixes). We distinguish three kinds of morphological processes, *viz.* inflection (e.g., adding the plural *"es"* in *"leuk⊕o⊕cyt⊕es"*,[1] derivation (e.g., attaching the derivation suffix *"ic"* in *"leuk⊕o⊕cyt⊕ic"*), and composition (e.g., in *"leuk⊕em⊕ia"*). Morphological analysis is concerned with the reverse processing of morphological variants, i.e., deflection (or lemmatization), dederivation and decomposition. The goal is to map all occurring morphological variants to some canonical base form(s) — e.g., *'leuk'* or *'cyt'* in the examples from above.

Medical terminology, on which we focus here, is further characterized by a typical mix of Latin and Greek roots and the corresponding host language, e.g., as evidenced by "neuroencephalomyelopathy", "glucocorticoid", "pseudohypoparathyroidism". This may also surface in some languages, e.g., German, as mild orthographic variations such as with *Karzinom* and the equivalent *Carcinom*. Obviously, dealing with such phenomena is crucial for medical information retrieval, in particular, for a system that maps free text to a controlled indexing vocabulary such as MESH.

## Interlingual Morpho-Semantic Normalization

In order to deal with such morphological problems in an IR scenario, we developed a document pre-processing engine which takes plain English, German and Portuguese texts as input and transforms them in three steps, *viz.* orthographic, morphological and semantic normalization (cf. Figure 1).

During orthographic normalization all capitalized characters from input documents are reduced to lower-case characters. Additionally, language-specific character substitutions are made (e.g., for German *'ß'* → *'ss'*, *'ä'* → *'ae'*, *'ö'* → *'oe'*, *'ü'* → *'ue'* and for Portuguese *'ç'* → *'c'*, *'ú'* → *'u'*, *'õ'* → *'o'*). This step eases the matching of (parts of) text tokens and entries in the lexicons.

For each source language, we provide a *subword lexicon* as background knowledge for morphological normalization. Each one contains morpheme-like entries (22,000 subwords for German and English, 14,000 for Portuguese). Based on such a lexicon, the system segments the orthographically normalized input stream into a sequence of semantically plausible subwords. The results are then checked for morphological plausibility using a finite-state automaton in order to reject invalid segmentations (e.g., ones without stems or beginning with a suffix). If there are ambiguous valid readings or incomplete segmentations (due to missing entries in the lexicon), a series of heuristic rules are applied, which prefer those segmentations with the longest match from the left, the lowest number of unspecified segments, etc.

For semantic normalization, we extended the subword lexicon by a *subword thesaurus*, in which intra- and interlingual semantic equivalence classes are defined, e.g., the one composed of English *"kidney"*, German *"niere"*, and Latin *"nephr"*. Each semantically relevant sublexical unit produced by the morphological segmentation is replaced by its corresponding *morpho-semantic class identifier* (MID), which represents all subwords assigned to one particular class. The result is a morpho-semantically normalized document in a language-independent, interlingual representation.

[1]'⊕' denotes the string concatenation operator.

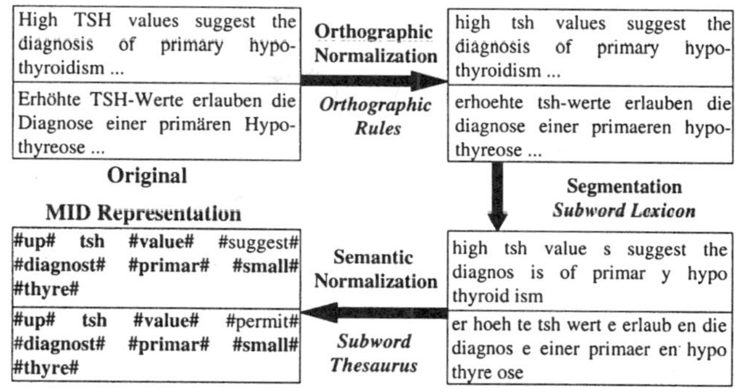


Figure 1: Morpho-Semantic Normalization Pipeline

In Figure 1, bold-faced MIDs co-occur in both document fragments. A comparison of the original natural language documents at the beginning of the pipeline and their interlingual representation at the very end already reveals the degree of (hidden) similarity uncovered by the overlapping MIDs.

During the construction of the subword thesaurus, we faced many of the notorious problems one encounters in the field of cross-language information retrieval, *viz.* ambiguity when translating terms, intralingual synonymy and homonymy. In our approach, multiple entries connected to a single MID express intralingual synonymy and interlingual translation. Ambiguous terms are linked to their respective equivalence classes by a special thesaurus link, producing a sequence of their related MIDs.

In practice, after three person years of construction on the medical subword lexicons and the thesaurus, their growth has almost reached the end at the level of 58,000 subwords connected to 28,500 equivalence classes, in total.

## Learning Indexing Patterns

In the following section, we describe a statistical, a heuristic and a hybrid approach to automatically identifying English MESH entries as document descriptors for English, as well as German and Portuguese documents, given sets of *a priori* assigned index terms to English documents. In the MESH (2001), descriptors are organized in a conceptual hierarchy. In its 2002 version (which we use), over 20,500 so-called main headings occur as potential descriptors.[2]

The particularity of our approach of assigning descriptors to documents is based on an interlingua representation for the documents as well as the indexing vocabulary. Using this representation (generated by the normalization procedures described the previous section) is advantageous in that we are able to train our indexing system on texts written in one language (English) and test it on documents of another, up until now unseen, languages. This approach allows the processing of documents in any language covered by the lexicons.

We start with a sample of 35,000 medical abstracts ($word_1 \ldots word_m$ in Figure 2, step A) taken from the set of approximately 350,000 new entries stored in MEDLINE in

[2]Publication Types and special descriptors such as Subheadings, Chemical Supplementary Terms, Age Groups, Check Tags and Geographics are not considered in our experiments.

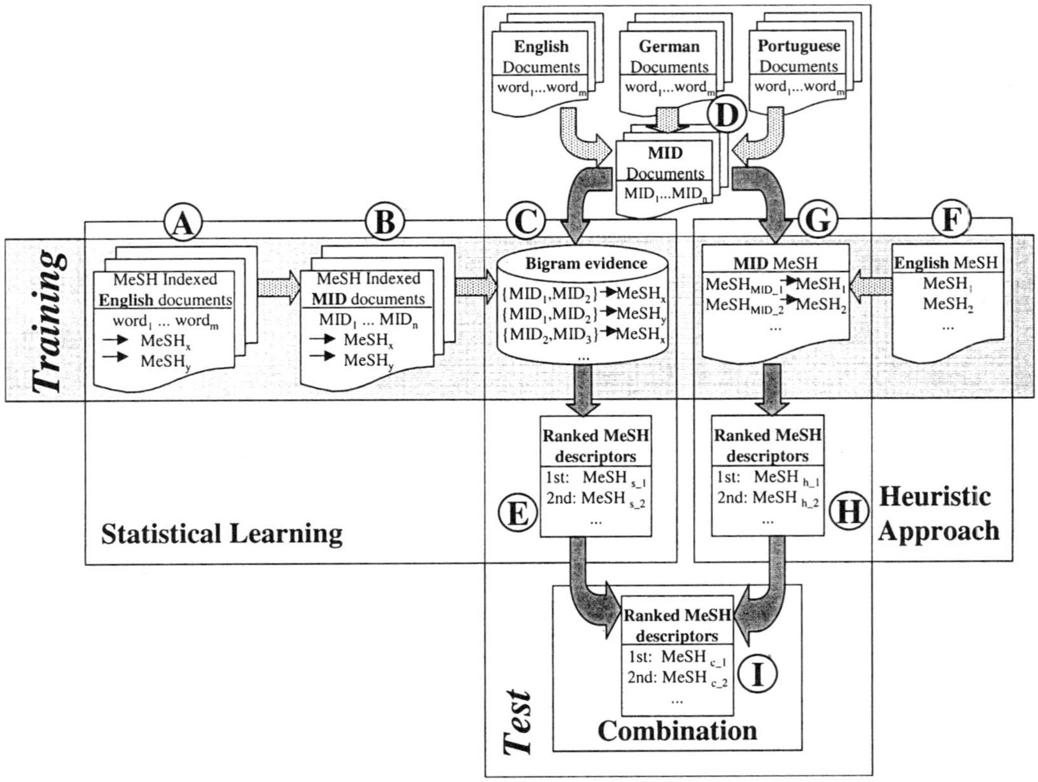


Figure 2: Architecture of the Combined Indexing System

$$w(MeSH_i \mid MID_1, ..., MID_n) = log \prod_{j=1}^{n-1} \begin{cases} \frac{P(MID_j, MID_{j+1} \mid MeSH_i)}{P(MID_j, MID_{j+1})} & \text{, if defined} \\ 1 & \text{, otherwise} \end{cases}$$

Figure 3: Estimating the Conditional Weighting Value of a MESH Descriptor Given $n$ Morpho-Semantic Class Identifiers (MIDs)

2002, to which English MESH main headings have already been assigned manually ($MeSH_x$ and $MeSH_y$ in Figure 2, step A). After morphological normalization, each natural language document is represented by a sequence of morpho-semantic class identifiers ($MID_1 \ldots MID_n$ in Figure 2, step B), while still preserving the original MESH index terms assigned to it. Based on that representation we employ a Bayesian approach which ignores the *a priori* probabilities of the descriptors. Thus, statistical evidence for class identifier (MID) bigrams is basically computed by counting their frequency of co-occurrence in the training corpus with individual (manually supplied) MESH entries (Figure 2, step C). That is how indexing patterns are learned.

In the test phase, we aim at identifying MESH terms as valid descriptors for unseen normalized documents (cf. Figure 2, step D), and we rank these terms by their weighting values ($w$ as defined in Figure 3). Given a document which contains $n$ class identifiers (MIDs), the conditional weighting value for $MeSH_i$, a particular MESH main heading, is computed with the product of the computed conditional probabilities $P$ of the MID bigrams in the text that co-occur with the descriptor $MeSH_i$ in the training set, divided by the *a priori* probability of the corresponding text bigrams in the training collection, if both probabilities can be observed. The denominator of the weighting function takes into account the fact that infrequent terms have a greater explanatory power for a given entity when faced with large quantities of data, therefore increasing the weighting value for that entity. If no bigram that is currently being processed appears in the training data, or if it is not associated with the current descriptor $MeSH_i$, it remains neutral (multiplication by 1).

We treat MID bigrams in an unordered way. They are defined as a set of MIDs that co-occur within a document window of two text tokens, regardless of the original sequence of words that license the set of MIDs. This is due to the fact that in German and English, the MID order changes when genitives or prepositions come into play, as with *"femoral neck fracture"* vs. *"fractured neck of femur"* corresponding to *["#femur#", "#nuchal#", "#fractur#"]* vs. *["#fractur#", "#nuchal#", "#femur#"]*. Finally, all identified MESH descriptors, $MeSH_{s\_1}$, $MeSH_{s\_2} \ldots$, are ranked according to their weighting value (Figure 2, step E).

## MESHing Document Representations

The indexing patterns identified with the methodology from the previous section are the backbone for the retrieval performance of our system. In the course of retrieval experiments, however, we also found that some heuristic add-ons were helpful to further increase the system's performance. In this section, we describe some of these heuristics and a hybrid approach, which combines the learned indexing patterns with these heuristics to automatically identify MESH entries as document descriptors.

In the heuristic approach, we just rely on the MESH Thesaurus and a collection of (non-indexed) documents. Based on suitable criteria, a fully automatic MESH indexing of the documents is computed. Unlike the learning method, no prior indexing of documents is necessary. In the training phase, all English MESH main headings, $MeSH_1$, $MeSH_2$, etc., (cf. Figure 2, step F) undergo the morpho-semantic normalization procedure. Thus, all words from the main headings which are covered by the English subword lexicon are substituted by their corresponding unique MIDs resulting in morpho-semantically normalized representations, $MeSH_{MID\_1}$, $MeSH_{MID\_2}$, etc., which are linked to the original MESH descriptors (Figure 2, step G).

In the test phase, English, German and Portuguese documents, defined by a sequence $word_1 \ldots word_m$, are processed by the morphological engine which generates for each document an identifier sequence, $MID_1 \ldots MID_n$, at the interlingua level (Figure 2, step D). Afterwards, heuristic rules (some of them already proposed by NLM's indexing initiative (Aronson *et al.* 2000)) are applied to the normalized test documents. In essence, this means that each MESH descriptor, whose normalized representation contains at least one of the MIDs in the document, is retrieved. Next, each normalized MESH descriptor is assessed against the normalized text by computing diverse factors. We confine ourselves to the most important metrics:

- **Longest Match Factor:** On the level of MIDs, individual MESH descriptors, which appear as single entries, can also appear as part of other MESH entries. For example, the German technical term *"Bauchschmerzen"* (*"abdominal pain"*) that appears in a text and is normalized to the MIDs *"#abdom#"* and *"#pain#"* is, amongst others, associated with the MESH entries "Abdominal Pain" (*["#abdom#", "#pain#"]*), "Abdomen" (*["#abdom#"]*) and "Pain" (*["#pain#"]*). If two or more normalized MeSH descriptors can be merged into one longer MESH descriptor, the latter is preferred over its constituents.
- **Phrase Factor:** The number of different MIDs in a phrase that match the MIDs in a normalized descriptor is called *MID number*. In addition, we consider the phrase interval of a normalized descriptor as the span between the first and the last MID associated with this descriptor in a phrase. Then, the *phrase factor* is defined as the ratio of MID number and phrase interval. The Portuguese phrase *"o fígado do paciente foi transplantado"* (*"the patient's liver was transplanted"*), e.g., will be transformed into *["#hepat#", "#patient#", "#transplant#"]*. Given the normalized descriptor for "liver transplantation" ("#hepat#", "#transplant#"), the corresponding MID number is 2, and the phrase interval amounts to 3. Therefore, the phrase factor equals $2/3$.
- **Entry Factor:** The *entry factor* is the MID number divided by the number of MIDs of the associated descriptor. For example, the German noun phrase *"noduläre Hyperplasie"* (*"nodular hyperplasia"*) is normalized to *["#nodul#", "#above#", "#plast#"]* and the MESH descriptor "Focal Nodular Hyperplasia" to *["#focal#", "#nodul#", "#above#", "#plast#"]*. The corresponding entry factor is $3/4$.
- **Title Factor:** A descriptor found in the title will be ranked higher than others.

Finally, all possible descriptors are ordered according to a weighted average of the above (and other) metrics ($MeSH_{h\_1}$, $MeSH_{h\_2} \ldots$ in Figure 2, step H).

We also pool the results of the statistical learning of indexing patterns and the heuristic add-ons in order to find out whether a combined effort performs better than any of the two in isolation. Thereupon, we merged both approaches in the following way. Firstly, all descriptors that are ranked in the top thirty by *both* of the methods are put at the top of the result list ($MeSH_{c\_1}$, $MeSH_{c\_2} \ldots$ in Figure 2, step I). After the first $k$ positions ($30 \geq k$) have been filled that way, the remaining positions are incrementally generated by the following rule: The two entries at the top of the output of the statistical approach are alternately incorporated into the final result, followed by one entry of the heuristic approach, until both lists (maximum length: 100 terms) are exhausted. Previous experiments have shown that this empirically motivated procedure leads to much more favorable results than a formal one, e.g., by multiplying the weights from the different weighting functions.

## Evaluation Scenario

For our evaluation, we selected abstracts from English, German and Portuguese medical journals. English and Portuguese texts were taken from PUBMED, the online interface of the MEDLINE database. German articles came from SpringerLink (`http://link.springer-ny.com/`), an online library for medicine which contains dozens of medical journals. We chose those journals which are linked to MEDLINE. Manually assigned MESH identifiers were also extracted from PUBMED.

We then randomly assembled text collections for the training phase (35,000 English abstracts for the statistical learning of indexing patterns from the English corpus) and the test phase (4,000 abstracts from the English/German corpus and due to limited availability, only 800 abstracts from the Portuguese corpus).

The data acquired during the training phase were then used for the indexing of English, German and Portuguese documents. The abstracts were automatically processed according to the methods described in the previous sections and the indexing results were evaluated against the manually supplied MESH main headings. This data serves as the *de facto* gold standard for our experiments (similar to the study of the indexing initiative of the NLM (Aronson *et al.* 1999)). Unfortunately, human indexings in MEDLINE are not really consistent. Funk & Reid (1983) measured 48.2% interrater agreement with regard to manually assigned MESH main-heading for English abstracts (only 41.5% for German abstracts). Obviously, such inconsistencies in the test collection will also affect the validity of our evaluation results when we take this data as the gold standard.

### Evaluation Results

Table 1 depicts the precision and recall values for the chosen test scenarios. For each of the three languages we considered the top 5, 10 and 40 ranked descriptors. These cut-off layers were previously introduced by Aronson *et al.* (1999) and we adopt them in order to more accurately compare the results.

| Cut Off | Method | English | | German | | Portuguese | |
|---|---|---|---|---|---|---|---|
| | | Prec | Rec | Prec | Rec | Prec | Rec |
| 5 | Heuristic | 32.7 | 18.5 | 25.9 | 16.9 | 21.6 | 17.5 |
| | Statistical | 34.3 | 18.6 | 28.2 | 18.1 | 18.7 | 14.1 |
| | Combined | 41.7 | 23.2 | 33.2 | 21.5 | 25.7 | 20.0 |
| 10 | Heuristic | 23.0 | 25.2 | 17.7 | 22.8 | 14.3 | 22.3 |
| | Statistical | 24.9 | 26.3 | 19.9 | 25.0 | 13.1 | 19.2 |
| | Combined | 30.2 | 32.8 | 23.3 | 29.7 | 17.6 | 26.8 |
| 40 | Heuristic | 8.6 | 36.4 | 6.5 | 32.9 | 5.6 | 33.9 |
| | Statistical | 10.4 | 42.5 | 8.4 | 41.7 | 5.8 | 33.9 |
| | Combined | 12.8 | 52.9 | 9.6 | 47.7 | 7.1 | 42.0 |

Table 1: Precision/Recall (Prec/Rec) Table for Different Languages and Indexing Methods at Different Cut-off Points

When focusing on the combined approach and considering the top five descriptors, our procedure already retrieves 23% of all relevant MESH terms for English (22% for German, 20% for Portuguese) at a precision rate of 42% (33% and 26%, respectively). Looking at the top 40 of the system-generated descriptors, precision for English drops to 13% (10% for German, 7% for Portuguese), whilst recall increases to 53% (48% and 42%, respectively).

Figure 4 summarizes the resulting precision/recall values for the different languages for the top 5, 10, 20, etc. up to the top 100 proposed descriptors using the combined indexing procedure. The crossing of the curves indicate that, on the average, ten MESH descriptors were manually assigned to the abstracts of the test collection. With recall values ranging between 27% and 33% for each of the languages for the top ten assigned descriptors, results seem to be not so shiny. However, when we compare these values to the average agreement of *human* indexers (for English 4.82 MESH descriptors out of ten, for German only 4.15 (Funk & Reid 1983)) our system derives 1.54 less descriptors on the average for English (68.1%) and only 1.18 less for German (71.6%) in a *fully automatic* indexing environment.

Considering the human indexing agreement for English as baseline for all of the three languages we achieve 68% for English, 62% for German and 56% for Portuguese. Keeping in mind that the processing of German and Portuguese abstracts was not part of the training phase, these results are still promising.

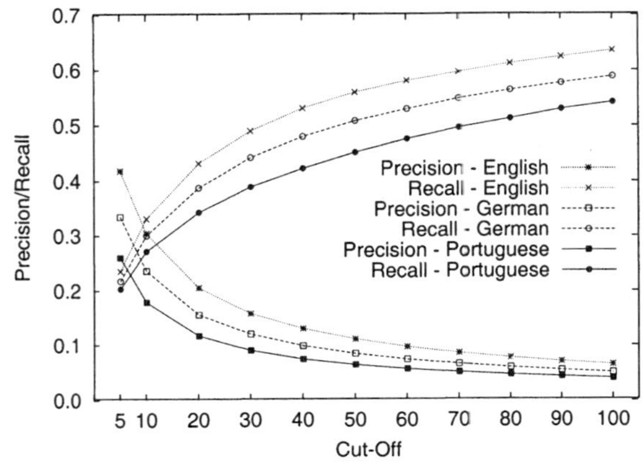


Figure 4: Precision/Recall Graphs for the English, German and Portuguese Indexing Task at Different Cut-off Points (Combined Indexing Method)

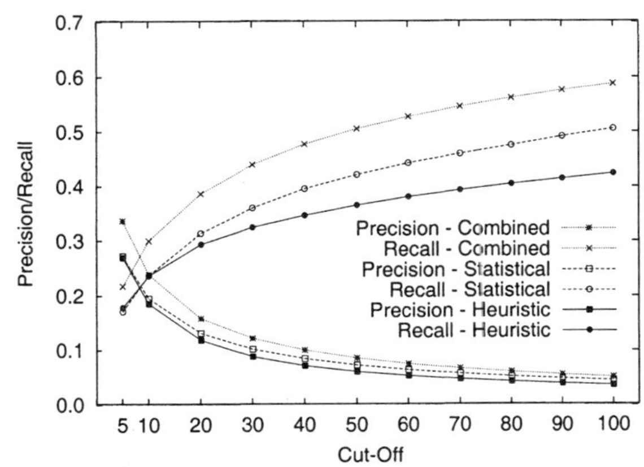


Figure 5: Precision/Recall Graphs for the Different Indexing Procedures at Different Cut-off points Averaged Over Three Languages (English, German, and Portuguese)

We also examined the different contributions of the two basic approaches we pursue. With the exception of Portuguese, in isolation, the statistical learning approach always significantly outperforms the heuristic one, for all languages at all cut-off points with respect to recall and precision. The learned indexing patterns are, therefore, the driving force for the performance of the system. Pooling both approaches, however, yields additional, mostly substantial benefits.

To summarize, Figure 5 shows the resulting precision/recall value pairs for the different indexing methods for the top 5, 10, 20, etc. up to the top 100 proposed descriptors averaged over the three languages we dealt with.

## Related Work

The (monolingual) MESH mapping methods proposed by NLM's indexing initiative (Aronson *et al.* 2000; 1999) reach

29% recall (top 5) and 61% recall (top 40)[3] on a small test corpus comprised of 200 MEDLINE abstracts (our data is 23% and 53% recall, respectively). In previous studies, when we focused on a smaller subset of MEDLINE documents covering clinical disciplines only, we observed similar results. The loss of performance in this study indicates that the lexicon has to be further adapted to non-clinical topics, e.g., public health, since we now take a much more comprehensive sample of MEDLINE into account.

In Eichmann et al.'s system (Eichmann, Ruiz, & Srinivasan 1998) and in the SAPHIRE International server (Hersh & Donohoe 1998) for cross-language IR, multilingual user queries are transformed into entries of the UMLS Metathesaurus in order to retrieve suitable documents (cf. also Aronson (2001)). These mapping approaches have much in common with our heuristic indexing procedure which is, however, clearly outperformed by the statistical learning method.

Sebastiani (2002) points out that any content-based indexing method that incorporates some machine learning algorithm (e.g., probabilistic or decision tree classifiers) does better than methods without any learning device. Various experiments carried out on the REUTERS-21578 corpus, the most widely used benchmark collection in automated indexing, showed that the combination of different indexing methods seems to generally perform the best. These considerations are also backed up by our results.

## Conclusions

We have investigated the use of large quantities of indexing knowledge as available for English medical documents and its transfer to non-English documents for which no such data is available. Our approach is based upon the supply of manually created subword lexicons and a conceptual interlingua linked to these language-specific lexicons. After automatic lexical analysis, indexing patterns are automatically learned from interlingual text representations. The subsequent assignment of English document descriptors to English, German and Portuguese texts is also achieved without any manual intervention. Based on evidence from our experiments, we may cautiously conclude that our approach is a reasonable way to go (still keeping in mind the fragile gold standard on which our results rest).

The methodology we use for learning indexing patterns is a standard Bayesian approach. The methodological news we have to offer is two-fold. First of all, the combined effort of statistical and heuristic methods beats a purely statistical approach. Secondly, pattern learning is not only based on the literal word (n-gram) level, but incorporates the level of light-weight ontologies, as well. The latter provides us with a conceptual interlingua which is crucial for the language-mapping we focus on.

Concerning the generality of our approach, medical lexicons for any natural language are certainly much more constrained in terms of lexico-semantic ambiguities than the general language lexicon (as witnessed by the ambiguity rates, e.g., in the WORDNET lexical database (Fellbaum 1998)). At the same time, the need for developing a home-grown medical lexicon becomes apparent after an inspection of WORDNET. Although some medical terminology can be found there, it is by no means adequately covered. While the development of the newly developed subword thesaurus has almost been completed for English and German, the Portuguese version still needs further curation.

[3]Including Check Tags and Age Groups, which are easier to identify.

## Acknowledgments

This work was funded by *Deutsche Forschungsgemeinschaft*, grant Klar 640/5-1. We thank our Brazilian colleagues, Percy Nohama & Roosewelt Leite de Andrade, for the acquisition and maintenance of the Portuguese lexicon.

## References

Aronson, A. R.; Bodenreider, O.; Chang, H. F.; Humphrey, S. M.; Mork, J. G.; Nelson, S. J.; Rindflesch, T. C.; and Wilbur, W. 1999. The indexing initiative. In *A Report to the Board of Scientific Counselors of the Lister Hill National Center for Biomedical Communications.*

Aronson, A. R.; Bodenreider, O.; Chang, H. F.; Humphrey, S. M.; Mork, J. G.; Nelson, S. J.; Rindflesch, T. C.; and Wilbur, W. J. 2000. The NLM indexing initiative. In *AMIA 2000 – Proceedings of the Annual Symposium of the American Medical Informatics Association*, 17–21. Los Angeles, CA, November 4-8, 2000. Hanley & Belfus.

Aronson, A. R. 2001. Effective mapping of biomedical text to the UMLS Metathesaurus: The METAMAP program. In *AMIA 2001 – Proceedings of the Annual Symposium of the American Medical Informatics Association*, 17–21. Washington, D.C., November 3-7, 2001. Hanley & Belfus.

Eichmann, D.; Ruiz, M. E.; and Srinivasan, P. 1998. Cross-language information retrieval with the UMLS metathesaurus. In *SIGIR'98 – Proceedings of the 21st Annual International ACM SIGIR Conference on Research and Development in Information Retrieval*, 72–80. Melbourne, Australia, August 24-28, 1998. ACM.

Fellbaum, C., ed. 1998. WORDNET*: An Electronic Lexical Database*. MIT Press.

Funk, M. E., and Reid, C. A. 1983. Indexing consistency in MEDLINE. *Bulletin of the Medical Library Association* 71(2):176–183.

Hersh, W. R., and Donohoe, L. C. 1998. SAPHIRE International: A tool for cross-language information retrieval. In *AMIA'98 – Proceedings of the 1998 AMIA Annual Fall Symposium*, 673–677. Orlando, FL, November 7-11, 1998. Hanley & Belfus.

Hersh, W. R.; Hickman, D. H.; Haynes, B.; and McKibbon, K. A. 1994. A performance and failure analysis of SAPHIRE with a MEDLINE test collection. *Journal of the American Medical Informatics Association* 1(1):51–60.

MESH. 2001. *Medical Subject Headings*. Bethesda, MD: National Library of Medicine.

UMLS. 2003. *Unified Medical Language System*. Bethesda, MD: National Library of Medicine.

Sebastiani, F. 2002. Machine learning in automated text categorization. *ACM Computing Surveys* 34(1):1–47.

# Interactive Information Extraction with Constrained Conditional Random Fields

**Trausti Kristjansson**
Microsoft Research
Redmond, Washington
traustik@microsoft.com

**Aron Culotta**
Dept. of Computer Science
University of Mass. Amherst
culotta@cs.umass.edu

**Paul Viola**
Microsoft Research
Redmond, Washington
viola@microsoft.com

**Andrew McCallum**
Dept. of Computer Science
University of Mass. Amherst
mccallum@cs.umass.edu

**Abstract**

Information Extraction methods can be used to automatically "fill-in" database forms from unstructured data such as Web documents or email. State-of-the-art methods have achieved low error rates but invariably make a number of errors. The goal of an *interactive information extraction* system is to assist the user in filling in database fields while giving the user confidence in the integrity of the data. The user is presented with an interactive interface that allows both the rapid verification of automatic field assignments and the correction of errors. In cases where there are multiple errors, our system takes into account user corrections, and immediately propagates these constraints such that other fields are often corrected automatically.

Linear-chain conditional random fields (CRFs) have been shown to perform well for information extraction and other language modelling tasks due to their ability to capture arbitrary, overlapping features of the input in a Markov model. We apply this framework with two extensions: a constrained Viterbi decoding which finds the optimal field assignments consistent with the fields explicitly specified or corrected by the user; and a mechanism for estimating the confidence of each extracted field, so that low-confidence extractions can be highlighted. Both of these mechanisms are incorporated in a novel user interface for form filling that is intuitive and speeds the entry of data—providing a 23% reduction in error due to automated corrections.

## Introduction

A recent study showed that as part of the process of gathering and managing information, currently 70 million workers, or 59% of working adults in the U.S., complete forms on a regular basis. Filling in forms is tedious, error-prone and time-consuming. In many cases, the data that is used to populate the fields of the form is already available in computer readable form.

The goal of this work is to reduce the burden on the user to the largest extent possible, while ensuring the integrity of the data entered into the system. One typical example is the entry of contact addresses from on-line sources such as email messages or Web pages. There are more than 20 fields in a contact database, including last name, first name, address, city, state, phone, etc. As we will show, it is possible to create automatic systems which will extract over 90% of these fields correctly from a diverse set of complex sources. Given this low error rate, the first goal of a good user interface is to display the extracted fields so that they can be verified rapidly. The second goal is to allow for the rapid correction of incorrect fields. It is important to realize that the fields are extracted as an interdependent set. Given the name "Charles Stanley" it is likely that the first name is Charles and the last name is "Stanley." But, the opposite is possible as well. Given the error that the two names have been switched, naive correction systems require two corrective actions. In the *interactive information extraction* system described below, when the user corrects the first name field to be "Stanley," the system then automatically changes the last name field to be "Charles." We call this capability *correction propagation*.

From the perspective of user interface design, there are a number of goals, including reducing cognitive load, reducing the number of user actions (clicks and keystrokes), and speeding up the data acquisition process. An important element that is often overlooked is the confidence the user has in the integrity of the data. This is crucial to the usability of the application, as users are not tolerant of (surprising) errors, and will discontinue the use of an automatic semi-intelligent application if it has corrupted or misclassified information. Unfortunately such factors are often hard to quantify.

An interactive form filling system is quite different from the batch processing of data, such as for warehouse data cleaning (Borkar, Deshmukh, & Sarawagi 2000). In batch processing the set of fields extracted are determined directly and are optimized for low error rates. In contrast interactive information extraction (IIE) puts additional requirements on the information extraction system. To facilitate a natural user experience, the information extraction system must display low confidence fields and make optimal use of any corrections that the user has made.

There are a number of statistical approaches for information extraction (IE) that are more or less suited to this paradigm. The most common engineering approach is to build a set of regular expressions that extract the fields in question. Regular expressions are a poor match for interactive information extraction since they cannot estimate confidence, nor can they naturally incorporate user labels and corrections. Maximum Entropy Classifiers are potentially quite powerful, since they allow for the introduction of arbitrary, potentially dependent, features. Maximum entropy classifier can also estimate the confidence in decisions. However, each field extracted using a maximum entropy model is estimated independently. For this reason the potential for correction propagation is minimal. Conditional Random Fields, a generalization both of maximum entropy models and hidden Markov models, allow for the introduction of arbitrary non-local features and capture the dependencies between labels. CRFs have been shown to perform well on information extraction tasks (McCallum & Li 2003; Pinto *et al.* 2003; McCallum 2003; Sha & Pereira 2003), and are well-suited for interactive information extraction since the confidence of the labels can be estimated and there is a natural scheme for optimally propagating user corrections.

There are two contributions of this paper. The first contribution is the introduction of the interactive information extraction framework. This includes a user interface that highlights the label assigned to each field in the unstructured document visually while flagging low confidence labels. The interface also allows for rapid correction using "drag and drop." Finally, the interface supports the propagation of field corrections, so that one correction will often correct many errors.

The second contribution is a pair of new algorithms for the estimation of field confidences in CRFs and for the incorporation of constraints into the Viterbi decoding process. In this case the constraints come from corrections to incorrect fields or from the new field labels added by the user.

The remainder of this paper describes each contribution in turn. We then describe a set of experiments in the domain of contact address entry. In these experiments we compare the performance of several well known algorithms against CRFs. We then investigate the effectiveness of constrained Viterbi decoding after correcting the least confident error.

## User Interaction Models

The idea explored in this paper is that of populating the fields of a contact database, sometimes called a Digital Address Book. With the increase of personal digital devices such as personal digital assistants (PDAs), and cell phones, there is increasing demand for better tools for contact entry.

### User Interfaces for Information Extraction

Figure 1 shows a user interface that facilitates interactive information extraction. The fields to be populated are on the left side, and the source text was pasted by the user into the right side. The information extraction system extracts text segments from the unstructured text and populates the corresponding fields in the contact record. This user interface is designed with the strengths and weaknesses of the information extraction technology in mind. Some important aspects are:

- The UI displays visual aids that allow the user to quickly verify the correctness of the extracted fields. In this case color-coded correspondence is used (e.g. blue for all phone information, and yellow for email addresses). Other options include arrows or floating overlayed tags.
- The UI allows for rapid correction. For example, text segments can easily be grouped into blocks to allow for a single click-drag-drop. In the contact record at the left, fields have drop down menus with other candidates for the field. Alternatively the interface could include "try again" buttons next to the fields that cycle through possible alternative extractions for the field until the correct value is found.
- The UI immediately propagates all corrections and additions by the "constrained Viterbi" procedure described below.
- The UI visually alerts the user to fields that have low confidence. Furthermore, in the unstructured text box, possible alternatives may be highlighted (e.g. alternate names are indicated in orange)

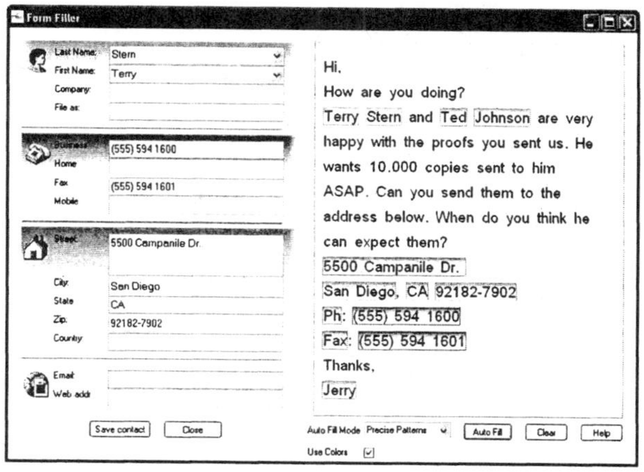


Figure 1: A user interface for entry of contact information. The user interface relies on interactive information extraction. If a user makes a correction, the interactive parser can update other fields. Notice that there are 3 possible names associated with the address. The user is alerted to the ambiguity by the color coding.

Using a well-defined probabilistic model, such as CRF's, we can correctly calculate confidence estimates for each field assignment. Estimation of confidence scores is discussed in the section "Confidence Estimation."

Confidence scores can be utilized in a UI in a number of ways. Field assignments with relatively low confidence can be visually marked. If a field assignment has very low confidence, and is likely to be incorrect; we may choose not to fill in the field at all. The text that is most likely to be assigned to the field can then be highlighted in the textbox (e.g. in orange).

Another related case is when there are multiple text segments that are all equally likely to be classified as e.g. a name, then this could also be visually indicated (as is done in Figure 1).

### User Interaction Models

For the purposes of quantitative evaluation we will simulate the behavior of a user during contact record entry, verification, and correction. This allows for a simpler experimental paradigm that can more clearly distinguish the values of the various technical components. A set of user studies will be reported elsewhere.

A large number of user interaction models are possible given the particulars of the interface and information extraction engine. Here we outline the basic models that will be evaluated in the experimental section.

**UIM1:** The simplest case. The user is presented with the results of automatic field assignment and has to correct all errors (i.e. no correction-propagation).

**UIM2:** Under this model, we assume an initial automatic field assignment, followed by a single randomly-chosen manual correction by the user. We then perform correction-propagation, and the user has to correct all remaining errors manually.

**UIM3:** This model is similar to UIM2. We assume an initial automatic field assignment. Next the user is asked to correct the *least confident incorrect field.* The user is visually alerted to the fields in order of confidence, until an error is found. We then perform correction-propagation and the user then has to correct all remaining errors manually.

**UIMm:** The user has to fill in all fields manually.

### Performance Evaluation

The goal in designing a new application technology is that users see an immediate benefit in using the technology. Assuming that perfect accuracy is required, benefit is realized if the technology increases the time efficiency of users, or if it reduces the cognitive load, or both. Here we introduce an efficiency measure, called the Expected Number of User Actions, which will be used in addition to standard IE performance measures.

**The Expected Number of User Actions:** The *Expected Number of User Actions* (ENUA) measure is defined as the number of user actions (e.g. clicks) required to correctly enter all fields of a record. The Expected Number of User Actions will depend on the user interaction model. To express the Expected Number of User Actions we introduce the following notation: $P_i(j)$ is the probability distribution over the number of errors $j$ after $i$ manual corrections. This distribution is represented by the histogram in Figure 2.

Under UIM1, which does not involve correction propagation, the Expected Number of User Actions is:

$$\text{ENUA} = \sum_{n=0}^{\infty} nP_0(n) \tag{1}$$

where $P_0(n)$ is the distribution over the number of incorrect fields (see Figure 2).

In models UIM2 and UIM3 the Expected Number of User Actions is

$$\text{ENUA}_1 = (1 - P_0(0)) + \sum_n nP_1(n). \tag{2}$$

where $P_0(0)$ is the probability that all fields are correctly assigned initially and $P_1(n)$ is the distribution over number of incorrect fields in a record after one field has been corrected. The distribution $P_1$ will depend on which incorrect field is corrected, e.g. a random incorrect field is corrected under UIM2 whereas the least confident incorrect field is corrected under UIM3. The subscript 1 on $ENUA_1$ indicates that correction-propagation is performed once.

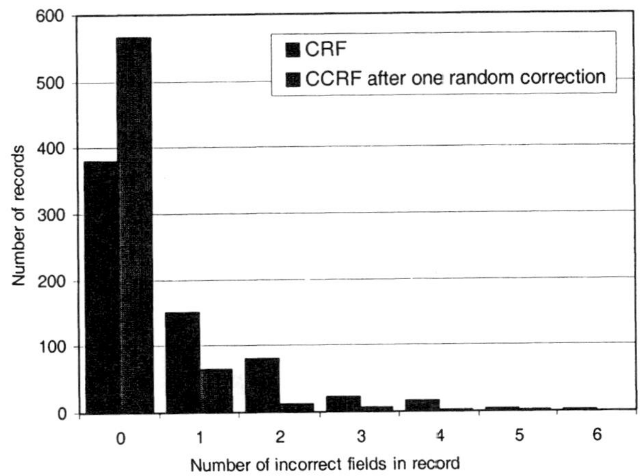


Figure 2: Histogram, where records fall into bins depending on how many fields in a record are in error. Solid bars are for CRF before any corrections. The shaded bars show the distribution after one random incorrect field has been corrected. These can be used to estimate $P_0(n)$ and $P_1(n)$ respectively.

## Constrained Conditional Random Fields

Conditional random fields (Lafferty, McCallum, & Pereira 2001) are undirected graphical models used to calculate the conditional probability of values on designated output nodes given values on designated input nodes. In the special case in which the designated output nodes of the graphical model are linked by edges in a *linear chain,* CRFs make a first-order Markov independence assumption among output nodes, and thus correspond to finite state machines (FSMs). In this case CRFs can be roughly understood as conditionally-trained hidden Markov models, with additional flexibility to effectively take advantage of complex overlapping features.

Let $\mathbf{o} = \langle o_1, o_2, ... o_T \rangle$ be some observed input data sequence, such as a sequence of words in a document, (the values on $T$ input nodes of the graphical model). Let $\mathcal{S}$ be a set of FSM states, each of which is associated with a label, (such as a label LASTNAME). Let $\mathbf{s} = \langle s_1, s_2, ... s_T \rangle$ be some sequence of states, (the values on $T$ output nodes). CRFs define the conditional probability of a state sequence given an input sequence as

$$p_\Lambda(\mathbf{s}|\mathbf{o}) = \frac{1}{Z_\mathbf{o}} \exp\left(\sum_{t=1}^{T} \sum_k \lambda_k f_k(s_{t-1}, s_t, \mathbf{o}, t)\right), \tag{3}$$

where $Z_{\mathbf{o}}$ is a normalization factor over all state sequences, $f_k(s_{t-1}, s_t, \mathbf{o}, t)$ is an arbitrary feature function over its arguments, and $\lambda_k$ is a learned weight for each feature function. The normalization factor, $Z_{\mathbf{o}}$, involves a sum over an exponential number of different possible state sequences, but because these nodes with unknown values are connected in a graph without cycles (a linear chain in this case), it can be efficiently calculated via belief propagation using dynamic programming. Inference to find the most likely state sequence (very much like Viterbi algorithm in this case) is also a simple matter of dynamic programming.

Maximum aposteriori training of these models is efficiently performed by hill-climbing methods such as conjugate gradient, or its improved second-order cousin, limited-memory BFGS (Sha & Pereira 2003).

In order to facilitate the user interaction model, we need to clamp some of the hidden variables to particular values. Doing so results in the constrained Viterbi algorithm for CRFs, described below.

For HMMs, the Viterbi algorithm (Rabiner 1989) is an efficient dynamic programming solution to the problem of finding the state sequence most likely to have generated the observation sequence. Because CRFs are conditionally trained, the CRF Viterbi algorithm instead finds the most likely state sequence given an observation sequence,

$$\mathbf{s}^* = \operatorname*{argmax}_{\mathbf{s}} \; p_\Lambda(\mathbf{s}|\mathbf{o}).$$

To avoid an exponential-time search over all possible settings of $\mathbf{s}$, Viterbi stores the probability of the most likely path at time $t$ which accounts for the first $t$ observations and ends in state $s_i$. Following the notation of (Rabiner 1989), we define this probability to be $\delta_t(s_i)$, where $\delta_0(s_i)$ is the probability of starting in each state $s_i$, and the induction step is given by:

$$\delta_{t+1}(s_i) = \max_{s'} \left[\delta_t(s') \exp\left(\sum_k \lambda_k f_k(s', s_i, \mathbf{o}, t)\right)\right]. \tag{4}$$

The recursion terminates in

$$p^* = \operatorname*{argmax}_i [\delta_T(s_i)]$$

We can backtrack through the dynamic programming table to recover $\mathbf{s}^*$.

Constrained Viterbi alters Eq. 4 such that $s^*$ is constrained to pass through some subpath $C = \langle s_t, s_{t+1} \ldots \rangle$. These constraints $C$ now define the new induction is $\delta_{t+1}(s_i) =$

$$\begin{cases} \max\limits_{s'} \left[\delta_t(s') \exp\left(\sum\limits_k \lambda_k f_k(s', s_i, \mathbf{o}, t)\right)\right] & \text{if } s_i = s_{t+1} \\ 0 & \text{otherwise} \end{cases} \tag{5}$$

for all $s_{t+1} \in C$. For time steps not constrained by $C$, Eq. 4 is used instead.

In the context of interactive form filling, the constraints $C$ correspond to a set of observations (an address field) manually corrected by the user. Upon correction, the system runs Constrained Viterbi to find the best path that conforms to the corrected field. In addition to correcting the field the user indicates, this process may also change the predicted states for observations *outside* of the corrected field. This is because the recursive formulation in Eq. 5 can affect optimal paths before and after the time steps specified in $C$.

## Confidence Estimation

To estimate the confidence the CRF has in an extracted field, we employ a technique we term *Constrained Forward-Backward* (Culotta & McCallum 2004). The Forward-Backward algorithm is similar to the Viterbi algorithm: instead of choosing the maximum state sequence, Forward-Backward evaluates all possible state sequences given the observation sequence.

The "forward values" $\alpha_{t+1}(s_i)$ are recursively defined similarly to Eq. 4, except the max is replaced by a summation. Thus we have

$$\alpha_{t+1}(s_i) = \sum_{s'} \left[\alpha_t(s') \exp\left(\sum_k \lambda_k f_k(s', s_i, \mathbf{o}, t)\right)\right]. \tag{6}$$

Furthermore, the recursion terminates to define $Z_{\mathbf{o}}$ in Eq. 3:

$$Z_{\mathbf{o}} = \sum_i \alpha_T(s_i) \tag{7}$$

The Constrained Forward-Backward algorithm calculates the probability of any sequence passing through a set of constraints $C = \langle s_q \ldots s_r \rangle$, where now $s_q \in C$ can be either a positive constraint or a *negative* constraint. A negative constraint constrains the forward value calculation *not* to pass through state $s_q$.

The calculations of the forward values can be made to conform to $C$ in a manner similar to the Constrained Viterbi algorithm. If $\alpha'_{t+1}(s_i)$ is the constrained forward value, then $Z'_{\mathbf{o}} = \sum_i \alpha'_T(s_i)$ is the value of the *constrained lattice*. Our confidence estimate is equal to the normalized value of the constrained lattice: $Z'_{\mathbf{o}}/Z_{\mathbf{o}}$.

In the context of interactive form filling, the constraints $C$ correspond to an automatically extracted field. The positive constraints specify the observation tokens labelled inside the field, and the negative constraints specify the boundary of the field. For example, if we use states names B-TITLE and I-JOBTITLE to label tokens that begin and continue a JOBTITLE field, and the system labels observation sequence $\langle o_2, \ldots, o_5 \rangle$ as a JOBTITLE field, then $C = \langle s_2 =$ B-JOBTITLE, $s_3 = \ldots = s_5 =$ I-JOBTITLE, $s_6 \neq$ I-JOBTITLE$\rangle$.

## Experiments

For training and testing we collected 2187 contact records (27,560 words) from web pages and emails and hand-labeled 25 classes of data fields.[1] Some data came from pages containing lists of addresses, and about half came from disparate

[1]The 25 fields are: FIRSTNAME, MIDDLENAME, LASTNAME, NICKNAME, SUFFIX, TITLE, JOBTITLE, COMPANYNAME, DEPARTMENT, ADDRESSLINE, CITY1, CITY2, STATE, COUNTRY, POSTALCODE, HOMEPHONE, FAX, COMPANYPHONE, DIRECTCOMPANYPHONE, MOBILE, PAGER, VOICEMAIL, URL, EMAIL, INSTANTMESSAGE

|  | Token Acc. | F1 | Prec | Rec |
|---|---|---|---|---|
| CRF | *89.73* | 87.23 | 88.24 | 86.24 |
| MAXENT | 88.43 | 84.84 | 85.09 | 84.95 |

Table 1: Token accuracy and field performance for the Conditional Random Field based field extractor, and the Maximum Entropy based field extractor.

web pages found by searching for valid pairs of city name and zip code.

The features consisted of capitalization features, 24 regular expressions over the token text (e.g. CONSTAINSHYPHEN, CONTAINSDIGITS, etc.), character n-grams of length 2-4, and offsets of these features within a window of size 5. We also used 19 lexicons, including "US Last Names," "US First Names," "State names," "Titles/Suffixes," "Job titles," and "Road endings." Feature induction was not used in these experiments.

We implemented five machine learning methods to automatically annotate the contact records. All models were trained on a random subset of 70% of the data and tested on the remaining 30%. Table 1 shows the performance for the two baseline methods. Column 1 lists the token accuracy (the proportion of tokens labeled correctly), and columns 2-4 list the segmentation performance at the field level, where F1 is the harmonic mean of recall and precision. CRF is the conditional random field classifier described earlier. MAXENT is a conditional maximum entropy classifier. The experiments do not include any user feedback. Notice that the token error rate of the CRF system is about 11% lower than that of the MaxEnt system.

In the following sections, we start by discussing results in terms of the Expected Number of User Actions. Then we discuss results that highlight the effectiveness of correction-propagation and utilization of confidence scores respectively.

## User Interaction Evaluation

The standard information retrieval metrics do not adequately capture the performance of an Interactive Information Extraction system. In this paper we have proposed a metric called the Expected Number of User Actions.

Table 2 shows the Expected Number of User Actions for the different algorithms and User Interaction Models. In addition to the CRF and MAXENT algorithms, Table 2 shows results for CCRF, which is the constrained conditional random field classifier presented in this paper.

The baseline user interaction model (UIM1) where IE is used to populate the fields and the user corrects all remaining errors is expected to require 0.73 user actions per record. Notice that manual entry of records is expected to require on average 6.31 user actions to enter all fields. This is about 8.6 times more user actions.

We see the advantages of correction-propagation in CCRMs when an arbitrary incorrect field is corrected (UIM2), over the baseline (i.e. not using correction propagation (UIM1)) in the second row of Table 2. The ENUA drops to 0.63, which is a relative drop in ENUA of 13.9%. In

|  | ENUA | Change |
|---|---|---|
| CRF – (UIM1) | 0.73 | baseline |
| CCRF – (UIM2) | 0.63 | **-13.9%** |
| CCRF – (UIM3) | 0.64 | -11.3% |
| MAXENT – (UIM1) | 0.94 | +29.0% |
| Manual – (UIMm) | 6.31 | +770.0% |

Table 2: The Expected Number of User Actions (ENUA) to completely enter a contact record. Notice that Constrained CRF with a random corrected field reduces the Expected Number of User Actions by 13.9%.

comparison, manual entry requires over 10 times more user actions.

Confidence estimation is used in UIM3. Recall that in this user interaction model the system assigns confidence scores to the fields, and the user is asked to correct the least confident *incorrect* field.

Interestingly, correcting a random field (ENUA = 0.63) seems to be slightly more informative for correction-propagation than correcting the least confident erroneous field (ENUA = 0.64).

While this may seem surprising, recall that a field will have low confidence if the posterior probability of the competing classes is close to the score for the chosen class. Hence, it only requires a small amount of extra information to boost the posterior for one of the other classes and "flip" the classification. We can imagine a contrived example where there are two adjacent incorrect fields. In this case, we should correct the *more* confident of the two to maximize correction propagation. This is because the field with lower confidence requires a smaller amount of extra information to correct its classification.

Under UIM3, the user may be required to verify a number of correct fields before an incorrect field is found, since the model may have least confidence in correct fields.

Another way of assessing the effectiveness of the confidence measure is to ask how effective is it at directing the user to an incorrect token. In our experiments with CCRFs, the number of records that contained one or more errors was 276. The least confident field was truly incorrect in 226 out of those 276 records. Hence, confidence estimation correctly predicts an erroneous fields 81.9% of the time. If we instead choose a token at random, then we will choose an incorrect token in 80 out of the 276 records, or 29.0%. In practice, the user does not initially know where the errors are, so confidence estimates can be used effectively to direct the user to incorrect fields.

The ENUA metric does not take into account the time it takes the user to scan the record and find incorrect fields. It is difficult to assess this without extensive user studies, where different strategies and visual cues are compared.

## Correction Propagation

To examine the effectiveness of correction propagation, Table 3 shows the token accuracy of CCRF on contact records containing errors in at least two fields. One field is corrected by the user, with the hope that correction propagation will

| total accuracy before correction | 72.02 |
|---|---|
| total accuracy after correction | **87.12** |
| uncorrected accuracy before correction | 79.50 |
| uncorrected accuracy after correction | **84.30** |

Table 3: Correction propagation results for CCRF on sequences with errors in at least two fields. Error reduction is 23% for uncorrected tokens.

automatically fix errors in other fields. Here, total accuracy is the token accuracy for the entire contact record, and uncorrected accuracy is the token accuracy of tokens not corrected by the user. Note that these accuracies are naturally lower than in Table 2 because we are only examining records with multiple errors.

These results show that having the user correct one field results in a 23% reduction in error in the remaining fields. This additional error reduction is a boon to users since they do not have to perform these corrections manually.

### Confidence Estimation

In the preceding discussion, the goal of IIE has been to correctly fill in all fields of each record. A different scenario arises if we wish to reduce the labelling error rate of a large amount of data but we do not need the labelling to be error free. If we have limited man-power, we would like to maximize the efficiency or information gain from the human labeller.

This user interaction model assumes that we allow the human labeller to verify or correct a single field in each record, before going on to the next record.

As before the constrained conditional random field model is used, where Constrained Forward-Backward is used to predict the least confident extracted field. If this field is *incorrect*, then CCRF is supplied with the correct labelling, and correction propagation is performed using Constrained Viterbi. If this field is *correct*, then no changes are made, and we go on to the next record.

The experiments compare the effectiveness of verifying or correcting the least confident field i.e. CCRF - (L.CONF), to verifying or correcting an arbitrary field i.e. CCRF - (RANDOM).

Finally, CMAXENT is a Maximum Entropy classifier that estimates the confidence of each field by averaging the posterior probabilities of the labels assigned to each token in the field. As in CCRF, the least confident field is corrected if necessary.

Table 4 show results after a single field has been verified or corrected. Notice that if a random field is chosen to be verified or corrected, then the token accuracy goes to 91.7%, which is only a 19.2% reduction in error rate. If however, we verify or correct only the least confident field, the error rate is reduced by 56.18%.

This difference illustrates that reliable confidence prediction can increase the effectiveness of a human labeller. Also note that the 56% error reduction CCRF achieves over CRF is substantially greater than the 27% error reduction between CMAXENT and MAXENT.

| | Error Reduction | F1 | Prec | Rec |
|---|---|---|---|---|
| CCRF - (L. CONF.) | **56.2%** | 94.45 | 94.84 | 94.06 |
| CCRF - (RANDOM) | 19.2% | 89.72 | 90.72 | 88.75 |
| CMAXENT | 27.2% | 89.4 | 90.34 | 88.48 |

Table 4: Token accuracy and field performance for interactive field labeling. CCRF - (L. CONF.) obtains a 56% reduction in error over CRF, and a 46% reduction in error over CCRF - (RANDOM).

| | Pearson's r | Avg. Precision |
|---|---|---|
| Constrained FB | **0.531** | **98.0** |
| Random | -0.02 | 87.99 |
| WorstCase | - | 71.48 |

Table 5: Constrained Forward-Backward confidence estimation performs substantially better than baseline approaches.

To explicitly measure the effectiveness of the Constrained Forward-Backward algorithm for confidence estimation, Table 5 displays two evaluation measures: Pearson's $r$ and average precision. Pearson's $r$ is a correlation coefficient ranging from $-1$ to 1 which measures the correlation between a confidence score of a field and whether or not it is correct.

Given a list of extracted fields ordered by their confidence scores, average precision measures the quality of this ordering. We calculate the precision at each point in the ranked list where a correct field is found and then average these values. WORSTCASE is the average precision obtained by ranking all incorrect fields above all correct fields. Both Pearson's $r$ and average precision results demonstrate the effectiveness of Constrained Forward-Backward for estimating the confidence of extracted fields.

## Related Work

This paper is the first of which we are aware that uses interactive information extraction with constraint propagation and confidence prediction to reduce human effort in form-filling. Several other efforts have studied efficient ways to interactively *train* an extraction system, which would later run without human interaction, for example (Cardie & Pierce 1998; Caruana, Hodor, & Rosenberg 2000).

Methods to visually link related components in a user interface have been explored, for example (Becker & Cleveland 1987; Swayne, Cook, & Buja 1991). The XGobi system uses color coding and "brushing" to indicate associations in various types of high dimensional data.

Many common word processors use visual cues to direct the users attention to possible errors in spelling and grammar. In (Miller & Myers 2001) the authors use a similar strategy, based on outlier detection.

Others have implemented systems for information extraction from free-text address blocks, however none using an interactive method. Borkar, Deshmukh, & Sarawagi (2000) obtains high accuracy using a HMM on a simpler and more limited set of fields (HouseNum, PO Box, Road, City, State, ZIP) ,which usually appear in very regular form. Similarly,

Bouckaert (2002) extracts the components of author affiliations from articles of a pharmaceutical journal.

Confidence prediction itself is also an under-studied aspect of information extraction—although it has been investigated in document classification (Bennett 2000), speech recognition (Gunawardana, Hon, & Jiang 1998), and machine translation (Gandrabur & Foster 2003). Much of the previous work in confidence estimation for information extraction comes from the active learning literature. For example, Scheffer, Decomain, & Wrobel (2001) derive confidence estimates using hidden Markov models in an information extraction system, however, they do not estimate the confidence of entire fields, only singleton tokens. The token confidence is estimated by the difference between the probabilities of its first and second most likely labels, whereas our Constrained Forward-Backward (Culotta & McCallum 2004) considers multi-token fields, and the full distribution of all suboptimal paths. Scheffer, Decomain, & Wrobel also explore an idea similar to Constrained Forward-Backward to perform Baum-Welch training with partially labelled data, wherein a limited number of labels provide constraints. However, these constraints are again for singleton tokens only. Constrained Viterbi has been used previously in bioinformatics to find sub-optimal alignments of RNA sequences (Zuker 1991).

## Conclusion and Future Work

We have introduced a new system for assisting users when entering database records from unstructured data. We exploit CRFs to pre-populate the database fields and allow natural user interaction where the system takes into account any corrections by the user. This is done by correction-propagation using the Constrained Viterbi algorithm in CRFs. Note that correction-propagation can be applied to any relational model. By calculating confidence estimates and highlighting low confidence field assignments, we help the user spot any incorrect fields. We have shown that both of these methods are quite useful. Using the system, the Expected Number of User Actions per record has been dramatically reduced, from 6.31 for manual entry to 0.63 or more than 10-fold.

### Acknowledgments

We would like to thank David Parkinson for providing labelling and parsing tools and valuable discussions. This work was supported in part by the Center for Intelligent Information Retrieval, the Central Intelligence Agency, the National Security Agency, the National Science Foundation under NSF grant #IIS-0326249, and by the Defense Advanced Research Projects Agency, through the Department of the Interior, NBC, Acquisition Services Division, under contract #NBCHD030010.

## References

Becker, R. A., and Cleveland, W. S. 1987. Brushing scatterplots. *Technometrics* 29:127–142.

Bennett, P. N. 2000. Assessing the calibration of naive bayes' posterior estimates. Technical Report CMU-CS-00-155, Computer Science Department, School of Computer Science, Carnegie Mellon University.

Borkar, V. R.; Deshmukh, K.; and Sarawagi, S. 2000. Automatically extracting structure from free text addresses. In *Bulletin of the IEEE Computer Society Technical committe on Data Engineering*. IEEE.

Bouckaert, R. 2002. Low level information extraction: A bayesian network based approach. In *Proc. TextML 2002*.

Cardie, C., and Pierce, D. 1998. Proposal for an interactive environment for information extraction. Technical Report TR98-1702.

Caruana, R.; Hodor, P.; and Rosenberg, J. 2000. High precision information extraction. In *KDD-2000 Workshop on Text Mining*.

Culotta, A., and McCallum, A. 2004. Confidence estimation for information extraction. In *Proceedings of the Human Language Technologies Conference (to appear)*.

Gandrabur, S., and Foster, G. 2003. Confidence estimation for text prediction. In *Proceedings of the Conference on Natural Language Learning (CoNLL 2003)*.

Gunawardana, A.; Hon, H.; and Jiang, L. 1998. Word-based acoustic confidence measures for large-vocabulary speech recognition. In *Proc. ICSLP-98*, 791–794.

Lafferty, J.; McCallum, A.; and Pereira, F. 2001. Conditional random fields: Probabilistic models for segmenting and labeling sequence data. In *Proc. 18th International Conf. on Machine Learning*, 282–289. Morgan Kaufmann, San Francisco, CA.

McCallum, A., and Li, W. 2003. Early results for named entity recognition with conditional random fields, feature induction and web-enhanced lexicons. In Hearst, M., and Ostendorf, M., eds., *HLT-NAACL*. Edmonton, Alberta, Canada: Association for Computational Linguistics.

McCallum, A. 2003. Efficiently inducing features of conditional random fields. In *Nineteenth Conference on Uncertainty in Artificial Intelligence (UAI03)*.

Miller, R. C., and Myers, B. A. 2001. Outlier finding: focusing user attention on possible errors. In *UIST*, 81–90.

Pinto, D.; McCallum, A.; Wei, X.; and Croft, W. B. 2003. Table extraction using conditional random fields. In *SIGIR '03: Proceedings of the Twenty-sixth Annual International ACM SIGIR Conference on Research and Development in Information Retrieval*.

Rabiner, L. 1989. A tutorial on hidden markov models. In *IEEE*, volume 77, 257–286.

Scheffer, T.; Decomain, C.; and Wrobel, S. 2001. Active hidden markov models for information extraction. In *Advances in Intelligent Data Analysis, 4th International Conference, IDA 2001*.

Sha, F., and Pereira, F. 2003. Shallow parsing with conditional random fields. In Hearst, M., and Ostendorf, M., eds., *HLT-NAACL: Main Proceedings*, 213–220. Edmonton, Alberta, Canada: Association for Computational Linguistics.

Swayne, D. F.; Cook, D.; and Buja, A. 1991. Xgobi: Interactive dynamic data visualization in the x window system. *Proceedings of the ASA Section on Statistical Graphics*.

Zuker, M. 1991. Suboptimal sequence alignment in molecular biology: Alignment with error analysis. *Journal of Molecular Biology* 221:403–420.

# Identification and Tracing of Ambiguous Names: Discriminative and Generative Approaches

**Xin Li** **Paul Morie** **Dan Roth**
Department of Computer Science
University of Illinois, Urbana, IL 61801
{xli1,morie,danr}@uiuc.edu

## Abstract

A given entity – representing a person, a location or an organization – may be mentioned in text in multiple, ambiguous ways. Understanding natural language requires identifying whether different mentions of a name, within and across documents, represent the same entity.

We present two machine learning approaches to this problem, which we call the "Robust Reading" problem. Our first approach is a discriminative approach, trained in a supervised way. Our second approach is a generative model, at the heart of which is a view on how documents are generated and how names (of different entity types) are "sprinkled" into them. In its most general form, our model assumes: (1) a joint distribution over entities (e.g., a document that mentions "President Kennedy" is more likely to mention "Oswald" or " White House" than "Roger Clemens"), (2) an "author" model, that assumes that at least one mention of an entity in a document is easily identifiable, and then generates other mentions via (3) an appearance model, governing how mentions are transformed from the "representative" mention.

We show that both approaches perform very accurately, in the range of $90\% - 95\%$ $F_1$ measure for different entity types, much better than previous approaches to (some aspects of) this problem. Our extensive experiments exhibit the contribution of relational and structural features and, somewhat surprisingly, that the assumptions made within our generative model are strong enough to yield a very powerful approach, that performs better than a supervised approach with limited supervised information.

## Introduction

Reading and understanding text requires the ability to disambiguate at several levels, abstracting away details and using background knowledge in a variety of ways. One of the difficulties that humans resolve instantaneously and unconsciously is that of reading names. Most names of people, locations, organizations and others, have multiple writings that are being used freely within and across documents.

The variability in writing a given concept, along with the fact that different concepts may have very similar writings, poses a significant challenge to progress in natural language processing. Consider, for example, an open domain question answering system (Voorhees 2002) that attempts, given a question like: "When was President Kennedy born?" to search a large collection of articles in order to pinpoint the concise answer: "on May 29, 1917." The sentence, and even the document that contains the answer, may not contain the name "President Kennedy"; it may refer to this entity as "Kennedy", "JFK" or "John Fitzgerald Kennedy". Other documents may state that "John F. Kennedy, Jr. was born on November 25, 1960", but this fact refers to our target entity's son. Other mentions, such as "Senator Kennedy" or "Mrs. Kennedy" are even "closer" to the writing of the target entity, but clearly refer to different entities. Even the statement "John Kennedy, born 5-29-1941" turns out to refer to a different entity, as one can tell observing that the document discusses Kennedy's batting statistics. A similar problem exists for other entity types, such as locations and organizations. Ad hoc solutions to this problem, as we show, fail to provide a reliable and accurate solution.

This paper presents two learning approaches to the problem of *Robust Reading*, compares them to existing approaches and shows that an unsupervised learning approach can be applied very successfully to this problem, provided that it is used along with strong but realistic assumptions on the nature of the use of names in documents.

Our first model is a discriminative approach that models the problem as that of deciding whether any two names mentioned in a collection of documents represent the same entity. This straightforward modelling of the problem results in a classification problem – as has been done by several other authors (Cohen, Ravikumar, & Fienberg 2003; Bilenko & Mooney 2003) – allowing us to compare our results with these. This is a standard pairwise classification task, under a supervised learning protocol; our main contribution in this part is to show how relational (string and token-level) features and structural features, representing transformations between names, can improve the performance of this classifier.

Several attempts have been made in the literature to improve the results by performing some global optimization, with the above mentioned pairwise classifier as the similarity metric. The results of these attempts were not conclusive and we provide some explanation for why that is. We prove that, assuming optimal clustering, this approach reduces the error of a pairwise classifier in the case of two classes (corresponding to two entities); however, in the more general case, when the number of entities (classes) is greater than 2, global optimization mechanisms could be worse than pairwise classification. Our experiments concur with this. However, as we show, if one first splits the data in some coherent way – e.g., to groups of documents originated at about the same time period – this can aid clustering significantly.

This observation motivates our second model. We developed a global probabilistic model for *Robust Reading*, detailed in (Li, Morie, & Roth 2004). Here we briefly illustrate one of its instantiations and concentrate on its experimental study and a comparison to the discriminative models. At the heart of this approach is a view on how documents are generated and how names (of different types) are "sprinkled" into them. In its most general form, our model assumes: (1) a joint distribution over entities, so that a document that mentions "President Kennedy" is more likely to mention "Oswald" or "White House" than "Roger Clemens"; (2) an "author" model, that makes sure that at least one mention of a name in a document is easily identifiable (after all, that's the author's goal), and then generates other mentions via (3) an appearance model, governing how mentions are transformed from the "representative" mention.

Our goal is to learn the model from a large corpus and use it to support *Robust Reading*. Given a collection of documents we learn the model in an *unsupervised* way; that is, the system is not told during training whether two mentions represent the same entity. We only assume, as in the discriminative model above, the ability to recognize names, using a named entity recognizer run as a preprocessor.

Our experimental results are somewhat surprising; we show that the unsupervised approach can solve the problem accurately, giving accuracies ($F_1$) above 90%, and better than our discriminative classifier (obviously, with a lot more data). In the rest of the paper, we further study the discriminative and generative model in an attempt to provide explanations to the success of the unsupervised approach, and shed light on the problem of Robust Reading and hopefully, many related problems. Our study addresses two issues: (1) Learning Protocol: A supervised learning approach is trained on a training corpus, and tested on a different one, necessarily resulting in some degradation in performance. An unsupervised method learns directly on the target corpus. The difference, as we show, is significant. (2) Structural assumptions: we show that our generative model benefits from the assumptions made in designing it. This is shown by evaluating a fairly weak initialization of model parameters, which still results in a model for *Robust Reading* with respectable results. We leave open the question of how much data is required for a supervised learning methods before it can match the results of our supervised learner.

There is little previous work we know of that directly addresses the problem of Robust Reading in a principled way, but some related problems have been studied. From the natural language perspective, there has been a lot of work on the related problem of coreference resolution (Soon, Ng, & Lim 2001; Ng & Cardie 2003; Kehler 2002) – which aims at linking occurrences of noun phrases and pronouns, typically occurring in a close proximity within a short document or a paragraph, based on their appearance and local context. In the context of databases, several works have looked at the problem of record linkage - recognizing duplicate records in a database (Cohen & Richman 2002; Hernandez & Stolfo 1995; Bilenko & Mooney 2003; Doan *et al.* 2003). Specifically, (Pasula *et al.* 2002) considers the problem of identity uncertainty in the context of citation matching and suggests a probabilistic model for that. One of the few works we are aware of that works directly with text data and across documents, is (Mann & Yarowsky 2003), which considers one aspect of the problem – that of distinguishing occurrences of *identical* names in different documents, and only of *people* (e.g., do occurrences of "Jim Clark" in different documents refer to the same person?).

The rest of this paper first presents the experimental methodology and data used in our evaluation; it then presents the design of our pairwise name classifier, a comparison to other classifiers in the literature, and a discussion of clustering on top of a pairwise classifier. Finally, we present the generative model and compare the discriminative and generative approaches along several dimensions.

## Experimental Methodology

In our experimental study we evaluated different models on the problem of robust reading for three entity types: People (Peop), Locations (Loc) and Organizations (Org). We collected $8,000$ names from randomly sampled 1998-2000 New York Times articles in the TREC corpus (Voorhees 2002) (about $4,000$ personal names[1], $2,000$ locations and $2,000$ organizations). The documents were annotated by a named entity tagger for these entity types. The annotation was then manually corrected and each name mention was labelled with its corresponding entity by two annotators. 5 pairs of training and test sets with 600 names in each data set are constructed for each of the three entity types by randomly picking from the $8,000$ names.

For the discriminative classifier, given a training set, we generated positive training examples using all co-referring pairs of names, and negative examples by randomly selecting (10 times that number of) pairs of names that do not refer to the same entity. The probabilistic model is trained using a larger corpus. The results in all the experiments in this paper are evaluated using the same test sets, except when comparing the clustering schemes. For a comparative evaluation, the outcomes of each approach on a test set of names are converted to a classification over all possible pairs of names (including non-matching pairs). Since most pairs are trivial negative examples, and the classification accuracy can always reach nearly 100%, only the set $M_p$ of examples that are predicated to belong to the same entity (positive predictions) are used in evaluation, and are compared with the set $M_a$ of examples annotated as positive. The performance of an approach is then evaluated by Precision $P = \frac{|M_p \bigcap M_a|}{|M_p|}$, Recall $R = \frac{|M_p \bigcap M_a|}{|M_a|}$, and $F_1 = \frac{2PR}{P+R}$. Only $F_1$ values are shown and compared in this paper.

[1]Honorifics and postfixes like "Jr." are parts of a personal name.

## A Discriminative Model

The *Robust Reading* problem can be formalized as pairwise classification: Find a function $f : N \times N \rightarrow \{0, 1\}$ which classifies two strings (representing entity writings) in the name space $N$, as to whether they represent the same entity (0) or not (1). Most prior work adopted fixed string similarity metrics and created the desired function by simply thresholding the similarity between two names. (Cohen, Ravikumar, & Fienberg 2003) compared experimentally a variety of string similarity metrics on the task of matching entity names and found that, overall, the best-performing method is a hybrid scheme (SoftTFIDF) combining a TFIDF weighting scheme of tokens with the Jaro-Winkler string-distance scheme. (Bilenko & Mooney 2003) proposed a learning framework (Marlin) for improving entity matching using trainable measures of textual similarity. They compared a learned edit distance measure and a learned vector space based measure that employs a classifier (SVM) with fixed measures (but not the ones mentioned above) and showed some improvements in performance.

We propose a learning approach, *LMR*, that focuses on representing a given pair of names using a collection of relational (string and token-level) and structural features. Over these we learn, for each entity type, a linear classifier, that we train using the SNoW (Sparse Network of Winnows (Carlson *et al.* 1999)) learning architecture. A feature extractor automatically extracts active features in a data-driven way for each pair of names. Our decision is thus of the form:

$$f(n_1, n_2) = \arg\max_{l \in \{0,1\}} f^l(n_1, n_2) = \arg\max_{l \in \{0,1\}} \sum_{i=1}^{k} w_{i,l} f_i \quad (1)$$

where $w_{i,l}$ is the weight of feature $f_i$ in the function $f^l$.

## Feature Extraction

An example is generated by extracting features from a pair of names. Two types of features are used: relational features representing mappings between tokens in the two names, and structural features, representing the structural transformations of tokens in one name into tokens of the other.

Each name is modelled as a partition in a bipartite graph, with each token in that name as a vertex (see Fig. 1). At most one token-based relational feature is extracted for each edge in the graph, by traversing a prioritized list of feature types until a feature is activated; if no active features are found, it goes to the next pair of tokens. This scheme guarantees that only the most important (expressive) feature is activated for each pair of tokens. An additional constraint is that each token in the smaller partition can only activate one feature. We use 13 types of token-based features. Some of the interesting types are:

- Honorific Equal: active if both tokens are honorifics and equal. An honorific is a title such as "Mr.", "Mrs.", "President", "Senator" or "Professor".
- Honorific Equivalence: active if both tokens are honorifics, not equal, but equivalent ("Professor", "Prof.").
- Honorific Mismatch : active for different honorifics.
- NickName: active if tokens have a "nickname" relation ("Thomas" and "Tom").

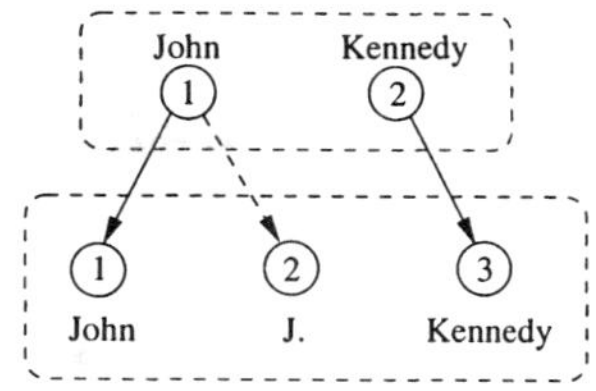


Figure 1: There are two possible features for token 1 in the smaller partition but only the higher priority Equality feature is activated.

| $F_1$(%) | Marlin | SoftTFIDF | LMR |
|---|---|---|---|
| Peop | 88.3 | 89.0 | **90.5** |
| Loc | 77.3 | 90.5 | **92.5** |
| Org | 78.1 | 87.7 | **93.0** |

Table 1: **Performance of Different Pairwise Classifiers in an Identical Setting.** Results are evaluated in the average $F_1$ value over the 5 test sets for each entity type with 600 names in each of them. The columns are different classifiers and LMR is our classifier. The learned classifiers are trained using corresponding training sets with 600 names.

- Equality: both names are equal.
- Edit Distance: the tokens have an edit-distance of 1.
- Symbol Map: one token is a symbolic representative of the other ("and" and "&").

Relational features are not sufficient, since a non-matching pair of names could activate exactly the same set of token-based features as a matching pair. Consider, for example, two names that are all the same except that one has an additional token. Our *structural* features were designed to avoid this phenomenon. These features encode information on the relative order of tokens between the two names, by recording the location of the participating tokens in the partition. E.g., for the pairs ("John Kennedy","John Kennedy") and ("John Kennedy", "John Kennedy Davis"), the active relational features are identical; but, the first pair activates the structural features "$(1, 2)$" and "$(1, 2)$", while the second pair activates "$(1, 3)$" and "$(1, \emptyset, 2)$".

## Experimental Comparison

Table 1 presents the average $F_1$ using three different pairwise classifiers on the 5 test sets we described before. The best results of each classifier using a uniform threshold for each entity type are shown here. The LMR classifier outperforms the non-learning SoftTFIDF classifier and the learned classifier (Marlin), under identical conditions.

Table 2 shows the contribution of our feature types to the performance of LMR. The *Baseline* classifier only uses string-edit-distance features and "Equality" features. The *Token-Based* classifier uses all relational token-based features while the *Structural* classifier uses, in addition, the

| $F_1$(%) | Baseline | Token-Based | Structural |
|---|---|---|---|
| Peop | 61.0 | 80.8 | 90.5 |
| Loc | 73.0 | 88.8 | 92.5 |
| Org | 82.2 | 88.3 | 93.0 |

Table 2: **Contribution of Different Feature Sets** The LMR classifier is trained with different feature sets using the 5 training sets. Results are evaluated in the average $F_1$ value over the 5 test sets for each entity type with 600 names in each of them.

structural features. Adding relational and structural features types is very significant, and more so to *People* due to the larger amount of overlapping strings in different entities.

## Does Clustering Help ?

There is a long-held intuition that using clustering on top of a pairwise classifier might reduce its error; several works (Cohen, Ravikumar, & Fienberg 2003; McCallum & Wellner 2003) have thus applied clustering in similar tasks. However, we prove here that while optimal clustering always helps to reduce the error of a pairwise classifier when there are two clusters (corresponding to two entities), in general, for $k$ classes and $k > 2$, it is not the case.

A typical clustering algorithm views data points $n \in N$ to be clustered as feature vectors $n = (f_1, f_2, \dots, f_d)$ in a $d$-dimensional feature space. A data point $n$ is in one of $k$ classes $C = \{C_1, C_2, \dots, C_k\}$. From a generative view, the observed data points $D = \{n_1, n_2, \dots, n_t\}$ are sampled i.i.d. from a joint probability distribution $P$ defined over tuples $(n, c) \in N \times C$ ($P$ is a mixture of $k$ models). A distance metric $dist(n_1, n_2)$ is used to quantify the difference between two points. Clustering algorithms differ in how they approximate the hidden generative models given $D$.

**Definition 1** *Given two i.i.d sampled data points* $(n_1, c_1)$ *and* $(n_2, c_2) \in N \times C$ *with only* $n_1, n_2$ *observed and* $c_1, c_2$ *hidden, and* $P_{N\times C}$*, the problem of Robust Reading is to find a function* $f : N \times N \to \{0, 1\}$ *which satisfies:*

$$f(n_1, n_2) = 0 \quad iff \quad c_1 = c_2 \tag{2}$$

**Definition 2** *The pairwise classification in this setting is:*

$$f_p(n_1, n_2) = 0 \quad \equiv \quad dist(n_1, n_2) \le T \tag{3}$$

*where* $T \ge 0$ *is a threshold. The clustering based decision:*

$$f_c(n_1, n_2) = 0 \equiv argmax_i p(n_1|C_i) = argmax_i p(n_2|C_i) \tag{4}$$

**Definition 3** *The error rate of the pair function* $f$ *is:*

$$err(f) = E_P(f(n_1, n_2) \neq I(n_1, n_2)) \tag{5}$$

*where* $I(n_1, n_2) = 0 \quad iff \quad c_1 = c_2; 1, \; otherwise.$

**Lemma 1** *Assume data is generated according to a uniform mixture of k Gaussians* $G = \{g_1, g_2, \dots, g_k\}$ *with the same covariance (i.e., a data point is generated by first choosing one of k models with probability* $p_k$ *(*$p_k = 1/k$*), and then sampling according to the i-th Gaussian chosen.), and suppose we find the correct k Gaussian distributions after clustering, then for* $k = 2$ *and* $\forall T$,

$$err(f_c) < err(f_p) \tag{6}$$

*However, this doesn't hold in general for* $k > 2$.

**Proof (sketch):**[2] It's easy to see that the probability density over tuples in $N \times C$ is $f(n, c_i) = \frac{1}{k} * g_i(n)$. The error rates $err(f_c)$ and $err(f_p)$ can be computed using the density function. Thus, for $k = 2$, we get $err(f_c) = \frac{1}{2} - \frac{1}{2}A^2$, where $A = \oint_R [g_1(X) - g_2(X)]dX$, and $R$ is the area in the feature space that satisfies $g_2(X) > g_1(X)$ $(X \in N)$. $R$ is a half space here. We also have:

$$\begin{aligned} err(f_p) = \quad & \tfrac{1}{2} - \tfrac{1}{2}\oint_R [g_2(X_1) - g_1(X_1)]dX_1 \times \\ & \oint_{M(X_1,T)} [g_2(X_2) - g_1(X_2)]dX_2 > err(f_c) \end{aligned}$$

where $M(X_1, T)$ is the sphere area in the feature space whose point X satisfies $dist(X_1, X) \le T$. This is so since $\oint_{M(X_1,T)} [g_2(X_2) - g_1(X_2)]dX_2 < \oint_R [g_2(X_2) - g_1(X_2)]dX_2$.

For $k > 2$, we can compute $err(f_c)$ and $err(f_p)$ in a similar way and compare them. We found that in this case, each can be smaller than the other in different cases. Specifically, when $\sum_{i=1}^{k} g_i(n) > 2 * g_j(n)$ for all $j$ and $n$, and $T \to 0$, we have $err(f_c) > err(f_p)$.

To study this issue experimentally, we designed and compared several clustering schemes for the *Robust Reading* task[3]. In a Direct clustering approach, we cluster named entities from a collection of documents with regard to the target entities, all at once. That is, the entities are viewed as the hidden classes that generate the observed named entities in text. The clustering algorithm used is a standard agglomerative clustering algorithm based on complete-link (which performed better than other clustering methods we attempted). The evaluation, column 2 of Table 3, shows a degradation in the results relative to pairwise classification.

Although, in general, clustering does not help, we attempted to see if clustering can be helped by exploiting some structural properties of the domain. We split the set of documents into three groups, each originated at about the same time period, and clustered again. In this case (columns Hier (Date) – Hierarchically clustering according to Dates), the results are significantly better than Direct clustering. We then performed a control experiment (Hier (Random)), in which we split the document set randomly into three sets of the same sizes as before; the deterioration in the results in this case indicate that exploiting the structure is significant.

The data set used here was different from the one used in other experiments. They were created by randomly selecting 600 names for each entity type from the documents of years $1998 - 2000$. The $1,800$ names for each entity type were randomly split into equal training and test set. We trained the LMR pairwise classifier for each entity type using the corresponding annotated training set and cluster the test set with LMR evaluated as a similarity metric.

## A Generative Model for Robust Reading

Motivated by the above observation, we describe next a generative model for *Robust Reading*, designed to exploit documents' structure and assumptions on how they are generated. The details of this model are described in (Li, Morie, & Roth 2004). Here we briefly describe one instantiation

[2]The assumption of Gaussian distributions can be relaxed.

[3]Given the activation values of the classifier, we define the distance metric as follows. Let $p, n$ be the positive and negative activation values, respectively, for two names $n_1$ and $n_2$; then, $dist(n_1, n_2) = \frac{e^n}{e^p + e^n}$.

| $F_1$ (%) | LMR | Direct | Hier. (Date) | Hier. (Random) |
|---|---|---|---|---|
| Peop | 81.9 | 78.6 | **79.9** | 76.7 |
| Loc | 89.6 | 88.1 | **88.4** | 88.8 |
| Org | 92.7 | 91.9 | **96.3** | 92.2 |

Table 3: **Best Performance of Different Clustering Approaches** (Various parameter settings, including different numbers of clusters were experimented within Direct Clustering.) 'LMR' represents our pairwise classifier. The other three columns are different clustering schemes. Results are evaluated by the $F_1$ values using the best threshold in experiments. The test set has 900 names for each entity type.

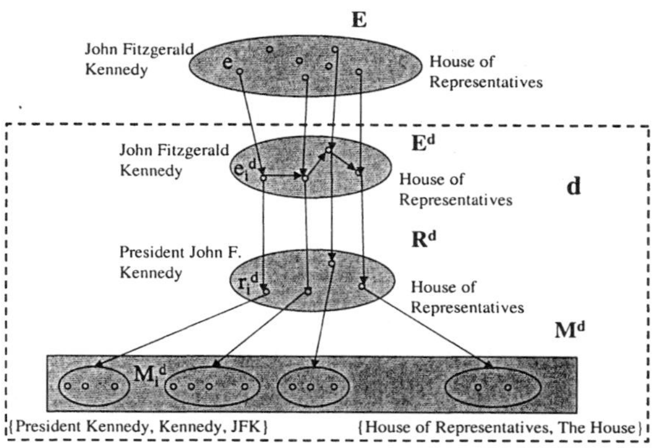


Figure 2: Generating a document

of the model (Model II there) and concentrate on its experimental study and a comparison to the discriminative models.

We define a probability distribution over documents $d = \{E^d, R^d, M^d\}$, by describing how documents are being generated. In its most general form the model has the following three components: (1) A joint probability distribution $P(E^d)$ that governs how entities (of different types) are distributed into a document and reflects their co-occurrence dependencies. (When initializing the model described here, we assume that entities are chosen independently of each other.) (2) One mention of a name in a document, a representative $r^d$ is easily identifiable and other mentions are generated from it. The number of entities in a document, $size(E^d)$, and the number of mentions of each entity in $E^d$, $size(M_i^d)$, are assumed in the current evaluation to be distributed uniformly over a small plausible range so that they can be ignored in later inference. (3) The *appearance probability* of a name generated (transformed) from its representative is modelled as a product distribution over relational transformations of attribute values. This model captures the similarity between appearances of two names. In the current evaluation the same appearance model is used to calculate both the probability $P(r|e)$ that generates a representative $r$ given an entity $e$ and the probability $P(m|r)$ that generates a mention $m$ given a representative $r$. Attribute transformations are relational, in the sense that the distribution is over transformation types and independent of the specific names. Fig. 2 depicts the generation process of a document $d$. Thus, in order to generate a document $d$, after picking $size(E^d)$ and $\{size(M_1^d), size(M_2^d), \ldots\}$, each entity $e_i^d$ is selected into $d$ independently of others, according to $P(e_i^d)$. Next,

| $F_1$ (%) | Marlin | SoftTFIDF | LMR | Generative |
|---|---|---|---|---|
| Peop | 88.3 | 89.0 | 90.5 | **95.1** |
| Loc | 77.3 | 90.5 | 92.5 | **87.8** |
| Org | 78.1 | 87.7 | 93.0 | **96.7** |

Table 4: **Discriminative and Generative Models** Results are evaluated by the average $F_1$ values over the 5 test sets for each entity type. "Marlin", "SoftTFIDF" and "LMR" are the three pairwise classifiers; "Generative" is the generative model.

| $F_1$ (%) | LMR | Generative (all) | Generative (unseen data) |
|---|---|---|---|
| Peop | 90.5 | 95.1 | 88.8 |
| Loc | 92.5 | 87.8 | 78.2 |
| Org | 93.0 | 96.7 | 84.2 |

Table 5: **Results of Different Learning Protocols for the Generative Model**. The table shows the results of our supervised classifier (LMR) trained with 600 names, the generative model trained with all the 8,000 names and the generative model trained with the part of 8,000 names not used in the corresponding test set. Results are evaluated and averaged over 5 test sets for each entity type.

the representative $r_i^d$ for each entity $e_i^d$ is selected according to $P(r_i^d|e_i^d)$ and for each representative the actual mentions are selected independently according to $P(m_j^d|r_j^d)$. Assuming conditional independency between $M^d$ and $E^d$ given $R^d$, the probability distribution over documents is therefore

$$\begin{aligned} P(d) &= P(E^d, R^d, M^d) = P(E^d)P(R^d|E^d)P(M^d|R^d) \\ &\sim \prod_{i=1}^{|E^d|}[P(e_i^d)P(r_i^d|e_i^d)] \prod_{(r_j^d, m_j^d)} P(m_j^d|r_j^d) \end{aligned}$$

after we ignore the size components.

Given a mention $m$ in a document $d$ ($M^d$ is the set of observed mentions in $d$), the key inference problem is to determine the most likely entity $e_m^*$ that corresponds to it. This is done by computing:

$$E^d = argmax_{E' \subseteq E} P(E', R^d, M^d|\theta), \quad (7)$$

where $\theta$ is the learned model's parameters. This gives the assignment of the most likely entity $e_m^*$ for $m$. And the probability of the document collection $D$ is: $P(D) = \prod_{d \in D} P(d)$.

The model parameters are learned in an unsupervised way given a collection of documents: that is, the information whether two mentions represent the same entity is unavailable during training. A greedy search algorithm modified after the standard EM algorithm is adopted here to simplify the computation. Given a set of documents $D$ to be studied and the observed mentions $M^d$ in each document, this

| $F_1$ (%) | Generative | Initial |
|---|---|---|
| Peop | 95.1 | 84.1 |
| Loc | 87.8 | 85.0 |
| Org | 96.7 | 92.1 |

Table 6: **Performance of Simple Initialization**. "Generative" – the generative model learned in a normal way. "Initial" – the parameters of the generative model initialized using some simple heuristics and used to cluster names. Results are evaluated by the average $F_1$ values over the 5 test sets for each entity type.

algorithm iteratively updates the model parameter $\theta$ (several underlying probabilistic distributions described before) and the structure (that is, $E^d$ and $R^d$) of each document $d$ by improving $P(D|\theta)$. Unlike the standard EM algorithm, in the E-step, it seeks the most likely $E^d$ and $R^d$ for each document rather than the expected assignment.

There is an initial step to acquire a coarse guess of document structures and to seek the set of entities $E$ in a closed collection of documents $D$. A local clustering is performed to group all mentions inside each document. A set of simple heuristics of matching attributes[4] is applied to computing the similarity between mentions, and pairs of mentions with similarity above a threshold are clustered together.

## A Comparison between the Models

We trained the generative model in an unsupervised way with all $8,000$ names. The somewhat surprising results are shown in Table 4. The generative model outperformed the supervised classifier for People and Organizations. That is, by incorporating a lot of unlabelled data, the unsupervised learning could do better. To understand this better, and to compare our discriminative and generative approaches further, we addressed the following two issues:

*Learning protocol*: A supervised learning approach is trained on a training corpus, and tested on a different one resulting, necessarily, in some degradation in performance. An unsupervised method learns directly on the target corpus. This, as we show, can be significant. In a second experiment, in which we do not train the generative model on names it will see in the test set, results clearly degrade (Table 5).

*Structural assumptions:* Our generative model benefits from the structural assumptions made in designing the model. We exhibit this by evaluating a fairly weak initialization of the model, and showing that, nevertheless, this results in a *Robust Reading* model with respectable results. Table 6 shows that after initializing the model parameters with the heuristics used in the EM-like algorithm, and without further training (but with the inference of the probabilistic model), the generative model can perform reasonably well.

## Conclusion

The paper presents two learning approaches to the "robust reading" problem – cross-document identification of names despite ambiguous writings. In addition to a standard modelling of the problem as a classification task, we developed a model that describes the natural generation process of a document and the process of how names are "sprinkled" into them, taking into account dependencies between entities across types and an "author" model. We have shown that both models gain a lot from incorporating structural and relational information – features in the classification model; coherent data splits for clustering and the natural generation process in the case of the probabilistic model.

The *robust reading* problem is a very significant barrier on our way toward supporting robust natural language processing, and the reliable and accurate results we show are thus very encouraging. Also important is the fact that our unsupervised model performs so well, since the availability of annotated data is, in many cases, a significant obstacle to good performance in NLP tasks.

In addition to further studies of the discriminative model, including going beyond the current noisy supervision (given at a global annotation level, although learning is done locally). exploring how much data is needed for a supervised model to perform as well as the unsupervised model, and whether the initialization of the unsupervised model can gain from supervision, there are several other critical issues we would like to address from the robust reading perspective. These include (1) incorporating more contextual information (like time and place) related to the target entities, both to support a better model and to allow temporal tracing of entities; (2) studying an incremental approach to learning the model and (3) integrating this work with other aspect of coreference resolution (e.g., pronouns).

[4]E.g., one example of a heuristics is: *If mention* $n_1$ *is a substring of mention* $n_2$*, then their similarity is* 0.8.


## Acknowledgment

This research is supported by NSF grants IIS-9801638, ITR IIS-0085836 and EIA-0224453, an ONR MURI Award and an equipment donation from AMD.


## References


Bilenko, M., and Mooney, R. 2003. Adaptive duplicate detection using learnable string similarity measures. In *KDD*.

Carlson, A.; Cumby, C.; Rosen, J.; and Roth, D. 1999. The SNoW learning architecture. Technical Report UIUCDCS-R-99-2101, UIUC Computer Science Department.

Cohen, W., and Richman, J. 2002. Learning to match and cluster large high-dimensional data sets for data integration. In *KDD*.

Cohen, W.; Ravikumar, P.; and Fienberg, S. 2003. A comparison of string metrics for name-matching tasks. In *IIWeb Workshop 2003*.

Doan, A.; Lu, Y.; Lee, Y.; and Han, J. 2003. Profile-based object matching for information integration. *IEEE Intelligent Systems* 18(5):54–59.

Hernandez, M., and Stolfo, S. 1995. The merge/purge problem for large databases. In *SIGMOD*.

Kehler, A. 2002. *Coherence, Reference, and the Theory of Grammar*. CSLI Publications.

Li, X.; Morie, P.; and Roth, D. 2004. Robust reading: Identification and tracing of ambiguous names. In *HLT-NAACL*.

Mann, G., and Yarowsky, D. 2003. Unsupervised personal name disambiguation. In *CoNLL*.

McCallum, A., and Wellner, B. 2003. Toward conditional models of identity uncertainty with application to proper noun coreference. In *IJCAI Workshop on Information Integration on the Web*.

Ng, V., and Cardie, C. 2003. Improving machine learning approaches to coreference resolution. In *ACL*.

Pasula, H.; Marthi, B.; Milch, B.; Russell, S.; and Shpitser, I. 2002. Identity uncertainty and citation matching. In *NIPS*.

Soon, W.; Ng, H.; and Lim, D. 2001. A machine learning approach to coreference resolution of noun phrases. *Computational Linguistics (Special Issue on Computational Anaphora Resolution)* 27:521–544.

Voorhees, E. 2002. Overview of the TREC-2002 question answering track. In *TREC*, 115–123.

# Text Classification by Labeling Words

**Bing Liu[1], Xiaoli Li[2], Wee Sun Lee[2] and Philip S. Yu[3]**

[1] Department of Computer Science, University of Illinois at Chicago. liub@cs.uic.edu
[2] Department of Computer Science, National University of Singapore. {lixl, leews}@comp.nus.edu.sg
[3] IBM T. J. Watson Research Center. psyu@us.ibm.com

### Abstract

Traditionally, text classifiers are built from labeled training examples. Labeling is usually done manually by human experts (or the users), which is a labor intensive and time consuming process. In the past few years, researchers investigated various forms of semi-supervised learning to reduce the burden of manual labeling. In this paper, we propose a different approach. Instead of labeling a set of documents, the proposed method labels a set of representative words for each class. It then uses these words to extract a set of documents for each class from a set of unlabeled documents to form the initial training set. The EM algorithm is then applied to build the classifier. The key issue of the approach is how to obtain a set of representative words for each class. One way is to ask the user to provide them, which is difficult because the user usually can only give a few words (which are insufficient for accurate learning). We propose a method to solve the problem. It combines clustering and feature selection. The technique can effectively rank the words in the unlabeled set according to their importance. The user then selects/labels some words from the ranked list for each class. This process requires less effort than providing words with no help or manual labeling of documents. Our results show that the new method is highly effective and promising.

## Introduction

The classic approach to building a text classifier is to first (often manually) label a set of training documents, and then apply a learning algorithm to build the classifier. This method is called *supervised learning*.

Manual labeling of a large set of training documents is a bottleneck of this approach as it is a time consuming process. To deal with this problem, (Nigam *et al.*, 2000; Blum & Mitchell, 1998) propose the idea of using a small labeled set of every class and a large unlabeled set for classifier building. (Denis, 1998; Liu *et al.*, 2002) also propose to learn from positive and unlabeled examples (without labeled negative examples). These research efforts aim to reduce the burden of manual labeling.

In this paper, we explore an alternative approach. Instead of asking the user to label a set of training documents, we ask him/her to provide some representative words for each class. These words and an unlabeled document set are then used to build a classifier. The main idea of the proposed approach is as follows: The user first provides a set of representative words for each class. These words are employed to identify a set of reliable documents for the class from the unlabeled set. This set of documents acts as the initial set of labeled training documents for the class. A classification algorithm is then applied to build a classifier. In this paper, we use the naïve Bayesian classification method (Lewis & Gale, 1994; McCallum & Nigam 1998a) and the Expectation Maximization (EM) algorithm (Dempster, Laird & Rubin, 1977) for classifier building[1].

The reason that this technique works is because the class of a text document essentially depends on the words that it contains. Most classification techniques use only words as features. Hence, if we can obtain a set of representative keywords for each class, we can extract an initial set of documents for the class by comparing the similarity of a document with the set of representative words of the class.

The key problem of the proposed approach is how to obtain a set of representative words for each class. One method is to ask the user to provide them. We tried this method with some success. However, a problem also revealed itself, i.e., it is hard for the user to provide a big number of keywords that are required for accurate learning. Thus, the issue is how to help users to provide a sufficient number of representative words for each class.

Clearly, it is not appropriate to list all the distinctive words in the unlabeled document set and to ask the user to select from them because the number of words is often too large (tens of thousand or more). It will be much better if the words can be ranked according to their importance or discriminative power. With this ranked list, it becomes a much easier task to select those important words for each class. The question is how to identify the set of important words automatically for an unlabeled document set (with no class information). We propose a novel approach to tackle the problem, which consists of three steps:

1. Cluster the unlabeled documents. This step aims at finding inherent clusters in the data. Each resulting cluster is treated as a category or class.



[1] The focus of this paper is to demonstrate the potential of learning without any labeled training documents. We believe that other classification techniques may also be used in this step.

2. Perform feature selection on the resulting clusters to identify those important words of each cluster. The result is a list of all words ranked according to their discriminative power of all the clusters/classes.
3. The user (or human expert) then inspects the ranked list of words to select a small set of representative words for each class of documents that he/she is interested in. We call this process *word labeling*.

Our experimental results show that the proposed technique is highly effective. The time taken to select the set of representative words is small.

## Related Work

Existing text classification techniques can be grouped into three types, *supervised learning*, *semi-supervised learning*, and *unsupervised learning* (or *clustering*). The proposed technique is related to but significantly different from all these existing approaches. We compare them below.

In *supervised learning*, a set of (often manually) labeled training documents of every class is used by a learning algorithm to build a classifier. Existing text classification techniques include the naive Bayesian method (Lewis & Gale 1994; McCallum & Nigam 1998a), support vector machines (SVM) (Vapnik, 95) and many others. As discussed in the Introduction, our technique is different. We only ask the user to select a set of important words for each class from a ranked list, rather than reading and labeling a set of documents, which requires more effort.

Due to the problem of manual labeling, *semi-supervised learning* is studied, which includes two main paradigms: (1) learning from a small set of labeled examples and a large set of unlabeled examples; and (2) learning from positive and unlabeled examples (with no labeled negative examples). Many researchers have studied learning in the first paradigm (e.g., Nigam *et al.*, 2000; Blum & Mitchell 1998; Bockhorst & Craven, 2002; Ghani, 2002; Goldman & Zhou, 2000). These are different from our work as we use no manually labeled examples.

In learning from positive and unlabeled examples, some theoretical studies and practical algorithms are reported in (Denis 1998, Liu *et al*, 2002; Yu, Han & Chang, 2002). Again, our proposed technique is different as it does not use any manually labeled documents.

Active learning is another method for reducing the number of labeled documents (McCallum and Nigam, 1998b). In active learning, the algorithm sequentially selects an example to be labeled next after receiving the labels for the previously selected examples. As in the other methods above, active learning requires the user to label documents, which is different from our approach.

The proposed work is also related to *unsupervised learning* or *clustering* (Jain & Dubes, 1988) and *constraint-based clustering* (e.g., Wagstaff *et al*, 2001). Although clustering is not commonly used for classification, its results can be employed as a classifier as follows: Given a new document, it is classified to the cluster (which represents a class) that is closest to it. This method, however, has two major shortcomings: (1) the accuracy is often low, and (2) the resulting clusters may not be what the user wants.

Recent work (e.g., (Basu, Banerjee & Monney, 2002)) tries to bring clustering closer to classification by using a small number of labeled documents as seeds to initialize *k*-means clustering. The original *k*-means algorithm selects initial seeds randomly. Again, our work is different. We only use clustering (and also feature selection) to help us to identify a set of important words in a text collection so that the user can select a set of representative words for each class.

In (McCallum & Nigam, 1999), a method is proposed to utilize user-specified keywords to help build classifiers. However, as we found in our experiments, it was very hard for the user to provide such keywords. This is similar to the well known problem of *knowledge acquisition* in building expert systems. Our technique can effectively assist the user to select a set of representative words.

## The Proposed Technique

This section presents the proposed technique. Given a set *U* of unlabeled documents, our technique has five steps.

Step 1: Cluster the documents in *U*.

Step 2: Perform feature selection on the clusters.

Step 3: Identify (by the user) a set of representative words for each class of documents that he/she is interested in.

Step 4: Automatically label an initial set of documents.

Step 5: Build the final classifier.

Below, we present these steps in turn.

### Clustering the Documents in the Unlabeled Set

This step finds inherent clusters in the unlabeled set. We use the popular *k*-means algorithm due to its efficiency, although other methods can also be applied. The inputs to *k*-means are the set *U* and the number of clusters *k*. Note that the value of *k* does not matter much in our case as long as it is not too small because we do not use the resulting clusters as the classifier. We only use them to help us identify some important words in *U*. In clustering, the cosine similarity metric from information retrieval (Salton & McGill, 1983) is used as the distance measure.

### Feature Selection

After clustering, *k* document clusters are produced. We treat each cluster as a distinctive class. This gives us a set of labeled documents of *k* classes. A feature selection technique from supervised learning is then applied to identify important words in each cluster.

There are many feature selection techniques for supervised learning (Yang & Pedersen, 1997). In this research, we utilize the entropy-based method. This method computes the information gain of each word and then ranks all the words in $U$ according to their gain values. Those words with higher gain values have higher discriminative power and are ranked higher. These top-ranked words are regarded as the important words in the unlabeled set $U$.

### Selecting Representatives Words for Each Class

This step is performed manually by the user. We assume that the user is familiar with the topics of the documents and also knows the classes that he/she is interested in.

Since the words are ranked according to their importance, the user simply inspects the top ranked words and decides which class each word belongs to. Note that a word can be selected as a representative word for more than one class. Although a word may be more important to one class than another, we tried to assign a weight to each class, but it was not effective. The user can also add additional words for any class that are not found at the top of the rank.

### Identifying Initial Documents for Each Class

Once a set of representative words is selected for each class $c_j \in C$ (= $\{c_1, c_2, \ldots, c_n\}$), the set of words is regarded as the *representative document* ($rd_j$) of class $c_j$. We then compare the similarity of each document $d_i$ in $U$ with each $rd_j$ using the popular cosine similarity metric (Salton & McGill, 1983) to automatically produce a set $L_j$ of *probabilistically* labeled documents for each class $c_j$.

The algorithm for this step is given in Figure 1. It works as follows. In lines 1-3, each unlabeled document $d_i$ in $U$ is compared with the representative document $rd_j$ of each class $c_j$ using the function *sim* (the cosine metric). $d_i$ is assigned to the class whose representative document is most similar to $d_i$ if the maximum similarity $s_r$ is greater than 0 (lines 4 and 5). That is, $d_i$ is included in $L_r$. Otherwise, $d_i$ is included in $RU$ (the set of *remaining unlabeled documents*) in line 6. Each document in $RU$ has 0 similarity with every $rd_j$ and is thus left unlabeled. In lines 7-15, we assign a probabilistic class label, $P(c_j|d_i) \leq 1$, to each document $d_i$ in $L_j$. We first rank the documents in $L_j$ based on their similarities. Each of the top $t$ percent of the documents is given $P(c_j|d_i) = 1$. Each of the remaining documents is given a class probability proportionally (lines 12-15) as they may not be as reliable as those top-ranked documents. $t$ is a parameter here. In our experiments, we tried $t$ with 16%, 50%, 84% and 100% (to be explained later) and found that its value does not matter much.

### Building the Classifier Using NB or EM

We build the final classifier using the naïve Bayesian (NB) technique and the EM algorithm. EM also uses NB as the base classifier. Below, we introduce them in turn.

**Naïve Bayesian (NB) Classification:** The basic idea of NB is to use the joint probabilities of words and classes to estimate the probabilities of classes given a document (McCallum & Nigan, 1998a; Lewis & Gale, 1994).

Inputs: $RD = \{rd_1, rd_2, \ldots, rd_n\}$, the set of representative documents of the classes, $c_1, c_2, \ldots, c_n$.
$U = \{d_1, d_2, \ldots d_m\}$, the set of unlabeled documents.
Output: $L = \{L_1, L_2, \ldots, L_n\}$, where $L_j$ is a set of labeled documents for class $c_j$. $L_j$ is initialized to {}.
$RU$, the set of remaining documents in $U$ that are not labeled with any class. It is initialized to {}.

1. **for** each $d_i \in U$ **do**
2.     **for** each $rd_j \in RD$ **do**
3.         $s_j = sim(d_i, rd_j)$;
4.     $s_r = \max(\{s_1, s_2, \ldots, s_n\})$;
5.     **if** $s_r > 0$ **then** $L_r = L_r \cup \{d_i\}$;
6.     **else** $RU = RU \cup \{d_i\}$;
7. **for** each $L_j \in L$ **do**
8.     Rank the documents in $L_j$ according to their similarity values in a descending order;
9.     Let $T_j$ be the set of $t$% top-ranked documents in $L_j$;
10.     **for** each $d_i$ in $T_j$ **do**
11.         $P(c_j|d_i) = 1$;
12.     Let *ms* be the minimal similarity of the documents in $T_j$;
13.     **for** each document $d_i$ in $L_j - T_j$ **do**
14.         $P(c_j|d_i) = d_i.sim / ms$; // $d_i.sim$ is the similarity of $d_i$
15.         $1 - P(c_j|d_i)$ is shared by other classes;

Figure 1: Labeling a set of documents automatically

In the NB formulation, each document in the labeled training set $D$ is considered as an ordered list of words. $w_{d_i,k}$ denotes the word in position $k$ of document $d_i$, where each word is from the vocabulary $V = \{w_1, w_2, \ldots, w_{|V|}\}$. The vocabulary is the set of all words considered in classification. There is also a set of pre-defined classes, $C = \{c_1, c_2, \ldots, c_n\}$. In order to perform classification, we compute the posterior probability $P(c_j|d_i)$, where $c_j$ is a class and $d_i$ is a document. Based on the Bayesian probability and the multinomial model, we have

$$P(c_j) = \frac{\sum_{i=1}^{|D|} P(c_j | d_i)}{|D|} \quad (1)$$

and with Laplacian smoothing,

$$P(w_t | c_j) = \frac{1 + \sum_{i=1}^{|D|} N(w_t, d_i) P(c_j | d_i)}{|V| + \sum_{s=1}^{|V|} \sum_{i=1}^{|D|} N(w_s, d_i) P(c_j | d_i)} \quad (2)$$

where $N(w_t,d_i)$ is the count of the number of times the word $w_t$ occurs in document $d_i$ and $P(c_j|d_i) \in \{0,1\}$ depending on the class label of the document.

Finally, assuming that the probabilities of words are independent given the class, we obtain the NB classifier:

$$P(c_j | d_i) = \frac{P(c_j) \prod_{k=1}^{|d_i|} P(w_{d_i,k} | c_j)}{\sum_{r=1}^{|C|} P(c_r) \prod_{k=1}^{|d_i|} P(w_{d_i,k} | c_r)} \quad (3)$$

To build a classifier for our purpose, NB will only use the set of labeled documents in each $L_i$. Those remaining unlabeled documents in $RU$ could not be used. The EM algorithm below is able to make use them.

**The EM Algorithm:** The EM algorithm is a popular class of iterative algorithms for maximum likelihood estimation for problems involving missing data (Dempster, Laird & Rubin, 1977). It is often used to fill the missing values in the data using existing values. Each iteration of EM consists of two steps, the E step and the M step. The E step basically fills in the missing values. The parameters are estimated in the M step after the missing data are filled. This leads to the next iteration of the algorithm. EM can be applied to our problem because the classes of the documents in *RU* (the remaining unlabeled documents) can be regarded as missing. The steps used by EM are identical to those used to build a NB classifier, equations (3) for the E step and equations (1) and (2) for the M step. Note that the probability of the class given the document takes the value in [0, 1] instead of {0, 1}.

Our algorithm, called NB-EM, is given in Figure 2. Initially, we use the labeled documents in *L* to build a NB classifier NB-C (line 1), which is then applied to classify the documents in *RU*. In particular, NB-C computes $P(c_i|d_j)$ of each document in *RU* (using equation (3)), which is assigned to $d_j$ as its new probabilistic class label. After every $P(c_i|d_j)$ is revised, a new classifier NB-C is built based on the new $P(c_i|d_j)$ values of the documents in *RU*, and the initially labeled documents in *L*. The next iteration starts. This iterative process goes on until EM converges (when the probability parameters stabilize).

NB-EM(L, RU)
1. Build an initial naive Bayesian classifier NB-C using the document set *L*;
2. **Loop** while classifier parameters change
3. **for** each document $d_j \in RU$
4. Compute $P(c_i \mid d_j)$ using the current NB-C;
5. Update $P(w_t|c_i)$ and $P(c_i)$ with the probabilistically assigned class for $d_j$ ($P(c_i|d_j)$) and *L* (a new NB-C is being built in the process);

Figure 2: The NB-EM algorithm

## Empirical Evaluations

**Datasets**: We used the 20 newsgroup collection[1] in our experiments, which are Usenet articles from 20 different newsgroups. The reason for using this collection is that its topics are general. We can find graduate students to act as human experts to select keywords. Each newsgroup in the collection has approximately 1000 articles. There are four (4) main categories, namely, *Science* (SCI), *Recreation* (REC), *Talk* (TALK) and *Computing* (COMP). Within each main category, there are 4 to 5 sub-categories. We build a classifier for the sub-categories within each main category. That is, each sub-category within a main category is regarded as a class. This gives us four (4) datasets, and each dataset has 4 or 5 classes.

For each dataset, we randomly selected 30% of the documents for testing, and the rest 70% for training.

**Evaluation measures**: We use accuracy as the main evaluation measure. Accuracy is adequate because every class in our four datasets has the same number (1000) of documents. We also used the F-score. However, its trends are similar to accuracy. Thus, its results are not included.

We now present the settings for each step of our technique.

**Clustering (step 1)**: We use the *k*-means algorithm. As mentioned earlier, the number of clusters *k* does not matter much for our technique. We purposely used $k = 7$ for every dataset, which is different from the actual number of classes of each dataset. We also experimented with *k* being the actual number of classes of each dataset. Those top-ranked words are very much the same as for $k = 7$.

**Feature selection and word ranking (step 2)**: We used the information gain (or entropy) based approach.

**Selecting representative words (step 3)**: Choosing representative words is a subjective task. Two students and one researcher were asked to serve as experts to choose representative words. Although they choose words independently, there is little difference in the words that they choose because they use the same ranking and most top keywords are obvious. Our experiments also show that slight differences in the selected words have almost no effect on the final classification results.

To test how many words are needed to produce good classifiers, we tried 5, 15, 20, and 30 words per class. We will see that additional words will not help.

**Labeling some training documents (step 4):** We experimented with different *t* settings (percent of documents in $L_j$ for each class $c_j$ that are given the class probability of 1, $P(c_j|d_i) = 1$). The rest of the documents in $L_j$ are given $P(c_j|d_i) < 1$ according to their similarity values. Those documents with $P(c_j|d_i) = 0$ for every class are in *RU* (the set of remaining unlabeled documents). We experimented with $t$ = 16%, 50%, 84%, and 100%. $t$ = 16% covers documents whose similarities are greater than one standard deviation above the mean similarity (these documents have the highest similarities). $t$ = 84% covers documents whose similarities are greater than one standard deviation below the mean similarity.

**Classifier building (step 5)**: Two classification methods, NB and EM, were experimented. EM was run 8 iterations for each dataset. After that, the results rarely change.

EM-Hard and EM-Soft: We experimented with two EM variations. (1) In each iteration of EM, we do not allow the class probability $P(c_j|d_i)$ of each document $d_i$ in $L_j$ (the set of labeled documents of class $c_j$) to change, but only allow the class probability of each document in *RU* to change. This method is called *EM-Hard.* (2) In each iteration, we allow $P(c_j|d_i)$ of each document $d_i$ in both $L_j$ and *RU* to change. This method is called *EM-Soft*.

**Experimental results:** Figure 3 shows the accuracy results of all datasets. In each chart (each dataset), the results are grouped according to different *t* values, 16%, 50%, 84% and 100%. For each *t*, we give the results of NB, EM-Hard and EM-Soft. The 4 bars in each group are the results of using 5, 15, 20, 30 representative words respectively.

---

[2] http://www.cs.cmu.edu/afs/cs/project/theo-11/www/naive-bayes/20_newsgroups.tar.gz

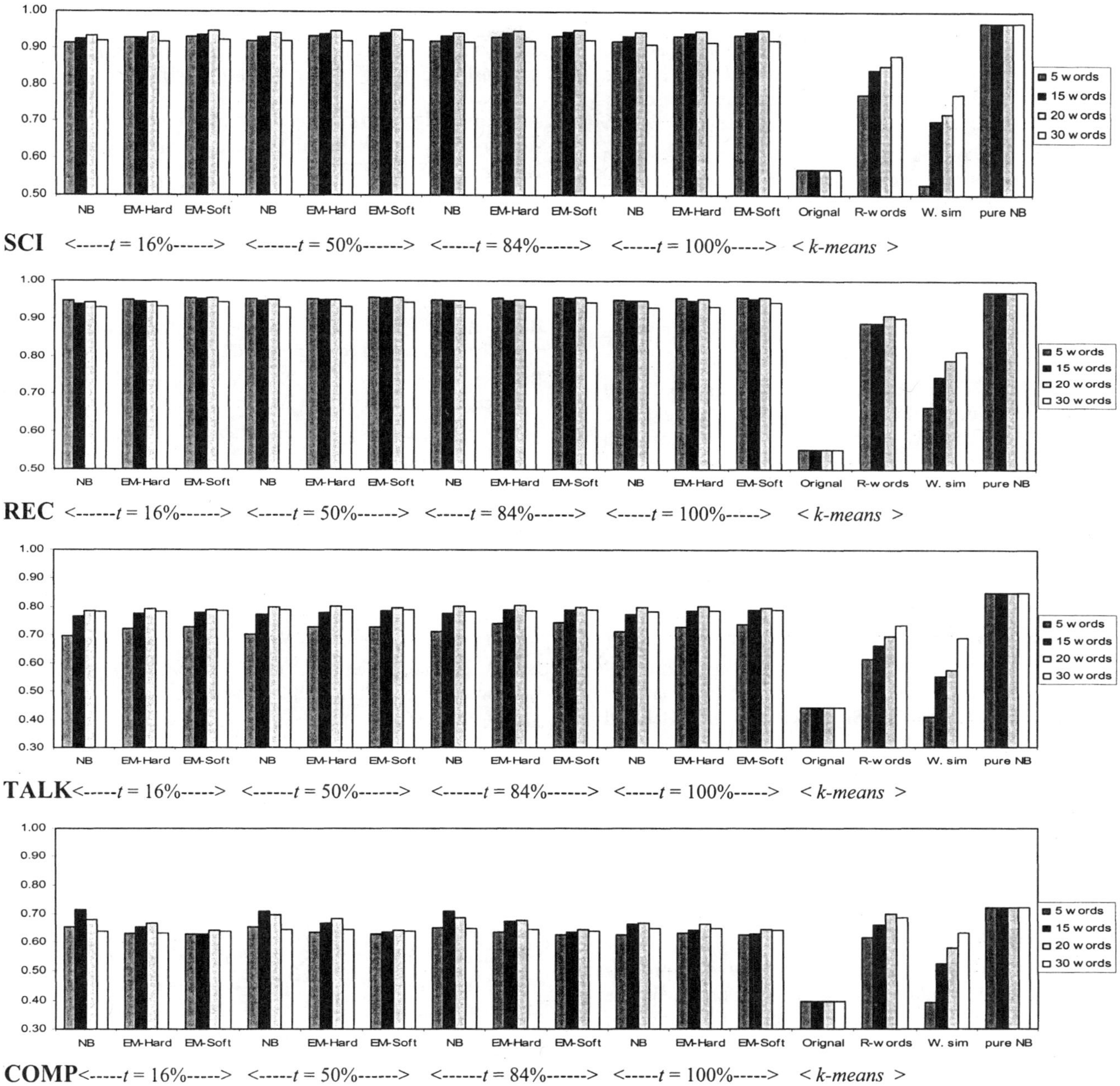


Figure 3: The accuracy results

*NB, EM-hard and EM-Soft*: We observe that these three methods all have similar results for all $t$ settings. Using 15 or 20 words for each class gives slightly better results in general with $t$ = 50%, 84% and 100%. For all $t$ values, the accuracy stabilizes or worsens after 20 words. This is because the additional words may not be as representative as the earlier words for each class.

EM based methods slightly outperform NB for the first three datasets. For dataset COMP, EM methods are slightly worse because the representative words for COMP are not as reliable as for other datasets. The representative words of COMP were the hardest to select because some classes of the dataset are similar. Thus, more EM iterations further blur the decision boundaries.

*k-means*: We also give two results for *k*-means. "*original*" standards for the original *k*-means with its initial $k$ seeds selected randomly. To allow fair comparison, we use the correct number of clusters $k$ for each dataset. The accuracy on the test set is obtained as follows. After *k*-means ends, for each test document $d$, we compute the similarity of $d$ with each cluster center. $d$ is assigned to the cluster that gives the highest similarity (using the cosine measure). After all test documents are assigned to clusters, we match the classes of the dataset with the clusters in such a way that gives the best accuracy. Due to the random nature of *k*-means the accuracies are the averaged values of 10 runs. Note that each row has the same value because representative words are not used.

"*R-words*" gives the results of *k*-means using the set of representative words as the initial cluster centers. From these two sets of results of *k*-means, we see that R-words outperforms the original *k*-means by a large margin.

Comparing with the results of NB and EM, we see that NB and EM methods are superior to clustering. This is especially true for smaller numbers of representative words. For dataset COMP, the results are similar. We believe that the selected representative words for this dataset are not as reliable as for the other datasets.

*W. sim*: It gives the accuracy results of using only the cosine similarity comparison with the representative words of each class. We compare the similarity of each test document *d* with the set of representative words of each class. *d* is assigned the class that gives the highest similarity value. If *d*'s similarity with every set of representative words is 0, *d* is assigned a random class. We observe that this technique is significantly worse than *k*-means using representative words as seeds, but better than the original *k*-means. It is also dramatically worse than the NB and EM-based approaches.

*Pure NB*: These are NB's accuracies in traditional classification, i.e., all the training documents are labeled with their original classes. Since we used fully labeled training data, thus all the results for each dataset are the same as they are not affected by the number of representative words. We observe that the accuracies of our proposed methods are very close to pure NB's accuracies. For datasets SCI, REC and COMP, the proposed methods are only about 2-3% worse and for dataset TALK, it is about 5% worse. This shows that our methods are highly effective considering that no manually labeled document is used.

**Time spent to select representative words**: The process of selecting representative words is not linear in the number of words. It gets harder with increasing number of words. The first 10 representative words for each class are generally easy to select. It takes around 5-10 minutes to choose 30 representative words for each class of a dataset. The time needed also depends on how different the classes are in the dataset. For example, for the first three datasets, it was very easy, and for the last dataset it was harder.

## Conclusions

This paper proposed a new approach to constructing text classifiers. Instead of labeling a large set of training documents as in traditional learning, the new method asks the user to label or select a set of representative words for each class from a list of ranked words. The ranking technique is based on clustering and feature selection. The set of words for each class and a set of unlabeled documents are used to build a classifier. We believe that selecting these words from a ranked list requires less user effort than labeling of a large set of documents. Our results demonstrated the effectiveness of this approach.

**Acknowledgments:** The work of Bing Liu is partially supported by the National Science Foundation under the NSF grant IIS-0307239.

## References

Basu, S., Banerjee, A., and Mooney, R. (2002). Semi-supervised clustering by seeding. *ICML-02.*

Blum, A., and Mitchell, T. (1998). Combining labeled and unlabeled data with co-training. *COLT-98.*

Bockhorst, J., and Craven, M. (2002). Exploiting relations among concepts to acquire weakly labeled training data. *ICML-02.*

Dempster, A., Laird, N. M. and Rubin. D. (1977). Maximum likelihood from incomplete data via the EM algorithm. *J. of the Royal Stat. Society*, B:39, 1-38.

Denis, F. (1998). PAC learning from positive statistical queries. *ALT-1998.*

Ghani, R. (2002). Combining labeled and unlabeled data for multiclass text categorization. *ICML-02.*

Goldman, S. and Zhou, Y. (2000). Enhancing supervised learning with unlabeled data. *ICML-00.*

Jain, A. K., and Dubes, R. C. (1988). *Algorithms for clustering data.* Englewood Cliffs, NJ: Prentice Hall.

Joachims, T. (1998). Text categorization with support vector machines: Learning with many relevant features. *ECML-98.*

Lewis, D., and Gale, W. (1994). A sequential algorithm for training text classifiers. *SIGIR-94.*

Liu, B., Lee, W. S., Yu, P., and Li, X. (2002). Partially supervised classification of text documents. *ICML-02.*

McCallum, A., and Nigam, K. (1998a). A comparison of event models for naïve Bayes text classification. *AAAI-98 Workshop on Learning for Text Categorization.*

McCallum, A., and Nigam. K. (1998b). Employing EM and pool-based active learning for text classification. *ICML-98.*

McCallum, A., and Nigam. K. (1999) "Text classification by bootstrapping with keywords, EM and shrinkage." *ACL Workshop on Unsupervised Learning in Natural Language Processing.*

Nigam, K., McCallum, A., Thrun, S., and Mitchell, T. (2000). Text classification from labeled and unlabeled documents using EM. *Machine Learning*, 39.

Salton, G. and McGill, M. (1983). *Introduction to Modern Information Retrieval.* McGraw-Hill.

Vapnik, V. *The nature of statistical learning theory*, 1995.

Wagstaff, K., Cardie, C., Rogers, S., and Schroedl, S. (2001). Constrained *k*-means clustering with background knowledge. *ICML-01.*

Yang, Y. and Pedersen J. P. (1997). A comparative study on feature selection in text categorization. *ICML-97.*

Yu, H., Han, J., Chang, K. (2002). PEBL: Positive example based learning for Web page classification using SVM. *KDD-02.*

# On the Relationship Between Lexical Semantics and Syntax for the Inference of Context-Free Grammars

**Tim Oates, Tom Armstrong, Justin Harris** and **Mark Nejman**
Department of Computer Science and Electrical Engineering
University of Maryland Baltimore County, Baltimore, MD 21250
{oates,arm1,jharri11,mnejma1}@umbc.edu

**Abstract**

Context-free grammars cannot be identified in the limit from positive examples (Gold 1967), yet natural language grammars are more powerful than context-free grammars and humans learn them with remarkable ease from positive examples (Marcus 1993). Identifiability results for formal languages ignore a potentially powerful source of information available to learners of natural languages, namely, *meanings*. This paper explores the learnability of syntax (i.e. context-free grammars) given positive examples and knowledge of lexical semantics, and the learnability of lexical semantics given knowledge of syntax. The long-term goal is to develop an approach to learning both syntax and semantics that bootstraps itself, using limited knowledge about syntax to infer additional knowledge about semantics, and limited knowledge about semantics to infer additional knowledge about syntax.

## Introduction

Learning formal languages from positive examples is a hard problem. If the language to be learned is finite and every string in the language is guaranteed to be presented at least once, the learner can memorize the strings that it sees. However, if the language can contain infinitely many strings and the learner is given a finite amount of time, then simple memorization will not work. The learner must generalize from the examples it sees. This is precisely the problem facing children learning their native language. For many important classes of languages, including regular and context-free, there are infinitely many languages that include any given set of positive examples. The challenge facing the learner is to avoid overgeneralization, to avoid choosing a language that contains the examples seen thus far and is a superset of the target language.

There is a handful of methods that are typically employed to avoid overgeneralization and establish learnability. If the learner knows that a given string is not in the target language, any overly general languages that include the string can be ruled out. A large number of learnability results reported in the literature depend on negative examples (Angluin 1987; Gold 1967; Oncina & Garcia 1992). In the absence of negative examples, learnability can follow from restrictions on the class of languages from which the target is drawn (Angluin 1982; Oates, Desai, & Bhat 2002; Koshiba, Makinen, & Takada 2000) or on the method for selecting examples (Denis, D'Halluin, & Gilleron 1996; Li & Vitanyi 1991). Establishing learnability for context-free languages is more difficult than for regular languages. A number of results on the learnability of context-free languages from positive examples require each string to be paired with its unlabeled derivation tree (Carrasco, Oncina, & Calera 1998; Oates, Desai, & Bhat 2002; Sakakibara 1992). Such a pair is called a *positive structural example*. An unlabeled derivation tree is a parse tree in which the non-terminal labels on interior nodes are not present.

The work reported in this paper is part of a larger effort aimed at understanding what is required to allow a robot to learn fragments of natural languages given qualitatively the same inputs available to children - utterances and sensory information about the physical context in which the utterances are heard. Children rarely receive negative examples (i.e. syntactically incorrect utterances marked as such), pay little attention when they do, and have only a few very weak proxies for negative examples (e.g. failure of a caregiver to respond to an utterance as expected) (Marcus 1993). Therefore, we focus on learning exclusively from positive examples, and on context-free languages because they are sufficiently expressive to represent large fragments of natural languages.

The key to our approach is to recognize that, in addition to hearing utterances, children have sensory access to the world around them. In particular, we assume that the lexicon contains word/meaning pairs, where the meanings have been established, for example, by some associative learning algorithm (Oates 2001; Roy 1999). The purpose of natural language communication is to share meanings. Therefore, the goal of the learner is to efficiently arrive at a compact representation of the language that makes it possible to determine which strings are in the language and what their meanings are.

According to Frege's principle of compositionality (Frege 1879), the meanings of phrases and sentences must be a function solely of the meanings of the words involved. Suppose rules for syntactic composition (i.e. productions in the grammar) are in a one-to-one correspondence with rules for semantic composition. For example, if the grammar for English has a syntactic production of the form `S` $\rightarrow$ `NP VP`, then there must be a corresponding semantic rule that says how to combine the meaning of an `NP` with the meaning of a `VP` to get the meaning of an `S`. Therefore, each syntactic parse tree has a structurally equivalent semantic parse tree. More importantly for this paper, each semantic parse tree, which specifies how the meanings of words and phrases are combined to yield the meaning of a sentence, has a structurally equivalent syntactic parse tree. We use lexical semantics to generate possible semantic parse trees, i.e. those that yield a coherent semantics for the sentence, and use these trees as input to an algorithm for learning context-free grammars from positive structural examples.

This paper explores the utility of lexical semantics with respect to inferring context-free languages from positive examples consisting solely of strings. Although unlabeled derivation trees are used by the learning algorithm, they are not part of its input. Rather, they are derived from lexical semantics. The main contributions are (1) the specification of a class of context-free grammars that can be learned from positive string examples and lexical semantics, and (2) a result on the learnability of lexical semantics given a context-free grammar. Our ultimate goal is to combine these two results into a system that uses lexical knowledge obtained via associative learning to infer some knowledge of syntax, and uses knowledge of syntax to infer additional lexical knowledge. Over time, such a system could bootstrap itself to increasingly complete knowledge of both syntax and semantics.

## Background

This section reviews one common algorithm for inferring context-free languages from positive structural examples and the $\lambda$-calculus, which is used to represent lexical and compositional semantics.

### Inferring Grammars from Positive Structural Examples

A *context-free grammar* (CFG) is a four-tuple $\{N, \Sigma, P, S\}$ where $N$ is a finite set of non-terminals, $\Sigma$ is a finite set of terminals, $P$ is a finite set of productions, and $S \in N$ is the start symbol. $N$ and $\Sigma$ are disjoint. A CFG is in Chomsky Normal Form (CNF) if all productions are of the form $X \rightarrow YZ$ or $X \rightarrow \sigma$, for $X, Y, Z \in N$ and $\sigma \in \Sigma$. For the remainder of this paper, the word *grammar* refers to a CFG in CNF.

Let $L(G)$ denote the language of grammar $G$. An unlabeled derivation tree (UDT) for $s \in L(G)$ is the derivation tree for $s$ with the non-terminal labels on the interior nodes removed. UDTs can be represented as parenthesized strings. For example, $(a(bc))$ and $((ab)c)$ are possible UDTs for string $abc$. In the first UDT, the string $bc$ is generated by some non-terminal, say, $X$, and the string $aX$ is generated by the start symbol.

A grammar is *reversible* if it is reset-free and invertible. A grammar is *reset-free* if $A \rightarrow XY$ and $B \rightarrow XY$ in $P$ implies $A = B$. A grammar is *invertible* if $X \rightarrow AY$ and $X \rightarrow BY$ in $P$ implies $A = B$. Sakakibara's algorithm (Sakakibara 1992) takes a set of positive structural examples

Table 1: A simple lexicon with semantics and semantic types.

| Lexeme | $\lambda$-calculus expression | Semantic type |
|---|---|---|
| Nathaniel | NATHANIEL | e |
| Isabel | ISABEL | e |
| loves | $\lambda$x $\lambda$y . LOVES(y,x) | <e, <e,*t* >> |
| rests | $\lambda$x . RESTS(x) | <e,t> |

and returns the reversible grammar that has the smallest language of all reversible grammars that contain the examples. The algorithm labels the root of each UDT with the start symbol and assigns unique labels to all interior nodes. The union of the productions in the newly labeled trees serve as the initial grammar. Since the generating grammar is known to be reversible, pairs of non-terminals that violate the reset-free and invertible properties are merged until no such pair exists, at which point the algorithm terminates. Let $GI(E)$ be the output of this algorithm on input $E$.

### Montague Grammar and the $\lambda$-Calculus

The first formal treatment of natural language semantics is typically attributed to Richard Montague. In three of his last papers, Montague introduced an intensional logic for representing the semantics of natural language strings (Dowty, Wall, & Peters 1981; Partee & Hendriks 1996). The semantics of words are represented as expressions in the $\lambda$-calculus which are (typically) functions. These functions take arguments and return values, both of which are also expressions in the $\lambda$-calculus. The semantics of strings are computed bottom-up by applying the $\lambda$-calculus expressions of lower-level constituents to one another. Table 1 shows a small lexicon in the Montague framework that will serve as a running example throughout the remainder of this section.

The $\lambda$-calculus is useful for exploring function descriptions and function application. It is a model suited for functional programming used in some languages (e.g. Lisp). Function descriptions are created by performing *lambda abstractions*. In lambda abstractions a variable argument is given scope and bound to a lambda operator. These anonymous functions can then be applied to other expressions.

Three rules are used to reduce $\lambda$-calculus expressions: $\alpha$-, $\beta$- and $\eta$- reductions. A $\lambda$-calculus expression, when fully reduced, will be a first-order logic expression. Let '*[x/y] z*' denote replacing instances of x with y in expression z. For any two arbitrary expression, a lambda operator may be bound to the same named variable in both. Performing an $\alpha$-reduction on one of the expressions results in a renaming of the variable to a unique name. When an expression is functionally applied to an argument expression it is called $\beta$-reduction. The first lambda-operator and variable are stripped off and the argument is substituted for each instance of the variable. The final operation removes lambda-operators which are bound to variables no longer found in the body of the expression.

For our purposes, and generally, the processes of abstraction and $\beta$-reduction are the most useful tools. Abstractions (i.e. functions) provide the representation for lexical semantics, and $\beta$-reductions are used to compute compositional semantics.

The following example shows the derivation of the meaning (an expression in first-order logic) of the UDT *(Nathaniel (loves Isabel))*. Note that there is ambiguity for any given pair inside a set of parentheses as to which is the function and which is the argument. For now, we assume the order of application is given and it is as follows: *loves* applies to *Isabel* and *loves Isabel* applies to *Nathaniel*.

1. (Nathaniel (loves Isabel)) = (NATHANIEL ($\lambda$x $\lambda$y . LOVES(y,x) ISABEL)
2. (NATHANIEL ($\lambda$x $\lambda$y . LOVES(y,x) ISABEL) $=>_\beta$ (NATHANIEL $\lambda$y . loves(y,ISABEL))
3. (NATHANIEL $\lambda$y . LOVES(y,ISABEL)) $=>_\beta$ loves(NATHANIEL,ISABEL)

From ordered function application we arrive at the standard English meaning of the string.

### Semantic Types

Every $\lambda$-calculus expression has a semantic type, and these types constrain how $\lambda$-calculus expressions compose with one another. Types are either basic or complex. Basic types are defined as *e*, entities (e.g. Nathaniel, Isabel), or *t*, truth values (e.g. true, false). Complex types, which represent types of functions, are defined recursively: if $\alpha$ and $\beta$ are types, then $< \alpha, \beta >$ is a type. Semantic types dictate the direction of function application (i.e. when applying a function of type $< \gamma, \delta >$, the argument to the function must have type $\gamma$). Take from Table 1 the types for *Isabel* and *rests*, e and <e,t> respectively. The order of application must be from *rests* to *Isabel* to properly compose.

Each expression in the $\lambda$-calculus, being a function description, has a parameter and return value. The semantic type of a function can be represented by $< \alpha, \beta >$ where $\alpha$ and $\beta$ are the semantic types of the parameter and return value respectively. There exists a many-to-one mapping between $\lambda$-calculus expressions and semantic types (e.g. *Nathaniel* and *Isabel* are both of type e).

## Learning Syntax Using Lexical Semantics

In this section we formally explore the utility of UDTs derived from semantic parse trees with respect to grammatical inference.

### Lexical Semantics Reducing Numbers of Parse Trees

How many semantically valid UDTs could there be for a string? For a string of length $n$, the number of possible UDTs is equal to the number of possible binary bracketings of that string. Catalan, an 18th century Belgian mathematician, posed a problem for finding the number of ways to compose factors in calculating products (Weisstein 2003). This problem is equivalent to finding the number of binary bracketings. Formally, C(n), the $n^{th}$ Catalan number, is $\frac{(2n)!}{(n!(n+1)!)}$. For strings of length $n$, the number of binary bracketings is equal to the $n-1^{th}$ Catalan number.

Table 2: A simple lexicon with semantic types.

| Lexeme | Semantic type |
|---|---|
| the | <<e,t>,<<e,t>,t>> |
| dog | <e,t> |
| cat | <e,t> |
| hates | <<<e,t>,t>, <e,t>> |

The number of possible parse trees for a string grows exponentially in the length of the string. From a learnability perspective, dealing with large numbers of trees for a single string is not easily handled. Given lexical types for terminal nodes, performing type checking on possible trees will rule out a subset of them as compositionally invalid. Type checking succeeds if after type composition over a tree for a string the root node has semantic type t. Bracketed strings of this form are called *semantically valid*.

Take, for example, the string $s$ = *the cat hates the dog* generated by some grammar. Given the length of $s$ is 5, C(4) = 14. Of the 14 possible parses, 3 are valid in terms of semantic composition: ((the cat) (hates (the dog)), ((the cat) hates) (the dog)) and ((((the cat) hates) the) dog). As shown above, a first order logic expression for the string can then be constructed following the application orderings for each of the three trees. In one case the expression denotes *the cat is the hater of the dog* and in others *the dog is the hater of the cat*. The following is a type-checking evaluation for one possible parse tree.

Take (the cat) in type form as (<<e,t>,<<e,t>,t>> $\rightarrow$ <e,t>) from Table 2. Performing the application in the order given (the cat) has type <<e,t>,t>. The type for (the dog) is clearly equivalent. The next bracket combines (hates (the dog)), thus the type is (<<<e,t>,t>,<e,t>> $\rightarrow$ <<e,t>,t>) resulting in a type of <e,t>. The final combination is between the types of (the cat) and (hates (the dog)) or (<<e,t>,t> $\rightarrow$ <e,t>). The root results in a t for this bracketing of the string.

### Computing Semantically Valid Parses

For string $s$, type $\alpha$, and grammar $G$, let $T(s)$, $T_\alpha(s)$, and $T_G(s)$ denote sets of unlabeled derivation trees. $T_G(s)$ is the set of trees that are possible given grammar $G$. $T(s)$ is the union of $T_G(s)$ for all grammars that generate $s$. Assuming that lexical semantics are given, $T_\alpha(s)$ is the restriction of $T(s)$ to those trees whose root have type $\alpha$. To use semantic parse trees to learn syntax, it must be possible to compute $T_\alpha(s)$ efficiently. We show that this is the case in what follows, starting from an efficient algorithm for computing $|T(s)|$.

The recurrence below can be used to compute $|T(s)|$ bottom up. $M$ is a zero-indexed $n \times n$ array, where $|s| = n$, and $M[i,j]$ is $|T(s[i \ldots j])|$, i.e. the number of possible UDTs for the substring of $s$ ranging from position $i$ to position $j$. Therefore, $|T(s)| = M[0, n-1]$.

$$M[i,i] = 1$$

$$M[i,j] = \sum_{l=2}^{n}\sum_{p=0}^{n-l}\sum_{q=0}^{l-2} M[p,p+q] * M[p+q+1,p+l-1]$$

Assuming the grammar is in CNF, the only way to generate a terminal is via a production of the form $X \longrightarrow \sigma$. Therefore, there is only one unlabeled derivation tree for each substring of $s$ of length 1 and $M[i,i] = 1$ for all $i$. All other entries are computed bottom-up via the second line in the recurrence. The first sum is over substring lengths, $l$, ranging from 2 to $n$. The second sum is over all starting positions, $p$, in $s$ of strings of length $l$. Together, $l$ and $p$ identify a substring of $s$, namely, $s[p \ldots p+l-1]$ that must have been generated by a production of the form $X \longrightarrow YZ$. The third sum is over all ways in which $Y$ and $Z$ can divide up that substring. For any such division, the number of trees for the substring is the product of the number of trees for the part $Y$ generates and the number of trees for the part that $Z$ generates.

Given lexical semantics, it is possible to compute $T_\alpha(s)$ using the recurrence below. Rather than $M$ being an $n \times n$ array, it is an $n \times n \times m$ array where $m$ is the number of distinct types that can label interior nodes in a semantic parse tree. Let $\delta(expr)$ take on value 1 if $expr$ is true, and 0 otherwise. Let $\texttt{typeof}(expr)$ return the type (an integer between 0 and $m-1$) of $expr$. Let @ denote function application.

$$M[i,i,t] = \delta(\texttt{typeof}(s[i \ldots i]) = t)$$

$$M[i,j,t] = \sum_{t_1,t_2}\sum_{l=2}^{n}\sum_{p=0}^{n-l}\sum_{q=0}^{l-2} M[p,p+q,t_1] * M[p+q+1,p+l-1,t_2] * \delta(\texttt{typeof}(t_1 @ t_2) = t \vee \texttt{typeof}(t_2 @ t_1) = t)$$

There is still only one unlabeled derivation tree for each substring of length 1, but the type of that tree is the type of the lambda expression for the meaning of the terminal. The outer sum in the second line of the recurrence is over all $m^2$ pairs of types. Given than $s[p \ldots p+l-1]$ will be split at offset $q$ (as established by the inner three sums), that split will yield a valid semantic parse only if the types of the two halves are compatible, i.e. if one can be applied to the other. If $t_1$ is the type of the left half and $t_2$ is the type of the right half, and applying $t_1$ to $t_2$ or applying $t_2$ to $t_1$ yields type $t$, then $M[i,j,t]$ is updated.

The recurrence above can be computed in $O(m^2 n^3)$ time. Note that $m$ will typically be a small constant because interior nodes can only be labeled by lexical types and types out of which lexical types are composed. Also, it is trivial to augment the computation so that $M$ can be used to extract all semantically valid parses of a given type. This is done by keeping a list of split points, $q$, for each $(i,j,t)$ that yield the desired type (i.e. $t$). This increases the storage required by a multiplicative factor of $n$.

## Using Semantically Valid Parse Trees to Learn Syntax

Our goal is to use lexical semantics and positive string examples to obtain positive structural examples that can be used to learn syntax. Clearly, if for every string in $L(G)$ there is a single semantically valid parse, then learning is straightforward. Later in this section we define a class of grammars for which this is the case. What happens, though, if there are multiple semantically valid parses for some string(s) in $L(G)$?

Let $E = \{s_1, s_2, \ldots\}$ be a set of strings. Let $T(E) = \cup_{s_i \in E} T(s_i)$, and let $T_G(E)$ and $T_\alpha(E)$ be defined similarly. Now consider grammar G for which $L(G) = \{xcd, xab, ycd, zab\}$ and $T_G(L(G)) = \{((xc)d), ((xa)b), (y(cd)), (z(ab))\}$. Suppose the type of $a$ and $c$ is $t$, and the type of all other lexical items is $< t, t >$. Then the semantically valid parses of the strings in $L(G)$ are as follows:

$$T_t(L(G)) = \{((xc)d), ((xa)b), (y(cd)), (z(ab)), (x(cd)), (x(ab)), ((yc)d), ((za)b)\}$$

For a reset-free grammar to generate these UDTs, the non-terminal that generates $cd$ must also generate $ab$ due to the trees $(x(ab))$ and $(x(cd))$. Coupled with the fact that $(y(cd))$ and $(z(ab))$ are in $L$, the grammar must also generate $(y(ab))$ and $(z(cd))$, neither of which are in $L(G)$. That is, learning a grammar based on all semantically valid parse trees can, in some cases, lead to overgeneralization.

Even so, given a sample of strings, $E$, from the language of some grammar, $G$, we can establish a few useful properties of the grammar learned from the structural examples contained in $T_t(E)$. For example, the language of that grammar will always be a subset of the language of the grammar learned from $E$ with the true UDTs. Somewhat more formally:

$$L(GI(T_G(E))) \subseteq L(GI(T_t(E)))$$

To see that this is true, first note that the output of $GI$ is independent of the order in which merges occur. It then suffices to show that the above holds for a single merge order. Suppose the merges performed by GI on $T_t(E)$ are precisely those performed on $T_G(E)$ up to the point where $GI(T_G(E))$ would terminate. If $GI(T_t(E))$ were to stop at this point, the language of the resulting grammar would be precisely $L(GI(T_G(E)))$ because it would contain all of the productions in $GI(T_G(E))$ plus productions that produce all and only the trees in $T_t(E) - T_G(E)$, and these trees correspond to strings in $E$ that are in $L(GI(T_G(E)))$. Additional merging required for $GI(T_t(E))$ to terminate can only add strings to the resulting language, so $L(GI(T_G(E))) \subseteq L(GI(T_t(E)))$.

## Lexically Unambiguous Parses

The previous section established that there exist grammars for which the language inferred using all semantically valid parses of the training examples is a superset of the language inferred using the true semantic parses of the training examples. This section defines a class of grammars for which every string in the language of such a grammar has a single semantically valid parse. For grammars in this class, lexical semantics ensure learnability.

For a given grammar $G$, let $right(X)$ be the set of terminals and non-terminals that can occur in the rightmost position of any string derivable in one or more steps from X.

Let $left(X)$ be defined analogously. Let $canapply(A, B)$ return true iff either $A$ is of the type $< \alpha, \beta >$ and $B$ is of the type $\alpha$ (i.e. $A$ can be applied to $B$) or $A$ is of the type $\gamma$ and $B$ is of the type $< \gamma, \delta >$ (i.e. $B$ can be applied to $A$).

**Theorem 1** *If for every production of the form $X \rightarrow YZ$ in grammar G neither condition 1 nor condition 2 below holds, then there is exactly one semantically valid parse of every string in the language generated by G.*

1. $\exists A \in right(Y) \bigcup \{Y\} \wedge \exists B \in left(Z)$ *s.t.* $canapply(A, B)$
2. $\exists A \in right(Y) \wedge \exists B \in left(Z) \bigcup \{Z\}$ *s.t.* $canapply(A, B)$

**Proof:** The proof will be by induction on the height of the derivation tree that generates the string. Because $G$ is in CNF, all productions are of the form $X \rightarrow YZ$ or $X \rightarrow \sigma$. Each non-terminal is generated by a tree of height one, and there is only one way to semantically parse any given non-terminal, so strings derived by a tree of height one have a single semantically valid parse. This is the base case. The inductive assumption is that all strings generated by a tree of height no more than $h$ have a single semantically valid parse.

Suppose some string has a derivation tree of height $h + 1$ and the string has multiple semantically valid parses. Let $X$ be the non-terminal that roots the derivation tree, and let $Y$ and $Z$ be the non-terminals that root it's left and right subtrees (i.e. the derivation tree was produced by expanding $X$ to $YZ$ via production $X \rightarrow YZ$). The subtrees rooted by $Y$ and $Z$ can have height at most $h$, so by the inductive assumption the strings they generate have a single semantically valid parse.

Therefore, the only way for the string generated by $X$ to have more than one semantically valid parse is for some non-terminal on the right edge of the tree generated by $Y$ to have a type that can be applied to the type of some non-terminal on the left edge of the tree generated by $Z$ (or vice versa). However, conditions 1 and 2 above explicitly disallow this, so there can be no string generated by a tree of height $h + 1$ with multiple semantically valid parses. Inductively, the theorem holds for strings generated by derivation trees of any height, i.e. all strings. □

The theorem above says that there is a class of grammars for which all strings have a single semantically valid parse. Grammars in this class can be learned by any algorithm that learns CFGs from unlabeled derivation trees.

## Semantic Type Inference

Until now we have assumed that the learning algorithm was given lexical semantics for all terminals. Now let us consider the case where we are given the UDTs and order of application for internal nodes for a sample of strings in a grammar. From this information we will demonstrate how all semantic types can be inferred using a minimal subset of semantic types.

Let X $\rightarrow$ Y Z be a production for which the meaning of $X$ is obtained by applying the meaning of $Y$ to the meaning of $Z$. Because the production obeys type constraints, if $X$ is of type $< \alpha, \beta >$ then $Y$ must be of type $\alpha$ and $X$ must be of type $\beta$. Types can be inferred for a given production in CNF in two ways. If the type of $Y$ is known, the types of $X$ and $Z$ can be inferred. If the types of $X$ and $Z$ are known, the type of $Y$ can be inferred. We assume that the start symbol has the same type for all strings. Consider the following grammar assuming left to right function application for all productions (e.g. assuming NP applies to VP and not vice versa):

$$
\begin{aligned}
\text{S} &\rightarrow \text{NP VP} \\
\text{NP} &\rightarrow \text{DET N} \\
\text{VP} &\rightarrow \text{TV NP} \\
\text{VP} &\rightarrow \text{IV}
\end{aligned}
$$

The start symbol, S, has semantic type of t. For this grammar, if we know the types of the elements of $\{\text{N} \bigcup \Sigma\}$ that are never used as functors in any production, we can infer the types of all other elements of $\{\text{N} \bigcup \Sigma\}$. For the above grammar the known types are of S, VP, N and IV. Knowing S and VP allows inference of NP, which then allows inference of DET using N, and inference of TV using VP and NP.

We say that non-terminal $Y$ *never applies* if it never occurs in a production $X \rightarrow YZ$ or $X \rightarrow ZY$ for which the meaning of $Y$ is applied to the meaning of $Z$ to obtain the meaning of $X$. The following theorem defines a subset of types that need to be known to ensure that all types are inferable.

**Theorem 2** *For any context-free grammar G in Chomsky Normal Form, given the types of all non-terminals that never apply, the types of all other non-terminals can be inferred.*

**Proof:** Let $G*$ be the directed graph created from grammar $G$ as follows. For each production of the form $X \rightarrow YZ$ add nodes labeled $X$, $Y$, and $Z$ to $G*$. If $Y$ applies to $Z$, add edges from node $Y$ to both node $X$ and $Z$. If $Z$ applies to $Y$, add edges from node $Z$ to both node $X$ and $Y$. Each node is marked as either known or unknown, depending on whether the type of the associated non-terminal is known. Nodes with out-degree zero correspond to non-terminals that never apply, and are therefore assumed to be known. All other nodes are initially marked unknown.

If all of the neighbors of a node are marked known, then its type can be inferred and the node marked known. This inference/marking step can be repeated until no new nodes are marked known. Because the number of unknown nodes decreases by at least one on each step, or the algorithm terminates, there can be no more than $O(|N|)$ iterations, each of which might need to do $O(|P|)$ work.

Suppose there exists a grammar $G$ for which all nodes in $G*$ are not marked known when the algorithm terminates. Let $X$ be the non-terminal associated with this node. If the type of $X$ cannot be inferred, then the type of at least one of its neighbors, call it $Y$, cannot be inferred. That is, there is path of length 1 from $X$ to a node whose type cannot be inferred. Likewise, because the type of $Y$ cannot be inferred, the type of at least one of its neighbors cannot be inferred, and this node lies on a path of length 2 from $X$. Inductively, there must be a node at the end of a path of length $n$ for all

$n \geq 0$ from $X$ whose type cannot be inferred. However, because a non-terminal's type cannot be defined (even partially) in terms of itself, all paths must terminate in a node with out-degree zero in $O(|N|)$ steps, and the types of all such nodes are known. This is a contradiction. Therefore, the theorem holds. □

The importance of theorem 2 is that words with types that never apply are typically those that refer to perceptually concrete aspects of the environment, such as nouns. That is, it is possible that an embedded learner might associatively learn the types of these words (Oates 2001; Roy 1999), and then use knowledge of syntax to infer the semantic types of all other words in the lexicon.

## Conclusion

This paper represents the first results of our inquiry into the relationship between meanings and learnability for context-free grammars. Theorem 1 established that there exists a class of grammars whose syntax can be learned from positive string examples and lexical semantics. Theorem 2 established that it is possible to infer lexical semantics given a grammar's syntax and a small number of lexical types.

The work most similar to ours reported in the literature is that of Tellier and her colleagues (Tellier 1998; Dudau-Sofronie, Tellier, & Tommasi 2001) who are also interested in the role of lexical semantics in grammatical inference. They propose an algorithm for inferring rigid categorial grammars given strings and their meanings, though the algorithm has exponential complexity and it is unclear (i.e. there is no proof) whether it converges to the target grammar or some grammar containing the target.

Future work will proceed in a number of directions. Ultimately, we want to develop algorithms that will iteratively use incomplete lexical knowledge to infer grammar fragments, and then use these fragments to infer more lexical knowledge. The goal is to have a learner that can provably converge on the correct lexicon and grammar by bootstrapping from some small amount of knowledge about lexical semantics obtained via associative learning.

An important result that we're currently working toward is an algorithm for inferring syntax when there are multiple semantically valid parse trees for one or more strings. One possible approach is to compute the corresponding semantics of each parse and use the fact that the learner is embedded in an environment to determine which parse is correct, i.e. which one refers to the current state of the world. An alternative approach might involve noticing when a merge would include strings in the grammar that are not observed.

## References


Angluin, D. 1982. Inference of reversible languages. *Journal of the Association for Computing Machinery* 29:741–765.

Angluin, D. 1987. Learning regular sets from queries and counterexamples. *Information and Computation* 75:87–106.

Carrasco, R. C.; Oncina, J.; and Calera, J. 1998. Stochastic inference of regular tree languages. *Lecture Notes in Computer Science* 1433:187–198.

Denis, F.; D'Halluin, C.; and Gilleron, R. 1996. PAC learning with simple examples. In *Symposium on Theoretical Aspects of Computer Science*, 231–242.

Dowty, D. R.; Wall, R. E.; and Peters, S. 1981. *Introduction to Montague Semantics*. Dordrecht: Reidel.

Dudau-Sofronie, D.; Tellier, I.; and Tommasi, M. 2001. From logic to grammars via types. In Popelínský, L., and Nepil, M., eds., *Proceedings of the 3rd Workshop on Learning Language in Logic*, 35–46.

Frege, F. L. G. 1879. Begriffschrift. In van Heijenoort, J., ed., *Frege and Godel: Two Fundamental Texts in Mathematical Logic (1970)*. Cambridge, MA: Harvard University Press.

Gold, E. M. 1967. Language identification in the limit. *Information and Control* 10:447–474.

Koshiba, T.; Makinen, E.; and Takada, Y. 2000. Inferring pure context-free languages from positive data. *Acta Cybernetica* 14(3):469–477.

Li, M., and Vitanyi, P. M. B. 1991. Learning simple concepts under simple distributions. *SIAM Journal of Computing* 20(5):911–935.

Marcus, G. F. 1993. Negative evidence in language acquisition. *Cognition* 46(1):53–85.

Oates, T.; Desai, D.; and Bhat, V. 2002. Learning k-reversible context-free grammars from positive structural examples. In *Proceedings of the Nineteenth International Conference on Machine Learning*.

Oates, T. 2001. *Grounding Knowledge in Sensors: Unsupervised Learning for Language and Planning*. Ph.D. Dissertation, The University of Massachusetts, Amherst.

Oncina, J., and Garcia, P. 1992. Inferring regular languages in polynomial updated time. In de la Blanca, N. P.; Sanfeliu, A.; and Vidal, E., eds., *Pattern Recognition and Image Analysis*. World Scientific.

Partee, B., and Hendriks, H. 1996. Montague grammar. In van Benthem, J., and ter Meulen, A., eds., *Handbook of Logic and Language*. Amsterdam: Elsevier Science and The MIT Press. 5–91.

Roy, D. 1999. *Learning Words from Sights and Sounds: a Computational Model*. Ph.D. Dissertation, MIT.

Sakakibara, Y. 1992. Efficient learning of context-free grammars from positive structural examples. *Information and Computation* 97:23–60.

Tellier, I. 1998. Meaning helps learning syntax. *Lecture Notes in Computer Science* 1433.

Weisstein, E. W. 2003. Catalan numbers. In *Eric Weisstein's World of Mathematics*.

# Distributed Representation of Syntactic Structure by Tensor Product Representation and Non-Linear Compression

**Heidi H. T. Yeung** **Peter W. M. Tsang**

City University of Hong Kong
Tat Chee Road, Kowloon Tong,
Kowloon, Hong Kong, China

### Abstract

Representing lexicons and sentences with the sub-symbolic approach (using techniques such as Self Organizing Map (SOM) or Artificial Neural Network (ANN)) is a relatively new but important research area in natural language processing. The performance of this approach however, is highly dependent on whether representations are well formed so that members within each cluster are corresponding to sentences or phrases of similar meaning. Despite the moderate success and the rapid advancement of contemporary computing power, it is still difficult to establish an efficient learning method so that natural language can be represented in a way close to the benchmark exhibited by human beings. One of the major problems is due to the general lack of effective method(s) to encapsulate semantic information into quantitative expressions or structures. In this paper, we propose to alleviate this problem with a novel technique based on Tensor Product Representation and Non-linear Compression. The method is capable of encoding sentences into distributed representations that are closely associated with the semantic contents, being more comprehensible and analyzable from the perspective of human intelligence.

## Introduction

In the early days, Symbolic and Sub-symbolic approaches were generally treated as 2 separated and competing fields in the realm of Artificial Intelligence. Apparently, neither of them seemed to be capable of attaining significant breakthrough on complicated task such as natural language understanding. Prince (1997) suggested that the integration of these 2 fields could possibly achieve graceful rewards when the combined effort was focused on the principle of optimization involving language grammar and cognitive architectures. In this paper, our scope of study is formal English which is one of the most common languages tackled in the research of Natural Language Processing (*NLP*). For clarity of explanation we shall present a brief introduction on the Symbolic and Sub-symbolic processing, and techniques for integrating these two approaches.



In the early stage of study in *NLP*, it had been assumed that a sentence, in its raw form, should be sufficient for processing and analysis. The result of this simple intuitive concept was soon found to be disappointing as phrases or sentences could vary dramatically even if they conveyed identical meaning. Later, researchers discover what human interpretation of natural language was largely derived from the sentence structures rather than the exact sequence of words. It was also in line with the rule-governed models that were adopted in linguistics research for defining the inter- and intra-relations between lexicons in formal languages.

Context-free grammar (*CFG*) was often considered as a fundamental paradigm for generating complete specifications of syntax in regular languages. It involves categories (titles of words with same syntactic meaning and phrases), productions (e.g. $NP \rightarrow ART, NBAR$ ), and parsers (algorithms for generating the complete syntactic structures with a given set of productions). An effective formulation of the *CFG* in linguistic studies was given by the Chomsky Normal Form (under constrained by X-bar scheme [Chomsky 1957]) which imposed constraints in the production rules to restrict the maximum number of siblings in any non-terminal nodes. An example of applying the X-bar scheme in parsing a sentence was illustrated in Figure 1.

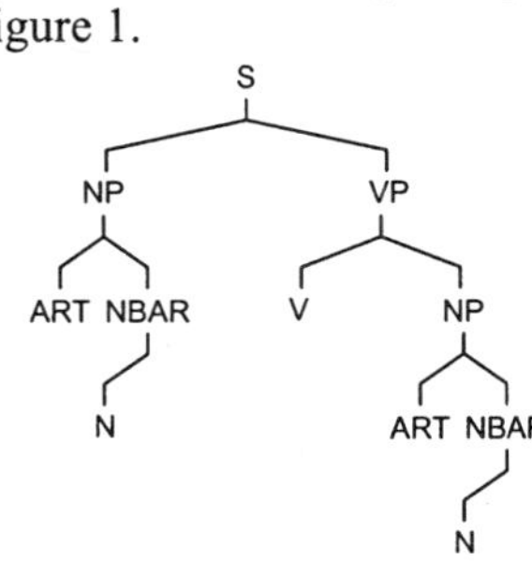


**Figure 1** The parse tree of the sentence "The man feeds the dog" where "The" = ART (Article), "Dog" and "Man" = N (Noun) and "Feeds" = V (Verb)

Sub-symbolic processing was based on the idea of cognitive science in expressing concepts, patterns, sequences or structures. Instead of deriving information explicitly from the hierarchical grouping of words and phrases in a parse tree, an implicit representation was built to encapsulate sentences to certain degree of abstraction. The task could be accomplished with an encoder, often implemented as an Artificial Neural Network (*ANN*) formed by a massive network of interconnecting processors. In the investigation of sub-symbolic processing in *NLP*, Elman (1990, 1991 & 1995), Miikkulaninen (FGREP, 1993) and Farkaš (SOM on lexicon cluster, 2001) proposed some well-known researches. Conclusively, the advantages of sub-symbolism were twofold. First, the approach enabled sentences to be represented in the form of holographic memories that were implicitly recorded in the synaptic connections of a massive network. The memory established for each learned sentence was robust towards lexical variations as long as the overall sequence was not substantial changed. Second, the learning process was performed in an autonomous and black-box fashion, avoiding the meticulous analytical procedures in symbolic processing. On the downside, the approach was relatively weak in modeling syntactic structures. In addition, methods based on *ANN* also inherited all its problems such as lengthy computation time and pre-mature termination in sub-optimal states even for small set of training samples.

A solution for the first problem was proposed by Pollack (1990) with the Recursive Auto-Associative Memory (*RAAM*). In this method, a collection of sentences were first decomposed into their corresponding parse trees and encoded in the form of multidimensional vectors. The latter were taken to train up a Recurrent Neural Network (*RNN*) via repetitive epochs of synaptic weight adjustment. Upon convergence, the syntactic structures of the sample sentences were memorized in the *RNN*. Later, Kwasny (1993, 1995) had introduced a simplified version of *RAAM* known as the Sequential RAAM (*SRAAM*). A different direction was suggested by Smolensky who adopted Tensor product to represent the symbolic structures in connectionist systems [Smolensky 1990]. In his approach, a concept was encoded into a compound or multiple-rank tensor by summing up (Boolean Addition) the outer product of each constituting components $v_{filter}$ and its corresponding role vector $v_{role}$, as

$$A_{Overall} = \sum v_{filter} \otimes v_{role} \tag{1}$$

Equation (1) resulted in an expression $A_{Overall}$ known as the Tensor Product Representation (*TPR*) that encapsulated the constituents of the concept as well as their infrastructure exhibited distributed representation properties (Figure 2). The method was much faster than those based on *ANN* as iterative computation was not required. Moreover, if the role vectors are linear independent of each other the *TPR* could be perfectly reverted back to all the constituents with the Unbinding Process [Smolensky 1990].

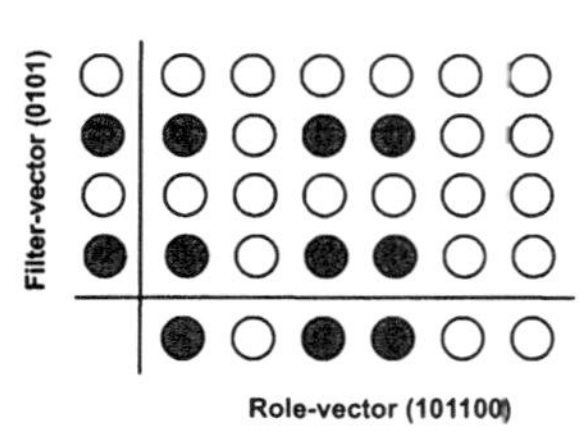


**Figure 2** The tensor formed with Filler-vector (0101) and Role vector (101100)

The major limitation of this approach was that the size of the *TPR* was unbounded, directly determined by the complexity of the concept as well as the quantity of constituents. This prohibited the use of this method in natural language representation when a fixed-size expression was required for representing an unbounded syntactic structure as Figure 3.

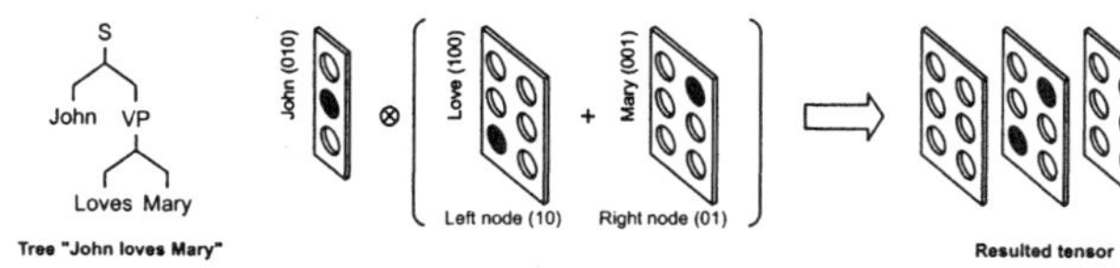


**Figure 3** The tensor product representation of syntactic structure

## Proposed encoding method - Tensor Product Representation with Non-linear Compression

In view of the above problems, we have developed a novel method based on Tensor Product with Non-Linear Compression so to translate sentences of varying length into fixed size representations. To start with, each unique category in a syntactic tree is mapped into a corresponding vector selected from an orthonormal basis. For clarity of description the following terminologies have been defined:

Let **T** and **G** denote the sets of tree and representation vectors, respectively. Following the Constraint Language for Attribute Trees CLAT($\mathcal{L}$) [Palm 1999], the first-order tree (e.g. Chomsky Normal Form) expression $t$ is given by

$$t = \delta^1\left(x_1, \pi_S^1\left(\{X_k\}_{k=2}^{k=c}\right)\right) \tag{2a}$$

$$\text{Sequence of children of node } x_1 = \{X_k\}_{k=2}^{k=c} \tag{2b}$$

where $x_1$ represents the root node of tree $t$ and $X_k$ is the unexpanded $k^{th}$ child (noted that a node may or may not contain a child) of its parent node. $\delta^1$ is the immediate dominance of $x_1$ to its sequence of children, and $\pi_s^1$ is the immediate sibling precedence among the sequence of children. In addition, $t$ may be a null collection $\sigma$ if it is a termination node.

Mapping from **T** to **G** is $\xi : \mathbf{T} \rightarrow \mathbf{G}$ and the mapping function $g = \xi_T(t, \varepsilon_1)$. $\varepsilon_j$ is the Level of Projection (*LoP*) of $j^{th}$ node in the tree and $\varepsilon_1 = 1$ is the starting node for $(\forall \varepsilon_j \in \mathbf{I}^+)$.

From the expression defining $t$ and the mapping function $g$, we have

$$g = \xi_T(t, \varepsilon_1) = \xi_T\left(\delta^1\left(x_1, \pi_S^1\left(\{X_k\}_{k=2}^{k=c}\right)\right), \varepsilon_1\right) \qquad (3)$$

The mapping function exhibited distributive properties, as

$$g = \xi_T(x_1, \varepsilon_1)\{\xi_T(X_k, \varepsilon_1 + 1)\}_{k=2}^{k=c}$$

$$g = \xi_T(x_1, \varepsilon_1)\left\{\xi_T\left(\delta^1\left(x_k, \pi_S^1\left(\{X_m\}_{m=c}^{m=c+n}\right)\right), \varepsilon_1 + 1\right)\right\}_{k=2}^{k=c} \qquad (4)$$

$\xi_T(x_j, \varepsilon_j)$ contains both the information of its category and the Level of Projection of the $j^{th}$ node in the tree. Each category is belonged to a specific unit vector ($e_i \in \mathbf{E}^d$ for $i^{th}$ category). The $j^{th}$ node in the tree is represented by its class vector $f_j \in \mathbf{E}^d$ which is an element of the set $\mathbf{E}^d$. Thus, the information encapsulated in the $j^{th}$ node can be expressed as $f_j = Rep(\xi_T(x_j, \varepsilon_j))$ with $\varepsilon_j = LoP(\xi_T(x_j, \varepsilon_j))$.

According to the original definition of *TPR* on syntactic structure, both nodes and branching information are deemed to be the elements contributing to the overall representation. This deviates from our approach where the *LoP* [Chomsky 1981] of the nodes is considered instead of the intra-relationships between them. To begin with, we define the set of vectors $r_k \in \mathbf{E}^{\max}$ to represent the *LoP* of the tree nodes. Suppose *max* is the maximum depth of an arbitrary tree structure, we have

$$r_\varepsilon = (\tilde{r}_1\, \tilde{r}_2 \ldots \tilde{r}_k \ldots \tilde{r}_{\max}) \text{ where } \tilde{r}_k = \begin{cases} 1 & k = \varepsilon \\ 0 & \text{otherwise} \end{cases} \qquad (5)$$

Next, the mapping $\Phi : \mathbf{G} \to \mathbf{U}$ is defined for associating the concept of a node and its *LoP*. For a tree consisting of $N$ nodes, the corresponding concepts can be concatenated through superimposition into a binary matrix given by

$$u = \Phi_G(g) = \Phi_G\left(\xi_T(x_1, \varepsilon_1)\{\xi_T(X_k, \varepsilon_1 + 1)\}_{k=2}^{k=c}\right)$$

$$u = \Phi_G(\xi_T(x_1, \varepsilon_1)) + \sum_{k=2}^{c} \Phi_G(\xi_T(X_k, \varepsilon_1 + 1)) \qquad (6a)$$

where $\Phi_G(\xi_T(\sigma, \varepsilon_j)) = \mathbf{0}$ and

$$\Phi_G(\xi_T(x_j, \varepsilon_j)) = Rep(\xi_T(x_j, \varepsilon_j)) \otimes r_{LoP(\xi_T(x_j, \varepsilon_j))} = f_j \otimes r_{\varepsilon_j} \qquad (6b)$$

From (6a) and (6b) a general form of the mapping $\Phi : \mathbf{G} \to \mathbf{U}$ for $N$ number of nodes in the tree can be expressed as

$$u = \Phi_G(g) = \sum_{j=1}^{N} f_j \otimes r_\varepsilon \qquad (7)$$

In the above derivations, it appears that the branching information has been neglected in building the representation. However, a closer look at (6a) reveals that the recursive expansion is in fact progressing through the nodes in a strict sequence defined by the hierarchical syntactic tree structure. The latter is derived from a parsing algorithm based on production rules and constraints governing the formation of language. For instance, the assertion of finite tree depth (non-recurrent relation), unique structure for individual sentence, and those nodes of the same category will not appear in the same *LoP*. All these imply that the branching information has been already been implicitly embedded in the representation.

The representation obtained in (7) is varying in size and difficult to be utilized by subsequent processes (a classifier, for instance) that accept fixed length inputs. To overcome this problem, we propose a novel method known as Non-linear Compression (*NLC*) for lossless compression of multiple-rank tensors to fixed-size vectors. In our method, a non-linear function ($\Theta : \mathbf{U} \to \mathbf{V}$) is defined to transform a vector into a scalar value.

In essence, suppose $a = (\tilde{a}_1\, \tilde{a}_2 \ldots \tilde{a}_k)$ (where $a \in \mathbf{I}^k$) is a vector to be converted and $\Omega(a, B)$ is the base-B transformation function ($B \in \mathbf{I}^+$). The transformation can result in either an integer $\Omega^+(a, B)$ or a floating-point value $\Omega^-(a, B)$. To avoid truncation error, we have chosen the latter to be the compression formula to convert an integer vector to a floating point value, as

$$\Omega^-(a, B) = \sum_{j=-\max}^{-1} \tilde{a}_{\max+j+1} B^j \qquad (8)$$

The compression is lossless and reversible if the $B^{-\max}$ can be perfectly represented within the precision of the processor (e.g. a computer). Otherwise, the data may be subject to certain degree of distortion depending on the extent of $k$. The base $B$ in the transformation is governed by the maximum discrete values that are defined within $a$. For binary vector, B is equals to 2.

The representation obtained in (7) can be expressed in the form of a two dimensional matrix. The row vector (fixed size) contains the category information of the tree and the column vector (variable size) encapsulates the *LoP* information. The latter is compressed into scalar value with the formula below:

$$\Theta_U(u) = \sum_{i=1}^{d} \Omega^-(u^{\mathrm{T}} \cdot e_i, B) \times e_i \quad \because u^{\mathrm{T}} = r_\varepsilon \otimes f_j \qquad (9)$$

The *LoP* of each category is extracted by dot product and the Base Transformation is applied on each of them. Finally, a value contributing to specific category vector and the representation is formed by summing all contributing category vectors. The 2 mapping functions can be integrated into a general form given by the mapping function ($\Psi : \mathbf{G} \to \mathbf{V}$):

$$\Psi_G(g) = \sum_{j=1}^{N} B^{-\varepsilon_j} \cdot f_j \qquad (10)$$

Using the Figure 1 as an example, the TP Representation with NLC is as Table 1 (B = 2).

**Table 1** TPR with NLC of "The man feeds the cat"

| S | NP | VP | NBAR | VBAR | ART | N | V |
|---|---|---|---|---|---|---|---|
| 0.5 | 0.375 | 0.25 | 0.1875 | 0.125 | 0.1875 | 0.09375 | 0.0625 |

Mathematically, an inverse transform for (9) is available as given by

$$\Phi_G(g) = \Theta_V^{-1}(\theta) = \sum_{i=1}^{d}\left(\Omega^{-1}\left(v \cdot e_i, B, \max\right) \otimes e_i\right) \qquad (11)$$

where $v = \Theta_U(u)$

Furthermore, the level of projection of the $i^{th}$ category in a tree can be extracted by the Unbinding Process, as

$$\Phi_U^{-1}(u,i) = [u]^{\mathrm{T}} \cdot e_i = \left[\sum_{j=1}^{N} f_j \otimes r_{\varepsilon_j}\right]^{\mathrm{T}} \cdot e_i = \sum_{j:f_j=e_i}^{N} r_{\varepsilon_j} \qquad (12)$$

According to (12), the tree can be recovered by back-tracking the nodes with reference to the parsing rules taken to construct the syntactic structures. Experimental results reveal that the full reconstruction can be achieved if the maximum depth of tree is less than 7 (cropping operation may be required for larger tree).

## Experiment results

We examine the characteristics of our approach with 3 experiments. Cluster analysis is one of the important tools to explore the features inside the representation [Pollack 1990] [Kwasny 1993, 1995] by grouping candidates of similar characteristics. To evaluate the proposed method, the *TPR* of 44 sentences and phrases with different structures are computed and further encoded with *NLC*. The representations are clustered according to their Euclidean distance the result is illustrated in Figure 4.

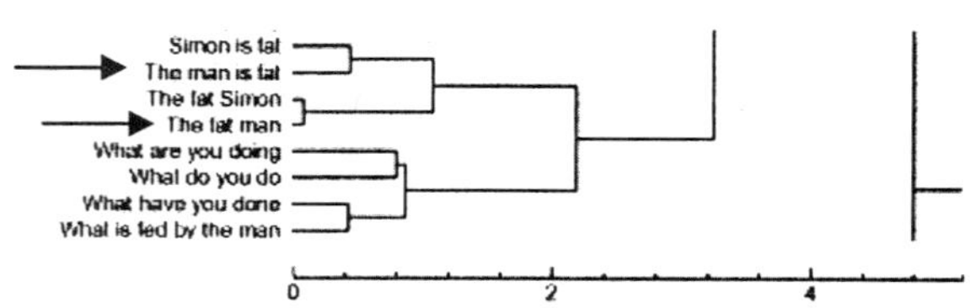


**Figure 4** Cluster result of representation of 44 generated sentences

It can be seen that the sentences have been grouped according to the similarity of structures and insensitive to the actual constituents and positioning of words. For example, "The man is fat" and "The fat man" are very similar as they have three words in common. However, out method has successfully identifying them as moderately different in structure.

We have also explored the effectiveness of our method in associating representations with their semantic information. A second experiment has been conducted following the works reported by Tsang and Wong (2002). In their experiment, the *RAAM* representations were built for a set of sentences and classified into frame-based semantics (e.g. AGENT_ACTION_PATIENT) with a three-layer Back-Propagation Neural Network (*BPNN*). We repeat the test with identical set of sentences and identical settings given below (Table 2):

**Table 2** Experiment parameters of second experiment

| Parameter | Value |
|---|---|
| Number of grammatical categories | 15 |
| Number of semantic frame types | 5 |
| Number of Parsing Rules | 18 |
| Size of hidden layer of BPNN | 12 |
| Number of training and testing sentences | 28 |
| BPNN Training epochs | 2000 |

Each sample sentence is presented in a shuffling manner to the *BPNN* for 100 times, each involving 2000 epochs of iterations. A plot of the average Root-Mean-Square (*RMS*) Error of M sentences and p output in BPNN against the number of iterations is plotted in Figure 5. The light and bolded lines illustrate results obtained with the representations constructed with *RAAM* and our method, respectively. It can be seen that throughout the entire training period, the *RMS* error is considerably lowered in our case except at the very beginning of the process. A very low error is finally reached (about 0.1893) with our approach whereas the system using RAAM is comparatively larger by ten times (about 1.04).

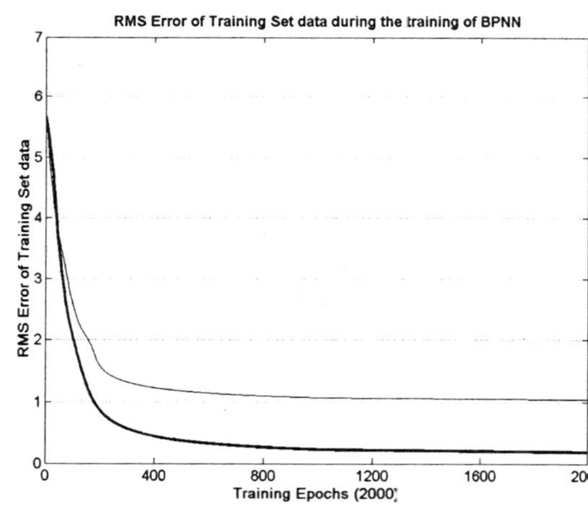


**Figure 5** RMS Error of classification during training BPNN using Tsang's data set

In addition, 100% of the training and test sentences are classified properly with the use of the *NLC-TP* representation whereas only a success rate of 85.71% is recorded in Tsang and Wong's article.

The experiment is further extended to classify 14 sentences that are similar to the samples but deviated in the syntactic arrangements. Representations obtained with our method exhibit excellent *graceful degradation*. For instance, "The man sleep" and "The fat man sleep" are both classified as AGENT-ACTION although the second sentence can easily be misinterpreted as ADJ-AGENT if the first three words are considered first. The word "fat" can be considered as a kind of noise which has been successfully discarded in the *NLC-TP* representation. The difference again, is clearly reflected with the *NLC-TP* representation. However, both of the above tests failed with the *RAAM* representation.

In order to examine the representational capacities and capabilities of our approach, we design the third experiment similar to the second one but it computes with a much larger grammatical data set which can handle the more complicated linguistic structures (e.g. tenses, negation & question) and a more powerful BPNN (with doubled hidden neurons) are involved shown as Table 3.

**Table 3** Experiment parameters of third experiment

| | |
|---|---|
| Number of grammatical categories | 44 |
| Number of semantic frame types | 39 |
| Number of Parsing Rules | 79 |
| Size of hidden layer of BPNN | 30 |
| Number of sample sentences | 91 |
| Number of test sentences | 50 |
| BPNN Training epochs | 2000 |

From the experimental results, the proposed representation seems much more compatible with BPNN than RAAM in terms of training stability and classifying correctness.

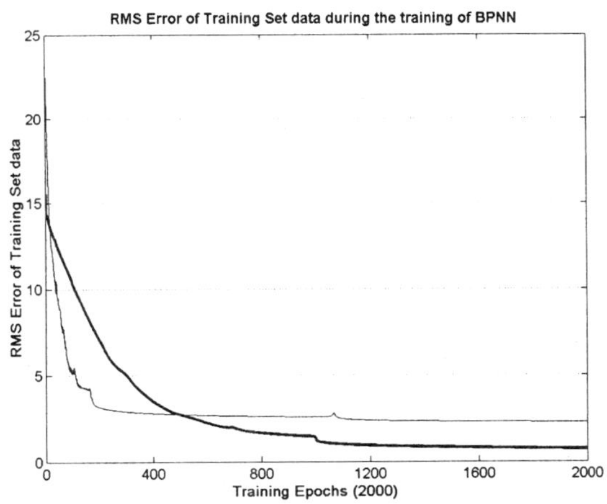


**Figure 6** RMS Error of classification during training BPNN with the larger data set

We plot the average case (not the best or worst one) of RMS Error converging progress of classifying the training sentences in to assigned semantic frame type as the same way as the second experiment does in Figure 6 above. In the first half of training epochs, a significant drop of RMS Error is experienced in the training using RAAM and the error value retains around 2.27 (about 0.025 per sentence). It is obviously trapped in a local minimum of error surface in pre-mature state. Again, the training with *NLC-TP* Representation converges in slower rates but a lower error state at 0.7176 (0.0079 per sentence) is finally reached with stable converging rates. At the mention of correctness of semantic type classification, the system with proposed representation classifies entire training set correctly but that with RAAM only achieve usually less than 70% successful rate.

Analogously, the set of testing sentences is designed for challenge the graceful degradation ability of the semantic extraction system. A difficult case is examined with the pair of sentences: "The cat would not be fed by the man" and "The cat would not be fed" that are rather similar at higher level of projection (from 5$^{th}$ level) but differ in the semantic frame type. The former is of type AGENT-INDIRECTACTION-PATIENT while the latter is a member of AGENT-INDIRECTACTION. The system with our representation recognizes this distinction with a clear sense (very low classification error). Nonetheless, that with RAAM representation is also failed this test as second experiment and it even cannot signify a most possible semantic type for the second sentence.

Comparing the classifying correctness on both second and third experiments, the results are generalized as Table 4a and 4b below averaging of 100 result sets. NLC-TP representation exhibits the overwhelming success in this semantic extraction application.

**Table 4a** Generalized results of second experiment for 100 result sets

| | RAAM | NLC-TPR |
|---|---|---|
| Lowest Error | 1.1412 | 0.1866 |
| Average Error per sentence | 0.0815 | 0.0133 |
| Correctness of Training Set (%) | 85.17 | 100 |
| Correctness of Testing Set (%) | 57.14 | 100 |
| Computation time (in terms of t) | 30 t | t |

**Table 4b** Generalized results of third experiment for 100 result sets

| | RAAM | NLC-TPR |
|---|---|---|
| Lowest Error | 2.1607 | 0.6082 |
| Average Error per sentence | 0.0237 | 0.0067 |
| Correctness of Training Set (%) | 69.23 | 100 |
| Correctness of Testing Set (%) | 32 | 94 |
| Computation time (in terms of t) | 100 t | t |

## Conclusions

In this paper we have developed a novel scheme based on Tensor Product and Non-linear Compression for encoding syntactic structures of English language into fixed size vector representations. The proposed method has a number of major advantages over existing approaches based on *RAAM*. First, the computing time is significantly reduced as *ANN* is not required in encoding the sentences. Second, the representations are stable as they are clustered according to the similarity of their corresponding syntactic structures, rather than the detail positioning or presence of individual words. Third, similar finding is obtained in the classification of representations into semantic categories through the use of Artificial Neural Network. Experimental results reflect that representations attained with our method are capable of extracting correct semantic from sentences even if they are absent in the training set. In addition considerably fewer amounts of iterations are required by the *ANN* to converge to a state with relatively lower *Mean Square Error* (*MSE*). These favorable results demonstrated the feasibility of the proposed method and its potential in real-time application on *NLP* such as Translation and Semantic Extraction.

## References


Kwasny, S. C., Kalman, B. L., & Chang, N. 1993. *Distributed Patterns as Hierarchical Structures.* Proceedings of the World Congress on Neural Networks, Portland, OR, July 1993, v. II, pp. 198-201.

Kwasny, S. C., & Kalman, B. L. 1995. *Tail-recursive distributed representations and simple recurrent neural networks.* Con. Sci., 7 (1), pp. 61-80.

Chomsky, N. 1957. *Syntactic structure.* The Hague, The Netherlands: Mouton.

Chomsky, N. 1981. *Lectures on Government and Binding.* Foris Publications, Dordrecht.

Costa, F., & Frasconi, P., & Lombardo, V., & Soda, G. 2003. Towards Incremental Parsing of Natural Language Using Recursive Neural Networks. Applied Intelligence 19, pp. 9-25

Elman, J. L. 1990. *Finding structure in time.* Cognitive Science, 14, 179-211.

Elman, J. L. 1991. *Distributed representations, simple recurrent networks, and grammatical structure.* Machine Learning, vol. 7, no. 2/3, pp. 195-226.

Elman, J. L., 1995. *Language as a dynamical system. Mind as Motion: Explorations in the Dynamics of Cognition,* Eds. R. F. Port and T. van Gelder, pages 195--225. MIT Press, Cambridge, MA, (cited in pages 23, 44).

Farkas, I., & Li, P. 2001. *A Self-Organizing Neural Network Model of the Acquisition of Word Meaning.* Proceedings of the 4th Int. Conf. on Cognitive Modeling, Fairfax, VA, pp. 67-72.

Miikkulainen, R. 1993. *Subsymbolic Natural Language Processing - An integrated model of scripts, lexicon, and memory.* MIT Press, Cambridge, MA, London.

Palm, A. 1999. *The expressivity of tree languages for syntactic structures.* The Mathematics of Syntactic Structure: Trees and Their Logics Eds. H. P. Kolb; U. Monnich, Mouton-de Gruyter. The theory of syntactic domains. Technical Report 75, Department of Philosophy, University of Utrecht. pp. 113-152

Pollack, J. B. 1989. *Implications of recursive distributed representations.* Technical report, OH 43210.

Pollack, J. B. 1990. *Recursive distributed representations. Artificial Intelligence*, 36, pp. 77-105.

Prince, A., & Smolensky, P. 1997. *Optimality: From neural networks to Universal Grammar.* Science, 275, 1604-1610.

Smolensky, P. 1990. *Tensor product variable binding and the representation of symbolic structures in connectionist systems.* Artificial Intelligence, pp. 46, 159-216.

Smolensky, P. 1994. *Grammar-based connectionist approaches to language.* Cognitive Science. Stabler, E.P. (1994). The finite connectivity of linguistic structure. Eds. C. Clifton, L. Frazier & K. Rayner, Perspectives on sentence processing (pp. 303--336). Hillsdale, NJ: Lawrence Erlbaum Associates.

Tsang, W. M., & Wong, C. K. 2002. *Extracting Frame Based Semantics from Recursive Distributed Representation - A Connectionist Approach to NLP.* IC-AI' 02.

# Perception

# Rapid Object Recognition from Discriminative Regions of Interest*

**Gerald Fritz, Christin Seifert, Lucas Paletta**
JOANNEUM RESEARCH
Institute of Digital Image Processing
Wastiangasse 6, A-8010 Graz, Austria
{gerald.fritz,christin.seifert,lucas.paletta}@joanneum.at

**Horst Bischof**
Graz University of Technology
Institute for Computer Graphics and Vision
Inffeldgasse 16/II, A-8010 Graz, Austria
bischof@icg.tu-graz.ac.at

## Abstract

Object recognition and detection represent a relevant component in cognitive computer vision systems, such as in robot vision, intelligent video surveillance systems, or multi-modal interfaces. Object identification from local information has recently been investigated with respect to its potential for robust recognition, e.g., in case of partial object occlusions, scale variation, noise, and background clutter in detection tasks. This work contributes to this research by a thorough analysis of the discriminative power of local appearance patterns and by proposing to exploit local information content to model object representation and recognition. We identify discriminative regions in the object views from a posterior entropy measure, and then derive object models from selected discriminative local patterns. For recognition, we determine rapid attentive search for locations of high information content from learned decision trees. The recognition system is evaluated by various degrees of partial occlusion and Gaussian image noise, resulting in highly robust recognition even in the presence of severe occlusion effects.

## Introduction

Research on visual object recognition and detection has recently focused on the development of local interest operators (Kadir & Brady 2001; Mikolajczyk & Schmid 2002; Obdrzalek & Matas 2002) and the integration of local information into occlusion tolerant recognition (Weber, Welling, & Perona 2000; Agarwal & Roth 2002; Fergus, Perona, & Zisserman 2003). Recognition from local information (part based recognition) serves several purposes, such as, improved tolerance to occlusion effects, or to provide initial evidence on object hypotheses in terms of providing starting points in cascaded object detection.

Previous work on the exploitation of local operator responses for recognition developed several viewpoints on how to advance from local to global information. (Weber, Welling, & Perona 2000) applied standard interest operators (Förstner, Harris) with the aim to determine localizable object parts for further analysis. (Weber, Welling, & Perona 2000) selected class related patterns from related fixed spatial configurations of recognizable operator responses. To avoid dependency on scale selection, (Kadir & Brady 2001; Mikolajczyk & Schmid 2002; Obdrzalek & Matas 2002) introduced interest point detectors that derive scale invariance from local scale saliency. These operators proved to further improve recognition from local photometric patterns, such as in (Fergus, Perona, & Zisserman 2003). While concern has been taken specifically with respect to issues of scale invariance (Lowe 1999; Kadir & Brady 2001), wide baseline stereo matching performance (Mikolajczyk & Schmid 2002; Obdrzalek & Matas 2002), or unsupervised learning of object categories (Weber, Welling, & Perona 2000; Agarwal & Roth 2002; Fergus, Perona, & Zisserman 2003), the application of interest point operators has not yet been investigated about the information content they provide with respect to object discrimination.

The key contribution of the presented work to local object recognition is, firstly, to provide a thorough analysis on the discriminative power of local appearances, and secondly, to exploit discriminative object regions to build up an efficient local appearance based representation and recognition methodology (Fig. 1). In contrast to the use of classifiers that determine discriminant features (e.g., (Swets & Weng 1996)) for recognition, our approach intends to make the actual local information content explicit for further processing. An information theoretic saliency measure is then used to construct the object model (Sec. 2) or to determine discriminative regions of interest for detection and recognition purposes (Sec. 3). In this work we focus on the investigation of the local information content, and how this leads to an early mapping to reject meaningless image regions. While this study primarily considers invariance to rotation of the object around the vertical axis as well as to translation (Sec. 5), we think that an extension to scale and (horizontal) rotation invariant local features (such as reported in (Lowe 1999) or (Mikolajczyk & Schmid 2002)) would be straight forward, by taking the discriminative potential of the features into account.

We propose in a first stage to localize discriminative regions in the object views from the Shannon entropy of a locally estimated posterior distribution (Sec. 2.1). In a sec-

---

*This work is funded by the European Commission's project DETECT under grant number IST-2001-32157, and by the Austrian Joint Research Project Cognitive Vision under sub-projects S9103-N04 and S9104-N04. This work has been carried out within the K plus Competence Center ADVANCED COMPUTER VISION.

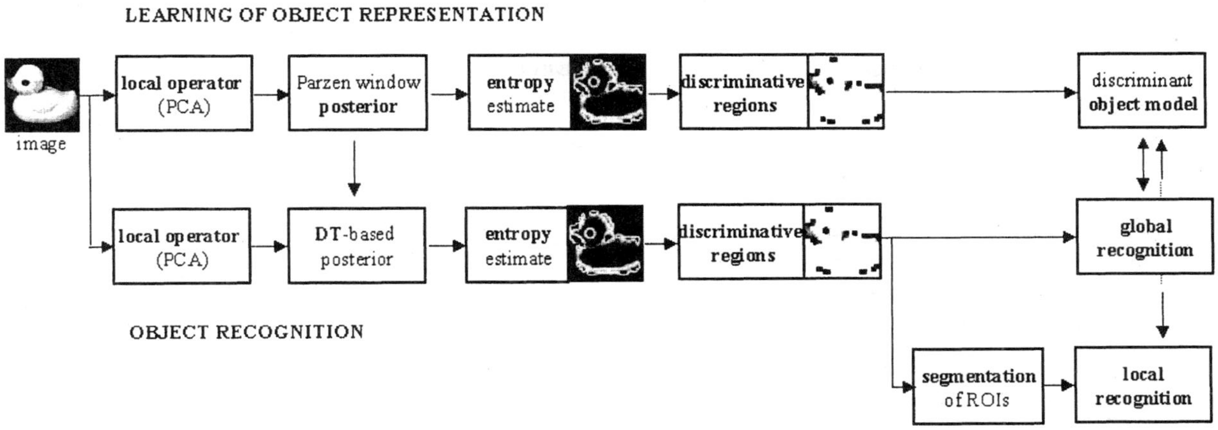


Figure 1: Concept of the entropy based recognition model. (Top) From a subspace feature selection (e.g., PCA) we compute the posteriors and the local information content. Responses of discriminative regions with entropy values below a predefi ned threshold are stored in the object model. (Bottom) For rapid object recognition, a decision tree outputs local entropy estimates. A global recognition method operates on the complete image. In contrast, individual discriminative regions can be segmented to provide a local recognition decision.

ond stage, we consequently derive object models in feature subspace from discriminative local patterns (Sec. 2.2). Object recognition is then exclusively applied to test patterns with associated low entropy. Identifi cation is achieved by majority voting on a histogram over local target attributions (Sec. 3). Rapid object recognition is supported by decision tree bases focus of attention on discriminative regions of interest (Sec. 4). The method is evaluated on images degraded with Gaussian noise and different degrees of partial occlusions using the COIL database (Sec. 5).

## Entropy-based object models

The proposed object model consists of projections of those local appearances that provide rich information about an object identity, i.e., *reference imagettes*[1] mapped into a subspace of the corresponding image matrix. Local regions in the object views that are both discriminative and robustly indicate the correct object label provide the reference imagettes for the object representation.

Note that discriminative regions correspond here to regions in the image that contain information with respect to object recognition. Feature extraction is here applied from principal component analysis and followed by an estimate of the local posterior to derive the local information content. In contrast to comparable work on the extraction of discriminative basis libraries (e.g., (Saito *et al.* 2002)) for an effi cient construction of feature subspaces, we specifi cally exploit the local information content value to derive effi cient thresholds for pattern rejection, with the purpose to determine both representation and region of interest.

[1]imagettes denote subimages of an object view (de Verdiére & Crowley 1998)

### Local distributions in subspace

We use a principal component analysis (PCA, (Murase & Nayar 1995)) calculated on local image windows of size $w \times w$ to form the basis for our local low dimensional representation. PCA maps imagettes $\mathbf{x}_i$ to a low dimensional vector $\mathbf{g}_i = \mathbf{E}\mathbf{x}_i$ by matrix $\mathbf{E}$ consisting of few most relevant eigenvectors of the covariance matrix about the imagette sample distribution $\mathbf{X} = \{\mathbf{x}_1, \ldots, \mathbf{x}_i, \ldots, \mathbf{x}_N\}$, $N$ is the total number of imagette samples.

In order to get the information content of a sample $\mathbf{g}_i$ in eigenspace with respect to object identifi cation, we need to estimate the entropy $H(O|\mathbf{g}_i)$ of the posterior distribution $P(o_k|\mathbf{g}_i)$, $k = 1 \ldots \Omega$, $\Omega$ is the number of instantiations of the object class variable $O$. The Shannon entropy denotes

$$H(O|\mathbf{g}_i) \equiv -\sum_k P(o_k|\mathbf{g}_i) \log P(o_k|\mathbf{g}_i). \tag{1}$$

We approximate the posteriors at $\mathbf{g}_i$ using only samples $\mathbf{g}_j$ inside a Parzen window (Parzen 1962) of a local neighborhood $\epsilon$, $||\mathbf{g}_i - \mathbf{g}_j|| \leq \epsilon$, $j = 1 \ldots J$. We weight the contributions of specifi c samples $\mathbf{g}_{j,k}$ - labeled by object $o_k$ - that should increase the posterior estimate $P(o_k|\mathbf{g}_i)$ by a Gaussian kernel function value $\mathcal{N}(\mu, \sigma)$ in order to favor samples with smaller distance to observation $\mathbf{g}_i$, with $\mu = \mathbf{g}_i$ and $\sigma = \epsilon/2$. The estimate about the Shannon entropy $\hat{H}(O|\mathbf{g}_i)$ provides then a measure of ambiguity in terms of characterizing the information content with respect to object identifi - cation within a single local observation $\mathbf{g}_i$.

### Discriminative object regions

It is obvious that the size of the local $\epsilon$-neighborhood will impact the distribution and thereby the recognition accuracy (Fig. 3, Sec. 5), highly depending on the topology of object related manifolds in subspace. One can construct

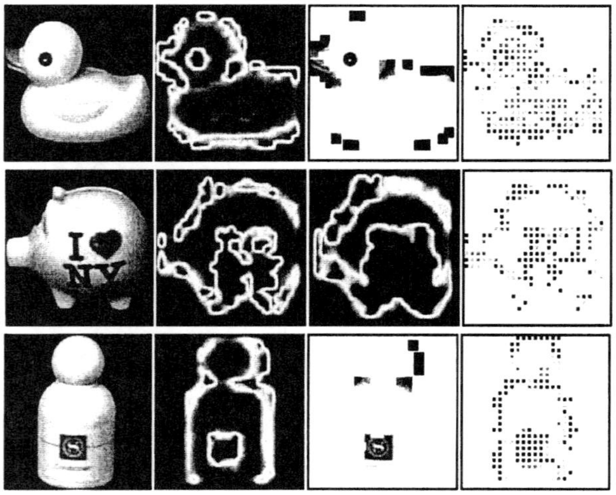


Figure 2: Sample COIL-20 objects (a) $o_1$, (b) $o_{13}$, (c) $o_{16}$ at view 0; each with - left to right - (i) original frame, (ii) entropy image (from 9x9 pixel imagettes; entropy coded color palette from low=blue to high=red), (iii) local appearances with $\Theta \leq 0.5$ in a,c (entropy image from 15x15 pixel imagettes in b), and (iv) accuracy-coded images (accuracy blue=true, white=false).

an entropy-coded image of an object view from a mapping of local appearances $\mathbf{x}_i$ to corresponding entropy estimates (Fig. 2 for characteristic objects of the COIL-20 database, Sec. 5). The individual images (from left to right) depict the original image, the color coded entropy image (from $9 \times 9$ pixel imagettes), corresponding imagettes with $\hat{H}(O|\mathbf{g}_i(\mathbf{x}_i)) \leq 0.5$, and associated images coding recognition accuracy (blue=correct, white=false). From these images it becomes obvious that regions containing specific texture and brightness contrasts provide highly discriminative information for recognition.

From discriminative regions we proceed to *entropy thresholded* object *representations*. The entropy coded images provide evidence that segmentation into discriminative regions and consequently exclusive usage of the associated reference points in eigenspace would provide sparse instead of extensive object representations (de Verdiére & Crowley 1998), in terms of storing only imagette information that is *relevant for classification* purposes. Object representations from local photometric patterns have been constructed either from extensive storage of all subspace (reference) points for k-nearest neighbor matching (de Verdiére & Crowley 1998), or from selected, cluster specific prototype points (Weber, Welling, & Perona 2000; Fergus, Perona, & Zisserman 2003) that necessarily convey uncertainty. In contrast, the proposed object model includes only *selected* reference points for nearest neighbor classification, storing exclusively those $\mathbf{g}_i$ with

$$\hat{H}(O|\mathbf{g}_i) \leq \Theta. \quad (2)$$

A specific choice on the threshold $\Theta$ consequently determines both storage requirements and recognition accuracy (Sec. 5). The question on how to practically select $\Theta$ must be answered in response to application related considerations, such as, requested recognition accuracy, etc. One recommended strategy to determine $\Theta$ would be to start with the $\Theta_{max}$, thereby requesting a maximum of resources, and then to gradually reduce $\Theta$ so that a critical limit will be empirically encountered.

To speed up the matching we use efficient memory indexing of nearest neighbor candidates described by the adaptive *K-d* tree method (Friedman, Bentley, & Finkel 1977).

## Object recognition from local information

The proposed recognition process is characterized by an entropy driven selection of image regions for classification, and a voting operation, as follows,

1. **Mapping** of imagette patterns into subspace (Sec. 2.1).
2. **Probabilistic interpretation** to determine local information content (Eq. 1).
3. **Rejection** of imagettes contributing to ambiguous information (Sec. 2.2).
4. **Nearest neighbor analysis** of selected imagettes within $\epsilon$-environment.
5. **Majority voting** for object identifications over a full image nearest neighbor analysis.

Each imagette pattern from a test image that is mapped to an eigenspace feature point is analysed for its entropy $\hat{H}(O|\mathbf{g}_i)$ with respect to object identification. In case this imagette would convey ambiguous information, its contribution to a global recognition decision would become negligible, therefore it is removed from further consideration. Actually, practice confirms the assumption that it is difficult to achieve a globally accurate object identification when multiple ambiguous imagettes 'wash out' any useful evidence on a correct object hypothesis (Paletta & Greindl 2003). The entropy threshold $\Theta$ for rejecting ambiguous test points in eigenspace is easily determined from the corresponding threshold applied to get the sparse model of reference points by Eq. 2. Selected points are then evaluated on whether they lie within the $\epsilon$-distance of any model reference point. In case several points are identified, the object class label of the nearest neighbor point is associated to the queried test point.

Object recognition on a set of imagettes is then performed on finding the object identity by majority voting on the complete set of class labels attained from individual imagette interpretations.

## Discriminative regions from decision trees

For the purpose of *rapid* object recognition and detection, we need a mapping of low computational complexity to perform a *focus of attention* on regions of interest (ROIs). These ROIs would then be fed into the recognition module (Sec. 3) for detailed analysis. Actually, this segmentation function would work in terms of a point of interest operator (POI) but be tuned from a discriminative objective function, i.e., entropy based. In order to keep complexity of the POI low, we do not use a neural network approach or a universal function estimator. In contrast, we provide rapid entropy estimates from a decision tree classifi er, assuming appropriate quantization of the entropy values into class labels. One expects from this tree to provide this estimate from a few attribute queries which would fundamentally decrease computation time per image for ROI computation.

**Estimation of entropy values** For a rapid estimation of local entropy quantities, each imagette projection is fed into the decision tree which maps eigenfeatures $\mathbf{g}_i$ into entropy estimates $\hat{H}$, $\mathbf{g}_i \mapsto \hat{H}(\Omega|\mathbf{g}_i)$. The C4.5 algorithm (Quinlan 1993) builds a decision tree using the standard top-down induction of decision trees approach, recursively partitioning the data into smaller subsets, based on the value of an attribute. At each step in the construction of the decision tree, C4.5 selects the attribute that maximizes the information gain ratio. The induced decision tree is pruned using pessimistic error estimation (Quinlan 1993).

**Rapid extraction of ROIs** The extraction of ROIs in the image is performed in 2 stages. First, the decision tree based entropy estimator provides a rapid estimate of local information content. Only eigenfeatures $\mathbf{g}_i$ with an associated entropy below a predefi ned threshold $\hat{H}(O|\mathbf{g}_i) < H_\Theta$ are considered for recognition (Sec. 3). These selected discriminative eigenfeatures are then processed by nearest neighbor analysis with respect to the object models and by majority voting according to the process described in Sec. 3.

## Experimental results

In order to perform a thorough analysis of the object recognition performance we applied the described methodology to images of the COIL-20 database (Murase & Nayar 1995).

**Eigenspace representation** Experiments were applied on 72 (test: 36) views of 20 objects of the COIL-20 database, for a total of 1440 (720) gray-scaled images with normalized size of $128 \times 128$ pixels. Analysis was performed with various imagette sizes: $9 \times 9$ (selected for further experiments), $15 \times 15$, and $21 \times 21$ pixels, resulting in larger discriminative regions (normalised per entropy maximum; e.g., in Fig. 2b) for larger imagette sizes. However, recognition errors due to partial occlusion positively correlate with imagette size. Imagettes were sampled by a step size of 5 pixels, giving a total of 603950 (301920) imagettes for training (test), excluding black background imagettes. Imagettes were projected into a 20-dimensional eigenspace.

**Local information content** For a local probabilistic interpretation of test imagettes, we searched for an appropriate threshold $\epsilon$ to determine the training samples in a local neighborhood (Sec. 2.1) that will be considered for the posterior estimation. Fig. 3 shows recognition rates (using a MAP classifi er and images degraded with 10% Gaussian noise, operated on all *single* imagettes) with various values for neighborhood $\epsilon$ and entropy threshold $\Theta$. This diagram shows that imagettes with high entropy $\Theta > 2$ dramatically

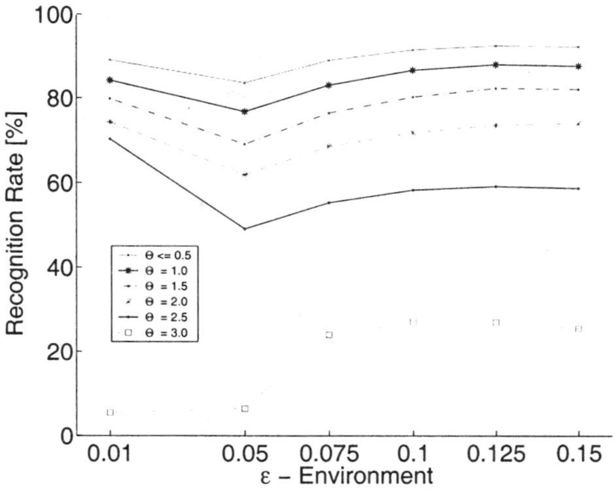


Figure 3: Recognition performance using MAP classifi cation on samples of a neighborhood $\epsilon$. Rejecting imagettes with entropy $\hat{H}(O|\mathbf{g}_i) > \Theta$, $\Theta = 2.0$, may dramatically increase accuracy of overall object recognition.

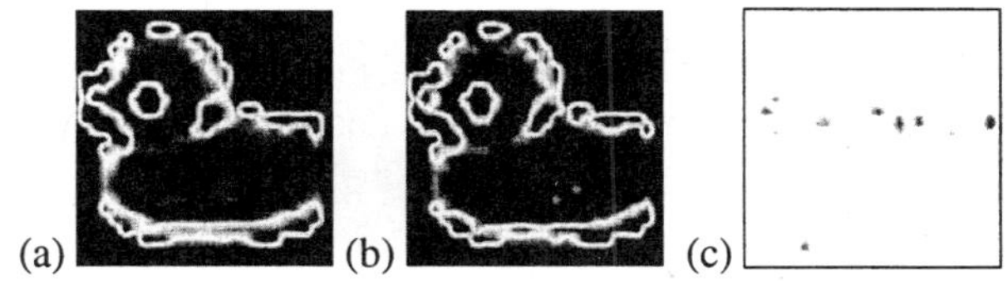


Figure 4: Estimation of entropy from decision trees. (a) Entropy estimation from Parzen windows $I_P$ (Sec. 2.1, color code see Fig. 2), (b) entropy estimation from decision tree $I_T$ (Sec. 4), (c) difference image $I_D = I_P - I_T$ (grayvalue coded for $[0, H_{max}]$ from white to black).

decrease the recognition rate. $\epsilon = 0.1$ was selected for best performance while not taking too many imagettes into account.

**Discriminative regions from decision trees** The decision tree was trained using eigenfeatures $\mathbf{g}_i$ of 50% of all extracted imagettes from the COIL-20 database and associated entropy estimates, determined from the Parzen window approach (Sec. 2.1). Entropy values were linearly mapped into equally spaced $N_H$ intervals $[(k-1)H_{max}/N_H, kH_{max}/N_H]$ for $k = 1..N_H$, $N_H = 5$ (Tab. 1). The error on the training set was determined 2.4%, the error on the test set 13.0%. This suffi ces to map eigenfeatures very effi ciently to corresponding entropy intervals (classes). Fig. 4 illustrates a typical decision tree based estimation of local entropy values. It demonstrates that discriminative regions can be represented highly accurately (Fig. 4b) from sequences of only $\approx 25$ attribute queries. A difference image (Fig. 4c) reflects the negligible errors and confi rms that discriminative regions can be both reliably and rapidly estimated from C4.5 decision trees.

| maps $\mapsto$ | $[0, H_{c_1})$ | $[H_{c_1}, H_{c_2})$ | $[H_{c_2}, H_{c_3})$ | $[H_{c_3}, H_{c_4})$ | $[H_{c_4}, H_{max}]$ |
|---|---|---|---|---|---|
| $[0, H_{c_1})$ | 38146 | 5546 | 2981 | 1425 | 218 |
| $[H_{c_1}, H_{c_2})$ | 1820 | 44418 | 1382 | 624 | 72 |
| $[H_{c_2}, H_{c_3})$ | 1495 | 2094 | 41989 | 2548 | 190 |
| $[H_{c_3}, H_{c_4})$ | 1036 | 1136 | 3725 | 40775 | 1644 |
| $[H_{c_4}, H_{max}]$ | 166 | 192 | 400 | 2709 | 44849 |

Table 1: Confusion map of the C4.5 decision tree based entropy estimation. The individual entropy intervals - denoted by classes $c_1 \cdots c_5$ - partitioning $[0, H_{max}]$ into equally large intervals (Sec. 5) are well mapped by the decision tree to corresponding output classes, providing an accurate estimation of the local entropy values (Fig. 4).

**Partial occlusion and Gaussian noise** For a thorough performance analysis in case of image corruption, we applied partial occlusion of $0 - 90\%$ and Gaussian noise to pixel brightness. For determining the occlusion area, we selected random center positions of the black occluding squared windows within the object regions, and computed the window size related to the total number of pixels attributed to a given object. This prevents from preferring specific object regions for occlusions, and assures that the object is actually occluded according to a given occlusion rate. Fig. 5 depicts sample entropy coded color images corrupted by various degrees of occlusion. The associated histograms on imagette based object label attribution illustrate that majority voting mostly provides a both accurate and robust decision on the object identity.

**Object recognition performance** The experiments on recognition rates from occlusion and noise demonstrate the superior performance of the entropy critical method as well as the associated majority voting classifier. Fig. 6 demonstrates best performance for an interpretation of a complete image that has been treated by small Gaussian noise = $10\%$. However, for detection issues we have to confine to local regions such as those segmented by entropy thresholding ($\Theta < \Theta_{max}$). Several models of entropy thresholding demonstrate the robustness of the system performance with respect to Gaussian noise = $50\%$ and for varying degrees of occlusions. Note that with an entropy critical selection of $30\%$ ($\Theta = 1.5$) out of all possible test imagettes an accuracy of $> 95\%$ is achieved despite a $70\%$ occlusion rate (blue). Considering instead *all* test imagettes for recognition (no selection), the performance would drop by more than $15\%$ (green; arrow)! To the knowledge of the authors, the entropy critical classifier is outperforming any comparable method in the literature, since comparable local recognition results have been achieved without noise only.

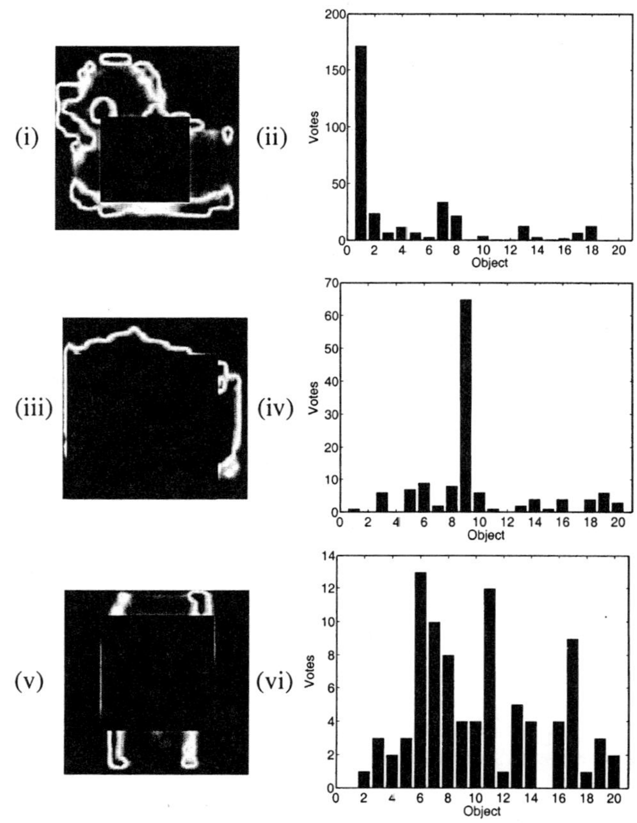


Figure 5: Samples of (top down) 40%, 80% and 60% occlusion on entropy coded images and associated histogram on imagette based object classes. Majority voting provided (top down) correct/correct/incorr. identification.

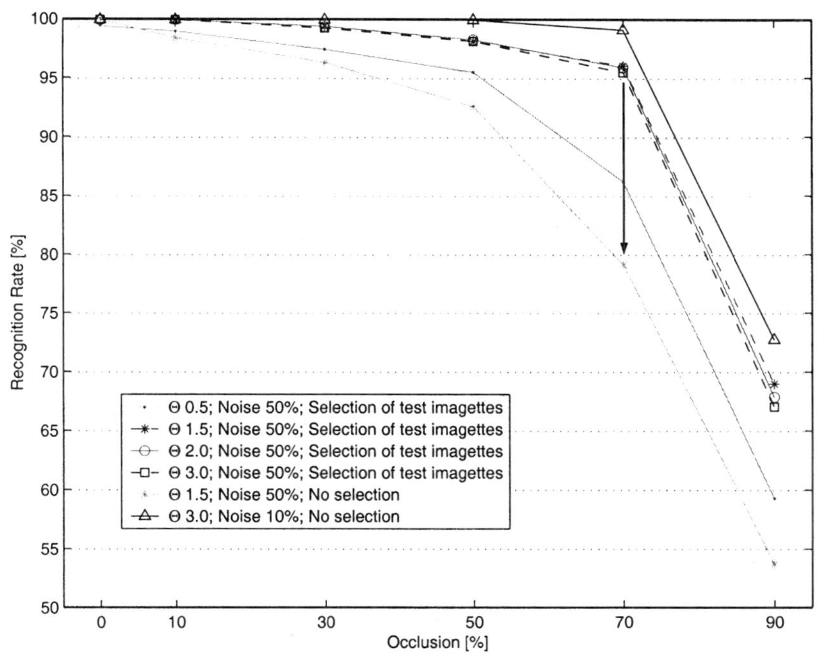


Figure 6: Resulting recognition performance for up to 90% occlusion rates and Gaussian noise of 50% (10%).

## Conclusions

This work represents a thorough statistical analysis of local discriminative information for object recognition applied to images of a well cited reference database. It demonstrates that the local information content of an image with respect to object recognition provides a favorable measure to determine both sparse object models and interest operators for detection. Focusing image analysis exclusively on discriminative regions will not only result in accelerated processing but even in superior recognition performance (Sec. 5). The methods potential for applications is in object detection tasks, such as in rapid and robust video analysis.

Future work will focus on fi nding appropriate methods to further thin out the sparse object model, and taking local topology in subspace into concern. Furthermore, ongoing work considers to develop a grouping mechanism that would locally segment promising regions of interest for detection with the goal of cascaded object detection.

## References


Agarwal, S., and Roth, D. 2002. Learning a sparse representation for object detection. In *Proc. European Conference on Computer Vision*, volume 4, 113–130.

de Verdiére, V. C., and Crowley, J. L. 1998. Visual recognition using local appearance. In *Proc. European Conference on Computer Vision*.

Fergus, R.; Perona, P.; and Zisserman, A. 2003. Object class recognition by unsupervised scale-invariant learning. In *Proc. IEEE Conference on Computer Vision and Pattern Recognition*, 264–271.

Friedman, J. H.; Bentley, J. L.; and Finkel, R. A. 1977. An algorithm for finding best matches in logarithmic expected time. *ACM Transactions on Mathematical Software* 3(3):209–226.

Kadir, T., and Brady, M. 2001. Scale, saliency and image description. *International Journal of Computer Vision* 45(2):83–105.

Lowe, D. 1999. Object recognition from local scale-invariant features. In *Proc. International Conference on Computer Vision*, 1150–1157.

Mikolajczyk, K., and Schmid, C. 2002. An affine invariant interest point detector. In *Proc. European Conference on Computer Vision*, 128–142.

Murase, H., and Nayar, S. K. 1995. Visual learning and recognition of 3-D objects from appearance. *International Journal of Computer Vision* 14(1):5–24.

Obdrzalek, S., and Matas, J. 2002. Object recognition using local affine frames on distinguished regions. In *Proc. British Machine Vision Conference*, 113–122.

Paletta, L., and Greindl, C. 2003. Context based object detection from video. In *Proc. International Conference on Computer Vision Systems*, 502–512.

Parzen, E. 1962. On estimation of a probability density function and mode. *Annals of Mathematical Statistics* 33:1065–1076.

Quinlan, J. 1993. *C4.5 Programs for Machine Learning*. San Mateo, CA: Morgan Kaufmann.

Saito, N.; R.R.Coifman; Geshwind, F.; and Warner, F. 2002. Discriminant feature extraction using empirical probability density estimation and a local basis library. volume 35, 2841–2852.

Swets, D., and Weng, J. 1996. Using discriminant eigenfeatures for image retrieval. *IEEE Transactions on Pattern Analysis and Machine Intelligence* 18(8):831–837.

Weber, M.; Welling, M.; and Perona, P. 2000. Unsupervised learning of models for recognition. In *Proc. European Conference on Computer Vision*, 18–32.

# Automatically Transforming Symbolic Shape Descriptions for Use in Sketch Recognition

**Tracy Hammond and Randall Davis**
MIT Computer Science and Artificial Intelligence Laboratory (CSAIL)
MIT Building 32-(239,237), 32 Vassar St.
Cambridge, MA 02139
{hammond,davis} at csail.mit.edu

## Abstract

Sketch recognition systems are currently being developed for many domains, but can be time consuming to build if they are to handle the intricacies of each domain. This paper presents the first translator that takes symbolic shape descriptions (written in the LADDER sketch language) and automatically transforms them into shape recognizers, editing recognizers, and shape exhibitors for use in conjunction with a domain independent sketch recognition system. This transformation allows us to build a single domain independent recognition system that can be customized for multiple domains. We have tested our framework by writing several domain descriptions and automatically created a domain specific sketch recognition system for each domain.

## Introduction

As pen-based input devices have become more common, sketch recognition systems are being developed for many domains such as mechanical engineering (Alvarado 2000), UML class diagrams (Hammond & Davis 2002), webpage design (Lin *et al.* 2000), architecture (Gross, Zimring, & Do 1994), GUI design (Caetano *et al.* 2002a; Lecolinet 1998), virtual reality (Do 2001), stick figures (Mahoney & Fromherz 2002), course of action diagrams (Pittman *et al.* 1996), and many others. These systems allow users to sketch a design, which is a more naturally interaction than a traditional mouse and palette tool (Hse *et al.* 1999). But sketch recognition systems can be quite time consuming to build if they are to handle the intricacies of each domain.

We propose that rather than build a separate recognition system for each domain, we instead build a single domain independent recognition system that can be customized for each domain. To build a sketch recognition system for a new domain, the developer would need only write a domain description, describing how shapes are drawn, displayed and edited. This description would then be transformed for use in the domain independent system. The inspiration for such a framework stems from work in speech recognition, which has been using this approach with some success (Zue & Glass 2000).



In our work, we transform a grammar into a domain recognizer of hand-drawn shapes. This is analogous to work done on compiler compilers, in particular visual language compiler compilers (Costagliola *et al.* 1995). A visual language compiler compiler allows a user to specify a grammar for a visual language, then compiles it into a recognizer which can indicate whether a arrangement of icons is syntactically valid. The main difference between this work and ours is that 1) ours handles hand-drawn images and 2) their primitives are the iconic shapes in the domain whereas our primitives are geometric.

In this paper we present the first translator that takes symbolic descriptions of how shapes are drawn, displayed, and edited in a domain and automatically transforms them into shape recognizers, editing recognizers, and shape exhibitors for use in a domain independent sketch recognition system. To succeed in our goal, we have created 1) LADDER(Hammond & Davis 2003), a symbolic language for describing how shapes are drawn, displayed, and edited in a domain, 2) a translator as described above, and 3) a simple domain independent recognition system that uses the newly translated components to recognize, display, and allow editing of the domain shapes. The implementation of this translator and domain independent sketch recognition system serves to show both that such a framework is feasible and that LADDER is an acceptable language for describing domain information.

The domain independent recognition system and transformer described here were designed to test whether we could in fact transform symbolic descriptions of a domain into active recognizers usable by a domain independent recognition system. Other work in our group is pursuing a more ambitious approach to both building a domain independent recognition system and studying the process of transforming descriptions into recognizers. Nevertheless, the work reported here does illustrate the plausibility of transforming descriptions into recognizers.

We have chosen a symbolic sketching language based on how shapes look rather than on features such as drawing speed, size of the bounding box, etc., (as in systems like (Rubine 1991; Long 2001)).We did this to ensure that symbols would be recognized if they looked the same, even if they weren't drawn in the same way (e.g., with a different number of strokes), allowing users to draw the shapes as they would naturally. A high-level symbolic language based on shape offers the added advantage in being easier to read and understand, facilitating identification and correction of errors in the description such as automatically checking if a shape is impossibly constrained (which would be difficult in a low-level languages such as (Jacob, Deligiannidis, & Morrison 1999)). Shape definitions primarily concern how shapes look, but may include other information helpful to the recognition process, such as stroke order or stroke direction.

Because different domains have different ways of displaying and editing the shapes in their domain, sketch recognition systems need to know how to edit and display the shapes recognized. This motivated us to create a language that allows developers to describe editing and display, as well as how the shapes look and are drawn.

Shape description languages have been created for use in architecture, diagram parsing, as well as within the field of sketch recognition itself. However, current shape description languages lack ways for describing editing (Stiny & Gips 1972; Futrelle & Nikolakis 1995; Bimber, Encarnacao, & Stork 2000; Mahoney & Frommerz 2002; Caetano *et al.* 2002b; Gross & Do 1996), display (Futrelle & Nikolakis 1995; Bimber, Encarnacao, & Stork 2000; Mahoney & Frommerz 2002; Caetano *et al.* 2002b; Gross & Do 1996), or non-graphical information, such as stroke order or direction (Stiny & Gips 1972; Futrelle & Nikolakis 1995; Bimber, Encarnacao, & Stork 2000).

## Framework Overview

Our goal is to make development of a sketch recognition system easier by enabling domain experts (rather than programmers) to describe the shapes to be recognized. Figure 1 gives an overview of the framework for our overall research effort: 1) a sketch description language, LADDER, 2) a translator that converts a domain description into components for use in conjunction with a domain independent sketch recognition system, and 3) a domain independent sketch recognition system that uses the newly generated components to recognize, edit, and display shapes in the domain. The domain description is transformed into shape recognizers, exhibitors, and editors which are used in conjunction with a domain independent recognition system to create a domain specific recognition system.

To create the domain specific recognition system, the developer writes a LADDER domain description consisting of multiple shape definitions. The left box of Figure 1 gives an example of an Arrow shape definition. The components and the constraints define what the shape looks like and are transformed into shape recognizers. The display section specifies how the shape is to be displayed when recognized and is transformed into shape exhibitors. The editing section specifies the editing behaviors that can be performed on the recognized shape and are transformed into editing recognizers.[1]

[1]The aliases section renames components or sub-components for ease of reference later.

LADDER supplies a number of predefined shapes, constraints, display methods, and editing behaviors. These predefined elements are hand-coded into the domain independent system, allowing it to recognize, display, and edit these predefined shapes. Recognition is carried out as a series of bottom up opportunistic data driven triggers in response to pen strokes.

The third box of Figure 1 shows the domain independent sketch recognition system, which contains hand-coded shape recognizers, editing recognizers, and shape exhibitors for the primitive shapes (line, ellipse, curve, arc, and point). This system also defines each of the constraints. The translator creates additional shape recognizers (which in turn call on the constraint functions), editing recognizers, and shape exhibitors. As each stroke is drawn, the system determines whether the stroke is an editing trigger for any shape. If not, it is taken to be part of the drawing, and is recognized as a collection of primitive shapes. The resulting primitives are added to the database, and the recognition module examines the database to attempt to combine the primitives into more abstract shapes. Specialized methods merge overlapping and connecting lines to account for primitives such as lines being drawn using more than one stroke. The display module then displays the result as defined by the domain description.

The domain independent recognition system, including the set of primitive shapes, constraints, display routines, and editing gesture handlers, and the links between them, provides a substantial foundation for the domain specific recognition system, helping to greatly simplify the translation process.

## Transformation

The translation process parses the description and generates code specifying how to recognize shapes and editing triggers as well as how to display the shapes once they are recognized and what action to perform once an editing trigger occurs. We describe the translation process in detail for each part of the shape definition.

### Generating Shape Recognizers

The job of the shape parser is to transform a shape definition into rules that recognize that shape. The shape definition specifies the components that make up the shape as well as the constraints on these components, including any requirements about stroke order or direction.[2] We use the Jess (Friedman-Hill 2001) rule engine for recognition.

Jess is a forward-chaining pattern/action rule engine for Java. In our system, Jess facts represent recognized drawn shapes. Each stroke is segmented into a point, line, curve,

[2]LADDER allows the user to specify both hard and soft constraints. Hard constraints must be satisfied for the shape to be recognized, but soft constraints may not be. Soft constraints can aid recognition by specifying relationships that usually occur. For instance, in the left box of Figure 1, we could have specified (draw-order shaft head1 head2) to specify that the the shaft of the arrow is commonly drawn before the head, but the arrow should still be recognized even if this is not satisfied. Our current implementation does not yet support soft constraints.

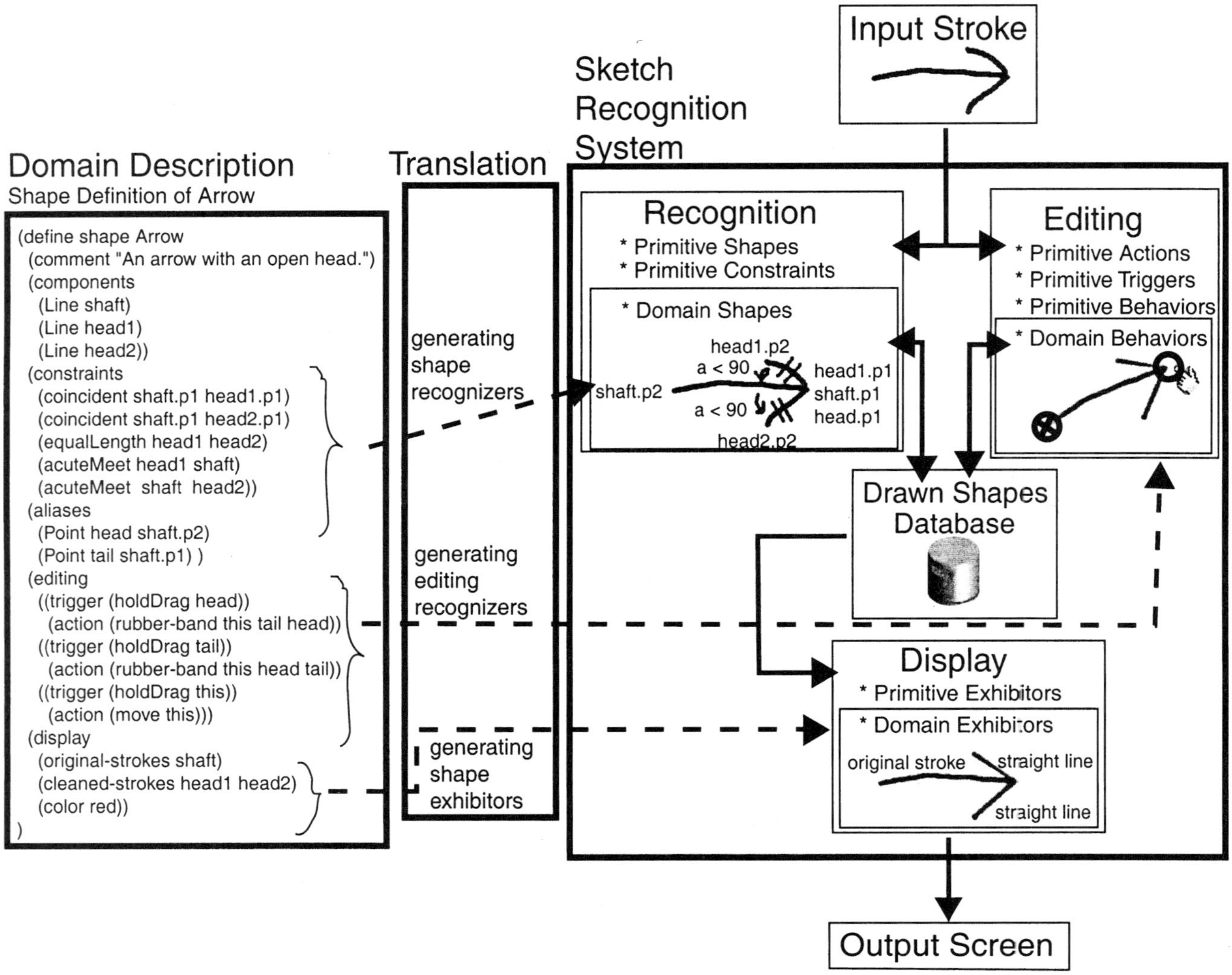


Figure 1: Framework Overview showing LADDER Domain Description, Translator, and Domain Independent Sketch Recognition System.

arc, ellipse, spiral, or some combination using techniques from (Sezgin 2001), and the primitive shapes are added to the Jess fact database. For instance, if a line is drawn, a fact is added of the form `(Line 342 23 24 25 10.6)`, where 342 indicates the line's ID, 23, 24, and 25 are the IDs of the endpoints and midpoint, and 10.6 indicates the length of the line.[3] An additional fact, `(Subshapes Line 342 342)`, is also sent to indicate the primitive shapes that make up the drawn shape.

Our domain shape recognizers are implemented as Jess rules. In the transformation process we create a rule whose pattern specifies the components of the shape and the constraints that must hold between the components.[4] An example of the rule generated for the arrow given in the left box in Figure1 is shown in Figure 2. The translation process is straightforward because of the foundation of primitives built into the domain independent system. The rule engine searches for all possible subsets of facts for the collection specified in its premise. In the case of Figure 1, the rule engine searches for three lines to make up the shaft, head1, and head2. The rule engine then tests whether the constraints hold for each subset. Then, for each collection of three lines labelled shaft, head1, and head2, the Jess engine will check that head1.p1 and shaft.p1 are coincident. Each LADDER constraint is defined as a Jess function to simplify transfor-

[3] Because we do not want to place any unspecified drawing order constraints, each line, arc, and curve is actually added twice to the Jess rule based system to take into account the fact that the endpoints may be assigned in either direction.

[4] The pattern also specifies that all components be distinct, to prevent the rule engine from returning three copies of the same line when trying to find an arrow.

```
(defrule ArrowCheck
  ;; get three lines
  ?f0 $<$- (Subshapes Line ?shaft \$?shaft_list)
  ?f1 $<$- (Subshapes Line ?head1 \$?head1_list)
  ?f2 $<$- (Subshapes Line ?head2 \$?head2_list)
  ;; make sure lines are unique
  (test (uniquefields \$?shaft_list \$?head1_list))
  (test (uniquefields \$?shaft_list \$?head2_list))
  (test (uniquefields \$?head1_list \$?head2_list))
  ;; get accessible components of each line
  (Line ?shaft ?shaft_p1 ?shaft_p2 ?shaft_midpoint ?shaft_length)
  (Line ?head1 ?head1_p1 ?head1_p2 ?head1_midpoint ?head1_length)
  (Line ?head2 ?head2_p1 ?head2_p2 ?head2_midpoint ?head2_length)
  ;; test constraints
  (test (coincident ?head1_p1 ?shaft_p1))
  (test (coincident ?head2_p1 ?shaft_p1))
  (test (equalLength ?head1 ?head2))
  (test (acuteMeet ?head1 ?shaft))
  (test (acuteMeet ?shaft ?head2))
  ;;deleted code: get line with endpoints swapped

=>  ;; FOUND ARROW (ACTION TO BE PERFORMED)
  ;; set aliases
  (bind ?head ?shaft_p1)
  (bind ?tail ?shaft_p2)
  ;; add arrow to sketch recognition system to be displayed properly
  (bind ?nextnum (addshape Arrow ?shaft ?head1 ?head2 ?head ?tail))
  ;; add arrow to Jess fact database
  (assert (Arrow ?nextnum  ?shaft ?head1 ?head2 ?head ?tail))
  (assert (Subshapes Arrow ?nextnum (union\$ \$?shaft_list
          \$?head1_list \$?head2_list)))
  (assert (DomainShape Arrow ?nextnum (time)))
  ;; remove Lines from Jess fact database for efficiency
  (retract ?f0) (assert (CompleteSubshapes Line ?shaft \$?shaft_list))
  (retract ?f1) (assert (CompleteSubshapes Line ?head1 \$?head1_list))
  (retract ?f2) (assert (CompleteSubshapes Line ?head2 \$?head2_list))
  ;;deleted code: retract line with endpoints swapped
)
```

Figure 2: Automatically Generated Jess rule for the arrow definition in the left box of Figure 1.

mation of a shape definition into a Jess rule.

If a shape is recognized (i.e., the rule pattern is satisfied), the rule action is fired. In the transformation process the rule action is specified to do three things: 1) add the new shape to the database of recognized shapes so it can be displayed correctly and edited; 2) add the new fact to the rule based system so more complicated shapes can be formed from it; 3) remove recognized components from the database. This last step improves efficiency at the expense of possibly missing some shape interpretations.

Jess then confirms that this newly created shape does not share any subcomponents with any other domain shape. If it does, then only one of the domain shapes will remain, either the shape containing more primitive components (Ockhams razor), or (in the case of a tie) the shape that was drawn first.

While the arrow example used throughout this paper is composed of a fixed number of components (3 lines), our architecture can also support shapes composed of a variable number of components, such as a polyline or polygon. A shape with a variable number of components is transformed into two Jess rules, the first recognizes the base case, and the second rule handles the recursive case. For example, the base case rule of a polyline recognizes a polyline consisting of two lines, while the recursive case rule recognizes a polyline consisting of an existing polyline and an additional line.

## Generating Editing Recognizers

The shape definition includes information on how a shape can be edited. The arrow definition from Figure 1 specifies three editing behaviors: dragging the head, dragging the tail, and dragging the entire arrow. Each editing behavior consists of a trigger and an action. Each of the three defined editing commands are triggered when the user places and holds their pen on the head, tail, or shaft, and then begins to drag the pen. The actions for these editing commands specify that the object should follow the pen either in a rubber band fashion for the head or tail of the arrow or by translating the entire shape.

The drawing panel watches for all of the possible editing triggers predefined in LADDER. When one occurs it calls the appropriate method to check if an editing behavior should occur. Each of the editing actions (such as translate, rotate, scale, rubber-band, or delete) is predefined for all shapes.

During the translation process, we transform all of the editing specifications of the shape definitions into one Java class. After a trigger first occurs (such as click or holdDrag), the Java class examines all of the viewable shapes with that trigger defined to see if an editing behavior has begun. For instance, holdDrag is defined as the pen initially resting on the screen for .4 seconds, and then dragging across the screen. After holdDrag is detected, the system looks to see if the pen is located over the head, tail, or shaft of an arrow. If not, the system treats the stroke as a drawing gesture. If there is a shape underneath the stylus that has that trigger specified, the editing action occurs. In our example, if the head of an arrow is underneath the pen, the arrow will rubber-band with the head following the path of the pen and the tail remaining fixed. [5]

## Generating Shape Exhibitors

The shape definition includes information on how a shape should be displayed once it is recognized. A shape or its components may be displayed in any color in four different ways: 1) the original strokes of the shape, 2) the cleaned up version of the shapes, where the best-fit primitives of the original strokes are displayed, 3) the ideal shape, which displays the primitive components of the shape with the constraints solved[6], or 4) another custom shape which specifies which shapes (line, circle, rectangle, etc.) to drawn and where. The arrow definition from Figure 1 specifies that the arrow should be displayed in the color red, that head1 and head2 should be drawn using cleaned-strokes (a straight line in this case), and that the shaft should be drawn using the original strokes.

LADDER has a number of predefined display methods, including color, original-strokes, and cleaned-strokes, which are hand-coded into the domain independent recognition system for use with all shapes. The domain independent recognition system also defines how to handle hierarchical display of shape, and provides generalized methods for al-

[5]Rubber-banding allows users to simultaneously rotate and scale and object, assuming a fixed rotation point is defined. This action has proved useful for editing arrows and other linking shapes.

[6]We currently solve only a subset of the constraints and are attempting to develop and integrate a more sophisticated geometric constraint solver.

tering the display of a shape, including translate, scale, and rotate.

During the transformation process we create a shape exhibitor (a Java class to display the shape) for each shape. This shape exhibitor specifies how the shape is to be drawn (original, cleaned, ideal, or custom). If the ideal strokes are to be drawn, the translator creates a method that displays the ideal strokes by attempting to solve the constraints of the shape (e.g., ensuring that points are coincident if the description indicates so) and then redraws the shape with the constraints solved. Likewise, if a custom display is defined, the translator creates a method that displays the specified shapes.

The shape exhibitor controls the displaying of the newly created shape and ensures that the components (e.g., the original strokes) are not drawn, but only the abstract shape (e.g., arrow) itself. The shape exhibitor keeps track of the location of the accessible components and aliases of a shape, which 1) can be used by the editing module to determine if an editing gesture is occurring, and 2) ensures that when a shape is moved or edited its components are moved or deleted with it. The shape exhibitor also keeps a original copy of each of the accessible components and aliases for use when scaling an object to ensure that we don't lose any precision after several scalings.

## Testing

To test our approach we have built and transformed domain descriptions for a variety of domains including UML class diagrams, flow charts, finite state machines, a simplified version of course of action diagrams, and a simple subset of 2-dimensional mechanical engineering diagrams. Figure 3 shows the variety of shapes recognized to date.

Figure 4, a flowchart of the domain independent recognition system described in this paper, was created using the flowchart domain sketch recognition system. The domain description specified that Actions, Decisions, Start/Ends should be displayed in blue and the Links in red, both using cleaned-strokes. [7]

## Related Work in our group

(Sezgin 2003) is working on a translation mechanism that can improve recognition efficiency using HMM techniques. (Alvarado 2003) is developing a more sophisticated domain independent recognition system using Bayesian networks to more effectively deal with the large amount of uncertainty present in messy hand-drawn sketches. (Veselova 2003) has developed a system to generate a symbolic shape definition from a single drawn example.

## Conclusions

### Future Work

We would like to improve our translator and domain independent recognition system to include the handling of soft constraints and continue to test it on additional domains. While we are attempting to make LADDER as intuitive as possible, shape definitions can be difficult to describe textually, and we would like to integrate work from (Veselova 2003) to automatically generated shape descriptions from a drawn example. However, even automatically generated shapes will need to be checked and modified. Thus we would like to create a GUI to debug a domain description, providing interfaces to test whether the shape is under-constrained (by automatically generating valid example shapes) or over-constrained (by allowing the user to draw several test examples).

### Contributions

We suggest an innovative framework for sketch recognition that uses a single, customizable domain independent recognition system for use with many domains. This paper presents the first translator which takes symbolic descriptions of how shapes are drawn, displayed, and edited in a domain and automatically transforms them into shape recognizers, editing recognizers, and shape exhibitors for use in a domain independent sketch recognition system. To accomplish this, we created 1) LADDER, a symbolic language for describing how shapes are drawn, displayed, and edited in a domain, 2) the translator described above, and 3) a simple domain independent recognition system that uses the newly translated components to recognize, display, and allow editing of the domain shapes. The implementation of this translator and domain independent sketch recognition system serves to show both that such a framework is feasible and that LADDER is an acceptable language for describing domain information.

[7] Text is also a primitive shape. Text can be entered using a keyboard or a handwriting recognizer GUI provided in Microsoft Tablet XP. The text appears at the last typed place.

## References

Alvarado, C. 2000. A natural sketching environmant: Bringing the computer into early stages of mechanical design. Master's thesis, MIT.

Alvarado, C. 2003. Dynamically constructed bayesian networks for sketch understanding. *Proceedings of the 3nd Annual MIT Student Oxygen Workshop.*

Bimber, O.; Encarnacao, L. M.; and Stork, A. 2000. A multi-layered architecture for sketch-based interaction within virtual environments. *Computer and Graphics: Special Issue on Calligraphic Interfaces: Towards a New Generation of Interactive Systems* 24(6):851–867.

Caetano, A.; Goulart, N.; Fonseca, M.; and Jorge, J. 2002a. JavaSketchIt: Issues in sketching the look of user interfaces. *Sketch Understanding, Papers from the 2002 AAAI Spring Symposium.*

Caetano, A.; Goulart, N.; Fonseca, M.; and Jorge, J. 2002b. Sketching user interfaces with visual patterns. *Proceedings of the 1st Ibero-American Symposium in Computer Graphics (SIACG02)* 271–279.

Costagliola, G.; Tortora, G.; Orefice, S.; and Lucia, D. 1995. Automatic generation of visual programming environments. In *IEEE Computer*, 56–65.

Do, E. Y.-L. 2001. Vr sketchpad - create instant 3d worlds by sketching on a transparent window. *CAAD Futures 2001, Bauke de Vries, Jos P. van Leeuwen, Henri H. Achten (eds)* 161–172.

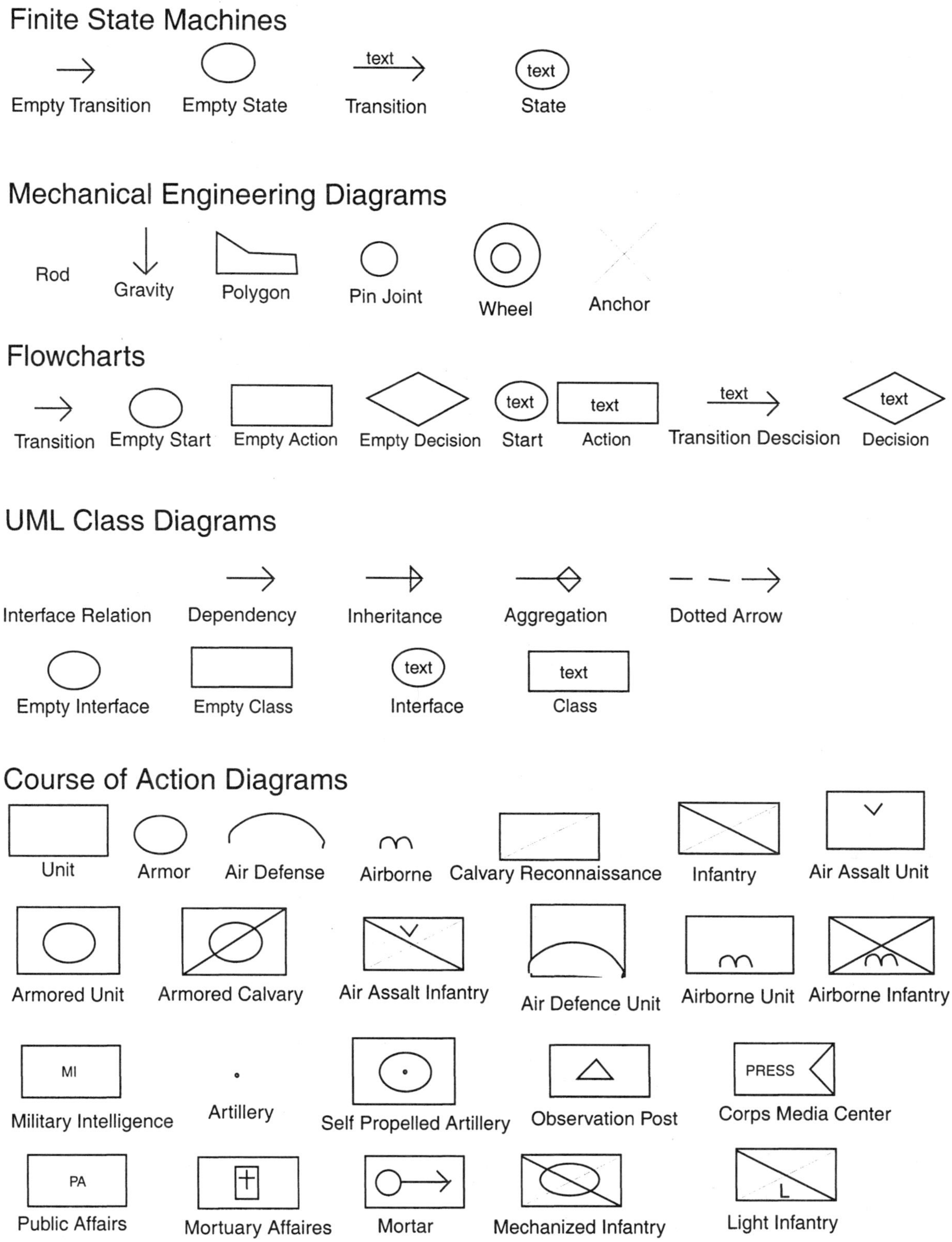


Figure 3: Domains and their shapes for which we have automatically generated sketch recognition systems.

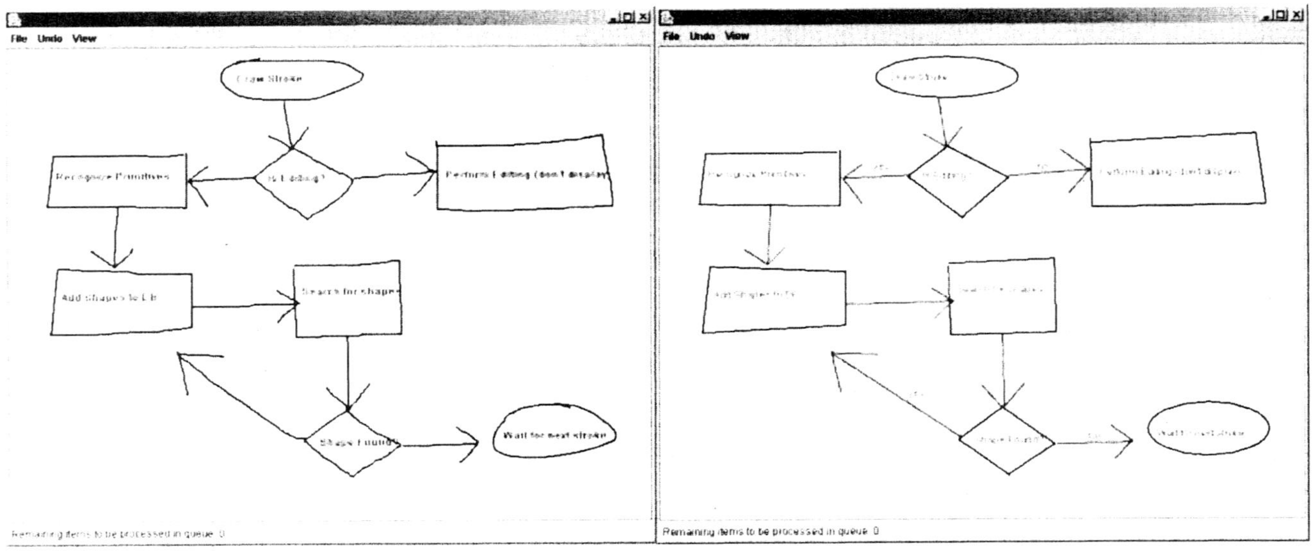


Figure 4: Flowchart of domain independent system drawn using system. Left side represents the original strokes. Right side represents the cleaned up drawing.

Friedman-Hill, E. 2001. Jess, the java expert system shell. http://herzberg.ca.sandia.gov/jess.

Futrelle, R. P., and Nikolakis, N. 1995. Efficient analysis of complex diagrams using constraint-based parsing. In *ICDAR-95 (International Conference on Document Analysis and Recognition)*, 782–790.

Gross, M. D., and Do, E. Y.-L. 1996. Demonstrating the electronic cocktail napkin: a paper-like interface for early design. *'Common Ground' appeared in ACM Conference on Human Factors in Computing (CHI)* 5–6.

Gross, M.; Zimring, C.; and Do, E. 1994. Using diagrams to access a case library of architectural designs. In Gero, J., and Sudweeks, F., eds., *Artificial Intelligence in Design '94*. Netherlands: Kluwer Academic Publishers. 129–144.

Hammond, T., and Davis, R. 2002. Tahuti: A geometrical sketch recognition system for uml class diagrams. *AAAI Spring Symposium on Sketch Understanding* 59–68.

Hammond, T., and Davis, R. 2003. Ladder: A language to describe drawing, display, and editing in sketch recognition. *Proceedings of the 2003 Internaltional Joint Conference on Artificial Intelligence (IJCAI)*.

Hse, H.; Shilman, M.; Newton, A. R.; and Landay, J. 1999. Sketch-based user interfaces for collaborative object-oriented modeling. Berkley CS260 Class Project.

Jacob, R. J. K.; Deligiannidis, L.; and Morrison, S. 1999. A software model and specification language for non-WIMP= user interfaces. *ACM Transactions on Computer-Human Interaction* 6(1):1–46.

Lecolinet, E. 1998. Designing guis by sketch drawing and visual programming. In *Proceedings of the International Conference on Advanced Visual Interfaces (AVI 1998).*, 274–276. AVI.

Lin, J.; Newman, M. W.; Hong, J. I.; and Landay, J. 2000. Denim: Finding a tighter fit between tools and practice for web site design. In *CHI Letters: Human Factors in Computing Systems, CHI 2000*, 510–517.

Long, A. C. 2001. *Quill: a Gesture Design Tool for Pen-based User Interfaces*. Eecs department, computer science division, U.C. Berkeley, Berkeley, California.

Mahoney, J. V., and Fromherz, M. P. J. 2002. Handling ambiguity in constraint-based recognition of stick figure sketches. *SPIE Document Recognition and Retrieval IX Conf., San Jose, CA*.

Mahoney, J. V., and Frommerz, M. P. J. 2002. Three main concerns in sketch recognition and an approach to addressing them. In *Sketch Understanding, Papers from the 2002 AAAI Spring Symposium*, 105–112. Stanford, California: AAAI Press.

Pittman, J.; Smith, I.; Cohen, P.; Oviatt, S.; and Yang, T. 1996. Quickset: A multimodal interface for military simulations. *Proceedings of the 6th Conference on Computer-Generated Forces and Behavioral Representation* 217–224.

Rubine, D. 1991. Specifying gestures by example. In *Computer Graphics*, volume 25(4), 329–337.

Sezgin, T. M. 2001. Feature point detection and curve approximation for early processing in sketch recognition. Master's thesis, Massachusetts Institute of Technology.

Sezgin, T. M. 2003. Recognition efficiency issues for freehand sketches. *Proceedings of the 3nd Annual MIT Student Oxygen Workshop*.

Stiny, G., and Gips, J. 1972. Shape grammars and the generative specification of painting and sculpture. In Freiman, C. V., ed., *Information Processing 71*. North-Holland. 1460–1465.

Veselova, O. 2003. Perceptually based learning of shape descriptions. Master's thesis, Massachusetts Institute of Technology, Cambridge, MA.

Zue, and Glass. 2000. Conversational interfaces: Advances and challenges. *Proc IEEE* 1166–1180.

# Large-Scale Map-Making

**Kurt Konolige**

SRI International
333 Ravenswood Avenue
Menlo Park, CA 94025
konolige@ai.sri.com

### Abstract

Current mapping algorithms using Consistent Pose Estimation (CPE) algorithms can successfully map areas of $10^4$ square meters, using thousands of poses. However, the computation to construct the map grows as $O(n \log n)$, so larger maps get increasingly difficult to build. We present an abstraction method for postponing the growth in computation. This method solves a much smaller problem in the space of the connection graph of the map.

## Introduction

In this paper we address one of the major goals of mobile robot research, the creation of a map from local sensor data collected as the robot moves around an unknown environment. Our emphasis is on the asymptotic behavior of the map creation algorithm, as the environments get very large. Current methods [Gutmann and Konolige 1999] are already capable of creating accurate, dense metric maps of environments of $10^4$ m$^2$, but have computational problems as the scale gets larger.

Current metric mapping methods are distinguished by whether they use features (usually called *landmarks*) or rely on dense surface information that does not distinguish features. In this paper, we remain agnostic about this issue; the only requirement is that the map is represented as a set of robot poses with *constraints* among them. The reason for this choice is that such a representation scales well as the area of the map grows, since it generally represents only local constraints among poses.

Another issue in map building is the difference between incremental and batch methods. During exploration, new information is added to the map in an incremental fashion, and the cost should be low (ideally, constant time), as only a small portion of the map would be modified. However, when the robot recognizes a previously-visited area, it may have to "close the loop," and change a large section of the map. Closing a large loop, and registering all the poses of a map, are the hard problems in map construction.

In this paper, we analyze the computational properties of the CPE method for loop closure and full map registration, by simulating very large scale maps, on the order of $10^5$ poses. These maps are several orders of magnitude larger than current mapping techniques can handle. The main results are:

- We provide an $O(n)$ algorithm for single loop closure, where $n$ is the number of poses along the loop.
- Multiple loop maps are harder to solve, but by noting the sparse matrix structure of CPE, we derive an efficient $O(n \log n)$ algorithm.
- We develop a refined algorithm that takes advantage of the structure of connections in a map to substantially postpone the $n \log n$ asymptote.

### Previous Work

Map making from a mobile robot is usually referred to as the SLAM (Simultaneous Localization and Mapping) problem. CPE is a SLAM method that uses constraints among local poses. As an alternative, Extended Kalman Filter (EKF) methods construct a large covariance matrix whose computational properties are poor at larger scales [Moutarlier and Chatila, 1989].

Recently there have been several efforts to develop EKF SLAM methods with good scaling properties. In [Newman et al. 2002], features and geometric constraints are used to merge partial maps created with SLAM techniques, using interesting geometric search techniques.

[Thrun et al. 2002] have developed a sparse matrix method for the information filter. They claim that the method scales linearly with the size of the map; however, it is difficult to determine if this is correct, since the limiting operation is sparse matrix inversion, which does not scale linearly in the general case.

[Leonard and Feder 2000] have a variation of SLAM that divides the world into submaps, so that the size of an update remains constant as the map grows.

[Guivant and Nebot 2001] also use a local update scheme, with local updates taking $O(n^2)$ time in the number of local features. Incorporation of local constraints into the global map, however, requires a complete calculation of the global EKF.

[Duckett et al. 2000] describe a system of linear constraints that has a network structure similar to the one described here; however, the convergence of the relaxation algorithm they propose is slow and inferior to the methods presented in this paper.

## Map Construction via Pose Constraints

In this section we review the CPE method of Lu and Milios, and investigate its computational properties in preparation for determining large-scale behavior.

### Lu-Milios Registration

We base our technique on the consistent pose registration paradigm of Lu and Milios [Lu and Milios 1997, Gutmann and Konolige 1999]. Figure 1 shows a set of poses from a mobile robot run, along with their scans from a laser range finder. The poses $X_i$ are the free variables of the system. For each pose, a set of *constraints* connect it to other poses. These constraints can arise from odometry between successive poses, from matching scans between poses, and from any other information relating the poses, including *a priori* information.

To put all the constraints into a common framework, we represent them in terms of local differences $D_{ij}$ between $X_i$ and $X_j$. The term $D_{ij}$ is a random variable with mean $\overline{D_{ij}}$ and covariance $C_{ij}$. Each constraint is a local spring, with a stiffness determined by $C_{ij}$. The optimal value for the poses is at the minimum energy of the constraint system. Lu and Milios phrase this condition in terms of a maximum likelihood:

$$\text{(1)} \qquad \underset{X_i}{\arg\max}\, P(D_{ij} \mid \overline{D_{ij}})$$

In the case of Gaussian covariance and mutually independent $D_{ij}$, this condition is equivalent to minimizing the Mahalanobis distance:

$$\text{(2)} \qquad \sum_{i,j} \left(D_{ij} - \overline{D_{ij}}\right)^T C_{ij}^{-1} \left(D_{ij} - \overline{D_{ij}}\right)$$

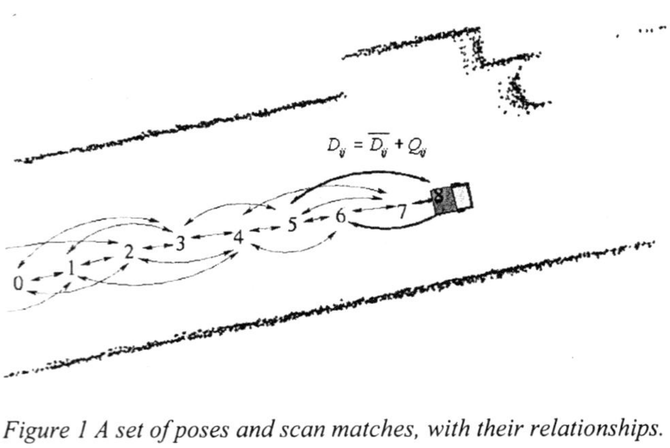


*Figure 1 A set of poses and scan matches, with their relationships.*

Frequently we will refer to this term as the *energy* of the system. Because the constraints are soft, the poses $X_i$ can be moved to accommodate new information. For example, suppose we know the relationship of two poses in Figure 2, along the sides of the long corridors. By adding this relationship as a constraint, the minimum energy system is distorted to conform to the relationship.

### Local Constraints

The energy equation (2) demands that constraints be expressed as differences between poses. Typically, these constraints arise from two sources:

1. *Odometry* between two successive poses of the robot.
2. *Matching* between two poses. If a sensor can see the same features from the two poses, then it is possible to derive an estimate of the position of the poses relative to each other. This estimate can take into account the error of the sensor in deriving the uncertainty between the two poses.

Global constraints can also be incorporated by establishing a fictional pose $O$ at the origin. If a pose $X$ has a global constraint, for example from GPS, then it can be expressed as the difference between $X$ and $O$.

Pose differences $D_{ij}$ are expressed in the origin of the pose $X_i$. Typically the difference is derived from an underlying measurement equation, which relates the measurement variables to pose coordinates. The measurement equation for a measurement $Z$ is represented as a function:

$$\text{(3)} \qquad X_j = f(X_i, Z)$$

The mean of the result is computed directly from the equation:

$$\text{(4)} \qquad \hat{X}_j = f(\hat{X}_i, \hat{Z}),$$

while the covariance is derived using the Jacobian $J(Z,X)$. Let $C_Z$ be the covariance of the measurement $Z$; then the covariance of the pose difference estimate is

$$\text{(5)} \qquad C_{ij} = J C_Z J^T$$

The most common measurement is angle and distance – for example, odometry and matching with range sensors can

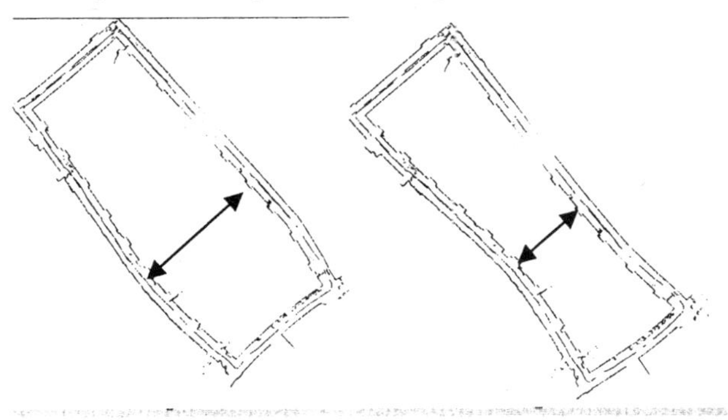

*Figure 2 Two deformations of a set of poses with minimum values of Equation (2), based on added constraints between two poses on the sides of the map. On the left the poses are pushed apart, on the right they are drawn together.*

both be represented this way. For this case, with distance $l$ and angle $\alpha$, we have:

$$f(X_i, Z) = \begin{bmatrix} x_i + l\cos(\theta_i + \alpha) \\ y_i + l\sin(\theta_i + \alpha) \end{bmatrix}$$

(6)

$$J_Z = \begin{bmatrix} \cos(\theta_i + \alpha) & -l\sin(\theta_i + \alpha) \\ \sin(\theta_i + \alpha) & l\cos(\theta_i + \alpha) \end{bmatrix}$$

Note that the expression for $J_Z$ and hence $C_{ij}$ is nonlinear, and the total energy function becomes nonlinear. In this case, there is no closed-form solution, and in general we will be able to find only local minima of the energy, using iterative linear methods.

### Iterative Linear Method

In the linear case, the energy function (2) constitutes an unconstrained quadratic optimization problem, which can be solved by direct methods [Lu and Milios 1997]. Let **X** be the vector of size $3n$ formed by stacking all the $X_i$. Then we can solve (2) by solving the following linear system:

(7) $\quad \mathbf{GX} = \mathbf{B}$,

where **G** is a $3n \times 3n$ matrix, and **B** is a constant vector of size $3n$.

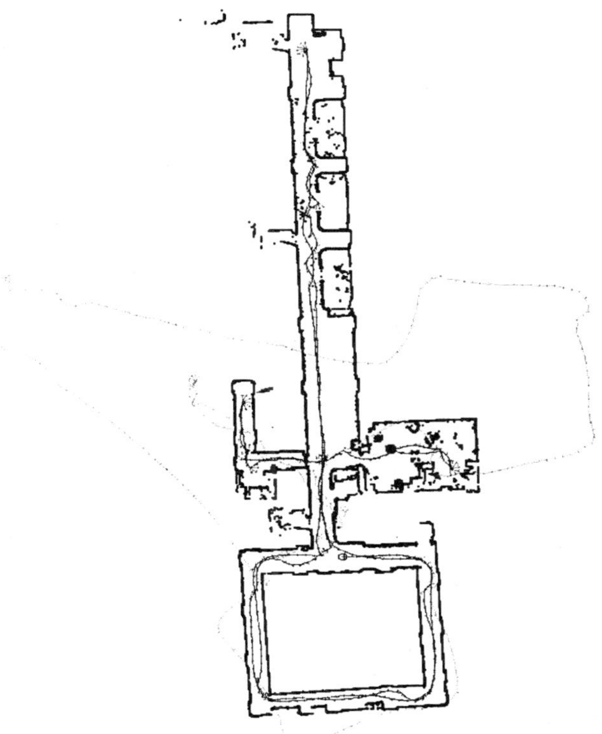

*Figure 3 Sample map built from 419 poses with 1109 links. The green line shows the robot position based on odometry.*

The elements of **G** are partitioned into 3x3 blocks $G_{ij}$, as follows:

$$G_{ii} = \sum_{j=0}^{n} C_{ij}^{-1}$$

(8)

$$G_{ij} = -C_{ij}^{-1}, \qquad i \neq j$$

The vector **B** consists of a stacked set of 3-vectors $B_i$, defined as:

(9) $$B_i = \sum_{j=0, j\neq i}^{n} C_{ij}\overline{D}_{ij}$$

If **G** is invertible, then the solution of the linear system gives the minimum energy solution of (2), when the covariances are linear. There is no proof yet that **G** is always invertible; however, in practice over many real and simulated mapping runs, **G** has always been invertible.

When the covariances are nonlinear, there is no direct reduction to the linear system (7). Instead, an approximate solution is found by linearizing the covariances using a Taylor series, solving the resulting linear system, and iterating the process. There are no guarantees that this method will converge, or that if it does, that the result is a global minimum. In fact it is easy to construct examples in which the system converges to a local minimum that is not globally optimal.

In building maps, the nonlinear system is typically well-behaved. Figure 3 shows an example mapping run of 418 poses and 1108 links; the poses are approximately 0.5 meters apart. The nonlinear system converges to a minimum after 3 steps of the linear solver; from inspection, this also appears to be the global minimum. Almost always the starting point for the nonlinear iteration is near to the solution, as forward matching aligns new poses before they are incorporated into the map [Gutmann and Konolige 1999]. The green line shows the unrestricted poses based on odometry, which would be harder to solve.

### Computational Properties

The key computation to solve the linear system is inverting the matrix **G**. In a straightforward algorithm this would take $O(n^3)$ time and storage, where $n$ is the number of variables (poses). But we can take advantage of the structure of **G** to improve on this result.

From inspection of Equation (8), **G** has the following form:

(10) $$\begin{bmatrix} G_{00} & & G_{02} & \cdots \\ & G_{11} & & \\ G_{02} & & G_{22} & \\ \vdots & & & \ddots \end{bmatrix},$$

where each of the submatrices $G_{ij}$ is 3x3. All of the diagonal blocks $G_{ii}$ are filled, but the off-diagonal elements

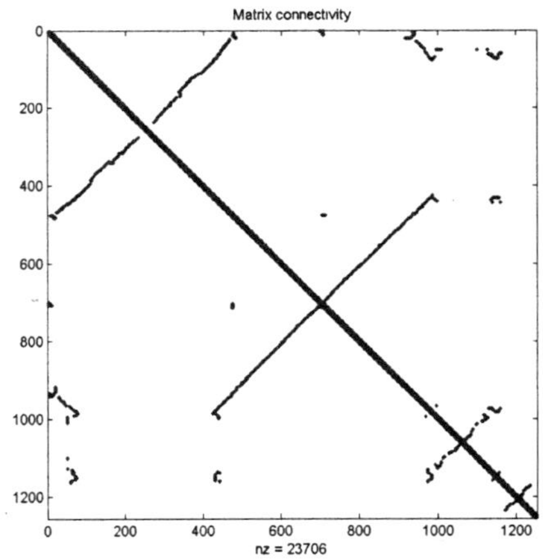


*Figure 4 Connectivity of the matrix* **G** *for the sample map.*

are sparsely populated – they occur only where there are links between poses that are not successors. Because of the locality of sensing, these links are limited to a neighborhood of a pose. For global constraints, there could also be a number of links from the origin pose $O$ to other poses. We will assume for the remainder of the paper that the number of links is at most a constant factor times the number of poses. Figure 4 shows the connectivity of matrix **G** for the example map of Figure 3. The off-diagonal elements are where the robot backtracked over previously-traversed areas. Only 1.5% of the matrix entries are non-zero.

The matrix **G** is positive, symmetric, and definite. The solution of choice for sparse systems of this type is the conjugate gradient (CG) method. CG is an iterative method that converges in at least $n$ iterations, where $n$ is the rank of **G**. With sparse matrices, CG requires storing only the sparse elements, and performs just one matrix-vector multiplication per iteration, so that the number of operations in the parse case is $O(n)$ per iteration. If there are $m$ iterations to convergence, then the whole process takes $O(nm)$ operations.

In the worst case, with $m = n$, CG is an $O(n^2)$ algorithm. To improve this result, it is important to reduce the number of iterations necessary for convergence. The *condition number* [Golub and Van Loan 1996] of **G** is a measure of how quickly CG will converge – numbers near 1 show a well-conditioned matrix, whose eigenvalues are similar. Unfortunately, **G** tends to have a small condition number for the mapping problem, since there can be large variations in the covariance matrix values for different links. For example, the condition number for the matrix of Figure 4 is $10^{13}$. The matrix is so poorly conditioned that roundoff error prevents it from converging without additional help.

To speed up convergence, **G** can be *preconditioned*, using a symmetric positive definite matrix **H**, to make it better conditioned – the Preconditioned Conjugate Gradient (PCG). One of the most useful preconditioners is the incomplete Cholesky factor [Golub and Van Loan 1996]. The complete Cholesky factor requires $O(n^3)$ computations, and perfectly preconditions **G**, so that it requires only 3 iterations to converge. By trading off completeness, we can get an approximate factor in $O(n)$ that still greatly speeds up convergence. For example, the number of iterations to solve the sparse linear system of Figure 4 can be reduced from 547 to 21, using an appropriate incomplete Cholesky factor.

For most mapping problems of a reasonable size (< 10K poses), the application of PCG is efficient enough to be used without modification. For example, the full map of Figure 3 is solved in under 0.8 seconds, in three PCG steps, with 21 iterations on each step. It should be noted that, because of the structure of the covariance matrices, the number of PCG steps to converge for the nonlinear problem is always 3, and we will consider the difficulty of the problem to be related to the computation of PCG.

With larger $n$, the number of iterations needed by PCG to converge will grow, and hence the overall computation is not linear in the number of poses. In typical sparse matrix PCG applications, the computation scales as $O(n \log n)$. This is the case for the mapping problem, as we show experimentally in the next section. In some applications, such as large differential modeling over regular grids, the structure of the matrix **G** is further exploited to produce linear scaling [Lackner and Menikoff 1998]. We seek similar results for the mapping problem over larger scales, so that the techniques just presented can be extended to truly large mapping applications.

## Linear Loop Closure

In constructing maps incrementally, most poses that are added cause relatively minor changes to the map, as in Figure 1, and can be incorporated without re-optimizing the whole map. When a loop is closed, by matching two poses that may initially be far apart (Figure 5), many poses can be affected, and at a minimum the poses comprising the loop must be optimized.

Loop closure in its simplest form involves a very sparse matrix **G**, with only one off-diagonal element from the matched poses. In this case, the PCG algorithm with incomplete Cholesky preconditioner exhibits only linear

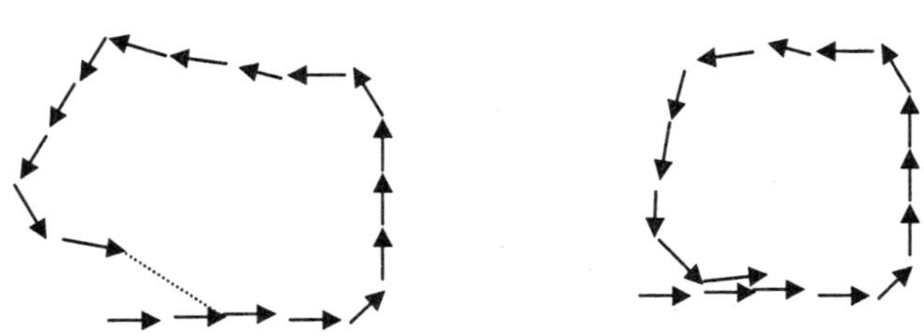

*Figure 5 Loop closure adds a constraint to close a loop. The associated matrix is fully diagonal, except for the matched closure poses.*

growth in computation as the number of poses increases. Figure 6 shows the results for simple loops with up to 15K nodes. To make sure the preconditioner is not adding more than linear time, we list the actual time spent in the computation as well as the number of PCG iterations. The iterations stayed constant at around 5 per PCG step, through 4 orders of magnitude of the problem size.

## Divide and Conquer Algorithm

It isn't surprising that simple loop closure is O($n$), since there is a divide-and-conquer algorithm for solving it exactly, in the linear case. Consider a chain of poses as in Figure 5, where the end points of the chain are fixed (they needn't be the same point, just fixed globally). Divide the chain in half, with the midpoint pose being $X_m$:

$$X_1 \quad X_2 \quad \cdots \quad X_m \quad X_{m+1} \quad \cdots \quad X_n .$$

Instead of solving the full system, we solve a reduced system consisting of just the three poses $X_1$ $X_m$ $X_n$. To find the covariance of the pose difference $D_{1m}$, we use the compounding property of chained covariances [Smith and Cheeseman 1987]. We already have the covariance $C_{12}$. To find $C_{13}$, we note that the pose differences add:

$$D_{13} = D_{12} + D_{23} .$$

The covariance of $D_{13}$ can be computed from the measurement equation (6) as:

$$(11) \qquad C_{13} = C_{12} + J(X_2, Z_2) C_Z J(X_2, Z_2)^T .$$

Continuing down the chain, the covariance $C_{1m}$ is computed, and similarly for $C_{mn}$. We solve the reduced system, and fix the pose $X_m$. Now there are two subproblems, which we solve in the same manner. Continuing recursively, finally we will have solved $n$ subproblems, but the complexity of the subproblems stays constant.

The compounding operations only contribute O($n$) computations, if they are done bottom-up. First the covariances $C_{13}$, $C_{35}$, ... are computed, then they are combined to produce $C_{15}$, $C_{59}$, etc. Thus, the complexity of the complete loop closure is O($n$).

The solution computed by divide-and-conquer will be exactly the same as solving the full linear system (6), if the constraints are linear. In the nonlinear case, both the linear system and the divide-and-conquer algorithm must be iterated to find a local minimum.

## Multi-loop Maps

In actual maps, there are multiple loop closures, depending on the size and structure of the environment, as well as the robot's motion. Multi-loop maps are harder to solve than the single-loop ones. We are interested in the asymptotic performance of a mapping algorithm at very large scales, and it is necessary to generate test cases for these scales. To represent large-scale maps in the abstract, we can generate a random 2D graph structure whose edges are chains of poses, and whose nodes are poses where the chains meet. Figure 7 shows a map of 1900 nodes. The map was created by dropping seeds randomly over the area, then growing the seeds until their borders touched. The distribution of edge lengths follows approximately a Poisson distribution.

We are interested in the the scaling behavior of the PCG algorithm under the following sets of conditions.

1. The node structure stays constant, and the number of poses in the edges grows with the map area.
2. The edges stay the same length, and the number of graph nodes grows proportionally with the map area.

These conditions represent the extremes of possible map structure changes with scaling. Condition (2) is more realistic, in that we expect the loop properties of the environment to remain relatively constant. In both cases, we expect PCG to have O($n$ log $n$) performance.

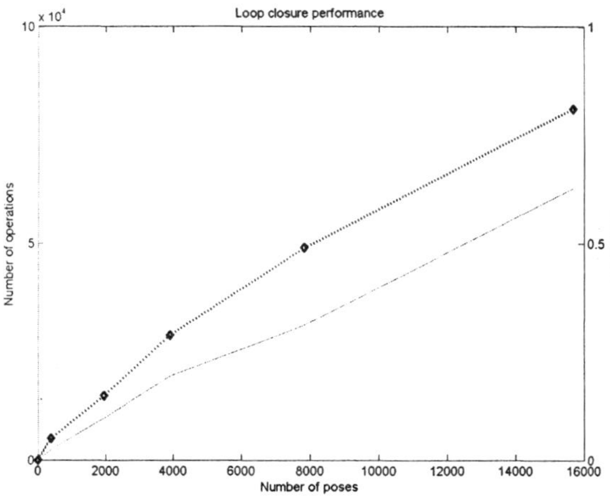


*Figure 6 Loop closure performance. CPU time for closure is given by the black line. Number of operations (iterations x nodes) is the blue line.*

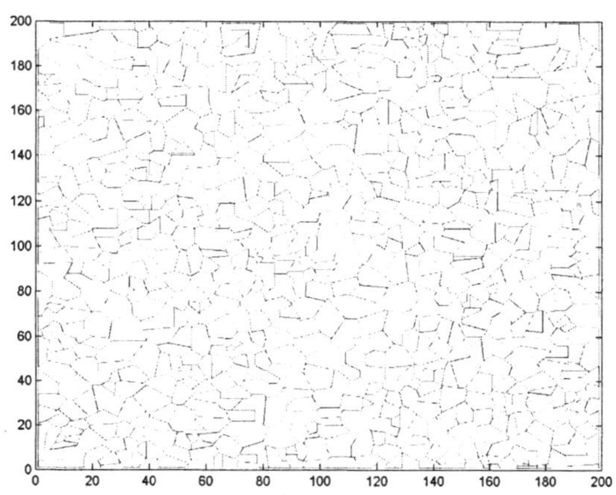


*Figure 7 Abstract map consisting of 1900 nodes connected by pose chains.*

## Structured PCG

For both conditions, we propose an algorithm that does sustantially better than PCG, by taking advantage of the structure of the connection graph, and exploiting the divide-and-conquer algorithm.

Consider the map $M$ represented in Figure 7, and note that the chain between two nodes $X_i$ and $X_j$ induces a constraint between these nodes. Since there are no outside links to the interior poses of the chain, the effect of the chain $X_i$ and $X_j$ can be represented by a single constraint, whose covariance is computed by compounding of the covariances of the individual links of the chain. The reduced map $M_R$ is formed by removing all chains and replacing them with the equivalent pose differences between the map nodes.

## Algorithm Structured PCG

Form the reduced map $M \Rightarrow M_R$.
Solve $M_R$ using PCG until convergence.
Fix the coordinates of the poses of $M_R$.
For each edge chain in $M$, solve the chain using PCG with fixed end poses.

Structured PCG performs the $O(n \log n)$ step on the reduced graph $M_R$, and thus we expect its performance to be superior to the standard PCG algorithm. The additional work to optimize the chains is linear in the total size of the chains, and hence the total number of poses.

Figure 8 shows how the two algorithms scale with increasing chain size, on the sample map with 1900 nodes. This is a log-log graph, so care must be taken in interpreting the shapes of the graphed results.

The upper line is the standard PCG algorithm. Even though it is an asymptotically straight line, its asymptotic behavior is $n \log n$.

The structured algorithm (bottom line) does much better, because it is just solving the reduced map. At the left-most point, the algorithms solve the same problem (chain size is 1). As the problem size grows, structured PCG spends less time solving the $O(n \log n)$ step, and just has to solve chains of poses, which is a linear operation. Hence, its asymptotic behavior is linear, and much more efficient than standard PCG.

For comparison, the middle line shows how PCG would perform if it *were* linear in the problem size, using the same number of iterations in PCG as needed for the initial problem. This clearly shows the efficiency of structured PCG, which factors out the solution of the interconnected nodes from the chains of links.

A more realistic assessment of performance comes from considering condition (2), where the map connectivity grows with map area, and the chains stay the same size (Figure 9). Here we picked a mean chain size of 12 poses. Most real-world environments would tend to have multiple loops, and the larger the area, the more loops they would have. For example, city streets have this characteristic.

The standard PCG algorithm (top line) exhibits the same $O(n \log n)$ growth, as the PCG iterations increase with problem size. Note that the PCG algorithm has essentially the same performance as it did in the previous fixed-structure case. The algorithm doesn't take advantage of any structural differences between the two types of problems. Again, for comparison the center line shows the PCG algorithm with fixed iterations (linear growth).

Unlike in the fixed structure case, the structured PCG algorithm now increases more rapidly as the problem size grows, because the reduced graph $M_R$ is growing, and this is the hard part of the solution. For any given problem size, though, structured PCG performs less work than the standard PCG algorithm, because it only solves the reduced

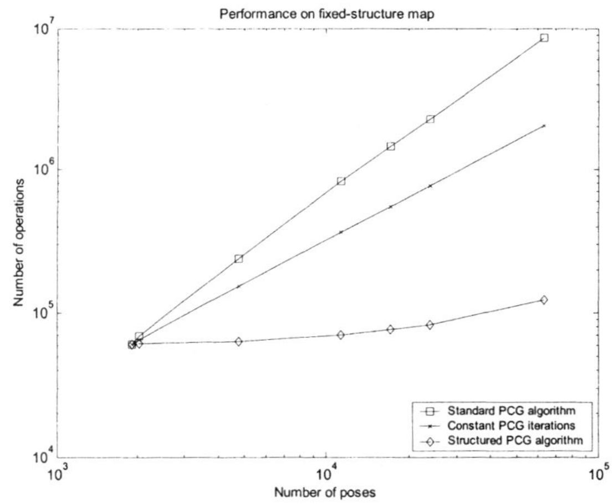


*Figure 8 Scaling performance of the standard and structured PCG algorithm. The middle line is the standard PCG algorithm with a fixed number of iterations (linear in node size).*

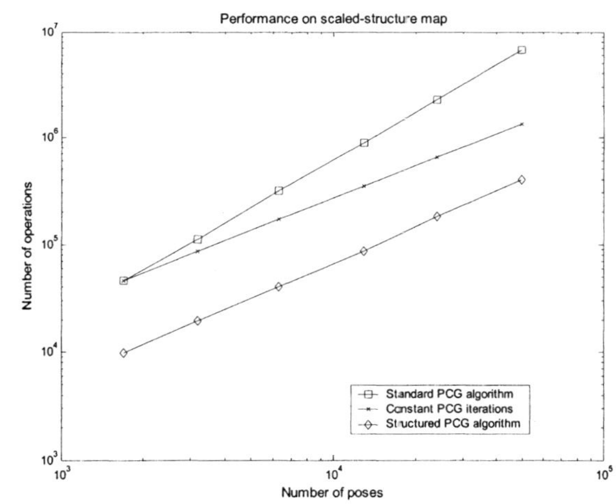


*Figure 9 Scaling performance of the algorithms as the chain size stays constant, and the map structure grows with map area. Chain size was fixed at 12 poses.*

graph. It also has better asymptotic behavior. Instead of $n$ log $n$, the reduced nature of the graph means that the asymptote is $(n/k)$ log $(n/k)$, where $n/k$ is the number of nodes in the reduced graph $M_R$.

We checked the computational behavior for both conditions by looking at the CPU time used. CPU time tracked the number of operations determined from PCG iterations. Interestingly, the CPU resources were quite modest – the largest problem, some 60K poses, used only 6.5 minutes of time on a standard PC.

## Conclusions

With the success of small-scale indoor and outdoor mapping, researchers are starting to turn their attention to the scaling behavior of their algorithms. In this paper, we determine this behavior for Consistent Pose Estimation methods, and show experimentally that O($n$ log $n$) can be expected by using PCG to solve the pose registration problem. A more sophisticated algorithm, structured PCG, can take advantage of the particular form of loops in mapping, to do better by several orders of magnitude. With suitable data sets, we can now hope to map areas comprising $10^5$-$10^6$ poses, and reasonably expect to cover a million square meters with such maps.

## References


T. Duckett, S. Marsland, and J. Shapiro. Learning globally consistent maps by relaxation. In *Proc. ICRA'2000*, pages 3841 - 3846, 2000.

G. H. Golub and C. F. Van Loan. *Matrix Computations*. John Hopkins University Press, 1996.

J. Guivant and E. Nebot. Compressed Filter for Real Time Implementation of Simultaneous Localization and Map Building. *Field and Service Robots 2001* June 2001, Finland.

Gutmann, J. S. and K. Konolige. Incremental Mapping of Large Cyclic Environments. In *CIRA 99*, Monterey, California, 1999.

K. Lackner and R. Menikoff. Multi-scale linear solvers for very large systems derived from PDES. In *Fifth Copper Mountain Conference on Iterative Methods*, April, 1998.

J.J. Leonard and H.J.S. Feder. A computationally efficient method for large-scale concurrent mapping and localization. In *Proceedings of the Ninth ISRR*, pages 169–176. Springer-Verlag, 2000.

Lu, F. and E. E. Milios. Globally consistent range scan alignment for environment mapping. *Autonomous Robots*, **4**(4), 1997.

P. Moutarlier and R. Chatila. An experimental system for incremental environment modeling by an autonomous mobile robot. *Proc. ISER-89*.

P.M. Newman, J.J. Leonard, J. Neira and J.D. Tardós: "Explore and Return: Experimental Validation of Real Time Concurrent Mapping and Localization". ICRA, May, 2002.

R. C. Smith and P. Cheeseman, *On the Representation and Estimation of Spatial Uncertainty*. The International Journal of Robotics Research **5**(4), pp. 56-68.

S. Thrun, D. Koller, Z. Ghahramani, H. Durrant-Whyte, and A. Y. Ng. Simultaneous Mapping and Localization with Sparse Extended Information Filters. *Proc. Algorithmic Foundations of Robotics*, Nice, 2002.

# A Multi-Resolution Pyramid for Outdoor Robot Terrain Perception

**Michael Montemerlo** and **Sebastian Thrun**
AI Lab, Stanford University
353 Serra Mall
Stanford, CA 94305-9010
{mmde,thrun}@stanford.edu


### Abstract

This paper addresses the problem of outdoor terrain modeling for the purposes of mobile robot navigation. We propose an approach in which a robot acquires a set of terrain models at differing resolutions. Our approach addresses one of the major shortcomings of Bayesian reasoning when applied to terrain modeling, namely artifacts that arise from the limited spatial resolution of robot perception. Limited spatial resolution causes small obstacles to be detectable only at close range. Hence, a Bayes filter estimating the state of terrain segments must consider the ranges at which that terrain is observed. We develop a multi-resolution approach that maintains multiple navigation maps, and derive rational arguments for the number of layers and their resolutions. We show that our approach yields significantly better results in a practical robot system, capable of acquiring detailed 3-D maps in large-scale outdoor environments.


## Introduction

This paper addresses the problem of robots navigating through unknown terrain. This problem arises in great many robot applications, such as planetary exploration (Matthies *et al.* 1995) and the exploration of abandoned mines (Ferguson *et al.* 2003). In such cases, a robot must rely on its sensors to determine the location of obstacles, so as to safely navigate through free space. In indoor environments, this is commonly achieved by assuming the world is planar and estimating a 2-D cross-section of the environment (Borenstein & Koren. 1991; Burgard *et al.* 2000; Simmons *et al.* 2000; Yamauchi *et al.* 1998). Outdoor environments require a 3-D analysis of the ground and possible obstacles that might protrude into navigable space (Hashimoto & Yuta 2003; Matthies & Grandjean 1992). Of particular importance are *negative* obstacles, characterized by the absence of supporting ground (e.g., holes) (Matthies *et al.* 1998) as well as obstacles that might protrude into the robot's workspace from far above the ground (e.g., overhangs) (Ferguson *et al.* 2003).

When modeling the navigability of terrain, one common approach is to extract a navigability assessment from sensor measurements (e.g., range scans), and to integrate these assessment over time using Bayes filters. To perform this integration, existing techniques partition the workspace into a grid, similar to the well-known occupancy grid map algorithm (Moravec 1988). For each grid cell, sensor measurements are integrated using Bayes rule to diminish the effect of sensor noise.

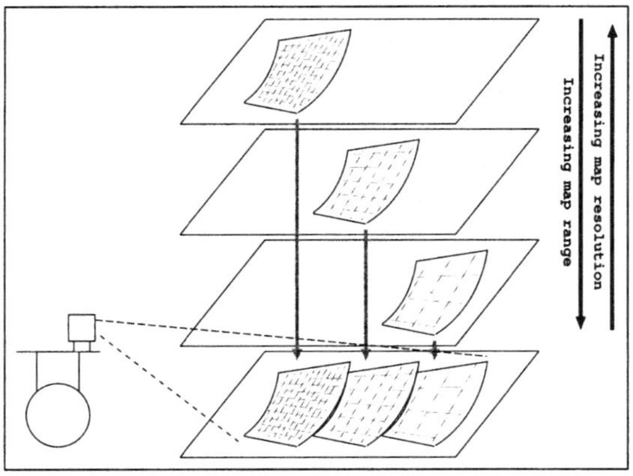


**Figure 1**: The terrain perception pyramid: terrain is modeled with multiple maps at differing resolutions, each sensitive to observations at different ranges.

Real-world terrain sensors have limited measurement resolution. For example, SICK laser range finders can only measure ranges with 0.5° accuracy; similar limitations exist for stereo camera systems and sonar sensors. Limited resolution can cause two problems with standard evidence grid algorithms:

1. First, the limited resolution may make it impossible to detect small obstacles at a distance. Obstacles like curbs or low-hanging wires can usually only be detected at close range. This is at odds with the ideal of Bayesian evidence integration in terrain grids: If evidence gathered at a distance *systematically* misses an obstacle, the grid may not change quickly enough when the robot is finally near the grid cell. As a result, the terrain model may miss obstacles, compromising the safety of the vehicle.
2. Second, limited sensor resolution makes it difficult to systematically find navigable terrain at a distance. As a result, a motion planner is either forced to make optimistic assumptions about the nature of terrain at a distance (with the obvious expense of having to replan when negative obstacles are encountered), or must remain confined to nearby regions that have been completely imaged.

The first limitation is the critical one that motivates our research, although our approach solves both of these problems.

The key insight in solving the first problem is to note that the range at which terrain is analyzed plays a *systematic* role in the robot's ability to detect obstacles. To make this dependence explicit, we propose to maintain multiple terrain maps, each sensitive to different, possibly overlapping sensor ranges. This is illustrated in Figure 1: Terrain observations are incorporated into the maps sensitive to the range at which the observation was acquired. Each map, thus, models the probability of obstacles *detectable at a particular range*. When combining maps for assessing the navigability of terrain, preference is given to shorter range maps; however, all maps participate in motion planning.

The use of multiple maps raises the issue of their resolution. As we will show in this paper, a variable resolution approach yields superior coverage to a fixed resolution approach. To derive an appropriate resolution, we will analyze the effect of measurement noise and limited resolution on the density of measurements, so that the maximum resolution is chosen at each level that guarantees that all grid cells are covered with high likelihood. The result of this analysis is a pyramid of terrain maps: Near the robot we have a fine-grained map sufficient for maneuvering the robot in close proximity to obstacles, whereas the map far from the robot is coarse, facilitating the task of motion planning. In extensive experiments, we show that the resulting approach is superior to existing terrain modeling approaches, in that it enhances the robot's safety while facilitating motion planning.

## Bayesian Techniques for Navigability

In this section we present our core Bayesian technique for constructing navigability maps of unknown terrain. The approach requires that the robot be equipped with a 3-D range finder. For a fixed resolution grid, this approach is identical to a previously published algorithm in (Ferguson *et al.* 2003). It forms the basis of the pyramid described in subsequent sections.

Suppose the robot acquires a 3-D range scan of its surrounding terrain. Each measurement is mapped into a $(x\ y\ z)$-coordinate using the obvious coordinate transformation. Whether or not a location $(x\ y)$ is navigable is determined by a simple geometric analysis; A location is navigable at height $z$ if the $z$-values of all measurements in the vicinity of $(x\ y)$ are either near each other (e.g., less than 5cm deviation), or are above the ground plane at a distance that exceeds the height of the robot. Either criterion is easily verified by a simple geometric analysis, as shown in (Ferguson *et al.* 2003).

The analysis of navigability results in a probability distribution $p(x_i \mid z_t)$ for each nearby location $x_i$, conditioned on the range scan $z_t$ (here $t$ denotes the time). Multiple measurements covering the same grid cell are then integrated using Bayes rule:

$$p(x_i \mid z_1, z_2, \ldots, z_T) = \frac{p(z_T \mid x_i, z_1, \ldots, z_{T-1})\, p(x_i \mid z_1, \ldots, z_{T-1})}{p(z_T \mid z_1, \ldots, z_{T-1})} \quad (1)$$

The "standard" derivation of the algorithm assumes that $x_i$ is a sufficient statistic of the past, hence we get

$$= \frac{p(z_T \mid x_i)\, p(x_i \mid z_1, \ldots, z_{T-1})}{p(z_T \mid z_1, \ldots, z_{T-1})} \quad (2)$$

and after another application of Bayes rule

$$= \frac{p(x_i \mid z_T)\, p(z_T)\, p(x_i \mid z_1, \ldots, z_{T-1})}{p(x_i)\, p(z_T \mid z_1, \ldots, z_{T-1})} \quad (3)$$

The navigability variable is binary—either a cell is navigable or not. Thus, we can invert the entire reasoning by substituting $\neg x_i$ for $x_i$:

$$p(\neg x_i \mid z_1, z_2, \ldots, z_T) = \frac{p(\neg x_i \mid z_T)\, p(z_T)\, p(\neg x_i \mid z_1, \ldots, z_{T-1})}{p(\neg x_i)\, p(z_T \mid z_1, \ldots, z_{T-1})} \quad (4)$$

If we now divide (3) by (4) and substitute $p(\neg x_i \mid \cdot) = 1 - p(x_i \mid \cdot)$ for arbitrary conditioning variables, we essentially obtain the standard grid mapping algorithm in (Moravec 1988), but here for navigability:

$$\frac{p(x_i \mid z_1, z_2, \ldots, z_T)}{1 - p(x_i \mid z_1, z_2, \ldots, z_T)} = \frac{p(x_i \mid z_T)}{1 - p(x_i \mid z_T)}\ \frac{1 - p(x_i)}{p(x_i)}\ \frac{p(\neg x_i \mid z_1, \ldots, z_{T-1})}{1 - p(\neg x_i \mid z_1, \ldots, z_{T-1})} \quad (5)$$

Or in log-form, with the recursion added out:

$$\log \frac{p(x_i \mid z_1, z_2, \ldots, z_T)}{1 - p(x_i \mid z_1, z_2, \ldots, z_T)} = \log \frac{p(x_i)}{1 - p(x_i)} + \sum_t \left[ \log \frac{p(x_i \mid z_t)}{1 - p(x_i \mid z_t)} + \log \frac{1 - p(x_i)}{p(x_i)} \right] \quad (6)$$

This update equation—which simply adds or subtracts evidence for the navigability from each grid cell—is at the core of classical techniques with a single navigability grid (Ferguson *et al.* 2003; Hashimoto & Yuta 2003), as well as our new approach that maintains a pyramid of grids at different resolutions.

The key problem of this update lies in its implicit independence assumption. Consider a grid cell $x_i$ that contains a non-navigable curb that can only be detected at close range. Measured from a distance, $p(x_i \mid z_t)$ will be smaller than the prior $p(x_i)$, hence

$$\frac{p(x_i \mid z_t)}{1 - p(x_i \mid z_t)} + \log \frac{1 - p(x_i)}{p(x_i)} \quad (7)$$

will be negative. Let this value be called $\alpha$. At close range, the robot can detect the obstacles; hence this expression turns into a positive value. Let us call this positive value $\beta$. The posterior will only indicate occupancy if the number of close range readings is at least $n\frac{-\alpha}{\beta}$, where $n$ is the number of long-range readings. Otherwise, the obstacle may be missed. Clearly, for any value of $\alpha$ and $\beta$, the approach can fail when the number of long-range readings is too large.

## Multi-Resolution Approaches

The central idea of our paper is to develop a pyramid of terrain models, in which each terrain model captures the occupancy from measurement data acquired at different ranges. These maps are defined through a sequence of distances

$$0 = d_0 < d_1 < d_2 < \ldots < d_N = \max \text{dist} \quad (8)$$

that partition the space of all distances at which the robot can perceive, up to its maximum range. Each interval $[d_n; d_{n+1})$ defines a map, that is, at any point in time, our approach only updates a grid cell in the $n$-th map if the actual distance of this cell to the sensor (at the time of measurement) falls into the interval $[d_n; d_{n+1})$. In this way, each range scan leads to updates at multiple maps.

The definition of the values $\{d_n\}$ requires some analysis, in that the issue of the grid resolution and the distance band to which each grid is tuned are closely intertwined. Our analysis will be carried out in two parts. First, we will derive a bound on the maximum resolution of each grid cell, which guarantees with high likelihood that all grid cells are covered. This bound sets the resolution levels at different ranges $d_n$; as to be expected, the resolution decreases with distance. The actual ranges $\{d_n\}$ that define the individual maps are then determined by an argument that ensures uniform spread of updates at all levels of the pyramid, which implies that all of the occupancy maps are similar in their resulting confidence.

## Upper Bound for the Grid Resolution

In this section, we will derive an upper bound on the resolution of each grid cell as a function of the distance to the robot, $d$. This bound is derived as a lower bound on the grid resolution. The bound is driven by three considerations: the effects of measurement noise, the vertical resolution, and the horizontal resolution of the range scanning device. Its rationale is that for exploration, we would like to guarantee coverage of each grid cell with high likelihood. Part of our analysis requires a flat ground. This is because the curvature in front of the robot is generally unknown a priori.

The bound assumes a range sensor with vertical angular resolution of $\phi$ (e.g., 1 degree) and horizontal angular resolution $\psi$, which is mounted at a fixed height $h$ on the robot. Let $r_\alpha$ be the correct measurement of a range finder pointed at the vertical angle $\alpha$, where $\alpha = 0$ denotes the horizontal direction. On a flat surface, the exact range $r_\alpha$ is obtained by the following equation

$$r_\alpha \quad = \quad \frac{h}{\sin \alpha} \tag{9}$$

Sensor measurements are, of course, noisy. The actual sensor measurement is a probabilistic function of $r_\alpha$. Let this distribution be denoted by $p(\hat{r}_\alpha \mid r_\alpha)$, where $\hat{r}_\alpha$ denotes the actual measurement. For our analysis, let us assume that the variance of this distribution is given by $\sigma_r^2$.

Let $d$ be the horizontal distance of a grid cell to the robot. The measurement noise causes noise in the distance at which ground is detected. The variance of this distance $d$ due to measurement noise is given by

$$\sigma_d^2 \quad = \quad \frac{\sigma^2}{1+(\frac{h}{d})^2} \tag{10}$$

where $\sigma^2$ is the variance of $p(\hat{r}_\alpha \mid r_\alpha)$. To see this, we note that the measurement angle at distance $d$ is

$$\alpha \quad = \quad \arctan \frac{h}{d} \tag{11}$$

Thus, range noise is projected onto surface noise in proportion to the cosine of this angle:

$$\begin{aligned} \cos \alpha \quad &= \quad \cos\left(\arctan \frac{h}{d}\right) \\ &= \quad \frac{1}{\sqrt{1+(\frac{h}{d})^2}} \end{aligned} \tag{12}$$

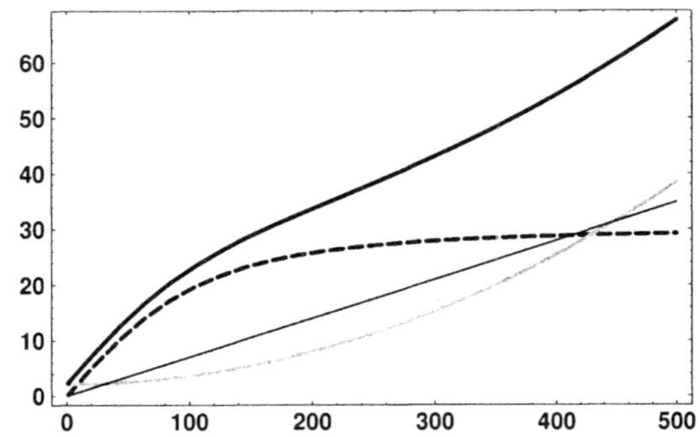


**Figure 2**: Lower bound on the grid cell size, for a range scanner with $\phi = 0.5°$ vertical resolution, $\psi = 2°$ horizontal resolution, and measurement noise $\sigma = 15$cm.

Since the variance is a quadratic function, the resulting variance on the ground is as stated in (10). For $d \gg h$, we have $\sigma^2 \approx \sigma_d^2$, suggesting a lower bound for the grid cell size that is asymptotically independent on the distance $d$.

This is quite different for the effect of limited angular resolution. Let $\phi$ be the vertical angular resolution of the sensor. Equation (11) specified the angle at which a point on the ground at distance $d$ is detected. This angle is a function of $d$. Its dependence on $d$ is characterized by the derivative

$$\left|\frac{\partial \alpha}{\partial d}\right| \quad = \quad \frac{h}{d^2+h^2} \tag{13}$$

Thus, for any (small) angular resolution $\phi$, we obtain

$$\Delta d \quad \approx \quad \phi \, \frac{(d^2+h^2)}{h} \tag{14}$$

where $\Delta d$ is the minimum vertical ground difference detectable by a sensor with resolution $\phi$. This value is of course only an approximation, since the function $\alpha$ is approximated using a linear function (first order Taylor expansion). However, for small $\phi$, this value gives us an accurate measure of the distance between ground detections due to sensor limitations. This value increases *quadratically* with the distance $d$.

The horizontal resolution of the scanner $\psi$ gives us the relation

$$\frac{\Delta d}{2d} \quad = \quad \arctan \frac{\psi}{2} \tag{15}$$

and hence

$$\Delta d \quad = \quad 2d \arctan \frac{\psi}{2} \tag{16}$$

which grows linearly in $d$.

Since resolution and noise effects are all worst-case additive, an appropriate lower bound for the grid cell size is

$$\delta(d) \quad = \quad \frac{\sigma}{\sqrt{1+(\frac{h}{d})^2}} + 2d \, \arctan \frac{\psi}{2} + \phi \, \frac{(d^2+h^2)}{h} \tag{17}$$

which consists of a constant, a linear, and a quadratic term.

Figure 2 illustrates the lower bound on the grid cell size, for a vertical resolution $\phi = 0.5°$, a horizontal resolution $\psi = 2°$, and a measurement noise variance $\sigma = 15$cm. The top curve is our additive lower bound, composed of the noise bound (dashed curve) that asymptotes into a constant, the linear horizontal resolution bound (thin line), and the resolution bound (gray curve) that grows quadratically. Within a range of up to five meters, the total bound is surprisingly close to a linear function. Beyond this range, it becomes quadratic.

As noted above, our analysis is based on the assumption of a flat ground. This assumption is adopted to reflect that the ground ahead of the robot is unknown. It is pessimistic in the face of an upward slope, in which case the density of measurements is larger than expected (hence the bound could be reduced). It is optimistic on downward-sloped ground, in which the resulting grid cells might not always be covered by at least one sensor measurement. In such situations, the robot will have to reduce its exploration speed so as to compensate the effects of reduced visibility in such terrain.

## The Pyramid

We have just devised a lower bound on the grid cell size depending on the range $d$ at which measurements are integrated. In this section, we will derive a rational argument for number and shape of the layers in our pyramid.

In determining the number of layers in the pyramid, we trade off the size of an obstacle that can be detected by the robot and the resolution and range at which it can be detected.

For a sensor with vertical resolution $\pi$, the ability to determine an obstacle of height $\Delta z$ depends on the distance $d$. This height is easily determined using the obvious geometric equation:

$$\frac{\Delta z}{2d} = \arctan\frac{\phi}{2} \tag{18}$$

This implies that the height of detectable obstacles depends linearly on the distance $d$, for a sensor with fixed resolution:

$$\Delta z = 2d \arctan\frac{\phi}{2} \tag{19}$$

This linear dependence suggests a linear decrease of grid resolution in the pyramid—this is at stark contract of an exponential structure of most pyramids in the field of computer vision. In particular, we propose an obstacle grid pyramid of resolutions $\Delta d, \gamma\Delta d, 2\gamma\Delta d, 3\gamma\Delta d, \ldots$, for a linear scaling parameter $\gamma$. With such a linear increase in resolution, the corresponding range for each layer is determined by the bound in (20):

$$d_i = \min_{\Delta d} \delta(d) < i\,\gamma\,\Delta d \tag{20}$$

While this bound is generally quadratic, within a measurement range of 5 meters the function is approximately linear. Thus, with appropriate choice of the pyramid resolution $\gamma$, we obtain a pyramid that scales linearly in resolution, and where each layer focuses on an approximately linear distance of cells near the robot.

In our experiments, we found that a "soft" boundary works better than a hard boundary on the association of ranges $d$ to a layer in the pyramid. In particular, when receiving range measurements that provide information on navigability at the distance $d$, the information integrated into the grid defined for the range $d_i$ is gated by a factor of

$$\exp\left\{-\tfrac{1}{2}\frac{(d-d_i)^2}{\sigma^2}\right\}\left[\log\frac{p(x_i \mid z_t)}{1-p(x_i \mid z_t)} + \log\frac{1-p(x_i)}{p(x_i)}\right]$$

**Figure 3**: The robotic vehicle is based on a Segway RMP, equipped with a vertically oriented SICK laser range finder mounted on an Amtec pan/tilt unit. The robot uses a highly tuned Inertial Measurement Unit and a GPS for localization.

This exponential decay leads to a smooth implementation of our distance-based multi-resolution grid approach.

## Experimental Setup

We recently developed a mobile robot system for 3-D mapping and navigation of outdoor environments. Our navigation algorithm is described elsewhere (Likhachev, Gordon, & Thrun 2003): In essence, this approach finds a path through the map that maximizes the progress to a target location while minimizing the risks of encountering non-navigable space.

Our robot, shown in Figure 3, is based on the Segway RMP mobile platform. The RMP is a computer-controlled version of the commercial Segway HT scooter. The robot is equipped with a SICK laser range finder mounted on an Amtec pan-tilt unit. The laser is swept back and forth in order to acquire 3-D scans of the robot's environment. The robot also incorporates a sophisticated Inertial Measurement Unit (IMU) and GPS for localization. By projecting the endpoints of the laser scans into 3-D according to the estimated position of the robot and the angle of the pan-tilt, the robot can construct clouds of 3-D points describing the world around the robot.

By integrating constraints from the IMU, GPS, and matches between laser scans, we are able to construct large-scale, globally consistent, 3-D maps of urban environments. A map of the center of Stanford campus over 600 meters wide is shown in Figure 4. While such maps are necessary for planning global routes from one location to another, the robot must also monitor the immediate surroundings of the robot to ensure safe motion. The navigation pyramid algorithm described in this paper was implemented as the local navigation layer on the Segway. Experiments were performed to validate the two advantages of the pyramid algorithm: robustness to limited spatial resolution, and improved sensor coverage.

The first experiment is shown in Figures 5 to 7. Figure 5 shows the robot standing at a distance from a set of stairs. At this distance the robot is not able to detect the stairs as an obstacle. Both the standard evidence grid algorithm and the pyramid algorithm generate terrain maps like the one shown in Figure 5. (All levels of the pyramid were chosen to have a fixed resolution for the purposes of comparison with the stan-

**Figure 4**: 3-D map of the center of the Stanford campus constructed by the Segway. The map is over 600 meters across, and was constructed from over 10 km of travel.

dard algorithm.) After standing still for several minutes, both algorithms describe the stairs area as being empty with high probability.

Subsequently, the robot was driven up to the stairs. At closer ranges, the stairs are detected as obstacles, but the standard evidence grid is unable to overcome the previous evidence describing the cells as free space. The resulting evidence grid, shown in Figure 6 does not contain the steps and would have resulted in a collision of the robot. The pyramid algorithm, on the other hand (Figure 7, was able to detect the stairs. As the robot moved closer to the stairs, the obstacles were incorporated into the shorter range layers of the terrain map.

The second experiment, pictured in Figures 8 and 9, shows an example of the effect of multi-resolution pyramids on mapping performance. Figure 8 shows a fixed resolution terrain map generated while the robot was approaching a gate. The localization of obstacles in the map is quite good, but the sweeping pattern of the laser leaves large holes in the terrain map. The abundance of holes makes it difficult to plan smooth local paths through this environment. Figure 9 shows the same scenario, except using a multi-resolution pyramid. Obstacles near the robot are precisely mapped, while obstacles in the distance are stored at low resolution. Furthermore, most of the holes in the terrain map have been filled.

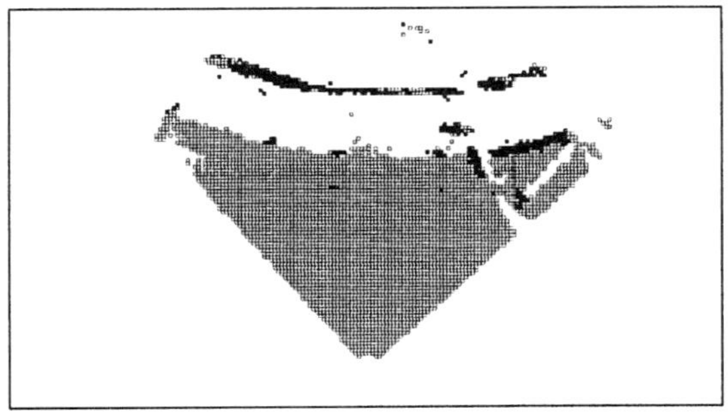

**Figure 5**: Watching the stairs from a distance, both algorithms create a similar terrain map with the stairs marked as free space.

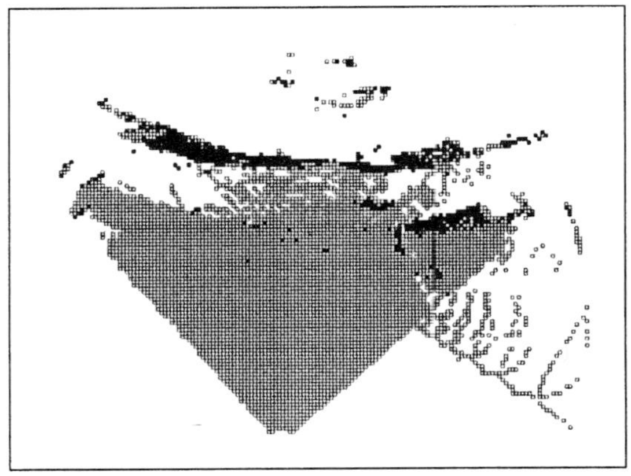

**Figure 6**: After the robot approaches the stairs, the standard occupancy grid algorithm is unable to overcome the previous negative evidence and the curb is not detected.

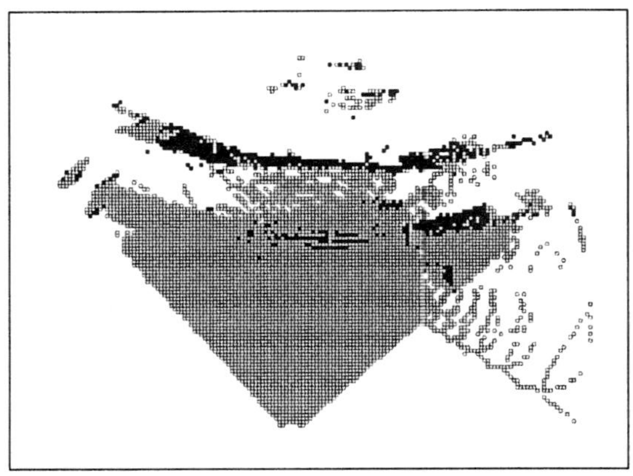

**Figure 7**: The pyramid approach is able to detect the stairs in time to safely avoid them.

## Conclusion

This paper proposed a pyramid approach to acquiring terrain models with mobile robots. The model was motivated by a key flaw in flat grid approaches to modeling the navigability of terrain; namely, that the ability of a sensor to detect obstacles varies with range. By integrating information into a single flat map, failures to detect obstacles at a distance are treated as random noise, and not what they actually are: the systematic effect of limited sensor resolution.

Our approach alleviates this problem by devising a hierarchy of maps, each tuned to a different sensor range (and hence a different sensor resolution). We derive a mathematical bound that provides a rational argument for determining the region covered by each map, and the granularity of the grid cells in each map. As a result, the map resolution decreases with the measurement range, which has the nice side effect that the resulting maps tend to have much higher coverage than common single-map approaches.

We have demonstrated our approach using an actual outdoor mobile robot system. Our system is based on a robotic Segway scooter, and has successfully acquired large-scale models of areas $1km^2$ in size. Our experiments demonstrate that our approach successfully identifies obstacles in situations where the

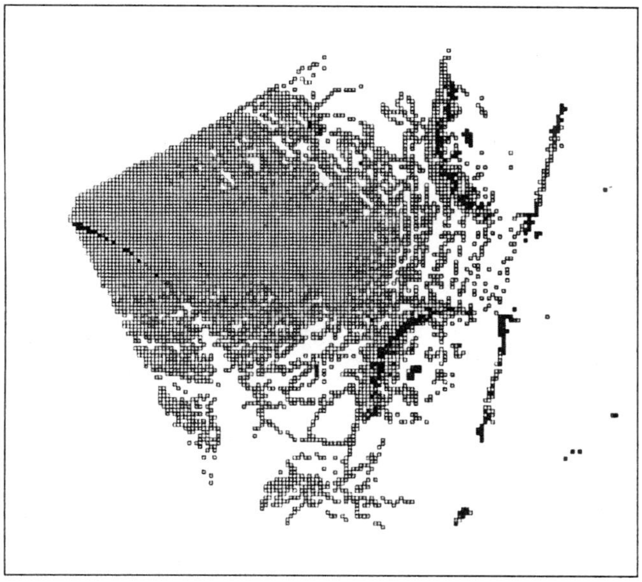

**Figure 8**: Model of the robot's surroundings using a fixed resolution grid. The large number of holes in the map makes motion planning difficult.

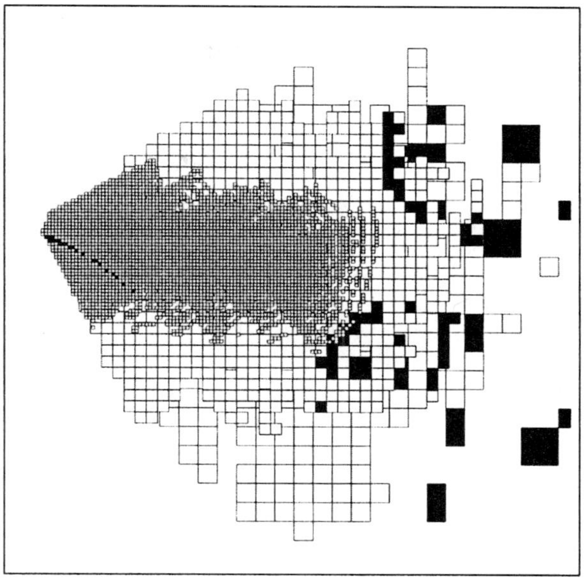

**Figure 9**: Multi-resolution pyramid model of the robot's surroundings. The majority of holes in the map are filled in. The terrain map close to the robot is very high resolution, while the area far from the robot is very coarse.

flat approach fails, and that it indeed leads to improved coverage in the resulting map. Computationally, our approach is only marginally more expensive than the single map approach, which should make our approach the method of choice for outdoor mobile robot navigation.

## Acknowledgements

This research is sponsored by by DARPA's MARS Program (Contract number N66001-01-C-6018), which is gratefully acknowledged.

## References

Borenstein, J., and Koren., Y. 1991. The vector field histogram – fast obstacle avoidance for mobile robots. *IEEE Journal of Robotics and Automation* 7(3):278–288.

Burgard, W.; Fox, D.; Moors, M.; Simmons, R.; and Thrun, S. 2000. Collaborative multi-robot exploration. In *ICRA*. San Francisco, CA: IEEE.

Ferguson, D.; Morris, A.; Hähnel, D.; Baker, C.; Omohundro, Z.; Reverte, C.; Thayer, S.; Whittaker, W.; Whittaker, W.; Burgard, W.; and Thrun, S. 2003. An autonomous robotic system for mapping abandoned mines. In Thrun, S.; Saul, L.; and Schölkopf, B., eds., *NIPS*. MIT Press.

Hashimoto, K., and Yuta, S. 2003. Autonomous detection of untraversability of the path on rough terrain for the remote controlled mobile robots. In *Proceedings of the International Conference on Field and Service Robotics*.

Likhachev, M.; Gordon, G.; and Thrun, S. 2003. ARA*: Anytime A* search with provable bounds on sub-optimality. In Thrun, S.; Saul, L.; and Schölkopf, B., eds., *NIPS*. MIT Press.

Matthies, L., and Grandjean, P. 1992. Stereo vision for planetary rovers: Stochastic modeling to near real-time implementation. *International Journal of Computer Vision* 8(1):71–91.

Matthies, L.; Gat, E.; Harrison, R.; Wilcox, B.; Volpe, R.; and Litwin, T. 1995. Mars microrover navigation: Performance evaluation and enhancement. *Autonomous Robots* 2(4):291–311.

Matthies, L.; Litwin, T.; Owens, K.; Rankin, A.; Murphy, K.; Coorobs, D.; Gilsinn, J.; Hong, T.; Legowik, S.; Nashman, M.; and Yoshimi, B. 1998. Performance evaluation of ugv obstacle detection with ccd/flir stereo vision and ladar. In *Proceedings of the Joint Conference on the Science and Technology of Intelligent Systems*.

Moravec, H. P. 1988. Sensor fusion in certainty grids for mobile robots. *AI Magazine* 9(2):61–74.

Simmons, R.; Apfelbaum, D.; Burgard, W.; Fox, D. an Moors, M.; Thrun, S.; and Younes, H. 2000. Coordination for multi-robot exploration and mapping. In *Proceedings of the AAAI National Conference on Artificial Intelligence*. Austin, TX: AAAI.

Yamauchi, B.; Langley, P.; Schultz, A.; Grefenstette, J.; and Adams, W. 1998. Magellan: An integrated adaptive architecture for mobile robots. Technical Report 98-2, Institute for the Study of Learning and Expertise (ISLE), Palo Alto, CA.

# Self-Organizing Visual Maps

**Robert Sim**
Department of Computer Science
University of British Columbia
2366 Main Mall
Vancouver, BC, V6T 1Z4

**Gregory Dudek**
Centre for Intelligent Machines
McGill University
3480 University St. Suite 409
Montreal, QC, H3A 2A7

### Abstract

This paper deals with automatically learning the spatial distribution of a set of images. That is, given a sequence of images acquired from well-separated locations, how can they be arranged to best explain their genesis? The solution to this problem can be viewed as an instance of robot mapping although it can also be used in other contexts. We examine the problem where only limited prior odometric information is available, employing a feature-based method derived from a probabilistic pose estimation framework. Initially, a set of visual features is selected from the images and correspondences are found across the ensemble. The images are then localized by first assembling the small subset of images for which odometric confidence is high, and sequentially inserting the remaining images, localizing each against the previous estimates, and taking advantage of any priors that are available. We present experimental results validating the approach, and demonstrating metrically and topologically accurate results over two large image ensembles. Finally, we discuss the results, their relationship to the autonomous exploration of an unknown environment, and their utility for robot localization and navigation.

## Introduction

This paper addresses the problem of building a map of an unknown environment from an ensemble of observations and limited pose information. We examine the extent to which we can organize a set of measurements from an unknown environment to produce a visual map of that environment with little or no knowledge of where in the environment the measurements were obtained. In particular, we are interested in taking a set of snapshots of the environment using an uncalibrated monocular camera, and organizing them to quantitatively or qualitatively indicate where they were taken which, in turn, allows us to construct a visual map. We assume that, at most, we have limited prior trajectory information, so as to bootstrap the process– the source of this information might be from the first few odometry readings along a trajectory, the general shape of the trajectory, information from an observer, or from a localization method that is expensive to operate, and hence is only applied to a small subset of the observation poses. While metric accuracy is of interest, our primary aim is to recover the topology of the ensemble. That is, to assure that metrically adjacent poses in the world are topologically adjacent in the resulting map.

The problem of automated robotic mapping is of substantial pragmatic interest for the development of mobile robot systems. The question of how we bootstrap a spatial representation, particularly a vision-based one, also appears to be relevant to other research areas such as computer vision and even ethology. Several authors have considered the use of self-organization in robot navigation (Takahashi *et al.* 2001; Beni & Wang 1991; Deneubourg *et al.* 1989; Selfridge 1962), often with impressive results. We believe this paper is among the first to demonstrate how to build a complete map of a real (non-simulated) unknown environment using monocular vision. We present quantitative data to substantiate this.

We approach the problem in the context of probabilistic robot localization using learned image-domain features (as opposed to features of the 3D environment) (Sim & Dudek 2001). To achieve this there are two steps involved: first, reliable features are selected and correspondences are found across the image ensemble. Subsequently, the quantitative behaviours of the features as functions of pose are exploited in order to compute a maximum-likelihood pose for each image in the ensemble. While other batch-oriented mapping approaches are iterative in nature (Thrun, Fox, & Burghard 1998; Kohonen 1984), we demonstrate that if accurate pose information is provided for a small subset of images, the remaining images in the ensemble can be localized without the need for further iteration and, in some cases, without regard for the order in which the images are localized.

### Outline

In the following section, we consider prior work related to our problem; in particular, approaches to self-organizing maps, and the simultaneous localization and mapping problem. We then proceed to present our approach, providing an overview of our feature-based localization framework, followed by the details of how we apply the framework to organize the input ensemble. Finally, we present experimental results on a variety of ensembles, demonstrating the accuracy and robustness of the approach.

## Previous Work

The construction of self-organizing spatial maps (SOM's) has a substantial history in computer science. Kohonen developed a number of algorithms for covering an input space (Kohonen 1984; 1995). While spatial coverage has been used as a metaphor, the problem of representing a data space in terms of self-organizing features has numerous applications ranging from text searching to audition. The problem of spanning an input space with feature detectors or local basis functions has found wide application in machine learning, neural nets, and allied areas. In much of this algorithmic work, the key contributions have related to convergence and complexity issues.

The issue of automated mapping has also been addressed in the robotics community. One approach to fully automated robot mapping is to interleave the map synthesis and position estimation phases of robot navigation (sometimes known as SLAM: simultaneous localization and mapping). As it is generally applied, this entails incrementally building a map based on geometric measurements (e.g. from a laser rangefinder, sonar or stereo camera) and intermittently using the map to correct the robot's position as it moves (Leonard & Durrant-Whyte 1991b; Yamauchi, Schultz, & Adams 1998; Davison & Kita 2001). When the motion of a robot can only be roughly estimated, a topological representation becomes very attractive. Early work by Kuipers and Byun used repeated observation of a previously observed landmark to instantiate cycles in a topological map of an environment during the mapping process (Kuipers & Byun 1987; 1991) . The idea of performing SLAM in a topological context was also been examined theoretically (Deng & Mirzaian 1996). The probabilistic fusion of uncertain motion estimates has been examined by several authors (cf, (Smith & Cheeseman 1986)) and the use of Expectation Maximization has recently proven quite successful although it still depends on estimates of successive robot motions (Shatkay & Kaelbling 1997; Thrun 1998; Choset & Nagatani 2001).

A closely related problem in computer vision is that of close-range photogrammetry, or structure-from-motion (SFM) (Longuet-Higgins 1981; Hartley & Zisserman 2000; Davison 2003), which involves recovering the ensemble of camera positions, as well as the full three-dimensional geometry of the scene that is imaged. In the case where a para-perspective camera model is assumed, the problem is linear and the solution can be computed directly.

The key difference between the SFM problem and inferring pose with a visual map is that a solution to the SFM problem is dependent on explicit assumptions about the optical geometry of the imaging apparatus. In the visual mapping framework we have avoided committing to any such assumptions, and as such the self-organizing behaviour exhibited in the experimental results is equally applicable to exotic imaging hardware, such as an omnidirectional camera.

## Visual Map Framework

Our approach employs an adaptation of the visual map framework described in (Sim & Dudek 2001). We review it here in brief and refer the reader to the cited work for further details.

The key idea is to learn visual features, parametrically describe them so that they can be used to estimate one's position (that is, they can be used for localization). The features are pre-screened using an attention operator that efficiently detects statistically anomalous parts of an image and robust, useful features are recorded along with an estimate of their individual utility.

In the localization context, assume for the moment that we have collected an ensemble of training images with ground-truth position information associated with each image. The learning framework operates by first selecting a set of local features from the images using a measure of visual attention, tracking those features across the ensemble of images by maximizing the correlation of the local image intensity of the feature, and subsequently parameterizing the set of observed features in terms of their behaviour as a function of the known positions of the robot.

The resulting *tracked features* can be applied in a Bayesian framework to solve the localization problem. Specifically, given an observation image $\mathbf{z}$, the probability that the robot is at pose $\mathbf{q}$ is proportional to the probability of the observation conditioned on the pose:

$$p(\mathbf{q}|\mathbf{z}) = \frac{p(\mathbf{z}|\mathbf{q})p(\mathbf{q})}{p(\mathbf{z})} \tag{1}$$

where $p(\mathbf{q})$ is the prior on $\mathbf{q}$ and $p(\mathbf{z})$ is a normalization constant. For a feature-based approach, we express the probability of the observation conditioned on the pose as a mixture model of probability distributions derived from the individual features:

$$p(\mathbf{z}|\mathbf{q}) = k \sum_{\mathbf{l}_i \in z} p(\mathbf{l}_i|\mathbf{q}) \tag{2}$$

where $\mathbf{l}_i$ is a detected observation of feature $i$ in the image and $k$ is a normalizing constant.

The individual feature models are generative in nature. That is, given the proposed pose $\mathbf{q}$, an expected observation $\mathbf{l}_i^*$ is generated by learning a parameterization $\mathbf{l}_i^* = F_i(\mathbf{q})$ of the feature, and the observation probability is determined by a Gaussian distribution centered at the expected observation and with covariance determined by cross-validation over the training observations. Whereas in prior work the parameterization was computed using radial basis function networks, in this work we construct the interpolants using bilinear interpolation of the observations associated with the nearest neighbour training poses, as determined by the Delaunay triangulation of the training poses. In this work, the feature vector $\mathbf{l}_i$ is defined as the position of the feature in the image:

$$\mathbf{l}_i = [x_i \; y_i] \tag{3}$$

Other scenarios might call for a different choice of feature vector.

A pose estimate is obtained by finding the pose $\mathbf{q}^*$ that maximizes Equation 1. It should be noted that the framework requires no commitment as to how uncertainty is represented or the optimization is performed. It should be noted, however, that the probability density for $\mathbf{q}$ might be multi-modal, and, as is the case for the problem at hand, weak priors on $\mathbf{q}$ might require a global search for the correct pose. For this work, we employ a multi-resolution grid decomposition of the environment, first approximating $p(\mathbf{q}|\mathbf{z})$ at a coarse scale and computing increasingly higher resolution grids in the neighbourhood of $\mathbf{q}^*$ as it is determined at each resolution.

## Self-Organization

We now turn to the problem of inferring the poses of the training images when ground truth is unavailable, or only partially available. The self-organization process involves two steps. In the first step, image features are selected and tracked, and in the second step the set of images are localized.

### Tracking

Tracking proceeds by considering the images in an arbitrary order (possibly, but not necessarily, according to distance along the robot's trajectory). An attention operator is applied to the first image $\mathbf{z}$ in the set[1], and each detected feature initializes a *tracking set* $T_i \in T$. The image itself is added to the ensemble set $E$. For each subsequent image $\mathbf{z}$, the following algorithm is performed:

1. A search is conducted over the image for matches to each tracking set in $T$, and successful matches are added to their respective tracking sets $T_i$. Call the set of successful matches $M$.
2. The attention operator is then applied to the image and the set of detected features $S$ is determined.
3. If the cardinality of $M$ is less than the cardinality of $S$, new tracked sets $T_i$ are initialized by elements selected from $S$. The elements are selected first on the basis of their response to the attention operator, and second on the basis of their distance from the nearest image position in $M$. In this way, features in $S$ which are close to prior matches are omitted, and regions of the image where features exist but matching failed receive continued attention. Call this new set of tracking sets $T_S$.

[1]We select local-maxima of edge-density.

4. A search for matches to the new tracking sets in $T_S$ is conducted over each image in $E$ (that is, the previously examined images), and the successful matches are added to their respective tracking set.
5. $T = T \cup T_S$
6. $E = E \cup \mathbf{z}$

The template used for by any particular tracking set is defined as the local appearance image of the initial feature in the set. We use local windows of 33 pixels in width and height. Matching is considered successful when the normalized correlation of the template with the local image under consideration exceeds a user-defined threshold.

When tracking is completed, we have a set of feature correspondences across the ensemble of images. The process is $O(kn)$ where $k$ is the final number of tracked sets, and $n$ is the number of images.

### Localization

Once tracking is complete, the next step is to determine the position of each image in the ensemble. For the moment, consider the problem when there is a single feature that was tracked reliably across all of the images. If we assume that the image feature is derived from a fixed 3D point in space, the motion of the feature through the image will be according to a monotonic mapping as a function of camera pose and the camera's intrinsic parameters. As such, the topology of a set of observation poses is preserved in the mapping from pose-space to image-space. While the mapping itself is nonlinear (due to perspective projection), it can be approximated by associating actual poses with a small set of the observations and determining the local mappings of the remaining unknown poses by constructing an interpolant over the known poses. Such an algorithm would proceed as follows:

1. Initialize $S = \{(\mathbf{q}, \mathbf{z})\}$, the set of (pose, observation) pairs for which the pose is known. Compute $D$, the parameterization of $S$ as defined by the feature learning framework.
2. For each observation $\mathbf{z}$ with unknown pose,
   (a) Use $D$ as an interpolant to find the pose $\mathbf{q}^*$ that maximizes the probability that $\mathbf{q}^*$ produces observation $\mathbf{z}$.
   (b) Add $(\mathbf{q}^*, \mathbf{z})$ to $S$ and update $D$ accordingly.

For a parameterization model based on a Delaunay Triangulation interpolant, updating the $D$ takes $O(\log n)$ amortized time, where $n$ is the number of observations in the model. The cost of updating the covariance associated with each model is $O(k \log n)$, where $k$ is the number of samples omitted during cross-validation.

In addition, the cost of finding the maximally likely pose with $D$ is $O(m \log n)$, where $m$ corresponds to the number of poses that are evaluated (finding a face in the triangulation that contains a point $\mathbf{q}$ can be performed in $\log n$ time.). Given $n$ total observations, the entire

Figure 1: The LAB scene, a 2.0m by 2.0m pose space.

algorithm takes $O(n(m+k+1)\log n)$ time. Both $m$ and $k$ can be bounded by constants, although in practice we typically bound $k$ by $n$.

In practice, of course, there is more than one feature detected in the image ensemble. Furthermore, in a suitably small environment, some might span the whole set of images, but in most environments, most are only visible in a subset of images. Finally, matching failures might introduce a significant number of outliers to individual tracking sets. Multiple features, and the presence of outlier observations are addressed by the localization framework we have presented; the maximum likelihood pose is computed by maximizing Equation 2, and the effects of outliers in a tracked set are reduced by their contribution to the covariance associated with that set.

When it cannot be assumed that the environment is small enough such that one or more feature spans it, we must rely on stronger priors to bootstrap the process.

In the following section we present experimental results on two image ensembles.

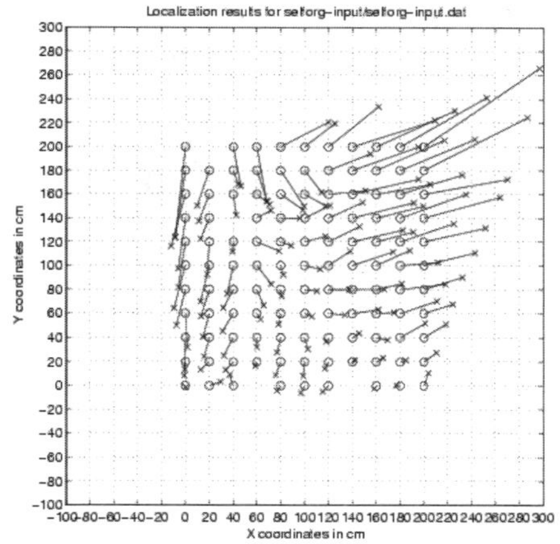


Figure 2: Self-organizing pose estimates plotted versus ground truth for the LAB scene.

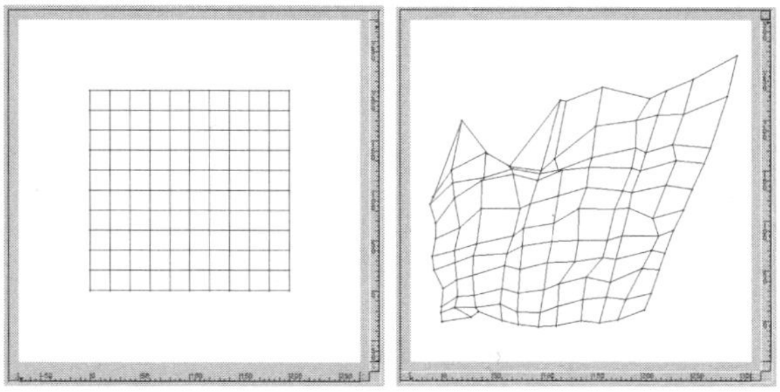

Figure 3: Ground truth, and the map resulting from the self-organizing process for the LAB scene.

## Experimental Results

### A Small Scene

For our first experiment, we demonstrate the procedure on a relatively compact scene. The LAB scene consists of an ensemble of 121 images of the scene depicted in Figure 1. The images were collected over a 2m by 2m environment, at 20cm intervals. Ground truth was measured by hand, accurate to 0.5cm.

Given the ensemble, the images were sorted at random and tracking was performed as described above, resulting in 91 useful tracked features. (A tracked feature was considered useful if it contained at least 4 observations). The localization stage proceeded by first providing the ground truth information to four images selected at random. The remaining images were again sorted at random and added, without any prior information about their pose, according to the methodology described in the previous section. Figure 2 depicts the set of inferred poses versus their ground truth positions. The four 'holes' in the data set at $(20, 200)$, $(40, 140)$, $(60, 0)$, and $(140, 0)$ correspond to the four initial poses for which ground truth was supplied. For the purposes of visualization, Figure 3 plots the original grid of poses, and beside it the same grid imposed upon the set of pose estimates computed for the ensemble.

In order to quantify the distortion in the resulting map, the lengths of the mapped line segments corresponding to the original grid were measured, and the average and standard deviation in the segment lengths was recorded. For the ground-truth mesh, the average and standard deviation segment length was 20cm and 0cm, respectively (assuming perfect ground truth). In the inferred map, the mean segment length was 24.2cm and the standard deviation was 11.5cm. These results demonstrate that the resulting map was slightly dilated and with variation in the segment lengths of about 11.5cm or 58% of 20cm on average.

While there is clearly some warping in the mesh, for the most part the topology of the poses is preserved.

### A Larger Scene

For our second experiment, we examine a larger pose space, 3.0m in width and 5.5m in depth, depicted in Figure 4. For this experiment, 252 images were collected at 25cm intervals using a pair of robots, one of which used a laser range-finder to measure the 'ground-truth' pose of the moving robot(Rekleitis *et al.* 2001).

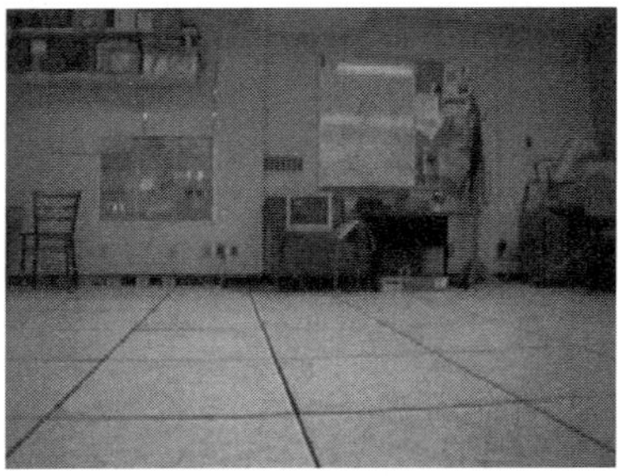

Figure 4: The second scene, a 3.0m by 5.5m pose space.

As in the previous experiment, tracking was performed over the image ensemble and a set of 49 useful tracked features were extracted. In this instance, the larger interval between images, some illumination variation in the scene and the larger number of input images presented significant challenges for the tracker, resulting in the smaller number of tracked features.

Given the size of the environment, no one feature spanned the entire pose space. As a result, it was necessary to impose constraints on the *a priori* known ground-truth poses, and the order in which the input images were considered for localization. In addition, a weak prior (i.e. having only a slight effect) $p(\mathbf{q})$ was applied as each image was added in order to control the distortion in the mesh.

Rather than select the initial ground-truth images at random, ground truth was supplied to the four images closest to the centre of the environment. The remainder of the images were sorted by simulating a spiral trajectory of the robot through the environment, intersecting each image pose, and adding the images as they were encountered along the trajectory. Figure 5 illustrates the simulated ground-truth trajectory through the ensemble. Finally, given the sort order, as images were added it was assumed that their pose fell on an annular ring surrounding the previously estimated poses. The radius and width of the ring was defined in terms of the interval used to collect the images. The computed *a priori* distributions over the first few images input into the map are depicted in Figure 6. The intent of using these priors was to simulate a robot exploring the environment along trajectories of increasing radius from a home position.

As in the previous section, Figure 7 plots the original grid of poses, and beside it the same grid imposed upon the set of pose estimates computed for the ensemble. Again, the positive $y$-axis corresponds to looming forward in the image, and as such the mesh distorts as features accelerate in image space as the camera approaches them. Note however, that as in the first experiment, the topology of the embedded poses is preserved for most of the grid.

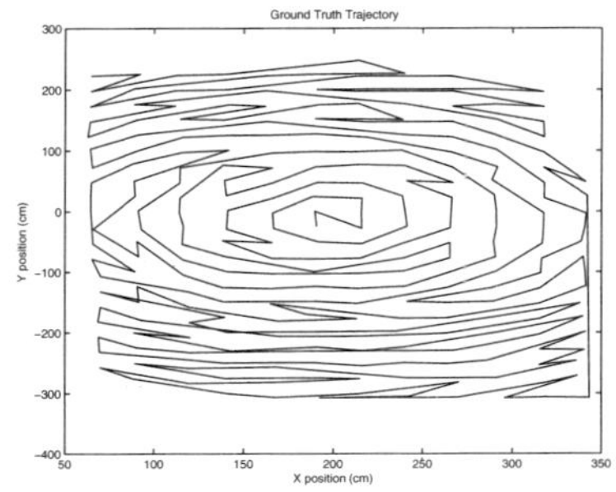


Figure 5: Ground truth simulated trajectory.

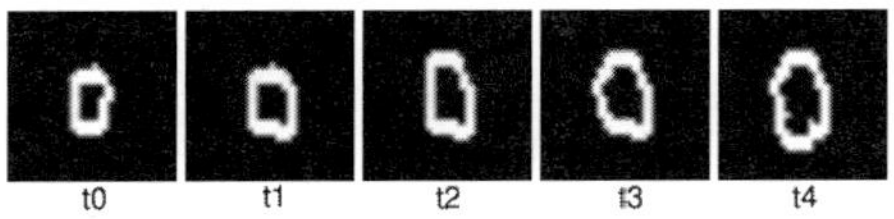


Figure 6: Evolution of the annular prior $p(\mathbf{q})$ over the first few input images. Each thumbnail illustrates $p(\mathbf{q})$ over the 2D pose space at time $t_i$.

## Discussion

We have demonstrated an approach to spatially organizing images of an unknown environment using little or no positional prior knowledge. The repeated occurrences of learned visual features in the images allows us to accomplish this. The visual map of the environment that is produced appears to be topologically correct and also demonstrates a substantial degree of metric accuracy and can be described as a locally conformal mapping of the environment. This representation can then be readily used for path execution, trajectory planning and other spatial tasks.

While several authors have considered systems that interleave mapping and position estimation, we believe ours is among the first to do this based on monocular image data. In addition, unlike prior work which typically uses odometry to constrain the localization process, we can accomplish this with essentially no prior estimate of the position the measurements are collected from. On the other hand, if some positional prior is available we can readily exploit it. In the second example shown in this paper we exploited such a prior. Even in this example, it should be noted that the data acquisition trajectory was one that did not include cycles. In general, cyclic trajectories (ones that re-visit previously seen locations via another route) will greatly improve the quality of the results; in fact they are prerequisite for many existing mapping and localization techniques, both topological and metric ones.

We believe that absence of a requirement of a position prior (i.e. odometry) makes this approach suitable for unconventional mapping applications, such as the integration of data from walking robots or from manually collected video sequences. Our ability to do this depends on the repeated occurrence of visual features

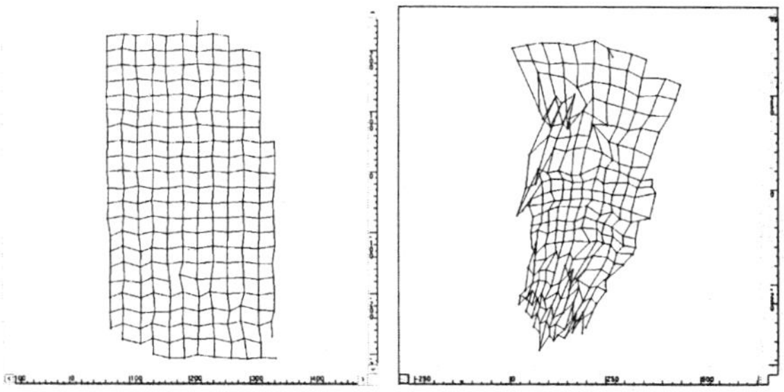

Figure 7: Ground truth, and the map resulting from the self-organizing process for the environment depicted in Figure 1.

in images from adjacent positions. This implies that successfully mapping depends on images being taken at sufficiently small intervals to assure common elements between successive measurements.

## References


Beni, G., and Wang, J. 1991. Theoretical problems for the realization of distributed robotic system. In *Proceedings of the IEEE International Conference on Robotics and Automation*, 1914–1920. Sacramento, CA: IEEE Press.

Choset, H., and Nagatani, K. 2001. Topological simultaneous localization and mapping (SLAM): Toward exact localization without explicit localization. *IEEE Transactions on Robotics and Automation* 17(2):125–137.

Davison, A. J., and Kita, N. 2001. 3D simultaneous localisation and map-building using active vision for a robot moving on undulating terrain. In *Proceedings of the IEEE Conference on Computer Vision and Pattern Recognition*, 384–391.

Davison, A. 2003. Real-time simultaneous localisation and mapping with a single camera. In *Proceedings of the IEEE International Conference on Computer Vision.*

Deneubourg, J.; Goss, S.; Pasteels, J.; Fresneau, D.; and Lachaud, J. 1989. Self-organization mechanisms in ant societies (ii): Learning in foraging and division of labor. In Pasteels, J., and Deneubourg, J., eds., *From Individual to Collective Behavior in Social Insects, Experientia Supplementum*, volume 54. Birkhauser Verlag. 177–196.

Deng, X., and Mirzaian, A. 1996. Competitive robot mapping with homogeneous markers. *IEEE Transactions on Robotics and Automation* 12(4):532–542.

Gross, H.; Stephan, V.; and Bohme, H. 1996. Sensory-based robot navigation using self-organizing networks and q-learning. In *Proceedings of the World Congress on Neural Networks*, 94–99. Lawrence Erlbaum Associates, Inc.

Hartley, R., and Zisserman, A. 2000. *Multiple View Geometry in Computer Vision.* Cambridge, United Kingdom: Cambridge University Press.

Kohonen, T. 1984. *Self-Organization and Associative Memory.* New York: Springer-Verlag.

Kohonen, T. 1995. *Self-organizing maps.* Berlin; Heidelberg; New-York: Springer.

Kuipers, B., and Beeson, P. 2002. Bootstrap learning for place recognition. In *Proceedings of the National Conference on Artificial Intelligence (AAAI)*, 174–180.

Kuipers, B. J., and Byun, Y. T. 1987. A qualitative approach to robot exploration and map-learning. In *Proceedings of the IEEE workshop on spatial reasoning and multi-sensor fusion*, 390–404. Los Altos, CA: IEEE.

Kuipers, B., and Byun, Y.-T. 1991. A robot exploration and mapping strategy based on a semantic hierachy of spatial representations. *Robotics and Autonomous Systems* 8:46–63.

Leonard, J. J., and Durrant-Whyte, H. F. 1991a. Simultaneous map building and localization for an autonomous mobile robot. In *Proceedings of the IEEE Int. Workshop on Intelligent Robots and Systems*, 1442–1447.

Leonard, J. J., and Durrant-Whyte, H. F. 1991b. Mobile robot localization by tracking geometric beacons. *IEEE Transactions on Robotics and Automation* 7(3):376–382.

Leonard, J. J., and Feder, H. J. S. 2000. A computationally efficient method for large-scale concurrent mapping and localization. In Hollerbach, J., and Koditschek, D., eds., *Robotics Research: The Ninth International Symposium*, 169–176. London: Springer-Verlag.

Longuet-Higgins, J. 1981. A computer algorithm for reconstructing a scene from two projections. *Nature* 293:133–135.

Rekleitis, I.; Sim, R.; Dudek, G.; and Milios, E. 2001. Collaborative exploration for the construction of visual maps. In *IEEE/RSJ/ International Conference on Intelligent Robots and Systems*, volume 3, 1269–1274. Maui, HI: IEEE/RSJ.

Selfridge, O. 1962. The organization of organization. In Yovits, M.; Jacobi, G.; and Goldstein, G., eds., *Self-Organizing Systems.* Washington D.C.: McGregor & Werner. 1–7.

Shatkay, H., and Kaelbling, L. P. 1997. Learning topological maps with weak local odometric information. In *Proceedings of the International Joint Conference on Artificial Intelligence (IJCAI)*, 920–929. Nagoya, Japan: Morgan Kaufmann.

Sim, R., and Dudek, G. 2001. Learning generative models of scene features. In *Proc. IEEE Conf. Computer Vision and Pattern Recognition (CVPR).* Lihue, HI: IEEE Press.

Smith, R., and Cheeseman, P. 1986. On the representation and estimation of spatial uncertainty. *International Journal of Robotics Research* 5(4):56–68.

Takahashi, T.; Tanaka, T.; Nishida, K.; and Kurita, T. 2001. Self-organization of place cells and reward-based navigation for a mobile robot. *Proceedings of the 8th International Conference on Neural Information Processing, Shanghai (China)* 1164–1169.

Thrun, S.; Fox, D.; and Burghard, W. 1998. A probabilistic approach to concurrent mapping and localization for mobile robots. *Autonomous Robots* 5:253–271.

Thrun, S. 1998. Finding landmarks for mobile robot navigation. In *Proceedings of the IEEE International Conference on Robotics and Automation*, 958–963.

Yamauchi, B.; Schultz, A.; and Adams, W. 1998. Mobile robot exploration and map building with continuous localization. In *Proceedings of the IEEE International Conference on Robotics and Automation*, 3715–2720. Leuven, Belgium: IEEE Press.

# Reconstruction of 3D Models from Intensity Images and Partial Depth

**Luz A. Torres-Méndez and Gregory Dudek**
Center for Intelligent Machines, McGill University
Montreal, Quebec H3A 2A7, CA
{latorres,dudek}@cim.mcgill.ca

**Abstract**

This paper addresses the probabilistic inference of geometric structures from images. Specifically, of synthesizing range data to enhance the reconstruction of a 3D model of an indoor environment by using video images and (very) partial depth information. In our method, we interpolate the available range data using statistical inferences learned from the concurrently available video images and from those (sparse) regions where both range and intensity information is available. The spatial relationships between the variations in intensity and range can be efficiently captured by the neighborhood system of a Markov Random Field (MRF). In contrast to classical approaches to depth recovery (i.e. stereo, shape from shading), we can afford to make only weak prior assumptions regarding specific surface geometries or surface reflectance functions since we compute the relationship between existing range data and the images we start with. Experimental results show the feasibility of our method.

## Introduction

This paper presents an algorithm for estimating depth information from a combination of color (or achromatic) intensity data and a limited amount of known depth data. Surface depth recovery is one of the classical standard vision problems, both because of its scientifi c and pragmatic value. The problem of inferring the 3D layout of space is a critical problem in robotics and computer vision, and is often cited as a signifi cant cognitive skill. In the vision community, solutions to such "shape from X" problems are often based on strong prior assumptions regarding the physical properties of the objects in the scene (such as matte or Lambertian reflectance properties). In the robotics community, such depth inference is often performed using sophisticated but costly hardware solutions.

While several elegant algorithms for depth recovery have been developed, the use of laser range data in many applications has become commonplace due to their simplicity and reliability (but not their elegance, cost or physical robustness). In robotics, for example, the use of range data combined with visual information, has become a key methodology, but it is often hampered by the fact that range sensors that provide complete (2-1/2D) depth maps with a resolution akin to that of a camera, are prohibitively costly. Stereo cameras can produce volumetric scans that are economical, but they often require calibration or produce range maps that are either incomplete or of limited resolution.

We seek to reconstruct suitable 3D models from sparse range data sets while simultaneously facilitating the data acquisition process. We present an effi cient algorithm to estimate 3D dense data from a combination of video images and a limited amount of observed range data. It has been shown in (Lee, Pedersen, & Mumford 2001) that although there are clear differences between optical and range images, they do have similar second-order statistics and scaling properties (i.e. they both have similar structure when viewed as random variables). Our motivation is to exploit this fact and also that both video imaging and *limited* range sensing are ubiquitous readily-available technologies while complete volume scanning remains prohibitive on most mobile platforms. Please note that we are not simply inferring a few missing pixels, but synthesizing a complete range map from as little as few laser scans across the environment.

Our method is based on learning a statistical model of the (local) relationship between the observed range data and the variations in the intensity image and use this model to compute unknown depth values. This can be regarded as a form of shape-from-shading (depth inference from variations in surface shading) based on statistical learning, although traditional shape-from-shading is quite different from this approach in its technical details. Here, we approximate the *composite* of range and intensity at each point as a Markov process. Unknown depth values are then inferred by using the statistics of the observed range data to determine the behavior of the Markov process. The presence of intensity where range data is being inferred is crucial since intensity provides knowledge of surface smoothness and variations in depth. Our approach learns that knowledge directly from the observed data, without having to hypothesize constraints that might be inapplicable to a particular environment.

## Previous Work

We base our range estimation process on the assumption that the pixels constituting both the range and intensity images acquired in an environment, can be regarded as the results of pseudo-random processes, but that these random processes exhibit useful structure. In particular, we exploit the assumption that range and intensity images are correlated, albeit in potentially complicated ways. Secondly, we assume that the variations of pixels in the range and intensity images are related to the values elsewhere in the image(s) and that these variations can be efficiently captured by the neighborhood system of a Markov Random Field. Both these assumptions have been considered before (Geman & Geman 1984; Efros & Leung 1999; Wei & Levoy 2000; Efros & Freeman 2001; Hertzmann *et al.* 2001), but they have never been exploited in tandem. Digital inpainting (Bertalmio *et al.* 2000; 2003; Criminisi, Perez, & Toyama 2003) is quite similar to our problem, although our domain and approach are quite different. In (Baker & Kanade 2002), a learned representation of pixel variation for perform resolution enhancement of face images. The processes employed to interpolate new high-resolution pixel data is quite similar in spirit to what we describe here, although the application and technical details differ significantly. The work in (Torralba & Freeman 2003; Freeman, Pasztor, & Carmichael 2003) on learning the relationships between intrinsic images is also related.

In prior work (Torres-Méndez & Dudek 2002), we performed reconstruction by inferring depth values using predetermined schedule over space, essentially walking a spiral from the boundary of a region towards the center. We have observed that reconstruction across depth discontinuities is often problematic as there is comparatively little constraint for probabilistic inference at these locations. Further, such locations are often identified with edges in both the range and intensity maps. Based on these observations, we have developed two important algorithmic improvements that have a dramatic effect on the quality of the results. In the present work, we modify the reconstruction sequence to first recover the values of those augmented voxels for which we can make the most reliable inferences. This leads to two critical algorithmic refinements: (1) as we recover augmented pixels we defer the reconstruction of augmented voxels close to intensity or depth discontinuities as much as possible, and (2) as we reconstruct we select those voxels for reconstruction that have the largest degree of boundary constraint (aside from those deferred by condition (1)).

Most of prior work on synthesis of 3D environment models uses one of either photometric data or geometric data (Debevec, Taylor, & Malik 1996; Hilton 1996; Fitzgibbon & Zisserman 1998) to reconstruct a 3D model of an scene. For example, in (Fitzgibbon & Zisserman 1998), a method is proposed to sequentially retrieves the projective calibration of a complete image sequence based on tracking corner and/or line features over two or more images, and reconstructs each feature independently in 3D. Their method solves the feature correspondence problem based on the fundamental matrix and tri-focal tensor, which encode precisely the geometric constraints available from two or more images of the same scene from different viewpoints.

Shape-from-shading is related in spirit to what we are doing, but is based on a rather different set of assumptions and methodologies. Such methods (Horn & Brooks 1989; Oliensis 1991) reconstruct a 3D scene by inferring depth from a 2D image; in general, this task is difficult, requiring strong assumptions regarding surface smoothness and surface reflectance properties.

Recent work has focus on combining information from the intensity and range data for 3d model reconstruction. Several authors (Pulli *et al.* 1997; El-Hakim 1998; Sequeira *et al.* 1999; Levoy *et al.* 2000; Stamos & Allen 2000) have obtained promising results. The work in (Pulli *et al.* 1997) addresses the problem of surface reconstruction by measuring both color and geometry of real objects and displaying realistic images of objects from arbitrary viewpoints. They use a stereo camera system with active lighting to obtain range and intensity images as visible from one point of view. The integration of the range data into a surface model is done by using a robust hierarchical space carving method. The integration of intensity data with range data has been proposed (Sequeira *et al.* 1999) to help define the boundaries of surfaces extracted from the 3D data, and then a set of heuristics are used to decide what surfaces should be joined. For this application, it becomes necessary to develop algorithms that can hypothesize the existence of surface continuity and intersections among surfaces, and the formation of composite features from the surfaces.

However, one of the main issues in using the above configurations is that the acquisition process is very expensive because dense and complete intensity and range data are needed in order to obtain a good 3D model. As far as we know, there is no method that bases its reconstruction process on having a small amount of intensity and/or range data and synthetically estimating the areas of missing information by using the current available data. In particular, such a method is feasible in man-made environments, which have inherent geometric constraints, such as planar surfaces.

## Methodology

Our objective is to infer a dense range map from an intensity image and a very sparse initial range data. At the outset, we assume that the intensity and range data are already registered. In practice, this registration could be computed as a first step, but we omit this in the current presentation. Note that while the process of inferring distances from intensity superficially resembles shape-from-shading, we do not depend on prior knowledge of reflectance or on surface smoothness or even on surface integrability (which is a technical precondition for most shape-from-shading methods, even where not explicitly stated). We solve the range data inference problem as an extrapolation problem by approximating the *composite* of range and intensity at each point as a Markov process. Unknown range data is then inferred by using the statistics of the observed range data to determine the behavior of the Markov process. Critical to the processes is the presence of intensity data at each point where range is being inferred. Intuitively, this intensity data provides at least two kinds of information: (1) knowledge of when the surface is smooth, and (2) knowledge of when there is a high probability of a variation in depth. Our approach learns that information from the observed data, without having to fabricate or hypothesize constraints that might be inapplicable to a particular environment.

We observed in previous experiments that the order of reconstruction highly influences the final result. In those experiments, we used a spiral-scan ordering, whose main disadvantage was the strong dependence from the previous assigned depth value. In the present work, our reconstruction sequence is to first recover the values of those locations for which we can make the most reliable inferences, so that as we reconstruct, we select those voxels for reconstruction that have the largest degree of boundary constraint. We have also observed that reconstruction across depth discontinuities is often problematic as there is comparatively little constraint for probabilistic inference at these locations. Further, such locations are often identified with edges in both the range and intensity maps. In this work we have incorporated edge information and, as we recover augmented voxels, we defer the reconstruction of augmented voxels close to intensity or depth discontinuities as much as possible.

## The Algorithm

We focus on our development of a set of **augmented voxels V** that contain intensity (either from grayscale or color images), edge (from the intensity image) and range information (where the range is initially unknown for some of them). Let $\Omega$ be the area of unknown range (i.e. the region to be filled). In our algorithm, the depth value $r$ of each augmented voxel $V_i \in \Omega$ is synthesized one at a time. We based our reconstruction sequence on the amount of reliable information surrounding the augmented voxel whose depth value is to be estimated, and also on the edge information. Thus, for each augmented voxel $V_i$, we count the number of neighbor voxels (in their 8-neighborhood system) with already assigned range and intensity. We start by synthesizing those augmented voxels which have more of their neighbor voxels already filled, leaving to the end those with an edge passing through them. After a depth value is estimated, we update each of its neighbors by adding 1 to their own neighbor counters. We then proceed to the next group of augmented voxels to synthesize until no more augmented voxels in $\Omega$ exist.

## MRFs for Range Synthesis

Markov Random Fields (MRFs) are used here as a model to synthesize range. Formally, an augmented voxel is defined as $\mathbf{V} = (\mathrm{I}, \mathrm{E}, \mathrm{R})$, where I is the matrix of known pixel intensities, E is a binary matrix (1 if an edge exists and 0 otherwise) and R denotes the matrix of incomplete pixel depths. We are interested only in a set of such augmented voxels such that one augmented voxel lies on each ray that intersects each pixel of the input image I, thus giving us a registered range image R and intensity image I. Let $Z_m = (x, y) : 1 \leq x, y \leq m$ denote the $m$ integer lattice (over which the images are described); then $\mathrm{I} = \{I_{x,y}\}$, $(x, y) \in Z_m$, denotes the gray levels of the input image, and $\mathrm{R} = \{R_{x,y}\}$, $(x, y) \in Z_m$ denotes the depth values. We model $\mathbf{V}$ as an MRF. Thus, we regard I and R as a random variables. For example, $\{\mathrm{R} = r\}$ stands for $\{R_{x,y} = r_{x,y}, (x, y) \in Z_m\}$. Given a *neighborhood system* $\mathcal{N} = \{\mathcal{N}_{x,y} \in Z_m\}$, where $\mathcal{N}_{x,y} \subset Z_m$ denotes the neighbors of $(x, y)$, such that, (1) $(x, y) \notin \mathcal{N}_{x,y}$, and (2) $(x, y) \in \mathcal{N}_{k,l} \Longleftrightarrow (k, l) \in \mathcal{N}_{x,y}$. An MRF over $(Z_m, \mathcal{N})$ is a stochastic process indexed by $Z_m$ for which, for every $(x, y)$ and every $v = (i, r)$ (i.e. each augmented voxel depends only on its immediate neighbors),

$$\begin{aligned} P(V_{x,y} = v_{x,y} \mid V_{k,l} = v_{k,l}, (k,l) \neq (x,y)) \\ = P(V_{x,y} = v_{x,y} \mid V_{k,l} = v_{k,l}, (k,l) \in \mathcal{N}_{x,y}), \quad (1) \end{aligned}$$

The choice of $\mathcal{N}$ together with the conditional probability distribution of $P(\mathrm{I} = i)$ and $P(\mathrm{R} = r)$, provides a powerful mechanism for modeling spatial continuity and other scene features. On one hand, we choose to model a neighborhood $\mathcal{N}_{x,y}$ as a square mask of size $n \times n$ centered at the augmented voxel location $(x, y)$. This neighborhood is causal, meaning that only those augmented voxels already containing information (either intensity, range or both) are considered for the synthesis process. On the other hand, calculating the conditional probabilities in an explicit form is an infeasible task since we cannot efficiently represent or determine all the possible combinations between augmented voxels with its associated neighborhoods. Therefore, we avoid the usual computational expense of sampling from a probability distribution (Gibbs sampling, for example), and synthesize a depth value from the augmented voxel $V_{x,y}$ with neighborhood $\mathcal{N}_{x,y}$, by selecting the range value from the augmented voxel whose neighborhood $\mathcal{N}_{k,l}$ most resembles the region being filled in, i.e.,

$$\mathcal{N}_{best} = \underset{(k,l) \in \mathcal{A}}{\mathbf{argmin}} \parallel \mathcal{N}_{x,y} - \mathcal{N}_{k,l} \parallel, \quad (2)$$

where $\mathcal{A} = \{\mathcal{A}_{k,l} \subset \mathcal{N}\}$ is the set of local neighborhoods, in which the center voxel has already assigned a depth value, such that $1 \leq \sqrt{(k-x)^2 + (l-y)^2} \leq d$. For each successive augmented voxel this approximates the maximum a posteriori estimate; $R(k, l)$ is then used to specify $R(x, y)$. The similarity measure $\parallel . \parallel$ between two generic neighborhoods $\mathcal{N}_a$ and $\mathcal{N}_b$ is defined as the weighted sum of squared differences (WSSD) over the partial data in the two neighborhoods. The "weighted" part refers to applying a 2-D Gaussian kernel to each neighborhood, such that those voxels near the center are given more weight than those at the edge of the window.

## Experimental Results

In this section we show experimental results conducted on data acquired in a real-world environment. We use ground truth data from two widely available databases. The first database [1] provides real intensity (reflectance) and range images of indoor scenes acquired by an Odetics laser range finder mounted on a mobile platform. The second database[2] provides color images with complex geometry and pixel-accurate ground-truth disparity data. We also show preliminary results on data collected by our mobile robot, which has a video camera and a laser range finder mounted on it. We start with the complete range data set as ground truth and then hold back most of the data to simulate the sparse sample of a real scanner and to provide input to our algorithm.

[1] http://marathon.csee.usf.edu/range/Database.html

[2] http://cat.middlebury.edu/stereo/newdata.html

This allows us to compare the quality of our reconstruction with what is actually in the scene. In the following, we will consider several strategies for subsampling the range data. In our experiments, we use the Canny edge detector (Canny 1986) for extracting the edges.

## Arbitrary shape of unknown range data

The first type of experiment involves the range synthesis when the unknown range data is of arbitrary shape. In particular, we show how the shape that contains the unknown range influences their estimation. In Figure 1a, two input range images (the two left images), and the input intensity with its corresponding edge information (the two right images), are given. The percentage of the missing area (shown in white) of both range images is 41.5% (6800 pixels). The perimeters however are different. Fig. 1b shows the synthesized range images (the two left images) and the ground truth range image (the right image) for comparison purposes.

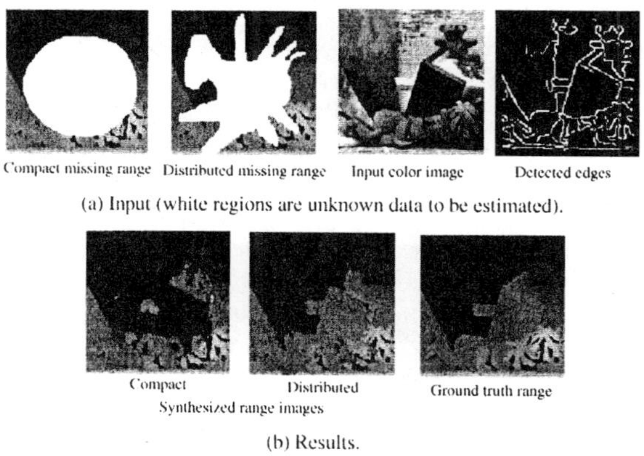


Figure 1: Results on two different shapes of unknown range with same area: 6800 pixels (41.5% of total image).

It can be seen that when synthesizing big areas of unknown range data, our algorithm performs better if the area is not compact, since combinations of already known range and intensity give more information about the geometry of the scene. In other words, the sample spans a broader distribution of range-intensity combinations.

## Range measurements with variable width along the $x-$ and $y-$ axis

This type of experiment involves the range synthesis when the initial range data is a set of stripes with variable width along the x- and y-axis of the intensity image. In the following experiments, 61% of the total area is unknown range. We conducted experiments on 32 images of common scenes found in a general indoor man-made environment using this case of subsampling. The smoothing parameter for edge detection was set to 0.8 in all examples. Due to space limitations, we are only showing 4 examples in Figure 2. The absolute value of each error is taken and the mean of those values is computed to arrive at the mean absolute residual (MAR)

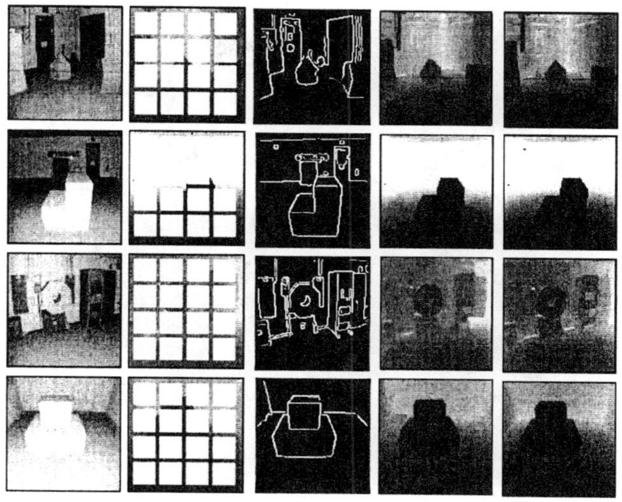

Figure 2: Examples on real data. The first two columns are the input intensity and range data, respectively. The area of missing range is 61%. The third column shows the edges detected in the input intensity. The synthesized results are shown in the fourth column and the ground truth range images are displayed in the last column for visual comparison.

error. The MAR errors from top to bottom are shown in Table 1. The approximated size of each scene is also given. We normalize the MAR error by dividing it by the scene size. This normalized MAR measure is a better indication of how large the error is according to the scene size. Computation time for these results using non-optimized code, is on the order of minutes on a generic PC's.

| | Ex. 1 | Ex. 2 | Ex. 3 | Ex. 4 |
|---|---|---|---|---|
| MAR Error (cms) | 8.58 | 13.48 | 11.39 | 7.12 |
| Approx. scene size (cms) | 600 | 800 | 500 | 400 |
| MAR/Depth | 0.017 | 0.021 | 0.024 | 0.048 |

Table 1: MAR errors of the cases shown in Figure 2.

We now show how color information can improve the synthesized results. Figure 3 displays in the first row, the grayscale and color images of the same scene, and to their right the input range data. The percentage of missing range is 61%. The size of the neighborhood is set to be 5x5 pixels. The synthesized results is shown in the second row together with the ground truth data for comparison purposes. It can be seen that there are some regions where color information may help in the synthesis process. For example, the chimney in the center of the image is separated from the background since they have different colors. This is hardly noticeable in the grayscale image.

Some preliminary results on data collected in our own building is presented next. We use a mobile robot with a video camera and a laser range finder mounted on it, to navigate the environment. For our application, the laser range finder was set to scan a 180 degrees field of view horizontally and 90 degrees vertically.

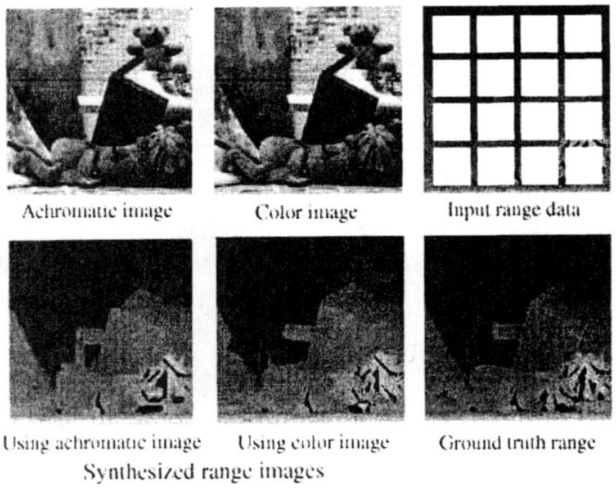


Figure 3: Results on achromatic and color images.

Figure 4 shows experimental results for a case where the input range data is a set of stripes along the x- and y-axis. The input intensity and the ground truth range data (for comparison purposes) are shown on the first row. Two examples are displayed in the second and third row. The left images show the input range images and the right images the synthesized range data after running our algorithm. For the first example, the area of unknown range is 62% of the total image and, for the second example, is 60%.

In general, the synthesized results are good in both cases. Our algorithm was capable of recovering the whole range of the image. There are, however, regions where the synthesis was not good. For example, regions containing surfaces that slope and whose surrounding neighborhoods lack of substantial intensity-range combinations to capture the underlying surface. The reconstruction in those regions becomes a difficult task since it is done from already seen depth values. A solution to this problem, which we are currently working on, is to use surface normal information to generate new depth values according to the type of surface being reconstructed. However, the results presented here demonstrate that this is a viable option to facilitate environment modeling.

## Summary and Conclusions

In this paper we have presented an approach to depth recovery that allows good quality scene reconstruction to be achieved in real environments. The method requires both an intensity images and set of partial range measurements input. In fact, the input range measurements are most effective if they are provided in the form of clusters of measurements scattered over the image. This form of sampling is best since it allows local statistics to be computed, but also provides boundary conditions at various locations in the image. While clumps per set are not available from most laser range scanners, swaths of data can be readily and efficiently extracted using laser scanners.

When we use color images in the reconstruction process, it appears that the fidelity of the reconstruction is somewhat improved over achromatic images. This appears to be due to the fact that the color data provides tighter constraint over where and how the interpolation process should be applied. At the same time, the higher dimensionality of the Markov Random Field model for color images may make the reconstruction problem more difficult in some cases.

We have also evaluated the performance of the reconstruction scheme using intensity data from a simple CCD camera and range data from a laser time of flight scanner (LIDAR) mounted near the camera. While these two sensors are mount close together, there remains an unavoidable stereo disparity between the two sensors. This is probably responsible for portion of the reconstruction error we observed. While this is slightly problematic it seems amenable to various solution techniques; in fact, it may be possible to exploit this disparity data as an additional form of stereo.

Critical to the performance of this method is the statistical similarity of the regions being reconstructed and the portions of the image used to define the Markov model. An open question is how to validate this statistical similarity which could be useful both to control and to validate the reconstruction process.

## Acknowledgements

We would like to thank the CESAR lab at Oak Ridge National Laboratory in Tennessee and the Stereo Vision Research Group at Middlebury College for making their range image databases available through their websites.
The first author gratefully acknowledges CONACyT for providing financial support to pursue her Ph.D. studies at McGill University.
We would like to thank also the Federal Centers of Excellence (IRIS) and NSERC for ongoing funding.

## References

Baker, S., and Kanade, T. 2002. Limits on super-resolution and how to break them. *IEEE Trans. on PAMI* 24(9):1167–1183.

Bertalmio, M.; Sapiro, G.; Caselles, V.; and Ballester, C. 2000. Image inpainting. In *SIGGRAPH*, 417–424.

Bertalmio, M.; Vese, L.; Sapiro, G.; and Osher, S. 2003. Simultaneous structure and texture image inpainting. In *IEEE CVPR*.

Canny, J. 1986. A computational approach to edge detection. *IEEE Trans. on PAMI* 8(6):679–698.

Criminisi, A.; Perez, P.; and Toyama, K. 2003. Object removal by examplar-based inpainting. In *IEEE CVPR*.

Debevec, P.; Taylor, C.; and Malik, J. 1996. Modeling and rendering architecture from photographs: A hybrid geometry and image-based approach. In *SIGGRAPH*, 11–20.

Efros, A., and Freeman, W. 2001. Image quilting for texture synthesis and transfer. In *SIGGRAPH*, 1033–1038.

Efros, A., and Leung, T. 1999. Texture synthesis by non-parametric sampling. In *ICCV (2)*, 1033–1038.

El-Hakim, S. 1998. A multi-sensor approach to creating accurate virtual environments. *Journal of Photogrammetry and Remote Sensing* 53(6):379–391.

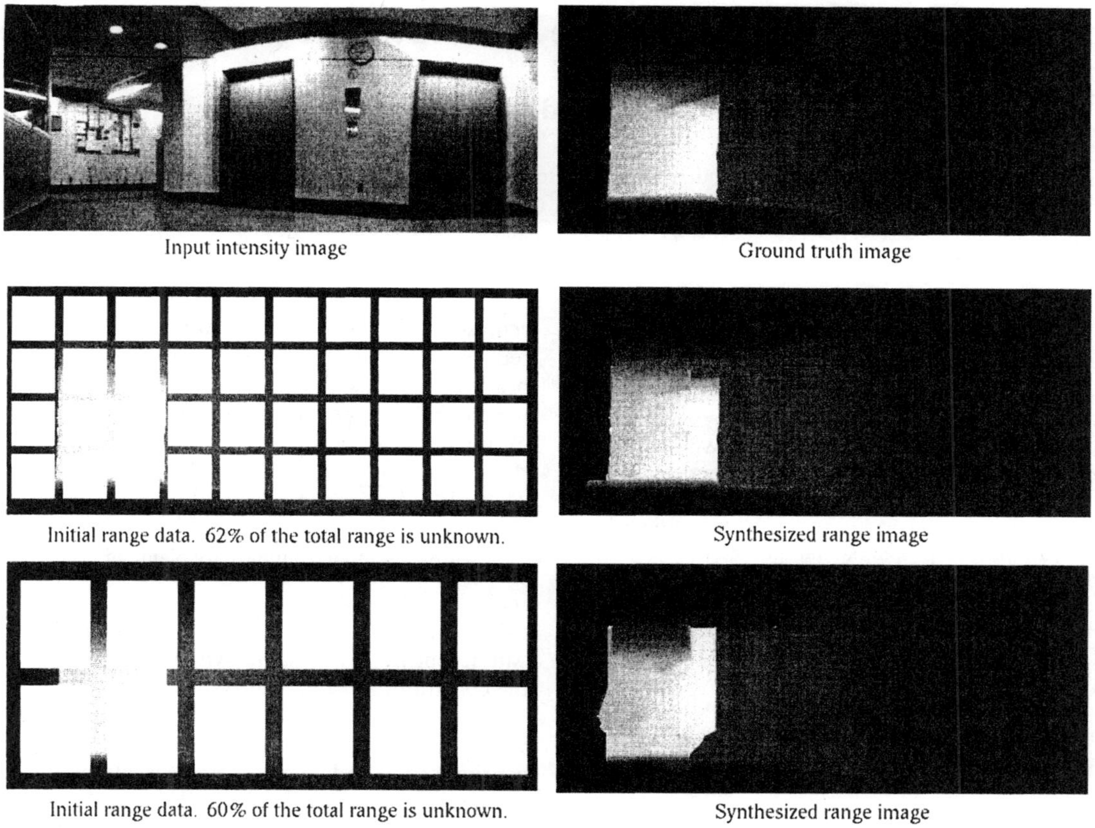


Figure 4: Results on real data collected from our mobile robot.

Fitzgibbon, A., and Zisserman, A. 1998. Automatic 3d model acquisition and generation of new images from video sequences. In *Proceedings of European Signal Processing Conference*, 1261–1269.

Freeman, W.; Pasztor, E.; and Carmichael, O. 2003. Shape recipes: scene representations that refer to the image. *Vision Sciences Society Annual Meeting* 25–47.

Geman, S., and Geman, D. 1984. Stochastic relaxation, gibbs distributions, and the bayesian restoration of images. *IEEE Trans. on PAMI* 6:721–741.

Hertzmann, A.; Jacobs, C.; Oliver, N.; Curless, B.; and Salesin, D. 2001. Images analogies. In *SIGGRAPH*.

Hilton, A. 1996. Reliable surface reconstruction from multiple range images. In *ECCV*.

Horn, B., and Brooks, M. 1989. *Shape from Shading*. MIT Press, Cambridge Mass.

Lee, A.; Pedersen, K.; and Mumford, D. 2001. The complex statistics of high-contrast patches in natural images. private correspondence.

Levoy, M.; Pulli, K.; Curless, B.; Rusinkiewicz, S.; Koller, D.; Pereira, L.; Ginzton, M.; Anderson, S.; Davis, J.; Ginsberg, J.; Shade, J.; and Fulk, D. 2000. The digital michelangelo project: 3d scanning of large statues. In *SIGGRAPH*.

Oliensis, J. 1991. Uniqueness in shape from shading. *Int. Journal of Computer Vision* 6(2):75–104.

Pulli, K.; Cohen, M.; Duchamp, T.; Hoppe, H.; McDonald, J.; Shapiro, L.; and Stuetzle, W. 1997. Surface modeling and display from range and color data. *Lecture Notes in Computer Science 1310* 385–397.

Sequeira, V.; Ng, K.; Wolfart, E.; Goncalves, J.; and Hogg, D. 1999. Automated reconstruction of 3d models from real environments. *ISPRS Journal of Photogrammetry and Remote Sensing* 54:1–22.

Stamos, I., and Allen, P. 2000. 3d model construction using range and image data. In *IEEE CVPR*.

Torralba, A., and Freeman, W. 2003. Properties and applications of shape recipes. In *IEEE CVPR*.

Torres-Méndez, L., and Dudek, G. 2002. Range synthesis for 3d environment modeling. In *IEEE Workshop on Applications of Computer Vision*, 231–236.

Wei, L., and Levoy, M. 2000. Fast texture synthesis using tree-structured vector quantization. In *SIGGRAPH*, 479–488.

# Perceptually Based Learning of Shape Descriptions for Sketch Recognition

**Olya Veselova and Randall Davis**

Microsoft Corporation, One Microsoft Way, Redmond, WA, 98052
MIT CSAIL, 32 Vassar St., Cambridge, MA, 02139
olyav@microsoft.com, davis@ai.mit.edu

**Abstract**

We are interested in enabling a generic sketch recognition system that would allow more natural interaction with design tools in various domains, such as mechanical engineering, military planning, logic design, etc. We would like to teach the system the symbols for a particular domain by simply drawing an example of each one – as easy as it is to teach a person. Studies in cognitive science suggest that, when shown a symbol, people attend preferentially to certain geometric features. Relying on such biases, we built a system capable of learning descriptions of hand-drawn symbols from a single example. The generalization power is derived from a qualitative vocabulary reflecting human perceptual categories and a focus on perceptually relevant global properties of the symbol. Our user study shows that the system agrees with the subjects' majority classification about as often as any individual subject did.

## 1 Introduction

We are interested in creating a generic sketch understanding mechanism that will allow more natural interaction with design tools in a variety of domains (e.g., mechanical engineering, military planning, logic design, etc.). This paper presents a learning system that is part of this larger effort. Our goal is to make teaching the system new shapes as natural as possible, ideally as easy as it is to teach new symbols to another person. Usually it is enough for people to see a symbol once to make a reasonable decision whether new drawings are instances of it, even without knowing its meaning. For example, would you recognize Figure 1b as an instance of the symbol in 1a?

Figure 1. a) Original symbol, b) New drawing.

For most people the answer is "yes" because 1b contains the same features they paid attention to in 1a. And people pay unequal attention to different features, so their recognition is undeterred by the differences between 1a and 1b. This is the goal of any learning system. Common approaches to learning (e.g., neural nets, SVMs) require training on numerous examples of a symbol seeking to "average out" the unimportant differences. We sought a representation and a generalization mechanism that would reduce the number of required training examples, preferably, to as few as one. The difficulty is knowing which features people perceive as relevant in that one example. Consider the symbol in Figure 2a:

Figure 2. Symbol from military planning.

In 2a lines L1, L4 and L5 are the same length. But people mostly notice only the equality of L4 and L5. Hence, they can accept 2b as the same symbol even though it violates the constraint L1=L4. The system's goal is to do the same. We turned to studies of human perception to understand what features people find relevant in a geometrical configuration, and created heuristics attempting to capture these perceptual biases. We used results from Goldmeier's perceptual similarity studies (Goldmeier 1972), Arnheim's book on art and visual perception (Arnheim 1974), and grouping principles described by the gestalt psychologists (Wertheimer 1923). Using these heuristics we built a system capable of learning descriptions of hand-drawn symbols from a single example. The description is phrased in terms of geometric primitives (lines and ovals) and constraints between them (connects, parallel, above, vertical, longer, etc.) The generalization power is derived from a qualitative vocabulary reflecting human perceptual categories and a focus on perceptually relevant global properties of the symbol – tension lines (defined below), obstruction, and grouping. Note that we focus on generalizing over variations that are not due to low-level noise and that would occur even with perfect lines, rectangles, ovals, and snap-to-grid (as in Figures 1 and 2). This alone presents a substantial challenge[1].

The recognition engine that will use our generated descriptions is still under development in our group, so we could not evaluate the final recognition accuracy. Instead, we measured how often our system agreed with people's perceptual judgments on near-perfect drawings. We asked several people to decide whether a given variation should be recognized as an instance of a new unfamiliar symbol and checked whether the description produced by the system would cause the same classification. On the whole



[1] The symbolic descriptions produced by our system will be used in a larger recognition engine with its own mechanism for dealing with low-level noise; see (Alvarado and Davis 2002).

data set, the system agreed with the majority vote 77% of the time. In comparison, a subject chosen randomly would agree with the majority 82% of the time. For cases with strong majority (>80% of the people voted the same) the system achieved 83% agreement (and a random person would get 91%). Section 4 describes the study in detail.

Because of several limitations (section 5) our system can't yet describe the full range of symbols in the domains of interest. We believe our preliminary results still show that using a representation and feature ranking built on knowledge about human perception adds considerable generalization power, allowing learning from one example.

## 2 Related Work

Of the large body of work supporting free-hand sketching, most relevant to this paper are systems attempting to recognize (i.e. give a categorical label to) the input. We are interested in two aspects of these systems: the representation and the learning mechanism. The choice of representation affects the descriptive power and the initial level of generalization. For learning, if the recognizers are trained (rather than created by hand), it is interesting to see what generalization techniques allow some systems to use fewer examples than others.

Some systems, like GRANDMA (Rubine 1991) or CALI (Fonseca, Pimentel, and Jorge 2002) use a set of global aggregate features (sum of angles, or properties of the bounding box, convex hull, etc.) to represent single-stroke gestures or simple shapes, and require over 50 training examples. Using only global features, like the ones in these systems, is not sufficient for capturing the detail of more complex symbols that we are interested in (e.g., Figure 1). Instead we needed to make explicit the properties of the individual parts of the symbol.

In several systems, the representation combines primitive shapes and higher level qualitative spatial relationships between them, similar to the ones in our system (Landay and Meyers 2001), (Gross and Do 2000), (Shilman et al. 2002). However, even if the low level shape recognizers can be trained, there is no mechanism for automatically learning which of the higher level relationships are important. They have to be picked out by the user from a fairly large list recorded by the system. In contrast, we focus on identifying the relevant subset automatically.

GeoRep (Feguson and Forbus 1999) produces descriptions of perfect line drawings in terms of geometric primitives and qualitative spatial relations between them. To generalize, it records only constraints between proximal elements, assuming only those constraints are visually important. Similarly, our system prefers local interactions. However, we found that interaction may be relevant even if two primitives are far away, as long as they are not separated visually by other primitives. We also take into account global alignments and grouping. We show that these are important to better capture perceptual relevancy.

(Calhoun et al. 2002) presents a system that is most similar to ours. It uses a semantic network to represent primitives (lines and arcs) and constraints between them (parallelism; angle between primitives, and intersections with their relative location). The system needs only a few examples to train each recognizer. The training filters out the relationships and properties appearing with low frequency. Different weights are assigned to different kinds of errors for recognition matching, reflecting different perceptual importance. These weights play the same role as the default relevance scores in our system. Yet our system has mechanisms to further adjust these scores, because we observed that the same type of constraint may have different perceptual importance depending on the global configuration of primitives.

In summary, similar to ours, several previous systems have used qualitative constraints for initial generalization. Our contribution is in ranking them and guiding further generalization by including heuristics about perception of the overall configuration of primitives in a symbol.

## 3 Approach

Our goal is to produce a symbolic description of a drawn symbol adequate for recognition, i.e. capturing just the relevant features. The input to the system is the user's strokes, segmented into simple geometric primitives (lines or ovals) (Sezgin, Stahovich, and Davis 2001). The output description includes these primitives and a set of geometric constraints between them. This section shows how the vocabulary of these constraints was determined and how the system decides which of all the constraints to keep. We also illustrate its operation on the symbol below:

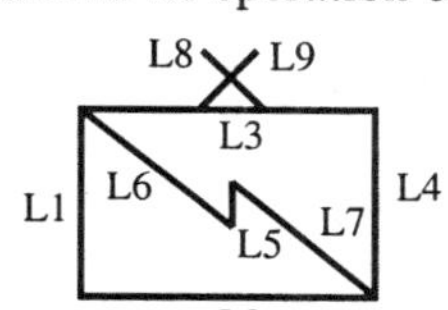


Figure 3. Symbol from military planning.

For this illustrative example, the system has previously learned the descriptions of the cross (L8, L9) and the rectangle (L1-L4), so it can identify them in the drawing.

### 3. 1 Qualitative Vocabulary

We have gained many insights from Goldmeier's work on perceived similarity of shapes (Goldmeier 1972), which shows how people are strongly biased to notice certain geometric properties and ignore others. Goldmeier identifies the relevant and irrelevant features by exploring their effect on perceived similarity. Figure 4 illustrates a typical experiment. Consider the shape in Figure 4a and ask yourself which of 4b and 4c is more similar to 4a.

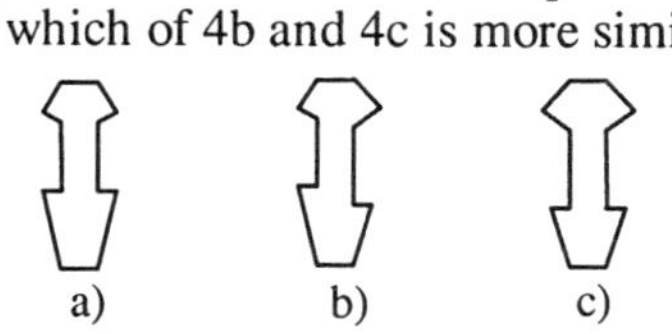


Figure 4. Which of b and c is more similar to a?

The majority of subjects chose c. Note that the left side of b is exactly the same as a. Even though in c all the lengths and angles are slightly changed, it is considered more similar because of preserved symmetry.

Goldmeier found that people attend to properties he calls *singularities*, i.e. special cases in the space of geometric configurations in the sense that small variations in them make a qualitative difference. One example is verticality: a vertical line rotated a little is no longer vertical. Symmetry is another example[1]. Goldmeier also showed that people are much less sensitive to variations in nonsingular properties, perceiving them as essentially the same state (Goldmeier 1982, p. 44). Thus we can reduce the description vocabulary to a few qualitative states that represent singularities and lump non-singular values together. For example, it is enough to describe a line as horizontal, vertical, or positively or negatively sloped.

Goldmeier's work mentions some singularities explicitly, like symmetry, parallelism, horizontality, verticality, and straightness. We have picked the rest of the vocabulary terms using our own introspection and relying on Goldmeier's definition of singularities as the "more regular, better, more unique" (Goldmeier 1982, p. 44), and as properties a change in which significantly alters the perception of the symbol. The table on the right lists the constraints we use.

In an input symbol we find all constraints expressible in this vocabulary, allowing for a small level of noise (like almost vertical or almost connected). For Figure 3, for example, the system identifies 92 constraints (in addition to those in the previously learned cross and rectangle). Sample constraints include: connects (L5 L6), parallel (L6 L8), vertical (L5), and above-centered (L3 L5).

## 3.2 Default Relevance Ranking

A second set of Goldmeier's experiments demonstrates that singular properties can have different perceptual importance, as illustrated below. In both figures, subjects were again asked which of b and c is more similar to a.

a) b) c)

Figure 5. Which of b and c is more similar to a?

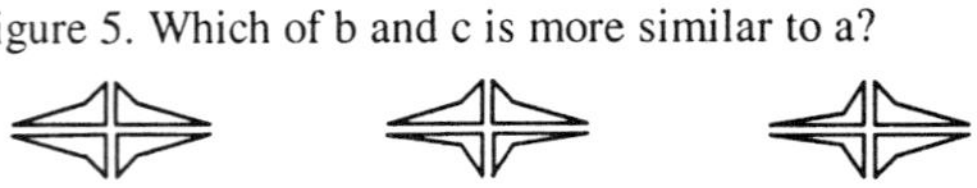

a) b) c)

Figure 6. Which of b and c is more similar to a?

In Figure 5, the majority of subjects chose c, while in Figure 6 the choice was b, even though the shapes in Figure 6 are simply rotated versions of Figure 5. In both cases, the viewers preferred the vertical axis of symmetry.

[1] We do not yet handle symmetry (or any $n$-ary constraints), but we use the example because it illustrates the larger point so simply and convincingly.

Goldmeier presents several similar experiments. However, they are not sufficient, for ranking all the constraints in our system. As a result, we had to use our own introspective analysis to find the relative perceptual importance of different constraints. We examined common symbols in several domains (military planning, mechanical engineering, etc.) and determined which symbol properties allowed the most variation without a large perceptual change to the symbol. The table below shows supported constraints in order of decreasing relevance, with singular constraints shown in bold.

| Constraints | Score |
|---|---|
| **Connects (for line endpoints)** | 1.0 |
| **Meets (i.e. T-intersection), intersects, tangent.** Inside, **inside-centered** | 0.95 |
| **Touches, overlaps (for ovals)** | 0.9 |
| **Horizontal, vertical (for lines)** | 0.8 |
| Pos- and neg-slope; above, below, right, left, upper-right, upper-left, lower-right, lower-left; **above-, and right-centered; parallel, perpendicular** | 0.7 |
| **Horizontal, vertical (for ovals);** elongated, **non-elongated; same-length, same-size** | 0.6 |
| longer, larger | 0.55 |

The scores reflect the default relative relevance, and were chosen to be spread in the upper half of the [0;1] interval. They are adjusted by the mechanisms described below.

## 3.3 Adjusting Relevance Scores

Goldmeier argues that the saliency of a given property depends on the overall configuration of the primitives in a shape. Observations we made in the course of this work helped us create heuristics for adjusting default relevance scores based on three global properties: obstruction, tension lines, and grouping. We describe these heuristics in the order that they are applied by the system.

**Obstruction.** In symbols with many parts attention seems to be focused on local interactions. Consider Figure 7a.

a) b) c)

Figure 7. b and c are parts of the pattern in a.

Figures 7b and 7c are parts of the pattern in 7a, yet the obvious parallelism of the lines in b is not noticeable when looking at a. The lines isolated in c, however, are more obviously parallel even in the original context in a. It is easier to pay attention to the local interaction of the lines in 2b because there are no other lines separating them. We try to approximate this effect by the notion of obstruction, which is measured by the number of geometric primitives between a given pair: $O(p_1, p_2)$. The system decreases the relevance of relative orientation, length, position, and size constraints by $0.15*O(p_1, p_2)*r$, where $r$ is the current relevance score[1]. For Figure 3, for example, this heuristic causes a large decrease of the relevance for the constraints like "parallel (L8 L6)" and "longer (L9 L5)," ensuring the system would accept the variation in Figure 12a.

**Tension Lines.** Arnheim argues in his work that people attend to regular alignments of geometric primitives, particularly horizontal and vertical alignments (Arnheim 1974). In Figure 8a the circle is perceived to be "out of balance," while placing it on one of the dashed lines in 8b would create a more "stable" configuration:

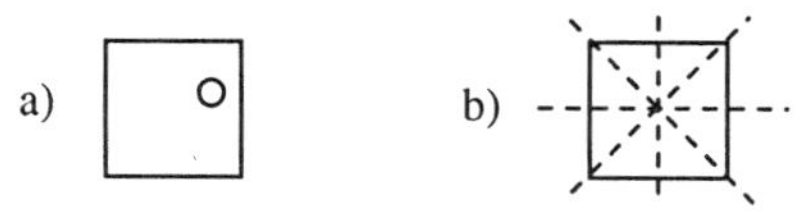


Figure 8. Regular alignments.

The alignments of corners of the square and the centers of its sides form a kind of perceptual grid that other elements are "pulled" toward. In our system, we call these alignments *tension lines*, defined in terms of alignments of line endpoints and midpoints. The system identifies a tension line wherever at least two such line points align horizontally or vertically (we do not yet support diagonal alignments). The system increases by $0.5*(1 - r)$ the current relevance $r$ of relative length, position, and orientation constraints that would break the tension lines if violated. For example, the relevance of the relative vertical positions of the lines L8, L9, L3 and L5 in Figure 3 is increased because their midpoints lie on a vertical tension line. This ensures that the example in Figure 12c would be rejected.
Note that this heuristic boosts some constraints that make parts of the symbol horizontally or vertically symmetrical, thus implicitly helping enforce some symmetry constraints.

**Grouping.** Finally, we also use observations of perceptual bias from the Gestalt psychologists, who noted that people tend to combine individual elements into a greater whole, grouping them by proximity, similarity, etc. (Wertheimer 1923). For example, Figure 9a is perceived as two rows of circles, rather than six individual circles. Properties of a row as a whole are perceptually more important than properties of its components. People do not tend to notice the vertical alignment of the circles in from each of the rows the way we do in Figure 9b.

Figure 9. Perceptual grouping.

The current implementation supports only two grouping principles: connectedness, determined by segmenting the symbol into connected components, and familiarity of shape, determined by looking for previously learned symbols as subparts of the new drawing. Figure 10 gives the group hierarchy for the symbol in Figure 3.

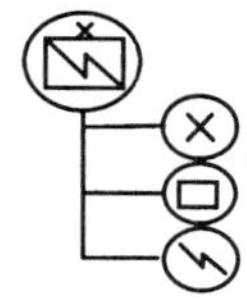

Group g1 connected-component
Group g2 object – cross
Group g3 object – rectangle
Group g4

Figure 10. Group hierarchy of the symbol.

The system decreases the relevance $r$ of relative orientation, length, position, and size constraints between primitives that belong to different groups by subtracting $0.4*r$. For example, it decreased the relevance of "same-length: (L6 L1) (L7 L4)," hence the variation in Figure 12b would be accepted according to the description.
After all the scores have been adjusted, only constraints ranking above 0.5 are included in the final description. For the example symbol, from 92 constraints initially found by the system only 34 remain in the description. Note that the description in Figure 11 refers to the previously learned descriptions for the cross and the rectangle, which are shown in the box.

GROUP HIERARCHY:
Group g1 connected-component: L1-L9
Group g2 object - cross: L9 L8
Group g3 object - rectangle: L1-L4
Group g4: L5 L6 L7

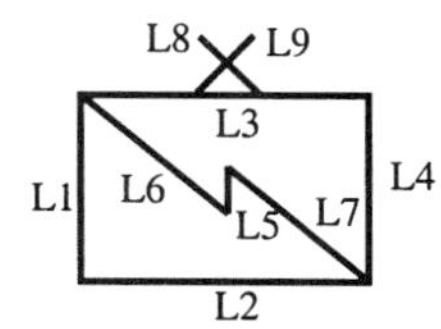


CONSTRAINTS
vertical: (L5)
neg-slope: (L7) (L6)
connects: (L5 L6) (L5 L7) (L4 L7) (L3 L6) (L7 L2) (L6 L1)
meets: (L9 L3) (L8 L3)
above-centered: (L5 L2) (L3 L5) (L9 L2) (L9 L3) (L9 L5) (L8 L2) (L8 L3) (L8 L5)
right-centered: (L5 L1)(L4 L5)
right: (L5 L6) (L7 L5)
upper-right: (L4 L7) (L3 L6) (L7 L2) (L6 L1)
parallel: (L7 L6)
longer: (L3 L6) (L3 L8) (L3 L9) (L2 L7) (L7 L5) (L6 L5)

CROSS:
intersects: (L8 L9)
pos-slope: (L9)
neg-slope: (L8)
same-length: (L8 L9)

RECTANGLE:
horizontal: (L3) (L2)
vertical: (L1) (L4)
above-centered: (L3 L2)
right-centered: (L4 L1)
upper-left: (L1 L2) (L3 L4)
upper-right: (L3 L1)(L4 L2)
same-length:(L3 L2) (L4 L1)
longer: (L2 L4) (L2 L1) (L3 L4) (L3 L1)

Figure 11. Final description for the symbol in Figure 3.

Figures 12 shows the variations that would be accepted and rejected respectively, according to this description:

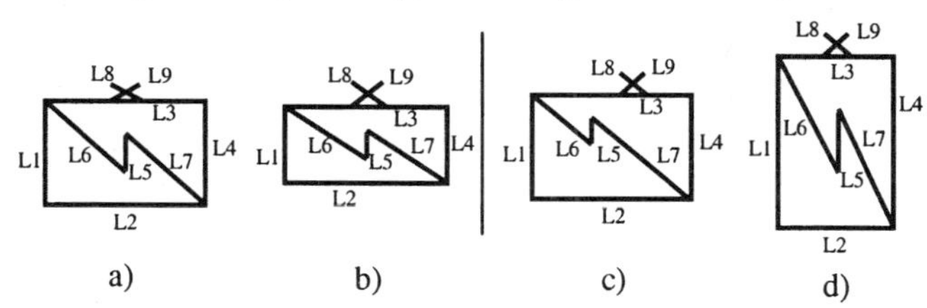


Figure 12. a), b) Variations that fit the system's description. c), d) Variations that contradict the description.

[1] The constants used in this and other formulas were determined empirically by examining resulting descriptions for symbols in various domains.

## 4 User Study and Evaluation

The ideal evaluation of the system would be to use the produced descriptions in a sketch recognition engine and test the recognition accuracy. However, the recognition engine in our group is still under development. As an alternative, we tested whether the system's descriptions would produce the same classifications of shapes as people would.

In our study 33 subjects were shown 9 unfamiliar symbols and 20 variations of each symbol. The variations were constructed using the system's descriptions produced for the 9 symbols by randomly picking a property from the description and varying it randomly to a large or a small degree. Half of the 20 variations were chosen to agree with the description and half contradicted it. This means that the description would cause a recognition engine to recognize half of these variations as the learned symbol. The subjects had to choose whether each variation should be recognized as the original symbol, even though on many examples the choice was somewhat difficult (e.g. like it would be for variations in Figure 12 on the original symbol in Figure 3). We forced a binary choice since ultimately this is the task that the system will have to face. Before voting on each variation, the subjects could look at the original symbol as long as they liked.

Given that our system relies only on geometric information, to ensure parity, we selected symbols from military planning, a domain most likely unfamiliar to the subjects and in which the symbols have little resemblance to the physical objects they stand for, preventing test subjects from relying on knowledge about the things represented (Figure 13).

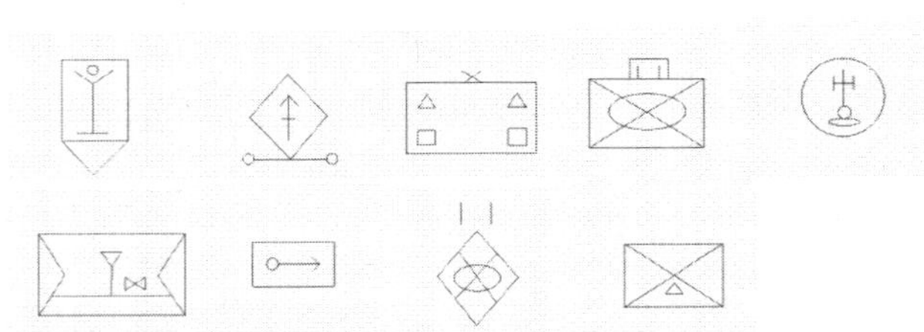

Figure 13. Symbols used for evaluation.

For each variation, we recorded the majority answer and the percentage of people who gave that answer (majority percentage). For almost 40% of the variations the subjects had high agreement – the majority percentage was above 90%. On more than half of data set the majority percentage was higher than 80%. For cases with highly divided opinions, it makes less sense to evaluate the performance of the system (i.e., level of agreement with people) since people did not agree with each other. Hence, we report the results for both the complete data set and for the variations with high agreement (i.e., with majority >= 80% and majority >= 90%).

Chart 1 shows the evaluation results. We measured the proportion of times that the system agreed with the majority answer, reported for different data subsets. For example, for the subset of the variations where the majority percentage exceeded 80%, the system agreed with the majority vote 83% of the time. Note that the baseline performance is 50%: the system would agree with people half of the time if it guessed randomly.

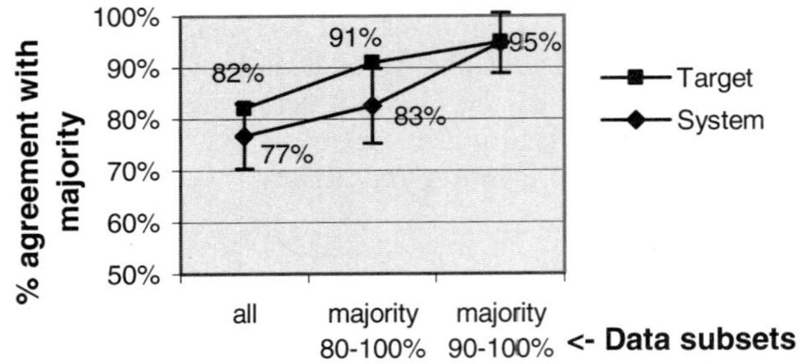


Chart 1. Evaluation results.

The "Target" marker shows the level of agreement that a person randomly selected from the subjects would achieve. Since we have focused on replicating people's perceptual biases, we should not expect the system to do better than this. The results show that system captured enough information about the symbol to perform significantly above chance level and to approach close to the target.

It is interesting to look at the disagreements. Most of the system's errors were false negatives, i.e. the system rejected a variation that most people would still recognize as the symbol. The issue was that people seemed to pay less attention to individual detail (aspect ratio, precise position, etc.) of the composing shapes in the symbol than the system biases accounted for.

Original symbol: Variation:

Majority vote: yes 89%
System: no

Figure 14. Example of a false negative error.

Most false positives stemmed from the lack of global symmetry detection and a lack of apparently perceptually relevant "must not" constraints for properties like touching, connection, or intersection.

Original symbol: Variation:

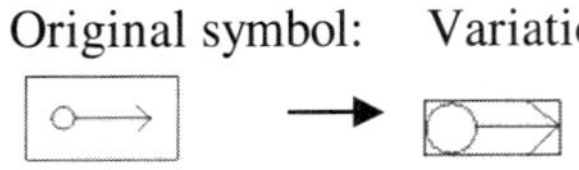

Majority vote: no 72%
System: yes

Figure 15. Example of a false positive error.

## 5 Limitations and Future Work

There are several limitations in the current system. The system currently supports only symbols composed of lines and ovals, and should eventually incorporate arcs and curves. This will require exploring what properties are perceptually salient for arcs and curves.

Our qualitative vocabulary lumps non-singular property values into one term and does not capture extreme degrees. For both a and b in Figure 16, for example, the system would describe the relative size of the circles as "larger o1 o2," making the descriptions identical. But these symbols appear quite different to human observers.

Figure 16. Perceptually different symbols.

As noted, the system doesn't handle "must not" constraints. Perhaps a possible solution is to treat the absence of the most perceptually relevant constraints (connects, touches, meets, etc.) in the description as required must-not's.

The system uses only pairwise constraints. We need to include support for constraints that involve several primitives, like symmetry, interval equality, or alignment of multiple elements. Without them it is impossible to represent configurations like the one in Figure 17.

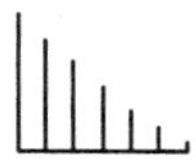

Figure 17. Symbol requiring alignment and interval equality.

The system records a fixed set of geometric primitives, so it is bound to overconstrain symbols that can have an arbitrary number of some elements:

Figure 18. Symbols with an arbitrary number of primitives.

Learning such configurations presents two challenges. The system has to be able to, first, identify a group of repeated components and, second, decide whether an arbitrary number of them was intended. Goldmeier's studies provide some hints on how this may be done. He has shown that when the repeated elements are small compared to the size of the symbol and there is a large number of them, people start perceiving them as material rather than form and become insensitive to the variation in number of such components. The difficult task is defining quantitatively the terms "small relative to the symbol size" and "large number of elements".

While these limitations show that the system is incomplete, the general approach of relying on perceptual biases seems sound, as it suggests potential solutions to some of the limitations.

## 6 Contributions

We have presented a system for learning shape descriptions. It guides the generalization from a single example using built-in knowledge of observations about human perception. The main sources of the generalization power are a qualitative vocabulary reflecting perceptual singularities, different relevance scores for different constraints, and score adjustment heuristics based on perceptually relevant global properties of the symbol.

Our initial implementation shows that it is possible to produce descriptions of structurally complex symbols from a single example. Our user study has shown that the system agreed with the majority perceptual judgment almost as well as a randomly chosen person would.

Future work on the system includes improving its descriptive ability by adding support for curves and parts with an arbitrary number of elements and by extending the vocabulary to support higher-level constraints like symmetry, interval equality, and multiple alignments. We believe that further exploration of perceptual biases may provide clues on how to achieve these extensions.

## 7 Acknowledgements


We thank sponsors of MIT Project Oxygen and Microsoft iCampus Project for funding of this research.


## References


Alvarado, C. and Davis, R. 2002. A Framework for Multi-Domain Sketch Recognition. Proc. of AAAI 2002 Spring Symposium: Sketch Understanding Workshop.

Arnheim, R. 1974. *Art and Visual Perception.* University of California Press.

Calhoun, T. F, Stahovich, T., Kurtoglu, L., and Kara, B., 2002. Recognizing multi-stroke symbols. Proc. of AAAI 2002 Spring Symposium: Sketch Understanding Workshop.

Ferguson, R. W. and Forbus, K. D., 1999. GeoRep: A Flexible Tool for Spatial Representation of Line Drawings. Qualitative Reasoning Workshop.

Fonseca, M. J., Pimentel, C., and Jorge, J. A. 2002. CALI: An Online Recognizer for Calligraphic Interfaces. Proc. of AAAI 2002 Spring Symposium: Sketch Understanding Workshop.

Goldmeier, E., 1972. Similarity in Visually Perceived Forms. *Psychological Issues*, Vol. 8, No. 1.

Goldmeier, E, 1982. *The Memory Trace: its formation and its fate.*

Gross, M. D. and Do, E. Y.-L., 2000. Drawing on the back of an Envelope: a framework for interacting with application programs by freehand drawings. Computers & Graphics 24(6): 835-849.

Landay, J. A. and Meyers, B. A., 2001. Sketching Interfaces: Toward More Human Interface Design. IEEE Computer. 34(3): pp. 56-64.

Rubine, D, 1991. Specifying Gestures by Example. Computer Graphics, Vol. 25, No. 4.

Sezgin, M., Stahovich, T., and Davis, R. 2001. Sketch Based Interfaces: Early Processing for Sketch Understanding. Proceedings of PUI.

Shliman, M., Pasula, H. Russel, S., and Newton, R. 2002. Statistical Visual Language Models for Ink Parsing. Proc. of AAAI 2002 Spring Symposium: Sketch Understanding Workshop.

Wertheimer, M., 1923. Translation in W. D. Ellis (ed.) *A Source Book of Gestalt Psychology.* New York: H. B. J., 1938.

# On the Integration of Grounding Language and Learning Objects

**Chen Yu and Dana H. Ballard**
Department of Computer Science
University of Rochester
Rochester, NY, 14620
{yu,dana}@cs.rochester.edu

**Abstract**

This paper presents a multimodal learning system that can ground spoken names of objects in their physical referents and learn to recognize those objects simultaneously from naturally co-occurring multisensory input. There are two technical problems involved: (1) the correspondence problem in symbol grounding – how to associate words (symbols) with their perceptually grounded meanings from multiple co-occurrences between words and objects in the physical environment. (2) object learning – how to recognize and categorize visual objects. We argue that those two problems can be fundamentally simplified by considering them in a general system and incorporating the spatio-temporal and cross-modal constraints of multimodal data. The system collects egocentric data including image sequences as well as speech while users perform natural tasks. It is able to automatically infer the meanings of object names from vision, and categorize objects based on teaching signals potentially encoded in speech. The experimental results reported in this paper reveal the effectiveness of using multimodal data and integrating heterogeneous techniques in machine learning, natural language processing and computer vision.

## Introduction

Intelligent machines, such as humanoid robots, are expected to be situated in users' everyday environments, communicate with users using natural language and provide services. To achieve this goal, machines must have the same perceptual and cognitive abilities as humans, such as visual object recognition and language understanding. However, sensory perception and knowledge acquisition of machines are quite different from those of human counterparts. The first difference is about *what* to learn. Machine learning is most often disembodied and focuses on manipulating symbols intelligently, but humans develop and learn based on their sensorimotor experiences with the physical environment. To mimic human perceptual abilities and ultimately build artificial embodied systems, a challenge in machine intelligence is how to establish a correspondence between internal symbolic representations and external sensory data, which is termed as the symbol grounding problem by Harnad (1990).



The second difference lies in *how* to learn. Researchers have tried different approaches to building intelligent machines (see a review in Weng *et al.*,2001). A knowledge-based system uses logic rules to represent the knowledge acquired from human experts and perform inference. A learning-based approach applies probabilistic models and then uses "spoon-fed" human-labeled sensory data to train the parameters of those models. In this way, the machine acquires some basic perceptual abilities, such as speech recognition (converting speech to text) and object recognition (converting visual signals into pre-defined labels). A relatively new approach termed *autonomous development* is proposed by several scientists in different fields (Weng *et al.* 2001). In this approach, a brain-like artificial embodied system develops based on real-time interactions with the environments by using multiple sensors and effectors. Although this approach shares many computational techniques with the learning-based one, these two are fundamentally different. In autonomous development, the machine continuously develops and learns to simulate the lifelong process of development and learning in humans (Thrun & Mitchell 1995). Thus, it does not need human involvement for segmenting and labeling data during the learning process. In contrast, most learning-based systems apply one-time training on labeled data and are not able to acquire any new capabilities after the training phase.

We report here on the first steps toward autonomous development and learning while focusing on grounding spoken language in sensory perception. People use words to refer to objects in the physical environment. To communicate with users and provide helps, a computational system also needs to know how to categorize instances of objects (visual object recognition) as well as map objects to linguistic labels. Despite intensive research in computer vision, the first problem is still an open issue due to practical reasons, such as the variations in lighting conditions in the environment. The second problem, termed *reference uncertainty* (Quine 1960), deals with finding the correspondence between words and perceptually grounded meanings from multiple co-occurrences of words and objects in a natural environment. To tackle these two problems, we develop a multimodal learning system that is situated in users' everyday environments wherein users introduce several objects to machines using natural language just like teaching their children or familiarizing newcomers with the environment. The system collects user-centric multisensory input consisting of visual and speech data, and automatically learns to build a word-world mapping in an unsupervised manner without human involvement. In addition, the system also learns to categorize objects based on the corresponding linguistic labels in speech.

## Related Work

The symbol grounding problem has been studied in the context of language acquisition in a number of recent works. The algorithm in Siskind (1995) was based on cross-situational learning and can successfully recognize various event types described by predicate logic. Regier (1996) proposed a connectionist system encoding domain-motivated structure, which was able to learn the meanings of prepositions (e.g., above, in, on and through). Steels & Vogt (1997) reported the experiments in which autonomous visually grounded agents bootstrap meanings and language through adaptive language games. They argued that language is an autonomous evolving adaptive system maintained by a group of distributed agents without central control and a lexicon may adapt to cope with new meanings that arise. Cohen *et al.* (2002) demonstrated that a robot can learn the denotational meanings of words from sensory data. Roy & Pentland (2002) used the correlation of speech and vision to associate spoken utterances with a corresponding object's visual appearance. The learning algorithm was based on cross-modal mutual information to discover words and their visual associations.

A relatively new topic termed anchoring (Coradeschi & Saffiotti 2003a) concerns grounding object names in sensory data and maintaining the word-world mapping to take into account the dynamic changes of sensory input. Different from the symbol grounding problem that aims at considering all kinds of symbols, anchoring focuses on a practical problem of connecting object names with visual objects in a physical environment. The recent progresses in anchoring can be found in the special issue of Robotics and Autonomous Systems on perceptual anchoring (Coradeschi & Saffiotti 2003b).

## System Overview

Figure 1 shows an overview of our system. The multisensory input consists of image sequences, each of which contains several objects in the scene, and speech that contains spoken names of objects. To achieve the goal of grounding object names and learning to categorize visual objects simultaneously, the system consists of the following three modules:

- **Natural language processing** first converts acoustic signals into transcripts, and then extracts a list of object name candidates using syntactic and semantic constraints.
- **Visual processing** detects scene changes in the video captured from a head-mounted camera. It then finds the objects from the scene. Next, visual features are extracted from objects and those perceptual representations are labeled with temporally co-occurring object name candidates to form many-to-many word-meaning pairs.
- **Multimodal integration** is the crucial step in which information from different modalities is integrated to discover word-object correspondences. In addition, linguistic information provides teaching signals to guide the grouping of visual features in their space. As a result, the system obtains not only a mapping of words to their grounded meanings extracted from visual perception, but also a better categorization of visual objects compared with unimodal clustering purely based on visual features.

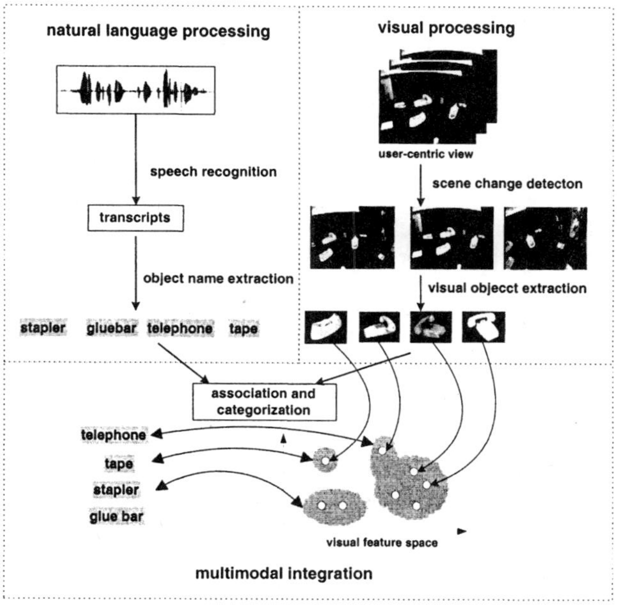


Figure 1: **Overview of the system.** Speech processing provides object name candidates based on speech recognition and natural language processing. Visual processing obtains a set of visual objects. The system associates object names with their visually grounded meanings and uses these linguistic labels to guide the categorization of objects in the visual feature space.

The following sections provide technical descriptions of the design and implementation of those subsystems in detail. The overall system is evaluated using the data that is collected when users perform natural tasks in everyday scenarios. The experimental setup is described and results are discussed.

## Natural Language Processing

Object name candidates are extracted from speech using lexical and grammatical analysis shown in Figure 2. First, the "Dragon Naturally Speaking" software is utilized for speech recognition. Given a spoken utterance consisting of several spoken words, the speech recognizer converts the continuous wave pattern into a series of recognized words by considering phonetic likelihoods and grammars. In practice, the recognition rate is above 90% in our experiments. We then extract the nouns from transcripts, which will be used as object name candidates. To do so, we first use the Link Grammar Parser (Sleator & Temperley 1993), a syntactic parser, to assign an input sentence with a syntactic structure consisting of a set of labeled links. The parser also labels the syntactic categories of the words in the sentence if they belong to nouns, verbs, or adjectives in the dictionary used by the parser. In this way, we discover a list of nouns from each sentence. Next, we apply two filters to get object name candidates as follows:

- The Oxford text archive text710 dictionary (Mitton 1992), which includes more than 70,000 words, is applied to spot proper nouns. A word is selected to be a name candidate if it is annotated as a countable noun or both countable and uncountable nouns in the dictionary.
- The WordNet (Fellbaum 1998), an electronic lexical database, is used to obtain underlying lexical concepts of candidate nouns. The system selects the nouns that belong to "physical object" or "entity".

The final list of object name candidates contains the words that satisfy both constraints.

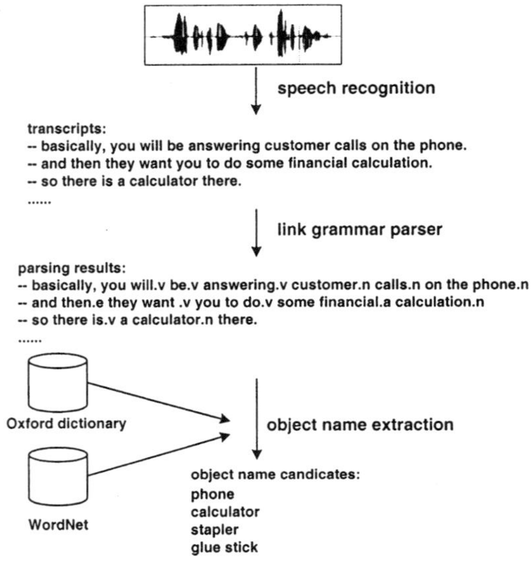


Figure 2: The acoustic signals are first converted into text. We then use syntactic and semantic constraints to obtain a list of object name candidates.

## Object Detection and Description

Image sequences are captured from a head-mounted camera to get a dynamic view of a speaker. We use a position sensor to track the motion of the speaker's head. At every time point that the head is stable, we capture a snapshot of the scene and label it with temporally co-occurring spoken utterances. One of the most challenges in computer vision is the segmentation of objects in a natural scene. This issue is easily handled in our experiment in which images have a simple uniform background. Figure 3 shows a sample of snapshot and the result of object segmentation using the method described in (Comanicu & Meer 2002). Next, each extracted object is represented by features including color, shape and texture properties. Based on the work of Mel (1997), we construct visual features of objects which are large in number, invariant to different viewpoints, and driven by multiple visual cues. Specifically, 64-dimensional color features are extracted by a color indexing method (Swain & Ballard 1991), and 48-dimensional shape features are represented by calculating histograms of local shape properties (Schiele & Crowley 2000). The Gabor filters with three scales and five orientations are applied to the segmented image. It is assumed that local texture regions are spatially homogeneous, and the mean and the standard deviation of the magnitude of the transform coefficients are used to represent an object in a 48-dimensional texture feature vector. The feature representations consisting of a total of 160 dimensions are formed by combining color, shape and texture features, which provide fundamental advantages for fast, inexpensive recognition. Most pattern recognition algorithms, however, do not work efficiently in high dimensional spaces because of the inherent sparsity of the data. This problem has been traditionally referred to as the dimensionality curse. In our system, we reduced the 160-dimensional feature vectors into 15-dimensional vectors by principle component analysis (PCA), which transforms the data in a lower dimensional subspace that contains as much of the variance in the data as possible.

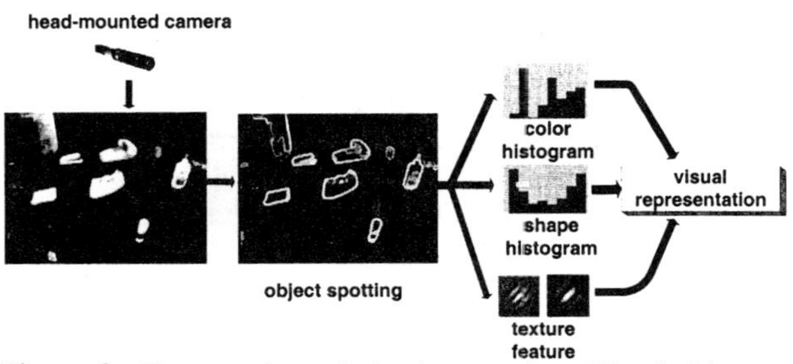


Figure 3: The overview of visual processing. Visual objects are segmented from the background scene and then multiple features are extracted to form perceptual representations.

## Generative Correspondence Model

Now we have object name candidates from the audio stream and perceptual representations of objects in the visual stream, which form many-to-many co-occurring word-meaning pairs shown in Figure 4. Machine learning techniques have been widely applied to process multimodal data. Most works focus on either the correspondence problem or the clustering problem. The correspondence problem deals with building a map between items from acoustic and visual data. In Duygulu *et al.* (2002), images were segmented into regions that are then classified into region types. A mapping between region types and the keywords in captions supplied with the images was then learned using a method based on machine translation. Wachsmuth & Sagerer (2002) used Bayesian networks to relate verbal and visual descriptions of the same object. Satoh *et al.* (1997) developed a mathematical description of co-occurrence measurement to associate names with faces that appear in televised news reports.

The multimodal clustering problem studies the influence of the data in one modality on another one based on the assumption that multisensory input is perfectly synchronized in time. de Sa & Ballard (1998) related this idea mathematically to the optimal goal of minimizing the number of misclassifications in each modality and applied it to derive an algorithm for two piecewise linear classifiers, in which one uses the output of the other as supervisory signals. Hofmann & Puzicha (1998) proposed several statistical models for analyzing the data that are joint occurrences of pairs of abstract objects from two finite sets.

Different from previous studies, we consider the correspondence and the clustering problems simultaneously. To build explicit correspondences between visual objects and words, we take a view of the data in term of a generative process. It first generates a latent variable, and then visual objects are generated based on the latent variable. Finally, words are generated conditioned on visual objects. This is because verbal descriptions are produced based on visual objects in the scene.

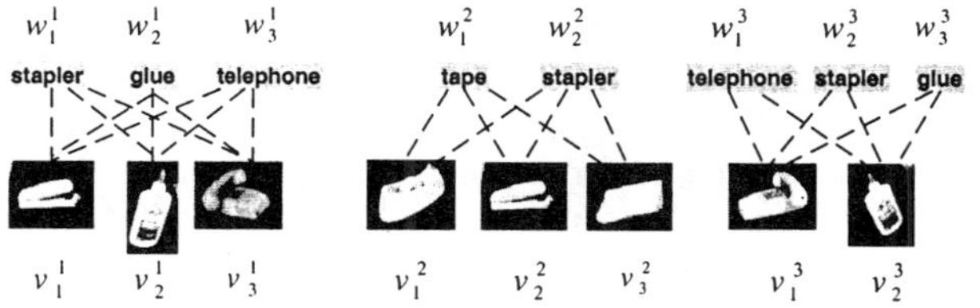


Figure 4: **Word learning.** The object name candidates in speech and co-occurring perceptual representations of objects are temporally associated to build possible lexical items.

Formally, we collect multiple pairs of co-occurring speech and visual data that can be represented by a set $S = \{S_1, S_2, ..., S_L\}$. Each $S_i (1 \leq i \leq L)$ consists of several linguistic items and visual features $\{w_1^i, w_2^i, ..., w_{m_i}^i, v_1^i, v_2^i, ..., v_{n_i}^i\}$, where $w_{m_i}^i$ represents a spoken word and $v_{n_i}^i$ is a visual feature vector extracted from an object's appearance. Given the data $S$, we need to maximize the log-likelihood expressed as follows:

$$\log P(S) \quad = \quad \sum_{i=1}^{L} \log P(S_i)$$

where

$$logP(S_i) \quad = \quad logP(w_1^i, w_2^i, ..., w_{m_i}^i, v_1^i, v_2^i, ..., v_{n_i}^i)$$
$$\approx \quad \log \prod_{n=1}^{n_i} p(v_n^i) \prod_{m=1}^{m_i} \sum_{n=1}^{n_i} p(w_m^i | v_n^i)$$

Two assumptions are made here. The first is that each individual object in a scene is generated independently. The second one claims that the influence of each object on a word is independent. Thus, the generative probability of a word given a visual scene equals to the sum of the condition probabilities of the word given each individual object in the scene. Now let us assume that the visual data is generated by a mixture model that consists of $K$ components. Specifically, a visual feature is generated by first selecting a mixture component according to the mixture weights $p(\alpha)$ (class prior probabilities), then having this selected mixture component to generate the visual feature according to its own parameters with the distribution $p(v_n^i|\alpha)$. In addition, we assume that $v_n^i$ and $w_m^i$ are independent given the latent label $\alpha$. Based on that, the log-likelihood can be expressed as:

$$\log \prod_{n=1}^{n_i} p(v_n^i) + \log \prod_{m=1}^{m_i} \sum_{n=1}^{n_i} \sum_{\alpha=1}^{K} p(w_m^i|\alpha) p(\alpha|v_n^i) \qquad (1)$$

To overcome the difficulties in maximizing a log of a sum, we introduce a set of latent variables and use the Expectation-Maximization (EM) algorithm (Dempster, Laird, & Rubin 1977) that will iteratively increase the likelihood and make it converge to a local maximum.

Let $R_{n\alpha}^i$ be an indicator variable to represent the unknown class $\alpha$ from which the observation $v_n^i$ is generated. A set of latent labels form a Boolean matrix $\{R_{n\alpha}^i\}_{n_i \times K}$ where $\sum_{\alpha=1}^{K} R_{n\alpha}^i = 1$, which indicates that only one item in each row is 1 and all others are 0. In this way, latent variables partition the visual data into $K$ clusters and can treated as additional unobserved data. We also need to introduce the other set of latent labels $\{Z^1, Z^2, ..., Z^L\}$, each of which is a Boolean matrix $\{Z_{nm}^i\}_{n_i \times m_i}$ indicating whether a word is generated by a specific visual feature in $i$th data pair with the constraint $\sum_{n=1}^{n_i} Z_{nm}^i = 1$. By treating $R$ and $Z$ as additional unobserved data, the complete data of the second item in Equation 1 is given by:

$$\sum_{m=1}^{m_i} \sum_{n=1}^{n_i} Z_{nm}^i \sum_{\alpha=1}^{K} R_{n\alpha}^i \log(p(w_m^i|\alpha) p(v_n^i|\alpha) p(\alpha))$$

As a result of introducing new latent variables, we decouple the parameters we want to estimate. In the E-step, the expected values of the posterior probabilities of $R_{n\alpha}^i$ and $Z_{nm}^i$ can be estimated as follows:

$$R_{n\alpha}^i = \frac{p(v_n^i|\alpha)p(\alpha)}{\sum_{k=1}^{K} p(v_n^i|k)p(k)} \qquad Z_{nm}^i = \frac{p(v_n^i|w_m^i)}{\sum_{\gamma=1}^{n_i} p(v_\gamma^i|w_m^i)} \qquad (2)$$

In the M-step, we calculate the derivative of Equation 1 using the estimated hidden variables and adding the normalization constraints by Lagrange multipliers. The class prior probability becomes as follow:

$$p(\alpha) = \frac{\sum_{i=1}^{L} \sum_{n=1}^{n_i} R_{n\alpha}^i (\sum_{m=1}^{m_i} Z_{nm}^i + 1)}{\sum_{k=1}^{K} \sum_{i=1}^{L} \sum_{n=1}^{n_i} R_{nk}^i (\sum_{m=1}^{m_i} Z_{nm}^i + 1)} \qquad (3)$$

For $p(v_n^i|\alpha)$, we use multidimensional Gaussian distributions over a number of visual features. We also assume the independence of the features and then enforce a block diagonal structure for the covariance matrix to capture the most important dependencies. Then the estimates of new parameters are as follows:

$$m_\alpha \quad = \quad \frac{\sum_{i=1}^{L} \sum_{n=1}^{n_i} R_{n\alpha}^i (\sum_{m=1}^{m_i} Z_{nm}^i + 1) v_n^i}{\sum_{i=1}^{L} \sum_{n=1}^{n_i} R_{n\alpha}^i (\sum_{m=1}^{m_i} Z_{nm}^i + 1)} \qquad (4)$$

$$\sigma_\alpha^2 \quad = \quad \frac{\sum_{i=1}^{L} \sum_{n=1}^{n_i} R_{n\alpha}^i (\sum_{m=1}^{m_i} Z_{nm}^i + 1)(v_n^i - m_\alpha)^2}{\sum_{i=1}^{L} \sum_{n=1}^{n_i} R_{n\alpha}^i (\sum_{m=1}^{m_i} Z_{nm}^i + 1)}$$

For linguistic data, $p(\alpha|w_m^i)$ is given by:

$$p(w_m^i|\alpha) = \frac{\sum_{i=1}^{L} \sum_{j=1}^{m_i} \sum_{n=1}^{n_i} Z_{nm}^i R_{n\alpha}^i \delta(w_m^i, w_j^i)}{\sum_{k=1}^{K} \sum_{i=1}^{L} \sum_{j=1}^{m_i} \sum_{n=1}^{n_i} Z_{nm}^i R_{nk}^i \delta(w_m^i, w_j^i)} \qquad (5)$$

where $\delta$ is the Kronecker delta function that equals to one if two arguments are the same or zero otherwise. $p(\alpha|w^i_m)$ indicates the probability of the word $w^i_m$ generated by the component $\alpha$. In the initialization, we use k-mean to cluster visual features and each cluster is assigned to one Gaussian. The mean and variance were computed based on the clustering results as well as the initial $R^i_{n\alpha}$. In addition, we calculate the co-occurrence of visual clusters and words and set the initial values of $Z^i_{nm}$. Then the EM-based algorithm performs the E-step and the M-step successively until convergence. In E-step, we compute the parameters of $p(v^i_n|\alpha)$ and $p(w^i_m|\alpha)$ by Equation (4) and (5). In M-step, we reestimate $R^i_{n\alpha}$ and $Z^i_{nm}$ using Equation (2).

## Experiment

Nine users participated in the experiments. They wore a head-mounted CCD camera to capture a first-person point of view. Visual data were collected at the resolution of 320 columns by 240 rows of pixels. Acoustic signals were recorded using a headset microphone at a rate of 22 kHz with 16-bit resolution. A Polhemus 3D tracker was utilized to acquire 6-DOF head positions at $40Hz$ to detect scene change. Users were seated at a desk on which there were nine office objects shown in Figure 3. They were given two tasks of introducing those objects to a newcomer (e.g. a human agent or a service robot recently purchased): (1) what are those objects and where are they located. (2) how to use those objects to accomplish the office task of writing down phone orders and maintaining purchasing records. They were asked to perform each task three times. Table 1 shows sample transcripts of these two tasks. Before the start of each trial, we randomly arranged the positions of objects and rotated them by $20^o$ to obtain images containing different sets of objects from different views. The system collected audio-visual pairs consisting of verbal descriptions and image sequences. The average length of the first task was 129 seconds and the second task was 186 seconds. The data collected from the first task formed Dataset 1 and Dataset 2 was made up of the data collected from the second task.

| Task 1<br>– I see on the table a glue stick.<br>– then in the front of me is a pink pencil sharpener.<br>that you can use to shape the pencil.<br>– in the back is a white stapler that is used to<br>put pieces of paper together.<br>...... |
|---|
| Task 2<br>– welcome to your first day of work.<br>– this is your desk and your job is to answer the phone<br>and take the orders.<br>– when taking orders over the phone, you write it down<br>on the pad of paper over there.<br>...... |

Table 1: Examples of natural descriptions

After learning, the system obtained grounded lexical items including the clusters of visual objects with their corresponding linguistic labels. To evaluate experimental results, we defined the following two measures for symbol grounding: (1) **symbol grounding accuracy** measures the percentage of the perceptual representations of objects which are correctly associated with linguistic labels. (2) **symbol spotting accuracy** measures the percentage of word-object pairs that are spotted by the computational system. This measure provides a quantitative indication about the percentage of grounded lexical items that can be successfully found. Table 2 shows the results of symbol grounding.

| | Dataset 1 | Dataset 2 |
|---|---|---|
| symbol grounding | 83.6% | 86.2% |
| symbol spotting | 81.9% | 82.5% |

Table 2: Results of symbol grounding

To evaluate the performance of categorizing visual objects, we compared our multimodal learning algorithm with several unimodal supervised and unsupervised methods that we ran on the same data set. The experiments were conducted using visual-only and audio-visual multimodal categorizations. For visual features, the clustering method based on Gaussian Mixture Model (GMM) was run which gave average accuracy of 66%. Moreover, Support Vector Machine (SVM) (Burges 1998) and Self-Organizing Map (SOM)(Vesanto & Alhoniemi 2000) were applied to visual data as supervised classification methods. Table 3 shows the comparison of all those methods. As we can see, the multimodal learning method yielded significantly better results than the performances achieved by the unsupervised learning methods. Moreover, the results showed that only using the multimodal information co-occurring in the environment is enough to give the categorization accuracy better than that of supervised SOM and within 7% of supervised SVM results. Considering the fact that our method deals with the correspondence and clustering problems simultaneously, these results are impressive. Note that the supervised methods provide benchmarks for evaluation and comparison, and we understand that more advanced classification methods could achieve better results for the same data set. However, the purpose of the experiments is to demonstrate the role of co-occurring data from multiple modalities in multimodal clustering. Specifically, we are interested in the possible improvement of performance in a fully unsupervised way by integrating more information at the sensory level. The limitation of this method is that a visual object and the corresponding spoken name are supposed to share the same latent node. Since some spoken words do not have visual correspondences, the algorithm tries to distribute them into several other nodes, which biases the estimates of parameters of those nodes. Thus, the algorithm has to fit some irrelevant data in this uniform structure.

## Conclusion

This paper presents a multimodal learning system that is able to not only ground spoken names of objects in visual perception but also learn to categorize visual objects using teaching

| | Dataset 1 | Dataset 2 |
|---|---|---|
| SOM (supervised) | 68.9% | 69.6% |
| SVM (supervised) | 85.5% | 87.2% |
| GMM (unsupervised) | 67.3% | 65.2% |
| multimodal | 79.9% | 80.9% |

Table 3: Results of categorization of visual objects

signals encoded in co-occurring speech. Our main motivation is to endow an autonomous system with the learning ability by being situated in user's everyday environments and processing multisensory data in an unsupervised mode.

The principal technical contribution of this paper is to explore the possibility of utilizing the spatio-temporal and cross-modal constraints of unlabeled multimodal data in the symbol grounding and clustering problems. Clustering is a descriptive task that seeks to identify homogeneous groups of objects based on the values of their attributes, which could be very difficult in dealing with sensory data. We show that the unimodal clustering problem can be fundamentally simplified by incorporating cross-modal cues. Also, we show that the EM algorithm extends readily to multimodal classification and that, importantly, the parametric forms of the individual modalities can be arbitrarily different in a general framework. Although the experiments reported in this paper focus on processing audio-visual data to ground language in visual perception, both the general principle and the specific algorithm are applicable to various applications in autonomous robot, multimodal interface, wearable computing, and multimedia index.

## References


Burges, C. J. C. 1998. A tutorial on support vector machines for pattern recognition. *Data Mining and Knowledge Discovery* 2(2).

Cohen, P. R.; Oates, T.; Beal, C. R.; and Adams, N. M. 2002. Contentful mental states for robot baby. In *Eighteenth national conference on Artificial intelligence*, 126–131.

Comanicu, D., and Meer, P. 2002. Mean shift: A robust approach toward feature space analysis. *IEEE Trans. Pattern Analysis Machine Intelligence* 24:603–619.

Coradeschi, S., and Saffiotti, A. 2003a. An introduction to the anchoring problem. *Robotics and Autonomous Systems* 43(2-3):85–96.

Coradeschi, S., and Saffiotti, A., eds. 2003b. *the special isssue on perceptual anchoring*, volume 42.

de Sa, V. R., and Ballard, D. 1998. Category learning through multimodality sensing. *Neural Computation* 10:1097–1117.

Dempster, A. P.; Laird, N. M.; and Rubin, D. B. 1977. Maximum likelihood from incomplete data via the em algorithm. *Journal of the Royal Statistical Society* 39(1):1–38.

Duygulu, P.; Barnad, K.; de Freitas, J.; and Forsyth, D. 2002. Object recognition as machine translation: learning a lexicon for a fixed image vocabulary. In *Proceedings of European Conference on Computer Vision*. Copenhagen: Springer.

Fellbaum, C., ed. 1998. *WordNet An Electronic Lexical Database*. MIT Press.

Harnad, S. 1990. The symbol grounding problem. *physica D* 42:335–346.

Hofmann, T., and Puzicha, J. 1998. Statistical models for co-occurrence data. Technical Report AI Memo 1625, Artificial Intelligence Laboratory, MIT.

Mel, B. W. 1997. Seemore: Combining color, shape, and texture histogramming in a neurally inspired approach to visual object recognition. *Neural Computation* 9:777–804.

Mitton, R. 1992. A computer-readable dictionary file based on the oxford advanced learner's dictionary of current english.

Quine, W. 1960. *Word and object*. Cambridge, MA: MIT Press.

Regier, T. 1996. *The Human Semantic Potential: Spatial Language and Constrained Connectionism*. MA: MIT Press.

Roy, D., and Pentland, A. 2002. Learning words from sights and sounds: A computational model. *Cognitive Science* 26(1):113–146.

Satoh, S.; Nakamura, Y.; ; and Kanade, T. 1997. Name-it: Naming and detecting faces in video by the integration of image and natural language processing. In *Proc. IJCAI'97*, 1488–1493.

Schiele, B., and Crowley, J. L. 2000. Recognition without correspondence using multidimensional receptive field histograms. *International Journal of Computer Vision* 36(1):31–50.

Siskind, J. M. 1995. Grounding language in perception. *artificial Intelligence Review* 8:371–391.

Sleator, D., and Temperley, D. 1993. Parsing english with a link grammar. In *Third International Workshop on Parsing Technologies*.

Steels, L., and Vogt, P. 1997. Grounding adaptive language game in robotic agents. In Husbands, C., and Harvey, I., eds., *Proc. of the 4th European Conference on Artificial Life*. London: MIT Press.

Swain, M. J., and Ballard, D. 1991. Color indexing. *International Journal of Computer Vision* 7:11–32.

Thrun, S., and Mitchell, T. 1995. Lifelong robot learning. *Robotics and Autonomous Systems* 15:25–46.

Vesanto, J., and Alhoniemi, E. 2000. Clustering of the self-organizing map. *IEEE Transactions in Neural Networks* 11(3):586–600.

Wachsmuth, S., and Sagerer, G. 2002. Bayesian Networks for Speech and Image Integration. In *Proc. of 18th National Conf. on Artificial Intelligence (AAAI-2002)*, 300–306.

Weng, J.; McClelland, J.; Pentland, A.; Sporns, O.; Stockman, I.; Sur, M.; and Thelen, E. 2001. Artificial intelligence: Autonomous mental development by robots and animals. *Science* 291(5504):599–600.

# Planning and Scheduling

# Generating Safe Assumption-Based Plans for Partially Observable, Nondeterministic Domains

**Alexandre Albore, Piergiorgio Bertoli**
ITC-IRST
Via Sommarive 18, 38050 Povo, Trento, Italy
{albore,bertoli}@irst.itc.it

### Abstract

Reactive planning using assumptions is a well-known approach to tackle complex planning problems for nondeterministic, partially observable domains. However, assumptions may be wrong; this may cause an assumption-based plan to fail. In general, it is not possible to decide at runtime whether an assumption has failed and is putting at danger the success of the plan; thus, plan execution has to be controlled taking into account every possible success-endangering assumption failure. The possibility of tracing such failures strongly depends on the actions performed by the plan. In this paper, focusing on a simple assumption language, we provide two main contributions. First, we formally characterize *safe* assumption-based plans, i.e. plans that not only succeed whenever the assumption holds, but also guarantee that any success-endangering assumption failure is traced by a suitable monitor. In this way, replanning may be triggered only when actually needed. Second, we extend the planner in a reactive platform in order to produce safe assumption-based plans. We experimentally show that safe assumption-based (re)planning is a good alternative to its unsafe counterpart, minimizing the need for replanning while retaining the efficiency in plan generation.

## Introduction

Planning for realistic domains, featuring nondeterministic action outcomes, initial state uncertainty and partial observability, is a very complex task. Using assumptions to restrict plan search in a reactive setting is a well-known approach to practically alleviate the complexity of the problem, allowing considerable scale-ups. However, assumptions taken during plan generation may turn out to be incorrect at plan execution time; if this event is not properly detected, an assumption-based plan may lead to an undesired state, or produce non-executable actions. Reactive architectures such as (Muscettola *et al.* 1998; Myers & Wilkins 1998; Singh *et al.* 2000) exploit monitoring components to trace the status of the domain; however, in general, due to the incomplete runtime knowledge on the domain state, it is not possible to decide whether an assumption is correct or not, and replanning must take place whenever a dangerous condition may have been reached because the assumption *might* be incorrect. When the assumption is actually correct, or it fails in a way not affecting the success of the plan, these replanning episodes are unnecessary and undesired; they could be avoided by faithfully tracing success-endangering assumption failures. Whether this is possible also depends on the actions performed by the plan. The plan generation components in current reactive systems, however, do not take into account such traceability issues; as a consequence, unnecessary replanning may occur, unless restricting to consider specific domains and assumptions that are "easily monitorizable" (see e.g. (Koenig & Smirnov 1997)).

In this paper we provide two main contributions. First, we formally define *safe* assumption-based plans, i.e. plans which not only reach the goal if the assumption holds, but also guarantee that any success-endangering assumption failure is traced, by performing actions that help the monitor inspect the domain status. Second, we implement a reactive planner exploiting safe assumption-based plan generation, extending the MBP planner inside the SYPEM platform (Bertoli, Cimatti, & Traverso 2003) .

Our experiments show that safe assumption-based (re)planning is a convenient alternative to its unsafe counterpart. It introduces no major overhead at plan generation time, thus retaining the benefit of assumption-based plan generation w.r.t. strong contingency planning, and minimizes the amount of needed replanning.

We first introduce some notation, and define the main components of our planning architecture. Then we define conditions establishing whether a plan is safe, and embed them in a forward chaining planning algorithm. We present an experimental analysis, and wrap up with conclusions and future work.

## Notation

We use the standard notation $\{x_1, \ldots, x_n\}$ for a set whose elements are $x_1, \ldots, x_n$. We indicate tuples with brackets, e.g. $\langle x, y\rangle$, and sequences with square brackets, e.g. $[x_1, \ldots, x_n]$. Sequences will be also indicated by overlines, e.g. $\overline{o}$ is a sequence; its length is $len(\overline{o})$. The n-th element of a sequence $\overline{o}$ is indicated with $\overline{o}^{(n)}$. Two sequences $\overline{o_1}$, $\overline{o_2}$ can be concatenated, written $\overline{o_1} \circ \overline{o_2}$.

## The Framework

In this work, we refer to a reactive architecture which exploits assumptions, coming e.g. from a database, see Fig. 1. At plan generation, assumptions are used to restrict the search that generates a plan that controls the domain. The domain is thought of as a generic system, responding to *actions* and whose internal state is only partially visible

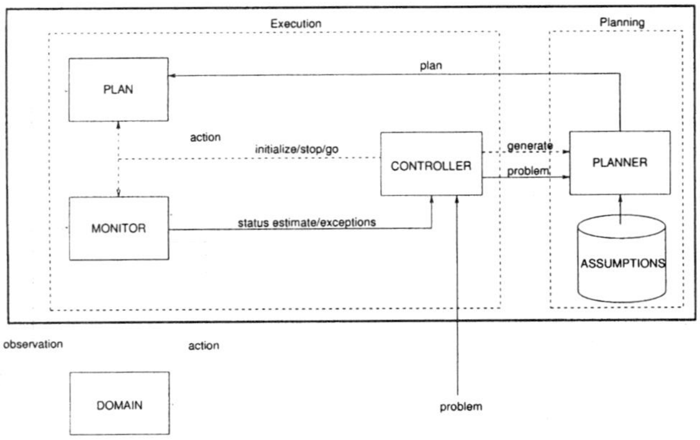


Figure 1: The framework.

through *observations*. The plan is an automaton; it controls the domain producing actions, based on the observations and on its internal status. At plan execution time, an automaton called a *monitor* gathers the actions applied on the domain, and its responses, to reconstruct estimates of the current domain status. Such estimates are used to evaluate whether the taken assumptions are compatible with the observed domain behaviour, and whether an action is safely executable. Based on this, replanning can be triggered, using the estimate as a new starting point.

We now provide more details on the components involved in plan execution and monitoring.

## Planning Domains

As in (Bertoli *et al.* 2003), a planning domain is defined in terms of its *states*, of the *actions* it accepts, and of the possible *observations* that the domain can exhibit. Some of the states are marked as valid *initial states* for the domain. A *transition function* describes how (the execution of) an action leads from one state to possibly many different states. Finally, an *observation function* defines which observations are associated with each state of the domain.

**Definition 1 (Planning domain)** *A* nondeterministic planning domain with partial observability *is a tuple* $\mathcal{D} = \langle \mathcal{S}, \mathcal{A}, \mathcal{U}, \mathcal{I}, \mathcal{T}, \mathcal{X} \rangle$*, where:*

- $\mathcal{S}$ *is the set of* states.
- $\mathcal{A}$ *is the set of* actions.
- $\mathcal{U}$ *is the set of* observations.
- $\mathcal{I} \subseteq \mathcal{S}$ *is the set of* initial states*; we require* $\mathcal{I} \neq \emptyset$.
- $\mathcal{T} : \mathcal{S} \times \mathcal{A} \rightarrow 2^{\mathcal{S}}$ *is the* transition function*; it associates with each current state* $s \in \mathcal{S}$ *and with each action* $a \in \mathcal{A}$ *the set* $\mathcal{T}(s,a) \subseteq \mathcal{S}$ *of next states.*
- $\mathcal{X} : \mathcal{S} \rightarrow 2^{\mathcal{U}}$ *is the* observation function*; it associates with each state s the set of possible observations* $\mathcal{X}(s) \subseteq \mathcal{U}$*, with* $\mathcal{X}(s) \neq \emptyset$.

*We indicate with* $[[o]]$ *the set of states compatible with the observation o:* $[[o]] = \{s \in \mathcal{S} : o \in \mathcal{X}(s)\}$. *Given a set of observations* $\mathcal{OF}$, $[[\mathcal{OF}]]$ *indicates the set of states compatible with some observation in* $\mathcal{OF}$.

*We say that action* $\alpha$ *is* executable *in state s iff* $\mathcal{T}(s,\alpha) \neq \emptyset$*; an action is executable in a set of states iff it is executable in every state of the set.*

**Example 1** 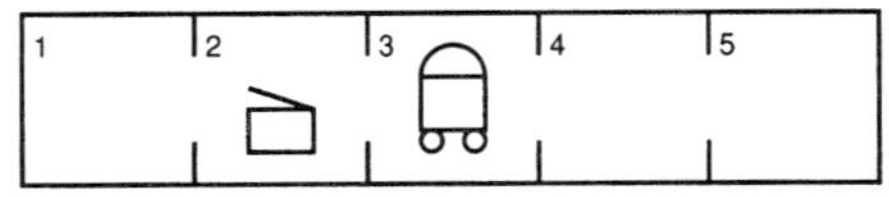


Figure 2: The printer domain.

Our domain model allows uncertainty in the initial state and in the outcome of action execution. Also, the observation associated with a given state is not unique. This allows modeling noisy sensing and lack of information.

*Consider the example depicted in Fig. 2. The domain involves a robot in a corridor of five rooms; a printer is in room number 2, and the robot may be initially in any room. The printer may be empty or full, and is initially empty. The states of the domain are* $1_e, 2_e, 3_e, 4_e, 5_e, 1_f, 2_f, 3_f, 4_f, 5_f$*, each corresponding to robot position and to a printer state.*

*Actions* $left$*,* $right$ *and* $refill$ *are available, with the obvious outcomes. The actions* $left$ *is executable on every state but* $1_e$ *and* $1_f$*;* $right$ *is executable on every state but* $5_e$ *and* $5_f$*. The action* $refill$ *that refills the printer is only executable when the state is* $2_e$.

*Three observations are available to the robot:* $wl$*,* $wr$*,* $wno$*, indicating that there is a wall to the left, to the right, or neither way. They hold iff the robot is in the leftmost, rightmost, or in the middle rooms respectively. That is, the observation function* $\mathcal{X}$ *associates* $\{wl\}$ *with states* $1_e$ *and* $1_f$*,* $\{wr\}$ *with states* $5_e$ *and* $5_f$*, and* $\{wno\}$ *with the remaining states.*

For ease of presentation, the example only features uncertainty in the initial state; however, this is enough to force reasoning on sets of possible states, or *beliefs*, the key difficulty in handling with nondeterminism.

## Goals, Assumptions, Plans

We consider reachability goals: a goal for a domain $\mathcal{D} = \langle \mathcal{S}, \mathcal{A}, \mathcal{U}, \mathcal{I}, \mathcal{T}, \mathcal{X} \rangle$ is a set of states $\mathcal{G} \subseteq \mathcal{S}$, and a problem is a pair $\langle \mathcal{D}, \mathcal{G} \rangle$, to be reached in a finite number of plan execution steps. For these problems, it is sufficient to consider acyclic plans that branch based on the sensed observation:

**Definition 2 (Plan)** *A plan for a domain* $\mathcal{D} = \langle \mathcal{S}, \mathcal{A}, \mathcal{U}, \mathcal{I}, \mathcal{T}, \mathcal{X} \rangle$ *is a nonempty set of pairs* $\langle \mathcal{OF}, \epsilon \rangle$ *and triples* $\langle \mathcal{OF}, \alpha, \pi \rangle$ *where:*

- $\mathcal{OF} \in 2^{\mathcal{U}}$*,* $\alpha \in \mathcal{A}$*, and* $\pi$ *is a plan.*
- $\epsilon$ *is the empty plan; when reached by the execution of a plan* $\pi$*, it indicates* $\pi$*'s termination.*

*Each pair and triple is called a branch of the plan. The sets of observations in the branches of a plan must cover* $\mathcal{U}$.

A plan is essentially an acyclic graph whose paths from the root to the leafs are sequences of the form $[\mathcal{OF}_1, \alpha_1, \ldots, \alpha_{n-1}, \mathcal{OF}_n]$, built by recursive concatenation of the observation sets and actions in the branches of the plan. We allow for some forms of syntactic sugar:

- We will use an if-then-else syntax to indicate plans with two branches; for instance, the plan $if\ \{o_1, o_2\}\ then\ \alpha_1; \pi_1\ else\ \alpha_2; \pi_2$ corresponds to $\{\langle \{o_1, o_2\}, \alpha_1, \pi_1 \rangle, \langle \mathcal{U} - \{o_1, o_2\}, \alpha_2, \pi_2 \rangle\}$.
- $\alpha; \pi$ is equivalent to $\{\langle \mathcal{U}, \alpha, \pi \rangle\}$

- $\epsilon.$ is equivalent to $\{\langle \mathcal{U}, \epsilon \rangle\}$, and $\alpha.$ is equivalent to $\alpha; \epsilon$.

**Example 2** *Here is a plan $P_0$ for the above domain:*

```
if wl
  then right; refill.
  else left; if wl
             then right; refill.
             else left; if wl
                        then right; refill.
                        else left; if wl
                                   then right; refill.
                                   else refill.
```

Given a planning problem, two key features for a plan are (1) its executability given possible initial states, and (2) whether the plan solves the problem, by ending its execution in a goal state. To provide these notions, we introduce the possible traces of the plan, i.e. the sequences of observations, actions and states that can be traversed executing the plan from an initial state.

**Definition 3 (Traces of a plan.)** *A trace of a plan is a sequence*

$$[s_0, o_0, \alpha_0, \ldots, s_{n-1}, o_{n-1}, \alpha_{n-1}, s_n, o_n, End]$$

*where $s_i, o_i$ are the domain state and associated observation at step $i$ of the plan execution, and $\alpha_i$ is the action produced by the plan at step $i$ on the basis of $o_i$ (and of the plan's internal state). The final symbol $End$ can either be $Stop$, indicating that the plan has terminated, or $Fail(\alpha)$, indicating execution failure of action $\alpha$ on $s_n$. A trace is a* failure trace *iff it terminates with $Fail(\alpha)$. A trace is a* goal trace *for a set of states $\mathcal{G}$ iff it is not a failure trace, and its final state is in $\mathcal{G}$. The predicate $Reaches(t, \mathcal{G})$ holds true on a trace $t$ iff $t$ is a goal trace for $\mathcal{G}$. We also indicate a trace with $\langle \overline{s}, \overline{o}, \overline{\alpha} \rangle$, splitting it into a state trace, an action sequence, and an observation trace, and omitting the final symbol.*

*We indicate with $Trs(\pi, s)$ the set of traces that can be generated by plan $\pi$ starting from a state $s$. This set can be easily built by recursion on the plan structure, taking into account executability of actions on the states. The set of traces $Trs(\pi, B)$ for plan $\pi$ starting from a belief $B$ is the union of the traces from every state $s \in B$.*

At this point, the notions of executability and solution can easily be provided as follows:

**Definition 4 (Executable plan)** *A plan $\pi$ is executable on state $s$ (on a set of states $B$) iff no failure trace exists in $Trs(\pi, s)$ ($Trs(\pi, B)$ resp.).*

**Definition 5 (Solution)** *A plan $\pi$ is a strong solution for a problem $\langle \mathcal{D}, \mathcal{G} \rangle$ iff every trace from $\mathcal{I}$ is a goal trace for $\mathcal{G}$:*

$$\forall t \in Trs(\pi, \mathcal{I}) : Reaches(t, \mathcal{G})$$

**Example 3** *Consider again the domain of Fig. 2, and plan $P_0$ from the previous example. The plan is a strong solution for the problem of reaching the filled printer status $2_f$, since $Trs(\pi_0, \{1_e, 2_e, 3_e, 4_e, 5_e\}) = \{t_1, t_2, t_3, t_4, t_5\}$, where:*

$$t_1 = [1_e, wl, right, 2_e, wno, refill, 2_f, wno, Stop],$$
$$t_2 = [2_e, wno, left] \circ t_1,$$
$$t_3 = [3_e, wno, left] \circ t_2,$$
$$t_4 = [4_e, wno, left] \circ t_3, \textit{and}$$
$$t_5 = [5_e, wr, left, 4_e, wno, left, 3_e, wno, left, 2_e, wno, refill, 2_f, wno, Stop]$$

Assumptions on the domain behaviour are used to simplify a problem, narrowing the search. In this paper, we consider assumptions that restrict the initial state of the domain:

**Definition 6 (Assumption)** *An assumption for a domain $\mathcal{D} = \langle \mathcal{S}, \mathcal{A}, \mathcal{U}, \mathcal{I}, \mathcal{T}, \mathcal{X} \rangle$ is a set of states $\mathcal{F} \subseteq 2^{\mathcal{S}}$, intended to restrict the possible initial states of $\mathcal{D}$ to $\mathcal{F} \cap \mathcal{I} \neq \emptyset$.*

The above notions of executable plan and solution plan lift naturally to take into account the assumptions:

**Definition 7 (Executable/Solution under assumption)** *A plan $\pi$ is executable for a set of states $B$ under assumption $\mathcal{F}$ iff it is executable for the set of states $B \cap \mathcal{F}$.*

*A plan $\pi$ is a strong solution for problem $\langle \mathcal{D}, \mathcal{G} \rangle$ under assumption $\mathcal{F}$ iff it is a strong solution for $\langle \mathcal{D}_A, \mathcal{G} \rangle$ where $\mathcal{D} = \langle \mathcal{S}, \mathcal{A}, \mathcal{U}, \mathcal{I}, \mathcal{T}, \mathcal{X} \rangle$ and $\mathcal{D}_A = \langle \mathcal{S}, \mathcal{A}, \mathcal{U}, \mathcal{I} \cap \mathcal{F}, \mathcal{T}, \mathcal{X} \rangle$.*

Naturally, executability under no assumptions implies executability under any assumption, but not vice versa. The same holds for the notion of solution: a plan which is a solution under a given assumption is not, in general, a solution, or even only executable.

**Example 4** *Consider again the printer domain, and consider the assumption $\{1_e, 2_e, 3_e\}$. Given this, the following plan $P_1$ is an assumption-based solution to fill the printer:*

```
if wl
  then right; refill.
  else left; if wl
             then right; refill.
             else refill.
```

*However, this plan is not a strong solution, nor executable. In fact, it is "dangerous to execute": if the assumption is wrong and the initial state is $4_e$, the sequence of actions $[left, refill]$ is attempted, which is not executable.*

## Monitoring

In order to monitor assumptions on initial states, and to produce the necessary information for replanning, we exploit *universal monitors*, defined in (Bertoli *et al.* 2003). A universal monitor is an automaton which embeds a faithful model of the domain, and evolves it on the basis of the received actions and observations, which constitute the I/O of the actual domain. In this way, at each execution step $i$, the monitor evolves, and provides as output, a belief $M_i$ on the domain status. The belief $M_i$ consists of the set of all states compatible with the domain behaviour observed up to step $i$, and with the domain being initially in some $s \in M_0$. Thus $M_i$ is empty if the domain behavior is not compatible with the initial state being in $M_0$, indicating that the domain status was initially outside $M_0$. Based on these properties, given a domain $\mathcal{D} = \langle \mathcal{S}, \mathcal{A}, \mathcal{U}, \mathcal{I}, \mathcal{T}, \mathcal{X} \rangle$, the output of a monitor whose initial belief is $\mathcal{I}$ can be used to check whether an action is guaranteed to be executable, and as a new initial belief for replanning. Moreover, given an assumption-based plan $\pi$ that reaches the goal iff the initial domain status belongs to $\mathcal{I}_\pi \subseteq \mathcal{I}$, a monitor whose initial belief is $\mathcal{I}_\pi$ can be used to detect whether the initial state is actually outside $\mathcal{I}_\pi$, preventing $\pi$'s success [1]. Thus the

[1] In general, an assumption-based solution $\pi$ for an assumption $\mathcal{F}$ may reach the goal $\mathcal{G}$ starting from a set of initial states

monitoring in our architecture exploits a pair of universal monitors, whose initial beliefs are $\mathcal{I}$ and $\mathcal{I}_\pi$ respectively.

## Generation of safe assumption-based plans

Our aim is to generate *safe* assumption-based plans, i.e. plans that guarantee that (a) whenever the assumption holds, the goal is reached, and (b) whenever an assumption failure inhibits success, this is signalled by the monitor, preventing possible execution failures (as opposed to *unsafe* assumption-based plans). These constraints can be restated based on traces, requiring that (a) any trace starting from $\mathcal{I} \cap \mathcal{F}$ is successful, and (b) any trace from $\mathcal{I} \cap \neg\mathcal{F}$ is either successful, or distinguishable from those from $\mathcal{I} \cap \mathcal{F}$ by monitoring. This can be formally expressed by defining the observation sequences compatible with an initial state/belief, given an action sequence $\overline{\alpha}$. For this purpose, we construct the observation sequences that may take place when executing $\overline{\alpha}$ starting from a state $s$. We first observe that $\overline{\alpha}$ induces a set of possible sequence of states traversed by the domain during the execution; in turn, each state sequence traversed by the domain can be associated with a set of possible observation sequences for it:

**Definition 8 (Induced state traces)** *Given an action sequence $\overline{\alpha} = [\alpha_1, \ldots, \alpha_n]$, the set of state traces induced by the execution of $\overline{\alpha}$ on s, is the set of state traces related to the execution of plan $\alpha_1; \ldots; \alpha_n$:*

$$sTraces(s, \overline{\alpha}) = \{\overline{s} : \langle \overline{s}, \overline{o}, \overline{\alpha} \rangle \in Trs(s, \alpha_1; \ldots; \alpha_n)\}$$

**Definition 9 (Compatible observations)** *Given a sequence of states $\overline{s}$, the set of compatible sequences of observations $\overline{\mathcal{X}}(\overline{s})$ is defined as follows:*

$$\overline{\mathcal{X}}(\overline{s}) = \{\overline{o} : \overline{o}^{(i)} \in \mathcal{X}(\overline{s}^{(i)})\}$$

**Definition 10 (Observations sequences compatible)** *with initial state/belief, given an action sequence.*

$$\overline{\mathcal{X}}_{\overline{A}}(s, \overline{\alpha}) = \bigcup_{\overline{s} \in sTraces(s,\overline{\alpha})} \overline{\mathcal{X}}(\overline{s})$$

$$\overline{\mathcal{X}}_{\overline{A}}(B, \overline{\alpha}) = \bigcup_{s \in B} \overline{\mathcal{X}}_{\overline{A}}(s, \overline{\alpha})$$

We can thus define safe plans, recalling that, given a trace $\langle \overline{s}, \overline{o}, \overline{\alpha} \rangle$, a monitor whose initial belief is $M_0$ detects whether $\overline{o} \notin \overline{\mathcal{X}}_{\overline{A}}(M_0, \overline{\alpha})$:

**Definition 11 (Safe assumption-based solution )** *A plan $\pi$ is a safe assumption-based solution iff:*

1. $\forall \langle \overline{s}, \overline{o}, \overline{\alpha} \rangle \in Trs(\pi, \mathcal{I} \cap \mathcal{F}) : Reaches(\langle \overline{s}, \overline{o}, \overline{\alpha} \rangle, \mathcal{G})$ *, and*
2. $\forall \langle \overline{s}, \overline{o}, \overline{\alpha} \rangle \in Trs(\pi, \mathcal{I} \cap \neg\mathcal{F}) : (Reaches(\langle \overline{s}, \overline{o}, \overline{\alpha} \rangle, \mathcal{G}) \vee \overline{o} \notin \overline{\mathcal{X}}_{\overline{A}}(\mathcal{I} \cap \mathcal{F}, \overline{\alpha}))$

**Example 5** *The strong plan $P_0$ from example 2 is safe for the assumption $\mathcal{F} = \{1_e, 2_e, 3_e\}$: in the case of success-endangering assumption failures (i.e. when the initial status is $4_e$ or $5_e$), executing $P_0$ cannot lead to any observation sequence identical to one which would stem by applying the same actions from $1_e$, $2_e$ or $3_e$. For instance, both starting from $3_e$ and $4_e$, the first two actions executed by $P_0$ are $[left, left]$; but in one case, the $wl$ observation holds true after that, while in the other it does not.*

*The assumption-based solution $P_1$ is not safe for the same assumption $\mathcal{F}$: both starting from $3_e$ and $4_e$, the same observations are produced before the hazardous $refill$ action is tried.*

*Consider the following plan $P_2$, which goes along $P_1$'s line but executes an additional $[left, right]$ sequence before filling the printer:*

```
if wl
  then right; refill.
  else left; if wl
            then right; refill.
            else left; right; refill.
```

*$P_2$ is a safe assumption-based solution: just as for $P_0$, monitoring will detect success-endangering assumption failures, since the actions produced by $P_2$ in those cases induce observation sequences incompatible with the domain being initially in $1_e$, $2_e$ or $3_e$. E.g. if the initial status is $4_e$, observation $wno$ holds after executing $[left, left]$, while $wl$ holds iff the status was $3_e$.*

We now use the above definitions to prune the search in a forward-chaining search algorithm. In particular, we consider the plan generation approach presented in (Bertoli, Cimatti, & Roveri 2001), where an and-or graph representing an acyclic prefix of the search space of beliefs is iteratively expanded: at each step, observations and actions are applied to a fringe node of the prefix, removing loops. Each node in the graph is associated with a belief in the search space, and with the path of actions and observations that is traversed to reach it. When a node is marked success, by goal entailment or by propagation on the prefix, its associated path is eligible as a path of a solution plan.

To constrain the algorithm to produce safe assumption-based plans, success marking of a node must also require that the associated path obeys a safety condition [2]. To achieve this, we evaluate safety considering the set of traces associated with a path, i.e. those traces traversing the path:

**Definition 12 (Traces associated with path)** *Given a path $\langle \overline{\mathcal{OF}}, \overline{\alpha} \rangle$ and a trace $\langle \overline{s}, \overline{o}, \overline{\beta} \rangle$, we say that the trace belongs to the path iff $\overline{\alpha} = \overline{\beta}$, and $\forall i \in \{1, \ldots, len(\overline{o})\} : \overline{o}^{(i)} \in \overline{\mathcal{OF}}^{(i)}$. Given a plan $\pi$, a path $p$ of $\pi$, and an initial set of states $B$, we write $Trs(p, B)$ to indicate the set of traces in $Trs(\pi, B)$ that belong to $p$.*

Thus, a path $p$ can be accepted as a part of a safe plan $\pi$ for problem $\langle \mathcal{D}, \mathcal{G} \rangle$ iff requirements 1 and 2 from Def. 11 are obeyed, replacing $\pi$ with $p$. Req.1 is easily computed symbolically by a $Exec_P$ operator that progresses the belief $\mathcal{I} \cap \mathcal{F}$ on the path $p$, obtaining the final belief for the path:

$$Exec_P(\mathcal{I} \cap \mathcal{F}, p) \subseteq \mathcal{G} \qquad (1)$$

Req.2 requires, instead, checking that for each non-success trace in $Trs(p, \mathcal{I} \cap \neg\mathcal{F})$ and each trace in $Trs(p, \mathcal{I} \cap \mathcal{F})$,

---

$\mathcal{I}_\pi \supseteq \mathcal{I} \cap \mathcal{F}$. $\mathcal{I}_\pi$ can be efficiently computed by symbolic backward simulation of $\pi$ from $\mathcal{G}$. The states in $\mathcal{I}_\pi / (\mathcal{I} \cap \mathcal{F})$ represent failures of $\mathcal{F}$ which do not affect the success of $\pi$.

[2] At the same time, loop checking is relaxed: a loop only takes place when the same belief *and* associated safety condition are met.

the observation components do not match. This can be extremely expensive, due to the huge number of paths. To avoid this expensive computation, we build the path annotation symbolically, by pruning at each step of the path those trace pairs that can be distinguished based on current observations. We achieve this by a function $EqPairs(B_1, B_2, p)$ which produces a set of pairs of beliefs, each implicitly associated with a sequence of observations $\overline{o} \in \overline{\mathcal{X}}_{\overline{A}}(B_1, p) \cap \overline{\mathcal{X}}_{\overline{A}}(B_2, p)$. Each pair overestimates the undistinguishable states originated by $\overline{o}$ starting from $B_1$ and $B_2$. As a special case, $EqPairs$ returns $\{\langle \mathcal{S}, \mathcal{S} \rangle\}$ to indicate that the executability of the path is not guaranteed, due to a possibly non-executable action (such as $refill$ in example 4). The results of $EqPairs(\mathcal{I} \cap \mathcal{F}, \mathcal{I} \cap \neg\mathcal{F}, p)$, can be used to state that no undetectable assumption failure (if any) evolves outside the goal, defining a sufficient *traceability* condition[3]:

$$\forall \langle B, B' \rangle \in EqPairs(\mathcal{I} \cap \mathcal{F}, \mathcal{I} \cap \neg\mathcal{F}, p) : B' \subseteq \mathcal{G} \quad (2)$$

The definition of $EqPairs$ exploits a $prune$ operator that, given a pair $\langle B_1, B_2 \rangle$ of nonempty beliefs, and a set of observations $\mathcal{OF}$, considers every observation $o \in \mathcal{OF}$ which may take place over both beliefs, and builds an associated belief pair restricting $B_1$ and $B_2$ to $o$, i.e. to those parts of $B_1$ and $B_2$ that cannot be distinguished if $o$ takes place:

$$prune(B_1, B_2, \mathcal{OF}) = \{\langle B_1 \cap [[o]], B_2 \cap [[o]] \rangle : o \in \mathcal{X}(B_1) \cap \mathcal{X}(B_2) \cap \mathcal{OF}\}$$

In particular, given a plan path $[\mathcal{OF}_0, \alpha_0, \mathcal{OF}_1, \ldots, \alpha_{n-1}, \mathcal{OF}_n]$, $EqPairs(B_1, B_2, p)$ is defined by repeatedly evolving the initial beliefs via the observations and actions in the path, and splitting them via the $prune$ operator:

- $EqPairs(B_1, B_2, [\mathcal{OF}_0] \circ p) = EqPairs_0(prune(B_1, B_2, \mathcal{OF}_0), p)$
- Let $bp = \{\langle B_1, B'_1 \rangle, \ldots, \langle B_n, B'_n, \rangle\}$ be a set of pairs of beliefs. Then:
  - $EqPairs_0(bp, []) = bp$
  - If, for some belief of $bp$, $\alpha$ is not executable, then $EqPairs_0(bp, [\alpha, \mathcal{OF}] \circ p) = \{\langle \mathcal{S}, \mathcal{S} \rangle\}$;
  - otherwise,

$$EqPairs_0(bp, [\alpha, \mathcal{OF}] \circ p) = EqPairs_0(\bigcup_{i=1..n} prune(\mathcal{T}(B_i, \alpha), \mathcal{T}(B'_i, \alpha), \mathcal{OF}), p)$$

Thus, a sufficient acceptance condition for a path inside a safe assumption-based plan conjoins conditions (1) and (2). As a further optimization, to avoid the blow-up in the size of the pairs set, belief pairs from $prune$ can be pairwise unioned. This further strengthens the traceability condition.

## Experimental evaluation

Our experiments intend to evaluate the overhead of adding safety conditions to plan generation, and the impact of safe plan generation within a reactive framework such as the one we presented. For these purposes, we obtained the SYPEM reactive platform (Bertoli, Cimatti, & Traverso 2003), and modified the MBP planner inside it so that it performs safe assumption-based plan generation. We name our MBP extension SAMBP (Safe Assumption-based MBP), and SAPEM the associated extension to SYPEM. No comparison is taken w.r.t. other systems, since, to the best of our knowledge, no other approach to generate safe-assumption based plans has been presented so far.

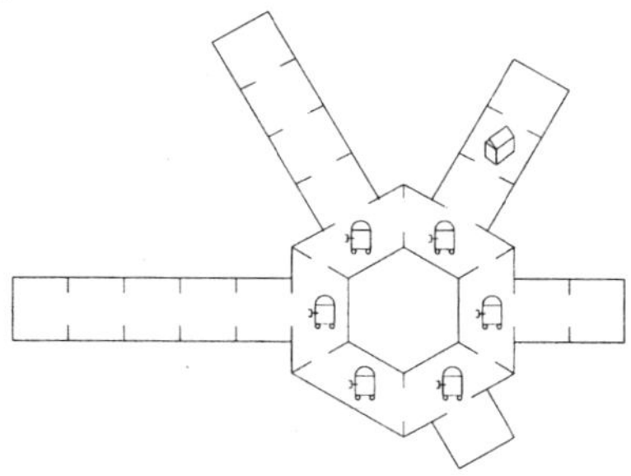

Figure 3: The test domain (for $N = 6$).

An instance of our test domain is shown in Fig. 3; it consists of a ring of $N$ rooms, where each room $n \neq 0$ is connected to a corridor of length $n$. In the middle of corridor connected to room $\lfloor N/2 \rfloor$, there is a printer which has to be refilled. The robot can be initially anywhere in the ring of rooms; it can traverse the ring by going left or right, step in or out from corridors, and fill the printer. Actions have the obvious applicability constraints, e.g. the robot cannot fill the printer unless at the printer's place. The robot is equipped with a "bump" sensor that signals whether it has reached the end of a corridor. We experiment with assumptions of different strength; in the weaker case (a1), we assume the robot can be anywhere in the ring; in (a2) we assume it is not in room 0; in (a3),(a4),(a5) we assume it is in a room within $\lfloor N/2 \rfloor \pm \Delta/2$, with $\Delta = \lfloor N/4 \rfloor$, $\Delta = 2$, and $\Delta = 0$ respectively. For any assumption, and for a range of sizes of the domain, we run the following tests on a 700 MHz Pentium III PC with 512 MBytes of memory:

1. Generation of unsafe assumption-based plans (by MBP, restricting the initial belief, see Def.9), and of safe assumption-based plans by SAMBP; we also generate strong plans for a reference;
2. Reactive plan generation and execution by SYPEM and SAPEM. We test every initial configuration where the assumption holds true, and every initial configuration where it fails (average timings are indicated with (ok) and (ko) resp.). To ease the comparison, we use no assumption when replanning.

Fig. 4 shows the results for assumptions (a3-a5); for assumptions (a1) and (a2), the behavior is essentially the same for every setting, converging to that of strong planning. Also, SYPEM and SAPEM always replan when the assumption fails, and their performance never differs for more than 20% (SAPEM scoring better); we collapse them for sake of clarity. Finally, since, when the assumption holds, SYPEM never replans, its behavior and performance coincides with that of SAMBP. We observe the following:

[3] Traceability is stronger than trace-based safety (Def. 11). Intuitively, it only distinguishes state traces based on their last state, and on traceability of their prefixes. That is, we pay space-saving with a limited form of incompleteness.

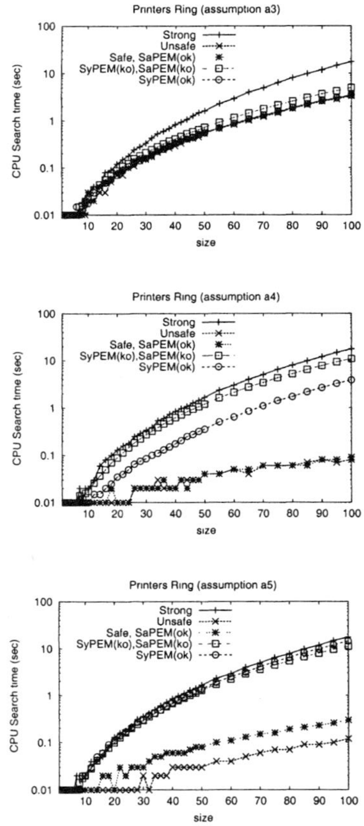


Figure 4: Experimental results for the printer domain.

- The overhead of safe plan generation vs. its unsafe counterpart is always limited. The bigger difference (within a factor of 3) takes place for the more restrictive assumption (a5), which, on the other side, is when assumptions are most effective to speed up the search, but unsafe assumption-based plans are most likely to fail. For weaker assumptions, (safe and unsafe) assumption-based plan generation tends to assimilate to strong planning, with no additional overhead paid by safe plan generation vs. its unsafe version.

- When the assumption holds, SAPEM avoids any replanning, while SYPEM has to replan considering possible assumption failures. The stronger the assumption, the more a SYPEM plan is likely to trigger replanning. In fact, for (a4) SYPEM replans 50% of the times, and for (a5) it replans 100% of the times. This reflects into SAPEM performing better than SYPEM. For weak assumptions, both systems tend towards the behavior of strong offline planning.

We obtained qualitatively similar results for a $31 \times 31$ maze positioning problem from (Bertoli, Cimatti, & Roveri 2001), considering assumptions related to the distance $D$ from the goal. The following table synthesizes the timings in seconds, and, for SYPEM, the percentage of cases in which useless replanning takes place, the assumption being actually true.

| Assum on $D$ | Unsafe | Safe, SAPEM(ok) | SYPEM(ok) | SYPEM(ko), SAPEM(ko) | Stg. |
|---|---|---|---|---|---|
| $\leq 10$ | 0.09 | 0.12 | 0.12 (19%) | 0.43 | 1.21 |
| $\leq 5$ | 0.02 | 0.03 | 0.11 (50%) | 0.50 | 1.21 |
| $\leq 4$ | 0.02 | 0.03 | 0.15 (71%) | 0.49 | 1.21 |
| $\leq 3$ | 0.02 | 0.02 | 0.20 (100%) | 0.49 | 1.21 |
| $\leq 2$ | 0.01 | 0.02 | 0.22 (100%) | 0.49 | 1.21 |
| $\leq 1$ | 0.01 | 0.02 | 0.23 (100%) | 0.50 | 1.21 |
| $= 0$ | 0.01 | 0.02 | 0.26 (100%) | 0.53 | 1.21 |

## Conclusions and future work

In this paper, we introduced safe assumption-based plan generation as a mean to minimize the amount of replanning required in a reactive setting using assumptions. Our experiments show that this is a viable way to effectively use assumptions in such setting, coupling the high efficiency of assumption-based plan generation with non-redundant replanning. Our work is related and complementary to those on diagnosability of controllers in (Cimatti, Pecheur, & Cavada 2003), where verification of diagnosability of a given controller is tackled given a set of admissible environment behaviors, simulating the behaviour of twin plants.

This work leads to several extensions. In particular, a more qualitative evaluation of plan safety may relax safety requirements for domains where poor or unreliable sensing makes "full" safety impossible; still, this could lead to plans which improve on unsafe plans by avoiding a substantial amount of useless replanning. Moreover, we are working at extending our concepts to a more expressive assumption language, exploiting LTL temporal logics.

## References


Bertoli, P.; A., C.; M., P.; and P., T. 2003. A Framework for Planning with Extended Goals under Partial Observability. In *Proc. of ICAPS'03*. AAAI Press.

Bertoli, P.; Cimatti, A.; and Roveri, M. 2001. Conditional Planning under Partial Observability as Heuristic-Symbolic Search in Belief Space. In *Proc. of ECP'01*.

Bertoli, P.; Cimatti, A.; and Traverso, P. 2003. Interleaving Execution and Planning via Symbolic Model Checking. In *Proc. of ICAPS'03 Workshop on Planning under Uncertainty and Incomplete Information.*

Cimatti, A.; Pecheur, C.; and Cavada, R. 2003. Formal verification of diagnosability via symbolic model checking. In *Proc. of IJCAI'03*.

Koenig, S., and Smirnov, Y. 1997. Sensor-Based Planning with the Freespace Assumption. In *Proc. of ICRA '97*.

Muscettola, N.; Nayak, P. P.; Pell, B.; and Williams, B. C. 1998. Remote Agent: To Boldly Go Where No AI System Has Gone Before. *Artificial Intelligence* 103(1-2):5–47.

Myers, K. L., and Wilkins, D. E. 1998. Reasoning about Locations in Theory and Practice. *Computational Intelligence* 14(2):151–187.

Singh, S.; Simmons, R.; Smith, T.; Stentz, A. T.; Verma, V.; Yahja, A.; and Schwehr, K. 2000. Recent progress in local and global traversability for planetary rovers. In *Proc. of ICRA-2000*. IEEE.

# Regrets Only! Online Stochastic Optimization under Time Constraints

**Russell Bent** and **Pascal Van Hentenryck**
Brown University, Providence, RI 02912
{rbent,pvh}@cs.brown.edu

**Abstract**

This paper considers online stochastic optimization problems where time constraints severely limit the number of offline optimizations which can be performed at decision time and/or in between decisions. It proposes a novel approach which combines the salient features of the earlier approaches: the evaluation of every decision on all samples (expectation) and the ability to avoid distributing the samples among decisions (consensus). The key idea underlying the novel algorithm is to approximate the regret of a decision $d$. The regret algorithm is evaluated on two fundamentally different applications: online packet scheduling in networks and online multiple vehicle routing with time windows. On both applications, it produces significant benefits over prior approaches.

## Introduction

Online scheduling and routing problems arise naturally in many application areas and have received increasing attention in recent years. Contrary to offline optimization, the data is not available a priori in online optimization. Rather it is incrementally revealed during algorithm execution. In many online optimization problems, the data is a set of requests (e.g., packets in network scheduling or customers in vehicle routing) which are revealed over time and the algorithm must decide which request to process next.

Online stochastic optimization under time constraints assumes the distribution of future requests, or an approximation thereof, is available for sampling. This is typically the case in many applications, where either historical data and predictive models are available. Moreover, it assumes that the time to make a decision is severely constrained, so that only a few offline optimizations can be performed at decision time and in between decisions. Online problems of this kind arise in many applications, including vehicle routing, taxi dispaching, packet scheduling, and online deliveries.

*One of the critical issues faced by online stochastic algorithms is how to use their time wisely, since only a few samples can be optimized within the time constraints.* In other words, the algorithm must find an effective approach to optimize the samples and extract information from their solutions in order to make more informed decisions. When time is not a factor, a traditional approach (see, e.g., (Chang, Givan, & Chong 2000)) consists of using an expectation algorithm: at time $t$, generate a number of samples, solve each sample once per available request $r$ by serving $r$ at $t$, and select the best request overall. Unfortunately, the expectation approach does not perform well under time constraints, since it must distribute its available optimizations across all requests. This issue was recognized and addressed in (Bent & Van Hentenryck 2004) where a consensus approach was proposed. Its key idea is to solve as many samples as possible and to select the request which is chosen most often in the sample solutions at time $t$. The consensus approach was shown to outperform the expectation method on online packet scheduling under time constraints. However, as decision time increases, the quality of the consensus approach levels off and is eventually outperformed by the expectation method. It is also possible to hybridize the expectation and consensus approaches but the resulting method loses some of the benefits of consensus under strict time constraints.

This paper reconsiders online stochastic optimization under time constraints and proposes a *regret* approach which truly combines the salient features of the consensus and expectation approaches. Like consensus (and unlike expectation), the regret approach avoids distributing the optimizations across the requests. Like expectation (and unlike consensus), the regret algorithm collects information on all requests for each optimization. Its key insight is to recognize that, in many applications, it is reasonably easy to approximate the regret of a request $r$, i.e., the cost of replacing the request served at time $t$ by $r$. As a consequence, once the regret is available, the best solution serving request $r$ at time $t$ for a given sample can be approximated without optimization. The regret approach was evaluated on online packet scheduling and online vehicle routing with time windows. On both applications, the regret algorithm exhibits significant benefits compared to earlier approaches. The key contributions of this paper can be summarized as follows:

1. It proposes a novel approach to online stochastic optimization under time constraints which outperforms prior approaches and combines their salient benefits.
2. It provides a fundamental insight about the relationship between the expectation and consensus approaches, a link missing in (Bent & Van Hentenryck 2004) and explaining why consensus was successful in online vehicle routing.

```
ONLINEOPTIMIZATION(H)
R ← ∅;
w ← 0;
for t ∈ H
do R ← AVAILABLEREQUESTS(R, t) ∪ NEWREQUESTS(t);
   r ← CHOOSEREQUEST(R, t);
   SERVEREQUEST(r, t);
   w ← w + w(r);
   R ← R \ {r};
```

Figure 1: The Generic Online Algorithm

3. It evaluates the regret approach on two radically different applications, i.e., online packet scheduling and vehicle routing, which are two extreme points in the spectrum of online stochastic optimization. On both applications, it provides significant benefits over earlier approaches.

## Online Stochastic Optimization

This section presents the online stochastic optimization framework. Although the framework is reasonably simple, it applies directly to a variety of applications (e.g., online packet scheduling) and can be easily adapted to more complex problems. Its main benefit is to crystallize the main focus of this paper: *how to use a limited number of offline optimizations to make more informed decisions.*

The framework assumes a discrete model of time. Its offline problem considers a time horizon $H = [\underline{H}, \overline{H}]$ and a number of requests $R$. Each request $r$ is associated with a weight $w(r)$ which represents the gain if the request is served. A solution to the offline problem serves a request $r$ at each time $t \in H$ and can be viewed as a function $H \rightarrow R$. Solutions must satisfy the problem-specific constraints which are left unspecified in the framework. The goal is to find a feasible solution $\sigma$ maximizing $\sum_{t \in H} w(\sigma(t))$.

In the online version, the requests are not available initially and become progressively available at each time step. The distribution, which is seen as a black-box, is also available for sampling. The online algorithms have at their disposal a procedure to solve, or approximate, the offline problem. However, at each time step, they may only use the offline procedure $\mathcal{O}$ times because of the time constraints. More precisely, the approaches presented herein are expressed in terms of the two black-boxes:

1. a function OPTIMALSOLUTION$(R, t)$ which, given a set $R$ of requests and a time $t$, returns an optimal solution for $R$ over $[t, \overline{H}]$;
2. a function GETSAMPLE$(H)$ returning a set of requests over horizon $H$ by sampling the arrival distribution.

Note that, in practice, it may not be practical to sample the distribution for the entire time horizon. As a consequence, we simply assume that the samples extend $\Delta$ time steps in the future, where $\Delta$ is an implementation parameter.

## Online Oblivious Algorithms

All the approaches described in this paper share the same overall structure which is depicted in Figure 1. The approaches only differ in the way they implement function CHOOSEREQUEST. The online optimization schema simply considers the set of available and new requests at each time step and chooses a request $r$ which is then served and removed from the set of available requests. Function AVAILABLEREQUEST$(R, t)$ returns the set of requests available for service at time $t$ and function SERVEREQUEST$(r, t)$ simply serves $r$ at time $t$ ($\sigma(t) \leftarrow r$). Subsequent sections specify the online algorithms, i.e., their implementations of function CHOOSEREQUEST. To illustrate the framework, here is how two oblivious algorithms, not using stochastic information, can be specified as instantiations of the generic algorithm. These algorithms serve as a basis for comparison.

**Greedy (G):** This heuristic serves the available request with highest weight. It can be specified formally as

```
CHOOSEREQUEST-G(R, t)
A ← READY(R, t);
return argmax(r ∈ A) w(r);
```

**Local Optimal (LO):** This algorithm chooses the next request to serve at time $t$ by finding the optimal solution for the available requests at $t$. It can be specified as

```
CHOOSEREQUEST-LO(R, t)
σ ← OPTIMALSOLUTION(R, t);
return σ(t);
```

## Online Stochastic Algorithms

We now review a number of existing stochastic algorithms.

**Expectation (E):** This is the primary method proposed by (Chang, Givan, & Chong 2000) for online packet scheduling. Informally speaking, the method generates future requests by sampling and evaluates each available requests against that sample. A simple implementation can be specified as follows:

```
CHOOSEREQUEST-E(R, t)
1  A ← READY(R, t);
2  for r ∈ A
3     do f(r) ← 0;
4  for i ← 1 ... O/|A|
5     do S ← R ∪ GETSAMPLE([t + 1, t + Δ]);
6        for r ∈ A
7           do σ ← OPTIMALSOLUTION(S \ {r}, t + 1);
8              f(r) ← f(r) + w(r) + w(σ);
9  return argmax(r ∈ A) f(r);
```

Line 1 computes the requests which can be served at time $t$. Lines 2-3 initialize the evaluation function $f(j)$ for each request $r$. The algorithm then generates a number of samples for future requests (line 4). For each such sample, it computes the set $R$ of all available and sampled request at time $t$ (line 5). The algorithm then considers each available request $r$ successively (line 6), it implicitly schedules $r$ at time $t$, and applies the optimal offline algorithm (line 7) using $S \setminus \{r\}$ and the time horizon. The evaluation of request $r$ is updated in line 8 by incrementing it with its weight and the score of the corresponding optimal offline solution $\sigma$. All scenarios are evaluated for all available request and the algorithm then returns the request $r \in A$ with the highest evaluation.

Observe Line 4 of Algorithm E which distributes the available offline optimizations across all available requests.

When $\mathcal{O}$ is small (due to the time constraints), each available request is only evaluated with respect to a small number of samples and hence the expectation method does not yield much information. This is precisely why online vehicle routing algorithms (Bent & Van Hentenryck 2001) do not use this method, since the number of requests is very large (about 50 to 100), time between decisions is limited, and the optimization is computationally demanding.

Note also that practical implementations of Algorithm E must be careful to avoid distributing the samples across similar requests and/or to avoid evaluating requests which are formally dominated by others. These problem-specific considerations can be encapsulated in function READY.

**Consensus (C):** We now turn to a consensus algorithm which uses stochastic information in a fundamental different way. Algorithm C was introduced in (Bent & Van Hentenryck 2004) as an abstraction of the sampling method used in online vehicle routing (Bent & Van Hentenryck 2001). Instead of evaluating each possible request at time $t$ with respect to each sample, algorithm C executes the offline algorithm on the available and sampled requests and to count the number of times a request is scheduled at time $t$ in each resulting solution. Then the request with the highest count is selected. Algorithm C can be specified as follows:

```
CHOOSEREQUEST-C(R, t)
1  for r ∈ R
2     do f(r) ← 0;
3  for i ← 1 ... O
4     do S ← R ∪ GETSAMPLE([t + 1, t + Δ]);
5        σ ← OPTIMALSOLUTION(S, t);
6        f(σ(t)) ← f(σ(t)) + 1;
7  return argmax(r ∈ R) f(r);
```

Observe line 5 which calls the offline algorithm with all available and sampled requests and a time horizon starting at $t$ and line 6 which increments the number of times request $\sigma(t)$ is scheduled first. Line 7 simply returns the request with the largest count. Algorithm C has several appealing features. First, it does not partition the available samples between the requests, which is a significant advantage when the number of samples is small and/or when the number of requests is large. Second, it avoids the conceptual complexity of identifying symmetric or dominated requests.

**Consensus+Expectation (C+E$_k$):** Algorithms E and C both have advantages and limitations. Algorithm C+E$_k$ attemps to combine their strengths while minimizing their drawbacks. Letting $\mathcal{O} = S_c + kS_e$, its key idea is to run algorithm C first to identify $k$ promising requests (using $S_c$ optimizations) and to run algorithm E to discriminate between them in a precise fashion (using $kS_e$ iterations).

**Limitations of Consensus** Figure 2 evaluates the various approaches on online packet scheduling under different time constraints (specified by the number of available offline optimizations). The figure exhibits a number of interesting points. First, it clearly shows that stochastic information pays off, since consensus is always significantly better than algorithms G and LO. Second, it shows that consensus significantly outperforms algorithm E when few offline optimizations are available. Third, it shows that consensus levels off and is dominated by algorithm E when the number of available optimizations increases. Finally, the hybrid algorithm exploits some of the benefits of C and E, but it is dominated by C when there are few offline optimizations available. Note also that the bottom line is the offline solution, i.e., a lower bound.

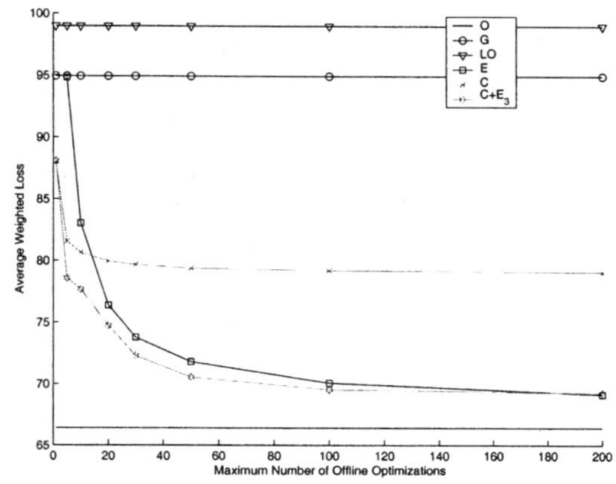


Figure 2: Existing Algorithms on Online Packet Scheduling

Consensus appears to have two main limitations. First, it is purely qualitative as it ignores the score of the optimal solutions. Second, it is extremely *elitist* in that only the optimal choice receives a credit for a given sample. The first limitation can be addressed by crediting the value of the optimal solution instead of incrementing a counter, i.e., replacing line 6 by $f(\sigma(t)) \leftarrow f(\sigma(t)) + w(\sigma)$; This "quantitative" consensus QC does not bring many benefits on the online packet scheduling and vehicle routing problems, where this modification seem to favor the best requests even more.

The real limitation of consensus is its *elitism*. Only the best request is given some credit for a given sample, while other requests are simply ignored. It ignores the fact that several requests may be essentially similar with respect to a given sample. Moreover, it does not recognize that a request may never be the best for any sample, but may still be extremely robust overall. *The fundamental issue is thus to determine if it is possible to gather that kind of information from the sample solutions without solving additional optimization problems.*

## The Regret Online Stochastic Algorithm

The key insight to resolve this issue lies in the recognition that, in many applications, *it is possible to quickly estimate the regret of a request r at time t*, i.e., the difference in objective value between the optimal solution $\sigma$ and the best solution serving request $r$ at time $t$.

**Definition 1 (Regret)** *Let $R$ be the set of requests at time $t$, $r \in$ READY$(R, t)$, and $\sigma =$ OPTIMALSOLUTION$(R, t)$. The regret of $r$ wrt $R$ and $t$, denoted by* REGRET$(R, t, r)$, *is defined as*

$$w(\sigma) - (w(r) + w(\text{OPTIMALSOLUTION}(R, t + 1))).$$

This paper assumes the availability of an application-specific regret function REGRETUB which provides an upper bound to the regret, i.e.,

$$\text{REGRETUB}(\sigma, R, t, r) \geq \text{REGRET}(R, t, r).$$

for $\sigma = \text{OPTIMALSOLUTION}(R, t)$. Of course, the computational complexity of REGRETUB is assumed to be negligible compared to the cost of the offline optimization.

Such regret approximations typically exist in practical applications. In an online facility location problem, the regret of opening a facility $f$ can be estimated by evaluating the cost of closing the selected facility $\sigma(t)$ and opening $f$. In vehicle routing, the regret of serving a customer $c$ next can evaluated by swapping $c$ with the first customer on the vehicle serving $c$. In packet scheduling, the regret of serving a packet $p$ can be estimated by swapping and/or serving a constant number of packets. In all cases, the cost of approximating the regrets is small compared to the cost of the offline optimization. The experimental sections discuss the regrets for specific applications in detail. Note that there is an interesting connection to local search, since computing the regret may be viewed as evaluating the cost of a local move for the application at hand. We are now ready to present the regret algorithm R:

```
CHOOSEREQUEST-R(R, t)
1  for r ∈ R
2     do f(r) ← 0;
3  for i ← 1 ... O
4     do S ← R ∪ GETSAMPLE([t + 1, t + Δ]);
5        σ ← OPTIMALSOLUTION(S, t);
6        f(σ(t)) ← f(σ(t)) + w(σ);
7        for r ∈ READY(R, t) \ {σ(t)}
8           do f(r) ← f(r) + (w(σ) − REGRETUB(σ, R, t, r));
9  return argmax(r ∈ R) f(r);
```

Its basic organization follows algorithm QC, the "quantitative" version of consensus. However, instead of assigning some credit only to the request selected at time $t$ for a given sample $s$, algorithm R (lines 7-8) uses the regret estimation to compute, each available request $r$, an approximation of the best solution of $s$ serving $r$ at time $t$, i.e.,

$$w(\sigma) - \text{REGRETUB}(\sigma, R, t, r).$$

As a consequence, every available request is given an evaluation value for every sample at time $t$ for the cost of (essentially) a single offline optimization. Observe that algorithm R performs $\mathcal{O}$ offline optimizations at time $t$.

## Relationships between E, C, R

The regret algorithm combines the salient features of the expectation and consensus algorithms. Like C (and unlike E), it considers $\mathcal{O}$ samples and avoids distributing the offline optimizations among the requests. Like E (and unlike C), each available request is evaluated for every sample. As a consequence, the algorithm combines the fundamental features of both approach and addresses their limitations.

The regret algorithm also establishes a clear relationship between the algorithms. Indeed, algorithm E is simply algorithm R with an exact regret, i.e.,

$$\text{REGRETUB}(\sigma, R, t, r) = \text{REGRET}(R, t, r).$$

Of course, an exact computation of the regret typically requires an offline optimization. Algorithm QC, the "quantitative" version of consensus, is simply algorithm R with the worst-case regret, i.e., $\text{REGRETUB}(\sigma, R, t, r) = w(\sigma)$. As a consequence, algorithms E and QC are two extreme instantiations in the spectrum of regret algorithms. Alternatively, algorithm E may be viewed as an ideal to achieve but time constraints make it impractical. Algorithm R then provides a general way to obtain fast approximations using regrets and QC is its worst-case instantiation.

Readers may wonder, as we did, why the "qualitative" version of consensus behaves so well in online vehicle routing and packet scheduling. The basic reason is that the difference between an optimal choice $\sigma(t)$ at time $t$ and another available choice $r$ is typically very small (we will come back to this issue later in the paper). It is over time that significant differences between the algorithms accumulate.

## Packet Scheduling

This section reports experimental results on the online packet scheduling problem was initially proposed by (Chang, Givan, & Chong 2000) to study the benefits of stochastic information on the quality of the schedules.

**Problem Description** The offline version can be specified as follows. We are given a set *Jobs* of jobs partitioned into a set of classes $C$. Each job $j$ is chararacterized by its weight $w(j)$, its arrival date $a(j)$, and its class $c(j)$. Jobs in the same class have the same weight (but different arrival times). We are also given a schedule horizon $H = [\underline{H}, \overline{H}]$ during which jobs must be scheduled. Each job $j$ requires a single time unit to process and must be scheduled in its time window $[a(j), a(j) + d]$, where $d$ is the same constant for all jobs (i.e., $d$ represents the time a job remains available to schedule). In addition, no two jobs can be scheduled at the same time and jobs that cannot be served in their time windows are dropped. The goal is to find a schedule of maximal weight, i.e., a schedule which maximizes the sum of the weights of all scheduled jobs. This is equivalent to minimizing weighted packet loss. More formally, assume, for simplicity and without loss of generality, that there is a job scheduled at each time step of the schedule horizon. Under this assumption, a schedule is a function $\sigma : H \rightarrow Jobs$ which assigns a job to each time in the schedule horizon. A schedule $\sigma$ is feasible if

$$\forall\, t_1, t_2 \in H : t_1 \neq t_2 \rightarrow \sigma(t_1) \neq \sigma(t_2)$$
$$\forall\, t \in H : a(\sigma(t)) \leq t \leq a(\sigma(t)) + d.$$

The weight of a schedule $\sigma$, denoted by $w(\sigma)$, is given by $w(\sigma) = \sum_{t \in H} w(\sigma(t))$. The goal is to find a feasible schedule $\sigma$ maximizing $w(\sigma)$. This offline problem can be solved in quadratic time $O(|J||H|)$.

**Experimental Setting** The experimental evaluation is based on the problems of (Chang, Givan, & Chong 2000; Bent & Van Hentenryck 2004), where all the details can be found. In these problems, the arrival distributions are specified by independent HMMs, one for each job class. The results are given for the reference 7-class problems and for an online schedule consisting of 200,000 time steps. Because

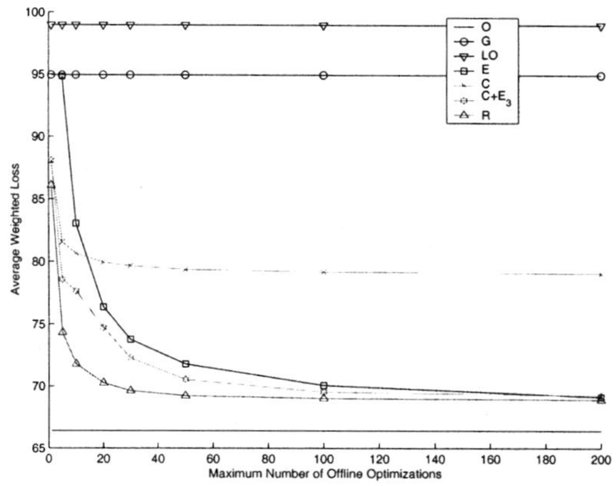


Figure 3: The Regret Algorithm on Packet Scheduling

it is unpractical to sample the future for so many steps, the algorithms use a sampling horizon of 50, which seems to be an excellent compromise between time and quality.

**The Regret Function** The online packet scheduling fits directly in the online stochastic framework of this paper. To evaluate the algorithms, it suffices to specify how to compute an upper bound to the regret. Our experimental evaluation uses a fast approximation based on a simple case analysis. Consider a job $r \in \text{READY}(R, t)$. If job $r$ is not scheduled (i.e., $r \notin \sigma$), the key idea is to try rescheduling $\sigma(t)$ instead of the job of smaller weight in $\sigma$. The regret becomes

$$\min(s \in [t, a(\sigma(t)) + d])\ w(\sigma(s)) - w(r)$$

since the replaced job is removed from $\sigma$ and $r$ is added to the schedule. In the worst case, the replaced job is $\sigma(t)$ and the regret is $w(\sigma(t)) - w(r)$. If job $r$ is scheduled at time $t_r$, the key idea is to select the best possible unscheduled job which may be scheduled at $t_r$. The regret now becomes

$$w(\sigma(t)) - \max(r \in U_r)\ w(u)$$

where $U_r = \{j \in \text{READY}(R, t_r) \mid j \notin \sigma\}$, since job $\sigma(t)$ is lost in the schedule and job $j$ is in the schedule already. Note that, in the best case, job $\sigma(t)$ is inserted at time $t_r$, in which case the regret is 0. This upper bound is $O(\max(d, |C|))$, which is sublinear in $|J|$ and $|H|$ and essentially negligible for this application.

**The Results** Figures 3 compares the various algorithms on the 7-class problems. The benefits of the regret algorithm are clearly apparent. Algorithm R indeed dominates all the other algorithms, including consensus (C) when there are very few offline optimizations (strong time constraints) and expectation (E) even when there are a reasonably large number of them, (weak time constraints).

## Vehicle Routing

We now evaluate the regret algorithm on a significantly more complicated problem: online multiple vehicle routing with time windows. This problem was studied initially in (Bent & Van Hentenryck 2001) to show the value of stochastic information in vehicle routing.

**Problem Formulation** The vehicle routing problems are specified formally in (Bent & Van Hentenryck 2001) where all the details can be found. Each problem contains a depot, a number of customer regions and a number of customer service requests from the regions. Each request has a demand, a service time, and a time window specified by an interval $[e, l]$, which represents the earliest and latest possible arrival times respectively. There are a number of identical vehicles available for use, each with capacity $Q$. A vehicle route starts at the depot, serves some customers at most once, and returns to the depot. The demand of a route is the summation of the demand of its customers. A routing plan is a set of routes servicing each customer exactly once. A solution to the offline VRPTW is a routing plan that satisfies the capacity constraints on the vehicle and the time window constraints of the requests. The objective is to find a solution maximizing the number of served customers. In the dynamic VRPTW, customer requests are not known in advance and become available during the course of the day. In general, a number of requests are available initially.

The online VRPTW is much more complicated than the online packet scheduling and does not fit directly in the stochastic framework presented earlier. First, decisions are triggered by two types of events: new customer requests and the arrival of a vehicle at a customer site. Second, a decision consists of choosing which customers to serve next on a given vehicle. Third, the online algorithm must decide whether to accept or reject customer requests immediately and must service the accepted requests. Finally, the VRPTW is a hard NP-complete problem whose instances are extremely difficult to solve optimally. Only 2 to 10 offline optimizations can be solved in between two events and the number of events is large (e.g., 50 different requests). Hence, the expectation method is not practical at all.

**Experimental Setting** The experimental results are based on the class-4 problems from (Bent & Van Hentenryck 2001), where all details can be found. They are derived from the Solomon benchmarks which are very challenging and involve 100 customers. The 15 instances exhibit various degrees of dynamism (i.e., the ratio between known and dynamic customers), different distributions of early and late requests, as well as time windows of very different sizes. Hence they cover a wide spectrum of possibilities and structures. The number of vehicles available for the dynamic algorithms was determined by solving the offline problems and adding two vehicles.

**The Stochastic Algorithm** The experimental evaluation is based on the MSA algorithm proposed in (Bent & Van Hentenryck 2001). This algorithm continously generates samples and "solves" the offline problems using large neighborhood search (LNS) (Shaw 1998). Plans are kept by the MSA algorithm as long as they are consistent with the decisions. This makes it possible to have a reasonable number of samples on which to base the decisions, since only very few samples can be solved in between events. This is due partly to the complexity of solving these complex vehicle routing problems and partly to the short time between events. In general, only a small number of samples (about 5) are avail-

| Prob | DOD | MSA$^c$ | MSA$^r$ |
|---|---|---|---|
| 20-20-60-rc101-1 | 46.3% | 3.00 | 3.48 |
| 20-20-60-rc101-2 | 45.8% | 4.32 | 4.84 |
| 20-20-60-rc101-3 | 50.0% | 3.24 | 3.46 |
| 20-20-60-rc101-4 | 45.6% | 5.08 | 5.38 |
| 20-20-60-rc101-5 | 47.4% | 6.08 | 5.72 |
| 20-20-60-rc102-1 | 59.0% | 1.10 | 1.94 |
| 20-20-60-rc102-2 | 57.5% | 3.66 | 3.70 |
| 20-20-60-rc102-3 | 56.0% | 4.12 | 3.60 |
| 20-20-60-rc102-4 | 52.0% | 2.58 | 3.12 |
| 20-20-60-rc102-5 | 57.6% | 2.88 | 2.90 |
| 20-20-60-rc104-1 | 76.1% | 13.38 | 11.26 |
| 20-20-60-rc104-2 | 75.6% | 13.86 | 12.16 |
| 20-20-60-rc104-3 | 76.1% | 10.64 | 8.98 |
| 20-20-60-rc104-4 | 72.2% | 14.32 | 9.42 |
| 20-20-60-rc104-5 | 74.4% | 13.38 | 10.20 |

Figure 4: Regret on Online Vehicle Routing

able to make a decision. *The main goal of our experimental evaluation is to evaluate two versions of the MSA algorithm: $MSA^c$ which uses consensus to choose the next customer on a given vehicle and $MSA^r$ which uses regret for the same decision.* The rest of the algorithm is left unchanged.

**The Regret Function** The regret function is simple and fast. Consider the decision of choosing which customer to serve next on vehicle $v$ and let $s$ be the first customer on the route $\sigma$ of vehicle $v$. To evaluate the regret of another customer $r$ on a vehicle $v$, the key idea is to determine if there is a feasible swap of $r$ and $s$ on $v$, in which case the regret is zero. Otherwise, if such a swap violates the time window constraints, the regret is 1. *The main benefit of this regret function is to recognize that some choices of customers are essentially equivalent.*

**Results** Table 4 depicts the results on the 15 instances of the Solomon benchmarks. Each instance is solved 50 times because of the nondeterministic nature of the sampling and LNS algorithms. The second column gives the degree of dynamism and the third and fourth columns report the number of missed customers by $MSA^c$ and $MSA^r$. The regret algorithm does not bring any benefit on the first two classes of problems with lower degrees of dynamism. *However, it produces some dramatic improvements on the third class of instances, where the degree of dynamism is high (about 70%) inducing stricter time constraints.* On this last class, the regret algorithm reduces the number of missed customers by about 35% on some problems and always produces reductions above 12%. This is a very interesting result, since consensus is particularly effective on these problems. Indeed, at a time $t$, the difference in the number of missed customers between a good and a bad choice is typically 1 and hence consensus is already a very good approximation of E. However, by recognizing "equivalent" choices, the regret algorithm further improves the approximation and produces significant benefits for the most time-constrained instances.

## Related Work

Online algorithms (e.g., (Fiat & Woeginger 1998)) have been addressed for numerous years but research has traditionally focused on techniques oblivious to the future and on competitive ratios (Karlin *et al.* 1988). It is only recently that researchers have begun to study how information about future uncertainty may improve the performance of algorithms. This includes scheduling problems (Chang, Givan, & Chong 2000), vehicle routing problems (Bent & Van Hentenryck 2001), (Cambell & Savelsbergh 2002) and elevator dispatching (Nikovski & Branch 2003) to name a few. Research on these problems has varied widely, but the unifying theme is that probabilistic information about the future significantly increases quality. The expectation method was the primary method used in (Chang, Givan, & Chong 2000), They also pointed out why POMDPs are too general for this class of problems. The consensus approach was motivated by online stochastic vehicle routing (Bent & Van Hentenryck 2001) and applied to online packet scheduling in (Bent & Van Hentenryck 2004).

## Conclusion

This paper proposed a novel algorithm for online stochastic optimization under time constraints. Like the consensus approach, the new regret algorithm solves as many samples as possible and avoids distributing them among requests. Like the expectation approach, it extracts information on all available requests for every sample by using an upper bound to the regret. The novel algorithm was evaluated on two very different applications, online packet scheduling and online vehicle routing, and was shown to outperform prior algorithms significantly in most cases. Moreover, the regret algorithm provides a fundamental insight in the relationships between the expectation and consensus approaches. This link, which was missing in earlier work, explains why consensus was so successful in online vehicle routing.

## Acknowledgment

This research is partially supported by NSF ITR Award DMI-0121495.

## References

Bent, R., and Van Hentenryck, P. 2001. Scenario Based Planning for Partially Dynamic Vehicle Routing Problems with Stochastic Customers. *Operations Research.* (to appear).

Bent, R., and Van Hentenryck, P. 2004. The Value of Consensus in Online Stochastic Scheduling. In *ICAPS 2004.*

Cambell, A., and Savelsbergh, M. 2002. Decision Support for Consumer Direct Grocery Initiatives. *Report TLI-02-09, Georgia Institute of Technology.*

Chang, H.; Givan, R.; and Chong, E. 2000. On-line Scheduling Via Sampling. In *AIPS'2000*, 62–71.

Fiat, A., and Woeginger, G. 1998. *Online Algorithms: The State of the Art.*

Karlin, A.; Manasse, M.; Rudolph, L.; and Sleator, D. 1988. Competitive Snoopy Caching. *Algorithmica* 3:79–119.

Nikovski, D., and Branch, M. 2003. Marginalizing Out Future Passengers in Group Elevator Control. In *UAI'03.*

Shaw, P. 1998. Using Constraint Programming and Local Search Methods to Solve Vehicle Routing Problems. In *CP'98*, 417–431.

# Assessing the Complexity of Plan Recognition

**Christopher W. Geib**

Honeywell Labs
3660 Technology Drive
Minneapolis, Minnesota 55418
christopher.geib@honeywell.com

**Abstract**

This paper presents a discussion of the theoretical complexity of plan recognition on the basis of an analysis of the number of explanations that any complete plan recognition algorithm must consider given various properties of the plan library. On the basis of these results it points out properties of plan libraries that make them computationally expensive.

## Introduction

Plan recognition is a well studied problem in the Artificial Intelligence literature. Following others, we distinguish between plan recognition/task tracking and goal identification. By plan recognition we mean the process of identifying not only the top level goal an agent is pursuing but also the plan that is being followed and the actions that have been done in furtherance of the plan.

The algorithms that have been used to address plan recognition range from, graph covering (Kautz 1986), to Bayes nets (Bui 2003, Horvitz 1998), to Probabilistic State Dependent Grammars (Pynadath 2000). While a significant amount of information is known about the complexity of these algorithms what has previously been lacking in the literature is a discussion of how hard the actual problem for an individual plan library is. Without a discussion of the complexity of the actual problem, we may find ourselves using very powerful algorithms to solve problems that are amenable to simpler algorithms.

The rest of this paper is organized as follows, we will discuss HTN plans as a representation for plan libraries and define an explanation for a given set of observations. Then, making sure to divorce ourselves from any particular plan recognition algorithm, we will discuss the complexity of a plan library in terms of the number of possible explanations licensed by a given set of observations and the features of the domain that control this. This will leave us in a position to make predictions about the difficulty any complete algorithm for plan recognition will have with a particular domain.



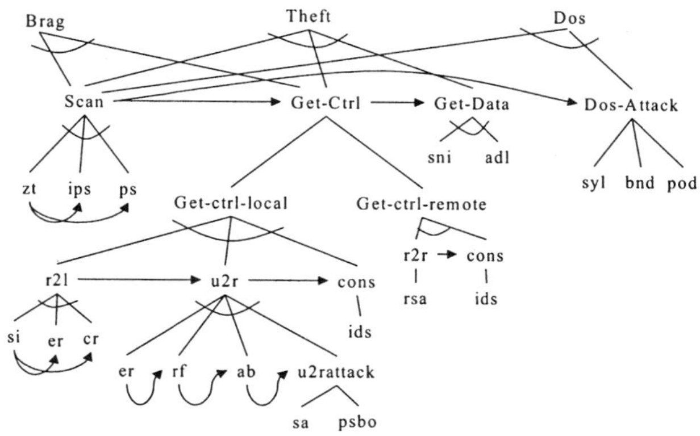


Figure 1: A small HTN plan library for a cyber security

## Modeling Plans and Explanations

Much of the past work in plan recognition has at least tacitly been based on simple hierarchical task networks (HTN) (Kutluhan, Hendler, and Nau 1994a, 1994b) as the representation for plans. Figure 1 is an HTN plan library represented as partially ordered and/or trees. In most plan recognition systems this kind of plan library is given to the system to define the set of plans it is expected to recognize. In the figure, interior "and nodes" representing plan decomposition (all the children must be performed for the parent to be achieved) are represented by an undirected arc across the lines connecting the parent node to its children. Interior "or nodes", which represent choice points in the plan (only one of the children must be performed to achieve the parent) do not have this arc. Finally, basic actions that are directly observable by a plan recognition system are shown as leaf nodes of the trees. Directed arcs represent ordering constraints between plan nodes. For example, in Figure 1, action **zt** must be executed before **ips** and **ps**. In this paper, we will be considering the complexity of plan recognition limited to plans that can be represented in this formalism.

We define an *explanation of a set of observations* as a minimal forest of instances of plan trees with expansions chosen for "or" nodes sufficient to allow an assignment of each observation to a specific basic action in the plan. For example, Figure 2 shows one of many possible

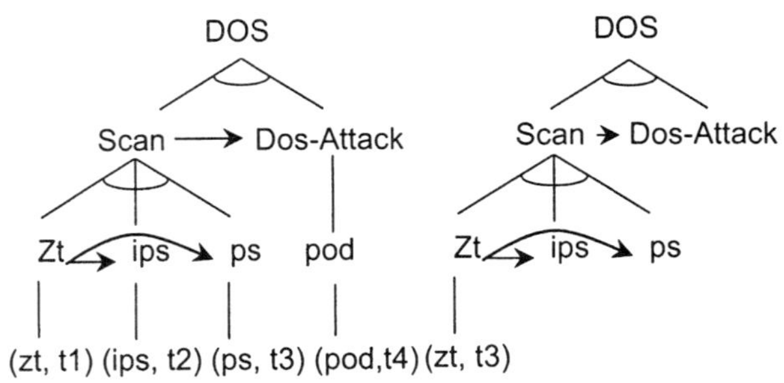


Figure 2: An Explanation

explanations for the set of observations (action, time pairs): {(zt, t1), (ips, t2), (zt, t3), (ps, t4), (pod, t5)} given the plan library shown in Figure 1. Note that the second Dos-Attack is not expanded in this explanation since it is not required to explain the observations. Also note that in this discussion we will be using an integer time notation.

Figure 2 shows two instances of the DOS (Denial of Service) goal being explained by this series of observations. Much research in plan recognition (Geib 2003, 2001a, 2001b, Goldman 1999, Goldman 1993) is committed to recognizing the interleaved execution of multiple goals that are active at the same time. In defining what is an acceptable explanation for a series for observations we will follow this tradition. What is less accepted in the research community is that plan recognition algorithms should consider multiple instances of the same goal as part of an explanation. Allowing multiple instances of the same goal makes the problem of plan recognition significantly harder, therefore we will provide a short justification for why algorithms must address this case.

### Multiple Instances of the Same Goal

Consider the cyber security domain from Figure 1. In the real world, it is common for a determined cyber attacker to launch multiple different attacks against a single host, and even multiple instances of the same attack, to achieve a single goal. This is done for a number of reasons: diversity of target susceptibility, attack success likelihood, and to create confusion, among others. Thus in this domain it is very common to see multiple instances of the same goal being pursued by different, very similar, or even identical instances of plans. The explanation presented in Figure 2 has remained agnostic about the specific Dos-Attack that will be launched, however since the **zt** (zone-transfer) observed at time **t3** is consistent with a second DOS goal any complete algorithm for plan recognition must consider the possibility that there are multiple interleaved instances of this goal being pursued by a single agent at the same time.

Having explicitly, stated that we will be looking at multiple interleaved goals and multiple instances of the same goal. It is worth noting some possible aspects of plan recognition that will not be covered in this discussion. Plans with explicit looping constructs, observations that contribute to more than one plan, domains that are only partially observable, questions of the certainty of a given observation, and the possible abandonment of plans, can all increase the number of viable explanations for a given set of observations and hence the complexity of the plan recognition task. A complete treatment of these issues are outside the scope of this paper, however, since they all result in increasing the number of possible explanations for a set of observations, this work can be seen as a lower bound on the complexity of plan recognition in domains that address these issues.

## Counting Explanations

We are interested in the worst case complexity of each problem domain. One way to examine the complexity of a domain to examine the maximal number of explanations that a given set of observations can have. Since any complete algorithm for plan recognition will have to examine all of the viable explanations for a given set of observations, this will give us a handle on the complexity of the domain. However, long sets of observations may result in more explanations than short sets. Therefore, we need to find a way to examine the complexity of the domain outside of a specific set of observations. That is, we are interested in identifying those plan properties that result in large sets of possible explanations. We will identify these properties by examining a single explanation, observing how the addition of a single observation changes the number of explanations that are licensed, and then identifying the properties of the plans in the explanation that enabled the changes.

One of the properties of an explanation is that each observation is assigned to a specific basic action. We will say an observation *explains* a basic action if it can be legally bound to the basic action within an explanation. Further, we define an *attachment point* as any basic action that does not have an observation assigned to it that could be explained by the current observation.

As with other highly constrained systems, the addition of a single observation can increase, decrease, or leave unchanged the number of explanations. That is, given an explanation, a new observation is either inconsistent with the explanation, in which case the number of explanations decreases, or it is consistent with the explanation in which case then number of explanation remains the same or increases.

In the following subsections we will examine the addition of an observation to a single explanation under various conditions and the effects it will have on the number of licensed explanations. We will first consider the simple case of observations that do not introduce new root goals to the explanation and then consider the case of adding observations that do.

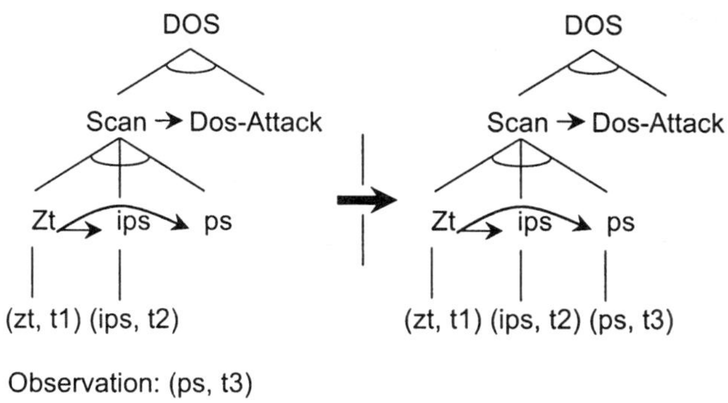


Figure 3: Left: an observation and explanation pair with a single point of attachment. Right: resulting explanation.

## No New Root Goals

We will break the case of observations that merely extend the root goals that are already in an explanation into two sub-cases. First we consider the case where there is only a single attachment point in the explanation for the observation. In this case, the observation is added, the explanation remains consistent and no new explanations need to be introduced. An example of this is shown in Figure 3. Note that if there were no basic actions the observation could explain then the explanation could be discarded and the number of explanations would decrease.

Second, we consider the more interesting case where there are multiple attachment points for the observation in the explanation. In this case, the number of consistent explanations is multiplied by the number of attachment points. A complete algorithm must consider the possible binding of the observation to each of the candidate attachment points resulting in multiple possible explanations.

Informal empirical evaluation of one complete, incremental plan recognition algorithm (Geib and Goldman 2003, 2001a, 2001b) over three different domains suggest that the most common cases that do not introduce new root goals are those where there is only a single possible attachment point. While there are many cases in these domains where multiple instances of the same basic action could have potentially resulted in multiple attachment points, the incremental nature of the algorithm and the restrictions imposed by ordering constraints within the plan libraries prevented it. Thus both theoretical and empirical analysis suggest that these are not the computationally expensive cases for plan recognition.

## New Root Goals the Simple Case

To discuss observations that introduce new goals, it will be helpful to define a *leader* as any basic action such that there exists a root goal in the plan library, such that, neither the basic action, nor any of its ancestors, is ordered after some other action within at least one possible plan for the root goal. Intuitively, a leader could be the first observed action within a plan for the designated goal. As in the case where no new goal is introduced it will be helpful to divide our discussion into two cases: the introduction of root goals and plans for them that have a single leader action and those that have multiple leader actions.

The introduction of single leader plans is very similar to the cases that do not introduce a new root goal. The number of explanations increases linearly with the number of root goals for which the action is a leader. Thus, it is actually only necessary to introduce a new explanation for each of the possible root goals that could be introduced by the action. In effect, each of the root goals for which the action is a leader can be seen as continually active attachment point. Figure 4 presents an example of this case.

## New Root Goals with Multiple Leaders

For the rest of this discussion, we will make a small alteration to the plan library that we have been using in our examples. For the rest of this discussion we will assume that the ordering constraints from **zt** to **ips** and **ps** have been deleted. That is **zt** is no longer the sole leader for all three of the root goals. Instead all three goals share the common set of unordered leaders {**zt, ips, ps**}.

The first observed leader for a root goal with multiple leaders is very similar to the previous case of a new goal with a single leader. The new observation only requires that the set of explanations be increased linearly in the number of root goals for which the observed action is a leader. In our example plan library, this means that observing any one of **zt**, **ips**, or **ps** will generate three explanations, one where the observed action contributes to a new instance of each of **DOS**, **Theft**, or **Brag.** This looks just like Figure 4 from the previous case. However, a very different thing happens when a second leader for the same root goal is seen.

Since the second observed leader for the root goal is unordered with respect to the first, we are no longer allowed to assume that it must be part of the same root goal. That is, we cannot be certain if the observation is contributing to an existing plan or if it is introducing a new goal. Thus if we are to consider all the possible explanations, we must consider both the possibility that the observation is contributing to the existing goal and that it is introducing a new root goal. An example of this is shown in Figure 5.

Now consider what happens when the third leader for this example is seen. We must consider three cases: 1) all three actions are contributing to the same goal, 2) that any two of them may be contributing to a single goal and the other to a second goal, and 3) that all three contribute to distinct root goal instances. On top of this all three of these cases must be enumerated for all goals that share the common leaders.

If we extend this case to have $m$ unordered leaders that are shared by $n$ root goals then, when we see all $m$ leaders we will be forced to consider the set of all subsets of the up to $m$ instances of the $n$ root goals and all the possible distributions of the $m$ leaders between them. Clearly this will grow quite fast, but having identified this as the case that will result in a large increase in the number of explanations, the question remains, how fast does this grow? Given a plan library that has a set of $m$ unordered leaders shared by $n$ plans. Then in the worst case where one of each of the unordered leaders is observed in a row, a single explanation will expand to exactly:

$$\sum_{i=i}^{m} \left\{ \begin{matrix} m \\ i \end{matrix} \right\} n^{i}$$

explanations. The summation captures the fact that the number of possible root goals varies from one to $m$. The first term in the summation represents the distribution of observed leaders to root goal instances, captured by Sterling's numbers of the second kind (Bogart 1990). This number is exactly the number of ways that the $m$ actions can be distributed to the $i$ root goals so that each goal has at least one action. The second term in the summation reflects the number of possible permutations of the root goals. To provide some intuition about the rate of growth of this function, consider the following. This function is bounded below by $n^m$ which is seen by considering the last term of the summation.

The function is also bounded above by $(mn)^m$. This can be seen by creating an alphabet of letters to assign to each observed unordered leader to tell us what goal it contributes to. Since we know that in the worst case there will be $m$ goals, each possible shared goal $\alpha$ is given $m$ letters $\alpha_1, \alpha_2, \ldots \alpha_m$ each one representing the possible goal instances of $\alpha$. This creates an alphabet of $mn$ letters. If each leader is given one letter to indicate which instance of which goal it contributes to. Since we are interested in the case of $m$ observations there are $(mn)^m$ such combinations. This represents an upper bound because, many of these combinations are not legal assignments of leaders to root goal instances. For example, none of the leaders could be assigned to contribute to the second instance of a particular goal unless there were already a first instance of the same goal, however, nothing in the construction of our alphabet or the assignment of letters to leaders prevents this.

$n^m$ represents significant growth in the number of explanations and will be a dominating source of complexity for the domain. Note that multiple instances of any one of the leaders will not have this kind of exponential growth. Consider the case of the following observations {(**zt**, 1), (**zt**, 2), (**zt**,3)}. Since any given instance of the root goals can only have one instance of **zt** we know that each of these observations must introduce a new root goal. Since they can't contribute to each other the set of explanations remains constant in size (introducing a new goal with each action.)

It is important to realize that while this problem is significantly amplified by having multiple root goals that share the unordered leaders, this problem occurs even when the leaders are not shared. Note that the exponent of this problem is the length of the unordered leader, not the number of goals sharing the leader. Thus the number of

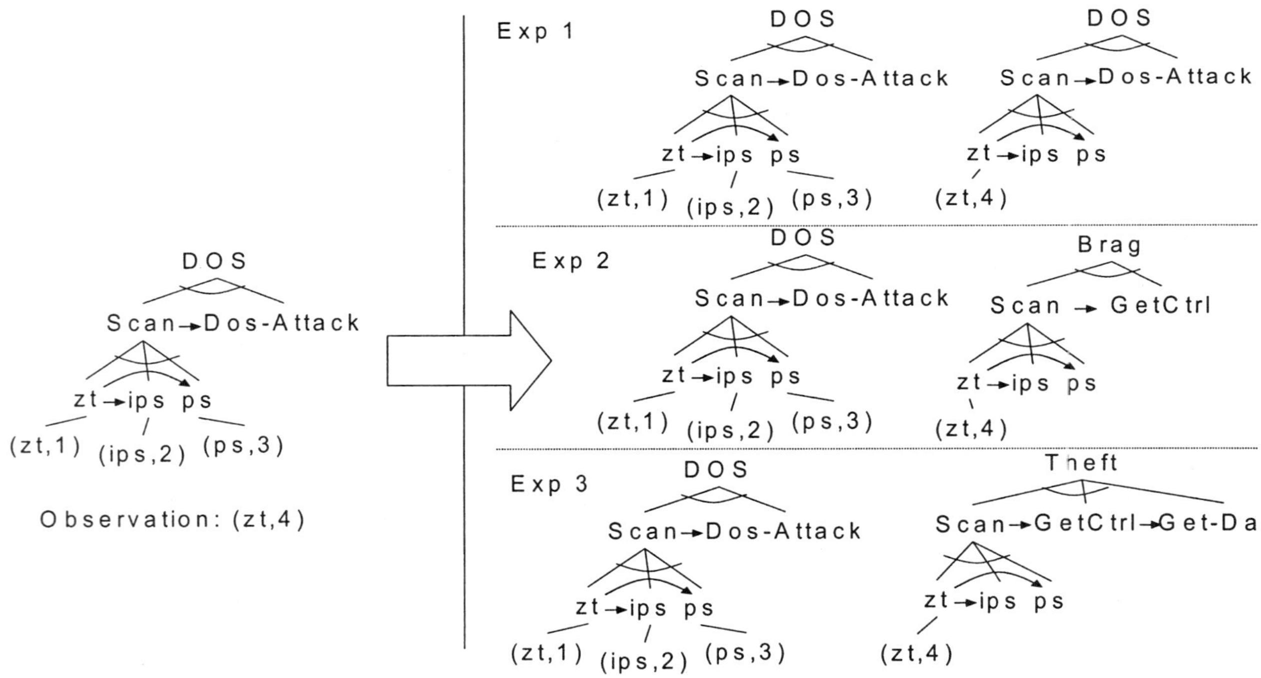


Figure 4: The Explanations that result from observing the single leader for three root goals

explanations will grow exponentially even if the leaders are not shared. That is, since, any complete algorithm will have to consider multiple instances of the same root goal, this problem will occur even for a single plan with unordered leaders, albeit to a lesser degree.

## Implications

To summarize, shared unordered leaders in a plan library have the potential to exponentially increase the number of explanations that have to be considered by any complete plan recognition algorithm. All other cases have, at worst, a increase in the number of explanations that is linear in the number of attachment points. Thus, plan libraries that have exceptionally large numbers of repeated actions or long shared unordered plan leaders will likely produce very large runtimes. Note that this shows that partial ordering of the plans can in fact have a more significant impact on the runtime of any plan recognition algorithm than even the sharing of actions across plans.

What is the most disheartening about this result is that this growth in the number of explanations will happen even when there is only a single instance of the root goal that is intended and a single set of the shared unordered leaders is executed. Encouragingly, in the case where there is only a single instance of one of the root goals being executed by the agent, once the leaders have all been executed a significant reduction of the number of explanations is possible. Given the ordering constraints that by definition end the unordered leaders, we can begin to eliminate explanations that involve multiple goals since they will be inconsistent. For example, consider the following set of observations: {(**ips**, 1), (**ps**, 2), (**zt**, 3), (**pod**, 4) again taken from the plan library of Figure 1 (with the initial ordering constraints removed between **zt**, **ips** and **ps**.). If we had just the unordered shared leaders the set of explanations would be quite large, however for the presence of the **pod** action to be legal within this plan library all three of the shared leaders must contribute to a single instance of the **scan** action. This allows us to eliminate all but one of the possible explanations.

Given these results some might be tempted to artificially introduce ordering into the plans in the library in order to reduce the number of possible explanations. One could enumerate all of the possible orderings for the shared unordered leaders, producing a plan library that had only shared ordered leaders. Of course in the end all this will do is push the implicit complexity of the ordering constraints into explicit complexity of the plan library itself. Further since all of the orderings must be enumerated and none of the complexity associated with multiple goals is addressed, this will not succeed in reducing the complexity of the problem.

### To Enumerate or Not

Beyond the conclusions about the properties of plan libraries that make plan recognition complex, these results shed light on the question of when to use which plan recognition algorithm. Some algorithms call for an explicit enumeration of the explanation space before seeing any of the observations (Bui 2003, Kautz 1986). Since the size of the explanation space depends on the number of observations that will be processed these approaches have often limited themselves to a single instance of each root goal. Further, as these results have shown, enumeration of the explanation space will require an exponential number

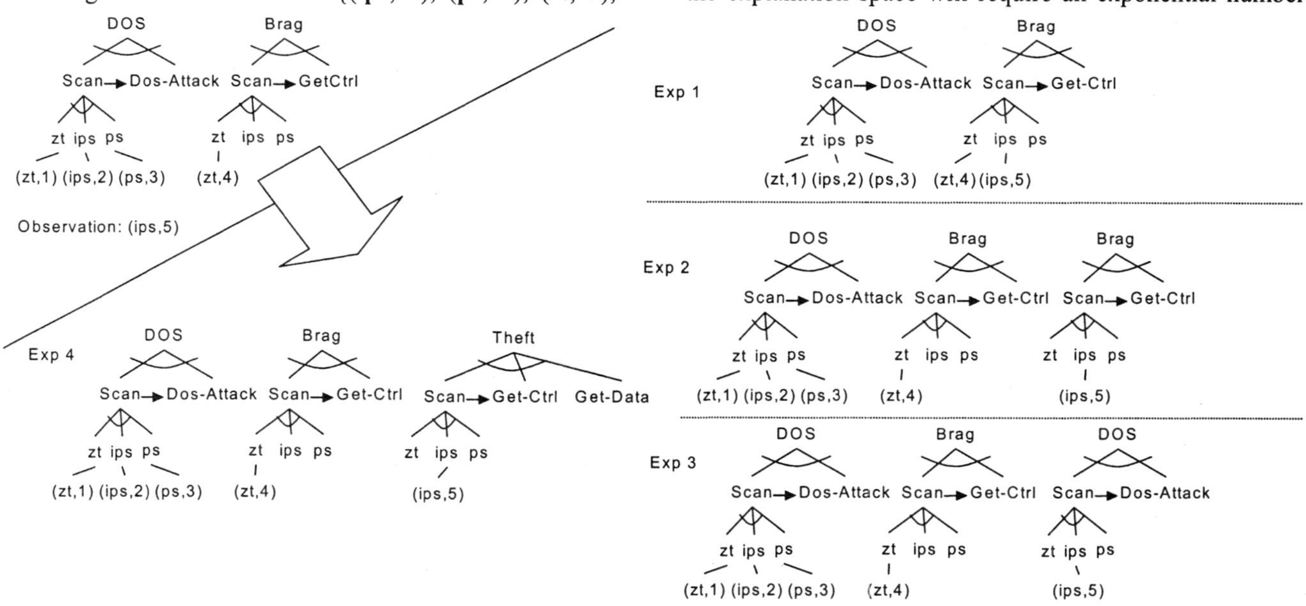


Figure 5:Upper Left: One of the explanations that explains an observation of the first unordered leaders. Lower Right: The four explanations required to explain the observation of the second unordered leader for the three root goals DOS, Brag, and Theft

of cases for some plan libraries. Thus these results should caution against such approaches to plan recognition in domains with shared unordered leaders. Instead, approaches that are incremental and only build those portions of the explanation space that are needed by the observations will be more effective.

## Conclusions

In this paper we have examined the way in which the set of possible explanations for a given set of observations grows in an effort to understand the complexity of complete plan recognition algorithms. We have demonstrated that the number of such explanations can grow exponentially in the number of root goals that share a common unordered prefix of actions.

These results have given us a concrete handle on those aspects of a plan library that may make it computationally difficult. Shared leaders are a result of having domains where many different plans for different goals have a "common prefix" of actions. Where the steps of such a prefix are unordered plan recognition will involve consideration of a large number of explanations.

This strongly argues that when given a choice, if a plan library must contain multiple plans for root goals with a common prefix that this prefix should be kept as short as possible and that ordering constraints should be introduced whenever possible within such a prefix.

### Acknowledgements

This material is based upon work supported by the Advanced Research and Development Activity (ARDA) under contract No. NBCHC030078.

## References

Bogart, K., 1990, *Introductory Combinatorics*, (2nd Ed.), Orlando, Fl., Harcourt Brace Jovanovich.

Bui, H., 2003, "A General Model for Online Plan Recognition," *Proceedings of IJCAI-2003.*

Geib, C., and Goldman, R., 2003, "Recognizing Plan/Goal Abandonment," *Proceedings of IJCAI-2003.*

Geib, C., and Goldman, R., 2001a, "Probabilistic Plan Recognition for Hostile Agents," *Proceedings of the FLAIRS01 Conference*, Key West.

Geib, C. and Goldman, R., 2001b, "Plan Recognition in Intrusion Detection Systems," *Proceedings of the DISCEX-II Conference.*

Goldman, R., Geib, C., and Miller, C., 1999, "A New Model of Plan Recognition," In *Proceedings of the 1999 Conference on Uncertainty in Artificial Intelligence.*

Goldman, R. and Charniak, E., 1993, "A Bayesian Model of Plan Recognition", *Artificial Intelligence*, vol 64(1)

Horvitz, E., Breese, J., Heckerman, D., Hovel, D., and Koos, R., 98, "The Lumiere Project: Bayesian User Modeling for Inferring the Goals and Needs of Software Users", *Proceedings of the Conference on Uncertainty in Artificial Intelligence (UAI-98).*

Kautz, H., and Allen, J., 1986, "Generalized Plan Recognition", *Proceeding of the National Conference on Aritficial Intelligence (AAAI-86).*

Kutluhan, E., Hendler, J. and Nau, D., 1994, "UMCP: A Sound and Complete Procedure for Hierarchical Task Network Planning," *Artificial Intelligence Planning Systems: Proceedings of the Second International Conference (AIPS-94)*, Chicago.

Kutluhan, E., Hendler, J. and Nau, D., 1994, "HTN Planning: Complexity and Expressivity," *Proceedings of the National Conference on Artificial Intelligence (AAAI-94).*

Poole, D., 1997, "The Independent Choice Logic for Modeling Multiple Agents Under Uncertainty," *Artificial Intelligence*, 94(1-2):7-56.

Pynadath, D., and Wellman, M., 2000, "Probabilistic State-Dependent Grammars for Plan Recognition", *Proceedings of the Conference on Uncertainty in Artificial Intelligence (UAI-2000).*

# Forward-Chaining Planning in Nondeterministic Domains

**Ugur Kuter**
Department of Computer Science,
University of Maryland,
College Park, MD 20742, USA
email: ukuter@cs.umd.edu

**Dana Nau**
Department of Computer Science and
Institute for Systems Research
University of Maryland,
College Park, MD 20742, USA
email: nau@cs.umd.edu

### Abstract

In this paper, we present a general technique for taking forward-chaining planners for deterministic domains (e.g., HSP, TLPlan, TALplanner, and SHOP2) and adapting them to work in nondeterministic domains. Our results suggest that our technique preserves many of the desirable properties of these planners, such as the ability to use heuristic techniques to achieve highly efficient planning.

In our experimental studies on two problem domains, the well-known MBP algorithm took exponential time, confirming prior results by others. A nondeterminized version of SHOP2 took only polynomial time. The polynomial-time figures are confirmed by a complexity analysis, and a similar complexity analysis shows that a nondeterminized version of TLPlan would perform similarly.

## Introduction

One of the biggest limitations of classical AI planning is the assumption of *determinism*: classical planner assumes that it knows the exact outcomes of the actions, so that for any given plan and initial state, the world will evolve along a single fully predictable path.

A more realistic assumption is that the world is *nondeterministic*: an action may have several possible outcomes, but we do not know in advance which one will occur. Unfortunately, this incurs a huge combinatorial explosion: a plan may have exponentially many different execution paths, and the planning algorithm must reason about all of them in order to find a plan that works despite the nondeterminism in the world.

Prior approaches for planning in nondeterministic domains have included model-checking techniques (Cimatti *et al.* 2003; Cimatti, Roveri, & Traverso 1998) and conformant-planning techniques (Smith & Weld 1998). Algorithms based on these approaches typically examine most or all of the states in the state space.

In deterministic planning domains, much work has been done on ways to improve the efficiency of planners by preventing them from visiting unpromising states. This work has been especially successful in planners based on forward chaining, such as HSP (Bonet & Geffner 1999), FF (Hoffmann & Nebel 2001), TLPlan (Bacchus & Kabanza 2000), TALplanner (Kvarnström & Doherty 2001), and SHOP2 (Nau *et al.* 2003). These planners know the current state at all times, which facilitates the use of some powerful pruning techniques—especially in hand-tailorable planners, in which the pruning techniques may be domain-specific.

In this paper, we present a way to transport these efficiency improvements over to nondeterministic planning. Our contributions are the following:

- A general technique for "nondeterminizing" forward-chaining planners, i.e., extending them to work in nondeterministic domains. This technique preserves soundness and completeness.
- Conditions under which a nondeterminized algorithm's time complexity is polynomially bounded by the time complexity of the deterministic version.
- Experimental comparisons of ND-SHOP2 (the nondeterminization of SHOP2) to the well known MBP algorithm, in two different domains. The experimental results show MBP's CPU time growing exponentially in the size of the problem, confirming the results in (Pistore, Bettin, & Traverso 2001), and ND-SHOP2's CPU time growing only polynomially.
- A complexity analysis confirming the experimental results for ND-SHOP2: its running time grows at $\Theta(n^4)$ in one domain and $\Theta(n^5)$ in the other. This level of performance is not restricted to ND-SHOP2: a similar complexity analysis shows that a nondeterminization of TLPlan would have similar growth rates.

## Definitions and Notation

Our definition of states, goals, operators, and actions (ground instances of operators) are the same as in classical planning, except that each operator (and thus each action) may have more than one possible result. A planning problem is a triple $P = (s_0, g, O)$, where $s_0$ is the initial state, $g$ is the goal, and $O$ is the set of operators. Recall that $s_0$ and $g$ vary from one problem to another, and $O$ remains fixed within a planning domain but varies from one domain to another.

We also use most of the same definitions used in nondeterministic planning domains. $\gamma(s,a)$, the *state-transition function* induced by the set of operators $O$, gives the set of all possible states that may result from applying the action $a$ to the state $s$, with $\gamma(s,a) = \emptyset$ if $a$ is not applicable to $s$. The planning domain is deterministic iff $|\gamma(s,a)| \leq 1\ \forall s \forall a$. A *policy* is a set $\pi = \{(s_i, a_i)\}_{i=1}^{k}$, where $k \geq 0$ is the size of the policy. The set of states in $\pi$ is $S_\pi = \{s \mid (s,a) \in \pi\}$. We require that for any state $s$, there is at most one action $a$ such that $(s,a) \in \pi$. The *execution structure* for $\pi$ is a directed graph $\Sigma_\pi$ whose nodes are all of the states that can be reached by executing actions in $\pi$, and whose edges represent the possible state transitions caused by actions in $\pi$. If there is a path in $\Sigma_\pi$ from $s_1$ to $s_2$, then we say that $s_1$ is a $\pi$-ancestor of $s_2$ and $s_2$ is a $\pi$-descendant of $s_1$. We use the usual definitions (Cimatti *et al.* 2003) of weak, strong, and strong-cyclic solutions for planning problems.

Researchers have often defined nondeterministic versions of well-known deterministic problems; we formalize this notion as follows. A planning problem $P' = (S_0, g, O')$ is a *nondeterministic version* of a deterministic planning problem $P = (s_0, g, O)$ if $s_0 \in S_0$ and $O$ is identical to $O'$ except that each operator in $O'$ may have additional sets of effects. These additional effects can be used to model action failures (e.g., a gripper drops what it is holding) and exogenous events (e.g., a road is closed).

## Nondeterminizing Forward Planners

We now describe a general technique for taking forward-chaining planners for deterministic planning domains, and *nondeterminizing* them, i.e., translating them into planners that find strong-cyclic solutions in nondeterministic domains. A policy $\pi$ is a *strong-cyclic solution* if every (finite or infinite) path in $\Sigma_\pi$ can be extended to a finite execution path that reaches to a goal state. We have also developed planners that produce weak and strong solutions; see (Kuter & Nau 2004) for details.

The basis of our approach is an abstract planning procedure FCP for deterministic domains, and a corresponding procedure ND-FCP for nondeterministic domains. Both are described below. If a planner $\Lambda$ can be described as an instance of FCP, then, ND-$\Lambda$, the corresponding instance of ND-FCP, will be the strong-cyclic nondeterminization of $\Lambda$. Using this technique, we have written strong-cyclic nondeterminizations of TLPlan (Bacchus & Kabanza 2000), SHOP2 (Nau *et al.* 2003), TALplanner (Kvarnström & Doherty 2001), and several other forward planners (see (Kuter & Nau 2004)).

As shown in Figure 1, FCP starts with an initial state $s_0$, and explores other states by successively choosing and applying planning operators until it reaches a state that satisfies the goal formula $g$. The *action-selection function* $\alpha(s)$ is used to prune the search space. It returns zero or more actions, which we will call the actions that *satisfy* $\alpha(s)$. Rather than trying all of the actions applicable to $s$, FCP only tries the ones that are applicable and satisfy $\alpha$.

```
Procedure FCP(s0, g, O, α);
  π ← ∅; s ← s0
  loop
    if s satisfies g then return(π)
    A ← {(s,a) | a is a ground instance of an operator
          in O, a is applicable to s, and a ∈ α(s)}
    if A = ∅ then return(failure)
    nondeterministically choose (s,a) ∈ A
    π ← π ∪ {(s,a)}
    s ← γ(s,a)
```

Figure 1: An abstract forward-chaining planning procedure for deterministic planning domains.

```
Procedure ND-FCP(S0, g, O', α')
  π ← ∅; S ← S0; solved ← ∅
  loop
    if S = ∅ then return(π)
    select a state s ∈ S and remove it from S
    if s satisfies g then insert s into solved
    else if s ∉ Sπ then
      A ← {(s,a) | a is a ground instance of an opera-
            tor in O', a is applicable to s, and
            a ∈ α'(s)}
      if A = ∅ then return(failure)
      nondeterministically choose (s,a) ∈ A
      π ← π ∪ {(s,a)}
      S ← S ∪ γ(s,a)
    else if s has no π-descendants in (S ∪ solved) \ Sπ
      then return(failure)
```

Figure 2: Nondeterminization of FCP. The underlines indicate how the coding from FCP is embedded in ND-FCP.

For example, in SHOP2, the search is controlled by a set of *methods* that decompose *tasks* into subtasks, and $\alpha(s)$ is the set of all actions $a$ applicable to $s$ such that $a$ can be produced by applying methods to the current task network. In TLPlan (Bacchus & Kabanza 2000), the search is controlled by a formula $\phi$ written in a modal logic called *Linear Temporal Logic (LTL)*. For each state $s$, $\alpha(s)$ is the set of all actions $a$ applicable to $s$ such that the successor state $\gamma(s,a)$ satisfies a *progressed formula*, $Progress(s, \phi)$.

Figure 2 shows ND-FCP, the strong-cyclic nondeterminization of FCP. Like FCP, ND-FCP plans forward from $S_0$, but the success criterion is more complicated. In FCP, a plan $\pi$ is a solution if its final state satisfies the goal condition $g$. In order for a policy in ND-FCP to be a solution, every state in $\pi$'s execution structure must have at least one $\pi$-descendant that satisfies the goal (a *solved* state in the pseudocode).

ND-FCP's action-selection function is analogous to

FCP's, and the action-selection function for a deterministic domain can generally be adapted to work in nondeterministic versions of the domain. As an example, recall that for TLPlan, the action-selection function $\alpha(s)$ for a planning domain $\mathcal{D}$ returns all actions applicable to $s$ such that $\gamma(s,a)$ satisfies $Progress(s,\phi)$, where $\phi$ is a search-control formula. If $\mathcal{D}'$ is a nondeterministic version of $\mathcal{D}$, then one possible action-selection function for ND-TLPlan is $\alpha'(s) = \{$all actions $a$ such that at least one state in $\gamma(s,a)$ satisfies $Progress(s,\phi)\}$. This trivial adaptation of $\alpha$ works correctly, but usually ND-TLPlan will perform more efficiently if we write an action-selection function that returns only some of the actions in $\alpha'(s)$.

## Theoretical Properties

It is not hard to show that FCP and ND-FCP are both sound (i.e., they do not return any plan that is not a solution), and that they are conditionally complete in the sense that they can find every solution whose actions satisfy the action-selection function.

We now establish an upper bound on the time complexity of a nondeterminized planning algorithm in a strongly connected planning domain. A planning domain is strongly connected if for any two states $s$ and $s'$, there exists a sequence of actions that reaches to $s'$ when executed in $s$. Such domains are not hard to find: some well-known examples from previous planning competitions include Blocks-World, Logistics, DriverLog, ZenoTravel, Depot, and Rover. Any nondeterminization of such a domain will also be strongly connected.

**Theorem 1** *Let $\Lambda$ be an instance of FCP. Suppose $\Lambda$ finds solution plans in time $O(\rho(|\pi|))$ in strongly-connected planning domains, where $|\pi|$ is the size of the solution plan and $\rho$ is a monotonic function. Then* ND-$\Lambda$ *finds solution policies in time $O(\rho(|\Sigma_{\pi'}|))$, where $|\Sigma_{\pi'}|$ is the size of execution structure for the solution policy returned by* ND-$\Lambda$.

**Corollary 1** *Under the conditions of Theorem 1, if the number of possible successors of each state is bounded by a constant, then* ND-$\Lambda$ *finds solution policies in time $O(\rho(|\pi'|))$, where $|\pi'|$ is the size of the solution policy.*

Note that every path in $\Sigma_{\pi'}$ can be extended to a finite execution path that reaches to a goal state in a strongly-connected domain. In domains that are not strongly connected, however, $\Sigma_{\pi'}$ may contain states that have no $\pi'$-descendants that satisfy the goals. We call such states as the *dead-end* states of $\Sigma_{\pi'}$.

The following complexity result holds even in planning domains that are not strongly connected:

**Theorem 2** *Let $\Lambda$ be an instance of FCP, and suppose that $\Lambda$'s running time is $O(\rho(|\pi|)$, where $|\pi|$ is the size of the solution plan returned by $\Lambda$, and $\rho$ is a monotonic function. Then* ND-$\Lambda$ *finds solution policies in average time $O(\rho(n) + \frac{xdn}{y}))$, where $n = |\Sigma_{\pi'}|$ is the size of the execution structure for the solution policy $\pi'$ returned by* ND-$\Lambda$, *$x$ the maximum number of state-action pairs that are added to any policy after* ND-$\Lambda$ *visits a dead-end state, $y$ is the maximum number of actions applicable to any state, and in every state $s$, $0 \leq d \leq y$ is the maximum number of actions applicable to $s$ that lead to a dead-end state.*

**Corollary 2** *Under the conditions of Theorem 2, if the number of possible successors of each state is bounded by a constant, then* ND-$\Lambda$ *finds solutions in average time $O(\rho(|\pi'|)+\frac{xd|\pi'|}{y}))$, where $|\pi'|$ is the size of the solution.*

## Experiments and Complexity Analysis

In order to perform an empirical evaluation of our theoretical results, we implemented ND-SHOP2, the nondeterminized version of SHOP2. We compared its performance and scalability for reachability goals with MBP (Bertoli *et al.* 2001), a well-known planning system for nondeterministic domains that is based on symbolic model checking techniques. In our comparisons, we used MBP's *Local Search* algorithm for finding strong-cyclic plans.[1] All of our experiments were run on an AMD Duron 900Mhz laptop computer running Linux RedHat 7.2 with 256MB memory.

Our first experimental domains was the Robot Navigation domain that was used for experimental evaluation of MBP in (Pistore, Bettin, & Traverso 2001). This domain is a variant of a similar domain described in (Kabanza, Barbeau, & St-Denis 1997). It consists of a building with 8 rooms connected by 7 doors. In the building, there is a robot and there are a number of packages in various rooms. The robot is responsible for delivering packages from their initial locations to their final locations by opening and closing doors, moving between rooms, and picking up and putting down the packages. The robot can hold at most one package at any time. To add nondeterminism, the domain also involves a "kid" that can close any of the open doors that are designated initially as "kid-doors."

We compared ND-SHOP2 and MBP with the same set of experimental parameters as in (Pistore, Bettin, & Traverso 2001): the number of packages $n$ ranged from 1 to 5, and the number of kid-doors $k$ ranged from 0 to 7. For each combination of $n$ and $k$, we generated 20 random problems, ran the planners on the problems, and averaged the CPU time for each planner.[2]

Figure 3 shows the results for $k = 7$ and $n = 1, \ldots, 5$; this illustrates the behavior of the algorithms as the size of the domain increases.

Our experimental results confirm the ones in (Pistore, Bettin, & Traverso 2001): in both their experiments and ours, MBP's CPU time grows exponentially (the logarithm of the data grows linearly) in the size

[1] We also tried using MBP's Global Search algorithm, but the Local Search algorithm ran faster.

[2] As in (Pistore, Bettin, & Traverso 2001), the CPU time for MBP's includes both its preprocessing and search times. Omitting the preprocessing times would not have significantly affected the results: they were never more than a few seconds, and usually below one second.

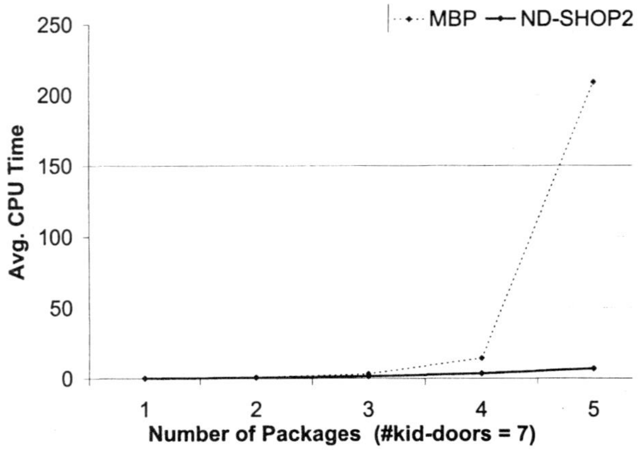


Figure 3: Average running times of ND-SHOP2 and MBP on Robot-Navigation problems, as a function of the number of packages. The number of kid-doors in the domain is fixed to 7.

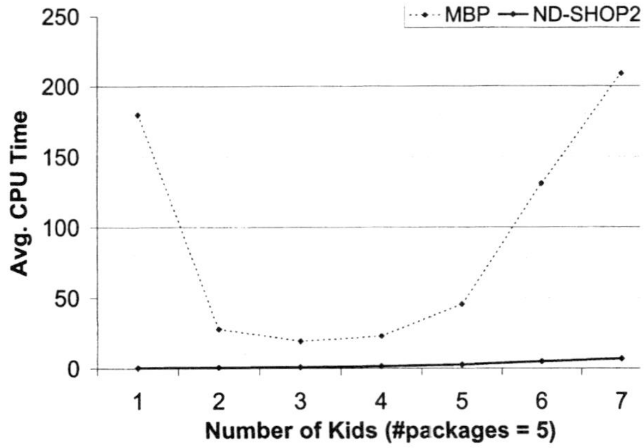


Figure 4: Average running times of ND-SHOP2 and MBP on Robot-Navigation problems, as a function of the number of kid-doors. The number of packages in the domain is fixed to 5.

of the problem. In contrast, the data for ND-SHOP2 show its CPU time growing polynomially, at only about $\Theta(n^4)$. Using the results in the previous section, we have confirmed that this is the correct growth rate for ND-SHOP2 in this domain.

To illustrate the scalability of the algorithms as the amount of nondeterminism increases, Figure 4 shows the results for $n = 5$ and $k = 1, \ldots, 7$. In each case, MBP takes one to two orders of magnitude more time than ND-SHOP2. The closest runtimes occurred at $k = 4$, where MBP is about 15 times slower than ND-SHOP2.

The reason for ND-SHOP2's fast performance relative to MBP is as follows. In the representation language for the Robot Navigation domain, a policy can say things along the lines of "if we are at door number 3 and it is open, then go through it," rather than having to give explicitly all of the exponentially many states of the world in which we're at door number 3 and the door is open. Because of this, problems in the robot-navigation domain have strong-cyclic solutions of linear size, and these are the solutions that ND-SHOP2 finds. Although MBP represents policies in a similar way, it apparently does not exploit this representation well enough to produce policies of polynomial size.

We also compared ND-SHOP2 and MBP on a nondeterministic version of the classical Blocks World domain. We introduced nondeterminism by allowing the operators to have three kinds of outcomes: (1) their traditional effects, (2) an operator may fail to change the state at all, and (3) an operator may fail by dropping the block onto the table.

Figure 5 shows the results of our experiments. Like before, each data point is the average of 20 random problems. For MBP, there are no data points for $n > 8$ because it was unable to solve any problems within the alloted time (30 minutes per problem). The logarithm of MBP's CPU time is linear; thus on this problem, like the other one, MBP takes exponential time.

Curve-fitting on ND-SHOP2's running time shows it growing at only about $\Theta(n^5)$, and a complexity analysis confirms this polynomial behaviour. The reasons are similar to the ones earlier: each time an operator puts a block in the wrong place, ND-SHOP2's methods tell it to pick it up and try again. As a result, ND-SHOP2 is guaranteed to produce a policy of size $O(n)$ where $n$ is the number of blocks. In contrast, MBP produces exponential-size policies that tell what to do in most of the states of the world.

It would also be possible to write nondeterministic versions of the blocks world with more complicated kinds of nondeterminism: for example, an operator could drop a block not just onto the table, but onto any clear block. We have not yet tested this case experimentally, but our complexity analysis shows that such an experimental study would yield results similar to the above. ND-SHOP2 would take polynomial time and space, although the space would this time be quadratic rather than linear (it would immediately pick up the fallen block again, but in the worst case there would be $O(n)$ different places to pick up this block from). MBP would take exponential time in the size of the problem, for the same reasons as before.

Although we have not implemented our pseudocode for ND-TLPlan, the nondeterminization of TLPlan, we have analyzed its complexity on the planning domains discussed in this section. The analysis shows that with appropriate control rules, it would perform similarly to ND-SHOP2 in these domains. The details of our complexity analyses can be found in (Kuter & Nau 2004).

## Related Work

One of the first approaches for planning in nondeterministic domains is the idea of *conditional planning*, which uses an extended form of STRIPS operators to have mutually-exclusive and conditional effects (Pryor & Collins 1996; Peot & Smith 1992). This approach

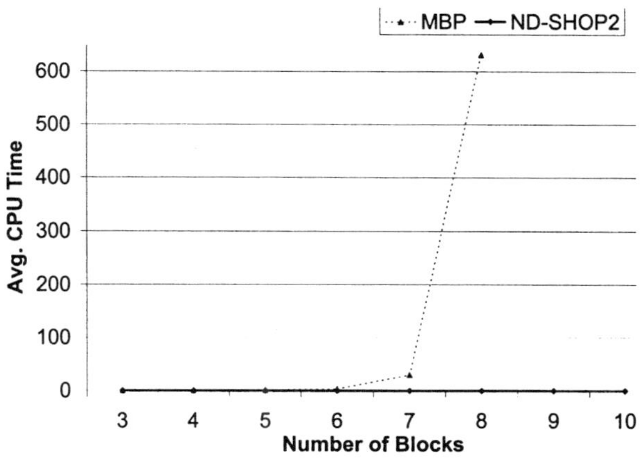


Figure 5: Average running times of ND-SHOP2 and MBP in the nondeterministic Blocks-World domain, as a function of the number of blocks.

does not scale up for complex planning domains.

The best-known approach for planning in nondeterministic domains is based on *symbolic model-checking* techniques (Cimatti *et al.* 2003; Cimatti, Roveri, & Traverso 1998; Daniele, Traverso, & Vardi 1999; Pistore, Bettin, & Traverso 2001). These works establish the notions of weak, strong, and strong-cyclic solution and algorithms based on symbolic techniques for finding such solution to nondeterministic planning problems. MBP (Bertoli *et al.* 2001) is an implementation of the ideas presented in these works.

Planning based on *Markov Decision Processes (MDPs)* (Boutilier, Dean, & Hanks 1999) also has actions with more than one possible outcome, but models the possible outcomes using probabilities and utility functions, and formulates the planning problem as an optimization problem. In MDPs, a policy is a total function from states to actions, whereas model-checking approaches allow a policy to be partial. For problems that can be solved either by MDPs or by model-checking-based planners, the latter have been empirically shown to be more efficient (Bonet & Geffner 2001).

Satisfiability and planning-graph based approaches have been extended to do planning in nondeterministic domains. To the best of our knowledge, the nondeterministic satisfiability-based planners (Castellini, Giunchiglia, & Tacchella 2003; Ferraris & Giunchiglia 2000)are limited to *conformant planning*, where the planner has nondeterministic actions and no observability. The planning-graph based techniques can address conformant planning and a limited form of partial-observabilitiy (Smith & Weld 1998; Weld, Anderson, & Smith 1998).

In deterministic planning domains, a key property of forward-chaining planners is that they know the current state at all times. This allows them to incorporate very powerful pruning techniques— particularly in hand-tailorable planners, in which the pruning techniques can be domain-specific. The domain-specific knowledge can be encoded into a planner in different forms. For example, HSP (Bonet & Geffner 1999) uses a heuristic function that allows the planner to choose the best successor state that can be reached by applying an action to the current state. Another heuristic-based planner, FF (Hoffmann & Nebel 2001), computes the heuristic values over the states by running a variation of the GRAPHPLAN algorithm (Blum & Furst 1997) on a *relaxed* instance of the input planning problems. TLPlan (Bacchus & Kabanza 2000) and TALplanner (Kvarnström & Doherty 2001) use different kinds of *temporal-logic formulas*. In SHOP2 (Nau *et al.* 2003), domain-specific knowledge is encoded as *task networks* which SHOP2 *decomposes* recursively until it reaches a task network in which all tasks can be directly executed.

Two planning approaches that can exploit search control in nondeterministic domains are RTDP (Bonet & Geffner 2000), which is based on greedy-search techniques, and SIMPLAN (Kabanza, Barbeau, & St-Denis 1997). SIMPLAN was developed for planning with reactive agents in nondeterministic domains for temporally-extended goals. We did not consider SIMPLAN for our experiments since to the best of our knowledge it cannot produce strong-cyclic solutions.

## Conclusions

During the past few years, some very efficient forward-chaining planners have been developed for planning in deterministic domains; there are many cases in which these planners can run in polynomial time. The goal of this paper has been to translate these advances in efficiency over to nondeterministic planning domains.

We have presented a general technique for taking forward-chaining planners for deterministic domains (e.g., HSP, TLPlan, TALplanner, and SHOP2), and *nondeterminizing* them to work in nondeterministic domains. The nondeterminization technique preserves soundness and completeness.

There are significant classes of nondeterministic planning problems in which the number of possible states is exponential but there are solutions whose execution structures have polynomial size. Our theoretical results suggest that in such domains, nondeterminizations of efficient deterministic planners may be able to do well.

The theoretical results are confirmed by our experiments and complexity analyses on two different problem domains. One of of these (Robot Navigation) has been used in several previous studies of planning in nondeterministic environments. In both problem domains, our experimental data show MBP's running time growing exponentially and ND-SHOP2's growing only polynomially. A complexity analysis for ND-SHOP2 confirms the latter result, and a complexity analysis for ND-TLPlan shows that it would perform similarly to ND-SHOP2 on these problems.

In the near future, we intend to improve our implementation of ND-SHOP2: for example, its implementation of ND-FCP's reachability tests is rather naive and can be done much more efficiently. We intend to test our approach on additional planning domains, extend it to deal with temporally extended goals, and perhaps to implement nondeterminizations of additional planners.

In the longer term, we hope to extend the theory of nondeterministic planning domains to encompass several of the kinds of problem features that can be handled by planners such as SHOP2 and TLPlan, such as numeric computations, axiomatic inference, and calls to external information sources and software packages. We also hope to develop a technique for translating planners for deterministic domains into planners for probabilistic domains.

## Acknowledgments

This work was supported in part by the following grants, contracts, and awards: Air Force Research Laboratory F30602-00-2-0505, Army Research Laboratory DAAL0197K0135, and Naval Research Laboratory N00173021G005. The opinions expressed in this paper are those of authors and do not necessarily reflect the opinions of the funders.

## References

Bacchus, F., and Kabanza, F. 2000. Using Temporal Logics to Express Search Control Knowledge for Planning. *Artificial Intelligence* 116(1-2):123–191.

Bertoli, P.; Cimatti, A.; Pistore, M.; Roveri, M.; and Traverso, P. 2001. MBP: A Model Based Planner. In *Proceedings of IJCAI Workshop on Planning under Uncertainty and Incomplete Information*, 93–97.

Blum, A. L., and Furst, M. L. 1997. Fast Planning Through Planning Graph Analysis. *Artificial Intelligence* 90(1-2):281–300.

Bonet, B., and Geffner, H. 1999. Planning as Heuristic Search: New Results. In *Proceedings of the European Conference on Planning (ECP)*, 360–372. Durham, UK: Springer-Verlag.

Bonet, B., and Geffner, H. 2000. Planning with Incomplete Information as Heuristic Search in Belief Space. In Chien, S.; Kambhampati, S.; and Knoblock, C., eds., *Proceedings of the International Conference on AI Planning Systems (AIPS)*, 52–61. Breckenridge, CO: AAAI Press.

Bonet, B., and Geffner, H. 2001. GPT: A tool for planning with uncertainty and partial information. In *Proceedings of the International Joint Conference on Artificial Intelligence (IJCAI)*, 82–87. Seattle, WA: Morgan Kaufmann.

Boutilier, C.; Dean, T. L.; and Hanks, S. 1999. Decision-Theoretic Planning: Structural Assumptions and Computational Leverage. *Journal of Artificial Intelligence Research* 11:1–94.

Castellini, C.; Giunchiglia, E.; and Tacchella, A. 2003. SAT-Based Planning in Complex Domains: Concurrency, Constraints and Nondeterminism. *Artificial Intelligence* 147(1–2):85–117. To appear.

Cimatti, A.; Pistore, M.; Roveri, M.; and Traverso, P. 2003. Weak, Strong, and Strong Cyclic Planning via Symbolic Model Checking. *Artificial Intelligence* 147(1–2):35–84.

Cimatti, A.; Roveri, M.; and Traverso, P. 1998. Strong Planning in Non-Deterministic Domains via Model Checking. In *Proceedings of the International Conference on AI Planning Systems (AIPS)*, 36–43. Pittsburgh, PA: AAAI Press.

Daniele, M.; Traverso, P.; and Vardi, M. 1999. Strong Cyclic Planning Revisited. In *Proceedings of the European Conference on Planning (ECP)*, 35–48. Durham, UK: Springer.

Ferraris, P., and Giunchiglia, E. 2000. Planning as Satisfiability in Nondeterministic Domains. In *AAAI/IAAI Proceedings*, 748–753. Menlo Park, CA: AAAI Press.

Hoffmann, J., and Nebel, B. 2001. The FF Planning System: Fast Plan Generation Through Heuristic Search. *Journal of Artificial Intelligence Research* 14:253–302.

Kabanza, F.; Barbeau, M.; and St-Denis, R. 1997. Planning Control Rules for Reactive Agents. *Artificial Intelligence* 95(1):67–113.

Kuter, U., and Nau, D. 2004. Using Forward-Chaining Planning for Generating Weak, Strong, and Strong-Cyclic Solutions in Nondeterministic Domains. Technical Report CS-TR-4580, Dept. of Computer Science, University of Maryland.

Kvarnström, J., and Doherty, P. 2001. TALplanner: A Temporal Logic-based Forward-chaining Planner. *Annals of Mathematics and Articial Intelligence* 30:119–169.

Nau, D.; Au, T.-C.; Ilghami, O.; Kuter, U.; Murdock, W.; Wu, D.; and Yaman, F. 2003. SHOP2: An HTN Planning System. *Journal of Artificial Intelligence Research* 20:379–404.

Peot, M., and Smith, D. 1992. Conditional Nonlinear Planning. In *Proceedings of the International Conference on AI Planning Systems (AIPS)*, 189–197. College Park, MD: AAAI Press.

Pistore, M.; Bettin, R.; and Traverso, P. 2001. Symbolic Techniques for Planning with Extended Goals in Nondeterministic Domains. In *Proceedings of the European Conference on Planning (ECP)*. Toledo, ES: Springer Verlag.

Pryor, L., and Collins, G. 1996. Planning for Contingency: A Decision-based Approach. *Journal of Artificial Intelligence Research* 4:81–120.

Smith, D. E., and Weld, D. S. 1998. Conformant Graphplan. In *AAAI/IAAI Proceedings*, 889–896. Menlo Park, CA: AAAI Press.

Weld, D. S.; Anderson, C. R.; and Smith, D. E. 1998. Extending Graphplan to Handle Uncertainty and Sensing Actions. In *AAAI/IAAI Proceedings*, 897–904. Menlo Park, CA: AAAI Press.

# Transport Logistics Planning with Service-Level Constraints

**Hoong Chuin LAU** and **Kien Ming NG** and **Xiaotao WU**
The Logistics Institute - Asia Pacific
National University of Singapore, 119260

## Abstract

In this paper, we study a logistics problem arising in military transport planning. A military organization operates a large fleet of vehicles in a depot to serve the requests of various operational units. Each request has a fixed start and end time, and is served by a prescribed number of vehicles. We address the following two problems: (1) how many vehicles are at least needed to meet a given service level of requests; and (2) suppose we allow each request to shift its start time by a constant duration, can all the requests be met? A Niche genetic algorithm, together with a hybridized variant, are applied to the problem.

## Introduction

The world is increasingly service-oriented and hence service constraints play an important role in business. In the military world, service constraints play an ever-increasing role in today's heightened security threats. In this paper, we consider a real-world transport logistics planning problem arising in a military organization. This problem is also prevalent in a logistics agency which services multiple clients, where service level constraints play an important role. The organization owns a large fleet of vehicles centralized in a depot to service requests from multiple operational units. A request has a start and end time, a weight and requires a number of vehicles. For simplicity, we assume that all vehicles are identical. The problem is to minimize the number of vehicles needed to meet a given service level constraint, or to maximize the number of served requests using a given number of vehicles. In the case where not all requests can be satisfied, a related interesting question is whether, by allowing some requests to be *shifted time-wise*, all requests can be satisfied with a certain fixed number of vehicles. The latter question is particularly important in the military context in achieving 100% operational readiness. Military commanders are interested to know whether, within a reasonable delay to their operations, they are able to guarantee full supply of resources. Without loss of generality, we assume that requests are to be shifted to a later time point.



In this paper, we study the complexity and algorithms for solving 2 major problems in this arena. We formulate the problems as integer programming models which render an exact solution approach, such as branch-and-bound (B&B), to solve them to optimality. However, such an exact solution approach may not be practical when tackling large problem instances as the solution process may take an exponential amount of time. It is also possible to apply genetic algorithms (GA) on the problems and solutions could then be obtained for large problem instances. But GAs may encounter the situation of being trapped in local optimality. To overcome the shortcoming of both approaches, we propose in this paper a hybrid algorithm that hybridize GA and B&B.

In the interest of space, the proofs of theorems and lemmas have been omitted in this version.

## Literature Review

Our problem is a generalization of what is commonly known as the problem of scheduling jobs with fixed start and end times. In graph theory, this problem is a generalization of the Dilworth's problem of finding a minimum chain decomposition of a given graph, which can be solved via a min-cost flow formulation. Examples of work in this area include the work of (Arkin & Silverberg 1987) and more recently, the online algorithms presented in (Woeginger 1994). Most of the literature emphasizes on jobs with single-resource requirement, because the problem exhibits very nice combinatorial structure (such as the property that the underlying matrix is totally unimodular). In this paper, we consider the multi-resource problem, and treat the single-resource problem as a special case.

In standard machine scheduling terminology, jobs are started and completed within job-specific release times and deadlines. To our knowledge however, little work has been done in the special case of allowing *constant* shifts of job start time, which, to some extent, seems to be an easier problem comparatively. In this paper, we show that this problem is NP-complete, even for shift of a single unit of time on jobs with equal release time and duration. This result is tight in the sense that the problem can be solved in polynomial time when jobs have single-resource requirement, even when they have arbitrary release times and due-dates (Simons 1983). Another example of work done in allowing shifts is due to (Gertsbakh & Stern 1978), who proposed an integer programming approach for the single-resource problem. There is a large collection of unreported related machine scheduling problems with release times and deadlines (see for example collection at (Brucker & Knust)), but suffices to say that most of these papers deal with different objective functions such as makespan and job-specific release times, which are not the concerns of this paper.

## Military Transportation Planning

For convenience, we say requests are *unweighted* when all the weights of the requests are equal, and *weighted* otherwise. A *unit* (or *single-vehicle*) request refers to one whose quantity of vehicles required is exactly 1. In this paper, unless otherwise specified, we consider the general problem of weighted, multi-vehicle requests.

We formally define the Military Transportation Planning (MTP) problem as the following optimization problem: Given a set of requests $R = \{1, \ldots, n\}$ indexed by $i$ over a planning period $T$ and an integer $k$, find the minimum number of vehicles needed to satisfy at least $k$ requests. This problem can be easily extended to the weighted case where the goal is to satisfy requests whose total weight is at least $k$. The dual optimization problem dMTP is also interesting: given an integer $m$, find the maximum weight (or number) of requests that can be satisfied using not more than $m$ vehicles.

We use a 2-D bar-chart to represent the requests, where the $x$-axis represents time, and the $y$-axis vehicles. Each request is represented as a horizontal bar from its start time to end time with height equals to the number of vehicles required.

### Mathematical Programming Formulation

Suppose there is a total of $n$ requests over a planning horizon of $T$ time periods, and we would like to fulfill $k$ requests, where $0 \leq k \leq n$. We let $q_i$, $s_i$, $t_i$, and $w_i$ be the quantity of vehicles required, the start time, the end time and the weight of request $i$ respectively, where $0 \leq i \leq n$. We define our decision variables to be $x_{i\ell}$ that represents the number of vehicles fulfilling request $i$ and then request $\ell$, where $0 \leq i, \ell \leq n, i \neq \ell$; and $y_i$ that takes a value of 1 if request $i$ is fulfilled, and 0 otherwise, where $0 \leq i \leq n$. We also denote the duration of request $i$ as $l_i = t_i - s_i$, and the number of the vehicles required by all the requests as $h = \sum_{i=1}^{n} q_i$.

Here, we introduce two additional "dummy" requests, i.e., request 0 and request $n+1$, to reflect the respective start and end of any feasible vehicle assignment to the physical requests. Thus, for any vehicle $j$, a feasible assignment to the requests would be of the form $0 \rightarrow j_1 \rightarrow j_2 \rightarrow \cdots \rightarrow j_p \rightarrow n+1$, where $p$, $j_1$, $j_2$, $\ldots$, $j_p \in \{1, 2, \ldots, n\}$, or $0 \rightarrow n+1$ indicating that the vehicle is not used at all. The mathematical programming formulation is then:

$$min \sum_{i=1}^{n} x_{0i} \tag{1}$$

such that

$$\sum_{\substack{\ell=1 \\ \ell \neq i}}^{n+1} x_{i\ell} \geq q_i y_i \quad (i = 1, 2, \ldots, n) \tag{2}$$

$$\sum_{\substack{\ell=0 \\ \ell \neq i}}^{n} x_{\ell i} - \sum_{\substack{r=1 \\ r \neq i}}^{n+1} x_{ir} = 0 \quad (i = 1, 2, \ldots, n) \tag{3}$$

$$\sum_{i=1}^{n} w_i y_i \geq k \tag{4}$$

$$(s_\ell - t_i) x_{i\ell} \geq 0 \quad (i = 1, 2, \ldots, n; \ell = 1, 2, \ldots, n,\ i \neq \ell) \tag{5}$$

$$x_{i\ell} \in \mathbb{Z}_{\geq 0} \quad (i = 0, 1, \ldots, n; \ell = 1, 2, \ldots, n+1,\ i \neq \ell) \tag{6}$$

$$y_i \in \{0, 1\} \quad (i = 1, 2, \ldots, n). \tag{7}$$

Equation (1) reflects the aim of minimizing the total number of vehicles used. Equation (2) ensures that a request is fulfilled only if the required number of vehicles are assigned to fulfil that request. Equation (3) is a conservation constraint ensuring that the total number of vehicles assigned for a particular request remains the same both before and after fulfilling a request. Equation (4) ensures that the weighted total number of requests satisfied meets the required level. Equation (5) is a constraint forcing variables $x_{i\ell}$ corresponding to an invalid sequence of fulfilling requests to assume a value of zero. Equations (6) and (7) are integrality constraints.

The number of integer decision variables required is easily verified to be $O(n^2)$ for this formulation.

### NP-Completeness of MTP

The MTP decision problem is NP-complete via a reduction from the Knapsack problem which is known to be NP-complete.

### Relationship between MTP and dMTP

Given a set of requests $R$, we can define parameterized MTP and dMTP problem instances as follows:

$$\text{MTP}(k) = min\{f(x) | g(x) \geq k\}. \tag{8}$$

$$\text{dMTP}(m) = max\{g(x) | f(x) \leq m\}. \tag{9}$$

where $f(x)$ and $g(x)$ are functions on a schedule $x$ counting the number of vehicles used and the number (weight) of requests satisfied respectively. Let $x^*$ and $y^*$ respectively denote an optimal solution for problems (8) and (9).

The following theorem relates problems (8) and (9).

**Theorem 1** *$f(x^*) = m$ if and only if: (1) $g(y^*) \geq k$; and (2) for all feasible schedules $y$ of dMTP$(m-1)$, $g(y) < k$.*

This theorem suggests that if we can solve the problem dMTP($m$), then simply by iterating from 1 to $m$ and checking if the number of satisfied requests has reached $k$, we can get the optimal value of problem MTP($k$). However, note that in the multi-vehicle case, since the value $q_i$ of each request $i$ is unbounded, this method suffers from high complexity issues if some requests require a large number of vehicles. For the single-vehicle case where $m = O(n)$, this method allows us to solve MTP by solving at most $n$ instances of dMTP.

Conversely, if we can solve the problem MTP($k$), then simply by iterating from $n$ down to 1, we can use the algorithm to solve dMTP($m$). This allows us to solve dMTP by solving at most $n$ instances of MTP, even for the multi-vehicle case.

**Special Case 1: 100% service level** This problem is to decide the minimum number of vehicles so that ALL requests can be fulfilled. The unit-request MTP problem can be solved by coloring of an interval graph, whose nodes represent the requests and edges represent overlapping time constraint. Interval graph coloring can be solved optimally in polynomial time, by known algorithms (such as (Gavril 1972)). Furthermore, since all requests need to be satisfied eventually, the multi-request MTP problem can easily be solved by treating each multi-vehicle request as multiple unit requests. The problem can be solved by applying a plane-sweep algorithm and the resulting time complexity is $O(n \log n + h)$ using $O(h)$ space.

**Special Case 2: $m = 1$** When there is only 1 vehicle (and therefore all requests are unit requests), dMTP is reduced to the Activity Selection Problem, which can be solved in $O(n)$ time via a greedy algorithm if endpoints are presorted: At each step, select a feasible activity (request) with earliest finish time with endpoints presorted such that it is compatible with already selected activities (requests). Even for the weighted case, dMTP can be solved by formulating it as a Shortest Path problem and applying Dijkstra's algorithm (Dijkstra 1959). With the corresponding graph constructed, which has $|E|$ edges and $|V|$ nodes, the complexity of Dijkstra's algorithm is $O(|E| + |V| \log |V|)$ (Fredman & Tarjan 1984). In our problem, with the interval graph constructed, $|V|$ is $O(n)$ and $|E|$ is $O(n^2)$, and hence the time complexity is $O(n^2)$.

**Special Case 3: Unit-requests** For the unit-request problem, we note that the minimum number of vehicles required is bounded from above by the number of requests $n$. Here, two results can be established.

1. (Arkin & Silverberg 1987) proposed a $O(n^2 \log n)$ time algorithm to solve the problem of scheduling $n$ jobs with fixed start and end times that maximizes the value of scheduled jobs on $m$ identical machines for any given $m$. Their approach is to model it as a min-cost flow problem. The above problem is actually the unit-request dMTP problem. Hence, by applying the same approach, the dMTP problem on a given value of $m$ can be solved by min-cost flows in $O(n^2 \log n)$ time (Papadimitriou & Steiglitz 1982). Note that the algorithm also implicitly solves all related dMTP instances greater than $m$, implying that when we choose $m = 1$, by Theorem 1, MTP can be solved with one iteration in $O(n^2 \log n)$ time.
2. When $m = 2$, the above situation can be improved. An $O(n^2)$ algorithm was proposed in (Hsiao *et al.* 1992) based on dynamic programming to solve the *maximum weight 2-independent set problem* on weighted interval graphs. Their approach can be generalized to $O(n^m)$ for finding an $m$-independent set. As dMTP on $m$ is equivalent to finding a maximum (weight) $m$-independent set, an $O(n^2)$ algorithm is found for $m = 2$, and in general, an $O(n^m)$ algorithm for arbitrary $m$. This means, by Theorem 1, that MTP can be solved in $\sum_{m=1}^{m^*} O(n^m) = O(n^{m^*})$ time. Thus, MTP instances with a minimum value of $m^* \leq 2$ can be solved in $O(n^2)$ time.

## MTP with Shifting (MTP-S)

We define the MTP with Shifting (MTP-S) problem as: given $n$ requests over a planning period $T$, and an integer $C$, find a schedule that satisfies ALL requests by allowing each request's start time to be shifted later by a duration not exceeding $C$ time units.

The unweighted MTP-S decision problem is NP-complete, even when $C = 1$ and all release times and durations are equal. The proof is a reduction from the 2-Partition problem which is known to be NP-Complete.

### Mathematical Programming Formulation

By introducing more variables, we can model MTP-S in a similar way. Since we can shift the start (and therefore the end) time by $C$, this is equivalent to each request having a release time $r_i$, deadline $d_i$ and an actual start time $s_i$, where $d_i = r_i + l_i + C$ and $l_i$ is the duration of request for $1 \leq i \leq n$.

It is then necessary to add the following constraints on the start time of each request:

$$r_i \leq s_i \leq r_i + C \quad (i = 1, 2, \ldots, n) \tag{10}$$

$$s_i \in \mathbb{Z}_{\geq 0} \quad (i = 1, 2, \ldots, n). \tag{11}$$

Since we would like to have all requests being satisfied, equation (4) can be omitted and (2) changed to

$$\sum_{\substack{\ell=1 \\ \ell \neq i}}^{n+1} x_{i\ell} = q_i \quad (i = 1, 2, \ldots, n) \tag{12}$$

Also, equation (5) would be modified to:

$$(s_\ell - s_i - l_i) x_{i\ell} \geq 0 \; (i = 1, 2, \ldots, n; \ell = 1, 2, \ldots, n, \; i \neq \ell). \tag{13}$$

If we define $z_{i\ell}$, for $1 \leq i, \ell \leq n$ and $i \neq \ell$ to be binary intermediate variables satisfying the following constraints:

$$x_{i\ell} \leq M z_{i\ell} \; (i = 1, 2, \ldots, n; \ell = 1, 2, \ldots, n, \; i \neq \ell) \tag{14}$$

$$s_\ell - s_i - l_i \geq M(z_{i\ell} - 1)$$
$$(i = 1, 2, \ldots, n; \ell = 1, 2, \ldots, n, i \neq \ell), \quad (15)$$

$$z_{i\ell} \in \{0, 1\} \ (i = 1, 2, \ldots, n; \ell = 1, 2, \ldots, n, i \neq \ell), \quad (16)$$

where $M = \max\{\max_i\{q_i\}, T\} + 1$ then it is easy to verify that equations (14), (15) and (16) could be used in place of equation (13), thereby removing the nonlinearities in the formulation of MTP-S.

In summary, the mathematical programming formulation of MTP-S is described by the minimization of equation (1) subject to the constraints (3), (6), (7), (10), (11), (12), (14), (15), and (16). The number of integer decision variables required is again $O(n^2)$ for this formulation. This formulation is similar in spirit to that of the vehicle routing problem with time windows (VRPTW) commonly seen in literature, such as (Fisher *et al.* 1997). Thus, it may be possible to adapt existing methods for handling the VRPTW to solve MTP-S, such as the Lagrangian relaxation approach in (Desrosiers *et al.* 1988).

## Genetic Algorithm for MTP-S Problem

In this section, we propose a genetic algorithm (GA) to solve the NP-hard MTP-S problem.

**Cumulative Request Histogram** Before presenting our proposed GA, we introduce the notion of a *request histogram.* By aggregating the 2-D graph representation of all requests, we derive a *Cumulative Request Histogram,* whose $x$-axis is the time period and $y$-axis is the total number of vehicles required by requests spanning each time period. Let $h_\ell$ denote the number of vehicles required at time period $l$. Let $CRH = (h_1, \ldots, h_\ell, \ldots, h_T)$ and $CRH_{max} = \max_{\ell=1}^{T} h_\ell$.

**Lemma 1** *For each $CRH$ with fixed actual start times (i.e. no shift allowed), we can construct a feasible schedule such that the number of vehicles used $m^*$ is equal to $CRH_{max}$ in polynomial time.*

This lemma is evident by inspecting the plane sweep algorithm presented in Special Case 1 that we need at most $CRH_{max}$ vehicles. The proof of optimality results from the observation that we need at least $CRH_{max}$ vehicles through the pigeon-hole argument. The computational complexity is $O(n \log n + h)$, as presented above.

The optimal schedule $CRH^*$ for MTP-S has the property that $CRH^*_{max} = \min\{CRH^k_{max} | k \in S\}$, where $S$ is the set of all possible $CRH$ resulting from fixing the actual start times of requests, and $CRH^k_{max}$ is the value of $CRH_{max}$ for the $k$-th $CRH$. Hence, by Lemma 1, we may generate a optimal schedule by simply enumerating all possible combinations of actual start times. Unfortunately, there is an exponential number (precisely $C^n$) of such combinations. In this paper, we adopt a Niche genetic algorithm which reduces the search space efficiently.

## Niche GA for MTP-S

Both experiments and analysis show that while the simple genetic algorithm is suitable for searching the optimum of unimodal functions in a bounded search space, it cannot find the multiple global maxima of a multimodal function (Goldberg 1989). This limitation can be overcome by a mechanism that creates and maintains several subpopulations within the search space in such a way that each maximum of the multimodal function can attract one of them. These mechanisms are referred to as "niching methods" in (Mahfoud 1999).

Our MTP-S problem is modeled as a multimodal function which has many optimal solutions. In fact, those $CRH$s with the same $CRH_{max}$ can be viewed as the same solutions, for the number of vehicles required is the same. Although we do not have to list all the optimal $CRH$s, since the search space is large, we still need a method to control the search efficiency. We adopt the niching idea here because it is useful to maintain population diversity and permit genetic algorithms to explore more search space so as to identify multiple peaks, whether optimal or otherwise.

There are several niching techniques in the literature. The fitness sharing method was proposed by Goldberg and Richardson (Goldberg & Richardson 1987) and the crowding method by DeJong (Jong 1975). The clearing idea used in this paper derives from the clearing procedure stated by Petrowski (Petrowski 1996). The basic idea is: instead of evenly sharing the available resources among the individuals of a subpopulation, the clearing procedure supplies these resources only to the best individuals of each subpopulation. In fact, we propose a variation of the clearing method which not only concerns the current population but the previous population as well. Thus, we need not worry about the crossover operation destroying the individuals located on the peaks found with a high probability.

**Coding** For the chromosome $\lambda = \{j_1, \ldots, j_i, \ldots, j_n\}$, where $j_i \in [0, 1, \ldots, C]$, $n$ is the number of requests and $C$ refers to the allowable time shift in the requests. This implies that the total solution space size is $C^n$.

**Fitness** The objective value $f(\lambda)$ for a particular chromosome $\lambda$ is the number of vehicles needed to fulfill all the requests when that chromosome is applied.

**Selection & Crossover** We use the *Roulette Wheel Selection* as our basic model (Goldberg 1989). Also and *elitist* model is then used for comparison where the best performing chromosome is exempt from mutation. We use *one-point crossover* in Niche GA.

**Mutation** Here, the *uniform mutation* operation with probability $p_m$ is used.

Suppose the chromosome is $\lambda = \{j_1, j_2, \ldots, j_n\}$ and $p$ is the selected mutation point, $1 \leq p \leq n$. After the uniform mutation operation, the new chromosome is $\lambda = \{j_1, j_2, \ldots, j'_p, \ldots, j_n\}$ where $j'_p = r \times C$ and $r$ is a random number from [0,1].

## Hybrid Approach

A pure Niche GA approach may still be inadequate in obtaining optimal or close-to-optimal solutions for certain problem instances. Here, we propose a hybrid algorithm that adapts the Niche GA method to make use of the strengths of an exact method. With the mathematical programming formulation, there are certainly many exact solution approaches that can produce the optimal solution though at the expense of computation time. For simplicity, we assume that our exact solution approach is a B&B method that is always generating feasible solutions with improving objective values if we apply it to the MTP-S problem. We start by running both Niche GA and B&B algorithms on an instance of the MTP-S problem. Each time the B&B algorithm returns a new feasible solution that is better than the current best solution of the Niche GA, we convert it into a corresponding chromosome, say $\lambda^*$.

For each gene $j_i$ of $\lambda^*$, we calculate the sum of hamming distance with that of all the chromosomes of the current population, and call it $dis(i)$, for $1 \leq i \leq n$. We then change the Niche GA parameters so that the resulting Niche GA algorithm will attempt to generate genes that are similar to that obtained by the B&B method. Thus, we can set the mutation probability $p_m[i]$ of each gene position to be $\frac{dis(i)}{PopSize}$, for $1 \leq i \leq n$, where *Popsize* is the size of the genetic population pool. But sometimes we do not want the offspring of the current generation to be similar as $\lambda^*$, especially at certain time periods where vehicles are densely scheduled. We can simply avoid this by setting a high mutation probability to the corresponding requests, i.e. $p_m[i] = 1$, for $1 \leq i \leq n$. We then proceed with running both the Niche GA and the B&B algorithms, and repeat the process with each new feasible solution returned by the B&B algorithm. The algorithm is terminated if either the B&B algorithm produces an optimal solution, or a prespecified iteration time limit is reached.

The reason for such a hybrid approach is that we are using the exact solution approach as a diversification strategy for the Niche GA algorithm. There has been literature on diversification strategies for GA algorithms (see e.g. (Ting *et al.* 2001)), but most of them are using heuristic or randomized techniques. A strong justification for our proposed approach is that we are in effect using an exact solution approach, which is guaranteed to obtain an optimal solution to the problem, to guide the diversification strategy. This will help prevent the Niche GA algorithm from getting iterates that are trapped in a local optimal solution. We can also interpret the process as the Niche GA algorithm "learning" from the intelligent search procedures used by an exact solution approach.

# Experimental Results

We experimented on two classes of data: practical data obtained from a military organization and randomly generated data.

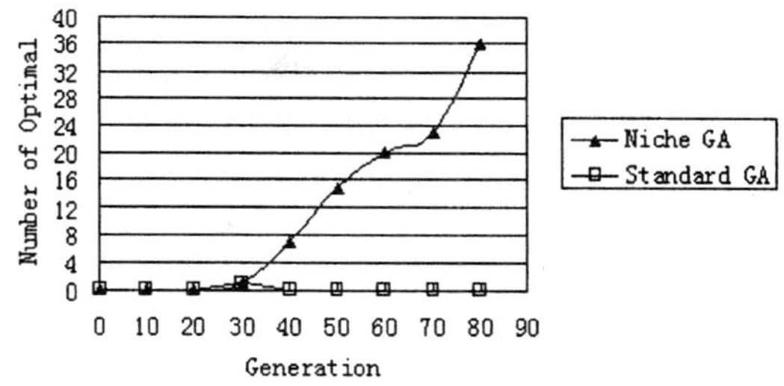


Figure 1: Population spread of Niche GA and Standard GA, with population size of 50

## Practical Data Generation and Results

We obtained a base case from a military organization and generated practical data sets around that case by carefully considering the distributions of data values on the number of time slots, number of vehicles, start and end times of a request, request quantity, and the total number of jobs spanning over the vehicle resources.

We compare the Niche GA and the exact integer programming (IP) model proposed above on a small data set D1 ($n$=240, $T$=365 units), with delay $C$ ranging from 1 to 5. Although both Niche GA and IP model obtain the optimal solution, the time taken for the IP model increases exponentially as the delay value increases, compared with linear scaleup for Niche GA.

We also did a comparison of the Niche GA and the Standard GA, using the same genetic operators. Figure 1 shows the number of individuals with optimal solutions as it varies from generation to generation. It can be seen that both Niche GA and Standard GA get the optimal solution in an early generation (both when generation = 30) due to the use of the $CRH$ technique which reduces the solution space. Also, we can see that the Niche GA has a much higher likelihood of obtaining other optimal solutions than the Standard GA.

## Random Data Generation and Results

Here, we generate data sets with known optimal solutions to verify the effectiveness of our Niche GA. The procedures of generating one data set cluster are:

1. Generate a rectangular histogram (that is the optimal $CRH$ for a data set cluster).
2. Partition the rectangle into small rectangles as requests (with random durations and quantities).
3. Shift each generated request with $k$ units forward, where $k \in [0, C]$ to generate the start and end time.
4. Change $C$ and go to step 3 in order to generate the next data set for this data set cluster.

We set each data set cluster to include 5 data sets, whose mean value of $C$ ranges from 1 to 5. It is trivial to see that these 5 data sets within the same data cluster share at least one identical optimal solution, which is the optimal $CRH$ generated.

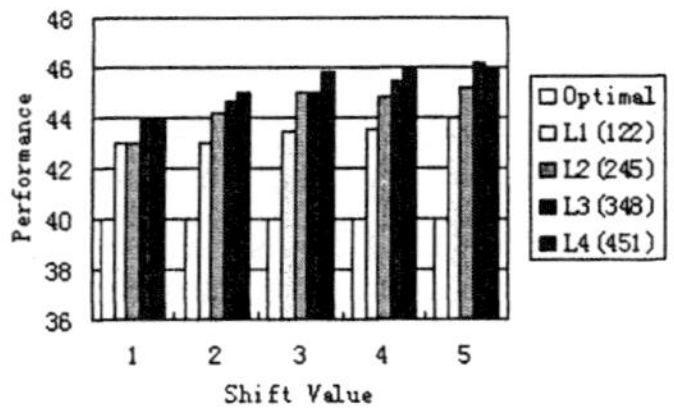


Figure 2: Performance of Niche GA on large data sets

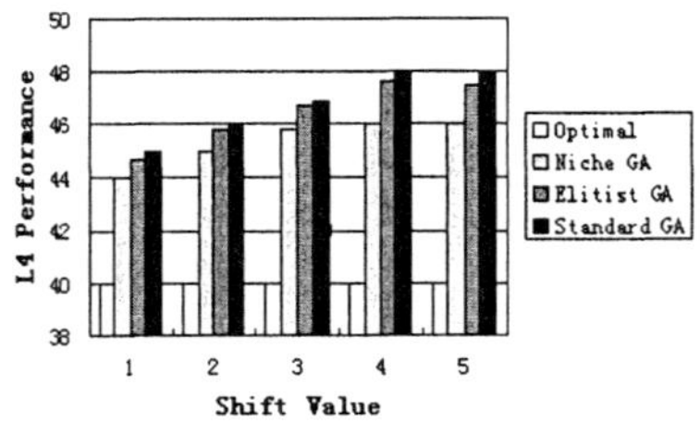


Figure 3: Performance of different GAs on L4

We experimented on 3 types of data sets (small, medium and large), with each type consisting of 4 data set clusters. Figure 2 shows the performance (number of vehicles required) of Niche GA on large data clusters $L1$ ($n = 122$), $L2$ ($n = 245$), $L3$ ($n = 348$), $L4$ ($n = 451$). It can be seen that Niche GA does not perform satisfactorily especially when $C$ is large. We also compared Niche GA with other GAs on data cluster $L4$. The average performance over 5 runs are reported in Figure 3. Compared with standard GA and Elitist GA, the Niche GA performs slightly better. In such cases, the search space is too large compared to the number of near optimal solutions. It is very hard to get the optimal solution because of very few optimal solutions (the worst case may only have one optimal $CRH$, i.e. with no symmetric cases included).

Given the poor performance of the Niche GA approach, we apply our proposed hybrid algorithm on the test data. In particular, we experimented with a test data set with size 62 requests and a shift of 5 time units, and it has an optimal solution of 20 vehicles. The pure Niche GA method is unable to get a solution that is better than 22 vehicles, while the B&B method takes a large number of iterations to obtain a solution that is less than 23 vehicles. With the hybrid algorithm, a solution of 21 vehicles can be obtained.

## Conclusion

In this paper, we studied a class of logistic problems. We have also developed mathematical programming models that allow exact solution approaches to produce intermediate solutions for intelligently influencing the GA's parameters. Future work is to extend this hybridization scheme to other classes of problems.

## References


E. M. Arkin and E. B. Silverberg, "Scheduling jobs with fixed start and end times", Disc. Appl. Math, 18(1), 1-8, 1987

P. Brucker and S. Knust, http://www.mathematik.uni-osnabrueck.de/research/OR/class/

J. Desrosiers, M. Sauvé and F. Soumis, "Lagrangian Relaxation Methods for Solving the Minimum Fleet Size Multiple Traveling Salesman Problem with Time Windows", Mgmt. Sc., 34(8), 1005-1022, 1988

E. W. Dijkstra, "A note on two problems in connexion with graphs", Numer. Math., 1, 269-271, 1959

M. L. Fredman and R. E. Tarjan, "Fibonacci heaps and their uses in improved network optimization algorithms", Proc. 25th IEEE Symp. on FOCS, 1984

M. L. Fisher, K. O. Jörnsten, O. B. G. Masden, "Vehicle Routing with Time Windows: Two Optimization Algorithms", Oper. Res., 45(3), 488-492, 1997

I. Gertsbakh and H. I. Stern, "Minimal Resources for Fixed and Variable Job Schedules", Oper. Res., 26(1), 68-85, 1978

F. Gavril, "Algorithms for Minimum Coloring, Maximum Clique, Minimum Covering by Cliques, and Maximum Independent Set of a Chordal Graph", SIAM J. Comput. 1(2), 180-187, 1972

D. E. Goldberg, J. Richardson, " Genetic Algorithms with Sharing of Multimodal Function Optimization", Proc. 2nd Int'l Conf. Genetic Algo., pp42-49, 1987

D. E. Goldberg, "Genetic algorithms in search, optimization and machine learning", Reading, Addison Wesley, 1989

J. Y. Hsiao, C. Y. Tang, R. S. Chang, "An Efficient Algorithm for Finding a Maximum Weight 2-Independent Set on Interval Graphs", Info. Proc. Lett., 43, 229-235, 1992

K. A. De Jong, "An analysis of the behavior of a class of genetic adaptive systems", PhD dissertation, University of Michigan, 1975

S. W. Mahfoud,"Niching Methods for Genetic Algorithms", PhD dissertation, University of Illinois Urbana-Champaign, 1995

C. H. Papadimitriou and K. Steiglitz, "Combinatorial Optimization: Algorithms and Complexity", Reading, Prentice-Hall, 1982

A. Petrowski, "A Clearing Procedure as a Niching Method for Genetic Algorithms", Proc. IEEE 3rd Int'l Conf. Evol. Comput. (ICEC), Nagoya, 1996

B. Simons, "Multiprocessor scheduling of unit-time jobs with arbitrary release times and deadlines", SIAM J., Computing, 12(2), 294-299, 1983

C.-K. Ting, S.-T. Li, C. Lee, "TGA: A new integrated approach to evolutionary algorithms", Proc. Congress on Evolutionary Computation, 917-924, 2001

G. Woeginger, "On-line scheduling of jobs with fixed start end times", Theo. Comp. Sci., 130, 5-16, 1994

# Distance Estimates for Planning in the Discrete Belief Space

**Jussi Rintanen**
Albert-Ludwigs-Universität Freiburg
Institut für Informatik
Georges-Köhler-Allee, 79110 Freiburg im Breisgau
Germany

### Abstract

We present a general framework for studying heuristics for planning in the belief space. Earlier work has focused on giving implementations of heuristics that work well on benchmarks, without studying them at a more analytical level. Existing heuristics have evaluated belief states in terms of their cardinality or have used distance heuristics directly based on the distances in the underlying state space. Neither of these types of heuristics is very widely applicable: often goal belief state is not approached through a sequence of belief states with a decreasing cardinality, and distances in the state space ignore the main implications of partial observability.

To remedy these problems we present a family of admissible, increasingly accurate distance heuristics for planning in the belief space, parameterized by an integer $n$. We show that the family of heuristics is theoretically robust: it includes the simplest heuristic based on the state space as a special case and as a limit the exact distances in the belief space.

## Introduction

Planning under partial observability is one of the most difficult planning problems because algorithms for finding plans have to – at least implicitly – address the incompleteness of the knowledge about the environment in which the plan execution will take place. The incompleteness of knowledge leads to the notion of belief states: depending on the type planning, belief states are either probability distributions on the state space, or, in the non-probabilistic versions of the partially observable planning problem, sets of states. In either case, the exponentially bigger size of the set of belief states – the belief space – in comparison to the state space is a major obstacle in achieving efficient planning.

Following the lead in classical planning (Bonet & Geffner 2001), also restricted types of planning in the belief space, most notably the planning problem without any observability at all (sometimes known as conformant planning), has also been represented as a heuristic search problem (Bonet & Geffner 2000). However, the implementation of heuristic search in the belief space is more complex than in classical planning because of the difficulty of deriving good heuristics. First works on the topic have used distances in the state space (Bonet & Geffner 2000) and cardinalities of the belief states (Bertoli, Cimatti, & Roveri 2001). On some types of problems these heuristics work well, but not on all, and the two proposed approaches have orthogonal strengths.

Many problems cannot be solved by blindly taking actions that reduce the cardinality of the current belief state: the cardinality of the belief state may stay the same or increase during plan execution, and hence the decrease in cardinality is not characteristic to belief space planning in general.

Similarly, distances in the state space completely ignore the most distinctive aspect of planning with partial observability: the same action must be used in two states if the states are not observationally distinguishable. A given (optimal) plan for an unobservable problem may increase the actual current state-space distance to the goal states (on a given execution) when the distance in the belief-space monotonically decreases, and vice versa. Hence, the state space distances may yield wildly misleading estimates of the distances in the corresponding belief space.

To achieve more efficient planning it is necessary to develop belief space heuristics that combine the strengths of existing heuristics based on cardinalities and distances in the state space. In this work we present such a family of heuristics, parameterized by a natural number $n$. The accuracy of the distance estimates improves as $n$ grows. As the special case $n = 1$ we have a heuristic based on distances in the state space, similar to ones used in earlier work. When the cardinality of the state space equals $n$, the distance estimates equal the actual distances in the belief space.

## Planning in the Belief Space

Let $S$ be a set of states. A planning problem $\langle I, O, G\rangle$ without observability is abstractly defined in terms of

1. an initial belief state $I \subseteq S$,
2. a set of operators $O$, each operator $o \in O$ associated with a transition relation $R_o \subseteq S \times S$ describing the possible transitions when $o$ is applied (the operators are nondeterministic and hence the transition relations are not restricted to partial functions), and
3. a set $G$ of goal states (the goal belief state).

In the special case of deterministic (classical) planning the set $I$ consists of one state and all the relations $R_o, o \in O$ are partial functions. The objective in deterministic planning is to find a sequence $o_1, \ldots, o_n$ of operators so that $s_0 R_{o_1} s_1 R_{o_2} s_2 \cdots s_{n-1} R_n s_n$ where $I = \{s_0\}$ and $s_n \in G$.

The state space is viewed as a graph $\langle S, R_1, R_2, \ldots, R_n \rangle$ with nodes $s \in S$ and sets $R_i$ of directed edges labeled with operators $o_i \in O$. Classical planning is finding a path from the initial state to one of the goal states.

In planning without observability (conformant planning), the objective is similarly to find a sequence of operators reaching a goal state, but because of the unknown initial state (equivalently, an initial state nondeterministically chosen from $I$) and the nondeterministic transitions, the intermediate stages during plan execution are not states, but sets of states, describing the sets of possible states at every stage of plan execution.

Belief states in the belief space are sets of states, that is, the belief space is the powerset of the state space. An operator $o$ maps a belief state $B$ to the belief state

$$\{s' \in S | s \in B, sR_o s'\}$$

if[1] for every $s \in B$ there is $s' \in S$ such that $sR_o s'$.

Similarly a labeled graph $\langle 2^S, R_1^b, R_2^b, \ldots, R_n^b \rangle$ can be constructed for the belief space. Here the set of directed edges $R_i^b$ are defined so that belief state $B$ is related to $B'$ by $R_i^b$ (that is $BR_i^b B'$) if $B$ is mapped to $B'$ by $o_i$. Like in classical planning, these relations $R_i^b$ are partial functions, and similarly to classical planning, planning without observability (conformant planning) is finding a path from the initial belief state $I$ to a belief state $G'$ such that $G' \subseteq G$.

## Algorithms

Planning in the belief space can be solved like a state-space search problem: start from the initial belief state and repeatedly follow the directed edges in the belief space to reach new belief states, until a belief state that is a subset of the goal states is reached.

When a heuristic search algorithm is used for avoiding the enumeration of all the belief states, then it is important to use some informative heuristic for guiding the search.

The most obvious heuristic would be an estimate for the distance from the current belief state $B$ to the set of goal states $G$. In the next section we discuss some admissible heuristics that are derived *from distances in the state space* that underlies the belief space. These are the most obvious heuristics one could use. The rest of the paper is dedicated to investigating more informative heuristics that are not directly derived from the distances in the state space.

## Distance Heuristics from the State Space

Research on conformant planning so far has concentrated on distance heuristics derived from the distances of individual states in the state space. The distance of a belief state is for example the maximum length of a shortest path from a constituent state to a goal state.

[1]This is the applicability condition, corresponding to the requirement that the preconditions of the operator is satisfied in every possible state of the belief state (precondition is part of the commonly used syntactic definitions of operators.)

Bonet and Geffner (2000) have used a related distance measure, the optimal expected number of steps of reaching the goal in the corresponding probabilistic problem. Bryce and Kambhampati (2003) have considered efficient approximations of state space distances.

The most obvious distance heuristics are based on the weak and strong distances in the state space. The weak distances of states are based on the following inductive definition. Sets $D_i$ consist of those states from which a goal state is reachable in $i$ steps or less.

$$\begin{aligned} D_0 &= G \\ D_{i+1} &= D_i \cup \{s \in S | o \in O, s' \in D_i, sR_o s'\} \end{aligned}$$

A state $s$ has *weak distance* $d \geq 1$ if $s \in D_d \backslash D_{d-1}$ and distance 0 if $s \in G$. This means that it is possible to reach one of the goal states starting from $s$ by a sequence of $d$ operators if the nondeterministic alternatives play out favorably. Of course, nondeterministic actions may come out unfavorably and a higher number of actions may be needed, or the goal may even become unreachable, but if it is possible that the goals are reached in $d$ steps then the weak distance is $d$.

Strong distances are based on a slightly different inductive definition. Now $D_i$ consists of those states for which there is a guarantee of reaching a goal state in $i$ steps or less.

$$\begin{aligned} D_0 &= G \\ D_{i+1} &= D_i \cup \{s \in S | o \in O, s' \in D_i, sR_o s', \\ &\qquad sR_o s'' \text{ implies } s'' \in D_i \text{ for all } s''\} \end{aligned}$$

A state $s$ has *strong distance* $d \geq 1$ if $s \in D_d \backslash D_{d-1}$ and strong distance 0 if $s \in G$.

Next we derive distance heuristics for the belief space based on state space distances. Both weak and strong distances yield an admissible distance heuristic for belief states, but strong distances are (not always properly) higher than weak distances and therefore a more accurate estimate for plan length.

**Definition 1 (State space distance)** *The* state space distance *of a belief state $B$ is $d \geq 1$ when $B \subseteq D_d$ and $B \not\subseteq D_{d-1}$, and it is 0 when $B \subseteq D_0 = G$.*

Even though computing the exact distances for a typical succinct representation of transition systems, like STRIPS operators, is PSPACE-hard, the much higher complexity of planning problems with partial observability still often justifies it: this computation would in many cases be an inexpensive preprocessing step, preceding the much more expensive solution of the partially observable planning problem. Otherwise cheaper approximations can be used.

## $n$-Distances

The essence of planning without observability is that the same sequence of actions has to lead to a goal state for every state in the belief state. The distance heuristics from the strong distances in the state space may assign distance 1 to both state $s_1$ and state $s_2$, but the distance from $\{s_1, s_2\}$ may be anywhere between 1 and infinite. The inaccuracy in estimating the distance of $\{s_1, s_2\}$ based on the distances of $s_1$

and $s_2$ is that the distances of $s_1$ and $s_2$ in the state space may be along paths that have nothing to do with the path for $\{s_1, s_2\}$ in the belief space. That is, the actions on these three paths may be completely different.

This leads to a powerful idea. Instead of estimating the distance of $B$ in terms of distances of states $s \in B$ in the state space $S$, let us estimate it in terms of distances of $n$-tuples of states in the product state space $S^n$, in which there is a transition from $\langle s_1, \ldots, s_n \rangle$ to $\langle s'_1, \ldots, s'_n \rangle$ if and only if there is an operator $o$ that allows a transition from $s_i$ to $s'_i$ for every $i \in \{1, \ldots, n\}$. Here the important point is that the transition between the tuples is by using the same operator for every component state. This corresponds to the necessity of using the same operator for every state, because observations cannot distinguish between them.

This leads to a generalization of strong distances. We define the distances of $n$-tuples of states as follows.

$$\begin{aligned} D_0 &= G^n \\ D_{i+1} &= D_i \cup \{\sigma \in S^n | o \in O, \sigma' \in D_i, \sigma R_o^n \sigma', \\ &\qquad \sigma R_o^n \sigma'' \text{ implies } \sigma'' \in D_i \text{ for all } \sigma''\} \end{aligned}$$

Here $R_o^n$ is defined by

$$\langle s_1, \ldots, s_n \rangle R_o^n \langle s'_1, \ldots, s'_n \rangle \text{ if } s_i R_o s'_i \text{ for all } i \in \{1, \ldots, n\}.$$

Now we can define the $n$-distance of a belief state as follows.

**Definition 2 ($n$-distance)** *Belief state $B$ has $n$-distance $d = 0$ if for all $\{s_1, \ldots, s_n\} \subseteq B$, $\langle s_1, \ldots, s_n \rangle \in D_0$ (this is equivalent to $B \subseteq G$.) Belief state $B$ has $n$-distance $d \geq 1$ if for all $\{s_1, \ldots, s_n\} \subseteq B$, $\langle s_1, \ldots, s_n \rangle \in D_d$ and for some $\{s_1, \ldots, s_n\} \subseteq B$, $\langle s_1, \ldots, s_n \rangle \notin D_{d-1}$. If the distance $d$ is not any natural number, then $d = \infty$.*

So, we look at all the $n$-element subsets of $B$, see what their distance to goals is in the product state space $S^n$, and take the maximum of those distances. Notice that when we pick the elements $s_1, \ldots, s_n$ from $B$, we do not and cannot assume that the elements $s_1, \ldots, s_n$ are distinct, for example because $B$ may have less than $n$ states. Of course, the definition assumes that $B$ has at least one state. The 1-distance of a belief state coincides with the state space distance defined in the previous section.

The motivation behind $n$-distances is that computing the actual distance of belief states is very expensive (as complex as the planning problem itself) but we can use an informative notion of distances for "small" belief states of size $n$.

Next we investigate the properties of $n$-distances. The first result shows that $n$-distances are at least as good an estimate as $m$-distances when $n > m$. This result is based on a technical lemma that shows that $m$-tuples from the definition of $m$-distances are included in the $n$-tuples of the definition of $n$-distances.

**Lemma 3 (Embedding)** *Let $n > m$ and let $D_0, D_1, \ldots$ be the sets in the definition of $m$-distances, and $D'_0, D'_1, \ldots$ the sets in the definition of $n$-distances.*

*Then for all $i \geq 0$, all belief states $B$ and all $\{s_1, \ldots, s_m\} \subseteq B$, if $\langle s_1, \ldots, s_m, s'_{m+1}, \ldots, s'_n \rangle \in D'_i$ where $s'_k = s_m$ for all $k \in \{m+1, \ldots, n\}$, then $\langle s_1, \ldots, s_m \rangle \in D_i$.*

*Proof:* By induction on $i$. Base $i = 0$: If $\{s_1, \ldots, s_m\} \subseteq B$ and $\langle s_1, \ldots, s_m, s_m, \ldots, s_m \rangle \in D'_0$ (state $s_m$ is repeated so that the number of components in the tuple is $n$), then $\langle s_1, \ldots, s_m, s_m, \ldots, s_m \rangle \in G^n$. Consequently, $\langle s_1, \ldots, s_m \rangle \in D_0 = G^m$.

Inductive case $i \geq 1$: We show that if $\langle s_1, \ldots, s_m, s_m, \ldots, s_m \rangle \in D'_i$, then there is an operator $o \in O$ such that for any states $s'_1, \ldots, s'_m$ such that $s_i R_o s'_i$ for all $i \in \{1, \ldots, m\}$, $\langle s'_1, \ldots, s'_m \rangle \in D_{i-1}$, and hence $\langle s_1, \ldots, s_m \rangle \in D_i$.

So assume $\langle s_1, \ldots, s_m, s_m, \ldots, s_m \rangle \in D'_i$. Hence there is an operator $o \in O$ such that for all $s'_1, \ldots, s'_n$ such that $s_i R_o s'_i$ for all $i \in \{1, \ldots, m\}$ and $s_m R_o s'_j$ for all $j \in \{m+1, \ldots, k\}$, the $n$-tuple $\langle s'_1, \ldots, s'_n \rangle$ is in $D'_{i-1}$. Now $\langle s'_1, \ldots, s'_m, s'_m, \ldots, s'_m \rangle \in D'_{i-1}$ because this tuple is one of those reachable from $\langle s_1, \ldots, s_m, s_m \ldots, s_m \rangle$, and hence by the induction hypothesis $\langle s'_1, \ldots, s'_m \rangle \in D_{i-1}$. Because this holds for all $s'_i$ reachable by $R_o$ from the corresponding $s_i$, we have $\langle s_1, \ldots, s_m \rangle \in D_i$. □

The embedding of $m$-distances in $n$-distances as provided by the lemma easily yields the result that $n$-distances are more accurate than $m$-distances when $n > m$.

**Theorem 4** *Let $d_n$ be the $n$-distance for a belief state $B$ and $d_m$ the $m$-distance for $B$. If $n > m$, then $d_n \geq d_m$.*

*Proof:* So assume that the $m$-distance of $B$ is $d_m$. This implies that there is $\{s_1, \ldots, s_m\} \subseteq B$ such that $\langle s_1, \ldots, s_m \rangle \notin D_{d_m - 1}$. Let $\sigma = \langle s_1, \ldots, s_m, s_m, \ldots, s_m \rangle$ where $s_m$ is repeated $n - m + 1$ times. By Lemma 3 $\sigma \notin D'_{d_m - 1}$. Hence there is $\{s_1, \ldots, s_m, s_m, \ldots, s_m\} \subseteq B$ such that $\langle s_1, \ldots, s_m, s_m, \ldots, s_m \rangle \notin D'_{d_m}$. Hence the $n$-distance $d_n$ of $B$ is greater than or equal to $d_m$. □

So, 2-distances are a better estimate for belief states than the estimate given by state space distances, and 3-distances are a better estimate than 2-distances, and so on.

For the last result we need another lemma, which we give without a proof. The lemma states that the components of the tuples in the sets $D_i$ may be reordered and replaced by existing components.

**Lemma 5** *Let $D_0, D_1, \ldots,$ be the sets in the definition of $n$-distances. Then if $\langle s_1, \ldots, s, s', \ldots, s_k \rangle$ is in $D_i$, then so is $\langle s_1, \ldots, s', s, \ldots, s_k \rangle$, and if $\langle s_1, s_2, s_3, \ldots, s_k \rangle$ is in $D_i$, then so is $\langle s_1, s_1, s_3, \ldots, s_k \rangle$.*

**Theorem 6** *Let the belief space be $2^S$, where the cardinality of the state space is $n = |S|$. Then the $n$-distance of $B$ equals the distance of $B$ in the belief space.*

*Proof:* Omitted because of lack of space. □

In summary, the accuracy of the $n$-distances grows as $n$ grows, and asymptotically when $n$ equals the number of states it is perfectly accurate.

In addition to including state space distances as a special case, the family of $n$-distances also takes into account the cardinalities of belief states, although only in a restricted manner as determined by the magnitude of $n$. Consider the belief state $B = \{s_1, s_2\}$. Its 2-distance is determined by the membership of the tuples $\sigma_1 = \langle s_1, s_2 \rangle$ (and symmetrically $\langle s_2, s_1 \rangle$), $\sigma_2 = \langle s_1, s_1 \rangle$, and $\sigma_3 = \langle s_2, s_2 \rangle$ in the sets $D_i$. The distance of $\sigma_1$ is at least as high as that of $\sigma_2$ and $\sigma_3$, because any sequence of actions leading to goals that is applicable for $\{s_1, s_2\}$ is also applicable for $s_1$ alone and for $s_2$ alone, and there might be shorter action sequences applicable for $s_1$ and $s_2$ but not for $\{s_1, s_2\}$. Therefore, any reduction in the size of a belief state, like from $\{s_1, s_2\}$ to $\{s_1\}$ would appropriately improve the $n$-distance estimate.

## Accuracy of the Heuristics

Preceding results show that the accuracy of $n$-distances increases as $n$ grows, reaching perfect accuracy when $n$ equals the cardinality of the state space. Can we demonstrate advantages of $n$-distances on concrete planning problems? We shed some light on this issue next, but the reader should note that the benchmarks used by us and others are rather simple and unlikely to reflect properties of more challenging problems. Consequently, this section just illustrates the impact the improved heuristics can have on different problems.

We have implemented a planner that does heuristic search in the belief space, and three heuristics for guiding the search algorithms implemented in this planner: the 1-distances, the 2-distances, and the cardinality of belief states. The first two heuristics are admissible, and can be used in connection with optimal heuristic search algorithms like A$*$. The third heuristic, size of the belief states, does not directly yield an admissible heuristic, and we use it only in connection with a search algorithm that does not rely on admissibility.

The planner is implemented in C and represents belief states as BDDs with the CUDD system from Colorado University. CUDD provides functions for computing the cardinality of a belief state. Our current implementation does not support $n$-distances for $n$ other than 1 and 2.

The search algorithms implemented in our planner include the optimal heuristic search algorithm A$*$, the suboptimal family of algorithms WA$*$[2], and suboptimal best-first search which first expands those nodes that have the lowest estimated remaining distance to the goal states.

The main topic to be investigated is the relative accuracy of $n$-distances, and as a secondary topic we briefly evaluate the effectiveness of different types of search algorithms and heuristics. We use the following benchmarks. Regrettably there are few meaningful benchmarks; all the interesting ones are for the more general problem of partially observable planning.

- Bonet and Geffner (2000) proposed one of the most interesting benchmarks for conformant planning so far, sorting networks (Knuth 1998). A sorting network consists of an ordered (or a partially ordered) set of gates acting on a number of input lines. Each gate combines a comparator and a swapper: if first input is greater than the second, then swap the values. The goal is to sort the input sequence. The sorting network always has to perform the same operations irrespective of the input, and hence exactly corresponds to planning without observability.

  Our size parameter is the number of inputs.
- In the empty room benchmark a robot without any sensors moves in a room to north, south, east and west and its goal is to get to the middle of the room. This is possible by going to north or south and then west or east until the robot knows that it is in one of the corners. Then it is easy to go to the goal position. The robot does not know its initial location.

  Size $n$ characterizes room size $2^n \times 2^n$.
- Our blocks world benchmark is the standard blocks world, but with several initial states and modified to be solvable without observability even when the initial state is not known. Operators are always applicable, but nothing happens if the relevant blocks are not accessible. The initial belief state consists of all the possible configurations of the $n$ blocks, and the goal is to build a stack consisting of all the blocks in a fixed order.
- The ring of rooms benchmark involves a round building with a cycle of $n$ rooms with a window in each that can be closed and locked. Initially the state of the windows and the location of the robot is unknown. The robot can move to the next room either in clockwise or counterclockwise direction, and then close and lock the windows. Locking is possible only if the window is closed. Locking an already locked window and closing an already closed window does not have any effect.

  The size parameter is the number of rooms.

There are other benchmarks considered in the literature, but their flavor is close to some of the above, and many can be easily reformulated as planning with full observability.

Table 1 makes a comparison on the accuracy of 1-distances and 2-distances on a number of problem instances. For each heuristic we first give the distance estimate for the initial belief state, followed by the percentage of the actual distance. The actual distance (= length of the shortest plan) was determined by A$*$ and is given in the last column.

As expected, on most of the problems 2-distances are strictly better estimates than 1-distances, and surprisingly, on one of the problems, the empty room navigation problem, the 2-distances equal the lengths of the shortest plans.

For the ring of room problems 1-distances and 2-distances are the same, and coincide with the actual shortest plan length. This is because of the simple structure of the problem and its belief space. It seems that 2-distances would also not provide an advantage over 1-distances on many other problems in which there are no dependencies between state variables with unknown values.

The sorting network problem is the most difficult of the benchmarks in terms of the relation between difficulty and number of state variables. Every initial state (combination of input values) in this benchmark can be solved by a sorting network with a small number of gates (more precisely $\lfloor \frac{n}{2} \rfloor$),

[2] We parameterize WA$*$ with $W = 5$, giving a 5 times higher value to the estimated remaining distance than to the distance so far, yielding solutions having cost at most 5 times the optimal.

| | 1-distance | | 2-distance | | exact |
|---|---|---|---|---|---|
| | len | % | len | % | len |
| sort02 | 1 | 1.00 | 1 | 1.00 | 1 |
| sort03 | 1 | 0.33 | 2 | 0.67 | 3 |
| sort04 | 2 | 0.40 | 3 | 0.60 | 5 |
| sort05 | 2 | 0.22 | 3 | 0.33 | 9 |
| sort06 | 3 | 0.25 | 4 | 0.33 | 12 |
| sort07 | 3 | 0.19 | 5 | 0.31 | 16 |
| sort08 | 4 | 0.16 | 6 | 0.32 | 19 |
| ring03 | 8 | 1.00 | 8 | 1.00 | 8 |
| ring04 | 11 | 1.00 | 11 | 1.00 | 11 |
| ring05 | 14 | 1.00 | 14 | 1.00 | 14 |
| ring06 | 17 | 1.00 | 17 | 1.00 | 17 |
| ring07 | 20 | 1.00 | 20 | 1.00 | 20 |
| BW02 | 2 | 0.67 | 3 | 1.00 | 3 |
| BW03 | 4 | 0.57 | 5 | 0.71 | 7 |
| BW04 | 6 | 0.46 | 8 | 0.62 | 13 |
| BW05 | 7 | 0.41 | 9 | 0.53 | 17 |
| emptyroom01 | 2 | 1.00 | 2 | 1.00 | 2 |
| emptyroom02 | 4 | 0.50 | 8 | 1.00 | 8 |
| emptyroom03 | 8 | 0.40 | 20 | 1.00 | 20 |
| emptyroom04 | 16 | 0.36 | 44 | 1.00 | 44 |
| emptyroom05 | 32 | 0.35 | 92 | 1.00 | 92 |

Table 1: Accuracy of 1-distances and 2-distances on a number of problem instances

which makes the 1-distances small. Increasing $n$ monotonically increases $n$-distances, but the increase is slow because for a small number of input combinations the smallest network sorting them all is still rather small, and as the number of input value combinations is exponential in the number of inputs, only a tiny fraction of all combinations is covered.

Table 2 gives runtimes on all combinations of search algorithm and heuristic. We only report the time spent in the search algorithm, ignoring a preprocessing phase during which BDDs representing 1-distances and 2-distances are computed. Computing 2-distances is more expensive than computing 1-distances because there are twice as many variables in the BDDs and the efficiency of BDDs decreases as BDDs grow. The higher accuracy of 2-distances is often reflected in the runtimes.

On the empty room problems, performance of A$*$ and 1-distances quickly deteriorates as room size grows, while with 2-distances A$*$ immediately constructs optimal plans even for bigger rooms. On sorting networks and WA$*$ 2-distances lead to a better performance because of its advantage over 1-distances in accuracy, but finding bigger optimal networks is still very much out of reach.

On all of the problems, best-first search is the fastest to find a plan, but plans were much longer on the empty room and blocks world problems, and slightly worse on sorting networks. For bigger sorting networks the cardinality heuristic combined with best-first is the best combination, as runtimes with the other heuristics and with A$*$ and WA$*$ grow much faster. We believe that our collection of benchmarks is too small to say conclusively anything general about the relative merits of the heuristics.

Interestingly, our planner with best-first search and the cardinality heuristic produces optimal sorting networks up to size 8 (Bonet and Geffner (2000) report producing networks until size 6 with an optimal algorithm), and for bigger networks the difference to known best networks is first relatively small, but later grows; see Table 3.

## Related Work

Bonet and Geffner (2000) were one of the first to apply heuristic state-space search to planning in the belief space. They used a variant of the state space distance heuristic considered by us, with the difference that they were addressing probabilistic problems and considered expected distances of states under the optimal probabilistic plan, instead of the non-probabilistic weak or strong distances.

Bryce and Kambhampati (2003) compute distances with Graphplan's (Blum & Furst 1997) planning graphs, and recognize that the smallest of the weak distances of states in a belief state – as is trivially obtained from planning graphs – is not very informative, and propose improvements based on multiple planning graphs: for a formula $\chi_1 \vee \chi_2 \vee \cdots \vee \chi_n$ describing a belief state, compute the estimate for each $\chi_i$ separately. Then an admissible estimate for the whole belief state is bounded from above by $\max_{i=1}^{n} \min_{s \in \sigma(\chi_i)} \delta(s)$ where $\sigma(\chi_i)$ is the set of states described by $\chi_i$, and $\delta(s)$ is the distance from state $s$ to a goal state. This is below the state space distances (1-distances) because minimization is used, not maximization. It may be difficult to do distance maximization with planning graphs as they do not represent most dependencies between state variables.

Smith and Weld's (1998) multiple planning graphs and especially their induced mutexes are related to our $n$-distances. They compute a kind of approximation of our $n$-distances, but as this computation is based on distances of state variable values as in the work by Bryce and Kambhampati, the approximation is not very good. With the multiple planning graphs there do not appear to be useful ways of controlling the accuracy parameter $n$, and Smith and Weld then essentially consider $n$ that equals the number of initial states for deterministic problems.

Haslum and Geffner (2000) have defined a family of increasingly accurate heuristics for classical deterministic planning. Their accuracy parameter $n$ is the number of state variables analogously to our parameter $n$ of states. However, they give approximations of distances in the state space (our 1-distances), not in the belief space, and many of the phenomena important for conditional planning, like nondeterminism, do not show up in their framework.

## Conclusions and Future Work

In this paper, we have presented a family of distance heuristics for planning in the belief space, and shown that this family behaves in a robust way, generalizes distance estimates based on distances in the state space, and asymptotically yields perfectly accurate estimates. Our experimental study on a number of benchmark problems indicates that on all problems considered, the estimates are a proper improvement over estimates based on state space distances, except when both are perfectly accurate.

| instance | A* | | | | WA* | | | | best first | | | | | |
|---|---|---|---|---|---|---|---|---|---|---|---|---|---|---|
| | 1-distance | | 2-distance | | 1-distance | | 2-distance | | 1-distance | | 2-distance | | cardinality | |
| | time | len | time | len | time | len | time | len | time | len | time | len | time | len |
| sort02 | 0.00 | 1 | 0.00 | 1 | 0.00 | 1 | 0.00 | 1 | 0.00 | 1 | 0.00 | 1 | 0.00 | 1 |
| sort03 | 0.00 | 3 | 0.00 | 3 | 0.00 | 3 | 0.00 | 3 | 0.00 | 3 | 0.00 | 3 | 0.00 | 3 |
| sort04 | 0.00 | 5 | 0.01 | 5 | 0.00 | 5 | 0.00 | 5 | 0.00 | 6 | 0.00 | 6 | 0.00 | 5 |
| sort05 | 0.12 | 9 | 0.15 | 9 | 0.13 | 9 | 0.07 | 9 | 0.00 | 10 | 0.01 | 10 | 0.00 | 9 |
| sort06 | 139.41 | 12 | 154.64 | 12 | 251.87 | 12 | 25.81 | 12 | 0.01 | 15 | 0.01 | 15 | 0.00 | 12 |
| sort07 | $> 2h$ | | $> 2h$ | | $> 2h$ | | $> 2h$ | | 0.01 | 21 | 0.01 | 20 | 0.01 | 16 |
| sort08 | $> 2h$ | | $> 2h$ | | $> 2h$ | | $> 2h$ | | 0.02 | 28 | 0.05 | 28 | 0.02 | 19 |
| ring03 | 0.01 | 8 | 0.01 | 8 | 0.00 | 8 | 0.00 | 8 | 0.00 | 8 | 0.00 | 8 | 0.01 | 8 |
| ring04 | 0.00 | 11 | 0.01 | 11 | 0.00 | 11 | 0.00 | 11 | 0.00 | 11 | 0.01 | 11 | 0.00 | 11 |
| ring05 | 0.01 | 14 | 0.03 | 14 | 0.01 | 14 | 0.04 | 14 | 0.01 | 14 | 0.03 | 14 | 0.01 | 14 |
| ring06 | 0.03 | 17 | 0.12 | 17 | 0.03 | 17 | 0.14 | 17 | 0.03 | 17 | 0.14 | 17 | 0.03 | 17 |
| BW02 | 0.00 | 3 | 0.00 | 3 | 0.00 | 3 | 0.00 | 3 | 0.00 | 3 | 0.00 | 3 | 0.00 | 3 |
| BW03 | 0.01 | 7 | 0.00 | 7 | 0.00 | 7 | 0.01 | 7 | 0.00 | 7 | 0.01 | 7 | 0.00 | 7 |
| BW04 | 0.71 | 13 | 0.93 | 13 | 0.04 | 13 | 0.06 | 14 | 0.02 | 14 | 0.04 | 14 | 0.03 | 14 |
| BW05 | 180.47 | 17 | 307.62 | 17 | 1.26 | 17 | 2.87 | 17 | 0.40 | 22 | 1.41 | 21 | 0.36 | 34 |
| emptyroom01 | 0.00 | 2 | 0.00 | 2 | 0.00 | 2 | 0.00 | 2 | 0.00 | 2 | 0.00 | 2 | 0.00 | 4 |
| emptyroom02 | 0.00 | 8 | 0.00 | 8 | 0.00 | 8 | 0.00 | 8 | 0.00 | 12 | 0.00 | 8 | 0.00 | 12 |
| emptyroom03 | 0.16 | 20 | 0.01 | 20 | 0.03 | 24 | 0.00 | 20 | 0.00 | 50 | 0.00 | 20 | 0.00 | 36 |
| emptyroom04 | 37.28 | 44 | 0.07 | 44 | 10.59 | 52 | 0.06 | 44 | 0.09 | 222 | 0.06 | 44 | 0.01 | 106 |
| emptyroom05 | $> 2h$ | | 0.92 | 92 | $> 2h$ | | 0.89 | 92 | 2.53 | 950 | 0.89 | 92 | 0.03 | 342 |

Table 2: Runtimes and plan sizes of a number of problem instances

| inputs | 2 | 3 | 4 | 5 | 6 | 7 | 8 | 9 | 10 | 11 | 12 | 13 | 14 | 15 | 16 |
|---|---|---|---|---|---|---|---|---|---|---|---|---|---|---|---|
| gates (best known) | 1 | 3 | 5 | 9 | 12 | 16 | 19 | 25 | 29 | 35 | 39 | 45 | 51 | 56 | 60 |
| gates (our planner) | 1 | 3 | 5 | 9 | 12 | 16 | 19 | 26 | 31 | 39 | 46 | 56 | 64 | 74 | 81 |

Table 3: Sizes of sorting networks found by best-first search and cardinality heuristic. Networks up to 8 inputs are optimal. From 9 on optimal network sizes are not known. Total runtime for 16 inputs is 5.81 seconds on a 800 MHz Pentium.

To make the use of 2-distances feasible on bigger problem instances a further investment in implementation techniques is needed. Most direct approach would be to give up exact computation of 2-distances. First, one could use generic approximation techniques for making BDDs smaller: compute a BDD of small size given upper and lower bounds for the Boolean function. Second, 2-distances can be approximated by abstracting half of the state variables away: for $\langle s_1, s_2\rangle$ ignore the even ones for $s_1$ and the odd ones for $s_2$.

So far we presented heuristics for the unobservable planning, but of course the main interest is in conditional planning with partial observability. The $n$-distances are not admissible for partially observable planning in general: increased observability decreases belief state distances. This will be addressed in future research.

## Acknowledgements

This work was partially funded by DFG grant RI 1177/2-1.

## References

Bertoli, P.; Cimatti, A.; and Roveri, M. 2001. Heuristic search + symbolic model checking = efficient conformant planning. In *Proceedings of the 17th International Joint Conference on Artificial Intelligence*, 467–472.

Blum, A. L., and Furst, M. L. 1997. Fast planning through planning graph analysis. *Artificial Intelligence* 90(1-2):281–300.

Bonet, B., and Geffner, H. 2000. Planning with incomplete information as heuristic search in belief space. In Chien, S.; Kambhampati, S.; and Knoblock, C. A., eds., *Proceedings of the Fifth International Conference on Artificial Intelligence Planning Systems*, 52–61. AAAI Press.

Bonet, B., and Geffner, H. 2001. Planning as heuristic search. *Artificial Intelligence* 129(1-2):5–33.

Bryce, D., and Kambhampati, S. 2003. Heuristic guidance measure for conformant planning. ICAPS'03 workshop on Planning under Uncertainty.

Haslum, P., and Geffner, H. 2000. Admissible heuristics for optimal planning. In Chien, S.; Kambhampati, S.; and Knoblock, C. A., eds., *Proceedings of the Fifth International Conference on Artificial Intelligence Planning Systems*, 140–149. AAAI Press.

Knuth, D. E. 1998. *Art of Computer Programming, Volume 3: Sorting and Searching*. Addison-Wesley Publishing Company.

Smith, D. E., and Weld, D. S. 1998. Conformant Graphplan. In *Proceedings of the Fifteenth National Conference on Artificial Intelligence (AAAI-98) and the Tenth Conference on Innovative Applications of Artificial Intelligence (IAAI-98)*, 889–896. AAAI Press.

# Continuous Time in a SAT-based Planner

**Ji-Ae Shin** and **Ernest Davis***
Courant Institute
New York University
{ jiae | davise }@cs.nyu.edu

### Abstract

The TM-LPSAT planner can construct plans in domains containing atomic actions and durative actions; events and processes; discrete, real-valued, and interval-valued fluents; and continuous linear change to quantities. It works in three stages. In the first stage, a representation of the domain and problem in an extended version of PDDL+ is compiled into a system of propositional combinations of propositional variables and linear constraints over numeric variables. In the second stage, the LPSAT constraint engine (Wolfman & Weld 2000) is used to find a solution to the system of constraints. In the third stage, a correct parallel plan is extracted from this solution. We discuss the structure of the planner and show how a real-time temporal model is compiled into LPSAT constraints.

**Keywords:** Propositional planning, LPSAT, continuous time, numerical quantities, processes.

## Introduction

Over the past decade, several new powerful engines for propositional satisfiability have become available and are now being used in a broad range of applications (Alessandro et al. 2002). One very successful application has been the development of *propositional planning,* in which a planning problem is compiled into a set of propositional constraints in such a way that a solution to the constraints demarcates a valid plan (Kautz & Selman 1992; Kautz & Selman 1996; Ernst et al. 1997; Kautz & Selman 1999).

Recently, a new class of inference engines (Wolfman & Weld 1999; Audemard et al. 2002; Barrett & Berezin 2004) has been developed for systems of propositional combinations of linear constraints over real-valued quantities. In this paper, we show that these can be used to extend propositional planning to many domains that involve real-valued quantities and continuous change.

The TM-LPSAT planner (Shin 2004) constructs plans in domains with the following features:

• The effects and preconditions of actions can involve discrete, real-valued, and interval-valued fluents.
• An action can change the value of a real-valued fluent either continuously, as a linear function of time, or discretely.
• An action may be either atomic or durative (taking place over an extended time interval).
• An action may take real- or interval-valued parameters.
• Actions may be concurrent.
• Exogenous events may occur. These can have the same types of preconditions and effects as atomic actions.
• Autonomous processes can be defined in the language.
• Reusable resources,both multiple-capacity and interval-valued, can be defined in the language.

TM-LPSAT has three modules. The *compiler* takes as input a domain and a problem description in PDDL+ (Fox & Long 2001; 2003) and outputs a set of constraints over propositional and numerical variables. The *LPSAT* constraint engine, developed by Wolfman and Weld (1999) , takes this set of constraints as input and outputs a solution, if one exists, in the form of an assignment to the variables. The *decoder* takes as input the assignment and outputs a correct plan. The overall system is thus a powerful and elegant planner for a wide range of problems.

In this paper[1], we present the encoding of real-time temporal model defined in PDDL+ Level 5 (Fox & Long 2001), consisting of atomic actions, exogenous events and autonomous processes.

## Foundations

The TM-LPSAT planner builds on three foundations: the theory of propositional planning, the LPSAT constraint engine, and the PDDL+ specification language.

### Propositional planning

In propositional planning, a planning problem in a domain with discrete actions and fluents[2] with discrete values is con-

*The research reported in this paper was supported in part by NSF grant IIS-0097537.


[1]We are preparing a paper that deals with the details of the encoding of a durative action, as defined in PDDL+ Levels 3 and 4. Due to space limitations, we do not discuss intervals or reusable resources here.

[2]Throughout this paper, we will use the word "fluent" in the temporal logic sense of "entity that takes on different values at different times" such as "on(blockA,blockB)", rather than meaning the particular PDDL construct of that name. Temporal logic "fluents" includes PDDL "predicates".

verted into a set of propositional constraints. This is done as follows:

- An upper bound N is guessed for the maximum number of steps in the plan. Time points are labelled 0 . . . N.
- The following propositional atoms are defined at each time point I:
  A. For each fluent F, for each possible value V of F, the statement that the value of F at time I is V.
  B. For each action A, the statement that A is executed at time I.
- The laws governing the domain are imposed by asserting every instance of every law at every moment of time. In classical planning domains the major categories of laws are: causal laws, domain constraints, and frame axioms.
- The problem is specified by stating that the start state holds at time 0 and that the goal state holds at time N.
- The constraints are fed to a propositional satisfiability engine. If the constraints can be solved, then the actions that are marked as occurring constitute a valid plan.

Propositional planners can be implemented easily and, with the current generation of satisfiability engines, quite effectively. Since their introduction in (Kautz & Selman 1992), they have been extensively studied (Kautz & Selman 1996; Kautz & Selman 1999), and various ways of formulating the constraints (Kautz et al. 1996; Ernst et al. 1997) have been compared. The major drawback is that large domains can lead to enormously large systems of constraints. Particularly dangerous are functions with many arguments; a fluent function or action function with $k$ arguments generates a collection of atoms of size exponential in $k$.

### The LPSAT program

The LPSAT constraint engine is composed from RelSAT a DPLL-based propositional solver, and Cassowary an incremental linear constraint solver. The input to LPSAT (Wolfman & Weld 1999) is a set of generalized clauses. Each clause is a disjunction; each disjunct is either a propositional literal or a linear equality or inequality over numeric variables. The program first looks for a propositional solution, treating each linear equation as a propositional atom, then tries to solve the set of equations that have been marked as true. If that set is inconsistent, then LPSAT adds a clause stating that these linear inequalities are not all true, and it looks for a new propositional solution. It goes back and forth between propositional and numerical mode until either finding a solution or establishing that no solution exists.

### PDDL+

PDDL (Planning Domain Definition Language) (McDermott 1998; 2000) is a declarative language for the definition of causal domains and planning problems. The basis of our work is PDDL+, which is the most recent extension to PDDL. PDDL+ comprises five levels. Level 1 contains discrete actions and fluents. Level 2 adds features for numeric quantities. Level 3 allows durative actions that cause discrete changes occurring at the beginning and at the end of the action. Level 4 allows durative actions that cause continuous changes throughout the occurrence of the action. (Levels 1 through 4 collectively comprise PDDL2.1 (Fox & Long 2003).) Level 5 (Fox & Long 2001), proposed but not approved by IPC (International Planning Competition) committee, is a real-time temporal model that includes atomic actions, exogenous events, and autonomous processes.

The input specification language for TM-LPSAT extends PDDL+ in that we allow actions to have real-valued parameters. For instance, there can be an action "scoop($N, C, B$)" of scooping up $N$ cups of flour from bin $B$ into cup $C$. PDDL2.1 excludes this (Fox & Long 2003) but their arguments do not strike us as cogent. Numerical parameters greatly increase the expressivity power of the language, and, in the LPSAT approach, impose no additional computational burden.

One restriction must be imposed on actions with numeric parameters: There cannot be two or more concurrent actions with the identical non-numeric parameters. For instance, we do not allow the actions "scoop(5,c1,b1)" and "scoop(2,c1,b1)" to be executed concurrently, though "scoop(5,c1,b1)" and "scoop(2,c2,b2)" may be concurrent. The restriction is reasonable because such numerical parameters are typically used in one of two ways. If the value of the parameter is assigned to a fluent – e.g. "scoop($N, C, B$)" results in the cup containing $N$ cups of flour — then two actions with different numeric parameters would be mutually exclusive. If the value of the parameter is used to increment a fluent — e.g. "scoop($N, C, B$)" results in adding $N$ cups of flour to cup $C$ — then two such concurrent actions scoop(5,c1,b1) and scoop(2,c1,b1) can be combined into a single action scoop(7,c1,b1). We have not found any cases where it would be reasonable and important to violate this restriction.

By virtue of this restriction, an action type is identified by the name of the functor and the non-numeric arguments. For example, we may speak of the action type "scoop(·,b1,c1)" (scooping some amount from b1 into c1) and be sure that at most one of these occurs at one time.

A few features of PDDL+ cannot be included in TM-LPSAT. First, TM-LPSAT cannot optimize a specified plan metric. Second, the language must be restricted so that, in any multiplication, all but one of the terms can be statically evaluated; and, in any division, the denominator can be statically evaluated. Otherwise, the result will be a non-linear equation that LPSAT cannot handle. Third, no non-linear expressions are allowed in any definitions. All other features of PDDL+ are included.

## Temporal ontology

We use a linear, real-valued time line. The representation used in the constraint language output by TM-LPSAT characterizes the time line in terms of the states of the world at a collection of *significant time points*. A significant time point is one where "something changes"; roughly speaking, some action, event, or process occurs, starts, or ends. In the intervals between significant time points, fluents are either constant, or, if they are numerical, they may undergo continuous change as a linear function of time. Every discontinuous change, or change in the derivative of a numerical fluent, occurs at a significant time point. Thus, there are two states associated with each time point T; the state *before* T and the state *after* T.

Each time point has a *clock time*, which is a non-negative real value. These clock times become numerical variables in the system of constraints set up by the compiler. It is possible, however, to have two distinct time points with equal clock times. This is used to accommodate the following situation: Suppose that action A is executed at time $T_i$, and has the effect of either causing fluent P to be true or making a discrete change to a numerical fluent. Suppose further that event E has triggering condition P or a numeric constraint satisfied by the discrete change. Then E should be executed immediately after A. We model that by positing that E is executed at time $T_{i+1}$, but that the clock time for $T_{i+1}$ is the same as the clock time for $T_i$. Note that event E *must* disable its own triggering condition; else there would have to be additional occurrences of E at $T_{i+2}$, at $T_{i+3}$, etc.; the result would be that the system of constraints would have no solution with finitely many time points.

An *atomic action* occurs instantaneously. An action is characterized by preconditions that must hold before the action and effects that hold after the action. For example, the action "turn on the faucet" has the precondition that the faucet is off and has the effect that the faucet is on.

An *event* is like an atomic action, except that, whereas an atomic action *may* occur if its preconditions hold (if the actor so chooses), an event *must* occur if its precondition hold. For example, the event "flood" has a precondition that the tub is full, the bathroom floor is dry, and that there is a process of inflow into the tub. It has the consequence that the bathroom floor is wet.

A *process* is active over an extended interval. It is characterized by preconditions and effects. The preconditions must hold through the interval; if the preconditions cease to hold, the process stops. The effects of a process are, in the language of (Forbus 1984), *direct influences* on numeric fluents. Specifically, each process has a fixed influence on some collection of real-valued fluents; the derivative of the fluent at a given time is the sum of its influences over all active processes and actions that influence it.

For example, the process "fillBath(B - bath; T - tap)" has the precondition that tap T is open and that the level of the bath is less than its capacity; and the constraint that T is a tap of B. (We assume, unrealistically, that flow will stop once the bath is full.) It has the effect of increasing level(B) at the rate flow(T). (We allow only taps that are fully on or off.) At any moment, the derivative of level(B) is the sum of the rates of the active fillBath processes.

PDDL+ permits concurrent actions under fairly restrictive conditions, designed to ensure that the actions do not interact, either destructively or synergistically. The actual condition imposed is one that can be computed easily and statically and that is sufficient, though not necessary, to ensure this non-interaction.

## Sample domain

The bath domain includes filling processes with different taps, a draining process, a flood event, and atomic actions of tapOn, tapOff, plugIn, plugOut, and addBubble. Filling processes can be concurrent with draining process. We can add bubble before the bath is half full. Thus, this domain can show concurrent continuous and discrete changes on the level of a bath.

```
(:process fillBath
 :parameters (?b - bath ?t - tap)
 :precondition (and (tap_on ?b ?t)
                    (<= (level ?b) (capacity ?b)))
 :effect (increase (level ?b) (* #t (flow ?b ?t))))
(:process drainBath
 :parameters (?b - bath)
 :precondition (and (not (plug_in ?b))
                    (> (level ?b) 0))
 :effect (decrease (level ?b) (* #t (draining_flow ?b)))
(:event flood
 :parameters (?b - bath)
 :precondition (and (exists (?t - tap) (tap_on ?b ?t))
                    (>= (level ?b) (capacity ?b))
                    (dry_floor ?b))
 :effect (not (dry_floor ?b)))
(:action addBubble
 :parameters (?b - bath ?q - real)
 :condition (and (exists (?t - tap) (tap_on ?b ?t))
                 (not (bubble_added ?b))
                 (<= (level ?b) (/ (capacity ?b) 2)))
 :effect (and (bubble_added ?b)
              (increase (level ?b) ?q)))
```

## Compilation to LPSAT constraints

We begin by guessing at an upper bound $N$ on the number of significant time points that will be needed to solve the problem. The significant time points are then $T_0 \ldots T_N$.

We define the following propositional atoms:

- For each time $T_i$, for each propositional fluent $F$, for each value $V$, the assertion that $F$ has value $V$ at $T_i$. We notate this "$F[T_i] = V$".
- For each time $T_i$, for each atomic action/event $E$, the assertion that $E$ occurs at $T_i$. (Note: An action/event is identified by the name of the action and the value of the non-numeric parameters, as discussed above.)
- For each time $T_i$, for each process[3] $P$, the assertion that $P$ is active at $T_i$. (This includes the time that $P$ starts but not the time when it terminates.)

We define the following numeric variables:

- The clock time of every significant time point $T_i$. We will denote this "c($T_i$)".
- For every time $T_i$, for every numeric fluent $Q$, the value of $Q$ *before* and *after* $T_i$. We notate these "$Q[T_i^-]$" and "$Q[T_i^+]$" respectively.

[3]The encoding assumes that two instances of the same process cannot be concurrent.

- For each numeric fluent $Q$, for each action or event $A$ that changes $Q$ incrementally (i.e. executes a discrete "increase" or "decrease") the amount of increase or decrease that an occurrence of $A$ makes to $Q$ at time $T_i$. This is denoted $\Delta(A, Q, T_i)$.
- For each numeric fluent $Q$, for each durative action or process $A$ that changes $Q$ continually, for each time $T_i$, the net change in $Q$ due to $A$ between $T_i$ and $T_{i+1}$. This is denoted $\Gamma(A, Q, T_i, T_{i+1})$.
- Let $A(P_1 \ldots P_k, Q_1 \ldots Q_m)$ be an action where $P_1 \ldots P_k$ are discrete parameters and $Q_1 \ldots Q_m$ are numeric parameters. Then, by the restriction mentioned above, at any particular time $T_i$, for any particular values $V_1 \ldots V_k$ of the discrete parameters, there is at most one valuation on the $Q_i$ for which an action of the form $A(P_1 \ldots P_k, Q_1 \ldots Q_m)$ begins at time $T_i$. The value of each such $Q_j$ before and after $T_i$ is a numeric variable.

We will use the following convention for labelling time-dependent terms:

- If a complex term $\alpha$ over fluents that appears in a precondition or on the right side of an assignment statement is evaluated using the values before a discrete change is made at time $T_i$, we will denote this evaluation as $\alpha[T_i^-]$. That is, it is evaluated with the values of propositional fluents from $T_{i-1}$ and the values of numeric fluents from *before* $T_i$.
- If a complex term $\alpha$ over fluents that appears in a precondition or effect is evaluated after a discrete change is made at time $T_i$, we will denote this evaluation as $\alpha[T_i^+]$. That is, it is evaluated using the values of propositional fluents from $T_i$ and the value of numeric fluents from *after* $T_i$.

A domain definition then gives rise to the following kinds of constraints (see (Shin 2004) for details):

**1. Atomic actions**
1.1: Effects:
1.1.1: If an effect of action $A$ is to assign term $\alpha$ to discrete or interval fluent $F$, then add the constraint
active$(A, T_i) \Rightarrow F[T_i] = \alpha[T_i^-]$.
1.1.2: If an effect of action $A$ is to assign term $\alpha$ to numeric fluent $F$, then add the constraint
active$(A, T_i) \Rightarrow F[T_i^+] = \alpha[T_i^-]$.
1.1.3: If an effect of action $A$ is to increase numeric fluent $Q$ by the term $\alpha$, then add the constraint
active$(A, T_i) \Rightarrow \Delta[A, Q, T_i] = \alpha[T_i^-]$.
$\neg$active$(A, T_i) \Rightarrow \Delta[A, Q, T_i] = 0$.
1.1.4: Let $A_1 \ldots A_k$ be all the action/events that can change numeric fluent $Q$ incrementally. Let $E_1 \ldots E_p$ be all the action/events that can assign to $Q$. Add the constraints:
$\neg$active$(E_1, T_i) \wedge \ldots \wedge \neg$active$(E_p, T_i) \Rightarrow$
$Q[T_i^+] = Q[T_i^-] + \sum_j \Delta[A_j, Q, T_i]$.
(Note that the terms in this sum can be determined statically.)
1.1.5: Conditional effects: If an effect of one of the above types is conditional on expression $\beta$ then add $\beta[T_i^-]$ as a conjunct on the left side of the above implication.
1.2: Preconditions: If action $A$ has preconditions $\beta$, then add the constraint: active$(A, T_i) \Rightarrow \beta[T_i^-]$.
1.3: Mutual exclusion: If action $A$ is mutually exclusive (mutex) with action or event $E$ then add the constraint
active$(A, T_i) \Rightarrow \neg$active$(E, T_i)$.
The rules for mutual exclusion are complex, but statically determined (Fox & Long 2003; Shin 2004).

**2. Events**
2.1: Effects: Same as for atomic actions.
2.2: Preconditions: Let $\beta$ be the preconditions of event $E$. Add the constraint: active$(E, T_i) \Leftrightarrow \beta[T_i^-]$
2.3: Immediate occurrence of events. Let $\beta$ be the preconditions of event $E$. Add the constraint:
$\beta[T_i^+] \Rightarrow c(T_{i+1}) = c(T_i)$.
PDDL+ requires an event to have at least one numerical constraint in its preconditions. This constraint ensures that the event is triggered with no time slip by discrete changes on numeric fluents.

**3. Processes**
3.1: Effects.
3.1.1: For each process $P$, for each quantity $Q$ influenced by $P$, let $\Phi$ be the influence of $P$ on the derivative of $Q$. Add the constraints
active$(P, T_i) \Rightarrow \Gamma(P, Q, T_i, T_{i+1}) = \Phi \cdot (c(T_{i+1}) - c(T_i))$.
$\neg$active$(P, T_i) \Rightarrow \Gamma(P, Q, T_i, T_{i+1}) = 0$.
3.1.2: For each quantity $Q$, let $P_1 \ldots P_m$ be the processes that potentially affect $Q$. Add the constraint
$Q[T_{i+1}^-] = Q[T_i^+] + \sum_j \Gamma(P_j, Q, T_i, T_{i+1})$.
3.2: Preconditions: Let $\beta$ be the preconditions for process $P$. Add the constraint
active$(P, T_i) \Leftrightarrow \beta[T_i^-] \vee \beta[T_i^+]$.
A process can be triggered either by continuous changes or by discrete changes.

**4. Frame Axioms**
4.1: Propositional fluents: For any fluent $F$ let $A_1 \ldots A_k$ be the actions and events that potentially change $F$. For each time $T_i$, for each value $V$ of $F$, add the constraint
$F[T_{i-1}] = V \wedge \neg$active$(A_1, T_i) \wedge \ldots \wedge \neg$active$(A_k, T_i)$
$\Rightarrow F[T_i] = V$.
4.2: Numerical fluents: No additional frame axioms are needed. If no processes that change $F$ are continuing between $T_i$ and $T_{i+1}$, then all the terms in the sum in equation 3.1.2 will be 0, so the equation will state that the quantity does not change. Likewise, if no actions or events occur that change $F$ at time $T_i$, then all the terms in the sum in equation 1.1.3 will be 0.

**5. Order on Significant Time-Points**
For each $T_i$, add the constraint $c(T_{i+1}) \geq c(T_i)$.

**6. Zero crossings**
One last type of constraint is trickier. This has to do with an event or process being triggered or terminated by a continuously changing numerical fluent attaining a particular value. Suppose that process P1 is active between times $T_a$ and $T_b$ and is steadily increasing the value of fluent Q; that process P2 will be triggered when Q reaches value V; and that this transition will occur at a time $T_x$ *between* $T_a$ and $T_b$. Suppose, further, that in the absence of P2, no significant change would occur between $T_a$ and $T_b$, so they would be consecutive significant time points. The problem is, how do we force the system of constraints to recognize the time point

$T_x$? That is, how can we prevent the system from accepting a solution in which $T_a$ and $T_b$ are consecutive time points and process P2 starts at time $T_b$? (Worse yet, consider a case where P2 is only triggered if Q is between V1 and V2; at time $T_a$ Q is less than V1 and at time $T_b$ Q is greater than V2. Then the system of constraints will discover that P2 is not triggered at time $T_a$ and not triggered at time $T_b$ and will conclude that it never occurs at all.)

The same thing can happen, in the reverse direction, with the termination of processes; we must make sure that they stop as soon as their continuation condition becomes false.

The solution rests on the fact that all numeric conditions are Boolean combinations of linear constraints, and that, within our domains, any numeric parameter that changes continuously is a linear function of time. Therefore, we can proceed as follows. First, we put every such condition that has to be checked over an interval into disjunctive normal form; that is, we express it as the disjunction of a collection of conjuncts. Further, we may assume that every numerical constraint has the form $Q(t) \geq 0$ where $Q(t)$ is a linear function of the numerical variables and of time $t$. Now, consider any such constraint $F_1 \wedge \ldots \wedge F_k \wedge Q_1 \geq 0 \wedge \ldots \wedge Q_m \geq 0$, where the $F_i$ are propositional expressions and the $Q_i$ are linear functions. The values of the $F_i$ do not change between two consecutive significant time points. (The $F_i$ will include conditions on the activity of processes and durative actions that affect the numeric quantities involved.) Depending on the context of the condition, we either have a case (such as the condition of an active process) where the conjunct is true at $T_i$ and we are interested in the first time when any of the numeric conjuncts becomes false; or a case (such as the precondition of an event) when the conjunct is false at $T_i$ and we are interested in the time when the last remaining numeric conjunct becomes true. Let us consider the second case; the first case is essentially a dual construction. Note that, at the time when $Q_j \geq 0$ becomes true, $Q_j = 0$ by continuity. Thus the time when $Q_j = 0$ is no earlier than $T_{i+1}$; thus $Q_j[T^-_{i+1}] \leq 0$. We therefore state the following constraints: For each significant time point $T_i$, for each such conjunction, for each conjunct $Q_j$, assert

$$[\wedge_p F_p[T_i]] \wedge Q_j[T^+_i] < 0 \wedge [\wedge_{p \neq j} Q_p[T^-_{i+1}] \geq 0] \Rightarrow Q_j[T^-_{i+1}] \leq 0.$$

This is just a continuity constraint over $Q_j$ of a form familiar from qualitative process theory (Forbus 1984); however, we are applying it to the complex terms $Q_j$ and restricting its application to those cases where it might make a difference in terms of triggering an event or process.

The effect of these constraint is, essentially, to generate the necessary intermediate time points by a sort of proof by contradiction, but a logic-based system such as TM-LPSAT has no trouble with proof by contradiction.

## Experimental Results[4]

There is no standard benchmark domain with continuous changes to use for performance comparison. We have some experimental results with toy domains. The domain used in Table 1 is a variation of the sample domain shown before. By distinguishing hot taps and cold taps, the goal includes constraints on the range of ratio of flows from hot taps to flows from cold taps, so that the desired bath temperature is achieved.

Since TM-LPSAT cannot optimize plans, the plan returned may have any number of steps, as long as the goal is satisfied. Table 1 shows the encoding size and processing times as the step increases.

Except pruning of the search space in a Graphplan style and Crawford's Compaction procedure, no other optimization is done with the current implementation of TM-LPSAT compiler. The times are measured on Linux 1.8 GHz Pentium IV processor with 512 MB RAM, averaged over 20 runs. The LPSAT engine is set to the option of learning and conflict-driven backjumping.

| No. of Steps | 5 | 10 | 15 |
|---|---|---|---|
| Total Time | 14.58 | 184.49 | 589.98 |
| Compaction Time | 0.09 | 0.4 | 0.94 |
| Solving Time | $14 \pm 4$ | $184 \pm 85$ | $582 \pm 225$ |
| Initial Statistics: | | | |
| No. of clauses | 339 | 769 | 1199 |
| No. of Boolean variables | 236 | 496 | 756 |
| No. of linear constraints | 136 | 296 | 456 |
| No. of real variables | 65 | 130 | 195 |
| After Compaction: | | | |
| No. of clauses | 329 | 724 | 1119 |
| No. of Boolean variables | 190 | 405 | 620 |
| No. of linear constraints | 121 | 256 | 391 |
| No. of real variables | 65 | 130 | 195 |
| No. of ground operators | 46 (59) | 101 (124) | 156 (189) |

Table 1: Filling the bath with multiple taps. Processing times are measured in seconds. The number inside of parenthesis in the last row shows the number of ground operators before pruning.

## Related Work

Obviously, TM-LPSAT is based on LPSAT (Wolfman & Weld 1999). The LPSAT planner both developed the constraint engine that we have used, and applied it to the metric planning in discrete time. The encoding of discrete changes on numeric fluents adopted in TM-LPSAT is almost the same as their encoding.

Among a number of early partial-order planners dealing with continuous changes to a limited extent, ZENO (Penberthy & Weld 1994) permitted a very general plan specification language, though its models of concurrency and of processes were less general than TM-LPSAT. Also, it was extremely slow; (Wolfman & Weld 2000) reports that ZENO was unable to solve even the simplest of the logistic problems that were used to test LPSAT.

McDermott (2003) has extended his estimated-regression planner, Optop, to deal with processes and continuous change. Unlike TM-LPSAT, his planner is not complete (ar-

[4]TM-LPSAT may be compared with McDermott's Optop; however, Optop is not available for comparison at this point.

guably an advantage, of course). It finds zero-crossings using binary search, so presumably it could easily be extended to non-linear functions; however, the current implementation has the same restriction as TM-LPSAT to linear functions with constant coefficients.

The best known study of processes in the AI literature is QP theory (Forbus 1984), which initiated a large body of research on physical reasoning with processes. This is at the extreme opposite end in terms of the language of quantities used; effects of processes are characterized purely in qualitative terms. A number of important ideas developed in this line of research have yet to be incorporated into the planning literature, such as indirect influences. Davis (1992) gives a logical analysis of QP theory.

## Conclusions and Future Work

As far as we know, TM-LPSAT is the first SAT-based planner that can reason about exogenous events and autonomous processes that cause continuous changes. It generates a parallel plan dealing with concurrent continuous and discrete changes. Preliminary experimentation on toy domains is reasonably encouraging this can be an effective framework for planning in continuous time over a wide range of problems.

In continuing this research, we hope to:

- Optimize both the process of compilation and the constraints output by compilation.
- Test the effectiveness of some engines other than LPSAT in solving the kinds of constraint systems generated by our compiler. MathSAT (Audemard et al. 2002) and CVCLite (Barrett & Berezin 2004) are both engines that can find solutions to propositional combinations of arithmetic constraints, so either of these could be used for this purpose.
- Study whether our methods for dealing with continuous change can be applied in the planning architectures based on Graphplan (Blum & Furst 1997).
- Add spatial reasoning by allowing region-valued fluents and motion as a process. If regions are restricted the polygons or polyhedra, either fully specified, or of a specified maximum complexity, and all motions are constant-velocity translations, then it should be possible to compile these domains into systems of linear constraints.

## Acknowledgments

We would like to thank Steven Wolfman and Daniel Weld for making their LPSAT program available for our research.

## References

Alessandro, A., Castellini, C., Giunchiglia, E., Giunchiglia, F., and Tacchella, A. 2002. SAT-Based Decision Procedures for Automated Reasoning: a Unifying Perspective. *Journal of Automated Reasoning* **28**.

Audemard, G., Bertoli, P., Cimatti, A., Kornilowicz, A., and Sebastiani, R. 2002. A SAT Based Approach for Solving Formulas over Boolean and Linear Mathematical Propositions. In *Proceedings of the International Conference of Automated Deduction.*

Barrett, C., and Berezin, S. 2004. CVC Lite: A New Implementation of the Cooperating Validity Checker. In *Proceedings of the International Conference on Computer Aided Verification.*

Blum, A. and Furst, M. 1997. Fast Planning through Planning Graph Analysis. *Artificial Intelligence* **97**.

Davis, E. 1992. Axiomatizing Qualitative Process Theory. In *Proceedings of the International Conference on Principles of Knowledge Representation and Reasoning.*

Ernst, M., Millstein, T., and Weld, D. 1997. Automatic SAT-Compilation of Planning Problems. In *Proceedings of the International Joint Conference on Artificial Intelligence.*

Forbus, K. 1984. Qualitative Process Theory. *Artificial Intelligence* **24**.

Fox, M., and Long, D. 2001. PDDL+ Level 5: An Extension to PDDL2.1 for Modelling Planning Domains Continuous Time-dependent Effects. Available at http://www.dur.ac.uk/d.p.long/competition.html.

Fox, M., and Long, D. 2003. PDDL2.1: An Extension to PDDL for Expressing Temporal Planning Domains. *Journal of Artificial Intelligence Research* **20**.

Kautz, H., and Selman, B, 1992. Planning as Satisfiability. In *Proceedings of the European Conference on Artificial Intelligence.*

Kautz, H., McAllester, D., and Selman, B. 1996. Encoding Plans in Propositional Logic. In *Proceedings of the International Conference on Principles of Knowledge Representation and Reasoning.*

Kautz, H., and Selman, B. 1996. Pushing the Envelope: Planning, Propositional Logic and Stochastic Search. In *Proceedings of the National Conference on Artificial Intelligence.*

Kautz, H., and Selman, B. 1999. Unifying SAT-based and Graph-based Planning. In *Proceedings of the International Joint Conference on Artificial Intelligence.*

McDermott, D. 1998. PDDL - the Planning Domain Definition Language. Available at http://www.cs.yale.edu/homes/dvm.

McDermott, D. 2000. The 1998 AI Planning Systems Competition. *AI Magazine* **21**.

McDermott, D. 2003. Reasoning about Autonomous Processes in an Estimated-Regression Planner. In *Proceedings of the International Conference on Automated Planning and Scheduling.*

Penberthy, J., and Weld, D. 1994. Temporal Planning with Continuous Change. In *Proceedings of the National Conference on Artificial Intelligence.*

Shin, J. 2004. TM-LPSAT: Encoding Temporal Metric Planning in Continuous Time. Ph.D. Dissertation, Dept. of Computer Science, New York University.

Wolfman, S., and Weld, D. 1999. The LPSAT Engine and its application to Resource Planning. In *Proceedings of the International Joint Conference on Artificial Intelligence.*

Wolfman, S., and Weld, D. 2000. Combining Linear Programming and Satisfiability Solving for Resource Planning. *Knowledge Engineering Review* **15**.

# Analogical Path Planning

**Saul Simhon** and **Gregory Dudek**
Centre for Intelligent Machines
McGill University
Montreal, Quebec
{saul,dudek}@cim.mcgill.ca

## Abstract

We present a probabilistic method for path planning that considers trajectories constrained by both the environment and an ensemble of restrictions or preferences on preferred motions for a moving robot. Our system learns constraints and preference biases on a robot's motion from examples, and then synthesizes behaviors that satisfy these constraints. This behavior can encompass motions that satisfy diverse requirements such as a sweep pattern for floor coverage, or, in particular in our experiments, satisfy restrictions on the robot's physical capabilities such as restrictions on its turning radius. Given an approximate path that may not satisfy the required conditions, our system computes a refined path that satisfies the constraints and also avoids obstacles. Our approach is based on a Bayesian framework for combining a prior probability distribution on the trajectory with environmental constraints. The prior distribution is generated by decoding a Hidden Markov Model, which is itself is trained over a particular set of preferred motions. Environmental constraints are modeled using a potential field over the configuration space.

This paper poses the requisite theoretical framework and demonstrates its effectiveness with several examples.

## Introduction

In motion planning (e.g. for a robot), we typically need to consider two types of constraints on the paths that can be taken: constraints imposed by the environment, and constraints imposed by the physical characteristics of the vehicle itself. In particular, *non-holonomic* constraints refer to limitations on the allowed derivatives of the path, and planning in the presence of such constraints in often difficult (an automobile is a commonplace example of a vehicle which such constraints, as it is unable to move perpendicular to the direction in which it is facing). Motion planning is typically complicated not only by the need to generate paths that satisfy various constraints, but also by the need to initially model whatever constraints may be imposed by a particular vehicle or task. Finding valid trajectories that satisfy both the mechanically imposed constraints and environmental constraints can be a difficult task. In this work, we present a method for "analogical path planning" wherein paths are generated by analogy with previous observed acceptable paths, and without an analytic model.



Our approach is based on accepting an input path (which may not satisfy the required constraints) and transforming it into an allowed path. The input path may be produced either by a person (e.g. as a sketch) or by an automated system; this request input path is referred to as a "goal path". The analogies that drive the system are learned from examples, where each example is composed of a pair of paths, an input and an output path fragment. These fragments depict a path fragment that might be requested, and the restricted (allowed) path that should be produced when such a request is made. Further, the constraints on the generated paths can be either hard constraints or probabilistic, and they may derive either from kinematic or dynamic constraints on the vehicle motion, or from other types of bias (for example, we might like to generate circuitous paths for our vehicle to determine if we are being followed by enemy spies).

Because our system learns from examples, it can be applied in a variety of domains. We avoid having to extract and analytically model constraints for each desired motion pattern or mechanical configuration that we may wish to control. Our object is that we should be able to demonstrate how a robot can move and subsequently the system would automatically produce new paths based on these motions. One area of application is tele-operated robots. A human can guide the robot to areas by simply sketching a coarse path. The system would then refine that path based on the learned specification of the robot and generate a new valid path analogous to the goal. Another application would be to complement high level planners to relieve them of the burden of non-holonomic (complex) path planning. Our system can take in as input such path generated by such planners and augment them to avoid objects while maintaining a particular behavior during motion.

Our approach consists of training a Hidden Markov Model for a set of examples that encode the analogies between pairs of *motion patterns* (output curve fragments) and *goal trajectories* (input curve fragments); each of these curve fragments is represented as a succession of tangent angles. The Hidden Markov Model learns local constraints on the sequence of tangents in the motion patterns in conjunction with their correlation to sample points in the goal trajectories. When producing new paths, these learned constraints are then combined with environmental constraints that bias the distribution of a Markovian Chain. At each step in the trajectory, we compute the posterior probability distribution of states in the

configuration space by combining a prior based on the learned fragments with a likelihood based on the input curve and the environmental constraints. Once the probability distribution over the entire input trajectory, the candidate path with maximum likelihood is chosen.

The paper is organized as follows. First we briefly review previous work. Then, we describe our approach to learning motion constraints. Then we present our method to generate novel motions from the learned constraints. We describe a general framework in combining the learned constraints with arbitrary biases and show cases using environmental and other constraints. Finally we present results and conclude.

## Related Work

There is a wide array of works by many authors that examine methods for path planning. One approach, similar in spirit to our work, is to provide stochastic models for maintaining and updating a distribution on predefined states (Thrun 2000; Simmons & Koenig 1995). These distributions generally reflect the likelihoods of a robot's pose or sensory information. Based on these likelihoods, a robot can make decisions on where to go next given a particular goal.

Another key ideas in the area is the notion of path planning under non-holonomic constraints. A classic approach to the application of non-holonomic constraints is to find an (optimal) unconstrained solution and then apply recursive constrained path refinement to the sub-regions to achieve an admissible plan (Latombe 1991). Dubins (Dubins 1957) and Reeds and Shepp (Reeds & Shepp 1990) on optimal trajectories. Much of this work deals with the quest for an optimal path (or trajectory) under a motion constraint which is expressed analytically (for example a derivative constraint). Prevalent solution techniques include analytic solutions (or expressions regarding their bounds), search methods that seek to optimize a path, and planners that start with a path of one form and seek to refine it. Similarly, jerky paths are sometimes smoothed using energy minimization methods (Singh & Leu 1989; Laumond *et al.* 1994).

This work shares that common spirit in that it takes an initial path as input and produces a refined path as its result. While traditional methods such as those cited above typically accomplish path refinement based on highly specialized constraints, typically in the domain of differential geometry, our methods learns from examples of acceptable paths. That is, the significant constraints or preferences are indicated by showing the appropriate refinements that should be applied in specific cases. This idea of learning to generalize specific examples to a broad ensemble of cases is, of course, the crux of classical machine learning (Mitchell 1997). There has also been some prior work on the relationship between learning and planning, most of this has dealt with more traditional plan formulation problems (Wang 1994) or on learning suitable cues that control or determine plan synthesis or execution (Engelson 1996).

## Learning Motion Behavior

Motion behaviors are learned from examples that show the way a path should behave given an goal (input) trajectory. Figure 1 shows a training set used to learn non-holonomic constraints corresponding to motion with a bounded turning angle (or radius of curvature). Each example in this set consists of an acceptable trajectory which is coupled to a goal trajectory (which is unacceptable on its own). For example, when our goal is to make a sharp right turn, the resulting path should be the smooth kinematically correct path. When our goal is to go straight while the robot is facing perpendicular, then the preferred path is a d-turn motion.

Given such a set, we train a two layer model. In one layer, local motion constraints are learned by examining the sequence of sample points in the acceptable paths. Then, in the other layer, the control function (the function describing a subset of valid trajectories given a goal) is learned by examining the correlation of the path sequence over valid trajectories with that of the goal trajectory. In general, we consider the training set as a set of examples that encompass a class of candidate trajectories for specific goals.

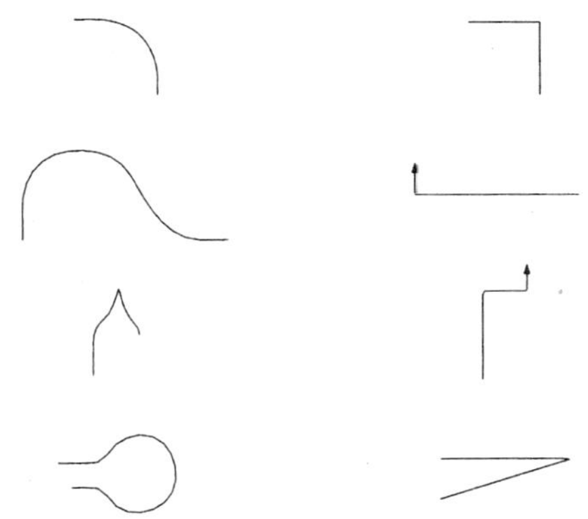

Figure 1: Samples of a training set simulating non-holonomic motions. Paths on the left display the constrained motions while paths on the right display the associated unconstrained goal path. Where specified, arrows indicate additional constraints on the direction of motion to account for the orientation of the robot. The full set consists of the above set at several rectilinear orientation.

Each example trajectory is represented by a parametric function $f(t, a)$ where $t$ is the arc-length of the path and $a$ is a path attribute. We use two attributes in out system; the shape of the path, as a sequence of the curve's tangent angles $\theta(t)$, and the facing direction of the robot axis $\phi(t)$. The shape $\theta(t)$ is represented over multiple scales using a wavelet decomposition $\theta(t, s)$ over the scale $s$. This allows us to efficiently capture large scale constraints on the paths, where one sample point in the higher scale represents a summary of several points in the low scales. Our examples are suitably normalized and sampled uniformly.

While other work (Simhon & Dudek 2003) has exploited a Hidden Markov Model (HMM) for path synthesis, the present paper is the first to consider environmental landmarks as well as constraints learned from examples. A

HMM is a two layer linear dynamic model. It models two primary components: 1) the transition probabilities of an underlying evolving system that is not directly observable and 2) the probabilistic effect that this underlying system has on observations. A HMM $\Lambda$ is defined as follows:

$$\Lambda = \{M, B, \pi\} \quad (1)$$

where $M$ is the transition matrix with transition probabilities on the hidden states, $p\{h_i(t) \mid h_j(t-1)\}$, B is the confusion matrix containing the probability that a hidden state $h_j$ would give rise to an observation $o_i$, $p\{o_i(t) \mid h_j(t)\}$, and $\pi$ is the initial distribution of the hidden states.

In our approach, the hidden states represent sample points from the preferred paths while the observations represent sample points from the goal paths. As such, the leaned transitions in the hidden layer impose local constraints on the succession of tangent angles and robot facing direction of a valid trajectory. Further, the learned relationship between the hidden layer and the observation layer identify what constraints should be applied given the current goal path (i.e. the conditional probability of the hidden states given the observation).

A HMM is trained from the statistics of the training set. The transition probabilities in $M$ are computed by counting the number of matches of successive sample points in the preferred paths. Similarly, the confusion probabilities in $B$ are computed by counting the number of matches of associated sample points from the preferred path and the goal path. The initial distribution $\pi$ is assumed uniform suggesting that at $t = 0$ all motions have equal likelihood. These constitute the learned priors of our system that are later used to produce valid motions over the configuration space and a goal.

The dimensionality of our state space is augmented in order to capture the multi-dimensional function $f(t, a)$. Thus, each state $h_i$ and $o_i$ is considered a multi-dimensional element. This allows us to capture multiple path attributes at various scales using only a single state (simulating a higher order Markov assumption).

## Generating Motions from Learned Constraints

Given the unconstrained goal trajectory, we wish to generate a new path that is consistent with the constraints of our trained HMM $\Lambda$. That is, the resulting motion should be consistent with the local constraints and input coupling seen in the examples. Decoding a HMM solves for the maximum likelihood hidden state sequence (our constrained motion) which best describes the given observation sequence (our goal trajectory). Let $\alpha = \{h(0), h(1), ..., h(T)\}$ denote the output path and let $\beta = \{o(0), o(1), ..., o(T)\}$ denote the coarse input path, we wish to solve the following:

$$\max p\{\alpha \mid \beta, \Lambda\}$$
$$or$$
$$\max_{h_i, \ldots h_n} p\{h(0), h(1), ..., h(T) \mid o(0), o(1), ..., o(T), \Lambda\} \quad (2)$$

One approach in solving for this (analogous to Variational Calculus techniques) is to evaluate a cost functional by accumulating local costs over the entire sample point sequence of a candidate solution. Then iterate over the solution space to minimize this total cost. This approach can become very inefficient in time and is subject to convergence pitfalls. Rather, our method consists of a dynamic programming technique which is more efficient in time, $O(n^2T)$ for $n$ states and $T$ sample points, and is guaranteed to converge. Although it is more memory intensive.

Our approach is based on the *Viterbi* algorithm for decoding a HMM. For each sample point in the sequence, we compute the distribution over **all** the hidden states (i.e. all paths). This is accomplished by first using the likelihoods of the confusion matrix to condition over the current observation. Then, we propagate that distribution to the next sequence point using the transition matrix likelihoods. For each state at sample point $t + 1$, we compute its posterior likelihood $\psi$ as follows:

$$\psi\{h_i(t)\} = p\{o(t) \mid h_i(t)\}\psi\{h_i(t)\}$$
$$\psi\{h_i(t+1)\} = \max_j[p\{h_i(t+1) \mid h_j(t)\}\psi\{h_j(t)\}] \quad (3)$$

The propagation phase is similar to the transition method used to generate a Markov Chain. However because our eventual goal is to uniquely specify each successive point, we do not sum over all possible transitions but rather only keep the maximum. Additionally, for each state, we store a back-pointer to the state in the previous iteration that put forward this maximum likelihood transition. Once we have iterated over the entire sequence of observations, we chose the state with maximum likelihood at time $T$ and then backtrack the sequence using the back-pointers. Backtracking is crucial for a consistent sequence. Rather than dealing with each sequence point independently, it considers the maximum likelihood transitions over the entire sequence.

Once we find the most likely sequence of tangent angles, we realize the path by computing the $(x, y)$ points using the uniform sampling rate and corresponding arc-length segments from training. Figure 2 and 3 show examples of goal trajectories and their resulting synthesized paths. Due to memory limitations in practice, we can not explicitly store the entire distribution over all possible sates $H_i$. Thus, we only keep the top candidate states and threshold candidates with low probability. Similarly, we cannot store all the prior likelihoods in a matrix but rather we must compute them on the fly by searching our training set and counting the number of matches.

### Likelihood Blurring

Rather than computing the likelihoods (of Equation 3) by searching for exact matches, we compute them based on the goodness of the matches. This is performed for both the transition and confusion likelihoods and is key in avoiding issues with quantization errors or observation mismatches. (Expecting the observations to match exactly with those in training is overly restrictive, in general, the input curve can be a noisy curve.)

For the transition likelihoods, we assume a Gaussian noise model with the variance empirically set. This variance provides a control on the *mixing* tendency of examples. The larger the variance, the more likely we are to accept transitions from one tangent angle to another, even if those tangent angles do not necessarily appear in sequence. We typically keep the variance very low (in the order of a half of a degree) to strongly enforce our motion constraints while avoiding issues with quantization errors.

For the confusion likelihoods, we use a Sigmoid distance metric. Using the Sigmoid function, we can suggest that for a given error range, the likelihood of matching is very similar but beyond that range, the likelihood decays exponentially. The Sigmoid shift parameter determines the amount of bias the input curve has over the distribution. A large value suggest that any input will match any state, reducing the impact of the input, while a small value will enforce the strength of the input conditional. The Sigmoid parameters are set empirically.

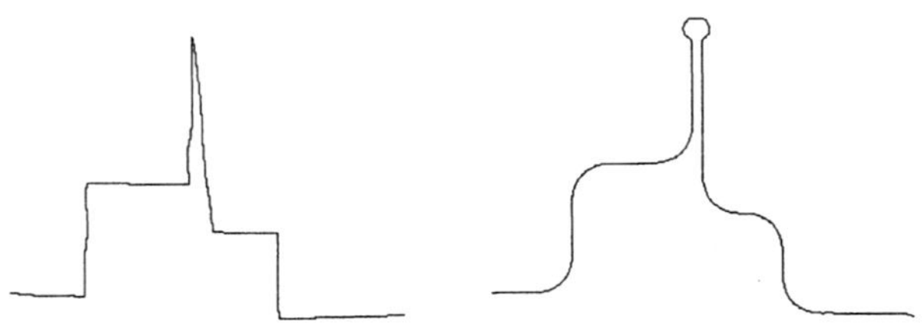

Figure 2: The left shows a coarse input path while the right shows the refined motion consistent with the learned nonholonomic constraints.

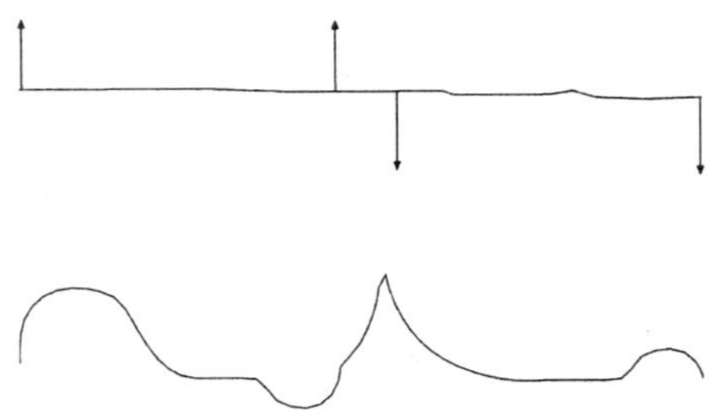

Figure 3: The top shows an example path with the desired robot axis facing directions (shown by arrows) and the bottom shows the resulting output path.

## Bayesian Path Reconstruction

Our goal is to reconstruct a *valid* path given a coarse goal trajectory. In our framework, there are several components that contribute to what we constitute a valid path. First, we must take into account the HMM such that the output is consistent with the training examples as described is section . Second, we require that the generated curve should stay near the input trajectory. (The HMM alone only constrains the tangent angles of the curve, it does not guarantee that the resulting path would stay near the input, Figure 4). Finally, the output curve should not go through or approach too close to obstacles in the environment. This combination of constraints can result in complex paths that would otherwise be difficult to determine using traditional analytical models.

The following lists the primary constraints of our system:

- The learned constraints of our HMM
  - local shape consistency with examples
  - control from the goal trajectory
- Distance to the goal trajectory
- Obstacles avoidance

We formalize this problem in a Bayesian framework such that it will become transparent to combine these (or other) constraints within the system. Our method is analogous to regularization techniques which are commonly used to reconstruct objects from partial data. The main idea in regularization methods is to minimize a cost functional that measures the distance between the data and the model in question and includes some additional constraints (such as smoothness) that bias the solution. It can be show that a probabilistic approach to regularization consists of maximizing the posterior likelihoods of a Bayesian model (Keren & Werman 1994; Szeliski 1989):

$$\max_{f \epsilon \mathcal{M}} P\{f \mid D\} \propto \max_{f \epsilon \mathcal{M}} p\{D \mid f\} p\{f \mid \mathcal{M}\} \qquad (4)$$

where $f$ is an object in class $\mathcal{M}$ and $D$ is the coarse data. Typically the *data model term* $P\{D \mid f\}$ assumes a Gaussian noise model and the *regularization term* $P\{f \mid \mathcal{M}\}$ is a prior that adds a bias toward smoother models.

Rather than having a fixed noise model or prior constraint, we learn these from examples and encode them in our HMM. It is easy to see that in a HMM, the confusion matrix represent an arbitrary *data model* ($p\{o_i(t) \mid h_j(t)\}$) and the transition matrix represent *priors* that biases solutions that are locally consistent with our training set. Thus, our HMM is analogous to a cost functional that generalizes to learned constraints.

Using the Bayesian framework, we can embed additional constraints over our HMM. In particular, we wish to include a bias for output curves that are closer to the goal trajectory and avoid obstacles. In general, we can regularize at each sample point using the desired biases as follows:

$$E\{h_i(t)\} = -log\{\psi(h_i(t))\} + \sum_k \lambda_k R_k(t, h_i) \qquad (5)$$

where $R_k(t)$ is the energy of a regularization constraint and $\lambda_k$ is the associated weight. This embeds the additional constraints within our model such that they are taken into account in the decoding phase. As such, the decoding algorithm can be thought of as an energy minimization algorithm.

### Magnetic Attraction

We include a bias that increases the likelihood of solutions that are closer to the goal trajectory. This simulates a magnetic attraction between the input path and the generated one. While this is an important additions to the system, we need to be careful in the amount of influence it exerts. In order to achieve the desired motion behavior learned in our HMM, it is still necessary for the output path to stray away at some distance. The amount of divergence allowed can be controlled by the weight of this energy term. (One may suggest ways to set $\lambda_{mag}$ based on the maximum divergence seen in the examples.) We can also relax this bias at the interior region of the path while enforcing it at the endpoints (for closure). We compute the regularization energy for magnetic bias as follows:

$$R_{mag}(t, h_i) = e^{|1-\frac{2t}{T}|}\, d^2 \quad (6)$$

where $t$ is the current sample point position, $T$ is the total sample points and $d$ is the distance between the goal and the candidate state $h_i$. At the endpoint of the path the relative weight of the energy term is higher than at regions within the path. As such, the bias term will have more influence at the endpoints and less at interior points.

At any given point in the sequence, we need to compute the distance $d$ between each candidate state and the associated point on the input curve. Thus, we augment the of the states to include auxiliary information that identifies the Cartesian co-ordinate. These dimensions are not used during the propagation or conditioning steps but are simply supplementary terms that store the required information. At $t = 0$ the auxiliary values are bootstrapped to the position of the input curve. Then, the co-ordinates of the states at the next iteration are computed by extrapolating their tangent from the co-ordinates of the previous state (identified by the back-pointer) using a suitable arc-length (based on the training sampling). Figure 4 shows example paths generated with and without the magnetic term. It can be seen how the output curve without the magnetic term diverges from the input while adding the magnetic term biases the result to stay closer to the input.

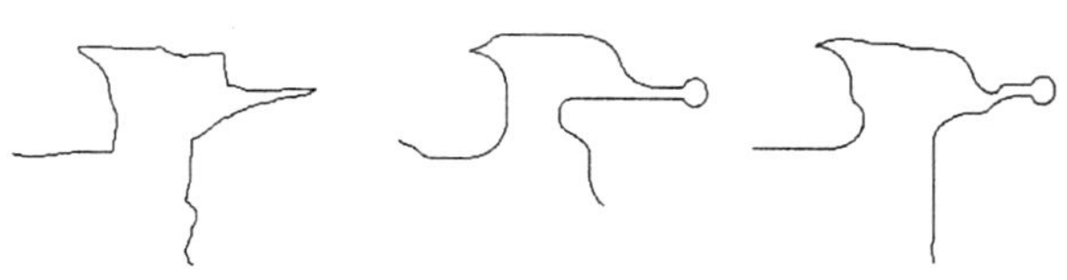

Figure 4: Example of magnetic attraction. The left path shows the goal trajectory, the middle shows the resulting output without the magnetic energy term and the right path shows the output with magnetic energy.

## Obstacle Avoidance

We compute a regularization constraints over the configuration space of the robot by applying a distance transform on obstacles in the environment. Akin to potential field methods, the transform generates an energy field over the environment. A suitable function would generate high energies at regions near the obstacles and low energies at regions far form obstacles. We compute the energy for a state as follows:

$$R_{obs}(t, h_i) = \max_{obs} \frac{1}{d_i} \quad (7)$$

where $d_i$ is the distance between the current candidate state and the $i^{th}$ obstacle. We choose the obstacle that produces the maximum energy over all the others. At position close to or on the obstacles, the energy goes to infinity while at areas further the energy decays to zero. The weight $\lambda_{obs}$ controls the amount of influence the obstacles have on the solution. Large value will coerce the robot to stay far from the obstacles while small values will allow the robot to reach closer to the obstacles, traveling through narrower regions.

We prepossess the environment and generate the field over a grid. To evaluate the energy for a state, we simply use its auxiliary parameter that identify the Cartesian co-ordinates and access the girds value. Figure 5 shows and field generated for a sample environment.

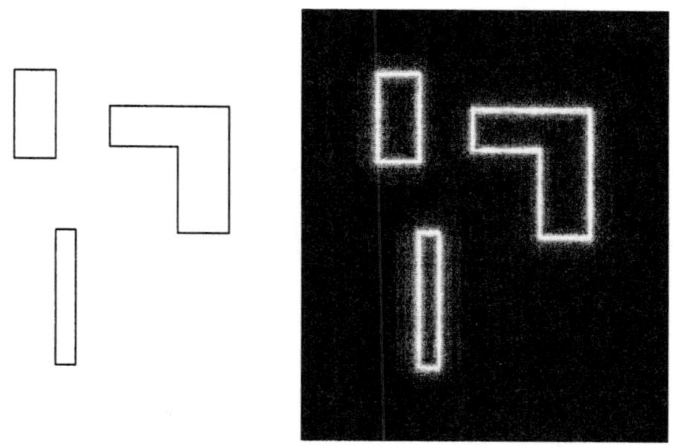

Figure 5: Example energy field. The left image shows the scene and the right image is a logarithmic plot of the energy field.

## Results

Figure 6 and 7 shows two example environments with the goal path (left) and the generated path (right). The goal path, sketched by a human operator, directs the robot too close to or through obstacles. It can be seen how the generated path avoids the obstacles while also maintaining the learned constraints.

Figure 8 shows an example of two generated paths from a goal path that goes through objects. The middle figure shows the result using a large value for the environment constraint weight while the left shows a small value. It can be seen that with a large value, the path stays further away from the obstacles while a small value allows the path so go through narrow regions. One noticeable issue here is that when the trajectory of the output path is much longer that the input path, the result does not reach the goal. This is due to the fact that we have not enough sample points in the goal trajectory. One approach to overcome this issue is to dynamically sam-

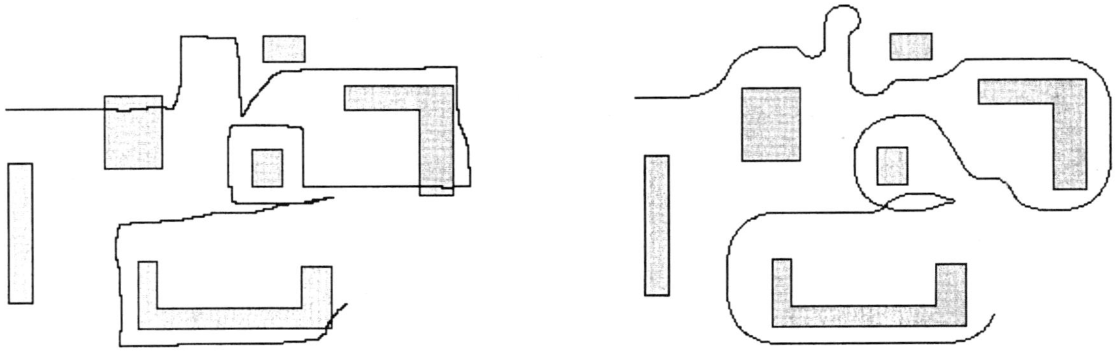

Figure 6: Example path synthesis. Left shows the input and right shows the output.

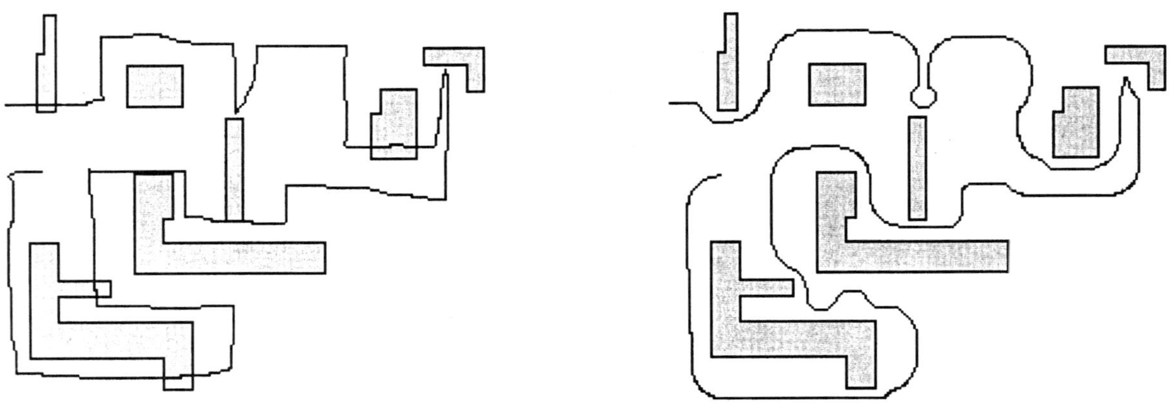

Figure 7: Example path synthesis. Left shows the input and right shows the output.

ple the goal path. This can be based on the projection of the resulting path onto the goal path.

## Conclusion and Future Work

We presented a method for analogical path planning. That is a method to generate paths that are analogical to both an input trajectory and a set of examples. The generated (analogical) paths maintain the local constraints expressing a desired motion preference. By formulating our Hidden Markov model in Bayesian terms, we were able to embed supplementary constraints such as proximity to input and obstacle avoidance.

One open problem that remains to be addressed is that of finding good values for the parameters that control the process. While this is performed empirically, we are currently examining how to set these values based on some initial conditions, such as a maximum divergence form the input or a minimum distance to the obstacles. In addition, another direction for future work is to examine applications of the method using related multiple curve signals, such as control for multi-robot navigation or some other correlated attributes.

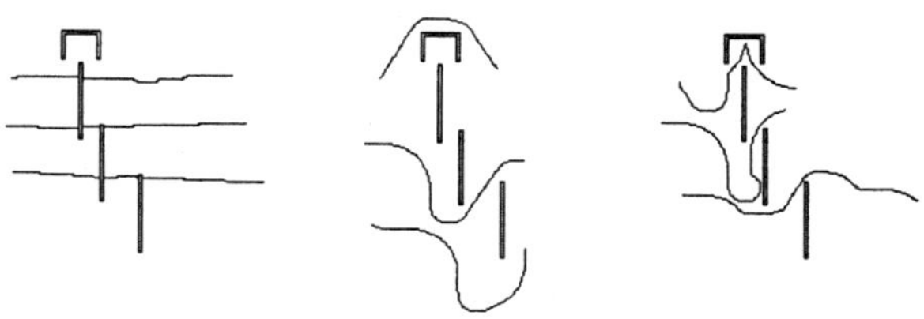

Figure 8: Example path synthesis going through a narrow region. Left shows the input. The middle figure shows the output using a large value for $\lambda_{obs}$ and right shows the output with a small value for $\lambda_{obs}$

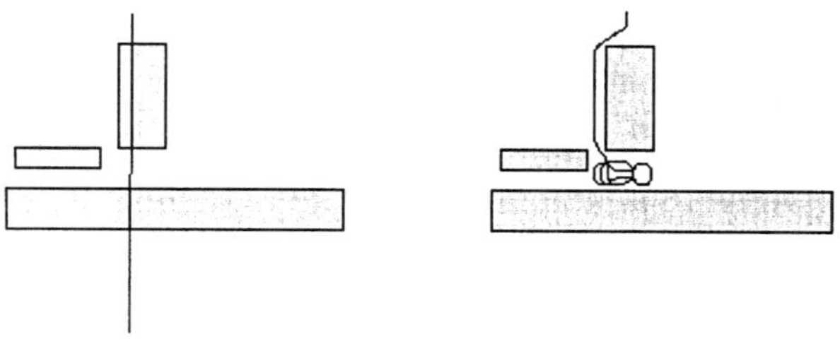

Figure 9: Example where the goal path goes through a large object. This causes the resulting path to be stuck behind the obstacle.

## References

Dubins, L. E. 1957. On curves of minimal length with a constraint on average curvature, and with prescribed initial and terminal positions and tangents. In *American Journal of Mathematics*, volume 79, 497–517.

Engelson, S. P. 1996. Learning robust plans for mobile robots from a single trial. In *AAAI/IAAI, Vol. 1*, 869–874.

Keren, D., and Werman, M. 1994. Bayesian interpolation. *ARPA Image Understanding Workshop.*

Latombe, J. 1991. *Robot Motion Planning*. Kluwer Academic Publishers.

Laumond, J.-P.; Jacobs, P. E.; Taix, M.; and Murray, R. M. 1994. A motion planner for nonholonomic mobile robots. In *IEEE Transactions on Robotics and Automation*, volume 10, 577–593.

Mitchell, T. 1997. *Machine Learning*. McGraw Hill.

Reeds, and Shepp, L. 1990. Optimal paths for a car that goes both forwards and backwards. In *Pacific Journal of Mathematics*, volume 145(2), 367–393.

Simhon, S., and Dudek, G. 2003. Path planning using learned constraints and preferences. In *Proceedings of the IEEE International Conference on Robotics and Automation.*

Simmons, R., and Koenig, S. 1995. Probabilistic robot navigation in partially observable environments. In *Proceedings of the International Joint Conference on Artificial Intelligence*, 1080–1087.

Singh, S., and Leu, M. C. 1989. Optimal trajectory generation for robotic manipulators using dynamic programming. In *ASME Journal of Dynamic Systems, Measurement and Control*, volume 109.

Szeliski, R. 1989. *Bayesian Modeling of Uncertainty in Low Level Vision*. Kluwer.

Thrun, S. 2000. Probabilistic algorithms in robotics. *AI Magazine* 21(4):93–109.

Wang, X. 1994. Learning planning operators by observation and practice. In *Artificial Intelligence Planning Systems*, 335–340.

# An Effective Algorithm For Project Scheduling With Arbitrary Temporal Constraints

**Tristan B. Smith**
CIS Department
University of Oregon
Eugene, OR 97403
tsmith@cs.uoregon.edu

**John M. Pyle**
On Time Systems, Inc.
1850 Millrace Drive, Suite 1
Eugene, OR 97403
john@otsys.com

## Abstract

The resource-constrained project scheduling problem with time windows (RCPSP/max) is an important generalization of a number of well studied scheduling problems. In this paper, we present a new heuristic algorithm that combines the benefits of squeaky wheel optimization with an effective conflict resolution mechanism, called bulldozing, to address RCPSP/max problems. On a range of benchmark problems, the algorithm is competitive with state-of-the-art systematic and non-systematic methods and scales well.

## Introduction

Project scheduling requires the assignment of resources and times to activities in a plan with the goal of makespan minimization. Such problems arise in a range of fields including construction, manufacturing, software development and a number of space applications. Because of their importance, many varieties of project scheduling problems have been well studied by the OR and AI communities.

Less attention has been paid to RCPSP/max problems. These generalize many of the well-known and well-studied classes of scheduling problems (including job-shop problems and their variants) through non-unary resource constraints and, most importantly, arbitrary temporal constraints. The latter permit both minimum and maximum time lags between activities to be represented. This allows a vast number of real-world constraints to be modelled, including fixed start times, releases and deadlines, set-up times, minimum and maximum overlaps, activities that must start or finish simultaneously, and shelf life constraints.

RCPSP/max problems have been tackled by both the AI and OR communities with most results achieved by the latter (Dorndorf, Pesch, & Phan-Huy 2000; Cesta, Oddi, & Smith 2002; Neumann, Schwindt, & Zimmerman 2003). Successful exact methods incorporate constraint propagation into a variety of branch and bound algorithms. Since these algorithms have limited scalability, a number of non-systematic methods, including tabu search, simulated annealing and genetic algorithms have also been developed.

In this paper, we describe how another heuristic approach, squeaky wheel optimization (SWO), can be applied effectively to RCPSP/max problems. The main component of SWO is a priority-based greedy schedule constructor. Search is used to find effective prioritizations for that constructor.

Arbitrary temporal constraints can cause problems for a greedy constructor since it is NP-hard to find any feasible schedule; if most prioritizations do not yield feasible schedules, SWO will be ineffective. Therefore, to increase the power of the greedy constructor, we have added a new conflict resolution mechanism, called bulldozing that allows the greedy constructor to move sets of activities later in a partial schedule to maintain feasibility. Finally, similar mechanisms move sets of activities earlier in a feasible schedule to allow shorter schedules to be discovered.

Our algorithm is compared with the best reported results in the OR and AI literature for benchmark RCPSP/max problems ranging from 10 to 500 activities. Competitive for all problem sizes, it begins to outperform most algorithms as problem size increases.

## The RCPSP/max Problem

An RCPSP/max problem contains a set $\{A_1, ..., A_n\}$ of activities and a set $\{R_1, ..., R_m\}$ of resources. Each activity $A_i$ has a start time $S_i$ and a duration $d_i$. Each resource has a maximum capacity $c_k$ and execution of each activity $A_i$ requires an amount $r_{ik}$ of resource $k$ for each time unit of execution. Binary precedence constraints $[T_{i,j}^{min}, T_{i,j}^{max}]$ enforce minimum ($T_{i,j}^{min}$) and maximum ($T_{i,j}^{max}$) time lags between the start times of activities $A_i$ and $A_j$.

The two constraints types of an RCPSP/max problem can be summarized as follows:

- **Precedence Constraints:** $T_{i,j}^{min} \leq S_j - S_i \leq T_{i,j}^{max}$
- **Resource Constraints:** $\Sigma_{\{i|S_i \leq t < S_i + d_i\}} r_{ik} \leq c_k, \forall t, \forall k$

A schedule is an assignment of a value to the start time $S_i$ of each activity. A schedule is *time-feasible* if it satisfies all precedence (temporal) constraints and is *resource-feasible* if it satisfies all resource constraints. A schedule that satisfies all constraints is *feasible*.

The goal of an RCPSP/max problem is to find a feasible schedule such that the project makespan, $MK = max_{1 \leq i \leq n}\{S_i + d_i\}$, is minimized. Unlike scheduling problems without both minimum and maximum time lags, even finding a feasible schedule for the RCPSP/max problem is NP-hard (Bartusch, Möhring, & Radermacher 1988).

## Solving RCPSP/max Problems

### Time Windows and Constraint Propagation

At the core of our algorithm is a greedy schedule constructor that selects a start times for each activity from a domain of possible values. We represent each such domain with a *time window*, $[ES_{A_i}, LS_{A_i}]$, representing all time points between the earliest and latest start times we wish to consider.

Temporally consistent time windows are efficiently maintained via well known constraint propagation techniques. In our algorithm, each window is initialized to $[0, horizon - d_i]$ (where *horizon* is the goal makespan) and then temporal constraint propagation achieves arc-consistency (Dechter, Meiri, & Pearl 1991).

Windows are updated during schedule construction. When a start time $t$ is selected for an activity $A_i$, the PLACEACTIVITY($A_i$,$t$) method will reduce windows as necessary to maintain temporal consistency. Similarly, when a start time is retracted (as we do in bulldozing), the UNPLACEACTIVITY($A_i$) method will expand windows if possible. These methods allow schedule construction to always produce time feasible schedules without the need for backtracking (Dechter, Meiri, & Pearl 1991).

While the above propagation considers only precedence constraints, the propagation of resource constraints can further reduce start time domains (Muscettola 2002; Laborie 2003).While some resource constraint propagation is clearly beneficial, it comes at a computational cost and limits the scalability of algorithms.

The algorithms we describe in this paper explicitly avoid resource constraint propagation as our intent is to show that search can be effective without it and to highlight the differences between our algorithm and others that have been proposed. However, there is no inherent reason for us to avoid resource constraint propagation and it could complement our approach.

### Squeaky Wheel Optimization

Squeaky Wheel Optimization (SWO) is an iterative approach to optimization that combines a greedy algorithm with a priority scheme (Joslin & Clements 1999). A number of results suggest that SWO can be applied effectively to a range of real-world problems and scales well (Joslin & Clements 1999; Chen, Fu, & Lim 2002).

Each iteration of the SWO algorithm can be divided into two stages: construction and prioritization. The construction stage takes a variable ordering and builds a solution using a greedy algorithm. In the prioritization stage, a variable is penalized with 'blame' depending on how well that variable was handled during construction. The updated priorities result in a new variable ordering for the next iteration.

The key to SWO is that elements that are handled poorly by the greedy constructor have their priority increased and are therefore handled sooner (and hopefully better) the next time ("The squeaky wheel gets the grease"). Over time, elements that are difficult to handle drift toward the top of the queue, those that are always easy to handle drift toward the bottom, and the rest settle somewhere in between.

A SWO implementation that uses the time window framework for the RCPSP/max problem, embedded in a binary search over possible horizons, is outlined here:

```
SWO(MaxIter)
1  counter ← 1
2  MK_best ← +∞
3  SETHORIZONLOWERBOUND
4  (P_1, ..., P_n) = initial priorities
5  for counter ← 1 to MaxIter
6      do feasible ← TRUE
7         for i ← 1 to n
8             do
9                A_i ← unscheduled activity with
                       highest P_i
10               if SCHEDULE(A_i) fails
11                  then feasible ← FALSE
12        if feasible
13          then MK_best ← MK_current
14               DECREASEHORIZON
15        if 10 iterations without feasible solution
16          then INCREASEHORIZON
17        (P_1, ..., P_n) = updated priorities
```

Line 3 and lines 14 through 16 perform a version of binary search over possible makespans, ranging from the resource-unconstrained lower bound to double the trivial upper bound.[1] Although not included in the pseudocode, our algorithm will quit if the minimum makespan is reached.

Line 4 initializes the priorities. Lines 7 to 11 make up the greedy schedule constructor and priorities are updated on line 17.

The basic SCHEDULE($A_i$) method is outlined below. It looks for the earliest time-feasible and resource-feasible place to start $A_i$. If none is found, resource constraints are ignored and $A_i$ is put at the earliest time-feasible start time $ES_{A_i}$.

```
SCHEDULE(A_i)
t ← earliest resource-feasible time for A_i
      in [ES_{A_i}, LS_{A_i}]
if t = NIL
   then PLACEACTIVITY(A_i, ES_{A_i})
        return FALSE
   else PLACEACTIVITY(A_i, t)
        return TRUE
```

**Example 1** *Consider the following three activity, one resource problem:*

- *Durations* $d_1 = d_2 = d_3 = 2$
- *Resource capacity* $r_1 = 2$
- *Resource requirements* $r_{11} = r_{21} = r_{31} = 1$

[1] $ub = \Sigma_{i=1}^{n} max(d_i, max(T_{i,j}^{min}))$ (Dorndorf, Pesch, & Phan-Huy 2000). We found that doubling this enabled bulldozing to find feasible schedules more easily.

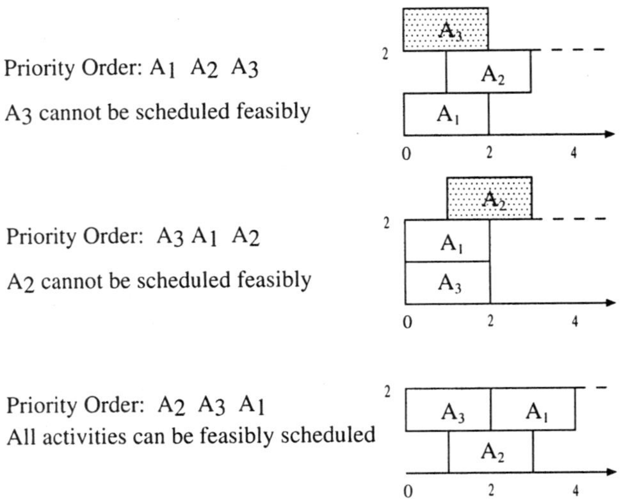


Figure 1: The third iteration of $SWO$ finds a feasible schedule. For illustration, an activity is moved to the beginning of the priority queue when it cannot be scheduled feasibly.

- *A constraint that $A_3$ must start exactly 1 unit before $A_2$. That is, $S_3 - S_2 = -1$ (or $T^{min}_{2,3} = T^{max}_{2,3} = -1$).*

*Figure 1 demonstrates $SWO$ beginning with the priority order $(A_1, A_2, A_3)$. Using this order, no resource-feasible time is available for $A_3$, its priority is increased and the priority order $(A_3, A_1, A_2)$ is obtained. On the second iteration, $A_2$ has the same problem. Finally, in the third iteration, the order $(A_2, A_3, A_1)$ leads to a feasible schedule with $MK = 4$. $SWO$ will then reduce the horizon to 3, recompute time windows and continue.*[2]

For initial priorities, we have chosen to use the $LS_{A_i}$ values calculated by the temporal constraint propagation (where the activity with the earliest $LS_{A_i}$ value gets the highest priority).

In our implementation, the priorities of activities that are not scheduled feasibly are increased by a constant amount. To add randomness, priorities of other activities are increased by a smaller amount with a small probability. Since binary search ensures that the horizon is less than the best makespan found, we know that on each iteration either a new best schedule will be found or at least one activity will have its priority changed.

## Bulldozing

In Example 1, we see how $SWO$ can find a feasible schedule by getting the three activities in the right priority order. For large or highly constrained problems, there can be many subproblems of this nature and it may be difficult for $SWO$ to get all of them right at the same time.

To avoid this potential problem and strengthen the greedy construction, we add a conflict-resolution method called bulldozing to the SCHEDULE method.

[2]Notice that this schedule is optimal. However, with only temporal constraint propagation, a schedule of length 3 cannot be ruled out and $SWO$ will continue to try to find one.

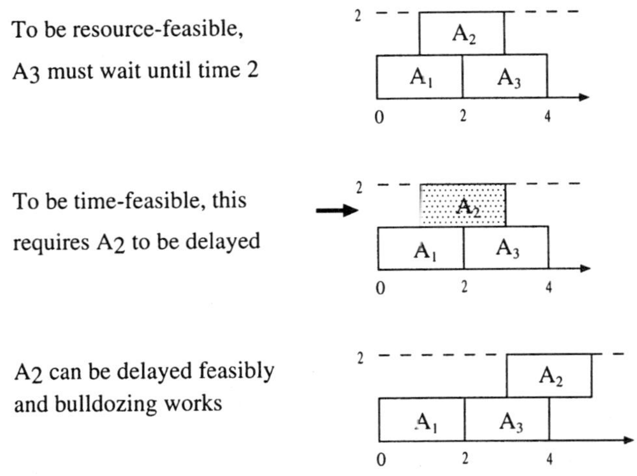


Figure 2: Bulldozing.

Bulldozing is inspired by the complication of maximum time lags. Without maximum time lags, a greedy algorithm can always find a feasible schedule since each $A_i$ can be postponed as long as necessary until resources are available. When there are maximum time lags, however, $A_i$ may not be able to be postponed long enough if activities that constrain it have been placed 'too early' (consider the first iteration of Example 1 where $A_3$ cannot be postponed long enough since it is constrained by $A_2$).

If such an $A_i$ is encountered, bulldozing will attempt to delay the activities that constrain it so that $A_i$ can be scheduled in the postponed position.

**Example 2** *Consider again the simple problem of Example 1. Figure 2 shows what happens if we add bulldozing to the constructor. Activities $A_1$ and $A_2$ are placed successfully. When $A_3$ is considered there is no feasible start time. Times $t \geq 2$ are resource-feasible but only time $t = 0$ is time-feasible since $A_3$ is constrained by the chosen start time for $A_2$. Therefore, we place $A_3$ at 2 and bulldoze $A_2$. Since $A_2$ can then be feasibly scheduled at time 3, bulldozing is successful and the resulting schedule is feasible.*

We get algorithm $SWO(B)$ by replacing SCHEDULE($A_i$) with SCHEDULEWITHDOZING($A_i, X$), a recursive procedure outlined below ($X$ is the set of activities that must be delayed; in the initial call, $X = \emptyset$). Instead of simply searching the current window $[ES_{A_i}, LS_{A_i}]$ for a feasible time, SCHEDULEWITHDOZING considers the larger interval $[ES_{A_i}, LS^{orig}_{A_i}]$ (where $LS^{orig}_{A_i}$ is the latest start of $A_i$ when no other activities are scheduled). If $t$ is not a feasible time or is before $LS_{A_i}$, the algorithm proceeds as before.

However, if the earliest resource-feasible time is outside of the current window but within the original window, bulldozing is invoked. Activity $A_i$ is placed at this potential start time and line 9 updates set $X$ with the activities that must be moved.[3] Each $A_j$ in this set is then unplaced (one

[3]These will be activities that forced $LS_{A_i} < t$ in the first place.

at a time) and a recursive SCHEDULEWITHDOZING($A_j$,$X$) call is made. If all activities can find new feasible start times, bulldozing succeeds. Otherwise, all delayed activities revert to their previous positions and $A_i$ is placed back at $ES_{A_i}$.

```
SCHEDULEWITHDOZING(A_i, X)
 1  t ← earliest resource-feasible time for A_i
          in [ES_{A_i}, LS^{orig}_{A_i}]
 2  if t = NIL
 3     then PLACEACTIVITY(A_i, ES_{A_i})
 4          return FALSE
 5     else if t ≤ LS_{A_i}
 6          then PLACEACTIVITY(A_i, t)
 7               return TRUE
 8          else PLACEACTIVITY(A_i, t)
 9               X ← X ∪ {A_j forced to move by A_i}
10  while X ≠ ∅
11     do A_k ← randomly selected element of X
12        UNPLACEACTIVITY(A_k)
13        if SCHEDULEWITHDOZING(A_k, X) fails
14          then UNDOALLBULLDOZING
15               UNPLACEACTIVITY(A_i)
16               PLACEACTIVITY(A_i, ES_{A_i})
17               return FALSE
```

The recursive nature of bulldozing means that more activities can be moved than the original set forced by $A_i$. In fact, we have observed that $A_i$ itself is often bulldozed further in attempts to settle on start times where all activities are resource-feasible. The reason seems to be that a highly constrained sub-problem may need to be moved out past other activities to fit. This is the motivation for selecting activities to bulldoze randomly on line 11; if a subset of activities proves difficult to schedule, attempts to reschedule them will be done in different orders.

This suggests a nice feature of bulldozing. If a problem has subsets of activities that are highly constrained, the subsets will be pushed out past other activities until they can be feasibly scheduled. It is interesting to note that in other work (Neumann, Schwindt, & Zimmerman 2003), RCPSP/max problems are explicitly divided into such subproblems that are solved separately and then combined into an overall solution. Bulldozing similarly isolates subproblems from the rest of the problem but does so only when subproblems prove difficult.

If there is a difficult subproblem, $SWO$ without bulldozing may also work because the activities involved are likely to move up in the priority queue and be scheduled before others. However, if there are multiple such subproblems, they will likely be jumbled together in the early part of the priority queue and SWO may have trouble fitting them all together. Bulldozing appears to overcome this problem.

Bulldozing can be considered a form of intelligent backtracking (Ginsberg 1993) since we unvalue and revalue the variables whose values contribute to an infeasible state. It also has the flavor of iterative repair algorithms that build schedules and then eliminate conflicts through local search. However, a key difference with local repair is that bulldozing is done with partial rather than complete schedules.

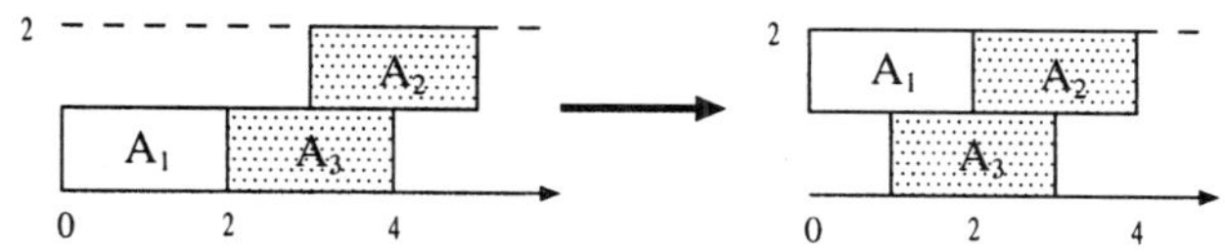


Figure 3: With refilling, $A_2$ and $A_3$ are bulldozed left and the makespan is reduced from 5 units to 4.

### Refilling

Consider our simple example once more. In Example 2, we see how bulldozing can allow feasible schedules to be constructed with priority queues that result in infeasible schedules without bulldozing. However, notice that the resulting schedule is not optimal. As shown in Figure 3, the two activities involved in bulldozing ($A_2$ and $A_3$) can be shifted left to fill in the space vacated by the bulldoze.

Algorithm $SWO(BR)$ results from adding two such 'refilling' pieces to the SCHEDULEWITHDOZING procedure:

1. **Left Bulldozing** After a successful bulldoze, an attempt is made to bulldoze the same set of activities back to earlier start times. This often works because of the space vacated by the bulldozed activities. This step is also bulldozing because the subset of activities considered may be highly constrained among themselves (hence the bulldoze in the first place). Therefore, it may not be possible to left-shift any of them individually but they may move as a group.
2. **Left Shifting** After a successful bulldoze, an attempt is made to left-shift activities that can take advantage of resources vacated by bulldozed activities. We simply consider each activity $A_i$ for which $S_i > ES_{A_i}$.

These refilling mechanisms are able to reduce the makespan of an already feasible schedule or partial schedule. When the horizon is small, they may also indirectly help the construction of more feasible schedules since they leave more room for activities that have yet to be scheduled.

**Example 3** *In the simple problem of Example 1, there are 6 possible priority orders. For $SWO$, 2 of them are both feasible and optimal. For $SWO(B)$, all 6 become feasible and 4 are optimal. Finally, for $SWO(BR)$, 6 are feasible and 5 are optimal.*

It is straightforward to show that each version of our algorithm is guaranteed to terminate in polynomial time and therefore cannot be guaranteed to find a feasible solution (since the problem is NP-hard).

## Experimental Results

We have tested our algorithms on five sets of benchmark problems (set A is divided into 3 subsets). All benchmarks were generated with ProGen/Max (Schwindt 1995) using a number of parameters to vary problem characteristics. Table 1 lists the benchmarks with the number of instances and how many are feasible as well as the number of activities and resources of each instance.

Our algorithm has been implemented in C++ and was run on a 1700 MHz Pentium 4. It uses well under 15 MB of memory on the largest problems.

Table 1: Benchmark names and parameters

| Set | $N_{instances}$ | $N_{feas}$ | $N_{act}$ | $N_{res}$ |
|---|---|---|---|---|
| *J10* | 270 | 187 | 10 | 5 |
| *J20* | 270 | 184 | 20 | 5 |
| *J30* | 270 | 185 | 30 | 5 |
| B | 1080 | 1059 | 100 | 5 |
| C | 120 | 119 | 500 | 5 |

Table 2: Results of schedule construction with all priority queues for feasible *J10* problems

| | $\%_{feas}$ | | | $\%_{opt}$ | | |
|---|---|---|---|---|---|---|
| Constructor | worst | avg | best | worst | avg | best |
| $SWO$ | 0 | 4 | 54 | 0 | 2 | 53 |
| $SWO(B)$ | 18 | 94 | 100 | 0.0002 | 7 | 100 |
| $SWO(BR)$ | 15 | 94 | 100 | 0.02 | 13 | 100 |

## Quality of the Greedy Constructor

For a SWO algorithm to be effective, it is crucial that the greedy constructor be capable of finding feasible and optimal solutions. We want to be confident that there are at least some (preferably many) priority orders from which optimal schedules will be produced. The *J10* problems are small enough that all $10! = 3628800$ possible priority queue permutations can be tried for each one.

In table 2, we see what percentage of those queues lead to feasible and optimal schedules using the constructors of our three versions of SWO. For both $\%_{opt}$ and $\%_{feas}$, we give the worst and best cases among all 187 feasible problems in *J10* as well as the average.

The benefits of strengthening the constructor are clear; bulldozing yields an enormous jump in the number of feasible schedules produced while refilling yields another jump in the number of optimal schedules produced. While the $SWO$ constructor fails to find any solution to 3 feasible problems, the other two find feasible solutions with at least 15% of the prioritizations for every feasible problem.[4]

Another consideration, of course, is time. On average, the $SWO(B)$ constructor took 3.2 times longer than that of $SWO$ and the $SWO(BR)$ constructor took twice again as long. Experiments suggest that these computational costs are worth paying.

## Benchmark Results

We compare $SWO(BR)$ with the best methods reported in the literature:

- $\mathbf{B\&B_{S98}}$ (Schwindt 1998) is a branch and bound algorithm that delays activities by adding precedence constraints.
- $\mathbf{B\&B_{D98}}$ (Dorndorf, Pesch, & Phan-Huy 2000) is a branch and bound algorithm that reduces the search space with a significant amount of resource constraint propagation.
- $\mathbf{B\&B_{F99}}$ (Fest *et al.* 1999) is a branch and bound algorithm that dynamically increases the release dates of some activities.
- **ISES** (Cesta, Oddi, & Smith 2002) is a heuristic algorithm that begins with all activities scheduled as early as possible and then iteratively finds and levels "resource contention peaks", by imposing additional precedence constraints and restarting.
- **KDE** (Cicirello 2003) improves upon priority rule methods by using models of search performance to guide heuristic based iterative sampling.

[4]It is unclear to us why the $SWO(BR)$ constructor did worse than the $SWO(B)$ one in the worst case.

Table 3: Results for benchmark problems

| Set | Algorithm | $\Delta_{LB}\%$ | $\%_{opt}$ | $\%_{feas}$ | Scaled $Cpu_{sec}$ |
|---|---|---|---|---|---|
| J10 | $SWO(BR)$ | 0.2 | 94.0 | 100 | 0.31 |
| | $B\&B_{S98}$ | 0.0 | 100 | 100 | - |
| | $ISES$ | 1.3[(a)] | 85.9 | 99.5 | 0.08 |
| J20 | $SWO(BR)$ | 4.9 | 66.4 | 100 | 0.63 |
| | $B\&B_{S98}$ | 4.3 | 85.3 | 100 | - |
| | $ISES$ | 5.4 | 64 | 100 | 0.53 |
| J30 | $SWO(BR)$ | 10.3 | 51.1 | 100 | 1.07 |
| | $B\&B_{S98}$ | 9.6[(a)] | 62.3 | 98.9 | - |
| | $ISES$ | 11.0 | 49.4 | 100 | 2.67 |
| B | $SWO(BR)$ | 6.8 | 64.2 | 100 | 1.85 |
| | $KDE$ | 4.6[(a)] | 63.8 | 99.9 | 1.97 |
| | $ISES$ | 8.0[(a)] | 63.2 | 99.9 | [(b)] |
| | $B\&B_{S98}$ | 9.6 | 63.7 | 100 | - |
| | $B\&B_{D98}$ | 4.6 | 73.1 | 100 | 3.49 |
| | $B\&B_{F99}$ | 7.0 | 72.5 | 100 | [(b)] |
| C | $SWO(BR)$ | 0.5 | 79.2 | 100 | 3.27 |
| | $B\&B_{D98}$ | 0.5[(a)] | 71.4 | 97.5 | 11.53 |
| | $B\&B_{F99}$ | 5.2 | 58.8 | 100 | [(c)] |

(a) Not directly comparable to other numbers since problems not feasibly solved are excluded.
(b) Cutoff of 11.8 seconds used but no average time reported.
(c) Cutoff of 23.6 seconds used but no average time reported.

For each of the above, results are available for a subset of the benchmark problems. The results from a number of algorithms that do less well than the above four algorithms are not reported. These include a genetic algorithm, tabu search, simulated annealing and priority rule based methods (Dorndorf, Pesch, & Phan-Huy 2000, see this paper for a summary of results).

For $SWO(BR)$, we report the average of 5 runs for each benchmark set. Each run was capped at 10 seconds (or 1000 iterations, whichever came first) in an attempt to ensure that we used no more computation time than other algorithms.

Results are summarized in table 3. Measure $\mathbf{\Delta_{LB}}\%$ gives the average relative deviation from the known lower bounds.

Measures $\%_{\mathbf{opt}}$ and $\%_{\mathbf{feas}}$ give the percentage of feasible problems for which optimal[5] and feasible solutions, respectively, were found. Finally, $\mathbf{Cpu_{sec}}$ gives the average computation time, scaled by processor speed. This last measure should only be used for rough comparisons since the algorithms were developed in different languages and run on different platforms.

Algorithm $SWO(BR)$ was able to find solutions to all 1733 feasible problems (on all 5 runs). The only other algorithm that does not miss feasible solutions is $B\&B_{F99}$, which does so at the expense of quality, especially on set $C$.

Not surprisingly, exact methods get the best results for small problems. $B\&B_{S98}$ is able to solve all *J10* problems optimally, does fairly well on the *J20* problems but already fails to find a number of feasible solutions to some of the problems in *J30*. $B\&B_{D98}$ is better able to handle larger problems and is by far the best algorithm on problem set $B$. However, when the number of activities is increased from 100 to 500 (set $C$), it fails to find all feasible solutions and solves fewer to optimality than $SWO(BR)$.

$SWO(BR)$ is also very competitive with the best non-systematic algorithms. It outperforms *ISES* on all metrics and on all problem sets. While *KDE* is significantly better on measurement $\mathbf{\Delta_{LB}}\%$, $SWO(BR)$ is slightly better than *KDE* on the other three dimensions.

Finally, in addition to scaling well in terms of relative solution quality, $SWO(BR)$ appears to scale effectively in terms of running time. For example, while *ISES* takes 33 times longer on *J30* than on *J10*, $SWO(BR)$ takes less than 4 times longer.[6] Similarly, $B\&B_{D98}$ takes 3.3 times longer on $C$ than on $B$; the difference for $SWO(BR)$ is under 2. It is unclear how *KDE* scales since results are only reported for problems of a single size.

## Concluding Remarks

We have described a new heuristic algorithm, $SWO(BR)$, for RCPSP/max problems. It uses bulldozing and refilling to improve the performance of greedy schedule construction in SWO. On a range of benchmarks $SWO(BR)$ is competitive with systematic and non-systematic state-of-the-art techniques. Able to consistently solve all feasible problems, it scales well, both in terms of solution quality and running time, relative to the best known OR and AI algorithms.

There are a number of ways $SWO(BR)$ could be improved. We have already mentioned that some resource constraint propagation should help guide SWO. Preliminary experiments using one of the consistency tests of Dorndorf et al. (Dorndorf, Pesch, & Phan-Huy 2000) give improvements for *J10* and *J20*. However, the benefits seem to be outweighed by the extra computational costs for the larger problem sizes.

It might be effective to incorporate $SWO(BR)$ into a meta-heuristic like tabu search (Chen, Fu, & Lim 2002, they find that tabu search combines well with SWO) or simulated annealing so that priority space is explored more intelligently; the current search is relatively unstructured.

Finally, $SWO(BR)$ should be tested on more difficult problems. While it didn't struggle with the above benchmarks, we do not know how it will do on problems that are larger or more difficult.

[5]Solutions that matched the lower bound or have been proven optimal by some algorithm.

[6]Of course, such comparisons must be taken with a grain of salt; running times depend partly on the cutoff times chosen.

## References

Bartusch, M.; Möhring, R. H.; and Radermacher, F. J. 1988. Scheduling project networks with resource constraints and time windows. *Annals of OR* 16:201–240.

Cesta, A.; Oddi, A.; and Smith, S. 2002. A constraint-based method for project scheduling with time windows. *Journal of Heuristics* 8(1):109–136.

Chen, P.; Fu, Z.; and Lim, A. 2002. The yard allocation problem. *AAAI-2002* 3–8.

Cicirello, V. A. 2003. *Boosting Stochastic Problem Solvers Through Online Self-Analysis of Performance*. Ph.D. Dissertation, The Robotics Institute, Carnegie Mellon Univ.

Dechter, R.; Meiri, I.; and Pearl, J. 1991. Temporal constraint networks. *Artificial Intelligence* 49:61–95.

Dorndorf, U.; Pesch, E.; and Phan-Huy, T. 2000. A time-oriented branch-and-bound algorithm for resource-constrained project scheduling with generalised precedence constraints. *Manag. Sci.* 46(10):1365–1384.

Fest, A.; Möhring, R. H.; Stork, F.; and Uetz, M. 1999. Resource constrained project scheduling with time windows: A branching scheme based on dynamic release dates. Technical Report 596, TU Berlin, Germany.

Ginsberg, M. L. 1993. Dynamic backtracking. *Journal of AI Research* 1:25–46.

Joslin, D. E., and Clements, D. P. 1999. Squeaky wheel optimization. *Journal of AI Research* 10:353–373.

Laborie, P. 2003. Algorithms for propagating resource constraints in AI planning and scheduling: Existing approaches and new results. *Artif. Intel.* 143(2):151–188.

Muscettola, N. 2002. Computing the envelope for stepwise constant resource allocations. In *CP 2002*, 139–154.

Neumann, K.; Schwindt, C.; and Zimmerman, J. 2003. *Project Scheduling with Time Windows and Scarce Resources*. Germany: Springer-Verlag.

Schwindt, C. 1995. ProGen/max: A new problem generator for different resource constrained project scheduling problems with minimal and maximal time lags. Technical report WIOR-449, Universitat Karlsruhe, Germany.

Schwindt, C. 1998. A branch-and-bound algorithm for the resource-constrained project duration problem subject to temporal constraints. Technical Report WIOR-544, Universitat Karlsruhe, Germany.

# Shortest Path Discovery Problems: A Framework, Algorithms and Experimental Results

**Csaba Szepesvári**
Computer and Automation Research Institute of the Hungarian Academy of Sciences
1111 Budapest XI. Kende u. 13-17.
e-mail: szcsaba@sztaki.hu

### Abstract

In this paper we introduce and study Shortest Path Discovery (SPD) problems, a generalization of shortest path problems: In SPD one is given a directed edge-weighted graph and the task is to find a the shortest path for fixed source and target nodes such that initially the edge-weights are unknown, but they can be queried. Querying the cost of an edge is expensive and hence the goal is to minimize the total number of edge cost queries executed. In this article we characterize some common properties of sound SPD algorithms, propose a particular algorithm that is shown to be sound and effective. Experimental results on real-world OCR task demonstrate the usefulness of the approach whereas the proposed algorithm is shown to yield a substantial speed-up of the recognition process.

## Introduction

Shortest path problem appear in many subproblems of artificial intelligence, e.g. in symbolic planning, parsing, vision, or speech recognition. Depending on the nature of additional assumptions made on the underlying search graph one gets fundamentally different problem types: the graph may be finite or infinite, or one might have additional initial knowledge about the solutions in the form of estimates of the cost-to-go function like in heuristic search, or the search might be interleaved with execution like in real-time search, etc. Recently there has been a growing interest in incremental search (or dynamic search) where one considers a sequence of related search problems and the goal is to speed up the overall process by reusing solutions to previous instances (Ramalingam & Reps 1996).

Less attention have been paid to another important aspect of search, namely that obtaining the costs of the edges might be a non-trivial process and the cost of this process may dominate the total cost of the algorithm. As an example consider segmentation lattice based character recognition systems when a path from the source node to the target node in the segmentation lattice represents a possible segmentation, the edges of the lattice are associated with certain segments (parts) of the image to be recognized and where the edge costs are e.g. proportional to the negated log-likelihood of a given segment representing some (any) character. Provided that one has upper and lower bounds on the widths of characters the segmentation lattice will have a particularly simple structure with the number of its edges growing at most linearly with the width of the image area to be recognized. The number of edges in such a graph is typically in the range of 1.5-5.0 times the number of characters on the image. When the recognizer must work even with degraded quality images or images that contain heavy clutter then the OCR component often needs to check many alternative interpretations of a single input image corresponding to alternative "binarizations". In such a case the time needed to recognize a single character for a difficult input can be substantially more expensive than to solve the full shortest path problem. In such cases the cost of finding the shortest path is clearly dominated by the cost of obtaining the costs associated with the edges.



In segmentation based speech recognition the situation is entirely analogous. Another example comes from hierarchical (symbolic or non-symbolic) planning when calculating the cost associated with an "edge" requires the solution of a subproblem. Thus, hierarchical planning algorithms might also benefit from minimizing the total number of edge-cost evaluations. A related example is the exploration of unsafe environments where one is interested in minimizing the number of dangerous exploration steps. One particular case is when robots are used to explore a minefield. In this case it is not the computational cost, but the probability of loosing the robot that is to be minimized. This example can again be casted as a SPD problem.

The article is organized as follows: In the next section we introduce the algorithmic framework and derive some common properties of SPD algorithms. Next we present an algorithm that we call "Greedy SPD" that in each step queries the cost of edges along the shortest path found using the current best estimate of the cost function. It is shown that this algorithm is sound and that it is not possible to uniformly improve the performance of this algorithm. In Section results of some experiments are presented on the task of recognizing vehicle license plates, where the proposed algorithm is shown to yield substantial savings in the total running time of recognition. Relation to previous work is discussed in Section , whilst conclusions are drawn in Section .

## Shortest Path Discovery Problems

### Framework

Consider the shortest path problem $P = (V, E, c, s, t)$, where $G = (V, E)$ is a finite directed graph, $V$, $E$ are the set of vertices and edges, respectively, $c : E \to \mathbb{R}$ is a function assigning costs (weights) to the edges of $G$, and where $s, t \in V$ are the source and target nodes, respectively. We further assume that the graph $G$ has at least one directed path from $s$ to $t$.

In the classical shortest path problem we are interested in finding the path connecting $s$ and $t$ with the least cost, where the cost of a path $\pi = (\pi_1, \ldots, \pi_n)$ is measured as the sum of the costs of the edges of the path:

$$c(\pi) = \sum_i c(\pi_i), \quad \pi_i \in E.$$

We shall denote by $\Pi(V, E, s, t)$ the set of paths in $G$ connecting $s$ and $t$, whilst $\Pi^*(V, E, c, s, t)$ shall denote the set of solutions of the shortest-path problem $(V, E, c, s, t)$.

In the case of SPDs one is given a shortest path problem instance $P$ and it is assumed that the costs of edges are initially unknown, but there exists a method `query` that can be used to query the cost of edges of $G$. The goal is to obtain a solution of $P$ with the least number of query calls. Algorithms that solve SPDs take a SPD problem instance (possibly extended with additional information) and return solution candidates.

**Definition 1** *An algorithm $\mathcal{A}$ for solving SPDs is* correct *if for all shortest path problem instances P when $\mathcal{A}$ terminates then it returns a solution of P. If an algorithm is correct and terminates in finite time for all problem instances then we call it* sound.

We shall call an edge *known* when its cost have been queried previously. The set of known edges is uniquely determined by the corresponding characteristic function $k : E \to \{0, 1\}$ that assigns 1 (0) to known (resp. unknown) edges. In what follows we shall refer to functions mapping the set of edges into the set $\{0, 1\}$ as *knowledge-functions*.

In what follows we shall assume that one is given an initial estimate of the edge costs, $c_0$ and a pair $(P, c_0)$ shall be called an SPD problem instance. The hope is that when $c_0$ is a good approximation of $c$ then it may be used in place of $c$ to guess optimal paths and ultimately to avoid querying the cost of some edges. When $c_0 \leq c$ we say that $c_0$ is an *admissible* estimate of $c$.[1]

From the point of view of input-output behavior an SPD algorithm may be represented as a function mapping SPD instances $(P, c_0)$ into paths of the graph underlying $P$. With a slight abuse of notation we shall use the same symbol to denote the algorithm and the function that it implements. Given a shortest path problem $P$ and an initial cost estimate $c_0$ we let $k_{\mathcal{A}}(P, c_0)$ denote the knowledge function that corresponding to the set of known edges at the time when algorithm $\mathcal{A}$ terminates.

[1]Here and in what follows $\leq$ will be used to denote the usual partial ordering of functions, too: $f \leq g$ iff $f(x) \leq g(x)$ holds for all $x$ from the common domain of $f$ and $g$.

The optimization criterion we are interested in can be defined as follows:

**Definition 2** *Let $\mathcal{A}$ be a sound algorithm and let $(P, c_0)$ be an SPD instance. Let $k = k_{\mathcal{A}}(P, c_0)$ and define $\|k\|_1 = \sum_{e \in E} k(e)$. We say that $\mathcal{A}$ is* optimally effective *on the SPD instance $(P, c_0)$ if for any other sound algorithm $\mathcal{A}'$ it holds that $\|k\|_1 \leq \|k'\|_1$, where $k' = k_{\mathcal{A}'}(P, c_0)$, i.e., the number of edges queried by $\mathcal{A}'$ is not smaller than the number of edges queried by $\mathcal{A}$.*

*We say that an SPD algorithm $\mathcal{A}$ is optimally effective if it is sound and if it is optimally effective on all problem instances $(P, c_0)$, where $c_0$ is any admissible initial cost estimate for the problem $P$.*

### The Fundamental Property of Correct SPD Algorithms

Fix a problem instance $P$. Let $k : E \to \{0, 1\}$ be an arbitrary knowledge function and define $c_k : E \to \mathbb{R}$ by

$$c_k(e) = \begin{cases} c(e), & \text{if } k(e) = 1; \\ c_0(e), & \text{if } k(e) = 0. \end{cases} \tag{1}$$

Note that $c_k$ gives the "best" available estimate of the cost of edges given the knowledge function $k$.

Before giving the main result of this section we shall need one more definition. Let $P$ be a shortest path problem. We call an edge $e$ of $P$ a *bottleneck* if all paths connecting $s$ and $t$ go through it. A graph is bottleneck free when it has no bottleneck edges. *In what follows we always assume that the graphs that we work with are bottleneck free.* Note that the cost of bottleneck edges need never be queried. Further, the identification of bottleneck edges does not require the knowledge of edge costs. Hence, the above assumption yields in no loss generality.

It should be fairly clear that a correct algorithm must query the cost of edges of the path that it returns. Further, it is also clear that a correct algorithm must return a shortest path given its best current estimate of the costs. The following theorem formalizes these observations and further it shows that the reverse statement holds as well:

**Theorem 1 (Fundamental property of SPD problems)** *Let $\mathcal{A}$ be an SPD algorithm that is designed to work with admissible initial cost estimates. The following statements are equivalent:*

1. *$\mathcal{A}$ is correct.*
2. *For all shortest path problems $P = (V, E, c, s, t)$ and admissible initial cost estimates $c_0$ if $k$ represents the state of edge-cost knowledge at the time when the algorithm stops and $\pi$ is the path returned by $\mathcal{A}$ then $k(e) = 1$ for all edges $e$ of $\pi$ and $\pi \in \Pi^*(V, E, c_k, s, t)$.*

*Proof.* Assume that (1) holds, but (2) does not hold. If (2) does not hold then either (i) $k(e) = 0$ for some $e \in \pi$, or (ii) $\pi \notin \Pi^*(V, E, c_k, s, t)$. In case (i) consider a modified problem $P'$ that is equal to $P$ in all respects except that $c(e)$ is replaced by some sufficiently large cost $g$. Since algorithm $\mathcal{A}$ has no knowledge of $c(e)$ it will return the same solution $\pi$. It should be clear that if $g > \max_\pi c(\pi)$ then $\pi$ cannot be optimal in $P'$. Hence algorithm $\mathcal{A}$ cannot be correct, which is a contradiction. Therefore we may assume that (i) does not hold, i.e., $k(e) = 1$ for all edges of $\pi$. Now assume that case (ii) holds true. Let $\pi' \in \Pi^*(V, E, c_k, s, t)$. Let us now define a problem instance $P'$ equivalent to $P$ in all respects except that $c(e)$ is redefined such that it is equal to $c_0(e)$ for all edges $e$ of $\pi'$ such that $k(e) = 0$. If no such edges exist then we let $P' = P$. Again, algorithm $\mathcal{A}$ will still return $\pi$ on $P'$. Therefore, by (i) we may assume that $k|_\pi \equiv 1$ (i.e. $k(e) = 1$ for all $e \in \pi$). Then $c(\pi') = c_k(\pi') < c_k(\pi) = c(\pi)$, which is a contradiction. This finishes the proof of (1)⇒(2).

Let us now consider the case (2)⇒(1): assume that (2) holds and let $\pi$ be the path returned by $\mathcal{A}$ on $P$. Take any other path $\pi'$ of $P$. Then $c(\pi') \geq c_k(\pi') \geq c_k(\pi) = c(\pi)$ since $k|_\pi \equiv 1$. This shows that $\pi$ is indeed an optimal path of $P$. □

The importance of this theorem is that it shows that an optimally effective algorithm can and should stop when the shortest path w.r.t. the best estimate of the cost has no unknown edges. This observation motivates the following definition:

**Definition 3** *Fix an SPD instance* $(P, c_0)$. *Then a knowledge function* $k : E \to \{0, 1\}$ *is called* terminating *if there exists a shortest path* $\pi$ *for the problem* $(V, E, c_k, s, t)$ *such that* $k|_\pi \equiv 1$.

It should be clear that if $k$ is terminating then for any $k' : E \to \{0, 1\}$ satisfying $k' \geq k$, $k'$ is also terminating.

## A Greedy Algorithm for Solving SPD Problems

Any SPD algorithm uniquely determines a sequence of knowledge functions. Naturally, the sequence of knowledge functions $\{k_n\}$ that an algorithm produces satisfies $k_n \leq k_{n+1}$. Actually, any reasonable algorithm would produce functions such that $k_n(e) < k_{n+1}(e)$ holds for at least one edge $e$, i.e., in each stage the algorithm queries the cost of at least one edge. Also, if $k_n$ is terminating it does not make any sense to query some more edges, hence reasonable SPD algorithms should terminate whenever they reach any terminating knowledge function. Therefore the behavior of reasonable SPD algorithms can be represented as a walk on the directed acyclic graph $G_K = (V_K, E_K, k_0, T)$, where $V_K$ is the set of all knowledge functions ($V_K = 2^E$), $(k_1, k_2) \in E_K$ iff $k_1 < k_2$, $k_0$ is the source node that satisfies $k_0 \equiv 0$ and $T$ is the set of terminating knowledge functions associated with $(P, c_0)$. The walk starts at $k_0$ and finishes whenever a node of $T$ is reached. It follows that any algorithm that constructs such a walk on $G_K$ is sound (termination within $|E|$ time steps follows since $k_n < k_{n+1}$ and the graph $G$ is assumed to be finite). The cost associated with an SPD algorithm that constructs the walk $k_0, k_1, \ldots, k_n$ is $\|k_n\|_1$. Hence, the performance of SPD algorithms can be lower bounded by $\min_{k \in T} \|k\|_1$.

Now, let us consider Algorithm 1 given below: In each iteration it computes a shortest path (ties should be broken in a deterministic manner) given its current knowledge and then queries the cost of all unknown edges along this path. Termination happens when the number of unknown edges belonging to the current shortest path equals to zero. It follows

**Algorithm 1** The Greedy SPD Algorithm

```
Input: (V, E, c_0, s, t)
for all e ∈ E do
   k(e) := 0
end for
repeat
   Let π ∈ Π*(V, E, c_k, s, t).
   u := 0
   for all e ∈ π do
      if k(e) = 0 then
         Call query(e), k(e) := 1
         u := u + 1
      end if
   end for
until u = 0
Return π
```

immediately from Theorem 1 that this algorithm is sound. The algorithm is greedy as it queries *all* the unknown edges. As an alternative one might decide to query edges along the best path one by one, hoping that querying the cost of some of these edges would already prove that the current solution is suboptimal. Then the ordering at which edges are queried becomes critical. In this article we focus only on the basic algorithm, leaving the study of its variants for further work. In what follows we shall call the set of edges that lie on some best path of $(V, E, c_k, s, t)$ the *set of critical edges given k*. The rest of the edges are called non-critical.

We now show that the performance of sound algorithms that query the cost of non-critical edges cannot uniformly dominate the performance of (sound) algorithms that query the cost of critical edges only. In order to see this consider a sound algorithm $\mathcal{A}$ that is known to query non-critical edges and in order to derive a contradiction assume that $\mathcal{A}$ dominates all sound algorithms that query the cost of critical edges only. We may assume that $\mathcal{A}$ always stops as soon as possible. Let $E^* = E^*(V, E, c_k, s, t)$ denote the set of critical edges given $k$, $P = (V, E, c, s, t)$ and $c_0$. By assumption, for some SPD instance $(P, c_0)$ algorithm $\mathcal{A}$ chooses to query edges outside of $E^*(V, E, c_k, s, t)$ at some stage of its execution. Let $(P, c_0)$ be such an SPD instance and let $n$ be the first stage when $\mathcal{A}$ queries some non-critical edges. Let the set of queried non-critical edges be $U_n$. Further, let $\pi \in \Pi^*(V, E, c_{k_n}, s, t)$ be a path such that $k|_\pi \not\equiv 0$. (By our assumption on $\mathcal{A}$ and Theorem 1 no path in $\Pi^*(V, E, c_{k_n}, s, t)$ can have all of its edges known at stage $n$.) Now define $P' = (V, E, c', s, t)$ such that

$$c'(e) = \begin{cases} c(e), & \text{if } k_n(e) = 1; \\ c_0(e), & \text{if } e \in \pi \text{ and } k_n(e) = 0; \\ \max(c(e), c(\pi) + 1), & \text{otherwise.} \end{cases}$$

It should be clear then that $\pi \in \Pi^*(V, E, c', s, t) \cap \Pi^*(V, E, c'_{k_n}, s, t)$ and $\pi$ is the unique optimal path of $P'$. Now let us consider the behavior of $\mathcal{A}$ on $(P', c_0)$. It is clear that at stage $n$ the state of algorithm $\mathcal{A}$ will be identical to its state when it was run on $(P, c_0)$. Therefore in time step $n$ algorithm $\mathcal{A}$ will still decide to query the edges in $U_n$. However, the unique optimal path in $P'$ is $\pi$ which has no edges in $U_n$, hence $\mathcal{A}$ queries edges of $U_n$ superfluously. Now, consider an algorithm $\mathcal{A}'$ that queries the cost of critical edges only. We may further assume that $\mathcal{A}'$ is such that it queries exactly the same set of edges up to stage $n$ as algorithm $\mathcal{A}$ (such an algorithm indeed exists since $n$ was the first time when $\mathcal{A}$ picked some non-critical edges). Without the loss of generality, we may assume that at stage $n$ $\mathcal{A}'$ chooses to query all the unknown edges along the path $\pi$. It follows then by the construction of $c'$ that $\mathcal{A}'$ terminates after the costs of these edges have been queried. Hence the cost of running $\mathcal{A}'$ on $(P', c_0)$ will be strictly less than that of $\mathcal{A}$. This shows that it is not possible to give a "clever" (and sound) algorithm that queries non-critical edges and which would uniformly dominate those (sound) algorithms that query only critical edges. This result is summarized in the following proposition:

**Proposition 1** *If $\mathcal{A}$ is a sound algorithm with a property such that for some SPD instances $(P, c_0)$ $\mathcal{A}$ queries non-critical edges during its execution then there exist a sound algorithm $\mathcal{A}'$ and an SPD instance $(P', c_0)$ such that $\mathcal{A}'$ queries only critical edges and $\|k_{\mathcal{A}'}(P', c_0)\|_1 < \|k_{\mathcal{A}}(P', c_0)\|_1$.*

Our next aim is to relax the condition $c_0 \leq c$. The next proposition shows that this can be done by appropriately redefining $c_k$ when a lower bound on the smallest non-zero difference of the cost of paths is known:

**Proposition 2** *Let $(P, c_0)$ be an SPD instance and let $k : E \to \{0, 1\}$. Assume that c is such that*

$$\min_{\pi,\pi' \in \Pi(V,E,s,t)} \{|c(\pi) - c(\pi')| : c(\pi) - c(\pi') \neq 0\} \geq 1. \tag{2}$$

*Further, assume that $c_0(e) > 0$ holds for all $e \in E$ and define $c_k^+(e) = c_0(e) + k(e)c(e)L_0, \quad e \in E$, where $L_0 \geq \operatorname{argmax}_{\pi \in \Pi(V,E,s,t)} c_0(\pi)$. Assume that for some $\pi \in \Pi^*(V, E, c_k^+, s, t)$, $k|_\pi \equiv 1$ holds true. Then $\pi$ is the solution of the SP problem $(V, E, c, s, t)$.*

*Proof.* Let $P, c_0, \pi, k, L_0$ be as defined above. Further, let $\pi'$ be an arbitrary path from $s$ to $t$ in $G = (V, E)$. Then $c_0(\pi) + c(\pi)L_0 = c_k^+(\pi) \leq c_k^+(\pi') \leq c_0(\pi') + c(\pi')L_0$. Rearranging the terms yields $(c(\pi) - c(\pi'))\, L_0 \leq c_0(\pi') - c_0(\pi) < L_0$, where we have used that $c_0(\pi') \leq L_0$ and that $c_0(e) > 0$ holds for all edges $e \in E$. Dividing both sides of this inequality by $L_0$ gives $c(\pi) - c(\pi') < 1$ or $c(\pi) < c(\pi') + 1$. Hence from (2) we conclude that $c(\pi) \leq c(\pi')$, which finishes the proof. □

Although the requirement that $c_0$ is a lower bound for $c$ is dropped, we still have condition (2) which might be hard to ensure unless e.g. the set of possible costs is discrete which is the case when e.g. the costs are integer valued. The proposition below shows a way to overcome this difficulty. The price we pay is that the solutions returned will not be optimal anymore:

**Proposition 3** *Fix an arbitrary $\epsilon > 0$. Let $(P, c_0)$ be an SPD instance and let $k : E \to \{0, 1\}$. Assume that $c_0(e) > 0$ holds for all $e \in E$ and let $c_k^+(e) = c_0(e) + L_0 k(e)c(e)/\epsilon, \quad e \in E$, where $L_0$ is as before. Assume that for some $\pi \in \Pi^*(V, E, c_k^+, s, t)$, $k|_\pi \equiv 1$. Then $\pi$ is an $\epsilon$-optimal solution of the SP problem $(V, E, c, s, t)$, i.e., for any path $\pi' \in \Pi(V, E, s, t)$, $c(\pi) < c(\pi') + \epsilon$.*

Figure 1: Original license plate image (with the detected license plate subimage framed) and the narrowest components found by the segmentation algorithm. Components are plotted in alternating colors/patterns. The segmentation boundaries are defined by the left and right edges of the narrowest components. Note that the segmentation algorithm successfully separated the letters 'H' and 'P'. However, the price is that it also cuts the stamp between the letters 'Z' and 'H' into two parts.

*Proof.* Let $\pi, \pi'$ be as in the conditions of the proposition. Analogously to the previous result we obtain $(c(\pi) - c(\pi'))\, L_0/\epsilon \leq c_0(\pi') - c_0(\pi) < L_0$. Dividing both sides by $L_0$ and rearranging the terms yields the desired inequality. □

## Experiments

The validity of the approach suggested, as well as the efficiency of the proposed algorithm was tested on a specific optical character recognition (OCR) problem, namely, the problem of recognizing the character strings on vehicle license plates. The proposed algorithm was built into a commercial system. Here we report experiments with this system.

Assume that the license plate was already found by a detector algorithm and the task is to decipher the characters on the "straightened", height and orientation normalized and cleaned plate. The segmentation lattice is produced as follows: A segmentation algorithm that considers various features measured on the image such as the peak to valley ratio identifies the boundaries that may separate characters. Any position between two neighboring pixel columns is a potential candidate for such a boundary. The exact description of this algorithm is out of the scope of the present paper, however we note that this algorithm typically yields an oversegmentation of the image. An example output of this algorithm for a license plate image is given in Figure 1.

The next step is to build the segmentation lattice (or graph) that will be the input of our algorithms. This graph is built as follows: We shall distinguish two types of vertices of the graph that we shall call 'white' and 'black'. White vertices correspond to boundaries on the image identified by the segmentation algorithm, whilst a black vertex is added for each candidate character region. First the skeleton of the

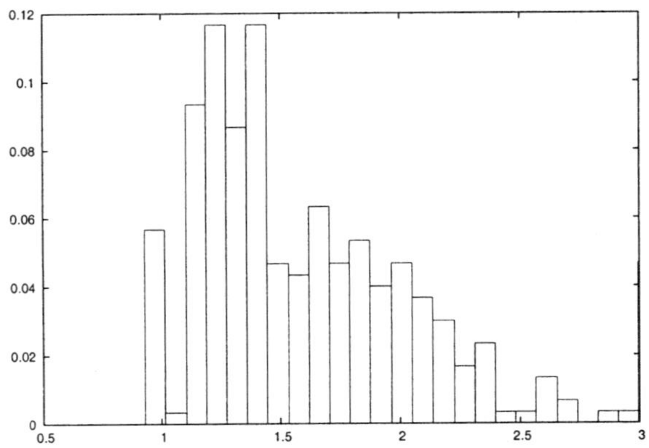


Figure 2: Histogram of the average number of black nodes per boundaries.

graph is built by adding all white vertices corresponding to all potential boundary points identified by the segmentation algorithm. No edges are added at this point. The source node, representing the 0th boundary position, and the target node representing the very last boundary position on the image are added in this step (they are white nodes). Next, all boundary point pairs that satisfy certain width constraints are considered. For a boundary pair whose corresponding vertices are $v_1$ and $v_2$, a black node, $v$, and the edges $(v_1, v)$ and $(v, v_2)$ are added to the graph. The reason of adding two edges instead of a single one is to separate the costs associated with the character region and that of the regions separating neighboring character regions. The distribution of the average number of black nodes per white nodes measured over a set of example images is shown below in figure 2.

The cost associated with character separating regions is obtained by means of some simple and quick calculations (the cost depends on e.g. the saturation of the corresponding region, if there exists a path from the top of the region to the bottom that does not cross any black pixels on the binarized image, etc.). The initial cost $c_0$ of a character region is set to $1 + c(R)$, where $c(R)$ depends on some other simple measures (e.g. width, aspect ratio, stroke width, existence of a white strip through the region, etc.). The idea is to penalize regions that have obviously 'wrong' features as opposed to regions that have no such trivial problems. Hence this estimate of the cost is undoubtedly a crude estimate of the true cost, but the hope is that it still should be able to guide the search process. Note that calculating this crude cost estimate is also cheap.

The solution of the recognition problem is defined as the path from the source to the target node that gives the minimal total cost, where costs are now defined as a function of the output of an optical character recognition component. In our case the OCR is built to recognize all the characters of the fonts of European license plates plus some special symbols (flags, arms, etc.). It is also capable of tolerating positioning errors up to the extent of a few pixels in all directions. The recognition component works on an appropriately binarized and cleaned image, but if the underlying imgae is highly cluttered and/or noise then the running time of the OCR component can increase substantially as it will consider alternative binarizations. This is the price that one has to pay to make the OCR component robust against substantial image noise and clutter. The cost of running the OCR component can be particularly high when many alternative "interpretations" (alignments, binarizations) exist. As a result, when due to some bad luck a non-license plate image is sent to the recognizer then the whole system may slow down. Hence the goal in this particular application is not merely to achieve a good average running time, but rather to achieve a good worst-case running time.

In our experiments we compared the performance of the Greedy SPD algorithm of the previous section with that of the algorithm that queries the costs of all the edges before starting the search for the shortest path. We shall call this algorithm the ALLCOSTS algorithm. The experiments were run on a Pentium IV 2.4GHz computer. Greedy SPD was run in the "approximate" mode with $\epsilon = 1E-5$.[2] For the purposes of these measurements we selected a one of our test sets of images that were used in assessing the performance of the various components of the system. This set consisted of 300 images that present both easy and difficult to recognize cases. We have measured factors like the number of vertices and edges of the segmentation graph, the total time to process the plate candidate, the time spent on calculating the costs, the number of queried edges and the number of iterations required by the Greedy SPD algorithm to return a solution.

Exploiting that the graph is acyclic, shortest path computations were implemented by the standard DAG shortest path algorithm that visits edges of the graph in reverse topological order. In the case of the Greedy SPD algorithm the topological ordering was obtained in the initialization phase since the structure of the graph is kept fixed in the process. Since the graphs are typically very small (typically having less than 50 vertices) we did not implement any further optimizations here (for larger graphs incremental search algorithms could prove to be useful). The ALLCOSTS algorithm used the same shortest path subroutines.

Figure 3 shows the scatter plot of the running time of the Greedy SPD algorithm plotted against that of the ALLCOSTS algorithm. It should be evident from the figure that Greedy SPD performs better in almost all cases than ALLCOSTS and it performs substantially better than ALLCOSTS in those situations when the running-time of ALLCOSTS is large (note the log scaling of the axes on the figure). As mentioned before the observed slow-down is due to the increased effort of the OCR component when it needs to process difficult to interpret regions. It can be concluded that in these cases Greedy SPD successfully cuts down the worst-case processing time, causing speed-ups in the order of 500-4000%. On the average the speed-up factor was found to be 260% on this set of images (it should be clear that all these numbers depend heavily on the set of images used). The cases when no speed-up was measured correspond to segmentation lattices that has a single path or just a very few

[2]The algorithm was not sensitive to the particular value of $\epsilon$.

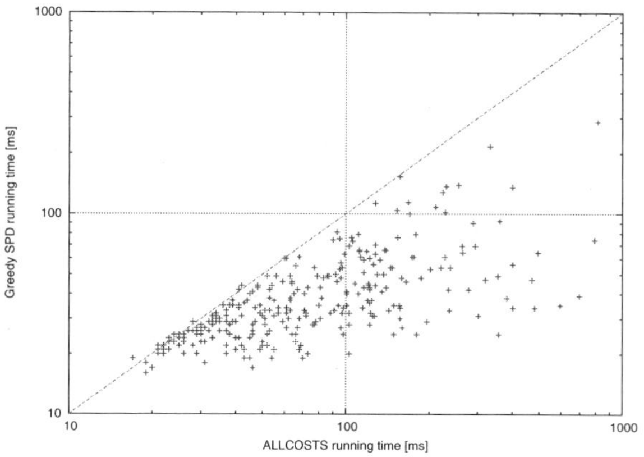


Figure 3: Scatter plot of the running time ALLCOSTS vs. the running time Greedy SPD. Note that both axis have log-scale.

paths from the source to the target. Note that the running time of the OCR component on a given region was found to be 3 ms on average, whilst the average running time of the shortest path algorithm was found to be less than 0.3 ms on average. On the average 80% of the edge cost were evaluated, with this percentage decreasing for the more difficult cases. Note that due to the choice of $c_0$, Greedy SPD will typically succeed at avoiding to send the most difficult to analyze characters to the OCR system – that can take longer time to process. Indeed it turned out that the average recognition time per region for those regions that were not sent to the OCR component when Greedy SPD was running then was 8.3ms, almost 3 times the time required by the OCR component to process 'normal' regions.[3]

We have also tried the version of the Greedy SPD algorithm that queries only the cost of the last unknown edge of the optimal path obtained. We have found no significant differences between the performances of these two versions.

## Related Work

Two recent branches of search research, real-time search and incremental search consider related, but still radically different aspects of search. Real-time (heuristic) search methods (e.g.(Korf 1990; Furcy & Koenig 2000)) interleave planning and plan execution. They are based on agent-centered search: the set of states considered in the search is restricted to those states that can be reached from the current state of the agent within a few number of action execution steps. Real-time search methods, like LRTA* (Korf 1990) iteratively refine their heuristic function that is used in the search. Their main advantage is that they can amortize the cost of obtaining the optimal cost-to-go functions over several search episodes and are thus capable of making decisions in "real-time" whilst still converging to optimality in the long run. Real-time search is similar to shortest path discovery in that both use heuristic functions to guide search and both can learn the true costs as the search proceeds. However, the optimality criterion used in SPD is radically different from that of used in real-time search (the total number of edge-costs queried vs. the number of suboptimal actions executed). Incremental search, e.g. (Ramalingam & Reps 1996; Frigioni, Marchetti-Spaccamela, & Nanni 2000) concerns the solution of a sequence of related search problems that are only slightly different from each other in ways that are communicated to the search algorithms. The SPD problem naturally gives rise to such a sequence of related search problems. However, in incremental search one is interested in quickly solving the actual search problem by reusing as much of the previous solutions as it is possible. Thus the optimality criteria of the two search problems are again rather different. It should be obvious that SPD algorithms might use incremental search algorithms as their subroutines when they need to recalculate the shortest path after the cost of some edges have been observed.

[3]Hence the cost assigned to evaluating an edge is not uniform as it was assumed in the previous sections. Extending the algorithms to such non-uniform cases looks like an important next step.

## Conclusions

We have introduced a new class of search problems, called Shortest Path Discovery Problems. An SPD instance is given by an underlying shortest path problem and an initial estimate of the costs of edges. Algorithms may query the cost of edges at any time in any order. The goal is to execute the least possible number of queries and return an optimal solution to the original shortest path problem. We have given necessary and sufficient conditions for an algorithm to be a sound SPD algorithm. We proposed an algorithm, Greedy SPD, that greedily explores all the edges of the current best path. It was shown that this algorithm is sound and we have argued that it is not possible to design a sound algorithm that would explore 'non-critical' edges and which would dominate the performance of algorithms that explore only 'critical' edges. Greedy SPD was extended to use non-admissible initial estimates at the price of returning only approximately optimal solutions. The utility of the approach was shown in a real-world experiment where Greedy SPD was shown to provide a speed-up of ca. 250%. In the particular example studied larger speed-up factors were measured in the more difficult cases.

## References

Frigioni, D.; Marchetti-Spaccamela, A.; and Nanni, U. 2000. Fully dynamic algorithms for maintaining shortest paths trees. *Journal of Algorithms* 34(2):251–281.

Furcy, D., and Koenig, S. 2000. Speeding up the convergence of real-time search. In *Proceedings of the National Conference on Artificial Intelligence*, 891–897.

Korf, R. 1990. Real-time heuristic search. *Artificial Intelligence* 42:189–211.

Ramalingam, G., and Reps, T. 1996. An incremental algorithm for a generalization of the shortest-path problem. *Journal of Algorithms* 21(2):267–305.

# Regression With Respect to Sensing Actions and Partial States

**Le-chi Tuan, Chitta Baral, and Xin Zhang**
Computer Science and Engineering
Arizona State University
Tempe, AZ 85287, USA
{lctuan,baral,xin.zhang}@asu.edu

**Tran Cao Son**
Computer Science Department
New Mexico State University
Las Cruces, NM 88003, USA
tson@cs.nmsu.edu

**Abstract**

In this paper, we present a *state-based regression function* for planning domains where an agent does not have complete information and may have sensing actions. We consider binary domains [1], and employ the 0-approximation (Son & Baral 2001) to define the regression function. In binary domains, the use of 0-approximation means using 3-valued states. Although planning using this approach is incomplete with respect to the full semantics, we adopt it to have a lower complexity. We prove the soundness and completeness of our regression formulation with respect to the definition of progression and develop a conditional planner that utilizes our regression function.

## Introduction and Motivation

An important aspect in reasoning about actions and in characterizing the semantics of action description languages is to define a transition function encoding the transition between states due to actions. This transition function is often viewed as a *progression* function in that it denotes the progression of the world by the execution of actions. The 'opposite' or 'inverse' of progression is referred to as *regression*.

Even for the simple case where we have only non-sensing actions and the progression transition function is deterministic, there are various formulations of regression. For example, consider the following. Let $\Phi$ be the progression transition function from actions and states to states. I.e., intuitively $\Phi(a, s) = s'$ means that if the action $a$ is executed in state $s$ then the resulting state will be $s'$. One way to define a regression function $\Psi_1$ is to define it with respect to states. In that case $s \in \Psi_1(a, s')$ will mean that the state $s'$ is reached if $a$ is executed in $s$. Another way regression is defined is with respect to formulas. In that case $\Psi_2(a, f) = g$, where $f$ and $g$ are formulas, means that if $a$ is executed in a state satisfying $g$ then a state satisfying $f$ will be reached.

For planning using heuristic search often a different formulation of regression is given. Since most planning research is about goals that are conjunction of literals, regression is defined with respect to a set of literals and an action. In that case the conjunction of literals (often specifying the goal) denotes a set of states, one of which needs to be reached. This regression is slightly different from $\Psi_2$ as the intention is to regress to another set of literals (not an arbitrary formula), denoting a sub-goal.

With respect to the planning language STRIPS, where each action $a$ has an add list $Add(a)$, a delete list $Del(a)$, and a precondition list $Prec(a)$, the progression function is defined as $Progress(s, a) = s + Add(a) - Del(a)$; and the regression function is defined as $Regress(conj, a) = conj + Prec(a) - Add(a)$, where $conj$ is a set of atoms. The relation between these two, formally proven in (Pednault 1986), shows the correctness of regression based planners; which in recent years through use of heuristics (e.g. (Bonet & Geffner 2001; Nguyen, Kambhampati, & Nigenda 2002)) have done exceedingly well on planning competitions.

*In this paper we are concerned with domains where the agent does not have complete information about the world, and may have sensing actions, which when executed do not change the world, but rather give certain information about the world to the agent.* As a result, plans may now no longer be simply a sequence of (non-sensing) actions but may include sensing actions and conditionals. Various formalisms have been developed for such cases (e.g. (Lobo 1998; Son & Baral 2001)) and progression functions have been defined. Also, the complexity of planning in such cases has been analyzed in (Baral, Kreinovich, & Trejo 2000). One approach to planning in the presence of incomplete information is conformant planning where no sensing action is used, and a plan is a sequence of actions leading to the goal from every possible initial situation. However, this approach proves inadequate for many planning problems (Son & Baral 2001), i.e., there are situations where sensing actions are necessary. In that case, one approach is to use belief states or Kripke models instead of states. It is shown that the total number of belief states is double exponential while the total number of 3-valued states is exponential in the number of fluents (Baral, Kreinovich, & Trejo 2000). Here, we pursue a provably less complex formulation with sensing actions and use 3-valued states. In this approach, we will miss certain plans, but that is the price we are willing to pay for reduced complexity. This is consistent with and similar to the considerations behind conformant planning. With that trade-off in mind, *in this paper we consider the 0-approximation*



[1] Due to space limitation, we do not present the results for non-binary domains here. Interested readers can find such results at http://www.public.asu.edu/~lctuan/TOCL/

*semantics defined in (Son & Baral 2001) and define regression with respect to that semantics.* We then formally relate our definition of regression with the earlier definition of progression in (Son & Baral 2001) and show that planning using our regression function will indeed give us correct plans. We then use our regression function in planning with sensing actions and show that, even without using any heuristics, our planner produces good results. To simplify our formulation, we only consider STRIPS like actions where no conditional effects are allowed.

In summary the main contributions of our paper are:

- A state-based regression function corresponding to the 0-approximation semantics in (Son & Baral 2001);
- A formal result relating the regression function with the progression transition function in (Son & Baral 2001);
- An algorithm that uses these regression functions to construct conditional plans with sensing actions;
- Implementation of this algorithm; and
- Illustration of the performance of this algorithm with respect to several examples in the literature.

**Related Work** Our work in this paper is related to different approaches to regression and planning in the presence of sensing actions and incomplete information. It differs from earlier formula regression such as (Pednault 1994; Reiter 2001; Son & Baral 2001) in that it is a state-based formulation and the other are formula based. Unlike the conditional planners (Peot & Smith 1992; Cimatti, Roveri, & Traverso 1998), our planner can deal with sensing actions similar to the planners in (Etzioni *et al.* 1992; Lobo 1998; Son, Tu, & Baral 2004; Weld, Anderson, & Smith 1998). However, it does not deal with nondeterministic and probabilistic actions such as the planners in (Bonet & Geffner 2001; Pryor & Collins 1996; Rintanen 2000; 2002). It is also not a conformant planner as in (Cimatti, Roveri, & Traverso 1998; Eiter *et al.* 2000). For these reasons, we currently compare our planner with those of (Son, Tu, & Baral 2004; Weld, Anderson, & Smith 1998).

## Background: 0-Approximation Semantics For A STRIPS-like Language

### Action and Plan Representation

We employ a STRIPS-like action representation (Fikes & Nilson 1971) and represent a planning problem by a tuple $P = \langle A, O, I, G\rangle$ where $A$ is a finite set of fluents, $O$ is a finite set of actions, and $I$ and $G$ encode an initial state and a goal state, respectively. A fluent literal is either a positive fluent $f \in A$ or its negation (negative fluent) $\neg f$. In this paper, we are interested in the planning problem in which $I$ and $G$ are sets of fluent literals. An action $a \in O$ is either a *non-sensing action* or a *sensing action* and is specified as follows:

- A non-sensing action $a$ is specified by an expression of the form

  `action` $a$ `:Pre` $Pre_a$ `:Add` $Add_a$ `:Del` $Del_a$

  where $Pre_a$ is a set of fluent literals representing the precondition for $a$'s execution, $Add_a$ and $Del_a$ are two disjoint sets of positive fluents representing the positive and negative effects of $a$, respectively; and
- A sensing action $a$ is specified by an expression of the form

  `action` $a$ `:Pre` $Pre_a$ `:Sense` $Sens_a$

  where $Pre_a$ is a set of fluent literals and $Sens_a$ is a set of positive fluents that do not appear in $Pre_a$.

To illustrate the action representation and our search algorithm, we will use a small example, a version of the "Getting to Evanston" from (Weld, Anderson, & Smith 1998). Figure (1) shows the actions of this domain.

| Non-sensing action | :Pre | :Add | :Del |
|---|---|---|---|
| goto-western-at-belmont | at-start | on-western<br>on-belmont | at-start |
| take-belmont | on-belmont, traffic-bad | on-ashland | on-western |
| take-ashland | on-ashland | at-evanston | |
| take-western | ¬traffic-bad, on-western | at-evanston | |

| Sensing action | :Pre | :Sense |
|---|---|---|
| check-traffic | True | traffic-bad |
| check-on-western | True | on-belmont |

Figure 1: Actions of the "Getting to Evanston" domain

The notion of a plan in the presence of incomplete information and sensing actions has been discussed in the literature (Levesque 1996; Son & Baral 2001). In this paper, we consider *conditional plans* that are formally defined as follows.

**Definition 1 (Conditional Plan)** .

- *An empty sequence of actions, denoted by* [ ], *is a conditional plan.*
- *If* $a$ *is a non-sensing action, then* $a$ *is a conditional plan.*
- *If* $a$ *is a sensing action,* $\varphi_1, \ldots, \varphi_n$ *are mutual exclusive conjunctions of fluent literals, and* $c_1, \ldots, c_n$ *are conditional plans, then so is*
  $$a; case(\varphi_1 \rightarrow c_1, \ldots, \varphi_n \rightarrow c_n).$$
- *if* $c_1, c_2$ *are conditional plans, then so is* $c_1; c_2$.
- *Nothing else is a conditional plan.*

### 0-Approximation

The 0-approximation in (Son & Baral 2001) is defined by a transition function $\Phi$ that maps pairs of actions and approximate states into sets of approximate states. An *approximate state* (or a-state) is a pair $\langle T, F\rangle$ where $T \subseteq A$ and $F \subseteq A$ are two disjoint sets of fluents. Intuitively, given an a-state $\sigma = \langle T, F\rangle$, $T$ (resp. $F$), denoted by $\sigma.T$ (resp. $\sigma.F$), is the set of fluents which are true (resp. false) in $\sigma$; and $f \in A \setminus (T \cup F)$ is unknown in $\sigma$. Alternatively, we can also view an a-state as the intersection of all states in a belief-state. Let $\sigma_1 = \langle T_1, F_1\rangle$ and $\sigma_2 = \langle T_2, F_2\rangle$ be two a-states. $\sigma_1 \cap \sigma_2 = \langle T_1 \cap T_2, F_1 \cap F_2\rangle$ is called the intersection of $\sigma_1$ and $\sigma_2$. We say $\sigma_1$ extends $\sigma_2$, denoted by $\sigma_2 \preceq \sigma_1$ if $T_2 \subseteq T_1$ and $F_2 \subseteq F_1$. $\sigma_1 \setminus \sigma_2$ denotes the set $(T_1 \setminus T_2) \cup (F_1 \setminus F_2)$. For a set of fluents $X$, we write $X \setminus \langle T, F\rangle$ to denote $X \setminus (T \cup F)$. To simplify the presentation, for a set of literals $L$, by $L^+$ and $L^-$ we denote the set of fluents $\{f \mid f \in L,\ f \text{ is a fluent}\}$ and $\{f \mid \neg f \in L,\ f \text{ is a fluent}\}$.

Given a fluent $f$ and an a-state $\sigma = \langle T, F\rangle$, we say that $f$ is true (resp. false) in $\sigma$ if $f \in T$ (resp. $f \in F$). $f$ (resp. $\neg f$) holds in $\sigma$ if $f$ is true (resp. false) in $\sigma$. $f$ is known (resp. unknown) in $\sigma$ if $f \in (T \cup F)$ (resp. $f \notin (T \cup F)$). A set $L$ of fluent literals holds in an a-state $\sigma = \langle T, F\rangle$ if every member of $L$ holds in $\sigma$. A set $X$ of fluents is known in $\sigma$ if every fluent in $X$ is known in $\sigma$. An action $a$ is *executable* in $\sigma$ if $Pre_a$ holds in $\sigma$. The transition function (for progression) is defined next.

**Definition 2 (Transition Function)** *For an a-state $\sigma = \langle T, F\rangle$ and an action a, $\Phi(a, \sigma)$ is defined as follows:*
- *if a is not executable in $\sigma$ then $\Phi(a, \sigma) = \{\bot\}$; and*
- *if a is executable in $\sigma$*
  - *if a is a non-sensing action: $\Phi(a, \sigma) = \{\langle T \setminus Del_a \cup Add_a, F \setminus Add_a \cup Del_a\rangle\}$;*
  - *if a is a sensing action: $\Phi(a, \sigma) = \{\sigma' | \sigma \preceq \sigma'$ and $Sens_a \setminus \sigma = \sigma' \setminus \sigma\}$.*

The function $\Phi$ can be extended to define the function $\Phi^*$ that maps each pair of a conditional plan $p$ and a-states $\sigma$ into a set of a-states, denoted by $\Phi^*(p, \sigma)$. Intuitively, $\Phi^*(p, \sigma)$ is the set of final a-states resulting from the execution of $p$ in $\sigma$. $\Phi^*$ is defined similarly to $\hat{\Phi}$ in (Son & Baral 2001).

Given a planning problem $P = \langle A, O, I, G\rangle$, the a-state representing $I$ is defined by $\sigma_I = \langle I^+ \cap A, I^- \cap A\rangle$. $\Sigma_G = \{\sigma \mid \sigma_G \preceq \sigma\}$, where $\sigma_G = \langle G^+ \cap A, G^- \cap A\rangle$, is the set of a-states satisfying the goal $G$. A *progression solution* to the planning problem $P$ is a conditional plan $p$ such that $\bot \notin \Phi^*(p, \sigma_I)$ and $\Phi^*(p, \sigma_I) \subseteq \Sigma_G$.

## Regression and Its Relation with Progression

In this section, we will present our formalization of a regression function, denoted by $Regress$, and prove its correctness. $Regress$ is a state-based regression function that maps a pair of an action and a set of a-states into an a-state. For this we introduce the notion of a *partial state* (or p-state) as a pair $[T, F]$ where $T$ and $F$ are two disjoint sets of fluents. Intuitively, a p-state $\delta{=}[T, F]$ represents a collection of a-states which extends the a-state $\langle T, F\rangle$. We denote this set by $ext(\delta)$ and call it *the extension set* of $\delta$. Formally, $ext(\delta) = \{\langle T', F'\rangle | T \subseteq T', F \subseteq F'\}$. $\sigma' \in ext(\delta)$ is called an extension of $\delta$. Given a p-state $\delta{=}[T, F]$, we say a p-state $\delta'{=}[T', F']$ is a partial extension of $\delta$ if $T \subseteq T', F \subseteq F'$.

The regression function will be defined separately for non-sensing actions and sensing actions. Since the application of a non-sensing action in an a-state results in a single a-state, the regression of a non-sensing action from a p-state should result into a p-state. On the other hand, as application of a sensing action in an a-state results in a set of a-states, the regression of a sensing action should start from a set of p-states and result into a p-state. Besides the regression should be sound (i.e., plans obtained through regression must be plans based on the progression) and complete (i.e., for each plan based on progression,using regression one should obtain that plan or an equivalent one) with respect to progression. To simplify the presentation, we define a partition of a set of fluents $X$ as a pair $(P, Q)$ such that $P \cap Q = \emptyset$ and $P \cup Q = X$. We begin with the applicability condition of non-sensing actions and then give the definition of their function $Regress$.

**Definition 3 (Applicability Condition - non-sensing action)** *Given a p-state $\delta = [T, F]$ and a non-sensing action a. We say that a is* applicable *in $\delta$ if (i) $Add_a \cap T \neq \emptyset$ or $Del_a \cap F \neq \emptyset$, and (ii) $Add_a \cap F = \emptyset$, $Del_a \cap T = \emptyset$, $Pre^+_a \cap F \subseteq Del_a$, and $Pre^-_a \cap T \subseteq Add_a$.*

The regression on a non-sensing action is defined next.

**Definition 4 (Regression - non-sensing action)** *Given a p-state $\delta = [T, F]$ and a non-sensing action a,*
- *if a is not applicable in $\delta$ then $Regress(a, \delta) = \bot$;*
- *if a is applicable in $\delta$ then $Regress(a, \delta) = [T \setminus Add_a \cup Pre^+_a, F \setminus Del_a \cup Pre^-_a]$.*

The regression function $Regress$ for non-sensing actions with respect to a set of p-states is defined as follows. $Regress(a, \{\delta_1, \ldots, \delta_n\}) = \{Regress(a, \delta_1), \ldots, Regress(a, \delta_n)\}$ where $\delta_1, \ldots, \delta_n$ are p-states and $a$ is a non-sensing action.

**Example 1 (Getting to Evanston - con't)** *The actions take_western and take_ashland are applicable in $\delta_0 = [\{$at-evanston$\}, \{\}]$. We have Regress(take_western, $\delta_0$) $= [\{$on-western$\}, \{$traffic-bad $\}]$ and Regress(take_ashland, $\delta_0$) $=$ $[\{$on-ashland$\}, \{\}]$*

We will now define $Regress$ for sensing actions. Recall that the execution of a sensing action $a$ in an a-state $\sigma$ requires that $a$ is executable in $\sigma$ and results in a set of a-states $\Phi(a, \sigma)$ whose member extends $\sigma$ by the set of fluents in $s_a \subseteq Sens_a$ and every $f \in Sens_a \setminus s_a$ holds in $\sigma$. This leads to the following definitions.

**Definition 5 (Properness)** *Let a be a sensing action, $\Delta = \{\delta_1, \ldots, \delta_n\}$ be a set of distinct p-states, and $\emptyset \neq X \subseteq Sens_a$ be a set of sensing fluents. We say that $\Delta$ is proper w.r.t X if (i) $Sens_a$ is known in $\Delta$; (ii) $n = 2^{|X|}$; (iii) for every partition $(P, Q)$ of X, there exists only one $\delta_i \in \Delta$ $(1 \leq i \leq n)$ s.t. $\delta_i.T \cap X = P$, $\delta_i.F \cap X = Q$; and (iv) for every $(1 \leq i \neq j \leq n)$, $\delta_i.T \setminus X = \delta_j.T \setminus X$, $\delta_i.F \setminus X = \delta_j.F \setminus X$. We call X a sensed set of $\Delta$ w.r.t a.*

**Lemma 1 (Sensed Set)** *Consider a sensing action a and a set of p-states $\Delta$. If there exists a sensed set of $\Delta$ w.r.t a then it is unique.*

Given a sensing action $a$ and a set of p-states $\Delta$, we denote $p(a, \Delta)$ as the unique sensed set of $\Delta$ w.r.t $a$; if there exists no sensed set w.r.t $a$ and $\Delta$, we write $p(a, \Delta) = \bot$.

**Definition 6 (Strong Applicability Condition - sensing action)** *Let a be a sensing action and $\Delta = \{\delta_1, \ldots, \delta_n\}$ be a set of p-states. We say that a is* strongly applicable *in $\Delta$ if (i) $p(a, \Delta) \neq \bot$; and (ii) $Pre^+_a \cap \delta_i.F = \emptyset$ and $Pre^-_a \cap \delta_i.T = \emptyset$.*

In the above definition, (i) corresponds to the fact that executing a sensing action $a$ in an a-state $\sigma$ results in a set of $2^{|p(a,\Delta)|}$ a-states that are represented by $2^{|p(a,\Delta)|}$ corresponding p-states of $\Delta$ where $p(a, \Delta)$ denotes the set of fluents that are not yet known, while $Sens_a \setminus p(a, \Delta)$ is already known when $a$ is executed; (ii) guarantees that $a$ must be executable prior to its execution.

Although this strong applicability condition guarantees the soundness of regression over sensing actions, it does not guarantee the completeness. We now provide a weaker applicability condition that guarantees both soundness and completeness of regression.

**Definition 7 (Applicability Condition - sensing action)** *Let $a$ be a sensing action and $\Delta = \{\delta_1, \ldots, \delta_n\}$ be a set of p-states. We say that $a$ is* applicable *in $\Delta$ if (i) there exists a set $\Delta'=\{\delta'_1, \ldots, \delta'_n\}$, where $\delta'_i$ is a partial extension of $\delta_i$ ($i = 1, \ldots, n$), such that $a$ is strongly applicable in $\Delta'$; and (ii) $Sens_a$ is known in $\Delta$.*

**Lemma 2 (Unique Sensed Set)** *Consider a sensing action $a$ and a set of p-states $\Delta$ such that $a$ is applicable in $\Delta$. Let $\Delta'=\{\delta'_1, \ldots, \delta'_n\}$, where $\delta'_i$ is a partial extension of $\delta_i$ ($i = 1, \ldots, n$), $\Delta''=\{\delta_1'', \ldots, \delta_n''\}$, where $\delta_i''$ is a partial extension of $\delta_i$ ($i = 1, \ldots, n$). If $p(a, \Delta') \neq \bot$ and $p(a, \Delta'') \neq \bot$ then $p(a, \Delta') = p(a, \Delta'')$.*

Given a sensing action $a$ and a set of p-states $\Delta$. If there exists a $\Delta'=\{\delta'_1, \ldots, \delta'_n\}$, where $\delta'_i$ is a partial extension of $\delta_i$ ($i = 1, \ldots, n$) such that $p(a, \Delta') \neq \bot$ then, by Lemma 2, $p(a, \Delta') = p(a, \Delta'')$ for all $\Delta'' = \{\delta_1'', \ldots, \delta_n''\}$, where $\delta_i''$ is a partial extension of $\delta_i$ ($i = 1, \ldots, n$) and $p(a, \Delta'') \neq \bot$. We refer to the set $p(a, \Delta')$ by $S_{a,\Delta}$. If there exists no such $p(a, \Delta')$, we write $S_{a,\Delta} = \bot$. Note that, from Definition 7, if $a$ is applicable in $\Delta$ then $S_{a,\Delta}$ is defined. In that case, we also often say that $a$ is applicable in $\Delta$ w.r.t $S_{a,\Delta}$ to make the applicability condition clearer from the context.

**Definition 8 (Regression - sensing action)** *Let $a$ be a sensing action and $\Delta = \{\delta_1, \ldots, \delta_n\}$ be a set of p-states.*

- *if $a$ is not applicable in $\Delta$, then $Regress(a, \Delta) = \bot$;*
- *if $a$ is applicable in $\Delta$, then $Regress(a, \Delta) =$ $[(\bigcup_{i=1}^n \delta_i.T) \setminus S_{a,\Delta} \cup Pre_a^+, (\bigcup_{i=1}^n \delta_i.F) \setminus S_{a,\Delta} \cup Pre_a^-]$.*

**Example 2 (Getting to Evanston - con't)** *Let $\Delta=\{\delta_1, \delta_2\}$ where $\delta_1$ = [{at-start, traffic-bad}, {on-western, on-belmont, on-ashland, at-evanston }] and $\delta_2$ = [{at-start}, {traffic-bad, at-evanston}].*

*We have that check-traffic is applicable in $\Delta$ w.r.t {traffic-bad} and that $Regress$(check-traffic, $\Delta$) = [{at-start)}, {on-western, on-belmont, on-ashland, at-evanston}].*

We now relate our regression function $Regress$ with the progression function $\Phi$.

**Proposition 1 (Non-sensing action)** *Let $\delta$ and $\delta'$ be p-states, let $a$ be a non-sensing action. If $Regress(a, \delta) = \delta'$ where $\delta' \neq \bot$, then for every $\sigma'' \in ext(\delta')$ we have that (i) $\bot \notin \Phi(a, \sigma'')$, and (ii) $\Phi(a, \sigma'') \subseteq ext(\delta)$.*

**Proposition 2 (Sensing action)** *Let $\Delta = \{\delta_1, \ldots, \delta_n\}$ be a set of p-states, $\delta'$ be a p-state, and $a$ be a sensing action. If $Regress(a, \Delta) = \delta'$ where $\delta' \neq \bot$, then for every $\sigma'' \in ext(\delta')$, we have that (i) $\bot \notin \Phi(a, \sigma'')$, and (ii) $\Phi(a, \sigma'') \subseteq ext(\delta_1) \cup \ldots \cup ext(\delta_n)$.*

We next extend $Regress$ to define $Regress^*$ that allows us to perform regression with respect to conditional plans.

**Definition 9 (Extended Regression Function)** *Let $\delta$ and $\{\delta_1, \ldots, \delta_n\}$ be a p-state and a set of p-states, respectively. The extended transition function $Regress^*$ is defined as follows:*

- *$Regress^*([\,], \delta) = \delta$;*
- *For a non-sensing action $a$, $Regress^*(a, \delta) = Regress(a, \delta)$;*
- *For a conditional plan $p = a; case(\varphi_1 \rightarrow c_1, \ldots, \varphi_n \rightarrow c_n)$,*
  - *if $Regress^*(c_i, \delta) = \bot$ for some $i$, $Regress^*(p, \delta) = \bot$*
  - *if $Regress^*(c_i, \delta) = [T_i, F_i]$ $i = 1, \ldots, n$, then $Regress^*(p, \delta) = Regress(a, \{R(c_1, \delta), \ldots, R(c_n, \delta)\})$ where $R(c_i, \delta) = [T_i \cup \varphi_i^+, F_i \cup \varphi_i^-]$ if $\varphi_i^+ \cap F_i = \emptyset$ and $\varphi_i^- \cap T_i = \emptyset$; otherwise, $R(c_i, \delta) = \bot$. Here, $\varphi_i^+$ and $\varphi_i^-$ denote the sets of fluents occurring positively and negatively in $\varphi_i$, respectively;*
- *For $p = c_1; c_2$, where $c_1, c_2$ are conditional plans, $Regress^*(p, \delta) = Regress^*(c_1, Regress^*(c_2, \delta))$; and*
- *$Regress^*(p, \bot) = \bot$ for every plan $p$.*

For a planning problem $P = \langle A, O, I, G \rangle$, let $\delta_G$ be the p-state $[G^+ \cap A, G^- \cap A]$, and $\Delta_I$ be the set of p-states such that for every $\delta \in \Delta_I$, $\sigma_I \in ext(\delta)$. (Recall that $\sigma_I$ is the a-state representing $I$ and $\Sigma_G$ is the set of a-states in which $G$ holds). A *regression solution* to the planning problem $P$ is a conditional plan $c$ that upon applying from the p-state $\delta_G$ will result to one of the p-states in $\Delta_I$. In other words, if $\bot \neq \delta = Regress^*(c, \delta_G)$ then $\delta$ is a p-state belonging to $\Delta_I$.

We now formalize the soundness of the regression solution with respect to the progression transition function $\Phi^*$.

**Theorem 3 (Soundness of Regression)** *For a planning problem $P = \langle A, O, I, G \rangle$ and a regression solution $p$ of $P$, then $\bot \notin \Phi^*(p, \sigma_I)$ and $\Phi^*(p, \sigma_I) \subseteq ext(\delta_G)$.*

We now proceed towards a completeness result. Intuitively our completeness result states that if a conditional plan can be found through progression we can also find a conditional plan through regression. The plan found through regression may not be the same one though. It will be one which does not have redundancies, both in terms of extra actions and extra branches. We now formalize these conditions. First we need the following notions. Given a sensing action $a$, a sub sensing action of $a$ is a sensing action $a'$ where $Pre_{a'} = Pre_a$ and $Sens_{a'} \subset Sens_a$.

**Definition 10 (Sub-plan)** *Let $c$ be a conditional plan. A conditional plan $c'$ is a sub-plan of $c$ if*

- *$c'$ can be obtained from $c$ by (i) removing an instance of a non-sensing action from $c$; (ii) replacing a sensing action $a$ with a sub sensing action $subSense(a)$ of $a$; or (iii) removing a case plan or a branch $\varphi_i \rightarrow c_i$ from a case plan in $c$; or*
- *$c'$ is a sub-plan of $c''$ where $c''$ is a sub-plan of $c$.*

**Definition 11 (Redundancy)** *Let $c$ be a conditional plan, $\sigma$ be an a-state, and $\delta$ be a p-state. We say that $c$ contains redundancy w.r.t $(\sigma, \delta)$ if*

- *$\bot \notin \Phi^*(c, \sigma)$ and $\Phi^*(c, \sigma) \subseteq ext(\delta)$; and*
- *there exists a sub-plan $c'$ of $c$ such that $\bot \notin \Phi^*(c', \sigma)$ and $\Phi^*(c', \sigma) \subseteq ext(\delta)$.*

For a non-empty set of fluents $S = \{f_1, ..., f_k\}$, a binary representation of $S$ is a formula of the form $l_1 \wedge \ldots \wedge l_k$ where $l_i \in \{f_i, \neg f_i\}$ for $i = 1, \ldots, k$. For a non-empty set of fluents $S$, let us denote $BIN(S)$ as the set of all different binary representations of $S$. We say a conjunction $\phi$ of literals is consistent if there exists no fluent $f$ such that $f$ and

$\neg f$ appear in $\phi$. A set of consistent conjunctions of literals $\chi = \{\varphi_1, \ldots, \varphi_n\}$ is said to span over $S$ if there exists a consistent conjunction of literals $\varphi \notin \chi$, such that:

1. $S \cap (\varphi^+ \cup \varphi^-) = \emptyset$ where $\varphi^+$ (resp. $\varphi^-$) denote the sets of fluents occurring positively (resp. negatively) in $\varphi$;
2. $\varphi_i = \varphi \wedge \psi_i$ where $BIN(S) = \{\psi_1, \ldots, \psi_n\}$.

We say that a set $\chi = \{\varphi_1, \ldots, \varphi_n\}$ is factorable if it spans over some non-empty set of fluents $S$.

**Lemma 4** *Let $\chi = \{\varphi_1, \ldots, \varphi_n\}$ be a non-empty set of consistent conjunctions of literals. If $\chi$ is factorable, then there exists a unique non-empty set of fluents $S$ such that $\chi$ spans over $S$.*

**Definition 12 (Possibly Regressable Case Plan)** *Given a case plan $p = a; case(\varphi_1 \rightarrow c_1, \ldots, \varphi_n \rightarrow c_n)$. We say that p is possibly regressable if (i) there exists a non-empty set $\emptyset \neq S_a \subseteq Sens_a$ and $\{\varphi_1, \ldots, \varphi_n\}$ spans over $S_a$, and (ii) for $1 \leq i \leq n$ $Sens_a \subseteq (\varphi_i^+ \cup \varphi_i^-)$.*

**Definition 13 (Possibly Regressable Conditional Plan)** *A conditional plan c is possibly regressable if every case plan occurring in c is possibly regressable.*

We now formulate the completeness result for regressable conditional plans that have no redundancy.

**Theorem 5 (Completeness of Regression)** *Let $P = \langle A, O, I, G\rangle$ be a planning problem. If c is a progression solution which is a possibly regressable conditional plan without redundancy w.r.t $(\sigma_I, \delta_G)$ then c is also a regression solution of P.*

We now present an algorithm that uses these regression functions to construct conditional plans with sensing actions.

## Conditional Planning Using Regression

In this section, we present a regression search algorithm for constructing conditional plans with sensing actions that makes use of the $Regress$ function described in the previous section. For a conditional plan $c$ and a p-state $\delta$, we call the pair $\langle c, \delta\rangle$ and *r-state*. For a set of r-states $X$, by $X_s$ we denote the set of all the p-states occurring in $X$. The main idea of the algorithm is as follows. At any step, we will maintain a set $N$ of r-states $\langle c, \delta\rangle$ such that $\delta = Regress^*(c, \delta_G)$. We print a solution if we find a r-state $\langle c, \delta\rangle \in N$ such that $\sigma_I \in ext(\delta)$ since $c$ would be one solution (Theorem 3). Otherwise, we regress from $N_s$ (the set of all the p-states occurring in $N$). This process involves the regression using non-sensing actions and sensing actions which are applicable in $N_s$. The algorithm will stop with failure if (i) we cannot regress from any p-state (or a set of p-states) in $N_s$; or (ii) no new p-state can be added to $N_s$. Below, we list the main steps of the algorithm:

Solve(P) where $P = \langle A, O, I, G\rangle$

1. Let $N = \{\langle [], \delta_G\rangle\}$ $(N_s = \{\delta_G\})$.
2. **Repeat**
3. If there exists some $\langle c, \delta\rangle \in N$ s.t. $\sigma_I \in ext(\delta)$ then prints $c$ as a solution.
4. Do one of the following:
   - **4.1** Find a $\langle c, \delta\rangle \in N$, a non-sensing action $a$ s.t. $a$ is applicable in $\delta$ and $\delta' = Regress(a, \delta) \notin N_s$. Add $\langle a; c, \delta'\rangle$ to $N$.
   - **4.2** Find a set $\Delta = \{\langle c_1, \delta_1\rangle, \ldots, \langle c_n, \delta_n\rangle\} \subseteq N$ and a sensing action $a$ such that $a$ is applicable in $\Delta_s$ w.r.t some $\emptyset \neq S_a \subseteq Sens_a$, i.e.: (i) $Sens_a$ is known in $\Delta_s$ and there exists a set $S_a = \{f_1, \ldots, f_k\} \subseteq Sens_a$, $2^k = n$; (ii) there exists an ordering of the set of conjunctions constructed using literals out of $S_a$, $\{\varphi_1, \ldots, \varphi_{2^k}\}$, such that $\varphi_i$ holds in $\delta_i'$ where $\delta_i'$ is a partial extension of $\delta_i$ and $a$ is strongly applicable in $\Delta' = \{\delta_1', \ldots, \delta_n'\}$ w.r.t $S_a$. If $\delta'{=}Regress(a, \Delta_s){\notin}N_s$, add $\langle a; case(\varphi_1{\rightarrow}c_1, \ldots, \varphi_n{\rightarrow}c_n), \delta'\rangle$ to $N$.
5. **Until** $N$ does not change.
6. Return NO SOLUTION.

Below, we demonstrate how our algorithm works.

**Example 3 (Getting to Evanston - con't)** *We have that $G = \{$ at-evanston$\}$ and the initial condition $I = \{$ at-start, $\neg$ on-western, $\neg$ on-belmont, $\neg$ on-ashland, $\neg$ at-evanston, $\}$. So, $\delta_G$ = [{ at-evanston }, {}]. The algorithm goes through the iterations (#I) in Figure (2).*

| #I | Action (a) | Regressed-from member of N |
|---|---|---|
| 0 | | $\langle [], \delta_G\rangle$ |
| 1 | $a_1$ =take-ashland | $\langle [], \delta_G\rangle$ |
| 2 | $b_1$ =take-western | $\langle [], \delta_G\rangle$ |
| 3 | $a_2$ =take-belmont | $\langle a_1, \delta 1_1\rangle$ |
| 4 | $b_2$ =goto-western-at-belmont | $\langle b_1, \delta 2_1\rangle$ |
| 5 | $a_3$ =goto-western-at-belmont | $\langle a_2; a_1, \delta 1_2\rangle$ |
| 6 | check-traffic | $\langle a_3; a_2; a_1, \delta 1_3\rangle$, $\langle b_2; b_1, \delta 2_2\rangle$ |

| #I | $Regress(a, \delta)$/$Regress(a, \Delta)$ | New member of N |
|---|---|---|
| 0 | | |
| 1 | $\delta 1_1$ = [{on-ashland}, {}] | $\langle a_1, \delta 1_1\rangle$ |
| 2 | $\delta 2_1$ = [{on-western}, {traffic-bad}] | $\langle b_1, \delta 2_1\rangle$ |
| 3 | $\delta 1_2$ = [{on-belmont, traffic-bad}, {}] | $\langle a_2; a_1, \delta 1_2\rangle$ |
| 4 | $\delta 2_2$ = [{at-start}, {traffic-bad}] | $\langle b_2; b_1, \delta 2_2\rangle$ |
| 5 | $\delta 1_3$ = [{at-start,traffic-bad}, {}] | $\langle a_3; a_2; a_1, \delta 1_3\rangle$ |
| 6 | $\delta 1_4$ = [{at-start}, {}] | $\langle p, \delta 1_4\rangle$ |

*where $\Delta = \{\delta_1, \ldots, \delta_n\}$ and $p = check\text{-}traffic; case(traffic\text{-}bad \rightarrow a_3; a_2; a_1, \neg\, traffic\text{-}bad \rightarrow b_2; b_1)$.*

Figure 2: Algorithm illustration

The following theorem establishes the correctness of our algorithm.

**Theorem 6** *For every $\langle c, \delta\rangle \in N$ where $N$ represents the search space of the planning algorithm, then $Regress^*(c, \delta_G) = \delta$.*

Since the algorithm search through all possible regression path, we have the following theorem.

**Theorem 7** *For a planning problem $P = \langle A, O, I, G\rangle$,*

- *if P has a regression solution then* **Solve**$(P)$ *will return a conditional plan; and*
- *if P has no regression solution then* **Solve**$(P)$ *will return NO SOLUTION.*

## Experimentation

We have experimentally compared our system with the two systems (Weld, Anderson, & Smith 1998; Son, Tu, & Baral 2004) in domains with *sensing actions and incomplete information* but did not compare our planner with (Pryor & Collins 1996) since the planner in (Weld, Anderson, & Smith 1998) is significantly better than that of (Pryor & Collins 1996). We also did not compare our system with others that deal with nondeterministic or probabilistic actions as our action representation does not have this capability.

We run our Java-based planner with three well known *domains with sensing actions: Cassandra, Bomb in the toilet, and Sickness domain.* These domains are obtained from the SGP distribution (Weld, Anderson, & Smith 1998). All experiments are run on a Compaq laptop 1.8Ghz CPU with 512 MbRAM. The experimental result (obtained without using heuristics) is presented in Figure (4). It is necessary to note that, Figure (4) is a crude comparison as the other two use static causal laws and boolean sensing fluents (e.g. in Bomb in the toilet domain) while ours uses multi-valued sensing fluents; and the Logic Programming based planner ($\pi(P)$) uses conditional effects but ours does not.

| Domains/ Problem | | aSense | | | $\pi(P)$ | SGP |
|---|---|---|---|---|---|---|
| | | preprocessing | search | total | | |
| **Cassandra** | a1-prob | 50 | 10 | **60** | 510 | 130 |
| | a2-prob | 50 | 10 | **60** | 891 | 60 |
| | a3-prob | 70 | 0 | **70** | 119 | 70 |
| | a4-prob | 60 | 220 | **280** | 1030 | 431 |
| | a5-prob | 30 | 10 | **40** | 130 | 20 |
| | a6-prob | 200 | 1392 | **1592** | 18036 | NA [2] |
| | a7-prob | 40 | 10 | **50** | 150 | 110 |
| **Bomb** | bt-1sa | 40 | 0 | **40** | 15812 | 751 |
| | bt-2sa | 40 | 10 | **50** | 18676 | 1161 |
| | bt-3sa | 40 | 10 | **50** | 18445 | 1512 |
| | bt-4sa | 200 | 10 | **210** | 22391 | 1892 |

Figure 4: Performance comparison (time in milliseconds).

## Conclusion and Future Work

In this paper, we used the 0-approximation semantics (Son & Baral 2001) and defined regression with respect to that semantics. We considered domains where an agent does not have complete information about the world, and may have sensing actions. We first started with domains having only Boolean fluents and formally related our definition of regression with the earlier definition of progression in (Son & Baral 2001). We showed that planning using our regression function would indeed give us correct plans. We then presented a search algorithm for generating conditional plans. Lastly, we presented preliminary experimental results and discussed difficulties we faced as well as future enhancements. To simplify our formulation, we used the STRIPS-like action representation and considered fluents with finite domains.

Our planner is sound, however the use of 0-approximation leads to its incompleteness w.r.t. the full semantics [3]. This is a trade-off to counter the higher complexity thus leading to the efficiency of search for plans. Other limitations due to state space regression are difficulties in handling static causal laws and conditional effects. To further improve the search efficiency, we have derived several heuristics by extending the work of (Bonet & Geffner 2001) to handle sensing actions. However, due to the space limitation, we do not present them here. We will include them in the full paper. An issue that needs to be addressed in the future is to find sufficiency conditions that would guarantee the completeness of our approach with respect to the full semantics. We also need to directly consider actions with conditional effects, nondeterministic actions, and static causal laws and develop regression operators for these cases.

[3]Note that 0-approximation reduces the complexity of the planning problem to $NP$

## Acknowledgement

This work was supported by NSF grant number 0070463 and NASA grant number NCC2-1232. Tran Cao Son was supported by NSF grants EIA-0130887 and EIA-0220590.

## References

Baral, C.; Kreinovich, V.; and Trejo, R. 2000. Computational complexity of planning and approximate planning in the presence of incompleteness. *AI-00* 122:241–267.

B. Bonet and H. Geffner. Planning with Incomplete Information as Heuristic Search in Belief Space AIPS-00, 52-61, 2000.

Bonet, B., and Geffner, H. 2001. Planning As Heuristic Search. *Artificial Intelligence* 129:5–33.

Cimatti, A.; Roveri, M.; and Traverso, P. 1998. Automatic OBDD-based Generation of Universal Plans in Non-Deterministic. AAAI-98, 875–891.

T. Eiter; W. Faber; N. Leone; G. Pfeifer; and A. Polleres. 2000. Planning under incomplete information. CL-2000, 807–821.

Etzioni, O.; Hanks, S.; Weld, D.; Draper, D.; Lesh, N.; and Williamson, M. 1992. An approach to planning with incomplete information. KR-92, 115–125.

Fikes, R., and Nilson, N. 1971. STRIPS: A new approach to the application of theorem proving to problem solving. *AI-71*.

Goldman, R., and Boddy, M. 1994. Conditional linear planning. Planning AIPS-94.

Levesque, H. 1996. What is planning in the presence of sensing. AAAI-96.

Lobo, J. 1998. COPLAS: a COnditional PLAnner with Sensing actions. Technical Report FS-98-02, AAAI.

Nguyen, X.L; Kambhampati, S., and Nigenda, R. 2002. Planning graph as the basis for deriving heuristics for plan synthesis by state space and CSP search. AIJ, 135(1-2):73–123.

Pednault, E. 1986. *Toward a Mathematical Theory of Plan Synthesis*. Ph.D. Dissertation.

Pednault, E. 1994. ADL and the state-transition model of actions. *Journal of Logic and Computation* 4(5):467–513.

Peot, M., and Smith, D. 1992. Conditional Nonlinear Planning. AIPS-92, 189–197.

Pryor, L., and Collins, G. 1996. Planning for contingencies: A decision-based approach. *JAIR-96*, 4:287–339.

Reiter, R. *KNOWLEDGE IN ACTION: Logical Foundations for Describing and Implementing Dynamical Systems*. MIT Press.

Rintanen, J. 2000. Constructing conditional plans by a theorem prover. *Journal of Artificial Intelligence Research* 10:323–352.

Rintanen, J. 2002. Backward Plan Construction for Planning with Partial Observability. Planning AIPS'02.

Scherl, R., and Levesque, H. 1993. The frame problem and knowledge producing actions. Artificial AAAI-93, 689–695.

Scherl, R., and Levesque, H. 2003. Knowledge, Action, and the Frame Problem. *Artificial Intelligence* 144(1-2).

Son, T., and Baral, C. 2001. Formalizing sensing actions - a transition function based approach. AIJ, 125(1-2):19–91.

Son, T.; Tu, P.; and Baral, C. 2004. Planning with Sensing Actions and Incomplete Information using Logic Programming. Logic LPNMR'04, 261–274.

Weld, D.; Anderson, C.; and Smith, D. 1998. Extending graphplan to handle uncertainity and sensing actions. AAAI 98.

# Effective Approaches for Partial Satisfaction (Over-Subscription) Planning

**Menkes van den Briel, Romeo Sanchez, Minh B. Do, and Subbarao Kambhampati***
Department of Computer Science and Engineering
Arizona State University, Tempe AZ, 85287-5406
{menkes, rsanchez, binhminh, rao}@asu.edu

## Abstract

In many real world planning scenarios, agents often do not have enough resources to achieve all of their goals. Consequently, they are forced to find plans that satisfy only a subset of the goals. Solving such partial satisfaction planning (PSP) problems poses several challenges, including an increased emphasis on modeling and handling plan quality (in terms of action costs and goal utilities). Despite the ubiquity of such PSP problems, very little attention has been paid to them in the planning community. In this paper, we start by describing a spectrum of PSP problems and focus on one of the more general PSP problems, termed PSP NET BENEFIT. We develop three techniques, (i) one based on integer programming, called *OptiPlan*, (ii) the second based on regression planning with reachability heuristics, called *AltAlt*$^{ps}$ , and (iii) the third based on anytime heuristic search for a forward state-space heuristic planner, called *Sapa*$^{ps}$ . Our empirical studies with these planners show that the heuristic planners generate plans that are comparable to the quality of plans generated by *OptiPlan*, while incurring only a small fraction of the cost.

## Introduction

In classical planning the aim is to find a sequence of actions that transforms a given initial state $I$ to some goal state $G$, where $G = g_1 \wedge g_2 \wedge ... \wedge g_n$ is a conjunctive list of goal fluents. Plan success for these planning problems is measured in terms of whether or not all the conjuncts in $G$ are achieved. In many real world scenarios, however, the agent may only be able to satisfy a subset of the goals. The need for such partial satisfaction might arise in some cases because the set of goal conjuncts may contain logically conflicting fluents, and in other cases there might just not be enough time or resources to achieve all of the goal conjuncts. Effective handling of partial satisfaction planning (PSP) problems poses several challenges, including an added emphasis on the need to differentiate between feasible and optimal plans. Indeed, for many classes of PSP problems, a trivially feasible, but decidedly non-optimal solution would be the "null" plan.

Despite the ubiquity of PSP problems, surprisingly little attention has been paid to the development of effective approaches in solving them. In this paper, we provide a systematic analysis of PSP problems. We will start by distinguishing several classes of PSP problems, and then focus on one of the more general classes, PSP NET BENEFIT. In this class, each goal conjunct has a fixed utility assigned to it, and each ground action has a fixed cost associated with it. The objective is to find a plan with the best *net benefit* (cumulative utility minus cumulative cost).

We investigate three customized algorithms for solving PSP NET BENEFIT. The first, called "*OptiPlan*", solves the problem by encoding it as an integer program (IP). *OptiPlan* builds on the work of solving planning problems through IP (Vossen *et al*, 1999), and uses a more involved objective function that directly captures the net benefit. The second and third approaches, called "*AltAlt*$^{ps}$ " and "*Sapa*$^{ps}$ ", model PSP in terms of heuristic search with cost-sensitive reachability heuristics. *AltAlt*$^{ps}$ builds on the AltAlt family of planners (Nguyen *et al*, 2001; Sanchez & Kambhampati 2003) that derive reachability heuristics from planning graphs. The main extension in *AltAlt*$^{ps}$ involves a novel approach for heuristically selecting upfront a subset of goal conjuncts that is likely to be most useful. Once a subset of goal conjuncts is selected, they are solved by a regression search planner with cost sensitive heuristics. *Sapa*$^{ps}$ is an extension of the forward state-space planner *Sapa* (Do & Kambhampati 2003). Unlike *AltAlt*$^{ps}$ , *Sapa*$^{ps}$ does not select a subset of goals up front but uses an anytime heuristic search framework in which goals are treated as "soft constraints". Any executable plan is considered a potential solution, with the quality of the plan measured in terms of its net benefit. The objective of the search is to find the plan with the highest net benefit. *Sapa*$^{ps}$ uses novel ways of estimating the $g$ and $h$ values of partial solutions, and uses them to guide an anytime A* search.

*OptiPlan* generates plans that are optimal for a given plan length. *Sapa*$^{ps}$ and *AltAlt*$^{ps}$ , while capable of generating globally optimal plans[1], focus on effective but inadmissible

*This paper is the result of merging two separate efforts–one on *OptiPlan* and *AltAlt*$^{ps}$ , and the other on *Sapa*$^{ps}$ . Authors names are listed in the reverse order of seniority. We thank Will Cushing, David Smith and the AAAI reviewers for many helpful comments. This research is supported in part by the NSF grant IIS-0308139 and the NASA grants NCC2-1225 and NAG2-1461.


[1]In theory, both *AltAlt*$^{ps}$ and *Sapa*$^{ps}$ can be made to generate

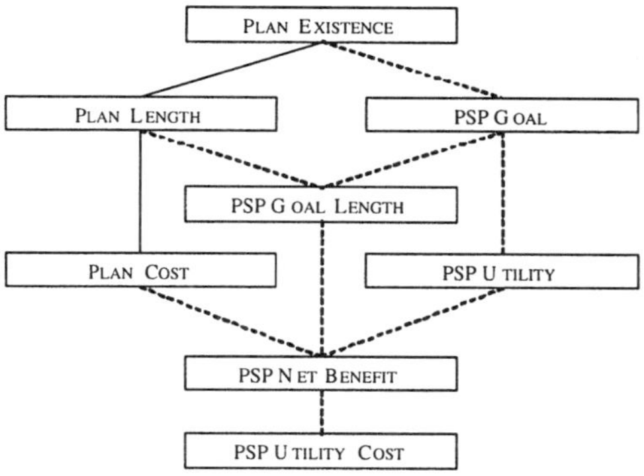


Figure 1: Hierarchical overview of several types of complete and partial satisfaction planning problems

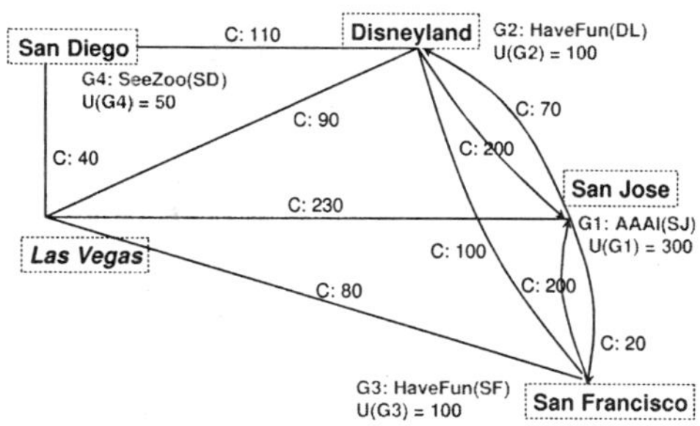


Figure 2: The travel example

heuristics for efficiency. Our empirical studies with these planners demonstrate that the heuristic planners *AltAlt*$^{ps}$ and *Sapa*$^{ps}$ can generate plans that are comparable to the quality of plans generated by *OptiPlan*, while incurring only a small fraction of the cost. The rest of this paper is organized as follows. In the next section, we give a taxonomy of PSP problems and discuss their complexity. In the following section, we describe how PSP problems can be modeled in *OptiPlan* through a more involved objective function. The next part of the paper describes the heuristic approaches for the PSP problem. We start with a discussion of cost-sensitive reachability heuristics, and then describe how they are used in qualitatively different ways in *AltAlt*$^{ps}$ and *Sapa*$^{ps}$. We then present an empirical study that compares the effectiveness of the various approaches. We will end with a discussion of the related work and conclusions.

## Definition and complexity

The following notation will be used: $F$ is a finite set of fluents and $A$ is a finite set of actions, where each action consists of a list of preconditions and a list of add and delete effects. $I \subseteq F$ is the set of fluents describing the initial state and $G \subseteq F$ is the set of goal conjuncts. Hence we define a planning problem as a tuple $P = (F, A, I, G)$. Having defined a planning problem we can now describe the following classical planning decision problems.

The problems of PLAN EXISTENCE and PLAN LENGTH represent the decision problems of plan existence and bounded plan existence respectively. They are probably the most common planning problems studied in the literature. We could say that PLAN EXISTENCE is the problem of deciding whether there exists a sequence of actions that transforms $I$ into $G$, and PLAN LENGTH is the decision problem that corresponds to the optimization problem of finding a minimum sequence of action that transforms $I$ into $G$.

The PSP counterparts of PLAN EXISTENCE and PLAN LENGTH are PSP GOAL and PSP GOAL LENGTH respectively. Both of these decision problems require a minimum number of goals that need to be satisfied for plan success.

Figure 1 gives a taxonomic overview of several types of complete (planning problems that require all goals to be satisfied) and partial satisfaction problems, with the most general problems listed below. Complete satisfaction problems are identified by names starting with PLAN and partial satisfaction problems have names starting with PSP.

Some of the problems given in Figure 1 involve action costs and/or goal utilities. Basically, PLAN COST corresponds to the optimization problem of finding minimum cost plans, and PSP UTILITY corresponds to the optimization problem of finding plans that achieve maximum utility. The problems of PSP NET BENEFIT is a combination of PLAN COST and PSP UTILITY, and PSP UTILITY COST is a generalization of PSP NET BENEFIT. Here we will formally define the decision problem of PSP NET BENEFIT and analyze its complexity. The corresponding optimization problem of finding a plan with maximum net benefit is the focus of this paper.

**Definition** PSP NET BENEFIT: Given a planning problem $P = (F, A, I, G)$ and, for each action a "cost" $C_a \geq 0$ and, for each goal specification $f \in G$ a "utility" $U_f \geq 0$, and a positive number $k$. Is there a finite sequence of actions $\Delta = \langle a_1, ..., a_n \rangle$ that starting from $I$ leads to a state $S$ that has net benefit $\sum_{f \in (S \cap G)} U_f - \sum_{a \in \Delta} C_a \geq k$?

**Example:** Figure 2 illustrates a simple example in which a student living in Las Vegas (LV) needs to go to San Jose (SJ) to present a AAAI paper. The cost of travelling is $C_{travel(LV,SJ)} = 230$. We assume that if the student arrives at San Jose, he automatically achieves the goal $g_1 = Attended\_AAAI$ with utility $U_{g_1} = 300$. The student also wants to go to Disneyland (DL) and San Francisco (SF) to have some fun ($g_2 = HaveFun(DL)$, $g_3 = HaveFun(SF)$) and to San Diego (SD) to see the zoo ($g_4 = SeeZoo(SD)$). The utilities for having fun in these places ($U_{g_2}$, $U_{g_3}$, $U_{g_4}$), and the travel cost of going from one place to the other are given in Figure 2. The goal of the student is to find a travel plan that gives him the best cost-utility tradeoff. In this example, the best plan is $P = \{travel(LV, DL), travel(DL, SJ), travel(SJ, SF)\}$ which achieves the goals $g_1, g_2$ and $g_3$, and ignores $g_4$.

**Theorem 1** PSP NET BENEFIT *is PSPACE-complete.*

**Proof** We will show that PSP NET BENEFIT is in PSPACE and we will polynomially transform it to PLAN EXISTENCE,

globally optimal plans. In the case of *Sapa*$^{ps}$, this involves using admissible heuristics, while for *AltAlt*$^{ps}$, we need to do both an exhaustive search over subgoal sets, and use admissible heuristics during search.

which is a PSPACE-hard problem (Bylander 1994).

PSP NET BENEFIT is in PSPACE follows from Bylander (1994). PSP NET BENEFIT is PSPACE-hard because we can restrict it to PLAN EXISTENCE by allowing only instances having $U_f = 0, \forall f \in F$, $C_a = 1, \forall a \in A$, and $k = -2^m$. This restriction obtains $\sum_{a \in \Delta} C_a \leq 2^m$, which is the condition for PLAN EXISTENCE. ∎

Given that PLAN EXISTENCE and PSP NET BENEFIT are PSPACE-hard problems, it should be clear that the other problems given in Figure 1 also fall in this complexity class. PSP NET BENEFIT does, however, foreground the need to handle plan quality issues.

## *OptiPlan*: An Integer Programming Approach

*OptiPlan* is a planning system that provides an extension to the state change integer programming (IP) model by (Vossen *et al*, 1999). The original state change model uses the complete set of ground actions and fluents; *OptiPlan* on the other hand eliminates many unnecessary variables simply by using Graphplan (Blum & Furst 1997). In addition, *OptiPlan* has the ability to read in PDDL files. In this respect, *OptiPlan* is very similar to the BlackBox (Kautz & Selman 1999) and GP-CSP (Do & Kambhampati 2001) planners but instead of using a SAT or CSP formulation, the planner uses an IP formulation.

The state change formulation is built around the state change variables $x_{f,l}^{add}$, $x_{f,l}^{pre-add}$, $x_{f,l}^{pre-del}$, and $x_{f,l}^{maintain}$. These variables are defined in order to express the possible state changes of a fluent, with $x_{f,l}^{maintain}$ representing the propagation of a fluent $f$ at level $l$. Besides the state change variables the IP model contains variables for actions, with $y_{a,l} = 1$ if and only if action $a$ is executed in level $l$.

It is quite straightforward to model PSP NET BENEFIT in *OptiPlan*, all we do is transfer goal satisfaction from the hard constraints to the objective function. In the case of maximizing net benefit the objective becomes:

$$\sum_{f \in G} U_f(x_{f,n}^{add} + x_{f,n}^{pre-add} + x_{f,n}^{maintain}) - \sum_{l \in L} \sum_{a \in A} C_a y_{a,l} \tag{1}$$

where $L = 1, ..., n$ is the set of plan step levels, $A$ is the set of actions, and $G$ the set of goal fluents.

*OptiPlan* will find optimal solutions for a given parallel length $l$, however, the global optimum may not be detected as there might be solutions of better quality at higher values of $l$.

## Heuristic Approaches: Preliminaries

In this section we describe *AltAlt*$^{ps}$ and *Sapa*$^{ps}$, the two heuristic search planners capable of handling PSP problems. Given that the quality of the plan for PSP problem depends on both the utility of the goals achieved and the cost to achieve them, these planners need heuristic guidance that is sensitive to both action cost and goal utility. Because only the execution costs of the actions and the achievement cost of propositions in the initial state (zero cost) are known, we need to do *cost-propagation* from the initial state through actions to estimate the cost to achieve other propositions, especially the top level goals. In *AltAlt*$^{ps}$ and *Sapa*$^{ps}$, this is done using the planning graph structure. In this section, we will first describe the cost propagation procedure over the planning graph as a basis for heuristic estimation in *AltAlt*$^{ps}$ and *Sapa*$^{ps}$. In subsequent sections, we discuss how *AltAlt*$^{ps}$ and *Sapa*$^{ps}$ use this information.

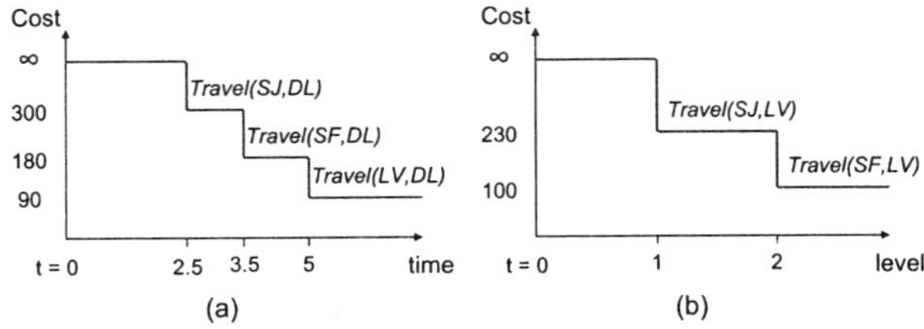


Figure 3: Cost function of goal $At(DL)$

### Cost-propagation to Estimate the Goal Achievement Costs

To estimate the overall benefit of achieving the goals, we can use the planning graph structure to propagate the cost of facts from the initial state through applicable actions until we can estimate the lowest cost to achieve the goals. Following (Do & Kambhampati 2003), we use cost functions to capture the way cost of achievement changes as the graph is expanded. In the following, we briefly review the procedure. (Note that the discussion below is done in the more general context of temporal planning; to apply it to classical planning scenarios, we need only assume that all actions have uniform durations).

The purpose of the cost-propagation process is to build the cost functions $C(f, t_f)$ and $C(a, t_a)$ that estimate the cheapest cost to achieve fluent $f$ at time (level) $t_f$ and the cost to execute action $a$ at level $t_a$. At the beginning ($t = 0$), let $S_{init}$ be the initial state and $C_a$ be the cost of action $a$ then[2]: $C(f, 0) = 0$ if $f \in S_{init}$, $C(f, 0) = \infty$ otherwise; $\forall a \in A : C(a, 0) = \infty$. The propagation rules are as follows:

- $C(f, t) = min\{C(a, t - Dur_a) + C_a) : f \in Eff(a)\}$
- Max-prop: $C(a, t) = max\{C(f, t) : f \in Prec(a)\}$
- Sum-prop: $C(a, t) = \Sigma\{C(f, t) : f \in Prec(a)\}$

The max-propagation rule will lead to an admissible heuristic, while the sum-propagation rule does not. In our travel example, assume that the student can only go to $SJ$ and $SF$ from $LV$ by airplane, which take respectively 1.0 and 1.5 hour. He can also travel by car from $LV$, $SJ$, and $SF$ to $DL$ in 5.0, 1.5 and 2.0 hours, respectively. Figure 3(a) shows the cost function for goal $g_2 = At(DL)$, which indicates that the earliest time to achieve $g_2$ is at $t = 2.5$ with the lowest cost of 300 (route: $LV \rightarrow SJ \rightarrow DL$). The lowest cost to achieve $g_2$ reduces to 180 at $t = 3.5$ (route:

[2] $C_a$ and $C(a, t)$ are different. If $a = Fly(SD, DL)$ then $C_a$ is the airfare cost and $C(a, t)$ is the cost to achieve preconditions of $a$ at $t$, which is the cost incurred to be at $SD$ at $t$.

$LV \rightarrow SF \rightarrow DL$) and again at $t = 5.0$ to 90 (direct path: $LV \rightarrow DL$). For the levelled planning graph, where actions are non-durative, Figure 3(b) shows the cost function for the fact $At(LV)$ assuming that the student is at $SJ$ in the initial state. At level 1, she can be at $LV$ by going directly from $SJ$ with cost 230. Then at level 2 she can at be $LV$ with cost 100, using route $SJ \rightarrow SF \rightarrow LV$.

There are many ways to terminate the cost-propagation process (Do & Kambhampati 2003): We can stop when all the goals are achievable, when the cost of all the goals are stabilized (i.e. guaranteed not to decrease anymore), or lookahead several steps after the goals are achieved. For classical planning, we can also stop propagating cost when the graph *levels-off* (Nguyen *et al*, 2001).[3]

## Cost-sensitive heuristics

After building the planning graph with cost information, both *AltAlt*$^{ps}$ and *Sapa*$^{ps}$ use variations of the relaxed plan extraction process (Hoffmann & Nebel 2001; Nguyen *et al*, 2001) guided by the cost-functions to estimate their heuristic values $h(S)$ (Do & Kambhampati 2003). The basic idea is to compute the cost of the relaxed plans in terms of the costs of the actions comprising them, and use such costs as heuristic estimates. The general relaxed plan extraction process for both *AltAlt*$^{ps}$ and *Sapa*$^{ps}$ works as follows: (i) start from the goal set $G$ containing the top level goals, remove a goal $g$ from $G$ and select a lowest cost action $a_g$ (indicated by $C(g,t)$) to support $g$; (ii) regress $G$ over action $a_g$, setting $G = G \cup Prec(a_g) \backslash Eff(a_g)$. The process continues recursively until each proposition $q \in G$ is also in the initial state $I$. This regression accounts for the positive interactions in the state $G$ given that by subtracting the effects of $a_g$, any other proposition that is co-achieved when $g$ is being supported is not counted in the cost computation. The relaxed plan procedure indirectly extracts a sequence of actions $R_P$ (the actions $a_g$ selected at each reduction), which would have achieved the set $G$ from the initial state $I$ if there were no negative interactions. The summation of the costs of the actions $a_g \in R_P$ can be used to estimate the cost to achieve all goals in $G$.

## *AltAlt*$^{ps}$ : Heuristic Search and Goal Selection

*AltAlt*$^{ps}$ is a heuristic regression planner that can be seen as a variant of *AltAlt* (Nguyen *et al*, 2001) equipped with cost sensitive heuristics using *Max-prop* rules (see previous section). An obvious, if naive, way of solving the PSP NET BENEFIT problem with such a planner is to consider all plans for the $2^n$ subsets of an *n-goal* problem, and see which of them will wind up leading to the plan with the highest net benefit. Since this is infeasible, *AltAlt*$^{ps}$ uses a greedy approach to pick the goal subset up front. The approach is sophisticated in the sense that it considers the net benefit of covering a goal not in isolation, but in the context of

[3]Stopping the cost propagation when the graph levels-off (i.e. no new facts or actions can be introduced into the graph) does not guarantee that the cost-functions are stabilized. Actions introduced in the last level still can reduce the cost of some facts and lead to the *re-activation* chain reaction process that reduce the costs of other propositions.

**Procedure** *partialize*($G$)
  $g \leftarrow getBestBenefitialGoal(G)$;
  **if**($g = NULL$)
    **return** Failure;
  $G' \leftarrow \{g\}; G \leftarrow G \setminus g$;
  $R^*_P \leftarrow extractRelaxPlan(G', \emptyset)$
  $B^*_{MAX} \leftarrow getUtil(G') - getCost(R^*_P)$;
  $B_{MAX} \leftarrow B^*_{MAX}$
  **while**($B_{MAX} > 0 \wedge G \neq \emptyset$)
    **for**($g \in G \setminus G'$)
      $G_P \leftarrow G' \cup g$;
      $R_P \leftarrow ExtractRelaxPlan(G_P, R^*_P)$
      $B_g \leftarrow getUtil(G_P) - getCost(R_P)$;
      **if**($B_g > B^*_{MAX}$)
        $g^* \leftarrow g; B^*_{MAX} \leftarrow B_g; R^*_g \leftarrow R_P$;
      **else**
        $B_{MAX} \leftarrow B_g - B^*_{MAX}$
    **end for**
    **if**($g^* \neq NULL$)
      $G' \leftarrow G' \cup g^*; G \leftarrow G \setminus g^*; B_{MAX} \leftarrow B^*_{MAX}$;
  **end while**
  **return** $G'$;
**End** *partialize*;

Figure 4: Goal set selection algorithm.

the potential (relaxed) plan for handling the already selected goals (see below). Once a subset of goal conjuncts is selected, *AltAlt*$^{ps}$ finds a plan that achieves such subset using its regression search engine augmented with cost sensitive heuristics. The goal set selection algorithm is described in more detail below.

## Goal set selection algorithm

The main idea of the goal set selection procedure in *AltAlt*$^{ps}$ is to incrementally construct a new partial goal set $G'$ from the top level goals $G$ such that the goals considered for inclusion increase the final net benefit, using the goals utilities and costs of achievement. The process is complicated by the fact that the net benefit offered by a goal $g$ depends on what other goals have already been selected. Specifically, while the utility of a goal $g$ remains constant, the expected cost of achieving it will depend upon the other selected goals (and the actions that will anyway be needed to support them). To estimate the "residual cost" of a goal $g$ in the context of a set of already selected goals $G'$, we compute a relaxed plan $R_P$ for supporting $G' + g$, which is biased to (re)use the actions in the relaxed plan $R'_P$ for supporting $G'$.

Figure 4 gives a description of the goal set selection algorithm. The first block of instructions before the loop initializes our goal subset $G'$,[4] and finds an initial relaxed plan $R^*_P$ for it using the procedure *extractRelaxPlan($G'$,$\emptyset$)*. Notice that two arguments are passed to the function. The first one is the current partial goal set from where the relaxed plan will be computed. The second parameter is the current relaxed plan that will be used as a guidance for computing

[4]$getBestBenefitialGoal(G)$ returns the subgoal with the best benefit, $U_g - C(g,t)$ tradeoff

the new relaxed plan. The idea is that we want to bias the computation of the new relaxed plan to re-use the actions in the relaxed plan from the previous iteration. Having found the initial subset $G'$ and its relaxed plan $R_P^*$, we compute the current best net benefit $B_{MAX}^*$ by subtracting the costs of the actions in the relaxed plan $R_P^*$ from the total utility of the goals in $G'$. $B_{MAX}^*$ will work as a threshold for our iterative procedure. In other words, we would continue adding subgoals $g \in G$ to $G'$ only if the overall net benefit $B_{MAX}^*$ increases. We consider one subgoal at a time, always computing the benefit added by the subgoal in terms of the cost of its relaxed plan $R_P$ and goal utility $B_g$. We then pick the subgoal $g$ that maximizes the net benefit, updating the necessary values for the next iteration. This iterative procedure stops as soon as the net benefit does not increase, or when there are no more subgoals to add, returning the new goal subset $G'$.

In our running example the original subgoals are $\{g_1 = AttendedAAAI,\ g_2 = HaveFun(DL),\ g_3 = HaveFun(SF),\ g_4 = SeeZoo(SD)\}$, with final costs $C(g,t) = \{230, 90, 80, 40\}$ and utilities U $= \{300, 100, 100, 50\}$ respectively. Following our algorithm, our starting goal $g$ would be $g_1$ because it returns the biggest benefit (e.g. 300 - 230). Then, $G'$ is set to $g_1$, and its initial relaxed plan $R_P^*$ is computed. Assume that the initial relaxed plan found is $R_P^* = \{travel(LV, DL), travel(DL, SJ)\}$. We proceed to compute the best net benefit using $R_P^*$ , which in our example would be $B_{MAX}^* = 300 - (200 + 90) = 10$. Having found our initial values, we continue iterating on the remaining goals $G = \{g_2, g_3, g_4\}$. On the first iteration we compute three different set of values, they are: (i) $G_{P_1} = \{g_1 \cup g_2\}$, $R_{P_1} = \{travel(LV, DL), travel(DL, SJ))\}$, and $B_{g_{P_1}} = 110$; (ii) $G_{P_2} = \{g_1 \cup g_3\}$, $R_{P_2} = \{travel(LV, DL), travel(DL, SJ), travel(LV, SF)\}$, and $B_{g_{P_2}} = 30$; and (iii) $G_{P_3} = \{g_1 \cup g_4\}$, $R_{P_3} = \{travel(LV, DL), travel(DL, SJ), travel(LV, SD)\}$, and $B_{g_{P_3}} = 20$. Notice then that our net benefit $B_{MAX}^*$ could be improved most if we consider goal $g_2$. So, we update $G' = g_1 \cup g_2$, $R_P^* = R_{P_1}$, and $B_{MAX}^* = 110$. The procedure keeps iterating until we consider goal $g_4$, which decreases the net benefit. The procedure returns $G' = \{g_1, g_2, g_3\}$ as our goal set. In this example, there is also a plan that achieves the four goals with a positive benefit, but it is not as good as the plan that achieves the selected $G'$.

## *Sapa$^{ps}$* : Heuristic Search using Goals as Soft Constraints

The advantage of the *AltAlt$^{ps}$* approach for solving PSP problems is that after committing to a subset of goals, the overall problem is simplified to the planning problem of finding the least cost plan to achieve all the goals. The disadvantage of this type of approach is that if the heuristics do not select the right set of goals, then we can not switch to another subset during search. In this section, we discuss an alternative method which models the top-level goals as "soft constraints." All executable plans are considered potential solutions, and the quality of a plan is measured in terms of its net benefit. The objective of the search is then to find a plan with the highest net benefit. To model this search problem in an A* framework, we need to first define the $g$ and $h$ values of a partial plan. The $g$ value will need to capture the current net benefit of the plan, while the $h$ value needs to estimate the net benefit that can be potentially accrued by extending the plan to cover more goals. Once we have these definitions, we need methods for efficiently estimating the the $h$ value. We will detail this process in he context of *Sapa$^{ps}$* , which does forward (progression) search in the space of states.

**g value:** In forward planners, applicable actions are executed in the current state to generate new states. For a given state $S$, let partial plan $P_P(S)$ be the plan leading from the initial state $S_{init}$ to $S$, and the goal set $G(S)$ be the set of goals accomplished in $S$. The overall quality of the state $S$ depends on the total utility of the goals in $G(S)$ and the costs of actions in $P_P(S)$. The $g$ value is thus defined as :

$$g(S) = \mathrm{U}(G(S)) - \mathrm{C}(P_P(S))$$

Where $\mathrm{U}(G(S)) = \sum_{g \in G(S)} \mathrm{U}_g$ is the total utility of the goals in $G(S)$, and $\mathrm{C}(P_P(S)) = \sum_{a \in P_P(S)} \mathrm{C}_a$ is the total cost of actions in $P_P(S)$. In our ongoing example, at the initial state $S_{init} = \{at(LV)\}$. Applying action $a_1 = travel(LV, DL)$ would leads to the state $S_1 = \{at(DL), g_2\}$ and applying action $a_2 = travel(DL, SF)$ to $S_1$ would lead to state $S_2 = \{at(SF), g_2, g_3\}$. Thus, for state $S_2$, the total utility and cost values are: $\mathrm{U}(G(S_2)) = \mathrm{U}_{g_2} + \mathrm{U}_{g_3} = 100 + 100 = 200$, and $\mathrm{C}(P_P(S_2)) = \mathrm{C}_{a_1} + \mathrm{C}_{a_2} = 90 + 100 = 190$.

**h value:** The $h$ value of a state $S$ should estimate how much additional net benefit can be accrued by extending the partial plan $P_S$ to achieve additional goals beyond $G(S)$. The perfect heuristic function $h^*$ would give the maximum net benefit that can be accrued. Any $h$ function that is an upper bound on $h^*$ will be admissible. Notice that we are considering the maximizing variant of A*. Before we go about investigating efficient $h$ functions, it is instructive to pin down the notion of $h^*$ value of a state $S$.

For a given state $S$, let $P_R$ be a plan segment that is applicable in $S$, and $S' = Apply(P_R, S)$ be the state resulting from applying $P_R$ to $S$. Like $P_P(S)$, the cost of $P_R$ is the sum of the costs of all actions in $P_R$. The utility of the plan $P_R$ according to state $S$ is defined as follows: $U(Apply(P_R, S) = U(G(S')) - U(G(S))$. For a given state $S$, the **best beneficial remaining plan** $P_S^B$ is a plan applicable in $S$ such that there is no other plan $P$ applicable in $S$ for which $U(Apply(P, S)) - C(P) > U(Apply(P_S^B, S)) - C(P_S^B)$. If we have $P_S^B$, then we can use it to define the $h^*(S)$ value as follows:

$$h^*(S) = U(Apply(P_S^B, S)) - C(P_S^B) \quad (2)$$

In our ongoing example, from state $S_1$, the most beneficial plan turns out to be $P_{S_1}^B = \{travel(DL, SJ), travel(SJ, SF)\}$, and $U(Apply(P_{S_1}^B, S_1)) = U_{\{g_1, g_2, g_3\}} - U_{\{g_2\}} =$

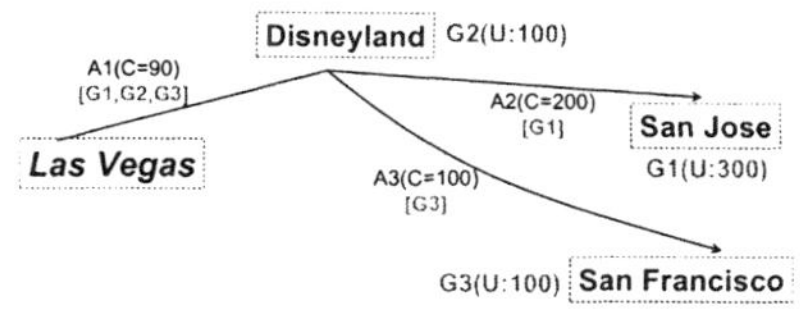


Figure 5: A relaxed plan and goals supported by each action.

$300+100+100-100=400$, $C(P^B_{S_1})=200+20=220$, and thus $h^*(S_1)=400-220=180$.

Computing $h^*(S)$ value directly is impractical as searching for $P^B_S$ is as hard as solving the PSP problem optimally. In the following, we will discuss a heuristic approach to approximate the $h^*$ value of a given search node $S$ by essentially approximating $P^B_S$ using a relaxed plan from $S$.

## Heuristic Estimation in *Sapa$^{ps}$*

Like *AltAlt$^{ps}$*, *Sapa$^{ps}$* also uses relaxed-plan heuristic extracted from the cost-sensitve planning graph (Do & Kambhampati 2003). However, unlike *AltAlt$^{ps}$*, in the current implementation of *Sapa$^{ps}$* we first build the relaxed plan supporting *all* the goals, then we use the second scan through the extracted relaxed plan to remove goals that are not beneficial, along with the actions that contribute solely to the achievement of those goals. For this purpose, we build the *supported-goals* list $GS$ for each action $a$ and fluent $f$ starting from the top level goals as follows:

- $GS(a)=\bigcup GS(f): f\in Eff(a)$
- $GS(f)=\bigcup GS(a): f\in Prec(a)$

Assume that our algorithm extracts the relaxed plan $f = R_P(S_{init}) = \{a_1 : travel(LV,DL), a_2 : travel(DL,SJ), a_3 : travel(DL,SF)\}$ (shown in Figure 5 along with goals each action supports). For this relaxed plan, action $a_2$ and $a_3$ support only $g_1$ and $g_3$ so $GS(a_2)=\{g_1\}$ and $GS(a_3)=\{g_3\}$. The precondition of those two actions, $At(DL)$, would in turn contribute to both these goals $GS(At(DL))=\{g_1,g_3\}$. Finally, because $a_1$ supports both $g_2$ and $At(DL)$, $GS(a_1)=GS(g_2)\cup GS(At(DL))=\{g_1,g_2,g_3\}$.

Using the supported-goals sets, for each subset $S_G$ of goals, we can identify the subset $SA(S_G)$ of actions that contribute only to the goals in $S_G$. If the cost of those actions exceeds the sum of utilities of goals in $S_G$, then we can remove $S_G$ and $SA(S_G)$ from the relaxed plan. In our example, action $a_3$ is the only one that solely contributes to the achievement of $g_3$. Since $C_{a_3}\geq U_{g_3}$, we can remove $a_3$ and $g_3$ from consideration. The other two actions $a_1,a_2$ and goals $g_1,g_2$ all appear beneficial. In our current implementation, we consider all subsets of goals of size 1 or 2 for possible removal. After removing non beneficial goals and actions (solely) supporting them, the cost of the remaining relaxed plan and the utility of the goals that it achieves will be used to compute an effective but inadmissible $h$ value.

## Search in *Sapa$^{ps}$*

The complete search algorithm used by *Sapa$^{ps}$* is described in Figure 6. In this algorithm, search nodes are categorized as follows:

```
State Queue: SQ={S_init}
Best beneficial node: N_B = ∅
Best benefit: B_B = 0
while SQ≠{}
    S:= Dequeue(SQ)
    if (g(S) > 0) ∧ (h(S) = 0) then
        Terminate Search;
    Nondeterministically select a applicable in S
        S' := Apply(a,S)
        if g(S') > B_B then
            Print BestBeneficialNode(S')
            N_B ← S';        B_B ← g(S')
        if f(S) ≤ B_B then
            Discard(S)
        else Enqueue(S',SQ)
end while;
```

Figure 6: Anytime A* search algorithm for PSP problems.

*Beneficial Node: $S$ is a beneficial node if $g(S)>0$.*

Thus, beneficial nodes $S$ are nodes that give positive net benefit even if no more actions are applied to $S$. In our ongoing example, both nodes $S_1,S_2$ are beneficial nodes. If we decide to extend $S_1$ by applying the action $a_3 = travel(DL,LV)$ then we will get state $S_3 = \{at(LV), HaveFun(DL)\}$, which is not a beneficial node ($g(S_3) = U_{g_2} - C_{\{a_1,a_3\}} = 100-180=-80$).

*Termination Node: $S_T$ is a termination node if: (i) $h(S_T)=0$, (ii) $g(S_T)>0$, and (iii) $\forall S: g(S_T)>f(S)$.*

Termination node $S_T$ is the *best* beneficial node in the queue. Moreover, because $h(S_T)=0$, there is no benefit of extending $S_T$ and therefore we can terminate the search at $S_T$. Notice that if the heuristic is *admissible*, then the set of actions leading to $S_T$ represents an optimal solution for the PSP problem.

*Unpromising Node: $S$ is a unpromising node if $f(S)\leq B_B$ with $B_B$ is the $g$ value of a best beneficial state found so far.*

The net benefit value of the best beneficial node ($B_B$) found during search can be used to set up the lower-bound value and thus nodes that have $f$ values smaller than that lower-bound can be discarded.[5]

As described in Figure 6, the search algorithm starts with the initial state $S_{init}$ and keeps dequeuing the best promising node $S$ (i.e. highest $f$ value). If $S$ is a termination node, then we stop the search. If not, then we extend $S$ by applying applicable actions $a$ to $S$. If the newly generated node $S' = Apply(a,S)$ is a beneficial node and has a better $g(S')$ value than the best beneficial node visited so far, then we print the plan leading from $S_{init}$ to $S'$. Finally, if $S'$ is not a unpromising node, then we will put it in the search queue $SQ$ sorted in the decreasing order of $f$ values. Notice that because we keep outputting the best beneficial nodes while conducting search (until a terminal node is found), this is an *anytime algorithm*. The benefit of this approach is that the

[5]Being a *unpromising node* is not equal to not being a *beneficial node*. A given node $S$ can have value $g(S)<0$ but $f(S)=g(S)+h(S)>B_B$ and is still promising to be extended.

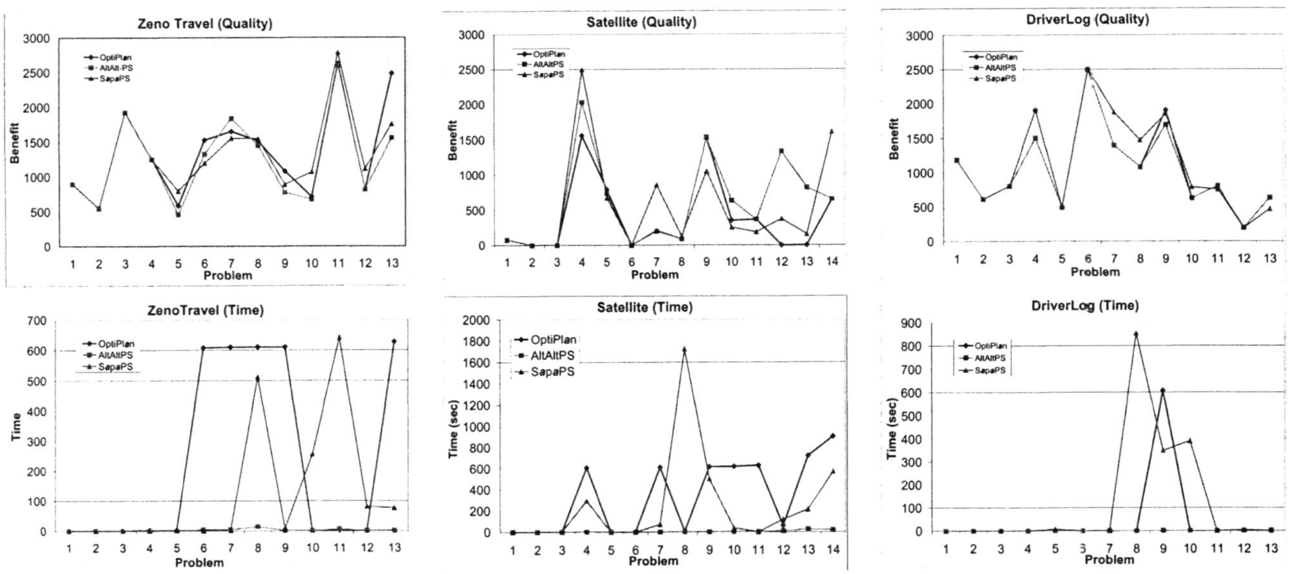


a) ZenoTravel domain b) Satellite domain c) DriverLog domain

Figure 7: Empirical evaluation

planner can return some plan with a positive net-benefit fast and keep on returning plans with better net benefit, if given more time to do more search.

Notice that the current heuristic used in *Sapa*$^{ps}$ is not admissible, this is because: (i) a pruned unpromising nodes may actually be promising (i.e. extendible to reach node $S$ with $g(S) > B_B$); and (ii) a termination node may not be the best beneficial node. In our implementation, even though weight $w = 1$ is used in equation $f = g + w * h$ to sort nodes in the queue, another value $w = 2$ is used for pruning (unpromising) nodes with $f = g + w * h \leq B_B$. Thus, only nodes $S$ with estimated heuristic value $h(S) \leq 1/w * h^*(S)$ are pruned. For the second issue, we can continue the search for a better beneficial nodes after a termination node is found until some criteria are met (e.g. reached certain number of search node limit).

## Empirical Evaluation

In the foregoing, we have described several qualitatively different approaches for solving the PSP problem. Our aim in this section is to get an empirical understanding of the cost-quality tradeoffs offered by this spectrum of methods.

Since there are no benchmark PSP problems, we used existing STRIPS planning domains from the last International Planning Competition (Long & Fox 2003). In particular, our experiments include the domains of Driverlog, Satellite, and Zenotravel. Utilities ranging from 100 to 600 were assigned to each of the goals, and costs ranging from 10 to 800 were assigned to each of the actions by taking into account some of the characteristics of the problem. For example, in the Driverlog domain, a driving action is assigned a higher cost than a load action. Under this design, the planners achieved around 60% of the goals on average over all the domains.

All three planners were run on a 2.67Ghz CPU machine with 1.0GB RAM. The IP encodings in *OptiPlan* were solved using ILOG CPLEX8.1 with default settings except that the start algorithm was set to the dual problem, the variable select rule was set to pseudo reduced cost, and a time limit of 600 seconds was imposed. In case that the time limit was reached, we denoted the best feasible solution as *OptiPlan*'s solution quality. Given that *OptiPlan* returns optimal solutions up to a certain level, we set the level limit for *OptiPlan* by post-processing the solutions of *AltAlt*$^{ps}$ to get the parallel length using techniques discussed in (Sanchez & Kambhampati 2003).

Figure 7 shows the results from the three planners. It can be observed that the two heuristic planners, *AltAlt*$^{ps}$ and *Sapa*$^{ps}$ , produce plans that are comparable to *OptiPlan*. In some problems they even produce better plans than *OptiPlan*. This happens when *OptiPlan* reaches its time limit and can not complete its search, or when the level given to *OptiPlan* is not high enough. When comparing the two heuristic planners, *AltAlt*$^{ps}$ is often faster, but *Sapa*$^{ps}$ usually returns better quality plans. The decrease on the performance of *AltAlt*$^{ps}$ could be due to the following reasons: either the greedy goal set selection procedure of *AltAlt*$^{ps}$ picks a bad goal subset upfront, or its cost-sensitive search requires better heuristics. A deeper inspection of the problems in which the solutions of *AltAlt*$^{ps}$ are suboptimal revealed that although both reasons play a role, the first reason dominates more often. In fact, we found that the goal set selection procedure tends to be a little bit conservative, selecting fewer subgoals in cases where the benefit gain is small, which means that our relaxed plan cost is overestimating the residual costs of the subgoals. To resolve this issue, we may need to account for subgoal interactions more aggressively in the goal set selection algorithm. The higher running time of *Sapa*$^{ps}$ is mostly due to the fact that it tries to search for multiple (better) beneficial plans and thus have higher number of search nodes. In many cases, it takes very short time to find the first few solutions but much more to improve the solution quality (even slightly). Moreover, the heuristic used in *Sapa*$^{ps}$ seems to be misleading in some cases (mostly in the Satellite domain) where the planner spends a lot of time switching between different search branches at the lower levels of the search tree before finding the promising one and go deeper.

## Related Work

As we mentioned earlier, there has been very little work on PSP in planning. One possible exception is the PYRRHUS planning system (Williamson & Hanks 1994) which considers an interesting variant of the partial satisfaction planning problem. In PYRRHUS, the quality of the plans is measured by the utilities of the goals and the amount of resource consumed. Utilities of goals decrease if they are achieved later than the goals' deadlines. Unlike the PSP problem discussed in this paper, all the logical goals still need to be achieved by PYRRHUS for the plan to be valid. It would be interesting to extend the PSP model to consider degree of satisfaction of the individual goals.

More recently, Smith (2003) motivated oversubscription problems in terms of their applicability to the NASA planning problems. Smith (2004) also proposed a planner for oversubscription in which the solution of the abstracted planning problem is used to select the subset of goals and the orders to achieve them. The abstract planning problem is built by propagating the cost on the planning graph and constructing the *orienteering* problem. The goals and their orderings are then used to guide a POCL planner. In this sense, this approach is similar to *AltAlt*$^{ps}$ ; however, the orienteering problem needs to be constructed using domain-knowledge for different planning domains.

Over-subscription issues have received relatively more attention in the scheduling community. Earlier work in scheduling over-subscription used greedy approaches, in which tasks of higher priorities are scheduled first (Kramer & Giuliano 1997; Potter & Gasch 1998). The approach used by *AltAlt*$^{ps}$ is more sophisticated in that it considers the residual cost of a subgoal in the context of an exisiting partial plan for achieving other selected goals. More recent efforts have used stochastic greedy search algorithms on constraint-based intervals (Frank *et al*, 2001), genetic algorithms (Globus *et al.* 2003), and iterative repairing technique (Kramer & Smith 2003) to solve this problem more effectively.

## Conclusions and Future Work

In this paper, we investigated a generalization of the classical planning problem that allows partial satisfaction of goal conjuncts. We motivated the need for such partial satisfaction planning (PSP), and presented a spectrum of PSP problems. We then focused on one general PSP problem, called PSP Net Benefit, and developed a spectrum of planners– *OptiPlan*, *AltAlt*$^{ps}$ and *Sapa*$^{ps}$ for it. Our empirical results show that the heuristic approaches are able to generate plans whose quality is comparable to the ones generated by the optimizing approach, while incurring only a fraction of the running time. The two types of heuristic planners can also complement each other. The heuristic techniques used in *AltAlt*$^{ps}$ can be employed in *Sapa*$^{ps}$ as an alternative to its current approach of heuristic evaluation of each search node. Our future work will extend our heuristic framework to more complex PSP problems. Of particular interest to us is handling partial satisfaction in metric temporal planning problems with resources. *Sapa*$^{ps}$ , developed on top of a temporal planner, is a promising candidate for this extension.

## References

Blum, A., and Furst, M. 1997. Fast planning through planning graph analysis. *Artificial Intelligence* 90:281–300.

Boutilier, C., Dean, T., and Hanks, S. 1999. Decision-Theoretic Planning: Structural assumptions and computational leverage. In *JAIR 11 (p.1-94)*

Bylander, T. 1994. The computational complexity of propositional STRIPS planning. In *AIJ* 69(1-2):165–204.

Do, M. and Kambhampati, S. 2003. Sapa: a multi-objective metric temporal planer. In *JAIR 20 (p.155-194)*

Do, M. and Kambhampati, S. 2001. Planning as Constraint Satisfaction: Solving the planning graph by compiling it into CSP. In *AIJ* 132(2):151–182.

Frank, J.; Jonsson, A.; Morris, R.; and Smith, D. 2001. Planning and scheduling for fleets of earth observing satellites. In *Sixth Int. Symp. on Artificial Intelligence, Robotics, Automation & Space.*

Globus, A.; Crawford, J.; Lohn, J.; and Pryor, A. 2003. Scheduling earth observing sateliites with evolutionary algorithms. In *Proc. Int. Conf. on Space Mission Challenges for Infor. Tech..*

Hoffmann, J. and Nebel, B. 2001. The FF planning system: Fast plan generation through heuristic search. In *JAIR 14 (p.253-302).*

Kautz, H., and Selman, B. 1999b. Blackbox: Unifying Sat-based and Graph-based planning. In *Proc. of IJCAI-99.*

Kramer, L. and Giuliano, M. 1997. Reasoning about and scheduling linked HST observations with Spike. In *Proc. of Int. Workshop on Planning and Scheduling for Space.*

Kramer, L. A., and Smith, S. 2003. Maximizing flexibility: A retraction heuristic for oversubscribed scheduling problems. In *Proc. of IJCAI-03.*

Long, D., and Fox, M. 1999. Efficient implementation of the plan graph in STAN. In *JAIR* 10:87–115.

Long, D. and Fox, M. 2003. The 3rd International Planning Competition: Results and analysis. In *JAIR 20 (p.1-59).*

Nguyen, X., Kambhampati, S., and Nigenda, R. 2001. Planning graph as the basis for deriving heuristics for plan synthesis by State Space and CSP search. In *AIJ 135 (p.73-123).*

Potter, W. and Gasch, J. 1998. A photo album of Earth: Scheduling Landsat 7 mission daily activities. In *Proc. of SpaceOps.*

Sanchez, R., and Kambhampati, S. 2003. Altalt-p: Online parallelization of plans with heuristic state search. In *JAIR 19 (p.631–657).*

Smith, D. 2003. The Mystery talk. *Planet Summer School*

Smith, D. 2004. Choosing objectives in Over-Subscription planning. In *Proc. of ICAPS-04.*

Vossen, T., Ball, M., and Nau, D. 1999. On the use of integer programming models in ai planning. In *Proc. of IJCAI-99*

Williamson, M., and Hanks, S. 1994. Optimal planning with a Goal-Directed utility model. In *Proc. of AIPS-94.*

# Branching and Pruning: An Optimal Temporal POCL Planner based on Constraint Programming*

**Vincent Vidal**
CRIL - Université d'Artois
rue de l'université - SP16
62307 Lens Cedex, FRANCE
vidal@cril.univ-artois.fr

**Héctor Geffner**
ICREA & Universitat Pompeu Fabra
Paseo de Circunvalacion 8
08003 Barcelona, SPAIN
hector.geffner@upf.edu

### Abstract

A key feature of modern optimal planners such as Graphplan and Blackbox is their ability to prune large parts of the search space. Previous Partial Order Causal Link (POCL) planners provide an alternative branching scheme but lacking comparable pruning mechanisms do not perform as well. In this paper, a domain-independent formulation of temporal planning based on Constraint Programming is introduced that successfully combines a POCL branching scheme with powerful and sound pruning rules. The key novelty in the formulation is the ability to reason about supports, precedences, and causal links involving actions that are not in the plan. Experiments over a wide range of benchmarks show that the resulting optimal temporal planner is much faster than current ones and is competitive with the best parallel planners in the special case in which actions have all the same duration.

## Introduction

The search for optimal plans, like the search for optimal solutions in many intractable combinatorial optimization problems, can be understood along two dimensions: the *branching scheme* used for expanding partial solutions, and the *pruning scheme* used for discarding them. Most AI planning frameworks can be understood in these terms. Optimal state-based planners, for example, branch by performing state regression or progression, and prune by comparing the estimated cost of the partial plans with a given bound (Haslum & Geffner 2000). Optimal SAT and CSP planners, on the other hand, branch by picking a variable and trying each of its values, pruning branches and domain values that lead to an inconsistency (Kautz & Selman 1999; Do & Kambhampati 2000). Pruning is a key operation in both cases: in the first, it is the result of the use of explicit lower bounds, in the second, of constraint propagation mechanisms and bounds encoded in the planning graph (Blum & Furst 1995). This pruning power distinguishes modern planners such as Graphplan from its predecessors (whether optimal or not). Indeed the main limitation of traditional Partial Order Causal Link (POCL) planners is that they provide an alternative branching scheme but no comparable pruning mechanisms. The result is that dead-ends are discovered late and the size of the search tree explodes much sooner.

Due to its expressive power, however, POCL planning remains an appealing framework for planning, and in particular temporal planning (Smith, Frank, & Jonsson 2000). The challenge is to close the performance gap that separates POCL planners from modern planners while retaining the optimality guarantees. In this paper, we undertake this challenge, extending a POCL temporal planner with powerful and sound pruning mechanisms based on a constraint programming formulation that integrates existing lower bounds with propagation rules that reason with supports, precedences, and causal links in novel ways. The experiments show that the resulting planner is faster than current optimal temporal planners and is competitive with current parallel planners in the special case in which action durations are all uniform.

A couple of remarks before proceeding. First, the formulation and implementation that we present is not completely general: we deal only with plans in which every (ground) action is executed at most once; plans that we call *canonical* (Geffner 2001). Canonical plans are thus halfway between full temporal planning and scheduling: while in scheduling typically every action is done *exactly once,* and in canonical planning it is done *at most once,* in full temporal planning, it may be done an arbitrary number of times. As we will see, for most benchmarks in sequential, parallel, or temporal planning, the optimal plans are canonical in this sense but they are not always so. Later on we will discuss briefly how to remove this assumption and preliminary results we have obtained in that direction.

The integration of heuristic functions in a POCL planning framework has been pursued recently in (Nguyen & Kambhampati 2001; Younes & Simmons 2003). However, no attempt at the generation of optimal plans is made in these proposals. Here we make use of some of the ideas in (Nguyen & Kambhampati 2001) like the use of structural mutexes for extending the notion of threats in POCL planning, and the use of disjunctive constraints for expressing the possible resolution of threats. Temporal POCL planners featuring constraint propagation mechanisms include IxTeT (Laborie & Ghallab 1995) and RAX (Jonsson *et al.*

---

*H. Geffner partially supported by Grant TIC2002-04470-C03-02, MCyT, Spain.

2000). These planners are more expressive than ours (e.g., in the use of resources), but their pruning mechanisms are weaker as they tend to reason about actions in the current partial plan only. Something similar occurs with formulations of POCL planning as Dynamic CSPs (Joslin & Pollack 1996). A previous CP approach to planning over various *specific* domains is given in (Van Beek & Chen 1999). We borrow some elements from this formulation, like the use of *distances* of various sorts, yet our approach is domain-independent. The broad ideas on which the current proposal is based have been outlined first in (Geffner 2001), and a preliminary implementation for parallel planning was reported earlier in (Palacios & Geffner 2002).

## Preview

In order to illustrate the capabilities of the proposed planner, let us consider the problem TOWER-$n$ where the task is to build a tower with $n$ blocks $b_1, \ldots, b_n$ in that order, $b_1$ on top, which initially lie all on the table. The single optimal plan for this problem involves picking each block $b_i$ from the table and stacking it on block $b_{i+1}$, in order, from $i = n - 1$ down to 1. The reasoning mechanisms underlying the proposed planner, that we call CPT, yield a solution to this problem *by pure inference and no search.* This is remarkable as the inferences are not trivial and existing optimal planners do not scale up well in this domain (see Table 1). How does CPT do it? First, it infers that each subgoal $on(b_i, b_{i+1})$ must be achieved by the action $stack(b_i, b_{i+1})$ and then that these actions must be ordered sequentially, $stack(b_{n-1}, b_n)$ first, then $stack(b_{n-2}, b_{n-1})$, and so on. CPT also infers that the first action cannot start earlier than $t = 1$, the second not earlier than $t = 3$, etc. Then, after setting the bound $B = 2(n - 1)$ on the makespan to the earliest starting time of the action $End$, it infers that the starting times of all actions must be set to their lowest possible values, and adds the actions $pick(b_i)$ at their correct times as a result of further reasoning that prunes the other possible supports and times.

| Problem | CPU time (sec.) | | | | Makespan |
|---|---|---|---|---|---|
| | CPT | BBOX | IPP | TP4 | |
| tower-8 | 0.33 | 2.95 | 0.05 | 17.68 | 14 |
| tower-9 | 0.64 | 7.28 | 0.11 | 887.7 | 16 |
| tower-10 | 1.01 | 13.6 | 0.38 | - | 18 |
| tower-11 | 1.69 | 28.2 | 2.26 | - | 20 |
| tower-12 | 3.61 | - | 15.35 | - | 22 |
| tower-13 | 5.83 | - | 123.78 | - | 24 |
| tower-14 | 9.70 | - | - | - | 26 |
| tower-15 | 13.65 | - | - | - | 28 |

Table 1: Results for TOWER-$n$ domain

Table 1 shows results for CPT in relation to other three modern planners: two optimal parallel planners, Blackbox (with Chaff) (Kautz & Selman 1999) and IPP (Koehler *et al.* 1997), and an optimal temporal planner TP4 (Haslum & Geffner 2001). While most domains are not like TOWER-$n$ and require search, the domain illustrates the strength of CPT inference mechanisms that often manage to prune the search space considerably. Over the next few sections we will see how this is achieved and how cost-effective these mechanisms are in other parallel and temporal domains.

## Background

The proposed scheme combines lower bounds, a branching scheme that parallels the one used in POCL planning, and a constraint-directed branch-and-bound search.

### Lower Bounds

A recent key development in AI planning is the use of *heuristic estimators* automatically extracted from problem encodings (McDermott 1996; Bonet, Loerincs, & Geffner 1997). A parameterized family of tractable admissible heuristics or lower bounds $h^m$, $m = 1, 2, \ldots$, for sequential and parallel planning is formulated in (Haslum & Geffner 2000). The heuristics $h^m$ recursively approximate *the cost of a set of atoms $C$ by the cost of the most costly subset of size $m$ in $C$.* For $m = 2$, in the parallel setting, $h^m$ is equivalent to the heuristic encoded in the planning graph. The $h^m$ heuristics are extended in (Haslum & Geffner 2001) to estimate *makespan* (completion time) in a temporal setting. The measures $h^m_T(C)$ are lower bounds on the time needed to make $C$ true from the initial situation. In CPT these heuristics are used in various ways.

### Branching

Branching in AI planning is most often discussed in terms of the *space* in which the search for plans is done, with state or directional planners searching in the space of *states*, and partial order planners searching in the space of *plans* (Kambhampati, Knoblock, & Yang 1995). All planners, however, can also be seen as searching in the space of plans, with directional planners taking advantage of a *decomposition property* by which a partial plan tail or head can be summarized by the state obtained by regressing the goal or progressing the initial state. This decomposition is not possible in non-directional partial plans as arising from POCL, SAT, or CSP formulations. In all cases, however, in order to search effectively for optimal plans it is necessary to detect and prune early partial plans that can only lead to solutions with cost exceeding a certain bound $B$. In state-based planners this is accomplished by comparing the bound $B$ with the value of an explicit evaluation function; in SAT and CSP formulations, this is achieved by means of clauses and constraints. Planning schemes based on POCL branching lack comparable pruning mechanisms and do not perform as well. Recent proposals like (Nguyen & Kambhampati 2001; Younes & Simmons 2003) extend POCL planning with guiding non-admissible heuristics but leave optimality considerations aside. Here we aim to achieve both good performance and optimality in the more general setting of temporal planning.

### Temporal Planning

A Strips temporal planning problem is a tuple $P = \langle A, I, O, G \rangle$ where $A$ is a set of ground atoms, $I \subseteq A$ and $G \subseteq A$ represent the initial and goal situations, and $O$ is the set of ground Strips operators, each with precondition, add, and delete list $pre(a)$, $add(a)$, and $del(a)$, and *duration* $dur(a)$. As in Graphplan, two actions $a$ and $a'$ interfere when one deletes a precondition or positive effect of the other. We follow the simple model of time in (Smith & Weld 1999), and define a valid plan as a plan where interfering actions do not overlap in time. We are interested in computing valid plans with minimum *makespan*. When all actions have uniform durations, the model reduces to the standard model of parallel planning.

## Temporal POCL Planning

Branching in POCL planning proceeds by picking a 'flaw' (open preconditions or threats) and trying each of the possible *repairs* (Weld 1994; Kambhampati, Knoblock, & Yang 1995). A state or partial plan in the resulting search space corresponds to a set of commitments represented by a tuple $\sigma = \langle Steps, Ord, CL, Open\rangle$, where $Steps$ is the set of actions in the partial plan, $Ord$ is a set of precedence constraints on $Steps$, $CL$ is a set of causal links, and $Open$ is a set of open preconditions (as in most current planners, we assume that all actions are grounded). A state is terminal if it is inconsistent (i.e., the ordering $Ord$ is inconsistent or contains flaws that cannot be fixed) or is a *goal* (is consistent and contains no flaws).

The adaptation of POCL branching to the temporal setting is rather direct (e.g., (Laborie & Ghallab 1995)). Here we consider a simple extension obtained by adding temporal variables $T(a)$ standing for the starting time of action $a$ for $a \in Steps$. These temporal variables have initial domains $T(Start) = 0$, $T(End) = B$, and $T(a) :: [0, B - dur(a)]$ where $B$ is the bound on the makespan ($Start$ and $End$ are the two 'dummy' actions used in POCL planning). The resulting states have the form $\sigma = \langle Steps, Ord_T, CL, Open, T(\cdot)\rangle$ where the qualitative precedence ordering $Ord$ is replaced by the temporal variables $T(a)$, $a \in Steps$, and the set $Ord_T$ of temporal constraints (the precedence ordering $Ord$ from classical POCL planning can be retained but is not strictly necessary).

As before, branching proceeds by picking a 'flaw' in a non-terminal state $\sigma$ and applying the possible repairs. *Open precondition flaws* $[p]a$ in $\sigma$ are solved by selecting an action $a'$ that supports $p$, and adding the causal link $a'[p]a$ to $CL$ and the temporal constraint $T(a') + dur(a') \leq T(a)$ to $Ord_T$. The action $a'$ is added to $Steps$ if $a' \notin Steps$ and in such case a variable $T(a')$ for $a'$ is created. Similarly, causal link *threats*, i.e., situations in which an action $a \in Steps$ may delete a condition $p \in del(a)$ in a causal link $a_1[p]a_2$ in $CL$, are solved by adding one of the temporal constraints $T(a) + dur(a) \leq T(a_1)$ or $T(a_2) + dur(a_2) \leq T(a)$ to $Ord_T$. A terminal state in the resulting space is either a state with an inconsistent set of temporal constraints (a *dead-end*) or a state with a consistent set of temporal constraints and no flaws (a *goal*).

The temporal constraints in $Ord_T$ form a Simple Temporal Problem (STP) (Dechter, Meiri, & Pearl 1991) whose consistency can be tested efficiently by applying a form of constraint propagation known as *bounds consistency* (Lhomme 1993), where the lower and upper bounds $T_{min}(a)$ and $T_{max}(a)$ of the variables $T(a)$ in constraints of the form $T(a) + dur(a) \leq T(a')$ are updated as $T_{max}(a) := \min[T_{max}(a), T_{max}(a') - dur(a)]$ and $T_{min}(a') := \max[T_{min}(a'), T_{min}(a) + dur(a)]$ until a fixed point is reached or a variable domain becomes empty.

With two additional provisions, it is possible to verify that the resulting branching scheme is *sound* and *complete*; i.e., terminal goal-states encode valid temporal plans $P$ with makespan $B$ where actions execute at their earliest possible times, and one such terminal goal state is generated when one such plan exists.

The two required provisions are the following. First, in the absence of a qualitative precedence ordering on actions as in POCL planning, we need to regard an action $a$ deleting the condition $p$ in a causal link $a_1[p]a_2$ as a *threat* when neither of the two temporal conditions $T_{min}(a) + dur(a) \leq T_{min}(a_1)$ and $T_{min}(a_2) + dur(a_2) \leq T_{min}(a)$ hold. This is because the lower bounds $T_{min}$ provide a consistent solution to a STP if the STP is consistent. Second, in accordance with the semantics, we need to ensure that interfering actions do not overlap in time. For that, let us say that a pair of interfering actions are *precondition-interfering* when one action deletes a precondition of the other, and are *effect-interfering* otherwise. It is then sufficient to branch also on a second class of threats; *mutex threats:* pairs of effect-interfering actions $a$ and $a'$ such that neither $T_{min}(a) + dur(a) \leq T_{min}(a')$ nor $T_{min}(a') + dur(a') \leq T_{min}(a)$ hold in $\sigma$. Such flaws are solved by adding to $Ord_T$ one of the temporal constraints $T(a) + dur(a) \leq T(a')$ or $T(a') + dur(a') \leq T(a)$.

Modern Constraint-Based Interval (CBI) planners (Jonsson *et al.* 2000; Smith, Frank, & Jonsson 2000) are based on similar ideas and are able to deal with more expressive languages. Yet, as in standard POCL and Dynamic CSP planners (Joslin & Pollack 1996), the following *performance problem* remains: pruning partial plans whose STP network is not consistent does not suffice to match the performance of modern planners. For this, *more powerful representations and inference methods for predicting that all STP networks in the way to the goal will become inconsistent* are needed.

## A Constraint Programming Formulation

The performance limitation of current constraint-based POCL planners arises mainly from their limitation *to reason about the actions in the current plan only.* Most often, nothing is inferred about an action $a$ until the action is considered for inclusion in the plan. Still, as we have seen in Section 2, a lot can be inferred about such actions including restrictions about their possible starting times and supporters. Some of this information can actually be inferred before any commitments are made; the lower bounds on the starting times of *all* actions as computed in Graphplan being one example. Yet this is not enough; if similar performance and optimality guarantees are to be achieved in the POCL setting, inferences that take advantage of the commitments made are also necessary. In order to perform such inferences, the representation of the space of possible commitments is crucial. We thus make two changes in relation to the temporal POCL planner above. First, we introduce and reason with variables that involve *all* the actions $a$ in the domain; not only those present in the current plan. And second, for all such actions we introduce variables $S(p, a)$ and $T(p, a)$ that stand for the possibly undetermined action supporting precondition $p$ of $a$ and the possibly undetermined starting time of such an action, and perform limited but useful forms of reasoning over such variables. A causal link $a'[p]a$ thus becomes a constraint $S(p, a) = a'$, which in turn implies that the supporter $a'$ of precondition $p$ of $a$ starts at time $T(p, a) = T(a')$.[1]

An important assumption that we make is that *no (ground) action $a$ in the domain occurs more than once in the plan.* This *canonicity assumption* allows us to collapse the notions of action and action occurrence, leading to a number of simplifications. At the same time, it is a meaningful extension of the more restrictive assumption often found in scheduling research where every action in the domain must occur exactly *once*. From a practical point of view, most current benchmarks, whether temporal or not, admit optimal solutions of this kind, as we will see below. Later on we will discuss ways for relaxing this restriction.

The basic CP formulation of the CPT planner is given in four parts: *preprocessing, variables, constraints, and branching.* After the preprocessing, the variables are created and the constraints are asserted and propagated. If an inconsistency is found, no valid plan for the problem exists. Otherwise, the constraint $T(End) = B$ for the bound $B$ set to the earliest possible starting time of the action $End$ (i.e.; $B = T_{min}(End)$) is asserted and propagated. The branching scheme then takes over and if no solution is found, the process restarts by retracting the constraint $T(End) = B$ and replacing it with $T(End) = B + 1$, and so on.

## Preprocessing

In the preprocessing phase, the planner computes the heuristic values $h^2_T(a)$ and $h^2_T(\{p, q\})$ for each action $a \in O$ and each atom pair $\{p, q\}$ as in (Haslum & Geffner 2001). The values provide lower bounds on the times to achieve the preconditions of $a$ and the pair of atoms $p, q$, from the initial situation $I$. In addition, we identify the *(structural) mutexes* as the pairs of atoms $p, q$ for which $h^2_T(\{p, q\}) = \infty$. We then say that an action $a$ *e-deletes* an atom $p$ when either $a$ deletes $p$, $a$ adds an atom $q$ such that $q$ and $p$ are mutex, or a precondition $r$ of $a$ is mutex with $p$ and $a$ does not add $p$ (in all cases $p$ is false after doing $a$; see (Nguyen & Kambhampati 2001)).

In addition, the simpler heuristic $h^1_T$ is used for defining *distances* between actions (Van Beek & Chen 1999) as follows. For each action $a \in O$, we compute the $h^1_T$ heuristic from an initial situation $I_a$ that includes all facts *except those that are e-deleted by $a$.* We then set the distances $dist(a, a')$ to the resulting $h^1_T(a')$ values. Clearly, these distances encode lower bounds on the *slack* that can be inserted between the completion of $a$ and the start of $a'$ in any legal plan in which $a'$ follows $a$.

The distances $dist(a, End)$ and $dist(a, Start)$ are defined in a slightly different way. The former are obtained by running a shortest-path algorithm over a 'relevance graph' where the nodes are the actions $a \in O$ and the action $End$ is the source node. An edge $a \longrightarrow a'$ in this graph means that $a'$ is 'relevant' to $a$ (namely that it adds a precondition $p$ of $a$) and its cost is given by $\delta(a', a) = dur(a') + dist(a', a)$. The distances $dist(a, End)$ are then set to the cost of the shortest-path connecting $End$ to $a$ in this graph. The distances $dist(Start, a)$ are set to $h^2_T(a)$.

## Variables and Domains

The state $\sigma$ of the planner is given by a collection of variables, domains, and constraints. As emphasized above, the variables are defined for each action $a \in O$ and not only for the actions in the current plan. Moreover, variables are created for each precondition $p$ of each action $a$ as indicated below. The domain of variable $X$ is indicated by $D[X]$ or simply as $X :: [X_{min}, X_{max}]$ if $X$ is a numerical variable. The variables, their initial domains, and their meanings are:

- $T(a) :: [0, \infty]$ encodes the starting time of each action $a$, with $T(Start) = 0$.
- $S(p, a)$ encodes the support of precondition $p$ of action $a$ with initial domain $D[S(p, a)] = O(p)$ where $O(p)$ is the set of actions in $O$ that add $p$
- $T(p, a) :: [0, \infty]$ encodes the starting time of $S(p, a)$
- $InPlan(a) :: [0, 1]$ indicates the presence of $a$ in the plan; $InPlan(Start) = InPlan(End) = 1$ (true)

In addition, the set of actions in the current plan is kept in the variable $Steps$; i.e., $Steps = \{a \mid InPlan(a) = 1\}$. Variables $T(a)$, $S(p, a)$, and $T(p, a)$ associated with actions $a$ which are not yet in the plan are *conditional* in the following sense: these variables and their domains are meaningful only under the assumption that they will be part of the plan. In order to ensure this interpretation, some care needs to be taken in the propagation of constraints as explained below.

## Constraints

The constraints correspond basically to disjunctions, rules, and temporal constraints, or their combination. Disjunctions are interpreted constructively: when one disjunct is false, the other is enforced. Similarly for rules: when the antecedent constraint holds, the consequent is enforced. The conditions under which a constraint is regarded as (necessarily) true or false in a state are determined by the nature of the constraint and the domains of the variables; roughly, a constraint is true (false) if it is true (false) for any possible assignment given the domains. E.g., $T(a) < T(a')$ is true if the variable domains are such that $T_{max}(a) < T_{min}(a')$ holds, is false if $T_{min}(a) \geq T_{max}(a')$ holds, and otherwise is *undetermined.*[2] Temporal constraints are propagated by

[1] Propositional 'causal' encodings of Strips planning problems have been formulated and analyzed in (Kautz, McAllester, & Selman 1996; Mali & Kambhampati 1999). Our encodings share a number of features with these formulations but are more compact due to the use of a temporal representation.

[2] Similarly, $T(a) = T(a')$ is true if $T_{min}(a) = T_{max}(a) = T_{min}(a') = T_{max}(a')$ holds, and is false if either $T(a) < T(a')$ or $T(a) > T(a')$ holds. The conditions for enumerated variables like $S(p, a)$ are similar; $S(p, a) = a'$ is true if $D[S(p, a)] = \{a'\}$

bounds consistency as indicated above. In constraints involving terms of the form $op_{a' \in D[S(p,a)]}$, information propagates *from* $S(p,a)$ but not *into* $S(p,a)$; propagation into such variables is achieved by explicit rules with variables $S(p,a)$ on the right hand side. The constraints apply to all actions $a \in O$ and all $p \in pre(a)$; we use $\delta(a, a')$ to stand for $dur(a) + dist(a, a')$.

- **Bounds:** For all $a \in O$, $T(Start) + dist(Start, a) \leq T(a)$ and $T(a) + dist(a, End) \leq T(End)$.
- **Preconditions:** Supporter $a'$ of precondition $p$ of $a$ must precede $a$ by an amount that depends on $\delta(a', a)$:

$$T(a) \geq \min_{a' \in [D(S(p,a)]} (T(a') + \delta(a', a))$$

- **Causal Link Constraints:** for all $a \in O$, $p \in pre(a)$ and $a'$ that e-deletes $p$, $a'$ precedes $S(p,a)$ or follows $a$

$$T(a') + dur(a') + \min_{a'' \in D[S(p,a)]} dist(a', a'') \leq T(p,a)$$

$$\vee \; T(a) + dur(a) + dist(a, a') \leq T(a')$$

- **Mutex Constraints:** For effect-interfering $a$ and $a'$

$$T(a) + \delta(a, a') \leq T(a') \; \vee \; T(a') + \delta(a', a) \leq T(a)$$

- **Support Constraints:** $T(p,a)$ and $S(p,a)$ related by

$$S(p,a) = a' \rightarrow T(p,a) = T(a')$$

$$\min_{a' \in D[S(p,a)]} T(a') \leq T(p,a) \leq \max_{a' \in D[S(p,a)]} T(a')$$

$$T(p,a) \neq T(a') \rightarrow S(p,a) \neq a'$$

$$T(a') + \delta(a', a) > T(a) \rightarrow S(p,a) \neq a'$$

The constraints involving the variables $S(p,a)$ and $T(p,a)$ are *lifted* in the sense that they apply to all possible supporters $a'$ of precondition $p$ of $a$. As mentioned above, the variables $T(a)$, $T(p,a)$, and $S(p,a)$ are *conditional* when $InPlan(a) = 1$ is neither true or false. They become *in-plan* variables when $InPlan(a) = 1$ becomes true, and *out-plan* variables when $InPlan(a) = 1$ becomes false. Constraints involving in-plan variables only are propagated as usual, and furthermore, an empty domain raises an inconsistency. Constraints involving an out-plan variable, on the other hand, are not propagated. Finally, and most importantly, constraints involving conditional variables associated with the *same action* $a$ and hence the same assumption (namely that $a$ will be part of the plan) are propagated but *only in the direction of the conditional variables.* This ensures that the domain of a conditional variable depends only on the assumption that that particular variable is in the plan and on no other assumption. As a result, *if the domain of a conditional variable associated with an action a becomes empty, it is inferred that the action a cannot be part of the current plan and not that the current partial plan is inconsistent.* More precisely, $InPlan(a)$ is set to 0 if the domain of a conditional variable associated with $a$ becomes empty, and in such case, the action $a$ is removed from the domain of all support variables $S(p, a')$ such that $a$ adds $p$. On the other hand, when $S(p, a') = a$ holds for some action $a'$ in the plan, $InPlan(a)$ is automatically set to 1. Conditional variables of this type in constraint programming have been considered in (Focacci & Milano 2001).

and is false if $a' \notin D[S(p,a)]$. In all cases, the constraint $\neg C$ is true (false) if $C$ is false (true). In CP, it is common to say that a constraint is *entailed* in a state rather than true (Van Hentenryck, Simonis, & Dincbas 1992). We also note that $T(a) < T(a')$ is true in our modified CP engine when $a' = End$, regardless of the domain of $T(a)$.

## Branching

The definition of 'flaws' parallels the one considered above for temporal POCL planning:

- **Support Threats:** $a'$ *threats a support* $S(p,a)$ when both actions $a$ and $a'$ are in the current plan, $a'$ e-deletes $p$, and neither $T_{min}(a') + dur(a') \leq T_{min}(p,a)$ nor $T_{min}(a) + dur(a) \leq T_{min}(a')$ hold.
- **Open Conditions:** $S(p,a)$ is an *open condition* when $|D[S(p,a)]| > 1$ holds for an action $a$ in the plan.
- **Mutex Threats:** $a$ and $a'$ constitute a *mutex threat* when both actions are in the plan, they are effect-interfering, and neither $T_{min}(a) + dur(a) \leq T_{min}(a')$ nor $T_{min}(a') + dur(a') \leq T_{min}(a)$ hold (two actions are effect-interfering in CPT when one deletes a positive effect of the other, and neither one *e-deletes* a precondition of the other).

Upon selecting a flaw in a state $\sigma$, a *binary split* is created which we denote as $[C_1; C_2]$ where $C_1$ and $C_2$ are constraints. The first child $\sigma_1$ of $\sigma$ is obtained by adding $C_1$ to $\sigma$ and closing the result under the propagation rules; the second child $\sigma_2$ of $\sigma$ is generated by adding the constraint $C_2$ instead, when the search beneath $\sigma_1$ fails. The binary splits generated for each type of flaw are as follows:

- A **Support Threat** $\langle a', S(p,a) \rangle$ generates the split $[T(a') + dur(a') + \min_{a'' \in D[S(p,a)]} dist(a', a'') \leq T(p,a); T(a) + \delta(a, a') \leq T(a')]$
- An **Open Condition** $S(p,a)$ generates the split $[S(p,a) = a'; S(p,a) \neq a']$ for a selected $a'$
- A **Mutex Threat** $\langle a, a' \rangle$ generates the split $[T(a) + \delta(a, a') \leq T(a'); T(a') + \delta(a', a) \leq T(a)]$

The branching scheme is sound and complete. Soundness follows from the validity of the plan $P$ obtained from a consistent state $\sigma$ with no flaws by scheduling the in-plan actions $a_i$ at the earliest possible times $t_i = T_{min}(a_i)$. Completeness in turn follows from the soundness of the propagation rules and the validity of the disjunctions $C_1 \vee C_2$ associated with the binary splits $[C_1; C_2]$.

**Branching heuristics** In each step, the selected flaw is a Support Threat (ST) if one exist, else an Open Condition (OC) if one exists, else a Mutex Threat (MT). The heuristic for selecting among the existing flaws is the following:

- **Support Threats** $\langle a', S(p,a) \rangle$ with minimum slack $\max[slack(a' \prec S(p,a)), slack(a \prec a')]$ selected first (Smith & Cheng 1993), where $slack(a \prec a')$ is $T_{max}(a') - (T_{min}(a) + \delta(a, a'))$ and $slack(a' \prec S(p,a))$ is $T_{max}(p,a) - (T_{min}(a') + \min_{a' \in [D(S(p,a)]} \delta(a', a))$

- **Open conditions** $S(p,a)$ selected latest first; i.e. maximizing the expression $\min_{a' \in D[S(p,a)]} T_{min}(a')$, splitting on the 'arg min' action $a'$ (i.e., creating the split $[S(p,a) = a'; S(p,a) \neq a']$.
- **Mutex Threats** $\langle a, a' \rangle$ selected as they are encountered

The heuristics for STs and OCs have a significant influence on performance but not so the heuristic for MTs (most often no MTs are left after removal of STs and OCs).

### Mutex Sets

The code incorporates an enhancement that helps in some domains without representing a significant overhead in others. It has to do with the idea of *mutex sets:* sets $M$ of actions *in the plan,* (not necessarily pairs) such that any two actions in $M$ are interfering. Since such actions cannot overlap, the time window associated with the set of actions $M$, $\max_{a \in M}(T_{max}(a) + dur(a)) - \min_{a \in M} T_{min}(a)$, must provide enough 'room' for scheduling all actions in $a \in M$ in sequence. Taking into account the pre-computed distances, a lower bound $\Delta(M)$ for the time needed for scheduling all actions in $M$ is given by

$$\sum_{a \in M} [dur(a) + \min_{a' \in M | a' \neq a} dist(a, a')] - \max_{\{a, a'\} \subseteq M} dist(a, a')$$

which expresses a lower bound on the time needed to schedule all the actions in $M$, one before another, except for the action scheduled last. With these lower bounds, we define the *Mutex Set* constraint as

$$\max_{a' \in M} T(a') - \min_{a'' \in M} T(a'') \geq \Delta(M)$$

and apply it to *some* mutex sets $M$ identified from the actions $Steps$ in the plan in a greedy fashion, as described below (computing the largest mutex sets in the plan seems too expensive). The idea of mutex sets is adapted from similar concepts used in constraint-based scheduling such as *edge-finding;* see (Carlier & Pinson 1989; Baptiste, Le Pape, & Nuijten 2001; Laborie 2003).

- **Global Mutex Sets** $M_i$ are built greedily as new actions are added to $Steps$. Initially a single mutex set $M_0$ with the $Start$ and $End$ actions is defined; then any time an action $a$ is added to $Steps$, $a$ is added to each existing mutex set $M_i$, $i = 0, \ldots, k$ such that $a$ is interfering with each action $a'$ in $M_i$, and a new mutex set $M_{k+1}$ is created with $a$ only when $a$ cannot be added to any existing mutex set. The mutex set constraint is enforced for each such set $M_i$.
- **Causal Link Mutex Sets** $M^-$ and $M^+$ are defined also for each 'causal link' $S(p,a)[p]a$ in the plan. Initially, these sets are empty, then when a new action $a'$ is added to the plan that e-deletes $p$ and cannot follow $a$ (resp. cannot precede $S(p,a)$), $a$ is added to $M^-$ (resp. to $M^+$) if $a$ is interfering with each action in $M^-$ (resp. in $M^+$). For these mutex sets $M^+$ and $M^-$, the following *CL Mutex Set constraint* is enforced, which unlike the mutex set constraint above, not only detects inconsistencies, but also prunes the bounds of the temporal variables $T(p,a)$ and $T(a)$:

$$\min_{a' \in M^-} T(a') + \Delta(M^-) \leq T(p,a) \ \wedge$$

$$T(a) + dur(a) \leq \max_{a' \in M^+} [T(a') + dur(a')] - \Delta(M^+)$$

In addition, for all $a'$ in the plan that e-delete $p$ that can follow $S(p,a)$ and precede $a$, we evaluate the consistency of the mutex set $M^- \cup \{a'\}$ (resp. $M^+ \cup \{a'\}$) if $a'$ is interfering with each action in $M^-$ (resp. $M^+$). If the set is inconsistent (i.e., it violates the mutex constraint), then it is inferred that $a'$ must follow $a$ (resp. must precede $S(p,a)$).

### Implementation

The CPT planner has been implemented using the Choco CP library (Laburthe 2000) that operates on top of the Claire programming language (Caseau, Josset, & Laburthe 1999) that compiles into C++. In early stages of the implementation, we wrote the constraints in Choco in a way that resembled the formulation above, yet we progressively moved to an implementation based on propagation rules that avoids unnecessary checks and triggerings, and speeds up the propagations. The current implementation is a collection of rules which are triggered by the event mechanism of Choco. Updates on lower bounds, upper bounds, and domain values are recorded in event queues, where similar events are 'collapsed'; e.g., if the lower bound of a variable $X$ is increased successively from 1 to 2, and then from 2 to 3 before the first event is dequeued, only one event is stored, stating that the lower bound of $X$ is increased from 1 to 3. When an event is dequeued, the relevant rules are triggered, performing the appropriate propagations (updates on variables constrained by the modified variables, ...). The only constraints not re-implemented in terms of rules are the dynamic constraints; namely those that are posted as a result of branching. We modified the Choco engine so that these constraints can be backtracked upon inconsistencies, and also for enforcing the semantics of conditional variables. As stated above, for the latter an empty domain does not raise an inconsistency but forces an action out of the plan. On temporal variables, the conditional behavior is obtained by handling those variables ourselves; support conditional variables, on the other hand, are treated as normal CP variables with a dummy action $\alpha$ added to their domains, with $D[S(p,a)] = \{\alpha\}$ meaning that $p$ cannot be supported by any action. The $InPlan(a)$ variables are not implemented as CP variables either; the information about the status of actions in the plan is compiled in the code of the propagation rules. The code incorporates optimizations which we lack the space to discuss here like the use of a larger set of (redundant but effective) 'threats' on which to branch. The code will be made available for download.

## Experimental Results

The experiments have been obtained using a Pentium IV machine running at 1.6Ghz, with 512Mb of RAM, under

Linux. The time limit for each problem is one hour. Table 3 compares CPT , Blackbox (with Chaff), IPP, and TP4 over parallel domains, while Table 4 compares CPT and TP4 over temporal domains. These are all optimal planners. The times in all cases include preprocessing. The parallel domains include blocks and logistic instances from the Blackbox distribution. The rest of the instances are from the 3rd Int. Planning Competition (Long & Fox 2003a). The tables show that CPT runtimes are close to Blackbox over the parallel domains, and can even solve problems like bw-large.c and satellite11 that Blackbox cannot solve (the good performance of CPT in blocks owes a lot to the use of mutex sets). CPT is sometimes slower than IPP but can solve many more problems while it clearly dominates TP4 over all parallel and temporal domains, and expands much fewer nodes (these are the numbers in parenthesis). As discussed in (Haslum & Geffner 2001), the problem of state-based temporal planners such as TP4 is their *branching factor* which may be exponential in the number of primitive actions in the domain. In CPT, the branching factor is two, and after every branching decision, a powerful pruning mechanism is applied.

As Table 2 shows, CPT seems to dominate also LPGP, a recent temporal planner that optimizes the number of steps in the plan rather than the makespan (Long & Fox 2003b). We only consider the instances reported for LPGP on a similar machine. The shorter makespans for LPGP in one domain (satellite), arise from slight differences in the semantics (namely, LPGP follows the PDDL2.1 semantics (Fox & Long 2003) where interfering actions may overlap, e.g., when preconditions do not have to be preserved throughout the execution of the action).

| Strips | CPU time (sec.) | | | | Makespan |
|---|---|---|---|---|---|
| problems | CPT | BBOX | IPP | TP4 | |
| bw.12step | 0.21 | 0.26 | 0.03 | 0.08 | 12 |
| bw.large.a | 0.44 | 1.13 | 0.07 | 0.08 | 12 |
| bw.large.b | 1.75 | 17.94 | 2.33 | - | 18 |
| bw.large.c | 231.22 | - | - | - | 28 |
| rocket.a | 0.28 | 0.38 | 7.97 | 44.20 | 7 |
| rocket.b | 0.24 | 0.45 | 11.95 | 31.83 | 7 |
| log.a | 0.70 | 0.47 | 781.13 | - | 11 |
| log.b | 0.90 | 0.91 | 2099.89 | - | 13 |
| log.c | 1.43 | 1.46 | - | - | 13 |
| log.d | 29.03 | 3.73 | - | - | 14 |
| zeno7 | 0.84 | 0.67 | 0.05 | 1.76 | 6 |
| zeno8 | 5.39 | 1.59 | 0.22 | 166.22 | 5 |
| zeno9 | 6.41 | 2.54 | 0.68 | - | 6 |
| zeno10 | 6.84 | 4.01 | 221.32 | - | 6 |
| zeno11 | 14.90 | 5.60 | 31.06 | - | 6 |
| zeno12 | 16.39 | 11.10 | - | - | 6 |
| zeno13 | 45.97 | 11.42 | - | - | 7 |
| driver7 | 0.24 | 0.24 | 0.15 | 22.98 | 6 |
| driver8 | 0.30 | 0.40 | 3.53 | 33.59 | 7 |
| driver9 | 1.46 | 1.55 | 11.26 | 2979.66 | 10 |
| driver10 | 1.02 | 1.00 | 17.06 | 1823.16 | 7 |
| driver11 | 4.33 | 2.67 | 2.26 | 1259.06 | 9 |
| satellite3 | 0.12 | 0.26 | 0.03 | 0.08 | 6 |
| satellite4 | 0.40 | 1.39 | 7.28 | 755.08 | 10 |
| satellite5 | 0.99 | 1.50 | 145.67 | - | 7 |
| satellite6 | 0.56 | 1.34 | 90.46 | - | 8 |
| satellite7 | 1.55 | 1.80 | 1039.23 | - | 6 |
| satellite8 | 101.18 | 235.13 | - | - | 8 |
| satellite9 | 8.52 | 4.68 | - | - | 6 |
| satellite10 | 185.90 | 42.35 | - | - | 8 |
| satellite11 | 22.51 | - | - | - | 8 |

Table 3: Results for parallel domains

## Discussion

We have developed a domain-independent optimal POCL temporal planner based on constraint programming that integrates existing lower bounds with novel representations and propagation rules that manage to prune the search space considerably. The experiments show that the resulting planner is faster than current optimal temporal planners and competitive with the best parallel planners. The formulation exploits the canonicity restriction that no (ground) action $a$ in the domain occurs more than once in the plan. This restriction allows us to collapse the notions of action and action occurrence, leading to a number of simplifications. We are currently working on a formulation that removes this restriction. The formulation is based on distinguishing *action types* from *action tokens*. Plans contain only action tokens which are all instances of the fixed set of action types defined by the initial set of operators. Action tokens are created dynamically from action types as in POCL planning; namely, as new action instances that support a selected open condition. In this setting, however, the creation of new instances takes the form of a 'cloning' operation: for the new instance $a'$ of type $a$, the variables $T(a')$, $S(p, a')$, and $T(p, a')$ are created as fresh copies of the variables $T(a)$, $S(p, a)$, and $T(p, a)$ with their corresponding domains, where $p$ is a precondition of $a$. In addition, the new token $a'$ is added as an independent action to all support domains that include the action type $a$. The resulting scheme can actually be seen as providing a lazy implementation of a planning domain with an infinite number of action instances, with the action types summarizing the domains of the action instances that have not been yet used in the plan. For the parallel domains, the performance degradation is moderate (runtimes do not appear to increase in more than 15% over the instances considered in this paper), while for temporal domains, it is greater (although the resulting planner still performs much better than current optimal planners). We are still tuning the non-canonical planner and plan to report the relevant details elsewhere.

## References

Baptiste, P.; Le Pape, C.; and Nuijten, W. 2001. *Constraint-Based Scheduling: Applying Constraint Programming to Scheduling Problems*. Kluwer.

Blum, A., and Furst, M. 1995. Fast planning through planning graph analysis. In *Proceedings of IJCAI-95*, 1636–1642.

Bonet, B.; Loerincs, G.; and Geffner, H. 1997. A robust and fast action selection mechanism for planning. In *Proceedings of AAAI-97*, 714–719. MIT Press.

Carlier, J., and Pinson, E. 1989. An algorithm for solving the job shop scheduling problem. *Management Science* 35(2).

Caseau, Y.; Josset, F. X.; and Laburthe, F. 1999. Claire: Com-

| | zeno4 | zeno5 | zeno6 | driver1 | rover1 | rover2 | rover3 | rover4 | satellite1 | satellite2 | satellite3 |
|---|---|---|---|---|---|---|---|---|---|---|---|
| CPT | 4.59 (522) | 3.83 (400) | 1.78 (323) | 0.06 (91) | 0.12 (53) | 0.07 (43) | 0.11 (53) | 0.09 (45) | 0.05 (46) | 0.95 (70) | 0.20 (34) |
| LPGP | 65.32 (740) | 43.83 (583) | 57.61 (350) | 0.33 (91) | 0.30 (55) | 0.24 (44) | 0.44 (58) | 0.40 (47) | 0.17 (41) | 24.15 (65) | 62.22 (29) |

Table 2: Comparison CPT vs. LPGP (CPU time in sec., makespan in parenthesis)

| Temporal problems | CPU time (sec.) (+number of states) CPT | TP4 | Makespan |
|---|---|---|---|
| zeno1 | 0.06 (2) | 0.05 (4) | 173 |
| zeno2 | 0.95 (892) | 1.23 (17124) | 592 |
| zeno3 | 0.50 (4) | 0.05 (618) | 280 |
| zeno4 | 4.59 (2233) | - | 522 |
| zeno5 | 3.83 (124) | 34.78 (595988) | 400 |
| zeno6 | 1.78 (54) | 6.03 (116715) | 323 |
| zeno7 | 77.58 (45187) | - | 665 |
| zeno8 | 265.93 (78044) | - | 522 |
| zeno9 | 1522.24 (432210) | - | 522 |
| zeno10 | 82.62 (12692) | - | 453 |
| zeno11 | 116.15 (874) | - | 423 |
| driver1 | 0.06 (6) | 0.05 (49) | 91 |
| driver2 | 734.98 (724327) | 458.19 (17444608) | 92 |
| driver3 | 0.12 (11) | 0.05 (621) | 40 |
| driver4 | 91.32 (54350) | - | 52 |
| driver5 | 0.40 (152) | - | 51 |
| driver6 | 111.10 (59702) | - | 52 |
| driver7 | 0.59 (103) | 20.79 (323963) | 40 |
| driver8 | - | - | - |
| driver9 | 493.91 (137716) | - | 92 |
| driver10 | 8.75 (1517) | - | 38 |
| satellite1 | 0.05 (5) | 0.05 (80) | 46 |
| satellite2 | 0.95 (1435) | 8.45 (712294) | 70 |
| satellite3 | 0.20 (26) | 0.05 (21143) | 34 |
| satellite4 | 4.36 (5257) | - | 58 |
| satellite5 | 2.32 (1191) | - | 36 |
| satellite6 | 0.82 (47) | - | 46 |
| satellite7 | 2.36 (325) | - | 34 |
| satellite8 | 3324.92 (827408) | - | 46 |
| satellite9 | 8.84 (516) | - | 34 |
| satellite10 | 2160.24 (261474) | - | 43 |

Table 4: Results for temporal domains


bining sets, search and rules to better express algorithms. In *Proceedings of the Int. Conf. on Logic Programming*.

Dechter, R.; Meiri, I.; and Pearl, J. 1991. Temporal constraint networks. *Artificial Intelligence* 49:61–95.

Do, M. B., and Kambhampati, S. 2000. Solving planning-graph by compiling it into CSP. In *Proc. AIPS-00*, 82–91.

Focacci, F., and Milano, M. 2001. Connections and integrations of dynamic programming and constraint programming. In *Proc. of the Int. Workshop on Integration of AI and OR techniques (CP-AI-OR'01)*.

Fox, M., and Long, D. 2003. PDDL2.1: An extension to PDDL for expressing temporal planning domains. *JAIR* 20.

Geffner, H. 2001. Planning as branch and bound and its relation to constraint-based approaches. Technical report, Universidad Simón Bolívar. At www.tecn.upf.es/~hgeffner.

Haslum, P., and Geffner, H. 2000. Admissible heuristics for optimal planning. In *Proc. AIPS-2000*, 70–82.

Haslum, P., and Geffner, H. 2001. Heuristic planning with time and resources. In *Proc. ECP-01*, 121–132.

Jonsson, A.; Morris, P.; Muscettola, N.; and Rajan, K. 2000. Planning in interplanetary space. In *Proc. AIPS-2000*, 177–186.

Joslin, D., and Pollack, M. E. 1996. Is "early commitment" in plan generation ever a good idea? In *Proc. AAAI-96*, 1188–1193.

Kambhampati, S.; Knoblock, C.; and Yang, Q. 1995. Planning as refinement search. *AI* 76(1-2):167–238.

Kautz, H., and Selman, B. 1999. Unifying SAT-based and Graph-based planning. *Proc. IJCAI-99*, 318–327.

Kautz, H.; McAllester, D.; and Selman, B. 1996. Encoding plans in propositional logic. In *Proc. KR'96*, 374–384.

Koehler, J.; Nebel, B.; Hoffman, J.; and Dimopoulos, Y. 1997. Extending planning graphs to an ADL subset. In Proc. ECP-97. Lect. Notes in AI 1348, 273–285.

Laborie, P., and Ghallab, M. 1995. Planning with sharable resources constraints. *Proc. IJCAI-95*, 1643–1649.

Laborie, P. 2003. Algorithms for propagating resource constraints in AI planning and scheduling. *AI* 143:151–188.

Laburthe, F. 2000. Choco: implementing a CP kernel. In *Proceedings CP-00, Lecture Notes in CS, Vol 1894*. Springer.

Lhomme, O. 1993. Consistency techniques for numeric CSPs. In *Proceedings IJCAI-93*, 232–238. Morgan Kaufmann.

Long, D., and Fox, M. 2003a. The 3rd international planning competition: Results and analysis. *JAIR* 20:1–59.

Long, D., and Fox, M. 2003b. Exploiting a graphplan framework in temporal planning. In *Proceedings ICAPS 2003*, 52–61.

Mali, A., and Kambhampati, S. 1999. On the utility of plan-space (causal) encodings. In *Proceedings AAAI-99*, 557–563.

McDermott, D. 1996. A heuristic estimator for means-ends analysis in planning. In *Proc. AIPS-96*.

Nguyen, X. L., and Kambhampati, S. 2001. Reviving partial order planning. In *Proc. IJCAI-01*.

Palacios, H., and Geffner, H. 2002. Planning as branch and bound: A constraint programming implementation. In *Proc. XXVIII Conf. Latinoamericana de Informática*, 239–251.

Smith, S., and Cheng, C. 1993. Slack-based heuristics for the constraint satisfaction scheduling. In *Proc. AAAI-93*, 139–144.

Smith, D., and Weld, D. 1999. Temporal planning with mutual exclusion reasoning. In *Proc. IJCAI-99*, 326–337.

Smith, D.; Frank, J.; and Jonsson, A. 2000. Bridging the gap between planning and scheduling. *Know. Eng. Review* 15(1).

Van Beek, P., and Chen, X. 1999. CPlan: a constraint programming approach to planning. In *Proc. AAAI-99*, 585–590.

Van Hentenryck, P.; Simonis, H.; and Dincbas, M. 1992. Constraint satisfaction using constraint logic programming. *Artificial Intelligence* 58(1–3):113–159.

Weld, D. S. 1994. An introduction to least commitment planning. *AI Magazine* 15(4):27–61.

Younes, B. L. S., and Simmons, R. G. 2003. VHPOP: Versatile heuristic partial order planner. *JAIR* 20:405–430.

# High-level Goal Recognition in a Wireless LAN

**Jie Yin** and **Xiaoyong Chai** and **Qiang Yang**
Department of Computer Science
Hong Kong University of Science and Technology
Clearwater Bay, Kowloon, Hong Kong, China
{yinjie, carnamel, qyang}@cs.ust.hk

## Abstract

Plan recognition has traditionally been developed for logically encoded application domains with a focus on logical reasoning. In this paper, we present an integrated plan-recognition model that combines low-level sensory readings with high-level goal inference. A two-level architecture is proposed to infer a user's goals in a complex indoor environment using an RF-based wireless network. The novelty of our work derives from our ability to infer a user's goals from sequences of signal trajectory, and the ability for us to make a trade-off between model accuracy and inference efficiency. The model relies on a dynamic Bayesian network to infer a user's actions from raw signals, and an N-gram model to infer the users' goals from actions. We present a method for constructing the model from the past data and demonstrate the effectiveness of our proposed solution through empirical studies using some real data that we have collected.

## Introduction

As the pervasive computing technology becomes more and more mature, different context-aware applications have emerged. A variety of techniques are now available for sensing the location of an individual using GPS devices, active badges, motion detectors, mobile phones and PDA's in wireless networks. Using these systems, an individual's location can be tracked in a pervasive computing environment. On observing a user's past and current mobile sensory readings, it is natural to ask: where is the user likely to visit in the next while? What is the user trying to do? What is the ultimate goal of the user?

The above questions are instances of inferring high-level user-behavior patterns from low-level sensory data through location-based plan recognition. Being able to accomplish this task is critical to many applications. For people suffering from various cognitive limitations in hospitals and care facilities, the technique can discover when a person's behavior is out of the norm and provide help in a timely manner (Patterson *et al.* 2003). For shoppers in a busy business environment such as a shopping mall, services and products can be offered not only according to the people's current location, but also according to their intended actions and goals.

Despite the potentially wide range of applications, location-based plan recognition remains a difficult task. One reason is that the location itself is often inferred from low-level sensory data, but often such data provides ambiguous information, making it impossible to obtain accurate estimation. This is particularly the case in a wireless LAN, in-door environment. Another source of difficulty is that the users' behavior is often inherently ambiguous. For example, a professor in an academic building may follow a route by which he walks through a sequence of hallways and then reaches some location in the office area. However, his intention and subsequent behavior can be quite different depending on not just his current location but his entire trace as well as the time and data of his activities. Depending on his goals he may wish to attend a seminar or to go to a printer.

In this paper, we address the problem of inferring a user's high-level goals from low-level mobile data in an indoor environment, where a wireless LAN is available. The novelty of our work can be seen from several aspects. First, in the pervasive computing literature, an important focus has been to determine and track a user's location from sensory data. Examples include the use of GPS, ultrasonic-based systems, infrared-based systems (Fox *et al.* 2002) and radio frequency (RF)- based systems (Bahl & Padmanabhan 2000; Youssef, Agrawala, & Shankar 2003; Ladd *et al.* 2002). Among these systems, the RF-based systems utilize an underlying wireless network to estimate the location of users, which has gained more attention recently, especially for indoor applications. Unlike infrared-based systems, RF-based techniques can provide more ubiquitous coverage, and do not require additional expensive hardware since many buildings are already equipped with IEEE 802.11b wireless Ethernet. Following this tradition, in our work, we utilize the data gathered from an RF-based wireless LAN. However, so far there has been a lack of study on the problem of inferring a user's high-level goals from low-level sensory data. In fact, as observed in (Patterson *et al.* 2003), having a good understanding about a user's high-level behavior patterns and goals will help in estimating the user's current locations.

Second, in the artificial intelligence area, recognizing complex high-level behavior has traditionally been the focus of plan recognition (Kautz & Allen 1986; Lesh & Etzioni 1995). A Bayesian network was used for plan recognition in story understanding in (Charniak & Goldman 1993). In (Blaylock & Allen 2003), a corpus-based N-gram model was proposed to predict the goal from a given sequence of command actions in the UNIX domain. In addition, other advanced stochastic models for recognizing high-level behavior were proposed such as Dynamic Bayesian Networks (DBNs) (Albrecht, Zukerman, & Nicholson 1998) and Probabilistic State Dependent Grammars (Pynadath & Wellman 2000). However, most of the work in plan recognition has been restricted to the high level for inference, and the challenge of dealing with low-level sensor models has not been addressed.

Only in recent years, attempts have been made to integrate high-level behavior models with low-level sensor models. The work of (Patterson *et al.* 2003) presented an approach by applying a Bayesian model to predict a user's transportation mode based on location readings from GPS devices in an urban environment. One feature of the GPS technology is that it can directly provide the information of locations more accurately. In contrast, in our problem, only RF-based signal-strength values from multiple sensor sources are available. Moreover, the signal itself is highly unstable and is affected by the environment to a large extent. Therefore, it is a challenging task to build a model that is both accurate and efficient using such noisy signals. Similarly, the activity maps developed in (Demirdjian *et al.* 2002) used computer vision to detect the users' non-transient behavior through spatial-temporal clustering.

In this paper, we present an architecture for inferring a user's high-level actions and goals from data obtained in the context of a popular RF-based wireless network in complex indoor environments. We build on the work of (Patterson *et al.* 2003), where a DBN is applied for inferring actions from traces of signals. On top of this framework, we provide a novel two-level hierarchy to enable the inference of goals from actions efficiently and accurately. Instead of directly applying a multi-level DBN model, which does not scale well for increasing numbers of goals, we provide a simple N-gram inference method for inferring goals from action sequences. We show that this model is more efficient than a monolithic DBN model, and is almost as accurate as a DBN model. One advantage of our architecture is that high-level, common sense knowledge can be easily incorporated into the reasoning process.

The rest of the paper is organized as follows. We begin by providing an overview of the problem domain. Then we present a DBN solution to the recognition problem. We then propose a two-level model that is more efficient but can achieve almost the same accuracy as the DBN. We describe experimental results in a real office environment. Finally we discuss conclusions and some directions for future work.

## Overview of Problem Domain

In this section, we first describe the problem domain in detail. The layout of the environment is shown in Figure 1. In the figure, several base stations with known Media Access Control (MAC) addresses are marked with double concrete circles.

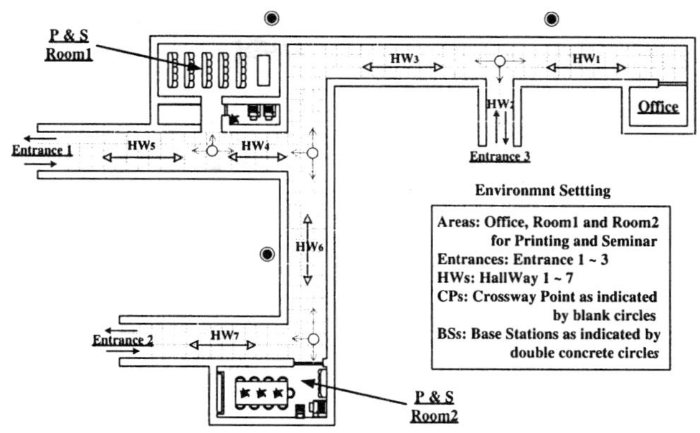


Figure 1: The Layout of Office Area

After collecting sequences of signals from the base stations and labelling each sequence with its intended goal, we obtain a database of a user's historic traces to achieve different goals as given in Table 1. Each trace, corresponding to a single goal, records a sequence of observed signals where each element of the trace is a vector. At each time instant $t_i$, the vector consists of several pairs of MAC addresses and signals from the corresponding base stations where the signals can be detected by a wireless device. For example, we can see from Table 1 that at the time point $t_2$, the signal-strength values of three base stations for the first trace are 56, 30 and 62, respectively.

| Trace # | Observed Signal Sequences | | | | Goal |
|---|---|---|---|---|---|
| | $t_1$ | $t_2$ | ... | $t_k$ | |
| 1 | (b1:57)<br>(b2:33)<br>(b3:51) | (b1:56)<br>(b2:30)<br>(b3:62) | (b1:55)<br>(b2:36)<br>(b3:56) | (b1:52)<br>(b2:62)<br>(b3:47) | $G_1$ |
| 2 | (b1:62)<br>(b2:57)<br>(b3:55) | (b1:39)<br>(b2:41)<br>(b3:32) | (b1:46)<br>(b2:45)<br>(b3:43) | (b1:41)<br>(b2:43)<br>(b3:27) | $G_2$ |

Table 1: An Example of Trace Database

A user's behavior model can be built based on these labelled historic sensory data. A user's behavior is represented as a sequence of actions to achieve a goal in the high level. There are 11 actions and 19 goals of a professor's behavior in this environment. To illustrate, examples of actions include "Walk-in-HW1", "Enter-Room1" and "Print". Out of the 19 goals, we illustrate using four examples of goals. $G_1$ = "Seminar-in-Room1": a professor leaves his office, walks through hallways HW1, HW3, HW4, and enters the P&S Room1 to attend a seminar there; $G_2$ = "Print-in-Room1": he follows the same route as before, but he goes to get some printed material from a printer in P&S Room1; $G_3$ = "Seminar-in-Room2": the professor leaves his office, walks through hallways HW1, HW3 and HW6 and then enters P&S Room2 for attending a seminar; $G_4$ = "Return-to-Office": he returns to his office after teaching a course via hallways HW5, HW4, HW3 and HW1.

The high-level goal-recognition problem is, given a new sequence of observed signals received from multiple base stations while a user is moving, infer the most probable high-level goal or intention of the user. For example, when a new sequence of signals $< (b_1 : 48)(b_2 : 60)(b_3 : 32) >< (b_1 : 45)(b_2 : 59)(b_3 : 35) > \ldots$ is observed, we would like to infer which goal the user is most probably pursuing currently, $G_1$ or $G_2$.

However, subject to reflection, refraction, diffraction and absorption by structures and even human bodies, the signal propagation suffers from severe multi-path fading effects in an indoor environment (Hashemi 1993). As a result, the signal-strength value received from the same base station varies with time even at a fixed location, and the number of base stations covering a location varies with time. Therefore, the goal- recognition problem is complicated due to the *noisy characteristics* of signals.

## DBN for Action and Goal Recognition

We first model the goal-recognition problem based on the framework of Dynamic Bayesian networks (DBNs) (Dean & Kanazawa 1989; Murphy 2002a). A DBN extends Bayesian networks by including a temporal dimension. It consists of a sequence of Bayesian networks to represent the world. At each time slice, exactly the same Bayesian network is used to model the dependencies among variables. In addition to the intra-slice connections in the Bayesian network, inter-slice connections are also required to represent temporal dependencies in consecutive time slices.

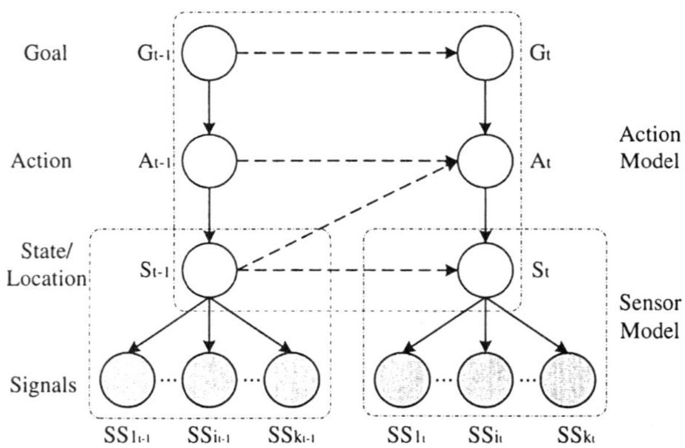


Figure 2: Two Time-slice DBN Model

The DBN model shown in Figure 2 is adopted to model our goal-recognition problem. It shows two time slices numbered $t$ and $t-1$ respectively in our behavior model. The shaded nodes $SSi_t$ represent the strength variables of signals received from multiple base stations, which are directly observable. All the other variables - the physical location $S_t$ of the user, the action $A_t$ the user is taking and the goal $G_t$ the user is pursuing - are hidden, with the values to be inferred from the raw signals. The dependencies among these nodes are shown in two kinds of directed links: solid links for intra-slice connections and dashed links for inter-slice connections. The network consists of two parts: a *sensor model* and *an action model*. At the bottom, a *sensor model* is used for location estimation based on sensory readings; while on the top, an *action model* is constructed for inferring actions and, subsequently, goals from the estimated locations. In the framework, two models are integrated by the location nodes that bridge the low-level evidence in terms of signal-strength values with the high-level actions and goals.

### Sensor Model

An important component of the DBN framework is the sensor model for estimating locations based on the signals received from multiple base stations. Regarding the DBN structure, in the time slice $t$, the links from the node $S_t$ in the location layer (states) to nodes $SS_{i_t}$ in the observation layer (signals) mean that the received signals are dependent on the actual physical location of the user in the current environment. The links are associated with probability distributions that reflect the uncertainty involved due to the noisy characteristics of the signals.

To build the sensor model, we model the world as a finite location-state space $\mathbb{S} = \{s_1, \ldots, s_n\}$ with a finite observation space $\mathbb{O} = \{o_1, \ldots, o_m\}$. The *sensor model* is defined to be a predicted model of the conditional probabilities $Pr(o_j|s_i)$, the likelihood of observing some sensory measurement $o_j \in \mathbb{O}$ at state $s_i \in \mathbb{S}$. The state space $\mathbb{S}$ is defined as a set of physical grid points on the floor map:

$$\mathbb{S} = \{s_1 = (x_1, y_1), \ldots, s_n = (x_n, y_n)\}.$$

An observation $o_j$ in the observation space $\mathbb{O}$ consists of a set of signal-strength measurements received from $k$ base stations respectively. We represent each observation $o_j$ at a particular state $s_i$ as a vector:

$$o_j =< (b_1, ss_1), \ldots, (b_k, ss_k) > .$$

where $b_p$ represents the $p$th base station and $ss_p$ is the average signal-strength value received from the $p$th base station.

Our on-site calibration revealed that it would be improper to impose some commonly used assumptions that use Gaussian or some other predefined statistical distributions to fit signal distribution, a point also made by (Roos *et al.* 2002). Therefore, we adopted a simpler but more robust scheme of directly sampling the conditional probabilities. We recorded the signal-strength values at each grid point $s_i$ and built a histogram of observed signal- strength values for each base station. A conditional probability $Pr(ss_p|b_p, s_i)$ was calculated for each base station, which is the probability that the base station $b_p$ has the average signal-strength value $ss_p$ at the state $s_i$. By making an independence assumption among signals from different base stations, we compute the conditional probability of receiving a particular observation $o_j$ at state $s_i$ as

$$Pr(o_j|s_i) = \prod_{p=1}^{k} Pr(ss_p|b_p, s_i).$$

### Action Model

After the sensor model is built, the next issue is to *automatically construct* the *action model* for inferring high-level actions and goals. In the DBN structure, the links from the node $G$ to the node $A$ mean that a goal is achieved by carrying out a sequence of actions, and the links from the node $A$ to the node $S$ mean that an action takes place in some locations. The action $A_t$ that a user takes at the time slice $t$ depends on his action $A_{t-1}$ and his location $S_{t-1}$ at the previous time slice, as well as the goal $G_t$ he is currently aiming at. By making use of the domain knowledge such as the number of location states, the number of actions and goals, we use an EM algorithm (Dempster, Laird, & B.Rubin 1977) on the training sequences of signals to learn the conditional probabilities among the nodes in the DBN.

## A Two-Level Recognition Model

Despite the power and flexibility of the DBN in providing a coherent modelling framework, a DBN model does suffer from certain disadvantages. Chiefly among them is that the complexity of the model is exponential in the number of hidden states. A large number of parameters need to be estimated and as a result a large data set is required to obtain statistically meaningful results. Therefore, to meet the needs of the real-time goal recognition, we wish to find a tradeoff between the expressive power of DBN and inference efficiency. We achieve this tradeoff in terms of several adaptations.

First, the users' behavior is often inherently ambiguous in our office environment. A typical example is that the activities taking place in the same location cannot be distinguished solely based on locations. Therefore, we introduce the concept of the time duration. In the framework of DBN, a semi-Markov structure can be appended to allow hidden states to have variable durations (Murphy 2002a). The basic idea is that each state emits a sequence of observations and the state duration can be specified. In a DBN, duration nodes can be added to explicitly represent how long a user has been in one state (Murphy 2002b). Although the conditional probability of these nodes is deterministic (counting the time steps spent in one state), inference is still linear in the maximum number of steps spent in a state. Therefore, to achieve the inference efficiency, we have to reduce the number of the sampled time points. However, this in turn has the damaging effect of reducing the accuracy.

Second, in order to achieve the tradeoff between accuracy and computational complexity, we propose a novel two-level architecture that separates the whole DBN model into two parts: a low-level DBN model and a high-level N-gram model. As shown in Figure 3, the low-level DBN model starts from the observation layer to the action layer. The high-level N-gram model is applied to infer the goals from actions. The N-gram-based inference is a simple and yet effective technique that has shown great success in natural language processing (NLP)(see, e.g. (Chen & Goodman 1996)).

Given a sequence of observations $o_1, o_2, \ldots, o_t$ obtained up to time $t$, the low-level DBN model is responsible for computing the most possible action sequence $A_1, A_2, \ldots, A_t$. This task is performed by using the junction tree algorithm (Murphy 2002a). After this, the next task is to infer the most likely goal. We define this task of *goal recognition* as follows: given an estimated action sequence

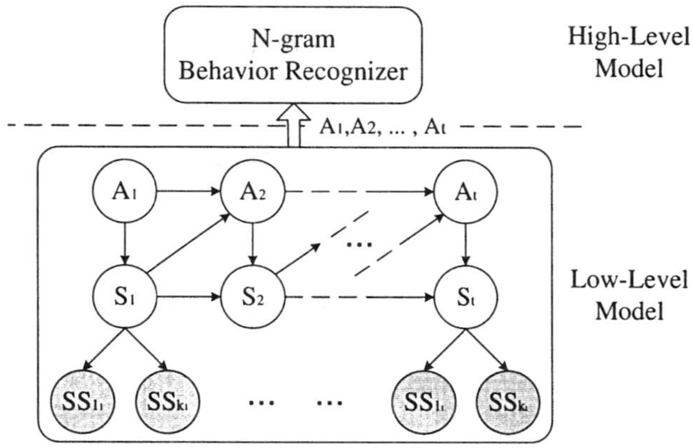


Figure 3: Two-Level Recognition Model

$A_1, A_2, \ldots, A_t$ obtained so far, infer the most likely goal $G^*$:

$$\begin{aligned} G^* &= \arg\max P(G|A_1, A_2, \ldots, A_t) \\ &= \arg\max P(G|A_{1:t}). \end{aligned}$$

By applying the Bayes' Rule, the above formula becomes:

$$\begin{aligned} G^* &= \arg\max \frac{P(A_{1:t}|G)P(G)}{P(A_{1:t})} \\ &= \arg\max P(A_{1:t}|G)P(G) \end{aligned}$$

where the term $P(A_{1:t})$ is a constant and can be dropped.

Since each action lasts for some duration, we can represent the action sequence in a more compact form: $A^1_{D_1}, A^2_{D_2}, \ldots, A^m_{D_m}$, where in each time segment $D_i$, the same action $A_i$ is taken. Note that the sum of durations $D_i$ is equal to the current time $t$: $\sum_{i=1}^m D_i = t$.

Furthermore, by using the Chain Rule, the calculation of $P(A_{1:t}|G)$ can be expanded as follows:

$$\begin{aligned} G^* = \ & \arg\max P(A^m_{D_m}|A^{m-1}_{D_{m-1}}, \ldots, A^1_{D_1}, G) \cdot \\ & P(A^{m-1}_{D_{m-1}}|A^{m-2}_{D_{m-2}}, \ldots, A^1_{D_1}, G) \cdots P(A^1_{D_1}|G). \end{aligned}$$

Since the estimation of these conditional probabilities are computationally expensive, we propose to use a simpler N-gram model: the action segment $A^i_{D_i}$ only depends on the goal $G$ and the $n-1$ action segments $A^{i-n+1}_{D_{i-n+1}}, \ldots, A^{i-1}_{D_{i-1}}$ preceding it. By further assuming that the transitions between actions are independent of action durations $D_i$, we get a Bigram model when $n = 2$ as follows:

$$\begin{aligned} G^* = \ & \arg\max P(G)P(A_1|G) \cdot \\ & \prod_{i=2}^{m} P(A_i|A_{i-1}, G) \prod_{i=1}^{m} P(D_i|A_i) \end{aligned}$$

where nonparametric nor parametric representations of time distribution can be used for $P(D_i|A_i)$. Initially, the goal recognition is solely based on the prior $P(G_i)$. After a period of time $t$, the expanded action sequence is inferred from the observations, and the goal is recognized by the above equation. The computational complexity is linear in the number of goals and in the length of an action sequence. An advantage of the proposed N-gram model is that the durations of actions can be explicitly and efficiently modelled.

## Experimental Evaluation

To test the validity of the model, we use the environment shown in Figure 1 as our testbed. The environment is modelled as a space of 99 states, each representing a 2-meter grid cell. Using the device driver and API we developed, the signals from base stations were recorded by an IBM laptop with a standard wireless Ethernet card. In our experiment, 8 out of 25 base stations were selected such that their signals occurred frequently and their signal-strength values were the strongest on average. We first collected 100 samples at each state, one per second, and these samples are used to estimate the sensor model. Then we collected about 570 traces for 19 goals of a professor's behavior in the office area.

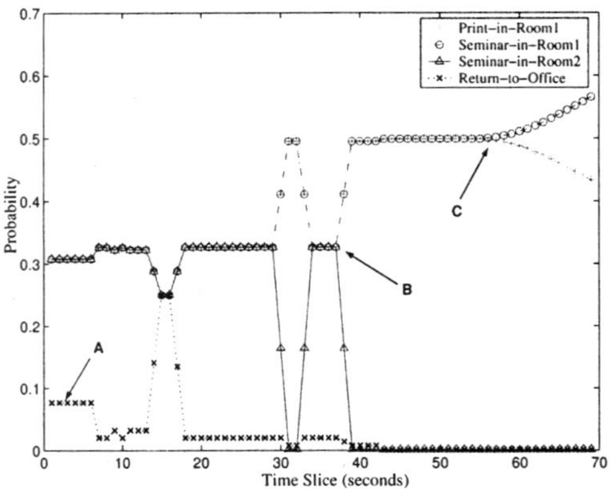


Figure 4: Behavior Recognition Example Using Four Out of the 19 Goals in Our Experiment

Figure 4 illustrates the recognition process of one trace belonging to the goal "Seminar-in-Room1", with respect to three other goals among the 19 goals. As shown in the figure, at the beginning, the probabilities of goals "Seminar-in-Room1", "Print-at-Room1" and "Seminar-in-Room2" are approximately equal since their starting points are the same, e.g. the office. However, one interesting point is that, at time point A, the probability of "Return-to-Office" is not equal to zero although its starting point is quite different from the other three goals. This is because the sensor model dominates the recognition result at the beginning since no much historic movement information can be used for smoothing at this point. As a result, it is unreliable to perform goal recognition solely based on the current location estimated from noisy signals. As time moves on, the probabilities of "Seminar-in-Room1" and "Print-in-Room1" increase when the user begins to take the action "Walk-in-HW4" at time point B.

A user's behavior patterns are often inherently ambiguous. Consider two goals happening in the same location such as "Seminar-in-Room1" and "Print-in-Room1". Since they can neither be distinguished based on the current location nor on the historic movement, a time-duration variable is introduced to distinguish them. For example, the time of attending a seminar is much longer than that of fetching some material from a printer. Therefore, the probability of "Seminar-in-Room1" is higher than "Print-in-Room1" *only after a certain period of time*. After time point $C$, the probability of "Seminar-in-Room1" is always the highest. Following (Blaylock & Allen 2003), we refer to time point $C$ as a *convergence point*, and the recognition process after $C$ is considered to *converge*.

To evaluate our experimental results, we use the following evaluation criteria (Blaylock & Allen 2003).

- *Efficiency*: Efficiency is measured in terms of the average processing time for each observation in our on-line goal recognition.
- *Accuracy*: For a certain goal, accuracy is defined as the number of correct recognition divided by the total number of recognition.
- *Convergence rate*: When applied to a specific goal, this criterion indicates the average number of observations, after which a recognized goal converges to the correct answer, over the average number of observations for those traces which converge. It measures how fast the recognition process of a goal converges to the correct answer.

We ran our experiments by doing a three-fold cross-validation over the collected traces. Figure 5 compares the inference efficiency of the whole DBN solution with that of the DBN+Bigram approach. Here *sampling interval* refers to the time interval during which the received signal-strength values are accumulated as one sample. Therefore, the length of traces decrease as the sampling interval increases. As shown in Figure 5, for both the whole DBN solution and the DBN+Bigram approach, the processing time for each observation decreases as the sampling interval increases. However, the DBN+Bigram approach is more efficient than the whole DBN solution for each sampling interval.

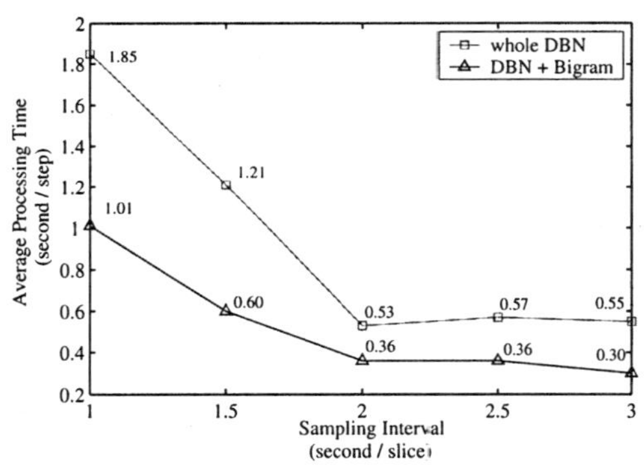


Figure 5: Comparison about the Average Processing Time for Each Observation

Table 2 shows the average recognition accuracy over 19 goals of the whole DBN and DBN+Bigram with respect to the sampling interval. The average accuracy decreases as the sampling interval increases. This is because when the sampling interval increases, the signal-strength values within a longer period of time will be accumulated into one observation corresponding to one time slice in the trace. This weakens the discriminative power of signals towards different locations, which in turn reduces the recognition accuracy. As can be seen from Table 2, the accuracy of DBN+Bigram is comparable to that of DBN.

| Interval (s) | 1 | 1.5 | 2 | 2.5 | 3 |
|---|---|---|---|---|---|
| Whole DBN (%) | 89.5 | 87.1 | 84.2 | 75.4 | 71.9 |
| DBN+Bigram (%) | 90.5 | 83.2 | 82.1 | 74.7 | 72.6 |

Table 2: Comparison about the Recognition Accuracy

Table 3 compares the convergence rate of the whole DBN solution with that of the DBN+Bigram approach. Due to the limited space, we only list the convergence rates of three goals and the average convergence rate of 19 goals. As can be seen from Table 3, the average convergence rate of DBN+Bigram is also comparable to that of DBN.

| | Whole DBN | DBN+Bigram |
|---|---|---|
| Entrance3-to-Office | 65.4% | 71.5% |
| Entrance1-to-Entrance3 | 82.3% | 82.0% |
| Seminar-at-Room2 | 84.0% | 82.2% |
| Average | 75.4% | 76.2% |

Table 3: Comparison about the Convergence Rate

## Conclusions and Future Work

We addressed the problem of inferring a user's high-level goals from low-level noisy signals in a complex indoor environment using an RF-based wireless network. We first model this problem based on the DBN framework. Then we propose a novel two-level architecture: in the low level, a DBN is used to infer the actions from signals; in the high level, an N-gram is used to infer the user's goals from actions. The experiments demonstrate that the two-level approach is more efficient than the whole DBN solution while the accuracy is comparable.

Our work can be extended in several directions. In this paper we assume that a user carrying out a sequence of actions is only aiming at achieve a single goal. However, a user can accomplish multiple goals within a single sequence of actions. In addition, we also wish to explore how to detect different behavior patterns of multiple users through plan recognition (Devaney & Ram 1998).

## Acknowledgements

The authors are supported by a grant from Hong Kong RGC and the Hong Kong University of Science and Technology. We thank Wong Wing Sing, To Ka Kui and Jin Yuan for helping us to collect the data.

## References

Albrecht, D.; Zukerman, I.; and Nicholson, A. 1998. Bayesian models for keyhole plan recognition in an adventure game. *User Modelling and User-adapted Interaction* 8(1–2):5–47.

Bahl, P., and Padmanabhan, V. N. 2000. RADAR: An in-building RF-based user location and tracking system. In *Proceedings of IEEE INFOCOM2000*, 775–784.

Blaylock, N., and Allen, J. 2003. Corpus-based statitical goal recognition. In *Proceedings of the 8th International Joint Conference on Artificial Intelligence*, 1303–1308.

Charniak, E., and Goldman, R. 1993. A Bayesian model of plan recognition. *Artificial Intelligence Journal* 64:53–79.

Chen, S. F., and Goodman, J. 1996. An empirical study of smoothing techniques for language modeling. In *Proceedings of the Thirty-Fourth Annual Meeting of the Association for Computational Linguistics*, 310–318.

Dean, T., and Kanazawa, K. 1989. A model for reasoning about persistentce and causation. *Artificial Intelligence* 93(1–2):1–27.

Demirdjian, D.; Tollmar, K.; Koile, K.; Checka, N.; and Darrell, T. 2002. Activity maps for location-aware computing. In *Proceedings of the IEEE WACV2002*.

Dempster, A. P.; Laird, N. M.; and B.Rubin, D. 1977. Maximum likelihood from incomplete data via EM algorithm. *Journal of the Royal Statistical Society Series B* 39:1–38.

Devaney, M., and Ram, A. 1998. Needles in a haystack: Plan recognition in large spatial domains involving multiple agents. In *Proceedings of AAAI1998*, 942–947.

Fox, D.; Hightower, J.; Liao, L.; and Schulz, D. 2002. Bayesian filtering for location estimation. *IEEE Pervasive Computing* 2(3):24–33.

Hashemi, H. 1993. The indoor radio propagation channel. volume 81, 943–968.

Kautz, H., and Allen, J. F. 1986. Generalized plan recognition. In *Proceedings of AAAI1986*, 32–38.

Ladd, A.; Bekris, K.; Marceau, G.; Rudys, A.; Kavraki, L.; and Wallach, D. 2002. Robotics-based location sensing using wireless ethernet. In *Proceedings of MOBICOM2002*.

Lesh, N., and Etzioni, O. 1995. A sound and fast goal recognizer. In *Proceedings of IJCAI95*, 1704–1710.

Murphy, K. 2002a. *Dynamic Bayesian Networks: Representation, Inference and Learning*. Ph.D. Dissertation, UC Berkeley.

Murphy, K. 2002b. Hidden semi-markov models(HSMMs). Technical report, MIT AI Lab.

Patterson, D. J.; Liao, L.; Fox, L.; and Kautz, H. 2003. Inferring high-level behavior from low-level sensors. In *Proceedings of UBICOMP2003*.

Pynadath, D. V., and Wellman, M. P. 2000. Probabilistic state-dependent grammars for plan recognition. In *Proceedings of the Sixteenth Conference on UAI*, 507–514.

Roos, T.; Myllymaki, P.; Tirri, H.; Misikangas, P.; and Sievanen, J. 2002. A probabilistic approach to WLAN user location estimation. *International Journal of Wireless Information Networks* 9(3):155–164.

Youssef, M.; Agrawala, A.; and Shankar, U. 2003. Wlan location determination via clustering and probability distributions. In *Proceedings of IEEE PerCom2003*.

# Qualitative Modeling

# Spatial Aggregation for Qualitative Assessment of Scientific Computations

**Chris Bailey-Kellogg**
Purdue Computer Science Dept.
250 N. Univ. St.
West Lafayette, IN 47907
cbk@cs.purdue.edu

**Naren Ramakrishnan**
2160L Torgersen Hall
Department of Computer Science
Virginia Tech, VA 24061
naren@cs.vt.edu

### Abstract

Qualitative assessment of scientific computations is an emerging application area that applies a data-driven approach to characterize, at a high level, phenomena including conditioning of matrices, sensitivity to various types of error propagation, and algorithmic convergence behavior. This paper develops a spatial aggregation approach that formalizes such analysis in terms of model selection utilizing spatial structures extracted from matrix perturbation datasets. We focus in particular on the characterization of matrix eigenstructure, both analyzing sensitivity of computations with spectral portraits and determining eigenvalue multiplicity with Jordan portraits. Our approach employs spatial reasoning to overcome noise and sparsity by detecting mutually reinforcing interpretations, and to guide subsequent data sampling. It enables quantitative evaluation of properties of a scientific computation in terms of confidence in a model, explainable in terms of the sampled data and domain knowledge about the underlying mathematical structure. Not only is our methodology more rigorous than the common approach of visual inspection, but it also is often substantially more efficient, due to well-defined stopping criteria. Results show that the mechanism efficiently samples perturbation space and successfully uncovers high-level properties of matrices.

## Introduction

A significant trend has recently developed in the numerical and scientific computing community, with researchers employing *data-driven* methodologies to assess broad, explicative features characterizing scientific computations. A typical application is in the analysis and "explaining away" of computations that may not be producing correct results. Such an approach is in stark contrast to the traditional focus on developing ever-stable numerical methods, to avoid the dangers of finite-precision computations. The philosophical shift is significant, since as Chaitin-Chatelin and Frayssé point out, "the aim is no longer to control the computing error, but rather to extract [high-level] meaning from results." (Chaitin-Chatelin & Frayssé 1996) Data-driven methodologies have been successfully applied in studying phenomena including conditioning of matrices, sensitivity to various types of error propagation, and algorithmic convergence behavior.



This approach to analysis of scientific computations has been labeled by one scientific computing group as *qualitative computing* (Chaitin-Chatelin & Traviesas 2002), and has many parallels to its namesake in the artificial intelligence community, particularly qualitative spatial reasoning in the style advocated by (Abelson *et al.* 1989). (1) It utilizes *imagistic reasoning*, expressing data in a suitable spatial context, and extracting and analyzing higher-level spatial structures in order to characterize, explain, or optimize a phenomenon of interest (Yip & Zhao 1996). Just as dynamical systems are qualitatively characterized with phase portraits (Yip 1991) and kinematic mechanisms in configuration spaces (Joskowicz & Sacks 1991), scientific computations are now characterized in perturbation and precision spaces. (2) It must harness *domain-specific knowledge*, here encoding the underlying mathematical structure, e.g. semantics arising from perturbation theory and computational invariants. Such information is important in order to discard spurious models of data, and to define rigorous acceptability criteria for models. (3) It should *integrate data collection and analysis*, focusing sample collection to gather information most useful for the key purpose of extracting qualitative insight. Intelligently closing-the-loop by interleaving sample selection and model assessment carefully exercises the degrees of freedom in collecting data in order to extract reinforcing interpretations that overcome noise and sparsity.

These facets present novel research issues when encountered in the context of assessing scientific computations. Our goal in this paper is to cast the assessment problem in a formal setting emphasizing qualitative model selection and iterative data collection. We do this within a spatial aggregation mechanism that identifies structures in the data, according to domain knowledge about the mathematical structure. To the best of our knowledge, this work presents the *first* systematic algorithms for performing complete imagistic analyses on matrix perturbation datasets (as opposed to relying on human visual inspection (Chaitin-Chatelin & Frayssé 1996)), and which interleave data collection and model evaluation until a high-confidence model is obtained. We first introduce the underlying problem domain and briefly survey background work in spatial aggregation, before describing our specific qualitative analysis mechanism. Results on important classes of matrix problems are then presented.

# Qualitative Assessment of Matrix Eigenstructure

Many tasks in scientific computing involve assessing the eigenstructure of a given matrix, i.e., determining the locations of eigenvalues, their multiplicities, and their sensitivities to perturbations. Eigenstructure helps characterize the stability, sensitivity, and accuracy of numerical methods as well as the fundamental tractability of problems. For instance, the eigenstructure of a matrix underlying the behavior of a harmonic oscillator gives valuable information about the vibration characteristics of the oscillator, as a function of forced inputs.

The *spectral portrait* has emerged as a popular tool for graphically visualizing eigenstructure in the complex plane; it displays how the eigenvalues of a matrix change as perturbations are introduced. The spectral portrait of a matrix $\mathcal{A}$ is defined as the map in the complex plane:

$$\Phi(z) = \log_{10} \|\mathcal{A}\|_2 \; \|(\mathcal{A} - zI)^{-1}\|_2, \qquad (1)$$

where $I$ is the identity matrix. The singularities of $\Phi$ are located at the eigenvalues of $\mathcal{A}$, and the analysis determines the sensitivity of computation to numerical imprecision by analyzing how the map decreases (from $\infty$) moving away from the eigenvalues. To see why, notice that when $z$ is an eigenvalue, the expression $(\mathcal{A} - zI)^{-1}$ is undefined because the determinant of $(\mathcal{A} - zI)$ is zero, and in such a case $\|(\mathcal{A} - zI)^{-1}\|_2$ is taken to be $\infty$. When $z$ is near an eigenvalue, $\|(\mathcal{A} - zI)^{-1}\|_2$ will be a large but finite number and can be expressed in terms of $\|\mathcal{A}\|_2$ as $\frac{1}{10^{-k}\|\mathcal{A}\|_2}$, for some $k$. Here, $\Phi(z)$ is simply given by $k$.

Why is the spectral portrait useful? Notice that the condition $\|(\mathcal{A} - zI)^{-1}\|_2 \geq \frac{1}{10^{-k}\|\mathcal{A}\|_2}$ describes the region enclosed by a level curve labeled $k$ in the spectral portrait. It can be proved (e.g., see (Chaitin-Chatelin & Frayssé 1996)) that such a region also denotes the eigenvalues of perturbed matrices $\mathcal{A} + E$ where $\|E\|_2 \leq 10^{-k}\|\mathcal{A}\|_2$. Hence the level curves in a spectral portrait correspond to perturbation magnitudes, and the region enclosed by a level curve contains all possible eigenvalues that are equivalent with respect to perturbations of the given magnitude. The above discussion will lead us to believe that the spectral portrait should consist of small circles around the eigenvalues, with radii given by $\Phi(z) = k$. For many matrices this is indeed true. Unfortunately, for other classes of matrices (known as 'non-normal' (Golub & Van Loan 1996)) this ideal behavior does not emerge, and this is where the graphical depiction of the spectral portrait becomes an invaluable tool.

Fig. 1(a) shows the spectral portrait of a non-normal matrix with eigenvalues at 1, 2, 3, and 4. The qualitative interpretations from such a portrait are several-fold. First, if the matrix is represented only to a certain (normwise) perturbation level, and we try to compute its eigenvalues, then we might obtain any point inside the region enclosed by the corresponding curve! The level curves summarize the extent to which we can afford loss of precision. Observe that at small perturbation levels, the spectral portrait is disconnected (which is desirable), but it gets connected at higher

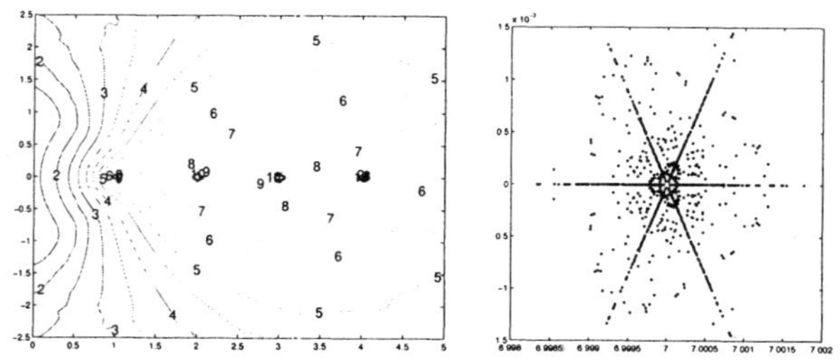

(a) (b)

Figure 1: Qualitative assessment of matrix eigenstructure by analysis of portraits in the complex plane. (a) Spectral portrait. Perturbation levels increase going outward from singularities at the (unperturbed) eigenvalues, and a curve surrounding multiple eigenvalues indicates a level of precision (labeled with negative logarithm base 10) beyond which those eigenvalues cannot be distinguished. Eigenvalues at 2 and 3 are the most sensitive to perturbation, but that at 4 becomes indistinguishable under a larger perturbation, and 1 merges under a very large perturbation. (b) Jordan portrait. Multiple positive and negative perturbations cause the computed eigenvalues to lie on the vertices of two slightly shifted polygons, yielding a star with degree twice the eigenvalue multiplicity. The six-fold symmetry of the star reveals a multiplicity of three for the eigenvalue at 1.

levels. Second, notice that there is a "drift" toward the eigenvalue at 1 as perturbations are increased. This gives important information about the "defectiveness" of the eigenvalues and the non-normality of the matrix. Finally, the spectral portrait suggests how iterative computations involving the matrix will converge; the defectiveness of the eigenvalues indicates that there might be periods of instability and/or periods of slow convergence.

Having determined the relationship between the eigenvalues at given perturbation levels, we typically desire to ascertain the (geometric) multiplicities of the eigenvalues, for further insight into matrix stability. This information is summarized in the so-called Jordan decomposition, whose direct computation is often difficult or impossible (Golub & Van Loan 1996). Once again, we can employ a data-driven approach, here determining the multiplicities by qualitatively assesing a different portrait in the complex plane, which we call a *Jordan portrait*. The Jordan portrait uses the property that, due to finite precision arithmetic, the *computed eigenvalues* will actually be the *true eigenvalues* of a suitably perturbed matrix. Specifically, the computed eigenvalues corresponding to an actual eigenvalue $\lambda_i$ under perturbation $\delta$ are given by:

$$\lambda_i + |\delta|^{\frac{1}{\rho_i}} e^{\frac{i\phi}{\rho_i}}, \qquad (2)$$

where $\lambda_i$ is of multiplicity $\rho_i$, and the phase $\phi$ of the perturbation $\delta$ ranges over $\{2\pi, 4\pi, \ldots, 2\rho_i\pi\}$ if $\delta$ is positive and over $\{3\pi, 5\pi, \ldots, 2(\rho_i + 1)\pi\}$ if $\delta$ is negative. These phase variations imply that the computed eigenvalues lie on the vertices of a regular polygon with $2\rho_i$ sides, centered on $\lambda_i$, and with diameter influenced by $|\delta|$. Therefore, qualitative analysis of the *symmetry* in a Jordan portrait that graph-

| |
|---|
| **Samples** Evaluate perturbation level (Eq. 1) for locations in complex plane, initially on a coarse uniform grid. |
| **Spatial aggregates** Aggregate interpolated samples with Delaunay triangulation. Construct iso-contour curves from connected points at same perturbation level. |
| **Correspondence** Establish analogy for connected points on different curves; abstract into curve merge events. |
| **Qualitative model** merge tree; constructed by tracking iso-contour correspondence outward from eigenvalues. For each pair of eigenvalues, evaluate model by separation and surroundedness. |
| **Sampling policy** Sample until absolute separation and absolute surroundedness are above limits, and relative values are converging. |

Table 1: Spatial aggregation for spectral portrait analysis.

| |
|---|
| **Samples** Perform random normwise perturbation (Eq. 2) at desired level. |
| **Spatial aggregates** Aggregate samples into triangles. Identify congruent triangles by geometric hashing. |
| **Correspondence** Establish analogy between congruent vertices; abstract as rotation. |
| **Qualitative model** polygon isomorphism; obtained by identifying rotations applicable to many points. Evaluate model by likelihood calculation. |
| **Sampling policy** Collect additional samples at same or subsequent perturbation level, until posterior distribution of models is peaked enough. |

Table 2: Spatial aggregation for Jordan portrait analysis.

ically *superimposes* numerous such perturbed calculations reveals the multiplicity $\rho_i$. For example, the Jordan portrait in Fig. 1(b) depicts a 6-gon around the eigenvalue at 1, hence indicating that the eigenvalue multiplicity is three.[1]

## Spatial Aggregation Mechanism

As the previous section illustrates, matrix eigenstructure can be characterized by imagistic analysis of responses to matrix perturbations. Our goal is to automatically and confidently extract high-level matrix properties through application of spatial reasoning. We develop here an integrated mechanism that abstracts perturbation data into spatial structures, quantitatively evaluates and compares models of matrix properties, and collects additional perturbation samples as needed. For spectral portraits, the analysis can be viewed as yielding a model we call a *merge tree* (Fig. 2, right), indicating for each pair of eigenvalues the perturbation level at which the iso-contours surrounding them merge. For Jordan portraits, our model is a *polygon isomorphism* (Fig. 3) capturing the symmetry of perturbations around an eigenvalue, and thereby revealing the multiplicity. The key components and knowledge for the spatial reasoning mechanism are summarized in Tabs. 1 and 2; detailed in the following subsections; and illustrated in Figs. 2 and 3.

[1]The 'noise' around the star is an artifact of the given matrix; while this 'hallucination' effect is not modeled in this paper, it can pose problems for automatic imagistic analysis.

### Extracting Spatial Structures

We ground our analysis mechanism in the Spatial Aggregation Language (SAL) (Bailey-Kellogg, Zhao, & Yip 1996; Yip & Zhao 1996; Zhao, Bailey-Kellogg, & Fromherz 2003), which defines a set of uniform operators and data types that exploit domain knowledge to identify structures in spatial data. SAL was developed in order to make explicit the reasoning performed by a number of successful AI applications (e.g., dynamical systems analysis (Yip 1991), kinematic mechanism analysis (Joskowicz & Sacks 1991)), and to provide a suitable vocabulary and mechanism for new applications. Subsequent reasoners utilized SAL in a number of different areas, including decentralized control design for thermal regulation (Bailey-Kellogg & Zhao 2001), object manipulation (Zhao, Bailey-Kellogg, & Fromherz 2003), weather data analysis (Huang & Zhao 1999), analysis of diffusion-reaction morphogenesis (Ordóñez & Zhao 2000), and identification of pockets underlying gradient fields (Bailey-Kellogg & Ramakrishnan 2001).

Two key aspects of SAL are particularly relevant here: use of a *spatial aggregate* representation identifying *relationships* among spatial objects in data, and exploitation of *domain knowledge* in uncovering these aggregates. The spatial aggregates in matrix eigenstructure analysis identify relationships among perturbations in portraits, and the domain knowledge coveys the underlying mathematical properties. We note that the matrices being studied are defined by different applications, so additional, specific knowledge about those domains could provide even more guidance; we do not pursue that here but focus on generic portrait analysis.

Our spectral portrait analysis algorithm groups perturbation samples into iso-contours and "tracks" these contours outward from eigenvalues through containment and merging events. The construction of iso-contours follows a stadard spatial aggregation paradigm; the tracking requires an extension discussed below. Samples are taken initially on a uniform grid, and isocontours extracted by interpolating locations at which desired perturbation levels are achieved. Spatial aggregates are computed by (1) localizing computation by aggregating interpolated points into a Delaunay triangulation (relating nearby objects); (2) grouping connected points in a perturbation level (relating similar objects); and (3) constructing curve objects for the groups of points (composing lower-level objects into higher-level objects).

Our Jordan protrait analysis algorithm groups perturbation samples into polygons and recognizes symmetry by a rotation aligning polygons. (The eigenvalue multiplicity is then apparent from the polygon degree.) As with spectral portraits, the first step follows a standard spatial aggregation approach, and the second requires extensions. Samples are taken by random normwise perturbation, and so appear "scattered" around the complex plane. The underlying mathematics indicates, however, that there is a structure in the portrait, such that, except for noise, points lie on vertices of regular polygons. In order to identify the polygon, we first group triples of points and compose them into triangles whose congruence will allow a subsequent analysis step to identify the symmetry defining the polygon.

In both cases, then, spatial aggregation groups samples

into some higher-level structure (iso-contours, triangles). The abstraction step allows further analyses to treat the objects "holistically," with more global properties (e.g. curvature and congruence) that aren't defined on mere sets of lower-level objects. In particular, the key to the applications studied here is *correspondence* relationships. Correspondence among level curves in spectral portraits reveals the merge events indicating when eigenvalues become indistinguishable. Similarly, correspondence among triangles of Jordan samples reveals the underlying symmetry. As an imagistic analysis aid, correspondence has been well studied in computer vision and pattern recognition. Our purpose here is to distill essential principles into the traditional SAL mechanism, exploiting the hierarchical composition of spatial aggregates, and demonstrating the effective use of such a correspondence mechanism in overcoming noise and sparisty in interpreting portraits.

In the context of SAL computations, it is easy to see that correspondence is intimately connected with locality and continuity, since close, similar parts of one object typically correspond to close, similar parts of another. Further, identification of sites at which this isn't true can be interesting events about which to reason (e.g. in the spectral portrait application, this distinguishes straight containment of iso-contours from merge events). Thus our correspondence mechanism leverages the fact that a SAL hierarchy composes lower-level objects into higher-level objects based on locality and continuity. Our mechanism has two key steps: (2) establish *analogy* as a relation among lower-level constituents of higher-level objects; (2) establish *correspondence* between higher-level objects as an *abstraction* of the analogy between their constituents.

**Definition 1 (Analogy)** *Given a set $L$ of lower-level SAL objects that have been composed into a set $H$ of higher-level objects, $l_i, l_j \in L$ is said to be an* analogous pair *with respect to $h_k, h_l \in H$ if $l_i \in h_k, l_j \in h_l$. An* analogy *is a relation $A$ on $L$ with respect to $H$ containing a subset of the possible analogous pairs.*

**Definition 2 (Correspondence)** *Given sets $L$ and $H$ and an analogy $A$ as in Definition 1, a* correspondence *on $H$ abstracting $A$ is a relation $M \subseteq H \times H$ defined for each pair of objects with analogous components in $A$, so that the objects can be transformed (approximately) onto each other.*

The analogy between constituents is well-defined only because of the context provided by the higher-level objects; higher-level correspondence then captures a more global view of the local matches. In spectral portrait analysis, analogy is defined for the interpolated samples on separate curves, connected by Delaunay edges. Correspondence then identifies pairs of curves with a strong set of analogies. In Jordan portrait analysis, analogy is defined by identifying (e.g. with geometric hashing) pairs of congruent triangles and mapping the vertices between each pair. Correspondence abstracts the analogy into a rotation such that analogous vertices map onto each other.

## Representing and Evaluating Models

Our goal is to identify and evaluate models explaining the perturbation data in terms of high-level matrix properties. The qualitative spatial models considered here capture spatial objects and their relationships, but do not otherwise impose any restrictions on how models are posited; in particular, a model could be derived by means other than SAL, and could be represented using a rich vocabulary of relationship types (e.g. (Cui, Cohn, & Randell 1992)). Given a model, derived either by the aggregation / correspondence mechanism or by some other means, we desire to decide how well the data support it, that is, to quantify confidence in the posited relationships. We employ a confidence function $f(M, d)$ to assess a qualitative spatial model $M$ in terms of a dataset $d$.

In a spectral portrait, a model encapsulates level curves and their merging relationships in the merge tree structure (can also be a forest), with leaves for eigenvalues, internal nodes for curves, and a parent function such that a parent's perturbation level is one larger than its child's. Such a model indicates, for each pair of eigenvalues, the magnitude of the smallest perturbation level at which they are equivalent. The dataset $d$ is a sampled grid of points in the complex plane, and we would like to ensure that the eigenvalues are definitely separate before their lowest common ancestor, and that the level curve for that ancestor definitely surrounds the eigenvalues. For each pair of eigenvalues $i$ and $j$, let $v$ be the level of the ancestor, and define $R_{i,v-1}$, $R_{j,v-1}$, and $R_{ij,v}$ to be the regions (sets of samples) containing respectively $i$, $j$, and both, as computed by region growing with samples of at most the given perturbation level. We measure the separation by the smallest number of samples on any grid walk between regions $R_{i,v-1}$ and $R_{j,v-1}$. We measure the surroundedness by the maximum flow on the grid for $R_{ij,v}$, from sources $R_{i,v-1}$ to sinks $R_{j,v-1}$ (i.e. strong connection between the regions).

In a Jordan portrait, the polygon isomorphism model relates pairs of vertices of two polygons. Such a model captures the symmetry relation of the sample points by the induced rotation $\theta$ around the eigenvalue $\lambda$, minimizing distance between related pairs. We can solve a straightforward least-squares problem for $\theta$ and $\lambda$, and calculate multiplicity $\rho$ as $180°/\theta$. The dataset $d$ is a random set of sample points in the complex plane, each of which can be viewed as an i.i.d. estimate of the eigenvalue. Thus we define the score $f(M, d)$ to be the likelihood $P(d|M)$. This likelihood can be simply given as $\Pi_k P(d_k|\lambda, \rho, \delta)$ where $\lambda$ and $\rho$ are the eigenvalue location and multiplicity as revealed by the model $M$, and $\delta$ is the perturbation level. The likelihood of each data element $d_k = a + ib$ is in turn assessed using Eq. 2, distributing probability mass of 1 among all vertices of the implied polygon mapping for the eigenvalue and perturbation level corresponding to point $d_k$. For instance, each vertex of the triangle isomorphism in Fig. 1(b) at a given perturbation level receives probability of $\frac{1}{6}$. This particular formulation of $f$ can be viewed as assessing the posterior of a model under a uniform prior over all models.

## Intelligently Collecting Additional Samples

Interleaving model generation, model assessment, and additional data collection steps can be viewed as causing a progressive peaking of the posterior distribution of models (under a probabilistic interpretation of model assessment). We treat data analysis in the simultaneous updating sense, although the Jordan portrait application lends itself to sequential updating (owing to the i.i.d. samples). In other words, with each additional data point, the analysis is performed over the entire dataset accumulated so far; this means that some models hastily ruled out in earlier stages could become relevant later. At some point, enough confidence is gained so that sampling can be stopped. Until that point, decisions must be made as to which additional samples to collect, under the degrees of freedom provided. A *sampling policy* defines the stopping criteria and sample selection strategy. It could be designed by optimization or based on heuristic considerations.

In the spectral portrait, data collection is driven by systematic global subsampling, where we begin with an uniform grid and the sampling strategy has the choice of expanding the grid (to ensure a merge tree rather than forest) or recursively subsampling (to gain more confidence). The design of the stopping criterion for the spectral portrait borrows from discretization refinement in numerical quadrature (Krommer & Ueberhuber 1998), where *pairs of formulas* with different levels of approximation are used so that one of the formulas is *expected* to yield more accuracy than the other, for most classes of problems. Between such successive applications, if the estimated answer doesn't change significantly, we declare to the model to be a sufficient approximation of the given function. Similarly, to assess the quality of the spectral portrait model, we evaluate the stability of merge and separation events, under the metrics provided by model assessment, with respect to additional subsampling.

In the Jordan portrait, data collection is driven by increasing the number of independent samples from which the multiplicity is estimated. The sampling strategy here must decide whether to sample (i) at the same perturbation level, (ii) at a higher perturbation level, or (iii) at the same perturbation level unless the number of posited models increased (thereby avoiding hallucination). Stopping criteria for the Jordan portrait assess the peakedness of the posterior distribution for $M$ and whether the log-likelihood score $f$ crosses a certain threshold (guaranteeing adequacy of a dataset before generalization).

## Results

We have applied the our qualitative analysis mechanism on the testbank of matrices described in (Chaitin-Chatelin & Frayssé 1996). These matrices are drawn from a variety of application domains such as hydrodynamics, stress analysis, control theory, fluid flow, and membrane transport phenomena. For want of space, we illustrate our results on only two matrices—*Rose* and *Brunet*—from this collection, highlighting the intuition behind the mechanism and performance results.

Fig. 2 illustrates the spectral portrait analysis for the $10 \times 10$ *Rose* matrix, motivated by the problem of determining the roots of the underlying characteristic equation. *A priori*, a double-factorial number of binary merge trees are possible, but the approach presented here eliminates almost all of them without even considering them. Instead, it considers only one plausible tree for a given number of samples, and decides whether or not the merge events captured in the tree can be clarified. Depending on model assessment, the mechanism then subsamples or expands, or halts. While some amount of correspondence is found even with the coarse initial grid (top of Fig. 2), the model is a forest and the model assessment yields low confidence (few separating points). As a result, our mechanism computes additional samples on a finer, larger grid (bottom of Fig. 2), yielding high confidence in the (correct) curve merge tree shown. The mechanism converges from this point when additional data are collected.

We have applied this approach to a variety of matrices (e.g., polynomial companion matrices, matrices from finite discretization of continuous models), with different numbers and spacings of roots. In each case, the correspondence mechanism correctly identifies the correct model with high confidence, essentially declaring that any other model that would be proposed would be highly inconsistent with the data, after 1–3 subsamples and 1–3 grid expansions.

Fig. 3 demonstrates the results of applying our Jordan portrait analysis with the $10 \times 10$ *Brunet* matrix. The top part uses a small set of sample points, while the bottom two parts use a larger set and illustrate a good vs. bad correspondence. As the number of samples increases, so does the risk of model "hallucination" — finding some subset of points that by chance happen to correspond, as in bottom of Fig. 3. This illustrates the importance of monitoring relative model confidence and controlling the sampling to avoid over-sampling.

We tested 10 matrices across 4–10 perturbation levels. To study the effect of sampling strategy, we organized data collection into rounds of 6–8 samples each and experimented with the three sample collection policies mentioned earlier. We varied a tolerance parameter for triangle congruence from 0.1 to 0.5 (effectively increasing the number of models posited) and determined the number of rounds needed to determine the Jordan form, for each of the sampling policies described earlier. Policy 1 required an average of 1 round at a tolerance of 0.1, up to 2.7 rounds at 0.5. Even with a large number of models proposed, additional data quickly weeded out bad models. Policy 2 fared better only for cases where policy 1 was focused on lower perturbation levels, and policy 3 was preferable only for the Brunet-type matrices. In other words, there is no real advantage to moving across perturbation levels! In retrospect, this is not surprising since our Jordan form computation treats multiple perturbations (irresp. of level) as independent estimates of eigenstructure.

The effectiveness of our spatial aggregation mechanism lies as much in the targeted use of domain knowledge as in the design of a suitable sampling policy, as revealed by the following count of feasible models:

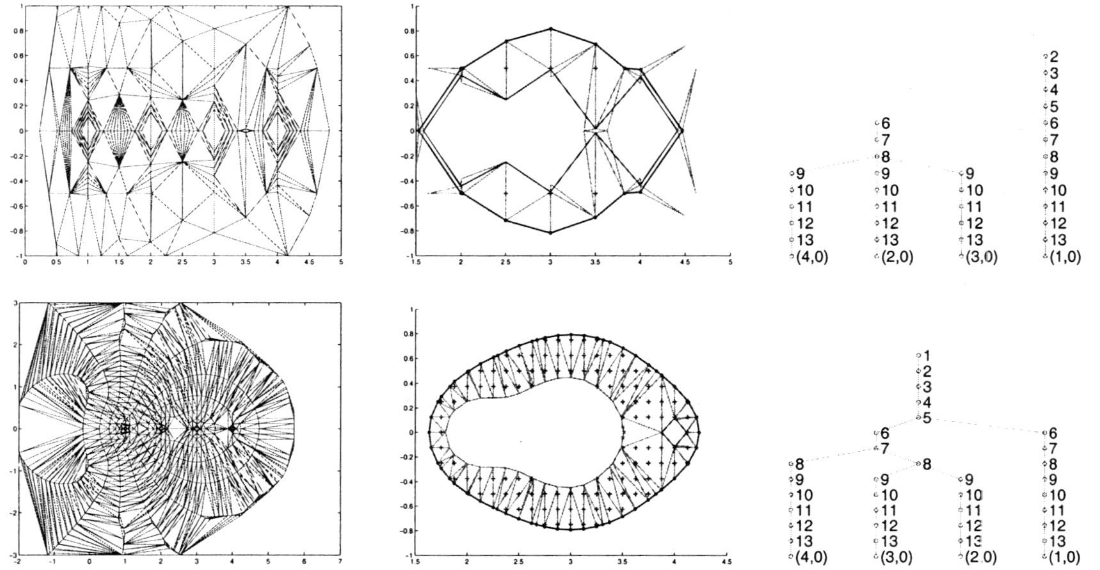

Figure 2: Example of *Rose* matrix spectral portrait analysis for (top) a small, coarse grid, and (bottom) an extended, subsampled grid. (left) Delaunay triangulation analogy for interpolated points comprising contours. (middle) Analogy at an example merge event; separating samples marked with "+". (right) Curve merge tree: eigenvalues at bottom; node for curves labeled with perturbation level. Merge events indicate at what perturbation level descendant eigenvalues are indistinguishable.

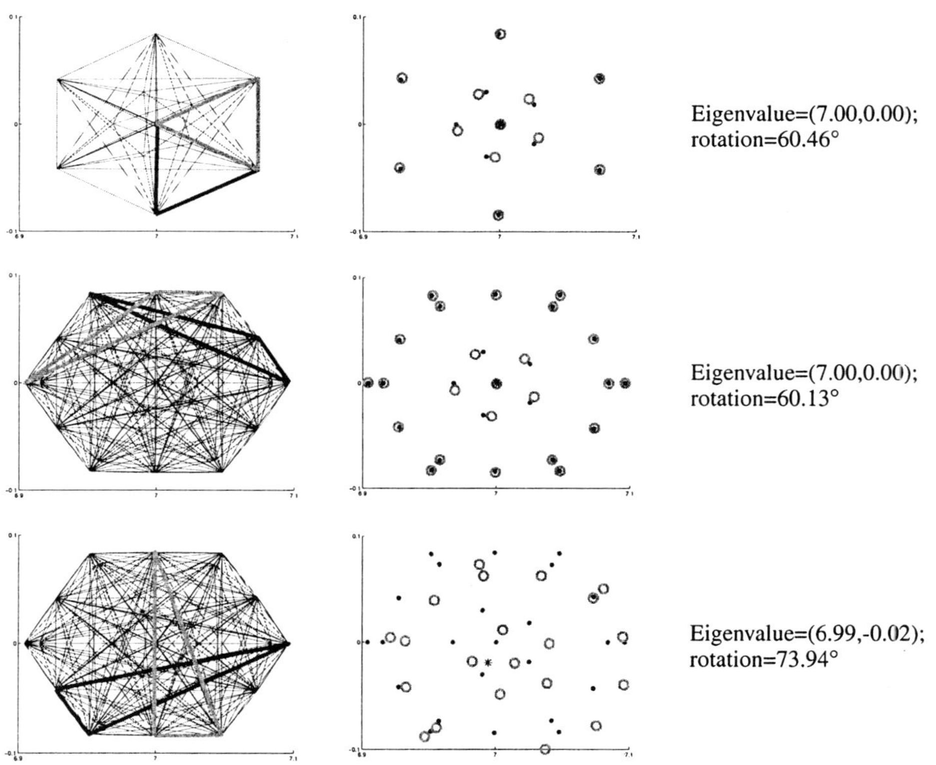


Figure 3: Example of *Brunet* matrix Jordan portrait analysis, for (top) small sample set; (middle) larger sample set; (bottom) larger sample set but lower-scoring model. (left) Approximately-congruent triangles. (middle) Evaluation of correspondence in terms of match between original (red dots) and rotated (green circles) samples. (right) Associated eigenvalue and rotation symmetry.

| *application* | *initial* | *round 1* | *round 2* | *round 3* |
|---|---|---|---|---|
| *spectral (Rose)* | 15 | 1 (forest) | 1 | 1 |
| *Jordan (Brunet)* | 1000 | 1 | 1 | 2 |

## Discussion

Automated imagistic reasoning, of the form presented here, is an important aid to reasoning about the quality, efficiency, and robustness of numerical computations involving matrices. Since matrix computations underly many areas of science and engineering (especially where linear models are employed), qualitative analysis of spectral portraits and Jordan portraits will play a central role in these domains.

The analysis of correspondence using our spatial aggregation mechanism is similar in spirit to that of (Huang & Zhao 1999) for weather data interpretation, and can be seen as a significant generalization, formalization, and application of techniques studied there for finding patterns in meteorological data. Similarly, our methodology captures and generalizes the computations employed in object recognition, allowing the body of research developed there to be applied to a broader class of applications, such as in scientific computing. This work is also very much philosophically aligned with work on structure-mapping (e.g. (Falkenhainer, Forbus, & Gentner 1989)), which seeks to develop a cognitively plausible theory and computationally efficient engine for analogical reasoning. The cited paper points out that "analogies are about relations rather than simple features." As with recent work from that same group (and others) on sketching (e.g. (Forbus, Tomai, & Usher 2003)), our mechanism applies this key insight to spatial reasoning; an important aspect of this paper is the integration of analogical relationships within the context of spatial aggregation relationships.

Similarly to compositional modeling (Falkenhainer & Forbus 1991), we advocate targeted use of domain knowledge, and as with qualitative/quantitative model selection (e.g. (Capelo, Ironi, & Tentoni 1998)), we seek to determine high level models for empirical data. Our focus is on problems requiring integrated qualitative model analysis and sampling to overcome sparsity and noise in spatial datasets. A possible direction of future work is to explore if the inclusion-exclusion methodology popular in grid algorithms (Bekas *et al.* 2001) can be fruitfully harnessed in a SAL-based framework. Our long-term goal is to study data collection policies and their relationships to qualitative model determination. The decomposable nature of SAL computations promises to both support the design of efficient, hierarchical algorithms for model estimation as well as provide a deeper understanding of the recurring roles that domain knowledge plays in spatial data analysis.

## Acknowledgements

We received very helpful comments for a preliminary version of this work (Bailey-Kellogg & Ramakrishnan 2003) at the 2003 Qualitative Reasoning Workshop, and would like to thank in particular Ron Ferguson, Ken Forbus, Liliana Ironi, Stefania Tentoni, and Feng Zhao. We also acknowledge the encouraging suggestions from Francoise Chaitin-Chatelin. This work was funded in part by grants from the National Science Foundation to CBK (IIS-0237654) and NR (EIA-9984317).

## References

Abelson, H.; Eisenberg, M.; Halfant, M.; Katzenelson, J.; Sacks, E.; Sussman, G.; Wisdom, J.; and Yip, K. 1989. Intelligence in scientific computing. *CACM* 32(5):546–562.

Bailey-Kellogg, C., and Ramakrishnan, N. 2001. Ambiguity-Directed Sampling for Qualitative Analysis of Sparse Data from Spatially Distributed Physical Systems. In *Proc. IJCAI*, 43–50.

Bailey-Kellogg, C., and Ramakrishnan, N. 2003. Active Data Mining of Correspondence for Qualitative Assessment of Scientific Computations. In *Proc. QR*, 23–30.

Bailey-Kellogg, C., and Zhao, F. 2001. Influence-Based Model Decomposition for Reasoning about Spatially Distributed Physical Systems. *AIJ* Vol. 130(2):pages 125–166.

Bailey-Kellogg, C.; Zhao, F.; and Yip, K. 1996. Spatial Aggregation: Language and Applications. In *Proc. AAAI*, 517–522.

Bekas, C.; Kokiopulou, E.; Koutis, I.; and Gallopoulos, E. 2001. Towards the Effective Parallel Computation of Matrix Pseudospectra. In *Proceedings of the International Conference on Supercomputing (ICS)*, 260–269.

Capelo, A.; Ironi, L.; and Tentoni, S. 1998. Automated Mathematical Modeling from Experimental Data: An Application to Material Science. *IEEE Transactions on Systems, Man, and Cybernetics* Vol. 28(3):pages 356–370.

Chaitin-Chatelin, F., and Frayssé, V. 1996. *Lectures on Finite Precision Computations*. SIAM Monographs.

Chaitin-Chatelin, F., and Traviesas, E. 2002. Qualitative Computing. In *Handbook of Numerical Computation*. SIAM.

Cui, Z.; Cohn, A.; and Randell, D. 1992. Qualitative simulation based on a logical formalism of space and time. In *Proc. AAAI*, 679–684.

Falkenhainer, B., and Forbus, K. 1991. Compositional Modeling: Finding the Right Model for the Job. *AIJ* Vol. 51(1-3):pages 95–143.

Falkenhainer, B.; Forbus, K.; and Gentner, D. 1989. The structure mapping engine: Algorithm and examples. *AIJ* 41:1–63.

Forbus, K.; Tomai, E.; and Usher, J. 2003. Qualitative spatial reasoning for visual grouping in sketches. In *Proc. QR*, 79–86.

Golub, G., and Van Loan, C. 1996. *Matrix Computations*. Johns Hopkins University Press. Third Edition.

Huang, X., and Zhao, F. 1999. Relation-Based Aggregation: Finding Objects in Large Spatial Datasets. In *Proc. IDA*.

Joskowicz, L., and Sacks, E. 1991. Computational kinematics. *AIJ* 51:381–416.

Krommer, A., and Ueberhuber, C. 1998. *Computational Integration*. SIAM.

Ordóñez, I., and Zhao, F. 2000. STA: Spatio-Temporal Aggregation with Applications to Analysis of Diffusion-Reaction Phenomena. In *Proc. AAAI*, 517–523.

Yip, K., and Zhao, F. 1996. Spatial Aggregation: Theory and Applications. *JAIR* Vol. 5:pages 1–26.

Yip, K. 1991. *KAM: A system for intelligently guiding numerical experimentation by computer*. MIT Press.

Zhao, F.; Bailey-Kellogg, C.; and Fromherz, M. 2003. Physics-based encapsulation in embedded software for distributed sensing and control applications. *Proceedings of the IEEE* 91:40–63.

# A Qualitative-Quantitative Methods-Based e-Learning Support System in Economic Education

**Tokuro Matsuo, Takayuki Ito and Toramatsu Shintani**
Dept. of Computer Science and Engineering ,
Graduate School of Engineering, Nagoya Institute of Technology.
Gokiso-cho, Showa-ku, Nagoya, Aichi, 466-8555, JAPAN.
{tmatsuo, itota, tora} @ics.nitech.ac.jp
http://www-toralab.ics.nitech.ac.jp/~ {tmatsuo, itota, tora}

### Abstract

This paper describes a new qualitative-quantitative simulator to help buyers learn how to make decisions when they purchase goods. In this paper, we propose an e-learning support system (LSDM) for assisting user decision making by applying artificial intelligence technology. When buyers purchase expensive items, they must carefully select these items from many alternatives. The learning support system provides useful information that assists consumers in purchasing goods. We employ qualitative simulations because the output simulation results are useful. Our system consists of a qualitative processing system and a quantitative calculation system. When users use the system, they first input information on the goods they want to purchase. The information input by users is used in the qualitative simulation. Next, they supply the details of their budgets, the rate of loans, and several other factors, on a form. The system then integrates the results of simulation and the user's input data and proposes plans to aid in their decision process. The system has several advantages: it can be used by simple input, the process of simulation is easy to understand, users can learn how to make decisions by trial and error, and the users can base their decision making on synthetic results.

## Introduction

Services (e.g., e-commerce and e-learning) using computers have made rapid progress in recent years and have been intensely investigated. E-learning has been recognized as a promising field in which to apply artificial intelligence technologies (Bredeweg & Forbus 2003)(Bredeweg & Winkels 1998)(Chen, Wang, & Yang 2002)(Forbus *et al.* 2001)(Weir 2002). We have developed an e-learning support system for assisting user decision making by applying artificial intelligence technology (Forbus 2002)(Russell & Norvig 1995). Our paper describes a system that combines qualitative and numerical information about a single system to help naive/end-users improve their purchasing decision-making skills.

The advantages of qualitative reasoning in education are as follows. Student knowledge is formed and developed through learning conceptual foundations. If there are any mechanisms in the (dynamic) system, the user can understand these mechanisms using qualitative methods. Generally, beginners(students) also understand dynamic systems through qualitative principles, rather than through mathematical formula. The contribution of our paper is the integration of theory, implementation and user perspectives.



When users purchase expensive items, they must make their selection carefully. In the current study, we focus on users purchasing an immovable item, such as a house or land (Matsuo, Ito, & Shintani 2004). When users purchase such items, they must take into account the price, the rate of a loan, their budget, and several other factors. Furthermore, it is important to know whether the value will increase or decrease in the future.

There are several important factors concerned with the item's price, for example, the exchange rate, tax system, economic indicators, and fiscal policies. Some factors cannot be expressed as quantitative values. A qualitative method is therefore used to simulate a trend in the price of the items. Such qualitative simulations output results as simple initial values (Nishida 1991). In our simulations, users can understand the mechanism and process of the simulations, because our qualitative methods consist of constructive graph models. On these models, causal factors are connected into a graph. In the simulation, node conditions on the graph change as time passes. Our system also uses quantitative calculation values concerned with total payments and so on. It can provide enough information for buyers to trade virtually. By using our system, users can learn how they should make decisions when they want to purchase expensive items.

The rest of the paper is organized as follows. Section 2 describes the outline of our e-learning support system (LSDM). In Section 3, we provide definitions and assumptions for the simulation. We show the formula for numerical calculation in the quantitative module. In Section 4, we describe an example of qualitative simulations using our system. In Section 5, we show the user interface of our system. We provide our concluding remarks in Section 6.

## The LSDM

In this section, we provide the outline of our e-learning support system for user decision making (LSDM). The system

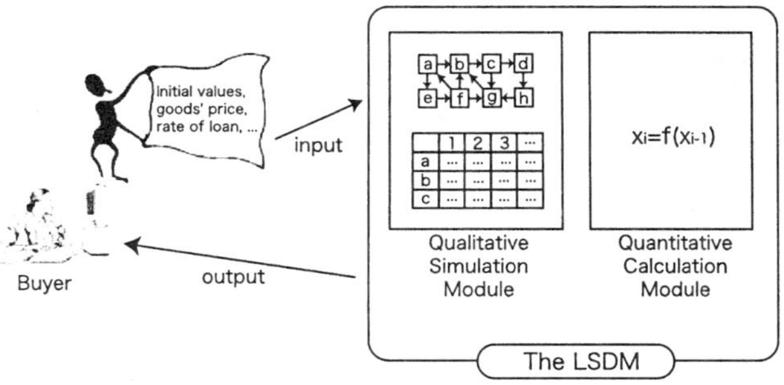


Figure 1: The Outline of LSDM

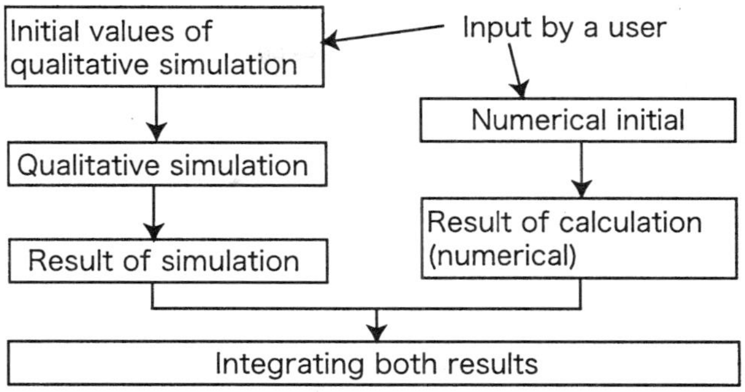


Figure 2: The Protocol of LSDM

consists of a qualitative simulation module and quantitative calculation module. We propose a learner support system for integrating both modules. The qualitative simulation uses qualitative methods in which calculating values are classified into cases, for example, "+", "0", or "-". The quantitative module is a numerical calculation using formulas. Our system provides the integrated results from which users can learn how or when they should purchase (expensive) immovable items.

In the following section, we first outline the system and explain the goal of our research. We then demonstrate the qualitative simulation and perform the numerical calculation.

## Outline of the LSDM

There has been much research on e-services using artificial intelligence technologies. We focus on an e-learning support system applying artificial intelligence technology when users want to purchase goods. The main goal of the LSDM is to support a conceptual understanding of economical systems and help/train users in their decision making. In recent years, there have been several studies about predicting stock and financial transactions. Most of these studies employ quantitative methods using certain complicated formulas. These studies have been developed as practical methods, but it is difficult for non-specialists to understand their mechanisms and the meaning of their calculations. The LSDM provides information for general users on how and when they should purchase goods.

Figure 1 shows a visual outline of the LSDM. First, a user inputs an initial value for the simulation, that is, the good's price, loan rates, total savings, and so on. Based on the user's input, the modules simulate a trend in the item's price and calculate the total payment. The results of the simulation and calculation are then integrated and given to the user. Finally, the LSDM displays purchase plans to assist the user's decision making. The simulation and calculation in the LSDM are based on the protocol shown in Figure 2.

## Qualitative Simulation Module

There are several methods for analyzing complex situations and the relations between cause and effect (Agell & Aguado 2001)(Asami, Takeuchi, & Otsuki 1997)(Hata, Ohkawa, & Komoda 1995). For example, a causal model using a directed graph is useful for analysis of complex situations, and we can observe dynamic behavior in the system (Kuipers 1994)(Ohkawa, Hata, & Komoda 1994). In this research, we developed an e-learning support system for assisting user decision making when making a major purchase (such as a house). There are some existing simulators, but they are severely limited because all possible outcomes are enumerated. The reason for not just adopting an off-the-shelf simulation method is the difference in task (i.e., generating plausible outcomes rather than all possible outcomes). The prices of immovable goods are influenced by many factors. Table 1 lists direct and indirect examples of these factors. The direct factors can be described in terms of the price of an immovable item, the loan rate, and the total amount of a user's savings. The indirect factors are the exchange rate, tax systems, business conditions, financing system for real estate properties (e.g., housing loans), and several others. Some factors can be calculated using numerical methods, but others cannot be calculated based on quantitative methods.

Table 1: An example of factors

| | |
|---|---|
| Direct factors | Price of immovable items (quantitative)<br>Total payments (quantitative)<br>Loan rate (quantitative)<br>Savings (quantitative)<br>Installments (quantitative)<br>etc. |
| Indirect factors | Exchange rate (quantitative)<br>Tax system (qualitative)<br>Business conditions (qualitative)<br>Financial system (qualitative)<br>etc. |

It is difficult to predict the price of an immovable item and its price trend in the future, by using quantitative (numerical) methods. Accordingly, LSDM employs a qualitative simulation by applying qualitative reasoning through artificial intelligence technology. Details of this qualitative simulation are given in Section 3.

### Numerical Calculation Module

The numerical module uses several mathematical formulas that are determined from the trend of an item's price, loan rates, and the buyer's savings. These factors are important for predicting a state in the future. Further, it is important for users to understand how much they must pay in total and how they plan to pay.

In the numerical calculation, one of the most important factors is the amount of money the user has saved and the price of the immovable item. When the savings are more than the price, the user can purchase the goods without price predictions. When the savings are less than the price, the user must determine how to pay the money using a loan. The next important factor is the rate of this loan. Here, it is assumed that the interest rate is fixed. When the rate is low, the total payment will be roughly equal to the purchase price (i.e., the case of no loan). However, if the rate is high and the balance is large, the buyer must pay a large amount of interest. Thus, the situation is complex depending on the terms.

The following is a simple example of a general formula used to calculate the total cost of a housing loan. Principal $G_0$ is defined as $G_0 = G$, where $G$ is the total loan amount. Principal $G_1$ is defined as $G_1 = (1+r)G_0 - X = (1+r)G - X$, where the 1st term, $r$, represents the loan rate and $X$ represents the amount of one payment. Generally, we can conduct the following formula in the $i$th term.

$$G_i = (1+r)^i G - \frac{(1+r)^i - 1}{r} X$$

It is assumed that the buyer pays in $N$ installments. Namely, the total repayment $G_N$ is zero after the $N$th term. When $G_N$ is zero, we can conduct the following equation.

$$0 = (1+r)^N G - \frac{(1+r)^N - 1}{r} X$$

$X$ is given by the following formula.

$$X = \frac{rG}{1 - \frac{1}{(1+r)^N}}$$

The LSDM provides information for users as a set of qualitative and quantitative simulated data. The users can comprehend the purchasing situation, and can purchase with appropriate strategy and decision making.

## Simulation Primer

The simulation primer uses a relation model between causes and effects expressed as a causal graph. Each node of the graph has a qualitative state value and each arc of the graph shows a trend in effects. The characteristics of the nodes and arcs are explained in this section.

### Qualitative States on Nodes

Each node has a qualitative state as time passes. We provide three sorts of qualitative state values on nodes.

**Def. 1** Qualitative state of factors

The qualitative state $[x(t)]$ is defined as given in Table 2. (node $x$ at time $t$.)

Table 2: Qualitative state

| $[x(t)]$ | Qualitative states |
|---|---|
| H | HIGH: In the next step, $[x(t)]$ is not higher than in the current step. |
| M | BOTH: In the next step, $[x(t)]$ is lower or higher than in the current step. |
| L | LOW: In the next step, $[x(t)]$ is not lower than in the current step. |

### State Trends Changing on Nodes

We define state trends changing on nodes that indicate the time differential. Three types of qualitative values are given.

**Def. 2** Changing trends of nodes

The qualitative changing state $[dx(t)]$ is defined as given in Table 3. (node $x$ at time $t$.)

Table 3: Qualitative changing state

| $[\delta x(t)]$ | Qualitative changing state |
|---|---|
| $I$ | $[x(t)]$ is increasing. |
| $S$ | $[x(t)]$ is stable. |
| $D$ | $[x(t)]$ is decreasing |

### Direction of Effects of Arcs

The direction of effects of arcs is defined by state trends changing on arcs. We show the direction of the effect nodes as influenced by the cause nodes. Two sorts of qualitative values are given.

**Def. 3** Direction of effects

$D(x, y)$ is the direction of the effects from node $x$ to node $y$, as defined in Table 4. The directions are classified into two categories.

### Transmission Speed of Effects on Arcs

Here, we define the transmission speed of effects from node $x$ to node $y$. The definition of the transmission speed is essentially different from Defs. 1 through 3. The speed depends on the causal model. The transmission speeds are distinguished between immediate($V_0$) and non-immidiate($V_n$).

Table 4: Direction of effects

| $D(x, y)$ | Direction of effects |
|---|---|
| $+$ | When $x$'s state value increases, $y$'s state value also increases. / When $x$'s state value decreases, $y$'s state value also decrease. |
| $-$ | When $x$'s state value decreases, $y$'s state value increases. / When $x$'s state value increases, $y$'s state value decreases. |

The $V_n$ is defined as follows. Time order $V_n$ of the transmission speed of effects from node $x$ to node $y$ is more than $V_n - 1$ and less than $V_n + 1$. This $n$ indicates the number of steps in the transmission delay. In our system, users can set up $n$ based on their own opinions. However, in this paper, we show and define the following simple set-up form for naive users.

**Def. 4** Transmission speed
The transmission speed $V(x, y)$ is classified in Table 5.

We assume that transmission speed $V_0$ is used on the arc from node $x$ to node $y$. When node $x$ is influenced by other nodes and changes to a qualitative value, node $y$ changes the value simultaneously, for example, the relations of wages and income. On the other hand, we assume that transmission speed $V_1$ is used on the arc from node $x$ to node $y$. When node $x$ is influenced by other nodes and changes to a qualitative value, node $y$ changes the value with a one-step delay, for example, the relations of quantities of consumption and quantities of product.

Table 5: Transmission speed

| $V(x, y)$ | Transmission speed |
|---|---|
| $V_0$ | Node $x$'s value gives an effect to node $y$'s value immediately. |
| $V_1$ | Node $x$'s value gives an effect to node $y$'s value slowly. |
| $V_?$ | The speed is unknown. |

## Integration of Multiple Effects on Nodes

The integration of multiple effects on nodes is defined as follows. Figure 3 shows an example of the integration. When there are multiple adjacent nodes connected to a node, the effects are defined by the following definition.

**Def. 5** Integration
When multiple nodes are connected to a node, the trends of effects are defined in Table 6. In the table, "?" means that the trends are not defined.

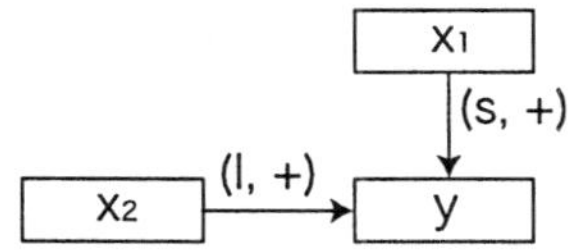


Figure 3: An example of the integration

Table 6: Integration of state values

| $+$ | $I$ | $S$ | $D$ |
|---|---|---|---|
| $I$ | $I$ | $I$ | ? |
| $S$ | $I$ | $S$ | $D$ |
| $D$ | ? | $D$ | $D$ |

| $-$ | $I$ | $S$ | $D$ |
|---|---|---|---|
| $I$ | $D$ | $D$ | ? |
| $S$ | $D$ | $S$ | $I$ |
| $D$ | ? | $I$ | $I$ |

# An Example of Qualitative Simulation

## A Model for Qualitative Simulation

The relation model for the qualitative simulation is explained in the following sections. Figure 4 shows the causal graph model for qualitatively predicting the major purchase price and the rate of a housing loan. Each arc has a characteristic $(D(x, y), V(x, y))$. This model was constructed according to Japanese economical statistics from 1975 to 1990. It should be noted that the model is based on the following assumptions.

- When GDP increases, wages increase.
- When income increases, the amount of consumption increases.
- When the amount of exports increases, stocks inventories decrease.
- When GDP decreases, a tax reduction system is conducted (reduced).

## An Example of Qualitative Simulation

Using the relation model and assumption given in Section 3.2, we conducted an experiment on the trend in the price of a major purchase (a house). The initial values for the simulation are based on the economical conditions in Japan in 1975. Table 7 shows the initial values. In the simulation, when a node's value cannot be determined by integration of multiple state values, the qualitative values are decided based on the number of "+"s(or "-"s). When the number of "+"s(or "-"s) is more than the threshold value (decided by the user), the qualitative value is decided as "+"(or "-"). On the other hand, when the number of "+"s(or "-"s) is not more than the threshold value, the qualitative value is decided at random. This operation is essential to output a single set of results.

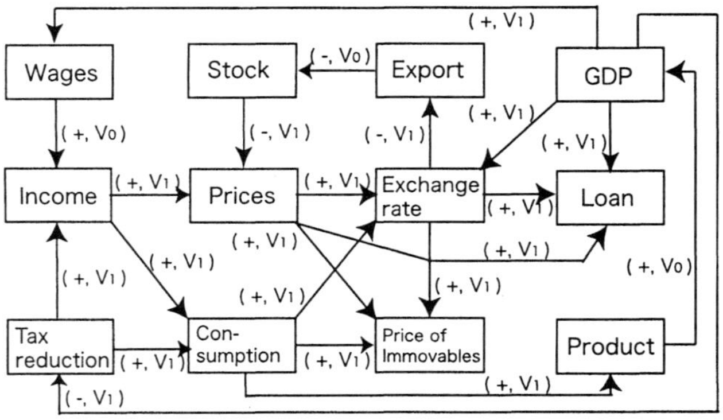


Figure 4: A model off the relation between factors

Table 7: Initial values for the qualitative simulation

| Trends | Factors (nodes) |
|---|---|
| Increasing | wage, income, price, consumption, export, exchange rate stock, product, GDP, loan rate |
| Decreasing | Tax reduction |

## User Interface

The LSDM's interface mainly consists of the input window and the output window in which a user can see the result of a simulation. Figure 5 shows a user interface in which the users make a relation model and input partial initial values for the qualitative simulation. The users decide arcs by inputting each node, such as "node A to node B". After that, to decide the characteristics of each node, the users select the attribute that is the direction ("+" or "-") of the effect of each arc. The users select the transmission speed of each arc from the radio buttons. To calculate the loans and payments, the users input their initial values into the text boxes of the interface in Figure 6. Based on the values input by the users, the quantitative module calculates the total payments, the number of divided repayments, and so on.

When the users fill out the form to simulate/calculate, the results of the simulation/calculation are shown as in Figure 7. The users view the result of the simulation and calculation as a graph. The simulation is conducted in 200 time steps. The horizontal axis represents time, while the vertical axis represents the price of the immovable items. In this case, using the above model and the initial values in Section 4, the immovable price and loan rate increase in the future. From the result of the simulation/calculation, we can predict that the user should not purchase the item in the future. Further, the system provides numerical information concerned with the total payments, including loans. The users can retry/re-simulate by pushing the improvement button. Thus, users learn how they should conduct their decision making through trial and error.

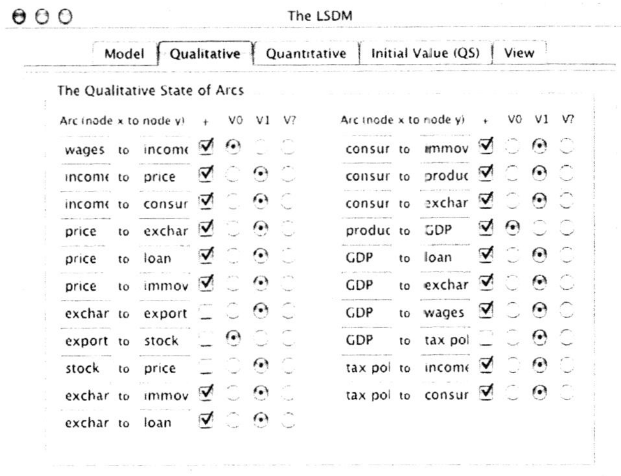


Figure 5: The LSDM 1

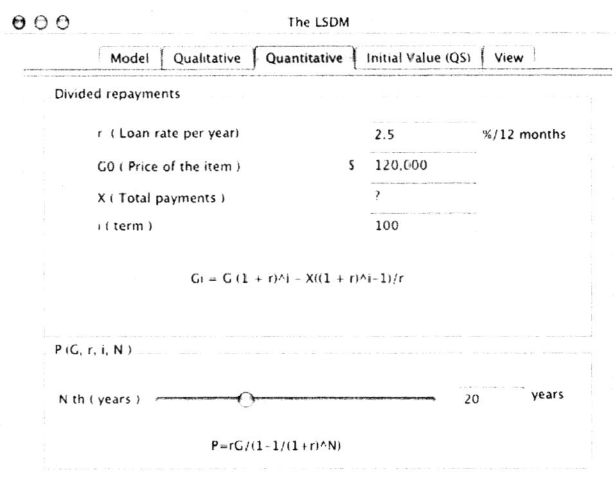


Figure 6: The LSDM 2

## Conclusion

In this paper, we proposed an e-learning support system (LSDM) for assisting user decision making by applying artificial intelligence technology. We employed qualitative simulations because the learners can understand conceptual foundation in economic dynamics by using the qualitative method. The LSDM consists of a qualitative processing system and a quantitative calculation system. The system integrates the results of simulation and the user's input data, and assists the user's decision process. The system has several advantages: it can be used by simple input, the simulation process is easy to understand, and the users can base their decision making on synthetic results.

Our future work includes development of the application as Web-based training (WBT) on the Internet.

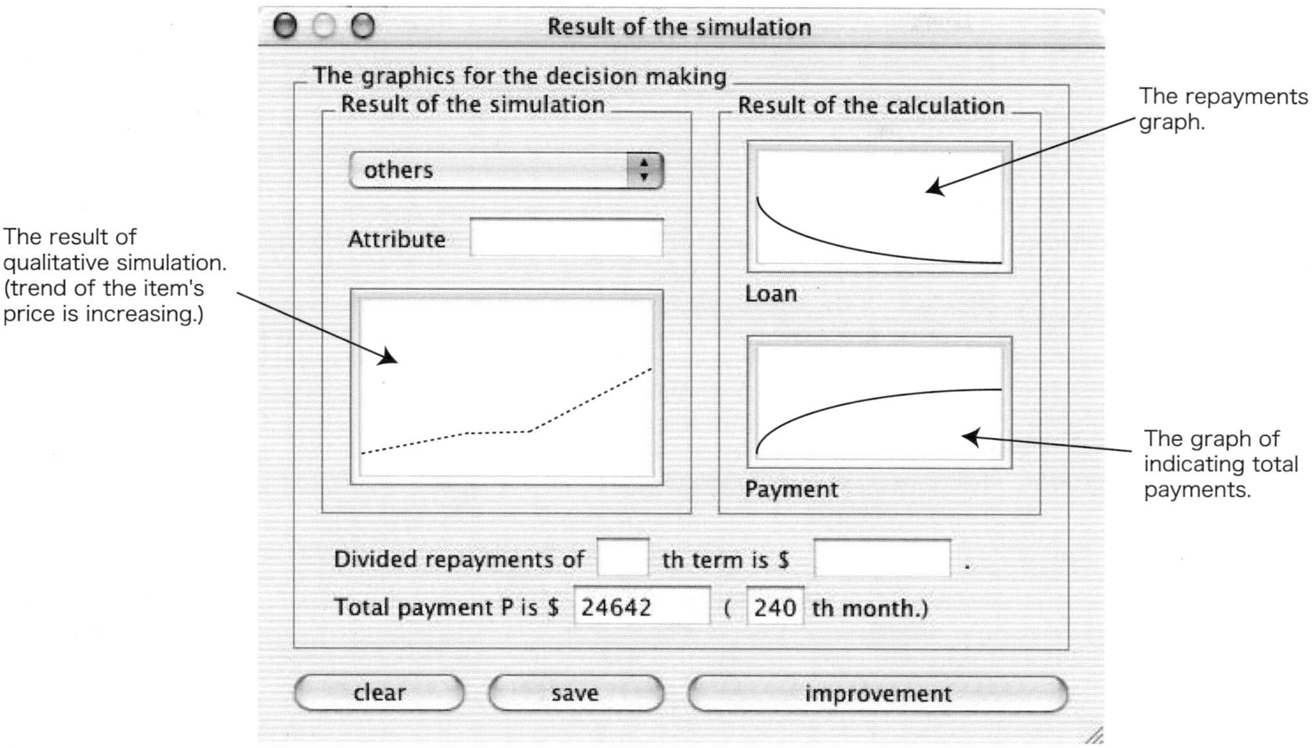


Figure 7: Result of the simulations

## References


Agell, N., and Aguado, C. J. 2001. A hybrid qualitative-quantitative classification technique applied to aid marketing decisions. In *the proceedings of 11th International Workshop on Qualitative Reasoning*.

Asami, K.; Takeuchi, A.; and Otsuki, S. 1997. A dialogue method for assisting students in understanding causalities in physical systems. *The Institute of Electronics, Information and Communication Engineers Transaction on Information and Systems, D-II* J80(10):2848–2859.

Bredeweg, B., and Forbus, K. 2003. Qualitative modeling in education. *AI magazine* Vol.24(4).

Bredeweg, B., and Winkels, R. 1998. Qualitative models in interactive learning environments. *Interactive Learning Environments* Vol.5.

Chen, S. A.; Wang, J.; and Yang, C. S. 2002. Constructing internet futures exchange for teach-ing derivatives trading in financial markets. In *the proceedings of International Conference on Computers in Education, Vol.2*, 1392–1395.

Forbus, K. D.; Carney, K.; Harris, R.; and Sherin, B. L. 2001. A qualitative modeling environment for middle-school students: A progress report. In *the proceedings of 11th International Workshop on Qualitative Reasoning*, 17–19.

Forbus, K. D. 2002. Helping children become qualitative modelers. *Journal of the Japanese Society for Artificial Intelligence* Vol.17(4).

Hata, S.; Ohkawa, T.; and Komoda, N. 1995. Backward simulation method in qualitative simulation. *IEEJ Transactions on Electronics, Information and Systems, Institute of Electrical Engineers of Japan* Vol.115-C(11).

Kuipers, B. 1994. *Qualitative Reasoning*. The MIT Press.

Matsuo, T.; Ito, T.; and Shintani, T. 2004. An e-learning support system for consumers based on qualitative simulation. *IPSJ SIG Technical Reports, Information Processing Society of Japan* Vol.2004(3).

Nishida, T. 1991. Qualitative reasoning and its application to intelligent problem solving. *IPSJ Magazine, Information Processing Society of Japan* Vol.32(2).

Ohkawa, T.; Hata, S.; and Komoda, N. 1994. Multiple time scaling qualitatives simulation using typical patterns. *IEEJ Transactions on Electronics, Information and Systems, Institute of Electrical Engineers of Japan* Vol.114(11).

Russell, S., and Norvig, P. 1995. *Artificial Intelligence - A Modern Approach-, Second Edition*. Pearson Education International.

Weir, R. S. G. 2002. The rigours of on-line student assessment lessons from e-commerce. In *the proceedings of International Conference on Computers in Education, Vol.2*, 840–843.

# Robotics

# Skill Acquisition and Use for a Dynamically-Balancing Soccer Robot

**Brett Browning, Ling Xu** and **Manuela Veloso**
Carnegie Mellon University
School of Computer Science
5000 Forbes Avenue, Pittsburgh, USA
brettb,mmv@cs.cmu.edu, lingx@andrew.cmu.edu *

### Abstract

Dynamically-balancing robots have recently been made available by Segway LLC, in the form of the Segway RMP (Robot Mobility Platform). We have addressed the challenge of using these RMP robots to play soccer, building up upon our extensive previous work in this multi-robot research domain. In this paper, we make three contributions. First, we present a new domain, called Segway Soccer, for investigating the coordination of dynamically formed, mixed human-robot teams within the realm of a team task that requires real-time decision making and response. Segway Soccer is a game of soccer between two teams consisting of both Segway riding humans and Segway RMPs. We believe Segway Soccer is the first game involving both humans and robots in cooperative roles and with similar capabilities. In conjunction with this new domain, we present our work towards developing a soccer playing robot using the RMP platform with vision as its primary sensor. Our third contribution is that of skill acquisition from a human teacher, where the learned skill is then used seamlessly during robot execution as part of its control hierarchy. Skill acquisition and use addresses the challenge of rapidly developing the low-level actions that are environment dependent and are not transferable across robots.

## Introduction

There has been considerable research into both human-robot interaction (Nicolescu & Mataric 2003), and multi-agent teams (Dias & Stentz 2002; Ferraresso *et al.* 2001; Kiat *et al.* 2001). Additionally, since the inception of RoboCup robot soccer (Asada *et al.* 2003), there has been considerable research into robot teams operating in adversarial environments. To our knowledge, however, there has been no work yet that combines these attributes; namely, to examine human-robot interaction within an adversarial, multi-robot setting where humans and robots are team members with similar capabilities and no clear role hierarchy.

We are developing a new game, which we call Segway Soccer, that aims to fill this void. Segway soccer is a game that requires mixed teams of humans and robots to cooperate to achieve the maximum reward in an adversarial task. To ensure interesting cooperation, both humans and robots are equipped with similar capabilities. We achieve this difficult task by requiring that both humans and robots use the same drive platform - the Segway platform developed by Segway LLC (Figure 1).

Our goal is to create a task that requires advanced robot intelligence, combined with robust human-robot interaction skills. We hope to extend the powerful aspects of RoboCup - competition, an adversarial domain requiring fast decisions, and a well understood task - to incorporate human-robot interaction. The need for this new domain lies in the lack of study for human-robot interaction where decisions need to be made quickly. As robots become more integrated into society, they will inevitably have to interact with humans and/or legacy robots in complex tasks. For some of these tasks, decisions may need to be made quickly and roles of both humans and robots may not be clearly defined a priori.

Figure 1: The Segway RMP (left and right) and HT (right) platforms developed by Segway LLC (http://www.segway.com).

In this paper, we describe our work towards developing a robot capable of participating in Segway soccer. As this new domain is set in the outdoors, compensating for variable lighting conditions and less structured environments, but still retaining the ability to make and act on decisions quickly is a challenging task. We describe our initial solutions to meet this challenge.

*This research was sponsored by the United States Army under Grant No. DABT63-99-1-0013. The content of the information in this publication does not necessarily reflect the position or the policy of the Defense Advanced Research Projects Agency (DARPA), the US Army or the US Government, and no official endorsement should be inferred.

The format of the paper is as follows. In the following section we describe the specifics of Segway soccer; its rules, structure, goals, and challenges. Following this we describe how to extend a Segway RMP to become a robot capable of playing soccer with vision as its primary sensor. We then focus on our third contribution, skill acquisition and use, leading to our empirical result, conclusions and future work.

## Segway Soccer

In this section, we concretely describe the game of Segway soccer. We begin by describing the unique features of the Segway platform that make the concept of human-robot teamwork feasible in a complex game such as soccer, before progressing to the game itself.

### Segway as a Platform for Robotics Research

The Segway platform, invented by Dean Kamen, is unique due to its combination of wheel actuators and dynamic balancing. For the robot version this imbues the robot with the novel characteristics of a fast platform, able to reach speeds of $3.5 m.s^{-1}$ and travel long ranges (on the order of kilometers), able to carry significant payloads, able to navigate in relatively tight spaces for its size, and provides the opportunity to mount sensors at a height comparable to human eye level. As it is derived from a commercial product, it is reliable and robust to damage. Finally, dynamic balancing offers a number of unique properties including low-pass filtering of perturbations by non-flat terrain, as well as a moderate level of compliance with collisions.

From the perspective of human-robot interaction, the Segway is unique in that its human and robot versions have identical physical capabilities. The only difference resides in different perception and cognition capabilities of humans versus robots. For exploring human-robot interaction in cooperative teams operating in adversarial tasks requiring real-time responses, this property is essential.

For control, the RMP presents a high-speed serial interface, using the automotive industry standard CAN bus. Although essentially identical to the human-ridable Segway HT, the robot version has a modified control algorithm enabling a connected laptop to send desired forward and rotational velocity commands. The RMP's onboard algorithms accelerate or decelerate the robot to achieve these commands. Finally, the robot provides feedback on its current state including full angular pose and velocity information. Physically, the robot appears as a table on wheels due to the addition of a large mass of approximately 50lbs at a height of about 50cm from the robot wheel base. This mass raises the robot's center of gravity thereby enabling the RMP to balance with a control loop operating at a realizable frequency.

### The Game

We have developed the domain of Segway soccer for investigating human-robot interaction. Segway soccer is a game between two teams playing on a grass field in an outdoor environment with an orange, size 5 soccer ball. Teams can consist of humans, robots, or a mix of humans and robots. Figure 2 shows the field structure. The field consists of a grass surface in an outdoor environment, where the size is scaled as a function of the number of team members so that with 11 players on each team it is a full-sized soccer field. Colored tubular markers are placed around the field to indicate the field boundary and goal locations. A human referee maintains control of the game and transmits signals verbally, for human consumption, and via wireless communication for the robots. The latter is achieved via an assistant referee armed with a laptop and a wireless network, an approach developed in robot soccer (Asada *et al.* 2003). Team members may be robots, humans, or robots and humans. In all cases, the Segway platform is used to ensure each team member has identical physical capabilities. Both humans and robots wear colored markers to allow easy team identification.

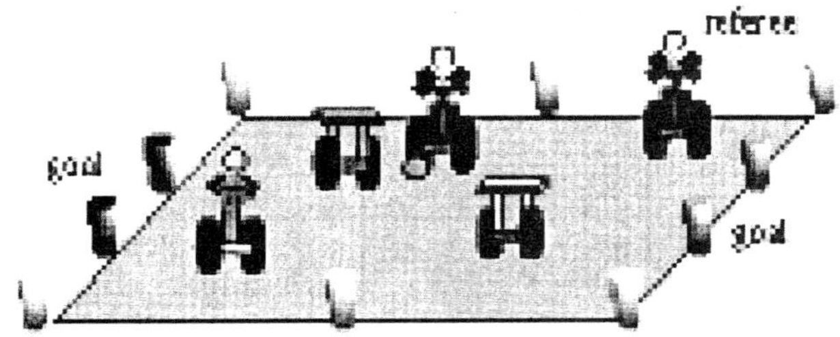

Figure 2: The Segway field. Teams consist of humans, robots, or robots and humans using the Segway platform, and an orange size 5 soccer ball.

As both Segway HT's and RMP's carry considerable mass, and are able to reach considerable speed, safety is a primary concern. To address this problem, the game follows a flow more familiar to Ultimate Frisbee[1]. When play begins, ball possession is decided with a coin toss. Thereafter, players gain possession based on proximity to the ball when it is "free". Once a player obtains possession, opponents must remain at least $3m$ away to prevent any unnecessary contact. Players are not allowed to move with the ball (i.e. dribble), and instead must pass the ball to one another for the team to maintain possession. A time limit on possession enforces how long a single player can retain the ball before passing to a teammate. When the ball is passed, the first player on any team to come within a specific distance of the ball when it comes to rest will gain possession. The same player cannot re-acquire possession of the ball until after another player has obtained possession. Possession is also changed if the ball is kicked out of bounds or if a goal is scored. Although primarily a safety measure, this rule also ensures that players must pass the ball to advance. As a direct consequence teamwork, rather than purely single robot skills, becomes essential. The goal of exploring intelligent teamwork is therefore achieved.

Although the rules as defined allow for a multi-agent, adversarial game to be played, they do not necessarily enforce human-robot interaction. If, for example, humans prove considerably more capable than their robot teammates, or vice-versa, one class of team members will dominate pos-

[1]Rules for Ultimate Frisbee can be found at http://www.upa.org

session leading to little human-robot interaction opportunities. Either case is undesirable. Our solution to this problem is to require that both a human and a robot be part of the sequence of passes leading to a goal score. How effective this solution is in the long term under competition conditions, remains to be seen.

## Developing a Segway Soccer Player

We now describe our work to develop a Segway RMP robot base capable of playing Segway soccer. As with any autonomous robot operating in a dynamic world, one must develop a *complete* system involving perception, cognition, and action inter-operating seamlessly with minimal response latency. In this section, we detail our contributions to achieving this goal which builds upon our prior work in this area.

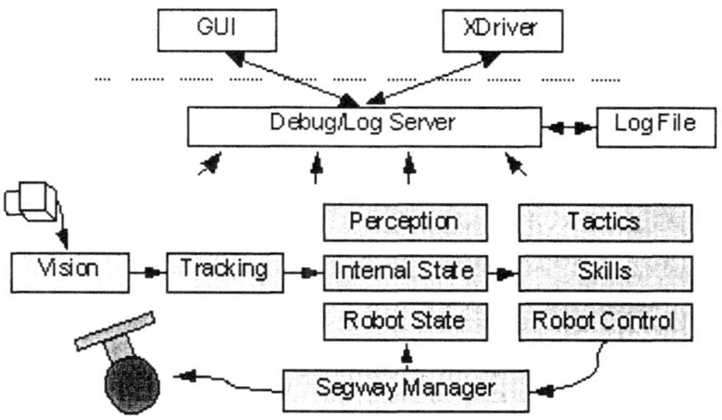


Figure 3: The control hierarchy used for the robot. The gray modules are the perception-cognition-action part of the system. The white are development infrastructure aids. Xdriver is the tele-operation program.

Figure 3 shows the complete control architecture for the RMP. The gray boxes show the main processing path that makes up perception, cognition, and action. In an environment occupied by other fast moving agents, the ability to perceive and respond to situational changes in minimum time is essential. Hence, it is critical to overall robot performance that the control loop formed by gray modules operate at full frame rate with minimum latency. The white boxes show the supporting development environment, which although not critical during execution play a central role in the pace of the development cycle and therefore in the robustness of the result. We now describe each major component and its role in the overall hierarchy, namely; perception, skills and tactics.

### Perception: Vision and Tracking

For environments like those the RMP operates in, there are few sensors that can compete with color vision for low cost, compact size, high information volume and throughput, and relatively low latency. Thus, our chosen path is decidedly vision centric where a color camera provides each robot with its only external sensor. Given the range of environments that the robot operates in – outdoors on grass fields, or indoors when the weather is poor – perception quickly becomes an overriding challenge. That is, to develop *fast* vision algorithms that provide the robot with timely, but relatively noise free information that is robust to variations in lighting intensity. To complicate issues, only a fraction of the available processing power is dedicated to vision as the remainder must be used for tracking, modeling, behaviors, navigation and motion control. Achieving these goals is one of the key challenges to be addressed for using the RMP. To our knowledge, there are no vision algorithms that offer all of these features.

A number of fast, color-based algorithms and freely available source libraries have been developed for static lighting conditions (e.g. (Bruce, Balch, & Veloso 2000)). However, these libraries do not as yet extend to variable, or changing lighting conditions. Our approach uses region growing (Adams & Bischof 1994), where seeds are first provided from any regions that found in the previous frame that were large enough. The remainder of the seeds are chosen uniformly. Each region is grown using a fixed homogeneity constraint based on the distance of the new color pixel in YUV space from the average color of the region grown thus far. That is, if the new pixel has color $c_j = (y_j, u_j, v_j)^T$, it is added to the region $R_i$ if it is a neighbor of an existing pixel in the region, $c_j \in \mathcal{N}(c_k)$, $c_k \in R_i$, and it is sufficiently close to the region mean, $(y_j - \hat{y}_i < \tau_y) \wedge (u_j - \hat{u}_i < \tau_u) \wedge (v_j - \hat{v}_i < \tau_v)$. The region mean is updated after each pixel addition and has the value $\hat{c}_i = |R_i|^{-1} \sum_{R_i} c_j$.

Once regions are identified and the summary statistics for each region are calculated, high level vision processing begins by identifying the regions that are potential objects of interest: the ball, field markers, teammates or opponents. Regions that are close to the color of interest, using a Euclidean distance metric and threshold, are labelled accordingly. That is for prototype $p$: $R^p = \{R_i | \, \|\hat{c}_i - c^p\| < \tau^p\}$. A region may be labeled as belonging to more than one class type. For each object of interest, the regions are then based on objects' expected geometric properties as in our earlier work (Lenser, Bruce, & Veloso 2001). Figure 4 shows an example of the vision processing and its output.

The goal of vision is to provide as many valid estimates of objects as possible (i.e. a low false-positive rate). Estimates of the global positions of the obstacles is derived using a lens distortion model, a pin-hole projective model for the camera, and knowledge of the robot's respective tilt angles. Tracking then fuses this information to track the most interesting objects of relevance to the robot. At the time of writing our current multi-hypothesis tracker is still under active development. Ongoing work is focused on developing a true probabilistic multi-hypothesis tracker (Bar-Shalom 1990).

### Robot Control Hierarchy

In our previous work we developed and thoroughly validated a hierarchical, behavior based control system called Skills-Tactics-Plays (STP) (Bruce *et al.* 2003 to appear) for adaptive multi-robot control in adversarial, highly dynamic environments. The architecture consists of Skills for low-level control policies, Tactics to encapsulate a complete single robot behavior, and Plays for team coordination. We have

Figure 4: The left image shows a raw image in an indoor scene, the right the resulting regions, with the identified ball region and yellow marker outlined with a bounding box.

applied the STP control hierarchy to the Segway problem. Here we focus on skills and tactics that encapsulate single robot behavior.

**Robot Control** At the lowest level of the hierarchy are motion control and obstacle free navigation, key components to any mobile robot. These modules are adapted versions of our prior work, (Bruce *et al.* 2003 to appear) and (Bruce & Veloso 2002), respectively, and will not be discussed in detail here. Above motion control are the skills, the building blocks of individual behavior.

**Skills** Each skill is a focused control policy for carrying out complex actions over some limited set of world states. For Segway soccer an example skill is the action to actually kick the ball, or to position behind a ball in order to kick it towards a target.

**Tactics** A tactic encapsulates a complete single robot behavior. An example tactic includes shooting the ball on goal, receiving the ball from a teammate, or defending the goal.

**Plays** A play encapsulates team behavior by encoding a sequence of tactics to be carried out by each team member (Bowling, Browning, & Veloso 2004 in press). Plays are beyond the scope of this paper.

Skills are the action primitives for tactics, thus a tactic consists of instantiating a sequence of skills to execute, in other words a finite state machine, where the sequence of execution depends upon how the perceived world state changes. Tactics affect the world by instantiating skills in sequence to execute and by passing each executing skill parameters derived from the world state to affect its operation as it executes. For example to shoot the ball at the goal, the shoot tactic executes a sequence of skills such as gotoBall, positionForKick, and when aimed at the target the final kick skill. Finally, following the usual behavior based approach (Arkin 1998), tactics and skills execute in parallel at frame rate (30Hz).

With only minor variations all of the tactics employed on the RMP were developed previously in (Bruce *et al.* 2003 to appear). At this high-level of behavior, the tactics evaluate the world and determine target points for kicking or moving. As most of the details of each action are contained in the underlying skills, we have found that the tactics transfer effectively from one platform to another completely different platform but for a very similar task. In contrast, the underlying skills are highly dependent up on the hardware and do not transition effectively. To avoid the necessity of redeveloping a new skill set, we followed the novel approach of developing skill acquisition systems for rapidly acquiring new skills through training by a human operator.

## Skill Acquisition and Use

Within the STP framework, skills form the closest interface to the physical robot hardware. Each skill, therefore, is highly dependent upon the physical properties of the robot and its environment and plays a major role in determining overall robot performance. The dependency of skills on the physical properties of robot and environment mean that skills rarely transfer well from one environment to the next, or from one robot platform to another, where deviations are the norm. When one considers that in practice, developing a skill requires considerable hand tweaking of control parameters, a notoriously error prone and time intensive operation, it seems apparent that some form of automated skill acquisition is needed.

One interesting approach to skill acquisition is reinforcement learning (e.g. (Bagnell *et al.* 2003)). Although there have been significant advancements in reinforcement learning, there are still a number of issues that must be address in order to learn effective robot control where *it could be used as a sub-component of an existing control hierarchy*. The primary limitation is that of long training time. Even the most advanced algorithms still take a considerable amount of time to achieve even moderate levels of performance.

### Approach

We have taken a different approach to skill acquisition, where skills commands are generated by generalizing from example trajectories provided by a human operator using tele-operation. There have been a number of examples in the literature (e.g. (Schaal & Atkeson 1998; Billard & Mataric 2001) and (Nicolescu & Mataric 2003)) where tele-operation or learning from observation has been effectively used to learn to execute a task thus motivating our approach. Our particular approach is inspired by two observations. First, it is usually relatively easy to tele-operate a wheeled robot, even a dynamically balancing one, through the approximate sequence of motions required to execute a skill. Second, skills developed by hand are often a direct, if complex, function mapping from sensory state to output commands. Our key assumption is that the commands given by the human operator are noisy samples from some fixed, but unknown function of the world state. The goal of skill acquisition is therefore to provide estimates of this function for world states experienced by the robot based on the provided samples.

There are numerous function approximation techniques that are available. However, we have focused our investigations on locally weighted regression (LWR) (Cleveland & Loader 1995). LWR provides robust function estimation using a minimal amount of training data, is able to generalize by interpolation across unseen inputs, and is amenable to fast, efficient implementations. All of these criteria are of importance to skill acquisition in the given setting. Additionally, LWR has a long, successful history of use in robot control problems (Atkeson, Moore, & Schaal 1997; Schaal & Atkeson 1998).

Our approach works in two phases; recording and playback. During the recording phase, a human operator guides the robot through a sequence motions by providing a sequence of commanded actions $a_i = \left(a_i^1, a_i^2, ..., a_i^k\right)^T$. A special purpose recording tactic stores the sent command $a_i$, as well as the corresponding relevant world state $x_i = \left(x_i^1, ..., x_i^d\right)^T$ for later recall. During playback, the skill uses these data-points to approximate the actions of the recording phase. The key assumption is that the recorded actions are sampled from some unknown function so that $a_i = f(x_i)$. During playback the skill approximates this function, using its samples, using LWR, such that i.e. $a(t) = \hat{f}(x(t))$ as the robot moves in the world. Concretely, we have:

$$a(t) = \hat{f}\left(x(t)\right) = \frac{\sum_i K\left(x(t), x_i\right) \cdot a_i}{\sum_i K\left(x(t), x_i\right)} \tag{1}$$

where $K(\cdot, \cdot)$ is a kernel function, which in practice is a Gaussian given by:

$$K\left(x(t), x_i\right) = e^{\frac{-(x(t)-x_i)^2}{2 \cdot h^2}} \tag{2}$$

### Implementation

There are three issues to implementing the LWR function approximation. The first is to provide for fast function approximation. Following the usual approach, we store the $x_i$'s in a Kd-tree for fast nearest neighbor search (Atkeson, Moore, & Schaal 1997). Additionally, we limit the horizon of the search to $H_{max} = sqrt\frac{2h^2}{lnK_{min}}$, for some predefined $K_{min}$, thereby limiting the extent of the evaluations of 1. Secondly, one must choose the so-called bandwidth parameter, $h$. We chose a global value of $h$ by hand. An alternative approach would be to use cross-validation, or a locally varying bandwidth parameter (Cleveland & Loader 1995). Although there are some arguments for the usefulness of the latter, in our current work it proved unnecessary. Finally, while LWR works well for interpolation, it is well recognized that it becomes unpredictable for extrapolation beyond the underlying data set, i.e. outside of the convex hull formed by the $x_i$'s. For robot control this can cause serious limitations. However, given that skills are by definition only defined over a sub-set of the state space, say $S_{skill}$, provided this set of states is a sub-set of the convex hull formed by the $x_i$'s no difficulties should occur. This is achieved by ensuring the skill training data covers $S_{skill}$. As a secondary safety measure, should the normalization factor in 1 be too small the output is set to the null vector and warning notifications are given.

## Experimental Results

All of the work described here has been fully implemented on the RMP platform. Moreover, all components of the system are fully integrated allowing execution at the full frame rate of 30Hz. Video demonstrations of the system in execution are available at *http://www.cs.cmu.edu/ robosoccer/segway*. While many sub-components have been built upon our previous extensive experiences with robot teams operating in dynamic environments, it was not possible to build upon our existing skill libraries developed for other platforms. The RMP's unique dynamic balancing means that short-term motions are distinctly different from a comparable differential drive robot. Thus, we have a practical need for effective skill acquisition and use.

All of the low-level skills operating on the RMP, except for the most trivial, utilize skill acquisition. However, to properly evaluate the performance of skill acquisition as described here, we made use of our small-size robots (Bruce *et al.* 2003 to appear) and high-fidelity simulator UberSim (Browning & Tryzelaar 2003), where accurate ground truth information is easily available. The robots were differential drive robots, but are statically balanced. We trained a skill using a hand-coded policy $\pi\left(x(t)\right)$ that drives the robot towards the ball. A hand coded policy was used instead of tele-operation in order to get a qualitative evaluation in execution performance. The skill was acquired using the training gathered training data and then evaluated on a previously unseen evaluation point that was inside the convex hull of the previously training trajectories. We then compared the performance of the acquired skill against the hand coded policy evaluated from the same location (see table 1).

**Training**
1. **for each** training point $x_j^{train}$
3. Execute $a(t) = \pi^{hc}(x(t))$ until goal reached
4. Record $(x(t), a(t))$ for learning

**Testing**
1. Load data points $x_i, a_i$
2. **for each** testing point $x_j^{test}$
3. Execute $a(t) = \hat{f}(x(t))$ until goal reached
4. Record $x^{acq}(t)$ for evaluation

**Evaluation**
1. **for each** testing point $x_j^{test}$
2. Execute $a(t) = \pi(x(t))$ until goal reached
3. Record $x^{hc}(t)$ for evaluation

Table 1: The evaluation procedure.

For learning, the state was encoded as the relative location of the ball as $x(t) = \left(b_x(t), b_y(t)\right)^T$. The commands were encoded as the forward and rotational speed, $a(t) = (v, \omega)^T$. The hand coded policy was used from existing, publicly available algorithms (Bruce *et al.* 2003 to appear). Figure 5 shows the comparison between the robot trajectories for the acquired skill ($x^{acq}(t)$) and the hand coded policy ($x^{hc}(t)$) for different starting conditions, with the ball located at $(0, 0)$. Twelve trajectories distributed over 4 grid points points with starting angles of 0, -90, and 90 degrees, were used to train the skill. Even with only a few examples, the acquired skill is able to show the appropriate operation

| Evaluation | Run 1 | Run 2 | Run 3 | Run 4 | Run 5 |
|---|---|---|---|---|---|
| Hand coded | 0.63 | 0.87 | 0.63 | 0.87 | 0.97 |
| Acquired | 0.70 | 0.77 | 0.60 | 0.97 | 1.03 |

Table 2: Comparison of the run time (in seconds).

with only minor amounts of error. Table 2 shows the difference in time to reach the goal for 5 of these runs.

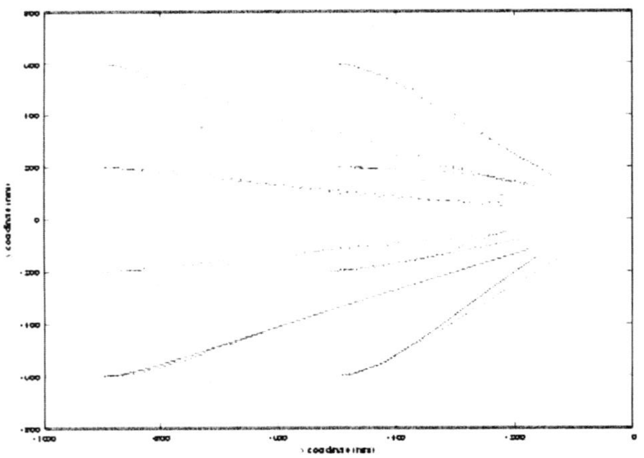

Figure 5: A comparison between trajectories from the acquired skill vs. the hand coded policy in simulation.

## Summary and Future Work

The Segway RMP and HT present a new and exciting robotics research platform. Based on this platform we have devised a new domain called Segway soccer for investigating human-robot interaction in real-time, adversarial tasks. We have developed the single robot capabilities to control an RMP in an outdoor environment. Specifically, we have developed robust outdoor vision, and extended our prior work with a skill-tactic-play control hierarchy. Our final contribution is a skill acquisition system for rapidly developing new skills through tele-operation.

## References


Adams, R., and Bischof, L. 1994. Seeded region growing. *IEEE Transactions on Pattern Analysis and Machine Intelligence* 16:641–647.

Arkin, R. 1998. *Behavior-Based Robotics*. MIT Press.

Asada, M.; Sklar, E.; Kaminka, G. A.; Obst, O.; Polani, D.; Browning, B.; Bonarini, A.; Fujita, M.; Christaller, T.; Takahashi, T.; and Tadokoro, S. 2003. An overview of robocup-2002 fukuoka/busan. *AI Magazine* 24(2):21–40.

Atkeson, C. G.; Moore, A. W.; and Schaal, S. 1997. Locally weighted learning. *Artificial Intelligence Review* 11(1-5):11–73.

Bagnell, J. A.; Kakade, S.; Ng, A.; and Schneider, J. 2003. Policy search by dynamic programming. In *Proceedings of Neural Information Processing Systems, NIPS 16*.

Bar-Shalom, Y. 1990. *Multitarget Multisensor Tracking: Advanced Applications*. Artech House.

Billard, A., and Mataric, M. 2001. Learning human arm movements by imitation: Evaluation of biologicallyinspired connectionist architecture. *Robotics and Autonomous Systems* 37:145–160.

Bowling, M.; Browning, B.; and Veloso, M. 2004, in press. Plays as effective multiagent plans enabling opponent-adaptive play selection. In *Proceedings of the International Conference on Automated Planning and Scheduling (ICAPS'04)*.

Browning, B., and Tryzelaar, E. 2003. Ubersim: A realistic simulation engine for robot soccer. In *Proceedings of Autonomous Agents and Multi-Agent Systems, AAMAS'03*.

Bruce, J., and Veloso, M. 2002. Real-time randomized path planning for robot navigation. In *Proceedings of IROS-2002*. An earlier version of this paper appears in the Proceedings of the RoboCup-2002 Symposium.

Bruce, J.; Balch, T.; and Veloso, M. 2000. Fast and inexpensive color image segmentation for interactive robots. In *Proceedings of IROS-2000*.

Bruce, J.; Bowling, M.; Browning, B.; and Veloso, M. 2003, to appear. Multi-robot team response to a multi-robot opponent team. In *Proceedings of ICRA'03, the 2003 IEEE International Conference on Robotics and Automation*.

Cleveland, W., and Loader, C. 1995. Smoothing by local regression: Principles and methods. Technical report, AT T Bell Laboratories, Murray Hill, NY.

Dias, M. B., and Stentz, A. 2002. Opportunistic optimization for market-based multirobot control. In *Proceedings of the IEEE/RSJ International Conference on Intelligent Robots and Systems IROS 2002*.

Ferraresso, M.; Ferrari, C.; Pagello, E.; Polesel, R.; Rosati, R.; Speranzon, A.; and Zanette, W. 2001. Collaborative emergent actions between real soccer robots. In Stone, P.; Balch, T.; and Kraetzschmar, G., eds., *RoboCup-2000: Robot Soccer World Cup IV*, 297–300. Berlin: Springer Verlag.

Kiat, N.; Ming, Q.; Hock, T.; Yee, Y.; and Yoh, S. 2001. Luckystar ii-team description paper. In Stone, P.; Balch, T.; and Kraetzschmar, G., eds., *RoboCup-2000: Robot Soccer World Cup IV*, 543–546. Berlin: Springer Verlag.

Lenser, S.; Bruce, J.; and Veloso, M. 2001. CMPack: A complete software system for autonomous legged soccer robots. In *Proceedings of the Fifth International Conference on Autonomous Agents*. Best Paper Award in the Software Prototypes Track, Honorary Mention.

Nicolescu, M., and Mataric, M. J. 2003. Natural methods for robot task learning: Instructive demonstration, generalization and practice. In *Proceedings of the Second International Joint Conference on Autonomous Agents and Multi-Agent Systems*, 241–248.

Schaal, S., and Atkeson, C. 1998. Constructive incremental learning from only local information. *Neural Computation* 10(8):2047–2084.

# Common Sense Data Acquisition for Indoor Mobile Robots

**Rakesh Gupta** and **Mykel J. Kochenderfer***
Honda Research Institute USA, Inc.
800 California Street, Suite 300
Mountain View, CA 94041
rgupta@hra.com, m.kochenderfer@ed.ac.uk

## Abstract

Common sense knowledge can be efficiently collected from non-experts over the web in a similar fashion to the Open Mind family of distributed knowledge capture projects. We describe the collection of common sense data through the Open Mind Indoor Common Sense (OMICS) website. We restrict the domain to indoor home and office environments to obtain dense knowledge. The knowledge was collected through sentence templates that were generated dynamically based on previous user input. Entries were converted into relations and saved into a database. We discuss the results of this online collaborative effort and describe two applications of the collected data to indoor mobile robots. We discuss active desire selection based on current beliefs and commands and a room-labeling application based on probability estimates from the common sense knowledge base.

## Introduction

The objective of this research is to enhance the intelligence of mobile robots so that they can autonomously accomplish tasks in a home or office environment. For these tasks, the robots must posses some common sense including knowledge about human desires, objects and their locations, and causality. Since common sense does not require expert knowledge, the data may be collected as part of a public online collaborative effort over the Internet.

Distributed online knowledge acquisition projects, such as those associated with the *Open Mind Initiative* (Stork 1999; 2000), have become quite popular. The Open Mind Common Sense project, led by Push Singh at the MIT Media Lab, has accumulated a corpus of 700,000 pieces of knowledge from 14,000 users (as of January 2004) over the past three years[1]. Other projects such as Open Mind Word Expert[2] and Open Mind 1001 Questions[3], have also been successful.

*Currently at Institute of Perception, Action and Behaviour, School of Informatics, University of Edinburgh, Edinburgh, United Kingdom.



[1]http://commonsense.media.mit.edu

[2]http://www.teach-computers.org/word-expert.html

[3]http://www.teach-computers.org/learner.html

This paper describes the Open Mind Indoor Common Sense (OMICS) project that became publicly available at the beginning of August 2003[4]. In the next section we describe the knowledge base framework and templates used to capture data. We then report on our results and experiences with working with online contributors. The next section of the paper discusses two applications that use this data. We discuss inference based on anticipating the desires of the users. We also describe a room-labeling application based on simulated object recognition and simulated room and object labels given by a user. Finally, we discuss our conclusions and future work.

## Data Collection Methods

In this section we first describe the framework of the knowledge base and the relations necessary to capture those types of common sense most useful to an indoor robot. We then describe how we built a website to capture this data in a user-friendly manner and how we converted the data into machine-understandable relations.

### Knowledge Representation

The framework of this work is *object-centric*. Robot activities involve perceiving the environment and acting upon it. What the robot knows about the environment must include what objects are present and their state. The robot must manipulate these objects in such a way so as to put them in some desired state to accomplish its goals. Hence, everything that the robot knows about the world and can do in the world is grounded in objects and their properties (or state).

The robot can observe properties of objects in its vicinity and it can perform actions that change the properties of objects. In this system, a statement is a pair $\phi = (o, p)$ where $o$ is some object and $p$ is an adjective describing the property. Statements may be thought of as assertions about the property of an object in the world or actions to be taken on an object to achieve a particular effect (actions are referred to by the effect they achieve.) For example, the statement (*cup-of-coffee*, *hot*) can mean "a cup of coffee is hot" or represent the action "make a cup of coffee hot." Using the same notation allows us to make connections between beliefs, desires, and intentions.

[4]http://openmind.hri-us.com

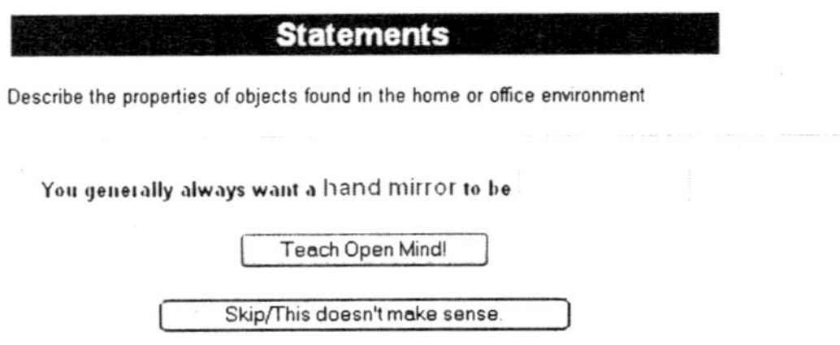


Figure 1: A template sentence.

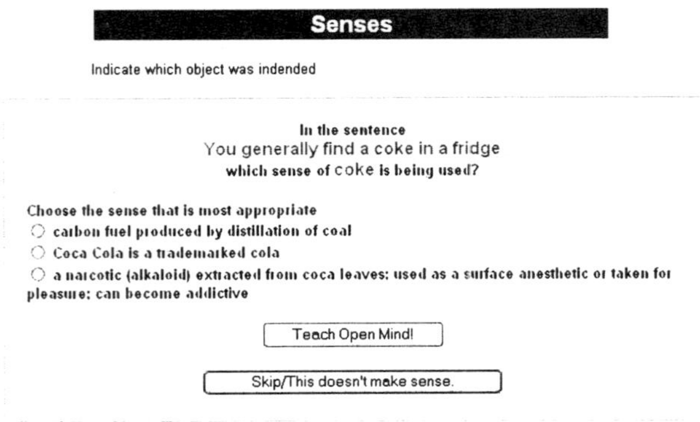


Figure 2: A word sense disambiguation form.

Our representation allows us to capture such common sense knowledge as: $(o_1, p_1)$ causes $(o_2, p_2)$. For example, the statement (*fan*, *on*) causes (*room*, *cool*). We also wish to capture knowledge about human desires such as $(o_1, p_1)$ indicating the human desire $(o_2, p_2)$. For example, the perception (*cup-of-coffee*, *cold*) indicates that the desire (*cup-of-coffee*, *hot*) be fulfilled.

At any given point in time, the robot observes a set of statements that are true and can execute a set of statements. Using the common sense knowledge about causality and desires as previously described, the general problem is to decide which statements to execute in order to achieve perceived goals.

Indeed, this object-centric representation is limited. It cannot express everything that first order logic with a large array of predicates can represent. In addition to making inference simpler, this "object-centric" representation makes it much easier to collect data from sentence templates.

## Activity Sentence Templates

We need some way to convert the common sense in the minds of non-expert users into relations in a knowledge base. Following the style of the Open Mind Common Sense website, we decided to use sentence templates. Users are prompted to fill in the blanks of sentences with words, as shown in figure 1.

Once a user logs on with their account, they are presented with a random activity. After a random number of entries for a particular activity, the system prompts them with a new activity. Users may also manually switch between the activities.

Different activities capture different types of knowledge. Below is a summary of some of the activities:

**Objects** In this activity, the user is asked to identify the types of objects commonly found in a home or office. The user may be prompted to type in an object name that comes to mind or simply label an image of an object. It is important to allow a user to simply type in any indoor object that comes to mind because we want to include all relevant objects in the database even if we do not have their picture.

Image labeling can link multiple labels to the same object (e.g. the labels "sofa" and "couch" might be both associated with "h0141.gif"). The images themselves can be used for training the object recognition system of the robot. When the website became public, the database initially contained a set of over 400 images of indoor objects selected by hand from a collection of stock photography.

**Statements** In the 'statements' activity, the user is prompted with a question such as, "You often want a fan to be ______." This activity pairs objects with properties in the knowledge base. The objects that appear in these sentence templates come from the objects entered by users in the other activities such as the 'objects' activity.

**Uses** This activity associates objects with their uses. For example, the user might be prompted with the form, "A hanger is used to ______." Again the objects come from user input.

**Causes** This activity captures causality. For example, a form might ask, "A computer is off when a ______ is ______." If the user enters a new object or a new object-property pair, it will be entered into the object or statement table. The object and property that makes up the first part of the sentence is formed dynamically by selecting a random object from the knowledge base.

**Desires** This activity helps the robot determine what needs to be done in various situations. A template form might ask, "You might want a fan to be blowing if you notice that your ______ has become ______."

**Locations** This activity associates objects with the rooms where they are typically found. For example, the user might be prompted with, "A room where you generally find a dinner table is the ______."

**Proximity** This activity associates objects with each other based on proximity. A sample form would be, "You generally find a frying pan in the same room as a ______."

**Senses** This activity disambiguates the intended sense of various objects entered into the database by other users. Figure 2 shows a sample form. The objects to disambiguate are selected from previous user entries and the senses are from WordNet (Miller 1995).

**People** This one describes the activities of people in a home or office (e.g. People eat food when they are hungry). The template form is, "People ______ when they ______."

**Paraphrase** This activity tries to capture multiple ways of interacting with the robot in natural language to accomplish a task. A sample template is "Another way to say heat the food in the microwave is ______."

**Tasks** This activity tries to capture the steps required to accomplish a task like making coffee, answering the phone etc. We prompt the user with 7 short natural language steps to accomplish the task. A sample template is "The task water indoor plants involves the steps: ______."

**Generalization** This activity tries to generalize upon previous entries in the knowledge base. Instead of having to individually specify that bananas, oranges, apples, etc. are commonly found in the kitchen, it would be useful to know that all kinds of fruit are found in the kitchen. If we know that fruit is found in the kitchen, we can use the WordNet hierarchy to infer that all of the hyponyms of fruit are found in the kitchen. An example of a prompt for this activity is the following: "Are all types of writing implement (a generalization of 'marker') commonly found in the study?"

**Freeform** This activity allows users to type in any form of common sense knowledge that might not be captured by any of the other activities. Although it is quite difficult to convert freeform sentences into useful relations, it provides us with a sense of the types of knowledge the general public would like an indoor robot to understand. Analysis of freeform sentences will later lead to the creation of new activities.

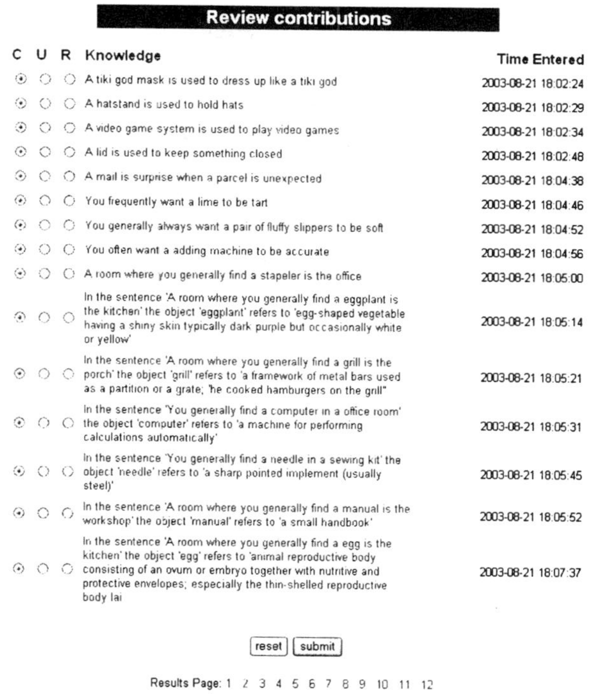

**Review contributions**

| C | U | R | Knowledge | Time Entered |
|---|---|---|---|---|
| ⦿ | ○ | ○ | A tiki god mask is used to dress up like a tiki god | 2003-08-21 18:02:24 |
| ⦿ | ○ | ○ | A hatstand is used to hold hats | 2003-08-21 18:02:29 |
| ⦿ | ○ | ○ | A video game system is used to play video games | 2003-08-21 18:02:34 |
| ⦿ | ○ | ○ | A lid is used to keep something closed | 2003-08-21 18:02:48 |
| ⦿ | ○ | ○ | A mail is surprise when a parcel is unexpected | 2003-08-21 18:04:38 |
| ⦿ | ○ | ○ | You frequently want a lime to be tart | 2003-08-21 18:04:46 |
| ⦿ | ○ | ○ | You generally always want a pair of fluffy slippers to be soft | 2003-08-21 18:04:52 |
| ⦿ | ○ | ○ | You often want a adding machine to be accurate | 2003-08-21 18:04:56 |
| ⦿ | ○ | ○ | A room where you generally find a stapeler is the office | 2003-08-21 18:05:00 |
| ⦿ | ○ | ○ | In the sentence 'A room where you generally find a eggplant is the kitchen' the object 'eggplant' refers to 'egg-shaped vegetable having a shiny skin typically dark purple but occasionally white or yellow' | 2003-08-21 18:05:14 |
| ⦿ | ○ | ○ | In the sentence 'A room where you generally find a grill is the porch' the object 'grill' refers to 'a framework of metal bars used as a partition or a grate; 'he cooked hamburgers on the grill" | 2003-08-21 18:05:21 |
| ⦿ | ○ | ○ | In the sentence 'You generally find a computer in a office room' the object 'computer' refers to 'a machine for performing calculations automatically' | 2003-08-21 18:05:31 |
| ⦿ | ○ | ○ | In the sentence 'You generally find a needle in a sewing kit' the object 'needle' refers to 'a sharp pointed implement (usually steel)' | 2003-08-21 18:05:45 |
| ⦿ | ○ | ○ | In the sentence 'A room where you generally find a manual is the workshop' the object 'manual' refers to 'a small handbook' | 2003-08-21 18:05:52 |
| ⦿ | ○ | ○ | In the sentence 'A room where you generally find a egg is the kitchen' the object 'egg' refers to 'animal reproductive body consisting of an ovum or embryo together with nutritive and protective envelopes; especially the thin-shelled reproductive body lai | 2003-08-21 18:07:37 |

[reset] [submit]

Results Page: 1 2 3 4 5 6 7 8 9 10 11 12

Figure 3: The review form used for administrators to commit, uncommit, or reject entries.

## Data Quality Review

It is important that there be some way of ensuring data quality since the data (such as names of objects and their properties) are used to generate new sentence templates. Sentence templates containing misspelled objects or objects that do not appear in a home or office environment would propagate errors in the knowledge base.

The completed sentence templates are stored in the database as raw sentences pending administrator review (see figure 3). It generally takes an administrator roughly half a minute to scan through a page with fifteen submissions. Once an administrator approves a set of entries, they are parsed into relations immediately. There is currently no need for part-of-speech tagging or lemmatization (as with the Open Mind Common Sense project) since the sentence templates are structured and designed in such a way that they implicitly cue the user as to what part-of-speech and tense they should use.

# Data Collection Results

To advertise the Open Mind Indoor Common Sense website, a message was sent to the Open Mind Initiative mailing list on August 5th. With no other direct advertising, within three weeks we had 190 users and 18,000 submissions with about 17,000 of them accepted. As of March 2004 we have over 400 users with 29,000 submissions with over 26,000 of them accepted.

We have had two weekly contests (lasting four weeks each) in August 2003 and February 2004 where the top contributor was awarded an Open Mind t-shirt. Other Open Mind projects have used similar contests to help motivate submissions. Winners were listed on the front page of the site.

## Observations

The OMICS site was publicly announced on August 5th and the first t-shirt prize was awarded August 6th. A significant portion of the entries were submitted within two days of the announcement. Prizes were also awarded on August 12, August 19, and August 26. In general, submissions were greater close to contest deadlines.

The quality of the data was actually quite good. About 10% of the submissions were rejected. Entries that were rejected tended to fall within one of the following categories:

- Misspelling: e.g. "A room where you generally find a exercise bike is the bym."
- Unclear or loose statements: e.g. "People cry when they can't get it."
- Outside the scope of home and office environments: e.g. "A trap is set when a predator is hunting."
- Nonsense: e.g. "You generally want a green light to be addressed to you."
- Inappropriate: e.g. suggestive or obscene

The 'causes' activity had the highest rejection rate. Deciding how one object affects another object proved to be difficult for some users. Interestingly, almost all word sense activities were answered correctly. Even users that entered

| Activity | Count |
|---|---|
| Objects | 5804 |
| Uses | 3517 |
| Locations | 3400 |
| Statements | 3394 |
| Proximity | 2547 |
| Freeform | 1696 |
| People | 1667 |
| Desires | 1792 |
| Causes | 1558 |
| Senses | 2349 |
| Generalization | 718 |
| Paraphrase | 351 |
| Tasks | 120 |
| Images | 55 |

Figure 4: The number of submissions for each activity.

*rogue* data in other activities generally entered the correct sense of the words in the 'sense' activity.

Users that appeared to have hostile intentions, indicated by sentence completions that were of a crude or sexual nature, also submitted useful data. Surprisingly, a few users that might be classified as malicious were among the top contributors of good data.

Figure 4 shows the ranking of the various activities and the number of submissions. Not surprisingly, users spent significantly more time on the 'objects' activity. This is probably because the 'objects' activity requires the least amount of thought and because it was the only activity that involved images. Although users were allowed to submit their own images of indoor objects, very few users actually did. The second contest in February 2004, with more emphasis on Generalization, Paraphrase, and Tasks activities had much fewer submissions (about 2000). Fewer submissions may be due to higher degree of difficulty, thought, and typing required for submissions.

### Feedback

Although we have received little feedback on the OMICS website, comments thus far have been largely positive. One of the weekly winners entered data with her seven-year-old son. She had the following to say about the site:

> As a teacher I think it is really great and put my son on it with me here at home—It was a great mom and kid project for several days. My little one who is 5 will be working on it too this week. It really forces us to do some critical thinking—the relationships and location section were great for him as were the free questions that he could come up with on his own.

Some users were concerned about their spelling errors and the spelling errors that were part of their sentence templates. Most grievous spelling errors were filtered out by the administrators, but some minor spelling errors were allowed into the database. Other users were concerned that the data they entered already existed in the database. One user commented:

> I still don't really know what to put in the *freeform* category, or what needs to be worked through to be the most help in the project (I'm guessing something like *computer & mouse* gets overused, while other objects go ignored?).

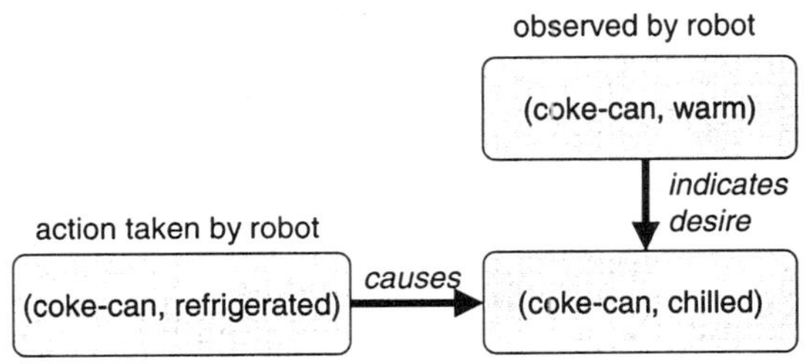


Figure 5: Example of using the OMICS knowledge base for active desire selection.

The general tone of the e-mails we received were positive and indicated a desire by the users to see the project succeed in making robots more intelligent.

## Data Applications

The data collected from the Open Mind family of projects have been applied to a wide variety of problems. Open Mind Word Expert has been applied to word sense disambiguation (Liu, Lieberman, & Selker 2003) and Open Mind Common Sense has been applied to textual affect sensing (Liu & Singh 2003). In this section, we describe two ways in which the data collected as part of OMICS is being used.

### Active Desire Selection

Our knowledge base can be used for common sense and practical reasoning using Belief-Desires-Intentions (BDI) theory. BDI was originally developed by Bratman (1987) and is founded upon established theory of rational action in humans.

Given causality relations, observations, and human commands, the robot can use the desires relations from the OMICS knowledge base to deduce active desires (goals). These desires can then be used in action selection using the Belief-Desire-Intention (BDI) architecture (Rao & Georgeff 1995; Wooldridge 1999).

Figure 5 shows an example of active desire selection. Here the robot observes from its sensors that a coke can is warm. From the desires relations, the robot knows that (*coke-can, warm*) $\rightarrow_d$ (*coke-can, chilled*), and hence that it should pursue an action that causes (*coke-can, chilled*). The robot, however, does not know how to directly cause (*coke-can, chilled*), so it looks into its list of causality implications. The robot sees that (*coke-can, refrigerated*) $\rightarrow$ (*coke-can, chilled*). Thus it can infer that by refrigerating the warm coke-can, it can be chilled, and therefore the robot can add that desire to its list of active desires.

### Topological Map with Room Labeling

Space can be labeled using terms that people typically use such as Large Conference Room, Small Conference Room,

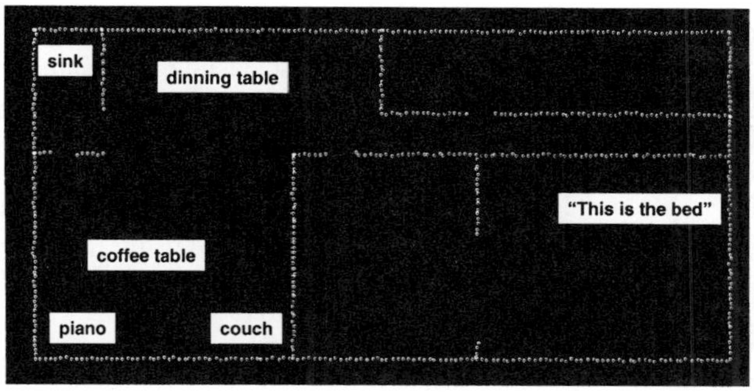


Figure 6: Room labeling showing input of simulated room and object labels at specific locations.

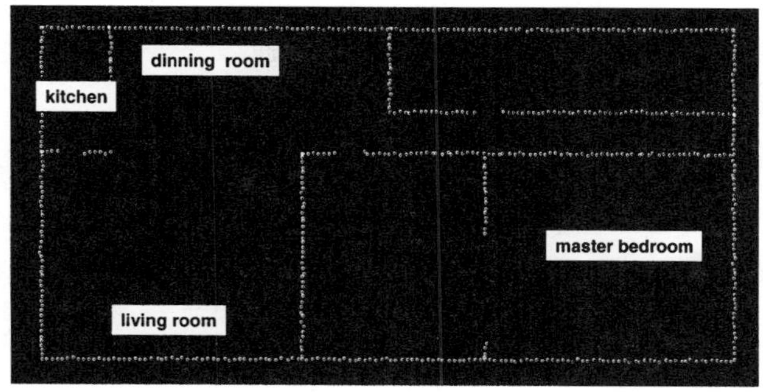


Figure 7: Room labeling showing output of our algorithm with most likely room labels and locations.

and Library. Information on the extent and connectivity of these regions can be used to generate a topological map with spatial labeling for providing natural interaction. This map can be used to plan a path to a specific room based on the current task.

We simulated data for a laser scanner to provide extent and connectivity 2D map information. Dots in figure 6 represent individual laser scan readings from a merged map generated during environment exploration. Humans provide a running description of the immediate surroundings as the robot explores a new home or office. These labels can be room types (e.g., *This is a kitchen* or *This is the living room*), or about objects (e.g., *This is a chair* or *This is a computer*). In addition, the robot might use an object recognition system to recognize objects with a confidence value given by the recognition system.

These simulated objects and room labels with associated probabilities (from a speech/object recognition system) and the 2D map are input to our system. We then use probability estimates given by statistical analysis of object location data from our knowledge base to label different rooms and open areas. We ran simulations to output topologically labeled maps of indoor home and office environments with different inputs.

In related work, Myers and Konolige (1992) generated and modified map layouts to reflect sentential information and common sense constraints for example:

- individuals own offices
- galleries or walkways are not owned by individuals
- reception is located at the entrance to the office

As shown in figure 6, we are given the walls and labels such as *This is the bed* and some objects recognized in the environment or pointed to by a user like sink, dining table, coffee table, piano and couch with an associated probability value. From this information, sensory data $D$, and the Open Mind Indoor Common Sense database we may compute the location probabilities.

These numbers can be used to compute the probability of the most likely room using Bayes' formula. Figure 7 shows the output of our algorithm. For example we have determined that based on available information, the most likely room label for the top-left room is the kitchen.

$P(\mathit{sink}|D) = 0.70$ (from object recognition)
$P(\mathit{microwave}|D) = 0.90$ (from speech recognition)
$P(\mathit{sink}|\mathit{kitchen}) = 0.13$ (estimated from OMICS)
$P(\mathit{microwave}|\mathit{kitchen}) = 0.11$ (estimated from OMICS)
$P(\mathit{sink}|\mathit{bedroom}) = 0.003$ (estimated from OMICS)
$P(\mathit{microwave}|\mathit{bedroom}) = 0.002$ (estimated from OMICS)

Further work will involve using laser data instead of simulated 2D maps. This data can also be extracted from cameras by building a sparse map of the unknown environment. Simulated place and object labels supplied by the user will be replaced by real data from a speech recognition system. Simulated object labels will be replaced by an object recognition system with associated confidence values.

**Probability Estimation from common sense knowledge base** The robot's sensory perceptions are combined with the priors and conditional probabilities for object location estimated from the common sense knowledge base to determine the most likely room label.

Given a set $\omega \in \Omega$ of rooms, objects $x_i$, and sensory data $D$, the robot sensory perception provides $P(x_i|D)$, and the location data in our knowledge base is used to estimate $P(x_i)$ and $P(x_i|\omega)$. The robot collects information about the objects in the room, perhaps through speech recognition (e.g. a human says "this is a chair") or through an object recognition system. These observations $D$ induce a conditional probability distribution $P(x_i|D)$ over the objects $x_i \in X$. We wish to combine these probability distributions with $P(x_i|\omega)$ and $P(x_i)$ probability estimations from our knowledge base to calculate the room that is most likely, namely:

$$\omega' = \arg\max_{\omega\in\Omega} P(\omega|D)$$

Let $\mathbf{x}$ denote a vector indicating the presence or absence of the objects $x_i$. Assuming a generative Bayesian model where $\omega$ influences $\mathbf{x}$ and $\mathbf{x}$ influences $D$, we calculate the joint distribution:

$$\begin{aligned} P(\omega, \mathbf{x}, D) &= P(\omega)P(x|\omega)P(D|\mathbf{x}) \\ &= \frac{P(\omega)P(\mathbf{x}|\omega)P(\mathbf{x}|D)P(D)}{P(\mathbf{x})} \end{aligned}$$

We use this to calculate the most likely room, $\omega'$:

$$\arg\max_{\omega\in\Omega} P(\omega|D)$$

$$= \arg\max_{\omega \in \Omega} \sum_{\mathbf{x}} P(\omega, \mathbf{x}|D)$$

$$= \arg\max_{\omega \in \Omega} \sum_{\mathbf{x}} \frac{P(\omega)P(\mathbf{x}|\omega)P(\mathbf{x}|D)}{P(\mathbf{x})}$$

$$= \arg\max_{\omega \in \Omega} P(\omega) \sum_{x_1} \frac{P(x_1|\omega)P(x_1|D)}{P(x_1)} \cdots \sum_{x_n} \frac{P(x_n|\omega)P(x_n|D)}{P(x_n)}$$

$$= \arg\max_{\omega \in \Omega} \ln P(\omega) + \sum_{i=1}^{n} \ln \sum_{x_i} \frac{P(x_i|\omega)P(x_i|D)}{P(x_i)}$$

Since the $x_i$'s are binary valued, the computational complexity is linear in the number of possible objects.

Our knowledge base contains a collection of tuples of objects and rooms. We estimate $P(x_i)$ by counting the number of times $x_i$ is mentioned in the database and dividing by the number of entries in the database. We estimate $P(x_i|\omega)$ by counting the number of times the tuple $(x_i, \omega)$ appears and dividing by the number of tuples that mention $\omega$, i.e. $P(x_i|\omega) = C(x_i, \omega)/C(\omega)$. However, this assigns zero probability to $P(x_i|\omega)$ in cases where the database never mentions the tuple $(x_i, \omega)$. This is rectified by using Lidstone's law to redistribute some of the probability mass assigned to the observed tuples to the unobserved tuples. Lidstone's law uses a parameter $\lambda < 1$ to control how much probability is distributed to unseen tuples. We then have

$$P(x_i|\omega) = \frac{C(x_i, \omega) + \lambda}{C(\omega) + \lambda n}$$

Unseen instances are assigned probability $\lambda/n$, where $n$ is the number of objects.

## Conclusions and Future Work

The Open Mind Indoor Common Sense project has successfully captured thousands of pieces of common sense knowledge about home and office environments. Our contributions to common sense data collection include the restriction of the domain to enhance the density of the knowledge, dynamic prompting of data based on prior data in the knowledge base, and object-centric data collection focusing on objects and their properties. We use comprehensive manual data review to ensure the quality of the collected knowledge.

The indoor home and office focus of our data collection and the structured activities have lead to a dense knowledge base. This knowledge base was useful in determining active desires from which actions could be selected. We computed probability estimates from our common sense knowledge base and used them in a Bayes formulation to compute the most likely room label given room and object labels with confidence levels. These labels were combined with a 2D map to build topologically labeled maps.

Distributed knowledge capture results in messy knowledge and one of the challenges is to convert this into a usable form. Further research will be required to clean up the data using statistical probability estimation techniques. Research is also required to represent, maintain and update this knowledge on a real robot.

Although the robot can use the common sense knowledge at a very high level to determine which desires to pursue, it is not yet intelligent enough to actually select and execute the mid-level actions that accomplish these desires. It remains to be seen how common sense can be used in the actual execution of various tasks, such as cleaning a bathtub. One might use the teleo-reactive program framework, as proposed by Nils Nilsson (1992; 1994), to accomplish such basic tasks as *make a cup of coffee hot* or *pop some popcorn.*

## Acknowledgments

This work was done while Mykel Kochenderfer was a summer intern at Honda Research Institute USA, Inc. The authors would like to thank David Stork and Push Singh for their helpful comments and suggestions. Nils Nilsson reviewed an earlier version of this paper and provided invaluable feedback. Thanks are also due to anonymous reviewers and the users of the Open Mind Indoor Common Sense website for their data and feedback.

## References

Bratman, M. 1987. *Intention, Plans, and Practical Reason.* Cambridge, MA: Harvard University Press.

Liu, H., and Singh, P. 2003. OMCSNet: A commonsense inference toolkit. Technical Report SOM02-01, MIT Media Lab Society Of Mind Group.

Liu, H.; Lieberman, H.; and Selker, T. 2003. Exploiting agreement and disagreement of human annotators for word sense disambiguation. In *Proceedings of the Seventh International Conference on Intelligent User Interfaces (IUI 2003)*, 125–132.

Miller, G. A. 1995. WordNet: A lexical database for english. *Communications of the ACM* 38(11):39–41.

Myers, K., and Konolige, K. 1992. Reasoning with analogical representations. In Nebel, B.; Rich, C.; and Swartout, W., eds., *Principles of Knowledge Representation and Reasoning: Proceedings of the Third International Conference (KR92).* San Mateo, CA: Morgan Kaufmann Publishers Inc.

Nilsson, N. J. 1992. Towards agent programs with circuit semantics. Technical Report STAN–CS–92–1412, Department of Computer Science, Stanford University, Stanford, CA 94305.

Nilsson, N. J. 1994. Teleo-reactive programs for agent control. *Journal of Artificial Intelligence Research* 1:139–158.

Rao, A. S., and Georgeff, M. P. 1995. BDI-agents: from theory to practice. In *Proceedings of the First Intl. Conference on Multiagent Systems.*

Stork, D. G. 1999. The Open Mind Initiative. *IEEE Expert Systems and Their Applications* 14(3):19–20.

Stork, D. G. 2000. Open data collection for training intelligent software in the open mind initiative. In *Proceedings of the Engineering Intelligent Systems (EIS2000).*

Wooldridge, M. 1999. Intelligent agents. In Weiss, G., ed., *Multiagent Systems: A Modern Approach to Distributed Artificial Intelligence.* Cambridge, MA, USA: The MIT Press. 27–78.

# Machine Learning for Fast Quadrupedal Locomotion

**Nate Kohl** and **Peter Stone**
Department of Computer Sciences, The University of Texas at Austin
1 University Station C0500, Austin, Texas 78712–1188
{nate,pstone}@cs.utexas.edu
http://www.cs.utexas.edu/~{nate,pstone}

### Abstract

For a robot, the ability to get from one place to another is one of the most basic skills. However, locomotion on legged robots is a challenging multidimensional control problem. This paper presents a machine learning approach to legged locomotion, with all training done on the physical robots. The main contributions are a specification of our fully automated learning environment and a detailed empirical comparison of four different machine learning algorithms for learning quadrupedal locomotion. The resulting learned walk is considerably faster than all previously reported hand-coded walks for the same robot platform.

## Introduction

The ability to deploy a fully autonomous robot in an unstructured, dynamic environment (the proverbial *real world*) over an extended period of time remains an open challenge in the field of robotics. Considerable progress is being made towards many components of this task including physical agility, power management, and on-board sensor technology. One such component that has drawn considerable interest recently is the ability for a robot to autonomously *learn* to improve its own performance (Ng *et al.* 2004; Bagnell & Schneider 2001; Zhang & Vadakkepat 2003). Despite this interest, considerable work remains due to the difficulties associated with machine learning in the real world.

Compared to other machine learning scenarios such as classification or action learning in simulation, learning on physical robots presents several formidable challenges, including the following.

**Sparse Training Data:** It is often prohibitively difficult to generate large amounts of data due to the maintenance required on robots, such as battery changes, hardware repairs, and, usually, constant human supervision. Thus, learning methods designed for physical robots must be effective with small amounts of data.

**Dynamical Complexity:** The dynamics of many robotic control tasks are too complex for faithful simulation to be possible. Furthermore, robots are inherently situated in an unstructured environment with unpredictable sensor and actuator noise, namely the real world. Thus, even when off-line simulation is possible, it can never be fully reflective of the target environment.

In this paper, we overcome these challenges for one concrete complex robot task, namely legged locomotion. Using a commercially available quadruped robot, we fully automate the training process (other than battery changes) and employ machine learning algorithms that are sufficiently data efficient to enable productive learning on physical robots in a matter of hours. The resulting learned walk is considerably faster than all previously reported hand-coded walks for the same robot platform.

This paper contributes both a specification of our fully automated learning environment and a detailed empirical comparison of four different machine learning algorithms for learning quadrupedal locomotion. The remainder of the paper is organized as follows. First, we introduce the parameterized walk which our learning process seeks to optimize. We then specify our four learning approaches, and follow with detailed empirical results. We close with a discussion of their implications and possible avenues for future work.

## A Parameterized Walk

The Sony Aibo ERS-210A is a commercially available robot that is equipped with a color CMOS camera and an optional ethernet card that can be used for wireless communication. The Aibo is a quadruped robot, and has three degrees of freedom in each of its four legs (Sony 2004).

At the lowest level, the Aibo's gait is determined by a series of joint positions for the three joints in each of its legs. An early attempt to develop a gait by Hornby et al. (1999) involved using a genetic algorithm to learn a set of low-level parameters that described joint velocities and body position.[1] More recent attempts to develop gaits for the Aibo have involved adopting a higher-level representation that deals with the trajectories of the Aibo's four feet through three-dimensional space. An inverse kinematics calculation is then used to convert these trajectories into joint angles.

Among higher-level approaches, most of the differences between gaits that have been developed for the Aibo stem from the shape of the loci through which the feet pass and the exact parameterizations of those loci. For example, a team from the University of New South Wales achieved the fastest known hand-tuned gait using the high-level approach described above with trapezoidal loci. They subsequently generated an even faster walk via learning (Kim & Uther 2003). A team from Germany created a flexible gait implementation that allows them to use a variety of different shapes of loci (Rofer *et al.* 2003), and the team from the University of Newcastle was able to generate high-velocity gaits using a genetic algorithm and loci of arbitrary shape (Quinlan, Chalup, & Middleton 2003).

Our team (UT Austin Villa, Stone *et al.* 2003) first approached the gait optimization problem by hand-tuning



[1]Developed on an earlier version of the Aibo.

a gait described by half-elliptical loci. This gait performed comparably to those of other teams participating in RoboCup 2003. The work reported in this paper uses the hand-tuned UT Austin Villa walk as a starting point for learning. Figure 1 compares the reported speeds of the gaits mentioned above, both hand-tuned and learned, including that of our starting point, the UT Austin Villa walk. The latter walk is described fully in a team technical report (Stone *et al.* 2003). The remainder of this section describes those details of the UT Austin Villa walk that are important to understand for the purposes of this paper.

| Hand-tuned gaits | | | Learned gaits | | |
|---|---|---|---|---|---|
| CMU (2002) | Austin Villa (2003) | UNSW (2003) | Hornby (1999) | UNSW (2003) | NUBots (2003) |
| **200** | **245** | **254** | **170** | **270** | **296** |

**Figure 1**: Maximum forward velocities of the best gaits (in mm/s) for different teams, both learned and hand-tuned.

The half-elliptical locus used by our team is shown in Figure 2. By instructing each foot to move through a locus of this shape, with each pair of diagonally opposite legs in phase with each other and perfectly out of phase with the other two (a gait known as a trot), we enable the Aibo to walk. Four parameters define this elliptical locus:

1. The length of the ellipse;
2. The height of the ellipse;
3. The position of the ellipse on the $x$ axis; and
4. The position of the ellipse on the $y$ axis.

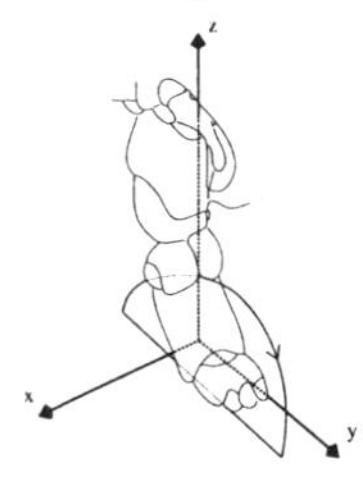

**Figure 2**: The elliptical locus of one the Aibo's feet. The half-ellipse is defined by length, height, and position in the $x$-$y$ plane.

Since the Aibo is roughly symmetric, the same parameters can be used to describe loci on both the left and right side of the body. To ensure a relatively straight gait, the length of the ellipse is the same for all four loci. Separate values for the elliptical height, $x$, and $y$ positions are used for the front and back legs. An additional parameter which governs the turning rate of the Aibo is used to determine the skew of all four ellipses in the $x$-$y$ plane, a technique introduced by the UNSW team (Hengst *et al.* 2001).[2] The amount of skew is determined by the product of the angle at which the Aibo wishes to move and this skew multiplier parameter.

The following set of 12 parameters define the Aibo's gait:

- The front locus (3 parameters: height, $x$-pos., $y$-pos.)
- The rear locus (3 parameters)
- Locus length
- Locus skew multiplier in the $x$-$y$ plane (for turning)
- The height of the front of the body
- The height of the rear of the body
- The time each foot takes to move through its locus
- The fraction of time each foot spends on the ground

[2]Even when walking directly forward, noise in an Aibo's motions occasionally requires that the four ellipses be skewed to allow the Aibo to execute small turns in order to stay on course.

During the American Open tournament in May of 2003,[3] UT Austin Villa used a simplified version of the parameterization described above that did not allow the front and rear heights of the robot to differ. Hand-tuning these parameters generated a gait with a velocity of 140 mm/s. After allowing the front and rear height to differ, the Aibo was tuned to walk at 245 mm/s in the RoboCup 2003 competition.[4] Applying machine learning to this parameter optimization process, however, allowed us to significantly improve the speed of the Aibos, as described in the following section.

## Learning the Walk

Given the parameterization of the walk defined in the previous section, our task amounts to a parameter optimization problem in a continuous 12-dimensional space. For the purposes of this paper, we adopt forward speed as the sole objective function. That is, as long as the robot does not actually fall over, we do not optimize for any form of stability (for instance in the face of external forces from other robots).

This optimization is performed from a computer that is connected via wireless ethernet to the Aibos. All of the policy evaluations take place on actual robots, without the use of a simulator. Previous attempts at learning Aibo gaits involved running each experiment directly on the Aibo, which imposed certain time limitations on the learning process (Kim & Uther 2003). A more decentralized approach allows us to distribute the learning process over multiple Aibos and prevents the loss of data due to battery swaps and mechanical failure. The only human intervention required during an experiment is replacing discharged batteries, an event which occurs about once an hour. We use three simultaneously walking Aibos for our experiments, but our approach scales naturally to arbitrary numbers of robots.

**Figure 3**: The training environment for our experiments. Each Aibo times itself as it moves back and forth between a pair of landmarks (A and A', B and B', or C and C').

We evaluate the efficacy of a set of parameters by sending those parameters to an Aibo and instructing it to time itself as it walks between two fixed landmarks (Figure 3). More efficient parameters result in a faster gait, which translates into a lower time and a better score. After completing a trial, the Aibo sends the resulting score back to the host computer and prepares itself for a new set of parameters to evaluate. Since there is significant noise in each trial, each set of parameters is evaluated three times. The resulting score for that set of parameters is computed by taking the average of the three trials.[5]

[3]`http://www.cs.cmu.edu/~AmericanOpen03/`

[4]Thanks to Daniel Stronger for hand-tuning the walks to achieve these speeds.

[5]There is video of the training process at: `www.cs.utexas.edu/~AustinVilla/legged/learned-walk/`

The following sections describe four machine learning algorithms that were implemented to perform the learning for this parameter optimization problem: a hill climbing algorithm, the amoeba algorithm, a genetic algorithm, and a policy gradient algorithm. For ease of comparison, we use some common notation in their presentation. Policies, denoted as $\pi$, are vectors of 12 parameters $\{\theta_1, \ldots, \theta_{12}\}$. Each algorithm evaluates $t$ policies per iteration of that algorithm, and will typically change the $j$th parameter of any policy by at most $\epsilon_j$ during any iteration.

## Hill Climbing

A hill climbing algorithm is one of the simplest ways to approach a parameter optimization problem. The $N$-dimensional hill climbing algorithm implemented for this work starts from an initial parameter vector $\pi = \{\theta_1, \ldots, \theta_N\}$ (where $N = 12$ in this case) and generates $t$ random policies in the vicinity of $\pi$. Each of these policies $\{R_1, R_2, \ldots, R_t\}$ is chosen such that each $R_i = \{\theta_1 + \Delta_1, \ldots, \theta_N + \Delta_N\}$ and each $\Delta_j$ is chosen randomly to be either $+\epsilon_j$, 0, or $-\epsilon_j$. After evaluating each $R_i$, the highest-scoring $R_i$ is chosen as a new starting point and the process is repeated. Pseudocode for this algorithm is provided in Figure 4.

```
π ← InitialPolicy
while !done do
   {R_1, R_2, ..., R_t} = t random perturbations of π
   evaluate( {R_1, R_2, ..., R_t} )
   π ← getHighestScoring({R_1, R_2, ..., R_t})
end while
```

**Figure 4**: Pseudocode for the hill climbing algorithm. During each iteration of the main loop $t$ policies are sampled near $\pi$. The highest-scoring policy is chosen as a new starting point, and the process is repeated.

## Amoeba

The downhill simplex (or "amoeba") algorithm is a multidimensional optimization method that involves moving a simplex of points through a high-dimensional space via a series of geometrical transformations (Press 1988). A *simplex* is a geometrical figure consisting of $N + 1$ points in an $N$ dimensional space. For example, in two dimensions a simplex is a triangle. The simplex of the amoeba algorithm is initially composed of $N + 1$ random policies in the vicinity of an initial policy $\pi$. These initial policies are generated in the same manner as the policies for the Hill Climbing algorithm, described above.

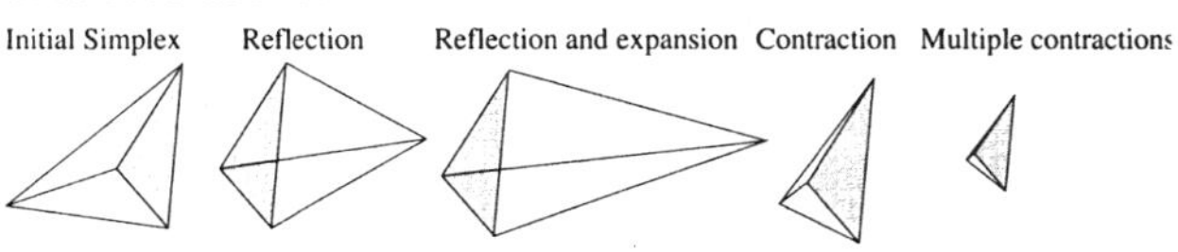


**Figure 5**: An example of the geometric transformations that would be used by the amoeba algorithm in three dimensions.

The amoeba algorithm then takes a series of steps, most of which simply reflect the lowest-scoring point of the simplex through the opposite face of the simplex. Most of these reflections preserve the volume of the simplex, which helps prevent the search process from stagnating around one policy. When possible, the amoeba algorithm expands the simplex. When the algorithm is faced with a narrow valley through which it must pass, all of the points of the simplex are contracted around its best point. After it has been contracted past a certain point, the simplex is re-initialized around the best point in a manner similar to how it is initialized at the start of the algorithm. An example of the geometric manipulations that would be performed on the simplex in three dimensions is given in Figure 5, and pseudocode for the amoeba algorithm is shown in Figure 6.

```
π ← InitialPolicy
Simplex ← N + 1 random perturbations of π
while !done do
  bestPoint ← determineBestPoint(Simplex)
  secondWorst ← determineSecondWorst(Simplex)
  score ← reflect(Simplex)
  if score > bestPoint.score                // good reflection, extend
  then
    reflectAndExpand(Simplex)
  else if score < secondWorst.score   // bad reflection, contract
  then
    score ← contract(Simplex)
    if score < secondWorst.score            // still bad, contract
    then
      if numContractions < MAX then
        contractAll(Simplex)
        numContractions++
      else
        Simplex = N + 1 perturbations of bestPoint //or reset
        numContractions = 0
      end if
    end if
  end if
end while
```

**Figure 6**: Pseudocode for the amoeba algorithm. A simplex undergoes various transformations in the search for an optimal policy.

## Genetic Algorithm

The standard genetic algorithm searches for an optimal policy by applying genetic operators to a population of policies. Policies that perform well are rewarded and proliferate through the population, whereas policies that perform poorly are removed from the population (Mitchell 1996). Our genetic algorithm maintains a population of $t$ policies, and uses the genetic operators of mutation and multi-point crossover to manipulate the policies in the population.

The population of policies is divided into a fixed number of species, where each species contains policies that are similar to each other. This technique, called *speciation*, allows the genetic algorithm to perform *explicit fitness sharing* (Goldberg & Richardson 1987). Explicit fitness sharing forces similar members of the same species to "share" one representative score, thereby penalizing species with a large number of policies. This allows new species to form even if they do not perform as well as other, larger, species.

The mutation operator acts on a policy $\pi$ by randomly altering each parameter of that policy $\theta_j$ with some probability $\rho$. The actual amount by which any parameter is altered is determined by drawing a number from a Gaussian distribution cut off after three standard deviations. The distribution is scaled to generate values between $-\epsilon_j$ and $+\epsilon_j$.

The crossover operator generates a new policy from two "parent" policies by performing multi-point recombination on the parameter strings of the two parents. An example of the crossover process is given in Figure 7.

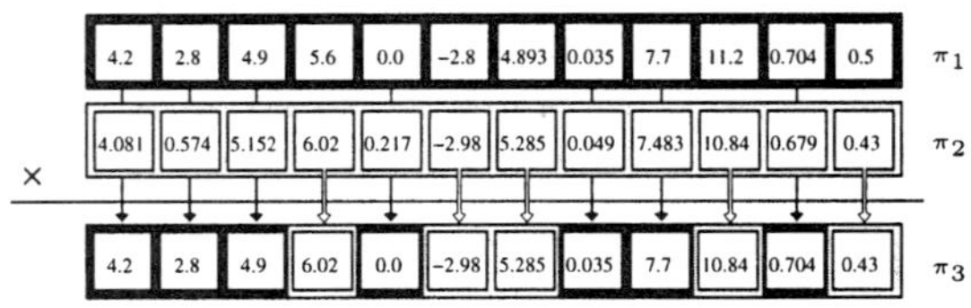


**Figure 7**: An example of the crossover operator for the genetic algorithm. A new policy ($\pi_3$) is created through multi-point recombination of two parent policies ($\pi_1$ and $\pi_2$).

## Policy Gradient Algorithm

Our implementation of the $N$-dimensional policy gradient algorithm builds on the hill climbing algorithm described above. Initially, a collection of $t$ policies is generated in the vicinity of an initial policy, $\pi$. Instead of focusing the search on the best policy at each step, however, the policy gradient algorithm estimates the gradient of the objective function in the parameter space and follows it towards a local optimum.

Since we do not know anything about the true functional form of the policy, we cannot calculate the gradient exactly. Furthermore, empirically estimating the gradient by sampling can be computationally expensive if done naively, given the large size of the search space and the temporal cost of each evaluation. Given the lack of accurate simulators for the Aibo, we are forced to perform the learning entirely on real robots, which makes efficiency a prime concern.

These concerns prompted us to develop an efficient method of estimating the policy gradient. This method can be considered a degenerate form of standard policy gradient reinforcement learning techniques (Sutton *et al.* 2000; Baxter & Bartlett 2001) in that the control policy is purely open loop and not a function of the robot's sensory input. Like these more general techniques, our approach will only converge towards a local optimum. In contrast, some action-value reinforcement learning algorithms, such as Q-learning provably converge to the globally optimal policy (Watkins 1989). However, Q-learning, which is designed for Markov decision processes, is not directly applicable to our problem, which features open-loop control and no notion of "state".

Our approach starts from an initial parameter vector $\pi = \{\theta_1, \ldots, \theta_N\}$ (where $N = 12$ in our case) and proceeds to estimate the partial derivative of $\pi$'s objective function with respect to each parameter. We do so by first evaluating $t$ randomly generated policies $\{R_1, R_2, \ldots, R_t\}$ near $\pi$, such that each $R_i = \{\theta_1 + \Delta_1, \ldots, \theta_N + \Delta_N\}$ and each $\Delta_j$ is chosen randomly to be either $+\epsilon_j$, 0, or $-\epsilon_j$. Each $\epsilon_j$ is a fixed value that is small relative to $\theta_j$.

After evaluating the speed of each $R_i$, we estimate the partial derivative in each of the $N$ dimensions. This is accomplished by grouping each $R_i$ into one of three sets for each dimension $n$:

$$R_i \in \begin{cases} S_{+\epsilon,n} & \text{if the } n\text{th parameter of } R_i \text{ is } \theta_n + \epsilon_n \\ S_{+0,n} & \text{if the } n\text{th parameter of } R_i \text{ is } \theta_n + 0 \\ S_{-\epsilon,n} & \text{if the } n\text{th parameter of } R_i \text{ is } \theta_n - \epsilon_n \end{cases}$$

We then compute an average score $Avg_{+\epsilon,n}$, $Avg_{+0,n}$, and $Avg_{-\epsilon,n}$ for $S_{+\epsilon,n}$, $S_{+0,n}$, and $S_{-\epsilon,n}$, respectively. These three averages give us an estimate of the benefit of altering the $n$th parameter by $+\epsilon_n$, 0, or $-\epsilon_n$. Note that in expectation, there will be $t/3$ of the $t$ policies with each of the three possible parameter settings, though there will be some random variation. We use these scores to construct an adjustment vector $A$ of size $N$, where

$$A_n = \begin{cases} 0 & \text{if } Avg_{+0,n} > Avg_{+\epsilon,n} \text{ and} \\ & \quad Avg_{+0,n} > Avg_{-\epsilon,n}, \\ Avg_{+\epsilon,n} - Avg_{-\epsilon,n} & \text{otherwise} \end{cases}$$

We normalize $A$ and multiply it by a scalar step-size $\eta$ (we used a value of $\eta = 2$ to offset the relatively small values of each $\epsilon_j$) so that our adjustment will remain a fixed size each iteration. Finally, we add $A$ to $\pi$, and begin the next iteration. Pseudocode for this policy gradient algorithm is shown in Figure 8.

```
π ← InitialPolicy
while !done do
  {R1, R2, ..., Rt} = t random perturbations of π
  evaluate( {R1, R2, ..., Rt} )
  for n = 1 to N do
    Avg+ε,n ← average score for all Ri that have
              a positive perturbation in dimension n
    Avg+0,n ← average score for all Ri that have a zero
              perturbation in dimension n
    Avg−ε,n ← average score for all Ri that have a
              negative perturbation in dimension n
    if Avg+0,n > Avg+ε,n and Avg+0,n > Avg−ε,n then
      An ← 0
    else
      An ← Avg+ε,n − Avg−ε,n
    end if
  end for
  A ← A/|A| * η
  π ← π + A
end while
```

**Figure 8**: Pseudocode for the $N$-dimensional policy gradient algorithm. During each iteration of the main loop $t$ policies are sampled near $\pi$ to estimate the gradient around $\pi$, then $\pi$ is moved by an amount of $\eta$ in the most favorable direction.

# Results

Figure 9 shows the progress of the four algorithms during training. Each curve is an average over 2 runs, and represents the best policy found at each instant in time. The genetic algorithm and amoeba algorithm were able to accomplish some learning and improve on the initial hand-tuned gait. The hill climbing and policy gradient algorithms yielded much better results, and both of these methods were able to offer better performance than our best hand-tuned walk. After 350 evaluations the policy gradient algorithm generated a gait that moved at 291 mm/s, faster than all current hand-tuned gaits and among the fastest learned gaits (in parallel with our work, a learned gait has been reported at 296 mm/s by Quinlan, Chalup, & Middleton, 2003).

Both the genetic algorithm and the amoeba algorithm performed fairly poorly, despite the fact that by many standards they would be considered to be more sophisticated algorithms than the hill climbing and policy gradient algorithms. To investigate this surprising result, we analyzed each algorithm in terms of the amount of the search space that each al-

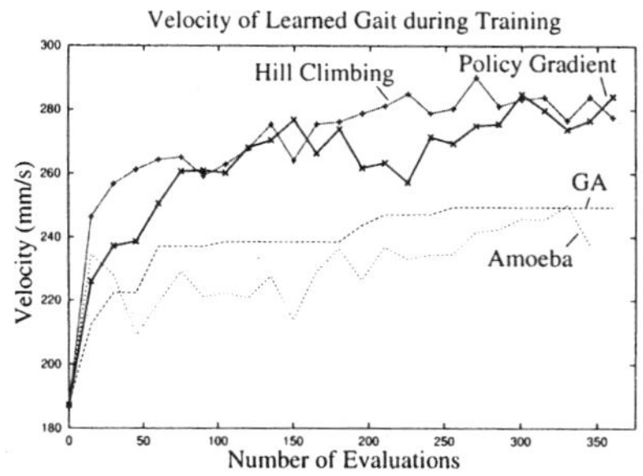


**Figure 9**: The velocity of the best gait from each iteration during training for the four methods. The policy gradient method was able to generate a gait that is faster than current hand-coded gaits and among the fastest learned gaits.

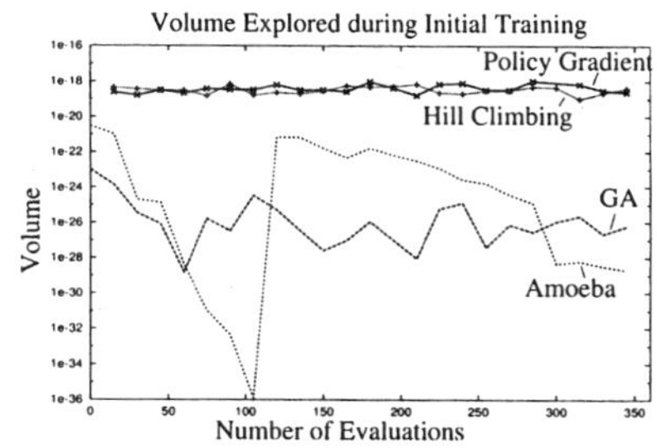


**Figure 10**: The amount of volume of the search space that each method explored during training. The genetic algorithm and the amoeba algorithm encompass much less volume than the hill climbing and policy gradient algorithms.

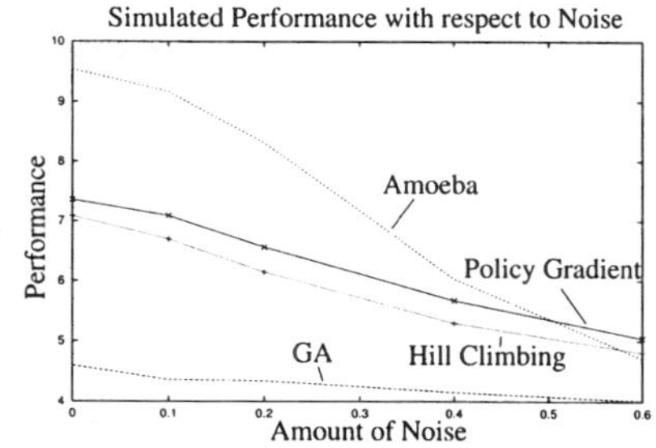


**Figure 11**: The performance of the four learning algorithms in a simulated domain. The performance of the amoeba algorithm is high when there is little noise in the objective function, but decreases rapidly as noise increases.

gorithm encompassed at each instant in time during training. This value was measured for each algorithm by computing the volume of a convex hull around all of the policies at a given point in time. The results of this analysis, which are shown in Figure 10, indicate that both the genetic algorithm and the amoeba algorithm suffer from rather low coverage rates, compared to the more successful hill climbing and policy gradient algorithms. In an effort to increase coverage for these two algorithms, we increased the mutation rate of the genetic algorithm and increased the rate at which the simplex was re-centered around the best policy for the amoeba algorithm. After these modifications, the performance of the genetic algorithm increased slightly and the performance of the amoeba algorithm improved to a level comparable to that of the hill climbing and policy gradient algorithms.

Despite these improvements, our results indicate that simpler algorithms perform as well as, or better than, more complicated algorithms in this domain. To further understand this phenomenon, we compared the four algorithms in an abstract simulation. We replaced our original objective function of maximizing forward velocity with an average over a set of ten mathematical functions with a variable amount of noise. Each of these functions had the same dimensionality as the original objective function (12 inputs and 1 output) and consisted of an arbitrarily chosen mix of constant, linear, trigonometric, and sigmoidal components. This set of functions was meant to represent a variety of different optimization problems, with the hope that lessons learned from the relative performance of algorithms on this simulated set of functions would translate to our target domain of velocity maximization for the Aibo. The results of this comparison, shown in Figure 11, show that while the amoeba algorithm performs well when there is little noise present, its performance drops sharply as the level of noise increases. This analysis suggests that our domain may be too noisy for the amoeba algorithm to perform at its best.

Note in Figure 9 that we stopped training each method after 350 evaluations, which amounted to just over 1000 field traversals in about 3 hours. Subsequent evaluations showed no further improvement, suggesting that the learning had plateaued in all cases.

## Discussion and Future Work

One of the useful aspects of automating the gait optimization process is that search algorithms often possess less bias than human engineers. For example, our gait was designed after a trot gait, where diagonally opposite legs strike the ground simultaneously. We assumed that the ideal trot gait would keep two feet on the ground at all times. Interestingly enough, the best learned gait defied our expectations by attempting to keep each foot on the ground only 43% of the time. By allowing the learning process to affect a large portion of the gait, we were able to discover parameter settings that we would not have likely found through hand-tuning.

On a similar note, recent work has suggested that due to mechanical limitations and environmental noise, the actual locus that each foot follows is significantly different than the requested half-elliptical locus (Stronger & Stone 2003). Given this discrepancy between the ideal locus and the real locus, a change in parameters describing the ideal locus may not have the intended effect on the real locus. This discrepancy could make hand-tuning difficult for humans, who expect a certain correspondence between parameters and their effects on the gait. Since the learning process is unaware of the semantics of the parameters, it might not suffer as much from discrepancies between the expected loci and the actual loci.

Another benefit of automated learning can arise in situations such that the robots are required to repeatedly switch surfaces. In RoboCup, the surfaces of different playing fields can vary widely in hardness and friction. Repeatedly tuning parameters by hand for each surface could consume a great deal of time from human engineers, whereas automatically learning parameters for various surfaces would require significantly less human effort.

One of the benefits of simple algorithms like the policy gradient algorithm and the hill climbing algorithm is that they could be considered a form of multi-robot learning, in that it would be relatively straightforward to implement these algorithms without the use of a central controller. Since the evaluations that each Aibo performs are generated randomly, the algorithm that each Aibo executes could be run almost completely independently of the other Aibos. The only requirement would be that each Aibo communicate the results of the evaluations that it performs to the other Aibos and that they have a common notion of the parameter $t$ which governs the number of policies evaluated per iteration. After finding out the results of $t$ evaluations, each robot could then independently perform the calculation to determine the next policy $\pi$ and continue with the next iteration. In contrast, more complicated algorithms like the amoeba algorithm require much stricter control over which policies are evaluated. Thus the robots would need to explicitly coordinate which policies they are to evaluate, and find a way to re-do evaluations that are interrupted by battery changes.

It is important to note that our implementations of all of the algorithms mentioned above require reasonable starting policies. Since we are not explicitly trying to find a stable gait, starting from an unstable gait can lead to mechanical failures that can make it difficult for the Aibos to make much progress. As a result, our method is probably not yet directly applicable to the problem of finding an initial stable walk (e.g. for a bipedal robot).

The fact that the amoeba algorithm performs relatively well given an absence of noise in our simulated experiments suggests that we could improve its performance on the Aibos by finding a way to reduce the noise associated with each evaluation. Possible methods to decrease the noise level include using more sensory input to determine the Aibo's location and averaging over more trials.

Since we distributed the learning process over multiple robots, the policies that we discovered were not tuned to any particular robot. While the hardware that the Aibos are made up of is theoretically homogeneous, cumulative wear and tear over time can lead to significant differences between robots. It is therefore possible that we could achieve further increases in performance by training individual Aibos to fine-tune their parameters.

Another possible avenue for future work involves broadening our analysis to include more existing optimization algorithms. Of particular interest are algorithms like Q2 (Moore *et al.* 1998) and PB1 (Anderson, Moore, & Cohn 2000) which were designed to work well in domains with sparse and noisy data. It would also be interesting to optimize fast omni-directional gaits. While the work presented in this paper has focused on maximizing velocity in a forward direction, methods similar to those presented here could be used to optimize turning gaits or gaits for movement in other directions.

## Conclusion

In this paper, we presented a comparison of four algorithms for learning a fast walk on a quadruped robot, namely the Aibo ERS-210A. All of the algorithms were able to improve over initial hand-tuned gaits, and the policy gradient algorithm was able to generate one of the fastest known walks on the Aibo: 291 mm/s. These algorithms allow distributed, efficient policy evaluation in the real world, with all learning happening on the robots. Video of the initial results, training process, and final results are all available on-line.[6]

## Acknowledgments

We would like to thank the members of the UT Austin Villa team, and Daniel Stronger in particular, for their efforts in developing the gaits and software mentioned in this paper. This research was supported in part by NSF CAREER award IIS-0237699.

[6] www.cs.utexas.edu/~AustinVilla/legged/learned-walk/

## References

Anderson, B.; Moore, A.; and Cohn, D. 2000. A nonparametric approach to noisy and costly optimization. In *International Conference on Machine Learning*.

Bagnell, J. A., and Schneider, J. 2001. Autonomous helicopter control using reinforcement learning policy search methods. In *International Conference on Robotics and Automation*.

Baxter, J., and Bartlett, P. L. 2001. Infinite-horizon policy-gradient estimation. *Journal of AI Research* 15:319–350.

Goldberg, D. E., and Richardson, J. 1987. Genetic algorithms with sharing for multimodal function optimization. 148–154.

Hengst, B.; Ibbotson, D.; Pham, S. B.; and Sammut, C. 2001. Omnidirectional motion for quadruped robots. In Birk, A. et al. eds., *RoboCup International Symposium, Lecture Notes in Computer Science, LNAI 2377*, 368. Springer.

Hornby, G. S.; Fujita, M.; Takamura, S.; Yamamoto, T.; and Hanagata, O. 1999. Autonomous evolution of gaits with the Sony quadruped robot. In Banzhaf, W. et al. eds., *Proceedings of the Genetic and Evolutionary Computation Conference*, volume 2, 1297–1304. Orlando, Florida, USA: Morgan Kaufmann.

Kim, M. S., and Uther, W. 2003. Automatic gait optimisation for quadruped robots. In *Australasian Conference on Robotics and Automation*.

Mitchell, M. 1996. *An Introduction to Genetic Algorithms*.

Moore, A.; Schneider, J.; Boyan, J.; and Lee, M. S. 1998. Q2: Memory-based active learning for optimizing noisy continuous functions. In Shavlik, J., ed., *Proceedings of the Fifteenth International Conference of Machine Learning*, 386–394. 340 Pine Street, 6th Fl., San Francisco, CA 94104: Morgan Kaufmann.

Ng, A. et al. 2004. Autonomous helicopter flight via reinforcement learning. In *Advances in Neural Information Processing Systems 17*. MIT Press. To Appear.

Press, W. H. 1988. *Numerical Recipes in C: the art of scientific computing*. Cambridge: Cambridge University Press.

Quinlan, M. J.; Chalup, S. K.; and Middleton, R. H. 2003. Techniques for improving vision and locomotion on the sony aibo robot. In *Proceedings of the 2003 Australasian Conference on Robotics and Automation*.

Rofer, T. et al. 2003. Germanteam robocup 2003. Tech report.

Sony. 2004. Aibo robot. www.sony.net/Products/aibo.

Stone, P. et al. 2003. UT Austin Villa 2003: A new RoboCup four-legged team. Technical Report UT-AI-TR-03-304, The University of Texas at Austin, Department of Computer Sciences, AI Laboratory. At http://www.cs.utexas.edu/home/department/pubsforms.shtml.

Stronger, D., and Stone, P. 2003. A model-based approach to robot joint control. Under Review. Available from http://www.cs.utexas.edu/~pstone/papers.html.

Sutton, R.; McAllester, D.; Singh, S.; and Mansour, Y. 2000. Policy gradient methods for reinforcement learning with function approximation. In *Advances in Neural Information Processing Systems*, volume 12, 1057–1063. The MIT Press.

Watkins, C. J. C. H. 1989. *Learning from Delayed Rewards*. Ph.D. Dissertation, King's College, Cambridge, UK.

Zhang, R., and Vadakkepat, P. 2003. An evolutionary algorithm for trajectory based gait generation of biped robot. In *Proceedings of the International Conference on Computational Intelligence, Robotics and Autonomous Systems*.

# Interleaving Temporal Planning and Execution in Robotics Domains

**Solange Lemai** and **Félix Ingrand***
LAAS/CNRS,
7 Avenue du Colonel Roche, F-31077 Toulouse Cedex 04, France
{*slemai,felix*}*@laas.fr*

## Abstract

Many autonomous systems such as mobile robots, UAVs or spacecraft, have limited resource capacities and move in dynamic environments. Performing on-board mission planning and execution in such a context requires deliberative capabilities to generate plans achieving mission goals while respecting deadlines and resource constraints, as well as run-time plan adaption mechanisms during execution. In this paper we propose a framework to integrate deliberative planning, plan repair and execution control in a dynamic environment with stringent temporal constraints. It is based on lifted partial order temporal planning techniques which produce flexible plans and allow, under certain conditions discussed in the paper, plan repair interleaved with plan execution. This framework has been implemented using the IxTeT planner and used to control a robotic platform.

## Introduction

The development of a complex autonomous system relies on the arrangement of the software components in a closed loop architecture, usually organized around two levels. A *decisional level* generates a plan of actions which achieves the mission goals, and executes this plan in a robust way. A *functional level*, interfaced with the hardware, executes the refined actions of the plan. The decisional level usually embeds a time-consuming planning process, as well as a time-bounded reactive execution process. We are interested in the key problem of defining how these two processes should interact to balance deliberation and reaction.

Various strategies have been applied so far. Some approaches propose the use of a strong executive, enhanced with deliberative capabilities. Procedural executives, such as TDL (Simmons & Apfelbaum 1998) or PRS (Ingrand *et al.* 1996), support action decomposition, synchronization, execution monitoring and exception handling. In PROPEL (Levinson 1995), and PropicePlan (Despouys & Ingrand 1999), the planner is used by the executive to anticipate by simulating subplans, or to generate a new subplan corresponding to the current situation. These systems provide mostly a reactive behavior, whereas a look-ahead far in the future is necessary to achieve a strong level of autonomy (e.g. to manage the level of a limited resource during the entire mission).

In the "batch planning" approach of the Remote Agent (Muscettola *et al.* 1998), planning and plan execution are two separate processes. The agent can perform replanning (but with long standby periods) and back to back planning.

Other approaches propose to interleave planning and execution in a continuous way. The planning process remains active to adapt the plan when new goals are added or to resolve conflicts appearing after a state update; and actions which are ready to be executed are committed to execution even if the plan is not yet completely generated. Examples include IPEM (Ambros-Ingerson & Steel 1988), based on the classical Partial Order Planning framework; ROGUE (Haigh & Veloso 1998), which has been deployed on mobile robots; or the multi-agent architecture CPEF (Myers 1999).

Still, very few approaches really take into account timing problems, such as actions with duration and goals with deadlines, and their effects on the planning and execution processes. Examples of temporal systems include CASPER and IDEA. In the CASPER system (Chien *et al.* 2000), state and temporal data are regularly updated and potential future conflicts are resolved using iterative repair techniques. However this approach does not handle conflicts which appear within the replanning time interval. The IDEA approach (Finzi, Ingrand, & Muscettola 2004) uses temporal planning techniques at any level of abstraction (mission planning as well as reactive execution). This system offers look-ahead abilities with flexible planning horizons and the use of a common language at any level of abstraction, but does not yet handle non-unary resources.

In this paper we propose a framework to integrate deliberative planning, plan repair and execution control that takes into account resource level updates and temporal constraints. These processes are embedded thanks to two interacting components which explicitly represent and reason about time: a temporal planner and a temporal executive. First the planner elaborates a complete plan. This plan is then run by the temporal executive following a cycle: integrate external messages, repair the plan if needed, decide to execute actions. This cycle enables interaction with the controlled system by taking into account runtime failures and timeouts, and updating the plan accordingly. Interleaving plan repair and execution is motivated by the facts that some parts of the plan may remain valid and executable, and that the plan can be temporally flexible and thus allow postponing and inserting actions. Plan repair uses non linear planning techniques under certain assumptions discussed in this paper. This framework assumes that the planning system has the following properties: a temporal representation based on state variables and a Partial Order Causal Link (POCL) planning process that generates flexible plans based on CSP managers, particularly the time-map relies on a Simple Temporal Network (STN) (Dechter,

*Part of this work was funded by a contract with CNES and ASTRIUM.

Meiri, & Pearl 1989). The proposed framework has been implemented in IxTeT-eXeC, using the planning system IxTeT.

The paper is organized as follows. The first section presents the general behavior of the IxTeT-eXeC system, especially the interactions between the executive and the controlled system, and briefly introduces the underlying planning system. The second section details the dynamic replanning framework and addresses the issues raised by the interleaving of planning and execution processes on the same plan. The last section illustrates the performances of IxTeT-eXeC on a rover exploration scenario involving goal deadlines and resource contention.

## Overview of the IxTeT-eXeC system

### General behavior

The key component in IxTeT-eXeC is the temporal executive (TeXeC) which interacts with the planner and the controlled system. It controls the temporal network to decide the execution of actions and maps the timepoints to their real execution time. The execution of an action $a$ with grounded parameters $p_a$, starting timepoint $st^a$, ending timepoint $et^a$, and identifier $i_a$ is started by sending the command (*START* $a$ $p_a$ $i_a$) to the controlled system. If the action is *non preemptive*, $et^a$ is not controllable, and TeXeC just monitors if $a$ is completed in due time. Otherwise $et^a$ is controllable. If the action did not terminate by itself, it is stopped with the command (*END* $i_a$) sent as soon as possible if $a$ is *early preemptive*, as late as possible if it is *late preemptive*.

TeXeC integrates in the plan the reports sent by the controlled system upon each action completion. A report returns the ending status of the action (*nominal*, *interrupted* or *failed*) and a partial description of the system state. If nominal, it contains just the final levels of the resources, if any, used by the action. Otherwise, it also contains the final values of the other state variables relevant to the action.

Besides completion reports, TeXeC reacts to two types of event: user requests to insert a new goal and sudden alterations of a resource capacity. Other situations that forbid further execution of the plan without plan adaptation are:

– *temporal failures* The STN constrains each timepoint $t$ to occur inside a time interval $[t_{lb}, t_{ub}]$. Thus two types of failure lead to an inconsistent plan: the corresponding event (typically, the end of an action) happens *too early* or *too late* (time-out).

– *action failure* The system returns a non nominal report.

– *resource level adjustment* If an action has consumed/produced more/less than expected, the plan may contain future resource contention.

TeXeC starts and controls the processes of plan adaptation. To take advantage of the temporal flexibility of the plan, the dynamic replanning strategy has two steps. A first attempt is to repair the plan while executing its valid part in parallel. If this fails or if a timepoint times out, the execution is aborted and IxTeT completely replans from scratch.

### The IxTeT planning system

IxTeT is a lifted POCL temporal planner based on CSPs (Laborie & Ghallab 1995). Its temporal representation describes the world as a set of *attributes*: logical attributes (e.g. robot_position(?$r$)), which are multi-valued functions of time, and resource attributes (e.g. battery_level()) over which borrowings, consumptions or productions can be specified. We note $LgcA$ and $RscA$, respectively the sets of logical and resource attributes. $LgcA_g$ and $RscA_g$ designate the sets of all possible instantiations of these attributes.

The evolution of a logical attribute value is represented through the proposition *hold*, which asserts the persistence of a value over a time interval, and the proposition *event*, which states an instantaneous change of values. The propositions *use*, *consume* and *produce* specify, respectively, the borrowing over an interval, the consumption or the production at a given instant of a given resource quantity.

```
task MOVE(?initL,?endL)(st,et){                     variable ?di,?du,?dist;
 ?initL,?endL in LOCATIONS;                          variable ?duration;
 event(ROBOT_POS():(?initL,IDLE_POS),st);            distance(?initL,?endL,?di);
 hold(ROBOT_POS():IDLE_POS,(st,et));                 distance_uncertainty(?du);
 event(ROBOT_POS():(IDLE_POS,?endL),et);             ?dist = ?di * ?du;
 event(ROBOT_STATUS():(STILL,MOVING),st);            speed(?s);
 hold(ROBOT_STATUS():MOVING,(st,et));                ?dist = ?s * ?duration;
 event(ROBOT_STATUS():(MOVING,STILL),et);            ?duration = et - st;
 hold(PTU_POS():FORWARD,(st,et));                    }latePreemptive
```

Figure 1: Example of action model.

An action (also called *task*) consists of a set of *events* describing the change of the world induced by the action, a set of *hold* propositions expressing required conditions or the protection of some fact between two events, a set of resource usages, and a set of constraints on the timepoints and variables of the action. An example is given in Figure 1.

A plan relies on two CSP managers. An STN handles the timepoints and their binary constraints (ordering, duration). The other CSP manages atemporal symbolic and numeric variables and their constraints (binding, domain restriction, sum, etc.). Mixed constraints between temporal and atemporal variables can also be expressed (e.g. $?dist\ = ?speed * (et - st)$) (see (Trinquart & Ghallab 2001)). These CSP managers compute for each variable a minimal domain which reflects only the necessary constraints in the plan.

The search explores a tree $\mathcal{T}$ in the partial plan space. In a POCL framework, a partial plan is generally defined as a 4-tuple $(A, C, L, F)$, where $A$ is a set of partially instantiated actions, $C$ is a set of constraints on the temporal and atemporal variables of actions in $A$, $L$ is a set of causal links[1] and $F$ is a set of flaws. A partial plan stands for a family of plans. A partial plan is considered to be a valid solution if all these plans are coherent, that is $F$ is empty.

The root node of $\mathcal{T}$ consists of: the initial state (initial values of all instantiated attributes), expected availability profiles of resources, goals to be achieved (desired values for specific instantiated attributes) and a set of constraints between these elements. The branches of $\mathcal{T}$ correspond to resolvers (new actions or constraints) inserted into the partial plan in order to solve one of its flaws. Three kinds of flaws are considered:

– *open conditions* are events or assertions that have not yet been established. Resolvers consist in finding an establishing event (in the plan or a new action) and adding a causal link that protects the attribute value between the establishing event and the open condition.

– *threats* correspond to pairs of *event* and *hold* which values are potentially in conflict. Such conflicts are solved by adding temporal or binding constraints.

– *resource conflicts* are detected as over-consuming sets of potentially overlapping propositions. Resolvers include insertion

[1]A causal link $a_i \xrightarrow{p} a_j$ denotes a commitment by the planner that a proposition $p$ of action $a_j$ is established by an effect of action $a_i$. The precedence constraint $a_i \prec a_j$ and binding constraints for variables of $a_i$ and $a_j$ appearing in $p$ are in $C$.

of resource production action, etc.
A planning step consists in detecting flaws in the current partial plan, selecting one, choosing a resolver in its associated list of potential resolvers and inserting it into the partial plan. This planning step is repeated until a solution plan is found. The algorithm is complete and the flaw and resolver choices are guided by diverse heuristics not discussed here.

The advantages of the CSP-based functional approach are numerous in the context of plan execution. Besides the expressiveness of the representation (handling of time and resources), the flexibility of plans (partially ordered and partially instantiated, with minimal constraints) is well-adapted to their execution in an uncertain and dynamic environment. Plans are further constrained at execution time. Finally, the planner, performing a search in the plan space, can be adapted to incremental planning and plan repair.

## Temporal plan execution and replanning

Interleaving partial order planning and execution may insert flaws in the plan. We formally define under which conditions such a partial plan remains executable.

### Definitions

We extend the previous definition of a partial plan to the definition of $P_t$: a **partial plan partially executed up to time *t*.**

**Definition 1** $P_t = (RA_t, FA_t, S_t, G_t, C_t, L_t, F_t)$.

$RA_t$ is the set of currently *running actions* ($a \in RA_t$ if $st^a_{ub} < t$ and $et^a_{ub} > t$), $FA_t$ is the set of *future actions* ($a \in FA_t$ if $st^a_{ub} \geq t$). $S_t$ represents the *state of the world* at time $t$. It is composed of 2 sets: $LgcS_t$ contains the last value of each attribute $la \in LgcA_g$,[2] $RscL_t$ contains the level at time $t$ of each resource $r \in RscA_g$. $G_t$ is the set of *goals* not yet completely achieved at time $t$ (and eventually not established)[3]. $C_t$ is the set of constraints on the variables appearing in $FA_t$, $RA_t$, $S_t$ and $G_t$. $L_t$ is the set of causal links supporting future actions. $F_t$ is the set of flaws present in the partial plan at time $t$.

The level of a resource at a certain time in the future cannot be computed, since it depends on the partial order of actions using this resource. But at time $t$ the past part of the plan is completely instantiated and linearized. Two cases have to be considered: if no running action modifies $r$, the exact level can be computed (case (1)); if at least one action in $RA_t$ requires the resource, only an estimate is available (case (2)).

In case (1), the exact level is computed in IxTeT according to formula (**a**). We note $C(r)$ the resource capacity. Let $p$ be a production, belonging to the action $a^p$, of a quantity $?q_p$ of the resource $r$ at time $t^p$ and $P(r)$ be the set of productions of resource $r$ in the plan. Similarly, $C(r)$ is the set of consumptions $c$, belonging to the action $a^c$, of a quantity $?q_c$ at time $t^c$, and $B(r)$ is the set of borrowings $b$, belonging to the action $a^b$, of a quantity $?q_b$ between $st^b$ and $et^b$. Then, if no running action modifies $r$, $RscL_t(r) = Lev^{past}_t(r)$ with: (**a**)

$$Lev^{past}_t(r) = C(r) + \sum_{\substack{p \in P(r)/t^p_{ub} < t \\ \text{and } a^p \notin RA_t}} ?q_p - \sum_{\substack{c \in C(r)/t^c_{ub} < t \\ \text{and } a^c \notin RA_t}} ?q_c$$

This level is a variable ranging over $[lev^{past}_{lb}, lev^{past}_{ub}]$.

In case (2), the uncertainty follows from the insufficient piece-wise constant model of the resource usage. The previous level definition is completed by an estimation of the level modification by the running actions ($Lev^{RA}(r)$) according to formula (**b**). The total amount produced, consumed or borrowed by an action is represented by a variable $?q$ in $[q_{min}, q_{max}]$. At a given time in the course of the action, the only information that the planner can deduce is that the amount produced/consumed up to now is in $[0, q_{max}]$ or that the amount borrowed is in $[q_{min}, q_{max}]$. An estimation of the level would then be: (**b**)

$$lev^{RA}_{min} \leq RscL_t(r) - Lev^{past}_t(r) \leq lev^{RA}_{max}$$

$$\text{with } lev^{RA}_{min} = - \sum_{c \in C(r)/a^c \in RA_t} q_{c_{max}} - \sum_{b \in B(r)/a^b \in RA_t} q_{b_{max}}$$

$$lev^{RA}_{max} = \sum_{p \in P(r)/a^p \in RA_t} q_{p_{max}} - \sum_{b \in B(r)/a^b \in RA_t} q_{b_{min}}$$

Finally, the level of a resource $r$ at time $t$ is comprised in the interval $[RscL_{lb}, RscL_{ub}]$ with, in case (1):

$$RscL_{lb} = lev^{past}_{lb}, RscL_{ub} = lev^{past}_{ub},$$

and in case (2):

$$RscL_{lb} = lev^{past}_{lb} + lev^{RA}_{min}, RscL_{ub} = lev^{past}_{ub} + lev^{RA}_{max}.$$

A timepoint in the temporal network may correspond to a goal timepoint or to an action starting or ending timepoint.

**Definition 2 (executable timepoint)** *A timepoint T is executable at time t if all timepoints $T^p$ that must directly precede it in the temporal network have already been executed ($T^p_{lb} = T^p_{ub} < t$) and if $t \in [T_{lb}, T_{ub}]$.*

A goal is instantaneously achieved or persistent (achieve and maintain a property between $st^g$ and $et^g$).

**Definition 3 (achievable goal)** *A goal $g$ is achievable at time $t$ if $st^g$ is executable and if $g \notin F_t$.*

Let $A^f_t$ be the set of actions that are involved in $F_t$.[4]

**Definition 4 (executable action)** *A future action $a$ is executable at time $t$ if its start timepoint is executable and if $a \notin A^f_t$.*

**Definition 5 (executable plan)** *A partial plan $P_t$ is executable at time $t$ if the constraint networks are consistent and if $RA_t \cap A^f_t = \emptyset$.*

### Execution cycle

The solution plan produced by the planner is run by the executive following a three phases "sense/plan repair/act" cycle. The executive wakes up when a message has been received, or when it is time to execute some timepoint or when a plan repair process is in progress. Let us call $ExecutingPlan$ the plan being executed. *Sensing* consists in integrating messages in $ExecutingPlan$ which may partially invalidate it. If

[2]In IxTeT, $LgcS_t$ contains the last executed *event* for each $la$.

[3]In IxTeT, a goal is represented by a grounded proposition $hold(GoalAtt(g) : GoalValue, (st^g, et^g))$. $G_t$ contains goals such that $et^g_{ub} \geq t$.

[4]The determination of $A^f_t$ is straightforward in the case of open conditions and resource conflicts. In a threat case, an action $a_k$ has effects in contradiction with the establishment of proposition $p$ by the causal link $a_i \xrightarrow{p} a_j$ and $(a_i \prec a_k \prec a_j)$ is consistent. $A^f_t$ contains $a_k$ and $a_j$.

$ExecutingPlan$ contains new flaws, a *plan repair* consists in keeping the structure of the plan (the ordering of actions) and taking advantage of the flexibility to try and find a solution plan. Planning is distributed on several cycles to allow reactivity to events and concurrent execution of the valid part. *Acting* consists in determining which timepoints have to be executed, processing them or detecting time-out. The user defines the maximum time allowed to the cycle, also called *timestep* ($ts$).

Distributing planning on several cycles raises two problems:
**On which plan relies the execution in the "act" part, especially if no solution has been found?** This plan has to be *executable*. At each planning step, the node is labeled if the current partial plan is *executable*. When the maximum time allowed to plan repair in the cycle is reached, the last labeled partial plan becomes $ExecutingPlan$.
**On which plan and which search tree relies the planning process in the next cycle?** If no decision has been made meanwhile (no timepoint execution, no message reception), the search tree can be kept as is and further developed during the next "plan repair" part. However, if the plan has been modified, a new search tree whose root node is the new $ExecutingPlan$ is used, and the planning decisions made in previous cycles are final.
The following subsections further detail the different phases of the cycle. Basically, all modifications made to $ExecutingPlan$ have to guarantee that an *executable* plan is available after each phase of the cycle. If this condition does not hold, the cycle is stopped and a complete replanning is mandatory. During a cycle without plan repair, $ExecutingPlan$ remains a solution plan.

## Message integration

A message can be: a report upon action completion, a new goal request or a notification of a capacity alteration.

**Report** A report is associated with the ending timepoint $et^a$ of the corresponding action $a$. If the message is received inside the bounds $[et^a_{lb}, et^a_{ub}]$, $et^a$ is set to the current time $t$ (equivalent to posting the constraint $(et^a - origin) = t$ in the STN). Otherwise, two situations arise. If there is no flexibility left in the plan, it is not executable anymore. Else, a new end timepoint, set to $t$ and constrained to occur before the executable timepoints, is created and the failed one is relaxed. The network is then recomputed. In IxTeT, such an operation keeps the network consistent since the only constraint that can be specified between two actions $a$ and $a'$ is a precedence constraint which upper bound is flexible: $(st^{a'} - et^a)$ in $]0, +\infty[$. If the report contains information about the state, $S_t$ is updated in the following way:

***Resource level -*** For each resource $r$, the report returns the current "real" level $l_r$. $RscL_t(r)$ is compared to $l_r$ and adjusted.
— If $l_r \in [RscL_{lb}, RscL_{ub}]$, the plan is consistent with reality. If the exact level can be computed (case (1) - see Definitions), its value is updated by adding the constraint $RscL_t(r) = l_r$.
— If $(l_r < RscL_{lb})$, the over-consumption is reflected on the plan by adding a consumption of quantity $c = RscL_{lb} - l_r$. In case (1), the new level $(RscL'_t(r) = RscL_t(r) - c)$ is updated by adding the constraint $RscL_t(r) = RscL_{lb}$, equivalent to $RscL'_t(r) = l_r$. If some running action modifies $r$ (case (2)), the part of the level due to past actions $(L^{past}_t(r))$ is updated by considering the worst case and adding the constraint $L^{past}_t(r) = lev^{past}_{lb}$.
— If $(l_r > RscL_{ub})$, the over-production is reflected on the plan by adding a production of quantity $p = l_r - RscL_{ub}$. Similarly, the level is updated by adding the constraint $RscL_t(r) = RscL_{ub}$ in case (1), and $L^{past}_t(r) = lev^{past}_{ub}$ in case (2).

The plan remains executable in case (1) since no running action is concerned by $r$, whereas conflicts may appear in case (2), requiring execution abortion. If the plan is executable, plan repair is requested in case of over-consumption and in case of over-production of a reservoir resource.

***State variables -*** $LgcS_t$ contains the last value for each instantiated logical attribute. If the report is nominal, $LgcS_t$ is updated with the effects of $a$ expected in the plan. Otherwise, it is updated with the values returned in the report. A value is not inserted if it leads to a non executable plan (threatens some proposition of a running action $a_r$). In that case and if $a_r$ is preemptive, its interruption is requested. Else, the value is inserted and causal links which contradict it are broken. This update leads to an executable plan with open conditions on which plan repair can be processed.

**Goal request** One specifies for each goal: a priority, a duration interval $I^d$, an estimation of its minimal achievement duration $d_{achiev}$ and a time interval $I^g$ for its start timepoint $st^g$. A goal is rejected if the following set of constraints is not consistent with the plan at current time $t$: $\{((et^g - st^g)$ in $I^d)$, $((st^g -$ origin$)$ in $I^g)$, $(st^g$-origin $\geq t + d_{achiev})\}$. Moreover the goal is constrained to occur after each running action $a$ such that the goal proposition threatens a proposition in $a$. A goal integration results in an executable plan with an open condition.

**Capacity alteration** As a consequence of an external event a resource capacity has increased or decreased by a quantity $q$. The capacity is updated. If the plan is not executable anymore, execution is aborted. Otherwise a plan repair is requested in case of decrease or increase of a reservoir resource.

**Causal links removal** After message integration, the plan may contain flaws (open conditions and/or resource conflicts) on a set of grounded attributes $Att^f$, possibly repaired thanks to the insertion of new actions. Let us consider $Att^i$ the set of the attributes appearing in the potentially inserted actions. Additional causal links, protecting propositions in the plan on attributes in $Att^i$, have to be broken to allow the insertion of these actions in the current plan structure.

The determination of $Att^i$ is based on information given by an abstraction hierarchy verifying the Ordered Monotonicity Property (Knoblock 1994; Garcia & Laborie 1995) and generated offline from the model description. Notably, this hierarchy points out the primary effects of an operator, which justify its insertion to solve a flaw. Let us call *main attributes* of an action the attributes appearing in its primary effects. $Att^i$, initialized with $Att^f$, is computed by searching the action operators for which at least one attribute $att_m$ in $Att^i$ is a main attribute. This operator is partially grounded (by binding its corresponding parameter with $att_m$) and the (eventually grounded) attributes appearing in the operator and not yet taken into account are added to $Att^i$. The algorithm proceeds recursively until a fixed point is reached.

Finally, the partial plan is executable and the sets of actions independent from the failures remain executable.

## Plan repair

The plan repair is similar to the IxTeT search process in the plan space. The root of the search tree $\mathcal{T}$ is $ExecutingPlan$, partially invalidated. $\mathcal{T}$ is developed according to an ordered depth first search strategy. Planning is distributed, if necessary, on several cycles and each time a new timepoint is inserted, it is constrained to occur after the end of the current cycle. Planning during one cycle is done one step at a time until it results in a dead-end (there is no solution), or a solution is found or a deadline is reached. This deadline corresponds to the share ($\mu$) of the timestep $ts$ allocated to the plan repair part (this parameter is tuned by the user).

Some aggregation mechanisms (corresponding to past forgetting) allow a reduction of the search space. In IxTeT, the establishing events are looked for in $LgcS_t$ and executed resource propositions are aggregated in one proposition.

This plan repair process is not guaranteed to find a valid plan, still it can avoid aborting execution and completely replanning at each failure. By invalidating only a part of the plan, the amount of decisions is rather limited and a repaired plan may be found in a few cycles. Plan repair is especially efficient and useful for temporally flexible plans and plans with some parallelism. This mechanism is also efficient to compensate for inadequate models of actions. Consider a move($L_1$,$L_2$) action, which is defined as a late preemptive action in the IxTeT-eXeC model. If the robot takes longer than expected in the model (e.g. due to obstacle avoidance), the action is interrupted. The controlled system returns the intermediate location $L_i$ and, if some temporal flexibility remains, a new move($L_i$,$L_2$) is immediately inserted and launched. This example is representative of the failures that frequently break plan execution.

## Action

Each timepoint is associated with an *execution time* $t_{exec}$. If $T$ is a start or goal timepoint, or an end timepoint of an early preemptive action, $t_{exec} = T_{lb}$. If $T$ is an end timepoint of a late preemptive action, $t_{exec} = T_{ub} - ts$. If $T$ is an end timepoint of a non preemptive action, $t_{exec} = T_{ub}$. During the "act" part, the executive determines the set of timepoints to execute during the current cycle ($ExecTPs$): these timepoints are executable and their execution time happens before the end of the cycle. $ExecTPs$ is updated after each timepoint execution to take into account newly executable timepoints. The detail of a timepoint execution depends on its type. If a goal is not achievable or if an action is not executable and if some flexibility remains, their execution is postponed. The execution time of a preemptive end timepoint is set when the corresponding report is received (expected in the next cycle). Finally, timeouts are detected when reports have not been received in time.

## Complete replanning

Let us call $P_{t_s} = (\emptyset, FA_{t_s}, S_{t_s}, G_{t_s}, C_{t_s}, L_{t_s}, F_{t_s})$ the plan obtained once execution is stopped. An initial plan is extracted from $P_{t_s}$ as:
$P_{t_i} = (\emptyset, \emptyset, S_{t_i}, G_{t_i}, C_{t_i}, \emptyset, F_{t_i})$, with
$S_{t_i} = S_{t_s}$, $G_{t_i} = \{g \in G_{t_s}/$*temporal constraints on g are coherent with current time*$\}$, $C_{t_i} = \{c \in C_{t_s}/$*c is a constraint just on variables appearing in* $S_{t_i}$ *and* $G_{t_i}\}$*(*$C_{t_i}$*notably contains constraints on origin and horizon timepoints)*, and $F_{t_i} = G_{t_i}$.

POCL planning can not be interrupted at any time and come up with an applicable plan. Still we have to guarantee that at the end of the replanning process, there remains enough time to execute the solution plan and meet the goal deadlines. We propose to add a specific flexible timepoint $T^{end}$ to $P_{t_i}$, that corresponds to the end of the planning process. $T^{end}$ is only constrained to occur between $t_i$ and the end of the horizon. Each time a new timepoint is inserted by the planning process, it is constrained to occur after $T^{end}$. Thus $T^{end}_{ub}$ decreases as new actions or new temporal constraints are added, and there is not enough time to execute the current plan if $T^{end}_{ub}$ < current time. Note however that $T^{end}_{ub}$ can increase when backtracking.

The strategy is then to plan one step at a time until it results in a dead-end, or a solution is found, or a time limit $l$ is reached. $l$ is defined as $l = T^{end}_{ub} - d$, $d$ being a *slack* duration to save enough time at the end of planning for cycle initialization. $l$ is updated after each planning step. Planning is stopped when $l$ is reached unless the next step corresponds to a backtrack node. In that case, and if the next step increases $l$, planning is pursued.

If planning is aborted without finding a solution, some goals are rejected and a new attempt is done. A new plan $P_{t_i}$ is extracted from $P_{t_s}$. At this point, some goals may have been rejected due to temporal constraints inconsistent with the current time. Otherwise, we abandon the goal with the lowest priority, and, if several goals have the same priority, the goal with the less flexibility for its achievement (this flexibility is computed as ($st^g_{ub}$ - $d_{achiev}$)). This criterion has been chosen to keep the goals that are more likely to be achieved in due course.

## Integration and example of scenario

IxTeT-eXeC has been integrated in the decisional level of the LAAS architecture (Alami *et al.* 1998) and used to control an iRobot ATRV. IxTeT-eXeC interacts with the user and the functional level through a procedural executive (OpenPRS). The plan execution is controlled by both executives as follows. TeXeC decides when to start or stop an action in the plan and handles plan adaptations. OpenPRS expands the action into commands to the functional level, monitors its execution and can recover from specific failures. It finally reports to TeXeC upon the action completion.

However, we face some difficulties to evaluate our work since there is no benchmark (involving time and resource issues) to apply the system to. We illustrate the performances of IxTeT-eXeC with an example of failure scenario for a simulated rover with an exploration mission. In such a domain, the quantitative effects and durations can be estimated in advance for planning but are accurately known only at execution time (e.g. the actual compression rate of an image or the actual duration of a navigation task), thus requiring regular updates and look-ahead capabilities to manage unforeseen situations and resource levels.

Goals are a list of targets to take a picture of, constraints correspond to deadlines and limited resources (memory storage, battery level). The planning model contains five actions: move, take_picture, move_ptu (change the orientation of the cameras through commands to the pan&tilt unit), download images (to free memory storage) and recharge battery (the robot stays still while solar panels recharge the battery). The sequence of actions to achieve a goal is: go to the target, change the camera orientation, take a picture.

IxTeT-eXeC is interfaced with the procedural system OpenPRS which simulates the robot state evolution. Figure 2 describes an example of IxTeT-eXeC reactivity to a scenario with multiple failures. The initial plan contains 5 goals ($g_1$,...,$g_5$). The third goal has a strict deadline and a higher priority. Since storage capacity is limited to 3 images, the plan contains a download action after $g_3$. The battery initial level is sufficient to complete the plan. The following events occur:

— ($e_1$) **action failure** - The first take picture fails, plan repair

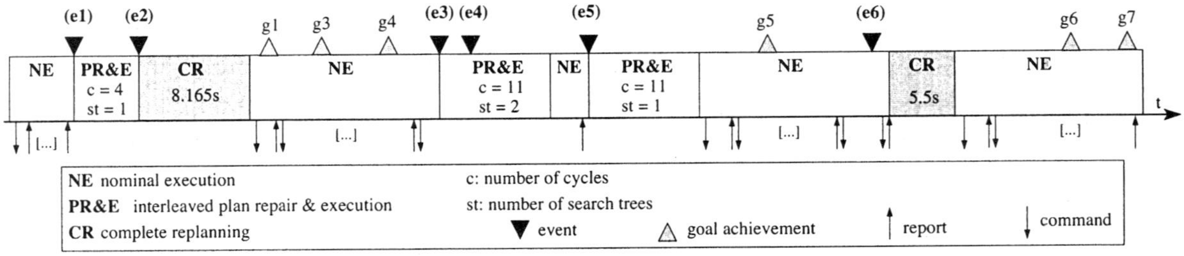


Figure 2: Example of scenario and reactions.

begins.
— ($e_2$) **timeout** - Due to $g_3$ deadline, the next executable time-point times out. After a complete replanning, $g_2$ has been removed. Further plan execution achieves $g_1$, $g_3$ and $g_4$.
— ($e_3$) **new goal** - During the download action, a new flexible goal $g_6$ is received. Plan repair begins.
— ($e_4$) **new goal** - A new goal $g_7$ is received 3s later. The repaired plan finally contains three goals not yet achieved.
— ($e_5$) **sub-production** - The download action has produced less than expected, the new level allows to take only two images. Plan repair leads to the insertion of a download action before the last take picture action.
— ($e_6$) **capacity alteration** During a move action, a sudden drop in battery level forbids the plan completion without recharging. Even if the current action completion is not directly threatened by the drop, it takes part in the future resource contention. Thus execution is aborted and a complete replanning leads to the insertion of an immediate recharge action. The plan can then be successfully completed. Note that the battery and memory storage levels are regularly adjusted. This example has been run on a Pentium IV, with $ts = 1.3s$ and $\mu = 61\%$. The average cycle duration during nominal execution is 0.22s.

## Conclusion and prospectives

We have presented the IXTET-EXEC system which combines a temporal lifted POCL planner with a temporal executive to integrate deliberative planning, execution monitoring and replanning while respecting real-time constraints. This approach cannot account for all the possible execution failures in all their generality, nevertheless, in many situations where some temporal and resource flexibility has been left, one can expect the presented repair techniques to greatly improve the overall performance of the system by:
— reducing the number of complete replannings,
— improving the system reactivity to unexpected events,
— taking into account new goals on the fly,
— managing the resources capacity changes,
— managing the uncertainty in the model description (actions duration, consumption/production).

Still, IXTET-EXEC effectiveness can be increased by improving replanning strategies (rejected goals selection, state update requests) and handling temporal non controllability earlier in the planning process and propagation algorithms (which may currently squeeze contingent durations). We plan to use the STNU framework and adapt the polynomial Dynamic Controllability Checking algorithms proposed in (Morris, Muscettola, & Vidal 2001). The current results are very encouraging and, providing we use proper heuristics for the planning process, we envision using this approach for more complex domains. More results are available in (Lemai 2004).

## References


Alami, R.; Chatila, R.; Fleury, S.; Ghallab, M.; and Ingrand, F. 1998. An architecture for autonomy. *IJRR*.

Ambros-Ingerson, J., and Steel, S. 1988. Integrating planning, execution and monitoring. In *National Conference on Artificial Intelligence*.

Chien, S.; Knight, R.; Stechert, A.; Sherwood, R.; and Rabideau, G. 2000. Using iterative repair to improve the responsiveness of planning and scheduling. In *National Conference on Artificial Intelligence*.

Dechter, R.; Meiri, I.; and Pearl, J. 1989. Temporal constraint networks. In *KR*.

Despouys, O., and Ingrand, F. 1999. Propice-plan: Toward a unified framework for planning and execution. In *ECP*.

Finzi, A.; Ingrand, F.; and Muscettola, N. 2004. Robot action planning and execution control. In *International Workshop on Planning and Scheduling for Space*.

Garcia, F., and Laborie, P. 1995. Hierarchisation of the search space in temporal planning. In *European Workshop on Planning*.

Haigh, K. Z., and Veloso, M. M. 1998. Planning, execution and learning in a robotic agent. In *AIPS*.

Ingrand, F.; Chatila, R.; Alami, R.; and Robert, F. 1996. PRS: A high level supervision and control language for autonomous mobile robots. In *International Conference on Robotics and Automation*.

Knoblock, C. 1994. Automatically generating abstractions for planning. *Artificial Intelligence* 68.

Laborie, P., and Ghallab, M. 1995. Planning with sharable resource constraints. In *IJCAI*.

Lemai, S. 2004. IXTET-EXEC: planning, plan repair and execution control with time and resource management. *PhD Thesis, INPT, LAAS-CNRS*.

Levinson, R. 1995. A general programming language for unified planning and control. *Artificial Intelligence* 76.

Morris, P. H.; Muscettola, N.; and Vidal, T. 2001. Dynamic control of plans with temporal uncertainty. In *IJCAI*.

Muscettola, N.; Nayak, P. P.; Pell, B.; and Williams, B. 1998. Remote agent : To boldly go where no ai system has gone before. *Artificial Intelligence* 103.

Myers, K. L. 1999. CPEF: Continuous planning and execution framework. *AI Magazine* 20(4):63–69.

Simmons, R., and Apfelbaum, D. 1998. A task description language for robot control. In *Conference on Intelligent Robotics and Systems*.

Trinquart, R., and Ghallab, M. 2001. An extended functional representation in temporal planning : towards continuous change. In *ECP*.

# Reinforcement Learning for a CPG-driven Biped Robot

**Takeshi Mori[1], Yutaka Nakamura[3,1], Masa-aki Sato[2,3], Shin Ishii[1,3]**
[1]Nara Institute of Science and Technology
Takayama 8916-5, Ikoma, Nara 630-0192
{tak-mori, yutak-na, ishii}@is.naist.jp
[2]ATR Computational Neuroscience Laboratories
Hikaridai 2-2-2, Seika, Soraku, Kyoto 619-0288
masa-aki@atr.jp
[3]CREST, JST

**Abstract**

Animal's rhythmic movements such as locomotion are considered to be controlled by neural circuits called central pattern generators (CPGs). This article presents a reinforcement learning (RL) method for a CPG controller, which is inspired by the control mechanism of animals. Because the CPG controller is an instance of recurrent neural networks, a naive application of RL involves difficulties. In addition, since state and action spaces of controlled systems are very large in real problems such as robot control, the learning of the value function is also difficult. In this study, we propose a learning scheme for a CPG controller called a CPG-actor-critic model, whose learning algorithm is based on a policy gradient method. We apply our RL method to autonomous acquisition of biped locomotion by a biped robot simulator. Computer simulations show our method is able to train a CPG controller such that the learning process is stable.

## Introduction

There have been many studies of locomotion robots (Hirai *et al.* 1998) (Buehler *et al.* 1998), but few of them achieved dynamic walking on irregular terrain. Although these studies employed precise models of environments, it is necessary for robots to be adapted to unknown environments when applied to real world problems (Morimoto & Doya 2001).

On the other hand, animal's movement show rapid adaptability to environmental changes and robustness to disturbances. Such a mechanism has been studied both in biological science and in engineering. Existing neurobiological studies have revealed that rhythmic motor patterns are controlled by neural oscillators referred as central pattern generators (CPGs) (Grillner *et al.* 1991), and this CPG mechanism is good for both adaptability and stability of animals.

Recently, there are many studies on locomotion or swimming robots controlled by CPG controllers, motivated by the animal's locomotion mechanism (human (Taga, Yamaguchi, & Shimizu 1991), mammal (Fukuoka, Kimura, & Cohen 2003), hexapod (Barnes 1998), salamander (Ijspeert 2001), or lamprey (Ekeberg 1993)). In (Fukuoka, Kimura, & Cohen 2003), robots realized flexible and robust locomotion even in unknown environments.

A CPG controller is composed of a kind of recurrent neural network (RNN), called the neural oscillator network. This controller receives a sensory feedback signal from a physical system (controlled system) and outputs a control torque to a physical system. Although there are connection weight parameters in the neural oscillator network, there is no design principle to determine their values. This problem can be regarded as the exploration of the optimal solution over the space of weight parameters, hence various learning methods will be helpful for the exploration. Actually, there exist studies in which genetic algorithm (GA) is employed to determine the weight values (Ogihara & Yamazaki 2001) (Ijspeert 2001). However, GA is not a learning scheme by individual robots but a scheme over generations of robot ensembles. Then, we propose in this article a reinforcement learning (RL) method to determine autonomously the weight values. In contrast to GA, RL is the learning framework based on individual trial and error, and has some analogy to the developmental process of animal's motor controls. As an example, an RL for a biped robot is analogous to a baby's acquisition of biped locomotion along its growth. The relationship of RL with the brain's motor learning has also been suggested (Fiorillo, Tobler, & Schultz 2003).

RL methods have been successfully applied to various Markov decision processes (MDPs) (Sutton & Barto 1998). They can be straightforwardly applied to controllers without internal states, a controller composed by a feedforward neural network for example. Because the 'policy' in such a case can be defined by a mapping from a state of the target system to a control signal. However, such a straightforward approach needs to acquire a high-dimensional policy when applied to real world problems like the control problem for a biped robot. The approximation problem for a policy or a value function then becomes high-dimensional. This makes the exploration problem of the optimal policy very difficult. Furthermore, the training of nonlinear function approximators in a high-dimensional space is also difficult, which will be problematic in the value learning. On the other hand, a CPG controller is beneficial for the robustness of a biped robot to various environmental changes, because the robot can be entrained to the rhythm inherent in the CPG. In addition, a control signal produced by a CPG controller is effectively restricted within the space determined by the inherent rhythmic patterns of the CPG controller. Then, the searching for the optimal policy becomes much easier than that without any restriction. The output patterns of a CPG controller can be changed by mainly tuning the connection weights in the neural oscillator network. The number of these parameters is often much smaller than that of the high-dimensional policy for the original control problem.

When we consider a naive application of RL to a CPG controller, however, the policy becomes unstationary, because a control signal depends not only on a state of the target system but also on an internal state of neurons constituting the CPG controller. Furthermore, the large amount of computation is usually required to train an RNN. In order to overcome these problems, we propose a new RL method called the CPG-actor-critic model. In this model, the variable part in the CPG controller is represented as a simple feedforward neural network, then it is not required to train the RNN as itself.

An RL is primarily formulated as to find the policy that minimizes the cost on an Markov decision process (MDP) (Sutton & Barto 1998). In conventional value-based RL methods, such as the $Q$ learning, the value function which represents cumulative cost toward the future for a state (and an action) is obtained. Then the policy is updated to minimize the value function over every state. In order to find the optimal policy, it is necessary to know the value function. In many real problems such as robot control, the computation of the correct value function or its function approximation (Sato & Ishii 1999) is difficult, analytically or numerically, because of the enormous size of the state and action spaces. Furthermore, it has been supposed that the convergence of these value-based RL methods is not guaranteed when employing function approximators, due to the effect of approximation errors (Bertsekas & Tsitsiklis 1996).

In our method, the learning scheme is based on a policy gradient method (Konda 2002). Policy gradient RL methods are not primarily based on value functions. In these methods, the policy parameter is updated based on the gradient of average cost with respect to the policy parameter, and it is possible to learn without value functions (Williams 1992). However, learning methods without value function take much computation time, then they had been less attractive. Recently, a new actor-critic method, i.e., a policy gradient method incorporating a value function, has been proposed, and its convergence was proved (Konda 2002). In this actor-critic method, a lower-dimensional projection of the value function is approximated instead of the true value function, because the policy gradient depends only on the projection. The approximation of the projection is often easier than that of the original one.

The training of our CPG-actor-critic model is based on this actor-critic method. Weights of connections within the CPG controller are optimized so as to control the biped robot simulator proposed by (Taga, Yamaguchi, & Shimizu 1991). Simulation results show that stable locomotion can be achieved by the CPG controller trained by our RL approach.

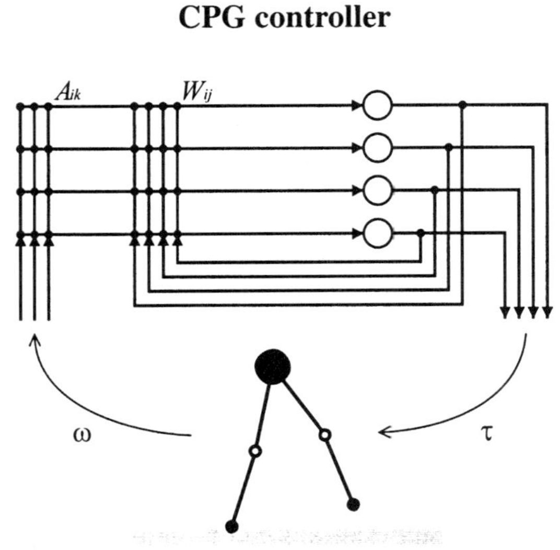


Figure 1: Control scheme using a CPG controller

The motion of a physical system like a biped robot is expressed as

$$\dot{\boldsymbol{x}} = F(\boldsymbol{x}, \boldsymbol{\tau}), \tag{1}$$

where $\boldsymbol{x}$ and $\dot{\boldsymbol{x}}$ denote the physical state and its time derivative, respectively. $\boldsymbol{\tau}$ denotes the control signal (torque) from the controller. $F(\boldsymbol{x}, \boldsymbol{\tau})$ represents the vector field of the dynamics.

The physical system is controlled by a CPG controller as depicted in Fig.1. The CPG controller is implemented as a neural oscillator network, and outputs a control signal $\boldsymbol{\tau}$ corresponding to neurons' states in the network. The CPG controller receives a sensory feedback signal $\boldsymbol{\omega}$ from the physical system.

The neural oscillator network is an instance of RNNs, and the dynamics of the $i$-th neuron is given by

$$\zeta_i \dot{\nu}_i = -\nu_i + I_i, \; y_i = G_i(\nu_i), \tag{2}$$

where $\nu_i, y_i, I_i$ and $\zeta_i$ denote the state, output, input, and time constant, respectively, of the $i$-th neuron. Output $y_i$ is calculated from state $\nu_i$ through the transfer function $G_i$. Actual function form for $G_i$ is described later.

Input $I_i$ is given by

$$I_i = \sum_j W_{ij} y_j + I_i^{ext} + B_i, \tag{3}$$

where the first term is the feedback input from the other neurons, the second term is the external input denoting the sensory feedback signal, and the third term is a bias. $W_{ij}$ represents the connection weight from the $j$-th neuron to the $i$-th neuron. The external input $I_i^{ext}$ is defined by

$$I_i^{ext} = \sum_k A_{ik} \omega_k, \tag{4}$$

namely, a sum of the sensory feedback signal $\boldsymbol{\omega}$ weighted by connection weight $\boldsymbol{A}_i$.

The control signal to the physical system, $\boldsymbol{\tau}$, is given by a weighted sum of the outputs of the CPG neurons:

$$\tau_n = \sum_i T_{ni} y_i, \tag{5}$$

where $T_{ni}$ represents the weight.

## CPG-actor-critic model

An actor-critic method is one of the popular RL methods (Sutton & Barto 1998). In this method, the actor is a controller that transforms an observation of the target system into a control signal. The critic predicts the cumulative or average cost toward the future when the current actor is used as a controller. The actor's parameter is updated so that the cost predicted by the critic becomes small.

When we try to apply the actor-critic method to the CPG controller, several difficulties arise. A naive application of the actor-critic method (Fig.2(a)) is not suited for training RNNs, because the critic's and actor's learning is usually based on temporally instantaneous errors called temporal difference (TD) errors. Training of an RNN needs the "error-back-propagation through time" (Sato 1990), which is not suited for on-line learning and needs heavy computation. Moreover, because a control signal $\boldsymbol{\tau}$ is generated by the CPG controller which has the internal dynamics given by equation (2), the total system coupled with the CPG controller has an dynamics:

$$(\dot{\boldsymbol{x}}, \dot{\boldsymbol{\nu}}) = F_{CPG-coupled-system}(\boldsymbol{x}, \boldsymbol{\nu}, \boldsymbol{\tau}, \boldsymbol{I}). \tag{6}$$

This equation shows the existence of a hidden state variable $\boldsymbol{\nu}$. This makes the policy, which is a function from a state to an action, not unique for any state; namely, the policy becomes unstationary. Since the policy gradient method we employ is formulated under the condition that the policy is stationary, its application to the learning task of an unstationary policy suffers from a remained variance. To formulate the learning scheme of the CPG controller as an MDP, it is profitable that the physical system and the neural oscillator network are regarded as a unified system, a CPG-coupled system (Fig.2(b)).

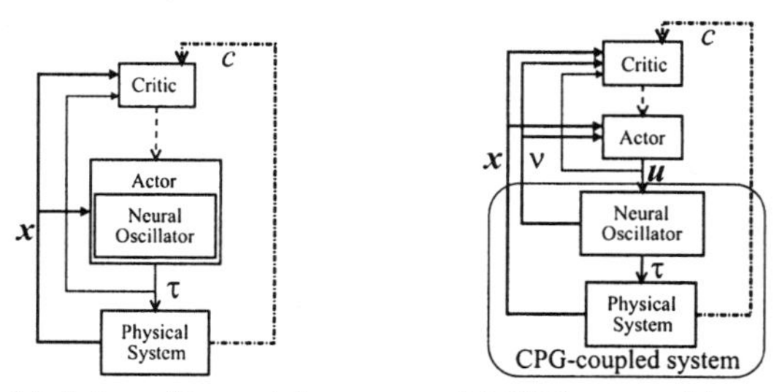


(a) Actor-critic model (b) CPG-actor-critic model

Figure 2: CPG-actor-critic model

In our method, the CPG controller is divided into two modules: the basic CPG and the actor, as depicted in Fig.3. The basic CPG is a neural oscillator network whose connection weight is $\boldsymbol{W}^{fix}$. The actor receives an input signal, which is a pair of an output of the basic CPG and a sensory

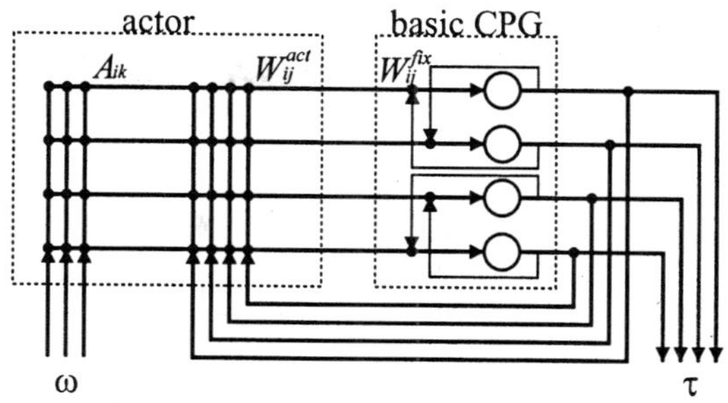


Figure 3: Actor and basic CPG

feedback signal, and outputs a control signal called an indirect control signal to the basic CPG. Corresponding to this separation, the input to the CPG neuron, $I_i$ (equation (3)), is divided into two parts:

$$I_i = I_i^{fix} + u_i \tag{7}$$

$$I_i^{fix} = \sum_j W_{ij}^{fix} y_j + B_i \tag{8}$$

$$u_i = \sum_j W_{ij}^{act} y_j + \sum_k A_{ik}\omega_k, \tag{9}$$

where $I_i^{fix}$ represents a feedback input from other neurons through the fixed mutual connection $\boldsymbol{W}^{fix}$ and the fixed bias input $\boldsymbol{B}$.

$\boldsymbol{u}$ is an indirect control signal and the output of the actor. The actor is a linear controller, and receives an output $\boldsymbol{y}$ of the basic CPG and a sensory feedback signal $\boldsymbol{\omega}$. The weight parameters $W_{ij}^{act}$ and $A_{ik}$ are adjustable, and are trained by RL. The control torque to the physical system is calculated by equation (5), and the weight parameter $\boldsymbol{T}$ is fixed. We call the architecture above the CPG-actor-critic model.

The CPG-actor-critic model has two aspects. From the control viewpoint, the CPG controller consists of the basic CPG and the actor (Fig.3), which cooperatively controls the physical system. From the RL viewpoint, the actor outputs an indirect control signal $\boldsymbol{u}$ to a CPG-coupled system which consists of the basic CPG and the physical system (Fig.2(b)). In the latter view, the actor is a linear controller without any mutual feedback connections, hence there is no need to train the RNN as itself. Another merit exists in this architecture, namely, the actor is trained as to modify the entrainment between the physical system and the basic CPG.

The critic observes the CPG-coupled system state, i.e., a basic CPG state $\boldsymbol{\nu}$ and a physical system state $\boldsymbol{x}$, and predicts the cumulative or average cost toward the future.

## Learning Algorithm

The CPG-actor-critic model is trained according to the actor-critic method based on the policy gradient method (Konda 2002). In the conventional value-based actor-critic method, the critic approximates the value function on the state and action spaces, and the actor parameter is improved to minimize the cumulative cost in each state according to the evaluation by the critic. In order to acquire the optimal actor parameter, therefore, the critic is required to approximate the value function with a high accuracy. In this case, the computation amount necessary for training the critic will increase as the state and action spaces become large, and inaccurate critic badly affects the actor's learning and makes the learning process unstable. In the policy gradient method, on the other hand, the actor is trained based on the gradient (policy gradient) of the average cost with respect to the policy parameter under a stationary condition, and the critic is used for efficiently estimating the gradient through the approximation of the value function. Roughly speaking, the policy is updated as follows; when the state transition from $s$ to $s'$ occurs by an action $u$, the action $u$ is positively (or negatively) reinforced, if the evaluation of this transition is larger (or smaller) than the expected one. The policy gradient indicates the direction of the policy parameter to realize such a reinforcement manipulation of actions.

At time $t$, the actor receives a basic CPG's output $\boldsymbol{y}_t$ and a sensory feedback signal $\boldsymbol{\omega}_t$ which is a transformation of $\boldsymbol{x}_t$, and outputs an indirect control signal $\boldsymbol{u}_t$ calculated by equation (9). The CPG-coupled system receives the actor output $\boldsymbol{u}_t$, and changes its state $(\boldsymbol{\nu}_t, \boldsymbol{x}_t)$ to $(\boldsymbol{\nu}_{t+1}, \boldsymbol{x}_{t+1})$ according to the dynamics of the basic CPG and the physical system, (1)-(8). After that, it is assumed that the critic receives an immediate cost $c(\boldsymbol{\nu}_t, \boldsymbol{x}_t, \boldsymbol{u}_t)$.

Subsequently, a state of the CPG-coupled system, $(\boldsymbol{x}, \boldsymbol{\nu})$, is simply denoted by $\boldsymbol{s}$. We formulate an MDP on the state space $\mathbb{S}$ and action space $\mathbb{U}$ of the CPG-coupled system, assuming the cost function is given by a mapping $c : \mathbb{S} \times \mathbb{U} \to \mathbb{R}$. $p(\boldsymbol{s}'|\boldsymbol{s}, \boldsymbol{u})$ represents the probability that the system changes its current state $\boldsymbol{s} \in \mathbb{S}$ to a next state $\boldsymbol{s}' \in \mathbb{S}$ when an action $\boldsymbol{u} \in \mathbb{U}$ is given.

A policy $\pi_{\boldsymbol{\theta}}(\boldsymbol{u}|\boldsymbol{s})$ defines the probability of an action $\boldsymbol{u}$ at a state $s$, where $\boldsymbol{\theta} \equiv \{\theta_i | i = 1, \cdots, M\}$ is a parameter vector. It is assumed that a stationary distribution $\eta_{\boldsymbol{\theta}}(\boldsymbol{s}, \boldsymbol{u})$ with respect to the state-action pair $(\boldsymbol{s}, \boldsymbol{u})$ exists under a fixed policy $\pi_{\boldsymbol{\theta}}$. Under these conditions, the objective of the MDP here is to obtain the optimal parameter $\boldsymbol{\theta}^{opt}$ that minimizes the average cost:

$$\bar{\alpha}(\boldsymbol{\theta}) = \int_{\boldsymbol{s} \in \mathbb{S}, \boldsymbol{u} \in \mathbb{U}} dsdu \; c(\boldsymbol{s}, \boldsymbol{u}) \eta_{\boldsymbol{\theta}}(\boldsymbol{s}, \boldsymbol{u}). \tag{10}$$

The gradient of the average cost $\bar{\alpha}(\boldsymbol{\theta})$ with respect to the parameter $\theta_i$ is given (Konda 2002) (Sutton *et al.* 2000) (Marbach & Tsitsiklis 2001) by

$$\frac{\partial}{\partial \theta_i} \bar{\alpha}(\boldsymbol{\theta}) = \int_{\boldsymbol{s} \in \mathbb{S}, \boldsymbol{u} \in \mathbb{U}} dsdu \; \eta_{\boldsymbol{\theta}}(\boldsymbol{s}, \boldsymbol{u}) Q_{\boldsymbol{\theta}}(\boldsymbol{s}, \boldsymbol{u}) \psi^i_{\boldsymbol{\theta}}(\boldsymbol{s}, \boldsymbol{u}), \tag{11}$$

where

$$\psi^i_{\boldsymbol{\theta}}(\boldsymbol{s}, \boldsymbol{u}) \equiv \frac{\partial}{\partial \theta_i} \ln \pi_{\boldsymbol{\theta}}(\boldsymbol{u}|\boldsymbol{s}). \tag{12}$$

Equation (11) is called the policy gradient, and suggests that the gradient of the objective function with respect to the policy parameter $\theta_i$ is calculated by the expectation of inner product between the $Q$ function and $\psi^i_{\boldsymbol{\theta}}(\boldsymbol{s}, \boldsymbol{u})$ over the stationary distribution. Then, it is not necessary to calculate the true $Q$ function, but its projection to the space spanned by $\{\psi^i_{\boldsymbol{\theta}}(s, u) | i = 1, \cdots, M\}$ is sufficient. Although the true $Q$ function may be a complex and high-dimensional mapping of $\mathbb{S} \times \mathbb{U} \to R$, the number of policy parameters is often smaller than the dimensionality of $\mathbb{S} \times \mathbb{U} \to R$, thus the approximation of the $Q$ function becomes much easier (Konda 2002).

In this method, the critic approximates the projected $Q$ function. A linear parametric model is employed as a function approximator:

$$Q^{\boldsymbol{r}}_{\boldsymbol{\theta}}(\boldsymbol{s}, \boldsymbol{u}) = \sum_{i=1}^{M} r_i \psi^i_{\boldsymbol{\theta}}(\boldsymbol{s}, \boldsymbol{u}), \tag{13}$$

where $\boldsymbol{r} \equiv \{r_i | i = 1, \cdots, M\}$ is a parameter vector of the critic. The critic is trained based on stochastic approximation with an eligibility trace, i.e., a TD($\lambda$) learning:

$$r_i \leftarrow r_i + \gamma \delta Z_i, \quad i = 1, \cdots, M. \tag{14}$$

Here $\delta$ is a TD-error:

$$\begin{aligned} \delta &= c(\boldsymbol{s}_{t+1}, \boldsymbol{u}_{t+1}) + Q^{\boldsymbol{r}_{t+1}}_{\boldsymbol{\theta}_{t+1}}(\boldsymbol{s}_{t+1}, \boldsymbol{u}_{t+1}) \\ &\quad - Q^{\boldsymbol{r}_t}_{\boldsymbol{\theta}_t}(\boldsymbol{s}_t, \boldsymbol{u}_t) - \alpha, \end{aligned} \tag{15}$$

where $\boldsymbol{Z} \equiv \{Z_i | i = 1, \cdots, M\}$ is the eligibility trace and performs responsibility assignment of the TD-error (Bradtke & Barto 1996), and $\alpha$ is the estimation of average cost.

Concurrently to this critic learning, actor parameter $\boldsymbol{\theta}$ is updated to minimize the objective function $\bar{\alpha}(\boldsymbol{\theta})$ according to the policy gradient. From equations (11) and (13), the following equation is derived:

$$\frac{\partial}{\partial \theta_i} \bar{\alpha}(\boldsymbol{\theta}) = \int_{\boldsymbol{s} \in \mathbb{S}, \boldsymbol{u} \in \mathbb{U}} dsdu \; \eta_{\boldsymbol{\theta}}(\boldsymbol{s}, \boldsymbol{u}) Q^{\boldsymbol{r}}_{\boldsymbol{\theta}}(\boldsymbol{s}, \boldsymbol{u}) \psi^i_{\boldsymbol{\theta}}(\boldsymbol{s}, \boldsymbol{u}). \tag{16}$$

$Q^{\boldsymbol{r}}_{\boldsymbol{\theta}}$ is calculated by the current critic, and the actor is trained by the gradient method using equation (16). The expectation with respect to $\eta_{\boldsymbol{\theta}}(\boldsymbol{s}, \boldsymbol{u})$ in equation (16) is approximated by using the empirical distribution $\{\boldsymbol{s}_t, \boldsymbol{u}_t\}, t = 1, 2, \cdots$. Concretely, the policy parameter $\theta_i$ is updated by

$$\theta_i \leftarrow \theta_i - \beta Q^{\boldsymbol{r}}_{\boldsymbol{\theta}}(\boldsymbol{s}, \boldsymbol{u}) \psi^i_{\boldsymbol{\theta}}(\boldsymbol{s}, \boldsymbol{u}), \tag{17}$$

where $\beta$ is the learning rate. The parameter update in the direction of the gradient of the average cost function, equation (16), is performed by repeating the individual update above. Namely, equation (17) is the stochastic gradient method for equation (16).

According to this method, the critic parameter may not converge, while the actor parameter converges because the actor's training is based on the long run average of the critic's output (Konda 2002). The behavior of the critic parameter will become more stable if the actor parameter is fixed for a certain period. Therefore, the actor's (critic's) parameter is fixed while the critic's (actor's) parameter is updated during a single learning episode in the experiments described below.

## Experiment

We apply our CPG-actor-critic model to a biped robot simulator (Taga, Yamaguchi, & Shimizu 1991). The objective of the simulation is to obtain a CPG controller that makes the robot simulator produce stable locomotion.

The biped robot is constructed by five links connected to each other, as depicted in Fig.4(a). The motions of these links are restricted in a sagittal plane. Link-1 is a point mass and representative of the upper body. Each leg consists of thigh (link-2,3) and shank (link-4,5), and has three joints, i.e., hip, knee and ankle. The length of thigh or shank is 0.5m or 0.6m, respectively. The robot is controlled by the torque $\tau_1 \cdots \tau_6$, each of which is applied to a single joint. When a shank is off the ground, the torque at the ankle joint is not generated. The action from the ground is modeled as a spring-damper model, and the reaction force occurs according to the displacement from the ground and the ankle velocity. (Taga, Yamaguchi, & Shimizu 1991).

A state of the biped robot is described by

$$\boldsymbol{x} = (x_1, h_1, a_2, a_3, a_4, a_5, \dot{x}_1, \dot{h}_1, \dot{a}_2, \dot{a}_3, \dot{a}_4, \dot{a}_5),$$

where $x_1$ and $h_1$ denote the horizontal and vertical coordinates of link-1, respectively, and $a_i$ represents the angle of link-$i$ from the vertical axis.

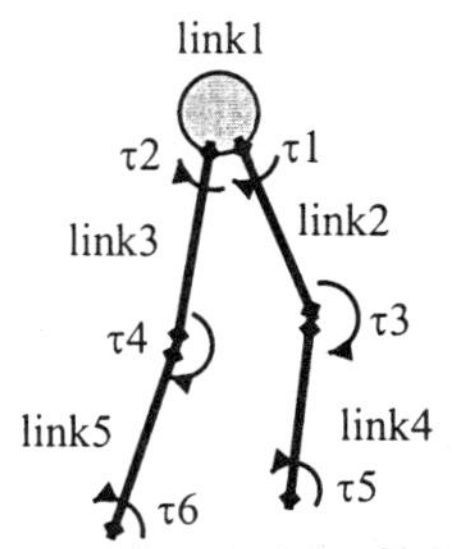

(a) Biped robot simulator

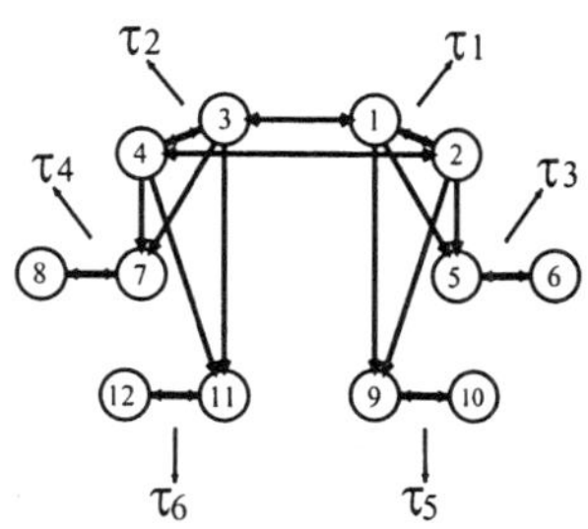

(b) Neural oscillator network

Figure 4: Structure of CPG-driven biped robot

The structure of the neural oscillator network, which constitutes the CPG controller, is also adopted from (Taga, Yamaguchi, & Shimizu 1991), as depicted in Fig.4(b). There are 24 neurons; the $i$-th and the $(i + 12)$-th neurons are called a primary neuron and a supplementary neuron, respectively. Each supplementary neuron is solely connected to its primary neuron by excitation-inhibition mutual connections. An output of the $i$-th primary neuron is given by $G_i(\nu_i) = \max(0, y_i)$, and an output of the $(i + 12)$-th supplementary neuron is given by the identical function. The weight of the mutual connection $\boldsymbol{W}^{fix}$ (equation (8)) is also adopted from (Taga, Yamaguchi, & Shimizu 1991). Without any sensory feedback signal, each neuron in the basic CPG outputs rhythmic signals autonomously. A combination of two primary neurons and two supplementary neurons $(2i-1, 2i, 2i+11, 2i+12, i = 1, \cdots, 6)$ behaves as a neural oscillator, and each neural oscillator is responsible for controlling the corresponding joint.

Torque $\tau_i$, which is applied to the $i$-th joint is calculated from the output of the CPG neurons:

$$\begin{aligned}\tau_i &= -T_i^F y_{2i-1} + T_i^E y_{2i} \ \ (i = 1, \cdots, 4)\\ \tau_i &= (-T_i^F y_{2i-1} + T_i^E y_{2i})\Xi_{i-1} \ \ (i = 5, 6),\end{aligned} \quad (18)$$

where $\Xi_{i-1}$ represents an indicator function of shank link-$i$ ($i$=4,5), i.e., $\Xi_i = 1$(or 0) when the link-$i$ touches (or, is off) the ground. $\tau_{1,2}, \tau_{3,4}$ and $\tau_{5,6}$ represent the torques applied to hip, knee and ankle, respectively. $T_i^F$ and $T_i^E$ represent weights of the flexor and extensor, respectively, and their values are fixed. A sensory feedback signal from the biped robot is $\boldsymbol{\omega} = \{a_2, a_3, a_4\Xi_4, a_5, \Xi_5, \Xi_4, \Xi_5, \dot{a}_4\Xi_4, \dot{a}_5\Xi_5\}$.

## Condition

The dynamics of the CPG-coupled system is calculated by the Runge-Kutta integration with time interval 0.0001 sec. The learning system observes the system state and outputs a control signal every 0.01 sec. The observation of each angular velocity is smoothed over the 0.01 sec. interval.

It is not desirable to make all parameters of the CPG controller variable, because the CPG controller uses the property that the motion of the physical system is entrained into the inherent rhythm of the CPG controller. In this experiment, we assume for simplicity that all mutual connection weights in the neural oscillator network are fixed, i.e., $W_{ij}^{act} \equiv 0$. We also assume that connection patterns from the sensory feedback signal to the CPG neurons have specific forms, as in (Taga, Yamaguchi, & Shimizu 1991):

$$\begin{aligned}I_1^{ext} &= \theta_1\omega_1 - \theta_2\omega_2 + \theta_3\omega_3 + \theta_4\omega_6,\\ I_3^{ext} &= \theta_1\omega_2 - \theta_2\omega_1 + \theta_3\omega_4 + \theta_4\omega_5,\\ I_5^{ext} &= \theta_5\omega_4, \ I_7^{ext} = \theta_5\omega_3,\\ I_9^{ext} &= -\theta_6\omega_3 - \theta_7\omega_4 - \theta_8\omega_7,\\ I_{11}^{ext} &= -\theta_6\omega_4 - \theta_7\omega_3 - \theta_8\omega_8,\\ I_{2i}^{ext} &= -I_{2i-1}^{ext} \ \text{for } i = 1, \cdots, 6,\end{aligned} \quad (19)$$

where $\{\theta_i | i = 1, \cdots, 8\}$ are elements of the connection weight $\boldsymbol{A}$ (equation (9)). The other elements of $\boldsymbol{A}$ are fixed at zero. The policy, which outputs an indirect control signal probabilistically to the CPG neurons, is given by a Gaussian distribution:

$$\mathcal{N}(\boldsymbol{\mu}, \theta_9), \quad (20)$$

where $\mu_i = I_{2i-1}^{ext} (i = 1, \cdots, 6)$ and $\theta_9$ are the mean and variance of the distribution, respectively. Then, the policy parameter $\{\theta_i | i = 1, \cdots, 9\}$ is adjusted by our RL method.

We assume that an immediate cost $c(\boldsymbol{\nu}_t, \boldsymbol{x}_t, \boldsymbol{u}_t)$ is determined only by the robot state at the next time step, $\boldsymbol{x}_{t+1}$, and defined as $\tilde{c}_{t+1}$:

$$\begin{aligned}\tilde{c}(\boldsymbol{x}) &= 0.1c_h(\boldsymbol{x}) + c_h'(\boldsymbol{x}) + 0.0002c_s(\boldsymbol{x}) \quad (21)\\ c_h(\boldsymbol{x}) &= -(h_1 - 0.9 - \min(h_4, h_5))\\ c_s(\boldsymbol{x}) &= \begin{cases} -\dot{x}_1 & \text{if } |\dot{x}_1| < 1\\ -\dot{x}_1/|\dot{x}_1| & \text{otherwise}\end{cases}\\ c_h'(\boldsymbol{x}) &= \begin{cases} (0.9 + c_h)^2 & \text{if } 0.9 + c_h > 0\\ 0 & \text{otherwise}\end{cases},\end{aligned}$$

where $h_i (i = 4, 5)$ represents the height of link-$i$. $c_h(\boldsymbol{x})$ encourages the robot not to fall down, and $c_s(\boldsymbol{x})$ encourages the robot to proceed to the forward direction. $c_h'(\boldsymbol{x})$ incurs a large penalty when the robot falls down.

The maximum period in one learning episode was 5 sec. (500 time steps). If the robot tumbled before 5 sec., the learning episode was terminated at that time. At the beginning of each learning episode, the state of the robot was initialized as a motion-less posture such that the two legs slightly opened, the states of whole neurons were initialized as $\mathbf{0}$, and the angles of the legs were selected randomly within a small range. At the beginning of the whole learning procedure, the critic parameter $\boldsymbol{r}$ was initialized simply as $\mathbf{0}$.

## Result

### Learning from the random initial value of the actor parameter

First, we examined whether the actor parameter that generates stable walking can be acquired by our learning scheme from a random initial value of the actor parameter with which the robot hardly walks.

**Learning from the actor parameter which hardly generates a walk** At the beginning of the learning procedure, the actor parameter $\boldsymbol{\theta}$ was randomly initialized around $\mathbf{0}$.

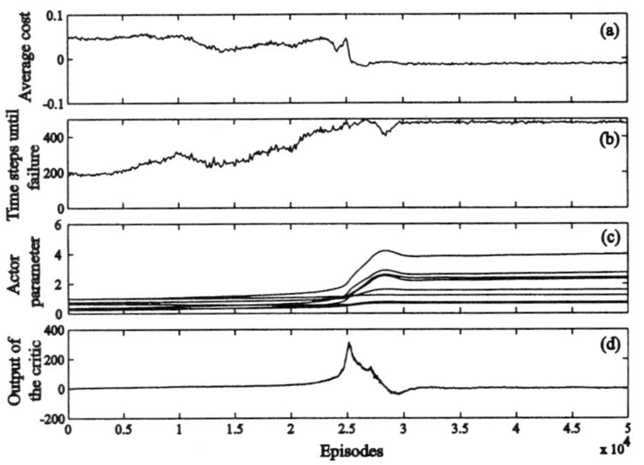


Figure 5: Learning curve

Fig.5 shows the learning curve until 50,000 learning episodes, where the horizontal axis denotes the number of learning episodes. Fig.5(a) shows the average cost in one time step. The average cost decreased almost monotonously, implying that the learning successfully proceeded. After about 25,000 learning episodes, a large drop off of the average cost was observed, suggesting a significant progress of the learning occurred. Fig.5(b) shows the number of time steps until failure, averaged over every 500 learning episodes. After about 30,000 learning episodes, a good CPG controller was acquired such that the robot seldom fell down. Fig.5(c) shows the actor parameter. After about 25,000 learning episodes, the parameter significantly changed, while after 30,000 learning episodes, it almost converged. Fig.5(d) shows the average output of the critic. Large values at around 25,000 learning episodes reflected the large drop off of the cost. When the critic's output was large, it caused large change of the actor parameter (equation (17)).

According to our cost design (equation (21)), a large penalty $c'_h$ is incurred when the robot falls down. Therefore, there is large difference in the cost per step between

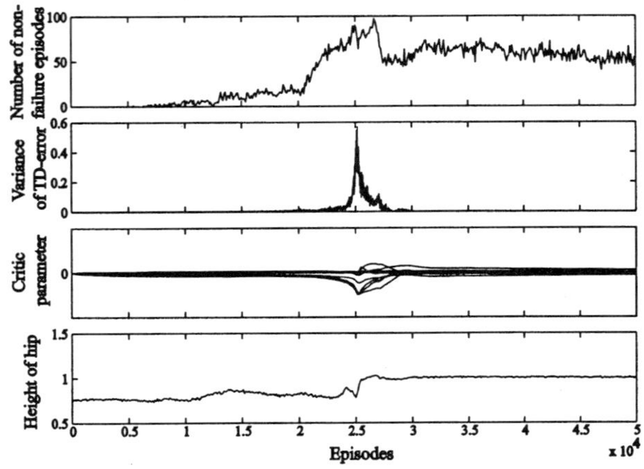


Figure 6: Analysis

learning episodes in which the robot falls down and does not fall down. According to the policy gradient method, the large difference between the actual and the expected value function causes the large gradient. Therefore, a large variance among episodes produces a large gradient which accelerates the learning. Fig.6 shows the detailed analysis of the learning curve in Fig.5. Fig.6(a) shows the number of learning episodes in which the robot does not tumble within every 100 episodes. The number of successful episodes increased after about 20,000 learning episodes. Concurrently to this increase, the variance of the TD-error became large (Fig.6(b)) and the critic's learning was accelerated (Fig.6(c)). Depending on this critic's learning, the actor learning is considered to also be accelerated (Fig.5(c)).

Fig.7(a) and Fig.7(b) show an example gait pattern before learning and that after learning, respectively. In order to evaluate the actor's performance, we repeated a test task in which the robot was initialized at a motion-less posture and was controlled until the robot tumbled or 1000 sec. elapsed. By using the CPG controller before learning, the robot walked for 1.9 sec. on average. By using the CPG controller after learning, on the other hand, the robot could walk for 30.9 sec. on average. The performance of the CPG controller was thus improved by our RL method. Among these 100 times tasks, however, stable walking for 1000 seconds was achieved only once, because the learning converged to a locally optimum solution.

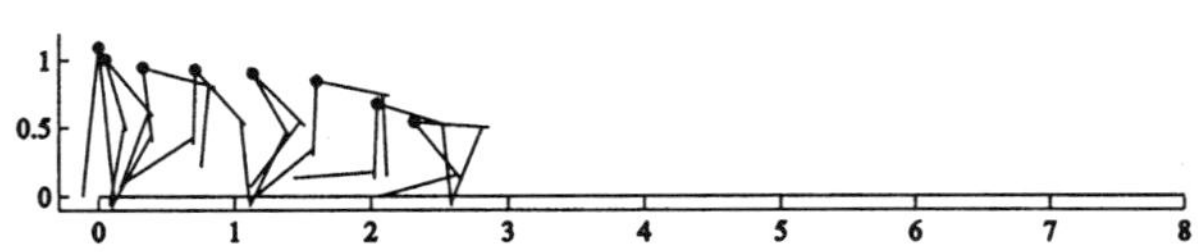

(a) Before learning

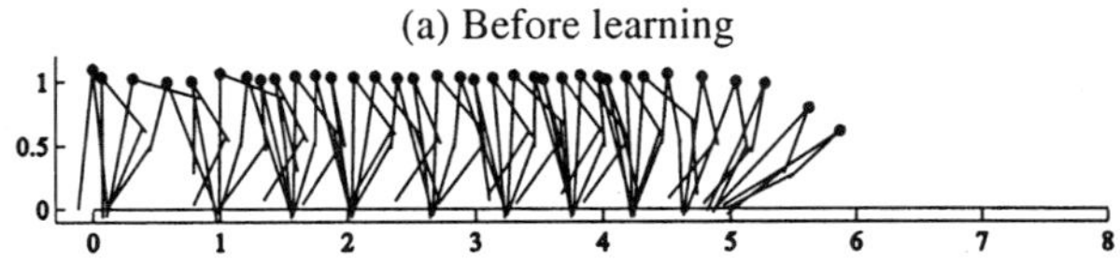

(b) After learning

Figure 7: Gait patterns

**Learning from the actor parameter acquired by the above learning** To escape from the local optimum, we then re-initialized the critic parameter, and trained the actor again. Fig.8 shows the learning curve until 150,000 learning episodes during this re-training. The vertical axis and the horizontal axis are the same as those in Fig.5. The average cost became temporally large after 25,000 learning episodes, but became eventually smaller than the initial value, as shown in Fig.8(a).

After this re-training, Fig.9 shows examples of gait patterns on a flat ground, an up-slope and a down-slope. Although the learning process proceeded on a flat ground, the robot was adapted flexibly to unknown environments, slopes. Before re-training, the number of successful test tasks in which the robot could walk stably for 1000 seconds was only one out of 100, while it became 84 after re-training. This result shows that a better CPG controller was acquired through this re-training process. The connection weights from the sensory feedback signal were $\boldsymbol{\theta}_{RL} = \{0.72, 0.73, 4.5, 1.3, 0.58, 3.7, 5.3, 2.3\}$, which were quite different from the hand-tuned parameter found in (Taga, Yamaguchi, & Shimizu 1991), $\boldsymbol{\theta}_{HT} = \{1.5, 1.0, 1.5, 1.5, 3.0, 1.5, 3.0, 1.5\}$.

The actor parameter converged to a local optimum in the previous experiment, and moreover there may be a lot of local optima or plateaus in the parameter space. By introducing perturbation to the value approximation due to the re-initialization of the critic parameter, the actor could find a better policy in the current experiment. Because the learning process is stable according to our learning scheme based on the policy gradient method, such a re-training is applicable in order to improve the policy.

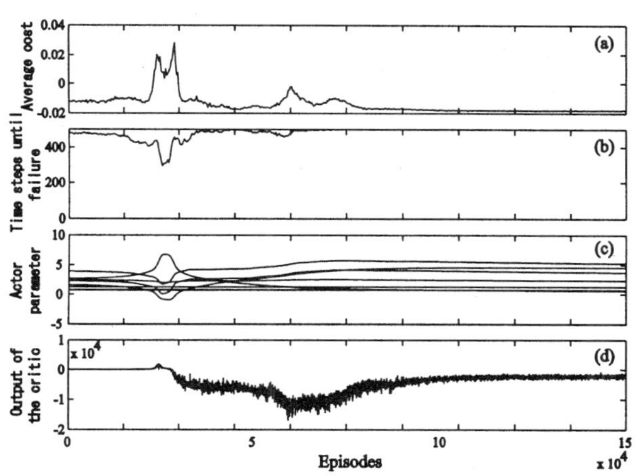


Figure 8: Re-training curve

## The comparison of RL and hand-tuned parameter

Next, we trained the CPG controller on a flat or a slope ground starting from the hand-tuned parameter $\boldsymbol{\theta}_{HT}$.

**Learning on a flat ground** After 50,000 learning episodes on a flat ground starting from the hand-tuned parameter $\boldsymbol{\theta}_{HT}$, the actor parameter was changed to $\boldsymbol{\theta}_{RL}^{flat} = \{1.46, 0.96, 1.39, 1.49, 2.73, 1.33, 2.72, 1.23\}$. In order to

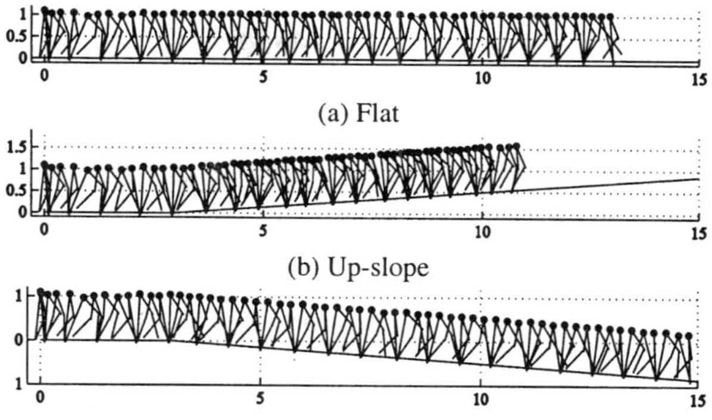

(a) Flat

(b) Up-slope

(c) Down-slope

Figure 9: Gait patterns after re-training

evaluate this parameter, we repeated a test task in which the robot was initialized to a motion-less posture and was controlled on a flat ground, and an up- or down-slope of 2.9 degrees until the robot tumbled or 20 sec. elapsed.

Table.1 shows the number of successful tasks in such 100 tasks controlled by $\boldsymbol{\theta}_{HT}$ and $\boldsymbol{\theta}_{RL}^{flat}$. They exhibited comparable performance because $\boldsymbol{\theta}_{HT}$ had already been a good controller, while $\boldsymbol{\theta}_{RL}^{flat}$ outperformed $\boldsymbol{\theta}_{HT}$ on up-slopes. $\boldsymbol{\theta}_{RL}^{flat}$ was robust to environmental disturbance such as up-slopes. Since the control signal is produced probabilistically (equation (20)) according to our RL scheme, the stochastic nature works similarly to the disturbance induced by the unknown environments. Then, it is considered that the robust policy against actual disturbance has been acquired.

Table 1: The performance comparison of $\boldsymbol{\theta}_{HT}$ and $\boldsymbol{\theta}_{RL}^{flat}$

| | $\boldsymbol{\theta}_{HT}$ | $\boldsymbol{\theta}_{RL}^{flat}$ |
|---|---|---|
| Flat | 94 | 96 |
| Up-slope | 17 | 44 |
| Down-slope | 95 | 95 |

**Learning on a slope** To evaluate the effect of environmental change in learning, the terrain was prepared as an up-slope of 5.7 degrees. After learning of 15,000 learning episodes, the actor parameter became $\boldsymbol{\theta}_{RL}^{slope} = \{1.51, 1.00, 2.55, 1.51, 1.66, 1.39, 2.87, 1.47\}$. In order to evaluate this parameter, we repeated a test task in which the robot was initialized to a motion-less posture and was controlled on a flat ground, and an up- or down-slope of 5.7 degrees until the robot tumbled or 20 sec elapsed (Table.2).

Table 2: The performance comparison of $\boldsymbol{\theta}_{HT}$ and $\boldsymbol{\theta}_{RL}^{slope}$

| | $\boldsymbol{\theta}_{HT}$ | $\boldsymbol{\theta}_{RL}^{slope}$ |
|---|---|---|
| Flat | 96 | 96 |
| Up-slope | 13 | 41 |
| Down-slope | 41 | 98 |

Although the performance on a flat ground did not show

any difference, the performance on slopes was much improved by $\theta_{RL}^{slope}$ on $\theta_{HT}$. The policy parameter which is suitable for walking on slopes has thus been acquired by our learning scheme. Moreover, although the learning episodes are carried out on up-slopes, the performance on down-slopes is also improved. The reason is probably similar to that of the improvement by $\theta_{RL}^{flat}$.

These two experiments suggest that a policy can be improved such to adapt to new environments according to our RL method.

## Discussion

In this article, we proposed an RL method for a CPG controller, called the CPG-actor-critic model, which is based on a policy gradient method. We applied our method to an automatic acquisition problem of biped locomotion. Simulation results showed the CPG controller was able to generate stable biped locomotion.

In our method, the policy parameter is supposed to converge to one of the local optima. In order to improve the policy by escaping from such a local optimum, we re-trained the actor parameter by re-initializing the critic's parameter, and then could obtain better one. Acquisition of the locomotion by human being may have such a process. The locomotion is unstable when a baby obtains it first, but is improved as it grows. It may be important to forget past successful experience to obtain a better control, when the learner is caught in a local optimum. We expect that the RL research provides some intuitions on the animal's developmental processes.

Although the simulation was successful, a lot of training episodes were still required. Therefore, it is difficult to apply the method directly to real robots; it is necessary to develop a more efficient algorithm which enables the robot to learn fast. Moreover, the CPG's internal weights were fixed and only sensory feedback connections were adjusted in the current study. It also remains a future study to adjust the weights of our CPG's internal connections by our CPG-actor-critic RL method.

## Acknowledgements

One of the authors (MS) is supported in part by the National Institute of Information and Communications Technology.

## References

Barnes, D. P. 1998. Hexapodal robot locomotion over uneven terrain. In *Proceedings of IEEE Conference on Control Applications*, 441–445.

Bertsekas, D. P., and Tsitsiklis, J. N. 1996. *Neuro-Dynamic Programming*. Athena Scientific.

Bradtke, S., and Barto, A. 1996. Linear least-squares algorithms for temporal difference learning. *Machine Learning* 22.

Buehler, M.; Battaglia, R.; Cocosco, A.; Hawker, G.; Sarkis, J.; and Yamazaki, K. 1998. Scout: A simple quadruped that walks, climbs and runs. In *Proceedings of the 1998 IEEE International Conference on Robotics & Automation*.

Ekeberg, Ö. 1993. A combined neuronal and mechanical model of fish swimming. *Biological Cybernetics* 69:363–374.

Fiorillo, C. D.; Tobler, P. N.; and Schultz, W. 2003. Discrete coding of reward probability and uncertainty by dopamine neurons. *SCIENCE* 299:1898–1902.

Fukuoka, Y.; Kimura, H.; and Cohen, A. H. 2003. Adaptive dynamic walking of a quadruped robot on irregular terrain based on biological concepts. *the International Journal of Robotics Research* 22:187–202.

Grillner, S.; Wallen, P.; Brodin, L.; and Lansner, A. 1991. Neuronal network generating locomotor behavior in lamprey: circuitry, transmitters, membrane properties and simulations. *Annual Review of Neuroscience* 14:169–199.

Hirai, K.; Hirose, M.; Haikawa, Y.; and Takenaka, T. 1998. The development of honda humanoid robot. In *Proceedings of the 1998 IEEE International Conference on Robotics & Automation*.

Ijspeert, A. J. 2001. A connectionist central pattern generator for the aquatic and terrestrial gaits of a simulated salamander. *Biological Cybernetics* 84:331–348.

Konda, V. R. 2002. Actor-critic algorithms, phd thesis. *Department of Electrical Engineering and Computer Science Massachusetts Institute of Technology*.

Marbach, P., and Tsitsiklis, J. N. 2001. Simulation-based optimization of markov reward processes. *IEEE Transactions on Automatic Control* 46:191–209.

Morimoto, J., and Doya, K. 2001. Acquisition of stand-up behavior by a real robot using hierarchical reinforcement learning. *Robotics and Autonomous Systems* 36:37–51.

Ogihara, N., and Yamazaki, N. 2001. Generation of human bipedal locomotion by a bio-mimetic neuro-musculo-skeletal model. *Biological Cybernetics* 84:1–11.

Sato, M., and Ishii, S. 1999. Reinforcement learning based on on-line em algorithm. In *Advances in Neural Information Processing Systems*, volume 11, 1052–1058.

Sato, M. 1990. A real time learning algorithm for recurrent analog neural networks. *Biological Cybernetics* 62:237–241.

Sutton, R., and Barto, A. 1998. *Reinforcement Learning: An Introduction*. MIT Press.

Sutton, R. S.; McAllester, D.; Singh, S.; and Mansour, Y. 2000. Policy gradient methods for reinforcement learning with function approximation. In *Advances in Neural Information Processing Systems*, volume 12, 1057–1063.

Taga, G.; Yamaguchi, Y.; and Shimizu, H. 1991. Self-organized control of bipedal locomotion by neural oscillators in unpredictable environment. *Biological Cybernetics* 65:147–159.

Williams, R. 1992. Simple statistical gradient following algorithms for connectionist reinforcement learning. *Machine Learning* 8:279–292.

# Advice Generation from Observed Execution: Abstract Markov Decision Process Learning

**Patrick Riley** and **Manuela Veloso***
Computer Science Department
Carnegie Mellon University
Pittsburgh, PA 15213-3891
pfr@cs.cmu.edu and mmv@cs.cmu.edu

**Abstract**

An advising agent, a coach, provides advice to other agents about how to act. In this paper we contribute an advice generation method using observations of agents acting in an environment. Given an abstract state definition and partially specified abstract actions, the algorithm extracts a Markov Chain, infers a Markov Decision Process, and then solves the MDP (given an arbitrary reward signal) to generate advice. We evaluate our work in a simulated robot soccer environment and experimental results show improved agent performance when using the advice generated from the MDP for both a sub-task and the full soccer game.

## Introduction

A coach agent provides advice to other agent(s) to improve their performance. We focus on a coach that analyzes past performance to generate advice. The synthesis of observed executions in a manner that facilitates advice generation is a challenging problem.

Observations that do not explicitly include the actions taken by the agents are an additional challenge. The intended actions must be inferred from observed behavior. In this paper we present algorithms to learn a model, including actions, based on such observations. The model is then used to generate executable advice for agents.

The areas of advice reception (e.g. Maclin & Shavlik 1996) and advice generation, in both Intelligent Tutoring Systems (e.g. Paolucci, Suthers, & Weiner 1996) and item recommendation (e.g. Shani, Brafman, & Heckerman 2002), have received attention in AI over many years. Our work in this paper further explores advice generation in the context of agent to agent advice.

In most coaching environments, it is impractical for the coach to provide advice only at the most detailed level of states and actions because of communication bandwidth or observability constraints. Further, in domains with large or continuous state spaces, abstraction can produce the necessary generalization. Constructing an abstract model of the environment is one way that a coach may generate advice. Markov Decision Processes (MDPs) are a well-studied formalism for modeling an environment and finding a good action policy. The use of state and action abstraction has gotten significant attention (Dearden & Boutilier 1997; Barto & Mahadevan 2003; Uther & Veloso 2002). Here we introduce an approach to construct an MDP that uses both state abstraction and temporally extended abstract actions.

The MDP is learned by observation of past performance of agents in the domain, considered as a series of states that do not include information about what (abstract) actions were performed. This type of data can be obtained by an external observer with no access to the internal processes of the agents. Domain knowledge is used to transform states to abstract states and then to attach actions to transitions, whose probabilities are estimated from observed data. This process of adding actions has much in common with past work in plan recognition from observation (Kautz 1991; Charniak & Goldman 1993).

We used a simulated robot soccer environment as the testbed. The presence of a coach agent makes the environment well suited to this research. Past work on coaching for this environment has mostly been on analysis of a particular team, with automated (Kuhlmann, Stone, & Lallinger 2004; Riley, Veloso, & Kaminka 2002; Visser & Weland 2004) or non-automated (Raines, Tambe, & Marsella 2000) advice generation. We present experimental results for a coach agent learning an MDP and improving performance for both a restricted part of the game and in full games.

## Learning an Abstract MDP from Observation

In this section we introduce our approach for creating a Markov Decision Process from observations. Our goal is to learn an *abstract* MDP. The main steps of the process are:

- Transform observations into sequences of abstract states.
- Create a Markov Chain based on the observed transition frequencies among the abstract states.
- Transform the Markov Chain to a Markov Decision Process (MDP) by associating transitions to actions based on a specification of the abstract actions to add.
- Add rewards to the MDP.

*This research was sponsored by Grants No. F30602-00-2-0549 and the Department of the Interior (DOI) - National Business Center (NBC) and the Defense Advanced Research Projects Agency (DARPA) under contract no. NBCHC030029. The content of this publication reflects only the position of the authors.

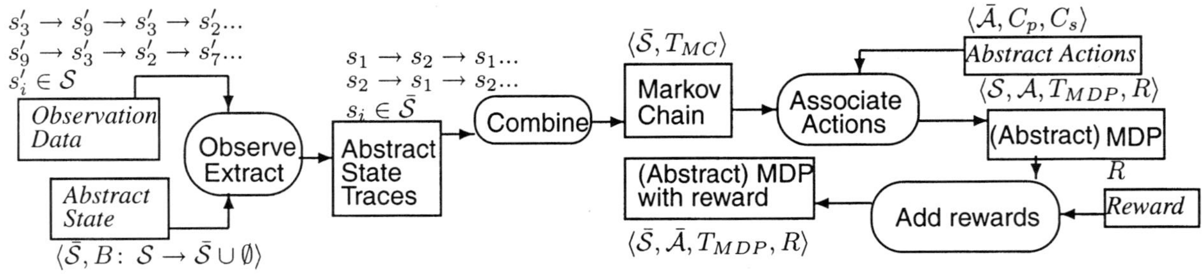


Figure 1: The process of a coach learning a Markov Decision Process from observation. The symbols are examples or types based on the formalism presented. The boxes with italics indicate information that must be provided for the system.

Figure 1 depicts the processes and data involved and we now describe the algorithms in detail.

## Observations to Markov Chain

There are two initial inputs to the process:

***Observation data*** consisting of sequences of observed states. These sequences can come from recordings of past performance or from online observation. Let $\mathcal{S}$ be the observed state space. The observation data is then a list of sequences of $\mathcal{S}$, or in other words, a list of $\mathcal{S}^*$.[1]

***State abstraction*** consisting of an abstract state space $\bar{\mathcal{S}}$, and an abstraction function $B\colon \mathcal{S} \to \bar{\mathcal{S}} \cup \emptyset$. Note that $B$ can map elements of $\mathcal{S}$ to the empty set, indicating there is no corresponding abstract state. Naturally, this specification can have a large impact on the overall performance on the system. While we currently use our domain expertise to specify the abstraction, learning techniques do exist which may provide useful abstractions (e.g. Schweitzer, Puterman, & Kindle 1985).

*Observe and extract* as shown in Figure 1 can then be implemented in terms of the above. $B$ is applied to every element of every sequence in the observation data. Any elements that map to $\emptyset$ are removed. *Observe and extract* outputs *abstract state traces* as a list of $\bar{\mathcal{S}}^*$.

Given the state traces, the *combine* algorithm produces a Markov Chain, a tuple $\langle \bar{\mathcal{S}}, T_{MC} \rangle$ where $\bar{\mathcal{S}}$ is the set of abstract states and $T_{MC}\colon \bar{\mathcal{S}} \times \bar{\mathcal{S}} \to \mathbb{R}$ is the transition function. $T_{MC}(s_1, s_2)$ gives the probability of transitioning from $s_1$ to $s_2$. Since the state space $\bar{\mathcal{S}}$ for the Markov Chain has already been given, just $T_{MC}$ must be calculated.

The *combine* algorithm estimates the transition probabilities based on the observed transitions. The algorithm calculates, for every pair of states $s_1, s_2 \in \bar{\mathcal{S}}$, a value $c_{s_1,s_2}$ which is the number of times a transition from $s_1$ to $s_2$ was observed. The transition function is then, $\forall s_1, s_2 \in \bar{\mathcal{S}}$:

$$T_{MC}(s_1, s_2) = \frac{c_{s_1,s_2}}{\sum_{s \in \bar{\mathcal{S}}} c_{s_1,s}} \qquad (1)$$

[1]The following notation will be used in the remainder of the paper. Sets will be set in script, e.g. $\mathcal{S}, \mathcal{N}$. The notation $\mathcal{S}^i$ is used to denote a sequence of $i$ elements of $\mathcal{S}$. $\mathcal{S}^*$ will denote $\cup_{i \in \mathbb{N}} \mathcal{S}^i$. The powerset of a set $\mathcal{S}$ will be denoted by $\mathcal{P}(\mathcal{S})$. Functions will be capital letters and in italics, e.g. $F$, $C$.

This estimation of $T_{MC}$ could possibly benefit from smoothing or clustering techniques to deal with problems of data sparsity. Our use of state abstraction already helps to deal with this somewhat and our experimental results demonstrate usefulness of the resulting model. More sophisticated estimation is an avenue for future work.

## Markov Chain to Markov Decision Process

Our algorithm now converts the Markov Chain into a Markov Decision Process. A Markov Decision Process is a tuple $\langle \bar{\mathcal{S}}, \bar{\mathcal{A}}, T_{MDP}, R \rangle$. $\bar{\mathcal{S}}$ is the set of abstract states, $\bar{\mathcal{A}}$ is the set of (abstract) actions, $T_{MDP}\colon \bar{\mathcal{S}} \times \bar{\mathcal{A}} \times \bar{\mathcal{S}} \to \mathbb{R}$ is the transition function, and $R\colon \bar{\mathcal{S}} \to \mathbb{R}$ is the reward function. Similar to a Markov Chain, the transition function $T_{MDP}(s_1, a, s_2)$ gives the probability of transitioning from $s_1$ to $s_2$ given that action $a$ was taken.

Shani, Brafman, & Heckerman (2002) also explain a mechanism for Markov Chain to Markov Decision Process conversion. However, for them the Markov Chain describes how the system acts with no agent actions. They use a simple proportional probability transform to add the actions. Here, the Markov Chain represents the environment with agent actions and we need to infer what those actions are.

In our approach, a set of abstract actions must be given as a set of transitions between abstract states, divided into primary and secondary transitions. The primary transitions represent the intended or normal effects of actions and the secondary transitions are other possible results of the action. This distinction is similar to Jensen, Veloso, & Bryant (2004).

We initially assign a zero reward function. Describing the algorithms for associating actions and transitions takes up the bulk of this section. We first illustrate the process using the example shown in Figure 2, then provide the full details.

Our algorithm processes each abstract state in turn. Figure 2(a) shows the state $s_0$ in the Markov Chain. It must be determined which actions can be applied in each state and how to assign the transitions and their probabilities to actions.

The transitions for the actions $a_0$, $a_1$, and $a_2$ are shown in Figure 2(b), with the primary transitions in bold. An action is added for a state if any of the action's primary transitions exist for this state. In Figure 2(c), actions $a_0$ and $a_1$ have been added, but $a_2$ has not (since its primary transition $s_0 \to s_4$ was not in the Markov Chain). Once an action has

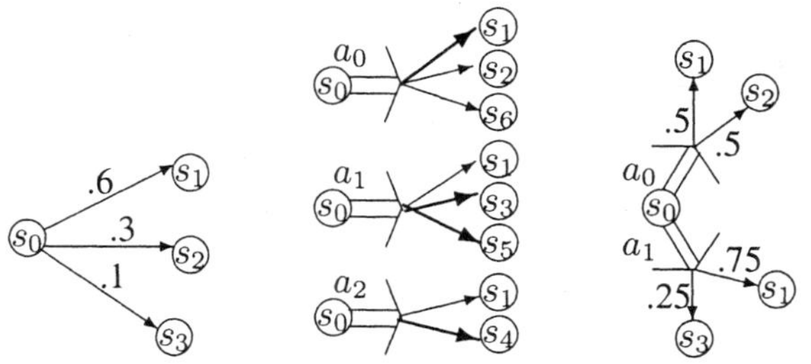

(a) Markov Chain (b) Actions (c) MDP

Figure 2: Associating actions with the transitions from one state in a Markov Chain to create a Markov Decision Process state

been added, all transitions in the Markov Chain which are primary or secondary transitions for the action are assigned to the action. It is fine for primary or secondary transitions that are part of the action definition to not be in the Markov Chain (e.g. the $s_0 \rightarrow s_6$ transition for $a_0$ and the $s_0 \rightarrow s_5$ for $a_1$). Once all actions have been processed, the probability mass for each transition is divided equally among all repetitions of the transition and the resulting distributions are normalized. For example, in Figure 2, the probability mass of 0.6 assigned to the $s_0 \rightarrow s_1$ transition is divided by 2 for the 2 repetitions. The transitions $s_0 \rightarrow s_1$ and $s_0 \rightarrow s_3$ have, respectively, probabilities 0.3 and 0.1 before normalization and 0.75 and 0.25 after normalization.

Formally, an abstract action set $\bar{\mathcal{A}}$ and functions giving the primary ($C_p\colon \bar{\mathcal{A}} \rightarrow \mathcal{P}(\bar{\mathcal{S}} \times \bar{\mathcal{S}})$) and secondary ($C_s\colon \bar{\mathcal{A}} \rightarrow \mathcal{P}(\bar{\mathcal{S}} \times \bar{\mathcal{S}})$) transitions must be given. We will calculate an unnormalized transition function $T'_{MDP}$ which will be normalized to $T_{MDP}$. The complete algorithm for adding actions to the Markov Chain is shown in Table 1.

For all $s \in \bar{\mathcal{S}}$
  Let $\mathcal{T} \subseteq \mathcal{P}(\bar{\mathcal{S}} \times \bar{\mathcal{S}})$ be the transitions from $s$
  $\mathcal{T} = \{\langle s, s_i\rangle \mid s_i \in \bar{\mathcal{S}}, T_{MC}(s, s_i) > 0\}$
  Let $\mathcal{N} \subseteq \bar{\mathcal{A}}$ be actions with primary transitions for $s$
  $\mathcal{N} = \{a \in \bar{\mathcal{A}} \mid C_p(a) \cap \mathcal{T} \neq \emptyset\}$
  For all $s_i \in \bar{\mathcal{S}}$
    Let $c_{s_i}$ be the number of actions for $s \rightarrow s_i$
    $c_{s_i} = |\{a \in \mathcal{N} \mid \langle s, s_i\rangle \in C_p(a) \cup C_s(a)\}|$
  For all $a \in \mathcal{N}$
    For all $\langle s, s_i\rangle \in C_p(a) \cup C_s(a)$
      $T'_{MDP}(s, a, s_i) = \dfrac{T_{MC}(s, s_i)}{c_{s_i}}$
  Add null action if needed (see text)
Normalize $T'_{MDP}$ to $T_{MDP}$

Table 1: Associating actions to convert a Markov Chain to an MDP.

As noted, a null action can be added. This occurs if a transition from the Markov chain is not part of any of the actions created for this state (i.e. if $c_{s_i} = 0$ and $T_{MC}(s, s_i) \neq 0$).

The definition of primary and secondary transitions and the algorithm above support situations in which the possible effects of an abstract action are known, but the probabilities of occurrence of the various results are not.

Once we have a Markov Decision Process, we can add additional rewards to whatever states desired. By changing the reward function, the learned Markov process can be used to produce different behaviors. This is explored further the in empirical section below.

## Learning In Simulated Robot Soccer

We used the Soccer Server System (Noda *et al.* 1998) as used in RoboCup (Kitano *et al.* 1997) as our implementation and testing environment. The Soccer Server System is a server-client system that simulates soccer between distributed agents. Clients communicate using a standard network protocol with well-defined actions. The server keeps track of the current state of the world, executes the actions the clients request, and periodically sends perceptions to the agents. Agents receive noisy information about the direction and distance of objects on the field (the ball, players, goals, etc.); information is provided only for objects in the field of vision of the agent. The agents communicate with the server at the level of actions like turn, dash, and kick. Higher level actions like passing or positioning on the field are implemented as combinations of these lower level actions.

There are eleven independent players on each side, as well as a coach agent who has a global view of the world, but whose only action is to send advice to the players.

This environment has a standard advice language called CLang, which is primarily rule based. Conditions are logical connections of domain specific atoms like ball and player location. Actions include the abstract soccer actions like passing and dribbling.

For the simulated soccer environment, only those states where an agent can kick the ball are represented in the abstract state space. We define the abstract state space in terms of a set of factors and values:

**GoalScore** 0,1,null, if we, they, or no one scored.

**DeadBall** 0,1,null, if it is our, their, or no one's free kick.

**BallGrid** Location of the ball on a discretized grid for the field (see Figure 3).

**BallOwner** 0,1,2, if no one, our, or their team owns the ball.

**PlayerOccupancy** Presence of teammate and opponent players in defined regions.

The regions for PlayerOccupancy for the opponents are shown in Figure 4. The regions are centered around the ball and oriented so that the right is always towards the attacking goal. The regions for our team are the same except that players which can currently kick the ball are ignored.

The abstract action space $\bar{\mathcal{A}}$ was constrained by the advice actions in CLang. CLang supports abstract actions like passing, dribbling, and clearing (kicking the ball away). All these actions can take a parameter of an arbitrary region of the field. Actions should correspond to changes in the abstract state space. Since many CLang actions involve ball movement, we chose to consider the ball movement actions with regions from the discrete grid of ball locations (see Figure 3) as the parameters.

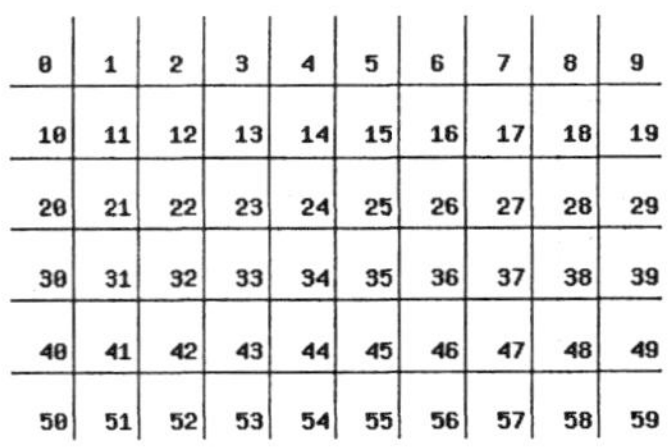


Figure 3: The regions for the BallGrid state factor

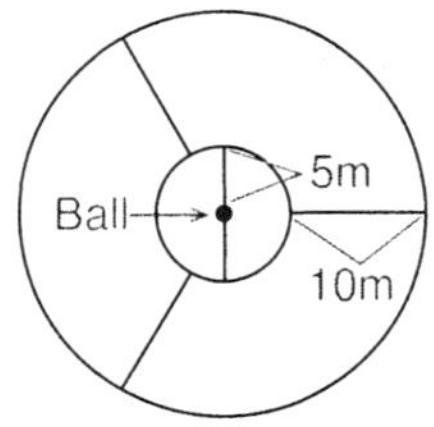


Figure 4: Player occupancy regions

To construct the $C_p$ and $C_s$ functions describing the primary and secondary transitions for the actions, we first classify the transitions (using the structured state representation discussed above). Then, these functions can be described in terms of the transition classes they represent, rather than writing out individual transitions. For example, we had transition classes including successful shots, kicks out of bounds, short passes, and failed passes.

### Markov Decision Process to Advice

The final set of algorithms go from a Markov Decision Process to advice. The first step is to solve the MDP. Since we have all transition probabilities, we use a dynamic programming approach (Puterman 1994). This algorithm gives us a $Q$ table, where for $s \in \bar{S}$ and $a \in \bar{A}$, $Q(s, a)$ gives the expected future discounted reward of taking action $a$ in state $s$ and performing optimally afterwords. An optimal policy (a mapping from $\bar{S}$ to $\bar{A}$) can be extracted from the $Q$ table by taking the action with the highest $Q$ value for a given state.

States and actions for advice must then be chosen. Advising about all states can overload the communication between the coach and agents (which is limited) and stress the computational resources of the agent applying the advice. Therefore, the scope of advice is restricted as follows:

- Remove states which don't have a minimum number of actions. For states with many possible actions, the agents will in general be in more need of advice from the coach. We experimented with different values here, but most of the time we only removed states without any actions.
- Remove states whose optimal actions can't be translated into the advice language.
- Only advise actions which are close to optimal. We only want to advise "good" actions, but we must be specific about what good means. We only advise actions which are within a given percentage of optimal for the given state.

Once the states and actions which to advise have been determined, they must be translated into the advice language.

### Advising In Simulated Robot Soccer

For simulated robot soccer, we pruned any action dealing with actions that the opponent takes. Clearly, we can not advise the agents to perform these actions.

After pruning, we are left with a set of pairs of abstract states and abstract actions. The advice is translated in to the CLang advice language. The goal is to structure the advice such that it can be matched and applied quickly at run time by the agents. We use the structured abstract state representation discussed above to construct a tree of CLang rules. At each internal node, one factor from the state representation is matched. At each leaf, a set of actions (for the abstract state matched along the path to the leaf) is advised.

## Empirical Validation

The learning and advice generation system is fully implemented for the SoccerServer (Noda *et al.* 1998). A version of the system described here made up the bulk of the Owl entry to the RoboCup 2003 coach competition. This section describes our empirical work in validating the system.

Throughout, we have used two different teams of agents which understand the advice language CLang: UTAustin Villa from the University of Texas at Austin (UTA) and the Wyverns from Carnegie Mellon University (CM).[2]

The data files, binaries, and configuration for all of these experiments can be found at the paper's online appendix: `http://www.cs.cmu.edu/~pfr/appendices/2004aaai.html`.

### Circle Passing

We constructed a sub-game of soccer in order to clearly evaluate the MDP learning from observed execution and the effect of automatically generated advice. While we are interested in modeling the entire soccer game, the number of factors affecting performance make it difficult to separately test effects.

We set up agents in a circle around the middle of the field and wrote a set of advice rules which cause the agents to pass in a circle, as shown in Figure 5. Stamina and offsides were turned off and dead balls were put back into play after 1 second. The goal was to use this data to learn a model which then be used to generate advice for a different team. This team would not know of the performance of the original team or even what the reward states in the model are. The goal was not to replicate this passing pattern, but to achieve the reward specified.

We ran 90 games of the UTA players executing this passing pattern. Note that because of noise in the environment, not every pass happens as intended. Agents sometimes fail to receive a pass and have to chase it outside of their normal positions. Kicks can be missed such that the ball goes in a direction other than intended or such that it looks like the agent is dribbling before it passes. These "errors" are important for the coach; it allows the coach observe other possible actions and results of the original advice.

We ran the process described above on the 90 games of data. Since there were no opponents on the field, the total possible size of the abstract state space was 5882 states. The effective state space size (states actually observed) was 346 states. Our algorithm produced a Markov Chain and a Markov Decision Process from this data.

[2]While both these institutions contributed agents for the official RoboCup2003 coachable team, the versions of the agents used here are updated from those official releases.

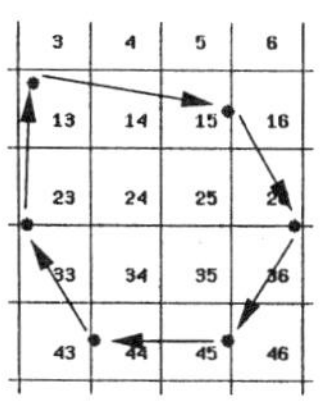


Figure 5: Locations and directions of passing for circle passing (cf Figure 3).

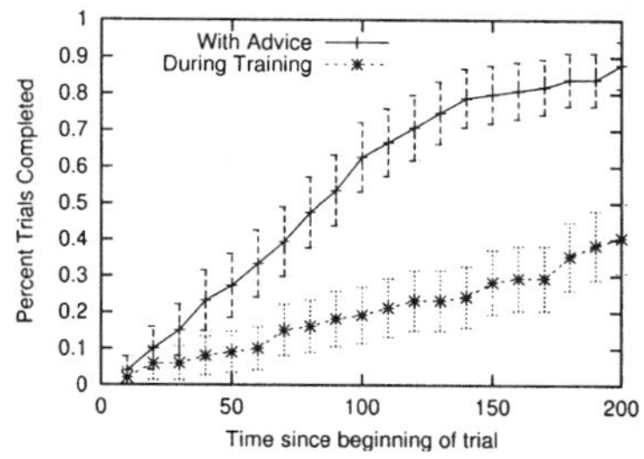


Figure 6: Time taken for trials in the reward cell 34 scenario. The intervals are 95% confidence intervals.

We experimented with adding different reward functions. In each case, reward was associated with all states in which the ball was in a particular grid cell (see Figure 5), namely:

**Cell 13** The cell where the upper left player usually stands.

**Cell 3** The cell immediately above the previous one. No agent would normally be here, but some passes and miskicks will result in agents being in this square.

**Cell 34** Near the middle of the field. Agents tend to move towards the ball (especially to try and receive a pass) so agents often end up in this cell during training.

**Cell 14** To the right of the upper left player. Since this is in the normal path between two players passing, the ball will frequently pass through this square. On a miskick, either one of the two closest agents could end up in that square with the ball.

There are other reasonable reward functions. We chose these to vary the degree to which the reward states were observed during training. Similar states around any one of the players would likely give similar results.

We ran with the CM agents receiving advice in each of these scenarios. Actions were sent if they were within 99.9% of optimal. We randomly chose 100 spots in the area around the players and for each of the eight cases (4 different rewards and training or with MDP advice) put the ball in each of those spots. The agents then ran for 200 cycles (20 seconds). A trial was considered a success if the agents got to any reward state in that time. The time bound is somewhat arbitrary as varying the time bound somewhat does not significantly affect the relative results. Further, the completion results at a particular time are easier to present and discuss that the full series of rewards received. Table 2 shows the results for the agents executing the learned advice for the four different reward cells. The "Training Success" line shows the percent of trials which completed during the initial UTA training games as a basis for comparison.

In all scenarios, the success percentage is higher with the MDP based advice. Figure 6 shows a different view of the reward cell 34 scenario. The $x$-axis is the time since the beginning of a trial and the $y$-axis is the percentage of the trials which received reward by that time. Graphs for the other scenarios are similar.

| Reward Grid Cell | 13 | 3 | 34 | 14 |
|---|---|---|---|---|
| # rew. states observed | 5095 | 211 | 1912 | 2078 |
| Training Success % | 53% | 4% | 40% | 44% |
| Advice Success % | 77% | 21% | 88% | 69% |

Table 2: Performance for circle passing. The first row shows the number of times a reward state was seen during training.

In all cases we see that agent execution is not perfect. This occurs for several reasons. Noise in the perception and execution can cause actions to fail and have undesired effects. Execution of some abstract actions (such as passing) requires more about the underlying states than what is expressed by the abstraction. In passing, another agent needs to be in or near the target location in order to receive the pass. Therefore, it can happen that the advised abstract action can not be done at this time.

The reward cell 3 scenario was the most difficult for the agents to achieve. It was also the set of reward states which was least often seen in training. More examples of transitions to reward states allow a better model to be created.

These experiments demonstrate that the coach can learn a model from observation which can then be used to improve agent performance. Changing the reward can allow the same transition model to be used to generate different advice. However, the more similar the training data is to the desired execution, the more effective the advice is in helping the agents achieve reward.

## Full Game

While the above experiments show that the MDP learning process described can extract a useful model and generate advice from it, providing advice for an entire soccer game is a larger and more challenging task. This section demonstrates that our coach can produce positive effects on a team's overall performance. While further experiments exploring the limits and general effectiveness would be useful, these results are still a compelling example of improvement.

Another advantage of the simulated robot soccer environment can also be leveraged here. Annual worldwide competitions have been held since 1997 with a number of smaller regional competitions over the last few years. Most of the logfiles from these competitions have been preserved and are publicly available. This is a wealth of data of many different teams playing. We used all the logfiles from RoboCup2001 and 2002, German Open 2002 and 2003, Japan Open 2002 and 2003, American Open 2003, and Australian Open 2003. This is a total of 601 logfiles. We also analyzed 1724 logfiles from our previous experiments with a number of past teams (Riley, Veloso, & Kaminka 2002).

While it may be better to only analyze games played between these particular teams or at least just involving this particular opponent, we wanted to take advantage of the wealth of past games available for analysis. Observing a range of performance should hopefully allow an understanding of the average case. While some of the knowledge learned could be internally inconsistent, we hope that most such cases will average out over time. Use of additional observations of the particular teams in order to refine the model is another avenue for further exploration.

Given the definition of the abstract state space above, there are 184442 possible states. After analysis, the MDP contained 89223 states. We associated a reward of 100 with our team scoring a goal and -100 for being scored upon. We also removed all transitions from these states. This allows for faster convergence of the dynamic programming because rewards do not have to be backed up through these states.

We tested two conditions: the CM team playing against Sirim (one of the fixed opponents in the RoboCup2003 coach competition) with and without the MDP based advice. With the MDP advice, actions were included if they were at least 96% of optimal. Each condition was run for 30 games. The results in Table 3 show that using the MDP improves the score difference by an average of 1.6 goals. This difference is significant at a $< 1\%$ level for a one-tailed $t$-test.

| | No MDP | With MDP |
|---|---|---|
| Score Difference | -4.6 [-5.3, -3.8] | -3 [-3.5, -2.5 ] |

Table 3: Mean score difference of CM playing Sirim. Score difference is CM's score minus Sirim's score. The interval shown is the 95% confidence interval.

While these results do not demonstrate the coached team moving from losing to winning, the results still show a significant improvement in performance. The overall performance of a simulated soccer team is a combination of many factors, including low level system timing and synchronization, implementation of basic skills like kicking and dribbling, and higher level strategy decisions. Coaching advice can only affect the last of these. As far as we are aware, our coach is the first for the simulated robot soccer environment that advises about such a large portion of the behaviors of the agents and does so in an entirely learned fashion.

## Conclusion

This paper has examined the problem of learning a model of an environment in order to generate advice. An MDP is learned based on observations of past agent performance in the environment and domain knowledge about the structure of abstract states and actions in the domain. The MDP learning process first creates a Markov Chain. Domain knowledge about actions is then used to successfully transform the Markov Chain into an MDP. Implementation was done in a simulated robot soccer environment. In two different scenarios, the advice generated from the learned MDP was shown to improve the performance of the agents.

This research provides a crucial step in agent to agent advice giving, namely the automatic generation of effective, executable advice from raw observations.

## References


Barto, A., and Mahadevan, S. 2003. Recent advances in hierarchical reinforcement learning. *Discrete-Event Systems Journal* 13:41–77.

Charniak, E., and Goldman, R. 1993. A Bayesian model of plan recognition. *Artificial Intelligence* 64(1):53–79.

Dearden, R., and Boutilier, C. 1997. Abstraction and approximate decision theoretic planning. *Artificial Intelligence* 89(1):219–283.

Jensen, R. M.; Veloso, M. M.; and Bryant, R. E. 2004. Fault Tolerant Planning: Toward Probabilistic Uncertainty Models in Symbolic Non-Deterministic Planning. In *ICAPS04*.

Kautz, H. A. 1991. A Formal theory of plan recognition and its implementation. In Allen, J. F.; Kautz, H. A.; Pelavin, R. N.; and Tenenberg, J. D., eds., *Reasoning About Plans*. Los Altos, CA: Morgan Kaufmann. chapter 2.

Kitano, H.; Tambe, M.; Stone, P.; Veloso, M.; Coradeschi, S.; Osawa, E.; Matsubara, H.; Noda, I.; and Asada, M. 1997. The RoboCup synthetic agent challenge. In *IJCAI-97*, 24–49.

Kuhlmann, G.; Stone, P.; and Lallinger, J. 2004. The champion UT Austin Villa 2003 simulator online coach team. In Polani, D.; Browning, B.; Bonarini, A.; and Yoshida, K., eds., *RoboCup-2003: Robot Soccer World Cup VII*. Berlin: Springer Verlag. (to appear).

Maclin, R., and Shavlik, J. W. 1996. Creating advice-taking reinforcement learners. *Machine Learning* 22:251–282.

Noda, I.; Matsubara, H.; Hiraki, K.; and Frank, I. 1998. Soccer server: A tool for research on multiagent systems. *Applied Artificial Intelligence* 12(2–3):233–250.

Paolucci, M.; Suthers, D. D.; and Weiner, A. 1996. Automated advice-giving strategies for scientific inquiry. In *ITS-96*, 372–381.

Puterman, M. L. 1994. *Markov Decision Processes*. New York: John Wiley & Sons.

Raines, T.; Tambe, M.; and Marsella, S. 2000. Automated assistant to aid humans in understanding team behaviors. In *Agents-2000*.

Riley, P.; Veloso, M.; and Kaminka, G. 2002. An empirical study of coaching. In Asama, H.; Arai, T.; Fukuda, T.; and Hasegawa, T., eds., *Distributed Autonomous Robotic Systems 5*. Springer-Verlag. 215–224.

Schweitzer, P. L.; Puterman, M. L.; and Kindle, K. W. 1985. Iterative aggregation-deaggregation procedures for discounted semi-Markov reward processes. *Operations Research* 33:589–605.

Shani, G.; Brafman, R. I.; and Heckerman, D. 2002. An MDP-based recommender system. In *UAI-2002*, 453–460.

Uther, W., and Veloso, M. 2002. TTree: Tree-based state generalization with temporally abstract actions. In *Proceedings of SARA-2002*.

Visser, U., and Weland, H.-G. 2004. Using online learning to analyze the opponent behavior. In Polani, D.; Bonarini, A.; Browning, B.; and Yoshida, K., eds., *RoboCup-2003: The Sixth RoboCup Competitions and Conferences*. Berlin: Springer Verlag. (to appear).

# Search

# Compressing Pattern Databases

**Ariel Felner** and **Ram Meshulam**
Computer Science Department
Bar-Ilan University
Ramat-Gan, Israel 92500
Email: {felner,meshulr1}@cs.biu.ac.il

**Robert C. Holte**
Computing Science Department
University of Alberta
Edmonton, Alberta, T6G 2E8, Canada
Email: holte@cs.ualberta.ca

**Richard E. Korf**
Computer Science Department
University of California
Los Angeles, CA 90095
Email: korf@cs.ucla.edu

**Abstract**

A pattern database is a heuristic function stored as a lookup table which stores the lengths of optimal solutions for instances of subproblems. All previous pattern databases had a distinct entry in the table for each subproblem instance. In this paper we investigate compressing pattern databases by merging several adjacent entries into one, thereby allowing the use of pattern databases that exceed available memory in their uncompressed form. We show that since adjacent entries are highly correlated, much of the information is preserved. Experiments on the sliding tile puzzles and the 4-peg Towers of Hanoi puzzle show that, for a given amount of memory, search time is reduced by up to 3 orders of magnitude by using compressed pattern databases.

## Introduction

Heuristic search algorithms such as A* and IDA* are guided by the cost function $f(n) = g(n) + h(n)$, where $g(n)$ is the actual distance from the initial state to state $n$ and $h(n)$ is a heuristic function estimating the cost from $n$ to a goal state. If $h(s)$ is "admissible" (i.e. is always a lower bound) then these algorithms are guaranteed to find optimal paths.

Pattern databases are heuristics in the form of lookup tables. They have proven very useful for finding lower bounds for combinatorial puzzles and other problems(Culberson & Schaeffer 1998; Korf 1997; Korf & Felner 2002).

The domain of a search space is the set of constants used in representing states. A *subproblem* is an abstraction of the original problem defined by only considering some of these constants. A *pattern* is a state of the subproblem. The *pattern space* for a given subproblem is a state space containing all the different patterns connected to one another using the same transition rules ("operators") that connect states in the original problem. A *pattern database* (PDB) stores the distance of each pattern to the goal pattern. A PDB is built by running a breadth-first search backwards from the goal pattern until the whole pattern space is spanned. A state $S$ in the original space is mapped to a pattern $S'$ by ignoring details in the state description that are not preserved in the subproblem. The value stored in the PDB for $S'$ is a lower bound (and thus serves as an admissible heuristic) on the distance of $S$ to the goal state in the original space since the pattern space is an abstraction of the original space.

The size of a pattern space is the number of patterns it contains. As a general rule, the speed of search is inversely related to the size of the pattern space used (Hernádvölgyi & Holte 2000). However, in (Holte *et al.* 2004) we showed that taking the maximum of a number of small PDBs is usually better than having one large PDB. Larger pattern spaces take longer to generate but that is not the limiting factor. The problem is the memory required to store the PDB. In all previous studies, the amount of memory needed for a PDB was equal to the size of the pattern space, because the PDB had one entry for each pattern. In this paper, we present a method for compressing a PDB so that it uses only a fraction of the memory that would be needed to store the PDB in its usual, uncompressed form. This permits the use of patterns spaces that are much larger than available memory, thereby reducing search time. We limit the discussion to a memory capacity of 1 gigabyte, which is reasonable in today's technology. The question we address in this paper is how to best use this amount of memory with compressed pattern databases. Experiments on the sliding tile puzzles and the 4-peg Towers of Hanoi puzzle show that search-time is significantly reduced by using compressed pattern databases.

## The 4-peg Towers of Hanoi Problem

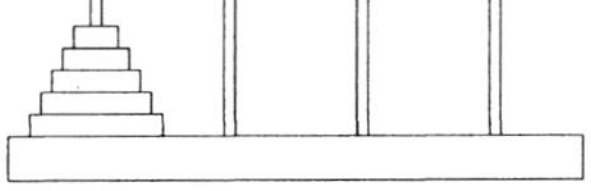

Figure 1: Five-disk four-peg Towers of Hanoi problem

The well-known 3-peg Towers of Hanoi problem consists of three pegs. The task is to transfer all the disks to the goal peg. Only the top disk on any peg can be moved and a larger disk can never be placed on top of a smaller disk. For the 3-peg problem, there is a simple recursive deterministic algorithm that provably returns an optimal solution. The 4-peg Towers of Hanoi problem (TOH4)(Hinz 1997) shown in Figure 1, is more interesting. There exists a deterministic algorithm for finding a solution, and a conjecture that it generates an optimal solution, but the conjecture remains unproven. Thus, systematic search is currently the only method guaranteed to find optimal solutions, or to verify the conjecture for problems with a given number of disks.

The domain of TOH4 has many small cycles, meaning there are many different paths between the same pair of states. For example, if we move a disk from peg A to peg B, and then another disk from peg C to peg D, applying these two moves in the opposite order will generate the same state. Therefore, any depth-first search, such as IDA*, will generate many nodes more than once and be hopelessly inefficient in this domain. Thus, we must use a search that prunes duplicate nodes. We used frontier-A* (FA*), a modification of A* designed to save memory (Korf & Zhang 2000). FA* only saves the open list and deletes nodes from memory once they have been expanded. In order to keep from regenerating closed nodes, with each node on the open list the algorithm stores those operators that lead to closed nodes, and when expanding a node those operators are not used.

## Pattern databases for TOH4

PDB heuristics are applicable to TOH4. Consider a 16-disk problem. We can build a PDB for the largest 10 disks by having an entry for each of the $4^{10}$ legal patterns of these 10 disks. The value of an entry is the minimum number of moves required to move all the disks in this 10-disk group from the corresponding pattern to the goal peg, assuming there are no other disks in the problem. Since there are exactly $4^n$ states for the $n$-disk problem, indexing this PDB is particularly easy, since each disk position can be represented by two bits, and any pattern of $n$ disks can be uniquely represented by a binary number $2n$ bits long. Given a state of the 16-disk problem, we compute the pattern for the 10-disk group and lookup the value for this configuration in the PDB. This value is an admissible heuristic for the complete 16-disk problem because a solution to the 16-disk problem must at least move the largest 10 disks to the goal.

A similar PDB can be built for the smallest 6 disks. Values from the 10-disk PDB and the 6-disk PDB can be *added* together to get an admissible heuristic value for the complete state since a complete solution must include a solution to the largest 10 disks problem as well as to the smallest 6 disks problem. This sum is a lower bound because the two groups are disjoint and their solutions only count moves of disks within their own group. The idea that costs of *disjoint* subproblems can be *added* was first used in (Korf & Felner 2002) for the tile puzzles and inspired this formalization.

Note that a PDB based on $n$ disks will contain exactly the same values for the largest $n$ disks or the smallest $n$ disks or any other $n$ disks. The reason is that only the relative sizes of the disks matter, and not their absolute sizes. Furthermore, a PDB for $n$ disks also contains a PDB for $m$ disks, if $m < n$. To look up a pattern of $m$ disks, we simply assign the $n - m$ largest disks to the goal peg, and then look up the resulting pattern in the $n$-disk PDB. Thus, in practice we only need a single PDB for the largest number of disks of any group of our partition. In our case, a 10-disk PDB contains both a PDB for the largest 10 disks and a PDB for the smallest 6 disks. In general, the most effective heuristic is based on

| Heuristic | Path | Avg h | Nodes | Seconds |
|---|---|---|---|---|
| Static 13-3 | 161 | 75.78 | 134,653,232 | 48.75 |
| Static 14-2 | 161 | 89.10 | 36,479,151 | 14.34 |
| Dynamic 14-2 | 161 | 95.52 | 12,827,732 | 21.56 |

Table 1: Results for the 16-disk problem

partitioning the disks into the largest groups that we can, thus building the largest PDB that will fit in memory. The largest PDB we can use with a gigabyte of memory is of 14 disks. This has $4^{14}$ entries and needs 256 megabytes at one byte per entry. The rest of the memory is needed for the open-list of FA*.

Given a PDB of 14 disks, there are two methods to use it for the 16-disk problem. The first is called *statically partitioned PDB*. In this method, we statically partition the disks into the largest 14 disks and the smallest 2 disks. This partition remains *static* for all the nodes of the search. The other method is called *dynamically partitioned PDB*. For each state we compute all 240 different ways of dividing the disks into groups of 14 and 2, look-up the database value for each, and return the maximum of these as the final heuristic value. Here, the exact partitioning to disjoint disks is *dynamically* determined for each state of the search on the fly. Table 1 has results for the standard initial state of the 16-disk problem. A 14-2 split is much better than a 13-3 split since the large PDB of 14 is more informed than the PDB of 13. For the 14-2 split, a dynamically partitioned heuristic is more accurate and the search generates fewer nodes (and therefore FA* requires less memory). Statically partitioned heuristics are much simpler to calculate and thus consume less overall time but generate more nodes. The static and dynamic partitioning methods can be applied in any domain where additivity of disjoint PDBs is applicable.

## Compressing cliques in pattern databases

Pattern databases in all previous studies have had one entry for each pattern in the pattern space. In this section, we describe methods for compressing pattern databases by merging the entries stored in adjacent positions of the lookup table. This obviously reduces the size of the pattern database, but the key to making this successful is that the merged entries should be very similar values. While this cannot be guaranteed in general, we show in this paper that it is the case for the state spaces and indexing functions that are used in our experiments.

Suppose that $K$ nodes of the pattern space form a clique. This means that all these nodes are reachable from each other by one edge. Thus, the PDB entries for these nodes will differ from one another by no more than 1, some will have a value $N$ and the rest will have value $N + 1$.

In permutation problems such as TOH4 or the tile puzzles where the operators move one object at a time, cliques usually exist where all objects are in the same location except one, which is often in a nearby location. Therefore, such cliques usually have nearby entries in the PDB. If we can identify a general structure of $K$ adjacent entries in the pattern database which store a clique of size $K$, we can squeeze the PDB as follows. Instead of storing $K$ entries for the different $K$ nodes we can have all these $K$ nodes mapped into one entry. This can be done in the following two ways:

**lossy compression** - Store the minimum of these $K$ nodes, $N$. The admissibility of the heuristic is preserved and the loss introduced is at most 1.

**lossless compression** - Store the minimum value for these $K$ nodes, $N$. Store also $K$ additional bits, one for each node of the clique, that will indicate whether the node's value is $N$ or $N+1$. This version will preserve the entire knowledge of the large PDB but will usually require less memory.

The existence of cliques in the pattern space is domain dependent. Furthermore, when cliques exist, their adjacency in the PDB depends on the indexing function used. Finally, in order for this technique to be applicable there must exist an efficiently computable indexing function into the compressed PDB. We do not assert that these conditions can be satisfied in all domains, but we believe they hold quite broadly, at least for the permutation-type domains that we study here. Note that with lossy compression, any block of nearby entries can be compressed and admissibility is still kept. With cliques, however, we are guaranteed that the loss of data will be at most 1.

For TOH4, the largest clique is of size 4. Consider a PDB based on a subproblem of $P$ disks, for example, the 10-disk PDB described above. Assume that the location of the largest $P-1$ disks is fixed and focus on the smallest disk which can be placed in 4 different locations. These 4 states form a clique of size 4 since the smallest disk can move among these 4 states in only 1 move. Thus, we can store a PDB of $P$ disks in a table of size $4^{P-1}$ (instead of $4^P$) by squeezing the 4 states of the smallest disk into one entry. If the PDB is built as a multi-dimensional array with $P$ indices where the last index corresponds to the smallest disk, then the only difference between these 4 states is their last index with the position of the smallest disk. Thus, they are stored in 4 adjacent entries.

In the compressed PDB, we will have $P-1$ indices for the largest $P-1$ disks and only one entry for the smallest disk instead of 4 entries in the original database. Lossy compression would store the minimum of these 4 entries and lose at most 1 for some of the entries. Alternatively, lossless compression can store 4 additional bits in each entry of the compressed database which will indicate for each location of the smallest disk whether the value is $N$ or $N+1$.

This idea can be generalized to a set of $K$ nodes with a diameter of $D$, i.e, each pair of nodes within the set have at least one connecting path consisting of $D$ or fewer edges (Note that a clique is a special case where $D = 1$). We can compress the set of nodes into only one entry by taking the minimum of their entries and lose at most $D$. Alternatively, for the lossless compression we need an additional $K \times log(D+1)$ bits to indicate the exact value. If the size of an entry is $M$ bits then it will be beneficial (memory-wise) to use this compression mechanism for sets of nodes with diameter of $D$ as long as $log(D+1) < M$.

For example for TOH4 this generalization applies as follows. We fix the position of largest $P-2$ disks and focus on the 16 different possibilities of the two smallest disks. These possibilities form a set of nodes with diameter 3, and it is easy to see that they are placed in 16 adjacent entries. Thus, we can squeeze these 16 entries to one entry and lose at most 3 for any state. Alternatively, we can add $2 \times 16 = 32$ bits to the one byte for the entry (for a total of 5 bytes) and store the exact values. This is instead of 16 bytes in the simple uncompressed database.

| TOH | h(s) | Avg h | D | Nodes | Time | Mem |
|---|---|---|---|---|---|---|
| $16^{14}_0$ | 119 | 89.10 | 0 | 36,479,151 | 14.34 | 256 |
| $16^{14}_1$ | 118 | 88.55 | 1 | 37,964,227 | 14.69 | 64 |
| $16^{14}_2$ | 116 | 87.74 | 3 | 40,055,436 | 15.41 | 16 |
| $16^{14}_3$ | 114 | 86.53 | 5 | 44,996,743 | 16.94 | 4 |
| $16^{14}_4$ | 110 | 84.80 | 9 | 45,808,328 | 17.36 | 1 |
| $16^{14}_5$ | 107 | 82.91 | 13 | 61,132,726 | 23.78 | 1/4 |
| $16^{14}_{1s}$ | 119 | 89.10 | 0 | 36,479,151 | 15.87 | 96 |

Table 2: Solving 16-disks with a pattern of 14 disks

## Experiments on the 4-peg Towers of Hanoi

As a first step we compressed the 14-disk PDB to a smaller size. Define a *compression degree of $z$* to denote a PDB that was compressed by storing all different positions of the smallest $z$ disks in one entry given that the rest of the disks are fixed. The amount of memory saved with a lossy compression degree of $z$ is $4^z$. We define $TOHx^y_z$ to denote a 4-peg Towers of Hanoi problem with $x$ disks that was solved by a PDB with $y$ disks compressed by a degree of $z$. For the 16-disk problem we define our PDBs by statically dividing the disks into two groups. The largest fourteen disks (disks 1-14) define the 14-disk PDB. The smallest two (disks 15 and 16) are in their own group and have a separate, uncompressed PDB with $4^2 = 16$ entries. To compute the heuristic for a state, the values for the state from the small PDB and the 14-disk PDB are added. Notice the difference between a 14-2 split where two separate PDBs are built (14 and 2) and a PDB of 14 compressed by a degree of 2 where the specific 14-disk PDB is compressed.

Table 2 presents results of solving the standard initial state (where all disks are initially located on one peg) of the 16-disk problem, which has an optimal solution of 161 moves. Different rows of the table correspond to different compression degrees of the 14-disk PDB. All but the last row represent lossy compression. The first row of Table 2 is for the complete 14-disk database with no compression while row 6 has a compression degree of 5. The third row for example, has a compressing degree of 2. In that case, the PDB only contains $4^{12}$ entries which correspond to the different possibilities of placing disks 1-12. For each of these entries, we take the minimum of all the 16 possibilities for disks 13 and 14 and have only one entry for them instead of 16.

The last column gives the size of the PDB in megabytes. The most important result here is that when compressing the PDB by a factor of $4^5 = 1024$, most of the information is not lost. Such a large compression increased the search effort by less than a factor of 2 for both the number of generated nodes

| TOH | Type | Avg h | Nodes | Time | M |
|---|---|---|---|---|---|
| $17_0^{14}$ | static | 90.5 | >393,887,912 | >421 | 256 |
| $17_0^{14}$ | dynam | 95.7 | 238,561,590 | 2501 | 256 |
| $17_1^{15}$ | static | 103.7 | 155,737,832 | 83 | 256 |
| $17_2^{16}$ | static | 123.8 | 17,293,603 | 7 | 256 |
| $18_2^{16}$ | static | 123.8 | 380,117,836 | 463 | 256 |

Table 3: Solving larger versions of TOH4

and for the time to solve a problem.

The last row represents lossless compression of the full 14-disk database by a degree of 1 where we stored 1 additional bit for each position of the smallest disk in the 14-disk group (#14). This needed 12 bits per 4 entries instead of the 32 bits in the uncompressed PDB (row 1). While the number of generated nodes is identical to row 1, the table clearly shows that it is not worthwhile to use lossless compression for TOH4 since it requires more time and more memory than lossy compression by a degree of both 1 and 2.

The maximum possible loss of data for lossy compression with a degree of $z$ – the diameter D – is presented in column $D$ of Table 2. This is the length of the optimal solution for a problem with $z$ disks, because the two farthest states with $z$ disks are those that have all disks on one different peg. The *Avg h* column with the average heuristic on all possible entries shows that on average, the loss was half the maximum. Note that the loss for the heuristic of the standard initial state is shown in the $h(s)$ column is exactly the maximum, $D$.

### Larger versions of the problem

With lossy compression we also solved the 17- and 18-disk problems. The shortest paths from the standard initial state are 193 and 225 respectively. Results are presented in Table 3. An uncompressed *statically partitioned* PDB of the largest 14 disks and the smallest 3 disks cannot solve the 17-disk problem since memory is exhausted before reaching the goal after 7 minutes (row 1). With an uncompressed PDB of 14 disks we were only able to solve the 17-disk problem with *dynamically partitioned* PDB (row 2).

The largest database that we could precompute when performing a breadth-first search backwards from the goal configuration was for 16 disks. Our machine has 1 gigabyte of memory. Thus, when tracking nodes with a bit map we need $4^{16}$ = 4 gigabits, half the size of our memory. Given the same amount of memory as the full 14-disk database, 256MB, we solved the 17-disk problem in 83 seconds with a 15-disk PDB compressed by a degree of 1, and in 7 seconds with a 16-disk PDB compressed by a degree of 2. This is an improvement of at least 2 orders of magnitude compared to row 1. The improvement is almost 3 orders of magnitude compared to the dynamic partitioning heuristic of the 14-disk PDB row 2. While a PDB of 16 disks compressed by a degree of 2 consumes exactly the same amount of memory as an uncompressed PDB of 14 disks it is much more informed as it includes almost all the data about 16 disks. With a 16-disk database compressed by a degree of 2 we were also able to solve the 18-disk problem in a number of minutes. Note that (Korf 2004) solved this problem in 16 hours when using the delayed duplicate detection (DDD) breadth-first search algorithm.

The system described above, is able to find a shortest path for any possible initial state of TOH4. However, one can do much better if a shortest path is only needed from the standard initial state where all disks are located on one peg (Hinz 1997). For this special initial state, one can only search half way to an intermediate state where the largest disk can move freely from its initial peg to the goal peg. In such a state all the other $n-1$ disks are distributed over the other two pegs. To complete the solution we apply the moves to reach such an intermediate state in the reverse order and interchange the initial and goal pegs. Based on this symmetry, (Korf 2004) was able to obtain a shortest path for the standard initial state with a DDD breadth-first search for TOH4 with up to 24 disks. However, this symmetry doesn't apply to arbitrary initial and goal states where a complete search must be performed to the goal state as our system does. Furthermore, his system needed tens of gigabytes and took 19 days.

## Experiments on the Sliding Tile Puzzles

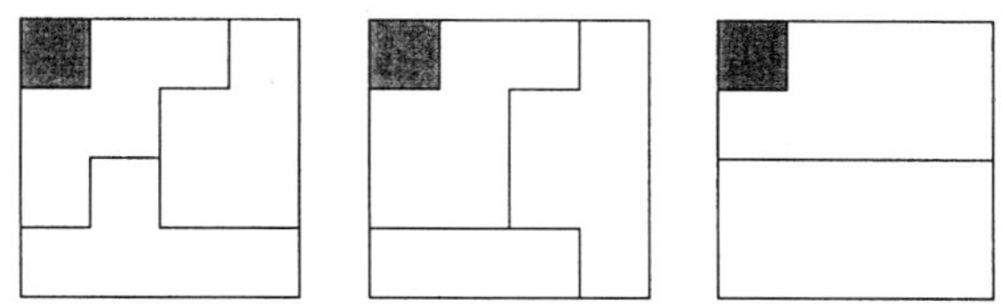

A 5-5-5 partitioning A 6-6-3 partitioning A 7-8 partitioning

Figure 2: Different disjoint databases for the Fifteen Puzzle

The best existing method for solving the tile puzzles uses disjoint pattern databases (Korf & Felner 2002). The tiles are partitioned into disjoint sets (subproblems) and a PDB is built for each set. The PDB stores the cost of moving the tiles in the given subproblem from any given arrangement to their goal positions. If for each set of tiles we only count moves of tiles from the given set, values from different disjoint PDBs can be *added* and are still admissible. An $x-y-z$ partitioning is a partition of the tiles into disjoint sets with cardinalities of $x$, $y$ and $z$. Figure 2 shows a 5-5-5, a 7-7-1 and a 7-8 disjoint partitioning of the 15-puzzle.

### Taking advantage of simple heuristics

In many domains there exists a simple heuristic, such as Manhattan distance (MD) for the sliding tile puzzles, that can be calculated very quickly. In these domains, a PDB can store just the addition above that heuristic. During the search we add values from the PDB to the simple heuristic.

For the tile puzzles we can therefore store just the addition above MD which correspond to conflicts and internal interactions between the tiles. These conflicts come in units of 2 moves, since if a tile moves away from its *Manhattan-distance path* it must return to that path again with a total of 2 additional moves to its MD. Compressing PDBs can greatly benefit from this idea. Consider a pair of adjacent entries in the PDB. While their MD is always different by one, the addition above the MD is most of the time exactly the same. Thus, much of the data is preserved when taking the minimum. In fact, for the 7-7-1 partition in Figure 2, we have found that more than 80% of the pairs we grouped stored exactly the same value.

| | | | |
|---|---|---|---|
| | 0 | 0 | 3 |
| 0 | 0 | 6 | 7 |
| 0 | 0 | 10 | 11 |
| 0 | 0 | 2 | 2 |

Figure 3: One pattern of the Fifteen puzzle

For example, consider the subproblem of $\{3,6,7,10,11\}$ shown in Figure 3. Suppose that all these tiles except tile 6 are located in their goal position and that tile 6 is not in its goal position. The values in Figure 3 written in location $x$ correspond to the number of steps above MD that the tiles of the subproblem must move in order to properly place tile 6 in its goal location given that its current location is $x$. For example, suppose that tile 6 is placed below tile 10 or tile 11. In that case tile 6 is in linear conflict with tiles 10 or 11 and one of them must move at least two more moves above MD. Thus we write the number 2 in these locations. For other locations we write 0 as no additional moves are needed. Locations where other tiles are placed are treated as *don't-care* as tile 6 cannot be placed at these locations. Note that most adjacent positions have the same value.

For TOH4, one can create a simple heuristic (similar to MD) concentrating on the number of moves that each disk must move. However, this heuristic is very inaccurate and proved ineffective in conjunction with PDBs.

## Storing PDB for the Tile Puzzles

While a multi-dimensional array of size $4^P$ is the obvious way to store a PDB for TOH4, there are two ways to store PDBs for the tile puzzles. Suppose for example, that we would like to store a PDB of 7 tiles for the 15-puzzle. There are $16 \times 15 \times \ldots \times 10$ different possible configurations to place these 7 tiles in 16 locations. A simple way would be to store a 7-dimensional array. This will need $16^7$ different entries but the access time is very fast. The other idea is to have a simple one-dimensional array of exactly $16 \times 15 \times \ldots \times 10$ entries, but use a complex mapping function in order to retrieve the exact entry of a given permutation. This is done as follows. The first tile can be located in 16 positions. The next tile can only be positions in 15 locations etc, The mapping function should calculate all these possibilities and return a unique value for each configuration. We refer to the first option as *simple mapping* and the second method as *packed mapping*.

For the simple mapping, there are 16 different entries for the last tile which correspond to the 16 different possible locations of the 15-puzzle. We divide the 16 locations into 8 pairs: (0,1), (2,3) ... (14,15). Instead of storing 16 entries for the last tile, we can store just 8 entries, one for each of these pairs. Thus, the size of the PDB will be $16^6 \times 8$ which is half the size of the original database. Since a legal move can only move one tile to a nearby location the largest clique in this puzzle is of size 2. By pairing neighboring locations of the last tile we take advantage of such cliques[1].

For the packed mapping it is a little more complicated. If the PDB is based on $k$ tiles, there are only $16 - k + 1$ entries for the last tile. For example, if $k = 7$ there are only 10 legal positions to place the last tile. If we use the same pairing mechanism described above then we can compress these 10 entries to 8 entries. This method will only be effective if the number of tiles is considerably smaller than half the size of the puzzle. For example, in the 24-puzzle, it will be efficient to compress 6 tiles even with the packed mapping.

| H | P | C | Nodes | Time | Mem | Av h |
|---|---|---|---|---|---|---|
| 1 7-8 | P | - | 136,288 | .081 | 576,575 | 44.75 |
| 1+ 7-8 | P | - | 36,710 | .034 | 576,575 | 45,63 |
| 1 7-7-1 | P | - | 464,977 | .232 | 57,657 | 43.64 |
| 1 7-7-1 | S | - | 464,977 | .058 | 536,870 | 43.64 |
| 1 7-7-1 | S | l | 565,881 | .069 | 268,435 | 43.02 |
| 1 7-7-1 | S | s | 487,430 | .070 | 268,435 | 43,59 |
| 2 7-7-1 | S | l | 147,336 | .021 | 536,870 | 43.98 |
| 2+ 7-7-1 | S | l | 66,692 | .016 | 536,870 | 44.92 |

Table 4: 15-puzzle results.

## Results on the Fifteen puzzle

Table 4 presents results on the 15-puzzle. All the values in the table are the average over the 1000 random initial states that were used in (Korf & Felner 2002). We used a 2.4GH pentium 4 with 1 gigabyte of main memory. The first column defines the heuristic. **1 7-7-1** means that we used only one 7-7-1 partitioning. **2 7-7-1** means that we used 2 different 7-7-1 partitionings and took their maximum as the heuristic. A **+** means that we also took the same partitioning and reflected it about the main diagonal. The second column indicates whether we used simple mapping (S) or packed mapping (P) and the next column indicates whether we used no compression (-), lossy compression (l) or lossless compression (s). The next columns present the number of nodes generated by IDA*, the average time in seconds, the amount of memory in K bytes (at one byte per entry) and the average initial heuristic. The time needed to precompute the PDB is traditionally omitted since one only needs to precompute it once and then solve as many problem instances as needed.

The first two rows present the same results of a 7-8 partitioning that was obtained by (Korf & Felner 2002) but on our current machine. Note that while (Korf & Felner 2002) report a running time of 0.027 seconds, exactly the same software took 0.034 seconds on our current machine which has a faster CPU. The reason is that hardware abilities of a given machine such as cache performance, memory-cpu data

[1]There are rare cases which only occur in 2.5% of the cases, where the above pairs are not a clique. This is due to the location of the blank tile (details are omitted). However, taking a minimum of any two values (even if they are not a clique) is always admissible.

exchange rate and internal hardware structure have a lot of influence on the actual overall running time.

The third and fourth rows present the results of the 7-7-1 database from Figure 2 but with the different mapping systems. Notice the time versus memory tradeoff here.

The fifth row gives the results of the 7-7-1 PDB after compressing each pair of entries described above into one entry with lossy compression. While the size of the PDB was reduced by a factor of 2, the overall effort was increased by no more than 20% in both the number of generated nodes and in the overall time. The next row presents results of the same 7-7-1 partitioning when we used lossless compression. While the number of generated node decreased by 15% from the lossy compression, the overall time increased a little. This is due to the additional constant time complexity of the bit handling of the lossless compression[2]. We have also tried to compress 4 adjacent entries of the PDB into one but this proved inefficient on the 15-puzzle as much data was lost.

The last two rows show the benefit of compression. The seventh row presents results when we took two different 7-7-1 partitionings, compressed them and took their maximum. This configuration uses the same amount of memory as one 7-7-1 partitioning of row 4 but solves the problem almost three times faster. It is also faster and uses less memory than the 7-8 partitioning (row 1). Finally, the last row also computes the reflection about the main diagonal of these two compressed databases and takes the maximum of the 4 different partitionings. This further reduced the running time and we now solve a problem in only 16 milliseconds. This is faster by a factor of two, and uses less memory, than the best 7-8 partitioning used in (Korf & Felner 2002) (row 2).

## Results on the 24-puzzle

The best existing heuristic for 24-puzzle is the 6-6-6-6 partitioning and its reflection about the main diagonal from (Korf & Felner 2002). We compressed the same 6-6-6-6 partitioning and found that like the 15-puzzle the lossy compression generated nearly 20% more nodes. However, with adding another 6-6-6-6 partitioning we could not achieve any significant reduction in the overall time. Due to geometrical attributes of the puzzle, the 6-6-6-6 partitioning and its reflection from (Korf & Felner 2002) are so good that adding another 6-6-6-6 partitioning (even without compressing anything) only achieves a small reduction in node generations which is not compensated by the time overhead.

We have also tried A 7-7-5-5 partitioning (and its refection) on this domain which could be stored in 1 gigabyte of memory if the 7-tile databases are compressed. Even without compressing, the number of generated nodes was not significantly different from the best 6-6-6-6 partitioning. The 6-6-6-6 partitioning of (Korf & Felner 2002) is probably the best 4-way partitioning of the 24-puzzle.

The only way to obtain a speedup in this domain is to compress larger databases such as an 8-8-8 partitioning. However, we need much more than 1 gigabyte to generate this database with breadth-first search, and that is beyond the scope of the current set of experiments.

[2]The reason that the number of generated nodes was not identical to the complete 7-7-1 partitioning is because as described above, in rare cases, two nearby entries are not a clique and differ by more than one. Thus, data is lost even with the lossless compression that we used.

## Conclusions and Future Work

We introduced a method that better utilizes memory by compressing PDBs and showed applications on the tile puzzles and on TOH4. In both domains significant compression was achieved, allowing larger pattern spaces to be used and search time to be considerably reduced. For the 15-puzzle and for TOH4 with arbitrary initial states we have the state of the art solvers. Our experiments confirm that given a specific amount of memory, $M$, it is better to compress larger PDBs into $M$ entries than to use an uncompressed PDB with $M$ entries. We have also showed two methods (i.e., static and dynamic) for partitioning disjoint patterns.

The memory limits imposed by using ordinary breadth-first search to generate very large pattern databases that are subsequently compressed might be overcome by using delayed duplicate detection (DDD)(Korf 2004). This is a method for performing best-first search which stores the open and/or closed lists on the disk. With DDD, one can run a breadth-first search on pattern spaces that are much larger than the available memory. Values from this breadth-first search can then be compressed to a database that can fit in memory. For example, one can run a breadth-first search for subproblems of 8 tiles for the 24-puzzle and then compress the values into 1 gigabyte of memory.

Future work will continue these ideas as follows. Advanced data structures (like a trie for the tile puzzles) might perform better than simple tables as they will have more flexibility with regards to what entries to compress. Another interesting approach would be to feed a learning system like a neural network with values from the PDB. Also, other ideas for having a selective PDBs which only keep important values can be developed.

## References

Hinz, A. 1997. The Tower of Hanoi, *Algebras and Combinatorics: Proceedings of ICAC'97*. 277–289

Culberson, J. C., and Schaeffer, J. 1998. Pattern databases. *Computational Intelligence* 14(3):318–334.

Hernádvölgyi, I. T., and Holte, R. C. 2000. Experiments with automatically created memory-based heuristics. *Proc. SARA-2000, Lecture Notes in Artificial Intelligence* 1864:281–290.

Holte, R.; Newton, J.; Felner, A.; Meshulam R.; and Furcy, D. 2004. Multiple pattern databases. *Proc. ICAPS-04*

Korf, R. E., and Felner, A. 2002. Disjoint pattern database heuristics. *Artificial Intelligence* 134:9–22.

Korf, R., and Zhang, W. 2000. Divide-and-conquer frontier search applied to optimal sequence alignment,. *Proc. AAAI-2000*, 910–916.

Korf, R. E. 1997. Finding optimal solutions to Rubik's Cube using pattern databases. *Proc. AAAI-97*, 700–705.

Korf, R. E. 2004. Best-fi rst frontier search with delayed duplicate detection *Proc. AAAI04*, San-Jose, Ca.

# A General Solution to the Graph History Interaction Problem

**Akihiro Kishimoto** and **Martin Müller**
Department of Computing Science, University of Alberta
Edmonton, Canada T6G 2E8
{kishi,mmueller}@cs.ualberta.ca

### Abstract

Since the state space of most games is a directed graph, many game-playing systems detect repeated positions with a transposition table. This approach can reduce search effort by a large margin. However, it suffers from the so-called Graph History Interaction (GHI) problem, which causes errors in games containing repeated positions. This paper presents a practical solution to the GHI problem that combines and extends previous techniques. Because our scheme is general, it is applicable to different game tree search algorithms and to different domains. As demonstrated with the two algorithms $\alpha\beta$ and df-pn in the two games checkers and Go, our scheme incurs only a very small overhead, while guaranteeing the correctness of solutions.

**Keywords:** GHI problem, df-pn algorithm, $\alpha\beta$ algorithm, Kawano's simulation

## Introduction

Heuristic search is an important topic in Artificial Intelligence. Search algorithms have many practical applications in areas such as theorem-proving, bio-informatics, and games. In particular, games have been regarded as useful test beds for search algorithms. Efficient search algorithms were shown to improve the strength of game-playing programs. Experiments in many different domains and with many different programs have shown a strong positive correlation between the depth of a search and the strength of a program. Therefore, programmers have invested a lot of effort to enhance the search performance of their programs.

One of the most valuable search enhancements is the *transposition table*, a large cache that keeps results of previous searches. A program can reach the same game state via a different path — a so called *transposition*. If the previously cached position was explored deeply enough, the search algorithm does not need to explore the position again. However, if the search space includes cycles, cached results may be unreliable because they ignore the path used to reach the position. This is the so-called GHI (Graph-History Interaction) problem (Palay 1983). In practice, so far programmers have either ignored the GHI problem, since they did not want to degrade the performance of their programs, or reduced the number of recognized transpositions in order to guarantee correctness. Our proposed solution completely solves the GHI problem with very small overhead.



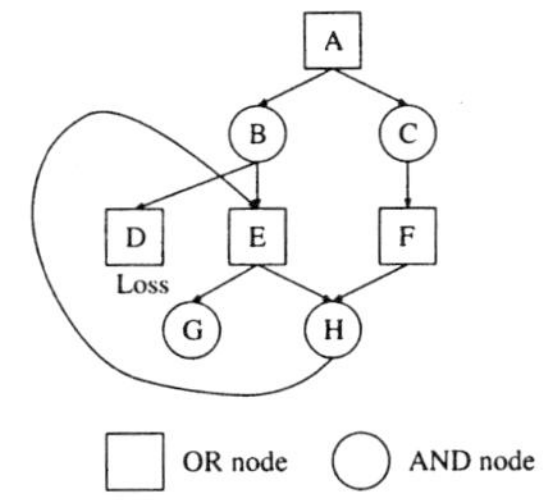


Figure 1: The GHI problem.

With the help of Figure 1 we explain the GHI problem for AND/OR trees. There are two scenarios in which the GHI problem can occur, depending on the rules of the game.

In the first scenario, which we call *first-player-loss*, a repetition is considered a loss for the *first player*, the player to play at the root node. Examples are checkmating problems in chess and shogi (tsume shogi), since a repetition does not help the first player who is trying to checkmate. Assume $D$ in the figure is a loss for the first player, and this result is stored in the transposition table. Let $G$ be a win for the first player. Then a search starting from $A$ in the following order leads to the wrong result:

1. Search $A \to B \to E \to H \to E$. A loss is stored in the table entry for $H$, because the position repetition cannot be avoided.
2. Search $A \to B \to D$. A loss is stored for AND node $B$.
3. Expand $A \to C \to F \to H$. A table look-up for $H$ retrieves a loss which is backed up to $F$ and $C$.
4. $A$ is now incorrectly labeled as a loss because losses are stored for both successors $B$ and $C$. However, $A$ is a win by the sequence $A \to C \to F \to H \to E \to G$.

In the first-player-loss scenario, the GHI problem only causes invalid disproofs (first-player losses). Programs can avoid the GHI problem, accepting a loss of performance, by not storing any disproofs caused by repetitions.

The other scenario for GHI, which we call *current-player-loss*, occurs when a repetition is declared to be a loss for the player who repeats the position. For instance, the situational super-ko (SSK) rule in Go declares that any move that repeats a previous board position is illegal. In this scenario, using a transposition table can lead to errors in both ways: it can change a loss into a win or a win into a loss. For example, in Figure 1, now assume that $G$ is a loss for the player to move at the root:

1. Search $A \rightarrow B \rightarrow E \rightarrow H$. $H$ is stored as a win because the opponent does not have a legal move at $H$.
2. Search $A \rightarrow C \rightarrow F \rightarrow H$. The win stored for $H$ is backed up and a win is stored for $C$ as well.
3. $A$ is now incorrectly labeled as a win since $C$'s table entry shows a win. However, $A$ is a losing position, since the sequences $A \rightarrow B \rightarrow D$, $A \rightarrow C \rightarrow F \rightarrow H \rightarrow E \rightarrow G$ and $A \rightarrow C \rightarrow F \rightarrow H \rightarrow E \rightarrow H$ all lose.

This scenario does not occur in checkmating problems where only one player's king is under attack. However, (van der Werf, van den Herik, & Uiterwijk 2003) point out that when using the SSK rule in Go, this scenario can lead to invalid proofs. In their work the problem is avoided by storing a separate hash entry for each path leading to a node. Unfortunately, this resulted in over 1,000 times larger searches when solving Go on a $4 \times 4$ board.

Avoiding the GHI problem is crucial, especially when one wants to declare that games are solved by programs. Since even a single flawed transposition table entry can lead to a completely wrong solution, correct techniques must be devised.

This paper describes a uniform solution to both aforementioned scenarios of the GHI problem. Our approach synthesizes and extends existing techniques. Our solution always guarantees correctness if all proven and disproven nodes are saved in the transposition table. The games of checkers, a first-player-loss scenario, and Go with the SSK rule, a current-player-loss scenario, are chosen to empirically measure the effectiveness of our approach. Since our idea does not depend on any algorithm-specific features, it can be applied to different game-tree search algorithms. We have chosen to implement our scheme for both the df-pn algorithm (Nagai 2002) and $\alpha\beta$ (Knuth & Moore 1975). Experimental results in these domains and algorithms show only a very small overhead compared to programs that ignore the GHI problem. In particular, since the only previous solution for the current-player-loss scenario was to give up all transpositions, which is very inefficient, our approach is the first attempt to handle the GHI problem with small overhead. Additionally, we empirically demonstrate that the GHI problem must be addressed since it does occur in practice.

The structure of this paper is as follows: First, the literature on the GHI problem is reviewed and the algorithms df-pn and $\alpha\beta$ are briefly explained. Then our solution to the GHI problem is described, followed by experimental results with both algorithms in Go and checkers, and some conclusions and future work.

## Previous Work on the GHI Problem

The GHI problem was first pointed out in (Palay 1983). Although two possible solutions were suggested, no implementation was provided. Campbell classified the GHI problem into two cases, *draw-first* and *draw-last*, and solved the GHI problem for the draw-first case (Campbell 1985). In the draw-first case, a score involving repetition is saved in the transposition table, and is later incorrectly retrieved for a position that does not involve repetition. In the draw-last scenario, a score not involving repetition is stored in the transposition table, and is later incorrectly used for a position involving repetition.

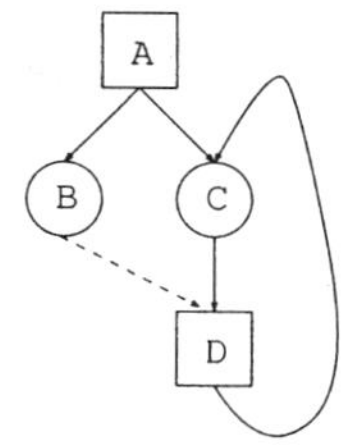

Figure 2: An example where BTA fails with the current-player-loss scenario.

(Breuker *et al.* 2001) proposed the *base-twin algorithm (BTA)* for solving the GHI problem in proof-number search. Since their implementation of BTA considered a draw to be a disproof, this model corresponds to the first-player-loss scenario in our framework. BTA uses a *possible-draw* mark combined with the depth of a node in the search graph to recognize repetitions. To find out at which depth a position causes repetitions, BTA splits repeated positions into two kinds of nodes: a *base* node to be explored and *twin* nodes which can have different values (i.e. possible-draw marks) than the base node. Possible-draw marks are propagated back to parents. When the root of the subtree that causes repetitions is detected, a real draw is stored in that root. Although Breuker *et al.* claim that BTA is a general solution to the GHI problem for best-first search, there are three issues that must be addressed:

- Since BTA was implemented for a best-first search algorithm that keeps an explicit graph in memory, it is an open question if BTA is applicable to depth-first search algorithms with limited memory.
- The cycle detection scheme in BTA does not work with the current-player-loss scenario. Figure 2 illustrates an example. $C$ is a node at the start of a repetition loop, but $C$'s value can not be uniquely determined without considering the path. $C$ via path $A \rightarrow C$ is a disproven node, since the last move in $A \rightarrow C \rightarrow D \rightarrow C$ is illegal. On the other hand, $C$ via path $A \rightarrow B \rightarrow D \rightarrow C$ is a proven node, since after this sequence the move to $D$ is a repetition for the opponent.
- All possible-draw marks are removed for each iteration of proof-number search. This is necessary in BTA since marks are path-dependent information. As long as a real draw is not stored, nodes causing repetitions must be explored again and again to mark possible-draws, resulting in a large overhead from tree reexpansion.

(Nagai 2002) proposes a solution to the GHI problem for df-pn. This modified df-pn is applied to tsume-shogi problems, a first-player-loss scenario. In Nagai's algorithm, df-pn first sets large thresholds of proof and disproof numbers at the root. In case of a repetition, df-pn simply returns to the parent node without storing a disproof. If a proof for the root is found, the proof tree is guaranteed to be repetition-free. However, if df-pn returns to the root by exceeding one of the large thresholds of proof and disproof numbers, df-pn re-searches by assuming that a move reaching the root is disproven. A similar repetition detection scheme is used at all interior nodes. One drawback of Nagai's approach is that it may take a long time for the proof or disproof numbers to exceed the preset threshold. If there is a large number of branches this approach is impractical for detecting disproofs with repetitions. Furthermore, Nagai's approach does not work with the current-player-loss scenario. Since this approach does not use any path information, it also cannot store two different path-dependent results for one node.

According to (Breuker *et al.* 2001), Thompson noticed that his tactical chess analyzer suffered from the GHI problem. He cured it for interior nodes by using a DCG (directed cyclic graph) representation and considering the history.

(Baum & Smith 1995) suggest a solution to the GHI problem for their best-first search algorithm. Their algorithm stores the whole DCG in memory and recognizes the case when a node reached through different paths must be split into two nodes to save different results. However, their idea was not implemented, and they concluded that a low storage algorithm would probably be too costly.

(Schijf, Allis, & Uiterwijk 1994) investigated proof-number search in domains where the search graph is a DAG (directed acyclic graph) or DCG. Schijf implemented three algorithms to deal with the GHI problem. However, two of these methods are inefficient, since they give up on using transpositions, while the third approach sometimes results in wrong disproofs.

## Overview of df-pn and $\alpha\beta$

### Depth-First Proof-Number Search

The depth-first proof-number algorithm df-pn (Nagai 2002) turns the best-first proof-number search (PNS) method (Allis, van der Meulen, & van den Herik 1994) into a depth-first search algorithm. Df-pn can expand less interior nodes and use a smaller amount of memory than PNS. Like PNS, it uses proof and disproof numbers and always expands a most-proving node. Df-pn utilizes local thresholds for both proof and disproof numbers, selects a most promising node, and performs iterative deepening until exceeding either one of the thresholds. Because df-pn is an iterative deepening method that re-expands interior nodes, the heart of the algorithm is its use of the transposition table. Whenever a node is explored, the transposition table is used to cache previous search efforts (i.e., proof and disproof numbers).

### The $\alpha\beta$ Algorithm

The $\alpha\beta$ algorithm (Knuth & Moore 1975) has been the most popular algorithm among game programmers. The algorithm utilizes a search window defined by two bounds, $\alpha$ and $\beta$, which represent lower and upper bounds on the minimax score of a game tree. The search window is narrowed during minimax search, and used for pruning subtrees if the score of a node is proven to be outside the window. Many variants and enhancements have been developed over the years, but a transposition table is almost always used.

## A New General Solution to the GHI Problem

Our solution utilizes two techniques: We encode path information using methods from (Zobrist 1970) and use Kawano's simulation technique (Kawano 1996) to search efficiently. The outline of our solution to the GHI problem is as follows: When a proven or disproven position stored in the transposition table is reached via a new path, instead of blindly retrieving the result, a search is performed to verify it. If the proof/disproof verifies, the result can be safely reused; otherwise the transposition table entry is treated as a different position. Kawano's simulation is used to reduce the search overhead. For efficiency, this approach requires a good scheme for storing and comparing paths, and a technique for minimizing the number of simulation calls.

### Duplicating Transposition Table Entries

In order to reuse the results of previous search efforts, unproven identical positions reached via different paths are considered to be transpositions. We reuse the values stored in the transposition table: proof and disproof numbers for df-pn, and minimax values for $\alpha\beta$. When position $A$ is proven via path $p$, the transposition table entry for $A$ is split into a *base* and a first *twin* table entry. A proof is stored in the twin table entry to indicate that $A$ is proven when reaching $A$ via $p$. If $A$ is proven via a different path $q$, another twin table entry for $q$ is created and the new proof is stored there. When reaching $A$ via a path other than $p$, the proofs of the twin table entries are simulated (see later). If at least one verifies then that proof is used; otherwise the information from the unproven base table entry is used in the search. Disproofs are handled in the same way.

### Encoding Paths

Identical positions reached via different paths can be differentiated by computing a signature of a path. A variant of the Zobrist function, which is used to hash a position into its corresponding transposition table key (Zobrist 1970), can be used to encode a path. In our implementation, each transposition table entry contains an additional 64-bit field to encode a signature of the path from the root to a position. Let *MaxMove* be the number of different moves in a game, and *MaxDepth* be the maximum search depth. A precomputed random table $R$ with *MaxMove*×*MaxDepth* 64 bit integers is prepared to encode a path. The sequence of moves to reach that position is encoded by a technique inspired by Zobrist's method. Let the path $p$ be $(m_1, m_2, \cdots, m_k)$, where $m_i$ are moves. Then $p$ is encoded as follows:

$$\text{code}(p) = R[m_1][1] \oplus R[m_2][2] \oplus \cdots \oplus R[m_k][k]$$

An important property of this path-encoding scheme is that the order of moves is not commutative, since the random table entries for the same move played at different depths are different. For example, the codes of the two paths $p_1 = (m_1, m_2, m_3)$ and $p_2 = (m_3, m_2, m_1)$ are not the same, since code($p_1$) $= R[m_1][1] \oplus R[m_2][2] \oplus R[m_3][3]$ is different from code($p_2$) $= R[m_1][3] \oplus R[m_2][2] \oplus R[m_3][1]$.

We note that the size of the random table is small enough for current hardware. For example, in our experiments on $19 \times 19$ Go, setting *MaxMove* = 362 and *MaxDepth* = 50 the size is about 140KB. In games with a large number of different possible moves, such as Shogi or Amazons, a move can be split into two or three partial moves, for example by separating the from-square information from the to-square information. This way *MaxMove* can be greatly reduced, while *MaxDepth* increases by a factor of 2 or 3.

## Invoking Simulation for Correctness

Tree *simulation* was invented by Kawano to effectively deal with useless interposing piece drops in tsume-shogi (Kawano 1996). Tanase applied this idea extensively in shogi, to reduce the overhead of calling the tsume-shogi solver within the normal $\alpha\beta$ search (Tanase 2000).

In AND/OR trees, which are the common concept on which both df-pn and $\alpha\beta$ are based, a *proof tree* $T$ provides a proof that a node $n$ is proven. Such a proof tree contains $n$, at least one child of each interior OR node of $T$, and all children of interior AND nodes of $T$. All terminal nodes of $T$ must be proven. A *disproof tree* $T$ which provides a disproof is defined in an analogous way.

Assume that $P$ is a proven node and $Q$ is a "similar" one that we want to prove. Simulation borrows moves from $P$'s proof tree to attempt a quick proof of $Q$. The winning move for each OR node in the proof tree is obtained from the transposition table of the proof tree of $P$. Likewise, *dual simulation* attempts to find a disproof.

Compared to a normal search, simulation requires much less effort to confirm whether a position is proven or not. Even with good move ordering, a newly created search tree is typically much larger than an existing proof tree. Also, since moves are borrowed from the transposition table at OR nodes, there is no need to invoke the move generator there.

Assume that position $A$ was proven via path $p$. If $A$ is reached via a different path $q$, we can check if $A$ via $q$ can be proven quickly by invoking simulation. A proof is borrowed from the twin table entry with path $p$. If a proof for $A$ via $q$ is verified, an additional twin table entry for the proof of $A$ via $q$ is created. If more than one twin table entry is available, they are tried one after another. However, since proof trees often have the same shape, it is rare that more than one tree simulation is needed. The analogous verification by dual simulation is tried to find disproofs.

## Reducing Simulation Calls

Since simulation incurs an overhead to assess the correctness of a transposition table entry, we devised a method to reduce the number of simulation calls. If a node is (dis)proven without detecting a repetition, that node can always be used as a transposition, since it is independent of the path taken by the search. In this case, the (dis)proof is stored directly in the base table entry, without creating a twin node. If another path leads to that position, this (dis)proof can be reused.

## Correctness of Our Solution

Assume that all proven and disproven nodes are stored in the transposition table. The following theorem guarantees correctness of the solutions:

**Theorem 1** *Our solution suffers neither from the draw-first nor from the draw-last case.*

For unproven nodes, our proposed solution might compute incorrect proof and disproof numbers for df-pn, and incorrect heuristic values for $\alpha\beta$ search. However, Theorem 1 guarantees that (dis)proofs returned by our approach are always correct. This theorem is proven for the case of df-pn in (Kishimoto & Müller 2004), and can be analogously proven for $\alpha\beta$ with some modifications (see the next section).

## Algorithm-Specific Implementation Details

**Df-pn** We made the following modifications to the original df-pn algorithm:

- Proof and disproof numbers in a base table entry are re-initialized to 1 whenever a (dis)proof is saved in a twin table entry. This is because df-pn tends to create large proof and disproof numbers before a (dis)proof is found, which made df-pn unable to solve some positions.
- As in (Nagai 2002), we initialize the thresholds of proof and disproof numbers at the root to $\infty - 1$, not $\infty$ as in the original df-pn algorithm. This is necessary to avoid the GHI problem at the root, since df-pn saves thresholds in the transposition table before expanding a node. If df-pn with our modification returns a proof number of 0 and a disproof number of $\infty$, or vice versa, it is a correct (dis)proof. Otherwise, df-pn returns the value *unknown*.

$\alpha\beta$ The following modifications are made:

- We modified the scheme for transposition table lookups. A normal transposition table entry contains a field that stores the depth searched below a node. If a transposition is recognized, the depth stored in the table entry is at least as deep as the depth that must be explored, and the table entry has a tight $\alpha\beta$ bound, then the table information is retrieved and no further search for that node is performed. We use this strategy only for unproven nodes. (Dis)proofs saved in the transposition table are always retrieved without checking the explored depth, since they are correct. This modification not only makes more use of the transposition table but also solves Campbell's draw-last case.
- Our current $\alpha\beta$ search uses only the three values (*win*, *unknown*, or *loss*). However, our solution works for the general case of more values in between *win* and *loss*. In our implementation of checkers, a draw is considered as a loss for the first player. To prove a draw, a second search must be performed in which a draw is regarded as a win for the first player. We note that determining a draw within a single search is not a trivial problem for the $\alpha\beta$ algorithm, since the values *draw* and *unknown* are incomparable. A

correct heuristic value can be obtained by performing a sequence of null window searches as in MTD(f) (Plaat *et al.* 1996).

### Game-Specific Implementation Details

**Go** Domain-specific enhancements from (Kishimoto & Müller 2003) are incorporated in our df-pn and $\alpha\beta$ implementations. $\alpha\beta$ performs iterative deepening, extends the search for forced moves, and searches the best move from a previous iteration first.

**Checkers** 8-piece endgame databases are incorporated to our df-pn and $\alpha\beta$ implementations. Scores obtained by database lookups are considered to be correct, because these scores are path independent. Simulation is not invoked for trees involving only database scores. The $\alpha\beta$ implementation performs a variable depth-first search with state-of-the-art enhancements.

## Experiments

### Setup

We applied the df-pn and $\alpha\beta$ algorithms to Go and checkers. We focused on the one-eye problem with situational super-ko in Go, a current-player-loss scenario. Checkers is a first-player loss scenario.

The experiments for programs ignoring and dealing with the GHI problem for both games were performed on an Athlon 2400MP with a 300 MB transposition table. All proven and disproven nodes are saved in the transposition table in both programs. 140 positions in Go and 200 positions in checkers were prepared. The time limit was set to 5 minutes per position in Go. In checkers the execution time was unstable because it is dominated by I/O to access the databases. Therefore, we did not limit the execution time here. Instead, the checkers searches were limited to 10 million node expansions per position.

### Results in Go

Tables 1 and 2 summarize the results for df-pn and $\alpha\beta$ in Go in terms of the number of problems solved and total node expansions. These statistics are collected from the two programs ignoring (IGNORE-GHI) and handling (HANDLE-GHI) the GHI problem. We could not test other approaches such as Nagai's in Go, since they do not handle the current-player-loss scenario. Both IGNORE-GHI and HANDLE-GHI solve the same subset of problems. However, IGNORE-GHI gave incorrect proof trees for two positions in df-pn and for three positions in $\alpha\beta$. Although the scores returned by IGNORE-GHI were correct, we conclude that it is important to have a scheme to handle the GHI problem, since GHI happens both in df-pn and $\alpha\beta$. Even if GHI does not appear in the final proof tree, it occasionally appears in the search. In the 136 problems solved, HANDLE-GHI in df-pn invoked simulation 648 times, explored 13,505 nodes by simulation, and discovered 190 flawed transposition table entries. In the 132 problems solved by $\alpha\beta$, HANDLE-GHI invoked simulation 12,005 times, explored

Table 1: Performance comparison between ignoring and dealing with the GHI problem for df-pn in Go. All statistics are computed for 136 problems solved by both program versions.

| Method Used | Number of problems solved | Total nodes | Total time (sec) |
|---|---|---|---|
| IGNORE-GHI | $134+2$ | 22,294,119 | 589 |
| HANDLE-GHI | 136 | 21,938,585 | 587 |

Table 2: Performance comparison for $\alpha\beta$ in Go. All the statistics are computed for 132 problems solved by both versions.

| Method Used | Number of problems solved | Total nodes | Total time (sec) |
|---|---|---|---|
| IGNORE-GHI | $129+3$ | 102,077,944 | 1,078 |
| HANDLE-GHI | 132 | 104,679,229 | 1,101 |

147,946 nodes by simulation, and detected 4,174 flawed entries. These numbers are conservative, because some incorrect proofs or disproofs may have been stored but never retrieved. The results show that HANDLE-GHI can avoid the GHI problem with negligible overhead in terms of expanded nodes and execution time. In our tests, HANDLE-GHI explored 2.5% extra nodes in $\alpha\beta$, and 1.5 % less nodes in df-pn. This is a very small price to pay for guaranteeing correctness.

### Results in Checkers

Table 3 gives the results for df-pn in checkers. We additionally implemented Nagai's solution (NAGAI) to the GHI problem (Nagai 2002). Of the 200 problems in the data set, NAGAI solved 138. IGNORE-GHI solved 144, including the 138 which NAGAI solved. However, IGNORE-GHI had incorrect disproofs in 18 cases, whereas NAGAI solves all problems correctly. HANDLE-GHI solves 143 problems correctly, including all 138 problems solved by NAGAI, some additional problems solved by IGNORE-GHI, plus some problems not solved by either of the other two methods. HANDLE-GHI solved 2 problems which IGNORE-GHI did not solve. IGNORE-GHI 'solved' 3 problems which our scheme did not solve, but only one of those problems was solved correctly. In these experiments, our solution has no overhead. It even expands slightly fewer nodes than IGNORE-GHI. Simulation again detects flawed transposition table entries. In the 138 problems solved by all programs, HANDLE-GHI invoked simulation 243,885 times with 970,373 node expansions and discovered 87,181 flawed transposition table entries. These numbers confirm that the GHI problem occurs in search. Some incorrect results were contained in the final disproof trees.

Table 4 shows the results for $\alpha\beta$. HANDLE-GHI solved all positions solved by IGNORE-GHI, plus one more. IGNORE-GHI returned incorrect disproofs for 8 positions.

Table 3: Performance comparison for df-pn in checkers. All statistics are computed for the subset of 138 problems solved by all program versions.

| Method Used | Problems solved | Total nodes |
|---|---|---|
| IGNORE-GHI | 126 + 18 | 129,006,133 |
| HANDLE-GHI | 143 | 128,082,295 |
| NAGAI | 138 | 137,888,627 |

Table 4: Performance comparison for $\alpha\beta$ in checkers. All statistics are computed for the subset of 111 problems solved by both program versions.

| Method Used | Problems solved | Total nodes |
|---|---|---|
| IGNORE-GHI | 103 + 8 | 119,289,609 |
| HANDLE-GHI | 112 | 116,673,224 |

In the 111 problems solved by both programs, HANDLE-GHI invoked simulation 22,536 times with 31,170 node expansions and detected 14,418 flawed entries. These numbers indicate that the GHI problem occurs in $\alpha\beta$ in checkers, but a bit less frequently than in df-pn.

In conclusion, since the GHI problem happens both in df-pn and $\alpha\beta$ in checkers, it is dangerous to ignore. Because our method not only incurs low overhead but also always returns correct answers, it is a worthwhile addition to any search engine susceptible to GHI.

Our method could be compared with Breuker's BTA. However, we note that BTA needs an explicit graph representation, and complicated operations to deal with repetitions. This causes a problem when BTA uses up available memory. On the other hand, our approach does not need any explicit graph representation. Unproven nodes can be replaced when the table becomes full. Breuker's scheme to detect real draws is specific to the first-player-loss scenario, and could be added to our framework.

## Conclusions and Future Work

In this paper, we presented a framework to solve an important open problem raised by (Palay 1983) 20 years ago. Our approach incurs very small overhead and is applicable to two algorithms df-pn and $\alpha\beta$. Therefore, we conclude that our solution to the GHI problem is practical and general.

An interesting topic for further consideration is the relation between the GHI problem with replacement and garbage collection schemes with limited memory. Since our algorithm currently needs to keep all proven and disproven nodes in memory, there is still an open question as to which nodes can be replaced or garbage-collected.

## Acknowledgments

We would like to thank Jonathan Schaeffer and Yngvi Björnsson for beneficial discussions and making their checkers code available. Nathan Sturtevant and Markian Hlynka read drafts of the paper and gave valuable comments. Financial support was provided by the Natural Sciences and Engineering Research Council of Canada (NSERC) and the Alberta Informatics Circle of Research Excellence (iCORE).

## References

Allis, L. V.; van der Meulen, M.; and van den Herik, H. J. 1994. Proof-number search. *Artificial Intelligence* 66(1):91–124.

Baum, E. B., and Smith, W. D. 1995. Best play for imperfect players and game tree search; part I - theory. Technical report, NEC Research Institute. Available at `http://citeseer.nj.nec.com/baum95best.html`.

Breuker, D. M.; van den Herik, H. J.; Uiterwijk, J. W. H. M.; and Allis, L. V. 2001. A solution to the GHI problem for best-first search. *Theoretical Computer Science* 252(1-2):121–149.

Campbell, M. 1985. The graph-history interaction: On ignoring position history. In *1985 Association for Computing Machinery Annual Conference*, 278–280.

Kawano, Y. 1996. Using similar positions to search game trees. In Nowakowski, R. J., ed., *Games of No Chance*, volume 29 of *MSRI Publications*, 193–202. Cambridge University Press.

Kishimoto, A., and Müller, M. 2003. Df-pn in Go: Application to the one-eye problem. In *Advances in Computer Games. Many Games, Many Challenges*, 125–141. Kluwer Academic Publishers.

Kishimoto, A., and Müller, M. 2004. A solution to the GHI problem for depth-first proof-number search. *Information Sciences*. To appear.

Knuth, D. E., and Moore, R. W. 1975. An analysis of alpha-beta pruning. *Artificial Intelligence* 6:293–326.

Nagai, A. 2002. *Df-pn Algorithm for Searching AND/OR Trees and Its Applications*. Ph.D. Dissertation, Department of Information Science, University of Tokyo.

Palay, A. J. 1983. *Searching with Probabilities*. Ph.D. Dissertation, Carnegie Mellon University.

Plaat, A.; Schaeffer, J.; Pijls, W.; and de Bruin, A. 1996. Best-First Fixed-Depth Minimax Algorithms. *Artificial Intelligence* 87(1-2):255–293.

Schijf, M.; Allis, L. V.; and Uiterwijk, J. W. H. M. 1994. Proof-number search and transpositions. *International Computer Chess Association Journal* 17(2):63–74.

Tanase, Y. 2000. Algorithms in ISshogi. In Matsubara, H., ed., *Advances in Computer Shogi 3*, 1–14. Kyouritsu Shuppan Press. In Japanese.

van der Werf, E. C. D.; van den Herik, H. J.; and Uiterwijk, J. W. H. M. 2003. Solving Go on small boards. *International Computer Games Association Journal* 26(2):92–107.

Zobrist, A. L. 1970. A new hashing method with applications for game playing. Technical report, Department of Computer Science, University of Wisconsin, Madison.

# Best-First Frontier Search with Delayed Duplicate Detection

**Richard E. Korf**
Computer Science Department
University of California, Los Angeles
Los Angeles, CA 90095
korf@cs.ucla.edu

### Abstract

Best-first search is limited by the memory needed to store the Open and Closed lists, primarily to detect duplicate nodes. Magnetic disks provide vastly more storage, but random access of a disk is extremely slow. Instead of checking generated nodes immediately against existing nodes in a hash table, delayed duplicate detection (DDD) appends them to a file, then periodically removes the duplicate nodes using only sequential disk accesses. Frontier search saves storage in a best-first search by storing only the Open list and not the Closed list. The main contributions of this paper are to provide a scalable implementation of DDD, to combine it with frontier search, and to extend it to more general best-first searches such as A*. We illustrate these ideas by performing complete breadth-first searches of sliding-tile puzzles up to the 3x5 Fourteen Puzzle. For the 4-peg Towers of Hanoi problem, we perform complete searches with up to 20 disks, searching a space of over a trillion nodes, and discover a surprising anomaly concerning the problem-space diameter of the 15 and 20-disk problems. We also verify the presumed optimal solution lengths for up to 24 disks. In addition, we implement A* with DDD on the Fifteen Puzzle. Finally, we present a scalable implementation of DDD based on hashing rather than sorting.

## Introduction

### Best-First Search

Best-first search (BFS) is an algorithm schema that includes as special cases breadth-first search, uniform-cost search or Dijkstra's algorithm (Dijkstra 1959), and A* (Hart, Nilsson, & Raphael 1968). BFS maintains a Closed list of nodes that have been expanded, and an Open list of nodes that have been generated but not yet expanded. Each cycle of the algorithm chooses an Open node of lowest cost, expands it, generating and evaluating its children, and moves it to Closed. Each child node is checked to see if the same state already appears on the Open or Closed lists. If so, only a single copy reached via a shortest path from the start is saved.

If the cost of a node is its depth, then BFS becomes breadth-first search. If the cost of a node $n$ is $g(n)$, the sum of the edge costs from the start to node $n$, then BFS becomes uniform-cost search or Dijkstra's algorithm (Dijkstra 1959). If the cost of a node is $f(n) = g(n) + h(n)$, where $h(n)$ is a heuristic estimate of the cost from $n$ to a goal, then BFS becomes A* (Hart, Nilsson, & Raphael 1968). Normally, BFS terminates when a goal node is expanded, but breadth-first search can terminate when a goal node is generated.

### The Problem

BFS stores every state it generates in either the Open or the Closed list. For problems where node expansion is relatively efficient, such as the ones discussed in this paper, BFS typically exhausts the available memory in a matter of minutes, terminating the algorithm. In some problems, this limitation can be avoided by depth-first searches (DFS) such as depth-first branch-and-bound (DFBnB), depth-first iterative-deepening (DFID), or iterative-deepening-A* (IDA*)(Korf 1985), which require space that is only linear in the search depth. Since DFS can't detect most duplicate nodes, however, it can generate exponentially more nodes than BFS. For example, in a rectangular-grid problem space, breadth-first search generates $O(r^2)$ nodes within a radius of $r$, while DFS generates $O(3^r)$ nodes, since each node has four neighbors, one of which is its parent.

To detect all duplicates, we must store large numbers of nodes. Disks with hundreds of gigabytes cost less than a dollar per gigabyte, a hundred times cheaper than memory. Furthermore, a 32-bit machine can only directly address four gigabytes of memory, but unlimited disk space. Disks cannot directly replace memory, however, since disk latency is about 5 milliseconds, or 100,000 times longer than memory latency. A disk behaves more like a sequential device such as a magnetic tape, with large capacity and high bandwidth, but only if it is accessed sequentially. To quickly detect duplicate states, however, nodes are usually stored in a hash table, which is designed for random access. Virtual memory doesn't help, because of the random access pattern.

## Prior Work

### Delayed Duplicate Detection

A solution to this problem, which we call *delayed duplicate detection* (DDD), was developed by (Roscoe 1994) in the context of breadth-first search for automatic verification. Rather than checking for duplicates as soon as a node is generated, it is simply appended to the Open list. At the end of each level of the search, the nodes on Open are sorted by their state representation, bringing duplicate nodes to adjacent positions, where they are eliminated. The sorted Open list is then merged with a sorted Closed list, deleting the closed nodes from Open, and producing a new sorted Closed list. Roscoe's implementation doesn't manipulate disk files, but works in main memory, relying on virtual memory to handle the overflow to disk. His system was run on problem spaces with up to ten million nodes. If the problem space is significantly larger than the capacity of main memory, however, the asymptotic I/O complexity of this algorithm is at least the size of the problem space times the depth of the breadth-first search. For the 20-disk 4-peg Towers of Hanoi problem, for example, the depth of a complete breadth-first search is 294 moves.

(Stern & Dill 1998) also implemented a breadth-first search with DDD in their model checker for hardware verification. They maintain a disk file of all states generated. When memory becomes full, the disk file of existing states is linearly scanned to eliminate duplicates from memory, and the new states remaining in memory are appended to the disk file, and to a separate queue of Open nodes. They report results on problems with just over a million states. Unfortunately, the I/O complexity of their algorithm also grows at least as fast as the size of the problem space times the search depth. In fact, its complexity is worse if a complete level of the search won't fit in memory, since in that case, the complete Closed list is scanned every time memory becomes full, in addition to the end of each level of the search.

### Frontier Search

Both of these schemes store all nodes generated in the search. Frontier search (Korf 1999; Korf & Zhang 2000) saves memory in any best-first search by storing only the Open list, and not the Closed list. In a breadth-first search, its space complexity is proportional to the maximum number of nodes at any depth, or the width of the problem space, rather than the total number of nodes in the space. In our experiments, these differed by as much as a factor of 46.

(Bode & Hinz 1999) implemented a form of breadth-first frontier search in memory for the 4-peg Towers of Hanoi, verifying the presumed optimal solution lengths for up to 17 disks. They save the nodes at the current depth, the prior depth, and the following depth. By contrast, our algorithm only stores two levels of the search at a time for the Towers of Hanoi, and one level for the sliding-tile puzzles.

## Graph Algorithms using External Storage

There exists a body of work in the theory community on graph algorithms using external storage. See (Katriel & Meyer 2003) for a recent and comprehensive treatment of this area. That work is focussed on explicit graphs, where all nodes and edges are stored on disk, and analyzing the asymptotic complexity of the algorithms, without implementations or experimental results. By contrast, we are concerned with implicit graphs defined by a successor function, and the performance of practical implementations.

## Overview

We first describe best-first search (BFS) with DDD in memory, and then consider using disk storage. We then show how to combine frontier search with DDD for breadth-first and uniform-cost search. The disk I/O complexity of our breadth-first frontier search with DDD scales linearly with the size of the state space. Unfortunately, DDD and frontier search can't be directly combined in A*. Using breadth-first frontier search with DDD, we compute the maximum optimal solution lengths for all sliding-tile puzzles up to the 3x5 Fourteen Puzzle, and confirm the presumed optimal solution lengths for the 4-peg Towers of Hanoi problem with up to 24 disks. By exhaustive search of the 4-peg Towers of Hanoi problems with up to 20 disks, we discover a surprising anomaly in the problem space diameter for 15 and 20 disks. The largest of these searches generate almost 4000 times more nodes than the previous state of the art. We solve a standard set of 100 random 15-puzzle instances using A* with DDD. Finally, we describe a scalable implementation of DDD based on hashing rather than sorting. Early versions of this work appeared in (Korf 2003b) and (Korf 2003a).

## Delayed Duplicate Detection in Memory

At first we assume that all nodes fit in memory, and that the cost of a child is never less than the cost of its parent. Define $bestf$ as the lowest $f = g + h$ cost among all Open nodes at any given time. BFS will expand all Open nodes of cost $bestf$, then increment $bestf$ to the next higher cost of any Open node, expand those nodes, etc.

BFS with DDD stores open and closed nodes intermixed in a single node list. Each iteration of our algorithm linearly scans the node list, expanding all nodes of cost $bestf$, and skipping nodes of lower or higher cost. For example, an iteration of breadth-first search will expand all nodes at a given depth. When a node is expanded, its children are generated, evaluated, and appended to the end of the node list, without checking for duplicates. If a child node has the same cost as its parent, the child will be appended to the end of the list, and expanded during the same iteration as the parent, when the scan reaches the child node.

Normally, duplicate detection is performed after each iteration. We sort the nodes by their state representation, using quicksort, since it sorts in place without additional memory. Sorting brings to adjacent locations any duplicate nodes representing the same state. Then, in a linear scan of the sorted node list, we remove all duplicate nodes, saving one copy of minimum $g$ value. During this scan, we also reset $bestf$ to the lowest cost of those nodes not yet expanded. We then start a new iteration, with the new value of $bestf$. Alternatively, duplicate elimination could be performed whenever memory becomes full.

If there are many unique node values, then a single iteration may expand all open nodes in a range of cost values. An appropriate range can be determined during the preceding duplicate scan. In that case, we terminate when we complete the first iteration that chooses a goal node for expansion.

If our cost function is non-monotonic, meaning that a child may have a lower cost than its parent, then we mark open nodes of cost less than $bestf$, so they are expanded when they are reached during the same iteration. Alternatively, after expanding a node, we can recursively expand all its descendents of cost less than or equal to $bestf$, appending them all to the end of the node list.

### Recovering the Solution Path

Once we find an optimal solution, we may want the actual solution path as well. Normally, this is done by storing with each node a pointer to its parent, and then following these pointers from the goal state back to the start state. Sorting the nodes moves them in memory, however, invalidating the pointers. Instead, with each node we store the operator that generated it from its parent, along a lowest-cost path to the node. Alternatively, if operators are invertible, we could store the operator that generates the parent from the child. Once we find a solution, we sort the node list again, but in decreasing order of $g$ value, rather than by state representation. We then scan the sorted list from the beginning, until we reach the goal node. We generate its parent state using the stored operator, and continue scanning the node list from the same point until we reach the parent node. When we reach the parent, we generate the grandparent state, etc, continuing until we reach the start state. If every edge has a positive cost, a parent node will always follow its children in the resorted node list, and hence we can reconstruct the entire solution path in one scan of the node list.

### Advantages of DDD in Memory

Even when storing all nodes in memory, there are several advantages of BFS with DDD over standard BFS. One is that DDD requires less memory per node, since it doesn't need pointers for a hash table or Open list. For the Fifteen Puzzle, for example, BFS with DDD needs less than half the memory per node of standard BFS.

A second advantage of BFS with DDD is that it may run faster than standard BFS, due to improved cache performance. A hash table spreads nodes uniformly over memory. By contrast, BFS with DDD scans the node list linearly, appending nodes to the end. Quicksort only accesses nodes at both ends of a list, and the purge phase linearly scans the sorted node list. Each of these steps exhibit good locality.

## BFS with DDD using Disk Storage

The main advantage of DDD, however, is that it allows us to store the node list on disk. We first give an overview of the algorithm. Think of the node list as a single file. We read this file sequentially, expanding nodes of cost $bestf$, and appending the children to the end of the file. When we've read the entire file, including nodes added during the current iteration, we sort it. Algorithms for sorting disk files are well-known (Garcia-Molina, Ullman, & Widom 2000). Finally, we sequentially scan the sorted file to remove duplicate nodes, and begin a new iteration.

To implement this efficiently, we start with a sorted node list in an input file, initially containing only the start node. We read this file sequentially, expanding those nodes of cost $bestf$. If a child has cost $bestf$ or less, it is recursively expanded, as are grandchildren of the same or lower cost, etc. In any case, all newly generated nodes are appended to a buffer in memory. When this buffer is full, the nodes are sorted by their state representation, duplicate nodes are deleted, saving one copy of lowest $g$ value, and the remaining nodes are written to an output file. We continue reading the input file, producing multiple output files. Each of these are sorted, and contain no duplicates within them, but duplicates will appear across different files.

We then merge all the sorted output files, together with the sorted input file, into one sorted file without duplicates, in a single multi-way merge. We initialize a heap with the first node in each file. At each cycle, the top node of the heap is removed, written to a new output file, and replaced in the heap by the next node from the file that it came from. During this process, duplicate nodes come together at the top of the heap, and are merged at that time, keeping a copy of lowest $g$ value. This process continues until all the output files, and the input file, have been exhausted. Then the next iteration of the search begins with the new output file as the input file. The virtue of a multi-way merge is that each node is only read once, and only one copy of each node is written once, in each sort-merge phase.

The algorithm alternates expansion and sort-merge phases, until an optimal solution is found. If we want the solution path itself, then the nodes are resorted into a single file in decreasing order of $g$ value. This file is then scanned linearly, looking for the goal node, then its parent, grandparent, etc, until the start node is reached.

The sort-merge algorithm described above could require up to twice as much disk space as necessary. When we read a node into memory, we no longer need it on disk, since it is stored until it is written to the new input file. However, most file systems don't allow deleting elements from a file as they are read. If the nodes in each output file and the old input file are uniformly distributed over the state space, we may not be able to delete any of these files until the entire sort-merge phase is almost complete, at which point all of these nodes, minus their duplicates, will have been written to the new input file. To avoid this problem, each "file" described above is actually broken up into a sequence of smaller file segments, so that we can delete an entire file segment as soon as it is read into memory.

The I/O complexity of this algorithm is on the order of the size of the search space times the number of expansion iterations. For a breadth-first search, this is no worse than the size of the space times its depth. It can be reduced by performing the initial expansion iterations without sorting and merging, until memory is full.

## Frontier Search

Frontier search (Korf 1999; Korf & Zhang 2000) is an independent way of implementing best-first search that saves memory by storing only the Open list and not the Closed list. We first describe the algorithm, and then show how to combine it with DDD. We assume here that all operators are invertible, i.e. the problem-space graph is undirected, but the algorithm applies to directed graphs as well.

Frontier search stores only the Open list, representing the frontier or boundary of the search, and deletes a node once it is expanded. The trick is to keep the search from "leaking" back into the expanded or interior region of the space. With each node, we store a *used* bit for each operator, to indicate whether the neighboring state reached by that operator has been expanded yet. For example, in the sliding-tile puzzles we need four bits for each state, one for each direction in which a tile could move. For the Towers of Hanoi, we need one bit for each peg, indicating the location of the last disk moved. When we expand a parent node, we only generate those children that are reached via unused operators, and delete the parent node from memory. In each child node, the operator that generates its parent is marked as used. We also look up each child state in the Open list. If a duplicate state is found, only the copy reached by a shortest path is kept, and any operator marked as used in any copy is marked as used in the retained copy. Since the Closed list is not stored, reconstructing the solution path requires some additional work, described in (Korf 1999; Korf & Zhang 2000).

The memory required by frontier search is proportional to the maximum size of the Open list, or the *width* of the search, rather than the size of the entire space. For example, the width of a rectangular grid space grows only linearly with the search radius, while the entire space grows quadratically. As another example, the maximum number of states at any depth of the $n$-disk, 3-peg Towers of Hanoi space is only $2^n$, while the entire space contains $3^n$ states.

## Combining Frontier Search with DDD

Since frontier search saves memory in best-first search, and DDD allows disk storage to be used, to maximize the size of problems we can solve we'd like to combine the two algorithms. While this combination is straightforward for breadth-first search and uniform-cost search, they cannot be easily combined in the case of A*. We begin with breadth-first frontier search with DDD.

### Breadth-First Frontier Search with DDD

In breadth-first frontier search with DDD, we merge duplicates at the end of each iteration, when all nodes at a given depth have been expanded. In the simplest case, the input file contains all nodes at depth $d$, and the output files contain nodes at depth $d+1$, since the used operator bits prevent generating nodes at depth $d-1$. We delete the input file when it's exhausted, and sort and merge the output files together.

Consider the square graph at left in Figure 1, where node $A$ is the start node. Node $A$ is expanded and then deleted, generating node $B$ with operator $w$ marked as used, and node $C$, with operator $x$ marked as used. In the next iteration, node $B$ is expanded and deleted, generating node $D$ with operator $y$ marked as used, and node $C$ is expanded and deleted, generating another copy of node $D$ with operator $z$ marked as used. In the sort-merge phase, these two copies of node $D$ are merged into a single copy, with operators $y$ and $z$ both marked as used. Since node $D$ has no more neighbors, the search would terminate at this point.

The I/O complexity of this algorithm is linear in the size of the search space. The first time a node is generated, it is stored until memory is full, then sorted and merged with any duplicates in memory, and written to a disk file. Once all the nodes at the current depth are expanded, a merge phase begins which will read the node back into memory, merge it with any duplicates from other files, and write it out to a single file. Finally, in the next expansion phase, it will be read back into memory, expanded and deleted. Thus each node is read twice and written twice. A given state can be represented by as many duplicate nodes as the branching factor of the problem, one from each of its neighbors. Since we assume a constant branching factor, the I/O complexity is still linear in the number of states in the problem space.

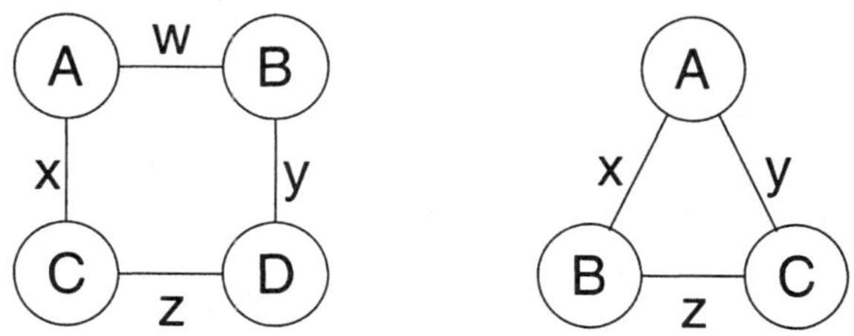


Figure 1: Example Graphs

This algorithm works fine in a graph where the lengths of all paths between any pair of nodes have the same parity. For example, for any pair of nodes in a sliding-tile puzzle, either all paths between them have odd length, or all have even length. In a triangle graph, however, such as that shown at right in Figure 1, there is a path of length one and of length two between any pair of nodes. The Towers of Hanoi problem space graphs contain many such triangles.

Consider our simple algorithm on the triangle in Figure 1, assuming that $A$ is the start node. Node $A$ is expanded and deleted, generating node $B$ with operator $x$ marked as used, and node $C$ with operator $y$ marked as used. In the next iteration, node $B$ is expanded and deleted, creating another copy of node $C$ with operator $z$ marked as used. These copies of node $C$ are not merged because we are in the middle of an iteration. Instead, the first copy of node $C$ is expanded and deleted, generating another copy of node $B$, with operator $z$ marked as used. At the end of this iteration, we have one copy each of nodes $B$ and $C$, each with operator $z$ marked as used. In the next iteration, both these nodes will be expanded and deleted, generating two copies of node $A$. In the following sort-merge phase, these two copies of node $A$ will be merged into a single copy with operators $x$ and $y$ marked as used, but if node $A$ had any other neighbors, it would be reexpanded.

This problem does not occur without DDD, since as soon as the second copy of node $C$ is generated, it would be immediately merged with the first copy, with both operators $y$ and $z$ marked as used. When we then tried to expand node $C$, the search would terminate.

To fix this problem, when expanding nodes at depth $d$, instead of deleting them, we write them to their own output file. At the end of the iteration, we sort and purge the nodes at depth $d$ together with the nodes at depth $d+1$, creating a single new input file with nodes at both depths. In the next iteration, as we scan the new input file, we expand and save the nodes at depth $d+1$, but delete the nodes at depth $d$. Essentially, we save two levels of the search at a time, rather than just one level, which is similar to a version of frontier search developed by (Zhou & Hansen 2003). This roughly doubles the amount of storage needed, but the I/O complexity is still linear in the size of the search space, since each node is now read three times and written twice.

### Frontier-A* with DDD

Even though both frontier search and DDD apply to A* individually, there is no obvious way to combine both methods with A*, without the search "leaking" back into the interior. In the example below, we adopt the constraints of the sliding-tile puzzles with the Manhattan distance heuristic. In particular, all edges have unit cost, all paths between any pair of nodes have the same parity, and the heuristic value of a child is either one greater or one less than that of its parent.

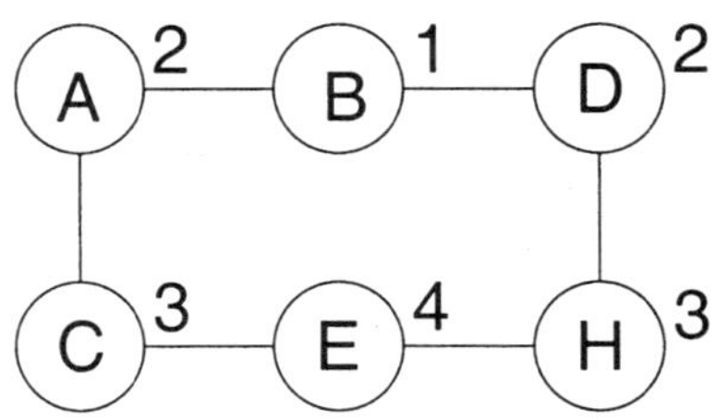


Figure 2: Failure of Frontier A* with DDD

Consider the graph in Figure 2, where node $A$ is the start state, and the numbers denote the heuristic values of the states. For the first iteration, $bestf = h(A) = 2$. Node $A$ is expanded, generating nodes $B$ and $C$, with $f(B) = 1+1 = 2$ and $f(C) = 1+3 = 4$. Since $f(B) = 2$, it is also expanded in the first iteration, generating node $D$ with $f(D) = 2+2 = 4$. The next iteration, with $bestf = 4$, expands nodes $C$ and $D$, generating nodes $E$ and $H$ with $f(E) = 2+4 = 6$ and $f(H) = 3+3 = 6$. In the next iteration, with $bestf = 6$, node $E$ is expanded, generating another copy of node $H$ with $f(H) = 3+3 = 6$. This duplicate node is not immediately detected, since we are in the middle of an iteration. The new copy of node $H$ is expanded in the same iteration, generating another copy of node $D$, with $f(D) = 4+2 = 6$. This copy of node $D$ is also expanded in this iteration, generating another copy of node $B$ with $f(B) = 5+1 = 6$, which is also expanded in this iteration, generating another copy of node $A$.

This last iteration reexpanded nodes that were first expanded several iterations previously. By extending the length of the cycle, we can construct examples where frontier-A* with DDD would "leak" arbitrarily far into the interior of the search. Thus, when applying DDD to A*, we cannot use frontier search, but have to store all closed nodes. This is not a major drawback, however, in problems where the number of nodes grows exponentially with cost, as in the sliding-tile puzzles with the Manhattan distance heuristic, for example. In such cases, the size of the closed list is often small compared to the size of the open list.

### Uniform-Cost Frontier Search with DDD

Fortunately, we can combine frontier search with DDD in uniform-cost search or Dijkstra's algorithm, if all edges have positive cost, and a sort-merge phase is performed after all nodes of the same cost have been expanded. This guarantees that the frontier cannot advance by more than one edge in any one place before duplicates are detected, preventing the search from leaking back into the interior.

## Experiments

We implemented breadth-first frontier search with DDD on sliding-tile puzzles and the Towers of Hanoi, and A* with DDD, but without frontier search, on the Fifteen Puzzle. In addition to finding optimal solutions and determining the diameter of a problem space, breadth-first search is also used in hardware and software verification, and for computing pattern database heuristics (Culberson & Schaeffer 1998).

### Complete Searches of Sliding-Tile Puzzles

The sliding-tile puzzle consists of a rectangular frame filled with square tiles except for one blank position. Any tile horizontally or vertically adjacent to the blank can be slid into that position. The task is to rearrange the tiles from some initial configuration to a particular goal configuration.

(Schofield 1967) first performed a complete breadth-first of the Eight Puzzle. We've extended this to all sliding-tile puzzles up to the $3 \times 5$ Fourteen Puzzle. The first column of Table 1 gives the $x$ and $y$ dimensions of the puzzle, and the second column shows the number of moves needed to reach all solvable states, which is the worst-case optimal solution length. The blank started in the center for the $3 \times 5$ puzzle, and in a corner in the other cases. The third column gives the number of solvable states, which is $(xy)!/2$, and the fourth column gives the width of the problem space, which is the maximum number of nodes at any depth. The horizontal line represents the previous state of the art.

| Size | Moves | Total States | Width of Space |
|---|---:|---:|---:|
| $2 \times 2$ | 6 | 12 | 2 |
| $2 \times 3$ | 21 | 360 | 44 |
| $2 \times 4$ | 37 | 20,160 | 1,999 |
| $3 \times 3$ | 31 | 181,440 | 24,047 |
| $2 \times 5$ | 55 | 1,814,400 | 133,107 |
| $2 \times 6$ | 80 | 239,500,800 | 13,002,649 |
| $3 \times 4$ | 53 | 239,500,800 | 21,841,159 |
| $2 \times 7$ | 108 | 43,589,145,600 | 1,862,320,864 |
| $3 \times 5$ | 84 | 653,837,184,000 | 45,136,428,198 |

Table 1: Complete Searches of Sliding-Tile Puzzles

Previously, the most efficient way to implement a complete breadth-first search was to allocate an array with one bit per state. A bit is set if and only if the corresponding state has already been generated. We implement the breadth-first search with a FIFO queue of nodes, either in memory or on disk, and use the bit array to reject duplicate nodes. We refer to this as a bit-state breadth-first search.

The $3 \times 4$ and $2 \times 6$ Eleven Puzzles were the largest we could search completely without DDD. We implemented the bit-state breadth-first search, a breadth-first frontier search, and a breadth-first frontier search with DDD. Bit-state breadth-first search required 15.25 minutes, breadth-first frontier search required 19.75 minutes, and breadth-first frontier search with DDD required 9.25 minutes, on a 440 Megahertz Sun Ultra 10 workstation. This shows that DDD can be useful even for problems that fit in memory.

To solve the $3 \times 5$ Fourteen Puzzle, we used symmetry by placing the blank at the center of the initial state, and rotating every state 180 degrees. This reduced the actual storage requirements by almost a factor of two. At 8 bytes per state, this problem required over 200 gigabytes of disk storage, and ran for almost 18 days on the above machine. Using this same symmetry, the bit-state breadth-first search would require over 38 gigabytes of memory for the bit array, plus over 168 gigabytes of disk space for the FIFO queue, since it must store a complete state representation for half the nodes in the width of the space. Frontier search without DDD would require over 168 gigabytes of memory.

Linear-space depth-first searches (DFS), which explore the problem-space tree, become increasingly inefficient with depth, since they can't detect most duplicate nodes. For example, in the Fourteen Puzzle graph, the number of states at each depth increases up to depth 51, then decreases to a single state at depth 84. The tree, however, continues to grow exponentially with a branching factor of just over two. Thus, a DFS to depth 84 would generate over $10^{25}$ nodes. Furthermore, DFS cannot detect the maximum search depth in a problem space.

## Complete Searches of 4-Peg Towers of Hanoi

The Towers of Hanoi problem consist of at least three pegs, and a set of different-size disks initially stacked on one peg. The task is to move all disks from the initial peg to a goal peg, subject to the constraints that only the top disk on any peg can move at one time, and a larger disk cannot be stacked on top of a smaller disk. For the well-known 3-peg Towers of Hanoi puzzle, there is a simple algorithm that provably generates a shortest solution, which is of length $2^{n-1}$ moves, where $nn$ is the number of disks.

The 4-peg Towers of Hanoi problem (Hinz 1999), is much more interesting. There is a deterministic algorithm to move all disks from one peg to another, and a conjecture that it is optimal (Frame 1941; Stewart 1941; Dunkel 1941), but the conjecture is unproven. Thus, systematic search is the only method guaranteed to find optimal solutions, or to verify the conjecture for a given number of disks.

We begin with exhaustive searches of these problem spaces, starting with all disks stacked on one peg. The three remaining pegs are symmetric. Given a particular state, we can generate up to five more equivalent states by permuting these three pegs. We represent each state by a canonical state in which the non-initial pegs are sorted by the size of their largest disk. This contributes almost a factor of six in performance (Bode & Hinz 1999).

Using this symmetry, we implemented breadth-first frontier search with DDD. Since the problem space contains path lengths of unequal parity between pairs of states, we save two levels at a time. We exhaustively searched all problems with up to 20 disks, and the results are shown in Table 2.

The first column gives the number of disks $n$, and the second column gives the minimum depth by which all legal states are generated, starting with all disks on one peg. The third column gives the number of states in the space, which is $4^n$. The last column gives the width of the space, or the maximum number of states at any depth. The actual numbers of nodes expanded are approximately one-sixth the numbers shown, due to symmetry. The 20-disk problem took over 18 days, using the algorithm described above.

The line under the 16-disk problem represents the state-of-the-art without DDD. In particular, using the bit-state breadth-first search described above, a 16-disk bit array requires $4^{16}/8$ or half a gigabyte of memory. The FIFO queue is stored on disk.

| Disks | Depth | States | Width |
|---|---|---|---|
| 1 | 1 | 4 | 3 |
| 2 | 3 | 16 | 6 |
| 3 | 5 | 64 | 30 |
| 4 | 9 | 256 | 72 |
| 5 | 13 | 1024 | 282 |
| 6 | 17 | 4,096 | 918 |
| 7 | 25 | 16,384 | 2,568 |
| 8 | 33 | 65,536 | 9,060 |
| 9 | 41 | 262,144 | 31,638 |
| 10 | 49 | 1,048,576 | 109,890 |
| 11 | 65 | 4,194,304 | 335,292 |
| 12 | 81 | 16,777,216 | 1,174,230 |
| 13 | 97 | 67,108,864 | 4,145,196 |
| 14 | 113 | 268,435,456 | 14,368,482 |
| 15 | 130 | 1,073,741,824 | 48,286,104 |
| 16 | 161 | 4,294,967,296 | 162,989,898 |
| 17 | 193 | 17,179,869,184 | 572,584,122 |
| 18 | 225 | 68,719,476,736 | 1,994,549,634 |
| 19 | 257 | 274,877,906,944 | 6,948,258,804 |
| 20 | 294 | 1,099,511,627,776 | 23,513,260,170 |

Table 2: Complete Searches of 4-Peg Towers of Hanoi

## Half-Depth Searches of 4-Peg Towers of Hanoi

In the standard problem of moving all disks from one peg to another, the initial and goal states are symmetric. To solve this problem, we must move the largest disk from the initial peg to the goal peg at some point, which requires distributing the remaining disks among the other two pegs. Once we find such a state, if we apply the same moves used to reach that state in the opposite order, but interchange the initial and goal pegs, we will complete the solution. Thus, we only have to search to half the solution depth, to the first state that distributes all but the largest disk on the two intermediate pegs (Bode & Hinz 1999). Using this symmetry precludes using most heuristic functions, since we don't know the actual distribution of the disks on the intermediate pegs.

Using both symmetries, we implemented breadth-first frontier search with DDD, and verified the presumed optimal solutions for all problems with up to 24 disks. The first column of Table 3 gives the number of disks, and the second column shows the optimal solution length. The third column gives the total number of states up to half the optimal solution depth, rounded up. The fourth column gives the number of states at that depth. Here we show the actual numbers of states generated, taking advantage of the problem symmetries. The 24-disk problem took almost 19 days to solve with a gigabyte of memory, and used almost 130 gigabytes of disk space. The largest problem that had been solved previously is the 17-disk problem (Bode & Hinz 1999), indicated by the horizontal line in the table. Concurrently with this work, (Felner *et al.* 2004) solved the 18-disk problem using frontier-A* with a pattern-database heuristic. Their algorithm applies to arbitrary initial and goal states.

| Disks | Moves | States | Width |
|---|---|---|---|
| 1 | 1 | 1 | 1 |
| 2 | 3 | 3 | 1 |
| 3 | 5 | 6 | 3 |
| 4 | 9 | 18 | 7 |
| 5 | 13 | 45 | 16 |
| 6 | 17 | 105 | 36 |
| 7 | 25 | 434 | 137 |
| 8 | 33 | 1,244 | 293 |
| 9 | 41 | 3,335 | 562 |
| 10 | 49 | 8,469 | 1,780 |
| 11 | 65 | 39,631 | 6,640 |
| 12 | 81 | 139,624 | 21,187 |
| 13 | 97 | 371,053 | 50,777 |
| 14 | 113 | 933,286 | 86,944 |
| 15 | 129 | 2,407,813 | 256,579 |
| 16 | 161 | 11,682,622 | 965,931 |
| 17 | 193 | 45,800,496 | 3,278,853 |
| 18 | 225 | 145,656,379 | 10,004,107 |
| 19 | 257 | 379,925,343 | 24,317,501 |
| 20 | 289 | 957,046,489 | 45,544,033 |
| 21 | 321 | 2,394,213,892 | 133,985,287 |
| 22 | 385 | 12,024,012,134 | 547,563,876 |
| 23 | 449 | 50,661,772,967 | 2,006,448,775 |
| 24 | 513 | 178,693,859,657 | 6,364,114,392 |

Table 3: Half-Depth Searches of 4-Peg Towers of Hanoi

The branching factor of the problem-space tree for this problem is about 3.766, assuming that we never move the same disk twice in a row. To find an optimal solution to the 9-disk problem, we would have to search to depth 20. $3.766^{20} \approx 3.29 \times 10^{11}$. Thus, the 9-disk problem is the largest that could be solved with a depth-first search, due to the proliferation of undetected duplicate nodes.

### A Very Surprising Anomaly

An incredibly astute reader might notice that in almost every case, the maximum search depth from a state with all disks on a single peg, shown in Table 2, is the same as the optimal number of moves needed to transfer all disks to another peg, shown in Table 3. For 15 disks, however, the optimal solution length is 129 moves, but there are 588 states at depth 130, starting with all disks on a single peg. For 20 disks, there are a total of $11,243,652$ states beyond the optimal solution length of 289 moves, up to a depth of 294. This result for 15 disks has been confirmed by about a half-dozen different implementations of breadth-first search, and the result for 20 disks has been confirmed by two different implementations. We have no explanation for this surprising anomaly, and leave it for future work.

### A* with DDD on the Fifteen Puzzle

We also implemented A* with DDD on the Fifteen Puzzle, with the Manhattan distance heuristic, but without frontier search. We used the set of 100 random solvable problem instances in (Korf 1985). With a gigabyte of memory, standard A* can store 35 million nodes, and can solve 83 of these problems. Frontier-A* without DDD uses the same amount of memory per node as standard A*, but only stores about half as many nodes. It can solve 93 of the 100 problems and runs about 38% slower than standard A*. A* with DDD can store 70 million nodes in the same amount of memory, and can solve 87 of these problems, but runs about three times slower than standard A*. Using disk storage, A* with DDD easily solves all the problems, and runs about five times slower than standard A*. To our knowledge, this is first time all these problems have been solved by A* with less than a gigabyte of memory. IDA* (Korf 1985) is still the preferred algorithm for this problem, however, since it uses only linear memory, and is very simple to implement.

## Duplicate Elimination Without Sorting

A large fraction of the CPU time of these algorithms is due to sorting. Sorting is not necessary to eliminate duplicate nodes, however, as shown by (Stern & Dill 1998). Here we present a duplicate elimination algorithm, based on hashing, which scales linearly with problem size.

The algorithm uses two hash functions that ideally are orthogonal, meaning that they hash most nodes to different values. As we expand each node in a breadth-first frontier search, we apply the first hash function to its children, and append each child to an output file dedicated to nodes with the same hash value. At the end of the expansion phase, any duplicate nodes occur only within the same file.

In the second phase, we iterate through each of the output files. For each file, we hash each node to a location in memory using the second hash function. Any duplicate nodes will hash to the same location and are merged. As we compact each file, we write its unique nodes to a new output file of nodes at the next depth. The next expansion phase then iterates through each of these files.

We implemented this method for the 4-peg Towers of Hanoi problem, and repeated the complete search experiments shown in Table 2. For this problem, we maintain two sets of files, one for the nodes at the current depth, and the other for the nodes at the next depth. For the second hash function we used the positions of the 14 smallest disks, and for the first hash function we used the positions of the larger disks. Thus, each file contains only states with the same configuration of the large disks. An advantage of this approach is that we never have to explicitly store the positions of the large disks, since it is uniquely determined by the file containing the states, and only have to store the positions of the 14 smallest disks, plus the used-operator bits.

The CPU time of our hashing-based implementation is less than half that of our sorting-based implementation. This is also true of total elapsed time for up to 17 disks, since only 15 pairs of files are needed, due to symmetry. For larger numbers of disks, however, the elapsed time is more than half the time of our sorting-based implementation. This appears to be due to reading and writing a large number of files, many of which contain relatively few nodes. For 20 disks, our current hashing-based implementation takes 11 days to run, compared to over 18 days for the sorting-based implementation, a speedup of over 41%.

## Summary and Conclusions

We presented an implementation of delayed duplicate detection (DDD) that scales up to large problems. For breadth-first search and uniform-cost search, we showed how to combine DDD with frontier search, which saves only the Open list, but DDD cannot be easily combined with frontier search for A*. We implemented breadth-first frontier search with DDD on sliding-tile puzzles and the 4-peg Towers of Hanoi. We performed complete breadth-first searches on all sliding-tile problems up to the $3 \times 5$ Fourteen Puzzle. We also performed complete searches of the 4-peg Towers of Hanoi problem with up to 20 disks, discovering a surprising anomaly in the 15 and 20-disk problems. In addition, we verified the presumed optimal solution lengths for the 4-peg Towers of Hanoi problems with up to 24 disks. These searches expand over three orders of magnitude more nodes than the previous state of the art. We also implemented A* with DDD, but without frontier search, solving all of a standard set of 100 Fifteen Puzzle instances. Finally, we presented an implementation of DDD that relies on hashing rather than sorting, which runs over 40% faster than our sorting-based implementation.

## Acknowledgments

This research was supported by NSF under grant No. EIA-0113313, by NASA and JPL under contract No. 1229784, and by the State of California MICRO grant No. 01-044. Thanks to Jianming He for independently verifying the 15-disk anomaly, and to Ariel Felner for helpful discussions concerning this research.

## References

Bode, J.-P., and Hinz, A. 1999. Results and open problems on the tower of hanoi. In *Proceedings of the Thirtieth Southeastern International Conference on Combinatoris, Graph Theory, and Computing*.

Culberson, J., and Schaeffer, J. 1998. Pattern databases. *Computational Intelligence* 14(3):318–334.

Dijkstra, E. 1959. A note on two problems in connexion with graphs. *Numerische Mathematik* 1:269–271.

Dunkel, O. 1941. Editorial noe concerning advanced problem 3918. *American Mathematical Monthly* 48:219.

Felner, A.; Meshulam, R.; Holte, R.; and Korf, R. 2004. Compressing pattern databases. In *Proceedings of the National Conference on Artificial Intelligence (AAAI-04)*, 1184–1189.

Frame, J. 1941. Solution to advanced problem 3918. *American Mathematical Monthly* 48:216–217.

Garcia-Molina, H.; Ullman, J. D.; and Widom, J. 2000. *Database System Implementation*. Upper Saddle River, N.J.: Prentice-Hall.

Hart, P.; Nilsson, N.; and Raphael, B. 1968. A formal basis for the heuristic determination of minimum cost paths. *IEEE Transactions on Systems Science and Cybernetics* SSC-4(2):100–107.

Hinz, A. M. 1999. The tower of hanoi. In *Algebras and Combinatorics: Proceedings of ICAC'97*, 277–289. Hong Kong: Springer-Verlag.

Katriel, I., and Meyer, U. 2003. Elementary graph algorithms in external memory. In *Algorithms for Memory Hierarchies, LNCS 2625*. Springer-Verlag. 62–84.

Korf, R., and Zhang, W. 2000. Divide-and-conquer frontier search applied to optimal sequence alignment. In *Proceedings of the National Conference on Artificial Intelligence (AAAI-2000)*, 910–916.

Korf, R. 1985. Depth-first iterative-deepening: An optimal admissible tree search. *Artificial Intelligence* 27(1):97–109.

Korf, R. 1999. Divide-and-conquer bidirectional search: First results. In *Proceedings of the International Joint Conference on Artificial Intelligence (IJCAI-99)*, 1184–1189.

Korf, R. 2003a. Breadth-first frontier search with delayed duplicate detection. In *Proceedings of the IJCAI03 Workshop on Model Checking and Artificial Intelligence*, 87–92.

Korf, R. 2003b. Delayed duplicate detection: Extended abstract. In *Proceedings of the International Joint Conference on Artificial Intelligence (IJCAI-03)*, 1539–1541.

Roscoe, A. 1994. Model-checking csp. In Roscoe, A., ed., *A Classical Mind, Essays in Honour of CAR Hoare*. Prentice-Hall.

Schofield, P. 1967. Complete solution of the eight puzzle. In Meltzer, B., and Michie, D., eds., *Machine Intelligence 3*. New York: American Elsevier. 125–133.

Stern, U., and Dill, D. 1998. Using magnetic disk instead of main memory in the mur(phi) verifier. In *Proceedings of the 10th International Conference on Computer-Aided Verification*, 172–183.

Stewart, B. 1941. Solution to advanced problem 3918. *American Mathematical Monthly* 48:217–219.

Zhou, R., and Hansen, E. 2003. Sparse-memory graph search. In *Proceedings of the International Joint Conference on Artificial Intelligence (IJCAI-03)*, 1259–1266.

# Temperature Discovery Search

**Martin Müller** and **Markus Enzenberger** and **Jonathan Schaeffer**
Department of Computing Science, University of Alberta
Edmonton, Canada T6G 2E8
{mmueller,emarkus,jonathan}@cs.ualberta.ca

**Abstract**

Temperature Discovery Search (TDS) is a new minimax-based game tree search method designed to compute or approximate the *temperature* of a combinatorial game. TDS is based on the concept of an *enriched environment*, where a combinatorial game $G$ is embedded in an environment consisting of a large set of simple games of decreasing temperature. Optimal play starts in the environment, but eventually must switch to $G$. TDS finds the temperature of $G$ by determining when this switch must happen. Both exact and heuristic versions of TDS are described and evaluated experimentally. In experiments with sum games in *Amazons*, TDS outperforms an $\alpha\beta$ searcher.

**Keywords:** Temperature Discovery Search, combinatorial games, $\alpha\beta$ algorithm, Go, Amazons

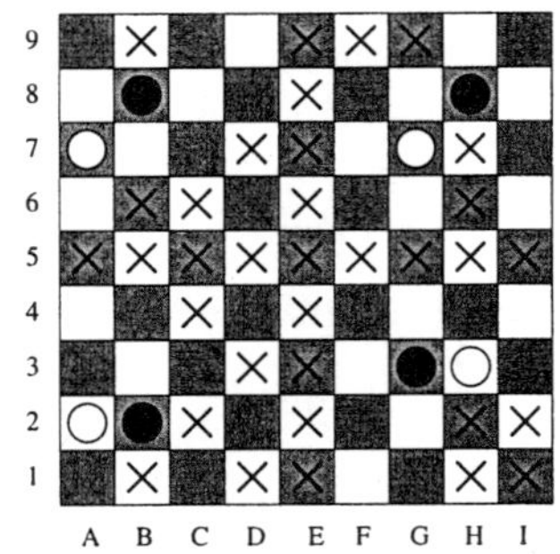


Figure 1: An *Amazons* position with four subgames of size $4 \times 4$ (Black to move)

## Introduction

The effort required to solve games by minimax search typically increases exponentially with the required search depth, even when all standard search enhancements are used (Schaeffer 1989). Improvements are possible for games that exhibit additional structure. One example are *combinatorial games* (Berlekamp, Conway, & Guy 1982), which can be broken down into a *sum* of independent *subgames*.

Go endgames can be analyzed as combinatorial games. They often consist of several independent fights to refine the boundaries of loosely surrounded territories. As another example, Figure 1 shows a position $G$ from the game of *Amazons* that decomposes into a sum of four subgames $G_1 + G_2 + G_3 + G_4$. In Amazons, playing pieces called amazons move like chess queens and try to block the other player by shooting arrows that block empty squares. Areas that become completely blocked from each other become independent subgames. In the figure, each of the four corners forms one subgame. Each corner is separated from the rest of the board by a solid wall of blocked squares.

One important goal of algorithms for combinatorial games is to replace global minimax search by local analysis of single subgames as much as possible. Because of the exponentially growing cost of search, and because the length of local move sequences is typically much shorter than playing out the whole sum game, even methods that perform substantial analysis of each local game can still be much faster than global search. For example, in Figure 1 there are several hundred legal moves and 39 empty squares, so the game can last up to 39 moves. Local analysis reduces both the width and the depth of the search by a factor of 4 or more. This is a massive reduction in the size of the search space.

An exact local search method that was applied to late-stage Go endgames is *decomposition search* (Müller 1999). Approximation algorithms must be used when the exact solution of local problems or the global combination of local solutions is too costly. Methods based on the concepts of *mean* and *temperature* (Berlekamp, Conway, & Guy 1982; Berlekamp 1996) can yield very good play, with bounded error. The mean of a subgame measures how advantageous for a player this game is "on average", when played as part of a sum of games. The temperature measures the urgency of playing first in a particular subgame. These two numbers are usually computed "bottom-up" by retrograde analysis, which requires building the complete local game graph.

This paper introduces *Temperature Discovery Search (TDS)*, a method for discovering the temperature of a local game by a forward minimax search. The method is more general and more practical than Kao's *Mean and Temperature Search* (Kao 2000). Kao's method applies to the restricted class of binary game trees, which allow only a single move for each player in a local game position. TDS has no such restriction. In many combinatorial games, including Go endgames and Amazons, there are local positions with many plausible moves for both players. Kao's method also requires a search to the end of the game, whereas TDS can be used as an approximation method with a given depth or time limit.

The contributions of this paper are:

- A novel use of AI search techniques to solve a problem in the domain of combinatorial games, and the novel use of combinatorial game theory to enhance the performance of an AI game-playing program.
- The first general *forward* search method to compute the mean and temperature of any finite loop-free combinatorial game.
- The first known systematic method to *approximate* mean and temperature by forward search.
- Several techniques to control the trade-off between speed and accuracy, and their empirical evaluation.
- A series of experiments in practical play of hot sum games, showing that TDS in combination with the *Hotstrat* algorithm convincingly outperforms an $\alpha\beta$ searcher.

## Combinatorial Games

A major difference between normal $\alpha\beta$ minimax search and local analysis of a sum game is that while $\alpha\beta$ solves a single optimization problem, in a sum game there is a trade-off between a local gain and the right to play first in another game. Combinatorial game theory analyzes subgames under the assumption that there are (many) other subgames around, and seeks to optimize the score in the sum game, not just in the current subgame. The gain from playing in one subgame must be compared against the potential loss from letting the opponent play first in the remaining subgames. Combinatorial game theory provides tools to quantify this trade-off. In a real-world sum game, the other subgames can be arbitrarily complex, and therefore evaluating the trade-offs precisely is hard. In contrast, a locally restricted $\alpha\beta$ search would optimize a player's local profit but ignore the trade-off. This leads to poor play in many situations.

A middle ground is represented by the concept of a standardized *enriched environment* (Berlekamp 1996), in which each subgame is analyzed. Traditionally, players are called Left, who prefers positive values, and Right, who prefers negative values. An enriched environment consists of many *elementary switches*, simple subgames of the form $v| - v$, with a large number of values $v$. In $v| - v$, Left to move can gain $v$, while Right to move can gain $-v$. The mean is $\mu(v| - v) = 0$ and the temperature is $t(v| - v) = v$ (Berlekamp, Conway, & Guy 1982). Sum games consisting only of switches are easy to play. Playing a switch with highest temperature $v$ is always an optimal move.

In a sum game consisting of a single, potentially complex, subgame $G$ plus an enriched environment, the trade-off now becomes much simpler to analyze: the choice is between playing in $G$ and playing the switch with highest value $v$ in the environment. If $v$ is very large, each player will take this profit rather than play in $G$. As the available values $v$ become smaller, eventually a player will prefer to move in $G$ instead.

For example, consider playing a game and having a choice of making a move (and thereby improving your position) or taking some money. How valuable is it to Left to have the right to move? Assume the money is a stack of coupons, of decreasing value \$10, \$9,... and the advantage Left gets by playing on the board is worth \$5 to Left. In this case Left would take the coupon, making the highest remaining coupon valued at \$9. Right would do a similar analysis, and conclude the position is (say) worth \$8, so Right takes the \$9 coupon leaving \$8 as the top coupon value. Nothing has changed on the board, so Left takes the \$8 coupon, leaving a \$7 top coupon. Now Right makes a move since moving is worth more (\$8) that taking the next coupon (\$7). If you view the coupon stack as being the value of moving in a different subgame, then the top value in the stack will decrease to the critical point where it becomes more profitable to move in the current game than to move in a different subgame. This critical point is a representation of how urgent it is to play in that subgame; this procedure finds a temperature where playing in the game is optimal.

Let $G$ be a finite loop-free combinatorial game and $p$ be a player. In the view of thermography (Berlekamp, Conway, & Guy 1982), a player should play in $G$ at a temperature $t(G)$. However, in so-called *sente* situations a player has a threat that makes it possible to play in $G$ at a higher temperature. Let $\hat{t}(G,p)$ be the highest temperature such that player $p$ can play in $G$ without a loss in the thermographic sense. For loop-free games, this means $p$ can play in $G$ at any temperature in the range $[t(G)\ ..\ \hat{t}(G,p)]$. For example, the game $G = 10|0||0$ has a temperature $t(G) = 0$, but $\hat{t}(G, Left) = 5$. Left's move to $10|0$ is a threat that *raises the temperature*. Left can play at any temperature $t$ in the range $[0,5]$. However, $\hat{t}(G, Right) = 0$, so Right should not play at a temperature above 0 here.

In the first phase of TDS, a single search is used to identify a first temperature estimate $t$, which is guaranteed to lie within the interval $[t(G)\ ..\ \hat{t}(G,p)]$. In a second phase, further searches are performed that successively lower the estimate $t$ until $t = t(G)$.

### Coupon Stacks

The concept of a *coupon stack* was introduced by Berlekamp in the context of analyzing Go endgames (Spight 2002). It is used to implement an enriched environment.

**Definition:** A *simple coupon stack* $C(t_{max}, \delta)$, where $t_{max} = n\delta$ for some integer $n \geq 0$, is the sum of elementary switches of temperatures $\delta, 2\delta, \cdots, t_{max}$. Each such switch is called a *coupon*. In $C(t_{max}, \delta)$, $t_{max} > 0$, either player can take the coupon of value $t_{max}$, which changes the score of the game by $t_{max}$ in the player's favor. The move leads to a smaller stack $C(t_{max} - \delta, \delta)$. A stack $C(0, \delta) = 0$ is said to be empty and neither player has a move.

A simple coupon stack $C = C(t_{max}, \delta)$ has temperature $t(C(t_{max}, \delta)) = t_{max}$ and mean $\mu(C(t_{max}, \delta)) = 0$. The *left score*, the minimax score with Left going first, is $V(C, Left) = \lceil \frac{n}{2} \rceil \delta$ and the *right score*, the minimax score with Right going first, is $V(C, Right) = -\lceil \frac{n}{2} \rceil \delta$.

In a sum $G + C$, an optimal player will play in $G$ only if $t(C) \leq \hat{t}(G,p)$. In the range $t(G) \leq t(C) \leq \hat{t}(G,p)$, playing in $C$ and playing in $G$ are both optimal.

Games played on a $19 \times 19$ Go board plus a coupon stack $C(20, \frac{1}{2})$ have been used in "Environmental Go" to gain insight into how professional players estimate the temperature of Go endgames (Spight 2002).

### Extended Coupon Stacks for Negative Temperatures

For games where all positions of temperature 0 or below can be evaluated statically, a simple coupon stack $C(t_{max}, \delta)$ is sufficient. However, in general play has to continue at negative temperatures down to $t = -1$. This situation can happen in games with difficult to evaluate endgame positions, such as Go or Amazons. One specific example are so-called *zugzwang* positions such as $-4|3 = 0$ where neither player wants to move.

**Definition:** An *extended coupon stack* $C_{-1}(t_{max}, \delta)$ can be constructed from a simple coupon stack $C(t_{max}, \delta)$ by adding coupons of value $0, -\delta, -2\delta, \cdots, -1$, followed by a sufficiently large number $k$ of further coupons of value -1, and a final coupon of value $-\frac{1}{2}$ as the bottom-most coupon. For any $\delta = \frac{1}{2m}$, with integer $m > 0$, this construction avoids bias and ensures that $V(C,p) = V(C_{-1},p)$ for both players $p$. The number $k$ of extra coupons should be chosen in a game-dependent way, large enough such that the final $-\frac{1}{2}$ coupon is never taken and the stack never becomes empty.

## Temperature Discovery Search

Temperature Discovery Search (TDS) is a standard $\alpha\beta$ minimax search of the sum of a game $G$ and a (simple or extended) coupon stack $C$. The important issue is how to use the information returned by the search to determine the mean and temperature of $G$.

### Searching a Sum Game $G + C$

The $\alpha\beta$ search process for TDS in a sum game $G + C$ proceeds as follows:

**Move generation** Possible moves in $G + C$ are all moves in $G$ plus one move in $C$, taking the top coupon (unless the stack is an empty simple coupon stack).

**Terminal Positions** Two types of positions are leaf nodes in the search: in a *normal terminal position* the value of $G$ can be statically recognized. In a *pseudo-terminal* position both players have taken a $-1$ coupon as their last move, indicating their unwillingness to continue play. Examples of such positions are *zugzwangs* such as $-4|3$, where both players would lose points by playing on.

**Evaluation** The evaluation of a position $G+C$, with player $p$ to play, is the sum of three components: evaluation of $G$, coupons taken, and remaining coupons in $C$.

1. Evaluation of $G$: Normal terminal positions are evaluated by their exact integer value. Nonterminal positions in $G$ can be evaluated by a heuristic evaluation function $h(G)$ to improve move ordering or enable heuristic TDS (see below). Pseudo-terminal positions are not evaluated heuristically by the playing program. Following the *simplicity rule* of combinatorial game theory (Berlekamp, Conway, & Guy 1982), such positions are assigned a value of 0.
2. Coupons taken: The evaluation is the sum of all coupons taken by Left minus the sum of all coupons taken by Right.
3. Remaining coupons: The evaluation is $V(C,p)$. This assumes that both players take the remaining coupons in turn, beginning with the player to move.

### Example

Figure 2 shows a local Amazons position $G$ with Black = Left to move first. The search of $G + C$ with an extended coupon stack $C = C_{-1}(t_{max} = \frac{17}{8}, \delta = \frac{1}{8})$ yields the minimax score $V(G + C, Left) = \frac{15}{8}$. This particular choice of $t_{max}$ and $\delta$ will be motivated in the description of Experiment 1 below. Taking a coupon of value $v$ is represented by $C(v)$ and an Amazons move by specifying the squares as **from – to × arrow**. The principal variation (best line of play–PV) for Figure 2 is:

**1.** $C(\frac{17}{8})$ **2.** $C(\frac{16}{8})$ **3.** $C(\frac{15}{8})$ **4.** $C(\frac{14}{8})$ **5.** $C(\frac{13}{8})$
**6.** $C(\frac{12}{8})$ **7.** $C(\frac{11}{8})$ **8. A2–A3×B2 9.** $C(\frac{10}{8})$ **10.** $C(\frac{9}{8})$
**11.** $C(\frac{8}{8})$ **12.** $C(\frac{7}{8})$ **13.** $C(\frac{6}{8})$ **14.** $C(\frac{5}{8})$ **15.** $C(\frac{4}{8})$
**16.** $C(\frac{3}{8})$ **17.** $C(\frac{2}{8})$ **18.** $C(\frac{1}{8})$ **19.** $C(0)$ **20.** $C(-\frac{1}{8})$
**21.** $C(-\frac{2}{8})$ **22.** $C(-\frac{3}{8})$ **23. C3–B4×C3.**

The value $\frac{15}{8}$ of the leaf position in this line is the sum of the final position value (White has 1 square; $-\frac{8}{8}$ from Black's point of view), the difference in coupon values (Black has $\frac{21}{8}$ more), and the value of the remaining coupons ($\frac{2}{8}$ in Black's favor). Most moves are coupon moves that lower the value of the coupon stack until at move 8 and again at move 23 it becomes advantageous for a player to make a move.

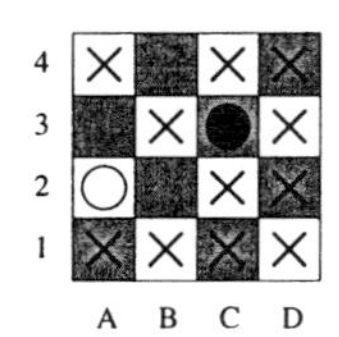

Figure 2: Example Amazons position (Black to move)

**Determining the mean:** Assume that $p$ is the player to move. According to a theorem in (Berlekamp 1996), if the value $\delta$ in $C$ is sufficiently small, then $V(G + C,p) = \mu(G) + V(C,p)$. Since $V(C,p)$ is known (see above), $\mu(G)$ can be determined. In the example, $V(C,\text{Left}) = \lceil\frac{17}{2}\rceil \cdot \frac{1}{8} = \frac{9}{8}$ (17 coupons split two ways, each of value $\frac{1}{8}$), $V(G+C,\text{Left}) = \frac{15}{8}$ and therefore $\mu(G) = \frac{15}{8} - \frac{9}{8} = \frac{3}{4}$.
**Determining the temperature:** Observe the move sequence in the principal variation returned by the search. If $t(C) > \hat{t}(G,p)$, then the first moves in the PV will all be

in $C$. At some time when $t(G) \leq t(C) \leq \hat{t}(G,p)$, the first move in $G$ will appear in the PV. This can be used as a starting point of an iterated search process to determine $t(G)$. $t(G)$ is the lowest temperature at which optimal play can switch from $C$ to $G$. In the example, the first move in $G$ was played between the coupons of value $t = \frac{11}{8}$ and $t - \delta = \frac{10}{8}$. The first estimate of $t(G)$ is set to $t$, since $t(G) \leq t$. If the minimax score stays the same even if the next lower coupon of value $t - \delta$ is played before the first move in $G$, then the temperature estimate can be lowered by $\delta$. To check this, TDS is modified to play all the coupons down to $C(t - \delta)$ before moves in $G$ is allowed. If the minimax score remains the same, then taking $C(t-\delta)$ first was not a loss, compared the previous search where $G$ was played before $C(t - \delta)$. Therefore the estimate can be decreased to $t := t - \delta$, and the process is repeated. Otherwise, if the minimax score changes, then taking $C(t - \delta)$ was nonoptimal, and the temperature is $t(G) = t$.

In the example, the first search returns $t = \frac{11}{8}$ by scanning the PV given above. In the second search, all coupons down to $C(t - \delta) = C(\frac{10}{8})$ are taken first. The minimax value of this search is also $\frac{15}{8}$, so $C(\frac{10}{8})$ was also an optimal play and the estimate is lowered to $t := t - \delta = \frac{10}{8}$. In the third search, coupons down to $C(\frac{9}{8})$ are taken first. The minimax value of this search is $\frac{13}{8}$, less than before. Taking the coupon $C(\frac{9}{8})$ before playing in $G$ was a loss. The temperature is $t(G) = t = \frac{10}{8}$.

### Heuristic TDS

Time- or depth-limited searches with TDS can be used to approximate the temperature of a game. As in any heuristic $\alpha\beta$ search, this introduces evaluation errors. Depending on the coupon stack used and the PV returned from the search, different outcomes are possible. Several searches with different coupon stacks may be required to find an approximate temperature.

Assume that TDS of a sum $G + C$ results in a PV consisting of k moves, $[m_1, \ldots, m_k]$. If the PV contains at least one move in $G$, determine $i$ such that $m_i$ is the first move in $G$. Otherwise, if all PV moves are in $C$, set $i = k + 1$. The outcome of a single search can be classified as follows:

**fail high** If either $i = k+1$ (all moves in the PV are coupon moves), or the last coupon of $C$ was played before any move in $G$.

**fail low** $m_1$ was played in $G$. The temperature of $G$ may be higher than $t(C)$.

**regular** Neither fail high nor fail low, $1 < i \leq k$. The PV starts with one or more moves in $C$ followed by a move in $G$.

The fail high and fail low cases require additional search(es) with a different stack to find the move to play.

### Hotstrat-TDS: a TDS-based Heuristic Sum Game Player

A simple way of using approximate temperatures in a playing program is to adapt the combinatorial game strategy of *Hotstrat* (Berlekamp, Conway, & Guy 1982), replacing the unknown exact temperatures by estimated temperatures computed by TDS. Given a sum game $G = G_1 + \ldots + G_n$, the temperature $t(G_i)$ of each subgame is estimated by TDS and a subgame $G_{hot}$ with highest estimated temperature is chosen.

A best move in $G_{hot}$ at temperature $t = t(G_{hot})$ is found by re-running TDS on $G_{hot}$ with a stack $C_{-1}(t, \delta)$. Move generation is modified to force the first move to be in $G_{hot}$, not in $C$.

As an optimization, since each move changes only one subgame, the temperature of the other unchanged subgames can be cached and reused for the upcoming moves. To try to avoid playing into zugzwang positions at the end of the game, when the temperature estimate of all subgames is $-1$, a simple global minimax search is performed.

As an example of how Hotstrat-TDS works, consider playing the four subgames in Figure 1. with Black to play. TDS approximates the temperatures of the four subgames as $t_{\text{top left}} = 2$, $t_{\text{top right}} = 1$, $t_{\text{bottom left}} = 3$, $t_{\text{bottom right}} = 0$. Therefore Hotstrat selects the bottom left as the hottest game, and TDS finds A2–B3×A3 as a best move on the board at temperature 3.

## Experiments

In the experiments, TDS is tested in the game of Amazons (Lieberum 2003). Amazons endgames are an ideal environment for evaluating this search method. Unlike Go, Amazons is a pure combinatorial game without the complications caused by *ko* (local position repetitions). Amazons is an attractive and difficult game on its own, with board positions that naturally split up into sum games in the course of a game. Furthermore, for small positions exact mean and temperature data is available in the form of databases. Using retrograde analysis, Theodore Tegos computed all Amazons positions on a subset of a $4 \times 4$ grid containing one amazon of each player (Tegos 2002).

All experiments were performed on a 2 GHz Athlon XP.

### Experiment 1: Comparing TDS with Exact Mean and Temperature Data

The following properties of Amazons were used to set up the first and second experiment: A $n$ point room containing 2 amazons has $n - 2$ empty points, limiting the maximum game length to $n - 2$ moves. In such a game, all means and temperatures must be integral multiples of $2^{3-n}$. The maximum possible temperature of these games is $n - 3$, so $t_{max} = n - 3 + \delta$ was used. According to (Berlekamp 1996), choosing $\delta = \frac{1}{2} \times 2^{3-n} = 2^{2-n}$ is sufficient to determine means and temperatures precisely.

The first experiment compares the mean and temperature computed by TDS against the exact database values from (Tegos 2002). For all 132 rooms with size 4, all 690 rooms of size 5 and all 3330 rooms of size 6, the TDS results for both mean and temperature agreed with the database values.

| $\delta \setminus$ Size | 4 | 5 | 6 |
|---|---|---|---|
| $\delta = 1$ | 0.155 /0 | 0.334 /0.086 | 0.306 /0.150 |
| $\delta = \frac{1}{2}$ | 0 /0 | 0.0029 /0.024 | 0.0099/0.020 |
| $\delta = \frac{1}{4}$ | **0 /0** | 0.0014 /0 | 0.0016/0.005 |
| $\delta = \frac{1}{8}$ | – | **0 /0** | 0.0008/0 |
| $\delta = \frac{1}{16}$ | – | – | **0 /0** |

Table 1: Average absolute errors of $t/\mu$

| $\delta \setminus$ Size | 4 | 5 | 6 |
|---|---|---|---|
| $\delta = 1$ | 1 /0 | 1.5 /0.75 | 1.5 /0.75 |
| $\delta = \frac{1}{2}$ | 0 /0 | 0.25 /0.25 | 0.375 /0.25 |
| $\delta = \frac{1}{4}$ | **0 /0** | 0.125 /0 | 0.125 /0.125 |
| $\delta = \frac{1}{8}$ | – | **0 / 0** | 0.0625/0 |
| $\delta = \frac{1}{16}$ | – | – | **0 /0** |

Table 2: Maximum errors of $t/\mu$

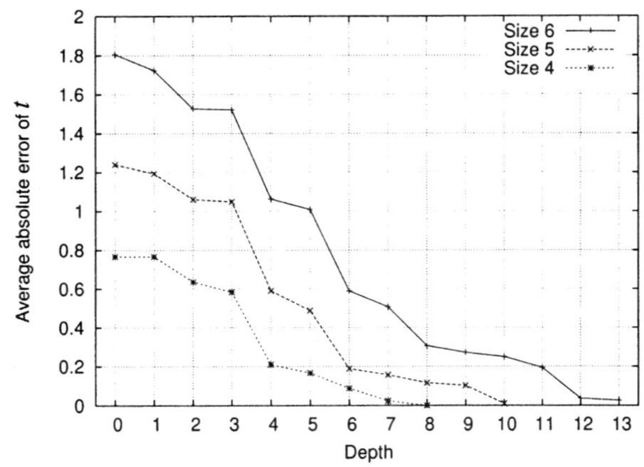


Figure 3: Average absolute errors of $t$ for depth-limited search for subgame sizes 4 to 6

### Experiment 2: Measuring the Effect of Increasing $\delta$

Tables 1 and 2 show the effects of using values of $\delta$ larger than $2^{2-n}$. Increasing $\delta$ introduces errors, but reduces the search depth and speeds up the search because far fewer coupons must be played. The experiments used all the rooms of size 4, 5 and 6 from the database. For each test position, two searches were performed, one for each player moving first. The mean and temperature estimates were set to the average of the two results, which greatly improved the accuracy. A table entry contains the error in the temperature estimate followed by the mean estimate. Table 1 shows the average absolute error and Table 2 the maximum error over the test sets.

The tables show a clear correlation between the size of $\delta$ and the accuracy of the computed means and temperatures. However, even for $\delta = \frac{1}{2}$ the average error is quite small.

### Experiment 3: Depth-limited Search

An alternate way of reducing the cost of a TDS search at the expense of some accuracy is to limit the search depth. In contrast to the previous experiments, the errors in the heuristic evaluation function $h(G)$ influence the result of these searches. Figure 3 shows the average absolute error of $t$ for fixed $\delta = \frac{1}{2}$ and varying search depth. As expected the average error decreases with deeper searches for two reasons. First, larger subgames need deeper searches because more board moves can be played in the subgame. Second, the maximum theoretically possible temperature grows with the size of the subgame and therefore a coupon stack with a higher $t_{max}$ has to be used.

### Experiment 4: Playing Sum Games against a Minimax Player

This experiment pits the Hotstrat-TDS player described above against a normal global $\alpha\beta$ search program in a sum of Amazons positions. Both programs share the same core $\alpha\beta$ search engine with standard performance enhancements and the same game-specific code such as move generation and evaluation function. The program used, *Arrow*, took third place at the Second Open Computer-Amazons Championship in 1999. Compared to the current top programs, it is weak in the opening and middle game, but competitive in the endgame phase due to its special endgame knowledge. Sums of small subgames have characteristics similar to endgame positions.

In the experiments, the number of subgames in a sum game varies from 2 to 6 in increments of 2, and the size of subgames from $4\times4$ to $6\times6$. Two amazons of different color and three arrows were placed on randomly chosen squares in each subgame. Figure 1 shows such a sum game, with four subgames of size $4 \times 4$. Usually, Amazons is played on a single $10 \times 10$ board with 4 amazons each.

For each combination of number and size of subgames, 200 random positions were created and played twice such that each player played each color once. Games were played under tournament-like conditions, but with a shorter time limit of 10 seconds per move. The score of a game is defined as the number of moves that the winning player can still make on the board when the opponent runs out of moves.

Table 3 shows the results. The average score of Hotstrat-TDS increases quickly with the number and the size of the subgames. In positions with two $4 \times 4$ subgames Hotstrat-TDS performs slightly worse than the global $\alpha\beta$ player. In this case the global search can search deeply enough to reach close to terminal positions, whereas the overhead of multiple searches for determining the temperature and best move with Hotstrat-TDS are a disadvantage here. In all other scenarios in this experiment, Hotstrat-TDS outperforms the global $\alpha\beta$ player. The advantage increases greatly as there are more and larger subgames.

Because of the reduced search width, local search in TDS can go deeper than global search. Even the simple approximation of the value of playing in a subgame by a single number, the estimated temperature, suffices to outplay global $\alpha\beta$ convincingly under tournament conditions. An alternative is to do local $\alpha\beta$ searches, to compute two local minimax values, one for each player going first, and then play a move in

| $N$ | $4 \times 4$ | $5 \times 5$ | $6 \times 6$ |
|---|---|---|---|
| 2 | −1.7(2.5) 43% | 1.2(5.7) 55% | 7.8(10.2) 67% |
| 4 | 2.3(4.9) 57% | 13.5(11.5) 69% | 41.2(18.3) 90% |
| 6 | 8.1(6.2) 72% | 32.5(15.3) 88% | 81.2(26.8) 96% |

Table 3: Game results depending on the number $N$ and the size of the subgames. Each entry shows the mean score, the standard deviation of the score and the percentage of wins

the subgame with the largest difference in minimax values. This is an inferior strategy, both experimentally and theoretically, for the reason outlined earlier, that it maximizes local profit but ignores global trade-offs.

Figure 4 illustrates some differences between Hotstrat-TDS and global $\alpha\beta$. In this position, there are several promising places to play. However, with a branching factor of several hundred and a 10 second time limit, $\alpha\beta$ search reaches only a search depth of 4 ply, and has to rely on a heuristic evaluation for many volatile positions. In contrast, TDS can search up to 9 ply locally. Even if many of these moves are coupon moves, the evaluations are closer to terminal positions, and they are all for the same local area, so they are more reliable for both reasons.

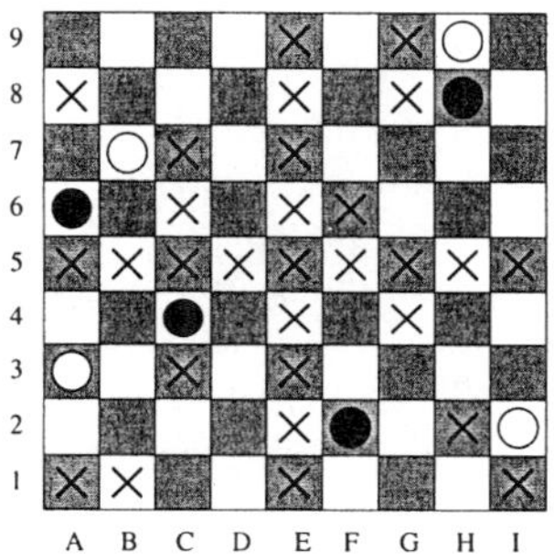


Figure 4: Sample game situation (Black to move)

## Conclusions and Future Work

TDS is the first *forward* search algorithm that can compute the mean and the temperature of a combinatorial game, as opposed to the usual bottom-up analysis. A major practical advantage of this method is that it can be used to approximate these values with high accuracy by resource-limited searches. TDS is shown to be successful both in its exact version and in practical play, where positions are too complex for exhaustive analysis. Even with a relatively large $\delta$ such as $\frac{1}{2}$, the approximation quality of TDS is excellent. One challenge for the future is to develop a mathematical analysis that explains these experimental results.

The main limitation of purely local search methods such as TDS is that they cannot always lead to globally optimal play. In particular, methods such as Hotstrat that compress information about a local game to a single number are limited in their performance. Given unlimited time, global search will eventually play optimally, while Hotstrat reaches a plateau once all temperatures are known exactly. A combination of local and global methods is necessary to further improve the performance.

TDS is applicable to any combinatorial game and is relevant for playing games that are sums of complex, hot subgames. One major future task is to apply it to Go endgames. The long term goal is to play real Go endgames at or beyond human professional level. The potential for such methods was shown in (Spight 2002), where computer-assisted human analysis uncovered several crucial errors in top-level human play.

The main technical problem in applying TDS to Go is that it must be extended to handle local *ko* repetitions. Berlekamp and Spight have developed interesting theoretical approaches to this problem (Berlekamp 1996; Spight 1999). One solution requires a coupon stack containing multiple copies of each switch. A direct implementation of these ideas will most likely be too slow in practice, so further research is needed.

## Acknowledgements

This research was supported by grants from NSERC, the Natural Sciences and Engineering Research Council of Canada, and iCORE, the Province of Alberta's Informatics Circle of Research Excellence. Theodore Tegos provided his databases of Amazons positions, which were invaluable for testing our implementation of TDS.

## References

Berlekamp, E.; Conway, J.; and Guy, R. 1982. *Winning Ways*. London: Academic Press. Revised version published 2001-2003 by AK Peters.

Berlekamp, E. 1996. The economist's view of combinatorial games. In Nowakowski, R., ed., *Games of No Chance: Combinatorial Games at MSRI*. Cambridge University Press. 365–405.

Kao, K. 2000. Mean and temperature search for Go endgames. *Information Sciences* 122(1):77–90.

Lieberum, J. 2003. An evaluation function for the game of Amazons. In van den Herik, J.; Iida, H.; and Heinz, E., eds., *Advances in Computer Games 10*, 299 – 308. Kluwer.

Müller, M. 1999. Decomposition search: A combinatorial games approach to game tree search, with applications to solving Go endgames. In *IJCAI-99*, 578–583.

Schaeffer, J. 1989. The history heuristic and the performance of alpha-beta enhancements. *IEEE Transactions on Pattern Analysis and Machine Intelligence* 11(11):1203–1212.

Spight, W. 1999. Extended thermography for multiple kos in Go. In van den Herik, H., and Iida, H., eds., *Computers and Games. Proceedings CG'98*, number 1558 in Lecture Notes in Computer Science, 232–251. Springer Verlag.

Spight, W. 2002. Go thermography - the 4/21/98 Jiang-Rui endgame. In Nowakowski, R., ed., *More Games of No Chance*. Cambridge University Press. 89–105.

Tegos, T. 2002. Shooting the last arrow. Master's thesis, University of Alberta.

# Simple Search Methods for Finding a Nash Equilibrium

**Ryan Porter** and **Eugene Nudelman** and **Yoav Shoham**
Computer Science Department
Stanford University
Stanford, CA 94305
{rwporter,eugnud,shoham}@cs.stanford.edu

### Abstract

We present two simple search methods for computing a sample Nash equilibrium in a normal-form game: one for 2-player games and one for $n$-player games. We test these algorithms on many classes of games, and show that they perform well against the state of the art– the Lemke-Howson algorithm for 2-player games, and Simplicial Subdivision and Govindan-Wilson for $n$-player games.

## Introduction

Game theory has had a profound impact on multi-agent systems research, and indeed on computer science in general. Nash equilibrium (NE) is arguably the most important concept in game theory, and yet remarkably little is known about the problem of computing a sample NE in a normal-form game. All evidence points to this being a hard problem, but its precise complexity is unknown (Papadimitriou 2001).

At the same time, several algorithms have been proposed over the years for the problem. In this paper, three previous algorithms will be of particular interest. For 2-player games, the Lemke-Howson algorithm (Lemke & Howson 1964) is still the state of the art, despite being 40 years old. For $n$-player games, until recently the algorithm based on Simplicial Subdivision (van der Laan, Talman, & van der Heyden 1987) was the state of the art. Indeed, these two algorithms are the default ones implemented in Gambit (McKelvey, McLennan, & Turocy 2003), the best-known game theory software. Recently, a new algorithm, which we will refer to as Govindan-Wilson, was introduced by (Govindan & Wilson 2003) and extended and efficiently implemented by (Blum, Shelton, & Koller 2003).

In a long version of this paper we provide more intuition behind each these methods. Here we simply note that they have surfaced as the most competitive algorithms for the respective class of games, and refer the reader to two thorough surveys on the topic (von Stengel 2002; McKelvey & McLennan 1996). Our goal in this paper is to demonstrate that for both of these classes of games (2-player, and $n$-player for $n > 2$) there exists a relatively simple, search-based method that performs very well in practice. For 2-player games, our algorithm performs substantially better than Lemke-Howson. For $n$-player games, our algorithm outperforms both Simplicial Subdivision and Govindan-Wilson.

The basic idea behind our search algorithms is simple. Recall that, while the general problem of computing a NE is a complementarity problem, computing whether there exists a NE with a *particular support*[2] for each player is a relatively easy feasibility program. Our algorithms explore the space of support profiles using a backtracking procedure to instantiate the support for each player separately. After each instantiation, they prune the search space by checking for actions in a support that are strictly dominated, given that the other agents will only play actions in their own supports.

Both algorithms order the search by giving precedence to supports of small size. Since it turns out that games drawn from classes that researchers have focused on in the past tend to have (at least one) NE with a very small support, our algorithms are often able to find one quickly. Thus, this paper is as much about the properties of NE in games of interest as it is about novel algorithmic insights.

We emphasize, however, that we are not cheating in the selection of games on which we test. Past algorithms were tested almost exclusively on "random" games. We tested on these too (indeed, we will have more to say about how "random" games vary along at least one important dimension), but also on many other distributions (24 in total). To this end we use GAMUT, a recently introduced computational testbed for game theory (Nudelman et al. 2004). Our results are quite robust across all games tested.

The rest of the paper is organized as follows. After formulating the problem and the basis for searching over supports, we describe our two algorithms. The $n$-player algorithm is essentially a generalization of the 2-player algorithm, but we describe them separately, both because they differ slightly in the ordering of the search, and because the 2-player case admits a simpler description of the algorithm. Then, we describe our experimental setup, and separately present our results for 2-player and $n$-player games. In the final section, we conclude and describe opportunities for future work.



[1]This work was supported in part by DARPA grant F30602-00-2-0598.

[2]The support specifies the pure strategies played with nonzero probability.

## Notation

We consider finite, $n$-player, normal-form games $G = \langle N, (A_i), (u_i) \rangle$:

- $N = \{1, \ldots, n\}$ is the set of players.
- $A_i = \{a_{i1}, \ldots, a_{im_i}\}$ is the set of actions available to player $i$, where $m_i$ is the number of available actions for that player. We will use $a_i$ as a variable that takes on the value of a particular action $a_{ij}$ of player $i$, and $a = (a_1, \ldots, a_n)$ to denote a profile of actions, one for each player. Also, let $a_{-i} = (a_1, \ldots, a_{i-1}, a_{i+1}, \ldots, a_n)$ denote this same profile excluding the action of player $i$, so that $(a_i, a_{-i})$ forms a complete profile of actions. We will use similar notation for any profile that contains an element for each player.
- $u_i : A_1 \times \ldots \times A_n \rightarrow \Re$ is the utility function for each player $i$. It maps a profile of actions to a value.

Each player $i$ selects a mixed strategy from the set $\mathcal{P}_i = \{p_i : A_i \rightarrow [0,1] | \sum_{a_i \in A_i} p_i(a_i) = 1\}$. A mixed strategy for a player specifies the probability distribution used to select the action that the player will play in the game. We will sometimes use $a_i$ to denote the pure strategy in which $p_i(a_i) = 1$. The support of a mixed strategy $p_i$ is the set of all actions $a_i \in A_i$ such that $p_i(a_i) > 0$. We will use $x = (x_1, \ldots, x_n)$ to denote a profile of values that specifies the size of the support of each player.

Because agents use mixed strategies, $u_i$ is extended to also denote the expected utility for player $i$ for a strategy profile $p = (p_1, \ldots, p_n)$: $u_i(p) = \sum_{a \in A} p(a) u_i(a)$, where $p(a) = \Pi_{i \in N} p_i(a_i)$.

The primary solution concept for a normal form game is that of Nash equilibrium. A mixed strategy profile is a Nash equilibrium if no agent has incentive to unilaterally deviate.

**Definition 1** *A strategy profile $p^* \in \mathcal{P}$ is a Nash equilibrium if:* $\forall i \in N, a_i \in A_i : \quad u_i(a_i, p^*_{-i}) \leq u_i(p^*_i, p^*_{-i})$

Every finite, normal form game is guaranteed to have at least one Nash equilibrium (Nash 1950).

## Searching Over Supports

The basis of our two algorithms is to search over the space of possible instantiations of the support $S_i \subseteq A_i$ for each player $i$. Given a support profile as input, Feasibility Program 1, below, gives the formal description of a program for finding a Nash equilibrium $p$ consistent with $S$ (if such an strategy profile exists).[3] In this program, $v_i$ corresponds to the expected utility of player $i$ in an equilibrium. The first two classes of constraints require that each player must be indifferent between all actions within his support, and must not strictly prefer an action outside of his support. These imply that no player can deviate to a pure strategy that improves his expected utility, which is exactly the condition for the strategy profile to be a Nash equilibrium.

[3] We note that the use of Feasibility Program 1 is not novel–it was used by (Dickhaut & Kaplan 1991) in an algorithm which enumerated all support profiles in order to find all Nash equilibria.

Because $p(a_{-i}) = \prod_{j \neq i} p_j(a_j)$, this program is linear for $n = 2$ and nonlinear for all $n > 2$. Note that, strictly speaking, we do not require that each action $a_i \in S_i$ be in the support, because it is allowed to be played with zero probability. However, player $i$ must still be indifferent between action $a_i$ and each other action $a'_i \in S_i$.

**Feasibility Program 1**

***Input***: $S = (S_1, \ldots, S_n)$, a support profile
***Output***: NE $p$, if there exists both a strategy profile $p = (p_1, \ldots, p_n)$ and a value profile $v = (v_1, \ldots, v_n)$ s.t.:

$$\forall i \in N, a_i \in S_i : \quad \sum_{a_{-i} \in S_{-i}} p(a_{-i}) u_i(a_i, a_{-i}) = v_i$$

$$\forall i \in N, a_i \notin S_i : \quad \sum_{a_{-i} \in S_{-i}} p(a_{-i}) u_i(a_i, a_{-i}) \leq v_i$$

$$\forall i \in N : \quad \sum_{a_i \in S_i} p_i(a_i) = 1$$

$$\forall i \in N, a_i \in S_i : \quad p_i(a_i) \geq 0$$

$$\forall i \in N, a_i \notin S_i : \quad p_i(a_i) = 0$$

## Algorithm for Two-Player Games

In this section we describe Algorithm 1, our 2-player algorithm for searching the space of supports. There are three keys to the efficiency of this algorithm. The first two are the factors used to order the search space. Specifically, Algorithm 1 considers every possible support size profile separately, favoring support sizes that are balanced and small. The motivation behind these choices comes from work such as (McLennan & Berg 2002), which analyzes the theoretical properties of the NE of games drawn from a particular distribution. Specifically, for $n$-player games, the payoffs for an action profile are determined by drawing a point uniformly at random in a unit sphere. Under this distribution, for $n = 2$, the probability that there exists a NE consistent with a particular support profile varies inversely with the size of the supports, and is zero for unbalanced support profiles.

The third key to Algorithm 1 is that it separately instantiates each players' support, making use of what we will call "conditional (strict) dominance" to prune the search space.

**Definition 2** *An action $a_i \in A_i$ is conditionally dominated, given a profile of sets of available actions $R_{-i} \subseteq A_{-i}$ for the remaining agents, if the following condition holds:* $\exists a'_i \in A_i \; \forall a_{-i} \in R_{-i} : \quad u_i(a_i, a_{-i}) < u_i(a'_i, a_{-i})$.

The preference for small support sizes amplifies the advantages of checking for conditional dominance. For example, after instantiating a support of size two for the first player, it will often be the case that many of the second player's actions are pruned, because only two inequalities must hold for one action to conditionally dominate another.

Pseudo-code for Algorithm 1 is given below. Note that this algorithm is complete, because it considers all support size profiles, and because it only prunes actions that are *strictly* dominated.

**Algorithm 1**

**for all** support size profiles $x = (x_1, x_2)$, sorted in increasing order of, first, $|x_1 - x_2|$ and, second, $(x_1 + x_2)$ **do**
  **for all** $S_1 \subseteq A_1$ s.t. $|S_1| = x_1$ **do**
    $A'_2 \leftarrow \{a_2 \in A_2$ not cond. dominated, given $S_1\}$
    **if** $\nexists a_1 \in S_1$ cond. dominated, given $A'_2$ **then**
      **for all** $S_2 \subseteq A'_2$ s.t. $|S_2| = x_2$ **do**
        **if** $\nexists a_1 \in S_1$ cond. dominated, given $S_2$ **then**
          **if** Feasibility Program 1 is satisfiable for $S = (S_1, S_2)$ **then**
            Return the found NE $p$

## Algorithm for N-Player Games

Algorithm 1 can be interpreted as using the general backtracking algorithm (see, e.g., (Dechter 2003)) to solve a constraint satisfaction problem (CSP) for each support size profile. The variables in each CSP are the supports $S_i$, and the domain of each $S_i$ is the set of supports of size $x_i$. While the single constraint is that there must exist a solution to Feasibility Program 1, an extraneous, but easier to check, set of constraints is that no agent plays a conditionally dominated action. The removal of conditionally dominated strategies by Algorithm 1 is similar to using the AC-1 to enforce arc-consistency with respect to these constraints. We use this interpretation to generalize Algorithm 1 for the $n$-player case. Pseudo-code for Algorithm 2 and its two procedures, Recursive-Backtracking and Iterated Removal of Strictly Dominated Strategies (IRSDS) are given below.[4]

IRSDS takes as input a domain for each player's support. For each agent whose support has been instantiated, the domain contains only that instantiated support, while for each other agent $i$ it contains all supports of size $x_i$ that were not eliminated in a previous call to this procedure. On each pass of the *repeat-until* loop, every action found in at least one support of a player's domain is checked for conditional domination. If a domain becomes empty after the removal of a conditionally dominated action, then the current instantiations of the Recursive-Backtracking are inconsistent, and IRSDS returns *failure*. Because the removal of an action can lead to further domain reductions for other agents, IRSDS repeats until it either returns *failure* or iterates through all actions of all players without finding a dominated action.

Finally, we note that Algorithm 2 is not a strict generalization of Algorithm 1, because it orders the support size profiles first by size, and then by a measure of balance. The reason for the change is that balance (while still significant) is less important for $n > 2$ than it is for $n = 2$. For example, under the model of (McLennan & Berg 2002), for $n > 2$, the probability of the existence of a NE consistent with a particular support profile is no longer zero when the support profile is unbalanced.

[4]Even though our implementation of the backtracking procedure is iterative, for simplicity we present it here in its equivalent, recursive form. Also, the reader familiar with CSPs will recognize that we have employed very basic algorithms for backtracking and for enforcing arc consistency, and we return to this point in the conclusion.

**Algorithm 2**

**for all** $x = (x_1, \ldots, x_n)$, sorted in increasing order of, first, $\sum_i x_i$ and, second, $max_{i,j}(x_i - x_j)$ **do**
  $\forall i : S_i \leftarrow NULL$   *//uninstantiated supports*
  $\forall i : D_i \leftarrow \{S_i \subseteq A_i : |S_i| = x_i\}$   *//domain of supports*
  **if** Recursive-Backtracking$(S, D, 1)$ returns a NE $p$ **then**
    Return $p$

**Procedure 1** Recursive-Backtracking

***Input***: $S = (S_1, \ldots, S_n)$: a profile of supports
  $D = (D_1, \ldots, D_n)$: a profile of domains
  $i$: index of next support to instantiate
***Output***: A Nash equilibrium $p$, or $failure$
**if** $i = n + 1$ **then**
  **if** Feasibility Program 1 is satisfiable for $S$ **then**
    Return the found NE $p$
  **else**
    Return $failure$
**else**
  **for all** $d_i \in D_i$ **do**
    $S_i \leftarrow d_i$
    $D_i \leftarrow D_i - \{d_i\}$
    **if** IRSDS$((\{S_1\}, \ldots, \{S_i\}, D_{i+1}, \ldots, D_n))$ succeeds **then**
      **if** Recursive-Backtracking$(S, D, i+1)$ returns NE $p$ **then**
        Return $p$
  Return $failure$

**Procedure 2** Iterated Removal of Strictly Dominated Strategies (IRSDS)

***Input***: $D = (D_1, \ldots, D_n)$: profile of domains
***Output***: Updated domains, or $failure$
**repeat**
  $changed \leftarrow false$
  **for all** $i \in N$ **do**
    **for all** $a_i \in d_i \in D_i$ **do**
      **for all** $a'_i \in A_i$ **do**
        **if** $\forall a_{-i} \in d_{-i} \in D_{-i}, u_i(a_i, a_{-i}) < u_i(a'_i, a_{-i})$ **then**
          $D_i \leftarrow D_i - \{d_i \in D_i : a_i \in d_i\}$
          $changed \leftarrow true$
          **if** $D_i = \emptyset$ **then**
            return $failure$
**until** $changed = false$
return $D$

| D1 | Bertrand Oligopoly | D2 | Bidirectional LEG, Complete Graph |
|---|---|---|---|
| D3 | Bidirectional LEG, Random Graph | D4 | Bidirectional LEG, Star Graph |
| D5 | Covariance Game: $\rho = 0.9$ | D6 | Cov. Game: $\rho \in [-1/(N-1), 1]$ |
| D7 | Covariance Game: $\rho = 0$ | D8 | Dispersion Game |
| D9 | Graphical Game, Random Graph | D10 | Graphical Game, Road Graph |
| D11 | Graphical Game, Star Graph | D12 | Graphical Game, Small-World |
| D13 | Minimum Effort Game | D14 | Polymatrix Game, Complete Graph |
| D15 | Polymatrix Game, Random Graph | D16 | Polymatrix Game, Road Graph |
| D17 | PolymatrixGame, Small-World | D18 | Uniformly Random Game |
| D19 | Travelers Dilemma | D20 | Uniform LEG, Complete Graph |
| D21 | Uniform LEG, Random Graph | D22 | Uniform LEG, Star Graph |
| D23 | Location Game | D24 | War Of Attrition |

Table 1: Descriptions of GAMUT distributions.

## Experimental Results

To evaluate the performance of our algorithms we ran several sets of experiments. All games were generated by GAMUT (Nudelman et al. 2004), a test-suite that is capable of generating games from a wide variety of classes of games found in the literature. Table 1 provides a brief description of the subset of distributions on which we tested.

A distribution of particular importance is the one most commonly tested on in previous work: D18, the "Uniformly Random Game", in which every payoff in the game is drawn independently from an identical uniform distribution. Also important are distributions D5, D6, and D7, which fall under a "Covariance Game" model studied by (Rinott & Scarsini 2000), in which the payoffs for the $n$ agents for each action profile are drawn from a multivariate normal distribution in which the covariance $\rho$ between the payoffs of each pair of agents is identical. When $\rho = 1$, the game is common-payoff, while $\rho = \frac{-1}{N-1}$ yields minimal correlation, which occurs in zero-sum games. Thus, by altering $\rho$, we can smoothly transition between these two extreme classes of games.

Our experiments were executed on a cluster of 12 dual-processor, 2.4GHz Pentium machines, running Linux 2.4.20. We capped runs for all algorithms at 1800 seconds. When describing the statistics used to evaluate the algorithms, we will use "unconditional" to refer to the value of the statistic when timeouts are counted as 1800 seconds, and "conditional" to refer to its value excluding timeouts.

When $n = 2$, we solved Feasibility Program 1 using CPLEX 8.0's callable library. For $n > 2$, because the program is nonlinear, we instead solved each instance of the program by executing AMPL, using MINOS as the underlying optimization package. Obviously, we could substitute in any nonlinear solver; and, since a large fraction of our running time is spent on AMPL and MINOS, doing so would greatly affect the overall running time.

Before presenting the empirical results, we note that a comparison of the worst-case running times of our two algorithms and the three we tested against does not distinguish between them, since there exist inputs for each which lead to exponential time.

### Results for Two-Player Games

In the first set of experiments, we compared the performance of Algorithm 1 to that of Lemke-Howson (implemented in Gambit, which added the preprocessing step of iterated removal of weakly dominated strategies) on 2-player, 300-action games drawn from 24 of GAMUT's 2-player distributions. Both algorithms were executed on 100 games drawn from each distribution. The time is measured in seconds and plotted on a logarithmic scale.

Figure 1(a) compares the unconditional median runtimes of the two algorithms, and shows that Algorithm 1 performs better on all distributions.[5] However, this does not tell the whole story. For many distributions, it simply reflects the fact that there is a greater than 50% chance that the distribution will generate a game with a pure strategy NE, which our algorithm will then find quickly. Two other important statistics are the percentage of instances solved (Figure 1(b)), and the average runtime conditional on solving the instance (Figure 1(c)). Here, we see that Algorithm 1 completes far more instances on several distributions, and solves fewer on just a single distribution (6 fewer, on D23). Additionally, even on distributions for which we solve far more games, our conditional average runtime is 1 to 2 orders of magnitude smaller.

Clearly, the hardest distribution for our algorithm is D6, which consists of "Covariance Games" in which the covariance $\rho$ is drawn uniformly at random from the range $[-1, 1]$. In fact, neither Algorithm 1 nor Lemke-Howson solved any of the games in another "Covariance Game" distribution in which $\rho = -0.9$, and these results were omitted from the graphs, because the conditional average is undefined for these results. On the other hand, for the distribution "CovarianceGame-Pos" (D5), in which $\rho = 0.9$, both algorithms perform well.

To further investigate this continuum, we sampled 300 values for $\rho$ in the range $[-1, 1]$, with heavier sampling in the transition region and at zero. For each such game, we plotted a point for the runtime of both Algorithm 1 and Lemke-Howson in Figure 1(d).[6] The theoretical results of (Rinott & Scarsini 2000) suggest that the games with lower covariance should be more difficult for Algorithm 1, because they are less likely to have a pure strategy Nash equilibrium. Nevertheless, it is interesting to note the sharpness of the transition that occurs in the $[-0.3, 0]$ interval. More surprisingly, a similarly sharp transition also occurs for Lemke-Howson, despite the fact that the two algorithms operate in unrelated ways. Finally, it is important to note that the transition region for Lemke-Howson is shifted to the right by approximately 0.3, and that, on instances in the easy region for both algorithms, Algorithm 1 is still an order of magnitude faster.

In the third set of experiments we explore the scaling behavior of both algorithms on the "Uniformly Random Game" distribution (D18), as the number of actions increases from 100 to 1000. For each multiple of 100, we generated 20 games. Because space constraints preclude an analysis similar to that of Figures 1(a) through 1(c), we instead plot in Figure 1(e) the *unconditional* average runtime over 20 instances for each data size, with a timeout counted as 1800s. While Lemke-Howson failed to solve any game with more than 600 actions and timed out on some 100-action games, Algorithm 1 solved all instances, and, without the help of cutoff times, still had an advantage of 2 orders of magnitude at 1000 actions.

### Results for N-Player Games

In the next set of experiments we compare Algorithm 2 to Govindan-Wilson and Simplicial Subdivision (which was implemented in Gambit, and thus combined with iterated removal of weakly dominated strategies). First, to compare performance on a fixed problem size we tested on 6-player,

[5]Obviously, the lines connecting data points across distributions for a particular algorithm are meaningless– they were only added to make the graph easier to read.

[6]The capped instances for Algorithm 1 were perturbed slightly upward on the graph for clarity.

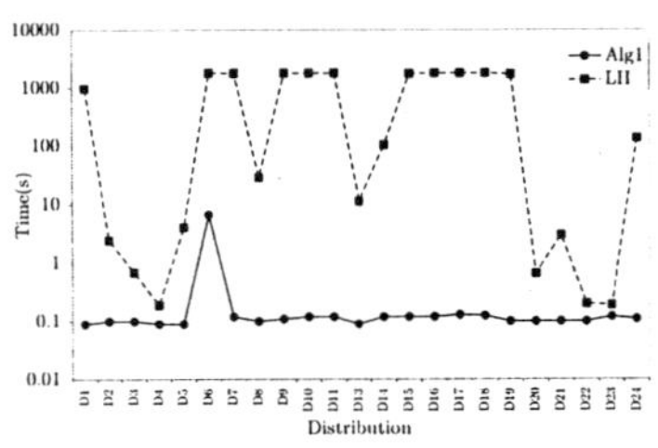


(a) Unconditional median runtime

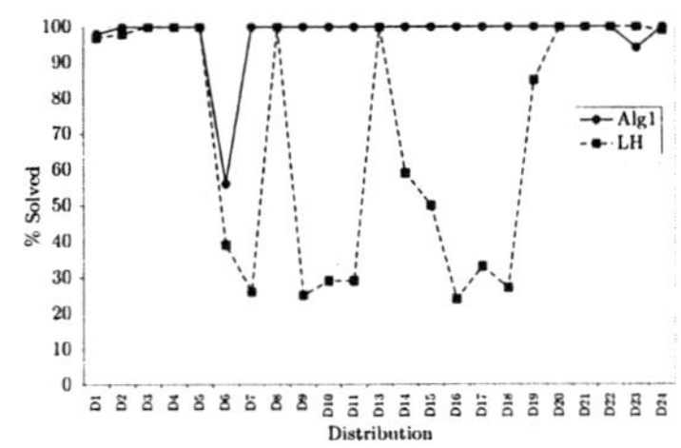


(b) Percentage solved

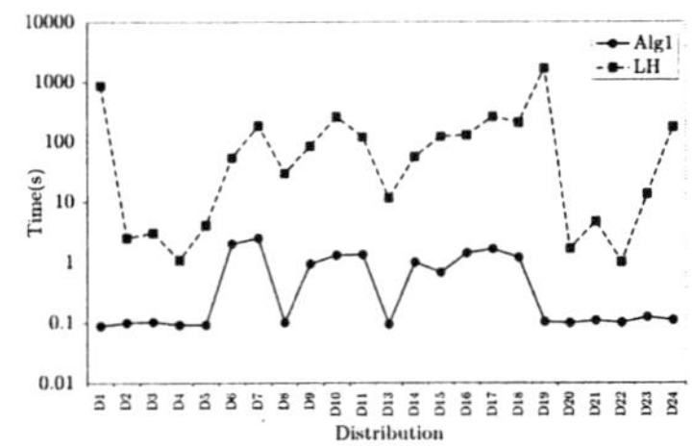


(c) Average time on solved instances

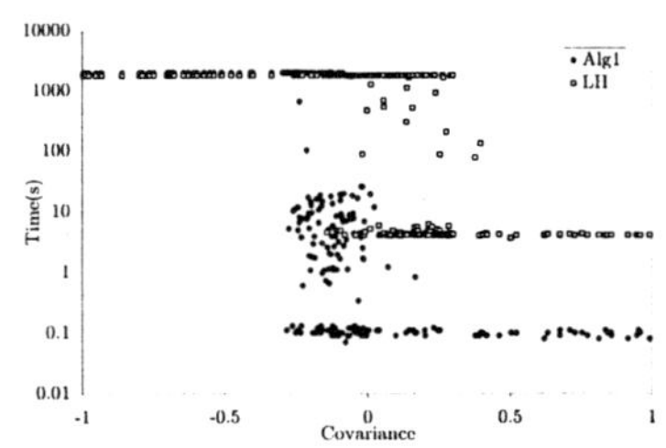


(d) Runtime vs. Covariance

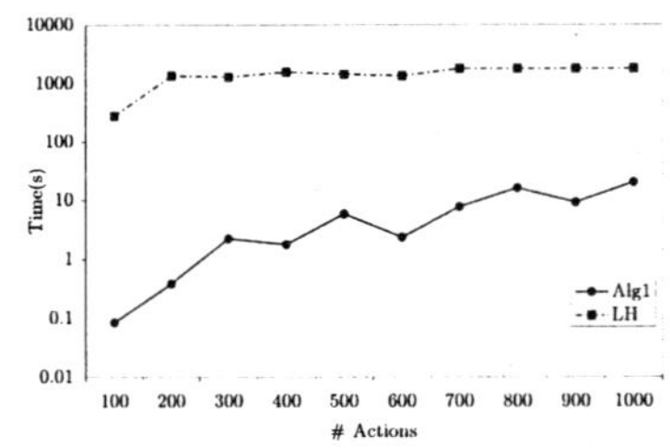


(e) Unconditional average vs. Actions

Figure 1: Comparison of Algorithm 1 and Lemke-Howson on 2-player games. Subfigures (a)-(d) are for 300-action games.

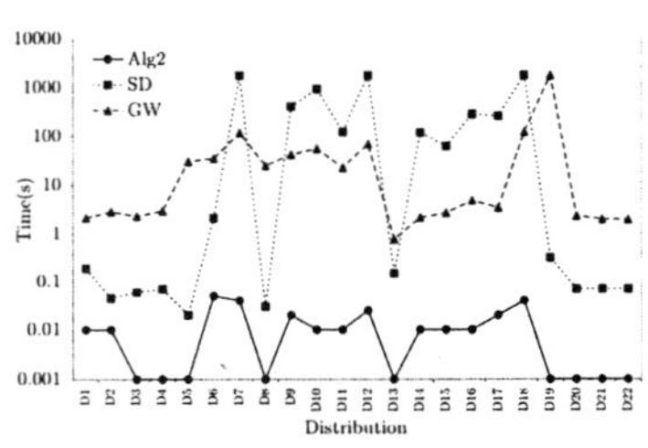


(a) Unconditional median runtimes

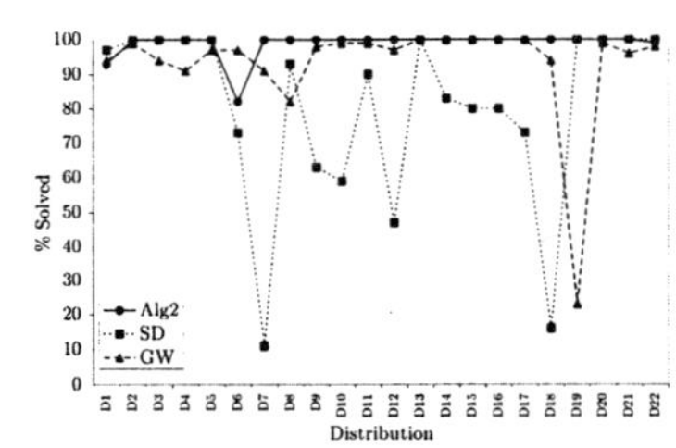


(b) Percentage solved

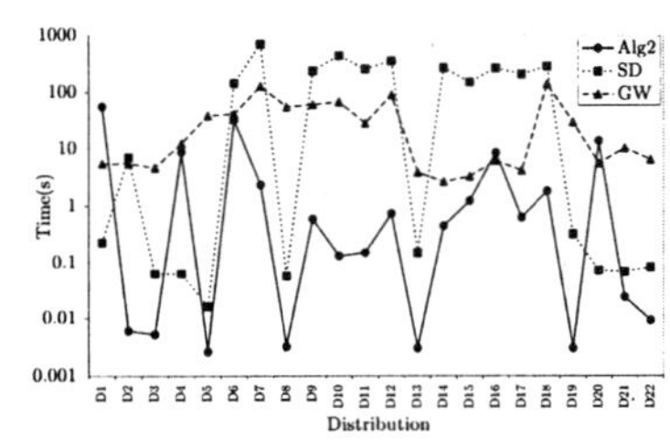


(c) Average time on solved instances

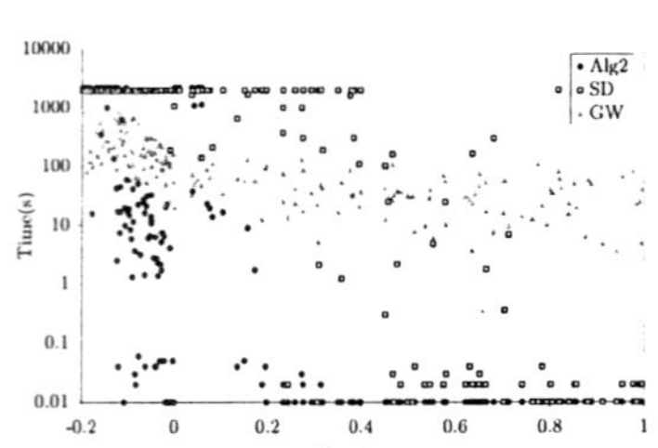


(d) Runtime vs. Covariance

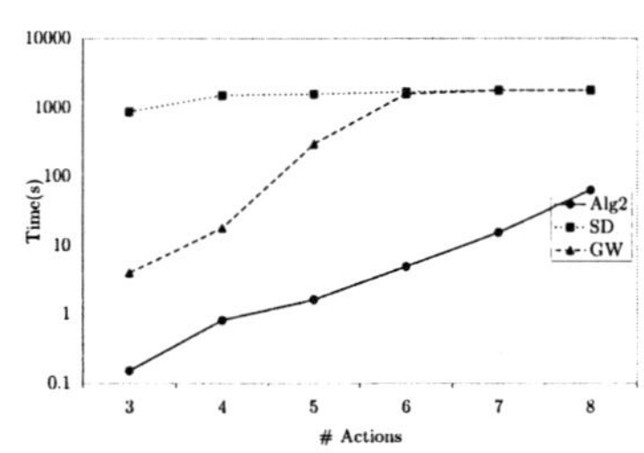


(e) Unconditional average runtime vs. Actions, on 6-player games

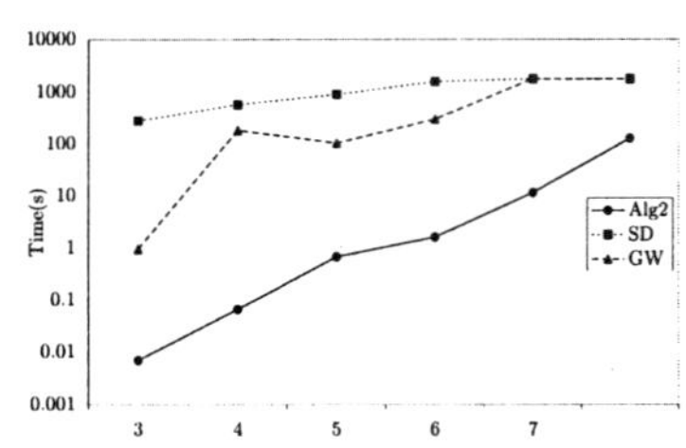


(f) Unconditional average runtime vs. Players, on 5-action games

Figure 2: Comparison of Algorithm 2, Simplicial Subdivision, and Govindan-Wilson. Subfigures (a)-(d) are for 6-player, 5-action games.

5-action games drawn from 22 of GAMUT's $n$-player distributions.[7] While the numbers of players and actions appear small, note that these games have 15625 outcomes and 93750 payoffs. Once again, Figures 2(a), 2(b), and 2(c) show unconditional median runtime, percentage of instances solved, and conditional average runtime, respectively. Algorithm 2 has a very low unconditional median runtime, for the same reason that Algorithm 1 did for two-player games, and outperforms both other algorithms on all distributions. While this dominance does not extend to the other two metrics, the comparison still favors Algorithm 2.

We again investigate the relationship between $\rho$ and the hardness of games under the "Covariance Game" model. For general $n$-player games, minimal correlation under this model occurs when $\rho = -\frac{1}{n-1}$. Thus, we can only study the range $[-0.2, 1]$ for 6-player games. Figure 2(d) shows the results for 6-player 5-action games. Algorithm 2, over the range $[-0.1, 0]$, experiences a transition in hardness that is even sharper than that of Algorithm 1. Simplicial Subdivision also undergoes a transition, which is not as sharp, that begins at a much larger value of $\rho$ (around $0.4$). However, the running time of Govindan-Wilson is only slightly affected by the covariance, as it neither suffers as much for small values of $\rho$ nor benefits as much from large values.

Finally, Figures 2(e) and 2(f) compare the scaling behavior (in terms of unconditional average runtimes) of the three algorithms: the former holds the number of players constant at 6 and varies the number of actions from 3 to 8, while the latter holds the number of actions constant at 5, and varies the number of players from 3 to 8. In both experiments, both Simplicial Subdivision and Govindan-Wilson solve no instances for the largest two sizes, while Algorithm 2 still finds a solution for most games.

## Conclusion and Future Work

In this paper, we presented two algorithms for finding a sample Nash equilibrium. Both use backtracking approaches (augmented with pruning) to search the space of support profiles, favoring supports that are small and balanced. Both also outperform the current state of the art.

The most difficult games we encountered came from the "Covariance Game" model, as the covariance approaches its minimal value, and this is a natural target for future algorithm development. We expect these games to be hard in general, because, empirically, we found that as the covariance decreases, the number of equilibria decreases, and the equilibria that do exist are more likely to have support sizes near one half of the number of actions, which is the support size with the largest number of supports.

One direction for future work is to employ more sophisticated CSP techniques. The main goal of this paper was to show that our general search method performs well in practice, and there are many other CSP search and inference strategies which may improve its efficiency. Another promising direction to explore is local search, in which the state space is the set of all possible supports, and the available moves are to add or delete an action from the support of a player. While the fact that no equilibrium exists for a particular support does not give any guidance as to which neighboring support to explore next, one could use a relaxation of Feasibility Program 1 that penalizes infeasibility through an objective function. More generally, our results show that AI techniques can be successfully applied to this problem, and we have only scratched the surface of possibilities along this direction.

[7]Two distributions from the tests of 2-player games are missing here, due to the fact that they do not naturally generalize to more than 2 players.

## References


Blum, B.; Shelton, C. R.; and Koller, D. 2003. A continuation method for Nash equilibria in structured games. In *IJCAI-03*.

Dechter, R. 2003. *Constraint Processing*. Morgan Kaufmann.

Dickhaut, J., and Kaplan, T. 1991. A program for finding Nash equilibria. *The Mathematica Journal* 87–93.

Govindan, S., and Wilson, R. 2003. A global newton method to compute Nash equilibria. In *Journal of Economic Theory*.

Lemke, C., and Howson, J. 1964. Equilibrium points of bimatrix games. *Journal of the Society for Industrial and Applied Mathematics* 12:413–423.

McKelvey, R., and McLennan, A. 1996. Computation of equilibria in finite games. In H. Amman, D. Kendrick, J. R., ed., *Handbook of Computational Economics*, volume I. Elsevier. 87–142.

McKelvey, R.; McLennan, A.; and Turocy, T. 2003. Gambit: Software tools for game theory, version 0.97.0.5. Available at http://econweb.tamu.edu/gambit/.

McLennan, A., and Berg, J. 2002. The asymptotic expected number of Nash equilibria of two player normal form games. Mimeo, University of Minnesota.

Nash, J. 1950. Equilibrium points in n-person games. *Proceedings of the National Academy of Sciences of the United States of America* 36:48–49.

Nudelman, E.; Wortman, J.; Shoham, Y.; and Leyton-Brown, K. 2004. Run the GAMUT: A comprehensive approach to evaluating game-theoretic algorithms. In *AAMAS-04*.

Papadimitriou, C. 2001. Algorithms, games, and the internet. In *STOC-01*, 749–753.

Rinott, Y., and Scarsini, M. 2000. On the number of pure strategy Nash equilibria in random games. *Games and Economic Behavior* 33:274–293.

van der Laan, G.; Talman, A.; and van der Heyden, L. 1987. Simplicial variable dimension algorithms for solving the nonlinear complementarity problem on a product of unit simplices using a general labelling. *Mathematics of Operations Research*.

von Stengel, B. 2002. Computing equilibria for two-person games. In Aumann, R., and Hart, S., eds., *Handbook of Game Theory*, volume 3. North-Holland. chapter 45, 1723–1759.

# Towards Efficient Sampling: Exploiting Random Walk Strategies

**Wei Wei, Jordan Erenrich, and Bart Selman**
Department of Computer Science
Cornell University
Ithaca, NY 14853
{weiwei, erenrich, selman}@cs.cornell.edu

### Abstract

From a computational perspective, there is a close connection between various probabilistic reasoning tasks and the problem of counting or sampling satisfying assignments of a propositional theory. We consider the question of whether state-of-the-art satisfiability procedures, based on random walk strategies, can be used to sample uniformly or near-uniformly from the space of satisfying assignments. We first show that random walk SAT procedures often do reach the full set of solutions of complex logical theories. Moreover, by interleaving random walk steps with Metropolis transitions, we also show how the sampling becomes near-uniform.

## Introduction

We consider the problem of sampling from the set of satisfying assignments ("models") of a propositional theory. Perhaps the best known methods for sampling from combinatorial spaces are Markov Chain Monte Carlo (MCMC) methods, such as the Metropolis algorithm and simulated annealing (Madras 2002; Metropolis *et al.* 1953; Kirkpatrick *et al.* 1983). These methods are based on setting up a Markov chain with a predefined stationary distribution. One can draw samples from the stationary distribution by running the Markov Chain for a sufficiently long time. Unfortunately, on many hard combinatorial problems, the Markov chain takes exponential time, in terms of problem size, before reaching its stationary distribution.

These methods can also be used to find optimal solutions to combinatorial problems. For example, simulated annealing (SA) uses the Boltzmann distribution as the stationary distribution. By lowering the temperature to near zero, the distribution becomes concentrated around the minimum energy states, which correspond to the solutions of the combinatorial problem under consideration. For example, to find a satisfying assignment of a propositional theory, one can use an energy function that assigns to each truth assignment an energy (or cost) equal to the number of violated logical constraints. Zero cost solutions correspond to satisfying assignments.

Unfortunately, standard SA on a propositional theory is of little practical use, because on theories of practical interest, SA at low temperature does not reach the stationary distribution in a reasonable number of steps. Several alternative local search methods have been discovered that find assignments for large and complex propositional theories, involving up to a million variables and several million constraints. These methods exploit properties of random walks. We will refer to them as random walk strategies.

An intriguing question to consider is whether these random walk strategies can also be used *to sample uniformly or near uniformly from the set of satisfying assignments of a propositional theory.* If so, this would have interesting implications for a wide range of probabilistic reasoning tasks, because of the close connections between sampling models from a propositional theory and probabilistic inference. In particular, if one could sample propopositional models efficiently, then one obtains an efficient method for Bayesian inference and a range of other forms of probabilistic reasoning. The full technical details on the connections between sampling from a logical theory and probabilistic reasoning are not overly complicated but not the focus of this paper. We refer to, e.g., (Roth 1996; Littman *et al.* 2001; Park 2002).

We will show that one can indeed exploit ideas from random walk based methods to obtain effective near-uniform sampling of the models of certain propositional theories. More specifically, we show that a random walk strategy which incorporates a greedy bias, called WalkSAT, samples nearly uniformly on several structured propositional theories. We will also see that on hard random formulas, WalkSAT does find all assignments, but the sampling is far from uniform. We then consider a hybrid strategy which interleaves simulated annealing (SA) steps and WalkSAT steps. This hybrid strategy restores the sampling to near uniform. See the scatterplots in Figure 1 for a preview of this result. Each data point corresponds to a solution of the theory (2531 total). The vertical axis gives the frequency with which each solution was reached. The top panel shows that the ratio between least frequent and most frequently found solutions for WalkSAT is around a factor of $10^4$; the bottom panel shows how interleaving simulated annealing steps reduces the non-uniformity by around a factor of 1,000 (a factor 10 between most frequent and least frequent remains). (Note that SA by itself can generally not reach any solution on these theories.) We also present a formal analysis in support of our empirical

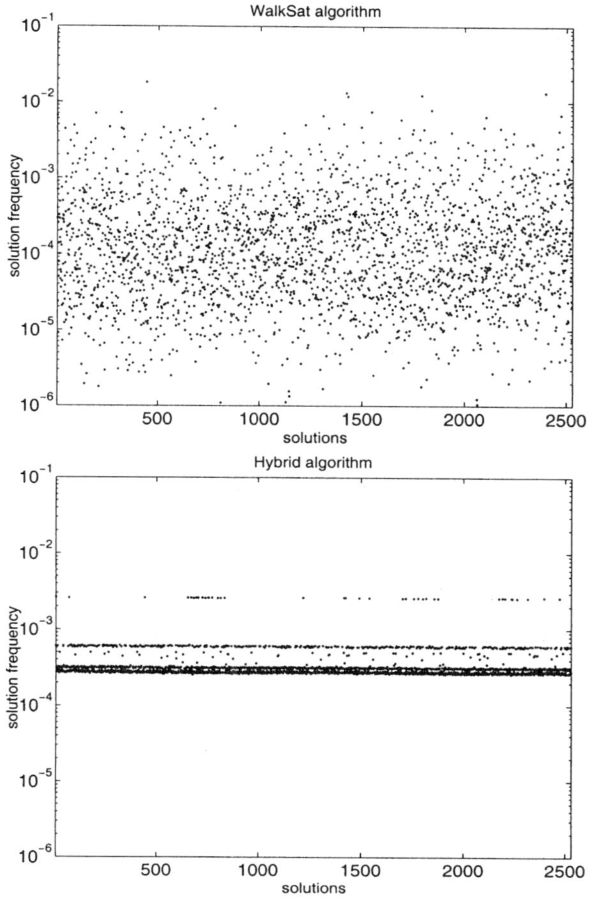


Figure 1: Sampling of hard random 3SAT instance. Top: Walksat. Bottom: Hybrid.

findings.

We believe that our results are a promising first step in the use of random walk strategies for sampling.

## Random Walk Strategies

Without loss of generality, we will assume that our propositional theory is given in Conjunctive Normal Form (CNF). That is, the theory consist of a conjunction (logical "and") of disjunctions. Each disjunction (also called a "clause") consists of the logical "or" of a set of literals, where each literal is a Boolean variable or its negation. The goal is to find a setting to the Boolean variables such that there is at least one literal in each disjunction that evaluates to `true`.

The problem of determining whether a CNF formula has a satisfying assignment is also referred to as the satisfiability or SAT problem. SAT is the prototypical NP-complete problem (Cook 1971). Therefore, it is generally believed that in the worst-case one has to search through the full space of all $2^N$ assignments to find a satisfying assignment if one exists, where $N$ is the number of Boolean variables of the theory. Because the SAT problem is NP-complete, it has a tremendous range of applications (Garey & Johnson 1979). The problem of counting the number of satisfying assignments is #P-complete (Valiant 1979), and believed to be significantly harder than NP-complete (again, worst-case).

We refer to a CNF formula with exactly $k$ literals in each clause as $k$-CNF; the associated satisfiability problem is referred to as $k$-SAT. For $k \geq 3$, the satisfiability problem is NP-complete. However, 2-SAT can be solved in linear time. Interestingly, counting the number of 2-SAT assignments is #P-complete. This suggests that counting is significantly harder than determining satisfiability.

A *random walk procedure* for satisfiability is a deceptively simple search technique. Such a procedure starts with a random truth assignment. Assuming this randomly guessed assignment does not already satisfy the formula, one selects one of the unsatisfied clauses at random, and flips the truth assignment of one of the variables in that clause. This will cause the clause to become satisfied but, of course, one or more other clauses may become unsatisfied. Such flips are repeated until one reaches an assignment that satisfies all clauses or until a pre-defined maximum number of flips are made. This simple strategy can be surprisingly effective. In fact, Papadimitriou (1991) showed that a pure (unbiased) random walk on an arbitrary satisfiable 2SAT formula will reach a satisfying assignment in $O(N^2)$ flips (with probability going to 1). More recently, Schoening (1999) showed that a series of short unbiased random walks on a 3-SAT problem will find a satisfying assignment in $O(1.334^N)$ flips (assuming such an assignment exists), much better than $O(2^N)$ for an exhaustive check of all assignments.

To gain some further insight into the behavior of random walk strategies for SAT, let us briefly consider an elegant argument introduced by Papadimitriou showing polytime behavior on 2SAT. Consider a satisfiable 2SAT formula $F$ on $N$ variables. Let $T$ denote a satisfying assignment of $F$. The random walk procedure starts with a random truth assignment, $T'$. On average, this truth assignment will differ from $T$ on the assignment of $N/2$ letters. Now, consider an unsatisfied clause in $F$ (if no such clause exists, then $T'$ is a satisfying assignment). Without loss of generality, we assume that the unsatisfied clause is of the form $(a \vee \neg b)$. Since this clause is unsatisfied, $T'$ must assign both literals in the clause to False (which means that $a$ is assigned False and $b$ True). Also, the satisfying assignment $T$ is such that at least one of the literals in the clause is assigned to True. Now, randomly select a variable in the clause and flip its truth value in $T'$. Since we have only two variables in the clause, we have at least a 50% chance of selecting the variable corresponding to the literal set to True in $T$. (Note that if $T$ satisfies exactly one literal in the clause, we will select that literal with 0.5 probability. If $T$ satisfies both literals, we select the "right" literal with probability 1.0.) It follows that with at least 50% chance, the Hamming distance of our new truth assignment to $T$ will be reduced by 1, and with at most 50% chance, we will have picked the wrong variable and will have increased the Hamming distance to the satisfying assignment. Finally, we appeal to a basic result for one-dimensional symmetric random walks, which says that after $L^2$ steps, the random walker will on average have traveled a distance of $L$ from the starting point. Given that our random walk starts a distance $N/2$ from the satisfying truth assignment $T$, after order $N^2$ steps, the walk will hit a satisfying assignment, with probability going to one. Note that although the walk may at first wander away from the satisfying assignment, it will "bounce off" the reflecting barrier at distance $N$. Also, our analysis is worst-case, *i.e.,* it holds for *any* satisfiable 2SAT formula.

It is instructive to consider what happens on a 3SAT formula, *i.e.*, a conjunctive normal form formula with 3 literals per clause. In this case, when flipping a variable selected at random from an unsatisfied clause, we may only have 1/3 chance of fixing the "correct" variable (assuming our satisfying assignment satisfies exactly one literal in each clause). This leads to a random walk heavily biased away from the solution under consideration. The theory of random walks tells us that reaching the satisfying assignment under such a bias would take an exponential number of flips. And, in fact, in practice we indeed see that a pure random walk on a hard random 3SAT formula performs very poorly.

However, we can counter this "negative" bias by considering the gradient in the overall objective function we are trying to minimize. The idea is that the gradient may provide the random walk with some additional information "pointing" towards the solution, and thus towards the right variable to flip. In SAT, we want to minimize the number of unsatisfied clauses. So, in selecting the variable to flip in an unsatisfied clause, we can bias our selection towards a variable that leads to the greatest decrease in the overall number of unsatisfied clauses. Introducing a bias of this form leads us to the WalkSAT algorithm and its variants. For the details of these algorithms, we refer to (Selman *et al.* 1994; McAllester *et al.* 1997). WalkSAT remains one of the most effective local-search style methods for SAT.

Table 1: Summary statistics from coverage experiments

| INST. | RUNS ($\times 10^6$) | HITS RARE | HITS COM | RATIO WSAT | RATIO HYBRID |
|---|---|---|---|---|---|
| RAND. | 50 | 53 | $9 \times 10^5$ | 17000 | 10 |
| LOG. | 1 | 84 | $4 \times 10^3$ | 50 | 17 |
| VERIF. | 1 | 45 | 318 | 7 | 4 |

## Sampling results

Given the effectiveness of current random walk style procedures for finding satisfying assignments, we now turn our attention to the question of how well such procedures can sample from the set of all satisfying assignments of a logical theory. Note that since the theory behind random walk SAT procedures relies on hitting an extremal point (corresponding to a solution) as quickly as possible, there is no a priori guarantee that we will reach all solutions or that we will sample from solutions uniformly. Contrast this with an equilibrium based sampling approach such as SA: using the number of unsatisfied clauses as a cost function and with temperature going to zero, SA is guaranteed to sample uniformly from the satisfying assignments, provided it approaches the stationary distribution (which is of course a problem in practice).

We consider a hard random 3-SAT instance, a more structured problem from a planning application, as well as a structured instance from microprocessor verification domain. In order to generate a random 3-SAT instance, we first created 100 uniform random 3-SAT instances, with 70 variables and 301 clauses (Mitchell *et al.* 1992). We chose an instance with 2531 solutions for our detailed experiments. (Relsat (Bayardo & Pehaushek 2000) was used to systematically generate all solutions.) For the logistics planning formula, we started with *logistics.d.cnf* available from Satlib with over $10^{10}$ solutions. To facilitate solution set sampling experiments, we added 52 unit clauses, constraining the instance to 1600 solutions. For the verification domain, we chose a formula from Miroslav Velev's formula suite SSS-SAT.1.0. We added 287 unit clauses to reduce the number of solutions to 6144.

Table 1 shows our experimental results for sampling solutions of these three instances. For the random 3-SAT (see row marked "rand."), logistic (row marked "log."), and verification (row marked "verif.") instances, we performed $50 \times 10^6$, $1 \times 10^6$, and $1 \times 10^6$ runs of WalkSAT, respectively. The first key observation is that WalkSAT ultimately finds every solution for all instances. So, apparently, in terms of "solution set coverage", the random walk strategy works already quite well. In Table 1, the column marked "hits rare" gives the number of times the rarest solution was reached; "hits com." gives the number of times the most common solution was found. The column marked "ratio Wsat" gives the ratio of hits of the most common to the rarest solution for the WalkSAT algorithm. So, for example, on the random instance, we see that the most frequently visited solution is sampled $1.7 \times 10^4$ times more often than the satisfying assignment that is sampled the least frequent. The sampling of the verification and planning formulas by WalkSAT is much more uniform (ratio of 7 and 50, respectively). The last column of the table shows how we can still significantly improve the sampling ratio by using a Hybrid sampling strategy. We discuss this strategy in the next section.

The scatterplot in the top panel of Figure 1 gives the actual solution frequency (#hits/#runs) for each of the 2531 solutions of the random formula. (One data point per solution.) The figure further confirms the results from Table 1: WalkSAT's solution sampling can be highly non-uniform. Notice the log scale on the y-axis: 4 orders of magnitude variance. The Kullback-Leibler(KL) divergence (Bishop 1995) between this data and uniform distribution is 1.2431. (A similar figure for the logistic problem shows the points in a relatively narrow band.)

## Improving uniformity: Hybrid strategy

In order to improve the uniformity of the sampling by WalkSAT, we explored a hybrid strategy. In this strategy, we select with probability $p$ a random walk style move and with probability $1 - p$, a simulated annealing step. We used fixed temperature annealing (*i.e.*, Metropolis) moves (Sait & Youssef 2000).[1] More specifically, for each SA move, we

[1]The temperature was tuned by hand to obtain the most uniform sampling. We used T = 0.1. The hybrid strategy is not very

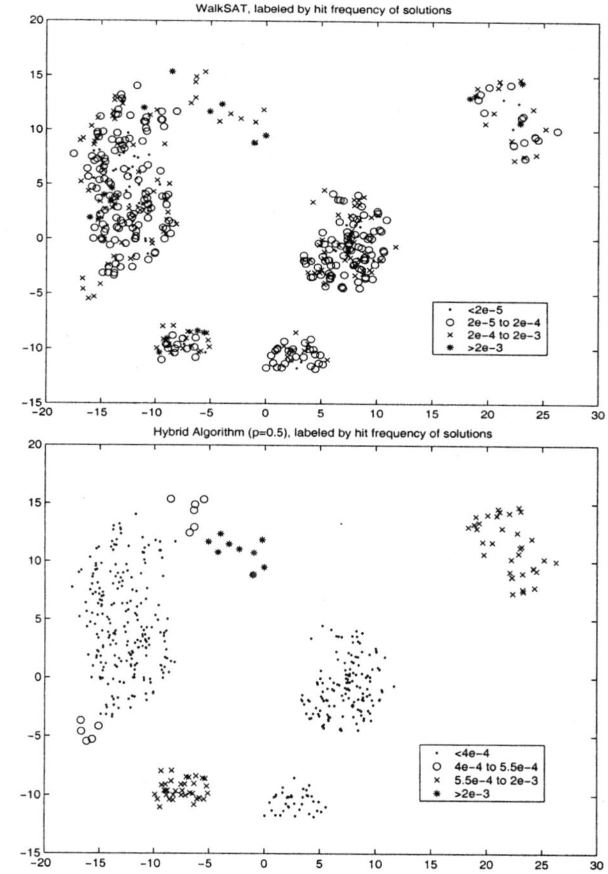


Figure 2: Solution space and the solution frequency for each solution.

consider a randomly selected neighbor of the current assignment. (A neighbor is an truth assignment that differs from the current truth assignment on a single letter.) When the neighbor satisfies the same or more clauses as the current assignment, the algorithm moves to the neighbor assignment. When the neighbor satisfies fewer clauses than the current assignment, we consider the $\Delta Cost$, which gives the decrease in the number of satisfied clauses. The algorithm moves with probability $e^{-\Delta Cost/Temp}$ to the neighbor (otherwise stays at the current assignment).

The bottom panel of Figure 1 gives our results. ($p = 0.5$; 5,000 steps of the mixed chain.) We see a dramatic improvement in the uniformity of sampling. The ratio between the most frequent and least frequently sampled solution is now around 10 (a factor 1000 improvement). The KL-divergence between the data and uniform distribution is reduced to 0.1495. The last column of Table 1 also shows significant improvements in uniformity for the two other domains. Apparently, the SA moves help make the sampling much more uniform. Note, however, that we do need WalkSAT transitions to actually reach solution states efficiently.

We further explored the interesting band structure of the

---

sensitive to the temperature setting.

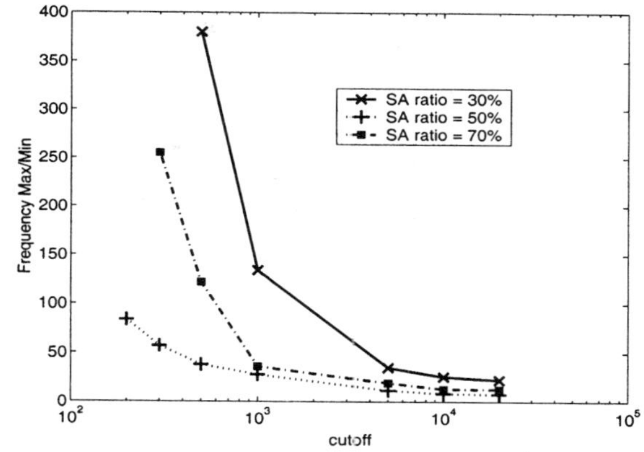


Figure 3: Ratio of least frequent versus most frequently sampled solution for hybrid.

bottom panel. We used a multi-dimensional scaling (Lee 2000) technique to project the high-dimensional solution space into two dimensions. Figure 2 shows the solution space with probabilities to reach each solution by WalkSAT and the Hybrid algorithm. (Not all datapoints are printed to make the figure readable in black and white.) Generally, the closer two solutions appear in the Figure 2, the closer they are in Hamming distance. We can see from the figure that the solutions form clusters. For the WalkSAT algorithm, the number of times a solution is reached varies considerably from solution to solution, even within a cluster. However, for the Hybrid algorithm, solutions within the same cluster are sampled with a similar frequency. This suggests that a Hybrid algorithm can move around a cluster quite effectively, thereby "smoothing" out the probabilities. Overall, the Hybrid method samples much more uniformly than WalkSAT by itself. (SA samples even less effective, because it often does not reach any solution.)

In Figure 3, we show how the effectiveness of the sampling depends on the choice of $p$. We give the ratio of the most frequent solution to the least frequent solution as a function of the number of steps taking in the hybrid chain. The figure shows that there is a clear optimal ratio: 50% SA moves is better than 30% or 70%. In fact, for 30% and 70%, it becomes difficult to measure the ratio when the chain runs only for a small number of steps (less than 200), because not all solutions are found on such short runs even after a million runs.

## Analysis

In this section, we present some analysis that illuminates the difference in sampling using a standard MCMC approach, such as SA, versus a random walk based strategy.

First, it is useful to highlight the fundamental difference between a Metropolis style algorithm and a random walk procedure for SAT. As we discussed, Papadimitriou showed that a random walk procedure for SAT will find a solution to any satisfiable 2CNF formula in $O(N^2)$ time, where $N$ is the number of variables in the formula. This is not the case for SA. (We will use SA as a prototypical example of an MCMC method.)

Consider a formula $F^\star$ of the following form: $a \vee c_1, a \vee c_2, \ldots a \vee c_n, \neg a \vee b, \neg a \vee \neg b$.

**Theorem 1** *SA at fixed temperature with probability going to 1 takes time exponential in $n$ to find a satisfying assignment of $F^\star$.*

The details of the proof are somewhat tedious. Informally, the argument goes as follows. There are two satisfying assignments of the formula. They both have $a$ assigned to `False`, in order to satisfy the last two clauses, and $c_1$ through $c_n$ assigned to `True` ($b$ can be assigned arbitrarily). We start with a random assignment. First assume that $a$ is assigned `True` in this assignment. Any proposed flips of the variables $c_1$ through $c_n$ will be accepted by SA because they do not create any new unsatisfied clauses (cost function does not increase). Flipping of $c_1$ through $c_n$ amounts to a random walk on an $n$-dimensional hypercube formed by these variables. In such a walk, the probability of reaching an area where only a small number of variables, say, $\sqrt{n}$ of them, are assigned `False` is exponentially vanishing. With a non-vanishing fraction of the variables in $c_1$ through $c_n$ assigned `False`, the probability that a proposal to flip $a$ to `False` will be accepted is exponentially small (note that temperature is fixed and $n$ goes to infinity), and finding the satisfying assignment takes exponential time. Informally, we are stuck in an area with local minima defined by $a$ set to `True`. If the search starts with $a$ assigned to `False`, with probability going to 1, it will be flipped to `True` in a polynomial number of flips, getting us to the previous scenario.

A random walk strategy finds a solution for $F^\star$ efficiently, since it is in 2CNF. Moreover, it will find the two satisfying assignments with equal probability due to symmetry in the formula. However, symmetry does of course not exist in all formulas. In fact, when the solution space is very asymmetrical, a random walk strategy can have vastly different probabilities of reaching different solutions. This is shown by considering the following formula $F^{\star\star}$ : $x \vee y_1, x \vee y_2, \cdots x \vee y_n, \neg y_n \vee y_1, \neg y_1 \vee y_2, \neg y_2 \vee y_3, \cdots \neg y_{n-1} \vee y_n$. The final $n$ clauses require $y_1$ through $y_n$ to adopt the same value. Therefore, this formula has exactly three assignments. They are $S_1 : x = 1, y_1 = y_2 = \cdots y_n = 0$, $S_2 : x = 1, y_1 = y_2 = \cdots y_n = 1$, and $S_3 : x = 0, y_1 = y_2 = \cdots y_n = 1$. (0 denotes `False` and 1 denotes `True`.) We will show that in a pure random walk algorithm, the last assignment is reached with an exponentially small probability. (The other two solutions are symmetric and are reached with probability $0.5(1-\epsilon)$, where $\epsilon$ is the probability of reaching $S_3$.)

**Theorem 2** *Pure random walk strategy on $F^{\star\star}$ reaches assignment $S_3$ with an exponentially small probability.*

One observation is that during pure random walk search on $F^{\star\star}$, if variable $x$ is ever assigned `True`, it will immediately satisfy all clauses in which it appears, so $x$ will never be flipped to `False` again during the entire search. To show that a solution with $x$ assigned `False` is rare, we only need to consider the case where $x$ is initially assigned `False`.

At the beginning of the search, we can expect about $\frac{n}{2}$ variables among $y_1$ through $y_n$ to be assigned `True`. Now we need to calculate the probability that the algorithm flips all of these $n$ variables to `True`, while not flipping the values of $x$. Note that during the search, if the $(n+i)$th clause is unsatisfied, variable $y_i$ must be `False`. Since $x$ is also `False`, the $i$th clause is also unsatisfied. This implies that before $x$ is flipped, at least half of the unsatisfied clauses come from the first $n$ clauses. The pure random walk algorithm at each step first picks an unsatisfied clause at random, then flips a random variable in that clause. So at each step, there is at least $\frac{1}{4}$ probability that variable $x$ is flipped. Since the number of steps needed is greater than $\frac{n}{2}$, the probability that $x$ is kept `False` in all these steps is less than $(\frac{3}{4})^{-\frac{n}{2}}$. This means that the probability of reaching $S_3$ with $x$ set to `False` is exponentially small.

So, in principle, MCMC methods such as SA sample uniformly from states with an equal cost value (number of unsatisfied clauses). However, Thm. 1, shows an example where reaching the stationary distribution (assume low temperature SA) takes exponential time, even on a 2-CNF formula. On the other hand, Random Walk (and its extension, WalkSAT) is much more effective at finding solutions but may sample quite non-uniformly (Thm. 2). This leads us to our Hybrid strategy introduced earlier. As we discussed, our empirical results show that the Hybrid strategy is indeed quite promising. Let us now try to obtain a better understanding as to why the hybrid strategy may work well. (At this point we do not have a full rigorous analysis of the hybrid strategy.)

By observing runs of the Hybrid algorithm, we found that the behavior can be characterized by two phases. Before the search finds a solution, the random walk strategy plays the dominant role. In this first phase, it is important to reach some solution. In Table 2, we compare the average number of steps it takes WalkSAT, Hybrid and SA algorithms to reach the first solution state. It shows that the Hybrid numbers are closer to the WalkSat numbers, and relatively far from the SA numbers. This is the first phase. (The table provides a good illustration of the limitations of a pure MCMC approach: it simply takes too long to reach any satisfying assignment.)

Table 2: Flips needed to reach first solution.

| INSTANCE | WALKSAT | HYBRID $p = 0.5$ | SA |
|---|---|---|---|
| RANDOM | 382 | 677 | 24667 |
| LOGISTIC | $5.7 \times 10^5$ | $15.5 \times 10^5$ | $> 10^9$ |
| VERIF. | 36 | 65 | 10821 |

After the algorithm reaches a solution, the search enters phase two where the SA moves dominate. In the second phase, the algorithm explores clusters of solutions. A cluster is a set of connected solutions, so that any two solutions within a cluster can be connected through a series of flips without leaving the cluster. In many domains of interest, solutions usually exist in clusters (Mézard *et al.* 2002). In phase two the algorithm behaves like SA because after the search enters a cluster of solutions, unsatisfied constrains no longer exist, and the random walk portion of the search is effectively turned off until an uphill move brings the search out of the cluster. Because SA has good properties in exploring a connected space, it samples near-uniformly and in practice often effectively explores the neighboring solution states.

SA has the following useful property when exploring a cluster of solutions:

**Theorem 3** *SA at zero temperature samples all solutions within a cluster uniformly.*

Consider the Markov Chain formed inside a cluster of satisfying assignments. For a node (satisfying assignment) $i$, the transition probability from $i$ to neighboring node $j$ inside the cluster is $\frac{1}{n}$. If the selected neighbor in outside the cluster, however, SA will not make the move since temperature is 0. Therefore there is a self cycle with probability $\frac{n-d_i}{n}$ for node $i$, where $d_i$ is the degree of node $i$ inside its cluster. (In other words, $d_i$ is the number of neighboring assignments (one truth value "flipped") of the current state that are also satisfying assignments.) This Markov chain is ergodic.

More formally, the transition matrix of the chain is $P = (p_{ij})$, where

$$p_{ij} = \begin{cases} \frac{1}{n}, & \text{if } i \text{ and } j \text{ neighbors in cluster;} \\ \frac{n-d_i}{n}, & \text{if } i = j; \\ 0, & \text{otherwise.} \end{cases}$$

The $i$th entry of $q \cdot P$ is $\frac{1}{n}\sum_{k=1}^{n} p_{ki} = \frac{1}{n}(d_i \cdot \frac{1}{n} + \frac{n-d_i}{n}) = \frac{1}{n}$ for all $i$. Therefore, $q = (\frac{1}{n}, \frac{1}{n}, \cdots, \frac{1}{n})$ is the stationary distribution of the underlying Markov chain.

A key question is how fast the stationary distribution is reached. This is determined by the mixing time. By using a Fourier analysis of the eigenvalues, one can show that the mixing time on a full hybercube is $O(n \log n)$, where $n$ is the number of dimensions. So, sampling from a full hypercube is very efficient. However, a cluster of satisfying assignments forms a subset of the hypercube and rigorous analysis of the mixing time of a subset of the nodes of a hypercube is beyond current analysis (Morris & Sinclair 1999). Our empirical observations suggest that SA samples quite effectively from the solution clusters.

Given the algorithm's ability to sample from a cluster nearly uniformly, the probability mass of a solution is very near to the ratio of the probability of reaching the cluster that the solution belongs to and the size of that cluster. Let $C$ denote a cluster of solutions, $P_C$ denote the probability of reaching the cluster, and $|C|$ denote the size of $C$. We have for the probability $P_a$ of reaching assignment $a$ in cluster $C$

$$\forall a \in C, P_a \simeq \frac{P_C}{|C|}$$

Ideally, if $P_C$ is proportional to $|C|$ for all clusters, this approach would achieve perfect sampling. However, this is not quite the case, which explains why our current hybrid does not sample fully uniformly. In particular, our empirical results show that larger clusters are reached with a higher probability, but not fully proportionally to their size. We are currently exploring other hybrid strategies that may further increase the uniformity of the sampling process.

## Conclusions

We have considered the problem of sampling satisfying assignments of Boolean satisfiability problems. This problem is closely related to various probabilistic reasoning tasks, and is believed to be much harder than the already intractable problem of finding a single satisfying assignment.

We have shown how random walk style procedures provide a promising technique for sampling from the set of satisfying assignments. These procedures can reach solution clusters for much larger problem instances than standard MCMC methods. Moreover, by using a hybrid strategy, we demonstrated how one can get reasonably uniform sampling in several problem domains. Our findings point to a promising research direction for the development of a new class of sampling techniques that combine random-walk style procedures with MCMC methods.

An interesting direction for future research is to adapt complete search methods, such as Davis-Putnam style procedures, for sampling. We are currently exploring such an approach.

## Acknowledgements

This work was supported in part by an Alfred P. Sloan Research Fellowship, a National Science Foundation Information Technology Research Grant IIS-0312910, and the Intelligent Information System Institute at Cornell University sponsored by Air Force Office of Scientific Research Grant F49620-01-1-0076.

## References

B. Aspvall, M. F. Plass, and R. E. Tarjan. A linear-time algorithm for testing the truth of certain quantified boolean formulas. *Information Processing Letters*, vol. 8, no. 3, pp. 121–123, 1979.

R. J. Bayardo, Jr. and J. D. Pehoushek. Counting Models Using Connected Components. In *Proc. AAAI-00*, 2000

C. M. Bishop, *Neural Networks for Pattern Recognition.* Oxford University Press, New York, pp. 58-59, 1995

S. A. Cook. The complexity of theorem proving procedures. In *Proc. Third Annual ACM Symposium on the Theory of Computing*, 1971.

M. R. Garey and D. S. Johnson. *Computers and Intractability*, W. H. Freeman and Company, 1979.

M. R. Jerrum, L. G. Valiant, V. V. Vazirani. Random Generation of Combinatorial Structures From a Uniform Distribution. *Theoretical Computer Science* 43, 169-188, 1986.

H. Kautz and B. Selman. Unifying SAT-based and Graph-based Planning. In *Proceedings of IJCAI-99*, Stockholm, 1999.

S. Kirkpatrick, C. D. Gelatt, Jr., M.P. Vecchi. Optimization by Simulated Annealing. *Science*, Number 4598, 1983.

M. D. Lee. Generating Multidimensional Scaling Representations. Software. Home page Michael Lee (software).

M. L. Littman, S. M. Majercik and T. Pitassi. Stochastic Boolean satisfiability. *Journal of Automated Reasoning*, Vol. 27, No. 3, 251-296, 2001.

N. Madras. *Lectures on Monte Carlo Methods*. Field Institute Monographs, Vol 16, 2002.

D. A. McAllester, B. Selman, and H. A. Kautz. Evidence for Invariants in Local Search. In *Proceedings of AAAI-97*, pages 321-326, 1997.

N. Metropolis, A. W. Rosenbluth, M. N. Rosenbluth, A. H. Teller and E. Teller. Equations of State Calculations by Fast Computing Machines. *J. Chem, Phys.* 21, 1087-1093, 1953.

M. Mézard, G. Parisi, and R. Zecchina. Analytic and Algorithmic Solution of Random Satisfiability Problems. *Science* 297, 812-815, 2002.

D. G. Mitchell, B. Selman, and H. J. Levesque. Hard and Easy Distributions of SAT Problems. In *Proceedings AAAI-92*, pages 459-465, 1992.

B. Morris, A. Sinclair. Random Walks on Truncated Cubes and Sampling 0-1 Knapsack Solutions. In *Proceedings FOCS-99*, pages 230-240, 1999.

C. H. Papadimitriou. On Selecting a Satisfying Truth Assignment. In *Proceedings of the Conference on the Foundations of Computer Science*, pages 163-169, 1991.

J. D. Park. MAP complexity results and approximation methods. In *Proceedings of the 18th Annual Conference on Uncertainty in AI (UAI)*, pages 388–396, 2002.

D. Roth. On the Hardness of Approximate Reasoning. *Artificial Intelligence* 82, 273-302, 1996.

S. M. Sait, H. Youssef, *Iterative Computer Algorithms with Applications in Engineering: Solving Combinatorial Optimization Problems*, Wiley-IEEE Computer Society Press, 2000.

U. Schoening. A Probabilistic Algorithm for k-SAT and Constraint Satisfaction Problems. In *Proceeedings of FOCS*, 1999.

B. Selman, H. Kautz, and B. Cohen. Local Search Strategies for Satisfiability Testing. *2nd DIMACS Challenge on Cliques, Coloring and Satisfiability*, 1994.

A. Sinclair. *Algorithms for Random Generation and Counting*. Birkhäuser, Boston. 1993.

L. G. Valiant. The Complexity of Enumeration and Reliability Problems. *SIAM Journal on Computing*, Vol. 8, No. 3, 410-421, 1979.

W. Wei and B. Selman. Accelerating Random Walks. In *Proc. CP-02*, 2002.

# Space-Efficient Memory-Based Heuristics

**Rong Zhou and Eric A. Hansen**
Department of Computer Science and Engineering
Mississippi State University
Mississippi State, MS 39762
{rzhou,hansen}@cse.msstate.edu

### Abstract

A memory-based heuristic is a heuristic function that is stored in a lookup table. Very accurate heuristics have been created by building very large lookup tables, sometimes called pattern databases. Most previous work assumes that a memory-based heuristic is computed for the entire state space, and the cost of computing it is amortized over many problem instances. But in some cases, it may be useful to compute a memory-based heuristic for a single problem instance. If the start and goal states of the problem instance are used to restrict the region of the state space for which the heuristic is needed, the time and space used to compute the heuristic may be substantially reduced. In this paper, we review recent work that uses this idea to compute space-efficient heuristics for the multiple sequence alignment problem. We then describe a novel development of this idea that is simpler and more general. Our approach leads to improved performance in solving the multiple sequence alignment problem, and is general enough to apply to other domains.

## Introduction

It is well-known that the performance of A* and other heuristic search algorithms depends on the quality of the heuristic that guides the search. An important trend in recent research is the development of memory-based heuristics that are pre-computed and stored in large tables, and map abstracted problem states to a lower bound on the cost for achieving the goal state (Korf 2000). Typically, the problem abstraction takes into account important subgoal interactions and results in highly accurate and effective heuristics that can significantly, and sometimes dramatically, reduce the number of nodes that must be expanded by A* to find an optimal solution path. Examples of memory-based heuristics include pattern databases used to solve permutation problems such as the Fifteen-Puzzle (Culberson & Schaeffer 1998), Twenty-Four Puzzle (Korf & Felner 2002), and Rubik's Cube (Korf 1997). The concept of a pattern database has been extended to STRIPS planning by Edelkamp (2002). And similar memory-based heuristics are used in solving the multiple sequence alignment problem using A* (Kobayashi & Imai 1998; Lermen & Reinert 2000; McNaughton *et al.* 2002).



A drawback of memory-based heuristics is that they typically take a long time to compute and a great deal of memory to store. The argument made is that the time and space complexity of computing the tables can be amortized over solving many instances of the problem. This argument reflects the fact that memory-based heuristics are typically computed for a fixed goal state, and all possible start states.

In this paper, we consider whether memory-based heuristics can be valuable for a single problem instance. Because a problem instance includes a start state as well as a goal state, a potential advantage of this approach is that the table only needs to be computed for the subset of states that may be explored by A* in searching for an optimal path from the start state to the goal state. Although the cost of computing a memory-based heuristic is not amortized over many problem instances, a table restricted in this way could be much smaller and potentially much easier to compute.

There are at least two kinds of domains in which this approach could be valuable. The first are domains with an arbitrary start state and an arbitrary goal state. Previous work on memory-based heuristics assumes an arbitrary start state and a fixed goal state. Although assuming a fixed goal state makes sense in some domains, such as sliding-tile puzzles and Rubik's Cube, it does not in many others. In heuristic-search planning, for example, it is typical for the goal state to vary with each problem instance, as well as for the start state to vary (Bonet & Geffner 2001). If it is difficult to compute a memory-based heuristic for a fixed goal state and all possible start states, it may be impossible to compute it for all possible goal states and all possible start states!

A second kind of domain in which it could be valuable to compute a memory-based heuristic for a single problem instance is a domain with a fixed start state and a fixed goal state. An important example of this kind of domain is the multiple sequence alignment problem (Carrillo & Lipman 1988). This problem can be viewed as a path-finding problem in an $n$-dimensional lattice where $n$ is the number of sequences, and A* has proven to be an effective method for finding optimal alignments. However, the most effective heuristic is a large table-based heuristic that stores optimal *sub-alignments*, that is, optimal alignments of subsets of the original set of sequences. The barrier to creating improved heuristics for this problem is the space-complexity of these tables. Computing an optimal sub-alignment for as few as three sequences can be extremely challenging.

Some recent work attempts to compute space-efficient sub-alignment heuristics for the multiple sequence alignment problem by leveraging the fact that there is a fixed start state and a fixed goal state, and most of the state space is unlikely to be visited in the course of searching for an optimal alignment (Kobayashi & Imai 1998; Lermen & Reinert 2000; McNaughton *et al.* 2002). We adopt the same strategy in this paper, but implement it in a novel way that is simpler and more general, and leads to improved performance.

## Memory-based heuristics

We begin this background section with a short review of the multiple sequence alignment problem, since it will be the focus of our computational results. Then we define the concept of a memory-based heuristic at a high level of abstraction, in order to clarify the relationship between previous work on pattern database heuristics in the AI community, and work on sub-alignment bounds (or heuristics) for multiple sequence alignment. We conclude this section with a review of previous work on computing space-efficient sub-alignment bounds.

### Multiple sequence alignment

The multiple sequence alignment problem is an important problem in computational biology. Given a set of DNA or protein sequences, and a cost function (defined by a substitution matrix and gap penalty), the problem is to insert gaps in such a way that matching characters in the sequences are aligned, and the overall cost (or score) of the alignment is minimized (or maximized). It is well-known that this problem can be formalized as a shortest-path problem in an $n$-dimensional lattice, where $n$ is the number of sequences to be aligned. However, the size of the state space is $l^n$, where $l$ is the length of the sequences and $n$ is the number of sequences, and a dynamic programming algorithm that solves the problem for the entire state space is limited to solving very small problems. A* has been shown to outperform other methods for finding optimal multiple sequence alignments because it can use an admissible heuristic to limit the number of states it needs to evaluate (Ikeda & Imai 1999; Kobayashi & Imai 1998; Yoshizumi, Miura, & Ishida 2000; Lermen & Reinert 2000; McNaughton *et al.* 2002). The effectiveness of A* depends on the quality of the heuristic that guides the search. For multiple sequence alignment using the sum-of-pairs cost function, Carillo and Lipman (1988) observed that the sum of the costs of all optimal pairwise sub-alignments is a lower bound on the cost of the optimal multiple alignment. From now on, we call this the *pairwise heuristic*. The time and space needed to compute the pairwise heuristic is very small.

Carillo and Lipman (1988) also suggested that more accurate lower-bound functions could be created by using higher-dimensional sub-alignments, that is, by aligning groups of more than two sequences. For example, consider the three possible pairwise alignments of three sequences. These three pairwise alignments can be replaced by a triple alignment of all three sequences. The triple alignment provides a tighter bound than the sum of the three pairwise alignments because it takes into account all possible interactions between the sequences. Thus, the pairwise heuristic can be improved by replacing three of its pairwise alignments with a triple alignment. A sub-alignment heuristic that uses just one or two triple alignments in combination with the remaining pairwise alignments can be very effective, and dramatically improves the performance of A*. The problem is that the space and time complexity for computing even one triple alignment can be prohibitive, if it is computed for the entire projected state space. Thus, sub-alignment bounds are a kind of memory-based heuristic, and techniques for computing memory-based heuristics more efficiently could improve the performance of A* in multiple sequence alignment.

### Simple memory-based heuristics

A memory-based heuristic is computed by projecting a search problem into an abstract state space that is small enough that an optimal cost function can be computed for all of its states and stored in a lookup table. Typically, the projection corresponds to a partial specification of the state. For example, if the state is defined by an assignment of values to variables, an abstract state corresponds to an assignment of values to a subset of the variables. Each abstract state corresponds to a set of states in the original search problem, and the optimal cost of the abstract state is a lower bound on the optimal cost of the corresponding states in the original search problem. Using the sliding-tile puzzle as an illustration, the puzzle state can be viewed as an assignment of locations to tiles. It can be projected into an abstract state space by considering only the location of a subset of the tiles.

In the literature on pattern databases, each projected (or abstract) state is called a pattern and the table that stores an optimal evaluation function for the projected state space is called a pattern database. A pattern database is traditionally computed backwards from the set of goal states by a dynamic programming algorithm that performs breadth-first traversal of the state space. Although a single pattern database can be useful, more informed heuristics can be obtained by combining several pattern databases based on different projections. As discussed by Culberson and Schaeffer (1998), the simplest way to combine them is as follows,

$$h(s) = \max_i h^*(s_i),$$

where $s_i$ denotes the projection of state $s$ into the abstract state space corresponding to projection $i$, and $h^*$ denotes the optimal evaluation function for the projected problem. The resulting heuristic is guaranteed to be admissible.

### Disjoint memory-based heuristics

A more effective heuristic can be obtained by summing over the pattern databases, as follows,

$$h(s) = \sum_i h^*(s_i).$$

But this heuristic is only admissible if the pattern databases are disjoint. Pattern databases are disjoint if each operator only affects one of the projected problems, ensuring that the sum of operator costs is admissible (Korf & Felner 2002). We now present an abstract theory of disjoint memory-based heuristics that is general enough to include previous work on disjoint pattern databases, as well as work on higher-dimensional sub-alignment bounds for the multiple sequence alignment problem.

We assume that a projection is created by partial specification of the state in the original problem. We define an *atomic projection* as the smallest partial specification such that each operator only affects the partially specified state (e.g., values assigned to the variables of the projected state). For many problem domains, it is straight forward to determine such an atomic projection. For instance, a single tile is an atomic projection in the sliding-tile puzzle domain; a (distinctive) pair of sequences is an atomic projection in the sum-of-pairs multiple sequence alignment domain.

Often, more accurate heuristics can be created by taking into account the interactions among atomic projections. One way to achieve this is to project the original problem into some larger projections that are made up of atomic ones. For example, we can consider a group of tiles instead of a single tile as a new projection. Grouping atomic projections gives rise to more accurate abstractions of the original problem, and can substantially improve the quality of the resulting heuristic. We use the set notation $P = \{p_i \mid p_i \in \{1, 2, \cdots, m\}\}$ to denote a grouping of atomic projections, where $m$ denotes the number of atomic projections of the original problem. This leads to the following definition.

**Definition 1** *A* disjoint partition *of the original problem is a collection of projection groups $P_1, P_2, \cdots, P_k$ such that $P_1 \cup P_2 \cup \cdots \cup P_k = \{1, \cdots, m\}$ and $P_i \cap P_j = \emptyset$ for all $i \neq j$.*

A memory-based heuristic that is created based on a disjoint partition of the original problem is called a *disjoint memory-based heuristic*. When each projection group contains a single element, we call it an *atomic disjoint partition*. Examples of heuristics based on atomic disjoint partitions include the well-known Manhattan-distance heuristic used in sliding-tile puzzles, and the pairwise heuristic used in multiple sequence alignment. In most cases, atomic disjoint partitions are easy to compute and have modest space complexity. But they are not as accurate as non-atomic disjoint partitions.

The fact that there can be more than one non-atomic disjoint partition of the original problem introduces an additional question – how to find the non-atomic disjoint partition that yields the most accurate memory-based heuristic. We employ the following simple criterion: choose the disjoint partition that maximizes the heuristic estimate of the start state among all such disjoint partitions. McNaughton et al. (2002) use a similar criterion in the context of multiple sequence alignment.

## Space-efficient sub-alignment heuristics

Because the multiple sequence alignment problem has a fixed start state and a fixed goal state, sub-alignment bounds (or heuristics) do not need to be computed for the entire projected state space. Several researchers have recognized this and suggested methods for computing a sub-alignment heuristic more efficiently based on this idea.

In recent work, McNaughton et al. (2002) introduce two ideas for computing triple alignments efficiently. First, they adopt the octree data structure as a compact representation of the projected state space, which in the case of three sequences is a cube. Second, they compute the values stored in the octree on demand, as needed by the A* search algorithm. As a result, values are not computed for much of the projected state space, and this significantly reduces the time and space complexity of computing a triple alignment.[1]

In Lermen and Reinert's (2000) implementation of A* for multiple sequence alignment, they adapt from Gupta *et al.* (1995) a technique called *face invalidity* to compute a triple alignment more efficiently. This technique assumes that any alignment path that passes through a projected state $s_i$ cannot be optimal, if the cost of the least-cost path through $s_i$ is greater than $h^*(s_i)+\delta$. It preserves admissibility only if $\delta$ is the difference between an upper and lower bound on the cost of an optimal solution to the original problem. Because it is infeasible to use a value of $\delta$ this large, they guess a reasonable value. This means the resulting heuristic is either not complete or not admissible. Kobayashi and Imai (1998) propose a similar technique for reducing the space complexity of sub-alignment bounds, but extend it to more than triple alignments. The technique we present in the following section is closely-related, and based on a similar intuition, but is simpler and more general, and preserves admissibility.

## Focused heuristic

We define a *focused memory-based heuristic* as a memory-based heuristic for a single problem instance, that is computed only for states that are projections of states in the original search space that could be explored by A* in solving the original search problem. In this section, we describe an algorithm that computes a focused memory-based heuristic and present a theoretical justification for it.

Recall that algorithms for computing a pattern database heuristic do so by using a dynamic programming method that traverses all of the projected state space in breadth-first order, beginning from the goal. Our algorithm for computing a focused memory-based heuristic also searches backwards from the goal. However, it uses A* to direct the search from the goal state backwards to the start state, and does not traverse the entire state space. For each node expanded by A* searching backwards from the goal state (and guided by a consistent heuristic), its g-cost represents the cost of a shortest path from this state to the goal state in the projected problem, and can serve as an admissible h-cost for the original search problem. The question is how to ensure that optimal g-costs are computed for the entire relevant region of the search space. In fact, if we terminate A* as soon as it finds an optimal solution path from the goal state to the start state in the projected state space, there is no guarantee that it has computed optimal g-costs for all relevant states.

[1]The idea of computing heuristic values on demand in order to limit storage was previously used by Holte et al. (1996), who also used A* in an abstract state space to compute the heuristic.

But note that we can *continue* to expand nodes after A* finds an optimal path from the goal state to the start state, in order to determine optimal g-costs (and thus admissible heuristics) for additional states. The question is how to determine when admissible heuristics have been computed for all relevant states. We ensure this by expanding all nodes in the projected search space with an f-cost less than or equal to an upper bound on the cost of an optimal solution path for the original problem. Informally, the reason this is sufficient is because the f-cost of each state in the projected problem space is a lower bound on the cost of an optimal path in the original search space that goes from the start state to the goal state via the state in the original state space that is mapped to this projected state.

An upper bound on the cost of an optimal solution path for a problem is given by the cost of any sub-optimal solution path, and there are several methods by which a sub-optimal solution can be computed quickly. For example, weighted A* search with a node evaluation function $f(n) = g(n) + w \times h(n)$, with weight $w > 1.0$, usually finds a solution quickly, and adjusting the weight adjusts a tradeoff between solution quality and search time.

**Theorem 1** *Let $U$ be an upper bound on the cost of the optimal solution to the original problem and let $f(s_i)$ be the f-cost in projected problem $i$ of projected state $s_i$. A memory-based heuristic only needs to be computed for $s_i$ if $f(s_i) < U$.*

**Proof:** Since the f-cost of a projected state $s_i$ provides a lower bound on the cost of the optimal solution to the projected problem $i$, which in turn is a lower bound on the cost of the optimal solution to the original problem, it follows that for any projected state whose f-cost exceeds $U$, it cannot lead to any better solution with cost lower than $U$ and thus can be safely ignored in the computation of memory-based heuristics.□

Thus, we compute a focused memory-based heuristic by using A* to search backwards from the goal to the start state, where A* is modified in a simple way: instead of terminating when an optimal solution path has been found, it terminates when the condition $f(s_i) < U$ is not satisfied for the currently-expanding state $s_i$. Because A* expands nodes in increasing order of f-cost when it uses a consistent heuristic, all remaining unexpanded states in the projected search space must have an f-cost equal to or greater than $U$, and thus cannot be relevant for the given problem instance.

This technique for computing a focused memory-based heuristic is particularly useful in computing a set of disjoint memory-based heuristics, that is, a disjoint pattern database. The following restriction of Theorem 1 applies only to disjoint pattern databases, but provides great computational leverage. Note that the left-hand side of the inequality in the following theorem is a projected lower bound, and the right-hand side of the inequality is a projected upper bound. Because the projected upper bound is very tight, the theorem provides a great deal of focus and significantly limits the region of the state space for which the memory-based heuristic is computed.

**Theorem 2** *Let $\Delta$ be the difference between an upper bound $U$ and a lower bound $L = \sum_i h(start_i)$ on the cost of an optimal solution to the original problem, where $h$ is a consistent heuristic and $start_i$ is the start state for the projected problem. A disjoint memory-based heuristic for projected problem $i$ only needs to be computed for projected state $s_i$ if $f(s_i) < h(start_i) + \Delta$.*

**Proof:** Recall that in disjoint memory-based heuristics, the cost of optimal solution to each projected problem can be added to obtain an admissible heuristic to the original problem. Therefore, similar to Theorem 1, it can be shown that a disjoint memory-based heuristic only needs to be computed for projected state $s_i$ such that $\sum_i f(s_i) < U$. So for any projection $j$, we have $f(s_j) < U - \sum_{i \neq j} f(s_i)$. Since $h$ is a consistent heuristic, thus $f(s_i) \geq h(start_i)$, it follows that

$$f(s_j) < U - \sum_{i \neq j} f(s_i) \leq U - \sum_{i \neq j} h(start_i).$$

Because $\sum_{i \neq j} h(start_i) = \sum_i h(start_i) - h(start_j)$, substitute this into the above inequality, we get

$$\begin{aligned} f(s_j) &< U - \sum_i h(start_i) + h(start_j) \\ &= U - L + h(start_j) \\ &= h(start_j) + \Delta. \end{aligned}$$

## Multi-resolution heuristic

Our technique for computing a focused memory-based heuristic can significantly reduce the time and space needed to compute the heuristic. But highly-accurate heuristics may still take a prohibitive amount of time and space to compute. To extend the applicability of this technique, we propose a method for further reducing the time and space needed to compute such heuristics, without significantly degrading their accuracy. It also preserves admissibility. This extension is motivated by the observation that not all values in a focused memory-based heuristic will be queried by the A* algorithm in solving the original problem.

Recall that computing a focused heuristic requires an upper bound which, in practice, usually overestimates the cost of an optimal solution. Let $\Delta^*$ denote the difference between the lower bound and the cost of an optimal solution to the original problem and note that $\Delta^* \leq \Delta$. Clearly, any node that deviates from the least-cost path in the projected problem by more than $\Delta^*$ will never be queried by the A* search algorithm in solving the original problem. Moreover, among the smaller set of projected states for which $f(s_i)$ is less than the projected cost of the optimal solution to the original problem, which can be potentially queried, some are much less likely to be queried than others during the course of the search, because they are farther from the optimal path.

To reduce the time and space complexity of computing a focused memory-based heuristic further, we introduce a real-valued parameter $\gamma \in [0, 1]$. Instead of using $\Delta$ to determine the projected upper bound used in computing the focused memory-based heuristic, we use $\gamma\Delta$. When $\gamma < 1$, not every memory-based heuristic value that is queried by

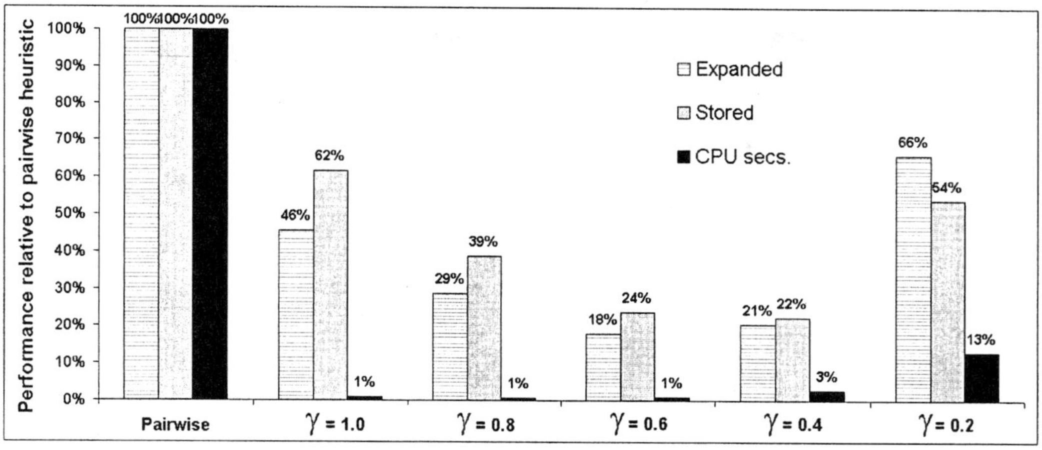


Figure 1: Performance of A* in aligning nine protein sequences, using a sub-alignment heuristic based on two quintuple alignments, with five different values of $\gamma$. Performance is relative to A* using the traditional pairwise heuristic.

A* in solving the original problem may be available. To preserve the admissibility of the heuristic, we propose a *multi-resolution heuristic*. If a heuristic value is unavailable in the focused memory-based heuristic because $\gamma < 1$, we supply a quickly-computed admissible heuristic instead. In the case of multiple sequence alignment, we use the pairwise heuristic whenever a higher-dimensional sub-alignment heuristic is not available. In practice, the $\gamma$-parameter causes the heuristic values that are most likely to be queried to be computed, because the values that are computed are for projected states closest to an optimal path in the projected state space. Moreover, in a disjoint memory-based heuristic, if a heuristic value is missing from one table (and an admissible but less accurate value is substituted), the overall heuristic value (the sum of the heuristic values in each table) can still be very accurate if heuristic values are present in the other tables. This is because the overall heuristic value is an "interpolation" of the heuristic values in all of the tables. In our experiments, we have found that only a small fraction of the heuristic values that could potentially be queried need to be computed, in order to have a heuristic function that is almost as good as one that stores all values. The $\gamma$ parameter provides a way of adjusting this tradeoff.

## Computational results

We implemented focused and multi-resolution sub-alignment heuristics for the multiple sequence sequence alignment problem, to measure their effect on the performance of A*. All experiments were performed on an UltraSparc II with a 300Mhz CPU and 2 gigabytes of RAM.

Figure 1 shows the average performance of A* in aligning nine protein sequences of length between 442 and 460, randomly selected from a set of similar protein sequences used in earlier experiments (Ikeda & Imai 1999; Yoshizumi, Miura, & Ishida 2000). The baseline for comparison is A* using the traditional pairwise heuristic. The focused heuristic we computed contains two *quintuple alignments*, and was computed for five different values of $\gamma$. Figure 1 shows how use of the focused heuristic improves the overall performance of A*. Note that the count of node expansions includes node expansions needed to compute the sub-alignment heuristic, as well as to solve the original problem using A*. This explains why a setting of $\gamma = 0.6$ results in the least number of total node expansions. Although a $\gamma$-value of less than 1.0 could result in more node expansions in solving the original problem (if the heuristic is less accurate), it requires fewer node expansions to compute the heuristic. A setting of $\gamma = 0.6$ optimizes this tradeoff. (Because node expansions in the projected state space are much faster than node expansions in the original state space, total node expansions is not well-correlated with CPU time.) Similarly, the storage shown in Figure 1 is the total space used to store the heuristic and to solve the problem using A*. Again, a setting of $\gamma = 0.6$ optimizes the tradeoff. The CPU time reported is the total time for computing the heuristic and for solving the problem using A*. It shows that our focused, multi-resolution memory-based heuristic improves overall problem-solving time by 100-fold, even when it is computed for a single problem instance.

We also compared the performance of A* with Partial Expansion using our focused, multi-resolution heuristic, to its performance using the octree heuristic. For this comparison, we used code made available by the developers of the octree heuristic (McNaughton *et al.* 2002). We first tested both heuristics in aligning various groups of five protein sequences from reference set 1 of BAliBASE (Thompson, Plewniak, & Poch 1999). Because the protein sequences are dissimilar, optimal alignment requires inserting many gaps and the problems are very challenging to solve. These alignment problems cannot be solved by A* using the pairwise alignment heuristic, since the number of expanded nodes quickly exceeds memory limits. But they can be solved using a more accurate sub-alignment heuristic that includes two triple alignments. We computed a heuristic that includes two triple alignments, using our focused method with a $\gamma$-value of 0.4, which appears to optimize performance.

The octree method stored heuristic values for 3 times as many projected states as our method. One reason for this is that it computes and stores some unnecessary heuristic values. But the primary reason is that the $\gamma$ parameter significantly reduces the number of projected states for which our method computes values. Although the octree heuristic stored 3 times as many states, it used 24% less memory to store these projected states, because the octree data structure allows much more efficient storage. The quality of the computed triple-alignment heuristic, measured by the number of partial expansions in aligning 5 sequences, is about the same for both methods. The $\gamma$-parameter does little to degrade the quality of our heuristic, and, using the $\gamma$-parameter, our heuristic can be computed in less than a quarter of the time it takes to compute the octree heuristic. In both cases, the time required to compute the heuristic is less than 5% of the time required by A* to solve the problem.

We also compared both heuristics in aligning 9 similar protein sequences from (Yoshizumi, Miura, & Ishida 2000). When averaged over 100 runs, the octree heuristic stored 40 times more projected states than our method, and used 8 times more memory. The focused heuristic took 25 times less time to compute the two quintuple alignments, which are also more accurate than multiple triple alignments. As a result, A* using our focused heuristic needed 40% fewer partial expansions than using the octree heuristic in aligning 9 sequences from this problem set.

The octree method can only be used to compute sub-alignment heuristics for multiple sequence alignment, because it requires a graphical representation of the search space, and most problems do not have such a property. Moreover, it is not obvious that it provides a practical approach to computing sub-alignments of more than three sequences. The reason is that an empty leaf of a $2^n$-ary tree needs to represent a subspace of dimensionality $n-1$. In a hextree, for example, leaf nodes would need to represent cubes, and this seems difficult to implement in a space-efficient way. Our method can not only be used to compute sub-alignments of any size, including quadruple and quintuple alignments, it can be used in computing memory-based heuristics for any other search problem.

Although our approach is fully general, it may not be equally effective in all domains. It will be most effective in domains where the projected bounds are tight enough that only a small fraction of the projected state space needs to be computed and stored to create the heuristic. Promising candidates include the class of search problems considered by Klein and Manning (2003).

## Conclusion

There has been much recent interest in using highly-accurate, memory-based heuristics to improve the performance of A*. It is possible to use the start and goal state of a problem instance to limit the time and space complexity of such heuristics, and this possibility has been explored in work on computing high-dimensional sub-alignment heuristics for the multiple sequence alignment problem. In particular, previous researchers have shown that the time it takes to compute a high-dimensional sub-alignment heuristic can be outweighed by the savings in search effort, even in solving a single instance of the multiple sequence alignment problem.

In this paper, we present a general method for computing space-efficient memory-based heuristics that has several advantages, and makes it possible to compute larger sub-alignments for use in solving more complex multiple sequence alignment problems. The method we present is simple and general, and could be used in computing memory-based heuristics for other search problems.

**Acknowledgments** We thank the anonymous reviewers for helpful comments. This work was supported in part by NSF grant IIS-9984952 and NASA grant NAG-2-1463.

## References

Bonet, B., and Geffner, H. 2001. Planning as heuristic search. *Artificial Intelligence* 129(1):5–33.

Carrillo, H., and Lipman, D. 1988. The multiple sequence alignment problem in biology. *SIAM J. Appl. Math.* 48(5):1073–1082.

Culberson, J., and Schaeffer, J. 1998. Pattern databases. *Computational Intelligence* 14(3):318–334.

Edelkamp, S. 2002. Symbolic pattern databases in heuristic search planning. In *Proc. of the 6th International Conference on Artificial Intelligence Planning and Scheduling*, 274–283.

Gupta, S.; Kececioglu, J.; and Schaffer, A. 1995. Improving the practical space and time efficiency of the shortest-paths approach to sum-of-pairs multiple sequence alignment. *Journal of Computational Biology* 2(3):459–472.

Holte, R.; Perez, M.; Zimmer, R.; and MacDonald, A. 1996. Hierarchical A*: Searching abstraction hierarchies efficiently. In *Proc. of the 13th National Conf. on Artificial Intelligence*, 530–5.

Ikeda, T., and Imai, H. 1999. Enhanced A* algorithms for multiple alignments: Optimal alignments for several sequences and k-opt approximate alignments for large cases. *Theoretical Computer Science* 210(2):341–374.

Klein, D., and Manning, C. 2003. Factored A* search for models over sequences and trees. In *Proceedings of the 17th International Joint Conference on Artificial Intelligence*, 1246–1251.

Kobayashi, H., and Imai, H. 1998. Improvement of the A* algorithm for multiple sequence alignment. In *Proceedings of the 9th Workshop on Genome Informatics*, 120–130.

Korf, R., and Felner, A. 2002. Disjoint pattern database heuristics. *Artificial Intelligence* 134(1–2):9–22.

Korf, R. 1997. Finding optimal solutions to Rubik's cube using pattern databases. In *Proceedings of the 14th National Conference on Artificial Intelligence*, 700–705.

Korf, R. 2000. Recent progress in the design and analysis of admissible heuristic functions. In *Proc. of the 17th National Conference on Artificial Intelligence*, 1165–1170.

Lermen, M., and Reinert, K. 2000. The practical use of the A* algorithm for exact multiple sequence alignment. *Journal of Computational Biology* 7(5):655–671.

McNaughton, M.; Lu, P.; Schaeffer, J.; and Szafron, D. 2002. Memory-efficient A* heuristics for multiple sequence alignment. In *Proc. of 18th National Conf. on Artificial Intelligence*, 737–43.

Thompson, J.; Plewniak, F.; and Poch, O. 1999. BAliBASE: A benchmark alignment database for the evaluation of multiple alignment programs. *Bioinformatics* 15(1):87–88.

Yoshizumi, T.; Miura, T.; and Ishida, T. 2000. A* with partial expansion for large branching factor problems. In *Proceedings of the 17th National Conference on Artificial Intelligence*, 923–929.

# Structured Duplicate Detection in External-Memory Graph Search

**Rong Zhou and Eric A. Hansen**
Department of Computer Science and Engineering
Mississippi State University
Mississippi State, MS 39762
{rzhou,hansen}@cse.msstate.edu

### Abstract

We consider how to use external memory, such as disk storage, to improve the scalability of heuristic search in state-space graphs. To limit the number of slow disk I/O operations, we develop a new approach to duplicate detection in graph search that localizes memory references by partitioning the search graph based on an abstraction of the state space, and expanding the frontier nodes of the graph in an order that respects this partition. We demonstrate the effectiveness of this approach both analytically and empirically.

## Introduction

Heuristic search in state-space graphs is a widely-used framework for problem solving in AI, but its scalability is limited by memory requirements. This has led to extensive research on how to use available memory efficiently in searching large state-space graphs.

The concept of "available memory" is ambiguous, since memory in most computer systems has a hierarchical structure in which fast, random-access internal memory is complemented by low-speed external memory, such as disk storage. Although external memory is vastly larger (and much cheaper) than internal memory, most heuristic search algorithms are designed to use internal memory only, and most research on memory-efficient heuristic search assumes a memory model in which access to all stored data items is equally fast. Algorithms that assume this memory model perform extremely poorly if external memory is used, since random access of external memory requires time-consuming I/O operations that are several orders of magnitude slower than random access of internal memory.

Some recent work begins to address this issue. Edelkamp and Schrödl (2000) consider use of virtual memory in A* graph search, and propose techniques that change the best-first order of node expansions in a way that improves reference locality and reduces the number of page faults in virtual memory. A more direct approach to limiting slow disk I/O is to design a search algorithm that explicitly manages access to external memory, since this approach can exploit knowledge of how the graph is structured, and is not limited by the size of virtual memory, which is usually much smaller than external memory. In the theoretical computer science community, there has been extensive research on external-memory algorithms, including development of external-memory breadth-first search algorithms for explicitly represented graphs (Munagala & Ranade 1999; Mehlhorn & Meyer 2002). In the AI community, Korf (2003a; 2003b) recently described an external-memory breadth-first search algorithm for implicitly represented graphs.

A key issue in designing an efficient external-memory graph search algorithm is *duplicate detection*. In graph search, the same node can be reached along different paths, and preventing redundant search effort requires storing already-visited nodes, so that the search algorithm can recognize when it encounters a node that has been already explored. Because duplicate detection potentially requires comparing each newly generated node to all stored nodes, it can lead to crippling disk I/O if already-explored nodes are stored on disk. All previous external-memory breadth-first search algorithms limit disk I/O by using a technique called *delayed duplicate detection* in which an entire set of nodes is expanded before performing any duplicate detection. In this paper, we introduce a new approach. Instead of delaying duplicate detection, we limit disk I/O by localizing memory references based on the structure of the search graph as revealed by a high-level abstraction of the state space. Computational results on challenging graph-search problems indicate that this approach, which we call *structured duplicate detection*, significantly limits disk I/O. For graphs with sufficient local structure, it allows graph-search algorithms to use external memory almost as efficiently as internal memory.

## Background

Development of external-memory algorithms for various computational problems is an active area of research. Because disk I/O is several orders of magnitude slower than random access of internal memory, the concept of *I/O complexity* has been introduced to analyze the performance of external-memory algorithms (Aggarwal & Vitter 1988). It assumes a two-level model of memory in which internal memory of size $M$ is supplemented by external memory, and an I/O operation moves data in blocks of size $B$ between internal memory and external memory, where $1 < B \leq M/2$. The I/O complexity of an algorithm is defined as the number of I/O operations it performs.

External-memory breadth-first search has been considered by several researchers. In the theoretical computer science community, researchers have focused on establishing bounds on its I/O complexity. A graph is assumed to be explicitly represented using adjacency lists and stored in external memory due to its large size. In searching explicit graphs, worst-case I/O complexity depends on the method of generating successor nodes as well as the method of duplicate detection, since adjacency lists must be read into internal memory to determine the successors of a node. Munagala and Ranade (1999) describe an external-memory breadth-first search algorithms that adopts an approach to successor generation that has linear complexity in the number of edges in the graph. Mehlhorn and Meyer (2002) achieve sublinear complexity for successor generation by a more sophisticated approach that involves partitioning the adjacency list based on a decomposition of the graph into connected subgraphs. Both algorithms use the same method of duplicate detection, called *delayed duplicate detection*, in which a set of nodes is expanded without performing duplicate detection, and the multi-set of generated successors is sorted and checked for duplicates in a single, more efficient operation. The algorithms alternate between these two steps.

1. *successor generation*, in which the algorithm generates successors for a set of nodes on the search frontier and appends these successors to a file (or files) in the order in which they are generated, without performing any duplicate detection, and
2. *delayed duplicate detection*, in which the file(s) of successor nodes are sorted (usually by an external-memory sort algorithm) based on their indices or state encodings, followed by a scan and compaction stage in which duplicate nodes in the sorted file(s) are eliminated.

In the AI community, Korf (2003a; 2003b) recently described an external-memory breadth-first search algorithm that uses the same method of delayed duplicate detection. His algorithm differs in two ways. First, he considers search in implicit graphs, in keeping with the standard AI approach to state-space search. An *implicit graph* is a compact representation of a graph in the form of a start node, a node expansion function that generates the immediate successors of a node, and a predicate that tests whether a node is a goal node. In searching implicit graphs, successor generation does not require disk I/O, and duplicate detection is the only source of I/O complexity.

A second difference is that Korf builds his external-memory breadth-first search algorithm on top of *frontier search*, a memory-efficient search algorithm that does not need to store a Closed list (Korf & Zhang 2000).

## Structured duplicate detection

We propose an alternative approach to duplicate detection in external-memory graph search that has some significant advantages over delayed duplicate detection. It can also be combined with delayed duplicate detection in some cases.

The central idea of our approach is to exploit the structure of a state-space graph in order to localize memory references during duplicate detection, and so we call the approach *structured duplicate detection*. As an example, consider the $(n^2 - 1)$ sliding-tile puzzle. When a new node is generated, it can only differ from its parent node with respect to the position of the "blank" by either one row or one column. Therefore, in checking for duplicates, it is not necessary to check stored nodes for which the position of the "blank" differs from that of the parent node by more than one row or one column. If we partition the set of stored nodes in this way, we can significantly limit the number of stored nodes that need to be checked to guarantee that all duplicates are found. We continue to use this motivating example in the following, to help explain the idea.

### Projection function and abstract state-space graph

Our approach is based on using a state-space projection function to decompose a state-space graph, and create an abstract state-space graph that reveals the local structure of the original graph at a high-level. State abstraction in heuristic search is well studied, and is used to create admissible heuristics and to organize hierarchical search (Holte *et al.* 1996). We use an approach to state abstraction that is very similar to previous approaches, but has a different purpose: localizing memory references in duplicate detection.

A state-space projection function is a many-to-one mapping from the original state space to an abstract state space, in which each abstract state corresponds to a set of states in the original state space. If a state $x$ is mapped to an abstract state $y$, then $y$ is called the *image* of $x$, and $x$ is called the *pre-image* of $y$. There are many ways to define a state-space projection function. A common approach is to ignore some state variables in the encoding of the problem. For example, a simple state-space projection function for the $(n^2 - 1)$ sliding-tile puzzle can be defined by ignoring the positions of all tiles and considering only the position of the "blank." In this case, an abstract state corresponds to all states with the same position of the "blank," and there are $n^2$ abstract states compared to $n^2!/2$ states in the original state space. State-space projection functions can be defined in a similar way for other search problems (Klein & Manning 2003).

Given a state-space graph and state-space projection function, an *abstract state-space graph* is constructed as follows.

1. The set of nodes, called *abstract nodes*, in the abstract state-space graph corresponds to the set of abstract states.
2. An abstract node $y'$ is a successor of an abstract node $y$ iff there exist two states $x'$ and $x$, such that
   a. $x'$ is a successor of $x$, and
   b. $x'$ and $x$ are preimages of $y'$ and $y$, respectively.

If $y = y'$, it means that the abstract node $y$ has a self loop.

For example, Figure 1(a) shows the nine possible positions of the "blank" in the Eight-puzzle. Figure 1(b) shows the abstract state-space graph created by the simple state-space projection function that maps a state into an abstract state based only on the position of the "blank." Each abstract node $B_i$ in Figure 1(b) corresponds to the set of states with the "blank" located at position $i$ in Figure 1(a).

### Duplicate-detection scope

Although transforming a state-space graph into an abstract state-space graph can result in exponential reduction in the

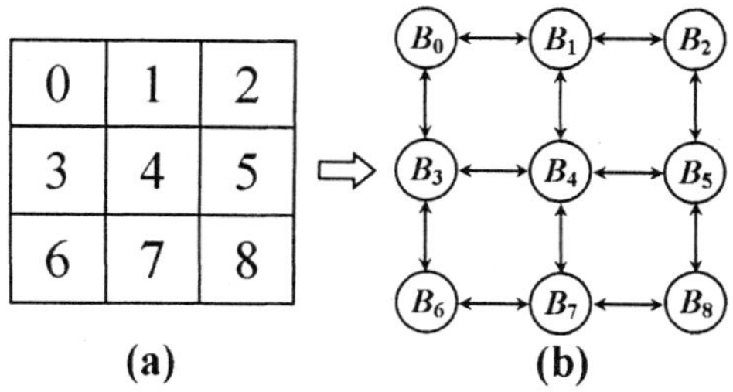


Figure 1: Panel (a) shows all possible positions of the "blank" for the Eight-puzzle. Panel (b) shows an example of an abstract state-space graph for the Eight-puzzle. This definition of the state-space projection function is based on the position of the "blank" only.

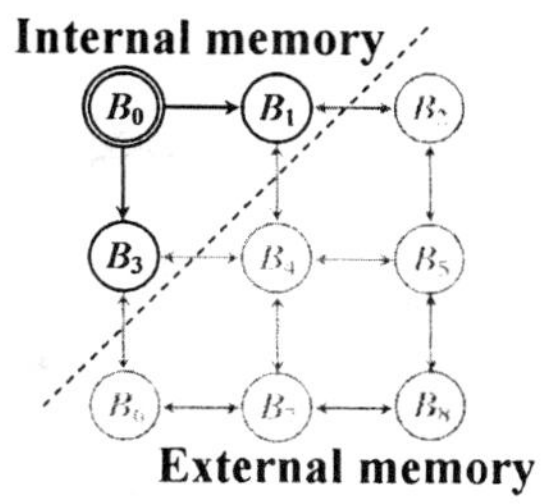


Figure 2: The duplicate-detection scope of nodes that are pre-images of abstract node $B_0$ includes nodes that are pre-images of abstract node $B_1$ or $B_3$. When expanding nodes that are pre-images of abstract node $B_0$, the search algorithm can use internal memory to store nodes that are pre-images of abstract node $B_0$, $B_1$, or $B_3$, and use external memory to store the rest of the nodes.

size of the graph, the local structure of the original state-space graph can be largely preserved. For example, abstract node $B_0$ in Figure 1(b) has only two successors; abstract nodes $B_1$ and $B_3$. This captures the fact that a single move of a tile can only change the position of the "blank" by either one column ($B_0 \rightarrow B_1$ in this case) or one row ($B_0 \rightarrow B_3$ in this case).

**Definition 1** *An abstract state-space graph has* local structure *if it has bounded out-degree.*

For the $(n^2 - 1)$ sliding-tile puzzle using this simple state-space projection function, the out-degree of the abstract state-space graph is bounded by 4, for every $n$.

The local structure of an abstract state-space graph can be used to restrict the scope of duplicate detection so that only a fraction of stored nodes needs to be checked for duplicates, while still guaranteeing that all duplicates are found. For example, when generating successors for nodes that are pre-images of abstract node $B_0$ in Figure 2, the algorithm only needs to check for duplicates against stored nodes that are pre-images of abstract node $B_1$ or $B_3$.

Let an abstract node $y = p(x)$ be the image of a node $x$ under a state-space projection function $p(\cdot)$ and let $successors(y)$ be the set of successor abstract nodes of $y$ in the abstract state-space graph.

**Definition 2** *The* duplicate-detection scope *of a node $x$ under a state-space projection function $p(\cdot)$ corresponds to the union of sets of stored nodes that are pre-images of an abstract node $y'$ such that $y' \in successors(p(x))$, that is,*

$$\bigcup_{y' \in successors(p(x))} p^{-1}(y')$$

*where $p^{-1}(y')$ is the set of stored nodes that are pre-images of $y'$.*

**Theorem 1** *The duplicate-detection scope of a node contains all stored duplicates of the successors of the node.*

*Proof*: Suppose that a node $x$ has a previously-generated successor node $x'$ that is not included in the duplicate-detection scope of node $x$. Let $y' = p(x')$ be the image of $x'$ under the state-space projection function $p(\cdot)$. According to Definition 2, we have $y' \notin successors(p(x))$. But according to the definition of an abstract state-space graph, if $x'$ is a successor of $x$, then $p(x')$ must be a successor of $p(x)$. In other words, $y' \in successors(p(x))$. Since this leads to a contradiction, Theorem 1 must hold. □

The concept of duplicate-detection scope can be very useful in external-memory graph search, because it suggests that a search algorithm use internal memory to store nodes within the duplicate-detection scope of a set of expanding nodes, and use external memory to store other nodes, when internal memory is full. Figure 2 illustrates this idea.

We use the term *nblock* to refer to a set (or "block") of nodes in the original state space that correspond to (i.e., are pre-images of) an abstract node. If an abstract state-space graph has local structure, then the duplicate-detection scope of any node consists of a bounded number of *n*blocks, and the largest duplicate detection scope can be a small fraction of the overall number of stored nodes. Note that the largest duplicate detection scope establishes a minimum internal-memory requirement for structured duplicate detection.

## Search using structured duplicate detection

We now describe how to integrate structured duplicate detection into a state-space search algorithm.

Similar to delayed duplicate detection, structured duplicate detection is used with a search algorithm that expands a set of nodes at a time, such that the underlying search strategy is consistent with expanding the nodes in this set in any order. This is straightforward in breadth-first search, where a set of nodes corresponds to all nodes in the same layer of the breadth-first search graph. (We later explain how it can apply to best-first search.) Given this set of nodes, structured duplicate detection determines an order of expansion that minimizes I/O complexity, by exploiting local structure revealed by the abstract state-space graph.

To support structured duplicate detection, the set of stored nodes (i.e., nodes in the Open and Closed lists) is partitioned based on an abstract state-space graph. Each *n*block in the partition consists of all stored nodes that are pre-images of the same abstract node (i.e., each *n*block corresponds to an abstract node). This local structure is exploited as follows.

First, nodes in the same *n*block are expanded together, i.e., consecutively. This improves locality of memory reference because all nodes in the same *n*block have the same duplicate-detection scope. But it leaves undetermined the order in which to consider *n*blocks. In general, if the duplicate-detection scopes of two *n*blocks are almost the same, they should be expanded close to each other, in order to minimize the number of possible I/O operations. *N*blocks correspond to abstract nodes, and abstract nodes that are neighbors in the abstract state-space graph tend to have similar duplicate-detection scopes. Therefore, we choose to expand *n*blocks in an order that reflects neighbor relations in the abstract state-space space graph. A simple way to do this is to expand the *n*blocks in an order that reflects a breadth-first traversal of the abstract state-space graph.

When internal memory is full, the search algorithm must remove from internal memory one or more *n*blocks that do not belong to the duplicate-detection scope of nodes currently being expanded. Immediately before expanding nodes in a different *n*block, it must check if some *n*blocks in their duplicate-detection scope are missing from internal memory, and if so, read them from external memory. Because reading an *n*block into internal memory often results in writing another *n*block to external memory, we refer to these pairs of read and write operations as *nblock replacements*.

Except for *n*blocks that are part of the duplicate-detection scope of nodes being expanded, any *n*block can potentially be moved from internal memory to external memory. Deciding which *n*blocks to remove is identical to the page-replacement strategy of virtual memory, except that now the unit of replacement is an *n*block instead of a page. Thus, we call it an *nblock-replacement strategy*. It is well-known that the optimal replacement strategy always removes the page (or *n*block) that will not be used for the longest time (Belady 1966). Implementing such a strategy is generally impossible, as it requires future knowledge of the order in which pages (*n*blocks) will be needed, and *least-recently-used* is often the best strategy in practice (Sleator & Tarjan 1985). However, it is possible to compute an optimal *n*block-replacement strategy in our case, since the order in which *n*blocks are expanded is given by the breadth-first traversal order of an abstract state-space graph.

Thus, given a set of nodes to expand, structured duplicate detection expands them in an order such that (1) nodes in the same *n*block are expanded together, (2) *n*blocks are considered in an order that reflects a breadth-first traversal of the abstract state-space graph, and, (3) when internal memory becomes full, selection of which *n*blocks to write to disk is based on a pre-computed optimal *n*block-replacement strategy, or else, the least-recently used strategy.

It it straightforward to use structured duplicate detection with breadth-first search, where the set of nodes being expanded is a layer of the breadth-first search graph. It is also possible to use it with a best-first search algorithm such as A*. In solving a search problem with many ties, the order in which A* expands nodes with the same $f$-value is non-deterministic, and structured duplicate detection can determine an order that minimizes I/O complexity. The $(n^2 - 1)$ sliding-tile puzzle is an example of a domain with many ties.

For search problems in which there are not many ties, it is possible to use structured duplicate detection as part of a slightly-modified version of A*, in which A* selects a set of nodes to expand containing nodes with almost the same $f$-value – for example, the best $k$ nodes on the Open list, where $k$ is a suitably large number. Structured duplicate detection can determine the order in which to expand this set of nodes. Although it may expand nodes in an order that is not strictly best-first, improved performance from structured duplicate detection may outweigh an increase in the number of nodes expanded. This modification of the best-first expansion order of A* to improve locality of memory references was previously proposed by Edelkamp and Schrödl (2000) as a way of improving use of virtual memory.

## I/O complexity

I/O complexity is the primary factor that affects the speed of external-memory algorithms. The I/O complexity of search in an implicit graph depends entirely on the I/O complexity of duplicate detection. The worst-case I/O complexity of delayed duplicate detection is $O(\frac{n+m}{B} \log_{\frac{M}{B}}(n+m))$, where $n$ is the number of nodes in the state-space graph, $m$ is the number of edges, $B$ is the size of a disk block, $M$ is the size of internal memory, and $O(\frac{x}{B} \log_{\frac{M}{B}} x)$ is the worst-case I/O complexity of externally sorting $x$ elements (Munagala & Ranade 1999).

For structured duplicate detection, we have this result.

**Theorem 2** *If every duplicate-detection scope fits in internal memory, the worst-case I/O complexity of structured duplicate detection is* $O(\frac{n}{B} \cdot E)$.

In this result, $E$ is the number of directed edges in the abstract state-space graph. (To keep the analysis simple, we consider an undirected edge as two reciprocally directed edges.) The theorem follows from the fact that $E$ is the worst-case number of *n*block replacements that must be done in traversing the abstract state-space graph, and the worst-case number of I/O operations needed per *n*block replacement is the size of the largest *n*block divided by the disk block size, where $n$ bounds the size of the largest *n*block.

The factor $\frac{1}{B}$ is the same in both analyses. Since an abstract state-space graph is typically exponentially smaller than the original state-space graph, the factor $E$ for structured duplicate detection is comparable to $\log_{\frac{M}{B}}(n+m)$ for delayed duplicated detection. The difference in I/O complexity is the difference between the factor $n+m$ for delayed duplicate detection, and the factor $n$ for structured duplicate detection. The presence of $n+m$ in the complexity analysis for delayed duplicate detection, in contrast to $n$ for structured duplicate detection, can be interpreted as a penalty for *delaying* duplicate detection, since it bounds the cardinality of the multi-set of successors that is generated by expanding a set of nodes *before* performing duplicate detection.

In a highly-connected graph, $m$ is *much* larger than $n$, and the penalty for delaying duplicate detection can be severe. It follows that delayed duplicate detection works best in sparse graphs. However, many important search problems do not have sparse graphs. An example is multiple sequence alignment, a motivating problem for frontier search (Korf & Zhang 2000). An advantage of structured duplicate detection is that it works equally well in sparse and highly-connected graphs.

| # | Sol | Int Mem | Ext Mem | Exp | Secs |
|---|---|---|---|---|---|
| 17 | 66 | 564,628 | 16,389,872 | 279,167,411 | 801 |
| 49 | 59 | 1,382,504 | 20,557,691 | 345,487,863 | 898 |
| 53 | 64 | 481,533 | 12,588,843 | 224,545,853 | 641 |
| 56 | 55 | 228,334 | 12,989,362 | 208,969,445 | 665 |
| 59 | 57 | 414,775 | 13,829,299 | 228,945,351 | 671 |
| 60 | 66 | 1,738,022 | 56,436,901 | 978,819,646 | 3,069 |
| 66 | 61 | 1,355,264 | 20,699,891 | 368,181,735 | 973 |
| 82 | 62 | 1,410,292 | 46,329,201 | 765,608,989 | 2,389 |
| 88 | 65 | 1,808,591 | 77,711,235 | 1,360,544,093 | 4,456 |
| 92 | 57 | 371,779 | 12,505,737 | 213,445,215 | 642 |

Table 1: Performance on the 10 most difficult instances of Korf's 100 random instances of the 15-puzzle. Columns show the instance number (#); solution length (Sol); peak number of nodes stored in internal memory (Int Mem); peak number of nodes stored in external memory (Ext Mem), number of node expansions (Exp), and running time in CPU seconds (Secs).

| Name | Cost | Int Mem | Ext Mem | Exp | Secs |
|---|---|---|---|---|---|
| 1aboA | 8,483 | 8K | 130K | 4,207K | 45 |
| 1amk | 33,960 | 29K | 555K | 31,704K | 373 |
| 1csy | 14,160 | 6K | 52K | 1,943K | 25 |
| 1ezm | 40,733 | 17K | 154K | 6,186K | 73 |
| 1gtr | 58,010 | 188K | 7,468K | 1,094,936K | 22,381 |
| 1idy | 7,888 | 19K | 415K | 10,246K | 110 |
| 1pfc | 15,718 | 12K | 153K | 6,600K | 71 |
| 1tis | 37,581 | 24K | 383K | 29,778K | 357 |
| 1wit | 13,979 | 53K | 1,513K | 80,591K | 1,192 |
| actin | 52,117 | 102K | 2,783K | 240,168K | 3,972 |

Table 2: Performance in aligning groups of 5 protein sequences from reference set 1 of BAliBASE (Thompson, Plewniak, & Poch 1999). Columns show name of instance, cost of optimal alignment, peak number of nodes stored in internal memory (in thousands), peak number of nodes stored in external memory (in thousands), number of node expansions (in thousands), and CPU seconds.

Unlike delayed duplicate detection, structured duplicate detection has a minimum internal-memory requirement. Theorem 2 holds only if every duplicate detection scope fits in internal memory. So, whether it holds depends partly on the size of internal memory, and partly on the locality of the graph, and how well it is captured in an abstract state-space graph. If the largest duplicate detection scope does not fit in internal memory, it is possible to combine structured duplicate detection with delayed duplicate detection. Given a set of nodes to expand, the set can be partitioned based on the abstract state-space graph, and delayed duplicate detection can be performed separately on the nodes in each *n*block, as a way of leveraging local structure to improve performance.

## Computational results

How efficiently the underlying graph-search algorithm uses internal memory has an effect on disk I/O, since it affects how much total memory is needed. For this reason, Korf (2003a; 2003b) built his external-memory graph search algorithm on top of frontier search, a very memory-efficient graph-search algorithm. In our experiments, we also combine structured duplicate detection with memory-efficient graph-search algorithms. A difference is that we consider heuristic search, whereas previous work on external-memory graph search considers breadth-first search only.

For the results in Tables 1 and 2, we ran the search algorithms in a mode that minimizes use of internal memory. So the peak amount of internal memory used corresponds to the minimum internal-memory requirements of the algorithms, using structured duplicate detection and a given abstraction of the state space. Ordinarily, the algorithms would use all available RAM before using disk. The algorithms were run on a 2.4GHz Intel Pentium with 2 gigabytes of RAM and a 7200RPM Seagate disk with 120 gigabytes of storage.

### Fifteen-puzzle

To solve the Fifteen puzzle, we use structured duplicate detection together with a breadth-first heuristic search algorithm that uses divide-and-conquer solution reconstruction, called Breadth-First Iterative-Deepening A* (Zhou & Hansen 2004). Unlike brute-force breadth-first search, this algorithm uses upper and lower bounds to prune nodes that cannot be part of an optimal solution. Table 1 shows how the algorithm performs on the 10 most difficult instances of Korf's 100 random instances of the 15-puzzle (Korf 1985).

We used a state-space projection function that groups together states based on the positions of tiles 15 and 8, plus the position of the "blank," creating an abstract state-space graph with $16 \cdot 15 \cdot 14 = 3360$ nodes. Based on this partition of the state space, structured duplicate detection reduces the internal-memory requirement of the search algorithm by a factor of between 16 and 58 times. In exchange, it increases running time by only about 24% in solving these examples. Using both structured duplicate detection and divide-and-conquer solution reconstruction, all 100 instances of the 15-puzzle are solved using no more than 42 megabytes of RAM, without ever re-expanding a node in the same iteration. Based on the number of distinct nodes expanded, A* would need 28 gigabytes of RAM just to store the Closed list in solving instance 88.

### Multiple sequence alignment

The multiple sequence alignment problem is an example of a search problem that cannot be solved efficiently using delayed duplicate detection because its search graph is very highly-connected. The search graph for the multiple sequence alignment problem is an $n$-dimensional hyperlattice, where $n$ is the number of sequences being aligned.

We implemented structured duplicate detection on top of a search algorithm called Sweep A*, which uses divide-and-conquer solution reconstruction to limit use of memory (Zhou & Hansen 2003).[1] We tested the resulting algorithm on a selection of difficult multiple sequence alignment problems from reference set 1 of BAliBASE, a widely-used benchmark (Thompson, Plewniak, & Poch 1999). All

[1]Sweep A* is a specialized search algorithm for multiple sequence alignment that expands nodes on a layer-by-layer basis, which makes it a good fit for structured duplicate detection. It is also very memory-efficient. For comparison, frontier search (Korf & Zhang 2000) cannot solve instances 1gtr, 1wit, or actin in Table 2 within 2 gigabytes of RAM, and uses an average of 25 times more memory than Sweep A* in solving the other instances.

problems involved aligning 5 protein sequences. Our cost function was a Dayhoff substitution matrix with linear gap penalty of 8, and we used a pairwise alignment admissible heuristic. To create an abstract state-space graph, we used a state-space projection function that ignores all but 3 sequences. This creates an abstract state space with $O(l^3)$ abstract nodes, where $l$ is the average length of a sequence, compared to $O(l^5)$ nodes in the original state-space graph.

Table 2 shows that structured duplicate detection reduces the internal-memory requirements of Sweep A* by a factor of between 10 and 40 times. Using disk, the algorithm needs only 20 megabytes of RAM to solve all instances in Table 2, including the space for the pairwise heuristic. Interestingly, the external-memory version of Sweep A* runs faster than an internal-memory version of Sweep A* that does not use structured duplicate detection, by an average of 72%! The reason is that structured duplicate detection runs faster in internal memory than un-structured duplicate detection due to locality of memory references, and this speedup outweighs the extra time for disk I/O. The speedup is more evident in multiple sequence alignment than the sliding-tile puzzle because the multiple sequence alignment search graph is much more highly-connected, which significantly increases the number of duplicates generated per node expansion.

### Speeding up internal-memory search

We emphasize that for both the Fifteen puzzle and multiple sequence alignment, structured duplicate detection improves the performance of internal-memory graph search, in addition to using external memory efficiently. This is because each time the search algorithm checks for duplicates, it only needs to check a small subset of the stored nodes. For the Fifteen puzzle, this leads to a 16% speedup in internal-memory performance. For multiple sequence alignment, it cuts the running time of internal-memory search in half. Again, the speedup is much greater for multiple sequence alignment because in a very highly-connected graph, many more duplicates are generated. This underscores a benefit of structured duplicate detection. Unlike delayed duplicate detection, it is more effective in highly-connected graphs, where the problem of duplicate detection is more crucial.

## Conclusion

We have introduced structured duplicate detection, a novel approach to localizing memory references in duplicate detection, and showed that it can reduce the I/O complexity of external-memory graph search, as well as increase the speed of duplicate detection in internal-memory search.

Structured duplicate detection has some advantages over delayed duplicate detection, the only previous approach to external-memory graph search. In particular, it is more effective in highly-connected graphs, and it can exploit local graph structure that is not considered by delayed duplicate detection. But structured duplicate detection and delayed duplicate detection can also be viewed as complementary approaches to reducing I/O complexity, and can be used together for difficult search problems. If a search algorithm can leverage enough locality in a state-space graph so that every duplicate-detection scope fits in internal memory, it is unnecessary to ever delay duplicate detection, and structured duplicate detection can manage external memory by itself. But if any duplicate-detection scope does not fit in internal memory (perhaps due to lack of sufficient local structure in the graph), structured duplicate detection by itself is not sufficient. Since delayed duplicate detection does not have a minimum memory requirement, it can be used in this case. Structured duplicate detection can be used together with delayed duplicate detection to improve its performance, by leveraging graph locality as much as possible.

**Acknowledgments** We thank the anonymous reviewers for helpful comments. This work was supported in part by NSF grant IIS-9984952 and NASA grant NAG-2-1463.

## References

Aggarwal, A., and Vitter, J. 1988. The input/output complexity of sorting and related problems. *Comm. of the ACM* 31(9):1116–27.

Belady, L. 1966. A study of replacement algorithms for virtual storage. *IBM Systems Journal* 5:78–101.

Edelkamp, S., and Schrödl, S. 2000. Localizing A*. In *Proc. of the 17th National Conference on Artificial Intelligence*, 885–890.

Holte, R.; Mkadmi, T.; Zimmer, R.; and MacDonald, A. 1996. Speeding up problem solving by abstraction: A graph-oriented approach. *Artificial Intelligence* 85(1–2):321–361.

Klein, D., and Manning, C. 2003. Factored A* search for models over sequences and trees. In *Proceedings of the 17th International Joint Conference on Artificial Intelligence*, 1246–1251.

Korf, R., and Zhang, W. 2000. Divide-and-conquer frontier search applied to optimal sequence alignment. In *Proceedings of the 17th National Conference on Artificial Intelligence*, 910–916.

Korf, R. 1985. Depth-first iterative deepening: An optimal admissible tree search. *Artificial Intelligence* 27:97–109.

Korf, R. 2003a. Breadth-first frontier search with delayed duplicate detection. In *Proceedings of the Workshop on Model Checking and Artificial Intelligence at IJCAI-03*, 87–92.

Korf, R. 2003b. Delayed duplicate detection: Extended abstract. In *Proceedings of the 17th International Joint Conference on Artificial Intelligence*, 1539–1541.

Mehlhorn, K., and Meyer, U. 2002. External-memory breadth-first search with sublinear I/O. In *Proceedings of the 10th Annual European Symposium on Algorithms*, 723–735.

Munagala, K., and Ranade, A. 1999. I/O-complexity of graph algorithms. In *Proceedings of the 10th Symposium on discrete algorithms*, 687–694. ACM-SIAM.

Sleator, D., and Tarjan, R. 1985. Amortized efficiency of list update and paging rules. *Communications of the ACM* 28:202–8.

Thompson, J.; Plewniak, F.; and Poch, O. 1999. BAliBASE: A benchmark alignment database for the evaluation of multiple alignment programs. *Bioinformatics* 15(1):87–88.

Zhou, R., and Hansen, E. 2003. Sweep A*: Space-efficient heuristic search in partially ordered graphs. In *Proc. of 15th IEEE International Conf. on Tools with Artificial Intelligence*, 427–434.

Zhou, R., and Hansen, E. 2004. Breadth-first heuristic search. In *Proceedings of the 14th International Conference on Automated Planning and Scheduling*.

# Uncertainty

# Stochastic Local Search for POMDP Controllers

**Darius Braziunas**
Department of Computer Science
University of Toronto
Toronto, ON M5S 3H5
*darius@cs.toronto.edu*

**Craig Boutilier**
Department of Computer Science
University of Toronto
Toronto, ON M5S 3H5
*cebly@cs.toronto.edu*

## Abstract

The search for finite-state controllers for partially observable Markov decision processes (POMDPs) is often based on approaches like gradient ascent, attractive because of their relatively low computational cost. In this paper, we illustrate a basic problem with gradient-based methods applied to POMDPs, where the sequential nature of the decision problem is at issue, and propose a new stochastic local search method as an alternative. The heuristics used in our procedure mimic the sequential reasoning inherent in optimal dynamic programming (DP) approaches. We show that our algorithm consistently finds higher quality controllers than gradient ascent, and is competitive with (and, for some problems, superior to) other state-of-the-art controller and DP-based algorithms on large-scale POMDPs.

## 1 Introduction

Partially observable Markov decision processes (POMDPs) provide a natural model for sequential decision making under uncertainty. Unfortunately, the application of POMDPs remains limited due to the intractability of current solution algorithms, especially those that use dynamic programming (DP) to construct (approximately) optimal value functions [16; 5]. One method for dealing with this bottleneck is to restrict the space of policies being considered, and devise techniques that search directly in that space. *Finite-state controllers (FSCs)* are the policy representation of choice in such work, providing a compromise between the requirement that action choices depend on certain aspects of observable history and the ability to easily control the complexity of policy space being searched.

While optimal FSCs can be constructed if no restrictions are placed on their structure [8], it is more usual to impose some structure that one hopes admits a good parameterization, and search through that restricted space. Among various techniques that search through a restricted policy space [12; 10; 18], *gradient ascent (GA)* has proven to be especially attractive because of its computational properties. GA has been applied to both the offline solution of POMDPs whose model is known [12] as well as the online reinforcement learning setting [13; 1]. We focus on known models.



One difficulty with gradient-based approaches, not surprisingly, is the ease with which they converge to local suboptima. Our experiences have demonstrated that GA, for example, has difficulty in problems where the *precise sequence* of actions taken is important for good performance. This is a common feature of stochastic planning problems to which POMDPs are often applied; they usually have different characteristics from navigational problems on which GA has often been tested. While various restrictions on policy space can be used to encode prior knowledge about a problem's solution [12], such restrictions may be hard to encode naturally, and such knowledge may be hard to come by.

In this paper, we describe an algorithm that searches for good controllers while remaining within the "local search" framework. Since finding an optimal fixed-size FSC is NP-hard [10; 12], we propose a *stochastic local search (SLS)* technique which, like GA, works in the space of FSCs, but uses very different heuristics to evaluate moves. *Belief-based SLS (BBSLS)* incorporates intuitions—used in the DP solution to POMDPs that work in belief-state value function space—that allow moves in different directions than those permitted by gradient-based methods. Specifically, BBSLS considers making moves that would be of high value when executed at some belief state, even though that belief state is not reachable given the current controller; since they do not improve controller value, such moves cannot be considered by GA. A tabu list is used to allow subsequent changes to the controller to adjust to this move. BBSLS is much less computationally intensive than DP methods, and provides a good compromise between full DP and the very restricted form of local search admitted by GA. Our empirical results suggest that our algorithm is competitive with recent state-of-the-art FSC and value-function-based methods such as BPI [15] and PBVI [14; 17], producing smaller, higher quality controllers, often significantly more quickly.

We begin in Section 2 with an overview of POMDPs. In Section 3 we first describe problems with GA that inspired our method, and then detail the BBSLS algorithm. Empirical results are provided in Section 4 that confirm various advantages over other algorithms, and we conclude with discussion of future research directions in Section 5.

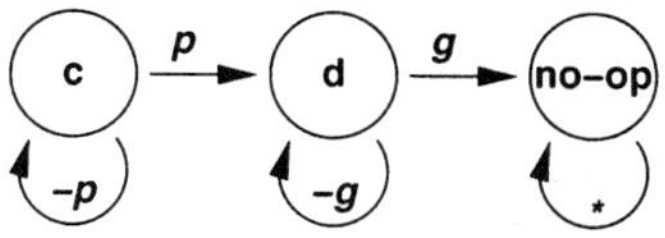


Figure 1: A simple FSC for a planning problem

## 2 Background and Notation

A POMDP is defined by: a set $\mathcal{S}$ of states; a set $\mathcal{A}$ of actions; a set $\mathcal{Z}$ of observations; a transition function $T$, where $T(s, a, s')$ denotes the probability $Pr(s'|s, a)$ of transitioning to state $s'$ when action $a$ is taken at state $s$; an observation function $Z$, where $Z(s, a, z)$ denotes the probability $Pr(z|s, a)$ of making observation $z$ in $s$ after performing $a$; and a reward function $R$, where $R(s, a)$ denotes the immediate reward associated with state $s$ and action $a$. We assume discrete state,[1] action and observation sets, and we focus on discounted, infinite horizon POMDPs with discount factor $0 \leq \gamma < 1$. When considering FSCs for POMDPs, we will assume an initial *belief state* $b_0$ denoting the initial distribution over states (where $b_0(s)$ is the probability of the initial state being $s$).

Let $H$ be the set of all finite *observable histories* (i.e., all finite sequences of action-observation pairs). A *stochastic policy* $\pi : H \mapsto \Delta(\mathcal{A})$ associates a distribution over actions with each history. A deterministic policy associates a single action with each $h \in H$. The *value* of policy $\pi$ at state $s$ is the expected sum of discounted rewards obtained by executing $\pi$ starting at state $s$:

$$V_\pi(s) = E(\sum_{t=0}^{\infty} \gamma^t R^t | \pi, s).$$

The expected value of $\pi$ is $b_0 \cdot V_\pi$ (viewing $V_\pi$ as an $|\mathcal{S}|$-vector).

The representation of a policy $\pi$ can take several forms. An indirect way of mapping histories into actions is to map *belief states* into actions: an agent's belief state comprises a sufficient statistic summarizing all relevant aspects of its history. An advantage of this approach is that instead of an infinite collection of discrete histories, one maps a continuous space $\Delta(\mathcal{S})$ into $\mathcal{A}$. Indeed, this mapping has nice properties and finite-horizon approximations of the optimal value function are piecewise linear and convex [16]. Unfortunately, methods that produce such representations (e.g., the Witness algorithm [4]) are often intractable, though approximation techniques like PBVI [14] can be used.

An FSC offers a different way of representing a policy $\pi$. A stochastic FSC $\langle \mathcal{N}, \psi, \eta \rangle$ comprises: $\mathcal{N}$, a finite set of *nodes*; $\psi$, an *action selection* function, where $\psi(n, a)$ denotes the probability with which $a \in \mathcal{A}$ is selected when the FSC is at node $n \in \mathcal{N}$; and $\eta$, a *transition function*, where $\eta(n, z, n')$ denotes the probability with which the FSC moves to node $n'$ given that it was at node $n$ after making observation $z \in \mathcal{Z}$. A *deterministic* FSC has deterministic action selection and node transition functions. While an FSC of a fixed size cannot generally represent an optimal policy, it offers a concise representation that can be exploited computationally. Figure 1 illustrates a 3-node, deterministic FSC. For each node $n$, $\psi$ dictates which action to take (stochastically) and, conditioned on the observation, $\eta$ prescribes which node to move to next. We sometimes refer to $\eta$ as an *observation strategy*. Later, we will also use the notion of a deterministic *conditional plan* $\sigma = \langle a, \nu \rangle$, where $a \in \mathcal{A}$ is an action to execute, and $\nu : \mathcal{Z} \mapsto \mathcal{N}$ is a deterministic observation strategy.

The original POMDP and an FSC $\pi$ induce a Markov chain whose states $\langle s, n \rangle$ are drawn from the cross-product $\mathcal{S} \times \mathcal{N}$. The value $V_\pi(s, n)$ of such a policy at $\langle s, n \rangle$ is:

$$V_\pi(s, n) = \sum_a \psi(n, a) R(s, a) + \gamma \sum_{a, z, s', n'} \psi(n, a) T(s, a, s') Z(s', a, z) \eta(n, z, n') V_\pi(s', n').$$

$V_\pi$ can be computed by solving this linear system. The value of $\pi$ given $b$ is $V_\pi(b, n) = \sum_s V_\pi(s, n) b(s)$, and for an initial $b_0$, the best initial node $n_0$ can be determined readily.

One can find good or optimal FSCs in several different ways. Hansen's policy iteration [8] uses DP to produce a sequence of (generally, increasingly large) FSCs that converge to optimality. *Bounded policy iteration (BPI)* [15] uses basic DP together with techniques for bounding the size of the FSC, resulting in an approximation method that scales much better than policy iteration. Various search techniques have been proposed as well that do not ensure optimality, but often yield good results in practice without the computational cost of policy iteration. Among these gradient ascent has proven very popular. We refer to Meuleau *et al.* [12] for details of a typical formulation; in that work, an FSC of fixed size is assumed and the gradient of $V_\pi(b_0, n_0)$ w.r.t. the policy parameters $\eta(n, z, n')$ and $\psi(n, a)$ is derived. Standard GA is then used to navigate through the space of bounded FSCs until a local optimum is found. Computational results on maze-like problems [12] and continuous navigation-style problems [1] suggest that GA can tackle problems that are generally considered unsolvable using exact DP techniques.

## 3 A Stochastic Local Search Technique

We now describe a new approach for solving POMDPs approximately using FSCs, based on the use of stochastic local search and a specific heuristic, that circumvents some of the difficulties of GA. We begin with a simple example that illustrates a common type of local optimum to which GA falls prey, and describe intuitions that would allow a local search technique to break out of such local optima. We then formalize these intuitions within our algorithm.

### 3.1 A Motivating Example

Consider a simple planning problem in which the optimal solution consists of performing action $c$ until the precondition $p$ for action $d$ is observed, then performing $d$ until goal $g$ is observed, and finally terminating (perhaps repeating some no-op).[2] Suppose further that: actions $c$ and $d$ are very costly, but

[1] Below, we will generalize our approach to continuous state POMDPs through the use of sampling.

[2] We assume the actions are stochastic and observations noisy. For instance, when $c$ is performed, it is not guaranteed to make $p$

the reward associated with the goal $g$ more than compensates for their expected costs; $d$ only achieves $g$ (with reasonable probability) if $p$ is true; $p$ is only made true by $c$; all other actions (at any state) have costs/rewards that are small relative to the costs/rewards of $c$, $d$, and $g$.

The optimal policy for this POMDP can be represented using the simple, deterministic 3-node FSC shown in Figure 1. If the action space is large enough, a random instantiation of this FSC is very unlikely to be optimal.[3] Suppose we attempt to solve this problem using GA, starting from some initial FSC, and suppose no node selects action $c$ or $d$ with significant probability. In this case, GA has no hope of finding the optimal FSC. Since the probability of $c$ being executed is small, the probability of $p$ being true at any belief state reachable using the current FSC is small; hence, increasing the probability of $d$ at any node will decrease controller value, preventing GA from moving in that direction. Similarly, since $d$ is unlikely to be executed, the value of increasing the probability of $c$ at any node is negative, preventing GA from moving in that direction. Indeed, the nature of this problem is such that GA will be forced to move *away* from the optimal FSC. The sequential nature of the problem, and the fact that optimal actions are *undesirable* unless their counterparts are in place, make the landscape very hard to navigate using (even stochastic) GA.

How could one avoid the difficulties GA faces on POMDPs of this type within the local search framework? Intuitively, action $d$ would be considered useful at a belief state in which precondition $p$ held. Unfortunately, since $c$ is never executed, such a belief state is unreachable given the current FSC. However, it is easy to verify that action $d$ is good at some belief state in the context of the current controller. More precisely, a conditional plan $\langle d, \nu \rangle$ installed at node $n$—where $\nu$ transitions to a terminal node if $g$ is observed, and back to $n$ otherwise—would have high value in any belief state where $p$ is sufficiently probable. As we will see, identifying the usefulness of this plan at *some* belief state $b$ is straightforward, requiring the solution of a simple linear program (LP). Our local search procedure will consider adjustments to the FSC of this type: if a plan has high value at some belief state $b$, even if it cannot be realized by the current controller, we will consider (stochastically) making that move (or adjusting the FSC parameters in that direction).

Of course, if we make this move by adjusting the parameters at node $n$ toward plan $\langle d, \nu \rangle$, we decrease the value of the FSC. Should we subsequently resort to moving in a direction that improves FSC value, we would naturally want to "undo" this move. Hence moves of this type will be held on a *tabu list* [7] for some period of time. This allows the algorithm a chance to "catch up" to the move. Specifically, since the plan at node $n$ has high value at belief states near $b$, by holding this node fixed, we give the FSC a chance to find a policy for the rest of the FSC that will induce this region of belief space at node $n$. In this example, by holding $n$ fixed, the plan $\langle c, \nu' \rangle$ at node $n'$—where $\nu'$ transitions to node $n$ if $p$ is observed, and back to $n'$ otherwise—will now look attractive (indeed, with $n$ fixed, GA would move in this direction). In a sense, this process simulates the reasoning inherent in value or policy iteration over belief space.

In the next sections, we make these intuitions more precise.

### 3.2 Algorithm Structure

Our *belief-based SLS algorithm (BBSLS)* stochastically adjusts the parameters of the fixed-size FSC at each iteration based on one of two criteria. The *moves* it makes consist of "installing" a deterministic conditional plan $\langle a, \nu \rangle$ at a node $n$: when such a move is made, the parameters of probabilistic FSC functions $\psi$ and $\eta$ at node $n$ are adjusted in the direction of the plan $\langle a, \nu \rangle$ to make action $a$ and transitions dictated by $\nu$ more likely. At each step, our SLS algorithm performs one or more *local* moves, followed by a sequence of *global* moves.

Local moves are designed to capture the basic intuitions described above, allowing BBSLS to break out of the types of local optima to which GA often falls prey. Intuitively, DP-inspired moves are considered, allowing policy choices to be made at unreachable belief states. By holding these moves on a tabu list, the rest of the controller is given a chance to "adjust" to these moves, by making these belief states reachable in order to attain higher value. Global moves correspond to direct stochastic hill-climbing, and are designed to increase controller value immediately, often taking advantage of earlier local moves. Thus, generally, in the local phase, we optimize for good, but potentially unreachable, belief states; in the global stage, we greedily improve the FSC value and make some of the belief regions considered in the local phase reachable.[4] Since the set of local and global moves is enormous, we need good ways of focusing on potentially useful moves. In each case, different techniques will be used. We now describe both phases in detail.

### 3.3 Local Moves

We first develop a heuristic for evaluating conditional plans. Let $\pi$ be a fixed FSC. The Q-function $Q^\sigma_\pi$ for a (deterministic) conditional plan $\sigma = \langle a, \nu \rangle$ is:

$$Q^\sigma_\pi(s) = R(s,a) + \gamma \sum_{\substack{s',n',\\ z|\nu(z)=n'}} T(s,a,s')Z(s',a,z)V_\pi(s',n').$$

Intuitively, this is the expected value of performing $a$ at $s$, moving to the controller node dictated by the resulting observation, then executing the controller from that point on. We define $Q^\sigma_\pi(b) = \sum_s Q^\sigma_\pi(s)b(s)$ for any belief state $b$.

Our aim is to rank plans $\sigma$ as possible moves in controller space according to a heuristic function $h(\sigma)$ that reflects *potential* value at belief states that might not be reachable from $b_0$ in the current FSC. Let $\Sigma_l$ be the set of plans from which we select local moves. For each $\sigma \in \Sigma_l$, we find a belief state

true; and detecting that $p$ is true is also noisy. Intuitively, the optimal policy would choose to execute $d$ only if $p$ is believed with sufficiently high probability; we assume that a single observation of $p$ makes this so.

[3]To keep things simple, we focus on a small two-step sequence; for longer sequences, typical of planning problems, the odds of a random FSC including any significant subsequence are negligible.

[4]BBSLS can be viewed as a form of *iterated local search* [9].

$b^\sigma$ such that the *difference* between the Q-value of $\sigma$ and the value of any current controller node is maximal. Define

$$\delta_\pi^\sigma = \max_b [Q_\pi^\sigma(b) - \max_n V_\pi(b, n)],$$

and let $b^\sigma$ be a belief state that maximizes this expression. The heuristic value of $\sigma$ is then simply $\delta_\pi^\sigma$, i.e., the maximal possible improvement over the current controller value (achieved at "witness" belief state $b^\sigma$). $\delta_\pi^\sigma$ can be computed by solving an LP with $|\mathcal{S}| + 1$ variables and $|\mathcal{N}|$ constraints.

With this heuristic in hand, local moves can be chosen. We first note that any plan $\sigma$ has the same Q-function $Q_\pi^\sigma$ regardless of the node at which it is installed. Because of this we break local move choice into two stages: plan evaluation (which plan $\sigma$ to install) and node selection (at which node to install the plan). The set of all conditional plans is generally too large to evaluate—we cannot compute $h(\sigma)$ for each $\sigma \in |\mathcal{A}||\mathcal{N}|^{|\mathcal{Z}|}$ for any but the smallest problems. Therefore, we restrict the set $\Sigma_l$ by using the Witness algorithm [4] to incrementally generate a (sub)set of *useful* plans that would improve controller value if we were to increase its size. We evaluate only such plans, and stochastically choose some $\sigma$ using a distribution that gives greater weight to plans with greater $h$-values. The distribution we use in our experiments is straightforward: since all $\delta_\pi^\sigma$ are positive, we simply normalize them to sum to one, and sample from the resulting probability distribution.

We place one other restriction on the choice of plan: no $\sigma$ is chosen whose witness belief state $b^\sigma$ is "near" the witness belief state of an existing node. If a new plan is chosen that has high value at some belief state near another for which a previously selected plan has high value, installing the new plan at a node will "waste" controller capacity by duplicating the function of the earlier plan. For this reason, we maintain a *belief tabu list* containing the witness belief states of the most recently selected plans. The distance between two belief states can be defined in a variety of ways. For our experiments, we used the belief discretization technique of Geffner and Bonet [6], but more suitable measures warrant further research.[5]

Finally, the selected $\sigma$ is *installed* (see above) at some node $n$ which is not on the *node tabu list*. Among non-tabu nodes, a node $n$ is randomly selected which is either unreachable from $n_0$ or leads to the greatest increase in value $b_0 \cdot V_\pi$. The latter choice directly increases controller value, while the former exploits unused controller capacity. The witness for $\sigma$ is associated with $n$, and $n$ is added to the tabu list.

Intuitively, in the local stage, we find plans that have high value at some belief states, even though they might not be reachable in the current FSC. Since the LP that computes $h(\sigma)$ also returns the witness $b^\sigma$, we record this as well. This information allows us to rule out other subsequent moves that duplicate the effect of $\sigma$ (which would waste controller capacity). It is also important to exploit unreachable nodes, since this helps avoid unused capacity; moves at unreachable nodes, since they have no impact on FSC value, would never be considered by GA (or in our global stage). Once a useful $\sigma$ has been installed at an unreachable node, there is incentive at subsequent iterations to link to this node.

### 3.4 Global Moves

In the global stage, we select moves that increase the overall controller value with respect to the initial belief state $b_0$. As with local moves, we consider a subset of deterministic plans $\Sigma_g$ as possible candidates. Each $\sigma \in \Sigma_g$ is evaluated based on its improvement in FSC value $b_0 \cdot V_\pi$ (much like GA) and the moves are chosen with probability related to their level of improvement. Since the objective of a global move is to increase controller value, we build the set of possible plans for consideration as follows. First, we simulate the controller to obtain a sample of *reachable* belief states and nodes.[6] For each belief state, we compute the best plan for that specific belief state (this can be done in time linear in controller size), and calculate the value of the controller that would result if the plan was installed at the corresponding node. We repeat as long as controller value increases.

The global stage is essentially a form of stochastic hill-climbing. While local moves instantiate nodes with plans that are useful for *some* belief states, we ultimately care about FSC value (w.r.t. $b_0$). Therefore, global moves are used to increase value. Such moves often link to the nodes instantiated with potentially useful plans in the local stage. In a sense, the global stage is used to verify the usefulness of moves proposed in the local stage.

### 3.5 The BBSLS Algorithm

The BBSLS algorithm is summarized in Table 1. At each iteration, the BBSLS algorithm executes one or more local moves, and a sequence of global moves. The parameters of the algorithm can be chosen to reflect problem structure. If there are many strong local basins of attraction, the number of local moves $l$ could be increased to facilitate an escape from local suboptima. Different approaches can be used to generate the set of candidate local moves $\Sigma_l$ (the witness method we use, described above, appears to work well).

The condition $C$ we use to terminate the execution of global moves is lack of improvement in controller value (as discussed above), though other conditions may be useful (e.g., a fixed number of steps). The parameters $k$ and $m$ in the global stage could be tuned based on the number of FSC nodes, POMDP states, and the discount factor. However, the default parameter values described in the next section proved to be adequate for our experiments. Finally, we have encoded the specific method of sampled reachable belief states within the algorithm as the method of constructing $\Sigma_g$; again, other ways to restrict the space of candidate moves could prove useful in specific settings.

BBSLS is an anytime algorithm. Empirically, because the global stage is essentially greedy optimization over reachable belief states, BBSLS quickly achieves (and exceeds) the performance of GA. The local stage runs in time polynomial in $|\mathcal{N}|, |\mathcal{S}|, |\mathcal{A}|, |\mathcal{Z}|$, and $|\Sigma_l|$, and the global stage

[5] Given an integer resolution $r > 0$ (we set $r = |\mathcal{S}|$ in our experiments), the probabilities $b(s)$ are discretized into $r$ levels. Two belief states $b, b'$ are close if their discretized representation is the same: $round(b(s) \cdot r)/r = round(b'(s) \cdot r)/r, \forall s \in \mathcal{S}$.

[6] This is done using $k$ runs of the controller (starting at $b_0, n_0$, randomly sampling transitions and observations) of $m$ steps each.

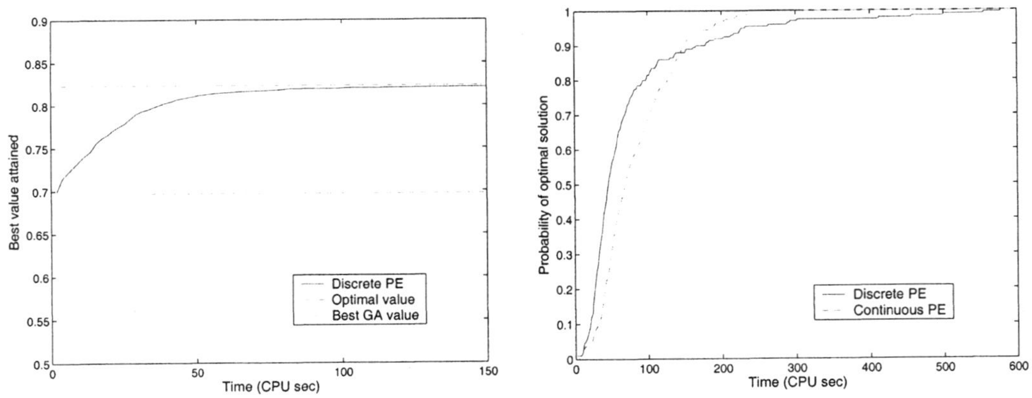


Figure 2: (a) Anytime performance of discrete PE; (b) RTDs for discrete (2.0 s/iter) and continuous (3.2 s/iter) PE.

While some search termination criterion is not met:

- Perform $l$ local moves:
  - create a set of candidate condition plans $\Sigma_l$;
  - *sample* a conditional plan $\sigma \in \Sigma_l$ according to the Q-value heuristic $h(\sigma)$ (plans with higher $h$-values are given greater weight in the sampling distribution) while ensuring that no node in the FSC already has a witness belief state $b^\sigma$;
  - randomly choose a non-tabu node $n$ which is either not reachable from $n_0$ (with probability $p_l$), or which leads to the highest increase in the FSC value when instantiated with the plan $\sigma$ (with probability $1 - p_l$);
  - execute the local move $\langle n, \sigma \rangle$, add the node $n$ to the move tabu list and the witness belief state $b^\sigma$ to the witness belief list.
- Perform global moves (until condition $C$ met):
  - run $k$ policy execution simulations for $m$ steps, starting from the initial node $n_0$ and belief state $b_0$, and record the belief states and nodes that were reached;
  - create the set of conditional plans that are optimal at the belief states visited during the previous step, and calculate the value (w.r.t. to the initial belief state $b_0$) of the controller that would result if a conditional plan from the set was installed at the corresponding node;
  - choose a move that leads to the highest increase in controller value. Make the selected move, and remove the witness belief state ascribed to the associated node.

Table 1: The BBSLS algorithm.

in time polynomial in $|\mathcal{N}|, |\mathcal{S}|, |\mathcal{A}|, |\mathcal{Z}|$, and $|\Sigma_g|$. Since $|\Sigma_l|, |\Sigma_g|, |\mathcal{N}|$ are controllable parameters, we can usually achieve a very good trade-off between solution quality and computation time.

## 4 Empirical Results

The following experiments illuminate various aspects of BBSLS and compare its performance to GA, PBVI, and BPI on examples drawn from the research literature.[7] Default algorithm parameters were: tabu list size equal to $|\mathcal{N}|/2$, $l = 1$, $p_l = 0.5$, $|\Sigma_l| = 10$; $k = 2$, $m = |\mathcal{N}|/2$. We used deterministic controllers on all problems except for Heaven/Hell. Generally, better performance can be achieved if parameters are tuned to specific problems.

The need for sequential policy structure is clearly evident in the small preference elicitation problem (PE) described in [2]. The objective is to optimally balance the cost of queries and the gain provided by the elicited utility information with respect to the quality of the final decision. We refer to [2] for a specification of the problem.

We tackle two variants of this problem. In the first, we discretize state space (possible utility functions) to six states and the number of actions (queries) to 14. In the second, the state space remains continuous. In both cases, an optimal FSC has 12 nodes. Good performance requires that a precise sequence of actions (queries) be executed before making a final decision. However, a default decision exists as a safe alternative for any belief state. Since asking queries before making a decision is initially costly, GA always converges to a safe, but suboptimal alternative. On the other hand, BBSLS is designed to avoid such local optima; for this small problem, it always finds the best global solution (which can be computed analytically). Figure 2 (a) plots the average value of the best 22-node FSC found by BBSLS (200 trials) and compares it to

[7] BBSLS was implemented in Matlab and run on Xeon 2.4GHz computers; linear programs were solved using CPLEX 7.1; GA used the quasi-Newton method with BFGS update and quadcubic line search from Matlab's Optimization Toolbox.

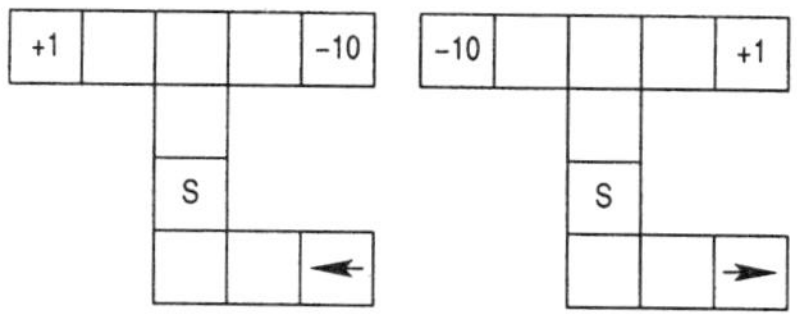


Figure 3: Heaven/Hell problem

the best GA value (measured on 10,000 random initial FSCs, each trial taking 3 seconds on average).

To solve a continuous POMDP with BBSLS, we *sample* $u$ states (utility functions) at each iteration (we set $u = 20$). We then calculate the observation function and the reward function for the sampled states. Although our work with continuous elicitation is at an early stage, the results are promising—because of added stochasticity, BBSLS finds optimal controllers even faster than in the discrete case. Figure 2 (b) shows *run-time distributions* (RTDs) for both the discrete and continuous versions of the PE problem, that is, plots of the empirical probability of finding an optimal FSC as a function of time.

In the Heaven/Hell (HH) POMDP [1; 6], an agent starts with equal probability in either the "left" or "right" worlds, and, because of partial observability, does not know which. The (left or right) arrow (Figure 3) conveys information about the location of "heaven" (positive reward); if the agent does not observe the arrow, it risks falling into "hell" (negative reward). After visiting heaven or hell, the agent is again placed in either the left or right world. It can observe the top and bottom cells in the center column, as well as non-zero reward locations. In [1; 6], both heaven and hell have symmetric rewards of +1 and -1. This allows GA methods some flexibility, since moving down from the start state (and acting randomly) is no worse than moving up (in expectation); there is no disincentive to adjusting a controller to move upward before the correct policy for the top part of the maze is discovered. Our experiments with 20-node controllers show that on symmetric HH, GA sometimes reaches a local optimum with value 0.8040 (100 trials, each 2.9 min on average). However, the optimal value is 8.641, achievable by an 8-node FSC. Furthermore, we can make this problem practically unsolvable by GA if we increase the hell penalty to -10 (Figure 3). GA always chooses (in 100 trials) the safe alternative (bumping into walls for zero reward), even though the optimal FSC has not changed. Our SLS procedure (stochastic FSC, $l = 2$, 12 trials) finds a near-optimal solution even in the asymmetric case: in 200 iterations (average time of 10.2 seconds per iteration), the average value attained is 6.93, and in 500 iterations an average value of 7.65 is achieved.

Hallway (60 states, 5 actions, 21 observations) and Hallway2 (92 states, 5 actions, 17 observations) are two domains of moderate size [11]. In Hallway, a 10-node FSC attains a value of 0.7 in 442 seconds, and eventually achieves 0.8 in 500 iterations (averaged over 13 trials). The best value reached by a 30-node FSC was 0.95. The best value reached by a 20-node FSC for Hallway2 problem was 0.34. For comparison, Q-MDP finds a policy with a value of 0.3444 for Hallway, and 0.097 for Hallway2 [3]. Our results are not directly comparable to those reported for recent state-of-the-art algorithms PBVI [14] or BPI [15] (due to different testing methods). However, an indirect comparison seems to indicate that BBSLS achieves similar performance on both hallway domains with much smaller controllers.

Finally, we compare the performance of BBSLS to BPI and PBVI on the large Tag domain [14], with 870 states, 5 actions, and 30 observations. Tag is based on the popular game of laser tag, where the goal is to search and tag a moving opponent. On this problem, GA converges to a local suboptimum of -20 (10-node FSC), and cannot be run with controllers having more than 20 nodes because of time and space constraints. PBVI achieves a value of -9.18 in 180,880 seconds with a policy of 1334 linear vectors (roughly comparable to a 1334-node controller); BPI finds a 940-node controller with the same value in 59,772 seconds; and, a modified version of PBVI described in [17] can find a solution with a value of -6.17 in 1670 seconds with 280 vectors. BBSLS attains similar or better performance faster than PBVI and BPI, and with many fewer nodes than any other algorithm. Figure 4 (a) shows results for 10- and 30-node controllers, averaged over 10 trials; Figure 4 (b) plots how the best value found is increasing for a 10-node FSC during a single best trial; it reaches -6.70 after 322 iterations. Average BBSLS performance gives controllers of somewhat better quality than BPI in the same amount of time, but of much smaller size. However, since BPI attempts to optimize policies with respect to all possible belief states, rather than just the initial belief state (like PBVI and BBSLS), this is not too surprising. The more appropriate comparison to PBVI (since both optimize w.r.t. an initial belief state) shows much better performance for BBSLS in terms of "controller size," and comparable performance in terms of policy quality. With respect to execution time, BBSLS is competitive with the PBVI, but modified PBVI finds high quality policies significantly faster. However, the BBSLS controllers are an order of magnitude smaller than the "controller" found by modified PBVI.

## 5 Concluding Remarks

Despite its computational attractiveness, GA for FSC search suffers from problems when faced with genuinely "sequential" POMDPs. Our BBSLS algorithm is designed to retain many of the computational properties of GA by remaining within the local search framework, but uses DP-style reasoning heuristically to explore a more appropriate controller neighborhood. Our experiments demonstrate that BBSLS consistently outperforms GA, and is superior in many respects to DP-based algorithms, such as PBVI and BPI, on recent benchmark problems.

There are a number of important directions we are currently pursuing. Refining our heuristics to enable further scaling is key among these. In addition, we are exploring methods that will allow BBSLS to be applied directly to factored POMDP representation (e.g., dynamic Bayes nets) so problems with exponentially larger state spaces can be tackled. Finally, we are investigating the use of BBSLS in practical preference elicitation problems, where continuous state,

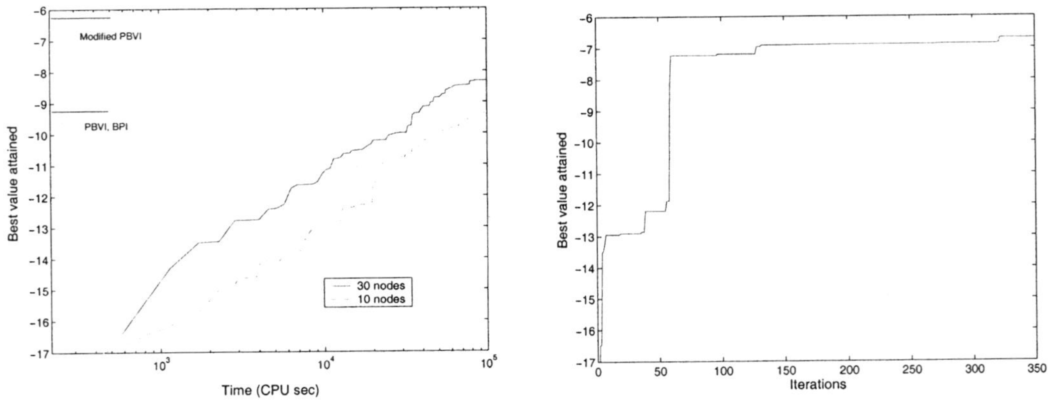


Figure 4: (a) Value vs. time for 10- and 30-node FSCs in Tag domain; (b) A specific trial, 10-node FSC.

action, and observation spaces present challenges to value-based POMDP solution methods.

## Acknowledgements

This research was supported by the Natural Sciences and Engineering Research Council (NSERC) and the Institute for Robotics and Intelligent Systems (IRIS). Thanks to Pascal Poupart for valuable discussions.

## References

[1] Douglas Aberdeen and Jonathan Baxter. Scalable internal-state policy-gradient methods for POMDPs. In *Proc. of ML-02*, pages 3–10, 2002.

[2] Craig Boutilier. A POMDP formulation of preference elicitation problems. In *Proc. of AAAI-2002*, pages 239–246, Edmonton, 2002.

[3] Anthony R. Cassandra. *Exact and Approximate Algorithms for Partially Observable Markov Decision Processes*. PhD thesis, Brown University, Providence, RI, 1998.

[4] Anthony R. Cassandra, Leslie Pack Kaelbling, and Michael L. Littman. Acting optimally in partially observable stochastic domains. In *Proc. of AAAI-94*, pages 1023–1028, Seattle, 1994.

[5] Anthony R. Cassandra, Michael L. Littman, and Nevin L. Zhang. Incremental pruning: A simple, fast, exact method for POMDPs. In *Proc. of UAI-97*, pages 54–61, Providence, RI, 1997.

[6] Hector Geffner and Blai Bonet. Solving large POMDPs by real time dynamic programming. In *Working Notes, Fall AAAI Symposium on POMDPs*, 1998.

[7] Fred Glover. Tabu search–part I. *ORSA Journal on Computing*, 1(3):190–206, 1989.

[8] Eric A. Hansen. Solving POMDPs by searching in policy space. In *Proc. of UAI-98*, pages 211–219, Madison, WI, 1998.

[9] Holger H. Hoos. *Stochastic Local Search—Methods, Models, Applications*. PhD thesis, TU Darmstadt, Darmstadt, Germany, 1998.

[10] Michael L. Littman. Memoryless policies: Theoretical limitations and practical results. In Dave Cliff, Philip Husbands, Jean-Arcady Meyer, and Stewart W. Wilson, editors, *Proceedings of the Third International Conference on Simulation of Adaptive Behavior*, Cambridge, MA, 1994. The MIT Press.

[11] Michael L. Littman, Anthony R. Cassandra, and Leslie Pack Kaelbling. Learning policies for partially observable environments: Scaling up. In *Proc. of ML-95*, pages 362–370, Lake Tahoe, 1995.

[12] Nicolas Meuleau, Kee-Eung Kim, Leslie Pack Kaelbling, and Anthony R. Cassandra. Solving POMDPs by searching the space of finite policies. In *Proc. of UAI-99*, pages 417–426, Stockholm, 1999.

[13] Nicolas Meuleau, Leonid Peshkin, Kee-Eung Kim, and Leslie Pack Kaelbling. Learning finite-state controllers for partially observable environments. In *Proc. of UAI-99*, pages 427–436, Stockholm, 1999.

[14] Joelle Pineau, Geoff Gordon, and Sebastian Thrun. Point-based value iteration: An anytime algorithm for POMDPs. In *Proc. of IJCAI-03*, pages 1025–1030, Acapulco, 2003.

[15] Pascal Poupart and Craig Boutilier. Bounded finite state controllers. In *Advances in Neural Information Processing Systems 16 (NIPS-2003)*, Vancouver, 2003.

[16] Richard D. Smallwood and Edward J. Sondik. The optimal control of partially observable Markov processes over a finite horizon. *Operations Research*, 21:1071–1088, 1973.

[17] Matthijs T. J. Spaan and Nikos Vlassis. A point-based POMDP algorithm for robot planning. In *IEEE International Conference on Robotics and Automation*, New Orleans, 2004. to appear.

[18] Marco Wiering and Juergen Schmidhuber. HQ-learning. *Adaptive Behavior*, 6(2):219–246, 1997.

# A Computational Study of the Kemeny Rule for Preference Aggregation

**Andrew Davenport** and **Jayant Kalagnanam**
IBM T.J.Watson Research Center, Yorktown Heights, New York, 10598
davenport@us.ibm.com, jayant@us.ibm.com

**Abstract**

We consider from a computational perspective the problem of how to aggregate the ranking preferences of a number of alternatives by a number of different voters into a single consensus ranking, following the majority voting rule. Social welfare functions for aggregating preferences in this way have been widely studied since the time of Condorcet (1785). One drawback of majority voting procedures when three or more alternatives are being ranked is the presence of cycles in the majority preference relation. The Kemeny order is a social welfare function which has been designed to tackle the presence of such cycles. However computing a Kemeny order is known to be NP-hard. We develop a greedy heuristic and an exact branch and bound procedure for computing Kemeny orders. We present results of a computational study on these procedures.

## Introduction

Preference aggregation concerns how to combine the preference rankings of a number of alternatives by a number of different voters into a single consensus (or society) ranking. The aggregation of preferences in this way arises in applications such as determining the winners of elections or sports tournaments (Truchon 1998), multi-criteria and word association queries in databases (Dwork et al. 2001), the ranking of suppliers by buyers during strategic sourcing and the combining of search results from multiple search engines in order to fight spam (Dwork et al. 2001).

The properties of social welfare functions for aggregating preferences have been studied by mathematicians since the 18$^{th}$ century, and it is well known that complications and paradoxes can arise when there are more than two alternatives to be ranked. Arrow's impossibility theorem (Arrow 1951) states that no non-dictatorial social welfare function can ever satisfy a set of desirable and compelling properties for fair elections simultaneously on all domains of preferences. The debate on the merits of different types of social welfare functions is still ongoing (Saari and Valognes 1998), however two classes of ranking methods have been widely studied. Positional methods, such as the Borda count (Borda 1781), assign points to each alternative, depending on how they are ranked by each voter. Candidates are then ordered in the consensus ranking according to the sum of their assigned points. Majority ranking methods determine an outcome in terms of the majority ranking for the alternatives: alternative $x$ is ranked ahead of alternative $y$ in the consensus ranking if more voters prefer $x$ to $y$. Positional methods such as the Borda count, while being very simple to compute, are considered to be highly manipulable and fail to satisfy important properties such as the independence of irrelevant alternatives (changes in individuals' rankings of "irrelevant" alternatives outside of a certain subset should have no impact on the societal ranking of this subset) and the Condorcet criterion (if some alternative is ranked ahead of all other alternatives by an absolute majority of voters, then it should be ranked first in the consensus ranking). Majority ranking methods such as Condorcet methods may be subject to cycles in the majority preference relation when there are more than two alternatives to be ranked, and thus may fail to select any winners at all (this is known as the Condorcet paradox (Condorcet 1785)).

The Kemeny rule (Kemeny 1959) has been proposed as a way of seeking a compromise ranking in the majority vote when there are cycles present in the majority preference relation. The Kemeny rule satsifies the Condorcet criterion and a weaker version of local independence of irrelevant alternatives. However the computational drawback of the Kemeny Rule is that is NP-hard to compute (Cohen, Schapire and Singer 1999; Dwork et al. 2001). This has discouraged the development of exact algorithms for computing Kemeny orders. Instead greedy heuristics (Cohen, Schapire and Singer 1999) or tractable multi-stage methods have been developed that combine both positional and majority voting methods (Black 1958; Dwork et al. 2001). A disadvantage of such approaches is that their theoretical properties are not known, and hence their outcomes can be unpredictable. Furthermore, NP-hardness is a only worst case complexity result which may not reflect the difficulty of solving problems which arise in practice. In the sections which follow we describe new exact and greedy heuristic procedures for computing Kemeny orders, and present results of an initial computational study into solving problems using these procedures.

## Notation

Let $X$ be a set of $m$ alternatives and $N$ be a set of $n$ voters. Each voter $j$ has weak order or ranking $r^j$ of the alternatives in $X$. Each element $r_j^s$ is the rank of voter $j$ of alternative $s$. A ranking with no tie for a rank is an order on $X$, which can be represented as a sequence $(s_1,\ldots,s_n)$ , where $s_i$ is the alternative with rank $i$. A *preference aggregation function* (also known as a social welfare function) maps a set of rankings $R$ (also referred to as a *profile of rankings*) into a single consensus ranking.

For each pair of alternatives $s$ and $t$ ranked by some profile of rankings $R$, we define $v_{st}$ as the number of voters expressing a preference for $s$ over $t$ in their individual rankings, that is $v_{st}(R) = | j \in N : r_s^j < r_t^j |$. If $v_{st} > v_{ts}$ we refer to $s > t$ as the *majority vote* and $t > s$ as the *minority vote* for $s$ and $t$. We represent a profile of rankings $R$ by a weighted, directed graph we call the *preference graph*. Each alternative in $X$ is represented by a node in the graph. Between each pair of nodes representing alternatives $s$ and $t$ is an edge of weight $v_{st}$.

We represent the strict majority relation by a simple, directed, weighted graph called the *strict majority graph*, which we also refer to more simply as the majority graph. There is an edge between each pair of nodes representing alternatives $s$ and $t$ iff $v_{st} > v_{ts}$. The weight of such an edge is $v_{st} - v_{ts}$. The weak majority relation is represented by the *weak majority graph*, which has an edge between each pair of nodes representing alternatives $s$ and $t$ iff $v_{st} \geq v_{ts}$. The weight of such an edge is $v_{st} - v_{ts}$.

## Majority voting and the Condorcet criterion

The *Condorcet criterion* (Condorcet 1785) states that if some alternative is ranked ahead of all other alternatives by an absolute majority of voters, then it should be ranked first in the consensus ranking. When such an alternative exists, it is called the *Condorcet winner*.

**Example 1:** *Consider the preferences expressed by the profile (A,B,C), (A,C,B), (B,A,C) (e.g. the 1[st] voter prefers A to B to C, the 2[nd] voter prefers A to C to B, the 3[rd] voter prefers B to A to C). The preferences for each of the pairwise rankings are:* $v_{AB}=2, v_{BA}=1, v_{BC}=2, v_{CB}=1, v_{AC}=3, v_{CA}=0$. *We have a majority of 1 vote for A > B, a majority of 1 vote for B > C and a majority of 3 votes for A > C.*

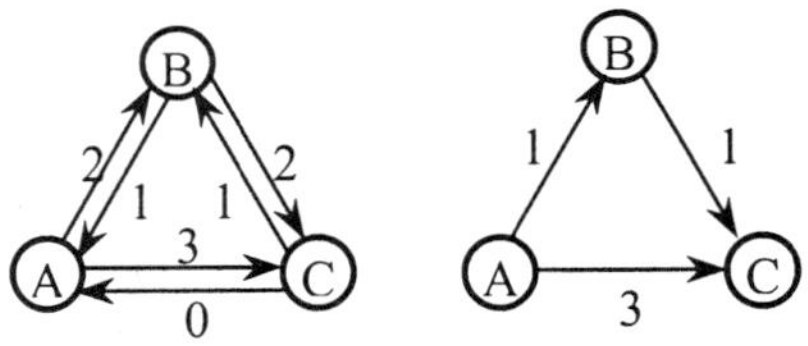


Figure 1: The preference graph (left) and majority graph (right) of the profile of Example 1

In Example 1 alternative $A$ is the Condorcet winner. Note that when there is a Condorcet winner, it can be found by identifying the node in the weak majority graph with an indegree of zero. However, there may not always be a Condorcet winner, as cycles may occur in the majority ranking of alternatives.

**Example 2:** *Consider the profile of rankings (A,B,C), (B,C,A), (C,A,B). There is a majority of 1 vote for A > B, a majority of 1 vote for B > C and a majority of 1 vote for C > A. This profile defines a cycle in the majority relation of A > B, B > C, C > A.*

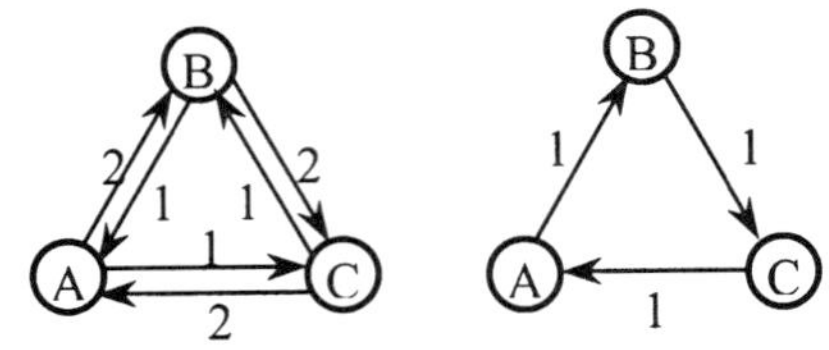


Figure 2: The preference graph (left) and majority graph (right) for the profile of Example 2

Cycles do occur in practice, even for quite small problems. For example, in a study of Olympic figure skating contests, cycles were found in competitions involving 9 out of 23 skaters (Truchon 1998). When cycles are present in the majority relation, the *extended Condorcet criterion* (Truchon 1998) gives a partial ordering of alternatives (with no cycles it gives a complete ordering). The extended Condorcet criterion states that if there is a partition $X_C$, $X_D$ of $X$ such that for any $s$ in $C$ and any $t$ in $D$ if the majority prefers $s$ to $t$ ($v_{st} > v_{ts}$) then $s$ must be ranked ahead of $t$ in the consensus ranking. One application of the Condorcet and extended Condorcet criteria is in fighting ``spam" in individual rankings (Dwork *et al.* 2001). However it has been shown that no positional method for aggregating preferences can ever satisfy either of these criteria (Young 1974).

Given some partial or complete consensus ranking of a profile of rankings $R$, we can enforce the extended Condorcet criterion on the ranking in the following way[1]:

**Algorithm 1:**

1. Identify all the maximal strongly connected components in the majority graph of $R$. Each strongly connected component of size > 1 node identifies a set of nodes which are involved in at least 1 cycle.
2. For each node $n$ in each component, consider all target nodes $m$ on all outgoing edges of $n$. If $m$ is not in the same component as $n$, add to the consensus ranking the ordering $s > t$, where $s$ is the alternative represented by node $n$ and $t$ is the alternative represented by node $m$.

Alternatives represented by nodes within non-trivial strongly connected components of the majority graph are involved in cycles, and will not be ordered by Algorithm 1. Kemeny (Kemeny 1959) proposed a way of breaking such cycles, using a notion of distance for orders. Given a total order $r$, a weak order $r^j$ and 2 alternatives $s$ and $t$, we define:

$$\delta_{st}(r, r^j) = \begin{cases} 1 & \text{if } r_s < r_t \text{ and } r_t^j \leq r_s^j \\ 0 & \text{otherwise} \end{cases}$$

and

$$\Delta(r, r^j) = \sum_{s \in X} \sum_{t \in X} \delta_{st}(r, r^j)$$

[1] A similar scheme is presented in (Cohen, Schapire and Singer 1999) and in (Dwork et al. 2001).

The value of $\delta_{st}(r, r^j)$ indicates whether there is a disagreement in the relative ranking of $s$ and $t$ between $r$ and $r^j$. $\Delta(r, r^j)$ measures the total number of disagreements between $r$ and $r^j$, and is referred to as the *Kendall tau distance* (Diaconis 1988). For complete orders, the Kendall tau distance is the ``bubble sort" distance: it gives the number of pairwise adjacent transpositions to transform one order into another. The distance between a complete order $r$ and a profile of rankings $R$ is given by $d(r, R) = \sum_{j=1..n} \Delta(r, r^j)$. A *Kemeny order* for a profile $R$ is an order $r$ which minimizes the distance $d(r, R)$ , i.e. an order which has the minimum number of disagreements with the pairwise rankings in the profile $R$. It has been shown that any Kemeny order satisfies the extended Condorcet criterion (Truchon 1998).

## Algorithm design

### Problem formulation

Given a (weak) majority graph $G_R$ of a profile of rankings $R$, we wish to compute a total order of the alternatives in $R$ taking into account as many of the majority preferences expressed by the edges in $G_R$ as possible. If $G_R$ is acyclic, a topological sort of the nodes in the graph will identify a Kemeny order of the alternatives. When $G_R$ contains cycles, it becomes necessary to remove some set of edges from $G_R$ such that the resulting graph is acyclic. To find a Kemeny order, the sum of the weights of the edges removed from the graph must be minimized. This problem is known as the minimum weight feedback edge set problem (Festa, Pardalos, and Resende 1999), and is known to be NP-hard. Feedback set problems have received considerable attention in recent years (Festa, Pardalos, and Resende 1999), especially with respect to approximation algorithms and tractable cases. However, as far as we are aware, there has been no work on exact approaches for finding optimal solutions to the weighted variant of the feedback edge set problem in directed graphs. In the sections which follow, we outline a new greedy heuristic and exact branch and bound approach for finding Kemeny orders, based on formulating the problem as minimum weight feedback edge set problem.

### Solution representation

We use a *solution graph* to represent orderings of alternatives that are established during a search procedure when constructing a Kemeny order. Each alternative in the set $X$ is represented by a node in the solution graph. A directed edge between a pair of nodes representing alteratives $s$ and $t$ indicates that in the solution $s$ is ranked ahead of $t$. A solution graph which is simple, directed, acyclic and where all nodes have degree of $|X|-1$ represents a complete ordering of the alternatives in $X$. The goal of the search procedure is to construct a solution graph representing a complete ordering which is a Kemeny order. A complete ordering can be obtained from the solution graph by performing a topological sort of the nodes in the graph.

We often want to compute a majority graph which takes into account the orderings that have been made in a solution graph, even if some of these orderings correspond to minority votes. Thus all edges in the solution graph have corresponding edges in the majority graph representing the same orderings, regardless of the majority votes for these alternatives. In the case where an edge in the solution graph corresponds to an ordering with a minority vote, the reverse edge in the direction of the majority vote will not be present in this modified majority graph.

### Greedy heuristic and branch and bound search

We have developed a simple greedy heuristic and an exact depth-first branch and bound procedure for computing Kemeny orders, based on constructing a solution by identifying orderings of pairs of alternatives and adding the corresponding edges to the solution graph. We use the following heuristic to select and order a pair of alternatives at each node of the search in both of these approaches: select the pair of alternatives which has the greatest difference between the majority and the minority vote for the different pairwise orderings and order the alternatives following the majority vote.

The greedy procedure simply follows this heuristic and applies propagation rules after each ordering is made, terminating when the solution graph represents a complete order. The branch and bound procedure performs a depth-first backtracking search, following the heuristic at each node and applying lower bounding procedures in addition to the propagation rules to prune the search. In the sections which follow we discuss the propagation rules and lower bounding techniques.

### Propagation

A solution is built up incrementally by adding edges to the solution graph. In order to ensure that the solution graph remains acyclic we maintain transitive closure of the graph after edges are added or deleted. Since the graph is directed and acyclic, we can use an efficient incremental algorithm that maintains transitive closure in time $O(n^2)$ for $n$ nodes in the graph.

The first step for both approaches is to run Algorithm 1 to satisfy the extended Condorcet criterion of the ordering. If there are no cycles in the majority graph, this step is sufficient to identify a Kemeny order. Otherwise, as edges are added to the solution graph during search, cycles may be broken in the majority graph that takes into account solution graph orderings (and new cycles may be created). We run Algorithm 1 as a propagation step on this majority graph. If there are new strongly connected components in the majority graph as a result of edges added to the solution graph, further orderings of alternatives may be added to the solution. Applying this propagation step every time an edge is added to the solution graph ensures that we only ever branch on orderings that are involved in some cycle in the majority graph associated with some solution graph.

### Lower bounding

A simple lower bound $LB_1$ on the Kemeny distance of a Kemeny order is the sum of the minority votes for every pair of alternatives:

$$LB_1 = \sum_{\forall s \in X} \sum_{\forall t \in X, s \neq t} \min(v_{st}, v_{ts})$$

This bound will be equal to the Kemeny distance of the Kemeny order when there are no cycles in the majority graph: in this case we can follow the majority vote in the Kemeny order for the ranking of all pairs of alternatives. When there are cycles, the bound can be strengthened during search by taking into account the orderings of the pairs of alternatives that have been fixed by the search procedure.

A stronger lower bound can be computed by determining a set of edge disjoint cycles in each strongly connected component of the majority graph (associated with some solution graph). Each edge disjoint cycle contains at least one edge representing a majority vote between a pair of alternatives which the Kemeny order must disagree with. The impact of disagreeing with the majority vote on the distance of the Kemeny order for some pair of alternatives $s$ and $t$ is $v_{st} - v_{ts}$, which is the weight of the edge between the nodes corresponding to the pair of alternatives in the majority graph. We can add, for each edge disjoint cycle, the minimum positive weight of the edges in the cycle to the bound $LB_1$ to form a stronger lower bound.

We simplify the lower bound computation by considering edge disjoint cycles containing only 3 nodes. This is motivated by the observations that (a) it is harder to compute a Kemeny order for profiles where there are no ties in the rankings between any pairs of alternatives[2] and (b) in a majority graph where there are no ties, there exists an edge between every pair of nodes in every non-trivial strongly connected component. When this is the case then every set of nodes involved in a cycle of length greater than 3 must contain a cycle of exactly length 3 on a subset of these nodes. An illustration of this proposition is given in Figure 3. Consider a cycle of length 4 between nodes $A$, $B$, $C$ and $D$. When there are no ties, there must be an edge in the majority graph between nodes $B$ and $D$. If this edge is directed from node $B$ to $D$ then we have the 3-cycle involving nodes $A$, $B$, $D$ (left, Figure 3). If the edge is oriented the reverse way, we have the 3-cycle involving nodes $B$, $C$, $D$ (middle, Figure 3). Finally, we consider the case where a cycle contains more than 4 nodes. The right graph in Figure 3 shows a cycle involving 5 nodes $A$, $B$, $C$, $D$, $E$. Consider the edge between nodes $A$ and $D$ which is not an edge of the 5-cycle. If this edge is directed from nodes $A$ to $D$ then we have the 3-cycle involving nodes $A$, $D$, $E$. Otherwise, the direction from $D$ to $A$ forms a 4-cycle involving nodes $A$, $B$, $C$, $D$ for which we have shown there must exist a 3-cycle on a subset of these nodes. A similar argument can be used to show that each cycle involving $n$ nodes ($n>3$) must contain a cycle involving either 3 or $n-1$ nodes.

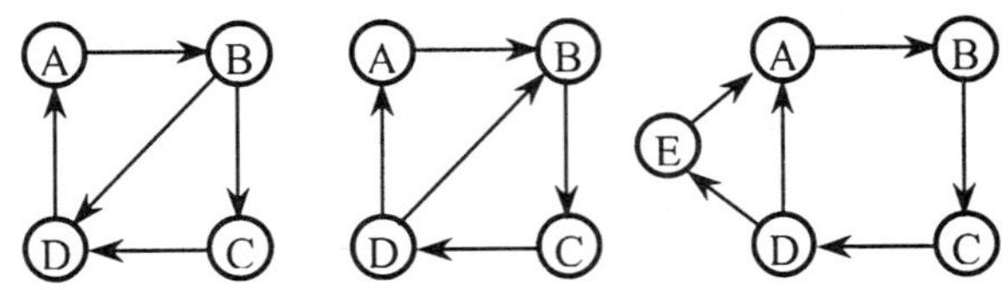


Figure 3: Illustration of 3-cycles in a majority graph.

We formulate the problem of computing edge disjoint 3-cycles in a strongly connected component of the majority graph as an iterative min-cost max-flow problem (Ahuja, Magnanti, and Orlin 1993). An example of the network formulation we use to solve this problem is given in Figure 4 for the majority graph illustrated in the left of Figure 3.

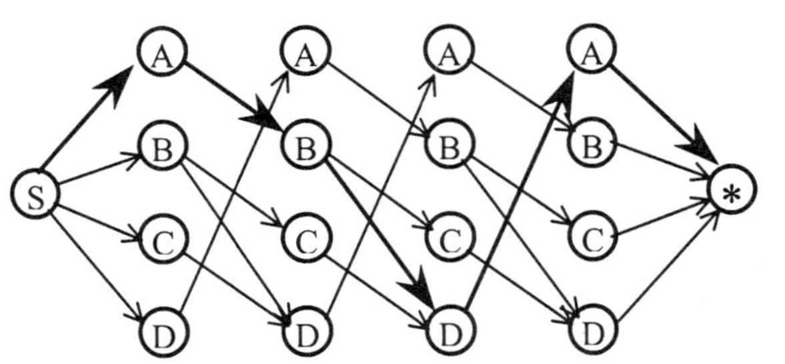


Figure 4: An example network formulation for the majority graph in the left of Figure 3.

The network has four layers of nodes, $l_1,\ldots,l_4$. In each layer there are $|X|$ nodes, where each node corresponds to a node in the majority graph. There is a directed edge between each pair of nodes in layers $l_i$ and $l_{i+1}$ in this network if there is a directed edge between the corresponding pair of nodes in the majority graph. The cost on each edge between the layers is some constant $K$ (e.g. the number of voters) minus the weight between the corresponding pair of nodes in the majority graph (we want to find cycles with the largest possible minimum edge cost in the majority graph). All nodes in layer $l_1$ are connected to the source node and all nodes in layer $l_4$ are connected to the sink node of the network. These connections all have a cost of 1. All minimum edge capacities are set to 0. The maximum capacities of all the edges between nodes in the layers are to set to 1. During each iteration we solve a min-cost max-flow problem to determine a set of paths through the network starting and ending at some common node in layers $l_1$ and $l_4$, representing a starting and ending point for a 3-cycle in the majority graph. For example, the highlighted edges

[2] This situation will always occur when we have an odd number of voters and all voters rank all alternatives.

in Figure 4 illustrate a path of length 3 starting at node $A$ in layer $l_1$ and ending at node $A$ in layer $l_4$. Such a path corresponds to the 3-cycle *(A, B, D, A)* in the majority graph in the left of Figure 3. In each iteration we select and fix the common starting and ending nodes $n_s$ and $n_e$ in layers $l_1$ and $l_4$ (e.g. node $A$ in Figure 4). The maximum number of 3-cycles $max_3$ that can be found from these nodes is the minimum of the out-degree of node $n_s$ and the in-degree of node $n_e$. We set the maximum capacity of the edge from the source node to the node $n_s$ and node $n_e$ to the sink node to $max_3$. We set the maximum capacities of all remaining edges from the source node to the layer $l_1$ nodes to 0. Similarly, we set the maximum capacities of all remaining edges between nodes in layer $l_4$ and the sink node to 0. The solution to the min-cost max-flow problem on this network specifies a set of paths through the network that correspond to a set of 3-cycles in the majority graph starting and ending at the fixed node. The value of the flow is the number of disjoint 3-cycles found in the corresponding majority graph. We determine, for each cycle found by the network flow solution, the lowest cost of all the edges in the cycle and add (the cost constant $K$ minus) this lowest cost to $LB_1$. Enumerating the paths can be achieved by solving multiple shortest path problems, one for each path in the network flow solution. Each shortest path computation can be performed with time complexity $O(n+m)$ for a directed acyclic graph with $n$ nodes and $m$ edges. Finally, at the end of each iteration, we delete all edges from the network which were found in the min-cost max-flow solution, to ensure that a single edge is only assigned to one 3-cycle. We have also observed that the order in which we perform the network flow iterations can have an impact on the number of 3-cycles that are found. For each node in the majority graph we determine the minimum and maximum of their in-degree and out degree. We sort the nodes by decreasing minimum of these degrees, breaking ties by decreasing maximum of these degrees, and perform the network flow iterations in this order.

The time to compute the min-cost max-flow solution of the network dominates the other parts of the procedure. This can be computed in time $O(m \log U(m+n\log n))$ for $n$ nodes of maximum degree $U$ and $m$ edges (Ahuja, Magnanti, and Orlin 1993). Since we may have up to $n$ iterations, the time complexity of this lower bounding procedure is $O(nm \log U(m+n\log n))$.

## Experiments

### Problem generation

We evaluated the algorithms on randomly generated problems. For each problem, we first generated a total order representing a consensus ordering of $m$ alternatives. We then generated a preference graph where each one of $n$ voters agrees with the consensus ordering regarding the ranking of every pair of alternatives with some consensus probability $p$. We generate problems with an odd number of voters, where each voter ranks all alternatives with no ties.

### Results

The first results we present explore the effect of varying the consensus probability and the number of voters on problem solving difficulty[3]. CPU time results for 15 alternatives are presented in Figure 5 (for all experiments, 500 problems are solved at each data point). As we increase the consensus probability, the CPU time required to find a Kemeny order decreases dramatically. When the consensus probability is over 0.7, most problems are solved without any search. Increasing the number of voters also makes problems easier to solve at higher consensus probabilities, but harder to solve at lower probabilities. We do not have an explanation for the phenomena at low probabilities. Figure 6 shows the difference in quality between the solution found by the greedy heuristic procedure and optimal solution found by branch and bound for the same set of problems. As we increase the number of voters and the consensus probability, the greedy heuristic finds better solutions. We have seen similar results for larger problems.

The encouraging aspect of these results is that although finding a Kemeny order can be very difficult for problems with very little consensus, it becomes much easier for problems with a reasonable amount of consensus that we would hope to find in real applications. One question which arises is: what are the range of problems we can solve to optimality by generating solutions with a greedy algorithm and comparing their Kemeny distance to the min-cost max-flow Kemeny distance lower bound? We compare here our greedy heuristic procedure with the greedy heuristic presented in (Cohen, Schapire, and Singer 1999) which has an approximation factor of 2[4]. Figures 7 and 8 present results exploring the deviation between the min-cost max-flow lower bound and the greedy heuristic solutions for finding Kemeny orders for problems with 50 alternatives. For 25 voters, we can prove optimality of most problems with consensus probability greater than 0.7 by comparing the solution of our greedy heuristic procedure with the lower bound. With only 5 voters, this consensus probability increases to around 0.9. The greedy procedure of Cohen et al. does less well at high probabilities, but finds better solutions at low probabilities. We have also seen similar results for problems with different numbers of alternatives.

---

[3] All experiments were run on a 1GHz Pentium III computer using C++ implementations of the algorithms

[4] The problem studied in (Cohen, Schapire, and Singer 1999) also allows voters to express degrees of preferences between alternatives.

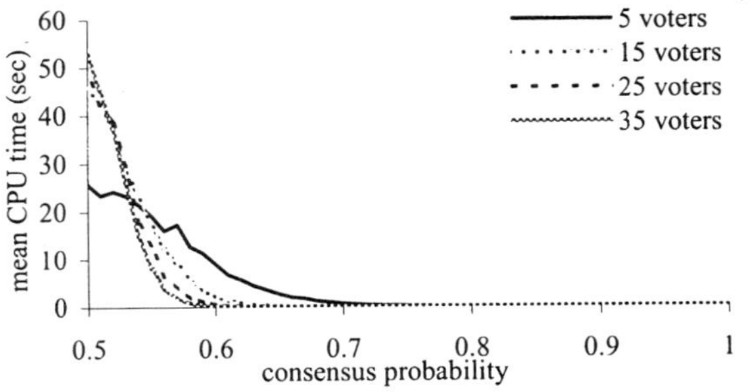


Figure 5: Mean CPU time to find optimal solutions for problems with 15 alternatives, using branch and bound.

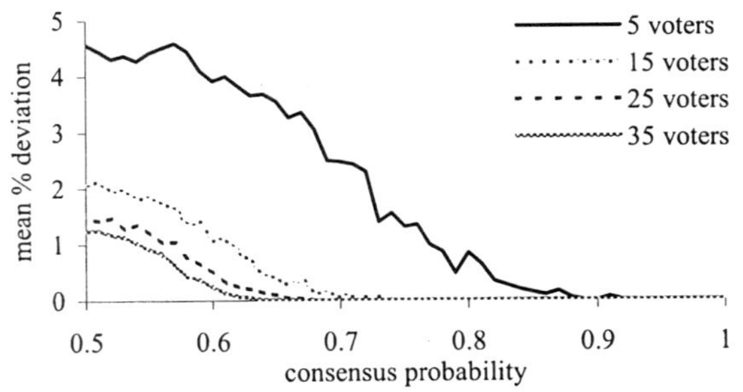


Figure 6: Mean % deviation of greedy heuristic procedure solutions from optimal, 15 alternatives.

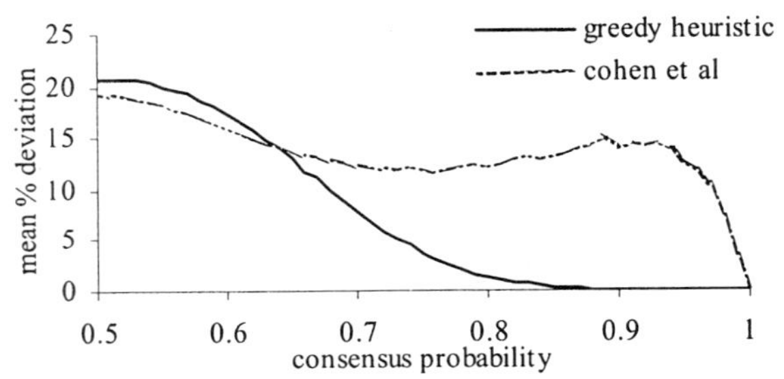


Figure 7: Mean % deviation of greedy solutions from lower bound, 50 alternatives, 5 voters.

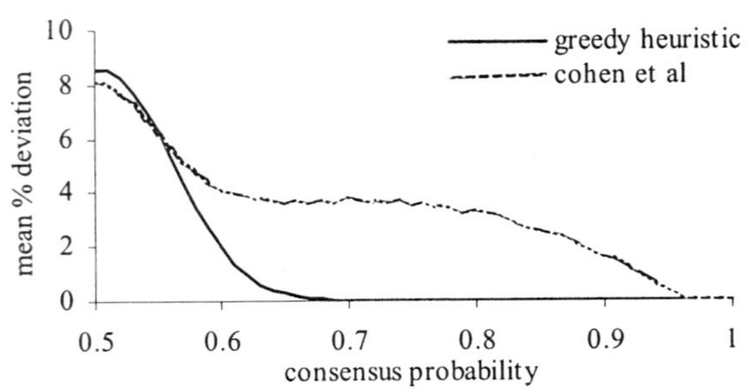


Figure 8: Mean % deviation of greedy solutions from lower bound, 50 alternatives, 25 voters.

## Conclusions

We have presented new exact and heuristic algorithms for aggregating preferences following the Kemeny rule. Results of a computational study indicate that computing Kemeny orders appears to be computationally expensive when there is very little consensus between voters. However we have found that when there is a reasonable degree of consensus, a Kemeny order can be found within a short amount of time. Furthermore, compared to multi-stage techniques that combine both positional and majority voting methods, the Kemeny orders found by these algorithms have well studied theoretical properties. Further research into improving lower bounding techniques may significantly extend the range of problems for which Kemeny orders can be found.

## References


Ahuja, K.; Magnanti, T.; and Orlin, J. 1993. *Network flows.* Prentice Hall.ISBN 0-13-617549-X.

Arrow, K. 1951. *Social Choice and Individual Values.* John Wiley, New York.

Black, D. 1958. *Theory of Committees and Elections.* Cambridge University Press.

Borda. 1781. Mémoire sur les élections au scrutin. In *Histoire de l'Académie Royale des Sciences.*

Cohen, W.; Schapire, R.; and Singer, Y. 1999. Learning to order things. *Journal of Artificial Intelligence Research* 10:213-270.

Condorcet. 1785. Essai sur l'application de l'analyse à la probabilité des décisions rendue à la pluralité des voix. In *Paris: Imprimerie royale.* Also reproduced in Condorcet, Sur les élections et autres textes, edited by O. de Bernon, Fayard, 1986.

Diaconis, P. 1988. *Group representation in probability and statistics.* IMS Lecture Series 11, Institute of Mathematical Statistics.

Dwork, C.; Kumar, R.; Naor, M.; and Sivakumar, D. 2001. Rank aggregation methods for the web. In *Proc. 10th WWW,* 613-622.

Festa, P.; Pardalos, P.; and Resende, M. 1999. Feedback set problems. In *Handbook of Combinatorial Optimization,* vol. 4. Kluwer Academic Publishers.

Kemeny, J. 1959.Mathematics without numbers. *Daedalus* 88:571-591.

Saari, D., and Valognes, F. 1998. Geometry, voting, and paradoxes.*Mathematics Magazine* 71(4):243-259.

Truchon, M. 1998. Figure skating and the theory of social choice. Technical Report Cahier 98-16, Centre de Recherche en Economie et Finance Appliquées, Université Laval, Canada.

Young, H. 1974. An axiomitization of Borda's rule. *Journal of Economic Theory* 9:43-52.

# PROBCONS: Probabilistic Consistency-based Multiple Alignment of Amino Acid Sequences

**Chuong B. Do, Michael Brudno, Serafim Batzoglou**

Department of Computer Science
Stanford University
Stanford, CA 94305
{chuongdo, brudno, serafim}@cs.stanford.edu

**Abstract**

Obtaining an accurate multiple alignment of protein sequences is a difficult computational problem for which many heuristic techniques sacrifice optimality to achieve reasonable running times. The most commonly used heuristic is progressive alignment, which merges sequences into a multiple alignment by pairwise comparisons along the nodes of a guide tree. To improve accuracy, consistency-based methods take advantage of conservation across many sequences to provide a stronger signal for pairwise comparisons. In this paper, we introduce the concept of *probabilistic consistency* for multiple sequence alignments. We also present PROBCONS, an HMM-based protein multiple sequence aligner, based on an approximation of the probabilistic consistency objective function. On the BAliBASE benchmark alignment database, PROBCONS demonstrates a statistically significant improvement in accuracy compared to several leading alignment programs while maintaining practical running times. Source code and program updates are freely available under the GNU Public License at http://probcons.stanford.edu/.

## 1 Introduction

Protein multiple alignments display patterns of sequence conservation by organizing homologous amino acids across different protein sequences in columns (see Figure 1). As sequence similarity often implies functional similarity, protein sequence comparisons have been crucial in many bioinformatics applications, including structure prediction (Jones 1999), phylogenetic analysis (Phillips et al. 2000), identification of conserved domains (Attwood 2002), and characterization of protein families (Sonnhammer et al. 1998). However, when the proportion of identities among amino acid matches falls below 30%, called the 'twilight zone' of protein alignments, the accuracies of most automatic sequence alignment methods drop considerably (Rost 1999, Thompson et al. 1999b). As a result, alignment quality is often the limiting factor in comparative modeling studies (Jaroszewski et al. 2002).

Progressive alignment approaches, which assemble complete multiple alignments by successive hierarchical pairwise steps, are commonly used for reasons of algorithmic efficiency (Feng and Doolittle 1987). Unfortunately, such strategies are highly prone to errors at early stages of the alignment. To combat this, consistency-based alignment techniques use shared homology with outgroup sequences to distinguish between evolutionary and coincidental sequence similarity, thus improving the quality of pairwise comparisons (Gotoh 1990, Morgenstern et al. 1998, Notredame et al. 2000).

```
---NAYCDEECKKG---AESGKCWY
-YDNAYCDKLCKDK--KADSGYCYW
-TAAGYCNTECTLK--KGSSGYCAW
LGKNDYCNRECRMKHRGGSYGYCYG
--GNEGCNKECKSY--GGSYGYCWT
```

Figure 1: A five-sequence multiple alignment example.

In this paper, we present PROBCONS, a protein multiple alignment tool that performs consistency-based progressive alignment while accounting for all suboptimal alignments with posterior-probability–based scoring. Other features of the program include the use of double affine insertion penalties, guide tree calculation via semi-probabilistic hierarchical clustering, optional iterative refinement, and unsupervised Expectation-Maximization (EM) training of gap parameters. On the BAliBASE (Thompson et al. 1999a) reference dataset, PROBCONS gives statistically significant improvements in alignment quality when compared to several leading alignment tools, including CLUSTALW (Thompson et al. 1994), DIALIGN (Morgenstern et al. 1998), and T-Coffee (Notredame et al. 2000), while maintaining comparable running times. Source code and updates for our system are publicly available under the GNU Public License at http://probcons.stanford.edu/.

### 1.1 Pair-HMMs and alignment

Given two sequences $x = x_1 \ldots x_{|x|}$ and $y = y_1 \ldots y_{|y|}$, a pairwise alignment indicates positions of each sequence that are considered to be functionally or evolutionarily related. Traditional edit-distance–based methods score an alignment as the sum of similarity values for aligned residues and length-dependent gap penalties for unaligned positions (Needleman and Wunsch 1970, Smith and

Waterman 1981). The similarity of specific residue pairs may be quantified with log-odds scores (Henikoff and Henikoff 1992), and affine gap parameters are generally estimated empirically (Vingron and Waterman 1994). For two sequences of length $L$, an optimal alignment may be computed in $O(L^2)$ time (Gotoh 1982) and $O(L)$ space (Myers and Miller 1988) via dynamic programming.

Pair hidden Markov models (HMMs) provide a natural probabilistic interpretation of alignment as a stochastic process in which two sequences are jointly generated according to a first-order Markov process. Typical pair-HMMs for alignment contain three states, including one match state that emits letters from $x$ and $y$ simultaneously according to a joint distribution for residue pairs, and two insert states that emit letters from one sequence at a time (Allison et al. 1992). A sequence of states that generates $x$ and $y$ corresponds uniquely to an alignment. Finally, the highest probability alignment can be computed with the Viterbi algorithm (Durbin et al. 1998).

Modeling an alignment as a pair-HMM confers several advantages. The alignment parameters obtain an intuitive probabilistic interpretation and can be trained using standard supervised or unsupervised maximum likelihood methods. Pair-HMMs, moreover, allow one to compute the *posterior probability*, $P(x_i \sim y_j \mid x, y)$, that particular positions $x_i$ and $y_j$ of the two sequences $x$ and $y$, respectively, will be matched in the final alignment.

### 1.2 Consistency-based alignment

Scoring a multiple alignment in a probabilistically rigorous and biologically motivated manner, and finding the optimal alignment once a scoring scheme has been specified, are not straightforward tasks. In practice, the ad hoc sum-of-pairs measure, which combines the projected pairwise scores for aligning all pairs of sequences (Carrillo and Lipman 1988), and its weighted variants (Altschul et al. 1989) are commonly used for scoring. Direct application of dynamic programming is too inefficient in the multiple sequence case, so many heuristic strategies use progressive alignment based on an evolutionary tree (Feng and Doolittle 1987), or iterative approaches including genetic algorithms (Notredame and Higgins 1996), simulated annealing (Kim et al. 1994), alignment to a profile HMM (Eddy 1995), or greedy assemblage of multiple segment-to-segment comparisons (Morgenstern et al. 1996). Progressive methods such as CLUSTALW are the most popular but are prone to errors in early stages of alignment. To combat this, post-processing steps such as iterative refinement (Gotoh 1996) may be applied.

Consistency-based schemes take the alternative view that "prevention is the best medicine." Note that for any multiple alignment, the induced pairwise alignments are necessarily consistent—i.e., given a multiple alignment of $x$, $y$, and $z$, if position $x_i$ aligns with position $z_k$ and position $z_k$ aligns with $y_j$ in the projected $x$-$z$ and $z$-$y$ alignments, then $x_i$ must align with $y_j$ in the projected $x$-$y$ alignment. Consistency-based techniques apply this principle in reverse, using alignments to intermediate sequences as evidence to guide the pairwise alignment of $x$ and $y$.

Gotoh (1990) first introduced consistency to identify anchor points for reducing the search space of a multiple alignment. A mathematically elegant reformulation of consistency in terms of boolean matrix multiplication was later given by Vingron and Argos (1991) and implemented in the program MALI, which builds multiple alignments from dot matrices (Vingron and Argos 1989). An alternative formulation of consistency was employed in the DIALIGN tool, which finds ungapped local alignments via segment-to-segment comparisons, determines new weights for these alignments using consistency, and assembles them into a multiple alignment by a greedy selection procedure (Morgenstern et al. 1996).

More recently, Notredame et al. (1998), introduced COFFEE, a new consistency-based objective function for scoring residue pairs in a pairwise alignment. In this approach, an alignment library is computed by merging consistent CLUSTALW global and LALIGN (Huang and Miller 1991) local pairwise alignments to form three-way alignments, which are assigned weights by percent identity. The score for aligning $x_i$ to $y_j$ is calculated by summing the weights of all alignments in the library containing that aligned residue pair. The program T-Coffee, which implements this objective function using progressive alignment based on pairwise maximum weight trace computations (Kececioglu 1993), has demonstrated superior accuracy on the BAliBASE test suite over competing methods, including CLUSTALW, DIALIGN, and PRRP (Gotoh 1996).

## 2 Computing pairwise alignments

To score an alignment between two sequences by using evidence from a third sequence, existing consistency-based methods rely on various heuristics for weighting consistency-derived information. DIALIGN uses the weight of the overlap shared between two consistent diagonals as a measure of consistency strength; T-Coffee uses alignment percent identity to determine weights for each residue pairing from two consistent alignments. No existing consistency-based alignment methods, however, use pair-HMM posterior probabilities, which give a per-position measure of alignment reliability that takes into account the effect of *all possible suboptimal alignments*. The combination of consistency and posterior-derived weights is the basis for probabilistic consistency.

In this section, we introduce the concept of probabilistic consistency with respect to calculation of two sequence alignments and describe an exact $O(L^3)$ method for computing an objective function based on this concept using triple-HMMs, where $L$ is the total length of the input sequences. As this method is computationally expensive in practice, we present an efficient $O(L^2)$ approximation of our objective function. In Section 3, we extend this approximation to the calculation of multiple alignments.

### 2.1 Definitions

As before, let $x$ and $y$ be two proteins represented as character strings in which $x_i$ is the $i$th amino acid of $x$. Given a pair-HMM, $M$, such as the one described in Section 1.1, each possible sequence of states for generating the sequences $x$ and $y$ corresponds to a *pairwise global alignment*. For an alignment $a$ of $x$ and $y$, we say $(i, j) \in a$ if positions $x_i$ and $y_j$ are aligned to each other in $a$.

Let $A_{x,y}$ denote the set of all possible pairwise global alignments of two sequences $x$ and $y$, and let $P(A_{x,y})$ be a probability distribution over all possible alignments, as specified by $M$. We denote the correct or true alignment of $x$ and $y$ (in an evolutionary or functional sense) as $a^*$. In the algorithms which follow, we assume that such an alignment $a^*$ exists and that $a^*$ was drawn from the distribution $P(A_{x,y})$.

Most alignment schemes build an "optimal" pairwise alignment by finding the highest probability alignment using the Viterbi algorithm. The resulting alignment reflects a global maximum of the probability distribution $P(A_{x,y})$ and may be highly sensitive to the exact parameters used in computing the alignment. In this work, we explore an alternative strategy that maximizes not the probability of an alignment but rather its *accuracy*, defined as

$$accuracy(a) = \frac{\sum_{(i,j)\in a} 1\{(i,j) \in a^*\}}{\min\{|x|,|y|\}},$$

where the indicator notation $1\{condition\}$ is equal to 1 if *condition* is true and 0 otherwise.

In general, however, $a^*$ is not known, so we instead maximize the expected accuracy of the reported alignment. To do this, we define the *posterior probability* of a match between $x_i$ and $y_j$ occurring in the true alignment as

$$P(x_i \sim y_j \mid x, y) = \sum_{a \in A_{x,y}} P(a) 1\{(i,j) \in a\}.$$

Note that under the assumption that the true alignment $a^*$ is drawn from the distribution $P(A_{x,y})$, the posterior probability may be considered the expectation value that a particular residue pairing is correct.

**Theorem 2.1**: *The expected accuracy of an alignment may be computed as*

$$E\{accuracy(a)\} = \frac{\sum_{(i,j)\in a} P(x_i \sim y_j \mid x, y)}{\min\{|x|,|y|\}}.$$

The proof of the theorem follows easily by applying linearity of expectations to the definition of accuracy.

We note that in many applications of HMMs, Viterbi is a superior choice to maximizing expected accuracy, because the resulting parse from the latter approach may fail to respect the relationships between highly correlated states in the HMM topology. In such a case, the highest expected accuracy parse will optimize local accuracy while creating a globally inconsistent parse. In the case of alignment, however, this is not the case as dependencies between states are not as prevalent; thus, per-position accuracy is a reasonable quantity to maximize.

### 2.2 Probabilistic consistency

In the process described above, computing the optimal expected accuracy involves finding the alignment for which the sum of the $P(x_i \sim y_j \mid x, y)$'s is maximal. Intuitively, the $P(x_i \sim y_j \mid x, y)$'s provide a quality score for determining the desirability of various position matches.

When a third homologous sequence $z$ is available, however, consistency provides a means for obtaining a better estimate for the quality of aligning $x_i$ and $y_j$. Given $P(A_{x,y,z})$, a joint distribution over all three sequence alignments of sequences $x$, $y$, and $z$, rather than using $P(x_i \sim y_j \mid x, y)$ values as quality scores, one may use the marginalized probabilities $P(x_i \sim y_j \mid x, y, z)$. We refer to the re-estimation of pairwise alignment probabilities based on three-sequence information as *probabilistic consistency*.

Note that the above computation may performed using a three-sequence HMM, for which evaluating posterior probabilities involves an $O(L^3)$ calculation using the forward and backward algorithms. For most sequences, however, a cubic running time is unacceptable. Thus, we employ the following heuristic "factorization":

$$P(x_i \sim y_j \mid x, y, z) \approx \sum_k P(x_i \sim z_k \mid x, z) P(z_k \sim y_j \mid z, y).$$

Admittedly, the independence assumptions required for such a transformation are in principle unjustified and do not account for alignments of $x_i$ and $y_j$ to gaps in $z$. Nevertheless, the transformation works well in practice, as seen in Section 4. From a computational perspective, the running time is reduced to approximately $O(L^2)$—normally, a position $x_i$ will align to only a few positions $z_k$, so the $P(x_i \sim z_k \mid x, z)$ values may be represented as a sparse matrix (and similarly for $P(z_k \sim y_j \mid z, y)$); thus, computing each $P(x_i \sim y_j \mid x, y, z)$ takes approximately constant time.

## 3 Computing multiple alignments

Thus far, we have described how to use pair-HMM–derived posterior probabilities to compute pairwise alignments of two sequences that maximize expected accuracy. Furthermore, we have introduced a heuristic approximation for obtaining consistency-based quality scores for aligning particular residue pairs when a third homologous sequence is present. In this section, we extend the pairwise alignment model to multiple alignment under a progressive scheme.

### 3.1 Progressive alignment

In the pairwise alignment case, an optimal expected accuracy alignment is calculated by applying the maximum weight trace algorithm (Kececioglu 1993) to a matrix consisting of the $P(x_i \sim y_j \mid x, y)$ values; a related scheme is used in the T-Coffee program.

For the multiple sequence case, we rely on a progressive alignment scheme using the guide tree calculated by hierarchical clustering of sequences by the method given in Section 3.2. Initially, progressive alignment proceeds by assigning each sequence to its corresponding leaf in the tree. If a node has exactly two leaves as children, then the sequences assigned to the children are aligned, the alignment is assigned to the node, the leaves are removed, and the process repeats until only a single node remains and all sequences have been aligned.

When aligning groups of sequences, we use a *sum-of-pairs* scheme in which the score of a multiple alignment is given by summing the expected accuracy for each possible projection of the multiple alignment to two sequences. Thus, we can find the optimal expected accuracy alignment of a group of sequences by a straightforward extension of the pairwise dynamic programming computation.

### 3.2 Guide tree calculation

Guide trees are computed in a greedy hierarchical manner. Given a set $S$ of sequences to be aligned, we denote the expected accuracy for aligning two sequences $x$ and $y$ as $E(x, y)$. Initially, each sequence is placed in its own cluster. Then, the two clusters $x$ and $y$ with the highest expected accuracy are merged to form a new cluster $xy$; we then define the expected accuracy of aligning $xy$ with any other cluster $z$ as $E(x, y)(E(x, z) + E(y, z)) / 2$. This process is repeated until only a single cluster remains.

### 3.3 The probabilistic consistency transformation

To align two sequences $x$ and $y$ given a set of multiple sequences, $S$, we would ideally estimate $P(x_i \sim y_j \mid S)$. In practice, we use the following heuristic decomposition:

$$P(x_i \sim y_j \mid S) \leftarrow \frac{1}{|S|} \sum_{z \in S} \sum_{k=1}^{|z|} P(x_i \sim z_k \mid x, z) P(z_k \sim y_j \mid z, y)$$

where we set $P(x_i \sim x_j \mid x)$ to 1 if $i = j$ and 0 otherwise.

In this sense, the approximate probabilistic consistency calculation may be viewed as a transformation that, given a set of all-pairs pairwise posterior probabilities, produces a new set of all-pairs pairwise posterior probabilities that have been adjusted to account for a single intermediate sequence. By *iterated applications* of the transformation, then, we can approximate the effect of accounting for more than one intermediate sequence at a time.

### 3.4 PROBCONS aligner

We implemented PROBCONS, an alignment tool based on the $O(L^2)$ approximate probabilistic consistency technique detailed above. Given sequences $x$ and $y$, the probability distribution over all possible global alignments is specified by a pair-HMM with states for emitting matched pairs of residues ($M$), short insertions in one sequence ($I_1^x$ and $I_1^y$), and long insertions in one sequence ($I_2^x$ and $I_2^y$). The allowed transitions and their associated probabilities are given in Figure 2.

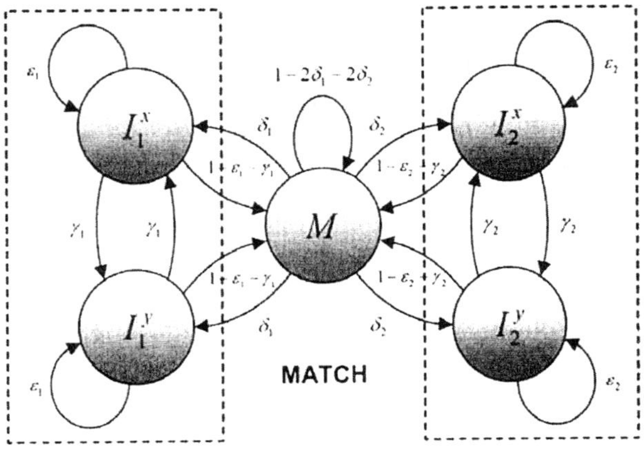


Figure 2: PROBCONS HMM topology. The transition parameters correspond to the probabilities of starting a new insertion ($\delta_1$ and $\delta_2$), continuing an insertion ($\varepsilon_1$ and $\varepsilon_2$), and switching between inserted sequences ($\gamma_1$ and $\gamma_2$). The initial probabilities for starting in a short or long insertion are given by $\pi_1$ and $\pi_2$ (not shown).

PROBCONS begins by computing all-pairs pairwise posterior probabilities, followed by two iterations of the probabilistic consistency transformation. One optional iteration of EM training over the sequences to be aligned is used to generate sequence-specific training parameters before the posteriors are calculated. After computing a guide tree as described above, a multiple alignment is generated using the progressive alignment procedure.

To further improve the quality of this alignment, 100 rounds of *iterative refinement* are applied; in this procedure, sequences of the multiple alignment are randomly partitioned into two groups (where each sequence is placed in the first group with probability 0.5), and the groups are realigned using the probabilistic consistency sum-of-pairs objective function. As the original multiple alignment can always be regenerated, the alignment score is guaranteed not to decrease.

## 4 Evaluation

To test the empirical performance of the PROBCONS aligner, we used the online BAliBASE 2.0 benchmark alignment database, a collection of 141 reference protein alignments consisting of structural alignments from the FSSP (Holm and Sander 1996) and HOMSTRAD (Mizuguchi et al. 1998) databases and hand-constructed alignments from the literature. The database is organized into five reference sets: Reference 1 consists of few equidistant sequences of similar length; Reference 2, families of closely-related sequences with up to three distant "orphan" sequences; Reference 3, equidistant divergent families; Reference 4, sequences with large N/C-terminal extensions; and Reference 5, sequences with large internal insertions.

| Algorithm | Ref 1 (82) SP | CS | Ref 2 (23) SP | CS | Ref 3 (12) SP | CS | Ref 4 (12) SP | CS | Ref 5 (12) SP | CS | Overall (141) SP | CS | Time (mm:ss) |
|---|---|---|---|---|---|---|---|---|---|---|---|---|---|
| CLUSTALW | 86.4 | 78.3 | 88.9 | 40.6 | 75.5 | 46.8 | 81.1 | 50.4 | 86.1 | 63.9 | 85.4 | 65.9 | **1:05** |
| DIALIGN | 81.3 | 71.4 | 85.0 | 27.9 | 68.6 | 34.8 | 91.2 | 81.9 | 94.1 | 84.5 | 82.8 | 63.2 | 3:04 |
| T-Coffee | 86.8 | 77.9 | 88.6 | 38.9 | 78.8 | 49.5 | 91.9 | 74.9 | 96.0 | 90.5 | 87.6 | 69.9 | 24:02 |
| PROBCONS | **90.3** | **83.2** | **91.5** | **48.9** | **85.1** | **63.1** | **95.2** | **85.7** | **98.2** | **92.4** | **91.1** | **76.9** | 8:26 |

Table 1: Comparison of BALIBASE performance for DIALIGN, CLUSTALW, T-Coffee, and PROBCONS. The time required to run on the entire BAliBASE data is reported. The best result in each column is shown in bold.

| Algorithm | CLUSTALW SP | CS | DIALIGN SP | CS | T-Coffee SP | CS | PROBCONS SP | CS |
|---|---|---|---|---|---|---|---|---|
| % unique best alignment | 12.1% | 9.9% | 3.5% | 5.7% | 14.2% | 14.2% | **51.8%** | **46.1%** |
| % best alignment | 19.9% | 21.3% | 13.5% | 19.1% | 30.5% | 34.0% | **68.1%** | **66.7%** |

Table 2: Percentage of alignments in which each method produced the (1) unique best alignment or (2) the best alignment (two or more methods achieved the same highest accuracy). The best results in each row are shown in bold.

| *s* | *c* | *ir* | *em* | Ref 1 (82) SP | CS | Ref 2 (23) SP | CS | Ref 3 (12) SP | CS | Ref 4 (12) SP | CS | Ref 5 (12) SP | CS | Overall (141) SP | CS | Time (mm:ss) |
|---|---|---|---|---|---|---|---|---|---|---|---|---|---|---|---|---|
| 1 | 0 | 0 | 0 | 87.7 | 79.3 | 89.1 | 36.2 | 83.4 | 52.3 | 86.5 | 63.0 | 96.2 | 85.9 | 88.2 | 69.1 | 2:45 |
| 2 | 0 | 0 | 0 | 87.8 | 79.3 | 89.8 | 41.5 | 83.3 | 52.6 | 86.6 | 63.9 | 95.2 | 83.4 | 88.2 | 69.9 | 5:08 |
| 2 | 1 | 0 | 0 | 89.1 | 81.4 | 91.2 | 47.3 | 85.5 | 62.3 | 90.5 | 73.2 | 97.5 | 90.5 | 90.0 | 74.3 | 5:29 |
| 2 | 2 | 0 | 0 | 89.4 | 81.8 | 91.5 | 48.9 | 85.1 | 63.1 | 90.5 | 73.2 | 98.2 | 92.4 | 90.2 | 75.0 | 5:54 |
| 2 | 2 | 100 | 0 | 90.3 | 83.2 | 91.5 | 48.9 | 85.1 | 63.1 | 95.2 | 85.7 | 98.2 | 92.4 | 91.1 | 76.9 | 8:26 |
| 2 | 2 | 100 | 1 | 90.6 | 83.5 | 91.7 | 49.5 | 85.3 | 63.8 | 95.2 | 85.7 | 98.2 | 92.4 | 91.4 | 77.2 | 14:14 |

Table 3: Comparison of BALIBASE performance for PROBCONS variants. The four parameters varied over these runs include: *s*, the number of insertion state pairs in the HMM topology; *c*, the number of consistency transformation applied; *ir*, the number of rounds of iterative refinement via randomized partitioning; and *em*, the number of unsupervised EM iterations used to train sequence-specific parameters for each set before aligning.

BAliBASE *core blocks*, regions for which reliable alignments are known to exist, comprise 58% of all residues in the database. To assess alignment quality, we used the ALN_COMPARE program (Notredame et al. 2000), which scores alignments against a reference according to both the *sum-of-pairs score* (SP), the percentage of aligned core block residue pairs which are also aligned in the reference, and the *column score* (CS), the percentage of aligned columns that are also aligned in the core blocks of the reference.

Emission probabilities for the PROBCONS HMM were estimated from the statistics used in generating the BLOSUM62 scoring matrix (Henikoff and Henikoff 1992). The remaining parameters, consisting of six transition ($\delta_1$, $\varepsilon_1$, $\gamma_1$, $\delta_2$, $\varepsilon_2$, $\gamma_2$) and two initial distribution probabilities ($\pi_1$, $\pi_2$) were obtained via unsupervised EM through two-fold cross validation.

### 4.1 Comparison against existing tools

We compared the results of the PROBCONS aligner to that of CLUSTALW 1.83, DIALIGN 2.2.1, and T-Coffee 1.37; default settings were used for all programs. From the results above (see Tables 1 and 2), PROBCONS shows a clear advantage over the other methods. Applying the Wilcoxon matched-pairs signed-ranks test over all 141 alignments indicated significant improvement over the other three methods (with $p < 10^{-6}$ for both SP and CS measures). In other experiments (results omitted for space reasons), we found no significant difference between the full $O(L^3)$ and the approximate $O(L^2)$ probabilistic consistency alignment procedures.

### 4.2 Comparison of PROBCONS variants

We also ran tests which showed that (1) using two insertion state pairs instead of one, (2) using iterative refinement, and (3) performing EM on each set before aligning to estimate better sequence-specific parameters all gave improvements in alignment quality (see Table 3).

## 5 Discussion

In this paper, we developed a framework for probabilistic consistency of alignments and implemented these ideas in the PROBCONS protein multiple alignment tool. Features of the program include (1) posterior probability scoring to account for suboptimal alignments, (2) the use of two insertion state pairs to model short and long insertions separately, (3) guide tree construction via expected accuracies rather than phylogenetic distance, (4) optimization of alignment expected accuracy rather than probability, (4) iterative refinement via a randomized partitioning strategy, and (5) unsupervised EM training for obtaining parameters. As demonstrated, PROBCONS provides a dramatic improvement in alignment quality over existing methods—achieving the highest scores on the BAliBASE alignment benchmark of any currently known alignment program—while maintaining practical running times. Source code and updates to the program are freely downloadable from http://probcons.stanford.edu/.

The potential applications of probabilistic consistency are not limited to protein alignments. Similar techniques may be used for DNA alignment, motif finding, and RNA structural prediction. In general, methods in which multiple sources of information are decomposed into pairwise relations are potential targets for this technique. We will continue developing these ideas, to unlock the full potential of the probabilistic consistency methodology.

## Acknowledgments

We thank Mahathi Mahabhashyam and Sandhya Kunnatur for help in program development. CBD was partly supported by a Siebel Fellowship. MB was partly supported by an NSF Graduate Fellowship. SB and CBD were supported in part by NSF grant EF-0312459.

## References

Allison, L., Wallace, C.S., Yee, C.N. 1992. Finite-state models in the alignment of macromolecules. *J Mol Evol* 35(1):77-89.

Altschul, S.F., Carroll, R.J., and Lipman, D.J. 1989. Weights for data related by a tree. *J Mol Biol* 207:647-653.

Attwood, T.K. 2002. The PRINTS database: a resource for identification of protein families. *Brief Bioinform* 3(3):252-263.

Carrillo, H. and Lipman, D. 1988. The multiple sequence alignment problem in biology. *SIAM J Appl Math* 48:1073-1082.

Durbin, R., Eddy, S., Krogh, A., and Mitchison, G. 1998. *Biological Sequence Analysis*. Cambridge UP, Cambridge.

Eddy, S.R. 1995. Multiple alignment using hidden Markov models. In *Proc 3rd International Conference on Intelligent Systems in Molecular Biology*, 114-120. Menlo Park, Calif.: AAAI Press.

Feng, D.F., and Doolittle, R.F. 1987. Progressive sequence alignment as a prerequisite to correct phylogenetic trees. *J Mol Evol* 25:351-360.

Gotoh, O. 1982. An improved algorithm for matching biological sequences. *J Mol Biol* 162:705-708.

Gotoh, O. 1990. Consistency of optimal sequence alignments. *Bull Math Biol* 52:509-525.

Gotoh, O. 1996. Significant improvement in accuracy of multiple protein sequence alignments by iterative refinement as assessed by reference to structural alignments. *J Mol Biol* 264:823-838.

Henikoff, S., and Henikoff, J.G. 1992. Amino acid substitution matrices from protein blocks. *Proc Nat Acad Sci USA* 89:10915-10919.

Holm, L., and Sander, C. 1996. Mapping the protein universe. *Science* 273:595-602.

Huang, X., and Miller, W. 1991. A time-efficient, linear space local similarity algorithm. *Adv Appl Math* 12:337-357.

Jaroszewski, L., Li, W., Godzik, A. 2002. In search for more accurate alignments in the twilight zone. *Prot Sci* 11(7):1702-1713.

Jones, D.T. 1999. Protein secondary structure prediction based on position-specific scoring matrices. *J Mol Biol* 292(2):195-202.

Kececioglu, J. 1993. The maximum weight trace problem in multiple sequence alignment. In *Proc 4th Symposium on Combinatorial Pattern Matching*, Springer-Verlag Lecture Notes in Computer Science 684:106-119.

Kim, J., Pramanik, S., and Chung, M.J. 1994. Multiple sequence alignment using simulated annealing. *Comput Appl Biosci* 10(4):419-426.

Mizuguchi, K., Deane, C.M., Blundell, T.L., and Overington, J.P. 1998. HOMSTRAD: a database of protein structure alignments for homologous families. *Prot Sci* 7:2469-2471.

Morgenstern, B., Dress, A., and Werner, T. 1996. Multiple DNA and protein sequence alignment based on segment-to-segment comparison. *Proc Nat Acad Sci USA* 93:12098-12103.

Morgenstern, B., Frech, K., Dress, A., and Werner, T. 1998. DIALIGN: finding local similarities by multiple sequence alignment. *Bioinformatics* 14:290-294.

Myers, E.W. and Miller, W. 1988. Optimal alignments in linear space. *Comput Appl Biosci* 4:11-17.

Needleman, S.B., and Wunsch, C.D. 1970. A general method applicable to the search for similarities in amino acid sequence of two proteins. *J Mol Biol* 48:443-453.

Notredame, C., and Higgins, D.G. 1996. SAGA: sequence alignment by genetic algorithm. *Nucleic Acids Res* 24:1515-1524.

Notredame, C., Higgins, D.G., and Heringa, J. 2000. T-Coffee: a novel method for multiple sequence alignments. *J Mol Biol* 302:205-217.

Notredame, C., Holm, L., and Higgins, D.G. 1998. COFFEE: An objective function for multiple sequence alignments. *Bioinformatics* 14(5):407-422.

Phillips, A., Janies, D., and Wheeler, W. 2000. Multiple sequence alignment in phylogenetic analysis. *Mol Phylogenet Evol* 16(3):317-330.

Rost, B. 1999. Twilight zone of protein sequence alignments. *Protein Eng* 12(2):85-94.

Smith, T.F., and Waterman, M.S. 1981. Identification of common molecular subsequences. *J Mol Biol* 147:195-197.

Sonnhammer, E.L.L., Eddy, S.R., Birney, E., Bateman, A., and Durbin, R. 1998. Pfam: multiple sequence alignments and HMM-profiles of protein domains. *Nucleic Acids Res* 26(1):320-322.

Thompson, J.D., Higgins, D.G., and Gibson, T.J. 1994. CLUSTAL W: improving the sensitivity of progressive multiple sequence alignment through sequence weighting, position-specific gap penalties and weight matrix choice. *Nucleic Acids Res* 22:4673-4680.

Thompson, J.D., Plewniak, F., and Poch, O. 1999a. BAliBASE: a benchmark alignment database for the evaluation of multiple alignment programs. *Bioinformatics* 15(1):87-88.

Thompson, J.D., Plewniak, F., and Poch, O. 1999b. A comprehensive comparison of multiple sequence alignment programs. *Nucleic Acids Res* 27(13):2682-2690.

Vingron, M., and Argos, P. 1991. Motif recognition and alignment for many sequences by comparison of dot matrices. *J Math Biol* 218:34-43.

Vingron, M., and Argos, P. 1989. A fast and sensitive multiple sequence alignment algorithm. *Comput Appl Biosci* 5(2):115-121.

Vingron, M, and Waterman, M.S. 1994. Sequence alignment and penalty choice: review of concepts, case studies and implications. *J Mol Biol* 235:1-12.

# Dynamic Programming for Partially Observable Stochastic Games

**Eric A. Hansen**
Dept. of Computer Science and Engineering
Mississippi State University
Mississippi State, MS 39762
hansen@cse.msstate.edu

**Daniel S. Bernstein and Shlomo Zilberstein**
Department of Computer Science
University of Massachusetts
Amherst, MA 01003
{bern,shlomo}@cs.umass.edu

### Abstract

We develop an exact dynamic programming algorithm for partially observable stochastic games (POSGs). The algorithm is a synthesis of dynamic programming for partially observable Markov decision processes (POMDPs) and iterated elimination of dominated strategies in normal form games. We prove that when applied to finite-horizon POSGs, the algorithm iteratively eliminates very weakly dominated strategies without first forming a normal form representation of the game. For the special case in which agents share the same payoffs, the algorithm can be used to find an optimal solution. We present preliminary empirical results and discuss ways to further exploit POMDP theory in solving POSGs.

## Introduction

The theory of stochastic games provides a foundation for much recent work on multi-agent planning and learning (Littman 1994; Boutilier 1999; Kearns, Mansour, & Singh 2000; Brafman & Tennenholtz 2002; Hu & Wellman 2003). A stochastic game can be viewed as an extension of a Markov decision process (MDP) in which there are multiple agents with possibly conflicting goals, and the joint actions of agents determine state transitions and rewards. Much of the literature on stochastic games assumes that agents have complete information about the state of the game; in this respect, it generalizes work on completely observable MDPs. In fact, exact dynamic programming algorithms for stochastic games closely resemble exact dynamic programming algorithms for completely observable MDPs (Shapley 1953; Filar & Vrieze 1997; Kearns, Mansour, & Singh 2000). Although there is considerable literature on partially observable Markov decision processes (POMDPs), corresponding results for partially observable stochastic games (POSGs) are very sparse, and no exact dynamic programming algorithm for solving POSGs has been previously described.

In this paper, we show how to generalize the dynamic programming approach to solving POMDPs in order to develop a dynamic programming algorithm for POSGs. The difficulty in developing this generalization is that agents can have different beliefs. As a result, it is not possible to solve a POSG by transforming it into a completely observable stochastic game over belief states, analogous to how a POMDP is solved by transforming it into a completely observable MDP over belief states. A different approach is needed. Our approach is related to iterative elimination of dominated strategies in normal form games, which also allows agents to have different beliefs. In fact, our approach can be viewed as a synthesis of dynamic programming for POMDPs and iterated elimination of dominated strategies in normal form games. We define a generalized notion of belief that includes uncertainty about the underlying state and uncertainty about other agent's future plans. This allows us to define a *multi-agent dynamic programming operator*. We show that the resulting dynamic programming algorithm corresponds to a type of iterated elimination of dominated strategies in the normal form representation of finite-horizon POSGs. This is the first dynamic programming algorithm for iterated strategy elimination. For the special case where all agents share the same payoff function, our dynamic programming algorithm can be used to find an optimal solution.

### Related work

A finite-horizon POSG can be viewed as a type of extensive game with imperfect information (Kuhn 1953). Although much work has been done on such games, very little of it is from a computational perspective. This is understandable in light of the negative worst-case complexity results for POSGs (Bernstein *et al.* 2002). A notable exception is reported in (Koller, Megiddo, & von Stengel 1994; Koller & Pfeffer 1997), in which the authors take advantage of the *sequence form* representation of two-player games to find mixed strategy Nash equilibria efficiently. In contrast to their work, ours applies to any number of players. Furthermore, our algorithms are focused on eliminating dominated strategies, and do not make any assumptions about which of the remaining strategies will be played.

For the special case of cooperative games, several algorithms have been proposed. However, previous algorithms do not guarantee optimality in general. If all agents share their private information, a cooperative POSG can be converted to a single-agent POMDP. There are also algorithms for solving cooperative POSGs with other forms of very specialized structure (Hsu & Marcus 1982; Becker *et al.* 2003). For general cooperative POSGs, algorithms such as those of Peshkin et al. (2000) and Nair et al. (2003) can be used, but they are only guaranteed to converge to local optima.

## Background

As background, we review the POSG model and two algorithms that we generalize to create a dynamic programming algorithm for POSGs: dynamic programming for POMDPs and elimination of dominated strategies in solving normal form games.

### Partially observable stochastic games

A *partially observable stochastic game* (POSG) is a tuple $\langle \mathcal{I}, \mathcal{S}, \{b^0\}, \{\mathcal{A}_i\}, \{\mathcal{O}_i\}, \mathcal{P}, \{R_i\} \rangle$, where,

- $\mathcal{I}$ is a finite set of agents (or controllers) indexed $1, \ldots, n$
- $\mathcal{S}$ is a finite set of states
- $b^0 \in \Delta(\mathcal{S})$ represents the initial state distribution
- $\mathcal{A}_i$ is a finite set of actions available to agent $i$ and $\vec{\mathcal{A}} = \times_{i \in \mathcal{I}} \mathcal{A}_i$ is the set of joint actions (i.e., action profiles), where $\vec{a} = \langle a_1, \ldots, a_n \rangle$ denotes a joint action
- $\mathcal{O}_i$ is a finite set of observations for agent $i$ and $\vec{\mathcal{O}} = \times_{i \in \mathcal{I}} \mathcal{O}_i$ is the set of joint observations, where $\vec{o} = \langle o_1, \ldots, o_n \rangle$ denotes a joint observation
- $\mathcal{P}$ is a set of Markovian state transition and observation probabilities, where $\mathcal{P}(s', \vec{o} | s, \vec{a})$ denotes the probability that taking joint action $\vec{a}$ in state $s$ results in a transition to state $s'$ and joint observation $\vec{o}$
- $R_i : \mathcal{S} \times \vec{\mathcal{A}} \to \Re$ is a reward function for agent $i$

A game unfolds over a finite or infinite sequence of stages, where the number of stages is called the *horizon* of the game. In this paper, we consider finite-horizon POSGs; some of the challenges involved in solving the infinite-horizon case are discussed at the end of the paper. At each stage, all agents simultaneously select an action and receive a reward and observation. The objective, for each agent, is to maximize the expected sum of rewards it receives during the game.

Whether agents compete or cooperate in seeking reward depends on their reward functions. The case in which the agents share the same reward function has been called a *decentralized partially observable Markov decision process (DEC-POMDP)* (Bernstein *et al.* 2002).

### Dynamic programming for POMDPs

A POSG with a single agent corresponds to a POMDP. We briefly review an exact dynamic programming algorithm for POMDPs that provides a foundation for our exact dynamic programming algorithm for POSGs. We use the same notation for POMDPs as for POSGs, but omit the subscript that indexes an agent.

The first step in solving a POMDP by dynamic programming (DP) is to convert it into a completely observable MDP with a state set $\mathcal{B} = \Delta(\mathcal{S})$ that consists of all possible beliefs about the current state. Let $b^{a,o}$ denote the belief state that results from belief state $b$, after action $a$ and observation $o$. The DP operator can be written in the form,

$$V^{t+1}(b) = \max_{a \in \mathcal{A}} \underset{s \in \mathcal{S}}{\;} b(s) \; R(s,a) + \underset{o \in \mathcal{O}}{\;} \mathcal{P}(o|s,a) V^t(b^{a,o}) \quad , \tag{1}$$

where $\mathcal{P}(o|s,a) = \sum_{s' \in \mathcal{S}} \mathcal{P}(s', o|s, a)$, and the updated value function is computed for all belief states $b \in \mathcal{B}$. Exact DP algorithms for POMDPs rely on Smallwood and Sondik's (1973) proof that the DP operator preserves the piecewise linearity and convexity of the value function. This means that the value function can be represented exactly by a finite set of $|\mathcal{S}|$-dimensional value vectors, denoted $\mathcal{V} = \{v_1, v_2, \ldots, v_k\}$, where

$$V(b) = \max_{1 \leq j \leq k} \underset{s \in \mathcal{S}}{\;} b(s) v_j(s). \tag{2}$$

As elucidated by Kaelbling et al. (1998), each value vector corresponds to a complete conditional plan that specifies an action for every sequence of observations. Adopting the terminology of game theory, we often refer to a complete conditional plan as a *strategy*. We use this interchangeably with *policy tree*, because a conditional plan for a finite-horizon POMDP can be viewed as a tree.

The DP operator of Equation (1) computes an updated value function, but can also be interpreted as computing an updated set of policy trees. In fact, the simplest algorithm for computing the DP update has two steps, which are described below.

In the first step, the DP operator is given a set $Q^t$ of depth-$t$ policy trees and a corresponding set $\mathcal{V}^t$ of value vectors representing the horizon-$t$ value function. It computes $Q^{t+1}$ and $\mathcal{V}^{t+1}$ in two steps. First, a set of depth $t+1$ policy trees, $Q^{t+1}$, is created by generating every possible depth $t+1$ policy tree that makes a transition, after an action and observation, to the root node of some depth-$t$ policy tree in $Q^t$. This operation will hereafter be called an *exhaustive backup*. Note that $|Q^{t+1}| = |\mathcal{A}||Q^t|^{|\mathcal{O}|}$. For each policy tree $q_j \in Q^{t+1}$, it is straightforward to compute a corresponding value vector, $v_j \in \mathcal{V}^{t+1}$.

The second step is to eliminate policy trees that need not be followed by a decision maker that is maximizing expected value. This is accomplished by eliminating (i.e., pruning) any policy tree when this can be done without decreasing the value of any belief state.

Formally, a policy tree $q_j \in Q_i^{t+1}$ with corresponding value vector $v_j \in \mathcal{V}_i^{t+1}$ is considered dominated if for all $b \in \mathcal{B}$ there exists a $v_k \in \mathcal{V}_i^{t+1} \setminus v_j$ such that $b \cdot v_k \geq b \cdot v_j$. This test for dominance is performed using linear programming. When $q_j$ is removed from the set $Q_i^{t+1}$, its corresponding value vector $v_j$ is also removed from $\mathcal{V}_i^{t+1}$.

The dual of this linear program can also be used as a test for dominance. In this case, a policy tree $q_j$ with corresponding value vector $v_j$ is dominated when there is a probability distribution $p$ over the other policy trees, such that

$$\sum_{k \neq j} p(k) v_k(s) \geq v_j(s), \forall s \in S. \tag{3}$$

This alternative, and equivalent, test for dominance plays a role in iterated strategy elimination, as we will see in the next section, and was recently applied in the context of POMDPs (Poupart & Boutilier 2004).

### Iterated elimination of dominated strategies

Techniques for eliminating dominated strategies in solving a POMDP are very closely related to techniques for eliminating dominated strategies in solving games in normal form. A game in normal form is a tuple $G = \{\mathcal{I}, \{D_i\}, \{V_i\}\}$, where $\mathcal{I}$ is a finite set of agents, $D_i$ is a finite set of strategies available to agent $i$, and $V_i : \vec{D} \rightarrow \Re$ is the value (or payoff) function for agent $i$. Unlike a stochastic game, there are no states or state transitions in this model.

Every strategy $d_i \in D_i$ is a *pure strategy*. Let $\delta_i \in \Delta(D_i)$ denote a *mixed strategy*, that is, a probability distribution over the pure strategies available to agent $i$, where $\delta_i(d_i)$ denotes the probability assigned to strategy $d_i \in D_i$. Let $d_{-i}$ denote a profile of pure strategies for the other agents (i.e., all the agents except agent $i$), and let $\delta_{-i}$ denote a profile of mixed strategies for the other agents. Since agents select strategies simultaneously, $\delta_{-i}$ can also represent agent $i$'s belief about the other agents' likely strategies. If we define $V_i(d_i, \delta_{-i}) = \sum_{d_{-i}} \delta_{-i}(d_{-i}) V_i(d_i, d_{-i})$, then

$$B_i(\delta_{-i}) = \{d_i \in D_i | V_i(d_i, \delta_{-i}) \geq V_i(d'_i, \delta_{-i}) \; \forall d'_i \in D_i\} \quad (4)$$

denotes the *best response function* of agent $i$, which is the set of strategies for agent $i$ that maximize the value of some belief about the strategies of the other agents. Any strategy that is not a best response to some belief can be deleted.

A dominated strategy $d_i$ is identified by using linear programming. The linear program identifies a probability distribution $\sigma_i$ over the other strategies such that

$$V_i(\sigma_i, d_{-i}) > V_i(d_i, d_{-i}), \forall d_{-i} \in D_{-i}. \quad (5)$$

This test for dominance is very similar to the test for dominance used to prune strategies in solving a POMDP. It differs in using strict inequality, which is called *strict dominance*. Game theorists also use *weak dominance* to prune strategies. A strategy $d_i$ is weakly dominated if $V_i(\sigma_i, d_{-i}) \geq V_i(d_i, d_{-i})$ for all $d_{-i} \in D_{-i}$, and $V_i(\sigma_i, d_{-i}) > V_i(d_i, d_{-i})$ for some $d_{-i} \in D_{-i}$. The test for dominance which does not require any strict inequality is sometimes called *very weak dominance*, and corresponds exactly to the test for dominance in POMDPs, as given in Equation (3). Because a strategy that is very weakly dominated but not weakly dominated must be *payoff equivalent* to a strategy that very weakly dominates it, eliminating very weakly dominated strategies may have the same effect as eliminating weakly dominated strategies in the *reduced normal form* representation of a game, where the reduced normal form representation is created by combining any set of payoff-equivalent strategies into a single strategy.

There are a couple other interesting differences between the tests for dominance in Equations (3) and (5). First, there is a difference in beliefs. In normal-form games, beliefs are about the strategies of other agents, whereas in POMDPs, beliefs are about the underlying state. Second, elimination of dominated strategies is iterative when there are multiple agents. When one agent eliminates its dominated strategies, this can affect the best-response function of other agents (assuming common knowledge of rationality). After all agents take a turn in eliminating their dominated strategies, they can consider eliminating additional strategies that may only have been best responses to strategies of other agents that have since been eliminated. The procedure of alternating between agents until no agent can eliminate another strategy is called *iterated elimination of dominated strategies*.

In solving normal-form games, iterated elimination of dominated strategies is a somewhat weak solution concept, in that it does not (usually) identify a specific strategy for an agent to play, but rather a set of possible strategies. To select a specific strategy requires additional reasoning, and introduces the concept of a Nash equilibrium, which is a profile of strategies (possibly mixed), such that $\delta_i \in B_i(\delta_{-i})$ for all agents $i$. Since there are often multiple equilibria, the problem of *equilibrium selection* is important. (It has a more straightforward solution for cooperative games than for general-sum games.) But in this paper, we focus on the issue of elimination of dominated strategies.

## Dynamic programming for POSGs

In the rest of the paper, we develop a dynamic programming algorithm for POSGs that is a synthesis of dynamic programming for POMDPs and iterated elimination of dominated strategies in normal-form games. We begin by introducing the concept of a normal-form game with hidden state, which provides a way of relating the POSG and normal-form representations of a game. We describe a method for eliminating dominated strategies in such games, and then show how to generalize this method in order to develop a dynamic programming algorithm for finite-horizon POSGs.

### Normal-form games with hidden state

Consider a game that takes the form of a tuple $G = \{\mathcal{I}, \mathcal{S}, \{D_i\}, \{V_i\}\}$, where $\mathcal{I}$ is a finite set of agents, $\mathcal{S}$ is a finite set of states, $D_i$ is a finite set of strategies available to agent $i$, and $V_i : \mathcal{S} \times \vec{D} \rightarrow \Re$ is the value (or payoff) function for agent $i$. This definition resembles the definition of a POSG in that the payoff received by each agent is a function of the state of the game, as well as the joint strategies of all agents. But it resembles a normal-form game in that there is no state-transition model. In place of one-step actions and rewards, the payoff function specifies the value of a strategy, which is a complete conditional plan.

In a normal form game with hidden state, we define an agent's belief in a way that synthesizes the definition of belief for POMDPs (a distribution over possible states) and the definition of belief in iterated elimination of dominated strategies (a distribution over the possible strategies of the other agents). For each agent $i$, a belief is defined as a distribution over $\mathcal{S} \times D_{-i}$, where the distribution is denoted $b_i$. The value of a belief of agent $i$ is defined as

$$V_i(b_i) = \max_{d_i \in D_i} \sum_{s \in \mathcal{S}, d_{-i} \in D_{-i}} b_i(s, d_{-i}) V_i(s, d_i, d_{-i}).$$

A strategy $d_i$ for agent $i$ is very weakly dominated if eliminating it does not decrease the value of any belief. The test for very weak dominance is a linear program that determines whether there is a mixed strategy $\sigma_i \in \Delta(D_i \setminus d_i)$ such that

$$V_i(s, \sigma_i, d_{-i}) \geq V_i(s, d_i, d_{-i}), \forall s \in \mathcal{S}, \forall d_{-i} \in D_{-i}. \quad (6)$$

These generalizations of the key concepts of belief, value of belief, and dominance play a central role in our development of a DP algorithm for POSGs in the rest of this paper.

In our definition of a normal form game with hidden state, we do not include an initial state probability distribution. As a result, each strategy profile is associated with an $|\mathcal{S}|$-dimensional vector that can be used to compute the value of this strategy profile for *any* state probability distribution. This differs from a standard normal form game in which each strategy profile is associated with a scalar value. By assuming an initial state probability distribution, we could convert our representation to a standard normal form game in which each strategy profile has a scalar value. But our representation is more in keeping with the approach taken by the DP algorithm for POMDPs, and lends itself more easily to development of a DP algorithm for POSGs. The initial state probability distribution given in the definition of a POMDP is not used by the DP algorithm for POMDPs; it is only used to select a policy after the algorithm finishes. The same holds in the DP algorithm for POSGs we develop. Like the POMDP algorithm, it computes a solution for all possible initial state probability distributions.

## Normal form of finite-horizon POSGs

Disregarding the initial state probability distribution, a finite-horizon POSG can be converted to a normal-form game with hidden state. When the horizon of a POSG is one, the two representations of the game are identical, since a strategy corresponds to a single action, and the payoff functions for the normal-form game correspond to the reward functions of the POSG. When the horizon of a POSG is greater than one, the POSG representation of the game can be converted to a normal form representation with hidden state, by a recursive construction. Given the sets of strategies and the value (or payoff) functions for a horizon $t$ game, the sets of strategies and value functions for the horizon $t+1$ game are constructed by exhaustive backup, as in the case of POMDPs. When a horizon-$t$ POSG is represented in normal form with hidden state, the strategy sets include all depth-$t$ policy trees, and the value function is piecewise linear and convex; each strategy profile is associated with an $|\mathcal{S}|$-vector that represents the expected $t$-step cumulative reward achieved for each potential start state (and so any start state distribution) by following this joint strategy.

If a finite-horizon POSG is represented this way, iterated elimination of dominated strategies can be used in solving the game, after the horizon $t$ normal form game is constructed. The problem is that this representation can be *much* larger than the original representation of a POSG. In fact, the size of the strategy set for each agent $i$ is greater than $|\mathcal{A}_i|^{|\mathcal{O}_i|^t}$, which is doubly exponential in the horizon $t$. Because of the large sizes of the strategy sets, it is usually not feasible to work directly with this representation. The dynamic programming algorithm we develop partially alleviates this problem by performing iterated elimination of dominated strategies at each stage in the construction of the normal form representation, rather than waiting until the construction is finished.

## Multi-agent dynamic programming operator

The key step of our algorithm is a *multi-agent dynamic programming operator* that generalizes the DP operator for POMDPs. As for POMDPs, the operator has two steps. The first is a backup step that creates new policy trees and vectors. The second is a pruning step.

In the backup step, the DP operator is given a set of depth-$t$ policy trees $Q_i^t$ for each agent $i$, and corresponding sets of value vectors $\mathcal{V}_i^t$ of dimension $|\mathcal{S} \times Q_{-i}^t|$.[1] Based on the action transition, observation, and reward model of the POSG, it performs an exhaustive backup on each of the sets of trees, to form $Q_i^{t+1}$ for each agent $i$. It also recursively computes the value vectors in $\mathcal{V}_i^{t+1}$ for each agent $i$. Note that this step corresponds to recursively creating a normal form with hidden state representation of a horizon $t+1$ POSG, given a normal form with hidden state representation of the horizon $t$ POSG.

The second step of the multi-agent DP operator consists of pruning dominated policy trees. As in the single agent case, an agent $i$ policy tree can be pruned if its removal does not decrease the value of any belief for agent $i$. As with normal form games, removal of a policy tree reduces the dimensionality of the other agents' belief space, and it can be repeated until no more policy trees can be pruned from any agent's set. (Note that different agent orderings may lead to different sets of policy trees and value vectors. The question of order dependence in eliminating dominated strategies has been extensively studied in game theory, and we do not consider it here.) Pseudocode for the multi-agent DP operator is given in Table 1.

The validity of the pruning step follows from a version of the optimality principle of dynamic programming, which we prove for a single iteration of the multi-agent DP operator. By induction, it follows for any number of iterations.

**Theorem 1** *Consider a set $Q_i^t$ of depth $t$ policy trees for agent $i$, and consider the set $Q_i^{t+1}$ of depth $t+1$ policy trees created by exhaustive backup, in the first step of the multi-agent DP operator. If any policy tree $q_j \in Q_i^t$ is very weakly dominated, then any policy tree $q' \in Q_i^{t+1}$ that contains $q_j$ as a subtree is also very weakly dominated.*

**Proof:** Consider a very weakly dominated policy tree $q_j \in Q_i^t$. According to the dual formulation of the test for dominance, there exists a distribution $p$ over policy trees in $Q_i^t \backslash q_j$ such that $\sum_{k \neq j} p(k) v_k(s, q_{-i}) \geq v_j(s, q_{-i})$ for all $s \in \mathcal{S}$ and $q_{-i} \in Q_{-i}^k$. (Recall that $v_j \in \mathcal{V}_i^t$ is the value vector corresponding to policy tree $q_j$.) Now consider any policy tree

[1]The value function $V_i^t$ of agent $i$ can be represented as a set $\mathcal{V}_i^t$ of value vectors of dimension $|\mathcal{S} \times Q_{-i}^t|$, with one for each strategy in $Q_i^t$, or as a set of value vectors of dimension $|\mathcal{S}|$, with one for each strategy profile in $Q_i^t \times Q_{-i}^t$. The two representations are equivalent. The latter is more useful in terms of implementation, since it means the size of vectors does not change during iterated elimination of dominated strategies; only the number of vectors changes. (Using this representation, multiple $|\mathcal{S}|$-vectors must be deleted for each strategy deleted.) The former representation is more useful in explaining the algorithm, since it entails a one-to-one correspondence between strategies and value vectors, and so we adopt it in this section.

$q' \in Q_i^{t+1}$ with $q_j$ as a subtree. We can replace instances of $q_j$ in $q'$ with the distribution $p$ to get a *behavioral strategy*, which is a stochastic policy tree. From the test for dominance, it follows that the value of this behavioral strategy is at least as high as that of $q'$, for any distribution over states and strategies of the other agents. Since any behavioral strategy can be represented by a distribution over pure strategies, it follows that $q'$ is very weakly dominated. □

Thus, pruning very weakly dominated strategies from the sets $Q_i^t$ before using the dynamic programming operator is equivalent to performing the dynamic programming operator without first pruning $Q_i^t$. The advantage of first pruning very weakly dominated strategies from the sets $Q_i^t$ is that it improves the efficiency of dynamic programming by reducing the initial size of the sets $Q_i^{t+1}$ generated by exhaustive backup.

It is possible to define a multi-agent DP operator that prunes strongly dominated strategies. However, sometimes a strategy that is not strongly dominated will have a strongly dominated subtree. This is referred to as an *incredible threat* in the literature. Thus it is an open question whether we can define a multi-agent DP operator that prunes only strongly dominated strategies. In this paper, we focus on pruning very weakly dominated strategies. As already noted, this is identical to the form of pruning used for POMDPs.

There is an important difference between this algorithm and the dynamic programming operator for single-agent POMDPs, in terms of implementation. In the single agent case, only the value vectors need to be kept in memory. At execution time, an optimal action can be extracted from the value function using one-step lookahead, at each time step. We do not currently have a way of doing this when there are multiple agents. In the multi-agent case, instead of selecting an action at each time step, each agent must select a policy tree (i.e., a complete strategy) at the beginning of the game. Thus, the policy tree sets must also be remembered. Of course, some memory savings is possible by realizing that the policy trees for an agent share subtrees.

## Solving finite-horizon POSGs

As we have described, any finite-horizon POSG can be given a normal form representation. The process of computing the normal form representation is recursive. Given the definition of a POSG, we successively compute normal form games with hidden state for horizons one, two, and so on, up to horizon $T$. Instead of computing all possible strategies for each horizon, we have defined a multi-agent dynamic programming operator that performs iterated elimination of very weakly dominated strategies at each stage. This improves the efficiency of the algorithm because if a policy tree is pruned by the multi-agent DP operator at one stage, every policy tree containing it as a subtree is effectively eliminated, in the sense that it will not be created at a later stage. We now show that performing iterated elimination of very weakly dominated strategies at each stage in the construction of the normal form game is equivalent to waiting until the final stage to perform iterated elimination of very weakly dominated strategies.

Input: Sets of depth-$t$ policy trees $Q_i^t$ and corresponding value vectors $\mathcal{V}_i^t$ for each agent $i$.

1. Perform exhaustive backups to get $Q_i^{t+1}$ for each $i$.
2. Recursively compute $\mathcal{V}_i^{t+1}$ for each $i$.
3. Repeat until no more pruning is possible:
   (a) Choose an agent $i$, and find a policy tree $q_j \in Q_i^{t+1}$ for which the following condition is satisfied: $\forall b \in \Delta(\mathcal{S} \times Q_{-i}^{t+1}), \exists v_k \in \mathcal{V}_i^{t+1} \backslash v_j$ s.t. $b \cdot v_k \geq b \cdot v_j$.
   (b) $Q_i^{t+1} \leftarrow Q_i^{t+1} \setminus q_j$.
   (c) $\mathcal{V}_i^{t+1} \leftarrow \mathcal{V}_i^{t+1} \setminus v_j$.

Output: Sets of depth-$t+1$ policy trees $Q_i^{t+1}$ and corresponding value vectors $\mathcal{V}_i^{t+1}$ for each agent $i$.

Table 1: The multi-agent dynamic programming operator.

**Theorem 2** *Dynamic programming applied to a finite-horizon POSG corresponds to iterated elimination of very weakly dominated strategies in the normal form of the POSG.*

**Proof:** Let $T$ be the horizon of the POSG. If the initial state distribution of the POSG is not fixed, then the POSG can be thought of as a normal form game with hidden state. Theorem 1 implies that each time a policy tree is pruned by the DP algorithm, every strategy containing it as a subtree is very weakly dominated in this game. And if a strategy is very weakly dominated when the initial state distribution is not fixed, then it is certainly very weakly dominated for a fixed initial state distribution. Thus, the DP algorithm can be viewed as iteratively eliminating very weakly dominated strategies in the POSG.□

In the case of cooperative games, also known as DEC-POMDPs, removing very weakly dominated strategies preserves at least one optimal strategy profile. Thus, the multi-agent DP operator can be used to solve finite-horizon DEC-POMDPs optimally. When the DP algorithm reaches step $T$, we can simply extract the highest-valued strategy profile for the start state distribution.

**Corollary 1** *Dynamic programming applied to a finite-horizon DEC-POMDP yields an optimal strategy profile.*

For general-sum POSGs, the DP algorithm converts the POSG to a normal form representation with reduced sets of strategies in which there are no very weakly dominated strategies. Although selecting an equilibrium presents a challenging problem in the general-sum case, standard techniques for selecting an equilibrium in a normal form game can be used.

## Example

We ran initial tests on a cooperative game involving control of a multi-access broadcast channel (Ooi & Wornell 1996). In this problem, nodes need to broadcast messages to each other over a channel, but only one node may broadcast at

| Horizon | Brute force | Dynamic programming |
|---|---|---|
| 1 | (2, 2) | (2, 2) |
| 2 | (8, 8) | (6, 6) |
| 3 | (128, 128) | (20, 20) |
| 4 | *(32768, 32768)* | (300, 300) |

Table 2: Performance of both algorithms on the multi-access broadcast channel problem. Each cell displays the number of policy trees produced for each agent. The brute force algorithm could not compute iteration 4. The numbers (in italics) shown in that cell reflect how many policy trees it would need to create for each agent.

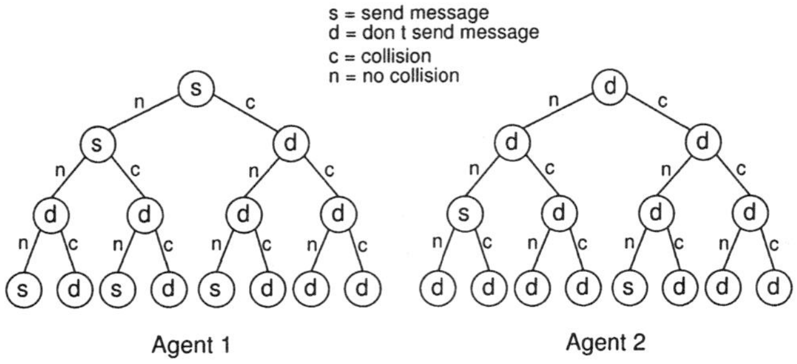


Figure 1: A pair of policy trees that is optimal for the horizon-4 problem when both message buffers start out full.

a time, otherwise a collision occurs. The nodes share the common goal of maximizing the throughput of the channel.

The process proceeds in discrete time steps. At the start of each time step, each node decides whether or not to send a message. The nodes receive a reward of 1 when a message is successfully broadcast and a reward of 0 otherwise. At the end of the time step, each node receives a noisy observation of whether or not a message got through.

The message buffer for each agent has space for only one message. If a node is unable to broadcast a message, the message remains in the buffer for the next time step. If a node $i$ is able to send its message, the probability that its buffer will fill up on the next step is $p_i$. Our problem has two nodes, with $p_1 = 0.9$ and $p_2 = 0.1$. There are 4 states, 2 actions per agent, and 2 observations per agent.

We compared our DP algorithm with a brute-force algorithm, which also builds sets of policy trees, but never prunes any of them. On a machine with 2 gigabytes of memory, the brute-force algorithm was able to complete iteration 3 before running out of memory, while the DP algorithm was able to complete iteration 4. At the end of iteration 4, the number of policy trees for the DP algorithm was less than $1\%$ of the number that would have been produced by the brute-force algorithm, had it been able to complete the iteration. This result, shown in Table 2, indicates that the multi-agent DP operator can prune a significant number of trees. However, even with pruning, the number of policy trees grows quickly with the horizon. At the end of the fourth iteration, each agent has 300 policy trees that are not dominated. Because the piecewise linear and convex value function consists of one $|S|$-vector for each pair of policy trees from the two agents, the representation of the value function requires $300^2$ $|S|$-vectors. In the fifth iteration, an exhaustive backup would create a value function that consists of $2 \cdot 300^4$ $|S|$-vectors, or more than 16 billion $|S|$-vectors, before beginning the process of pruning. This illustrates how the algorithm can run out of memory. In the next section, we discuss possible ways to avoid the explosion in size of the value function.

Figure 1 shows a pair of depth-4 policy trees constructed by the DP algorithm. In the case where the message buffers both start out full, this pair is optimal, yielding a total reward of 3.89.

## Future work

Development of an exact dynamic programming approach to solving POSGs suggests several avenues for future research, and we briefly describe some possibilities.

### Improving efficiency

A major scalability bottleneck is the fact that the number of policy trees grows rapidly with the horizon and can quickly consume a large amount of memory. There are several possible ways to address this. One technique that provides computational leverage in solving POMDPs is to prune policy trees incrementally, so that an exhaustive backup never has to be done (Cassandra, Littman, & Zhang 1997). Whether this can be extended to the multi-agent case is an open problem. Other techniques seem easier to extend. More aggressive pruning, such as pruning strategies that are *almost* very weakly dominated, can reduce the number of policy trees in exchange for bounded sub-optimality (Feng & Hansen 2001). The number of policy trees may be reduced by allowing stochastic policies, as in (Poupart & Boutilier 2004). Work on compactly represented POMDPs and value functions may be extended to the multi-agent case (Hansen & Feng 2000).

In addition, there exist POMDP algorithms that leverage a known start state distribution for greater efficiency. These algorithms perform a forward search from the start state and are able to avoid unreachable belief states. Whether some kind of forward search can be done in the multi-agent case is an important open problem.

### Extension to infinite-horizon POSGs

It should be possible to extend our dynamic programming algorithm to infinite-horizon, discounted POSGs, and we are currently exploring this. In the infinite-horizon case, the multi-agent DP operator is applied to infinite trees. A finite set of infinite trees can be represented by a finite-state controller, and policy iteration algorithms for single-agent POMDPs have been developed based on this representation (Hansen 1998; Poupart & Boutilier 2004). We believe that they can be extended to develop a policy iteration algorithm for infinite-horizon POSGs. Because our definition of belief depends on explicit representation of a policy as a policy tree or finite-state controller, it is not obvious that a value iteration algorithm for infinite-horizon POSGs is possible.

## Conclusion

We have presented an algorithm for solving POSGs that generalizes both dynamic programming for POMDPs and iterated elimination of dominated strategies for normal form games. It is the first exact algorithm for general POSGs, and we have shown that it can be used to find optimal solutions for cooperative POSGs. Although currently limited to solving very small problems, its development helps to clarify the relationship between POMDPs and game-theoretic models. There are many avenues for future research, in both making the algorithm more time and space efficient and extending it beyond finite-horizon POSGs.

**Acknowledgments** We thank the anonymous reviewers for helpful comments. This work was supported in part by the National Science Foundation under grants IIS-0219606 and IIS-9984952, by NASA under cooperative agreement NCC 2-1311, and by the Air Force Office of Scientific Research under grant F49620-03-1-0090. Daniel Bernstein was supported by a NASA GSRP Fellowship. Any opinions, findings, and conclusions or recommendations expressed in this material are those of the authors and do not reflect the views of the NSF, NASA or AFOSR.

## References

Becker, R.; Zilberstein, S.; Lesser, V.; and Goldman, C. V. 2003. Transition-independent decentralized Markov decision processes. In *Proceedings of the 2nd International Conference on Autonomous Agents and Multi-agent Systems*, 41–48.

Bernstein, D.; Givan, R.; Immerman, N.; and Zilberstein, S. 2002. The complexity of decentralized control of Markov decision processes. *Mathematics of Operations Research* 27(4):819–840.

Boutilier, C. 1999. Sequential optimality and coordination in multiagent systems. In *Proceedings of the 16th International Joint Conference on Artificial Intelligence*, 478–485.

Brafman, R., and Tennenholtz, M. 2002. R-MAX–a general polynomial time algorithm for near-optimal reinforcement learning. *Journal of Machine Learning Research* 3:213–231.

Cassandra, A.; Littman, M. L.; and Zhang, N. L. 1997. Incremental pruning: A simple, fast, exact method for partially observable Markov decision processes. In *Proceedings of the 13th Annual Conference on Uncertainty in Artificial Intelligence*, 54–61.

Feng, Z., and Hansen, E. 2001. Approximate planning for factored POMDPs. In *Proceedings of the 6th European Conference on Planning*.

Filar, J., and Vrieze, K. 1997. *Competitive Markov Decision Processes*. Springer-Verlag.

Hansen, E., and Feng, Z. 2000. Dynamic programming for POMDPs using a factored state representation. In *Proceedings of the 5th International Conference on Artificial Intelligence Planning and Scheduling*, 130–139.

Hansen, E. 1998. Solving POMDPs by searching in policy space. In *Proceedings of the 14th Conference on Uncertainty in Artificial Intelligence (UAI-98)*, 211–219.

Hsu, K., and Marcus, S. I. 1982. Decentralized control of finite state Markov processes. *IEEE Transactions on Automatic Control* AC-27(2):426–431.

Hu, J., and Wellman, M. 2003. Nash Q-learning for general-sum stochastic games. *Journal of Machine Learning Research* 4:1039–1069.

Kaelbling, L.; Littman, M.; and Cassandra, A. 1998. Planning and acting in partially observable stochastic domains. *Artificial Intelligence* 101:99–134.

Kearns, M.; Mansour, Y.; and Singh, S. 2000. Fast planning in stochastic games. In *Proceedings of the 16th Conference on Uncertainty in Artificial Intelligence (UAI-00)*, 309–316.

Koller, D., and Pfeffer, A. 1997. Representations and solutions for game-theoretic problems. *Artificial Intelligence* 94(1):167–215.

Koller, D.; Megiddo, N.; and von Stengel, B. 1994. Fast algorithms for finding randomized strategies in game trees. In *Proceedings of the 26th ACM Symposium on Theory of Computing*, 750–759.

Kuhn, H. 1953. Extensive games and the problem of information. In Kuhn, H., and Tucker, A., eds., *Contributions to the Theory of Games II*. Princeton University Press. 193–216.

Littman, M. 1994. Markov games as a framework for multi-agent reinforcement learning. In *Proceedings of the 11th International Conference on Machine Learning*, 157–163.

Nair, R.; Pynadath, D.; Yokoo, M.; Tambe, M.; and Marsella, S. 2003. Taming decentralized POMDPs: Towards efficient policy computation for multiagent settings. In *Proceedings of the 18th International Joint Conference on Artificial Intelligence*, 705–711.

Ooi, J. M., and Wornell, G. W. 1996. Decentralized control of a multiple access broadcast channel: Performance bounds. In *Proceedings of the 35th Conference on Decision and Control*, 293–298.

Peshkin, L.; Kim, K.-E.; Meuleau, N.; and Kaelbling, L. P. 2000. Learning to cooperate via policy search. In *Proceedings of the 16th International Conference on Uncertainty in Artificial Intelligence*, 489–496.

Poupart, P., and Boutilier, C. 2004. Bounded finite state controllers. In *Advances in Neural Information Processing Systems 16: Proceedings of the 2003 Conference*. MIT Press.

Shapley, L. 1953. Stochastic games. *Proceedings of the National Academy of Sciences of the United States of America* 39:1095–1100.

Smallwood, R., and Sondik, E. 1973. The optimal control of partially observable Markov processes over a finite horizon. *Operations Research* 21:1071–1088.

# Solving Concurrent Markov Decision Processes

**Mausam** and **Daniel S. Weld**
Dept of Computer Science and Engineering
University of Washington
Seattle, WA-98195
*{mausam,weld}@cs.washington.edu*

**Content areas: Markov Decision Processes, Planning**

### Abstract

Typically, Markov decision problems (MDPs) assume a single action is executed per decision epoch, but in the real world one may frequently execute certain actions in parallel. This paper explores *concurrent MDPs*, MDPs which allow multiple non-conflicting actions to be executed simultaneously, and presents two new algorithms. Our first approach exploits two provably sound pruning rules, and thus guarantees solution optimality. Our second technique is a fast, sampling-based algorithm, which produces close-to-optimal solutions extremely quickly. Experiments show that our approaches outperform the existing algorithms producing up to two orders of magnitude speedup.

## 1. Introduction

Recent progress achieved by planning researchers has yielded new algorithms that relax, individually, many of the classical assumptions. However, in order to apply automated planning to many real-world domains we must eliminate larger groups of the assumptions in concert. For example, (Bresina *et al.* 2002) notes that optimal control for a NASA Mars rover requires reasoning about uncertain, concurrent, durative actions and a mixture of discrete and metric fluents. While today's planners can handle large problems with *deterministic* concurrent durative actions, and semi-MDPs provide a clear framework for durative actions in the face of uncertainty, few researchers have considered concurrent, uncertain actions — the focus of this paper.

For example, a Mars rover has the goal of gathering data from different locations with various instruments (color and infrared cameras, microscopic imager, Mossbauer spectrometers *etc.*) and transmitting this data back to Earth. Concurrent actions are essential since instruments can be turned on, warmed up and calibrated while the rover is moving, using other instruments or transmitting data. Similarly, uncertainty must be explicitly confronted as the rover's movement, arm control and other actions cannot be accurately predicted.

We adopt the framework of *Markov decision processes* (MDPs) and extend it to allow multiple actions per decision epoch. In the traditional case of a single action per decision epoch, state-space heuristic search and dynamic programming have proven quite effective. However, allowing multiple concurrent actions at a time point will inflict an exponential blowup on all of these techniques.

In this paper we investigate techniques to counter this combinatorial explosion. Specifically, we extend the technique of *real-time dynamic programming* (RTDP) (Barto, Bradtke, & Singh 1995; Bonet & Geffner 2003) to handle concurrency, making the following contributions:

- We empirically illustrate the exponential blowup suffered by the existing MDP algorithms.
- We describe two pruning strategies (*combo-elimination* and *combo-skipping*), prove that they preserve completeness, and evaluate their performance.
- We describe a novel technique, *combo-sampling*, that produces a speedup of an order of magnitude. Although this technique sacrifices solution optimality, we show that for a wide range of problems, combo-sampling produces solutions that are quite close to optimal.

## 2. Background

Planning problems under probabilistic uncertainty are often modeled using Markov Decision Processes (MDPs). Different research communities have looked at slightly different formulations of MDPs. These versions typically differ in objective functions (maximising reward *vs.* minimising cost), horizons (finite, infinite, indefinite) and action representations (DBN *vs.* parametrised action schemata). All these formulations are very similar in nature, and so are the algorithms to solve them. Though, the methods proposed in the paper are applicable to all the variants of these models, for clarity of explanation we assume a particular formulation of an MDP as follows.

Following (Bonet & Geffner 2003), we define a *Markov decision process* as a tuple $\langle \mathcal{S}, \mathcal{A}, \mathcal{P}r, \mathcal{C}, \mathcal{G}, s_0, \gamma \rangle$ in which

- $\mathcal{S}$ is a finite set of discrete states.
- $\mathcal{A}$ is a finite set of actions. An applicability function, $Ap : \mathcal{S} \rightarrow \mathcal{P}(\mathcal{A})$, denotes the set of actions that can be applied in a given state ($\mathcal{P}$ represents the power set).
- $\mathcal{P}r : \mathcal{S} \times \mathcal{A} \times \mathcal{S} \rightarrow [0, 1]$ is the transition function. We write $\mathcal{P}r(s'|s, a)$ to denote the probability of arriving at state $s'$ after executing action $a$ in state $s$.

State variables : $x_1, x_2, x_3, x_4, p_{12}$

| Action | Precondition | Effect | Probability |
|---|---|---|---|
| toggle-$x_1$ | $\neg p_{12}$ | $x_1 \leftarrow \neg x_1$ | 1 |
| toggle-$x_2$ | $p_{12}$ | $x_2 \leftarrow \neg x_2$ | 1 |
| toggle-$x_3$ | true | $x_3 \leftarrow \neg x_3$ | 0.9 |
| | | no change | 0.1 |
| toggle-$x_4$ | true | $x_4 \leftarrow \neg x_4$ | 0.9 |
| | | no change | 0.1 |
| toggle-$p_{12}$ | true | $p_{12} \leftarrow \neg p_{12}$ | 1 |

Goal : $x_1 = 1, x_2 = 1, x_3 = 1, x_4 = 1$

Figure 1: Probabilistic STRIPS definition of a simple MDP with potential parallelism

- $\mathcal{C} : \mathcal{A} \rightarrow \Re^+$ is the cost model[1].
- $\mathcal{G} \subseteq \mathcal{S}$ is a set of absorbing goal states.
- $s_0$ is a start state.
- $\gamma \in [0, 1]$ is the discount factor. If $\gamma = 1$ our problem is known as the *stochastic shortest path problem.*

We assume full observability, and we seek to find an optimal, stationary policy — *i.e.*, a function $\pi$: $\mathcal{S} \rightarrow \mathcal{A}$ that minimises the expected discounted cost (over an infinite horizon) incurred to reach a goal state. Note that any *value function*, $J$: $\mathcal{S} \rightarrow \Re$, mapping states to the expected cost of reaching a goal state defines a policy as follows:

$$\pi_J(s) = \underset{a \in Ap(s)}{\operatorname{argmin}} \left\{ \mathcal{C}(a) + \gamma \sum_{s' \in \mathcal{S}} \mathcal{P}r(s'|s, a) J(s') \right\}$$

The *optimal* policy derives from a value function, $J^*$, which satisfies the following pair of *Bellman equations.*

$$J^*(s) = 0, \text{ if } s \in \mathcal{G} \text{ else}$$

$$J^*(s) = \min_{a \in Ap(s)} \left\{ \mathcal{C}(a) + \gamma \sum_{s' \in \mathcal{S}} \mathcal{P}r(s'|s, a) J^*(s') \right\} (1)$$

For example, Figure 1 defines a simple MDP where four state variables ($x_1, \ldots, x_4$) need to be set using toggle actions. Some of the actions, *e.g.*, toggle-$x_3$ are probabilistic.

Various algorithms have been developed to solve MDPs. *Value iteration* is a dynamic programming approach in which the optimal value function (the solution to equations 1) is calculated as the limit of a series of approximations, each considering increasingly long action sequences. If $J_n(s)$ is the value of state $s$ in iteration $n$, then the value of state $s$ in the next iteration is calculated with a process called a *Bellman backup* as follows:

$$J_{n+1}(s) = \min_{a \in Ap(s)} \left\{ \mathcal{C}(a) + \gamma \sum_{s' \in \mathcal{S}} \mathcal{P}r(s'|s, a) J_n(s') \right\}$$

Value iteration terminates when $\forall s \in \mathcal{S}$, $|J_n(s) - J_{n-1}(s)| \leq \epsilon$, and this termination is guaranteed for $\epsilon > 0$. Furthermore, the sequence of $\{J_i\}$ is guaranteed to converge to the optimal value function, $J^*$, regardless of the initial values. Unfortunately, value iteration tends to be quite slow, since it explicitly updates every state, and $|\mathcal{S}|$ is exponential in the number of domain features. One optimization restricts search to the part of state space reachable from the initial state $s_0$. Two algorithms exploiting this *reachability analysis* are LAO* (Hansen & Zilberstein 2001) and our focus: RTDP (Barto, Bradtke, & Singh 1995).

RTDP, conceptually, is a lazy version of value iteration in which the states get updated in proportion to the frequency with which they are visited by the repeated executions of the greedy policy. Specifically, RTDP is an anytime algorithm that simulates the greedy policy along a single trace execution, and updates the values of the states it visits using Bellman backups. An RTDP *trial* is a path starting from $s_0$ and ending when a goal is reached or the number of updates exceeds a threshold. RTDP repeats these trials until convergence. Note that common states are updated frequently, while RTDP wastes no time on states that are unreachable, given the current policy. RTDP's strength is its ability to quickly produce a relatively good policy; however, complete convergence (at every state) is slow because less likely (but potentially important) states get updated infrequently. Furthermore, RTDP is not guaranteed to terminate. *Labeled RTDP* fixes these problems with a clever labeling scheme that focusses attention on states where the value function has not yet converged (Bonet & Geffner 2003). Labeled RTDP is guaranteed to terminate, and is guaranteed to converge to the optimal value function (for states reachable using the optimal policy) if the initial value function is admissible.

## 3. Concurrent Markov Decision Processes

Extending traditional MDPs to *concurrent MDPs, i.e.* allowing multiple parallel actions, each of unit duration, requires several changes. Clearly, certain actions can't be executed in parallel; so we adopt the classical planning notion of mutual exclusion (Blum & Furst 1997) and apply it to a *factored* action representation: *probabilistic STRIPS* (Boutilier, Dean, & Hanks 1999). Two actions are *mutex* (may not be executed concurrently) if in any state 1) they have inconsistent preconditions, 2) they have conflicting effects, or 3) the precondition of one conflicts with the (possibly probabilistic) effect of the other. Thus, non-mutex actions don't interact — the effects of executing the sequence $a_1; a_2$ equals those for $a_2; a_1$.

**Example:** Continuing with Figure 1, toggle-$x_1$, toggle-$x_3$ and toggle-$x_4$ can execute in parallel but toggle-$x_1$ and toggle-$x_2$ are mutex as they have conflicting preconditions. Similarly, toggle-$x_1$ and toggle-$p_{12}$ are mutex as the effect of toggle-$p_{12}$ interferes with the precondition of toggle-$x_1$.

**Cost model:** An *action combination*, $A$, is a set of one or more actions to be executed in parallel. The cost model $\mathcal{C}$ is now a function, $\mathcal{C} : \mathcal{P}(\mathcal{A}) \rightarrow \Re^+$, *i.e.* the domain is the *power-set* of actions. Note that unless there exists a combination $A$, such that $\mathcal{C}(A) < \sum_{a \in A} \mathcal{C}(\{a\})$, the optimal policy from the single-action MDP would be optimal for the concurrent case as well. However, we believe that in many domains most combinations do obey the inequality. Indeed, the inequality always holds when the cost of a combination includes both *resource* and *time* components. Here, one can define the cost model to be comprised of two parts:

[1]Indeed, all our techniques except Theorem 1 allow costs to be conditioned on states as well as actions.

- $t$ : Time taken to complete the action.
- $r$ : Amount of resources used for the action.

Assuming additivity, we can think of cost of an action $\mathcal{C}(a) = t(a) + r(a)$, to be sum of its time and resource usage. Hence, the cost model for a combination of actions in terms of these components would be defined as:

$$\mathcal{C}(\{a_1, a_2, ..., a_k\}) = \sum_{i=1}^{k} r(a_i) + \max_{i=1..k}\{t(a_i)\}$$

For example, a Mars rover might incur lower cost when it preheats an instrument while changing locations than if it executes the actions sequentially, because the makespan is reduced while the energy consumed does not change.

**Applicability Function:** The applicability function, $Ap(s)$, for concurrent MDPs now has range $\mathcal{P}(\mathcal{P}(\mathcal{A}))$; it is redefined in terms of our original definition, now denoted $Ap_1$. $Ap(s) = \{A \subseteq \mathcal{A} | \forall a, a' \in A,\ a, a' \in Ap_1(s) \land \neg\text{mutex}(a, a')\}$

**Transition Function:** Let $A = \{a_1, a_2, \ldots, a_k\}$ be an action combination applicable in $s$. Since the actions don't interact, the transition function may be calculated as follows:

$$\mathcal{P}r(s'|s, A) = \sum_{s_1, s_2, \ldots s_k \in \mathcal{S}} \cdots \sum \mathcal{P}r(s_1|s, a_1)\mathcal{P}r(s_2|s_1, a_2) \ldots \mathcal{P}r(s'|s_k, a_k)$$

**Bellman equations:** Finally, instead of equations (1), the following set of equations represents the solution to a concurrent MDP:

$J^*(s) = 0$, if $s \in \mathcal{G}$ else

$$J^*(s) = \min_{A \in Ap(s)} \left\{ \mathcal{C}(A) + \gamma \sum_{s' \in \mathcal{S}} \mathcal{P}r(s'|s, A) J^*(s') \right\} \quad (2)$$

These equations are the same as in a traditional MDP, except that instead of considering single actions for backup in a state, we need to consider all applicable action combinations. Thus, only this small change must be made to traditional algorithms (*e.g.*, value iteration, LAO*, Labeled RTDP). However since the number of action combinations is exponential in $|\mathcal{A}|$, efficiently solving a concurrent MDP requires new techniques. Unfortunately, there is no easy structure to exploit, since an optimal action for a state from a classical MDP solution may not even appear in the optimal action combination for a concurrent MDP. In the next section, we describe two provably-sound pruning techniques that speed policy construction; then in Section 5, we present fast sampling methods which generate near-optimal policies.

## 4. Pruned RTDP

Recall that during a trial, labeled RTDP performs Bellman backups in order to calculate the values of applicable actions (or in our case, action combinations) and then chooses the best action (combination); we now describe two pruning techniques that reduce the number of backups to be computed. Also, let $Q(s, A)$ be the expected cost incurred by executing action combination $A$ in state $s$ and then following the greedy policy, *i.e.*

$$Q_n(s, A) = \mathcal{C}(A) + \gamma \sum_{s' \in \mathcal{S}} \mathcal{P}r(s'|s, A) J_{n-1}(s')$$

A Bellman update can thus be rewritten as:

$$J_n(s) = \min_{A \in Ap(s)} Q_n(s, A)$$

**Combo Skipping:** Since the number of applicable action combinations can be exponential, we'd like to prune suboptimal combinations. The following theorem (proved in (Mausam & Weld 2004)) imposes a lower bound on $Q(s, A)$ in terms of the costs and the $Q$-values of single actions.

**Theorem 1** *Let $A = \{a_1, a_2, \ldots, a_k\}$ be an action combination which is applicable in state $s$.*

$$Q(s, A) \geq \gamma^{1-k} Q(s, \{a_1\}) + \mathcal{C}(A) - \left( \sum_{i=1}^{k} \gamma^{i-k} \mathcal{C}(\{a_i\}) \right)$$

**Corollary 2** *Let $\lceil J_n(s) \rceil$ be an upper bound of $J_n(s)$. If*

$$\lceil J_n(s) \rceil < \gamma^{1-k} Q_n(s, \{a_1\}) + \mathcal{C}(A) - \left( \sum_{i=1}^{k} \gamma^{i-k} \mathcal{C}(\{a_i\}) \right)$$

*then, $A$ cannot be optimal for state $s$ in this iteration.*

Corollary 2 justifies a pruning rule, *combo-skipping*, that preserves optimality in any iteration algorithm that maintains value function monotonicity. This is powerful because all Bellman-backup based algorithms preserve monotonicity when started with an admissible value function. To apply combo-skipping, one must compute all the $Q(s, \{a\})$ values for single actions $a$ that are applicable in $s$; it is useful to precompute the summation of discounted costs, *i.e.* $\left(\sum_{i=1}^{k} \gamma^{i-k} \mathcal{C}(\{a_i\})\right)$, for all possible combinations. In the undiscounted case, this computation reduces to the simple sum of costs. To calculate $\lceil J_n(s) \rceil$ one may use the optimal combination for state $s$ in the previous iteration ($A_{opt}$) and compute $Q_n(s, A_{opt})$. This value gives an upper bound on the value $J_n(s)$.

Theorem 1 and Corollary 2 are valid for any ordering of $a_i$'s. But in order to skip the most combinations, we must maximise the right-hand side. In practice, the following heuristic suffices: choose $a_1$ to be the $a_i$ with maximal $Q(s, a_i)$ and order other actions in order of increasing cost.

**Example:** In Figure 1, let $\gamma$=1. Let a single action incur unit cost, and let the cost of an action combination be: $\mathcal{C}(A) = 0.5 + 0.5|A|$. Let state $s = (1,1,0,0,1)$ represent the ordered values $x_1 = 1$, $x_2 = 1$, $x_3 = 0$, $x_4 = 0$, and $p_{12} = 1$. Suppose, after the $n^{th}$ iteration, the value function assigns the values: $J_n(s) = 1$, $J_n(s_1{=}(1,0,0,0,1)) = 2$, $J_n(s_2{=}(1,1,1,0,1)) = 1$, $J_n(s_3{=}(1,1,0,1,1)) = 1$. Let $A_{opt}$ for state $s$ be {toggle-$x_3$, toggle-$x_4$}. Now, $Q_{n+1}(s, \{\text{toggle-}x_2\}) = \mathcal{C}(\text{toggle-}x_2) + J_n(s_1) = 3$ and $Q_{n+1}(s, A_{opt}) = \mathcal{C}(A_{opt}) + 0.81 \times 0 + 0.09 \times J_n(s_2) + 0.09 \times J_n(s_3) + 0.01 \times J_n(s) = 1.69$. So now we can apply Corollary 2 to skip combination {toggle-$x_2$, toggle-$x_3$} in this iteration, since using toggle-$x_2$ as $a_1$, we have $\lceil J_{n+1}(s) \rceil = Q_{n+1}(s, A_{opt}) = 1.69 \leq 3 + 1.5 - 2 = 2.5$.

Experiments in Section 6 show that combo-skipping yields considerable savings. Unfortunately, combo-skipping has a weakness — it prunes a combination for only a *single iteration*. In contrast, our second rule, *combo-elimination*, prunes irrelevant combinations altogether.

**Combo Elimination:** We adapt the action elimination theorem from traditional MDPs (Bertsekas 1995) to prove a similar theorem for concurrent MDPs.

**Theorem 3** *Let $A$ be an action combination which is applicable in state $s$. Let $\lfloor Q^*(s, A) \rfloor$ denote a lower bound of $Q^*(s, A)$. If $\lfloor Q^*(s, A) \rfloor > \lceil J^*(s) \rceil$ then $A$ is never the optimal combination for state $s$.*

In order to apply the theorem for pruning, one must be able to evaluate the upper and lower bounds. By using an admissible value function when starting RTDP search (or in value iteration, LAO* *etc.*), the current value $J_n(s)$ is guaranteed to be a lower bound of the optimal cost; thus, $Q_n(s, A)$ will also be a lower bound of $Q^*(s, A)$. To calculate an upper bound of the optimal $J^*(s)$, one may solve the MDP (*e.g.*, using labeled RTDP) while forbidding concurrency. This is much faster than solving the concurrent MDP, and yields an upper bound on cost, because forbidding concurrency restricts the policy to use a strict subset of legal action combinations.

**Example:** Continuing with the previous example, let $A$={toggle-$x_2$} then $Q_{n+1}(s, A) = \mathcal{C}(A) + J_n(s_1) = 3$ and $\lceil J^*(s) \rceil = 2.222$ (from solving MDP forbidding concurrency). As 3 > 2.222, $A$ can be eliminated for state $s$ in all remaining iterations.

Used in this fashion, combo-elimination requires the additional overhead of optimally solving the single-action MDP. Since algorithms like RTDP exploit state-space reachability to limit computation to relevant states, we do this computation incrementally, as new states are visited by our algorithm.

Combo-elimination also requires computing the current value of $Q(s, A)$ (for the lower bound of $Q^*(s, A)$); this differs from combo-skipping which avoids this computation. However, once combo-elimination prunes a combination, it never needs to be reconsidered. Thus, there is a tradeoff: should one perform an expensive computation, hoping for long-term pruning, or try a cheaper pruning rule with fewer benefits? Since $Q$-value computation is the costly step, we adopt the following heuristic: "First, try combo-skipping; if it fails to prune the combination, attempt combo-elimination". We also tried some other heuristics, such as: 1) If some combination is being skipped repeatedly, then try to prune it altogether with combo-elimination. 2) In every state, try combo-elimination with probability $p$. Space precludes presenting our experimental results, but neither alternative performed significantly better, so we kept our original (lower overhead) heuristic.

Since combo-skipping does not change any step of labeled RTDP and combo-elimination removes provably sub-optimal combinations, *pruned* labeled RTDP maintains convergence, termination, optimality and efficiency, when used with an admissible heuristic.

## 5. Sampled RTDP

Since the fundamental challenge posed by concurrent MDPs is the explosion of action combinations, sampling is a promising method to reduce the number of Bellman backups required per state. We describe a variant of RTDP, called *sampled RTDP*, which performs backups on a random set of action combinations[2], choosing from a distribution that favors "likely combinations." We generate our distribution by: 1) using combinations that were previously discovered to have low $Q$-values (recorded by *memoizing* the best combinations per state, after each iteration); 2) calculating the $Q$-values of all applicable single actions (using current value function) and then biasing the sampling of combinations to choose the ones that contain actions with low $Q$-values. This approach effectively manages the exploration / exploitation tradeoff.

**Termination and Optimality:** Since the system doesn't consider every possible action combination, sampled RTDP is not guaranteed to choose the best combination to execute at each state. As a result, even when started with an admissible heuristic, the algorithm may assign $J_n(s)$ a cost that is greater than the optimal $J^*(s)$ — *i.e.*, the $J_n(s)$ values are no longer admissible. If a better combination is chosen in a subsequent iteration, $J_{n+1}(s)$ might be set a lower value than $J_n(s)$, thus sampled RTDP is not *monotonic*. This is unfortunate, since admissibility and monotonicity are important properties required for termination[3] and optimality in labeled RTDP; indeed, sampled RTDP loses these important theoretical properties. The good news is that it is extremely useful in practice. In our experiments, sampled RTDP usually terminates quickly, and returns values that are extremely close to the optimal.

**Improving Solution Quality:** We have investigated several heuristics in order to improve the quality of the solutions found by sampled RTDP.

- **Heuristic 1:** Whenever sampled RTDP asserts convergence of a state, do not immediately label it as converged (which would preclude further exploration (Bonet & Geffner 2003)); instead first run a complete backup phase, using all the admissible combinations, to rule out any easy-to-detect inconsistencies.

- **Heuristic 2:** Run sampled RTDP to completion, and use the value function it produces, $J^s()$, as the initial heuristic estimate, $J_0()$, for a subsequent run of pruned RTDP. Usually, such a heuristic, though inadmissible, is highly informative. Hence, pruned RTDP terminates quite quickly.

- **Heuristic 3:** Run sampled RTDP before pruned RTDP, as in Heuristic 2, except instead of using the $J^s()$ value function directly as an initial estimate, scale linearly downward — *i.e.*, use $J_0() := cJ^s()$ for some constant $c \in (0, 1)$. Hopefully, the estimate will be admissible (though there is no guarantee). In our experience, $c = 0.9$ suffices, and the run of pruned RTDP yields the optimal policy very quickly.

[2] A similar action sampling approach was also used in (Zhang & Dietterich 1995) in the context of space shuttle scheduling to reduce the number of actions for value function computation.

[3] To ensure termination we implemented the policy: *if number of trials exceeds a threshold, force monotonicity on value function.* This will achieve termination but will reduce quality of solution.

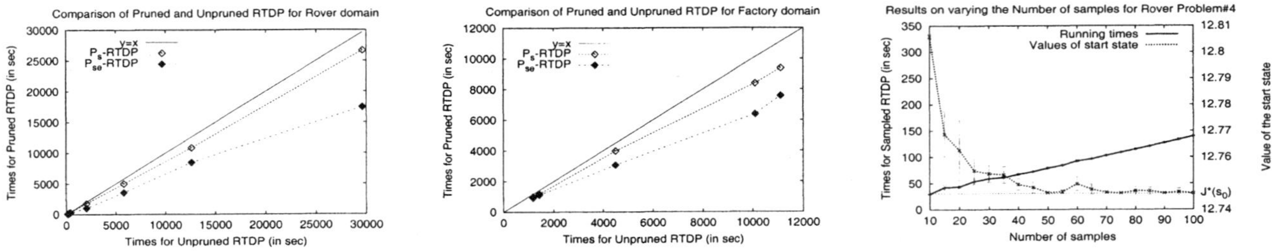


Figure 2: (a,b): Pruned vs. Unpruned RTDP for Rover and Factory domains respectively. Pruning non-optimal combinations achieves significant speedups on larger problems. (c) : Variation of quality of solution and efficiency of algorithm (with 95% confidence intervals) with the number of samples in Sampled RTDP for one particular problem from the Rover domain. As number of samples increase, the quality of solution approaches optimal and time still remains better than $P_{se}$-RTDP (which takes 259 sec. for this problem).

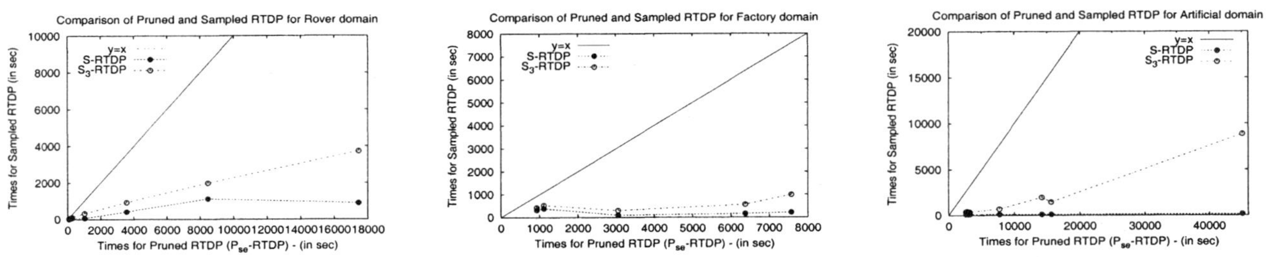


Figure 3: (a,b,c): Sampled vs Pruned RTDP for Rover, Factory and Artificial domains respectively. Random sampling of action combinations yields dramatic improvements in running times.

Experiments showed that Heuristic 1 returns a value function that is close to optimal. Adding Heuristic 2 improves this value moderately, and Heuristic 3 invariably returns the optimal solution.

## 6. Experiments

We tested our algorithms on problems in three domains. The first domain was a probabilistic variant of NASA Rover domain from the 2002 AIPS Planning Competition, in which there are multiple objects to be photographed and various rocks to be tested with resulting data communicated back to the base station. Cameras need to be focussed, and arms need to be positioned before usage. Since the rover has multiple arms and multiple cameras, the domain is highly parallel. The cost function includes both resource and time components, so executing multiple actions in parallel is cheaper than executing them sequentially[4]. We generated problems with 20-30 state variables having up to 81,000 reachable states and average number of applicable combinations per state ($Avg(Ap(s))$) up to 2735.

We also tested on a probabilistic version of a factory domain with multiple subtasks (*e.g.*, roll, shape, paint, polish *etc.*), which need to be performed on different objects using different machines. Machines can perform in parallel, but not all are capable of every task. We tested on problems with 26-28 state variables and around 32000 reachable states. $Avg(Ap(s))$ ranged between 170 and 2640.

Finally, we tested on an artificial domain similar to Figure 1 but much more complex. In this domain, some Boolean variables need to be toggled; however, toggling is probabilistic in nature. Moreover, certain pairs of actions have conflicting preconditions and thus, by varying the number of mutex actions we may control the domain's degree of parallelism. All the problems in this domain had 19 state variables and about 32000 reachable states, with $Avg(Ap(s))$ between 1024 and 12287.

We used Labeled RTDP, as implemented in GPT, as the base MDP solver. We implemented various algorithms, unpruned RTDP ($U$-RTDP), pruned RTDP using only combo skipping ($P_s$-RTDP), pruned RTDP using both combo skipping and combo elimination ($P_{se}$-RTDP), sampled RTDP using Heuristic 1 ($S$-RTDP) and sampled RTDP using both Heuristics 1 and 3, with value functions scaled with 0.9. ($S_3$-RTDP). We tested all of these algorithms on a number of problem instantiations from our three domains, generated by varying the number of objects, degrees of parallelism, and distances to goal.

We observe (Figure 2(a,b)) that pruning significantly speeds the algorithm. But the comparison of $P_{se}$-RTDP with $S$-RTDP and $S_3$-RTDP (Figure 3(a,b,c)) shows that sampling has a dramatic speedup with respect to the pruned versions. In fact, pure sampling, $S$-RTDP, converges extremely quickly, and $S_3$-RTDP is slightly slower. However, $S_3$-RTDP is still much faster than $P_{se}$-RTDP. The comparison of qualities of solutions produced by $S$-RTDP and $S_3$-RTDP *w.r.t.* optimal is shown in Table 1. We observe that solutions produced by $S$-RTDP are always nearly optimal. Since the error of $S$-RTDP is small, scaling it by 0.9 makes it an admissible initial value function for the pruned RTDP;

[4]For details on the domain, refer to `http://www.cs.washington.edu/ai/concurrent/NasaRover.pddl`

| Problem | $J(s_0)$ ($S$-RTDP) | $J^*(s_0)$ (Optimal) | Error |
|---|---|---|---|
| Rover1 | 10.7538 | 10.7535 | <0.01% |
| Rover2 | 10.7535 | 10.7535 | 0 |
| Rover3 | 11.0016 | 11.0016 | 0 |
| Rover4 | 12.7490 | 12.7461 | 0.02% |
| Rover5 | 7.3163 | 7.3163 | 0 |
| Rover6 | 10.5063 | 10.5063 | 0 |
| Rover7 | 12.9343 | 12.9246 | 0.08% |
| Art1 | 4.5137 | 4.5137 | 0 |
| Art2 | 6.3847 | 6.3847 | 0 |
| Art3 | 6.5583 | 6.5583 | 0 |
| Fact1 | 15.0859 | 15.0338 | 0.35% |
| Fact2 | 14.1414 | 14.0329 | 0.77% |
| Fact3 | 16.3771 | 16.3412 | 0.22% |
| Fact4 | 15.8588 | 15.8588 | 0 |
| Fact5 | 9.0314 | 8.9844 | 0.56% |

Table 1: Quality of solutions produced by Sampled RTDP

indeed, in all experiments, $S_3$-RTDP produced the optimal solution.

Figure 4(a,b) demonstrates how running times vary with problem size. We use the product of the number of reachable states and the average number of applicable action combinations per state as an estimate of the size of the problem (the number of reachable states in all artificial domains is the same, hence the x-axis for Figure 4(b) is $Avg(Ap(s))$). From these figures, we verify that the number of applicable combinations plays a major role in the running times of the concurrent MDP algorithms. In Figure 4(c), we fix all factors and vary the degree of parallelism. We observe that the speedups obtained by $S$-RTDP increase as concurrency increases. This is a very encouraging result, and we can expect $S$-RTDP to perform well on large problems involving high concurrency, even if the other approaches fail.

In Figure 2(c), we present another experiment in which we vary the number of action combinations sampled in each backup. While solution quality is inferior when sampling only a few combinations, it quickly approaches the optimal on increasing the number of samples. In all other experiments we sample 40 combinations per state.

## 7. Related Work

(Meuleau *et al.* 1998) and (Singh & Cohn 1998) deal with a special type of MDP (called a factorial MDP)[5] that can be represented as a set of smaller weakly coupled MDPs — the separate MDPs are completely independent except for some common resource constraints, and the reward and cost models are purely additive. They describe solutions in which these sub-MDPs are independently solved and the sub-policies are merged to create a global policy. Thus, concurrency of actions of different sub-MDPs is a by-product of their work. Singh & Cohn present an optimal algorithm (similar to our combo-elimination), whereas Meuleau *et al.*'s domain specific heuristics have no such guarantees.

All of the work in Factorial MDPs assumes that a weak coupling exists and has been identified, but factoring an MDP is a hard problem in itself. In contrast, our algorithm can handle strongly coupled MDPs and does not require any sub-task decomposition as input.

(Rohanimanesh & Mahadevan 2001) investigate a special class of semi-MDPs in which the action space can be partitioned by (possibly concurrent) *Markov options*. They propose an algorithm based on value-iteration, but their focus is calculating joint termination conditions and rewards received, rather than speeding policy construction. Hence, they consider *all* possible Markov option combinations in a backup. Although their model supports options with varying durations, it is restricted in several ways. First, they require the user to specify all possible options (as well as to define the effects of actions). Second, they assume different constraints on concurrency: i) they omit condition 3 of our mutex definition (Section 3), hence they are subject to race conditions, and ii) their definition restricts some well-defined types of concurrency[6] which may preclude finding optimal solutions, which our methods *would* find. Finally, they only experiment on a single, small problem with 400 states.

NASA researchers have developed techniques for solving a harder version of the Rover domain (*e.g.*, with uncertain continuous effects). They propose a *just-in-case* scheduling algorithm, which incrementally adds branches to a straight-line plan. While their work is more general than ours, their solution is heuristic and it is unclear how closely their policies approximate optimality (Bresina *et al.* 2002; Dearden *et al.* 2003). It would be exciting to combine their methods with ours, perhaps by using their heuristic to guide $S$-RTDP.

Recently, Younes and Simmons (2004) have developed a generic test and debug approach which converts a continuous time MDP into a deterministic planning problem. The optimal plan of the deterministic problem is converted back into a policy which can then be repaired if any failure points are identified.

Fast generation of parallel plans has also been investigated in (deterministic) classical state space based planning scenarios. (Edelkamp 2003) presents an anytime algorithm that repeatedly creates sequential plans of increasing lengths, and schedules the actions in the plan concurrently using "critical path analysis". This approach is based on the observation that any parallel plan to a goal can be serialised into a valid serial plan to the goal and vice versa. However, this observation is not true in the probabilistic version of the problem as a parallel policy may not be serialisable to a serial policy.

AltAlt$^p$ builds greedy parallelisations within the state space heuristic regression search coupled with *pushing up* the current actions if they can be parallelised with some earlier nodes of the search tree (Nigenda & Kambhampati 2003). Unfortunately, its heuristics draw heavily from planning graph constructions that have not been as effective

[5]Guestrin, Koller and Parr (2001) have investigated similar representations in the context of multiagent planning.

[6]In their model, two options, $o_a$ and $o_b$, may not be executed concurrently if there exist actions, $a \in o_a$ and $b \in o_b$, which have 1) inconsistent preconditions or 2) conflicting effects. This is overly conservative because the option's *policies* might guarantee that $a$ and $b$ are never executed concurrently.

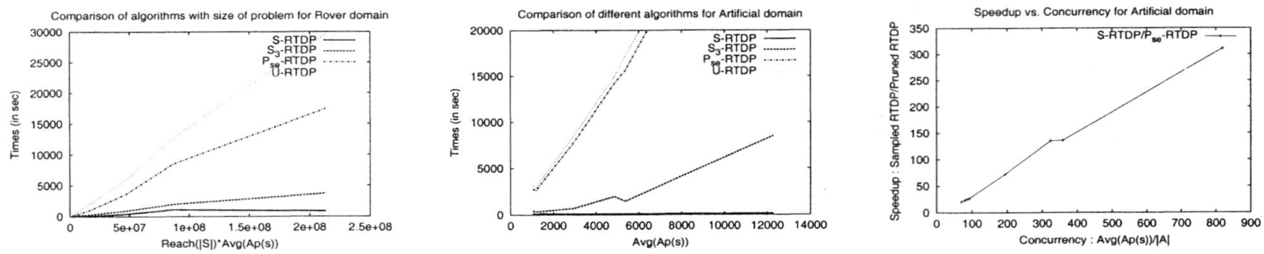


Figure 4: (a,b): Comparison of different algorithms with size of the problems for Rover and Artificial domains. As the problem size increases, the gap between sampled and pruned approaches widens considerably. (c): Relative Speed vs. Concurrency for Artificial domain.

in probabilistic problems. Secondly, as AltAlt$^p$ performs greedy action selection, it is not guaranteed to find an optimal plan.

## 8. Conclusions and Future Work

This paper formally defines the concurrent MDP problem and describes two algorithms to solve them. *Pruned RTDP* relies on combo-skipping and combo-elimination; with an admissible initial value function, it is guaranteed to converge to an optimal policy and is faster than plain, labeled RTDP on concurrent MDPs. *Sampled RTDP* performs backups on a random subset of possible action combinations; when guided by our heuristics, it converges orders of magnitude faster than other methods and produces optimal or close-to-optimal solutions. We believe that our sampling techniques will be extremely effective on very large, concurrent MDP problems. Moreover, our sampling and pruning techniques are extremely general and can be applied to other base algorithms like value iteration, LAO* *etc.* Thus, we believe our methods will extend easily to solve concurrent MDPs with rewards, non-absorbing goals, and other formulations.

In the future, we wish to prove error bounds on $S$-RTDP and to modify it so that its convergence is formally guaranteed. Concurrent reinforcement learning may also benefit from our sampling techniques. We also hope to extend our methods to include durative actions, and continuous parameters.

## Acknowledgements

We are thankful to Blai Bonet and Sumit Sanghai for their inputs at various stages of this research. We also thank David Smith, Subbarao Kambhampati, Stanley Kok, Julie Letchner, Benson Limketkai, Jayant Madhavan, and Parag for giving useful comments on an earlier draft of the paper. We thank the reviewers for their worthy comments and suggestions on the paper. This work was supported by National Aeronautics and Space Administration (Award NAG 2-1538), National Science Foundation (Award IIS-0307906), and Office of Naval Research (Award N00014-02-1-0932).

## References

Barto, A.; Bradtke, S.; Singh, S. 1995. Learning to act using real-time dynamic programming. *Artificial Intelligence* 72:81–138.

Bertsekas, D. 1995. *Dynamic Programming and Optimal Control.* Athena Scientific.

Blum, A., and Furst, M. 1997. Fast planning through planning graph analysis. *Artificial Intelligence* 90(1–2):281–300.

Bonet, B., and Geffner, H. 2003. Labeled RTDP: Improving the convergence of real-time dynamic programming. In *ICAPS'03*, 12–21. AAAI Press.

Boutilier, C.; Dean, T.; and Hanks, S. 1999. Decision theoretic planning: Structural assumptions and computational leverage. *J. Artificial Intelligence Research* 11:1–94.

Bresina, J.; Dearden, R.; Meuleau, N.; Smith, D.; and Washington, R. 2002. Planning under continuous time and resource uncertainty : A challenge for AI. In *UAI'02*, 77–84.

Dearden, R.; Meuleau, N.; Ramakrishnan, S.; Smith, D. E.; and Washington, R. 2003. Incremental Contingency Planning. In *ICAPS'03 Workshop on Planning under Uncertainty and Incomplete Information*, 38–47.

Edelkamp, S. 2003. Taming numbers and duration in the model checking integrated planning system. *Journal of Artificial Intelligence Research* 20:195–238.

Guestrin, C.; Koller, D.; and Parr, R. 2001. Multiagent planning with factored MDPs. In *NIPS'01*, 1523–1530. The MIT Press.

Hansen, E., and Zilberstein, S. 2001. LAO*: A heuristic search algorithm that finds solutions with loops. *Artificial Intelligence* 129:35–62.

Mausam, and Weld, D. 2004. Solving concurrent Markov decision processes. TR 04-03-03, University of Washington, Department of Computer Science and Engineering. Available at `ftp://ftp.cs.washington.edu/pub/ai/`.

Meuleau, N.; Hauskrecht, M.; Kim, K.-E.; Peshkin, L.; Kaelbling, L.; Dean, T.; and Boutilier, C. 1998. Solving very large weakly coupled Markov Decision Processes. In *AAAI'98*, 165–172.

Nigenda, R. S., and Kambhampati, S. 2003. Altalt-p: Online parallelization of plans with heuristic state search. *Journal of Artificial Intelligence Research* 19:631–657.

Rohanimanesh, K., and Mahadevan, S. 2001. Decision-Theoretic planning with concurrent temporally extended actions. In *UAI'01*, 472–479.

Singh, S., and Cohn, D. 1998. How to dynamically merge Markov decision processes. In *NIPS'98*. The MIT Press.

Younes, H. L. S., and Simmons, R. G. 2004. Policy generation for continuous-time stochastic domains with concurrency. In *ICAPS'04*. AAAI Press.

Zhang, W., and Dietterich, T. G. 1995. A reinforcement learning approach to job-shop scheduling. In *IJCAI'95*. Morgan Kaufmann. 1114–1120.

# Low-cost Addition of Preferences to DTPs and TCSPs

**Bart Peintner and Martha E. Pollack**
Computer Science and Engineering
University of Michigan
Ann Arbor, MI 48109 USA
{bpeintne, pollackm}@eecs.umich.edu

### Abstract

We present an efficient approach to adding soft constraints, in the form of preferences, to Disjunctive Temporal Problems (DTPs) and their subclass Temporal Constraint Satisfaction Problems (TCSPs). Specifically, we describe an algorithm for checking the consistency of and finding optimal solutions to such problems. The algorithm borrows concepts from previous algorithms for solving TCSPs and Simple Temporal Problems with Preferences (STPPs), in both cases using techniques for projecting and solving component sub-problems. We show that adding preferences to DTPs and TCSPs requires only slightly more time than corresponding algorithms for TCSPs and DTPs without preferences. Thus, for problems where DTPs and TCSPs make sense, adding preferences provides a substantial gain in expressiveness for a marginal cost.

## Introduction

Over the last decade, efficient algorithms have been developed for reasoning with a variety of temporal networks, which range in complexity from Simple Temporal Problems (STPs) and Temporal Constraint Satisfaction Problems (TCSPs) (Dechter, Meiri, & Pearl 1991) to Disjunctive Temporal Problems (DTPs) (Stergiou & Koubarakis 2000). Attention has been paid to checking networks for consistency, finding solutions, and correctly dispatching the steps in plans described by such networks. Only recently, though, has effort been made to increase the expressiveness of temporal networks. The two major extensions include uncertainty, i.e., the modeling of stochastic or uncontrollable events (Morris, Muscettola, & Vidal 2001; Tsamardinos, Pollack, & Ramakrishnan 2003), and preferences, i.e., the representation of soft constraints in addition to the hard constraints typical in temporal networks (Khatib *et al.* 2001; 2003). Where previous work has addressed the addition of preferences to STPs, in this paper we focus on adding preferences to DTPs and their subclass TCSPs.

Hard constraints in temporal networks specify the allowable temporal distances between time points in a network. For example, $X_2 - X_1 \in [5, 10]$ specifies that time point $X_2$ must occur 5-10 units after $X_1$. Adding preferences to a temporal network involves assigning to each constraint a preference function that maps each temporal distance value to a preference value. Preferences allow a knowledge engineer to designate some temporal differences as more desirable than others. With preferences, the problem is changed from simply finding a consistent assignment for time points to finding an optimal assignment.

The latest work on preferences in temporal networks provides a polynomial-time algorithm for checking the consistency of and finding an optimal assignment for STPs with semi-convex preference functions[1] (Khatib *et al.* 2003). The notion of optimality used in that work is called Weakest Link Optimality (WLO). With WLO, the preference value of an entire solution is set to the minimal (worst) preference value for any part of the solution, and hence the optimal solution is the one that makes the best worst assignment; i.e., it is a maximin decision criterion (Wald 1950). In this paper, we adopt the WLO approach, and present an algorithm for checking the consistency of and finding a WLO solution for DTPs with Preferences (DTPPs) and TCSPs with Preferences (TCSPPs). The algorithm borrows concepts from previous algorithms for solving STPs with Preferences (STPPs) and TCSPs, in both cases using techniques for projecting and solving component sub-problems. We demonstrate that the added expressivity provided by preferences is computationally inexpensive. Specifically, we show that our algorithm not only falls into the same complexity class as the corresponding hard-constraint algorithms, but that the *added* cost of handling such preferences is worst case polynomial in the number of time points in the network.

After a brief review of temporal networks, we motivate the need for preferences with an example. We then present a modified version of an algorithm for solving standard TCSPs, and extend it to one that handles both TCSPPs and DTPPs. Finally, we analyze the algorithm's complexity and present future work.

## Background

A Simple Temporal Problem (STP) is a pair $< X, C >$, where the elements $X_i \in X$ designate time points, and $C$ is a set of binary constraints of the following form:

$$X_j - X_i \in [a_{ij}, b_{ij}].$$

[1] Their definition of a semi-convex function is one in which, for all $Y$, the set $\{X : f(X) \geq Y\}$ forms an interval.

A *solution* to an STP is an assignment of values to each time point such that all constraints are satisfied. An STP is said to be *consistent* if at least one solution exists. Consistency-checking in a STP can be cast as an all-pairs shortest path problem: the STP is consistent iff there are no negative cycles in the all-pairs graph. This check can be performed in $|X|^3$ time. A by-product of this check is the *minimal network*, which is the tightest representation of the STP constraints that still contains all solutions present in the original network. A single solution can be extracted from the minimal network in $|X|^2$ time (Dechter, Meiri, & Pearl 1991).

To extend an STP to an STP with preferences (STPP), one adds to each constraint a preference function that maps each value in the interval identified by that constraint to a *preference value*, a quantitative measure of the value's desirability. Hence the constraints in an STPP have the following form:

$$< X_j - X_i \in [a_{ij}, b_{ij}], f_{ij} : x \in [a_{ij}, b_{ij}] \rightarrow \Re > .$$

A Temporal Constraint Satisfaction Problem (TCSP) extends an STP by allowing multiple intervals in constraints:

$$X_j - X_i \in \{[a_{ij1}, b_{ij1}], ..., [a_{ijn}, b_{ijn}]\}.$$

This expresses the constraint that the distance between $X_i$ and $X_j$ must be in one of the intervals listed. The extra expressiveness comes at a high cost: determining consistency for a general TCSP is NP-hard (Dechter, Meiri, & Pearl 1991). Note that a TCSP constraint can be viewed as a disjunction of STP constraints over the same two time points: $X_j - X_i \in [a_{ij1}, b_{ij1}] \vee X_j - X_i \in [a_{ij2}, b_{ij2}] \vee \ldots$ A standard way of checking the consistency of a TCSP is to view it as a collection of component STPs, where, intuitively, each component STP is defined by selecting one STP constraint (i.e., one interval) from each TCSP constraint. Checking the consistency of the TCSP then amounts to searching for a consistent component STP, since a solution to a component STP will also be a solution to the complete TCSP.

A Disjunctive Temporal Problem (DTP) (Stergiou & Koubarakis 2000) removes the binary restriction of TCSPs, resulting in constraints with the following form:

$$(X_{j1} - X_{i1} \in [a_{i1j1}, b_{i1j1}]) \vee (X_{j2} - X_{i2} \in [a_{i2j2}, b_{i2j2}]) \vee \cdots \vee (X_{jn} - X_{in} \in [a_{injn}, b_{injn}]).$$

Clearly, the TCSP is a subcase of the DTP in which $X_{j1} = X_{j2} = \ldots X_{jn}$, and $X_{i1} = X_{i2} = \ldots X_{in}$. As with a TCSP, the standard way to solve a DTP is to extract component STPs, by selecting one disjunct from each constraint, and searching for a consistent component STP.

To our knowledge, there has not been previous work on extending TCSPs and DTPs to handle preferences. It is clear, however, what the form of such an extension should be: each individual disjunct of a TCSP or DTP constraint is given an associated preference function that maps the values in the identified interval to preference values.

## Example

To motivate the need for preferences we describe an example from the domain of Autominder, a system that uses DTPs to manage the daily plans for persons with memory impairment (Pollack *et al.* 2003). An elderly woman must exercise for 30 uninterrupted minutes in late afternoon (3-6pm) and take heart medication shortly after. A friend will visit from 4:30 to 5, so it is best if the exercise occurs well before the visit, to allow for cool-down, or else after it. The task is to model this scenario with a temporal network and use consistency-checking to determine when to begin exercising and when to take the medicine. The example has seven time points to model: a temporal reference point (TRP), which is used for stating absolute (clock-time) constraints; and the start and end of the Exercise, TakeMeds, and Visit actions.

| | | |
|---|---|---|
| Time Points: | TRP (3pm): | $TRP$ |
| | Exercise: | $E_S$, $E_E$ |
| | TakeMeds: | $T_S$, $T_E$ |
| | Visit: | $V_S$, $V_E$ |
| Constraints: | $T_S - E_E \in [5, 20]$ | |
| | $V_S - E_E \in [5, \infty] \vee E_S - V_E \in [0, \infty]$ | |
| | $V_S - TRP = 90$ | |
| | $V_E - V_S = 30$ | |
| | $E_S - TRP \in [0, \infty]$ | |
| | $E_E - TRP \in [-\infty, 360]$ | |
| | $E_E - E_S = 30$ | |

Figure 1: DTP encoding of the Autominder example.

Figure 1 shows a DTP encoding of this example. The first constraint states that TakeMeds must start 5 to 20 minutes after Exercise, the second expresses when Exercise can occur relative to the visit, the third constrains the starting time of the visit, and so on. Consider the first constraint. We assume its parameters are chosen by a medical expert who understands the effects of the medicine in relation to exercise. In the DTP, the interval [5, 20] represents the allowable time difference between finishing the Exercise action and starting the TakeMeds action. Any other time, say 4, 21, or -30, is not allowed and represents an inconsistency or failure in the DTP. Notice that in a DTP, a difference of -30 is no worse than a difference of 4; both are considered failures.

When specifying bounds on time differences, the expert must reason about a trade-off: a wider set of bounds increases the likelihood that the entire DTP is consistent, while narrower bounds keeps actions closer to their ideal times. Therefore, specifying good bounds requires knowledge about the underlying relationship *and* how the bounds will affect the rest of the network. This type of situation motivates the need for preferences. The doctor may want to express that the ideal time difference between Exercise and TakeMeds is the interval [5,10); that the intervals [3,5) and [10,20) are almost as good; and that the intervals [0,3) and [20, 25] are acceptable, but not preferable. This could be implemented by attaching a preference function $f$ to the first constraint in the DTP, such that $f([5,10)) = 3, f([3,4)) = 2, f([10,20)) = 2, f([0,3)) = 1$, and $f([20,25]) = 1$. Expressing preferences in this way avoids the trade-off mentioned above. The expert can express the local relationship without regard to its affect on the DTP as a whole.

Our example encoding can also be improved by adding preferences to the disjunctive (second) constraint, which states that Exercise must finish at least 5 minutes before the visitor arrives *or* anytime after the visitor leaves. We may want to elaborate this to say that finishing at least 15 minutes ahead is most desirable; finishing 10 minutes early is the next preference and is equivalent to exercising after the visitor leaves; and finishing only 5 minutes before the visitor arrives has the lowest preference of all allowed possibilities. To encode this set of preferences, we would use two preference functions. Let $f$ be associated with the first disjunct of the constraint; then $f([15,\infty)) = 3, f([10,15)) = 2$, and $f([5,10)) = 1$. Similarly, let $g$ be associated with the second disjunct, which assigns the value 2 to the entire interval for that disjunct: $g([0,\infty]) = 2$. By default, each preference function assigns a value of 0 to all disallowed points.

In this example, the preference functions were step functions, mapping intervals to each preference level. In general, however, any function, discrete or continuous, that maps temporal differences to preference values is acceptable.

## Solving DTPs

As noted above, DTPs (and TCSPs) can be viewed as collections of component STPs, and solving a DTP (or TCSP) can thus be achieved by searching for a consistent component STP. This insight underlies the Forward and Go-Back algorithm of Dechter *et al.* (1991). Although this algorithm was originally designed to solve TCSPs, it applies directly to DTPs as well, since it does not exploit the fact that the constraints in a TCSP are binary. In fact, the approach of searching for component STPs is the basis of most modern DTP-solving algorithms (Stergiou & Koubarakis 2000; Oddi & Cesta 2000; Tsamardinos & Pollack 2003). Consequently, in the reminder of the paper, we shall refer only to DTPs; the reader should keep in mind that everything we write also applies to the special case of TCSPs.

The Forward and Go-back algorithm works by searching the space of partial component STPs within a given DTP, where a partial STP consists of single STP constraints extracted from a subset of the DTP constraints. It builds the STPs one constraint at a time, adding a constraint if the current set is consistent, and backtracking otherwise, looking for complete component STPs that are consistent. (A component STP is complete if it includes a disjunct from every constraint in the original DTP.) The original version of the algorithm found *all* consistent component STPs, and returned a network consisting of the union of their minimal networks. For many applications, however, it suffices to find the minimal network of a single consistent component STP.

Figure 2 shows the Forward and Go-back algorithm modified in two ways. First, it returns the minimal network of the first consistent STP found. Second, the bookkeeping aspects of the algorithm have been modified to enable it to be extended to an algorithm that solves DTPs with preferences. Because of these bookkeeping modifications, a line-by-line comparison of our version of the algorithm with the original one reveals few similarities, but in fact they search through the space of component STPs in the same order.

The algorithm operates on a DTP represented as a list of $n$ DTP constraints, each of which is itself a set of STP constraints; by definition $S_i$ is the number of STP constraints (i.e., the number of disjuncts) in the $i^{th}$ DTP constraint. Thus each DTP constraint is defined as $D_i = \{\mathrm{STPC}_1, \ldots, \mathrm{STPC}_{\mathrm{S_i}}\}$, where $\mathrm{STPC_k}$ is an STP constraint and $i$ ranges from 1 to $n$. A vector *select*[ ] stores the indices of the STP constraints currently under consideration in the algorithm; if $select[j] = k$, then the $k^{th}$ disjunct of $D_j$ is included in the current partial STP. The vector is initialized to 0's, meaning no disjuncts are selected at the algorithm's start. If $select[\,] = \{2, 1, 0, 0\}$, it identifies a partial STP composed of the second disjunct in $D_1$ and the first disjunct in $D_2$. Constraints $D_3$ and $D_4$ are not included.

```
Solve-DTP(i)
1. select[i] = select[i] + 1; // Choose next disjunct in constraint i
2. if select[i] > S_i // If true, no more disjuncts in constraint i
3.     begin
4.       if i = 1 return failure // no solution
5.       select[i] = 0; //Reset disjunct in this constraint
6.       Solve-DTP(i-1); // Try next disjunct in previous constraint
7.     end
8. if Consistent-STP(D_1(select[1]), ..., D_i(select[i]))
9.     begin
10.      if i = n return Minimal Network of selected STP
11.      Solve-DTP(i+1); // Add another constraint
12.    end
13. else
14.    Solve-DTP(i); // Try the next interval in this constraint
```

Figure 2: Solve-DTP, a modified version of the Forward and Go-back algorithm. (Dechter, Meiri, & Pearl 1991)

The algorithm uses one internal function, Consistent-STP, which checks an STP for consistency. The external call to Solve-DTP should pass in the integer '1' for i, indicating that it starts the search with the first DTP constraint.

Line 1 of the algorithm chooses the next disjunct for constraint $D_i$ by incrementing the constraint's index. If the index goes out of bounds (line 2), lines 4-6 remove $D_i$ from the current component STP, and backtrack to try the next disjunct of the previous constraint $D_{i-1}$.

Line 8 checks the consistency of the partial STP defined by the *select*[ ] vector. If it is both consistent and complete (line 10), then a solution has been found. If consistent but not complete, then the algorithm is called recursively to find a disjunct from the next DTP constraint $D_{i+1}$ (line 11). If inconsistent, the method is called again with current constraint $D_i$ so that its next disjunct can be considered (line 14).

The algorithm's time complexity depends on the number of component STPs in the DTP, which in turn depends upon the number of DTP constraints and the number of disjuncts in each. If the DTP contains $|X|$ time points and $n$ constraints with a maximum of $k$ disjuncts, there exists $O(k^n)$ STPs to check for consistency. In the worst case, where no consistent STP exists, the total complexity is $O(k^n * |X|^3)$.

## Solving STPPs

As noted earlier, recently an algorithm has been developed for finding optimal solutions to STPPs (STPs with preferences) with semi-convex preference functions (Khatib *et al.* 2001; 2003). Like the algorithm for solving DTPs, this algorithm works by searching a space of projected STPs. This time, however, the projected STPs (of the STPP) are defined by the preference functions associated with each STPP constraint. Specifically, given an STPP constraint $< X_j - X_i \in [a,b], f : x \in [a,b] \rightarrow \Re >$, for every preference level $p$ we can project a constraint of the form $X_j - X_i \in [c,d]$, where the interval $[c,d] = \{x : f_{ij}(x) \geq p\}$. If $f_{ij}$ is semi-convex, the projected points will always form at most a single interval, resulting in an STP constraint. Moreover, there will be at most a single complete projected STP at level $p$.

To find a weakest-link optimal solution to an STPP, one can search for the maximum $p$ such that there exists a consistent projected STP at preference level $p$. If preference levels are discretized into the set $A$, a binary search through preference levels will find the consistent STP with the highest preference level in $\log(|A|) * |X|^3$ time.

## Extending the algorithm to handle DTPPs

Our approach to finding WLO-optimal solutions to DTPPs (and TCSPPs) combines the idea of projecting component STPs from DTPs with the idea of projecting networks with hard temporal constraints from those with preferences. At a high level, the algorithm has two phases, as illustrated in Figure 3. In the first, the preference values in the DTPP are discretized and a set of DTPs is projected from the DTPP—one DTP for each preference value. As explained below, this is done in a manner similar to that of the STPP algorithm. In the second phase, an attempt is made to solve each DTP by searching for a consistent component STP. The goal is to find the DTP with highest preference value that is consistent.

To project a DTP at preference level $p$ from a DTPP, we use an approach analogous to that of projecting an STP from an STPP: each *disjunct* $< X_j - X_i \in [a,b], f_{ij} >$ is projected to $X_j - X_i \in [c,d]$ where $[c,d] = \{x : f_{ij}(x) \geq p\}$. Note that just as projecting an STPP constraint to a given preference level produces an STP constraint, projecting a DTPP constraint to a given level produces a set of disjunctive STP constraints, i.e., a DTP constraint. Consequently, a projection of a DTPP to preference level $p$ is a single DTP, which we label $\text{DTP}^p$.

Figure 4 provides an example; for ease of illustration, the example is actually a TCSPP constraint, but the process is identical for general DTPP constraints. The set of disjuncts produced by projecting constraint $i$ at preference level p is stored in $D_i^p$, while the number of disjuncts is stored in $S_i^p$;

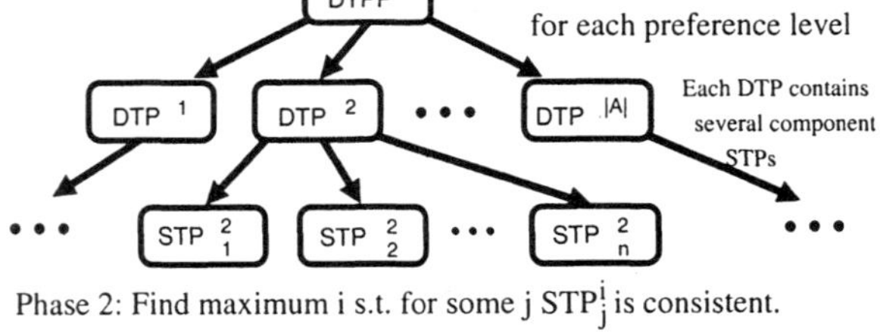


Figure 3: The two phases of solving a DTPP

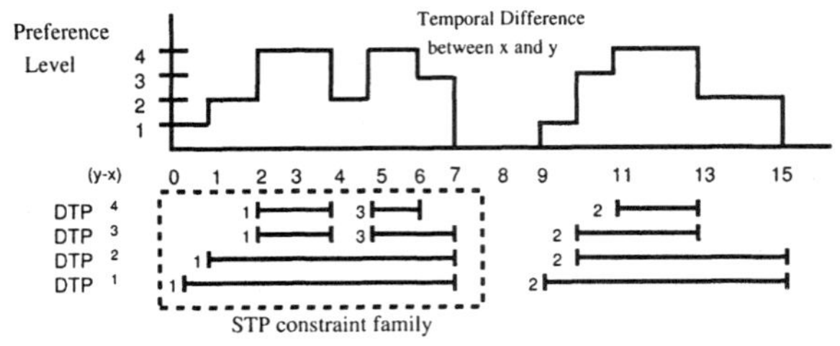


Figure 4: A DTPP (actually a TCSPP) constraint containing two disjuncts projected onto 4 DTP constraints. Each interval is labeled with the index assigned during projection.

the superscript $p$ is necessary because we do not restrict preference functions to be semi-convex, allowing DTPs at different levels to have different numbers of disjuncts (see Figure 4). Whenever a disjunct splits, as in levels 2 and 3 in Figure 4, the projection algorithm must assign one the index of the original interval and assign an unused index to the other.

The projection phase produces a set of $|A|$ DTPs, where $|A|$ is the number of discrete preference levels. Notice in Figure 4 that each disjunct of the DTPP constraint produces multiple STP constraints, which we label an STP constraint *family*. Within a family each constraint is *tighter* than members at lower levels, meaning, the set of temporal difference values allowed by the constraint is a subset of those allowed by members at lower levels. We can define these terms for entire STPs as well: $\text{STP}_1$ is *tighter* than $\text{STP}_2$ if each constraint in $\text{STP}_2$ corresponds to a unique tighter constraint in $\text{STP}_1$; and $\text{STP}_1$ is *related* to $\text{STP}_2$ if each constraint in $\text{STP}_2$ has a constraint family member in $\text{STP}_1$.

These definitions allow us to describe two properties of the projected DTPs that make our algorithm efficient. First, each component STP of $\text{DTP}^p$ will be related to and tighter than a component STP of each $\text{DTP}^q$ for $q < p$. Because an STP has a solution if any tighter STP does, we obtain the Downward Consistency property:

**Property 1** ***Downward Consistency.*** *If there is a consistent component STP in* $\text{DTP}^p$*, then there is a consistent STP for every* $\text{DTP}^q$ *for all* $q < p$.

The converse property is Upward Inconsistency:

**Property 2** ***Upward Inconsistency.*** *If a component STP of* $\text{DTP}^q$ *is inconsistent, then any related component STP of* $\text{DTP}^p$ *for* $p > q$ *will also be inconsistent.*

This property holds because the higher-level STP constraints are tighter than the lower-level STP constraints belonging to the same family. If no solution exists in an STP, no tighter version of that STP will contain a solution.

The upward inconsistency property allows us to prune away a large part of the search space each time an inconsistent STP is found. For example, if the algorithm finds an inconsistent STP at preference level 1, then it can prune away all related higher-level STPs.

The algorithm for the first phase depends on the original form of the preference function and the discrete prefer-

```
Solve-DTPP-Main(dtpp)
1. Let D = constraints in dtpp
2 ∀i,∀p. [D_i^p, S_i^p] = project(D_i, p)
3. bestSolution = Ø;
4. Solve-DTPP(1, 1)

Solve-DTPP(i, p)
1. if p > |A| return bestSolution; // Solution found at highest p-level.
2. select[i] = select[i] + 1; // Choose next disjunct in constraint i
3. if select[i] > S_i^p // If true, there are no more disjuncts in constraint i
4.     begin
5.       if i = 1 return bestSolution; // no solution at this p-level
6.       select[i] = 0;
7.       Solve-DTPP(i-1, p); // Try next interval in previous constraint
8.     end
9. if Consistent-STP(D_1^p(select[1]), ..., D_i^p(select[i]))
10.    if i = n
11.      begin
12.        bestSoln = Minimal Network of selected STP
13.        p = p + 1;
14.        select[i] = select[i] - 1;
15.        Solve-DTPP(i, p); // Try related STP at higher preference level
16.      end
17.    else
18.      Solve-DTPP(i+1, p); // Add another constraint
19.else
20.    Solve-DTPP(i, p);// Try the next interval in this constraint
```

Figure 5: Algorithm for Solving DTPPs. Bold lines indicate differences between Solve-DTP and Solve-DTPP.

ence levels chosen. For most reasonable forms of preference functions (e.g. piecewise linear), this step is inexpensive compared to the second step of the algorithm, which involves searching through the projected DTPs to find the one with highest preference value that is consistent. This is done using the technique of searching for a conistent component STP from within the projected DTPs.

The entire algorithm is shown in Figure 5. After projecting DTPs from the input DTPP, it searches through partial component STPs within the lowest level DTP until it finds a consistent STP. Once a solution is found, the search moves to the next preference level. At the new level, the search starts with an STP that is related to the consistent one just found at the level below. At each level, the solution found (the minimal network of the consistent component STP) is stored as 'bestSolution'. The search ends when no solution is found for a given level. There is no need to search higher levels in this case, as the upward inconsistency property ensures that it is not possible for a solution to exist at one.

The initial call to `Solve-DTPP` starts the search at the first DTP constraint and at preference level 1. The algorithm behaves exactly like Solve-DTP until it finds the first solution (line 11). It then stores the solution, moves up one preference level, and tries a related STP at the higher level (lines 12-15). This continues until a solution is found at the highest level (line 1) or no more solutions are found (line 5).

When the algorithm moves up one preference level, it does not search the entire space of STPs at that level: it "skips" STPs that are related to the STPs already searched at lower levels[2]. Operationally, this skipping is enacted by leaving the *select*[ ] indexes unchanged during the shift to the higher level[3]. The upward inconsistency property tells us that skipping these STPs is justified, since they are tighter than STPs already found to be inconsistent at lower levels.

## Analysis

A simple algorithm for solving DTPPs is to run Solve-DTP (*not Solve-DTPP*) for the DTP projected at the highest preference level and decrement the level until a solution is found. This algorithm would have an O($|A|*$ *complexity*(Solve-DTP)) worst case run time, where *complexity*(Solve-DTP) is the complexity of solving the largest of the $|A|$ DTPs. A slight improvement can be made by performing a binary search through the preference levels, reducing the worst case complexity to O($(log|A|)$ $*$ *complexity*(Solve-DTP)).

Unlike these two simple algorithms, however, our algorithm does not require multiple calls to the Solve-DTP procedure. It modifies the procedure to achieve a time complexity of O($|A|$ $*$ *complexity*(Solve-STP) $+$ *complexity*(Solve-DTP)); hence the additional cost of preferences over hard DTPs is at most $|A|*|X|^3$. To understand why this is so, notice that only two pieces of code were added to Solve-DTP to produce Solve-DTPP. The first addition (line 1) does not affect the trajectory through the search space; it simply checks for an exit condition. The second addition (lines 11-16) executes only after a valid solution for a level is found. These lines store the solution, increment the preference level, and continue the search with a *related* STP one preference level higher. Since Solve-DTPP moves to the next preference level each time it finds a consistent STP, it will find at most $|A|$ consistent STPs and will thus make at most $|A|-1$ more STP consistency checks ($|X|^3$ time) than would Solve-DTP on the largest of the $|A|$ DTPs. Our analysis focuses on the *additional* cost of adding preferences over solving a hard DTP, and supports our claim that for problems where DTPs make sense, preferences can be added for a marginal cost.

### Improving Efficiency

The shape of preference functions can greatly influence the additional cost of handling preferences. Consider Figure 6. In this network, consisting of only two constraints, the DTP at level 2 contains 9 STPs, whereas the DTP at level 3 contains only 1. If a solution exists at level 3, then starting at level 1 using Solve-DTPP may require up to 11 STPs to be checked for consistency, where starting at the solution level would only require a single check.

The general issue here is that the number of component STPs in the largest DTP may be much larger than the number in the solution level DTP. Since the algorithm may search the largest DTP completely before reaching the solution level, our claim that cost of adding preferences is at most $|A|*|X|^3$ greater than the time needed for the largest DTP, while true, is misleading. Fortunately, this issue can be addressed by careful assignment of indices during the

[2]We should note that *some* related STPs are not skipped, because intervals can split as the preference level increases.

[3]Lines 14 and 2 cancel each other out to produce no change.

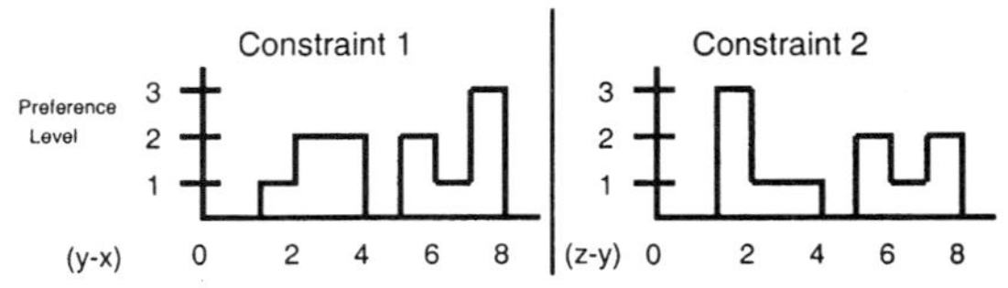


Figure 6: DTPP constraints whose lower level DTPs have much greater complexity than the upper level DTP.

projection step of the algorithm. When a disjunct $I$ splits into $I_1$ and $I_2$, the one that persists to the highest preference level should be assigned the lower index. This causes the algorithm to search STPs related to the top-level STPs first. Using this strategy, a stronger claim can be made: the cost of adding preferences is at most $|A| * |X|^3$ greater than the time needed for solving the *solution-level* DTP.

A second approach to increasing efficiency takes advantage of the relationship between STPs at adjacent preference levels. If a solution to a DTPP exists at the highest preference level, the algorithm as presented must find solutions at all lower levels before reaching the optimal one. However, by intersecting the constraints of an STP $S$ at level $k + 1$ with the minimal network of the unique STP related to it at level $k$, we obtain information that may allow us to immediately determine whether $S$ is consistent or inconsistent, thereby obviating the need to run the check. If the intersection produces an empty set, then $S$ is guaranteed to be inconsistent. On the other hand, if the intersection returns the minimal network of the STP at level $k$, then $S$ is guaranteed to be consistent. In both cases, a consistency check is unnecessary. The average savings derived from this technique depends on the shape of the preference functions. For example, a rectangle or steep-sloped rhombus may often produce the second case (immediate determination of consistency).

Further increases in efficiency can be obtained by exploiting techniques that have been developed for pruning the search space of TCSPs and DTPs, including Conflict-Directed Backjumping, Semantic Branching, Removal of Subsumed Variables, and No-good Recording (Tsamardinos & Pollack 2003). Each of these methods can be incorporated with few modifications into the Solve-DTP algorithm, and, although we do not provide adequate explanation in this paper, they can similarly be adopted into Solve-DTPP.

Finally, note that because it starts its search at the lowest preference level, Solve-DTPP has an anytime quality. In practice, since DTPs at lower levels are less tight, it will be easier to find a solution at a lower level. The algorithm can be interrupted anytime after the first solution is found if available computation time is exhausted. Given that general DTPs are NP-Hard, this is an important property.

## Future Work

The Solve-DTPP algorithm, like the STPP algorithm in (Khatib *et al.* 2001), provides solutions with Weakest Link Optimality, meaning that it finds solutions whose lowest preference constraint is maximal. For a given problem, several solutions of equal value can exist, some of which may dominate others, meaning although the lowest preference constraint for each solution is at the same level, all constraints of one is satisfied at equal or greater level than the other. For semi-convex STPPs, an algorithm has been developed to remove all dominated solutions, leaving a set of Pareto optimal solutions for that STPP (Khatib *et al.* 2003). It would be useful to develop a similar algorithm for DTPPs.

An empirical comparison between solving tractable DTP problems and DTPPs randomly generated from them would provide a characterization of the impact of the various efficiency strategies described in the previous section, as well as the usefulness of Solve-DTPP's anytime property.

## Acknowledgements

We would like to thank Robert Morris for useful discussions on this topic. The material presented in this paper is based upon work supported by the U.S. Air Force Office of Scientific Research (FA9550-04-1-0043), the National Science Foundation (IIS-0085796), and the Defense Advanced Research Projects Agency, through the Department of the Interior, NBC, Acquisition Services Division (NBCHD030010).

## References

Dechter, R.; Meiri, I.; and Pearl, J. 1991. Temporal constraint networks. *Artificial Intelligence* 49:61–95.

Khatib, L.; Morris, P.; Morris, R.; and Rossi, F. 2001. Temporal constraint reasoning with preferences. *17th International Joint Conference on AI* 1:322–327.

Khatib, L.; Morris, P.; Morris, R.; and Venable, K. B. 2003. Tractable pareto optimal optimization of temporal preferences. *18th International Joint Conference on AI* 1:1289–1294.

Morris, P.; Muscettola, N.; and Vidal, T. 2001. Dynamic control of plans with temporal uncertainty. In *Proceedings of the 17th International Joint Conference on AI*, 494–499.

Oddi, A., and Cesta, A. 2000. Incremental forward checking for the disjunctive temporal problem. In *Proceedings of the 14th European Conference on AI*, 108–112.

Pollack, M. E.; Brown, L.; Colbry, D.; McCarthy, C. E.; Orosz, C.; Peintner, B.; Ramakrishnan, S.; and Tsamardinos, I. 2003. Autominder: An intelligent cognitive orthotic system for people with memory impairment. *Robotics and Autonomous Systems* 44(3-4):273–282.

Stergiou, K., and Koubarakis, M. 2000. Backtracking algorithms for disjunctions of temporal constraints. *Artificial Intelligence* 120:81–117.

Tsamardinos, I., and Pollack, M. E. 2003. Efficient solution techniques for disjunctive temporal reasoning problems. *Artificial Intelligence* 151(1-2):43–90.

Tsamardinos, I.; Pollack, M. E.; and Ramakrishnan, S. 2003. Assessing the probability of legal execution of plans with temporal uncertainty. In *Proceedings of the ICAPS03 Workshop on Planning under Uncertainty and Incomplete Information*.

Wald, A. 1950. *Statistical Decision Functions*. Wiley, New York.

# $m$CP Nets: Representing and Reasoning with Preferences of Multiple Agents

**F. Rossi** and **K. B. Venable**
Dept. of Mathematics
University of Padova
Padova, Italy
{frossi,kvenable}@math.unipd.it

**T. Walsh**
Cork Constraint Computation Centre
University College Cork
Cork, Ireland
tw@4c.ucc.ie

**Abstract**

We introduce $m$CP nets, an extension of the CP net formalism to model and handle the qualitative and conditional preferences of multiple agents. We give a number of different semantics for reasoning with $m$CP nets. The semantics are all based on the idea of individual agents voting. We describe how to test optimality and preference ordering within a $m$CP net, and we give complexity results for such tasks. We also discuss whether the voting schemes fairly combine together the preferences of the individual agents.

## Introduction and Motivation

In many situations, we need to represent and reason about the simultaneous preferences of several agents, and to aggregate such preferences (see for example (Yager 2001)). As a motivating example, suppose you invite three friends round for dinner. Alice prefers fish to beef. Bob, on the other hand, prefers beef to fish. Finally, Carol is like Alice and prefers fish to beef. What do you cook? Both choices are Pareto optimal. If you cook fish then changing to beef will be more preferred by Bob, but less preferred by Carol and Alice. Similarly, changing from beef to fish will be more preferred by Alice and Carol, but less preferred by Bob. However, fish is perhaps the "best" choice according to a majority ordering as it is the preferred choice for both Alice and Carol, whilst beef is the preferred choice for only Bob.

Which wine do you serve with the main course? Alice, Bob and Carol are fortunately more consistent here. If it is fish then they all prefer white wine to red. However, if it is beef, then they all prefer red wine to white. Finally, do you serve cheese or dessert? Even though you are happy to serve everyone their own choice of cheese or dessert, you must still determine and reason about your friends' preferences. For example, if his girlfriend Alice has cheese, Bob prefers cheese to dessert. However, if his girlfriend Alice has dessert, he will not be able to resist so he prefers dessert to cheese.

This example demonstrates that multiple agents may have some features in common but not all (e.g. the main dish is common to all but the choice of cheese or dessert is not), that there may no longer be a single optimal solution, that there can be several definitions of optimality (e.g. Pareto optimal *versus* a majority dominance), that preferences may be conditional (e.g. the preference for wine depends on the choice of the main course) and dependent on the features of other agents (e.g. Bob's preference for dessert or cheese depends on Alice's choice for dessert or cheese). We therefore propose a framework for representing and reasoning with such preferences.



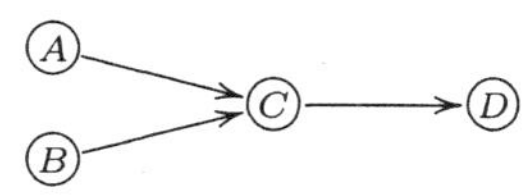



Figure 1: The dependency graph of the example CP net.

The paper is structured as follows. We first describe CP nets, a general purpose framework for representing and reasoning with qualitative and conditional preferences (Boutilier *et al.* 1999). We then introduce partial CP nets, an extension of the formalism which we use to represent the preferences of a single agent. By combining together several partial CP nets, we obtain a $m$CP net which can represent the preferences of multiple agents. We give a semantics for $m$CP nets based on the idea of the individual agents voting. Different voting schemes yield different preference orderings. We then describe how to test optimality and preference dominance, and we compute the complexity of such tasks. We also discuss whether the voting schemes fairly combine together the preferences of the individual agents.

## Background: CP nets

In many applications, it is natural to express preferences via generic qualitative (usually partial) preference relations over variable assignments. For example, it is often more intuitive to say "I prefer red wine to white wine", rather than "Red wine has preference 0.7 and white wine has preference 0.4". The former statement provides less information, but does not require careful selection of preference values. Moreover, we often wish to represent conditional preferences, as in "If it is meat, then I prefer red wine to white". Qualitative and conditional preference statements are thus useful components of many applications.

CP nets (Boutilier *et al.* 1999) are a graphical model for compactly representing conditional and qualitative preference relations. They exploit conditional preferential independence by structuring an agent's preferences under the *ceteris paribus* assumption (e.g. under the "ceteris paribus" or "all other things being equal" assumption). Informally, CP nets are sets of *conditional ceteris paribus (CP)* preference statements. For instance, the statement *"I prefer red wine to white wine if meat is served."* asserts that, given two meals that differ *only* in the kind of wine served *and* both containing meat, the meal with a red wine is preferable to the meal with a white wine. Many philosophers and AI researchers (Doyle & Wellman 1994) have argued that many of our preferences are of this type.

CP nets bear some similarity to Bayesian networks. Both utilize directed graphs where each node stands for a domain variable, and assume a set of features $\mathbf{F} = \{X_1, \ldots, X_n\}$ with finite, discrete domains $\mathcal{D}(X_1), \ldots, \mathcal{D}(X_n)$. For each feature $X_i$, each user specifies a set of *parent* features $Pa(X_i)$ that can affect her preferences over the values of $X_i$. This defines a dependency graph in which each node $X_i$ has $Pa(X_i)$ as its immediate predecessors. Given this structural information, the user explicitly specifies her preference over the values of $X_i$ for *each complete outcome* on $Pa(X_i)$. This preference is assumed to take the form of total (Boutilier *et al.* 1999) or partial order over $\mathcal{D}(X)$.

For example, consider a CP net with the dependency graph given in Figure 1, whose features are $A$, $B$, $C$, and $D$, with binary domains containing $f$ and $\overline{f}$ if $F$ is the name of the feature, and with the preference statements as follows: $a \succ \overline{a}$, $b \succ \overline{b}$, $(a \wedge b) \vee (\overline{a} \wedge \overline{b}) : c \succ \overline{c}$, $(a \wedge \overline{b}) \vee (\overline{a} \wedge b) : \overline{c} \succ c$, $c : d \succ \overline{d}$, $\overline{c} : \overline{d} \succ d$. Here, statement $a \succ \overline{a}$ represents the unconditional preference for $A = a$ over $A = \overline{a}$, while statement $c : d \succ \overline{d}$ represents $D = d$ is preferred to $D = \overline{d}$, given that $C = c$.

How do we reason with such CP statements? The semantics of CP nets depends on the notion of a worsening flip. A worsening flip is a change in the value of a variable to a value which is less preferred by the CP statement for that variable. For example, in the CP net of Fig. 1, passing from $abcd$ to $ab\overline{c}d$ is a worsening flip since $c$ is better than $\overline{c}$ given $a$ and $b$. We say that one outcome $\alpha$ is better than another outcome $\beta$ (written $\alpha \succ \beta$) iff there is a chain of worsening flips from $\alpha$ to $\beta$. This definition induces a strict partial order over the outcomes. In general, there may be many optimal outcomes. However, in acyclic CP nets, there is only one.

Several types of queries can be asked about CP nets. First, given a CP net, what are the optimal outcomes? For acyclic CP nets, such a query is answerable in linear time (Boutilier *et al.* 1999): we forward sweep through the CP net, starting with the unconditional variables, following the arrows in the dependency graph and assigning at each step the most preferred value in the preference table. For instance, in the CP net of Figure 1 above, we would choose $A = a$ and $B = b$, then $C = c$ and then $D = d$. The optimal outcome is therefore $abcd$. The same complexity also holds for testing whether an outcome is optimal since an acyclic CP net has only one optimal outcome. We can find this optimal outcome (in linear time) and then compare it to the given one (again in linear time).

The second type of query is a dominance query. Given two outcomes, is one better than the other? Unfortunately, this query is NP-hard even for acyclic CP nets (Domshlak & Brafman 2002), Whilst tractable special cases exist, there are also acyclic CP nets in which there are exponentially long chains of worsening flips between two outcomes. In the CP net of Figure 1, $\overline{a}b\overline{c}\overline{d}$ is worse than $abcd$.

## Partial CP nets

We first introduce partial CP nets. These will be used to represent the preferences of the individual agents in a $m$CP net. A partial CP net is one in which certain features may not be ranked. Intuitively, this means that the agent is indifferent to the values of such features. The presence of non ranked features is needed since an agent's preferences may depend on another agent's preferences (e.g. Bob's preference for dessert or cheese depends on Alice's choice).

Partiality requires us to relax the semantics slightly. A *worsening flip* in a partial CP net is the change in the value of a variable $A$ such that:

- if $A$ is ranked, the flip is worsening in the CP table of $A$;
- if $A$ is not ranked, it is worsening in the CP tables of all features that depend on $A$.

For example, if $A$ is not ranked, and for $B$ we have $a : b \succ \overline{b}$ and $\overline{a} : \overline{b} \succ b$, then passing from $ab$ to $\overline{a}b$ is a worsening flip as we go from the best ranked position to the worst.

In addition to worsening flips, we now also have *indifferent* and *incomparable* flips. Indifferent flips are all those flips of a non-ranked variable such that, for each CP table of the features that depend on this feature, they are neither improving nor worsening. Suppose $A$ is not ranked, $B$ has three values, and we have the CP statement $a : b_1 \succ b_2 \succ b_3$ and $\overline{a} : b_3 \succ b_2 \succ b_1$. Then, passing from $ab_2$ to $\overline{a}b_2$ is an indifferent flip. Incomparable flips are all those flips which are neither worsening, nor improving, nor indifferent. For example, if $A$ is not ranked, for $B$ we have $a : b \succ \overline{b}$ and $\overline{a} : \overline{b} \succ b$, and for $C$ we have $\overline{a} : c \succ \overline{c}$ and $a : \overline{c} \succ c$, passing from $abc$ to $\overline{a}bc$ is an incomparable flip.

Each agent represents their preferences by a partial CP net. An agent prefers outcome $\alpha$ to outcome $\beta$ (written $\alpha \succ \beta$) iff, in their partial CP net, there is a chain of flips from $\alpha$ to $\beta$ where each flip is worsening or indifferent, and there is at least one worsening flip. This ordering is again a strict partial ordering. However, outcomes can now also be incomparable and indifferent. An agent is indifferent between outcomes $\alpha$ and $\beta$ (written $\alpha \approx \beta$) iff at least one chain of flips between them consists only of indifferent flips. This requires the outcomes to differ only for the values of non-ranked features (e.g. $ab_2 \approx \overline{a}b_2$). Similarly one outcome $\alpha$ is incomparable to another $\beta$ (written $\alpha \bowtie \beta$) iff it is not the case that $\alpha \succ \beta$, $\beta \succ \alpha$ or $\alpha \approx \beta$ (e.g. $ab_3 \bowtie ab_1$).

Partial CP nets can have more than one *optimal outcome* even if their dependency graphs are acyclic: there is one for each possible outcome of the non-ranked features. Finding one of the optimal outcomes in an acyclic partial CP net is linear: it is enough to choose any value for the non-ranked features, and to perform the forward sweep for the remaining features. Optimality testing in acyclic partial CP nets is also linear since, given an outcome, it is enough to set the non-ranked features to the values given by the outcome, and then perform the forward sweep from here. If the resulting outcome is the same as the given one, it is optimal, otherwise it is not.

Given a partial CP net and two outcomes, checking if one dominates another is as difficult as for CP nets. Checking indifference is instead $O(kn)$, where $n$ is the size of the net and $k$ is the number of non-ranked features, assuming a constant time to access a CP table. For each non-ranked feature, we need to check whether flipping it is indifferent for all features depending on it (there may be $O(n)$ of them).

## $m$CP nets

We now put together several partial CP nets to represent the preferences of multiple agents. A **$m$CP net** is a set of $m$ partial CP nets which may share some features, such that every feature is ranked by at least one of the partial CP nets. Graphically, an $m$CP net is obtained by combining the graphs of the partial CP nets so we have one occurrence of each shared feature. For simplicity, we assume that the partial CP nets in a $m$CP net are acyclic. We leave it as future work to see what happens when we relax this assumption. The "$m$" in $m$CP net stands for both multiple agents and the number of agents. Thus, a 3CP net is a $m$CP net in which $m = 3$. Note that a CP net is a 1CP net. Hence, $m$CP nets (with $m = 1$) immediately inherit all the complexity results for regular CP nets.

Each feature in a partial CP net $N$ of an $m$CP net is shared, visible or private. Private features are ranked in $N$ only, and are not visible to other partial CP nets. Visible features for $N$ are those used in the conditions of $N$ but not ranked there. Shared features are ranked in $N$ and also in at least one other of the partial CP nets. For example, Bob's conditional preference on cheese or dessert can be represented within Bob's partial CP net as follows: $c_A : c_B \succ \overline{c_B}$ and $\overline{c_A} : \overline{c_B} \succ c_B$ where $C_B$ is the private feature in Bob's partial CP net representing his preference for cheese or desert, and $C_A$ is the visible feature for Bob from Alice's partial CP net representing her preference for cheese or desert.

An outcome for an $m$CP net is an assignment to all the features in all the partial CP nets to values in their domains. This outcome induces an outcome for each single partial CP nets forming the overall $m$Cp net, by eliminating all the features which do not belong to the partial CP net.

## Voting semantics

We will reason about a $m$CP net by querying each partial CP net in turn and collecting together the results. We can see this as each agent "voting" whether an outcome dominates another. We can obtain different semantics by collecting these votes together in different ways. Many of these semantics may be useful in a distributed setting, or when there are privacy issues. We do not need to know all the preferences of each partial CP net. We may just have to ask if anyone votes against a particular outcome.

The semantics we propose are based on known concepts, like Pareto optimality, lexicographic ordering, and quantitative ranking. Therefore the value of our proposal is more in the embedding of such semantics in the context of $m$CP nets, where indifference and incomparability coexist, rather than in their concept.

Given a $m$CP net and two outcomes $\alpha$ and $\beta$, let $S_\succ$, $S_\prec$, $S_\approx$ and $S_{\bowtie}$ be the sets of agents who say, respectively, that $\alpha \succ \beta$, $\alpha \prec \beta$, $\alpha \approx \beta$, and $\alpha \bowtie \beta$. Note that it is not possible for $|S_\succ| = |S_\prec| = |S_{\bowtie}| = 0$ (i.e. for every agent to be indifferent). Given any two outcomes, some agent must order them or say they are incomparable.

**Pareto.** This semantics is one of consensus. We say that one outcome $\alpha$ is better than another $\beta$ (written $\alpha \succ_p \beta$) iff every agent says that $\alpha \succ \beta$ or $\alpha \approx \beta$. That is, $\alpha \succ_p \beta$ iff $|S_\prec| = |S_{\bowtie}| = 0$. Two outcomes are incomparable iff they are not ordered either way. An outcome is Pareto optimal iff no other outcome is better. Consensus is a stringent test (see (Ephrati & Rosenschein 1996) for the properties of a consensus approach in a multi-agent scenario), and outcomes will often be incomparable as a consequence.

**Majority.** An alternative criterion is just that a majority of the agents who are not indifferent vote in favor. We say that one outcome $\alpha$ is majority better than another $\beta$ (written $\alpha \succ_{maj} \beta$) iff $|S_\succ| > |S_\prec| + |S_{\bowtie}|$. Two outcomes are majority incomparable iff they are not ordered either way. An outcome is majority optimal iff no other outcome is majority better.

**Max.** A weaker criterion is that more agents vote in favor than against or for incomparability. We say that one outcome $\alpha$ is max better than another $\beta$ (written $\alpha \succ_{max} \beta$) iff $|S_\succ| > \max(|S_\prec|, |S_{\bowtie}|)$. Two outcomes are max incomparable iff they are not ordered either way. An outcome is max optimal iff no other outcome is max better.

**Lex.** The next semantics we consider assumes the agents are ordered in importance. If the first agent orders two outcomes then this is reflected in the final outcome. However, if they are indifferent between two outcomes, we consult the second agent, and so on. We say that one outcome $\alpha$ is lexicographically better than another $\beta$ (written $\alpha \succ_{lex} \beta$) iff there exists some distinguished agent such that all agents higher in the order say $\alpha \approx \beta$ and the distinguished agent says $\alpha \succ \beta$. Two outcomes are lexicographically incomparable iff there exists some distinguished agent such that all agents higher in the ordered are indifferent between the two outcomes and the outcomes are incomparable to the distinguished agent. Finally, an outcome is lexicographically optimal iff no other outcome is lexicographically better.

**Rank.** The last semantics eliminates incomparability. Each agent ranks each outcome. Given a partial CP net, the rank of an outcome is zero if the outcome is optimal, otherwise it is the length of the shortest chain of worsening flips between one of the optimal outcomes and it. We say that one outcome $\alpha$ is rank better than another $\beta$ (written $\alpha \succ_r \beta$) iff the sum of the ranks assigned to $\alpha$ is smaller than that assigned to $\beta$. Two outcomes are rank indifferent iff the sum of the ranks assigned to them are equal. Either two outcomes are rank indifferent or one must be rank better than the other. Finally, an outcome is rank optimal iff no other outcome is rank better.

## Basic properties

The Pareto, Lex and Rank semantics define strict orderings. By comparison, neither the Majority or Max semantics induce a strict ordering. More precisely, the following properties can be proved.

**Theorem 1** *$\succ_p$, $\succ_{lex}$ and $\succ_r$ are transitive, irreflexive, and antisymmetric. Thus they induce strict partial orders. $\succ_{maj}$ and $\succ_{max}$ are irreflexive and antisymmetric but may be not transitive.*

The five relations are closely related. We say that one binary relation $R$ subsumes another $S$ iff $xRy$ implies $xSy$. We say that one binary relation $R$ strictly subsumes another $S$ iff $R$ subsumes $S$ but not vice versa. Finally, we say that two binary relations are incomparable iff neither subsumes the other.

**Theorem 2** *$\succ_p$ strictly subsumes $\succ_{maj}$, $\succ_{lex}$ and $\succ_r$. Similarly, $\succ_{maj}$ strictly subsumes $\succ_{max}$. Any other pair of relations is incomparable.*

Figure 2 shows the subsumption schema over the five relations.

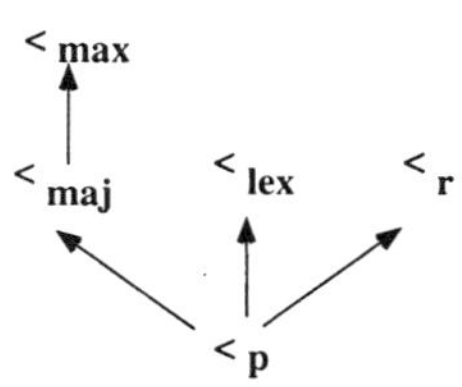


Figure 2: Implications among the six relations corresponding to the voting semantics.

Given two outcomes, we can therefore first try to compare them with $\succ_p$. If they are incomparable, we have three options: either we try to compare them with $\succ_{maj}$ and if they remain incomparable with $\succ_{max}$, or we try to compare them with $\succ_{lex}$, or we try to compare them with $\succ_r$. All options enlarge the set of pairs of outcomes which are comparable. However, only the last option (comparing them with $\succ_r$) is guaranteed to order any two outcomes.

Notice that in all the five relations, except Rank, it is not possible for two outcomes to be indifferent, since we assume that each feature is ranked by at least one of the partial CP nets, while indifference in the qualitative relations (Pareto, Max, Majority, and Lex) means indifference for everybody.

## Optimality

From these subsumption results, the following relationships immediately hold between the various optimal outcomes. For example:

- a majority, lexicographical or rank optimal outcome is necessarily Pareto optimal. However, the reverse is not true. For instance, a Pareto optimal outcome is not necessarily rank optimal.
- A max optimal outcome is necessarily majority optimal, but the reverse is not true.

Similarly, from the incomparability results, we can deduce incomparability also for the respective optimal outcomes.

A fundamental question is whether any optimal outcomes exist. While this is obvious for relations which induce a finite strict order like Pareto, it is not immediately obvious for all of the relations. Nevertheless, optimal outcomes always exist for them. The main reason for this result is that all relations are antisymmetric (see Theorem 1), and thus there can be no cycles in the ordering.

Notice that the set of Pareto optimal outcomes does not necessarily coincide with the set of outcomes which are optimal for all the CP nets. In fact, if an outcome is optimal for all, then it is Pareto optimal. However, the converse is not true in general. For example, consider the set of optimal outcomes of a single partial CP net. If they are all incomparable (no matter if they are not optimal for the other CP nets), then they are also Pareto optimal for the $m$CP net.

We will now give several results on testing optimality and finding optimal outcomes. We assume that there are $n$ binary features in the $m$CP net, $k$ in the largest partial CP net, and $l$ maximum number of visible features in a partial CP net.

To test if an outcome is Pareto optimal, we need to compare ($O(2^k)$) the given outcome with all other outcomes ($O(2^n)$) in all partial CP nets ($m$). Similarly for Max and Majority. For lexicographical optimality, we check if the given outcome is optimal for the first agent ($O(k)$). If it is not, it is not lexicographically optimal. If it is, then, for any optimal outcome of the first agent to which it is indifferent (there may be $2^l$ of them), we must ask the second agent if the given outcome is better ($O(2^k)$). If also the second agent is always indifferent, we must turn to the next agent and so on ($m$ agents). Finally, for rank optimality, we need to first rank all outcomes for each partial CP net. To do this, we start with the optimal ones, which are $O(2^l)$ and have rank 0, and for each of them we build the flipping sequence to any other of the outcomes (which are $2^k$). Then, for each outcome ($2^n$), we compute the global rank by summing the ranks in each partial CP net (the rank tables have $2^k$ elements) and we check that the rank of the given outcome is minimal.

Summarizing, testing optimality is easy for Lex if the size of the partial CP nets ($k$) is bounded, and it is difficult for Pareto, Majority, Max and Rank.

**Theorem 3** *Testing optimality has the following complexity:*

- *for Pareto, Majority and Max: $O(m2^{n+k})$ time;*

- *for Lex:* $O(m2^{l+k})$;
- *for Rank:* $O(m2^{l+k} + 2^n m2^k) = O(m2^{n+k})$.

We now consider the problem of finding an optimal outcome. For Majority, we need to compare ($O(2^k)$) all outcomes ($2^n$) to all other outcomes ($O(2^n)$ in all partial CP nets ($m$). To find a max optimal outcome, we must do the same steps as for Majority. To find a lexicographically optimal outcome, we compute all the optimal outcomes for the first agent ($O(k2^l)$), and then we do the same steps as for testing optimality ($O(m2^l 2^k)$) for each one of them (they can be $2^l$). For Pareto optimality, since lexicographically optimals are also Pareto optimals, the complexity is the same as for Lex. To find a rank optimal outcome, we need to perform the same steps as for testing optimality, except that we don't have to compare with the given outcome. However, this does not change the overall complexity. To summarize, finding an optimal outcome is easy for Pareto and Lex if the size of the partial CP nets ($k$) is bounded, and it is difficult for Majority, Max and Rank. Thus, with respect to optimality testing, Pareto now falls into the easy category.

**Theorem 4** *Finding an optimal outcome has the following complexity:*

- *for Majority and Max:* $O(m2^{2n+k})$;
- *for Lex and Pareto:* $O(m2^{2l+k})$; *the same complexity holds also to find all optimal outcomes, not just one;*
- *for Rank:* $O(m2^{n+k})$ *(for the first optimal outcome, linear for the others).*

## Dominance

We again assume that there are $n$ binary features in the $m$CP net, $k$ in the largest partial CP net, and $l$ visible features.

**Theorem 5** *Given two outcomes, testing if one dominates the another has the following complexity:*

- *for Pareto, Majority, Max, and Lex:* $O(m2^k)$;
- *for Rank:* $O(m2^{n+k})$.

To determine if $O_1 \succ_p O_2$, we must test whether $O_1 \succ O_2$ or $O_1 \approx O_2$ for all $m$ partial CP nets. Each of these tests takes at most $O(2^k)$ time. To determine if $O_1 \succ_{maj} O_2$, we must also test whether $O_1 \succ O_2$ for all $m$ partial CP nets. Only the last test may give us the required majority. Similarly, to determine if $O_1 \succ_{max} O_2$, we must test whether $O_1 \succ O_2$ for all $m$ partial CP nets. Even for Lex, in the worst case, we must check dominance or indifference in all CP nets, since it may be that they are indifferent for all partial CP nets except the last one. For Rank, a brute force algorithm would rank all outcomes and then compare the ranks of the given two. This takes $O(m2^{n+k})$ as explained above for testing Rank optimality. Thus, although Rank gives us a quantitative ordering, it is easier to test dominance in the qualitative semantics (Pareto, Majority, Max, and Lex). In fact, if the number and size of the partial CP nets are bounded, it takes constant time.

The fact that Majority and Max may be not transitive implies that for such semantics we cannot optimize any dominance test exploiting the transitive property. Thus, while in the worst case the complexity is the same as for Pareto and Lex, in practice dominance testing can be much easier for such two semantics.

## Fairness

Having cast our semantics for $m$CP nets in terms of voting, it is appropriate to ask if Arrow's theorem (Arrow 1986) about the impossibility of a fair electoral system applies. Are we fairly combining together the preferences of the individual agents? Observe that, a $m$CP net (and its constituent partial CP nets) can represent preference, indifference and incomparability. By comparison, the votes in an election only express preference and indifference, whilst the election result only expresses society's preference. In addition, partial CP nets can only represent orderings which decompose into independent conditional CP statements, whereas voters in an election can order their votes in any way. As a result, Arrow's theorem does not immediately apply to $m$CP nets.

In short, Arrow's theorem states that no voting system which totally orders three or more candidates can be fair. That is, no voting system cam be free, transitive, independent to irrelevant alternatives, monotonic and non-dictatorial (Arrow 1986). We will adapt these terms to our scenario. We say that a voting semantics for $m$CP nets is **free** iff it is possible to represent any possible ordering of the outcomes. Note that 1CP nets cannot directly represent all possible orderings. For instance, no CP net can represent $ab \succ \bar{a}\bar{b} \succ a\bar{b} \succ \bar{a}b$. However, by combining together features, CP nets can represent any ordering. To return to the last example, we would have to replace the two binary features by a single feature with four values. We say that a voting semantics is **transitive** iff the ordering it defines is transitive. Note that the ordering within each partial CP net in a $m$CP net is transitive by construction. We say that a voting semantics is **independent to irrelevant alternatives** iff the ordering between two outcomes only depends on how the partial CP nets vote on these two outcomes; their votes on other outcomes do not matter. We say that a voting semantics is **monotonic** iff if one agent changes from $\beta \succ \alpha$ or $\beta \approx \alpha$ to $\alpha \succ \beta$ then $\alpha$ cannot become less preferred. Finally, we say that a voting semantics is **non-dictatorial** iff the ordering depends on more than one particular agent. Note that, in assessing if there is a dictator, we ignore incomparability and only consider outcomes which are ordered or indifferent. For example, if one agent says that all outcomes are incomparable, then according to the Pareto semantics, all outcomes are incomparable. However, we do not consider this agent to be a dictator as she does not force any of her *preferences* on the rest. We will say that a semantics for $m$CP nets is **fair** iff it satisfies all five definitions above.

It is possible for $m$CP nets to be fair. For example, the Pareto semantics satisfies all five of these properties. The Pareto semantics is transitive, since it is a strict order. Whether one outcome is better, indifferent or incomparable to another only depends on how each agent votes on these two outcomes. Hence, the Pareto semantics is independent to irrelevant alternatives. The Pareto semantics is also monotonic since improving the preference for an outcome in one partial CP net can only move this up the ordering or leave it in the same place. Finally, the Pareto semantics is non-dictatorial as the ordering clearly depends on more than one particular agent.

On the other hand, none of the other semantics are fair. Majority and Max may be not transitive (see Theorem 1). Proofs that the Majority and Max semantics are free, independent to irrelevant alternatives monotonic and non-dictatorial are similar to those for the Pareto semantics. To show that the Lex semantics may be dictatorial, suppose that the first agent orders all her outcomes. Then this agent will dictate the final outcome. Proofs that the Lex semantics are free, transitive, independent to irrelevant alternatives and monotonic are similar to those for the Pareto semantics.

To show that the Rank semantics may not be independent to irrelevant alternatives, suppose $\alpha \succ_r \beta$. That is, the sum of the ranks assigned to $\alpha$ is less than that assigned to $\beta$. By introducing irrelevant alternatives, we can increase the rank of $\alpha$ so that its rank is larger than $\beta$. Proofs that the Rank semantics are free, transitive, monotonic and non-dictatorial are similar to those for the Pareto semantics.

The following theorem summarizes these results over the five semantics.

**Theorem 6** *The Pareto semantics is free, transitive, independent to irrelevant alternatives, monotonic and non-dictatorial. The Majority and Max semantics are free, independent to irrelevant alternatives, monotonic and non-dictatorial, but may not be transitive. The Lex semantics is free, transitive, independent to irrelevant alternatives and monotonic, but may be dictatorial. The Rank semantics is free, transitive, monotonic, and non-dictatorial but may not be independent to irrelevant alternatives.*

Whilst the Pareto semantics is fair, this comes at a price. The Pareto semantics orders fewer outcomes than the Majority, Max, Lex or Rank semantics. If we wish to order two outcomes, we may therefore have to sacrifice some aspect of fairness.

## Comparison

The following table summaritzes the main properties of the semantics considered in this paper for $m$CP nets. In particular, we show whether the semantics yields a strict order or not, we compare the complexity of testing optimality and dominance, and of finding an optimum. Finally, we also indicate whether the semantics is fair or not. This table lets us compare the five semantics easily.

For example, Lex is the semantics to choose if we don't care about fairness and it is reasonable to order the agents. On the other hand, Pareto is the best in terms of complexity (except for optimum testing). However, as it looks for a consensus among all agents, it orders the fewest pairs of outcomes. Max and Majority ordering are less desirable in terms of complexity, since only dominance testing is easy (under certain assumptions). Moreover, they are equal with respect to fairness criteria. Since Majority subsumes Max, Majority has more optimal outcomes and a weaker ordering. Finally, the Rank semantics has bad complexity, and is not fair. This bad complexity seems a result of merging the qualitative nature of CP nets with the quantitative spirit of a rank. Note that this complexity is only seen the first time two outcomes are ordered, and subsequent queries can be answered in linear time.

| | Pareto | Maj | Max | Lex | Rank |
|---|---|---|---|---|---|
| S.O. | yes | no | no | yes | yes |
| Test opt. | diff | diff | diff | e-k | diff |
| Find opt. | e-k | diff | diff | e-k | diff |
| Dominance | e-k<br>c-m | e-k<br>c-m | e-k<br>c-m | e-k<br>c-m | diff |
| Fairness | yes | no | no | no | no |

Table 1: Comparison among the five semantics. Legenda: S.O. = strict order, diff = difficult, e-k = easy if k bounded, c-m = constant if m bounded).

## Conclusions and Future Work

We have introduced $m$CP nets, an extension of the CP net formalism to represent the qualitative and conditional preferences of multiple agents. We have given a number of different semantics for reasoning with $m$CP nets. The semantics are all based on the idea of individual agents voting. We then described how to test optimality and preference. We also discussed whether the voting schemes fairly combine together the preferences of the individual agents.

We would like to explore distributed $m$CP nets. We have assumed so far that decision making is coordinated in some central place. However, in many applications, decision making is more distributed. An additional direction for further research is the extension of our work to CP nets where it is possible to partially order the values of a feature. In this paper we have considered the case in which one either totally orders the values or it does not order them at all.

## References


Arrow, K. 1986. Rationality of self and others in an economic system. *Journal of Business* Vol. 59 (4).

Boutilier, C.; Brafman, R.; Hoos, H.; and Poole, D. 1999. Reasoning with conditional ceteris paribus preference statements. In *UAI-99*, 71–80.

Domshlak, C., and Brafman, R. 2002. Cp-nets - reasoning and consistency testing. In *KR-02*, 121–132.

Domshlak, C.; Rossi, F.; Venable, K.; and Walsh, T. 2003. Reasoning about soft constraints and conditional preferences: complexity results and approximation techniques. In *IJCAI-03*.

Doyle, J., and Wellman, M. 1994. Representing preferences as ceteris paribus comparatives. In *AAAI Spring Symposium on Decision-Making Planning*, 69–75.

Ephrati, E., and Rosenschein, J. S. 1996. Deriving consensus in multiagent systems. *Artifi cial Intelligence* 87:21–74.

Yager, R. R. 2001. Fusion of multi-agent preference orderings. *Fuzzy Sets and Systems* 117:1–12.

# Extending CP-Nets with Stronger Conditional Preference Statements

**Nic Wilson**
Cork Constraint Computation Centre
Department of Computer Science, University College Cork, Cork, Ireland
n.wilson@4c.ucc.ie

### Abstract

A logic of conditional preferences is defined, with a language which allows the compact representation of certain kinds of conditional preference statements, a semantics and a proof theory. CP-nets can be expressed in this language, and the semantics and proof theory generalise those of CP-nets. Despite being substantially more expressive, the formalism maintains important properties of CP-nets; there are simple sufficient conditions for consistency, and, under these conditions, optimal outcomes can be efficiently generated. It is also then easy to find a total order on outcomes which extends the conditional preference order, and an approach to constrained optimisation can be used which generalises a natural approach for CP-nets. Some results regarding the expressive power of CP-nets are also given.

## Introduction

CP-nets (Boutilier *et al.* 1999; a) is a formalism for compactly expressing conditional preferences in multivariate problems. They involve statements of the form: $u : x > x'$, where $x, x'$ are values of a variable $X$ and $u$ is an assignment to a set of variables $U$ (called *parents of* $X$). The interpretation is that given $u$, $x$ is (strictly) preferred to $x'$, *all else being equal* (*ceteris paribus*); that is, for all assignments $s$ to the other variables $S$, $sux$ is preferred to $sux'$, where e.g., $sux$ is the outcome (complete assignment) $\alpha$ such that $\alpha(X) = x$, $\alpha(U) = u$ and $\alpha(S) = s$. A set of such statements generates a preference relation on complete tuples, and consistency corresponds to the induced preference relation being acyclic, and hence being a (strict) partial order. An acyclic CP-net involves a set of such statements structured in a particular way, so that the parent-child relation on variables is acyclic. This condition ensures consistency. They also possess a number of other attractive properties.

However, CP-nets are quite restrictive in the kinds of preference statements that they can represent. The *ceteris paribus* statements they are based upon express a very natural kind of preference, but a rather weak one. An agent will sometimes want to express much stronger statements such as $x$ *is preferred to* $x'$ *irrespective of the values of other variables*, where the variable $X$ is the most important variable, and, for example, $x'$ represents a value which should be avoided if at all possible. CP-nets cannot generally express such statements (in a compact way).

This paper develops a formalism along similar lines to CP-nets, but where a richer language of preference statements can be expressed: stronger conditional preference statements as well as the usual CP-nets *ceteris paribus* statements, and also allowing locally partially ordered preferences. The language consists of statements of the form $u : x > x' \, [W]$, (where $W$ is a subset of $S$) which represents that for all assignments $w, w'$ to $W$ and assignments $t$ to $S - W$, $tuxw$ is preferred to $tux'w'$. So, given $u$ and any $t$, $x$ is preferred to $x'$ irrespective of the values of $W$. CP-nets *ceteris paribus* statements are represented by such statements with $W = \emptyset$, and the strong conditional preference statement in the previous paragraph corresponds to $\top : x > x' \, [V - \{X\}]$, where $V$ is the set of all variables. As in CP-nets, this is a compact representation: each statement typically corresponds to many preferences between outcomes.

Key properties of CP-nets generalise naturally for this formalism. In particular:

— the semantics and complete proof theory;

— there is still a simple and efficient algorithm for generating an optimal outcome;

— there are simple sufficient conditions for consistency based on acyclicity of variable order;

— there exists an efficient algorithm for picking a subset of the optimal solutions, when the set of outcomes is constrained.

The next section introduces the formalism, which can be viewed as a simple logic of conditional preferences. A semantics is given and also a complete proof theory, based on 'swapping sequences' which is the natural generalisation of flipping sequences in CP-nets. The following section examines the relative expressivity of the language as compared with CP-nets. It shows how CP-nets can be represented within the language; however, this stronger kind of preference statement, which can be used, for example, to construct a lexicographic order on outcomes, is not expressible within the language of CP-nets (or TCP-nets).

Some of the main technical results in the paper use what we call a partial conditional lexicographic (pcl) order on outcomes, which is similar to a standard lexicographic order except that it allows the importance ordering on variables to be only partial, and allows the value orderings to be partial, and conditional on the values of more important variables. If a set $\Gamma$ of preference statements satisfies a local consistency property and the associated relation on variables is acyclic then the induced preference order $>_\Gamma$ is dominated by a pcl order, which implies consistency, as pcl orders are strict partial orders. Generating outcomes in an order consistent with a pcl order is easy, just as it is for a standard lexicographic order; this can then be used, for example, in a constrained optimisation algorithm to generate some of the optimal (i.e., maximal) outcomes with respect to $>_\Gamma$, as discussed in the penultimate section along with other applications of the results.

## A Logic of Conditional Preferences

In this section a logic of conditional preferences is defined, with a language, semantics and a kind of proof theory. It is strongly related to a system defined in (Lang 2002), where general complexity results are derived. As we will see later, CP-nets can be expressed within this language. The logic has a somewhat restrictive language, but the restrictions entail some nice properties, generalising properties of CP-nets.

**The Language.** Let $V$ be a set of variables. For each $X \in V$ let $\underline{X}$ be the set of possible values of $X$. For subset of variables $U \subseteq V$ let $\underline{U} = \prod_{X \in U} \underline{X}$ be the set of possible assignments to $U$. A *complete tuple* or *outcome* is an element of $\underline{V}$, i.e., an assignment to all the variables. For complete tuple $\alpha$ and partial tuple $u \in \underline{U}$, we may write $\alpha \models u$ to mean that $\alpha$ projected to $U$ gives $u$, which can also be written as $\alpha(U) = u$.

The language $\mathcal{L}_V$ (abbreviated to $\mathcal{L}$) consists of all statements of the form $u : x > x' \, [W]$, where $u$ is an assignment to a set of variables $U \subseteq V$ (i.e., $u \in \underline{U}$), $x, x'$ are different values of a variable $X \notin U$, and $W$ is some subset of $V - U - \{X\}$. The assignment to the empty set of variables is written $\top$. If $\varphi$ is the statement $u : x > x' \, [W]$, we may write $u_\varphi = u$, $U_\varphi = U$, $x_\varphi = x$, $x'_\varphi = x'$, $W_\varphi = W$ and $T_\varphi = V - (\{X\} \cup U \cup W)$.

Subsets of $\mathcal{L}$ are called *conditional preference theories* (on $V$). For $\varphi = u : x > x' \, [W]$, let $\varphi^*$ be the set of pairs of outcomes $\{(tuxw, tux'w') : t \in \underline{T_\varphi}, w, w' \in \underline{W}\}$. Such pairs $(\alpha, \beta) \in \varphi^*$ are intended to represent a preference for $\alpha$ over $\beta$, and $\varphi$ is intended as a compact representation of the preference information $\varphi^*$. Informally, $\varphi$ represents that, given $u$ and any $t$, $x$ is preferred to $x'$, irrespective of the assignments to $W$. For conditional preference theory $\Gamma \subseteq \mathcal{L}$, define $\Gamma^* = \bigcup_{\varphi \in \Gamma} \varphi^*$. $\Gamma^*$ represents a set of preferences. We assume here that preferences are transitive, so it is then natural to define order $>_\Gamma$, induced on $\underline{V}$ by $\Gamma$, to be the transitive closure of $\Gamma^*$. In the next section it is shown that CP-nets can be represented in terms of statements $u : x > x' \, [W]$ with $W = \emptyset$.

Note that conditional preference theories allow locally partially ordered preferences: we do not need to assume that we can elicit a total order on the values of a variable given each assignment to its parents. This kind of representation of conditional preferences is very flexible as regards elicitation: we can reason with an arbitrary subset $\Gamma$ of the language $\mathcal{L}$, so we can accept any conditional preference statements (of the appropriate form) that the agent is happy to give us (however, to maintain consistency, we may insist on the conditional preference theory $\Gamma$ having particular properties, such as the conditions of Corollary 1 below). More statements can be added later, and, because the logic is monotonic, all of our previous deductions from $\Gamma$ will still hold, in particular whether one outcome is preferred to another

We will associate with a conditional preference theory $\Gamma$ a pair of binary relations on the set of variables $V$. Let $H(\varphi) = \{(Y, X_\varphi) : Y \in U_\varphi\}$ and let $H(\Gamma) = \bigcup_{\varphi \in \Gamma} H(\varphi)$; this can be thought of as a directed graph, which contains edge $(Y, X)$ if and only if there is some conditional preference statement $\varphi \in \Gamma$ which makes the preferences for $X$ conditional on $Y$. Let $G(\varphi) = H(\varphi) \cup \{(X_\varphi, Z) : Z \in W_\varphi\}$, and define $G(\Gamma) = \bigcup_{\varphi \in \Gamma} G(\varphi)$. $G(\Gamma)$ is $H(\Gamma)$ with extra edges $(X, Z)$ when there is some $\varphi \in \Gamma$ representing some preference for values of $X$ irrespective of the value of $Z$.

**Example.** I'm planning a holiday. I can either go next week ($\mathtt{n}$) or later in the year ($\mathtt{l}$). I've decided to go either to Oxford ($\mathtt{o}$) or to Manchester ($\mathtt{m}$), and I can either fly ($\mathtt{f}$) or drive and take a car ferry ($\mathtt{d}$). So there are three variables, $X_1$, $X_2$ and $X_3$, where $\underline{X_1} = \{\mathtt{l}, \mathtt{n}\}$, $\underline{X_2} = \{\mathtt{m}, \mathtt{o}\}$ and $\underline{X_3} = \{\mathtt{d}, \mathtt{f}\}$. Firstly, I'd prefer to go next week irrespective of the choices of the other variables, as I could do with a break soon. This can be represented by statement $\varphi_1$ which equals $\top : \mathtt{n} > \mathtt{l} \, [\{X_2, X_3\}]$. This represents a set $\varphi_1^*$ of pairs of outcomes $(\mathtt{n}w_1, \mathtt{l}w_2)$, where $w_1$ and $w_2$ are both arbitrary assignments to the set of variables $\{X_2, X_3\}$; e.g., $w_1 = \mathtt{mf}$ and $w_2 = \mathtt{of}$ gives the pair $(\mathtt{nmf}, \mathtt{lof})$ indicating the preference of $\mathtt{nmf}$ over $\mathtt{lof}$. $\varphi_1$ is a compact way of representing the 16 pairs in $\varphi_1^*$. Secondly, all else being equal, I'd prefer to go to Oxford rather than Manchester. This is represented by the statement $\varphi_2$ which equals $\top : \mathtt{o} > \mathtt{m} \, [\emptyset]$. This is an unconditional *ceteris paribus* statement. It represents set $\varphi_2^*$ of pairs of outcomes $(x_1 \mathtt{o} x_3, x_1 \mathtt{m} x_3)$ meaning outcome $x_1 \mathtt{o} x_3$ is preferred to $x_1 \mathtt{m} x_3$, where $x_1$ is any value of $X_1$ and $x_3$ is any value of $X_3$.

My preferences on variable $X_3$ are conditional. I'd prefer to fly rather than drive unless I go later in the year to Manchester, when the weather will be warmer and a car would be useful for touring around. This can be represented by conditional preference statements $\varphi_3$, $\varphi_4$ and $\varphi_5$ defined as follows. $\varphi_3$ is $\mathtt{n} : \mathtt{f} > \mathtt{d} \, [\emptyset]$, and $\varphi_4$ is $\mathtt{o} : \mathtt{f} > \mathtt{d} \, [\emptyset]$. $\varphi_5$ is $\mathtt{lm} : \mathtt{d} > \mathtt{f} \, [\emptyset]$, representing $\varphi_5^*$ which consists of the single preference of $\mathtt{lmd}$ over $\mathtt{lmf}$.

Let $\Gamma = \{\varphi_1, \ldots, \varphi_5\}$. $G(\Gamma)$ equals the total order on variables, $\{(X_1, X_2), (X_1, X_3), (X_2, X_3)\}$, and $H(\Gamma) = \{(X_1, X_3), (X_2, X_3)\}$. The statement $\varphi_1$ cannot be represented in a CP-net on $V = \{X_1, X_2, X_3\}$. The others all can as they involve empty $W$ and they express locally totally ordered preferences.

The induced partial ordering $>_\Gamma$ on outcomes can

be shown to be the transitive closure of: $\texttt{nof} >_\Gamma \{\texttt{nod}, \texttt{nmf}\} >_\Gamma \texttt{nmd} >_\Gamma \texttt{lof} >_\Gamma \texttt{lod} >_\Gamma \texttt{lmd} >_\Gamma \texttt{lmf}$, so that $>_\Gamma$ is almost a total order, with only the pair of outcomes nod and nmf not being ordered.

**Semantics.** We define models of $\mathcal{L}$ to be strict total orders on $\underline{V}$, i.e., irreflexive[1] transitive binary relations $>$ on $\underline{V}$ such that for all $\alpha$ and $\beta$ in $\underline{V}$, with $\alpha \neq \beta$, either $\alpha > \beta$ or $\beta > \alpha$.[2] For such a total order $>$, we say $> \models \varphi$ if and only if $> \supseteq \varphi^*$, so that $>$ is a model of $\varphi = u : x > x' [W]$ if and only if for all $t \in \underline{T}$ and $w, w' \in \underline{W}$, $tuxw > tux'w'$. For $\Gamma \subseteq \mathcal{L}$ we say $> \models \Gamma$ if and only if for all $\varphi \in \Gamma$, $> \models \varphi$, which is if and only if $> \supseteq \Gamma^*$. For $\Gamma \subseteq \mathcal{L}$ and $\varphi \in \mathcal{L}$, we define the semantic entailment relation by $\Gamma \models \varphi$ if and only if $> \models \varphi$ for all $>$ such that $> \models \Gamma$. For $\alpha, \beta \in \underline{V}$ we also say that $\Gamma \models (\alpha, \beta)$ if $\alpha > \beta$ holds for all models $>$ of $\Gamma$. We say that $\Gamma$ *is consistent* if it has a model, i.e., if there exists strict total order $>$ with $> \models \Gamma$. The construction of semantic entailment relation $\models$ ensures that it is monotonic.

In the example, $\Gamma$ is consistent; in fact, there are two total orders $>$ on outcomes which satisfy $\Gamma$ (i.e., contain $>_\Gamma$); they only differ according to whether they have $\texttt{nod} > \texttt{nmf}$ or $\texttt{nmf} > \texttt{nod}$.

**Proof theory.** Let $\alpha, \beta \in \underline{V}$ be two outcomes. We say that $\beta$ *is a worsening swap from* $\alpha$ with respect to conditional preference theory $\Gamma$ if and only if $(\alpha, \beta) \in \Gamma^*$, i.e., iff there exists $\varphi = (u : x > x' [W]) \in \Gamma$ such that $\alpha \models u$, $\beta \models u$, $\alpha(X) = x$, $\beta(X) = x'$, and $\alpha(T_\varphi) = \beta(T_\varphi)$. We say that $\beta$ *can be reached from* $\alpha$ *with a worsening swapping sequence* (with respect to $\Gamma$) if there exists a sequence $\alpha = \alpha_1, \ldots, \alpha_l = \beta$ with for each $k = 1, \ldots, l-1$, $\alpha_{k+1}$ is a worsening swap from $\alpha_k$, i.e., $(\alpha_k, \alpha_{k+1}) \in \Gamma^*$. Clearly, then $(\alpha, \beta)$ is in the transitive closure $>_\Gamma$ of $\Gamma^*$. Conversely, if $(\alpha', \beta')$ is in the transitive closure of $\Gamma^*$ then there exists a sequence $\alpha' = \alpha_1, \ldots, \alpha_l = \beta'$ with for each $k = 1, \ldots, l-1$, $(\alpha_k, \alpha_{k+1}) \in \Gamma^*$. In fact we have the following result which is a soundness and completeness result for worsening swapping sequences.

**Theorem 1** *Let $\Gamma$ be a conditional preference theory on $V$ and let $\alpha, \beta \in \underline{V}$ be outcomes. Then $\alpha >_\Gamma \beta$ if and only if there exists a worsening swapping sequence with respect to $\Gamma$ from $\alpha$ to $\beta$. Also $\Gamma$ is consistent if and only if $>_\Gamma$ is irreflexive. If $\Gamma$ is consistent then $\Gamma \models (\alpha, \beta)$ if and only if $\alpha >_\Gamma \beta$.*

## CP-nets and Expressibility

In this section we show how CP-nets can be expressed as conditional preference theories, using statements $u : x > x' [W]$ with $W = \emptyset$. It is also shown that the language is a good deal more expressive than CP-nets.

[1]Relation $>$ on set $A$ is irreflexive if and only if for all $a \in A$, it is not the case that $a > a$. It is acyclic if and only if its transitive closure is irreflexive, so that there are no cycles $a > a' > a'' > \cdots > a$.

[2]Binary relation $\succ$ on set $\underline{V}$ is defined to be a subset of $\underline{V} \times \underline{V}$; the notations "$(\alpha, \beta) \in \succ$" and "$\alpha \succ \beta$" are used interchangeably.

### Expressing CP-nets in the language

A *CP-net over* $V$ is defined (see (Boutilier *et al.* 1999) and especially definitions 1, 2 and 3 of (Boutilier *et al.* a)) to be a pair $N = (H, \mathrm{CT})$ where $H$ is a (binary) relation on $V$ (which is conventionally thought of as a directed graph) and CT is a function which assigns a *conditional preference table* to each variable $X \in V$. The conditional preference table $\mathrm{CT}(X)$ is defined to be a function which assigns to each[3] $u \in \underline{\mathrm{Pa}_H(X)}$ a strict total order $\succ_u^X$ on $\underline{X}$.

Let $>$ be a (strict) total order on $\underline{V}$. Let $X$ be a variable and let $u \in \underline{\mathrm{Pa}_H(X)}$ be an assignment to the parents of $X$. Let $T = V - \mathrm{Pa}_H(X) - \{X\}$. $>$ is said to satisfy $\succ_u^X$ if $tux > tux'$ holds for all $t \in \underline{T}$ and for all $x, x' \in \underline{X}$ such that $x \succ_u^X x'$.

$>$ is said to satisfy CP-net $N = (H, \mathrm{CT})$ if for all $X \in V$, and all $u \in \underline{\mathrm{Pa}_H(X)}$, $>$ satisfies $\succ_u^X$ (where $\succ_u^X = \mathrm{CT}(X)(u)$). CP-net $N$ is said to be satisfiable if there exists some $>$ which satisfies $N$. There is a simple sufficient condition for satisfiability of a CP-net $N$: that its associated relation $H$ is acyclic.

For CP-net $N$ define relation $\succ_N$ on $\underline{V}$ as follows. For $\alpha, \beta \in \underline{V}$, $\alpha \succ_N \beta$ if and only if $\alpha > \beta$ for all total orders $>$ satisfying $N$. Therefore $\succ_N$ is the intersection of all $>$ satisfying $N$.

For $X \in V$ and $u \in \underline{\mathrm{Pa}_H(X)}$, let $\Gamma_N^{X,u} \subseteq \mathcal{L}$ be the set of statements $\{(u : x > x' [\emptyset]) : x, x' \in \underline{X}, x \succ_u^X x'\}$. Let conditional preference theory $\Gamma_N$ be the union of sets $\Gamma_N^{X,u}$ over all $X \in V$ and $u \in \underline{\mathrm{Pa}_H(X)}$. Note that the construction of $\Gamma_N$ is linear in the size of the conditional preference table.[4] Now, $> \models \Gamma_N^{X,u}$ if and only if $>$ satisfies $\succ_u^X$. So $> \models \Gamma_N$ if and only if $>$ satisfies $N$. Using Theorem 1 this leads to:

**Proposition 1** *Let $N$ be a CP-net, and $\Gamma_N \subseteq \mathcal{L}$ (as defined above) be its associated conditional preference theory. Then $N$ is satisfiable if and only if $\Gamma_N$ is consistent. If $N$ is satisfiable, then $>_{\Gamma_N} = \succ_N$.*

This shows that a CP-net can be represented within the language $\mathcal{L}$, with the same associated order on outcomes.

### Representing lexicographic orders

For set of variables $V$, a lexicographic order on $\underline{V}$ involves an ordering $X_1, \ldots, X_n$ of the variables $V$, and for each $X_i$ a total order $>_i$ on the set of values $\underline{X_i}$ of $X_i$. Define relation $>_{lex}$ as follows. For $\alpha, \beta \in \underline{V}$, $\alpha >_{lex} \beta$ if and only if $\alpha \neq \beta$ and $\alpha(X_i) >_i \beta(X_i)$, where $X_i$ is the first variable (i.e., with minimal $i$) such that $\alpha(X_i) \neq \beta(X_i)$. The lexicographic order $>_{lex}$ is a strict total order on $\underline{V}$.

The following proposition shows that lexicographic orders can be represented by conditional preference theories, i.e., for any lexicographic order $>_{lex}$, there exists $\Gamma$ such that its associated order $>_\Gamma$ equals $>_{lex}$.

[3]$\mathrm{Pa}_H(X)$, the parents of $X$ with respect to $H$, is the set of all $Y$ such that $(Y, X) \in H$.

[4]If the domain of variable $X$ is large, one might represent total order $\succ_u^X$ by a sub-relation whose transitive closure is $\succ_u^X$; the sub-relation could then also be used in the definition of $\Gamma_N^{X,u}$.

**Proposition 2** *For each variable $X_i$, let $\Gamma_i$ be the set of all statements $\top : x > x' [\{X_{i+1}, \dots, X_n\}]$, where $x, x' \in \underline{X_i}$ are such that $x >_i x'$. Let $\Gamma = \Gamma_1 \cup \cdots \cup \Gamma_n$. Then the associated order $>_\Gamma$ equals $>_{lex}$.*

The following lemma is useful for revealing the limited expressiveness of CP-nets (and TCP-nets (Brafman, Domshlak, & Shimony 2002)). We say that $\alpha$ *covers* $\beta$ with respect to a (transitive) relation $\succ$ on $\underline{V}$ if $\alpha \succ \beta$ and there does not exist $\gamma \in \underline{V}$ with $\alpha \succ \gamma \succ \beta$.

**Lemma 1**

(i) *Let $\Gamma$ be a conditional preference theory. Suppose $\alpha$ covers $\beta$ with respect to $>_\Gamma$. Then $\beta$ is a worsening swap from $\alpha$.*

(ii) *Let $N$ be a CP-net. Suppose $\alpha$ covers $\beta$ with respect to $\succ_N$. Then $\alpha$ and $\beta$ differ on precisely one variable. In other words, there exists $X \in V$ with $\alpha(X) \neq \beta(X)$ and for all $X' \in V - \{X\}$, $\alpha(X') = \beta(X')$.*

(iii) *Let $M$ be a TCP-net, with associated relation $\succ_M$ (so that $\gamma \succ_M \delta$ if and only if $\gamma \succ \delta$ is a consequence of $M$). Suppose $\alpha$ covers $\beta$ with respect to $\succ_M$. Then $\alpha$ and $\beta$ differ either on one variable or on two variables.*

All three parts follow easily from the appropriate completeness theorems for swapping/flipping sequences: Theorem 1 above for (i); Theorem 8 (the CP-nets completeness result for flipping sequences) of (Boutilier *et al.* a) for (ii); and for (iii): the TCP-nets completeness result: see lemma 5 of (Brafman, Domshlak, & Shimony 2002). For example, to prove (iii): $\alpha$ covers $\beta$ with respect to $\succ_M$ implies, by lemma 5 of (Brafman, Domshlak, & Shimony 2002), that there exists a worsening flipping sequence from $\alpha$ to $\beta$; but since $\alpha$ covers $\beta$, there can be no element in the sequence between $\alpha$ and $\beta$, so $\beta$ is a worsening TCP-net flip from $\alpha$. Therefore $\alpha$ and $\beta$ differ on either one or two variables, according to whether it's a CP-flip or an I-flip (see definition 4 of (Brafman, Domshlak, & Shimony 2002)).

In the example, there are a pair of outcomes, nmd and lof, which are consecutive in the preference order $>_\Gamma$ that differ on all three variables. The lemma then implies that the preferences in the example cannot be represented by a CP-net or TCP-net, i.e., there's no CP-net or TCP-net $N$ on $V$ with $>_N = >_\Gamma$.

A consequence of the above lemma is that, except in some trivial cases, if $N$ is a CP-net or a TCP-net, then $\succ_N$ is never a lexicographic order. This is because lexicographic orders on $n$ variables include consecutive elements that differ on all $n$ variables (assuming the domain of each variable has more than one element). To illustrate this, consider the case of boolean variables and the order on complete tuples being just the usual order of binary numbers. Then $(1, 0, 0, \dots, 0)$ and $(0, 1, 1, \dots, 1)$ are consecutive in the order, but they differ on all the variables. Therefore, by the lemma the order cannot be generated by a CP-net if $n > 1$ and the order cannot be generated by a TCP-net if $n > 2$.

**Proposition 3** *Let $>_{lex}$ be a lexicographic order (as defined above) on $\underline{V}$, where the domain of each variables contains more than one element, i.e., for all $X \in V$, $|\underline{X}| > 1$. Then (a) if $|V| > 1$, there exists no CP-net $N$ on $V$ with $\succ_N = >_{lex}$; (b) if $|V| > 2$, there exists no TCP-net $M$ on $V$ with $\succ_M = >_{lex}$.*

## Representing stronger conditional preferences

Lexicographic orders are a very special type of order, but the kind of statements they represent can be natural. Let $\succ$ be a strict partial order (i.e., a transitive irreflexive relation) on $\underline{V}$. Let $X \in V$ and $W \subseteq V - \{X\}$ and let $T = V - \{X\} - W$, so that $\{X\}$, $W$ and $T$ partition $V$. Let $>_X$ be a non-empty partial order on $\underline{X}$. We say $X$ (unconditionally) dominates $W$ with respect to $(\succ, >_X)$ if the following condition holds: for $\alpha, \beta \in \underline{V}$, $\alpha \succ \beta$ holds whenever $\alpha$ and $\beta$ are such that: $\alpha(X) >_X \beta(X)$ and $\alpha(T) = \beta(T)$. In particular, if $X$ dominates $W = V - \{X\}$ with respect to $(\succ, >_X)$, then a sufficient condition for $\alpha \succ \beta$ is $\alpha(X) >_X \beta(X)$. This is a stronger form of preference statement than *ceteris paribus* statements. It represents a situation where the value of variable $X$ is much more important than the values of any other variable; we prefer any outcome that does better on variable $X$.

This kind of condition is naturally represented within the language $\mathcal{L}$. Let $\Theta = \{(\top : x > x' [W]) : x >_X x'\}$. Then, if $\Gamma \supseteq \Theta$, $X$ dominates $W$ with respect to $(>_\Gamma, >_X)$. Such statements can be used to represent a lexicographic order, as shown above.

This type of variable dominance is not at all natural for CP-nets and TCP-nets, as the following two propositions indicate. But it is easy to construct consistent $\Gamma$ which satisfy the hypotheses of the two propositions (e.g., $\Gamma = \Theta$ for the representation $\Theta$ above), or extensions of $\Theta$, in particular, a lexicographic order).

**Proposition 4** *Consider any satisfiable CP-net $N$ on $V = \{X_1, \dots, X_n\}$ $(n \geq 2)$ such that $X_2$ has no parents and $|\underline{X_2}| > 1$ with associated order $\succ_N$ on $\underline{V}$. Then for no (non-empty) $>_1$ on $\underline{X_1}$ is it the case that $X_1$ dominates $\{X_2, \dots, X_n\}$ with respect to $(\succ_N, >_1)$.*

In the example, $X_1$ dominates $\{X_2, X_3\}$ with respect to $(>_\Gamma, >_1)$, where n $>_1$ l; also $X_2$ has no parents. The proposition then implies (without looking at the level of outcomes) that there's no CP-net $N$ on $V$ with $\succ_N = >_\Gamma$. It also implies that the same would hold if we were to change the preferences on $X_3$ in any way.

There is a similar result for TCP-nets:

**Proposition 5** *Consider any TCP-net $M$ on $V = \{X_1, \dots, X_n\}$ $(n \geq 3)$ such that $X_2$ has no parents and $X_3$ has no parents, $|\underline{X_2}|, |\underline{X_3}| > 1$ and the associated relation $\succ_M$ on $\underline{V}$ is acyclic. Then for no total order $>_1$ on $\underline{X_1}$ is it the case that $X_1$ dominates $\{X_2, \dots, X_n\}$ with respect to $(\succ_M, >_1)$.*

**Generating precisely a total order on outcomes** We finish this section with an expressibility result that can be proved with the help of Theorem 2 and Lemma 1, illustrating how hard it is to generate a CP-net associated to a total order of outcomes. (However, one should not usually expect an agent's preferences to generate a total order, so this should not be considered as a damning criticism of CP-nets.) It shows that once one removes the obvious symmetries concerned with variable and value ordering, there is a unique CP-net on a set of boolean variables which generates a total order of outcomes. This contrasts with the situation for conditional preference theories, where there are precisely $2^{2^n-n-1}$ total orders $>$ with maximum element $(1,1,\ldots,1)$ on $\underline{V}$ with are equal to some $>_\Gamma$, for $\Gamma$ such that $G(\Gamma)$ is consistent with the variable ordering $X_1,\ldots,X_n$.

**Proposition 6** *There is a unique CP-net $N$ on boolean variables $V = \{X_1,\ldots,X_n\}$ satisfying the following properties: (i) the CP-net order $\succ_N$ is a total order of outcomes with maximum element $(1,\ldots,1)$; (ii) the variable ordering is consistent with the relation $H$ on $V$ associated with $N$, i.e., $(X_j, X_i) \in H$ implies $j < i$.*

It can be shown furthermore that $H$ is maximally large: $H = \{(X_j, X_i) : j < i\}$ so that the parents set $\text{Pa}(X_i)$ of $X_i$ is $\{X_1,\ldots,X_{i-1}\}$. The conditional preference tables (when written out explicitly) are therefore of exponential size. They can be expressed compactly as follows: for each $i = 1,\ldots,n$, and assignment $u$ to $\text{Pa}(X_i)$, $1 \succ_u^{X_i} 0$ if and only if $u$ (viewed as a sequence of boolean values) contains an even number of zeros.

## Ensuring Consistency

The main purpose of this section is to give simple and natural sufficient conditions for a conditional preference theory to be consistent. There is a clear necessary condition, which we call local consistency, based on considering each variable separately (that always holds for CP-nets). The main result of this section is that given $G(\Gamma)$ is acyclic, $\Gamma$ is consistent if and only if $\Gamma$ is locally consistent. (This generalises the acyclicity condition for CP-nets since, for CP-nets, the relations $G$ and $H$ (of the corresponding conditional preference theory) are equal.) To prove this we use a more general form of lexicographic order, which we call a pcl order: a partial conditional lexicographic order. It is like a lexicographic order except that the importance order between variables need only be a partial order, and the order on values of a variable can be partial and conditional on the values of more important variables. A pcl order is a strict partial order. We show that for any locally consistent conditional preference theory $\Gamma$ such that $G(\Gamma)$ is acyclic, the associated order $>_\Gamma$ on outcomes is a subrelation of a pcl order; this then implies that $>_\Gamma$ is irreflexive, so $\Gamma$ is consistent by Theorem 1.

### Local consistency

In certain cases, it's clear that $\Gamma$ is not consistent, by just looking at local conditions: if there's a sequence of worsening swaps from some $\alpha$ to itself, which just change the values of a single variable $X$.

Fix conditional preference theory $\Gamma$ on $V$, and consider outcome $\alpha \in \underline{V}$ and variable $X \in V$. Say that pair $(x, x')$ of values of $X$ *is validated by* $\alpha$ if there exists some statement $(u : x > x' \, [W]) \in \Gamma$ with $\alpha \models u$ (i.e., $u$ is a projection of $\alpha$). Define relation $>_\alpha^X$ on $\underline{X}$ to be the transitive closure of the set of all pairs $(x, x')$ validated by $\alpha$. We say that $\Gamma$ is *locally consistent* if for all $\alpha$ and $X$, $>_\alpha^X$ is irreflexive.

If $\Gamma$ were not locally consistent then there would exist outcome $\alpha$, variable $X$ and a sequence $x_1,\ldots,x_k$ of values of $X$ with associated statements in $\Gamma$, $(u_i : x_i > x_{i+1} \, [W_i])$, such that $\alpha \models u_i$, and $\alpha(X) = x_1 = x_k$. This would give a worsening swapping sequence from $\alpha$ to $\alpha$ (only involving changing variable $X$), thus implying that $\Gamma$ is not consistent, by Theorem 1. Therefore local consistency is a necessary condition for consistency.

The set of statements $\Gamma$ in the example is easily seen to be locally consistent. However, if $\varphi_5$ were changed to $\varphi_5' = \mathtt{m} : \mathtt{d} > \mathtt{f} \, [\emptyset]$ then $\Gamma$ would no longer be locally consistent as $\varphi_5'$ and $\varphi_3 = \mathtt{n} : \mathtt{f} > \mathtt{d} \, [\emptyset]$ would give conflicting preferences for $X_3$ under the conditions $\mathtt{nm}$. Let $\alpha = \mathtt{nmd}$. Then $>_\alpha^{X_3}$ is not irreflexive since $\mathtt{d} >_\alpha^{X_3} \mathtt{f}$ using $\varphi_5'$ and $\mathtt{f} >_\alpha^{X_3} \mathtt{d}$ using $\varphi_3$, so $\mathtt{d} >_\alpha^{X_3} \mathtt{d}$. $\Gamma$ would no longer be consistent as $>_\Gamma$ is no longer irreflexive: we have $\mathtt{nmd} >_\Gamma \mathtt{nmf} >_\Gamma \mathtt{nmd}$ so $\alpha >_\Gamma \alpha$.

For $X \in V$, let $U_X = \text{Pa}_{H(\Gamma)}(X)$ be the parents[5] of $X$ with respect to $H(\Gamma)$. Then $>_\alpha^X$ equals $>_\beta^X$ whenever $\alpha(U_X) = \beta(U_X)$, so for any $u \in \underline{U_X}$ we can define relation $>_u^X$ to be $>_\alpha^X$ for any $\alpha$ such that $\alpha(U_X) = u$. Local consistency can then be expressed in terms of these relations: $\Gamma$ *is locally consistent if and only if for all $X \in V$ and $u \in \underline{U_X}$, $>_u^X$ is irreflexive.*

Often checking local consistency will be easy; in particular, when the sets $\text{Pa}_{H(\Gamma)}(X)$ are small (as in intended applications of CP-nets) one can efficiently construct each relation $>_u^X$ explicitly. (CP-nets assume these $>_u^X$ relations have already been computed, or directly elicited; they are also assumed to be total orders, so local consistency is guaranteed.) To give another example, when all the variables are binary, local consistency can be determined in time proportional to $|\Gamma|^2|V|$.

### Partial conditional lexicographic orders

For $\alpha, \beta \in \underline{V}$, define $\Delta(\alpha, \beta)$ to be the set of variables where $\alpha$ and $\beta$ differ, i.e., $\{X \in V : \alpha(X) \neq \beta(X)\}$. For relation $G$ on $V$, let $G^\circ$ be the transitive closure of $G$, and for $U \subseteq V$, define $\min_{G^\circ}(U)$ to be $\{X \in U : \forall Y \in U, (Y, X) \notin G^\circ\}$, that is, the set of undominated variables in $U$ with respect to $G^\circ$, i.e., the set of variables in $U$ which have no ancestors in $U$ (with respect to $G$). If $G$ is acyclic then for any non-empty $U$, $\min_{G^\circ}(U)$ is non-empty.

A pcl structure on set of variables $V$ is defined to be a tuple $\langle G, H, \{\succ_u^X : X \in V, u \in \underline{\text{Pa}_H(X)}\}\rangle$, where $G$ and $H$ are acyclic relations on $V$ with $G \supseteq H$, and for each variable $X \in V$, and each $u \in \underline{\text{Pa}_H(X)}$, $\succ_u^X$ is a (possibly empty) strict partial order (a transitive irreflexive relation) on $\underline{X}$. Associated with a pcl structure $p$ is a binary relation $\succ_p$ on $\underline{V}$, called the *pcl order*, given as follows:

For $\alpha, \beta \in \underline{V}$, $\alpha \succ_p \beta$ if and only if $\alpha \neq \beta$ and for all $X \in \min_{G^\circ}(\Delta(\alpha, \beta))$, $\alpha(X) \succ_u^X \beta(X)$, where $u = \alpha(\text{Pa}_H(X))$ (which equals $\beta(\text{Pa}_H(X))$ since any variable $Y$ in $\text{Pa}_H(X)$ is an element of $\text{Pa}_G(X)$ so is not in $\Delta(\alpha, \beta)$ by minimality of $X$, so $\alpha(Y) = \beta(Y)$).

[5]The set of parents $\text{Pa}_H(X)$ of $X$ with respect to relation $H$ is defined to be the set of all $Y$ such that $(Y, X)$ is in $H$.

The idea is that $\min_{G^\circ}(\Delta(\alpha, \beta))$ is the set of most important variables where $\alpha$ and $\beta$ differ. $\alpha$ is preferred to $\beta$ if $\alpha$ is better than $\beta$ on each of these variables. A standard lexicographic order compares two outcomes $\alpha$ and $\beta$ by considering the most important variable $X$ on which $\alpha$ and $\beta$ differ, and preferring $\alpha$ to $\beta$ if $\alpha(X)$ is preferred to $\beta(X)$. So a pcl order generalises a standard lexicographic order by allowing: (i) there to be more than one best variable on which $\alpha$ and $\beta$ differ, because $G^\circ$ is only a partial order; and (ii) the local preference of $\alpha(X)$ over $\beta(X)$ to be partial and conditional on some of the earlier variables.

**Proposition 7** *For any pcl structure $p$, the associated order $\succ_p$ is transitive.*

Hence $\succ_p$ is a partial order, since it is also irreflexive.

**Generating a Partial Conditional Lexicographic Order from $\Gamma$.** If $\Gamma$ is locally consistent and such that $G(\Gamma)$ is acyclic then we can generate a pcl structure from $\Gamma$. Abbreviate $\mathrm{Pa}_{H(\Gamma)}(X)$ to $U_X$. For each variable $X \in V$, and each $u \in \underline{U_X}$, define relation $\succ_u^X$ on $\underline{X}$ to be just $>_u^X$ (see Local Consistency section). Because $\Gamma$ is locally consistent, each $\succ_u^X$ is a (strict) partial order, so $\langle G(\Gamma), H(\Gamma), \{\succ_u^X : X \in V, u \in \underline{U_X}\}\rangle$ is a partial conditional lexicographic structure, and we write the associated order $\succ_p$ as $\succ_{p(\Gamma)}$.

With the example, we have e.g., the following conditional preferences for $X_3$: $\succ_{\mathtt{no}}^{X_3} = \succ_{\mathtt{nm}}^{X_3} = \succ_{\mathtt{lo}}^{X_3}$ defined by $\mathtt{f} \succ_{\mathtt{no}}^{X_3} \mathtt{d}$, and also $\mathtt{d} \succ_{\mathtt{lm}}^{X_3} \mathtt{f}$. The relation $\succ_{p(\Gamma)}$ is in this case a total order, which extends $>_\Gamma$ with the additional preference $\mathtt{nod} \succ_{p(\Gamma)} \mathtt{nmf}$, because variable $X_2$ is more important than $X_3$ according to $G(\Gamma)$. As we see below, it is a general result that $\succ_{p(\Gamma)}$ extends $>_\Gamma$. It is also the case that given conditional preference theory $\Gamma \subseteq \mathcal{L}$, we can extend $\Gamma$ to a set $\overline{\Gamma}$ making the associated ordering on outcomes equal to the pcl ordering.

Fix $\Gamma \subseteq \mathcal{L}$. For $\varphi = (u : x > x'\,[W]) \in \Gamma$ let $\overline{\varphi}$ be $(u : x > x'\,[W'])$ where $W'$ is the set of descendants of $X$ in $G(\Gamma)$ (i.e., the set of variables $Y$ such that $(X, Y)$ is in the transitive closure of $G(\Gamma)$). Define $\overline{\Gamma} = \{\overline{\varphi} : \varphi \in \Gamma\}$.

**Theorem 2** *If $\Gamma$ is locally consistent and $G(\Gamma)$ is acyclic then $\succ_{p(\Gamma)} = \succ_{p(\overline{\Gamma})} = >_{\overline{\Gamma}} \supseteq >_\Gamma$.*

The most important part of this theorem is the result that $\succ_{p(\Gamma)} \supseteq >_\Gamma$, i.e., that if $\alpha >_\Gamma \beta$ then $\alpha \succ_{p(\Gamma)} \beta$. This can be proved by showing that $\succ_{p(\Gamma)} \supseteq \Gamma^*$, which implies the result, since $\succ_{p(\Gamma)}$ is transitive (by Proposition 5) and $>_\Gamma$ is the transitive closure of $\Gamma^*$.

If locally consistent conditional preference theory $\Gamma$ is such that $G(\Gamma)$ is acyclic then by Theorem 2 $\succ_{p(\Gamma)} \supseteq >_\Gamma$ which implies that $>_\Gamma$ is irreflexive since $\succ_{p(\Gamma)}$ is irreflexive, and hence by Theorem 1, $\Gamma$ is consistent. So we have the following result (since local consistency is a necessary condition for consistency), which generalises the consistency result for acyclic CP-nets (i.e., CP-nets whose associated relation $H$ is acyclic).

**Corollary 1 (Consistency)** *Let conditional preference theory $\Gamma$ be such that $G(\Gamma)$ is acyclic. Then $\Gamma$ is consistent if and only if $\Gamma$ is locally consistent.*

This shows that, as long as $\Gamma$ is chosen so that the associated order $G(\Gamma)$ on variables is acyclic, and the local consistency property is confirmed, then $\Gamma$ is guaranteed to be consistent and the associated order on outcomes will be irreflexive (and hence acyclic). It gives an agent considerable flexibility in making their preference statements, without risking inconsistency.

## Further Applications

We consider some further consequences of our results.

**Choosing a total order compatible with $\Gamma$** For some applications, one does not need to determine $>_\Gamma$ precisely; it is sufficient to be able to list outcomes in an order compatible with $>_\Gamma$, i.e., compatible with the preferences expressed by $\Gamma$. Theorem 2 shows that this is easy (given that $\Gamma$ is locally consistent and $G(\Gamma)$ is acyclic), since we can pick an ordering compatible with $\succ_{p(\Gamma)}$, and hence compatible with $>_\Gamma$. We list the variables in an order $X_1, \ldots, X_n$ compatible with $G(\Gamma)$ and we extend each local partial order relation $>_u^X$ to a total order on $\underline{X}$ (this can be done implicitly using a default ordering on $\underline{X}$). We can then generate outcomes lexicographically: to start with, we pick the best value $x_1$ of $X_1$ first and then pick the best value $x_2$ of $X_2$ conditional on $x_1$, etc. Note that it is also very easy to check, for this total order $>$, if $\alpha > \beta$ for outcomes $\alpha$ and $\beta$.

**Finding optimal (maximal) outcomes** Clearly, one can use the above algorithm to efficiently find an outcome which is $>_\Gamma$-maximal. It can also be done more directly. Assume that $H(\Gamma)$ is acyclic and $\Gamma$ is locally consistent (actually, the latter condition can be considerably weakened; c.f. the proof of Theorem 2 in (Domshlak *et al.* 2003)). Write $V$ as $\{X_1, \ldots, X_n\}$ where the variable ordering is consistent with $H(\Gamma)$. We say that $x' \in \underline{X_i}$ *is undominated given $y$* if there does not exist statement $u : x > x'\,[W]$ in $\Gamma$ such that $y \models u$ (i.e., such that $u$ is a projection of $y$). We can generate (without backtracking) a (in fact, any) $>_\Gamma$-maximal outcome $\alpha$ as follows: for $i = 1, \ldots, n$, we let $\alpha(X_i) = x'$ for any $x' \in \underline{X_i}$ undominated given $(\alpha(X_1), \ldots, \alpha(X_{i-1}))$ (local consistency ensures that there always is such an $x'$). This can be done in time approximately linear in the size of $\Gamma$.

**Constrained Optimisation** The approach to constrained optimisation described in (Boutilier *et al.* b) can be easily generalised to finding maximal outcomes with respect to $>_\Gamma$ that satisfy a set of constraints. Furthermore, the following result shows that each outcome which is $\succ_{p(\Gamma)}$-maximal among those satisfying a set of constraints, is also maximal with respect to $>_\Gamma$.

**Corollary 2 (of Theorem 2)** *Let $\Gamma$ be a locally consistent conditional preference theory such that $G(\Gamma)$ is acyclic. For $\Omega \subseteq \underline{V}$, if $\alpha$ is $\succ_{p(\Gamma)}$-maximal in $\Omega$ then $\alpha$ is $>_\Gamma$-maximal in $\Omega$.*

Finding the $\succ_{p(\Gamma)}$-maximal outcomes satisfying a set of constraints is relatively easy. In particular, we can modify the complete algorithm given in section 3.1 of (Boutilier *et al.* b) by replacing each (generally hard) dominance test

$\alpha \succ_N \beta$ by the test $\alpha \succ_{p(\Gamma)} \beta$, which is easy because of the lexicographic-style construction of $\succ_{p(\Gamma)}$. To determine if $\alpha \succ_{p(\Gamma)} \beta$ or not, we consider the set $\Delta(\alpha, \beta)$ of all variables on which $\alpha$ and $\beta$ differ; we find all variables $X$ which are minimal in $\Delta(\alpha, \beta)$ with respect to the transitive closure of $G(\Gamma)$, and we check the local condition $\alpha(X) >_u^X \beta(X)$, where $u = \alpha(\mathrm{Pa}_H(X))$.

For moderate to large problems, often even the number of $\succ_{p(\Gamma)}$-maximal outcomes will be very large, so that we can enumerate more than enough $\succ_{p(\Gamma)}$-maximal outcomes; in such cases there may be little advantage in using the much less efficient complete algorithm. These remarks of course also apply when we restrict to CP-nets.

**Searching for Swapping Sequences** If one wants to prove that $\alpha >_\Gamma \beta$, one may well need to search for a worsening swapping sequence from $\alpha$ to $\beta$. Since these generalise flipping sequences, this can be a hard problem, as shown in (Boutilier *et al.* a; Brafman & Domshlak 2002). The following proposition is useful in restricting the swaps that one need consider, as only certain variables need be changed.

**Proposition 8 (prefix and suffix fixing)** *Let conditional preference theory $\Gamma$ be locally consistent and such that $G = G(\Gamma)$ is acyclic. Suppose $\alpha >_\Gamma \beta$. Define $R$ to be the set of variables $X \in V$ such that $\alpha(X) = \beta(X)$ and for all ancestors $Y$ in $G$ of $X$, $\alpha(Y) = \beta(Y)$. Define $S$ to be the set of variables $X \in V$ such that $\alpha(X) = \beta(X)$ and for all descendants $Z$ in $G$ of $X$, $\alpha(Z) = \beta(Z)$. Then there exists a worsening swapping sequence from $\alpha$ to $\beta$ in which the values of $R \cup S$ remain constant. Furthermore, in any worsening swapping sequence $\alpha = \alpha_1, \ldots, \alpha_l = \beta$ the values of $R$ remain constant, i.e., for all $k = 1, \ldots, l$, and for all $X \in R$, $\alpha_k(X) = \alpha(X) = \beta(X)$.*

This means that when searching for a worsening swapping sequence from to $\alpha$ to $\beta$ we need only consider swaps that don't change the values of $R \cup S$. Suffix fixing generalises the CP-nets property described in (Boutilier *et al.* 1999; a). Prefix fixing also generalises a property of CP-nets, and can be seen to be revealing regarding the structure of $>_\Gamma$.

## Conclusion

In this paper, a logic of conditional preferences is defined, with a language which allows the compact representation of certain kinds of statements of conditional preference. It is shown that the language can express CP-nets, and that the semantics and proof theory generalise those of CP-nets. The formalism also generalises other important properties of CP-nets; maximal outcomes can be efficiently generated, and there are simple sufficient conditions for consistency. It is also easy, under such conditions, to find a total order on outcomes compatible with the conditional preference order, and a similar approach to constrained optimisation can be used as for CP-nets. Along the way, a number of results were given illustrating the restrictive expressive power of CP-nets and TCP-nets.

Despite being a substantially more expressive language than CP-nets, it is still quite restrictive (with these restrictions allowing some good properties). There are many natural ways of augmenting the language to allow the compact representation of other kinds of preferences. For example, one could allow statements of the form $u : s > s'\,[W]$ where $s$ and $s'$ are assignments to a set of variables $S$, rather than just a single variable $X$. One could allow statements of the form $u : s > *\,[W]$ meaning that conditional on $u$, $s$ is the most preferred assignment of variables $S$. The language might also be extended to allow the representation of indifference between values or partial tuples.

This paper has focused mainly on CP-nets rather than their extension TCP-nets. (Wilson 2004) considers the relationship with TCP-nets, which can be expressed with statements $u : x > x'\,[W]$ with $|W| = 0$ or 1, and derives similar results to this paper under weaker acyclicity conditions.

## Acknowledgements

This work has received support from Science Foundation Ireland under Grant 00/PI.1/C075. I am grateful to Rick Wallace, Paul Snow and Barry O'Sullivan for helpful discussions.

## References

Boutilier, C.; Brafman, R. I.; Domshlak, C.; Hoos, H.; and Poole, D. CP-nets: A tool for reasoning with conditional *ceteris paribus* preference statements. *To appear in JAIR.*

Boutilier, C.; Brafman, R. I.; Domshlak, C.; Hoos, H.; and Poole, D. Preference-based constrained optimization with CP-nets. *To appear in Computational Intelligence, Special Issue on Preferences.*

Boutilier, C.; Brafman, R. I.; Hoos, H. H.; and Poole, D. 1999. Reasoning with conditional ceteris paribus preference statements. In *Proceedings of the Fifteenth Conference on Uncertainty in Artificial Intelligence (UAI99)*, 71–80.

Brafman, R. I., and Domshlak, C. 2002. CP-nets—reasoning and consistency testing. In *Proceedings of the Eighth International Conference on Principles of Knowledge Representation and Reasoning (KR2002).*

Brafman, R. I.; Domshlak, C.; and Shimony, E. 2002. Introducing variable importance tradeoffs into CP-nets. In *Proceedings of the Eighteenth Conference on Uncertainty in Artificial Intelligence (UAI02).*

Domshlak, C.; Rossi, F.; Venable, K.; and Walsh, T. 2003. Reasoning about soft constraints and conditional preferences: complexity results and approximation techniques. In *Proc. IJCAI03.*

Lang, J. 2002. From preference representation to combinatorial vote. In *Proceedings of the Eighth International Conference on Principles of Knowledge Representation and Reasoning (KR2002)*, 277–288.

Wilson, N. 2004. Consistency and optimisation for conditional preferences. *Unpublished report.*

# Solving Generalized Semi-Markov Decision Processes using Continuous Phase-Type Distributions

**Håkan L. S. Younes** and **Reid G. Simmons**
School of Computer Science
Carnegie Mellon University
Pittsburgh, PA 15213, USA
{lorens, reids}@cs.cmu.edu

**Abstract**

We introduce the generalized semi-Markov decision process (GSMDP) as an extension of continuous-time MDPs and semi-Markov decision processes (SMDPs) for modeling stochastic decision processes with asynchronous events and actions. Using phase-type distributions and uniformization, we show how an arbitrary GSMDP can be approximated by a discrete-time MDP, which can then be solved using existing MDP techniques. The techniques we present can also be seen as an alternative approach for solving SMDPs, and we demonstrate that the introduction of phases allows us to generate higher quality policies than those obtained by standard SMDP solution techniques.

## Introduction

We are interested in modeling and solving stochastic decision processes with asynchronous events and actions, where the delay from when an event or action is enabled until it triggers can be governed by an arbitrary positive distribution. While each of the aspects of stochastic decision processes listed above have been individually addressed in research on decision theoretic planning, no existing approach deals with all aspects simultaneously.

Guestrin, Koller, & Parr (2002) show how factored MDPs can be used to handle concurrent actions, but only for sets of actions executed in synchrony. Continuous-time MDPs (Howard 1960) can be used to model asynchronous systems, but are restricted to events and actions with exponential delay distributions. Semi-Markov decision processes (SMDPs) (Howard 1971) lift the restriction on delay distributions, but cannot model asynchrony.

We therefore introduce the *generalized* semi-Markov decision process (GSMDP), based on the GSMP model of discrete event systems (Glynn 1989), as a model for asynchronous stochastic decision processes. A GSMDP, unlike an SMDP, can remember if an event enabled in the current state has been continuously enabled in previous states without triggering. This is key in modeling asynchronous processes, which typically involve events that race to trigger first in a state, but the event that triggers first does not necessarily disable the competing events. For example, if we boil water for tea while simultaneously toasting bread, the fact that the bread pops out of the toaster first does not mean that we have to start over with the tea. Intuitively, a GSMDP can be viewed as the composition of asynchronous SMDPs.



In order to solve a GSMDP, we propose an approximation scheme that transforms an arbitrary GSMDP into a continuous-time MDP. Each non-exponential delay distribution in the GSMDP is approximated by a continuous *phase-type distribution* (Neuts 1981). This yields a continuous-time MDP, which in turn can be transformed into a discrete-time MDP using a technique called *uniformization* (Jensen 1953). Consequently, by using our proposed approximation scheme, we can approximately solve any GSMDP using standard MDP solution techniques. We will show that phase-type distributions are a practical tool for solving GSMDPs and SMDPs, and that our approach can produce policies of higher quality for SMDPs than standard techniques, because the introduction of phases indirectly allows us to take into account the time spent in a state.

## Generalized Semi-Markov Decision Processes

The generalized semi-Markov process (GSMP), first introduced by Matthes (1962), is an established formalism in queuing theory for modeling continuous-time stochastic discrete event systems (Glynn 1989). We add a decision dimension to the formalism by distinguishing a subset of the events as controllable and adding rewards, thereby obtaining the generalized semi-Markov *decision* process (GSMDP).

### A Model of Stochastic Discrete Event Systems

Consider a computer that can be in one of two states labeled up and $\neg$up. Imagine an event, crash, that can cause a transition at a random point in time from the up state to the $\neg$up state, with the delay being governed by some positive distribution $G$. For example, if $G$ is the uniform distribution $U(0,1)$, then the time a computer remains up before crashing is uniformly distributed in the interval $(0,1)$. A system consisting of a single such computer can be modeled as a semi-Markov process. Figure 1(a) shows the state transition diagrams for two identical processes modeling two computers running asynchronously.

Now, assume the two computers are connected to each other in a network. If we view the network as a single stochastic process, we get the state transition diagram in Figure 1(b). Note that for continuous delay distributions, the probability is zero that two events trigger at exactly the same time, so there is no direct transition from state $\mathrm{up}_1 \wedge \mathrm{up}_2$ to state $\neg\mathrm{up}_1 \wedge \neg\mathrm{up}_2$. The resulting process is, in general, no longer a semi-Markov process. To see why, consider the scenario in which all events have a $U(0, 1)$ delay distribution and after $0.2$ time units the $\mathrm{crash}_1$ event triggers in state $\mathrm{up}_1 \wedge \mathrm{up}_2$, causing a transition to state $\neg\mathrm{up}_1 \wedge \mathrm{up}_2$. Note that $\mathrm{crash}_2$, which is enabled in the new state, has already been enabled for $0.2$ time units, as it was enabled in the previous state without triggering. Consequently, the delay distribution for $\mathrm{up}_2$ is not $U(0, 1)$ at this point, but $U(0, 0.8)$. In general, the delay distribution of an event at a particular point in time can depend on the entire execution history, and this history dependence cannot be captured by a semi-Markov process without augmenting the state space. However, the composite process is, without modifications to the state space, a *generalized* semi-Markov process (GSMP).

A GSMP consists of a set of states $S$ and a set of events $E$. At any point in time, the process occupies a state $s \in S$ in which a subset $E_s$ of the events are enabled. With each event $e$ is associated a distribution $G_e$, governing the time until $e$ triggers if it remains enabled, and a next-state probability distribution $p_e(s'|s)$. The enabled events race to trigger first, and the event that triggers causes a transition to a state $s' \in S$ according to the next-state probability distribution for the triggering event. A GSMP is equivalent to a continuous-time Markov chain if all delay distributions are exponential.

To formally define the semantics of a GSMP, we associate a real-valued clock $c_e$ with each event that indicates the time remaining until $e$ is scheduled to occur. The process starts in some initial state $s$ with events $E_s$ enabled. For each enabled event $e \in E_s$, we sample a trigger time according to the distribution $G_e$ and set $c_e$ to the sampled value. Let $e^*$ be the event in $E_s$ with the smallest clock value, i.e. $e^* = \arg\min_{e \in E_s} c_e$. The event $e^*$ becomes the triggering event in $s$. When $e^*$ triggers after $c_{e^*}$ time units in $s$, we sample a next state $s'$ according to $p_{e^*}(s'|s)$ and update each clock $c_e$ for $e \in E_{s'}$ as follows: $c'_e = c_e - c_{e^*}$ if $e \in E_s \setminus \{e^*\}$, otherwise $c'_e$ is sampled from $G_e$. In other words, events that remain enabled without triggering are not rescheduled in $s'$, while the triggering event and newly enabled events are. The specified procedure is repeated with $s = s'$ and $c_e = c'_e$ so long as $E_s \neq \emptyset$.

Before we discuss actions, policies, and rewards for GSMDPs, we need to introduce the concept of an *execution path*. An execution path $\sigma$ for a GSMP is a sequence

$$\sigma = s_0 \xrightarrow{t_0, e_0} s_1 \xrightarrow{t_1, e_1} s_2 \xrightarrow{t_2, e_2} \ldots$$

with $s_i \in S$, $e_i \in E_{s_i}$, and $t_i > 0$ being the sojourn time in state $s_i$ before event $e_i$ triggers a transition to state $s_{i+1}$. An execution path is finite if a state $s_i$ along the path is absorbing (i.e. $E_{s_i} = \emptyset$), in which case we set $t_i = \infty$ ($e_i$ is undefined). The length of an execution path equals the number of state transitions along the path, which can be infinite. An execution path for a GSMP up to state $s_i$ contains sufficient information to characterize the future execution behavior of the process.

## Actions, Policies, and Rewards

Given a GSMP with event set $E$, we identify a set $A \subset E$ of controllable events, or *actions*. The remaining events are called *exogenous events*. Actions differ from exogenous events in that they can be disabled at will in a state, while an exogenous event $e$ always remains enabled in a state $s$ if $e \in E_s$. For a given state $s$, a *policy* $\pi$ picks the action in the set of potentially enabled actions $A \cap E_s$ to be enabled in $s$, or a special action $a_\infty$ representing idleness and meaning that only exogenous events should be enabled in $s$. We allow the action choice to depend not only on the current state, but on the entire execution history up to the current choice point including the time spent in the current state. Thus, a policy is a mapping from partial execution paths and non-negative real numbers to actions.

In addition to actions, we need rewards to fully specify a GSMDP. We assume a traditional reward structure with a lump sum reward $k(s, e, s')$ associated with the transition from state $s$ to $s'$ caused by the triggering of event $e$, and a continuous reward rate $c(s, a)$ associated with action $a$ being enabled in $s$. Since policies can switch actions at arbitrary time points, reward rates can vary over time in a given state.

For a fixed policy $\pi$, we define the discounted value of an execution path $\sigma$ of length $n$ (possibly infinite) by

$$v_\alpha^\pi(\sigma) \equiv \sum_{i=0}^{n} e^{-\alpha T_i} \biggl( e^{-\alpha t_i} k(s_i, e_i, s_{i+1}) + \int_0^{t_i} e^{-\alpha t} c(s_i, \pi(\sigma_{\le i}, t))\, dt \biggr),$$

where $T_0 = 0$ and $T_i = \sum_{j=0}^{i-1} t_j$ for $i > 0$, and $\sigma_{\le i}$ is the prefix of $\sigma$ up to and including state $s_i$. The parameter $\alpha$ is the *discount rate*, and can be interpreted as the rate of a termination event with exponential delay distribution (Howard 1960). We now define the expected infinite-horizon discounted reward for $\pi$, given that execution starts in state $s$ at time 0, by

$$v_\alpha^\pi(s) \equiv E_s^\pi[v_\alpha^\pi(\sigma)]. \tag{1}$$

Here, $E_s^\pi[\cdot]$ denotes the expectation with respect to the probability measure induced by policy $\pi$ over the set of execution paths starting in state $s$. The objective is to find a policy $\pi$ maximizing the expectation in (1). We propose to do so by first approximating the GSMDP with a continuous-time MDP using phase-type distributions.

## Continuous Phase-Type Distributions

The memoryless property of the exponential distribution plays a key role in the analytical tractability of continuous-time Markov chains and MDPs. Erlang (1917) was the first to consider a generalization of the exponential distribution that preserves much of its analytic tractability. The Erlang distribution introduces $n$ sequential *phases*, with the time spent in phase $i$ being exponentially distributed with rate $\lambda$. A stochastic process with Erlang distributed sojourn times is Markovian if phase is included in state descriptions.

The Erlang distribution is a special case of the class of continuous *phase-type distributions* (Neuts 1981). A ran-

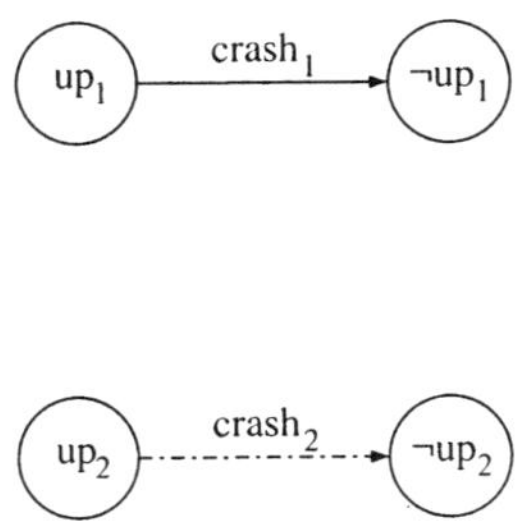


(a) Two asynchronous processes.

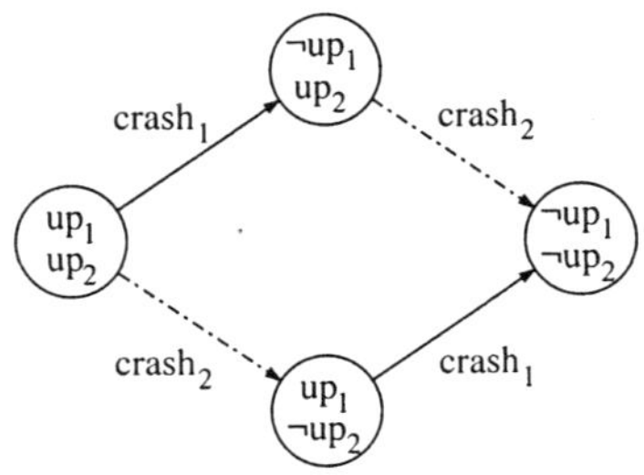


(b) Composite system.

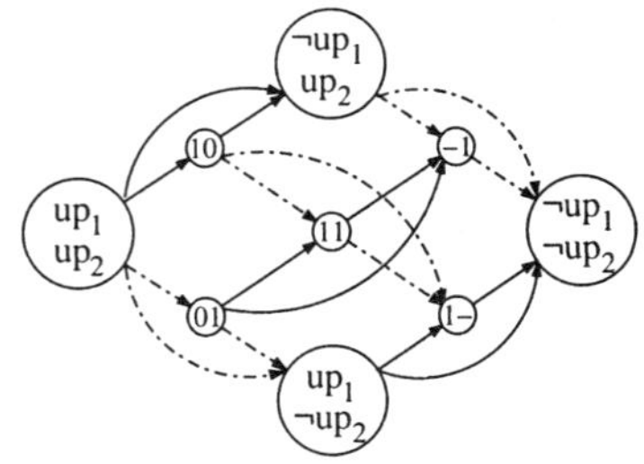


(c) Composite system with phase transitions.

Figure 1: State transition diagrams for stochastic processes modeling a network of computers. The rightmost diagram includes additional states to record the phase of the events. The first digit represents the phase of $\mathrm{crash}_1$ and the second digit the phase of $\mathrm{crash}_2$. A dash ("–") means that the event associated with the phase is disabled in the state.

dom variable associated with a continuous phase-type distribution of order $n$ represents the time to absorption in an $n$-state Markov chain and has the cumulative distribution function $1-\boldsymbol{\alpha}e^{\boldsymbol{T}t}\boldsymbol{e}$, where the $n$-dimensional row vector $\boldsymbol{\alpha}$ is the initial distribution of the Markov chain, $\boldsymbol{T}$ is its $n \times n$ infinitesimal generator matrix, and $\boldsymbol{e}$ is an $n$-dimensional column vector of ones.

There exist numerous techniques for approximating a general distribution $G$ with a continuous phase-type distribution $PH$. The most straightforward technique is the *method of moments*, where the objective is to find $\boldsymbol{\alpha}$ and $\boldsymbol{T}$ such that the first $k$ moments of $G$ and $PH$ match. The $i$th moment of a distribution $G$ is defined as $\mu_i \equiv E[X^i]$, where $X$ is a random variable with distribution $G$. Two useful concepts are the *mean* of a distribution ($\mu_1$) and the *coefficient of variation* ($cv^2 \equiv \mu_2/\mu_1^2 - 1$). Note that $cv^2 = 1$ for the exponential distribution.

When using the method of moments, it is desirable to match as many moments of $G$ as possible, but we will typically need more phases to match more moments. More phases means a larger state space, so there is a tradeoff between accuracy and complexity of the approximate model.

We can match a single moment using an exponential distribution with rate $1/\mu_1$ but this typically yields a poor approximation of $G$. A better approximation is obtained by matching the second moment as well. For $G$ with $cv^2 \geq 1/2$, this can be accomplished by using a two-phase Coxian distribution (Figure 2(a)) with parameters $\lambda_1 = 2/\mu_1$, $\lambda_2 = 1/(\mu_1 \cdot cv^2)$, and $p = 1/(2 \cdot cv^2)$ (Marie 1980). For example, a Weibull distribution $W(1, 1/2)$ with scale parameter 1 and shape parameter $1/2$ ($\mu_1 = 2$ and $cv^2 = 5$) can be approximated by a two-phase Coxian distribution ($\lambda_1 = 1$, $\lambda_2 = 1/10$, and $p = 1/10$). If $W(1, 1/2)$ is the delay distribution for both $\mathrm{crash}_1$ and $\mathrm{crash}_2$ in Figure 1(b), then Figure 1(c) is the Markov chain approximating the original GSMP obtained by approximating each delay distribution with a phase-type distribution.

If $cv^2 < 1/2$, we match the first two moments by using a generalized Erlang distribution (Figure 2(b)) with parameters $n = \lceil 1/cv^2 \rceil$, $p = 1 - (2n \cdot cv^2 + n - 2 - \sqrt{n^2 + 4 - 4n \cdot cv^2})/(2(n-1)(cv^2+1))$, and $\lambda = (1-p+np)/\mu_1$ (Sauer & Chandy 1975; Marie 1980). For example, a uniform distribution $U(0, 1)$ ($\mu_1 = 1/2$ and $cv^2 = 1/3$) can be approximated by a three-phase generalized Erlang distribution with $p = 1$ and $\lambda = 6$.

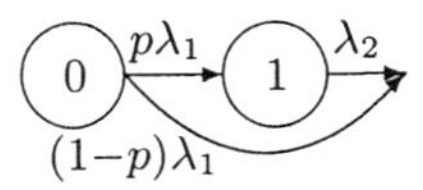


(a)

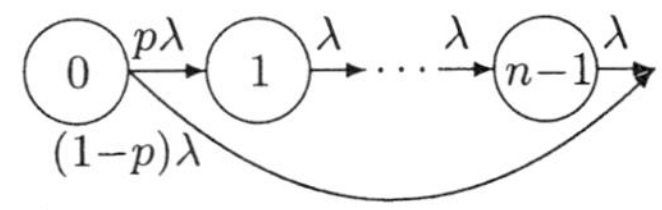


(b)

Figure 2: (a) Two-phase Coxian distribution; (b) $n$-phase generalized Erlang distribution.

More recently, Osogami & Harchol-Balter (2003) have presented a closed-form solution for matching the first three moments of any positive distribution using an Erlang distribution followed by a two-phase Coxian distribution. Later in this paper, we compare the quality of policies obtained by matching one, two, and three moments of each non-exponential distribution in a model. Better policies are generally obtained by increasing the number of matching moments, but at the cost of larger state spaces.

## Solution Method

To solve a GSMDP, we first convert it into a discrete-time MDP, which can be solved using standard techniques such as value iteration. The resulting policy is then translated into a policy for the GSMDP.

### From GSMDP to Discrete-Time MDP

We note that if all events of a GSMDP are Markovian (i.e. have exponential delay distribution) then the GSMDP is simply a continuous-time MDP. By using phase-type distributions, we can replace each non-Markovian event in the GSMDP with one or more Markovian events, thereby obtaining a continuous-time MDP that approximates the original GSMDP. The continuous-time MDP can be turned into

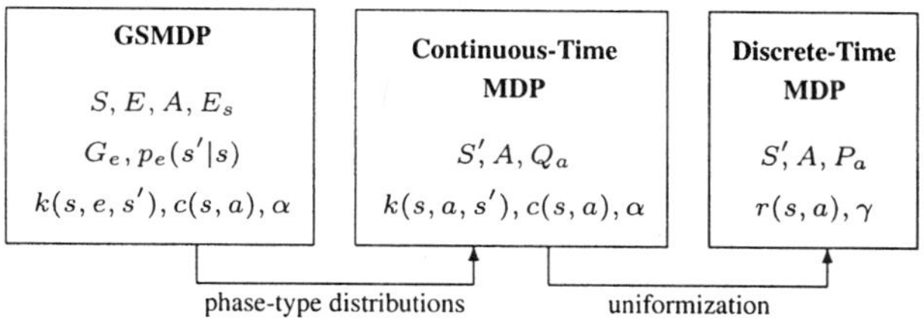


Figure 3: From GSMDP to discrete-time MDP.

a discrete-time MDP using uniformization, described below. The complete process of transforming a GSMDP into a discrete-time MDP, detailed below, is outlined in Figure 3.

We assume a factored representation of the state space with state variables $V$, and associate an enabling condition $\phi_e$ with each event $e \in E$ such that $s \models \phi_e$ iff $e \in E_s$ for all $s \in S$. We also assume that $p_e(s'|s)$ is implicitly represented by an effect formula $\mathit{eff}_e$ for each $e \in E$, for example using the effect formalism described by Rintanen (2003). Thus, a GSMDP event $e$ is represented by a triple $\langle \phi_e, G_e, \mathit{eff}_e \rangle$.

For each non-Markovian event $e$ with delay distribution $G_e$, we find a phase-type distribution of order $n_e$ approximating $G_e$. We add a phase variable $s_e$ to $V$ for each event $e$ with $n_e > 1$ and replace $e$ with one or more Markovian events. For example, if we match two moments, we get a phase-type distribution defined in terms of $n_e$, $p_e$, $\lambda_1^e$, and $\lambda_2^e$ ($\lambda_2^e = \lambda_1^e$ if $n_e > 2$). If $n_e > 2$ we add the event $\langle \phi_e \wedge s_e \in [1, n-2], \mathit{Exp}(\lambda_1), s_e \leftarrow s_e + 1 \rangle$. The following events are added for all values of $n_e$:

$$\langle \phi_e \wedge s_e = 0, \mathit{Exp}(p_e \lambda_1^e), s_e \leftarrow 1 \rangle$$
$$\langle \phi_e \wedge s_e = 0, \mathit{Exp}((1-p_e)\lambda_1^e), \mathit{eff}_e \wedge s_e \leftarrow 0 \rangle$$
$$\langle \phi_e \wedge s_e = n_e - 1, \mathit{Exp}(\lambda_2^e), \mathit{eff}_e \wedge s_e \leftarrow 0 \rangle$$

We associate the transition reward $k(s,e,s')$ with the last two events and zero transition reward with the other events, which represent pure phase transitions.

An event $e = \langle \phi_e, \mathit{Exp}(\lambda_e), \mathit{eff}_e \rangle$ by itself represents a continuous-time Markov chain having an infinitesimal generator matrix $Q_e$ with elements

$$q_{ij} = \begin{cases} 0 & \text{if } i \not\models \phi_e \\ p_e(j|i)\lambda_e & \text{if } i \models \phi_e \text{ and } i \neq j \\ -(1 - p_e(i|i))\lambda_e & \text{if } i \models \phi_e \text{ and } i = j \end{cases},$$

where $p_e(s'|s)$ is the next-state probability distribution induced by $\mathit{eff}_e$. A set of asynchronous events $E$ represents a continuous-time Markov chain with $Q_E = \sum_{e \in E} Q_e$, and we call $\sum_{e \in E} \lambda_e$ the *exit rate* of $E$.

Let $E'$ be the set of events obtained from the original set of events $E$ for the GSMDP through the translation process described above, and let $E'_e \subset E'$ be the events derived from the original GSMDP event $e$. The set $A' = \{e' \in E'_e | e \in A\}$ represents all Markovian events associated with GSMDP actions. We compute infinitesimal generator matrices $Q_\infty = \sum_{e \in E' \setminus A'} Q_e$ for the idle action $a_\infty$ and $Q_a = Q_\infty + \sum_{e \in E'_a} Q_e$ for each action $a \in A$, and we define the exit rate $\lambda_a$ of an action as the sum of exit rates for the events factored into $Q_a$. The matrices $Q_\infty$ and $Q_a$ for each $a \in A$, together with the expected transition rewards $k(s,a,s') = \sum_{e \in (E' \setminus A') \cup E'_a} k(s,e,s')\lambda_e/\lambda_a$ and reward rates $c(s,a)$ (reward rates are independent of phase and remain unmodified), constitute a continuous-time MDP with action space $A \cup \{a_\infty\}$ and state space $S'$ defined by the state variables $V$ and phase variables $s_e$ for each non-Markovian GSMDP event $e \in E$.

The obtained continuous-time MDP approximates the original GSMDP, and can be solved by first transforming it into a discrete-time MDP using *uniformization*. This technique, introduced by Jensen (1953) as a technique for analyzing continuous-time Markov chains and implicitly used by Howard (1960) for solving continuous-time MDPs, allows us to use regular solution methods for discrete-time MDPs, such as value iteration, to solve continuous-time MDPs. Puterman (1994) gives an excellent description of the uniformization process, to which we refer the reader for details. In brief, we choose a uniformization constant $q \geq \max_{a \in A \cup \{a_\infty\}, i \in S'} -q_{ii}^a$. We derive transition probability matrices $P_a = I + Q_a/q$ for the discrete-time MDP, where $I$ is the identity matrix of the same dimension as $Q_a$. The expected discounted reward between decision epochs for the discrete-time MDP becomes $r(s,a) = \sum_{s' \in S'} p_a(s'|s)k(s,a,s') + c(s,a)/(\alpha + \lambda_a)$, where $p_a(s'|s)$ is an entry in $P_a$ and $\lambda_a$ is the exit rate for $a$ as defined above. Finally, we derive a discount factor $\gamma = q/(q+\alpha)$.

## Policy Execution

The execution history of a GSMDP can be represented by a set of real-valued variables, one for each event $e \in E$ representing the time $e$ has been continuously enabled without triggering. The phases we introduce when approximating a GSMDP with a continuous-time MDP can be thought of as a randomized discretization of the time events have remained enabled. For example, approximating $G$ with an $n$-phase Erlang distribution with parameters $p$ and $\lambda$ represents a discretization of the time $G$ has been enabled into $n$ random-length intervals. The length of each interval is a random variable with distribution $\mathit{Exp}(\lambda)$. A policy for the continuous-time MDP with phase transitions is therefore approximately a mapping from states and the times events have been enabled to actions for the original GSMDP.

Phase transitions are not part of the original model, so we have to simulate them when executing the policy obtained for the approximate model. When a GSMDP event or action $e$ becomes enabled during execution, we sample a first phase transition time $t_1$ for the phase-type distribution used to approximate $G_e$. If $e$ remains enabled for $t_1$ time units without triggering, we increment the phase associated with $e$ and sample a second phase transition time $t_2$. This continues until $e$ triggers or is disabled, in which case the phase is reset to zero, or we reach the last phase, in which case the phase does not change until $e$ triggers or is disabled. The action choice can change every time a simulated phase transition occurs, although phase transitions do not change the actual state of the process. This allows us to take the time we have spent in a state into account when selecting which action to enable. We will see in the next section that this will permit us to obtain better policies than if we switched the enabled action only at actual state transitions.

## Empirical Evaluation

We have implemented a basic GSMDP planner based on the transformation procedure outlined in Figure 3. Our implementation uses multi-terminal BDDs (MTBDDs, also known as ADDs) (Fujita, McGeer, & Yang 1997) to represent matrices and vectors. The discrete-time MDPs that result from the transformation are solved using value iteration, essentially using the same approach as Hoey *et al.* (1999).

Our first test case is a variation of Howard's "the Foreman's Dilemma" (Howard 1960), where we have a machine that can be working ($s_0$), failed ($s_1$), or serviced ($s_2$). A failure event with delay distribution $G$ is enabled in $s_0$ and causes a transition to $s_1$. Once in $s_1$, the repair time for the machine has distribution $Exp(1/100)$. The foreman can at any time in $s_0$ choose to enable a service action with delay distribution $Exp(10)$. If this action triggers before the failure event, the system enters $s_2$ where the machine is being serviced with service time distribution $Exp(1)$. Given reward rates $c(s_0) = 1$, $c(s_1) = 0$, and $c(s_2) = 1/2$, independent of action choice, and no transition rewards, the problem is to produce a service policy that maximizes expected infinite-horizon discounted reward in $s_0$.

We can model this problem as an SMDP, noting that the probability of the service action triggering before the failure event is $p_{02} = 1 - \int_{t_0}^{\infty} 10e^{-10(t-t_0)}F(t)\,dt$ (where $F(t)$ is the cumulative distribution function for $G$) if we enable the service action after $t_0$ time units in $s_0$. We can solve the SMDP using the techniques described by Howard (1971), but then we can choose to enable the action in $s_0$ only immediately ($t_0 = 0$) or not at all ($t_0 = \infty$). Alternatively, we can express the expected reward in $s_0$ as a function of $t_0$ and use numerical solution techniques to find the value for $t_0$ that maximizes the expected reward. Depending on the shape of $F(t)$, both of these approaches may require numerical integration over semi-infinite intervals.

Figure 4 plots the expected reward as a percentage of the optimal expected reward for policies obtained using standard SMDP solution techniques as well as our proposed technique for approximating a (G)SMDP with an MDP using phase-type distributions. The optimal value and the value for the SMDP solution were computed using MATLAB, while the other values were computed by simulating execution of the policy generated by our GSMDP planner and taking the average value over 5000 samples. We used $\alpha = -\log 0.95$ as the discount factor. The two graphs are for different choices of the failure time distribution $G$ ($U(5, x)$ for left graph and $W(1.6x, 4.5)$ for right).

We can see that the SMDP solution is well below the optimal solution because it has to enable the action either immediately, or not at all, in $s_0$. For small values of $x$, the optimal SMDP policy is to enable the action in $s_0$, but as $x$ increases so does the expected failure time, so for larger $x$ it is better not to enable the action because it allows us to spend more time in $s_0$ where the reward rate is highest. The performance of the policy obtained by matching a single moment of $G$ is almost identical to that of the SMDP solution. This policy is also restricted to either enabling the action immediately or nor at all in $s_0$. Due to the approximation of $G$, the performance is slightly worse around the point where the optimal SMDP policy changes. We can see that by increasing the number of moments that are matched, we can increase the quality of the policy. Note the number of phases varies with $x$ for $U(5, x)$, but is constant for $W(1.6x, 4.5)$, which explains why the curves in the right graph are smoother than in the left. The only exception is for lower values of $x$ in the right graph. In this case, the phase-type distribution we obtain underestimates the probability that failure occurs at a very early stage, so the enabling of the action comes later than needed to perform well. In general, however, matching more moments gives us better policies, mainly because the phases that are introduced allow us to take into account the fact that $G$ is not memoryless, and so delay the enabling of the action in $s_0$ accordingly.

Our second test case is a system administration problem based on the computer network system introduced earlier in this paper (cf. Guestrin, Koller, & Parr 2002). To make it a decision problem, we add a reboot action for each machine $m_i$, which can be enabled if $m_i$ is not up. The reward rate for a state is equal to the number of machines that are up. The delay distributions for the reboot actions are all set to $U(0, 1)$, while $Exp(1)$ was chosen for the crash events.

Figure 5 plots the expected discounted value of the policy ($\alpha = -\log 0.95$) obtained by our GSMDP planner when matching between one and three moments of non-exponential delay distributions. We see that by matching two or three moments, we can obtain a policy that performs noticeably better than the policy obtain by matching only a single moment. By matching a single moment, we can select to enable a reboot action based only on which machines are currently not up, and the resulting policy reboots $m_i$ before $m_j$ if $i < j$. In contrast, the policy obtained when matching two or three moments keeps a reboot action enabled if it is in a phase other than zero, because it is then expected to trigger soon. While the first test case illustrated that phases can result in better policies by delaying the enabling of an action in a state, this test case illustrates that phases can help by keeping an action enabled if it has already been enabled for some time.

By matching more moments, we increase the accuracy of the approximation, but we also increase the state space. In terms of planning time, a larger state space means a solution will take longer to obtain. Matching more moments typically also results in a larger uniformization constant, which translates to a slower convergence for value iteration. Thus, as one can expect, better policies are obtained at the price of longer solution times. For the system administration domain with $n$ machines, $|S|$ is $2^n$, $(n{+}1)2^n$, and $(1.5n{+}1)2^n$ when matching one, two, and three moments, respectively. The uniformization constant is $n + 1$, $n + 5$, and approximately $n + 17$, respectively. With our implementation, it takes 4–12 times longer to solve the model obtained by matching two moments than the model obtained by matching only a single moment.

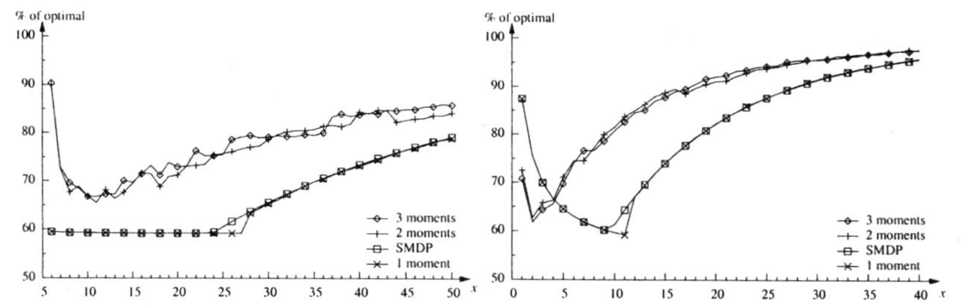


Figure 4: Policy value, as a percentage of the optimal value, obtained using different solution techniques for a variation of "the Foreman's Dilemma" with the failure time distribution $G$ being $U(5, x)$ (left) and $W(1.6x, 4.5)$ (right).

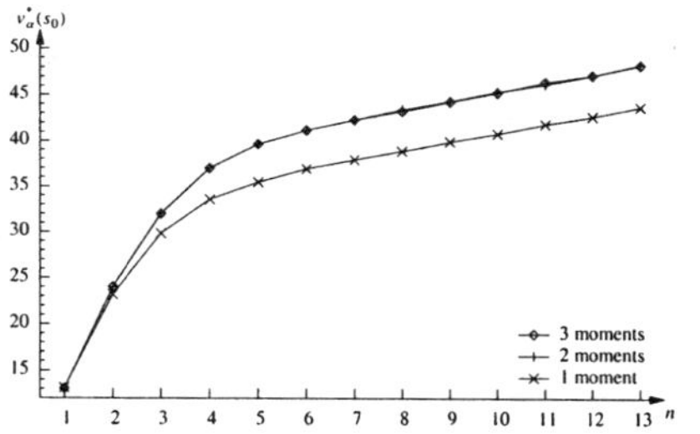


Figure 5: Expected discounted reward for the system administration problem with $n$ machines using phase-type distributions.

## Discussion

The generalized semi-Markov decision process is a natural model for stochastic systems with asynchronous events and actions. The main contribution of this paper has been a general technique for approximating a GSMDP with an MDP by the use of phase-type distributions. We have shown that the approximation technique is useful not only for solving GSMDPs, but also for generating policies for SMDPs. Phases allow us to take into account the time spent in a state when selecting actions, which can result in better policies than by using standard SMDP techniques. In addition, the approximation technique is not tied to any specific solution technique for MDPs. This makes the approach very general and allows one to easily take advantage of novel MDP solution techniques when solving GSMDP, including approximate solution methods.

**Acknowledgments.** Thanks to Vu Ha and David Musliner for insightful comments on an early draft.

This paper is based upon work supported by DARPA and ARO under contract no. DAAD19–01–1–0485, and a grant from the Royal Swedish Academy of Engineering Sciences (IVA). The U.S. Government is authorized to reproduce and distribute reprints for Governmental purposes notwithstanding any copyright annotation thereon. The views and conclusions contained herein are those of the authors and should not be interpreted as necessarily representing the official policies or endorsements, either expressed or implied, of the sponsors.

## References

Erlang, A. K. 1917. Solution of some problems in the theory of probabilities of significance in automatic telephone exchanges. *The Post Office Electrical Engineers' Journal* 10:189–197.

Fujita, M.; McGeer, P. C.; and Yang, J. C.-Y. 1997. Multi-terminal binary decision diagrams: An efficient data structure for matrix representation. *Formal Methods in System Design* 10(2/3):149–169.

Glynn, P. W. 1989. A GSMP formalism for discrete event systems. *Proceedings of the IEEE* 77(1):14–23.

Guestrin, C.; Koller, D.; and Parr, R. 2002. Multiagent planning with factored MDPs. In *Advances in Neural Information Processing Systems 14: Proc. 2001 Conference*. Cambridge, MA: The MIT Press. 1523–1530.

Hoey, J.; St-Aubin, R.; Hu, A.; and Boutilier, C. 1999. SPUDD: Stochastic planning using decision diagrams. In *Proc. Fifteenth Conference on Uncertainty in Artificial Intelligence*, 279–288. Morgan Kaufmann Publishers.

Howard, R. A. 1960. *Dynamic Programming and Markov Processes*. New York, NY: John Wiley & Sons.

Howard, R. A. 1971. *Dynamic Probabilistic Systems*, volume II. New York, NY: John Wiley & Sons.

Jensen, A. 1953. Markoff chains as an aid in the study of Markoff processes. *Skandinavisk Aktuarietidskrift* 36:87–91.

Marie, R. 1980. Calculating equilibrium probabilities for $\lambda(n)/C_k/1/N$ queues. In *Proc. Performance '80*, 117–125. ACM Press.

Matthes, K. 1962. Zur Theorie der Bedienungsprozesse. In *Trans. Third Prague Conference on Information Theory, Statistical Decision Functions, Random Processes*, 513–528. Publishing House of the Czechoslovak Academy of Sciences.

Neuts, M. F. 1981. *Matrix-Geometric Solutions in Stochastic Models: An Algorithmic Approach*. Baltimore, MD: Johns Hopkins University Press.

Osogami, T., and Harchol-Balter, M. 2003. A closed-form solution for mapping general distributions to minimal PH distributions. In *Proc. 13th International Conference on Modelling Techniques and Tools for Computer Performance Evaluation*, volume 2794 of *LNCS*, 200–217. Springer.

Puterman, M. L. 1994. *Markov Decision Processes: Discrete Stochastic Dynamic Programming*. New York, NY: John Wiley & Sons.

Rintanen, J. 2003. Expressive equivalence of formalism for planning with sensing. In *Proc. Thirteenth International Conference on Automated Planning and Scheduling*, 185–194. AAAI Press.

Sauer, C. H., and Chandy, K. M. 1975. Approximate analysis of central server models. *IBM Journal of Research and Development* 19(3):301–313.

# User Modeling

# Exploring more Realistic Evaluation Measures for Collaborative Filtering

**Giuseppe Carenini, Rita Sharma**
Computer Science Dept. University of British Columbia
2366 Main Mall, Vancouver, B.C. Canada V6T 1Z4
carenini,rsharma@cs.ubc.ca

**Abstract**

Collaborative filtering is a popular technique for recommending items to people. Several methods for collaborative filtering have been proposed in the literature and the quality of their predictions compared in empirical studies. In this paper, we argue that the measures of quality used in these studies are based on rather simple assumptions. We propose and apply additional measures for comparing the effectiveness of collaborative filtering methods which are grounded in decision-theory.

[**keywords:** information agents, human-computer interaction, recommender systems, evaluation]

## Introduction

Recommenders are computer systems designed to help people find preferred items within a very large set of available alternatives, such as movies, books and news. Collaborative filtering (CF) is a technique used by recommenders to make predictions on how a user will rate a particular item, given his or her ratings on other items and given other people's ratings on various items including the one in question. CF has been an active area of research in recent years both in AI and HCI. Several collaborative filtering algorithms have been suggested, ranging from binary to non-binary ratings, and from implicit to explicit ratings (Resnick *et al.* 1994; Shardanand & Maes 1995),(Breese, Heckerman, & Kadie 1998), (Pennock *et al.* 2000), (Sharma & Poole 2001). Of all these algorithms, the most recent and most successful ones are based on a probabilistic approach.

(Breese, Heckerman, & Kadie 1998) presented the first attempt to perform a comprehensive evaluation of all the algorithms that had appeared in the literature up to that time. They compared each algorithm's performance according to two measures of prediction accuracy that have since become a standard for evaluating CF algorithms: the Mean Absolute Error (MAE) and the ranked scoring (RS). MAE has become especially popular. It has been used to evaluate new probabilistic CF algorithms (Sharma & Poole 2001), (Pennock *et al.* 2000) as well as techniques for eliciting ratings in CF (Rashid *et al.* 2002). In this paper, we examine the tacit assumptions underlying MAE and RS. MAE equates recommendation quality with the accuracy of the algorithm prediction of how a user will rate a particular item. The problem with this approach is that it makes an unrealistic assumption on how recommenders are used in practice. Users of a recommender are not prediction checkers. Rather, they use predictions to make decisions. So, a measure of recommendation quality should take into account the outcomes of the users' decisions. To address this problem, we propose a new measure for comparing CF algorithms which is grounded in decision-theory. Our new measure attempts to compute how useful a recommendation will be for the user by taking into account a user-specific *threshold* for accepting a recommendation. Also, we note that our new measure presents interesting similarity with RS (the other performance measure commonly used in CF). Based on this observation, we uncover tacit assumptions underlying RS and we conclude that our new measure can be effectively used to define a more plausible RS.

## CF and its Evaluation

### Filtering Problem and Notation

Let $N$ be the number of users and $M$ be the total number of items in the database. $S$ is an $N \times M$ matrix of all user's ratings for all items; $S_{ui}$ is the rating given by user $u$ to item $i$. Ratings are typically on a cardinal scale with $m$ values (e.g., $0, \ldots, 5$ in the movie domain). In collaborative filtering, $S$, the user-item matrix is generally very sparse since each user will only have rated a small percentage of the total number of items. Under this formulation, the collaborative filtering problem becomes predicting those $S_{ui}$ which are not defined in $S$, the user-item matrix. The user for whom we are predicting a rating is called the active user $a$.

### Algorithms for CF

Initial CF algorithms (Resnick *et al.* 1994; Shardanand & Maes 1995), referred in (Breese, Heckerman, & Kadie

1998) as memory based, predict the active user ratings as a *similarity-weighted sum* of the other users' ratings, with the most successful similarity measure being *correlation* (Breese, Heckerman, & Kadie 1998). Recently, AI researchers have investigated model based algorithms for CF. Model based algorithms build a model of the data and use the model for prediction. Breese et al. (Breese, Heckerman, & Kadie 1998) proposed and evaluated two probabilistic models: *cluster models* and *Bayesian networks*. Pennock et al. (Pennock *et al.* 2000) introduced another probabilistic model based CF algorithm called *personality diagnosis* (*PD*). And finally, (Sharma & Poole 2001) proposed a probabilistic approach based on a *noisy sensor model.*

## Evaluation Strategy and Measures

Typically, a machine learning *training and test set* approach is used to evaluate the accuracy of CF algorithms. In this approach, the dataset of users and their ratings is divided into two: a *training set* and a *test set.* The *training set* is used as the CF dataset. The *test set* is used to evaluate the accuracy of the CF algorithm. When testing is performed, each user from the test set is treated as the *active* user. The ratings by each test user are divided into two sets: $I_a$ and $P_a$. The set $I_a$ contains ratings that are treated as observed ratings. The set $P_a$ contains the ratings that the CF algorithm attempts to predict by using both the observed ratings ($I_a$) and the training set.

The Mean Absolute Error (MAE) is the most commonly used measure to evaluate the accuracy of CF algorithms. Let the number of predicted ratings in the test set for the active user be $n_a$; then the MAE for that user is given as follows:

$$MAE_a = \frac{1}{n_a} \sum_{j \in P_a} |o_{a,j} - p_{a,j}|$$

where $o_{a,j}$ is user $a$'s observed rating for item $j$ and $p_{a,j}$ is user $a$'s predicted rating for item $j$. The MAE reported in CF evaluations is the average MAE for all users in the test set. Notice that the lower the MAE, the more accurate the collaborative filtering algorithm is.

A second, less commonly used measure of recommendation quality is the ranked scoring (RS). This measure assumes that the recommender presents a recommendation to the user as a list of items ranked by their predicted ratings. As described in (Breese, Heckerman, & Kadie 1998), RS assesses the expected utility of a ranked list of items, by multiplying the utility of an item for the user by the probability that the item will be viewed by the user. The utility of an item is computed as the difference between its observed rating and the default or neutral rating $d$ in the domain (which, they suggest, can be either the midpoint of the rating scale or the average rating in the dataset), while the probability of viewing decays exponentially as the rank of items increases. Formally, the RS of a ranked list of items sorted according to the index j in order of declining $p_{a,j}$[1] is:

$$RS_a = \sum_j max(o_{a,j} - d, 0) * \frac{1}{2^{(j-1)/(\alpha-1)}}$$

The first term computes the utility of the item in the $j^{th}$ position of the list, whereas the second term computes the probability of the user viewing that item (see (Breese, Heckerman, & Kadie 1998) for details on this second term). The RS reported in CF evaluations combines the $RS_a$s for all the users in the test set:

$$RS = 100 \sum_a \frac{RS_a}{RS_a^{max}}$$

where $RS_a^{max}$ is the utility of the best possible ranked list for user $a$ (i.e., the utility of the ranked list that the recommender would generate if it knew all the $o_{a,j}$). Notice that the higher the RS, the more accurate the collaborative filtering algorithm is.

Table 1: MAE scores on the EachMovie data for *Noisy-Best* (Noisy sensor model), *PD* (Personality Diagnosis) and *Correl* (Correlation) - Note: lower scores are better.

| *Algorithm* | *Protocol* | | | |
|---|---|---|---|---|
| | *AllBut1* | *Given10* | *Given5* | *Given2* |
| Noisy-Best | **.893** | **.943** | **.974** | **1.012** |
| PD | .964 | .986 | 1.016 | 1.039 |
| Correl | .999 | 1.069 | 1.145 | 1.296 |

## Evaluation results using MAE and RS on the Eachmovie database[2]

Table 1 shows the results of a recent comparison of CF algorithms based on MAE (Sharma & Poole 2001)[3]. The algorithms were tested on the same subset of the EachMovie database as used by (Breese, Heckerman, & Kadie 1998) and (Pennock *et al.* 2000), consisting of 1,623 movies, 381,862 ratings, 5,000 users in the training set, and 4,119 users in the test set. Ratings in the EachMovie database are elicited on an integer scale from zero to five. In the table, *AllBut1* means that the test set $P_a$ for each test user contains a single randomly selected rating and the observed set $I_a$ contains the rest of the ratings. In contrast, *GivenX* means that $X$ ratings are randomly placed for each test user in the observed set $I_a$, while the rest of the ratings are placed in the test set $P_a$. As shown in the

[1](Breese, Heckerman, & Kadie 1998) says that items are sorted in order of declining $o_{a,j}$, but we believe that was a typo because the recommender cannot present a list ordered by the true ratings.

[2]http://research.compaq.com/SRC/eachmovie/

[3](Sharma & Poole 2001) proposed two algorithms based on a noisy sensor model. In the table, we report only the performance of the best one, that we call Noisy-Best.

Table 2: RS scores on the EachMovie data when $d$ is equal to 2.5 (the midpoint of the 0-5 rating scale) and 3.04 (the average rating of the dataset) - Note: higher scores are better.

| *Algorithm* | *d* | *Protocol* | | | |
|---|---|---|---|---|---|
| | | *AllBut1* | *Given10* | *Given5* | *Given2* |
| Noisy-Best | *2.5* | **77.42** | **76.82** | **76.80** | **74.09** |
| PD | *2.5* | 69.58 | 69.20 | 69.08 | **75.72** |
| Correl | *2.5* | **76.81** | 71.17 | 67.86 | 59.70 |
| Noisy-Best | *3.04* | **72.49** | **71.91** | **71.90** | **68.74** |
| PD | *3.04* | 63.18 | 62.78 | 62.71 | **70.66** |
| Correl | *3.04* | **71.89** | 65.53 | 61.88 | 52.94 |

table, *Noisy-Best* performed better than *PD* and *Correlation* in all these settings. And since *Correlation* had been shown to either perform similarly or outperform (with respect to MAE) all other CF methods studied in (Breese, Heckerman, & Kadie 1998) (e.g., Bayesian Networks), it appears that *Noisy-Best* is the best performing CF algorithm according to MAE (when tested on the EachMovie database).

We also compared CF algorithms with respect to the RS measure. Table 2 shows the results of this comparison. *Noisy-Best* performed similarly or outperformed *PD* and *Correlation* in most settings (more later on statistical significance). Notice that these are new results, because neither (Sharma & Poole 2001) nor (Pennock *et al.* 2000) considered RS. As we did for MAE, the algorithms were tested on the same dataset and following the same procedure used by (Breese, Heckerman, & Kadie 1998). However, for *Correlation* (the only algorithm that both we and (Breese, Heckerman, & Kadie 1998) investigated) we obtained rather different results (our RS for *Correlation d=2.5* is in the 67-77 interval while RS for the same protocol in (Breese, Heckerman, & Kadie 1998) is in the 23-43 interval). We are not quite sure of the source of the discrepancy. Randomization cannot be the culprit because the differences are quite large. Therefore, this issue requires further investigation. Nevertheless, since in (Breese, Heckerman, & Kadie 1998) *Correlation* had been shown to either perform similarly or outperform all other CF methods studied with respect to RS, it appears that *Noisy-Best* is overall the best performing CF algorithm also according to RS (when tested on the EachMovie database).

Tables 1 and 2 also summarize the statistical significance of the results. In each protocol, the score(s) of the algorithm(s) that significantly outperformed the other algorithms is(are) in bold. In Table 1 statistical significance was based on randomized paired sample tests ($p < .05$) (Sharma & Poole 2001), while in Table 2 it was based on ANOVA with the Bonferroni procedure at 90% confidence level (as in (Breese, Heckerman, & Kadie 1998)).

## Exploring New Evaluation Measures

Although MAE has become a standard metric for comparing CF algorithms, we argue that it is based on an unrealistic assumption about what it means for a recommendation to be effective. MAE relies on viewing the recommendation process as a machine learning problem, in which recommendation quality is equated with the accuracy of the algorithm's prediction of how a user will rate a particular item. This perspective is missing a key aspect of the recommendation process. The user of a recommender system is engaged in deciding whether or not to experience an item (e.g., whether or not to watch a movie). So, the value of a recommendation critically depends on how the recommendation will impact the user decision making process and only indirectly on the accuracy of the recommendation. For illustration, consider a user who will watch only movies whose predicted rating $p_{a,j}$ is greater than 3.5. Now, consider the following two predictions for that user:

*(i)* $p_{a,j} = 0$; when $o_{a,j} = 2$; (Absolute Error = 2)

*(ii)* $p_{a,j} = 3$; when $o_{a,j} = 4$; (Absolute Error = 1)

The Absolute Error in *(i)* is greater than the one in *(ii)*. However, in terms of user decision quality, *(i)* leads to a good decision because it entails that the user will avoid watching a movie that she would not have liked, while *(ii)* leads to a poor decision, because it entails that the user will miss a movie that she would have enjoyed.

The key point of this example is that in measuring the quality of a recommendation we should take into account the criterion used by the user in deciding whether or not to accept the recommendation. When the recommendation is provided as a predicted rating, a simple plausible criterion is a user specific threshold in the range of possible ratings. The user will accept a recommendation when the prediction is greater than the threshold.

More formally, let $\theta_a$ be a user specific threshold (in the range of possible ratings) such that:

$p_{a,j} \geq \theta_a \Rightarrow select(a, j)$

where, as before, $p_{a,j}$ is user $a$'s predicted rating for item $j$, and $select(a, j)$ means that user $a$ will select item $j$ (e.g., the user will watch the movie).

Then, the quality of a recommendation $p_{a,j}$, which we call User Gain (UG), can be defined as:

$$UG(p_{a,j}) = \begin{cases} o_{a,j} - \theta_a & \text{if } p_{a,j} \geq \theta_a \\ \theta_a - o_{a,j} & \text{otherwise} \end{cases}$$

where, as previously defined, $o_{a,j}$ is user $a$'s observed rating for item $j$.

The first condition covers the situation in which, since the prediction is greater than the threshold, the user will decide to experience the item and will enjoy it to the extent that its true rating is greater than the threshold. The second condition covers the situation in which the user will decide not to experience the item. In this case, the user will gain to the extent that the item's true rating is smaller than the threshold.

Similarly to $\text{MAE}_a$, we can also define the active user Mean User Gain ($\text{MUG}_a$) as:

$$MUG_a = \frac{1}{n_a} \sum_{j \in P_a} UG(p_{a,j})$$

and MUG as the average $\text{MUG}_a$ for the test set

A comparison between the UG measure and the $RS_a$ measure (see section on CF evaluation strategy and measures) reveals that the two measures are interestingly related. And, we argue, UG can be effectively used to improve $RS_a$. In $RS_a$, the utility of an item is computed as $max(o_{a,j} - d, 0)$. If we substitute in this expression $d$ (the default rating) with $\theta_a$ (the user's threshold) and we admit negative utilities (by removing the $max$ operator), the utility computed in $RS_a$ is the same as the one computed in the first condition of UG (i.e., when $p_{a,j} \geq \theta_a$). Now let's examine these transformations and their effect in order.

- $\theta_a$ is just a more adequate version of $d$. While $d$ is a neutral rating for the dataset [4], $\theta_a$ is a neutral rating for the active user decision strategy.
- If the user experiences an item whose true rating is below $\theta_a$ she will be disappointed. So, it is sensible to admit negative utilities.

Now, why is $RS_a$ covering only the first condition of UG? We believe the underlying assumption is that, since the ranked list is presenting the items with the highest predicted rating in the dataset, for all these items $p_{a,j}$ is assumed to be greater than $\theta_a$. However, when that is not necessarily the case a more comprehensive definition of $RS_a$ would be:

$$RS_a^{UG} = \sum_j UG(p_{a,j}) * \frac{1}{2^{(j-1)/(\alpha-1)}}$$

In order to evaluate a CF algorithm, the $RS_a^{UG}$s for all the users in the test set need to be combined. Unfortunately, we cannot apply the same formula we used in RS to combine all the $RS_a$ because $RS_a^{UG}$ can be negative and this would lead to unintuitive results. A preliminary more intuitive way to combine the $RS_a^{UG}$s is simply to compute their average. We call this summary measure $RS^{UG}$. Notice that the higher the $RS^{UG}$, the more accurate the collaborative filtering algorithm is.

As a final note, we discuss how previous attempts to use MAE by taking into account the user decision process did not really address the core of the problem. Shardanand and Maes (Shardanand & Maes 1995) and Pennock et al. (Pennock *et al.* 2000) proposed that the accuracy of a CF algorithms should be evaluated only on items whose observed ratings are extreme (very high or very low). The supposition is that, most of the time, people are interested in suggestions about items they might like or dislike, but not about items they are unsure of. Pennock et al. (Pennock *et al.* 2000) defined the extreme ratings as those which are 0.5 above and 0.5 below the average rating in the dataset. In light of our analysis of MAE, this proposal is clearly problematic. Since intuitively $\theta_a$s should correspond to non-extreme ratings (more on this in the following section), errors on items with non-extreme ratings are more likely to lead the user to make poor decisions (e.g., watching movies she will not enjoy). So, if you wanted to use MAE trying to take into account the user decision process, you should focus on non-extreme ratings, rather than on extreme ones.

[4]Typically, $d$ is either the midpoint of the rating range or the average of all ratings in the dataset (2.5 and 3.04 respectively in the Eachmovie database). So, $d$ may not have any relation with any user decision criterion.

Again, assume that for any movie you can get a reliable rating tailored to your preferences on a scale from 0 to 5 (where 0 means an awful movie and 5 means a great movie).

Would you go to a movie-theater (and spend ~10$) to watch a movie with rating 1 ?

Yes Not sure No

Would you go to a movie-theater (and spend ~10$) to watch a movie with rating 5 ?

Yes Not sure No

.................... *(same question for all remaining ratings: 2, 3 and 4)*

Figure 1: Portion of the questionnaire to assess $\theta_a$

## Elicitation Study

The $\text{MUG}_a$ measure relies on a user specific threshold $\theta_a$, which determines whether the user will choose to experience an item given its predicted rating. Thus, in order to apply UG in any domain, you need either to elicit $\theta_a$ from all users, or to elicit $\theta_a$ from a sample of users and then use the sample to compute a $\hat{\theta}$ that can be used as a default $\theta_a$ for all users [5]. To obtain a reasonable $\hat{\theta}$ for the movie domain, we have performed a user study in which participants filled out a questionnaire about their preferences and decision strategies in that domain.

The questionnaire was first checked with a few pilot participants and then was administered to 27 participants (students and faculties at UBC). Of these 27, 5 were eliminated from the study because of procedural faults. The questionnaire consists of two parts: one to elicit the user specific $\theta_a$; the other to elicit the user utility function (in the decision-theoretic sense) for movie ratings. The reason for assessing the user's utility function was to obtain further independent support for the estimate of $\hat{\theta}$.

Figure 1 shows the part of the questionnaire that assesses $\theta_a$. We left the definition of the ratings as general as possible *"..where 0 means an awful movie and*

[5]$\hat{\theta}$ should not be confused with the $d$ in RS. $\hat{\theta}$ is based on a user decision criterion, while $d$ only depends on the dataset.

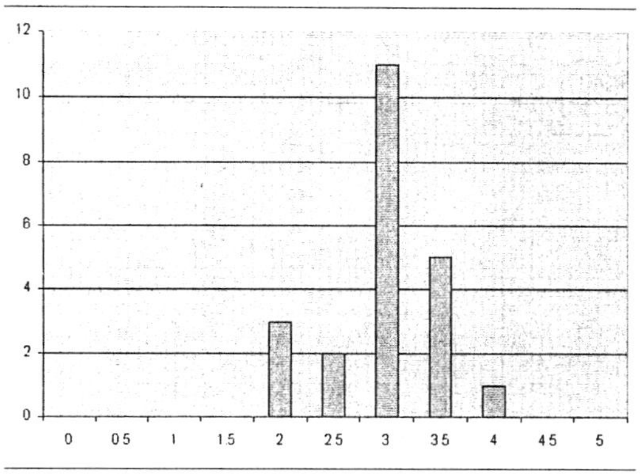

Figure 2: Counts for values of $\theta_a$.

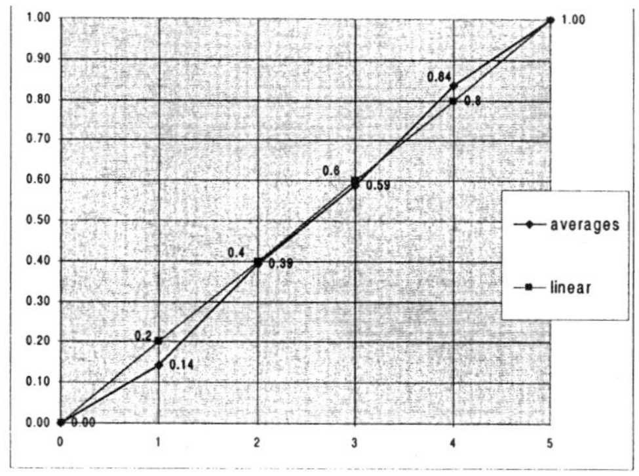


Figure 3: A comparison between a linear utility function and the one computed by averaging for each rating the utility of all participants.

*5 means a great movie"* to preserve as much as possible the generality of the assessment. In interpreting the participant answers, we applied the following schema. If the participant marks "not sure" for a certain rating, $\theta_a$ is assigned that rating. Whereas, if the participant does not mark any rating as "not sure", then $\theta_a$ is assigned the midpoint between the highest rating for which the participant answered "no" and the lowest rating for which the participant answered "yes". The results of the analysis of this portion of the questionnaire are shown in Figure 2. The mean of our sample for $\theta_a$ is 2.98. So, we assume 2.98 as a reasonable estimate for $\hat{\theta}$ in the movie domain.

A second portion of the questionnaire elicited the participants' utility function for movie ratings. This was based on the classic probability-equivalent (PE) procedure.

The outcomes of the utility elicitation process are summarized in Figure 3. The figure compares a linear utility function with what we call the "average" utility function for our participants. This function is computed by averaging for each rating the utility of all participants.

When aggregated in this way, the users' utility functions provide independent evidence on the position of $\hat{\theta}$ on the rating scale. Several studies in behavioral decision theory have shown that people are $risk-adverse$ (their utility function is concave) when they believe they are gaining, while they are $risk-seeking$ (their utility function is convex) when they believe they are losing (Clemen 1996). Figure 3 indicates that people on average believe they are gaining when they watch a movie whose rating is greater than 3 (the average utility function is concave) and believe they are losing when they watch a movie whose rating is less than 2 (the average utility function is convex). Thus, a reasonable $\hat{\theta}$ must lie in that interval.

## Applying MUG and RS$^{UG}$

We have applied MUG and RS$^{UG}$ in comparing the same three CF algorithms that were compared with MAE in (Sharma & Poole 2001) and that we compared with RS in this paper. As it was the case for (Sharma & Poole 2001), we run our testing on the EachMovie database. This database specifies the user-item matrix, but does not provide any information on user specific $\theta_a$s. Therefore, we used the default estimates we obtain from our elicitation study. $\hat{\theta} = 2.98$ was used in all the experiments.

Table 3: MUG scores on the EachMovie data. Note: scores are expressed on the $[-max(\hat{\theta}, 5 - \hat{\theta}), +max(\hat{\theta}, 5 - \hat{\theta})]$ rating interval ([-2.98,+2.98] in our experiments) and higher scores are better.

| *Algorithm* | *Protocol* | | | |
|---|---|---|---|---|
| | *AllBut1* | *Given10* | *Given5* | *Given2* |
| Noisy-Best | 0.71 | **0.70** | **0.62** | **0.52** |
| PD | 0.58 | 0.54 | 0.52 | 0.09 |
| Correl | **0.78** | 0.60 | 0.52 | 0.37 |

Results for MUG and RS$^{UG}$ are shown in Table 3 and Table 4 respectively. In all these tables, as we did before, in each protocol, the score(s) of the algorithm(s) that significantly outperformed the other algorithms are in bold. Statistical significance was based on ANOVA with the Bonferroni procedure at 90% confidence level (as in (Breese, Heckerman, & Kadie 1998)).

Let us start by examining the results for MUG in Table 3. *Noisy-Best* is the best performer in all protocols except for *AllBut1*, in which *Correlation* is the best. When these results are compared with what was obtained with MAE (see Table 1), the most noticeable difference is that in the *AllBut1* protocol *Correlation* is the winner for MUG, whereas it was the loser for MAE. The explanation for this (which we verified empirically) is that in the *AllBut1* protocol *Correlation* is the most precise algorithm in predicting movies whose observed

Table 4: $RS^{UG}$ scores on the EachMovie data. Note: the maximum value for this measure in our experiments was 1.72 (which is the average of the utilities of the best possible ranked list for all users in the test set) - higher scores are better.

| *Algorithm* | *Protocol* | | | |
|---|---|---|---|---|
| | *AllBut1* | *Given10* | *Given5* | *Given2* |
| Noisy-Best | **1.04** | **0.96** | **0.95** | **0.83** |
| PD | 0.77 | 0.73 | 0.71 | 0.35 |
| Correl | **1.04** | 0.75 | 0.61 | 0.43 |

value is close to $\hat{\theta}$ (i.e., observed-value= 3). And UG, by definition, is more sensitive to errors in that proximity.

The results for $\mathrm{RS}^{UG}$ mirror the ones that were obtained for RS. This is not surprising given that we had to use $\hat{\theta}$ instead of user-specific $\theta_a$s and given how close $\hat{\theta}$ was to the neutral rating of the dataset [6]. In detail, *Noisy-Best* is the best performer for $\mathrm{RS}^{UG}$ in all protocols with *Correlation* performing at the same level in the *AllBut1* protocol. A plausible explanation for *Correlation* performing less well in $\mathrm{RS}^{UG}$ than in MUG is the following. In RS-measures items are ranked with respect to their predicted value. This ranking is then used to weight the utility gain of each prediction, with more weight given to higher ranked items. Since *Correlation* is more precise only in predicting movies whose observed value is close to $\hat{\theta}$, it will be more precise only in predicting items that will tend to be ranked in the middle of the ranking and therefore will tend to be modestly weighted. As a result, the advantage of *Correlation* in MUG plays a more limited role in $\mathrm{RS}^{UG}$.

In general, we claim the outcomes of our evaluation using MUG and $RS^{UG}$ are more valuable than the ones presented in previous studies using MAE and RS, because MUG and $RS^{UG}$ are arguably more realistic measures of recommendation quality than MAE and RS.

## Conclusions and Future Work

Performance measures for testing algorithms should be based on realistic assumptions on how the output of those algorithms is used in practice. Algorithms for CF predict how a user will rate a particular item and these predictions are used by users to decide whether or not to select that item. Thus, performance measures for CF should take into account how predicted ratings influence the user's decision.

We noted that MAE, the most popular performance measure for CF, is inadequate in this respect, because it focuses exclusively on the accuracy of the predictions, without consideration for their influence on the user decision. To overcome this limitation, we have proposed the new measure of performance MUG that tries to quantify how much a user is going to gain from decisions based on CF predictions.

[6]But this may not be the case for other datasets or domains

We have shown that UG (the basic component of MUG) presents interesting similarity with RS, another performance measure commonly used in CF, and we have described how UG can be used to define a more plausible RS.

We have also presented the results of a user study in which we elicited from actual users their decision thresholds and their utility functions in the movie domain. This information was then used in performing a comparative evaluation of CF algorithms with respect to our new measures of recommendation quality. The main outcome of this evaluation is that while according to MAE *Noisy-Best* is the top performer in all protocols, according to MUG *Correlation* wins in the *AllBut1* protocol. As for $RS^{UG}$, the results mirror the ones obtained for RS. However, this may change if user-specific utility thresholds are used.

We envision at least two future extensions for our research. First, we plan to collect a new dataset that includes not only the user/rating matrix but also user specific $\theta_a$s. On this dataset, it will be possible to evaluate CF algorithms with MUG without having to rely on a default threshold. A second direction, we intend to pursue, consists of applying our new measures to both other CF algorithms (e.g., Bayesian Networks) and other datasets (e.g., the Nielsen TV viewing dataset) in order to verify the generality of our findings.

## References


Breese, J. S.; Heckerman, D.; and Kadie, C. 1998. Empirical ananlysis of predictive algorithms for collaborative filtering. In *Proc. of the 14th Conf. on Uncertainity in AI*, 43–52.

Clemen, R. T. 1996. *Making Hard Decisions.* Belmont CA: Duxbury Press, 2nd edition edition.

Pennock, D. M.; Horvitz, E.; Lawrence, S.; and Giles, C. L. 2000. Collaborative filtering by personality diagnosis: A hybrid memory-and model-based approach. In *Proc. of the 16th Conf. on Uncertainty in AI*, 473–480.

Rashid, A.; Albert, I.; Cosley, D.; Lam, S.; McNee, S.; Konstan, J.; and Riedl, J. 2002. Getting to know you: learning new user preferences in recommender systems. In *Proc. of the Int. Conf. on Intelligent User Interfaces*, 127–134.

Resnick, P.; Iacovou, N.; Suchak, M.; Bergstrom, P.; and Riedl, J. 1994. Grouplens: An open architecture for collaborative filtering of netnews. In *Proc. of Conf. on Computer Supported Cooperative Work*, 175–186.

Schafer, J. B.; Konstan, J.; and Riedl, J. 1999. Recommender system in e-commerce. In *Proc. of the ACM Conf. on E-Commerce (EC-99)*, 158–166.

Shardanand, U., and Maes, P. 1995. Social information filtering: Algorithms for automating "word of mouth". In *Proc. of ACM CHI'95 Conf. on Human Factors in Computing Systems*, 210–217.

Sharma, R., and Poole, D. 2001. Symmetric collaborative filtering using the noisy sensor model. In *Proc. of the 17th Conf. on Uncertainty in AI*, 488–495.

# Mining Opinion Features in Customer Reviews

**Minqing Hu and Bing Liu**

Department of Computer Science
University of Illinois at Chicago
851 South Morgan Street
Chicago, IL 60607-7053
{mhu1, liub}@cs.uic.edu

**Abstract**

It is a common practice that merchants selling products on the Web ask their customers to review the products and associated services. As e-commerce is becoming more and more popular, the number of customer reviews that a product receives grows rapidly. For a popular product, the number of reviews can be in hundreds. This makes it difficult for a potential customer to read them in order to make a decision on whether to buy the product. In this project, we aim to summarize all the customer reviews of a product. This summarization task is different from traditional text summarization because we are only interested in the specific features of the product that customers have opinions on and also whether the opinions are positive or negative. We do not summarize the reviews by selecting or rewriting a subset of the original sentences from the reviews to capture their main points as in the classic text summarization. In this paper, we only focus on mining opinion/product features that the reviewers have commented on. A number of techniques are presented to mine such features. Our experimental results show that these techniques are highly effective.

## Introduction

With the rapid expansion of e-commerce, more and more products are sold on the Web, and more and more people are buying products on the Web. In order to enhance customer satisfaction and their shopping experiences, it has become a common practice for online merchants to enable their customers to review or to express opinions on the products that they buy. With more and more common users becoming comfortable with the Internet, an increasing number of people are writing reviews. As a consequence, the number of reviews that a product receives grows rapidly. Some popular products can get hundreds of reviews at some large merchant sites. This makes it very hard for a potential customer to read them to help him or her to make a decision on whether to buy the product.

In this research, we propose to study the problem of *feature-based opinion summarization* of customer reviews of products sold online. The task is performed in two steps:

1. Identify the features of the product that customers have expressed opinions on (called *opinion features*) and rank the features according to their frequencies that they appear in the reviews.
2. For each feature, we identify how many customer reviews have positive or negative opinions. The specific reviews that express these opinions are attached to the feature. This facilitates browsing of the reviews by potential customers.



We give a simple example to illustrate. Assume that we summarize the reviews of a particular digital camera, *digital_camera_1*. Our summary looks like the following:

*Digital_camera_1*:
  picture quality:
    Positive: 253 <individual reviews>
    Negative: 6 <individual reviews>
  size:
    Positive: 134 <individual reviews>
    Negative: 10 <individual reviews>
  …

*picture quality* and *size* are opinion features. There are 253 customer reviews that express positive opinions about the picture quality, and only 6 that express negative opinions. <individual reviews> points to the specific reviews that give positive (or negative) comments about the feature.

With such a feature-based opinion summary, a potential customer can easily see how the existing customers feel about the digital camera. If he/she is very interested in a particular feature, he/she can drill down by following the <individual reviews> link to see why existing customers like it or what they complain about.

Our task is clearly different from traditional text summarization (Radev and McKeown. 1998; Hovy and Lin 1997) in a number of ways. First of all, our summary is structured rather than another (but shorter) free text document as produced by most text summarization systems. Second, we are only interested in features of the product that customers have opinions on and also whether the opinions are positive or negative. We do not summarize the reviews by selecting or rewriting a subset of the original sentences from the reviews to capture their main points as in traditional text summarization.

In this paper, we only focus on the first step of the review summarization. That is, we aim to mine product features that the reviewers have commented on. The second step of determining whether an opinion is positive or negative will be discussed in a subsequent paper as it is quite involved.

A question that one may ask is "why not ask the merchant or the manufacturer of the product to provide a list of features?" This is a possible approach. However, it has a number of problems: (1) It is hard for a merchant to provide the features because he/she may sell a large number of products. (2) The words used by merchants or the manufacturer may not be the same as those used by common users of the product although they may refer to the same features. This causes problem in identifying what the customers are interested in. Furthermore, customers may comment on the lack of certain features of the product. (3) Customers may comment on some features that the manufacturer has never thought about, i.e., unexpected features. (4) The manufacturer may not want users of its product to know certain weak features.

This paper proposes a number of techniques based on data mining and natural language processing methods to mine opinion/product features. Our experimental results show that these techniques are highly effective.

## Related Work

Our work is mainly related to two areas of research, text summarization and terminology identification. The majority of text summarization techniques fall in two categories: template instantiation and text extraction. Work in the former framework includes (DeJong 1982), (Tait 1983), and (Radev and McKeown 1998). They focus on the identification and extraction of certain core entities and facts in a document, which are packaged in a template. This framework requires background analysis to instantiate a template to a suitable level of detail. It is thus not domain independent (Sparck-Jones 1993a, 1993b). Our technique does not fill in any template and is domain independent.

The text extraction framework (Paice 1990; Kupiec, Pedersen, and Chen 1995; Hovy and Lin 1997) identifies some representative sentences to summarize the document. Over the years, many sophisticated techniques were developed, e.g., strong notions of topicality (Hovy and Lin 1997), lexical chains (Barzilay and Elhadad 1997), and discourse structures (Marcu 1997). Our work is different as we do not extract those most representative sentences, but only identify and extract those specific product features and the opinions related with them.

Kan and McKeown (1999) propose a hybrid approach that merges template instantiation with sentence extraction. (Boguraev and Kennedy 1997) also reports a technique that finds a few very prominent expressions, objects or events in a document and use them to help summarize the document. Again, our work is different as we need to find all product features in a set of customer reviews regardless whether they are prominent or not.

Most existing works on text summarization focuses a single document. Some researchers also studied summarization of multiple documents covering similar information. Their main purpose is to summarize the similarities and differences in the information contents of these documents (Mani and Bloedorn 1997). Clearly, our work is related but different.

In terminology identification, there are basically two techniques for discovering terms in corpora: symbolic approaches that rely on syntactic description of terms, namely noun phrases, and statistical approaches that exploiting the fact that the words composing a term tend to be found close to each other and reoccurring (Jacquemin and Bourigault 2001; Justeson and Katz 1995; Daille 1996; Church and Hanks 1990). However, using noun phrases tends to produce too many non-terms, while using reoccurring phrases misses many low frequency terms, terms with variations, and terms with only one word. Our association mining based technique does not have these problems, and we can also find infrequent features by exploiting the fact that we are only interesting in features that the users have expressed opinions on.

Our feature-based opinion summarization system is also related to (Dave, Lawrence and Pennock 2003), in which a semantic classifier of product review sentences is built using a training corpus. However, their system does not mine product features. In addition, our work does not need a training corpus to build a summary.

## The Proposed Techniques

Figure 1 gives an architectural overview for our opinion summarization system. The system performs the summarization in two main steps: feature extraction and opinion orientation identification. The inputs to the system are a product name and an entry page for all the reviews of the product. The output is the summary of the reviews as the one shown in the introduction section.

Given the inputs, the system first downloads (or crawls) all the reviews, and puts them in the review database. The feature extraction function, which is the focus of this paper, first extracts "hot" features that a lot of people have expressed their opinions on in their reviews, and then finds those infrequent ones. The opinion orientation identification function takes the generated features and summarizes the opinions of the feature into 2 categories: positive and negative. In Figure 1, POS tagging is the part-of-speech tagging (Manning and Schütze 1999) from natural language processing. Below, we discuss each of the functions in feature extraction in turn. We will not discuss the final step "Opinion orientation identification" as it is not the focus of this paper and it is complex and involved (it will be described in a subsequent paper). Nevertheless, a brief introduction of the step will be given in a later section.

### Part-of-Speech Tagging (POS)

Before discussing the application of part-of-speech tagging from natural language processing, we first give some example sentences from some reviews to describe what kinds of opinions that we will handle.

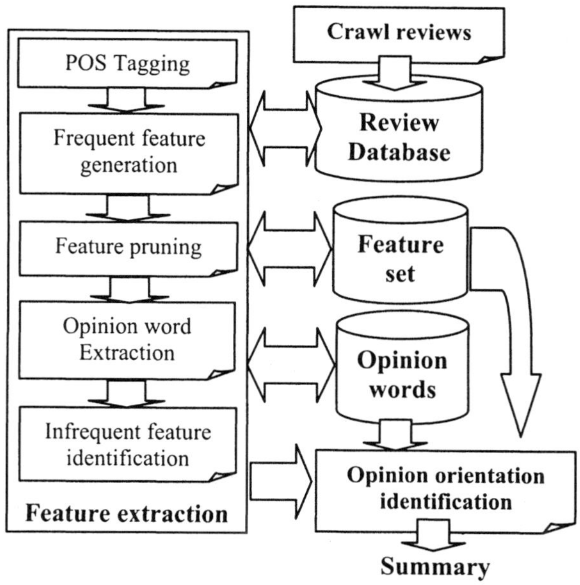


Figure 1: The opinion summarization system

Our system aims to find what people like and dislike about a given product. Therefore how to find out the product features that people talk about is an important step. However, due to the difficulty of natural language understanding, some types of sentences are hard to deal with. Let us see some easy and hard sentences from the reviews of a digital camera:

*"The pictures are very clear."*

*"Overall a fantastic very compact camera."*

In the first sentence, the user is satisfied with the picture quality of the camera, *picture* is the feature that the user talks about. Similarly, the second sentence shows that *camera* is the feature that the user expresses his/her opinion. While the features of these two sentences are explicitly mentioned in the sentences, some features are implicit and hard to find. For example,

*"While light, it will not easily fit in pockets."*

This customer is talking about the *size* of the camera, but the word "size" is not explicitly mentioned in the sentence. To find such implicit features, semantic understanding is needed, which requires more sophisticated techniques. However, implicit features occur much less frequent than explicit ones. Thus in this paper, we focus on finding features that appear explicitly as nouns or noun phrases in the reviews. To identify nouns/noun phrases from the reviews, we use the part-of-speech tagging.

In this work, we use the NLProcessor linguistic parser (NLProcessor 2000), which parses each sentence and yields the part-of-speech tag of each word (whether the word is a noun, verb, adjective, etc) and identifies simple noun and verb groups (syntactic chunking). The following shows a sentence with the POS tags.

```
<S> <NG><W C='PRP' L='SS' T='w' S='Y'> I </W>
</NG> <VG> <W C='VBP'> am </W><W C='RB'>
absolutely </W></VG> <W C='IN'> in </W> <NG>
<W C='NN'> awe </W> </NG> <W C='IN'> of </W>
<NG> <W C='DT'> this </W> <W C='NN'> camera
</W></NG><W C='.'> . </W></S>
```

The NLProcessor system generates XML output. For instance, <W C='NN'> indicates a noun and <NG> indicates a noun group/noun phrase.

Each sentence is saved in the review database along with the POS tag information of each word in the sentence.

A transaction file is then created for the generation of frequent features in the next step. In this file, each line contains words from a sentence, which includes only pre-processed nouns/noun phrases of the sentence. The reason is that other components of a sentence are unlikely to be product features. Here, pre-processing includes the deletion of stopwords, stemming and fuzzy matching. Fuzzy matching (Jokinen and Ukkonen 1991) is used to deal with word variants or misspellings. For example, "autofocus" and "auto-focus" actually refer to the same feature. All the occurrences of "autofocus" are replaced with "auto-focus".

## Frequent Features Generation

This step is to find features that people are most interested in. In order to do this, we use association rule mining (Agrawal and Srikant 1994) to find all frequent itemsets. In our context, an itemset is a set of words or a phrase that occurs together.

Association rule mining is stated as follows: Let $I = \{i_1, \ldots, i_n\}$ be a set of items, and $D$ be a set of transactions (the dataset). Each transaction consists of a subset of items in $I$. An *association rule* is an implication of the form $X \rightarrow Y$, where $X \subset I$, $Y \subset I$, and $X \cap Y = \varnothing$. The rule $X \rightarrow Y$ holds in $D$ with confidence $c$ if $c\%$ of transactions in $D$ that support $X$ also support $Y$. The rule has support $s$ in $D$ if $s\%$ of transactions in $D$ contain $X \cup Y$. The problem of mining association rules is to generate all association rules in $D$ that have support and confidence greater than the user-specified minimum support and minimum confidence.

*Mining frequent occurring phrases*: Each piece of information extracted above is stored in a dataset called a *transaction* set/file. We then run the association rule miner, CBA (Liu, Hsu and Ma 1998), which is based on the Apriori algorithm in (Agrawal and Srikant 1994). It finds all frequent itemsets in the transaction set. Each resulting frequent itemset is a possible feature. In our work, we define an itemset as frequent if it appears in more than 1% (minimum support) of the review sentences.

The Apriori algorithm works in two steps. In the first step, it finds all *frequent itemsets* from a set of *transactions* that satisfy a user-specified *minimum support*. In the second step, it generates rules from the discovered frequent itemsets. For our task, we only need the first step, i.e., finding frequent itemsets, which are candidate features. In addition, we only need to find frequent itemsets with three words or fewer in this work as we believe that a product feature contains no more than three words (this restriction can be easily relaxed).

The generated frequent itemsets, which are also called candidate *frequent features* in this paper, are stored to the feature set for further processing.

### Feature Pruning

Not all frequent features generated by association mining are useful or are genuine features. There are also some uninteresting and redundant ones. Feature pruning aims to remove these incorrect features. We present two types of pruning below.

**Compactness pruning**: This method checks features that contain at least two words, which we call *feature phrases*, and remove those that are likely to be meaningless.

In association mining, the algorithm does not consider the position of an item (or word) in a transaction (or a sentence). However, in a natural language sentence, words that appear together and in a specific order are more likely to be meaningful phrases. Therefore, some of the frequent feature phrases generated by association mining may not be genuine features. The idea of compactness pruning is to prune those candidate features whose words do not appear together. We use distances among the words in a candidate feature phrase (itemset) to do the pruning.

**Definition 1**: *compact phrase*

- Let $f$ be a frequent feature phrase and $f$ contains $n$ words. Assume that a sentence $s$ contains $f$ and the sequence of the words in $f$ that appear in $s$ is: $w_1$, $w_2$, ..., $w_n$. If the word distance in $s$ between any two adjacent words ($w_i$ and $w_{i+1}$) in the above sequence is no greater than 3, then we say $f$ is *compact* in $s$.
- If $f$ occurs in $m$ sentences in the review database, and it is compact in at least 2 of the $m$ sentences, then we call $f$ a *compact feature phrase*.

For example, we have a frequent feature phrase *"digital camera"* and three sentences from the review database contain the phrase:

*"I had searched for a digital camera for 3 months."*

*"This is the best digital camera on the market"*

*"The camera does not have a digital zoom"*

The phrase *digital camera* is compact in the first two sentences but not compact in the last one. However, it is still a compact phrase as it appeared compactly two times.

For a feature phrase and a sentence that contains the phrase, we look at the position information of every word of the phrase and check whether it is compact in the sentence. If we could not find two compact sentences in the review database, we prune the feature phrase.

**Redundancy pruning:** In this step, we focus on removing redundant features that contain single words. To describe redundant features, we have the following definition:

**Definition 2** *p-support (pure support)*

*p-support* of feature *ftr* is the number of sentences that *ftr* appears in as a noun or noun phrase, and these sentences must contain no feature phrase that is a superset of *ftr*.

p-support is different from the general support in association mining. For example, we have feature *manual*, with the support of 10 sentences. It is a subset of feature phrases *manual mode* and *manual setting* in the review database. Suppose the support of the two feature phrases are 4 and 3 respectively, the two phrases do not appear together in any sentence, and all the features appear as noun/noun phrases. Then the p-support of *manual* would be 3. Recall that we require the feature to appear as a noun or noun phrase as we do not want to find adjectives or adverbs as features.

We use the minimum p-support to prune those redundant features. If a feature has a p-support lower than the minimum p-support (in our system, we set it to 3) and the feature is a subset of another feature phrase (which suggests that the feature alone may not be interesting), it is pruned. For instance, *life* by itself is not a useful feature while *battery life* is a meaningful feature phrase. In the previous example of *manual,* which has a p-support of 3, it is not pruned. This is reasonable considering that *manual* has two senses as noun meaning "references" and adjective meaning "of or relating to hands". Thus all the three features, *manual*, *manual mode*, *manual setting*, could be interesting.

### Opinion Words Extraction

Opinion words are words that people use to express a positive or negative opinion. Observing that people often express their opinions of a product feature using opinion words that are located around the feature in the sentence, we can extract opinion words from the review database using all the remaining frequent features (after pruning). For instance, let us look at the following two sentences:

*"The strap is horrible and gets in the way of parts of the camera you need access to."*

*"After nearly 800 pictures I have found that this camera takes incredible pictures."*

In the first sentence, *strap*, the feature, is near the opinion word *horrible*. And in the second example, feature *picture* is close to the opinion word *incredible.*

Following from this observation, we can extract opinion words in the following way:

- For each sentence in the review database, if it contains any frequent feature, extract the nearby *adjective.* If such an adjective is found, it is considered an opinion word. A nearby adjective refers to the adjacent adjective that modifies the noun/noun phrase that is a frequent feature.

As shown in the previous example, *horrible* is the adjective that modifies *strap*, and *incredible* is the adjective that modifies *picture*.

We use stemming and fuzzy matching to take care of word

variants and misspellings. In this way, we build up an opinion word list, which is used below.

### Infrequent Feature Identification

Frequent features are the "hot" features that people are most interested in for a given product. However, there are some features that only a small number of people talked about. These features can also be interesting to some potential customers. The question is how to extract these infrequent features? Considering the following sentences:

*"Red eye is very easy to correct."*

*"The camera comes with an excellent easy to install software"*

*"The pictures are absolutely amazing"*

*"The software that comes with it is amazing"*

Sentences 1 and 2 share the same opinion word *easy* yet describing different features: sentence 1 is about *red eye*, sentence 2 is about the *software*. Assume that *software* is a frequent feature in our digital camera review database. *red eye* is infrequent but also interesting. Similarly, *amazing* appears in both sentences 3 and 4, but sentence 3 is about *picture* while sentence 4 is about the *software*.

From the examples, we see that people use the same adjective words to describe different subjects. Therefore, we could use the opinion words to look for features that cannot be found in the frequent feature generation step.

In the opinion words generation step, we use frequent features to find adjacent opinion words that modify the features. In this step, we use the known opinion words to find those *nearby* features that opinion words modify. In both steps, we utilize the observation "opinions tend to appear closely together with features". We extract infrequent features using the following procedure:

- For each sentence in the review database, if it contains no frequent feature but one or more opinion words, find the *nearest* noun/noun phrase of the opinion word. The noun/noun phrase is then stored in the feature set as an infrequent feature.

We use the *nearest* noun/noun phrase as the noun/noun phrase that the opinion word modifies because that is what happens most of the time. Since finding the corresponding noun/noun phrases that an opinion word modifies requires natural language understanding, which is difficult with only POS tags, we use this simple heuristic method to find the nearest noun/noun phrase instead. It works quite well.

A problem with the infrequent feature identification using opinion words is that it could also find nouns/noun phrases that are irrelevant to the given product. The reason for this is that people can use common adjectives to describe a lot of subjects, including both interesting features that we want and irrelevant subjects. Considering the following,

*"The salesman was easy going and let me try all the models on display."*

*salesman* is not a relevant feature of a product, but it will be found as an infrequent feature because of the nearby opinion word *easy*.

This, however, is not a serious problem since the number of infrequent features, compared with the number of frequent features, is small. They account for around 15-20% of the total number of features as obtained in our experimental results. Infrequent features are generated for completeness. Moreover, frequent features are more important than infrequent ones. Since we rank features according to their p-supports, those wrong infrequent features will be ranked very low and thus will not affect most of the users.

**Opinion Sentence Orientation Identification:** After opinion features have been identified, we determine the semantic orientation (i.e., positive or negative) of each opinion sentence. This consists of two steps: (1) for each opinion word in the opinion word list, we identify its semantic orientation using a bootstrapping technique and the WordNet (Miller *et al.* 1990), and (2) we then decide the opinion orientation of each sentence based on the dominant orientation of the opinion words in the sentence. The details are presented in a subsequent paper.

## Experiments

We have conducted experiments on the customer reviews of five electronics products: 2 digital cameras, 1 DVD player, 1 mp3 player, and 1 cellular phone. The two websites where we collected the reviews from are Amazon.com and C|net.com. Products in these sites have a large number of reviews. Each of the reviews includes a text review and a title. Additional information available but not used in this project, include date, time, author name

Table 1: Recall and precision at each step of the system

| Product name | No. of manual Features | Frequent features (association mining) | | Compactness pruning | | P-support pruning | | Infrequent feature identification | |
|---|---|---|---|---|---|---|---|---|---|
| | | Recall | Precision | Recall | Precision | Recall | Precision | Recall | Precision |
| Digital camera1 | 79 | 0.671 | 0.552 | 0.658 | 0.634 | 0.658 | 0.825 | 0.822 | 0.747 |
| Digital camera2 | 96 | 0.594 | 0.594 | 0.594 | 0.679 | 0.594 | 0.781 | 0.792 | 0.710 |
| Cellular phone | 67 | 0.731 | 0.563 | 0.716 | 0.676 | 0.716 | 0.828 | 0.761 | 0.718 |
| Mp3 player | 57 | 0.652 | 0.573 | 0.652 | 0.683 | 0.652 | 0.754 | 0.818 | 0.692 |
| DVD player | 49 | 0.754 | 0.531 | 0.754 | 0.634 | 0.754 | 0.765 | 0.797 | 0.743 |
| **Average** | **69** | **0.68** | **0.56** | **0.67** | **0.66** | **0.67** | **0.79** | **0.80** | **0.72** |

and location (for Amazon reviews), and ratings.

For each product, we first crawled and downloaded the first 100 reviews. These review documents were then cleaned to remove HTML tags. After that, NLProcessor is used to generate part-of-speech tags. After that, our system is applied to perform feature extraction.

To evaluate the discovered features, a human tagger manually read all the reviews and produced a manual feature list for each product. The features are mostly explicit in opinion sentences, e.g., *pictures* in *"the pictures are absolutely amazing"*. The implicit features such as *size* in *"it fits in a pocket nicely"* are also easy to identify by the human tagger. Column "No. of manual features" in Table 1 shows the number of manual features for each product.

Table 1 gives all the precision and recall results. We evaluated the results at each step of our algorithm. In the table, column 1 lists each product. Columns 3 and 4 give the recall and precision of frequent feature generation for each product, which uses association mining. The results indicate that the frequent features contain a lot of errors. Using this step alone gives poor results, i.e., low precision. Columns 5 and 6 show the corresponding results after compactness pruning is performed. We can see that the precision is improved significantly by this pruning. The recall stays steady. Columns 7 and 8 give the results after pruning using p-support. There is another dramatic improvement in the precision. The recall level has almost no change. The results from Columns 4-8 demonstrate clearly the effectiveness of these two pruning techniques. Columns 9 and 10 give the results after infrequent feature identification is done. The recall is improved dramatically. The precision drops a few percents on average. However, this is not a major problem because the infrequent features are ranked rather low, and thus will not affect most users.

In summary, with the average of recall of 80% and the average precision of 72%, we believe that our techniques are quite promising, and can be used in practical settings.

## Conclusion

In this paper, we proposed a number of techniques for mining opinion features from product reviews based on data mining and natural language processing methods. The objective is to produce a feature-based summary of a large number of customer reviews of a product sold online. We believe that this problem will become increasingly important as more people are buying and expressing their opinions on the Web. Our experimental results indicate that the proposed techniques are effective in performing their tasks. In our future work, we plan to further improve these techniques. We also plan to group features according to the strength of the opinions that have been expressed on them, e.g., to determine which features customers strongly like and dislike. This will further improve the feature extraction and the subsequent summarization.

**Acknowledgements.** This work is supported by the National Science Foundation under the grant IIS-0307239.

## References

Agrawal, R. and Srikant, R. 1994. "Fast algorithm for mining association rules." *VLDB'94*, 1994.

Barzilay, R., and Elhadad, M. 1997. Using lexical chains for text summarization. *ACL Workshop on Intelligent, scalable text summarization.*

Boguraev, B., and Kennedy, C. 1997. Salience-based content characterization of text documents. *In Proceedings of the ACL Workshop on Intelligent Scalable Text Summarization.*

Church, K. and Hanks, P. 1990. Word association norms, mutual information and lexicography. *Computational Linguistics*, 16(1) : 22-29.

Daille. 1996. Study and Implementation of Combined Techniques for Automatic Extraction of Terminology. *The Balancing Act: Combining Symbolic and Statistical Approaches to Language Processing.* MIT Press, Cambridge

Dave, K., Lawrence, S., and Pennock, D., 2003. Mining the Peanut Gallery: Opinion Extraction and Semantic Classification of Product Reviews. *WWW-2003.*

DeJong, G. 1982. An Overview of the FRUMP System. *Strategies for Natural Language Parsing*. 149-176

Hovy, E., and Lin, C.Y. 1997. Automated Text Summarization in SUMMARIST. *ACL Workshop on Intelligent, Scalable Text Summarization*

Jacquemin, C., and Bourigault, D. 2001. Term extraction and automatic indexing. In R. Mitkov, editor, *Handbook of Computational Linguistics*. Oxford University Press.

Jokinen P., and Ukkonen, E. 1991. Two algorithms for approximate string matching in static texts. In A. Tarlecki, (ed.), Mathematical Foundations of Computer Science.

Justeson, J. S., and Katz, S.M. 1995. Technical Terminology: some linguistic properties and an algorithm for identification in text. *Natural Language Engineering* 1(1):9-27.

Kan, M. and McKeown, K. 1999. Information Extraction and Summarization: Domain Independence through Focus Types. *Columbia University Technical Report CUCS-030-99.*

Kupiec, J., Pedersen, J., and Chen, F. 1995. A Trainable Document Summarizer. *SIGIR-1995.*

Liu, B., Hsu, W., Ma, Y. 1998. Integrating Classification and Association Rule Mining. *KDD-98*, 1998.

Mani, I., and Bloedorn, E., 1997. Multi-document Summarization by Graph Search and Matching. *AAAI-97.*

Manning, C. and Schütze, H. 1999. *Foundations of Statistical Natural Language Processing*, MIT Press. May 1999.

Marcu, D. 1997. From Discourse Structures to Text Summaries. *ACL Workshop on Intelligent, Scalable Text Summarization.*

Miller, G., Beckwith, R, Fellbaum, C., Gross, D., and Miller, K. 1990. Introduction to WordNet: An on-line lexical database. *International Journal of Lexicography*, 3(4):235-312.

NLProcessor – *Text Analysis Toolkit.* 2000. http://www.infogistics.com/textanalysis.html

Paice, C. D. 1990. Constructing Literature Abstracts by Computer: techniques and prospects. *Information Processing and Management* 26:171-186.

Radev, D. and McKeown, K. 1998. Generating natural language summaries from multiple on-line sources. *Computational Linguistics*, 24(3):469-500, September 1998.

Sparck-Jones, K. 1993a. Discourse Modeling for Automatic Text Summarizing. *Technical Report 290*, University of Cambridge.

Sparck-Jones, K. 1993b. What might be in a summary? *Information Retrieval* 93: 9-26.

Tait, J. 1983. *Automatic Summarizing of English Texts.* Ph.D. Dissertation, University of Cambridge.

# Just How Mad Are You? Finding Strong and Weak Opinion Clauses

**Theresa Wilson**
Intelligent Systems Program
University of Pittsburgh
Pittsburgh, PA 15260
twilson@cs.pitt.edu

**Janyce Wiebe** and **Rebecca Hwa**
Department of Computer Science
University of Pittsburgh
Pittsburgh, PA 15260
{wiebe,hwa}@cs.pitt.edu

## Abstract

There has been a recent swell of interest in the automatic identification and extraction of opinions and emotions in text. In this paper, we present the first experimental results classifying the strength of opinions and other types of subjectivity and classifying the subjectivity of deeply nested clauses. We use a wide range of features, including new syntactic features developed for opinion recognition. In 10-fold cross-validation experiments using support vector regression, we achieve improvements in mean-squared error over baseline ranging from 57% to 64%.

## Introduction

There has been a recent swell of interest in the automatic identification and extraction of attitudes, opinions, and sentiments in text. Strong motivation for this task comes from the desire to provide tools and support for information analysts in government, commercial, and political domains, who want to be able to automatically track attitudes and feelings in the news and on-line forums. How do people feel about the latest camera phone? Is there a change in the support for the new Medicare bill? A system that could automatically identify and extract opinions and emotions from text would be an enormous help to someone sifting through the vast amounts of news and web data, trying to answer these kinds of questions.

Researchers from many different areas of AI have been working on the automatic identification of opinions and related tasks. To date, most such work has focused on classification at the document or sentence level. Document classification tasks include picking out editorials from among news articles and classifying reviews as positive or negative. A common sentence level task is to classify sentences as subjective or objective.

However, for many applications, just identifying opinionated sentences may not be sufficient. In the news, it is not uncommon to find two or more opinions in a single sentence, or to find a sentence containing opinions as well as factual information. An information extraction system trying to distinguish between factual information (which should be extracted) and non-factual information (which should be discarded or labeled uncertain) would find it helpful to be able to pinpoint the particular clauses that contain opinions. This ability would also be important for multi-perspective question answering, which aims to present multiple answers to the user based on opinions derived from different sources, and for multi-document summarization systems, which need to summarize differing opinions and perspectives.

Many applications would benefit from being able to determine not just whether something is opinionated but also the *strength* of the opinion. Flame detection systems want to identify strong rants and emotional tirades, while letting milder opinions pass through. Information analysts need to recognize changes over time in the virulence expressed by persons or groups of interest, and to detect when rhetoric is heating up, or cooling down.

This paper presents the first research in automatic opinion or sentiment classification to classify the clauses of every sentence in the corpus. Also, where other research has focused on distinguishing between subjective and objective or positive and negative language, we address the task of classifying the *strength* of the opinions and emotions being expressed in individual clauses, considering clauses down to four levels deep. A strength of *neutral* corresponds to the absence of opinion and subjectivity, so our strength classification task subsumes the task of classifying language as subjective versus objective.

Because the variety of words and phrases that people use to express opinions is staggering, a system limited to a fixed vocabulary will be unable to identify opinionated language over a broad range of discourse. A broad-coverage approach will require knowledge of subjective language that is truly comprehensive in scope. In this spirit, we use a wide range of features for the experiments in this paper—new syntactic clues that we developed for opinion recognition, as well as a variety of subjectivity clues from the literature. We found that these features can be adapted to the task of strength recognition, and that the best classification results are achieved when all types of features are used.

We present experiments in strength classification using boosting, rule learning, and support vector regression. In 10-fold cross validation experiments, we achieve significant improvements over baseline mean-squared error and accuracy for all algorithms.

## Strong and Weak Subjective Expressions

Subjective expressions are words and phrases that express opinions, emotions, sentiments, speculations, etc. A general covering term for such states, from (Quirk et al., 1985), is *private state*, "a state that is not open to objective observation or verification." There are three main ways that private states are expressed in language: direct mentions of private states, speech events expressing private states, and *expressive subjective elements* (Banfield, 1982). An example of a direct private state is "fears" in (1). An example of a speech event expressing a private state is the one referred to by "continued" in (2).

**(1)** "The US fears a spill-over," said Xirao-Nima.

**(2)** "The report is full of absurdities," he continued.

Sentence (2) also contains an example of an expressive subjective element, namely "full of absurdities". With expressive subjective elements, sarcasm, emotion, evaluation, etc. are expressed through the way something is described or through particular wording. The subjective *strength* of a word or phrase is the strength of the opinion, emotion, or other private state that it expresses.

### An Annotated Corpus of Opinions

In 2003, the Multi-perspective Question Answering (MPQA) corpus of opinion annotations (Wilson and Wiebe, 2003) was released. In the corpus, individual expressions are marked that correspond to explicit mentions of private states, speech events, and expressive subjective elements. A key aspect of the annotation project was that annotators were asked to judge all expressions in context. The result is an amazing variety of annotated expressions. Out of all the subjective expressions marked in the MPQA corpus, fully 53% are unique strings.

Each expression that is marked is characterized by a number of attributes: who is expressing the opinion, who or what is the target of the opinion, the type of attitude expressed by the opinion, and, key for our purposes, its subjective strength. In the annotation scheme, strength is marked as one of four values: *neutral*, *low*, *medium*, and *high*.[1] *Neutral* refers to the absence of opinion. Sentence (3) gives examples of strength annotations in the MPQA corpus.

**(3)** President Mohammad Khatami of Iran, whose attempt at reforms have gotten American <*low*>support</>, <*high*>accused</> the United States of "<*high*>warmongering</>."

Inter-annotator agreement for strength ratings is challenging. It is not unusual for two annotators to identify the same expression in the text, but to differ in how they mark the boundaries. This in turn affects how they judge the strengths of the annotations. For example, (4) below shows how the same subjective phrase was judged by two annotators.

**(4a)** <*high*>imperative for harmonious society</>

**(4b)** <*medium*>imperative</> for <*medium*>harmonious</> society

Also, different people have different mental scales for what they consider strong and weak. *Low* strength to one annotator might be *medium* to another. For the annotations in the MPQA corpus, no specific attempt was made to align the strength scales of the different annotators.

Because of these challenges, as expected, absolute percent agreement for strength judgments on expressions is not high, on average 61%. However, measuring how often two annotators agree in their *ordering* of annotations by strength yields an average pairwise agreement of 95%, computed as follows. Let $S_A$ and $S_B$ be the sets of annotations identified by annotators A and B respectively. If a pair of annotations, $a \in S_A$ and $b \in S_B$, overlap, then $a$ and $b$ are a *matched pair*. Let $S_{AB}$ be all possible combinations of matched pairs $ab$. Given two matched pairs $(ab)_i$ and $(ab)_j$ from $S_{AB}$, A and B agree on the ordering if:

$$strength(a_i) \geq strength(a_j) \land strength(b_i) \geq strength(b_j)$$

or

$$strength(a_i) \leq strength(a_j) \land strength(b_i) \leq strength(b_j)$$

Let $M$ be the number of matched pairs for which A and B agree on the ordering. Then, $agreement = \frac{M}{|S_{AB}|}$.

### Exploring Strength

An examination of the annotated data shows not only that a huge variety of expressions have been marked, but that strong subjectivity in particular is expressed in many different ways. We can think of some words that are clearly strong, such as "reckless" and "praise", as well as obvious modifications to these that increase or decrease their strength, as in "not reckless", "very reckless" and "high praise." It is unlikely, though, that expressions like "rhetorical petards" and "hell-bent" readily come to mind, both of which are marked in the annotations.

Expressions marked *high* often contain words that are very infrequent. For example, the word "petards" appears only once in the corpus. Collocations like "at all" add punch to an expression, as in, "at all costs" and "not true at all." It is also important to have knowledge of patterns like "expressed <direct-object>," which can generalize to many different phrases, such as "expressed hope," "expressed concern," "expressed gratitude," and "expressed some understanding." Also, there are syntactic modifications and syntactic patterns that have subjective force. Besides those patterns that merely intensify a subjective word, for example "very <ADJECTIVE>", we find patterns that have a cumulative effect on strength: "terrorist and extremist," and "criticize and condemn." The clues used later in the strength classification experiments contain examples of all these kinds of subjective phenomena.

As can be seen from earlier example (3), sentences are often complex, with opinions of differing strengths being expressed by perhaps two or more agents. In (3), there is low-strength support being expressed by the United States, as well as high-strength negative accusations coming from Khatami. In the MPQA corpus, 31% of sentences are made up of clauses that differ in strength by two or more strength

[1] *High* actually breaks down into *high* and *extremely-high* ratings. The *extremely-high* ratings are folded into the *high* ratings, rather than being treated as a separate rating, because they are rare.

ratings. This highlights the need to identify opinions at the clause level, as we do in our experiments.

Many other researchers are interested in polarity, another attribute of subjective language. We find some interesting interactions between polarity and strength in the data. The annotators were asked to judge the polarity of expressions that they marked, using an attribute called *attitude-type* that has values *positive*, *negative*, and *other*. The annotations show that annotators are often not comfortable with *positive* and *negative*: 22% of all *attitude-type* labels are *other*. However, the annotations also reveal that the stronger the expression, the clearer the polarity. Only 8% of the high-strength annotations are marked as *other*, while 39% of the low-strength annotations are so marked. In addition to stronger expressions having clearer polarity, stronger expressions of opinions and emotions also tend to be more negative in this corpus. Only 33% of low-strength annotations are negative, compared to 78% of high-strength annotations. These observations lead us to believe that the strength of subjective expressions will be informative for recognizing polarity, and vice versa.

## Subjectivity Clues

In this section, we describe the information that we use for automatic strength classification. In addition to a wide variety of previously established subjectivity clues, we introduce a collection of new syntactic clues that are correlated with subjective language.

### Previously Established Types of Clues

Previous work in subjectivity identification has supplied the research community with a large stable of subjectivity clues. These clues (**PREV**) include words and phrases culled from manually developed resources, others learned from annotated data, and others learned from unannotated data.

Due to the broad range of clues and their sources, the set of **PREV** clues is not limited to a fixed word list or to words of a particular part of speech. The clues from manually developed resources include entries from (Levin, 1993; Ballmer and Brennenstuhl, 1981), Framenet lemmas with frame element *experiencer* (Baker et al., 1998), adjectives manually annotated for polarity (Hatzivassiloglou and McKeown, 1997), and subjectivity clues listed in (Wiebe, 1990). Clues learned from annotated data include distributionally similar adjectives and verbs (Wiebe, 2000) and n-grams (Dave et al., 2003; Wiebe et al., 2001). From unannotated data, we have extraction patterns and subjective nouns learned using two different bootstrapping algorithms and a set of seed words (Riloff et al., 2003; Riloff and Wiebe, 2003). Finally, low-frequency words, which require no training to identify (Wiebe et al., 2001), are also used as clues.

A few of the **PREV** clues require more explanation. First, extraction patterns are lexico-syntactic patterns typically used by information extraction systems to identify relevant information. Riloff and Wiebe (2003) show that AutoSlog-TS, an algorithm for automatically generating extraction patterns, is able to find extraction patterns that are correlated

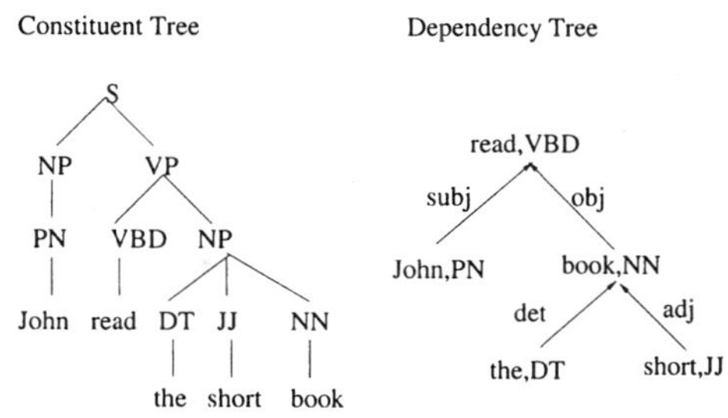


Figure 1: The constituent tree for "John read the short book" is on the left, and the dependency representation is on the right.

with subjectivity. An example of a subjective extraction pattern is *<subj> dealt blow*, which matches phrases like "the mistake dealt a stiff blow to his pride."

Interestingly, low-frequency words are informative for subjectivity recognition. We use low frequency words as clues; we consider a word to have low frequency if it appears $\leq 3$ times in the document containing it plus a 1-million word corpus of news articles. In addition, we use n-gram clues from (Wiebe et al., 2001) that have fillers matching low-frequency words. When these clues were learned, the fillers matched low frequency words in the training data. When used during testing, the fillers are matched against low-frequency words in the test data. Examples of such n-grams are *<LowFreq-verb> and <LowFeq-verb>* and *so <LowFreq-adj>*.

### Syntax Clues

The syntactic clues are developed by using a mostly-supervised learning procedure. The training data is based on both a human annotated (the MPQA) corpus and a large unannotated corpus in which sentences are automatically identified as subjective or objective through a bootstrapping algorithm (Riloff and Wiebe, 2003). The learning procedure consists of three steps.

First, we parse the training sentences in the MPQA corpus with a broad-coverage lexicalized English parser (Collins, 1997). The output constituent trees are automatically converted into their dependency representations (Xia and Palmer, 2001). In a dependency representation, every node in the tree structure is a surface word (i.e., there are no abstract nodes such as NP or VP), but each word may have additional attributes such as its part-of-speech (POS) tag. The parent word is known as the *head*, and its children are its *modifiers*. The edge between a parent and a child node specifies the grammatical relationship between the two words (e.g., *subj*, *obj*, and *adj*). Figure 1 shows the dependency parse tree for a sentence, along with the corresponding constituent representation, for comparison. For this study, we use 48 POS tags and 24 grammatical relationships.

Next, we form five classes of syntactic clues from each word $w$ in every dependency parse tree.

**root**$(w, t)$**:** word $w$ with POS tag $t$ is the root of a dependency tree (i.e., the main verb of the sentence).

**leaf**($w, t$)**:** word $w$ with POS tag $t$ is a leaf in a dependency tree (i.e., it has no modifiers).

**node**($w, t$)**:** word $w$ with POS tag $t$.

**bilex**($w, t, r, w_c, t_c$)**:** word $w$ with POS tag $t$ is modified by word $w_c$ with POS tag $t_c$, and the grammatical relationship between them is $r$.

**allkids**($w, t, r_1, w_1, t_1, \ldots, r_n, w_n, t_n$)**:** word $w$ with POS tag $t$ has $n$ children. Each child word $w_i$ has POS tag $t_i$ and modifies $w$ with grammatical relationship $r_i$, where $1 \leq i \leq n$.

For each class specified above, we also consider less specific variants that back off to only POS tags. For example, $bilex(t, r, t_c)$ considers the cases in which any word with a POS tag $t$ is modified by a word with POS tag $t_c$ with grammatical relationship $r$.

Finally, we evaluate the collected clues. A clue is considered to be *potentially useful* if more than $x\%$ of its occurrences in the MPQA training data are in phrases marked as subjective, where $x$ is a parameter tuned on development data (in our experiments, we chose $x = 70\%$). Potentially useful clues are further categorized into one of three *reliability* levels. First, a useful clue is *highly reliable* if it occurs frequently in the MPQA training data. For those that occur fewer than five times, we check their reliability on the larger corpus of automatically identified subjective and objective sentences. Clues that do not occur in the larger unannotated corpus are considered *not very reliable*. Clues that occur in the subjective set at least $y$ times more than in the objective set are considered *somewhat reliable* ($y$ is tuned on the development data and is set to 4 in our experiments), and the rest are rejected as not useful clues.

## Feature Organization

Given the large number of **PREV** and **SYNTAX** clues, we are faced with the question of how best to organize them into features for strength classification. We tried a representation in which each clue is a separate feature, but it gave poor results. Instead, we adopt the strategy from (Riloff et al., 2003) of aggregating clues into sets, and creating one feature per set. The value of each feature is the number of instances in the sentence or clause of all the members of the set.

We define 29 features for the **PREV** clues reflecting how they were presented in the original research. For example, there are two features for the polar adjectives in (Hatzivassiloglou and McKeown, 1997), one for the set of positive adjectives and one for the set of negative adjectives. These 29 features are collectively called **PREV-type** in the experiments below. In addition, we define 15 features for the **SYNTAX** clues. For example, one feature represents the set of highly-reliable *bilex* clues. These features are called **SYNTAX-type**.

Although the above sets of subjectivity clues were selected because of their correlation with subjective language, they are not necessarily geared to discriminate between strong and weak subjectivity, and the groupings of clues into sets were not created with strength in mind. We hypothesized that a feature organization that takes into consideration the potential strength of clues would do better for strength classification.

To adapt the clues to strength classification, we use the annotations in the training data to filter the clues and organize them into new sets based on strength. For each clue $c$ and strength rating $s$, we calculate the $P(strength(c)) = s$ as the probability of $c$ being in an annotation of strength $s$. For $s = neutral$, this is the probability of $c$ being in a neutral-strength annotation or in no annotation at all. If $P(strength(c)) = s \geq T$, for some threshold $T$, we put $c$ in the set for strength $s$. In our experiments, we set $T = (P(strength(word)) = s) + 0.25$ or 0.95 if $(P(strength(word)) = s) + 0.25 \geq 1$. The value 0.25 was determined using experiments on a small amount of development data, held out from the experiment data for parameter tuning. It is possible for a clue to be in more than one set.

When **PREV** and **SYNTAX** clues are used in this feature organization they are called **PREV-strength** and **SYNTAX-strength** .

## Experiments in Automatic Strength Classification

It is important to classify the strength of clauses, but pinpointing subjectivity at deeper levels can be challenging because there is less information to use for classification. To study the feasibility of automatically classifying clauses by their subjective strength, we conducted a suite of experiments in which a strength classifier is trained based on the features previously described. We wished to confirm three hypotheses. First, it is possible to classify the strength of clauses, for those that are deeply nested as well as those at the sentence level. Second, classifying the strength of subjectivity depends on a wide variety of features, including both lexical and syntactic clues. Third, organizing features by strength is beneficial.

To test our hypotheses, we performed the experiments under different settings, varying three factors: the learning algorithm used to train the classifiers, the depth of the clauses to be classified, and the types of features used. We vary the learning algorithm to explore its effect on the classification task. In our studies, the three machine learning algorithms are boosting, rule learning, and support vector regression. For boosting, we use BoosTexter (Schapire and Singer, 2000) AdaBoost.HM with 1000 rounds of boosting. For rule learning, we use Ripper (Cohen, 1995). For support vector regression we use SVMlight (Joachims, 1999) and discretize the resulting output into the ordinal strength classes. These algorithms were chosen because they have successfully been used for a number of natural language processing tasks.

We vary the depth of clauses to determine the effect of clausal depth on system performance. In our experiments, clauses are determined based on the non-leaf verbs in the parse tree, parsed using the Collins parser and converted to the dependency representation described earlier. For example, sentence (5) has three clauses, corresponding to the verbs "driven," "refused," and "give."

**(5)** They were driven out by rival warlord Saif Ullah,

who has refused to give up power.

The clause defined for "driven" (level 1) is the entire sentence; the clause for "refused" (level 2) is "has refused to give up power"; and the clause for "give" (level 3) is "to give up power."

The gold standard strength ratings of sentences and clauses are based on the individual expression annotations: the strength of a sentence or clause is defined to be the highest strength rating of any expression in that sentence or clause.

In setting up experiments for classifying nested clauses, either clauses of the same or different levels may be classified in the training and testing phases. In the experiments below, the training examples are always entire sentences regardless of the clause level being classified during testing. Preliminary results showed that this configuration is better than training and testing at the same level.

All experimental results reported are averages over 10-fold cross validation using 9313 sentences from the MPQA corpus. Significance is measured using a 1-tailed t-test. For each experiment, both mean-squared error and classification accuracy are given. Although raw accuracy is important, not all misclassifications should be weighted equally for the task of strength classification. If the true strength of a sentence or clause is *high*, classifying it as *neutral* (off by 3) is a much worse error than classifying it as *medium* (off by 1). Mean-squared error captures this distinction, and, for this task, it is perhaps more important than accuracy as a metric for evaluation. If $t_i$ is the true strength of sentence $i$, and $p_i$ is the predicted strength of sentence $i$,

$$\text{mean-squared error (MSE)} = \frac{1}{n}\sum_{i}^{n}(t_i - p_i)^2$$

where $n$ is the number of sentences or clauses being classified.

## Classification Results

Tables 1 and 2 show strength classification results for clauses of depth 1–4. Table 1 gives results for BoosTexter and Table 2 gives results for Ripper and SVMlight.

The first row of Table 1 gives MSE and accuracies for a baseline classifier that chooses the most frequent class. Note that the distribution changes for clauses at different levels, giving higher baseline accuracies for more nested levels. The remaining rows in Table 1 show the BoosTexter results using different sets of features. Row 2 gives the results for a classifier trained using bag-of-words (**BAG**), where the words in each sentence are given to the classification algorithm as features. Rows 3 and 4 give the results for classifiers using **PREV-type + SYNTAX-type** features and **PREV-strength + SYNTAX-strength** features. The next two rows give the results for combining the two feature organizations with bag-of-words. The last row of the table shows the results when the **SYNTAX-strength** features are excluded from the best experiment.

The results for strength classification are promising for clauses at all levels of nesting. In Table 1, all of the improvements over baseline in MSE and accuracy are significant. The experiment in row 6 using **BAG + PREV-strength + SYNTAX-strength** features gives the best results. The improvements in MSE over baseline range from 48% to 60%, and the improvements in accuracy range from 23% to 79%. Table 2 rows 1 and 3 give the results for the same feature set using Ripper and SVMlight. Note that BoosTexter and Ripper are non-ordinal classification algorithms, whereas support vector regression takes into account ordinal values. This difference is reflected in the results. The results are comparable for BoosTexter and Ripper (MSE is not significantly different; BoosTexter has slightly better accuracy). Although accuracies are lower, the regression algorithm achieves much better MSE, improving 10% to 20% over BoosTexter and 57% to 64% over baseline, coming closer to the true strength at all levels[2].

The best experiments (Table 1 row 6 and Table 2 rows 1 and 3) use all the features, supporting our hypothesis that using a wide variety of features is effective. For boosting, the improvements over bag-of-words are significant (compare rows 2 and 6 in Table 1): from 20% to 25% for MSE and from 7% to 12% for accuracy. Results for Ripper and SVMlight (not shown) are similar. The new syntax clues contribute information over and above bag-of-words and the previous clues. For all learning algorithms and all clause levels, removing the syntax clues results in a significant difference in MSE (compare rows 6 and 7 in Table 1, rows 1 and 2 in Table 2, and rows 3 and 4 in Table 2). The differences in accuracy are also significant, with the exception of BoosTexter levels 1 and 2 and Ripper level 4.

Turning to feature organization, we see that organizing features by strength is beneficial. Comparing rows 3 and 4 in Table 1, the strength-based organization shows significant improvements across the row. Row 6 improves over row 5 for all values. All differences except for levels 3 and 4 MSE are significant. Results for Ripper and SVMlight using the strength-based feature organization (not given) show similar improvements.

## Related Work

Research in automatic opinion and sentiment recognition includes distinguishing subjective from objective language (Yu and Hatzivassiloglou, 2003; Riloff et al., 2003; Riloff and Wiebe, 2003), distinguishing positive from negative language (Yu and Hatzivassiloglou, 2003; Turney and Littman, 2003; Pang et al., 2002; Dave et al., 2003; Nasukawa and Yi, 2003; Morinaga et al., 2002), and recognizing particular types of attitudes (Gordon et al., 2003; Liu et al., 2003). Ours are the first results to automatically distinguishing between not only subjective and objective (*neutral*) language, but among weak, medium, and strong subjectivity as well. Researchers who have identified opinions below the sentence level have restricted their attention to particular words and phrases (Turney and Littman, 2003; Pang et al., 2002; Dave et al., 2003; Nasukawa and Yi, 2003; Morinaga et al., 2002; Gordon et al., 2003; Liu et al., 2003). In contrast, this paper presents the first work classifying nested clauses in all sentences in the corpus.

[2]In future work we plan to experiment with more sophisticated ordinal regression algorithms (Herbrich et al., 1999).

| | level 1 | | level 2 | | level 3 | | level 4 | |
|---|---|---|---|---|---|---|---|---|
| | MSE | Acc | MSE | Acc | MSE | Acc | MSE | Acc |
| (1) baseline | 1.921 | 30.8 | 2.749 | 41.8 | 2.538 | 45.9 | 2.507 | 48.3 |
| (2) BAG | 1.234 | 50.9 | 1.390 | 53.1 | 1.534 | 53.6 | 1.613 | 53.0 |
| (3) PREV-type + SYNTAX-type | 1.135 | 50.2 | 1.267 | 53.4 | 1.339 | 54.7 | 1.410 | 55.5 |
| (4) PREV-strength + SYNTAX-strength | 1.060 | 54.1 | 1.180 | 56.9 | 1.258 | 57.9 | 1.269 | 60.3 |
| (5) BAG + PREV-type + SYNTAX-type | 1.069 | 52.0 | 1.178 | 54.8 | 1.267 | 55.9 | 1.321 | 56.8 |
| (6) **BAG + PREV-strength + SYNTAX-strength** | **0.991** | **55.0** | **1.111** | **57.0** | **1.225** | **57.5** | **1.211** | **59.4** |
| (7) BAG + PREV-strength | 1.081 | 54.1 | 1.205 | 56.0 | 1.364 | 55.4 | 1.363 | 57.0 |

Table 1: Classification results using BoosTexter.

| | | level 1 | | level 2 | | level 3 | | level 4 | |
|---|---|---|---|---|---|---|---|---|---|
| | | MSE | Acc | MSE | Acc | MSE | Acc | MSE | Acc |
| Ripper | (1) **BAG + PREV-strength + SYNTAX-strength** | **1.004** | **53.2** | **1.138** | **55.3** | **1.220** | **55.9** | **1.244** | **57.8** |
| Ripper | (2) BAG + PREV-strength | 1.230 | 50.7 | 1.347 | 53.5 | 1.458 | 54.3 | 1.459 | 56.6 |
| SVMlight | (3) **BAG + PREV-strength + SYNTAX-strength** | **0.793** | **48.3** | **0.979** | **36.3** | **1.071** | **32.1** | **1.084** | **29.4** |
| SVMlight | (4) BAG + PREV-strength | 0.849 | 43.5 | 1.164 | 31.2 | 1.300 | 27.4 | 1.346 | 25.2 |

Table 2: Classification results using Ripper and SVMlight.

Automatic opinion extraction is being applied in a number of interesting applications. Tong (2001) tracks sentiment timelines in on-line discussions. Many researchers classify reviews as positive and negative (Turney and Littman, 2003; Pang et al., 2002; Dave et al., 2003; Nasukawa and Yi, 2003; Morinaga et al., 2002). Others perform automatic analyses of product reputations (Morinaga et al., 2002; Nasukawa and Yi, 2003; Yi et al., 2003). Das and Chen (2001) examine the relationship between public sentiment in message boards and stock prices. All such applications would benefit from the rich subjectivity analysis performed by our system.

## Conclusions

This paper presents promising results in identifying opinions in deeply nested clauses and classifying their strengths. We use a wide range of features, including new syntactic features. In 10-fold cross-validation experiments using boosting, we achieve improvements over baseline mean-squared error ranging from 48% to 60% and improvements in accuracy ranging from 23% to 79%. Experiments using support vector regression show even stronger mean-squared error results, with improvements ranging from 57% to 64% over baseline. Applications such as question answering and summarization will benefit from the rich subjectivity analysis performed by our system.

## Acknowledgments

We would like to thank the reviewers for their helpful comments, Paul Hoffmann for programming support, and Adam Lopez for providing his dependency grammatical relationship labeling program. This work was supported in part by the National Science Foundation under grant IIS-0208798.

## References

C. Baker, C. Fillmore, and J. Lowe. 1998. The Berkeley framenet project. In *Proceedings of the COLING-ACL.*

T. Ballmer and W. Brennenstuhl. 1981. *Speech Act Classification: A Study in the Lexical Analysis of English Speech Activity Verbs.* Springer-Verlag.

Ann Banfield. 1982. *Unspeakable Sentences.* Routledge and Kegan Paul, Boston.

William Cohen. 1995. Learning trees and rules with set-valued features. In *Proceedings of the Twelfth International Conference on Machine Learning (ICML-95).*

Michael Collins. 1997. Three generative, lexicalised models for statistical parsing. In *Proceedings of the 35th Annual Meeting of the Association for Computational Linguistics (ACL-97)*, pages 16–23.

S. R. Das and M. Y. Chen. 2001. Yahoo! for Amazon: Opinion extraction from small talk on the web. In *Proceedings of the 8th Asia Pacific Finance Association Annual Conference.*

Kushal Dave, Steve Lawrence, and David M. Pennock. 2003. Mining the peanut gallery: Opinion extraction and semantic classification of produce reviews. In *Proceedings of the 12th International World Wide Web Conference (WWW2003).* Web Proceedings.

Andrew Gordon, Abe Kazemzadeh, Anish Nair, and Milena Petrova. 2003. Recognizing expressions of commonsense psychology in English text. In *Proceedings of the 41st Annual Meeting of the Association for Computational Linguistics (ACL-03)*, pages 208–215.

Vasileios Hatzivassiloglou and Kathy McKeown. 1997. Predicting the semantic orientation of adjectives. In *Proceedings of the 35th Annual Meeting of the Association for Computational Linguistics (ACL-97)*, pages 174–181.

Ralf Herbrich, Thore Graepel, and Klaus Obermayer. 1999. Support vector learning for ordinal regression. In *Proceedings of the 9th International Conference on Artificial Neural Networks.*

T. Joachims. 1999. Making large-scale SVM learning practical. In B. Scholkopf, C. Burgess, and A. Smola, editors,

*Advances in Kernel Methods – Support Vector Learning*. MIT-Press.

Beth Levin. 1993. *English Verb Classes and Alternations: A Preliminary Investigation*. University of Chicago Press, Chicago.

H. Liu, H. Lieberman, and T. Selker. 2003. A model of textual affect sensing using real-world knowledge. In *Proceedings of the International Conference on Intelligent User Interfaces (IUI-2003)*.

S. Morinaga, K. Yamanishi, K. Tateishi, and T. Fukushima. 2002. Mining product reputations on the web. In *Proceedings of the 8th ACM SIGKDD International Conference on Knowledge Discovery and Data Mining (KDD-2002)*.

T. Nasukawa and J. Yi. 2003. Sentiment analysis: Capturing favorability using natural language processing. In *Proceedings of the 2nd International Conference on Knowledge Capture (K-CAP 2003)*.

Bo Pang, Lillian Lee, and Shivakumar Vaithyanathan. 2002. Thumbs up? Sentiment classification using machine learning techniques. In *Proceedings of the Conference on Empirical Methods in Natural Language Processing (EMNLP-2002)*, pages 79–86.

Randolph Quirk, Sidney Greenbaum, Geoffry Leech, and Jan Svartvik. 1985. *A Comprehensive Grammar of the English Language*. Longman, New York.

Ellen Riloff and Janyce Wiebe. 2003. Learning extraction patterns for subjective expressions. In *Proceedings of the Conference on Empirical Methods in Natural Language Processing (EMNLP-2003)*, pages 105–112.

Ellen Riloff, Janyce Wiebe, and Theresa Wilson. 2003. Learning subjective nouns using extraction pattern bootstrapping. In *Proceedings of the 7th Conference on Natural Language Learning (CoNLL-2003)*, pages 25–32.

Robert E. Schapire and Yoram Singer. 2000. BoosTexter: A boosting-based system for text categorization. *Machine Learning*, 39(2/3):135–168.

Richard Tong. 2001. An operational system for detecting and tracking opinions in on-line discussions. In *Working Notes of the SIGIR Workshop on Operational Text Classification*, pages 1–6.

P. Turney and M. Littman. 2003. Measuring praise and criticism: Inference of semantic orientation from association. *ACM Transactions on Information Systems (TOIS)*, 21(4):315–346.

Janyce Wiebe, Theresa Wilson, and Matthew Bell. 2001. Identifying collocations for recognizing opinions. In *Proceedings of the ACL-01 Workshop on Collocation: Computational Extraction, Analysis, and Exploitation*, pages 24–31.

Janyce Wiebe. 1990. *Recognizing Subjective Sentences: A Computational Investigation of Narrative Text*. Ph.D. thesis, State University of New York at Buffalo.

Janyce Wiebe. 2000. Learning subjective adjectives from corpora. In *Proceedings of the Seventeenth National Conference on Artificial Intelligence (AAAI-2000)*, pages 735–740.

Theresa Wilson and Janyce Wiebe. 2003. Annotating opinions in the world press. In *Proceedings of the 4th ACL SIGdial Workshop on Discourse and Dialogue (SIGdial-03)*, pages 13–22.

F. Xia and M. Palmer. 2001. Converting dependency structures to phrase structures. In *Proceedings of the Human Language Technology Conference (HLT-2001)*.

J. Yi, T. Nasukawa, R. Bunescu, and W. Niblack. 2003. Sentiment analyzer: Extracting sentiments about a given topic using natural language processing techniques. In *Proceedings of the 3rd IEEE International Conference on Data Mining (ICDM-2003)*.

Hong Yu and Vasileios Hatzivassiloglou. 2003. Towards answering opinion questions: Separating facts from opinions and identifying the polarity of opinion sentences. In *Proceedings of the Conference on Empirical Methods in Natural Language Processing (EMNLP-2003)*, pages 129–136.

# Innovative Applications of Artificial Intelligence

# Innovative Applications of Artificial Intelligence

## *Deployed Applications*

# Tenth Anniversary of the Plastics Color Formulation Tool

**William Cheetham**

1 Research Circle
Niskayuna, NY 12309
cheetham@research.ge.com

### Abstract

Since 1994 GE Plastics has employed a case-based reasoning tool that determines color formulas which match requested colors. This tool, called FormTool, has saved GE millions of dollars in productivity and material (i.e. colorant) costs. The technology developed in FormTool has been used to create an on-line color selection tool for our customers called ColorXpress Select. A customer innovation center has been developed around the FormTool software.

## Introduction

With headquarters in Pittsfield, Massachusetts and technical facilities, manufacturing sites and sales locations on five continents, GE Plastics (GEP) produces many of the world's best known and most widely used polymers. In offices and factories ... in hospitals, homes and schools ... on the road and in outer space, products made with GE materials make life simpler, safer and more comfortable for people every day. The plastic GE creates can be made any color that is requested by a customer. Plastic is colored by adding pigments while the plastic is manufactured. In order to determine the correct formulas for our customers, a Case-Based Reasoning (Watson 1997) tool called FormTool was started in 1994.

### Prior Art in Color Matching for Plastics

Determining the colorants and loading levels that can be added to plastic so the plastic matches a given color is a difficult problem for multiple reasons. First, the number of combinations of possible colorants is very large. Four to seven colorants are selected from thirty to fifty potential colorants. Second, for each set of possible colorants the amount of each colorant also needs to be determined. Third, there is currently no accurate method to predict the color produced when a set of colorants are added to plastic. Unlike paint, where light primarily reflects off of the surface, in plastics a significant percentage of light penetrates the surface, reacts with the internal structure of the plastic, and can exit the plastic a color that depends on that internal structure. Fourth, a given formula can appear different in different lighting conditions (natural sunlight vs. florescent lighting). Fifth, different base plastics have different starting colors (e.g. clear, white, gray), so the same set of colorant will likely produce a different color in different grades of plastic. GEP makes hundreds of different grades of plastic. Because of these difficulties, selecting the colorants and loading levels for a color formula was previously either accomplished by using human working experience or computationally expensive computer programs. There are commercially available computer programs that can calculate the colorant loading proportions for a color formula that matches a color standard. Since these programs perform an exhaustive search, they require a user to select a subset of the allowable colorants. Usually five to seven are selected out of the thirty to fifty possible colorants. Since the final formula will usually consist of four or five colorants, the users have to make the critical decision of which colorants to select for the search, which often produces a non-optimal solution. Furthermore, it does not take into consideration other important attributes of a color match, such as the cost of the colorants.

We mentioned above that there is no exact algorithm for predicting the color produced by a given set of colorants and loadings. However, the Kubelka-Munk theory (Billmeyer, 1981) can be used to produce an approximation of the color produced by a set of colorants and loadings. This theory describes how the absorption and scattering of colorants in a material are related to the visible color of the material. Each colorant contributes to the absorption and scattering of the material and its contribution is proportional to the amount of it present in the system multiplied by an absorption and scattering coefficient for that colorant. Our system uses Kubelka-Munk theory.

## Description of Color Matching Process

GEP provides a color matching service to customers. Customers submit a physical sample of the color they want and GEP either finds a close match from their color library or formulates a new color to meet the customer's needs. GEP currently has over 50,000 previously matched colors on file and performs approximately 4,000 color matches per year. In the past, when GEP performed a custom color match and formula development, there is a significant cost to GEP and the turnaround for the customer average 2 weeks. We looked for ways to reduce this cost and shorten the turnaround time.

Selecting the colorants and loading levels for a color formula was previously accomplished by using a combination of human working experience and computationally expensive computer programs. Figure 1 shows the color matching process that was in place. The process starts with a color matcher inspecting the color request for the type of plastic, physical color standard supplied by customer, and special properties requested. The matcher would then compare the customer's color standard with previous color chips that were stored in a filing cabinet. The filing cabinet held about 2,000 plastic chips that were about 2" by 3" by 1/8", sorted by color. The matcher would select the most similar color from the filing cabinet. Each chip was labeled and another filing cabinet held a formula card for each chip. The matcher would then inspect the physical chip selected from the filing cabinet to determine if it matched the color and special properties requested by the customer. If it did match, then the formula that was associated with the selected chip would be used for the customer and the match is finished. If the best chip from the filing cabinet was not a satisfactory match, then the matchers used experience along with commercially available computer programs to adapt the colorant loadings. The new loadings would be used to create a small chip containing the adapted loadings. This chip would be compared with the standard. If it was acceptable the adapted formula would be used for the customer and the chip would be placed in the filing cabinet for future reference. If the color was unacceptable then the formula would be adapted repeatedly until an acceptable formula was obtained.

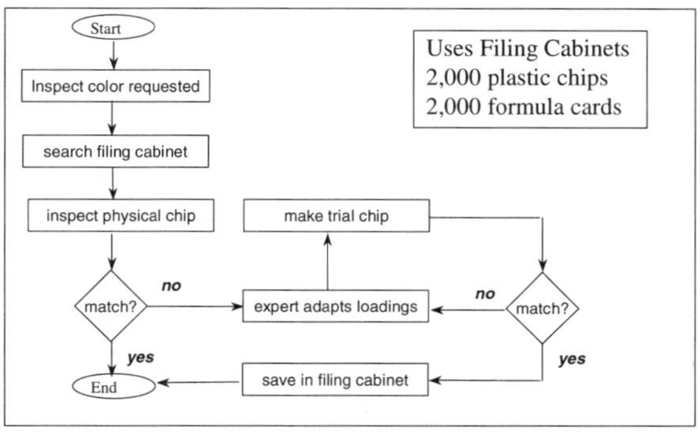


**Figure 1: Color Matching Process**

## FormTool Description

The color matching system consists of a spectrophotometer attached to a personal computer as shown in Figure 2. The spectrophotometer is used to determine a numerical representation of a color, called a reflectance curve. The reflection curve shows the percentage of light reflected by a color at each wavelength of the visible spectra (i.e. 400nm to 700nm). A spectrophotometer reads the reflectance of an object at 31 points equally spaced along the visible spectrum. Comparing two spectra is done by calculating the sum of differences or sum of squared differences between two curves over all 31 points in the visible spectrum. The personal computer contains the case-base and case-based reasoning software, called FormTool. Each case in the case-base contains a reflectance curve and a list of pigments and loadings used to create that color. FormTool is described below.

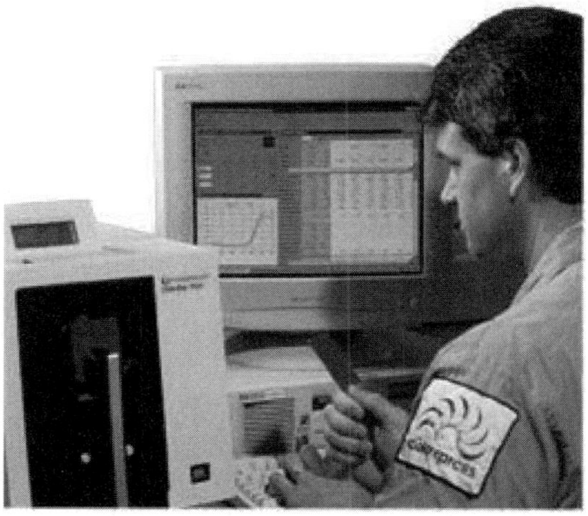

**Figure 2: FormTool on PC with Spectrophotometer**

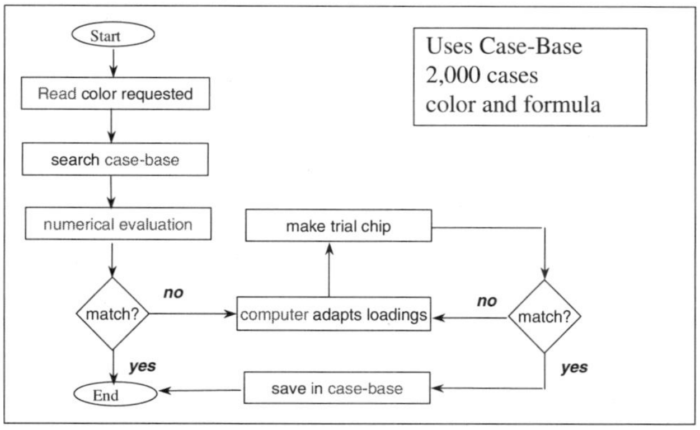


**Figure 3: Automated Color Matching Process**

The existing color matching process already followed the CBR methodology so the automated CBR process is very similar to the original color matching process and is shown in Figure 3. The color matcher places the physical color standard in the spectrophotometer and reads the spectrum of the color standard into the color matching system. Next, the color matcher enters key information such as the resin and grade of material in which to generate the match. FormTool then searches its case-base of previous matches for the "best" previous match and adjusts those previous matches to produce a match for the new standard. There are multiple criteria that the color match must satisfy

- The color of the plastic must match the standard under multiple lighting conditions,
- There must be enough pigments to hide the color of the plastic,
- The cost of colorant formula should be as low as possible,

- Only a limited amount of light can be transmitted through the plastic (optical density), and
- The color should not change when the plastic is molded at different temperatures.

The color matcher looks at the physical standard from this previous match and determines if it is acceptable for the application and customer. If the match is not acceptable, FormTool then adapts this previous match so that it more closely matches the requested color and application. The color matcher then makes a physical chip using the adapted formula. If this new match is acceptable then the adapted loadings are saved into the database and the match is finished. If the match is not acceptable then the user can decide to do one of two things:

1) Manually or automatically adjust the color loadings (manual), or
2) Switch to a different previous match as the starting point for this color match (search database)

After one of these is done the cycle continues until a match is found. When the "End" oval is reached, a formula has been obtained that gives the "best" color match and balance of all other important properties.

## Case Selection

This section describes a method to evaluate the quality of a specific color formula. A selection process that uses this method to evaluate a formula can be used to find the formula that will reproduce a specified color and meet all desired attributes for the application of the specified color. A nearest neighbor retrieval is used. However, the nearest neighbor must be determined by evaluating the degree of match in all of the attributes described above. This evaluation needs to provide a consistent meaning of an attributes similarity throughout all attributes. The consistency is achieved through the use of fuzzy linguistic terms, such as Excellent, Good, Fair, and Poor, which are associated with measured differences in an attribute. Any number of linguistic terms can be used. A fuzzy preference function (Mendel 1995) is used to calculate the similarity of a single attribute of a case with the corresponding attribute of the subject, see Figure 4. In this figure, a difference of 1 unit in the values of that attribute for the subject and comparable would be considered excellent, a difference of 2 would be good, 3 would be fair, and 4 would be poor. This rating is then transformed into the fuzzy preference function in Figure 4.

The result of using fuzzy preference functions is a vector, called the fuzzy preference vector. The vector contains a fuzzy preference value for each attribute. The values in this vector can be combined, through weighted aggregation, to produce a robust similarity value. The use of fuzzy preference functions allows for smooth changes in the result when an attribute is changed unlike the large changes that are possible when step functions are used.

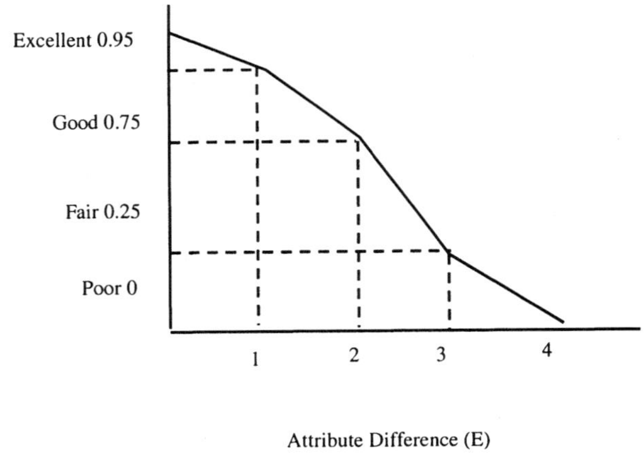


**Figure 4: Fuzzy Preference Function**

A fuzzy preference function is used to transform a quantifiable value for each attribute into a qualitative description of the attribute that can be compared with the qualitative description of other attributes. A fuzzy preference function allows a comparison of properties that are based on entirely different scales such as cost, measured in cents per pound, and spectral curve match, measured in reflection units. Based on discussions with experts and work to classify previous matches into various sets of linguistic terms we found that there was enough precision in our evaluation of the similarity of the attributes to have four linguistic terms. Table 1 shows the linguistic terms and the numeric similarity score that corresponds to each term.

**Table 1: Global Preference Function Scale**

| Fuzzy Rating | Maximum Score | Minimum Score |
|---|---|---|
| Excellent | 1 | 0.95 |
| Good | 0.94 | 0.75 |
| Average | 0.74 | 0.25 |
| Poor | 0.24 | 0 |

Fuzzy preference functions were created for each of the following attributes of the color match

- Color similarity,
- Total colorant load,
- Cost of colorant formula,
- Optical density of color, and
- Color shift when molded under normal and abusive conditions.

For more details on the case selection see (Cheetham and Graf, 1997).

## Case Adaptation

Most formulas that are retrieved need some adaptation. The similarity calculation described above is used to guide the adaptation. Adaptation is done by repeatedly varying the loadings of the colorants in the formula retrieved and evaluating the new similarity. Kubelka-Munk theory is used as part of the similarity calculation and provides a formula for predicting the color change from modifying the loadings of the colorants. Having a function that can accurately evaluate the effect of an adaptation is the key to performing the correct adaptation.

### Hardware and Software Used

The hardware selection was limited to the hardware that was currently available in the color-matching lab. So, FormTool's hardware consists of a spectrophotometer attached to a personal computer running Windows 95. The spectrophotometer is used to determine a numerical representation of a color, called a reflectance curve. The reflection curve shows the percentage of light reflected by a material at each wavelength of the visible spectra (i.e. 400nm to 700nm). A typical color spectrophotometer reads the reflectance of an object at 31 points equally spaced along the visible spectrum. Two spectra are compared by calculating the sum of squared differences, between two curves over all 31 points in the visible spectrum.

The software used to create FormTool required a little more evaluation. Existing case-based reasoning tools were researched. The one that appeared to have the most promise in was ART IM. We created a quick prototype in ART IM, but found that ART IM, in 1994, did not allow the flexibility of case selection needed. Furthermore, GE Plastics systems support would not be able to maintain an ART IM application after it was created. We needed to use tools that could be supported after FormTool was created. A custom development using a Visual Basic front end connected with C++ code for adaptation routines was selected. The case-base was later stored in a Microsoft access database.

## Use of AI Technology

FormTool was one of the first AI systems to fully implement the CBR process as described in (Aamdot 1994). When a new color is matched, the case selection algorithms "Retrieve" a set of close matches to that color and related attributes. The "Reuse" of those cases is done by the adaptation algorithms based on color theory. The "Revision" phase is performed by a human who makes a sample batch of the color formula suggested by FormTool. If that formula is proven correct then the solution is confirmed. If the confirmed solution is significantly different that all cases in the current case base, uses different colorants or is greater than a set color difference in Lab color space, then the solution is "Retained" by the case base. It was very convenient that the existing process exactly used the CBR methodology before this project was started.

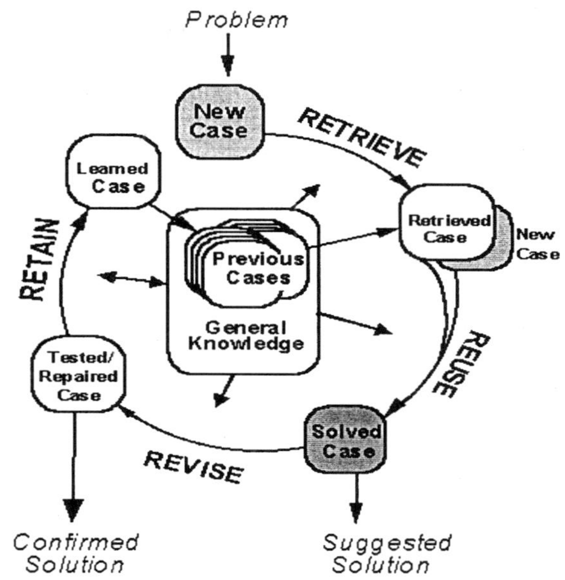


**Figure 5: CBR process from Aamodt**

## Application Use and Payoff

FormTool has been in constant use since its introduction in 1995. During 2004 it was used for an average of 130 custom color matches per week. The following benefits have resulted from using FormTool.

### Color Matcher Productivity

The average number of test chips that are created in the Revise phase has decreased from 4.2 to 2.7 per color match. This is an average reduction of 4.5 hours per color match. Since over 5000 color matches are performed per year, this saves 22,500 hours of work per year. The custom color match is a free service for our customers, so the cost of these 22,500 hours would directly reduce our profits. Saving the time directly adds to our bottom line.

### Pigment Cost Reduction

Pigments are the most expensive component in plastic. If the amount of pigment that is needed can be reduced then the difference in the cost of the pigment and the cost of the plastic would be saved. This could be a few cents per pound. FormTool's adaptation algorithms were designed to determine the minimum pigment loading that would allow for correct manufacturing of the color desired.

Another way to reduce pigment cost is to use cheaper pigments. Different pigments have different properties and different costs. For example, some red pigments are twice as expensive as other red pigments. The most expensive pigments are usually the easiest to use in a color match. FormTool's case selection algorithms select the best previous match based on cost, and other factors, in addition to the color of the case.

Part of the testing for FormTool that was conducted in 1994 was re-matching 100 colors that had already been matched but still were being manufactured. FormTool found lower cost matches for 64 of the 100 colors. The new formulas were substituted for the old, more costly, formulas. For each of these colors we tracked the number of pounds that were manufactured with the new formula. The cost savings can be calculated by multiplying the difference in cost by the volume for each color then taking the sum for all 64 colors. This was done near the end of 1994. The cost savings were $200,000 in 1994, $1.2 million in 1995, and $1.5 million in 1996. FormTool was used for new matches from 1995 onward. The colorant cost savings for years after 1996 are conservatively estimated at an average of $2.4 million per year.

These cost savings had a critical impact on the Parkersburg plant. Before FormTool, the plant was loosing over a million dollars per year and was slated for closure. This shutdown would have put 100 people out of work in an area where jobs were scarce. Since FormTool and other measures allowed the plant to start making a profit it was not closed and those people did not lose their jobs.

### Global Color Consistency

GE has plastics manufacturing sites throughout the world. The consistency of the colors we produce is important to our customers. FormTool has been used to share color formulas. Also, if some pigments are not available in one location, FormTool's case selection can automatically substitute the unavailable pigments with the closest available pigments. This has helped provide globally consistent colors.

A separate tool was created to allow the color matchers to manage the case-base and list of available colors. The manager tool allows the following functionality.

- Import a case base from another location
- Numerically determine the visual properties of a pigment for use in adaptation
- Specify which pigments are available for use
- Specify the price of each pigment.

### Other Tool Development

The case adaptation algorithms were used to create a tool for controlling the color produced by a manufacturing line, called LineTool. When colors are manufactured they do not always come out as planned because of many factors. LineTool can determine how to adjust a color that is not exactly on target. It produces a list of pigments that should be added to bring the manufacturing line back on target.

### Speed of Color Match

The speed of the color match was very important to many of our customers. For example, if a cell phone maker needed to add a month of time to their development cycle in order to get the various pieces of plastic in the casing to match, they might miss their target date for product release. FormTool reduced the time needed for a color match. This allowed the color matchers to eliminate the backlog of color matches. Since less experience was needed to perform a color match, resources could easily be added when a spike in demand was received and shifted to other work when there was low demand. Because of the benefits mentioned, the average time from receiving a color match request to creating the formula was reduced by two thirds. At the current writing, 2004, FormTool is used in the countries shown in gray in Figure 6.

**Figure 6: Countries with FormTool in Use**

## Application Development and Deployment

The software engineering paradigm used was the spiral development process. Two developers created the first version of FormTool in less than one year for a total cost of $300K. The first version only worked for one family of plastic, Cycolac, which was manufactured Parkersburg. The initial deployment was only to the West Virginia site. At the system's first demonstration, the manager paying for the project asked the developers to rematch a red color that had just been matched and had not started use in production. FormTool found a match that saved GE $50K on that year's production of that color.

The two developers continued working on FormTool and related projects for the next two years. During these years features were added, a maintenance tool was created, new families of plastics were supported, and FormTool was transitioned to other site in the United States. It was more difficult to transition FormTool to a new site than we expected. Each site had a different color match process. We needed to standardize these processes before FormTool could be transitioned. This standardization involved determining what was the best process, modifying FormTool to meet this process if needed, and convincing people to adopt this process. We recruited a local expert at each site to be the person in charge of FormTool at that site. The expert's tasks included installing updates, distributing locally added cases, and training others at their site in how to use FormTool.

Globalization of the tool was performed in 1997. The user interface was modified to be in either English or French. The case-base was changed from a local version, which needed user intervention to be updated with downloads of new cases, to a centralized database. In 1998, maintenance of FormTool was transitioned from the two developers to the Information Technology group of GE Plastics.

The creation of FormTool paved the way for other AI tools. In 1996 LineTool was created to help operators of the plastics manufacturing line adjust the color of a batch that is being produced. If samples indicated the color was not correct then a slightly modified version of FormTool was used to determine what pigments to add in order to bring the batch back to the correct color.

In 1997 ColorXpress Select was created as an on-line color selection tool for GE's customers, http://www.gecolorxpress.com/. The case-base from FormTool was used as a color palate that our customers can browse, request samples, and order online. When a customer used this tool it completely eliminated the need for a color match and reduced the time needed for the customer to get their match completed. Any item selected has already been matched and a sample can be sent FedEx to the customer in less than 48 hours. The web page for selecting a formula is shown in Figure 7.

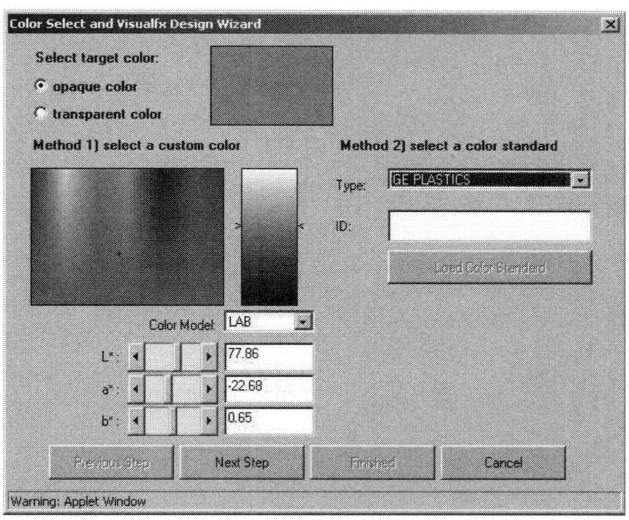


**Figure 7: ColorXpress Select Web Page**

In order to select a formula a customer first selects the resin type, opaque or transparent. Then they can select a custom color by specifying the color desired on the rainbow display or selecting a color standard by specifying the type and ID of the existing standard. If a point in the rainbow display is selected, the values of that point are placed in the numeric color value boxes. When the "Next Step" button is clicked the case selection algorithm will be executed and another screen will show the nine closest matches to the desired color. If a satisfactory match can not be found then a custom match request can be submitted and FormTool is used off-line to create the color formula. The formula created for the custom match will eventually be available on ColorXpress Select.

ColorXpress Select has been in use since 1999. It is one of the first customer service tools that GE Plastics has made available over the web. Tools like this have simplified the process for customers to submit orders over the web. GE now leads the plastic industry in on-line sales. The on-line dollar sales of GE Plastics are greater than the book sales of Amazon.com.

In 1998, the cost savings from FormTool and ColorXpress Select allowed GE Plastics to invest in another method for customers to select colors. In early 2000 GE Plastics opened a new $10 million ColorXpress center to help designers and marketers quickly create custom colors and special effects for plastics. The 4000 square foot center in Selkirk, N.Y. brings together all of the resources needed to select and develop custom colors and produce color chips, pellet samples, and prototype parts in a single day.

The idea behind the ColorXpress center is that in a competitive marketplace the color, texture, and style of a product can be a differentiating feature. An example of this is the Apple iMac computer. The ColorXpress center provides a location where customers can go through the CBR process of selecting a color face-to-face with a GE color matcher. The color matcher helps the customers refine the look and special effects of their products. This one-day service is only now available because of the FormTool system, which is the key tool used in the center. Before FormTool most color matches took over two days. Now, most matches take a day or less.

**Figure 8: ColorXpress Center Chip Room**

The case-base in the ColorXpress center is a color-chip room where three walls are filled with 20,000 baseball-card size colored plastic chips, see Figure 8. Three sets of overhead lights - incandescent, fluorescent and daylight – show the chips color varies under different lighting conditions.

Development included creating documentation, training manuals, tutorials, and submitting patents on various algorithms in FormTool. The U.S. Patent and Trademark office has granted GE four patents on various aspects of the color matching process described here.

- U.S. Patent No. 5,668,633; Method and System for Formulating a Color Match
- U.S. Patent No. 5,720,017; System and Method for Formulating a Color Match Using Color Keys
- U.S. Patent No. 5,740,078; Method and System for Determining Optimum Colorant Loading Using Merit Functions
- U.S. Patent No. 5,841,421; Method and System for Selecting a Previous Color Match from a Set of Previous Matches.

## Maintenance

The FormTool case-base originally resided in a Microsoft Access database format and requires minimal maintenance. The main responsibility of the site experts was to update and backup the database and send new local cases for distribution to other sites using FormTool. The database is now in Oracle and this job is automated by having one global case-base.

New cases are automatically added to the database each time a color match is performed and saved. Filtering algorithms are run just before adding a new case to make sure that is in fact a non-redundant case. This has made it possible to keep the case-base database optimized as it grows with time.

Functionality has been built into the software to allow color specialists to add new pigments and dyes to the tool. This process involves producing a number of color batches used to characterize the optical properties of the pigment or dye that are then saved in the tool to be used in the case-adaptation algorithms. Additionally, the site expert has the responsibility to enter the rules for each pigment or dye. These rules include which product grade it can be used in and at what minimum and maximum concentrations. However, since new pigments or dyes are added infrequently, this does not consume much time of the color specialists. A visual basic maintenance tool was created to assist the site expert in these tasks.

## Conclusion

FormTool is considered a huge success at General Electric due to the project's financial return on investment. It is also considered a technology achievement due to its early use of the CBR methodology, the number of patents obtained, and the opportunities for other systems it has created.

## References


Aamodt, A., 1994. Case-Based Reasoning: Foundational Issues, Methodological Variations, and System Approaches, AICOM, Vol. 7, No. 1.

Billmeyer, F., 1981. Principles of Color Technology: Second Edition, John Wiley & Sons, New York.

Cheetham, W., Graf, J., 1997. Case-Based Reasoning in Color Matching. Lecture Notes in Computer Science, Vol. 1266. Springer-Verlag, Berlin Heidelberg New York pp 1–12.

Mendel, J., 1995. Fuzzy Logic Systems for Engineering: A Tutorial, Proceedings of the IEEE, Vol. 83, no. 3.

Watson, I., 1997. Applying Case-Based Reasoning: Techniques for Enterprise Systems, San Francisco, Cal.: Morgan Kaufmann Publishers

# The General Motors Variation-Reduction Adviser: Deployment Issues for an AI Application

**Alexander P. Morgan[1], John A. Cafeo[2], Kurt Godden[1], Ronald M. Lesperance[1], Andrea M. Simon[1], Deborah L. McGuinness[3] and James L. Benedict[3]**

[1] GM R&D Center, MC 480-106-359, Manufacturing Systems Research Lab, 30500 Mound Rd., Warren, MI 48090-9055, {alexander.p.morgan, ronald.m.lesperance, kurt.godden, andrea.m.simon}@gm.com

[2] GM R&D Center, MC 480-106-256, Vehicle Analysis and Dynamics Lab, 30500 Mound Rd., Warren, MI 48090-9055, john.cafeo@gm.com

[3] McGuinness Associates, 20 Peter Coutts Circle, Stanford, CA 94305, {dlm, jbenedict}@mcguinnessassociates.com

**Abstract**

The General Motors Variation-Reduction Adviser is a knowledge system built on case-based reasoning principles that is currently in use in a dozen General Motors Assembly Centers. This paper reviews the overall characteristics of the system and then focuses on various AI elements critical to support its deployment to a production system. A key AI enabler is ontology-guided search using domain-specific ontologies.

## 1. Introduction

The Variation-Reduction Adviser (VRA) is a knowledge system for automotive assembly plants whose goal is to support quality improvement activities for assembly line processes. (Cafeo *et al.*, 2001; Morgan *et al.*, 2001) The primary use of the VRA is to improve communication in the plants and between plants to assist with problem-solving necessary to keep the line producing the highest quality products. Our original prototype was tested by a "dimensional management" team working on "variation reduction" problems in a plant. Currently, other teams including "paint," "maintenance," and "general assembly" are testing it at various plant locations, so its range of application includes a whole cluster of related assembly-plant domains. While its original name reflected the specific focus on dimensional analysis for variation reduction, we have kept this name and broadened its interpretation following the principle of *kaisan,* that all improvements in process can be viewed as "variation reduction."

The VRA was originally conceived as a case-based reasoning (CBR) system (Leake, 1996) and retains case-based features. Its failure as a pure CBR system for social reasons is one of the interesting aspects of this application. That this failure induced us to introduce an ontology-guided search (OGS) functionality not originally planned is another interesting aspect. In this paper, we will focus on the AI perspective of our business task, pointing out the problems being addressed, some challenges encountered in the field, our solution strategy, and an evaluation of the value added by the system.

There are, of course, recognized relationships between various aspects of knowledge management and AI. See, for example, the survey (Smith and Farquhar 2000). AI has been used for planning in manufacturing; for example, DLMS (Rychtyckyj 1999) and "The Stamping Adviser" (Leake *et al.* 1999). The VRA is more closely related to problem-solving systems; for example, Ford's eBPR (Kwiecien *et al.* 2001), Schlumberger's Eureka/InTouch (McDermott *et al.* 2000), and Xerox PARC's Eureka (Bobrow and Whalen 2002). All of these have common elements with the VRA of best practices, peer-to-peer sharing, and diagnosis, as well as some commonality in their choice of AI tools. The main differences include the VRA's focus on manufacturing (including its community-of-practice-specific diagnostic ontologies) and the fact that its "best practice" functionality is peer moderated rather than "managed." We lack the space here to compare these various systems at length.

The VRA prototype is currently in production use in about twelve GM Assembly Centers. The original system is in English, but there is a Spanish version in use in two Mexican plants, and a German version is being tested.

## 2. Task Description

The VRA addresses two primary issues with respect to plant production. First, there are many people working on tasks across multiple shifts, and these people must communicate about their progress and problems. The second is that plants need to maintain a record of updates to equipment and work done. The VRA fulfills both these needs, which are relatively short term in nature. The combination of these two types of entries, when viewed from a longer perspective enable the VRA to also function as a lessons-learned system for assembly plants, providing a "memory" for solutions and a repository from which "best practices" can be extracted.

## 3. Application Description

The VRA architecture includes viewing and authoring subsystems, with a variety of domain-friendly features, support functions, a database of entries, and search and summarization functions. Also included are database and ontology maintenance functions. The VRA is organized around "entries." Each entry has some attribute values (entered via pull-down lists) and also a block of free text. Graphical attachments are optional, but useful. See (Morgan *et al.* 2003) for screen shots and a fuller description of the user interface. The application is currently being converted from Microsoft Visual Basic/Access to a web-based version with more powerful database and search support. We have been assisted in this by members of the PARC scientific staff, who joined the project in 2003 to assist with in-plant social-technical analyses and with this web-based transition.

The key AI elements are the case-based features and the elements of the domain-specific ontologies and ontology-guided search. These are discussed further in the following two sections.

## 4. Uses of AI Technology: CBR

The VRA was originally conceived as a classic feature-vector-based diagnostic case-based reasoning (CBR) system. It was quickly realized, however, that a strict feature-based CBR model would not work because of the complexity of the problem-solving process. This is described in Section 4.1. The system based on the model in Section 4.1 became version 0 (VRA-0) of our system, described below. In response to user feedback, we developed VRA-1, which is VRA-0 weakly linked to a communication log. After VRA-1 was further tested, a new version, VRA-2, was created. In (Morgan *et al.*, 2003), the evolution from VRA-0 to VRA-2 is detailed. Here we only sketch this evolution and note the main AI features.

### 4.1 A Case Structure for a Complex Diagnostic Environment

Consider a diagnostic environment in which, for each case, a small subset of a large set of symptoms can arise. Some of these symptoms will be the results of tests. These tests are not performed in any fixed order, but at the discretion of the technicians. No particular subset of tests is always performed. A case consists of symptoms, results of tests, results of inspections (a kind of test), results of actions (*e.g.*, replace a part), resolving actions and ultimately the root causes. This formulation fits our domain and also that of the National Semiconductor case structure described in (Watson, 2002, Chapter 3).

A fixed-length feature vector cannot capture a case because: (1) the attribute values are naturally grouped (by symptom, test, etc.), so that there are repetitions of values for the same attribute that must be properly associated with each other; (2) cases do not have a natural fixed length; (3) there is a time sequence for these groupings of attribute values that has physical significance and that changes from case to case. A case needs to be a reasonable summary of what happened as symptoms, tests, inspections, and results occurred, a comprehensible record that a person can read and understand. Thus, for VRA-0, we devised the following structure: a case is defined to be a sequence of observations. Observations are classified into a finite number of types. Each type is represented by a templated sentence. These sentences capture symptoms, results of tests, actions, resolutions and a few other types. A vector of attribute values represents each type of observation, where the values are the fillers of the slots of the templated sentence. Thus, a case is a sequence of observations of various types, and the types occur in no particular order, although they are taken from a finite set of types. This formal structure seems to be detailed enough to capture the important aspects of the diagnostic process, and it is vastly more structured than free text. Similarity between cases is built up from similarity between values of attributes and similarity between observations. See (Morgan *et al.*, 2003) for details.

### 4.2 A Knowledge Structure Emphasizing Communication Over Problem Solving

After using VRA-0, the users asked us to provide them with a log environment, in which a few categorizing attributes may be selected via pull-down menus, and then the user is free to enter content as a block of text. This log system began as a supplement to the CBR system (creating VRA-1). However, it quickly became a focal point of the implemented system. In fact, the log flourished while the CBR system languished. The users found significant benefit in having a distributed online mechanism for capturing semi-structured input of daily events. They could not make much use of the CBR system for recovering previously solved problems, however, because they would not author enough cases to "boot strap" the archive.

The next version of the VRA, VRA-2, thus focused on the communications and log aspects of the system. One way of describing this evolution is moving from the context of CBR with a focus on structural similarity to that of computer-supported cooperative work (CSCW) with a focus on communication [see (Ackerman, 2003)] and simple natural language input. This could be viewed as a movement away from structured AI as a primary solution strategy. However, VRA-2 has seen a technology pull for a different kind of AI, in requests for a smart search capability. That is, the original desire to recover solutions to problems, when the problems re-occur, remains. Users want to be able to find previous cases similar to a current problem, even though they are unwilling to contribute more case-authoring effort than making entries in a written log book. Originally, the CBR structure facilitated the retrieval of past similar cases. VRA-2 does not have the symptom information captured in a structured way, but this CBR recall function may be "salvaged" via OGS. Our solution uses ontologies (see McGuinness 2002) as a way of encoding context and symptoms. This is exploited when we process queries in a query expansion style (see McGuinness 1999) to yield a functionally smarter search capability.

The core of the VRA-2 observation is a free-text block, in which any number of sentences might be written. Attached to this free text are classifying attributes, whose values are chosen by the user from pull-down menus. Here, some structure is restored, but users cannot enter symptom descriptions from the pull down menus. This kind of interface was the one required to maintain a satisfied user base. Although we would have liked an interface that allowed users to input more structure, that kind of interface was not operational in our plant settings. Thus, much of the content in our database is available only as unstructured text. In particular, the symptoms of the problem are described only in the text. Thus, the clarity of knowledge capture and the structured similarity search of VRA-0 are lost in VRA-2.

The socio-technical interplay here is interesting. Although there were some technical challenges, the core reasons for evolving from VRA-0 to VRA-2 were social: the users did not think they had the time to author cases, and it was not feasible to create a dedicated group of case authors. More details concerning the system evolution and the social and technological issues influencing the evolution are in (Morgan et al, 2003). The users, however, were enthusiastic about using the VRA as a communication tool, as it was recognized that this immediately helped daily work. Since the elements of cases were being captured in partially structured log entries, we decided that this database of log entries might still function as a lessons-learned archive (the original purpose of the CBR system), if a sufficiently "smart" search engine could be devised. The next section describes the VRA needs for ontology-guided search and our solution path.

## 5 Uses of AI Technology: Ontology-Guided Search

The VRA achieved striking early acceptance while functioning essentially only as a communication tool. Its primary everyday impact was to facilitate communication across shifts of staff, and it had the added value of being available from multiple workstations, thereby replacing the single written logbook. While it has had significant impact providing improved communication, it is also a problem-solving tool. Previous entries in the database that have relevance to new issues can be found. It can also be searched to provide automatic report generation about problems and work items over particular time periods, by plant, by zone, and by worker or work area.

The current VRA allows several versions of simple string-based search. However, the user community specifically requested the ability to locate references to concepts and log entries that are "related" to their search terms, either for search queries that fail to retrieve any exact string matches or for queries that do return results but have additional closely related concepts that may also be relevant for the user. For these reasons, we have constructed an OGS engine to infer structure and inter-relationships on the free text without requiring the user to take on the additional burden of more complicated data entry. While an alternative might be to capture user entries in a controlled, semi-structured language, based on previous GM work on controlled languages (Godden, 1998), we believe that this would place too great a burden on users even if the VRA had a built-in controlled language checker. Another alternative would be to depend upon markup information generated either by automatic tools or humans and then search on the meta information. However, GM deployments have found that users are unwilling to do manual markup. Additionally, automatic markup tools might provide some assistance both in generating background ontologies and in providing automatic markup. While Clear Forest and other similar tools have useful entity identification and extraction capabilities, they are primarily used for text analysis and mining, and do not contribute substantially to our initial work in ontology creation and use. We are, however, actively evaluating such tools for follow-on research regarding the identification of causes and corrections of plant issues described in VRA user logs.

Prior work using data that was contracted to be marked up using controlled vocabularies (using either manual or automatic techniques) was found to be inconsistent and inadequate for dependable searches (McGuinness 2000). Thus, while our work will use meta tagging information if available, it does not count on this meta information. An anonymous reviewer adds "Schlumberger worked on automatic meta-data collection in 2001-02 and eventually concluded that the available systems did not eliminate the need for a manually generated taxonomy."

Our approach uses ontologies we built from the starting points available from within the company and driven by the needs of our application. We did not take an approach that utilizes automatically generated taxonomies. As has been pointed out in other literature (e.g., Delphi, 2002), automatically generated taxonomies can require large data sets for training as well as having control and accuracy issues and, while they may have benefits of scaling and certain kinds of efficiency, the tradeoffs were not seen to be of benefit to our effort.

The supporting domain ontologies facilitate intelligent search of unstructured text. Seven interrelated ontologies comprising approximately 200 concepts have already been seeded for the first OGS prototype, including:

- Process elements – tooling, robots, operators, transfer mechanisms, welding, anything used to make a vehicle that is not a part of the vehicle.
- Process issues – e.g. robot failures.
- Parts, subassemblies, and part features - *Parts* are individually inventoried items that make up the vehicle, e.g., the left front door handle. *Subassemblies* are specific to the manufacturing process. *Part features* include commonly referred to items such as the door ring that are abstractions of various parts and subassemblies.
- Single part issues – relate to only one vehicle component, e.g. a ding in a fender
- Multiple part issues – relate to two or more parts, especially misalignments, unsatisfactory gaps, malformations of joints between parts.
- Data analysis – results of analysis of measurement data generated by optical and mechanical gages.
- Plant locations – zones and stations organized topologically or functionally

These initial ontologies include common terms and morphological variants used in the plants. The ontologies contain information found in log entries, synonyms and common misspellings, as well as a canonical form of each concept. For each ontology, we capture subclass relationships between concepts (e.g. 'Hood' is a subclass of 'Panel') as well as "part-of" relationships (e.g. 'Tailgate' is part-of a truck 'Box'). Additionally we capture various semantic properties of the concepts such as front vs. rear position as well as indications of the source of the concept, person who entered the concept into the ontology, etc.

The initial ontology built for enhanced retrieval focuses on subclass, synonym, and containment relationships along with meta information for ontology evolution. We have done some additional design work on using more sophisticated ontologies with expanded property information including more value restrictions, cardinality, enumerated filler sets, etc. At present, the ontologies are being maintained in the Protégé-2000 environment and deployed into the VRA in RDF format. We may convert to OWL in the future if user feedback indicates the need for greater expressive power.

The initial search algorithm for the VRA uses both the *subclass* and *part-of* relations, but this could expand in future versions as usage analysis is performed. Synonyms in the target text are normalized to a canonical form during the search before comparison is made with the ontology. After exploiting this simple similarity-based retrieval for terms from background ontologies, we will evaluate how well the retrieval is doing, and we do not anticipate the need for any full or partial parsing of the natural language text. We expect results similar to those found in PChip (McGuinness, 1999) and FindUR (McGuinness, 2000). In those applications, we found improved recall with little degradation of precision. Thus, without OGS, simple textual searches typically missed relevant information because the documents (in this case, the log entries) were short and contained few words to search on. When ontology-enhanced search was used, queries were expanded to include more words to search for and thus, relevant documents could be found. Since the documents being searched were in a limited domain, there were few problems with multiple senses of words introducing problems that hurt precision. In our database, case entries are similar – the textual fields do not contain long descriptions and the content is limited to plant assembly information. In the full range of FindUR deployments, query expansion was done along a range of complexity. The simplest deployments used subclass relationships only and more sophisticated search interfaces leveraged domain and range information, value restrictions, cardinality, disjoint class information, enumerated sets, roles and subrole hierarchies. When interface requirements were such that they demanded more expressive and precise query manipulation, the additional ontological information was leveraged effectively. When however interfaces were required that simply used straight text input, the simpler ontologies were used as background information. We are exploring a similar deployment strategy here.

Evaluation criteria for search include:

- Impact on precision and recall using individual ontologies.
- Review of structure modification requests. (For example, it is not clear in advance how important

term relationships will be, compared to raw occurrences of terms.)

- Review of user interface concerns regarding user-suggested updates, as cited below.
- Review of requests to evaluate if patterns emerge, conflicts arise, ontologies become stable, etc.

## 6 Application Use and Payoff

The VRA has been deployed in one plant for about four years and in nine plants for over one year, with new installations in an additional two plants. In each plant where it is deployed, the VRA is used daily. For example, at the GM truck plant in Silao, Mexico, the Dimensional-Engineering Team begins their daily morning meeting with a review of the previous day's entries. About 10 entries are created per day per shift in the plants where it is installed.

A formal business case was created to quantify the benefits and payoff of the VRA, and we will sketch the elements of this business case here. The business case presents evidence that the VRA is a mechanism for *cost avoidance*, a more systemic concept than *cost savings*. Scenarios are constructed about "events" that generate cost. Formulas estimate how using the VRA reduces these costs. The frequency of the events over a time period (like a year) is estimated. The result is a dollars/year estimate of cost avoidance generated by using the VRA.

For the VRA we had three scenarios:

1. "Wasted Time in Connecting" In this scenario, we envision an exchange between two team members in which there is wasted time, say, via "telephone tag" or by losing notes that have to be recovered or by forgetting to respond to a request or other such "slips" that can occur when everybody is busy and doing a number of things at the same time.

2. "Continuous-Improvement Problem Solving" Typically, this includes two types of activities: (1) reducing process variation and (2) resolving small issues not likely to require *rework* (adjustments to a vehicle before it can be released from the factory).

3. "Crisis Problem Solving" The events for this scenario are "breakdowns" that cause definite warranty or rework until they are solved. These problems generally get a lot of attention when they occur. Solving these, definitely and directly, improves the productivity of the plant and the overall quality of the vehicle output. Additionally, since warranty claims quantitatively decrease customer loyalty, fixing this problem also addresses customer loyalty.

The first two scenarios have to do with moving the work process to a less wasteful state. The third scenario has to do with returning the current state of the work process to its normal operating conditions.

In the first two scenarios, jobs are done quicker and less time is wasted. This *time savings* is converted to a dollar figure by multiplying by a wages/hour estimate. Here we could have left the savings in *hours* rather than converting to *dollars*. In a company where contracts fix most wage costs, it may not be realistic to convert time savings to dollars, as if wages could be "saved." However, this device of converting time to money might be accepted as a metaphor for the value of saved time, without interpreting it literally.

In the third scenario, the value of avoiding rework, warranty costs, and lost sales are converted to dollars via economic models. Additionally, lowered warranty usage translates to higher customer satisfaction and a higher percentage of return customers. Establishing a rigid analytical justification for the assumptions in such models and for values of their parameters is difficult, and we made do with "best guess" estimates in combination with some quantitative market research numbers which were available. Even with the variability of the evaluation parameters, using conservative scenarios showed considerable cost avoidance.

## 7 Application Development and Deployment

The development process began at the GM Research and Development Center. It was noticed that complex dimensional-management problems were being solved daily in the assembly plants without any systematic record being kept of this problem-solving activity. This suggested a CBR system, and a first prototype was constructed at the R&D Center. Its evolution under user feedback is described in Section 4. Four researchers working approximately 20 hours/week each, with the cooperation of 2 or 3 plant engineers over a year yielded essentially the "final" prototype, using Microsoft Visual Basic and Access. Since then, there have been many evolutionary changes and a process to convert the code to a web-based system.

Currently, a software supplier is working with us on a "production hardened" version of the web-based code. The cost of basic development was the salaries of the involved parties. As the project matured, suppliers have been involved with completing and hardening the code, which has involved further cost. Most of the difficulties encountered in this project have to do with the human-computer interface and in fitting the system into the plant workflow and sharing patterns. Here is a list of some of the practical lessons learned from our experience designing, developing, and deploying the VRA.

- The interface for input and retrieval in our plant settings needed to appear simple and natural. Thus, a natural language input and output format was required.
- While structured case information may be seen to have future value from retrieval and reporting perspectives, this was not viewed to have enough benefit to offset the perceived burden of authoring case information in a structured format.
- The exact form of the user interfaces and their supporting structures cannot be worked out "in advance." Rather, the user community must be given the opportunity to try out prototypes and have them modified based on experience. This is consistent with the grassroots development process noted in (Morgan, 2002).
- Improved communication is received with more immediate enthusiasm than providing a problem-solving tool, whose usefulness takes time to establish.

While we hoped the incentive of being able to re-use the solutions to previously solved problems would be enough to motivate the users to author structured cases, we found this was not so. They would use the system only via natural language input. Thus, our only options were to have authors or editors separate from the users (impossible in our setting) or to provide a mechanism that provides some access to the structure and content implicit in the free text fields. We believe that our ontology-based approach to smart search is an appropriate reaction to the environment we find in our plants and offers a place for AI technology to provide value and impact in industrially-deployed plant communication and retrieval systems.

## 8 Maintenance

Once an application is dependent upon a background set of knowledge, it becomes important to have an evolution environment for obtaining, checking, and maintaining the knowledge. For example, a new interface to support OGS will allow a user to make a suggestion to add a term to a particular ontology. We are currently investigating the requirements for such an interface. The suggestion log would then be submitted to an internal ontology owner for approval and incorporation into the next version.

Both academic and industrial work has been done on ontology evolution environments that this project can draw on. In a paper entitled "Industrial Strength Ontology Management" (Das *et al.*, 2001), a list of ontology management requirements is provided that we endorse and include in our evolution plan:

- Scalability, Availability, Reliability and Performance
- Ease of Use by domain literate people
- Extensible and Flexible Knowledge Representation
- Distributed Multi-User Collaboration
- Security Management
- Difference and Merging
- XML Interfaces
- Internationalization, including support for multiple languages
- Versioning

Over time, as analysis is done on the size, usage, and updating requirements of the ontologies, we will create an ontology evolution environment that addresses the concerns listed above that are most important to the GM deployments. We anticipate ease of use, availability, and multi-user collaboration to be the most important initial concerns. However, difference/merging, versioning, extensibility, and internationalization will become more important as the VRA has a longer life and is deployed in more varied locations. As already noted, the VRA application is available in English, Spanish and German. Maintaining versions in different languages obviously has ontology implications.

The VRA will continue in the near term to be guided by the research group, but our plan is for the plant data managers (one per plant) to handle the day-to-day management of each plant system, while a few selected managers will control the ontology maintenance process. Each GM vehicle model is manufactured for a period of years, so the knowledge refresh process can have an evolutionary flavor. The "model changeover" process will use the VRA as a diagnostic aid, and this will prime the knowledge base as new vehicles are produced.

## 9 Summary and Discussion

Working closely with the GM Assembly Centers, we have deployed an AI-based knowledge system, the Variation-Reduction Adviser, which has accomplished measurable benefits for the GM vehicle-assembly process. As a result, the system is being deployed to all assembly centers, and it is in daily use in all the centers in which it is currently deployed.

The system underwent a considerable degree of restructuring based on user feedback. This feedback focused on the perceived burden of authoring structured cases. An ontology-guided search mechanism has been designed to allow free-text case authoring, while maintaining the use of the case base as a solved-problems archive.

The success of the system is due to its ability to address everyday needs for communication in ways superior to previous processes. This capability is our explanation for the significant user pull for the VRA and is the main reason we believe for its success.

The "knowledge management" nature of the VRA is more in the class of "light weight" and "grassroots" diagnostic systems, such as Xerox PARC's Eureka, rather than more "managed" systems (as noted in Section 1). Commercially available technology for automatically capturing meta-data (e.g., Clear Forest, Stratify, or Interwoven's Meta-Tagger) typically have their greatest success under conditions different from this application, although they were considered. Protégé was our choice for an ontology management tool, preferable to taxonomy-focused systems (Wordmap, Inxight), since we have more than simple taxonomies to manage. (Note our use of "part-of" as well as "isa" relations.)

Corporate policy does not allow us to specify the ontology, the details of its implementation, the algorithm for OGS, or other material judged to offer GM a competitive advantage. However, the essential features are outlined, especially in Section 5, so that the essence of our approach is clearly revealed.

AI was critical to the success of this deployed application. Both the CBR inspiration and the functionality of OGS were essential to frame and drive the system toward its eventual user acceptance and its suitability to its dual functions in communication and problem-solving. It is now being considered as a model at GM for shops where problem-solving teams must collaborate, share, and remember, both within and across communities of practice.

Our practical lessons learned from this application were listed in Section 7, but the fundamental lesson – applicable to any business process – is the "grassroots development process." The users must be listened to aggressively, and the system changed to fit their work practices. Knowledge as "communication" is received, understood, and managed much more intuitively than knowledge as "gems." Best practices are valuable, but connecting with peers is essential.

## Acknowledgements

We appreciate support from the GM Flint Assembly Center: Dave Coumes, Dave Holland, Gene Morrison, Dan Rach, and Nathan Grzymkowski. We also acknowledge support from GM Dimensional Engineering: Glenn Pacer, Gary Telling Tony Grix, and Richard Grimes. We acknowledge the PARC scientists who joined us in 2003: Jack Whalen, Erik Vinkhuyzen, Robert Moore, Robert Cheslow, and Danny Bobrow. Finally, we would like to thank the anonymous reviewers for several useful suggestions.

## References

Ackerman, Mark S. 2003. The Intellectual Challenge of CSCW: The Gap Between Social Requirements and Technical Feasibility, to be published in *Human-Computer Interaction*. Available at www.eecs.umich.edu/~ackerm/.

Bobrow, D. and Whalen, J. 2002. "Community Knowledge Sharing in Practice: The Eureka Story," *Reflections*, Vol. 4, No. 2., 47-59.

Cafeo, J. A.; Gibbons, D. I.; Lesperance, R. M.; Morgan, A. P.; Sengir, G. H.; Simon, A. M. 2001. Capturing Lessons Learned for Variation Reduction in an Automotive Assembly Plant. In *Proc. 14th Int. Fla. AI Research Soc. Conf.*, 89-92. AAAI Press, Menlo Park, Calif.

Das, A.; Wu, W.; McGuinness, D. 2002. Industrial Strength Ontology Management. In Cruz, Decker, Euzenat, McGuinness, eds. *The Emerging Semantic Web.* IOS Press.

Delphi Group. Taxonomy and Content Classification: Market Mileston Report. April 2002.

Godden, K. 1998. Controlling the Business Environment for Controlled Language. In *Procs. of the 2nd Intl Workshop on Controlled Language Applications.* Carnegie Mellon University.

Kwiecien, S.; Kramek, B.; Aiello, S.; Moola, M.; and Swarup, S. 2001. "Best Practice Replication: The Evolution of KM at Ford Motor Company," *Knowledge Management*, Vol. 5, No. 3, Oct. 2001.

Leake, D. ed. 1996. *Case-Based Reasoning: Experiences, Lessons, and Future Directions.* AAAI Press, Menlo Park, California and The MIT Press, Cambridge, Mass.

Leake, D.; Birnbaum, L.; Hammond, K.; Marlow, C.; and Yang, H. 1999. "Integrating Information resources: A Case Study of Engineering Design Support." In. *Proc. 3rd Int. Conf. on Case-Based Reasoning*. ICCBR 1999. Seeon Monastery, Germany, July 1999, Proceedings, 482-496.

McDermott, R.; O'Dell, C.; Hubert, C. 2000. *Building and Sustaining Communities of Practice: Final Report*, APQC, *www.apqc.org/portal/apqc/site/store*

McGuinness, D. 1999. Ontology-enhanced Search for Primary Care Medical Literature. In Proc. Int. Medical Informatics Assoc. Working Group 6 - Medical Concept Representation and Natural Language Processing Conference, Phoenix, Arizona, December 16-19, 1999.

McGuinness, D. 2000. Conceptual Modeling for Distributed Ontology Environments, In the Proceedings of the Eighth International Conference on Conceptual Structures: Logical, Linguistic, and Computational Issues (ICCS 2000), August 14-18, 2000, Darmstadt, Germany.

McGuinness, D. 2002. Ontologies Come of Age. In Fensel, Hendler, Lieberman, Wahlster, eds. *Spinning the Semantic Web: Bringing the World Wide Web to its Full Potential.* MIT Press.

Morgan, A. P.; Cafeo, J. A.; Gibbons, D. I.; Lesperance, R. M.; Sengir, G. H.; Simon, A. M. 2001. CBR for Dimensional Management in a Manufacturing Plant. In. *Proc. 4th Int. Conf. on Case-Based Reasoning*. ICCBR 2001. Vancouver, BC, Canada., 597-610.

Morgan, A. P.; Cafeo, J. A.; Gibbons, D. I.; Lesperance, R. M.; Sengir, G. H.; Simon, A. M. 2002. The General Motors Variation-Reduction Adviser: An Example of Grass Roots Knowledge Management Development. *Int. J. Intelligent Systems in Accounting, Finance, & Management* 11:269-276.

Morgan, A. P.; Cafeo, J. A.; Gibbons, D. I.; Lesperance, R. M.; Sengir, G. H.; Simon, A. M. 2003. The General Motors Variation-Reduction Adviser: Evolution of a CBR System. In *Proc. 5th Int. Conf. on Case-Based Reasoning.* ICCBR 2003. Trondheim, Norway, Springer (2003) 306-318.

Rychtyckyj, Nester 1999. "DLMS: Ten Years of AI for Vehicle Assembly Process Planning." In *Proc. 11th Conf. on Innovative Applications of Artificial Intelligence.* July 18-22, 1999, Orlando, Florida, 821-828

Smith, Reid; Farquhar, Adam 2000. "The Road Ahead for Knowledge Management: An AI Perspective," *AI Magazine*, Winter 2000, 17-40.

Watson, Ian 2002. *Applying Knowledge Management: Techniques for Building Corporate Memories* Morgan Kaufman, New York.

# Making Better Recommendations with Online Profiling Agents

**Danny Oh, Chew Lim Tan**
School of Computing
National University of Singapore
3 Science Drive 2
Singapore 117543
+65 6874 2900

dannyoh@marcuria.com, tancl@comp.nus.edu.sg

## Abstract

In recent years, we have witnessed the success of autonomous agents applying machine learning techniques across a wide range of applications. However, agents applying the same machine learning techniques in online applications have not been so successful. Even agent-based hybrid recommender systems that combine information filtering techniques with collaborative filtering techniques have only been applied with considerable success to simple consumer goods such as movies, books, clothing and food. Complex, adaptive autonomous agent systems that can handle complex goods such as real estate, vacation plans, insurance, mutual funds, and mortgage have yet emerged. To a large extent, the reinforcement learning methods developed to aid agents in learning have been more successfully deployed in offline applications. The inherent limitations in these methods have rendered them somewhat ineffective in online applications. In this paper, we postulate that a small amount of prior knowledge and human-provided input can dramatically speed up online learning. We will demonstrate that our agent HumanE – with its prior knowledge or "experiences" about the real estate domain - can effectively assist users in identifying requirements, especially unstated ones, quickly and unobtrusively.

## Categories and Subject Descriptors

I.2.11 [**Distributed Artificial Intelligence**]: Intelligent agents.

## General Terms

Design, Reliability, Experimentation, Human Factors.

## Keywords

Inference, intelligent agents, electronic profiling, personalization, user preferences, reinforcement learning, interactive learning, experience.



## 1. INTRODUCTION

Electronic profiling agents have been deployed with considerable success in certain agent-based recommender systems, namely, information filtering (IF) systems, collaborative filtering (CF) systems and hybrid recommender systems.

Unfortunately, the successes of these systems have been restricted to simple consumer goods such as movies, books, clothing and food. When the IR and/or CF techniques plus other reinforcement learning methods are applied in online applications for complex consumer products such as real estate, vacation plans, insurance, mutual funds, and mortgage, they fail to enjoy much success.

This is because many reinforcement learning implementations assume that the agent developed knows nothing about the environment to begin with, and that the agent must gain all of its information by exploration and subsequent exploitation of learned knowledge.

When dealing with a real, complex online system such as a large-scale real estate listing and brokerage application, however, this approach is simply not practical. Typically, the state space is too large to explore satisfactorily within the lifetime of the agent (much less within the attention time-span of typical online users).

Worse still, making "random" exploratory recommendations can frustrate and disappoint the user, potentially causing the user to abandon the system totally.

Accumulated knowledge in the form of memories and experiences allows humans to go about performing daily tasks. In the real world, we often go to a human real estate agent for assistance in selling or acquiring real estate properties. We naturally expect the agent to be an expert in the real estate domain, and hence able to offer suitable advice and recommendations. Certainly, we do not expect the real estate agent to have no knowledge about the real estate domain.

Hence, in order to take our prior knowledge (which are often implicit) and incorporate them into a reinforcement learning framework, we have examined in this work the idea of supplying the agent with an initial policy about the real estate domain in the HumanE agent ("HumanE").

## 2. BETTER RECOMMENDATIONS WITH HUMANE

### 2.1 Difficulties in Developing Profiling Agents for Complex Domains

The main problems encountered when developing online profiling agents for complex multi-dimensional domains can be summarized as below:

- Assumption that the agent knows nothing and must acquire its knowledge through exploration and subsequent exploitation of learned knowledge results in slow agent learning for complex domains and makes online implementation difficult
- Difficult to give an agent large amount of application-specific and domain-specific knowledge
- Difficult to encode this knowledge in an abstract language
- Difficult to transfer agent knowledge and the control architecture for building agents for other applications
- Difficult to maintain the individual rules in the agent rule base over time
- Static agent knowledge (i.e. cannot be customized to individual user habits and preferences)
- Making "random" exploratory recommendations can frustrate and disappoint the user
- Difficult to allow for serendipitous discoveries of user preferences
- Difficult to obtain user trust when an interface agent is very sophisticated, qualified and autonomous from the start
- Too much data is required in an online setting for typical learning methods (e.g. reinforcement-learning methods)

### 2.2 Practical Approach

We strongly believe that practical agent learning for online applications is possible by integration with human-supplied knowledge. This is because humans can provide a lot of help to assist agents in learning, even if humans cannot perform the task very well. Humans can provide some initial successful trajectories through the space. Trajectories are not used for supervised learning, but to guide the learning methods through useful parts of the search space leading to efficient exploration of the search space.

Online profiling agents can be bootstrapped from a human-supplied policy which basically gives some sample trajectories. The purpose of the policy is to generate "experiences" for the agents. This policy can be hand-coded by domain experts. It need not be optimal and may be very wrong. The policy shows the agents "interesting" parts of the search space.

Our online profiling agent, HumanE, is based on the aforementioned approach and it offers users the opportunity to find products that will best meet their requirements. HumanE guides users through a product selection process. Users get to specify information about their individual requirements and restrictions by creating and refining their profiles.

Based upon the profile (and initial policy if the profile is newly created), HumanE offers an initial selection of products. Users can then select from these matching products to view more detailed product information such as product features. HumanE also tries to be helpful by providing products that are newly added as well as products that are popular among other users.

To refine the profile, users can specify which features are desirable or undesirable through an intuitive and friendly interface, and HumanE will offer a new selection of products matching the revised profile. If no matching products are found, users can backtrack to their previous profile.

### 2.3 Design Assumption

Our design approach assumes that the entire user experience is an iterative process of browsing and meaningful user feedback. The approach has in fact been adopted successfully by similar systems such as RentMe [2, 3], CASA [7] and Apt Decision [12]. As the user is actively involved throughout the entire profile creation process, the user can react independently to every feature of the real estate offerings.

### 2.4 Domain Analysis

To test the feasibility of the proposed learning model, we chose the real estate domain. As the agent needed to have built-in knowledge about the domain, we analyzed online and offline apartment advertisements to determine the standard apartment features for the local real estate domain.

Next, we considered how people choose apartments. After examining the features, we concluded that some of them (e.g. district, type, price) were pivotal to the final choice of apartment. That is, most people would reject an apartment if the value for a crucial feature were not to their liking. Other features (e.g. bridge, underpass, swimming pool) were less pivotal. All this domain knowledge went into HumanE.

In addition, we examined two destinations of apartment seekers: real estate websites and human real estate agents, to determine what knowledge we could glean from those interactions.

#### *2.4.1 Real Estate Websites*

Many real estate websites adopt either the pure browsing metaphor [14] or the search-like metaphor [13]. One problem is that users are expected to enter many specific details about their ideal apartment. Another problem is that they must enter their preferences when they visit a new site and each time they visit the site. This is because there is no option to save multiple sets of preferences for a single site.

#### *2.4.2 Humane Real Estate Agents*

We consider how people deal with the ambiguity and imprecision of real world decisions. For example, when a customer interacts with a real estate agent, the customer may react in a variety of ways not limited by answers to explicitly posed questions. The agent's description will typically contain many details not asked for originally by the customer. The success of the interaction is determined largely by the agent's ability to infer unstated requirements and preferences from the responses. Near-miss examples establish whether the ostensible constraints are firm or flexible. Good agents are marked by their ability to converge quickly on a complicated set of constraints and priorities.

### *2.4.3 Transferring Domain Knowledge*

Much of the work done for HumanE would transfer well into any domain in which the user could browse the features of a complex object. That is, objects such as calling plans, mutual funds, homes, computers, vacation plans, or cars would work well, but simple consumer goods such as clothing or food would not. Transferring the agent into another domain would require the services of a subject matter expert who could identify salient features of the complex objects in the domain, alter the program to work with those features and determine which features were crucial to the final decision. After testing on a suitable list of objects, the "new" agent could be released.

# 3. LEARNING APPROACH

## 3.1 Introduction

The proposed two-phase learning approach has been tested successfully in past research on robotics [16]. Kaelbling et. al. found that robots using reinforcement learning learnt better when they were provided prior knowledge about their environment using a supplied initial policy. The policy generated example trajectories through the state-action space and showed the robot areas of high rewards and low rewards. After the robot had acquired a suitable amount of information through this initial phase of learning, the reinforcement learning system took control of the robot. Usually by this time, the robot had learned enough to make more informed exploration of the environment.

In this work, we adapt a similar approach when building a agent-based online real estate system. To do so, we consider each user decision as a trajectory in the search space much like the trajectories in the robot motion.

## 3.2 Initial Profile vs Initial Policy

Initial profile refers to the profile that is created at the very beginning of the learning approach. The initial profile contains only the user-defined preferred district, desired apartment type, and price.

Initial policy refers to the set of trajectory samples that show HumanE areas of high rewards and low rewards in the search space.

## 3.3 Constituents of a Profile

The main objective of HumanE is to create a user profile (or simply called a profile) to store user preferences and to assist the user to refine his or her profile intelligently using the supplied learning approach. In our scenario, a profile stores both static and dynamic (learned) user preferences in the form of desired and undesired apartment features. Examples of apartment features include "high floor", "near MRT", "marble floor", etc.

## 3.4 Overview of the Learning Approach

We have adopted a two-phase learning approach for HumanE. In the first phase of learning, HumanE learns by reinforcement, observation and takes actions that arise from a supplied initial policy. This mode of learning will last for one iteration of the profile refinement process (i.e. the iterative process of viewing apartments and selecting/ranking desired and undesired features). In the second phase, HumanE learns by reinforcement and observation. The content of the initial policy is dynamic as it is updated without human intervention from the actions taken by HumanE.

In the first phase of learning, HumanE learns by reinforcement, observation and takes actions that arise from a supplied initial policy. This mode of learning will last for one iteration of the profile refinement process (i.e. the iterative process of viewing apartments and selecting/ranking desired and undesired features). In the second phase, HumanE learns by reinforcement and observation. The content of the initial policy is dynamic as it is updated without human intervention from the actions taken by HumanE.

Figure 1 depicts the workflow of the two-phase learning approach.

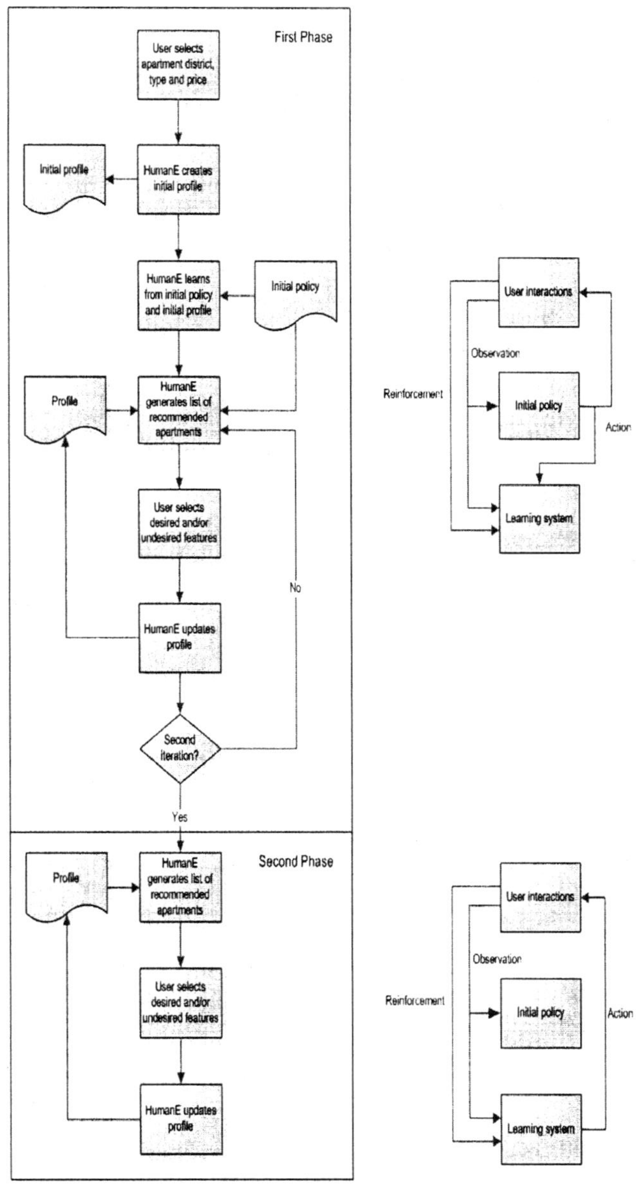


Figure 1. Workflow for the two-phase learning approach

## 3.5 Phase One Learning

In phase one learning, HumanE initially learns and takes action from a supplied initial policy. This occurs right after when an initial profile is created. Using the information stored within the supplied initial policy and initial profile, HumanE learns the locations of desired (high rewards) and undesired (low rewards) apartments in the search space that match the user preferences stored in the initial profile.

### *3.5.1 Learning from an Initial Policy*

To emulate some of the inference power a human real estate agent might have, we have incorporated an initial policy to enhance the interactive learning ability of the agent. Basically, an initial policy is a XML file that stores information about which apartment features are generally considered as desirable and undesirable.

In HumanE, the initial policy is stored in a file named "Bootstrap.xml". Figure 2 shows the content of this file.

```
<?xml version="1.0" encoding="utf-8" ?>
<features>
  <item id="desired" value="1,4,8,98"/>
  <item id="undesired" value="23,24,43"/>
</features>
<desired>
  <district>
    <item id="1"
value="15,45,92,123,280,410,488,523,677,712"/>
    ......
  </district>
</desired>
<undesired>
  <district>
    <item id="1"
value="23,34,52,166,232,359,390,416,509,682"/>
    ......
  </district>
</undesired>
```

Figure 2. Initial policy used in HumanE

The first piece of information encoded in the initial policy as shown above is the list of features generally considered as desirable and undesirable features. The attribute "id" denotes the attribute name and the attribute "value" refers to the value of the attribute "id".

The second piece of information encoded is the list of top ten most popular apartments per district. The attribute "id" denotes the attribute name which in this case refers to the district id. The attribute "value" refers to the value of the attribute "id" i.e. the apartment id of the top ten most popular apartments per district. The third piece of information encoded is the list of top ten most unpopular apartments per district. The attribute "id" denotes the attribute name which in this case refers to the district id. The attribute "value" refers to the value of the attribute "id" i.e. the apartment id of the top ten most unpopular apartments per district.

Coupling with the information stored in the initial profile, the initial policy will generate certain "interesting" trajectories through the search space, showing HumanE areas of high (popular apartments) and low (unpopular apartments) rewards. These trajectories and associated rewards are then used in this first, passive phase of learning.

As shown in Figure 1, the bootstrapping process occurs after the creation of the initial profile. Here, HumanE observes the states and rewards being generated and bootstraps this information into its "memory". In our domain, the areas of high rewards are those apartments which have at least half of the "desired" features as specified in the initial policy.

On the other hand, the areas of low rewards are those apartments which have at least half of the "undesired" features as specified in the initial policy. We have labeled each feature as either "desired" or "undesired" based on commonsense rules.

In short, this corresponds to a real-life situation in which a human real estate agent always has in mind a small number of real estate properties that he or she knows that are popular or unpopular by virtue of the features they had.

The initial policy will show HumanE where the locations of potentially "desired" and "undesired" apartments based on the profile. For example, if the user has specified in the profile that the features desired are "MRT", "Schools" and "High Floor", then HumanE will search for matching apartments that have a combination of the following criteria:

- All desired features as stated in the profile ("MRT", "Schools" and "High Floor").
- More than half of the desired features as stated in the initial policy (e.g. "MRT", "Bus Stop", "Lift Level", "Mid Floor", "Good View", and "Windy").
- Less than half of the undesired features as stated in the initial policy (e.g. "Playground", "Rubbish Dump", "Low Floor", "Blocked View", and "Facing Afternoon Sun").

Coupling with the information stored in the initial profile, the initial policy will generate certain "interesting" trajectories through the search space, showing HumanE areas of high (popular apartments) and low (unpopular apartments) rewards. These trajectories and associated rewards are then used in this first, passive phase of learning.

Therefore, HumanE is able to generate a larger but potentially interesting set of matching apartments. This gives the user an opportunity to learn about apartments that do not exactly match the initial profile but may be of interest to him. In this way, HumanE allows for the serendipitous discoveries of new user preferences without the danger of random, unguided "exploratory" recommendations.

### *3.5.2 Reinforcement Learning using a Multidimensional Utility Function*

After HumanE has generated a list of recommended apartments, it adopts reinforcement learning as the next learning technique to learn user preferences. It learns a multidimensional utility function on states (or histories) and uses it to select actions that maximize the expected utility of their outcomes. The reinforcement learning approach is used through the entire profile refinement process. In this way, the multidimensional utility function is able to capture past profile changes (i.e. the agent remembers history information) and incorporate the knowledge learned into a simple representation to be used by the matching algorithm.

#### *3.5.3 Learning by Observation*

To augment the serendipitous discoveries of apartments which can be of potential interest to the user, we have implemented the "favourites" and "views" functions. First, the user can specify an apartment to be added to a "favourites" list for a particular profile. Second, the user can select an apartment to develop the profile or simply to view more details about it.

As part of the matching process, HumanE selects the top ten apartments which are the top "favourites" and widely "viewed". This encourages the user to make more serendipitous discoveries of apartments which the user may be interested in. The assumption taken here is that there is a high possibility that a typical user may be interested in apartments which are generally considered by other users to be "good".

#### *3.5.4 Matching Algorithm*

HumanE employs a matching algorithm that is based on the concept of property relaxation. It uses a sequence of built-in rules when searching for matching apartments. If no matching apartments can be found, HumanE displays the apartments listed in the "top ten most popular apartments per district" information contained in the initial policy for the district specified in the profile.

### 3.6 Phase Two Learning

The purpose of having the initial policy in phase one learning is simply to generate experiences of the world which is tantamount to incorporating prior knowledge into HumanE. After a suitable amount of information has been acquired in the bootstrapping process, the second phase of learning takes over where HumanE learns primarily using reinforcement learning and learning by observation. Usually by this time, HumanE is more "knowledgeable" which allows for more informed exploration of the search space.

### 3.7 Benefits of Proposed Learning Approach

One of the main reasons why many reinforcement learning implementations fail to achieve much success for complex goods is that it is assumed that the agent developed knows nothing about the environment to begin with and that the agent must gain all of its information by exploration and subsequent exploitation of learned knowledge.

When dealing with a real, complex online system such as a large-scale real estate listing and brokerage application, however, this approach is simply not practical. Typically, the search space is too large to explore satisfactorily within the lifetime of the agent (much less within the attention time-span of typical online users). Worse still, making "random" exploratory recommendations can frustrate and disappoint the user, potentially causing the user to abandon the system totally.

For example, Apt Decision [12] suffers from the possibility that the user may get frustrated and disappointed if no suitable recommendations are found during the initial use of the system. This scenario can result as the Apt Decision agent has no prior knowledge about the real estate domain and cannot make good recommendations initially. Moreover, the agent needs time to learn the user's preferences from scratch and the time taken could be significantly long enough to cause the user to give up on the agent.

Another example is the SurfJet Agent [15] which is an intelligent assistant (much like HumanE) that acts as an autonomous learning agent. It is non web-based and uses an interest profile to perform searches on the Internet for articles on the user's behalf. SurfJet is able to make more accurate and useful searches as compared to traditional searching techniques as the user can give it a profile describing many of his or her interests, including how interesting (or uninteresting) each item is and how they relate to each other. However, SurfJet does not store any prior knowledge and rely solely on the iterative process of user feedback and profile refinement to make increasing accurate recommendations. Making good recommendations in the early stages of learning could be difficult and, like Apt Decision, a considerable amount of time may be spent to train SurfJet to understand a user's stated and unstated interests. It is likely that many users may not be prepared to commit that kind of time and effort to train the agent until it is sufficiently capable of making fairly good recommendations.

Accumulated knowledge in the form of memories and experiences allows humans to go about performing daily tasks. In the real world, we often go to a human real estate agent for assistance in selling or acquiring real estate properties. We naturally expect the agent to be an expert in the real estate domain, and hence able to offer suitable advice and recommendations. Certainly, we do not expect the real estate agent to have no knowledge about the real estate domain.

Hence, in order to take our prior knowledge (which are often implicit) and incorporate them into a reinforcement learning framework, we have examined the idea of supplying HumanE with an initial policy about the real estate domain and in this section, we have briefly described the learning approach which we are confident that it can aid profiling agents in making better recommendations faster with the ultimate aim of soliciting greater satisfaction, confidence and trust from users. We will support our claims using experimental results and the details can be found in the next section.

## 4. EXPERIMENTAL ANALYSIS

### 4.1 Methodology

The following sections outline the methodology used for the experiments conducted with HumanE and our testers.

#### *4.1.1 Metrics*

There are four dimensions to measure HumanE's ability to increase customer satisfaction:

- Number of profile changes
- Time taken to create a profile
- Ease of use

- Performance

### 4.1.2 Test data

To ensure the realistic nature of the experiments to be conducted, we painstakingly created our test data set from more than eight hundred actual real estate ad postings from both offline and online sources.

## 4.2 Experimental Design

Basically, we want to test whether our proposed learning approach with the use of initial policy contributes to better performance for web profiling agents. Based on the findings in [8, 9], we decided to use survey research in our experimental design. In addition, our experimental design is also strongly influenced by the findings from [6, 10] especially in the area of web page evaluation.

We invited one hundred and fifty genuine real estate buyers to evaluate HumanE based on the chosen metrics. Most testers were of the age between late twenties to fifty years old. This coincided with the age range where most people would consider buying apartments and would genuinely be interested in using HumanE as an intelligent assistant during the searching and selection of apartments.

We also took into consideration the occupational profiles of the testers. We wanted to avoid having many IT professionals as our testers and they would naturally be more IT-savvy and might be inclined to rate HumanE more favourably due to its sophisticated mechanics.

Another factor we considered was the size of the test groups. The size of each test group should be sufficiently large to allow for more precision in the analysis of the test results. On the other hand, we did not want the test groups to be overly large as the returns in terms of the accuracy of the test results could be diminishing as the test group size grew.

The evaluation process consisted of the following three tests:

- First test: Test HumanE without learning approach
- Second test: Test HumanE with learning approach without initial policy
- Third test: Test HumanE with learning approach with initial policy

We assigned fifty different testers to each test. We could not repeat the three tests for the same group of testers as they might be influenced by the earlier test data. To obtain consistent feedbacks from the three groups of testers, we gave the testers some guidelines to follow when giving answers.

For example during the measurement of the "ease of use" and "performance" metrics, we instructed the testers to give their answers based on the following definitions:

| **Scale** | **Number of times a tester requests for help or asks questions on the use of HumanE** |
|---|---|
| Very Bad | >10 |
| Bad | 10 – 8 |
| Neutral | 7 – 6 |
| Good | 5 – 3 |
| Excellent | 2 – 0 |

Table 1. Scale definitions for "ease of use" metric

| **Scale** | **Time taken to return match-ing apartments (sec)** |
|---|---|
| Very Bad | >60 |
| Bad | 60 – 30 |
| Neutral | 29 – 21 |
| Good | 20 – 11 |
| Excellent | 10 – 0 |

Table 2. Scale definitions for "performance" metric

Before the actual evaluation took place, we gave the testers a quick introduction on how to use HumanE. To ensure the objectiveness of the testers' assessments, we chose not to be directly involved throughout the evaluation process (except the scalability test). Instead, a test coordinator with adequate knowledge of HumanE was asked to conduct the experiment.

Typically, the main method to show that a variable affects the outcome is to hold all other variables constant while changing only that variable. Preferably the experiment should be conducted in such a way that the users do not know the state of the variable so that they are unable to help the result even if they want to. Thus to ensure the accuracy of the test results, an identical interface was used to test HumanE 1) without, 2) with the learning approach (excludes initial policy) and 3) with the learning approach (includes initial policy) while the user was not informed of whether HumanE was learning or not.

The objective of each test is to allow the tester to arrive at a satisfactory profile. Each tester was asked to select his or her desired apartments using HumanE's web interface. The test was considered completed when the user declared that he or she was satisfied with the list of desired apartments stored in the "favourites" list. Subsequently, the user was allowed to keep the profile created by printing out a hard copy of the "favourites" list. In each of the three tests, the user was not told whether HumanE was used in helping him or her develop the profile.

The user went through the entire profile creation process without much intervention from the test coordinator. The only assistance that was provided by the test coordinator was to clarify some questions asked by a few users pertaining to navigation and program operation.

At the end of each test, the values of the five metrics were recorded. For the "ease of use" and "performance" metrics, each tester was asked to rate them from a scale of one to five (i.e. 1: Very Bad, 2: Bad, 3: Neutral, 4: Good, 5: Excellent) for the three tests. For each test, the values for the "time taken to create a profile" and "number of profile changes" metrics were recorded and computed by HumanE. Since HumanE recorded the login time and logoff time for each tester, HumanE was able to compute the value for the "time taken to create a profile" metric by subtracting the logoff time from the login time. And because every profile modification was recorded, HumanE was able to provide the value of the "number of profile changes" metric for each tester.

## 4.3 Experimental Results

The results from the experiments conducted are tabulated in the following figures:

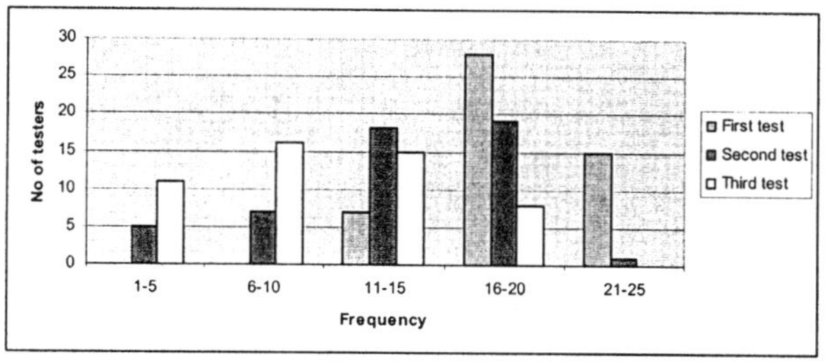


Figure 3. Test result summary for "number of profile changes" metric

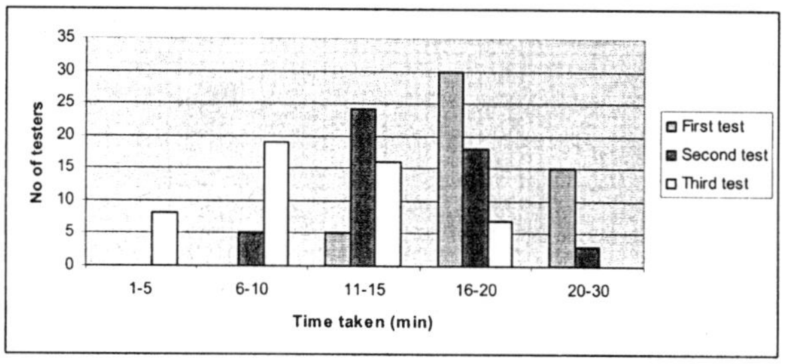


Figure 4. Test result summary for "time taken to create a profile" metric

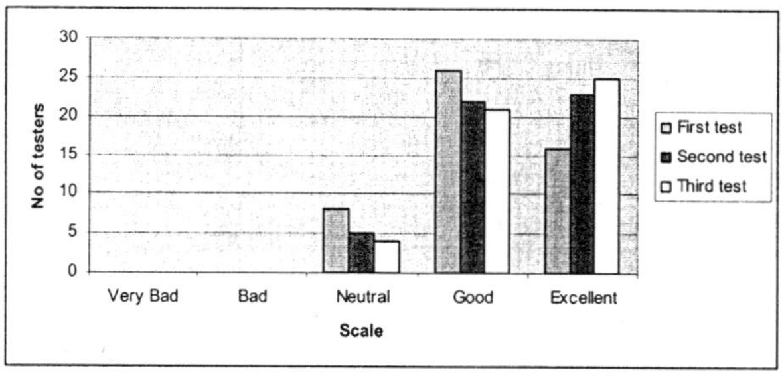


Figure 5. Test result summary for "ease of use" metric

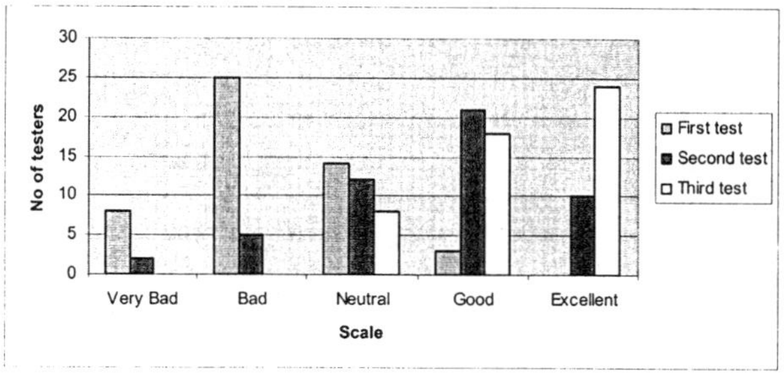


Figure 6. Test result summary for "performance" metric

## 4.4 Discussion

The test results for the first test for the "number of profile changes" metric showed that most testers took eleven to twenty-five profile changes before converging on a satisfactory profile. The test results for the second test for the "number of profile changes" metric showed some improvement as most testers took eleven to twenty searches. The test results for the third test for the "number of searches" metric showed further improvement as most testers took one to fifteen searches. Thus, it is evident that testers tend to make less number of profile changes with HumanE's assistance and even lesser number when HumanE becomes more intelligent with the supply of the initial policy.

Similarly, the time taken to create a satisfactory profile decreased as we introduced a more intelligent HumanE with each test. The test results for the first test for the "time taken to create a profile" metric showed that most testers took sixteen to thirty minutes while most testers in the second test took less time i.e. from eleven to twenty minutes. However, the testers from the third test took the least time as most of them spent six to fifteen minutes. Thus, it is clear that HumanE can reduce the time taken by users when creating and refining their profiles.

The test results for the three tests for the "ease of use" metric are quite similar indicating that almost all of the testers are happy with using HumanE regardless of whether the learning system with or without the initial policy was present or not. Hence, it is safe to say that using HumanE can result in increased customer satisfaction during the apartment selection process.

The test results for the "performance" metric for the first test apparently showed that majority of the testers were not satisfied with the average quality of the "recommended apartments" shown to them for selection and the average response time taken to display an apartment listing. Quite a number of them perceived HumanE as a search engine for apartment listings and they were not satisfied with the perceived browsing metaphor which is offered by typical search engines. Even though many testers were fairly happy that they were given complete control over the entire profile creation process, they also voiced out their displeasure of having to make many tedious profile changes before converging on a good profile. On the other hand, the test results for the second test and the third test showed that the majority of testers preferred to use HumanE to assist them during the apartment selection process. Obviously, the use of HumanE can increase customer satisfaction.

In summary, the experimental results showed that the use of HumanE for complex multidimensional domains such as real estate can result in higher customer satisfaction as it can learn faster via a supplied initial policy and is able to elicit trust from users through its user-friendly interface, quality recommendations and excellent performance.

# 5. FUTURE WORK

The development of HumanE will continue to evolve particularly in a different domain i.e. vacation plans. In future versions of HumanE, we would like to incorporate some of the following features to improve its usefulness.

- Refine the initial policy refining algorithm based on the results obtained using more sophisticated data mining tools.
- The ability to ask the user questions in natural language, allow the user to enter the response in natural language, and finally understand the response obtained for profile refinement.
- The ability to seek advice from users with similar profiles via email, interpret the reply so as to refine the profile.
- The ability to submit user profile to multiple domain-specific web sites, and show the user the results online. The agent will also need to parse and understand the listing obtained for profile refinement.

## 6. CONCLUSION

HumanE addresses the problem of poor learning when implementing online implementation of large-scale autonomous agent-based recommender systems for several complex domains through the use of a supplied initial policy which allows it to make more "knowledgeable" exploratory recommendations.

We feel that existing implementations of interactive learning method for online systems are simply impractical as the state-action space is simply too large for the agent to explore within its lifetime. This is further exacerbated by the short attention time-span of typical online users.

It seems easier and more intuitive for the application developer to specify what the agent should be doing and to let it learn the fine details of how to do it. The key strength of our approach is that, by incorporating an initial policy or prior knowledge, HumanE is able to provide better recommendations within a shorter time span.

This is because the initial policy has generated some experiences or knowledge about the real estate domain which HumanE can use throughout the interactive learning process. No longer does the user need to face an agent that does not know anything about the task to be completed. We believe that this approach is far more practical and effective than current implementations [1, 4, 5, 11].

We also postulate, contrary to the experimental results obtained from past research [16], that a good initial policy is critical to the success of HumanE from a reward perspective as the user usually takes less time to build a good profile. Good initial policies head directly for the goal state and they typically do not expose much of the state-space, since their trajectories through it are much more directed. This behavior is actually quite desirable as most online users generally have little patience and want to see a good profile built quickly.

Finally, transferring the work done here to another different domain such as vacation plans, insurance, mutual funds, and mortgages would not require a rocket scientist. The main requirement would be to find a domain expert who would be able to identify the key features of the complex objects in the domain. Creating an initial policy would require the identification of "good" and "bad" features and the classification of features into loosely connected groups.

## 7. REFERENCES


[1] Brooks, R.A. (1986), A robust layered control system for a mobile robot. IEEE Journal of Robotics and Automation 2:14-23.

[2] Burke, D., Hammond, K. J., and Young, B. C. (1997). "The FindMe Approach to Assisted Browsing," IEEE Expert, pp. 32-40, July-August 1997.

[3] Burke, D., Hammond, K. J., and Young, B. C. (1997). "The FindMe Approach to Assisted Browsing," IEEE Expert, pp. 32-40, July-August 1997.

[4] Franklin, Stan and Graesser, Art: Is it an Agent, or just a Program? A Taxonomy for Autonomous Agents, Proceedings of the Third International Workshop on Agent Theories, Architectures, and Languages, Springer-Verlag, 1996.

[5] Decision Support Systems and Intelligent Systems, Efraim Turban and Jay E. Aronson. Copyright 1998, Prentice Hall, Upper Saddle River, NJ.

[6] Evaluating Websites URL: http://trochim.human.cornell.edu/WebEval/webeval.htm

[7] Gao X., Sterling L. (1998). Classified Advertisement Search Agent (CASA): a knowledge-based information agent for searching semi-structured text. Proceedings of the Third International Conference on the Practical Application of Intelligent Agents and Multi-Agent Technology, pp. 621-624.

[8] K. Kraemer (ed.), The Information Systems Research Challenge: Survey Research Methods, K. Kraemer (ed.), Boston: Harvard Business School, 1991, pp 299-315.

[9] Newsted, P. R., W. Chin, O. Ngwenyama, and A. Lee, "Resolved: Surveys have Outlived their Usefulness in IS Research," Panel presented at the 1996 International Conference on Information Systems, December 17, 1997 ,Cleveland, Ohio.

[10] Pinsonneault, A. & K. Kraemer, "Survey research methodology in management information systems," Journal of Management Information Systems, Fall, 1993, pp 75-105.

[11] Schneiderman, B., Direct Manipulation: A Step Beyond Programming Languages, IEEE Computer, Vol. 16, No. 8, pp. 57-69, 1983.

[12] Shearin, S. and Lieberman, H. Intelligent Profiling by Example, in Proceedings of Conference on Intelligent User Interfaces, ACM Press, 2001.

[13] Singapore-Real-Estate URL: http://www.singapore-real-estate.com/

[14] SingaporeResidentialProperties URL: http://www.singapore residentialproperties .com/

[15] SurfJet Agent URL: http:// www.leptonicsystems.com/surfjet/

[16] William D. Smart and Leslie Pack Kaelbling, "Effective Reinforcement Learning for Mobile Robots," Proceedings of the IEEE International Conference on Robotics and Automation, 2002.

# Ergonomics Analysis for Vehicle Assembly Using Artificial Intelligence

**Nestor Rychtyckyj**

Ford Motor Company
Manufacturing Engineering Systems
Rouge Office Building
Dearborn, MI 48121
nrychtyc@ford.com

### Abstract

In this paper we discuss a deployed application at Ford Motor Company that utilizes AI technology for the analysis of potential ergonomic concerns at our assembly plants. The manufacture of motor vehicles is a complex and dynamic problem and the costs related to workplace injuries and lost productivity due to bad ergonomic design can be very significant. We have developed two separate ergonomic analysis systems that have been integrated into the process planning for manufacturing system at Ford known as the Global Study and Process Allocation System (GSPAS). GSPAS has become the global repository for standardized engineering processes and data for assembling all Ford vehicles, including parts, tools and standard labor time. One of the more significant benefits of GSPAS is the use of a controlled language, known as Standard Language, which is used throughout Ford to write the process assembly instructions. AI is already used within GSPAS for Standard Language validation and direct labor management. The work described here shows how we built upon our previous success with AI to expand the technology into the new domain of ergonomics analysis.

## Introduction

At the 6[th] Annual Applied Ergonomics Conference held in Dallas, TX in March of 2003, the Institute of Industrial Engineers (IIE) awarded the "Ergo Cup" in Training & Education to Ford Motor Company for the GSPAS Ergonomics Application (Ergo Solutions 2003). Ford Motor Company has been utilizing an integrated process planning system since 1990 to standardize the process sheet writing, create work allocations for the plant floor and to estimate labor time accurately. This system, formerly known as the Direct Labor Management System (DLMS) (Rychtyckyj 1999) is a knowledge-based system that utilizes a semantic network knowledge representation scheme. DLMS utilizes techniques from natural language processing, description logics and classification-based reasoning to generate detailed plant floor assembly instructions from high-level process descriptions. This system also provides detailed estimates of the labor content that is required from these process descriptions. Techniques such as machine translation and evolutionary computation were integrated into DLMS to support knowledge base maintenance and to deploy DLMS to Ford's assembly plants that do not use English as their main language.

The process sheet is the primary vehicle for conveying vehicle assembly information from the central engineering functions to the assembly plants. It contains specific information about work instructions and describes the parts and tools required for the build process. The work that is required to build the vehicle according to the process sheet instructions is then be allocated among the available personnel. Work allocation requires a precise means of measuring the labor time that is needed for any particular task. The DLMS system interprets these instructions and generates a list of detailed actions that are required to implement these instructions at the assembly plant level. These work instructions, known as "allocatable elements", are associated with MODAPTS (MODular Arrangement of Predetermined Time Standards) codes that are used to calculate the time required to perform these actions. MODAPTS codes are widely utilized as a means of measuring the body movements that are required to perform a physical action and have been accepted as a valid work measurement system (Carey et al. 2001). For example, the MODAPTS code for moving a small object with only a hand is M2; utilizing the arm gives a code of M3. The MODAPTS codes are then combined to describe an entire sequence of actions. MODAPTS codes are then converted into an equivalent time required to perform that action.

Subsequently the ergonomics engineers would manually inspect the process sheets for possible ergonomic problems. Since there may be 1000 or more process sheets for every single type of vehicle that Ford manufactures, this manual type of inspection was very labor intensive and time-consuming. An ergonomics engineer would spend upwards of two weeks in manually inspecting each process build instruction for a vehicle.

In an effort to streamline this process we developed a system that would automate the inspection of process sheets for ergonomics concerns. This work resulted in the development of an artificial intelligence system for ergonomic analysis within GSPAS that checks for two types of potential ergonomics issues: "red" and "warning". Process sheets that are flagged as "red" will not be sent to the assembly plants until those errors are corrected. Process sheets that are flagged with "warning" messages are released to the assembly plants; however, the ergonomic specialists have the opportunity to check and approve these issues through the use of a system that was built specifically for this application.

The Ergonomics system was developed and deployed to production in April of 2002. Since that time, more than 1100 process sheets with ergonomics problems were stopped by the AI system from going into production at the assembly plants. This has already resulted in a savings of over $17,000,000 in injury cost avoidance as the high risk processes never made it to the plant floor. These calculations are based on the type of injuries prevented and the direct cost associated per injury for each type of ergonomic problem.

In this paper, we discuss how artificial intelligence technology was used to prevent potential ergonomic problems at our assembly plants with significant benefits in reducing workplace injuries and time lost by workers. Section 2 discusses the problem of ergonomics analysis for manufacturing. Section 3 provides a detailed description of the ergonomics analysis that is being performed by the system. We discuss the application of AI technology in Section 4. An analysis of the benefits provided by our system is given in section 5. The application deployment and maintenance is discussed in Section 6.

## Problem Description

The proactive Ergonomics group within Vehicle Operations at Ford Motor Company is responsible for the launch of all future vehicles with ergonomically correct assembly. This team starts working as early as four years before the vehicle is launched to develop standardized ergonomic strategies for vehicle assembly and design. This work includes checking the process build instructions for every vehicle for potential ergonomic issues. A complete ergonomics analysis would include the following:

- Check the assembly work instruction to determine what type of physical action is being described: (ex. LOAD, POSITION, OBTAIN) and what the frequency of the work is.
- Check the assembly work instruction to determine what object is being manipulated (ex. BRACKET ASSEMBLY INNER)
- Check the assembly work instruction in Standard Language to determine what parts and tools are needed for this operation.
- Check the associated parts and determine what part is being used and the weight of that part.
- Check the associated tools and determine the properties of the tool to see how it impacts the operation.

The manufacturing build instructions are written in Standard Language, which is a "controlled language" that was developed specifically at Ford. Standard Language has been in use at Ford since the early 1990s and is used worldwide by Ford engineers to describe the assembly process for virtually all vehicle programs. A controlled language defines a set of explicit restrictions and constraints on the grammar, lexicon and style of the document being produced. The major aim of these constraints is to reduce the ambiguity, redundancy, size and complexity of the language that is being written. A specific type of verb, known as a Standard Language verb, was used as the basis of Standard Language usage. Each Standard Language verb (we currently have 134) was carefully defined to represent a specific action and was used as the main driver for a Standard Language element or sentence. Only one Standard Language verb is valid per element and the resulting actions from a process instruction are based on the interaction between the verb, the object, any modifiers and the tools and parts that are used in the element. The ergonomics engineers identified those verbs that are associated with potential risk factors (force, frequency and posture). Thresholds were assigned to each trigger verb to assess the level of risk based in part on the force and frequency associated with the element. A sample of a process sheet is given in Figure 1.

**Process Sheet Written in Standard Language**
TITLE: ASSEMBLE IMMERSION HEATER TO ENGINE
10 OBTAIN ENGINE BLOCK HEATER ASSEMBLY FROM STOCK
20 LOOSEN HEATER ASSEMBLY TURNSCREW USING POWER TOOL
30 APPLY GREASE TO RUBBER O-RING AND CORE OPENING
40 INSERT HEATER ASSEMBLY INTO RIGHT REAR CORE PLUG HOSE
50 ALIGN SCREW HEAD TO TOP OF HEATER
TOOL 20 1 P AAPTCA TSEQ RT ANGLE NUTRUNNER
TOOL 30 1 C COMM TSEQ GREASE BRUSH
PART 10 1 01 7499 01 S-011201 B ENGINE BLK HEATER ASSY

Figure 1: Sample GSPAS Process Sheet

In this example, the ergonomics engineer would need to determine if this process sheet has any potential ergonomics concerns. In element 10 the engineer determined that the OBTAIN operation requires an operator to get a "engine block heater assembly" part from the part bin and walk back to his station. This could potentially cause a concern if the part weighed above a certain threshold; therefore the engineer would need to look up the weight of the part. If the part weighed more than a certain threshold (in this case 35 pounds) the engineer would also need to check if a "lift assist" type tool was assigned to this element. If there were no lift assist tool assigned, the engineer would flag this job as having an ergonomic concern due to the excessive weight that the operator would need to carry.

As stated previously, this type of manual analysis was unfeasible due to the sheer volume of data that needed to be analyzed. Potential ergonomics problems that were not flagged before they reached the assembly plant floor would need to be fixed at the plant and this would entail additional delay and expense. Therefore, our challenge in this project was to develop an automated method that could flag potential ergonomics concerns before they reached the assembly plant.

## Ergonomics Analysis for Manufacturing

All of the manufacturing process sheet information at Ford is already processed through an AI-based system; therefore we already have a description-logics based knowledge base, an inference engine and a rule base in place. The ergonomic engineers at Ford Motor Company provided us with the details and description of what type of concerns needed be identified and this knowledge was added to the GSPAS knowledge base. The structure of the knowledge included both rules and concepts that provided specific details about potential ergonomics concerns.

Ergonomic analysis of process sheets in Standard Language is done at two different levels. The artificial intelligence system in GSPAS checks each process sheet for elements that violate certain "red" ergonomic conditions as identified by the ergonomics engineers. Any such violation requires the process engineer to rewrite the element(s) that have Ergonomics errors and resubmit the sheet for AI validation. The process sheet does not validate correctly and cannot be released to the assembly plant until all of the ergonomics errors are corrected.

There are three classes of ergonomics errors that the AI system checks for: frequency errors, tooling torque violations and heavy part violations. A frequency violation is triggered when the element describes repetitive actions for a particular operation that exceed a predetermined threshold. The "ergonomics frequency" error is based on the Standard Language verb that is used in the element and the number of times that a particular operation needs to be done. The information about each verb and its associated frequency condition is stored in the knowledge base and can be easily updated. For example, the following element will trigger an ergonomics error.

```
HANDSTART 10 BOLTS will return an error:
The number of times <TEN> verb <HANDSTART>
is performed exceeds the ergonomic limit
<8>.
```

The processor must rewrite this element so that the number of bolts is changed from 10 to 8 or less and then revalidate the process sheet. This will usually require that the element be split into two or more separate elements that do not violate this ergonomics condition. Splitting the offending element into two separate elements (each containing 5 "Hand-start" operations) does not change the amount of work that needs to be done. However, since the work is now split up it will probably be assigned to two separate operators.

A tool torque violation is triggered when a power tool with a torque above a certain threshold is assigned to an element using a particular Standard Language verb and a tool to mitigate the additional torque is not assigned to that element. The Ergonomics Analysis system reads and verifies that the tool assigned to the element belongs to the class of tools that can handle the high installation torque. This analysis is based on several factors: a comparison of the tool description, checking the tool description with the information that is available inside the AI knowledge base and checking the tool number.

A part weight violation is triggered when the operator is assigned a part that weighs more than a maximum weight and a lift assist is not assigned to that element. The processor must assign a lift assist tool to this element in order to validate it. The ergonomics analysis must consider several factors in determining if this element is in violation of the ergonomics constraints. First, the system must analyze the Standard Language sentence to determine what part description in the sentence is actually being lifted by the operator as a sentence may contain multiple parts. For example, the following Standard Language sentence contains three potential part descriptions:

```
LOAD THE FRONT BUMPER INTO STATION WITH
PALLET TRANSFER SYSTEM
```

The AI parser must recognize the fact that the "front bumper" is the only part that is actually being loaded and that the weight of the other two items is irrelevant. Each element in Standard Language has a number of parts assigned to it; these parts are loaded into GSPAS from the Worldwide Engineering Releasing System (WERS). Each part in WERS contains a prefix and suffix as well as a part description. There may be upwards of 100 parts and their various revisions assigned to a single Standard Language element. The ergonomics analysis system selects the most up-to-date part from the list of available parts and tries to match the WERS part description to the part description that is specified in Standard Language. This part matching is based on the following rules:

- Match the head noun in the Standard Language description with the same term in the part description from WERS. The "head noun" is the last and main noun in a sequence of terms. For example, the description "STATION WAGON LOAD FLOOR LOCK CYLINDER" has a head noun of "CYLINDER". This is the noun that is searched for in the WERS part description.

- Standard Language allows for the use of size adjectives that modify a part description at the end of the description. The term "front bumper large" signifies to the system that the process engineer needs to override the existing size of the "bumper assembly" with a "large" size. In this case, the head noun is "large" and the Ergo Analysis tool will ignore this size when finding the head noun search term. In this example, the head noun will be "bumper".
- The ergonomic analysis tool will also ignore generic terms such as "assembly", "front", and "rear" in determining what the head noun should be.
- The WERS part descriptions often contain extra punctuation & abbreviations that will cause the part matching to fail. The ergo analysis tool filters out the punctuation and special characters before making any comparisons. Abbreviations are checked against the GSPAS knowledge base, and substitutions are made before the comparison takes place. For example, the term "brkt" is converted to "bracket" before any comparisons are made.

Nevertheless, the matching of the part description from Standard Language with the part descriptions from WERS still misses some matches and potential ergonomics violations for lifting. These misses are caused by the ambiguity that is inherently present in natural language. The following list shows some of the cases where part matching still has problems and our proposed solutions:

- The part description in Standard Language and the part description in WERS refer to the same part, but they use a synonym rather than the exact part match. For example, "glass" & "windshield" may refer to the same part, but they do not use the same terminology. A straight comparison will not match these as describing the same part. Our solution to this is two-fold: we can make one term a synonym of the other as we already check for synonyms or we can modify our knowledge base so that both "glass" & "windshield" belong to the same class of parts and have the same properties.
- There is no direct correlation between the terms in Standard Language and WERS. We have analyzed all the terminology in WERS and have found that about 13% of these terms are not found in Standard Language. This list contains some misspellings as well as terms, acronyms and abbreviations that are not in Standard Language and will not match up properly. The correct terms will need to be added into Standard Language, and it may be necessary to use a spellchecker to correct the misspelled terms that can be fixed.
- We are currently just checking the head noun from Standard Language against the list of terms in the part description without doing any analysis on the part description itself. For example, the following Standard Language element "ROUTE THE WIRE THROUGH THE HARNESS" is matched up against the part description "PART WIRE HARNESS". In this case the part "WIRE" in Standard Language matches up with the term "WIRE" in the part description even though they don't represent the same part. We will need to parse the WERS part descriptions in order to analyze the phrase and find the appropriate head noun for comparison. This will require us to add additional Standard Language terminology and modify the parser to handle the types of phrases that are used in the WERS part descriptions.

## Ergonomics "WARNING" Processing

The ergonomics "red" conditions that were discussed in the previous section prevent the process instructions from being released to the assembly plants. We also developed a system to check for ergonomic conditions of less severity that are known as "warning" messages. A process sheet that has "warnings" can get released to the assembly plant; however, the warning messages are reviewed by the ergonomics engineers and either approved as being acceptable or flagged as "requiring action". Those that require action will be sent back to the process engineers for correction.

There are also three classes of ergonomics warnings that the AI System checks for: frequency warnings, force warnings and "always flagged" warnings. These warning conditions differ from the error conditions in the thresholds that are assigned to trigger each condition. For example, a frequency violation may trigger a warning at a level of 6, but an error is not triggered until it reaches a level of 12.

A frequency warning is triggered when the element describes repetitive actions for a particular operation that exceed a predetermined threshold. The "ergonomics frequency" warning is based on the Standard Language verb that is used in the element and the number of times that a particular operation needs to be done. A force warning is triggered when the operator is assigned a part that weights more than a maximum weight and a lift assist is not assigned to that element.

An "always flagged" warning is triggered whenever a particular Standard Language verb is used, regardless of the tools or parts that are assigned to this element. In Standard Language a verb may be defined in terms of another verb; for example, the POSITION verb also includes a GRASP in it. Therefore trying to position a part that weighs more then 10 pounds will also trigger an ergonomics warning because the part must be grasped before it can be positioned.

## Uses of AI Technology

The ergonomics analysis tool in use at Ford makes use of the following AI technologies: description logics, natural language processing and rule-based processing. The heart of our AI system is the knowledge base that utilizes a semantic network model to represent all of the automobile assembly planning information. The use of a semantic network as part of knowledge representation system is also known as "Description Logics". A Description Logic implementation known as CLASSIC has been successfully used at AT&T to develop telecommunication equipment configurators (McGuiness and Patel-Schneider 1998). The DLMS implementation of Description Logic is based on the KL-ONE knowledge representation language (Brachman & Schmolze 1985). There are over 10,000 concepts represented and each concept may have up to 45 properties or attributes depending on the context of the object being represented. This knowledge base contains information about the parts, tools, ergonomics triggers, work descriptions and all the other knowledge that is relevant to building a car at Ford. Description logics enable us to maintain and modify the knowledge base despite the dynamic changes that are present in the automobile industry. In an average year about 8% of our knowledge base is updated in order to keep current with changes in the manufacturing processes.

Natural language processing techniques are integrated with the knowledge base to represent the technical language of manufacturing process planning in the automobile industry. As discussed in the previous section, we need to be able to match part descriptions that are have multiple written representations, but represent one single part. This includes dealing with acronyms, synonyms, abbreviations, misspellings, misplaced punctuation and other problems inherent in natural language. The rule-based component of our application consists of modeling the knowledge about potential ergonomics concerns into rules and interact with the knowledge base.

We have found that the combination of using a controlled language, such as Standard Language, in conjunction with a description logics based knowledge structure has allowed us to maintain the knowledge base without requiring any wholesale rewriting of rules. This basic architecture has been proven to be an excellent choice for the long-term maintenance of knowledge bases that represent a very dynamic problem domain such as auto manufacturing (Rychtyckyj and Reynolds 2000).

## Application Use and Payoff

The ergonomics analysis tool has been deployed at Ford for approximately two years. The impact of this system can be summarized as follows:

- The automation of the ergonomics "red" processing stopped over 1100 process sheets with potential ergonomics problems from reaching the assembly plants.
- The automation of the ergonomics "warning" processing reduced the workload of the ergonomics engineers by 20% due to the fact that they did not have to review as many potential concerns as before.
- The engineers that wrote the process sheets became aware of ergonomics concerns and started writing their process sheets to address these concerns before they were flagged by the system.
- Ergonomics is a vital concern to both Ford and the UAW. All of the process improvements that have been described in this paper, including the use of MODAPTS, Standard Language and ergonomics analysis have been supported by both management and the UAW.
- The use of ergonomics triggers for manufacturing assembly would not be limited to Ford Motor Company. Most manufacturing companies have their own systems for dealing with process build instructions and some utilize controlled languages for this task including Boeing (Wojcik, Halmback and Hoard 1998) and Caterpillar (Kamrath and Adolphson 1998).

The quantifiable benefits of the system include cost savings of over $17 million dollars in terms of avoiding injury costs associated with the "red" triggers as well as reducing the number of "warning" triggers that need to be manually inspected by 20%. However, the benefits of this application to Ford Motor Company are much more significant than those numbers. The avoidance of health and injury problems makes the workplace safer for our employees and improves the morale of our workforce. In addition, this system has convinced our ergonomics engineers that the application of AI can help make their job easier and improve their efficiency. The hardware and software was already in place and our main investment was the time spent by the developers and the ergonomics engineers. The benefits of this system, both quantifiable and indirect, were significantly higher than the development costs and this system has been a very successful industrial application of AI.

## Application Development and Deployment

The artificial intelligence development for our applications here at Ford Manufacturing Engineering Systems is based on the Hewlett-Packard UNIX (HP-UX) platform utilizing the Lispworks and Knowledgeworks tool from Xanalys Corporation (Xanalys 1998). We have found that this tool provides a flexible and powerful development environment while providing access to our

Oracle database through an SQL interface. In addition, this tool provides the capability to create a Graphical User Interface (GUI) through the CLIM (Common Lisp Interface Manager) package and easy communication to other systems and platforms. The integration of Lispworks and Knowledgeworks with our existing Oracle databases has been very successful in terms of throughput and accuracy. Our AI system makes thousands of database transactions every day and this is all accomplished with an average response time of about 8 seconds for each AI process sheet validation.

The development of the ergonomics analysis system for process validation took about 2 months with a team of 2 developers as well as additional time provided by the ergonomics specialists. We added the additional functionality and rules needed to represent the ergonomic analysis through a combination of KnowledgeWorks rules, LISP code, concepts and their associated properties into our knowledge base. The Ergonomic "hard" constraints (e.g. lifting thresholds, verbs to check, etc) are all contained in our knowledge base and can easily be modified. The AI system reads the required information from an Oracle database, does the required processing and writes the results back into the Oracle database.

Maintenance of this system is made much simpler by the use of a knowledge base that uses a Description Logics framework. Any changes that need to be made to the knowledge base can be quickly made through a graphical Knowledge Base Manager (KBM) and then migrated to the production environment. We have also developed a suite of regression tests that are run and validated before any changes are moved to production. In addition, the knowledge base contains built-in edit checking functionality that validates the entries that are being added to specific slots and attributes for different classes of concepts.

## Conclusions

In this paper we discussed two applications of ergonomics analysis that are being used at Ford. There is no question that ergonomics is a critical factor in manufacturing and needs to be addressed at the earliest point possible. Our ergonomics analysis tool has made it possible to analyze the assembly work before it reaches the assembly floor for potential ergonomics violations. This ergonomics analysis of process sheets identifies problem concerns in the area of frequency and repetitive issues, excessive tool torque and the lifting of heavy parts without some form of mechanized lift assists. In the future, we plan to increase the performance of the existing systems with additional part matching capabilities and expand the ergonomics analysis to catch other types of potential problems.

## Acknowledgements

I would like to thank the following people for their knowledge and expertise in developing this system: Allison Stephens, Brian Carroll, and David Adams. A special note of thanks is given to Mike Rosen for his work on this application. I would also like to thank Erica Klampfl and Samy Uthurusamy for their invaluable assistance in the preparation of this paper.

## References

Brachman, R., Schmolze, J. (1985), "An Overview of the KL-ONE Knowledge Representation System." *Cognitive Science* 9(2): 171-216.

Carey, Farrell, Hui, and Sullivan (2001), *Heyde's Modapts: A Language of Work.* Heyde Dynamics PTY LTD.

Ergo Solutions Magazine (2003), "Ford Motor Company Team Wins 2003 Ergo Cup Top Honors for Training & Education", May 2003 (www.ergosolutionsmag.com)

Kamrath, C., Adolphson, E., (1998), "Controlled Language for Multilingual Document Production: Experience with Caterpillar Technical English" in the *Proceedings of the Second International Workshop on Controlled Language Applications (CLAW 98),* May 21-22, 1998, Language Technologies Institute, Carnegie Mellon University, Pittsburgh, PA, pp. 51-61.

McGuiness, D. and Patel-Schneider, P. (1998). "Usability Issues in Knowledge Representations Systems", *Proceedings of the Fifteenth National Conference on Artificial Intelligence*, 608-614. Menlo Park, CA: AAAI Press.

Rychtyckyj, N., (1999), "DLMS: Ten Years of AI for Vehicle Assembly Process Planning", *AAAI-99/IAAI-99 Proceedings*, Orlando, FL, July 18-22, 1999, pp. 821-828, AAAI Press.

Rychtyckyj, N., and Reynolds, R., (2000), "Long-Term Maintenance of Deployed Knowledge Representation Systems", *Proceedings of the Seventh International Conference on the Principles of Knowledge Representation and Reasoning*, April 12-17, 2000, Breckenridge, CO, pp. 494-504, Morgan Kaufmann Publishers.

Wojcik, R., Holmback, H., Hoard, J.,(1998), "Being Technical English: An Extension of AECMA SE Beyond the Aircraft Maintenance", in *Proceedings of the Second International Workshop on Controlled Language Applications (CLAW 98),* May 21-22, 1998, Language Technologies Institute, Carnegie Mellon University, Pittsburgh, PA, pp. 114-123.

Xanalys Corporation, (1998), "LispWorks Reference Manual, version 4.1.

# Innovative Applications of Artificial Intelligence

## *Emerging Applications*

# The KOJAK Group Finder: Connecting the Dots via Integrated Knowledge-Based and Statistical Reasoning

**Jafar Adibi, Hans Chalupsky, Eric Melz and Andre Valente**

USC Information Sciences Institute
4676 Admiralty Way, Marina del Rey, CA 90292
Email: {adibi, hans, melz, valente}@isi.edu

### Abstract

Link discovery is a new challenge in data mining whose primary concerns are to identify strong links and discover hidden relationships among entities and organizations based on low-level, incomplete and noisy evidence data. To address this challenge, we are developing a hybrid link discovery system called KOJAK that combines state-of-the-art knowledge representation and reasoning (KR&R) technology with statistical clustering and analysis techniques from the area of data mining. In this paper we report on the architecture and technology of its first fully completed module called the KOJAK Group Finder. The Group Finder is capable of finding hidden groups and group members in large evidence databases. Our group finding approach addresses a variety of important LD challenges, such as being able to exploit heterogeneous and structurally rich evidence, handling the connectivity curse, noise and corruption as well as the capability to scale up to very large, realistic data sets. The first version of the KOJAK Group Finder has been successfully tested and evaluated on a variety of synthetic datasets.

## Introduction

The development of information technology that could aid law enforcement and intelligence organizations in their efforts to detect and prevent illegal and fraudulent activities as well as threats to national security has become an important topic for research and development. Since the amount of relevant information, tips, data and reports increases daily at a rapid pace, analyzing such data manually to its full potential has become impossible. Hence, new automated techniques are needed to take full advantage of all available information.

One of the central steps in supporting such analysis is link discovery (LD), which is a relatively new form of data mining. Link discovery can be viewed as the process of identifying complex, multi-relational patterns that indicate potentially illegal or threat activities in large amounts of data. More broadly, it also includes looking for not directly explainable connections that may indicate previously unknown but significant relationships such as new groups or capabilities (Senator, 2002) .



Link discovery presents a variety of difficult challenges. First, data ranges from highly unstructured sources such as reports, news stories, etc. to highly structured sources such as traditional relational databases. Unstructured sources need to be preprocessed first either manually or via natural language extraction methods before they can be used by LD methods. Second, data is complex, multi-relational and contains many mostly irrelevant connections (connectivity curse). Third, data is noisy, incomplete, corrupted and full of unaligned aliases. Finally, relevant data sources are heterogeneous, distributed and can be very high volume.

To address these challenges we are developing a hybrid link discovery system called KOJAK that combines state-of-the-art knowledge representation and reasoning (KR&R) technology with statistical techniques from the area of data mining. Using KR&R technology allows us to represent extracted evidence at very high fidelity, build and utilize high quality and reusable ontologies and domain theories, have a natural means to represent abstraction and meta-knowledge such as the interestingness of certain relations, and leverage sophisticated reasoning algorithms to uncover implicit semantic connections. Using data or knowledge mining technology allows us to uncover hidden relationships not explicitly represented in the data or findable by logical inference, for example, entities that seem to be strongly related based on statistical properties of their communication patterns.

The full KOJAK system contains a variety of experimental LD components such as an abductive, logic-based Pattern Finder to identify complex patterns of interest in the evidence and a Connection Finder to identify interesting and unusual entities and connections (Lin & Chalupsky 2003). In this paper we only report on the architecture and technology of its first fully completed module called the KOJAK Group Finder (GF). The Group Finder is capable of finding hidden groups and group members in large evidence databases. Our group finding approach addresses a variety of important LD challenges, such as being able to exploit heterogeneous and structurally rich evidence, handling the connectivity curse, noise and corruption as well as the capability to scale up to very large, realistic data sets. The first version of the KOJAK Group Finder has been successfully tested and evaluated on a variety of synthetic datasets.

## The Group Detection Problem

A major problem in the area of link discovery is the discovery of hidden organizational structure such as groups and their members. There are of course many organizations and groups visible and detectable in real world data, but we are usually only interested in detecting certain types of groups such as organized crime rings, terrorist groups, etc. Group detection can be further broken down into (1) discovering hidden members of *known groups* (or group extension) and (2) identifying completely *unknown groups*.

A known group (e.g., a terrorist group such as the RAF) is identified by a given *name* and a set of known members. The problem then is to discover potential additional hidden members of such a group given evidence of communication events, business transactions, familial relationships, etc. For unknown groups neither *name* nor known members are available. All we know are certain suspicious individuals ("bad guys") in the database and their connection to certain events of interest. The main task here is to identify additional suspicious individuals and cluster them appropriately to hypothesize new real-world groups, e.g., a new money laundering ring. While our techniques address both questions, we believe group extension to be the more common and important problem.

Another important problem characteristic that influenced our solution approach concerns the data. Evidence available to law enforcement organizations is split into *primary* and *secondary* sources. Primary evidence is lower volume, high reliability, usually "owned" by the organization and can be searched and processed in arbitrary ways. Secondary evidence is usually not owned by the organization (e.g., might come from news articles or the Web), is higher volume, might only be searchable in restricted ways and might be associated with a cost (e.g., access might require a warrant). Our group detection approach needs to take these different characteristics into account to keep cost at a minimum and properly handle access restrictions to secondary data sources.

## The KOJAK Group Finder

The KOJAK Group Finder is a hybrid logic-based/statistical LD component designed to solve group detection problems. It can answer the following questions:

- How likely is P a member of group G?
- How likely are P and Q members of the same group?
- How strongly connected are P and Q?

Figure 1 shows the general architecture. The system takes primary and secondary evidence (stored in relational databases) as input and produces group hypotheses (i.e., lists of group members) as output. The system works in four phases. First, a logic-based group seed generator analyzes the primary evidence and outputs a set of seed groups using deductive and abductive reasoning over a set of domain patterns and constraints. Second, an information-theoretic mutual information model finds likely new candidates for each group, producing an extended group. Third, the mutual information model is used to rank these likely members by how strongly connected they are to the seed members. Fourth, the ranked extended group is pruned using a threshold to produce the final output.

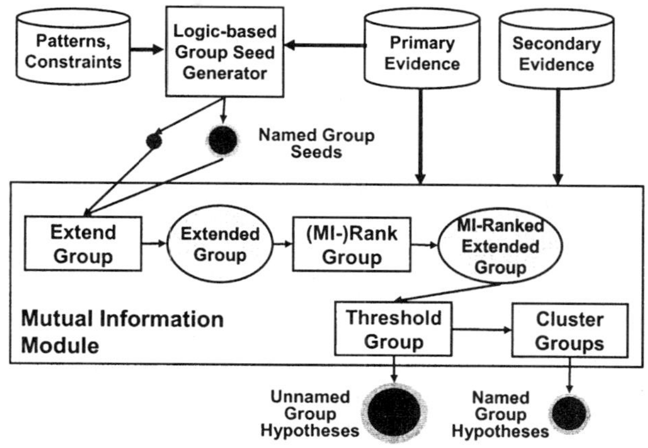


**Figure 1: KOJAK Group Finder Architecture.**

The processing for known and unknown groups is somewhat different at the beginning and end of the process. First, the seed generation for unknown groups is different, since there is less information available. Second, the generation of unknown groups involves an extra step because the extended groups need to be clustered to eliminate duplicates before the thresholding step.

The logic-based seed generation module is based upon the PowerLoom™ knowledge representation & reasoning system (PowerLoom, 2003). The mutual information module was implemented in the Matlab programming language. The modules are integrated by combining the C++ translation of PowerLoom and the C translation of the Matlab modules into a single program. Evidence databases are stored in MySQL and accessed from both Matlab and PowerLoom via ODBC. The primary and secondary evidence databases uses a very general evidence schema developed as part of DARPA's Evidence Extraction and Link Discovery (EELD) program (Senator, 2002) which should make it easy to transition to different domains.

### The Need for a Hybrid Approach

Link discovery is a very challenging problem. It requires the successful exploitation of complex evidence that comes in many different types, is fragmented, incomplete, uncertain and very large-scale. LD requires reasoning with abstractions, e.g., that **brother-of** and **husband-of** are both subtypes of a **family-relation**, temporal and spatial reasoning, e.g., that cities are subregions of counties which are subregions of states, etc., common-sense type inferences, e.g., that if two people bought tickets for the same event, they probably were at one point in close spatial proximity in the same city, and constrained search, e.g., one might want to look more closely at people who joined a company around the same time a suspect joined. The knowledge and ontologies needed for these types of inferences are very naturally modeled in a symbolic, logic-based approach as done in the logic-based seed generator of the KOJAK Group Finder. However, LD also needs detection and reasoning with statistical phenomena such as communication patterns, behavior similarity, etc., which requires cumulative analysis of evidence that cannot be done in logic but is most effectively done in specialized models such as our mutual information component. Such models, on the other hand, are not well-suited for the representation of complex domains and usually assume some data normalization and simplification. Given these characteristics of the problem, using a hybrid approach that combines the strengths of multiple paradigms is a natural choice. How these two approaches work together for the KOJAK Group Finder is described below.

## Logic-Based Seed Generation

The first phase of the KOJAK group detection process is the generation of seed groups. Each seed group is intended to be a good hypothesis for one of the actual groups in the evidence data, even though the number of seed members known or inferable for it might be significantly less than its actual members. The reasons for using this logic-based, seeded approach are threefold. First, the information in primary and secondary evidence is incomplete and fragmented. By "connecting the dots" via logical inference we can extract information that is not explicitly stated and our statistical methods would not be able to infer. Second, because the MI model needs to analyze access-restricted secondary data, it needs good initial focus such as seed groups of "bad guys" in order to query the data selectively. The seeded approach therefore dramatically reduces data access cost as well as MI-processing time. Third, logical reasoning can apply constraints to the information available as well as rule out or merge certain group hypotheses.

To generate seed groups we use the PowerLoom KR&R system to scrub every piece of available membership information from primary evidence (which is smaller volume, less noisy and can be searched arbitrarily). Given the size of primary evidence data we are working with (O(10,000) individuals and O(100,000) assertions) we can simply load it directly from the EDB into PowerLoom using its database interface and a set of import axioms.

The process of finding seeds is different for known and unknown groups. For known groups, we start with a query to retrieve existing groups and their explicitly declared members. We then employ a number of logic rules to infer additional group members by connecting data that is available but disconnected. For example, in the synthetic datasets available to us members of threat groups participate in exploitation cases (meant to model threat events such as a terrorist attack). To find additional members of a group we can look for exploitations performed by a group that have additional participants not explicitly known to be members of the group. The PowerLoom definition below for the relation memberAgentsByParticipation formalizes this type of reasoning (memberAgents relates a group and its members; deliberateActors relates groups or people to an event):

```
(DEFRELATION memberAgentsByParticipation ((?g Group) (?p Person))
  :<= (AND (Group ?g)
           (Person ?p)
           (FAIL (memberAgents ?g ?p))
           (EXISTS (?c) (AND (ExploitationCase ?c)
                             (deliberateActors ?c ?g)
                             (deliberateActors ?c ?p)))))
```

For unknown groups, we use rules to look for patterns on events to find seeds. The basic idea is to find teams participating in threat events that no (known) group is known to be responsible for. Since people who participate in a threat event are part of a threat group, teams of people who are found to jointly participate in a threat event that cannot be attributed to a known group can be used as seeds for unknown groups. Note, however, that such teams may be subsets of one of the known groups or that two or more of the teams may be part of the same unknown group. For that reason, it is vital to use merging techniques later to combine teams (or their extended groups) if appropriate.

The logic module can also check constraints to help in the merging of hypotheses. For example, a strong hint that two groups may be the same is that their members participated in the same exploitation events. The rule below finds groups who participated in a given exploitation event indicating a potential duplicate group hypothesis if more than one group is found:

```
(DEFRELATION groupHasMemberWhoParticipatedInEvent
                ((?g Group) (?e VulnerabilityExploitationCase))
  :<= (AND (Group ?g) (VulnerabilityExploitationCase ?e)
           (EXISTS ?p (AND (Person ?p)
                           (OR (memberAgents ?g ?p)
                               (memberAgentsByParticipation ?g ?p))
                           (deliberateActors ?e ?p)))))
```

The use of memberAgentsByParticipation shows that these rules not only encode complex queries but also interconnect to build a real domain model. There are about 50 complex rules of this type that are specific to group discovery. Even though the synthetic dataset used in our experiments was designed to be relatively poor in link types and attributes, the data is still quite complex. It contains 72 entity types (22 of which are actually instantiated) and 107 relations and attributes (25 of which are actually instantiated in the data). These entity and relation types are further organized by an ontology (developed by Cycorp) whose upward closure from the entity and relation types in the data contains a hierarchy of about 620 concepts (or classes) and 160 relations. Adding this to the O(100,000) assertions representing the evidence we have a fairly large and complex knowledge base to work with.

While the examples given above are specific to the synthetic group discovery domain, the approach is general and applicable to other areas. Evidence data will always be fragmented. Such fragmentation is usually easy to handle by a human analyst, but it can be a big obstacle for an automated system. Using a logic-based model of the domain is a very powerful approach to overcome this problem and connect evidence fragments in useful ways.

## Finding Strong Connections Via a Mutual Information Model

After exploiting the various explicit and implicit evidence fragments given in the EDB to generate a seed group, we try to identify additional members by looking for people that are strongly connected with one or more of the seed members. To find two strongly connected entities, we need to aggregate the many other known links between them and statistically contrast those with connections to other entities or the general population. This cannot be done via a logic-based approach and instead is achieved via an information-theoretic mutual information model.

The mutual information model can identify entities strongly connected to a given entity or a set of entities and provide a ranked list based on connection strength. To do this it exploits data such as individuals sharing the same property (e.g., having the same address) or being involved in the same action (e.g., sending email to each other). Since such information is usually recorded by an observer we refer to it as evidence. Time is often also an important element of evidence and is also recorded in the EDB. Without loss of generality we only focus on individuals' actions in this paper, but not on their properties.

We transform the problem space into a graph in which each node represents an entity (such as a person) and each link between two entities represents the set of actions (e.g., emails, phone calls etc.) they are involved in. For each node we represent the set of its actions with a random variable, which can take values form the set of all possible actions. Figure 2 illustrates this concept. There are four people and three possible actions: sending *Email*, making a *Phone Call* and participating in a *Meeting*. When a person is not involved in any of the above-mentioned actions we indicate that with the empty action φ. For example, we can represent $P_1$'s actions with the random variable $X_1$ which takes values from the set $\{E, P, M, \varphi\}$ at any given time.

Most individuals in the LD evidence space are connected to each other either directly or indirectly. For example, two people may eat at the same restaurant, drink coffee at the same cafe and take the same train to work every day without any strongly meaningful connection. On the other hand, three individuals may be strongly connected if they engage in atypical phone call patterns.

To address this problem we measure the *mutual information* (MI) between the random variables representing individuals' activities. MI is a measure of the dependence between two variables. If the two variables are independent, the MI between them is zero. If the two are strongly dependent, e.g., one is a function of another; the MI between them is large. We therefore believe that two individuals' mutual information is a good indicator whether they are in fact strongly connected to each other or not compared to the rest of the population.

There are other interpretations of MI, for example, as the stored information in one variable about another

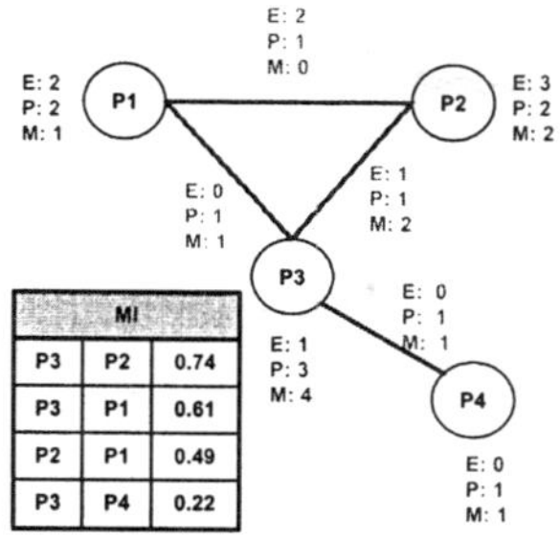


| MI | | |
|---|---|---|
| P3 | P2 | 0.74 |
| P3 | P1 | 0.61 |
| P2 | P1 | 0.49 |
| P3 | P4 | 0.22 |

| Time | Action | P1 | P2 | P3 | P4 |
|---|---|---|---|---|---|
| 1 | P1 Email P2 | E | E | Φ | Φ |
| 2 | P3 Phone Call P4 | Φ | Φ | P | P |
| 3 | P2 Meeting P3 | Φ | M | M | Φ |
| 4 | P1 Email P2 | E | E | Φ | Φ |
| 5 | P2 Email P3 | Φ | E | E | Φ |
| 6 | P1 Phone Call P3 | P | Φ | P | Φ |
| 7 | P1 Phone Call P2 | P | P | Φ | Φ |
| 8 | P2 Meeting P3 | Φ | M | M | Φ |
| 9 | P3 Meeting P4 | Φ | Φ | M | M |
| 10 | P1 Meeting P3 | M | Φ | M | Φ |
| 11 | P2 Phone Call P3 | Φ | P | P | Φ |

**Figure 2: MI Example. P1, P2, P3 and P4 represent people. E, P and M stand for *Email*, *Phone Call* and *Meeting* respectively. The table on the right shows activities among individuals and the table on the left shows the MI among them.**

variable or the degree of predictability of the second variable by knowing the first. Clearly, all these interpretations are related to the same notion of dependence and correlation. The *correlation function* is another frequently used quantity to measure dependence. The correlation function is usually measured as a function of distance or time delay between two quantities. It has been shown that MI measures the more general (non-linear) dependence while the correlation function measures linear dependence (Li, 1990). Therefore, MI is the more accurate choice to measure dependence. One of the important characteristics of MI is that it does not need actual variables values to be computed, instead it only depends on the distribution of the two variables. In classical information theory (Shannon, 1948) MI between two random variables $X$ and $Y$ is defined as:

$$MI(X;Y) = \sum_x P(x) \sum_y P(y \mid x) . \log\left( P(y \mid x) \Big/ \sum_x P(x)P(y \mid x) \right)$$

where $P(x)$ is the $Prob(X = x)$, $P(y)$ is the $Prob(Y = y)$ and $P(y \mid x)$ stands for $Prob(Y = y \mid X = x)$. In addition, $MI(X;Y) = H(Y) - H(Y|X) = H(X) - H(X|Y)$, where the conditional entropy $H(X|Y)$ measures the average uncertainty that remains about $X$ when $Y$ is known (see (Adibi et al. 2004) for more details about the MI model).

## Group Expansion via Mutual Information

Given that we can use the mutual information calculation to find strongly connected individuals, we can exploit this capability to expand the seed groups provided in phase 1 by the logic-based KR&R module. This expansion is done in the following steps:

(1) For each seed member in a seed group we retrieve all activities it participates in from primary and secondary data and add any new individuals found to the group. This step therefore expands the seed group graph by one level. Note, that we obey query restrictions for secondary data and only ask one focused query per seed member.

(2) Now we view the expanded group as the universe and compute MI for each connected pair in the graph.

(3) Next we look for individuals that either have high MI score with one of the seed members or with all seed

members when viewed as a single "super individual". Members whose score is below a certain (fairly lax) user-defined threshold are dropped from the list.

(4) In this step the MI engine repeats the whole procedure by expanding the expanded group from the previous step one more level and recalculates MI for the new graph. For known groups we stop here and pass the result to the final thresholding step.

(5) For unknown groups we usually have much smaller seed sets and therefore repeat the previous step one more time to achieve appropriately-sized group hypotheses.

The group expansion procedure is performed for each seed group generated by the KR&R module and generates an MI-ranked list of possible additional members for each seed group. This list is initially kept fairly inclusive and needs to undergo proper thresholding before it can be reported to a user or passed on to another LD component.

## Threshold Selection and Thresholding

The result of the process described above is a list of extended groups where members are ranked by their mutual information scores. In order to produce and report a definite result on which members we believe are actually part of the group, we need to cut the ordered list at some threshold. The problem is how to set the threshold so that we get "good" (or even "optimal") recall and precision for a particular application scenario. We used an empirical method that selects a threshold for a dataset based on an empirical analysis of a number of groups in different types of datasets. This method is discussed further in the section describing the experimental results. The good news is that (1) our group detection process generates a very selective ranking (i.e., we reach high recall fairly early) and (2) in real-world situations a good ranking is often more important than picking the best possible cutoff, since human analysts might be willing to accept a certain number of false positives in order to maximize the number of true positives they are after.

## Handling Noise Via a Noisy Channel model

So far we assumed that we are capable to observe all evidence accurately. However, such accuracy occurs rarely in real world databases. We therefore consider the following kinds of noise in the formulation of our model:

**Observability (Negative Noise):** This factor describes how much of the real data was observable. Not all relevant events that occur in the world will be observed or reported and might therefore not be known to LD components.

**Corruption:** This type of noise varies from typos to misspelled names all the way to intentional misinformation.

The negative noise phenomenon has been discussed extensively in the communication literature. We adopt the view of a classical noisy channel scenario where a sender transmits a piece of information to a receiver. The transmission goes through a channel with certain noise properties. In our domain we view the ground truth (GT) as the "sender" and the evidence database (EDB) as the "receiver". While in a noiseless environment information is recorded in the EDB without error, in a noisy environment we have a noisy channel, which may alter every piece of evidence transmitted through it with some small probability *p(noise)*. For instance, negative noise occurs if there is a phone call in the ground truth but no record of it in the EDB. Corruption occurs, for example, if there is no phone call in the ground truth but a record indicating one in the EDB. The MI framework is a natural fit for such model. Figure 3 illustrates a noisy channel for a given phone call.

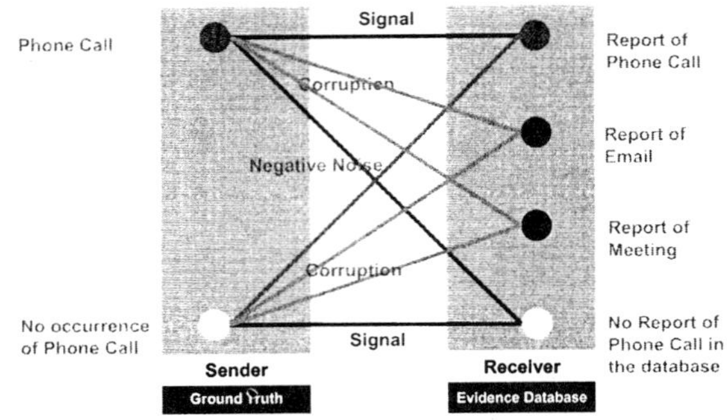


**Figure 3: Noise model for a given "Phone Call"**

## Complexity and Dataset Scale

Real-world evidence data sets can be very large and we have to make sure that our techniques scale appropriately. The largest synthetic datasets we have analyzed so far contained O(100,000) events and O(10,000) individuals. Running the KOJAK GF on such a dataset takes roughly 5 minutes for the logic-based seed generation and about 10-20 minutes to run the MI engine on a 2Ghz Pentium-IV desktop with 1Gb of RAM. Runtime for the MI engine varies depending on the overall connectivity of the data. While this is perfectly acceptable at the moment, we will eventually need to handle datasets that are at least two orders of magnitude larger, so let us look a bit closer at the architecture and algorithm complexity involved.

The complexity of the MI model is relatively low. The MI engine expands only a limited number of nodes in the problem space starting from the seed members of a group. How many individuals are considered depends on how deeply we grow the link graph to build an extended group. So far, one to two levels have been sufficient. Computing MI between two individuals is $O(N*M)$ where $N$ is the average number of people connected to a given individual and $M$ is the average number of links a person is involved in. Unless $N$ and $M$ grow significantly with larger datasets, the overall complexity is primarily dependent on the number of threat groups we are looking for.

To be able to handle such large datasets in the logic-based seed generation phase, we built a new database access layer into PowerLoom that allows us to easily and transparently map logic relations onto arbitrary database tables and views. By using these facilities we can keep smaller data portions such as the primary data in main memory for fast access and processing, while keeping potentially very large secondary data sets in an RDBMS from where we page in relevant portions on demand. Particular attention was paid to be able to offload large join processing to the RDBMS wherever possible to avoid doing it inefficiently tuple-by-tuple in PowerLoom. This gives us an architecture where we use a traditional RDBMS for storage and access to very large datasets but enrich it with a deductive layer that allows us to formulate more complex queries where necessary. The complexity of the resulting system depends heavily on the nature of the queries and domain rules used which so far has proven to be manageable. For example, the current system uses an ontology with about 800 concept and relation definitions and about 50 complex, non-taxonomic rules that link evidence fragments without any performance problems.

## Experimental Set-Up

We have applied the KOJAK Group Finder to a wide variety of synthetic data. Access to real world databases has been a main concern in AI, machine learning and data mining communities in the past. The LD community is not an exception in this matter. In particular, since the LD goal is to relate people, place and entities, it triggers privacy concerns. The balance between privacy concerns and the need to explore large volumes of data for LD is a difficult problem. These issues motivate employing synthetic data for performance evaluation of LD techniques.

### Synthetic Data

For the purpose of evaluating and validating our techniques, we tested them on synthetic datasets developed by Information Extraction & Transport, Inc. within the EELD Program (Silk 2003, Schrag 2003). These synthetic datasets were created by running a simulation of an artificial world. The main focus in designing the world was to produce datasets with large amounts of relationships between agents as opposed to complex domains with a large number of entity properties.

From the point of view of group detection, the artificial world consists of *individuals* that belong to *groups*. Groups can be *threat groups* (that cause *threat events*) or *non-threat-groups*. Targets can be exploited (in threat and non-threat ways) using specific combinations of resources and capabilities; each such combination is called a *mode*. Individuals may have any number of capabilities or resources, belong to any number of groups, and participate in any number of exploitations at the same time. Individuals are *threat* individuals or *non-threat* individuals. Every threat individual belongs to at least one threat group. Non-threat individuals belong only to non-threat groups. Threat groups have only threat individuals as members. Threat individuals can belong to non-threat groups as well. A group will have at least one member qualified for any capability required by any of its modes. Non-threat groups carry out only non-threat modes.

The evidence available in the dataset for our analysis consists of two main types of information:

| Number of entities | 10,000 |
|---|---|
| Number of Links | 100,000 |
| Number of Distinct Threat Pattern | 20 |
| Lowest Signal to clutter ratio | 0.3(-5 db) |
| Lowest Signal to Noise Ratio | .008(-21 db) |
| Observability | 50%-100% |
| Corruption of Evidence | 0-25% |

**Table 1: Synthetic Data Characteristics**

(1) *Individual and group information.* The existence of most individuals and some of the groups is available directly in the evidence. The groups available in the evidence are known or named groups discussed earlier.

(2) *Activities from individuals.* Individuals participate in activities related to resources, capabilities and events. Much like in the real world, information about those activities is not available directly, but rather indirectly as transactions (e.g., phone calls or email messages).

### Synthetic Data Characteristics

One of the key advantages of using a simulated world is that we are able to test our system against a wide range of datasets. In other words, we are able to create datasets with (almost) arbitrary characteristics, and therefore better understand the potential and limitations of our techniques.

Some of the features used in defining the datasets are in Table 1. The values displayed are typical for the datasets we used in our evaluation; each dataset employs different values for each of these features. Of particular interest are observability (how much of the artificial world information is available as evidence), corruption (how much of the evidence is changed before being reported) and clutter (how much irrelevant information that is similar to the information being sought is added to the evidence).

### Evaluation Metrics

The quality of groups we find can be measured with traditional precision and recall metrics defined as follows: Given a proposed group $G$ with $g$ members which matches an answer group $A$ with $a$ members, and given that of the $g$ proposed members only $c$ are correct, precision $P=c/g$ and recall $R=c/a$. Another metric that helps us analyze precision and recall in aggregate is the $F$-measure:

$$F = \frac{(b^2 + 1)PR}{b^2 P + R}$$

The $F$-measure both requires and allows us to specify the desired trade-off between precision and recall through the $b$ variable. A value of $b$=1 indicates that precision and recall are equally important; $b$ = 2 means that recall is twice as important as precision, etc. That is, using the $F$-measure allows users of our module to specify their own desired trade-offs in terms of $b$.

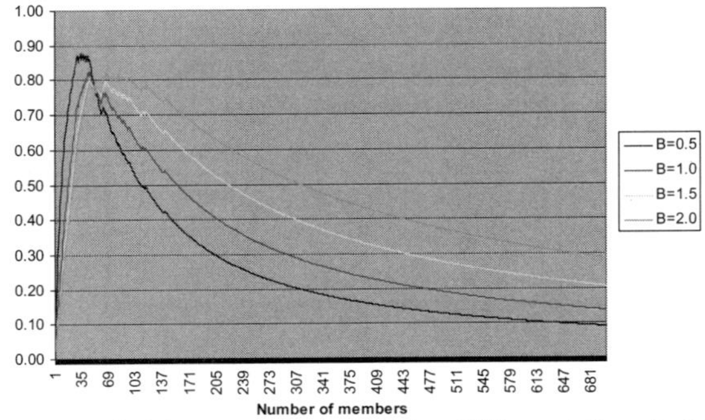


**Figure 4: *F*-measure curves for different thresholds for a typical group.**

## Experimental Results

### Overall empirical properties

Figure 4 shows a typical set of *F*-measure curves for different thresholds. An important property is that our *F*-measure curves have maximums (and thus optimums). Notice also that *F*-measure curves for higher values of *b* have wider "peaks", which means they are more "forgiving" in threshold selection (a given variation of threshold provokes a smaller variation in F-measure.)

### Threshold Analysis

Focusing on the *F*-measure, we defined an empirical model that allowed us to predict good threshold values for a given type of dataset. Datasets vary in many dimensions, in particular on their levels of observability, corruption, and clutter. Our goal was to define a model parametric on these dataset dimensions.

One key initial step is to define the base for the model. Possible bases include the average size of the groups we are looking for (if sufficiently known), the size of extended group and the size of the seed group. Our empirical analysis indicated that the best alternative is to use the size of extended group as a basis for defining the threshold. We found that the ratio between the real size of the group we would be looking for and the size of the extended group we created as a hypothesis varies little and is usually around 11%-14%. Another advantage is that this measure is organic to the mutual information model, that is, no additional information is needed.

The empirical model consists of defining one specific threshold (as a percentage of the extended group size) for each type of dataset. We used thirteen types of datasets that employed combinations of different values for the parameters in Table 1. We then analyzed the *F*-measure curves to find optimums for each *b*-value (i.e., trade-off between precision and recall) and type of dataset. For example, for a *b* of 1, we predicted a threshold of 8% for a baseline dataset, 6% for a dataset with more clutter, 9% for a dataset with low observability and 3% for a dataset with both additional clutter and low observability. These thresholds are then used to predict the best threshold for a new dataset of a particular type.

| | | Logic Module | | KOJAK Group Finder | | | | |
|---|---|---|---|---|---|---|---|---|
| Data set | Number of Groups | Avg. Precision | Avg. Recall | Avg. Precision | Precision Variance | Avg. Recall | Recall Variance | Avg. F-Measure (b=1.5) |
| Plain | 14 | 1 | 0.53 | 0.81 | 0.005 | 0.87 | 0.010 | 0.85 |
| High clutter | 11 | 1 | 0.53 | 0.59 | 0.010 | 0.86 | 0.014 | 0.74 |
| Low observability | 16 | 1 | 0.52 | 0.70 | 0.004 | 0.72 | 0.026 | 0.71 |
| Both | 19 | 1 | 0.50 | 0.88 | 0.005 | 0.66 | 0.011 | 0.75 |

**Table 2: Scores for applying the KOJAK Group Finder to datasets of increasing complexity (known groups only).**

### Results

We have applied KOJAK to 26 datasets of varying complexity and characteristics. Table 2 shows some sample metrics for four datasets. Since there are many groups in each dataset we provide mean and variance values for precision and recall among all groups in a dataset. The average *F*-measure for known groups varies between 0.71 and 0.85. Note that the differences in the properties of the datasets cause the best *F*-measure to be obtained with different recall and precision values. This shows that "harder" datasets, where precision drops more steeply require lower thresholds that yield lower recalls and higher precision values. A more detailed analysis with ROC curves is presented in (Adibi et al. 2004).

Table 2 also compares the KOJAK results against a baseline of using only the logic module. The results show that the logic module is very accurate (precision = 1), meaning all members found are provably correct. However, since the evidence is incomplete the logic module achieves a maximum recall of about 50%.

We also evaluated our threshold prediction model. We found that the average *F*-measure for these datasets compares to the optimum *F*-measure obtained by using the best possible threshold for each group would result only in a difference of around 6%. In other words, the threshold model only "misses" 6% of whatever was available in the extended groups.

## Related Work

Link discovery (LD) can be distinguished from other techniques that attempt to infer the structure of data, such as classification and outlier detection. Classification and clustering approaches such as that of Getoor et al. (2001) try to maximize individual similarity within classes and minimize individual similarity between classes. In contrast, LD focuses on detecting groups with strongly connected entities that are not necessarily similar. Outlier detection methods attempt to find abnormal individuals. LD, on the other hand, identifies important individuals based on networks of relationships. Additionally, outlier techniques require large amounts of data including normal and abnormal cases, and positive and negative noise. This is inappropriate for LD applications that need to detect threats with few or no available prior cases.

Mutual information has also been used in other domains such as finding functional genomic clusters in RNA expression data and measuring the agreement of object models for image processing (Butte, 2000).

Our work can be distinguished from other group detection approaches such as Gibson, (1998) and Ng, (2001) by three major characteristics. First, GF is unique since it is based on a hybrid model of semantic KR&R and statistical inference. There are very few approaches that use semantic information. Second, in our approach each type of relation (link) is valuable and treated differently, in contrast to work in fields such as Web analysis and social networks. Third, with our technique, multiple paths between individuals or groups (direct or indirect) imply a strong connection which is different from techniques which focus on finding chains of entities.

The work closest to our own is that of Jeremy Kubica et al. (Kubica, 2002; Kubica, 2003) that uses a probabilistic model of link generation based on group membership. The parameters of the model are learned via a maximum likelihood search that finds a Gannt Chart that best explains the observed evolution of group membership. The approach has a strong probabilistic foundation that makes it robust in the face of very low signal-to- noise ratios.

Another recent approach to the LD problem is the use of probabilistic models (Cohn, 2001; Friedman, 1999; Getoor, 2001). Kubica et al. (2001) present a model of link generation where links are generated from a single underlying group and then have noise added. These models differ significantly from ours since we do not assume a generative model of group formation, but rather probabilistically determine each entity's membership.

## Conclusion and Future Work

In this paper we introduced the KOJAK Group Finder (GF) as a hybrid model of logic-based and statistical reasoning. GF is capable of finding potential groups and group members in large evidence data sets. It uses a logic-based model to generate group seeds and a multi-relational mutual information model to compute link strength between individuals and group seeds. Noise and corruption are handled via a noisy channel model. Our GF framework is scalable and robust, and exhibits graceful degradation in the presence of increased data access cost and decreased relational information. The Group Finder is best-suited for problems where some initial information or group structure is available (e.g. finding hidden members of existing groups vs. detecting completely new groups) which is a common case in many real world applications. Group detection is useful for law enforcement, fraud detection, homeland security, business intelligence as well as analysis of social groups such as Web communities.

There are several lines of ongoing and future work, such as, determining group leaders by measuring their entropy, use of temporal information for more focused access to relevant information as well as employing sampling and data streaming techniques to deal with very large datasets.

**Acknowledgments**. This research was sponsored by the Defense Advance Research Projects Agency and Air Force Research Laboratory, Air Force Materiel Command, USAF, under agreement number F30602-01-2-0583. The views and conclusions contained herein are those of the authors and should not be interpreted as necessarily representing the official policies or endorsements, either expressed or implied, of DARPA, AFRL or the U.S. Government.

## References

Adibi, J., Valente, A., Chalupsky, H. & Melz, E. (2004). Group detection via a mutual information model. Submitted to *KDD 2004*.

Butte, A. & Kohane, I. (2000). Mutual information relevance networks: Functional genomic clustering using pairwise entropy measurements. *Pacific Symposium on Biocomputing*. Honolulu, Hawaii.

Cohn, D. & Hofmann, T. (2001). The missing link: a probabilistic model of document content and hypertext connectivity. *Advances in Neural Information Processing Systems* 13: 430–436.

Friedman, N., Getoor, L., Koller, D. & Pfeffer, A. (1999). Learning probabilistic relational models. *IJCAI 1999*, San Francisco, Morgan Kaufmann Publishers.

Getoor, L., Segal, E., Taskar, B., & Koller, D. (2001). Probabilistic models of text and link structure for hypertext classification. *IJCAI 2001 Workshop on Text Learning: Beyond Supervision*. Seattle, Washington.

Gibson, D., Kleinberg, J. & Raghavan, P. (1998). Inferring Web communities from link topology. In *Proceedings of the Ninth ACM Conference on Hypertext and Hypermedia*. New York, ACM Press.

Kubica, J., Moore, A., Cohn, D. & Schneider, J. (2003). Finding underlying connections: a fast method for link analysis and collaboration queries. *International Conference on Machine Learning (ICML)*.

Kubica, J., Moore, A., Schneider, J. & Yang, Y. (2002). Stochastic link and group detection. *Eighteenth National Conference on Artificial Intelligence (AAAI)*.

Li, W. (1990). Mutual information functions versus correlation functions. *Journal of Statistical Physics* 60: 823-837.

Lin, S. & Chalupsky, H.. Using unsupervised link discovery methods to find interesting facts and connections in a bibliography dataset. *SIGKDD Explorations*, 5(2): 173-178, December 2003

Ng, A., Zheng, A. & Jordan, M. (2001). Link analysis, eigenvectors and stability. *IJCAI 2001*.

PowerLoom (2003). www.isi.edu/isd/LOOM/PowerLoom.

Schrag, R. et. al. (2003). EELD Y2 LD-PL Performance Evaluation, Information Extraction and Transport, Inc.

Senator, T. (2002). Evidence Extraction and Link Discovery, *DARPA Tech 2002*.

Shannon, C. (1948). A Mathematical Theory of Communication. *Bell System Tech. Journal* 27: 379-423.

Silk, B. & Bergert, B. (2003). EELD Evidence Database Description, Information Extraction and Transport, Inc.

# Detecting and Eliminating the Cascade Vulnerability Problem from Multilevel Security Networks using Soft Constraints*

**Stefano Bistarelli**
Dipartimento di Scienze
Università di Chieti-Pescara, Italy
bista@sci.unich.it
Istituto di Informatica e Telematica, C.N.R.
Pisa, Italy
stefano.bistarelli@iit.cnr.it

**Simon N. Foley** and **Barry O'Sullivan**
Department of Computer Science
University College Cork
Ireland
{s.foley,b.osullivan}@cs.ucc.ie

## Abstract

The security of a network configuration is based, not just on the security of its individual components and their direct interconnections, but it is also based on the potential for systems to interoperate indirectly across network routes. Such interoperation has been shown to provide the potential for cascading paths that violate security, in a circuitous manner, across a network. In this paper we show how constraint programming provides a natural approach to expressing the necessary constraints to ensure multilevel security across a network configuration. In particular, soft constraints are used to detect and eliminate the cascading network paths that violate security. Taking this approach results in practical advancements over existing solutions to this problem. In particular, constraint satisfaction highlights the set of all cascading paths, upon which we can compute in polynomial time an optimal reconfiguration of the network and ensure security.

## Introduction

The composition of secure systems is not necessarily secure. A user may be able to gain unauthorized access to an object by taking a circuitous access route across individually secure but interoperating systems (Foley 2000; Gong & Qian 1994). Determining security is based not just on the individual system authorization mechanisms but also on how the systems are configured to interoperate. For example, if Alice is permitted to have access to Bob's files on the Administration system, and Clare is permitted access Alice's files on the Sales system, then is it safe to support file sharing between these systems? The extent of system interoperation must be limited if the administration security policy states that Clare is not permitted access to Bob's (administration) files.

The *cascade vulnerability problem* (TNI 1987) is concerned with secure interoperation, and considers the *assurance risk* of composing multilevel secure systems that are evaluated to different levels of assurance according to the criteria specified in (TNI 1987). The transitivity of the multilevel security policy upheld across all secure systems ensures that their multilevel composition is secure; however, interoperability and data sharing between systems may increase the risk of compromise beyond that accepted by the assurance level. For example, it may be an acceptable risk to store only secret and top-secret data on a medium assurance system, and only classified and secret data on another medium assurance system: classified and top-secret data may be stored simultaneously only on 'high' assurance systems. However, if these medium assurance systems interoperate at classification secret, then the acceptable risk of compromise is no longer adequate as there is an unacceptable cascading risk from top-secret across the network to classified.

Existing research has considered schemes for *detecting* these security vulnerabilities and for *eliminating* them by reconfiguring system interoperation. While detection of some security vulnerability (Millen & Schwartz 1988; Horton & others 1993; Fitch & Hoffman 1993; Gong & Qian 1994) can be easily achieved, their optimal elimination is NP-complete (Horton & others 1993; Gritalis & Spinellis 1998; Gong & Qian 1994).

We present an approach to using constraints (Dechter 2003) for reasoning about secure interoperation. Constraint solving is an emerging software technology for modeling and solving large-scale optimization problems (Wallace 1996). Constraints have been successfully applied to a number of problems in computer security (Bharadwaj & Baras 2003; Bistarelli & Foley 2003; Pierro, Hankin, & Wiklicky 2002; Bella & Bistarelli 2001). However, the cascade vulnerability problem, and secure interoperation in general, have not been studied in the context of constraints.

The approach that we present in this paper represents a paradigm shift in the modeling, detection and elimination of the cascade problem. We present a constraint model that provides a natural description of an arbitrary multilevel secure network. Any solution to the model represents a cascading path through the network, providing significantly more information on its vulnerabilities than the existing approaches, and providing a basis for eliminating the cascade vulnerability problem. Previous approaches (Fitch & Hoffman 1993; Horton & others 1993) detect a single cascading

*This work has received partial support from the Italian MIUR project "Constraint Based Verification of Reactive Systems" (COVER), from Enterprise Ireland under their Basic Research Grant Scheme (Grant Number SC/02/289) and their International Collaboration Programme (Grant Number IC/2003/88) and the Boole Centre for Research in Informatics, UCC, under the HEA-PRTLI scheme.

path in polynomial time, but correcting the cascade in an optimal way is NP-complete. Using a constraint model, we can rely on a significant body of successful techniques from the field of constraint processing for finding the set of cascading paths with reasonable effort, which once found, can be eliminated in polynomial time. These results are applicable to secure interoperation in general.

## Background

### The Cascade Problem

Figure 1 gives an example of a multilevel secure (MLS) network configuration with a cascade vulnerability problem (Fitch & Hoffman 1993).

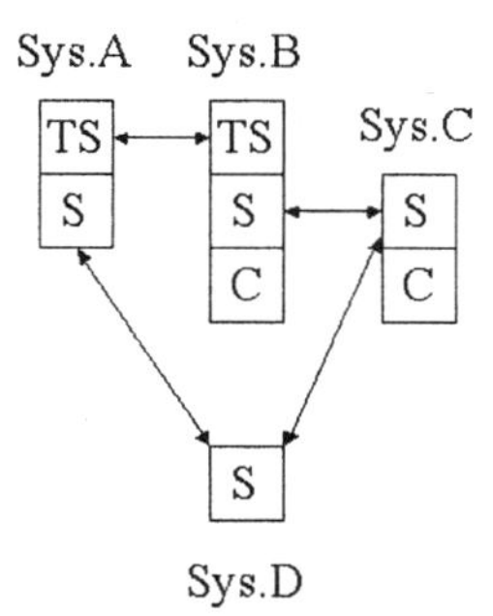


| Assurance Ratings | |
|---|---|
| System | Level |
| Sys.A | B2 |
| Sys.B | B3 |
| Sys.C | B1 |
| Sys.D | C2 |

Figure 1: Network configuration with a potential cascade problem.

The network is comprised of multilevel secure systems Sys.A, Sys.B, Sys.C and Sys.D storing classified ($C$), secret ($S$) and top-secret ($T$) information as depicted in Figure 1. Each system is accredited according to levels of assurance C2<B1<B2<B3 from (TNI 1987; TCSEC 1985). For example, Sys.B is used to simultaneously store $C$, $S$ and $T$ information and, therefore, (according to (TNI 1987; TCSEC 1985)) must be evaluated at level B3 or higher, reflecting the high level of confidence that must be placed in the secure operation of the system. This is to counter the risk of an attacker compromising the system and copying $T$ information to $C$. Sys.D, on the other hand, has been evaluated at the lowest level of assurance C2 and, therefore, may be used only to store single level data.

However, the security-level interoperability defined by the system connections in Figure 1 results in a cascade vulnerability across the network. There is a risk that an attacker who has the ability to compromise security on B2 or lower assured systems can copy $T$ to $S$ on Sys.A, to $S$ on Sys.D to $S$ to $C$ on Sys.C. This is contrary to the criteria requirement that the level of assurance that $T$ cannot be copied to $C$ should be B3 or higher. This requirement is met by the individual systems but not as a result of their interoperation. A generalized form of the cascade problem is defined as follows.

**MLS** A multilevel secure system enforces a lattice-based security policy $L$ of security levels that has ordering relation $\leq$. Given $x, y : L$ then $x \leq y$ means that information may flow from level $x$ to level $y$, for example, $C \leq S \leq T$.

**Assurance Levels** Security criteria define a lattice, $\mathcal{A}$, of assurance levels with ordering $\leq$. Given $x, y : \mathcal{A}$, then $x \leq y$ means that a system evaluated at $y$ is no less secure than a system evaluated at $x$, or alternatively, that an attacker that can compromise a system evaluated at $y$ can compromise a system evaluated at $x$. Let $\mathcal{S}$ define the set of all system names. We define $accred : \mathcal{S} \rightarrow \mathcal{A}$ where $accred(s)$ gives the assurance level of system $s : \mathcal{S}$, and is taken to represent the minimum effort required by an attacker to compromise system $s$.

**Acceptable Risk** Security evaluation criteria also define an acceptable risk function $risk : L \times L \rightarrow \mathcal{A}$, such that given $l, l' : L$ then $risk(l, l')$ defines the minimum acceptable risk of compromise from $l$ to $l'$; it represents the minimum acceptable effort required to 'compromise security' and copy/downgrade information from level $l$ to level $l'$. Without any loss of generalization we assume that there is no security enforcement at the lowest assurance level **0**, and thus, if $l \leq l'$ then $risk(l, l') = \mathbf{0}$. For example, function $risk$ encodes the assurance matrix from (TNI 1987; TCSEC 1985) as $risk(C, S) = risk(C, T) = risk(S, T) = 0$ [C2], $risk(S, C) = 1$ [B1], and so forth.

**Evaluated Systems** Individual systems must be assured higher than the minimum acceptable risk to compromise the data they store. If a system $s$ can hold information at levels $l$ and $l'$ then $risk(l, l') \leq accred(s)$.

**Network Model** A node is a pair $(s, l)$ and represents the fact that system $s$ can hold information at level $l$. A system is a collection of nodes that represent the data it holds. For example, in Figure 1, Sys.A is represented by nodes $(Sys.A, S)$ and $(Sys.A, T)$. A network of systems is a weighted graph of these nodes according to how they are connected. An $w$-weighted arc from $(s, l)$ to $(s', l')$ means that it requires minimum $w$ effort to directly copy information at level $l$ held on system $s$ to level $l'$ on system $s'$.

**Cascading Risks** Arcs are used to represent direct flows within a system and interoperation links between systems. A flow $l \leq l'$ that is permitted on system $s$ is represented as a (assurance) **0**-weighted arc from $(s, l)$ to $(s, l')$; if a flow is not permitted between levels $l$ and $l'$ that are held on system $s$ then it is represented as an arc weighted as $accred(s)$ from $(s, l)$ to $(s, l')$.

A link from system $s$ to $s'$ that connects $l$-level information is represented as a **0**-weighted arc from $(s, l)$ to $(s', l)$—all other pairs $(s, l)$ to $(s', l)$ not related in this way are either represented as having no arc, or an arc with the maximum assurance value **1**.

Given pairs $(s, l)$ and $(s, l')$ we then define $effort((s, l), (s', l'))$ as the minimum effort required to compromise the network and copy/downgrade level $l$ information held on system $s$ to level $l'$ information on system $s'$. As an example, in Figure 1, $effort((Sys.A, T), (Sys.C, C)) = B2$ via the path through $Sys.D$.

**Cascade Freedom** We require that for any systems $s$,$s'$ and levels $l$,$l'$ then $risk(l, l') \leq effort((s, l), (s', l'))$. Given a path in the network from $(s, l)$ to $(s', l')$, then its cascade weighting is the maximum weight that directly connects any two nodes on the path. This reflects the minimum effort that will be required by an attacker to copy information from $(s,l)$ to $(s',l')$ by using this path. $effort((s,l),(s',l'))$ is the minimum of the cascade weightings for all paths that connect $(s,l)$ to $(s',l')$.

### Soft Constraints

Several formalizations of the concept of *soft constraints* are currently available. In the following, we refer to the one based on c-semirings (Bistarelli, Montanari, & Rossi 1997) which can be shown to generalize and express many of the others (Bistarelli *et al.* 1999).

Soft constraints associate a qualitative or quantitative value either with the entire constraint or with each assignment of its variables. More precisely, they are based on a semiring structure $S = \langle A, +, \times, \mathbf{0}, \mathbf{1} \rangle$ and a set of variables $V$ with domain $D$. In particular the semiring operation $\times$ is used to combine constraints together, and the $+$ operator for projection.

Technically, a *constraint* is a function which, given an assignment $\eta : V \longrightarrow D$ of the variables, returns a value of the semiring. So $\mathcal{C} = \eta \longrightarrow A$ is the set of all possible constraints that can be built starting from $S$, $D$ and $V$ (values in $A$ are interpreted as level of preference or importance or cost). Using the levels, we can order constraints: to say that $c_1$ is better then $c_2$ we will write $c_1 \sqsupseteq c_2$.

When using soft constraints it is necessary to specify, via suitable combination operators, how the level of preference of a global solution is obtained from the preferences in the constraints. The combined weight of a set of constraints is computed using the operator $\otimes : \mathcal{C} \times \mathcal{C} \rightarrow \mathcal{C}$ defined as $(c_1 \otimes c_2)\eta = c_1\eta \times_S c_2\eta$. Moreover, given a constraint $c \in \mathcal{C}$ and a variable $v \in V$, the *projection* of $c$ over $V - \{v\}$, written $c \Downarrow_{(V-\{v\})}$ is the constraint $c'$ s.t. $c'\eta = \sum_{d \in D} c\eta[v := d]$.

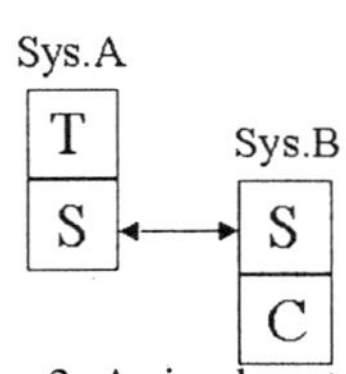

Figure 2: A simple network.

## Modeling MLS Networks

Consider a network $N = \{A, B, C, \ldots\}$ of a finite arbitrary number $n$ of systems. In our constraint model, this network of $n$ nodes is represented using $2 \times n$ *system-node variables*. Each system-node variable $S_i^s$ and $S_i^d$, for $i := 1 \ldots n$ can be instantiated to be one system of the network. Each of the possible flows of information among the systems of the network are represented by a specific instantiation of the variables $S_1^s$,$S_1^d$,$S_2^s$,$S_2^d$,...,$S_n^s$,$S_n^d$. In particular, the instantiation of the pair of nodes $S_i^s$ and $S_i^d$, for $i := 1 \ldots n$, represents the flow from the source $S_i^s$ to the destination $S_i^d$ inside the $i$-th System in the specific path. Similarly, instantiation of $S_i^d$ and $S_{i+1}^s$, for $i := 1 \ldots n-1$ represents the flow among the the $i$-th and the $i+1$-th System in the specific instantiated path.

Consider for instance the network $N = \{A, B\}$ represented in Figure 2 involving two systems, $A$ and $B$, with system $A$ handling information at level Top-Secret ($T$) and Secret ($S$), and system $B$ handling information at level Secret ($S$) and Confidential ($C$). We can model this instance by using 4 system-node variables: $S_1^s$,$S_1^d$,$S_2^s$,$S_2^d$.

### System-Node Variable Domains

The domain of each system-node variable defines the set of possible security levels available on each system. In particular, each *source* variable $S_i^s$ contains domain elements marked with $s$, and each *destination* variable $S_i^d$ contains domain elements marked with $d$.

The network in Figure 2 has in our model 4 variables $S_1^s, S_1^d, S_2^s, S_2^d$ with domain $D(S_i^s) = \{T_A^s, S_A^s, S_B^s, C_B^s\}$, with $i := 1, 2$, and $D(S_i^d) = \{T_A^d, S_A^d, S_B^d, C_B^d\}$, with $i := 1, 2$.

In general, when the network contains $n > 2$ systems, we also need to be able to deal with paths of length $k < n$. To do this, we need to extend the domain of each system-node variable, $S_i^?$ (where ? stands alternatively for $s$ and $d$), for any $i > 2$, with some artificial elements. More precisely, we extended the domain $D(S_i^?)' = D(S_i^?) \cup \{*_1^?, *_2^?, \ldots, *_{i-2}^?\}$. These $*$ elements are added to deal with paths shorter than $n$. This is necessary because solving a Soft CSP (SCSP) requires finding an assignment for each variable in the SCSP and we may want to represent paths shorter than the number of nodes in the network.

### Modeling each System

The constraint on each system defines three classes of system flows.:

- $Flow_{permitted}$ represents the information flows permitted by the policy at each node;
- $Flow_{risk}$ represents the information flows that are not permitted by the policy, but for which there is a risk of flow if the system became compromised;
- $Flow_{invalid}$ represents all the remaining flows which are not valid (i.e. that are impossible for the given network).

Between each pair of system-node variables $S_i^s$ and $S_i^d$ for each system $i$, we define a soft constraint, $c_{(S_i^s, S_i^d)}$, that gives a weight to each possible (permitted or risk) flow within system $i$. Various semirings could be used to represent the network and the associated policy. We use the following semiring in this paper, although our results are general and are not limited to this particular semiring:

$$S_{cascade} = \langle \mathbb{N}, min, max, +\infty, 0 \rangle.$$

Given this semiring, the constraint $c_{(S_i^s, S_i^d)}$ representing the flow inside system $i$ is defined as follows:

$$c_{(S_i^s, S_i^d)}(s,d) = \begin{cases} accred(S_i) & (s,d) \in Flow_{risk} \\ & \text{(risk flows)} \\ 0 & (s,d) \in Flow_{permitted} \\ & \text{(permitted flows)} \\ +\infty & \text{otherwise.} \\ & \text{(invalid flows)} \end{cases}$$

Recall that $accred(S_i)$ is the accreditation value of System $i$. For example, given the MLS policy ordering $C \leq S \leq T$, then we have

$$\begin{aligned} Flow_{permitted} &= \{(T^s_A, T^d_A), (S^s_A, S^d_A), (S^s_A, T^d_A), \\ &\quad (S^s_B, S^d_B), (C^s_B, C^d_B), (C^s_B, S^d_B)\} \\ Flow_{risk} &= \{(T^s_A, S^d_A), (S^s_B, C^d_B)\} \end{aligned}$$

and the $Flow_{invalid}$ set contains all the remaining tuples.

Since the domain of the variables $S^?_i$ (where ? stands for $s$ and $d$) has been extended with the elements $\{*^?_1, *^?_2, \ldots, *^?_{i-2}\}$, we have also to consider these "artificial" values. In particular, we extend the definition of each constraint $c_{(S^s_i, S^d_i)}$ as follows:

$$c_{(S^s_i, S^d_i)}(s,d) = \begin{cases} 0 & (s,d) \in \{(*^s_1, *^d_1), \ldots, (*^s_{i-2}, *^d_{i-2})\} \\ & \text{(Artificial permitted flows)} \\ +\infty & \text{otherwise} \\ & \text{(Artificial invalid flows)} \end{cases}$$

### Modeling the Network

Flow constraints between systems result in two classes of network flows:

- $Network_{permitted}$ represents information flows permitted by the connection policy between each system and represents direct synchronization flows between systems;
- $Network_{invalid}$ represents the absence of direct connection between the systems.

Between each pair of systems, $S_i$ and $S_{i+1}$, we define a soft constraint, $c_{(S^d_i, S^s_{i+1})}$, that defines the possible synchronizations between systems $i$ and $i+1$. Note that these constraints are defined between the destination system-node variable of the first system, $S^d_i$, and the source system-node variable of the second system, $S^s_{i+1}$. The constraint $c_{(S^d_i, S^s_{i+1})}$ representing the synchronization flows between system $i$ and $i+1$ can be defined as follows:

$$c_{(S^d_i, S^s_{i+1})}(d,s) = \begin{cases} 0 & (d,s) \in Network_{permitted} \\ & \text{(Policy permitted synchronization)} \\ +\infty & \text{otherwise.} \\ & \text{(invalid synchronization)} \end{cases}$$

For example, constraint $Network_{permitted}$ for Figure 2 is defined as follows.

$$Network_{permitted} = \{(S^d_A, S^s_B), (S^d_B, S^s_A)\}$$

Note that the model does not consider assurance risks for connections: this can be achieved, if desired, by explicitly modeling the connections by their components (for example, a link encryption device) and corresponding assurance levels.

When connecting systems $S^d_i$ and $S^s_{i+1}$ it is also necessary to consider the constraints imposed by the artificial elements $*^?_i$. The definition of each constraint $c_{(S^d_i, S^s_{i+1})}$ is extended as follows:

$$c_{(S^d_i, S^s_{i+1})}(d,s) = \begin{cases} 0 & (d,s) \in \{(*^d_1, *^s_2), \ldots, (*^d_{i-3}, *^s_{i-2})\} \\ & \cup \{(\sharp, *^s_1) \text{s.t. } \sharp \in D(S^d_i)\} \\ & \text{(Artificial permitted synchronization)} \\ +\infty & \text{otherwise} \\ & \text{(Artificial invalid synchronization)} \end{cases}$$

The extension of this constraint is slightly different to the previous system-level constraints. In particular, it enables us to model the connection between the last real domain element in the path and the first $*^s_1$-element.

In addition to ensuring that systems are configured in a valid way, we also need to ensure that no two pairs of system-node variables represent the same system. This ensures that our model does not capture cyclic paths. Therefore, we need to post an *alldifferent* (Regin 1994) constraint amongst all the variables in the model. An *alldifferent* constraint ensures that all variables over which it is defined take on different values.

The solution of the defined SCSP, $E$, that is all the solution with level lower than $+\infty$, represents all of the possible paths through the system. The semiring level associated with each path gives a measure of the effort required to compromise the network using that specific path.

## Detecting Cascade Vulnerabilities

To determine whether or not there exists a cascade vulnerability problem we need to compare the effort required to compromise the network with the risk of compromising the system as a whole. Therefore, we introduce a set of *risk* constraints, $R = \{r_{(S^s_1, S^d_i)} | i \in \{2, \ldots, n\}\}$. The weight of each instance of $r_{(S^s_1, S^d_i)}$ represents the risk associated with the path from $S^s_1$ to $S^d_i$. The cost of each tuple in these constraints is defined as follows:

$$r_{(S^s_1, S^d_i)}(s,d) = \begin{cases} 0 & \text{if } d = *^d_i, \\ risk(s,d) & \text{otherwise.} \end{cases}$$

The set of solutions of the SCSP $E$ (that is the Effort-CSP defined above) whose associated semiring level is lower than $+\infty$ represents the set of paths through the network. The semiring level associated with each solution-path of $E$ represents the minimum *effort* required to compromise the network, while the combination of the constraints in $R$ (the Risk-CSP), gives the risk for all the paths. Therefore, a cascading path can be identified as any path $\eta$ where the risk associated with the path exceeds the effort to compromise it, i.e. where the following constraint is satisfied:

$$\bigotimes R\eta > \bigotimes E\eta$$

Therefore, by adding the above constraint to our constraint model, the existence of a solution to that model indicates that here exists a cascading path. Furthermore, the set of solutions provides the set of cascading paths. This provides us with a basis upon which we can set about removing the cascade vulnerability problem from the network by eliminating all solutions from the model.

## An Example

In this section we encode the network example described in Figure 1 within the proposed constraints model. Figure 3 depicts the structure of the constraint relationships in this model. We first present an example of how our model identifies a cascade-free path, before we present an example of detecting a cascading path.

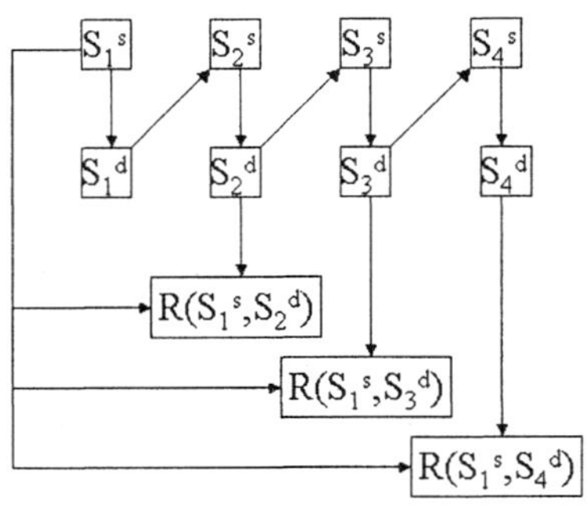

Figure 3: A constraint Model Structure.

For the purposes of the examples, the risk lattice is assumed to be as follows: $risk(C,S) = risk(C,T) = risk(S,T) = 0$, $risk(S,C) = 1$, $risk(T,S) = 2$, $risk(T,C) = 3$.

Figure 3 presents the structure of the constraint model for an example from (Fitch & Hoffman 1993). Our model comprises 8 system-node variables, $S^s_1, S^d_1, S^s_2, S^d_2, S^s_3, S^d_3, S^s_4$, and $S^d_4$, and 3 risk variables, $r_{(S^s_1,S^d_2)}, r_{(S^s_1,S^d_3)}$ and $r_{(S^s_1,S^d_4)}$. The domain of each system-node variable, $D(S^?_i)$, is: $\{T^?_A, S^?_A, T^?_B, S^?_B, C^?_B, S^?_C, C^?_C, S^?_D\}$ (where ? stands alternatively for $s$ and $d$) and $i := 1, \ldots, 4$. Note that we also extend each domain using $*^?_i$ values as described above, but don't show this here for conciseness.

### A Cascade-free Path

Consider the following path through the network:

$$\eta = [S^s_1 := T^s_A, S^d_1 := T^d_A, S^s_2 := T^s_B, S^d_2 := S^d_B, S^s_3 := S^s_C, S^d_3 := C^d_C, S^s_4 := *^s_1, S^d_4 := *^d_1]$$

This scenario is illustrated in Figure 4.

Evaluating the cascade detection constraint we get the following, proving that this path is cascade-free:

$$\bigotimes R\eta > \bigotimes E\eta \equiv 3 > 3 \equiv False$$

### A Cascading Path

Consider the following path through the network, depicted in Figure 5:

$$\eta = [S^s_1 := T^s_A, S^d_1 := S^d_A, S^s_2 := S^s_D, S^d_2 := S^d_D, S^s_3 := S^s_C, S^d_3 := C^d_C, S^s_4 := *^s_1, S^d_4 := *^d_1]$$

Evaluating the cascade detection constraint we get the following, characterizing a cascading path:

$$\bigotimes R\eta > \bigotimes E\eta \equiv 3 > 2 \equiv True$$

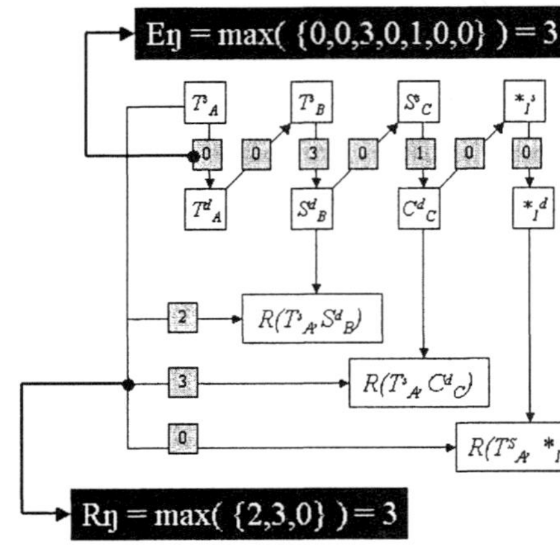


Figure 4: Cascade-free Path.

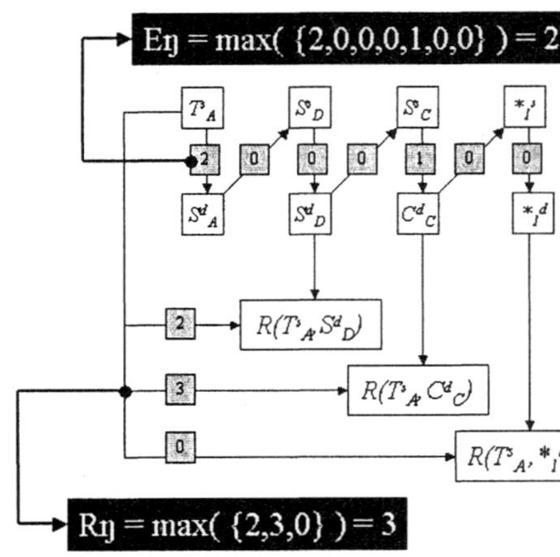


Figure 5: Cascading Path.

## Eliminating Cascade Vulnerabilities

Clearly, in order to eliminate the cascade vulnerability problem from an MLS network we need to remove all cascading paths through it. However, by breaking links (connections) between systems, the services provided by the network are affected. Therefore, when eliminating the cascade vulnerability problem we require that the number of links to be broken is minimal.

The set of solutions to the constraint model presented earlier provides all the cascading paths in the network. Therefore, in order to remove all cascade vulnerabilities from the network, we need to eliminate all solutions to the constraint model. Central to our approach to eliminating cascading paths is the notion of a *minimal cascading path.*

**Definition 1 (Minimal Cascading Path)** *A minimal cascading path, $\eta$, is a path involving a sequence of assignments to system-node variables that is not a sub-sequence of another cascading path. Note that we ignore the artificial values $*^?_i$.*

Recall that the set of solutions to the constraint model not only contains all minimal cascading paths, but also all of their extensions. Thus, in order to focus attention on the causes of the cascade vulnerabilities we must limit ourselves to the set of minimal cascading paths. These can be obtained from the set of solutions in polynomial-time.

Each minimal cascading path has a very important property; namely, that it is sufficient to remove one link on the path in order to remove the cascading effect associated with it.

**Theorem 1** *Given a minimal cascading path $\eta$, removing any of the links on that path removes the cascading effect along that path.*

Therefore, given the set of minimal cascading paths, we simply apply the following simple steps in order to remove the minimal number of links to eliminate the cascade vulnerability problem:

1. we maintain a counter for each link involved in the set of minimal cascading paths we need to remove;
2. we remove the most common link (the link with the highest counter), thus removing all minimal cascading paths involving that link;
3. we update the link counters built in Step 1 to reflect the effect of reducing the set of minimal cascading paths that we need to consider;
4. we continue removing links and updating the link counters until all cascading paths have been removed.

This is a polynomial-time procedure, for which the following can be easily proven:

**Theorem 2 (Soundness)** *The network we obtain from applying the procedure is cascade free.*

**Theorem 3 (Optimality)** *The number of links that are removed from the network is minimal.*

## Conclusion

In this paper we have presented a new approach to detecting and eliminating the cascade vulnerability problem in multilevel secure systems based on soft constraints. These results demonstrate the usefulness of constraints as a general purpose modeling technique for security.

The approach we present in this paper represents a paradigm shift in the modeling, detection and elimination of the cascade problem. In particular, our constraint model provides a natural and declarative description of an arbitrary multilevel secure network. Any solution to the model represents a cascading path, which provides significantly more information regarding the vulnerabilities in the network than the existing approaches. The set of solutions to the proposed constraint model provides a basis for removing the cascade vulnerability problem. Previous approaches (Fitch & Hoffman 1993; Horton & others 1993) detect a single cascading path in polynomial time, but correcting the cascade in an optimal way is NP-complete. As described above, detecting all paths in the constraint model is NP-complete, however their optimal elimination is polynomial.

While constraint solving is NP-complete in general, this has not detracted from its uptake as a practical approach to solving many real-world problems (Wallace 1996). Using a constraint model, we can rely on a significant body of successful techniques for finding the set of cascading paths, which once found, can be eliminated in polynomial time. In this paper we explored the cascade vulnerability problem in the context of interoperating multilevel secure systems. We expect that it is straightforward to generalize these results to cascades within secure interoperation in general (Foley 2000; Gong & Qian 1994).

## References


Bella, G., and Bistarelli, S. 2001. Soft Constraints for Security Protocol Analysis: Confidentiality. In *Proc. of PADL'01*, LNCS 1990, 108–122.

Bharadwaj, V., and Baras, J. 2003. Towards automated negotiation of access control policies. In *Proc. of IEEE Workshop Policies for Distributed Systems and Networks*, 77–80.

Bistarelli, S., and Foley, S. 2003. Analysis of integrity policies using soft constraints. In *Proc. of IEEE Workshop Policies for Distributed Systems and Networks*, 77–80.

Bistarelli, S.; Fargier, H.; Montanari, U.; Rossi, F.; Schiex, T.; and Verfaillie, G. 1999. Semiring-based CSPs and Valued CSPs: Frameworks, properties, and comparison. *CONSTRAINTS: An international journal. Kluwer* 4(3).

Bistarelli, S.; Montanari, U.; and Rossi, F. 1997. Semiring-based Constraint Solving and Optimization. *JACM* 44(2):201–236.

Dechter, R. 2003. *Constraint Processing*. Morgan Kaufmann.

Fitch, J. A., and Hoffman, L. J. 1993. A shortest path network security model. *Computers and Security* 12(2):169–189.

Foley, S. 2000. Conduit cascades and secure synchronization. In *ACM New Security Paradigms Workshop*.

Gong, L., and Qian, X. 1994. The complexity and composability of secure interoperation. In *Proceedings of the Symposium on Security and Privacy*, 190–200. Oakland, CA: IEEE Comp. Soc. Press.

Gritalis, S., and Spinellis, D. 1998. The cascade vulnerability problem: The detection problem and a simulated annealing approach to its correction. *Microprocessors and Microsystems* 21(10):621–628.

Horton, R., et al. 1993. The cascade vulnerability problem. *Journal of Computer Security* 2(4):279–290.

Millen, J., and Schwartz, M. 1988. The cascading problem for interconnected networks. In *4th Aerospace Computer Security Applications Conference*, 269–273.

Pierro, A. D.; Hankin, C.; and Wiklicky, H. 2002. On approximate non-interference. In *Proc. of Workshop on Issues in the Theory of Security*. IFIP WG1.7.

Regin, J.-C. 1994. A filtering algorithm for constraints of difference in csps. In *Proceedings AAAI-94*, 362–367.

TCSEC. 1985. Computer security requirements – guidance for applying the department of defense trusted computer system evaluation criteria in specific environments. Technical Report CSC-STD-003-85, National Computer Security Center. Orange Book.

TNI. 1987. Trusted computer system evaluation criteria: Trusted network interpretation. Technical report, National Computer Security Center. Red Book.

Wallace, M. 1996. Practical applications of constraint programming. *Constraints* 1(1–2):139–168.

# The U.S. National Football League Scheduling Problem

**Bistra N. Dilkina** and **William S. Havens**
Intelligent Systems Lab
Simon Fraser University
Burnaby, British Columbia
Canada V5A 1S6
and
Actenum Corp.
Vancouver, British Columbia
{bnd, havens}@cs.sfu.ca

### Abstract

We describe the problem of scheduling the television broadcasts of the U.S. National Football League (NFL). Unlike traditional round-robin tournament scheduling, the NFL problem involves assigning games to broadcast slots under various complex constraints while attempting to satisfy a set of user preferences. As well, a mixed-initiative functionality was required to allow the user to control and assist in the scheduling process. A prototype system was developed for the NFL which produced schedules satisfying many of these constraints and preferences. In this paper, we provide an overview of the constraint solving methodology employed and the implementation of the NFL prototype system.

## Introduction

Sports league scheduling is very important for both professional and amateur sports alike. Obtaining good "playable" schedules under a myriad of league and logistics constraints is extremely difficult yet essential to the success of the league. Thus developing practical techniques for this problem is a very important research area.

Sports league scheduling is particularly interesting type of constraint satisfaction problem (CSP) which has attracted significant research interest (Henz 1999; Nemhauser & Trick 1998). The CSP, in general, and sports scheduling, in particular, are NP-hard requiring exponential computing time in the size of the problem. Developing algorithms capable of solving large instances of these problems has proven to be extremely difficult.

In this paper, we report on the research and development of a prototype system (called *NFLSched*) to solve a very large and difficult sports league scheduling problem for the U.S. National Football League (NFL). This problem differs from the usual round-robin league scheduling in significant ways. The NFL problem is very large comprising 32 teams which play 256 games in a 17 week broadcast schedule. Indeed, the matches (games) are already known ahead of time by agreement between the teams and television broadcast networks. What must be scheduled is the assignment of games to broadcast slots while satisfying a large number of diverse constraints and maximizing a set of preferences.



Furthermore, it was desired to intimately involve the user in the scheduling process. The NFL wants to be able to "tweak" schedules during the scheduling process to obtain preferred broadcasts of particular games in particular slots in the schedule while continuing to satisfy the hard "playability" constraints. Thus the NFL problem is a mixed-initiative constraint optimization problem.

The NFL scheduling system is required by the league's Broadcasting Department to produce their regular season game schedules. The Broadcasting Department works with the four major U.S. television networks (ABC, CBS, FOX and ESPN) to obtain a broadcast schedule acceptable to all parties. The NFL desired that the scheduling application be able to (sub)optimally schedule professional football games given multiple (and often conflicting) broadcast, physical and fairness constraints. Additionally, the system must support building flexible network game packages and be able to modify the rules and constraints as necessary to find preferred playable schedules which are acceptable to both the NFL teams and the broadcast networks.

Previously, the league schedules were produced by a human expert. But the complexity of the problem has increased (both in size and type of constraints) necessitating automation. Earlier attempts at exhaustive backtrack search for completing (and verifying) partial schedules were unsuccessful. Thus the NFL requested proposals for developing a new mixed-initiative league scheduling application. Of the approximately forty respondents, two groups were selected to build prototype applications. Our NFLSched application was one of these two successful solutions.[1] The application was designed and implemented in a very short 10 week time frame using a proprietary constraint programming environment called ReSolver developed by Actenum.

Our analysis is that the underlying CSP is critically constrained. Many of the constraints reflect the business relationships between the NFL and the television networks. These constraints are often mutually conflicting requiring that "playable" solutions actually break a significant number of these constraints. Our approach to this problem has been to exploit the mixed-initiative capabilities of ReSolver. In particular, we have designed a system which involves the

[1] The other system was developed by a collaboration of Sengen of Marlton, New Jersey and ILOG S.A. of Paris, France.

user (human scheduler) directly in the scheduling process. Both the user and the system work together to search for playable solutions but always under user control. The user can explore different solution possibilities, adding and removing constraints and preferences as the search proceeds. Thus schedules can be produced which include as many desirable properties as possible while still being feasible (playable).

In the remainder of this short paper, we describe the NFL problem in more detail and characterize it as a mixed-initiative constraint satisfaction problem with preferences. Next we describe the constraint solving methodology used to search for solutions to the problem. Some practical details of the NFLSched application are also provided including the essential mixed-initiative (tweaking) functionality. Finally, we conclude with the status of the prototype, the lessons learned and the need for mixed-initiative tools like NFLSched to assist users in finding good solutions to very hard complexity problems.

## Problem Description

The NFL league has two divisions: NFC and AFC of 16 teams each for a total of 32 teams. Each team plays 16 games during the season both within its division and across divisions. So each team will play 8 home games and 8 away games against the same 8 opponents. The actual pairings of teams into games is decided before the scheduling begins. There are a total of 256 games played across both divisions in the full season. The season lasts 17 weeks with each team playing at most once per week. Each team necessarily will have a "bye" week once during the season which must occur between weeks 3-10 of the season.

The four broadcast networks (CBS, FOX, ESPN, and ABC) divide the games among their respective television shows. CBS and FOX both purchase blocks of 128 games each. Some of these are resold to the ESPN and ABC networks. The broadcast slots comprise Monday Night Football (ABC), ESPN games, FOX/CBS Sunday Double Headers, CBS Sunday and FOX Sunday games. The number of games per slot varies from week to week depending on the match-ups, geography and other constraints. For example, there may be between 0 and 2 games broadcast by ESPN per week while CBS may broadcast between 4 and 7 simulcast regional games on any particular Sunday.

## Constraint Satisfaction Problem Definition

The NFL league scheduling problem involves creating a schedule such that a set of games is assigned to television network timeslots with limited capacities within a 17 week season. The NFL season is a combination of two types of problems: constraint satisfaction and optimization. It involves hard constraints, those that need to be fulfilled by any schedule that would be acceptable, and soft constraints, those desirable properties that not need be necessarily fulfilled. Hence the most preferred solution will satisfy all hard constraints and break the least possible number of soft constraints.

Formally defined, a Constraint Satisfaction Problem (CSP), is a triple $(V, D, C)$, where $V = \{v_1, ..., v_n\}$ is a set of variables with corresponding finite domains of possible values for each variable $D = \{D_1, ..., D_n\}$ and $C$ is a set of k-ary hard constraints. A k-ary constraint defines the allowed combinations of values for a subset of k variables $(v_1, ..., v_k)$ from $V$. A solution to a CSP consists of assigning a value to each variable so that all constraints are satisfied.

The soft constraints, which arise in any real-life problem, account for the quality of the solution. NFL has a number of soft rules that bring penalty points to any solution that does not satisfy them. Finding the best fulfillment of these rules is an optimization problem.

The constraints defined by the NFL are complex, involving many varibles and over various characterstics (games, teams, timeslots) of the schedule. In addition, in our analysis they critically constrain the solution space. Hence, modeling this problem adequately was very difficult. We considered several CSP models for the NFL Scheduling problem: a grid of variables, the 32 teams *versus* the 17 weeks, assigning the opponent away teams (the usual model for Round-Robin schedules); a grid of the home teams *versus* away teams, assigning the timeslots, *et cetera*. We note that there are exactly 92 possible broadcasting timeslot types based on the week, network and broadcast time combinations. Each game needs to be assigned a timeslot. However, since the broadcast rights to each game are predetermined by the NFL ahead of time, each game can only be played in the timeslots of the owning network, which are usually one timeslot time per week such as the ESPN broadcast. Only the doubleheader games of FOX and CBS can be played in two different timeslots in a week. Thus, almost all games variables have 17 possble timeslot type assignments. In fact, we exploit the fact that several games, such as the Monday Night Football games, have fixed or almost fixed timeslots. This reduces the research space, however, our estimate of its size is still approximately $10^{40}$. Since each game has the home team and away team attributes, it was easy to express constraints over teams by simply selecting the games that involved these teams. In additional timeslot capacity constraints (such as CBS Sunday can show between 4 and 7 games in a week) were easily expressed over only the games that could be played in the given timeslot type. This model was selected because it compares to the other models in search space size, however it provides for easier incorporation of the various types of constraints and avoids composite values for variables.

## Pre-Defined Constraints and Scoring Rules

The search for candidate solutions is guided by league-specified constraints and scoring rules. Basically, the scheduling constraints determine the playability of a candidate schedule, while the scoring rules quantify the quality of the schedule.

### Stadium Blocks

Stadium blocks are used to determine when each stadium is available for home games: unavailable (hard); available but other events make playing there undesirable (soft); the stadium is available but other events may require the game to be moved (swap). The stadium blocks on the home team of a game determines when it can be played.

### Home/Away Spacing

Home/away spacing constraints can be constructed to ensure that all teams play a reasonable home/away pattern over the course of the season. There are a number of home/away spacing constraints including:

- Teams cannot play 3 consecutive home/away games during weeks 1-5
- Teams cannot play 3 consecutive home/away games during weeks 15-17
- Teams may play 1 set of 3 consecutive home/away games during weeks 4-16, but the schedule will receive 1 penalty point (Soft constraint)
- Teams must play at least 2 home/away games every 6 weeks
- Teams must play at least 4 home/away games every 10 weeks
- Teams cannot play 4 consecutive home/away games

### Opponent Spacing

When teams play each other twice in a season, as is the case for divisional opponents, the preference is for the two games to be spaced reasonably far apart. Ideally, the games should be at least 6 weeks apart with at least one game after the 8th week of the season:

- Any two opponents may only play 1 game every 8 weeks (at least 1 would have to be after week 8). If this constraint is violated, the schedule receives 1 penalty point. (Soft constraint)
- Any two opponents may only play 1 game every 3 weeks (cannot be violated).

### Shared Hometowns

For teams that share a stadium (New York Giants / New York Jets), the schedule imposes constraints that the two teams may not play at home on the same day.

In addition, for the teams that share a local viewing audience (New York Giants / New York Jets, San Francisco 49ers / Oakland Raiders) the schedule ensures that the two teams:

- Do not play at the same time
- Do not play on the same network (i.e. CBS or FOX) on the same afternoon

## Scheduling Strategy

The mixed-initiative paradigm involves the user in the solving process at several levels. The user can dynamically add and remove new constraints to the problem description. For example he may wish to enforce one of the preferences as a hard constraint. However, a human user can easily overconstrain the problem by adding additional constraints. Unfortunately most constructive methods do not support explanations (Jussein & Lhomme 2002) and nogood learning but are based on the tree search paradigm. Thus, such a method would simply report a failure to find a solution without any insight for the user about what went wrong.

Further, given the domain expertise in sport scheduling which is hard to convey to the programmers or incorporate in the CSP model, a user interaction during the search process itself can greatly facilitate finding the most desirable schedules (a property that cannot be fully grasped by the formal preferences). However, constructive search does not readily support dynamic constraint addition and retraction during the search process. In addition, working with the partial schedule produced during constructive search is hard because of the hidden hard constraints over the remaining unassigned variables.

All of these characteristics of the NFL problem called for a local search solution which works on a full (although) inconsistent assignment. In this environment, the user could work together with the search algorithm to fix the inconsistent parts of the schedule by manually (re)assigning variables. We developed a new hybrid constraint solving schema, called *systematic local search* (Havens & Dilkina 2004), which retains some systematicity of constructive search. Our method backtracks through a space of complete but possibly inconsistent solutions while supporting the freedom to move arbitrarily under heuristic guidance.

There has been various recent research into hybrid search schemes which combine desirable aspects of constructive and local search methods (Freuder & Wallace 1992; Ginsberg & McAllester 1994; Jussein & Lhomme 2002; Lynce, Baptista, & Marques-Silva 2001; Minton *et al.* 1990; Morris 1993; Prestwich 2001). In the work reported here extends these methods. The scheme operates from a nearly complete instantiation of values to variables (Ginsberg & McAllester 1994; Prestwich 2001). Forward checking of both assigned and unassigned variables is performed (Prestwich 2001). In this process we maintain a count of the number of constraints disallowing each domain value of every variable. Thus reassignment of a variable only involves subtracting the effects of the previous assignment and adding the effects of the new assignment to all neighbour variables. The hill-climbing gradient is the number of constraint violation. Using the minconflict heuristic (Minton *et al.* 1990), every variable chooses the value with the least constraint violations. This notion of a maximally consistent solution relaxes the requirement that the constructed partial solution remain consistent (Freuder & Wallace 1992).

The drawback of local search methods is that they suffer from local maxima and cycling. Different diversification methods have been developed to avoid these undesirabe effects such as simulated annealing, tabu lists(Glover 1990), random restart(Selman, Levesque, & Mitchell 1992), etc. These work extremely well especially on problems with adequate solution density.

Given that the NFL problem is critically constrained, we desire not only diversification but also some amount of systematicity that will guarantee that large portion of the search space is explored and that revisiting of old solutions is rare. In our schema, systematicity is enforced using a nogood cache of known inconsistent variable assignments (Ginsberg & McAllester 1994; Havens 1997; Jussein & Lhomme 2002; Stallman & Sussman 1977). These inconsistent variable assignments represent the violating constraint tuples at each local maximum as explicit new constraints guaranteeing that the local maximum will not be revisted in the future.

The nogoods provide the diversification needed to break away from local maximum and at the same time the use of randomized (arbitrary) backtracking (Gomes, Selman, & Kautz 1998; Jussein & Lhomme 2002; Lynce, Baptista, & Marques-Silva 2001; Yokoo 1994) preserves the freedom to move for every assigned variable.

Our Maximal Constraint Solving schema searches heuristically through a space of maximally consistent variable assignments while backtracking on assignments which are not acceptable solutions. It discards the maintenance of a totally consistent partial solution. Variables use value ordering heuristics to choose a *maximal assignment* from their live domain of allowed values (i.e. assignments not prevented by a known nogood). If no allowed values remain for some variable then that variable induces a nogood and backtracks. When all variables have chosen a maximal assignment, these assignments constitute a *maximal solution*. Such a solution is a mutual local maxima for every variable. If the maximal solution does not exhibit full consistency then the solution induces nogoods and again the system backtracks.

The systematic local search algorithm is listed in Figure 1. Given a set of variables, $V$, and constraints, $C$, $solve(V, C)$ returns the first solution, $\alpha$, whose assignments satisfy each constraint in $C$. The algorithm operates as follows. In the initial global assignment, $\alpha$, (line 2) every variable is unassigned. The loop beginning in line 3 is repeated until every variable assignment in $\alpha$ is assigned the best value (MAXIMAL) and is still allowed (in line 13). Then the solution, $\alpha$, is returned in line 14. While every variable is not MAXIMAL (line 4), a variable, $x$, is chosen via the variable ordering heuristic, $select(V)$. Then the variable, $x$, is assigned the best allowed domain element. However, if an *empty nogood* is ever derived (line 7) then the algorithm returns failure indicating that no solution exists.

When every variable is MAXIMAL, the current global assignment, $\alpha$, is a maximal solution but may not be a consistent solution. Beginning in line 9, for every constraint, $c \in C$, which is not satisfied, a new nogood, $\lambda_\perp$, is derived from $c$ and added to the nogood cache, $\Gamma$ in line 11.[2]

The use of nearly complete instantiation of variables, of nogood recording and explanations allowed for the mixed initiative paradigm in which the user could stop the engine at any time and look at the current state of the solution and constrain additionally the schedule thus guiding the engine towards feasible solutions. In addition, once a playable solution is found the user could modify it, and hence breaking

[2]Without an infinite nogood store, the algorithm stills remains incomplete since it does not systematically cover the entire search space.

```
1  function solve(V, C) {
2    α =all variables unassigned
3    repeat {
4      while (α ≠ MAXIMAL) {
5        let x = select(V);
6        assign(x);
7        if empty nogood is derived return noSolution;
8      }
9      ∀c ∈ C s.t. c is inconsistent {
10       λ⊥ = failure(c);
11       add λ⊥ to Γ, the nogood store;
12     }
13   } until (α = MAXIMAL);
14   return α;
15 }
```

Figure 1: The *solve* algorithm finds a consistent solution of the variables $V$ for the constraints $C$.

some constraints, and then the search algorithm would try to find the closest feasible solution incorporating the user decisions by iteratively fixing the broken constraints by following again the minconflict gradient. We provided a simple integration of soft constraint in the prototype by allowing users to dynamically add these constraints to the problem and try to find feasible solutions to the further constrained problem.

## Application Description

Our solution consists of three (3) separate modules:

- The Database Module - used for storing scheduling data, constraints, scoring rules, and completed solutions
- The User Interface Module - an easy to use GUI for defining any number of global or team-specific scheduling constraints
- The Intelligent Interactive Search (IIS) Module - an interactive scheduling grid for generating, modifying or 'tweaking, viewing, and printing candidate schedules

### Database Module (Schedules, Constraints, Scoring)

The database module, which is Oracle based, maintains all data pertinent to the scheduling application. It is connected to both the User Interface Module and the IIS Module and contains four independent datasets: scheduling parameters, pre-defined scheduling constraints and scoring rules, interactive constraints, and completed schedules.

Each of these datasets contains two uniquely defined indexes, [Season] and [Scenario], which allow users to create and isolate data for any number of "what-if" situations complete with names, date/time stamps, security levels, etc.

Handling these datasets independently allows users to:

- Apply different scoring schemes to current/past schedules
- Interactively modify or "tweak" schedules

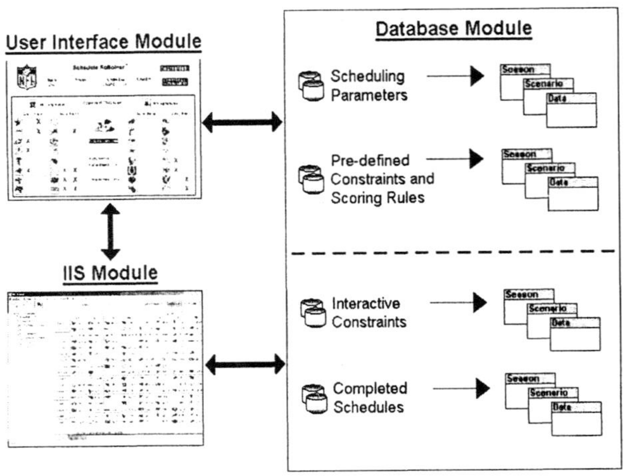


Figure 2: Application Architecture

### User Interface Module

The schedule definition parameters are the datasets required to build the scheduling framework. They include:

- Season data: Schedule weeks, bye allocation, etc.
- Team data: Team logos, divisional & conference alignments, home/away opponents, etc.
- Network data: Network slots, package requirements, allowable game/slot combinations, etc.

In addition to tying together the Database Module and the IIS Module, the User-Interface Module or "front-end" allows users to:

- Construct the schedule definition requirements and data required for a new season or "what if" scenario
- Modify schedule-definition parameters such as season data, team data, and network data
- Modify scheduling constraints and scoring rules

### Intelligent Interactive Search Module

The Intelligent Interactive Search (IIS) Module is the interface between the user and the search engine. It allows users to:

- Initiate the search for solutions
- Add aditional constraints
- Interact with the schedule during search
- Save/Restore schedules

It provided the user with different views of the schedule that made it easier to assess it and interact with it. The views are:

- Games: a grid of game cells including the home and away team, the network and asigned timeslot
- Teams vs. Weeks: 2 grids for the 2 divisions respectively of 16 teams vs. 17 weeks. Each cell included the opponent in the game played by the team in the given week (or 'bye'), the status (home or away), the network, and timeslot
- Networks vs. Weeks: the list of games owed by the particular network played in the given week

### Pre-Defined vs. Interactive Constraints

Our proposed solution allows users to define two different types of constraints: pre-defined and interactive. Essentially, pre-defined constraints are used for general schedule requirements, and are constructed using the User Interface Module, while interactive constraints are used for tuning schedules in the IIS Module. The scheduling constraints and scoring rules datasets will be used to guide the scheduling application towards playable and fair "initial" schedules, which may then be tweaked by the user.

The User Interface Module allows users to construct any number of pre-defined constraints and scoring rules that affect stadium blocks, home/away spacing, opponent spacing, game spacing (rest days), shared hometowns, network appearances, game parings, and general fairness rules.

In addition, many of these constraints and scoring rules are "dialable", meaning that they may be adjusted or turned off for any or all of the teams, depending on the scheduling scenario.

Intelligent Interactive Search system offers the user the ability to explicitly specify the date or network of any match-up (or range of match-ups) during the interactive process. The details of these interactive constraints are stored in a dataset and can be can be disabled at any time as desired.

### Schedule Interaction

Our proposed solution allows users to interactively add/remove/modify constraints as a way of exploring the solution space to ultimately to find "better" schedules (keeping in mind that better schedules do not always correspond with lower scores). The search engine uses the existing solution as a starting point and searches for solutions that observe the modified constraints.

Any of the following constraint changes may be made interactively to help the user improve upon a found schedule:

- Changes to stadiums blocks or the forcing of bye weeks
- "Manual" game assignments
- Global or team-specific changes to home/away spacing, divisional opponent spacing, game pairing or fairness constraints
- Changes to allowable game/slot options

## Application Development and Evaluation

The appication was developed using *Java* 2 1.3 with *Swing*$^{TM}$ components using *Borland JBuilder*$^{TM}$ 7 under different operating systems(Sun Microsystems, Macintosh and Windows). The CSP model and search sheme were implemented in *ReSolver*$^{TM}$, a constraint programming library owed by Actenum Corporation.

The *NFLsched* prototype was build with extremely limited resources: only 10 weeks of development time, 5 programmers and a sports scheduling consultant [3]. The modeling of the problem and the definition of the constraints from the NFL specifications required domain expertise that the development team lacked in the beginning. The longest and hardest development stage was designing the search algorithm. In addition, an important part was designing meaningful graphical interface that allowed the user to visualize the schedule from different perspectives and conviniently interact with it.

The system was able to find within 1 to 2 hour playable schedules of preference quality around 30 when run on an COMPAQ 1.6G MHz PC with 500MB RAM. However, we estimate that when used by a domain expert it can find schedules faster and of better quality. It was tested on the season scheduling data from 2002 provided by NFL at the start of the development period. Finally, the NFLSched application was compared in performance to the other prototype system on the scheduling data for 2003 provided one day in advance of the testing date. Both systems were run as a batch solver and both were able to find feasible solutions in about one hour. The mixed-initiative capabilities of our system were not used in the trial test and the final contract was awarded to our competitor.

The prototype developed provides easy interface for entering the season data such as games selected, network rights, hard constraints, etc. The mixed-initiative functionality and dynamic constraint support allows for easy experimentation with different rules, preference scoring, for intimate particiaption in the scheduling process and use of human exprtise. In particular, satisfying additional broadcast preferences would have substantial monetary advantage.

## Conclusion

In this short paper, we provided a specification of the NFL scheduling problem, its model as a constraint optimization problem, and the description of a prototype scheduling application. Our solution used the constraint programming paradigm applying techniques both from Artificial Intelligence and Operations Research such as constraint propagation, nogood learning and inference, and local search.

The development of this prototype required the innovation of a new hybrid search schema, described in detail in (Havens & Dilkina 2004). In addition, it raised important research issues that have not been currently adequately addressed such as mixing hard satisfaction constraints with soft constraints or preferences. There has been recent work on solving soft CSPs, but not for what one can call *'hybrid' CSP*, which have the two distinct categories of constraints, those that necessarily must hold and those that could be unpreferably broken. We discovered that the mixed-initiative paradigm calls for further understanding and research in the area of explanations (Jussein & Lhomme 2002).

Despite the complexity and the unusual nature of this sport scheduling problem, we were successful at building a functional prototype that can find playable schedules for the NFL league.

[3] Rick Stone, President of Optimal Planning Solutions

## References


Freuder, E., and Wallace, R. 1992. Partial constraint satisfaction. *Artificial Intelligence* 58:21–70.

Ginsberg, M., and McAllester, D. 1994. Gsat and dynamic backtracking. In *proc. 4th Int. Conf. on Principles of Knowledge Representation and Reasoning*.

Glover, F. 1990. Tabu search: a tutorial. *Interfaces* 20:74–94.

Gomes, C.; Selman, B.; and Kautz, H. 1998. Boosting combinatorial search through randomization. In *proc. Fifteenth National Conference on Artificial Intelligence*, 431–437. AAAI Press.

Havens, W., and Dilkina, B. 2004. A hybrid scheme for systematic local search. In *proc. Seventeenth Canadian Conference on Artificial Intelligence*.

Havens, W. 1997. Nogood caching for multiagent backtrack search. In *proc. AAAI-97 Constraints and Agents Workshop*.

Henz, M. 1999. Constraint based round robin tournament planning. In *proc. Sixteenth International Conference on Logic Programming*, 545–557. MIT Press.

Jussein, N., and Lhomme, O. 2002. Local search with constraint propagation and conflict-based heuristics. *Artificial Intelligence* 139:21–45.

Lynce, I.; Baptista, L.; and Marques-Silva, J. P. 2001. Stochastic systematic search algorithms for satisfiability. In *proc. LICS Workshop on Theory and Applications of Satisfiability Testing (LICS-SAT)*.

Minton, S.; Johnston, M.; Phillips, A.; and Laird, P. 1990. Minimizing conflicts: a heuristic repair method for constraint satisfaction and scheduling problems. *Artificial Intelligence* 58:161–205.

Morris, P. 1993. The breakout method for escaping from local minima. In *proc. AAAI-93*, 40–45.

Nemhauser, G., and Trick, M. 1998. Scheduling a major college basketball conference. *Operations Research* 46(1):1–8.

Prestwich, S. 2001. Local search and backtracking vs nonsystematic backtracking. In *proc. AAAI 2001 Fall Symposium on Using Uncertainty within Computation*.

Selman, B.; Levesque, H.; and Mitchell, D. 1992. A new method for solving hard satisfiability problems. In *proc. 10th National Conf. on Artificial Intelligence*, 440–446.

Stallman, R., and Sussman, G. 1977. Forward reasoning and dependency-directed backtracking in a system for computer-aided circuit analysis. *Artificial Intelligence* 9:135–196.

Yokoo, M. 1994. Weak commitment search for solving constraint satisfaction problems. In *proc. AAAI-94*, 313–318.

# VModel: A Visual Qualitative Modeling Environment for Middle-school Students


**Kenneth D. Forbus**
Qualitative Reasoning Group
Northwestern University
1890 Maple Avenue
Evanston, IL, 60201, USA
forbus@northwestern.edu

**Karen Carney**
Qualitative Reasoning Group
Northwestern University
1890 Maple Avenue
Evanston, IL, 60201, USA
k-carney@northwestern.edu

**Bruce L. Sherin**
School of Education
and Social Policy
Northwestern University
2115 N. Campus Drive
Evanston, IL, 60201, USA
bsherin@northwestern.edu

**Leo C. Ureel II**
Qualitative Reasoning Group
Northwestern University
1890 Maple Avenue
Evanston, IL, 60201, USA
ureel@cs.northwestern.edu



### Abstract

Learning how to create, test, and revise models is a central skill in scientific reasoning. We argue that qualitative modeling provides an appropriate level of representation for helping middle-school students learn to become modelers. We describe Vmodel, a system we have created that uses visual representations that enables middle-school students to create qualitative models. Software coaches use simple analyses of model structure plus qualitative simulation to provide feedback and explanations. This system has been used in several studies in Chicago Public School classrooms, using curricula developed in collaboration with teachers. We discuss the design of the visual representation language, how Vmodel works, and evidence from school studies that indicate it is successful in helping students.


## Introduction

Modeling is a central skill in scientific reasoning. Learning to formulate, analyze, test, and revise models is a crucial aspect of understanding science, and critical to helping students become active, lifelong learners. Supporting students in articulating models of a domain, and refining them through experience, reflection, and discussion with peers and teachers, can lead to deeper, systematic understanding of science [5]. However, modeling is often treated as an art. Since modeling formalisms have traditionally been associated with creating mathematical models and deriving numerical results, they have been relatively inaccessible to younger students, such as middle school students.

Qualitative reasoning formalisms provide the expressive power needed to capture the intuitive, causal notions of many human mental models [9]. This includes expressing aspects of modeling not handled by traditional formalisms, e.g., conditions of applicability and other types of modeling knowledge. However, the predicate calculus based formalisms typically used in QR work provide a serious entry barrier to their use by children.

Our solution to this problem is to develop a *visual representation language*, based on concept maps, that provides a student-friendly way to express qualitative models, and software that helps students create and refine qualitative models. This paper describes the visual language and our modeling software Vmodel which uses it. We start by motivating our approach. The design and software architecture of Vmodel is outlined next, focusing on its ontology, supports for the modeling process, and coaching. Evidence that suggests Vmodel helps students learn from classroom experiments is summarized. We close by describing related work and future plans.

## Approach

Why do we want students to become modelers? (1) Models provide a means to externalize thought. External representations help reduce working memory load, allowing students to work through more complex problems. External representations also help them present their ideas for discussion and collaboration, an important aspect of learning among young students [3]. (2) The process of modeling itself is valuable. It forces students to articulate relationships between entities and dependencies between their beliefs. This is important for both understanding the phenomenon being modeled but also in developing a broader understanding of complex, interrelated systems, an important goal in the AAAS standards [1]. The idea that a change in one variable may have far-reaching and unforeseen consequences is missing from many science curricula. The qualitative causal relationships developed by the QR community provide an appropriate level of expressive power for achieving this goal. (3) Modeling provides students with practice in using formal representations, a skill they will need for mastering mathematics and programming. It provides them with a source of experience in the creative, liberating power of a technical vocabulary. Qualitative modeling, being grounded in everyday experience, can provide a bridge to more complex symbolic formalisms.

Given that we want to make students into modelers, how do we do it? Graphical external representations, coupled with computer support, can provide powerful ways for people to communicate and collaborate. Many graphical external representations have been created to aid students. They can be grouped into three families: (1) *Concept Map notations*. Concept maps [20,4] describe structural and functional properties and relationships between entities and

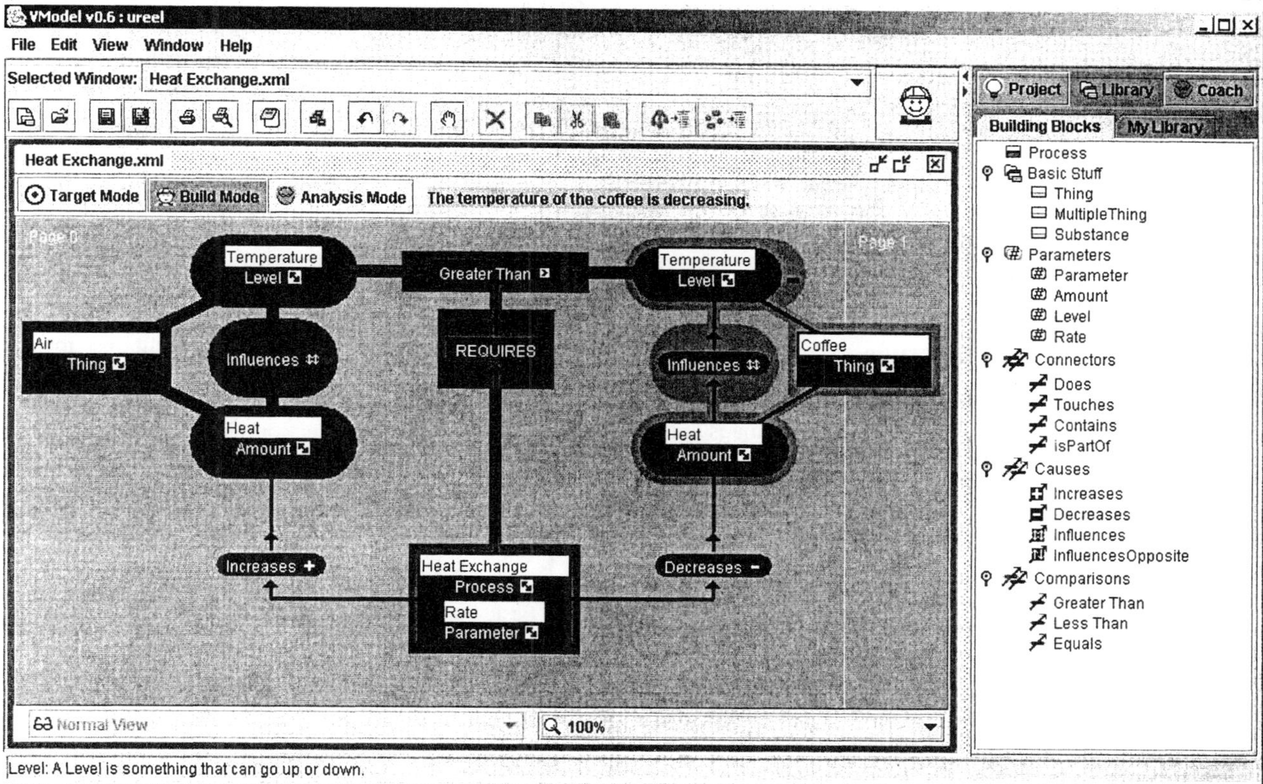


**Figure 1: The Vmodel interface**

ideas. Typically, concept maps express global or time-invariant information. (2) *Dynamical Systems notations*. Forrester's version of system dynamics [14], Bond graphs, and software systems such as STELLA [15] and Model-It [16] provide graphical languages for expressing differential equations for continuous systems. (3) *Argumentation environments*. Belvedere [22] and the Collaboratory Notebook [8] are examples of software that use graphical conventions to help students gather, create and reason about evidence and arguments for and against hypotheses.

Each of these notations expresses some aspects of modeling, but none of them alone is sufficient. For example, concept maps adhere to minimal structural or semantic requirements. Although in theory they can be used to express anything, the lack of standardized semantics makes it difficult for students to understand each other's concept maps and extremely difficult to create software that detects whether or not maps are well-formed [4,21]. Dynamical system notations do not express the conditions under which a given model is applicable. Argumentation environments treat as atomic what would be whole complex structures in notations, which limits their ability to scaffold students in detailed explorations.

Even taken together, these notational families and curricula based on them neglect two key issues in understanding the art of modeling: (1) *The importance of broadly-applicable principles and processes*. Existing educational modeling systems treat each modeling task as a new problem, with no connection to other situations. This misses any opportunity to help students see that the same principles and processes operate across a broad range of situations. For example, the basic idea of heat flow is relevant to chemistry, biology, atmospheric physics and many other areas that, on the surface, appear unrelated. Existing modeling systems do not help students see the importance of creating a systematic body of knowledge (as scientists do), as opposed to a series of ad hoc explanations concerning specific systems. (2) *Qualitative understanding of behavior*. Modeling systems tend to be numerical (e.g., STELLA), although sometimes including a qualitative layer on top to simplify model creation (e.g., Model-It). Understanding numerical data plots as depicting behavior is an important skill, but providing all the data needed to run a numerical model can distract students from understanding the causal phenomena in the situation. In addition, the level of mathematics necessary to make a model of any reasonably complex phenomenon may be out of reach for a young student. Mathematics shifts the representation away from the basic level entities a student might naturally attend to. For example, a mathematical model necessitates students simultaneously representing all influences in a single equation or set of equations. This may be beyond the student. In addition, a student may not be able to easily interpret outcomes couched in mathematical terms or to debug wrong models.

The theories, representations, and reasoning techniques developed in qualitative reasoning research provide most of the pieces needed to address these problems. Enabling and encouraging students to create their own domain theories should help them understand the broad applicability of scientific principles and processes. Qualitative modeling provides both the formalisms for expressing intuitive, causal models and the reasoning techniques needed to generate predictions and explanations from them for helping students see the consequences of their ideas. Making these formalisms available through a visual notation makes this power accessible to young students.

## The design and architecture of VModel

We have created a visual modeling tool for conceptual modeling that combines good ideas from concept maps and dynamical systems notations into a qualitative modeling environment. The basic organization uses concept maps, but with some very strong restrictions. As usual, nodes represent entities and properties of entities. However, each node has a specified type, such as `Thing` or `Process`, drawn from the system's ontology. As usual, links represent relationships. However, the labels used on links are drawn from a fixed set of relationships.

These restrictions provide a clearer semantics than traditional concept maps have. In traditional concept maps, any path of whatever length is intended to be a proposition, i.e., a natural-language statement that is true about what is being described. With our restrictions, links in our concept maps can be identified with propositional logic statements involving binary relations.[1] This makes software coaching more feasible than in traditional concept maps. Figure 1 shows the interface and a model.

These constraints address the tradeoff between providing freedom of expression versus scaffolding for students. Providing their own names for entities and properties enables them to express their ideas more accurately (e.g., "temperature" versus "hotness" versus "cold"). Requiring students to select a general type for entities and properties helps coaching software figure out which is which, and avoids the need to do natural language understanding on their typed phrases. Restricting links to a fixed set of relationships provides a powerful scaffold for students, ensuring that their ideas are at least in the ballpark in terms of form of argument[2]. It also forces students to enter a community of modelers, enabling their ideas to be compared and contrasted with those of others more easily.

The other basic feature of our design is the use of a *Model Library*. All of the models a student builds are included in their Model Library. The Model Library also contains extensions they create to the entity ontology, based on their modeling of specific situations, i.e., a simple form of domain theory. This encourages students to generalize across situations. A student's Model Library thus represents their evolving understanding, providing a portfolio and support for reflection.

The underlying ontology used in Vmodel is that of qualitative process theory [12]. Systems and phenomena are modeled via sets of entities with continuous parameters, whose relationships are expressed using a causal, qualitative mathematics, where processes provide an explicit notion of mechanism. Although QP theory was designed to capture everyday adult intuitions about the physical world, creating a student-friendly visual notation was one of the major design challenges in Vmodel.

In the rest of this section, we describe Vmodel's ontology, the Model Library, workflow, and coaching.

| Entities | | Relationships | |
|---|---|---|---|
| Processes: | | Connectors: | |
| | Process | | Does |
| | | | Touches |
| Basic Stuff: | | | Contains |
| | Thing | | isPartOf |
| | Multiple-Thing | | |
| | Substance | Controllers: | |
| | | | Requires |
| Parameters: | | | |
| | Parameter | Comparisons: | |
| | Amount | | Greater than |
| | Level | | Less than |
| | Rate | | Equals |
| | | Causes: | |
| | | | Increases |
| | | | Decreases |
| | | | Influences |
| | | | InfluencesOpposite |

**Table 1: The Vmodel ontology**

### The Vmodel Ontology

Table 1 illustrates the basic ontology used in Vmodel. The contents are more or less familiar in AI representation practice, although some of the names have been changed to be kid-friendly, based on our classroom experiences.

There are three kinds of entities. Processes represent the QP theory notion of physical process. Basic Stuffs represent objects (Thing, e.g., an elephant), groups (Multiple-Thing, e.g., a population) and substances (e.g., water) in the world. Parameters represent the QP theory notion of quantity. As a form of scaffolding, we include subclasses for extensive parameters (Amount), intensive parameters (Level), and rates (Rate), since these are fundamental distinctions that middle-school students are unclear on, but must master. An unspecified type (Parameter) is also provided to support brainstorming.

The astute reader will notice that there is no relationship in the ontology presented to students that links a quantity

---

[1] This restriction to binary relations entails no loss of expressivity for two reasons. First, higher-arity relationships can be expressed via reification. Second, the use of compositional relationships such as influences enables the assembly of more complex statements by underlying reasoning systems.

[2] For example "Pixies do it" and other anthropomorphic arguments are simply not expressible.

to an entity. In Vmodel such links are unlabelled, because (a) they are extremely common, (b) we never found a concise term and explanation that didn't confuse students, and (c) students are perfectly happy not articulating this connection, given the intimate nature of the relationship between an entity and its continuous properties. An unlabelled line is used to relate an entity and a parameter of it, which in the interface is introduced by a right-click menu on the entity itself.

Connectors provide a small vocabulary of relationships to express configural information (e.g., Touches, Contains, isPartOf). The relationship Does is used when a process is considered to be part of some entity (e.g., a stomach does digestion). The conditions for a process are expressed using Controllers, i.e., the Requires relationship. The Requires relationship links a physical process to a relationship (cf. Figure 1).

Value information about parameters is expressed via comparisons, i.e., Greater Than, Less Than, and Equals. Given the curricula we have examined, we have not yet seen a requirement for $\leq$ or $\geq$.

Causes express QP theory's qualitative mathematics of influences. Influences are particularly appropriate because of their compositional nature: Each influence can be stated as a link, and the set of such links provides the set of influences on a parameter in a student's model.

Finding student-friendly names for these relationships took considerable experimentation. Here are the names we have found that work reasonably well:

- Increases/Decreases: Indicates an integral connection between two parameters, i.e., heat flow decreases the heat of its source and increases the heat of its destination. These are QP theory's direct influences, with Increases $\equiv$ I+ and Decreases $\equiv$ I-.
- Influences/InfluencesOpposite: Indicates functional dependence between two parameters, i.e., the heat of something determines its temperature. These are QP theory's indirect influences, with Influences $\equiv \propto_{Q+}$ and InfluencesOpposite $\equiv \propto_{Q-}$.

In early classroom trials, we experimented with an extended vocabulary that included relationships that didn't make a commitment to the sign (i.e., $\propto_{Q*}$) and relationships didn't make a commitment to the direction of causal relationship between two parameters. The intent was to allow students to first articulate and then refine their partial understandings. In practice, students using weaker relationships rarely refined them, hence their elimination.

Vmodel is designed to be very general, in order to handle a wide variety of phenomena and so be relevant to a broad range of middle-school topics. Consequently, we allow certain aspects of the ontology to be extended. For example, teachers and curriculum developers are allowed to extend the vocabulary of Connectors as desired. We can allow this since Vmodel's reasoning software does not exploit the specific semantics of these vocabulary items. However, the rest of the relational vocabulary is fixed, since these terms are used in Vmodel's reasoning. Teachers and curriculum designers can also "seed" the Model Library with new entities and processes, using the same capabilities available to students, as described below.

## The Model Library

The true power of modeling arises when students can use concepts they developed in earlier exercises to tackle more complex problems. Few modeling tools explicitly support this kind of reuse and abstraction, but we believe that it encourages the systematization of a student's knowledge. For example, maintaining a library of models and abstractions derived from them should facilitate transfer of ideas from one situation to another.

The Model Library contains two kinds of information. First, it includes a *portfolio* of all of the modeling projects a student (or a group of students) has tackled. The ability to refer back to previous exercises promotes reflection. The second kind of information in the model library is a catalog of entities and processes that the student has extracted from previous models to use as parts for future models. Adding an entity to the Model Library simply copies a template containing that entity, all of its quantities, and all relationships between those properties. Using the new entity in a subsequent model simply copies that piece of map into the current model. Adding a process to the Model Library causes a general template to be created. The participants of the process are identified by using any Requires links and causal relationships involving the process' rate parameter, and these participants are replaced by variables. When this template is used in a new model, these variables appear as diamonds, which can be dragged onto other elements of the model to "wire in" the process instance into the model. Thus students can accumulate a general library of physical processes.

One simplification we have made to keep Vmodel usable by middle-school students is to only allow a single level of extension to the process and entity ontologies. Ideally, one might want to have a full lattice of classes, with multiple layers. We have found that middle-school students are struggling with the idea of representing continuous properties via parameters. Thus it seems unwise to burden them with additional subtleties at this stage.

## Supporting the modeling process

Modeling involves several different activities. We communicate and support this by organizing the software among several modes, each of which corresponds to a modeling activity. These are *stating the problem*, *modeling*, and *analysis*. We describe each in turn.

**Problem statement.** Students are always asked to identify how one specific continuous parameter of the system will change (i.e., increase, decrease, or remain constant), the *modeling target*. A model is successful when its qualitative simulation produces the predicted result and yields a plausible explanation. We discovered through experimentation that such structuring is very important for students. Otherwise, they tend to treat modeling as a "brain dump", putting in everything that they can think of.

**Modeling.** The Build mode in the interface is where students create and edit their concept map, using the representations outlined above. Their specific prediction about a change in a parameter, based on their model target, is made here as well. Most of the student's time is spent in Build mode.

**Analysis**. The Analysis mode is where students analyze their model through simulation and reflection. Upon entering analysis mode, the students' model is analyzed via qualitative simulation. The qualitative simulation method we use is extremely simple. Every process instance in a model must be active. Therefore we can identify all directly influenced parameters by finding all the increases/decreases links, and resolve them using the laws of QP theory. If there is an ambiguity, due to conflicting direct influences, it is resolved by asking the student for the outcome. Influence resolution continues by propagating changes through indirect influences, until directions of change for all parameters have been found. (Uninfluenced parameters are of course unchanging, as per QP theory.)

While simple, this qualitative simulation method is very appropriate for middle-school modeling tasks. We only deal with a single (tacit) qualitative state, avoiding the complexity of branching behaviors and envisioning. All rates are tacitly assumed to be positive. These assumptions suffice for the vast majority of the examples that middle-school students deal with. Resolving ambiguous influences via asking the student is straightforward and easy for them to understand. Unfortunately, this means the software cannot support discussion of relative magnitudes and when effects can be neglected. On the other hand, we have seen little need for such discussions so far.

The results of qualitative simulation are provided to the student in terms of a textual explanation. For example, this explanation is generated from a model of heating water in a microwave oven:

- There is the process of Heating which
    - Increases the Heat of Water that is INCREASING and which
    - Influences the Temperature of Water that is INCREASING

The generated text serves several pedagogical purposes. First, it encourages students to name and decompose their entities properly, since the templates include conventions such as "*<quantity>* of *<entity>*". This overcomes a student tendency to lump things together by relying on their language skills (e.g., "Trixie eating does eating." grates, even though the fragment of concept map that gives rise to the statement at first did not.) Second, it illustrates the process that students should follow when reasoning with causal models on their own. This point is reinforced by animation used during qualitative simulation, where the quantity currently being considered is highlighted and intermediate results are displayed as graphical annotations on the student's model.

## Supporting students in modeling

We have built in a number of supports to help students learn modeling. The most basic is an embedded HTML-based help system, which provides answers to questions about the software, modeling (e.g., How do I know when I am done?), and the representation system. Most of the interface design was driven by scaffolding needs. For example, when a Process is created, it always includes inside itself a Rate parameter, since every process must have one (see Figure 1). Similarly, the use of "skins" to provide visual cues for grouping helps deal with complex maps. Each entity is assigned a unique color, and the skin grows to include every quantity of it. Moreover, the skin for a process expands to include the Requires link and the antecedent relationship it links to.

Through several years of experimentation in schools, we found two kinds of software coaching to be useful. The first concerns structural properties of models, and the second concerns the qualitative simulation of the model. We discuss each in turn.

**Structural Coaching:** Students learning the visual notation often have trouble with its syntax and grammar, i.e., what kinds of relationships can be used to connect what sorts of elements. We call the coach for this the Builder. The Builder uses a simple set of rules to identify when they are using modeling elements incorrectly, when a more appropriate modeling element is available, or when there are missing elements or inconsistencies in their model. For example, two of the Builder's rules, stated in English, are: "A direct influence relationship must be connected between the rate of a process and any type of parameter" and "No type of parameter can have both a direct influence and an indirect influence as input."

In addition to scaffolding the student in modeling, the Builder also acts as a gate-keeper for Analysis mode. That is, the student cannot proceed until the Builder is satisfied. This prevents the qualitative simulator from having to deal with models that do not satisfy the constraints of QP theory (which of course is a different issue from whether or not the model's contents are correct).

The Builder indicates when it finds a problem in two non-intrusive ways. First, an icon always depicts the state of the Builder. The default icon is smiling, but as the student's model accumulates errors, it is replaced by a puzzled-looking icon. If a large number of errors are made, a frowning icon is used. Second, parts of the model that are implicated in problems are highlighted in red. Students can query the coach as to the nature of the problem(s) by clicking on the coach icon or by right-clicking on the indicated modeling element. The coach responds by displaying its analysis of the current state of the model. It is important that the coach be non-intrusive because editing a model often involves temporary inconsistencies.

**Analysis Coaching:** When the student enters analysis mode, another coach, the Professor, becomes available. The Professor provides help in interpreting the results of their simulation. For example, if there is a mismatch between the student's prediction and the results of the simulation, this is noted as part of the text generated along with the simulation, e.g.,

**Model Check**

Level Temperature

- You predicted that Temperature would be DECREASING but instead it is INCREASING

with the offending parameter highlighted in red. Like the Builder, the Professor is depicted by icons indicating various degrees of contentment or alarm, depending on the student's results.

## Classroom experiences

The classroom portion of this research has been conducted as part of the NSF Center for Learning Technologies in Urban Schools, (LeTUS) a partnership involving Northwestern University, University of Michigan, and the Chicago and Detroit Public School systems. The Center developed inquiry-based middle school science curricula. These curricula were developed in *work circles*, a collaborative organization that involves researchers, teachers, and school administrators in developing and adapting materials for classroom settings. This joint development arrangement provided invaluable feedback and supports experiments in a variety of urban schools

We helped CPS teachers develop two curricula. One curriculum concerns heat and temperature, in which students consider alternate energy resources for homes (cf. [18]). In collaboration with Marcia Linn's group at Berkeley, we added complementary simulation-based activities to their successful thermal curriculum [19]. These activities use self-explanatory simulators [13] to allow students to explore the outcomes of design choices in making a solar house. The other curriculum concerns ecosystems, using as a hook the creation of a life support system for a Mars colony. This provides an arena for students to explore the requirements of life and how ecosystems work, using simulation experiments.

Our design process for the visual notation was guided by pencil and paper studies we carried out in CPS classrooms. The first pilot studies with the software took place in Winter and Spring of 2001, in a bilingual magnet school in Chicago. Eleven sixth graders (aged eleven and twelve) worked together, in groups of two or three, creating models related to the Mars curriculum. The task was initially posed in terms of relationships between two species (e.g., grass and antelopes) and students were asked to extend their models to handle new species. The second and third studies (Fall 2001/Winter 2002, Spring 2003) also used the Mars curriculum. In a seventh-grade classroom, students completed a combination of class-wide and small-group modeling exercises to plan an ecosystem from scratch. Students working in small groups were asked to discuss and justify their models in front of the entire class. Data was collected via videotaping, clinical interviews, and portfolios of models constructed.

Since this paper is about the design and architecture of Vmodel, we focus on results that bear on these choices. In particular, between the second and third studies, we added most of the modeling process supports (e.g., the model target) and the qualitative simulator.

- *Naturalness of the visual language.* After some tuning, student questions tend to focus on contents of the models, rather than on how to use the primitives of the modeling language. However, that does not mean that they always used these concepts correctly. In the first two studies, 67% (198/296) of boxes and 44% (113/258) of arrows were used correctly. In the third study, correct box use rose to 74% (222/298) and correct arrow use rose to 96% (221/230).
- *Structure of causal chains.* Prior to introducing stronger coaching, student models exhibited a variety of flaws in their causal models. Causal paths were often short, with several disconnected paths rather than a single path explaining a change. Student would often leave out processes and attempt to specify direct entity-to-entity relationships, rather than articulating the specific quantities involved. After introducing stronger coaching, student causal paths became longer and more focused on explaining changes specified in the target.

These observations suggest that qualitative simulation and coaching are actually providing significant value in Vmodel. Is Vmodel helping students learn modeling? Here the analysis of data is still in progress, but the results so far are very encouraging:

- *Generalization in modeling.* Even though there have not been many opportunities yet in the curriculum to make generalizations based on their models, we are finding that students do indeed start exploiting abstractions. One student for instance, used their model of gazelles and grass to model the interaction between lions and gazelles via the appropriate substitutions. This is not an easy thing for students to grasp. In one classroom discussion, students were working out what to name a model they had created that described an astronaut's weight gain or loss in terms of their caloric intake and their exercise and metabolic needs. Could the model be used to explain more than just astronauts? How could it be made truly general, if it wasn't already? One girl ventured "I think it should be called 'the calorie cycle' because you could take out ASTRONAUT and replace it with DOG, and that model would explain both." That is the kind of insight that we want them all to attain.

Unfortunately, we are also finding some places where further improvements could be made:

- *Comparison and reflection were lacking.* Students often viewed their model as finished when "both coaches were happy." This is not surprising given how work is structured in middle-school classrooms. Similarly, students sometimes viewed reusing models from their library as "cheating."

• *Causal map redundancy.* Students are able to use physical process descriptions correctly. However, they sometimes include extra statements that summarize the result of influence chains in a particular situation. For instance, they might have that the rate of predation of gazelles by lions is influenced by the population of lions, and that the rate of predation decreases the population of gazelles, which is a correct partial description of predation. But they will often add an additional relationship between population of gazelles and population of lions, in an attempt to summarize the effect of the mechanism.

We discuss our plans for tackling these problems next.

## Plans for additional coaching

We are designing an analogy-based [11] coaching facility to provide feedback based on normative models. (Normative models are authored using the same software, so that teachers and curriculum developers can add content without us being involved.) The candidate inferences of a comparison of a student model to a normative model can provide suggestions for what a student might want to think about in order to improve their model [7].

On the other hand, there are infrastructure difficulties. Students working in schools with network connections will be able to use an email facility built into the software. Unfortunately, many classrooms are not so endowed, and in those cases we resort to carrying a floppy or laptop back with us to get the data, or asking the teacher to email student work to us later using their personal accounts. Even if every classroom were networked, we would continue to use email, rather than web-based, coaching for scalability. One does not expect an instant reply to an email message, whereas a web server that does not respond instantly is annoying. Our collaborating teachers find this model reasonable because students will only be working a small part of any typical day on science activities, and that time will be spent in discussions as well as computer work.

For people unconstrained by such computational resource limitations, we are planning a knowledge entry and analysis tool based on VModel with supercharged modeling and analysis capabilities. We plan to merge VModel-like concept mapping with our open-domain sketching system, sKEA [10]. To this we will attach a domain-independent, mixed-initiative Socratic tutor, which will provide students and engineers with a companion with whom they can engage in a dialogue for assistance in model development and analysis.

## Related Work

We know of two projects that are very similar to ours in both spirit and approach. One is the UWF Quorum project [4,21], which used concept maps to let student express and share a wide variety of ideas, both within their schools and with students in other countries. Quorum's success encouraged us to consider the use of restricted concept maps as a visual notation for qualitative modeling. Their use of an "artificial idiot", the Giant, is a different approach to coaching than ours, where we use a simple version of the persona effect [17] to make feedback more palatable for students. The second is "Betty's Brain" at Vanderbilt [2], where they are using qualitative representations in concept maps to foster learning. The task they use, of "teaching" Betty (their software) by building concept maps so that Betty can produce explanations, is inspired. Their domain-specific qualitative modeling framework uses tables for composing discrete values to provide qualitative simulation. Our qualitative modeling framework is richer, incorporating physical processes and a student-extendable ontology. We also support the creation of new abstractions from student models, unlike the Vanderbilt software.

## Discussion

This paper summarizes our effort to create a representational system with computer support that enables middle-school students to learn to be modelers. By using qualitative representations as a formal semantics for a restricted concept map language, we have created a visual notation for building models in terms of conceptual knowledge, rather than requiring mathematics as traditional modeling systems do. Vmodel provides scaffolding that helps students learn to build causal models with it. Software coaches to help students avoid the modeling equivalent of grammatical errors, and using qualitative simulation, helps the student reason through their models.

Our school studies provide evidence that we have been successful in helping students become modelers. We are particularly encouraged by spontaneous uses of the visual qualitative language by students outside of the software; it suggests that this way of looking at the world is becoming a habit of mind, something that they, not the software, own. While Vmodel is aimed at middle-school students, we believe that this combination will be very useful for a wide range of students. One of our hypotheses, which cannot be tested until Vmodel spreads further through the schools, is that having better conceptual models will facilitate later learning of mathematics and mathematical modeling.

Educationally, bringing modeling into science curricula more broadly has the potential to help students become full-fledged modelers, engaged in the joy of unraveling complex phenomena rather than frustrated by memorizing mountains of isolated facts.

Our vision for modeling environments is that they should become as natural for modelers as word processors are to writers and spreadsheets are to accountants. Ideally, they can be used in all stages of modeling, from gathering and summarizing the phenomenon to be explained to initial model formulation to refinement via testing the consequences of the model against data. Most modeling tools focus on later, quantitative-oriented tasks in the modeling process. Given our target audience of middle-school students, Vmodel focuses exclusively on conceptual modeling. But one can imagine using it as part of a larger suite of tools that encompass the whole modeling process, for both learning and professional work.

## Acknowledgements

This research is supported by the National Science Foundation under the REPP program. Rob Harris provided additional programming assistance. We have had the invaluable support of several Chicago Public Schools teachers in developing curricula, and thank them for allowing us to use their classrooms for testing purposes. These teachers are Beverly Miller, Deborah Rogers-Green, Adam Dorr, Carol Scafide, Kiesha Korman, Carlos Rodrigues, and Judy Whitcomb.

## References

1. American Association for the Advancement of Science (1989) Science for all Americans: a Project 2061 reports on literacy goals in science, mathematics, and technology. Washington, D.C., American Association for the Advancement of Science

2. Biswas, G., Schwartz, D., Bransford, J. & The Teachable Agents Group at Vanderbilt. Technology Support for Complex Problem Solving: From SAD Environments to AI. In Forbus, K. and Feltovich, P. (Eds.) 2001 *Smart Machines in Education: The coming revolution in educational technology*. AAAI Press.

3. Brown, A. L., Campione, J. C: Guided Discovery in a Community of Learners. *Classroom Lessons: Integrating Cognitive theory and classroom practice* Cambridge MA., MIT Press 229-270

4. Cañas A. J., Ford K. M., Brennan J., Reichherzer T., Hayes P.1995. Knowledge Construction and Sharing in Quorum. World Conference on Artificial Intelligence in Education, Washington DC, July.

5. Collins, A. 1996. Design issues for learning environments. In S. Vosniadou, E.D. Corte, R. Glaser, & H. Mandl (Eds.) *International perspectives on the design of technology-supported learning envrionments* (pp 347-362). Mahwah, NJ: Erlbaum.

6. Collins, A. and Ferguson, W. 1993. Epistemic Forms and Epistemic Games: Structures and Strategies to Guide Inquiry. *Educational Psychologist*, March, 1993.

7. Collins, A., & Stevens, A. L. (1982). Goals and strategies of inquiry teachers. In R. Glaser (Ed.), *Advances in instructional psychology* (Vol. 2, pp. 65-119). Hillsdale, NJ: Erlbaum.

8. Edelson, D. C., Pea, R. D., & Gomez, L. M. (1996, April). The Collaboratory Notebook: Support for Collaborative Inquiry. Communications of the ACM, 39, 32-33.

9. Forbus, K. and Gentner, D. 1997. Qualitative mental models: Simulations or memories? *Proceedings of the Eleventh International Workshop on Qualitative Reasoning*, Cortona, Italy.

10. Forbus, K. and Usher, J. 2002. Sketching for knowledge capture: A progress report. *IUI'02*, January 13-16, 2002, San Francisco, California.

11. Forbus, K., Gentner, D. and Law, K. 1995. MAC/FAC: A model of Similarity-based Retrieval. *Cognitive Science*, 19(2), April-June, pp 141-205.

12. Forbus, K. Qualitative Process theory. *Artificial Intelligence*, **24**, 1984.

13. Forbus, K. and Falkenhainer, B. "Self-explanatory simulations: An integration of qualitative and quantitative knowledge", AAAI-90, August, 1990.

14. Forrester, Jay W. *System Dynamics and K – 12 Teachers.* Lecture: University of Virginia School of Education, May 30, 1996.

15. High Performance Systems, STELLA software, http://www.hps-inc.com/

16. Jackson, S., Stratford, S.J., Krajcik, J.S. and Soloway, E. (1996). A Learner-Centered Tool for Students Building Models. Communications of the ACM, 39(4), 48 - 50.

17. J. Lester et al., "*The persona effect: Affective impact of animated pedagogical agents*," in Proc. Human Factors Comput. Syst., Mar. 1997, pp. 359--366.

18. Linn, M.C., Houses in the Desert. http://wise.berkeley.edu/WISE/about/houses/

19. Linn, M. C. & Songer, N. B. (1991). Teaching thermodynamics to middle school students: What are appropriate cognitive demands? Journal of Research in Science Teaching, 28(10), 885-918

20. J.D. Novak and D.B. Gowin, *Learning How To Learn*, New York: Cambridge University Press. 1984.

21. The Giant: A Classroom Collaborator, Reichherzer, T. R., Cañas, A. J., Ford, K. M., Hayes, P. J., Workshop on Pedagogical Agents of the Fourth International Conference on Intelligent Tutoring Systems (ITS), San Antonio, 1998, pp. 83-86.

22. Suthers, D. & Jones, D. (1997). An architecture for intelligent collaborative educational systems. *AI-Ed 97, the 8th World Conference on Artificial Intelligence in Education,* Kobe Japan, August 20-22, 1997.

# SOFIA's Choice: An AI Approach to Scheduling Airborne Astronomy Observations

**Jeremy Frank** and **Michael A. K. Gross*** and **Elif Kürklü**†
NASA Ames Research Center
Mail Stop N269-3
Moffett Field CA 94035-1000
{frank,ekurklu}@email.arc.nasa.gov, mgross@mail.arc.nasa.gov

## Abstract

We describe an innovative solution to the problem of scheduling astronomy observations for the Stratospheric Observatory for Infrared Astronomy, an airborne observatory. The problem contains complex constraints relating the feasibility of an astronomical observation to the position and time at which the observation begins, telescope elevation limits and available fuel. Solving the problem requires making discrete choices (e.g. selection and sequencing of observations) and continuous ones (e.g. takeoff time and setting up observations by repositioning the aircraft). The problem also includes optimization criteria such as maximizing observing time while simultaneously minimizing total flight time. We describe a method to search for good flight plans that satisfy all constraints. This novel approach combines heuristic search, biased stochastic sampling, continuous optimization techniques, and well-founded approximations that eliminate feasible solutions but greatly reduce computation time.

## Introduction

The Stratospheric Observatory for Infrared Astronomy (SOFIA) is NASA's next generation airborne astronomical observatory. The facility consists of a 747-SP modified to accommodate a 2.5 meter telescope. SOFIA is expected to fly an average of 140 science flights per year over it's 20 year lifetime, and will commence operations in early 2005. The SOFIA telescope is mounted aft of the wings on the port side of the aircraft and is articulated through a range of 20° to 60° of elevation. The telescope has minimal lateral flexibility; thus, the aircraft must turn constantly to maintain the telescope's focus on an object during observations. A significant problem in future SOFIA operations is that of scheduling Facility Instrument (FI) flights in support of the SOFIA General Investigator (GI) program. GIs are expected to propose small numbers of observations, and many observations must be grouped together to make up single flights. Approximately 70 GI flight per year are expected, with 5-15 observations per flight.

The scope of the flight planning problem for supporting GI observations with the anticipated flight rate for SOFIA makes the manual approach for flight planning daunting. There has been considerable success in automating observation scheduling for ground-based telescopes (Bresina 1996), space-based telescopes such as Hubble Space Telescope (Johnston & Miller 1994), Earth Observing Satellites (Potter & Gasch 1998) and planetary rovers (Smith 2004). However, the SOFIA flight planning problem differs from these problems in a variety of ways. Observations are feasible over large, continuous regions of space and time. The motion of the aircraft is governed by differential equations, and the aircraft can be flown in any direction for any length of time to enable an observation. The principal feasibility condition for observations is a nonlinear function over the solution to the equations of motion. As a consequence of these factors, even though SOFIA has a "closed tour" constraint that makes it appear similar to problems such as the Traveling Salesperson Problem, there are no fixed waypoints to define routes. Also, the SOFIA problem cannot be characterized only by discrete decisions. The complexity of the differential equations and feasibility constraints makes it difficult to find good heuristics, and the expense of solving the differential equations impacts solver performance.

In this paper, we describe a combination of heuristic search, biased stochastic sampling, approximations and continuous optimization methods to produce an algorithm that efficiently finds good solutions to the SOFIA flight planning problem. The rest of the paper is organized as follows. We first formally describe the problem of planning GI flights, the constraints on flight plans, and the optimization criteria used to compare valid flight plans. We then briefly describe the search algorithm used to construct good flight plans, which combines heuristic search with stochastic sampling. Initial experiments with this algorithm indicate that it spends much of its time deciding what observation to schedule next. We then describe a combination of well-founded approximations and continuous optimization techniques that allow us to eliminate a large number of expensive computations while still finding good flights. We describe experiments to validate the approach. Finally, we conclude and discuss future work.

## SOFIA's Choice

The SFPP (Single Flight Planning Problem) consists of a number of observation requests, a flight day, and a takeoff and landing airport. The objective is to find a flight plan that maximizes the summed priority of the observations performed while obeying the constraints governing legal flights. The aircraft can perform two different classes of activities during a flight. *Flight-legs* require tracking an object and

*Universities Space Research Association
†QSS Group, Inc.

are only legal if the object is within the telescope elevation limits throughout the observation. *Dead-legs* can be used to reposition the aircraft to enable flight-legs, but no observations are performed. A distinguished class of dead-legs are used to take off and return to the landing airport.

The input to the SFPP consists of a set of observation requests, each consisting of the Right Ascension (RA) and Declination (Dec), observation duration, priority, earliest start time and latest end time; a flight date; initial fuel load; earliest takeoff time and latest landing times; and the designated takeoff and landing airports (which need not be the same). The primary objective is to find a flight plan that maximizes the summed priority of the observations of the observations performed. A secondary criteria is to maximize efficiency (the proportion of the flight spent performing observations). Since it is intractable to find the best possible plan, we limit ourselves to searching for *good* plans that perform many observations of high priority. Solving the SFPP requires selecting the set of observations to service, ordering them and inserting necessary dead-legs.

Unlike traditional scheduling problems studied in the AI and OR communities, the principle constraint links the position of the aircraft and the time an observation begins to the telescope elevation required to see the object. There are few absolute temporal constraints on individual observations and also few relative temporal constraints between observations. However, there are numerous combinations of positions and times at which observations are infeasible. While it is possible to make observations feasible by repositioning the aircraft or delaying the observation, poorly chosen orderings can lead to inefficient flights with few scheduled observations.

## Constraints on Valid Flights

In this section we elaborate on the various constraints on valid solutions to the SFPP. The constraints linking aircraft motion and observation feasibility are the most important component of the problem, so we describe them in detail here. (This description differs from that in previous work (Frank & Kürklü 2003) in that it is simpler and more accurate.) If an observation is scheduled, then it must be performed for the requested duration without interruption. As we will see, the elevation depends on the coordinates of the object being observed, the position of the aircraft, and the time. SOFIA can view objects between 20° and 60° of elevation; checking this constraint requires first computing the aircraft's ground track throughout the course of the observation. Figure 1 shows the interaction between the object's position in the sky at a particular time, the aircraft's ground track, and the telescope elevation. The Earth is modeled as an oblate spheroid $\mathbf{E}$, whose surface is defined by the equation $\frac{x^2}{a^2} + \frac{y^2}{a^2} + \frac{z^2}{c^2} = 1$ where $c < a$.

Let $\mathbf{p}$ be the aircraft's current position, and $\theta$ be the (Sidereal) time that the aircraft is at $\mathbf{p}$. Let $\vec{\mathbf{S}}$ be the vector from the center of $\mathbf{E}$ to $\mathbf{p}$. Let $\vec{\mathbf{T}}$ be the vector defining the vector to an astronomical object $o$, and $\mathbf{P}$ as the plane tangent to $\mathbf{E}$ at $\mathbf{p}$. Let $\hat{\mathbf{i}}, \hat{\mathbf{j}}, \hat{\mathbf{k}}$ be the unit vectors in the $x, y, z$ directions respectively. Let $\vec{\mathbf{N}}$ be the vector normal to $\mathbf{P}$: $\vec{\mathbf{N}} = \frac{p_x}{a^2}\hat{\mathbf{i}} + \frac{p_y}{a^2}\hat{\mathbf{j}} + \frac{p_z}{c^2}\hat{\mathbf{k}}$ (Note that $\vec{\mathbf{S}}$ and $\vec{\mathbf{N}}$ are generally not parallel since $\mathbf{E}$ is a spheroid.) Let $\vec{\mathbf{T_P}}$ be the projection of $\vec{\mathbf{T}}$ onto $\mathbf{P}$; this is the *object azimuth* at $\mathbf{p}$, and is given by

$$\vec{\mathbf{T_P}} = \vec{\mathbf{T}} - \frac{\vec{\mathbf{T}}\vec{\mathbf{N}}}{||\vec{\mathbf{N}}||^2}\vec{\mathbf{N}} \tag{1}$$

Let $\vec{\mathbf{V}}$ be the desired heading of the aircraft. The observatory must track the object inducing $\vec{\mathbf{T}}$, subject to the constraint that the angle between $\vec{\mathbf{V}}$ and $\vec{\mathbf{T_P}}$ is 270°, because the telescope points out the left-hand side of the aircraft. Let $\mathbf{R}_{\vec{\mathbf{N}}}(\mathbf{270°})$ be a rotation matrix that rotates a vector 270° around $\vec{\mathbf{N}}$, and $v$ be the airspeed of the aircraft; then

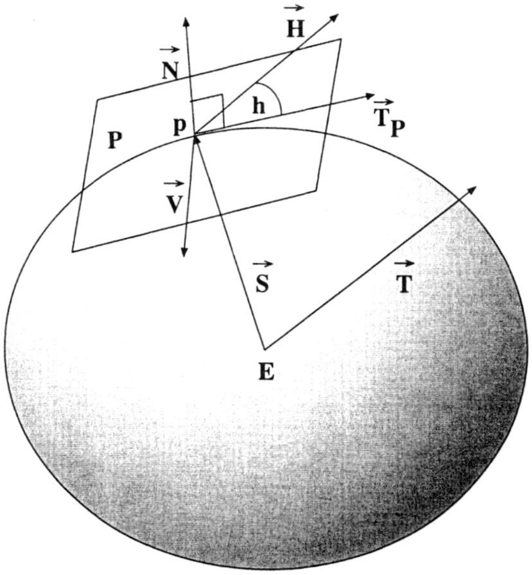


Figure 1: The Cartesian formulation of the instantaneous equations of motion of the aircraft and the elevation. We have exaggerated the spheroid $E$.

$$\vec{\mathbf{V}} = v\mathbf{R}_{\vec{\mathbf{N}}}(\mathbf{270°})\frac{\vec{\mathbf{T_P}}}{||\vec{\mathbf{T_P}}||} \tag{2}$$

Let $\vec{\mathbf{H}}$ be the elevation vector with respect to $\mathbf{P}$. We also require the angle $h$ between $\vec{\mathbf{H}}$ and $\vec{\mathbf{T_P}}$ obey the constraint $20° \leq h \leq 60°$ throughout an observation. Most targets are sufficiently far from Earth that we can assume $\vec{\mathbf{H}} = \vec{\mathbf{T}} + \vec{\mathbf{S}}$ From vector calculus we then get the equation for the elevation $h$:

$$h = \cos^{-1}\left(\frac{\vec{\mathbf{H}}\vec{\mathbf{T_P}}}{||\vec{\mathbf{H}}||\ ||\vec{\mathbf{T_P}}||}\right) \tag{3}$$

$\vec{\mathbf{T}}$ is a function of $o$ and $\theta$; this is because the Earth rotates on its axis. The vector $\vec{\mathbf{T}}$ traces a circle of radius $x^2 + y^2 =$

$\frac{c^2-d}{c^2}$, where $d = |\frac{\delta}{90^\circ}|$ in 24 hours (see (Meeus 1991) for an explanation of this).

The instantaneous change in $\mathbf{p}$ as the aircraft tracks $o$ is $\frac{d\mathbf{p}}{d\theta} = \vec{\mathbf{V}}$. Since $\vec{\mathbf{V}}$ is a function of $\vec{\mathbf{T}}$, it is a function of $o, \mathbf{p}$ and $\theta$. Solving for the ground track is necessary to compute $h$ and check the elevation constraints. It is worth noting that this formulation also makes it easy to add the effect of winds by adding the appropriate vectors to $\vec{\mathbf{V}}$, and also correct for aircraft pitch by rotating about $\vec{\mathbf{V}} \times \vec{\mathbf{N}}$, but we omit these for brevity. The ground track and elevation constraints are solved using $5^{th}$-order Runge-Kutta (Ferziger 1981) with error-adaptive step sizing.

The telescope is carried aboard a Boeing 747-SP aircraft. The fuel consumption of each engine depends on the aircraft weight, outside air temperature, drag, initial altitude and final altitude. The fuel consumption constraints are represented in a lookup table provided by Boeing; space precludes describing the fuel consumption constraint in more detail. A gridded wind and temperature model is available to correct the ground track in the face of winds and provide data for calculating fuel consumption.

```
ForwardPlanner()
# F is (initially empty) current flight plan
Select takeoff time
while not done
   # E is (initially empty) set of feasible observations
   for each unscheduled observation o
     if Feasible(o, F)
       v=Evaluate(o, F)
       Add (o, v) to E
   end for
   if E is not empty
     Use values v to select e from E
     Extend F by e; empty E
   else done
return F
end
```

Figure 2: A sketch of the SFPP Flight Planning Algorithm.

## Algorithm Description

Figure 2 describes ForwardPlanner, an algorithm for solving the SFPP (previously described in (Frank & Kürklü 2003)). ForwardPlanner combines progression based search, heuristics and stochastic sampling, resulting in a fast, incomplete randomized algorithm. An observation $o$ is considered feasible at time $\theta$ and position $\mathbf{p}$ if there is a *dead-leg* of duration $\leq D$ after which the observation stays within the elevation limits for the required duration of the observation, and the aircraft can fly to the landing airport after the observation is finished. ($D$ is an operational constraint, and is not strictly speaking an algorithm parameter.) The function Feasible() performs a search for the *shortest dead-leg* that satisfies these conditions. Each feasible observation $o$ is evaluated by constructing a short extension to the flight plan; this is performed by Evaluate(), as shown in Figure 3. After adding $o$ to the flight plan, up to $K$ additional observations are added to the flight plan. This "lookahead" is performed

```
Evaluate(o, F)
# K is the maximum extension
Extend F by o
repeat K times
   # L is the (initially empty) set of feasible observations
   for each unscheduled observation q not in F
     if Feasible(q)
       w=value of extending F by q
       Add (q, w) to L
   end for
   Use values w to select f from L
   Extend F by f; empty L
end repeat
v is value of F
return v
```

Figure 3: A sketch of the Evaluation method of the Forward-Planner Algorithm. The flight plan is extended by an observation $o$, the best possible flight plan possible after adding $o$ is approximated by adding up to $K$ additional observations.

to estimate the best flight plan possible after adding observation $o$. These short extensions are evaluated to estimate the value of the best plan conditioned on adding the observation $o$. When ForwardPlanner() decides how to extend a flight plan or Evaluate() conducts its lookahead, the candidates are evaluated using a heuristic. This heuristic is a weighted sum of the *priority* of the observations performed so far, the *efficiency* (ratio of time spent observing to total flight time) of the (incomplete) flight, the estimated time to return to the designated landing airport, and the total time spent in turns. (Details on the heuristics can be found in (Frank & Kürklü 2003)). The heuristic rank of each observation is treated as the mass of a probability distribution used to select the next observation. This technique is similar to Heuristic Biased Stochastic Sampling (HBSS), a technique used for scheduling ground based telescopes (Bresina 1996). This means that the "best" candidate need not be selected at any stage of the process, but has the highest probability of being selected next. This has proved to be an effective strategy when using inexpensive but somewhat inaccurate heuristics. The process of evaluating the feasible observations and adding the next observation to a flight is shown in Figure 4.

The principal cost of this algorithm is in the calls to Feasible(), where many flight-legs and dead-legs are constructed to test the conditions on object elevation. Let $N$ be the number of observation requests, let $K$ be the lookahead depth, and let $M$ be the maximum number of observations that can be in any flight plan. Then the algorithm makes $O(N^2KM)$ calls to Feasible(); a proof of this appears in (Frank & Kürklü 2003).

## Improving Algorithm Performance

Stochastic sampling approaches like the one employed in ForwardPlanner typically require many trials to find a good solution. The faster each trial is, the faster a good solution can be found. The predictive power of the heuristics is also

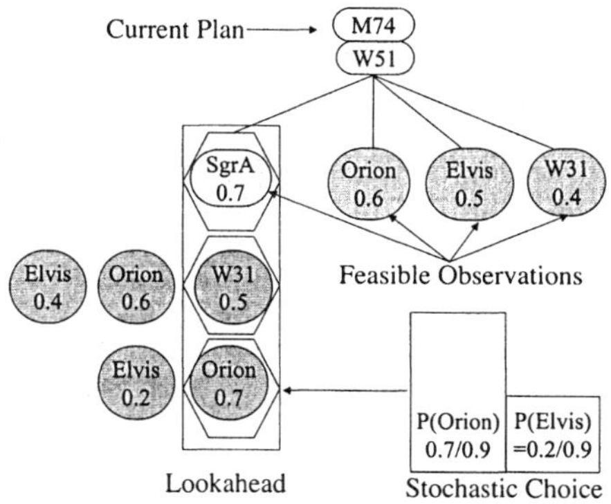


Figure 4: ForwardPlanner's search. At each step, all feasible observations are considered as the next observation in the plan. For each feasible observation, an extension of the plan is built using lookahead. The extensions are evaluated to determine which observation to perform next (the numbers inside each feasible observation.) The values are used to construct a probability distribution used to choose the next observation; each choice is indicated by a hexagon.

important, but not the focus of this paper. Our investigation into the first version of ForwardPlanner algorithm revealed that we spend a considerable amount of time deciding which observations are feasible, and most of this feasibility testing is performed in the lookahead phase of Evaluate() (in Figure 3). Feasibility testing is done by performing a brute force search for a short dead-leg. In the worst case, this requires ForwardPlanner to construct a very large number of legs; a typical number is $500,000$, evenly split between flight-legs and dead-legs. This is true even though the dead-leg duration is discretized and limited, as are the heading choices for the enabling dead-leg.

In this section we describe how to change the solution methodology to reduce the cost of checking feasibility without sacrificing performance. First we describe a modification to the ForwardPlanner that *restricts* the set of plans that can be built, increasing speed with only a small impact on the value of the flight plans found. We then show how to replace the expensive brute force search for dead-legs by a continuous optimization problem whose solutions are the desired dead-legs, again increasing speed with minimal performance impact.

## Restricting the Set of Plans

The call to Feasible() may require a large number of expensive checks to ensure that the aircraft can return to the landing airport. In some cases, a short dead-leg enabling an observation makes it impossible to return home, while a longer dead-leg both enables the observation and allows the aircraft to return to the landing airport. However, SOFIA will normally take off and land at the same airport, so the aircraft will trivially be in range of the landing airport for at least half the flight.

We change the call to Feasible() as follows: first, we find the shortest dead leg that enables the observation for the desired duration. If the aircraft can return to the landing airport after completing *both* this dead-leg and the observation, then the observation is feasible, otherwise it is not feasible. We next postpone the check until *after* deciding to add an observation to the flight plan (after the step Extend $F$ by $e$ in Figure 2.) If the aircraft can't return to the landing airport after performing the chosen observation and its shortest enabling dead-leg, then it is discarded and another observation is chosen to extend the flight. This will reduce the expected number of checks significantly when most observations are feasible. Some observations previously considered feasible will not pass this check, and so the set of flight plans that can be produced by the algorithm is *restricted.* However, this restriction will reduce the value of the flight plans found only when *high priority* observations are excluded late in the flight. In practice we find comparable flight plans after making this modification with a modest increase in speed. In the interests of brevity, we do not report these results.

## A Condition for the Shortest Dead-Leg

Even after reducing the number of checks to ensure that the aircraft can land, brute force search is still required to find the shortest dead-leg that enables an observation. However, we can take advantage of the new restricted feasibility condition by defining a function whose zeros correspond to the shortest dead-leg enabling the observation. This subproblem can be efficiently solved by using zero-finding algorithms such as Newton's Method. Because the resulting formulation allows us to search the full continuous space of dead-legs, we avoid discretizing the search space to enable brute-force search, and may also find *shorter* dead-legs.

Using the new conditions on object feasibility, the dead-leg construction phase of the feasibility check requires finding the heading and duration of the shortest dead-leg that enables the observation for a sufficient amount of time. A dead-leg may be necessary for one of two reasons: an observation is not visible at the current position and time, or an observation is not visible for long enough. We will treat these cases separately.

Consider the *feasible region* of an observation $o$ at time $\theta$. This region is the set of positions on the Earth from which the observation is visible, and is the annulus defined by two circles centered at the nadir position of $o$ whose radii are the *coelevation* limits of the telescope (in SOFIA's case, the radii of these circles are $30°$ and $70°$). Suppose the aircraft position $\mathbf{p}$ is outside the feasible region at time $\theta$. We want the aircraft to be in the feasible region after completing the dead-leg, either by making the object rise or set by changing position. Now, the shortest leg would put the aircraft on the *boundary* of the feasible region, as opposed to anywhere strictly inside it. This means that the object elevation $h$ will equal one of the two elevation limits after flying the dead-leg. If the aircraft begins inside the inner circle of the annulus, then we want the object to be precisely at the the upper telescope elevation limit of $60°$, while if it is outside the outer circle, we want the object to be at the lower telescope elevation limit of $20°$.

If the object was fixed relative to the ground, flying directly towards or away from the object would maximize the rate of change of the object elevation. However, the object (and therefore the feasible region) appears to move across the Earth as the Earth rotates. A dead-leg that tracks the object as it moves would not minimize the flight distance. We use the following intuition: we search for a dead-leg that *ends* with the aircraft flying either directly towards or directly away from the object to be observed. Intuitively, this is the correct policy when the object is nearly in view, or near the end of longer dead-legs. Observatory policy will normally prevent dead-legs longer than a few tens of minutes, so this intuition will likely produce very short, if not "locally optimal" dead-legs.

Suppose flying a dead-leg with initial heading $b$ for duration $d$ results in aircraft heading vector $\vec{\mathbf{V_d}}$ at the aircraft's new position. The angle $r$ between $\vec{\mathbf{V_d}}$ and the object azimuth at the new position $\vec{\mathbf{T_P}}$ is given by:

$$r = \cos^{-1}\left(\frac{\vec{\mathbf{V_d}}\vec{\mathbf{T_P}}}{||\vec{\mathbf{V_d}}||\,||\vec{\mathbf{T_P}}||}\right) \quad (4)$$

Thus, we have the following problem: find $b, d$ such that $F_1(b,d) = \langle f_1(b,d), f_2(b,d)\rangle = \langle 0,0\rangle$ where $f_1(b,d) = r$ i.e. the difference between the object azimuth and the final heading of the aircraft after flying the dead-leg defined by $b, d$, and $f_2(b,d) = e - h$ is the difference between the final object elevation and the telescope elevation limit $e$ closest to the initial object elevation.

Now consider the case where the object violates the elevation limits at some point during the observation, regardless of whether or not it is initially visible. We see that the flight track exits the annulus (and possible re-enters it later on). In this case, we can set up a function very similar to that we used when the observation was initially outside the feasible region. We now want to find $b, d$ such that $F_2(b,d) = \langle f_1(b,d), f_3(b,d)\rangle = \langle 0,0\rangle$, where $f_3(b,d)$ is the difference between the *extreme* object elevation achieved during the flight-leg and the telescope elevation limit violated during the observation. The intuition behind this is that the dead-leg we wish to fly should just barely nudge the ground track of the flight-leg inside the feasible region. $f_1$ remains the same. Figure 5 shows a situation in which we would zero $F_2$ while searching for a dead-leg. Initially, the aircraft could not observe the object without the elevation exceeding the upper elevation limit, whose boundary is shown. However, it is possible to fly a 10 minute dead-leg to a new position, from which the maximum elevation achieved during the flight-leg does not exceed the elevation limits.

Unlike the previous case, where we only needed to compute the heading and object elevation at the end of the dead leg, we now must find either the minimum or maximum of the elevation over the course of the flight-leg. We perform binary search over the ground track to find the extreme of the object elevation.

In both cases, we have now reduced the problem of finding the shortest dead-leg to the problem of finding a zero of a function, which can be solved efficiently using a variety of methods as long as $F$ satisfies some simple conditions.

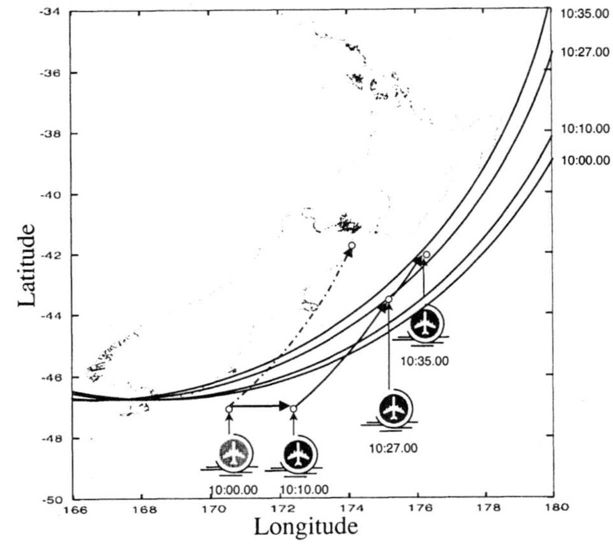


Figure 5: Flying a short dead-leg to enable an observation. The feasible region boundary shown is the upper elevation limit. In this case we would zero $F_2$ to search for the dead-leg enabling this observation. The aircraft's initial location is shown at 10:00:00. The dead-leg lasts 10 minutes, after which the flight-leg begins. At 10:27:00 the object elevation achieves a maximum; the figure also shows the feasible region at 10:27:00, and shows that the elevation limits are not violated by the flight-leg. The flight leg ends at 10:35:00.

## Properties of the dead-legs

The behavior of zero-finding algorithms depends on how many zeros $F$ has and how they are distributed. Also, the resulting dead-legs may not be feasible given other constraints on how the aircraft flies. We now analyze the zeros of the functions $F_1$ and $F_2$ and their corresponding dead-legs.

First of all, we observe that there are a countably infinite number of zeros of both $F_1$ and $F_2$. This does not pose a serious problem; these zeros are widely separated, and some require that the aircraft fly all the way around the world multiple times. The dead-leg duration restriction imposed by the ForwardPlanner algorithm will eliminate long dead-legs. However, Newton's Method might not find the shortest dead leg, and either incorrectly conclude that some observation is not feasible or return a suboptimal dead-leg.

Also, not all zeros correspond to valid dead-legs. For example, a dead leg whose duration is negative is impossible for the aircraft to fly. Also, short dead-legs may violate the minimum turn duration of the aircraft. A standard rate turn for a 747 is 180 degrees in 2 minutes. If the heading change and duration of the dead-leg violate this constraint, then the minimum dead-leg is impossible to achieve, but a longer dead leg might enable the leg. Under these circumstances, Newton's Method would incorrectly report that an observation is infeasible. Despite these potential drawbacks, this approach imposes no limitations on the heading or durations of the dead-legs, so it might find dead-legs that could not be found by discretizing dead-leg durations and headings.

## Finding dead-legs By Zeroing

In this section we will describe how to find dead-legs by zeroing $F_1$ and $F_2$.

### Newton's Method and Cramer's Rule

Newton's Method is our choice for finding the zeros of $F_1$ and $F_2$. It is simple to implement and very fast (Gill, Murray, & Wright 1981). Newton's Method requires an initial guess for the zero; let this be denoted $b_0, d_0$ with future iterates denoted $b_i, d_i$ . For functions $F$ of 2 inputs and 2 outputs, the method proceeds as follows:

1. Compute $F(b_i, d_i) = \langle f_1(b_i, d_i), f_2(b_i, d_i)\rangle \equiv \langle f_1, f_2\rangle$
2. Compute the Jacobian (matrix of partial derivatives):
$$J = \begin{pmatrix} \frac{\partial f_1}{\partial b}(b_i, d_i) & \frac{\partial f_1}{\partial d}(b_i, d_i) \\ \frac{\partial f_2}{\partial b}(b_i, d_i) & \frac{\partial f_2}{\partial d}(b_i, d_i) \end{pmatrix} \equiv \begin{pmatrix} p & q \\ r & s \end{pmatrix}$$
3. Compute the determinant of $J : |J| = ps - qr$. If this is smaller than error tolerance $t$ then set $|J| = t$ (preserving the sign of $|J|$).
4. Compute the Cramer's Rule update: $db = \frac{f_2 q - f_1 s}{|J|}$ and $dd = \frac{f_1 p - f_2 r}{|J|}$
5. Set $b_{i+1} = b_i + db$ and $d_{i+1} = d_i + dd$
6. If $\langle b_{i+1}, d_{i+1}\rangle \approx \langle 0, 0\rangle$ or step limit reached, then halt, otherwise go to step 1.

Directly calculating the derivatives of the functions $F_1$ and $F_2$ is difficult because of the gridded wind model that influences the ground track, which in turn influences the elevation (remember, the elevation is a function of time and position). Consequently, we use finite differencing to compute all of our derivatives numerically (Gill, Murray, & Wright 1981). Zeroing $F_1$ only requires constructing the dead-leg preceding an observation, because evaluating $F_1$ only requires the heading and the object elevation at the end of the dead-leg. Zeroing $F_2$ requires constructing both the dead-leg and the flight-leg, because evaluating $F_2$ requires the extreme elevation of the object during the flight-leg. Of the available schemes, we chose forward differencing over centered differencing because of the smaller number of function evaluations required. Forward differencing requires evaluating $F$ a total of 3 times to compute the partial derivatives. Thus, zeroing $F_1$ requires 3 dead-leg constructions per step, and zeroing $F_2$ requires 3 dead-leg constructions and 3 flight-leg constructions per step.

### The Initial Guess

Algorithms like Newton's Method are highly sensitive to the closeness of the initial guess to the actual zero of the function. Newton's Method has *quadratic convergence* near a zero, which (roughly) means that the number of correct digits in the guesses doubles at each step. The brute-force dead-leg search does a blind search over possible headings and durations, so the number of correct digits in each guess improves by only a constant factor (at best) each step. Thus, using this methodology to find dead-legs should be an obvious performance win. However, we must make good initial guesses to benefit from rapid convergence.

Guessing the initial heading requires determining how an object's elevation is changing, and choosing the flight direction to make the elevation change correctly. Guessing the initial dead-leg duration requires estimating the change in elevation that the dead-leg must achieve, and then estimating the rate of change of the elevation during the dead-leg. Suppose that either the object is below the lower elevation limit and rising or above the elevation limits and setting. In this case we zero $F_1$. If the target is initially too high we want it to set faster. In this case we want to fly away from it, i.e. we guess $b_0 = A_f - 180°$. Similarly, if the object is initially too low, we want it to rise faster, so we want to fly towards it, i.e. we guess $b_0 = A_f$. Now suppose the object is moving out of the feasible region. In these cases we zero $F_2$. If the object initially is rising, either it will rise continuously or eventually set. We want to make it rise slower initially, set faster later, or both. In any case, we want to fly away from the object, so we guess $b_0 = A_f - 180°$. If the object is initially setting, either it continually sets or sets then rises; we either want it to set slower, rise faster, or both. In any case, we want to fly towards the object, so we guess $b_0 = A_f$. Only at high latitudes is it possible for an object to move into and then out of the feasible region; under these circumstances, we zero $F_2$. We might also find after successfully zeroing $F_1$ that we must zero $F_2$.

Guessing the duration is somewhat more complex. Calculating the maximum required change in elevation $\Delta h$ at the current position and time is simple once we have calculated the test-leg. However, we have to account for the rate of change of the elevation both as a function of time, and the change in position as the aircraft flies. Define $r_e$ as the equatorial radius of the Earth, $\phi_p$ as the latitude component of the aircraft's location $\mathbf{p}$, and $v$ as the aircraft's estimated ground-speed. We compute the instantaneous vectors of the aircraft's ground speed and Earth's rotation, then use the law of cosines to determine the aggregate effect on the object elevation, resulting in the following guess: $v_{rot} = \frac{2.0\pi r_e}{24.0\phi_p}$ and $d_0 = \frac{\Delta h r_e}{\sqrt{v^2 + v_{rot}^2 + 2.0v\sin(b_0)}}$.

### Matters of Convergence

Newton's Method depends on the function being zeroed to obey some properties to guarantee convergence. Our functions do not obey these properties all of the time, and so Newton's Method occasionally fails to converge.

Newton's Method is "non-local", in the sense that it can generate any point in $\Re^2$ during any step. Thus, if $F$ is not defined on every element of $\Re^2$, Newton's Method may fail to converge to a solution even if one exists. $F_1$ and $F_2$ are not well defined for sufficiently short or long dead-leg durations. The problem with long durations is due to the built-in nature of the fuel model. Essentially, if a Newton step requires the aircraft to fly long enough that it would run out of fuel, we can't evaluate the ground track of the flight-leg. The problem with short durations has been explained above. Thus, convergence of Newton's method may be interrupted if any intermediate step violates one of these conditions. This is a problem because it is conceivable that the zero found by Newton's method can correspond to a legitimate supporting dead-leg even if an iteration of Newton's method corresponds to an impossible dead-leg. If the function or the derivatives can't be evaluated during Newton's Method, our only option is to truncate the feasibility check and report that the observation is not feasible. Additionally, we could find Newton's Method failing to converge after a large number of steps; we thus use a cutoff value to terminate search. In practice, we found few instances when Newton's Method could not establish the feasibility of an observation and using the brute-force approach could do so.

## Empirical Results

In this section we describe experiments designed to test the value of using Newton's Method to speed up the feasibility check for ForwardPlanner.

### Sample Problems

We used 24 of the problem instances described in (Frank & Kürklü 2003) to determine the utility of our new techniques. We restricted our attention to the "Single Day" instances; these contain between 6 and 11 observations. The priorities of all observations are identical, and all observations can be scheduled on a designated flight day. Thus, the principal goal is to find an efficient flight with all of the observations scheduled. The amount of lookahead influences the number of leg-construction steps required to compute the heuristics; for these experiments we set the lookahead depth to 4. The maximum dead-leg duration was set to 4 hours. For the brute-force search, we used a dead-leg duration increment of 1 minute and a heading increment of 7.5°. For Newton's Method we used a step cutoff of 150 and error tolerance $t = 10^{-6}$. The step parameters used in forward differencing were: $s_1 = 0.01°$ and $s_2 = 60$ seconds. Experiments were run on a Sun Workstation with dual 600 MHz CPUs and 2048 Mb memory. The aircraft takeoff weight was fixed at 210,000 pounds of fuel for all flights; this typically gives about 10 hour flights. The altitude was fixed at 35,000 feet. We ran ForwardPlanner 20 times with each of the two feasibility methods. We compare the CPU times and the best flight efficiency results for the cases in which both approaches found a plan with all observations scheduled.

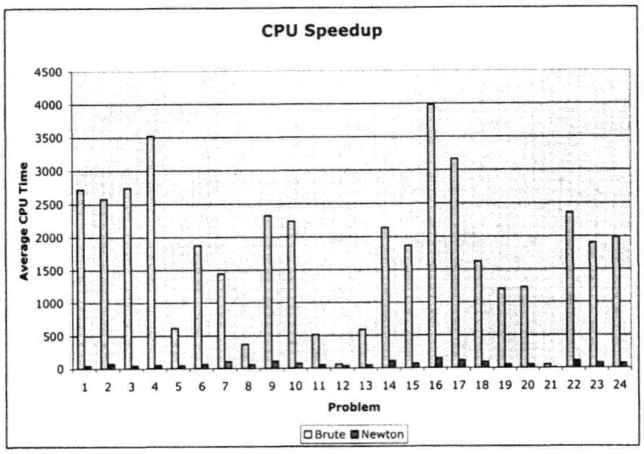


Figure 6: Performance improvements.

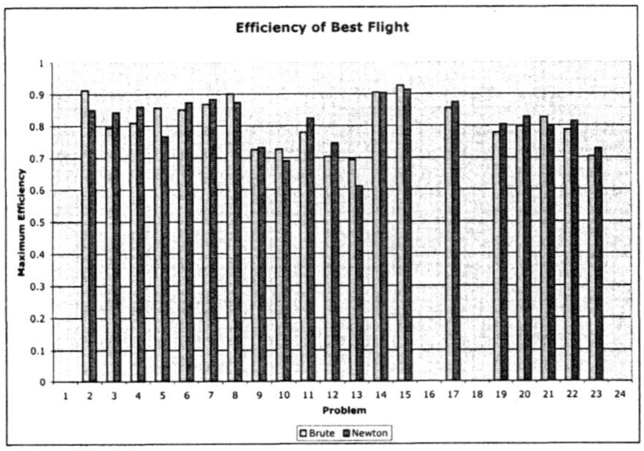


Figure 7: Efficiency of the best flights.

Figure 6 shows the average time to construct a single flight plan, contrasting the brute force and Newton's method driven feasibility checks. The speedups realized when using Newton's Method to check feasibility are dramatic for all but a small number of very short (4 observations) flight plans. In only 4 instances was either version of ForwardPlanner unable to schedule all observations to establish feasibility. Figure 7 shows the maximum efficiency of the 20 flight plans constructed for the cases where both versions of ForwardPlanner were able to schedule all observations. We see that the efficiencies are quite comparable; thus, eliminating solutions has not resulted in worse flight plans.

To see how the reduction in the number of legs corresponded to computational improvements, we analyzed a small number of flights from each of the takeoff airports. We compared the number of flight-legs and dead-legs constructed using the brute-force dead-leg search approach and Newton's Method for establishing feasibility over 20 runs. The results are shown in Figure 8. We see that the number of leg construction steps is dramatically reduced, leading consistently to increased speed. The speedup factor is typically smaller than the reduction in the number of legs constructed due to differences in the time required to construct flight-legs versus dead-legs, and added overhead resulting from the rest of Newton's Method such as the search for the minimum or maximum elevation required when zeroing $F_2$.

| Problem | Flight-legs (B) | (N) | Dead-legs (B) | (N) | CPU Speedup |
|---|---|---|---|---|---|
| 1 | 366,416 | 3,824.5 | 365,108 | 5,221.55 | 68x |
| 2 | 326,840 | 5,854.4 | 324,890 | 5,577.75 | 40x |
| 3 | 326,396 | 5,078.35 | 323,615 | 4,337.6 | 31x |
| 5 | 66,391.1 | 2972.45 | 64,877.1 | 1737.6 | 13x |
| 6 | 222,304 | 4,242.5 | 223,116 | 6,158.9 | 29x |

Figure 8: Comparison of Newton's Method and Brute Force method of establishing observation feasibility on a small set of sample problems.

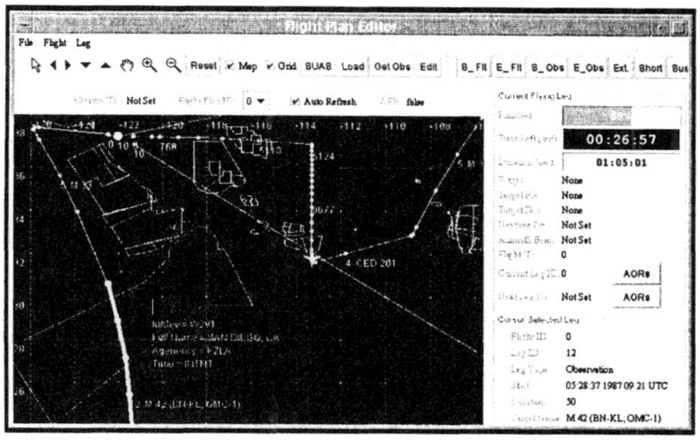


Figure 9: The SOFIA Flight Management System GUI.

## SOFIA Flight Management

The SOFIA Flight Management System shown in Figure 9 is a software tool suite designed to facilitate the planning of flights. ForwardPlanner is fully integrated with all other software tools used to manage the flight plannning process for SOFIA. Users can construct inputs for SFPPs by assembling lists of observation requests and selecting flight days. Flight plans produced by ForwardPlanner can be displayed and superimposed on a variety of different maps, including Special Use Airspace (SUA) boundaries. The graphical display includes pop-ups with information about the observation and the aircraft performance during the indicated leg. The user can also display lists of scheduled and rejected observations in summary tables. Finally, users can simulate flight plans in a number of ways to test their robustness to uncertain conditions.

## Conclusions and Future Work

We have described an application of AI techniques to the problem of scheduling astronomy observations on an airborne telescope. The resulting problem has complex interacting constraints, discrete and continuous decisions, as well as competing optimization criteria. We reduced the number of expensive observation feasibility checks by a novel combination of well-founded approximations and continuous optimization. Despite the fact that these assumptions eliminate some feasible flight plans, the new algorithms dramatically increase the speed of the algorithm at little cost in terms of the value of the flight plans produced. The resulting increase in speed improved the overall performance of the original heuristic-driven stochastic sampling approach. This approach can be employed for other planning and scheduling problems with mixtures of discrete and continuous variables. By analyzing the nature of the continuous decisions, it may be possible to reduce the set of options for these decisions to the solutions of an optimization problem that can be solved efficiently.

There are additional constraints that must be accounted for by ForwardPlanner prior to deployment. First, the aircraft must not cross any Special Use Airspace (SUA) zones. While these zones are relatively sparse, they may generally force longer dead-legs in flight plans. More importantly, the observation requests will have constraints on line-of-sight water vapor that must also be satisfied. The existing weather predictions will include estimated water vapor, which further constrains the aircraft's trajectory, and will also generally lead to longer dead-legs. Handling these constraints will impose further requirements on the feasibility check, potentially requiring new approaches to ensure that good flight plans can be produced quickly.

## Acknowledgments


We would like to thank Karen Gundy-Burlet and the anonymous reviewers for their comments and insights. We would also like to thank Lan Lin for the Flight Management screen shot. This work was funded by the SOFIA Projects Office and by the NASA Intelligent Systems Program.


## References


Bresina, J. 1996. Heuristic-biased stochastic sampling. In *Proceedings of the 13th National Conference on Artificial Intelligence.*

Ferziger, J. 1981. *Numerical Methods for Engineering Applications.* John Wiley and Sons.

Frank, J., and Kürklü, E. 2003. Sofia's choice: Scheduling observations for an airborne observatory. *Proceedings of the* $13^{th}$ *International Conference on Automated Planning and Scheduling.*

Gill, P.; Murray, W.; and Wright, M. 1981. *Practical Optimization.* Academic Press.

Johnston, M., and Miller, G. 1994. Spike: Intelligent scheduling of the hubble space telescope. In Zweben, M., and Fox, M., eds., *Intelligent Scheduling.* Morgan Kaufmann Publishers.

Meeus, J. 1991. *Astronomical Algorithms.* Willmann-Bell, Inc.

Potter, W., and Gasch, J. 1998. A photo album of earth: Scheduling landsat 7 mission daily activities. In *Proceedings of the International Symposium Space Mission Operations and Ground Data Systems.*

Smith, D. 2004. Choosing objectives in over-subscription planning. *Proceedings of the* $14^{th}$ *International Conference on Automated Planning and Scheduling.*

# A Comparison of Techniques for Scheduling Earth Observing Satellites

**Al Globus**
CSC at NASA Ames

**James Crawford**
NASA Ames

**Jason Lohn**
NASA Ames

**Anna Pryor**
NASA Ames

## Abstract

Scheduling observations by coordinated fleets of Earth Observing Satellites (EOS) involves large search spaces, complex constraints and poorly understood bottlenecks; conditions where stochastic algorithms are often effective. However, there are many such algorithms and the best one to use is not obvious. Here we compare multiple variants of the genetic algorithm, hill climbing, simulated annealing, squeaky wheel optimization and iterated sampling on ten realistically-sized model EOS scheduling problems. Schedules are represented by a permutation (non-temperal ordering) of the observation requests. A simple, greedy, deterministic scheduler assigns times and resources to each observation request in the order indicated by the permutation, discarding those that violate the constraints created by previously scheduled observations. Simulated annealing performs best and random mutation outperforms a more 'intelligent' mutator. Furthermore, the best mutator, by a small margin, was a novel approach we call 'temperature-dependent swap' that makes large changes in the early stages of the search and smaller changes towards the end.

## Introduction

Approximately 60 scientific and commercial Earth Observing Satellites (EOS) circle the globe collecting images. Nearly all of these satellites are chronically oversubscribed, i.e., there are far more observation requests than can possibly be satisfied. Scheduling systems are used to satisfy as many of these requests as possible, favoring those with higher priority. Currently, each satellite is separately scheduled with manual coordination. As the number of satellites grows this will become increasingly inefficient.

The EOS observation scheduling problem is characterized by multiple complex constraints, including power, thermal, data capacity, and the limited time each satellite spends over each target. Some EOS satellites can make hundreds of observations per day, each request may have dozens of imaging opportunities a week, and request backlogs often number in the thousands. Thus, finding an optimal or near-optimal schedule involves searching a very large space. In general, the size and complexity of the space precludes a complete search.

EOS scheduling is an example of an oversubscription scheduling problem; meaning there are more requests for a resource than can be satisfied, insuring that some requests remain unfulfilled. Such problems include scheduling planetary probes, telescopes, the deep space network, wind tunnels and other test facilities. These problems involve allocation of expensive resources, often with complex constraints and prioritized tasks. Poor schedules will result in under-utilization of expensive facilities and thus a substantial waste of money, often taxpayer dollars. There are a number of scheduling algorithms that address oversubscription problems in general or EOS scheduling in particular, but few systematic comparisons between them.

Our study compares thirteen scheduling algorithms including variants of stochastic hill climbing (Baluja 1995), simulated annealing (Kirkpatrick, Gelatt, & AndVecchi 1983), the genetic algorithm (Holland 1975), squeaky wheel optimization (Joslin & Clements 1999), and iterated sampling (ISAMP) (Crawford & Baker 1994). HIll climbing and simulated annealing mutate a single schedule looking for an optimum, the difference being that hill climbing is strictly greedy whereas simulated annealing will occasionally take backwards steps attempting to avoid local optima. We test both steady-state and generational genetic algorithms, both population-based techniques. Random mutation and crossover operators are used as well as 'squeaky' mutators which try to make intelligent changes to the schedule. One of the mutation operators, temperature-dependent swap described below, is novel. It marginally outperformed purely random mutation. ISAMP is effectively random search.

Stochastic algorithms, particularly the genetic algorithm (GA), have been used to schedule a wide variety of tasks. For example, Syswerda and Palmucci scheduled the U.S. Navy's System Integration Test Station laboratory for F-14 jet fighters using a GA with a permutation of tasks representation and a fast greedy scheduler to place tasks, one at a time, in the schedule (Syswerda & Palmucci 1991). This work motivated our research. Philip Husbands provides a good, if somewhat dated, survey of GA for scheduling problems (Husbands 1994).

Computational scheduling techniques have been applied to the EOS scheduling problem by several authors, including:

1. Sherwood (Sherwood *et al.* 1998) used ASPEN (Chien *et al.* 2000), a general purpose scheduling system, to simulate automation of scheduling for NASA's EO-1 satellite.
2. Potter and Gasch (Potter & Gasch 1998) described a clever algorithm for scheduling NASA's Landsat 7 satellite featuring greedy search forward in time with fixup to free resources for high priority observation.
3. Lamaitre's group has examined EOS scheduling issues including comparison of multiple techniques. See, for example, (Lamaitre, Verfaillie, & Bataille 1998), (Bensana, Lemaitre, & Verfaillie 1999) and (Lamaitre *et al.* 2000).
4. Wolfe and Sorensen (Wolfe & Sorensen 2000) compared three algorithms on the window-constrained packing problem, which is related to EOS scheduling. They found that the genetic algorithm produced the best schedules, albeit at a significant CPU cost.
5. Smith and collaborators (Smith, Engelhardt, & Mutz 2001) used ASPEN to schedule a radar satellite.
6. Our group has published earlier results in (Globus *et al.* 2002) and (Globus *et al.* 2003).

In the next section we describe the scheduling problem and our model of it. A description of the scheduling techniques follows. The nature and results of our computational experiments are then presented along with a discussion of results and conclusions.

## EOS Scheduling Problem

We first describe the real EOS scheduling problem. Then we describe the ten model problems used in this experiment.

EOS scheduling attempts to take as many high-priority observations as possible within a fixed period of time with a fixed set of satellite-born sensors. For example, the Landsat 7 satellite scheduler is considered to have done a good job if 250 observations are made each day. EOS scheduling is complicated by a number of important constraints. Potin (Potin 1998) lists some of these as:

1. Revisit limitations. Observation targets must be within sight of the satellite. EOS satellites travel in fixed orbits, usually about 800 km above the surface which take 100 minutes to circle the Earth one time. These orbits pass over any particular place on Earth at limited, although predictable, times; so there are only a few observation windows (and sometimes none) for a given target within a given time period.
2. Time required to take each image. Most Earth observing satellites take a one-dimensional image and use the spacecraft's orbital motion to sweep out the area to be imaged. For example, a Landsat image requires 24 seconds of orbital motion.
3. Limited on-board data storage. Images are typically stored on a solid state recorder (SSR) until they can be sent to the ground.
4. Ground station availability. The data in the SSR are sent to the ground (SSR dumps) when the satellite passes over a ground station. Ground station windows are limited as with any other target.
5. Transition time between look angles (slewing). Some instruments are mounted on motors that can point side-to-side (cross-track). These motors can wear out so slewing should be minimized.
6. Pointing angle. The highest resolution images are taken when the target is directly below the satellite (nadir pointing). Other pointing angles are sometimes required for special purposes.
7. Power availability. Most satellites have very restrictive power budgets.
8. Thermal control. As satellites pass in and out of the Earth's shadow the thermal environment changes radically. This places constraints on sensor use.
9. Coordination of multiple satellites. In particular, assigning image collection responsibility appropriately.
10. Cloud cover. Some sensors cannot see through clouds.
11. Stereo pair acquisition or multiple observations of the same target by different sensors or the same sensor at different times.

To make confident statements about the best method to solve a set of real-world problems it is not enough to solve randomly generated problems. Watson and his collaborators at Colorado State University (Watson *et al.* 1999) examined the performance of a number of algorithms on model job-shop problems. They found that although sophisticated algorithms performed very well on random problems, they did poorly if the problems were modified to exhibit structure based on real-world problems. Simple algorithms performed better on the more realistic problems.

To take this effect into account, although our model problems contain randomly generated observation targets, these are limited to land areas, the satellites are in realistic orbits, and our model problems implement all of Potin's constraints except the last two.

Table 1 contains the variable parameters of the model problems. Each problem consists of one to three satellites in Sun-synchronous orbit (one in which the equator is crossed at the same local time each orbit) for one week. Multiple satellites are spaced ten minutes apart along the same orbit. Each satellite carries one sensor mounted on a cross-track slewable motor that can point up to 24 degrees to either side of nadir (nadir is straight down).

| problem | satellites | | | observations | | | | weights | | |
|---|---|---|---|---|---|---|---|---|---|---|
| name | number | SSR | slew (°/sec) | number | time (sec) | SSR use | priority | $w_p$ | $w_s$ | $w_a$ |
| 1 | 1 | 75 | 2 | 1934 | 24 | 1 | 1-6,50 | 1 | 0.01 | 0.02 |
| 2 | 3 | 50 | 2 | 6041 | 36 | 1,3,5 | 1-6,50 | 1 | 0.01 | 0.50 |
| 3 | 3 | 50 | 2 | 6114 | 24 | 1,3,5 | 1-6,50 | 1 | 0.01 | 0.00137 |
| 4 | 3 | 75 | 2 | 6114 | 24 | 1,3,5 | 1-6,50 | 1 | 0.01 | 0.02 |
| 5 | 3 | 50 | 10 | 6041 | 36 | 1,3,5 | 1-51,5 | 1 | 0.5 | 0.02 |
| 6 | 3 | 75 | 2 | 6114 | 24 | 1,5,8 | 1-16,50 | 1 | 0.10 | 0.20 |
| 7 | 3 | 75 | 2 | 5465 | 48 | 1,5,8 | 1-16,50 | 1 | 0.10 | 0.20 |
| 8 | 3 | 75 | 2 | 5465 | 48 | 1,3,5 | 1-6,50 | 1 | 0.01 | 0.02 |
| 9 | 2 | 75 | 2 | 3995 | 24 | 1,3 | 1-6,50 | 1 | 0.01 | 0.02 |
| 10 | 3 | 100 | 1 | 6041 | 36 | 1,10,25 | 1-6,50 | 1 | 0.1 | 0.7 |

Table 1: Variable parameters of the EOS scheduling problems tested. The first column is the problem name. The next three columns relate to the satellties: the number of satellites, the size of the SSR in arbitrary units, and the slew rate. The next four columns relate to the observations: the number of observation targets the satellites could see, the time necessary for each observation, the SSR used by each observation and the priority of the observations. Where there is more than one number in the SSR column the values are evenly divided among the observation targets. The format of the priority column is lowest-highest, numberOfLevels. 'numberOfLevels' is the number of distinct priority levels divided evenly among the observation requests. The last three columns are the weights used in the fitness function (see Equation 1).

Each problem is assigned $2100n$ observation targets randomly generated on land, where $n$ is the number of satellites. This is a bit more than Landsat is expected to take. Each target is assumed to lie in the center of a rectangle whose size depends on the observing time. Not all of these targets will be visible during the one week period, so the effective number of targets is less than $2100n$. The longer the observation time required per target the fewer targets will be observable. Any satellite is allowed to make any observation. Each observation target counted in Table 1 is within view of a satellite at least once, usually several times and sometimes over twenty. Orbits and observation windows were determined by the free version of the Analytical Graphics Inc.'s Satellite Tool Kit, also known as the STK (see www.stk.com). The STK uses highly accurate orbital determination methods.

There is one ground station in Alaska. Whenever a satellite comes within sight of the ground station it is assumed to completely empty its SSR, which is then available for additional observation storage. There are approximately 75 SSR dumps per spacecraft during a week. Since some orbits are over oceans and all targets are on land, some SSR dump opportunities are wasted on an empty, or nearly empty, SSR.

We model power and thermal constraints using so-called duty cycle constraints, the approach taken by Landsat 7. A duty cycle constraint requires that a sensor not be turned on for longer than a maximum time within any interval of a certain length. Our model problem uses the Landsat 7 duty cycles. Specifically, a sensor may not be used for more than:

1. 34 minutes in any 100 minute period,
2. 52 minutes in any 200 minute period, or
3. 131 minutes in any 600 minute period.

The fitness (quality) of each schedule is determined by a weighted sum (smaller values indicate better fitness):

$$F = w_p \sum_{O_u} P_o + w_s S + w_a A \quad (1)$$

where $F$ is the fitness, $O_u$ is the set of unscheduled observation requests, $P_o$ is an observation's priority, $S$ is the mean time spent slewing for all scheduled observations, $A$ is the mean off-nadir pointing angle for all scheduled observations, $w$ stands for weight. The weights actually used are in Table 1.

Using a weighted sum for the fitness function allows placing more or less importance on the images taken, wear and tear on the slew motor, and the resolution of the images taken.

## Scheduling Algorithms

This study compares thirteen stochastic search algorithms. The search techniques were hill climbing, simulated annealing, steady state and generational genetic algorithms, and ISAMP (essentially random search). By using a more intelligent mutation operator, these algorithms (except ISAMP) become variants of squeaky wheel optimization (Joslin & Clements 1999). In squeaky wheel optimization, those observations that are not scheduled are given a high likelihood of being involved in mutation.

Our work focuses on *permutation-based* (Syswerda & Palmucci 1991) approaches to scheduling problems. The key insight underlying such approaches is that if we could greedily schedule EOS observation requests in an optimal order then we would produce an optimal schedule.[1] Thus, a greedy scheduler allows us to search the space of permutations rather than the space of schedules. This change of representation has two key advantages. First, and most important, the greedy scheduler can take any permutation and produce a feasible (though generally sub-optimal) schedule. This means that mutation and crossover operations never stray into infeasible space. This is in contrast to methods that search in the space of schedules. These must work hard to maintain feasibility, or find ways to assign infeasible schedules a fitness that guides search (i.e., infeasible schedules cannot all be assigned the same fitness). Second, if there are many possible times at which observations can be scheduled it is often the case that the space of possible permutations is significantly smaller than the space of possible schedules.

Thus, we represent a schedule as a permutation or arbitrary, non-temporal ordering of the observations. The observations are scheduled one at a time in the order indicated by the permutation. In psuedo-code:

```
int[] permutation = permute(1-numObservations)
for(int i = 1; i <= numObservations; i++)
    if (observation at permutation[i]
                not violate current constraints)
        schedule observation at permutation[i]
```

A simple, greedy, deterministic scheduler assigns resources to observations in the order indicated by the permutation. This produces a set of timelines with all of the scheduled observations, the time they were taken, and the resources (SSR, sensor, slew motor setting) used. The greedy scheduler assigns times and resources to observations using earliest-first scheduling heuristics without violating constraints. If an observation cannot be scheduled without violating the current constraints (those created by scheduling observations from earlier in the permutation), the observation is left unscheduled.

The first greedy scheduler we implemented employed earliest-first heuristics starting at $time = 0$. For observations that could be taken at several different times (windows), the earliest window that did not violate current constraints was chosen. We discovered that better schedules are generated if, for each observation, 'earliest-first' starts at some initial time chosen by search rather than $time = 0$.

The initial time, set randomly at first, is generally different for each observation request. The greedy scheduler starts at the initial time and looks forward for a constraint-free window where the observation can be scheduled. If none is found before the end of time, the scheduler then goes to $time = 0$ and continues the search, stopping if the initial time is reached. The time each observation is scheduled (or, if unscheduled, what time 'earliest-first' search started) is stored and preserved by mutation and crossover. The extra scheduling flexibility may explain why this approach works better than earliest-first starting at $time = 0$.

Constraints are enforced by representing sensors, slew-motors and SSRs as timelines. Scheduling an observation causes timelines to take on appropriate values (i.e., in use for a sensor, slew motor setting, amount of SSR memory available) at appropriate times. These timelines are checked for constraint violations as the greedy scheduler attempts to schedule additional observations.

The simplest technique tested was ISAMP, which is essentially a random search. With ISAMP, 100,000 schedules are generated from random permutations with random start times for each observation for the greedy scheduler. The rest of the techniques start with 1, 100, or 110 random permutations and generate 100,000 new permutations (children) from old permutations (parents) with mutation and/or crossover. The techniques tested were:

1. Hill climbing (Hc)[2], which starts with a single randomly generated permutation. This permutation (the parent) is mutated to produce one new permutation (a child) which, if the child represents a more fit schedule than the parent, replaces the parent.
2. Simulated annealing (Sa), which is similar to hill climbing except that less fit children replace the parent with probability $p = e^{\frac{-\triangle F}{T}}$. $\triangle F$ is the fitness and $T$ is an artificial temperature. The temperature starts at 100 (arbitrary units) and is multiplied by 0.92 every 1000 children (100,000 children are generated per job).
3. A steady-state tournament selection genetic algorithm (Gs), in which parents are chosen from a population of 100 schedules. Parents are chosen by a tournament where the most fit of two randomly selected schedules becomes the parent. Children replace one member of the population, chosen by randomly selecting two schedules and replacing the least fit.
4. A generational elitist genetic algorithm (Gg), which is identical to Gs except that for each generation the 10 most fit schedules are copied into a second population. Then another 100 schedules are generated from the old population and placed in the new population choosing parents with the same tournament selection method. Once the new population is complete, the old is discarded and the process repeated.

Each search technique (except ISAMP) was tested with three mutation operators:

1. Random swap (Sr)[3]. Two permutation locations are chosen at random and the observation requests

[1] We should note that proving optimality for a permutation-based method requires a detailed analysis of the constraints and optimization criteria of the domain as well as the details of the greedy scheduler.

[2] These abbreviations are used in the figures.

[3] Abbreviations are concatenated to indicate the complete technique. For example, HcSr indicates hill climbing using random swap mutation.

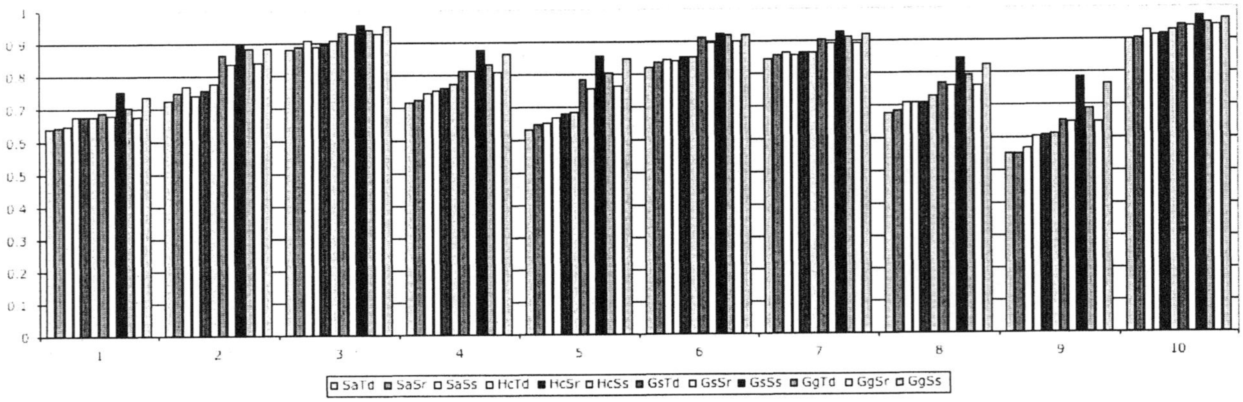


Figure 1: Relative fitness of all techniques on all problems normalized by ISAMP fitness. The vertical axis is the mean fitness divided by the equivalent ISAMP fitness for the same problem. The mean is taken from the most fit schedules for each of 32 jobs for each technique. Lower values indicate better fitness. The horizontal axis is the technique. Color/shade indicates the problem. Sa = simulated annealing, Hc = hill climbing, Gs = steady state genetic algorithm, Gg = generational genetic algorithm, Td = temperature-dependent swap, Sr = random swap, Ss = squeaky shift. For example, on problem 9 simulated annealing with temperature-dependent swap (SaTd) had a mean best fitness 55% of ISAMP on the same problem, whereas in problem 4 the fitness was 71% of ISAMP.

swapped, with 1-15 swaps (chosen at random) per mutation. Earlier experiments (Globus *et al.* 2003) determined that allowing more than one swap improved scheduling.

2. Temperature-dependent swap (Td). Here the number of swaps (1-15) is still chosen at random but with a bias. Early in the search a larger number of swaps tends to be used, and later in the search fewer swaps are performed. This is analogous to the 'temperature' dependent behavior of simulated annealing. The choice of the number of swaps is determined by a weighted roulette wheel where the weights vary linearly as search proceeds. Weights start at $n$ and end at $16 - n$ where $n$ is the number of swaps. In the beginning of search, temperature-dependent swap allows large jumps to find a deep local well. Near the end of search the schedule is close to the minima and the smaller mutations are more likely to move downhill. This technique is novel.

3. Squeaky shift (Ss). This implements squeaky wheel optimization. The mutator shifts 1-15 (randomly chosen) 'deserving' observations earlier in the permutation. Early in the permutation an observation is more likely to be scheduled since fewer other observations will have been scheduled to create constraints. Each observation to shift forward is chosen by a tournament of size 50, 100, 200, or 300 (chosen at random each time). The observation is always chosen from the last half of the permutation. The position-to-shift-in-front-of is chosen by a tournament of the same size (each time) and is guaranteed to be at a location at least half-way towards the front of the permutation (starting at the 'deserving' observation). Of the observations randomly selected to participate in the tournament, the most deserving to move earlier in the permutation is determined by the following characteristics (in order):

   (a) unscheduled rather than scheduled
   (b) higher priority
   (c) later in the permutation

   The position-to-shift-in-front-of tournament looks for the opposite characteristics. The details of this technique are novel.

We tested a number of other mutation operators in preliminary experiments (Globus *et al.* 2003). The ones examined in this experiment performed the best.

In the case of the genetic algorithms, half of all children are created by mutation and the other half by crossover. Crossover combines two parents to create a child. The crossover operator is called position-based crossover (Syswerda & Palmucci 1991). Roughly half of the permutation positions are chosen at random (50% probability per position). The observations in these positions are copied from the father to the same permutation location in the child. The remaining observations fill in the child's other permutation positions in the order they appear in the mother. For example:

```
mother:  5 4 3 2 1
father:  1 2 3 4 5
choose:  x     x x
child:   1 3 2 4 5
```

We also tested heuristic-biased stochastic sampling (HBSS) (Bresina 1996) with contention heuristics (Frank *et al.* 2001), an algorithm proposed for the EOS observation scheduling problem. This technique is not permutation based. HBSS uses dynamic heuristics to

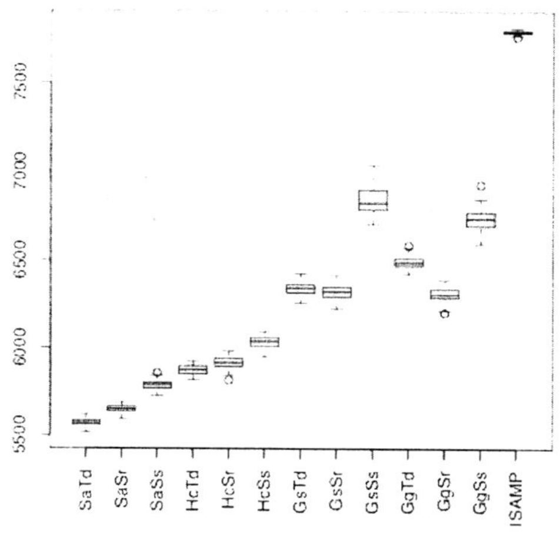


Figure 2: Fitness distribution comparison for all techniques on problem 4. Results on the other nine problems are similar. The vertical axis is fitness (lower values are better), the horizontal axis technique. The boxes indicate the second and third quartiles. The line inside the box is the median and the whiskers are the extent of the data. Outliers are represented by small circles.

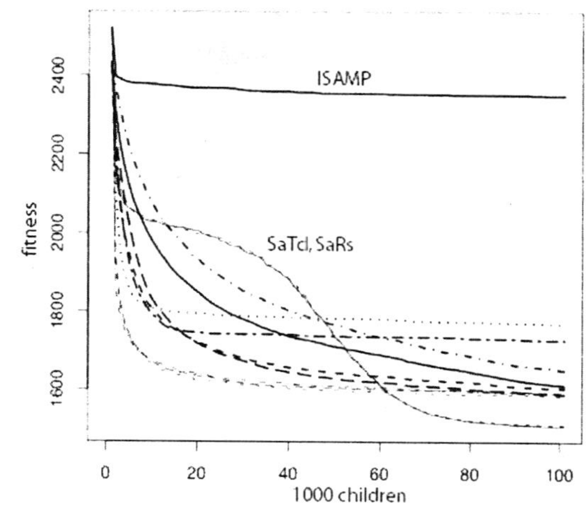


Figure 3: Search history on problem 1. Results on the other nine problems are similar. The vertical axis is the median fitness of the most fit individuals in each of 32 jobs for each technique. The horizontal axis is the number of schedules generated (children). The lines are the techniques. ISAMP, SaTd, and SaSr are labeled. Note that the best techniques (simulated annealing with variations of random swap) do poorly after only 20,000-50,000 children, but are by far the best by 100,000 children.

repeatedly choose the next observation request to place in the timelines and which observation window to use. The contention data from which the heuristics are calculated must be updated as observations are scheduled, an expensive process. HBSS was hundreds of times slower than the permutation-based techniques, required far more memory, and produced very poor schedules.

## Experiment

To find the best algorithm for the model problems we compared a total of thirteen techniques. These were ISAMP and every combination of the four search techniques crossed with the three mutation operators. Thirty-two jobs with identical parameters (except the random number seed) were run for each algorithm. Each job generated approximately 100,000 schedules (the GA jobs generated slightly more). Most jobs ran in 2-3 hours on a modern Linux Pentium processor with plenty of memory (no swapping or paging to disk). We did not notice major differences in the CPU time required for the various techniques.

In any study of this kind it is always possible that the results would have been different if one algorithm or another had used a different set of parameters (population size, temperature schedule, hill-climbing restarts, etc.). The number of potential combinations is literally astronomical and one must, in the interest of finishing within the lifetime of the universe, choose some set to test. For the same reason, the reader's favorite technique may have been left out.

We spent considerable time in preliminary experiments searching for good GA parameters and some time looking for the best restart schedule for hill climbing. However, the simulated annealing cooling schedule used for this paper was the first we tried. The population size was chosen after many jobs with random population sizes were examined. The best results appeared around population = 100. Several restart regimes where examined for hill climbing but the differences were generally not statistically significant. The simulated annealing cooling schedule was set such that considerably less fit schedules could win near the beginning of search but by the end of search simulated annealing became almost pure hill climbing. From the beginning simulated annealing out-performed all other techniques so we never felt a need to improve the cooling schedule; this could only increase simulated annealing's lead. We also ran preliminary experiments to choose the number of mutation swaps and other parameters common to several techniques. Most of the differences observed in the results were statistically significant by both t-test and ks-test, with confidence levels usually far above 99%. The raw data are available on request.

## Results and Discussion

Figure 1 compares the algorithm's fitness performance for all problems, normalized by ISAMP's performance so all results are in the range 0-1. The rising slope of the bars within each problem indicates that simulated annealing was best, followed closely by hill climbing. The genetic algorithms performed quite a bit worse on all problems. The differences are not academic. The best techniques schedule hundreds more observations than the worst on most of the model problems.

Figure 2 compares fitness for all jobs and all techniques on problem 4. Results for the other nine problems are similar. Note that the range of fitness values within jobs running the same technique is very small. Thus, almost all of the differences are statistically significant by the t-test and ks-test. In most cases, the probability that the distributions are different is >> 99%.

Simulated annealing performance benefits from a proof of optimality, at least for an infinitely slow cooling schedule. Hill climbing is vulnerable to local minima, but performs nearly as well as simulated annealing, suggesting that there are local optima but their depth is not greatly different. Both hill climbing and simulated annealing outperform both variants of the genetic algorithm. This does not appear to be caused by poor choice of GA parameters. Rather, the EOS scheduling problem appears to favor exploitation over exploration.

The tight distribution of fitness values around the median (see Figure 2) also suggests that all jobs found the same minimum or that, if the fitness landscape is multi-modal as the Sa vs Hc results suggest, most minima must be about the same. Since both hill climbing and simulated annealing spend all of their time on a single individual and the GA must spread its search over a population, GA does less exploitation and loses. It is possible that a smaller population and/or larger tournament size could reduce this effect. The population size was, however, selected on the basis of preliminary experiments.

Examining Figures 1 and 2 carefully, we see that temperature-dependent swap (Td) performs better than random swap (Sr) for simulated annealing and hill climbing and worse for the steady state and generational GAs, although not by much. In units of ISAMP mean fitnes, the differences were 0.01 for simulated annealing, 0.0067 for hill climbing, 0.01 for steady state GA, and 0.027 for generational GA averaged over all problems. Thus, temperature-dependent swap is a bad idea for GA but of some value for the better techniques. These differences were usually, but not always, statistically significant.

The squeaky shift mutator performs worse than the other mutation operators, particularly for the genetic algorithms. Relative to temperature-dependent swap (in units of ISAMP mean fitness) Ss is 0.024 worse for simulated annealing, 0.015 for hill climbing, 0.05 for steady state GA and 0.024 for generational GA. This suggests that squeaky shift is smart in the wrong way.

In preliminary experiments we also tried having the squeaky operator swap, rather than shift, observations. The shift operator performed the better. However, neither squeaky operator matches random swap. If random outperforms intelligent, then clearly intelligence is being poorly applied. We do not understand the dynamics of permutation-space scheduling in any fundamental way, and do not know if the dynamics are similar for different problems. Until a better understanding is reached, the random swap operators – with an optional decrease in the number of swaps as search proceeds – appear best.

Figure 3 shows the fitness for all techniques as a function of the number of children generated for problem 1. Note the rapid improvement for all techniques in the beginning, with ISAMP quickly leveling out. Most techniques then show an elbow shape, rapid improvement followed by a transition to very slow improvement. However, the best two techniques, simulated annealing with random swap or temperature-dependent swap, have a different shape. They actually perform worse than everything but ISAMP between 20,000 and 50,000 children. Thus, if we had run our experiment for 50,000 children we would have quite different results. All techniques have small slopes at 100,000 children so we do not expect the results to change with longer runs. The curves for most other problems had a similar shape, although the best simulated annealing techniques were rarely worse than all others (except ISAMP) in the 20,000-50,000 children range.

## Conclusions

We compared thirteen different permutation-space search techniques on ten realistically-sized EOS scheduling problems. Simulated annealing outperformed hill climbing which, in turn, substantially outperformed the genetic algorithm. Simple random swap mutation outperformed the more 'intelligent' squeaky mutation. Reducing the number of random swaps as the search proceeds further improved performance for simulated annealing and hill climbing, but only slightly. Strategies that explore widely at first then narrow the search and focus on exploitation later in evolution, such as simulated annealing and temperature dependent swap, appear best suited for this problem. Other algorithm either get stuck at worse local minima or spend insufficient resources in exploitation.

Future EOS scheduling applications, at least those choosing a permutation representation, should strongly consider simulated annealing with either random swap or temperature-dependent swap mutation. These are simple to implement, fast, and appear to be superior for EOS observation scheduling.

An important follow-up to our work would be an equally thorough study of non-permutation methods; those that search in the space of all possible schedules. We conjecture that the simplicity of local search in permutation-space (particularly the fact that we do not need to search in infeasible space) will lead permutation-based methods to dominate. However, this conjecture can only be evaluated by a head-to-head comparison of the best permutation-based and schedule-based search algorithms.

## Acknowledgements

This work was funded by NASA's Computing, Information, & Communications Technology Program, Advanced Information Systems Technology Program (contract AIST-0042), and by the Intelligent Systems Program. Thanks to Greg Hornby and Bonnie Klein for reviewing this paper and to Jennifer Dungan, Jeremy Frank, Robert Morris and David Smith for many helpful discussions. Finally, thanks to the developers of the excellent Colt open source libraries for high performance scientific and technical computing in Java.

## References

Baluja, S. 1995. An empirical comparison of seven iterative and evolutionary function optimization heuristics. Technical Report CMU-CS-95-193, Carnegie Mellon University.

Bensana, E.; Lemaitre, M.; and Verfaillie, G. 1999. Earth observation satellite management. *Constraints* 4(3):293–399.

Bresina, J. 1996. Heuristic-biased stochastic sampling. In *Proceedings of the Thirteenth National Conference on Artificial Intelligence.*

Chien, S.; Rabideau, G.; Knight, R.; Sherwood, R.; Engelhardt, B.; Mutz, D.; Estlin, T.; Smith, B.; Fisher, F.; Barrett, T.; Stebbins, G.; and Tran, D. 2000. Aspen - automating space mission operations using automated planning and scheduling. In *SpaceOps 2000, Toulouse, France, June 2000.*

Crawford, J. M., and Baker, A. B. 1994. Experimental results on the application of satisfiability algorithms to scheduling problems. In *Proceedings of the Twelfth National Conference on Artificial Intelligence.*

Frank, J.; Jonsson, A.; Morris, R.; and Smith, D. 2001. Planning and scheduling for fleets of earth observing satellites. In *Proceedings of the 6th International Symposium on Artificial Intelligence, Robotics, Automation and Space 2001.*

Globus, A.; Crawford, J.; Lohn, J.; and Morris, R. 2002. Scheduling earth observing fleets using evolutionary algorithms: Problem description and approach. In *Proceedings of the 3rd International NASA Workshop on Planning and Scheduling for Space.*

Globus, A.; Crawford, J.; Lohn, J.; and Pryor, A. 2003. Scheduling earth observing satellites with evolutionary algorithms. In *Conference on Space Mission Challenges for Information Technology (SMC-IT).*

Holland, J. H. 1975. *Adaptation in Natural and Artificial Systems.* Oakland,CA: University of Michigan Press.

Husbands, P. 1994. Genetic algorithms for scheduling. *AISR Quarterly* (89).

Joslin, D. E., and Clements, D. P. 1999. Squeaky wheel optimization. *Journal of Artificial Intelligence Research* 10:353–373.

Kirkpatrick, S.; Gelatt, C. D.; and AndVecchi, M. 1983. Optimization by simulated annealing. *Science* 220(4598):671–680.

Lamaitre, M.; Verfaillie, G.; Frank, J.; Lachiver, J.; and Bataille, N. 2000. How to manage the new generation of agile earth observation satellites. In *Proceedings of the International Symposium on Artificial Intelligence, Robotics and Automation in Space.*

Lamaitre, M.; Verfaillie, G.; and Bataille, N. 1998. Sharing the use of a satellite: an overview of methods. In *SpaceOps 1998.*

Potin, P. 1998. End-to-end planning approach for earth observation mission exploitation. In *SpaceOps 1998.*

Potter, W., and Gasch, J. 1998. A photo album of earth: Scheduling landsat 7 mission daily activities. In *SpaceOps 1998.*

Sherwood, R.; Govindjee, A.; Yan, D.; Rabideau, G.; Chien, S.; and Fukunaga, A. 1998. Using aspen to automate eo-1 activity planning. In *Proceedings of the 1998 IEEE Aerospace Conference.*

Smith, B.; Engelhardt, B.; and Mutz, D. 2001. Reducing costs of the modified antarctic mapping mission through automated planning. In *Fourth International Symposium on Reducing the Cost of Spacecraft Ground Systems and Operations, 2001.*

Syswerda, G., and Palmucci, J. 1991. The application of genetic algorithms to resource scheduling. In *Proceedings of the Fourth International Conference on Genetic Algorithms*, 502–508.

Watson, J.-P.; Barbulescu, L.; Howe, A. E.; and Whitley, D. 1999. Algorithm performance and problem structure for flow-shop scheduling. In *AAAI/IAAI*, 688–695.

Wolfe, W. J., and Sorensen, S. E. 2000. Three scheduling algorithms applied to the earth observing systems domain. *Management Science* 46(1):148–168.

# Branching Storylines in Virtual Reality Environments for Leadership Development

**Andrew Gordon, Mike van Lent, Martin van Velsen, Paul Carpenter, and Arnav Jhala**

The Institute for Creative Technologies, The University of Southern California
13274 Fiji Way, Marina del Rey, CA 90292 USA
{gordon, vanlent, vvelsen, carpenter}@ict.usc.edu, ahjhala@unity.ncsu.edu

### Abstract

Simulation-based training is increasingly being used within the military to practice and develop the skills of successful soldiers. For the skills associated with successful military leadership, our inability to model human behavior to the necessary degree of fidelity in constructive simulations requires that new interactive designs be developed. The ICT Leaders project supports leadership development through the use of branching storylines realized within a virtual reality environment. Trainees assume a role in a fictional scenario, where the decisions that they make in this environment ultimately affect the success of a mission. All trainee decisions are made in the context of natural language conversations with virtual characters. The ICT Leaders project advances a new form of interactive training by incorporating a suite of Artificial Intelligence technologies, including control architectures, agents of mixed autonomy, and natural language processing algorithms.

## Computer-based Leadership Development

The success of organizations and their missions can often be attributed to the leadership aptitude of its members. Many of the traits and skills needed to be an effective leader are learned only through experience. Organizations such as the US Army view strong leadership ability as essential to their success, and have devoted substantial training resources toward leadership development. The broadening of the types of missions that soldiers are assigned and the new responsibilities of junior officers and enlisted soldiers has increased the need for leadership development within the Army, encouraging them to explore the use of computer-based training to supplement more traditional classroom-based instruction.

To date, most of the Army's computer-based training involves the use of constructive simulations, where soldiers practice the planning and execution of missions in simulated environments. In these simulations, predictive models of physical and character behavior are used to calculate the effects of trainee decisions, allowing for low-stakes practice and evaluation of a soldier's performance. However, the skills associated with successful leadership are tightly coupled with the subtleties of human behavior, involving intellectual flexibility, adaptability, and a capacity for operating in ambiguous and stressful environments. While some research efforts are beginning to incorporate more comprehensive models of human behavior in Army training simulations (e.g. Rickel et al., 2002), the fidelity of these behavior models have not yet achieved the level necessary for training across the broad range of leadership skills.

Hill et al. (2003) developed an alternative to constructive simulations for computer-based leadership development that used a case-analysis model of instruction. In their TLAC-XL application, trainees analyzed a challenging leadership scenario presented as a short video production, and engaged in an after-action analysis with a virtual mentor and virtual characters from the fictional storyline. While scripted cinematic sequences demonstrated that fictional scenarios could be constructed that promote deep and relevant discussion about leadership, the case-analysis approach did not allow the soldiers being trained to practice making leadership decisions for themselves in a learn-by-doing environment.

### The ICT Leaders Project

The ICT Leaders Project, a collaboration between the University of Southern California's Institute for Creative Technologies and Paramount Pictures, is a research effort aimed at allowing trainees to practice making leadership decisions in the context of complex fictional scenarios realized in a virtual reality environment. In our first prototype, the user plays the role of a US Army captain commanding a company of soldiers on a peacekeeping mission in Afghanistan. The situation, which parallels the story described in Hill et al. (2003), involves providing security for a food distribution operation. Rather than relying on scripted video, however, the ICT Leaders project presents the story and fictional scenario in a virtual reality environment based on a commercial game engine, where cinematic scenes are interwoven among conversations with animated virtual soldiers and civilians in the environment.

The user experience in the ICT Leaders application is structured around a series of scripted cinematic scenes rendered in the virtual environment of the game engine. These scenes move the storyline forward and present challenging leadership problems where a decision needs to be made by the user. These problems are always presented

Figure 1. The ICT Leaders Project

to the user by storyline characters, and the primary user interaction involves text-based conversations with these characters. The user has the opportunity to raise questions and make comments concerning the problem, but in order to move the storyline forward the user must present a decision to the virtual character. The choice that the user makes has a direct effect on how the storyline unfolds, where different choices cause the experience to follow different paths in a branching storyline structure. In all, there are 63 decisions that make up the branch points of our current application prototype, and each decision in the storyline has been motivated by a specific leadership point. These leadership points were identified through directed interviews with experienced company commanders. Each point challenges the expectations that novices have when adopting a leadership role.

The ICT Leaders project uses a commercial game engine, Epic Game's Unreal Tournament 2003, to create the virtual environment for the user experience. Using the standard "mod" editor that ships with this product, we have created a system that is very far removed from the original first person shooter design. This approach has allowed us to take advantages of advances in technology within the computer game industry and collaborate effectively with other research groups that use this same platform for their research prototypes.

A screen shot of the ICT Leaders application is presented in Figure 1.

## AI Application Advancements

The ICT Leaders project draws on previous work in a number of fields to extend two technology areas: story-based training simulations and video game engines. The ICT Leaders application is the result of a novel combination of these technologies as well as innovative applications of artificial intelligence (AI) techniques. By combining the branching storyline structures used in story-based training simulations with a rich virtual world realized using a commercial game engine, the ICT Leaders application immerses users into a rich training context while keeping the experience focused on pedagogical training objectives. This combination capitalizes on the strengths of both approaches, improving the level of immersion of story-based training simulations and the degree of pedagogically relevant user interaction in video games. The ICT Leaders application incorporates a story management agent that controls the current state of the user experience within this branching storyline structure, and monitors the users decisions to support virtual mentoring and after-action review.

The ICT Leaders application utilizes AI-controlled non-player characters, divided into two categories with different levels of AI fidelity for each. Background characters move through the world and perform actions autonomously based on a library of behaviors. The behavior of foreground characters is more tightly constrained by the underlying branching storyline. Using natural language, the user interacts with these foreground characters via a text-based interface, enabled by AI natural language processing techniques. This is contrast to current commercial video games, where the standard approach to incorporating natural language is to have the user select an utterance from a short menu of possibilities. This standard approach is undesirable from a leadership development perspective, as the user will not have a list of choices when faced with real-life leadership dilemmas. By incorporating contemporary statistical text classification techniques, the ICT Leader application gives users the challenge of deciding what to say while retaining the ability to respond appropriately given the context of the situation.

The next five sections of this paper describe each of the various AI-related technologies used in the ICT Leaders application to create an effective training application for leadership development within the US Army. First, the branching storyline structures that underlie the user experience are discussed. Second, a mixed-fidelity approach to AI-based virtual characters is described. Third, we describe the statistical natural language processing techniques used to support natural language dialogue with the virtual characters in the environment. Fourth, we discuss a capacity for virtual mentoring in the application to support the leadership training objectives. Fifth, we describe the multi-agent control architecture that manages the flow of interaction between heterogeneous software components. A preliminary evaluation of the ICT Leaders project is then briefly discussed, followed by some directions for future research within the context of this project.

## Branching Storylines

The user experience of the ICT Leaders application can best be compared to the classic *Choose-your-own-adventure* paperback novels published by Bantum Books (Packard, 1979), but where decisions are made in the context of text-based conversations rather than by multiple choice. While branching storylines of this sort have been used in computer-based training applications for many decades, the ICT Leaders project employs a particular method of authoring branching storylines called *Outcome-driven Simulations* developed at Northwestern University's Institute for the Learning Sciences in the 1990s (Gordon, 2004). As an alternative to traditional constructive simulations, Outcome-driven Simulations are branching storylines where every decision that a trainee makes in the training experience is motivated by a specific training point, and where the consequences of every action will lead the trainee to pedagogically important outcomes.

The methodology for authoring Outcome-driven Simulations begins with the identification of training points through the collection of anecdotes from experienced practitioners of the skill to be trained (Ferguson et al., 1992; Johnson et al., 2000). For the ICT Leaders project, 63 anecdotes were collected from experienced US Army captains who had been company commanders. Each of these anecdotes was analyzed to identify its underlying point, which we formulated as expectations that were violated by the experience as retold by the practitioner (as in Schank & Abeleson, 1995). These points were then recast as decisions to be made in hypothetical situations, where the choice that a person would take hinges on whether or not they believe the point expressed in the anecdote. These decision formulations were the basis for each branch point in the resulting branching storyline, and each hypothetical situation was instantiated in the context of a fictional situation that grounds the user experience. In the ICT Leaders project, this fictional situation is a security mission for a food distribution operation in Afghanistan to be conducted by a US Army company of soldiers.

After instantiating decision formulations into the fictional context, an overall branching storyline was constructed by connecting the choices available in each decision formulation with the situations presented in another, where every path through the branching storyline is a coherent narrative. While many possible branching storyline topologies are possible in Outcome-driven Simulations, the 63 decision formulations in the ICT Leaders project were arranged as an ordered sequence of five trees, representing five chapters in a larger narrative. Within each chapter, 12-14 decisions are arranged with exactly two choices per decision and with an average of 4 different decisions for any given path through the chapter. Each of the last choices in the chapter leads to the first decision in the subsequent chapter, except for the fifth chapter, which has many unique final outcomes. This structure allows the branching storyline in the ICT Leaders project to have roughly 20 trainee decisions for any given route through the full application.

Rather than presenting the trainee with a list of choices at every decision point, as was done in previous Outcome-driven Simulations, users of the ICT Leaders applications indicate their choices in the context of natural language conversations with the virtual storyline characters. After being presented with a situation by a virtual character, the user is allowed to type free-text statements, either to ask questions, make comments about the situation, or to indicate a choice that they wish to make. To support this natural language interaction, statistical machine learning techniques are used to identify the features of the user text that are most predictive of the class of the user utterance, causing the story to move forward in the case of choices and informative responses from the virtual characters in the case of questions or comments.

An example of the type of user interaction supported by this approach follows, in which a user must make a leadership decision regarding the appropriateness of the current mission plan. Presented as text here, this example is realized as a fully animated sequence of camera and virtual character actions in the virtual world that we have created within Unreal Tournament 2003.

**Situation**: *The user, playing the role of Captain Young, the company commander, is engaged in discussion with his First Sergeant, Jones, and Command Sergeant Major*

*Pullman, who accompanying the Captain during the mission on a related Civil Affairs task.*

**Pullman**: Captain, I don't want to go stepping on any toes, but I was looking over your terrain. I'm sure this site got chosen because of the road access. But it's sure got some problems. I would encourage you to bump up your security perimeter eastward, and put more distance between the wire and the road. [...]

**Jones**: Captain, myself along with the XO and the platoon leaders, we put a lot of thought into this configuration. Not saying the CSM has an inferior plan, but company personnel collaborated very closely in strategy and tactics.

**Pullman**: Captain, your First Sergeant heads a great team, but if you make these changes, it'll pay off. Just give it some thought. [exits]

**Jones**: Captain, would you like changes made to the security perimeter?

**User**: `Jones, don't you think that these changes are a good idea?`

**Jones**: Captain, I'm sure the CSM will tell you plans get changed all the time. I just think there was some real good collaboration on the prep for this operation.

**User**: `Jones, are you suggesting that making these changes might be bad for the morale of the soldiers?`

**Jones**: Speaking freely, sir, I think letting the CSM waltz in and dictate tactics is a bad idea. This company should be rewarded for its good work here.

**User**: `Yes, but the CSM has a lot of experience. Let's see if we can incorporate his advice into our plan.`

**Jones**: I'll get right on it, Captain. This company prides itself on its flexibility.

Having made the decision to incorporate the advice of the CSM, the conversation ends and the next decision situation in the branching storyline structure is presented to the user. This particular dilemma was motivated by an anecdote from an experienced Army captain who emphasized the importance of sticking with the plans that were generated collaboratively by those who are actually going to execute them. The choice made the user in this example runs counter to this teaching point. By tracking the choices that are made within the Outcome-driven Simulation, users can be prompted to reflect on these choices in an after-action review component at the end of the experience.

## Mixed-fidelity AI Agents

There are two classes of agents in ICT Leaders: scripted agents and autonomous agents. Scripted agents are essential to the progression of the story. The autonomous agents fill the role of the background characters. Although the background characters are not essential to the story, they provide a much richer, realistic environment, which is necessary to properly engage the user in the evolving situation.

Both types of agents are written using Unreal Tournament's built-in object-oriented scripting language, UnrealScript. Complex agent behaviors were realized by inheriting and modifying the existing bot code that is used to control the non-player characters in the original commercial version of the game. Such primitive behaviors include path planning, turning to face the direction the agent is moving, and obstacle avoidance, among many others. Although the high-level behaviors of the existing bots did not meet our specific needs, they were easily replaced with new behaviors while leaving the more primitive behaviors intact. Using inheritance, we were able to concentrate on the development of higher-level behaviors.

### Scripted Character Agents

Scripted agents were developed to play the major character roles in the story with which the user can communicate. Like Hollywood screen actors, these agents are required to perform actions at pre-defined locations at specific times in order to present the fictional situation as an engaging narrative. These actions include the animated delivery of pre-recorded audio clips, gesture and gaze control in single-party and multi-party dialogs, and interacting with the virtual physical environment through scripted body animations. Although many of the primitive bot behaviors were retained, the majority of these character actions were carefully scripted during the authoring process.

In authoring the ICT Leaders application, one of the major problems we dealt with concerned the exact timing of the scripted behavior of these agents, particularly with respect to the delivery of pre-recorded audio clips. An audio clip that is played even half a second too soon may overlap with the previous line that was delivered, while playing it a half of a second too late results in too much of a pause in-between the spoken lines. Problems in timing can easily be compared to watching a movie where the soundtrack is mis-cued with the film. To avoid the distractions that this would cause, fine adjustments in timing of scripted action were made on a subjective basis.

Other timing problems arose due to variation and uncertainty within the virtual environment of the commercial game engine. For example, it is sometimes difficult to predict how long it will take an agent to arrive at a destination in the virtual world due to variations in the path selected by the low-level AI path-planning algorithm or due to variations in processor speed of the computer running the application. In this case, we chose a solution that is analogous to traditional filmmaking practices, where we kept the scripted agents located nearby, just out of view of the camera, whenever they were not part of the current scene. By keeping them physically close, the variance in the timings due to navigating the environment were kept to a minimum.

### Autonomous Character Agents

Autonomous agents were used to give a sense of life to the virtual environment. These agents are analogous to the extras that are used on a movie set. They do not have spoken dialog lines to deliver and are not required to be at any specific location at any specific time during the course of any given scene. In the ICT Leaders project, a wide assortment of autonomous characters were necessary to convincingly visualize a food distribution operation being supported by company of 120 US Army soldiers. Without the portrayal of soldiers patrolling ridge tops, working on fencing surrounding the food distribution site, or standing guard at security checkpoints, the experience would be greatly diminished.

As with movie extras, the primary responsibility of fully autonomous agents in the ICT Leaders applications is to avoid being a distraction from the main action of the scene. Some level of sophistication was necessary, however, to avoid the appearance of mindless repetitive action. For example, a soldier working on fences for crowd control in the background of a scene can be distracting if they are simply looping over a single animation without ever moving around the environment. Accordingly, behavioral control algorithms were authored for a wide range of classes of background characters in the ICT Leaders application, including the following:

- Soldiers working on fences for crowd-control
- Military Police soldiers guarding security checkpoints
- Soldiers patrolling ridgelines
- Soldiers simply moving around the environment
- Afghan civilians in the area of the food distribution site

Each type of background character in the application is completely autonomous, controlled by customized behavior specification tailored to the specific role of the agent in the story. For example, soldiers working on fences for crowd control select among one of the animations corresponding to working on a fence, loop over the animation for a random amount of time, move to another location along the layout of the fencing in the terrain model, and then repeat this behavior. Other roles played by autonomous agents are programmed similarly.

As is the case with the scripted agents, the low-level behaviors of the autonomous agents are inherited from the existing bot code. This includes path-planning behaviors used to move agents around the virtual environment. Although path nodes for navigation are placed manually in the terrain model, it is impossible to predict the exact paths that agents will take. Occasionally one of the autonomous agents moving around the environment will walk closely behind a scripted agent in a scene with which the user is engaged in conversation. Since care was taken when placing the path nodes, the path the autonomous character takes does not interrupt the scene. Instead, a much more positive impact is realized, where the seemingly close interaction between scripted and autonomous characters makes the environment seem much more alive to users.

## Natural Language Processing

The natural language interaction component of the ICT Leaders project is supported by statistical natural language processing algorithms, where each decision point in the branching storyline is coupled with one text classifier trained to route user inputs into one of some number of utterance classes. We employed a Naïve Bayesian classification algorithm (George & Langley, 1995) implemented in the WEKA open source machine learning toolkit (Witten & Eibe, 1999). Training data and user inputs are encoded as large feature vectors, where each dimension in the vector corresponds to one of all of the single words (unigrams) and adjacent pairs of words (bigrams) seen in the training data. These feature vectors are constructed without using stop-list filters, without truncating the feature space, by ignoring punctuation and variation in case, and using features counts for feature values.

Hill et al. (2003) employed the same text classification approach that we use in the ICT Leaders project, and reported percentage accuracy rates averaging 65.72% given small training data sets averaging 194 instances across 13 classes. To compensate for the small training data sets that are likely to be collected and tagged over the course of the ICT Leaders project lifecycle, we are experimenting with an approach that has trainees classify their own utterances in the context of using the application. Instead of immediately selecting the class of highest confidence as the best classification of the user utterance, the ICT Leaders application collects the top three most likely classifications, and presents to the user a paraphrase of each class in a pop-up list. The user is then asked to select among this list of three choices which paraphrase best characterizes the utterance they have typed, or to select none-of-the-above. In selecting the most appropriate paraphrase, the user interface informs a centralized language processing service that performs the classification of the verification selection, and the original user text is then treated as additional training data in support of the verified class. It remains an open research question as to the effectiveness of this approach, and whether user verification of classifications can be legitimately used as additional training data to improve the statistical text classification performance. An evaluation of the relative merits of this approach will be conducted after enough user-verified data has been collected.

## Virtual Mentoring

The ICT Leaders application includes a virtual mentor that occasionally interjects suggestions to assist the user. The virtual mentor is not a character in the scenario but acts as an assistant offering comments and suggestions. The virtual mentor's comments appear as text in a pop-up window in the lower left corner of the screen shown in

Figure 1. While these interjections risk breaking the user's immersion in the scenario, their timing is carefully designed to occur only when the user is already having difficulties that threaten the immersion or when the user repeatedly fails to understand the intended leadership points. These two instances highlight the two ways the virtual mentor guides the user.

First, the virtual mentor steps in when the user enters a phrase that the natural language processor cannot match to any of the pre-defined choices. This could be caused by the user not understanding the decision before him, the entering of a phrase that is not easily classified into one of the pre-defined utterance classes, or when the appropriate utterance isn't in the three classes with the highest confidence. In the current system the virtual mentor has no means of determining the specific cause of the problem. To compensate, the virtual mentor covers all possibilities by interjecting a pre-authored comment giving the user clear guidance as to the allowable choices and expected phrasing of each. While this approach quickly and easily gets the user back on track, there is a risk that users will take advantage of these interjections in order to quickly identify what they need to say to move the story forward, without considering the leadership issue at hand. Future work may lead to the development of a virtual mentor that can determine the underlying cause of the problem and offer more tailored advice that doesn't uncover too much about the available choices.

The second situation in which the virtual mentor steps in to assists the user only occurs when the user is going through the experience for the second time (or any subsequent time). If the user makes the choice that is counter to the point of the original leadership anecdote at a decision point in one run and then in a later run reaches the same decision point and makes the same decision, again countering the leadership anecdote, the virtual mentor interjects to steer the user towards the choice that supports the leadership anecdote. The fact that the user has repeatedly made the choice countering the leadership point suggests the user doesn't understand the point and is in danger of reinforcing a misconception. The virtual mentor interrupts the user's choice with an explanation of the leadership point and the supporting choice and gives the user a chance to take back the decision that was just made. By breaking the flow of the experience and forcing the student to think about the decision, the virtual mentor can prevent the user from reinforcing a decision that counters the intended leadership point. Still, users have the option of ignoring the advice of the virtual mentor and sticking with their choices if, for example, they are trying to explore specific parts of the branching storyline.

## Control Architecture

A service-based approach was used in the ICT Leaders application to coordinate a variety of heterogeneous software components that were originally designed to operate as stand-alone systems. By implementing each

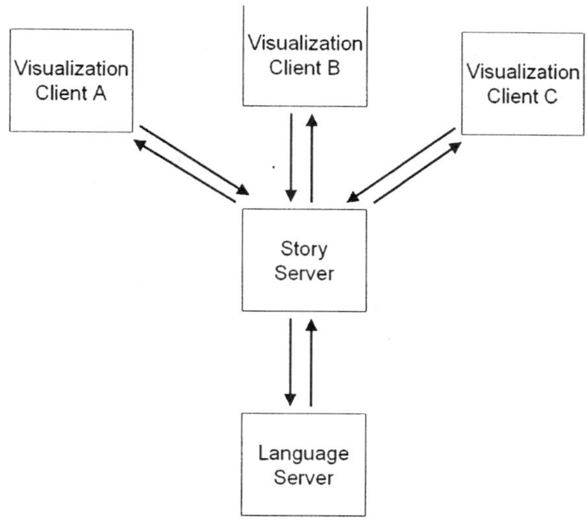


Figure 2. Distributed Control Architecture

component as a service or wrapped to become a service, the collection of these components could serve each of the functional requirements of the system. Three primary services comprise the ICT Leaders application. First, a visualization service presents the user with a view onto the virtual world and provides a user interface for interaction on this virtual stage. Second, a story management service controls the ordering of scenes presented to users by tracking their location through the branching storyline structure that underlies the experience, taking into account the decisions that users make. Third, a language processing service is used to interpret the natural language text given by users, providing to the story management service an indication of the best classification of each statement. Figure 2 diagrams the flow of information among these three service types.

The use of blackboard-style control architectures has become more prominent in heterogeneous agent-based systems, particularly in interactive multimedia applications (Vaysburd & Birman, 1997; Johanson & Fox, 2002; Hill et al., 2003). However, the linear flow of information and a lack in need of asynchronous event handling in the ICT Leaders application has allowed us to return to a more traditional functional control architecture.

### Visualization Service

Visualization services in the ICT Leaders application provide each of the functions necessary to present to the user a view of the virtual environment. To reduce production costs and to capitalize on advancement in computer graphics within the commercial game industry, the ICT Leaders project used a modified version of Epic Games' Unreal Tournament 2003 as its visualization environment. The most important factor in selecting this software platform for visualization services was the ability to modify nearly all aspects of the commercial version of the game using a object-oriented scripting language and editing tools that ship with this commercial product. The

Liquid Narrative group at North Carolina State University had adopted this software platform for the development of their Mimesis system (Young et al., 2004), and we used the tools developed by this research group to control simulation events within Unreal Tournament 2003 from processes running outside of the game engine.

### Story Management Service

The selection of events to be visualized within the virtual world is handled by a dedicated story management service running outside of the game engine. This service, which simultaneously handles multiple visualization clients, tracks the users' locations within the underlying branching storyline structure. The primary information that is communicated to the story management service is the text that is typed by users in the course of conversations with virtual characters in the visualization service. The story management service identifies the appropriate classifier to be used to process this text, a service that is then delegated to a separate language processing service. The results of this language processing service are then passed through the story management service to be verified by the user in the visualization service, where the user is asked to choose which classification best paraphrases the statement that they made. When this result is given to the story management agent, the location of the user within the branching narrative is updated, the next scripted scene is triggered, and the process repeats itself.

### Language Processing Service

The language processing service has the responsibility of classifying text passed to it from the story management service to identify which of a fixed set of expected utterance classes best characters the user's statement. Each of these classes corresponds to a possible decision or virtual character response in the underlying branching storyline. After a user confirms which classification best represents what was originally stated, this confirmation is used as training data for future classifications by the language processing service.

### Interaction Flow

All communication among the participating software services is encapsulated in XML messages, and is designed to be an expandable notation for a wide range of narrative events. The expressive nature of these formalisms are particular important for the visualization service, where the XML being parsed serves as a generic visualization representation. Each time the story management service communicates with a visualization client, a high-level scene description, formatted in XML, is being passed. By authoring an expressive XML schema for these messages, the ICT Leaders applications supports modularity among the services, which may be switched with new designs as our research efforts continue.

## Preliminary Evaluation

Two types of evaluations are scheduled for the ICT Leaders project. Formative evaluations with members of our target training population (junior US Army officers) will be conducted in early 2004 to assess the usability of the ICT Leaders application. Summative evaluations, aimed at determining the effectiveness of the application for the purpose of leadership development in the US Army, will be conducted with members of our target training population in the summer of 2004.

Preliminary formative evaluations of the ICT Leaders application have been conducted with students and an instructor of a university Army ROTC program, where a group of undergraduates collectively used the application under the supervision of the instructor. These evaluators navigated the user interface and storyline without difficulty, and tended to discuss the most appropriate choice given a decision situation with each other rather than engaging the virtual characters in prolonged dialogs. These group discussions were supported by subtle interventions on the part of the instructor, yielding a effective mix of both human and virtual mentoring.

## Future Work

In the production of interactive virtual environments for training applications there is a need for the development of automated and semi-automated tools for designers and creative artists that aid them in generating immersive and affective worlds. Following the production process used in developing the branching storyline for the ICT Leaders application, generalized tools could be built for rapid development of similar training applications. This project also motivates research in the development of computational models of techniques and rules followed by Hollywood filmmakers who have been successful in visual storytelling. At each step in the production process of this application we have identified potential areas for future work.

### Creating the Branching Storyline

In writing the story, tools that help a writer quickly build and visualize sequences of interactive and non-interactive action make the overall experience more coherent for the user. Other research groups have developed systems for automated generation of stories in interactive virtual environments (Magerko & Laird, 2003; Young et. al., 2004). These automated story generation systems could be used for the generation of complex scenarios for training applications.

### Autonomous Characters

For providing ambience to the virtual world, characters in the virtual world have behaviors that make them look believable. Tools for defining such behaviors and agents would save a lot of time in the production process. Semi-automated tools that convert script directives to character actions could be developed.

### Autonomous Camera Control and Lighting

Training soft skills like leadership require the virtual environments to have expressive lighting and shot composition for communicating the importance and consequences of the decisions that are made by the user. With the increase in geometric complexity of the training environments there is a need to incorporate work in the field of expressive autonomous lighting (Seif El-Nasr, 2003) and camera control (Jhala, 2004). We are developing semi-automated tools that could be used by designers of such training applications with automated lighting design and shot sequences that could be structured to the preferences of the user.

## Acknowledgments

This paper was developed with funds of the Department of the Army under contract number DAAD 19-99-D-0046. Any opinions, findings and conclusions or recommendations expressed in this paper are those of the authors and do not necessarily reflect the views of the Department of the Army.

## References

Ferguson, W., Bareiss, R., Birnbaum, L., & Osgood, R. 1992. ASK systems: an approach to the realization of story-based teachers. *Journal of the Learning Sciences* 1, 95-134.

George, J. & Langley, P. 1995. Estimating continuous distributions in Bayesian classifiers. *Proceedings of Eleventh conference on uncertainty in Artificial Intelligence*. 338-345, San Mateo, CA: Morgan Kaufmann.

Gordon, A. 2004. Authoring Branching Storylines for Training Applications. *Proceedings of the Sixth International Conference of the Learning Sciences (ICLS-04), Santa Monica, CA.*

Hill, R., Douglas, J., Gordon, A., Pighin, F., & van Velsen, M. 2003. Guided Conversations About Leadership: Mentoring with Movies and Interactive Characters. *Proceedings of the Fifteenth Innovative Applications of Artificial Intelligence Conference*, pp. 101-108.

Jhala A. 2004. Intelligent Cinematic Camera Control for Dynamic Narratives, *Master's Thesis, Department of Computer Science, North Carolina State University.*

Johanson B. & Fox A. 2002. The Event Heap: A Coordination Infrastructure for Interactive Workspaces. *Proceedings of the 4th IEEE Workshop on Mobile Computing Systems & Applications*

Johnson, C., Birnbaum, L., Bareiss, R., and Hinrichs, T. 2000. War stories: harnessing organizational memories to support task performance. *Intelligence* 11(1), 16-31. New York: ACM Press.

Magerko, B. & Laird, J. E., 2003. Building an Interactive Drama Architecture, *1st International Conference on Technologies for Interactive Digital Storytelling and Entertainment*, Darmstadt, Germany, March 24 – 26.

Rickel, J., Gratch, J., Hill, R., Marsella, S., Traum, D., & Swartout, W. 2002. Toward a New Generation of Virtual Humans for Interactive Experiences, *IEEE Intelligent Systems*, July/August 2002, pp. 32-38.

Schank, R. & Abelson, R. 1995. Knowledge and memory: The real story. In R. Wyer (ed) Advances in Social Cognition, Vol. 8. Mahwah, NJ: Lawrence Erlbaum Associates. pp 1-86.

Seif El-Nasr, M. & Horswill, I. 2003. Real-Time Lighting Design for Interactive Narrative. *Proceedings of the 2003 International Conference on Virtual Storytelling.*

Vaysburd A. & Birman K. 1997. Building Reliable Adaptive Distributed Objects with the Maestro Tools. *Proceedings of the Workshop on Dependable Distributed Object Systems, OOPSLA'97, Atlanta, GA.*

Witten, I. & Frank, E. 1999. *Data Mining: Practical Machine Learning Tools and Techniques with Java Implementations*. San Francisco: Morgan Kaufmann.

Young, R. Michael, Riedl, Mark, Branly, Mark, Jhala, Arnav, Martin, R.J. and Saretto, C.J., *An architecture for integrating plan-based behavior generation with interactive game environments*, to appear in *The Journal of Game Development*, March 2004.

# The Independent LifeStyle Assistant™ (I.L.S.A.): AI Lessons Learned

**Karen Zita Haigh, Liana M. Kiff,**
Janet Myers, Valerie Guralnik, Christopher W. Geib, John Phelps, Tom Wagner
*Honeywell Laboratories, 3660 Technology Drive, Minneapolis, MN 55418*
{karen.haigh,liana.kiff}@honeywell.com

**Abstract**

The Independent LifeStyle Assistant™ (I.L.S.A.) is an agent-based monitoring and support system to help elderly people to live longer in their homes by reducing caregiver burden. I.L.S.A. is a multiagent system that incorporates a unified sensing model, situation assessments, response planning, real-time responses and machine learning. This paper describes the some of the lessons we learned during the development and six-month field study.

## 1 Introduction

Historically, 43% of Americans over the age of 65 will enter a nursing home for at least one year. We have been developing an alternative: an automated monitoring and caregiving system called *Independent LifeStyle Assistant*™ (I.L.S.A.) [9; 10; 12]. Researchers and manufacturers are developing a host of home automation devices that will be available in the near future. I.L.S.A.'s concept is to integrate these individual devices, and augment them with reasoning capabilities to create an intelligent, coherent, useful assistant that helps people enjoy a prolonged, independent lifestyle.

From January to July 2003, we field tested I.L.S.A. in the homes of eleven elderly adults. The I.L.S.A. field test was designed to complete an end-to-end proof-of-concept. It included continuous data collection and transmission via security sensors installed in the home, data analysis, information synthesis, and information delivery to I.L.S.A. clients and their caregivers. The test concentrated on monitoring two of the most significant Activities of Daily Life: medication and mobility. All ADL-based monitoring was performed by family caregivers.

This paper describes the system we built, outlines the field study, and then describes the major lessons we learned relating to AI technology:

- Agents
- Developing and making use of an ontology
- Automated Reasoning
- Integration

Haigh *et al* [9] describe many additional lessons learned, including client selection, system configuration, and usability.



## 2 System Description

The main goal of the field test was to demonstrate the complete cycle of I.L.S.A. interactions: from sensors to data transmission to reasoning to alerts and home control.

We selected our initial feature set based on their importance ranking, the ability to exercise the full range of technical capabilities of the I.L.S.A. architecture, and the need to learn more about a particular area. The ability to implement and appropriately support a robust test application was the final determining factor. The system we field tested had the following significant features:

- Passive Monitoring: basic mobility, occupancy, medication compliance, sleeping patterns.
- Cognitive Support: reminders, date/time of day.
- Alerts and Notifications: auto contacting caregivers (by telephone).
- Reports: summary reports of client behavior.
- Remote access to information (Internet or telephone)
- Control: modes (on/off).

Other capabilities and features were tested in the lab.

### 2.1 Architecture

Because clients age, and technology changes, I.L.S.A. had to be rapidly deployable, easy to configure, and easy to update. To meet these requirements, we decided to use an agent-oriented approach [10]. An agent-based architecture would provide modularity, distribution, functional decoupling, and dynamic discovery of capability. It would also make our ontology explicit. We selected JADE as our environment [1].

The agents in the system included device controllers, domain agents, response planners, and system management. One of each of the following agents were created for each human client: Medication, Mobility, Modes (on/off), Reminders, ResponseCoordinator, MachineLearning. The sketch in Figure 1 shows sample capabilities.

Exactly one each of the following agents was created on the server (one server for all the human clients): PhoneAgent, Platform, Database. In the research system, we explored task tracking (Section 5.1), machine learning techniques (Section 5.3) and several more domain agents.

The hardware employed in the I.L.S.A. field test consisted of readily available Honeywell home automation and control products. The Honeywell Home Controller served as the backbone for communicating sensor events out of the home.

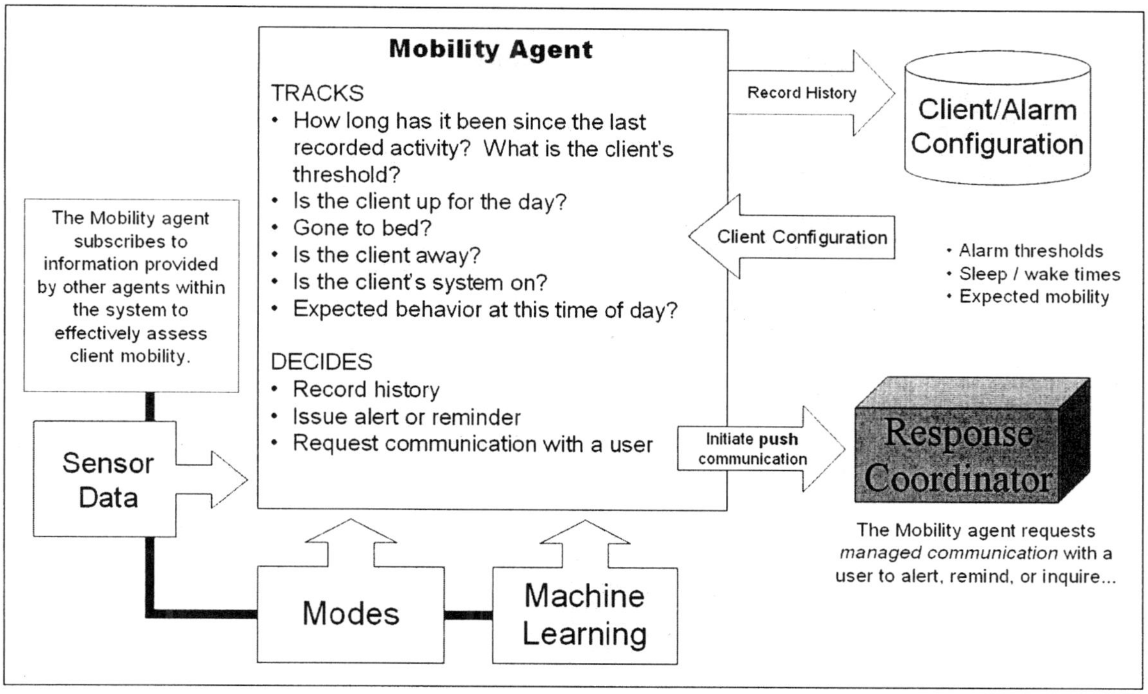


Figure 1: The Mobility agent tracks the client's activity.

## 2.2 Field Study Environments

We installed I.L.S.A. in the homes of four system engineers, and eleven elderly clients. From July 2001 through December 2001 we installed four systems in engineers' homes, and focused on hardware configuration to determine which sensors were most effective. No reasoning components or user interfaces were included in these deployments.

Beginning January 2003, we installed I.L.S.A. into the homes of eleven elders and collected data through July 2003. We limited the number of sensors in the elders' homes for reasons of cost and concerns about privacy—for example, it would have been difficult to find appropriate test subjects who would accept a system with a toilet flush sensor. Each test home had from four to seven sensors, including one medication caddy and several motion detectors. Two installations had a contact switch and pressure mat at the exit door.

## 2.3 User Interface

Elderly clients were equipped with Honeywell Web Pads™ with wireless access to the Internet over a broadband connection. Through the Web interface, the elders could display reminders, medication schedules & status, mobility summary, on/off controls and information about their caregivers. Figure 2 shows a sample web page for the elderly client. I.L.S.A. could also deliver reminders to the elder by phone.

Caregivers could access I.L.S.A. data about their client/family member with their normal ISP Web connection. The caregiver Web interface allowed the caregiver to view and acknowledge alerts, view general ADL status (including historical trends for medication and mobility, view and edit prescription and medication schedule, and set up scheduled reminders and personalized activity alerts.

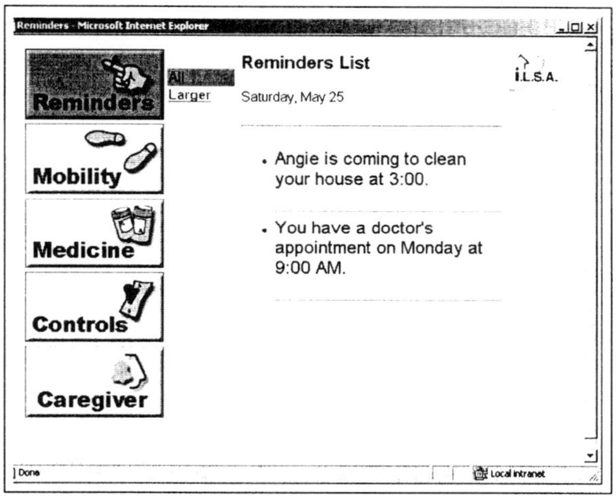


Figure 2: A sample webpage from the elder user interface.

Alerts and reminders could be delivered by telephone. In addition, a dial-in telephone interface allowed caregivers to get abbreviated status reports and record and schedule reminders for the elder.

# 3 Lessons: Agents

In addition to meeting I.L.S.A. requirements, we expected the agent-based approach to provide the following benefits [10]:

**Multi-Person Development.** Development of independent agents could be assigned to independent developers.

**Scalability.** We expected that The distributed architecture would support a much more scalable system.

**Robustness and Reliability.** Distributed processing and control would mean that the system would not crash with a local single point of failure.

**Testing and debugging.** Independent agents could be independently tested.

Agent-based approaches to system development are still relatively new. Robust infrastructures for applying this technology to a real-world system are not commercially available; research prototypes are not yet fully reliable and are mostly unsupported. There was considerable risk in basing the I.L.S.A. field test on this cutting-edge infrastructure.

I.L.S.A. was one of the first agent-based systems seen by "real" people outside the lab. As a result, we identified several risks and pitfalls in developing agent-based systems that had not been previously identified. We also describe new ways to address and mitigate these risks.

### 3.1 Lesson #1: Multi-Person Development

Since each I.L.S.A. agent performs a single role, we expected to facilitate rapid deployment of the system by assigning development of each agent to a separate software engineer. During the design stage we discovered that the agents could not be developed independently of each other. Even though each agent is responsible for a single task, many tasks are related to those of other agents. For example, when a *Medication* domain agent generates a reminder to take a medication, it is processed by the *ResponseCoordinator*, which coordinates interactions over multiple domain agents. It is then delivered to the client by the *Phone* agent. All three agents share a single goal—delivering a medication reminder to elder—and must be able communicate with each other *as well as the expected portions of the system.*

To support inter-agent communication, the development team needed to resolve such issues as communication protocols, recovery from failures or exceptions in agent conversations, and ontology development for semantic information exchange. Each time a protocol changes in one agent, many other agents also need to change.

In I.L.S.A.s tightly coupled system, the promise of independent development did not materialize. Agents needed to communicate with each other much more frequently than we had anticipated, and so resolving these issues required a great deal of coordination among team members and added considerable overhead to development time.

### 3.2 Lesson #2: Scalability

The I.L.S.A. system needs to handle a large number of clients, but current agent technology does not address scalability in any meaningful way. We noted three particular challenges for future agent system development.

First, to provide controlled access to client data, we implemented a database agent that performed all data read and write operations. While this approach insured database consistency, it also meant that the database agent could become a localized bottleneck. One approach to solving this problem is to have multiple, "specialized" databases.

Second, we had to determine how to properly scope each agent—hoping to build lightweight agents while keeping agent coordination and communication tractable. We therefore decomposed the message delivery task between the *ResponseCoordinator* and the device agents (see [15] for more). This innovative structure allowed us to decouple protocols for delivering different types of messages from the details of the message mediums. For example, the system could have multiple *Phone* agents and an *Email* agent.

Because reminders for different items (for example, two medications) can be issued at the same time, we designed the delivery protocols to multiplex such reminders for delivery as one message. We put this capability in the *ResponseCoordinator* agent so the system could handle multiple devices, each with its own dedicated agent. Because a reminder could be received by *ResponseCoordinator* right after it dispatched the previous reminder to the *Phone* agent, multiple messages were still delivered. To overcome this issue, we replicated the delivery protocol in the *Phone* agent, defeating the purpose of decoupling protocols. A *cancel* message would not have been an appropriate solution, because then it is possible that no message would ever be delivered.

Finding an effective scoping and decoupling of capabilities is extremely challenging, and becomes more so as the system grows. Our hope for "straightforward" scalability will not be possible until agent technology develops much stronger and more scalable mechanisms for enforcing (logical) protocols.

Finally, when we chose an agent-oriented approach, we expected to use a small set of agents for the basic functionality of each installation of I.L.S.A. Each installation could then be customized by adding specialized agents. As client requirements or technology capabilities evolved, agents could be replaced with different versions.

While all agent-based systems encounter complications with new agents, they are more severe in a tightly coupled agent system like I.L.S.A. We discovered that developing new agents required *extensive* re-development of the existing system. As new agents are added, new functionalities and interfaces need to be added to existing agents: you cannot simply plug in a new agent. These issues are compounded by multi-person development and also increase testing effort.

### 3.3 Lesson #3: Robustness and Reliability

One benefit of the multi-agent approach is that it is distributed; however, this approach does not preclude the system from having a single point of failure. Notably, the system has several agents to provide services for other agents. Some of these service agents (e.g. *Database*, the *ResponseCoordinator*, or *Platform*) are more critical than others; if one of them fails, the whole system fails. Failures of less critical service agents (e.g. *Phone*, *UnexpectedActivity*) severely limit functionality. If a "non-service" domain agent (e.g. *Medication*, *Mobility*) fails, other parts of the system still work, although this reduces the usefulness of the system. Redundant capabilities (both software and hardware) is one way to address this reliability problem; however, the designer will need to carefully consider how to not generate redundant (read "irritating") messages to the users.

In I.L.S.A., the promise of inherent robustness from distributed computation did not hold true. Certain capabilities need to be centralized (e.g. communication with the elder) and this centralization is guaranteed to make system design difficult. An agent-based approach is unlikely to be appropriate when capabilities need to be centralized.

In a system where reliability is critical, it is important to design for persistence over restarts. For example, many of I.L.S.A.s domain agents needed a concept of recent history to make interaction decisions. If the system failed or was rebooted for some reason, agents had to reconstruct their history. Different agents reasoned over different windows of activity, hence only localized approaches to solving this problem are appropriate.

### 3.4 Lesson #2: Testing and Debugging

The requirement that every system needs to be thoroughly tested was noticeably more pronounced in the agent-based system than it would have been in a monolithic system. The ability to communicate "freely" with other agents meant that every possible interaction needed to be tested and verified; in a monolithic system, however, interactions between components are much more controlled, and testing can be focussed on the single point of change. With each new agent, the entire system had to be thoroughly tested to check behavioral and data coherence.

The extent to which the agents communicate and work together resulted in significant complications for debugging. Current agent technology does not provide adequate support to localize bugs: an error generated by an agent does not necessarily identify the root cause of the problem. Errors can propagate from agent to agent through communication channels, making it difficult to identify the agent at fault.

As a side effect of inadequate support for enforcing logical protocols throughout the system, we often found that we had to fix the same bug in multiple agents. It was also hard, with the multi-person development team, to know who had found time to implement the new protocol, and who had not. Often, this led to finding the same error during multiple, independent testing sessions, and therefore multiple, independent hunts for the same bug.

### 3.5 A Final Note

The agent-based approach promised a highly open and flexible system. We learned that this approach still requires a very rigorous software development process and many challenges are yet to be addressed by the agent research community. Agent based systems will need to focus much more strongly on scalability, debugging, and reliability issues before they will emerge from the lab.

We believe that the development issues we faced will be shared by any system in which agents work cooperatively toward a common goal. The more centralized that capabilities need to be, the more likely that an agent-based approach is inappropriate.

## 4 Lessons: Ontology

The Consolidated Home Ontology in Protégé (CHOP) serves two primary purposes. First, it is a common vocabulary for I.L.S.A.-related concepts, and their relationships. Second, in conjunction with a program code generator, CHOP produces an agent communication interface between I.L.S.A.'s agent-based system components.

CHOP is an ontology containing over 800 distinct concepts. It was developed with Protégé [7], a popular visual ontology construction tool. CHOP was derived from two upper ontologies, Cyc [3] and the Suggested Upper Merged Ontology (SUMO) [13; 14]. CHOP contains concepts including support for agent configuration, logging monitoring results to a long-term store, client and environment states, and status communication.

In addition to clarifying the meaning of terms and objects in a system, the power of a formal ontology is that it may be used as the basis to automatically generate portions of code that are otherwise tedious. I.L.S.A.'s inter-agent communication depended upon Java classes that were auto-generated from the ontology. Taken to the furthest extreme, many system artifacts can be automatically generated using a formal ontology, including communications interfaces in multiple implementation languages, database schema, and other formal interfaces such as database access routines.

Useful lessons we derived from the creation and use of CHOP include:

- Designing one ontology for multiple purposes may mean trading lack of duplication for a steeper development learning curve.
- Don't waste ontological development effort supporting concept taxonomy or attributes that are not dictated by the application, even if they are relevant to the domain.
- In developing a taxonomy, be conscientious about cross-cultural compatibility.

While the use of ontologies is not novel in software design, existing ontologies did not cover the eldercare domain. While it is incomplete, CHOP represents a promising starting point for developing a reusable ontology for knowledge-based home assistance systems. We will be presenting CHOP to the Center for Aging Services and Technologies (CAST) [2] Electronic Health and Wellness Records task group. The CAST group is working on recommendations for the Health Level Seven (HL7) [11] medical record standard regarding long-term assisted care.

Researchers interested in obtaining a copy of the ontology can send email to the authors of this paper.

## 5 Lessons: Automated Reasoning

At the outset of the program, a major focus was on using high-level reasoning to provide an intelligent monitoring system. We intended to build three main components: situation assessment and task tracking, response generation, and machine learning. Experiments in the engineers' homes validated our hypothesis that this domain is very complex and lends itself very well to advanced reasoning techniques.

### 5.1 Lesson #1: Situation Assessment and Task Tracking

A significant risk for a monitoring system like I.L.S.A. is accurate recognition of activity. Sensors are noisy, inaccurate, and low quality. It is a significant challenge to assess the situation and recognize what activities are occurring.

Our task tracking system was based on the Probabilistic Hostile Agent Task Tracker (PHATT) [5]. At the beginning of the program, we recognized that PHATT had a number of capabilities not available in other task tracking systems, making it uniquely suited to this domain. Continuing our research on I.L.S.A., we reached the following list of requirements for task tracking systems in this kind of domain:

**Abandoning Plans:** All people abandon plans at one time or another: they forget what they are doing, get distracted, or decide explicitly to abandon a goal.

**Unobservable actions:** Not all elders are willing to have their actions observed by an assistant system and may try to hide their actions. This unobservable action stream is a significant challenge.

**Failed Actions:** People will often try to achieve a goal but fail. This information is extremely useful in this domain.

**Partially Ordered Plans:** People frequently work on multiple goals at the same time. The task tracker must be able to recognize interleaved plans.

**Actions used for multiple effects:** Often one action can achieve multiple effects; the task tracker must be able to handle this kind of *overloaded* action.

**World state:** Different factors in the environment can significantly affect the likelihood of the elder adopting different goals.

**Multiple hypotheses:** One set of actions might be contributing to more than one plan. The task tracker needs to provide a ranked list of different possibilities.

In the lab, using data from the four richly-sensored engineer homes, we demonstrated the importance of each of these requirements. Geib [4] describes these requirements in more detail. Geib and Goldman [6] describe the specific extensions made under I.L.S.A. funding to PHATT to incorporate reasoning about abandoned goals.

The PHATT-based intent recognition component was removed from the I.L.S.A. field study because, in an effort to reduce the deployment cost for the elders in the field study, I.L.S.A. focused on a reduced set of low-cost sensors. To fully realize the potential of the task tracking system, more extensive and higher level sensor information is required.

## 5.2 Lesson #2: Response Generation

Response generation deals with 1) deciding *how* to respond to a given situation that exists with the elderly, and 2) *coordinating* all responses that may occur at any given moment.

Domain agents decide how to respond to a situation in a *context-free* manner. That is, they generate appropriate responses only within the context of their expertise; they do not take into account responses that other domain agents may be generating. Responses fall into four categories: reminders, notifications, alerts, and alarms. Each response category is defined by specific protocols and priorities that I.L.S.A. must follow.

Excessive and inaccurate alerts are a significant risk for this kind of monitoring system. In our field study excessive no-motion alerts were a major cause of client and caregiver dissatisfaction. In a few cases early in our test, they created a small amount of panic when an elder forgot to "turn I.L.S.A. off" when leaving the apartment. A secondary and very real risk is that the bad alerts will cause real alarms to be ignored ("never cry wolf").

The context-free messages must be prioritized, timely, and coordinated. Messages cannot be lost in a flood, and elders (and their caregivers) must not be overwhelmed. We chose to coordinate responses centrally rather than giving domain agents distributed access to devices. The centralized approach allows us to ensure that submission of important messages is *context-aware*:

- All responses from all domain agents must be presented on one set of devices, to one set of recipients. If we allowed domain agents to access devices directly, the recipients could be overwhelmed. Imagine receiving a dozen phone calls for different reminders at 9:00am; we wanted to merge these reminders into a single call.
- I.L.S.A. must recognize message priorities. Allowing domain agents to have distributed access to devices could cause important messages to be lost or delivered too late. For example, if the elder were to fall, the emergency call to a caregiver might be delayed behind a reminder to eat lunch.

For more detailed discussion refer to Wagner *et al.* [15].

## 5.3 Lesson #3: Machine Learning

Success in this domain requires that I.L.S.A. capture complex interactions among devices, the environment, and humans, and be particularly responsive to constant changes. Currently these systems are very inflexible, and their initial configuration is labor intensive. To adapt to changes in the client or in the environment (inevitable in this domain), we must reprogram the system. Reprogramming adds to the cost of the system and presents an inconvenience to the client.

We explored three machine learning techniques to assess their impact on I.L.S.A.'s actual operating environment:

**Patterned behaviour profiles** [8]: build models of which sensor firings correspond to which activities, in what order, and at what time.

**Unexpected Activity** : raise alerts if activity occurs when it is probabilistically unlikely.

**Schedules** : learn schedule information for regular activities in the clients home (e.g. medication, wake/sleep, occupancy)

Results of our analysis showed that Machine Learning is a useful enhancement to even the simplest system. At a minimum, machine learning techniques can learn schedules and provide long-term activity trends. Given a rich sensor suite, machine learning techniques can learn complex models of the environment, the elder, other people, and even the effectiveness of its own devices. These models can then be used by the system to improve its assessments and responsiveness. Machine learning techniques allow a system:

1. to tune itself to the operating environment, greatly reducing the amount of tuning and knowledge acquisition required at setup.

2. to respond to changes in the users and the domain, directly reducing maintenance costs.
3. to capture the user's preferences, enhancing usability.

Two main barriers remain: evaluation and automatic incorporation of learned models into the system.

It was not possible to gather ground-truth information for I.L.S.A. because users were not willing to either note every activity or be constantly videotaped. Our evaluations were based on "eyeballing" results for plausibility and then observing whether changed system behavior was more or less acceptable to the elders and their caregivers. While short-term ground truth can be gathered, researchers will need to develop good techniques for long-term evaluation.

Currently, the elder-care industry will not accept a system that does not have a human-in-the-loop; many other industries have regulations that explicitly prohibit automatic modifications. Our approach of presenting the results to a human before incorporating them into the system was well-accepted but is unlikely to scale to a larger community of users in its current form.

## 6 Conclusion

I.L.S.A., in its form as an agent-based system, has been retired. Using an agent-based system, contrary to our expectations, *significantly* added to the development effort. I.L.S.A. had many capabilities that needed to be centralized, and therefore it is clear to us that pursuing a simpler route would have saved us time, money, and frustration—a single-threaded, component-oriented architecture may have been a better approach.

If we continue research on the Independent LifeStyle Assistant, we will create a new software platform using the knowledge we gained during this program. The largest technical barriers we perceive are:

- further development, testing and verification of intelligent automation within this domain;
- development of a more effective medication management system, including 360-degree pharmaceutical services;
- development of effective and comfortable methods of communication between the system and the elderly clients.

We view the I.L.S.A. program as a success because of the following significant achievements:

- We successfully prototyped a passive monitoring system for elders in their own homes.
- We have a much better understanding of what constitutes an *acceptable* monitoring system for elders and, in particular, disproved some of the assumptions made about "technophobic" elders [9]. Through our Knowledge Acquisition effort, we learned what factors affect elders' independence and identified technology opportunities. We improved the understanding of factors that impede the delivery and acceptance of assistive technologies, and also improved our ability to overcome these factors.
- We validated the importance of artificial intelligence technologies to support a broad customer base in widely varied and unstructured environments. Notably, we have validated the importance of machine learning as a technique to mitigate expensive installations and ongoing adaptation (Section 5.3).

## Acknowledgments

The authors would like to thank the contributions of the entire Honeywell I.L.S.A. team, as well as Dr. Kathleen Krichbaum, United Health Care, Presbyterian Homes and Services, and LifeLine Systems, Inc. We also acknowledge the support of the Advanced Technology Program at the National Institute of Science and Technology, U.S. Department of Commerce under agreement #70NANBOH3020.

## References

[1] F. Bellifemine, A. Poggi, and G. Rimassa. JADE: A FIPA-compliant agent framework. In *Proceedings of The Practical Applications of Intelligent Agents and MultiAgent Technology (PAAM)*, pages 97–108, 1999. http://sharon.cselt.it/projects/jade/.

[2] Center for Aging Services Technologies. Available from: www.agingtech.org, 2003 [cited 3-Sept-2003].

[3] Cyc. Available from: www.cyc.com/, 2003 [cited 3-Sept-2003].

[4] C. W. Geib. Problems with intent recognition for elder care. In *Proceedings of the AAAI-02 Workshop "Automation as Caregiver"*, pages 13–17, 2002.

[5] C. W. Geib and R. P. Goldman. Probabilistic plan recognition for hostile agents. In *Proceedings of the FLAIRS 2001 Conference*, 2001.

[6] C. W. Geib and R. P. Goldman. Recognizing plan/goal abandonment. In *Proceedings of IJCAI 2003*, 2003.

[7] J. H. Gennari, M. A. Musen, R. W. Fergerson, W. E. Grosso, M. Crubézy, H. Eriksson, N. F. Noy, and S. W. Tu. The evolution of Protégé: An environment for knowledge-based systems development. Technical Report SMI-2002-0943, Stanford University.

[8] V. Guralnik and K. Z. Haigh. Learning models of human behaviour with sequential patterns. In *Proceedings of the AAAI-02 workshop "Automation as Caregiver"*, pages 24–30, 2002.

[9] K. Z. Haigh, L. M. Kiff, J. Myers, V. Guralnik, K. Krichbaum, J. Phelps, T. Plocher, and D. Toms. The Independent LifeStyle Assistant™ (I.L.S.A.): Lessons learned. Technical Report ACS-P03-023, Honeywell Laboratories, 3660 Technology Drive, Minneapolis, MN 55418, December 2003.

[10] K. Z. Haigh, J. Phelps, and C. W. Geib. An open agent architecture for assisting elder independence. In *The First International Joint Conference on Autonomous Agents and Multi-Agent Systems (AAMAS)*, pages 578–586, 2002.

[11] Health Level 7. Available from: www.hl7.org/, 2003 [cited 3-Sept-2003].

[12] The Independent LifeStyle Assistant™. Available from: www.htc.honeywell.com/projects/ ilsa, 2003.

[13] I. Niles and A. Pease. Origins of the IEEE Standard Upper Ontology. In *Working Notes of the IJCAI-2001 Workshop on the IEEE Standard Upper Ontology*, August 2001.

[14] Suggested Upper Merged Ontology. Available from: ontology.teknowledge.com/, 2003 [cited 3-Sept-2003].

[15] T. A. Wagner, V. Guralnik, and J. Phelps. Achieving global coherence in multi-agent cargiver systems: Centralized versus distributed response coordination in I.L.S.A. In *Proceedings of the AAAI-02 Workshop on "Automation as Caregiver"*, pages 100–105, 2002.

# Identifying Terrorist Activity with AI Plan Recognition Technology

**Peter A. Jarvis, Teresa F. Lunt*, and Karen L. Myers**

Artificial Intelligence Center
SRI International
333 Ravenswood Avenue
Menlo Park, CA 94025, USA.
Peter.Jarvis@sri.com Karen.Myers@sri.com

Palo Alto Research Center*
3333 Coyote Hill Road
Palo Alto, CA 94304, USA
tlunt@parc.com

**Abstract**

We describe the application of plan recognition techniques to support human intelligence analysts in processing national security alert sets by automatically identifying the hostile intent behind them. Identifying the intent enables us to both prioritize and explain the alert sets for succinct user presentation. Our empirical evaluation demonstrates that the approach can handle alert sets of as many as 20 elements and can readily distinguish between false and true alarms. We discuss the important opportunities, for future work, that will increase the cardinality of the alert sets supported by the system to the level demanded by a deployable application. In particular, we outline opportunities to bring the analysts into the process and the opportunities for heuristic improvements to the plan recognition algorithm.

**Keywords:** Plan Recognition, Intelligence Analysis.

## Introduction

Events in the United States during 2001 tragically demonstrated the nation's vulnerability to acts of terrorism. U.S. security agencies had information available at that time that could have been used to thwart the World Trade Center attack. However, it was not utilized as it was residing within the ocean of other intelligence leads then under consideration [U.S. Senate Report 2002].

Significant research has focused on the problem of uncovering the critical pieces of intelligence information that can be used to thwart an attack from a large body of intelligence leads [DISCEX 2003]. The data mining approaches that have been explored for this purpose can sift through vast quantities of information, but suffer from a high false alarm rate and do not help analysts link together separate facts and events [Ning & Dingbang 2003].

We have developed a proof-of-concept prototype for a tool to automate the analysis currently undertaken by humans by exploiting plan recognition techniques from the artificial intelligence community. Our thesis is that we can significantly improve the quality of the information passed to human analysts if we can automatically discover a significant causal coherence between disparate activities. Our analysis can also aid in the explanations of hypotheses by presenting them in the context of the evidence.



We structure this paper as follows. We first present our Computer Aided Plan Recognition (CAPRe) architecture. We then describe the modeling framework that we use to represent terrorist behavior before detailing the plan recognition algorithm we have developed to match observations with the model. Our experimental section evaluates the performance of the system on alert sets with range of signal-to-noise properties. We close by reflecting on what we have learned and define avenues that must be explored by future work before the capability can be deployed in an operational setting.

## Computer-Aided Plan Recognition (CAPRe) Architecture

Our approach, illustrated in Figure 1, involves specifying *a priori* attack templates that are compared against observables to infer whether a particular attack matching one or more templates might be under way. The templates also support the anticipation of future steps so that data collection can be directed, and early interventions to interfere with the plan are possible.

## Attack Templates

CAPRe's attack template library contains a description of attack activities structured hierarchically with a specification of the conditions under which they can be combined. The library forms a description of the action physics for a particular application domain that can be used to construct plan instances tailored to specific target requirements, not a library of known attack plan cases.

We draw on the rich hierarchical action representation developed and refined in the automated planning community during the past 30 years (Fikes and Nilsson 1971, Tate 1977). These representations have found application in areas as diverse as spacecraft control (Muscettola et al. 1997) and oil spill response planning (Bienkowski et al. 1994). Figure 2 presents a sampling of the templates in our library for terrorist attacks on a national infrastructure. A template contains information organized into the following slots:

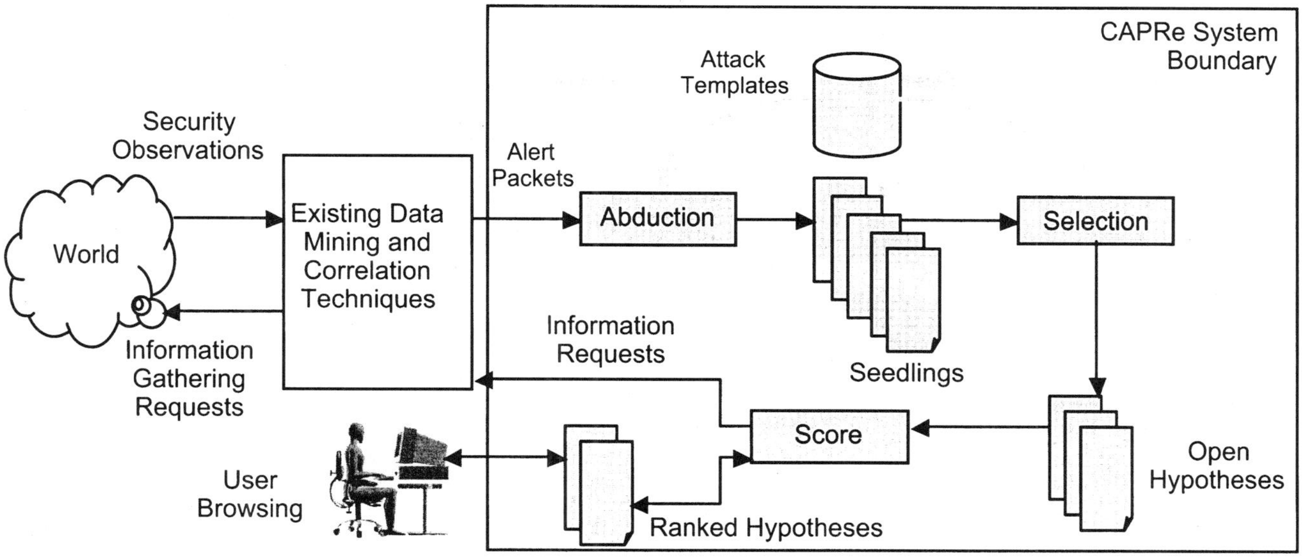


**Figure 1: CAPRe Architecture**

**:template** Physical_Attack
**:purpose** destroy(?group ?target)
**:tasks**
1. reconnaissance(?group ?target)
2. prepare_attack(?group ?target)
3. attack(?group ?target);

**:orderings** 1 > 3, 2 > 3;
**:end_template**

**:template** Reconnaissance_of_Target
**:vars** group ?group, target ?target;
**:purpose** reconnaissance(?group ?target)
**:tasks**
1. recon_security(?group ?target)
2. recon_structure(?group ?target);

**:end_template**

**:template** Research_Structure
**:purpose** recon_structure(?group ?target)
**:tasks**
1. obtain_structural_plans (?target ?group)
2. take_job (?group ?target)
3. structural_engineering_training (?group);

**:conditions** member(?person ?group);
**:effects** retrieved_blue_prints(?person ?group) :at 1.
hr_records(?group ?target) :at 2.
enrollment(?group ?engineering_school) :at 3.
**:end_template**

**Figure 2: Example Templates**

- **:vars** - variables that provide typed parameter descriptions for a template
- **:purpose** - the overall purpose of the template
- **:tasks** - set of labeled lower-level tasks to be performed to achieve the purpose
- **:orderings** - temporal constraints on the execution of actions defined in terms of task labels
- **:preconditions** constraints on the execution of a task (e.g., valid driver's license required to rent a car)
- **:effects** - changes to the world that result from the execution of tasks within a template

We define three properties on each task and effect within a template[1]. Each property can take the value *high*, *medium*, or *low*. While more complicated schemes are possible, we decided that this simple scheme would be the most accessible to our user community.

- **Frequency** of the occurrence of a task or effect in normal behavior. For example, car rentals are assigned a *high* frequency, while missing person reports are assigned a *low* frequency.
- **Accuracy** of normal observations of a task or effect. For example, missing person reports are *highly* accurate, while a witness's recollection of a suspicious car's license tag is generally *low* accuracy.
- **Gathering Cost** records the cost of making an observation. Accessing an online database is considered a *low* cost, while an observation that demands a door-to-door search by law enforcement officials is a *high*-cost operation.

Frequency and accuracy properties are exploited during the plan recognition process to score hypotheses or to filter observation lists. Cost is used during the information-gathering planning phase to determine the cost benefit of a particular information-gathering action.

[1]We have omitted these properties from Figure 2 because of space constraints.

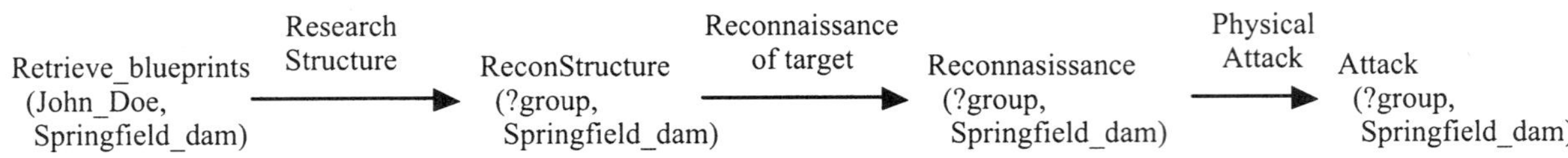


**Figure 3: Example Seedling**

## Plan Recognition Process

We first provide an overview of our plan recognition process before describing each element in detail. The broad approach is adapted from our earlier work on abductive plan sketch completion (Myers 1997).

### Process Overview

Informally, the plan recognition task is to take a set of observed actions and world state changes and a collection of (attack) templates and produce a set of plans that offer potential explanations for the observations within the template set.

Consider the observation *retrieved_blueprints (John_Doe, Springfield_dam)* in the context of the templates shown in Figure 2. We can work backward from this observation through the *research structure* template to conclude that the group of which Mr. Doe is a member is attempting to obtain control information about the Springfield dam. Working back another two steps, we can explain the control information attempt as part of the broader reconnaissance component of a physical attack on this dam. Figure 1 labels this reasoning as the abductive phase of the plan recognition activity that results in a set of *seedling* explanations for each observation.

The *selection* phase of the plan recognition activity takes the set of seedlings generated for all observations and seeks subsets that can be combined consistently with respect to the templates. For example, if we had observed another individual with links to the same organization as Mr. Doe enrolling in an engineering school, then we could combine these two observations to form an *open hypothesis*. If Mr. Doe and this new individual were associated with two different organizations, then these seedlings would not be able to be combined as they violate the *member* precondition in the *Research_Structure* template.

We now describe these two phases in more detail.

### Seedling Generation

We use an abductive inference procedure to identify the *seedling hypotheses* that provide candidate explanations for a set of observed activities A. Each seedling hypothesis tops out in an element of the goal space, *G,* for a domain model. While *G* could be defined explicitly, we use the set of template purposes that do not appear as tasks in templates. *Destroy(?group, ?target)* is one example member of *G* that is shown in Figure 2.

**Definition 1 (Seedling)** The seedling for a task α is the set of labeled linear graphs:

$$A \xrightarrow{O_n,\sigma_n} G_n \xrightarrow{O_{n-1},\sigma_{n-1}} G_{n-1} \xrightarrow{O_{n-2},\sigma_{n-2}} \ldots \xrightarrow{O_1,\sigma_1} G_1$$

where $G_1 \in G$, and $O_j$ is a template with purpose $G_j$ and a subtask T such that $\sigma_j$ is a most general unifier of T and $(G_{j+1})^{\beta}$, for $\beta = \cup_{n \geq i \geq j} \sigma_j$ and $A = G_{n+1}$.

Consider the following observation set:

*{retrieved_blue_prints(doe_corp, springfield_dam), enrollment(john_smive, springfield_eng_school), retrieved_blue_prints(doe_corp, sand_dam }.*

Figure 3 shows the seedlings that will be generated for these observations given the template set shown in Figure 2. Technically, this figure should show variable bindings, but we have simplified the presentation to the propositional case.

Implementing a seedling generation procedure is simple given the above definition. The only concern is the runtime of the procedure. We define the *abstraction factor* for a task *T* to be the number of template schema subtasks that unify with *T.* We define α to be the maximum abstraction factor for all the tasks in a domain definition. Let $l_A$ be the difference in abstraction level between observations *A* and the most abstract goal in the goal space *G.* The sum

$$\sum_{a \in \text{observation}} \alpha^{la}$$

(where ε =) is a loose upperbound on the construction time for the seedling explanations for a set of observations.

We show empirically the time spent in the seedling generation phase in our experiment section. While a procedure with exponential bounds is cause for concern, we have found in practice that typical domain definitions contain 8 to 10 abstraction levels, and the abstraction factor rarely exceeds 6 (Myers 1997).

We provide two mechanisms that allow the user to influence the seedling generation process. The *frequency filter* parameter allows the user to specify the maximum occurrence frequency of the observations that should be considered. This allows the user to filter out high- or medium-frequency events. The user can also specify classes of events and effects to ignore.

### Seedling Selection

The selection phase seeks to combine the seedlings generated in the first phase to form a set of open hypotheses with each member offering an explanation of the intent behind a cluster of seedlings.

Figure 3, all three seedlings would be clustered into a single seedling group, *SG*, as they share the common *destroy* top-level predicate. We now iterate through the powerset of each seedling group (ignoring those of cardinality < 2 and generating the set incrementally) to identify the seedlings that can be combined. The powerset of *SG* that we consider consists of the following sets:

1. {blue_prints_springfield, engineering_training_smive}
2. {blue_prints_springfield, blue_prints_sand}
3. {blue_prints_sand, engineering_training_smive}
4. {blue_prints_springfield, engineering_training_smive, blue_prints_sand}

Corresponding seedling steps can be combined to form an open hypothesis if the following conditions are satisfied:

- The purpose statements unify.
- The steps use a common template.
- All constraints in the template are satisfied.
- The bindings entailed by the purpose and task statements across the steps are consistent.

The combination process starts with the top-level step of each seedling in the set under consideration. Consider the members of Set 1. The top-level steps can be combined as the combination conditions are satisfied. Now consider the members of Set 2. The top steps of these two seedlings cannot be combined, as the binding for the *target* variable is inconsistent across the seedlings. Return to Set 1; the combination process continues by considering the next steps in each seedling under consideration. A valid open hypothesis is produced if all steps in all seedlings could be combined.

Figure 4 shows the open hypothesis produced by combining the members of Set 1. While the group behind the attack is not named, the template constraints state that Doe Corp and the individual known as Smive are associated with the group behind the attack.

The concern with the composition procedure, as with the seedling construction phase, is the computational complexity of the procedure. The size of a power set of $n$ elements is $2^n$.

We carefully structure our search and exploit search pruning to maximize the activity cluster size that we can consider. Our primary strategy is to search through the powerset of seedlings in ascending cardinality order. This strategy has several advantages. First, we can terminate our search as soon as we find a cardinality level with no open hypotheses. Second, we can use a no-good learning strategy. Once we have found a set of seedlings that cannot combine, we can prune all other sets that contain that set as a subset. We show the benefit of no-good learning in the experiments section.

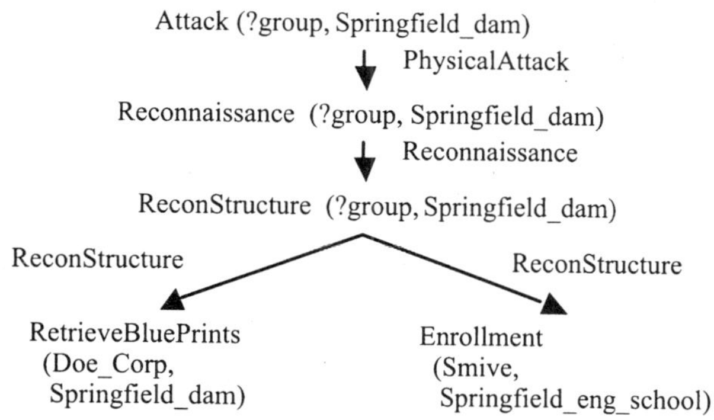


**Figure 4: Example Open Hypothesis**

## Implementation

We have implemented a prototype of our CAPRe architecture in Java. Figure 5 shows the user interface to this system. The top pane displays the current open hypotheses with observations bolded. The left and center bottom panels allow the user to control the seedling generation and compositions process and the scoring function used to sort the open hypotheses. We currently support a simple scoring scheme that rates open hypotheses according to the number of observations that support them. The bottom right panel displays the constraint on the currently selected hypotheses.

Our current implementation includes only the plan recognition portion of the architecture. Implementing and evaluating the generation of information-gathering plans is left for further work.

## Experiments

Our empirical evaluation of the CAPRe implementation examined the performance of the system on a range of alert sets. We focused on variations in the following properties of alert sets:

- **Number of alerts** is the total number of alerts in a set.
- **Signal-to-noise ratio** is the number of alerts in a set that are part of a malicious plan (the target plan) divided by the total number of false alerts in the set.
- **Noise coherence** refers to the maximum number of false alerts in a set that can be combined consistently to form a coherent attack plan.

Table 1 presents the results of our empirical examination of CAPRe. The input alert sets were crafted by hand to include evidence for a target hypothesis together with noise with the appropriate signal-to-noise and coherence properties. We recorded both the runtime of the system and the position of the target hypothesis within the sorted list of hypotheses identified for each set.

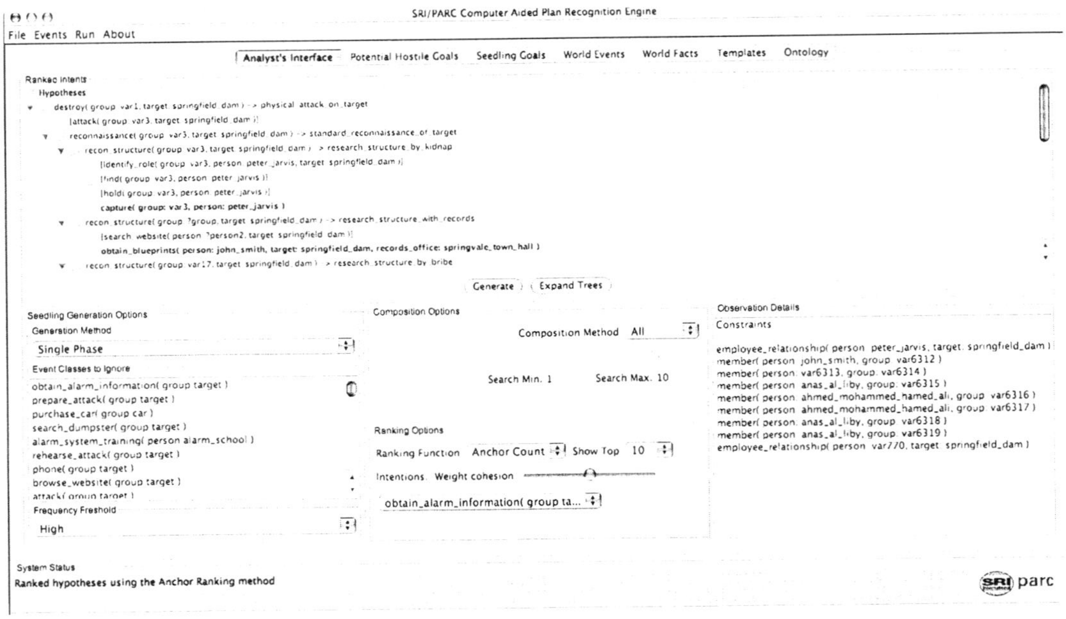


**Figure 5: CAPRe User Interface**

| Maximum Noise Coherence | | 1 | | | 4 | | | 8 | | |
|---|---|---|---|---|---|---|---|---|---|---|
| No. Events | Signal/ Noise | 1/3 | 1/1 | 3/1 | 1/3 | 1/1 | 3/1 | 1/3 | 1/1 | 3/1 |
| 8 | **Time** | 0:00:00.1 | 0:00:00.1 | 0:00:00.1 | 0:00:00.1 | 0:00:00.1 | 0:00:00.1 | 0:00:00.1 | 0:00:00.1 | 0:00:00.1 |
| | **Rank** | **1/7** | **1/5** | **1/3** | 3/3 | **1/2** | **1/2** | 2/2 | *Joint 1st* | **1/2** |
| 16 | **Time** | 0:00:00.7 | 0:01:00.4 | 0:01:26.0 | *0:00:01.7* | 0:01:02 | 0:01:25.9 | 0:03:06.1 | 0:01:00.1 | 0:00:23.8 |
| | **Rank** | **1/13** | **1/9** | **1/4** | *Joint 1st* | **1/3** | **1/2** | 3/3 | *Joint 1st* | **1/2** |
| 20 | **Time** | 0:00:09.7 | 2:27:02.4 | 0:47:34.0 | 0:00:06.3 | 0:47:28.2 | 0:48:19.4 | 0:28:01.0 | 0:48:20.5 | 0:54:59.4 |
| | **Rank** | **1/16** | **1/12** | **1/8** | 5/5 | **1/4** | **1/3** | 3/3 | **1/2** | **1/2** |
| 25 | **Time** | 0:19:49.3 | * | * | * | * | * | * | * | * |
| | **Rank** | **1/19** | * | * | * | * | * | * | * | * |

**Table 1: Experimental Results**

Apple PowerMac G5 1.8 GHz, 500 MB RAM. * denotes no result after 12 hours.

We sorted the set of hypotheses by the number of seedlings combined to generate hypotheses. The more seedlings composed to form a hypothesis the higher its support, and therefore the higher its score.

Examining Table 1 reveals that the time CAPRe takes to identify intent increases exponentially with the number of events in an alert set. This is the behavior that we predicted from the appreciation that our seedling composition step must consider the powerset of the seedlings explanation generated for an alert set. CAPRe is currently limited to alert sets of about 20 actions on state-of-the-art hardware.

The noise coherence and signal-to-noise ratio properties of alert sets affected both the runtime and accuracy of CAPRe. Consider first the group of three results with a noise coherence of 1. In this case, noise cannot mislead the recognition process as each mistaken hypothesis can be supported by only one alert. In this situation, CAPRe consistently ranks the target hypothesis first. When we move to alerts with a noise coherence of 4, CAPRe ranks incorrect hypotheses higher when the signal-to-noise ratio favors the noise. The target hypothesis is ranked first again when the signal-to-noise ratio is 1 or favors the signal. When the noise coherence is adjusted to 8, the results show that it becomes increasingly difficult for CAPRe to correctly identify the target hypothesis. This is understandable, as the noise has become coherent and is dwarfed in cases where it outnumbers or equals the target activities.

We draw two conclusions from the experiments. First, the runtime performance degrades exponentially with alert set size, and for practical purposes 20 alerts is the limit. Second, the accuracy of the system falls off as the cohesion of the noise exceeds that of the actual attack activity.

## Summary and Further Work

We have introduced the CAPRe architecture for automating the deep analysis of security alert clusters in order to reduce the load on human security analysts. Our proof-of-concept demonstration illustrates that the technology is capable of recognizing the intent behind events in an alert set and of presenting that intent succinctly to a human user. Our empirical investigation concluded that the technology could process alert clusters of as many as 20 actions and demands that noise (false alerts) be less casually coherent than the components of the attacks.

Further work is needed to move CAPRe to a position where it is ready for operational deployment. We recommend that further work focus on the following three areas:

- **Real Alert Sets:** CAPRe has benefited from a close development relationship with the intelligence community. However, it is essential that future work have access to actual or at least analyst-generated alert sets. Research can then focus on addressing the issues raised by actual rather than projected signal-to-noise ratios and coherence factors.
- **Mixed-Initiative Paradigm:** the number of seedlings generated for an alert set is the critical factor in determining the runtime of the composition phase. Intelligence analysts often have deep insights into the attack activity in progress and events that are supporting false conclusions. Future work should explore a mixed initiative approach where seedlings are presented in a digestible form to the analysts for filtering.
- **Heuristic Development:** We propose to explore two approaches to improving the algorithmic performance of CAPRe. First, we will explore the information-gathering planning concept defined in the architecture to enable us to perform plan recognition on only low-frequency actions in an alert cluster before examining the cluster for alerts that support the set of hypotheses generated. This approach would have the key benefit of reducing the number of seedlings generated for an alert set. Second, we will explore the inclusion of probabilities of observing template tasks given a template purpose in a way similar to that used by Goldman et al. (1999). We will use this information to rank seedlings according to the probability that the observation supports the goal of each. A simple cutoff strategy can then be used to prune unlikely seedlings and again reduce the number of seedlings passed into the computationally expensive combination phase.

## References


Bienkowski, M., des Jardins, M., and Desimone, R., 1994. SOCAP: System for Operations Crisis Action Planning. In Proceedings of the ARPA/Rome Lab 1994 Knowledge-Based Planning and Scheduling Initiative Workshop, February.

DISCEX 2003, Proceedings of the DARPA Information Survivability Conference and Exposition (DISCEX'03) 0-7695-1897-4/03, IEEE.

Goldman, R., Geib, C., and Miller, C., 1999. A New Model of Plan Recognition. In Proceedings of the Conference on Uncertainty in Artificial Intelligence, pp. 245-254.

Fikes, R., and Nilsson, N., 1971. STRIPS: A New Approach to the Application of Theorem Proving to Problem Solving, *Artificial Intelligence*, Vol. 5, No. 2, North-Holland publishing Co., Amsterdam, Netherlands.

Myers, K., 1997. Abductive Completion of Plan Sketches. In Proceedings of the Fourteenth National Conference on Artificial Intelligence (AAAI-97), AAAI Press, Menlo Park, CA.

Muscettola, N., Smith, B., Fry, C., Chien, S., Rajan, K., Rabideau, G., and Yan, D., 1997. In Proceedings of the IEEE Aerospace Conference, Aspen, CO.

Ning, P., and Dingbang, X., 2003. Adapting Query Optimization Techniques for Efficient Intrusion Alert Correlation. In proceedings of the 17th IFIP WG 11.3 Working Conference on Data and Application Security.

Tate. A., 1977. Generating Project Networks. In Proceedings of the International Joint Conferences on Artificial Intelligence, pp. 888-893.

U.S. Senate Select Committee on Intelligence and U.S. House Permanent Select Committee on Intelligence, 2002. Joint Inquiry Into Intelligence Community Activities Before and After the Terrorist Attacks of September 11, 2001. *S. Rept. No. 107-351*, December. http://www.gpoaccess.gov/serialset/creports/911.html. Accessed October 8, 2003.



**Acknowledgments**

The authors thank Tom Garvey and other members of SRI's AI Center who have commented on this work. The DARPA Cyber Panel program through subcontract MP201427 under contract N66001-03-C-8004 supported the work.

# A Robotic Wayfinding System for the Visually Impaired

**Vladimir Kulyukin*** **Chaitanya Gharpure** **Pradnya Sute**

**Nathan De Graw** **John Nicholson**

Department of Computer Science
Utah State University
Logan, UT 84322
vladimir.kulyukin@usu.edu

### Abstract

We present an emerging indoor assisted navigation system for the visually impaired. The core of the system is a mobile robotic base with a sensor suite mounted on it. The sensor suite consists of an RFID reader and a laser range finder. Small passive RFID sensors are manually inserted in the environment. We describe how the system was deployed in two indoor environments and evaluated by visually impaired participants in a series of pilot experiments.

## Introduction

The inability to navigate unfamiliar environments remains a key barrier to equal access for the 11.4 million visually impaired people in the United States (LapLante & Carlson 2000). This inability denies the visually impaired adequate access to many buildings, impedes their use of public transit, and makes their integration into local communities difficult. Thus, there is a significant need for assisted navigation systems that help the visually impaired overcome the navigation barrier, especially in unfamiliar environments, where conventional aids, such as white canes and guide dogs, are of limited use.

Over the past three decades, considerable R&D effort has been dedicated to navigation devices for the visually impaired. Benjamin, Ali, and Schepis (Benjamin, Ali, & Schepis 1973) built the C-5 Laser Cane. The cane uses optical triangulation with three laser diodes and three photo-diodes as receivers. Bissit and Heyes (Bissit & Heyes 1980) developed the Nottingham Obstacle Detector (NOD), a hand-held sonar device that gives the user auditory feedback with eight discrete levels. Shoval et al. developed the NavBelt, an obstacle avoidance wearable device equipped with ultrasonic sensors and a wearable computer (Shoval, Borenstein, & Koren 1994). The NavBelt produces a 120-degree wide view ahead of the user. The view is translated into stereophonic audio directions. Borenstein and Ulrich (Borenstein & Ulrich 1994) built GuideCane, a mobile obstacle avoidance device for the visually impaired. GuideCane consists of a long handle and a ring of ultrasonic sensors mounted on a steerable two-wheel axle.

More recently, a radio frequency identification (RFID) navigation system for indoor environments was developed at the Atlanta VA Rehabilitation Research and Development Center (Ross 2001; Ross & Blasch 2002). In this system, the blind users' canes are equipped with RFID receivers, while RFID transmitters are placed at hallway intersections. As the users pass through transmitters, they hear over their headsets commands like "turn left," "turn right," and "go straight." The Haptica Corporation has developed Guido©, a robotic walking frame for people with impaired vision and reduced mobility (www.haptica.com). Guido© uses the onboard sonars to scan the immediate environment for obstacles and communicates detected obstacles to the user via speech synthesis.

While the existing approaches to assisted navigation have shown promise, they have had limited success for the following reasons. First, many existing systems increase the user's navigation-related physical load because they require that the user wear additional and, oftentimes substantial, body gear (Shoval, Borenstein, & Koren 1994), which contributes to physical fatigue. The solutions that attempt to minimize body gear, e.g., the C-5 Laser Cane (Benjamin, Ali, & Schepis 1973) and the GuideCane (Borenstein & Ulrich 1994), require that the user abandon her conventional navigation aid, e.g., a white cane or a guide dog, which is not acceptable to many visually impaired individuals. Second, the user's navigation-related cognitive load remains high, because the user makes all final wayfinding decisions. While device-assisted navigation enables visually impaired individuals to avoid immediate obstacles and gives them simple directional hints, it provides little improvement in wayfinding over white canes and guide dogs. Limited communication capabilities also contribute to the high cognitive load.

*This research has been supported, in part, by the National Science Foundation Grant IIS-0346880, a Community University Research Initiative Grant (CURI) from the State of Utah, and by a New Faculty Research grant from Utah State University.

Finally, few assisted navigation technologies are deployed and evaluated in their target environments over extended time periods. It is this lack of deployment and evaluation that makes it difficult for assistive technology (AT) practitioners to compare different solutions and choose the one that best fits the needs of a specific individual.

## Can Robot-Assisted Navigation Help?

Yes, it can. First, the amount of body gear carried by the user is significantly minimized, because most of it can be mounted on the robot and powered from on-board batteries. Thus, robotic bases offer solutions to two of the hardest problems in assisted navigation: hardware miniaturization and portable power supply. Consequently, the navigation-related physical load is reduced. Second, the delegation of such key wayfinding capabilities as localization and path planning to the robot reduces the user's cognitive load. Third, the robot can interact with other people in the environment, e.g., ask them to yield or receive instructions. Fourth, robotic guides can carry useful payloads, e.g., suitcases and grocery bags. Finally, the user can use robotic guides in conjunction with her conventional navigation aids, e.g., white canes and guide dogs.

Are all environments suitable for robotic guides? No. There is little need for such guides in familiar environments where conventional navigation aids are adequate. However, unfamiliar indoor environments that are dynamic and complex, e.g., airports and conference centers, are a perfect niche for robotic guides. Guide dogs, white canes, and other navigation devices are of limited use in such environments, because they cannot help their users localize and find paths to useful destinations.

The idea of robotic guides is not new. Horswill (Horswill 1993) used the situated activity theory to build Polly, a mobile robot guide for the MIT AI Lab. Polly used lightweight vision routines that depended on textures specific to the lab. Thrun et al. (Thrun et al. 1999) built Minerva, a completely autonomous tour-guide robot that was deployed in the National Museum of American History in Washington, D.C. Burgard et al. (Burgard et al. 1999) developed RHINO, a close sibling of Minerva's, which was deployed as an interactive tour guide in the Deutsches Museum in Bonn, Germany. Unfortunately, these robots do not address the needs of the visually impaired. The robots depend on the users' ability to maintain visual contact with them, which cannot be assumed for the visually impaired. Polly has very limited interaction capabilities: the only way users can interact with the system is by tapping their feet. To request a museum tour from RHINO (Burgard et al. 11999), the user must identify and press a button of a specific color on the robot's panel. The approach on which Polly is based requires that a robot be evolved by its designer to fit its environment not only in terms of software but also in terms of hardware. This makes it difficult to produce replicable solutions that work out of the box in a variety of environments. Autonomous solutions like RHINO and Minerva require substantial investments in customized engineering to become and remain operational. For example, RHINO must run 20 parallel processes on 3 on-board PCs and 2 off-board SUN workstations connected via a customized Ethernet-based point-to-point socket communication protocol. Even with these high software and hardware commitments, RHINO reportedly experienced six collisions over a period of forty-seven hours, although each tour was less than ten minutes long (Burgard et al. 1999).

## A Robotic Guide

We have built and deployed a prototype of a robotic guide for the visually impaired. Its name is RG, which stands for "robotic guide." Our basic research objective is to alleviate localization and navigation problems of purely autonomous approaches by incrementing environments with inexpensive and reliable sensors that can be placed in and out of environments without disrupting any indigenous activities. Effectively, the environment becomes a distributed tracking and guidance system (Kulyukin & Blair2003; Kulyukin, Gharpure, & De Graw 2004) that consists of stationary nodes, e.g., sensors and computers, and mobile nodes, e.g., robotic guides.

Additional requirements are: 1) that the instrumentation be fast, e.g., two to three hours, and require only commercial off-the-shelf (COTS) hardware components; 2) that sensors be inexpensive, reliable, easy to maintain (no external power supply), and provide accurate localization; 3) that all computation run onboard the robot; and 4) that human-robot interaction be both reliable and intuitive from the perspective of the visually impaired users. The first two requirements make the systems that satisfy them replicable, maintainable, and robust. The third requirement eliminates the necessity of running substantial off-board computation to keep the robot operational. In emergency situations, e.g., computer security breaches, power failures, and fires, off-board computers are likely to become dysfunctional and paralyze the robot if it depends on them. The fourth requirement explicitly considers the needs of the target population.

### Scope limitations

Several important issues are currently beyond the project's scope. First, we do not address the issue of navigating large open spaces, e.g., large foyers in hotels. While a few recent references in the literature suggest that ultrasonic sensors could be used to address this issue (Addlesee et al. 2001), the proposed solutions are sketchy and are evaluated in carefully controlled, small lab environments. Thus, we assume that all environments in which RG operates have walls, hallways, aisles, T- and X-intersections, and solid and static objects, e.g., vending machines, that the onboard sensors can detect. Second, robotic guides prototyped by RG are not meant for individual ownership. Rather, we expect institutions, e.g., airports and large chain stores, to purchase such guides and operate them on the premises in the future. Third, the wayfinding technology proposed in this project could potentially assist sighted people with cognitive and mobile disabilities in navigating unfamiliar environments. While we intend to pursue these possibilities in the future, the target population for this project is visually impaired individuals (no more than light perception), at least 16 years of age, ambulatory, with no serious speech impediments, hearing problems, or cognitive disabilities. Finally, robotic guides prototyped by RG are not meant for outdoor navigation.

## Hardware and software

RG is built on top of the Pioneer 2DX robot platform (www.activmedia.com). The platform has three wheels, 16 ultrasonic sonars, 8 in front and 8 in the back, and is equipped with three rechargeable Power Sonic PS-1270 onboard batteries that can operate for up to five hours at a time.

What turns the platform into a robotic guide is a Wayfinding Toolkit (WT) mounted on top of the platform and powered from the on-board batteries. The WT currently resides in a PCV pipe structure attached to the top of the platform. The WT includes a laptop connected to the platform's microcontroller. The communication between the laptop and the microcontroller is done through a usb to serial cable.

The laptop interfaces to a radio-frequency identification (RFID) reader through another usb to serial cable. The TI Series 2000 RFID reader is connected to a square 200mm by 200mm RFID RI-ANT-GO2E antenna that detects RFID sensors (tags) placed in the environment. We currently use TI RFID Slim Disk tags. These tags can be attached to any objects in the environment or worn on clothing. They do not require any external power source or direct line of sight to be detected by the RFID reader. They are activated by the spherical electromagnetic field generated by the RFID antenna with a radius of approximately 1.5 meters. Each tag is programmatically assigned a unique ID. Finally, the laptop is connected to a LMS 200 laser range finder from the SICK corporation (www.sick.com) mounted on the front of the robot. A dog leash is attached to the battery bay handle on the back of the platform. The upper end of the leash is hung on a PCV pole next to the RFID antenna's pole. Visually impaired individuals follow RG by holding onto that leash. Eventually, when we find a satisfactory solution to the hardware miniaturization problem, we may be able to mount the WT directly on the guide dog and take advantage of a natural vision system.

As a software system, RG is based on Kupiers' Spatial Semantic Hierarchy (SSH) (Kupiers 2000). The SSH is a framework for representing spatial knowledge. It divides spatial knowledge of autonomous agents, e.g., people and robots, into four levels: the control level, causal level, topological level, and metric level. The control level consists of low level mobility laws, e.g., trajectory following and aligning with a surface. The causal level represents the world in terms of views and actions. A view is a collection of data items that an agent gathers from its sensors. Actions move agents from views to views. For example, a robot can go from one end of a hallway (start view) to the other end of the hallway (end view). The topological level represents the world's connectivity, i.e., how different locations are connected. The metric level adds distances between locations.

The control level is implemented with the following low-level routines all of which run on the laptop: follow-wall, turn-left, turn-right, avoid-obstacles, go-thru-doorway, pass-doorway, and make-u-turn. In selecting the routines, we tried to find a minimal action set that can be used in many standard indoor environments. These routines are written in the behavior programming language of the ActivMedia Robotics Interface for Applications (ARIA) system from ActivMedia Robotics, Inc. These behaviors draw on well understood indoor navigation techniques of the potential fields approach (Murphy 2000). Thus, in RG, sensor readings are converted into attractive and repulsive vectors that are summed to decide where the robot should go next.

RFID-based localization allows the robot to overcome the problem of local minima that many potential fields approaches experience in the absence of reliable localization, because the robot can generate a necessary direction vector on the basis of its current location. The laptop also runs two other software components: 1) a speech recognition and synthesis engine that enables RG to receive and synthesize speech and 2) a path planner. The advantages and disadvantages of speech-based interaction are discussed in the next section.

The Path Planner realizes the causal and topological levels of the SSH. The Planner's knowledge base represents an aerial view of the environment in which RG operates. Currently, the knowledge base consists of tag connectivity graphs, tag to destination mappings, and low-level action scripts associated with specific tags.

Specifically, the environment is represented as a graph where nodes represent the RFID tags and the edges represent the actions required to travel from one tag to another. Views consist of sonar and laser range finder readings and the IDs of the RFID tags currently detectable. Thus, detecting a tag can trigger a specific behavior, e.g., move through a doorway and align with a right wall. The Planner uses the standard breadth first search algorithm to find a path from one location to the other. A path plan is a sequence of tag numbers and action sequences at each tag.

## Human-Robot Interaction

Humans can interact with RG through speech, wearable keyboard, and GUIs. Speech-based and keyboard-based interactions are intended for visually impaired individuals. GUIs are intended for system administrators. Speech is received by RG through a wireless microphone placed on the user's clothing. Speech is recognized and synthesized with Microsoft Speech API (SAPI) 5.1, which is freely available from www.microsoft.com/speech. SAPI includes the Microsoft English SR Engine Version 5, a state-of-the-art Hidden Markov Model speech recognition engine. The engine includes 60,000 English words, which we found adequate for our purposes. SAPI couples the Hidden Markov Model speech recognition with a system for constraining speech inputs with context-free command and control grammars. The grammars constrain speech recognition sufficiently to eliminate user training and provide speaker-independent speech recognition. Grammars are defined with XML Data Type Definitions (DTDs).

RG interacts with its users and people in the environment through speech and audio icons. An audio icon is a non-verbal sound that can be readily associated with a specific object, e.g., the sound of water bubbles associated with a water cooler. For example, when RG is passing a water cooler, it can either say "water cooler" or play an audio file with sounds of water bubbles. We added audio icons to the system because, as recent research findings indicate (Tran, Letowski, & Abouchacra 2000), speech perception can be slow and prone to block ambient sounds from the environment. On the other hand, associating objects and events with non-speech audio messages requires training or the presence of a universally accepted mapping between events and objects and sounds. Since no such mapping is currently available, our assumption is that the user can quickly create such a mapping.

## Pilot Experiments

We deployed our system for a total of approximately fifty hours in two indoor environments: the Assistive Technology Laboratory (ATL) of the Utah State University (USU) Center for Persons with Disabilities and the USU Computer Science Department. The ATL occupies part of a floor in a building on the USU North Campus. The floor has an area of approximately 14,000 square feet. The floor contains 6 laboratories, two bathrooms, two staircases, and an elevator. The CS Department occupies an entire floor in a multi-floor building. The floor's area is 21,600 square feet. The floor contains 23 offices, 7 laboratories, a conference room, a student lounge, a tutor room, two elevators, several bathrooms, and two staircases.

Forty RFID tags were deployed at the ATL and one hundred tags were deployed at the CS Department. Once the destinations were known, it took one person 20 minutes to deploy the tags and about 10 minutes to remove them at the ATL. The same measurements at the CS Department were 30 and 20 minutes, respectively. The tags were attached to objects with regular scotch tape. The creation of the knowledge base took one hour at the ATL and about 2 hours at the CS Department. In both environments, one administrator first walked around the area with a laptop and recorded tag-destination associations. Then the administrator associates specific robotic actions with tags. RG was first deployed and tested by the project's team at the ATL, the smaller of the two environments, and then deployed at the CS Department for the pilot experiments with visually impaired participants.

Our pilot experiments involved five visually impaired participants, one participant at a time, over a period of two months. The five participants were selected from the target population: three participants were completely blind and two participants could perceive only light. The participants had no speech impediments, hearing problems, or cognitive disabilities. Two participants were dog users; the other three used white canes. The participants were asked to use RG to navigate to three distinct locations (an office, a lounge, and a bathroom) at the USU Computer Science Department. All participants were new to the environment and had to navigate approximately 40 meters to get to all destinations. In communication and audio perception experiments, we tested the participants' ability to communicate with RG through speech and the participants' audio perception preferences, i.e., whether they preferred to be notified of events and objects in the environment through speech or audio icons. The exit interviews showed that the participants really liked the system and thought it was a very useful navigation aid in unfamiliar environments. They especially liked the idea that they did not have to give up their white canes and guide dogs to use RG.

### Navigation

All five participants reached the assigned destinations. However, they expressed concerns about RG's slow speed and movement jerkiness. RG's speed was 0.5 m/s, which is below normal walking speeds of 1.2-1.5 m/s. Since at the time of the pilot study, the laser range finder had not yet been integrated into the WT, RG's navigation was based on sonar sensors, which are sometimes unreliable due to specular reflection and cross talk. In addition, since the effective range of the sonars is 2.5 meters, we had to adjust the speed of the robot so that it could stop in time to avoid bumping into people in hallways. The jerky movements occurred when the sonars either underestimated or overestimated the distances to the closest objects. For example, once when the robot followed a right wall and two of its right sonars told it that the wall was 50 centimeters (cm) further than it actually was, the robot turned right to better align itself with the wall, which caused jerkiness.

Another structural improvement suggested by the visually impaired participants in our pilot study was to replace the dog leash with a more static plastic pole similar to a white cane. This suggestion was made by the white cane users. It is interesting that the two dog users liked the dog leash, but said they would not mind a more static holder.

### Speech-based communication

Our first human-robot communication experiment tested the feasibility of using speech as a means of input for humans to communicate with the robot. Each participant was asked to speak approximately sixty phrases while wearing a headset that consisted of a microphone and one headphone. The phrase list was a list of standard phrases that a person may say to a robotic guide in an unfamiliar environment, e.g., "go to the bathroom," "where am I?" etc. Each phrase was encoded as a context-free command and control grammar rule in SAPI's XML-based grammar formalism. Each participant was positioned in front of a computer running SAPI. The test program was written to use SAPI's text-to-speech engine to read the phrases to the participant one by one, wait for the participant to repeat a phrase, and record a recognition result (speech recognized vs. speech not recognized) in a database. This experiment was repeated in two environments: noise-free and noisy. The noise-free environment did not have any ambient sounds other than the usual sounds of a typical office. To simulate a noisy environment, a long audio file of a busy bus station was played on another computer in the office. All five participants were native English speakers and did not train SAPI's speech recognition engine on sample texts.

We found that the average percentage of phrases recognized by the system in the noise-free environment was 38%, while the average percentage of recognized phrases in the noisy environment was 40.2%. While the level of ambient noise in the environment did not seem to affect the system's speech recognition, in both environments fewer than 50% of phrases were correctly recognized. Even worse, on average, 20% of spoken phrases were incorrectly recognized by the system. For example, when one participant made two throat clearing sounds, the system recognized the sound sequence as the phrase "men's room."

The statistics were far better for the participants understanding phrases spoken by the computer. The average percentage of speech understood in the noise-free environment was 83.3%, while the average percentage of phrases understood in the noisy environment was 93.5%. Clearly, in the second trial (the noisy environment), the participants were more used to SAPI's speech synthesis patterns. These results suggest that speech appears to be a better output medium than input.

Another problem with speech recognition occurs when the person guided by RG stops and engages in conversation with someone. Since speech recognition runs continuously, some phrases said by the person are erroneously recognized as route directives, which causes RG to start moving. For example, once RG erroneously recognized a directive and started pulling its user away from his interlocutor until the user's stop command pacified it. In another situation, RG managed to run a few meters away from its user, because the user hung the leash on the PCV pole when he stopped to talk to a friend of his in a hallway. Thus, after saying "Stop," the user had to grope his way along a wall to RG, standing a few meters away.

As was argued elsewhere (Kulyukin 2004), it is unlikely that these problems can be solved on the software level until there is a substantial improvement in the state-of-the-art speech recognition. Of course, one could add yes-no route change confirmation interactions. However, since unintended speech recognition is frequent, such interactions could become annoying to the user. Therefore, we decided to seek a wearable hardware solution. Specifically, we are exploring human-robot interaction through a wearable keyboard. Many wearable keyboards now fit in the palm of one's hand or can be worn as badges. We are currently experimenting with a small Belkin© keypad that directly interfaces to the WT laptop. When a guided person stops to talk to someone, one button push disables the speech recognition process for the duration of the conversation. Similarly, when the guided person clears her throat and RG misinterprets it as a command, one button push can tell RG to ignore the command and stay on the route. Potentially, the wearable keyboard may replace speech recognition altogether. The obvious advantage is that keyboard-based interaction eliminates the input ambiguity problems of speech recognition. One potential disadvantage is the learning curve required of a human participant to master the necessary key combinations. Another potential disadvantage is restrictions on the quality and quantity of interactions due to the small number of keys. Additional experiments with human participants are needed to determine the validity of these speculations.

### Audio perception

We conducted audio perception experiments with all five participants to test whether they preferred speech to audio icons, e.g., a sound of water bubbles, to signify different objects and events in the environment and how well participants remembered their audio icon selections. The participants used the tool to associate events and objects, e.g., water cooler to the right, approaching left turn, etc., with three audio messages: one speech message and two audio icons. There were seven different objects, e.g., elevator, vending machine, bathroom, office, water cooler, left turn, and right turn. This small number was chosen to eliminate steep learning curves.

Each object was associated with two different events: *at* and *approaching*. For example, one can be at the elevator or approaching the elevator. The audio icons available for each event were played to each participant at selection time. The following statistics were gathered: 1) percentage of accurately recognized icons; 2) percentage of objects/events associated with speech; 3) percentage of objects/events associated with audio icons; 4) percentage of objects/events associated with both. The averages for these experiments were: 1) accurately recognized icons (93.3%); 2) objects/events associated with speech (55.8%); 3) objects/events associated with icons (32.6%); 4) objects/events associated with both (11.4%). The analysis of the audio perception experiments showed that two participants were choosing audio preferences essentially at random, while the other three tended to follow a pattern: they chose speech messages for at events and audio icons for approaching events or vice versa. The experiments also showed that the participants tended to go either with speech or with audio icons, but rarely with both. The experiments did not give a clear answer as to whether visually impaired individuals prefer to be notified of objects/events via speech or audio icons. Further work is needed on a larger sample to answer this question on a statistically significant level.

## Conclusion

We presented an assisted navigation system for the visually impaired. The system consists of a mobile robotic guide and small RFID sensors embedded in the environment. The system allows visually impaired individuals to navigate in unfamiliar indoor environments and interact with the robotic guide via speech, sound, and wearable keyboard.

The main question addressed by our research is the feasibility of robot-assisted navigation in indoor environments instrumented with inexpensive passive sensors. So, is indoor robot-assisted navigation feasible? While our experiments show that the technology has promise, the answer to this question cannot be given either negatively or affirmatively at this point. The benefits of autonomous systems, such as RG, increase with longer deployments. Only through longer deployments can one answer how easy it is to maintain the system over extended time periods and whether the target environment accepts the technology sociologically. Our deployments have not been sufficiently long to answer either question.

A major barrier to long-term deployment is the unwillingness of real target environments, e.g., airports, to agree to the exploratory long-term deployments (two to three months) of assistive technologies. Only after this barrier is overcome, both sociologically and technologically, will we be able to render a definite verdict on the feasibility of indoor robot-assisted navigation.

## References


Addlesee, M.; Curwen, R.; Hodges S.; Newman J.; Steggles P.; and Ward A. 2001. Implementing a Sentient Computing System. *IEEE Computer*, August: 2-8.

Benjamin, J. M.; Ali, N. A.; and Schepis, A. F. 1973. A Laser Cane for the Blind. In *Proceedings of San Diego Medical Symposium*, San Diego, CA.

Bissit, D. and Heyes, A. 1980. An Application of Biofeedback in the Rehabilitation of the Blind. *Applied Ergonomics*, 11(1):31-33.

Borenstein, J. and Ulrich, I. 1994. The GuideCane – A Computerized Travel Guide for the Active Guidance of Blind Pedestrians. In *Proceedings of IEEE International Conference on Robotics and Automation.* San Diego, CA.

Burgard, W.; Cremers, A.; Fox, D.; Hahnel, D; Lakemeyer G.; Schulz, D.; Steiner, W.; and Thrun, S. 1999. Experiences with an Interactive Museum Tour-Guide Robot. *Artificial Intelligence* (114):3-55.

Horswill, I. 1993. Polly: A Vision-Based Artificial Agent. In *Proceedings of the 11th Conference of the American Association for Artificial Intelligence (AAAI-93).* Washington, DC.

Kulyukin, V. and Blair, M. 2003. Distributed Tracking and Guidance in Indoor Environments. In *Proceedings of the Conference of Rehabilitation Engineering and Assistive Technology Society of North America (RESNA-2003).* Atlanta, GA.

Kulyukin, V.; Gharpure, C.; and De Graw, N. 2004. A Robotic Guide for the Visually Impaired. In *Proceedings of the AAAI Spring Symposium on Interaction between Humans and Autonomous Systems over Extended Operation.* Palo Alto, CA.

Kulyukin, V. 2004. Human-Robot Interaction through Gesture-Free Spoken Dialogue. *Autonomous Robots*, 16(3), to appear.

Kupiers, B. 2000. The Spatial Semantic Hierarchy. Artificial Intelligence, 119:191-233.

LaPlante, M. and Carlson, D. 2000. *Disability in the United States: Prevalence and Causes.* U.S. Department of Education, National Institute of Disability and Rehabilitation Research.

Murphy, R. 2000. *Introduction to AI Robotics.* Cambridge, MA: MIT Press.

Ross, D. and Blasch, B. 2002. Development of a Wearable Computer Orientation System. *IEEE Personal and Ubiquitous Computing*, 6:49-63.

Ross, D. 2001. Implementing Assistive Technology on Wearable Computers. IEEE Intelligent Systems, May:2-8.

Shoval, S.; Borenstein, J.; and Koren, Y. 1994. Mobile Robot Obstacle Avoidance in a Computerized Travel for the Blind. In *Proceedings of the IEEE International Conference on Robotics and Automation.* San Diego, CA.

Thrun, S.; Bennewitz, M.; Burgard, W.; Cremers, A.; Dellaert, F.; Fox, D.; Hahnel, D.; Rosenberg, C.; Roby, N.; Schutle, J.; and Schultz, D. 1999. Minerva: A Second Generation Mobile Tour-Guide Robot. In *Proceedings of the IEEE International Conference on Robotics and Automation (ICRA-99).* Antwerp, Belgium.

Tran, T.; Letowski, T.; and Abouchacra, K. 2000. Evaluation of Acoustic Beacon Characteristics for Navigation Tasks. *Ergonomics*, 43(6):807-827.

# Machine Learning for Adaptive Image Interpretation

**Ilya Levner** and **Vadim Bulitko**
Department of Computing Science
University of Alberta
Edmonton, Alberta T6G 2E8, CANADA
{ilya|bulitko}@cs.ualberta.ca

**Abstract**

Automated image interpretation is an important task with numerous applications. Until recently, designing such systems required extensive subject matter and computer vision expertise resulting in poor cross-domain portability and expensive maintenance. Recently, a machine-learned system (ADORE) was successfully applied in an aerial image interpretation domain. Subsequently, it was re-trained for another man-made object recognition task. In this paper we propose and implement several extensions of ADORE addressing its primary limitations. These extensions enable the first successful application of this emerging AI technology to a natural image interpretation domain. The resulting system is shown to be robust with respect to noise in the training data, illumination, and camera angle variations as well as competitively adaptive with respect to novel images.

**Keywords:** machine learning, Markov decision models in vision, adaptive image interpretation, remote-sensing, forest mapping, natural resource inventory.

## 1 Problem formulation

Forest maps and inventories have become a critical tool for wood resource management (planting and cutting), ecosystem management and wild-life research. Unfortunately, forest mapping at the level of individual trees is a continuous and costly undertaking. Canada alone has an estimated 344 million hectares of forests to inventory on a 10-20 year cycle (Pollock 1994).

At these scales, ground-based surveys and inventories are not feasible. Researchers have therefore turned to developing automated systems to produce forest maps from airborne images and LIDAR 3D data sources. The final goal is to measure the type (species), position, height, crown diameter, wood volume and age class for every tree in the survey area.

The task of large-scale forest mapping from aerial images presents formidable challenges, including: (i) massive amounts of high-resolution data, in order to recognize and measure individual tree crowns, (ii) construction and maintenance of (and providing access to) very large databases; Canada alone has an estimated $10^{11}$ trees, (iii) geo-referencing of airborne images for validation purposes, (iv) orthorectification of aerial images, particularly given that elevation maps are often unavailable at the accuracy required. Of a particular interest are the challenges created by the image content, including variations in sun and camera angle and the resulting shadow and tree crown overlap. These challenges have been known to have an adverse effect on special purpose algorithms for individual tree identification (Culvenor 2002). In fact, the task is substantially challenging even to expert human interpreters resulting in up to 40% error in comparison to ground-based surveys (Gougeon & Leckie 2003).

Figure 1: A fragment of an aerial image taken over a spruce plot is shown on the left. The right image is the desired interpretation with spruce canopies labeled in white. It is provided as a part of the training set.

In this paper we focus on the tree labeling problem as a first step towards an overall solution. Namely, we consider pixel-level labeling of aerial tree images (Figure 1). For each aerial image the task is therefore to identify all pixels belonging to canopies of trees of a certain kind. In the illustrations throughout the paper, we label spruce canopies. In each image such pixels are labeled in white while the rest of the image is labeled in black.

The rest of the paper is organized as follows: we survey special purpose tree canopy labeling systems and their shortcomings in section 2. Section 3 then presents a domain-independent approach in which a control policy over the space of vision operators is machine-learned. Our innovative applications of the AI technology are presented in section 4 with the empirical evaluation following in section 5. A discussion of the generalizability of the system and the current and future research directions conclude the paper.

## 2 Related research: special purpose systems

A number of approaches have been proposed for creating forest inventories from aerial images. Image-based (model-free) approaches use simplifying assumptions about forest images. For example, (Gougeon & Leckie 2003; Pinz 1991) use a token-based recognition approach which assumes a high level of contrast between the tree crown and the surrounding area. They deal with canopy feature extraction almost exclusively in terms of finding image features which evidence different types of tree canopies. A current example of this approach is ITC system (Gougeon & Leckie 2003) where tree canopies are detected and classified by a mixture of "valley-finding" (low intensity iso-contours), peak intensity detection (Wulder, Niemann, & Goodenough 2000b; 2000a) and texture, structure and contextual image features. This falls within traditional image segmentation and region labeling strategies where there is no explicit need to model features in terms of known tree attributes or specific 3D geometric models. Consequently, the approach is designed to apply where there are sufficiently spatially separated trees. Unfortunately, the performance can degrade significantly as such methods are applied to naturally occurring dense forests with overlapping tree crowns.

Another approach uses example-based image models. The underlying idea is to compare pre-specified tree crown image(s) with the image at hand. Typically such methods, e.g., (Murgu 1996), have a collection of example tree crowns which they match to the image. Drawbacks of such approaches include the need to collect a very large database of templates to account for differences in tree species, size, the slant of the terrain and illumination.

Model-based approaches take advantage of an explicit model of tree crowns to match with images. While minimizing the amount of image feature processing, elementary image features are used to hypothesize large numbers of regions for matching with 3D CAD tree models via computer graphics methods. For example, the STCI system (Pollock 1994) uses a template matching approach, however, unlike the example-based approaches discussed above, the crown templates are synthesized from a tree crown model. The upper part of a tree crown (known as "sun crown") is modelled as a generalized ellipsoid of revolution and ray-tracing techniques are used to generate templates (Larsen & Rudemo 1997). Model-based approaches typically rely on detecting image features such as crown peaks and normally use pre-generated templates to match projected models with image data. The latter technique can require generation of many templates for different slant angles, tree types, etc. Additionally, model-based methods use simple shadow models and simplified 3D CAD models typically representing the canopy envelope only and are often unable to deal with natural variations in foliage and branches and the resulting irregular canopy boundaries.

## 3 Machine learning approach

All of the approaches reviewed in the previous section are promising, at least in a laboratory setting, but share some common drawbacks. First, they were carefully crafted in a development process that required both time and expertise. More importantly, this development process exploited domain properties, such as whether the trees are separated or have overlapping canopies, whether the ground is flat or mountainous, or whether the forest has a homogeneous or heterogeneous species composition. Similarly, assumptions about the properties and position of the sensor are also integrated in the system design. As a result, these systems work within a narrow set of operating conditions, and cannot be applied under other conditions without re-engineering.

The challenges of the tree inventory problem are not unique in the realm of image interpretation. Thus, rather than crafting yet another domain-specific approach we present a general method of automated development of image interpretation systems with the following objectives: (i) rapid system development for a wide class of image interpretation tasks; (ii) low demands on subject matter, computer vision, and AI expertise on the part of the developers; (iii) accelerated domain portability, system upgrades, and maintenance; (iv) adaptive image interpretation wherein the system adjusts its operation dynamically to a given image; (v) user-controlled trade-offs between recognition accuracy and resources utilized (e.g., time spent).

These objectives favor the use of readily available off-the-shelf image processing libraries (IPL). However, the domain independence of such libraries requires an intelligent domain-specific policy to control the application of library operators. Operation of such a control policy is a complex and adaptive process. It is complex in that there is rarely a one-step mapping from image data to object label; instead, a series of operator applications is required to bridge the gap between raw pixels and semantic labels. Examples of the operators include region segmentation, texture filters, and the construction of 3D depth maps. Image recognition is an adaptive process in the sense that generally there is no fixed sequence of actions that will work well for most images (Bulitko *et al.* 2003).

The success of this approach to image interpretation therefore depends on the solution to a control problem: for a given image, what sequence of actions will most effectively and reliably detect the regions of interest?

Recently, a system called ADaptive Object REcognition (ADORE) became the first system to learn a complex domain-specific control policy for roof recognition in aerial photographs (Draper, Bins, & Baek 2000). As with many vision systems, it identified objects (in this case buildings) in a multi-step process. Raw images were the initial input data, while image regions containing identified buildings constituted the final output data; in between the data could be represented as intensity images, probability images, edges, lines, or curves. ADORE modelled image interpretation as a Markov decision process, where the intermediate representations were continuous state spaces, and the vision procedures were actions. The goal was to learn a dynamic control policy that selects the next action (i.e., image processing operator) at each step so as to maximize the quality of the final image interpretation. To demonstrate its general applicability, ADORE was subsequently ported to another domain (recognizing objects in office scenes) in another labo-

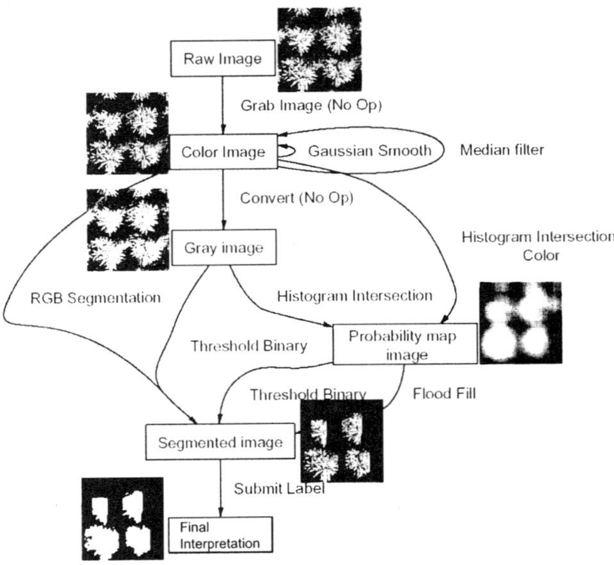


Figure 2: A fragment of the state-action graph used in our experiments. States are labeled with their vision data types and have forest samples shown next to them. Common vision operators are shown as the arcs.

ratory (Draper, Ahlrichs, & Paulus 2001).

## 4 Innovative applications of AI technology

One of the contributions of this paper is to apply this emerging technology to the forest mapping domain, using it for the first time to recognize natural (as opposed to man-made) objects (i.e., tree canopies). More significantly, we propose and empirically evaluate solutions to ADORE's three primary limitations. First, ADORE learned recognition strategies from training samples – but only after a human expert had selected the features that describe each intermediate level of representation. This process is effort-consuming and requires computer vision and domain expertise. Second, using the history-free Markov decision process model for selecting computer vision operators proved to be deficient in both applications of ADORE. Third, ADORE processed each image as a whole, which reduces interpretation quality while dealing with highly non-uniform images.

As in the case of ADORE, we begin with the Markov decision process (MDP) as the basic mathematical model by casting the IPL operators as the MDP actions and the results of their applications as the MDP states. Figure 2 presents a fragment of the state-action graph. The system operates in two modes as follows. During the *off-line training stage*, available subject matter expertise is encoded as a collection of training images with the corresponding desired interpretation (the so called ground truth). Figure 1 demonstrates an example of such (input image, ground truth label) pair for the forest mapping domain. Then off-policy reinforcement learning with deep backups and no bootstrapping is used to acquire a value function (Sutton & Barto 2000). At first, all feasible length-limited sequences of IPL operators are applied to each training image. The resulting interpretations are evaluated against the domain expert provided ground

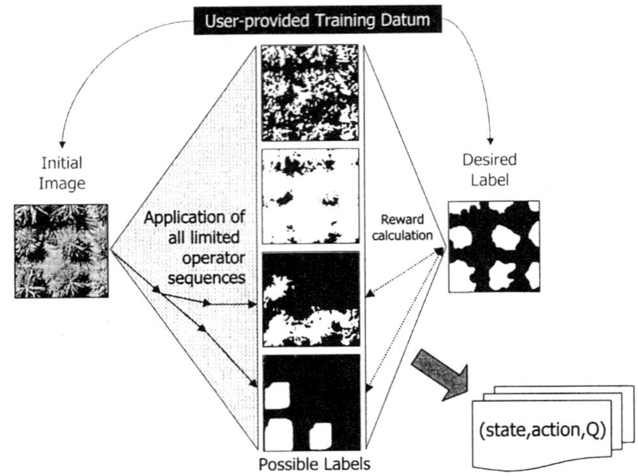


Figure 3: Off-line training stage: all limited-length operator sequences are applied to each training image. The resulting image interpretations are evaluated against the desired label. Action-state rewards are then computed.

truth as shown in Figure 3. We use a pixel-level similarity scoring metric defined as the ratio of the number of pixels labeled as the target class (e.g., spruce) by both the system and the expert to the total number of pixels labeled as the target class by either one of them. According to such a metric, an interpretation identical to the user-supplied label scores 1 while a totally disjoint interpretation will get a score of 0.

The interpretation scores are then "backed up" along the IPL operator sequences using dynamic programming. As a result, the value function $Q : S \times A \to \mathbb{R}$ is computed for the expanded states $S' \subset S$ and applied actions $A' \subset A$. The value of $Q(s, a)$ corresponds to the best interpretation score the system can expect by applying operator $a$ in state $s$ and acting optimally thereafter. In reinforcement learning terms, we are representing the task as a finite horizon non-discounted problem wherein all intermediate rewards are zero except these collected by outputting an image interpretation. The latter is a positive reward proportional to the quality of the interpretation. The term $Q$ comes from Watkins' Q-learning (Watkins 1989).

The collected training set of Q-values $\{[s, a, Q(s, a)]\}$ samples a tiny fraction of the $S \times A$ space. Correspondingly, we use function approximation methods to extrapolate the value function onto the entire space. Features $f$ are extracted off the raw (large) states $S$ to make the approximation feasible. In this paper we use Artificial Neural Networks as the Q-function approximator.

During the *on-line interpretation stage*, the system receives a novel image and proceeds to interpret it as shown in Figure 4. Namely, the value function learned off-line now guides the control policy to apply vision operators from the IPL library. Several control policies are possible ranging from greedy policies that select the next action $a$ so as to maximize $Q(s, a)$ in each state $s$ to static policies that always apply the same sequence of vision operators regardless of the input image (Levner *et al.* 2003b).

The "least-committment" control policy we use addresses

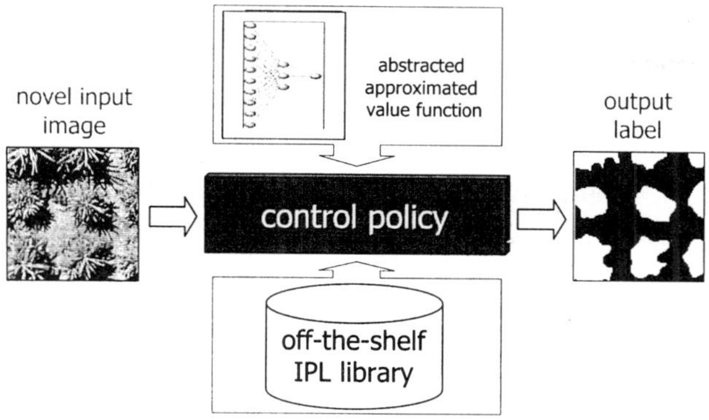


Figure 4: On-line operation: the control policy uses an approximate value function to select the best sequence of operators from an IPL library. As the result, an image interpretation label is produced.

the first two shortcomings of ADORE. First, it applies all limited feasible sequences of operators to the input image $s_0$. Once the set of possible image interpretations $\{s_1, \ldots, s_N\}$ is computed, the policy uses the label of each interpretation $s_i$ to extract features from the original input image $s_0$. The resulting composite feature vectors $f_{s_i}(s_0)$ are used with the machine-learned value function to select the most promising interpretation $s_{i^*}$ as follows: $i^* = \arg\max_i Q(f_{s_i}(s_0), submit)$. In other words, the policy selects the interpretation $s_{i^*}$ that is expected to bring the highest reward when submitted (i.e., output as the system's interpretation of the input image).

This technique eliminates ADORE's need to design high-quality features for every processing level as they are now required for the initial color image and the final binary interpretation only. Additionally, extracting features from the initial image provides a context for the features extracted off a candidate interpretation thereby addressing ADORE's loss of performance due to history-free Markov features.

Finally, before interpreting a novel image, we partition it into regular rectangular tiles. Each tile is processed independently by the control policy. The resulting interpretations (one per tile) are then assembled into a single interpretation of the original image. This technique greatly increases flexibility of the system by allowing it to use different operators on different parts of a non-uniform image thereby addressing the third primary drawback of ADORE.

## 5 Empirical evaluation

In the following sections we evaluate the approach with respect to several key attributes of a successful image interpretation system: overfitting-free training on real-world data, robustness to noise in the training data, and robustness to variance in illumination conditions, camera angles, and inter-image differences.

In the tests we use the least-commitment policy with an Artificial Neural Network as the function approximator over 192 color histogram based features. Cross-validation error was monitored during the training process to guard against overfitting. The operator library contained approximately 100 common vision operators similar to the ones found in Intel OpenCV library. The parameters of each operator were tabulated in regular intervals so that invoking such an operator actually applied all parameterized instantiations of it.

Longer operator sequences have been shown to increase the interpretation quality at the cost of an exponential increase in the running time (Bulitko *et al.* 2003). In the experiments presented in this paper we capped the system at the shortest non-trivial sequence length (four).

### 5.1 Performance on spruce canopy images

In order to demonstrate the adaptive nature of the learned policy we compared its performance to the static operator sequence with the best mean performance on the training data (henceforth called 'best static policy'). Thirty four 256x256 pixel aerial images were acquired with an RGB camera over spruce plots. A fragment of a typical image is shown in Figure 1. We employed the standard leave-one-out cross-validation technique by training on a subset of 33 images and testing on the left-out image. This process was repeated $\binom{34}{33}$ times for all combinations of the training images. The mean pixel-level similarity score of the machine-learned policy was $0.54$ with the standard deviation of $0.14$ while the best static policy scored $0.46 \pm 0.13$. Figure 5 demonstrates on-line performance of the machine-learned and best static policies relative to the perfect control policy (i.e., the policy gaining the highest possible score on each image). On most of the 34 cross-validation images, the machine-learned policy produced a nearly optimal sequence achieving $93.6 \pm 15.5\%$ of the perfect policy's score. Substantial variation in the interpretation difficulty among the images left the best static policy at $81.6 \pm 19.7\%$.

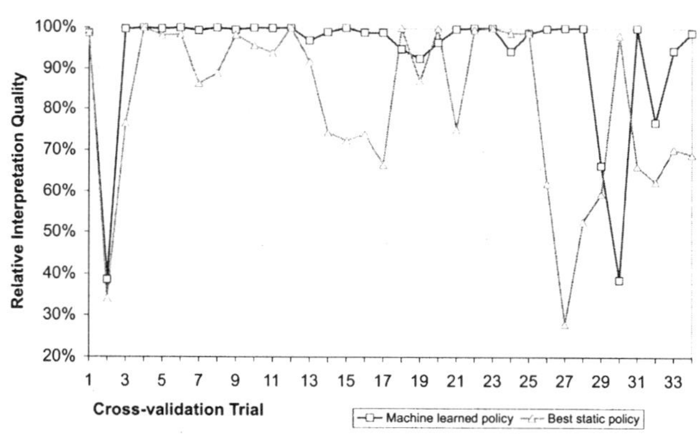


Figure 5: On-line interpretation: machine-learned policy adapts to different images frequently selecting the perfect operator sequence.

It is worth noting that the pixel-based similarity metric we use is a very strict measure penalizing every single pixel mislabeled. At the same time, missing individual pixels is not critical in the overall forest mapping framework since the desired tree parameters, such as crown diameter, position, and species, can be recovered even from an imperfect but proportional label. Since the tree parameter estimation module is not yet operational, we presented the interpretations our system produced to silviculture specialists and solicited their feedback. The current level of performance was deemed promising for tree parameter extraction. An interesting case is shown in Figure 6 wherein the system was able to label spruce canopies "drowned" in the surrounding vegetation better than a human interpreter.

Figure 6: Shown on the left is the original image with three small spruce canopies "drowned" in surrounding young aspen. The human interpreter labeled only one of them (lower left corner of the image). The system was able to label two canopies (right image).

## 5.2 Robustness to noise in training data

The tedious and time-consuming nature of manual image labeling inevitably leads to interpretation errors. One study (Gougeon & Leckie 2003) found the tree count error to be between 10-40% relative to ground surveys. Therefore, it is important to establish the extent to which our learning model is robust with respect to noise in manually labeled training data. Pending an extensive study involving a panel of human forest interpreters and ground-based surveys, we present the robustness results with simulated training data labeling errors. Namely, we used the same 34-image spruce canopy set but this time perturbed the corresponding training labels. The two common types of human interpretation errors are labeling several neighboring tree canopies as one and missing a tree canopy completely. We simulated these errors via eroding and dilating the training labels by approximately 30%. Eroding an interpretation significantly distorts the desired canopy labels often reducing a single canopy label to a collection of disjoint pixels. On the other hand, dilation enlarges the labels sometimes merging two neighboring canopy labels into one as illustrated in Figure 7.

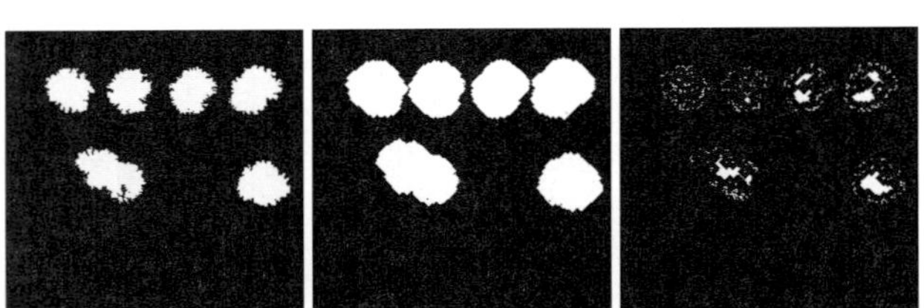

Figure 7: Noise in the training data: the true label (left), a dilated label joining neighboring canopies together (middle), an eroded label missing full canopies (right).

Training on the dilated and eroded labels reduced the performance of the machine-learned control policy to $85.6 \pm 24.2\%$ of the perfect policy (corresponding to the pixel-level similarity score of $0.49 \pm 0.17$). The static policy scored $82.3 \pm 19.4\%$ of the perfect policy ($0.47 \pm 0.13$ in the absolute terms). As we used the same leave-one-out cross-validation technique, the results suggest certain robustness to training data noise.

## 5.3 Robustness to changes in illumination

Large-scale forest mapping is a continuous undertaking resulting in the images acquired at different times of day and different seasons. The consequent changes in illumination can lead to significant performance degradation in systems fine-tuned for a specific set of images (Culvenor 2002). Additionally, low sun angles can result in canopies "missing" in shadows cast by taller trees. Pending a large scale experiment with multiple aerial acquisitions of the same forest plot at different times of day and different seasons, we conducted a smaller scale study using synthetic data. Namely, a scene with two types of trees (six trees of each type) was computer ray-traced at every hour between 7 o'clock in the morning and 5 o'clock in the evening (the most likely data acquisition times for real forests). As the sun traversed the sky, the rendered shadows and undergrowth illumination varied significantly (Figure 8).

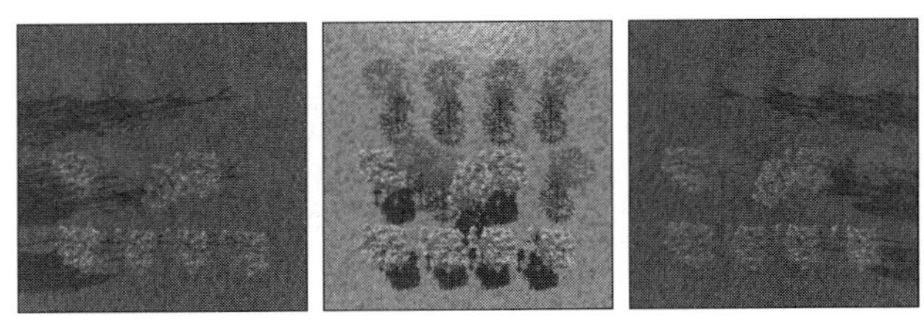

Figure 8: Effects of the sun position: 7am (left), noon (middle), 5pm (right).

We then administered the leave-one-out cross-validation procedure by training the system on 10 out of 11 images and testing it on the remaining image. The process was repeated 11 times for all sets of training images. The results in Figure 9 indicate that the machine-learned policy is robust to image variations resulting from different sun positions. On the other hand, the best fixed operator sequence achieved the optimal interpretation only on the 9am image. Cumulatively, the machine-learned policy scored $94 \pm 9.5\%$ of the perfect policy while the best static policy was at $63.8 \pm 21.6\%$.

## 5.4 Robustness to camera angle variations

Another difficulty with remote sensing vision systems lies with the fact that the sensor (camera) can be at different angles when the images are acquired. This can happen due to aircraft maneuvers, turbulence, and other reasons. In forest mapping nadir angles are generally preferred as low-angle images can be plagued with overlapping canopies (Figure 10).

In this experiment we measured the robustness of machine-learned and best static control policies to increasingly off-nadir camera angles. The synthetic scene from the sun angle experiments was re-used but rather than varying the sun position we changed the camera angle from nadir to significantly slanted in five steps. Figure 11 suggests that

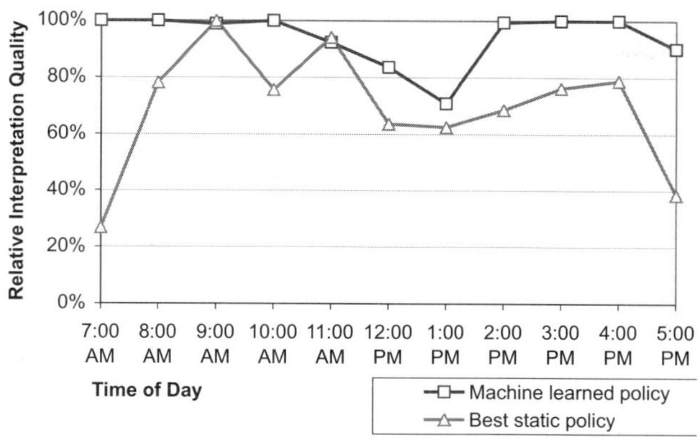


Figure 9: Performance of machine-learned and best static policies on images acquired at different times of day.

Figure 10: Effects of off-nadir camera angles.

the machine-learned policy demonstrates some robustness to varying camera angles. It scored $93.5 \pm 14.5\%$ of the perfect policy whereas the best static policy achieved $79.1 \pm 44.1\%$.

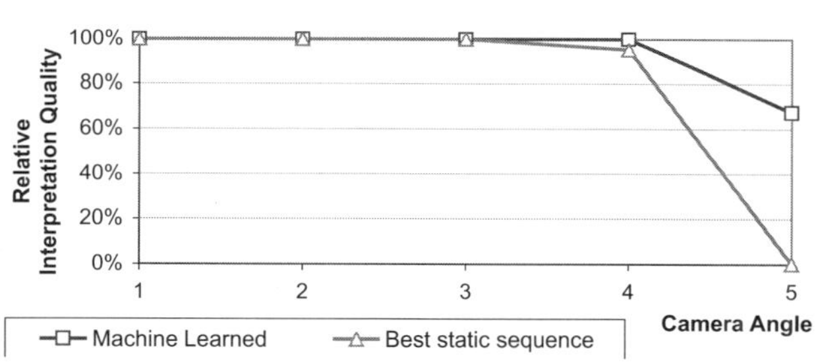


Figure 11: Machine-learned and best static policies on images acquired at increasingly off-nadir camera angles.

## 5.5 Adaptivity to novel images

Natural forests are inherently diverse in terms of tree species, canopy sizes, and foliage conditions. Consequently, even images of a simple composition stand taken within a hundred feet of each other can be vastly dissimilar as shown in Figure 12. Therefore, the ability to adapt to a novel image radically different from the training data is a crucial factor in the success of a forest mapping system.

In order to evaluate the robustness of the presented approach we compared it with a state-of-the-art system based on a trainable hierarchical hidden Markov tree (HHMT) model (Cheng, Caelli, & Ochoa 2002). We first gauged its performance on forest images with moderate variance such as parts of a single image. The HHMT-based system demonstrated an impressive mean pixel-level similarity score of 0.71 (compared to our system's score of 0.58).

Figure 12: Two diverse images acquired in a close spatial proximity.

We then selected two substantially diverse and images (parts of which are shown in Figure 12). One of the images (shown left in the figure) was considerably more difficult due to the dense deciduous vegetation enveloping the spruce trees. In each of the two trials both systems were trained on one of the two images and tested on the other. The HHMT-based system had the mean pixel-level similarity score of 0.1. At the same time our approach scored 0.25. This initial experiment suggests a certain degree of adaptivity of the MDP-based approach and warrants further studies.

# 6 Discussion and future work

Conventional ways of developing image interpretation systems usually require a significant subject matter and computer vision expertise from the developers. The resulting systems are expensive to upgrade, maintain, and port to other domains.

In this paper we present an emerging AI technology with the aim of automating development of image interpretation systems. Our extensions of the state-of-the-art MDP-based machine-learned system ADORE address its three primary drawbacks. First, by partitioning input images our system can interpret uniform regions of a non-uniform image independently. Second, as high-quality interpretations are tightly coupled with the input image thereby violating the history-free Markov assumption, our control policy extracts features off the initial image as well as the candidate interpretation. Finally, our least-commitment policy does not rely on high-quality features for all processing levels thereby increasing the interpretation quality as well as portability of the system.

Cumulatively, the three extensions enabled the first application of an MDP-based vision system to interpretation of natural (as opposed to man-made) objects. The preliminary experiments presented in this paper suggest that the approach is robust with respect to noise in the training data, variable illumination and camera angles as well as high variation between training and testing images.

The initial success encourages further automation of the system. In particular, we are presently investigating automated methods of feature selection (Levner *et al.* 2003a). When successful, they will eliminate computationally expensive application of all operator sequences as some sequences will be discarded dynamically. We have also had initial success with automated techniques for operator parameter tuning and selection (Bulitko, Lee, & Levner 2003).

This is expected to result in significant computational savings as only a fraction of the operator set will have to be executed on- and off-line. Ensemble learning and boosting methods have recently seen success in classification and regression. We are presently developing extensions of such methods to control policies (Li *et al.* 2003). Finally, a more adaptive image splitting and interpretation merging procedure is under development and is expected to replace the current regular tiling scheme.

On the application side, the system is presently considered for deployment at an Alberta government natural resources office within the next several months. It will be evaluated with respect to identification of forest fire burn boundaries and validation of commercial thinning practices. Being domain-independent, our approach is already being tested for brain tumor detection in magnetic resonance imaging (MRI) scans in cooperation with the Alberta Cross Cancer Institute.

## Acknowledgements

Bruce Draper participated in the initial system design and contributed to an early draft of the related research section. We appreciate help of Li Cheng, Terry Caelli, Lihong Li, Greg Lee, Dave McNabb, Ken Greenway, Rongzhou Man, Joan Fang, Dorothy Lau, Russ Greiner, Jane Hilderman, Guanwen Zhang, and Albert Murtha. The funding was generously provided by NSERC, iCORE, the University of Alberta, and the Alberta Ingenuity Centre for Machine Learning.

## References

Bulitko, V.; Lee, G.; Levner, I.; Li, L.; and Greiner, R. 2003. Adaptive image interpretation : A spectrum of machine learning problems. In *Proceedings of the ICML Workshop on The Continuum from Labeled to Unlabeled Data in Machine Learning and Data Mining*, 1–8.

Bulitko, V.; Lee, G.; and Levner, I. 2003. Evolutionary algorithms for operator selection in vision. In *Proceedings of the 7th Joint Conference on Information Sciences : the 5th International Workshop on Frontiers in Evolutionary Algorithms*, 359–362.

Cheng, L.; Caelli, T.; and Ochoa, V. 2002. A trainable hierarchical hidden markov tree model for color image segmentation and labeling. In *Proceedings of the International Conference on Pattern Recognition.*

Culvenor, D. 2002. Tida: an algorithm for the delineation of tree crowns in high spatial resolution remotely sensed imagery. *Computers & Geosciences* 28(1):33–44.

Draper, B.; Ahlrichs, U.; and Paulus, D. 2001. Adapting object recognition across domains: A demonstration. In *Proceedings of International Conference on Vision Systems*, 256–267.

Draper, B.; Bins, J.; and Baek, K. 2000. ADORE: adaptive object recognition. *Videre* 1(4):86–99.

Gougeon, F., and Leckie, D. 2003. Forest information extraction from high spatial resolution images using an individual tree crown approach. Technical report, Pacific Forestry Centre.

Larsen, M., and Rudemo, M. 1997. Using ray-traced templates to find individual trees in aerial photos. In *Proceedings of the 10th Scandinavian Conference on Image Analysis*, volume 2, 1007–1014.

Levner, I.; Bulitko, V.; Li, L.; Lee, G.; and Greiner, R. 2003a. Automated feature extraction for object recognition. In *Proceedings of the Image and Vision Computing New Zealand conference*, 309–313.

Levner, I.; Bulitko, V.; Li, L.; Lee, G.; and Greiner, R. 2003b. Towards automated creation of image interpretation systems. In Gedeon, T., and Fung, L., eds., *Lecture Notes in Artificial Intelligence (LNAI)*, volume 2903. Berlin, Heidelberg: Springer-Verlag. 653–665.

Li, L.; Bulitko, V.; Greiner, R.; and Levner, L. 2003. Improving an adaptive image interpretation system by leveraging. In *Proceedings of the 8th Australian and New Zealand Conference on Intelligent Information Systems*, 501–506.

Murgu, D. 1996. Individual tree detection and localization in aerial imagery. Master's thesis, Department of Computer Science, University of British Columbia.

Pinz, A. 1991. A computer vision system for the recognition of trees in aerial photographs. In *J.C.Tilton (ed.), Multisource Data Integration in Remote Sensing*, 111–124.

Pollock, R. 1994. A model-based approach to automatically locating tree crowns in high spatial resolution images. In Desachy, J., ed., *Image and Signal Processing for Remote Sensing.*

Sutton, R., and Barto, A. 2000. *Reinforcement Learning: An Introduction.* MIT Press.

Watkins, C. 1989. *Learning from Delayed Rewards.* Ph.D. Dissertation, Kings College, Cambridge University.

Wulder, M.; Niemann, K.; and Goodenough, D. 2000a. Error reduction methods for local maximum filtering. In *The Proceedings of the 22nd Symposium of the Canadian Remote Sensing Society.*

Wulder, M.; Niemann, K.; and Goodenough, D. 2000b. Local maximum filtering for the extraction of tree locations and basal area from high spatial resolution imagery. *Remote Sensing of Environment* 73:103–114.

# AI Characters and Directors for Interactive Computer Games

Brian Magerko, John E. Laird, Mazin Assanie, Alex Kerfoot, Devvan Stokes

University of Michigan
1101 Beal Ave.
Ann Arbor, MI 48109-2110
magerko, laird, mazina, akerfoot, stokesd @umich.edu

## Abstract

We are creating an environment for investigating the role of advanced AI in interactive, story-based computer games. This environment is based on the Unreal Tournament (UT) game engine and the Soar AI engine. Unreal provides a 3D virtual environment, while Soar provides a flexible architecture for developing complex AI characters. This paper describes our progress to date, starting with our game, Haunt 2, which is designed so that complex AI characters will be critical to the success (or failure) of the game. It addresses design issues with constructing a plot for an interactive storytelling environment, creating synthetic characters for that environment, and using a story director agent to tell the story with those characters.

## Introduction

To date, every successful computer game is an existence proof that you can create good games without human-level AI. Our research is focused on determining whether or not the addition of human-level AI can facilitate the creation of new types of games: games where the AI characters are central to the player's experience. Our current work builds on previous research on AI in games where the AI characters were enemies for actions games such as Quake 2 and the characters had many of the same capabilities as human players, including the ability to use many tactics, create internal maps of the level, and anticipate their enemy's behavior (Laird 2001). Although action games such as Quake are one of the most popular game genres, there are inherent limits in the complexity of the behaviors required to create compelling bots that are essentially computerized punching bags. Furthermore, these types of games limit the human gaming experience to violent interactions with other humans and bots, ignoring many other types of more subtle social interactions. Therefore, we are currently working to develop non-violent plot-driven computer games where we really need complex AI characters and directors.

Ours is but one approach in the growing field of *interactive drama,* which strives to provide a narrative experience to a human player that has a strong connection between the player's actions and the story (Laurel 1986). Our approach to plot-driven games assumes that there is a single human player that is the focus of the game, as in the Holodeck of Star Trek, The Next Generation. The player moves through the game, performing actions in the world. The story is defined by challenges and conflicts that arise from interactions with the other (synthetic) characters that populate the world. In order to ensure that the player's experience is a coherent story, we do not want to rely on arbitrary interactions that may or may not arise between the player and the synthetic characters. Instead, we propose relying on a pre-written script that is available to a computer director. It becomes the responsibility of a computer director to ensure that the script is followed during the game experience so that a coherent narrative is experienced by the player. In order to support an immersive and realistic experience, the synthetic characters must be responsive to the interaction of their body with the environment, their goals, their knowledge of the world they inhabit, their own personal history, their interactions with human players, and real-time advice from a director.

To explore the development of computer-based directors and characters, we are building on one of the oldest genres of computer games, sometimes called interactive fiction or adventure games, where the human player must overcome obstacles and solve puzzles in pursuit of some goal – games such as Adventure, Zork, Bladerunner, and the Monkey Island series. One weakness of the traditional adventure games is that the behavior of non-player AI characters is scripted; therefore, the interactions with them are stilted and not compelling. One of our challenges is to create AI characters whose behaviors are not only human-like but also lead to engaging game play.

In this paper we describe our initial results in developing human-level AI characters and directors within computer games. Our challenge is to demonstrate that for at least one genre, human-level AI can make a difference so that with human-level AI, the game play is qualitatively different (and still entertaining). This paper covers the following: the overall software architecture, our initial script/game scenario, the design of the physiology and sensing of our characters which in turn forces us to support a combination of goal-driven and environmentally-driven behavior, and the structure of the story director. We then conclude with a look forward to future research problems.

## Our Story: Haunt 2

The game we are creating in Unreal Tournament has the player taking on the persona of a ghost trapped in a bed & breakfast. The human player's goal as the "ghost" is to determine what happened to it (it was murdered), who murdered it, and then bring the murderer to justice. The ghost is severely limited in its ability to manipulate the environment. It can move throughout the building (through walls even), but it can't move or manipulate objects, nor can it talk to other characters, but it can appear and disappear. These constraints force the player to entice, cajole, threaten, or frighten the AI characters into manipulating the objects in the world, which in turn forces us to develop AI characters that have enough "intelligence" to make these social manipulations possible and realistic. Initially we are avoiding issues with natural language understanding and using a small fixed grammar for communication.

To provide more interaction, the ghost is able to "possess" an AI character as long as the AI character isn't too scared. Possession allows the player, as the ghost, to see some of the AI characters' thought processes and influence its decisions when the AI character does not have a strong bias. However, whenever the ghost influences a decision, it feels a bit weird to the AI character, raising the possessed character's level of anxiety. The ghost can maintain possession of relatively calm characters; too much manipulation leads to the ghost being expelled from the AI characters. In order to make the possession fun and engaging, we will have to develop characters whose internal processing appears human-like to a player possessing them

## Requirements for Haunt 2

When considering our system design in the context of building an interactive drama, there are six main requirements we strive to fulfill:

1. **Generalizable design**: Our goal is not to build a specific game, but to explore research issues and then to develop solutions that can be applied more generally. The design needs to be modular so that individual components can be independently developed. Moreover, we are exploring approaches where an author can easily change the current story, add new characters, or create an entirely new plot. The system described in this paper should be applicable to the telling of many narratives; Haunt 2 is merely one of those many.
2. **Flexible, efficient system**: The software architecture should be low-cost, and easy to develop and use.
3. **Believable behavior**: Synthetic characters have to exhibit behavior that is dramatically and realistically believable, whether in performing a simple action such as picking up a drink because they are thirsty, or having more complicated interactions with other characters, the player, or the world.
4. **Directability**: The synthetic characters should be able to receive story direction from an exterior agent that is responsible for the narrative. Each synthetic character will need to balance the story's goals with its individual personal goals, giving preference to the story. However, even when responding to direction, the characters must generate behavior that is coherent, in character, and thus believable.
5. **Fully-structured story**: Our goal is to create experiences in which complete dramatic stories can be experienced, which is in contrast to systems that depend on a story, or at least the story's structure, to emerge. Initially, we are assuming that the story is created by a human author and that the content in the story is structured according to the author's desires.
6. **Interactive player experience**: Although there is a pre-defined story, the user's action should have significant impact on the details of how the story unfolds. Different player behaviors within the environment should elicit different, however so slightly, narratives. If the player executes some series of actions that are unexpected or go against the plot, the system should mediate the differences to elicit a coherent narrative.

We address how these requirements relate to Haunt 2 in the following sections.

## System Software Design

To support the development, experimentation, and evaluation of our AI characters, we need a game environment that is flexible and efficient (requirement 2):

- Flexible and low-cost development:
  We should use existing game software and development tools (level and character editors) whenever possible. The underlying software should be easily modifiable so that we can test out alternative designs.
- Support a full debugging/development environment:
  Our design should support all of our existing debugging and development tools for creating AI characters.
- High performance:
  We should not sacrifice performance in the AI engine or in its interface to the game. We should support a large number of AI characters in the game without sacrificing graphics performance. We should be able to run the game and the AI engine on a single laptop.

We achieved flexibility and low cost in the game environment by following in the footsteps of other projects (NCSU: Mimesis (Young 2001), ESC Online (Martin 2001), Deus Ex, Gamebots (Kaminka et al. 2002)) and using the Unreal Tournament (UT) engine. UT provides an off-the-shelf 3D game engine that can be easily extended. A copy of Unreal Tournament costs about ~$20. Moreover there are many free level editors available for creating your own virtual environment; furthermore, the game physics and interface are coded in a powerful internal scripting language (Unrealscript) that is completely accessible.

Each AI character is implemented as rules in Soar (Newell 1990). The characters share the same basic knowledge base to support interacting with the world and other characters; however, specific characters have different physiology (see below), goals and background knowledge.

Designing the interface between the environment and the AI engine is challenging because of two often contradictory goals: high performance and supporting a powerful development environment. Achieving high performance usually demands that the AI engine run as an embedded application in the same process as the game environment, eliminating access to a powerful development environment. In an attempt to finesse these problems, we have developed a high-level interface that is really three low-level interfaces. The high-level interface hides the differences at the low-level so that the user can select from among the three low-level interfaces at run time without requiring any changes to the game engine and the AI engine. The overall interface is called Soar General Input/Output (SGIO) (Laird et al. 2002) and is a domain independent interface between the Soar AI engine and an external environment – in our case Unreal Tournament. SGIO supports across-machine and across-process communication via sockets, allowing us to use our full development environments. For high performance, SGIO supports the direct embedding of multiple copies Soar within the UT process using a C API.

This project builds directly on related work for modeling human behavior in military simulation that shares the same core infrastructure, which consists of UT, SGIO, Soar, and navigation knowledge (Wray and Laird 2002). Although there are many components in common, the other research emphasized encoding military doctrine and tactics with very short but intense interactions among human participants and AI characters. There was no notion of story or director.

## AI Characters as Actors

For the AI characters to be believable (requirement 3), they must have many general cognitive capabilities including perception, internal reasoning, and acting in the world. In Haunt 2, each character has a long-term knowledge base, implemented as rules in Soar, perceptual and motor systems, and a simple model of physiology. The current situation is represented declaratively in working memory, which holds what is perceived from sensors (including physiology), current goals and operators, and the character's understanding of the current situation. The long-term knowledge can be broken down into situation-assessment knowledge that reactively classifies sensor data into relevant categories, and task knowledge, which is organized hierarchically as a set of operators. The operators cover both abstract tasks, such as exploring the Inn, and more primitive tasks such as talking to other actors (using a set of templates) or manipulating objects in the world.

### AI Character Physiology

A critical part of making the actors believable is having them respond to their environment. Although one possible way to implement this is for the synthetic actors to "act" as if they have needs and drives; however, our approach is to give them a synthetic physiology so that they have needs and drives. For example, in Haunt 2 the characters that are cold (and have no other pressing needs or goals) will go into the parlor room, where there is a fire to warm them up. Similarly, a thirsty character may ask the innkeeper for a drink. The game will push our research to integrate the knowledge-based, goal-oriented reasoning that we have concentrated on in the past, with emotions, personality, and physical drives that have been used in simple, knowledge-lean agents in other systems (e.g. the Oz project (Loyall and Bates 1997), Gratch's work at ICT (Gratch and Marsella 2001), and the Sims (Macedonia 2000)).

To support the physical drives, we have extended Unreal Tournament so that all of our characters have a model of physiological responses to the environment and to their internal processing. Moreover, the environment has attributes that influence the physiology of the characters. For example, just as games have a measure of ambient light level, we have added ambient temperature. Different regions of the game have different ambient temperatures; outside it is very cold and inside it is moderately cold, although when a fire is lit in the fireplace, it is very warm near the fire. All of the physiological properties serve as input into the AI characters; that is, the characters are aware of their values. However, the character can only indirectly change them by the actions it performs. For example, the characters have a body temperature that can be raised by exertion, by changing the clothes they wear, or by moving to different regions of the level that have different temperature levels, such as near the fire. Changes in one of these attributes can affect others, so that a significant drop in body temperature can make them more tired.

Physiological effects that we have implemented include: temperature, exertion, fatigue, sleepiness, hunger, and thirst. There are other attributes that impact a character's actions, such as its strength, speed and dexterity. Commercial computer games have had complex physiological effects for the human player's character as well as many character attributes (an important part of role-playing games). For example, the Sims has a set of attributes for the computer characters which drives their behavior. We are attempting to extend the set to be more comprehensive and to explore the interplay between physiological drives and goal-driven behavior, which other systems in interactive drama lack.

### Environmental Sensing and Action

As in our previous work with Quakebots (Laird 2001), we are committed to giving our characters realistic sensing and actions in their environments. However, this is challenging because of the difficulty of sensing walls (and doors) in these environments. To enable sensing of the rooms, we annotate the map with regions that give the name of each room so that the characters can directly sense which room they are in. We are creating nodes in the map that are placed at important locations (doors, windows). The characters use these nodes for navigation between rooms, but move more freely within a room based on their sensing of objects and other characters.

### Autonomy and Directability

The agents in Haunt 2 are first and foremost autonomous; they can move about in the synthetic world on their own, gathering knowledge and attempting to fulfill whatever their current goals are. The characters are at a base-level defined by their goal-oriented behaviors. This way of viewing our agent design in an interactive drama follows Mateas and Stern's view of *strongly autonomous* characters (Mateas and Stern 2000). However, as they point out, using strongly autonomous agents for storytelling can be problematic. Characters performing in a drama may base some of their decisions on their internal state and personal goals, but should give priority to doing the proper actions given the current state of the story. There have been attempts to create interactive dramas that employ a director agent to monitor the story state, which makes use of low-bandwidth communications with the characters to occasionally give them directions to alter their behavior, thus performing story elements (Weyhrauch 1997; Young 2001). There have also been projects focused on *weakly autonomous* agents that have high-bandwidth communications with the director (Mateas and Stern 2002). In this design, the director has more control (and responsibility) to continually monitor all of the agents and provide them with detailed directions. This allows for a finer grain of control over the agents, with the goal being to create a more coherent presentation of the drama, but requires much more communication and forces more complexity into the director.

In order to fulfill both design requirements 3 and 4, we have opted towards a hybrid approach for incorporating synthetic characters in Haunt 2's plot. The characters are *semi-autonomous*, which follows closest to the philosophy laid out by Blumberg and Galyean (1997). In Haunt 2, we imbue the characters with autonomous behaviors that the director can manage using high-level directions for major plot points of the story, with the characters executing the directions on their own. However, the director also has the ability to drill down and give low-level direction when the details really matter. This approach is possible because long-term knowledge in Haunt 2 characters is defined by a hierarchy of operators, which includes a range of general operators to very specific ones that execute atomic actions. The director can give very general commands (e.g. "be social") that correspond to abstract operators, or very specific ones ("move to area X, face the Jon character, and perform dialogue line 126) that execute lower-level agent behaviors. This design allows for flexibility in the story representation not seen in other interactive drama approaches; the story author can write story events with *a varying degree of specificity*, which we discuss later in the paper.

With this design, a synthetic character's performance can be the result of story direction from the director, the dynamic selection of a new internal goal based on new inputs, a change in the agent's physiology, or most likely some combination of these affects. In the end, the story dictates an agent's performance, which in turn is coordinated by the director. The story author can make use of a character's knowledge or physiology as a tool in telling the story he wishes to tell. The next section discusses the director and its relationship with the story and synthetic characters.

## Story Director

As mentioned above, our approach to interactive drama centers around building semi-autonomous agents that perform actions largely dependent on director commands. Drama managers have been used in varying ways in other interactive narrative projects as well (Weyhrauch 1997; Young 2002; Mateas and Stern 2002; Blumberg and Galyean 1995). There are also alternative systems that rely mainly on autonomous behaviors or predefined dramatic principles to elicit an interesting story (Sgorous 1999; Cavazza, Charles and Mead 2002). The story director in Haunt 2 uses player prediction to determine if the player's actions will endanger the plot. It is this capability that distinguishes it most from other interactive narrative systems, such the MIMESIS architecture developed by the Liquid Narrative Group (Young 2001).

MIMESIS uses a fully-structured plot, represented as a partial-order plan, and either incorporates unplanned player actions into the story or avoids them altogether if incorporating them is infeasible. What Mimesis, as well as other interactive narrative approaches, does not address is the preemptive alteration of the story state in subtle ways to avoid problematic actions in the future. Other approaches to this problem have taken a more modular approach to plot construction (Mateas and Stern 2002; Weyhrauch 1997; Sgorous 1999). They rely on heuristically choosing plot elements as the player moves through the space of possible stories. While these approaches provide a greater number of possible story orderings, our design focuses on providing different possible plot content from one experience to the other with the game. This section will discuss the story representation used to encode the plot content, how that representation is used by the director and actors, and how player prediction fits into our design.

The story used in Haunt 2 is written by a human author and given as an initial input to the director (requirement 4). The representation used is similar to that in a partially-order plan. A story's scene can be broken down into atomic events called *plot points*, which can be partially-ordered to construct a scene. A plot point represents some important, story-relevant change in the world. Each plot-point can be split into a set of preconditions and postconditions. The preconditions describe what has to be in true in the world in order for this plot point to be relevant. The postconditions describe what actions should take place once these conditions are met. Just as in any real-time dramatic experience, timing is important. We also provide a special precondition, called a *timing constraint*, for plot points that indicate a specific time or range of times that the other preconditions must be met by. We have found this structured approach to be particularly sensible when considering creating an interactive narrative for teaching or training applications, when creating an experience where realism and interactivity are important, but also that specific teaching goals are met (Magerko and Laird 2002).

The Haunt 2 Bed & Breakfast story begins with the player awakening from a brutal murder at the bed & breakfast as a ghost. He knows little about where he is, or even who the murderer is, so he begins by exploring the house, invisible and immaterial. His first encounter with the characters in the building is overhearing a conversation between Sally and the Innkeeper in the main lobby. Figure 1 illustrates how this event would be represented in the story structure. It describes that both Sally and the Innkeeper should be in the same room and that the player is within earshot. Another more modular way this plot point could be written would be to tell the characters to "engage in small talk," and let them pick out of a set of pre-written dialogues. One of the director's roles is to step through the plot and give characters their "cues" for different performances (e.g. dialogue, a new goal, or information). Therefore, the director will notice when the conditions are met for this plot point and move the plot forward by directing the relevant characters to perform specific lines of dialogue.

If the player behaves precisely as the author expected when constructing the plot, then the story will be told without any problems. One of the main issues that arises when working with a fully-structured plot is that the player, and plausibly the synthetic characters, can execute actions in the world that threaten a future plot point's preconditions from being met. For example, if the player explores the house for longer than two minutes, then the preconditions in the plot point in Figure 1 would be violated. This problem introduces one of the director's main roles: giving direction to either the world or to the synthetic characters to change their state or their behavior to encourage the satisfying of some precondition(s). In our current representation, the director's commands are not directly connected to the individual preconditions, but are

| preconditions | postconditions |
|---|---|
| Location( Sally, x )<br>Location( Innkeeper, x )<br><br>Proximity(Player, Sally, 2)<br><br>Timing( <= 2 min. ) | Talk(Sally, Innkeeper, small_talk)<br><br>Talk(Innkeeper, Sally, small_talk) |

Figure 1: An example plot point in Haunt 2.

categorized by the type of situation for which they are applicable. For instance, if a *proximity* precondition, as in Figure 1, is unfulfilled when the plot point's timing constraint is violated, then a director action that addresses the positions of characters relative to the player may be chosen (e.g. a director command labeled "proximity to player" which would order Sally and the Innkeeper to move closer to the player before engaging in small talk). Some director commands may be general across narratives or types of stories, but it is up to the author of the story to write any needed director commands and have them fit in with the overall narrative. Future work may focus on what sets of strategies for different situations would be appropriate, and how to choose between them.

Requirement 6 reflects the common goal in interactive drama systems to create a narrative that hinges on the player's actions; different player actions should yield different narratives. In terms of story representation, we try to meet this goal within the constraints of having a fully-structured plot along two axes: *content variability* and *temporal variability* (Magerko 2003). Content variability refers to "what happens in a story" being different across experiences. Temporal variability refers to when those things happen.

In our representation, plot points are partially-ordered by the author. The preconditions for a given plot point can only be considered after all of the preconditions of the points that temporally proceed that point have been met and their postconditions performed. This allows for some temporal variability between experiences, but is constrained by our earlier-stated requirement for having a fully-structured plot. There have been less structured approaches to representation that are more flexible in providing temporal variability (Mateas and Stern 2002; Weyhrauch 1997; Sgorous 1999).

Content variability is an issue brought up far less in interactive drama systems, in part due to the fact that if a system has a high degree of temporal variability, the player is likely to see different plot content between experiences. Systems such as MIMESIS or Façade provide mechanisms for choosing between different pre-written plot points at run-time, but the content of those plot points themselves is fixed; "who," "what," and "where" go unchanged. In Haunt 2, we make a simple, but effective, design choice in allowing the story author to leave plot content uninstantiated when it is given to the director.

Another role of the director is to recognize missing plot content and instantiate it properly. For example, the final plot point of our scene in Haunt 2 is shown in Figure 2. At this point, the player has discovered his dead body in the library, and has helped another character stumble upon it. Which character the player ends up with in the final scene depends on who the player has decided to coax into the room with him (e.g. by materializing and scaring them out of the lobby and into the library). A variable can be shared across plot points, allowing for the instantiation of a variable early on the plot to affect plot content throughout the rest of the narrative. Therefore, the variable representing which character should discover the body alongside the player could be shared with earlier plot points, or bound by the director based on the player's previous experiences (e.g. instantiate the variable to be the character the player has gathered the least information about and then direct that character to find its way to the dead body). This representational feature is a very simple example of a significant strength of our story representation: it creates a strong connection between the player's interactions with the world and the story that they experience. The author has the flexibility with this representation to be as exact or as vague as he wishes to be with the use of temporal ordering, content variables, and abstract agent operators.

| preconditions | postconditions |
|---|---|
| Location( Sally, x )<br>Location( Innkeeper, x ) | Talk(Sally, Innkeeper, small_talk) |
| Proximity(Player, Sally, 2) | Talk(Innkeeper, Sally, small_talk) |
| Timing( <= 2 min. ) | |

Figure 2: Ending plot point for Haunt 2.

In requirement 5, we commit to a fully-defined plot structure, as opposed to dynamically creating structure (Mateas and Stern 2002; Sgorous 1999; Weyhrauch 1997). This commitment gives our system the capability to make use of a predictive model of player behavior. The director can run an internal simulation of player behavior and hypothesize about whether or not the story can reach completion in a coherent, timely manner. The player model is implemented as an internal rule-based simulation within the director. The long-term memory of the model is written as production rules in a similar fashion as the synthetic characters are defined, like implementing the top-level operators *listen* or *explore*. As the player moves through the world, the director hypothesizes what declarative knowledge he is acquiring through his experiences. It also keeps an up-to-date internal structure describing the state of the world. Periodically, the director runs a simulation of the user model and the world state, observing what new knowledge the player might gather and what actions he might take. The next step is to have the modeling triggered by events, such as the player moving into a new room, acquiring some knowledge, or too much time passing.

If the model is a success, it means that the player is predicted to execute actions that encourage or at the very least don't hinder the story from progressing from the current story state to the conclusion. Model failure indicates that there is some precondition on a plot point that is being threatened by predicted player action. Model failure is the same as a precondition being violated by some player or character action; the annotated director actions are executed to attempt to ensure that the state of the world is focused back on achieving this particular condition. For example, before trying to coax one of the characters into the library to discover the dead body, the player has to know a) that the body exists, b) that the room exists, and c) that the body is in that room. The director queries the model, asking "based on the current hypothesis of player knowledge, will the player behave in a manner that will keep the plot from continuing?" In this example, if the player is missing any of the above knowledge, the model is likely to fail; the player model will execute a series of irrelevant actions and violate a timing constraint. The user model that we employ is a simple one, designed to show that user prediction is a useful module in an interactive drama architecture. Future work would involve revising the model using experimental data. We will also investigate choosing different directions for when the model fails as opposed to when an action in the actual environment violates the plot specification.

## Conclusions & Future Work

This research has gone from the initial desire of exploring the development of human-level AI agents, to pursuing that desire within the context of computer games, to embedding AI agents as actors and directors. We have followed this with the creation of an environment for developing the AI agents. We have sufficient implementations of these agents so that the actors can perform actions on their own as well as take actions sent by the director. The director monitors the agents, the player, and the plot, reasons about how they may interact in the future, and sends directions to the agents based on that reasoning and any story elements that are currently applicable. We are at a stage where we have demonstrated the feasibility of this overall approach, and now the real fun begins as we can explore the deeper research issues that arise in developing more capable actors and directors and extending the system to a complete story that can be played by human users.

The primary research problem we are pursuing with the actors is focused on improving their ability to manage the tension between carrying out their own goals and responding to commands from the director. To maintain believability, the actors must not only stay in character, but also appear to have coherent behavior. If the Innkeeper receives a command to offer a drink to the player who is across the room, the Innkeeper should not immediately abandon his current activity, such as pouring a drink for another customer, and then shouting at the player. Instead, the Innkeeper must replan its actions, determining when it can smoothly incorporate the new direction while still maintaining coherent behavior (Assanie 2002).

Our current plans for the director include having it not only model the player's actions and respond to problems when they arise, but also to anticipate when the player is unable to move forward in the story. When predicting player behavior, the director asks "Is the player likely to move the plot along?" If the answer is "no" to this question, the director currently stops there and acts on that result. A more intelligent approach to the design would be to have a second, complete search of the possible story futures and ask "Is it even *possible* for the story to be completed?"

Some action may have been executed, either by the player or a synthetic character, which prevents the story from ever reaching a conclusion. Knowing whether or not the story's end can actually be reached could be a key piece of information for the director in deciding what direction to give the characters. If there is a relatively short path to the next plot point, the director's decision may be different than if there were only a single, long path or none at all.

Our future work in Haunt 2 will not only focus on evaluating the system once it is in a more mature state, but also on developing methodologies for such an evaluation. It is hard to categorize how much more entertaining or "fun" a system is. We intend to instead rely on fulfilling the reasonable design requirements we have laid out for our view of an interactive narrative, as well as conducting experiments on the effectiveness of story direction. The director's effectiveness can be evaluated in terms of how often temporal constraints are violated by players (i.e. how often plot flow lags because of player behavior) and how often the player executes actions that threaten preconditions of future plot points. If the prediction model is effective, these measures will be lower than the same system with player prediction removed form the director's capabilities.

We plan on extending our story beyond a single scene to a complete interactive drama (on the order of 20-30 minutes of game play). The player should be able to replay the experience several times with noticeable differences in the narrative each time due to different plot instantiations, character behavior choices, and player behavior. That will stress all components of the system and let us evaluate whether or not this approach to incorporating human-level AI into computer games can be successful.

## References


Assanie, M. 2002. *Directable Synthetic Characters,* AAAI 2002 Spring Symposium Series: Artificial Intelligence and Interactive Entertainment.

Blumberg, B. and Galyean, T. 1995. *Multi-level Direction of Autonomous Characters for Real-Time Virtual Environments.* In Proceedings of SIGGraph 1995.

Blumberg, B. and Galyean T. 1997. *Multi-level Control for Animated Autonomous Agents: Do the Right Thing...Oh, Not that.* In Creating Personalities for Synthetic Actors, Ed. R. Trappl and P. Petta, Springer.

Cavazza, M., Charles, F., and Mead, S. 2002. *Sex, Lies, and Video Games: an Interactive Storytelling Prototype.* AAAI 2002 Spring Symposium Series: Artificial Intelligence and Interactive Entertainment.

Gratch, J. and Marsella, S. 2001. *Tears and Fears: Modeling emotions and emotional behaviors in synthetic agents.* In *Proceedings of the 5th International Conference on Autonomous Agents,* Montreal, Canada, 278-285.

Kaminka, G. A., Schaffer, S.; Sollitto, C., Adobbati, R., Marshal, Andrew N., Scholer, Andrew, S., and Tejada, S. 2002. *GameBots: the ever-challenging multi-agent research test-bed.* In Communications of the ACM. Vol. 45, No. 1.

Laird, J. E. 2001. *It knows what you're going to do: Adding anticipation to a Quakebot.* Proceedings of Agents 2001, 385-292, Montreal, CA.

Laird, J. E., Assanie, M., Bachelor, B., Benninghoff, N., Enam, S., Jones, B., Kerfoot, A., Lauver, C., Magerko, B., Sheiman, J., Stokes, D., and Wallace, S. 2002. *A Test Bed for Developing Intelligent Synthetic Characters.* AAAI 2002 Spring Symposium Series: Artificial Intelligence and Interactive Entertainment.

Laird, J. E., A. Newell, Rosenbloom, P.S. 1987. *Soar: An architecture for general intelligence.* Artificial Intelligence 33(3), 1-64.

Laurel, B. 1986. *Toward the Design of a Computer-Based Interactive Fantasy System.* Ph.D. diss., Drama Department, Ohio State University.

Loyall, A. B. and Bates, J. 1997. *Personality-Rich Believable Agents That Use Language.* Proceedings of the First International Conference on Autonomous Agents, Marina del Rey, California, 106-113.

Macedonia, M. 2000. *Using Technology and Innovation to Simulate Daily Life*, Computer, 110-112.

Magerko, B. and Laird, J.E. 2002. *Towards Building an Interactive Training Simulator,* In the Proceedings of the Eleventh Conference on Computer-Generated Forces and Behavior Representation, Orlando, FL.

Magerko, B. 2003. *Building an Interactive Drama Architecture.* 1st International Conference on Technologies for Interactive Digital Storytelling and Entertainment, Darmstadt, DE.

Martin, M. 2001. *EscOnline: a Venue for Believable Agents.* AAAI 2001 Spring Symposium Series: Artificial Intelligence and Interactive Entertainment.

Mateas, M. and A. Stern. 2002. *A Behavior Language for Story-Based Believable Agents.* AAAI 2002 Spring Symposium Series: Artificial Intelligence and Interactive Entertainment.

Newell, A. 1990. *Unified Theories of Cognition.* Cambridge, Massachusetts, Harvard University Press.

Sgorous, N. M. 1999. *Dynamic Generation, Management, and Resolution of Interactive Plots.* Artificial Intelligence, 107, 29-62.

Weyhrauch, P. 1997. *Guiding Interactive Drama*. Ph.D. diss., Dept. of Computer Science, Carnegie Mellon.

Wray, R. E., Laird, J. E., Nuxoll, A., and Jones, R. M 2002. *Intelligent Opponents for Virtual Reality Training.* Inter-service/Industry Training, Simulation, and Education Conference (I/ITSEC), Orlando, FL.

Young, R. M. 2001. *An Overview of the Mimesis Architecture: Integrating Intelligent Narrative Control into an Existing Gaming Environment.* AAAI 2001 Spring Symposium Series: Artificial Intelligence and Interactive Entertainment, March 2001: AAAI Technical Report SS 01-02, 77-81.

# Agent-based Simulation of Geo-Political Conflict

**Glenn Taylor[1], Richard Frederiksen[1], Russell R. Vane, III[2], Edward Waltz[2]**

[1]Soar Technology, Inc., 3600 Green Court Suite 600, Ann Arbor, MI 48103
[2]General Dynamics – Advanced Information Systems, 1400 Key Blvd, Suite 700, Arlington, VA 22209
glenn@soartech.com, rdf@soartech.com, russ.vane@gd-ais.com, ed.waltz@gd-ais.com

**Abstract**

The intelligence analysis task of anticipating crises and providing decision makers with reasonable (supportable, explainable) possible futures is extremely difficult. To perform this task, a team of analysts must consider the political, economic, and military aspects of national governments and non-governmental organizations. This paper describes an agent-based simulation framework, the Advanced Global Intelligence and Leadership Experiment (AGILE), for building executable models for conducting regional analysis. AGILE is a full-featured simulation framework that enables the specification of simulation parameters, models and agents, lets the user define and run simulations under varying conditions, and enables post-run analysis of the results. In this paper, we describe the system implementation, and some examples of its use in a pseudo-operational setting.

## Introduction

Intelligence analysis includes abductive processes, in which analysts propose alternative competing hypotheses to explain current evidence. Long-term analysis of foreign nations requires the analysis of state interactions, especially where those interactions lead to instability, crisis, or conflict. In order to explore potential future scenarios, an analyst must understand the political, economic, military, diplomatic, and social aspects of those countries, with special focus on the major decision-makers and their motivations, capabilities, and tendencies.

This already difficult task is compounded by many circumstances. The information available to analysis is typically sparse, and buried within a vast amount of irrelevant, and often intentionally misleading, information. The analytic process is resource bounded – too few analysts must analyze a large amount of information in a short timeframe. In considering multiple hypotheses, limited resources may lead to considering only the most likely few, which might eliminate low-probability, high-impact hypotheses. While some regions have been analyzed for years, regional instability and regime change may require analysts to quickly familiarize themselves with new decision-makers in the regions.

Several tools and techniques are currently available to an analyst to help perform the task of state and leadership analysis, including social network analysis, role-playing ("Red Teaming") and wargaming. However, most of these techniques are performed manually, with only basic tools such as databases and search engines used to assist. Recent government R&D programs for the intelligence community have focused on dealing with the overwhelming amount of information available to analysts, such as text summarization, query answering, and information retrieval, as illustrated by programs such as NIMD (ARDA 2002a) and AQUAINT (ARDA 2002b). Less attention has been paid to providing tools to help analysts with the abductive reasoning processes used in the analysis of feasible future scenarios.

This paper describes an implemented system meant to address this shortcoming. The Advanced Global Intelligence Leadership Environment (AGILE) is a simulation environment in which analysts may model the dynamics of a geopolitical crisis, and play out the kind of role-playing and wargaming that is typically conducted manually. AGILE enables a team of analysts to make explicit their tacit assumptions about a state leadership in the form of an executable agent-based model, and use that model to generate and analyze hypotheses about interacting nations. This work focuses not only on the capabilities of the simulation system, but also how the system fits into a larger analytic process. As such, a significant portion of this effort is in making the system usable and intuitive to intelligence analysts. This work is very much along the lines of scenario planning (Schwartz 1991) and fits within work on the practice of intelligence analysis (Heuer 1999).

## System Overview

AGILE is a complete simulation environment, where a user can set up, run, and analyze simulations meant to represent a particular region in the world. In order to reflect the analytic process of exploring possible scenarios, we have developed AGILE to provide intelligence analysts with a "simulation workspace" for encoding knowledge, generating hypotheses, and drawing conclusions to support their reasoning. Specifically, AGILE is designed to meet the following goals:

- Support abductive reasoning about complex nation-state relationships
- Allow analysts to model nation-state interactions and processes at a high level of abstraction
- Support the collaborative nature of intelligence analysis

The national-strategic level of interest to regional analysis has been one of our overriding design considerations. Rather than being focused on making precise predictions about future events, regional analysis is interested in larger trends, toward crisis or conflict. Low-level, tactical behaviors are less important when trying to understand these trends. As with any simulation, the goal is to model at a reasonable level of abstraction, ignoring unnecessary details, without sacrificing meaning or clarity. The design of AGILE has been greatly influenced by these ideas. For example, in our simulations built to date, numerical models represent high-level, aggregate information such as average military tension in a region, or gross domestic product trends. Similarly, agents tend to represent aggregate decision-making entities such as branches of a government, rather than individual decision-makers.

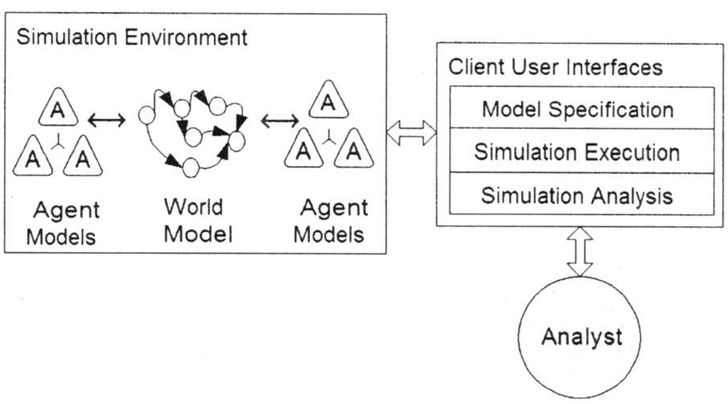


**Figure 1: AGILE high-level architecture**

AGILE is composed of three major components: a world model for simulating processes in the environment; agents (and their interactions) for simulating decision-making; and a graphical user interface that allows specification, execution, and analysis of the simulation (see Figure 1). The simulation environment consists of multiple countries (represented as groups of agents) interacting through the world model.

For simplicity, we have designed AGILE to run as a turn-based simulation, with two phases: the world model processes and updates its state, then the agents go through decision-making and post actions to the world model. After all agent decision-making is complete, the world model processes the agent actions, and the cycle repeats. The simulation runs for a user-specified number of turns before completing. Each turn corresponds roughly to a week of activity. Currently, the both the world model and the agents operate deterministically.

The typical process of running a simulation includes specifying the model's initial conditions, and then (via built-in wizards) defining variations on those initial conditions, such that a wide array of simulations can be quickly generated to explore a large space of possible scenarios. This variation also enables the user to account for uncertainties in the starting conditions, and supports a kind of sensitivity analysis on the models. AGILE currently allows automatic parametric variation of at most two initial world model conditions, and arbitrary manual variation of any system parameters, including initial conditions, agents and events.

The following subsections describe the major components of AGILE in detail, and how they serve to meet the objectives outlined earlier.

## World Model

The world model (WM) represents the governing rules of geopolitical conflict, and provides the environment for agent interaction. The WM computes change over time, and maintains state from turn to turn. The WM can be composed of sub-models; the instance we describe later is composed of sub-models that correspond to economic, military, diplomatic, and social domains. Most importantly, the WM defines how all of the domains are interconnected. For example, if the level of nationalistic propaganda from Country A is very high, the apprehension level in Country B may rise, which, in turn, may dampen the Country B's economy. These model dependencies allow us to reflect the deep interconnections between nations in a region.

The world model is a well-defined, separable component within the system architecture, and can be replaced by models of different fidelity. We have developed an infrastructure for defining many different instances and types of world models, including numeric, symbolic, agent-based or hybrid models, to act as the underlying engine for the AGILE simulation. However, to date, we have built only numerical world models, composed of variables and their relationships.

During the world model update phase of a turn, the variable values are updated, and changes are propagated to other affected variables based on the WM definition. A subset of the variables in the WM serves to define actions for agent activity (an action is simply a change to a single variable in the world model). In addition to fielding the actions of the agents, the world model allows the injection of exogenous events – timed changes to the system that are not the result of agent modifications. For instance, an earthquake can be modeled using an event to modify regional effects, such as lowered stock markets and heightened economic apprehension. Events also let the user model simple forces external to the particular target countries without having to add several agents to model a country; for example, in the models described below, we model the presence of the US military as events, instead of by creating a suite of US agents.

## Agent Models

Agents embody decision-making aspects of nation-state interaction, and are the driving force behind the dynamics of the system. We adopt here a strong notion of agency, as given by (Bratman 1987), who defines agents as autonomous entities that maintain goals, knowledge, beliefs, and obligations, and can interact with their environment and with other agents. The agent system is built using the Soar agent architecture (Rosenbloom et al. 1993), a general architecture for intelligent systems, which provides mechanisms for problem solving, knowledge inferencing, and goal-directed behavior. Soar has been used successfully to model a wide variety of human behavior, including behavior for military simulation (Tambe et al. 1995; Hill et al. 1997; Jones et al. 1999; Taylor et al. 2001). We selected Soar as the basis for the agents in this system due to its track record in representing complex, human-like decision-making.

While Soar, as a general agent system, provides many capabilities, we do not expect the end-users to be experts in developing knowledge-based systems. Therefore, we must allow a user to describe agents in familiar terms, such as goals, beliefs, and relationships to other agents. For our system, it was necessary to abstract away from the low-level details of Soar programming by exposing only the artifacts necessary to specify an agent. In order to do this, we essentially developed an agent architecture on top of the basic Soar architecture. The result is the two-tier architecture shown in Figure 2.

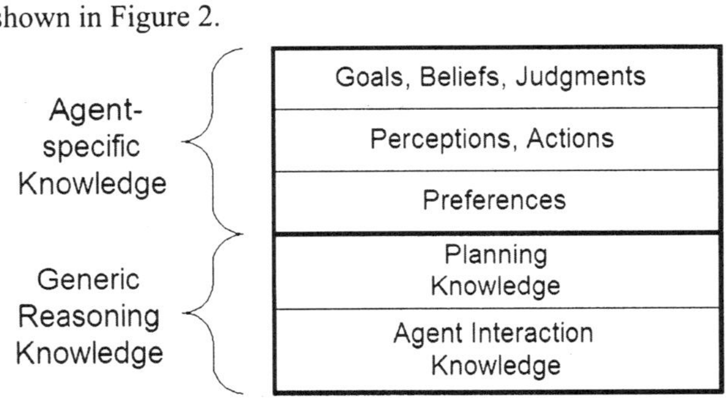


**Figure 2: Agent knowledge architecture**

The bottom layer consists of capabilities that govern the basic behavior of an agent in its environment and within a group, including low-level message handling, action execution, goal monitoring and management, belief inferencing, and plan generation and execution. This layer is essentially the same for every agent defined in this system (though there are some differences based on role). The upper layer is the data for the lower layer – it contains the knowledge that specializes an agent's behavior to a certain domain of activity. There are five basic types of knowledge defined in the upper tier:

- The actions available to the agent
- The agent's goals and preferences
- Beliefs to help the agent determine appropriate values for actions (action beliefs)
- Beliefs for the agent to determine the effects actions have on the world model (cause-effect beliefs)
- Beliefs for evaluating states, including the current and future projected states (judgment beliefs)

The basic agent activity revolves around meeting goals: an agent senses information from the world model, evaluates the current state, including what goals are met and unmet, plans for any activities that might help meet its unmet goals, and executes actions to meet its goals. Am agent's particular domain-specific knowledge guides the basic problem-solving process. Figure 3 below shows the execution cycle of an agent, with the knowledge that is applied at each step. Because the base architecture is still Soar, knowledge in both of the upper and lower tier is ultimately in the form of rules; the user specifies knowledge in the upper layer in an architecture-neutral format, and that knowledge is translated to Soar rules automatically.

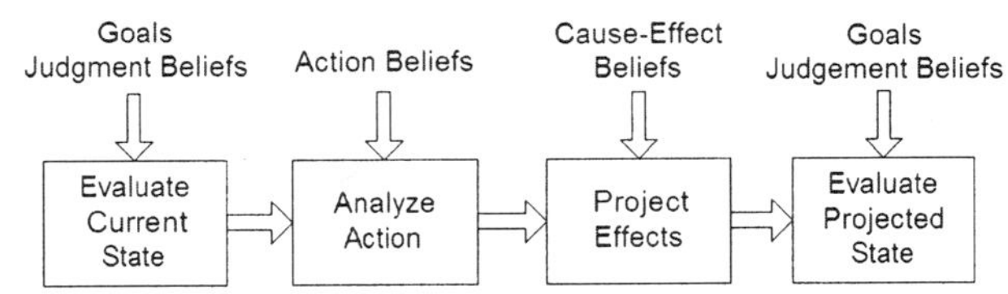


**Figure 3: A single agent's decision-making process**

Each country may be composed of multiple agents acting as a group to solve problems. Within a group, each agent has a specialty role, and acts within a larger group decision-making context. Each agent role roughly corresponds to a sub-domain of the world model. There is no limit to the number of countries in a model, and so no limit to the number of agents within the system – however, the system enforces a policy that no two agents can have write access to the same world model variables.

We have so far implemented only a single organization structure, which we have called the "management" style of decision-making – a single moderator (the "leader") and any number of subordinates ("advisors"). In this organization, each advisor maintains a level of influence with the leader, and the leader gives more deference to the suggestions of agents with higher influence. An advisor's most important unsatisfied goal is nominated as an issue to the leader, who collects issues from the entire group (and itself), and prioritizes them by order of agent influence. One at a time, each issue is then suggested to the whole group for problem solving – all the agents in the group can suggest a way to deal with the issue. The leader collects all of the suggested actions, and selects the one that looks most promising, partly based on influence of the suggesting agent. This selected action is then passed through a review process, in which each agent in the group is allowed to vote for or against that action, based on analyzing the action against its own goals and beliefs. The leader tallies all these votes, and if the action passes the review, the agent that suggested it schedules that action for execution. This process continues until all of the suggested issues have been dealt with for a given turn. Figure 4 illustrates the lead-advisor relationship. This multi-agent action selection and review process is similar in spirit to the FIPA Contract Net Protocol (FIPA 2002), except that all participants in this process are stakeholders, and so have a say in whether an activity happens or not. In fact, all inter-group communication in AGILE is governed by a set of well-defined communicative acts that reflect the role distinctions of leader and advisors.

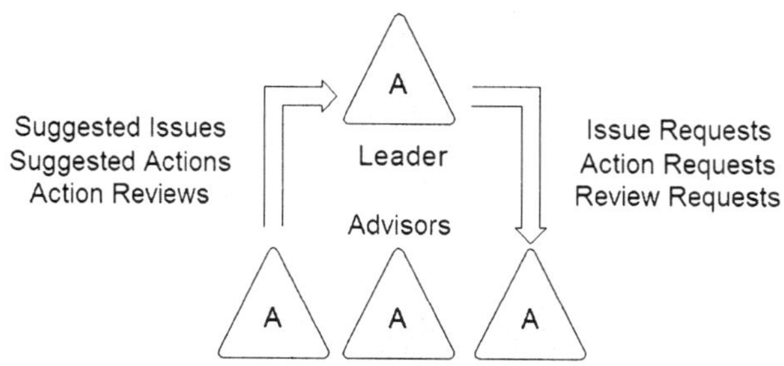


**Figure 4: AGILE's muti-agent organization**

In addition to intra-country communication, agents in one country can interact explicitly with agents in another by means of diplomatic communications. Two countries can establish diplomatic agreements in which both sides agree to change some goal or activity; for example, limiting the presence of foreign troops near the border or putting a cap on the tariff levels imposed on goods. These agreements begin as requests for one country to change its behavior, which enters into the normal within-country decision-making process as a new issue. If both sides have such requests, and both sides find the terms amenable, a formal agreement is established, and new goals are formed on both sides to accommodate it.

We have adopted the metaphor of beliefs, desires, and intentions to describe the characteristics of agents and how they behave in their environments. However, we have not adopted the full extent of the BDI paradigm as described in (Rao and Georgeff 1991). Instead, we have found that describing agents in terms such as beliefs and desires (goals), similar to what is described in (Dennett 1987), has an intuitive appeal, and finds resonance with our users. While Soar-based models have not traditionally been described in these terms, it is not unreasonable to do so, especially in this case where we have built a knowledge architecture atop the traditional Soar architecture to support these artifacts directly.

## Graphical User Interface

The primary purpose of the AGILE graphical user interface is to provide an environment within which an analyst can generate and test hypotheses in simulation. Within this environment, the analyst can create and modify agents, agent groups, world models, and pre-defined events; quickly set up and run multiple simulations; and analyze the results. The user can also annotate artifacts in the system, such as with comments or references, in order to fit the model into the larger analytic process. As analysis is ultimately a collaborative process, the user can also share these artifacts with other analysts, including model components (agents, world models), results, and annotations. For the discussion here, there are two major relevant GUI capabilities: the specification of simulation parameters, especially agent behavior; and understanding simulation results, especially the agents' decision-making processes.

Because of the two-tier organization of the agent as described earlier, the user only needs to specify the information in the upper tier, since the underlying processes are the same for all agents, and are not exposed to the user. The user must define the actions, goals, and beliefs for an agent, all in terms of the variables defined in the world model. Additionally, the user specifies descriptions for each of these knowledge types, which are used later in the explanation of the results. The GUI assists in this entire process, using various interfaces to simplify what could otherwise be quite complicated.

As an example, suppose the user wishes to define an agent to manage the diplomatic affairs of a country. Suppose also the world model contains, among other things, a variable called Propaganda representing the diplomatic rhetoric level toward another country, with value range (0.0, 1.0). The Propaganda level directly effects the Apprehension level of the economy – high Propaganda means high Apprehension. The user assigns this action to the Diplomat, and creates an accompanying belief that says how to change the Propaganda level under different conditions. The user then assigns a goal to the Diplomat agent to keep the Propaganda level below 0.5, otherwise too much Apprehension dampens the overall economy, and has a diminishing effect on the other country. Next, the user creates agent beliefs that describe the relationship between Propaganda and Apprehension, so the agent will know how to judge the effects of applying the action to the world model. The agents we have developed so far require only a few such goals and accompanying beliefs in order to exhibit interesting behavior. There is no real limit to the number of beliefs and goals an agent can have; however, since goals currently correspond only to variables in the world model, there is typically a correlation between the number of goals an agent will have, and the number of variables in the world model for which it is concerned.

After a simulation has been run, the GUI allows the user to analyze the results in order to relate them back to the analyst's original hypotheses. We have developed a variety of displays for the different types of data generated by the simulation. For example, the results of multi-variation runs can be displayed by a 3-dimensional surface, and the dynamics of the world model are easily described as 2-

dimensional timelines, with each variable shown as a single graph covering the duration of the simulation. Two types of agent information overlays annotate the 2-dimensional timeline: regions of the parameter space covered by agent goals, and changes in world model variables that were the direct result of agent actions and events.

Another level of detail describes the agent activity using textual descriptions in "narratives." Summary narratives include information about the decision-making within a country, turn-by-turn including the issues that were brought up and how they were dealt with. Detailed narratives show information about a decision on an agent-by-agent basis, where agent activity is given side-by-side in columns – which issues were suggested, what actions were suggested to fix that issue, how the agents reviewed other actions, and which action was finally selected and executed (see Figure 5). To give further insight, this narrative also links to details about the precise beliefs an agent applied when making these choices.

| | China Diplomat | China Military |
|---|---|---|
| Propose Actions | ***Assess Status***<br><br>*Belief:* If Taiwan statehood too high, increase propaganda to militant levels (Propaganda)<br>*details*<br><br>*Goal:* Want Taiwanese Statehood Low<br><br>***Propose Action***<br>Set Propaganda to -0.094<br>(L) | ***Assess Status***<br><br>*Belief:* Increased forced incidents to lower statehood (Military_Incident_Intensity)<br>*details*<br><br>*Goal:* Want Taiwanese Statehood Low<br><br>***Propose Action***<br>Set Military_Incident_Intensity to 1.25<br>(L) |

**Figure 5: Snapshot of Detailed Narrative Swimlanes**

All of the results displays, from the 3d surface plots, to the 2d timelines, down to the individual agent decision calculus, are interconnected to allow the user to drill down for more detail about a particular simulation. This ability to easily navigate to any level of detail enables the user to quickly understand the full dynamics of the simulation.

## Evaluation

We have used AGILE to model a few scenarios for testing and for demonstrating its capabilities to potential users. First, with the help of analysts, we modeled a particular historical scenario, the 1995-1996 Taiwan Straits Crisis, based on open source data, to see if AGILE was able to model the important events. Later, we staged a hypothetical crisis between China and Taiwan in 2005, and worked with analysts in a simulated Red Team to use AGILE as the workspace for their hypothesis generation and testing.

### Taiwan Straits Crisis of '95-'96

This scenario detailed the largely diplomatic conflict that ensued over the Chinese perception that Taiwan was making a bid for independence. The crisis involved rising diplomatic and military tensions, including Chinese missile test firings across the Taiwan Straits as a way to subtly threaten Taiwan into backing down on its perceived move toward independence.

In order to model these events, we developed a simple numerical world model that captures the relationships and interconnections between economic, social, military, and diplomatic processes. We created a mapping from the historical record into the terms of the simulation in order to create a reference model of events for comparison. The reference model captures the historical data at the same level of abstraction as the simulation, so we can compare historical cases against simulation outputs. The important variables we modeled included the China's level of perceived Taiwanese independence, the movement of troops into and out of the theater, the level of military incidents in the Straits, the diplomatic rhetoric level (propaganda), and economic indicators such as GDP and apprehension. Additionally, we included the presence of US troops as part of the numeric model, since we were not interested in US decision-making in this exercise. We then developed a set of agents, five for each of China and Taiwan – one for each of the four world model domains, and one leader – and assigned those agents with the goals and beliefs that were suggested by our data sources. A major Chinese goal was keeping Taiwanese independence in check without going to war; a major Taiwanese goal was to see how high it could raise its perceived independence without invoking a drastic response from China.

We initialized the world model with historically informed parameters, and generated a parametric variation space around the initial conditions to account for our uncertainties in those parameters. We ran each simulation for 65 turns (equivalent to weeks) to match the rough span of time taken by the actual historical events. Using this multi-simulation method of 100 simulations, we were able to generate a wide range of system behaviors, a handful of which matched quite closely to the actual historical events, and whose underlying rationale fit well against the historical data. Figure 6 represents a comparison of the reference model we created (left) against the results of a single simulation run (right). A visual comparison of the reference versus evaluation models demonstrates the close similarities exhibited by the agent behavior and the model dynamics. We have begun to develop tools that help identify these individual runs within the multiple simulations. One example is the Interesting Run Finder, which allows the user to find simulation runs that match certain criteria, such as when a variable's value falls within a defined range. Qualitative descriptors in the model definition identify meaningful ranges of values – for

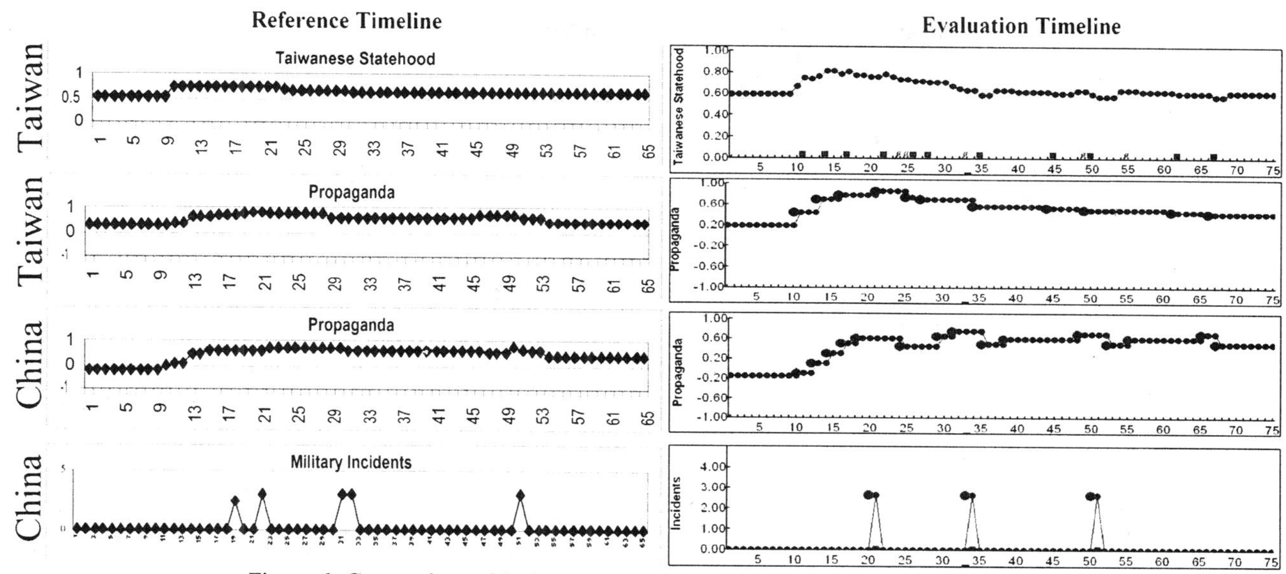


**Figure 6: Comparison of Reference Model to '95-'96 Taiwan Straits Crisis Model**

example, in this model, values of Military Intensity above 0.8 would indicate those runs in which full war broke out.

Encouraging was the fact that with fairly simple agent models (roughly 5-10 goals, 40-50 beliefs, and 5 basic actions per agent), and a fairly simple world model (about 15 interconnected variables), we were able to achieve quite rich, believable system behavior. This initial combined model took roughly one month's time of a software developer to build, test, simulate, and analyze the results. We have not yet run usability tests with end-users, so we do not know how this would translate to the field.

## China-Taiwan 2005

In this exercise, the analysts imagined a future scenario where the current Taiwanese president had won a second term in office, and Taiwan's Democratic People's Party had introduced to the legislature an enabling bill for a future referendum on national independence. The goal was to exercise the model's ability to explore what-if scenarios and suggest believable possible futures for analysis. Using the same world model as in the previous example, the analysts suggested initial conditions and brainstormed on the mindsets of the major decision-making entities, which we translated into viable agent beliefs and goals. Over the course of three days, the analysts would suggest changes to the base model as what-if scenarios, which we encoded into the model, and then ran as simulations whose results were presented the following morning.

Figure 7 illustrates Chinese military activity as multi-run surfaces taken from the economics excursions of the exercise. Each surface represents a set of parametrically varied initial conditions for the world model, and each grid location on surface a represents the maximum value of the Chinese Military Incidents variable over a single simulation run – essentially showing China's use of military force to quell Taiwanese moves toward independence. The four surfaces reflect different agent economic beliefs and goals. As the series progresses, both China and Taiwan increase their level of concern about the economic aspects of their relationship. *(a)* shows the base run for the exercise, indicating generally high military incidents; *(b)* displays the results of increasing the influence of the Taiwanese Economic advisor, with an effect of decreased military incidents; *(c)* shows the effects of adding an additional belief to the Taiwanese Economic advisor to dislike Taiwanese Propaganda increases; and *(d)* displays the results of making every Chinese actor consider (at a medium importance level) the economic effects of their actions. These results indicate that Chinese military coercion decreases as the importance of the economic interests increase. This corresponded to the analysts' hypothesis

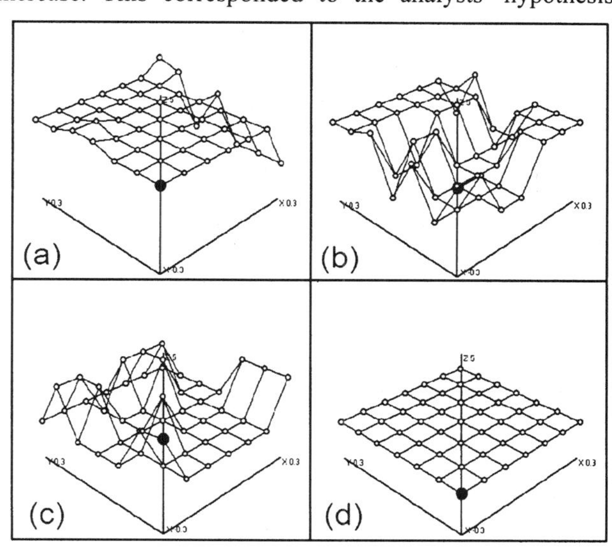


**Figure 7: Multi-simulation surfaces showing the effect of growing economic importance on China's military actions**

that China has resisted military invasion of Taiwan because of possible negative economic consequences. As with the previous example, we used the Interesting Run Finder to identify runs of interest to the analysts.

We have not yet conducted a thorough quantitative evaluation of these models. The next step forward will be traditional verification and validation—does the built model match the analyst's theory, and does that theory describe the real world? So far, we have only used face validation by intelligence analysts as a technique for validating the example models, to see that they "make sense." However, face validation is fraught with problems, due to the complexity of the system and human biases. Quantitative evaluation, on the other hand, can be done at multiple levels, from looking at just the numeric outputs from the world model (to know that the system dynamics are valid), to validation of the agent's knowledge and decision-making processes. Human behavior validation is known to be a difficult problem, and while face validation is the most widely used method, other methods have been suggested (DMSO 2001). In the absence of data at the same abstract level as the model (as is the case here), raw historical data can be re-cast into abstract simulation terms as a reference model. From this, we can perform regression testing against the system output. It must be noted, however, that the abstraction from historical data into a reference model is itself subject to interpretation and bias, so one must be careful in comparing to abstracted reference data or any other selective data set. In the case of the Taiwan Straits crisis, there is little data available in a form that could be compared against the output of the abstract model. Likewise, we have not found other models of the Taiwan Straits scenario against which we might evaluate the results of our models. Validation in general remains a challenging problem for these types of systems. Because we intend AGILE to be deployed to analysts, we expect to include extensions to help users evaluate the goodness of the models they build.

## Discussion

The process of modeling real phenomena in simulation is always challenging, especially as the level of abstraction goes up – the ability to map from reality to an abstract model and back is often considered a black art. This seems especially true when modeling human decision-making. As with any simulation, there are tradeoffs between usability, fidelity, abstraction, explainability, and predictability. The constraint that analysts need to specify agent behavior illustrates this tradeoff. This constraint impacted the design of our agent system, which effectively limits the types of agents a user can specify in AGILE. That is, whatever capabilities are present in the lower tier of agent definition are the only capabilities the user can exploit when specifying the behavior of an agent. We expect that some new capabilities in the agent would require new types of knowledge for agent specification, potentially complicating the job for the user. We have begun to understand some of these tradeoffs, but finding a multi-dimensional "sweet spot" remains a challenge.

In building a system like this, it is very easy to fall into a rut of designing something that makes sense to its designers but not its intended users. Not everyone thinks in the same way, so a display that makes sense to an engineer may not be intuitive to an intelligence analyst. Therefore, it is critically necessary to stay in active engagement with these users, to ensure we answer their needs directly, rather than our interpretation of their needs. This is certainly not a new idea, but a project such as this, where it is difficult to get time with our potential end-users, only reinforces its importance.

While working directly with analysts, we have encountered a range of responses to AGILE. Some users were not familiar with computer simulation as a support tool, so did not see a clear benefit to this approach. Others were reluctant to adopt a technology they perceived as possibly supplanting them. Others still were put off by the overhead of setting up and maintaining the simulations over time. Those who saw the benefit of the tool wanted to obtain it immediately, even in an unfinished state, as they saw its benefit not only as a simulation tool, but also as a way to encode and relate their own knowledge to an analysis problem. This only serves to illustrate that the challenges in building new tools are seldom solely technical or scientific.

## Relationship to other work

Certainly the idea of using agent-based simulation for what-if analysis is not new – there is a rich literature on decision-making models for military simulation (Pew and Mavor 1998). However, little work has been done in agent-based modeling of national-strategic decision-making, where the military is but one component. Furthermore, agents in simulation have traditionally been difficult to employ, and specifying agent behavior for these domains is still regarded as something of an art. Much of our effort here has been in finding a good balance between the native capabilities of the agent and the ease in user specification of agent behavior

The agent system we describe here has taken inspiration from multiple sources, especially from the Multi-Agent Systems community (Casti 1996; Epstein and Axtell 1996) and organizational modeling (Prietula et al. 1998; Carley et al. 2001). Our approach can perhaps be described as a middle ground between the very simple agents of Complex Adaptive Systems (CAS), and much more sophisticated agent behavior, such as those traditionally built using cognitive architectures like Soar. In fact, CAS has been used to model some nation-level phenomena such as policy evolution (Axelrod 1997). However, our focus has been on the decision-making calculus of organizations and their members, rather than on the evolution of system behavior. Therefore, AGILE agents are more sophisticated than CAS agents. Our placement in that spectrum is driven by the need for the agents to be, on the one hand, simple to specify and employ, and on the other hand, still capable of rich, goal-directed behavior that is transparent and explainable to the user.

## Summary and Future Work

We have developed an agent-based simulation framework called AGILE intended for use by intelligence analysts engaged in understanding the complex relationships in geopolitical conflict. AGILE allows intelligence analysts to hypothesize about the relationships between countries, and to explore events and decisions leading up to conflict. Analysts can encode in these models their knowledge about the workings of the target countries, including the major decision-makers, and in this process make explicit their tacit assumptions about the target. This enables them to more readily share their conclusions and results with other analysts. Where, previous to this work, analysts used static formats such as databases and text reports, the idea of building executable models for estimation represents a new paradigm for intelligence analysis.

While we have not yet deployed AGILE to analysts for everyday use, we have engaged them at various points in the development process, to help us build and validate these models, to demonstrate the system, and to elicit their feedback. Based on those interactions, we are currently improving the system capabilities at all levels to more effectively implement the process of hypothesis generation and testing using an agent-based simulation environment. Overall, this effort has demonstrated the richness of the intelligence analysis domain for future AI research.

## Acknowledgements

This work was funded by the US Government. We would like to thank our sponsors and the entire AGILE development team for their dedication to this program over the last four years.

## References

ARDA (2002a). Novel Intelligence From Massive Data (NIMD), Advanced Research and Development Activity.

ARDA (2002b). Advanced Question and Answering for Intelligence, Advanced Research and Development Activity.

Axelrod, R. (1997). The Complexity of Cooperation: Agent-Based Models of Competition and Collaboration. Princeton, NJ, Princeton University Press.

Bratman, M. (1987). Intention, Plans, and Practical Reason. Cambridge, MA, Harvard University Press.

Carley, K. M., J.-S. Lee and D. Krackhardt (2001). "Destabilizing Networks." Connections **24**(3): 31-34.

Casti, J. (1996). Would-Be Worlds: How Simulation Is Changing the Frontiers of Science, John Wiley & Sons.

Dennett, D. C. (1987). The Intentional Stance. Cambridge, MA, The MIT Press.

DMSO (2001). VV&A Recommended Practices Guide, Department of Defense Modeling and Simulation Office.

Epstein, J. M. and R. Axtell (1996). Growing Artificial Societies: Social Science from the Bottom Up. Cambridge, MA, MIT Press.

FIPA (2002). FIPA Contract Net Interaction Protocol Specification. http://www.fipa.org/specs/fipa00029/. [Web document], Foundation for Intelligent Physical Agents.

Heuer, R. J., Jr. (1999). Psychology of Intelligence Analysis. Washington, DC, Center for the Study of Intelligence.

Hill, R. W., J. Chen, J. Gratch, P. S. Rosenbloom and M. Tambe (1997). Intelligent Agents for the Synthetic Battlefield: A Company of Rotary Wing Aircraft. Ninth Conference on Innovative Applications of Artificial Intelligence, AAAI Press.

Jones, R. M., J. E. Laird, P. E. Nielsen, K. J. Coulter, P. G. Kenny and F. V. Koss (1999). "Automated Intelligent Pilots for Combat Flight Simulation." AI Magazine **20**(1): 27-42.

Pew, R. and A. Mavor, Eds. (1998). Modeling Human and Organizational Behavior: Application to Military Simulations. Washington, DC, National Academies Press.

Prietula, M., K. M. Carley and L. Gasser, Eds. (1998). Simulating Organizations: Computational Models of Institutions and Groups. Menlo Park, CA, AAAI Press.

Rao, A. S. and M. P. Georgeff (1991). Modeling Rational Agents within a BDI-Architecture. Second International Conference on Principles of Knowledge Representation and Reasoning, San Mateo, CA, Morgan Kaufmann Publishers.

Rosenbloom, P. S., J. E. Laird and A. Newell, Eds. (1993). The Soar Papers: Research on Integrated Intelligence. Cambridge, MA, MIT Press.

Schwartz, P. (1991). The Art of the Long View: Planning for the Future in an Uncertain World. New York, NY, Doubleday.

Tambe, M., W. L. Johnson, R. M. Jones, F. M. Koss, J. E. Laird, P. S. Rosenbloom and K. B. Schwamb (1995). "Intelligent Agents for Interactive Simulation Environments." AI Magazine **16**(1): 15-39.

Taylor, G., F. Koss and P. E. Nielsen (2001). Special Operations Forces IFORS. Tenth Conference on Computer Generated Forces and Behavioral Representation, Norfolk, VA.

# Artemis: Integrating Scientific Data on the Grid


**Rattapoom Tuchinda, Snehal Thakkar, Yolanda Gil, and Ewa Deelman**

USC Information Sciences Institute
4676 Admiralty Way, Suite 1001
Marina Del Rey, CA 90292
{pipet, thakkar, gil, deelman}@isi.edu



## Abstract

Grid technologies provide a robust infrastructure for distributed computing, and are widely used in large-scale scientific applications that generate terabytes (soon petabytes) of data. These data are described with metadata attributes about the data properties and provenance, and are organized in a variety of metadata catalogs distributed over the grid. In order to find a collection of data that share certain properties, these metadata catalogs need to be identified and queried on an individual basis. This paper introduces Artemis, a system developed to integrate distributed metadata catalogs on the grid. Artemis exploits several AI techniques including a query mediator, a query planning and execution system, ontologies and semantic web tools to model metadata attributes, and an intelligent user interface that guides users through these ontologies to formulate queries. We describe our experiences using Artemis with large metadata catalogs from two projects in the physics domain.


## Introduction

Scientific data analysis is quickly moving to realms that require efficient management of data repositories in the petabyte scale [National Virtual Observatory project (NVO)[1]; Laser Interferometer Gravitational Wave Observatory (LIGO)[2]; Earth System Grid (ESG)[3]; Southern California Earthquake center (SCEC)[4]]. Grid technologies [Foster and Kesselman 99; Foster et al 01] are used to manage distributed resources: compute, data, instruments etc across organizational boundaries. Middleware, such as the Globus Toolkit[5], enable the discovery of remote resources and access to them in a secure fashion. Grids support the distributed management of large data sets through secure and efficient data transfer, storage resource management, and data replica management. Grids also enable distributed, large-scale, computation and data intensive analysis. Grids are very dynamic: the availability of the resources may vary significantly over time.

Although grids make many large data repositories available, integrating them in a highly dynamic distributed environment is a challenge. Metadata catalogs address some of these problems by supporting queries to data based on metadata attributes of the files and managing collections of data as well as versioning and provenance information [Moore et al 01, Singh et al 03]. Mediator techniques can be used to integrate diverse data sources [Levy 2000] but have not been used in grid environments that are extremely dynamic. Data sources can appear, be temporarily unavailable or disappear, change contents or access mechanism, and migrate to different locations. These changes are not only at the implementation and installation level, but also at the conceptual level in terms of the metadata used to describe and index their contents. As scientists model scientific phenomena and analyze large data sets, they generate new data products that need to be described using possibly new metadata that needs to be incorporated in the repository. In addition to operating in this very dynamic environment, scientific applications need to support a high degree of heterogeneity in the data. This is because they are often multidisciplinary efforts that integrate results from complementary observations and analysis of the same underlying phenomenon. That phenomenon may be described in different ways in different disciplines or modeling environments.

This paper describes Artemis, a query formulation and planning system that enables users to easily query metadata catalogs on the grid. It includes a query mediator based on planning techniques that dynamically updates its domain model, and an ontology-based query formulation system that helps a user create and refine queries interactively based on the current contents of the repositories. Artemis is integrated with an existing Metadata Catalog Service (MCS), which is based on the widely used Globus toolkit for grid computing. We have evaluated Artemis with data from two different scientific domains.

Artemis illustrates the potential of Artificial Intelligence techniques for data integration on the grid, and complements prior work on Pegasus, a workflow generation and mapping system for grid computing [Blythe et al 03; Deelman et al 03 Gil et al 04]. As Pegasus continues to be used in a variety of scientific domains to



[1] http://www.us-vo.org
[2] http://ligo.caltech.edu
[3] http://www.earthsystemgrid.org
[4] http://www.scec.org/cme
[5] http://www.globus.org

map, manage and execute workflows with hundreds of thousands of jobs and terabytes of data products [Deelman et al 04], the need to provide grids with a system like Artemis becomes more immediate.

The paper begins by outlining the key problems to be addressed in dynamic heterogeneous query planning. After describing Artemis in detail, we discuss our experiences to date integrating data from real scientific applications and the future extensions that are needed to support data integration on the grid.

## Motivation

Science today is conducted in a collaborative fashion. In order to enable scientific discovery, collaborations encompass numerous researchers sharing computation, data and network resources, and instruments. Additionally, scientists share their applications and data not only in the raw form, but processed in some fashion.

Because of the size of the data, terabytes today, and petabytes in the near future, data is often distributed and replicated in the environment. Additionally, metadata—descriptive data about particular data products—is often stored and queried separately from the data itself. The metadata may be distributed as well. For example, in the case of the LIGO scientific collaboration that encompasses scientists from the US LIGO as well as the GEO[6] efforts (a British-German gravitational-wave detector experiment) scientists share the data collected independently in the US and in Europe. Each of the experiments: LIGO and GEO publish their data and their metadata to the Grid independently of the other experiments. Additionally, even after publication, the LIGO and GEO metadata may evolve independently of each other.

In order to conduct cross-correlation studies between the LIGO and GEO data, scientists need to discover the necessary data products in distributed metadata catalogs. However, it may be difficult for a LIGO researcher to fully understand the GEO metadata. After identifying the desired data products through the metadata queries, researchers can locate and access the corresponding data.

The metadata being published by experiments is often not the definitive set of descriptive attributes. As the understanding of the data collected increases, the attributes may change or may be augmented to include the new information. For example, it is often the case that raw data is of no scientific value unless it is carefully calibrated. Calibration is not an easy process and is often iterative. Consequently, the metadata changes as the calibrations are updated.

The LIGO/GEO metadata integration problem is in some sense simple, because the metadata comes from the same discipline. More complex issues arise when the metadata crosses discipline boundaries. For example, a gravitational wave scientist may want to identify potential objects in the sky based on a hypothesis that these particular objects (such as pulsars for example) can be a potential source of gravitational waves. In order to identify these sources, the scientist may want to search astronomy databases. Astronomy data sets are published by different entities (representing a particular telescope or mission for example) and include diverse metadata. Thus, a gravitational-wave scientist needs to be able to locate, query, and interpret these astronomy-specific distributed metadata sources.

[6] http://www.geo600.uni-hannover.de/

In summary, three key problems need to be addressed:

- **Dynamic updates of sources:** A given metadata catalog may change over time not only in content, but also in the definitions and structure of the metadata. Each time a scientist processes data or runs a simulation, new data is generated that may need to be described with attributes that did not exist before in the catalog. New metadata types are continually being incorporated.
- **Integrating multiple sources:** Answering a single user request may require a sequence of queries to various catalogs as well as integrating intermediate results.
- **Bridging user requirements and system metadata across disciplines:** Users that are expert in a certain scientific discipline may need to access data in other sciences but may be unfamiliar with the terms and structure of the metadata. Metadata for different scientific disciplines or groups are naturally defined or structured differently, and are continuously and asynchronously redefined or restructured as scientific advances take place. This accentuates the already challenging problem of mapping a user's terms to the terms that are known to the system.

The next section describes our approach to address these challenges integrating several Artificial Intelligence techniques that include query mediation, planning, ontologies, semantic web languages and tools, and intelligent user interfaces.

## Artemis: An Interactive Query Mediator for Distributed Metadata Catalogs

We developed Artemis, an interactive query planning system that integrates metadata catalogs available on the grid. Figure 1 shows the architecture of the Artemis system. The goal of the Artemis system is to enable the user to easily query various objects stored in different data sources. Metadata catalogs, such as the Metadata Catalog Service (MCS) [Singh et al 03] store the metadata about different objects in different data sources on the grid. Artemis utilizes data integration techniques in conjunction with an interactive query builder to enable the user to easily create complex queries to obtain objects that match user criteria.

In this section, first we briefly discuss the MCS. Next, we describe the process of dynamically generating various data models based on the information from the Metadata Catalog Services. Then, we show how the Prometheus mediator is used in the Artemis system. Finally, we explain an interactive query building component of the Artemis system termed MCS Wizard.

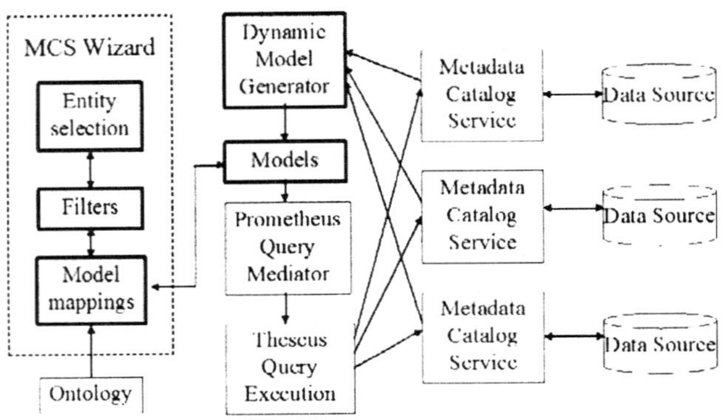


Figure 1. The Architecture of Artemis. The components in the lighter boxes are pre-existing modules, while the components in the darker boxes are developed specifically for Artemis. Note that Artemis is capable of integrating an arbitrary number of data sources

## Metadata Catalog Services

Artemis utilizes the Metadata Catalog Service (MCS) [Singh et al 03] that has been developed as part of the Grid Physics Network (GriPhyN)[7] and NVO projects. The aim of these projects is to support large-scale scientific experiments. MCS is a standalone catalog that stores information about logical data items (e.g., files). It also allows users to aggregate the data items into collections and views. MCS provides system-defined as well as user-defined attributes for logical items, collections and views. One distinguishing characteristic of MCS is that users can dynamically define and add metadata attributes. MCS can also provide the names of the user-defined attributes. As a result, different MCS instances can be created with alternative contents. In our implementation, we assume that different MCS instances contain disjoint information. This assumption is not necessary for Artemis as it can handle replicated metadata, rather, it is dictated by the difficulty of maintaining the consistency of updates in a wide area network, which is typically part of a grid's networking infrastructure. For example, if two MCS instances contain the same information, when one MCS is updated the second one should be updated at the same time. Guaranteeing this level of consistency is very expensive in the wide area network and is beyond the scope of this work. Each data item in an MCS is described with a set of metadata expressed as attribute-value pairs. Some attributes are common metadata, such as creation date, name, author, etc (see for example, the Dublin Core[8]). Other attributes represent user-defined metadata and are typically specific to the domain and the contents of the files. Additionally, the set of attributes can be different for each item.

An MCS can be queried for files by specifying values for any attribute. In addition to items, the MCS can be queried for collections and views. Collections are usually created to group related items together. For example, if one experiment results in ten items, a collection can be created for those items. All items in the collection may have their own metadata. In addition, a collection can have its own metadata as well. Collections usually represent an organization of the data imposed by the data publisher and may carry authorization information. Views are similar to collections but rather than being defined by the data publisher, they are defined by users based on their own grouping of items. As such, views do not impose authorization constraints on the items they contain. Both collections and views may have a hierarchical structure.

The MCS architecture is very flexible because it easily supports the addition of new content with novel metadata that was not previously defined in the MCS. This flexibility presents a challenge to the problem of integrating multiple MCS sources for two reasons:

- **Rapidly changing metadata:** Since new items, views and collections can be added to an MCS at any time and each may contain a new type of attribute, it is not possible to define a model of the contents of an MCS a priori. This is one of the novel issues addressed in our work in integrating the mediator. Although mediators have mechanisms to handle dynamic data sources, MCS content varies more rapidly.
- **Lack of semantic specifications of metadata attributes:** the current MCS architecture does not include mechanisms to attach semantic information to the metadata attributes within an MCS (other than their type—string, integer, etc.,) or to indicate definitions shared across multiple MCS instances. Metadata such as the time interval for an observation with an instrument may be expressed in a variety of ways such as a start and end times, or as a start time and duration, or duration, etc. The same attribute may also be stored with different names. When several MCS instances are available, a user has to analyze their metadata attributes by hand and formulate different queries as appropriate for each of them.

[7] http://www.griphyn.org/index.php

[8] http://dublincore.org/documents/dces

We address the first issue by dynamically creating models of the information available in various Metadata Catalog Services. We address the second issue by using ontologies to describe, map, and organize metadata information. The next section describes the process of dynamically generating models of the metadata.

## Dynamic Model Generation

The dynamic model generator creates a relational model of the entities available in the metadata catalogs. As we described earlier the Metadata Catalog Service utilizes an object-oriented model to allow the user to associate different metadata with each item in the catalog. While the object-oriented model provides user with a greater flexibility by allowing them to define arbitrary metadata attributes for any item, the data integration techniques target mainly relational models. Thus, in our work, the dynamic model generator first needs to create a relation domain model for the mediator by querying various metadata catalogs specified in the metadata layer.

Domain models are generated dynamically in four steps:

1. For each entity type supported by the MCS instances (e.g. items, collections, and views) Artemis queries all the MCS instances and finds all the attribute types.
2. For each entity type Artemis creates a domain predicate and sets its arguments to the list of attributes found in the previous step.
3. For each MCS and entity type Artemis creates a source predicate whose arguments are the list of attributes for the given entity type in that MCS. It also adds the *Itemname* attribute to the source arguments. The *Itemname* attribute is returned to the user, so the user can obtain the item from the Grid using the *Itemname*.

The original MCS did not support the queries described in step 1 above. As a result of the Artemis project, the MCS API was extended to accommodate this functionality.

Artemis creates domain rules for the mediator to relate the source predicates from step 3 to the domain predicates from step 2. If the MCS does not have some attributes in the attribute list Artemis uses a constant "empty" to denote the missing attribute.

For example, consider two simplified Metadata Catalog Services shown in Table 1.[9]

| MCS | Object Type | Attributes |
|---|---|---|
| MCS 1 | Item | keyword, starttime, endtime |
| MCS 2 | Item | ci, about, sttime, etime |

**Table 1: Example of two MCS instances.**

[9] For simplicity, we assume just one entity type. Both MCS and Artemis can support multiple entity types.

MCS 1 contains metadata for objects of type item. The metadata is described by the following attributes: keyword, starttime, endtime. Similarly MCS 2 also contains metadata for objects of type item. However, the metadata in MCS 2 is described by different attributes. The dynamic model generator creates the following domain model for the mediator.

```
items(keyword, starttime, endtime,ci,about, sttime, etime)
:-
  Mcs1items(keyword, starttime, endtime)^
  (ci = "empty")^
  (about = "empty")^
  (sttime = "empty")^
  (etime = "empty")

items(keyword, starttime,endtime,ci, about, sttime, etime)
:-
  Mcs2items(ci, about, sttime, etime)^
  (keyword = "empty")^
  (starttime = "empty")^
  (endtime = "empty")
```

The domain model states that objects of type item can be queried based on the following attributes: *keyword, starttime, endtime, ci, about, sttime*, and *etime*. The attribute list is a combination of attributes of both MCS instances. Furthermore, to obtain information about the objects of type item, Artemis needs to query both MCS instances and then it needs to construct the union of the resulting objects.

In general, MCS catalogs can be updated at any time. The frequency of updates can depend on the type of application and/or situation. For example, astronomy metadata may not vary too frequently once it is curated and published by the collaboration to the broad astronomy community. However, it may change often soon after the data is collected by a telescope, when it is made available to the researchers that are part of the initial collaboration.

Currently, Artemis regenerates the domain model for each query. However, as the number of metadata catalogs grows, it may become very expensive to regenerate the domain model for each query. In the future, Artemis may query individual MCS instances to find out whether there have been new attributes added and only then regenerate its model. Alternatively the MCS can be augmented with the capability to send out notifications to subscribed systems when changes to the attribute definitions are made.

## Mapping Models to Ontology

The model mapping module shown in Figure 1 is used to attach semantics to the models generated by the dynamic model generator. This step is very important as it enables the user to compose the query using the terms in the ontology. This module generates the mappings between the terms defined in the metadata catalogs and the concepts represented in an ontology by interactively asking the user to map different terms from the model to the concepts in the ontology. The model mapping module is currently limited in scope. Much research is still needed to fully support semantic interoperability and semantic data integration, but we believe that current technology may already have a great impact by improving the current state of the art of metadata services on the grid.

The model mapping module can include several alternative ontologies, each with its own scope and expressive power. Each ontology contains a set of associated mappings of the attributes in each MCS to the terms in that ontology. For each primitive type in an ontology, there exist predicates that specify the types of constraints that can be used in queries for that type. For example, a query over a numeric type can specify comparison or range constraints. If an attribute is mapped to a numeric type in the ontology then only such queries are semantically valid.

In our current implementation, we create the mappings and the predicates manually. An important area of future work is to create them dynamically. As users add new metadata attributes to an MCS, they should be required to provide additional information that can be used to create the necessary mappings. This will require a tighter integration of the model mapping module with the MCS architecture, and will require modifications to the API specification of the current MCS. We anticipate that this will be a complex process but one that could have significant impact for the scientist utilizing the grid system. We can illustrate the process using the example shown in Table 1. The user may elect to use an ontology that contains the concepts: *keyword, city*, and *time-range*. The user then needs to specify that the concept *keyword* maps to the keyword *attribute* in MCS 1 and the attribute *about* in MCS 2. Similarly, the city concept maps to the ci attribute in MCS 2. Finally, the starttime, endtime, sttime, and etime attributes map to the time-range concept.

We have used semantic web languages and tools to develop the model mapping component. The ontologies are expressed in OWL[10]. We use Jena's[11] RDQL to query the ontology about its contents, for example for the hierarchical structure of the ontology. The interactive query formulation system described next generates questions for users based on the contents of the ontologies, and helps them formulate queries for the Prometheus mediator based on the mappings between the models and the ontologies.

## Data Integration using Prometheus

Artemis uses Prometheus, a mediator system that supports uniform access to heterogeneous data sources, including web services, web sources, and databases [Thakkar et al 03]. Prometheus uses planning techniques to expand a given query into a set of operations that specify how to access the appropriate data sources.

[10] http://www.w3.org/TR/2002/WD-owl-guide-20021104/
[11] http://jena.sourceforge.net/

The Prometheus mediator receives the user's query in a form of a query on the domain predicates. This query is received from the user interface. The mediator utilizes the given query and the domain model generated by the dynamic model generator to obtain a datalog program to answer the user query. As various metadata catalogs may be widely distributed in the wide area, some catalogs may take a long time to respond to the query. Therefore, it is important to query the metadata catalogs in parallel. The Prometheus mediator utilizes the Theseus execution engine [Barish and Knoblock 03] to efficiently execute the generated datalog program. The Theseus execution engine has a wide variety of operations to query databases, web sources, and web services. Theseus also contains a wide variety of relational operations, such as, selection, union, or projection. Furthermore, Theseus optimizes the execution of an integration plan by querying several data sources in parallel and streaming data between operations.

In the original MCS, the user had to query each individual MCS in turn and combine the results by hand. With Artemis, the user can seamlessly query across the various MCS catalogs and obtain combined results. The desired result set can be further refined through the Artemis interface. For example, if the first query returns too many objects, the user may want to add additional constraints on the attribute values. In the original MCS the user would have to again query all the catalogs with the new query. However, with Artemis, the constraint can be directly applied to the initial results. The burden of issuing the new queries is shifted from the user to the system.

Using this domain model, the mediator system can answer queries to obtain items, views, or collections that satisfy the query. However, the mediator requires that the queries are formulated in terms of its domain model and therefore in terms of the MCS metadata attributes that will be unfamiliar to users. The interactive query formulation system that we describe next addresses this problem.

## Interactively Composing Queries using MCS Wizard

Artemis includes the MCS Wizard, an interactive query builder based on the idea in the Agent Wizard [Tuchinda and Knoblock 04]. The Agent Wizard allows users to build a complex agent by guiding users through a list of questions. The MCS Wizard follows a similar approach. To generate a set of simplified questions to pose to the user, the MCS Wizard takes the model generated by the dynamic model generator and exploits the previously created ontology.

Figure 2 shows the sequence of steps in the MCS Wizard. The MCS Wizard begins its interaction with the user by asking what ontology they would like to use and what type of object (items, collections, views) they would like to query. Based on the response, it helps the user formulate the query by navigating through the class hierarchy and the predicates that can be used to define the query expressions. The user is guided through the classes until the query is specified in terms of the classes that have mappings to attributes that exist in the MCS instances.

The MCS Wizard then queries the mediator and presents the user with the answers. The MCS Wizard allows the user to refine the query if the results retrieved are not satisfactory. This is an important capability since queries are likely to return empty results because users will typically be unfamiliar with the contents of the MCS catalogs. An important area for future extension of the MCS Wizard is to generate guidance to the user in terms of how to reformulate or relax the query in order to find relevant contents by analyzing the intermediate results generated by the mediator.

To illustrate the user interaction with MCS wizard we use an example scenario where the user would like to find all objects present in the two MCS instances described in Table 1 that contain atmospheric data. In the first step, the user picks the ontology containing the concepts: *keyword, city*, and *time-range*. Next, the user picks the object type *item* and specifies the mapping between the attributes and the concepts in the ontology. Next, the MCS Wizard asks which concepts the user wants to query on. The user picks for example the concept *keyword* and specifies that the keyword must contain the term *atmospheric data*. The MCS Wizard generates the following queries for the Prometheus mediator:

Q1(keyword, starttime,endtime,ci, about, sttime, etime):-
items(keyword, starttime,endtime,ci, about, sttime, etime)^
(keyword contains 'atmospheric data')

Q1(keyword, starttime,endtime,ci, about, sttime, etime):-
items(keyword, starttime,endtime,ci, about, sttime, etime)
(about contains 'atmospheric data')

The query states that the mediator should find all items that have an attribute *keyword* containing atmospheric data or an attribute *about* atmospheric data. The Prometheus mediator queries both MCS instances and finds the relevant objects. The MCS Wizard shows the relevant objects to the user.

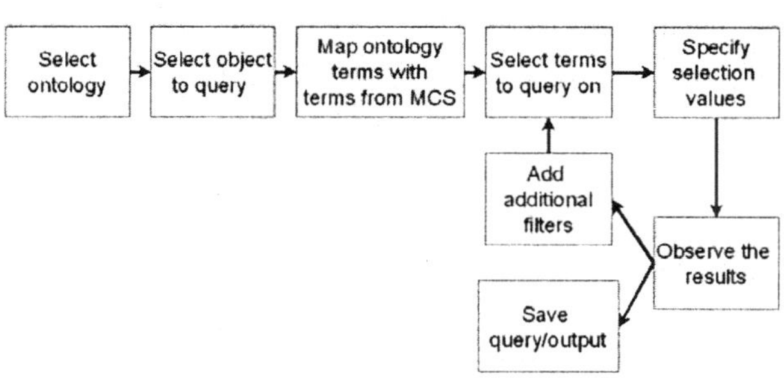


Figure 2. Building a query using MCS Wizard

## Experiences to Date with Scientific Data Sources

We evaluated the effectiveness of our system by integrating 12 MCS services. These MCS catalogs contained information from three different systems: ESG, LIGO, and National Imagery and Mapping Association (NIMA)[12] Feature Vector data information covering different areas of the world. The NIMA Feature Vector data consists of 17,000 files that provide information about different feature vectors, such as road networks and railroad networks in different areas. We added this data to increase the complexity of the system. In total, the 12 MCS services contained information about 30,000 different files. On an average, each file had 50 attributes. Our goal was to be able to allow users to easily query for different files with different metadata using a simple interface.

We created our own ontology in OWL to define domain specific attributes as well as spatial attributes. We used an existing time ontology [Pan 2004] to map temporal attributes. This ontology mapped attribute names from different MCS instances with attribute names more familiar to users. Once the ontology and the mappings were created, Artemis users were able to build queries using terms from the ontology.

To test that Artemis would work even when metadata in MCS instances were updated or one of the services went down, we manually added metadata to one of the MCS services as Artemis was running. Then, we used the Artemis system to build a new query. During the dynamic model generation Artemis recognized the addition of the new MCS and built a domain model that included the new metadata.

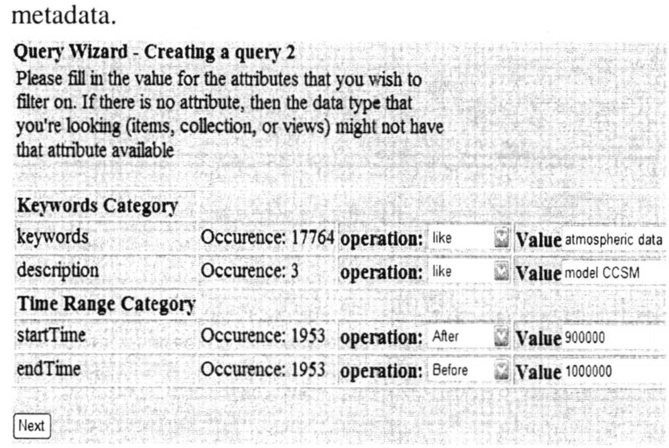


Figure 3. User interaction with MCS wizard

Figure 3 shows an example interaction aimed at finding a set of items that has "atmospheric data" in the *keywords* attribute, contains "model CCSM" in the *description*

[12] http://www.nima.mil

attribute, and has *starttime* and *endtime* of the data between 900000 and 1000000. First, the user picks *item* as the type of entity from the list of entity types (e.g., *items, views*, and *collections*). Next, the user selects terms from the ontology on which the user wants to put conditions. Next, the user is presented with a set of options to create filters on selected terms (e.g., *keywords* with filter operation "contains" on "atmospheric data", *description* with filter operation "contains" on "model CCSM") as shown in Figure 3. The time range query component is specified through the *starttime*'s operation "After" and the *endtime*'s operation "Before." The MCS wizard then formulates and sends the corresponding query to the mediator. The resulting list of items returned from the mediator is shown to the user. The user then has the option to either save the list of item names or to further refine the query.

If a user were to query the items based on three terms in the ontology, the user would need, on average, twelve simple mouse clicks in the MCS wizard interface to obtain the results. If the user were to perform these queries without using the Artemis system, the user would have to formulate separate query expressions to each of the MCS services. Furthermore, using Artemis, the user only needs to know the terms in the ontology instead of having to know attribute names from each of the 12 MCS instances. Overall, our experiences have shown that Artemis is able to cope with the three challenges outlined in the paper.

## Related Work

The myGrid project [Wroe et al 03] is developing and exploiting semantic web technology to describe and integrate a wide range of services in a grid environment. Data sources are modeled as semantic web services, and are integrated through web service composition languages. The result is a workflow that may include not only steps to access to data sources as in Artemis, but also as simulation or other data processing steps. The workflows are generated by instantiating pre-defined workflow templates, while Artemis generates the entire set of access queries to the different data sources automatically and dynamically.

In [Ludäscher et al 03], the authors describe a mediator-based system that utilizes the semantics of the data exported by the data sources to integrate the data. A key assumption in that work is that the data sources export the semantics of the data. However, as we showed earlier, the MCS contains very weak semantic information. Thus, Artemis is not only responsible for integrating data from various MCS instances, but also assigning semantics to data from various MCS instances.

Recently, view integration researchers have developed various systems to integrate information from various data sources. A good survey of the view integration techniques is available in [Levy 2000]. Traditionally, view integration systems assume that a domain model is given by domain experts to the mediator system. In our case, the Artemis system automatically generates the domain model by reading information from various MCS instances.

## Conclusions and Future Work

We described Artemis, a system that integrates distributed metadata catalogs in grid computing environments. Artemis exploits several AI techniques including a query mediator, a query planning and execution system, as well as ontologies and semantic web tools, and intelligent user interfaces. Artemis can automatically generate models of the data sources in order to dynamically incorporate new metadata attributes as they appear in the catalogs when new data items are added to the collection. Artemis isolates the users from the complexity of using distributed heterogeneous catalogs. It does so by providing interactive assistance to formulate valid, integrated queries using a single ontology that is automatically mapped to the particular metadata of each catalog.

We also plan to convert the existing system into a service. The Prometheus mediator and the Agent Wizard are already available as web services. The MCS is also implemented as either a web or grid service. Once Artemis is converted to the grid service, the user will be able to check status of their requests, by checking status of the service. This feature would be very useful when the number of MCS is very large as the user queries may take a long time to execute.

Another important improvement would be to add query reformulation capabilities to the mediator, so that it will be able to exploit the ontologies to reformulate queries.

An interesting test for Artemis will be the National Virtual Observatory (NVO) project, where a diversity of catalog services exist or are being created to store data collected from various telescopes. The catalog services will include not only MCS-based services but also other catalogs that will have a different structure. The architecture of Artemis and its mediator system are well suited to support heterogeneity of data sources. A single access point to such a large heterogeneous collection of data would enable rapid analysis of astronomy observations.

Scientific end-to-end workflows should integrate both data retrieval and data analysis steps. Artemis could provide the former, while the Pegasus system [Deelman et al 04] could provide the latter. The Artemis mediator already has mechanisms for robust execution of queries, while these capabilities are still being incorporated into Pegasus. Combining the capabilities of both systems to generate complete workflows will be an important area of future research.

Ideally, end users would want to query the collection using their own ontologies and definitions. The grid has much need for semantic web technology to support individual and community-based descriptions of data in a distributed setting. With systems like Artemis illustrating the added value and ultimate potential of Artificial

Intelligence techniques for data integration, the grid community is more likely to embrace this technology. This adoption would satisfy the requirements posed by complex and ambitious applications, scientific and otherwise.

## Acknowledgements

We would like to thank Gurmeet Singh for the development and setup of MCS and Craig Knoblock for useful comments on the paper.

This material is based upon work supported in part by the National Science Foundation, under Award No. IIS-0324955, in part by the Air Force Office of Scientific Research under grant number F49620-01-1-0053, in part by a gift from the Microsoft Corporation, and in part by the National Science Foundation under grants ITR-0086044 (GriPhyN), AST0122449 (NVO) and EAR-0122464 (SCEC/ITR). The views and conclusions contained herein are those of the author and should not be interpreted as necessarily representing the official policies or endorsements, either expressed or implied, of any of the above organizations or any person connected with them.

## References

Annis, J., Zhao, Y., Voeckler, J., Wilde, M., Kent, S. and Foster, I., Applying Chimera Virtual Data Concepts to Cluster Finding in the Sloan Sky Survey. in *Supercomputing*. 2002. Baltimore, MD.

Barish, G. and C.A. Knoblock. An Expressive and Efficient Language for Information Gathering on the Web. Proceedings of the Sixth International Conference on AI Planning and Scheduling (AIPS-2002) Workshop: Is There Life Beyond Operator Sequencing? - Exploring Real-World Planning. 2002. Toulouse, France.

Berners-Lee, T., James Hendler and Ora Lassila. "The Semantic Web" *Scientific American*, May 2001.

Blythe, J., Deelman, E., Gil, Y., and Kesselman, C. "Transparent Grid Computing: A Knowledge-Based Approach". Proceedings of the Fifteenth Annual Conference on Innovative Applications of Artificial Intelligence (IAAI), August 2003, Acapulco, Mexico.

Deelman, E., Blythe, J., Gil, Y., Kesselman, C., Mehta, G., Patil, S., Su, M., Vahi, K. Pegasus: Mapping Scientific Workflows onto the Grid. To appear in the Proceedings of across Grid EU Conference, 2004.

Deelman, E., Blythe, J., Gil, Y., Kesselman, C., Mehta, G.,Vahi, K., Blackburn, K., Lazzarini, A., Arbree, A., Cavanaugh, R., and Koranda, S. Mapping Abstract Complex Workflows onto Grid Environments, Journal of Grid Computing, Vol.1, no. 1, 2003, pp. 25-39.

Foster, I. and C. Kesselman, Eds. *The Grid: Blueprint for a New Computing Infrastructure*. 1999, Morgan Kaufmann.

Foster, I., C. Kesselman, and S. Tuecke, The Anatomy of the Grid: Enabling Scalable Virtual Organizations. *International Journal of High Performance Computing Applications*, 2001. 15(3): p. 200-222.

Gil, Y., Deelman, E., Blythe, J., Kesselman, C., and Tangmunarunkit, H., Artificial Intelligence and Grids: Workflow Planning and Beyond. IEEE Intelligent Systems Special Issue on E-Science, Vol. 19, No. 1, Jan/Feb 2004.

Gil, Y., De Roure, D., and Hendler, J. (Eds) Guest Editor's Introduction to the IEEE Intelligent Systems Special Issue on E-Science, Vol. 19, No. 1, Jan/Feb 2004.

Levy, A., Logic-Based Techniques in Data Integration, in Logic Based Artificial Intelligence, J. Minker, Ed. 2000, Kluwer Publishers.

Ludäscher, B., Gupta, A., and Martone M. E. A Model-Based Mediator System for Scientific Data Management, B. In T. Critchlow and Z. Lacroix, editors, Bioinformatics: Managing Scientific Data. Morgan Kaufmann, 2003.

Moore R. W., *Boisvert, R., and Tang, P,* Data Management Systems for Scientific Applications. *"The Architecture of Scientific Software," pp. 273-284, Kluwer Academic Publishers,* 2001.

Pan, F. and J.R. Hobbs. Time in OWL-S. To Appear In Proceedings of the AAAI Spring Symposium, 2004.

Singh, G., S. Bharathi, A. Chervenak, E. Deelman, C. Kesselman, M. Manohar, S. Patil, and L. Pearlman. A Metadata Catalog Service for Data Intensive Applications. Proceedings of the Supercomputing Conference, November 2003.

Thakkar, S. and C.A. Knoblock. Efficient Execution of Recursive Integration Plans. Proceeding of 2003 IJCAI Workshop on Information Integration on the Web. 2003. Acapulco, Mexico.

Thakkar, S., J.-L. Ambite, and C.A. Knoblock. A view integration approach to dynamic composition of web services. In Proceedings of 2003 ICAPS Workshop on Planning for Web Services. 2003. Trento, Italy.

Tuchinda, R. and C.A. Knoblock. AgentWizard: Building Information Agents by Answering Questions. Proceedings of the 2004 International Conference on Intelligent User Interfaces. 2004. Portugal.

Wroe, C., R. Stevens, C. Goble, A. Roberts, and M. Greenwood. (2003). "A Suite of DAML+OIL ontologies to describe bioinformatics web services and data". To appear in *Journal of Cooperative Information Science.*

# An Explainable Artificial Intelligence System for Small-unit Tactical Behavior

**Michael van Lent**
The Institute for Creative Technologies, The University of Southern California
13274 Fiji Way, Marina del Rey, CA 90292 USA
vanlent@ict.usc.edu

**William Fisher, Michael Mancuso**
Quicksilver Software, Inc.
Irvine, CA USA
bfisher@quicksilver.com, mmancuso@quicksilver.com

**Abstract**

As the artificial intelligence (AI) systems in military simulations and computer games become more complex, their actions become increasingly difficult for users to understand. Expert systems for medical diagnosis have addressed this challenge though the addition of explanation generation systems that explain a system's internal processes. This paper describes the AI architecture and associated explanation capability used by Full Spectrum Command, a training system developed for the U.S. Army by commercial game developers and academic researchers.

## Introduction

Full Spectrum Command (FSC) is a "commercial platform training aid" developed by the USC Institute for Creative Technologies and Quicksilver Software, Inc. for the U.S. Army. A commercial platform training aid is a computer game designed not for entertainment, but as a training tool to achieve a targeted training objective. Like most video games and training simulations, Full Spectrum Command includes a significant artificial intelligence (AI) system that controls the behavior of the user's subordinate units and the opposing forces. This complex AI system, which controls up to 200 entities and uses 60% of the CPU's processing cycles, is an excellent example of game industry AI technology, a branch of AI little studied by the academic research community. In addition, Full Spectrum Command includes an Explainable AI (XAI) feature that is the result of an academic research effort motivated by previous work in systems such as Mycin (Shortliffe 1976), Debrief (Johnson 1994), and the Explainable Expert System (Swartout, Paris and Moore 1994). The goal of this paper is to describe the XAI system and its application in Full Spectrum Command. However, this requires an understanding of the AI system in FSC that controls the Non-Player Characters (NPCs) (i.e. the computer controlled soldiers). This NPC AI is interesting in its own right as an example of a game industry AI system, including the methodologies and technologies employed by game developers.

Video games are probably the largest commercial applications of artificial intelligence today. Many video game reviews, in magazines or on the web, use the quality of a game's AI as a major criterion for evaluation. Most game developers list "AI Programmer" as a job title and game technology conferences include numerous talks on advances in AI technology. While a number of researchers are working to apply research techniques to video games (Laird and van Lent 2001, Young et. al., 2004), few researchers have studied and reported on the AI techniques being developed by the video game industry. Describing FSC's NPC AI system will providing one example of an AI system developed by a commercial game developer.

In the military modeling and simulation community the academic AI research community is well-represented and state-of-the-art AI technologies are being used in many systems (Laird, Jones and Neilsen 1994). Interestingly, in both games and military simulations as the AI systems get more complicated and generate more complex behaviors a new problem arises. The correlation between a player or human controller's orders and the AI-controlled entity's behavior sometimes becomes less obvious as the AI becomes more sophisticated. One solution is to extend the AI systems so they can explain their behavior either during execution or after the fact. Ideally, this Explainable AI can present the user with an easily understood chain of reasoning from the user's order, through the AI's knowledge and inference, to the resulting behavior.

Full Spectrum Command includes an Explainable AI system that allows the user to click on any subordinate soldier during the after-action review phase of the game and ask that soldier questions about the current behavior of its platoon. In addition, the Explainable AI identifies key events to be highlighted in the after-action review.

The next section of this paper describes the Full Spectrum Command commercial platform training aid.

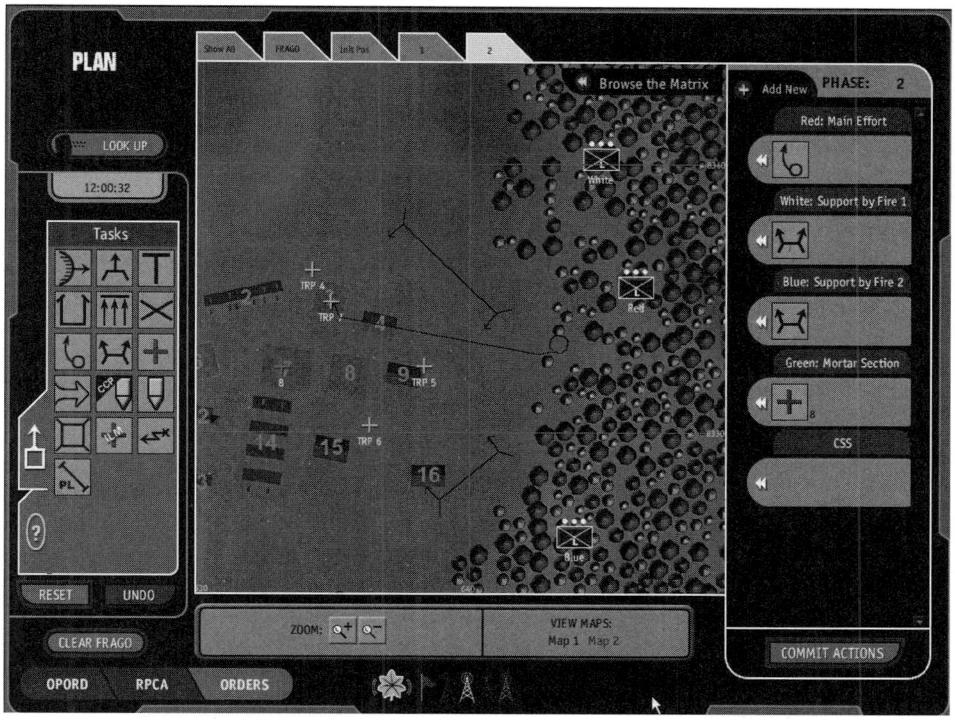


Figure 1: The execution matrix development screen from the planning phase. The column on the right is one phase of an execution matrix populated with a task for each of four platoons. A fifth platoon has no task assigned.

The following section gives a detailed overview of the game's AI system. The next section describes the Explainable AI system in more detail and fits it into the context of previous work on explanation systems. The fifth section details the deployment of Full Spectrum Command and provides some feedback and evaluation results. Finally, the last section describes a number of directions for future research that could improve the effectiveness of the Explainable AI system.

## Full Spectrum Command

Unlike traditional video games, which are designed for entertainment and profitability, Full Spectrum Command is designed to train and exercise the cognitive skills involved in commanding a light infantry company. However, this doesn't mean that FSC isn't entertaining. Entertainment is used as a powerful tool to increase the application's effectiveness as a training system. Because FSC is engaging, soldiers spend more time using the training aid and even choose to train in their free time.

Full Spectrum Command is a Windows XP application that requires a 2GHz Pentium 4 processor, 512 MB of system RAM, and a GeForce4 graphics accelerator with 128 MB of video RAM. In the training aid the user is placed in the role of a U.S. Light Infantry Company Commander with the rank of Captain. The user controls about 120 soldiers who are divided into 3-5 platoons and associated elements. The FSC missions focus on urban combat against an asymmetric opponent (i.e. terrorists and insurgents who don't wear uniforms or fight as an organized military unit). The game's virtual environment recreates the physical urban combat training site located at Ft. Benning, GA. Called the McKenna MOUT (Military Operations, Urban Terrain) site, this is where light infantry company commanders conduct live training exercise in urban combat. Our virtual McKenna can be populated with up to 80 civilians and opposing soldiers and configured for daytime or nighttime missions.

Full Spectrum Command's game-play is most similar to the Real Time Strategy (RTS) game genre which includes games such as Warcraft and Age of Empires. In RTS games the player acts as a commander controlling the gathering of resources, production of units, and issuing orders to these units in battles against one or more opponent commanders. In most RTS games the player views the world from a top-down or "God's eye" view.

Full Spectrum Command differs from traditional RTS games in a number of key ways. First, FSC doesn't include the resource gathering and unit production aspects of most RTS games. In the game, as in real life, company commanders begin each mission with an assigned company of soldiers that may or may not be at full strength. A "mission" in FSC proceeds in three phases: planning, execution, and after-action review. In the planning phase the user reads the operation order (the goal and details of the assigned mission), organizes the composition of his forces, and creates an initial plan for the entire mission.

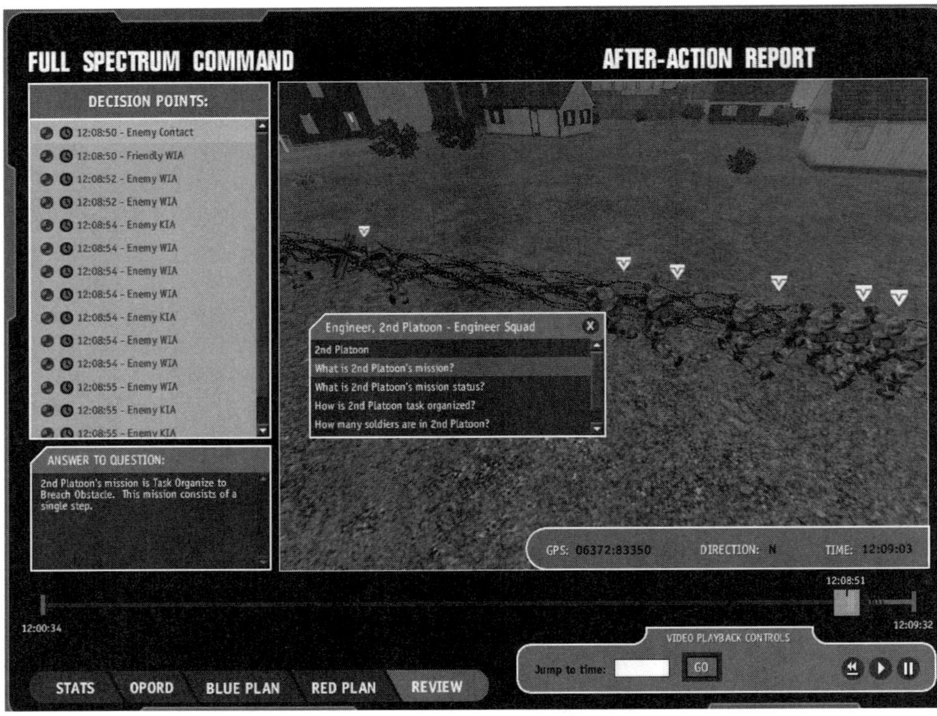


Figure 2: The mission playback screen from a Full Spectrum Command after-action review session.

This plan is represented as an "execution matrix" which includes a row for each sub-unit of the company (each platoon) and a column for each time-based phase of the mission plan (see Figure 1). "Go codes" (key words called over the radio) or pre-defined time stamps are set up to coordinate the actions of the platoons and transition between phases of execution. Once the plan is complete the user moves on to the execution phase by clicking the "Execute" button.

In the execution phase the user monitors the behavior of his soldiers as they carry out the execution matrix, gathers information about the location, composition and actions of the opposing soldiers, and modifies the initial plan by issuing "on the fly" orders called fragmentary orders or Fragos. Unlike the God's eye view of traditional RTS games, the user in FSC must monitor the battle and adjust his plan from the first-person perspective of the company commander's avatar in the game world, which is sometimes fairly far away from the action. This includes the possibility that the user's avatar will be killed which results in immediate mission failure. During the execution phase the user moves around the environment, sends and receives radio transmissions from both subordinate and superior units, monitors the actions of his soldiers and the opposition, and issues Fragos to modify his initial plan. An important part of the company commander's job is maintaining "situational awareness" – a clear mental model of what is happening in the simulated world. This includes recognizing when the mission objective has been achieved or when the company is incapable of achieving the mission.

The final phase of Full Spectrum Command is the after-action review (AAR). Both the military (Morrison and Meliza 1999) and educational researchers (Katz and Lesgold 1994) have identified the importance of post-problem reflection. During the AAR the user and an instructor are provided with a new set of user interfaces and tools designed to help uncover what happened, why it happened, and how the user could have done better. The AAR interfaces include a mission statistics screen, an operation order review screen, a screen that presents the user's initial plan for review, a similar screen that presents the opponent's plan for review, and a mission playback screen. From an AI perspective the most interesting components of the after-action review is the mission playback screen.

The mission playback screen gives the user and instructor the ability to replay the mission with controls to pause, rewind and fast forward the playback (see Figure 2). Unlike the execution phase, the user views the playback through a God's eye camera that can move freely to see what was happening at any point in the game at any time.

The Explainable AI system enhances this playback capability in two ways. First, a set of rules extracts key events from the mission log and represents these as hash marks on a mission time line. Places on the time line where these event and decision hash marks are tightly grouped are often particularly important points in the replay. The user can scroll along the time line and view some details of each hash mark including buttons to jump to the time and location of that event or decision. The second enhancement the XAI system provides is the capability to click on any AI-controlled soldier in the playback window and access a pop-up menu of questions that can be asked of that soldier. The content of these questions and the corresponding answers, as well as the key events and decision points, will be described in more detail during the discussion of the XAI system later in this paper.

## The AI System

There are two artificial intelligence systems in Full Spectrum Command. The Non-Player Character (NPC) AI controls the behavior of the player's subordinate units, the opposing force, and any civilians during the execution phase. The Explainable AI (XAI) works during the after-action review phase to extract key events and decision points from the playback log and allow the NPC AI controlled soldiers to explain their behavior in response to the questions selected from the XAI menu. In order to describe the application of the explainable AI research in Full Spectrum Command it is necessary to first provide an overview of the NPC AI which the XAI seeks to explain. A description of the NPC AI is also interesting as an example of an artificial intelligence system developed not by academic researchers but by commercial game developers. While the underlying ideas have similarities to a number of AI research areas their realization is driven by the processing, memory, and development effort constraints of industry developers.

The NPC AI in Full Spectrum Command is divided into two AI subsystems; a Control AI and a Command AI (see Figure 3). The Command AI and Control AI software modules act as cooperative, event-driven message handlers. The simulation sends a stream of event messages to the Control AI which determines if each event requires an immediate reaction (i.e. return fire or take cover). If so, the Control AI responds with an action notification. Depending on the event type the Control AI may pass the event to the Command AI which generates higher-level tactical behavior. Because the Command AI operates in a separate processing thread, it can take additional time to generate more complex behavior based on a database of task knowledge.

The Control AI is responsible for reactive behavior and low level actions of individual soldiers and, in some cases, the smallest unit or grouping of soldiers (a four soldier Fire Team). It manages all low level decision-making and reactive behaviors (e.g. path planning, find cover, return fire) for NPC Objects. The Command AI is responsible for the behavior of the higher echelon units such as platoons (about 30 to 50 soldiers in 3-5 squads), squads (typically 9 soldiers in two fire teams plus a squad leader), and the fire team behavior not covered by the Control AI. The Command AI manages all strategic level decision making functions (e.g. task selection, task assignment, and unit organization). The Control AI is integrated into the application's basic simulation loop along with standard game components such as rendering, user input and physics simulation. To maintain an acceptable frame rate the

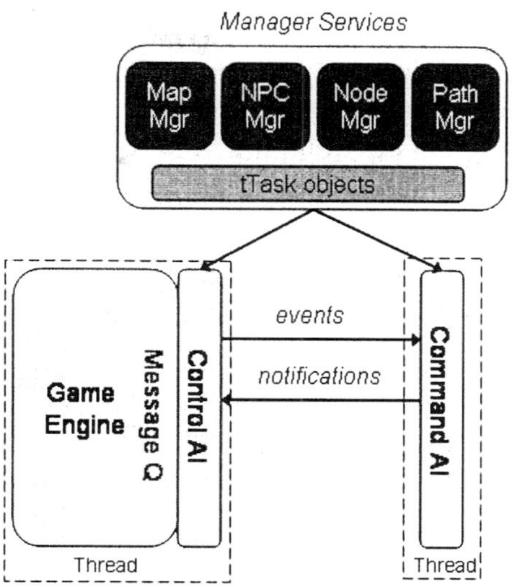


Figure 3: The structure of the AI systems in Full Spectrum Command.

simulation needs to cycle through this loop at least 30 times a second placing strict time constraints on each component of the loop. Thus the Control AI must generate NPC behaviors, not only quickly, but in a consistently predictable number of milliseconds. The Command AI runs in a separate processing thread from the simulation loop and therefore can take more time to generate higher level unit behavior without impacting the simulation loop and frame rate. Both the Control AI and the Command AI interact with a series of manager services to sense and act on the state of the simulation. These services include an NPC manager, a task manager, a map manager a node manager, and a path manager.

In each cycle through the simulation loop the Control AI is called to execute the atomic actions of the Control AI's current set of tasks. These atomic actions include moving a soldier or fire team to a new location, changing a soldier's stance (standing, kneeling, prone) or firing a soldier's weapon. The majority of the Control AI's time is spent on path planning for moving soldiers to new locations. Full Spectrum Command's map includes an embedded navigation graph stored in the map manager. NPCs moving through the environment are actually moving from node to node along the edges of this graph. The graph is carefully constructed so that an NPC that moves along the edges of the graph will never collide with a barrier in the game world. Thus, the path planning code doesn't need to know anything about the locations of buildings, trees and other barriers in the game world. All this spatial information is implicitly represented in the navigation graph. The navigation graph was developed by an automated graph generation algorithm with a great deal of fine tuning by the developers. This is a common approach to path planning in the game industry that has the advantage of very efficient path planning through an A* search over the navigation graph. The navigation graph does require some additional storage, beyond the polygonal map representation used by the graphics renderer, and fine tuning the graph is a time consuming process. First person shooter games, such as Quake and Unreal Tournament, usually include fully automated navigation graph generation which allows users to easily develop and modify maps without having to embed their own navigation graphs. The transfer of such computationally intense tasks from run time to compile time is key to the success of this implementation strategy.

The Control AI changes the stance of an NPC soldier by simply updating the state of that NPC in the NPC manager which in turn changes how the character is rendered by the graphics engine. Weapon firing is decided when a line of sight calculation determines that an NPC has spotted an opposing soldier. The Command AI sends a message to the Control AI calling for a fire action and specifying a shooter NPC and a target NPC. The fire-at-enemy action notification is then sent by the Control AI to the simulation. The outcome of the weapons fire is determined by a statistical "combat calculator" that takes into account factors such as range, shooter and target stance, weapon type, and the target's body armor.

The Command AI, running in a separate thread, takes as input the platoon-level tasks assigned by the user, the task knowledge stored in the task manager, and a constantly updated list of events passed from the simulation thread through the Control AI to the Command AI. Full Spectrum Command tasks are organized into a task hierarchy containing N total tasks in M levels. At the top of the task hierarchy are N platoon-level tasks, such as clear-building, move-to-checkpoint, and execute-supporting-fire, and M high-level tasks used only by the opposing force (or OPFOR), such as shoot-and-scoot and ambush. As described previously, during the planning phase of FSC the user creates an execution matrix that assigns one of these platoon-level tasks to each platoon for each phase of the mission. Similarly, for each mission the mission designer creates an execution matrix assigning tasks for each OPFOR unit. The Command AI takes each top-level task and decomposes it into sub-tasks, sub-sub-tasks and so on. Each time a task is decomposed the Control AI breaks the associated unit into sub-units and assigns a sub-task to each unit.

For example, when a platoon begins a clear-building task the Command AI will decompose that task into two sub-tasks; secure-building-perimeter and assault-building. The platoon will be broken into two parts, in this case a single security squad and a multiple squad assault unit. The security squad will be assigned the secure-building-perimeter tasks while the assault unit will be assigned the assault-building tasks. The assault-building task will then be further decomposed into one or more clear-floor tasks, one for each floor of the building. The assault unit will be divided into floor clearing units (typically squads), who are then assigned to clear the floors in a specific order, one at a time. The clear-floor task for the initial floor will be divided again into multiple clear-room tasks, assigned to fire teams, with each clear-room task resulting in a set of movement orders for the individual soldiers to achieve "positions of dominance" within that room. Once the first room is cleared that fire team becomes available and can be assigned to another clear-room task on the same floor. In decomposing the tasks and forces the Command AI generally follows U.S. Army doctrine although some deviations do occur due to difficulties in getting subject matter experts to agree on an interpretation of the doctrine and constraints on the development timeline. While these differences aren't apparent when observing the resulting behavior they will have ramifications for the explainable AI.

Events in Full Spectrum Command consist of a set of pre-conditions, a set of goal conditions, and a set of task abandonment conditions. In addition, each task includes a list of child tasks in the task hierarchy and is associated with a C++ function that is called to execute the task. A task is executed when it is invoked by a parent task (or directly from the user's initial plan) and its pre-conditions are satisfied by the events passed to the Command AI. When a task is executed its C++ function is called which performs the unit and task decomposition and/or sends an action notification to the Control AI. If a task's abandonment conditions are met the Command AI stops executing the task and a report is sent to the user. For example, if too many soldiers are wounded or killed a unit may become "combat ineffective" in which case the remaining soldiers will seek cover and a radio report to the user will report that the unit has taken heavy casualties.

## Explainable AI in Games and Simulations

As the previous description makes clear, the behavior of the individual NPCs in Full Spectrum Command starts with the user's platoon-level orders but is the result of a number of unit and task decomposition mixed with the reactive behavior of the Control AI. Other video games and military simulation systems include similarly complex processes to generate entity level behavior from orders to larger groups or units. As these AI systems have become more complex their inner workings have become less obvious to users. In training simulations, this can result in users who feel their orders don't really affect the NPC's behavior or users who may try to place blame for failure on the AI systems rather than their own orders.

### Related Work

Interestingly, the problem of explaining the internal processing of an AI system has been previously considered by the research community only in a different context. Medical diagnosis expert systems, such as Mycin (Shortliffe, 1976) used a complex set of rules to diagnose illness and suggest treatments based on patient statistics and test results. Early on the developers of these systems realized that doctors weren't willing to accept the expert system's diagnosis on faith. As a result these systems were designed not only to diagnose an illness but also provide explanations of how the diagnosis was generated. Explanation systems have also been applied to educational applications such as teaching LISP programmers to improve their code (Swartout, Paris and Moore 1994) and to assist knowledge engineer with debugging description logics (McGuinness and Borgida 1995).

One previous effort in the military simulation field is the Debrief system (Johnson, 1994). Debrief allows Soar agents to justify their actions in the TacAirSoar tactical air combat domain (Laird, Jones and Nielsen 1994). Debrief uses Soar's built in learning mechanism to continually store the agent's state during a mission. During the after action review (or debriefing) the system can recall the state of the agent at various points during the mission and experiment with different modifications to that state to determine which aspects of the state were critical to the agent's next decision. By performing this analysis Debrief can report the critical attribute values that resulted in the agent's decision. Debrief can also justify an agent's internal beliefs through a similar process of recalling an agent's state and examining how the agent's beliefs change in response to changes to state attribute values. Debrief explanations are presented through structured natural language phrases and graphical displays of aircraft positions. Debrief makes use of a number of Soar-specific mechanisms, such as chunking, and thus isn't directly applicable to systems not based on Soar. However, the underlying idea of logging an agent's behavior and examining that log during the after-action review to extract critical state features and explanations was influential in the development of the XAI system for Full Spectrum Command.

## Explainable AI in Full Spectrum Command

The Explainable AI system in Full Spectrum Command logs the activities of the NPC AI system during the execution phase and uses that log during the after-action review phase. The log consists of a long sequence of AI events records each with an associated time stamp. The events that are recorded in the log include:

**Weapon Fire**: generated when an NPC shoots at another NPC. Records the weapon type, range, shooter and target details, chance to hit, hit result (did the shooter hit) and the effect of the shot on the target.

**Unit Generation**: generated when the player or NPC AI creates a new unit (i.e. the player creates a fourth platoon within the company or the NPC AI decomposes a platoon into squads). Records the unit id, parent unit's id, formation, unit purpose (security, assault, guard...), NPC count, task assignment, status (idle, waiting, active), leader id, and whether the unit is in position or on the move.

**Unit Update**: generated when the details of a unit are modified by the player or NPC AI. Records the aspects of a unit that could be changed which are formation, unit purpose, task assignment, status and in-position. NPC count doesn't change since wounded or killed NPC are still considered part of the unit.

**Task Generation**: generated when a unit is assigned a new task (i.e. clear-building is decomposed into secure-building-perimeter and assault-building). Records task id, id of the unit to which the task is assigned, task status (complete, incomplete, inactive) and parent task id.

**Task Update**: generated when the details of a task are modified (i.e. records that secure-building-perimeter is completed). Records the task id and task status which is the only detail of a task that can change.

A typical mission in FSC will take between 30 minutes and two hours and will generate a log consisting of thousands or tens of thousands of AI event records. These records are continually streamed to the hard drive as part of the after-action review file generated for each mission.

At the beginning of the after-action review phase the AI log is read from the hard drive and the XAI system reads through all the records. During this initial pass the XAI system gathers mission statistics and a list of important events to support the after-action review process. The mission statistics gathered includes mission duration, casualty statistics and ammo usage statistics. While gathering these statistics doesn't involve any AI technique, the information logged for the XAI is the easiest place to gather this data.

During this first pass through the logged AI events the system also gathers a list of important events that should be highlighted for the user. These events are indicated by hash marks on a mission time line displayed at the bottom of the mission playback screen (see Figure 2). The key event hash marks are color coded according to which side the event relates (blue for the user's units, red for enemy units and white for civilians). The XAI system detects nine types of key event:

- Friendly Soldier Killed in Action (KIA)
- Friendly Soldier Wounded in Action (WIA)
- Enemy Soldier Killed in Action
- Enemy Soldier Wounded in Action
- Civilian Killed in Action
- Civilian Wounded in Action
- Friendly Unit First Contact with the Enemy
- Platoon Task Started
- Platoon Task Completed

The KIA and WIA events are a subset of the logged Weapon Fire records in which the effect of the fire is a killed or wounded NPC. The platoon task started and completed events are a subset of the logged Task Generation and Task Completion records in which the unit associated with the task is a platoon. The XAI system has the capability to also include squad and fire-team level task events. However, as a Company Commander the user should be focusing on the activities of the platoons which are his immediate subordinate units. Finally, a "First Contact with the Enemy" event is generated from a Weapon Fire record that represents the first time an NPC in the associated unit has fired on the enemy.

The third job of the XAI system is to explain the behavior of the platoons during the mission playback. As the user moves through the mission playback the XAI system moves through the logged AI records to maintain the current state of each unit and task. Similar to Debrief, the XAI system uses the logged information to recall the state of the NPC AI at any point during the mission. Unlike Debrief, the XAI system doesn't perform "what if" simulations but does allow the user to inquire about the status of tasks and units. On the playback screen the user can click on any friendly NPC to pop up a menu of questions the user can select to inquire about the current behavior of that NPC's platoon. Early versions of the XAI system included questions and explanations of squad and fire-team level behaviors. However, these were later removed in part to focus the user on the behavior of the platoons and in part because the explanations uncovered aspects of the NPC behavior that doesn't match U.S. Army doctrine. Limiting the user to a menu of pre-defined questions ensures that the system can answer the posed question.

The questions and answers are presented in English. Each question and answer has an associated sentence (or multi-sentence) template that is filled in with the details of the specific situation. The questions available to the user describe the platoon's current task, the status of that task, and the parameters that might affect task execution. These questions and the associated explanations are presented in English. These questions are:

**What is the platoon's mission?** The answer describes the platoon's top-level task and how that task is decomposed into the next level of sub-tasks. An example answer might be "2nd platoon's mission is clear building. This mission consists of two steps: secure building perimeter and assault building."

**What is the platoon's mission status?** The answer describes the status of the platoon's top-level task (active, complete, waiting) and the status of each sub-task. An example answer might be "2nd platoon's clear building task is active. 1st squad's secure building perimeter task is active. 2nd squad's assault building tasks is waiting."

**How is the platoon task organized?** The answer describes how the platoon is decomposed into the next level of sub-units and the number of soldiers in each sub-unit. An example answer might be "2nd platoon is task organized into 3 squads. 1st squad has 9 soldiers. 2nd squad has 9 soldiers. 3rd squad has 7 soldiers."

**How many soldiers are in the platoon?** The answer describes the total number of soldiers in the platoon and how many of these soldiers have been wounded or killed. An example answer might be "2nd platoon has 25 soldiers. Of these 2 soldiers are KIA and 1 soldier is WIA."

**What is the platoon's ammo status?** The answer describes the ammo status of the platoon as green (less than 75% of ammo has been used), red (more than 75% of ammo has been used), or black (no ammo remaining) for each weapon type. An example answer might be "2nd platoon is ammo status black for heavy weapons and ammo status red for light weapons."

## Preliminary Deployment and Evaluation

Full Spectrum Command has been deployed for evaluation purposes in the Infantry Captain's Career Course (ICCC) at the Infantry School at Ft. Benning. Starting in the summer of 2002 beta versions were used in classroom exercises to teach concepts such as execution matrix development and battlefield synchronization. The final software was delivered in February 2003 and has been in use since. In addition, Full Spectrum Command was used in Afghanistan by U.S. soldiers tasked with training Captains in the newly created Afghan National Army.

In 2003 the Army Research Institute conducted an evaluation of the pedagogical effectiveness of Full Spectrum Command. Although the evaluation wasn't designed to explicitly test the NPC AI or XAI, some of the results provide indirect feedback on these systems. Soldiers who used FSC in the context of the ICCC were asked to rank the "relative importance of FSC fidelity" in a number of different areas. The most important area of fidelity was "tactical blue force" or the NPC AI of the soldier's subordinate units. The second most important area of fidelity was "tactical red force" or the NPC AI of the opponent units. Overall 88% of the soldiers indicated that the fidelity of FSC was "excellent" or "adequate." Taken together these results suggest that the soldiers were watching the NPC AI closely and most found it to be acceptable. Overall 60% of the soldiers felt FSC has high training value while 18% of the soldiers felt it has little or no training value. Unfortunately, the XAI was not explicitly mentioned in the results of the evaluation. As discussed in the following section, a separate evaluation is planned that will focus on the effectiveness of the XAI in answering user's questions and determining how the system should be extended to better support FSC's training objectives.

Currently Full Spectrum Command is used by approximately 20% of the instructors who teach the ICCC. This number is likely to increase as more computers with the appropriate graphics accelerator cards are obtained and more instructors are trained to use the training aid. An expanded and improved version of Full Spectrum Command, called FSC 1.5, is currently under development. This second round of development is being funded by the Singapore Armed Forces in collaboration with the U.S. Army.

## Future Work

The current NPC AI and XAI systems have a number of limitations that provide fertile ground for future work. Probably the greatest limitation with the NPC AI is the difficulty in modifying the map and internal behaviors. This has become particularly apparent during the development of FSC 1.5 as we attempt to modify the NPC AI to follow the doctrine of the Singapore Armed Forces.

A more modular NPC AI system that includes an automated spatial reasoning system that can automatically generate a navigation graph would make adding new maps, tactics and doctrine much easier. To this end we are in the process of developing a standard software interface between the simulation system and key components. This standard interface will modularize these components and allow different AI systems to be swapped in and out. This effort will start with the Command AI, the map/navigation graph manager, and adding a new strategic AI module described below. Ideally, this will result in a version of Full Spectrum Command that serves as a research testbed in which different ideas and approaches can be compared and evaluated with respect to fidelity, flexibility, processing demands, and ease of development.

For the XAI, an immediate next step is to evaluate the current explanation capability to determine if it meets the needs of the users. This evaluation should include both testing of the FSC XAI component and an exploration of common types of explanations that occur in after-action reviews of live and simulated training exercises. The fundamental limitation of the XAI is the depth of the explanations it can provide. The current XAI system is limited to explaining how the pre-existing task knowledge was applied. Unfortunately, this task knowledge defines how each task should be carried out, but doesn't include any deeper knowledge about why each task should be approached in the specified way. For example, the clear-building task indicates that the secure-building-perimeter sub-task should be completed before starting the assault-building sub-task but no information on why this constraint is necessary. The NPC AI performs these steps by rote without any knowledge of why it is important to secure the perimeter. As a result the XAI system can't answer questions such as "Why do I need to secure the perimeter before I assault the building?"

Previous research into explanation systems have identified this problem and suggested a number of solutions. The obvious solution, encoding additional knowledge into each task providing the underlying motivation, is unwieldy. It requires an additional, and not insignificant, step each time a task is developed or modified. A more promising solution is to encode the domain's motivating first principles and use an automated planning approach to develop behaviors in response to specific task or mission goals. Because the system is compiling behaviors from first principles, the deeper "why" questions can be answered by retracing the behavior generation process. Although this approach is more complex it has a number of advantages. Behavior knowledge and explanations are generated by the same process from the same source and are guaranteed to match. Once a domain's first principles are encoded they are likely to apply to a wide range of goals and behaviors. It is easier to validate the behaviors once the first principles are defined. Finally, the automated planner might find a range of behaviors that can achieve the same task goals increasing the variability of NPC behavior.

## Acknowledgments

This paper was developed with funds of the Department of the Army under contract number DAAD 19-99-D-0046. Any opinions, findings and conclusions or recommendations expressed in this paper are those of the authors and do not necessarily reflect the views of the Department of the Army.

## References

Johnson, W. L., 1994. Agents that learn to explain themselves. In *Proceedings of the Twelfth National Conference on Artificial Intelligence*, pgs. 1257—1263.

Katz, S. and Lesgold, A. 1994. Implementing post-problem reflection within coached practice environments. In *Proceedings of the East-West International Conference on Computer Technologies in Education*. Crimea, Ukraine. Pgs. 125-130.

Laird, J. E., Jones, R. and Nielsen, P. E. 1994. Coordinated behavior of computer generated forces in TacAir-Soar. In *Proceedings of the Fourth Conference on Computer Generated Forces and Behavioral Representation*. Orlando, FL.

Laird, J. E. 2000 It Knows What You're Going to Do: Adding Anticipation to a Quakebot. AAAI 2000 Spring Symposium Series: Artificial Intelligence and Interactive Entertainment, AAAI Technical Report SS00 -02.

Laird, J. E. and van Lent, M. 2001. Human-Level AI's Killer Application: Interactive Computer Games. *AI Magazine*, Volume 22 (2), pgs. 15-25.

McGuinness, D. L. and Borgida, A. 1995. Explaining Subsumption in Description Logics. In *Proceedings of the 14th International Joint Conference on Artificial Intelligence*, Montreal, Canada, August 1995.

Morrison, J. E. and Meliza, L. L. 1999. Foundations of the After Action Review Process. U.S. Army Research Institute for the Behavioral and Social Sciences Special Report #42.

Shortliffe, E. H. 1976. *Computer-based Medical Consultations: MYCIN*. Elsevier, New York.

Swartout, W. R., Paris, C. L., and Moore, J. D. 1994. *Design For Explainable Expert Systems*. IEEE Expert, Volume 6, Number 3, pages 58-64.

Young, R. M., Riedl, M., Branly, M., Jhala, A., Martin, R. J. and Saretto, C. J. 2004. An architecture for integrating plan-based behavior generation with interactive game environments, *The Journal of Game Development,* Volume 1 (1).

# An Application View of COORDINATORS Coordination Managers for First Responders*

**Thomas Wagner** **John Phelps** **Valerie Guralnik** **Ryan VanRiper**
Honeywell Laboratories
John.Phelps@honeywell.com

### Abstract

COORDINATORs are coordination managers for fielded first responders. Each first response team is paired with a COORDINATOR coordination manager which is running on a mobile computing device. COORDINATORs provide decision support to first response teams by reasoning about who should be doing what, when, with what resource, in support of which other team, and so forth. COORDINATORs respond to the dynamics of the environment by (re)coordinating to determine the right course of action for the current circumstances. COORDINATORs have been implemented using wireless PDAs and proprietary first responder location tracking technologies. This paper describes COORDINATORs, the motivation for them, the underlying agent architecture, implementation issues, and first response exercises.

**Track: Emerging Applications**
**Topic Area: Software Agents**

## Introduction

COORDINATORs are coordination managers for fielded first responders such as fire fighters. They provide decision support for first response teams and the incident commander by reasoning about mission structures, resource limitations, time considerations, and *interactions* between the missions of *different teams* to decide who should be doing what, and when, so as to get the best overall result. COORDINATORs provide global team activity optimization – helping the teams to respond to the dynamics of the environment and to act in concert, supporting one another, as appropriate for the current circumstances. When the situation changes, the COORDINATORs communicate, evaluate the implications of change, and potentially decide (or suggest, depending on their role) on a new course of action for the teams.

* Effort sponsored by the Defense Advanced Research Projects Agency (DARPA) and the Air Force Research Laboratory (AFRL) under agreement number F30602-03-C-0010 and by Honeywell International under project numbers I10155-AB and I10133-AC. The U.S. Government is authorized to reproduce and distribute reprints for Governmental purposes notwithstanding any copyright annotation thereon. Disclaimer: The views and conclusions contained herein are those of the authors and should not be interpreted as necessarily representing the official policies or endorsements, either expressed or implied, of the Defense Advanced Research Projects Agency (DARPA), the Air Force Research Laboratories, the U.S. Government or Honeywell International.


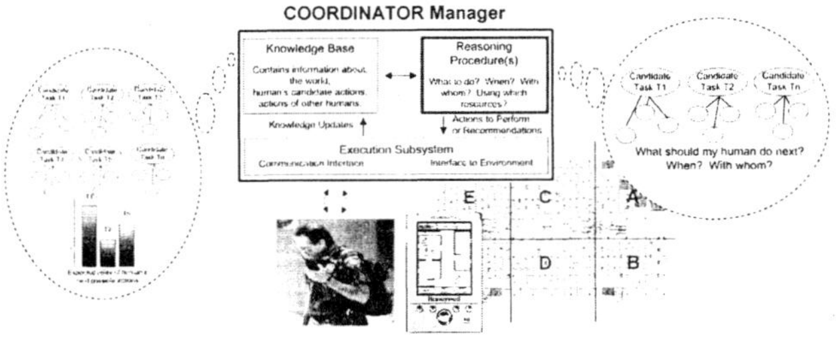


Figure 1: COORDINATORs Help First Responders Coordinate Joint Action By Reasoning About Tasks and Interactions

The underpinnings of COORDINATORs are TÆMS agents (Decker 1995; Wagner, Guralnik, & Phelps 2003a; 2003b; Lesser, Horling, & et al ) equipped with a new coordination module derived from the coordination keys (Wagner, Guralnik, & Phelps 2003a) technology. This means that each distributed COORDINATOR is able to reason about complex mission task structures and communicate with other coordinators to determine who should be supporting whom, when, in order to save the most lives, make the best use of assets or resources, reduce risk to the response teams, and so forth. An application-centric view of an indivudal COORDINATOR is shown in Figure 1. A network of COORDINATORs is shown in Figure 2.

Implementationally, COORDINATORs have been constructed using off-the-shelf wireless PDAs and are currently being ported to more specialized wearable computing devices. COORDINATORs also leverage a Honeywell proprietety asset location technology (akin to RF id tags) to track the physical location of first response teams, victims, and important resources such as a wall cutting saw or a multistory portable ladder. A screen snapshot of a PDA-based coordinator is shown in Figure 3. The screen is showing the location of the teams with its owner team's schedule arranged across the top.

COORDINATORs are implemented and functioning and have been experimented with using staged first response exercises. However, this project and the work described here is only the potential starting point for COORDINATORs and technology that supports human activity coordination.

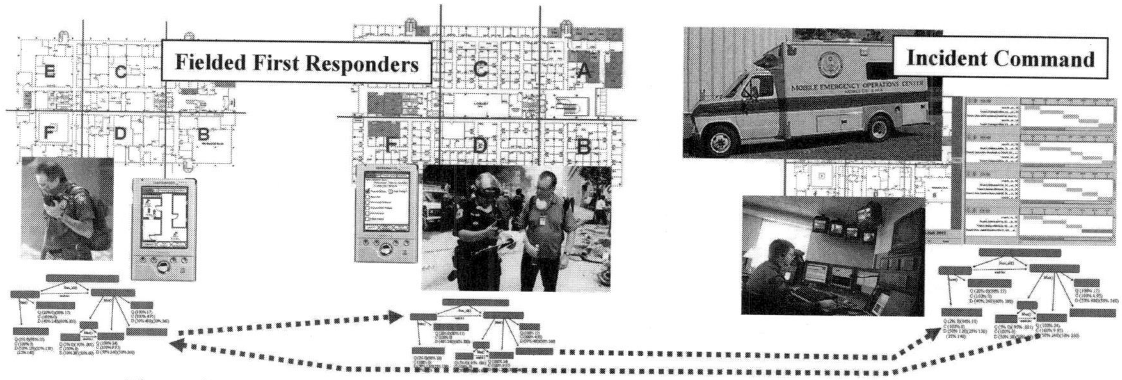


Figure 2: A Network of COORDINATORs Handling Task Coordination Between Responders

DARPA (Defense Advanced Projects Research Agency) is exploring the possibility of creating a larger effort in coordination which would lead to *cognitive* COORDINATORs that learn to improve, reason about organizational structures when decision making, reason about change in the environment, and exhibit other advanced reasoning capabilities.

Note that throughout this paper we use the term "first responder" to mean personnel ranging from fire fighters to emergency medical teams. For the details of this project, however, we have focused primarily on the needs of the fire fighters and the incident commander because we were able to get domain expertise in that area.

In this paper we discuss the first response domain, the motivation for COORDINATORs, and a few underlying business development issues. We then provide architectural and technical details of COORDINATORs and discuss human-based first response exercises using COORDINATORs.

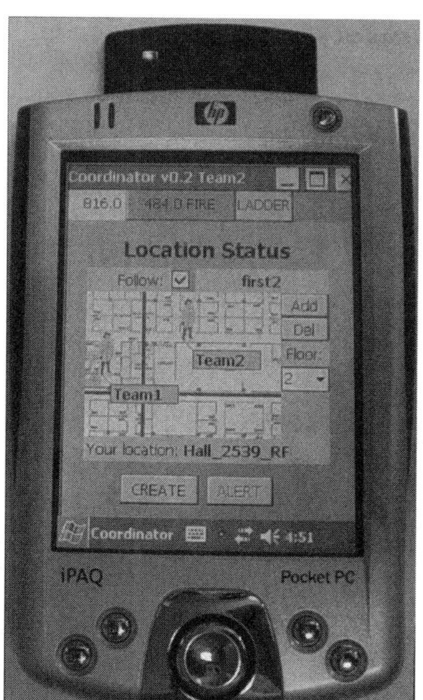


Figure 3: A Single COORDINATOR Running on an Off-The-Shelf Wireless PDA

## Motivation and Business Concepts

COORDINATORs are for large-scale first response team coordination. To frame the problem space, imagine a large-scale crisis event such as a terrorist attack, at a large facility such as a university campus or a petrochemical plant, with multiple concurrent incidents, and multiple organizations or teams responding. In situations such as this, effective response requires coordination between the first response teams. They must act both in concert, supporting each others' efforts (and attempting not to hinder one another), and individually, carrying out their own different assignments. In this environment, the situation is changing in real-time and there is often not very much *a priori* information available. This means that the teams and the incident commander must form and adapt their plans online as the situation unfolds. Currently, this process is carried out using walkie-talkies and the teams rely heavily on the incident commander to provide high-level coordination. The problem is that reasoning about who should be doing what, and when, in a large scale situation is very difficult for humans. (Consider the number of hours per week one spends simply scheduling meetings.) Add-in that the situation is highly dynamic and that change requires timely evaluation and response. Then factor-in the crisis element – flames, explosions, and human lives at stake. Human decision making in these situations translates into high levels of cognitive load, coarse approximation in reasoning, and, from a factual evaluation standpoint, suboptimal coordination. This is a situation in which decision support technologies can help make better decisions, faster, with a greater attention to detail (finer grain of coordination), and with a (near) optimal utilization of teams and resources. The goal of COORDINATORs is to enable the human responders and the incident commander to focus on the human-hard problems and to offload coordination reasoning on to the automated coordination managers.

This concept has been well received by experts in fire, security, and first response, as well as by other customers for military or industrial applications. Keep in mind, however, that the technical vision motivating COORDINATORs is *long term*. This concept is still very far away from something that could be used by first responders in the field. Consider the device level issues alone – heat, moisture, *steam*, darkness, device interaction in a loud setting while wearing

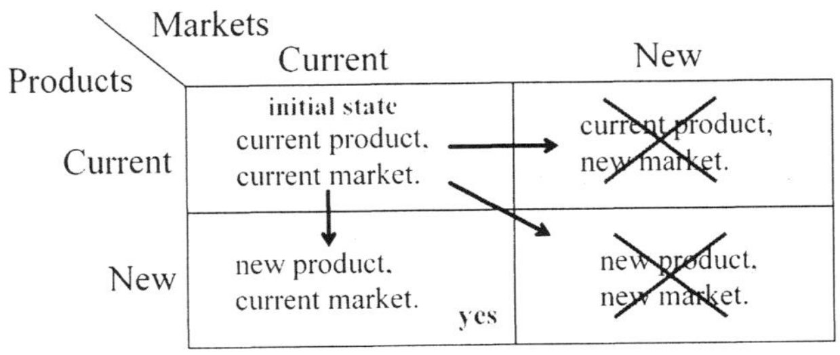

Figure 4: Ansoff's Product/Market Expansion Grid

gloves and carrying equipment, device power, ad-hoc networking/connectivity, are just a few of the areas that must come together before this concept is fully viable. These issues *are* being addressed by other research communities but interaction with experts and our own product divisions has made it clear that this vision is still several years away from deployment.

Another important tool when developing a new technology concept like COORDINATORs is Ansoff's product-market-expansion grid, shown in Figure 4. The general idea is that the current or present market/product mix is in the upper-left hand side and expansion moves from that point to one of the other spaces in the grid. The move that most business people will balk at is the move from the upper-left to the lower-right. This means creating a new product and trying to sell it in a new market. This is regarded as a risky proposition because they are not working from a position of strength. As a technical person, developing a concept that moves a company into that lower-right box means that investment may be very difficult to obtain. On the other hand, a move from the upper-left to the upper-right is a move that business development people endorse. This means taking a current product and developing a new market for it. This is an instance of expansion from a strength. However, this expansion movement is generally of little use to those developing technical concepts because, by definition, we are generally creating new products and new ideas. The one expansion avenue open to work like COORDINATORs is to keep the company in its existing market (movement from upper-left to lower-left) but to develop a new product for that market. Whether or not COORDINATORs actually makes the move to the lower-left is a matter of some debate – partially because the entire first response / homeland defense market is in a state of flux. What is helpful when developing a concept like COORDINATORs is to hit on multi-purpose use – something that is an enabler on a day-to-day basis as well as something that has value in first response and crisis situations. Whether COORDINATORs for first response will achieve product status in the distant future is far from predictable.

## Agents, Architecture, and Implementation

COORDINATORs are based-on TÆMS agents (Decker 1995; Wagner, Guralnik, & Phelps 2003a; 2003b; Lesser, Horling, & et al ). The name TÆMS stands for *Task Analysis Environment Modeling and Simulation* though in its present day usage TÆMS is best regarded as a hierarchical modeling language used to represent complex task networks and interactions between different agents. TÆMS-based components, such as the DTC agent scheduler (Wagner, Garvey, & Lesser 1998; Wagner & Lesser 2001; Raja, Lesser, & Wagner 2000) then reason about these complex task networks to decide on a course of action for the agent. TÆMS enables TÆMS-based technologies to be used in many different domains because, as with any modeling language, it provides a layer of abstraction away from the domain details. Figure 5 shows a single TÆMS agent as constructed for COORDINATORs. From a high-level, each TÆMS agent contains sophisticated control problem solving modules that reason about tasks, task interactions, interactions that span agents, time deadlines, resource constraints, and so forth to decide who should be doing what, and when, so as to optimize the activities of a group of distributed agents. The details of how the technologies operate are beyond the scope of this paper, though more information can be found in papers on TÆMS (Decker 1995; Lesser, Horling, & et al ), DTC agent scheduling (Wagner, Garvey, & Lesser 1998; Wagner & Lesser 2001; Raja, Lesser, & Wagner 2000), GPGP agent coordination (Decker 1995; Decker & Li 1998; Lesser *et al.* 1998), in a different COORDINATORS paper (Wagner *et al.* 2004), and in the aircraft service team coordination application (Wagner, Guralnik, & Phelps 2003a).

From the larger MAS system view, each COORDINATOR has a single TÆMS agent to which it is linked via wireless 802.11b network, as shown in Figure 6. In the future, we envision the TÆMS agents themselves running on portable computing devices but the processing requirements of a TÆMS agent are too great for current PDAs and wearable computers (shrinking the TÆMS agent requirements has not be explored to conserve resources). The current COORDINATOR system architecture has each wireless PDA connecting to a TÆMS agent back-end – the PDA agent is essentially an interface stub that communicates as needed with the TÆMS agents. Each TÆMS agent in turn may communicate with other TÆMS agents to coordinate the activities of different teams (exchange local information, negotiate over task interactions, determine who should be doing what, and when). When the system is running in simulation mode (as it is generally as we have few buildings to actually burn for experimental purposes), agent commu-

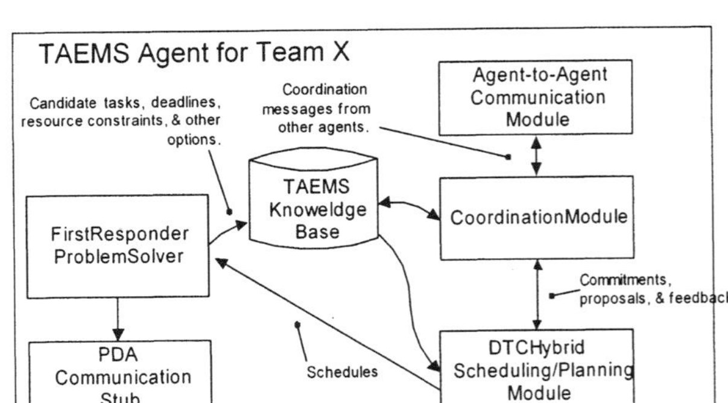

Figure 5: A Single TÆMS Agent / the Core of a COORDINATOR

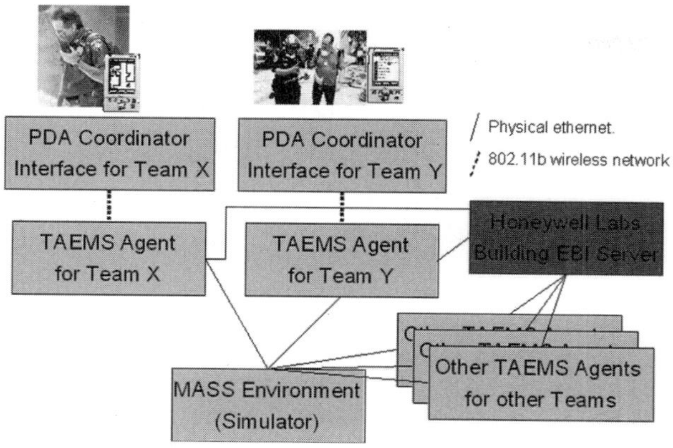


Figure 6: Overview of the MAS Architecture of a Network of COORDINATORs

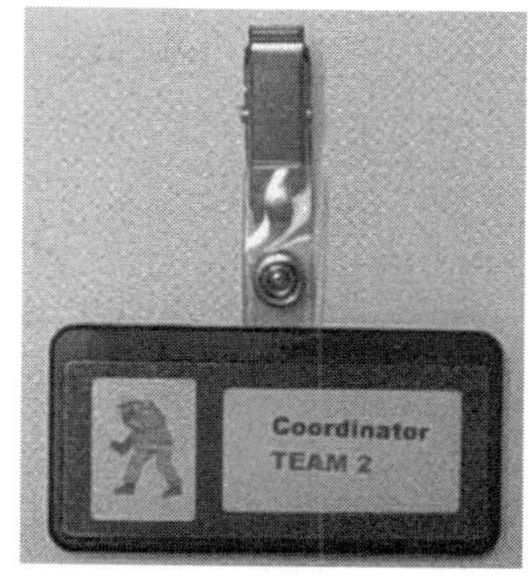


Figure 7: Locater Tag Tracks Humans/Assets & Their Locations

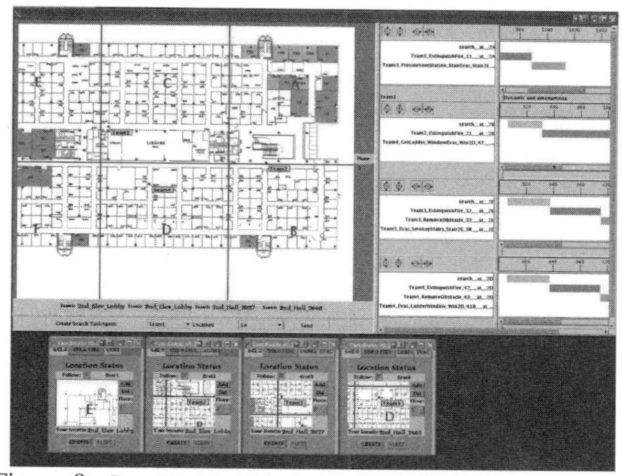

Figure 9: Java Enables Displaying Both "Mobile" Device Side Interfaces and Centralized Command on a Single Workstation

nication is routed through the MASS (Vincent, Horling, & Lesser 2001) simulation environment (as shown in the figure). Each TÆMS agent also communicates with the Honeywell Lab's building EBI server. The EBI server is a commercial proprietary technology for controlling building systems and for tracking assets within a facility. For instance, managers within the building wear asset location tags so that they can be located as needed. In the COORDINATORs system, first responders are tagged so they can be tracked through the facility and so the teams can see visually where other teams are located and track each other's movements using the PDAs and digitized maps. The incident commander COORDINATOR (another TÆMS agent supports it) can also track team movements using the asset location technology. The addition of situational icons, e.g., locations of known fires, is planned for future implementation. Obviously, the information gathered from the tracking system could also be fed into other automated reasoning modules in a more comprehensive COORDINATOR, e.g., one that provides path planning or intelligent evacuation support using the information. These ideas have not been explored in any meaningful way to date. An asset location tag is shown in Figure 7. The tag uniquely identifies a person or an asset by sending a signal to receiver units which are distributed throughout the building. Location of the party in question is determined by proximity to a given receiver. In many modern office buildings / facilities, such tagging is commonplace and becoming more so. Note that there are many other location technologies that might be used in systems like COORDINATORs, including GPS and cellular-based triangulation (both of which generally perform poorly indoors).

COORDINATORs are implemented in a combination of Java and C++. The reasoning components, e.g., the DTC agent scheduling module, rely on the Java Agent Framework (JAF) and the MASS simulation environment (Vincent, Horling, & Lesser 2001) to provide inter-component glue/messaging/execution and inter-agent message transport. The JAF infrastructure includes a Java representation of TÆMS. DTC, the major C++ component, uses its own internal TÆMS representation. As discussed, the TÆMS agents themselves run on linux-based workstations while the PDA interactions are managed by Java-based "agent-lets" or stubs. The advantage of this design and these platform choices is that we do not need the PDAs to run the rest of the system – the PDA-side Java applications can simply be run under linux and connected to using a physical network, as shown in Figure 9. This facilitates testing, experimentation, and debugging.

The user interfaces developed for COORDINATORs attempt to strike a good balance between research/development cost and functionality. Recall that we regard these devices as demonstration vehicles – for actual deployment a different device is needed and user interaction will most likely *not* be based on stylus manipulation. Figure 8 shows the steps necessary to create a rescue mission. The data entered via pull- down menu and check box selection serves to fill-in the details of an existing mission template. We are experimenting with speech recognition, heads-up displays, and wearable computers as a way to facilitate more natural environment-embedded interaction.

## Coordination and First Response Exercises

While a detailed example of first responder coordination in COORDINATORs is beyond the scope of this paper (one can be found in (Wagner *et al.* 2004)), the critical conceptual point is that coordination requires reasoning about tasks and interactions. That is, understanding how one team's tasks

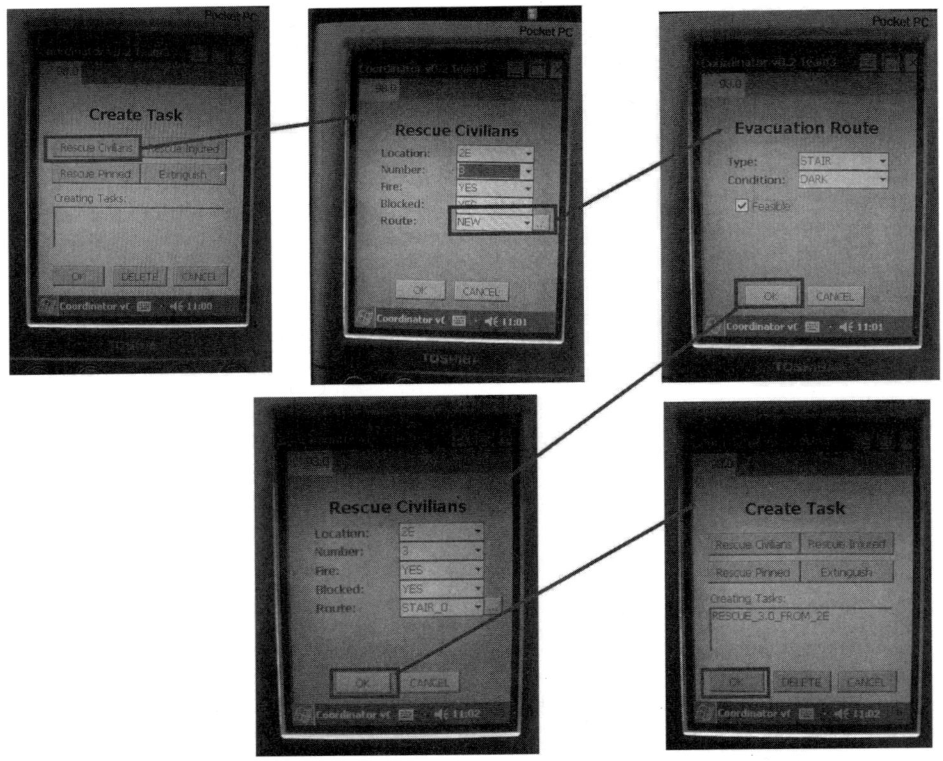


Figure 8: Creating a Rescue Mission By Instantiating a Mission Template

interact with those of other teams. These interactions require cohesive choice (everyone selecting the "right" way to perform tasks) and temporal sequencing (everyone must do their actions at the "right times"). From a high-level, coordination is about deciding *who should be doing what*, and *when*, so as to get the best overall result for the *current* circumstances. The idea behind COORDINATORs is that they continuously evaluate change in the situation or in the mission and decide how the teams should adapt and respond. COORDINATORs are a technology intended for *online* use which means they must respond in "soft" real-time and cannot rely on algorithms requiring exponential search. A small example of a coordination episode is shown in Figure 10. At this point in time (in a larger scenario), $Team_2$'s COORDINATOR has negotiated with $Team_3$'s COORDINATOR for $Team_2$ to support $Team_3$'s evacuation efforts by providing secondary lighting for a darkened stairwell. Later in the same scenario, due to new deadlines imposed by the potential for explosions elsewhere in the facility, the COORDINATORs must renegotiate and consider alternatives – $Team_2$ winds up supporting $Team_3$ by providing a net for window evacuation instead of lighting for stairwell evacuation.

In terms of evaluation, arguably the most important overall evaluation question for COORDINATORs is whether they improve the performance of first responders. In a perfect world with unlimited resources, one might design a set of experiments in which first responders engage in a series of first response episodes both with and without COORDINATORs providing support. In each case, one would like to measure specific metrics like number of lives saved, number of assets saved, time required to perform the mission tasks, number of responders necessary to address the situation, amount of risk incurred by the responders and the civilians, etc. In this perfect world, one would have buildings to burn and the ability to recreate, verbatim, scenarios so that the measurement and comparison could be one-to-one.

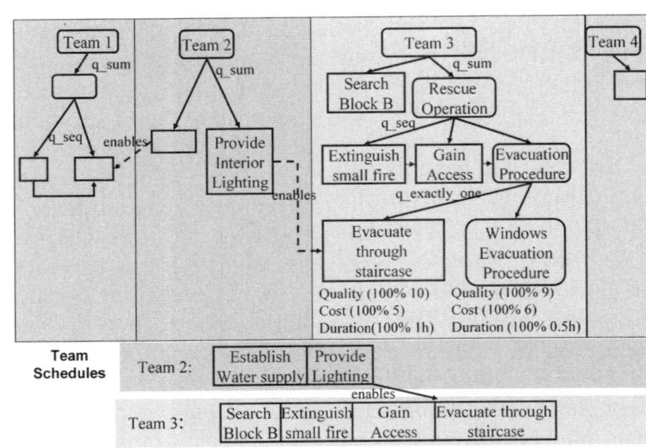


Figure 10: A Single Slice of Larger Coordination Episode: Tasks and Schedules Reflect $Team_2$'s Support of $Team_3$

Not living in a perfect world, we elected to use a somewhat more economic approach. To evaluate COORDINA-

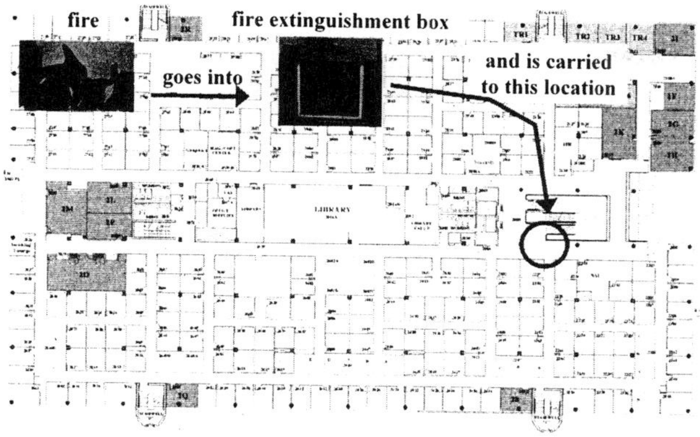


Figure 11: Domain Work is Carried Out With Props

TORs from an application view, rather than simply evaluating the performance of the underlying technology (e.g., time required for coordination), we staged first response exercises and had human performers take the role of first responders. Note that the lessons learned from this process are anecdotal but are also more meaningful as an early viability test of the concept.

In the exercises there are four teams and an incident commander (IC). The scenario is set in a petrochemical plant though the plant is mapped back onto the Honeywell Lab's building. During the exercise, responders must move around the building, perform situation assessment tasks, respond to the situations they discover, and coordinate to rescue civilians. The scenario is setup in such a way that teams must coordinate in order to rescue the civilians. Failure to do so results in (simulated) loss of life – a metric that can be tabulated.

To assess the benefits of having COORDINATORs, we first deploy the teams on the first response exercise using walkie-talkies for communication (they are also equipped with stop-watches and building maps to make the simulation more complete). After the walkie-talkie exercise, during which loss of (prop) life is recorded, the teams are rotated and the scenario run again, this time with COORDINATORs providing automated support.

In doing this exercise, we rapidly discovered the degree to which humans are overwhelmed when faced with lots of temporal and task related data that is in a state of constant change. The initial plan was to host VIPs and to have a VIP take the role of incident commander – the individual who generally handles coordination in the walkie-talkie exercise. Not only was the IC task too difficult for the VIPs, it was too difficult for most of the research team members. In practice, only someone who had memorized the flow of events in the exercise could help the teams to rescue all the civilians. We resorted to this model in order to get human performers through the walkie-talkie exercise at all.

Thus VIPs and visitors (with varying degrees of domain expertise) generally took the role of first response teams. At the start of the scenario, the teams are deployed by the IC and given situation assessment tasks. In enacting the scenario, at this point teams move throughout the building and go to assigned zones (generally conference rooms). To simulate the situation assessment task, we created a series of props representing the situation. For instance, a first response team might find fire props, debris props, and a civilian prop pinned by a girder prop. This would indicate that a civilian was trapped and that the fire needed to be put out and the debris cleared before the girder could be cut away. Cutting the girder also requires some other team (generally) to fetch a power saw from the simulated truck. In the exercise, props are reinforced by staging data sheets that describe the situation textually and explicitly cull out resource needs and potential temporal issues (e.g., "you must evacuate these civilians before the adjacent wall collapses at time T=40").

Because fielded first responders must coordinate while carrying out domain tasks, we also require our first response stand-ins to carry out simulated domain tasks. In general, this translates into putting props into one another and moving them physically throughout the building. Figure 11 illustrates the process of putting out a small fire. To extinguish the fire, it goes into a *fire extinguishment box* and the box must then be carried to a staging area on a specific floor of the building. Similarly, evacuation of an injured civilian requires that the civilian prop be put into the gurney prop box, a box that must be fetched from the staging area, and then the gurney box must be put into a stairwell box (if that is the exit route chosen) and the stairwell box carried to the staging area.

Dynamics are introduced into the environment using secondary envelopes on which is printed a time at which they are to be opened. Thus teams may coordinate, decide on a course of action, then open an envelope and discover that the situation has changed (e.g., a ceiling fell-in) and then they must recoordinate to adapt to the new situation.

As one might guess from the description, human performers generally fared poorly during this exercise. Only with an expert IC who knew the complete scenario *a priori* and had figured out exactly who should be supporting whom, and when, could get both the teams and the cardboard civilians out of the facility in time. What is more interesting is that the stress incurred by the human performers during the exercise was pronounced and observable even to the non-expert. Trying to battle one's props while processing all the cross chatter on the walkie-talkie and interact with the IC proved to be a difficult task even without the heat, smoke, sound, and inherent danger of a crisis situation. Few performers were able to coordinate properly. Few were able to evaluate their mission structures properly. Not once did a guest team make it through the scenario with the optimal course of action chosen. Notable among our VIPs was a Honeywell VP who processed the temporal data without hand drawn Gantt charts and who carried the props with great vigor while barking commands into his walkie-talkie. (Confidence in management rose a fraction during this episode.)

In contrast to the walkie-talkie scenario, the run with COORDINATORs handling the activity coordination is almost boring – despite the scenario being run at a faster clock rate. In the COORDINATOR scenario, the teams perform situation assessment and describe their situation to the COORDINATORs. The COORDINATORs then handle all of the

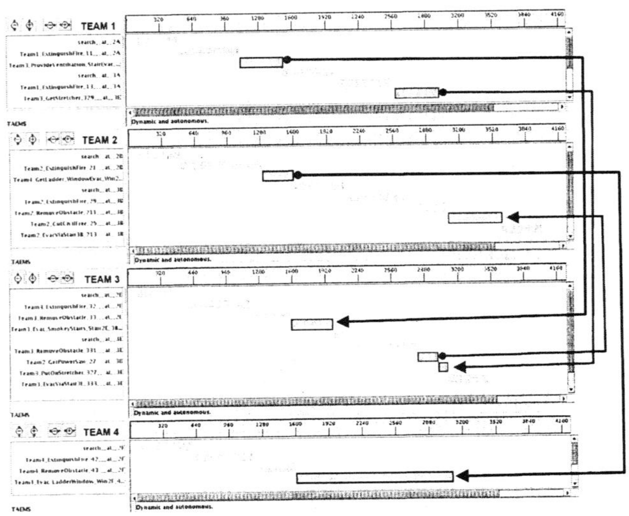


Figure 12: After the Exercise, First Response Stand-ins are Debriefed by Being Shown the Optimal Course of Action and the Choices They Made

exchange of local information, the analysis, and the formation of commitments. Teams are then informed of what they should be doing, when, who will be supporting them, and so forth.

After both exercises, the VIPs are then debriefed and shown a simplified Gantt chart, Figure 12, of the major coordination points and support needs of the different teams. While the evidence gathered during these exercises is anecdotal, the reaction of our visitors, some with first response and military domain expertise, has served to reinforce our belief that this line of work is valuable. In practice, the "fog of war" caused by flames, screaming, smoke, etc., makes a set of tasks that humans have difficulty with under normal circumstances nearly impossible. Information exchange and coordination analysis should be off-loaded from the humans to automated assistants that are better equipped to reason precisely and respond in a (near) optimal and timely fashion.

## Unaddressed Research Issues, Limitations, and Future Work

In this paper, we have presented COORDINATORs, discussed the motivation behind them, and identified a few important business development concepts. We have also described the underlying TÆMS agent technology and described the anecdotal experimentation with COORDINATORs.

COORDINATORs relate to several areas of prior art. The electronic elves (Chalupsky *et al.* 2002) project underscored the value of using a portable computing device as a front end for a more complex, agent-based, support system. The use of GPS tracking in e-elves also affirmed our interest in leveraging Honeywell asset tracking technologies in COORDINATORs. Our work differs from e-elves in that the reasoning and information exchange is all distributed – in theory no agent has a complete view of the activities of the other agents. COORDINATORs also differs in the type of task/temporal analysis required to coordinate complex mission structures. In a sense, COORDINATORs are more narrowly scoped than e-elves but require deeper analysis technology. The use of agents and portable computing devices to disseminate information to, and collect information from, aircraft repair teams (Shehory *et al.* 1999) also contributed intellectually to COORDINATORs. Interfacing with the building systems and displaying digital maps, along with team location, information is a concept that relates naturally with this prior work. Another area is the work done in using TÆMS agents to support aspects of distributed collaborative design processes (Decker & Lesser 1995). Though there are differences, e.g., grainsize and response time requirements, the underlying technical problems are probably members of the same class or related classes.

While this paper has described the COORDINATORs project, we have not dealt overmuch with research issues (more technical details appear in (Wagner *et al.* 2004)). Hard problems are abundant in COORDINATORs. At the most basic level, distributed activity coordination from partial views in a (soft) real-time setting is an extremely difficult problem – particularly given the degree of complexity needed to represent mission tasks and their interactions. This the reason for the "nearly optimal" terminology in this paper. Most techniques that we have developed to date are approximate, e.g., the keys coordination mechanism (Wagner, Guralnik, & Phelps 2003a). Another hard issue is how to provide a centralized command-and-control interface to a network of COORDINATORs that are inherently distributed. Through our interaction with domain experts it became clear that we needed to support and leverage the incident commander, not replace him/her. A related issue is how to support mixed modes of decision making – COORDINATORs need to be able to (learn to) make decisions for their teams in some circumstances and in others need to consult their team members (or the IC) directly. This might involve advanced situation assessment or reasoning about what the team is currently doing, the importance of the decision at hand, the existence of other options, the response time required for the decision, and so forth. Another issue hereto unaddressed is the classic question of "where do the models come from?" Our assumption is that we can create a library of templates and then instantiate them at run time – possibly asking the IC or the responders to adapt the missions to the current situation. This is time consuming and will require the right interfaces, right mission editing tools, etc., in order to make it feasible (our current tools could be improved). Even if these issues can be resolved, they are still predicated on the assumption that missions can be generalized and they repeat (the hypothesis that this is the case is based on the current day existence of *response plans* and standardized procedures). Another area of future work involves organizational structures – reasoning about decision making procedures and following proper organizational structure, and decision making protocols, for both COORDINATORs and humans.

In the future, we plan to explore some of the underlying

technical issues in COORDINATORs in greater depth. For instance, the coordination algorithm used here has not been evaluated in the small and it is known to have some unaddressed issues, e.g., considering load balancing when tasking. The next steps for this work will also be partially influenced by DARPA interests and Honeywell interests. This work was partly funded by DARPA's IPTO office as an exploratory project in coordination. Their interest is in creating greatly enhanced *cognitive* COORDINATORs that not only solve all the core problems well, but that learn and adapt over time, reason about organizational structure and military decision making when coordinating, and are scalable by learning to control their own problem solving (learning with whom to coordinate, learning which coordination decisions are important, etc.). From the cognitive COORDINATOR perspective, the COORDINATORs discussed here should be viewed as an early prototype of things to come and what is possible in this problem space.

## Acknowledgments

Victor Lesser's group at UMASS is an industrial affiliate of Honeywell and a subcontractor on the COORDINATORs project. TÆMS has a long history and has involved many researchers, including: Victor Lesser, Keith Decker, Alan Garvey, Tom Wagner, Bryan Horling, Regis Vincent, Ping Xuan, Shelley XQ. Zhang, Anita Raja, Roger Mailler, and Norman Carver. We would also like to acknowledge the efforts of the other Honeywell Lab's project team who performed first hand interviews with fire marshals and first responders. These include Tom Plocher, Walt Heimerdinger, Tony Faltesek, and Michelle Raymond. This work was partially supported by DARPA's IPTO office, through AFRL, and by Honeywell International. We would like to thank Ron Brachman, Barbara Yoon, Zach Lemnios, John Beane, Mike Lynch, and Andrew Berezowski for their support.

## References

Chalupsky, H.; Gil, Y.; Knoblock, C.; Lerman, K.; Oh, J.; Pynadath, D.; Russ, T.; and Tambe, M. 2002. Electric Elves: Agent Technology for Supporting Human Organizations. *AI Magazine* Summer.

Decker, K. S., and Lesser, V. R. 1995. Coordination assistance for mixed human and computational agent systems. In *Proceedings of Concurrent Engineering 95*, 337–348. McLean, VA: Concurrent Technologies Corp. Also available as UMASS CS TR-95-31.

Decker, K., and Li, J. 1998. Coordinated hospital patient scheduling. In *Proceedings of the Third International Conference on Multi-Agent Systems (ICMAS98)*, 104–111.

Decker, K. S. 1995. *Environment Centered Analysis and Design of Coordination Mechanisms*. Ph.D. Dissertation, University of Massachusetts.

Lesser, V.; Decker, K.; Wagner, T.; Carver, N.; Garvey, A.; Neiman, D.; and Prasad, N. 1998. Evolution of the GPGP Domain-Independent Coordination Framework. Computer Science Technical Report TR-98-05, University of Massachusetts at Amherst. A longer version of this paper will appear in the Journal of Autonomous Agents and Multi-Agent Systems in 2003.

Lesser, V.; Horling, B.; and et al. The TÆMS whitepaper / evolving specification. http://mas.cs.umass.edu/research/taems/white.

Raja, A.; Lesser, V.; and Wagner, T. 2000. Toward Robust Agent Control in Open Environments. In *Proceedings of the Fourth International Conference on Autonomous Agents (Agents2000)*.

Shehory, O.; Sycara, K.; Sukthankar, G.; and Mukherjee, V. 1999. Agent aided aircraft maintenance. In *Proceedings of the Third International Conference on Autonomous Agents (Agents99)*, 306–312.

Vincent, R.; Horling, B.; and Lesser, V. 2001. An agent infrastructure to evaluate multi-agent systems: The java agent framework and multi-agent system simulator. In Wagner, T., and Rana, O., eds., *Infrastructure for Agents, Multi-Agent Systems, and Scalable Multi-Agent Systems, Lecture Notes in AI*. Springer. 102–127.

Wagner, T., and Lesser, V. 2001. Design-to-Criteria Scheduling: Real-Time Agent Control. In Wagner/Rana., ed., *Infrastructure for Agents, Multi-Agent Systems, and Scalable Multi-Agent Systems*, LNCS. Springer-Verlag. Also appears in the 2000 AAAI Spring Symposium on Real-Time Systems and a version is available as University of Massachusetts Computer Science Technical Report TR-99-58.

Wagner, T.; Phelps, J.; Guralnik, V.; and VanRiper, R. 2004. Coordinators - coordination managers for first responders. In *To appear in the proceedings of the 3rd International Joint Conference on Autonomous Agents and Multi-Agent Systems (AAMAS04)*.

Wagner, T.; Garvey, A.; and Lesser, V. 1998. Criteria-Directed Heuristic Task Scheduling. *International Journal of Approximate Reasoning, Special Issue on Scheduling* 19(1-2):91–118. A version also available as UMASS CS TR-97-59.

Wagner, T.; Guralnik, V.; and Phelps, J. 2003a. A key-based coordination algorithm for dynamic readiness and repair service coordination. In *Proceedings of the 2nd International Conference on Autonomous Agents and Multi-Agent Systems (AAMAS2003), 2003.* Nominated for most novel application award.

Wagner, T.; Guralnik, V.; and Phelps, J. 2003b. Software Agents: Enabling Dynamic Supply Chain Management for a Build to Order Product Line. *International Journal of Electronic Commerce Research and Applications, Special issue on Software Agents for Business Automation* 2(2):114–132.

# Towards Autonomic Computing: Adaptive Job Routing and Scheduling

**Shimon Whiteson and Peter Stone**
Department of Computer Sciences
The University of Texas at Austin
1 University Station, C0500
Austin, TX 78712-0233
{*shimon,pstone*}@*cs.utexas.edu*
http://www.cs.utexas.edu/~{shimon,pstone}

**Abstract**

Computer systems are rapidly becoming so complex that maintaining them with human support staffs will be prohibitively expensive and inefficient. In response, visionaries have begun proposing that computer systems be imbued with the ability to configure themselves, diagnose failures, and ultimately repair themselves in response to these failures. However, despite convincing arguments that such a shift would be desirable, as of yet there has been little concrete progress made towards this goal. We view these problems as fundamentally *machine learning* challenges. Hence, this article presents a new network simulator designed to study the application of machine learning methods from a system-wide perspective. We also introduce learning-based methods for addressing the problems of job routing and scheduling in the networks we simulate. Our experimental results verify that methods using machine learning outperform heuristic and hand-coded approaches on an example network designed to capture many of the complexities that exist in real systems.

## Introduction

Computer systems are rapidly becoming—indeed some would say have already become—so complex that maintaining them with human support staffs will be prohibitively expensive and inefficient. Nonetheless, most computer systems today are still built to rely on static configurations and can only be installed, configured, and re-configured by human experts.

In response, visionaries have begun proposing that computer systems be imbued with the ability to configure themselves, diagnose failures, and ultimately repair themselves in response to these failures. The resulting shift in computational paradigm has been called by different names, including *cognitive systems* (Brachman 2002) and *autonomic computing* (Kephart & Chess 2003), but the underlying motivation and goal is remarkably similar.

However, despite convincing arguments that such a shift would be desirable, as of yet there has been little concrete progress made towards this goal. There has been preliminary progress on adaptive system *components* such as network routing (Boyan & Littman 1994; Caro & Dorigo 1998; Clark *et al.* 2003; Itao, Suda, & Aoyama 2001). But to our knowledge, there has not been any previous work on improving system performance from a system-wide perspective.

We view these goals as fundamentally *machine learning* challenges. For entire systems to be able to self-configure, self-diagnose failures, and repair themselves, there will need to be machine learning components at multiple levels, including the operating systems, databases, and networking modules. Furthermore, individual computers and local systems will need to adapt their interactions with remote systems whose connectivity and computing capabilities may vary unpredictably.

This article introduces a simulator designed to facilitate the study of machine learning in enterprise systems and reports on our initial experiments in this domain. These experiments underscore key complexities that arise when optimizing routing and scheduling in such networks. We present machine learning approaches to address these challenges.

The remainder of this article is organized as follows. The next section provides background on our network simulator and the particular network we use in all our experiments. After that, we detail methods for optimizing routing and scheduling and present the results of experiments evaluating these methods. Finally, we discuss the implications of these results and highlight some opportunities for future work.

## Background

This section introduces the simulator that we use as the substrate system for our research as well as a detailed example network that is the setting for the experiments presented in this article.

### The Simulator

To pursue our research goals, we need a high-level simulator that is capable of modeling the relevant types of interactions among the many different components of a computer system. While detailed simulators exist for individual system components, such as networks, databases, etc., we were unable to locate any simulator that models system-wide interactions. Therefore, we have designed and implemented a system that simulates the way a computer network processes user requests from a high-level perspective.

The simulator represents a computer network as a graph: nodes represent machines or users and links represent the communication channels between them. Users create jobs that travel from machine to machine along links until all of their steps are completed. When a job is completed, it is assigned a score according to a given *utility function*, which depends on how much time the job took to complete. The utility function may vary depending on the type of job or the user who created it. The job's score is added to the simulation's global, cumulative score, which the agents controlling the network are trying to maximize.

The simulator includes the following components:

**Nodes:** A node is a component of the network that is connected to other nodes via links. There are two primary types of nodes: users and machines.

**Users:** Users are special nodes who create jobs and send them to machines for processing. Once a job is completed, it is returned to the user, who computes its score.

**Machines:** A machine is a node that can complete portions of a job. Each type of machine is defined by the set of steps it knows how to complete.

**Links:** A link connects two nodes in the network. It is used to transfer jobs and other packets between nodes.

**Packets:** A packet is a unit of information that travels between nodes along links. The most common type of packet is a job, described below, but nodes can create other types of packets in order to communicate with other nodes about their status.

**Jobs:** A job is a series of steps that need to be completed in a specified order. Completing these steps could require the job to travel among several machines. A system usually has several types of jobs which differ in the list of steps they require for completion.

**Steps:** A step is one component of a job. Each step can only be carried out by a subset of machines in the network. For example, the retrieval of information in response to a database query must happen at a database server.

A simulation proceeds for a specified number of discrete timesteps. At each timestep, machines can allocate their CPU cycles towards the completion of steps on the jobs in its possession, packets can be sent along links, and packets can arrive at new nodes.

We believe that this simulator provides a valuable testbed for new approaches to autonomic computing because it captures many of the real world problems associated with complex computer systems while retaining the simplicity that makes experimental research feasible.

## An Example Network

All of the experiments presented in this article were performed on the network depicted in Figure 1. In this network, the users (the CEO and Intern) can check their mail or perform database queries via a web interface. Two load balancers do not complete any steps but make important decisions about how to route jobs.

There are two types of jobs that the users create: Mail Jobs and Database Jobs. Each Mail Job consists of the following three steps: 1) Web Step (work = 50), 2) Mail Step

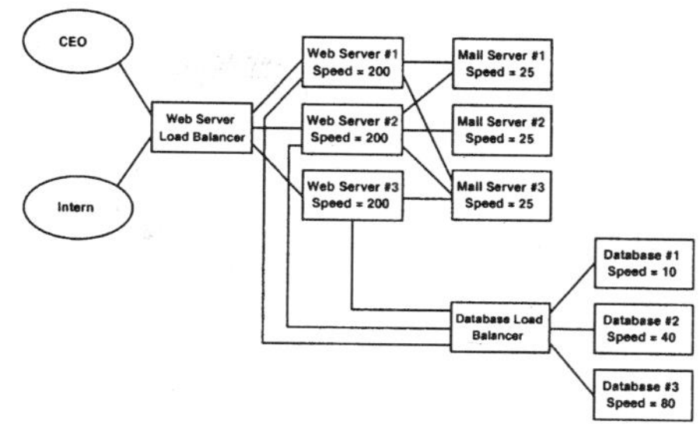


Figure 1: The network used in our experiments. Ovals represent users, rectangles represent machines, and the lines between them represent communication links. The speed of each is the number of CPU cycles it can execute in one turn.

(work = 100), and 3) Web Step (work = 50). The work associated with each step is simply the number of CPU cycles required to complete the step. As one might expect, only Web Servers can complete Web Steps and only Mail Servers can complete Mail Steps. A Database Job is identical except that its second step is a Database Step (work = 200).

In this article, we explore ways of applying machine learning techniques to the problems of routing and scheduling jobs efficiently. The network just described, although abstract, nonetheless captures the essential difficulties posed by such optimization problems. For example, each Database has a different speed, which means that if the Database Load Balancer routes jobs randomly, it will overload the slower Databases and underload the faster ones. Even if we take machine speed into account, routing on this network is far from trivial. Consider a Web Server that wishes to forward a Mail Job to a Mail Server. Since there is no load balancer governing the Mail Servers, the Web Server must pick directly from among the Mail Servers to which it is connected. Doing so optimally requires considering not just the speed of each Mail Server but also how busy that server is completing jobs sent by other Web Servers. Since the connections between Web and Mail Servers are not just incomplete but also uneven (i.e. some Web Servers are connected to more Mail Servers than others), determining this is not easy. Similarly, the Web Server Load Balancer cannot consider only the relative speed of a Web Server to which it is considering routing a Mail Job. It must also consider how much access that Web Server has to Mail Servers and how busy those Mail Servers are.

**Load Updates** Every five timesteps, each machine sends a Load Update to each of its neighbors. Load Updates indicate how many jobs a machine already has in its queue. While Load Updates incur network traffic overhead, their contents can help an intelligent router make better decisions.

**Job Creation** At each timestep, each user chooses randomly between creating one or two new jobs. For each job, it chooses randomly between a Mail Job and a Database Job. The creation of new jobs by each user is subject to an important restriction: each user must remain below a maximum number of incomplete jobs (set to fifty in our experiments). When a user is at this maximum, it does not create any new jobs until older jobs are completed. This simple method of generating jobs models features of real user behavior: users tend to reduce their use of networks that are overloaded and the creation of new jobs depends on the completion of older ones. For example, a user typing a document on a slow terminal is likely to stop typing momentarily when the number of keystrokes not reflected on the screen becomes too great. In addition, this demand model allows us to easily test our methods on a network that is busy but not overloaded. Any demand model that is not tied to the system's capacity is likely to either under or over utilize network resources. In the former case, weak methods may still get good performance since there is spare capacity (i.e. a ceiling effect). In the latter case, even good methods will perform badly because the available resources, regardless of how they are allocated, are insufficient to meet demand. Our demand model, by striking a balance between these alternatives, allows us to more effectively compare methods of optimizing the network's performance.

**Utility Functions** The ultimate goal of our efforts is to improve the network's utility to its users. In the real world, that utility is not necessarily straightforward. While it is safe to assume that users always want their jobs completed as quickly as possible, the value of reducing a job's completion time is not always the same. Furthermore, each user may have a different importance to the system.

In order to capture these complexities, we assign different utility functions, shown in Figure 2, to our two users. Jobs created by the intern are scored according to the following function:

$$U(t) = \begin{cases} -t/10, & if\ t<75 \\ -10t+742.5, & otherwise \end{cases}$$

where $t$ is the job's completion time. By contrast, jobs created by the CEO are scored by the function

$$U(t) = \begin{cases} -10t, & if\ t<75 \\ -t/10-742.5, & otherwise \end{cases}$$

The crucial feature of these metrics is that they do not have constant slope. Hence, the change in utility that the system reaps for reducing the response time of a job is not constant. As explained below, this feature gives rise to the complications that make intelligent scheduling non-trivial. Though our experiments study only this particular pair of metrics, our algorithms are designed to work with arbitrary functions of completion time, so long as they are monotonically decreasing.

## Method

In this section, we present our approach to developing intelligent routers and schedulers for networks like the one detailed above. Due to the complications described above, achieving good performance in such a network using fixed algorithms and hand-coded heuristics is very difficult and prone to inflexibility. Instead, we use reinforcement learning to develop routers and schedulers that are efficient, robust, and adaptable. The rest of this section explains the details of our approach to these two problems.

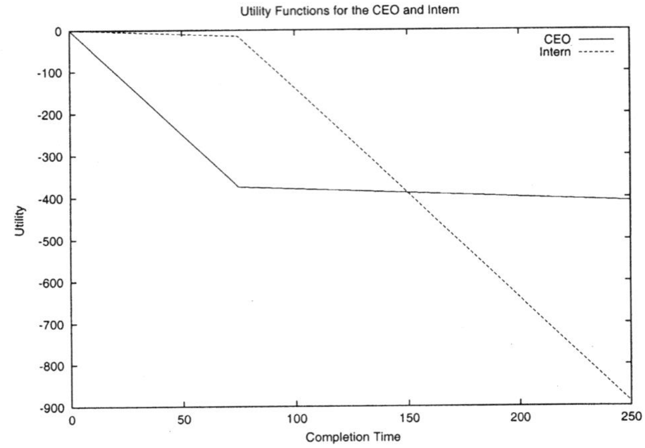


Figure 2: Utility Functions for the CEO and Intern.

### Routing

As traditionally posed, the packet routing problem requires a node in a network to decide to which neighboring node to forward a given packet such that it will reach its destination most quickly. In the network simulation described above, each machine faces a similar but not identical problem each time it finishes processing a job. When it is unable to complete the next step required by the job, it must search among its neighbors for machines that can complete that step (or that can forward the job to machines that can complete it). If more than one neighbor qualifies, the machine should make the choice that allows the job to be completed as quickly as possible.

In both our task and the traditional routing problem, the router tries to minimize the travel time of a packet given only local information about the network. However, in the traditional problem the goal is only to get the packet from its source to a specified destination. In our domain, this goal is not relevant. In fact, since a job returns to its creator when it is complete, the source and destination are the same. Instead, we want the job to travel along a path that allows the appropriate machines to complete its various steps in sequence and return to its creator in minimal time.

In this section, we present three ways of addressing this modified routing problem: a random method, a heuristic method, and a method, called Q-routing, based on reinforcement learning.

**Random Router** As its name implies, the random router forwards jobs to a machine selected randomly from the set of contenders $C$. A neighboring machine is a contender if it is capable of completing the job's next step. If no such machines exist, then $C$ is the set of all neighbors who can forward the job to a machine that can complete its next step. In the random router, the probability that a given job will be forwarded to a specific contender $c \in C$ is:

$$P_c = \frac{1}{|C|}$$

where $|C|$ is the size of $C$. Despite its simplicity, the random router is not without merit. For example, if all the neighbors have the same speed and do not receive load from anywhere else, the random router will keep the load on those neighbors evenly balanced. Of course, it does not address any of the complications that make routing a non-trivial problem and hence we expect it to perform poorly in real world scenarios.

**Heuristic Router** Without the aid of learning techniques or global information about the network, a heuristic router cannot be expected to perform optimally. However, it can do much better than the random router by exploiting the available local information, like the speed of its neighbors, to make routing decisions. Hence, our experiments also test a heuristic in which the likelihood of routing to a given neighbor is in direct proportion to that neighbor's speed. That is, for each $c \in C$,

$$P_c = \frac{speed(c)}{\sum_{c' \in C} speed(c'))}$$

This algorithm ignores both the load these neighbors might be receiving from other machines and the status of any machines the job might be sent to later. Hence, it acts as a myopic load balancer.

**Q-Router** Despite the distinctive features of our version of the routing problem, techniques developed to solve the traditional version can, with modification, be applied to the task faced by machines in our simulation. In this article, we adapt one such technique, called Q-routing (Boyan & Littman 1994), to improve the performance of our network. Q-routing is an on-line learning technique in which a reinforcement learning module is inserted into each node of the network.

In Q-routing, each node $x$ maintains a table of estimates about the *time-to-go* of packets if they are routed in various ways. Each entry $Q_x(d, y)$ is an estimate of how much additional time a packet will take to travel from $x$ to its ultimate destination $d$ if it is forwarded to $y$, a neighbor of $x$. If $x$ sends a packet to $y$, it will immediately get back an estimate $t$ for $x$'s time-to-go, which is based on the values in $y$'s Q-table:

$$t = min_{z \in Z} Q_y(d, z)$$

where $Z$ is the set of $y$'s neighbors. With this information, $x$ can update its estimate of the time-to-go for packets bound for $d$ that are sent to $y$. If $q$ is the time the packet spent in $x$'s queue and $s$ is the time the packet spent traveling between $x$ and $y$, then the following update rule applies:

$$Q_x(d, y) = (1 - \alpha)Q_x(d, y) + \alpha(q + s + t)$$

where $\alpha$ is a learning rate parameter (0.7 in our experiments). In the standard terms of reinforcement learning (Sutton & Barto 1998), $q+s$ represents the instantaneous reward (cost); $t$ is the estimated value of the next state, $y$.

By bootstrapping off the values in its neighbors' Q-tables, this update rule allows each node to improve its estimate of a packet's time-to-go without waiting for that packet to reach its final destination. This approach is based directly on the Q-learning method (Watkins 1989). Once reasonable Q-values have been learned, packets can be routed efficiently by simply consulting the appropriate entries in the Q-table and routing to the neighbor with the lowest estimated time-to-go for packets with the given destination.

***State Representation.*** To make Q-routing more suitable for our unique version of the packet routing problem, we must change the state features on which learning is based. Instead of simply using the job's destination, we use three features that indicate in what general direction the job is headed, what machine resources it will likely tax if routed in a particular way, and what priority it will be given by subsequent schedulers: 1) the type of the job, 2) the type of the next step the job needs completed, and 3) the user who created the job. In addition, we want a fourth state feature that allows the router to consider how much load is already on the neighbors to which it is considering forwarding a job. We could add a state feature for every neighbor that represents the current load on that machine. However, this would dramatically increase the size of the resulting Q-table, especially for large, highly-connected networks, and could make table-based learning infeasible. Fortunately, almost all of those state features are irrelevant and can be discarded. Since we are trying to estimate a job's time-to-go if it is routed to a given machine, the only information that is relevant is the load on *that particular machine*. Hence, we use an action-dependent feature (Stone & Veloso 1999). As the name implies, action-dependent features cause an agent's state to change as different actions are considered. In this case, our action-dependent feature always contains the current load on whatever neighbor we are considering routing to. The load on all other neighbors is not included and hence the Q-table remains very small.

***Update Frequency.*** The original formulation of Q-routing specifies that each time a node receives a packet it should reply with a time-to-go estimate for that packet. However, it is not necessarily optimal to do so every time. In fact, the frequency at which such updates are sent represents an important trade-off. The more often a reply is sent, the more reliable the router's feedback will be and the more rapidly it will train. However, if replies are sent less often, then more network bandwidth is reserved for jobs, instead of being clogged with administrative updates. In our implementation, replies are sent with a 0.5 probability, which we determined through informal experimentation to be optimal.

***Action Selection.*** Like other techniques based on reinforcement learning, Q-routing needs an exploration mechanism to ensure that optimal policies are discovered. If the router always selects the neighbor with the lowest time-to-go, it may end up with a sub-optimal policy because only the best neighbor's estimate will ever get updated. An exploration mechanism ensures the router will sometimes select neighbors other than the current best and hence eventually correct sub-optimalities in its policy. Our implementation uses $\epsilon$-greedy exploration (Sutton & Barto 1998), with $\epsilon$ set to 0.05. In $\epsilon$-greedy exploration, the router will, with probability $\epsilon$, select a neighbor randomly; with probability $1 - \epsilon$ it will select the currently estimated best neighbor.

## Scheduling

The routing techniques discussed above all attempt to minimize the time that passes between the creation and completion of a job. However, this completion time is only indirectly related to the score, which it is our goal to maximize. The score assigned to any job is determined by the utility function, which can be different for different types of jobs or users. The only requirement is that the function decrease monotonically with respect to completion time (i.e. users never prefer their jobs to take longer).

At first, this monotonicity constraint may seem to make the routing approach sufficient on its own: if we are minimizing the completion time, we must be maximizing the score. However, this is true only in the very limited case where all jobs have the same importance. When jobs are governed by different utility functions, minimizing the completion time of less important jobs can be dramatically suboptimal because it uses network resources that would be better reserved for more important jobs. In this sense, the Q-routing technique explained above has a greedy approach: it attempts to maximize the score of a given job (by minimizing its completion time) but does not consider how doing so may affect the score of other jobs.

In principle, this shortcoming could be addressed by revising the values that the Q-router learns and bases its decisions on. For example, if the Q-values represented global utility instead of time-to-go, the router would have no incentive to favor the current job and could eventually learn to route in a way that maximizes global utility, even at the expense of a particular job's time-to-go. However, such a system would have the serious disadvantage of requiring each node to have system-wide information about the consequences of its actions, whereas the current system is able to learn given only feedback from immediate neighbors.

Another alternative would be to change the router's action space. Currently, an action consists of routing a particular job to some neighbor. Instead, each action could represent a decision about how to route *all* the jobs currently in the machine's queue. While such a system would reduce the router's myopia, it would create a prohibitively large action space. Given a queue of length $n$ and a set of $m$ neighbors, there would be $m^n$ possible actions!

Given these difficulties, we believe the challenges posed by complicated utility functions are best addressed, not by further elaborating our routers, but by coupling them with intelligent schedulers. Schedulers determine in what order the jobs sitting at a machine will be processed. They decide how the machine's CPU time will be scheduled. By determining which jobs are in most pressing need of completion and processing them first, intelligent schedulers can maximize the network's score even when the utility functions are asymmetric.

**FIFO Scheduler** The default scheduling algorithm used in our simulator is the *first-in first-out* (FIFO) technique. In this approach, jobs that have been waiting in the machine's queue the longest are always processed first. More precisely, the scheduler chooses the next job to process by selecting randomly from the set $J_l$ of jobs that have been waiting the longest. If $time(j)$ is the time that job $j$ arrived at the machine and $J$ is the set of waiting jobs, $J_l$ is determined as follows:

$$J_l = \{j \in J \mid time(j) \leq time(j'), \forall j' \in J\}$$

The FIFO algorithm does nothing to address the complications that arise when jobs have different importance.

**Priority Scheduler** An alternative heuristic that does address these concerns is a *priority scheduler*. This algorithm works just like the FIFO approach except that each job is assigned a priority. When allocating CPU time, the priority scheduler examines only those jobs with the highest priority and selects randomly from among the ones that have been waiting the longest. In other words, the priority scheduler selects jobs randomly from the following set:

$$\begin{aligned} J_l = \{j \in J \mid \quad & time(j) \leq time(j') \land \\ & priority(j) \geq priority(j'), \quad \forall j' \in J\} \end{aligned}$$

If all the utility functions are simply multiples of each other, the priority scheduler can achieve optimal performance by assigning jobs priorities that correspond to the weight of their utility function. However, when the utility functions are truly different, the problem of deciding which jobs deserve higher priority becomes much more complicated and the simplistic approach of the priority scheduler breaks down.

**Insertion Scheduler** To develop a more sophisticated approach, we need to formulate the problem more carefully. Every time a new job arrives at a machine, the scheduler must choose an ordering of all the $n$ jobs in the queue and select for processing the job that appears at the head of that ordering. Of the $n!$ possible orderings, we want the scheduler to select the ordering with the highest utility, where utility is the sum of the estimated scores of all the jobs in the queue. Hence, to develop an intelligent scheduler, we need to decide 1) how to estimate the utility of an ordering and 2) how to efficiently select the best ordering from among the $n!$ contenders.

The utility of an ordering is the sum of the constituent jobs' scores and a given job's score is a known function of completion time. Thus, the problem of estimating an ordering's utility reduces to estimating the completion time of all the jobs in that ordering. A job's completion time depends on three factors: 1) how old it was when it arrived at the current machine, 2) how long it will wait in this machine's queue given the considered ordering, and 3) how much additional time it will take to complete after it leaves this machine. The first factor is known and the second factor is easily computed given the speed of the machine and a list of the jobs preceding this one in the ordering. The third factor is not known but can be estimated using machine learning. In fact, the values we want to know are exactly the same as those Q-routing learns. Hence, if the scheduler we place in each machine is coupled with a Q-router, no additional learning is necessary. We can look up the entry in the Q-table that corresponds to a job of the given type. Note that this estimate improves over time as the Q-router learns.

Once we can estimate the completion time of any job, we can compute the utility of any ordering. The only challenge that remains is how to efficiently select a good ordering from among the $n!$ possibilities. Clearly, enumerating each possibility is not computationally feasible. If we treat this task as a search problem, we could use any of a number of optimization techniques (e.g. hill climbing, simulated annealing, or genetic algorithms). However, these techniques also require significant computational resources and the performance gains offered by the orderings they discover are unlikely to justify the CPU time they consume, since the search needs to be performed each time a new job arrives. Given these constraints, we propose a simple, fast heuristic called the *insertion scheduler*. When a new job arrives, the insertion scheduler does not consider any orderings that are radically different from the current ordering. Instead, it decides at what position to insert the new job into the current ordering such that utility is maximized. Hence, it needs to consider only $n$ orderings. While this restriction may prevent the insertion scheduler from discovering the optimal ordering, it nonetheless allows for intelligent scheduling of jobs, with only linear computational complexity, that exploits learned estimates of completion time.

## Results

To evaluate our routing and scheduling methods, we ran a series of experiments on the example network described above. Figure 3 shows the result of the first set of experiments, in which our three routing methods — random routing, heuristic routing, and Q-routing — are each employed in conjunction with a FIFO scheduler in simulations that run for 20,000 timesteps. In each case, the simulation runs for another 20,000 "warmup" steps before timestep #0 to get the network load up to full capacity before tallying scores. In the case of Q-routing, a random router is used during the warmup steps; Q-routing is turned on and begins training only at timestep #0. At timestep #10,000, a network catastrophe is simulated in which Web Server #1, Mail Server #1, and Database #3 simultaneously go down and remain down for the duration of the run. At any point in the simulation, the score for each method represents a uniform moving average over the scores received for the last 100 completed jobs. The scores are averaged over 25 runs.

The graph clearly indicates that routing randomly is dramatically suboptimal. The heuristic router, which routes in proportion to the speed of its neighbors, performs much better. Using a t-test, we verified that the heuristic router's advantage is significant with 95% confidence after timestep #1,000. The Q-routing method, whose initial policy lacks even the primitive load balancing of the random router, starts off as the worst performer but improves rapidly and plateaus with a higher score than the heuristic. This difference is significant with 95% confidence after timestep #4,000. Both the Q-router and the heuristic router are able to respond gracefully to the loss of machines in the middle of the simulation (the reason for the heuristic router's robustness is discussed in the following section); the Q-router maintains its superiority afterwards. The random router, however, suffers a major loss of performance from the sudden change in network configuration.

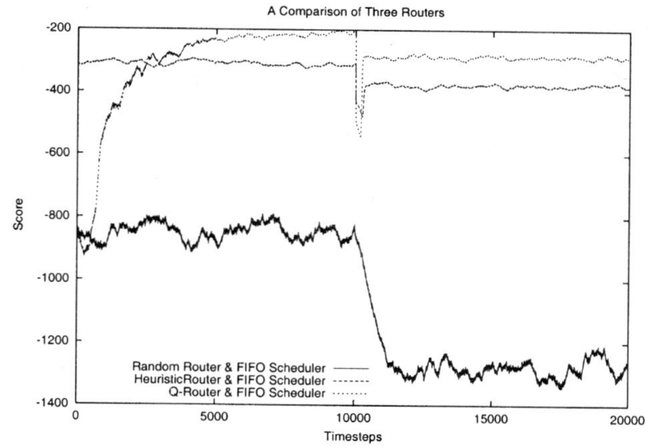


Figure 3: A comparison of three routing methods. A network catastrophe occurs at timestep #10,000.

Figure 4 shows the results of a second set of experiments. These experiments are identical to the first except that three different schedulers—the FIFO scheduler, the priority scheduler, and the insertion scheduler—are tested, all in conjunction with our best router, the Q-router.

The FIFO scheduler, which ignores complications that arise from the utility functions, performs relatively poorly, while the priority and insertion schedulers fare much better. The insertion scheduler, by capitalizing on the information learned in each machine's Q-table, obtains scores that are approximately 20% higher than those of the priority scheduler. A t-test verified that these differences are significant with 95% confidence after timestep #4,000. Since all of these runs use Q-routing, they all recover from the network catastrophe at timestep #10,000.

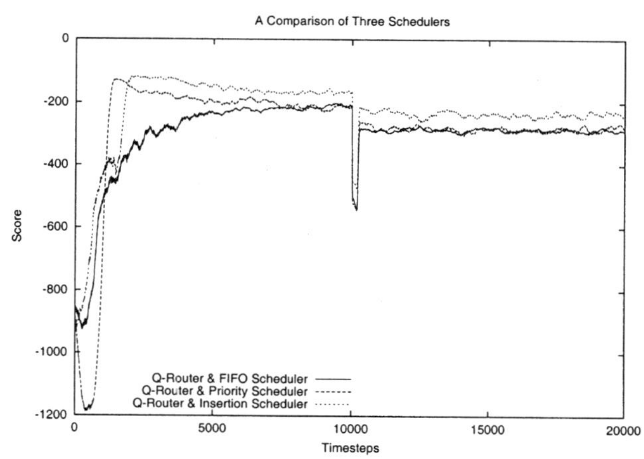


Figure 4: A comparison of three scheduling methods. A network catastrophe occurs at timestep #10,000.

Note that these results compare only five of the nine possible combinations of routers and schedulers. Two of the remaining combinations (pairing insertion schedulers with random or heuristic routers) are infeasible since the insertion scheduler depends on estimates from the Q-router and cannot function in its absence. The other two combinations (pairing priority schedulers with random or heuristic routers) performed worse in our experiments and are omitted from the graphs for the sake of clarity.

## Discussion

Our experimental results indicate that machine learning methods offer a significant advantage in optimizing the performance of complicated networks. Both the router and scheduler placed in each machine benefit substantially from the time-to-go estimates discovered through reinforcement learning. Furthermore, the best performance is achieved only by placing intelligent, adaptive agents at more than one level of the system: the Q-router and the insertion scheduler perform better together than either could apart. Hence, they benefit from a sensible division of optimization tasks; the router routes jobs efficiently and balances load throughout the network while the scheduler prioritizes those jobs whose effect on the score will be most decisive.

One of the chief advantages of the reinforcement learning techniques we employ is that they learn on-line, while the system is running. Unlike off-line methods, our system is never locked in to a specific policy but can continually adapt to changes in network topology or shifts in user demand. The superior recovery of Q-routing after machines have been ablated, when compared to random routing, verifies the worth of this feature. However, Q-routing, while continuing to get the best performance, does not recover more gracefully than the heuristic router, which uses no learning at all. Though initially surprising, this result makes sense after a careful consideration of the heuristic policy. Because the heuristic router does not learn, nothing in its policy is tuned to the current status of the network. Hence, adapting to changes is easier. So long as the heuristic router gets updated information about the state of its neighbors (which can be provided via Load Updates without learning), its policy remains viable. Since Q-routing's policy depends highly on the current configuration, it faces a greater task of adaptation when that configuration changes. In this light, it is not surprising that the heuristic router suffers little degradation in performance after a sudden system change. Instead, it is remarkable that our system, despite a greater burden to adapt, is able to recover just as robustly.

## Future Work

In ongoing research, we hope to use machine learning to determine what network topology gives optimal performance. In the research presented here, network performance is optimized given a certain network configuration; the structure of the network is not within the learner's control. We hope to develop a system in which machine learning helps determine the most efficient structure of the network when it is designed, upgraded, or repaired.

Our on-going research goal is to discover, implement, and test machine learning methods in support of autonomic computing at all levels of a computer system. Though this initial work is all in simulation, the true measure of our methods is whether they can impact performance on real systems. Whenever possible, our design decisions are made with this fact in mind. Ultimately we plan to implement and test our autonomic computing methods, such as Q-router and insertion scheduler, on real computer systems.

## Conclusion

The three main contributions of this article are: 1) a concrete formulation of the autonomic computing problem in terms of the representative task of enterprise system optimization, 2) a new fully implemented and tested vertical simulator designed to abstractly represent all aspects of a computer system, and 3) adaptive approaches to the job routing and scheduling problems in this simulator that out-perform reasonable benchmark policies.

The research presented in this article indicates that machine learning methods can offer a significant advantage for routing and scheduling jobs on complex networks. It also provides evidence of the value of combining intelligent, adaptive agents at more than one level of the system. Together these results provide hope that machine learning methods, when applied repeatedly and in concert, can produce the robust, self-configuring, and self-repairing systems that tomorrow's computing needs will demand.

## Acknowledgments

We would like to thank IBM for a generous faculty award to help jump-start this research. In particular, thanks to Russ Blaisdell for valuable technical discussions and to Ann Marie Maynard for serving as a liaison. This research was supported in part by NSF CAREER award IIS-0237699. Finally, we would like to thank Gerry Tesauro for his insightful suggestions about Q-routing.

## References

Boyan, J. A., and Littman, M. L. 1994. Packet routing in dynamically changing networks: A reinforcement learning approach. In Cowan, J. D.; Tesauro, G.; and Alspector, J., eds., *Advances in Neural Information Processing Systems*, volume 6, 671–678. Morgan Kaufmann Publishers, Inc.

Brachman, R. J. 2002. Systems that know what they're doing. *IEEE Intelligent Systems* 17(6):67–71.

Caro, G. D., and Dorigo, M. 1998. AntNet: Distributed stigmergetic control for communications networks. *Journal of Artificial Intelligence Research* 9:317–365.

Clark, D. D.; Partridge, C.; Ramming, J. C.; and Wroclawski, J. 2003. A knowledge plane for the internet. In *Proceedings of ACM SIGCOMM*.

Itao, T.; Suda, T.; and Aoyama, T. 2001. Jack-in-the-net: Adaptive networking architecture for service emergence. In *Proc. of the Asian-Pacific Conference on Communications*.

Kephart, J. O., and Chess, D. M. 2003. The vision of autonomic computing. *Computer* 41–50.

Stone, P., and Veloso, M. 1999. Team-partitioned, opaque-transition reinforcement learning. In Asada, M., and Kitano, H., eds., *RoboCup-98: Robot Soccer World Cup II*. Berlin: Springer Verlag. Also in *Proceedings of the Third International Conference on Autonomous Agents*, 1999.

Sutton, R. S., and Barto, A. G. 1998. *Reinforcement Learning: An Introduction*. Cambridge, MA: MIT Press.

Watkins, C. J. C. H. 1989. *Learning from Delayed Rewards*. Ph.D. Dissertation, King's College, Cambridge, UK.

# Synthetic Adversaries for Urban Combat Training

**Robert E. Wray**

Soar Technology, Inc.
3600 Green Court Suite 600
Ann Arbor MI 48105
wray@soartech.com

**John E. Laird, Andrew Nuxoll, Devvan Stokes, Alex Kerfoot**

University of Michigan
1101 Beal Ave.
Ann Arbor, MI 48109-2110
laird, anuxoll, dstokes, akerfoot@umich.edu

**Abstract**

This paper describes requirements for synthetic adversaries for urban combat training and MOUTBots, a prototype application. The MOUTBots use a commercial computer game to define, implement and test basic behavior representation requirements and the Soar architecture as the engine for knowledge representation and execution. We describe how these components aided the development of the prototype and present an initial evaluation against competence, taskability, fidelity, variability, transparency, and efficiency requirements.

## Introduction

Offensive urban combat is one of the most difficult tasks soldiers perform. Urban combat is characterized by building-to-building, room-to-room fighting. Frequent training is an essential element in reducing casualties. However, training in urban environments is costly and restricted to physical mockups of buildings and small towns. The Office of Naval Research's Virtual Training & Environments (VIRTE) program is developing immersive virtual trainers for military operations on urbanized terrain (MOUT). In this trainer, four-person fire teams of U.S. Marines will be situated in a virtual urban environment and tasked to clear a building, possibly containing enemy soldiers. Virtual opponents are required to populate the environment and challenge the trainees.

This paper describes the general requirements for opponents and our development of synthetic adversaries to meet them. The agents are built using the Soar cognitive architecture and they interface to a commercial game engine that served as an initial development environment. In order to simplify the behaviors that needed to be encoded in the prototype, we have initially focused on MOUT behaviors within a building.

### Requirements for Synthetic Adversaries

This application has six major high-level requirements:

1. **Competence:** The adversaries must perform the tactics and missions humans perform in this domain. For this application, the adversaries' goal is to defend a small multi-storied building in teams of 2-5 using assault weapons and grenades. The agents must move through the environment, identify tactically relevant features (such as escape routes), and communicate and coordinate with other agents.
2. **Taskability:** The agents must be able to be assigned new missions for different training scenarios and they must change their objectives during an exercise.
3. **Observational fidelity:** The agents do not have to model accurately all aspects of human behavior. Instead, they must model those aspects of human behavior that are observable and relevant to training.
4. **Behavior variability:** The agents must not be predictable so that the trainees are exposed to many diverse experiences. By experiencing many different situations and opponent behaviors, unexpected situations will be minimized in real life.
5. **Transparency:** To allow "after action review," opponents should be able to explain why they went into a particular room, or retreated at some juncture in the scenario. Explanations are much easier to generate in systems that use transparent representations that map directly to understood terms.
6. **Minimal computational footprint:** This application is targeted for personal computers, with a majority of the computational processing reserved for graphics and physics modeling. Thus, synthetic adversaries will be allocated only a small time slice in system execution.

## Related Work

Possibly the most advanced examples of embedding synthetic agents in military simulations are TacAir-Soar and RWA-Soar. These systems emulate the behavior of military personnel performing missions in fixed-wing and rotary-wing aircraft and have been used in large-scale military training exercises (Jones et al., 1999; Tambe et al., 1995). TacAir-Soar and RWA-Soar agents are completely autonomous, making decisions based on their awareness of the surrounding environment, commands received from other entities, and their extensive knowledge of military doctrine and tactics. They have the ability to pursue mission objects alone, or they can participate in larger groups made up of other synthetic agents or even human teammates participating via simulators (Laird, Jones, & Nielsen, 1998). The research described here builds on that prior research and extends it to the specific requirements of the creating adversaries for MOUT training. The four most important areas of differentiation are:

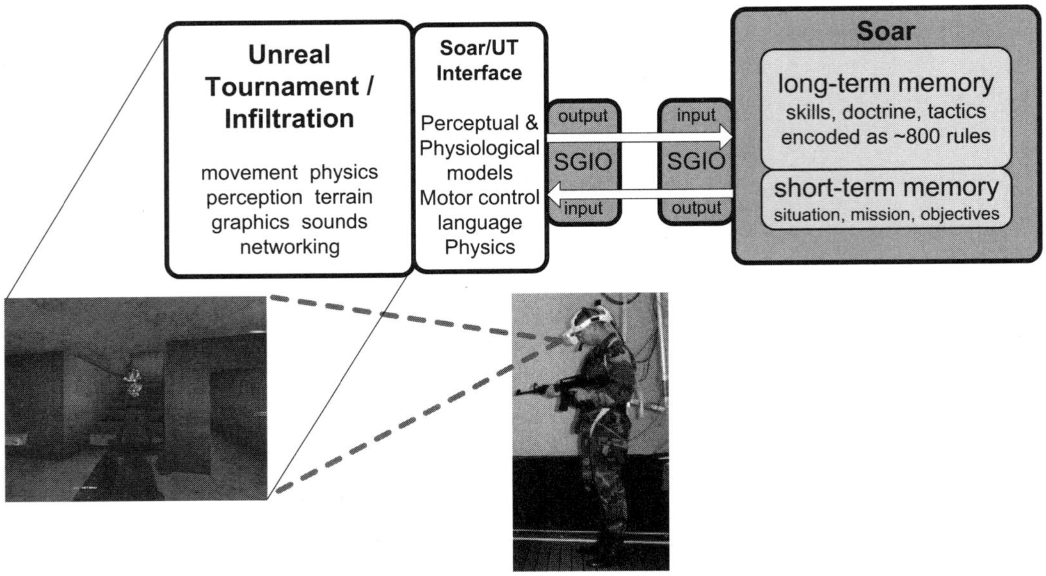


Figure 1. The MOUTBot System Architecture

1. **Compressed time scale**: In TacAir-Soar and RWA-Soar, the decision cycle could vary from .25 to .5 seconds without significant degradation in observable behavior. For MOUT, reaction times must be on the order of .1 seconds to support realistic behavior (e.g., avoid running into walls). Missions in TacAir-Soar and RWA-Soar were on the order of an hour, while for the MOUT domain, scenarios transpire in minutes.
2. **Loose mission structure, teamwork and coordination:** Missions could be very complex in the air domain with multiple phases to each mission. In addition, a complex hierarchical command structure, set by military doctrine, coordinated teamwork. For some missions, over 30 aircraft could be flying together. In the MOUT domain, the missions consist mostly of defending specific rooms, with some individual missions. Only small numbers of agents work together and there is little or no time for complex communication and preplanned coordination. In fact, one surprise was that the types of coordination required of the adversaries was so minimal, that using the coordination schemes developed for the air agents (Tambe, 1997) was unnecessary.
3. **Indoor spatial reasoning:** In the air domain, fine-grained spatial reasoning about terrain is unnecessary. For indoor combat, agents must understand room geometry of as well as the total topology of a building in order to set up attacks, ambushes, and retreats.
4. **Behavior variability:** In the air domain, the overall complexity of the virtual environment provided sufficient variability so that the behavior of TacAir-Soar agents was not predictable. However, this application requires a training environment where the trainees can be exposed to the same general situation many times. As a result, variability in behavior is much more important than in TacAir-Soar.

Another implementation of synthetic adversaries has been developed using ACT-R (Best, Lebiere, & Scarpinnatto, 2002). Their emphasis was to demonstrate the feasibility of using ACT-R for controlling synthetic characters and fine-grained spatial representations; our application was directly geared to the requirements of deployment.

Many commercial computer games simulate military combat (America's Army, Operation Flashpoint, Full Spectrum Warrior). The adversaries in these games are usually scripted or based on simple finite-state machines. Thus, they have limited autonomy, little ability to reason on the spatial aspects of tactical situations, and can be too predictable, possibly leading to negative training. However, more autonomous individual adversaries have also been developed for first-person perspective interactive computer games (Adobbati, Marshall, et al 2001; Laird, 2001a). These "bots" play "deathmatches", where the rules and weapons are significantly different than MOUT engagements. They do not meet the list of requirements listed above (no individual missions, limited coordination, behavior not constrained by real-world military doctrine and tactics). However, there is significant overlap in some of the underlying capabilities, enough so that the system described here was based in part on a bot developed in Soar to play Quake (Laird, 2001a, 2001b).

## Overall System Design

This section introduces *MOUTBots*, the autonomous, intelligent opponents developed to meet the requirements. Here, we briefly review supporting technologies and describe the overall system architecture.

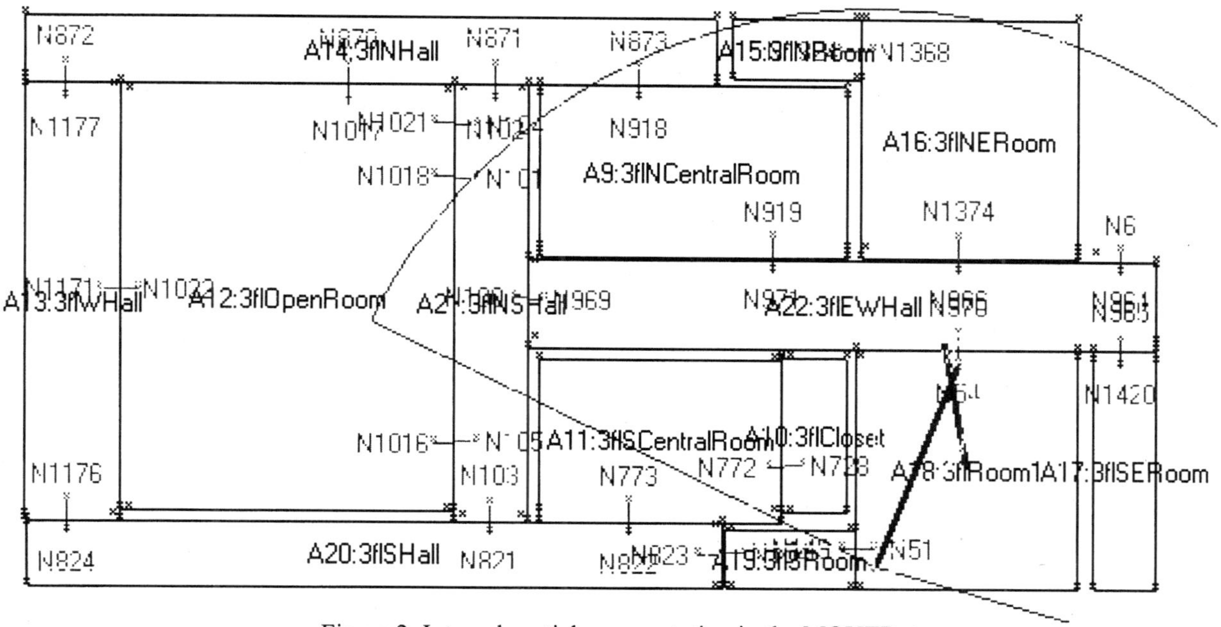


Figure 2. Internal spatial representation in the MOUTBots

## Simulation Environment: Unreal Tournament

Figure 1 presents the system architecture. The simulation environment is realized in an extension of the commercial computer game Unreal Tournament (UT) called Infiltration[1]. The UT-Soar-Interface simulates the perception and motor actions of our agents in the environment and is connected to Soar via Soar General Input/Output (SGIO). Each agent is run as an independent copy of Soar, the cognitive component of a MOUTBot. Soar knowledge is encoded as rules. All of the agents are run on a single computer, with the human players running on their own computers, networked together.

Unreal Tournament is an off-the-shelf extendable 3D game engine that supports networked play. Infiltration provides graphics and models of modern weapons (e.g., M-16 rifles), more sophisticated models of the impact of wounds, and representations of modern army uniforms and equipment. All game physics and the game interface are coded in an internal scripting language. Using UT's environment editor, we created a synthetic training environment (a 3 story building with a variety of rooms and hallways) that presented the breadth of training situations as recommended by our subject matter experts.

## Perception and Motor Control Module

We extended Infiltration to include more complete models of perception and motor actions. Visual perception is challenging because of the difficulty of sensing walls (and doors) in simulation environments. Processing the internal Unreal data structures to detect walls, doors and other environmental features would be computationally prohibitive. To circumvent these challenges, we introduced a number of simplifications based on an annotated map.

Figure 2 illustrates an example map. Each agent receives an annotated map with nodes that define the boundaries of each room. This allows an agent to determine the room in which it is located. Nodes are also placed in the map at connections (doors, windows) between areas. The MOUTBots use the nodes to build up a topological map of the building. The interface supports the motor actions required by adversaries, including walking, running, shooting (aiming, firing, reloading), grenade throwing, as well as postures other than standing (crouching, kneeling).

## Cognitive Architecture: Soar

The cognitive component of the synthetic adversaries is implemented in the Soar cognitive architecture (Laird, Newell, & Rosenbloom, 1987; Newell, 1990). In Soar, all long-term knowledge is encoded as production rules, while the current situation (perception, situational awareness, mission information, and goals) is encoded in declarative data structures comprising its state. The rules in Soar match against the state and propose operators to apply to the current situation. Primitive operators send commands to the motor system. Complex operators are dynamically converted to subgoals that are then pursued by once again having rules select and apply operators in the subgoals, eventually resulting in operators that execute primitive actions. Recent versions of Soar now also include belief and goal maintenance mechanisms (Wray & Laird, 2003a). These mechanisms improve robustness and simplify

[1] Unreal Tournament was developed by Epic Games. Infiltration was developed by Sentry Studios.

knowledge development, contributing to our ability to encode a complex behavior system quickly.

## Meeting the Requirements

The MOUTBot consists of over 25 major data structures and 800 production rules (which implement 120 operators). This section outlines some of the knowledge encoded in the MOUTBots and how this knowledge is applied to generate behavior, addressing each of the above requirements.

### Competence

To create competent adversaries for MOUT training, we studied available literature (field manuals and historical accounts) and interviewed experts. We discovered there is little written doctrine for urban combat defense, so we relied heavily on human subject matter experts (SMEs). We developed synthetic adversaries that could play many different roles: defending a room, acting as a sentry (by watching through a window), defending a hallway, and acting as the leader of the group – giving commands to reposition, retreat or attack. As the project progressed, the training application began to focus on scenarios of only a single fire team of four trainees. Because attackers prefer at least a 3-to-1 force ratio for urban attack, these scenarios require only two adversaries working together to provide an appropriate training experience. However, our implemented system also supports larger scenarios with teams of five to eight adversaries defending a building.

In order to perform the required missions, the MOUTBots required the following capabilities:

- Situational awareness
  - Categorize situation: available weapons, ammo, enemy, health, level of incoming fire, etc.
  - Record/manage information about threats and friendly units
  - Identify tactically relevant topology of building
- Movement
  - Move within room, to door ways, and through doorways (run and walk)
  - Compute paths between rooms; determine visibility between rooms, note types of rooms, exits, etc.
  - Explore buildings and create an internal map
- Weapons handling & management
  - Reload, unjam weapon
  - Choose weapon based on situation
- Perform specific mission
  - Change mission on command from leader
  - Abandon mission
- Appropriate tactical and mission response
  - Atack with gun and grenade (and rocks)
  - Retreat/Hide and pop out
  - Defend a room
  - Roam
  - Watch for enemy entry (sentry)
  - Surrender
- Communication & coordination via realistic messages

This knowledge is represented as elaborated objects in memory and operators (implemented via production rules).

**Objects.** The agent uses object data structures to maintain situation awareness during execution of a scenario. For example, the **threat** data structure is used to maintain awareness about enemy (i.e., trainee) contacts. The threat structure includes information about the status of the threat and current or last known location. Additional situation-specific information may also be elaborated. For example, for a visible threat, the threat's body position, its direction of movement, whether or not it is firing, its egocentric location with respect to the agent (near, far; left, right; etc.) will be asserted. In some situations when the agent cannot directly observe a known threat, it may make (simple) predictions about the possible movement of the enemy which are stored with the threat information.

The building map is the most complex object maintained by the MOUTBot. The MOUTBot creates its map by exploring the building before an engagement. It uses map nodes to build an internal representation of the location and extent of rooms, doors, and windows. Figure 2 shows a visualization of the MOUTBot's internal representation of the map. The bot is in the lower right corner facing northeast. The semi-circle shows the bots potential visible areas (it can not see through walls). Nodes (represented as asterisks) are embedded in the map. The agent uses these nodes to define walls (black lines) and connections between rooms. The agent determines navigable areas within rooms (gray lines). During exploration, the MOUTBot also analyzes the map to determine paths between rooms, which are critical for some of its tactical analysis of threats and safe retreat paths. The MOUTBot can engage an enemy without a full map; however, because many of the tactics are dependent on map information, its behavior will be severely degraded without it. Thus, the image in Figure 2 is built up by the agent from its own exploration of the building environment.

Other important objects include **mission**, a description of the current mission and the achievement of objectives; and **self**, the current assessment of the agent's capabilities including health, available weapons, as well as any customizations that differentiate this agent from others.

**Operators.** Operators are used to take action in the world, establish goals, and record persistent facts about the current situation. For example, the **reload** operator performs an action in the environment. The MOUTBots do not count rounds as they are expended (in contrast to Dirty Harry, but in agreement with our experts). **Reload** is proposed after the agent attempts to fire and receives an error message from the simulator. This error message corresponds to the "click" of a trigger to an empty chamber. When reload is selected, a rule sends the **reload** command to the simulator. The simulator will respond by playing an animation representing the reloading of the weapon and providing additional rounds to the weapon (assuming the agent has additional rounds available). During this time, the agent can do additional reasoning, but it cannot perform any other actions in the world. The reload error message can trigger other actions beside **reload**. For example, if a threat is near, other operators will be proposed so that the agent might choose to seek cover before reloading.

**Record-threat** is an example of an operator that maintains situation awareness by internally recording information, in this case, about other agents it has observed. It is invoked whenever a threat is encountered that the agent has not previously encountered, when it is loses contact with an agent (e.g., if the agent passes by a doorway), and when it encounters an agent it has encountered previously. The action of the **record-threat** operator is to add to or update the **threat** object with information about the enemy agent. In the current MOUTBot, the agent discriminates between individual enemies and makes no mistakes due to misclassification of a threat (e.g. fratricide), although introducing human error would require relatively simple elaborations of the model.

The **Retreat** operator requires many primitive actions spread out over time. When **retreat** is selected, a subgoal is automatically created (because there are not rules to directly apply it). In the subgoal, there are additional operators that perform the necessary actions, including determining where the greatest threat is (shown as the red line in Figure 2), picking a door to retreat through (away from the threat), abandoning the current objective, moving to a new room and then determining what objective should be pursued in that room (such as defending the room or further retreating). Some of these actions require subgoals as well (such as moving to a new room), and a subgoal stack is dynamically created. The dynamic context switching required by the MOUTBots did not require elaborate knowledge representations because Soar now includes mechanisms that dynamically capture dependencies between goals and performs the context switching via architectural mechanisms (Wray & Laird, 2003a).

## Taskability

All agent knowledge (and consequently behavior) is independent of the specific mission and scenario; the same set of rules is used for all scenarios and all agents. In order to define specific scenario with unique roles for different MOUTBots, a user creates explicit mission tasking within a single "mission specification" production rule. This mission specification allows the user to indicate teammates, fire teams, and a commander(s), the type of mission (defensive/offensive), each MOUTBot's role in the mission (defend area/roam/sentry), initial areas to defend, places to which to retreat, and the type and direction of expected threats. Moreover, the leader MOUTBot can issue a limited set of commands to change the missions of other bots. For example, if there is an agent performing the sentry mission, once it sights an enemy approaching the building and informs others of the approaching threat, it might be instructed to move to another area and defend that area, causing it to terminate the sentry objective and initiate a defend objective.

## Observational Fidelity

We did not attempt to make the MOUTBots as realistic as possible. The MOUT environment has many behavioral elements to consider for representation, among them doctrine and tactical knowledge, spatial and temporal knowledge, coordination and communication with other entities, courage and cowardice, indecision, leadership, startle responses, reaction to light, noise, smoke, debris, emotion, mood, physiological moderators, etc. The observational fidelity requirement provided a critical guide for determining what to represent among this imposing list. We concentrated on those elements observable to trainees as well as fundamental behaviors such as tactically appropriate movement, weapons handling, and communication. This focus allowed us to simplify non-observable behaviors. For example, trainees should not generally be able to observe opponents at-ease in a MOUT situation; thus, MOUTBots "at-ease" simply stand without moving, fidgeting, etc. Observational fidelity also allowed us to avoid detailed internal models when the behavioral role of the model is minimal. For example, although we implemented a fairly sophisticated ray-tracing model of peripheral vision, a plane-based model of visual perception was indistinguishable at the level of behavior from the ray-tracing model. Although it did not fully represent the complexities of human peripheral vision, the simpler model required significantly less computational resources.

Observational fidelity also mandates that any behavior that is observable should be represented. Thus, agents must not "cheat" (as in common in commercial computer games). Agents are limited by the terrain; they do not transport to other locations, disappear in firefights, etc. Additionally, they must coordinate as actual human combatants do, by shared, common knowledge, observation, and communication when necessary. This requirement also means that their behavior can be disrupted in the same way human behavior is and it means that the agents will make mistakes. For example, if one member of a MOUTBot fire team decides to exit after observing an enemy, it is possible that his partner may have not sighted the enemy and may miss his retreat, unless these events are communicated.

Figure 3. An example of variability in the MOUTBots: Choosing a location from which to defend

## Behavior Variability

A difference in observed behavior when entities are placed in essentially the same situations is the essence of behavior variability. Capturing variability in synthetic entities is important because it prepares the trainee for the variability inherent in human behavior in the real world. As project SMEs stressed, it is critical to expose trainees to the breadth of skill levels in the opponent forces. Untrained forces may behave in ways that are non-optimal and even dangerous for themselves; however trainees must be prepared to quickly respond to such behavior with appropriate tactics, even if they would not use them against a highly trained opponent.

For this project, we focused on behavior variability in individual agents. If a single agent has little or no variability in its behavior, it becomes predictable, and a trainee may attempt to "game" an opponent inappropriately. Rather than modeling detailed knowledge differences that lead to different choices or potential sources of variability, our goal was to create mechanisms that better support variability in decision making within the agent architecture. Our hypothesis is that, long-term, it will be less expensive to introduce factors that influence the decision making process that can be generalized over many applications rather than attempting to program (or have an agent learn) knowledge differences. These *variability parameters* can be used to generate within-subject and across-subject variability without having to model the sources of variability explicitly. This hypothesis assumes that there are human behavior moderators that lead to variability, even when the knowledge of human participants is (more or less) the same.

Normally, we would encode the best or good choices for a specific situation. For example, one might only use a grenade at dynamic tactical junctures, or when faced with overwhelming firepower. Following this approach, multiple agents in the simulation and across multiple runs of the simulation all would exhibit similar behaviors. They would not use grenades until tactically appropriate situations. In reality, soldiers make different choices.

We extended Soar's basic knowledge representation and modified the Soar decision process to support more varied option selection. Productions that propose and prefer operators now include a numeric value, indicating a "probability" of selection when compared to other, equally preferable choices. When the options available are all equally preferable, the values for each option are averaged and then a random choice made from the normalized probability distribution of the averaged values.

This new selection mechanism requires a broader knowledge base than is strictly necessary. When variability is desired, the knowledge engineer must identify a range of options rather than one. For example, in the MOUTBots, target selection was initially based on proximity, which is a valid, realistic algorithm for selecting targets. To improve variability, we need to encode multiple target selection strategies and define simple probability distributions among these different strategies. In the long-term, agent development may focus on much more comprehensive efforts to describe and codify behaviors across many classes of subjects.

We implemented this simple within-subject approach to greater variation in decision making. Figure 3 shows an example of the resulting variability in the MOUTBots. In this scenario, two MOUTBots move to corner positions in the room. Agents also choose a body position (standing, crouched, prone) appropriate for the position. For example, at positions near the covered doors, agents will stand or crouch, but not go prone. The figure shows some of the possible positions that the agents will take, given repeated execution of the identical scenario. Variability also plays a role in more dynamic decision making. For example, the agents have knowledge to recognize some tactically appropriate situations in which to use a grenade. The grenade selection knowledge was also encoded for regular engagements with a low probability. Thus, the user can be surprised when the MOUTBots unexpectedly throw a grenade, increasing unpredictability in the user experience.

This new mechanism is still being evaluated and, at this point, we can not claim that this design for variability in decision making provides human-like decision making. This is an empirical question and will require both data on human variability as well as experimentation to determine how it provides/fails to provide human-like variability.

### Transparency

Because Soar is a symbolic architecture, its knowledge can be readily understood by non-technical users. For example, a MOUTBot goal might be to defend a room; a user could find a "defend-room" goal among the Soar agent's active goals. Although this representation facilitates transparency, alone it does not achieve it because some knowledge of the run-time aspects of the architecture is needed to extract this information. For the MOUTBot development, we used an application specific visualization tool that provides users the ability to see an agent's map of its terrain, where it believes other friendly and enemy agents are located, its desired movement and targeting goals, and a fine-grained view of its near-field environment (e.g., whether it was adjacent to a wall). Figure 2 showed a representation of the map portion of the tool. For a fielded application, we could couple the Soar agents with a tool specifically designed to bridge the gap between the transparency of Soar's representation and the extraction of this information from the agents themselves (Taylor et al, 2002), making it much easier for non-technical users to understand the decisions and behavior of Soar agents.

### Minimal Computational Footprint

A significant direction Soar development over the past decade has been improving its performance and it has run as many as twenty simple bots in UT while maintaining the game's frame rate.(Laird et al., 2002). For the MOUTBot application, as mentioned previously, we used observational fidelity as a criterion for simplifying the models of perceptions and actions that would increase computational overhead. Another significant element of the MOUTBot's efficiency is the SGIO interface. SGIO provides both a socket interface for development and an option to compile Soar directly into other applications. Using the compiled connection, we were able to run 5 independent agents while maintaining a game frame rate of 20 Hz on a 1GHz Pentium III laptop with ½ GB RAM. While we did not perform more specific stress tests, this performance was more than acceptable for the target application, because only 1 or 2 MOUTBots were needed.

## Limitations and Future Work

The MOUTBot is a prototype, a first approximation of the tremendous behavior space of this domain. It has a number of limitations, four of which are outlined below.

1. **Integration with higher-fidelity simulations**: Some behavior simplifications were dictated by Unreal Tournament's simulation limitations, rather than fundamental limits in the approach. For example, UT represents entity bodies as cylinders, rather than as articulating components. While there are some animations that show specific body movements (aiming, reloading, walking), it was not feasible to simulate realistically ones that were not (such as turning the head or communicating with gestures). When MOUTBots are integrated with a simulator that provides more fine-grained representations of the body, they will need to be extended or combined with other, existing technologies to capture the kinematics of body movement and to make control decisions over these features.
2. **Robust models of spatial reasoning**: The MOUTBots are dependent on the nodes embedded in the Unreal Tournament maps. As described previously, the agents need representations of walls and doors. In simulators where these representations are available, more general models of space and the ability to comprehend and predict concealment and cover locations will be required.
3. **Fault tolerant execution**: Extensions to the agent are needed so that it can better handle failures itself. In particular, the current agent lacks common sense knowledge that would allow it to reflect about its situation when it found itself unable to execute its desired task. Such models exist (e.g., Nielsen et al, 2002), so this problem is more of a knowledge integration challenge than a basic research problem.
4. **Requirements analysis & behavior validation**: Even with the behavior variability solutions described above, competent behavior covers only a narrow part of the overall behavior space. Fanaticism, "less" competent behaviors (possibly representing poorly trained guerillas or novices), additional errors in judgment and perception, etc. all could be modeled. In order to justify their cost, these extensions require a thorough understanding of user requirements in specific training applications. We attempted to obtain some of this information by presenting the MOUTBots at various stages during development to subject matter experts. These demonstrations resulted in valuable feedback (e.g., early demos led us to concentrate on variability as an overall requirement). However, we recognize the need for more formal

validation techniques that would allow knowledge engineers to evaluate agent behaviors more directly and quickly. Some recent progress has been made towards this goal, using the current MOUTBot prototype as a testbed (Wallace & Laird, 2002).

## Conclusions

Achieving intelligent opponents that are fully autonomous, believable, and interactive, while exhibiting a variety of behaviors in similar circumstances, will require much additional research and development. However, we made significant progress towards these goals. Using computer game technology allowed us to develop the prototype MOUTBot entities without a high fidelity simulator. The Soar cognitive architecture provided efficient execution, allowing a full complement of opponents to run with the simulation on standard PC hardware. Soar also facilitated knowledge reuse, resulting in greater breadth, depth, and realism in behaviors. We also developed a general framework for supporting behavioral variability, and implemented portions of this framework in Soar. Thus, the MOUTBots, by combining the strengths of human behavior representation and computer game technology, demonstrate that realistic, autonomous, embodied intelligent agents can meet the requirements of interactive, virtual training.

## Acknowledgments

This work was sponsored by the Office of Naval Research, VIRTE Program, contracts N00014-02-C-003 and N00014-02-1-0009. Kelly McCann and K.C. Pflugler provided expert opinion about urban combat behaviors. Portions of this work were reported previously (Wray, Laird, et al 2002; Wray & Laird 2003). The authors thank Randolph Jones and Jens Wessling for help in the development of the MOUTBot and associated software.

## References

Adobbati, R., Marshall, A. N., Kaminka, G., Scholer, A., & Tejada, S. (2001). *Gamebots: A 3D Virtual World Test-Bed For Multi-Agent Research.* Paper presented at the 2nd International Workshop on Infrastructure for Agents, MAS, and Scalable MAS, Montreal, Canada.

Best, B. J., Lebiere, C., & Scarpinnatto, K. C. (2002). *Modeling Synthetic Opponents in MOUT Training Simulations Using the ACT-R Cognitive Architecture.* Paper presented at the 11th Conference on Computer Generated Forces and Behavior Representation, Orlando.

Jones, R. M., Laird, J. E., Nielsen, P. E., Coulter, K. J., Kenny, P. G., & Koss, F. V. (1999). Automated Intelligent Pilots for Combat Flight Simulation. *AI Magazine, 20*(1), 27-42.

Laird, J. E. (2001a). *It Knows What You're Going To Do: Adding Anticipation to a Quakebot.* Paper presented at the Fifth International Conference on Autonomous Agents (Agents 2001), Montreal, Canada.

Laird, J. E. (2001b). Using a Computer Game to Develop Advanced AI. *Computer, 34*(7), 70-75.

Laird, J. E., Assanie, M., Bachelor, B., Benninghoff, N., Enam, S., Jones, B., Kerfoot, A., Lauver, C., Magerko, B., Sheiman, J., Stokes, D., & Wallace, S. (2002, March). *A Test Bed for Developing Intelligent Synthetic Characters.* Paper presented at the AAAI 2002 Spring Symposium: Artificial Intelligence and Interactive Entertainment.

Laird, J. E., Jones, R. M., & Nielsen, P. E. (1998). *Lessons learned from TacAir-Soar in STOW-97.* Paper presented at the Seventh Conference on Computer Generated Forces and Behavioral Representation, Orlando, Florida.

Laird, J. E., Newell, A., & Rosenbloom, P. S. (1987). Soar: An architecture for general intelligence. *Artificial Intelligence, 33*(3), 1-64.

Newell, A. (1990). *Unified Theories of Cognition.* Cambridge, Massachusetts: Harvard University Press.

Nielsen, P., Beard, J., Kiessel, J., & Beisaw, J. (2002). *Robust Behavior Modeling.* Paper presented at the 11th Computer Generated Forces Conference.

Tambe, M. (1997). Towards Flexible Teamwork. *Journal of Artificial Intelligence Research (JAIR), 7*, 83-124.

Tambe, M., Johnson, W. L., Jones, R. M., Koss, F. M., Laird, J. E., Rosenbloom, P. S., & Schwamb, K. B. (1995). Intelligent Agents for Interactive Simulation Environments. *AI Magazine, 16*(1), 15-39.

Taylor, G., Jones, R. M., Goldstein, M., Fredericksen, R., & Wray, R. E. (2002). *VISTA: A Generic Toolkit for Agent Visualization.* Paper presented at the 11th Conference on Computer Generated Forces and Behavioral Representation, Orlando.

Wallace, S. A., & Laird, J. E. (2002). *Toward Automatic Knowledge Validation.* Paper presented at the Eleventh Conference on Computer Generated Forces and Behavioral Representation, Orlando, Florida.

Wray, R. E., & Laird, J. E. (2003a). An architectural approach to consistency in hierarchical execution. *Journal of Artificial Intelligence Research, 19*, 355-398.

Wray, R. E., & Laird, J. E. (2003b, May). *Variability in Human Behavior Modeling for Military Simulations.* Paper presented at the Conference on Behavior Representation in Modeling and Simulation, Scottsdale, AZ.

Wray, R. E., Laird, J. E., Nuxoll, A., & Jones, R. M. (2002). *Intelligent Opponents for Virtual Reality Training.* Paper presented at the Inter-service/Industry Training, Simulation, and Education Conference (I/ITSEC), Orlando.

# CaBMA: Case-Based Project Management Assistant

**Ke Xu & Héctor Muñoz-Avila**
Department of Computer Science and Engineering,
19 Memorial Drive West
Lehigh University
Bethlehem, PA, 18015, USA
{kex2, munoz}@cse.lehigh.edu

## Abstract

We are going to present an implementation of an AI system, CaBMA, built on top of a commercial project management tool, MS Project™. Project management is a business process for successfully delivering one-of-a kind products and services under real-world time and resource constraints. CaBMA (for: Case-Based Project Management Assistant) provides the following functionalities:

- It captures cases from project plans
- It reuses captured cases to refine project plans and generate project plans from the scratch
- It maintains consistency of pieces of a project plan obtained by case reuse
- It refines the case base to cope with inconsistencies resulting from capturing cases over a period of time

CaBMA adds a knowledge layer on top of MS Project™ to assist the user with his project management tasks.

## 1 Introduction

Project management is a business process for successfully delivering one-of-a kind products and services under real-world time and resource constraints (PMI, 1999). In previous work (Muñoz-Avila et al, 2002), a knowledge-layer for project management was proposed; the core idea of the proposal, called Knowledge-Based Project Planning (KBPP), was to reuse cases containing pieces of project plans when creating new project plans.

In this paper, we report on CaBMA, the first implementation of knowledge-based project planning on a commercial project management tool. CaBMA addresses the following issues that we encountered while implementing the idea of case reuse on top of a commercial project management tool, MS Project™.

The first issue was how to populate the case base. Do we assume that domain experts create the cases? Knowledge acquisition is a problem frequently faced when using intelligent problem-solving techniques in real-world situations. Over the years, intelligent systems were developed but not used because it was not feasible to feed such systems with adequate knowledge. The first component of CaBMA extracts cases automatically from user interactions with MS Project™. By doing so, the knowledge acquisition effort becomes transparent to the user. Cases captured are generalizations of project plans. The main advantage of this generalization is that it increases the opportunities for reusing the cases.

The second issue results from the automated case capture procedure. Situations arise where multiple cases may be applicable to the same part of a project plan and any of them is reusable. Thus, a case may not be reused in the same context from which it was captured. Depending on the domain, reusing a different case may yield an incorrect solution. In such situations, we say that the case capture procedure is not sound relative to the captured solutions. These inconsistencies are a result of the generalization procedure during the case capture. However, if cases are not generalized, a very large case base will be required to obtain an adequate coverage. The second component of CaBMA refines the case base over time. This revision process is performed when potential conflicts between the new and the existing cases are identified.

The third issue emerged during early trials with CaBMA. We identified a problem that is due to the use of knowledge-based approaches in interactive environments such as MS Project™. When the user requests CaBMA to complete parts of a project plan, the system responds by identifying applicable cases and reusing them. Case applicability is determined based on elements of the current project plan. The problem may arise if the user later changes some of these elements. An inconsistency occurs when cases previously reused are no longer applicable. We refer to these inconsistencies as case reuse inconsistencies (Xu & Muñoz-Avila, 2003b). These can be seen as a kind of semantic inconsistencies and are complementary to the syntactical inconsistencies that MS Project™ can detect, which refer to the over-allocation of resources. The third component of CaBMA keeps track of all modifications being performed to the current project plan. These

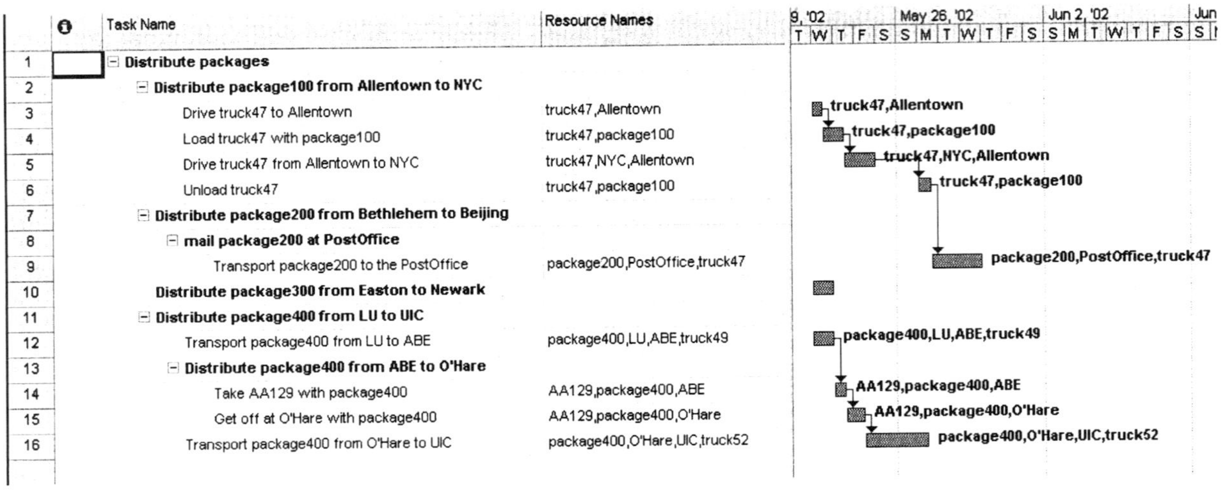


**Figure 1:** Snapshot of a WBS on MS Project™

modifications include user edits and CaBMA-made changes. Edits that may result in case reuse inconsistencies will trigger a propagation process by this component. Any inconsistencies detected are pointed out for the user in a non-intrusive manner allowing him/her to decide at what point he/she wants to deal with them.

The paper continues by describing project management (Section 2). After that, we present the architecture of CaBMA. The next three sections (Section 4-6) discuss the case reuse, the consistency control, and the case-base refinement components. Then we discuss related work and finally, in Section 8, we make some final remarks.

## 2 Project Management

Project management involves 6 activities: (1) Creating a work breakdown structure, (2) Identifying/incorporating task dependencies, (3) Estimating task and project duration, (4) Identifying, estimating, and allocating resources, (5) Estimating overall project costs or budget, and (6) Estimating uncertainties and risks associated with tasks, their schedules, and resources.

Tools for project management support the user on each of these phases. For example, MS Project™ allows user edits to a work breakdown structure (WBS). Figure 1 shows a snapshot of a WBS in MS Project™. The task *distribute-packages* is decomposed into four subtasks (Task Name column): *Distribute package100 from Allentown to NYC*, *Distribute package200 from Bethlehem to Beijing*, *Distribute package300 from Easton to Newark*, and *Distribute package400 from ABE to O'Hare*. Some tasks, called activities, represent concrete actions. For example, *Drive truck47 to Allentown* is an activity. Tasks have assigned resources (Resource Name column). For example, the task *Distribute truck47 to Allentown* has two assigned resources: *truck47* and *Allentown*. Finally, tasks have ordering relations among them (the column with schedules). For example, the task *Drive truck47 to Allentown* occurs before the task *Load truck47 with package100*. More generally, there are three kinds of relations in a WBS:

- Task - subtask relations
- Task - resource assignment relations
- Task- task ordering relations

Thus, creating a WBS also provides information about the six project management activities.

## 3 Overview of the System

Knowledge-based project planning advocates assisting project managers in the development of a WBS by using hierarchical (HTN) planning techniques (Muñoz-Avila et al, 2002). This approach is based on the observation that WBS has a one-to-one correspondence with the hierarchical task networks (HTNs; (Erol et al, 1994)).

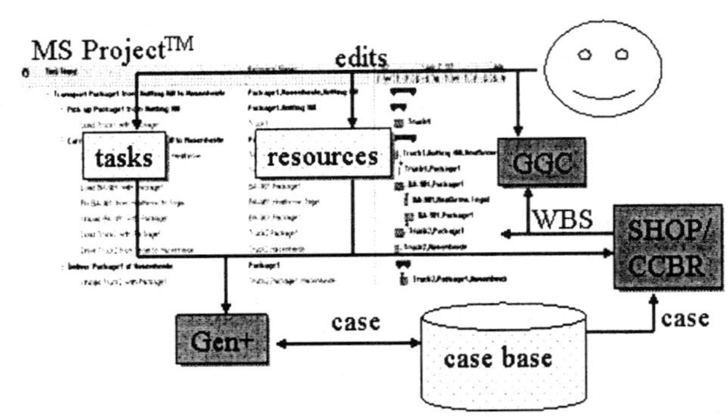


**Figure 2:** Information flow in CaBMA

Figure 2 depicts the information flow in CaBMA. First, the user edits a project plan in MS Project™. For the purposes of our work, this means that the user edits tasks, relations, and the available resources in the WBS. The user selects to store part or the whole WBS generated. Gen+ stores one or more cases in the case base and may refine existing cases if necessary. The user can at any time select a task in the WBS and ask CaBMA to generate a decomposition for that task. SHOP/CCBR is the component of CaBMA that reuses cases. As the user edits some parts of the WBS may become inconsistent relative to the reused cases. GGC keeps track of edits performed by the user and reused cases. GGC alerts the user of potential inconsistencies in an unobtrusive manner. We will now explain each component in detail.

## 4 SHOP/CCBR

A case contains one-level decompositions in the WBS and is defined as a 4-tuple (h,ST,R,<), where:

- h is the task decomposed
- ST are the subtasks decomposing h
- R are the resources required to apply the case
- < is a set of ordering relations between the subtasks

Cases represent generalizations of WBSs. That is, cases contain variables instead of the original elements mentioned in the WBS. For example, in place of the element package23, cases use the variable ?package23 (variables are denoted with a question mark).

A case (h,ST,R,<) is reused to decompose a task t in a current project plan if t is an instance of h and the resources in R can be instantiated to resources in the current project plan. For example, Table 1 shows the case reused to decompose the task *Distribute package100 from Allentown to NYC* from Figure 1. The variable instantiation that makes this case applicable is:

{?package23 → package100, ?Easton → Allentown, ?NYC → NYC, ?truck12 → truck47}.

**Table 1: A generalized case**

| Task: |
|---|
| distribute ?package23 from ?Easton to ?NYC |
| Resources: |
| city ?Easton |
| package ?package23 |
| city ?NYC |
| truck ?truck12 |
| Subtask: |
| Drive ?truck12 to ?Easton |
| Load ?truck12 with ?package23 |
| Drive ?truck12 from ?Easton to ?NYC |
| Unload ?truck12 |

The case reuse algorithm that we implemented is the SiN algorithm (Munoz-Avila et al, 2001). SiN integrates the HTN planning as in the SHOP system (Nau et al, 1999) and case-based reasoning as in the NaCODAE conversational CBR (CCBR) system (Aha and Breslow, 1998). To decompose tasks, SiN uses SHOP's methods and NaCoDAE/HTN's cases. At any point of time, either SHOP or NaCODAE is decomposing tasks and will yield control to the other one if it reaches a compound task that it cannot decompose.

The SiN algorithm is implemented in the CaBMA's component called SHOP/CCBR. This component extends SHOP while mimicking the CCBR style interactions of NaCoDAE. The main advantage of SHOP/CCBR over SiN is that it allows simultaneous consideration of cases and methods to decompose a task instead of SiN's approach of considering either cases or methods but not both at the same time. An important point is that SHOP/CCBR does not require either methods or operators to generate task decompositions. That is, SHOP/CCBR can use cases only to generate task decompositions. This is crucial in the context of project planning, where a complete knowledge base might not be available.

## 5 Goal Graph Component (GGC)

When the user orders CaBMA to complete parts of a project plan, the system responds by determining applicable cases and reusing them. Case applicability is determined based on two factors: the task being completed and the available resources. A problem may arise if the user later changes the available resources and/or the task. An inconsistency occurs when cases previously reused are no longer applicable. We refer to these inconsistencies as case reuse inconsistencies.

To deal with case reuse inconsistencies, we implemented the Goal Graph Component (GGC). GGC is built on top of the Redux architecture, which is a Justification Truth Maintenance System (JTMS) for dealing with planning contingencies (Petrie, 1992). GGC keeps track of all modifications being performed to the current project plan in a data structure called the Goal Graph (GG). These modifications include user edits and case reuse episodes. Edits that may result in case reuse inconsistencies will trigger a JTMS propagation process in GG. Any inconsistencies detected are displayed to the user in a non-intrusive manner, allowing him/her to decide at what point he/she wants to deal with them. Redux has two crucial properties: first, Redux can propagate the effects of user edits automatically. Second, Redux has a sound JTMS propagation mechanism that ensures the detection of all inconsistent pieces of the project plan.

Redux combines the theory of Justification-based Truth Maintenance System (JTMS) and Constrained Decision Revision (CDR). In a Truth Maintenance System (TMS), assertions (called nodes) are connected via a tree-like network of dependencies. The combination of JTMS and CDR provides the ability to perform dependency-directed backtracking and to identify pieces of the plan that are affected by the changes. The main advantage of GGC is twofold. First, GGC propagates the effects of the changes on the fly. Second, GGC is sound; it ensures detection of all affected pieces of the plan. As a result, the affected pieces of the plan can be repaired without having to re-plan from the scratch.

Redux represents relations between goals, operators and decisions. A goal g is decomposed into subgoals G by applying an operator o. The assignments A indicate changes in the plan caused by applying o to decompose g. A decision is a 4-tuple (g, G, o, A). As different operators may be applicable, the choice of an operator represents a backtracking point and it is represented as a decision. Given a goal g, a conflict set is a pair of the form (g, (D1, .., Dn)), where (D1, .., Dn) is the collection of decisions for g. A decision is rejected if its associated operator is rejected. The reasons for rejections are explicitly represented as justifications, which are a list of assignments. GG is a structure representing goals, conflict sets and subgoals.

We mapped elements from a project plan into Redux (See Table 2). Since tasks are decomposed into subtasks, tasks and subtasks are mapped into goals. Resources and orderings between tasks/activities are mapped into assignments because they represent changes in the plan. SHOP/CCBR's cases and methods are mapped into the Goal Graph's operators.

**Table 2: Mapping of Project Plans into Redux**

| **Project Plan** | **Redux** |
|---|---|
| Task, Subtask | Goal |
| resources | Assignment |
| Task, activities ordering | Assignment |
| Case, Method | Operator |

With this mapping, we can generate the GG automatically during project planning sessions with MS Project™. Every change in the project plan causes a change in GG. For example, if the user removes truck47 from the list of resources in the project plan shown in Figure 1, recall that the decomposition of the task *Distribute package100 from Allentown to NYC* was made using the case from Table 1. In this situation, the condition *truck ?truck12* of the case is no longer satisfied. CaBMA uses special icons to mark the tasks that may be inconsistent. These icons are annotated with the justification for the inconsistency. Notice that other tasks may become inconsistent as well. Using the JTMS-propagation mechanism of GG allows the identification of these tasks and their associated justifications.

## 6 The Gen+ Component

Gen+ is the module of CaBMA responsible for capturing cases from the project plan and refining the case base over time.

A WBS can be seen as a collection of one-level decompositions. Each one-level decomposition refines a single task into (sub)tasks and/or activities. The whole collection decomposes the most high-level tasks (i.e., tasks having no parent tasks) into activities (i.e., the non-decomposable elements of the WBS). In our approach, each one-level decomposition is stored as a single case. The alternative could have been cases that contain several decomposition levels or even a complete WBS. There are some trade-offs that we consider:

- Cases containing several decomposition levels or the complete WBS provide a better or complete picture of the overall plan. Their main drawback is that the case re-usability is limited. As more levels are added, more constraints should be considered to assess the applicability of the WBS in new situations.
- Cases containing one-level decomposition give no overall picture of the plan. Their main advantage is that they can be reused in several situations as cases from different WBS can be combined. For example, it is possible to decompose a task with a case captured from one WBS and to decompose one of the subtasks with a case captured from another WBS.

We decided to store only one-level decompositions in our cases to maximize the re-usability of the cases.

Another question that we explored was whether to store concrete cases (containing only constants) or generalized cases (replacing the constants with variables) in the case base. The problem of using generalized cases is that they might not correctly model the target domain. That is, If X= {?x1, ...., ?xn} is the set of the variables in a generalized case, there might be instantiations of X that do not reflect the behavior of the target domain. On the other hand, using concrete cases reduces the coverage of the case base. We would require one case for each possible task in the domain. If there is a maximum of n tasks, with an average number of arguments, m, and each argument can take an average number of instantiations, v. The minimum number of cases required will be $n*m^V$, one for each possible task. Notice that this is only the minimum number of the possible number of cases. Since we compute similarity on the conditions for determining applicability of a case to a given task, we may need more than one case for each task to obtain a better coverage.

**Table 3: A captured generalized case**

| |
|---|
| Task:<br>distribute ?package100 from ?Allentown to ?NYC<br>Resources:<br>city ?Allentown<br>package ?package200<br>city ?NYC<br>truck ?truck47<br>Subtask:<br>Drive ?truck47 to ?Allentown<br>Load ?truck47 with ?package100<br>Drive ?truck47 from ?Allentown to ?NYC<br>Unload ?truck47 |

Our answer to this question was to combine these two alternatives. Given a case CA = (:case h C ST <), we replace each parameter with a unique variable, ?ψ only if the type of the parameter is known. Otherwise, the parameter is not replaced with a variable and is viewed as a constant. In addition, we add the following constraints as conditions of the case:

- For each two different variables, ?x and ?y, of the same type, we add the constraint: *different ?x ?y*
- For each constant, c, and each variable, ?x, we add the constraint: *different ?x c*

As an example, Table 3 shows the case that is learned from the decomposition of the task *Distribute package100 from Allentown to NYC* from the WBS depicted in Figure 1.

By capturing generalized cases, CaBMA increases the coverage of the knowledge base. However, generalized cases may contain (1) redundant cases and (2) instantiations that are inconsistent with the target domain.

The first problem can be easily solved by ensuring that a new case will not be added if it matches an existing case in the case base. A case NC matches a case CA if there is a substitution θ such that NCθ = CA. For example, the case in Table 3 matches the case in Table 1, and, thus, would not be added to the case base.

The second problem is difficult to address because it is unfeasible to provide a domain model in the context of project planning. Thus, the only way to ascertain possible inconsistencies is by learning from the differences between the cases as they are captured over time. For this purpose, the Gen+ component revises previously acquired cases when a new case is captured. This revision process is performed when potential conflicts between the new and the existing cases are identified.

We found that it is possible that the order in which the cases are captured will determine which cases will be reused. However, Gen+ is still sound relative to the captured solutions. That is, if S is a solution for a problem P and (P, S) is used to learn generalized cases in a case base, then S will be generated as a solution whenever P is given as a problem. This property is a weak version of soundness for planning procedures. We cannot ensure that every solution generated is correct in the target domain unless we make some stronger assumptions (e.g., (Muñoz-Avila et al, 2001)). Still, this property guarantees soundness for those problems whose solutions have been previously captured.

**Table 4: A concrete solution and the corresponding Gen+ case**

| Case 1 | Case 2 |
|---|---|
| Task:<br>deliver ?e ?d ?o<br>Resources:<br>deliverCompany ?fd<br>equipment ?e<br>depot ?d<br>office ?o<br>Subtask:<br>contract ?fd ?e ?d ?o | Task:<br>deliver ?e ?d ?o<br>Resources:<br>deliverCompany ?fd<br>equipment ?e<br>depot ?d<br>office ?o<br>depot ?d1<br>truck ?t<br>different ?d ?d1<br>Subtask:<br>contract ?fd ?e ?d1 ?o<br>internalDeliver ?t ?e ?d1 ?o |

We illustrate the idea of the case revision process with an example in a supply-chain domain. For a detailed discussion of the case revision algorithm, please see (Xu & Muñoz-Avila, 2003a). Table 4 shows two generalized cases. Case 1 is a generalized solution for delivering an equipment ?e from office depot ?d to office location ?o. The solution indicates contracting a delivery company ?fd to do the job. Case 2 accomplishes the same task but has more requirements. It uses a delivery company ?fd to transport the equipment to an intermediate depot location ?dl and then uses transportation means ?t to make the final delivery.

Suppose that Case 1 is added first in the case base and that Case 2 is added afterwards. The problem is that if the same situation used to generate Case 2 occurs, Case 1 may be retrieved instead. The reason is that any situation satisfying Case 2 must also satisfy Case 1 because the resources in Case 1 are a subset of the resources in Case 2. Gen+ modifies Case 1 and Case 2 to ensure that this will not happen. The resulting changes are illustrated in Table 5. A new case, Case 3, is added, having the same task as the original Cases 1 and 2. Case 3 has a new, unique subtask vT ?fd ?e ?d ?o. This subtask is used as task for the new Case 1 and Case 2. This subtask links the new Case 1 and 2 to Case 3. The new Case 1 has negated conditions that ensure that it will not be selected when the new Case 2 is applicable.

Although the case revision process is cumbersome, it is transparent to the user. The user never sees the cases directly, but only the resulting decompositions. In addition, we modified SHOP/CCBR so that new task names such as "VT" in Table 5 are skipped. The reason is that these tasks were added artificially for the case refinement procedure, but have no meaning in the actual domain.

**Table 5: Refinement of Case 1 with Gen+**

| Case 3 | Case 1 | Case 2 |
|---|---|---|
| Task:<br>deliver ?e ?d ?o<br>Condition:<br>deliverCompan y ?fd<br>equipment ?e<br>depot ?d<br>office ?o<br>Subtask:<br>vT ?fd ?e ?d ?o | Task:<br>vT ?fd ?e ?d ?o<br>Condition:<br>¬deliverCompan y ?ud<br>different ?d ?d1<br>¬depot ?d1<br>¬truck ?t<br>Subtask:<br>contract ?fd ?e ?d ?o | Task:<br>vT ?fd ?e ?d ?o<br>Condition:<br>deliverCompany ? ud<br>depot ?d1<br>truck ?t<br>different ?d ?d1<br>Subtask:<br>contract ?fd ?e ?d 1 ?o<br>internalDeliver ?t ?e ?d1 ?o |

## 7 Related Work

The RealPLAN system advocates the separation of planning from resource allocation (Srivastava & Kambhampati, 1999). RealPLAN is inspired by project planning. As opposed to CaBMA, RealPLAN uses standard planning techniques for plan generation, and, thus, requires a domain model to generate the plans. Nevertheless, the idea of the separation of planning and resource allocation is compatible with our approach for project planning.

Providing tools for knowledge acquisition has been a frequently studied research topic. For example, in the EXPECT project (Blythe et al, 2001), an integrated suit of intelligent interfaces is used to capture knowledge. The EXPECT project shows that by integrating these interfaces, it is possible to elicit the context of the user actions, which enhances the knowledge acquisition capabilities. The main difference is that CaBMA does not use ad-hoc interfaces to capture knowledge, instead, it captures the cases from the interactions of the user with MS Project™.

CaMeL allows the automatic elicitation of methods from cases (Elgami et al, 2002). A similar process, developed by Carrick and Cunningham (Carrick and Cunningham, 1993), can elicit rules from cases. In our work, we study the automatic acquisition of cases, which is a complementary problem to those two approaches.

## 8 Final Remarks

We presented CaBMA, a case-based planning assistant built on top of MS Project™. CaBMA assists the project manager by providing suggestions for refining tasks in the current WBS, using experience captured from previous project planning episodes. CaBMA consists of three main components. The first component is Gen+, which captures cases automatically. To increase the coverage of the case base, cases are generalized from task decompositions in the WBS. However, this may result in problems due to the generalization process. Gen+ also provides a procedure to refine the cases over time. The second component is SHOP/CCBR. This component follows a HTN planning paradigm for case reuse. As user edits may violate applicability conditions of the cases, the third component, GGC, detects such inconsistencies and indicates them to the user in an unobtrusive manner. CaBMA adds a knowledge layer on top of MS Project™ to assist the user with the project management tasks.

Although CaBMA has not been deployed yet, we have made targeted evaluations for some of its components. We performed an experimental evaluation to see the impact of the overhead in Gen+ as a result of adding new cases (Xu & Muñoz-Avila, 2003a), we observed the effects of adding more cases to the coverage of the case base (Muñoz-Avila et al, 2002), and we monitored the effects of GGC's propagations in MS Project™ (Xu & Muñoz-Avila, 2003b).

## References


Aha, D.W., and Breslow, L Refining conversational case libraries. In: Proceedings of the Fourth European Workshop on Case-Based Reasoning (EWCBR-98). Providence, RI: Springer. 1998.

Blythe, J., Kim, J., Ramachandran, S., and Gil, Y. An Integrated Environment for Knowledge Acquisition. In: Proceedings of the International Conference on Intelligent User Interfaces 2001.

Erol, K., Nau, D., & Hendler, J. HTN planning: Complexity and expressivity. In: Proceedings of the Twelfth National Conference on Artificial Intelligence (pp. 123-1128). Seattle, WA: AAAI Press, 1994.

Hanney, K., & Keane, M. T. Learning Adaptation Rules From a Case-base. August. In I. Smyth & B. Faltings (Eds.), Advances in Case-Based Reasoning. Amsterdam: Springer Verlag, 1996.

Ilghami, O., Nau, D.S., Muñoz-Avila, H., & Aha, D.W. (2002) CaMeL: Learning Methods for HTN Planning. To appear in Proccedings of the The Sixth International Conference on AI Planning & Scheduling (AIPS'02), 2002.

Ke, X. & Muñoz-Avila, H. CBM-Gen+: An Algorithm for Reducing Case Base Inconsistencies in Hierarchical and Incomplete Domains. To appear in Proceedings of ICCBR-03. Springer, 2003a.

Ke, X. & Muñoz-Avila, H. Maintaining Consistency in Project Planning Reuse. To appear in Proceedings of ICCBR-03. Springer, 2003b.

Mukammalla, S. & Muñoz-Avila, H. Case Acquisition in a Project Planning Environment. In proceedings of the Sixth European Conference on Case-Based Reasoning (ECCBR-02). Springer, 2002.

Muñoz-Avila, H., Aha, D.W., Nau D. S., Breslow, L.A., Weber, R., & Yamal, F. SiN: Integrating Case-based Reasoning with Task Decomposition. To appear in Proceedings of the Seventeenth International Joint Conference on Artificial Intelligence (IJCAI-2001). Seattle, WA: AAAI Press, 2001.

Muñoz-Avila, H., Gupta, K., Aha, D.W., Nau, D.S. Knowledge Based Project Planning. To appear in Knowledge Management and Organizational Memories. 2002.

Nau, D., Cao, Y., Lotem, A., & Muñoz-Avila, H. SHOP: Simple hierarchical ordered planner. Proceedings of the Sixteenth International Joint Conference on Artificial Intelligence (IJCAI-99). Stockholm: AAAI Press, 1999.

Petrie, C. (1992). Constrained decision revision. In *Proceedings of AAAI-92*. AAAI Press.

Project Management Institute (PMI). (1999). PMI's A Guide to the Project Management Body of Knowledge (PMBOK® Guide). Technical Report. Release No.: PMI 70-029-99. Project Management Institute.

Srivastava, B., Kambhampati, S. Scaling up Planning by teasing out Resource Scheduling. Tech. Report ASU CSE TR 99-005. Arizona State University, 1999.

# Automatic Generation of Artistic Chinese Calligraphy


**Songhua Xu**
CAD & CG State Key Lab of China, Zhejiang University; Department of Computer Science & Information Systems, The University of Hong Kong

**Francis C.M. Lau**
Department of Computer Science & Information Systems, The University of Hong Kong

**Kwok-Wai Cheung**
Department of Computer Science, Hong Kong Baptist University

**Yunhe Pan**
CAD & CG State Key Lab of China, Zhejiang University

Figure 1: A single character in many styles; the first row is the training examples, and the other rows were automatically generated by our system.


### Abstract

We introduce a novel intelligent system which can generate new Chinese calligraphic artwork that meets certain aesthetic requirements automatically. In the machine learning phase, parametric representations of existent calligraphic artwork are derived from input images of calligraphy. Using a six-level hierarchical representation, the acquired knowledge is organized as a small structural stroke database, which is then exploited by a constraint-based analogous reasoning component to create artwork in new styles. A set of geometric constraints is proposed and incorporated into the system for rejecting the aesthetically unacceptable results. The combination of knowledge from various input sources creates a huge space for the intelligent system to explore and produce new calligraphy.


## Introduction

Chinese calligraphy is among the finest and most important of all Chinese art forms, and an inseparable part of Chinese history. It can convey not just what is explicitly in the written message but also the emotions of the writer. The very delicate aesthetic effects achievable by Chinese calligraphy are generally considered to be unique among all calligraphic arts. The most common use of calligraphic art in the digital world is creating typographic or artistic fonts for display or printing, for which Knuth has done some pioneering work (1979). In (Blum & Wed 1967), the authors gave a detailed analysis of the writing effects that hairy brushes can produce. For artistic rendering, researchers have tried to model the brush used in calligraphy, such as (Strassmann 1986) where the brush is modeled as a collection of bristles which evolve over the course of the stroke.

In this paper, we propose a methodology for automatically generating novel artistically appealing Chinese calligraphy artwork based on a small number of training samples from existing calligraphic artwork. In particular, we adopt shape analysis techniques to recover the shapes of the training examples, and represent them using a hierarchical parameterization. An analogous reasoning process is proposed to align the shape representations of the training examples, and then to generate novel calligraphy artwork. The process takes into consideration aesthetics expressed in the form of geometric constraints of the constructive elements to filter out aesthetically unacceptable candidates. To demonstrate the feasibility of the proposed methodology, we have implemented a prototype system which is able to generate brand new Chinese calligraphic artwork fully automatically when given as input a small training set (typically below 10). To the best our knowledge, there has not been any published work on the same approach. A related research is (Ramalho & Ganascia 1994)'s work on the simulation of creativity in jazz performance, in the sense that it is also an attempt to model artistic activities using analogous reasoning.

The structure of the paper is as follows. Section 2 presents the formulation for the problem of "artistic calligraphy generation" and provides an overview of the system architecture. Section 3 describes the hierarchical and parametric representation for modeling the shape of Chinese characters as well as the extraction of their representation. Section 4 explains the proposed analogical reasoning process for automatic generation of new Chinese calligraphic characters. Section 5 discusses how aesthetics in terms of geometrical constraints can be incorporated in the system in order to weed out unacceptable candidates for the final output of the artwork. Section 6 gives the experimental results and

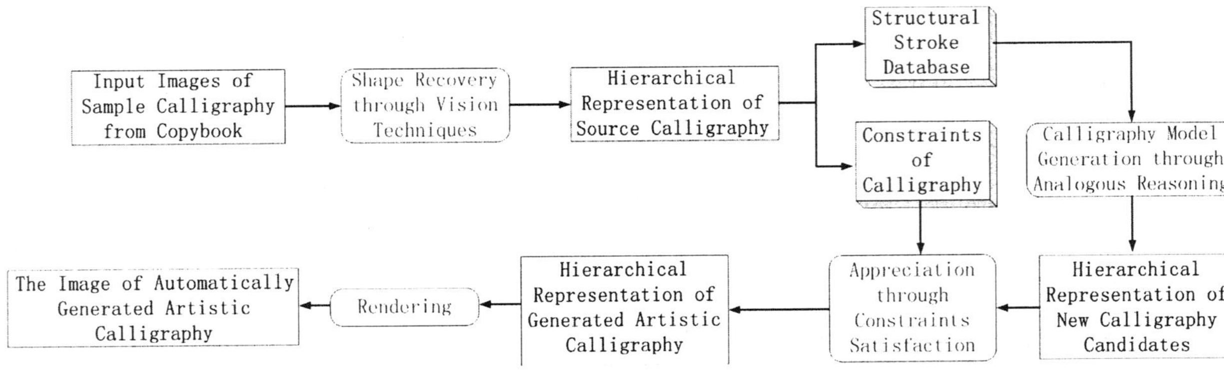


Figure 2: Architecture of our intelligent calligraphy generation system.

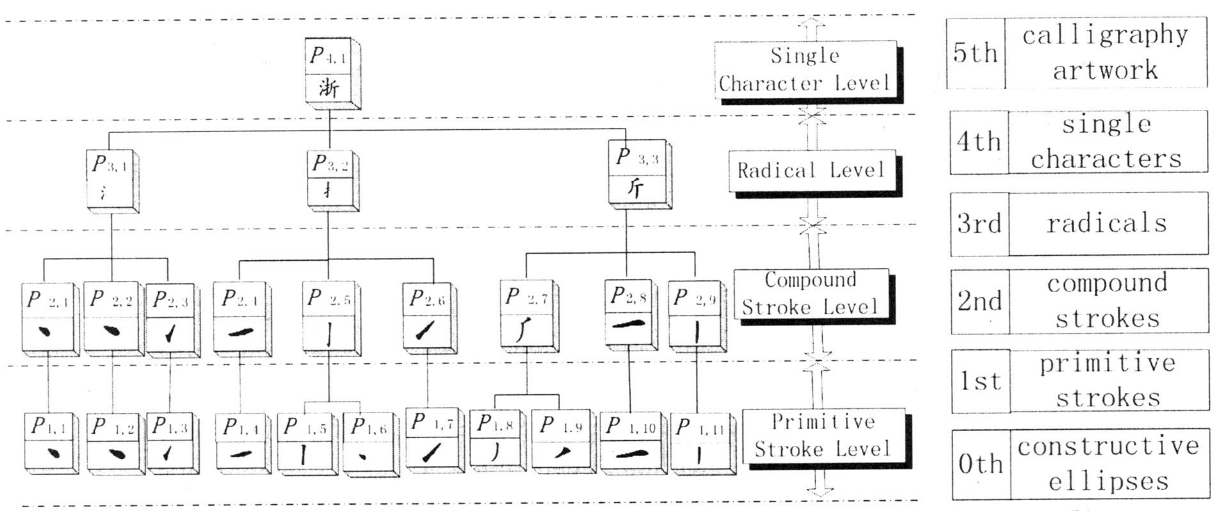


(a) (b)

Figure 3: (a) Hierarchical representation of a Chinese character (only four levels are shown). (b) Six-level hierarchical representation of calligraphy.

suggests some possible directions for future research.

## Problem Formulation and Overall System Architecture

Our approach to solving the problem of generating new calligraphy based on some given training samples consists of three major steps: *shape decomposition*, *reference model generation from examples*, and *novel calligraphy generation*.

**Calligraphic shape decomposition.** Let $\mathcal{P}$ denote a model family, each spanned by a parameterization $\mathbf{E}$ for representing the class of interested shapes (Chinese characters in our case), and let $\mathbf{C}_i$ denote the image of the $i$-th training example. *Shape decomposition* (or recovery) is equivalent to the problem of identifying the model $\mathbf{P}$ in $\mathcal{P}$ and a corresponding set of parameters $\mathbf{E}^*$ to instantiate a model $\mathcal{P}(\mathbf{E}_i)$ as a best fit for $\mathbf{C}_i$. If $\mathcal{P}$ is a hierarchical composition of shape primitives, $\mathbf{E}$ will also be hierarchical and the recovery process becomes that for a shape decomposition problem. In our context, the process is equivalent to character stroke segmentation/extraction.

**Calligraphy model generation from examples.** Given a set of $n$ models $\{\mathbf{P}_i\}$, each corresponding to one of the training examples, a family of novel shape models $\mathbf{P}(\omega)$ can be defined by *blending* the $n$ model instances, $\{\mathbf{P}_i\}$. For the blending, an optimal match computed based on shape information is needed. An analogous reasoning process (intuitively, a kind of interpolation/extrapolation) is adopted for the model blending. Note that the newly derived shape family is parameterized by a set of blending parameters, $\omega$, to control the contribution of each training example.

**Novel calligraphy generation.** Given $\mathbf{P}(\omega)$ and a set of aesthetically related geometrical constraints, $\Theta$, on the primitive shapes, novel calligraphy can be generated by identifying some $\omega$ which can satisfy $\Theta$ in such a way that only aesthetically acceptable calligraphy artwork will be selected.

Figure 2 shows the overall architecture of the proposed intelligent calligraphy generation system. At the heart of the system is an analogous reasoning component that creates new calligraphy based on training examples and satisfying all the aesthetic constraints. In our experiments, the training examples come from printed "copybooks". Our simulated analogous reasoning process is essentially data prediction (either interpolation or extrapolation) subject to the aesthetical constraints.

## Hierarchical and Parametric Representation

The earliest Chinese characters are pictographs, which project meanings through shapes and images in an intuitive fashion. Over time, these characters gradually became symbols. It can be easily observed that many basic features occur in different Chinese characters frequently. To take advantage of this representation redundancy, we employ a hierarchical representation for Chinese characters. The hierarchical approach extends also to the level of calligraphy artwork.

### Hierarchical Representation

We decompose a Chinese calligraphy artwork into six levels: constructive ellipse level, primitive stroke level, compound stroke level, radical level, single-character level, and complete artwork level (see Figure 3(b)). Via this six-level framework, a Chinese calligraphy artwork is represented parametrically. The parametric representations of the calligraphic artwork at all levels altogether form the parameter space $\mathbf{E}$ for the ensuing reasoning process to generate aesthetically acceptable novel calligraphy artwork.

Figure 3(a) shows the hierarchical representation of the Chinese character "zhe". The lower-level elements will be promoted to the next upper level (e.g., the primitive stroke $\mathbf{P}_{1,1}$ in Figure 3(a) becomes the compound stroke $\mathbf{P}_{2,1}$ at the next upper level) if they cannot be combined with other elements at the same level. Similarly, it is possible for a radical to degrade to a compound stroke, and then to a primitive stroke. With this promotion and degradation arrangement, a uniform six-level hierarchy can result, which will be needed in the calligraphy generation phase.

### Six Levels of Parametric Representation

We denote the $i$-th constructive element at the $k$-th level as $\mathbf{P}_{k,i}$, and its corresponding shape parameters in matrix form as $\mathbf{E}_{k,i}$. If $k \geq 1$, $\mathbf{P}_{k,i}$ must be composed of one or more constructive elements in one level down; we call the latter sub-constructive elements. All the information needed for the composition of $\mathbf{P}_{k,i}$ is stored in $\mathbf{T}_{k,i}$, the *topological constructor* of $\mathbf{P}_{k,i}$. Also, we denote $\overline{\mathbf{P}}_{k,i}$ the bounding box of the image space that the element $\mathbf{P}_{k,i}$ occupies, that is, $\overline{\mathbf{P}}_{k,i} \triangleq \{\overline{\mathbf{P}}_{k,i}.h, \overline{\mathbf{P}}_{k,i}.w, \overline{\mathbf{P}}_{k,i}.x, \overline{\mathbf{P}}_{k,i}.y\}$, where $\overline{\mathbf{P}}_{k,i}.h$ is the box's height, $\overline{\mathbf{P}}_{k,i}.w$ the box's width, and $(\overline{\mathbf{P}}_{k,i}.x, \overline{\mathbf{P}}_{k,i}.y)$ the box's center. All the coordinates are in the world coordinate system.

At the 0-th level of the hierarchical representation, the artwork is viewed as a collection of ellipses, denoted as $\mathbf{P}_0$. These ellipses are called the "constructive ellipses" of the artwork (Figure 3(b)). For each constructive ellipse denoted as $\mathbf{P}_{0,i}$, let $(x_i, y_i)$ be the center and $a_i$ and $b_i$ the lengths of its major and minor axes respectively. Then, the "image" of the artwork $\mathbf{C}$ will be rendered as the regions in the image space that are covered by the collection of the constructive ellipses. This representation is inspired by the Blum model (Blum & Wed 1967), in which a zonary area is defined through an ellipse moving along a predefined curve.

An element at a level higher than the zero-th level, say $\mathbf{P}_{k+1,l} \forall k > 0$, is composed of $N_{k+1,l}$ elements at the next lower level, from $\mathbf{P}_{k,l_1}, \cdots, \mathbf{P}_{k,l_{N_{k+1,l}}}$. The corresponding shape matrix $\mathbf{E}_{k+1,l}$ is derived by concatenating the matrices $\mathbf{E}_{k,l_1}, \cdots, \mathbf{E}_{k,l_{N_{k+1,l}}}$ column by column in sequence. Since the parametric representation of a constructive ellipse is a $4 \times 1$ matrix, the proposed concatenation at the higher levels will produce matrices having exactly four rows. Each row of the matrix formed is called a *field* of the element's parametric representation. Different fields of an element can be separately reasoned on.

### Calligraphic Shape Decomposition

This is the process in which the hierarchical and parametric representations are extracted from training examples—images of calligraphy artwork.

**Extracting Levels 0–1 Elements** To extract the constructive ellipses from a training example, we first compute the skeleton of the calligraphy artwork. This is called "character skeletonization" in pattern recognition. Once the skeletons of the primitive strokes are identified, each pixel on these discrete curves is taken as the center of an ellipse, and the biggest ellipse that can fit into the stroke area is computed.

**Extracting Levels 2–3 Elements** We identify compound strokes and radicals by analyzing the spatial relation between the primitive and compound strokes at higher levels through shape grammar productions. The shape grammar production that yields the highest overall confidence will be applied for the stroke composition.

**Extracting Level 4 Elements.** To extract the constructive elements at level 4, we need to determine which radicals belong to the same character, and whether the radicals are degraded or not. This is the well-known and frequently occurring problem of "character segmentation" in pattern recognition research. In our system, we use projection analysis to account for possible slanting of the characters in order to segment the characters that are in a calligraphy artwork, like what is done in (Yanikoglu & Sandon 1994).

## Calligraphic Model Generation From Examples

### Principles of Calligraphic Model Generation

In 1975, Simon pointed out that design and creation is a class of problems having a character of synthesis (Simon 1975). Keane (Keane 1988) applied analogical mechanisms to problem solving. Our approach of generating new calligraphy using training examples is also based on an analogical reasoning process (**ARP**). One can understand the adopted

ARP as synthesizing a novel shape model by blending together some known ones. To support the blending, shape primitives mapping between models is typically needed and thus also forms part of the adopted **ARP**.

In principle, the **ARP** can be applied at different levels of the hierarchy and different artistic effects will result. Assume the **ARP** is applied to $\mathbf{P}_{k,l}$, the $l$-th constructive element on the $k$-th level of the hierarchical representation. And we have $n$ different versions of $\mathbf{P}_{k,l}$: $\mathbf{P}^1_{k,l}$, $\cdots$, $\mathbf{P}^n_{k,l}$, which are derived from the $n$ training examples and considered as the knowledge sources in the **ARP**. We also denote the result of the **ARP** as $\mathbf{P}^r_{k,l}$.

The general mathematic principle we adopted in the **ARP** can then be stated as Eq.(1), where $\omega^i$ $(i = 1, \cdots, n)$ is the analogous reasoning intensity for $\mathbf{P}^i_{k,l}$.

$$\mathbf{P}^r_{k,l} = \sum_{i=1}^{n} \omega^i \mathbf{P}^i_{k,l} \tag{1}$$

The suggested **ARP** is essentially either an interpolation or an extrapolation process. That is, $\omega^i$ is the interpolation or extrapolation weight for $\mathbf{P}^i_{k,l}$ with the constraint that $\sum_{i=1}^{n} \omega^i = 1$. In our intelligent calligraphy generation system, all the analogous reasoning intensities can be adjusted by the user manually through a graphical interface. Our system is also equipped with a component to generate random perturbations for the analogous reasoning intensities to be used for generating new calligraphy with aesthetic constraint satisfaction.

## New Calligraphy Generation System

In this subsection, we reveal more details on how we construct our system based on the general principle of calligraphic model generation as discussed above.

In our implemented system, computation on $\mathbf{P}^i_{k,l}$ is carried out by operating its matrix-form parametric representation $\mathbf{E}^i_{k,l}$. Obviously, to apply Eq.(1), the dimensions of the shape matrices $\mathbf{E}^i_{k,l}$ must all be identical. Otherwise a correspondence problem would appear, which is similar to the mapping issue in analogous reasoning.

Thus we need to equalize the dimensions of the reasoning sources. That is, if $\mathbf{P}_{k,s}$ and $\mathbf{P}_{k,t}$ are knowledge sources in the **ARP**, their shape matrix representations $(\mathbf{E}_{k,s})_{4\times n_1}$ and $(\mathbf{E}_{k,t})_{4\times n_2}$ must satisfy the condition that $n_1 = n_2$. Recall that each element has four fields, and thus four rows for $\mathbf{E}_{k,s}$ and $\mathbf{E}_{k,t}$ respectively. For shape matrices with different dimensions, which correspond to the cases of similar strokes having different numbers of constructive ellipses, the **ARP** can be made possible by computing a correspondence or match between $\mathbf{P}_{k,s}$ and $\mathbf{P}_{k,t}$. Here, we define an equalization operator, $\nabla^g_t$, which converts a matrix with any number of columns into a new matrix with $t$ columns based on "key columns" in the original matrix.

To instantiate the equalization operator $\nabla^g_t$, we first derive a discrete planar curve composed of the centers of all the constructive ellipses that $\mathbf{P}^i_{k,l}$ contains, which is denoted as $\mathbf{C}^i_{k,l}$. In our case, the derived curve is actually the skeleton of the component $\mathbf{P}^i_{k,l}$. If $\mathbf{C}^i_{k,l}$ has $v + 1$ key points, with their occurrences in the curve being the sequence $u_0$, $u_1$, $\cdots$, $u_v$, the "key columns" in the matrix $\mathbf{E}_{k,l_i}$ are selected as the $u_0$, $u_1$, $\cdots$, $u_v$-th columns. We use the algorithm in (Zhu & Chirlian 1995) to extract critical points on the planar curve as the key points. Based on the key columns computed for all the shape matrices of the training examples, the correspondence among them can readily be set up.

In the **ARP**, we assume the shape of a constructive element written in the font style "Kai" (GB2312) as used in recent versions of Microsoft Word to be the standard shape of an element. For each reasoning source $\mathbf{P}_{k,l}$ in the **ARP**, we denote its associated standard constructive element as $\mathbf{P}^{std}_{k,l}$ and its matrix form parametric representation as $\mathbf{E}^{std}_{k,l}$. Note that because the syntax of the component $\mathbf{P}_{k,l}$ has already been extracted in the calligraphy shape decomposition phase, we can easily identify the correspondent $\mathbf{P}^{std}_{k,l}$ for each $\mathbf{P}_{k,l}$ by their syntax. We then compute the distance $\mathbf{F}_{k,l}$ by which the shape of $\mathbf{P}^i_{k,l}$ differs from that of $\mathbf{P}^{std}_{k,l}$, as expressed in (2). $\mathbf{F}^i_{k,l}$ is used as the feature of $\mathbf{P}^i_{k,l}$ in our **ARP**.

$$\mathbf{F}^i_{k,l} \triangleq \mathbf{E}^i_{k,l} \ominus \mathbf{E}^{std}_{k,l} \tag{2}$$

$\ominus$ can simply be implemented as a minus operator between matrices, as what is currently done in our prototype system. More delicate feature extraction strategies are likely to yield better reasoning results.

The weighting associated with the $s$-th field of the $i$-th source knowledge on the $k$-th level, i.e., the $i$-th training example ($\mathbf{P}^i_{k,l}$), is denoted as $\omega^i_{l,s}$. We call $\omega^i_{l,s}$ $(s = 1, \cdots, 4)$ the reasoning intensity of $\mathbf{P}^i_{k,l}$ in the **ARP**. Then the order set of analogous reasoning intensities, $\omega^i_{l,s}, s = 1, \cdots, 4$ forms the "viewpoint sequence" of the **ARP**: $\varpi = \{\omega^i_{l,s} | i = 1, \cdots, n; s = 1, \cdots, 4\}$. It is so called as different orders of presenting the training examples will yield different calligraphy results.

To derive $\mathbf{F}_{k,r}$, the features of the reasoning result via the **ARP**, we take the reasoning intensity $\omega^i_{l,s}$ against the $s$-th field of the $i$-th reasoning source $\mathbf{P}^i_{k,l}$ as the weight for the $s$-th row of the feature matrix $\mathbf{F}^i_{k,l}$ in an interpolation/extrapolation process $(s = 1, \cdots, 4;\ i = 1, \cdots, n)$. This means that $\mathbf{F}^i_{k,l}$s are the entities that are actually interpolated/extrapolated. The interpolation/extrapolation process we employed to simulate the **ARP** is in the form of Eq.(3).

$$\mathbf{F}_{k,r} = \oslash(\mathbf{F}^1_{k,l}, \cdots, \mathbf{F}^n_{k,l}, \varpi) \tag{3}$$

where $\oslash$ is the analogous reasoning mechanism simulation operator, which is currently implemented as an interpolation/extrapolation process in our prototype system. If all the intensities of reasoning sources fall within $(0, 1)$, namely $0 \le \omega^i_{l_s} \le 1$ $(s = 1, \cdots, 4;\ i = 1, \cdots, n)$, the **ARP** is simulated using an interpolation process; otherwise it is simulated using an extrapolation process. From a psychological point of view, if $\exists \omega^i_{l_s} < 0$, the **ARP** reflects the inverse reasoning of brain activity; if $\exists \omega^s_{l_i} > 1$, the **ARP** represents positive exaggeration of brain activity; and if $n \ge 3$, the **ARP** mimics combined thinking activity.

Finally by adding back the shape of $\mathbf{P}_{k,r}^{std}$, the standard constructive element associated with the reasoning result $\mathbf{P}_{k,r}$ in the **ARP**, we obtain the parametric representation $\mathbf{E}_{k,r}$ of $\mathbf{P}_{k,r}$ as indicated by Eq.(4), where $\mathbf{E}_{k,r}^{std}$ is the matrix-form parametric representation of the shape of $\mathbf{P}_{k,r}^{std}$. In the equation, the operator $\oplus$ applies the reverse function of the operator $\ominus$. Since in our system, $\ominus$ is simply implemented as a minus operator between matrices, $\oplus$ is realized as an addition operator between matrices in our software prototype.

$$\mathbf{E}_{k,r} = \mathbf{F}_{k,r} \oplus \mathbf{E}_{k,r}^{std} \tag{4}$$

Note that the **ARP** can be applied not only to the matrix representations of all the reasoning sources by evaluating a series of matrix operations simulating the **ARP**, but also to the topological constructors of all the reasoning sources. Some simple **ARP** simulation operators for topological constructors are: arithmetic mean, geometric mean and harmonic mean.

## Generating Artistic Calligraphy

Before accepting the generated artwork candidates, a filtering step is needed to make sure that they meet some aesthetic requirements. These requirements were derived by learning from the training examples.

### Extracting Aesthetic Constraints from Training Examples

**Measuring Overlapping between Constructive Elements** Needed for a quantifiable constraint on aesthetics is the concept of *degree of overlapping* between two constructive elements. The degree of overlapping indicates the spatial relationship between the elements and can be used to direct the process of generating the upper-level constructive elements from the lower-level ones.

Let the bounding boxes of two constructive elements **a** and **b** be denoted as $\bar{\mathbf{a}}$ and $\bar{\mathbf{b}}$. Three types of overlapping between **a** and **b**, as given in (5), can be defined, namely, the $x$ dimensional overlapping $\vartheta_x(\mathbf{a}, \mathbf{b})$, the $y$ dimensional overlapping $\vartheta_y(\mathbf{a}, \mathbf{b})$, and the area overlapping $\vartheta_s(\mathbf{a}, \mathbf{b})$.

$$\begin{cases} \vartheta_x(\mathbf{a}, \mathbf{b}) \triangleq (\bar{\mathbf{a}}.x - \bar{\mathbf{b}}.x)/(\bar{\mathbf{a}}.w + \bar{\mathbf{b}}.w) & (5.1) \\ \vartheta_y(\mathbf{a}, \mathbf{b}) \triangleq (\bar{\mathbf{a}}.y - \bar{\mathbf{b}}.y)/(\bar{\mathbf{a}}.h + \bar{\mathbf{b}}.h) & (5.2) \\ \vartheta_s(\mathbf{a}, \mathbf{b}) \triangleq (I(\mathbf{a}) \cap I(\mathbf{b}))/(I(\mathbf{a}) \cup I(\mathbf{b})) & (5.3) \end{cases} \tag{5}$$

In (5.3), $I(\mathbf{a})$ and $I(\mathbf{b})$ are the areas in the image space that the constructive elements **a** and **b** take up; $I(\mathbf{a}) \cap I(\mathbf{b})$ and $I(\mathbf{a}) \cup I(\mathbf{b})$ are the intersection and union of these two areas, respectively.

**Structure Matrix of a Constructive Element** Based on the three types of overlapping just defined, we can represent in a compact form the spatial overlapping of a constructive element's composing components (at a lower level) using what we call *structure matrices*. Recall $\mathbf{P}_{k+1,l}$ is composed of $m$ constructive elements $\mathbf{P}_{k,l_1}, \cdots, \mathbf{P}_{k,l_m}$ in the next lower level. Three structure matrices, $\theta_x(\mathbf{P}_{k+1,1})$, $\theta_y(\mathbf{P}_{k+1,1})$, and $\theta_s(\mathbf{P}_{k+1,1})$, can be defined to represent the structure (the spatial relationship of it composing components) of $\mathbf{P}_{k+1,l}$, as given in Eq.(6). the three matrices are essentially made up of degrees of $x, y$ dimensional and area overlapping between every pair of $\mathbf{P}_{k,l_i}$ and $\mathbf{P}_{k,l_j}$.

$$\begin{cases} \theta_x(\mathbf{P}_{k+1,1}) \triangleq (\theta_x^{i,j})_{m \times m}; & \theta_x^{i,j} = \vartheta_x(\mathbf{P}_{k,l_i}, \mathbf{P}_{k,l_j}) \\ \theta_y(\mathbf{P}_{k+1,1}) \triangleq (\theta_y^{i,j})_{m \times m}; & \theta_y^{i,j} = \vartheta_y(\mathbf{P}_{k,l_i}, \mathbf{P}_{k,l_j}) \\ \theta_s(\mathbf{P}_{k+1,1}) \triangleq (\theta_s^{i,j})_{m \times m}; & \theta_s^{i,j} = \vartheta_s(\mathbf{P}_{k,l_i}, \mathbf{P}_{k,l_j}) \\ \quad (i = 1, \cdots, m; \; j = 1, \cdots, m) & \end{cases} \tag{6}$$

### Constraint Satisfaction for Calligraphy Generation

Based on the structure matrices of the $m$ training examples computed according to Eq.(6), we can derive constraint matrices for the **ARP** needed for the generation of artistic calligraphy artwork. Without loss of generality, we discuss how to derive two representative $x$-dimensional constraint matrices from the set of matrices $\theta_x(\mathbf{P}_{k,l_1}), \cdots, \theta_x(\mathbf{P}_{k,l_m})$. The two representative constraint matrices correspond to the matrix of the maximum tolerable structure $\theta_x^{max}$ and that of the minimum tolerable structure $\theta_x^{min}$. Assume that each of $\mathbf{P}_{k,l_1}, \cdots, \mathbf{P}_{k,l_m}$ is composed of $m$ constructive elements of the next lower level. Then, $\theta_x^{max}$ and $\theta_x^{min}$ are both $m \times m$ dimensional matrices. In $\theta_x^{max}$, the element $\theta_x^{max}(i,j)$ is the maximum value of all the $n$ elements in the $i$-th row and the $j$-th column of $\theta_x(\mathbf{P}_{k,l_1}), \cdots, \theta_x(\mathbf{P}_{k,l_n})$. Similarly, $\theta_x^{min}(i,j)$ is the minimum value of all the elements in the $i$-th row and the $j$-th column of $\theta_x(\mathbf{P}_{k,l_1}), \cdots, \theta_x(\mathbf{P}_{k,l_n})$. The use of the two constraint matrices in the **ARP** is intuitive. During the **ARP**, when the system automatically generates a new constructive element $\mathbf{P}_{k,r}$, the $x$-dimensional structure matrix of this element is computed as $\theta_x(\mathbf{P}_{k,r})$. The system will output this newly generated constructive element only if $\theta_x(\mathbf{P}_{k,r})$ is greater than $\theta_x^{min}$ under the tolerance $\tau^{min}$ and no larger than $\theta_x^{max}$ under the tolerance $\tau^{max}$. We say a matrix is larger (resp. smaller) than another matrix under a certain tolerance $\tau$ only if all of its elements are at least (resp. at most) $\tau$ times that of the corresponding elements in another matrix and these other elements are non-zero. In our experiments, we set $\tau^{max} = 0.8$ and $\tau^{min} = 1.2$. Similarly, we also derive $\theta_y^{min}$, $\theta_y^{max}$, $\theta_s^{min}$, $\theta_s^{max}$ to constrain the randomly generated intensities of the **ARP** to forbid the system to output a calligraphy that violates the aesthetic constraints extracted from training examples.

The constraints of the **ARP** can be relaxed in order to allow for results with new styles that cannot be easily imagined. From a computational psychology's perspective, relaxing or ignoring the constraints in our analogous reasoning process corresponds to the creative brain activity of a calligraphist performing cursive and running style writing. End users can also interactively adjust these two thresholds according to their preferences. The best values of the two thresholds are a matter of the reviewer's personal aesthetic taste.

## Experimental Results and Discussions

Given limited space here, we can only show a small sample of the results here. Figure 1 shows the results from the

Figure 4: A "couple" in many styles. (a) The training examples. (b)–(k) Some selected results generated by our system.

**ARP** being applied to a single character using six training examples as the reasoning source and linear interpolation in the analogous reasoning process. Figure 4 shows the results at the single-character level using five examples and a non-linear interpolation process. The results demonstrate that our approach can yield different new styles after having digested some existing styles. Note the consistency in style among characters within the same newly generated calligraphic piece. To verify that the system was indeed able to generate quality outputs, we invited a group of judges consisting of six amateur calligraphists with at least more than two years' writing experience and four professional calligraphists including a professor major at calligraphy in an art school. They cast votes on the calligraphic artwork generated by the system. If an artwork received more than seven votes, it was considered a new acceptable calligraphic artwork. The result: they considered most of our generated calligraphy to be acceptable.

Our thesis has been that with the parametric hierarchical knowledge representation of Chinese calligraphy, a system can be built to create new Chinese calligraphic artworks in a variety of styles fully automatically and in real time, and the system would need as input only a limited number of printed calligraphic artwork samples.

Although we focus on automatic generation of Chinese calligraphy in this paper, the lure and challenge of automatic generation of artistic calligraphy is not the exclusive problem for Chinese. So an immediate future work item would be to extend our algorithm to cover calligraphy in more languages. Another future direction is to add a feedback component behind the constraint satisfaction component to automatically tune the component to use the best thresholds in the constraint satisfaction.

## References

Blum, H., and Wed, W. 1967. Model for the perception of speech and visual form. volume 10 of 2, 119–122. Cambridge, Massachusetts: MIT Press.

Keane, M. 1988. Analogical mechanisms. In *Artificial Intelligence Review*, volume 2, 229.

Knuth, D. 1979. *Tex and Metafont: New Directions in Typesetting*. Providence, R.I.: American Mathematical Society, and Bedford, Mass.: Digital Press.

Ramalho, G., and Ganascia, J.-G. 1994. Simulating creativity in jazz performance. In *National Conference on Artificial Intelligence*, 108–113.

Simon, H. 1975. Style in design. In *Spatial Synthesis in computer Aided Building Design, Edited by C.M. Eastman*. London: Applied Science Pub.

Strassmann, S. 1986. Hairy brushes. In *Proceedings of the 13th Annual Conference on Computer Graphics and Interactive Techniques*, 225–232. ACM Press.

Yanikoglu, B., and Sandon, P. 1994. Recognizing off-line cursive handwriting. In *Proc. Computer Vision and Pattern Recognition*, 397 – 403.

Zhu, P., and Chirlian, P. 1995. On critical point detection of In *IEEE Trans. Pattern Analysis and Machine Intelligence*, volume 17 of *8*, 737–748.

# Student Abstracts

# A Correspondence Metric for Imitation

**R. Amit** and **Maja Matarić**
Computer Science Department
University of Southern California
Los Angeles, California 90089–0781
Email: {amitr|mataric}@cs.usc.edu

## Introduction

Learning by imitation is a powerful form of learning. Different forms of imitation, like mimicry, copying, response facilitation, etc. have been studied extensively (Miklosi 1999). Recent research in robotics has begun to explore imitation as a means to allow complex robots, like humanoid robots, acquire new skills (Swinson & Bruemmer 2000).

One of the key issues in imitation learning is the *correspondence problem*. This problem concerns the answer to the question: *what action sequence of the imitator is similar to that of the demonstrator and how similar it is?* The notion of "similarity" has remained subjective thus far. Robotics research in imitation has mostly focussed on action learning and classification, and not on the correspondence problem. Our aim is to develop a generalized metric that provides a scalar measure of dissimilarity/distance between any given pair of action sequences. This, we expect would be a uniform means to evaluate imitation in agents. The metric can also be used as a part of the action selection mechanism in an imitator agent.

## Related work

Nehaniv et al. (Nehaniv & Dautenhahn 2000; 2001) have provided a formal framework for the correspondence problem. Within this framework, Alissandrakis et al. (Alissandrakis, Nehaniv, & Dautenhahn 2002) have explored multiple metrics. These have however been specific to the particular agents and problems considered.

Pomplun et al. (Pomplun & Matarić 2000) have used four different metrics to evaluate imitation of arm movements. These metrics used scaled and time-normalized Euclidean distance. These are specific to the experiment, and cannot be used as a general metric for correspondence.

Research in object recognition has resulted in the development of metrics that compare object silhouettes (Liu & Geiger 1999; Sebastian, Klein, & Kimia 2001). These methods are not directly extendable to motions or actions of articulated agents.



## The Approach

We consider agents as simple open kinematic chains. We represent each chain as a *tree*, termed *kinematic tree* or *k-tree*. We introduce the following definitions.

**Definition 1 (k-tree)** *A* kinematic tree *or* k-tree *is an encoding of an open kinematic chain such that every link in the kinematic chain is represented by a unique edge in the k-tree.*

**Definition 2 (Pose)** *A* pose $p$ *of a k-tree* $t$ *is an assignment of the ordered pair* $\langle n_i, l_i \rangle$ *to every edge* $e_i$ *of* $t$. $n_i$ *is a unit normal that is the orientation of the link, represented by* $e_i$*, in the world coordinate frame.* $l_i$ *is the length of the link represented by* $e_i$.

**Definition 3 (Homeomorphic pose class)** *A* homeomorphic pose class $P$ *is a set of poses such that for any pair of poses* $p, q \in P$*, if* $t_p$ *is the k-tree of* $p$ *and* $t_q$ *the k-tree of* $q$ *then* $t_p$ *and* $t_q$ *are* homeomorphic.

We have developed an algorithm that computes a distance measure between a pair of poses that belong to a homeomorphic pose class. The algorithm first partitions the edges of each k-tree into disjoint sets. Based on the presence of a common minimal homeomorph for the two trees, the algorithm pairs the edge sets of the two k-trees. A distance measure, based on the summed squared difference of the instantaneous slopes is then used to compute the dissimilarity between individual pairs. The distance between the two poses is the sum of all the dissimilarity measures. The distance thus computed imposes a *pseudometric* over the homeomorphic pose class. Our algorithm thus provides a measure of dissimilarity between poses which can be used toward estimating pose correspondence.

## Experimental Validation

In order to experimentally test the metric, we require agents with differing kinematic structures such that their poses belong to the same pose class. We chose to use three different agents for the purpose, a Sony AIBO (Figure 1) robot dog, a human, and a simulated dolphin-like structure (Figure 2).

Pose information for the AIBO was obtained by converting the joint angle values obtained from the software onboard to orientations in a world coordinate frame. For the human, digital images of the subject in various postures

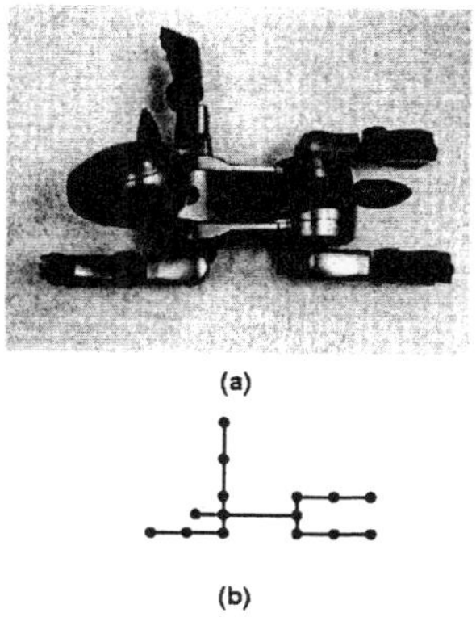

Figure 1: (a) Sony AIBO and (b) its k-tree representation

were captured and limb orientations were extracted and then encoded into *poses* (Figure 3).

For the experiments, we used 16 poses for each of the three agents for a total of 48 poses. All-pairs distances of the poses were computed based on the pseudometric. Figure 4 shows some closest pose pairs between agents.

We are currently extending the correspondence algorithm to allow comparisons between time-extended actions. Actions result in continuous curves in pose space, and hence comparisons can be made between curves.

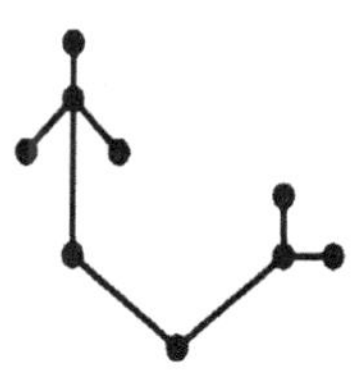

Figure 2: k-tree of the dolphin-like skeleton

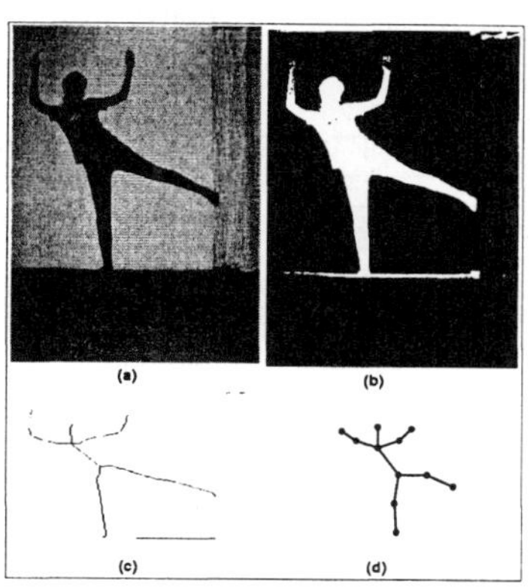

Figure 3: (a) Captured image (b) Image after background subtraction (c) Image after skeletonization (d) Computed pose

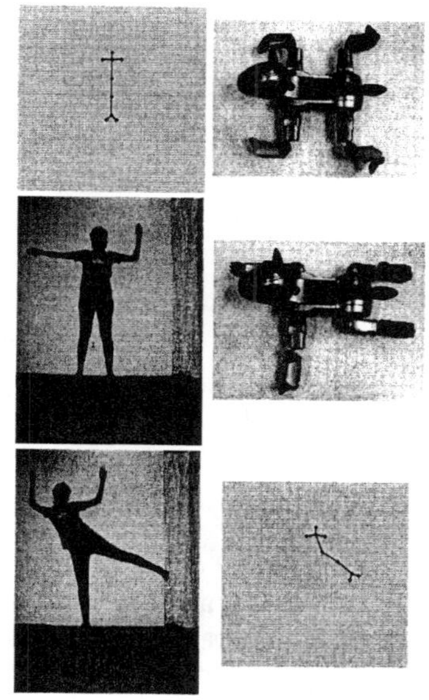

Figure 4: Top row: Closest AIBO pose to the dolphin pose; middle row: Closest AIBO pose to the human pose; bottom row: Closest dolphin pose to the human pose

## References


Alissandrakis, A.; Nehaniv, C. L.; and Dautenhahn, K. 2002. Imitating with alice: Learning to imitate corresponding actions across dissimilar embodiments. *IEEE Transactions on Systems, Man, and Cybernetics—Part A: Systems and Humans* 32(4):482–496.

Liu, T.-L., and Geiger, D. 1999. Approximate tree matching and shape similarity. *7th International Conference on Computer Vision* 456–462.

Miklosi, A. 1999. The ethological analysis of imitation. *Biological Review* 74:347–374.

Nehaniv, C. L., and Dautenhahn, K. 2000. Of hummingbirds and helicopters: An algebraic framework for interdisciplinary studies of imitation and its applications. *Interdisciplinary Approaches to Robot Learning, World Scientific Series in Robotics and Intelligent Systems* 24, World Scientific Press:136–161.

Nehaniv, C. L., and Dautenhahn, K. 2001. Like me? – measures of correspondence and imitation. *Cybernetics and Systems: An International Journal* 32(1-2):11–51.

Pomplun, M., and Matarić, M. 2000. Evaluation metrics and results of human arm movement imitation. In *First IEEE-RAS International Conference on Humanoid Robotics (Humanoids-2000).*

Sebastian, T.; Klein, P.; and Kimia, B. 2001. Recognition of shapes by editing shock graphs. *IEEE International Conference on Computer Vision* 755–762.

Swinson, M. L., and Bruemmer, D. J., eds. 2000. *IEEE Intelligent Systems*, volume 15(4).

# Fuzzy Induction in Dynamic User Profiling for Information Filtering

**Rafal A. Angryk and Costin Barbu**

Electrical Engineering and Computer Science Department
Tulane University, New Orleans, LA, 70118
{angryk, barbu}@eecs.tulane.edu

In this paper we investigate the role of the user profile in information filtering and we introduce a novel algorithm for learning the user profile based on user's initial profile and on a queries' interpretation using fuzzy generalization (Angryk and Petry 2003). Thousands of documents are usually retrieved by search engines for a given query during an information search on WWW. One way to prune irrelevant documents is to take advantage of the user's implicit interests to filter the documents returned by the search engine, or to reformulate the query based on these interests.

One of the common representations of the documents (and queries) in information retrieval is based on the vector hyperspace model (Salton and McGill 1993). We are using the expanded version of Salton's vector space model introduced by Barbu and Simina (2003) for its effectiveness in computing the dynamics of the user profile. In contrast with the classical vector space model, this recent model, time-words vector hyperspace, has an additional temporal dimension. The coordinates of the documents and queries vectors are calculated using the traditional TF-IDF technique. Only the queries have a temporal dimension (current interest weight) which is set to a preset positive initial value that decays in time, suggesting that some specific user interests could decrease as time goes on. The user's categories of interest are computed based on a novel approach using Fuzzy Concept Hierarchies (FCH) extracted from the WordNet[1] ontology. An FCH is built for each of the query's keywords, using their hypernym chains provided by WordNet. A sub-unitary membership degree (weight) is assigned for each of the edges of the hierarchy via a bottom-up approach, from the lowest level concept (initial keyword) to the more abstract one. The assignment of the weights is performed according to the following two conditions:

*1) The sum of weights assigned to the links outgoing from the original keyword has to be equal to unity.*

*2) The sum of weights from all links incoming to each node in the FCH has to be equal to the sum of weights in all outgoing edges.*

The user category of interest is found by intersecting keywords generalization models for each query. For each of the generalization paths ending at the same abstract concept we calculate the Average Generalization Path Value (AGPV) as the average of the products of the paths' weights, and choose the abstract with the largest value as the category of interest. An example of extracting the user category of interest given the *Query* = *{Shrimp, Chardonnay}* is illustrated in Figure 1. The Average Generalization Path Value was computed for both abstract concepts: *Food* and *Organism*. $AGPV_{Food}$ was obtained by taking into consideration the path weights' product on the chains: *Shrimp – Food* and *Chardonnay – Food*. $AGPV_{Organism}$ was calculated employing the path weights' product on the chains *Shrimp - Organism* and *Chardonnay – Organism*. The abstract Food was selected as the category of interest since $AGPV_{Food} > AGPV_{Organism}$.

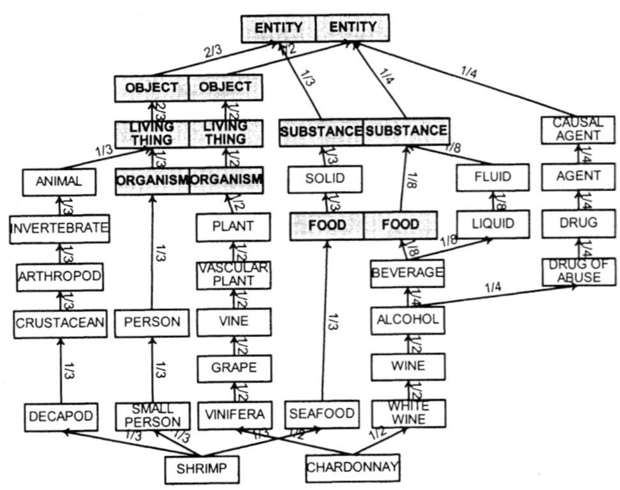


Figure 1. Intersection of Fuzzy Concept Hierarchies for *Query* = *{Shrimp, Chardonnay}*

The rate of interest change $\alpha_i$ computed as the cosine similarity between two sequential query feature vectors $Q_i$

[1] WordNet is an on-line lexical reference system available at: http://www.cogsci.princeton.edu/cgi-bin/webwn1.7.1

and $Q_{i-1}$ proved to be an effective measure of user's profile dynamics (Barbu and Simina 2003). We have modeled the user behavior by developing an adaptive algorithm for dynamic learning of the user profile (Figure 2). The scheme proposed in this work keeps track of both the user's Recent and Long-Term Profiles. The input of the algorithm is a query ($Q_i$) and the output is one or more triplets (Category $C_i$, Current Interest Weight $W_i$, Rate of Interest Change $\alpha_i$).

**LearnUserProfile($Q_i$) => updated profile P**

1. For each query $Q_i = \{t_{1i}, t_{2i}, t_{3i}, ..., t_{ki}\}$, where $k = 1...M$ and $t_{ki}$ are the keywords of $Q_i$
2. Compute the Rate of Interest Change $\alpha_i$ between $Q_i$ and $Q_{i-1}$
3. Extract the generalized Category $C_i$ via fuzzy induction method on keywords' hypernym chains
4. Insert Category $C_i$, to the Recent Profile together with the Current Interest Weight $W_i$ (preset to a positive initial value $W$) and with the Rate of Interest Change $\alpha_i$
5. If Rate of Interest Change $\alpha_i > \alpha_{threshold}$ (= 0.6) then increase the Current Interest Weight of Category $C_i$ by a positive value $\Delta W$ : $W_i = W + \Delta W$
6. Sort the triplets ($C_i$, $W_i$, $\alpha_i$) from the Recent Profile in ascending order of the Current Interest Weight $W_i$.
7. Decrease all $W_i$ from Recent Profile by a temporal decay factor $\theta$
8. If $W_i < 0$ then move ($C_i$, $W_i$, $\alpha_i$) to the Long Term Profile
9. Return Updated User Profile.

Figure 2. User Profile Learning algorithm

Experimental results are presented in Table 1. The filtering process is performed based on the Relevance Score determined as the cosine similarity between the User Profile feature vector and the feature vectors of the documents retrieved by a classical search engine (i.e. Yahoo).

| | No Profile Filtering | Total Profile Filtering | Recent Profile Filtering |
|---|---|---|---|
| Total Number Documents Retrieved | 31,356,000 | 256 | 11,756 |
| Accuracy in Top 10 Documents Retrieved | 36.33 % | 41.25 % | 70.66% |
| Accuracy in Top 20 Documents Retrieved | 28 % | 31 % | 65 % |

Table 1. Experimental results (on average) for various filtering methods on a set of queries

Our preliminary results demonstrate that the information filtering effectiveness is significantly improved by using the User Recent Profile as opposed to existing approaches that consider the total profile (Balabanovic 1997, Chen and Sycara 1998, Widyantoro et al. 1999). We plan to extend our work by integrating the background knowledge available in WordNet with a more specialized ontology in order to accommodate queries with brand names.

## References


Angryk, R., and Petry, F. 2003. Data Mining Fuzzy Databases Using Attribute-Oriented Generalization. In Proceedings of the Third IEEE International Conference on Data Mining, 8-15. Melbourne, FL.: IEEE Computer Society.

Angryk, R., and Petry, F. 2003. Consistent Fuzzy Concept Hierarchies for Attribute Generalization. In *Proceedings of the IASTED International Conference on Information and Knowledge Sharing*, 158-163. Scottsdale, AZ.: ACTA Press.

Barbu, C., and Simina, M. 2003. Information Filtering Using the Dynamics of the User Profile. In *Proceedings of the 16th International Florida Artificial Intelligence Research Society Conference*, 245-249, St. Augustine, FL.: AAAI Press.

Balabanovic, M. 1997. An Adaptive Web Page Recommendation Service. In *Proceedings of the First International Conference on Autonomous Agents.* 378 – 385, New York. N.Y.: ACM Press.

Chen, L., and Sycara, K. 1998. WebMate: Personal Agent for Browsing and Searching. In *Proceedings of the Second International Conference on Autonomous Agents*, 132-139. New York. N.Y.: ACM Press.

Cubero J. C., Medina J.M., Pons O.and Vila M.A. 1999. Data Summarization in Relational Databases Through Fuzzy Dependencies, *Information Sciences,* 121(3-4): 233-270.

Lee D.H., and Kim M.H.1997. Database Summarization Using Fuzzy ISA Hierarchies. *IEEE Transactions On Systems, Man, and Cybernetics* - part B, 27(1): 68-78.

Lee M. 2001. Mining Generalized Fuzzy Quantitative Association Rules with Fuzzy Generalization Hierarchies. In *Proceedings of the Joint 9th IFSA World Congress and 20th NAFIPS International Conference*, 2977 - 2982. Vancouver, Canada: IEEE.

Mock, K. J. 1996. Hybrid-Hill-Climbing and Knowledge-based Techniques for Intelligent News Filtering. *In Proceedings of the Thirteenth National Conference on Artificial Intelligence and the Eighth Innovative Applications of Artificial Intelligence Conference.* 48-53. Menlo Park, California: AAAI Press

Salton, G., and McGill, M. J. 1993. *Introduction to Modern Information Retrieval.* New York. N. Y.: McGraw-Hill.

Voorhees, E.M. 1993. Using WordNet to Disambiguate Word Senses for Text Retrieval. In *Proceedings of the 16th Annual International ACM-SIGIR Conference on Research and Development in Information Retrieval*, 171-180. Pittsburgh, PA: ACM Press.

Widyantoro, D. H., Yin J., El Nasr, M., S., Yang, L., Zacchi, A. and Yen J. 1999. Alipes: A Swift Messenger in Cyberspace. In *1999 AAAI Proceedings of the Spring Symposium on Intelligent Agents in Cyberspace*, 62-67. Palo Alto, CA: AAAI Press.

# Semantically Guiding a First-Order Theorem Prover with a Soft Model

**Arnold Binas**
Department of Computer Science
Texas A&M University
College Station, TX 77843-3112
Tel: 979-862-6801
arnold-binas@neo.tamu.edu

**John Slaney**
Computer Science Laboratory, RSISE
The Australian National University
Canberra, ACT, Australia
John.Slaney@anu.edu.au

Various versions of our first-order logic theorem prover SCOTT have been developed over the past decade to employ the concept of semantic guidance for improving the underlying system OTTER by McCune (Slaney, Lusk, & McCune 1994; Hodgson & Slaney 2001; 2002). We introduce our latest attempt to speed up OTTER's proof search, Softie. While the various SCOTTs consulted an ordinary constraint solver to gain information about the problem to be solved, Softie is implemented from scratch and uses a solver capable of handling soft constraints.

The first-order theorem prover OTTER searches for refutation proofs by the means of the *given clause algorithm*, which partitions the clauses of a problem into the *usable list* (UL) and the *set of support* (SOS). So-called *given clauses* are selected from the SOS, moved to the UL, and react under inference rules to generate new clauses (McCune 1994). While OTTER uses purely syntactic criteria to select the next given clause, SCOTT bases that decision on the truth-values of clauses in several models of a subset of the problem's clauses. The models are supplied by the constraint solver FINDER (Slaney 1994). As the goal of a refutation proof search is to arrive at the empty clause, clauses false in the guiding model are preferred as next given clauses. This approach is known as the *false preference strategy*.

When dealing with hard constraints, multiple models improve the quality of semantic guidance, but their maintenance is very costly. The new Softie uses a guiding model that is generated by SFINDER, a version of FINDER that handles soft constraints. While the underlying idea of semantic guidance remains the same as in previous versions of SCOTT, Softie is built from scratch and maintains a single, largely soft model of almost the whole current UL.

The figure below illustrates the basic workings of Softie. The SOS is partitioned into buckets to differentiate both between lengths of clauses and their truth-values in the current model. A new given clause is selected from the SOS mostly[1] using the false preference strategy, incorporated into SFINDER's model, and used by OTTER to generate new clauses. The new clauses that OTTER generates are tested against the current model and put into the appropriate buckets of the SOS. Testing a clause against the current model is relatively cheap as the model is very small (we use a domain of only around three elements). The process is then repeated until the empty clause has been derived and a proof found.

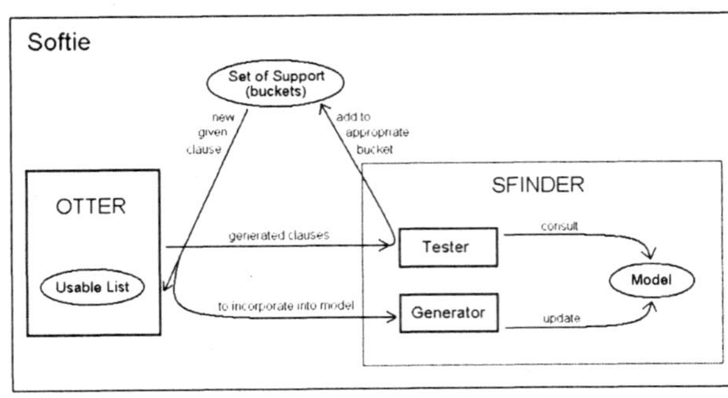


As its predecessor FINDER, SFINDER uses a generic sort with a finite domain for all variables and functions in the theory it is modeling. In Softie's proof search, the clauses initially in the UL (before the proof search starts) are treated by SFINDER as hard constraints to give the model a general direction. In most cases, the clauses in the initial UL are consistent with each other as they are axioms, so a model is still guaranteed to be found. Clauses that are selected as given clauses during the proof search are then added to the set of clauses being modeled. Due to the way SFINDER works, only so-called short clauses can be incorporated into the model as soft constraints. The number of literals a clause can have and still be considered short is set as a parameter in Softie. All selected given clauses that are short are incorporated into the model as soft constraints. Treating the constraints imposed by short clauses as soft opens a way to consider a larger portion of the problem's clauses while still finding a model. Whenever a new clause is true in the current model, it is added without any changes to the model. Otherwise, a new model including the new clause is sought. Thus, SFINDER always supplies Softie with a model that satisfies as many instances as possible, fitting the model to most of the UL clauses and making it more representative of the problem. As another parameter in Softie, SFINDER is given a time limit after which it returns the best model found up to that point.

Softie has been tested with various parameter settings on



[1] Every now and then a clause is selected without semantic guidance to ensure the completeness of the approach.

several eligible problems from the CADE-18 ATP System Competition (Sutcliffe & Suttner 2002) and compared to runs of its underlying system OTTER on the same set of problems. At this early stage, the results are mixed, yet encouraging. While there are problems that OTTER solves within a time limit of ten minutes that Softie cannot solve in that period, there are several problems that Softie solves in well under ten minutes and which OTTER cannot prove in the given time. For harder problems that both systems solve within the time limit, Softie generally takes fewer given clauses before finding a proof than OTTER, which indicates that the semantic guidance is successfully focusing the search. In many cases, however, that comes at a high cost in time spent on the model searches, effectively causing Softie to take longer than OTTER for many problems. These experiments show that Softie is headed in the right direction, but it is far from finished. However, it is already many times faster than the previous versions of SCOTT. A major potential improvement we plan to implement in the future is for Softie to utilize its guiding model not only for the false preference strategy, but also for *semantic resolution* (Slagle 1967). Under this approach, clauses in the UL are labeled with a truth-value as well. Semantic resolution then calls for at least one parent of each newly generated clause to be false in the guiding model. Other areas of future work include tuning the various settings and details of the clause selection algorithm as well as making Softie learn features of problems and thereby enabling it to adapt to different problem classes autonomously.

The presented system exposes the potential of using soft models in semantically guided theorem proving. We consider it a good start in further exploring how to speed up the proof search of contemporary first-order provers.

## Acknowledgements

This work was supported by the National ICT Australia. National ICT Australia is funded through the Australian Government's *Backing Australia's Ability* initiative, in part through the Australian Research Council.

## References

Hodgson, K., and Slaney, J. 2001. System Descrption: SCOTT-5. In *Proc. First International Joint Conference on Automated Reasoning*, 443–447. Berlin, Heidelberg: Springer Verlag.

Hodgson, K., and Slaney, J. 2002. TPTP, CASC and the Development of a Semantically Guided Theorem Prover. *AI Communications* 15(2):135–146.

McCune, W. W. 1994. OTTER 3.0 Reference Manual and Guide. Technical Report, ANL-94/6, Argonne National Laboratory.

Slagle, J. R. 1967. Automatic Theorem Proving With Renamable and Semantic Resolution. *Journal of the Association for Computing Machinery* 14(4):687–697.

Slaney, J.; Lusk, E. L.; and McCune, W. 1994. SCOTT: Semantically Constrained Otter System Description. In *Proc. 12th Conference on Automated Deduction*, 764–768. Berlin, Heidelberg: Springer Verlag.

Slaney, J. 1994. FINDER: Finite Domain Enumerator (System Description). In *Proc. 12th Conference on Automated Deduction*, 798–801. Berlin, Heidelberg: Springer Verlag.

Sutcliffe, G., and Suttner, C. 2002. The CADE-18 ATP System Competition. Retrieved April 1, 2004 from the World Wide Web
`http://www.cs.miami.edu/~tptp/CASC/18/`.

# Metrics for Finite Markov Decision Processes

**Norm Ferns**
School of Computer Science
McGill University
Montréal, Canada, H3A 2A7
(514)398-7071 ext 09183
nferns@cs.mcgill.ca

**Prakash Panangaden**
**Doina Precup**
School of Computer Science
McGill University
Montréal, Canada, H3A 2A7
prakash@cs.mcgill.ca
dprecup@cs.mcgill.ca

Markov decision processes (MDPs) offer a popular mathematical tool for planning and learning in the presence of uncertainty (Boutilier, Dean, & Hanks 1999). MDPs are a standard formalism for describing multi-stage decision making in probabilistic environments. The objective of the decision making is to maximize a cumulative measure of long-term performance, called the *return*. Dynamic programming algorithms, e.g., value iteration or policy iteration (Puterman 1994), allow us to compute the optimal expected return for any state, as well as the way of behaving (policy) that generates this return. However, in many practical applications the state space of an MDP is simply too large, possibly even continuous, for such standard algorithms to be applied. A typical means of overcoming such circumstances is to partition the state space in the hope of obtaining an "essentially equivalent" reduced system. One defines a new MDP over the partition blocks, and if it is small enough, it can be solved by classical methods. The hope is that optimal values and policies for the reduced MDP can be extended to optimal values and policies for the original MDP.

The notion of equivalence for stochastic processes is problematic because it requires that the transition probabilities agree *exactly*. This is not a robust concept, especially considering that usually, the numbers used in probabilistic models come from experimentation or are approximate estimates; what is needed is a quantitative notion of equivalence. In our work we provide such a notion via semimetrics, distance functions on the state space that assign distances quantifying "how equivalent" states are. These semimetrics could potentially be used as a new theoretical tool to analyze current state compression algorithms for MDPs, or in practice to guide state aggregation directly. The ultimate goal of this research is to efficiently compress and analyze continuous state space MDPs. Here we focus on finite MDPs, but note that most of our results should hold, with slight modifications, in the context of continuous state spaces.

Recent MDP research on defining equivalence relations on MDPs (Givan, Dean, & Greig 2003) has built on the notion of strong probabilistic bisimulation from concurrency theory. Bisimulation was introduced by Larsen and Skou (1991) based on ideas of Park (1981) and Milner (1980). Roughly speaking, two states of a process are deemed equivalent if all the transitions of one state can be matched by transitions of the other state, and the results are themselves bisimilar. The extension of bisimulation to transition systems with rewards was carried out in the context of MDPs by Givan, Dean and Greig (2003). Suppose $M = (S, A, \{r_s^a | s \in S, a \in A\}, \{P_{ss'}^a\})$ is a given finite MDP consisting of a finite state space, a finite action space, numerical rewards (for convenience assumed constrained to the unit interval), and transition probabilities, respectively. *Stochastic bisimulation* is the largest relation on $S$ that satisfies the following property: it is an equivalence relation and states are equivalent precisely when for each action they share the same expected immediate rewards and 1-step transition probabilities to equivalence classes, i.e. $s \sim s' \iff \forall a \in A.(r_s^a = r_{s'}^a$ and $\forall C \in S/\sim.(P_s^a(C) = P_{s'}^a(C)))$. Here $\sim$ denotes the bisimulation equivalence relation and $S/\sim$ denotes the resulting quotient space.

We quantify the notion of bisimulation in terms of bisimulation semimetrics (henceforth "metrics"), which assign distance zero to states precisely when those states are bisimilar. Our goal is to construct a class of bisimulation metrics useful for MDP state compression. Specifically, we require such metrics to be easily computable and to provide information concerning the optimal values of states. However, it is not hard to show that the bisimulation metric that assigns distance 1 to states that are not bisimilar satisfies both requirements, while possessing no more distinguishing power than that of bisimulation itself. So we additionally require that metric distances should vary smoothly and proportionally with differences in rewards and differences in probabilities. Formally, we will construct bisimulation metrics via a metric on rewards and a metric on probability functions (called a probability metric). The choice of metric on rewards is an obvious one: we simply use the usual Euclidean distance. However, there are many ways of defining useful probability metrics (Gibbs & Su 2002). Two of the most important for our purposes are the Kantorovich metric and the total variation metric. They lead to two classes of bisimulation metrics.

Our original bisimulation metrics use the Kantorovich metric, whose origins lie in the theory of mass transportation. Suppose $d$ is a metric on $S$. Consider two copies of the state space, one in which states are labeled as supply nodes, and the other in which states are labeled as demand nodes. Each supply node has a supply whose value is equal to the probability mass of the corresponding state under probability function $P$. Each demand has a value equal to the probability mass of the corresponding state under probability function $Q$. Furthermore, imagine there is a transportation arc from each supply node to each demand node, labeled with a cost equal to the distance of the corresponding states under $d$. This constitutes a transportation network. A flow with respect to this network is an assignment of quantities to be shipped along each arc subject to the conditions that the total flow leaving a supply node is equal to its supply, and the total flow entering a demand node is equal to its demand. The cost of a flow along an arc is the value of the flow along that arc multiplied by the cost assigned to that arc. The goal of the Kantorovich optimal mass transportation problem is to find the best total flow for the given network, i.e. the flow of minimal cost. If we denote by $T_K(d)$ the Kantorovich metric, then the distance assigned to $P$ and $Q$, $T_K(d)(P, Q)$, is the cost of the optimal flow. It is known to be computable in strongly polynomial time.

The associated bisimulation metric, $d_{fix}$, is given by $d_{fix}(s, s') = \max_{a \in A}(c_R|r_s^a - r_{s'}^a| + c_T T_K(d_{fix})(P_s^a, P_{s'}^a))$ where $c_R$ and $c_T$ are fixed positive weights that sum to 1, i.e. it is a (unique) fixed-point metric. It is based on similar fixed-point metrics developed in the context of labeled Markov systems, roughly MDPs without rewards in (Desharnais *et al.* 1999) and (Desharnais *et al.* 2002). Like those, these metrics can be iteratively computed in time polynomial in the sizes of the state space and the action space, and can be equivalently formulated in terms of a real-valued modal logic characterizing bisimulation.

An alternative bisimulation metric, $d_\sim$, comes from replacing in the above equation the Kantorovich metric by one based on the total variation distance. We take the bisimulation probability metric $T_B$ to be defined as $T_B(P, Q) = \frac{1}{2}\sum_{C \in S/\sim} |P(C) - Q(C)|$. Its calculation involves computing the stochastic bisimulation partition, which can be done iteratively in polynomial time (Givan, Dean, & Greig 2003). We then define $d_\sim(s, s') = \max_{a \in A}(c_R|r_s^a - r_{s'}^a| + c_T T_B(P_s^a, P_{s'}^a))$.

Both bisimulation metrics assign distances between 0 (bisimilar) and 1 (not bisimilar), giving a measure of "how bisimilar" two states are. They are related by $d_{fix} \leq d_\sim$ under a pointwise ordering and are in some sense the tightest and loosest smooth bisimulation metrics of the given form, respectively. Moreover, we can show that the optimal value function for $M$, $V^*$, is Lipschitz continuous for each. Specifically, $c_R|V^*(s) - V^*(s')| \leq d_{fix}(s, s') \leq d_\sim(s, s')$ provided the discount factor $\gamma \leq c_T$ (Ferns 2003). In particular, this shows that the more bisimilar two states are, the closer are their optimal values. Such results are extendable to a particular aggregate MDP, allowing us to similarly bound the difference between the optimal value of a state in $M$ and the optimal value of its equivalence class in the aggregate in terms of the bisimulation distances.

Both metrics have advantages and disadvantages. Computation of $d_{fix}$ does not require that the exact bisimulation partition be computed. Moreover, extending these metrics to continuous state space models in which rewards are uniformly bounded looks very promising. On the other hand, iteratively computing the Kantorovich metric (as is required for the overall computation) while requiring only polynomially many operations is still very time consuming. By contrast, $d_\sim$ is relatively fast to compute (as the bisimulation partition itself can be quickly computed). On the other hand since its computation relies on computing the exact bisimulation partition, which is subject to numerical inaccuracy, it may be numerically unstable. Nevertheless, for these reasons and more we argue that while the Kantorovich based bisimulation metrics are theoretically pleasing, the total variation based metrics are more pleasing in practice, and provide empirical results. The bulk of this work can be found in (Ferns 2003).

## References


Boutilier, C.; Dean, T.; and Hanks, S. 1999. Decision-theoretic planning: Structural assumptions and computational leverage. *Journal of Artificial Intelligence Research* 11:1–94.

Desharnais, J.; Gupta, V.; Jagadeesan, R.; and Panangaden, P. 1999. Metrics for labeled markov systems. In *International Conference on Concurrency Theory*, 258–273.

Desharnais, J.; Gupta, V.; Jagadeesan, R.; and Panangaden, P. 2002. The metric analogue of weak bisimulation for probabilistic processes. In *Logic in Computer Science*, 413–422. Los Alamitos, CA, USA: IEEE Computer Society.

Ferns, N. 2003. Metrics for markov decision processes. Master's thesis, McGill University. URL: `http://www.cs.mcgill.ca/~nferns/mythesis.ps`.

Gibbs, A. L., and Su, F. E. 2002. On choosing and bounding probability metrics.

Givan, R.; Dean, T.; and Greig, M. 2003. Equivalence notions and model minimization in markov decision processes. *Artif. Intell.* 147(1-2):163–223.

Larsen, K., and Skou, A. 1991. Bisimulation through probabilistic testing. *In Information and Computation* 94:1–28.

Milner, R. 1980. *A Calculus of Communicating Systems*. Lecture Notes in Computer Science Vol. 92. Springer-Verlag. MIL r 80:1 1.Ex.

Park, D. 1981. Concurrency and automata on infinite sequences. In *Proceedings of the 5th GI-Conference on Theoretical Computer Science*, 167–183. Springer-Verlag.

Puterman, M. L. 1994. *Markov Decision Processes: Discrete Stochastic Dynamic Programming*. John Wiley & Sons, Inc.

# Robust Solutions for Constraint Satisfaction and Optimization

**Emmanuel Hebrard***
Cork Constraint Computation Centre
University College Cork, Ireland.
email: e.hebrard@4c.ucc.ie

### Abstract

Super solutions are solutions in which, if a small number of variables lose their values, we are guaranteed to be able to repair the solution with only a few changes. In this paper, we stress the need to extend the super solution framework along several dimensions to make it more useful practically. We demonstrate the usefulness of those extensions on an example from jobshop scheduling, an optimization problem solved through constraint satisfaction. In such a case there is indeed a trade-off between optimality and robustness, however robustness may be increased without sacrificing optimality.

## Introduction

Many AI problems may be modeled as constraint satisfaction and optimization problems. However, the real world is subject to change: machines may break, drivers may get sick, stock prices increase or decrease, etc. In such cases, our solutions to the problems may "break". In this context, one may want a solution to be robust, that is able to remain valid despite changes. Supermodels were introduced in (Ginsberg, Parkes, & Roy 1998) as a framework to measure inherent degrees of solution stability. They are propositional satisfiability models such that we are guaranteed to have a close alternative solution in case of breakage. This notion extends to constraint satisfaction: an $(a, b)$-*super-solution* ((Hebrard, Hnich, & Walsh 2004)) is a solution to a constraint satisfaction problem (CSP) such that the loss of the values of at most $a$ variables in $S$ can be repaired by assigning other values to these variables, and modifying the assignment of at most $b$ other variables. We call this new solution (with at most $a + b$ variables reassigned) a *repair solution*. Consider the following CSP:

$$A < B < C \quad A, B, C \in [1..4]$$

$\langle A : 1, B : 2, C : 4\rangle$ is a $(1, 1)$-super-solution since for any loss of value of any single variable, another solution may be found by changing at most one other variable. For instance, a break on A is repaired by the following solution:

$$\langle A : 2, B : 3, C : 4\rangle$$

*supported by Science Foundation Ireland and an ILOG grant.


The problem of determining the existence of a super-solution has been proved to be NP-complete for a fixed $a$ (Hebrard, Hnich, & Walsh 2004), as well as for supermodels of SAT theories (Ginsberg, Parkes, & Roy 1998).

Our aim is to be able to "constrain" a problem in a such way that a solution has the good properties of robustness we need. The approach taken in (Hebrard, Hnich, & Walsh 2004) was to explore in depth the simplest case, namely $(1, 0)$-super-solutions, i.e., solutions where the loss of a value taken by any variable may be repaired (the variable is reassigned) without changing the rest of the solution. An efficient algorithm based on the notion of super-consistency was introduced. The next step is to bring all $(a, b)$-super-solutions to the constraint satisfaction framework. Furthermore, in practice, we may know how the problem is likely to break, or how we may repair it. We explore here some extensions of the framework to take this knowledge into account. We classify those extentions as follows:

- **Break and repair set:** restrictions on the set of variables that may break, or may participate to a repair.
- **Alternative value:** restrictions on the alternative value given to a "broken" variable.
- **Value and variable:** restrictions on the reassignments required when "repairing" a break, either concerning the values or the variables.

## Algorithm and Extensions

Constraint solving often involves search and inference. Local consistency is used to prune values in future variables' domains and and backtrack when a domain wipe-out occurs. We introduce an algorithm for finding $(a, b)$-super-solutions based the Maintain Arc-Consistency (MAC) algorithm (Sabin & Freuder 1994)(Bessiere & Regin 1996). On top of MAC's backtrack search, our algorithm fails also if the current partial assignment is not "repairable",i.e., the partial assignment is not a super-solution of the CSP restricted to the assigned variables, thus cutting branches which wouldn't have been cut by MAC. This algorithm returns both the super-solutions and the repair solutions.

However, super-solutions alone are unable to model all the criteria of robustness one might want a solution to possess. For instance, consider the jobshop scheduling problem (jsp). A jsp involves a set of jobs and a set of machines. Each job is a sequence of activities, where each activity has a duration for its execution on one of the machines. The objective is to schedule the activities such that their order is respected, no machine is required by two activities that overlap, and the makespan, i.e., the interval from the starting point of the first activity, and ending point of the last, is minimized.

A jsp can be formulated as a CSP, with one variable for each activity, and a domain size equal to the makespan minus its duration. To find the minimal makespan, one starts with the makespan equal to a lower bound and increase it till a solution exists.

The following figure represents a jsp with 4 jobs and 4 machines. Bars are activities, organized in jobs. Their length are proportional to their duration. Each job's activities have the same border (respectively solid, dashed, dotted, dash and two dots), whilst colors correspond to machines.

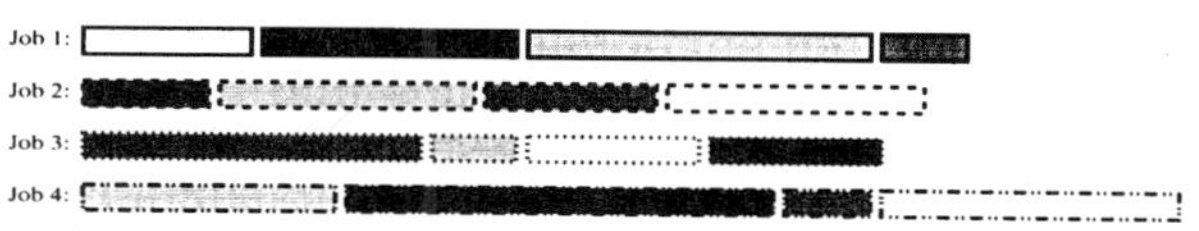


The second figure shows an optimal solution.

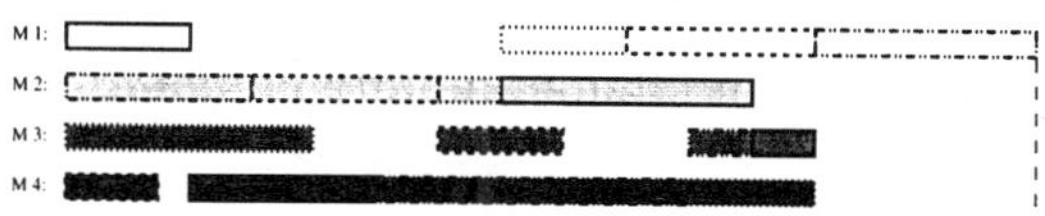


Activities are now scheduled on each machine. One may argue that this solution is not robust. Indeed activities are tightly grouped and a "break" on a machine, and the subsequent delay, may trigger further delays in the schedule. Now, consider a $(1, 0)$-super-solution for this instance:

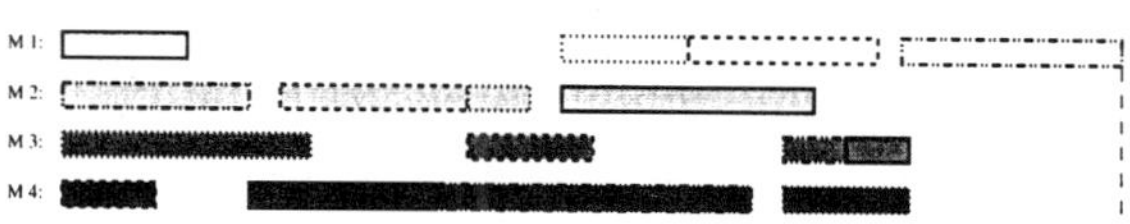


It's important to say that until now no assumption were made about the problem solved, and about what might be a robust solution to that problem. Nevertheless, with a small increase in the makespan, we observe that a super-solution for a jsp contains more slacks between activities, making it more robust. However, this is not really satisfying. Indeed, the values are time points, the breakages are known only when they occur, thus we might want to change only events in the future. The next figure shows a super-solution with this (alternative value) restriction:

This solution is clearly more robust than the first one. However, the makespan increase is relatively important. One alternative, which ensures a smaller makespan is to optimize the *repairability*, i.e, the proportion of repairable variables. For instance, suppose that we don't want the makespan to increase by more than two time units. The next figure shows a solution with optimal repairability (i.e., more robust) whilst the makespan length is restricted:

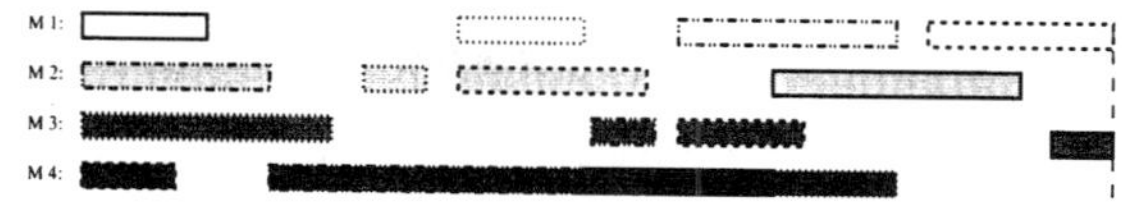


There are a number of such improvements upon classical super-solution that we can gather from our knowledge of the problem. For instance, some machines may be reliable, one would then restrict the break-set accordingly. Moreover, the slacks should be linked to the duration for repairing a particular machine, this can be done by restricting the alternative values.

Another example is the instruction scheduling problem, where primitive instructions of a program are to be scheduled in order to minimize the time complexity of the program while keeping its semantic. When we model this problem, a variable can take the value "NOP", which stands for "no operation". Whilst a breakage may happen on any variable, one assigned to "NOP" cannot break. When some variables are set to such an assignment, no witness of repairability is required. Note that super-solutions offers no real difficulties to adapt to the optimization framework. However, it's not surprising that one has to sacrifice optimality in order to achieve robustness. An alternative is to optimize the *repairability* of a solution, that is the proportion of repairable breaks, without giving up optimality, or at least bounding the loss. More generally we have now a multi-criteria optimization problem.

## Conclusion

We claim that super-solutions offer a useful framework to obtain more robust solution to constraint satisfaction or optimization problems. They are often a good starting point for characterizing robustness, without requiring any knowledge of the problem. However, we showed that integrating specific information about a problem can lead to much better results. In our future work we plan to define and implement a library of useful predicates and optimization criteria that can be used and combined in order to easily post robustness constraints. Our algorithm would simply use the appropriate predicates to check the validity of any repair. Then we would like to use this framework to obtain robust solutions of real problems subject to uncertainty.

## References

Bessiere, C., and Regin, J.-C. 1996. MAC and combined heuristics: Two reasons to forsake FC (and CBJ?) on hard problems. In *Proceedings CP'96*, 61–75.

Ginsberg, M.; Parkes, A.; and Roy, A. 1998. Supermodels and robustness. In *Proceedings AAAI'98*, 334–339.

Hebrard, E.; Hnich, B.; and Walsh, T. 2004. Super solutions in constraint programming. In *Proceedings CPAIOR'04 (to appear)*.

Sabin, D., and Freuder, E. 1994. Contradicting Conventional Wisdom in Constraint Satisfaction. In Borning, A., ed., *Proceedings CP'94*, volume 874, 10–20.

# Generation of Emotional Behavior for Non-Player Characters -- Development of *EmoBot* for Quake II --

**Tye Hooley, Bart Hunking, Mike Henry and Atsushi Inoue**

Department of Computer Science
Eastern Washington University
Cheney, WA 99004-2412
{thooley, ainoue}@ewu.edu

## Introduction to *EmoBot*

Recent technology advances in computer game industries demand a development of high-level artificial intelligence. This trend motivates the International Game Developers' Association to develop a special interest group (SIG) in artificial intelligence (IGDA 2003) and the roundtable of 'AI in Computer Games' at the Game Developers Conference (GDC 2003). According to the IGDA SIG, high-level artificial intelligence is defined by the realization of more attractive humanistic features within computer games, such as believable and interesting non-player characters (NPCs) that perform complex reasoning and learning in order to exhibit emotions.

Similarly, the AAAI 2000 Spring Symposium on AI and Interactive Entertainment discussed issues concerning the generation of human-like characteristics for computer games and toys. Reflecting industrial demands and being inspired by contributions from AAAI symposiums, a set of intelligent agents named *EmoBot* was developed to generate emotional behaviors for NPCs (Laird 2000; Wilson 2000). *EmoBot* is embedded within an open-source first-person shooter computer game, ID Software's *Quake II*. The following provides a short overview of the AI engine in *Quake II* (Hooley 2003):

> *Quake II* by ID Software uses a simplistic state-machine approach to its artificial intelligence. ... An objective can be interpreted as a "state." Bots start out with their objective as the world, which signifies the bot will follow pre-determined actions such as guarding or patrolling. Once the bot is aware of a player, the bot's objective becomes that player.

*EmoBot* fabricates emotional behavior with fuzzy logic in the extended logic programming language: *FRIL* -- *F*uzzy *R*elational *I*nference *L*anguage (Baldwin, et. al. 1995). The deployment of fuzzy logic is primarily justified by the fuzziness of personality, and its great success in control applications analogous to *EmoBot* tasks.



## Description of Computational Model

*EmoBot* is realized as a knowledge-based agent that generates emotional behavior as reactions to a momentary perception of game variables (**Figure 1**).

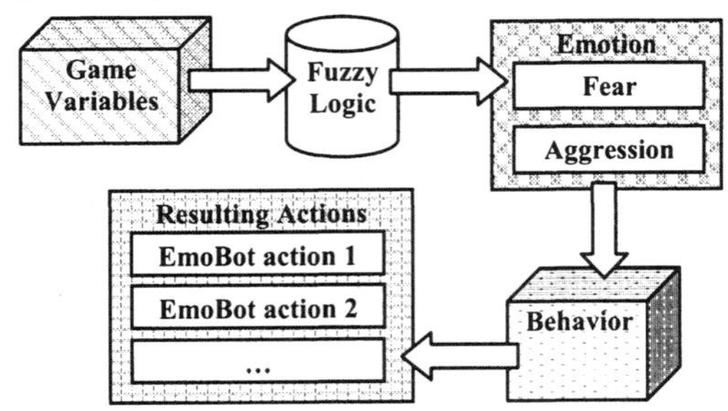


Figure 1—*EmoBot* Overview

## Representation of Emotions: EFA Space

States of emotion are represented as values in the three-dimensional Cartesian space, called *EFA* space (where EFA stands for *E*xtroversion, *F*ear and *A*ggression) deployed in the Artificial Emotion Engine™ (Wilson 2000). For simplicity and insignificant relevancy of the extroversion in first-person shooter games such as *Quake II*, *EmoBot* determines its reaction by taking two of the three dimensions into account: Fear and Aggression (FA space). Additionally, variations of mapping game variables onto two dimensions (i.e. representation of a personality) can also be considered as a replacement to the extroversion dimension.

## Environment Perception: Game Variables

There are six game variables (specific to *Quake II*) used for momentary perception of the environment by *EmoBot*:

1. NPC health: {bad, fair, good}
2. NPC damage: {low, medium, high}
3. Player health: {bad, fair, good}
4. Player damage: {low, medium, high}
5. Distance: {near, medium, far}
6. Angle: {small, medium, large}

Each variable is partitioned by three fuzzy sets associated

with linguistic labels. Each fuzzy set corresponds to perception agents. An example is provided below (**Figure 2**):

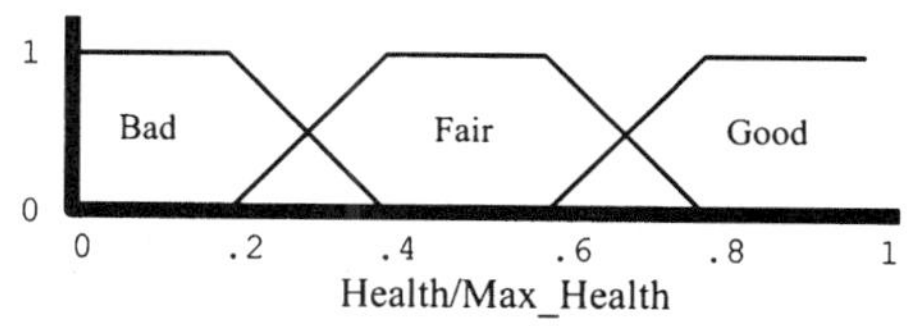


Figure 2—A Fuzzy Partition

## Personality: Fuzzy Logic Rules

Fuzzy logic is used to determine a corresponding state of emotion based upon a mapping from perceptions of the environment. Below, the following example mappings are configured by simple fuzzy rules such that underlined linguistic expressions correspond to fuzzy sets and boldfaced logical operators are standard fuzzy logic operators:

**IF** bot-health IS bad **AND** player-health IS bad
  **THEN** fear IS medium
**IF** bot-health IS bad **AND** player-health IS fair
  **THEN** fear IS high
**IF** bot-health IS bad **AND** player-health IS good
  **THEN** fear IS high

Mappings represent personality traits of a NPC, which is analogous to an individual's characteristics (e.g. solders with ample experience may feel less fear in a battle field). Additionally, perceptions represented as fuzzy rules may be uniquely configured to each NPC.

## Emotional Behaviors: Partitions in FA Space

Emotional behaviors are determined according to a partition defined on the FA space. Each partition represents a behavioral state corresponding to a set of emotions. Currently, *EmoBot* implements a granularity of six partitions (**Figure 3**):

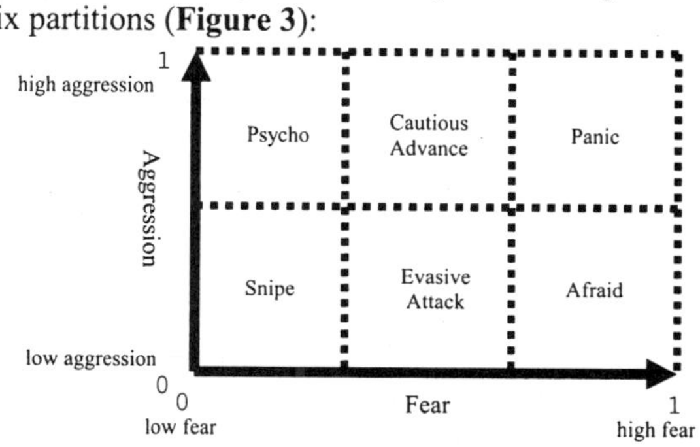


Figure 3—Behavioral States in FA Space

Based upon the NPCs personality and current game states, fuzzy inference yields a specific coordinate within FA space by means of the underlying computational model within FRIL, called Support Logic Programming and Mass Assignment Theory. This is consistent with the standard fuzzy inference as well as probabilistic reasoning. Finally, the coordinate is projected onto the partitioned space to determine the emotional behavior.

## Generation of Actions

Action(s) for each emotional behavior was intuitively defined; please see the list below for details:

1. Psycho: Sprint towards player and attack.
2. Snipe: Shoot from a distance.
3. Cautious Advance: Shoot and slowly advance towards player.
4. Evasive attack: Jump from side-to-side and shoot.
5. Panic: Freeze and run in random directions (The NPC cannot do anything because of fear).
6. Afraid: Run in the opposite direction of the player.

Currently, they are statically embedded within *Quake II* game.

## Preliminary Project Results

Despite the simplicity of the emotional behavior model (six states, six game variables as inputs), *EmoBot* adds a significant difference to the behaviors of NPCs, as opposed to traditional *Quake II* AI. Furthermore, *EmoBot* illustrates the usefulness of fuzzy logic and demonstrates its positive potentials as a basis for the high-level artificial intelligence in computer games.

Future research may include an adaptive *EmoBot*, where fuzzy partitions of emotional behaviors blend actions.

## References

Baldwin, J. F.; Martin, T. P.; Pilsworth, B. 1995. FRIL: Fuzzy and Evidential Reasoning in AI. Research Studies Press. (on-line manual): http://www.enm.bris.ac.uk/ai/martin/downloads/FrilResources.html)

Game Developers Conference. 2003. Conference Archive. http://www.gdconf.com/archives/2003/

International Game Developers' Association. 2003. Artificial Intelligence SIG. http://www.igda.org/ai/.

Laird, J. 2000. It Knows What You're Going To Do: Adding Anticipation to a Quakebot. AAAI Spring Symposium. http://www.qrg.northwestern.edu/aigames.org/2000papers.html

Hooley, T. 2003. Game AI Overview (a course write-up). http://penguin.ewu.edu/class/ai/modules.03/gameai/

Wilson, I. 2000. The Artificial Emotion Engine™, Driving Emotional Behavior. AAAI Spring Symposium. http://www.qrg.northwestern.edu/aigames.org/2000papers.html

# Knowledge State Reconsideration: Hindsight Belief Revision*

**Frances L. Johnson** and **Stuart C. Shapiro**
Department of Computer Science and Engineering; Center for Cognitive Science;
Center for Multisource Information Fusion; SNePS Research Group
University at Buffalo, The State University of New York
201 Bell Hall, Buffalo, NY 14260-2000, USA
*{flj | shapiro}@cse.buffalo.edu*

As a knowledge representation and reasoning (KRR) system gathers and reasons about information, it has to update its belief space to maintain consistency. Some belief change operations it can perform include expansion (addition with no consistency checking), contraction (aka removal or retraction), revision (consistent prioritized addition), and consolidation (elimination of *any and all* inconsistencies). Whether belief change operations are performed on theories (Alchourrón, Gärdenfors, & Makinson 1985) or bases (Nebel 1989; Hansson 1991; 1993b), with ideal agents or those that are resource-bounded (Wassermann 1999; Williams 1997), there is no doubt that the order of operations typically affects the makeup of the resulting belief base.

If a KRR system gains *new* information that, in hindsight, might have altered the outcome of an earlier belief change decision, the earlier decision should be re-examined. We call this operation *reconsideration*, and the result is an optimal belief base regardless of the order of previous belief change operations.

For this paper, we assume a global decision function is used in the belief change operations, and it will favor retaining the most preferred beliefs as determined by a preference ordering ($\succ$) that is irreflexive, anti-symmetric and transitive (referred to here as an IAT-preference ordering).[1] Any base can be represented as a sequence of beliefs in order of decending preference: $B = p_1, p_2, \ldots, p_n$, where $p_i$ is preferred over $p_{i+1}$ ($p_i \succ p_{i+1}$).

This work proposes maintaining a knowledge state ($KS$) which is defined as follows: $KS = \langle B, B^{\cup}, \succ \rangle$, where $B$ is the current belief base[2], $B^{\cup}$ is the set of all beliefs that have ever been in the belief base at any time (effectively, the union of all past and current bases), and $\succ$ is the preference ordering relation for the beliefs in $B^{\cup}$.

*This work was supported in part by the US Army Communications and Electronics Command (CECOM), Ft. Monmouth, NJ through Contract #DAAB-07-01-D-G001 with Booze·Allen & Hamilton. The authors appreciate the insights and feedback of the SNePS Research Group.


[1] An ordering that is not anti-symmetric is more realistic, but requires more discussion than this format allows.

[2] Assuming a foundations approach where base beliefs have independent justification (Hansson 1993a).

We define reconsideration of a knowledge state $KS$ (denoted $KS\circledast$) as: $KS\circledast = \langle B^{\cup}!, B^{\cup}, \succ \rangle$, where ! is a consolidation operation (Hansson 1991; 1997).

The goal of reconsideration is to obtain an optimal base. Given a $KS = \langle B, B^{\cup}, \succ \rangle$, $B = p_1, p_2, \ldots, p_n$ is optimal if it is consistent and there is no $B' = q_1, q_2, \ldots, q_m$ s.t. $B' \subseteq B^{\cup}$, $B'$ is consistent, and either $B \subset B'$ or $\exists q_i$ s.t $q_i \succ p_i$ and $p_1, p_2, \ldots, p_{i-1} = q_1, q_2, \ldots, q_{i-1}$.

We assume a system using reconsideration would use the non-prioritized revision of semi-revision (Hansson 1997), where $B$ revised by the belief $p$ is defined as $(B \cup \{p\})!$. A belief being added must survive on its own merits.

As a result of reconsideration, beliefs retracted in an earlier belief change operation might be recovered, and some current beliefs might be retracted.

**Example1:** If we believe that Ty graduated Tufts Medical School ($p$) and infer that he is well-educated ($q$, using the base belief $p \rightarrow q$), we might disregard someone's comment that Ty does not seem well-educated ($\neg q$). Upon being told that $p$ is a false statement, reconsideration would return $\neg q$ to our belief base, since there is no *current* reason to disbelieve it.

This is much like the recovery postulate for contraction ($\div$) followed by expansion ($+$) of a deductively closed belief set $K$ (aka theory): $K \subseteq (K \div p) + p$ (Alchourrón, Gärdenfors, & Makinson 1985).

For those opposed to the recovery postulate: consider that any beliefs recovered through reconsideration were, originally, *base* beliefs with *independent justification*. They were removed solely because of some additional base belief that has since been removed. In hindsight, it is wise to return them to the base provided no other obstruction exists.

Believing that Ty is not well-educated ($\neg q$) just because he did not graduate Tufts Med School is reasonable, because we were *told* $\neg q$ and no longer have evidence to the contrary. If the order of operations that added then removed $p$ had been reversed, $\neg q$ would never have been removed.

It should also be noted that reconsideration works equally well for relevance logics, where believing both $p$ and $q$ does not typically infer $p \rightarrow q$.

**Example2:** If we start with the base $B1$ as described in Figure 1, the addition of $\neg p$ (where $\neg p \succ p$) forces the retraction of $p$. NOTE: Most systems would stop here. Reconsideration produces the following changes: (1) $\neg q$ re-

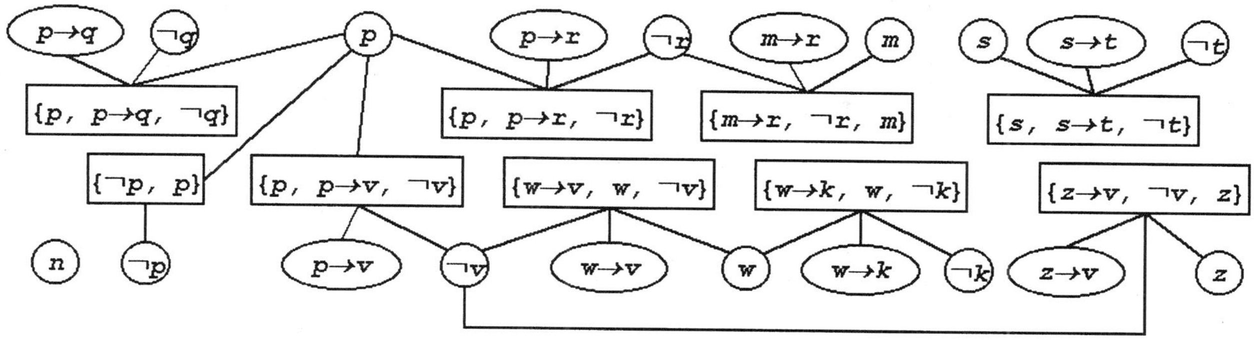


Figure 1: A graph showing the elements of $B^{\cup}$ (circles/ovals) of a KS connected to their inconsistent sets (rectangles). If $\neg p$ was not yet added to the base, and we had an IAT-preference ordering that ordered the beliefs in the following sequence from most to least preferred: $p, p \rightarrow q, p \rightarrow r, m \rightarrow r, s \rightarrow t, w \rightarrow v, w \rightarrow k, p \rightarrow v, z \rightarrow v, n, \neg r, w, s, \neg v, m, z, \neg q, \neg t, \neg k$, then the optimal base would be $B1 = \{p, p \rightarrow q, p \rightarrow r, m \rightarrow r, s \rightarrow t, w \rightarrow v, w \rightarrow k, p \rightarrow v, z \rightarrow v, n, w, s, m, z\}$.
The semi-revision addition of $\neg p$ (preferred over $p$) followed by reconsideration is described in Example2.

turns to the base, and (2) $\neg r$ returns to the base with the simultaneous removal of $m$[3].

The "recovery for bases" flavor of reconsideration is seen if we discover that the ordering of $p$ and $\neg p$ was incorrect: actually $p \succ \neg p$. Reconsideration would return $p$, remove $\neg p$, remove $\neg q$, and remove $\neg r$ while returning $m$ to the base. The resulting base would be $B1$.

One algorithm for reconsideration in a TMS (Forbus & De Kleer 1993) might be to place all inconsistent sets on a priority queue in decreasing order of their culprits (least preferred beliefs). Processing each set, $S$, in turn (provided $S \subseteq$ the current base) by retracting its culprit would result in a literal reconsideration ($B^{\cup}!$). All beliefs not retracted during this process would be in the base of the resulting KS.

The implementation of reconsideration, however, does not require an actual consolidation over all $B^{\cup}$. Recalling Example2, a dependency-directed reconsideration (DDR) algorithm that determines that $\neg v$ cannot return to the base (due to its being the culprit for the inconsistent set $\{w \rightarrow v, w, \neg v\}$) would prune off the examination of the inconsistent sets containing $\neg k$ and $z$. The inconsistent set containing $s$ could also be ignored, because it is not connected to $p$ in any way. This latter case is representative of the possibly thousands of unrelated inconsistent sets for a typical belief base which *would* be checked during the literal $B^{\cup}!$ operation, but are ignored by DDR.

For some KRR systems, maintaining $B^{\cup}$ and its inconsistent sets would require additional memory usage, but TMS systems are already storing this information. Specifically, ATMS systems do this to enable reasoning in multiple contexts (Forbus & De Kleer 1993; Martins & Shapiro 1983). Some concession to limited resources may be needed (e.g. permanently remove oldest retracted beliefs).

Although incorporating reconsideration into a system's belief change operations will increase runtime, it is worth implementing, because (1) it allows sequential operations of belief change without concern for operation order and (2) it provides an optimal base from which to reason.

[3]Because $\neg r \succ m$.

## References


Alchourrón, C. E.; Gärdenfors, P.; and Makinson, D. 1985. On the logic of theory change: Partial meet contraction and revision functions. *The Journal of Symbolic Logic* 50(2):510–530.

Forbus, K. D., and De Kleer, J. 1993. *Building Problem Solvers.* Cambridge, MA: MIT Press.

Hansson, S. O. 1991. *Belief Base Dynamics.* Ph.D. Dissertation, Uppsala University.

Hansson, S. O. 1993a. Reversing the Levi identity. *Journal of Philosophical Logic* 22:637–669.

Hansson, S. O. 1993b. Theory contraction and base contraction unified. *Journal of Symbolic Logic* 58:602–625.

Hansson, S. O. 1997. Semi-revision. *Journal of Applied Non-Classical Logic* 7:151–175.

Martins, J. P., and Shapiro, S. C. 1983. Reasoning in multiple belief spaces. In *Proceedings of the Eighth International Joint Conference on Artificial Intelligence.* San Mateo, CA: Morgan Kaufmann. 370–373.

Nebel, B. 1989. A knowledge level analysis of belief revision. In Brachman, R. J.; Levesque, H. J.; and Reiter, R., eds., *Proceedings of the First International Conference on Principles of Knowledge Representation and Reasoning (KR'89)*, 301–311.

Wassermann, R. 1999. *Resource-bounded Belief Revision.* Ph.D. Dissertation, University of Amsterdam, Amsterdam, The Netherlands.

Williams, M.-A. 1997. Anytime belief revision. In *Proceedings of the Fourteenth International Joint Conference on Artificial Intelligence.* San Mateo, CA: Morgan Kaufmann. 74–79.

# Utilizing Internal State in Multi-Robot Coordination Tasks

**Chris Jones** and **Maja J Matarić**
Computer Science Department, University of Southern California
941 West 37th Place, Los Angeles, CA 90089-0781 USA
http://robotics.usc.edu/interaction/research/projects/chris-project.php
{cvjones|mataric}@usc.edu

## Introduction and Related Work

The success of a task-achieving multi-robot system (MRS) depends on effective coordination mechanisms to mediate the robots' interactions in such a way that a given task is achieved. In the MRS community, many elegant coordination mechanisms have been empirically demonstrated. However, there is a lack of systematic procedures for the synthesis of coordinated MRS. In this paper, we address this issue by presenting a principled framework suitable for describing and reasoning about the intertwined entities involved in any task-achieving MRS – the task environment, task definition, and the capabilities of the robots themselves. Using this framework, we present a systematic procedure by which to synthesize controllers for robots in a MRS such that a given sequential task is correctly executed. The MRS is composed of homogeneous robots capable of maintaining internal state but not capable of direct inter-robot communication. This systematic approach to the synthesis of coordinated MRS permits formal identification of the benefits and limitations of MRS composed of robots maintaining internal state and when other types of controllers may become necessary, such as those using communication.

The most relevant related work includes work on finding optimal policies in partially observable stochastic domains (Cassandra, Kaelbling, & Littman 1994). In MRS, the study of information invariants (Donald 1995) addresses the problem of determining information requirements for performing robot tasks. The work presented here builds upon our previous results on automated synthesis of controllers using internal state (Jones & Matarić 2003) by addressing the issue of uncertainty in sensing and action. Our work presented in (Jones & Matarić 2004) presents results on the synthesis of stateless controllers which are communicative but stateless. In the multi-agent systems community, the issues addressed in (Pynadath & Tambe 2002) and (Stone & Veloso 1999) are related to ours in that they are systematically studying the role different control characteristics play in coordinated systems.



## Definitions and Notation

The *world* is the domain in which the MRS performs a given task. We assume the world is Markovian and the state is an element of the finite set $S$ of all possible states. An action $a$ performed in the world by a single robot $r$ is drawn from the finite set $A$ of all possible actions. An *observation* $x$ made by robot $r$, drawn from the finite set of all observations $X$, consists of accessible information external to the robot and formally represents a subset of the world state. Given a world state $s$ at time $t$, a robot $r$ making observation $x$ and executing action $a$, and a world state $s'$ at time $t+1$, we define a probabilistic world state transition function as $P(s,x,a,s') = Pr(S^{t+1} = s'|S^t = s, X_r^t = x, A_r^t = a)$. We note that the world state transition function involves an observation because the tasks we consider are spatial in nature and the physical location where an action is performed is just as important as the action itself. We define a *task*, assumed to be Markovian, as a set of $n$ ordered world states $T_s = \{s_0, s_1, ..., s_n\}$ which must be progressed through in sequence. We assume the initial state of the world is $s_0$. We define *correct task execution* to be the case where for all task states $s_i \in T_s$, $i < n$ the only actions executed by any robot are those that transition the world state to $s_{i+1}$. Once the world state is $s_n \in T_s$ the task is terminated. Therefore, we define an observation and action pair for a robot, $x$ and $a$, to be correct for task state $s_i$ if $P(s_i, x, a, s_{i+1}) > 0$. We assume that an observation $x$ and action $a$ cannot be correct for more than one task state. The probabilistic *observation function* $O(s,x) = Pr(X_r^t = x|S^t = s)$ gives the probability observation $x$ will be made in state $s$ by a robot $r$. Furthermore, we assume that an observation $x$ may only be made at one physical location in the world in a state $s$. A robot's internal state value $m$ at any time is a member of the finite set $M = \{m_0, m_1, ..., m_p\}$. Two probabilistic functions define a robot $r$'s behavior in the world, known collectively as the robot's *controller*. The controller is comprised of an *action function* $A(x,m,a) = Pr(A_r^t = a|X_r^t = x, M_r^t = m)$ and an *internal state transition function* $L(m,x,m') = Pr(M_r^{t+1} = m'|X_r^t = x, M_r^t = m)$. Although the controller is modeled with probabilistic functions for generality, in this paper these functions will always be either 0 or 1.

## Principled Controller Synthesis

Leveraging the formalism presented above, Figure 1 presents a controller synthesis procedure consisting of four phases. The first phase (lines 2-3) synthesizes an action function for a baseline stateless controller which contains a rule for each action in the task, but there is no guarantee the task will be performed in the correct sequence.

The second phase (lines 4-6) initializes some relevant variables. The variable $X_a(s_i)$ contains the set of all observations $x$ for which there exists an action $a$ such that $x$ and $a$ are correct for state $s_i$, for all $s_i \in T_s$. The set $V_a(s_i)$ will contain the index of the internal state value (i.e., 0 represents $m_0$) that a robot will need to have in order to execute an action in state $s_i$, for all $s_i \in T_s$. Initially, all values in $V_a$ are assigned the same internal state value $m_0$ – this is equivalent to not using any internal state at all. Lastly, the set $O_a(s_i)$ will contain the observation, if any, that will be used to transition the internal state value in state $s_i$, for all $s_i \in T_s$. Initially, all values in $O_a$ are $NULL$ as no internal state transitions are defined at this point.

The third phase (lines 7-12) identifies situations in which internal state can be used to improve coordination and assigns appropriate values to the sets $V_a$ and $O_a$. The basis for determining when internal state can be used to improve coordination is in identifying task states where an observation $x$ in $X_a(s_j)$, where $x$ and some action $a$ are correct for $s_j$, can also be made in some earlier task state $s_i$ for which $x$ and $a$ are not correct. We note that our synthesis method does not deal with the situation where there exists a task state $s_p$ which occurs *later* than $s_j$ and $O(s_p, x) > 0$, where $x$ and $a$ are not correct for $s_p$.

The fourth phase (lines 13-18) synthesizes the final controller by augmenting the stateless controller synthesized in the first phase. This is accomplished by adding the internal state transition function and appropriately modifying the action function such that an action is not executed unless the robot's current internal state value is appropriate. The internal state transition function is constructed (lines 14-15) by mapping the internal state value $m_{V_a(s_i)-1}$ and observation $O_a(s_i)$ to the next internal state value of $m_{V_a(s_i)}$, for all $s_i \in T_s$. The action function is modified (lines 16-17) such that for each rule of the action function $A(x, m_0, a) = 1$ where $x$ and $a$ are correct for a state $s_i$ is modified to become $A(x, m_{V_a(s_i)}, a) = 1$, where $m_{V_a(s_i)}$ is the required internal state value for task state $s_i$ as determined in the third phase. All probabilities not explicitly declared are 0.

(1) procedure Synthesize_Controller()<br>
(2) for all $s_i \in T_x, a \in A, x \in X(O(s_i, x) > 0 \wedge P(s_i, x, a, s_{i+1}) > 0)$ do<br>
(3) $A(x, m_0, a) = 1$

(4) for all $s_i \in T_s$ do<br>
(5) $X_a(s_i) = \{x_0, x_1, \ldots, x_n\}$ s.t. $\forall x \in X_a(s_i) \exists a (O(s_i, x) > 0 \wedge A(x, m_0, a) = 1)$<br>
(6) $V_a(s_i) = 0; O_a(s_i) = NULL$

(7) for all $s_i, s_j \in T_s (i < j)$ do<br>
(8) if $\exists x \in X_a(s_j)(O(s_i, x) > 0)$ then<br>
(9) for $s_k = s_j$ downto $s_{i+1}$ do<br>
(10) if $\exists z \nexists s_u (O(s_k, z) > 0 \wedge u < (i+1) \wedge O(s_u, z) > 0)$ then<br>
(11) $O_a(s_k) = z$<br>
(12) $\forall s_w (w >= k) \rightarrow V_a(s_w) = V_a(s_w) + 1$

(13) for all $s_i \in T_s$ do<br>
(14) if $O_a(s_i) \neq NULL$ then<br>
(15) $L(m_{V_a(s_i)-1}, O_a(s_i), m_{V_a(s_i)}) = 1$<br>
(16) for all $x \in X_a(s_i), a \in A(A(x, m_0, a) = 1)$ do<br>
(17) $A(x, m_0, a) = 0; A(x, m_{V_a(s_i)}, a) = 1$<br>
(18) end procedure Synthesize_Controller

Figure 1: Controller synthesis procedure.

## Experimental Validation

We experimentally validate our controller synthesis procedure in a multi-robot construction domain, through extensive physically-realistic simulations and on a limited set of real-robot experiments. The construction task requires the sequential placement of a series of cubic colored bricks into a planar structure. Each robot's sensing capabilities limit it to sensing only a limited profile of the current construction at any given time. Additional details on the multi-robot construction domain can be found in (Jones & Matarić 2004).

We performed 300 experimental trials in simulation for a specific construction task made up of 7 bricks. The synthesized controller correctly executed the construction task in 31.5% of the trials. We note that there exists significant uncertainty in sensing and imperfect actions, and in the absence of such uncertainties, the synthesized controller would be gauranteed to correctly execute the task. For comparison, the stateless controller from the first phase of the synthesis procedure resulted in only 0.9% of the trials resulting in correct task execution. A limited number of successful real-robot experiments were performed to verify that any assumptions we made are reasonable and realistic. The experiments were also performed to show that our formalism and synthesis method are not merely abstract concepts but have been successfully implemented on real systems and capture the difficult issues involved in real-world embodied MRS.

## References


Cassandra, A.; Kaelbling, L. P.; and Littman, M. 1994. Acting optimally in partially observable stochastic domains. In *Proceedings of the Twelfth National Conference on Artificial Intelligence*, 1023–1028.

Donald, B. R. 1995. Information invariants in robotics. *Artifical Intelligence* 72(1–2):217–304.

Jones, C., and Matarić, M. 2003. Towards a multi-robot coordinaton formalism. In *Proc. of the Workshop on the Mathematics and Algorithms of Social Insects*, 60–67.

Jones, C., and Matarić, M. 2004. Communication in multi-robot coordination. Technical report, University of Southern California Center for Robotics and Embedded Systems, CRES-04-001.

Pynadath, D., and Tambe, M. 2002. Multiagent teamwork: Analyzing the optimality and complexity of key theories and models. In *International Joint Conference on Autonomous Agents and Multi-Agent Systems*, 873–880.

Stone, P., and Veloso, M. 1999. Task decomposition, dynamic role assignment, and low-bandwidth communication for real-time strategic teamwork. *Artificial Intelligence* 110(2):241–273.

# Generating "Random" 3-SAT Instances with Specific Solution Space Structure

**Pushkin R. Pari, Jane Lin, Lin Yuan** and **Gang Qu**
Department of Electrical and Computer Engineering
University of Maryland, College Park, Maryland 20742
{pushkin,janelin,yuanl,gangqu}@eng.umd.edu

## Introduction

Generating good benchmarks is important for the evaluation and improvement of any algorithm for NP-hard problems such as the Boolean satisfiability (SAT) problem. Carefully designed benchmarks are also helpful in the study of the nature of NP-completeness . Probably the most well-known and successful story is the discovery of the phase transition phenomenon (Cheeseman, Kanefsky, and Taylor 1991). More recently, (Achlioptas et al. 2000) pointed out the importance of generating satisfiable problem instances.

In this abstract, we consider how to create 3-SAT formulas that look like random but with specific solution structures. In particular, we show that random 3-SAT formulas do not have their solutions distributed randomly in the solution space and we further develop generators to build random 3-SAT formulas with randomly distributed solutions or fixed number of solutions.

## Is a 3-SAT Formula Random

There are two groups of SAT benchmarks: random SAT instances and those encoded from problems in other fields (Hoos and Stuzle, 2000). Arguably the most interesting and best studied one is the *random k-SAT* model, where each instance consists of clauses uniformly selected from all the possible clauses of the same length (Franco and Paull 1983).

Now we ask the reverse problem: *given a 3-SAT formula (or a family of formulas), determine whether it belongs to the random 3-SAT model.* Clearly it is impossible to repetitively generate random 3-SAT instances and check whether it matches the given one. Therefore, we need to extract properties from the random 3-SAT model and see whether the given 3-SAT formulas possess the same properties.

The 'Suite I' curve in Figure 1 represents the average occurrence of each variable from 50,000 50-variable 218-clause 3-SAT generated randomly based on (Franco and Paull, 1983). The other three curves represent 100 instances for three different families of 3-SAT formulas with the same number of variables and clauses. One can conclude that benchmark IV (represented by curve 'Suite IV') is not random while the other two seem to be random.

Other metrics for the randomness include: the distribution of average occurrence of each literal, each pair of variables/literals, total number of negated/unnegated variables, and the ratio of clauses with 0/1/2/3 negated variables. Such characteristics can be easily computed for the random 3-SAT model for a fixed clause-to-variable ratio and verified by extracting from large amount of random 3-SAT instances. Similar to Figure 1, benchmarks I, II and III have very similar behavior on all these criteria. This suggest to us that both II and III belong to the random 3-SAT model. However, they are created artificially to embed certain properties to the solution space.



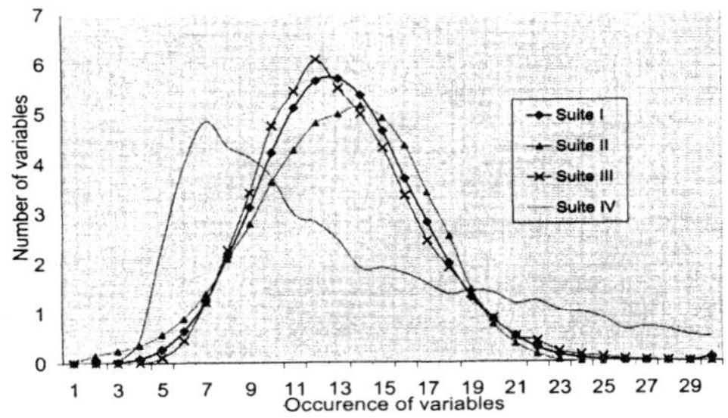


Figure 1: Clause randomness of 3SAT instances.

## Benchmarking with Structured Solution Space

We first create clauses based on the given solution space structure and then fine tune these clauses to make them "random" while preserving the desired properties. We show how this is performed by the example benchmark suites II and III in Figure 1. Recall that all the instances will have 50 variables and 218 clauses so they can be readily compared with the uniform random 3-SAT model.

**SAT instance with given number of solutions**

Our goal is to generate random-like 3-SAT formulas on $n$ variables with $m$ clauses and $S$ solutions.

Phase I: generating a random core.

1. generate a uniform random 3-SAT formula with $n$ variable and $m$ clauses.
2. randomly select $k$ variables, $\{v_1, v_2, \cdots, v_k\}$ and delete the rest of the variables from the formula.
   This gives us a random SAT with $k$ variables consisting of 1-, 2-, and 3-literal clauses, which we refer to as random *core*.
3. find all the solutions to the core by either using a SAT solver or a simple exhaustive search.We can afford this by making $k$ small ($k = 10$ in our experiments).

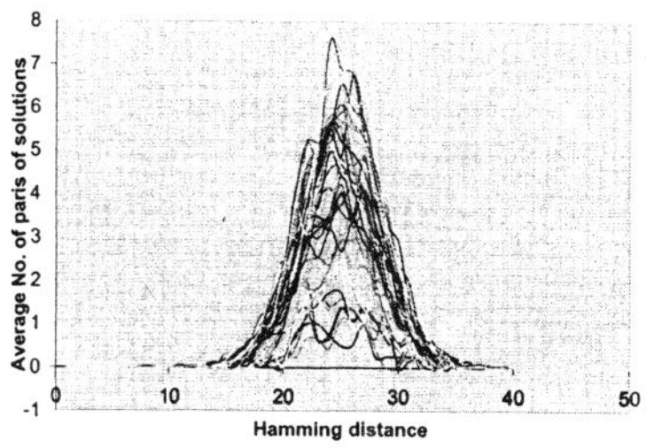


Figure 2: Solution randomness of randomly selected solutions.

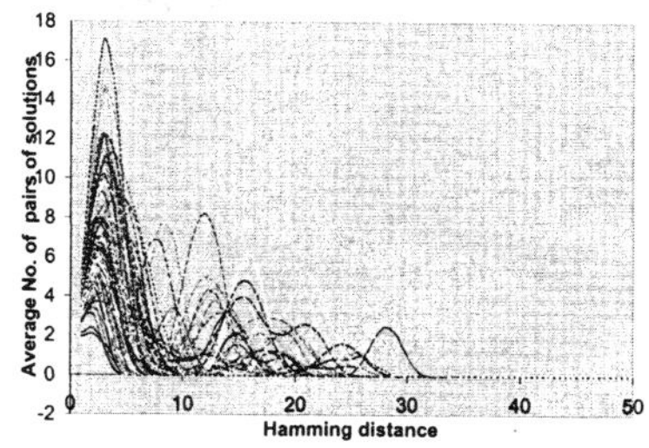


Figure 3: Solution randomness of uniform random 3-SAT instances.

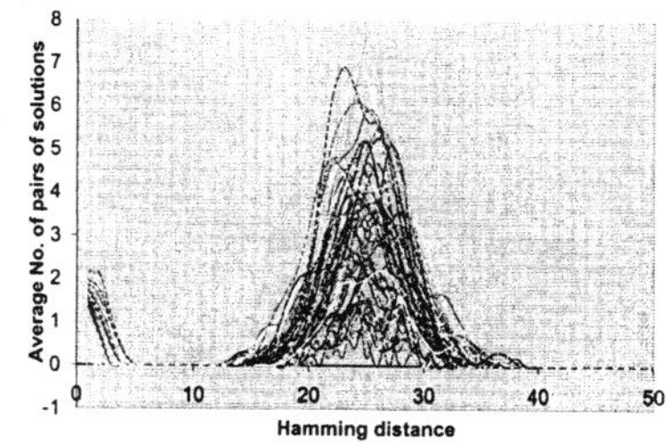


Figure 4: Solution randomness of benchmark suite III.

Phase II: adding the remaining variables to the core.

For each of the rest $n - k$ variables, we add them one by one to the core while tracking the solution database. For a variable $v_i (i = k+1, k+2, \cdots, n)$, we explain how to add literal $v_i$ into the core, the negated literal $v_i'$ is added in the same fashion. When $i$ is close to $n$, we pay special attention to make sure that the total number of clauses will be $m$ and the total number of solutions will be $S$ as required.

1. update the solution database. By introducing variable $v_i$, the number of solutions will be doubled.
2. based on the occurrence distribution of each literal, determine $C$, the occurrences of $v_i$; $C_2$ ( and $C_1$), the number of times $v_i$ will appear in a 2-literal (and single literal) clause consists of the first $i - 1$ variables.
3. randomly select $C_2$ 2-literal clauses and add literal $v_i$ to make them 3-literal clauses. Eliminate solutions that fail to satisfy any of these newly created 3-literal clauses. If the size of the solution database is over $\frac{S}{2}$ or still far below $\frac{S}{2}$ when $i$ is close to $n$, fine tune the selections of the 2-literal clauses.
4. add literal $v_i$ to $C_1$ randomly selected single literal clauses; and introduce $C - C_2 - C_1$ single clauses with variable $v_i$ only. Later variables will make these new 2-literal and single literal clauses eventually 3-literal clauses.

We have successfully generated 100 formulas using this approach with the total number of solutions varying from 1 to 5,000, the same range as we have observed from the 50,000 uniform random 3-SAT instances. These instances pass all the randomness test we listed in the previous section.

**SAT instance with randomly distributed solutions**

The uniform random 3-SAT model does not guarantee that the solutions are randomly distributed. One evidence is the so-called *backbone*, variables that remain constant in all the solutions (Singer, Gent, and Smaill 2000).

To get a quantitative measurement of the solution randomness, we solve the SAT formula for all the solutions and then compute the Hamming distance between each pair of solutions. Figures 2-4 plot the average number of pairs with the same Hamming distance for 100 sets of solutions, with each set contains 10-64 solutions, over three different families. In Figure 2, the solutions are selected randomly and we see the perfect bell shape of the normal Gaussian distribution. Figure 3 is based on uniform random 3-SAT formulas, where we need about 1,000 instances to find 100 instances with solutions in the range of 10-64. Figure 4 is drawn based on instances we generate to have the 10-64 solutions "randomly" distributed. Figure 4 looks much more similar to Figure 2 than Figure 3, which implies that the formulas we generate have random solutions in terms of the pairwise Hamming distance. Furthermore, the formula's randomness has also been tested as shown in Figure 1. Due to space limitation, we briefly mention the procedure of how to build the benchmarks in Figure 4 without elaborating the details.

We start with $k$ randomly selected solutions and then find *local clauses* that all the $k$ solutions satisfy. By the term *local clauses*, we mean clauses consists of literals only from 10 pre-selected random variables. These clause will eliminate part of the non-solutions. We repeat this for about 100 times to ensure the randomness of clauses and the elimination of all non-solutions. Next, we remove the redundancy from clauses. A clause $\mathcal{C}$ in formula $\mathcal{F}$ is *redundant* if $\mathcal{F} = \mathcal{F} \backslash \mathcal{C}$, the formula obtained by removing $\mathcal{C}$ from $\mathcal{F}$. Whether $\mathcal{C}$ is redundant can be determined by checking the satisfiability of formula $\mathcal{C}'(\mathcal{F} \backslash \mathcal{C})$. After removing all the redundancy, we observe that there are around 180 clauses left. We then gather the statistical information about this formula and add extra clauses to make the total number of clauses 218 and make the formula look as "random" as possible.

The existence of solutions with extremely small Hamming distance (around 2-4) in Figure 4 is due to the fact that it becomes almost impossible to eliminate all the non-solutions when large number of solutions are selected randomly. We compensate this by selecting 10-20 random solution and including their neighbors as solutions if the desired number of solutions is large.

## References

Achlioptas, D., Gomes, C. Kautz, H., and Selman, B. 2000. Generating satisfiable problem instances. In *Proceedings of the Tenth National Conference on Artificial Intelligence, Menlo Park, California,* 256–261.

Cheeseman, P.; Kanefsky, B., and Taylor, W.M. 1991. Where the Really Hard Problems Are. In *Proceedings of the Twelfth International Joint Conference on Artificial Intelligence, Sidney, Australia,* 331–337.

Franco, J. and Paull, M. 1983. Probabilistic analysis of the Davis Putnam procedure for solving the satisfiability problem. In *Discrete Applied Mathematics,* 5:77-87.

Hoos, H.H. and Stuzle, T. 2000. SATLIB: An Online Resource for Research on SAT. In *SAT 2000 (ed. I.P. Gent, H.V. Maaren, and T. Walsh,* pp. 283-292, IOS Press.

Singer, J., Gent, I., and Smaill, A. 2000. Backbone Fragility and the Local Search Cost Peak. In *Journal of Artificial Intelligence Research,* 12: 235-270

# Occam's Razor and a Non-syntactic Measure of Decision Tree Complexity

**Goutam Paul**

Department of Computer Science, SUNY Albany
1400 Washington Avenue, NY 12222
Email: goutam@cs.albany.edu, Web: http://www.cs.albany.edu/~goutam

Occam's razor, attributed to the fourteenth century English philosopher William of Occam, states: "plurality should not be assumed without necessity." The machine learning interpretation of Occam's razor is that if two models have the same performance on the training set, choose the simpler. Decision tree learning widely uses Occam's razor. Popular decision tree generating algorithms are based on information gain criterion which inherently prefers shorter trees (Mitchel 1997). Furthermore, decision tree pruning is common regardless of the splitting criterion. Experiments suggest that shorter trees indeed have better generalization accuracy (*GA*), typically estimated by a validation set prediction accuracy. However, some case studies show evidence apparently against Occam's razor. Recently, Webb (1996) has built C4.5X, a version of C4.5 decision tree classifier (Quinlan 1993) with a postprocessor, which adds more nodes and branches to the tree generated by basic C4.5. He showed that though C4.5 and C4.5X have identical training set accuracies, the generalization accuracy over some datasets is better for C4.5X. But Webb's argument is based on the traditional syntactic complexity measure (number of nodes) of decision trees. In this paper, we explore a non-syntactic measure of decision tree complexity using the notion of Kolmogorov Complexity (Kolmogorov 1965) and show that in this measure the complexity of C4.5X tree is less than that of C4.5 tree on average. Hence, according to our measure of complexity, C4.5X does not violate Occam's razor.

The Kolmogorov Complexity $K_U(X)$ of an object $X$ (typically represented by a binary string) is the shortest possible description $l_{\min}$ (represented by another binary string) of $X$ under a fixed universal description method $U$. We can think of each description method as a Turing machine and each description as a program. When the Turing machine executes its input program string, it generates the object string as the output. Since the Kolmogorov Complexity of the same object in two different universal Turing machines is bounded by some constant independent of the object (Li & Vitanyi, 1997), it is a measure of intrinsic complexity of the object, unlike information theoretic complexity measures of an object's source (Shanon 1948). Hence, we can omit the subscript $U$ and simply write $K(X)$. We can extend the definition above from a single object to two or more objects by encoding the set of objects into a single string in such a way so that the machine can parse it into a set of description strings for the individual objects (Li & Vitanyi, 1997). If the set of objects is $\{X_1, X_2,\ldots, X_k\}$, we denote the Kolmogorov Complexity of this set by $K(X_1, X_2,\ldots, X_k)$.

If there are $m$ independent attributes, we can represent each instance as a point in an $m$-dimensional instance space. Each test of attribute places a hyperplane in the instance space parallel to that attribute axis. Thus a decision tree $T$ with $k$ leaf nodes induces a partitioning of the instance space into $k$ blocks $B_1, B_2,\ldots, B_k$, where block $B_i$ is the set of instances belonging to the leaf node $i$, $i=1,2,\ldots,k$. The hyperplanes placed by all the attribute-tests occurring along the path from the root node to the leaf node $i$ mark the boundaries of the set of instances $B_i$. We define the *K-complexity* of a decision tree $T$ for a data set as $C(T)=K(B_1, B_2,\ldots, B_k)$. Our measure is non-syntactic in the sense that it does not consider the parameters of the model, rather it considers the partitions of the instance space as induced by the model.

The Kolmogorov complexity of an object is incomputable. There are formal approximations using bounded measures such as Levin Complexity (Zvonkin & Levin 1970). In this paper, we employ the less formal approach of using the length of the compressed object after applying a fixed compression technique. Similar approach has been adopted by the Kolmogorov Complexity community for measuring similarity between strings (Cilibrasi & Vitanyi 2003). We have concatenated the blocks together with an additional newline character as a delimiter between the instances of one block and those of the next and then applied the Linux "compress" utility.

To compare with Webb's result, we have used the same experimental set-up as described in his paper (Webb 1996). The result of our experiments on four datasets is

| | | Pima | Iris | New Thyroid | Glass |
|---|---|---|---|---|---|
| **Average Training Set Error (%)** | **R** | 15.12 | 1.7 | 1.486 | 0 |
| | **X** | 15.12 | 1.7 | 1.486 | 0 |
| **Average Test Set Error (%)** | **R** | 26.812 | 6.464 | 7.688 | 3.057 |
| | **X** | 26.478 | 5.564 | 7.432 | 3.483 |
| **Average Tree Size (Number of Nodes)** | **R** | 49.9 | 8.2 | 14.2 | 11 |
| | **X** | 72.14 | 14.34 | 22.12 | 15.58 |
| **Average K-complexity** | **R** | 2706.04 | 502.21 | 617.28 | 1280 |
| | **X** | 2705.98 | 503.17 | 616.13 | 1278.81 |
| **% times R and X partitioning differs** | | 98 | 92 | 84 | 96 |
| **% times Occam's Razor Holds** | | 72 | 76 | 83 | 80 |

Table 1: Comparison of Regular C4.5 and Webb's C4.5X: "R" means regular C4.5 and "X" means Webb's extended C4.5

summarized in Table 1. For all of these data sets, the more syntactically complicated C4.5X tree returns better predictive accuracy than the C4.5 tree. Except for Iris, the Kolmogorov Complexity of the test set partitioning averaged over 100 experiments (random divisions of the data into training and test set) is less for C4.5X than for regular C4.5. We define Occam's razor as holding, if and only if for two classifiers $T_i$ and $T_j$, either $C(T_i) \leq C(T_j)$ and $GA(T_i) \geq GA(T_j)$, or $C(T_i) \geq C(T_j)$ and $GA(T_i) \leq GA(T_j)$, otherwise we say Occam's razor fails. As the table shows, out of 100 experiments, more than 70% support Occam's razor in all the datasets including Iris.

We have measured the complexity of partitioning on the test set, rather than on the training set. This is so because C4.5 and C4.5X produce the same partitioning on the training set and both have the same training set accuracies. However, our complexity measure is generic. We can also measure the complexity based on partitioning on the training set, when we are considering two different decision tree generating algorithms having different training set partitioning.

Our $K$-complexity measure of decision trees has two potential applications. First, we can choose between two or more decision trees based on the minimum complexity criterion. Secondly, we can perform prediction on an unknown test instance $x$ as follows. Let $\{B_1, B_2, \ldots, B_k\}$ be the partitioning of the training set. Let $E_i = B_i \cup \{x\}$ and $j = \text{argmin}_{i=1,2,\ldots,k}\{K(E_i) - K(B_i)\}$. We can set the class label of $x$ to be the most occurring class label amongst the instances in block $B_j$, i.e. the block having the least increase in complexity. We plan to further explore these applications in our future work.

We also intend to compare MML/MDL approach with our work. Traditional message length formulations of decision tree learning were purely syntactic (Quinlan & Rivest 1989, Wallace & Patrick 1992). However, recently people have shown close relationship between MML/MDL and Kolmogorov Complexity in general (Wallace & Dowe 1999, Vitanyi & Li 2000).

## References


Mitchell T. M., *Machine Learning*, McGraw Hill, 1997

Webb G. I., "Further Experimental Evidence against the Utility of Occam's Razor," *Journal of Artificial Intelligence Research,* 4 (1996) 397-417

Quinlan J. R., *C4.5: programs for Machine Learning*, Morgan Kaufman (1993)

Kolmogorov A. N., "Three approaches to the quantitative definition of information," *Problemi Peredachi Informatsii* (Problems of Information Transmission) 1 (1965) 3-11.

Li M., Vitanyi P., *An Introduction to Kolmogorov Complexity and Its Applications*, Springer (1997)

Shannon C. E., "The Mathematical Theory of Communication," U. of Illinois Press, Urbana, IL (1948)

Zvonkin A. K., Levin L. A., "The Complexity of finite objects and the Algorithmic Concepts of Information and Randomness," *Russian Math. Surveys*, 25:6 (1970), 83-124

Cilibrasi R., Vitanyi P., "Clustering by compression," CWI manuscript (2003), Available from *http://homepages.cwi.nl/~paulv/kolmcompl.html*

Quinlan J. R., Rivest R., "Inferring Decision Trees Using the Minimum Description Length Principle," *Information & Computation* 80 (1989), 227-248

Wallace C. S., Patrick J. D., "Coding Decision Trees," *Technical Report 91/153* (1992), Monash U., Australia

Wallace C., Dowe D., "Minimum Message Length and Kolmogorov complexity," *Computer Journal*, 42:4 (1999), 270-283

Vitanyi P., Li M., "Minimum Description Length Induction, Bayesianism, and Kolmogorov Complexity," *IEEE Transactions on Information Theory*, IT-46:2(2000), 446-464

# Discriminating Among Word Meanings By Identifying Similar Contexts

**Amruta Purandare** and **Ted Pedersen**
Department of Computer Science
University of Minnesota
Duluth, MN 55812
{pura0010,tpederse}@d.umn.edu
http://senseclusters.sourceforge.net

**Abstract**

Word sense discrimination is an unsupervised clustering problem, which seeks to discover which instances of a word/s are used in the same meaning. This is done strictly based on information found in raw corpora, without using any sense tagged text or other existing knowledge sources. Our particular focus is to systematically compare the efficacy of a range of lexical features, context representations, and clustering algorithms when applied to this problem.

## Introduction

The goal of word sense discrimination is to group multiple instances of a word/s into clusters, where each cluster represents a distinct meaning of that word/s. For example, we might wish to differentiate among sentences containing the word *line* that refer to a *product line* versus those that refer to a *telephone line*. Or, we might wish to identify which instances of *bat* and *club* refer to a stick used for hitting. Thus, word sense discrimination seeks to identify different words that refer to the same meaning (synonyms), and also discover the different senses of a given word.

Word sense discrimination is often based on the premise that words that are used in similar contexts will tend to have similar meanings (Miller & Charles 1991). This allows word sense discrimination to be reduced to the problem of finding classes of similar contexts such that each discovered class represents a word sense. Two very distinct approaches that rely on this premise have been proposed by (Pedersen & Bruce 1998) and (Schütze 1998). We compare a number of their techniques via an experimental evaluation, and propose extensions to these methods based on these results.

Our strategy is to represent the contexts in which words occur using a variety of lexical features that are easy to identify in large corpora. As a result our approach conveniently scales to larger data since no manually annotated text is required. These contexts are then converted into similarity or vector spaces which can then be clustered using a variety of different algorithms. The objective of our research is to determine which combinations of features, context representations, and clustering algorithms result in better word sense discrimination.



## Context Representation

We maintain a separation between the instances to be discriminated (i.e., the test data) and the data from which features are selected (i.e., the training data). This allows us to explore variations in the training data while maintaining a consistent test set, and also avoid any limitations that might be caused by selecting features from test data when discriminating a small number of instances.

We identify various lexical features in the training data using a combination of frequency counts and measures of association. These features include unigrams, bigrams, and co-occurrences. Unigrams are individual words that occur with high frequency, while bigrams are strongly associated pairs of words that occur within a few positions of each other. Co-occurrences are strongly associated unordered pairs of words that include the word to be discriminated.

Once the features are selected, each word to be discriminated is represented in terms of the features that directly occur in the surrounding context, loosely following (Pedersen & Bruce 1998). We refer to this as a first order context vector representation, since the vector represents the immediate context in which the word to be discriminated occurs.

We also represent context indirectly with a second order context vector representation, as suggested by (Schütze 1998). This technique creates first order vectors for the individual words that occur in a context, and then averages those together to create a generalized vector that captures second order relationships among words in that context.

## Clustering

Vector space clustering algorithms directly use the vector representations of the contexts as their input. However, similarity space algorithms require a similarity matrix that provides the pair–wise similarities between the given contexts.

In both similarity and vector space, we have used a hierarchical agglomerative clustering algorithm with the average link criteria function, and a hybrid algorithm called bisected K-means that combines the partitional K-means algorithm with hierarchical divisive clustering.

We do not know a-priori the number of possible senses to be discriminated. Hence, in our experiments, we specify an upper limit on the number of clusters to be discovered. Our belief is that a successful sense discrimination algorithm will automatically discover approximately the same number of clusters as actual senses for a word, and that the excess clusters will contain very few instances and can be safely discarded without fear of affecting overall performance.

## Experimental Results

We have carried out experiments using the *line*, *hard*, and *serve* sense–tagged corpora, each of which has approximately 4,000 instances. We have also used a subset of the words from the sense–tagged SENSEVAL-2 corpus. These represent much smaller quantities of data, since there are 50–200 sense tagged instances for each word. We evaluate our results in terms of precision and recall, which measure the degree to which the discovered clusters correspond with the true word senses as indicated by the sense–tags.

Experimental results described in (Purandare 2003) and (Purandare & Pedersen 2004b) show that bigrams and co-occurrences with high degrees of association according to the log–likelihood ratio prove to be particularly useful. We have also found that the first order context representation results in more accurate discrimination when discriminating the larger *line*, *hard* and *serve* corpora. The second order representation performs better when given smaller corpora such as the SENSEVAL-2 words.

We hypothesize that the sparseness of the features in smaller corpora causes the first order methods to perform poorly, while second order methods are able to better identify features when given limited data. However, both representations lead to very sparse representations regardless of the corpora size. As such we are experimenting with Singular Value Decomposition (SVD) to reduce sparsity and convert the word level feature space into a conceptual semantic space, as is done in Latent Semantic Analysis (Landauer, Foltz, & Laham 1998).

## Future Work

In our experiments to date, our training data has consisted of instances of the word/s to be discriminated. Thus, the training and test data are fairly homogeneous, and focus on the particular word to be discriminated. We plan to conduct experiments where the features are selected from a huge corpus that is not specific to the words being discriminated. We will draw from a variety of sources, including the British National Corpus, the English GigaWord Corpus, and the Web.

Our motivation is that huge corpora will provide more generic co–occurrence information about words without regard to a particular word to be discriminated. It is not clear if this will be more effective than our current approach, which captures co–occurrence behavior in the immediate context of the word to be discriminated.

We are also developing a method to attach descriptive labels to the discovered clusters. These labels will define the sense of the cluster, and will be based on the most characteristic features of the instances that belong to that cluster. We will then map the discovered clusters to established dictionary senses by matching the automatically derived labels to the existing definitions. This will allow us to associate our clusters with an existing sense inventory, making it possible to perform fully automatic word sense disambiguation that does not rely on any manually annotated text.

## Conclusions

We have conducted an extensive comparative analysis of word sense discrimination techniques using first order and second order context vectors, where both can be employed in similarity and vector space. We conclude that for larger amounts of homogeneous data such as the *line, hard* and *serve* data, the first order context vector representation and average link clustering algorithm as proposed by (Pedersen & Bruce 1998) is most effective. We believe this is the case because in a large sample of data, it is very likely that the features that occur in the training data will also occur in the test data, making it possible to represent test instances with fairly rich feature sets.

When given smaller amounts of data like the SENSEVAL-2 words, second order context vectors and a hybrid clustering method such as repeated K–means perform better. We believe that this occurs because in small and sparse data, direct first order features are seldom observed in both the training and the test data. However, the indirect second order co–occurrence relationships that are captured by these methods provide sufficient information for discrimination to proceed.

## Acknowledgments

This research is supported by a National Science Foundation Faculty Early CAREER Development Award (#0092784).

All of the experiments described in this paper were conducted using version 0.47 of the SenseClusters package (Purandare & Pedersen 2004a), which is freely available from SourceForge.

## References

Landauer, T.; Foltz, P.; and Laham, D. 1998. An introduction to latent semantic analysis. *Discourse Processes* 25:259–284.

Miller, G., and Charles, W. 1991. Contextual correlates of semantic similarity. *Language and Cognitive Processes* 6(1):1–28.

Pedersen, T., and Bruce, R. 1998. Knowledge lean word sense disambiguation. In *Proceedings of the Fifteenth National Conference on Artificial Intelligence*, 800–805.

Purandare, A., and Pedersen, T. 2004a. Senseclusters - finding clusters that represent word senses. In *Proceedings of the Nineteenth National Conference on Artificial Intelligence*.

Purandare, A., and Pedersen, T. 2004b. Word sense discrimination by clustering contexts in vector and similarity spaces. In *Proceedings of the Conference on Computational Natural Language Learning*.

Purandare, A. 2003. Discriminating among word senses using mcquitty's similarity analysis. In *Proceedings of the HLT-NAACL 2003 Student Research Workshop*, 19–24.

Schütze, H. 1998. Automatic word sense discrimination. *Computational Linguistics* 24(1):97–123.

# A Bayes Net Approach to Argumentation

**Sabyasachi Saha and Sandip Sen**
Department of Mathematical & Computer Sciences
The University of Tulsa
{sahasa, sandip}@ens.utulsa.edu

### Abstract

Argumentation-based negotiation approaches have been proposed to present realistic negotiation contexts. This paper presents a novel Bayesian network based argumentation and decision making framework that allows agents to utilize models of other agents. Our goal is to use Bayesian networks to capture the opponent model through an incremental learning process and use the model to generate more effective arguments to convince the opponent to accept favorable contracts.

## Introduction

Automated negotiation has drawn significant attention in multiagent systems research (Kraus, Sycara, & Evenchik 1998; Jennings *et al.* 2001). Agents are typically assumed to have correct and complete knowledge of preferences, and the negotiation context as well as agents' preferences are held constant during the course of negotiation. In real-life negotiation scenarios, however, individual preferences are not static. Agents might also have incorrect beliefs about the world or may not be cognizant about all pertinent attributes. In such situations, agents can influence each other by argumentation to influence their belief state.

Most existing argumentation based negotiation frameworks are logic or rule-based (Kraus, Sycara, & Evenchik 1998; Parsons, Sierra, & Jennings 1998; Rahwan, Sonenberg, & Dignum 2003). While these approaches provide a formal framework with provable properties, we believe there is a need for alternative frameworks that can better capture the uncertainty and complexity of real-life negotiations. In particular, the factors influencing an agent's decisions may be incompletely known and be gradually revealed to a negotiator. Accordingly, negotiation frameworks should incorporate approximate opponent models represented in a form that can capture complex relationships between domain attributes and can be efficiently updated based on information revealed during negotiation.

The specific research questions we are interested in include the following:

• When processing an offer or a counter-offer, what decision mechanisms should an agent use to decide whether to accept a proposal, argue about its last proposal, or generate a new proposal?
• How are arguments for negotiation generated/selected?
• Should an agent try to persuade the other agent by reward, threat, etc.
• How does the agent's model of the opponent influence its argumentation and proposals?
• How and when does an agent update its belief about the other agent or about the negotiation issues based on received arguments and offers?



We propose to use a Bayesian network model (Jensen 1996) to represent the influences of different factors on agent decisions. An agent's knowledge of such causal factors and their relative importance is captured in the topology of the network as well as the prior and conditional probability assignments. Initial approximate knowledge of an agent is incrementally refined based on actual negotiation experiences. We focus on the decision mechanism that allows a modeling agent to use its knowledge represented as a Bayesian network to determine negotiation offers and select arguments to influence the opponent to accept offers that has been rejected. The goal is to use the Bayes net model of the opponent to select and manipulate the negotiation context to maximize the chance of a preferred offer being accepted by the other party.

## Architecture and Decision procedure

We present the decision architecture of the agents in Figure 1. We have proposed the use of Bayesian networks for representing the *Opponent's belief model.* We group the arguments into different categories such as *conflict-arg, emphasizing-arg, persuasive-arg* and *justification.* We will illustrate the different arguments using the scenario of a travel agent who is contacted by a buyer agent to purchase an airline ticket. *Conflict-arg* is an argument that is presented if there is a conflict in belief about some variable and the opponent rejects this agent's earlier proposal for the "wrong belief" about this variable. For example, the buyer agent rejects an offer by the travel agent citing the reason that the corresponding airline has a poor luggage handling reputation. The travel agent uses a *conflict-arg* to contradict this belief. *Emphasizing-arg* is an argument to emphasize particular attributes in the offer to influence the opponent to accept

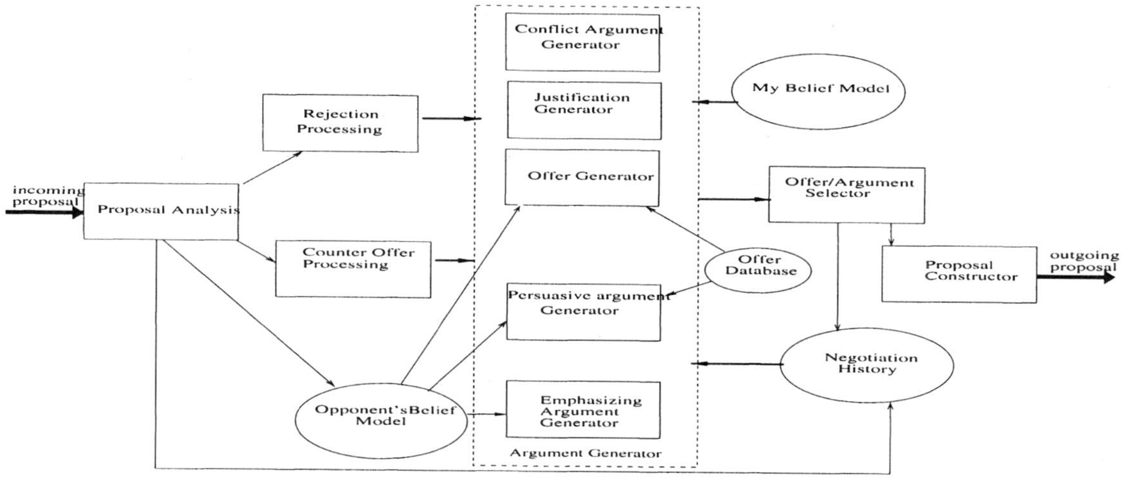


Figure 1: Decision Architecture of the arguing agent.

the previous offer. For example, suppose the buyer agent rejects an offer from the travel agent because of the extended waiting time in the transit. The travel agent can emphasize the 5-star accommodation provided during the wait. This attribute is not new to the offer but was not highlighted prior to this point in the negotiation process. A *justification* is used to reinforce the agent's previous offer by introducing auxilliary information about that offer. Suppose the buyer agent was rejecting the offer because of high price. The travel agent justifies the high price factor by citing the current peak travel season. *Persuasive-arg* is an argument that shows threat or reward to persuade the opponent to accept the offer. For example, the travel agent can offer a rebate of $100 for the next purchase if the buyer accepts the current offer.

For brevity, our decision mechanism for the argument (or proposal) generation based on the architecture shown in Figure 1 is summarized in the following steps:

1. Receive proposal from the opponent.
2. Analyze whether it is a counter proposal or rejection or counter argument. Update own belief model and opponent's belief model.
3. In case the opponent shows a "wrong" belief to reject previous proposal, the agent generates *conflict-arg*. Though it does not repeat an argument if it is presented earlier.
4. If there it is possible to justify the reason for which the other agent has rejected the previous proposal then *justification* is generator to justify its stand.
5. Otherwise, the agent computes based on the opponent's belief model, the expected utilities of the following options: (a) generating *emphasizing-arg* which is to emphasize the other facilities in the previous offer which was not explicit in the set of issues, (b) different persuasive arguments (*persuasive-arg*) like *threat* or *reward*, (c) the best counter offer and the utility of the opponent's offer. Finally choose argument or offer that produces maximum expected utility.

We have outlined a framework using which an opponent model can be used to generate arguments that are likely to convince the opponent to accept proposed offers. The use of Bayes nets allow us to formally capture the complex interrelationships between domain issues and their influence on the opponent's decisions. Such models allow agents to efficiently arrive at profitable negotiated settlements. Such models can also be updated based on negotiation history and can serve as useful repositories for dealing with steady customers.

We have presented an asymmetric negotiation model, with a knowledgeable domain expert interacting with a user agent. We plan to extend this model for peer-to-peer level interaction scenarios where both the agents can trade arguments. In particular we are interested in applying such techniques in P2P environments for resource procurement and exchange.

**Acknowledgements:** This work has been supported in part by an NSF award IIS-0209208.

## References

Jennings, N.; Faratin, P.; Parsons, A. R. L. S.; Sierra, C.; and Wooldridge, M. 2001. Automated negotiation: prospects, methods and challenges. *International Journal of Group Decision and Negotiation* 10(2):199–215.

Jensen, F. 1996. *An Introduction to bayesian Networks*. UCL Press and Springer Verlag.

Kraus, S.; Sycara, K.; and Evenchik, A. 1998. Reaching agreements through argumentation: a logical model and implementation. *AI Journal* 104(1-2):1–69.

Parsons, S.; Sierra, C.; and Jennings, N. R. 1998. Agents that reason and negotiate by arguing. *Journal of Logic and Computation* 8(3):261–292.

Rahwan, I.; Sonenberg, L.; and Dignum, F. 2003. Towards interest-based negotiation. In *Proc. AAMAS 2003*, 773–780.

# Identifying an Object that Is Perceptually Indistinguishable from One Previously Perceived

**John F. Santore and Stuart C. Shapiro**
Department of Computer Science and Engineering
and Center for Cognitive Science
University at Buffalo, The State University of New York
201 Bell Hall Box 602000
Buffalo, NY 14260-2000

## Introduction

People often encounter objects that are perceptually indistinguishable from objects that they have seen before. When this happens, how do they decide whether the object they are looking at is something never before seen, or if it is the same one they encountered before? To identify these objects people surely use background knowledge and contextual cues. We propose a computational theory of identifying perceptually indistinguishable objects(PIOs) based on a set of experiments which were designed to identify the knowledge and perceptual cues that people use to identify PIOs. By identifying a PIO, we mean deciding which individual object is encountered, not deciding what category of objects it belongs to. In particular, identifying a PIO means deciding if the object just encountered is a new, never before seen object, or if it has been previously encountered, which previously perceived object it is.

Our agent's beliefs and reasoning are based on an intensional representation (Maida & Shapiro 1982). Intensional representations model the sense (Frege 1892) of an object rather than the object referent, itself. The terms of our representation language, SNePS (Shapiro & the SNePS Implementation Group 2002; Shapiro & Rapaport 1992), denote mental entities. Some such entities are propositions; others are abstract ideas; others are the agent's "concepts" or "ideas" of objects in the world. This is important for the task of identifying PIOs, because before the identification task is complete, the agent may have two mental entities, $e_1$ and $e_2$, that it might or might not conclude correspond to the same object in the world.

## The base cases in the identification of PIOs

**What is a base case.** Experiments with human subjects showed that there are four conditions under which human subjects find the identification of PIOs to be very easy. We'll call these four conditions the base cases of the identification task. Subjects tried to put themselves into a position where they could use one or more base case to identify the PIOs in the experiment.

When the computational agent identifies a PIO using a base case, it does not form a new mental entity for the object and then try to reason if it already knows about this same object already. The agent only creates new entities as needed for cognizing information (Maida & Shapiro 1982). The object that the agent is perceiving is either *the one* that it has seen before, or a new object. If the object is *the one*, then the agent ought to use the original mental entity for it and not conceive of something new which the agent then believes really refers to the same object. If the object is a new one, a new mental entity is created for the new object.

**Base case 1: Simultaneous perceptions.** If an agent perceives two PIOs in its sensory field at the same time, the agent can trivially conclude that the two are not the same object.[1]

**Base case 2: Objects with a unique appearance.** If the agent believes that an object has a unique appearance and the agent never sees more than one such PIO at a time, then the agent can instantly identify the object as soon as the agent perceives an object with that appearance. The agent can and ought to use its original entity for the object in this case.

**Base case 3: Immobile objects.** Immobile objects are defined here as those objects which cannot move or be moved. We're also including those objects which humans think about as not being movable such as a house or a park bench bolted to the ground.

The location of an immobile object is the most important feature to identify immobile PIOs since the location doesn't change. Either the agent knows about an immobile object of this kind at this location already, or the agent has never encountered an object like this at this location, so the object must be a new one.

Correct use of this base case depends on an agent correctly identifying its current location. Subjects were vulnerable to mistaking one room for another if the two looked similar. Kuipers and his colleagues (Kuipers & Beeson 2002) call this sort of mistake "perceptual aliasing" when discussing its implications for robotic agents. When agents fall victim to perceptual aliasing, use of location to identify immobile objects is fallible.

[1] We are ignoring the use of illusions with mirrors and other deliberate attempts to make a single object appear to be multiple objects.

**Base Case 4: Continuous viewing.** Pollock (1974) has discussed reidentification of objects, a subproblem of identifying PIOs. He notes that an object under continuous observation can be reidentified at a later time as the same object, stating that "continuity of appearance is a logical reason for reidentification."

Continuous viewing of an object also appeared in the human subjects trials as a base case for identifying PIOs. This ease of identification of objects while under continuous observation seems to be implicitly assumed in Coradeschi and Saffiotti's (2003) *Track* functionality.

## A General Algorithm for PIO identification

To identify an object with description *D*, just encountered by agent *A, A* should first decide if it has ever seen anything that looks like D before. If not, then the object is a newly encountered object. If *A* has seen something that looks like *D* before, then *A* then checks the base cases of identifying PIOs. If there is only one thing with description *D* visible to *A* now, and *A* believes that there is only one thing $e_1$ that looks like *D,* and *A* has only seen one such object before, *A* assumes that it has encountered $e_1$ again. Otherwise, if objects that look like *D* are immobile, *A* must decide if it has seen an $e_1$ at the same location before, if so, then the object is $e_1$, else the object is something new. Otherwise, if *A* believes that it has continuously viewed an $e_1$ as it traveled to the place that A now sees the object, *A* believes that the object is $e_1$. If none of these base cases hold, then for each place that *A* currently sees an object with description *D, A* should create a new mental entity $e_2$. With each $e_2$, *A* should consider if that $e_2$ actually refers to the same object in the world as some previously conceived entity $e_1$.

We make a simplifying assumption at this point: that a moving object will move at a constant speed. When trying to decide if $e_2$ refers to the same entity as $e_1$ *A* first considers the rate of movement of each. If the rates are not the same then $e_1$ and $e_2$ refer to different objects. If *A* doesn't know the rate of movement, *A* cannot make an informed decision about the identity of $e_1$ and $e_2$. Next *A* checks to see if the distance that $e_1$ could have traveled is less than the shortest path (that *A* knows about) between the place it last saw $e_1$ and the place *A* sees $e_2$. If so, then $e_1$ and $e_2$ refer to different objects. Next *A* should consider if it believes that the motivations and capabilities that it believes $e_1$ has would disallow $e_1$ from being in the place that $e_2$ is currently being encountered. If so $e_1$ and $e_2$ refer to different objects. At this point, A should consider if the possible range of $e_1$ is larger than an environment specific constant ("it could be almost anywhere by now"). If so, then *A* cannot decide with certainty if $e_1$ and $e_2$ refer to the same object. Otherwise *A* should decide if $e_1$ and $e_2$ are coreferential given that only a short distance could be traveled.

When there is only a short possible distance to travel, the agent can now make the closed world assumption. Since an object moves at a constant speed, any other object that might be mistaken for the object being identified will also move at the same speed, and thus be restricted to a small travel distance of its own. So *A* now checks to see if it knows of any other PIOs except for $e_1$ and $e_2$ that could reach the place where $e_2$ is now. If not, then it assumes that $e_1$ and $e_2$ are coreferential. Otherwise, if $e_1$ was headed toward the place $e_2$ is now seen but no other PIOs were, then *A* assumes that $e_1$ and $e_2$ are coreferential. If there is another PIO headed in the same direction, *A* can't be sure if $e_1$ and $e_2$ are coreferential. If none of the above cases hold, the agent will assume that $e_1$ and $e_2$ are not coreferential.

## Conclusions and Future Work

We have presented a cognitively plausible computational method of identifying PIOs. We are currently implementing this algorithm in a simulated robot(Santore & Shapiro 2003). The simulated robot will then be tested on the same tasks as the human subjects to gauge the performance of the algorithm.

## References


Coradeschi, S., and Saffioti, A. 2003. An introduction to the anchoring problem. *Robotics and Autonomous Systems* 43(2-3):85–96.

Frege, G. 1892. *On Sense and Nominatum.* 85–102.

Kuipers, B., and Beeson, P. 2002. Bootstrap learning for place recognition. In *Proceedings of the Eighteenth International Joint Conference on Artificial Intelligence (IJCAI-02)*, 174–180. San Francisco, CA: Morgan Kaufmann.

Maida, A. S., and Shapiro, S. C. 1982. Intensional concepts in propositional semantic networks. *Cognitive Science* 6(4):291–330.

Pollock, J. 1974. *Knowledge and Justification.* Princeton University Press.

Santore, J. F., and Shapiro, S. C. 2003. Crystal cassie: Use of a 3-d gaming environment for a cognitive agent. In Sun, R., ed., *Papers of the IJCAI 2003 Workshop on Cognitive Modeling of Agents and Multi-Agent Interactions*, 84–91. Menlo Park, CA: AAAI Press.

Shapiro, S. C., and Rapaport, W. J. 1992. The SNePS family. *Computers and Mathematics with Applications* 23(2-5):243–275.

Shapiro, S. C., and the SNePS Implementation Group. 2002. *SNePS 2.6 User's Manual.* Department of Computer Science and Engineering, University at Buffalo, The State University of New York, Buffalo NY.

# Evaluating Consistency Algorithms for Temporal Metric Constraints

**Yang Shi** , **Anagh Lal** , and **Berthe Y. Choueiry**
Constraint Systems Laboratory
Computer Science & Engineering
University of Nebraska-Lincoln
Email: {yshi, alal, choueiry}@cse.unl.edu

**Abstract**

We study the performance of some known algorithms for solving the Simple Temporal Problem (STP) and the Temporal Constraint Satisfaction Problem (TCSP). In particular, we empirically compare the Bellman-Ford (BF) algorithm and its incremental version (incBF) by (Cesta & Oddi 1996) to the △STP of (Xu & Choueiry 2003a). Among the tested algorithms, we show that △STP is the most efficient for determining the consistency of an STP, and that incBF combined with the heuristics of (Xu & Choueiry 2003b) is the most efficient for solving the TCSP. We plan to improve △STP by exploiting incrementality as in incBF and other new incremental algorithms.

## 1 Introduction

Many planning and scheduling applications rely on an efficient handling of temporal information. We study two networks of metric constraints: the Simple Temporal Problem (STP) and the Temporal Constraint Satisfaction Problem (TCSP). An STP (Figure 1) is defined by a graph $G = (V, E, I)$ where $V$ is a set of vertices $t_i$ representing time

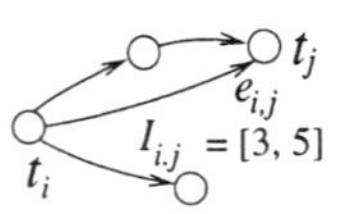


Figure 1: *STP*

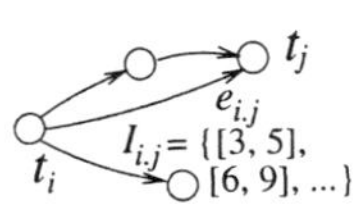


Figure 2: *TCSP*

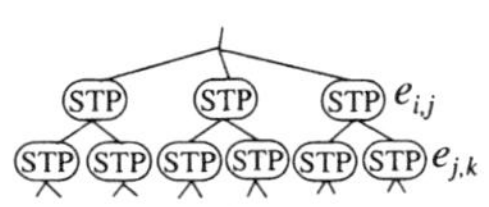


Figure 3: *Meta-CSP*

points; $E$ is a set of directed edges $e_{i,j}$ representing constraints between two time points $t_i$ and $t_j$; and $I$ is a set of constraint labels for the edges. A constraint label $I_{i,j}$ of edge $e_{i,j}$ is a *unique* interval $[a, b]$, $a$ and $b \in \mathbb{R}$, and denotes a constraint of bounded difference $a \leq (t_j - t_i) \leq b$. We assume that there is at most one constraint between any two vertices $e_i$ and $e_j$ and that the constraint $e_{i,j}$ labeled $[a, b]$ can also be referred to as the constraint $e_{j,i}$ labeled $[-b, -a]$. A TCSP (Figure 2) is defined by a similar graph $G = (V, E, I)$, where each edge label $I_{i,j} = \{l_{ij}^1, l_{ij}^2, \ldots, l_{ij}^k\}$ is a *set* of disjoint intervals denoting a disjunction of constraints of bounded differences between $t_i$ and $t_j$. The consistency of the STP can be determined in polynomial time. Solving the TCSP is **NP**-complete and can be done by expressing the TCSP as a meta-CSP and solving it with backtrack search (Dechter, Meiri, & Pearl 1991). Every node in the tree for solving the meta-CSP (Figure 3) is an STP that must be tested for consistency. Thus, it is important to solve the STP efficiently. In this paper, we compare empirically the performance of various algorithms for solving the STP and TCSP. We plan to extend our approach to the Disjunctive Temporal Problem (Stergiou & Koubarakis 2000).



## 2 Background

The following algorithms can be used to determine the consistency of an STP: directional path consistency (DPC) (Dechter 2003), △STP (Xu & Choueiry 2003a), Floyd-Warshall (FW) and Bellman-Ford (BF) (Cormen, Leiserson, & Rivest 2001). In (Xu & Choueiry 2003a) we showed that △STP consistently outperforms FW, outperforms DPC on sparse graphs, and is comparable to DPC on dense graphs. We did not cover BF. Cesta and Oddi (1996) introduced an incremental version of BF (incBF) but did not test it on the TCSP. In (Xu & Choueiry 2003b) we showed that △STP outperforms FW and DPC on the TCSP, and proposed △STP-TCSP that dramatically improves search performance by combining △STP and two new heuristics (EdgeOrd and NewCyc). In this paper, we achieve two tasks: (1) Compare BF and △STP for solving the STP, and (2) Compare incBF and △STP for solving the TCSP.

## 3 Algorithms tested & experiments

A known technique for enhancing the performance of solving a Constraint Satisfaction Problem (CSP) is to decompose the graph of the CSP into biconnected components according to its articulation points[1], independently solve each component, then combine the results. This technique (AP) provides an upper bound, in the size of the largest biconnected component, to the search effort (Freuder 1985). We integrated AP in each one of the tested solvers except for △STP in which AP is implicit. For the TCSP, we used △AC of (Choueiry & Xu 2004) as a preprocessing step for filtering the constraints. We compared the algorithms listed in Table 1 for solving the STP and the TCSP on randomly generated problems, measuring averages of CPU time, the number of constraint checks CC, and the number of nodes visited NV (for TCSP). We used the random generators of

[1]An articulation point of a graph is a vertex whose removal disconnects the graph into its biconnected components.

(Xu & Choueiry 2003b), varying constraint density $d$ in [2%, 90%], where $d = \frac{|E|-e_{min}}{e_{max}-e_{min}}$, $e_{max}$=$(\frac{|V|(|V|-1)}{2})$, and $e_{min}$=$(|V| - 1)$. Below we summarize the three experiments, which lead to the ranking shown in Table 1. The first experiment compares STP solvers. We used STP instances of 50 nodes and generated 100 instances per density value. The results are shown in Figure 4. The second experiment compares TCSP solvers. We used problems with 10 nodes and 3 to 5 intervals per node, and generated 600 instances per density value. (The size of the meta-CSP grows exponentially in the number of nodes in the TCSP, thus limiting the size of tested instances.) We tested finding both the first solution and all solutions to the TCSP (i.e., the minimal network), but report in Figure 5 only the latter because the difference in behavior is more significant. Similar results hold for NV and CPU time. Table 2 shows the average CC gain of the best strategy and its lower limit (LL) and upper limit (UL) with 95% confidence, where the gain is the difference of the values for the last two algorithms in Table 1. Table 2 shows a high instability for $d \in [2\%, 10\%]$. The third experiment justifies the unreliability of these results. We computed the cumulative averages of the performance measures as the sample size increases. Figure 6 shows that, for small values of $d$, the average of CC is not stable when the sample size is below 400 samples. Hence results for these density values are not statistically significant.

| Algorithm | STP | TCSP |
|---|---|---|
| FW+AP | worse | worse |
| DPC+AP | good | OK |
| BF+AP | OK | – |
| △STP | best | – |
| incBF+AP | – | good |
| △STP+EdgeOrg+NewCyc | – | better |
| incBF+AP+EdgeOrg+NewCyc *(new)* | – | best |

Table 1: *Ranking according to performance.*

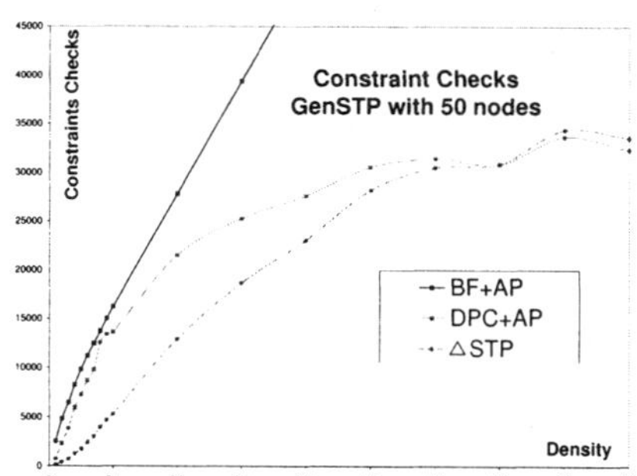


Figure 4: *Constraint checks for selected STP solvers.*

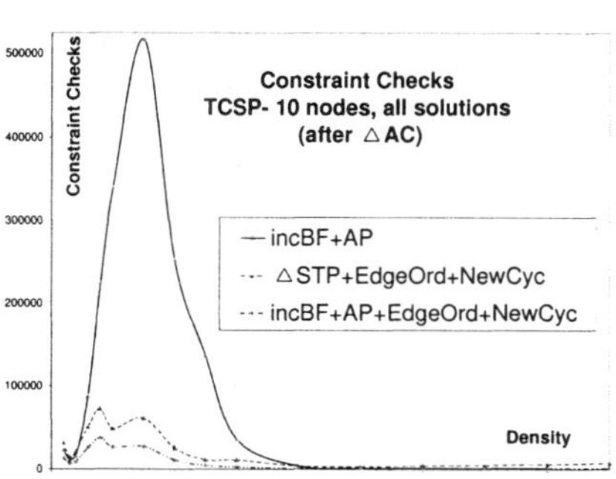


Figure 5: *Constraint checks for selected TCSP solvers.*

| $d$ | △ STP CC×$10^3$ | IncBF CC×$10^3$ | Gain CC×$10^3$ LL | Average | UL |
|---|---|---|---|---|---|
| 0.02 | 45.61 | 14.77 | 5.39 | 30.84 | 56.29 |
| 0.04 | 17.51 | 7.56 | 5.06 | 9.95 | 14.84 |
| 0.06 | 51.66 | 24.30 | 3.45 | 27.35 | 51.24 |
| 0.08 | 83.38 | 50.74 | 4.86 | 32.63 | 60.41 |
| 0.10 | 50.31 | 26.24 | 20.29 | 24.07 | 27.84 |
| 0.15 | 75.92 | 37.61 | 20.52 | 38.30 | 56.08 |
| 0.20 | 28.09 | 12.03 | 10.74 | 16.06 | 21.38 |

Table 2: *incBF+AP vs. △STP, both including EdgeOrg+NewCyc.*

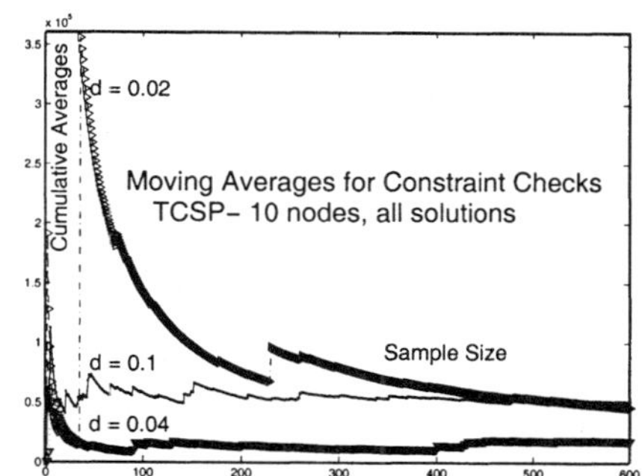


Figure 6: *Moving averages for* CC *for the TCSP.*

## 4 Conclusions

We tested empirically the behavior of various algorithms for solving temporal networks. We showed that the performance of incBF for solving the TCSP can be significantly improved when combined with the heuristics proposed in (Xu & Choueiry 2003b). In the future, we plan to exploit the incrementality feature of incBF and of other new algorithms indicated to us by the reviewers. This research is supported by NSF CAREER Award #0133568.

## References

Cesta, A., and Oddi, A. 1996. Gaining Efficiency and Flexibility in the Simple Temporal Problem. In *TIME 96*.

Choueiry, B., and Xu, L. 2004. An Efficient Consistency Algorithm for the Temporal Constraint Satisfaction Problem. In *Submitted to AI Communications*.

Cormen, T.; Leiserson, C.; and Rivest, R. L. 2001. *Introduction to Algorithms*. McGraw-Hill & MIT Press.

Dechter, R.; Meiri, I.; and Pearl, J. 1991. Temporal Constraint Networks. *AIJ* 49:61–95.

Dechter, R. 2003. *Constraint Processing*. Morgan Kaufmann.

Freuder, E. 1985. A Sufficient Condition for Backtrack-Bounded Search. *JACM* 32 (4):755–761.

Stergiou, K., and Koubarakis, M. 2000. Backtracking Algorithms for Disjunctions of Temporal Constraints. *AIJ* 12- (1):81–117.

Xu, L., and Choueiry, B. 2003a. A New Efficient Algorithm for Solving the Simple Temporal Problem. In *TIME-ICTL 03*, 212–222. IEEE Press.

Xu, L., and Choueiry, B. 2003b. Improving Backtrack Search for Solving the TCSP. In *CP 03*, 754–768. LNCS 2833.

# Mixed-Initiative Workflow Composition

**Marc Spraragen**

University of Southern California / Information Sciences Institute
4676 Admiralty Way, Marina del Rey, CA 90292 USA +1 310 448 9197
marcs@isi.edu

Complex applications in many areas, including scientific computations and business-related systems, are represented as computational workflows composed out of multiple components. There are several approaches that help a user compose these workflows. Some composition systems implement a user-system interactive approach (Kim, Spraragen, and Gil 2004). These systems are useful for expressing user preferences during composition; however, they can be tedious to use if a large number of tasks are needed in the workflow, as composition is done one step at a time, manually. Another approach to workflow composition is full automation, which aims to eliminate unnecessary user interaction during composition (Blythe et al. 2003), (Myers et al. 2003). This approach is efficient, but is not ideal if user preferences need to be expressed during composition.

Our approach combines the strengths of manual and automatic approaches into mixed-initiative workflow composition. This combined approach uses automated planning techniques, while also incorporating user preferences during composition. Our approach is implemented in a new system, AutoCAT, by combining an interactive workflow editor (Composition Analysis Tool or CAT) (Kim, Spraragen, and Gil 2004) and a planner, Prodigy (Veloso et al. 1995).

CAT enables users to manually compose workflows by adding and removing tasks, and by linking the tasks together in order to supply data (i.e., linking task outputs) to the workflow's user-defined end results. Using AI planning principles, CAT checks the workflow for possible composition errors introduced by a user. For instance, the workflow's links are checked for correctness (e.g., "flight number" task output linked to "driver license number" task input is incorrect), and checks for unnecessary workflow tasks (for example, if the workflow's only end result is "flight reservation", then a "real estate service" task is unnecessary). CAT's approach also involves searching a knowledge base of task types in order to suggest to the user the next composition steps that should be taken (for example, "Suggestion: remove the real estate service task"). CAT also lets the user choose one out of several similar tasks (e.g., "do you want to add Travelocity flight reservation task, or Orbitz?") to add to the workflow. Lastly, CAT's knowledge base contains abstract task types, for example "abstract flight reservation task," which can be included in a workflow as placeholders. CAT will then suggest that users specialize abstract tasks; one such suggestion might be "specialize abstract flight reservation task to Travelocity or Orbitz."

AutoCAT extends CAT by incorporating Prodigy's automatic workflow completion. AutoCAT takes a partial workflow created by the user, and sends it to Prodigy. The representation of the workflow in Prodigy defines the problem's initial state as every task output from a workflow (i.e., all effects), and the goal state as every task input from the workflow (i.e., all preconditions). Prodigy processes the problem, while referencing AutoCAT's knowledge base for the available task types that can be added to the workflow. Prodigy then returns the shortest sequence of operators (i.e., tasks), based on the initial state, which supplies all necessary effects to achieve the goal state (if such a sequence exists). During planning, if Prodigy reaches a state where more than one similar operator can be applied, it will return the most specific common parent of these operators, as specified in the knowledge base's task ontology (e.g., Prodigy will choose "abstract flight reservation service" instead of choosing between Travelocity or Orbitz). AutoCAT incorporates the tasks from Prodigy into the workflow, and then presents the completed workflow to the user in case he/she wants to make further changes.

AutoCAT provides mixed-initiative workflow completion and correction for users, by the following interaction (available at any point during composition).

1) The user composes a partial workflow manually.
2) Algorithms in AutoCAT automatically remove incorrect links and unnecessary tasks from the workflow.
3) Prodigy is invoked to complete the workflow, and returns a sequence of tasks to AutoCAT (including abstract tasks).

4) AutoCAT formulates suggestion choices for specializing the abstract tasks.
5) AutoCAT returns the completed workflow, and suggestions, to the user.
6) The user applies suggestions or further composes the workflow manually.

The work outlined above demonstrates how mixed-initiative composition can help users compose workflows. An existing system, PASSAT, has been successful in a similar mixed-initiative approach using hierarchical task network (HTN) planning models (Myers et al. 2003), while AutoCAT uses operator-based planning models instead of HTN. Our future work will include user tests of AutoCAT. We will compare these results with results from previous and future user evaluations of CAT, in part to analyze AutoCAT's efficiency and user-friendliness with respect to CAT.

## References

Blythe, J., et al. 2003. The Role of Planning in Grid Computing. In *Proceedings of the Thirteenth International Conference on Automated Planning and Scheduling*, 153-163. Menlo Park, Calif.: AAAI Press.

Kim, J., Spraragen, M., and Gil, Y. 2004. An intelligent assistant for interactive workflow composition. In *Proceedings of the Ninth International Conference on Intelligent User Interfaces*, 125-131. New York, New York: ACM Press.

Myers, K., et al. 2003. A Mixed-initiative Framework for Robust Plan Sketching. In *Proceedings of the Thirteenth International Conference on Automated Planning and Scheduling*, 256-266. Menlo Park, Calif.: AAAI Press.

Veloso, M., et al. 1995. Integrating Planning and Learning: The PRODIGY Architecture. *Journal of Theoretical and Experimental Artificial Intelligence,* 7(1):81-120.

# Mobile Agent-Based Search for Service Discovery on Dynamic Peer-to-Peer Networks

**Evan A. Sultanik***
eas28@cs.drexel.edu

Dynamic multi-agent planning has many shortcomings in real-world domains. Specifically, it is not clear how services can be discovered and located in dynamic non-fault-tolerant networks. Examples of such include multi-hop ad hoc wireless and dynamic peer-to-peer networks. The nature of ad hoc and peer-to-peer networks inherently imposes the restriction of communication to one's "neighbors." Therefore, communication over multiple hops in the network is difficult without facilities such as ad hoc routing. In these networks, the problem of locating a service is compounded when services themselves can be mobile.

In some domains mobile agents can be service providers. For example, consider a group of helicopters deployed on a battlefield, as in the synthetic aircraft domain (Tambe 1998). A certificate authority might be required for secure communication between helicopters; this server could be encapsulated by a mobile agent capable of reasoning about the network (Artz, Peysakhov, & Regli 2003). The agent might then continuously migrate to portions of the network with low volatility. For instance, the agent might migrate to helicopters less likely to be removed from the network. To improve performance and minimize latency, heuristics for such migration might include proximity to the geographic center of the group or association with the centroid of the network topology graph. Therefore a method for pro-actively tracking the location of services in dynamic networks is required.

No fixed memory deterministic algorithm can locate a service in a network in a fixed amount of time (Kirousis *et al.* 2000). We propose a fixed-memory randomized method for approximating the location of a service in a dynamic network with a probabilistic certainty in a fixed amount of time.

Deploying a set of service monitoring agents to randomly walk the hosts of a dynamic peer-to-peer network can provide an accurate means of service discovery. The agents' task environment, a dynamic peer-to-peer network, is stochastic, dynamic, and continuous; there exists a delay between actual topology changes and the propagation of knowledge of these changes throughout the network. The agents do not have a goal, per se; their sole purpose is to randomly walk the network gathering information. Agents' percepts are comprised solely of the set of services available at the current host and the set of hosts neighboring the current host. Agents' actions are comprised solely of hopping to a neighbor host from their current host. At each host agents query for services, storing these data in memory (along with a timestamp). The agents' itineraries are dictated by the network; successor hosts for migration are selected randomly from the set of available neighbor hosts in the network. The agents' itineraries are dictated by the network; successor hosts for migration are selected randomly from the set of available neighbor hosts in the network.

Each host on the network is assumed to have a local state description represented by a tuple containing the following elements:

- $\nu$ - probability an agent will be at host $h$;
- $\eta$ - number of instances of a service $s$;
- $|\mathcal{H}|$ - cardinality of the set of hosts;
- $|\mathcal{A}|$ - cardinality of the set of agents;
- $\ell$ - average time needed for an agent to hop from one neighbor to another; and

Many of these elements need neither be calculated nor known a priori; they can be inferred from or provided by the service monitoring agents.

This approach has three important advantages over other alternatives, such as naïve message passing and broadcast:

1. a minimum of network bandwidth is used, and bandwidth usage scales linearly; this is an important issue for resource-constrained mobile devices and large-scale peer-to-peer networks;
2. services need not register themselves; and
3. properties of random walks are relatively easy to mathematically model and likewise make inferences upon.

Intuitively, the less frequently a host is visited by service discovery agents that have seen a service in some period of time, the less likely that service is currently available. Exploiting properties of random walks, such as limiting distributions, we have developed a mathematical formulation of agent movement in the network and an algorithmic technique for approximating the parameters of the formulation. Using this model, we can predict the availability of services with a high level of accuracy. This allows for time-critical reasoning and probabilistic inferences to be made upon the agent system.

Our current focus is on using our method for propagating service location information throughout the network as a

*Advised by Dr. William Regli

heuristic for mobile agent-based search. For example, each host could cache the data brought to them by the random walking service discovery agents. In doing so, each host would develop an index (or "belief") of the locations of services. These beliefs will become more accurate in conjunction with a host's proximity to the service. Therefore these beliefs, along with the timestamp of when the agent last saw the service, can be used as a hill climbing search heuristic when tracking down the service.

Our current research is focusing on the feasibility, admissibility, and accuracy of this heuristic, and its integration into the Secure Wireless Agent Testbed (SWAT) (Sultanik *et al.* 2003). This includes live tests with a dozen resource-constrained mobile computing devices, communicating over an ad hoc wireless network.

## References


Artz, D.; Peysakhov, M.; and Regli, W. 2003. Network meta-reasoning for information assurance in mobile agent systems. In *Proceedings of the Eighteenth International Joint Conference on Artificial Intelligence*, 1455–57.

Kirousis, L. M.; Kranakis, E.; Krizanc, D.; and Stamatiou, Y. C. 2000. Locating information with uncertainty in fully interconnected networks. In *International Symposium on Distributed Computing*, 283–296.

Sultanik, E.; Artz, D.; Anderson, G.; Kam, M.; Regli, W.; Peysakhov, M.; Sevy, J.; Belov, N.; Morizio, N.; and Mroczkowski, A. 2003. Secure mobile agents on ad hoc wireless networks. In *The Fifteenth Innovative Applications of Artificial Intelligence Conference*. American Association for Artificial Intelligence.

Tambe, M. 1998. Implementing agent teams in dynamic multi-agent environments. *Applied Artificial Intelligence* 12(2–3):189–210.

# Finding Redundant Constraints in FSM Minimization

**Lin Yuan, Pushkin R. Pari** and **Gang Qu**
Department of Electrical and Computer Engineering
University of Maryland, College Park, Maryland, 20742
{yuanl,pushkin,gangqu}@eng.umd.edu

## Introduction

Finite state machine (FSM) is a computation model that consists of a finite set of states, a start state, an input alphabet, and a transition function that defines the next state and/or outputs based on the current state and input symbols.

Finding an equivalent FSM with minimal number of states is generally referred as *state minimization* or *state reduction* (SR) problem. State minimization is an effective approach in logic synthesis to optimize sequential circuit design in terms of area and power(Kam, 1997). The SR problem of FSM is NP-complete and can be treated as a special case of the Constraint Satisfaction Problem(CSP) where the transition function defines all the constraints that need to be satisfied.

Interestingly, we observe that not all the constraints are required to obtain a given SR solution. Identifying the redundancy in the FSM will be useful in the following occasions. First, it helps to understand the nature of the NP-complete SR problem and to build FSM benchmarks to test the effectiveness of SR solvers. Second, the redundancy can be utilized to hide information and thus provide security protection to the FSM. Simulation results on real life FSMs reveal the existence of extremely rich redundancy.

## Motivational Example

Consider an incompletely specified FSM represented by state transition graph(STG) in Figure 1. Each node in the graph represents one state. Each (directed) edge indicates a state transition and the attributes carried by the edge specify the input/output associated with the transition. For example, the edge from node 4 to node 6 with "1/0" means that on input "1", the system moves from state 4 to state 6 and outputs "0". An edge without ending state represent the case when the next state of that transition is a *don't care*. This FSM can be minimized to an FSM with only four states and the solution is not unique. Figure 2 gives the STG of one solution, while another solution in this case is: A={1,4,7}, B={2,5}, C={3,6}, and D={8}.

Surprisingly, if we keep all the output values and only five transitions (the edges with a dot) in Figure 1, the minimized FSM remains the same. In another word, this implies that these conditions are sufficient to obtain this specific solution. The other transitions specified in the original FSM are *redundant* in the sense that their absence (i.e., changing the next states of these transitions from *specific states* to *don't care states*) will have no impact on the final state minimization solutions.



## Problem Formulation

Given an FSM and a solution to the SR problem, a transition in the original FSM is *redundant* if the given solution can still be obtained after we replace the next state of this transition by a don't care (we call this the *removal* of this transition). A *maximal redundant set* (MRS) is a set of redundant transitions that can be removed without affecting the given SR solution, but removing one more transition will not preserve this solution.

We will show in next section that finding an MRS can be converted to the problem of finding a truth assignment to a SAT formula with maximal number of 1s.

## Finding Maximal Redundant Set

Figure 3 depicts the state transition table, another representation of FSM, for the same FSM given in Figure 1. Each table entry specifies the next state and the output given the current state (which row this entry is in) and the input (which column this entry is in). For each entry with a specific next state (i.e., not don't care), we introduce a Boolean variable $x_i$ and stipulate that $x_i = 1$ means the entry is redundant. The clauses in the SAT formula are created as follows.

First, we compute all the compatible sets of the given FSM. Recall that i) two states are *compatible* if they have the same output values whenever they are both specified and their next states are also compatible whenever they are both specified; and ii) a *compatible set* is a set of states that are compatible pairwise. The essence of the SR problem is to include all the states using the minimal number of compatible sets.

Next, we examine each pair of states that are not compatible according to the given SR solution to make sure that we include sufficient constraints in the FSM specification to distinguish them. If there exists some input value on which the two states output different values (e.g., states $s1$ and $s2$ on input $i = 1$), then they are not compatible and no information on their next states is required. If, however, when the

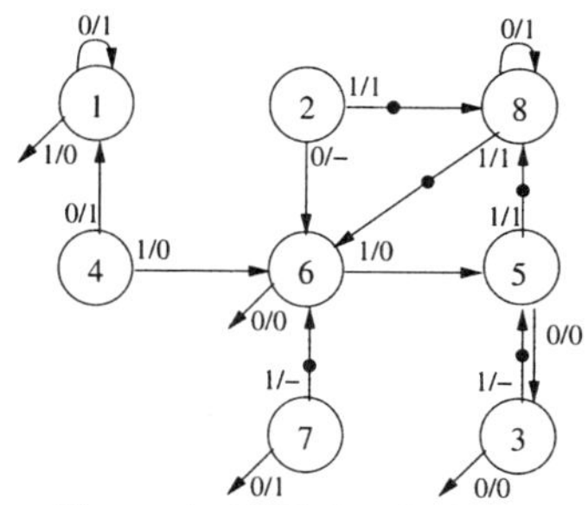

Figure 1: STG for the FSM.

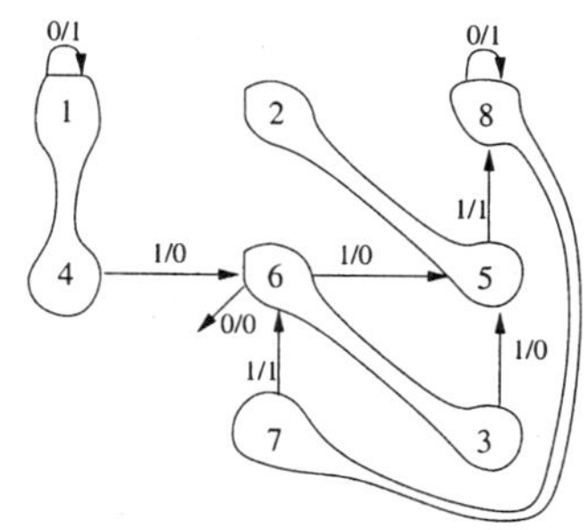

Figure 2: STG for the reduced FSM.

| | Next State In=0 | Next State In=1 | Output In=0 | Output In=1 |
|---|---|---|---|---|
| 1 | 1 ($x_1$) | - | 1 | 0 |
| 2 | 6 ($x_2$) | 8 ($x_3$) | - | 1 |
| 3 | - | 5 ($x_4$) | 0 | - |
| 4 | 1 ($x_5$) | 6 ($x_6$) | 1 | 0 |
| 5 | 3 ($x_7$) | 8 ($x_8$) | 0 | 1 |
| 6 | - | 5 ($x_9$) | 0 | 0 |
| 7 | - | 6 ($x_{10}$) | 1 | - |
| 8 | 8 ($x_{11}$) | 6 ($x_{12}$) | 1 | 1 |

Figure 3: State table for the FSM.

two states, for every input value, either have the same output value or at least one has a don't care as its output, then we need the information on their next states to distinguish them. Take states $s2$ and $s3$ for instance, the only way to distinguish them is to make both transitions $x_3$ and $x_4$ non-redundant, which can be done by including the expression $x_3'x_4'$ into the SAT formula.

A more complicated example is the pair of states $s2$ and $s8$. Their respective next states $s6$ and $s8$ are not compatible and we need the presence of both transitions $x_2$ and $x_{11}$ or $x_3$ and $x_{12}$ to distinguish them. This can be conveniently enforced by the following Boolean expression (in CNF format)

$$\begin{aligned} & x_2'x_{11}' + x_3'x_{12}' \\ (DeMorgan) \Rightarrow & (x_2 + x_{11})(x_3 + x_{12}) \\ (Distributive) \Rightarrow & x_2x_3 + x_2x_{12} + x_{11}x_3 + x_{11}x_{12} \\ (DeMorgan) \Rightarrow & (x_2' + x_3')(x_2' + x_{12}')(x_{11}' + x_3')(x_{11}' + x_{12}') \end{aligned}$$

As a result, for the FSM in Figure 1 and its SR solution in Figure 2, we have the following SAT instance:

$$\mathcal{F} = x_3'x_4'x_{10}'(x_2' + x_3')(x_3' + x_{11}')(x_2' + x_{12}')(x_{11}' + x_{12}')x_8'$$

For variables that do not appear in this formula (such as $x_1$), we can safely assume that their corresponding transitions are redundant. Clearly, finding the MRS becomes equivalent to finding a solution to the corresponding SAT formula such that the number of variables assigned to be '1' is maximized. An exact algorithm is to formulate it as an integer linear programming(ILP) problem which has been discussed in (Aloul *et al.* 2002). Practically, one can also simply solve the SAT formula multiple times, each solution represents one MRS, and pick the one with the maximal 1s.

## Results and Discussion

We consider FSM benchmarks from the MCNC suite of sequential circuits (Yang 2002). For each FSM, we use *stamina* from the logic synthesis package SIS (Sentovich & others 1992) to obtain a solution to the SR problem. We then generate the SAT instance and solve it by a SAT solver *zchaff* (Moskewicz *et al.* 2001) and ILP solver *CPLEX*(ILO 2002). We report the redundancy of each FSM benchmark in Table 1. The 2nd and the 3rd columns give the number of states and transitions in the original FSM; the next two columns report the number of redundant constraints identified by ILP solver and the percentage in the original constraints; the last

Table 1: Redundant constraints in FSM benchmarks

| FSM | states | orig. constr. | cplex | | zchaff | |
|---|---|---|---|---|---|---|
| | | | redun | ratio | redun | ratio |
| donfile | 24 | 96 | 96 | 100% | 96 | 100% |
| ex2 | 19 | 72 | 27 | 38% | 15 | 21% |
| ex3 | 10 | 36 | 19 | 53% | 10 | 28% |
| ex5 | 9 | 32 | 19 | 59% | 9 | 28% |
| ex7 | 10 | 36 | 20 | 56% | 14 | 39% |
| example | 6 | 24 | 24 | 100% | 24 | 100% |
| lion9 | 9 | 25 | 12 | 48% | 12 | 48% |
| modulo12 | 12 | 12 | 12 | 100% | 12 | 100% |
| s27 | 6 | 96 | 88 | 92% | 85 | 89% |
| s8 | 5 | 80 | 80 | 100% | 80 | 100% |
| train11 | 11 | 25 | 5 | 20% | 3 | 12% |
| opus | 10 | 176 | 176 | 100% | 176 | 100% |
| beecount | 7 | 51 | 36 | 71% | 34 | 67% |
| bbara | 10 | 160 | 36 | 23% | 33 | 21% |
| mark1 | 15 | 240 | 129 | 54% | 128 | 53% |

two columns show the similar result obtained by the SAT solver. One can see that both the ILP and SAT solvers manage to find very rich redundancy (from 12% to 100% with an average of 66%). Most of the 100% redundancy occurs when the original FSM is minimized to a single state FSM.

In sum, we introduce the concept of redundancy in FSM specification and formulate the problem as finding a SAT solution with maximal number of 1s. We expect to find some more real-world applications where this redudant information can be utilized.

## References


Aloul, F.; Ramani, A.; Markov, I. L.; and Sakallah, K. A. 2002. Generic ilp versus 0-1 specialized ilp. In *IEEE/ACM International Conference on Computer Aided Design*, 450–457.

ILOG Inc. 2002. *ILOG AMPL CPLEX System Version 8.0 Use Guide.*

Moskewicz, M. W.; Madigan, C. F.; Zhao, Y.; Zhang, L.; and Malik, S. 2001. Chaff: Engineering an efficient sat solver. In *The 38th ACM/IEEE Design Automation Conference*, 530–535.

Sentovich, E. M., et al. 1992. Sis: A system for sequential circuit synthesis. Technical report, Electronics Research Laboratory, University of California, Berkeley.

Yang, S. 2002. Synthesis and optimization benchmarks user guide. Technical report, ftp://mcnc.mcnc.org.

# SIGART/AAAI Doctoral Consortium

# Semi-supervised Clustering with Limited Background Knowledge

**Sugato Basu**
Email: sugato@cs.utexas.edu
Address: Department of Computer Sciences, University of Texas at Austin, Austin, TX - 78712, USA

## Thesis Goal

In many machine learning domains, there is a large supply of unlabeled data but limited labeled data, which can be expensive to generate. Consequently, semi-supervised learning, learning from a combination of both labeled and unlabeled data, has become a topic of significant recent interest. Our research focus is on semi-supervised clustering, which uses a small amount of supervised data in the form of class labels or pairwise constraints on some examples to aid unsupervised clustering. Semi-supervised clustering can be either constraint-based, i.e., changes are made to the clustering objective to satisfy user-specified labels/constraints, or metric-based, i.e., the clustering distortion measure is trained to satisfy the given labels/constraints. Our main goal in this thesis is to study constraint-based semi-supervised clustering algorithms, integrate them with metric-based approaches, characterize some of their properties and empirically validate our algorithms on different domains, e.g., text processing and bioinformatics.

## Background

Existing methods for semi-supervised clustering fall into two general approaches that we call *constraint-based* and *metric-based* methods.

In constraint-based approaches, the clustering algorithm itself is modified so that user-provided labels or constraints are used to get a more appropriate clustering. Previous work in this area includes modifying the clustering objective function so that it includes a term for satisfying specified constraints (Demiriz, Bennett, & Embrechts 1999), and enforcing constraints to be satisfied during the cluster assignment in the clustering process (Wagstaff *et al.* 2001).

In metric-based approaches, an existing clustering algorithm that uses a particular distortion measure is employed; however, the measure is first trained to satisfy the labels or constraints in the supervised data. Several distortion measures have been used for metric-based semi-supervised clustering, including Jensen-Shannon divergence trained using gradient descent (Cohn, Caruana, & McCallum 2003), Euclidean distance modified by a shortest-path algorithm (Klein, Kamvar, & Manning 2002), or Mahalanobis distances trained using convex optimization (Bar-Hillel *et al.* 2003; Xing *et al.* 2003).

However, metric-based and constraint-based approaches to semi-supervised clustering have not been adequately compared in previous work, and so their relative strengths and weaknesses are largely unknown.

An important domain that motivates the semi-supervised clustering problem is the clustering of genes for functional prediction. For most organisms, only a limited number of genes are annotated with their functional pathways, with the majority of the genes still having unknown functions. Categorization of these genes into functional groups using gene microarray data, phylogenetic profiles, etc. is a natural semi-supervised clustering problem. Clustering (with model selection to choose the right number of clusters) is more well suited to this domain than classification, since the number of functional classes is not known a priori. Moreover background knowledge, available in the form of functional pathway labels (KEGG, GO) or constraints over some of the genes (DIP), could easily be incorporated as supervision to improve the clustering accuracy.

## Progress

In our first work, we showed how supervision in the form of labeled data can be incorporated into clustering (Basu, Banerjee, & Mooney 2002). The labeled data were used to generate seed clusters for initializing model-based clustering algorithms, and constraints generated from the labeled data were used to guide the clustering process towards a partitioning similar to the user-specified labels. We showed that the K-Means algorithm is equivalent to an EM algorithm on a mixture of $K$ Gaussians under assumptions of identity covariance of the Gaussians, uniform mixture component priors and expectation under a particular type of conditional distribution. This underlying model helps us to prove convergence guarantees for the proposed label-based semi-supervised clustering algorithms.

Next, we showed that semi-supervised clustering with pairwise *must-link* and *cannot-link* constraints has an underlying probabilistic model – a Hidden Markov Random Field (HMRF) (Basu, Banerjee, & Mooney 2004). In this work, we also outlined a method for selecting maximally informative constraints in a query-driven framework for pairwise constrained clustering. In order to maximize the utility of the limited supervised data available in a semi-supervised setting, supervised training examples should be, if possible, *actively* selected as maximally informative ones rather than chosen at random. This would imply that fewer constraints will be required to significantly improve the clustering accuracy. To this end, a new algorithm was developed to actively select good pairwise constraints for semi-supervised clustering, using an active learning strategy based on farthest-first traversal. The proposed scheme has two phases: (a) explore the given data to get pairwise disjoint non-null neighborhoods, each belonging to a different cluster in the underlying true categorization of the data, within a small number of queries, and (b) consolidate this cluster structure using the remaining queries, to get better centroid estimates.

In recent work, we have shown that the HMRF clustering model is able to incorporate any Bregman divergence (Banerjee *et al.* 2004) as the clustering distortion measure, which allows using the framework with such common distortion measures as KL-divergence, I-divergence, and parameterized squared Mahalanobis distance. Additionally, cosine similarity can also be used as the clustering distortion measure in the framework, which makes it useful for directional datasets (Basu, Bilenko, & Mooney 2004). For all such measures, minimizing the semi-supervised clustering objective function becomes equivalent to finding the maximum *a posteriori* probability (MAP) configuration of the underlying HMRF.

We have also developed a new semi-supervised clustering approach that unifies constraint-based and metric-based techniques in an integrated framework (Bilenko, Basu, & Mooney 2004). This algorithm trains the distortion measure with each clustering iteration, utilizing both unlabeled data and pairwise constraints. The formulation is able to learn individual metrics for each cluster, which permits clusters of different shapes. This work also explores metric learning for feature generation (in contrast to simple feature weighting), which we empirically demonstrate to outperform current state-of-the-art metric learning algorithms, under certain conditions.

In all these projects, experiments have been performed on both low dimensional UCI datasets and high dimensional text data sets, using KMeans and EM as the baseline clustering algorithms.

## Proposed Research

In future, we want to study the following aspects of semi-supervised clustering, in decreasing order of priority:

(1) Semi-supervised approaches for finding *overlapping* clusters in the data. This is especially relevant for gene clustering in the bioinformatics domain, since genes often belong to multiple functional pathways.

(2) The feasibility of semi-supervising other clustering algorithms, e.g., spectral clustering, agglomerative clustering, etc. We are currently exploring semi-supervised versions of kernel-based clustering, which would be useful for datasets that are not linearly separable.

(3) Application of the semi-supervised clustering model to other domains apart from UCI datasets and text. We are currently focusing on two domains: (a) search result clustering of web search engines, e.g., Google, and (b) clustering of gene microarray data in bioinformatics.

(4) Effect of noisy or probabilistic supervision in pairwise constrained clustering. This study will be especially important for deploying our proposed semi-supervised clustering algorithms to practical settings, where background knowledge would be in general noisy.

(5) Model selection using both unsupervised data and the limited supervised data, for automatic selection of number of clusters in semi-supervised clustering. Most model selection criteria in clustering are only based on unsupervised data – we want to explore whether supervised data available in the form of labels or constraints can be used to select the number of clusters more effectively.

(6) Theoretical study of the relative benefits of supervised and unsupervised data in semi-supervised clustering, similar to the analysis of (Ratsaby & Venkatesh 1995).

## References


Banerjee, A.; Merugu, S.; Dhillon, I. S.; and Ghosh, J. 2004. Clustering with Bregman divergences. In *Proc. of the 2004 SIAM Intl. Conf. on Data Mining (SDM-04)*.

Bar-Hillel, A.; Hertz, T.; Shental, N.; and Weinshall, D. 2003. Learning distance functions using equivalence relations. In *Proc. of 20th Intl. Conf. on Machine Learning (ICML-2003)*, 11–18.

Basu, S.; Banerjee, A.; and Mooney, R. J. 2002. Semi-supervised clustering by seeding. In *Proc. of 19th Intl. Conf. on Machine Learning (ICML-2002)*, 19–26.

Basu, S.; Banerjee, A.; and Mooney, R. J. 2004. Active semi-supervision for pairwise constrained clustering. In *Proc. of the 2004 SIAM Intl. Conf. on Data Mining (SDM-04)*.

Basu, S.; Bilenko, M.; and Mooney, R. J. 2004. A probabilistic framework for semi-supervised clustering. In submission, available at `http://www.cs.utexas.edu/~ml/publication`.

Bilenko, M.; Basu, S.; and Mooney, R. J. 2004. Integrating constraints and metric learning in semi-supervised clustering. In *Proc. of 21st Intl. Conf. on Machine Learning (ICML-2004)*.

Cohn, D.; Caruana, R.; and McCallum, A. 2003. Semi-supervised clustering with user feedback. Technical Report TR2003-1892, Cornell University.

Demiriz, A.; Bennett, K. P.; and Embrechts, M. J. 1999. Semi-supervised clustering using genetic algorithms. In *Artificial Neural Networks in Engineering (ANNIE-99)*, 809–814.

Klein, D.; Kamvar, S. D.; and Manning, C. 2002. From instance-level constraints to space-level constraints: Making the most of prior knowledge in data clustering. In *Proc. of 19th Intl. Conf. on Machine Learning (ICML-2002)*, 307–314.

Ratsaby, J., and Venkatesh, S. S. 1995. Learning from a mixture of labeled and unlabeled examples with parametric side information. In *Proc. of the 8th Annual Conf. on Computational Learning Theory*, 412–417.

Wagstaff, K.; Cardie, C.; Rogers, S.; and Schroedl, S. 2001. Constrained K-Means clustering with background knowledge. In *Proc. of 18th Intl. Conf. on Machine Learning (ICML-2001)*, 577–584.

Xing, E. P.; Ng, A. Y.; Jordan, M. I.; and Russell, S. 2003. Distance metric learning, with application to clustering with side-information. In *Advances in Neural Information Processing Systems 15*, 505–512. Cambridge, MA: MIT Press.

# Learnable Similarity Functions and Their Applications to Clustering and Record Linkage

**Mikhail Bilenko**
Department of Computer Sciences
University of Texas at Austin
1 University Station C0500
Austin, TX 78712-1188, USA
mbilenko@cs.utexas.edu

Many problems in machine learning and data mining depend on distance estimates between observations, e.g., instance-based classification, clustering, information retrieval, and record linkage in databases. However, the appropriate notion of similarity can vary depending on the particular domain, dataset, or task at hand. Consequently, a large number of functions that compute similarity between objects have been developed for different data types, varying greatly in their expressiveness, mathematical properties, and assumptions (Gusfield 1997; Duda, Hart, & Stork 2001). Additionally, there exists a substantial body of research on feature space transformations that attempt to provide a more salient representation of data than the original feature space, e.g. Principal Component Analysis (Jolliffe 1986) and Locally Linear Embedding (Saul & Roweis 2003).

All of these techniques make certain assumptions about the optimal representation of data and its influence on computing similarity which may or may not be applicable for specific datasets and tasks. Therefore, it is desirable to learn accurate similarity functions from training data to capture the correct notion of distance for a particular task at hand in a given domain. Recently, several approaches have been suggested for training such functions using *pairwise relations* between instances, e.g. pairwise equivalence (Ristad & Yianilos 1998; Cohen & Richman 2002), common cluster membership (Xing *et al.* 2003), and relative comparisons (Schultz & Joachims 2004). These approaches have shown improvements over traditional similarity functions for different data types such as vectors in Euclidean space, strings, and database records composed of multiple text fields. While these initial results are encouraging, there still remains a large number of similarity functions that are currently unable to adapt to a particular domain. In our research, we attempt to bridge this gap by developing both *new learnable similarity functions* and methods for their *application to particular problems* in machine learning and data mining.

In preliminary work, we proposed two learnable similarity functions for strings that adapt distance computations given training pairs of equivalent and non-equivalent strings (Bilenko & Mooney 2003a). The first function is based on a probabilistic model of edit distance with affine gaps (Gusfield 1997), a widely used character-based metric. The second function is a variant of cosine similarity that utilizes a Support Vector Machine (SVM) classifier (Vapnik 1998) to discriminate between similar and dissimilar string pairs. As opposed to their *static* analogs, these similarity functions *adapt* to a particular domain using training examples and produce more accurate similarity estimates as a result.



These string similarity functions were inspired by the *record linkage* problem, which is the task of identifying semantically equivalent database records that are syntactically different. Record linkage is one of the key tasks in data cleaning since presence of unidentified duplicate records violates data integrity principles. Information integration from multiple sources also relies on record linkage methods because information describing the same entity must be linked across sources. We developed a system, MARLIN (Multiply Adaptive Record Linkage using INduction), that we used as a testbed for evaluating learnable string similarity measures on the record linkage task. MARLIN incorporates learnable string metrics in a two-layer learning framework where multiple string distances are combined to identify duplicate database records. MARLIN was used to experimentally demonstrate that learnable string distances improve over traditional distance functions on a number of real-world record linkage datasets (Bilenko & Mooney 2003a).

Prior research on active learning has demonstrated that the learning process can be facilitated by intelligent selection of informative training examples from a pool of unlabeled data. Because training data for learnable similarity functions is typically composed of object pairs, selecting meaningful training examples presents unique challenges that are distinct from traditional active learning methods in classification. Based on initial experiments with MARLIN, we proposed two strategies for selectively collecting pairwise training data, static-active sampling and weakly-labeled selection, that facilitate training of adaptive similarity functions for the record linkage task (Bilenko & Mooney 2003b).

Another important application that can benefit from using learnable similarity functions is clustering. While traditionally clustering has been viewed as an unsupervised learning problem, recently there has been increasing attention to *semi-supervised clustering*, where limited supervision is provided to obtain better grouping of data (Wagstaff *et al.* 2001; Xing *et al.* 2003). In initial work on employing learnable distance functions in clustering, we developed the MPCK-MEANS algorithm, which is a semi-supervised variant of unsupervised K-means clustering. MPCK-MEANS utilizes training data in the form of pairwise constraints in a unified framework that encompasses cluster initialization, constraint satisfaction, and learning individual parameterized Mahalanobis distances for each cluster. Our initial results have shown that using both distance metric learning and cluster seeding with constraints leads to improvements over unsupervised clustering as well as over the individual methods in isolation (Bilenko, Basu, & Mooney 2004). In recent work, we have presented a probabilistic framework for semi-supervised clustering, HMRF-KMEANS, which generalizes MPCK-MEANS to other distance measures including Bregman divergences and cosine similarity while presenting a view of semi-supervised clustering as the task of label assignment in Hidden Markov Random Fields (Basu, Bilenko, & Mooney 2004).

While these initial results are encouraging, there is a number of open avenues for future research in developing and applying learnable similarity functions. Following are several directions that appear most promising to pursue in the near future.

We plan to extend the vector-space string similarity based on pairwise classification with SVMs by incorporating alternative vector-space representations that go beyond simple tokenization, e.g. string subsequence kernels (Lodhi *et al.* 2002). Additionally, we intend to modify SVM training methods to avoid overly aggressive feature selection performed by traditional SVM algorithms.

While our initial learnable model for string edit distance with affine gaps uses Hidden Markov Models in a generative framework, we will attempt to model string edit distance using undirected graphical models such as Conditional Random Fields (Lafferty, McCallum, & Pereira 2001). Because of the greater representational power of such models, we hope that this research will lead to edit distances that go beyond sequential character alignment and incorporate long-range dependencies.

Finally, we hope to extend usage of learnable similarity measures beyond record linkage to related information integration tasks, information extraction and schema mapping (Doan, Domingos, & Halevy 2001), and combine these tasks in a single cohesive framework. Because all of these tasks involve identifying equivalent objects represented differently, employing adaptive similarity functions in a unified framework could improve accuracy on the individual tasks as well as for the overall information integration process.

We hope that progress in these directions will lead to new learnable similarity functions that will advance the state-of-the-art in clustering and information integration. We believe that usefulness of learnable distance measures stretches far beyond the applications outlined here, and this research will lay the groundwork for developing and applying learnable similarity functions in other areas such as vision and information retrieval.

## References


Basu, S.; Bilenko, M.; and Mooney, R. J. 2004. A probabilistic framework for semi-supervised clustering. In submission, available at http://www.cs.utexas.edu/~ml/publication.

Bilenko, M., and Mooney, R. J. 2003a. Adaptive duplicate detection using learnable string similarity measures. In *Proceedings of the Ninth ACM SIGKDD International Conference on Knowledge Discovery and Data Mining (KDD-2003)*, 39–48.

Bilenko, M., and Mooney, R. J. 2003b. On evaluation and training-set construction for duplicate detection. In *Proceedings of the KDD-03 Workshop on Data Cleaning, Record Linkage, and Object Consolidation*, 7–12.

Bilenko, M.; Basu, S.; and Mooney, R. J. 2004. Integrating constraints and metric learning in semi-supervised clustering. In *Proceedings of 21st International Conference on Machine Learning (ICML-2004)*.

Cohen, W. W., and Richman, J. 2002. Learning to match and cluster large high-dimensional data sets for data integration. In *Proceedings of the Eighth ACM SIGKDD International Conference on Knowledge Discovery and Data Mining (KDD-2002)*.

Doan, A.; Domingos, P.; and Halevy, A. 2001. Reconciling schemas of disparate data sources: A machine-learning approach. In *Proceedings of the 2001 ACM SIGMOD International Conference on Management of Data*, 509–520. Santa Barbara, CA: ACM Press.

Duda, R. O.; Hart, P. E.; and Stork, D. G. 2001. *Pattern Classification*. New York: Wiley, second edition.

Gusfield, D. 1997. *Algorithms on Strings, Trees and Sequences*. New York: Cambridge University Press.

Jolliffe, I. T. 1986. *Principal Component Analysis*. New York: Springer-Verlag.

Lafferty, J.; McCallum, A.; and Pereira, F. 2001. Conditional random fields: Probabilistic models for segmenting and labeling sequence data. In *Proceedings of 18th International Conference on Machine Learning (ICML-2001)*.

Lodhi, H.; Saunders, C.; Shawe-Taylor, J.; Cristianini, N.; and Watkins, C. 2002. Text classification using string kernels. *Journal of Machine Learning Research* 2:419–444.

Ristad, E. S., and Yianilos, P. N. 1998. Learning string edit distance. *IEEE Transactions on Pattern Analysis and Machine Intelligence* 20(5):522–532.

Saul, L., and Roweis, S. 2003. Think globally, fit locally: unsupervised learning of low dimensional manifolds. *Journal of Machine Learning Research* 4:119–155.

Schultz, M., and Joachims, T. 2004. Learning a distance metric from relative comparisons. In *Advances in Neural Information Processing Systems 16*.

Vapnik, V. N. 1998. *Statistical Learning Theory*. John Wiley & Sons.

Wagstaff, K.; Cardie, C.; Rogers, S.; and Schroedl, S. 2001. Constrained K-Means clustering with background knowledge. In *Proceedings of 18th International Conference on Machine Learning (ICML-2001)*, 577–584.

Xing, E. P.; Ng, A. Y.; Jordan, M. I.; and Russell, S. 2003. Distance metric learning, with application to clustering with side-information. In *Advances in Neural Information Processing Systems 15*, 505–512. Cambridge, MA: MIT Press.

# Flexible Decision-Making in Sequential Auctions

**Gangshu Cai**
Operations Research and Computer Science
North Carolina State University
gcai@unity.ncsu.edu

## Introduction

It is quite common that items are sold sequentially in a series of auctions. For example, in the Seattle Fur Exchange, approximately eighty percent of pelts are auctioned sequentially (Lambson & Thurston 2003). On eBay, there are thousands of identical or similar items that are sold sequentially.

A sequential auction is a combination of individual auctions. Each individual auction, which we call a component auction, can be any type of auction, such as a first-price, sealed-bid auction. In this thesis, I assume that there are $q$ items for sale in a sequence of auctions, $K$. There are $n$ agents, $n > q$, competing for these $q$ items. Each agent has single-unit demand and will leave if it wins one item. Agents have incomplete information; each agent knows its own true valuation; however, it knows only a distribution function of other agents' valuations. After each auction, all bidders' bids are revealed, a practice which is common on eBay and other e-commerce sites.

The intention of decision-making in sequential auctions is to find the optimal solutions for agents in the sequence of auctions as a whole. One myopic approach is to treat sequential auctions as a collection of independent auctions. However, as pointed out by Engelbrecht-Wiggans and Weber (Engelbrecht-Wiggans & Weber 1979), this kind of approach may be inappropriate in the general case. A better approach is to model sequential auctions as a game and find the equilibrium strategies.

There is a voluminous theoretical literature on finding equilibria in sequential auctions. However, these models lack flexibility and a re-analysis is necessary even for a slightly different model. On the other hand, the vast number of trading opportunities and the increasingly fluid markets bolster the need for automated trading support in the form of *trading agents*—software programs that participate in electronic markets on behalf of a user. Simple bidding tools, like eSnipe[1] and AuctionBlitz[2], enable bidders to automate submission of bids. However, these tools lack the sophistication that bidders require when faced with a plethora of auctions possibly occurring in a sequence. The need for economic efficiency and computational efficiency leads to the question:

> Can we design a flexible decision-making system for sequential auctions so that an agent can find the equilibrium strategies efficiently and automatically?

I develop a multi-dimensional sequential auction design space based on Wurman, et al.'s classification, which includes three dimensions: bidding rules, clearing policy, and information revelation policy (Wurman, Wellman, & Walsh 2001). The flexible decision-making system is designed to automatically generate strategies for different models with a specification of the parameters. In next section, I present an approach to generate strategies for sequential auctions with discrete strategy spaces. In the following section, I provide two conjectures and discuss an algorithm to compute strategies for sequential auctions with continuous strategy spaces.

## Completed Work

### The Monte Carlo Approximation (MCA) Approach

For incomplete information games, we may use Harsanyi's transformation (Harsanyi 1967 8) to translate an incomplete information game into an imperfect information game. However, due to the infinite possible valuations for each agent, the computability of the Harsanyi transformation is limited. In this thesis, I investigate the use of Monte Carlo sampling to generate heuristic bidding policies for the incomplete information game with agents having discrete strategy spaces. The approach to the problem can be summarized as follows:

1. Create a sample complete-information game by drawing a set of valuations for other bidders.
2. Solve for a Nash equilibrium of the sample game.
3. Update the agent's bidding policy.

The first step is straightforward Monte Carlo sampling. The second step is the subject of the following two paragraphs. To update the agent's bidding policy, I take the weighted sum of the equilibrium solutions across all sample games (Cai & Wurman 2003).

The default representation of this game in extensive form is to expand each of the leaves with an appropriate subgame. A subgame is any part of the game tree that begins with a singleton information set. However, it is useful to identify



[1] http://www.esnipe.com

[2] http://www.auctionblitz.com

the game structure of individual auctions. Given that the bidders have complete information, all subgames with the same players remaining have the same solution(s). Thus, a single-unit, sealed-bid (component) auction with $n$ agents has at most $n$ *unique* subgames—one for each possible set of non-winners. Our agent's approach is essentially *dynamic programming*, and equivalent to standard backward induction with caching. The agent solves all possible smallest component games, and recursively constructs higher-order subgames until it solves the root game.

This leveraged structure enables significant computational savings. The component form representation is exponential in the number of agents and the number of bidding choices. However, the total number of nodes in our leveraged structure required to express the game is exponentially less than in the full expansion (Cai & Wurman 2003). For example, five-agent, four-item sequential single-unit auctions with five bid choices and random tie-breaking require only 1931 nodes to encode in the component form, compared to the 4.5 billion required for the naive expansion.

## Empirical Results

To evaluate the efficacy of the approach, I simulated several market configurations in which I varied the bidding rules, the functional form of the valuation distributions, the form of the update equation, and the strategies of the other bidders.

In the experiments, I measure the utility for our agent, the social welfare, and the revenue achieved by the seller. The performance of the MCA strategy is quite close to that of the subgame perfect equilibrium both when the other agents play perfectly and when they construct their own MCA strategies. This result indicates that the approximation technique generates policies that perform quite well in this environment (Cai & Wurman 2003).

A perfect Bayesian equilibrium (PBE) is defined in terms of beliefs at decision points in the game, and requires that an equilibrium policy be consistent with those beliefs. The MCA policy at a node implicitly captures the agent's beliefs about which opponent valuations would explain the fact that the agent arrived at a particular decision point in the game tree. I have shown that MCA strategies converge to the average policy of PBE (Cai 2003).

## Proposed Work

I expect to complete three threads of related research. The first one involves showing the relevance of different MCAs to PBE. A successful proof of the convergence of MCA strategies to PBE would validate the significance of using the MCA approach to compute equilibria in sequential auctions. In a previous report (Cai 2003), I introduce another policy update function. This function is a weighted update function in which I add utility to the policy update function to allow more weight to those bids which yield more utility. My preliminary analysis lends support to a conjecture:

**Conjecture 1.** *For a class of sequential-auction games, the weighted MCA strategies converge to PBE.*

The second and third threads are related to sequential auctions with continuous strategy spaces. Weber's model (Weber 1983) is a classic sequential auction model with continuous strategy spaces, in which the auctioneer announces only the winner and its bid. However, solutions change when we simply change the announcement rule. On the basis of some preliminary analyses, I conjecture:

**Conjecture 2.** *In a single-unit demand, independent private value sequential auction model with incomplete information and a price quote in which the auctioneer announces the bids of all agents after each auction, there does NOT exist an equilibrium in pure strategies.*

Most literature on sequential auctions is aimed at finding equilibria in pure strategies. The second conjecture suggests that there might be some sequential auction models, in which pure strategy equilibria do not exist, and moreover, this is the type of auction prevalent on the Internet.

In the third thread, I plan to design an algorithm to generate strategies for sequential auctions with continuous strategy spaces. One approach is to discretize the continuous strategy spaces so that we may use the previous MCA approaches to approximate a solution. Another approach could be a heuristic algorithm by combining best response and search algorithms under a leveraged structure similar to the MCA approach for models with discrete strategy spaces.

## Conclusion and Contribution

This thesis has the potential to contribute to both computer science and economics. The computer science contribution lies chiefly in the development of automatic and efficient algorithms for solving sequential auction games. The economic contribution is the theoretic analysis of the existence of equilibrium in sequential auctions and the relevance of MCAs to PBE for a class of sequential auction models.

## References

Cai, G., and Wurman, P. 2003. Monte Carlo approximation in incomplete-information, sequential-auction games. *Decision Support Systems*. Forthcoming.

Cai, G. 2003. Flexible decision-making in sequential auctions: A dissertation proposal. North Carolina State University.

Engelbrecht-Wiggans, R., and Weber, R. J. 1979. An example of a multi-object auction game. *Management Science* 25:1272–1277.

Harsanyi, J. C. 1967-8. Games with incomplete information played by bayesian players. *Management Science* 14:159–182,320–334,486–502.

Lambson, V. E., and Thurston, N. K. 2003. Sequential auctions: Theory and evidence from the seattle fur exchange. A working paper.

Weber, R. J. 1983. Multiple-object auctions. In Engelbrecht-Wiggans, R.; Shubik, M.; and Stark, R. M., eds., *Auctions, Bidding and Contracting: Uses and Theory*. New York University Press. 165–91.

Wurman, P. R.; Wellman, M. P.; and Walsh, W. E. 2001. A parametization of the auction design space. *Games and Economic Behavior* 35:304–338.

# A Framework for Optimal Sequential Planning in Multiagent Settings

**Prashant J. Doshi***
Dept. of Computer Science
Univ of Illinois, Chicago, IL 60607
pdoshi@cs.uic.edu

## Introduction

Research in autonomous agent planning is gradually moving from single-agent environments to those populated by multiple agents. In single-agent sequential environments, partially observable Markov decision processes (POMDPs) provide a principled approach for planning under uncertainty. They improve on classical planning by not only modeling the inherent non-determinism of the problem domain, but also by producing "universal" plans or policies which represent complete control mechanisms. We are motivated by these reasons to generalize POMDPs from their traditional single-agent application setting to an environment populated by several interacting autonomous agents.

The formalism of Markov decision processes has been extended to multiple agents previously, giving rise to stochastic games or Markov games. Other extensions of POMDPs to multiple agent environments have also appeared and are called DEC-POMDPs (Bernstein *et al.* 2002) in the literature. Both these formalisms employ the solution concept of Nash equilibria. Specifically, solutions are plans (policies) that are in mutual equilibrium with each other. However, while Nash equilibria are useful for describing a multiagent system when, and if, it has reached a stable state, this solution concept is not sufficient as a general control paradigm. The main reasons are that there may be multiple equilibria with no clear way to choose among them (non-uniqueness), and the fact that equilibria do not specify actions in cases in which agents believe that other agents may not act according to their equilibrium strategies (incompleteness). Furthermore, at present, researchers have inadequate understanding of the intermediate stages before Nash equilibrium is reached.

In this thesis, we present a new framework called Interactive POMDPS (I-POMDPs) for optimal planning by an agent interacting with other autonomous agents in a sequential environment and maximizing its reward that depends on joint actions of all agents. As expected, the generalization of POMDPs from a single-agent setting to multiple agents is not trivial. In addition to maintaining beliefs about the physical environment, each agent must also maintain beliefs about the other agents: their sensing capabilities, beliefs, preferences, and intentions. Analogously to POMDPs, each agent will locally compute its actions that optimize its preferences given what it believes in. The resulting control paradigm complements and generalizes the traditional equilibrium approach in that, if the agent believes that other agents will act according to an equilibrium, then it will also act out its part of the equilibrium. However, if it believes that other agents will diverge from equilibrium, then it will choose the appropriate optimal response. The unique aspect of I-POMDPs is that, by prescribing actions based on the agent's belief about other agents' beliefs and parameters, an agent maintains a possibly infinitely nested interactive belief system.

*Joint work with my advisor Piotr Gmytrasiewicz



## Interactive POMDPs

The proposed framework attempts to bring together game-theoretic solution concepts of equilibrium and decision-theoretic control paradigms such as policies as put forward by frameworks like POMDPs. The conceptual pieces of our framework are similar to those of POMDPs, thereby facilitating its easy adoption by the research community for multi-agent settings. In the next few paragraphs, we briefly discuss our framework, its properties, and preliminary results.

For simplicity of presentation let us consider an agent, $i$, that is interacting with one other agent, $j$. An *interactive POMDP* of agent $i$, *I-POMDP*$_i$, is:

$$\textit{I-POMDP}_i = \langle IS_i, A, T_i, \Omega_i, O_i, R_i \rangle$$

where:

• $IS_i$ is a set of **interactive** states defined as $IS_i = S \times \Theta_j$, where $S$ is the set of states of the physical environment, and $\Theta_j$ is the set of possible intentional models of agent $j$. An intentional model of $j$ is, $\theta_j = \langle b_j, A, \Omega_j, T_j, O_j, R_j, OC_j \rangle$ where $OC_j$ is agent $j$'s optimality criterion, together with the assumption that agent $j$ is Bayesian rational. For the sake of simplicity, let us rewrite $\theta_j$ as, $\theta_j = \langle b_j, \widehat{\theta}_j \rangle$ where $\widehat{\theta}_j$ is the agent $j$'s *frame*. Agent $j$'s belief is a probability distribution over the states of the world and the models of the agent $i$, $b_j \in \Delta(S \times \Theta_i)$. Each interactive state of agent $i$ therefore contains possibly infinitely nested beliefs over others' types and their beliefs about others. This nesting may be terminated by assuming that at some arbitrary level, an agent (say $i$) models the other agent (say $j$) using a *no-information* model – $i$ considers all of $j$'s actions to be equally likely.

• $A = A_i \times A_j$ is the set of joint moves of all agents.

• $T_i$ is a transition function $T_i : IS_i \times A \times IS_i \rightarrow [0, 1]$ which describes results of agents' actions. Actions can change the physical state, as well as the frames of other agents, for example by changing their observation function.

• $\Omega_i$ is the set of agent $i$'s observations.

• $O_i$ is an observation function $O_i : IS_i \times A \times \Omega_i \rightarrow [0, 1]$.

• $R_i$ is defined as $R_i : IS_i \times A \rightarrow \mathbf{R}$. We allow the agent to have preferences over physical states and models of other agents, but usually only the physical state will matter.

In a manner similar to POMDPs, we can show that agent's beliefs over their interactive states are *sufficient statistics* i.e. they fully summarize the agent's observable histories. Furthermore, we propose the following equation which captures the belief update process of an agent modeled as an I-POMDP.

$$\begin{aligned} b_i^t(is^t) = \ & \beta \int_{IS^{t-1}} \sum_{a_j^{t-1}} Pr(a_j^{t-1}|\theta_j^{t-1}) O_i(is^t, a^{t-1}, o_i^t) \\ & \times \sum_{o_j^t} \tau_{\theta_j^t}(b_j^{t-1}, a_j^{t-1}, o_j^t, b_j^t) T_i(is^{t-1}, a^{t-1}, is^t) \\ & \times O_j(is_j^t, a^{t-1}, o_j^t) db_i^{t-1}(is^{t-1}) \end{aligned}$$

Here $is = (s, \theta_j)$, $is_j = (s, \theta_i)$, $b_j^{t-1}$ and $b_j^t$ are the belief elements of $\theta_j^{t-1}$ and $\theta_j^t$, $\beta$ is a normalizing constant, $O_j$ is the observation function in $\theta_j^t$, and $Pr(a_j^{t-1}|\theta_j^{t-1})$ is the probability of other agent's action given its model.

Though our proposed belief update has a lot in common with that of POMDPs, two important differences manifest due to the multiagent application setting. First, since the predicted state of the environment depends on the actions performed by both agents, a probability measure on the other agent's actions ($Pr(a_j^{t-1}|\theta_j^{t-1})$) must be obtained. Second, changes in the models of the other agent must be included in the update. Specifically, update of the other agent's beliefs due to its observations ($\tau_{\theta_j^t}(b_j^{t-1}, a_j^{t-1}, o_j^t, b_j^t)$) is included. A formal derivation of our belief update appears in (Gmytrasiewicz & Doshi 2004). We note that this update *recurses* through the entire belief nesting, with the recursion bottoming out when a no-information model is encountered.

The local policy of each agent is computed by solving the associated I-POMDP using value iteration. Agent $i$'s optimal action, $a^*$, for the case of infinite horizon criterion with discounting, is an element of the set of optimal actions for the belief state, $OPT(\theta_i)$, which is defined as:

$$OPT(\theta_i) = \underset{a_i \in A_i}{argmax} \Big\{ \int_{IS} ER_i^{a_j}(is, a_i) db_i(is) + \gamma \sum_{o_i \in \Omega_i} Pr(o_i|a_i, b_i) U(\langle SE_{\theta_i}(b_i, a_i, o_i), \widehat{\theta}_i \rangle) \Big\}$$

where, $ER_i^{a_j}(is, a_i) = \sum_{a_j} R_i(is, a_i, a_j) Pr(a_j|\theta_j)$

It turns out that, as in POMDPs, the value function is piecewise linear and convex (PWLC) w.r.t. the belief. Additionally, the sequence of value functions converges as the horizon approaches infinity. However, both these properties hold in the case of a finite belief nesting only. By establishing these critical properties, we can apply the wide array of POMDP solution techniques to I-POMDPs as well.

We have applied the I-POMDP framework to the multi-agent tiger game (Tambe *et al.* Aug 2002). Our preliminary results have shown that an agent's policy changes as its belief about the other agent's beliefs changes. For example, if the agents are operating as a team (coordination is rewarded), and if agent $i$ believes that agent $j$ likely believes that the tiger is behind the left door, then $i$ gives preference to opening the right door. However, if $i$ believes that $j$ likely believes that the tiger is behind the right door, then $i$ prefers opening the left door. In addition to modeling multiple agents as a team, we have also modeled them as enemies, and as being neutral towards each other.

## Future Work

We have adopted a two-stage approach towards my thesis research. The first stage involved developing the framework, identifying and formalizing its properties and solution techniques, and conducting preliminary experiments on interesting problem domains. High computational complexity of solving I-POMDPs forces us to search for efficient approximation techniques. The second stage of this thesis will concentrate on developing these approximation techniques.

A promising approximation technique seems to be stochastic sampling methods such as particle filters. Particle filters utilize Monte Carlo sampling to approximate a belief state, and propagate it forwards in time. As frequently is the case when it comes to Bayesian update methods, here over the space of possible models of agents, the choice of the "right" prior arises. To address this issue we have turned to algorithmic probability and Kolmogorov complexity (Li & Vitanyi 1997).

## Conclusion

We have proposed a new framework, called Interactive POMDPs, for optimal sequential decision-making in multi-agent settings. Our framework is applicable to autonomous agents operating in partially observable environments, who locally compute actions they should execute to optimize their preferences given what they believe. I-POMDPs infuse decision-theoretic planning with notions of game theory thereby blending strategic and long term planning into a single framework. We have established its definition, its properties, and gathered some preliminary empirical data. Future work will revolve around developing approximate solution techniques that will tradeoff complexity with the quality of the solution, and performing more experimentation.

## References


Bernstein, D. S.; Givan, R.; Immerman, N.; and Zilberstein, S. 2002. The complexity of decentralized control of markov decision processes. *Mathematics of Operations Research.*

Gmytrasiewicz, P., and Doshi, P. 2004. A framework for sequential optimality in multiagent settings. Technical Report UIC-AIL-TR05, University of Illinois at Chicago.

Li, M., and Vitanyi, P. 1997. *An Introduction to Kolmogorov Complexity and its Applications.* Springer.

Tambe, M.; Nair, R.; Pynadath, D.; and Marsella, S. Aug 2002. Towards computing optimal policies for dec-pomdps. In *AAAI Workshop on Game and Decision Theoretic Agents.*

# User-Sensitive Text Summarization
## Thesis Summary

**Noemie Elhadad**
Computer Science Department
Columbia University
New York, New York 10027
noemie@cs.columbia.edu

## Introduction

Text summarization has emerged as an increasingly established field over the course of the past ten years. We may soon reach a stage where researchers will be able to design, and provide everyday users with, robust text summarization systems. Users of text summarization are many and range from the Internet surfers lacking the time to locate and digest all the latest news available on the web to scientists unable to keep pace with the burgeoning number of technical publications who must, nonetheless, be familiar with the latest findings in their fields.

Given texts to summarize, there is no *a priori* criteria for determining relevance for the summary. When humans summarize texts, they identify relevant information that they think will be of interest to the readers. Summarization is not only a function of the input documents but also of the reader's mental state: who the reader is, what his knowledge before reading the summary consists of, and why he wants to know about the input texts. This fact has been long acknowledged by both the psycho-linguistic and the computational-linguistic communities. However, both communities agree that trying to model the reader's mental state is far too complicated, if not entirely impossible. Given this dilemma, most of the computational linguistic research in summarization has assumed that the "reader variable" is a constant and has focused on defining a general notion of salience, valid for all readers.

In my thesis, I investigate strategies to take user characteristics into account in the summarization process. Acquiring a user model is by itself a wide subject of research. I do not focus on ways to acquire a user model, and I assume that there is an existing user model in my framework. Rather, my focus is on the challenges entailed in incorporating knowledge about the user into summarization strategies and providing the user with a text relevant to his needs.

In my work, two types of user tailoring are examined: *individualized*, i.e., the specific facts in which the reader is interested, and *class-based*, i.e., the degree of expertise of the reader. My research framework consists of PERSIVAL, a digital library that provides tailored access to medical technical literature for both physicians and patients. When treating a specific patient, physicians will want to keep abreast of the latest findings that pertain to that patient. Likewise, patients may want to access the latest findings that are relevant to their medical situation but may be hindered by the jargon commonly used in technical medical texts. My summarizer attempts to provide both types of users with tailored syntheses of the findings reported in clinical studies. Such tailoring is accomplished at the *individual* level by taking advantage of the existing patient record in the digital library. The summarizer will also adapt the language in which the summary is generated by using *class-based* information, i.e., whether the user is a physician or a patient.



## Summaries and the Users' Interests

There are several challenges in incorporating individual-based modeling. The first one consists of deciding which stages of the summarization process should be affected by the individual characteristics of the user; should it occur when selecting the content to include in the summary, when organizing the selected bits of information, and/or when choosing verbalizations? The second challenge is to determine the degree of abstraction and inference needed to achieve satisfactory modeling. Given input texts to summarize and a patient record composed of many reports in textual format, one must choose a representation of the information conveyed both in the input and the patient record that allows for efficient and accurate matching of information.

One contribution of my thesis work is to show how individual characteristics can determine what content should be included in the summary. While this has been investigated in information retrieval and traditional semantic-to-text generation, incorporating the user in the selection of content from textual input is a novel approach for summarization. Individual modeling takes place at the content selection stage; it is the place where the user's interests have most impact on the output summary. The summarizer selects the findings that pertain to the user's characteristics. This is achieved in a simple fashion thanks to an adequate representation of the input texts and the patient record. Using information extraction techniques and relying on an existing ontology, the summarizer operates over a data-structure called *content item* that is between full-semantic analysis and agnostic extracted text. This representation enables the use of simple matching strategies between the user model and the input texts.

At the current stage of my thesis work, I have designed and implemented a multi-document summarizer which generates tailored summaries of clinical studies (Elhadad *et al.* 2004). It is integrated into the overall PERSIVAL digital library. It tailors its output based on the record of the patient under care. Using information extraction techniques, *content items* are extracted at the sentence level from the input articles. Each content item represents a finding reported in a clinical study. It contains extracted pieces of information (namely, a set of parameters and a relation which links them) and meta-information (such as article and sentence numbers in which the finding was reported). The content items are then filtered against the patient record using a simple strategy. The strategy was reviewed and approved by the medical experts working on the PERSIVAL project. Next, the content items are organized: they are first merged into blocks of semantically related items using clustering. The similarity measure used for clustering is based on features of the content items: the more parameters two content items have in common, the more similar they are. Repetitions are identified as identical content items and contradictions are identified as content items with identical parameters but with contradictory relations. Once the blocks are produced, each block is then assigned a priority weight based on salient features of its content items. This determines the order in which the blocks will be displayed in the summary. The summary itself is obtained by using phrasal generation, relying on the verbalization used by the input articles of the different content items. The resulting summary is a coherent and fluent re-generated (not extracted) text. The filtering against the patient record allows for the individual tailoring. To date the language the summarizer generates is targeted at physicians. I now plan to focus on generating summaries that are appropriate to users with a different level of expertise, such as patients.

## Summaries and the Users' Expertise Level

I model the generation as a text simplification process. Given a summary originally produced for expert users, the goal is to generate a simplified version readable by lay users. Text simplification is an incipient field of computational linguistics, and many challenges presently exist. While most of the content is already selected in the original summary, not all the pieces of information should be included in the simplified version. Some details might be too technical for instance, and including them in a simplified version would only confuse the reader. Conversely, it might be necessary to introduce additional content such as background knowledge to enhance the reader's comprehension. Wording is obviously affected by the simplification process, whether one looks at the syntactic or lexical level.

I propose to approach the simplification process as applying a set of rewriting rules which affect both the technical lexical items and the technical sentences as whole. I plan to learn the rewriting rules by relying on a comparable corpus of technical texts and their simplified versions targeted at lay users. Lexical rules will include term simplification and definition insertion, while sentence rules will consist of paraphrasing the input sentence into a lay equivalent.

The first step is to collect instances of technical/lay sentence pairs from the comparable corpus automatically so that learning on many instances can be done. In preliminary work (Barzilay & Elhadad 2003), we have designed an algorithm for aligning sentences in comparable texts, such as encyclopedia articles written for children and adults. Our method relies on a simple lexical similarity measure and the automatically identified topical structure of typical articles. However, in the medical domain, new challenges arise: there is very little lexical similarity between technical and lay texts, and the topical structure is harder to induce automatically. I plan to investigate ways to adapt the algorithm to these new challenges.

The next step will be to learn the actual rewriting rules. For lexical rewriting rules, I will investigate ways to choose between alternative verbalizations of technical terms based on their frequency counts in lay and technical corpora. I plan to research when a definition is needed for a specific term and how it can be inserted into the simplified text. At the sentence level, I plan to investigate methods for unsupervised acquisition of the rewriting rules based on the automatically aligned comparable corpus.

Finally, I plan to evaluate my summarizer overall both with physicians and lay users. For physicians, I plan to assess whether the summaries help them access relevant information efficiently. Working with cognitive scientists members of the PERSIVAL team, we have set up a set of medical scenarios in which physicians have to find some information in the literature in order to treat a specific patient. We plan to compare how easy it is for the physicians to find the relevant information when presented with (a) the summarizer's output, (b) a modified version of the summarizer which does not tailors for individual content, or (c) results of a search. For lay users, I plan to evaluate whether their comprehension is eased by the simplification. In the planned user study, lay users will be presented with a technical summary or its lay version and a set of comprehension questions. To date, I have evaluated individual components of my summarizer, such as the content extraction and the content filtering module. The evaluation of the sentence alignment and the validity of the rewriting rules is planned work.

## Acknowledgments

I would like to thank Kathleen McKeown, Regina Barzilay and Smaranda Muresan for the useful discussions. This work is supported by the National Science Foundation Digital Library Initiative Phase II Grant No. IIS-98-17434.

## References

Barzilay, R., and Elhadad, N. 2003. Sentence alignment for monolingual comparable corpora. In *Proceedings of Empirical Methods in Natural Language Processing (EMNLP)*, 25–32.

Elhadad, N.; Kan, M.-Y.; Klavans, J.; and McKeown, K. 2004. Customization in a unified framework for summarizing medical literature. *Journal of Artificial Intelligence in Medicine*. to appear.

# Connecting Cognitive and Physical Worlds with Dynamic Cost Function Definition

**Jamie Lennon**

University of Maryland
Department of Aerospace Engineering
College Park, MD 20742
lennon@aic.nrl.navy.mil

### Abstract

Our goal is to mesh the symbolic reasoning capabilities of a cognitive model with the constrained optimization possibilities inherent in optimal controls. We plan to develop and test such a system for several different dynamical models in environments of differing certainty and differing efficiency requirements.

## Problem Description

We desire an intelligent robot that can reason, plan ahead, and make decisions based on its goals, its environment, and the desires of any teammates it might have. A cognitive model capable of symbolic inference can, with a large enough rules set and world information, do this for us. It can make judgment calls not only about what actions it should undertake, but *how* it should perform them - quickly, efficiently, cautiously, aggressively. Furthermore, given feedback, it could fine-tune these behaviors. They exist on a spectrum, after all. "Less aggressively" is not necessarily the same as "cautiously." A "less aggressive" behavior can still be far more reckless than the "least cautious" behavior.

These behaviors, illustrated with possibly emotionally loaded words, are simply stereotypes of classes of trajectories. An "aggressive driver" is one who drives quickly, leaves little clearance between his vehicle and others, and engages in rapid accelerations between and within lanes. We interpret these dynamic characteristics of the vehicle's motion as aggression, regardless of the actual emotional state of the driver. (This is different from the research presented in (Velasquez 1999), where simulated emotions actually trigger reactive behaviors). A "cautious driver" would have different characteristics. He might still drive very quickly on a highway, but would leave larger clearances between his car and others, and would maintain a more constant speed with fewer and more gradual accelerations. How can we elicit these characteristics in position, velocity, and acceleration in a variety of domains?

In an aerospace context, for example, we may be dealing with a military air vehicle on a mission through hostile territory. A reconnaissance mission would be flown in a very different manner than a bombing run.

Most existing path planners (Latombe 1991) would need to augment their states to handle more than just path (position only), and be able to compute full trajectories that are optimal with respect to our desired characteristics. The states are likely to quickly become unmanageable, and the resolution on the solution may be poor if discretization is decreased as a result of state explosion. Happily, the field of optimal controls (Kirk 1970) uses the calculus of variations to compute continuous, full-state trajectories. Additionally, the technique allows constraints to be placed on the trajectories. These can include, for example, system dynamics (including real-world concerns such as motor saturation), resulting in a path that the agent is guaranteed to be able to follow. They can also include a multi-term cost function that will allow us to elicit our various behaviors. This is an offline planning technique that is both mathematically rigorous and provably optimal, at the expense of computational complexity. It is therefore quite different from the work done in (Santamaria and Ram 1997), which is for fast, reactive behaviors that do not have a global perspective.

Our optimal control cost function contains three terms: fuel use, clearance from obstacles, and time. Prior to this work, relative cost function weights were set in an ad hoc fashion, often determined experimentally. While we will develop our basic behavior-eliciting weights experimentally, we are working toward rules to dictate weight adjustment "within" as well as "between" behaviors. Perhaps the most analogous work is the hybrid dynamical systems approach taken by (Aaron et al 2002). In this work on low-level navigation, a dynamic "comfort level" is used to adjust the weighting parameters of repulsor fields surrounding environmental obstacles. This is another reactive method, and it does not attempt to calculate or minimize any costs.

Selection of the weights returns us to the cognitive model. Systems like Soar (Newell 1990), EPIC (Kieras and Meyer 1997) and ACT-R (Anderson and Lebiere 1998) all try to model not only the end result of human cognition, but also the process by which those results are reached. Not only can high-level planning be accomplished, but in theory the implementation should be very "human-like," making user interface more intuitive. This is very desirable if we have a human user critiquing trajectories returned by the system, who may give feedback such as, "No, be more careful." We chose to use ACT-R, although the other architectures could be adopted as well. In ACT-R, procedural rules fire in the presence of certain "chunks" of symbolic declarative memory. This is a serial system, using the bottleneck as a point of coordination among different cognitive modules. This makes it a very attractive option for implementing on a hardware system. Finally, ACT-R also has an extension, ACT-R/S, which supports spatial awareness, which we may leverage to extend the work (see Proposed Plan, below).

Given the agent's current goals, its environment, its state, and possibly other factors, the cognitive model is well-equipped to decide both the actions it needs to take and how it should perform them. "How" is linked to a weight set, which is then passed to the optimal controls trajectory planner. The trajectory planner then returns a trajectory that displays the dynamic characteristics sought by the cognitive model.

## Proposed Plan of Research

Our first step has been to characterize three "extreme" weight sets, where one of the three weights dominated the cost function. Using a numeric solver (Matlab's bvp4c) and a simple dynamic model, we generated sample curves for one and for five obstacles. Certain experimental parameters - for instance, the height and extent of the potential field used to create a penalty for approaching an obstacle - have been determined. Single-obstacle results generalized well to a multi-obstacle field.

Our next steps in the optimal controls side of the research are to extend the problem for free end time, to characterize behaviors resulting from less "extreme" weight sets, and then to group the weights into behaviors, so that they can be adjusted by the cognitive model.

When the optimal control trajectory planner is well-characterized, it will be time to begin programming the cognitive model. This will include extensive rules for recognizing features in the environment and how they impact goal acquisition. We also seek to add a domain-specific understanding of fuel economy: space satellite maneuvers, for example, must be more fuel-thrifty than easily refueled aircraft or ground robots. Further, we want the cognitive model to be able to collaborate with a human user, making adjustments to the trajectory based on the human's inputs.

Finally, we would like to leverage some of the perspective-taking work done at the Naval Research Laboratory (Trafton et al. 2004), enabling the agent to recognize a "hostile" obstacle and then to take cover behind a "good" obstacle.

## Metrics

We will perform a complexity analysis of the algorithms used to compute the optimal trajectories. We expect that worst-case examples will be too costly to run in real-time, but hope that average cases can be run on the order of seconds. Replanning in the field becomes a more tenable position in that case.

To compare our work with others', we will develop at least two dynamic models: a wheeled ground robot and an autonomous spacecraft. We will test the system across environments with varying degrees of uncertainty, as well as cases where fuel conservation is more or less important. We expect to find crossover points where, on one side, a regime of reactive behaviors is more successful, and on the other, the optimal trajectory planner is superior.

## Acknowledgements

would like to thank my advisor, Dr. Ella Atkins, for her continuing guidance and direction. This work was performed at the Naval Research Laboratory under funding from the Office of Naval Research under work order N0001404WX30001.

## References

Aaron, E., Sun, H., Ivancic, F., and Metaxas, D. 2002. A hybrid dynamical systems approach to intelligent low-level navigation. In *Proceedings of Computer Animation 2002*: 154-163.

Anderson, J.R. and Lebiere, C. 1998. The Atomic Components of Thought. Mahwah, NJ: Lawrence Erlbaum.

Kieras, D., and Meyer, D.E. 1997. An overview of the epic architecture for cognition and performance with application to human-computer interaction. *Human Computer Interaction* 12: 391-438.

Kirk, D.E. 1970. Optimal Control Theory: An Introduction. Englewood Cliffs, NJ: Prentice-Hall, Inc.

Latombe, J.C. 1991. Robot Motion Planning. Norwell, MA: Kluwer Academic publishers.

Newell, A. 1990. Unified Theories of Cognition. Cambridge, MA: Harvard University Press.

Ram, A., Arkin, R., Boone, G., and Pearce, M. 1994. Using genetic algorithms to learn reactive control parameters for autonomous robotic navigation. *Adaptive Behavior* 2(3): 277-304.

Santamaria, J.C. and Ram, A. 1997. Learning of Parameter-Adaptive Reaction Controllers for Robotic Navigation. In *Proceedings of the World Multiconference on Systemics, Cybernetics, and Informatics.*

Trafton, J.G., Schultz, A.C., Perzanowski, D., Bugajska, M.D., Adams, W., Cassimatis, N.L., and Brock, D.P. 2004. Children and robots learning to play hide and seek. *Cognitive Systems Research*, under review.

Velasquez, J.D. 1999. An emotion-based approach to robotics. In *Proceedings of the 1999 IEEE/RSJ International Conference on Intelligent Robots and Systems*: 235-240.

# Interesting Instance Discovery in Multi-Relational Data

Shou-de Lin
Information Sciences Institute, University of Southern California
4676 Admiralty Way, Suite 1001,Marina Del Rey, CA, 90292
sdlin@isi.edu
Advisor: Dr. Hans Chalupsky

The general area of machine discovery focuses on methods to use computers to perform or assist discovery tasks. Herbert Simon described it as "gradual problem-solving processes of searching large problem spaces for **incompletely defined goal objects**" [Simon, 1995, p.171]. Today machine discovery research falls into two major categories, scientific discovery and knowledge discovery and data mining (KDD). In this paper we propose a new research direction that lies somewhere in-between these two trends: we call it **interesting instance discovery (IID)** which aims at discovering interesting instances in large, multi-relational datasets.

There are three important characteristics for IID research: (1) Unlike scientific discovery and KDD, it aims at the discovery of particular interesting *instances* as opposed to general laws or patterns. (2) It is dealing with multi-relational data instead of numeric data that is best described as a relational graph or a semantic net. In such a network nodes represent objects and links represent relationships between them – see Figure 1 for an example of such a network from a bibliography domain. (3) Similar to KDD, it also focuses on data that are too large and complex to be analyzed manually by humans.

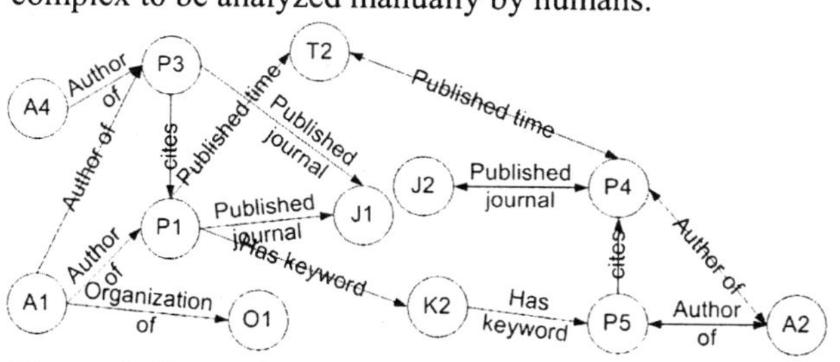


**Figure 1: Example multi-relational dataset from a bibliography domain represented as a graph**

The main challenge of IID arises from the fact that the term "interestingness" is vague so there is no consensus on how it can be measured. Therefore it is hard to find unbiased training examples for learning. This incompletely defined goal object makes IID a discovery problem instead of an easier supervised learning problem. In addition, the lack of universally accepted interestingness measures also creates a difficult problem on how to evaluate and verify the results of an IID program.

Our primary research goals try to address these challenges. They are as follows:

1. Investigate unbiased, universal features that (at least partially) can capture the "meaning" or essential characteristics of instances (i.e. the nodes and links in the network as shown in Figure 1) in multi-relational data.
2. Research how such features can be exploited to identify interesting instances.
3. Explore methodologies to verify IID results.

## Potential Applications for IID

We believe that interesting instances play an important role in many areas such as fraud detection, intrusion detection, criminal investigation or homeland security. Since illegal and covert activities are generally less frequent and more unusual than normal activities, we believe that they are more likely to generate "interesting" evidence. Therefore, an interesting entity or event might be a good indicator for a dangerous threat, a credit card fraud, an unauthorized computer intrusion, etc. To identify those special entities, we need a methodology that aims at identifying interesting *instances* instead of patterns. This is particularly important, since in situations such as the ones described above, we will often need to find things without knowing exactly what to look for.

More generally, we believe that interesting instances could serve as "inspirations" in the inspiration-driven discovery process depicted in Figure 2. In this process people first have some problems in mind but have no clear idea what a solution could be. Suddenly they notice something interesting (we call it inspiration) that triggers the formulation of some hypothesis (or potential solution). One then has to usually look for verification to either prove or disprove the hypothesis. Inspirations play an important role in this discovery process and history shows that interesting instances have often served as the inspiration for discoveries. For example, the various types of bird beaks Darwin saw on Galapagos triggered his idea of natural selection.

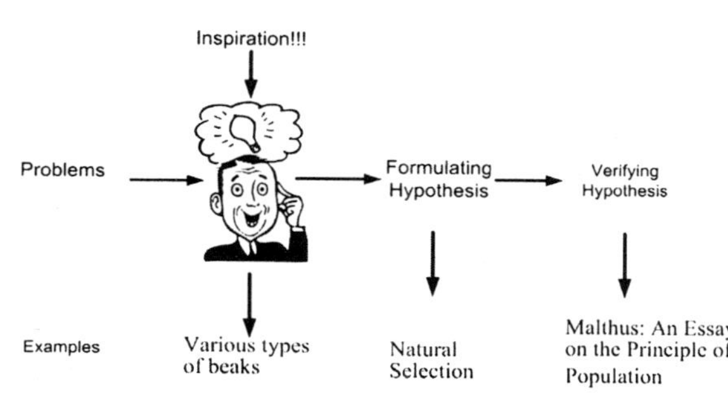


**Figure 2: The process of inspiration-driven discovery**

## Potential Solutions for IID

So far we have developed two unsupervised methods to address our first and second research goals. To find interesting instances without training examples, we need to think about what could be the general characteristics that make one instance more interesting than another. Here are two potential solutions:

(1) A node is interesting if it carries different, abnormal semantics compared to others [Lin & Chalupsky, 2003b].

(2) A path (or loop) is interesting if it is rare, or, if it occurs extremely frequently [Lin & Chalupsky, 2003a].

The challenge for (1) is how to capture the semantics of a node as well as to identify the ones with abnormal semantics. We observe that each path surrounding or emanating from a node carries certain semantics of the node and we quantify that by computing the statistical "contribution" of each type of path for a given node participating in it. We then find abnormal nodes by looking for outliers in the contribution domain. The basic idea is that a node is abnormal if it contributes differently than others with respect to the types of paths in which it participates.

The challenge for (2) is that in fact each path occurs exactly once in the network, thus they are all equally rare. We therefore define the rarity of a path as the reciprocal of "similar" paths in the network, and our program provides the users four different choices for path similarity.

In general we tried to tackle this problem by integrating insights from both symbolic and statistical AI. The logic representation for an instance is applied to generate feature sets and we then compute their influence statistically to use as feature values.

## Verification of IID Results

The lack of training examples and the incompletely defined goal object are two intrinsic characteristics that distinguish a discovery problem from a learning problem. These make a discovery problem not only more difficult to carry out but also to evaluate and verify its results. In IID we encounter a chicken and egg dilemma, since if there were unbiased ways to judge whether an instance is interesting or not, one could simply implement them to search for the solution. Lack of such universally agreed upon measures, however, prevents us from verifying discovered results directly. Since evaluation of IID results is still important, we want to investigate several indirect ways that could strengthen our belief in the validity of our IID system:

1. Rediscovery: The spirit of rediscovery lies in the verification of the methodology itself. Since there is no gold standard for verifying the results, one detour we can take is to check whether the methodology itself is applicable to a similar domain or data for which we have a better understanding. We have applied this method in the past by showing that our IID method could discover pre-defined events of interest (e.g., gang wars) in a synthetic dataset about organized crime.

2. Explanation-based discovery: The idea of this approach is to develop discovery systems that not only produce the discovered results but also generate explanation (in natural language or other human-understandable form) describing how and why the program discovered the results.

3. Minimum description length (MDL): MDL is widely applied to guide learning methods and might have similar uses for discovery. The basic idea behind it is that we prefer to store information in as little capacity as possible. The MDL criteria for verifying discovered pattern prefers simple patterns that cover the majority of data. We are investigating whether this idea can also be applied to verify IID results.

4. Exploiting independent sources: Knowledge can be represented in various forms as well as acquired from difference sources. Take the sentence "a bachelor is male" for example: one could prove it true by logical reasoning based on a certain existing ontology. Or one could say it is correct, since of a 1000 people asked 99% agreed with it. Or one could claim it is correct because there are 9 relevant documents generated by Google when using "bachelor is male" as a keyword. This shows that logical inference, statistic evidences or the Web could all serve as different ways to verify a particular piece of knowledge. Similarly, to verify a discovered result, one can try to explain the results from these views whichever are independent of the discovery methods. For example, in [Lin & Chalupsky, 2003b] we tried to verify our results on the KDD Cup 2003 bibliography dataset by (1) manually checking the semantics (note that our IID program does not understand the semantics of those relationships as human beings do) and (2) by trying to find supporting evidence on the Web.

## Summary

We proposed a new discovery problem called interesting instance discovery, which has applications in many areas such as homeland security or scientific discovery. Difficult challenges are what it means for an instance to be interesting as well as how to verify discovered results, but initial results show promising success [Lin & Chalupsky, 2003b]. Other issues we want to address are automatic explanation of results, how to handle temporal information and noise as well as scalability of our algorithms.

## References

[Lin & Chalupsky, 2003a] S. Lin and H. Chalupsky. "Unsupervised Link Discovery in Multi-relational Data via Rarity Analysis". In *Proceedings of the Third IEEE International Conference on Data Mining (ICDM '03)*. 2003.

[Lin & Chalupsky, 2003b] S. Lin and H. Chalupsky "Using Unsupervised Link Discovery Methods to Find Interesting Facts and Connections in a Bibliography Dataset". *SIGKDD Explorations*, 5(2): p.173-178. December 2003.

[Simon, 1995] H. Simon. "Machine Discovery". *Foundations of Science*, 1(2), p.171-200. 1995.

# Adaptive Algorithms for Routing and Traffic Engineering in Stochastic Networks

**Sudip Misra and B. John Oommen**

School of Computer Science
Carleton University, Ottawa, Ontario, Canada K1S5B6
E-mail: smisra_@scs.carleton.ca, oommen@scs.carleton.ca

**Abstract**

In this paper we report some of the research endeavors we are embarking on as part of the Doctoral research of the first author. We have already completed an investigation of some of the existing algorithms in the areas of Network Routing and Traffic Engineering, and we propose superior algorithms that would adapt to the changes in the environment in which they operate. In this attempt, we intend to use the theory of Learning Automata (LA) (Narendra and Thathachar, 1989; Obaidat *et al.* 2002) to address the problems we are investigating.

## Introduction

The primary goal of the proposed Doctoral research is to address some of the (serious) shortcomings present in existing Network Routing and Traffic Engineering Algorithms. We also hope to propose theoretically and empirically superior algorithms using suitable Artificial Intelligence (AI) techniques that would adapt to the changes in the environment in which they will operate. We propose to use LA to tackle these problems.

LA (Narendra and Thathachar, 1989; Obaidat *et al.* 2002) have been traditionally used to model biological learning systems. They have also been used for learning an optimal action out of several possible actions, which a random Environment offers. Upon choosing an action the learning automaton is either rewarded or penalized by the environment with a certain probability. As time progresses, the automaton eventually attempts to choose the best possible action. Learning is accomplished by actually interacting with the Environment and processing its responses to the actions that are chosen, while gradually converging toward an ultimate goal. The learning loop involves two entities, the *Random Environ*ment (RE) and a *Learning Automaton*.



Because of the vastness and diversity of the problems in the area of Networks, in the proposed research, to start with, we plan to address the following fundamental, yet challenging problems.

### Dynamic Algorithms for Single Source Shortest Path Tree Computation

The Single Source Shortest Path Problem consists of finding shortest paths from one node to all others in a network. This problem becomes interesting in dynamic scenarios where the topology and structure of the network constantly changes – i.e., the network links are inserted and dropped-drown from the graph, and the link-costs are continuously randomly changing. Several research papers exist in the literature for solving the problem in scenarios that are not very realistic in computer networks. The relatively difficult, but more realistic network scenarios are fully dynamic, i.e., where the routing algorithms should handle multiple heterogeneous changes in the structure of the networks, besides the changes in the link-costs. This has received very limited attention by researchers (Frigioni *et al.*, 2000; Ramalingam and Reps, 1996).

Prior to our work, there has been no solution for the dynamic single source shortest path problem using LA. In the past, LA solutions of various other problems have shown superior results. In this regard, we have already investigated this problem, and proposed superior LA-based solutions, when compared to the currently available ones. Our algorithms (Misra and Oommen, 2004) are the best known so far for solving the dynamic single source shortest path problem. The algorithm has been rigorously experimentally evaluated, and has been found to be a few orders of magnitude superior to the algorithms available in the literature. In particular, it can be used to find the shortest path within the "statistical" average network, which converges irrespective of whether there are new changes in link-costs or not. On the other hand, the existing algorithms will fail to exhibit such a behavior and would recalculate the affected shortest paths after each link-cost update. We have also designed and tested a new set of learning algorithms for maintaining software path routes using the theory of Generalized Pursuit Learning that pursues a set of actions at any time instant, instead of a single action. This set of algorithms has also demonstrated superiority of performance, when compared to the other algorithms.

### Dynamic Algorithms for All-Pairs Shortest Paths Problem

The problem of determining the All-pairs Shortest Paths Problem concerns finding shortest paths between all-pairs of vertices in a network. As in the previous problem, we propose to solve, using LA, the dynamic version of the problem where the topology and structure of the network constantly change when links go up and down randomly in a network, and the edge weights change randomly. Two popular existing dynamic all-pairs shortest path algorithms are described in (Cicerone *et al.*, 2003; Demetrescu and Italino, 2003).

### Adaptive QoS Routing Algorithms

Quality of Service (QoS) Routing Algorithms are concerned with selecting routing paths while meeting strict end-to-end service requirements involving resource constraints, while achieving optimum throughput in the network. Two basic considerations in QoS Routing in integrated services packet switched networks concern: (1) routing traffic with bandwidth guarantees, and (2) routing traffic with delay guarantees. Some of the algorithms proposed for solving the latter problems are: Widest-Shortest Path (WSP) (Guerin *et al.*, 1997), Shortest-Widest Path (SWP) (Wang and Crowcroft, 1996), and the Shortest-Distance Path (Bellman, 1958; Dijkstra, 1959) solutions.

We propose to solve this problem using LA under dynamic scenarios where the network links constantly go up and down, and the link-costs change randomly.

### Network Traffic Engineering Algorithms

The above-mentioned QoS Routing algorithms, viz., WSP, SWP, do not provide routing decisions considering the underlying traffic distribution in a network, and therefore can lead to under-utilization of network resources. Two recent Traffic Engineering Algorithms, which have gained widespread popularity are (1) Minimum Interference Routing Algorithm (MIRA) (Kodialam and Lakshman, 2000), and (2) Profile Based Routing (PBR) (Suri *et al.*, 2003). Both the algorithms are complex and are computationally intensive and are based on minimum-interference theory, and the multi-commodity flows.

In this research, we also propose to devise a relatively simpler LA-based Traffic Engineering algorithm for enabling the dynamic routing of bandwidth-guaranteed flows in carrier and ISP networks. The devised algorithm will hopefully perform better than the existing algorithms in terms of the amount of bandwidth routed, the number of requests rejected, and the amount of link capacities wasted.

## References


Bellman, R. 1958. On a Routing Problem. *Quart. Appl. Math* 16:87-90.

Cicerone, S., Stefano, G.D., Frigioni, D., and Nanni, U. 2003. A Fully Dynamic Algorithm for All-Pairs Shortest Paths. *Theoretical Computer Science* 297:83-102.

Dijkstra, E.W. 1959. A Note on two Problems in Connection with Graphs. *Numerische Math.* 1:269-271.

Demetrescu, C., and Italino, G.F. 2003. A New Approach to Dynamic All Pairs Shortest Paths. In Proc. 35th Annual ACM Symposium on Theory of Computing, 159-166. San Diego, USA.

Frigioni, D., Marchetti-Spaccamela, A., Nanni, U. 2000. Fully Dynamic Algorithms for Maintaining Shortest Paths Trees. *Journal of Algorithms* 34:251-281.

Guerin, R., Orda, A., and Williams, D. 1997. Qos Routing Mechanisms and OSPF Extensions. In Proceedings of the Global Internet Miniconference. Phoenix, Arizona, USA.

Kodialam, M., and Lakshman, T.V. 2000. Minimum Interference Routing with Applications to MPLS Traffic Engineering. In Proc. *IEEE INFOCOM,* 884-893. Tel Aviv, Israel.

Misra, S., and Oommen, B.J. 2004. Stochastic Learning Automata-Based Dynamic Algorithms for the Single-Source Shortest Path Problem. In Proc. of IEA/AIE'04. Ottawa, Ontario, Canada. Forthcoming.

Narendra, K.S., and Thathachar, M.A.L. 1989. *Learning Automata.* New Jersey: Prentice-Hall.

Ramalingam, G., and Reps, T. 1996. On the Computational Complexity of Dynamic Graph Problems. *Theoretical Computer Science* 158:233-277.

Obaidat, M.S., Papadimitriou, G.I., and Pomportsis, A.S. 2002. Learning Automata: Theory, Paradigms and Applications. *IEEE Trans. Syst., Man., and Cybern.* 32:706-709.

Suri, S., Waldvogel, M., Bauer, D., and Warkhede, P.R. 2003. Profile-Based Routing and Traffic Engineering. *Computer Communications* 26:351-365.

Wang, Z., and Crowcroft, J. 1996. Quality-of-Service Routing for Supporting Multimedia Applications. *IEEE Journal of Selected Areas in Communications* 14:1228-1234.

# Inducing Constraint-based Grammars using a Domain Ontology

**Smaranda Muresan**
Department of Computer Science
Columbia University
smara@cs.columbia.edu

In many knowledge intensive applications, there is a critical need to populate knowledge bases rapidly and to keep them up to date. Since the World Wide Web is a large source of information that continuously is being updated, a solution is to automatically acquire knowledge from text, which requires language understanding in a smaller or grater degree. The need for "rapid" text-to-knowledge acquisition imposes some critical conditions on the methods used: scalability and adaptability. Thus, there is a need to move from handcrafted grammars and hand-build systems to learning methods. However, most statistical and learning techniques have been applied only to restricted domains (e.g., air travel domain) or tasks (e.g., information extraction where the knowledge is limited to *a priori* relations and entities), reducing the variety of the acquired knowledge.

This thesis presents a framework for domain specific text-to-knowledge acquisition, with focus on medical domain. The main challenge of this domain is the abundance of linguistic phenomena that require both syntactic and semantic information in order to "understand" the meaning of the text, and thus to acquire knowledge. Examples include prepositional phrases, coordinations, noun-noun compounds and nominalizations, phenomena which are not well covered by existing syntactic or semantic parsers.

In my thesis, I propose a relational learning framework for the induction of a constraint-based grammar able to capture both syntax and aspects of meaning in an interleaved manner from a small number of semantically annotated data. The novelty of this framework is the learning method based on an ordered set of examples. This approach to learning follows the argument that language acquisition is an incremental process, in which simpler rules are acquired prior to complex ones. Several new theoretical concepts need to be tied together in order to make the approach feasible and theoretically sound: 1) a type of constraint-based grammar, called *lexicalized well-founded grammar*, which is learnable and able to capture large fragments of natural language; 2) a semantic representation, which we call *semantic molecule* that can be linked to the grammar and is simple enough to allow the relational learning of the grammar; 3) a small ordered set of semantically annotated examples, called *representative examples*, which is used as our training data; and 4) an ontology-based semantic interpretation encoded as a constraint at the grammar rule level ($\Phi_{onto}$), which refrains from full logical analysis of meaning, known to be intractable. On the application side, the grammar learning is used for rapid acquisition of medical terminological knowledge from text.

**Semantic molecule.** Given a natural language expression, $w$, we denote by $w\prime = h \bowtie b$ the semantic molecule of $w$, where $h$ is the head acting as a valence for semantic composition, and $b$ is the body acting as the semantic representation of $w$. The head is represented as a one level feature structure (i.e., feature values are atomic), while the body is a Canonical Logical Form given as a flat semantic representation, similar with Minimal Recursion Semantics (MRS). Unlike MRS, it uses as semantic primitives a set of frame-based atomic predicates of the form: *concept.attr=concept*, suitable for the interpretation on the ontology: *concept* corresponds to a frame in the ontology and *attr* is a slot of the frame, encoding either a property or a relation. For example, for the adjective "chronic" we have the following semantic molecule:

$$\begin{bmatrix} cat & a \\ head & X \\ mod & Y \end{bmatrix} \bowtie [X.isa = chronic, Y.Has\_prop = X]$$

The *cat* attribute (i.e., syntactic category), is mandatory for each molecule head, and is used as principle for grammar lexicalization. The composition of semantic molecules occurs at the grammar rule level via a constraint, $\Phi_{comp}$.

**Lexicalized Well-Founded Grammar and Representative Examples.** A *lexicalized well-founded grammar (LWFG)* is a Context-Free Grammar enhanced with a set of partial ordering relations among the nonterminals and with a set of semantic molecules associated with the set of terminals. $LWFG$ has the following properties: 1) the set of nonterminals is well-founded; 2) every nonterminal symbol is a left-hand side in at least one ordered nonrecursive rule, i.e. it is greater than all nonterminals from the right-hand side; 3) the empty string cannot be derived from any nonterminal symbol; and 4) all substrings, $w$ derived from a nonterminal have the same category (*cat*) of their semantic molecules, $w\prime$. Based on the first property the concept of representative examples can be defined, as given below, and the bottom up induction of the grammar is guaranteed. The second and the third properties ensure the termination condition for the induction process, while the last property guides the predicate invention during learning through the attribute *cat* of the semantic molecule's head.

For a $LWFG$, $G$, the *representative set*, $E_R$ of the sublanguage $E \subseteq L(G)$ has been defined and computed, such that: 1) $E_R$ is small (i.e., its size is smaller than the size of the set of grammar production rules); 2) $E_R$ is ordered based on the partial ordering relation among the nonterminals; and 3) if $G$ covers $E_R$, the grammar covers the sublanguage $E$. The $LWFG$ Induction Theorem in (Muresan, Muresan, & Klavans 2004) showed that $E_R$ can be used as a small semantic treebank for the bottom-up induction of a $LWFG$.

We encode the *lexicalized well-founded grammar* in the Definite Clause Grammar formalism, where each nonterminal is augmented with a semantic molecule, and each rule is augmented with two constraints: one for semantic composition, $\Phi_{comp}$, and one for ontological validation, $\Phi_{onto}$.

$$A(w, h \bowtie b) \Rightarrow B_1(w_1, h_1 \bowtie b_1), \ldots, B_n(w_n, h_n \bowtie b_n): \\ w = w_1 \ldots w_n,\ b = b_1, \ldots, b_n, \\ \Phi_{comp}(h, h_1, \ldots, h_n),\ \Phi_{onto}(b)$$

$\Phi_{comp}(h, h_1, \ldots, h_n)$, which is rule specific, is learned together with the grammar rule, based on the information stored both in the head and the body of the semantic molecules (but applied only to the heads). $\Phi_{onto}(b)$ is built based on a meta-interpreter with *freeze* (Muresan, Potolea, & Muresan 1998), asserting/validating the information from the body of the semantic molecules into/on the ontology.

**Learning Framework.** The induction of the constraint-based grammar is done incrementally, using a relational learning framework based on Inverse Entailment. Unlike other relational learning methods that use randomly-selected examples and for which the class of efficiently learnable rules is limited, our algorithm learns from an ordered set of representative examples, allowing a polynomial efficiency for more complex rules. Moreover, the size of this set is small and thus our algorithm is able to learn when no large annotated treebanks can be easily built. For each representative example a cover set algorithm performs two steps: 1) the most specific constraint rule generation using a robust bottom-up active chart parser and 2) the generation of the final hypothesis based on the most specific rule generalization using a set of heuristics. The process continues iteratively until all the representative examples are covered. The algorithm is linear on the length of the learned hypothesis.

**Input**: representative example $(w, w\prime)$:
(chronic # disease, [cat=n,head=Y] $\bowtie$
[X.isa=chronic,Y.Pn=X,Y.isa=disease])

Most specific constraint rule:
N1(h $\bowtie$ b) $\Rightarrow$ Adj(h1 $\bowtie$ b1), Noun(h2$\bowtie$ b2):
$\Phi_{comp}(h, h1, h2), \Phi_{onto}(b)$

**Output**: final grammar rule
N1(h $\bowtie$ b) $\Rightarrow$ Noun(h1 $\bowtie$ b1) : $\Phi_{comp}(h, h1), \Phi_{onto}(b)$
N1(h $\bowtie$ b) $\Rightarrow$ Adj(h1 $\bowtie$ b1), N1(h2 $\bowtie$ b2):
$\Phi_{comp}(h, h1, h2), \Phi_{onto}(b)$

The learning engine uses both annotated and unannotated sets of examples. First, the cover set algorithm is based only on the representative set that is semantically annotated (pairs of strings and their semantic molecules). During the generation of the final hypothesis, weakly annotated (only chunked), and optionally unannotated examples are used for the performance criteria in choosing the best rule. Also negative examples are used, if needed, given also as weakly annotated data.

During learning background knowledge is used, containing: 1) the ontology, 2) the lexicon that specifies for each word its concept in the ontology and its semantic molecule, 3) the previously learned grammar and 4) the previously learned compositional semantic constraints.

**Building a Terminological Knowledge Base.** In my thesis, the constraint-based grammar induction framework is applied to build a medical terminological knowledge base. I focus on definitions as my corpus since they are a rich source of conceptual information. This corpus is automatically extracted from on-line articles using our system DEFINDER (Muresan & Klavans 2002). Using the learned grammar and a bottom-up active chart parser, the definitions are semantically parsed. Ideally, a definition should contain the necessary and sufficient conditions to place a concept within a conceptual system. In this ideal setting after semantic parsing, a definition can be asserted to the knowledge base through the use of our meta-interpreter. However, a challenge of our corpus is that it is heterogeneous, containing many definitions for the same medical term. My solution is to merge these definitions, process in which I identify similarities and differences. After the merging process the definition is added to the knowledge base.

## Current Status and Plan for Completion

To date, the constraint-based grammar induction framework is implemented and has been applied to a fragment of the definitional corpus (e.g., complex noun phrases with prepositional phrases, active/pasive forms of verbs, coordinations). Moreover, the formal specification of the new theoretical concepts together with the proof of the $LWFG$ Induction Theorem was published in (Muresan, Muresan, & Klavans 2004).

Currently I am extending the grammar coverage to noun-noun compounds and nominalizations. I plan to implement a statistical refinement algorithm that will be applied after the grammar learning. I will evaluate the grammar induction given different settings: 1) with and without ontology constraints; 2) with and without statistical refinement.

The merging algorithm needs to be implemented. I plan to evaluate it using human judgments (for redundant and missing information). I will also perform an evaluation for identification of paraphrases by comparison to an existing state-of-the art paraphrase identification system.

## References

Muresan, S.; Muresan, T.; and Klavans, J. 2004. Inducing Constraint-based Grammars from a Small Semantic Trebank. In *Proceedings of AAAI Spring Symposium on Language Learning:An Interdisciplinary Perspective*. Stanford Univ., CA.

Muresan, T.; Potolea, R.; and Muresan, S. 1998. Amalgamating CCP with Prolog. *Scientific Journal of Politechnics University, Timisoara* 43(4).

Muresan, S., and Klavans, J. L. 2002. A Method for Automatically Building and Evaluating Dictionary Resources. In *Proceedings of LREC 2002*.

# Capturing User Intent for Information Retrieval

**Hien Nguyen**
Computer Science and Engineering Department
University of Connecticut
371 Fairfield Rd., Unit 2155 , Storrs, CT 06269-1155
hien@cse.uconn.edu

## Abstract

We study the problem of employing a *cognitive user model* for information retrieval in which *knowledge* about a user is captured and used for improving retrieval performance and user satisfaction. In this proposed research, we improve retrieval performance and user satisfaction for information retrieval by building a user model to capture *user intent* dynamically through analyzing behavioral information from retrieved relevant documents, and by combining captured user intent with the elements of an information retrieval system. We use decision theoretic principles and bayesian networks for building this model. The novelties of our approach lie with the fine-grained representation of the model, the ability to learn user knowledge incrementally and dynamically, the integration of user intent and system elements for improving retrieval performance and the unified evaluation framework to assess the accuracy of user intent captured and effectiveness of our model.

## Problem Statement

We study the problem of employing a *cognitive user model* for information retrieval in which *knowledge* about a user is captured and used for improving retrieval performance and user satisfaction. The problem of employing a user model for information retrieval has been investigated since the late 80s (Brajnik, Guida, & Tasso 1987) to address the difficulty of traditional information retrieval which is to satisfy a user's information needs by retrieving information with good quality quickly. It has many applications from information filtering, and text recommendation systems (e.g (Balabanovic 1998; Billsus & Pazzani 2000)). This problem is well-known for the challenges it poses to Information Retrieval (IR), and User Modeling (UM) communities. We have identified four primary challenges of this problem which are (i) *non-observability* of user knowledge (ii) *uncertainty* in modeling user interactions (ii) *vagueness* of a user's information needs (iv) and *dynamics* of user knowledge which changes over time as a result of new information, and temporal factors. These challenges come from the main problem of modeling a user in information seeking. Unfortunately, traditional IR does not offer a way to overcome these challenges because its framework supported very little users' involvement (Saracevic 1996). The thesis of this proposed research is *to improve retrieval performance and user satisfaction for IR by building a user model to capture user intent dynamically through analyzing behavioral information of retrieved relevant documents, and combine it with the elements of an IR system.* Our methodologies for this research are (i) to combine system-centered approaches and user-centered approaches by taking advantage of well-established evaluation frameworks in IR, and using the strength of knowledge representation techniques in artificial intelligence (AI) to build this model. As pointed out in (Saracevic, Spink, & Wu 1997), so far there has been a little crossover between IR and AI communities with regards to building user models for IR; and (ii) to create an unified evaluation framework which combines IR procedures with human computer interaction (HCI) usability testing to evaluate this model. We use decision theoretic (DT) principles and Bayesian networks (BNs) for building this model because the process of elicitation of user's preferences has long been studied in decision theory (Keeney & Raiffa 1976). BNs (Pearl 1988) offer a mathematically sound and intuitive representation to capture uncertainty which is a key factor in modeling a user. We seek to address the following questions:

- What factors of user intent should be captured? How can we capture, represent and use them for improving retrieval performance and user satisfaction?
- How can we combine user intent with elements of an IR system to maximize retrieval performance and user satisfaction?
- How do we evaluate the accuracy, and the effectiveness of our user model?

## Our approach

### User model architecture

We hypothesize that by decomposing user intent into 3 components: interests, preferences and context, our user model will help an IR system better adapt to the user than a model containing each factor alone. We refer to our user model as the *IPC user model* (Santos, Nguyen, & Brown 2001; Santos *et al.* 2003a; 2003b). In our model, we capture, represent and use the information on *what* a user is currently interested in (the Interests); *how* a query needs to be constructed (the Preferences) and *why* the user dwells on a search topic (the Context) to modify a user's queries pro-actively. We capture the Context, the Interests, and the Preferences aspects of a user's intent with a *context network* (*C*), an *interest set* (*I*), and a *preference network* (*P*). A context network (C) is a directed acyclic graph (DAG) that contains *concept nodes* and *relation nodes*. We construct *C* dynamically by finding the intersections of all retrieved relevant documents. Each element of *I* consists of an *interest concept* and *interest level*. We use a spreading activation algorithm on *C* to reason about a new *I*. We use a Bayesian network to represent *P* because of its expressiveness, and power of modeling uncertainty. *P* is used to represent a user's preferences over a class of tools used to modify a query. *P* is updated when a user gives feedback based on the frequency of tools used in the past. An original query graph is modified by adding relation and concept nodes from *C* given current *I* and tools inferred by *P*. In summary, *C* contains the knowledge used for modifying a user's query while *I* and *P* contain information to determine which knowledge should be included. In other words, we disambiguate a user's information needs by using information from *I, P, C*.

### Evaluation

The main questions needed to be answered in this evaluation are: (1) How accurate is the user intent that has been captured? (2) How competitive is the improvement obtained by using our user model compared with the improvement obtained by existing approaches? and (3) How effective is our user model is in terms of improving user satisfaction? In our initial study (Santos *et al.* 2003b), we evaluate the effects of our user model with regards to retrieval performance using a medical database with 521 records, over a set of 35 queries. This evaluation showed that precision and recall of the system with a user model are at least as good as without a user model. In some cases, it is actually better. In the pilot usability testing (Santos *et al.* 2003b), however, we were unable to find a significant effect of the user model on user or task efficiency. The main reasons are (i) small database and (ii) opaqueness of the system's behaviors.

## Future work

Our user model helps the target IR system adapt to the user's interests, preferences and context. Some difficulties may arise such as: degrading in retrieval performance due to a user's poor domain knowledge and difficulty in retrieving *new* information which contradicts with a user's interests. Fortunately, the target IR system consists of some elements containing built-in domain and system knowledge (e.g indexing scheme). Therefore, we propose to combine user intent and the elements of an IR system in a decision theoretic framework for improving retrieval performance and user satisfaction. The raw architecture of the proposed model takes user intent (*IPC model*), elements of an IR system, and the goal representing a user's purpose of using the IR system (e.g recall-driven or precision-driven) as inputs and formulates a decision tree which can be used to predict what is the best move for the user. The challenges for this task include (i) which attributes and values should be included and (ii) how to determine utility functions to maximize the effectiveness of our user model. We compare the effectiveness of our user model approach against Ide dec-hi with term frequency inverted document frequency using popular collections in IR such as CRANFIELD, NPL, MEDLINE, CACM, and TREC disks. The challenge here is to maintain the consistency, scalability and robustness of our approach for both small and large collections. Lastly is the extension of our usability testing which uses the results from the pilot study in (Santos *et al.* 2003b). The novelty of our future work is the combination of *system-centered* and *user-centered* approaches for representation and evaluation of our user model.

**Acknowledgement** This work was supported in part by the Advanced Research and Development Activity (ARDA)—U.S. Government. Any opinions, findings and conclusions or recommendations expressed in this material are those of the authors and do not necessarily reflect the views of the U. S. Government

## References

Balabanovic, M. 1998. Exploring versus exploiting when learning user models for text recommendation. *User Modeling and User-Adapted Interaction* 8:71–102.

Billsus, D., and Pazzani, M. J. 2000. User modeling for adaptive news access. *Journal of User Modeling and User-Adapted Interaction* 10:147–180.

Brajnik, G.; Guida, G.; and Tasso, C. 1987. User modeling in intelligent information retrieval. *Information Processing and Management* 23(4):305–320.

Keeney, R. L., and Raiffa, H. 1976. *Decision with Multiple Objectives: Preferences and Value Tradeoffs*. John Wiley and Sons.

Pearl, J. 1988. *Probabilistic Reasoning in Intelligent Systems: Networks of Plausible Inference*. Morgan Kaufmann, San Mateo, CA.

Santos, E.; Nguyen, H.; Zhao, Q.; and Hua, W. 2003a. User modelling for intent prediction in information analysis. In *Proceedings of the HFES-03*, 1034–1038.

Santos, E.; Nguyen, H.; Zhao, Q.; and Pukinskis, E. 2003b. Empirical evaluation of adaptive user modeling in a medical information retrieval application. In *Proceedings of the ninth User Modeling Conference*, 292–296.

Santos, E.; Nguyen, H.; and Brown, S. M. 2001. Kavanah: An active user interface information retrieval application. In *Proceedings of 2nd Asia-Pacific Conference on Intelligent Agent Technology*, 412–423.

Saracevic, T.; Spink, A.; and Wu, M. 1997. Users and intermediaries in information retrieval: What are they talking about? In *Proceedings of the 6th International Conference in User Modeling*, 43–54. Springer-Verlag Inc.

Saracevic, T. 1996. Relevance reconsidered. In *Proceedings of the Second International Conference on Conceptions of Library and Information Science: Integration in Perspective. Copenhagen: The Royal School of Librarianship*, 201–218.

# A Metric for the Evaluation of Imitation

**Amit Ramesh**
Computer Science Department
University of Southern California
Los Angeles, California 90089–0781
Email: amitr@cs.usc.edu

## Introduction

Stick out your tongue at a toddler and she will likely imitate by sticking out her tongue. Imitation is a very common and natural form of learning ubiquitous in humans. Dolphins and some species of apes also show imitative abilities, but only humans are attributed with 'true' imitation that enables the acquisition of entirely novel skills (Miklosi 1999). Imitation learning has become a very attractive topic for robotics researchers with the recent advent of humanoid robots and other highly articulated systems (Schaal 1999). Various research groups are working on the problem of endowing robots with the ability to learn and acquire new skills by imitation through demonstration (Atkeson & Schaal 1997; Billard & Matarić 2001; Ijspeert, Nakanishi, & Schaal 2001; Jenkins, Matarić, & Weber 2000; Matarić 2001; Nicolescu & Matarić 2001; Schaal 1997; 1999).

One of the primary issues in imitation is finding corresponding actions. When a dolphin nods its head to imitate the nod of its human instructor, it has somehow figured out what action is the one that best corresponds to the demonstration. Similarly, when a child claps her hands to imitate an adult, she has successfully deduced the action that closely corresponds to what the adult did. In both of these cases, the imitators were able to sieve through their motor programs and select a suitable action sequence. This suggests the presence of an intrinsic measure of similarity between actions, which leads us to the *correspondence problem*. The correspondence problem asks the question: "how similar is an action sequence to the demonstration?". This problem lies at the very core of imitation.

Despite the significance of this problem in imitation, there is almost no work to date in robotics that explicitly addresses it. The bulk of imitation research in robotics has focused on recognition of actions and learning and execution of motor programs. The correspondence problem has largely been implicitly "solved" by making use of very specific heuristic criteria appropriate for the considered task.

We are specifically interested in addressing the correspondence problem in imitation. Our aim is to develop a comprehensive *correspondence metric* that can provide a scalar measure of dissimilarity/distance between any pair of action sequences executed by agents with similar or different embodiments. By developing such a metric, we intend to provide a standardized means to quantitatively evaluate imitation. The metric can also be employed for action selection by an imitating agent. In addition, it can also benefit learning agents by serving as a gradient in action space.

The correspondence metric could also have applications in a wider range of domains. For example, it is directly relevant to animation research in synthesizing believable motion. It is also relevant to physical therapy, where it can be used to automatically monitor and evaluate the progress of patients. In the domain of reconfigurable robots, it may prove useful in the transfer of action strategies from one configuration to another very different in form.

## The Approach

We plan to address the correspondence problem by developing a metric that geometrically compares any two action sequences and provides a scalar measure of dissimilarity. In imitation, however, the notion of similarity is not purely geometric but also rests on the intentionality of the demonstrator. For example, in a task like reaching, only the end-point trajectory or even the end point itself, is of significance. Thus an effective similarity measure must ignore differences in all other limb and joint values between the demonstrator and the imitator. In order to make the metric comprehensive and incorporate the notion of intention, we plan to have a weighting mechanism that can be suitably instantiated to bias the metric based on what is significant in the demonstrator's action sequence. Aside from spatial variability, as in the example above, intentionality may also be reflected in temporal variability. The temporal profile of the action sequence may or may not be of significance in the demonstration. In order to address this issue, we plan to make the correspondence metric decomposable into spatial and temporal components. The temporal component can thus be selectively included in the dissimilarity computation.

In order to keep the metric sufficiently general, two additional properties are desirable, (1) reference frame independence: the two agents are not required to be in a common reference frame; and (2) scale invariance: scaling of any one agent does not affect the dissimilarity measure. The first property automatically implies translational and rotational invariance.

We are approaching the problem of developing the correspondence metric by first developing a *pose metric* that provides dissimilarity measures between static postures/poses of agents. We will then extend it to the comparison of action sequences.

In order to compare poses of agents, we require a uniform representation to encode them. We have chosen to treat agents as open kinematic chains, and therefore encode their structure in a *tree* termed *kinematic tree* or *k-tree*. We have introduced the following definitions.

**Definition 1 (k-tree)** *A* kinematic tree *or* k-tree *is an encoding of an open kinematic chain such that every link in the kinematic chain is represented by a unique edge in the k-tree.*

**Definition 2 (Pose)** *A* pose $p$ *of a k-tree* $t$ *is an assignment of the ordered pair* $\langle n_i, l_i \rangle$ *to every edge* $e_i$ *of* $t$. $n_i$ *is a unit normal that is the orientation of the link, represented by* $e_i$*, in the world coordinate frame.* $l_i$ *is the length of the link represented by* $e_i$.

**Definition 3 (Homeomorphic pose class)** *A* homeomorphic pose class $P$ *is a set of poses such that for any pair of poses* $p, q \in P$*, if* $t_p$ *is the k-tree of* $p$ *and* $t_q$ *the k-tree of* $q$ *then* $t_p$ *and* $t_q$ *are* homeomorphic.

We have developed a pose distance algorithm that takes a pair of poses from a homeomorphic pose class as input, and computes a distance measure between the poses. The algorithm first realigns the two poses and brings them to a common reference frame, then partitions the edges of the individual k-trees of the two poses, then uses the underlying homeomorphism between the k-trees of the two poses to find matchings between the partitions of the k-trees. Dissimilarity measures are computed between every such pair and these are summed up to obtain the dissimilarity measure for the pair of poses. The distance measure computed by the pose distance algorithm satisfies properties (1) and (2) desired of the correspondence metric. We have successfully applied the pose metric across various poses of a human, the Sony AIBO dog, and a simulated dolphin-like skeleton.

We have recently used multi-dimensional scaling (MDS) followed by principal component analysis (PCA) to project poses as distributions on a common space. We are investigating the use of transportation cost functions in order to provide measures of pose distance without the homeomorphic pose class constraint.

## Related Work

Nehaniv et al. (Nehaniv & Dautenhahn 2000; 2001) have used abstract algebra as a means to formalize the correspondence problem. Their work provides an abstraction where, given elementary correspondences, one can employ a suitable metric and analyze more complex sequences. The metric is crucial to the process of determining correspondences, but their work does not address the issue of determining a metric. Alissandrakis et al. (Alissandrakis, Nehaniv, & Dautenhahn 2002; 2003) have explored some metrics for this formal framework and applied them to different agents. However these metrics are only suitable to the specific problem considered. We are interested in developing a generalized metric that can be applied to different domains.

## References

Alissandrakis, A.; Nehaniv, C. L.; and Dautenhahn, K. 2002. Imitating with alice: Learning to imitate corresponding actions across dissimilar embodiments. *IEEE Transactions on Systems, Man, and Cybernetics—Part A: Systems and Humans* 32(4):482–496.

Alissandrakis, A.; Nehaniv, C. L.; and Dautenhahn, K. 2003. Synchrony and perception in robotic imitation across embodiments. *IEEE International Symposium on Computational Intelligence in Robotics and Automation* 32(4):923–930.

Atkeson, C. G., and Schaal, S. 1997. Robot learning from demonstration. *International Conference on Machine Learning* 12–20.

Billard, A., and Matarić, M. J. 2001. Learning human arm movements by imitation: Evaluation of biologically-inspired connectionist architecture. In *Robotics and Autonomous Systems*, volume 37:2-3, 145–160.

Ijspeert, A. J.; Nakanishi, J.; and Schaal, S. 2001. Trajectory formation for imitation with nonlinear dynamical systems. In *Proceedings of the IEEE/RSJ International Conference on Intelligent Robots and Systems (IROS 2001)*, 752–757.

Jenkins, O. C.; Matarić, M. J.; and Weber, S. 2000. Primitive-based movement classification for humanoid imitation. In *First IEEE-RAS International Conference on Humanoid Robotics (Humanoids-2000)*.

Matarić, M. J. 2001. Visuo-motor primitives as a basis for learning by imitation: Linking perception to action and biology to robotics. In Dautenhahn, K., and Nehaniv, C., eds., *Imitation in Animals and Artifacts*, 392–422. MIT Press.

Miklosi, A. 1999. The ethological analysis of imitation. *Biological Review* 74:347–374.

Nehaniv, C. L., and Dautenhahn, K. 2000. Of hummingbirds and helicopters: An algebraic framework for interdisciplinary studies of imitation and its applications. *Interdisciplinary Approaches to Robot Learning, World Scientific Series in Robotics and Intelligent Systems* 24, World Scientific Press:136–161.

Nehaniv, C. L., and Dautenhahn, K. 2001. Like me? – measures of correspondence and imitation. *Cybernetics and Systems: An International Journal* 32(1-2):11–51.

Nicolescu, M., and Matarić, M. J. 2001. Learning and interacting in human-robot domains. *Special Issue of IEEE Transactions on Systems, Man, and Cybernetics, Part A: Systems and Humans* 31(5):419–430.

Schaal, S. 1997. Learning from demonstration. *Advances in Neural Information Processing Systems* 9:1040–1046.

Schaal, S. 1999. Is imitation learning the route to humanoid robots? *Trends in Cognitive Sciences* 3(6):233–242.

# Planning and Verification for Stochastic Processes with Asynchronous Events

**Håkan L. S. Younes**
Computer Science Department
Carnegie Mellon University
Pittsburgh, PA 15213, USA
lorens@cs.cmu.edu

**Abstract**

We consider a general model of stochastic discrete event systems with asynchronous events, and propose to develop efficient algorithms for verification and control of such systems.

## Introduction

Dynamic systems consisting of concurrent interacting processes present a broad spectrum of uncertainty, including uncertainty in the occurrence of exogenous events and the outcome of actions selected by a control policy. In this work, we are concerned with stochastic discrete event systems with asynchronous events, and where the delay from when an event is enabled until it triggers is governed by an arbitrary positive distribution.

As an example, consider a network of computers. Each computer can be in one of two states: working or failed. Failure is caused by the triggering of an exogenous event, with the time from when a computer starts working until it fails being a random variable associated with some positive distribution, for example a Weibull distribution.

In addition to exogenous events, we can have controllable events (actions) that can be enabled or disabled at will by a control policy. For the network of computers, we could introduce a reboot action for each computer that can restore a failed computer to the working state. Given a system of this type, we are interested in generating a control policy for the system satisfying some objective, which can be to either satisfy a formula in a temporal stochastic logic or to maximize expected reward.

We conjecture that asynchronous stochastic decision processes with general delay distributions exhibit sufficient structure as to allow computationally tractable algorithms for policy generation. We will prove this by developing efficient algorithms for probabilistic and decision theoretic planning with complex stochastic domain models. As part of this effort, we will also consider the problem of verifying properties of stochastic discrete event systems, and we will develop scalable verification algorithms for such systems.

The problem of planning under uncertainty has been addressed by researchers in operations research, artificial intelligence (AI) and control theory, among others. Numerous approaches have been proposed, but current methods for planning under uncertainty cannot handle the full generality of the model we are considering. Guestrin, Koller, & Parr (2002) have shown that factored Markov decision processes (MDPs) can be used to handle concurrent actions, but this approach is restricted to sets of actions executed in synchrony. Continuous-time MDPs (Howard 1960) can be used to model asynchronous systems, but are restricted to events and actions with exponential delay distributions. Semi-Markov decision processes (SMDPs) (Howard 1971) lift the restriction on delay distributions, but cannot model asynchrony.

We adopt the generalized semi-Markov process (GSMP), first introduced by Matthes (1962), as our domain model. The GSMP is an established formalism in queuing theory for modeling continuous-time stochastic discrete event systems (Glynn 1989). Intuitively, a GSMP can be viewed as the composition of concurrent semi-Markov processes, and is a natural model for systems with asynchronous components.



## Accomplishments to Date

The idea of probabilistic planning with GSMP domain models was first explored by Younes & Musliner (2002) in an effort to extend CIRCA (Musliner, Durfee, & Shin 1995)—an architecture for real-time control—to handle stochastic information in the form of probability distributions over event trigger times. CIRCA generates control policies incrementally, using a verifier module to ensure that each expansion of a policy remains safe relative some safety constraints specified by the user. Younes & Musliner developed a plan verification algorithm for GSMP domain models based on sequential acceptance sampling (Wald 1945).

The plan verification algorithm was later generalized by Younes & Simmons (2002) to handle time-bounded properties expressed in CSL (Aziz *et al.* 2000; Baier *et al.* 2003), a logic formalism for expressing temporal and probabilistic properties of stochastic systems. Younes *et al.* (2004) compare this statistical approach for CSL model checking with numerical solution techniques for continuous-time Markov chains based on uniformization (Baier *et al.* 2003) and show that the statistical approach scales better with an increase in the size of the state space, while the numerical approach is less sensitive to decreases in error tolerance.

A general framework for policy generation in continuous-time stochastic domains with asynchronous events and actions was presented by Younes, Musliner, & Simmons (2003) based on the Generate, Test and Debug paradigm (Simmons 1988). The test step is carried out using the statistical verification algorithm mentioned above making it possible to plan for arbitrary time-bounded CSL goals. Concrete techniques for representing and generating initial policies using an existing deterministic temporal planner, robust sample path analysis techniques for extracting failure scenarios, and efficient policy repair techniques were presented in a followup paper (Younes & Simmons 2004a). These techniques have been implemented in TEMPASTIC, a novel planner accepting domain descriptions in an extension of PDDL developed by Younes (2003) and using VHPOP (Younes & Simmons 2003) as a deterministic planner.

## Remaining Research Effort

While TEMPASTIC represents a step towards practical planning algorithms for complex stochastic domains with asynchronous events, there is still work to be done to improve its efficiency. We need to develop heuristics for selecting failure scenarios that best will guide the search towards a policy satisfying a given CSL goal. We are also exploring ways to improve the efficiency of the verification algorithm, including distributed algorithms.

In addition to research on probabilistic planning, we are pursuing decision theoretic approaches as well. For this purpose, we will introduce the generalized semi-Markov decision process (GSMDP) as a model for decision theoretic planning with asynchronous events and actions. We need to develop practical policy generation algorithms for GSMDPs, and are currently exploring various possible directions for this research. In a recent paper (Younes & Simmons 2004b) we propose using phase-type distributions (Neuts 1981) to approximate general distributions in the GSMDP model, which enables us to use standard MDP techniques to approximately solve GSMDPs. We also expect Monte Carlo integration and value function approximation using nearest neighbor learning, previously used for solving partially observable MDPs (Thrun 2000), to be useful for solving GSMDPs.

## References


Aziz, A.; Sanwal, K.; Singhal, V.; and Brayton, R. 2000. Model-checking continuous-time Markov chains. *ACM Transactions on Computational Logic* 1(1):162–170.

Baier, C.; Haverkort, B. R.; Hermanns, H.; and Katoen, J.-P. 2003. Model-checking algorithms for continuous-time Markov chains. *IEEE Transactions on Software Engineering* 29(6):524–541.

Glynn, P. W. 1989. A GSMP formalism for discrete event systems. *Proceedings of the IEEE* 77(1):14–23.

Guestrin, C.; Koller, D.; and Parr, R. 2002. Multiagent planning with factored MDPs. In *Advances in Neural Information Processing Systems 14: Proc. 2001 Conference*. Cambridge, MA: The MIT Press. 1523–1530.

Howard, R. A. 1960. *Dynamic Programming and Markov Processes*. New York, NY: John Wiley & Sons.

Howard, R. A. 1971. *Dynamic Probabilistic Systems*, volume II. New York, NY: John Wiley & Sons.

Matthes, K. 1962. Zur Theorie der Bedienungsprozesse. In *Trans. Third Prague Conference on Information Theory, Statistical Decision Functions, Random Processes*, 513–528. Publishing House of the Czechoslovak Academy of Sciences.

Musliner, D. J.; Durfee, E. H.; and Shin, K. G. 1995. World modeling for the dynamic construction of real-time control plans. *Artificial Intelligence* 74(1):83–127.

Neuts, M. F. 1981. *Matrix-Geometric Solutions in Stochastic Models: An Algorithmic Approach*. Baltimore, MD: Johns Hopkins University Press.

Simmons, R. G. 1988. A theory of debugging plans and interpretations. In *Proc. Seventh National Conference on Artificial Intelligence*, 94–99. AAAI Press.

Thrun, S. 2000. Monte Carlo POMDPs. In *Advances in Neural Information Processing Systems 12: Proc. 1999 Conference*. Cambridge, MA: The MIT Press. 1064–1070.

Wald, A. 1945. Sequential tests of statistical hypotheses. *Annals of Mathematical Statistics* 16(2):117–186.

Younes, H. L. S., and Musliner, D. J. 2002. Probabilistic plan verification through acceptance sampling. In *Proc. AIPS-02 Workshop on Planning via Model Checking*, 81–88.

Younes, H. L. S., and Simmons, R. G. 2002. Probabilistic verification of discrete event systems using acceptance sampling. In *Proc. 14th International Conference on Computer Aided Verification*, volume 2404 of *LNCS*, 223–235. Springer.

Younes, H. L. S., and Simmons, R. G. 2003. VHPOP: Versatile heuristic partial order planner. *Journal of Artificial Intelligence Research* 20:405–430.

Younes, H. L. S., and Simmons, R. G. 2004a. Policy generation for continuous-time stochastic domains with concurrency. In *Proc. Fourteenth International Conference on Automated Planning and Scheduling*. AAAI Press.

Younes, H. L. S., and Simmons, R. G. 2004b. Solving generalized semi-markov decision processes using continuous phase-type distributions. In *Proc. Nineteenth National Conference on Artificial Intelligence*. AAAI Press.

Younes, H. L. S.; Kwiatkowska, M.; Norman, G.; and Parker, D. 2004. Numerical vs. statistical probabilistic model checking: An empirical study. In *Proc. 10th International Conference on Tools and Algorithms for the Construction and Analysis of Systems*, volume 2988 of *LNCS*, 46–60. Springer.

Younes, H. L. S.; Musliner, D. J.; and Simmons, R. G. 2003. A framework for planning in continuous-time stochastic domains. In *Proc. Thirteenth International Conference on Automated Planning and Scheduling*, 195–204. AAAI Press.

Younes, H. L. S. 2003. Extending PDDL to model stochastic decision processes. In *Proc. ICAPS-03 Workshop on PDDL*, 95–103.

# Intelligent Systems Demonstrations

# Intelligent Systems Demonstration: The Secure Wireless Agent Testbed (SWAT)

**Gustave Anderson** and **Andrew Burnheimer** and **Vincent Cicirello*** and **David Dorsey** and **Saturnino Garcia** and **Moshe Kam** and **Joseph Kopena** and **Kris Malfettone** and **Andy Mroczkowski** and **Gaurav Naik** and **Max Peysakhov** and **William Regli** and **Joshua Shaffer** and **Evan Sultanik** and **Kenneth Tsang** and **Leonardo Urbano** and **Kyle Usbeck** and **Jacob Warren**
Department of Computer Science and Department of Electrical and Computer Engineering
Drexel University, 3141 Chestnut Street
Philadelphia, PA 19104

## Abstract

We will demonstrate the Secure Wireless Agent Testbed (SWAT), a unique facility developed at Drexel University to study integration, networking and information assurance for next-generation wireless mobile agent systems. SWAT is an implemented system that fully integrates: 1) mobile agents, 2) wireless ad hoc multi-hop networks, and 3) security. The demonstration will show the functionality of a number of decentralized agent-based applications, including applications for authentication, collaboration, messaging, and remote sensor monitoring. The demonstration will take place on a live mobile ad hoc network consisting of approximately a dozen nodes (PDAs, tablet PCs, and laptops) and hundreds of mobile software agents.

## Description of the SWAT

The Secure Wireless Agent Testbed (SWAT) is a unique facility developed at Drexel University to study integration, networking and information assurance for next-generation wireless mobile agent systems (Sultanik *et al.* 2003). It is the only implemented system that fully integrates: 1) mobile agents, 2) wireless ad hoc multi-hop networks, and 3) security.

In the SWAT infrastructure, mobile agents manage keys, assess network traffic patterns, analyze host behaviors, revoke access rights for suspicious agents, users, or hosts, adaptively re-route traffic at the network layer to improve the information integrity of the overall system, and provide the implementation framework for a number of decentralized user applications, including authentication, collaboration, messaging, and remote sensor monitoring. SWAT is currently able to support industrial-strength, fielded, mobile agent architectures that include, but are not limited to, the Extendable Mobile Agent Architecture (EMAA) from Lockheed Martin's Advanced Technology Laboratories (Lentini *et al.* 1998) and Cougaar (BBN Technologies 2003). The agent-based applications of the SWAT currently include: a group display GUI that shows a list of all members in a user group, and tracks the creation, joining, and leaving of groups; a secure, multi-group whiteboard application that enables users to communicate notes and map annotations within their groups; an application that employs agents to carry secure audio communications similar to two-way radios; agent-based network and resource monitoring; among others.

SWAT enables agents to reason about and react to network dynamics (Artz, Peysakhov, & Regli 2003). It is implemented for ad hoc network environments, in which hosts have the ability to dynamically identify routes and forward packets between hosts that are not within direct wireless range of each other and which may require multi-hop ad hoc routes. In the SWAT framework, agents are able to modify the network state, make decisions about their itineraries based on network topology, and adapt their communication modalities to avoid network congestion. SWAT is not limited to any particular ad hoc routing protocol. Currently, there are few wireless ad hoc routing algorithms that have been deployed live; most have only been simulated. For this reason, SWAT has created the Topology-based Secure Ad hoc Routing (TSAR) Protocol which is an authenticated and encrypted, proactive routing protocol that supports secure multi-hop routes (Artz *et al.* 2003).

SWAT addresses the need for a mobile agent information assurance framework that includes cryptography and the ability for different groups of agents to generate secure communications channels within the overall agent community. Agents must be able to reason about security groups and communications in a manner that allows them to adapt to a dynamic security environment in which hosts may become compromised, networks may get attacked, and malicious agents may need to be identified and contained. SWAT provides agents with secure multi-layer, agent-to-agent group communication on resource-constrained devices. The security framework uses a combination of symmetric and public-key cryptography to support encrypted communication at both the network and the agent application layers, including support for secure group communication. To accomplish this, established security technologies have been integrated into SWAT. SWAT is the first complete integration of tools for key generation and management; secure group communication; user revocation through the use of a security mediator; and en/decryption of traffic on the network layer. The cryptographic tools integrated in the current implementation of SWAT include: CLIQUES, the Tree Group Diffe-Hellman (TGDH) algorithm, Spread (Amir & Stanton

*Contact author: cicirello@cs.drexel.edu

1998), Secure Spread (Amir *et al.* 2002), a SEcurity Mediator (SEM) (Boneh *et al.* 2001), and IPSec.

Each host in the SWAT is an integration of the agent system, the network, and security infrastructure. The agent framework contains both mobile agents, and static agents (services). The security components of a host include group key management, and group membership revocation, enforced by a security mediator. The agent framework is connected to the security components, enabling an agent (or the whole agent system) to join or leave a group, with the permission to join controlled by the security mediator. The network components enable secure point-to-point communication for the agent framework, as well as reliable group communication for the security components. Point-to-point communication is implemented using standard TCP/IP and is secured using IPSec. All network communication is routed through a multi-hop ad hoc routing protocol on a wireless network.

The SWAT infrastructure consists of PDAs (mostly HP iPAQs), tablet PCs, and laptops on an 802.11b wireless network with ad hoc routing. SWAT is developed on the Familiar Linux distribution, using the Intel Strong Arm architecture found within the HP iPAQ h3800 series PDAs. A similarly configured Linux environment exists for the x86 architecture, to incorporate other portable devices to the testbed such as laptop and tablet PCs. SWAT makes use of Cisco Systems' Aironet 350 series PCMCIA cards across all platforms. We have selected the Aironet cards based on empirical studies, demonstrating that the Aironet cards have the best performance in ad hoc mode compared to network cards of other brands.

## Demonstration Scenarios

SWAT is currently being tested and validated in a number of practical scenarios. The main functional objective of SWAT is to provide users with tools for distributed, mobile, collaborative work and communication. There are many practical applications of such a system (e.g., police personnel at a sports event, medical personnel at an accident scene, emergency responders to a natural disaster). One possible SWAT application may be in the homeland security domain, where first-responders react to civil emergencies and "bring their own network." Using SWAT they will be able to communicate and transfer information more effectively, and in ways not possible with existing technologies.

Throughout the conference Demo Program, SWAT will be demonstrated continuously. A demonstration will begin with a large set of hosts in the staging area, familiarizing the audience with the platforms. After a review of the equipment, we shall demonstrate group functionality through group creation and "join" and "leave" operations. Certain SWAT demonstrators wielding wireless components would leave the area, and demonstrate use of the whiteboard application. The whiteboard application will also show the integration of GPS as a backdrop for notations sent to group members (given adequate GPS radio signal reception inside the building). Two-way radio communication features will be used to show coordination, and for demonstrating secure routing of messages according to group structure. Revocation functionality will be demonstrated through the revocation of agents and users both within the staging area, and away "in the field". Streaming video and audio will be sent from remote hosts to the staging area, and hosts may be "knocked out of commission" as they suffer power and network failures. Different host topologies will be demonstrated in order to impose network "stresses" on the routing protocol and on the network-aware reasoning agents. A Sharp Zaurus handheld PDA will attempt to decipher transmissions and disturb operation of the secure SWAT network.

## References


Amir, Y., and Stanton, J. 1998. The spread wide area group communication system. Technical Report CNDS-98-4, The Center for Networking and Distributed Systems, John Hopkins University. http://www.cnds.jhu.edu/publications/.

Amir, Y.; Kim, Y.; Nita-Rotaru, C.; and Tsudik, G. 2002. On the performance of group key agreement protocols. In *Proceedings of the 22nd IEEE International Conference on Distributed Computing Systems*. An extended version is available as Technical Report CNDS-2001-5.

Artz, D.; Burnheimer, A.; Regli, W.; and Kam, M. 2003. The topology-aware secure ad hoc routing protocol. Technical report, Department of Computer Science, Drexel University.

Artz, D.; Peysakhov, M.; and Regli, W. 2003. Network meta-reasoning for information assurance in mobile agent systems. In *Proceedings of the Eighteenth International Joint Conference on Artificial Intelligence*, 1455–1457.

BBN Technologies. 2003. Cougaar architecture document. http://docs.cougaar.org.

Boneh, D.; Ding, X.; Tsudik, G.; and Wong, M. 2001. A method for fast revocation of public key certificates and security capabilities. In *Proceedings of the 10th USENIX Security Symposium*, 297–308.

Lentini, R.; Rao, G. P.; Thies, J. N.; and Kay, J. 1998. Emaa: An extendable mobile agent architecture. In *AAAI Workshop on Software Tools for Developing Agents*.

Sultanik, E.; Artz, D.; Anderson, G.; Kam, M.; Regli, W.; Peysakhov, M.; Sevy, J.; Belov, N.; Morizio, N.; and Mroczkowski, A. 2003. Secure mobile agents on ad hoc wireless networks. In *Proceedings of the 15th Innovative Applications of Artificial Intelligence Conference (IAAI-03)*, 129–136.

# Multi-agent System Development: Design, Runtime, and Analysis

**K. S. Barber, J. Ahn, K. Fullam, T. Graser, N. Gujral, D. C. Han, D. N. Lam, R. McKay, J. Park, M. Vanzin**

The Laboratory for Intelligent Processes and Systems
Electrical and Computer Engineering
The University of Texas at Austin
{barber, jsahn, kfullam, graser, ngujral, dhan, dnlam, rmckay, jisun, vanzin}@lips.utexas.edu

## Introduction

Dynamic and unexpected events are defining characteristics of numerous application domains. These environments often require decision-makers to solve many problems with insufficient time and resources. To effectively assess options, decision-makers require situation analysis and decision-support tools that model the dynamism of these environments to make rapid, robust decisions. Autonomous agents and multi-agent systems satisfy these requirements for decision-making in dynamic environments.

Developing a multi-agent system (MAS) is a challenging task, considering sophisticated agent interactions and uncertain environmental dynamics and domain requirements. This demonstration addresses the comprehensive development process for multi-agent systems; illustrating tools for the initial design of the agent system, the capabilities encoded in the individual agents, and analysis tools that enhance developer comprehension of system behavior.

## Design Tools

Two design activities supported by this research are categorization and comparison of agent technologies under a common ontology and construction of agent architectures through the selection of technologies that fulfill the designer's requirements. Developing agent systems requires the proper selection of agent technologies where selection is based on adherence to the agent architecture structure and satisfaction of domain and installation requirements. MAS designers are guided by specific desired "competencies" (capabilities) in the context of a particular domain, for the entire system and/or a particular agent. Thus, agent technologies (e.g., belief revision, organization, planning, etc.) are developed or selected for a MAS by considering their application to a particular domain and their ability to fulfill desired competencies.

The Technology Portfolio Manager (TPM) allows a designer to view and compare agent technologies with respect to both competencies provided and domains supported (Barber et al. 2004). The TPM is populated with four sets of information and the relationships between these sets: agent competencies, agent infrastructure services, domain tasks in a particular domain (in this case UAV surveillance) and agent technologies. Furthermore, the tool allows the designer to interrogate the repository from the perspective of: (1) technologies (displaying related domain tasks and competencies satisfied by the selected technologies), (2) domain tasks (displaying related competencies and technologies capable of delivering selected domain tasks), and (3) agent competencies (displaying related domain tasks and technologies capable of satisfying the selected competencies). The TPM provides the designer with a tool for browsing a repository of agent technology specifications allowing the designer to evaluate how well different technologies map to the desired agent competencies or infrastructure services.

The Designer's Agent Creation and Analysis Toolkit (DACAT) aids the designer in constructing agent designs based on the agent competencies (Barber and Lam, 2003b). Metrics such as component complexity and cohesion are prescribed to evaluate and compare agent designs based on agent competencies. Tasks and task dependencies resulting from inclusion of respective competencies in the agent architecture (design) can be analyzed and improved. This type of structural analysis can be performed during the architecting process to assist in forming agent components, during development (when more dependency details are known), or as a method to survey existing agent architectures.

## Runtime – Agent Competencies

This demonstration also illustrates some novel methods (technologies loaded in TPM) for fulfilling agent competencies, such as belief maintenance and action selection, in the domain of UAV surveillance of military targets.

Accurate beliefs are required for an agent to correctly select actions. This demonstration presents a belief revision algorithm (Fullam 2003) based on information valuation "policies" accounting for information source reliability, information corroboration, information source certainty, and information timeliness. An algorithm based on policies for information valuation provides justification for derived beliefs by identifying influential policies as reasons why more valuable information is given priority over less valuable information. This research makes a major contribution toward producing quality beliefs for decision-making by examining information quality assessment in terms of a number of factors, not only information source reliability. In addition, basing information valuation on logical policies promotes traceability in algorithm construction. Justification for derived beliefs is provided, a useful feature for any domain in which humans are the ultimate decision-making authority.

In addition to the underlying belief revision algorithm, the organization of the agents affects which beliefs are adopted or revised. To maintain autonomy, an agent should control formation of its beliefs. The degree of an agent's belief autonomy is its degree of dependence on others to build its beliefs, which can be controlled by selecting the most appropriate agents on which to rely. Large, open environments make finding the most appropriate information sources difficult since agents may only know about a limited number of sources and sources may enter and leave the system. Finding partners can be facilitated by decomposing the agents in a system into small groups so that the scale and openness can be efficiently managed within the group. The partner-finding process benefits from trustworthiness information with respect information quality assurance, increasing the agents' goal achievement probability (Barber and Park, 2004).

Agents should behave in a rational manner, meaning an agent should perform actions that enable it to achieve its goals. Action selection is complicated by the existence of multiple goals of different priorities and interaction with other agents. In order to account for all these factors in the UAV demonstration, action selection is performed in a decision-theoretic fashion. Goal priorities are represented in the expected rewards obtained through goal achievement while agent coordination is performed through transformations on the reward and cost structure the agent uses in its action selection process (Barber and Han, 2003).

## Analysis Tools

Software comprehension is the analysis of the implementation and extraction of a design, which ideally should be equivalent to the original design. In addition to extracting a design, software comprehension for MAS involves understanding the behaviors of the constituent agents with respect to their individual goals. Knowing the reasons for agent behaviors in the implementation is important for the development of MAS because those behaviors must agree with designed behaviors. The Tracing Method can be used to validate the implemented behaviors against the designed behaviors as well as facilitating agent software comprehension (Barber and Lam, 2003a).

The Tracer tool aims to automate the developer's task of analyzing run-time data and relating it to models of agent structure and behavior. The method involves logging agent behavior during execution and associating the log entries and run-time data with agent concepts in the design models. As a result, the agent concepts (e.g., beliefs about the current state of the environment) are instantiated with run-time data. Explanations of run-time agent behavior can be generated using abductive reasoning on this connection between the implementation and design models.

Agent software comprehension can be performed as soon as the initial implementation is done to verify that the agents are performing basic tasks correctly. During and after implementation, agent comprehension can be used to help debug the implemented MAS and to insure that the agents are behaving as expected and for the right reasons.

## Acknowledgements

This research was funded in part by the Defense Advanced Research Projects Agency and Air Force Research Laboratory, Air Force Materiel Command, USAF, under agreement number F30602-00-2-0588. The U.S. Government is authorized to reproduce and distribute reprints for Governmental purposes notwithstanding any copyright annotation thereon. The views and conclusions herein are those of the authors and should not be interpreted as necessarily representing the official policies or endorsements, either expressed on implied, of the Defense Advanced Research Projects Agency (DARPA), the Air Force Research Laboratory, or the U.S. Government.

## References

Barber, K. S. and Han, D. C. 2003. *Decision-Theoretic Action Selection for Interacting Planning Agents*, Technical Report, TR2003-UT-LIPS-003, Laboratory for Intelligent Processes and Systems, The University of Texas at Austin.

Barber, K. S.; Ahn, J; Gujral, N; Lam, D. N.; and Graser, T. 2004. *Technology Portfolio Manager*, Technical Report, TR2004-UT-LIPS-007, Laboratory for Intelligent Processes and Systems, The University of Texas at Austin.

Barber, K. S. and Lam, D. N. 2003a. Enabling Abductive Reasoning for Agent Software Comprehension. In *Proceedings of the IJCAI-03 Workshop on Agents and Automated Reasoning*, 7-13.

Barber, K. S. and Lam, D. N. 2003b. Specifying and Analyzing Agent Architectures using the Agent Competency Framework. In *Proceedings of the 15th International Conference in Software Engineering and Knowledge Engineering*, 232-239.

Barber, K. S. and Park, J. 2004. Finding Partners to Form Information Sharing Networks in Open Multi-Agent Systems. In *Proceedings of the The 17th Florida Artificial Intelligence Research Symposium.* Forthcoming.

Fullam, K. (2003) An Expressive Belief Revision Framework Based on Information Valuation, Master's Thesis, The University of Texas at Austin.

# Visual Odometry Using Commodity Optical Flow

**Jason Campbell[†‡], Rahul Sukthankar[†‡], Illah Nourbakhsh[‡]**

[†] Intel Research Pittsburgh
417 South Craig Street, Suite 300
Pittsburgh, PA 15213
jason.d.campbell@intel.com, rahul.sukthankar@intel.com

[‡] Carnegie Mellon University, The Robotics Institute
5000 Forbes Ave
Pittsburgh, PA 15213
jasoncam@ri.cmu.edu, rahuls@ri.cmu.edu, illah@ri.cmu.edu

**Abstract**

A wide variety of techniques for visual navigation using robot-mounted cameras have been described over the past several decades, yet adoption of optical flow navigation techniques has been slow. This demo illustrates what visual navigation has to offer: robust hazard detection (including precipices and obstacles), high-accuracy open-loop odometry, and stable closed-loop motion control implemented via an optical flow based visual odometry system. This work is based on 1) open source vision code, 2) common computing hardware, and 3) inexpensive, consumer-quality cameras, and as such should be accessible to many robot builders.

## Demo Overview

Optical flow field and camera ego-motion estimation have been the subject of much research for over 30 years, but this research has seen limited use. For many years this could be attributed to the high computational cost of the known techniques, but modern PCs and embedded systems have been sufficiently powerful to enable real-time optical flow analyses for several years now. Other potential reasons why optical navigation has not seen wider application may include the mathematical and coding complexity of implementing a robust vision system, and a lack of understanding about the high quality of information available via the technique.

This demonstration is designed to explore (and give participants a chance to explore) the practicality and potentially high quality of an optical flow navigation system based on 1) readily available open source vision code, 2) common computing hardware, and 3) consumer-quality cameras. The capabilities of this visual navigation system include robust hazard detection (precipices and obstacles), high-accuracy open-loop "visual odometry", and stable closed-loop motion control. As part of the demonstration, participants will arrange a variety of hazards (obstructions, precipices) for a tabletop mobile robot equipped with a USB webcam as its only sensor. The robot will show robust detection of any hazards put in its way and, in the absence of a hazard, demonstrate robotic positioning accuracy to better than 1% of distances traveled and better than 5 degrees in orientation, in spite of any (accidental or experimenter-induced) wheel slip. Participants may also vary parameters in the vision system (in particular, frame rate and resolution) and observe the effect on overall system performance in order to gain a better appreciation of the design-time tradeoffs required by different environments, velocities, and types of movement.

**Figure 1: Robot poised near a drop-off to illustrate precipice detection. The visual navigation system demonstrated can reliably detect a cliff even when similar colors and textures appear at both the bottom and the top of the precipice (such as in this photo). The robot pictured has two cameras, but only the lower one, pointing roughly 30° below horizontal, is in use.**

## Related Work

This is by no means the first robot to use visual sensing to control motion! As long ago as 1976, Hans Moravec and Donald Gennery used feature tracking algorithms to perform visual servoing/course correction on the Stanford Cart (Gennery and Moravec 1976). Since then many research robots have explored more sophisticated forms of visual sensing. One recent example has been the CMU

Autonomous Helicopter Project, which uses an on-board visual navigation system based on optical flow techniques (Amidi 1996).

Early work on visual navigation focused on the extraction of an optical flow field from a time-sequence of images. For a survey of such algorithms, see (Barron et al. 1994) which remains the definitive comparison study in the area. This study highlighted the gradient-based image matching technique proposed in (Lucas and Kanade 1981) as effective across both synthetic and real-world image sequences, a conclusion other researchers have reached less formally as they have chosen to base further work on this algorithm. Recently, an efficient form of the Lucas-Kanade technique (Bouguet 1999) has become widely available as part of the OpenCV computer vision library[1] (Bradski 2000). OpenCV also incorporates image acquisition and processing functions suitable for commonly available cameras and so offers a relatively complete package for those wishing to apply the Lucas-Kanade technique. This demo system uses the Lucas-Kanade functions in OpenCV to capture video frames and extract the optical flow field from each pair of frames.

Once an optical flow field has been obtained for a sequence of images, a further analysis is required to estimate camera ego-motion corresponding to the flow field. From a research perspective this problem typically has been viewed as just one component of a more general problem termed "structure-from-motion" or SFM. Ego-motion estimation and SFM are challenging because they seek to recover 3-D information from a 2-D projection, and to do so an algorithm must treat multiple observations of movement in the 2-D images as one or more sets of simultaneous equations. The resulting sets of equations are often both highly over-determined and subject to ill conditioned inputs. Statistical methods such as least-median-of-squares or RANSAC have been proposed to help screen out outliers and segment flow fields (Bab-Hadiashar and Suter 1996). An additional complication arises in that some solution techniques may fail when presented with flow fields corresponding to the common case of 2-D rotational and translational movement along a flat floor, or when the tracked points all lie in a single plane (Torr et al. 1998). The visual odometry system demonstrated adopts several simpler techniques (calculating median feature displacements and evaluating the consistency of feature vectors over time) which allow quick but surprisingly accurate estimates to be made of incremental and total distance traveled / angle turned / floor geometry by assuming the robot is traveling in only two dimensions over a predominantly flat floor.

[1] http://www.intel.com/research/mrl/research/opencv/

## References


Amidi, O. 1996. An Autonomous Vision-Guided Helicopter. Ph.D. Thesis, Electrical & Computer Engineering Department, Carnegie Mellon University.

Barron, J. L., Fleet, D. J., and Beauchemin, S. S. 1994. Performance of Optical Flow Techniques. The International Journal of Computer Vision 12(1):43–77.

Bab-Hadiashar A., Suter D. 1996. Robust Optic Flow Estimation Using Least Median of Squares. In Proceedings of the IEEE International Conference on Image Processing, 513–516.

Bouguet, Jean-Yves 1999. Pyramidal Implementation of the Lucas-Kanade Feature Tracker, OpenCV Documentation, Micro-processor Research Labs, Intel Corporation.

Bradski, G. 2000. Programmer's tool chest: The OpenCV library. *Dr. Dobbs Journal*, November 2000.

Gennery, D. and Moravec, H. 1976. Cart Progress Report, Stanford University (unpublished). http://cart.frc.ri.cmu.edu/users/hpm/project.archive/robot.papers/1976/nasa1.txt

Lucas, B.D., and Kanade, T. 1981. An Iterative Image Registration Technique with an Application to Stereo Vision. In Proceedings of 7th International Joint Conference on Artificial Intelligence, 674–679.

Torr, P.H.S., Zisserman, A. and Maybank, S. 1995. Robust Detection of Degenerate Configurations for the Fundamental Matrix. In Proceedings of the Fifth International Conference on Computer Vision, 1037–1042.

# Engineering Open Multi-Agent Systems as Electronic Institutions

**M. Esteva, D. de la Cruz, B. Rosell, J. Ll. Arcos, J. A. Rodríguez-Aguilar, G. Cuní**
IIIA-CSIC Campus UAB
08193 Bellaterra, Spain
{marc,davdela,rosell,arcos,jar,cuni}@iiia.csic.es

## Abstract

In this demo we focus on the engineering of open multi-agent systems as electronic institutions. Electronic institutions are a formalism to define the rules which structure agent interactions, establishing what agents are permitted and forbidden to do. We present a set of tools that support the specification, analysis and execution of institutions, as well as the implementation of agents. Our methodology allows for a successive refinement approach to multi-agent systems engineering.

## Introduction

Multi-agent systems (MASs, henceforth) are harder to design than centralised systems, and tools and methods to support their development are in urgent need. Specially when we consider open MAS populated by self-interested heterogeneous (human and software) agents representing different parties. Hence, it seems apparent the need for introducing regulatory structures establishing what agents are permitted and forbidden to do. We advocate that such regulatory structures can be defined as *electronic institutions* (or e-institutions for shorter) (Esteva 2003) that shape the environment wherein agents interact by introducing sets of artificial constraints that articulate their interactions. Engineering electronic institutions can be regarded as engineering environments (from totally open to normative) for open agent societies as illustrated in figure 1.

In this demo we present a method and support tools for engineering MAS based on the notion of electronic institutions. Next we detail the steps to be followed when engineering and subsequently executing institutions. Furthermore, in the demo we demonstrate the software tools that support all the steps from the specification of an institution to its final deployment.

In what follows we detail the different steps of our methodology, identifying which tool(s) give(s) support to each one (detailed and illustrated in figure 2):

1. *Electronic institution specification.* Electronic institutions can be graphically specified with the aid of ISLANDER (Esteva, de la Cruz, & Sierra 2002) (Best prototype paper award at the First Joint International Conference on Autonomous Agents and Multiagent Systems AAMAS 2002). It allows for the definition of a common ontology, all the interactions that agents may have, and the consequences of such interactions. The result is a precise description of the kinds and order of messages that the components of the MAS can exchange, along with a collection of norms to regulate agents' actions. The tool permits th graphical specification of some of the components, facilitating the work of institution designers. The specifications obtained using the ISLANDER editor are based on the formalisation of e-institutions presented in (Esteva 2003). Notice that the specification of an e-institution focus on the macro-level (societal) aspects of electronic institutions, instead of the micro-level (internal) aspects of agents.



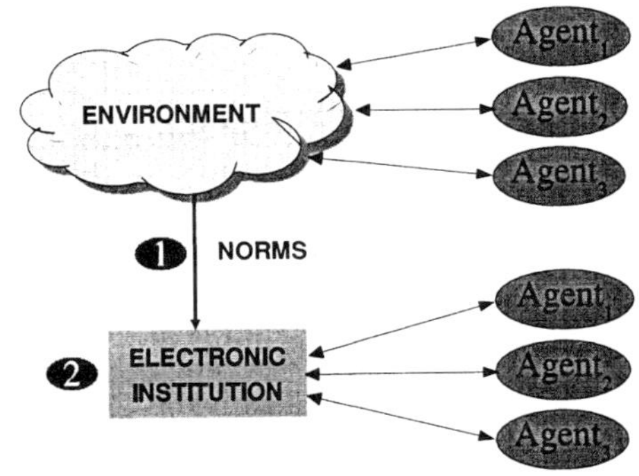


Figure 1: Open systems engineering. A vision

2. *Verification.* Once specified an institution, it should go through a verification process to verify it, before open it to participating agents. This step is twofold. There is a first verification process focusing on static, structural properties of the e-institution specification. A second verification process follows concerned with the expected dynamic properties of the e-institution at work.

   (a) The static verification of e-institutions amounts to checking the structural correctness of specifications. For instance, to check that interaction protocols are correctly specified. This process is also supported by the ISLANDER editor.

   (b) We advocate that the dynamic verification of e-

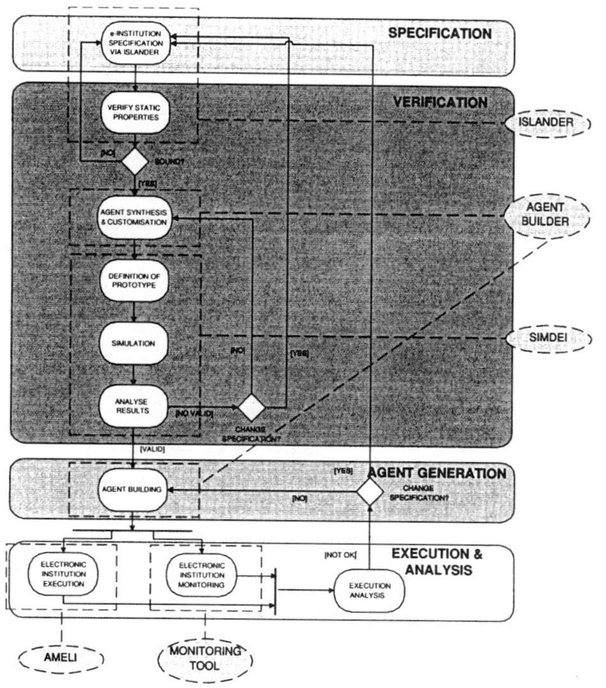


Figure 2: Overview of a Methodology for Engineering MASs

institutions should be done by means of simulation, with the aim of verifying the dynamic properties of the specified institution. This process starts with the definition of different types of agents for the specified institution. In order to facilitate this task we have developed an *agent builder* capable of generating, from a specification, an agent skeleton depending on the roles and interactions in which the agent may participate. In order to completely define an agent, the generated skeleton must be filled up by agent designers with decision making mechanisms. Once agents have been implemented, simulations of the e-institution can be ran using the SIMDEI simulation tool. This simulation tool for electronic institutions has been developed over REPAST (REPAST URL ). It permits to run simulations with different populations of agents. The institution designer should analyse the results of the simulation and return to step one, if they differ from the expected ones.

3. *Agent generation.* Once the institution specification is validated, it can be make open for agent participation. At this points agent designers should must implement their agents. We want to remark that we do not impose restrictions on the type of agents which can participate in the institution. Agent designers can choose the language and architecture that is better to fulfil their goals, as well as, the use of any software tool that facilitates their work. However, we believe that it is important to give support to this process, and the agent builder can be used by agent designers in this stage to implement their agents. Nowadays the agent builder permits the development of agents in JAVA in a defined architecture. In next future we plan to extend it to permit to define agents in different languages and architectures.

4. *Execution & Analysis.* An electronic institution define a normative environment that shapes agent interactions. As an institution will be populated at execution time by heterogeneous and self interested agents we can not expect that this agents will behave according to the institutional ruled encoded in the specification. For this purpose, the institution is executed via an infrastructure which facilitates agents interactions while enforcing the institutional rules, the so-called *AMELI* (Esteva *et al.* 2003; 2004). The implemented infrastructure is of general purpose, as it can interpret any ISLANDER specification. Therefore, it must be regarded as domain independent, and it can be used in the deployment of any specified institution without any extra codification. The infrastructure keeps the execution state and uses it, along with the institution specification to validate the actions that agents want to undertake. Hence, the execution of the e-institution starts out by running the infratructure containing the specification. Thereafter, external agent may enter the institution and they can interact with other agents in the institution via the infrastructure. An institution execution can be monitored by a monitoring tool that we have developed. The monitoring tool shows in graphical interface the events occurring during the institution execution. It can be used for debugging the institution execution to detect agents' misbehaviours.

As a summary, we want to point out that in this demo we will show all the steps that lead from the institution specification to its execution and monitoring.

**Acknowledgements**
The research reported in this paper is partially supported by the Spanish CICYT project Webi2 (TIC2003-08763-C02-01).

## References

Esteva, M.; Rosell, B.; Rodríguez-Aguilar, J. A.; and Arcos, J. L. 2003. Social layer middleware for electronic institutions. In *Proceedings of the First European Workshop on Multi-agent Systems.*

Esteva, M.; Rosell, B.; Rodríguez-Aguilar, J. A.; and Arcos, J. L. 2004. Ameli: An agent-based middleware for electronic institutions. In *Third International Joint Conference on Autonomous Agents and Multiagent Systems (AAMAS 2004).*

Esteva, M.; de la Cruz, D.; and Sierra, C. 2002. Islander: an electronic institutions editor. In *Proceedings of AAMAS 2002*, 1045–1052.

Esteva, M. 2003. *Electronic Institutions: from specification to development.* IIIA PhD Monography. Vol. 19.

REPAST URL. http://repast.sourceforge.net/.

# iBundler: An Agent-based Decision Support Service for Combinatorial Negotiations

**A.Giovannucci, J.A.Rodríguez-Aguilar**
IIIA-CSIC Campus UAB
Bellaterra, Spain
{andrea,jar}@iiia.csic.es

**Jesús Cerquides**
Dept. de Matemàtica Aplicada i Anàlisi
Universitat de Barcelona
Barcelona, Spain
{cerquide@maia.ub.es}

**A. Reyes, F. X. Noria**
Intelligent Software Components, S.A.
Edificio Testa, C/ Alcalde Barnils, 64-68 A
08190 Sant Cugat del Vallès, Barcelona, Spain
{toni,fxn}@isoco.com

**Abstract**

Negotiation events in industrial procurement involving multiple, highly customisable goods pose serious challenges to buying agents when trying to determine the best set of providing agents' offers. Typically, a buying agent's decision involves a large variety of constraints that may involve attributes of a very same item as well as attributes of multiple items. In this paper we describe *iBundler*, an agent-aware negotiation service to solve the winner determination problem considering buyers' and providers' constraints and preferences.

## Introduction

Consider the problem faced by a buying agent when negotiating with providing agents. In a negotiation event involving multiple, highly customizable goods, buying agents need to express relations and constraints among attributes of different items. Not forgetting the provider side, providing agents may also wish to impose constraints or conditions over their offers. Once a buying agent collects all offers, he is faced with the burden of determining the winning offers. We have implemented *iBundler* (introduced in (Rodríguez-Aguilar *et al.* 2003) and thoroughly described in (Giovannucci *et al.* 2004)) with the aim to relieve buying agents from solving such a problem. *iBundler* is an agent-aware decision support service acting as a combinatorial negotiation solver (solving the winner determination problem) for both multi-item, multi-unit negotiations and auctions. The service can be employed by both buying agents and auctioneers in combinatorial negotiations and combinatorial reverse auctions respectively. Furthermore, it extends current combinatorial auction (CA) models by accommodating both operational constraints and attribute-value constraints. At this aim, new ontological issues have been considered in order to empower the expressiveness offered by negotiation objects and offers to incorporate buyers' and providers' business constraints. Its deployment over the Agentcities (http://www.agentcities.org) network was awarded the prize of the Best Application of the 2003 Agentcities Worldwide Agent Technology Competition.

## iBundler Service Features

As we explained above buyers and providers need to express their business rules. In the following we make explicit the support offered by *iBundler* to express buyers constraints:

**Negotiation over multiple items.** A negotiation event is usually started with the preparation of a request for quotation (RFQ) form, which details the requirements.

**Offer aggregation.** An RFQ item can be multiply sourced.

**Business sharing constraints** to restrict the number of providers that may have each RFQ item awarded.

**Constraints over single items.** Every RFQ item is described by a list of negotiable attributes. Since: a) there exists a degree of flexibility in specifying each of these attributes (e.g. several values are acceptable); and b) multiple offers referring the very same item can be finally accepted; buyers need to impose constraints over attribute values.

**Constraints over multiple items.** In daily industrial procurement, accepting certain configuration for one item might affect the configuration of a different item (e.g. to ensure compatibility between products). Hence, buyers need to express constraints and relationship between attributes of different RFQ items.

**Specification of providers' capacities.** Buyers cannot risk to award contracts to providers beyond their capabilities. At this aim, they must require to have providers' capacities per item declared.

Analogously, providers are endowed with a rich bidding language as follows:

**Multiple bids per item.** Providers might be interested in offering alternate sub-conditions/configurations for the very same good, i.e., offering alternatives for a same request. A common situation is to offer volume-based discounts. This means that a provider submits several offers and each offer only applies for a minimum (maximum) number of units.

**Combinatorial offers.** Economy efficiency is enhanced if providers are allowed to offer (bid on) combination of goods. They might lower the price, or improve service assets if they achieve to get more business.

**Multi-unit offering.** Each provider requires to specify his willingness to sell over/below a minimum/maximum number of units.

**Homogeneous combinatorial offers.** Combinatorial offering may produce inefficiencies when combined with multi-unit offering. Thus a provider may wind up with an award of a small number of units for a certain item, and a large number of units for a different item, being both part of the very same offer (e.g. 10 chairs and 200 tables). It is desirable for

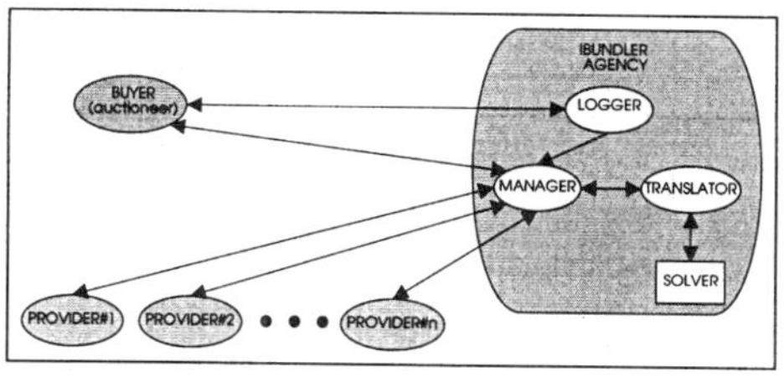


Figure 1: Architecture of the *iBundler* agency

providers to be able to specify homogeneity with respect to the number of units for complementary items.

**Packing constraints.** It is often not possible to serve an arbitrary number of units. Thus, providers require to specify their packing sizes.

**Complementary and exclusive offers.** Providers usually submit XOR bids, i.e., exclusive offers that cannot be simultaneously accepted. A second type of constraint, AND, allows to express volume-based discounts (e.g. first 1000 units at $2.5 p.u. and then $2 each).

## iBundler implementation

The *iBundler* service has been implemented as an agency composed of agents and software components that cooperatively interact to offer a negotiation support service. The service can be employed by both buyers and auctioneers. Figure 1 depicts the components of the agency along with the fundamental connections of buyers and providers with the service. Next we make explicit the main functionality of its members:

**[Logger agent].** It represents the interface of the *iBundler* agency to the world. It manages the access to the agency for both buyers and providers.

**[Manager agent].** Agent devoted to providing the solution of the problem of choosing the set of bids that best matches a user's requirements. It offers the following services: brokering service to forward buyers' requirements (RFQs) to selected providers; collection of bids; winner determination in a combinatorial negotiation/auction; and award of contracts on behalf of buyers. Furthermore it bundles each RFQ and its bids into a negotiation problem to be conveyed to the Translator agent; and extracts the solution to the negotiation problem handled back by the Translator agent.

**[Translator agent].** It is in charge of translating problems expressed in FIPA compliant format into XML format, understandable by the Solver component, and vice versa.

**[Solver component].** The XML specification is parsed into an MIP formulation and solved using available MIP solvers. Our formulation of the problem (Giovannucci *et al.* 2004) can be regarded as similar to the binary multi-unit combinatorial reverse auction winner determination problem with side constraints (Sandholm *et al.* 2002). Expressing the problem as an MIP problem with side constraints enables its resolution by standard algorithms and commercially available software. With these considerations in mind the Solver component has been modelled and implemented as a mixed integer program(MIP) problem: a version using ILOG CPLEX 7.1 in combination with SOLVER 5.2; and another version using iSOCO's Java MIP modeler —that integrates GLPK (http://www.gnu.org/directory/GNU/glpk.html).

Our design manages to separate concerns among the three members of the agency. On the one hand, the Manager is strictly devoted to coordination; it represents the façade of the service. Besides, since every negotiation requested by a buyer makes the agency create an instance of the Manager, the service can cope with scalability issues. Thus, if the service is heavily accessed, Managers can synchronise to queue tasks for the Translator. This is in charge of relieving both Managers and Solver from the burden of translating FIPA-compliant specifications into the XML language required by Solver. Notice too that Solver has been implemented as a software component because it was intended to serve for two purposes: as the core component of the *iBundler* agency, and as the winner determination component in a commercial sourcing application (Rodríguez-Aguilar *et al.* 2004).

To implement the *iBundler* agency we used the following technologies: JADE (http://sharon.cselt.it/projects/jade) as the software tool to implement agents, and as the platform where the agency resides and Tomcat 4.1 (http://jakarta.apache.org/tomcat/) as J2EE server to build web interfaces for human traders. The ontology was defined with the aid of *Protege 2000* (http://protege.stanford.edu) and the conversion from ontological objects to Java classes was realized via the *beangenerator* Protege 2000 plug-in (http://www.swi.psy.uva.nl/usr/aart/beangenerator).

## Contributions

The implementation of *iBundler* contributes along two main directions. On the one hand, we have incorporated actual-world side constraints to the winner determination problem for combinatorial negotiations. On the other hand, we have realized a new ontology that accommodates both operational constraints and attribute-value constraints for buying and providing agents, offering a highly-expressive bidding language.

## References

Giovannucci, A.; Rodríguez-Aguilar, J. A.; Reyes-Moro, A.; Noria, F. X.; and Cerquides, J. 2004. Towards automated procurement via agent-aware negotiation support. In *AAMAS 2004.* http://www.iiia.csic.es/ andrea/papers/aamas-ibundler.pdf.

Rodríguez-Aguilar, J. A.; Giovanucci, A.; Reyes-Moro, A.; Noria, F. X.; and Cerquides, J. 2003. Agent-based decision support for actual-world procurement scenarios. In *2003 IEEE/WIC International Conference on Intelligent Agent Technology.*

Rodríguez-Aguilar, J. A.; Reyes-Moro, A.; López-Sánchez, M.; and Cerquides, J. 2004. Enabling assisted strategic negotiations in actual-world procurement scenarios. *Electronic Commerce Research.* (forthcoming).

Sandholm, T.; Suri, S.; Gilpin, A.; and Levine, D. 2002. Winner determination in combinatorial auction generalizations. In *First Joint Conference on Autonomous Agents and Multiagent Systems (AAMAS'02)*, 69–76.

# Domain-Independent Reason-Enhanced Controller for Task-ORiented systems - DIRECTOR

**Darsana P. Josyula**[1], **Michael L. Anderson**[2] and **Don Perlis**[1,2]
(1) Department of Computer Science
(2) Institute for Advanced Computer Studies
University of Maryland, College Park, MD 20742
{darsana, anderson, perlis}@cs.umd.edu

In today's market, different systems (e.g., camera, microwave etc.) exist that can perform specialized tasks. However, users find it frustrating to learn how to operate these task-oriented systems (TOSs) in a manner that suits their needs. If a single agent can interface users with different TOSs, then the users need not learn how to interact with each TOS separately; instead, they just need to learn how to interact with one agent. In addition, if the agent is rational, users can flexibly adapt the operation of the TOSs by interacting with the agent.

For example, consider a pool controller that can accept commands to heat a pool, stop heating, and provide the temperature. A user interacting directly with such a system will have to issue the appropriate commands when required. By integrating a rational interfacing agent with such a system, the user could tell the agent to heat the pool every Saturday at 10:00 am and maintain the temperature around $35^{o}C$ until 1:00 pm. The agent will then issue appropriate commands to the pool controller at the required times.

For such an interfacing agent to effectively control different TOSs it should have the capability not only to translate a user request into a TOS instruction, and to issue that instruction to the TOS at the appropriate time(s), but also to track the effect of those commands and to detect any perturbations, such as contradictory information, or a difference between expected and actual outcomes.

We are developing such a perturbation tolerant, domain-independent interfacing agent (Anderson, Josyula, & Perlis 2003; Josyula, Anderson, & Perlis 2003) by modeling the beliefs, desires, intentions, expectations and achievements of the agent. The current version of the agent has been successfully integrated with and tested on six different TOSs.

Our agent is built on a logical engine (ALFA - Active Logic For Agents) based on Active Logic (Elgot-Drapkin & Perlis 1990; Purang *et al.* 1999; Purang 2001). ALFA can keep track of the evolving time, handle contradictory information and distinguish between desires, intentions and expectations that are achievable and those that are not. Therefore, our agent based on ALFA can rationally deliberate *despite* having deadlines and contradictory beliefs, desires or other mental attitudes. In addition, it can allocate its resources to satisfy achievable goals, resist attempting unachievable goals (until they become achievable) and ignore achieved goals.



## Architecture

A general architecture for a rational interfacing agent for task-oriented systems is shown in Fig 1. In DIRECTOR (an acronym for a Domain-Independent Reason-Enhanced Controller for Task-ORiented systems), the KB stores the beliefs (domain-specific as well as general), desires, intentions, expectations and achievements of the agent. Given an utterance, the **parser** asserts a syntactic structure of the utterance in the KB.

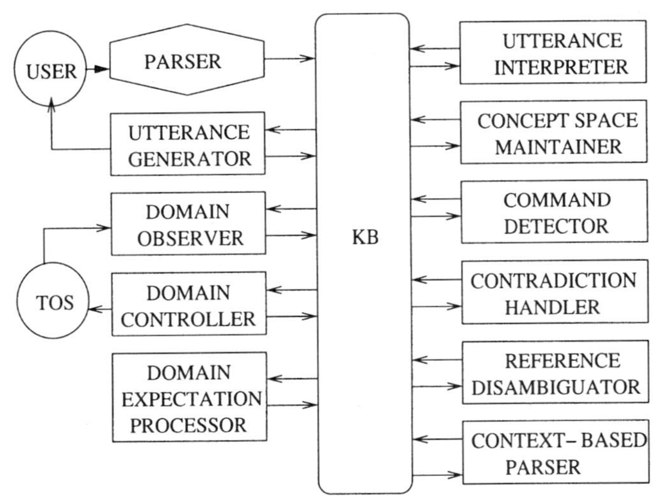


Figure 1: DIRECTOR Architecture

The **Utterance Interpreter** first checks whether there is a valid parse available. If the parse is not valid, then it creates a desire to parse the utterance using the **Context-based Parser**.

Once there is a valid parse available, the **Utterance Interpreter** creates a desire to identify the command in the utterance. The Command Detector identifies the command in a user utterance using the parse and the list of valid commands available in the KB. Once the Detector asserts the command associated with an utterance in the KB, the Interpreter uses the syntax and semantics of the command (from the KB) to determine the objects associated with the command. In case, the object references in the utterance parse are ambiguous, the interpreter creates a desire to determine the referents for the ambiguous object references.

For each ambiguous object reference, the **Reference Disambiguator** first introspects to determine whether the reference can be disambiguated using the current contents of the KB. If introspection does not resolve the referent, then the Disambiguator creates a desire to get help from either the user or the TOS. For instance, for the ambiguous expression *"the Chicago train"*, the Disambiguator first introspects to determine the referent. If introspection fails to identify the referent, then a desire is created to get help from the TOS. (Thus, the agent could ask the TOS for the current train at Chicago, if it already knows that the expression *"the Chicago train"* refers to the train that is currently at Chicago.) If both introspection and interaction with the TOS fail to provide a referent, then the Disambiguator will create a desire to ask the user for clarification.

**Utterance Generator** executes the intentions of producing utterances. For questions type of utterances, an expectation about the user's response is created and represented in the KB. This expectation is used by the Context Based Parser to parse user responses.

**Domain Controller** executes the intentions of sending valid instructions to the TOS. If there is an anticipated result (in the KB) associated with an instruction, then an expectation for that result is created in the KB, when that instruction is issued to the TOS. Once the Domain Controller executes an intention, it creates a desire to inform the user about the action that it is taking.

For each expectation that the Domain Controller produces, the **Domain Expectation Processor** initiates an observation to confirm that expectation, if such an observation action has not been initiated already.

While Domain Controller *sends* instructions to the TOS, its counterpart - **Domain Observer** - *receives* information from the TOS. The information about the format of the TOS outputs and the expectations created by the Domain Controller are used to interpret the observations that the Domain Observer receives.

The **Concept Space Maintainer** makes modifications to the belief space of the KB. These changes include additions, modifications and deletions; correspondingly learning, belief revision and unlearning respectively is achieved. Once the Concept Space Maintainer executes an intention, it creates a desire to inform the user about the action that it has taken.

When a contradiction occurs in the KB, the **Contradiction Handler** notes the contradiction and tries to resolve the contradiction. How the contradiction is resolved depends on the type of contradiction. When enough information is not available to fix an inconsistency, the contradiction handler will create a desire to get help from the user to fix the inconsistency.

## Implementation

We have implemented the DIRECTOR architecture in an interfacing agent - ALFRED (Active Logic for Reason-Enhanced Dialog). ALFRED interprets the user requests and creates desires to accomplish the requests. Based on its knowledge and availability of time and resources, it creates and executes intentions to achieve the requests. Since ALFRED does not interact with the real world, the only way it can determine whether an instruction that it issued to a TOS has resulted in the desired action is by confirming it from either the user or the TOS. In order to make this determination, ALFRED creates an expectation regarding the outcome, based on available knowledge, whenever it initiates an action and compares the actual result with the expected outcome.

The current version of ALFRED can translate a user request to a valid action request, for either the TOS to perform a task or for ALFRED to update its Knowledge Base. In addition, it can learn alternative names for existing TOS commands, ALFRED commands or domain objects via user instructions. ALFRED can also interface with different TOSs by merely changing the initial Knowledge Base.

Alfred has been tested on the following domains:

- Simulated Pool: Alfred controls the temperature settings of a pool based on user needs.
- Movie Player: Alfred plays different movies based on user requests.
- Toy Train: Alfred moves various trains to different cities based on user requests.
- Simulated House: Alfred controls different appliances in a house based on user needs.
- Home Designer: Alfred helps the user create and move different objects in a house model.
- Chess Player: Alfred plays chess for the user by sending the user requested moves to a chess program.

## References

Anderson, M. L.; Josyula, D.; and Perlis, D. 2003. Talking to Computers. In *Proceedings of the Workshop on Mixed-Initiative Intelligent Systems at the Eighteenth International Joint Conference on Artificial Intelligence (IJCAI-03)*.

Elgot-Drapkin, J., and Perlis, D. 1990. Reasoning Situated in Time I: Basic Concepts. *Journal of Experimental and Theoretical Artificial Intelligence* 2(1):75–98.

Josyula, D. P.; Anderson, M. L.; and Perlis, D. 2003. Towards Domain-independent, Task-oriented, Conversational Adequacy. In *Proceedings of the Eighteenth international Joint Conference on Artificial Intelligence (IJCAI-03)*, 1637–1638.

Purang, K.; [Josyula], D. P.; Traum, D.; Andersen, C.; and Perlis, D. 1999. Practical Reasoning and Plan Execution with Active Logic. In *Proceedings of the IJCAI-99 Workshop on Practical Reasoning and Rationality*, 30–38.

Purang, K. 2001. Alma/Carne: Implementation of a Time-situated Meta-reasoner. In *Proceedings of the Thirteenth International Conference on Tools with Artificial Intelligence (ICTAI-01)*, 103–110.

# Agent-Based Modeling with Social Networks for Terrorist Recruitment

**Teresa H. Ko** and **Nina M. Berry**
Embedded Reasoning Institute
Sandia National Laboratories
{thko,nmberry}@sandia.gov

### Abstract

The Seldon model combines concepts from agent-based modeling and social network analysis to create a computation model of social dynamics for terrorist recruitment. The underlying recruitment model is based on a unique hybrid agent-based architecture that contains simple agents (individuals such as *expatriates*) and abstract agents (conceptual entities such as *society* and *mosques*). Interactions between agents are determined by multiple social networks which form and dissipate according to the actions of the individual. We have implemented a Java-based toolkit to evaluate the dynamics of social behavior and the specific dynamics associated with terrorist recruitment described by expert social scientists, creating an architecture for simple adaptation to other group phenomenon.

## Introduction

The Seldon project takes its name from Hari Seldon, the fictitious originator of "psycho-history" in Isaac Asimov's Foundation stories. In those stories, Seldon was able to employ a deep knowledge of history, the social sciences, and mathematics to forecast large-scale and long-term trends in the development of civilization. Only large-scale forecasting was possible; in fact, the major tension in the stories stems from the unexpected role of a single unique individual, born long after Seldon's death, who threatens to disrupt Seldon's calculations and destroy the plans he based upon them (Berry *et al.* 2003).

Today, psycho-history remains a science fiction fantasy. However, computational tools are now emerging that allow short-term modeling of tightly-constrained, complex social interactions. Unlike psycho-history, these tools cannot reliably be used to predict the future. Nevertheless, they may illuminate dynamics that can help us anticipate the broad consequences of the complex interactions of social forces that will arise in our efforts to combat terrorism.

We present a terrorist recruitment model based on a unique approach to computational social simulation by combining both agent-based modeling techniques and social networks analysis in order to capture the underlying social dynamics of terrorist recruitment.

## Our Model

The model consists of agents and the social networks that bind them together. The model contains two categories of agents: individual agents, a traditional computation agent used to represent a human, and abstract agents, a conceptual agent used to incorporate social concepts into the model. The terrorist model has two types of individual agents: an *expatriate*, a foreign national who is isolated from the community and terrorist organizations, and a *bridge*, a foreign national who has the ability to connect an expatriate with a terrorist organization. The three types of abstract agents are the *society*, the *mosque*, and the *clique*. The *society* captures the culture in which these agents reside encompassing societal concepts such as the willingness to accept foreigners in their world. The *mosque* represents the religious and social gathering place for expatriates. The *clique* encapsulates the group dynamics of individuals who are all close friends with one another.

Individuals belong to social networks which vary dynamically from day to day. There is a prevalent world network which all individuals are a member of and smaller networks derived from past interactions and abstract agents. There are five networks within our model: the *world* network (which connects everyone together), the *mosque* network (which connects an individual with other individuals attending the same mosque), the *acquaintance* network, the *strong bonds* network, and the *clique* network (which all captured different levels of relationships between individuals). By varying an individual's interactions within different networks, the types of friendships that form (i.e., within a mosque vs. throughout the world, the number of bonds vs. the strength of the bond) illuminate the underlying dynamics of different social scenarios.

We have used homophyly as an underlying mechanism for bond formation and stickiness to an abstraction. The more similar two expatriates are, the more likely they will create a stronger bond or reinforce an existing bond. This concept between simple agents has been extended further to capture how committed simple agents are to a concept. In this case, we used homophyly between an expatriate and the mosque it is currently attending in conjunction with the homophyly between an expatriate and their fellow attendees. If similar enough over time, an expatriate's commitment causes them to be virtual stuck to that particular mosque.

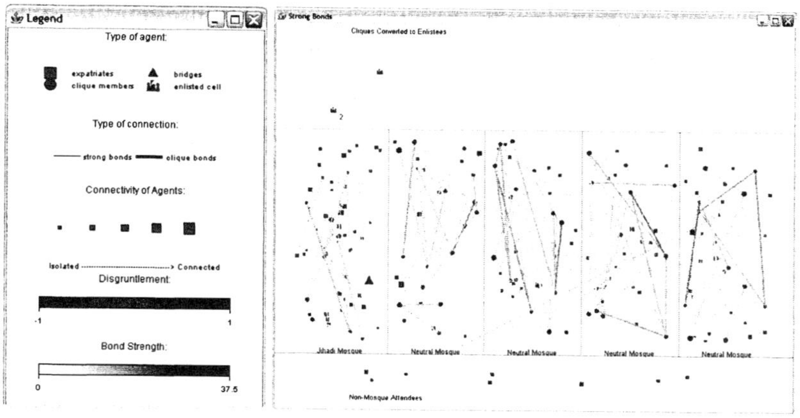


Figure 1: Snapshot of a simulation run. Expatriates are visualized by squares of varying size, representing their disgruntlement and relative isolation, respectively. Strong bonds are visualized by an edge where the strength of the bond is shown through the gradation of the edge. Cliques are distinguished from other agents by circles rather than squares and thick lines between members.

## A Simulation

We have converted the research done by Marc Sageman (Sageman 2004) into a computation model describing a path for an expatriate to become an enlistee of the terrorist camps. Expatriates are initialized as neutral entities that are completely isolated. They flow in and out of different mosques attempting to finds friends. Through random interactions within the world and the mosques, expatriates begin to form acquaintances with others similar to themselves. Over time, the bonds between some expatriates become strong enough to be considered friends. Cliques naturally begin to form among the expatriates. At the same time, the disgruntlement (a measure of dissatisfaction with the current living status) of expatriates changes through their interactions with the abstract agents and individuals. To enlist an expatriate into a terrorist organization, three things need to be true simultaneously:

- the expatriate must belong to a clique
- the clique must be disgruntled enough to consider a terrorist organization, and
- a bridge must be willing to confide to the expatriate its connection to the terrorist organization.

If all these conditions are satisfied, the entire clique is enlisted and journeys to a terrorist training camp.

Figure 1 shows a snapshot of a simulation run which contains expatriates in all stages of the path to a terrorist camp. In this simulation, there are 200 expatriates and one bridge. Expatriates can choose to attend five different mosques, a jihadi mosque which influences expatriates to be disgruntled and four neutral mosques which influences expatriates to be slightly above neutral. There is a sharp division between expatriates attending the neutral mosques and the jihadi mosque. In addition to being influenced by a mosque, an expatriate is also more likely to continue to attend a mosque that is similar to itself. These two aspects result in the jihadi mosque having very disgruntled attendees and the neutral mosques having neutral to happy attendees. In this simulation run, cliques tend to form within a single mosque due to an expatriate's high percentage of time spent interacting with members of its mosque's network. The bridge has successfully converted two disgruntled cliques that originated from the jihadi mosque.

By varying the parameters of our model, we have investigated which dynamics have the greatest impact on reducing terrorist camp enlistment. Among the most effective means are creating a more tolerant city, reducing interactions within the acquaintance network, and increasing the requirements for establishing friendship.

## Conclusion

We have presented a novel approach to agent-based modeling by incorporating conceptual agents which enable higher-level concepts while providing individual agents that exhibiting socialized behavior. We have merged the concept of multiple dynamic social networks into agent-based social simulations increasing the flexibility and accuracy of social simulations. These concepts have been applied to the domain of terrorist recruitment enabling greater understanding of the underlying dynamics of social behavior and possible mitigating strategies.

## References

Berry, N.; Ko, T.; Lee, M.; Moy, T.; Pickett, M.; Smrcka, J.; Turnley, J.; and Wu, B. 2003. Computational social dynamic modeling of group recruitment. Technical Report SAND2003-8754, Sandia National Laboratories.

Sageman, M. 2004. Understanding terrorist networks. Technical report, University of Pennsylvania.

# Mobile Emergency Triage Support System

**Wojtek Michalowski**
University of Ottawa
136 Jean Jacques Lussier St.
Ottawa, Ontario K1N 6N5, Canada
wojtek@management.uottawa.ca

**Roman Slowinski** and **Szymon Wilk**
Poznan University of Technology
Piotrowo 3a
60-965 Poznan, Poland
{roman.slowinski, szymon.wilk}@cs.put.poznan.pl

## Abstract

We are designing and developing a mobile clinical decision support system, known as MET (Mobile Emergency Triage), for supporting emergency triage of different types of acute pain presentations. MET needs to interact with an existing hospital information system, run on handheld computing devices and be suitable for operation in weak connectivity conditions (with unstable connections between mobile clients and a server). The MET system captures necessary hospital data, allows for patients' data entry and provides triage support. By operating on handheld computers, it fits to the regular clinical workflow without introducing any hindrances and disruptions. It supports triage anytime and anywhere, directly at the point of care, and can be used as an electronic patient chart that facilitates structured data collection.

## General Design

The MET system (http://www.mobiledss.uottawa.ca) is a mobile clinical decision support system supporting Emergency Department (ED) triage of various types of acute pain presentations. Clinical knowledge is explicitly presented in the form of decision rules that are inferred from past clinical experience, and the system works as a "helper" (or debiaser (Silverman 1992)). It helps to avoid biases and mistakes during patient triage by presenting possible management outcomes together with the strength of the recommendation, reflecting the uncertainty inherent in clinical reasoning. The system has a modular and open architecture with separate clinical modules associated with various acute pain problems, so it can be easily extended to handle new presentations. MET offers triage support anytime and anywhere, irrespective of the stage in the process of patient management. Moreover, it is integrated with the electronic patients' record system (EPRS) to extract data collected during registration and to allow clinicians to transfer results of the ED examination to the EPRS after triaging a patient.

## Mobile Component Design

Weak connectivity (i.e., unstable connection between client and server) calls for the extended client-server architecture



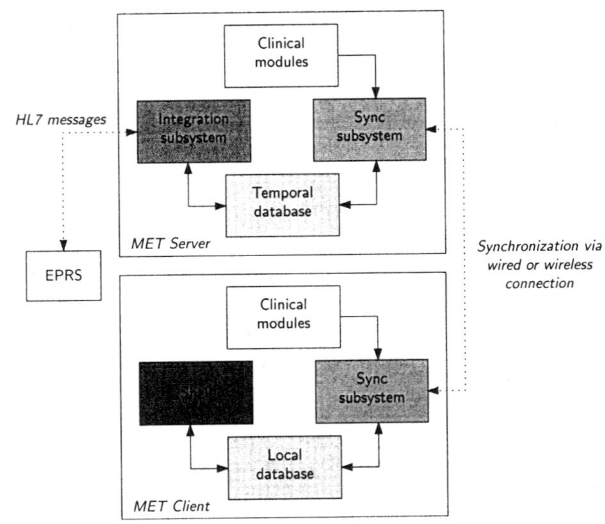


Figure 1: General architecture of the MET system

(Jing, Helal, & Elmagarmid 1999), where a client takes over some functions of a server when a connection is not available. The computer architecture of the MET system is presented in Figure 1.

The MET server integrates via the integration subsystem with the EPRS. It also communicates with clients using the sync subsystem to exchange patients' data and to send necessary clinical modules associated with specific presentations (i.e., the modules are stored on the server and executed on the client side). Clinicians use the MET client to collect clinical data, to support triage decisions, to synchronize data with the server and to retrieve required clinical modules.

We assume that the client must be able to support triage without the need to contact the server. Therefore, this necessitates storing the triage support component and a local patient database.

Unlike with classical knowledge-based systems, where data entered by the experts and case data supplied by the users are stored in the same knowledge base, the MET system maintains the case data in a separate database to simplify management of the clinical modules and facilitate data synchronization with the server.

The MET server communicates with the EPRS using HL7 (Health Level 7) protocol (Quinn 1999). HL7 is the standard of exchanging information between medical applications. It specifies the format and content of exchanged data, however, it defines neither how messages are passed between applications nor how applications store and process these messages. This flexibility allows one to experiment with various network protocols (e.g., TCP/IP or FTP) and to integrate diverse systems without extensive modifications.

By integrating with the EPRS, the MET system saves clinicians from repeating the mundane task of entering demographic data and presenting complaint that are normally collected and entered into the EPRS during registration. Moreover, by sending back values collected during the examination in the ED, the MET system can be also considered as an electronic extension of a patient's chart, allowing for structured and convenient data collection and storage in an electronic format. As reported in the literature, this feature alone leads to improved management (Guerlain *et al.* 2001; Glass *et al.* 2002). Further, because of the design solutions discussed above, the MET system can be introduced into virtually every ED without any updates to the existing network (i.e., a wireless network is not required).

## Knowledge Discovery

A retrospective chart review was done, using the records of 606 patients with abdominal pain, seen during the 1997–2002 period in the ED of the Children's Hospital of Eastern Ontario (Ottawa, Ontario). The ED chart of each patient was reviewed with special reference to 12 clinical symptoms, signs, and tests (attributes) and the discharge diagnosis. Reliance on the discharge diagnosis guarantees that the actual clinical outcomes, not the decisions made by the ED staff, are used for developing and evaluating the decision model for early triage.

It is usual that data collected as part of a retrospective chart review contains a significant number of missing values. The analysis of those clinical symptoms and signs that have missing values is very important. Clearly, they should not be discarded (a common approach in other studies was to remove from further analysis the attributes with a number of missing values above a certain threshold), as their importance depends on the context in which they are evaluated.

In this study, the data set created from the patients' charts was studied for regularities using knowledge discovery method based on the original idea of rough sets (Pawlak 1991). This method, described in (Slowinski, Greco, & Matarazzo 2004) is well suited to deal with partially missing and inconsistent data. It permits to assess the relevance of each attribute by means of the Shapley value (Shapley 1953). The method, implemented in ROSE system (Predki & Wilk 1999), was used to analyze medical data set for the regularities. At this point ED physicians were consulted and asked to validate the obtained results.

The information about the relevance of each attributes as indicated by respective Shapley value was considered in the process of generating decision rules. In order to check if all clinical attributes should be used to create robust rules, we iteratively tested subsets of attributes distinguished according to Shapley values, starting with top ones and ending with all twelve. The rules were tested retrospectively on how well they could classify a patient presenting with an abdominal pain complaint. The classification accuracy was estimated through the validation tests. Robustness of obtained rules confirmed our earlier findings (Michalowski *et al.* 2001) and allowed us to use them to develop a decision model for the MET system.

The MET system described here was prospectively evaluated during 6 months long clinical trial in the ED of the Children's Hospital of Eastern Ontario.

## References


Glass, A.; Pijnenburg, B.; Lijmer, J.; Bogaard, K.; de Roos, M.; Keeman, J.; Butzelaar, R.; and Bossuyt, P. 2002. Comparison of diagnostic decision rules and structured data collection in assessment of acute ankle injury. *Canadian Medical Association Journal* 6:727–733.

Guerlain, S.; LeBeau, K.; Thompson, M.; Donnelly, C.; McClelland, H.; Syverud, S.; and Calland, J. 2001. The effect of a standardized data collection form on the examination and diagnosis of patients with abdominal pain. In *Proceedings of the Human Factors and Ergonomics Society 45th Annual Meeting*, 1284–1289.

Jing, J.; Helal, A.; and Elmagarmid, A. 1999. Client-server computing in mobile environments. *ACM Computing Surveys* 31(2):115–157.

Michalowski, W.; Rubin, S.; Slowinski, R.; and Wilk, S. 2001. Triage of the child with abdominal pain: A clinical algorithm for emergency patient management. *Journal of Paediatrics and Child Health* 6:23–28.

Pawlak, Z. 1991. *Rough sets: Theoretical aspects of reasoning about data.* Kluwer Academic Publishers.

Predki, B., and Wilk, S. 1999. Rough set based data exploration using rose system. In Ras, Z., and Skowron, A., eds., *Foundations of Intelligent Systems*. Springer-Verlag. 172–180.

Quinn, J. 1999. An HL7 (Health Level Seven) overview. *Journal of American Health Information Management Association* 7:32–34.

Shapley, L. 1953. A value for n-person games. In Kuhn, H., and Tucker, A., eds., *Contributions to the Theory of Games II*, 307–317. Princeton University Press.

Silverman, B. 1992. Building a better critic - recent empirical results. *IEEE Intelligent Systems* 7(2):18–25.

Slowinski, R.; Greco, S.; and Matarazzo, B. 2004. Rough set based decision support. In Burke, E., and Kendall, G., eds., *Introductory Tutorials on Optimization, Search and Decision Support Methodologies*. Kluwer Academic Publishers. chapter 16.

# CMRadar: A Personal Assistant Agent for Calendar Management

**Pragnesh Jay Modi, Manuela Veloso, Stephen F. Smith, Jean Oh**
Department of Computer Science
Carnegie Mellon University
Pittsburgh PA 15213
{pmodi,mmv,sfs,jeanoh}@cs.cmu.edu

## Introduction

One of the more compelling visions for agents research is the development of "personal assistant agents" that are tasked with making people and organizations more efficient by autonomously handling routine tasks on behalf of their users (Maes 1994) (Mitchell *et al.* 1994) (Chalupsky *et al.* 2001). Most recently, several researchers including ourselves have embarked on a large research project, called The Radar Project (Radar 2004), whose overall goal is to develop a personalized agent that is able to assist its user in a wide range of everyday tasks. Within this larger project, we are concerned with the more focused task of managing a user's calendar. While isolated aspects of calendar management have been investigated before (Sen & Durfee 1998), in this paper, we present CMRadar, a *complete* agent with capabilities ranging across the full spectrum of calendar management, from natural language processing of incoming scheduling-related emails, to making autonomous scheduling decisions, to negotiating with other users, to user interfacing and visualization. Although many research issues remain, we believe CMRadar is the first end-to-end agent for automated calendar management.

A key contribution of the design of CMRadar is the specification of a basic representation, called a Template, for communicating calendar scheduling related information. The Template data structure is used as the language for the communication between the components in CMRadar and as the "glue" that binds them together. In addition, Templates are also used to normalize unformatted natural language emails into a machine readable format. We offer the Template data structure as a flexible approach to the general design of a meeting scheduling agent.

The CMRadar architecture contributes a modular design in which the core scheduling functions of the agent are separated from the multiagent aspects of calendar management. Rather than an approach that tightly couples schedule optimization and negotiation, CMRadar has a separate Manager component which handles the sending and receiving of messages from other agents and more generally, manages the negotiation with others. The Manager then communicates via Templates with a separate Scheduler component that handles the core optimization problems. We found that this modular architecture facilitates the integration of existing scheduling systems and indeed, a core component of CMRadar is the Ozone scheduler (Smith, Lassila, & Becker 1996) originally designed for and used in several real-world logistics planning domains.

The primary underlying emphasis of the Radar project is to learn to improve performance, adapt to unexpected situations and to customize to different users. The emphasis on learning is reflected in our design of the CMRadar architecture in which all components read and write data to a central knowledge base that can be used by a separate learning process to provide feedback to the decision making components (see Figure 1). Indeed, it is the need to collect real-world data to support learning that drives our development of a complete end-to-end agent.

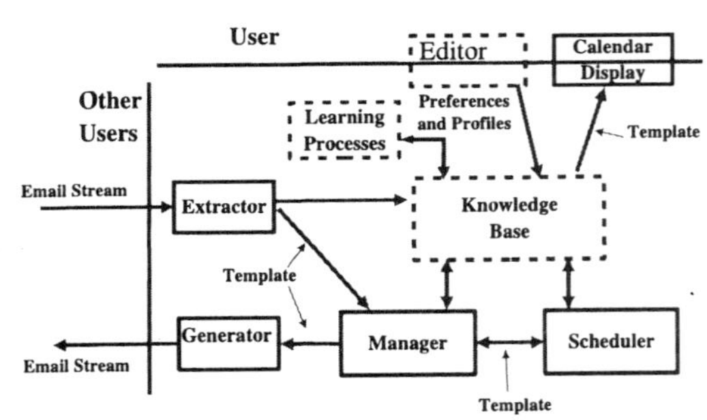


Figure 1: Architecture of a single user's CMRadar

## The CMRadar Agent

Our CMRadar is developed as a personalized agent that interacts with other users or agents. Figure 1 shows the overall architecture of CMRadar with its functional modules. Dotted lines represent components not yet implemented. We present two main modules in detail in this paper in the coming sections, namely the Manager and the Scheduler. We now overview the complete architecture, briefly describing each of the modules.

**Extractor:** We assume that multiagent interaction in calendar meeting scheduling occurs through email message exchange. The Extractor is responsible for parsing email messages into a *template* normalized format representing the meeting request or reply to a request. The email messages can be sent directly by other Radar agents or by users in natural language. We have followed research on applying state-of-the-art natural language parsing techniques,[1] as well as successfully defining and applying special purpose parsing rules for language specific to meeting scheduling.[2]

**Manager:** Calendar management is in its essence a multiagent problem as meetings involve more than one person. The Manager module in CMRadar explicitly handles the multiagent aspects of calendar management, including flexible negotiation with other agents and control of email threads. Meeting scheduling is a complex process dependent on many factors, and different users schedule meetings with other users according to many different strategies. We view this variety of possible multiagent interactions similar to a *playbook* approach that we have previously developed in robot soccer (Bowling, Browning, & Veloso 2004). The Manager can represent and reason about several different multiagent (team) strategies and learn to select the ones that are more effective when interacting with other specific agents.

**Scheduler:** The core task of meeting scheduling involves determining which times for the meetings. The Scheduler module in CMRadar handles all the time analysis. It receives (or initiates) a specific request for a meeting and returns the user's time availability by considering the user's preferences and its calendar with different kinds of commitments. Calendar management is handled by the Scheduler under a rich set of soft and hard constraints, and agents can reason about truthfully and rationally about their preferences towards optimizing the general social welfare. [3]

**Calendar Data and Display:** A human user is used to maintaining a calendar using the existing available COTS calendars. Our Calendar Data and Display module aims at having CMRadar use the same calendar programs. The current system is integrated with MS Outlook as shown in Figure 2. [4]

**Learning** Although not yet part of the system, learning is necessary because obtaining ill-structured user preferences and customizing behavior to different users by hand is infeasible. The agent must acquire much of its required knowledge about its specific user over time through experience. The current CMRadar, as we present in this paper, is the base step towards a complete CMRadar agent which will be truly a learning agent.

[1] We thank Donna Gates, Lori Levin, and Benjamin Han for their NLP work.

[2] We thank Kerry Hannan for her NLP work.

[3] We thank Elisabeth Crawford for her initial work on addressing this problem under a game theoretical approach.

[4] We thank Andrew Faulring and Brad Meyers for the integration of CMRadar with MS Outlook.

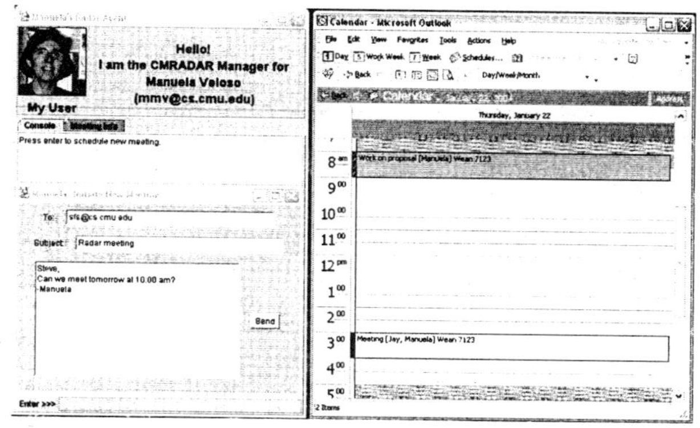


Figure 2: A single user's CMRadar integrated with MS Outlook

## Acknowledgments

This work is supported by the Defense Advanced Research Projects Agency (DARPA) under Contract No. NBCHC030029. We thank the following people for their work on CMRadar: Andrew Faulring, Brad Meyers, Kerry Hannan, Lawrence Lee, Akiva Leffert, Elisabeth Crawford, Donna Gates, Benjamin Han, and Lori Levin.

## References

Bowling, M.; Browning, B.; and Veloso, M. 2004. Plays as effective multiagent plans enabling opponent-adaptive play selection. In *Proceedings of the International Conference on Automated Planning and Scheduling (ICAPS'04)*.

Chalupsky, H.; Gil, Y.; Knoblock, C.; Lerman, K.; Oh, J.; Pynadath, D.; Russ, T.; and Tambe, M. 2001. Electric elves: Applying agent technology to support human organizations. In *Proceedings of Innovative Applications of Artificial Intelligence Conference*.

Maes, P. 1994. Agents that reduce work and information overload. *Communications of the ACM* 37(7).

Mitchell, T. M.; Caruana, R.; Freitag, D.; McDermott, J.; and Zabowski, D. 1994. Experience with a learning personal assistant. *Communications of the ACM* 37(7):80–91.

Radar. 2004. "www.radar.cs.cmu.edu".

Sen, S., and Durfee, E. H. 1998. A formal study of distributed meeting scheduling. In *Group Decision and Negotiation*, volume 7, 265–289.

Smith, S.; Lassila, O.; and Becker, M. 1996. Configurable, mixed-initiative systems for planning and scheduling. In Tate, A., ed., *Advanced Planning Technology*. Menlo Park: AAAI Press.

# Centibots: Very Large Scale Distributed Robotic Teams

**Charlie Ortiz, Kurt Konolige, Regis Vincent, Benoit Morisset, Andrew Agno, Michael Eriksen**
SRI International

**Dieter Fox, Benson Limketkai, Jonathan Ko, Benjamin Steward, Dirk Schulz**
University of Washington

## Problem and Related Work

In this paper, we describe the development of Centibots, a framework for very large teams of robots that are able to perceive, explore, plan and collaborate in unknown environments. Teams consist of approximately 100 robots which can be deployed in unexplored areas and which can efficiently distribute tasks among themselves; the system also makes use of a mixed initiative mode of interaction in which a user can easily influence missions as necessary. In contrast to simulation-based systems which abstract away aspects of the environment for examining component technologies, our design reflects an integrated, end-to-end system.

The experiments described here involve the coordinated deployment of $\approx$ 100 robots in three successive stages: (1) a mapping stage involving the coordinated exploration of the environment while simultaneously constructing a very high accuracy occupancy map using laser range finders; (2) a search stage in which the environment is exhaustively searched for a predefined object of interest (OOI); and (3) an intruder detection stage in which robots are distributed throughout the environment to "guard" the OOI by continuously sensing the environment for human intruders. This stage included recharging a portion of the robots to prove the system could continue indefinitely. Previous work has largely focused on isolated aspects of our system, including multi-robot exploration (Burgard *et al.* 2000), architecture(Gerkey & Matarić 2003), task allocation(Nair, Tambe, & Marsella 2003), coordination(Modi *et al.* 2003), and human interaction(Tews, Mataric, & Sukhatme 2003). In addition to integrating all these aspects into a working system, we had to make advances in various technical and system engineering areas, as described in the next section.

## Technical Approach

**Mapping and exploration** We developed novel decision-theoretic algorithms for robot teams to effectively coordinate mapping. Key challenges are that the robots can start from multiple, unknown locations; communication is not guaranteed; and there is no central coordination of the mapping process. We have used a multi-robot version of Lu-Milios mapping, together with novel Bayesian learning algorithms,



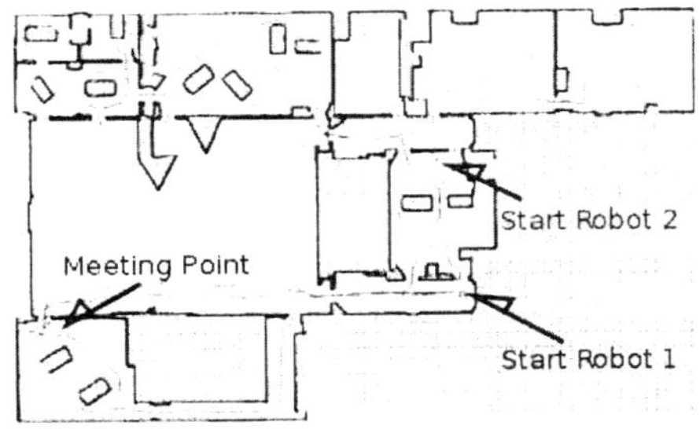


Figure 1: Map and paths during exploration. The robots start exploring from different, unknown locations. After finding a good hypothesis for their relative locations, they meet at the meeting point, merge their maps, and continue coordinated exploration under limited communication.

to solve this difficult problem (Lu & Milios 1997). If not in communication, each robot is able to explore on its own. Otherwise, the robots coordinate their exploration strategies, estimate and actively verify their relative locations (if unknown), and merge their sensor data into a globally consistent map (Ko *et al.* 2003) (also see figures 1, 2).

**Spatial reasoning** We extended current methods of spatial reasoning to associate spatial regions with team goals. A topological graph is abstracted from a Voronoi diagram and labelled with metadata to enable reasoning about movement, placement and coordination of robots. See figure 3.

**Robot teams** We developed an adaptive team organization for scalable distributed control based on the dispatcher metaphor. Robots can take on tasks as needed, request help for a task, and cause new tasks to be created. The dispatcher can run on any system in the network to facilitate the necessary coordination.

**Wireless communication** For effective information flow under a constantly changing network topology, we developed a short range communications system and used the existing Jini(Waldo 1999) system over a dynamically reconfiguring multihop, ad-hoc network(Ogier *et al.* 2002). In addition, the mixed initiative interface and the spatial reasoning could be used to create a network backbone when necessary.

**Mixed-initiative interface** We developed new mixed initiative methods for single users to track and influence missions involving hundreds of robots. The robots can be con-

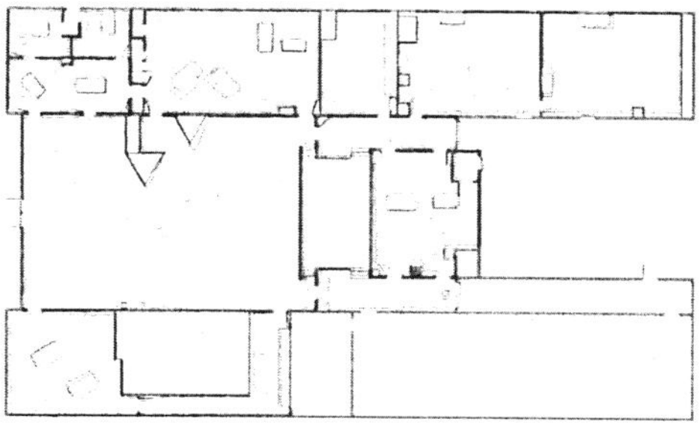

Figure 2: Generated map (free space in light gray) overlayed with a CAD model (in dark gray) of the building. The CAD model was generated from manual measurements by a third party. Map edges overlap in black.

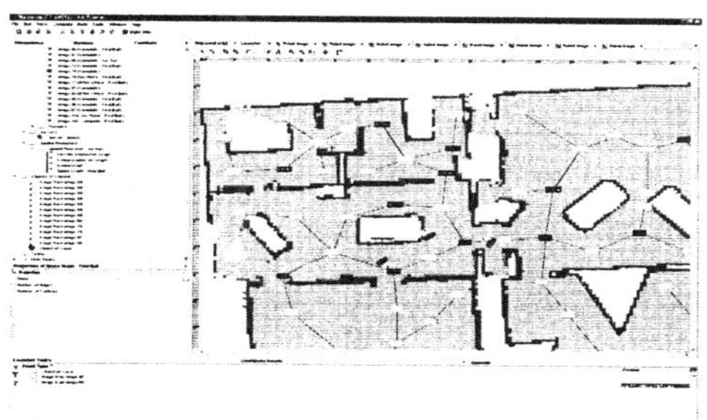

Figure 3: Mixed initiative interface with the graph structure extracted from the occupancy map. Robots are assigned to graph nodes based on the expected utility for the overall task.

trolled from the level of individual motion commands to task based behavior as part of a group. Robot groups may be constructed and reconstructed dynamically. When needed, groups can be manually reassigned tasks.

## Experiments

The Centibots project is unique in having an experimental validation conducted by an outside group. For a week in January 2004, the Centibots were tested at a $700m^2$ building in Ft. A.P. Hill, Virginia. We had no access to one third of the environment until the beginning of the experiments. The system was tested under controlled conditions, with a single operator in charge of the robot team via our mixed initiative interface. The evaluation criteria varied by stage. For mapping, these included time to create a map, topological accuracy, and percent of area mapped. For searching, the criteria were time to locate OOI(s), positional accuracy, topological accuracy, and false detections. For the protection stage, the criteria were detection, and time to first detection.

There were four 'standard' runs, going through the three stages: mapping, searching and guarding. For single robot mapping, two runs with single mappers yielded 22 and 26 minutes running time, with 100% topological accuracy for both, and 97 and 98% area accuracy. For two robots mapping, two runs yielded 17 and 19 minutes, 100% topological accuracy, with 96% area accuracy. For searching, the OOI was found in the first three runs with 100% topological accuracy with mean error in position of the OOI of 14cm. The times to find the OOI were 34, 71 and 16 minutes. The OOI was not found in the fourth run after 53 minutes of searching. One and two false positive occurred in tests two and four, respectively. For guarding, each run consisted of four separate intrusions. The detection percentages for the four runs were: 75, 50, 25[1], 100%. The average times to first detection for each run were 8, 8, 8 and 48 seconds. There was one false positive in the first run. The number of robots used for the last two stages were: 66, 55, 43 and 42.

Experiments were also performed on isolated stages of the system. For mapping, three robots were used, with the same start location. This resulted in a 1.41 times improvement in the time to map compared to the average standard run. For two mappers with different start positions, the time to map worsened by a factor of 0.82. The accuracy for both cases was the same as in the standard run, up to 1%.

For searching, five OOIs were placed. All five were detected after approximately one hour, but communications failures led to two of these detections not being reported to the command center in a reasonable fashion. Also, a rapid launch experiment was devised to determine the speed at which robots could be deployed. For this, 37 robots were deployed in 555 seconds (one robot/15 seconds).

## References


Burgard, W.; Moors, M.; Fox, D.; Simmons, R.; and Thrun, S. 2000. Collaborative multi-robot exploration. In *ICRA*.

Gerkey, B. P., and Matarić, M. J. 2003. Multi-Robot Task Allocation: Analyzing the Complexity and Optimality of Key Architectures. In *Proc. of the IEEE Intl. Conf. on Robotics and Automation (ICRA)*.

Ko, J.; Stewart, B.; Fox, D.; Konolige, K.; and Limketkai, B. 2003. A practical, decision-theoretic approach to mutirobot mapping and exploration. In *IROS*.

Lu, F., and Milios, E. 1997. Globally consistent range scan alignment for environment mapping.

Modi, P.; Shen, W.; Tambe, M.; and Yokoo, M. 2003. An asynchronous complete method for distributed constraint optimization. In *Proceedings of Autonomous Agents and Multi-Agent Systems, 2003*.

Nair, R.; Tambe, M.; and Marsella, S. 2003. Role allocation and reallocation in multiagent teams: Towards a practical analysis. In *Proceedings of Autonomous Agents and Multi-Agent Systems*.

Ogier, R.; Templin, F.; Bellur, B.; and Lewis., M. 2002. Topology broadcast based on reverse-path forwarding. IETF Internet Draft (work in progress).

Tews, A.; Mataric, M.; and Sukhatme, G. 2003. A scalable approach to human-robot interaction. IEEE International Conference on Robotics and Automation, Taipei, Taiwan, 2003.

Waldo, J. 1999. The Jini architecture for network-centric computing. *Communications of the ACM* 42(7):76–82.


[1] A misconfigured track filter was at work for this result, and was fixed before the next run

# WordNet::Similarity - Measuring the Relatedness of Concepts

**Ted Pedersen**
Department of Computer Science
University of Minnesota
Duluth, MN 55812
tpederse@d.umn.edu

**Siddharth Patwardhan**
School of Computing
University of Utah
Salt Lake City, UT 84102
sidd@cs.utah.edu

**Jason Michelizzi**
Department of Computer Science
University of Minnesota
Duluth, MN 55812
mich0212@d.umn.edu

http://search.cpan.org/dist/WordNet-Similarity
http://wn-similarity.sourceforge.net

### Abstract

WordNet::Similarity is a freely available software package that makes it possible to measure the semantic similarity or relatedness between a pair of concepts (or word senses). It provides six measures of similarity, and three measures of relatedness, all of which are based on the lexical database WordNet. These measures are implemented as Perl modules which take as input two concepts, and return a numeric value that represents the degree to which they are similar or related.

## Introduction

Measures of similarity quantify how much two concepts are alike, based on information contained in an *is–a* hierarchy. For example, an *automobile* might be considered more like a *boat* than a *tree*, if *automobile* and *boat* share *vehicle* as a common ancestor in an *is–a* hierarchy.

The lexical database WordNet is particularly well suited for similarity measures, since it organizes nouns and verbs into hierarchies of *is–a* relations. In version 2.0, there are nine noun hierarchies that include 80,000 concepts, and 554 verb hierarchies that are made up of 13,500 concepts.

*Is–a* relations in WordNet do not cross part of speech boundaries, so WordNet–based similarity measures are limited to making judgments between noun pairs (e.g., *cat* and *dog*) and verb pairs (e.g., *run* and *walk*). While WordNet includes adjectives and adverbs, these are not organized into *is–a* hierarchies so similarity measures can not be applied.

However, concepts can be related in many ways beyond being similar to each other. For example, a *wheel* is a part of a *car*, *night* is the opposite of *day*, *snow* is made up of *water*, a *knife* is used to cut *bread*, and so forth. As such WordNet provides additional (non–hierarchical) relations such as *has–part*, *is–made–of*, *is–an–attribute–of*, etc. In addition, each concept (or word sense) is described by a short written definition or gloss.

Measures of relatedness are based on these additional source of information, and as such can be applied to a wider range of concept pairs. For example, they can cross part of speech boundaries and assess the degree to which the verb *murder* and the noun *gun* are related. They can even measure the relatedness of concepts that do not reside in any *is–a* hiearchy, such as the adjectives *violent* and *harmful*.



## Similarity Measures

Three similarity measures are based on path lengths between concepts: *lch* (Leacock & Chodorow 1998), *wup* (Wu & Palmer 1994), and *path*. The *lch* measure finds the shortest path between two concepts, and scales that value by the maximum path length in the *is–a* hierarchy in which they occur. *wup* finds the path length to the root node from the least common subsumer (LCS) of the two concepts, which is the most specific concept they share as an ancestor. This value is scaled by the sum of the path lengths from the individual concepts to the root. The measure *path* is equal to the inverse of the shortest path length between two concepts.

The three remaining similarity measures are based on *information content*, which is a corpus–based measure of the specificity a concept. These measures include *res* (Resnik 1995), *lin* (Lin 1998), and *jcn* (Jiang & Conrath 1997). The *lin* and *jcn* measures augment the information content of the LCS of two concepts with the sum of the information content of the individual concepts. The *lin* measure scales the information content of the LCS by this sum, while *jcn* subtracts the information content of the LCS from this sum (and then takes the inverse to convert it from a distance to a similarity measure).

By default, the information content of concepts is derived from the sense–tagged corpus SemCor. However, there are utility programs available in WordNet::Similarity that compute information content from untagged corpora such as the Brown Corpus, the Penn Treebank, the British National Corpus, or any given corpus of plain text.

WordNet::Similarity supports two hypothetical root nodes that can be turned on and off. When on, one root node subsumes all of the noun concepts, and another subsumes all of the verb concepts. This allows for similarity measures to be applied to any pair of nouns or verbs. If the hypothetical root nodes are off, then concepts must be in the same *is–a* hierarchy for a similarity measurement to be taken.

## Measures of Relatedness

There are three relatedness measures supported in WordNet::Similarity: *hso* (Hirst & St-Onge 1998), *lesk* (Banerjee & Pedersen 2003), and *vector* (Patwardhan 2003). The *hso* measure is path based, and classifies relations in WordNet as having direction. For example, *is-a* relations are upwards, while *has–part* relations are horizontal. It establishes the relatedness between two concepts by trying to find a path between them that is neither too long nor that changes direction too often.

Each concept (or word sense) in WordNet is defined by a short gloss. The *lesk* and *vector* measures use the text of that gloss as a unique representation for the underlying concept. The *lesk* measure assigns relatedness by finding and scoring overlaps between the glosses of the two concepts, as well as concepts that are directly linked to them according to WordNet.

The *vector* measure creates a co–occurrence matrix from a corpus made up of the WordNet glosses. Each content word used in a WordNet gloss has an associated context vector. Each gloss is represented by a *gloss vector* that is the average of all the context vectors of the words found in the gloss. Relatedness between concepts is measured by finding the cosine between a pair of gloss vectors.

## Using WordNet::Similarity

WordNet::Similarity is implemented with Perl's object oriented features. It uses the WordNet::QueryData package (Rennie 2000) to create an object representing WordNet. There are a number of methods available that allow for the inclusion of existing measures in Perl source code, and also for the development of new measures.

When an existing measure is to be incorporated into a Perl program, an object of that measure must be created via the *new()* method. Then the *getRelatedness()* method can be called for a pair of word senses that appear in WordNet, and their similarity or relatedness value will be returned.

WordNet::Similarity can also be utilized via a command line interface provided by the utility program *similarity.pl*. This allows a user to run the measures interactively for specific pairs of concepts when given in *word#pos#sense* form. For example, *car#n#3* refers to the third WordNet noun sense of *car*. It also allows for the specification of all the possible senses associated with a *word* or *word#pos* combination. In addition, there is a web interface that is based on this utility.

Regardless of how it is run, WordNet::Similarity supports detailed tracing that shows a variety of diagnostic information specific to each of the different kinds of measures. For example, for the measures that rely on path lengths (*lch, wup, path*) the tracing shows all the paths found between the concepts. Tracing for the information content measures (*res, lin, jcn*) includes both the paths between concepts as well as the least common subsumer. Tracing for the *hso* measure shows the actual paths found through WordNet, while the tracing for *lesk* shows the gloss overlaps in WordNet found for the two concepts and their nearby relatives. The *vector* tracing shows the word vectors that are used to create the gloss vector of a concept.

We have incorporated WordNet::Similarity into a generalized approach to word sense disambiguation that is based on semantic relatedness (Patwardhan, Banerjee, & Pedersen 2003). This is implemented in the SenseRelate package (*http://senserelate.sourceforge.net*). The premise of this algorithm is that the sense of a word can be determined by finding which of its senses is most related to the possible senses of its neighbors. We are now exploring the use of similarity and relatedness measures in evaluating the lexical choice component of a text generation system.

## Acknowledgments

This work has been partially supported by a National Science Foundation Faculty Early CAREER Development award (#0092784), and by a Grant-in-Aid of Research, Artistry and Scholarship from the Office of the Vice President for Research and the Dean of the Graduate School of the University of Minnesota.

WordNet::Similarity is distributed under the Gnu Public License (GPL). It is freely available from the Comprehensive Perl Archive Network and SourceForge.

## References

Banerjee, S., and Pedersen, T. 2003. Extended gloss overlaps as a measure of semantic relatedness. In *Proceedings of the Eighteenth International Joint Conference on Artificial Intelligence*, 805–810.

Hirst, G., and St-Onge, D. 1998. Lexical chains as representations of context for the detection and correction of malapropisms. In Fellbaum, C., ed., *WordNet: An electronic lexical database*. MIT Press. 305–332.

Jiang, J., and Conrath, D. 1997. Semantic similarity based on corpus statistics and lexical taxonomy. In *Proceedings on International Conference on Research in Computational Linguistics*, 19–33.

Leacock, C., and Chodorow, M. 1998. Combining local context and WordNet similarity for word sense identification. In Fellbaum, C., ed., *WordNet: An electronic lexical database*. MIT Press. 265–283.

Lin, D. 1998. An information-theoretic definition of similarity. In *Proceedings of the International Conference on Machine Learning*.

Patwardhan, S.; Banerjee, S.; and Pedersen, T. 2003. Using measures of semantic relatedness for word sense disambiguation. In *Proceedings of the Fourth International Conference on Intelligent Text Processing and Computational Linguistics*, 241–257.

Patwardhan, S. 2003. Incorporating dictionary and corpus information into a context vector measure of semantic relatedness. Master's thesis, Univ. of Minnesota, Duluth.

Rennie, J. 2000. WordNet::QueryData: a Perl module for accessing the WordNet database. http://search.cpan.org/dist/WordNet-QueryData.

Resnik, P. 1995. Using information content to evaluate semantic similarity in a taxonomy. In *Proceedings of the 14th International Joint Conference on Artificial Intelligence*, 448–453.

Wu, Z., and Palmer, M. 1994. Verb semantics and lexical selection. In *32nd Annual Meeting of the Association for Computational Linguistics*, 133–138.

# PRECISE on ATIS: Semantic Tractability and Experimental Results

**Ana-Maria Popescu** **Alex Armanasu** **Oren Etzioni** **David Ko** **Alexander Yates**
University of Washington
Department of Computer Science and Engineering
Box 352350
Seattle, Washington 98195–2350
etzioni@cs.washington.edu

## Abstract

The need for Natural Language Interfaces to databases (NLIs) has become increasingly acute as more and more people access information through their web browsers, PDAs, and cell phones. Yet NLIs are only usable if they map natural language questions to SQL queries *correctly* — people are unwilling to trade reliable and predictable user interfaces for intelligent but unreliable ones. We describe a reliable NLI, PRECISE, that incorporates a modern statistical paser and a semantic module. PRECISE provably handles a large class of natural language questions correctly. On the benchmark ATIS data set, PRECISE achieves 93.8% accuracy.

## Introduction

Research on Natural Language Interfaces to databases (NLIs) has tapered off since the mid 1980's (Androutsopoulos, Ritchie, & Thanisch 1995). Yet more and more non-technical people access an increasingly complex array of databases through their web browsers and PDAs, making NLIs that reliably map English questions to SQL statements increasingly desirable.

PRECISE pushes the boundaries of NLI research in several ways. It is a "transportable" NLI in that it minimizes manual, database-specific configuration. Second, it incorporates the important advances made by statistical parsers over the last two decades, using semantic information to override syntactic information in cases where it knows how to correct parser mistakes. And third, PRECISE is built on a theoretical foundation that identifies a class of *Semantically Tractable* (ST) questions for which PRECISE is always correct, given correct syntactic and lexical information. Thus PRECISE is making progress, both theoretically and experimentally, on the goal of a reliable NLI.

## Terminology and Theory

In an NLIDB, interpretations of a sentence are SQL statements. By giving a set of lexical constraints, semantic constraints, and syntactic constraints, we define what it means for an SQL statement to be a *valid interpretation* of a question. Our theoretical goal is to find classes of questions for which we can provably identify all the valid interpretations. While understanding natural language questions in general may be regarded as an "AI-complete" problem, questions like "What are the Chinese restaurants in Seattle?" are relatively easy to understand. Thus we have defined the class of ST questions, and we have shown that PRECISE always returns exactly the set of valid interpretations for any ST question, given correct syntactic and lexical information. (Etzioni *et al.* 2004)



## PRECISE in Action

Consider the following question $q_1$ at the beginning of a dialog: "What are the flights from Boston to Chicago on Monday?"

**Non-elliptical Sentence Interpretation.** First, the system derives a set of word attachment constraints from $q_1$'s parse tree. For example, "flight" is attached to "Boston" through preposition "from." The *tokenizer* produces a single tokenization of this question `(what, is, flight, from, boston, to, chicago,on,Monday)` and computes the token attachment function. PRECISE efficiently retrieves the set of matching database elements for every token from the *lexicon*. The *matcher* reduces the problem of satisfying the semantic constraints imposed by the valid interpretation definition to a graph matching problem and solves it efficiently with the Maxflow algorithm. The *query generator* takes the attachment information, the mappings of sentence tokens to database elements, the solution to the graph match, and a set of valid join paths between pairs of relations (as defined by the database administrator), and it constructs an SQL statement that obeys the semantic, syntactic, and lexical constraints identified by the inputs.

**Elliptical Fragment Interpretation** Now consider a follow-up question $q_2$, "from Boston to Atlanta?" PRECISE uses the *default*, *replacement* and *merging* operations to understand elliptical questions. The *default* operation consists of adding a wh-token to a tokenization of $q_2$, and it is the only one used when interpreting an elliptical sentence as a stand-alone utterance. The other two operations make use of the notion of *parallel* tokens: informally, tokens from two different sentences are parallel if they have the same token type and participate in *compatible* attachment constraints. The tokens `atlanta` and `boston` in $q_2$ and $q_1$, respectively, are not parallel because different

| System Setup | PRECISE | PRECISEL |
|---|---|---|
| $Parser_{ORIG}$, *No Over-rides* | 61.7% | 60.1% |
| $Parser_{ORIG}$, *Over-rides* | 89.5% | 85.3% |
| $Parser_{ATIS}$, *No Over-rides* | 92.2% | 88.1% |
| $Parser_{ATIS}$, *Over-rides* | 93.8% | 89.1% |
| $Parser_{CORRECT}$, *Over-rides* | 95.1% | 91.3% |

Table 1: **Impact of Parser Enhancements. The PRECISE column records the percentage of questions where the small set of SQL queries returned by PRECISE contains the correct query; PRECISEL refers to the questions correctly interpreted if PRECISE is forced to return exactly one SQL query.** $Parser_{ORIG}$ **is the original version of the parser,** $Parser_{ATIS}$ **is the version re-trained for the ATIS domain, and** $Parser_{CORRECT}$ **is the version whose output is corrected manually. *Over-rides* refer to the automatic use of semantic over-rides to correct parser errors.**

prepositions mediate their attachment, whereas `atlanta` and `chicago` are parallel because they have similar types and compatible attachment constraints. The *replacement* operation substitutes $q_2$ tokens for parallel $q_1$ tokens. In the merging operation, if there are tokens in $q_2$ that are not parallel to any in $q_1$ (or vice versa), they are kept as part of the final tokenization $T'_{q_2}$. Here are possible tokenizations $T'_{q_2}$, computed using the replacement and merging operations described above: $T'_{q_2}$=`what, fare, from, boston, to, atlanta, on, monday`, $T'_{q_2}$=`what, fare, from, boston, to, atlanta`.

## Experimental Evaluation

Previously, we measured the practical impact of our theoretical framework by assessing the first version of our system on hundreds of natural language questions compiled by researchers at U.T. Austin (Tang & Mooney 2001) - we obtained 100% precision and approximately 80% recall. We then evaluated our system on the well-known ATIS dataset. The scoring set contains 445 context-independent sentences and 287 context-dependent sentences. There are 9 elliptical context-independent questions and 15 elliptical context-dependent questions. PRECISE was able to interpret ??? out of the 445 sentences in the A dataset. The rest were intractable either due to parser error (how many???) or due to intractability of ellipsis. 9 sentences were incorrectly interpreted. PRECISE correctly handles all 15 elliptical context-dependent sentences. The accuracy on transcribed text input on the A set is 93.8%, which is comparable to the response error rate of the best ATIS systems (see Table2).

| Precise | AT&T | CMU |
|---|---|---|
| 93.8% | 96.2% | 96.2% |

Table 2: **Response error rate comparison:** PRECISE **vs. highest-performing ATIS systems.**

In another series of experiments, we tested how the behavior of PRECISE changed according to the quality of the syntactic information it was provided with (see Table 1). We measured PRECISE's accuracy using the Charniak parser, the Charniak parser retrained on questions from the ATIS domain, and manually corrected syntactic information. Overall, the results improved from 61.7% accuracy to 95.1% accuracy as the parser improved.

## Related Work

There have been a great number of systems built for the ATIS domain. Semantic parser-based systems (Seneff 1992; Ward & Issar 1996) used manually-crafted, context-free semantic rules to fill slots in semantic frames. Stoachastic model-based systems (Levin & Pieraccini 1995) require a fully annotated corpus to build a reliable model. PRECISE's, on the other hand, uses a set of domain-independent semantic constraints and existing parsing technology so that it is more portable than both kinds of systems while performing comparably on ATIS.

Mooney's learning approach to database interfaces requires a great deal of hand tagged sentences, and it emphasizes recall over precision by attempting to interpret sentences with unknown words. As far as handling ellipsis is concerned, most previous work (such as (Crouch 1995; Dalrymple, Shieber, & Pereira 1991)) deals with verb phrase ellipsis and only tangentially mentions noun phrase elliptical fragments. (Carbonell 1983) requires a semantic grammar, so the application cannot easily be ported to another domain and processes only a subset of the elliptical fragments PRECISE can handle.

## References


Androutsopoulos, I.; Ritchie, G. D.; and Thanisch, P. 1995. Natural Language Interfaces to Databases - An Introduction. In *Natural Language Engineering, vol 1, part 1*, 29–81.

Carbonell, J. 1983. Discourse pragmatics and ellipsis resolution in task-oriented natural language interfaces. In *Proceedings of the 21st Annual Meeting of the Association for Computational Linguistics*, 164–168.

Crouch, R. 1995. Ellipsis and quantifi cation: A substitutional approach. In *Proceedings of the Seventh Conference of the European Chapter of the Association for Computational Linguistics*, 229–236.

Dalrymple, M.; Shieber, S.; and Pereira, F. C. N. 1991. Ellipsis and higher-order unifi cation. *Linguistics and Philosophy* 14(4):399–452.

Etzioni, O.; Popescu, A.; Armanasu, A.; Yates, A.; and Ko, D. 2004. Semantically tractable questions and follow-up questions in the atis data. In *Submitted to Coling-2004*.

Levin, E., and Pieraccini, R. 1995. Chronus, the next generation. In *Proceedings of the DARPA Speech and Natural Language Workshop*, 269–271.

Seneff, S. 1992. Robust parsing for spoken language systems. In *Proceedings of the IEEE International Conference on Acoustics, Speech and Signal Processing*.

Tang, L., and Mooney, R. 2001. Using multiple clause constructors in inductive logic programming for semantic parsing. In *Proceedings of the 12th European Conference on Machine Learning (ECML-2001), Freiburg, Germany*, 466–477.

Ward, W., and Issar, S. 1996. Recent improvements in the cmu spoken language understanding system. In *Proceedings of the ARPA Human Language Technology Workshop*, 213–216.

# SEM-Ether: Semantic Web based Pervasive Computing Framework - Integrating Web, Devices and People

**Sushil Puradkar, Sachin Singh, Chintan Patel, Kartik Vishwanath, Rahul Gupta, Yugyung Lee**

School of Computing and Engineering, University of Missouri – Kansas City
{shpgzd, sbs7vc, copdk4, kvktb, rgxq2, leeyu}@umkc.edu

### Abstract

Pervasive computing aims to build an aggregated environment around a user by knitting diverse computing and communicating devices and software services into a single homogeneous unit. Our work is to develop a Pervasive computing framework which harnesses the power of Semantic Web and Web Services, facilitating the development of effective and intelligent Pervasive environments. This paper presents a high level view of the framework and how different Pervasive services can be built on this framework

## Introduction

Computers have become part of daily lives of people and are becoming increasingly dependent on traditional computers and other networked computing mobile devices. Though the intention of these devices is to help people in improving the way they do their work, it happens that these devices are more intrusive in terms of increased overheads of managing information distributed across them and the context of interaction with these devices. We need these computing devices to seamlessly integrate into our daily activities by creating a collective environment around a user managing the distributed information a single amassed information and managing the context of interaction across the physical devices. The computing environment around us should proactively tailor and present itself depending upon specific role, location, preferences and similar context parameters for a given individual.

Pervasive Computing is an effort towards achieving the vision of invisible computing fabric around us. The target is to create smart homes, smart offices with intelligent computing devices connected through reliable network that would recognize and adapt accordingly to users and help them to smoothly carry on their tasks without explicit commands.

Current research in Pervasive computing has been much localized, in sense the current Pervasive computing systems [1] [2] have been demonstrated in restricted environment with several assumptions about devices and information representation. Our goal is to remove the barriers of representation and devices communication by using Semantic Web as a mechanism for a generic Pervasive Computing Framework that extends beyond a particular room or organization. Semantic Web provides standardized [3] representation mechanisms that allow automated reasoning and representation of information and services over Web.

## The SEM-Ether Approach

Our solution is to use Ontological representations for User profiles, context, preferences and Semantic Web service based wrappers for physical devices and information services. Depending upon the user event, the Pervasive Computing Framework, SEM-Ether, would execute service planner that invokes and composes different services depending upon the event and user profile. With such approach, we can easily envision a global Pervasive Computing framework where different computing devices in different environments or locations would recognize the user and provide appropriate services.

We have developed a prototype for SEM-Ether that demonstrates the intended goals and shows the feasibility for the proposed approach. Integrating some common computing devices such as PDAs, Cell phones and personal computers, we show how the system actually functions and interacts seamlessly with the user. To bring out the effectiveness of the framework, we have implemented the framework for several scenarios. We intend to give a demonstration for the selected scenarios and show how new scenarios can be dynamically added to the framework.

## Architectural Description

The major focus in the design of SEM-Ether has been to make it simple and easily implemented to allow wider acceptance and usage. We show a high level architecture diagram for the framework in Fig 1. The Event Handler is a central key component that is responsible for capturing various user-events, such as the "User-In" event when a user enters the environment. Current implementation of Event Handler has been as a Web Service that is invoked by the event generated by the client. The Event Handler invokes the Service Planner which essentially interfaces Semantic Web and has modules for parsing the Semantic User Profile and invoking Semantic Web services. The semantic user profile is annotated information about a user which stores various aspects of the users, like his history, likes/dislikes, medical information. We foresee that in future, user would 'host' their marked up profiles on 'profile servers' analogous to the user web pages of today's Web.

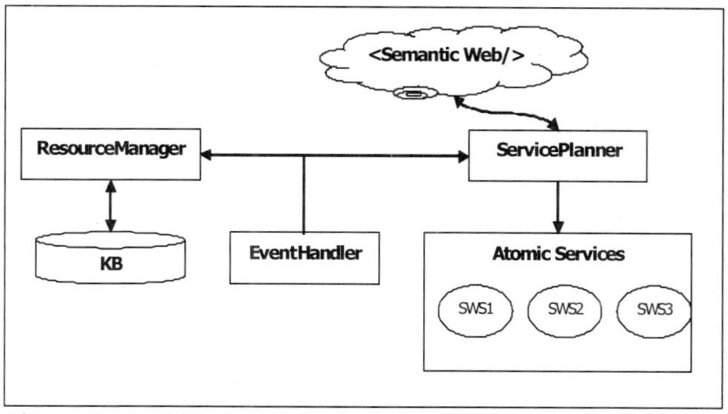


Figure 1. Architecture Diagram

The base of the Pervasive system is a set of Atomic Services that abstract local devices such as a printer or software services like scheduling software. These atomic services are presented as Web Services and are marked up semantically. The Resource Manager stores the information about the resources; hardware or software, part of the given environment in the local KB. The User event is caught by the Event Handler and processed by the Service Planner which fetches the corresponding user context parameters and provides a required service to the user by discovering and composing the available set of local atomic services. The planner also interfaces Semantic Web services over Web. The Service Planner invokes a set of atomic services which takes inputs from user's context and current resource settings and the complete task is accomplished.

## Scenarios

We demonstrate the working of the SEM-Ether using several interesting scenarios:

a) **Pervasive Music**: The framework recognizes the user, fetches the user profile from the Web which stores information about user's favorite songs. In this scenario the context is defined by the user's location, user's music preferences and the system policies. The system fetches user's favorite song from the atomic service which provides it or from the external services using Web Service. It then selects the atomic audio service to play the song on the speakers nearest to the user.

b) **Pervasive Buddies**: The system keeps track of the users present in environment. When a new user enters into the environment, the system fetches his/her user profile from Web and checks his/her buddy list (Fig. 2). If any of his/her buddies is present in the environment then the system alerts the user and his/her buddy. The device used to alert these users depends on the context. The system can send message on user's device like his/her PDA or cell phone or can flash a message on his/her computer.

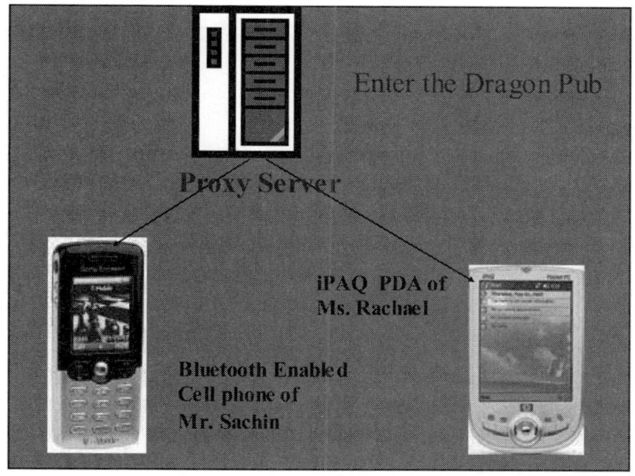


Figure 2. Buddy-Alert: SEM-Ether notifies the presence of buddies on their respective devices.

c) **Pervasive Phone**: The phony service is an intelligent telephone call forwarding service which forwards the telephone call depending on user's current location in the environment. We have also defined policies that govern the call forwarding service. Hence if user is busy with some high priority activity then the system redirects the call to an appropriate person or gives dynamic message to the caller, depending on the context. Since the framework is exposed as Web Service to the external world and user profile is always updated with the user's current location, the system is also capable of handling call forwarding across different Pervasive environments.

d) **Pervasive Scheduling**: User schedule is an integral part of semantic user profile. The system monitors user schedule as long as the user present in the environment. If any task is scheduled in the user's calendar then the system takes an appropriate action to execute related service to that event or informs the user about the event by sending notification to the device which the user is currently using. The user schedules can be updated and referred to irrespective of the environment he/she is currently in.

## References

[1] The Official Oxygen Brochure., http://www.oxygen.lcs.mit.edu/publications/Oxygen.pdf

[2] Project Aura at CMU http://www-2.cs.cmu.edu/~aura/

[3] Word Wide Web Consortium http://www.w3c.org

# SenseClusters - Finding Clusters that Represent Word Senses

**Amruta Purandare** and **Ted Pedersen**
Department of Computer Science
University of Minnesota
Duluth, MN 55812
{pura0010,tpederse}@d.umn.edu
http://senseclusters.sourceforge.net

**Abstract**

SenseClusters is a freely available word sense discrimination system that takes a purely unsupervised clustering approach. It uses no knowledge other than what is available in a raw unstructured corpus, and clusters instances of a given target word based only on their mutual contextual similarities. It is a complete system that provides support for feature selection from large corpora, several different context representation schemes, various clustering algorithms, and evaluation of the discovered clusters.

## Introduction

Most words in natural language have multiple possible meanings that can only be determined by considering the context in which they occur. Given instances of a target word used in a number of different contexts, word sense discrimination is the process of grouping these instances into clusters that refer to the same word meaning. Approaches to this problem are often based on the strong contextual hypothesis of (Miller & Charles 1991), which states that *two words are semantically related to the extent that their contextual representations are similar*. Hence the problem of word sense discrimination reduces to that of determining which contexts of a given target word are related or similar.

SenseClusters creates clusters made up of the contexts in which a given target word occurs. All the instances in a cluster are contextually similar to each other, making it more likely that the given target word has been used with the same meaning in all of those instances. Each instance normally includes two or three sentences, one of which contains the given occurrence of the target word.

SenseClusters was originally intended to discriminate among word senses. However, the methodology of clustering contextually (and hence semantically) similar instances of text can be used in a variety of natural language processing tasks such as synonymy identification, text summarization and document classification. SenseClusters has also been used for applications such as email sorting and automatic ontology construction.



## Feature Selection

SenseClusters distinguishes among the different contexts in which a target word occurs based on a set of features that are identified from raw corpora. SenseClusters uses the Ngram Statistics Package (http://ngram.sourceforge.net), which is able to extract surface lexical features from large corpora using frequency cutoffs and various measures of association.

SenseClusters currently supports the use of unigram, bigram, and co-occurrence features. Unigrams are individual words that occur above a certain frequency cutoff. These can be effective discriminating features if they are shared by a minimum of two contexts, but not shared by all contexts. Very common non-content words are excluded by providing a stop–list.

Bigrams are pairs of words that occur above a given frequency cutoff and that have a statistically significant score on a test of association. There may optionally be intervening words between them that are ignored. Co–occurrences are unordered word pairs that include the target word. In effect co–occurrences localize the scope of the unigram features by selecting only those words that occur within some number of positions from the target word.

SenseClusters allows for the selection of lexical features either from a held out corpus of training data, or from the same data that is to be clustered, which we refer to as the test data. Selecting features from separate training data is particularly useful when the amount of the test data to be clustered is too small to identify interesting features.

## Context Representation

Once features are selected, SenseClusters creates a vector for each test instance to be discriminated where each selected feature is represented by an entry/index. Each vector shows if the feature represented by the corresponding index occurs or not in the context of the instance (binary vectors), or how often the feature occurs in the context (frequency vectors). This is referred to as a first order context vector, since this representation directly indicates which features make up the contexts. Here we are following (Pedersen & Bruce 1997), who likewise took this approach to feature representation.

(Schütze 1998) utilized second order context vectors that represent the context of a target word to be discriminated by taking the average of the first order vectors associated with the unigrams that occur in that context. In SenseClusters we have extended this idea such that these first order vectors can also be based on co–occurrence or bigram features from the training corpus.

Both the first and second order context vectors represent the given instances as vectors in a high dimensional word space. This approach suffers from two limitations. First, there may be synonyms represented by separate dimensions in the space. Second, and conversely, a single dimension in the space might be polysemous and associated with several different underlying concepts. To combat these problems, SenseClusters follows the lead of Latent Semantic Analysis (Landauer, Foltz, & Laham 1998) and allows for the conversion of word level feature spaces into a concept level semantic space by carrying out dimensionality reduction with Singular Value Decomposition (SVD). In particular, the package SVDPACK (Berry *et al.* 1993) is integrated into SenseClusters to allow for fast and efficient SVD.

## Clustering

Clustering can be carried out using either a first or second order vector representation of instances. SenseClusters provides a seamless interface to CLUTO, a Clustering Toolkit (Karypis 2002), which implements a range of clustering techniques suitable for both representations, including repeated bisections, direct, nearest neighbor, agglomerative, and biased agglomerative.

The first or second order vector representations of contexts can be directly clustered using vector space methods provided in CLUTO. As an alternative, each context vector can be represented as a point in similarity space such that the distance between it and any other context vector reflects the pairwise similarity of the underlying instances.

SenseClusters provides support for a number of similarity measures, such as simple matching, the cosine, the Jaccard coefficient, and the Dice coefficient. A similarity matrix created by determining all pairwise measures of similarity between contexts can be used as an input to CLUTO's clustering algorithms, or to SenseClusters' own agglomerative clustering implementation.

## Evaluation

SenseClusters supports evaluation of the clusters it discovers via external and internal evaluation techniques.

When an external gold standard clustering of the instances is available, SenseClusters builds a confusion matrix that shows the distribution of the known senses in each of the discovered clusters. A gold standard most typically exists in the form of sense–tagged text, where each sense tag can be considered to represent a different cluster that could be discovered. SenseClusters finds the mapping of gold standard senses to discovered clusters that would result in maximally accurate discrimination. The problem of assigning senses to clusters becomes one of re-ordering the columns of the confusion matrix to maximize the diagonal sum. Thus, each possible re-ordering shows one assignment scheme and the sum of the diagonal entries indicates the total number of instances in the discovered clusters that would be in their correct sense given that alignment. This corresponds to several well known problems, among them the Assignment Problem in Operations Research and finding the maximal matching of a bipartite graph.

When gold standard data is not available, SenseClusters relies on CLUTO's internal evaluation metrics to report the intra-cluster and inter-cluster similarity. There is also a graphical component to CLUTO known as gCLUTO that provides a visualization tool. In unsupervised word sense discrimination, the user will usually not know the actual number of senses ahead of time. One possible solution to this problem is to request an arbitrarily large number of clusters and rely on such visualizations to discover the true number of senses. In future work, we plan to support mechanisms that automatically determine the optimal number of clusters/senses to be found.

## Acknowledgments

This work has been partially supported by a National Science Foundation Faculty Early CAREER Development award (Grant #0092784).

SenseClusters is an open source software project that is freely distributed under the GNU Public License (GPL) via http://senseclusters.sourceforge.net/

SenseClusters is an ongoing project, and there are already a number of published papers based on its use (e.g., (Purandare 2003), (Purandare & Pedersen 2004)).

## References

Berry, M.; Do, T.; O'Brien, G.; Krishna, V.; and Varadhan, S. 1993. SVDPACK (version 1.0) User's Guide. Technical Report CS-93-194, University of Tennessee at Knoxville, Computer Science Department.

Karypis, G. 2002. CLUTO - a clustering toolkit. Technical Report 02-017, University of Minnesota, Department of Computer Science.

Landauer, T.; Foltz, P.; and Laham, D. 1998. An introduction to Latent Semantic Analysis. *Discourse Processes* 25:259–284.

Miller, G., and Charles, W. 1991. Contextual correlates of semantic similarity. *Language and Cognitive Processes* 6(1):1–28.

Pedersen, T., and Bruce, R. 1997. Distinguishing word senses in untagged text. In *Proceedings of the Second Conference on Empirical Methods in Natural Language Processing*, 197–207.

Purandare, A., and Pedersen, T. 2004. Word sense discrimination by clustering contexts in vector and similarity spaces. In *Proceedings of the Conference on Computational Natural Language Learning*.

Purandare, A. 2003. Discriminating among word senses using Mcquitty's similarity analysis. In *Proceedings of the HLT-NAACL 2003 Student Research Workshop*, 19–24.

Schütze, H. 1998. Automatic word sense discrimination. *Computational Linguistics* 24(1):97–123.

# CAMEO : Modeling Human Activity in Formal Meeting Situations

**Paul E. Rybski, Fernando de la Torre, Raju Patil, Carlos Vallespi, Manuela Veloso, Brett Browning**
Robotics Institute,Carnegie Mellon University
5000 Forbes Ave.,Pittsburgh, PA 15213
Email: {prybski,ftorre,raju,cvalles,veloso,brettb}@cs.cmu.edu

### Abstract

We present CAMEO, the Camera Assisted Meeting Event Observer, which is a physical awareness system designed for use by an agent-based electronic assistant. CAMEO is used to observe formal meeting environments and infer the activities of people attending them.

## Introduction

We have recently engaged on the challenging development of an agent to assist users in everyday office-related tasks. In particular, the agent needs to keep track of the state of their users so it can anticipate the user's needs and proactively address them. To address this challenge, we have developed CAMEO, the Camera Assisted Meeting Event Observer (Rybski *et al.* 2004), which is a physical awareness system designed for use by an agent-based electronic assistant. CAMEO addresses the problem of extracting and reasoning about high-level features from real-time and continuous observation of a meeting environment. Contextual information about meetings and the interactions that take place within them are used to define Dynamic Bayesian Network classifiers to effectively infer the state of the users as well as a higher-level state of the meeting. CAMEO is part of a larger effort called CALO (Cognitive Agent that Learns and Organizes) to develop an enduring personalized cognitive assistant that is capable of helping humans handle the many daily business/personal activities in which they engage. CAMEO is intended to be used in a manner similar to a speaker/video phone for a conference call.

## The CAMEO System

CAMEO is an omni-directional camera system consisting of four or five firewire cameras (CAMEO supports both configurations) mounted in a circle, as shown in Figure 1. The individual data streams coming from each of the cameras are merged into a single panoramic image of the world. The cameras are connected to a Small Form-Factor 3.0GHz Pentium 4 PC that captures the video data and does the image processing.

Faces are detected using an algorithm by Schneiderman and Kanade (Schneiderman & Kanade 1998) which is a



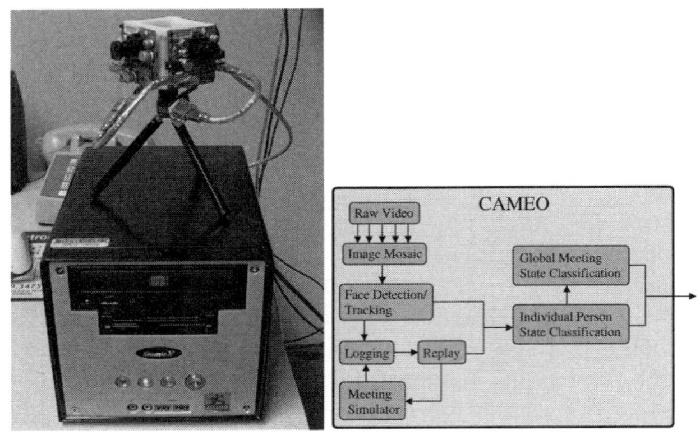


Figure 1: CAMEO consists a panoramic vision system and a small-form-factor PC. CAMEO processes video from its camera to locate people and classify their actions.

parts-based method for classification of image regions into "face" and "non-face" regions. It explicitly models and estimates the joint statistics of local appearance and position on the face and the statistics of local appearance in the visual world. by using approximately a million patterns to represent local appearance and counts the frequency of occurrence of these patterns over a large set of training images to compute the probabilities. Once detected, the faces are classified by computing a distance metric between sets of tracked faces and the new faces. Matches are those that have the smallest distance. The metric is computed by taking the SVD of the image sets and computing the weighted sum of the most significant eigenvectors. The relative displacements of the face's centroid are used as features for the person action recognition system. Finally, a color histogram of the person's face and torso is learned to allow the person to be tracked from frame to frame regardless of whether their face is visible to CAMEO.

The panoramic video stream is scanned for human activity by identifying the positions of human faces found in the image. This low-level visual information is fed into a Dynamic Bayesian Network (Murphy 2002) (DBN) classifier system. The classifier determines the state of the individual people in the meeting. These individual person state esti-

(a) Positions of faces detected by CAMEO with the Schneiderman and Kanade algorithm.

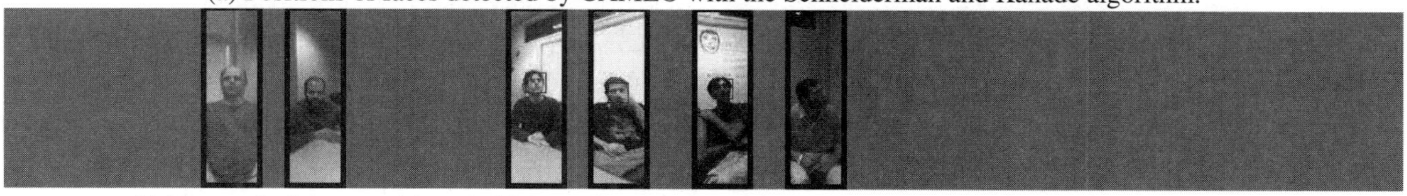

(b) The tracked face positions (with bounding box to capture the body) as stored by the tracking system.

(c) Synthesized facial data from a simulated meeting whose parameters were learned from real data.

Figure 2: Several data gathering and representation layers in CAMEO.

mates are then used to infer high-level state estimates of the meeting itself. Our approach makes use of a very specific set of contextual information regarding the meeting domain to generate the Bayesian classification system, rather than attempting to solve the general image understanding problem.

## Inferring Human Activity

Inferring the state of activities in a meeting takes place at two levels. The first level is the state classification of the individual people attending the meeting. The second level is classification of global meeting state, which is done after the individual states of the people are determined. Instead of attempting to solve the image understanding problem purely from data, we construct a set of Dynamic Bayesian Network classifiers from *a priori* knowledge about meetings and how interactions between people in those meetings.

In order to determine the state of each person in the meeting, a Dynamic Bayesian Network (DBN) model of a Hidden Markov Model (HMM) (Rabiner 1989) is created with a single discrete hidden node and a single continuous-valued observation node. Given a sequence of real-valued state observations from the meeting, the above DBN inference algorithm is used to infer the state of each person from data.

The state transition function for the DBN's hidden state is defined by a simple finite state machine model of a person's behavior. Example states for an individual person's actions include: stand, standing , sit, sitting, and walking. The conditional probability distribution for the hidden node are either hand-coded or learned from collecting statistics from CAMEO's observations. The global state of the meeting is determined by examining all of the states of the individual meeting participants. Allowable state transitions are defined as a first-order (fully-observable) Markov model which takes into account a minimum duration for a state transition.

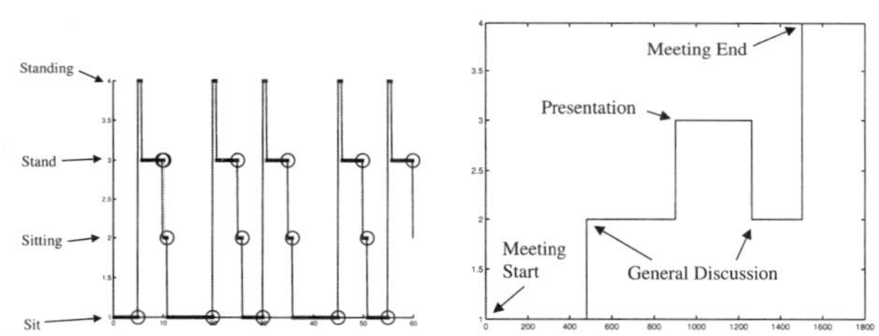


Figure 3: Classified states from a single person (left) as well as the global state of the meeting (right).

## References

Murphy, K. 2002. *Dynamic Bayesian Networks: representation, Inference and Learning*. Ph.D. Dissertation, UC Berkeley, Computer Science Division.

Rabiner, L. R. 1989. A tutorial on Hidden Markov Models and selected applications in speech recognition. *Proceedings of the IEEE* 77(2):257–286.

Rybski, P. E.; de la Torre, F.; Patil, R.; Vallespi, C.; Veloso, M. M.; and Browning, B. 2004. Cameo: The camera assisted meeting event observer. In *International Conference on Robotics and Automation*.

Schneiderman, H., and Kanade, T. 1998. Probabilistic modeling of local appearance and spatial relationships for object recognition. In *Proceedings of the IEEE Conference on Computer Vision and Pattern Recognition*, 45–51.

# A Robotic Model of Human Reference Resolution

**Matthias Scheutz**(*) and **Virgil Andronache**(*) and **Kathleen Eberhard**(**)
(*) Department of Computer Science and Engineering
(**) Department of Psychology
University of Notre Dame, Notre Dame, IN 46556, USA
mscheutz,vandrona,keberhar@nd.edu

### Abstract

Evidence from psychology suggests that humans process definite descriptions that refer to objects present in a visual scene incrementally upon hearing them, rather than constructing explicit parse trees after the whole sentence was said, which are then used to determine the referents. In this paper, we describe a real-time distributed robotic architectures for human reference resolution that demonstrates various interactions of auditory, visual, and semantic processing components hypothesized to underlie human processes.

## Introduction

Processing natural language sentences in typical AI algorithms involves a syntactic analysis of the sentence, followed by the construction of one or more parse trees, for each of which the assignment of meaning can subsequently be attempted. This approach, however, can lead to a large number of possible unnecessary parse trees, especially, for simple instructions like "Put the red block on the blue block on the green block on the yellow block..." (e.g., the red block could be on the blue, and should be put green block on top of a yellow block), where referents can be incrementally restricted based on the context in which the sentences is encountered. Evidence from psychology suggests that humans, rather than constructing explicit parse trees, use an incremental method for determining the referents of such expressions based on context that is available to them.

In this paper, we use experimental results from studies with humans as a basis for the development of a robotic architecture that verifies the method of reference resolutions hypothesized for humans. Moreover, we demonstrate a parallel implementation of the proposed architecture, which shows the real-time interactions of auditory, visual, and semantic processing components in the architecture framework APOC (Scheutz forthcoming).

## A Model of Human Reference Resolution

The domain under consideration is a simple *Blocks World Domain*, in which blocks of different color can be stacked (e.g., see the left part of Figure 1). Blocks can exhibit one of the following relationships: they can be *on*, *under*, or *next-to* other blocks, or they can be *single* (i.e., without any immediately adjacent block). In this domain, it is easily possible to arrange situations, where referential expressions are ambiguous. For example, "the red block" fails to pick out a referent if there are two or more red blocks in a scene. However, if "the red block" is followed by "on the blue block", and if there is only one red block on a blue block, the unique reference can be established.



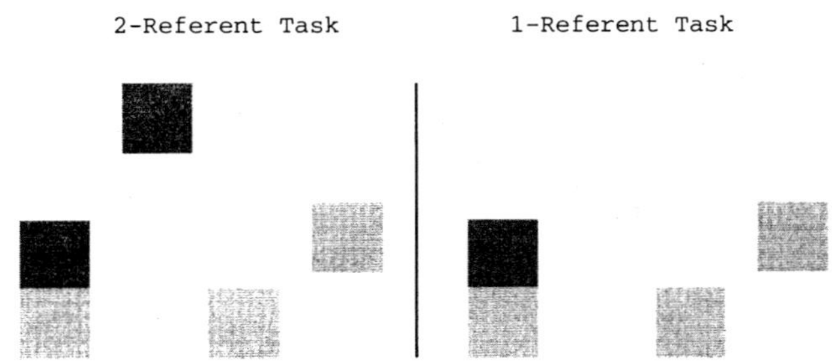


Figure 1: The overall setup of the experiment for the resolution of referents in instructions like "Put the red block on the orange block on the blue block."

In our model we consider sentences like the following: "Put the red block on the orange block on the blue block". Syntactically, this sentence has two parse trees, which can be expressed logically as follows: PUT(REDBLOCK,ON(ORANGEBLOCK,BLUEBLOCK)) or PUT(ON(REDBLOCK,ORANGEBLOCK),BLUEBLOCK). Suppose we are given the environment on the left in Figure 1. Starting with the first parse tree, the resolution of the reference of ON(ORANGEBLOCK,BLUEBLOCK)) fails as there is no orange block on a blue block. Consequently, in a typical computational approach, this parse tree is discarded and the tree will be considered (if it exists). In the above case, the reference to ON(REDBLOCK,ORANGEBLOCK) succeeds.

Interestingly, this method based on all possible parse trees is not the way humans resolve reference when the referents are visually co-present. Rather, humans seem to resolve reference incrementally–without building explicit parse trees and using backtracking to build an alternative tree if the previous one fails: upon hearing "red" in the above sentence and scenario, they build a set of possible referents $PR(red)$, which at this point contains two red blocks. Since the set is not a singleton, the subsequent words are taken to specify constraints on $PR$ and thus to belong to the same referential phrase. Hence, upon hearing "on" a constraint will be instantiated that limits the referents in $PR(red)$ based on the set $PR(orange)$, which will be formed upon hearing "orange". Since the newly formed set $PR(on(red, orange))$ is a singleton, the referent, which is the argument for "put" has been established to be the single element in $PR(on(red, orange))$. Hence, subsequent words are not taken to be part of the definite description anymore.

Now consider a situation depicted on the right in Figure 1, where the referent of "the red block" is uniquely specified. Taking again the above sentence "Put the red block on the orange block on the blue block", a classical parser would produce the unique parse PUT(ON(REDBLOCK,ORANGEBLOCK),BLUE). Hence, there is no ambiguity as to what the sentences seems to ask for. Yet, for human subjects, this sentences causes problems, because according to the above described algorithm reference to a unique object is established upon hearing "red", at which point "on" is taken to belong to "put". Consequently, the second argument of "put", i.e., the location at which to place the red block, is taken to be the referent of "orange". Although this is a set with two possible referents, the precondition of "put"–that no block can be on top of a target of the *put action*–eliminates the orange block underneath the red block, and thus reduces the set of possible referents for "orange" to a singleton (namely, the orange block on the right). Hence, at this point, all the information is present that allows subjects to carry out the put action. Yet, the sentence has not finished, but rather the additional, but seemingly superfluous phrase "on the blue block" is heard. At this point, human subjects attempt to make sense of that phrase. While some subjects interpret it as another put action (after having put the red block from the orange block on the left onto the orange block on the right), others simply ignore it.

## Model and Architecture

Several psychological experiments have established the above effect (e.g., (Tanenhaus et al. 1995)) and suggest the above algorithm described for the human behavior. In particular, the assumption is that resolving reference is an incremental process that does not depend on prior established parse trees, which, if a conflict is encountered, are discarded to build alternative trees (if possible). The architecture that implements the above algorithm is depicted in Figure 2.

Each rectangle indicates a component type, whose function is indicated by its label. While some types only have one instance in the virtual machine (e.g., speech recognition), others can have multiple ones (e.g., blob tracking). For space reasons, we can only briefly sketch the functionality of the architecture.

Lexical items are processed in real-time using *Sphinx 2* (see HTTP://WWW.SPEECH.CS.CMU.EDU/SPHINX/). The recognized words are passed to the word analysis node, which ensures that only one word at a time is processed (this node effectively "wraps" the Sphinx system within APOC).

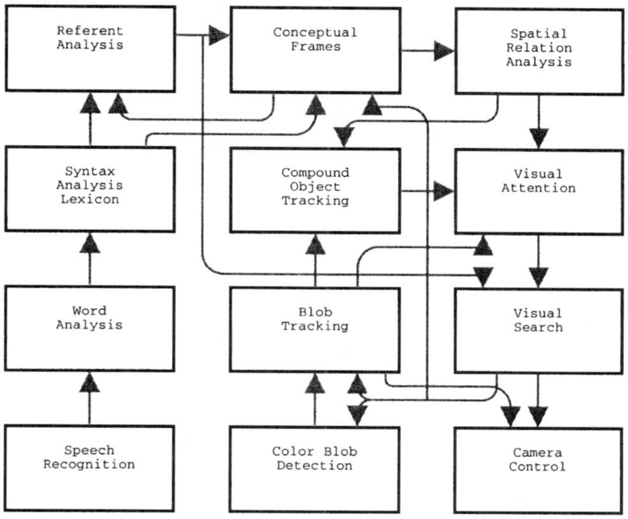


Figure 2: A high-level view of the components employed in the architecture used in the reference resolution task.

The syntactic analysis looks up the word in a lexicon and either initiates a referential analysis (if a referential expression is expected), or instantiates the associated conceptual frame, if it exists (e.g., as in the case of "put"), which will pass control to the referential analysis to obtain its arguments. The referential analysis influences the visual search, which will look for items that match the meaning of the expression built so far. This process involves the instantiation of trackers that lock onto recognized objects in the visual scene, from which more complex trackers can be built based on relational, spatial properties obtained from spatial analysis (e.g., "on"). The visual attention node focuses on one of possibly many trackers (in the cases considered here this is always the one closest to the last focus of attention). Complex trackers, in this architecture, are the "meaning" of relational terms that denote relationship among primitive objects (such as color blocks) as represented by instantiated trackers. When a referent has been uniquely determined, the referential analysis passes control back to the instantiated conceptual frame, which then either expects more arguments, or, if complete, triggers an action (not depicted here). During the whole process, all components are concurrently active, and the camera is moving, if necessary, in such a way as to keep all trackers within the camera's view. While all components could run on separate computers, in the experimental tests the whole architecture was run autonomously on a ActivMedia Pioneer Peoplebot.

## References


Scheutz, M. (forthcoming) "APOC - An Architecture Framework for Complex Agents." In Darryl Davis. *Visions of Mind.* Idea Group Inc.

Tanenhaus, M. K., Spivey-Knowlton, M. J., Eberhard, K. M., & Sedivy, J. C. 1995 Integration of visual and linguistic information in spoken language comprehension *Science*, 268, 1632-1634.

# SCoT: a Spoken Conversational Tutor

**Karl Schultz, Brady Clark, Heather Pon-Barry, Elizabeth Owen Bratt, Stanley Peters**

Center for the Study of Language and Information – Stanford University
Stanford, California 94305
{schultzk, bzack, ponbarry, ebratt, peters}@csli.stanford.edu

### Abstract

We describe SCoT, a Spoken Conversational Tutor, which has been implemented in order to investigate the advantages of natural language in tutoring, especially spoken language. SCoT uses a generic architecture for conversational intelligence which has capabilities such as turn management and coordination of multi-modal input and output. SCoT also includes a set of domain independent tutorial recipes, a domain specific production-rule knowledge base, and many natural language components including a bi-directional grammar, a speech recognizer, and a text-to-speech synthesizer. SCoT leads a reflective tutorial discussion based on the details of a problem solving session with a real-time Navy shipboard damage control simulator. The tutor attempts to identify and remediate gaps in the student's understanding of damage control doctrine by decomposing its tutorial goals into dialogue acts, which are then acted on by the dialogue manager to facilitate the conversation.

## Dialogue Management

Our overall framework attempts to separate the purely linguistic parts of dialogue interaction from the knowledge of tutoring. Thus, capabilities such as turn management, construction of a structured history of the dialogue, and appropriate use of discourse markers are part of the dialogue manager's general conversational intelligence. Our dialogue manager coordinates input from the user, interprets this input as a dialogue move(s), updates the dialogue context, and delivers speech and graphical output to the user according to a plan specified by the tutor.

The Architecture for Conversational Intelligence makes use of several recent ideas in dialogue modeling, described in detail in (Lemon 2001). It creates and updates an information state corresponding to a notion of dialogue context. Dialogue moves (e.g., an assertion) update information state and can be initiated by either the user or the system. A dialogue move might send a user response to the system, elicit an assertion by the system, or prompt a follow-up question.

The dialogue manager itself includes the following dynamically updated components: a *Dialogue Move Tree* containing a structured history of dialogue moves and 'threads', plus a list of 'active nodes' determining possible interpretations of user input; an *Activity Tree* representing a hierarchical structure of activities initiated by the system or the user; a *System Agenda* of issues to be raised; *Salience Groups* for objects referenced recently; and a *Modality Buffer* for storing gestures to be resolved.



## Conversational Tutoring

The main purpose of SCoT is to investigate the value of natural language in tutoring, especially speech and multi-modal gesture. SCoT is a reflective tutor, and takes as input the details of a problem solving session from DC-Train (Wilkins 2000), a real-time Navy shipboard damage control simulator. This simulator is also speech-driven, taking advantage of many of the natural language components described below, though it has a dialogue management system that is much less complex. The initial plan for a dialogue is created by taking a DC-Train session and feeding an analysis of it from the knowledge representation into the tutorial recipes.

### Tutoring Recipes

The tutorial recipes outline how to decompose a tutorial goal into other recipes or dialogue actions. They are written according to the scripting language set forth in Gruenstein (2002) and primarily consist of two groups: those corresponding to high level tutorial plans and those for responding to a specific student utterance. The recipes are responsible for creating an initial dialogue plan by examining a student's performance and identifying knowledge areas that need attention. They describe how to use information from the student assessment and the dialogue history to appropriately steer the conversation.

### Knowledge Representation

The domain knowledge is represented as production rules acting on a working memory. The tutor can query this for procedural explanations about how to solve a problem. Justifications for each step in a solution are currently only derived from rule preconditions, and not a justification for each precondition. We are still working on how to use a more robust declarative structure for more descriptive justifications, especially for rule preconditions. In other words *why* a precondition exists, not merely *that* it exists.

### Multi-modal Gesture

Gestures are a large part of typical human-to-human interaction and the more we allow a student and a tutor to interact within a common workspace the more effective the dialogue interaction becomes (Clark 1996). This capability also lifts a considerable burden from the tutor since the tutor doesn't always need to formulate a full textual description for everything it is trying to convey. Making use of a 3-D model of a Navy ship from DC-Train the tutor is able to point out locations on the ship and easily create a context for discussing a problem (e.g., a burning compartment). The student is also able to point and highlight within this display, but only at specified times.

### Work in Progress

We are also working on a student model and a robust language generation component. The student model assigns a probability to each rule in the knowledge representation based on evidence seen during a problem solving session with DC-Train as well as evidence during dialogue. The language generation component takes a set of feature-value pairs which map onto particular logical forms and are then sent through Gemini (see Grammar section) to be turned into an utterance.

## Speech Interaction

In creating any system which interacts with a user via natural language, especially spoken language, special attention is needed for the extra language components. The goal of accurate speech recognition dictates many of the developmental choices, particularly what phrases will be understood. To understand a user takes the combination of a powerful speech recognizer in addition to a robust parser, both of which depend on a hand-built grammar. There are fewer language restrictions for the text-to-speech, however creating a high quality audio voice takes a fair amount of effort. We discuss each of these below.

### Grammar: Gemini

The Gemini NLP system (Dowding et al. 1993) uses a single unification grammar both for parsing strings of words into logical forms (LFs) and generating sentences from LF inputs, e.g., the question "What happened next?" has the LF: (ask(wh([past,happen]))). Therefore SCoT understands a student through deep semantic processing, which enables us to get a very precise and detailed understanding of student utterances. This is key to understanding the dialogue intentions of a student (e.g., a question; an answer).

### Speech Recognition: Nuance

Another major aspect of understanding a user is the speech recognizer. Nuance takes the Gemini grammar and creates a recognition model of expected utterances using its built-in understanding of phonetics. The grammar, therefore, will bias the recognizer towards correct understanding by limiting the input to that which is pertinent to tutoring and the specific domain being tutored. However, this can have the unintended side effect of turning an out-of-grammar utterance into something in-grammar, which typically leads to problems. This is why a well engineered grammar is key to good language understanding.

### Text-To-Speech: Festival and Festvox

We have seen from testing SCoT that likeability is highly correlated with the quality of the voice output, regardless of content. The Festival text-to-speech system can turn any text into audio, however it has too much of a 'computer-sounding' voice and at present lacks the clarity and subtle inflections of a real human voice. One solution we have to this is to use the Festvox add-in to Festival, which allows the developer to create a more natural sounding voice. It is a non-trivial process, which involves recording a large number of utterances within the desired domain. These are analyzed by a speech recognizer with their text representation, and a voice is created which can generate audio within the language coverage of utterances recorded.

## Acknowledgements

This work is supported by the Department of the Navy under research grant N000140010660, a multidisciplinary university research initiative on natural language interaction with intelligent tutoring systems.

## References

Lemon, O.; Gruenstein, A.; and Peters, S. 2002. Collaborative Activities and Multi-tasking in Dialogue Systems. *Traitement Automatique des Langues (TAL)*, 42(2):131-154, special issue on dialogue.

Gruenstein, A. 2002. Conversational Interfaces: A Domain-Independent Architecture for Task-Oriented Dialogues, M.S. Thesis, Symbolic Systems, Stanford Univ.

Dowding, J.; Gawron, J.; Appelt, D.; Bear, J.; Cherny, L.; Moore, R.C.; and Moran, D. 1993. *Gemini*: A Natural Language System for Spoken Language Understanding. *Proceedings of the 31st Annual Meeting of the Association for Computational Linguistics*. Columbus, OH.

Wilkins, D. C.; and Sniezek, J. A. 2000. The DC-SCS Supervisory Control Systems for Ship Damage Control: Volume 1 - Design Overview, Knowledge Based Systems Report, UIUC-BI-KBS-2000-03, Beckman Institute, University of Illinois.

Clark, Herbert H. 1996. *Using Language*. Cambridge: Cambridge University Press.

# Intelligent Agents for Coalition Search and Rescue Task Support

**Austin Tate, Jeff Dalton, Clauirton de Siebra, Stuart Aitken**
*Artificial Intelligence Applications Institute (AIAI), University of Edinburgh, Edinburgh EH8 9LE, UK*
*{a.tate, j.dalton, c.siebra, s.aitken}@ed.ac.uk*

**Jeffrey M. Bradshaw, Andrzej Uszok**
*Institute for Human and Machine Cognition (IHMC), 40 S. Alcaniz, Pensacola, FL 32501, USA*
*{auszok, jbradshaw}@ihmc.us*

http://www.aiai.ed.ac.uk/project/cosar-ts/demo/isd/

### Abstract

The Coalition Search and Rescue Task Support demonstration shows cooperative agents supporting a highly dynamic mission in which AI task planning, inter-agent collaboration, workflow enactment, policy-managed communications, semantic web queries, semantic web services matchmaking and knowledge-based notifications are employed.

## Introduction

The Coalition Search and Rescue Task Support (CoSAR-TS) project is integrating AIAI's I-X planning and collaboration technology, IHMC's KAoS policy and domain management agent services, and semantic web services of various kinds. Search and rescue operations by nature require the kind of rapid dynamic composition of available policy-constrained services making it a good use case for Semantic Web technologies. Other participants in the application include BBN Technologies, SPAWAR, AFRL, and Carnegie Mellon University.

## CoSAR-TS Scenario

The scenario is set in the Binni domain used for multi-national research in Command and Control (Rathmell, 1999). It begins with an event that reports a downed airman in the Red Sea between the coastlines of two fictional nations: Binni (to the West) and Arabello (to the East). In this initial scenario it is assumed that excellent location knowledge is available, and that there are no local threats to counter or avoid in the rescue. The airman reports his own injuries via his suit sensors. Next is an investigation of the facilities available to rescue the airman. There will be three possibilities: a US ship-borne helicopter; a Gaoan helicopter from a land base in Binni; or a patrol boat situated off the Arabello coastline. Finally, there is a process to establish available medical facilities for the specialized injury reported using the information provided about the countries in the region. Arabello's hospital is best placed to provide the facilities, due to the fact that it has the necessary treatment facilities for burns. But the selection of the rescue resource is policy-constrained since no Gaoan helicopters may enter Arabello airspace.

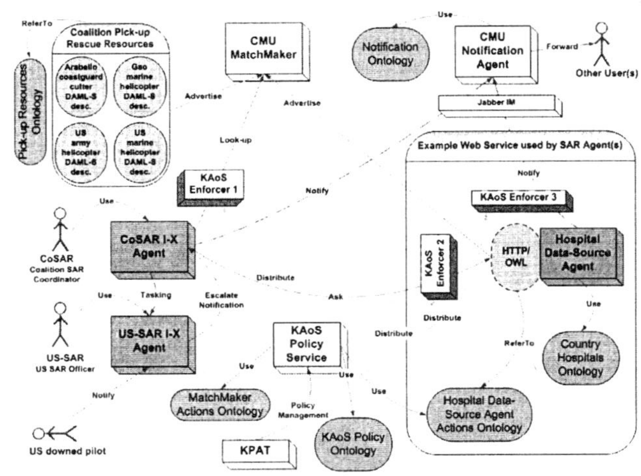


Figure 1: CoSAR-TS Components

Figure 1 shows the agents used in the demonstration, representing the roles and functions of the Coalition SAR coordinator, US SAR officer, hospital information provider, SAR resource provider and a Notification Agent. The Coalition SAR Coordinator and US SAR Officer each has an I-X process panel, which can be used for messaging concerning collaborative activity, and is also used to select, refine and execute a suitable standard operating procedure or plan. A query is made on a BBN Technologies semantic web service of OWL-encoded facts about country medical infrastructure. The selection of a SAR resource is made using the CMU Semantic Matchmaker to find a suitable service. These lookups obey policies set by the IHMC KAoS Policy Administration Tool (KPAT). Finally, the CMU Notification Agent uses knowledge of the recipients to make notifications to hospital administrators or pilots.

## I-X Technology

I-X Process Panels (http://i-x.info - Tate, 2003) can provide task support by reasoning about and exchanging with other agents and services any combination of Issues, Activities, Constraints and Annotations (in the <I-N-C-A> ontology). I-X can therefore provide collaborative task support and exchange of structured messages related to plans, activity and the results of such activity. These types of information can be exchanged with other I-X panels and with other tools using OWL, RDF or other languages.

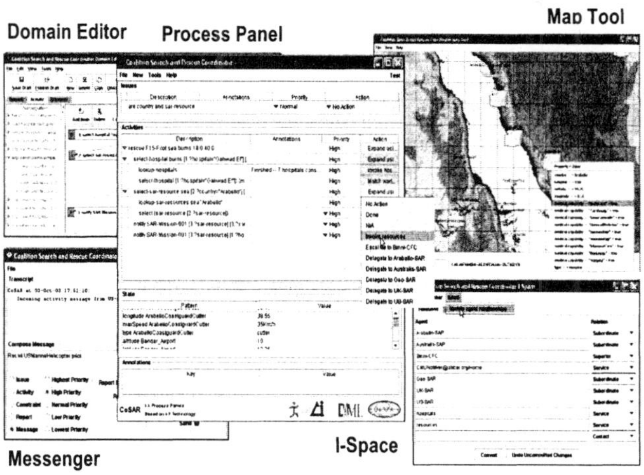


Figure 2: I-X Process Panel and Associated Tools

Figure 2 shows an I-X Process Panel (I-P$^2$) and associated I-X Tools. I-X can make use of multiple communications methods ranging from simple XML instant messaging (e.g. via Jabber) to sophisticated policy constrained agent communications environments (e.g. CoABS Grid, KAoS). The I-Space tool maintains agent relationships. The relationships can be obtained from agent services such as KAoS. I-X Process Panels can also link to semantic web information and web services though an I-Q query adaptor.

I-X includes a process editor for creating process models (I-DE) to populate the domain model and an AI planner (I-Plan) that can compose a suitable plan for the given tasks when provided with a library of standard operating procedures or processes, and knowledge of other agents or web services that it may use. I-Plan can support hierarchical plan creation, precondition achievement, consistent binding of multiple variables, temporal constraint checking, etc.

## KAoS Technology

Figure 3 shows the KAoS Policy Administration Tool (http://www.ihmc.us/research/projects/KAoS/ - Uszok et al. 2003). Through it, policies constraining usage of resources and agents' actions are inserted into the system. The policies are expressed using OWL. This allows the use of Description Logic reasoning algorithms to perform sophisticated queries and analysis of policies; supported by Stanford University's Java Theorem Prover (JTP) inferencing engine. Loading relevant application specific ontologies can dynamically extend the KAoS Services. The layer of guards and enforcers integrated with the application facilitates the enforcement of the policies.

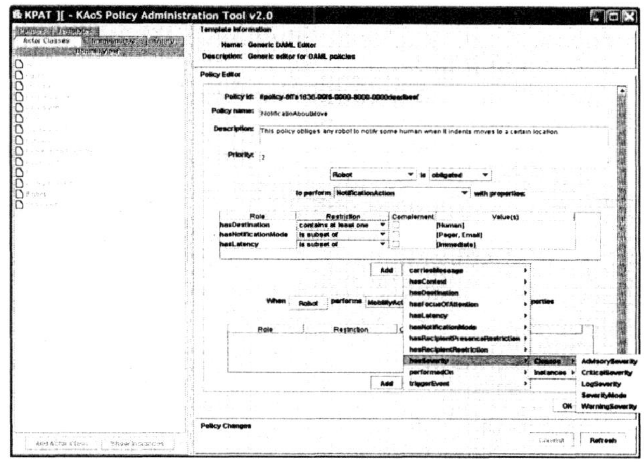


Figure 3: KAoS Policy Administration Tool

## Acknowledgements

This material is based on research sponsored by the Defense Advanced Research Projects Agency (DARPA) and US Air Force Research Laboratory under agreement numbers F30602-00-2-0577 and F30602-03-2-0014. The U.S. Government, IHMC, and the University of Edinburgh are authorized to reproduce and distribute reprints and on-line copies for their purposes notwithstanding any copyright annotation hereon. The views and conclusions contained herein are those of the authors and should not be interpreted as necessarily representing the official policies or endorsements, either expressed or implied, of other parties.

## References

Rathmell, R.A. (1999) A Coalition Force Scenario 'Binni - Gateway to the Golden Bowl of Africa', in Proceedings of the International Workshop on Knowledge-Based Planning for Coalition Forces, (ed. Tate, A.) pp. 115-125, Edinburgh, Scotland, 10-11 May 1999.

Tate, A. (2003). Coalition Task Support using I-X and <I-N-C-A>. Proceedings of the Third International Central and Eastern European Conference on Multi-Agent Systems (CEEMAS 2003), 16-18 June, Prague, Czech Republic, LNAI 2691. (pp. 7-16). Berlin: Springer.

Uszok, A., Bradshaw, J. M., Jeffers, R., Suri, N., Hayes, P., Breedy, M. R., Bunch, L., Johnson, M., Kulkarni, S., & Lott, J. (2003). KAoS policy and domain services: Toward a description-logic approach to policy representation, deconfliction, and enforcement. Proceedings of Policy 2003. Como, Italy.

# The Autonomous Sciencecraft Experiment Onboard the EO-1 Spacecraft

**Daniel Tran, Steve Chien, Rob Sherwood, Rebecca Castano, Benjamin Cichy, Ashley Davies, Gregg Rabideau**

Jet Propulsion Laboratory, California Institute of Technology
4800 Oak Grove Dr.
Pasadena, CA 91109
Firstname.Lastname@jpl.nasa.gov

**Abstract**

The Autonomous Sciencecraft Experiment (ASE), currently flying onboard the Earth Observing-1 (EO-1) spacecraft, integrates several autonomy software technologies enabling autonomous science analysis and mission planning. The experiment demonstrates the potential for future space missions to use onboard decision-making to respond autonomously to capture short-lived science phenomena. The AAAI software demonstration will consist of two sections: a real-time display of an ASE-commanded ground contact from the EO-1 spacecraft, and a simulation of the full ASE autonomous science-response scenario.

## Introduction

The Autonomous Sciencecraft Experiment (ASE) [Chien et al., 2003] is currently flying onboard NASA's Earth Observing-1 (EO-1) spacecraft. Uploaded in the Fall of 2003, ASE has successfully commanded EO-1 operations and enabled autonomous retargeting to capture dynamic science events. ASE is currently executing a series of ambitious science-response scenarios scheduled for completion in the Fall of 2004. The ASE onboard flight software includes several autonomy components:

1. *Onboard science processing algorithms.* Science analysis algorithms process onboard image data to detect science events and suggest reactions to maximize science return.
2. *Onboard planning and scheduling software.* The Continuous Activity Scheduling Planning Execution and Replanning (CASPER) [Chien et al., 2000] system generates mission operations plans from goals uplinked by the EO-1 Science Team or inserted by the onboard science analysis module. The model-based planning algorithms enable rapid response to a wide range of operations scenarios based on models of spacecraft constraints.
3. *Robust execution software.* The Spacecraft Command Language (SCL) expands the CASPER mission plans to low-level spacecraft commands. SCL monitors the execution of the plan and has the flexibility and knowledge to perform improvements in execution as well as local responses to anomalies.

Building autonomy software for space missions presents a number of key challenges:

1. *Limited, intermittent communications.* EO-1 has eight ten-minute communications opportunities per day. This means that the spacecraft must be able to operate for long periods of time without supervision.
2. *Complex subsystems and controls.* A typical spacecraft has thousands of components carefully engineered to survive the rigors of space.
3. *Limited observability.* Bandwidth and onboard processing constraints limit the availability of engineering telemetry. Onboard software and ground operations teams must be able to operate the spacecraft on limited information.
4. *Limited computing resources.* An average spacecraft CPU offer 25 MIPS and 128 MB RAM – far less than a typical personal computer. The EO-1 team allocated 4 MIPS for all of the ASE software.
5. *High stakes.* A typical space mission costs hundreds of millions of dollars, any failure has significant economic impact.

ASE on EO-1 demonstrates an integrated autonomous mission using onboard science analysis, replanning, and robust execution. ASE performs intelligent science data processing, editing, and spacecraft retargeting, leading to a reduction in data downlinked and an increase in science return. These capabilities enable radically different missions with significant onboard decision-making allowing novel science opportunities. The paradigm shift toward highly autonomous spacecraft will enable future

NASA missions to achieve significantly greater science returns with reduced risk and reduced operations cost.

## Live ASE Contact from EO-1

The first part of the demonstration will showcase a live contact from the EO-1 spacecraft *commanded onboard by ASE*. Telemetry from the spacecraft will be displayed remotely from the EO-1 Mission Operations Center at Goddard Spaceflight Center. The real-time telemetry stream will display the commands currently executing onboard EO-1 and the status of each ASE software component. During the demonstration ASE will downlink engineering and science data by issuing spacecraft commands to achieve the following objectives:

1. Point the X-Band phased-array antenna at the groundstation one minute prior to acquisition of signal (AOS).
2. At AOS, power on both transceivers and configure S-Band for a 2 Mbit downlink rate.
3. Command the onboard solid state recorder to playback mode and begin streaming science data over the X-Band link.
4. Initiate the dumping of engineering data over S-Band.
5. Initiate the playback of the spacecraft event log through S-Band.
6. At loss of signal (LOS), turn off the S-Band transceiver, stop streaming science data, and begin streaming fill data.
7. Ten seconds after LOS, power down the X-Band transceiver and return the solid state recorder to standard operations mode.

A typical EO-1 contact lasts between 10 and 15 minutes.

## Full Autonomous Science Scenario

The second part of the demonstration will simulate an ASE mission scenario. During this demonstration ASE will command a software simulation of the EO-1 spacecraft to image science targets, process and analyze onboard image data, and re-plan operations based on science results.

The demonstration will highlight the following capabilities of ASE:

1. *Autonomous Execution*. CASPER will generate a mission plan using an uplinked set of high-level goals requesting science observations and data downlinks. SCL will convert these plans to sequences of spacecraft commands and issue these commands to EO-1.
2. *Dynamic Event Tracking*. The onboard science analysis algorithms will detect an erupting volcano in one of the requested observations, and as a result recommend a follow-on observation.
3. *Data Editing*. During the analysis of another science observation, the analysis algorithms will determine an unacceptable percentage of cloud-obscured data. Based on this analysis the ASE software will recommend deleting this image and imaging an alternate target.
4. *Onboard Replanning*. CASPER will modify the onboard schedule to respond to the science analysis recommendations to insert new observations and delete low-value data from onboard storage.

## Acknowledgement

Portions of this work were performed at the Jet Propulsion Laboratory, California Institute of Technology, under a contract with the National Aeronautics and Space Administration.

We would like to acknowledge the important contributions of Nghia Tang and Michael Burl of JPL, Dan Mandl, Stuart Frye, and Stephen Ungar of GSFC, Jerry Hengemihle and Bruce Trout of Microtel LLC, Jeff D'Agostino of the Hammers Corp., Seth Shulman and Robert Bote of Honeywell Corp., Jim Van Gaasbeck and Darrell Boyer of ICS, Michael Griffin and Hsiao-hua Burke of MIT Lincoln Labs, Ronald Greeley, Thomas Doggett, and Kevin Williams of ASU, and Victor Baker and James Dohm of University of Arizona.

## References

S. Chien, B. Cichy, S. Schaffer, D. Tran, G. Rabideau, R. Bote, Dan Mandl, S. Frye, S. Shulman, J. Van Gaasbeck, D. Boyer, "Validating the EO-1 Autonomous Science Agent", *Working notes of the Workshop on Safe Agents*, AAMAS-2003.

S. Chien, et al. (2003) Autonomous Science on EO-1, I-SAIRAS, 7th Symposium on Artificial Intelligence, Robotics and Automation in Space, Nara, Japan, May 2003.

S. Chien, R. Knight, A. Stechert, R. Sherwood, and G. Rabideau, "Using Iterative Repair to Improve Responsiveness of Planning and Scheduling," *Proceedings of the 5th Intl. Conference on AI Planning and Scheduling*, Breckenridge, CO, April 2000.

A.G. Davies, R. Greeley, K. Williams, V. Baker, J. Dohm, M. Burl, E. Mjolsness, R. Castano, T. Stough, J. Roden, S. Chien, R. Sherwood, "ASC Science Report," August 2001. (available at ase.jpl.nasa.gov).

# Online Semantic Extraction by Backpropagation Neural Network with Various Syntactic Structure Representations

**Heidi H. T. Yeung**

City University of Hong Kong
Tat Chee Road, Kowloon Tong,
Kowloon, Hong Kong, China

### Summary of Demonstration

The sub-symbolic approach on Natural Language Processing (NLP) is one of the mainstreams in Artificial Intelligence. Indeed, we have plenty of algorithms for variations of NLP such as syntactic structure representation or lexicon classification theoretically. The goal of these researches is obviously for developing a hybrid architecture which can process natural language as what human does. Thus, we propose an online intelligent system to extract the semantics (utterance interpretation) by applying a 3-layer back propagation neural network to classify the encoded syntactic structures into corresponding semantic frame types (e.g. AGENT_ACTION_PATIENT). The results are generated dynamically according to training sets and user inputs in webpage-form. It can diminish the manipulating time while using extra tools and share the statistical results with colleagues in clear and standard forms.

## Implementation

This intelligent system is implemented with JAVA which is an object-oriented and multiplatform programming language. During the development stage, the programs can be simply tested in console mode with using IDE provided by SUN. Later, the well-designed *Java Service Page* (JSP) as the interactive user interface to link those classes as *Java Beans* with the support of Apache Tomcat server.

We use three connectionist-based encoders to represent the syntactic structures: Recursive Auto-Association Memories (RAAM) [Pollack 1990], Sequential RAAM [Kwasny 1993] and Tensor product representation with Non-linear Compression (our proposed representational algorithm). There is a main program "NLP" which includes all procedures in the semantic extraction and training processes. The flows of semantic extraction procedures are based on Tsang's and Wong's (2002) design.



## Functionalities

First, a three layer back-propagation neural network (BPNN) is trained with a set of training sentences and expected semantic frame types as the procedures shown in the flowchart below. The training performance and the classification results of both training and testing sentences are listed systematically and graphically.

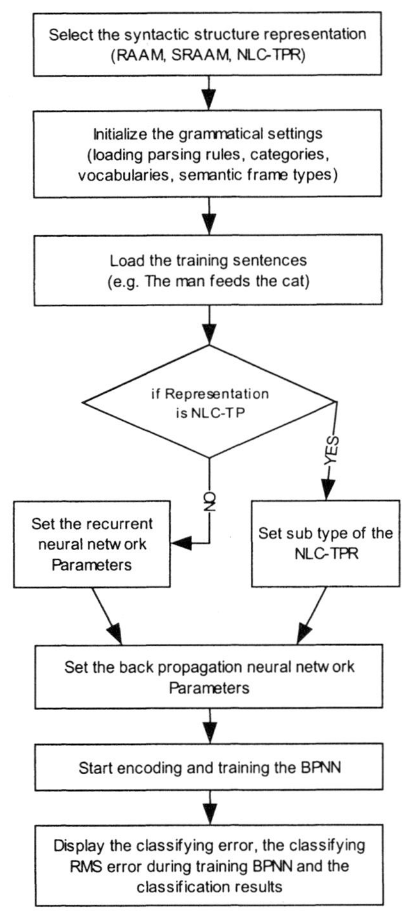


**Figure 1** Flowchart of training the BPNN

To test the classifying performance of BPNN, user can input the grammatical sentence with the interactive interface provided. The interface will result the plots of the output layer activation of BPNN and the determined semantic frame type. If the expected type is chosen, the classification error is also calculated as a reference.

After the training of BPNN, the latest data will be stored as the references and the 4 types of results can be revised from the system.

1) Encoding Progress – Real time plots of the Root-mean-square (RMS) Error of the recurrent NN during training for RAAM and SRAAM
2) Classifying Progress – Real time plots of the RMS Error of the BPNN during training for different data sets and syntactic structure representations.
3) Cluster Results – The syntactic structure representations and the BPNN hidden activation of training sentences are clustered in the distance map as Postscript files for different data sets and syntactic structure representations.
4) Classifying Results – The output layer activations of BPNN are tabled against both training and testing sentences for different data sets and syntactic structure representations.

## Special Features

Making use of the dynamic properties in *Macromedia Flash Movie*, we create 3 SWF documents for graphical display. One of them is for plotting the Root-mean square errors in output layers of recurrent neural network for RAAM and SRAAM and that of BPNN during training shown in Figure 2.

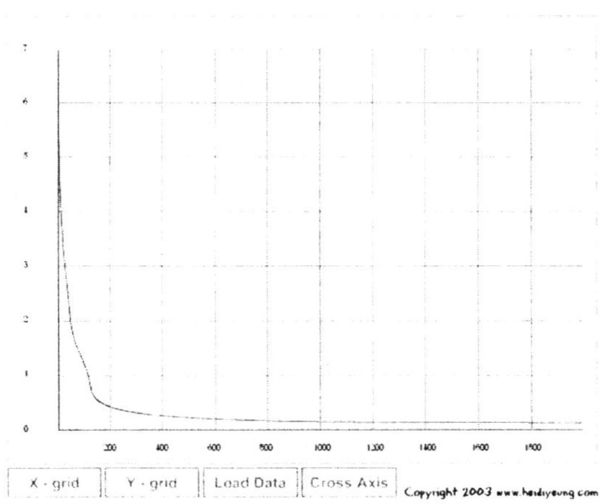


**Figure 2** Classifying progress display

The second one is the activation plots for BPNN output layer activation as below.

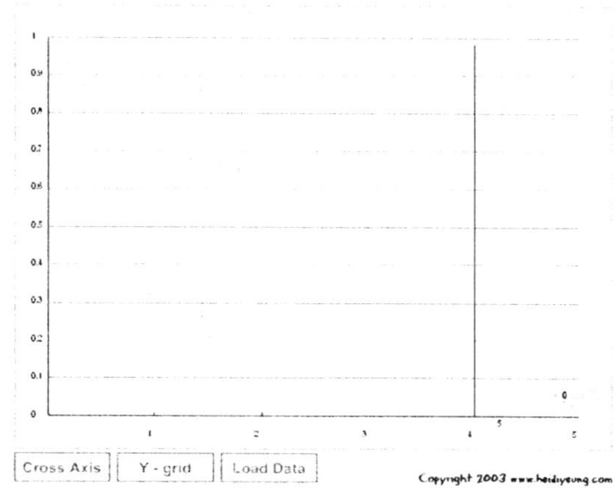


**Figure 3** Output layer activation of BPNN

The tree from is previewed with the last Flash movie in Figure 4.

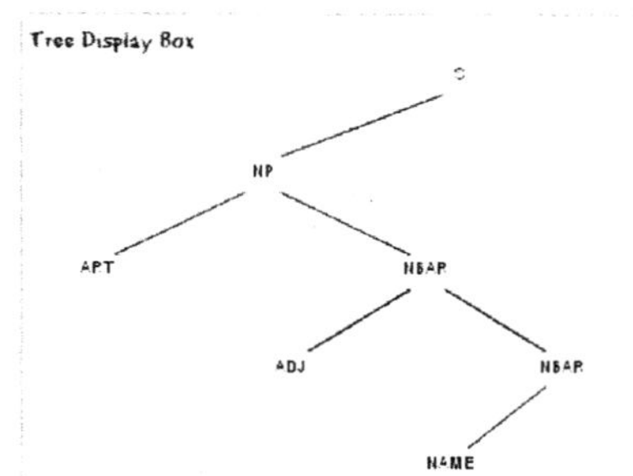


**Figure 4** Tree display

The cluster results of memories and BPNN hidden layer activations are generated and stored in server side. Then, a Java class invokes the Cluster Application and Postscript Generating Program in operating system.

## References

Kwasny, S. C., Kalman, B. L., & Chang, N. 1993. *Distributed Patterns as Hierarchical Structures*. Proceedings of the World Congress on Neural Networks, Portland, OR, July 1993, v. II, pp. 198-201.

Pollack, J. B. 1990. *Recursive distributed representations. Artificial Intelligence*, 36, pp. 77-105.

Tsang, W. M., and Wong, C. K. 2002. *Extracting Frame Based Semantics from Recursive Distributed Representation - A Connectionist Approach to NLP*. IC-AI' 02.

This System is powered by *Apache Tomcat 4.1, Macromedia Flash MX*

# Responsive Information Architect: A Context-Sensitive Multimedia Conversation Framework for Information Seeking

**Michelle Zhou Keith Houck Rosario Uceda-Sosa Shimei Pan**
**Min Chen[†] Vikram Aggarwal James Shaw**

IBM T. J. Watson Research Center
19 Skyline Drive
Hawthorne, NY 10532
imi@us.ibm.com

† Now with Oracle

## 1. MOTIVATION AND BACKGROUND

Information seeking, such as searching for a particular vacation package or looking for a Christmas gift online, is almost a routine task in our daily life. However the seeking process can often be very difficult and time consuming due to the following three main reasons. First users must face many choices because of the sheer volume of data that has been made available. Second, traditional GUI-based data access and navigation models are very limited when dealing with large and complex information spaces. Specifically, a pure GUI-based system is not flexible enough to allow users to express complex data queries that may involve multiple data linkages. For example, it would be very difficult to handle user queries, such as *"find me 3 days/2 nights vacation packages to a destination with an average annual temperature at least over 70F*". In addition, most current access/navigation models are context insensitive. Continuing the above example, most systems would not be able to understand any follow up queries, such as *"how about just to those cities in Europe*". Users may also get lost when facing too many choices or get stuck if there is no data satisfying their criteria. Third, existing systems normally organize and present the retrieved information in a one-size-fits-all format, which may not be easily understood or digested by the users.

To address all the above issues and better aid users in their information seeking process, we are building a context-sensitive framework, called **Responsive Information Architect** (RIA), which engages users in automatically generated multimedia conversations. Unlike existing information browsing paradigm that forces users to explore information following pre-defined paths (e.g., GUI menus), RIA allows users to express their information requests flexibly using a mixture of input modalities, including speech, text, and gesture. Using a rich context, such as conversation history and data semantics, RIA is capable of understanding user inputs, including these complex data queries (e.g., *"tell me about cities in the north along Hudson with at least 5000 people"*), abbreviated inquiries (e.g., *"what about golf courses"*), or imprecise requests (e.g., inaccurate gesture inputs). By tracking and learning from user navigation patterns, RIA is also able to aid users in navigating large and complex information space intelligently. In particular, RIA can help users to refine their queries by indicating the most effective navigation path when there is too much data retrieved, or to automatically relax user queries by recommending the most similar data when no data matches user criteria. In addition, to provide users with a customized presentation of retrieved information, RIA automatically synthesizes a multimedia tour of information on the fly using graphics, speech, and video.

Here we focus on demonstrating RIA capabilities from three aspects: 1). Supporting complex data queries in context, 2). System-guided query refinement and query relaxation, and 3). Customized multimedia information presentation.

## 2. DEMONSTRATION

Currently RIA framework is embodied in a real estate application, RealHunter™, which aims to help users search for residential properties. RealHunter™ operates on the housing data subscribed from the Westchester board of realtors Multiple Listing Service. In addition to the housing data, RealHunter™ also provides users with other related information, such as city, school, and transportation.

**Support complex data queries in context.** During an information seeking process, different users may employ different searching strategies and choose different navigation paths (e.g., finding a suitable city first before querying about the houses or vice versa). Moreover, users may link several data concepts together to locate the desired targets. For example, query *"find houses in cities in the north along Hudson River"* intends to use the city to constrain the house set. Queries mentioned above may be translated into traditional relational database queries. However, it would require users to explicit specify from which table the data be retrieved and exactly how the database joins be formed, not mentioning it does not allow abbreviated queries, such as *"how about cities in the south"*. To support a diverse array of user queries, RIA allows users to express their data requests flexibly in a natural language format (e.g., by typing). As will be demonstrated, RIA can interpret a wide variety of data queries, which may be inherently complex, spanning multiple data concepts and data attributes, explicitly or implicitly. As shown in Figure 1, queries such as *"show colonials in school districts with at least 95% stu-*

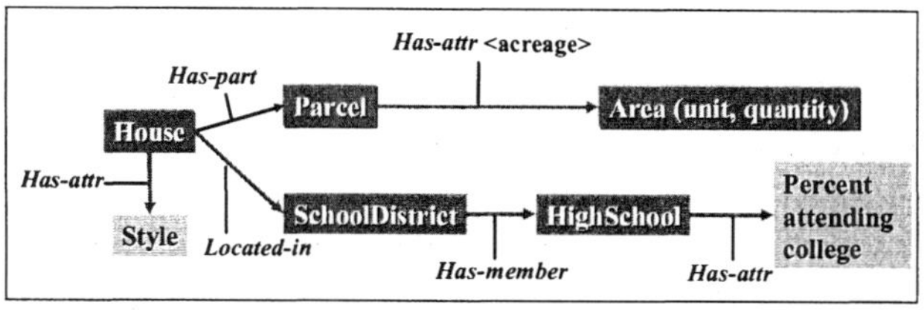


Figure 1. An ontology fragment used in RIA depicting the relationships between different data concepts and attributes.

*dents attending college"*, involves figuring out the relations among different data concepts without users' explicitly articulating them. We also demonstrate that RIA supports abbreviated queries within context. For example, given a follow-up query to the above request *"how about over 90%"*, RIA can figure out that the user intends to substitute the school criterion by changing the percentage attending college. Similarly, given a follow-up query, such as *"just those with brick siding"*, RIA understands that the user is further constraining the house set with additional house constraints (i.e., constraining the siding material).

**System-guided data navigation.** There are two common situations where users can easily get lost or get stuck. First, upon a user request, there may be too much data satisfying the user query. In this case, users may not know which is the best path for them to further narrow down the data set. On the opposite, for a given user query, there may be nothing that meet the user constraints. In this case, users may want to know whether there exist alternatives that are close enough to match their preferences. To address these two problems, RIA builds a user preference space that records a static user profile, and also dynamically tracks/updates user preferences as the conversation unfolds. As will be shown in our demo, using the user preference space, RIA is able to indicate the most efficient navigation path when there is too much data and recommend the similar data entities when no data is retrieved.

**Customized multimedia information presentation.** To present the retrieved data in a way that is customized to user preferences, the underlying data characteristics, and the available media capabilities, RIA automatically synthesizes a multimedia presentation of information by considering a number of factors on the fly. First, RIA uses a set of factors, including the specified user profiles, the retrieved data volume, and the current user query, to decide what pertinent content to be presented. For example, similar user queries may result in different presentations based on different user profiles: Figure 2(a) outlines financial information such as house price and tax, while Figure 2(b) presents information relevant to house size (e.g., square footage and lot size) and amenity (e.g., air conditioning, fuel). During this process, RIA also considers the proper organization of the content (e.g., the number of bedrooms and the number of bathrooms are always presented together whenever possible), and the availability of the required medium. For example, if there is no visual medium available, RIA would not select the city boundary (e.g., Chappaqua boundary in Figure 2). After determining the content, RIA assigns a proper medium to each piece of content by considering three factors: medium suitability (how suitable a medium is for a given piece of data, e.g., visual medium is more suitable for presenting spatial data), medium capability (whether a suitable medium is capable of presenting the desired information), and medium availability (whether a particular medium is currently available). As indicated in Figure 2, RIA uses speech to convey the total number of houses retrieved, and uses text/graphics to describe each house and the relevant city information (i.e., Chappaqua).

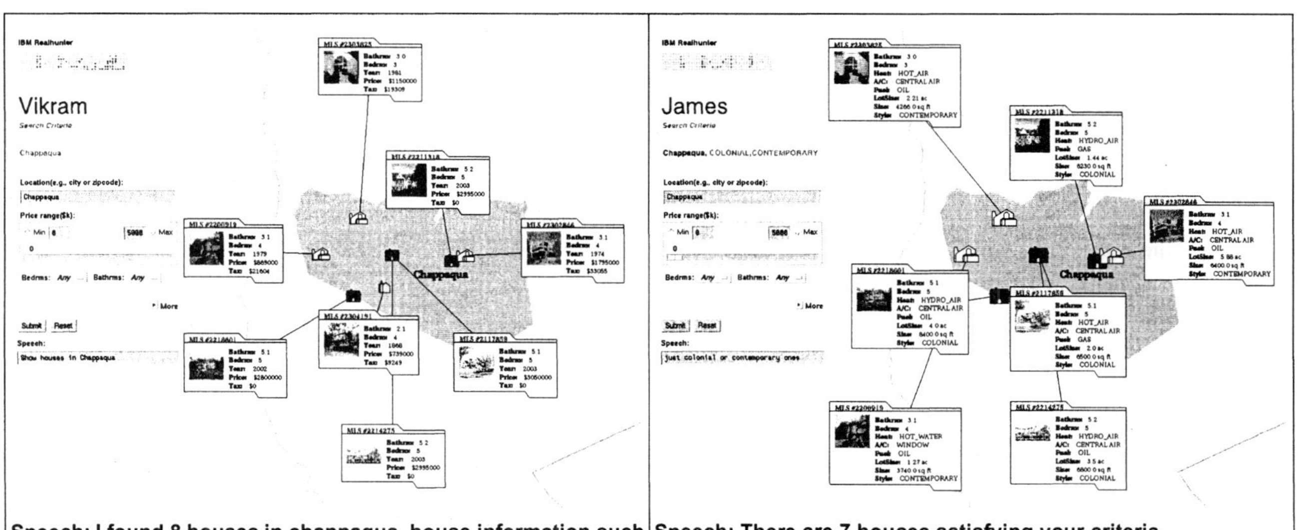


| **Speech: I found 8 houses in chappaqua, house information such as the price is shown on the screen.** | **Speech: There are 7 houses satisfying your criteria.** |
|---|---|
| (a) User profile: Financial/Exterior/Interior with 8 houses retrieved | (b) User profile: Size/Amenity with 7 houses retrieved. Note that house style is given as it is part of current user inquiry. |

Figure 2. Different presentations created for different situations.

# Index